US History
INTERACTIVE

SAVVAS
LEARNING COMPANY

Social Studies Reimagined

To start, download the free **BouncePages** app on your smartphone or tablet. Simply search for the BouncePages app in your mobile app store. The app is available for Android and IOS (iPhone®/iPad®).

Make your book come alive! Activate your digital interactivities directly from the page.

To launch the myStory video look for this icon.

To activate more interactivities look for this icon. BOUNCE to Activate

1. **AIM** the camera over the image so it is easily viewable on your screen.
2. **TAP** the screen to scan the page.
3. **BOUNCE** the page to life by clicking the icon.

Savvas Learning Company LLC, 15 East Midland Avenue, Paramus, NJ 07652

SAVVAS
LEARNING COMPANY

ISBN-13: 978-1-418-33230-3
ISBN-10: 1-418-33230-5
6 22

Authors and Partners

United States History Authors

Emma J. Lapsansky-Werner

Emma J. Lapsansky-Werner is Emeritus Professor of History and Curator of the Quaker Collection at Haverford College. "Retired" after thirty years at Haverford, she continues to teach and consult there. After receiving her doctorate from the University of Pennsylvania, she taught at Temple University for almost two decades. Dr. Lapsansky-Werner authored and coauthored over thirty books and/or articles on American social history, especially on African American, Quaker, and Pennsylvania history. She has consulted with PBS, with the Smithsonian and other museums, and lectures widely on these topics. Recent publications include *Quaker Aesthetics,* coauthored with Ann Verplanck, (University of Pennsylvania Press); *Back to Africa: Benjamin Coates and the Colonization Movement in America, 1848–1880,* coedited with Margaret Hope Bacon (Penn State University Press), and *Struggle For Freedom,* a textbook on African American history, coauthored with Gary B. Nash and Clayborne Carson (Pearson). Since 2015, she has contributed to anthologies on Quaker and Pennsylvania history (Oxford University Press, Cambridge University Press), and consults for the National Park Service. She lives in Wynnewood, PA.

Peter B. Levy

Peter B. Levy is a Full Professor in the Department of History at York College of Pennsylvania, where he teaches a wide variety of courses in American history. He received his B.A. from the University of California, Berkeley, and his Ph.D. from Columbia University. Dr. Levy's recent publications include *The Great Uprising: Race Riots in Urban America during the 1960s; The Seedtime, The Work, and The Harvest: New Perspectives on the Black Freedom Struggle in America,* co-edited by Jeffrey Littlejohn and Reginald Ellis; and *Civil War on Race Street: The Civil Rights Movement in Cambridge, Maryland.* He lives in Towson, Maryland.

Randy Roberts

Randy Roberts is the 150th Anniversary Professor and Distinguished Professor of History at Purdue University. An award-winning author, his primary research areas are sports and popular culture, and he has written, co-written, and edited more than 30 books. He has also won numerous teaching awards, including the Carnegie Foundation for the Advancement of Teaching as Indiana Professor of the Year. Among his work are books on Jack Johnson, Jack Dempsey, Joe Louis, Oscar Robertson, Bear Bryant, Joe Namath, Muhammad Ali, Malcolm X, Mickey Mantle, John Wayne, Ronald Reagan, American sports, the Alamo, Pearl Harbor, and Vietnam. Some of his most recent books include *A Team for America: The Army-Navy Game That Rallied a Nation* and *War Fever: Boston, Baseball, and America in the Shadow of the Great War,* co-authored with Johnny Smith. Roberts has served as a consultant and on-camera commentator for PBS, HBO, and History Channel. He lives in Lafayette, Indiana, with his wife Marjie.

Alan Taylor

Alan Taylor is the Thomas Jefferson Memorial Foundation Chair at the University of Virginia. He earned his Ph.D. in history from Brandeis University and did a postdoctoral fellowship at the Institute of Early American History and Culture in Williamsburg, Virginia. He teaches courses in early American history and the history of the American West. Dr. Taylor is the author of eight books, including *The Internal Enemy: Slavery and War in Virginia, 1772–1832,* which won the 2014 Pulitzer Prize for American history, and *American Colonies* and *William Cooper's Town,* which won the Bancroft and Beveridge prizes, as well as the 1996 Pulitzer Prize for American history.

Program Partners

NBC LEARN

NBC Learn, the educational arm of NBC News, develops original stories for use in the classroom and makes archival NBC News stories, images, and primary source documents available on demand to teachers, students, and parents. NBC Learn partnered with Savvas to produce the myStory videos that support this program.

Constitutional Rights Foundation Educate. Participate.

Constitutional Rights Foundation is a nonprofit, nonpartisan, community-based organization focused on educating students about the importance of civic participation in a democratic society. The Constitutional Rights Foundation is the lead contributor to the development of the Civic Discussion Topic Inquiries for this program.

Reviewers & Academic Consultants

Textbook Academic Consultants

Paul Apodaca
Professor American Studies
Chapman University
Orange, California

Christy Clark-Pujara
Associate Professor and Director of Graduate Studies
Department of Afro-American Studies
University of Wisconsin-Madison
Madison, Wisconsin

Stephen F. Knott
Professor, Department of National Security Affairs
United States Naval War College
Newport, Rhode Island

Jeffery Long, Ph.D.
Professor of Religion and Asian Studies
Elizabethtown College
Elizabethtown, Pennsylvania

Gordon Newby
Professor of Islamic, Jewish and Comparative Studies
Department of Middle Eastern and South Asian Studies
Emory University
Atlanta, Georgia

Jill Ogline Titus
Associate Director, Civil War Institute
Gettysburg College
Gettysburg, Pennsylvania

Audrey Peterson
Associate Director
Office of Communications and Marketing, Brooklyn College
Former Editor-in-Chief, American Legacy Magazine

Mark Peterson
Associate Professor
Department of Asian and Near Eastern Languages
Brigham Young University
Provo, Utah

William Pitts
Professor, Department of Religion
Baylor University
Waco, Texas

Benjamin Ravid
Professor Emeritus of Jewish History
Department of Near Eastern and Judaic Studies
Brandeis University
Waltham, Massachusetts

Harpreet Singh
College Fellow
Department of South Asian Studies
Harvard University
Cambridge, Massachusetts

Christopher E. Smith, J.D., Ph.D.
Professor
Michigan State University
MSU School of Criminal Justice
East Lansing, Michigan

John Voll
Professor of Islamic History
Georgetown University
Washington, D.C.

Michael R. Wolf
Associate Professor
Department of Political Science
Indiana University-Purdue University Fort Wayne
Fort Wayne, Indiana

Project Imagine: United States History

Program Hosts

Keith Hughes
Instructional Technology Coach, Buffalo Public Schools
Adjunct Professor of New Literacies, Graduate School of Education, University at Buffalo (SUNY)

Kezia Pearson
Educator, Buffalo Public Schools

Academic Consultants

Keith Huxen
Senior Director of Research and History
The National World War II Museum

Alan M. Kraut
University Professor of History and Fellow
Migration Policy Institute
American University

John Olszowka, Ph.D.
Professor of History
Mercyhurst University

Audrey Peterson
Associate Director of News and Information
Brooklyn College

Heather Marie Stur, Ph.D.
General Buford Blount Professor of Military History
Fellow, Dale Center for the Study of War & Society
University of Southern Mississippi

Jesse Tarbert, Ph.D.
Visiting Assistant Professor of History
Loyola University, Maryland

Jill Ogline Titus
Associate Director, Civil War Institute
Gettysburg College
Gettysburg, Pennsylvania

Program Contributors

HAI | History Associates Incorporated

Social Studies Today

Social studies is more than the story of the past.

It's how we shape our world today. It's seeing how yesterday's stories change our perspective on today. And in today's fast-paced world, it's essential.

Welcome to the next generation of interactive social studies!

Savvas' new *Interactive Social Studies* program was created in collaboration with educators, social studies experts, and students nationwide. The program uses tested best practices to engage students in social studies content through current events, dynamic technology, active classroom strategies, inquiry-based learning and more, so students are college- and career-ready.

The Program Includes:

- Inquiry-focused projects, civic discussions, and document analysis questions that develop content and skills mastery in preparation for real-world challenges.
- Essential Questions, personal myStory videos, Connections to Today and current events to spark interest and increase long-term understanding for students.
- Higher-level content with differentiation tools to support students' access to complex text, acquire core content knowledge, and tackle rigorous questions.
- Digital activities on Savvas Realize that are dynamic, flexible, and use the power of technology to bring social studies to life.

>> **Go online to learn more and see the program overview video.**

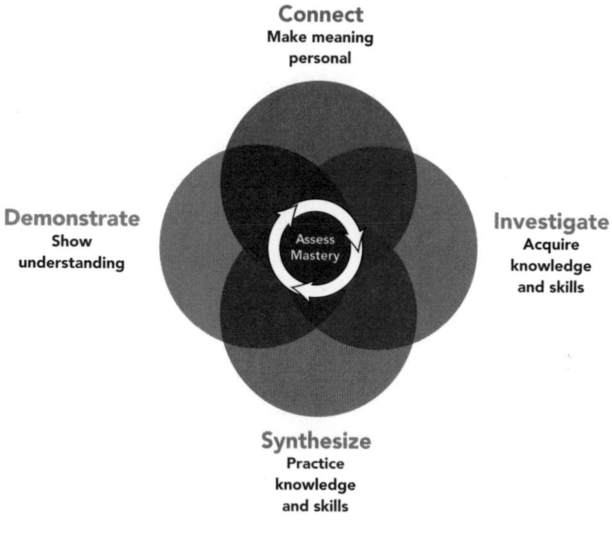

SAVVAS realize™

The digital course on Realize!

The program's digital course on Realize puts rich and engaging content, embedded assessments with instant data, and flexible tools at your fingertips.

Connect: Make Meaning Personal

CONNECT! Students will begin *Interactive Social Studies* by engaging in the topic story and connecting it to their own lives.

>> **Connections to Today** brings the past to the present. Students will be introduced to a topic by seeing how history influenced today. Educators will find more resources on the Savvas Realize course.

>> Instruction begins with an **Essential Question**. These thought-provoking questions engage students and introduce the Topic.

>> Developed in partnership with NBCLearn, the **My Story** videos help students connect to the Topic content by the personal story of an individual whose life is related to the content students are about to learn.

QUEST! INQUIRY

>> **Quest Inquiry activities** include projects, civic discussions, and document-based activities. Students will demonstrate their knowledge of the topic and practice real-world skills by creating presentations, videos, conduct discussions, and more.

INVESTIGATE! Step two of *Interactive Social Studies* allows students to investigate the topic story through a number of engaging features as you learn the content.

>> **Active Classroom Strategies** integrated in the daily lesson plans help to increase in-class participation, raise energy levels and attentiveness, all while engaging in the story. These 5–15 minute activities have you use what you have learned to draw, write, speak, and decide.

project Imagine

>> Be Part of History with ***Project Imagine*** digital immersive experiences. These dynamic activities are found in key topics to reinforce students' understanding of history and increase historical empathy.

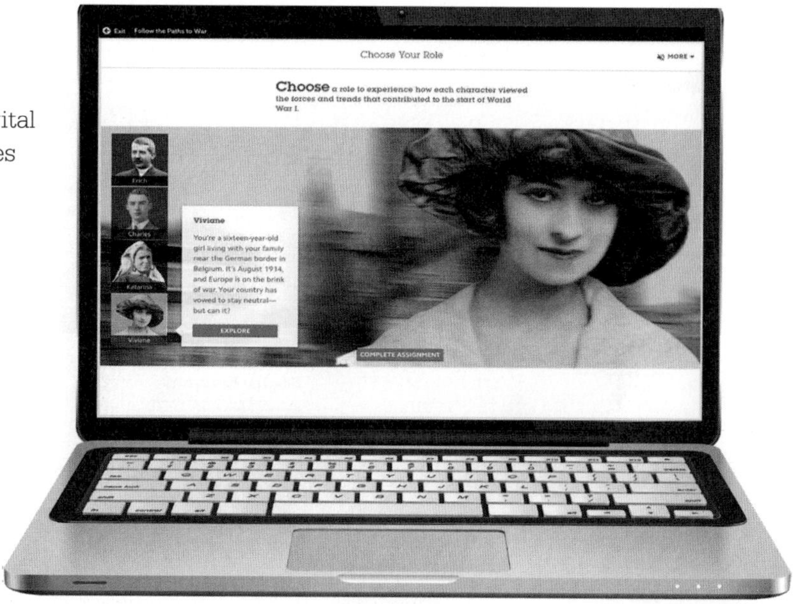

Listenwise

>> Connect through Current Events! We've partnered with **Listenwise** to bring you daily news updates to help bring what's happening outside your classroom into your daily instruction.

Investigate

>> Feel like you are a part of the story with **interactive 3-D models, primary sources, maps, and more.**

>> Reinforce content with **leveled lesson summaries** and **lesson video recaps** found on the Savvas Realize course.

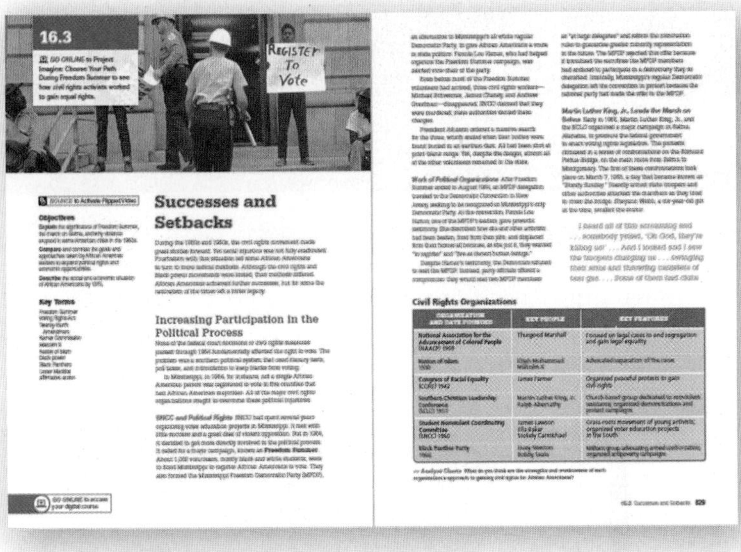

>> Learn content by reading narrative text online or in a printed Student Edition.

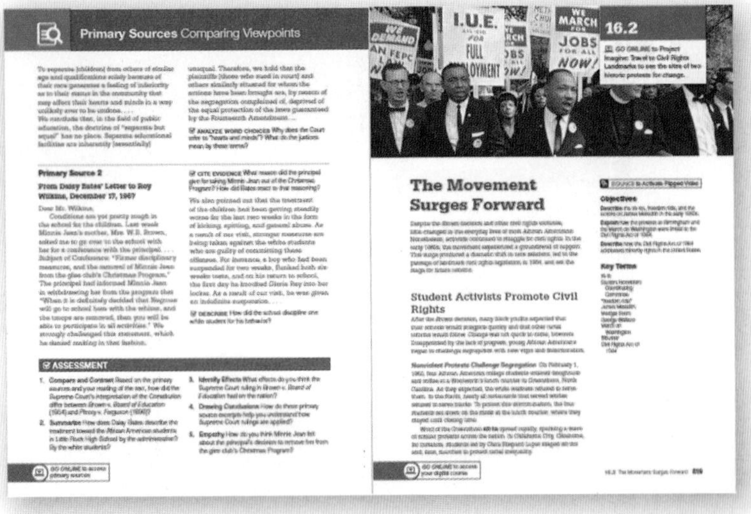

>> See history from a different perspective. **Comparing Viewpoints** provides students with contrasting primary sources to understand all sides of history.

Synthesize: Practice Knowledge and Skills

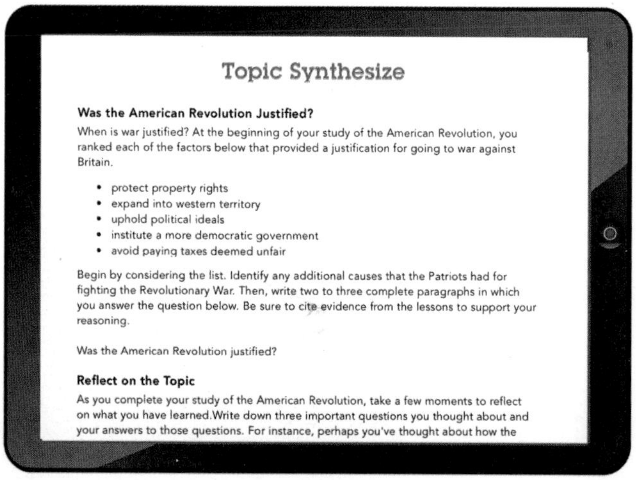

SYNTHESIZE!

In step three of the Mastery System, pause to reflect on what you learn and revisit an essential question.

Demonstrate: Show Understanding

DEMONSTRATE! The final step of *Interactive Social Studies* is to demonstrate understanding of the content.

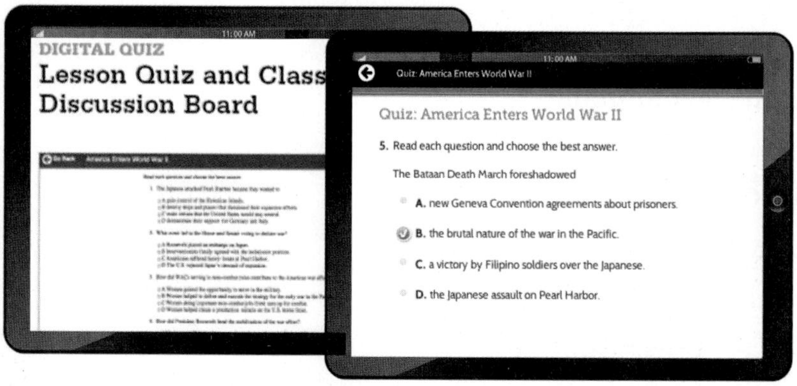

>> **Assessment:** At the end of each lesson and topic, demonstrate understanding through Lesson Quizzes, Topic Tests, and Topic Inquiry performance assessments. Topics Tests are available in three different content levels so educators can reach all students.

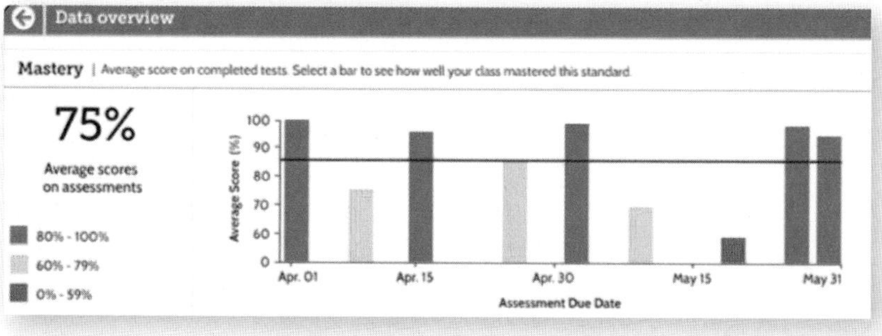

>> **Class and Data** features on Realize make it easy to use students' data to show if time is needed to re-teach or move ahead.

Table of Contents

Topic 1 America's Cultural Roots (Prehistory–1783) 1

Topic 2 England's American Colonies (1607–1754) 42

GO ONLINE to access the eText, videos, Interactive Primary Sources, Biographies, and Project Imagine immersives designed to bring key moments in history to life.

Topic 3 The American Revolution (1754–1783) 88

Topic 4 Establishing the New Nation (1781–1789) 130

Table of Contents

Topic 5 The Early Republic (1789–1840) 162

Topic 6 Reshaping America in the Early 1800s (1800–1860) 222

GO ONLINE to access the eText, videos, Interactive Primary Sources, Biographies, and Project Imagine immersives designed to bring key moments in history to life.

Topic 7 Sectional Divisions and Civil War (1846–1865) 270

Topic 8 Reconstruction (1865–1877) 334

Table of Contents

Topic 9 Industry and Immigration (1865–1914) 372

Topic 10 Challenges in the Late 1800s (1865–1900) 426

GO ONLINE to access the eText, videos, Interactive Primary Sources, Biographies, and Project Imagine immersives designed to bring key moments in history to life.

Table of Contents

Topic 12 World War I and the 1920s (1914–1929) 534

GO ONLINE to access the eText, videos, Interactive Primary Sources, Biographies, and Project Imagine immersives designed to bring key moments in history to life.

Topic 13 The Great Depression and the New Deal (1928–1941) 610

Table of Contents

Topic 14 World War II (1931–1945) 670

Topic 15 Postwar America (1945–1960) 750

GO ONLINE to access the eText, videos, Interactive Primary Sources, Biographies, and Project Imagine immersives designed to bring key moments in history to life.

Table of Contents

GO ONLINE to access the eText, videos, Interactive Primary Sources, Biographies, and Project Imagine immersives designed to bring key moments in history to life.

Topic 19 America in the 1980s and 1990s (1980–1999) 954

Topic 20 America in the Twenty-First Century (2000–Today) 1006

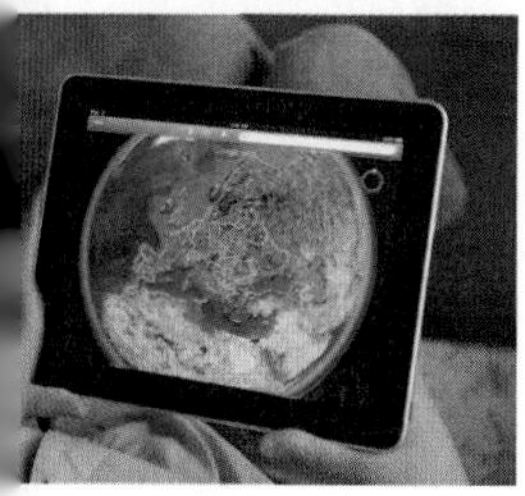

Print Resources

Primary Source Excerpts

GO ONLINE to access the eText, videos, Interactive Primary Sources, Biographies, and Project Imagine immersives designed to bring key moments in history to life.

Print Resources

GO ONLINE to access the eText, videos, Interactive Primary Sources, Biographies, and Project Imagine immersives designed to bring key moments in history to life.

Print Resources

Timelines

GO ONLINE to access the eText, videos, Interactive Primary Sources, Biographies, and Project Imagine immersives designed to bring key moments in history to life.

Maps

Print Resources

GO ONLINE to access the eText, videos, Interactive Primary Sources, Biographies, and Project Imagine immersives designed to bring key moments in history to life.

Charts, Graphs, and Tables

Print Resources

GO ONLINE to access the eText, videos, Interactive Primary Sources, Biographies, and Project Imagine immersives designed to bring key moments in history to life.

Infographics

GO ONLINE to access the eText, videos, Interactive Primary Sources, Biographies, and Project Imagine immersives designed to bring key moments in history to life.

Digital Resources

project Imagine GO ONLINE for immersive experiences and rich primary sources.

Immigration, 1870–1914
- Decision Tree: Give Your Son A Better Life
- 360° Exploration: Explore Immigrant Life in New York City
- Interactive Map and Timeline: Build a New Life
- Opinion Poll: Should You Stay or Leave?
- Role Play: Define Your Identity as an American

The 1920s
- Decision Tree: Enjoy the Roaring 20s
- Role Play: Adjust to Changing Times for Women
- Interactive Map and Timeline: Explore African American Life
- Opinion Poll: Should Prohibition be Repealed?

The Great Depression and the New Deal
- Role Play: Survive the Great Depression
- Interactive Map and Timeline: Experience the Dust Bowl
- Decision Tree: Work to End the Depression
- 360° Exploration: See the New Deal in Action
- Opinion Poll: Does FDR Deserve a Third Term?

World War II
- Role Play: Join the War Effort
- Interactive Map and Timeline: Follow News from the Battle Front
- Decision Tree: Do Your Part on the Home Front
- 360° Exploration: Tour a Japanese American Incarceration Camp
- Opinion Poll: Advise Truman on the Atomic Bomb

The Civil Rights Movement
- Interactive Map and Timeline: Witness Milestones in the Civil Rights Movement
- Role Play: Work as an Investigative Reporter
- 360° Exploration: Travel to Civil Rights Landmarks
- Decision Tree: Choose Your Path During Freedom Summer
- Opinion Poll: Weigh the Evidence on the Black Power Movement

The Vietnam War
- Interactive Map and Timeline: Explore America's Road to War in Vietnam
- 360° Exploration: Witness the Fighting in Vietnam
- Decision Tree: Investigate how the War Divided Americans
- Opinion Poll: Do You Support Nixon's Strategy in Vietnam?
- Role Play: Experience the Legacy of the Vietnam War

Interactivities

Interactive 3-D Models
- Seafaring Techniques, Topic 1 Lesson 3
- Plymouth Plantation, Topic 2 Lesson 2
- Early 19th Century Textile Mill, Topic 5 Lesson 4
- The Cotton Gin, Topic 5 Lesson 5
- The Covered Wagon, Topic 6 Lesson 1
- The Battle at Gettysburg, Topic 7 Lesson 6
- Living in a Tenement, Topic 9 Lesson 5
- Nineteenth-Century Sod House, Topic 10 Lesson 2
- Trench Warfare, Topic 12 Lesson 1
- The B-24 Liberator, Topic 14 Lesson 4
- Space Shuttle Science, Topic 19 Lesson 2
- The World Today, Topic 20 Lesson 4

Interactive Before and After
- The Growth of San Francisco, Topic 6 Lesson 3
- Atlanta Reconstructed, Topic 8 Lesson 2
- Hiroshima, Topic 14 Lesson 6
- Suburban Sprawl—1950s to the Present, Topic 15 Lesson 6
- Johnson's Great Society, Topic 16 Lesson 5

Interactive Cartoons
- The Horse "America" Throwing His Master, Topic 3 Lesson 2
- The Embargo Act of 1807, Topic 5 Lesson 2
- Forcing Slavery Down the Throat of a Freesoiler, Topic 7 Lesson 2

GO ONLINE to access the eText, videos, Interactive Primary Sources, Biographies, and Project Imagine immersives designed to bring key moments in history to life.

- Worse Than Slavery, Topic 8 Lesson 3
- A Different Kind of Knight, Topic 9 Lesson 3
- Teapot Dome Scandal, Topic 12 Lesson 5

Interactive Charts

- Spanish and French Exploration and Colonization of North America, Topic 1 Lesson 4
- Colonial Conflicts in New England, Topic 2 Lesson 2
- Advantages and Disadvantages of the British and Colonists, Topic 3 Lesson 4
- Trade with Great Britain, Topic 4 Lesson 1
- The Great Compromise, Topic 4 Lesson 2
- The Federal System, Topic 4 Lesson 3
- Viewpoints on Ratification, Topic 4 Lesson 3
- Federalists versus Republicans, Topic 5 Lesson 1
- Key Cases of the Marshall Court, Topic 5 Lesson 6
- Andrew Jackson versus the World, Topic 5 Lesson 7
- The Spanish Borderlands, Topic 6 Lesson 1
- Compare Viewpoints: The Annexation of Texas, Topic 6 Lesson 2
- Analyzing Primary Sources on Women's Rights, Topic 6 Lesson 6
- Causes and Effects of Sectional Issues in the 1800s, Topic 7 Lesson 1
- South Carolina Declaration of Causes of Secession, Topic 7 Lesson 3
- Causes and Effects of the Civil War, Topic 7 Lesson 7
- Comparing Viewpoints on Reconstruction, Topic 8 Lesson 1
- The Cycle of Poverty, Topic 8 Lesson 2
- The Courts, Business, and Labor Regulation, Topic 9 Lesson 2
- Major Strikes of the Late 1800s, Topic 9 Lesson 3
- Immigration, 1870–1910, Topic 9 Lesson 4
- Gold and Silver Rushes, Topic 10 Lesson 2
- Gridlock in Congress in the Late 1800s, Topic 10 Lesson 3
- The Populist Party, Topic 10 Lesson 4
- Roosevelt and Wilson, Topic 11 Lesson 4
- Reasons for American Expansionism, Topic 11 Lesson 5
- Points of View on American Expansionism, Topic 11 Lesson 6
- American Attitudes Toward Involvement in World War I, Topic 12 Lesson 1
- The Great Migration, Topic 12 Lesson 2
- Should the U.S. Join the League of Nations?, Topic 12 Lesson 3
- Rural and Urban Life, Topic 12 Lesson 7
- Causes of the Great Depression, Topic 13 Lesson 1
- Evaluate the U.S. Economy in the 1920s, Topic 13 Lesson 1
- Left and Right Opposition to the New Deal, Topic 13 Lesson 4
- Roosevelt's Leadership, Topic 13 Lesson 5
- Jewish Populations in Europe, 1933–1950, Topic 14 Lesson 7
- Experience the Cold War, Topic 15 Lesson 3
- Opposing Views on Affirmative Action, Topic 16 Lesson 3
- Challenges of Escalation, Topic 17 Lesson 2
- Doves and Hawks, Topic 17 Lesson 3
- Environmental Protection Versus Economic Development, Topic 18 Lesson 4
- Key Events of the Watergate Scandal, Topic 18 Lesson 5
- The Supreme Court and Social Issues of the 1970s, Topic 18 Lesson 6
- Two Views—Liberal and Conservative, Topic 19 Lesson 1
- Identifying Political Views, Topic 19 Lesson 2
- Reagan's Leadership, Topic 19 Lesson 3
- Checks and Balances in Action, Topic 19 Lesson 5
- Long-Term Health of Entitlements, Topic 20 Lesson 1
- Checks and Balances Among Branches of Government, Topic 20 Lesson 2
- Presidential Election of 2008, Topic 20 Lesson 2
- COVID-19 Comes to the United States, Topic 20 Lesson 3

Interactive Galleries

- Artifacts of West African Kingdoms, Topic 1 Lesson 2
- The Renaissance, Topic 1 Lesson 3
- Effects of American Silver and Gold on the Spanish Economy, Topic 1 Lesson 4
- James Oglethorpe and the Founding of Georgia, Topic 2 Lesson 1
- Problems Faced by Jamestown, Topic 2 Lesson 1
- Puritan Values and Society, Topic 2 Lesson 2
- The Middle Colonies, Topic 2 Lesson 3
- Africans Become African Americans, Topic 2 Lesson 4
- A New Kind of Society, Topic 2 Lesson 5
- Freedom of the Press, Topic 2 Lesson 6
- Roots of Democracy, Topic 2 Lesson 6
- Important People of the American Revolution, Topic 3 Lesson 2
- Thomas Paine and Common Sense, Topic 3 Lesson 3

Digital Resources

- The Northwest Territory, Topic 4 Lesson 1
- Delegates of the Constitutional Convention, Topic 4 Lesson 2
- On the Trail with Lewis and Clark, Topic 5 Lesson 2
- The Closed World of the Plantation, Topic 5 Lesson 5
- American Art of the Mid-1800s, Topic 5 Lesson 6
- The California Gold Rush, Topic 6 Lesson 3
- Mid-Nineteenth Century Reform Movements, Topic 6 Lesson 4
- Religious and Spiritual Movements of the Early 1800s, Topic 6 Lesson 4
- Resisting Slavery, Topic 6 Lesson 5
- The Movement to End Slavery, Topic 6 Lesson 5
- African Americans and the Civil War, Topic 7 Lesson 4
- The Road to the Emancipation Proclamation, Topic 7 Lesson 4
- New Ways of Waging War, Topic 7 Lesson 5
- Sherman's March to the Sea, Topic 7 Lesson 6
- Lincoln's Assassination, Topic 7 Lesson 7
- Reconstruction-Era Political Groups, Topic 8 Lesson 2
- Major Inventions in the 1800s, Topic 9 Lesson 1
- Captains of Industry, Topic 9 Lesson 2
- Contributions of Immigrants to American Culture, Topic 9 Lesson 4
- Growth of Cities, 1870–1900, Topic 9 Lesson 5
- Leisure Activities at the Turn of the Century, Topic 9 Lesson 6
- Mexican and Chinese American Contributions to the West, Topic 10 Lesson 2
- Thomas Nast, Topic 10 Lesson 3
- Legacy of Populism, Topic 10 Lesson 4
- The Triangle Shirtwaist Factory Fire, Topic 11 Lesson 1
- Key Figures in the Women's Rights Movement, 1848–1920, Topic 11 Lesson 2
- Reform Groups Today, Topic 11 Lesson 3
- National Land Conservation, Topic 11 Lesson 4
- U.S. Economic Expansion in Hawaii, Topic 11 Lesson 5
- Media and the Spanish-American War, Topic 11 Lesson 6
- The Panama Canal, Topic 11 Lesson 7
- Constitutional Issues During World War I, Topic 12 Lesson 2
- Standard of Living in the 1920s, Topic 12 Lesson 4
- The Prohibition Era, Topic 12 Lesson 6
- Key Figures of the Harlem Renaissance, Topic 12 Lesson 8
- Effects of the Dust Bowl, Topic 13 Lesson 2
- Life During the Great Depression, Topic 13 Lesson 2
- Enduring New Deal Programs, Topic 13 Lesson 3
- Entertainment in the Depression Era, Topic 13 Lesson 6
- The New Deal and Culture, Topic 13 Lesson 6
- Characteristics of Totalitarianism, Topic 14 Lesson 1
- Life Under Nazi Rule, Topic 14 Lesson 1
- Battle of Britain, Topic 14 Lesson 2
- Norman Rockwell's Four Freedoms, Topic 14 Lesson 2
- Americans Mobilize for War, Topic 14 Lesson 3
- The War in North Africa, Topic 14 Lesson 4
- The War in the North Atlantic, Topic 14 Lesson 4
- African Americans and World War II, Topic 14 Lesson 5
- The Experience of Japanese Internment, Topic 14 Lesson 5
- D-Day, Topic 14 Lesson 6
- Inside a Nazi Concentration Camp, Topic 14 Lesson 7
- The Nuremberg Trials: What is a War Crime?, Topic 14 Lesson 8
- World War II and the U.S. Economy, Topic 14 Lesson 8
- The Berlin Airlift Saves a City, Topic 15 Lesson 1
- Cold War Technological Advance, Topic 15 Lesson 3
- Red Scare Culture, Topic 15 Lesson 4
- Postwar Entrepreneurs, Topic 15 Lesson 5
- Medical Advances of the Postwar Era, Topic 15 Lesson 6
- The Spread of Rock-and-Roll, Topic 15 Lesson 7
- Fighting for Justice, Topic 16 Lesson 1
- Nonviolent Protest Through History, Topic 16 Lesson 1
- Separate but Equal?, Topic 16 Lesson 1
- Nonviolent Strategies in the Civil Rights Movement, Topic 16 Lesson 2
- The Election of 1960, Topic 16 Lesson 4
- The Warren Court, Topic 16 Lesson 5
- America Enters Vietnam, Topic 17 Lesson 1
- The Living Room War, Topic 17 Lesson 3
- Remembering Vietnam Veterans, Topic 17 Lesson 4
- Culture of the Counterculture, Topic 18 Lesson 1
- Generation Gap Issues, Topic 18 Lesson 1
- Case Study—Grape Boycott, Topic 18 Lesson 3
- The Fight for American Indian Rights, Topic 18 Lesson 3
- The Fall of Communism in Europe, Topic 19 Lesson 3
- Evaluate the U.S. Role in the World Bank, Topic 19 Lesson 4

GO ONLINE to access the eText, videos, Interactive Primary Sources, Biographies, and Project Imagine immersives designed to bring key moments in history to life.

- The Persian Gulf War, 1991, Topic 19 Lesson 4
- The Gun Debate, Topic 19 Lesson 5
- Fighting al Qaeda Worldwide, Topic 20 Lesson 2
- Efforts to Manage the Environment, Topic 20 Lesson 4

Interactive Graphs

- Immigration to the United States, 1820–1850, Topic 5 Lesson 5
- 1950s Prosperity Sparks Growth, Topic 15 Lesson 5
- Women in the Workforce, Topic 18 Lesson 2

Interactive Illustrations

- The Lowell System, Topic 5 Lesson 4
- Hardships on the Home Front, Topic 7 Lesson 5
- Turn-of-the-Century Department Store, Topic 9 Lesson 6
- Goals of Social Progressivism, Topic 11 Lesson 1
- Ford's Innovation—The Assembly Line, Topic 12 Lesson 4
- Technology Changes Home Life, Topic 12 Lesson 7
- Free Enterprise Spreads Technological Innovation, Topic 19 Lesson 5

Interactive Maps

- Diversity of the 13 Colonies, Topic 2 Lesson 4
- Comparing the English Colonies, Topic 2 Lesson 5
- Battles of the French and Indian War, Topic 3 Lesson 1
- North America, 1775–1783, Topic 3 Lesson 4
- The War of 1812, Topic 5 Lesson 3
- Canals, Roads, and Railroads, 1840–1850, Topic 5 Lesson 4
- Trails to the West, Topic 6 Lesson 1
- Growth of the United States, 1783–1853, Topic 6 Lesson 2
- The Underground Railroad, Topic 7 Lesson 1
- Territories Open to Slavery, Topic 7 Lesson 2
- Key Turning Points of the Civil War, Topic 7 Lesson 6
- Railroads Spur Economic Development in Cities, Topic 9 Lesson 1
- Major Indian Wars, 1861–1886, Topic 10 Lesson 1
- U.S. Interventions in Latin America, Topic 11 Lesson 7
- Key Battles Fought by Americans in World War I, Topic 12 Lesson 3
- PWA & WPA Projects, Topic 13 Lesson 5
- Military Action, 1930–1939, Topic 14 Lesson 1
- Axis Aggression in Europe, 1936–1941, Topic 14 Lesson 2
- Japanese Aggression, December 1941–June 1942, Topic 14 Lesson 3
- Surprise Attack on Pearl Harbor, Topic 14 Lesson 3
- World War II in Europe, 1942–1945, Topic 14 Lesson 6
- World War II in the Pacific 1942–1945, Topic 14 Lesson 6
- Europe in 1942 and 1950, Topic 14 Lesson 8
- Phases of the Korean War, Topic 15 Lesson 2
- Global Cold War, 1946–1956, Topic 15 Lesson 3
- Demographic Trends of the 1950s, Topic 15 Lesson 7
- Violent Conflicts During the Civil Rights Era, Topic 16 Lesson 3
- Superfund Sites, Topic 18 Lesson 4
- Nixon's Foreign Policy, Topic 18 Lesson 5
- U.S. Foreign Affairs under George H.W. Bush, Topic 19 Lesson 4
- United States and the Middle East, 2001–2010, Topic 20 Lesson 1

Interactive Timelines

- American Indian Cultures, Topic 1 Lesson 1
- Turning Points of the American Revolution, Topic 3 Lesson 4
- The Trail of Tears, Topic 5 Lesson 7
- The Early Women's Rights Movement, Topic 6 Lesson 6
- Early Battles of the Civil War, Topic 7 Lesson 3
- Legislative Acts Affecting Native Americans, Topic 10 Lesson 1
- The Women's Rights Movement, 1848-Today, Topic 11 Lesson 2
- African American Reform Movement, 1895–1915, Topic 11 Lesson 3
- Buildup to War, Topic 12 Lesson 1
- Anti-Immigration Sentiment in the 1920s, Topic 12 Lesson 6
- African American Achievers of the 1920s, Topic 12 Lesson 8
- Milestones in Social Security, Topic 13 Lesson 4
- U.S. Response to Soviet Aggression, Topic 15 Lesson 1
- Red Scare and the Government, Topic 15 Lesson 4
- Riding for Freedom, Topic 16 Lesson 2
- Confronting Cuba, Topic 17 Lesson 1
- 1968: The Whole World Is Watching, Topic 17 Lesson 3
- Final Years of the Vietnam War, Topic 17 Lesson 4
- The Fight for the Equal Rights Amendment, Topic 18 Lesson 2
- Iran Hostage Crisis, Topic 18 Lesson 6
- Presidential Elections, 1964–1980, Topic 19 Lesson 1

Digital Resources

Core Concepts

Culture
- What Is Culture?
- Families and Societies
- Language
- Religion
- The Arts
- Cultural Diffusion and Change
- Science and Technology

Geography
- The Study of Earth
- Geography's Five Themes
- Ways to Show Earth's Surface
- Understanding Maps
- Earth in Space
- Time and Earth's Rotation
- Forces on Earth's Surface
- Forces Inside Earth
- Climate and Weather
- Temperature
- Water and Climate
- Air Circulation and Precipitation
- Types of Climate
- Ecosystems
- Environment and Resources
- Land Use
- People's Impact on the Environment
- Population
- Migration
- Urbanization

Government
- Foundations of Government
- Political Systems
- Political Structures
- Conflict and Cooperation
- Principles of American Government

Civics
- Citizenship and Naturalization
- Responsibilities of Citizens
- Traits of Good Citizens
- Addressing Societal Problems
- Accuracy in Civic Life

History
- How Do Historians Study History?
- Measuring Time
- Historical Sources
- Archaeology and Other Sources
- Historical Maps

Economics
- Economics Basics
- Economic Process
- Economic Systems
- Economic Development
- Trade
- Money Management

Personal Finance
- Your Fiscal Fitness: An Introduction
- Budgeting
- Checking
- Investments
- Savings and Retirement
- Credit and Debt
- Risk Management
- Consumer Smarts
- After High School
- Taxes and Income

Landmark Supreme Court Cases

- *Korematsu* v. *United States*
- *Marbury* v. *Madison*
- *McCulloch* v. *Maryland*
- *Gibbons* v. *Ogden*
- *Worcester* v. *Georgia*
- *Dred Scott* v. *Sandford*
- *Plessy* v. *Ferguson*
- *Schenck* v. *United States*
- *Brown* v. *Board of Education*
- *Engel* v. *Vitale*
- *Sweatt* v. *Painter*
- *Mapp* v. *Ohio*
- *Hernandez* v. *Texas*
- *Gideon* v. *Wainwright*
- *Wisconsin* v. *Yoder*
- *Miranda* v. *Arizona*
- *White* v. *Regester*
- *Tinker* v. *Des Moines School District*
- *Roe* v. *Wade*
- *Baker* v. *Carr*
- *Grutter* v. *Bollinger*
- *Edgewood* v. *Kirby*
- *Texas* v. *Johnson*
- *National Federation of Independent Businesses et al.* v. *Sebelius et al.*
- *Mendez* v. *Westminster* and *Delgado* v. *Bastrop*

GO ONLINE to access the eText, videos, Interactive Primary Sources, Biographies, and Project Imagine immersives designed to bring key moments in history to life.

Selected Interactive Primary Sources

See the course for a full list of Interactive Primary Sources.

- The Magna Carta
- The Destruction of the Indies, Bartolomé de Las Casas
- Mayflower Compact
- English Petition of Right
- English Bill of Rights
- Two Treatises of Government, John Locke
- The Spirit of Laws, Baron de Montesquieu
- The Social Contract, Jean-Jacques Rousseau
- The Interesting Narrative of the Life of Olaudah Equiano
- "Give Me Liberty or Give Me Death," Patrick Henry
- "Remember the Ladies," Abigail Adams
- Common Sense, Thomas Paine
- The Wealth of Nations, Adam Smith
- Declaration of Independence
- Virginia Declaration of Rights
- Virginia Statute for Religious Freedom, Thomas Jefferson
- "To His Excellency, General Washington," Phillis Wheatley
- Articles of Confederation
- Anti-Federalist Papers
- The Federalist No. 10, James Madison
- The Federalist No. 39, James Madison
- The Federalist No. 51
- The Federalist No. 78, Alexander Hamilton
- Northwest Ordinance
- Iroquois Constitution
- Declaration of the Rights of Man and the Citizen
- Farewell Address, George Washington
- Debate Over Nullification, Webster and Calhoun
- Democracy in America, Alexis de Tocqueville
- 1836 Victory or Death Letter from the Alamo, Travis
- Texas Declaration of Independence
- Declaration of Sentiments and Resolutions
- The Communist Manifesto: Karl Marx and Friedrich Engels
- "Ain't I a Woman?," Sojourner Truth
- Uncle Tom's Cabin, Harriet Beecher Stowe
- "A House Divided," Abraham Lincoln
- First Inaugural Address, Abraham Lincoln
- Declaration of Causes: February 2, 1861
- Emancipation Proclamation, Abraham Lincoln
- Gettysburg Address, Abraham Lincoln
- Second Inaugural Address, Abraham Lincoln
- Red Cloud's Speech at Cooper Union, 1870
- "I Will Fight No More Forever," Chief Joseph
- How the Other Half Lives, Jacob Riis
- The Pledge of Allegiance
- Preamble to the Platform of the Populist Party
- Atlanta Exposition Address, Booker T. Washington
- "The White Man's Burden," Rudyard Kipling
- The Jungle, Upton Sinclair
- Hind Swaraj, Mohandas Gandhi
- The Fourteen Points, Woodrow Wilson
- Two Poems, Langston Hughes
- All Quiet on the Western Front, Erich Maria
- The Revolution Betrayed, Leon Trotsky
- Four Freedoms, Franklin D. Roosevelt
- Anne Frank: The Diary of a Young Girl, Anne Frank
- Charter of the United Nations
- "The Sinews of Peace," Winston Churchill
- Universal Declaration of Human Rights
- Autobiography, Kwame Nkrumah
- Inaugural Address, John F. Kennedy
- Silent Spring, Rachel Carson
- "I Have a Dream," Martin Luther King, Jr.
- "Letter From Birmingham Jail," Martin Luther King, Jr.
- State of the Union address, Lyndon Johnson
- State of the Union address, Gerald Ford
- "Tear Down This Wall," Ronald Reagan
- State of the Union address, William Jefferson Clinton
- "Glory and Hope," Nelson Mandela
- A Thousand Points of Light, George H. W. Bush
- State of the Union address, George W. Bush
- 16th Birthday Speech at the United Nations, Malala Yousafzai
- COVID-19 Briefing, Dr. Tedros Adhanom Ghebreyesus
- Speech at the United Nations Climate Action Summit, Greta Thunberg

Digital Resources

Selected Biographies

See the course for a full list of Biographies.

- Abigail Adams
- John Adams
- John Quincy Adams
- Samuel Adams
- Susan B. Anthony
- James Armistead
- Crispus Attucks
- Moses Austin
- Stephen F. Austin
- James A. Baker III
- Emily Greene Balch
- William Blackstone
- Simón Bolívar
- Napoleon Bonaparte
- Chief Bowles
- Omar Bradley
- John Brown
- John C. Calhoun
- Andrew Carnegie
- César Chávez
- Wentworth Cheswell
- George Childress
- Winston Churchill
- Henry Clay
- Bill Clinton
- Jefferson Davis
- Martin De León
- Green DeWitt
- Frederick Douglass
- Dwight Eisenhower
- James Fannin
- James L. Farmer, Jr.
- Charles Finney
- Benjamin Franklin
- Milton Friedman
- Betty Friedan
- Margaret Fuller
- Bernardo de Gálvez
- Hector P. Garcia
- John Nance Garner
- William Lloyd Garrison
- King George III
- William Gladstone
- Henry B. González
- Raul A. Gonzalez, Jr.
- Mikhail Gorbachev
- William Goyens
- Ulysses S. Grant
- José Gutiérrez de Lara
- Alexander Hamilton
- Hammurabi
- Warren Harding
- Vaclav Havel
- Friedrich Hayek
- Jack Coffee Hays
- Patrick Henry
- Adolf Hitler
- Oveta Culp Hobby
- James Hogg
- Sam Houston
- Kay Bailey Hutchison
- Andrew Jackson
- John Jay
- Thomas Jefferson
- Lyndon B. Johnson
- Anson Jones
- Barbara Jordan
- Justinian
- John F. Kennedy
- John Maynard Keynes
- Martin Luther King, Jr.
- Marquis de Lafayette
- Mirabeau B. Lamar
- Robert E. Lee
- Abraham Lincoln
- John Locke
- Niccolò Machiavelli
- James Madison
- John Marshall
- George Marshall
- Karl Marx
- George Mason
- Mary Maverick
- Jane McCallum
- Joseph McCarthy
- James Monroe
- Charles de Montesquieu
- Dwight L. Moody
- Edwin W. Moore
- Gouverneur Morris
- Moses
- Lucretia Mott
- Benito Mussolini
- José Antonio Navarro
- Chester A. Nimitz
- Richard M. Nixon
- Barack Obama
- Sandra Day O'Connor
- Thomas Paine
- Quanah Parker
- Charley Parkhurst
- Rosa Parks
- George Patton
- John J. Pershing
- John Paul II
- Robert Purvis
- Sam Rayburn
- Ronald Reagan
- Charles Remond
- Hiram Rhodes Revels
- Harriet Hanson Robinson
- John D. Rockefeller
- Franklin D. Roosevelt
- Theodore Roosevelt
- Lawrence Sullivan Ross
- Haym Soloman
- Antonio Lopez de Santa Anna
- Phyllis Schlafly
- Erasmo Seguín
- Juan N. Seguín
- Roger Sherman
- Adam Smith
- Alexander Solzhenitsyn
- Joseph Stalin
- Elizabeth Cady Stanton
- William Graham Sumner
- Billy Sunday
- Raymond L. Telles
- Alexis de Tocqueville
- Hideki Tojo
- William B. Travis
- Harry Truman
- Sojourner Truth
- Lech Walesa
- Mercy Otis Warren
- George Washington
- Daniel Webster
- Theodore Weld
- Lulu Belle Madison White
- William Wilberforce
- Laura Ingalls Wilder
- James Wilson
- Woodrow Wilson
- Lorenzo de Zavala
- Mao Zedong

GO ONLINE to access the eText, videos, Interactive Primary Sources, Biographies, and Project Imagine immersives designed to bring key moments in history to life.

21st Century Skills

- Identify Main Ideas and Details
- Set a Purpose for Reading
- Use Context Clues
- Analyze Cause and Effect
- Categorize
- Compare and Contrast
- Draw Conclusions
- Draw Inferences
- Generalize
- Make Decisions
- Make Predictions
- Sequence
- Solve Problems
- Summarize
- Analyze Media Content
- Analyze Primary and Secondary Sources
- Compare Viewpoints
- Distinguish Between Fact and Opinion
- Identify Bias
- Analyze Data and Models
- Analyze Images
- Analyze Political Cartoons
- Create Charts and Maps
- Create Databases
- Read Charts, Graphs, and Tables
- Read Physical Maps
- Read Political Maps
- Read Special-Purpose Maps
- Use Parts of a Map
- Ask Questions
- Avoid Plagiarism
- Create a Research Hypothesis
- Evaluate Web Sites
- Identify Evidence
- Identify Trends
- Interpret Sources
- Search for Information on the Internet
- Synthesize
- Take Effective Notes
- Develop a Clear Thesis
- Organize Your Ideas
- Support Ideas With Evidence
- Evaluate Existing Arguments
- Consider & Counter Opposing Arguments
- Give an Effective Presentation
- Participate in a Discussion or Debate
- Publish Your Work
- Write a Journal Entry
- Write an Essay
- Share Responsibility
- Compromise
- Develop Cultural Awareness
- Generate New Ideas
- Innovate
- Make a Difference
- Work in Teams
- Being an Informed Citizen
- Paying Taxes
- Political Participation
- Serving on a Jury
- Voting

Atlas

- The United States: Political
- The United States: Physical
- The World Political
- Africa: Political
- Africa: Physical
- Asia: Political
- Asia: Physical
- Europe: Political
- Europe: Physical
- North and South America: Political
- North and South America: Physical
- Australia, New Zealand, and Oceania: Political-Physical
- The Arctic: Physical
- Antarctica: Physical

Celebrate Freedom

DECLARATION OF INDEPENDENCE

When it issued the Declaration of Independence in 1776, the Continental Congress did more than announce the separation of the 13 American colonies from Great Britain. It also summed up the most basic principles that came to underlie American government. This section, the preamble, is sometimes called the "social contract" section. You can read the words at right.

The Declaration, largely written by Thomas Jefferson, is one of the most important documents in the history of the world. It not only declared the independence of a colony from its mother country—thereby setting a precedent for other oppressed peoples around the world to do the same—it also established the first government of, by, and for the people.

The ideas expressed in the Declaration of Independence also had a profound effect on later developments in American history. You will notice the relationship of the ideas behind the Declaration of Independence to the American Revolution, the writing of the U.S. Constitution, including the Bill of Rights, and the movements to end slavery and to give women the right to vote. You'll see how the United States became a nation of immigrants, with its rich diversity of people, and the ways this development relates to the ideas of the Declaration of Independence.

Read the first three paragraphs of the Declaration of Independence. Then recite words from the Declaration of Independence quoted at the right. Consider their meaning and then answer these questions.

"We hold these Truths *to be self-evident, that all Men are created equal, that they are endowed by their Creator with certain unalienable Rights, that among these are Life, Liberty and the Pursuit of Happiness. That to secure these Rights, Governments are instituted among Men, deriving their just Powers from the Consent of the Governed."*

—Declaration of Independence

ASSESSMENT

1. **Identify Central Idea** According to the preamble (right) of the Declaration of Independence, why do people form governments?
2. **Predict** What concepts in this passage would eventually be used to justify ending the practice of slavery in the United States?
3. **Apply Information** Identify two ways that your federal, state, or local government protect the rights to life, liberty, or the pursuit of happiness.

CONSTITUTION DAY ASSEMBLY

September 17 is Constitution Day, and your school may hold an assembly or other celebration in honor of the day. As part of this celebration, your teacher may ask you to participate in planning and holding a Constitution Day assembly.

Organize As a class, create the basic plan for your assembly. Discuss the following:

1. When and where should the assembly take place?
2. How long should it take? Should you plan on a short program taking a single class period or a longer program?
3. Who should be involved? Will other classes or other grades take part? Will you invite outsiders, such as parents or people from the community?
4. What activities might be included?

Plan After your discussion, divide the class into committees to complete jobs such as getting permission from the school administration, preparing a program, inviting any guests, advertising the plan beforehand, and blogging about it afterward.

Give thought to the types of activities that might be included in the assembly. You might invite a guest speaker from your community. You might run an essay contest among students and have the winners read their essays during the assembly. Some students might prepare a video presentation about the Bill of Rights. Others might write and perform a skit about what the Declaration of Independence or U.S. Constitution mean to them.

Consider asking those who present speeches, essays, videos, or skits to address this question: What are the key tenets or principles of American democracy?

For additional support, go to the Social Studies Resource Center on Realize and refer to the Constitution Day Resources, including the Celebrate Freedom documents and the Declaration of Independence.

Communicate Present your Constitution Day assembly. After the assembly is over, discuss the event with the class. Ask yourselves questions such as these:

1. How well was the assembly planned and organized? What improvements could we have made?
2. How would you rate each of the presentations or other activities of the assembly?
3. Was the audience engaged?
4. How effectively did the class work together?

Your school may hold a Constitution Day assembly like the one shown here.

Primary Source Index by State

Please Note: This index does not include hundreds of primary sources included in the program that are considered national in nature, such as magazine articles, nationally popular songs, and national speeches.

Key to Location of Sources

IPS (Interactive Primary Sources) These sources can be found in the Interactive Primary Sources folder on the online course table of contents.

PI (Project Imagine Sources) These sources can be found in two ways:

1. Enter the Source Title in the Search Tool function on Realize.

2. From the online course table of contents, open the Project Imagine folder and then the Primary Source Library folder.

PSRG (Primary Source Reading Guide Sources) These sources can be found in the Primary Source Reading Guide student workbook.

Q (Quest Inquiry Sources) These sources can be found in the Quest Inquiry folder for the designated Topic.

ST (Student Text Sources) These sources can be found in the indicated Topic and Lesson within the print student text or in the online eText.

Type	Source Title	Date	Location of Source
Alabama			
Memoir	Memoirs of Mrs. Clay, of Alabama, Covering Social and Political Life in Washington and the South, 1853–66	Published 1904	**PSRG** Topic 7, Source 2
Photograph	Little Nettie Photograph, Alabama Canning Co., Bayou La Batre, by Lewis Hine	February 1911	**PI** Immigration, Build a New Life, 1910
Sheet Music	W.C. Handy, The St. Louis Blues	1914	**PI** Immigration, Define Your Identity as an American, Chloe
Photograph	Alabama textile worker	early 1900s	**ST** Topic 9, Lesson 1
Data	Education Infographic, Getting an Education, early 1900s	early 1900s	**PI** The 1920s, Adjust to Changing Times for Women, Ada
Photograph	Tuskegee University, Tuskegee	no date	**PI** The 1920s, Adjust to Changing Times for Women, Ada
Newspaper Article	Voting Rights Testimony, “Charges of Negro Stir Committee,” *Evening Star,* Washington, D.C.	December 29, 1920	**PI** The 1920s, Explore African American Life, Fighting Back
Video	Tuskegee Institute Video, Tuskegee Institute Movable School Instruction Video	1921	**PI** The 1920s, Adjust to Changing Times for Women, Ada
Photograph	Nine African American young men, known as “the Scottsboro Boys” in the Jefferson County jail, Birmingham, Alabama	March 4, 1931	**PI** The Great Depression and the New Deal, Survive the Great Depression, Clarence
Letter	Child Labor Letter, from Mrs. David Smoot to Alabama Governor Benjamin Miller	July 13, 1933	**PI** The Great Depression and the New Deal, Work to End the Depression
Photograph	Segregated Barbecue, F.M. Gay’s annual barbecue	Circa 1930–1941	**PI** Immigration, Define Your Identity as an American, Chloe
Newsreel	Bombing of Germany Video, African American pilots in the 332nd Fighter Group (Tuskegee Airmen)	unknown	**PI** World War II, Follow News from the Battle Front, 1944
Letter	From Jo Ann Robinson, Women’s Political Council President to Mayor W.J. Gayle, Montgomery, Alabama	May 21, 1954	**PSRG** Topic 16, Source 1; **PI** Civil Rights, Work as an Investigative Reporter, Montgomery Bus Boycott
Police Report	Rosa Parks’s Arrest, Police Report on Rosa Park’s Arrest, Montgomery	December 1955	**PSRG** Topic 16, Source 1; **PI** Civil Rights, Work as an Investigative Reporter, Montgomery Bus Boycott
Photograph	Rosa Parks boards a desegrated bus, Montgomery	December 26, 1956	**PSRG** Topic 16, Source 1; **PI** Civil Rights, Work as an Investigative Reporter, Montgomery Bus Boycott
Notes	Rosa Parks’s Arrest, Rosa Parks’s Notes after her arrest	undated	**PSRG** Topic 16, Source 1; **PI** Civil Rights, Work as an Investigative Reporter, Montgomery Bus Boycott
Photograph	Photograph of the Bus Boycott, African Americans walk to work instead of taking buses, Montgomery	1956	**PI** Civil Rights, Work as an Investigative Reporter, Montgomery Bus Boycott

Primary Source Index by State (continued)

Type	Source Title	Date	Location of Source
Photograph	Montgomery Bus Boycott Photograph, Carpooling During the Montgomery Bus Boycott, Alabama	February 1956	**PI** Civil Rights, Witness Milestones in the Civil Rights Movement, A Movement Begins
Photograph	Montgomery Bus Boycott Photograph, Dr. King being booked by city police after his arrest for his role in the boycott, Alabama	Feburary 1956	**PI** Civil Rights, Witness Milestones in the Civil Rights Movement, A Movement Begins
Photograph	Rosa Parks's Arrest, Parks is fingerprinted by police, Montgomery	February 22, 1956	**PI** Civil Rights, Work as an Investigative Reporter, Montgomery Bus Boycott
Speech	Speech Ending the Bus Boycott, "Statement on Ending the Bus Boycott," Martin Luther King, Jr.	December 20, 1956	**PI** Civil Rights, Work as an Investigative Reporter, Montgomery Bus Boycott
Article	"A Freedom Rider Speaks His Mind," Jimmy McDonald, *Freedomways*	Spring 1961	**PI** Civil Rights, Witness Milestones in the Civil Rights Movement, Early Campaigns
Photograph	Segregationists firebomb a freedom bus, Anniston, Alabama	May 14, 1961	**PI** Civil Rights, Work as an Investigative Reporter, Freedom Rides
Photograph	Freedom Riders Susan Hermann, Etta Simpson and Frederick Leonard rest at a bus station in Birmingham, Alabama	May 20, 1961	**PI** Civil Rights, Work as an Investigative Reporter, Freedom Rides
Photograph	Freedom Rider Jim Zwerg after being attacked by segregationists in Montgomery, Alabama	1961	**PI** Civil Rights, Work as an Investigative Reporter, Freedom Rides
Photograph	The National Guard escorts the Freedom Riders on their bus	1961	**PI** Civil Rights, Witness Milestones in the Civil Rights Movement, Early Campaigns
Photograph and Statue	Police Tactics, Civil Rights demonstrator attached by police dogs, Birmingham, Alabama	May 3, 1963	**PI** Civil Rights, Travel to Civil Rights Landmarks, Birmingham
Photograph	Peaceful demonstrators are sprayed by police with fire hoses, Birmingham, Alabama	May 3, 1963	**PI** Civil Rights, Witness Milestones in the Civil Rights Movement, Political Victories
Photograph	Children's Crusade, Police lead children to jail after their arrest, Birmingham, Alabama	May 4, 1963	**PI** Civil Rights, Travel to Civil Rights Landmarks, Birmingham
Newspaper Article	Birmingham Church Bombing Article, *The Troy Record,* Troy, New York	September 16, 1963	**PI** Civil Rights, Travel to Civil Rights Landmarks, Birmingham
Photographs	Birmingham Church Bombing Photographs, Birmingham, Alabama	various	**PI** Civil Rights, Travel to Civil Rights Landmarks, Birmingham
Video	Police Action Against Birmingham Campaign Protesters	1963	**PI** Civil Rights, Travel to Civil Rights Landmarks, Birmingham
Letter	"Letter from Birmingham Jail," Martin Luther King, Jr.	1963	**ST** Topic 16, Lesson 2; Topic 16 Primary Source feature; **IPS; PI** Civil Rights, Travel to Civl Rights Landmarks, Birmingham
Photograph	Alabama Governor George Wallace attempts to block the integration of the University of Alabama	1963	**ST** Topic 16, Lesson 2
Poster	Voting Poster, Alabama Voting Rights poster	no date	**PI** Civil Rights, Choose Your Path During Freedom Summer
Photograph	Demonstrators from the Student Nonviolent Coordinating Committee (SNCC) urge blacks to register to vote, Selma, Alabama	October 7, 1964	**PI** Civil Rights, Choose Your Path During Freedom Summer
Video	Bloody Sunday Footage, Associated Press	March 7, 1965	**PI** Civil Rights, Choose Your Path During Freedom Summer
Book	Excerpt from *Selma, Lord, Selma,* about a confrontation on the Edmund Pettus Bridge, Sheyann Webb	March 7, 1965	**ST** Topic 16, Lesson 3
Video	March Participants Footage, Interviews with Selma to Montgomery Marchers	March 23, 1965	**PI** Civil Rights, Witness Milestones in the Civil Rights Movement, Political Victories

Primary Source Index by State (continued)

Type	Source Title	Date	Location of Source
Photograph	Selma to Montgomery civil rights march	1965	**PSRG** Topic 16, Source 4
Photograph	Marchers Carry Flags, Selma to Montgomery	March 1965	**PI** Civil Rights, Witness Milestones in the Civil Rights Movement, Political Victories
Photograph	Martin Luther King, Jr., Coretta Scott King, John Lewis, Selma to Montgomery	March 1965	**PI** Civil Rights, Witness Milestones in the Civil Rights Movement, Political Victories
Photograph	Poll watchers observe voters in Tuskegee, Alabama	May 31, 1966	**ST** Topic 16, Lesson 3
Video	The Children's Crusade, Excerpt from Interview with Freeman Hrabowski, Birmingham, Alabama	2011	**PI** Civil Rights, Travel to Civil Rights Landmarks, Birmingham
Video	Selma Anniversary Speech, President Barack Obama Delivers Remarks on the Fiftieth Anniversary of the Selma Marches	March 7, 2015	**PI** Civil Rights, Choose Your Path During Freedom Summer
Arizona			
Photograph	Congress Street, Tucson	1890s	**PI** Immigration, Build a New Life, 1890
Photograph	Mexican Miner Photographs, mine workers, Morenci	circa 1890	**PI** Immigration, Build a New Life, 1900
Newspaper	*El Fronterizo* Newspaper, Tucson	January 30, 1897	**PI** Immigration, Build a New Life, 1890
Photograph	Mexican Miner Photographs, Housing for Mexican mine workers, Morenci	circa 1900	**PI** Immigration, Build a New Life, 1900
Photograph	Navajo Indians on the Bosque Redondo reservation in present-day Arizona and eastern New Mexico	unknown	**ST** Topic 10, Lesson 1
Photograph	Navajo CCC workers, Tuba City, Arizona	unknown	**PI** The Great Depression and the New Deal, See the New Deal in Action, Shenandoah
Photograph	Hoover Dam	unknown	**PI** The Great Depression and the New Deal, See the New Deal in Action, Hoover Dam
Photographs	Hoover Dam, High Scalers, Native Americans, blasting, Ragtown, Boulder City	unknown	**PI** The Great Depression and the New Deal, See the New Deal in Action, Hoover Dam
Video	Boulder Dam, U.S. Department of the Interior	1937	**PI** The Great Depression and the New Deal, See the New Deal in Action, Hoover Dam
Photograph	Navajo Code Talkers, Corporal Henry Blake, Jr., (left) and Private First Class George H. Kirk, Marine Signal Unit	December 1943	**PI** World War II, Follow News from the Battle Front, 1942
Photograph	Official checking Departure list, Gila River Incarceration camp, Arizona	1945	**PI** World War II, Tour a Japanese American Incarceration Camp
Arkansas			
Letter	African American Work Letter, from Reverend W. M. Henry to John T. Clark, Altheimer, Arkansas	December 22, 1922	**PI** The 1920s, Explore African American Life, Moving North
Photograph	Sharecropper plows a field	1935	**PI** The Great Depression and the New Deal, Survive the Great Depression, Clarence
Poster	War Stamp and Bond Drive, Rohwer War Relocation Center, McGehee, Arkansas	unknown	**PI** World War II, Tour a Japanese American Incarceration Camp, Daily Life
Book excerpt	*Take Your Choice: Separation or Mongrelization,* Theodore G. Bilbo	1946	**PI** Civil Rights, Work as an Investigative Reporter, Little Rock School Desegregation
Photograph	Elizabeth Eckford at Little Rock High School in Little Rock, Arkansas	1957	**ST** Topic 16, Lesson 1

Primary Source Index by State (continued)

Type	Source Title	Date	Location of Source
Photograph	National Guard troops protect African American students entering Little Rock High School	1957	**ST** Topic 16, Lesson 1
Speech	Address on Little Rock, President Dwight D. Eisenhower	1957	**ST** Topic 16, Lesson 1
Photograph	Troops protect African American students entering Little Rock Central High School	1957	**PI** Civil Rights, Work as an Investigative Reporter, Little Rock School Desegregation
Newspaper Article	Little Rock Newspaper Coverage, Front Page of the *Arkansas Democrat*	September 4, 1957	**PI** Civil Rights, Work as an Investigative Reporter, Little Rock School Desegregation
Video	Presidential Statement, President Dwight Eisenhower	September 1, 1957	**PI** Civil Rights, Work as an Investigative Reporter, Little Rock School Desegregation
Video	Little Rock Nine Account, Ernest Green's Account of Integrating Little Rock High School	no date	**PI** Civil Rights, Work as an Investigative Reporter, Little Rock School Desegregation
Letter	Daisy Bates' Letter to Roy Wilkins	December 17, 1957	**ST** Topic 16 Primay Source feature; **PI** Civil Rights, Work as an Investigative Reporter, Little Rock School Desegregation
Military Report	Situation Report to President Eisenhower, On Little Rock High School	February 1, 1958	**ST** Topic 16 Primay Source feature; **PI** Civil Rights, Work as an Investigative Reporter, Little Rock School Desegregation
Photograph	Fighting Desegregation, white segregationist rally at state capitol	1959	**ST** Topic 16 Primay Source feature; **PI** Civil Rights, Work as an Investigative Reporter, Little Rock School Desegregation
California			
Engraving	The Laundry of the Palace Hotel, San Franciso	1800s	**PI** Immigration, Should You Stay or Leave?
Letter	Chinese Merchants' Letter, to Chief of Police H.H. Ellis, San Francisco	June 30, 1876	**PI** Immigration, Should You Stay or Leave?
Photograph	Chinese workers on the Oregon and California Railroad	late 1800s	**PI** Immigration, Should You Stay or Leave?
Advertisement	California Advertisement	late 1800s	**PI** Immigration, Give Your Son a Better Life
Data	Chinese Immigrant Jobs and Wages, Average Pay and Occupations	1880; 1885–1886	**PI** Immigration, Should You Stay or Leave?
Illustration	Chinese Culture in America, Theatrical Performances in Chinatown, San Francisco, Harper's Weekly	1883	**PI** Immigration, Should You Stay or Leave?, Legacy
Fine art	China Town, San Francisco, by Robert F. Blum	circa 1890	**PI** Immigration, Should You Stay or Leave?, Legacy
Book	Description from a party that left South Bend, Indiana for the California gold rush, David Rohrer Leeper, "The Argonauts of '49"	First printed 1894	**ST** Topic 6, Lesson 3
Photograph	Anaheim School Photograph, First Grade Class, Anaheim Central School	1898	**PI** Immigration, Build a New Life, 1890
Photograph	Chinese Segregated School	unknown	**PI** Immigration, Build a New Life, 1890
Article	Sanitary Laws Article, *San Francisco Call*	November 23, 1901	**PI** Immigration, Should You Stay or Leave?
Article	Chinese Exclusion Article, *San Francisco Call*	December 3, 1901	**PI** Immigration, Should You Stay or Leave?, Legacy

Primary Source Index by State (continued)

Type	Source Title	Date	Location of Source
Photograph	Yosemite National Park, California; President Theodore Roosevelt and John Muir	1903	**ST** Topic 11, Lesson 4
Biography	Biography of Lee Chew, "The Biography of a Chinaman," Independent	1903	**PI** Immigration, Should You Stay or Leave?
Letter	Letter to a Lost Love, August Aalto to Hilma Aerila	April 27, 1906	**PI** Immigration, Give Your Son a Better Life
Poster	Anti-Japanese Poster, San Francisco	June 1, 1913	**PI** Immigration, Should You Stay or Leave?, Legacy
Photograph	Angel Island Poetry, Angel Island Immigration Station	early 1900s	**PI** Immigration, Should You Stay or Leave?, Legacy
Legal Contract	Chinese Six Companies Contract, agreement hiring watchmen to protect Chinese businesses and homes, San Francisco	January 1, 1910	**PI** Immigration, Should You Stay or Leave?
Photograph	Mexican American Photographs, Sisters in front of train backdrop, Los Angeles	1912	**PI** Immigration, Build a New Life, 1910
Photograph	Mexican American Photographs, Lopez Brothers, First and Utah streets, Los Angeles	1916	**PI** Immigration, Build a New Life, 1910
Photograph	Herlinda Lopez and Verlinda Silva Clark (child), First Street, Los Angeles	1916	**PI** Immigration, Build a New Life, 1910
Photograph	Mexican American Photographs, Marcelo Lopez and passengers in a car decorated for the Fourth of July, Los Angeles.	1918	**PI** Immigration, Build a New Life, 1910
Photograph	A window fashion display at the McCormick-Saeltzer department store, Redding	circa 1925	**PI** The 1920s, Adjust to Changing Times for Women, Lillian
Photograph	Woman protests immigration raids, Los Angeles	unknown	**PI** The Great Depression and the New Deal, Work to End the Depression
Photograph	San Diego Civic Center (San Diego County Administration Building)	unknown	**PI** The Great Depression and the New Deal, See the New Deal in Action, San Diego
Photograph	Hobo, by Dorothea Lange, Los Angeles County, CA	unknown	**PI** The Great Depression and the New Deal, Survive the Great Depression, Jack
Photograph	Exterior of Union Station, Los Angeles	unknown	**PI** The Great Depression and the New Deal, Survive the Great Depression, Maria
Photograph	Friends and family wave goodbye as Mexicans are deported at train station in Los Angeles	1931	**PI** World War II, Join the War Effort, Francisco
Telegram	Deportation Telegram, from C. P. Visel to Colonel Arthur M. Woods, Los Angeles, California	January 6, 1931	**PI** The Great Depression and the New Deal, Survive the Great Depression, Maria; **PSRG** Topic 13, Source 1
Photograph	Deportation Photograph, People boarding a train from Los Angeles to Mexico, Los Angeles	August 1931	**PI** The Great Depression and the New Deal, Survive the Great Depression, Maria
Photograph	Mexicans at train station to return to Mexico	1932	**PI** The Great Depression and the New Deal, Survive the Great Depression, Maria
Letter	From Pablo Guerrero to the Los Angeles County Clerk,	May 28, 1934	**PI** The Great Depression and the New Deal, Survive the Great Depression, Maria; **PSRG** Topic 13, Source 2
Photograph	Federal Art Project mural, Coit Tower, San Francisco, California	1934	**ST** Topic 13, Lesson 6
Photographs	Dorothea Lange photographs, migrants in California	various	**PI** The Great Depression and the New Deal, Experience the Dust Bowl, 1937–1939
Mosaic	WPA Mosaic, Municipal Auditorium, Long Beach, CA	1938	**PI** The Great Depression and the New Deal, See the New Deal in Action, San Diego

Primary Source Index by State (continued)

Type	Source Title	Date	Location of Source
Sculpture	Guardian of Water by Donal Hord, San Diego Civic Center	1939	**PI** The Great Depression and the New Deal, See the New Deal in Action, San Diego
Murals	WPA Murals, "Agriculture" and "Conservation," by Jean Goodwin and Arthur Ames, San Diego Civic Center	1939	**PI** The Great Depression and the New Deal, See the New Deal in Action, San Diego
Postcard	Wilshire Boulevard, Los Angeles	1941	**PI** World War II, Join the War Effort, Annie
Interview	Women Factory Workers Inteview, Meet the Girls Who Keep 'Em Flying, Frank J. Taylor, *Saturday Evening Post*	1942	**PI** World War II, Join the War Effort, Ruth
Photograph	African American Worker Photos, Luedell Mitchell and Lavada Cherry, El Segundo Plant, Douglas Aircraft Company	unknown	**PI** World War II, Join the War Effort, Annie
Photograph	African American Worker Photos, Welder -trainee Josie Lucille Owens, Kaiser Shipyards, Richmond, California	unknown	**PI** World War II, Join the War Effort, Annie
Photograph	African American Worker Photos, Welders Alivia Scott, Hattie Carpenter, and Flossie Burtos, Kaiser Shipyards, Richmond, California	unknown	**PI** World War II, Join the War Effort, Annie
Photograph	Women work on A-20 attack bombers, Douglas Aircraft, Long Beach, California	1942–1945	**PI** World War II, Join the War Effort, Ruth
Photograph	Dance at a California incarceration camp	1942–1945	**PI** World War II, Tour a Japanese American Incarceration Camp, Daily Life
Letter	Fusa Tsumagara to Miss Clara Breed, Librarian at San Diego Public Library, Santa Anita Assembly Center, Arcadia, California	May 1942	**PI** World War II, Tour a Japanese American Incarceration Camp, Daily Life
Photograph	Buildings at Spreckels Sugar Company, Woodland, California	November 24, 1942	**PI** World War II, Join the War Effort, Francisco
Photograph	Japanese Americans board a bus bound for Manzanar Incarceration Camp	1942	**PI** World War II, Tour a Japanese American Incarceration Camp, Incarceration
Photograph	Barracks at Manzanar Incarceration camp, Inyo County, California	1942	**PI** World War II, Tour a Japanese American Incarceration Camp, Daily Life
Photograph	Boys reading comic books, Tule Lake Relocation Center, Newell, California	1942	**PI** World War II, Tour a Japanese American Incarceration Camp, Daily Life
Photograph	Guard tower at Manzanar Incarceration Camp, Inyo County, California	unknown	**PI** World War II, Tour a Japanese American Incarceration Camp, Incarceration
Photograph	Basketball game, Manzanar Incarceration Camp, Inyo County, California	unknown	**PI** World War II, Tour a Japanese American Incarceration Camp, Daily Life
Photograph	High School Biology class, Manzanar Incarceration camp, Ansel Adams, Inyo County, California	1943	**PI** World War II, Tour a Japanese American Incarceration Camp, Daily Life
Yearbook	Manzanar High School Yearbook, Manzanar Incarceration camp, Ansel Adams, Inyo County, California	1943–1944	**PI** World War II, Tour a Japanese American Incarceration Camp, Daily Life
Photograph	Los Angeles police arrest a group of young Mexican Americans following the "zoot suit riots."	1943	**ST** Topic 14, Lesson 5
Article	"The West Can Pull Out of Berlin Proudly," Los Angeles Times	September 2, 1948	**PSRG** Topic 15, Source 3
Photograph	Post-war suburban development, Lakeland Park, California	1950s	**ST** Topic 15, Lesson 5
Photograph	Stokely Carmichael speaking at the University of California at Berkeley	October 29, 1966	**ST** Topic 16, Lesson 3; **PI** Civil RIghts, Weigh the Evidence on the Black Power Movement

Primary Source Index by State (continued)

Type	Source Title	Date	Location of Source
Speech	Nomination acceptance speech, John F. Kennedy, delivered in Los Angeles, California	July 15, 1960	**ST** Topic 16, Lesson 4
Letter	"From Bobbie Lou Pendergrass, Santa Ana California to President John F. Kennedy"	February 18, 1963	**ST** Topic 17, Primary Source feature; **PI** Vietnam, Explore America's Road to War in Vietnam, U.S. Involvement Grows, 1961–1963
Photograph	Demonstrators march in support of the Vietnam War, Oakland, California	November 1965	**PI** Vietnam, Investigate How the War Divided Americans
Video	Black Panther Party Film, Bobby Seale , Huey Newton, Oakland, California	October 1966	**PI** Civil RIghts, Weigh the Evidence on the Black Power Movement
Poster	Concert poster, The Grateful Dead, San Francisco	1966	**ST** Topic 18, Lesson 1
Flyer	Noncooperation flyer, We Refuse to Serve	1967	**PI** Vietnam, Investigate How the War Divided Americans
Newspaper Article	Black Panther Party Article, "Black Panthers Stun Assembly," Wat Takeshita, *Daily Independent Journal,* San Rafael, California	May 3, 1967	**PI** Civil RIghts, Weigh the Evidence on the Black Power Movement
Photograph	Black Panther members and sympathizers demonstrate their support for leader Huey Newton as he stands trial for the murder of an Oakland police officer in Alameda County, California.	1968	**ST** Topic 16, Lesson 3
Photograph	Mexican Americans in East Los Angeles protest against discrimination	August 29, 1970	**PI** Vietnam, Investigate How the War Divided Americans
Flyer	Black Panther Party Initiatives, Free Bags of Groceries, Oakland and Berkeley, California	March 29–31, 1972	**PI** Civil Rights, Witness Milestones in the Civil Rights Movement, An Era Ends
Photograph	Black Panther Party Initiatives, Sickle Cell Testing, Oakland, California	March 1972	**PI** Civil Rights, Witness Milestones in the Civil Rights Movement, An Era Ends
Photograph	Marine wives at Camp Pendleton, California await the return of Vietnam prisoners of war	February 12, 1973	**PI** Vietnam, Experience the Legacy of the Vietnam War, Heather
Photograph	Former POW Lieutenant Colonel Robert L. Stirm is welcomed home, Travis Air Force Base, Fairfield, California	March 1973	**PI** Vietnam, Experience the Legacy of the Vietnam War, Heather
Speech	Speech by Representative Norman Mineta, House of Representatives	1987	**PI** World War II, Tour a Japanese American Incarceration Camp, Daily Life
Audio Interview	Interview with Bracero Worker, Agustín Martínez Olivares, (discusses work in Monterrey, California)	2003	**PI** World War II, Join the War Effort, Francisco
Statue	Vietnamese Boat People Memorial, Westminster Memorial Cemetery, Orange County, California	2009	**PI** Vietnam, Experience the Legacy of the Vietnam War, Hien
Colorado			
Newspaper Article	Mexican Repatriation Article, "Colorado Aliens Face Deportation," *New York Times*	March 31, 1935	**PI** World War II, Join the War Effort, Francisco
Video	Dust storm	1938	**PI** The Great Depression and the New Deal, Experience the Dust Bowl, 1933–1934
Photograph	Farmer inspects his crop	1938	**PI** The Great Depression and the New Deal, Experience the Dust Bowl, 1937–1939
Photograph	Grasshoppers cover the sidewalk in Colorado Springs	unknown	**PI** The Great Depression and the New Deal, Experience the Dust Bowl, 1933–1934
Photograph	Girls' Reserves Victory Dolls, Jane Nagai, left, and Boots Sotomura, right, Granada Relocation Center, Camp Amache, Colorado	unknown	**PI** World War II, Tour a Japanese American Incarceration Camp, Daily Life

Primary Source Index by State (continued)

Type	Source Title	Date	Location of Source
Photograph	Choral group, Granada Relocation Center, Camp Amache, Colorado	1942	**PI** World War II, Tour a Japanese American Incarceration Camp, Daily Life
Photograph	Decorating Christmas tree, Granada Relocation Center, Camp Amache, Colorado	1943	**PI** World War II, Tour a Japanese American Incarceration Camp, Daily Life
Interview	Deportation Interview, Emma Gomez Martinez, Boulder County Latino History Project	Recorded 2013	**PI** The Great Depression and the New Deal, Survive the Great Depression, Maria
Connecticut			
Document	Regulations at Yale College	1745	**ST** Topic 2, Lesson 5
Video	Italian American Video, *The Making of an American,* Connecticut State Board of Education	1920	**PI** Immigration, Define Your Identity as an American, Emilio
Delaware			
Photograph	Newsboys on a stoop at 4th & Market Streets, by Lewis Hine, Wilmington, Delaware	May 1910	**PI** Immigration, Define Your Identity as an American, Patrick
Florida			
Photograph	Cigar Industry Photographs, V. M. Ybor Cigar Factory, Tampa	1882	**PI** Immigration, Build a New Life, 1880
Photograph	Cigar Industry Photographs, Workers at Scale Strike in Tampa	1899	**PI** Immigration, Build a New Life, 1880
Photograph	Cigar Industry Photographs, Cigar factory strikers, Tampa	1899	**PI** Immigration, Build a New Life, 1880
Newspaper	Motor Vehicle Safety Article, "Don't Hold Your Girl and Drive", *Miami Daily Metropolis*	December 22, 1922	**PI** The 1920s, Enjoy the Roaring 20s
Photograph	Women Golfers, Coral Gables Country Club	1920s	**PI** The 1920s, Adjust to Changing Times for Women, Helen
Essay	"How It Feels to Be Colored Me", Zora Neale Hurston	1928	**PI** The 1920s, Adjust to Changing Times for Women, Ada
Letter	To the Mothers of Female Students at the University of Miami From B.F. Ashe, President	December 28, 1928	**PI** The 1920s, Adjust to Changing Times for Women, Helen
Photograph	Zora Neale Hurston	unknown	**PI** The 1920s, Adjust to Changing Times for Women, Ada
Photograph	Overseas Highway, PWA, Florida Keys	unknown	**PI** The Great Depression and the New Deal, See the New Deal in Action, Hoover Dam
Georgia			
Liithograph	Savannah, Georgia settlement	unknown	**ST** Topic 2, Lesson 1
Letter	Letter from William T. Sherman to James Calhoun, mayor of Atlanta	September 12, 1864	**ST** Topic 7, Lesson 6
Speech	The State of Georgia, Hiram Revels	March 16, 1870	**ST** Topic 8, Primary Source feature
Speech	Atlanta Exposition Address, Booker T. Washington	1895	**ST** Topic 8, Lesson 3; **ST** Topic 11, Primary Source feature; **IPS**
Photograph	African Americans under a Pavilion	about 1900	**PI** Immigration, Define Your Identity as an American, Chloe
Newspaper Article	Voting Rights Testimony, "Charges of Negro Stir Committee," *Evening Star,* Washington, D.C.	December 29, 1920	**PI** The 1920s, Explore African American Life, Fighting Back
Speech	Franklin D. Roosevelt, speech at Oglethorpe University, Brookhaven, Georgia	May 22, 1932	**ST** Topic 13, Lesson 3
Photograph	Church service in the Negro church, Woodville, Greene County, Georgia	October 1941	**PI** The Great Depression and the New Deal, Survive the Great Depression, Clarence
Recording	Johnson Tape on Vietnam; Taped Conversation Between President Johnson and Georgia Senator Richard Russell	May 27, 1964	**PI** Vietnam, Explore America's Road to War in Vietnam, The War Escalates, 1963–1964

Primary Source Index by State (continued)

Type	Source Title	Date	Location of Source
Letter	Martin Luther King, Jr. Letter, "It Is Not Enough to Condemn Black Power"	October 1966	**PI** Civil Rights, Weigh the Evidence on the Black Power Movement
Photograph	Martin Luther King, Jr.'s Funeral Procession, Atlanta, Georgia	April 9, 1968	**PI** Civil Rights, Witness Milestones in the Civil Rights Movement, An Era Ends
Photograph	Poor People's Campaign members march through Atlanta	May 10, 1968	**ST** Topic 16, Lesson 3
Hawaii			
Quote	On the attack on Pearl Harbor, Corpsman James F. Anderson, aboard the hospital ship USS Solace	December 7, 1941	**ST** Topic 14, Lesson 3
Photograph	The *USS Arizona* sinks following the attack on Pearl Harbor	December 7, 1941	**ST** Topic 14, Lesson 3
Letter	Letter from Guy Vecera, Hawaii	December 1941	**PI** World War II, Follow News from the Battle Front, 1941; **PRSG** Topic 14, Source 1
Photograph	Japanese photograph taken during the attack on Pearl Harbor, Hawaii	December 7, 1941	**PI** World War II, Follow News from the Battle Front, 1941
Photograph	USS West Virginia, burning as a result of Japanese attack on Pearl Harbor, Hawaii	December 7, 1941	**PI** World War II, Follow News from the Battle Front, 1941
Interview	Women Factory Workers Inteview, Meet the Girls Who Keep 'Em Flying, Frank J. Taylor, *Saturday Evening Post*	1942	**PI** World War II, Join the War Effort, Ruth
Photograph	Japanese American Soldiers, 100th Infantry Battalion, Training at Camp Shelby, Mississippi	1943	**PI** World War II, Follow News from the Battle Front, 1944
Idaho			
Letter	Farm Loan Letter, Mollie Bostic to Senator W.E. Borah, Boise	March 25, 1922	**PI** The 1920s, Adjust to Changing Times for Women, Mary; **ST** Topic 12, Primary Source feature
Radio Address	Fireside Chat, Franklin Roosevelt, mentions Boise Valley, Idaho	October 12, 1937	**PI** The Great Depression and the New Deal, See the New Deal in Action, Shenandoah
Letter	Italian Campaign Letter, Minoru Masuda to wife in Minidoka Incarceration camp, Hunt Idaho, Italy	June 1944	**PI** World War II, Follow News from the Battle Front, 1944
Illinois			
Speech	Regarding the Mexican-American War, Abraham Lincoln, Represenative from Illinois	January 12, 1848	**PSRG** Topic 6, Source 3
Speech	"A House Divided," Abraham Lincoln, Springfield, Illinois	June 16, 1858	**IPS**
Poster	Haymarket Affair Broadside, Chicago	1886	**PI** Immigration, Build a New Life, 1880
Newspaper	Frank Leslie's Illustrated Newspaper, Haymarket Riot	May 15, 1886	**PI** Immigration, Build a New Life, 1880
Letter	Traveling in Steerage Letter, Berta Kingestad to her family, Malta, Illinois	June 20, 1886	**PI** Immigration, Make a Better Life for Your Son
Photograph	The "White City," Chicago	1893	**ST** Topic 9, Lesson 5
Photograph	Vendors on Maxwell Street, Chicago	1906	**PI** Immigration, Define Your Identity as an American, Rachel
Text	*The Jungle,* Upton Sinclair	1906	**ST** Topic 11, Primary Source feature; **IPS**
Photograph	Association House, Indoor baseball team, Chicago	1909	**PI** Immigration, Define Your Identity as an American, Rachel
Photograph	Singing Class, Hull House, Chicago	1910	**PI** Immigration, Define Your Identity as an American, Rachel

Primary Source Index by State (continued)

Type	Source Title	Date	Location of Source
Artifact	Patriotic Yiddish Sheet Music, "Long Live the Land of the Free" music by Joseph Rumshinsk, lyrics by Solomon Smulewitz, New York	1911	**PI** Immigration, Define Your Identity as an American, Rachel
Photograph	Chicago Hebrew Institute, Physical Education Class	1914	**PI** Immigration, Define Your Identity as an American, Rachel
Photograph	Christian Prayer Group Photo, Marcy House, Chicago	circa 1915	**PI** Immigration, Define Your Identity as an American, Rachel
Advertisement	*Chicago Defender,* Ad for male workers needed in Milwaukee, Wisconsin	December 1917	**PI** Immigration, Define Your Identity as an American, Chloe
Letter	Temperance Letter, from Alfred Fowler (Springfield, IL) to Senator Wesley Jones, Washington, D.C.	April 1, 1920	**PI** The 1920s, Should Prohibition Be Repealed?
Newspaper Article	Ideas on Women Who Work Article, "The Inquiring Reporter," *Chicago Daily Tribune,* Chicago	April 25, 1922	**PI** The 1920s, Adjust to Changing Times for Women, Helen
Photograph	African American family newly arrived in Chicago from the South	1922	**PI** The 1920s, Explore African American Life, Moving North
Article	"Spring to See Greatest Migration in History," *Chicago Defender*	February 20, 1925	**PSRG,** Topic 12, Source 2
Letter	Temperance Letter, Letter from Alfred Fowler to Senator Wesley Jones	April 1, 1920	**PI** The 1920s, Should Prohibition Be Repealed?
Audio Recording	Louis Armstrong Jazz Song, "Muskrat Ramble," performed by Louis Armstrong and his Hot Five	1926	**PI** The 1920s, Explore African American Life, Raising Voices
Photograph	Louis Armstrong Hot Five band	unknown	**PI** The 1920s, Explore African American Life, Raising Voices
Campaign pin	Oscar de Priest For Congress campaign pin	circa 1928–1934	**PI** The 1920s, Explore African American Life, Fighting Back
Photograph	Women at Northwestern University, Evanston	1929	**PI** The 1920s, Adjust to Changing Times for Women, Lillian
Newspaper	Oscar De Priest Article, "Oscar De Priest Sworn In," *The New York Amsterdam News*	April 17, 1929	**PI** The 1920s, Explore African American Life, Fighting Back
Photograph	Soup kitchen, Chicago	1931	**PI** The Great Depression and the New Deal, Survive the Great Depression, Jack
Photograph	Soup kitchen, lower level of Wacker Drive, Chicago	unknown	**PI** The Great Depression and the New Deal, Survive the Great Depression, Clarence
Photo	Jane Addams, Hull House	1935	**ST** Topic 11, Lesson 1
Poster	Louis Armstrong and His Orchestra, Collinsville, Illinois	August 6, 1937	**PI** The 1920s, Explore African American Life, Raising Voices
Report	Franck Report, Memorandum on "Political and Social Problems" from Members of the Metallurgical Laboratory of the University of Chicago,	June 12, 1945	**PI** World War II, Advise Truman on the Atomic Bomb, Franck Report
Magazine Article	Jet Magazine Article, "Nation Horrified by Murder," *Jet*	September 15, 1955	**PI** Civil Rights, Witness Milestones in the Civil Rights Movement, A Movement Begins
Photograph	Emmett Till's mother, Mamie Bradley, cries over her son's casket, Chicago, Illinois	1955	**PI** Civil Rights, Witness Milestones in the Civil Rights Movement, A Movement Begins
Photograph	Protestors outside the Democratic National Convention, Chicago	August 1968	**ST** Topic 17, Lesson 3
Photograph	Black Panther Party headquarters after being damaged by the police, Chicago, Illinois	Summer 1969	**PI** Civil Rights, Weigh the Evidence on the Black Power Movement, The Legacy of Black Power

Primary Source Index by State (continued)

Type	Source Title	Date	Location of Source
Speech, Video	President Obama Victory Speech, Barack Obama	November 4, 2008	**PI** Civil Rights, Witness Milestones in the Civil Rights Movement, Work Continues
Video	Excerpts From Interview With Arthur T. Baltazar, Chicago, Veterans History Project	Recorded December 9, 2014	**PI** Vietnam, Experience the Legacy of the Vietnam War, Heather
Indiana			
Book	Description from a party that left South Bend, Indiana for the California gold rush; David Rohrer Leeper, "The Argonauts of '49"	First printed 1894	**ST** Topic 6, Lesson 3
Photograph	Girls making baskets, basket factory, Evansville	October 1908	**PI** Immigration, Build a New Life, 1900
Speech	Wilkie Campaign Speech, Address Accepting the Republican Presidential Nomination, Elwood, Indiana	August 17, 1940	**PI** The Great Depression and the New Deal, Does FDR Deserve a Third Term?
Iowa			
Letter	Immigrant Farmer Letter, Herman Berghuis, Orange City	1882	**PI** Immigration, Build a New Life, 1880
Silent film	"Hoover Campaigning Silent Film, President Hoover Campaigns in Des Moines (Iowa)"	1932	**PI** The Great Depression and the New Deal, Experience the Dust Bowl, 1929–1932
Article	Iowa Penny Auction Article, "A Farmer Learns Direct Action," Ferner Nuhn, Nation,	March 8, 1933	**PI** The Great Depression and the New Deal, Experience the Dust Bowl, 1935–1936
Photograph	Iowa Penny Auction	unknown	**PI** The Great Depression and the New Deal, Experience the Dust Bowl, 1935–1936
Photograph	Women on lunch break, Chicago & Northern Western Railway Company, by Jack Delano, Clinton, Iowa	April 1943	**PI** World War II, Join the War Effort, Ruth
Letter	D-Day Letter, George Montgomery, France	June 1944	**PI** World War II, Follow News from the Battle Front, 1944
Kansas			
Poem	Claude McKay Poem, "America," published in *Harlem Shadows*	1922	**PI** Immigration, Define Your Identity as an American, Chloe
Photograph	Family and Wheat harvest, Sedgwick, Kansas	1931	**PI** The Great Depresssion and the New Deal, Experience the Dust Bowl, 1929–1932
Memoir	Black Sunday Memoir, The Black Sunday of April 14, 1935, Pauline Winkler Grey, Kansas Historical Society	unknown	**PI** The Great Depresssion and the New Deal, Experience the Dust Bowl, 1935–1936
Photograph	Black Sunday, Rolla, Kansas	April 14, 1935	**PI** The Great Depresssion and the New Deal, Experience the Dust Bowl, 1935–1936
Photograph	Black Sunday, Dodge City, Kansas	April 14, 1935	**PI** The Great Depresssion and the New Deal, Experience the Dust Bowl, 1935–1936
Photograph	Sunbonnet Sue Flour Sacks, by Margaret Bourke-White	1939	**PI** The Great Depresssion and the New Deal, Survive the Great Depression, Irene
Newspaper column	"My Day" Column, Eleanor Roosevelt, Evening Sun, Kansas and Nebraska	November 4, 1939	**PI** The Great Depresssion and the New Deal, Experience the Dust Bowl, 1933–1934
Letter	Letter to the Pittsburgh Courier from James G. Thompson of Wichita, Kansas	January 31, 1942	**ST** Topic 14, Lesson 8

Primary Source Index by State (continued)

Type	Source Title	Date	Location of Source
Court Decision	Supreme Court Opinion, Chief Justice Earl Warren, Opinion of the Court, Brown v. Board of Education of Topeka, Shawnee County, Kansas	1954	**PI** Civil Rights, Witness Milestones in the Civil Rights Movement, A Movement Begins
Kentucky			
Photograph	One-room school for African Americans; Anthoston, Kentucky	1916	**ST** Topic 11, Lesson 3
Song	Labor Union Song, "Which Side Are You On?" composed by Florence Reece, performed by Pete Seeger	1931	**PI** The Great Depression and the New Deal, Work to End the Great Depression
Louisiana			
Photograph	Migrant workers, winter in Dunbar Louisana	July 1909	**PI** Immigration, Build a New Life, 1910
Photograph	Sharecropper's cabin, interior	unknown	**PI** The Great Depresssion and the New Deal, Survive the Great Depression, Clarence
Audio Recording	Senator Huey Long Radio Address, "Our Plundering Government"	February 10, 1935	**PI** The Great Depresssion and the New Deal, Does FDR Deserve a Third Term?
Photograph	Huey Long	circa 1935	**PI** The Great Depresssion and the New Deal, Does FDR Deserve a Third Term?
Photograph	Ieshia Evans protests, Baton Rouge, Louisiana	July 9, 2016	**PI** Civil Rights, Witness Milestones in the Civil Rights Movement, Work Continues
Maine			
Letter	Radio Letter, Annie Oaks Huntington to Florence Windom, Lane's End, Waterford	June 1924	**PI** The 1920s, Adjust to Changing Times for Women, Mary
Maryland			
Speech	To the Maryland State Legislature, Luther Martin	November 29, 1787	**IPS**
Artifact	Baseball card, John McGraw, Baltimore National League team	1890s	**PI** Immigration, Define Your Identity as an American, Patrick
Photograph	Migrant workers, Bottomley Farms, near Baltimore	July 1909	**PI** Immigration, Build a New Life, 1910
Political Cartoon	"A Step in the Right Direction," Workers Wanted Regardless of Color, Baltimore, Maryland	May 1942–January 1943	**PI** World War II, Join the War Effort, Annie
Award	National Security Award, Revere Copper and Brass, Inc. Baltimore Division	September 1, 1944	**PI** World War II, Do Your Part on the Home Front
Photograph	Nonviolent Training and Protests, Gloria Richardson, Chairman of the Cambridge Non-Violent Action Committee (far right) watches as sit-in demonstrators Johnny Weeks, (far left), James Lewis, (front center), and Dwight Campbell (back center) are arrested after refusing to leave the Dizzyland Restaurant, Cambridge, Maryland	July 10, 1963	**PI** Civil Rights, Work as an Investigative Reporter, Greensboro Sit-Ins
Photograph	Middle East peace talks, Camp David, Frederick County, Maryland	1978	**ST** Topic 18, Lesson 6
Agreement	Camp David Accords, Camp David, Frederick County, Maryland	September 19, 1978	**ST** Topic 18, Lesson 6
Photograph	Protests against police violence toward Freddie Gray, Baltimore, Maryland	April 29, 2015	**PI** Civil Rights, Weigh the Evidence on the Black Power Movement
Massachusetts			
Document	The Mayflower Compact	November 1620	**IPS**
Painting	John Winthrop, Govenor of the Massachusetts Bay Colony	unknown	**ST** Topic 2, Lesson 2

Primary Source Index by State (continued)

Type	Source Title	Date	Location of Source
Sermon	"A Model of Christian Charity," John Winthrop	1630	**ST** Topic 2, Lesson 2
Journal	*Of Plymouth Plantation,* William Bradford	1630–1651	**ST** Topic 2, Primary Source
Pamphlet	*The Simple Cobler of Aggawam in America,* Nathaniel Ward	1647	**PSRG,** Topic 2, Source 2
Sermon	"Sinners in the Hands of an Angry God," Jonathan Edwards	1741	**ST** Topic 2, Lesson 6
Letter	Letter from Anne Hulton to Elizabeth Lightbody	June 30, 1768	**ST** Topic 3, Primary Source feature
Engraving	Boston Massacre, Paul Revere	1770	**ST** Topic 3, Lesson 1
Letter	Letter from Abigail Adams to Mercy Otis Warren	December 5, 1774	**ST** Topic 3, Primary Source feature
Letter	Letter from Abigail Adams to John Adams	March 31, 1776	**IPS**
Engraving	Shays' Rebellion, Springfield, Massachusetts	1787	**ST** Topic 4, Lesson 1
Speech	Massachusetts ratifying convention, Amos Singletary	1788	**ST** Topic 4 Assesment
Speech	Massachusetts ratifying convention, Jonathan Smith	1788	**ST** Topic 4 Assesment
Pamphlet	Pamphlet against slavery, *Appeal to the Colored Citizens of the World,* David Walker	1829	**ST** Topic 6, Lesson 5
Newspaper	*The Liberator,* founded by Boston abolitionist William Lloyd Garrison	1831	**ST** Topic 6, Lesson 5
Debate	"Debate over Nullification," Daniel Webster and John C. Calhoun	March 1833	**IPS**
Petition	Petition to the Massachusetts Legislature on the state of prisons, Dorothea Dix	1843	**ST** Topic 6, Lesson 4
Speech	Speech at Lake Mohonk, Massachusetts Senator Henry Dawes	1883	**Q** Document D, Topic 1
Artifact	Baseball card, Michael "King" Kelly, Boston	circa 1887–1890	**PI** Immigration, Define Your Identity as an American, Patrick
Letter	A Letter Home to Ireland, Mary Ann Rowe, Dedham	October 29, 1888	**PI** Immigration, Build a New Life, 1880
Photograph	Domestic servants doing laundry	circa 1905	**PI** Immigration, Build a New Life, 1880
Autobiography	Russian Immigrant Autobiography, The Promised Land, Mary Antin	1912	**PI** Immigration, Define Your Identity as an American, Rachel
Poem	Claude McKay Poem, "If We Must Die," *The Liberator,* Boston	July 1919	**PI** The 1920s, Explore African American Life, Raising Voices
Interview	Italian American Interview, Roland Damiani, Beverly	February 15, 1939	**PI** Immigration, Define Your Identity as an American, Emilio
Artifact	Baseball, Autographed by Babe Ruth	unknown	**PI** The 1920s, Enjoy the Roaring 20s
Speech	Roosevelt Campaign Speech, Boston, Massachusetts	October 1940	**PI** The New Deal and the Great Depression, Does FDR Deserve a Third Term?
Michigan			
Photograph	Melting Pot Ceremony, Ford English School, Detroit	July 4, 1917	**PI** Immigration, Build a New Life, 1911
Video	Ford English School Video, Immigrants Learning English at the Ford English School, Ford Motor Company	1918	**PI** Immigration, Build a New Life, 1910
Photograph	Ford Production Line Photograph, Rouge Plant, Dearborn	May 1923	**PI** The 1920s, Explore African American Life, Moving North
Video	Model T Advertisement, Ford Motion Picture Laboratories	1924	**PI** The 1920s, Enjoy the Roaring 20s
Photograph	Traffic jam, Lafayette at Third Street, Detroit	unknown	**PI** The 1920s, Enjoy the Roaring 20s

Primary Source Index by State (continued)

Type	Source Title	Date	Location of Source
Speech	Defense of Henry Sweet Speech, Closing Arguments of Defense Attorney Clarence Darrow in the trial of Henry Sweet, Detroit	1925	**PI** The 1920s, Explore African American Life, Enduring Violence
Photograph	Ossian Sweet	unknown	**PI** The 1920s, Explore African American Life, Enduring Violence
Photograph	Home of Ossian Sweet, Detroit	unknown	**PI** The 1920s, Explore African American Life, Enduring Violence
Photograph	Michigan Farmer Stands by the Family Car	1928	**PI** The 1920s, Enjoy the Roaring 20s
Data	Auto Workers in Detroit	1920–1930	**PI** The 1920s, Explore African American Life, Moving North
Photograph	Man with sign asking for work, Detroit	1930	**PI** The Great Depression and the New Deal, Work to End the Depression
Quote	Striking auto workers, Flint, Michigan	January 1936	**ST** Topic 13, Lesson 4
Photograph	Chrysler's Tank Arsenal, Detroit, Michigan	unknown	**ST** Topic 14, Lesson 3
Letter	"Letter to Eleanor Roosevelt from Sylvia Tucker, Detroit, Michigan"	1941	**ST** Topic 14, Primary Source feature
Letter	Liberation of Dachau Letter, Harold Porter, Germany	May 1945	**PI** World War II, Follow News from the Battle Front, 1945
Letter	Concerned Citizen Letter, To Eleanor Roosevelt from Sylvia Tucker, Detroit, Michigan	unknown	**PI** World War II, Do Your Part on the Home Front
Photograph	Students march for civil rights and equality for all Americans, University of Michigan	1960	**ST** Topic 16, Lesson 2
Speech	Great Society Speech, President Johnson, University of Michigan	May 22, 1964	**ST** Topic 16, Lessson 5
Photograph	Race riot, Detroit, Michigan	1967	**ST** Topic 16, Lesson 3
Photograph	Teach-in at the University of Michigan	1970	**PI** Vietnam, Investigate How the War Divided Americans
Audio	Reflecting on the Teach-Ins Audio Recording, University of Michigan Professors Discuss Teach-In Movement	2015	**PI** Vietnam, Investigate How the War Divided Americans
Minnesota			
Artifact	Bible, Fort Snelling Sunday School	1883	**PI** Immigration, Build a New Life
Photograph	Minnesota Immigrant Photographs, St. Anthony Chapter of Turners	circa 1890	**PI** Immigration, Build a New Life, 1890
Artifact	Minnesota Immigrant Photographs, Hymnal, Westminster Chinese Sunday School, Minneapolis	unknown	**PI** Immigration, Build a New Life, 1892
Artifact	Minnesota Immigrant Photographs, Ribbon, Ancient Order of the Hibernians, Brainerd	March 29, 1898	**PI** Immigration, Build a New Life, 1891
Photograph	Temperance Images, Women of Madison, Minnesota Picket for Temperance	circa 1917	**PI** The 1920s, Should Prohibition be Repealed?
Autobiography	Story of an Norwegian Immigrant, Andreas Ueland	1929	**PI** Immigration, Give Your Son a Better Life
Letter	Saying Goodbye to Mother Account, Letter from Leslie E. Paul, Duluth (Minnesota), in Errol Lincoln Uys, *Riding the Rails*	1933	**PI** The Great Depression and the New Deal, Surviving the Great Depression, Jack
Letter	Farm Family Letter, Arney Family to President Roosevelt and Eleanor Roosevelt, Bagley, Minnesota	August 10, 1934	**PI** The Great Depression and the New Deal, Experience the Dust Bowl, 1933–1934
Audio	Army Nurse Interview, Excerpts From Diane Carlson Evans Interview Transcript, Vietnam Archive Oral History Project	Recorded May 1, 2004	**PI** Vietnam, Experience the Legacy of the Vietnam War, Robert

Primary Source Index by State (continued)

Type	Source Title	Date	Location of Source
Mississippi			
Declaration	A Declaration of the Immediate Causes which Induce and Justify the Secession of the State of Mississippi from the Federal Union	January 9, 1861	**PSRG** Topic 7, Source 1
Photograph	Vicksburg cave shelters	1863	**ST** Topic 7, Lesson 6
Letter	Letter from William G. Christie at Vicksburg	June 6, 1863	**ST** Topic 7, Primary Source feature
Memoir	*My Cave Life in Vicksburg,* Mary Ann Webster Loughborough	1864	**ST** Topic 7, Primary Source feature
Sheet Music	W.C. Handy, The St. Louis Blues	1914	**PI** Immigration, Define Your Identity as an American, Chloe
Audio	Gospel Song, "The United States Needs Prayer, Everywhere," composed by Sister McCreasy McKissick, performed by Lulu Morris and members of the African Methodist Church, Recorded by Herbert Halpert, Tupelo, Mississippi	May 1939	**PI** The Great Depression and the New Deal, Surviving the Great Depression, Clarence
Photograph	Japanese American Soldiers, 100th Infantry Battalion, Training at Camp Shelby, Mississippi	1943	**PI** World War II, Follow News from the Battle Front, 1944
Magazine Article	Jet Magazine Article, "Nation Horrified by Murder," *Jet*	September 15, 1955	**PI** Civil Rights, Witness Milestones in the Civil Rights Movement, A Movement Begins
Photograph	The National Guard escorts the Freedom Riders on their bus	1961	**PI** Civil Rights, Witness Milestones in the Civil Rights Movement, Early Campaigns
Photographs	Freedom Rider mugshots, Jackson, Mississippi	1961	**PI** Civil Rights, Work as an Investigative Reporter, Freedom Rides
Pamphlet	Freedom Riders Speak for Themselves, News & Letters	November 1961	**PSRG** Topic 16, Source 2; **PI** Civil Rights, Work as an Investigative Reporter, Freedom Rides
Letter	Voter Intimidation Letter, Charles R. McLaurin to President Kennedy, Ruleville, Mississippe	September 21, 1962	**PI** Civil Rights, Choose Your Path During Freedom Summer
Literacy Test	Voter Registration Literacy Test, Mississippi Voter Application and Literacy Test	1962	**PI** Civil Rights, Choose Your Path During Freedom Summer
Photograph	James Meredith integrates the University of Mississippi	1962	**Topic** 16, Lesson 2
Photograph	Sit-in Protesters Attacked in Jackson, Mississippi	May 28, 1963	**PI** Civil Rights, Witness Milestones in the Civil Rights Movement, Early Campaigns; **PI** Civil Rights, Work as an Investigative Reporter, Greensboro Sit-Ins
Photograph	Voter Intimidation, Black citizens filling out voter registration forms beneath sign saying their names will be published in the newspaper, Hattiesburg, Mississippi	January 22, 1964	**PI** Civil Rights, Choose Your Path During Freedom Summer
FBI Missing Poster	Freedom Summer Volunteers Andrew Goodman, James Earle Chaney, Michael Henry Schwerner, Philadelphia, Mississippi	June 21, 1964	**PI** Civil Rights, Witness Milestones in the Civil Rights Movement, Political Victories
Posters	Freedom Candidate Poster, Mississippi Freedom Democratic Party Posters	1964	**PI** Civil Rights, Choose Your Path During Freedom Summer
Speech	Speech Before the Credentials Committee, Democratic National Convention, Fannie Lou Hamer	August 1964	**PSRG** Topic 16, Source 3
Data	Voter Registration Statistics, Mississippi Congressional Districts	August 1, 1964	**PI** Civil Rights, Choose Your Path During Freedom Summer

Primary Source Index by State (continued)

Type	Source Title	Date	Location of Source
Audio and Photograph	Democratic Convention Speech, Speech Before the Credentials Committee, Democratic National Convention, Fannie Lou Hamer	August 22, 1964	**PI** Civil Rights, Choose Your Path During Freedom Summer
Photograph	Freedom school conducting class in literacy, history, and voter registration, Ruleville, Mississippi	Summer 1964	**PI** Civil Rights, Choose Your Path During Freedom Summer
Flyer	Freedom Community Center Flyer, Shaw, Mississippi	Summer 1964	**PI** Civil Rights, Choose Your Path During Freedom Summer
Photograph	Freedom School, Jackson, Mississippi	Summer 1964	**PI** Civil Rights, Choose Your Path During Freedom Summer
Pamphlet	Freedom Primer, No. 2, Mississippi	1964	**PI** Civil Rights, Choose Your Path During Freedom Summer
Photograph	A black man enters a segregated movie theatre in Belzoni, Mississippi	unknown	**PI** Civil Rights, Witness Milestones in the Civil Rights Movement, A Movement Begins
Poem, Photograph	Freedom School Poem, "Fight On Little Children," Edith Moore, *Freedom School Poetry,* SNCC, McComb, Mississippi	1965	**PI** Civil Rights, Choose Your Path During Freedom Summer
Speech	Mourning Mother's Speech, An Address by Fannie Lee Chaney, Meridian Mississippi, *Freedomways*	1965	**PI** Civil Rights, Choose Your Path During Freedom Summer
Photograph	The March Against Fear Photographs, (left to right) Willie Ricks, Bernard Lee, Martin Luther King Jr., Stokely Carmichael, Andrew Young, and Hosea Williams, Mississippi	June 1, 1966	**PI** Civil Rights, Witness Milestones in the Civil Rights Movement, An Era Ends
Photograph	The March Against Fear Photographs, James Meredith after being shot, Hernando, Mississippi	June 6, 1966	**PI** Civil Rights, Witness Milestones in the Civil Rights Movement, An Era Ends
Photograph	Martin Luther King, Jr. with Younger Leaders of SNCC, CORE, Hernando, Mississippi	June 7, 1966	**PI** Civil Rights, Weigh the Evidence on the Black Power Movement
Photograph	The March Against Fear Photographs, crowds at end of March, outside Jackson, Mississippi	June 26, 1966	**PI** Civil Rights, Witness Milestones in the Civil Rights Movement, An Era Ends
Video	SNCC Volunteer Interview, Excerpt of Interview with Hollis Watkins	November 9, 1985	**PI** Civil Rights, Choose Your Path During Freedom Summer
Missouri			
Photograph	Union soldier of the 33rd Missouri	unknown	**ST** Topic 7, Lesson 3
Article	"Corruption and Reform in St. Louis," Lincoln Steffens and Claude Wetmore, McClure's Magazine	October 1902	**ST** Topic 11, Lesson 1
Sheet Music	W.C. Handy, The St. Louis Blues	1914	**PI** Immigration, Define Your Identity as an American, Chloe
Photograph	President Wilson on a speaking tour to promote the League of Nations, St. Louis, Missouri	1919	**ST** Topic 12, Lesson 3
Photograph	Negro National League Photos, Kansas City Monarchs, Missouri	circa 1922	**PI** The 1920s, Explore African American Life, Fighting Back
Newspaper article	Prohibition Crime Article, "Our Crime Wave," The Democrat-Argus, Caruthersville, Missouri	June 5, 1931	**PI** The 1920s, Should Prohibition Be Repealed?
Serial Novel	An Unemployed Girl Serial Novel, "Wanted—Love! The Story of an Unemployed Girl," Ethelda Bedford, *Daily Capital News,* Jefferson City, Missouri	May 20, 1932	**PI** The Great Depression and the New Deal, Survive the Great Depression, Jack
Photograph	Missouri family, 1937	1937	**ST** Topic 13, Lesson 2
Speech	"Sinews of Peace," Winston Churchill, given at Westminster College, Fulton, Missouri	1946	**ST** Topic 15, Primary Source feature

Primary Source Index by State (continued)

Type	Source Title	Date	Location of Source
Nebraska			
Speech	Regarding the Treatment of Indians on Reservations, Susette La Flesche	1881	**PSRG** Topic 10, Source 2
Artifact	Swedish Immigrant Chest, Nebraska	1887	**PI** Immigration, Give Your Son a Better Life
Political Platform statement	Preamble to the Platform of the Populist Party, adopted at its national convention in Omaha, Nebraska	1892	**IPS; ST** Topic 10, Primary Source feature
Interview	Homesteader Inteview, Mrs. John Donnelly on Pioneer Life	November 1938	**PI** Immigration, Build a New Life, 1870; **PSRG** Topic 9, Source 4
Newspaper column	"My Day" Column, Eleanor Roosevelt, Evening Sun, Kansas and Nebraska	November 4, 1939	**PI** The Great Depresssion and the New Deal, Experience the Dust Bowl, 1933–1934
Interview	Flour Sack Dresses Interview, Herman Goertzen Wessels Living History Farm	unknown	**PI** The Great Depression and the New Deal, Surviving the Great Depression, Irene
Photograph	New Deal Shelter Belt, southwest of Lincoln, Nebraska	unknown	**PI** The Great Depresssion and the New Deal, Experience the Dust Bowl, 1933–1934
Interview	Tumbleweed Interview, Alvin and Delbert Apetz, Wessels Living History Farm	unknown	**PI** The Great Depression and the New Deal, Experience the Dust Bowl, 1933–1934
Letter	Invasion of Italy Letter, Vera Lee to family in Lewellen, Nebraska	November 1943	**PI** World War II, Follow News from the Battle Front, 1943
Letter	Battle of Saipan Letter, Harold Moss to family in Minatare, Nebraska	July 1944	**PI** World War II, Follow News from the Battle Front, 1944
Nevada			
Photograph	Hoover Dam	unknown	**PI** The Great Depression and the New Deal, See the New Deal in Action, Hoover Dam
Photographs	Hoover Dam, High Scalers, Native Americans, blasting, Ragtown, Boulder City	unknown	**PI** The Great Depression and the New Deal, See the New Deal in Action, Hoover Dam
Video	Boulder Dam, U.S. Department of the Interior	1937	**PI** The Great Depression and the New Deal, See the New Deal in Action, Hoover Dam
Interview	Dust Storm Interview, Ernest Williams, University of Nevada, Las Vegas	Recorded March 26, 2004	**PI** The Great Depresssion and the New Deal, Experience the Dust Bowl, 1933–1934
New Jersey			
Photograph	Sandlot Baseball game, Newark	1915	**PI** Immigration, Define Your Identity as an American, Patrick
Poster	Atlantic City Postcards, Steel Pier, Atlantic City	1920	**PI** The 1920s, Enjoy the Roaring 20s
Postcard	Atlantic City Postcards, The Chalfonte-Haddon Hall Hotel, Atlantic City	circa 1920	**PI** The 1920s, Enjoy the Roaring 20s
Postcard	Atlantic City Postcards, Atlantic City	1923	**PI** The 1920s, Enjoy the Roaring 20s
Article	"A Negro in the CCC," Luther Wandall, *The Crisis*	August 1935	**PI** The Great Depression and the New Deal, See the New Deal in Action, Shenandoah
Photograph	Entrance to Lincoln Tunnel, PWA	unknown	**PI** The Great Depression and the New Deal, See the New Deal in Action, Hoover Dam
Telegram	Battle of the Bulge Telegrams, To family of Robert M. Cafarelli, North Bergen, New Jersey	January 22, 1945	**PI** World War II, Follow News from the Battle Front, 1944

Primary Source Index by State (continued)

Type	Source Title	Date	Location of Source
Photograph	VJ Day, Newark, New Jersey	August 18, 1945	**PI** World War II, Follow News from the Battle Front, 1945
Photograph	Members of Freedom Democratic Party holding up sketches of three slain civil rights leaders (L-R): Andrew Goodman, James Chaney and Michael Schwerner, during Democratic National Convention, Atlantic City, New Jersey	August 1, 1964	**PI** Civil Rights, Choose Your Path During Freedom Summer
Audio and Photograph	Democratic Convention Speech, Speech Before the Credentials Committee, Democratic National Convention, Fannie Lou Hamer,	August 22, 1964	**PI** Civil Rights, Choose Your Path During Freedom Summer
Video Interview	Black Power Leaders Interviews, Junius Williams, Amiri Baraka, Henry Hampton Collection, Washington University Library	Unknown	**PI** Civil Rights, Weigh the Evidence on the Black Power Movement
New Mexico			
Photograph	Navajo Indians on the Bosque Redondo reservation in present-day Arizona and eastern New Mexico	unknown	**ST** Topic 10, Lesson 1
Photograph	CCC workers at Bandelier National Monument	unknown	**PI** The Great Depression and the New Deal, See the New Deal in Action, Shenandoah
Video	Testing of first atom bomb, Operation Trinity, New Mexico	July 16, 1945	**PI** World War II, Advise Truman on the Atomic Bomb, Interim Comittee Notes; ST Topic 14, Lesson 6
New York			
Text	"New Netherlands," Reverend Isaac Jogues	1644	**ST** Topic 2, Lesson 3
Letter	From the Dutch West India Company to Peter Stuyvesant, Governor of New York	1663	**ST** Topic 2 Assessment
Document	Federalist Paper 10, James Madison	November 23, 1787	**IPS; Q** Topic 4, Document D
Diary	*A Narrative of Some of the Adventures, Dangers and Sufferings of a Revolutionary Soldier, Interspersed with Anecdotes of Incidents that Occurred Within His Own Observation,* Joseph Plumb Martin	1830	**PRSG,** Topic 3, Source 2
Editorial	Manifest Destiny editorial, John L. O'Sullivan, New York Morning News	December 27, 1845	**ST** Topic 6, Lesson 1
Cartoon	The Seneca Falls Convention in New York	1848	**ST** Topic 6, Lesson 6
Document	Declaration of Sentiments and Resolutions, Elizabeth Cady Stanton at the Seneca Falls Convention	July 1848	**IPS**
Speech	*Independence Day Speech,* Frederick Douglass, Rochester, New York	1852	**ST** Topic 6, Primary Source feature
Newspaper article	Frank Leslie's Illustrated Newspaper	July 2, 1887	**PI** Immigration, Give Your Son a Better Life
Book	*How the Other Half Lives,* Jacob Riis	1890	**ST** Topic 11, Primary Source feature
Song (audio)	Immigrant Communities, Maggie Murphy's Home	1890	**PI** Immigration, Explore Immigrant Life in New York City
Photograph	Immigrant Communities, Students at school in Little Italy, by Jacob Riis	c. 1890	**PI** Immigration, Explore Immigrant Life in New York City
Photograph	Physicians Examine Men, Ellis Island	unknown	**PI** Immigration, Give Your Son a Better Life
Map excerpt	Immigrant Communities, Immigrant Groups in Manhattan	1895	**PI** Immigration, Explore Immigrant Life in New York City
Photograph	St. Francis Xavier Church, New York City	1897	**PI** Immigration, Define Your Identity as an American, Chloe

Primary Source Index by State (continued)

Type	Source Title	Date	Location of Source
Photograph	Children riding tricycles, Ellis Island, by Jacob Riis	circa 1900	**PI** Immigration, Define Your Identity as an American, Rachel
Document	The Origins of the Confederation of the Five Nations; Iroquois Leaders	1900	**ST** Topic 1, Primary Source
Photograph	Mulberry Street with Italian signs, New York City	1900	**PI** Immigration, Define Your Identity as an American, Emilio
Artifact	Baseball card, John McGraw, New York Giants	1902	**PI** Immigration, Define Your Identity as an American, Patrick
Article	Sweatshop Article, "The Story of a Sweatshop Girl: Sadie Frowne," *Independent*	September 25, 1902	**PI** Immigration, Build a New Life, 1900; **ST** Topic 9, Primary Source feature
Photograph	Soy Kee Company, Chinatown, New York City	1903	**PI** Immigration, Should You Stay or Leave?
Video	New York City Fish Market, by Thomas A. Edison, Inc.	1903	**PI** Immigration, Explore Immigrant Life in New York City
Newspaper article	Kishinev Pogrom Article, *Sun*	May 15, 1903	**PI** Immigration, Give Your Son a Better Life
Photograph	The Educational Alliance, Men's basketball team, New York City	1904	**PI** Immigration, Define Your Identity as an American, Rachel
Photograph	W.E.B. Du Bois and other founding members of the Niagara Movement attended the Niagara Conference	1905	**ST** Topic 11, Lesson 3
Photograph	Jewish Americans celebrate the Jewish New Year	1905–1915	**PI** Immigration, Define Your Identity as an American, Rachel
Film	Arrival at Ellis Island	1906	**PI** Immigration, Give Your Son a Better Life
Video	The Skyscrapers of New York, American Mutoscope and Biograph Company	1906	**PI** Immigration, Explore Immigrant Life in New York City
Postcard	Essex and Hester Streets, New York City	1907	**PI** Immigration, Give Your Son a Better Life
Photograph	John Hayes, London Olympic Games	1908	**PI** Immigration, Define Your Identity as an American, Patrick
Photograph	President Roosevelt Poses with Olympic Team	1908	**PI** Immigration, Define Your Identity as an American, Patrick
Newspaper article	Olympic Team Article, President Greets Olympic Athletes, *New York Times*	September 1, 1908	**PI** Immigration, Define Your Identity as an American, Patrick
Photograph	Chinatown, New York City	1909	**PI** Immigration, Should You Stay or Leave?
Photograph	English class at New York's Italian House	circa 1909	**PI** Immigration, Define Your Identity as an American, Emilio
Photograph	Children's Aid Society, Christmas, Italian House, New York City	circa 1909	**PI** Immigration, Define Your Identity as an American, Emilio
Photograph	Children's Aid Society, Junion Drum Corps, Italian House, New York City	circa 1909	**PI** Immigration, Define Your Identity as an American, Emilio
Photograph	Italian House, Printing Trade class, New York City	circa 1909	**PI** Immigration, Define Your Identity as an American, Emilio
Photograph	The Educational Alliance, Americanization Day, New York City	1910	**PI** Immigration, Define Your Identity as an American, Rachel
Photograph	Chidren's Cooking Class Photo, Educational Alliance, New York City	1910	**PI** Immigration, Define Your Identity as an American, Rachel
Artifact	IAAC Emblem, Irish American Athletic Club, Queens, New York	1910	**PI** Immigration, Define Your Identity as an American, Patrick
Photograph	Children's Aid Society, Learning Italian, Italian House, New York City	circa 1910	**PI** Immigration, Define Your Identity as an American, Emilio

Primary Source Index by State (continued)

Type	Source Title	Date	Location of Source
Photograph	Italian House, Women learn homemaking skills, New York City	circa 1910	**PI** Immigration, Define Your Identity as an American, Emilio
Photograph	Italian House library, New York City	circa 1910	**PI** Immigration, Define Your Identity as an American, Emilio
Photograph	Immigrants at Work, Children removing shells from nuts, by Lewis Hine	c. 1910–1924	**PI** Immigration, Explore Immigrant Life in New York City
Photograph	Immigrant Communities, Children play ball, by Lewis Hine	c. 1910–1925	**PI** Immigration, Explore Immigrant Life in New York City
Photograph	Immigrants at Work, Garment industry, by Lewis Hine	c. 1910–1925	**PI** Immigration, Explore Immigrant Life in New York City
Photograph	Firefighters fight to extinguish the fire at the Triangle Shirtwaist Factory	1911	**ST** Topic 11, Lesson 1
Letter	Polish Immigrant Letter, Aleksandra Rembiénska to her family, Brooklyn, NY	October 14, 1911	**PI** Immigration, Give Your Son a Better Life
Photograph	Immigrants with Their Bags, on a Dock, Ellis Island (New York)	1912	**PI** Immigration, Give Your Son a Better Life
Photograph	Coney Island	1912	**ST** Topic 9, Lesson 6
Sheet Music	W.C. Handy, The St. Louis Blues	1914	**PI** Immigration, Define Your Identity as an American, Chloe
Photograph	Irish football match, Celtic Park, Queens, New York	July 26, 1914	**PI** Immigration, Define Your Identity as an American, Patrick
Photograph	Street vendor in Little Italy, New York City	unknown	**PI** Immigration, Define Your Identity as an American, Emilio
Postcard	Times Square at Night, New York City	1920s	**PI** The 1920s, Enjoy the Roaring 20s
Postcard	Yankee Stadium, Bronx, New York City	1920s	**PI** The 1920s, Enjoy the Roaring 20s
Photograph	The Capitol theatre, New York City	1920s	**PI** The 1920s, Enjoy the Roaring 20s
Photograph	Harlem nightclubs	1920s	**ST** Topic 12, Lesson 8
Photograph	People on the street in Harlem, New York	1920s	**ST** Topic 12, Lesson 8
Photograph	Lynching Banner at NAACP Headquarters, New York City	1920s	**PI** Explore African American Life, Enduring Violence
Photograph	Gwendolyn Bennett with friends, Harlem	1920s	**PI** Explore African American Life, Raising Voices
Data	Population of Harlem, African American and White	1920 and 1930	**PI** Explore African American Life, Raising Voices
Photograph	UNIA Representatives in a parade, Harlem, New York City	1920	**PI** The 1920s, Explore African American Life, Fighting Back
Document	Declaration of Negro Rights, Declaration of Rights of the Negro Peoples of the World, UNIA, New York	August 13, 1920	**PI** The 1920s, Explore African American Life, Fighting Back
Letter	William Allen White, letter to the editor of the *New York World*	1921	**ST** Topic 12, Lesson 6
Poem	Claude McKay Poem, "America," published in *Harlem Shadows*	1922	**PI** Immigration, Define Your Identity as an American, Chloe
Photograph	Marcus Garvey, New York City	1922	**PI** The 1920s, Explore African American Life, Fighting Back
Newspaper Article	Mothers of Flappers Article, "Mother Not to Blame for Flappers Flapping," *Evening World,* New York City	February 3, 1922	**PI** The 1920s, Adjust to Changing Times for Women, Helen
Newspaper article	Murray's is Raided, *New York Herald*	May 27, 1922	**PI** The 1920s, Enjoy the Roaring 20s
Audio Recording	Bessie Smith Song, "Down Hearted Blues," recorded in New York City	1923	**PI** Explore African American Life, Raising Voices
Artifact	Baseball, Autographed by Babe Ruth	no date	**PI** The 1920s, Enjoy the Roaring 20s

Primary Source Index by State (continued)

Type	Source Title	Date	Location of Source
Photograph	Young women in Harlem Dance the Charleston	unknown	**PI** Explore African American Life, Raising Voices
Photograph	Langston Hughes, Harlem	1924	**PI** Explore African American Life, Raising Voices
Poem	Langston Hughes Poem, "I, Too," *The Weary Blues,* Knopf	1926	**PI** Explore African American Life, Raising Voices
Cartoon	"The National Gesture," Clive Weed, *Judge*	1926	**PI** The 1920s, Should Prohibition Be Repealed?
Postcard	Traffic Tower, 5th Ave and 42nd Street, New York City	late 1920s	**PI** The 1920s, Enjoy the Roaring 20s
Book cover	*Home to Harlem,* by Claude McKay	1928	**PI** Explore African American Life, Raising Voices
Speech	Al Smith Acceptance Speech, Al Smith's Address of Acceptance at the State Capitol, Albany (New York)	August 22, 1928	**PI** The 1920s, Should Prohibition Be Repealed?
Newspaper article	Yankees Win Title, Daily News, New York City	October 10, 1928	**PI** The 1920s, Enjoy the Roaring 20s
Video	Duke Ellington Film, Duke Ellington Orchestra, Harlem, New York City	1929	**PI** The 1920s, Enjoy the Roaring 20s
Newspaper	Oscar De Priest Article, "Oscar De Priest Sworn In," *The New York Amsterdam News*	April 17, 1929	**PI** The 1920s, Explore African American Life, Fighting Back
Newspaper headline	Brooklyn Daily Eagle	October 24, 1929	**ST** Topic 13, Lesson 1
Photograph	Outside the New York Stock Exchange	October 29, 1929	**ST** Topic 13, Lesson 1
Newsreel	Breadline Newsreel, Starving Thousands Fill Bread Line in Unemployed Crisis, Universal Newspaper Newsreel	April 9, 1930	**PI** The Great Depression and the New Deal, Experience the Dust Bowl, 1929–1932
Photograph	Empire State Building under construction, New York City	1931	**ST** Topic 12, Lesson 4
Photograph	Women's International League for Peace and Freedom, New York City	1932	**PI** The 1920s, Adjust to Changing Times for Women, Helen
Speech	President Herbert Hoover at Madison Square Garden	October 1932	**Q** Topic 13, Document A
Newspaper Article	Repeal Revenue Article, "$2,000,000,000 Saving by Dry Repeal Seen," *New York Times*	October 30, 1932	**PI** The 1920s, Should Prohibition Be Repealed?
Photograph	People in New York celebrate Repeal of Prohibition	1933	**PI** The 1920s, Should Prohibition Be Repealed?
Letter	New York Citizen Letter, J. F. Bando to President Roosevelt, Brooklyn, New York	March 13, 1933	**PI** The Great Depression and the New Deal, Does FDR Deserve a Third Term?
Memoir	On the experience of arriving at Ellis Island, Edward Corsi, *In the Shadow of Liberty*	1935	**ST** Topic 9, Lesson 4
Letter	Letter from New York Girls to President Roosevelt, Homer, New York	1935	**PI** The Great Depression and the New Deal, See the New Deal in Action, Shenandoah
Photograph	Dining Hall, University of Buffalo	unknown	**PI** The Great Depression and the New Deal, Survive the Great Depression, Maria
Sculpture	Mother Goose, Frederick Roth, Central Park, New York City	1938	**PI** The Great Depression and the New Deal, See the New Deal in Action, San Diego
Photograph	Fifth Avenue Looking North from Just Below 42nd Street, New York City	1940s	**PI** World War II, Join the War Effort, Ruth
Magazine Article	African American Worker's Article, "What My Job Means to Me," Leotha Hackshaw, *Opportunity*	1943	**PI** World War II, Join the War Effort, Annie

Primary Source Index by State (continued)

Type	Source Title	Date	Location of Source
Photograph	Victory Garden Photograph, Children's School Victory Gardens, New York City	1944	**PI** World War II, Do Your Part on the Home Front
Document	Dispatch Bearer Instructions, Boy Scouts Adirondack Council of New York	unknown	**PI** World War II, Do Your Part on the Home Front
Photograph	Americans celebrate the end of World War II, New York City	August 1945	**ST** Topic 14, Lesson 6
Interview (audio)	Interview with Dora Maisler, Triangle Shirtwaist Factory fire	April 12, 1957	**PI** Immigration, Explore Immigrant Life in New York City
Newspaper Article	Freedom Ride Article, "Freedom Ride," *CORE-Lator*	May 1961	**PI** Civil Rights, Work as an Investigative Reporter, Freedom Rides
Newspaper Article	Birmingham Church Bombing Article, *The Troy Record,* Troy, New York	September 16, 1963	**PI** Civil Rights, Travel to Civil Rights Landmarks
Application	Freedom Summer Volunteers, Andrew Goodman, Freedom Summer Application	April 1964	**PI** Civil Rights, Witness Milestones in the Civil Rights Movement, Political Victories
Video Interview and Speech	Malcolm X Interview and Speech in New York	October 1964	**PI** Civil Rights, Weigh the Evidence on the Black Power Movement
Letter	NAACP Letter, Letter to NAACP Supporters Regarding Black Power, Roy Wilkins	October 1966	**PI** Civil Rights, Weigh the Evidence on the Black Power Movement
Photograph	Anti-draft protestors, New York City	October 1967	**ST** Topic 17, Lesson 3
Book cover	The Pentagon Papers in book form, based on the *New York Times* investigative reports	1971	**PI** Vietnam, Experience the Legacy of the Vietnam War, Lucia
Article	"A Vietnam Veteran Stills Audience With Rebuke," New York Times	May 30, 1979	**PI** Vietnam, Experience the Legacy of the Vietnam War, Robert
Photograph	Air traffic control strikers, New York's LaGuardia Airport	August 1981	**ST** Topic 19, Lesson 2
Song (audio), Photograph	"Rise 'n' Shine," Kool Moe Dee, featuring Chuck D and KRS-One	1991	**PI** Civil Rights, Witness Milestones in the Civil Rights Movement, Work Continues
Photograph	Million Hoodies March in memory of Trayvon Martin, New York City	March 21, 2012	**PI** Civil Rights, Witness Milestones in the Civil Rights Movement, Work Continues
North Carolina			
Painting	*Painting of the Town of Pomeiock,* John White	1585	**PSRG** Topic 1, Source 2
Speech	Speech at the North Carolina Ratifying Convention, James Iredell	July 1788	**PSRG** Topic 4, Source 3
Letter	Nancy Mangum to North Carolina Governor Zebulon Vance on conditions in the state	1863	**ST** Topic 7, Lesson 5
Photograph	Railroad car for African Americans only, Fayetteville	unknown	**PI** The 1920s, Explore African American Life, Moving North
Oral History	Stringing Tobacco Bags Account, "Mary Smith," Works Progress Administration, Federal Writers' Project	1938	**PI** The Great Depression and the New Deal, Surviving the Great Depression, Clarence
Photograph	A man stands outside a segregated waiting room at a bus station in Durham, North Carolina	unknown	**PI** Civil Rights, Witness Milestones in the Civil Rights Movement, A Movement Begins
Photograph	The Greensboro Four (from left to right): David Richmond, Franklin McCain, Ezell Blair, Jr., Joseph McNeil	Feburary 1, 1960	**PI** Civil Rights, Work as an Investigative Reporter, Greensboro Sit-Ins
Photograph	Joseph McNeil, Franklin McCain, Billy Smith, and Clarence Henderson wait for service on the second day of their sit-in at Woolworth's, Greensboro, North Carolina	February 2, 1960	**PI** Civil Rights, Work as an Investigative Reporter, Greensboro Sit-Ins

Primary Source Index by State (continued)

Type	Source Title	Date	Location of Source
Letters	Letters to the Advisory Committee, Letters from Greensboro Citizens to the Advisory Committee on Community Relations	February–March 1960	**PI** Civil Rights, Work as an Investigative Reporter, Greensboro Sit-Ins
Video	Woolworth Sit-In Film, Segregation Protest at Woolworth Store, Greensboro, North Carolina	1960	**PI** Civil Rights, Witness Milestones in the Civil Rights Movement, Early Campaigns
Speech	""From a Lunch Counter Stool," James Lawson, at Shaw University in Raleigh, North Carolina"	1960	**ST** Topic 16, Lesson 2
Newspaper Editorial	"Nixon and His New Indo-China War," Craig Wilson, Technician (North Carolina State University's student newspaper)	May 1, 1970	**PI** Vietnam, Do You Support Nixon's Strategy in Vietnam?, Cambodia Editorial
Audio Recording	Greensboro Four Interview, Interview with Joseph McNeil, Greensboro Public Library	October 14, 1979	**PI** Civil Rights, Work as an Investigative Reporter, Greensboro Sit-Ins
Photograph	People protest the death of Keith Scott, Charlotte, North Carolina	September 22, 2016	**PI** Civil Rights, Witness Milestones in the Civil Rights Movement, Work Continues
North Dakota			
Photograph	Wetzel family prays for rain on their farm, Bismarck, North Dakota	1930s	**PI** The Great Depression and the New Deal, Experience the Dust Bowl, 1935–1936
Diary	Dust Bowl Diary, Ann Marie Low	August 1, 1934	**PI** The Great Depression and the New Deal, Experience the Dust Bowl, 1933–1934
Photograph	President Roosevelt visits a North Dakota farmer	1936	**PI** The Great Depression and the New Deal, Experience the Dust Bowl, 1933–1935
Ohio			
Poster	Board of Education Poster, Cleveland, Ohio	1917	**PI** Immigration, Giver Your Son a Better Life
Photograph	League of Women Voters, Cincinatti, Ohio	1920s	**PI** The 1920s, Adjust to Changing Times for Women, Lillian
Photograph	Twentieth annual session of the NAACP in Cleveland, Ohio	1929	**ST** Topic 12, Lesson 6
Photograph	NAACP Junior Auxiliary Delegates, Cleveland, Ohio	1929	**PI** The 1920s, Explore African American Life, Fighting Back
Artifact	Exchange Credit Coupon, Yellow Spring, Ohio	1934	**PI** The Great Depression and the New Deal, Surviving the Great Depression, Irene
Letter	Ohio Citizen Letter, Raymond E. Click to President Roosevelt, Prospect, Ohio	April 30, 1935	**PI** The Great Depression and the New Deal, Does FDR Deserve a Third Term?
Video	Recruitment of Women Film, Dayton, Ohio	unknown	**PI** World War II, Join the War Effort, Ruth
Identification Card	Sam Harsh, Civilian Defense Messenger ID Card	June 11, 1942	**PI** World War II, Do Your Part on the Home Front
Telegram	Battle of the Bulge Telegrams, Lieutenant Carroll Sammetinger, to family in Lima, Ohio from Prisoner of War Camp in Germany	December 25, 1944	**PI** World War II, Follow News from the Battle Front, 1944
Photograph	African Americans protest against Vietnam, Cleveland, Ohio	1965	**PI** Vietnam, Investigate How the War Divided Americans
Photograph	Protest March in Cleveland, Ohio	1965	**PSRG** Topic 17, Source 3
Video	Reaction to King's Assassination, Cleveland Mayor Carl Stokes Reacts to the Assassination of Dr. Martin Luther King, Jr.	April 1968	**PI** Civil Rights, Witness Milestones in the Civil Rights Movement, An Era Ends

Primary Source Index by State (continued)

Type	Source Title	Date	Location of Source
Article	"Lonely Wife Keeps Vigil for U.S. Flier Captured by Viet Cong," Beverly Beyette, The Cincinnati Enquirer	November 7, 1968	**PI** Vietnam, Experience the Legacy of the Vietnam War, Heather
Letters	Kent State Letters, Letters from an Ohio taxpayer and from Greg Baker to the President of Kent State Student Body	May 1, 1970	**PI** Vietnam, Investigate How the War Divided Americans
Photograph	Kent State shootings, Kent, Ohio	May 4, 1970	**ST** Topic 17, Lesson 4
Oklahoma			
Photograph	"Rioters burned the homes of African Americans in Tulsa, Oklahoma"	1921	**ST** Topic 12, Lesson 4
Article	Tulsa Race Massacre Article, "The Eruption of Tulsa," Walter F. White, *Nation*	June 29, 1921	**PI** The 1920s, Explore African American Life, Enduring Violence
Photograph	African American being arrested, Greenwood, Tulsa	circa 6/1/1921	**PI** The 1920s, Explore African American Life, Enduring Violence
Photograph	Armed White Men and African Americans	circa 6/1/1921	**PI** The 1920s, Explore African American Life, Enduring Violence
Photograph	African American victim, Greenwood (sensitive content)	circa 6/1/1921	**PI** The 1920s, Explore African American Life, Enduring Violence
Photograph	Greenwood buildings in flames, Tulsa, Oklahoma	circa 6/1/1921	**PI** The 1920s, Explore African American Life, Enduring Violence
Photograph	Will Rogers	circa 1930	**PI** The 1920s, Enjoy the Roaring 20s
Interview	Tumbleweed Interview, Alvin and Delbert Apetz, Wessels Living History Farm	unknown	**PI** The Great Depression and the New Deal, Experience the Dust Bowl, 1933–1934
Photograph	Workers plant shelterbelt trees on an Oklahoma farm	unknown	**PI** The Great Depression and the New Deal, Experience the Dust Bowl, 1933–1934
Song	Woodie Guthrie Song, "So Long, It's Been Good to Know Yuh," composed and recorded by Woody Guthrie	1935	**PI** The Great Depression and the New Deal, Experience the Dust Bowl, 1935–1936
Letter	Rains Return Letter, Caroline Henderson to Eli Jaffe	December 20, 1938	**PI** The Great Depression and the New Deal, Experience the Dust Bowl, 1935–1936
Photograph	Alfred P. Murrah Federal Building, Oklahoma City	April 1995	**ST** Topic 19, Lesson 5
Oregon			
Speech	"I Will Fight No More Forever," Chief Joseph	October 5, 1877	**IPS**
Photograph	Cannery Laborers Photograph, Chinese Workers in Astoria Cannery	circa 1900	**PI** Immigration, Build a New Life, 1880
Photograph	Cannery Laborers Photograph, Chinese Workers at the Bon Bon Salmon Cannery, Astoria	circa 1900	**PI** Immigration, Build a New Life, 1880
Photograph	An American Indian family, Warm Springs Reservation, Oregon	unknown	**ST** Topic 10, Lesson 1
Photograph	Farm for sale	1930s	**ST** Topic 13, Lesson 2
Photograph	Two Girls in private residence, Portland Assembly Center, Oregon	1942	**PI** World War II, Tour a Japanese American Incarceration Camp, Daily Life
Pennsylvania			
Letter	George Washington to his mother, about an ambush near Fort Duquesne	1755	**ST** Topic 3, Lesson 1
Newspaper	Pennsylvania Journal	1765	**ST** Topic 3, Lesson 1

Primary Source Index by State (continued)

Type	Source Title	Date	Location of Source
Article	Centinel Number 1, Philadelphia *Independent Gazetteer*	1787	**Q** Topic 4, Document E
Address	"The Address and Reasons of Dissent of the Minority of the Convention of the State of Pennsylvania to their Constituents," William Findley, Robert Whitehall, John Smilie; published in *The Pennsylvania Packet and Daily Advertiser*	December 1787	**IPS**
Speech	Gettysburg Address, Abraham Lincoln	November 19, 1863	**ST** Topic 7, Primary Source feature; **IPS**
Letter	Letter to the President, Horace W. Pitkin to Grover Cleveland regarding the Chinese Exclusion Act, Philadelphia	September 19, 1888	**PI** Immigration, Should You Stay or Leave?
Pamphlet	African American Voting Pamphlet, What a Colored Man Should Do to Vote	circa 1900	**PI** Immigration, Define Your Identity as an American, Chloe
Artifact	Baseball card, Honus Wagner, Pittsburgh Pirates	circa 1909	**PI** Immigration, Define Your Identity as an American, Patrick
Photograph	"Women workers in a cigar factory near Pittsburgh, Pennsylvania"	early 1900s	**ST** Topic 11, Lesson 2
Photograph	Italian shops on 8th and Christian Streets, South Philadelphia	circa 1920	**PI** Immigration, Define Your Identity as an American, Emilio
Yearbook	University Yearbook, University of Pennsylvania	1921	**PI** The 1920s, Adjust to Changing Times for Women, Lillian
Photograph	Members of Delta Sigma Theta, University of Pennsylvania	December 1921	**PI** The 1920s, Adjust to Changing Times for Women, Ada
Letter	African American Work Letter, from Reverend W. M. Henry to John T. Clark, Altheimer, Arkansas (mentions Nashville, TN and Pittsburgh, PA)	December 22, 1922	**PI** The 1920s, Explore African American Life, Moving North
Photograph	Negro National League Photos, Philadelphia Hilldale club	October 1924	**PI** The 1920s, Explore African American Life, Fighting Back
Photograph	Child labor in a coal mine, South Pittston, Pennsylvania	unknown	**PI** The Great Depression and the New Deal, Work to End the Depression
Photograph	"Double V" Campaign Photo, The Ink Spots On Stage holding sheet music for 'A Yankee Doodle Tan', Savoy Ballroom (Hill City Auditorium), Pittsburgh, Pennsylvania	1942	**PI** World War II, Join the War Effort, Annie
Letter	Letter to the Pittsburgh Courier from James G. Thompson of Wichita, Kansas	January 31, 1942	**ST** Topic 14, Lesson 8
Photograph	African American Worker Photos, Bertha Stallworth inspecting end of 40mm artillery cartridge, Frankford Arsenal, Philadelphia	unknown	**PI** World War II, Join the War Effort, Annie
Poster and Letter	Army-Navy E Award, Hershey Chocolate Corp., Hershey, Pennsylvania	December 30, 1944	**PI** World War II, Do Your Part on the Home Front
Rhode Island			
Book	*The Bloudy Tenent of Persecution for Cause of Conscience,* Roger Williams	1644	**PSRG** Topic 2, Source 1
Letter	Letter from William Rotch, Sr. to Moses Brown	November 1787	**PSRG** Topic 4, Source 4
South Carolina			
Painting	A View of Charleston, *South Carolina;* Thomas Mellish	18th century	**ST** Topic 2 Opener
Speech	Viewpoint on Article 7, Section 4, Charles Pinckney	January 1788	**PSRG** Topic 4, Source 4
Debate	"Debate over Nullification," Daniel Webster and John C. Calhoun	March 1833	**IPS**

Primary Source Index by State (continued)

Type	Source Title	Date	Location of Source
Declaration	Declaration of the Immediate Causes Which Induce and Justify the Secession of South Carolina From the Federal Union	December 20, 1860	**ST** Topic 7, Lesson 3
Newspaper	Newspaper headline announcing secession, Charleston, South Carolina	1860	**ST** Topic 7, Lesson 3
Photograph	Charleston, South Carolina	1865	**ST** Topic 8, Lesson 1
Speech	Address by Reverend E.J. Adams	March 19, 1867	**ST** Topic 8, Primary Source feature
Newspaper Article	Voting Rights Testimony, "Charges of Negro Stir Committee," *Evening Star,* Washington, D.C.	December 29, 1920	**PI** The 1920s, Explore African American Life, Fighting Back
Poem	Claude McKay Poem, "America," published in *Harlem Shadows*	1922	**PI** Immigration, Define Your Identity as an American, Chloe
Photograph	First aid training for CCC enrollees at Camp F-6, Enoree District Sumter National Forest, Newberry County, South Carolina	unknown	**PI** The Great Depression and the New Deal, See the New Deal in Action, Shenandoah
South Dakota			
Photograph	"A Golden Work," Hydroulic [sic] mining at Rockdrville [i.e. Rockerville], South Dakota	1889	**ST** Topic 6, Lesson 3
Interview	Black Elk Speaks: Being the Life Story of a Holy Man of the Oglala Sioux, as told through John G. Neihardt	1932	**PSRG** Topic 10, Source 4
Photograph	The aftermath of a dust storm in Dallas, South Dakota.	1936	**PI** The Great Depression and the New Deal, Experience the Dust Bowl, 1933–1934
Tennessee			
Photograph	Fisk Jubilee Singers, by J.W. Black	1872	**PI** Immigration, Define Your Identity as an American, Chloe
Photograph	Fisk University, Choir and Organ	1899	**PI** Immigration, Define Your Identity as an American, Chloe
Photograph	A boy named Eb Snow, near Nashville	circa 1901	**PI** Immigration, Define Your Identity as an American, Chloe
Receipt	State and County Poll Tax Receipt, Memphis	1903	**PI** Immigration, Define Your Identity as an American, Chloe
Photograph	African Americans hauling cargo to ships on the Mississippi River, Memphis	circa 1906	**PI** Immigration, Define Your Identity as an American, Chloe
Photograph	Fisk University Library	1908	**PI** Immigration, Define Your Identity as an American, Chloe
Audio	"Swing Low, Sweet Chariot" Fisk University Jubilee Quartet	December 1, 1909	**PI** Immigration, Define Your Identity as an American, Chloe
Sheet Music	W.C. Handy, The St. Louis Blues	1914	**PI** Immigration, Define Your Identity as an American, Chloe
Letter	African American Work Letter, from Reverend W. M. Henry to John T. Clark, Altheimer, Arkansas (mentions Nashville, TN and Pittsburgh, PA)	December 22, 1922	**PI** The 1920s, Explore African American Life, Moving North
Newspaper Article	Great Migration Article, "Spring to See Greatest Migration in History," *Chicago Defender,* Memphis, TN	February 20, 1925	**PI** The 1920s, Explore African American Life, Moving North
Photograph	Woman working in the wheel well of a Vultee "Vengeance dive bomber, Nashville	February 1, 1943	**PI** World War II, Join the War Effort, Ruth
Photograph	Racial tensions led to mass arrests of African Americans in Columbia, Tennessee	February 26, 1946	**ST** Topic 16, Lesson 1
Photograph	The balcony of the Lorraine Motel in Memphis, Tennessee; following the assassination of Dr. Martin Luther King, Jr.	April 14, 1968	**ST** Topic 16, Lesson 3

Primary Source Index by State (continued)

Type	Source Title	Date	Location of Source
Photograph	Carla Thomas, Concert	1973	**PI** Civil Rights, Weigh the Evidence of the Black Power Movement
Audio Interview	Freedom Rides Interview, Diane Nash, Blackside Inc., Washington Univ. Libraries Film and Media Archive	1985	**PI** Civil Rights, Work as an Investigative Reporter, Freedom Rides
Texas			
Letter	Letter from the Alamo, Texan Commander William B. Travis	February 24, 1836	**IPS**
Document	Texas Declaration of Independence	March 2, 1836	**IPS**
Document	A Declaration of Causes, Texas Secession Convention	2 February 1861	**IPS**
Advertisement	International & Great Northern Railroad Advertisement	circa 1880	**PI** Immigration, Give Your Son a Better Life
Photograph	School ruined in the Galveston Hurricane	1900	**ST** Topic 11, Lesson 1
Newspaper	The Jewish Herald	September 9, 1909	**PI** Immigration, Give Your Son a Better Life
Photograph	Refugees from Veracruz, Mexico await transportation to Galveston	1914	**PI** Immigration, Give Your Son a Better Life
Letter	Chicago Defender Letter, Letter from an African American from Port Arthur, Texas to the Chicago Defender, published in The Journal of Negro History	1917	**PI** Immigration, Define Your Identity as an American, Chloe
Photograph	Female Athletes at the University of Texas	1920s	**PI** The 1920s, Adjust to Changing Times for Women, Lillian
Newspaper Article	Voting Rights Testimony, "Charges of Negro Stir Committee," *Evening Star,* Washington, D.C.	December 29, 1920	**PI** The 1920s, Explore African American Life, Fighting Back
Receipt	Poll Tax Receipt, San Antonio	1931	**PI** The 1920s, Explore African American Life, Fighting Back
Interview	German Texas Pioneers Interview, Mrs. Amelia Steward Christoffer	1930s	**PI** Immigration, Build a New Life, 1870
Photograph	Walter Ballard, Hardeman County, Texas	1933	**PI** The Great Depression and The New Deal, Surviving the Great Depression, Jack
Photograph	CCC Company 888, showing African American members segregated, Mission Tejas State Park, Weches, Texas,	October 1934	**PI** The Great Depression and the New Deal, See the New Deal in Action, Shenandoah
Photograph	Dust storm, Stratford, Texas	1935	**ST** Topic 13, Lesson 2
Song	Woodie Guthrie Song, "So Long, It's Been Good to Know Yuh," composed and recorded by Woody Guthrie	1935	**PI** The Great Depression and the New Deal, Experience the Dust Bowl, 1935–1936
Photograph	Black Sunday storm bears down on Spearman, Texas	April 14, 1935	**PI** The Great Depression and the New Deal, Experience the Dust Bowl, 1935–1936
Newspaper Article	Rainmaker Article, "Thornton to Bombard Sky for Moisture," *Pampa Daily News,* Texas,	May 1, 1935	**PI** The Great Depression and the New Deal, Experience the Dust Bowl, 1935–1936
Fine Art	Alexandre Hogue, Drought Survivors	1936	**PI** The Great Depression and the New Deal, Experience the Dust Bowl, 1935–1936
Court decision	Smith v. Allwright, U.S.	1944	**PSRG** Topic 8, Source 3
Photograph	"President Kennedy and his wife ride with Texas Governor John Connally and his wife in the presidential motorcade through Dallas, Texas"	November 22, 1963	**ST** Topic 16, Lesson 4

Primary Source Index by State (continued)

Type	Source Title	Date	Location of Source
Letter	Letter from Stephen Daniel to his Parents, Waco Texas	1968	**PI** Vietnam, Witness the Fighting in Vietnam, The Jungle
Interview	Hobo Interview, Walter Ballard about Riding the Rails, Wessels Living History Farm, Hardeman County, Texas	1984	**PI** The Great Depression and The New Deal, Surviving the Great Depression, Jack
Utah			
Photograph	"People celebrate the completion of the Transcontinental Railroad, Promontory, Utah"	1869	**ST** Topic 10, Lesson 2
Photograph	Immigrants in Utah Photographs, Roma man and children	December 19, 1906	**PI** Immigration, Build a New Life, 1900
Photograph	Immigrants in Utah Photographs, Copperfield Mercantile Company	1908	**PI** Immigration, Build a New Life, 1900
Photograph	Immigrants in Utah Photographs, Parade with Italian lodge members, Bingham	1909	**PI** Immigration, Build a New Life, 1900
Photograph	Ogden High School, PWA, Odgen, Utah	1937	**PI** The Great Depression and the New Deal, See the New Deal in Action, Hoover Dam
Vermont			
Photograph	Ida Fuller of Ludlow, Vermont, with Social Security check	1930s	**ST** Topic 13, Lesson 4
Painting	Rosie the Riveter, Norman Rockwell	1943	**PI** World War II, Join the War Effort, Ruth
Interview	Italian Shed Owner Interview, Giacomo Tonazzi	August 12, 1940	**PI** Immigration, Build a New Life, 1910
Virgnia			
Book	Nova Britannia: Offering Most Excellent fruites by Planting in Virginia, Robert Johnson	1609	**ST** Topic 2 Assessment
Document	Virginia Resolves, Patrick Henry	May 29, 1765	**ST** Topic 3, Lesson 1
Speech	"Give Me Liberty or Give Me Death," Patrick Henry	March 1775	**IPS**
Document	Virginia Declaration of Rights, George Mason	Adopted June 12, 1776	**IPS**
Statute	Virginia Statute for Religious Freedom, Thomas Jefferson	1786	**IPS; ST** Topic 4, Primary Source feature
Notes	Notes on the Debates in the Federal Convention, James Madison	1787	**PSRG** Topic 4, Source 1
Essay	"Letter from the Federal Farmer to the Republican," Richard Henry Lee	October 1, 1787	**IPS**
Essay	Federalist Paper 10, James Madison	November 23, 1787	**IPS; Q** Topic 4, Document D
Essay	Federalist Paper 39, James Madison	January 18, 1788	**IPS**
Document	Federalist Paper 51, James Madison	February 8, 1788	**IPS**
Diary	*A Narrative of Some of the Adventures, Dangers and Sufferings of a Revolutionary Soldier, Interspersed with Anecdotes of Incidents that Occurred Within His Own Observation,* Joseph Plumb Martin	1830	**PRSG** Topic 3, Source 4
Speech	Excerpt from speech given by a delegate at the Virginia legislature, Niles' Weekly Register, vol. 43	September 8, 1832	**ST** Topic 6 Assessment
Letter	Letter from Robert E. Lee to his sister regarding his resignation from the United States Army	April 20, 1861	**ST** Topic 7, Lesson 3
Photograph	Richmond munitions factory	Civil War era	**ST** Topic 7, Lesson 5
Photograph	Battlefield at Fredericksburg	1862	**ST** Topic 7, Lesson 6

Primary Source Index by State (continued)

Type	Source Title	Date	Location of Source
Account	Appeal to the Eastern District of Virginia, Richmond, Milton Claiborne Nicholas	1870	**PSRG** Topic 8, Source 2
Letter	Attack by the Ku Klux Klan Letter, Letter from Rampy J. Burdick, (Erving, VA) to Attorney General John G. Sargeant, (Washington, D.C.)	March 3, 1928	**PI** The 1920s, Explore African American Life, Enduring Violence
Photograph	Turk Mountain Overlook, Shenandoah National Park	unknown	**PI** The Great Depression and the New Deal, See the New Deal in Action, Shenandoah
Postcard	Skyline Drive, Shenandoah National Park	unknown	**PI** The Great Depression and the New Deal, See the New Deal in Action, Shenandoah
Photograph	Big Meadows Lodge, Shenandoah National Park	unknown	**PI** The Great Depression and the New Deal, See the New Deal in Action, Shenandoah
Letter	Battle of Bataan Letter, Vernon D. Hobbs, Philippines (to Richmond, Virginia)	December 1941–February 1942	**PI** World War II, Follow News from the Battle Front, 1942
Letter	Segregation Letter, Letter from Robert Leon Bacon to Governor Stanley, Richmond, Virginia	December 5, 1955	**PI** Civil Rights, Witness Milestones in the Civil Rights Movement, A Movement Begins
Photograph	Nonviolent Training and Protests, NAACP Volunteer Training, Petersburg, Virginia	May 1, 1960	**PI** Civil Rights, Work as an Investigative Reporter, Greensboro Sit-Ins
Washington D.C.			
Speech	Monroe Doctrine, James Monroe, address to Congress	December 2, 1823	**ST** Topic 5, Lesson 6
Speech	On the Indian Removal Act, President Andrew Jackson, message to Congress	December 6, 1830	**ST** Topic 5, Lesson 7
Speech	First Inaugural Address, Abraham LIncoln	March 1861	**IPS**
Photograph	President Abraham Lincoln at his second inauguration	March 1865	**ST** Topic 8, Lesson 1
Speech	Second Inaugural Address, Abraham Lincoln	March 1865	**IPS; ST** Topic 8, Lesson 1; **ST** Topic 8, Primary Source feature
Photograph	Union troops victory parade in Washington, D.C.	May 1865	**ST** Topic 8, Lesson 1
Speech	"Peace Without Victory," Woodrow Wilson address to Congress	January 22, 1917	**ST** Topic 12, Lesson 3
Speech	The Fourteen Points, Woodrow Wilson speech to Congress	January 8, 1918	**ST** Topic 12, Primary Source feature
Photograph	Ku Klux Klan March in Washington, DC	1920s	**PI** The 1920s, Explore African American Life, Enduring Violence
Letter	Temperance Letter, from Alfred Fowler (Springfield, IL) to Senator Wesley Jones, Washington, D.C.	April 1, 1920	**PI** The 1920s, Should Prohibition Be Repealed?
Newspaper Article	Voting Rights Testimony, "Charges of Negro Stir Committee," *Evening Star,* Washington, D.C.	December 29, 1920	**PI** The 1920s, Explore African American Life, Fighting Back
Photograph	Salvation Army House Girls, Washington, DC	1921	**PI** The 1920s, Adjust to Changing Times for Women, Helen
Advertisement	Anti-Lynching Advertisement, "The Shame of America," NAACP, *Evening Star,* Washington, D.C.,	November 23, 1922	**PI** The 1920s, Explore African American Life, Enduring Violence
Letter	Attack by the Ku Klux Klan Letter, Letter from Rampy J. Burdick, (Erving, VA) to Attorney General John G. Sargeant, (Washington, DC)	March 3, 1928	**PI** The 1920s, Explore African American Life, Enduring Violence

Primary Source Index by State (continued)

Type	Source Title	Date	Location of Source
Video	Hunger March Silent Documentary, The National Hunger March, Workers Film and Photo League	1931	**PI** The New Deal and the Great Depression, Survive the Great Depression, Jack
Telegram	Deportation Telegram, from C. P. Visel to Colonel Arthur M. Woods, Los Angeles, California to Washington, D.C.	January 6, 1931	**PI** The Great Depression and the New Deal, Survive the Great Depression, Maria
Newspaper Article	Unemployment Newspaper Article, "Colored Jobless Growing Restless," Associated Press, *Evening Star*	June 11, 1931	**PI** The Great Depression and the New Deal, Survive the Great Depression, Clarence
Photograph	Veterans outside the U.S. Capitol	1932	**ST** Topic 13, Lesson 3
Quote	Evalyn McLean, Washington, D.C., resident	1932	**ST** Topic 13, Lesson 3
Video	Bartering film, Footage of Bartering in Washington, D.C.	1933	**PI** The Great Depression and the New Deal, Survive the Great Depression, Irene
Film	New Deal Promotional Film, for the National Recovery Administration, Metro-Goldwyn-Mayer	1933	**PI** The Great Depression and the New Deal, Work to End the Great Depression
Speech	Roosevelt Repeal Speech, President Franklin Roosevelt's Speech to Congress (Prohibition)	March 13, 1933	**PI** The 1920s, Should Prohibition Be Repealed?
Debate	Minimum Wage Debate, Arguments For and Against a Minimum Wage, Frances Perkins, Franklin Roosevelt, Joint Hearings Before Congress	1934, 1937, 1938	**PI** The Great Depression and the New Deal, Work to End the Great Depression
Film	National Recovery Act Film, The March of Time, RKO Pictures/20th Century Fox	1935	**PI** The Great Depression and the New Deal, Work to End the Great Depression
Photograph	Lincoln Memorial Dust Photograph, Dust Falling on the Lincoln Memorial	March 1935	**PI** The Great Depression and the New Deal, Experience the Dust Bowl, 1935–1936
Newsreel	Social Security Newsreel, Applications for Old Age Security, Pathé News and the Social Security Board	1936	**PI** The Great Depression and the New Deal, Work to End the Great Depression
Documentary film	Dust Bowl Documentary, The Plow That Broke the Plains, written and directed by Pare Lorentz, sponsored by the U.S. Resettlement Administration	1936	**PI** The Great Depression and the New Deal, Experience the Dust Bowl, 1935–1936
Poster	Social Security for families, Social Security Act Amendments	1939	**PI** The Great Depression and the New Deal, Work to End the Great Depression
Newsreel	Conservation Work Newsreel, Emergency Conservation Work, United States Department of the Interior/National Park Service	1939	**PI** The Great Depression and the New Deal, Work to End the Great Depression
Pamphlet	War Production Drive Pamphlet, Official Plan Book	1942	**PI** World War II, Join the War Effort, Louis
Newsreel	Scrap Metal Newsreel, "Salvage," Office of War Information/Bureau of Motion Pictures	1942	**PI** World War II, Do Your Part on the Home Front
Photograph	Paper Drive Photograph, Scrap Salvage Campaign, Victory Program, Washington, D.C.	1942	**PI** World War II, Do Your Part on the Home Front
Pamphlet	Citizens Defense Corps Booklet, Office of Civilian Defense	1942	**PI** World War II, Do Your Part on the Home Front
Audio	Fireside Chat, Franklin D. Roosevelt	February 23, 1942	**PI** World War II, Join the War Effort, Louis
Video	War Manpower Commission Video, Manpower, Office of War Information	1943	**PI** World War II, Join the War Effort, Louis
Chart	Food Points Value Chart, Rationing, Office of Price Administration,	1943	**PI** World War II, Do Your Part on the Home Front
Video	Government Rationing Animation, Point Rationing of Foods, Office of War Information/ Bureau of Motion Pictures	1943	**PI** World War II, Do Your Part on the Home Front

Primary Source Index by State (continued)

Type	Source Title	Date	Location of Source
Photograph	Salvage Award Recognition, Dial Rawl, U.S. War Production Board	June 1943	**PI** World War II, Do Your Part on the Home Front
Memo	Memorandum from Henry Stimson, Secretary of War, to Harry S. Truman	July 2, 1945	**PI** World War II, Advise Truman on the Atomic Bomb
Speech	Truman Doctrine speech, President Harry S. Truman, Before a Joint Session of Congress	March 12, 1947	**ST** Topic 15, Lesson 1
Photograph	Diem Visits America	1957	**PI** Vietnam, Explore America's Road to War in Vietnam, Cold War Fears, 1953–1961
Speech	Inaugural Address, John F. Kennedy	January 20, 1961	**ST** Topic 16 Primary Source feature; **ST** Topic 17, Lesson 1; **IPS**
Article	"A Freedom Rider Speaks His Mind," Jimmy McDonald, *Freedomways*	Spring 1961	**PI** Civil Rights, Witness Milestones in the Civil Rights Movement, Early Campaigns
Speech/Audio	President John F. Kennedy Speech, Radio and Television Report to the American People on Civil Rights	June 11, 1963	**PI** Civil Rights, Witness Milestones in the Civil Rights Movement, Political Victories
Audio	Department of State Research Memo, Soviet Media Coverage of Racial Crisis in U.S.	June 14, 1963	**PI** Civil Rights, Travel to Civil Rights Landmarks, Birmingham
Audio and photograph	Jackie Robinson Interview, Educational Radio Network	1963	**PI** Civil Rights, Travel to Civil Rights Landmarks, Washington, D.C.
Audio	Firsthand Accounts of the 1963 March on Washington	August 28, 1963	**PI** Civil Rights, Travel to Civil Rights Landmarks, Washington, D.C.
Video	Film Footage of the March on Washington	August 28, 1963	**PI** Civil Rights, Travel to Civil Rights Landmarks, Washington, D.C.
Photograph	Marchers at the March on Washington, Capitol in the background	August 28, 1963	**PI** Civil Rights, Travel to Civil Rights Landmarks, Washington, D.C.
Photograph	Organizers of the March on Washington Photo, Martin Luther King, Jr., Floyd B. McKissick, Rev, Eugene Carson Blake, Washington, D.C.	August 28, 1963	**PI** Civil Rights, Travel to Civil Rights Landmarks, Washington, D.C.
Speech, Audio	"I Have a Dream," Dr. Martin Luther King, Jr. during the March on Washington"	August 28, 1963	**IPS; ST** Topic 16 Primary Source Feature; **PI** Civil Rights, Travel to Civil Rights Landmarks, Washington, D.C.
Photograph	Johnson Signs the Civil Rights Act Photograph	July 2, 1964	**PI** Civil Rights, Travel to Civil Rights Landmarks, Washington, D.C.
Photograph	Anti-Vietnam war protest, Washington, D.C.	October 21, 1967	**PI** Vietnam, Investigate How the War Divided Americans
Photograph	Former Vietnam POW Air Force Major Norman McDaniel arrives back in the United States, Andrews Air Force Base, Washington, D.C.	February 17, 1973	**PI** Vietnam, Experience the Legacy of the Vietnam War, Heather
Photograph	Watergate Committee Chair Senator Sam Ervin	1973	**ST** Topic 18, Lesson 5
Photograph	March for the Equal Rights Amendment, Washington, D.C.	1978	**ST** Topic 18, Lesson 2
Video	President Ronald Reagan's Remarks at Dedication of the Vietnam Veterans Memorial Statue	November 11, 1984	**PI** Vietnam, Experience the Legacy of the Vietnam War, Robert
Photograph	President Reagan and First Lady Nancy Reagan inaugural ball	January 1985	**ST** Topic 19, Lesson 2
Photograph	AIDS Memorial Quilt in Washington, D.C.	1987	**ST** Topic 19, Lesson 2
Speech	Speech by Representative Norman Mineta, House of Representatives	1987	**PI** World War II, Tour a Japanese American Incarceration Camp, Daily Life
Speech	Speech by President Ronald Reagan, H.R. 442 Signing Ceremony	1988	**PI** World War II, Tour a Japanese American Incarceration Camp, Daily Life

Primary Source Index by State (continued)

Type	Source Title	Date	Location of Source
Statue	Memorial honoring the women who served in Vietnam, Vietnam Veterans Memorial, National Mall	1993	**PI** Vietnam, Experience the Legacy of the Vietnam War, Lucia
Speech	President Obama at Georgetown University	June 25, 2013	**ST** Topic 20, Lesson 2
Photographs	Marches on Washington after 1963 Gallery, Various Marches	1987, 2009, 2018	**PI** Civil Rights, Travel to Civil Rights Landmarks, Washington, D.C.
Washington			
Photograph	City Street, Eastern view on Pike Street from 3rd Ave., Seattle, Washington,	circa 1930	**PI** The Great Depression and the New Deal, Survive the Great Depression, Jack
Photograph	Listen to President Roosevelt give his Fireside Chat	no date	**PI** The 1920s, Adjust to Changing Times for Women, Lillian
Photographs	Hooverville(s), Seattle, Washington	October 27, 1931	**PI** The Great Depression and the New Deal, Survive the Great Depression, Jack
Personal Account	Hooverville Personal Account, "The Story of Seattle's Hooverville," Jesse Jackson, *Social Trends in Seattle*	1938	**PI** The Great Depression and the New Deal, Survive the Great Depression, Jack; **ST** Topic 13, Primary Source feature
Interview	Unemployment Interview, Studs Terkel Interview with Ed Paulsen, Part 1	1930s; Recorded 1971	**PI** The Great Depression and the New Deal, Work to End the Great Depression
Photograph	Japanese family from Washington state waiting to be sent to an incarceration camp in California	1942	**ST** Topic 14, Lesson 5
Letter	Italian Campaign Letter, Minoru Masuda to wife in Minidoka Incarceration camp, Hunt Idaho, Italy	June 1944	**PI** World War II, Follow News from the Battle Front, 1944
Photograph	Black Panthers on the steps of the legislative building, Olympia, Washington	1969	**PI** Civil Rights, Weigh the Evidence on the Black Power Movement
West Virgnia			
Photograph	African American children exercise outside Pleasant Green School, near Marlinton, WV, by Lewis Hine	October 1921	**PI** The 1920s, Adjust to Changing Times for Women, Ada
Speech	Senator Joseph McCarthy, Wheeling West Virginia	February 9, 1950	**Q** Topic 15, Document C
Wisconsin			
Letter	Religion in the New World, Anonymous Norwegian Immigrant	December 1878	**PI** Immigration, Build a New Life, 1870
Advertisement	*Chicago Defender,* Ad for male workers needed in Milwaukee, Wisconsin	December 1917	**PI** Immigration, Define Your Identity as an American, Chloe
Letter and Photographs	Letter from Bob Winters to Helen Steele, CCC Camp, Loretta, Wisconsin	July 23, 1935	**PI** The Great Depression and the New Deal, See the New Deal in Action, Shenandoah
Painting	In the Dugout, Paul Clemens, Wisconsin Federal Art Project, WPA	1938	**PI** The Great Depression and the New Deal, See the New Deal in Action, San Diego
Photograph	African American Women working in Aircraft Manufacturing Plant, Milwaukee, Wisconsin	October 1942	**PI** World War II, Join the War Effort, Annie
Wyoming			
Interview	Amy Uno Ishii, Incarcerated at Heart Mountain, California State Oral History Project, Park County, Wyoming	1973	**PI** World War II, Tour a Japanese American Incarceration Camp, Incarceration
Photograph	Boy Scout leads Parade, Heart Mountain Incarceration Camp, Park County, Wyoming	unknown	**PI** World War II, Tour a Japanese American Incarceration Camp, Daily Life
Photograph	Ice Skating, Heart Mountain Incarceration Camp, Park County, Wyoming	unknown	**PI** World War II, Tour a Japanese American Incarceration Camp, Daily Life

Topic 1

America's Cultural Roots (Prehistory–1783)

ESSENTIAL QUESTION How Much Does Geography Affect People's Lives?

GO ONLINE to access the eText, videos, Interactive Primary Sources, Biographies, and other online resources.

Mississippian period (c. 800–1600) clay pot from Cahokia, Illinois

Connections to Today

When Europeans first came to the Americas, native peoples controlled every inch of the land. Today, Native Americans control only a small fraction of the United States, but many Native American nations retain real power on their land. Tribal governments own land, run police departments, and enforce their own laws. Still, the rights and powers of tribal governments are contested in many communities. What issues do you think arise when the rights of a Native American nation conflict with the power of a state government?

NBC LEARN

Learn about how Austin celebrates his heritage.

BOUNCE to Activate My Story Video

Topic 1 Overview

In this Topic you'll learn about the peoples of the Americas, their ways of life, and the ways European exploration and colonization affected their cultures. Look at the lesson outline and explore the timeline. As you study this Topic, you'll complete the Quest Inquiry.

LESSON OUTLINE	
1.1 The Peoples of the Americas	**1.3** Europeans Make Contact
1.2 The West Africans	**1.4** Spain and France in the Americas

Key Events in the Americas, A.D. 500–1700

500s
Maya city of Chichen Itza founded

1100
Cahokia's population reaches its peak

1492
Christopher Columbus sails to the Americas

1550s
Diseases reduce American Indian populations by hundreds of thousands

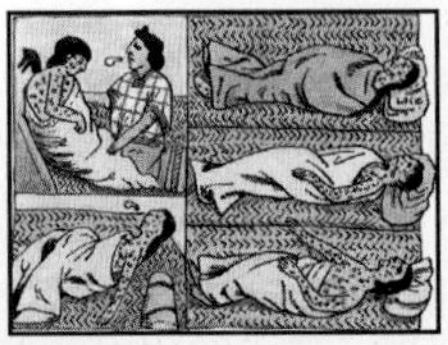

1680
Pueblos in New Mexico revolt against the Spanish

500 — 800 — 1100 — 1400 — 1700

QUEST! INQUIRY

Changing Perspectives on American Indians

How have conceptions of American Indians changed over time? In this Quest, you'll analyze historical documents and then write an essay about how American Indians have been perceived over time.

STEP 1
Discuss the ways American Indians have been viewed by themselves and others in the years since European contact. Make a list of questions about the perceptions of American Indians and their cultures.

STEP 2
Research to find answers to the questions. Analyze the documents relating to the historical study of American Indians. Compare and contrast their viewpoints and portrayals of American Indians.

STEP 3
Evaluate the sources and use the evidence and viewpoints to formulate conclusions. Then write an essay that states your conclusion and supports it with relevant facts.

STEP 4
Present your completed essay. Reflect on what you learned to form a carefully reasoned opinion on the historical study of American Indians.

GO ONLINE to access complete Quest materials

1.1

Cliff Palace pueblo, in what is now southern Colorado, contains nearly 220 rooms. The circular structures are kivas, which were large underground rooms used for religious ceremonies and political meetings.

BOUNCE to Activate Flipped Video

Objectives

Explain how American Indians may have come to North America.

Describe the process by which different American Indian groups and cultures developed.

Describe the major culture areas prior to the arrival of Europeans in North America.

Key Terms

ice age
migrated
Maya
Aztecs
adobe
Iroquois League

GO ONLINE to access your digital course

The Peoples of the Americas

The people who first inhabited North and South America found a land rich in resources and varied in geographic features. As they spread out across the land, they developed distinctive ways of living and surviving. Their cultures represent a central part of our heritage and history.

Early Inhabitants of the Americas

Scholars refer to the first humans to live in the Americas as Paleo-Indians. They think these people came from Siberia, a region in Asia that lies just across the narrow Bering Strait from Alaska. Scholars disagree, however, about when and how the Paleo-Indians arrived.

Migration to the Americas Until recently, most scholars insisted that the first Americans were hunters who arrived about 15,000 years ago. At that time, the world was experiencing an **ice age**, a period lasting thousands of years during which the Earth was covered by ice and glaciers. Much of the planet's seawater was frozen in polar ice caps.

Because of this, the sea level fell as much as 360 feet below today's level. The lower sea levels exposed a land bridge between Siberia and Alaska. Scholars believe Paleo-Indian hunters crossed this land bridge in pursuit of their favored prey—immense mammals such as mammoths, mastodons and giant bison.

However, recent discoveries have led some scholars today to question the land bridge theory. These scholars have developed the coastal route theory, suggesting that the first Americans **migrated**, or traveled, from Asia as many as 40,000 years ago.

These were coastal peoples who gathered wild plants and hunted seals and small whales. According to this view, the first people to arrive in the Americas arrived in small boats, eventually working their way down the west coasts of North and South America.

Climate Change Encourages Adaptation

Scholars do agree that about 12,000 to 10,000 years ago, the climate warmed. As temperatures rose, the polar ice melted and the oceans rose close to present-day levels.

Together, the warming climate and the spread of skilled Paleo-Indian hunters killed off the mammoths and other large mammals. Meanwhile, the environment became more diverse. The northern grasslands shrank while forests expanded northward.

Paleo-Indians adapted by relying less on hunting large mammals and more on fishing and on gathering nuts, berries, and roots. They also developed tracking techniques needed for hunting small, mobile animals such as deer, antelope, moose, elk, and caribou. The broader array of new food sources led to population growth. As the population grew, it expanded throughout the North and South American continents.

Diverse Cultures Emerge American Indians became culturally diverse as they adapted to their varying local climates and environments. Over time, their languages, rituals, mythic stories, and kinship systems became more varied. Eventually American Indians came to speak at least 375 languages, belonging to language families such as Athapaskan, Algonquian, Siouan, and Iroquoian. They belonged to an even larger number of ethnic groups, or nations.

In turn, these subdivided into many smaller groups that identified with a particular village or hunting territory. Each group was headed by a chief, who was usually advised by a council of elders.

Agriculture Emerges Some of these peoples learned how to domesticate wild plants so that they could be planted and grown for food. By about 8,000 years ago in central Mexico, American Indians developed three important crops using sophisticated techniques: maize (corn), squashes, and beans. The expanded food supply promoted population growth, which led to larger, permanent villages. In Mexico, some villages grew into great cities ruled by powerful chiefs. Residents built large pyramids topped with temples. By carefully studying the sun, moon, and stars, the Mexican peoples developed precise calendars of the seasons and the days. In eastern Mexico, the Olmec civilization led the way for the **Maya**. In the highlands of central Mexico, the **Aztecs** later became the most powerful people.

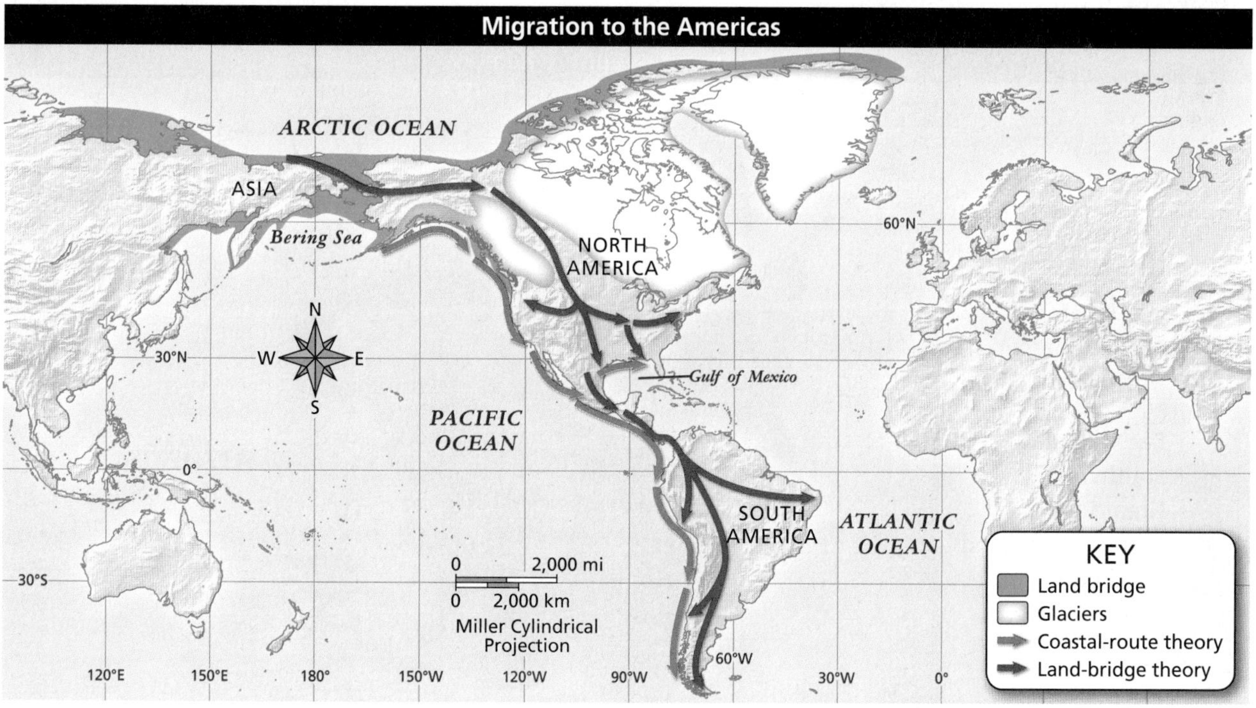

>> The first people to come to the Americas spread slowly across the continents. **Analyze Maps** What geographical features may have caused people to keep moving south?

BOUNCE to Activate Timeline

From Mexico, the methods of learning how to plant, cultivate, and harvest crops slowly spread northward. By about 1800 B.C., crop cultivation was common in parts of the American Southwest, Midwest, and Southeast.

In some places, people clung to a traditional mix of hunting, gathering, and fishing. Some lived in regions that were too cold or dry for farming, such as the frigid subarctic regions of Alaska, the Sierra Nevada, the Rocky Mountains, and the arid western Great Plains and Great Basin. In addition, coastal peoples in what is now California and the Pacific Northwest did not need to farm because their fishing—usually for salmon—and their gathering of nuts, seeds, and berries was so productive.

☑ **IDENTIFY MAIN IDEAS** Why do some scholars believe the ice age led to the migration of people to the Americas?

Early Cultures in North America

Early people grew in numbers and developed permanent villages in areas where farming was practiced. A little more than 2,000 years ago such villages began to appear in what would later become the United States.

The Southwest The first farming villages north of present-day Mexico emerged in the arid Southwest. There, the cultivation of crops required building ponds, dams, and ditches in order to irrigate, or bring water to, the fields. Building such complex systems required leadership by a group of priests and chiefs.

The Hohokams lived in the Gila and Salt river valleys of present-day southern Arizona. Over the course of their history, they built more than 500 miles of irrigation canals. The Hohokam irrigation canals were so elaborate that later peoples referred to the Hohokams as Canal Builders.

In their largest village, about 1,000 people inhabited row houses built of **adobe**, a type of sun-dried brick. Some of the houses were three stories tall.

The Ancestral Puebloans occupied the upland canyons in the Four Corners region at the intersection of what is now Arizona, New Mexico, Utah, and Colorado. At Chaco Canyon, the Ancestral Puebloans built an especially complex village that required 30,000 tons of sandstone blocks. This site became the center of the Ancestral Puebloan world. Some of the multistory dwellings, known as pueblos, rose five stories and had about 600 rooms.

Between A.D. 1100 and 1300, both the Hohokams and the Ancestral Puebloans experienced a severe crisis as a prolonged drought reduced crops. The resulting famine led to violence between rival villages that were competing for scarce resources.

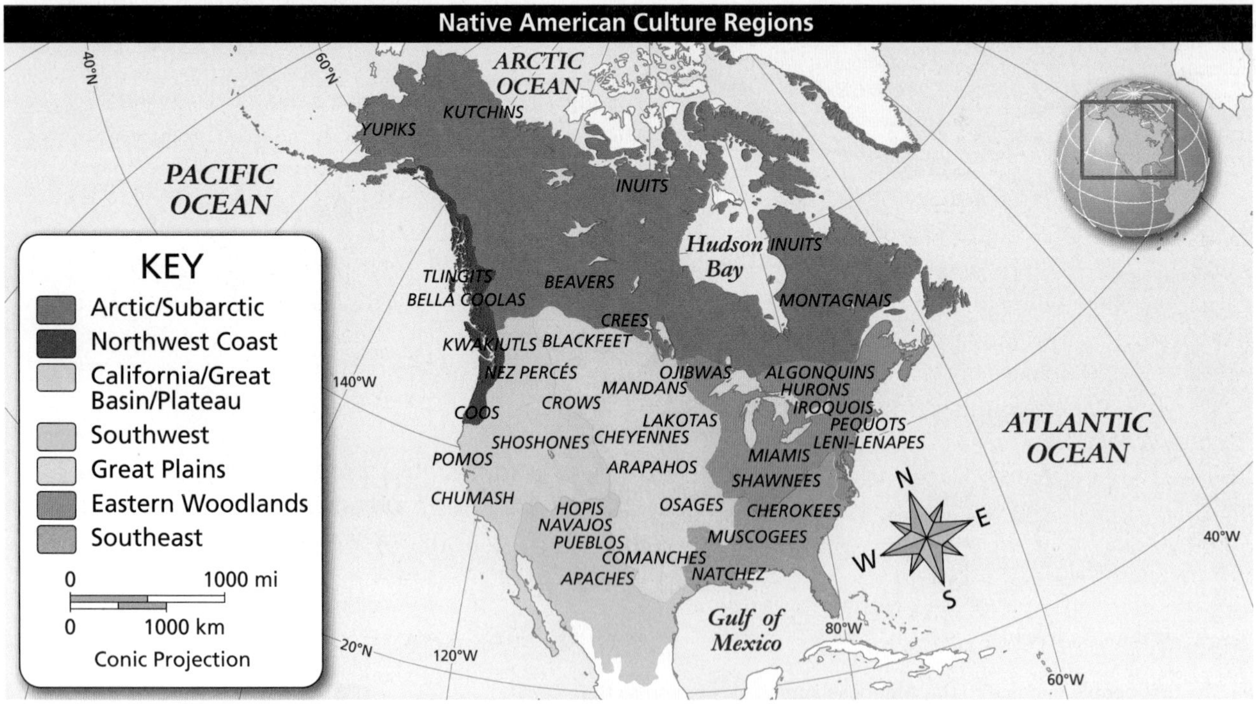

>> This map shows some of the larger Native American groups and the geographic regions they inhabited.

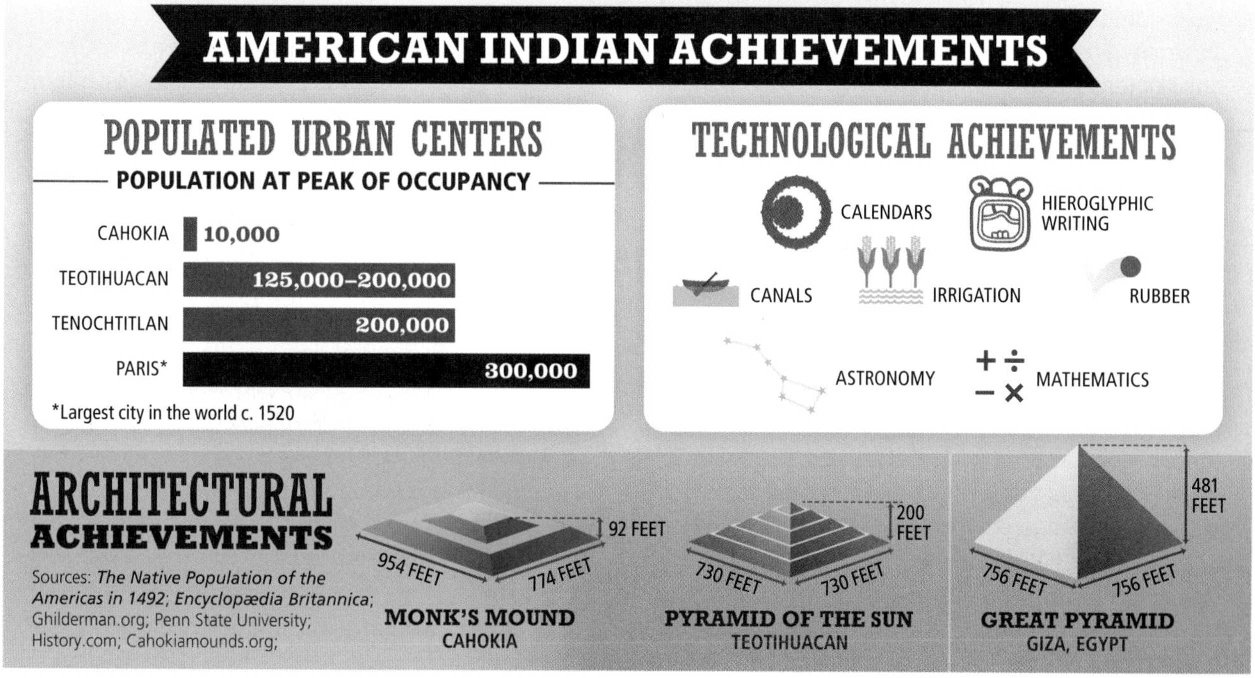

>> **Analyze Information** What details from this infographic support the claim that American Indians developed complex civilizations?

The crisis broke up both the Hohokam and Ancestral Puebloan villages. Most of the Ancestral Puebloans moved south and east in search of water. They resettled along the Rio Grande and Pecos River in present-day New Mexico. Today, they are known as the Pueblo peoples.

The Mississippians Unlike the arid Southwest, the Mississippi River valley has a humid and temperate climate. The Mississippi River collects the waters of wide-ranging tributaries, including the Ohio, Missouri, Arkansas, and Red rivers.

The people from this area, known as the Mississippians, were influenced by the great cultures of Mexico. They built large towns around central plazas, featuring pyramids made of earth. At the top of the pyramids, they built wooden temples that also served as the residences of chiefs.

The largest and wealthiest city of the Mississippian culture was at Cahokia in present-day southwestern Illinois. Cahokia benefited from being located near the confluence of the Missouri, Tennessee, Ohio, and Mississippi rivers. The site provided fertile soil and excellent trade connections with distant groups. At its peak in the year 1100, Cahokia had a population of at least 10,000 people and perhaps as many as 40,000. During the twelfth century, Cahokia's residents abandoned the city.

As in the Southwest, evidence suggests that an environmental crisis led to social conflict. The growing population had depleted the soil and decreased the number of deer. Hunger led to disease and to fighting among villages. Although Cahokia disappeared, Mississippian culture still thrived to the south at Moundville in Alabama, Etowah in Georgia, and Spiro in Oklahoma.

Early Peoples of the Great Plains Between the Rocky Mountains and the Mississippi River, the Great Plains is an immense, windy, and arid grassland in the heart of North America. The Great Plains receive only between 12 and 20 inches of rain a year. Only a few major rivers flow year-round. Instead of trees, drought-resistant grasses cover the land. Thus, grazing animals, especially the bison, favor the Great Plains. When Europeans first arrived, the Great Plains probably supported more than 20 million bison.

During the ninth century, some Mississippians moved westward up the major river valleys onto the Great Plains. They built villages and planted crops beside the rivers. In the hotter southern valleys, people lived in well-ventilated beehive-shaped houses made from wooden frames covered with grass thatch.

In colder northern valleys, villagers built log lodges well insulated with earth. In the summer, villagers ventured on foot onto the plains to hunt bison. While on the hunt, they lived in mobile camps. Their shelters were called tepees—cone-shaped tents of tanned bison hides stretched over a frame of cottonwood poles.

Great Plains villagers sometimes clashed with people they called the Apaches, who lived to the west and south. The Apaches spoke Athapaskan languages. Some were farmers, while others made a living through hunting and gathering, moving seasonally.

Some nomad bands established economic ties with the villagers of the valleys. The nomads traded bison meat and hides for maize, beans, squash, turquoise, pottery, and cotton blankets. The villagers would forgo this trade, however, when they lacked surplus food. Angered, the nomads raided the villages.

Eastern Woodlands Peoples The eastern region featured a vast forest atop rolling hills and a low range of mountains, the Appalachians. Many streams, rivers, and lakes drained this wooded land.

Stretching from eastern Texas to the Atlantic Ocean, the Southeast has mild winters and warm summers with plenty of rainfall. The Cherokees were the largest group in the Southeast. They lived in present-day western North Carolina and eastern Tennessee. Other people in the Southeast included Choctaws, Chickasaws, Natchez, and Creeks. Because of the long growing season, the Choctaws, the Creeks, and other southeastern groups were primarily farmers, but they also depended on hunting and fishing. They knew what plants to use to make rope, medicine, and clothing. Their main crops were corn, beans, squashes, and pumpkins.

Northeastern people developed into two major language groups: the Algonquians and the Iroquoians. The Algonquians occupied the Atlantic seaboard from present-day Virginia north to the mouth of the St. Lawrence River. The Iroquoians lived around Lake Ontario and Lake Erie and along the upper St. Lawrence River.

A chief difference between the two cultures lay in their housing. Algonquians lived in wigwams: oval frames between 10 and 16 feet in diameter that are made of saplings covered with bark sheets or woven mats.

Using similar materials, Iroquoians built larger multifamily longhouses, some more than 200 feet in length. In fact, when five Iroquoian-speaking peoples united to form a loose confederation, they called themselves the Haudenosaunee, or *People of the Longhouse.* This confederation—including the Mohawks, Oneidas, Onandagas, Cayugas, and Senecas—is known to historians as the **Iroquois League.**

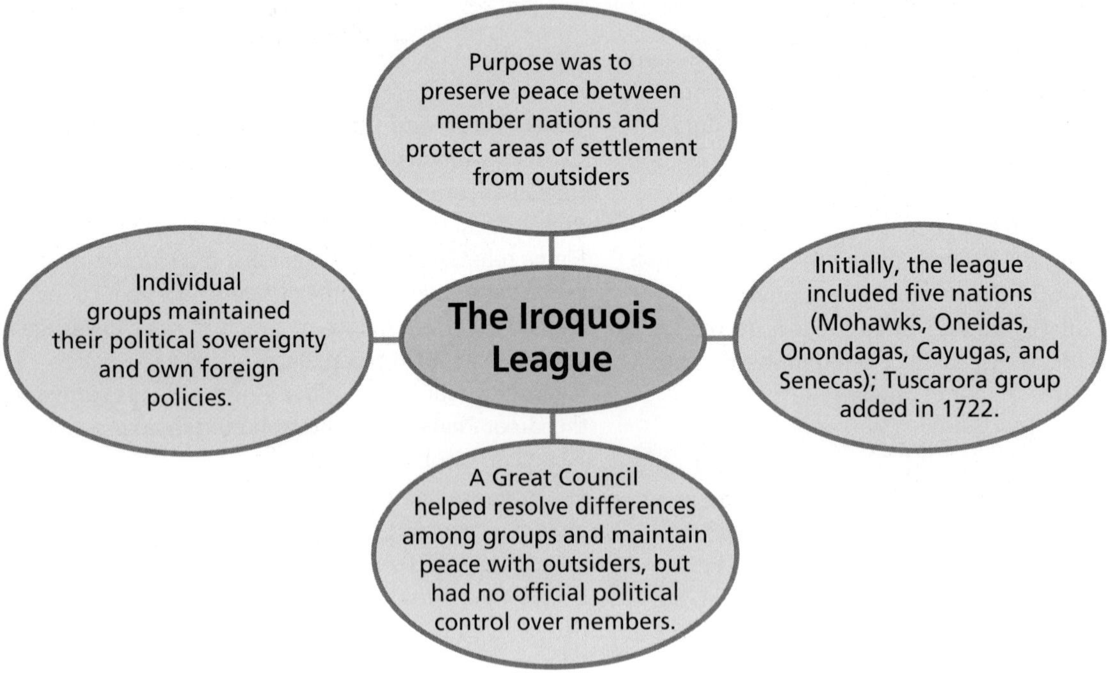

SOURCES: *Encyclopædia Britannica;* National Park Service; New York State Museum; University of Maryland, Baltimore County

>> **Analyze Information** What Iroquois League political ideals unified the confederation?

The Iroquois League was not a European-style nation. Lacking central authority, it was mainly a ritual forum for promoting peaceful cooperation among the member nations.

The Iroquois League's guiding law was a constitution, which was passed down by oral tradition.

> The Lords of the Confederacy of the Five nations shall be mentors of the people for all time. . . . Their hearts shall be full of peace and good will and their minds filled with a yearning for the welfare of the people of the Confederacy.
>
> —The Iroquois Constitution

Shared Cultural Characteristics Despite their cultural diversity, most American Indian groups shared several cultural features. For example, for most American Indian groups, political power was spread among many local chiefs with limited authority.

American Indians believed that spirits could be found in every plant, animal, rock, cloud, and body of water. If properly honored, the spirits could help people catch or grow what they needed. If offended, spirits might hide the animals or fish or destroy the corn crop. Spiritual leaders, called *shamans* by historians, mediated between their people and the spirit beings. They conducted rituals to promote hunts, secure crops, and protect warriors.

American Indians owned little private property. Some families owned garden plots and hunting territories, but they could not sell them. Most local land was considered a common resource for every resident to use.

There was a respectful equality among the various groups of American Indians. Usually, work was divided along gender lines. Men assumed more dangerous tasks, such as hunting and warfare. Women cared for the children, wove baskets, made pottery, prepared meals, and gathered food. If their people cultivated crops, that work also usually fell to women.

CHECK UNDERSTANDING What were three common cultural characteristics shared by most American Indians?

>> American Indian religious leaders, like this Hupa woman photographed in the 1920s, served their people's spiritual needs.

BOUNCE to Activate Map

ASSESSMENT

1. **Analyze Information** What theories do scholars have about when and why the earliest inhabitants of North and South America first arrived?
2. **Apply Concepts** How did climate change affect the Paleo-Indians of North and South America?
3. **Compare** How did the early people of the Southwest differ from those of the Mississippi region?
4. **Summarize** What type of government did the Iroquois League have?
5. **Categorize** Which cultural features did most American Indian groups share?
6. **Quest Connections** What evidence in this lesson demonstrates that Native Americans actively managed their environment?

Primary Sources

The Origins of the Confederation of the Five Nations

>> This engraving made by a French artist in the 1700s shows Dekanahwideh with leaders of the Iroquois nations.

You have read about the Iroquois League, a confederation of American Indian nations centered in northern New York state. Traditionally, credit for founding the league was given to the legendary figure Dekanahwideh, sometimes called the Peace Maker. Iroquois oral histories say that Dekanahwideh travelled from village to village spreading a message of peace and urging the five original Iroquois nations to unite.

There are several accounts of Dekanahwideh's life. The selections below come from a document compiled in 1900 by a committee of leaders of all the Iroquois nations. These excerpts begin before Dekanahwideh's birth, when a messenger brings his mother and grandmother word that the new baby will have a special destiny.

Primary Source

"It is the wish of the creator that you should bear a child, and when you will see the male child you shall call him Dekanahwideh. The reason you should give him that name is because this child will reveal to men-beings The Good Tidings of Peace and Power from Heaven and the Great Peace shall rule and govern on earth, and I will charge that you and your daughter should be kind to him because he has an important mission to perform in the world, and when he grows up to be a man do not prevent him from leaving home."

Then the old woman [Dekanahwideh's grandmother] asked the messenger, what office the child should hold.

The messenger answered and said: "His mission is for peace and life to the people both on Earth and in heaven."

PREDICT Will Dekanahwideh grow up to be a great king or a warrior? What is his special destiny?

The child grew up rapidly, and when he had become a young man he said: "The time has come when I should begin to perform my duty in the world. I will therefore begin to build my canoe and by tomorrow I must have it completed because there is work for me to do tomorrow when I go away to the eastward."

Then he began to build his canoe out of a white rock, and when he had completed it Dekanahwideh said: "I am now ready to go away from home and I will tell you that there is a tree on top of the hill and you shall have that for a sign whenever you wish to find out whether I shall be living or dead. You will take an axe and chop the tree and if the tree flows of blood from the cut, you will thereby know that I am beheaded and killed, but if you find no blood running away from the tree after you chopped a chip from it, then you may know that my mission was successful. The reason that this will happen is because I came to stop forever the wanton shedding of blood among human beings. . ."

Then the grandmother said "How are you going to travel since your canoe is made out of stone? It will not float."

Then Dekanahwideh said "This will be the first sign of wonder that man will behold; a canoe made out of stone will float. . . ."

DETERMINE MEANING What is unusual about Dekanahwideh's canoe? How might this be important to his mission?

Then he journeyed on a great way and went to another settlement. Here he inquired who their Royaner [lord, leader] was . . . and when they met, Dekanahwideh said, "Have you heard that the Good Tidings of Peace and Power are coming?" The lord then said: "I truly have heard of it."

Then Dekanahwideh asked him what he thought about it.

Then the lord [Hahyonhwatha] said, "Since I have heard of the good news I have been thinking about it and since then I have not slept." Then Dekanahwideh said, "It is now at hand – that which has been the cause of your sleeplessness. . . ."

USE CONTEXT CLUES Why has Lord Hahyonhwatha been unable to sleep?

Then the Lord Hahyonhwatha announced to his colleagues and people that they assemble to hear Dekanahwideh, and when they were assembled Hahyonhwatha asked Dekanahwideh what news he had for the people. Dekanahwideh answered that the proclamation of the Good Tidings of Peace and Power had arrived and that he had come on a mission to proclaim the Good News of Peace and Power that bloodshed might cease in the land, as the Creator, he had learned, never intended that such should ever be practiced by human beings. . . .

Then one of the chief warriors asked "What shall we do with the powerful tribes on the east and on the west of our villages who are always hostile to us?"

Then Dekanahwideh answered and said that the hostile nations referred to had already accepted the Good News of Peace and Power.

EXPLAIN What objection does the chief warrior give to accepting Dekanahwideh's message of peace?

ASSESSMENT

1. **Analyze Style and Rhetoric** How is the symbolism of a bleeding tree related to Dekanahwideh's mission?
2. **Make Inferences** According to Dekanahwideh, where does the message of peace come from? Why might this have been important to his listeners?
3. **Draw Conclusions** One of Lord Hahyonhwatha's chief warriors objects to the message of peace. How does his objection reflect an obstacle to peace in many situations?
4. **Summarize** How does Dekanahwideh answer the objection of one of Lord Hahyonhwatha's chief warriors? How does this show a way in which peacemaking can succeed?

GO ONLINE to access primary sources

1.2

Mali ruler Mansa Musa led a West African kingdom of immense wealth and power.

BOUNCE to Activate Flipped Video

Objectives

Describe the development and cultural characteristics of West Africa in the fifteenth century.

Summarize West African religions, culture, and society.

Explore the roots of the system of slavery practiced in the Americas.

Key Terms

Ghana
Mali
Mansa Musa
Songhai

The West Africans

The people and cultures of West Africa in the 1500s, like the region in which they lived, were incredibly diverse. Valuable natural resources and several key rivers encouraged West African kingdoms to develop prosperous trade networks that fueled growth.

The Kingdoms of West Africa

The Relationship Between Geography and Trade Western Africa is a varied land. An enormous desert—the Sahara—dominates the northern part. To the south of the Sahara lies a broad grassland, or savanna. South of this savanna is a lush region that is well watered by several major rivers, including the Niger and the Senegal. The West African landscape abounds with valuable natural resources—in particular, salt, found in the Sahara, and gold, located in the valleys along the Atlantic coast.

Hundreds of years ago, these resources provided for a thriving trade network among the people of West Africa. This trade revolved around certain trading towns that grew into great and powerful empires. The trading empires of West Africa commanded trading routes that linked the region with North Africa, the Mediterranean, and Asia. Trade promoted rich and thriving cultures.

Ghana Between A.D. 300 and 1500, three kingdoms rose and fell in West Africa. The earliest kingdom, **Ghana**, expanded from the Sahara to the Gulf of Guinea and from the Atlantic Ocean to the Niger River. Ghana rose to prominence around A.D. 800.

A thriving caravan trade with African peoples across the Sahara to Morocco resulted in extensive Muslim influence in North Africa. By the eleventh century, Ghana supplied much of the gold

GO ONLINE to access your digital course

for the Mediterranean region. The ancient kingdom had large towns, beautifully designed buildings, a system of commerce, and a complex political structure.

Foreign travelers recorded their accounts of Ghana's prominence, including the lavish lifestyle of Ghana's king in the eleventh century.

> The King adorns himself . . . wearing necklaces around his neck and bracelets on his forearms, and he puts on a high cap decorated with gold and wrapped in a turban of fine cotton. He sits in audience to hear grievances against officials in a domed pavilion around which stand ten horses covered with gold-embroidered materials.
>
> — Al-Bakri, *The Book of Routes and Realms*

Mali Emerges Attacks from the Almoravids, an alliance of peoples from the Sahara, eventually weakened Ghana's control of West African trade. The kingdom's power faded until, finally, Ghana was supplanted around A.D. 1200 by a new kingdom known as **Mali**. The most famous ruler of Mali was a king named **Mansa Musa**.

During his reign in the early 1300s, he expanded Mali's domain westward to the Atlantic coast and increased the role of Islam, a religious faith that spread slowly through North Africa in the early 700s, when the region was under Muslim conquest. His promotion of Islamic scholarship helped lead to the founding of the famous university at Timbuktu. This great center of learning and culture was known throughout the Islamic world. The kingdom of Mali weakened after the death of Mansa Musa in 1332.

The Rise of Songhai By the 1400s, another empire emerged: **Songhai**. The Songhai capital, Gao, grew rich as a trading center. Under the rule of Askia Muhammad, Songhai sustained an Islamic system of education based in the city of Timbuktu. Like Ghana and Mali, Songhai grew rich from trade. In 1468, Songhai's armies conquered Mali and its capital. As a result, Songhai became the most powerful and largest kingdom in West Africa. Eventually, however, military defeat resulted in the loss of Gao and the rest of the empire.

Additional Kingdoms In addition to the great empires of Ghana, Mali, and Songhai, West Africa also hosted smaller kingdoms. For example, to the

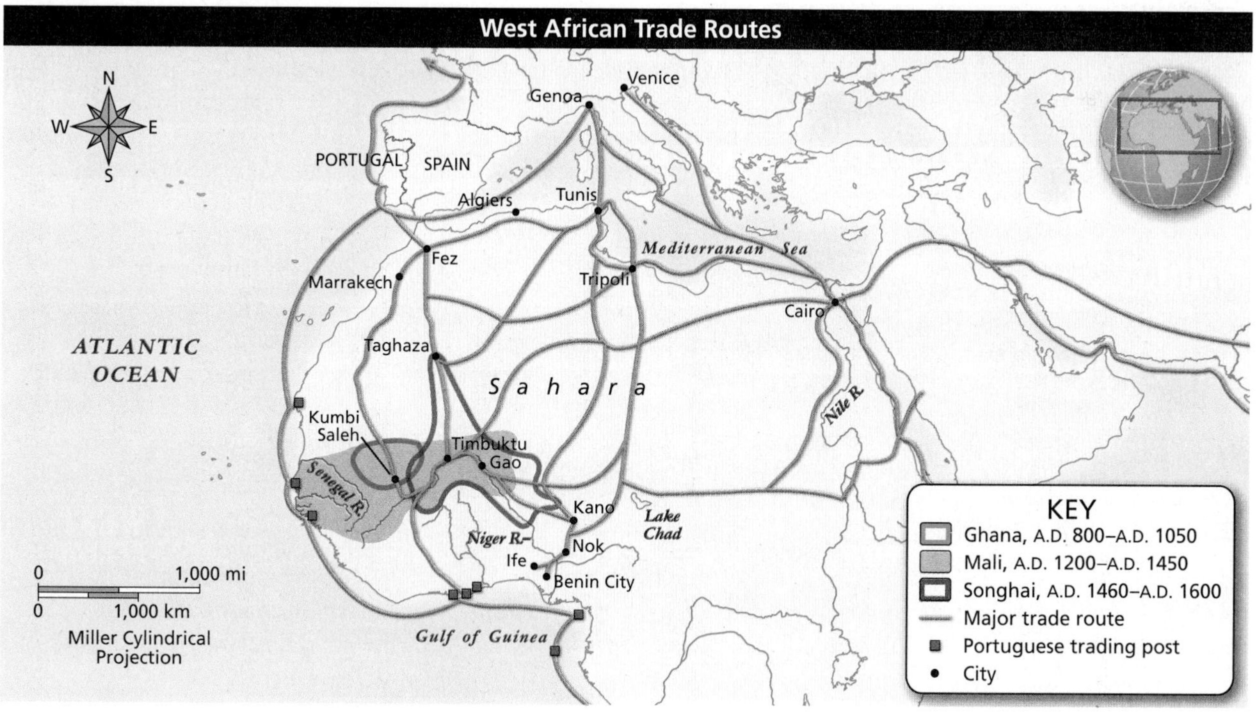

>> **Analyze Maps** Why was the location of West Africa so important to its role in international trade?

BOUNCE to Activate Gallery

south of Songhai, the kingdom of Benin occupied the tropical forest along the Gulf of Guinea. Known as "obas," the kings of Benin promoted art, especially sculptures in bronze or ivory. The Hausa people built seven cities in present-day Nigeria and Niger. Both became well known for producing beautiful cloth and for establishing extensive trade.

☑ **DESCRIBE** how the presence of resources such as gold and salt encouraged the development of great kingdoms in West Africa.

Characteristics of West African Societies

The peoples of West Africa, like the peoples of the Americas, were a diverse group with highly developed civilizations. Religious beliefs and family bonds were among the ways of life that reinforced a sense of community.

Religion in West African Societies West African spiritual beliefs varied. Caravans brought Islam across the Sahara to the people of the savanna. In many places, such as along the coast of the Gulf of Guinea, Africans held traditional beliefs. These involved a supreme creator supplemented by many spirit beings who inhabited every object and creature of the natural world. The people of West Africa believed, just as the American Indians did, that spirits lived in rain, trees, rocks, and animal life. Furthermore, these spirit beings could also intervene in human affairs. Therefore, the spirits were specially honored. Ancestors, too, became spirits of enduring influence in the extended families that formed the major support system of African society.

Land Ownership and Society Land did not belong to individuals as private property. Instead, land belonged to extended kinship networks derived from an ancient ancestor. Powerful kings could assign particular territories to favored officials to collect tribute from the peasants. But these favorites could not sell the land to others or pass it on to their heirs. Furthermore, the kings could readily replace these officials, reassigning that particular land to a new favorite. The peasants who worked the land could not be removed from it nor could they sell it or rent it to others. Often the people of a village worked the land in common and divided the harvest according to the number of people in each household. Holding enslaved people or having multiple wives, rather than property, determined one's wealth.

Slavery in West Africa As in other pre-modern societies, slavery was common in West Africa. In fact, human beings were frequently used as items of

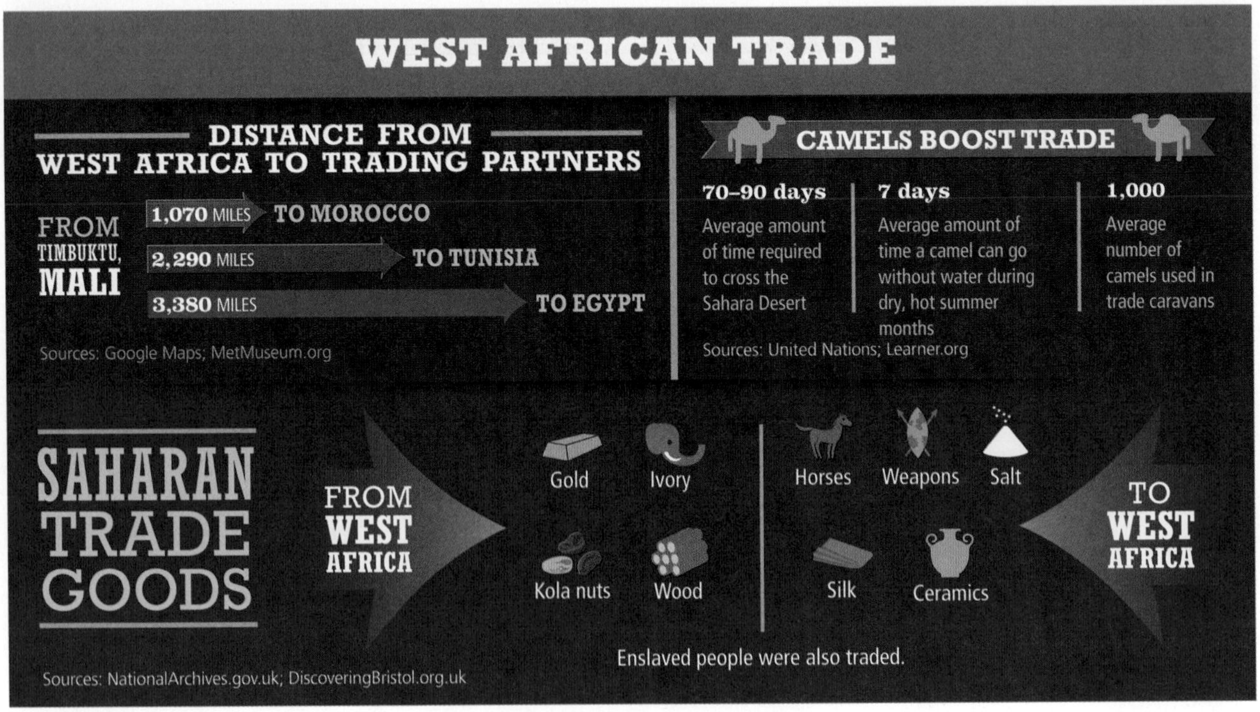

>> **Analyze Information** What inference can you make about how closely West African kingdoms were connected with the rest of the world? What details from the infographic support this inference?

Portuguese Exploration of West Africa, 15th Century

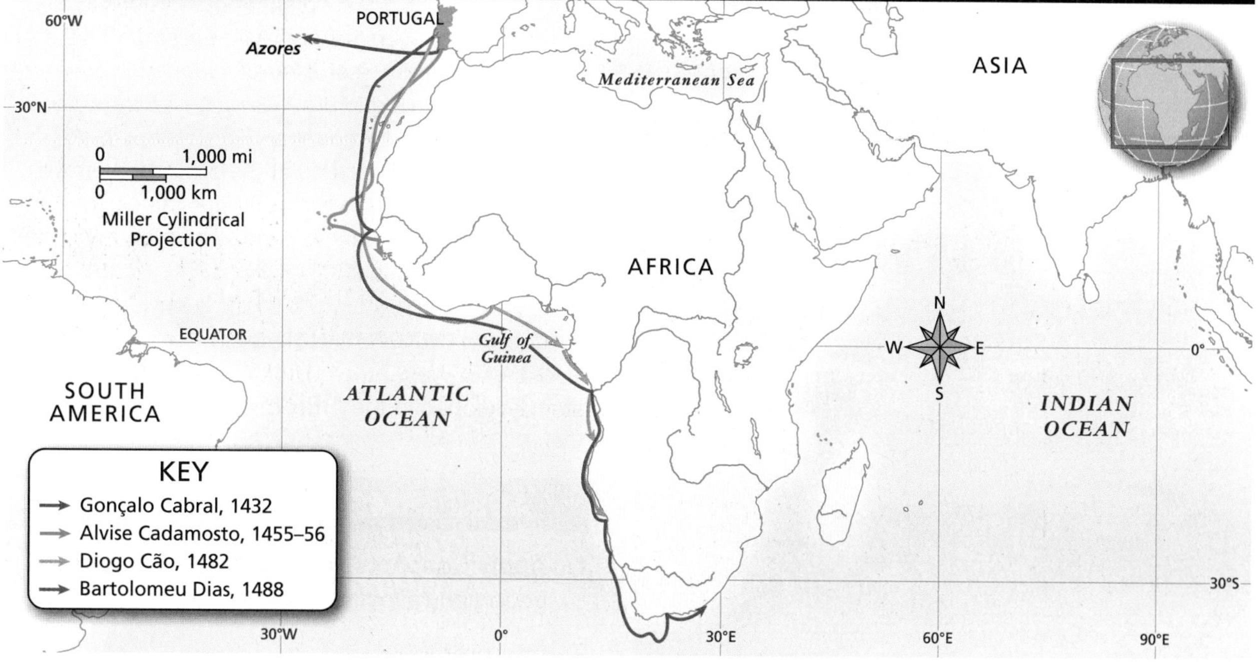

>> **Analyze Maps** In which regions of Africa would you most likely find a legacy of Portuguese trade influence today?

trade, along with gold, salt, ivory, and other valuable resources found in the region. West African rulers sold about 1,000 enslaved people annually to Arab traders, who carried them in caravans across the Sahara to the Mediterranean. The trade in enslaved people was an important part of West Africa's economy.

Slavery was a common fate for people who were conquered or captured during warfare. People who committed crimes or were otherwise found undesirable to the community might also be enslaved.

African slavery differed from the system that later developed in the Americas. It was not based on any idea of racial superiority and inferiority. Most enslaved people could not be routinely bought or sold.

Enslaved people in West Africa fell into one of two categories, domestic or captive. Most were domestic slaves. They could generally not be bought or sold, and had the right to marry. Their children had the right to inherit property, and if one parent were free, they might inherit an improved status as well. Captive slaves, by contrast, could be bought and sold as property. In fact, they were used as currency in some transactions.

Some enslaved people in Africa managed to become important officials and soldiers. Powerful kings relied on enslaved armies and enslaved officials to control local nobles. Successful enslaved commanders and officials could become wealthy from the rewards of their positions.

Portuguese Exploration in West Africa Located on the Atlantic Ocean and close to Africa, the country of Portugal was ideally situated to seek new trade routes and to expand European influence. Using new navigational tools, such as the compass, astrolabe, and the quadrant, the Portuguese ventured into the Atlantic Ocean and explored the coast of West Africa beginning in the 1400s.

When the Portuguese first sailed along the coast of Africa, they were largely interested in gold. As they began to extend their influence, Portuguese explorers established a profitable trade with the people of West Africa. They exported a variety of goods, including peppers, ivory, copper, and enslaved Africans. In this way, Europeans in the mid-1400s first became involved in the long-standing African trade in enslaved people.

To conduct their African trade, the Portuguese mariners needed the assent of the powerful West African kings. Commercial treaties permitted the Portuguese to construct fortified trading posts at key harbors along the coast. The forts served to keep away rival European vessels. Indeed, the Portuguese treated rivals harshly, confiscating their vessels and casting their crews into the ocean to drown.

>> Portuguese traders established large coastal forts like Elmina Castle from which to conduct the trade in enslaved people.

The Portuguese did not invent the trade in enslaved people, but they did greatly expand it. The first major European trading fort was established in 1482. It became a major trading center for enslaved people. By 1500, Europeans purchased about 1,800 enslaved Africans a year. This nearly doubled the previous trade of some 1,000 enslaved people between Arab traders and West African rulers.

Some enslaved people were shipped to Europe. Most, however, worked on sugar plantations located on the Madeira, Canary, and Azore islands. These were islands in the East Atlantic claimed in the 1400s by Iberian explorers. Growing numbers were sent across the Atlantic to labor on new plantations in the Americas. Thus began the brutal exploitation of West Africans enslaved by Europeans—a fate that would befall millions more African men and women in the centuries ahead.

CHECK UNDERSTANDING How did slavery as practiced in West Africa differ from the slavery that later developed in the Americas?

ASSESSMENT

1. **Apply Concepts** How did West Africa's geography affect its growth and development?
2. **Interpret** What led to the rise and fall of the kingdom of Ghana?
3. **Summarize** What were Mansa Musa's most important accomplishments as ruler of Mali?
4. **Distinguish** How was a person's wealth determined in ancient West Africa?
5. **Support Ideas with Evidence** What role did slavery play in West African culture before the arrival of the Europeans?
6. **Connections to Today** In the 1900s, two West African nations gained independence from European rule. They took the names *Ghana* and *Mali*. Why do you think they chose these names?

1.3

This 1519 portrait is one of many that claim to show famous navigator Christopher Columbus.

Europeans Make Contact

Europe in the 1400s experienced enormous cultural, economic, and technological changes. As new ideas swept the continent, some Europeans began to look beyond their shores to satisfy their growing ambitions. They were about to enter an age of discovery and exploration that would change not only Europe but much of the world as well.

BOUNCE to Activate Flipped Video

Objectives

Describe conditions in Europe in the fifteenth century.

Analyze how changes taking place in Europe shaped Europeans' worldview and helped lead to economic expansion.

Describe the major developments on the Iberian Peninsula at the end of the Middle Ages and the start of the Renaissance.

Explain the goals of Christopher Columbus and the consequences of his explorations.

Analyze how contact with Europeans affected the people of the Americas.

Key Terms

Middle Ages
Renaissance
reconquista
Prince Henry the Navigator
Bartolomeu Dias
Vasco da Gama
Christopher Columbus
John Cabot
Pedro Alvarez Cabral
Amerigo Vespucci
Ferdinand Magellan
conquistadors
Hernán Cortés
Moctezuma
Columbian Exchange

Change Sweeps Through Europe in the 1400s

The earlier years of the **Middle Ages**, which began with the collapse of the Western Roman Empire, were marked by the absence of an effective central government and the constant threat of famine, disease, and foreign invasion. However, as political stability returned, new institutions and ideas slowly took hold, and a new civilization emerged in Europe. By the 1400s, European sailors were beginning a dramatic new period of exploration fueled by the search for gold, spices, and wealth. Attempts to expand trade networks brought Europeans into contact with other peoples throughout the known world.

Agriculture Drives the Economy In the 1400s, the population of Europe was beginning to recover from the drastic effects of bubonic plague, known as the Black Death. During the 1340s, that epidemic had killed about a third of all Europeans. However, as populations recovered, the economic situation improved. Hand tools and draft animals sustained an economy that was overwhelmingly agricultural. The great majority of the people lived in the countryside. Cities, however, were growing, especially

GO ONLINE to access your digital course

in northern Italy and in the Netherlands. In the days before mechanized factories, the small-scale manufacturing of cloth, tools, weapons, and ceramics took place in the urban workshops of artisans. The cities also served as bases for the merchants.

>> An illustration from the *Grimani Breviary*, of the early 1500s, shows peasant farmers at work on an aristocrat's lands. **Analyze Primary Sources** What challenges did these farmers face?

A Divided Society Extremes of wealth and poverty characterized European society. A ruling elite of less than 5 percent of the population controlled almost all of the land. The most prestigious were aristocrats—people who had inherited social rank and title and, generally, landed estates worked by peasants. Less honored, but often wealthier, were the great merchants who shipped cargoes between cities for profit. The elite also included leaders of the Roman Catholic Church. A monarch—usually a king but sometimes a queen—reigned over the social pyramid in each kingdom.

Under the domination of this small elite class were the commoners. About three-fifths of western Europeans were working poor. In good years, they subsisted by farming on land rented from an aristocrat or by selling their labor. In hard times, many fell into the ranks of the beggars. The most prosperous commoners were middle-class families. They owned enough property to employ themselves as farmers, artisans, and shopkeepers. Such people, however, accounted for only a fifth of the population.

>> During the Middle Ages, European kingdoms engaged in near-continuous warfare. This illustration shows the 1415 Battle of Agincourt between the English and the French.

Kingdoms Fight for Power Western Europe was divided into a number of warring kingdoms. The most important were Castile, Portugal, France, and England. Each was ruled by a monarch who, in turn, depended on the elite class to do much of the governing. By waging war to conquer new territories, monarchs hoped to build their own power and to keep their often unruly aristocrats occupied.

☑ **CHECK UNDERSTANDING** Describe the social structure of European society during the 1400s.

Europe Expands its Influence

During the Middle Ages, the Church strictly controlled intellectual life. Church leaders sought to ensure that all thought adhered to their understanding of the world. Church leaders felt that everything worth knowing had either been discovered by the Greeks and Romans or recorded in the Bible. Those who pursued scientific discoveries that went against Church teachings risked prosecution for heresy by Church courts.

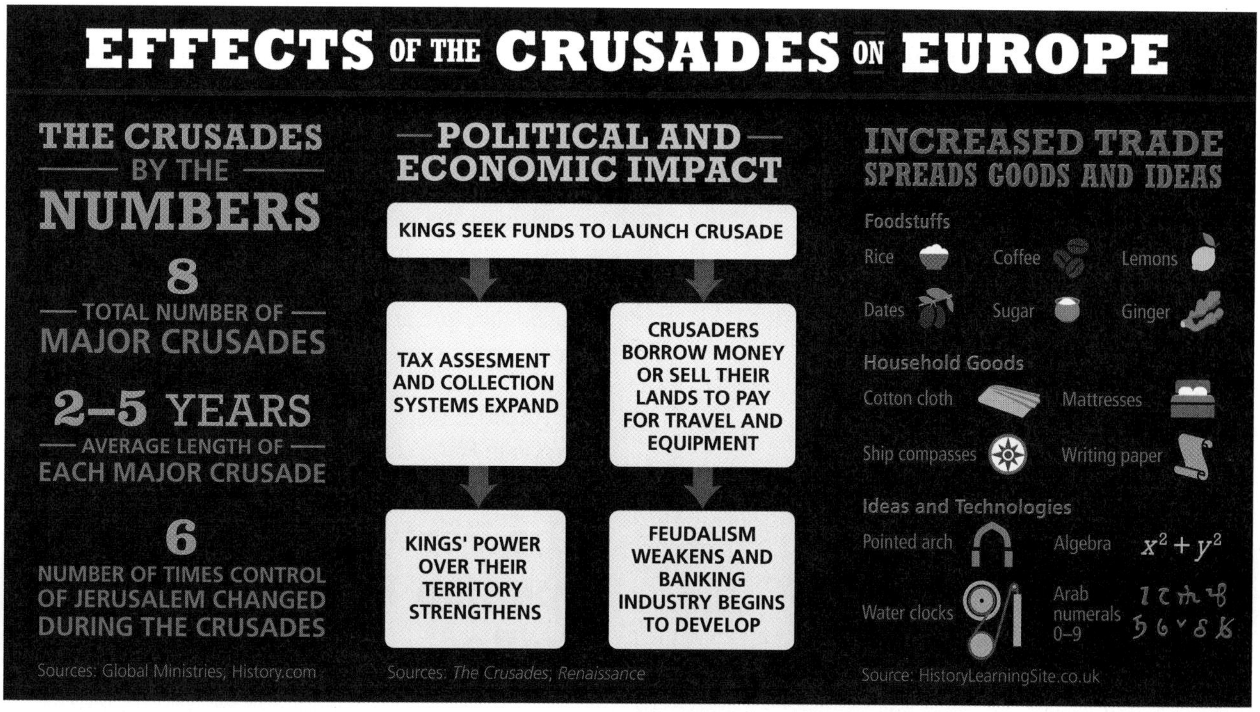

>> **Analyze Information** What negative effect did the Crusades have on Europe? What positive effect did they have?

Europe in the 1400s was in an era of rapid change. Though old ways of thinking persisted, many factors, especially rapidly widening trade, were broadening people's views of the world.

The Crusades Lead to Increased Trade In the latter half of the Middle Ages, European Christians and Southwest Asian Muslims fought one another in a series of religious wars known as the Crusades. The goal was to capture and hold Jerusalem and all of the Holy Land where Jesus had lived and died. In the end, the Muslims defeated the Christian Crusaders.

However there were other lasting effects of the Crusades that benefited the people of Europe. Europeans became aware of distant lands and different ways of life. Trade was encouraged. Crusaders returned home with goods and raw materials from the East, including silks, gems, and spices. Increasing demand for these products caused European traders to expand their businesses to Asia.

The Renaissance and New Ideas By the mid-1400s, a new era had begun in Europe. Known as the **Renaissance**, it featured renewed interest in learning and the advancement of the arts and sciences. During the Renaissance, trade with and awareness of the world beyond Europe expanded. This, in turn, produced wealth for the increasingly powerful nations of Europe. This wealth and power would fuel more explorations. The consequences for the people of Europe—and for the rest of the world—would be profound.

Popular literature reinforced the European longing for access to the fabled riches of India and China. During the fifteenth century, the development of the printing press lowered the cost and increased the volume of publishing. Books became available to more than the wealthy and leisured elite. The spread of literature helped promote the daring new Renaissance ideas of individualism and experimentation.

Readers especially delighted in vivid reports of the wealth and power of India and China. The most famous travel account came from Marco Polo, a thirteenth-century Italian merchant who had traveled across Asia to visit the emperor of China. Inspired by such accounts, Europeans longed to enlist Asian peoples and Asian wealth for a renewed crusade to capture the Holy Land.

Muslims Control the Trade Routes The Europeans, who were Christian, felt hemmed in by the superior wealth, power, and technology of their rivals and neighbors, the Muslims. Muslims followed the religion of Islam.

Dominated by the Ottoman Turks, the vast Muslim realm stretched across North Africa and around the southern and eastern Mediterranean

>> Prince Henry the Navigator helped make Portugal a leader in naval technology and exploration.

BOUNCE to Activate Gallery

>> This 1482 illustration shows a Portuguese caravel (left) and galley (right). The caravel's multiple sails made it easier to maneuver than earlier ships, like the galley.

BOUNCE to Activate 3D Model

Sea to embrace parts of Eastern Europe and Southwest Asia. The Muslim world also spread east through Central and Southeast Asia, and continued to expand. The Ottoman Turks even invaded southeastern Europe, capturing the strategic city of Constantinople in 1453. Within this vast Muslim world, long and relatively secure trade routes extended from Morocco to the East Indies and from Mongolia to West Africa. Reluctant to travel through Muslim lands, European traders had to find another way to reach the riches of the East.

☑ **RECALL** What were the characteristics of the European Renaissance in the fifteenth century?

The Portuguese and Spanish Explore New Routes

European expansionists found hope on the Iberian Peninsula of southwestern Europe. There, the kingdoms of Aragon, Castile, and Portugal were waging the ***reconquista*** (reconquest) to drive out the Muslim Moors who had ruled Iberia for centuries. In 1469, the marriage of Prince Ferdinand and Queen Isabella united Aragon and Castile to create "Spain." In 1492, Ferdinand and Isabella completed the *reconquista* by seizing Granada, the last Muslim stronghold in Iberia. Long and violent, the *reconquista* inspired a zealous crusading spirit for spreading the Christian faith.

Portuguese Technology and Navigators Facing the Atlantic Ocean and close to Africa, Spain and Portugal were well situated to seek new trade routes and to expand European influence. The Portuguese took the early lead in venturing out into the Atlantic. They relied on several new devices: the compass, the astrolabe, and the quadrant.

These innovations helped sailors determine their location and direction when beyond sight of land. Shipbuilders were producing sturdier ships capable of sailing hundreds of miles. A ship known as the caravel had a stern rudder, three masts, and a combination of square and triangular lateen sails.

Starting in 1419, **Prince Henry the Navigator** directed Portuguese efforts to sail into the Atlantic, spread Christianity, and reduce Muslim domination of trade. Henry founded a school of navigation and sponsored several expeditions down the coast of West Africa. By sailing southward, the Portuguese hoped to reach the sources of the gold, ivory, and enslaved people that Muslim merchants transported across the great Sahara.

Throughout the 1400s, the Portuguese continued to sail farther and farther from home. They sought a route around Africa's southern tip into the Indian Ocean. Then their ships could continue east in search of India, the East Indies, and eventually China.

In 1487, the Portuguese mariner **Bartolomeu Dias** learned how to use the counterclockwise winds of the South Atlantic to get around southern Africa. In 1498, **Vasco da Gama** exploited that discovery to reach India, opening an immensely profitable trade route. The Portuguese dominated the southern and eastern trade routes around Africa.

Spanish Mariners Sail West By default, in the late 1400s the Spanish looked westward into the open Atlantic. They took inspiration from the profitable discovery and exploitation earlier in the century of islands in the Atlantic—the Azores, Madeiras, and Canaries. Perhaps, they thought, similar islands could be found farther to the west. Furthermore, by leaping from one set of islands to another, perhaps mariners could one day reach the coveted coast of China.

Contrary to popular belief, fifteenth-century Europeans did not think that the world was flat. They did, however, worry that China lay too far away and that ships could not complete a voyage west over what they believed was a vast, open ocean.

☑ **IDENTIFY MAIN IDEAS** Why were the Portuguese venturing into the Atlantic Ocean?

Christopher Columbus Explores the Americas

With financial backing from Spain's monarchs, Isabella and Ferdinand, Christopher Columbus sailed west to the Americas. He then returned to conquer the land, exploit its wealth, and convert its people to Christianity. The colonization process launched by Columbus transformed the Americas, Europe, and Africa.

Christopher Columbus To pursue the western dream, Spain relied on an Italian mariner from the city of Genoa named **Christopher Columbus**. He sought a route to China not only to find a new trade route but as a means of reviving the Christian struggle against Islam. By converting the Chinese to Christianity, he hoped to recruit their people and use their wealth to assist Europeans in a new crusade.

Columbus dared the westward trip because he underestimated the size of Earth. He believed the planet was 18,000 miles around—almost 7,000 miles smaller than it actually is.

>> Europeans first established agricultural plantations on fertile islands near the coast of Africa such as the Azores.

Viking Stories Influence Columbus An experienced Atlantic mariner, as a young man Columbus had investigated stories about mysterious lands to the west. He may have sailed to Iceland. If so, he probably heard about the western discoveries by the Vikings from Scandinavia.

During the ninth and tenth centuries, Viking mariners had probed the North Atlantic to discover and colonize Iceland and then Greenland. From Greenland, some mariners reached the northeastern coast of North America. About the year 1000, they founded a little settlement on the northern tip of Newfoundland. But they soon abandoned it because of the site's isolation and conflict with American Indians.

Columbus Sails West In 1492, Queen Isabella and King Ferdinand of Spain provided 3 ships, 90 men, and most of the funding for Columbus's voyage west in search of China. After 33 days at sea, he reached what we now call the Bahamas. Turning south, Columbus found another set of islands. He supposed that these belonged to the East Indies, which lay near the mainland of Asia. Based on his mistaken notion, he referred to the people living on the islands as Indians, a name that has endured to this day.

The presence of native people did not stop Columbus from claiming the land for Spain. As the representative of a Christian nation, Columbus believed that he had the right and duty to dominate the people he found.

> They should be good servants and intelligent, for I observed that they quickly took in what was said to them, and I believe that they would easily be made Christians, as it appeared to me that they had no religion. I, our Lord being pleased, will take hence, at the time of my departure six natives. . . .
>
> —Journal of Christopher Columbus, October 1492

The Impact of Columbus's Voyage Columbus continued to explore the islands of the Caribbean. He established a fort on the island he called Hispaniola. Then, in early 1493, leaving a number of men to guard the fort, he returned to Spain.

Later that year, Columbus returned to the Caribbean to colonize Hispaniola. The new colony was supposed to produce profits by shipping gold, sugar, and enslaved American Indians to Spain. The Spanish planned to dominate the natives and forge an empire. Columbus was to be governor of the new Spanish territories.

Upon his return to Hispaniola, however, Columbus discovered that the local people had killed the men he had left behind to guard the fort. Columbus turned to force. Employing the military advantages of horses, gunpowder, and steel, Columbus killed and captured hundreds of local people on Hispaniola and the adjacent islands.

Unfortunately for Columbus, reports of his cruelty and mismanagement during his second and third expeditions prompted the king and queen to recall him in 1500. Columbus returned to Spain, was deprived of the governorship, but made a final expedition to the Americas before he died in 1506. The Spanish colonization of the Americas, however, continued.

Columbus had not reached Asia, as he believed, but he had found a source of riches that enabled European Christendom to grow more powerful and wealthy than the Muslim world. During the next three centuries, the mineral and plantation wealth of the Americas—produced by the labor of enslaved Africans—helped finance the expansion of European commerce. In turn, that commerce promoted the development of new technologies and the growth of military power.

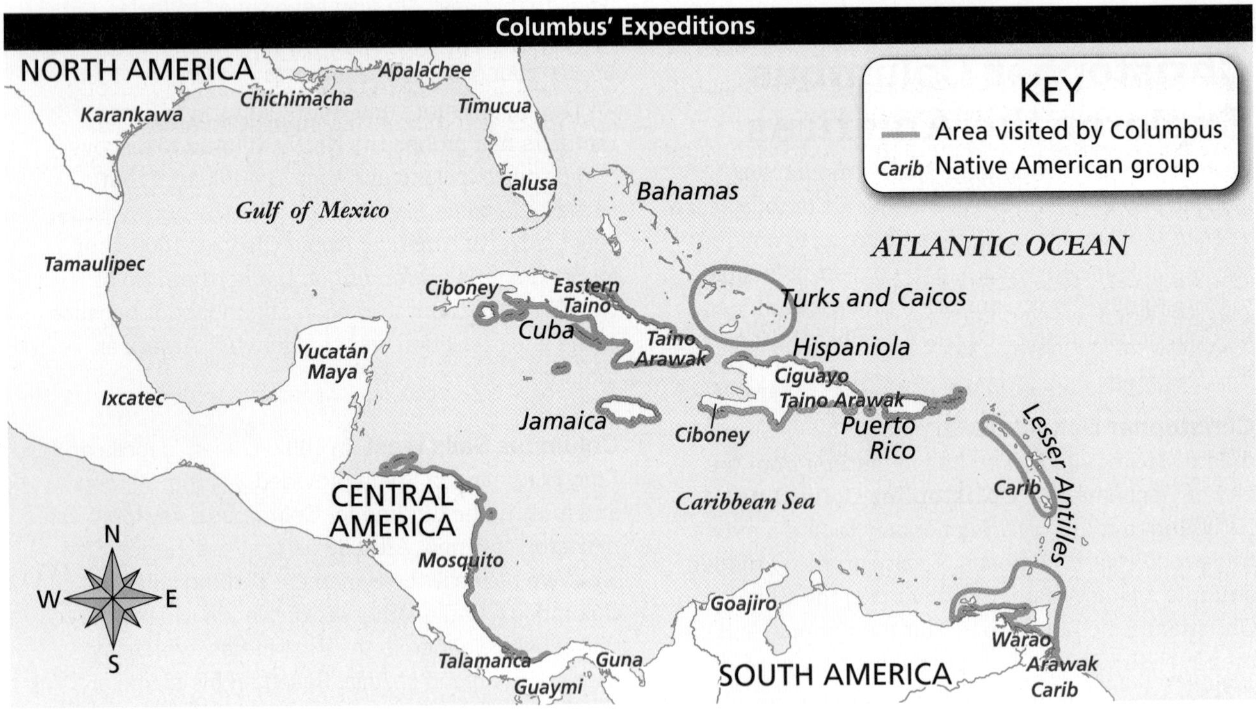

>> After his first voyage to the Americas in 1492, Columbus crossed the Atlantic three more times. **Analyze Maps** How much of the coast of the Americas did Columbus visit? How do you think this affected the accuracy of his reports?

Spain and Portugal Divide the Americas With the assistance of the pope, the Spanish and the Portuguese negotiated the 1494 Treaty of Tordesillas. They agreed to split ownership of the newly-encountered lands by drawing a north-south boundary line through the mid-Atlantic west of the Azores.

The Portuguese secured a monopoly to exploit the coast of Africa and the Indian Ocean. In return, the Spanish claimed Columbus's western lands. Further exploration later determined that South America bulged eastward beyond the treaty line, placing Brazil in the Portuguese sphere.

In dividing the world, no one bothered to consult the peoples of the Americas. The Iberians and the pope considered them pagan savages without any rights. The other European kings refused to honor the treaty, for they claimed an equal right to explore and exploit the new lands. But no European leaders thought that the original people of the Americas could, or should, be left alone in their former isolation.

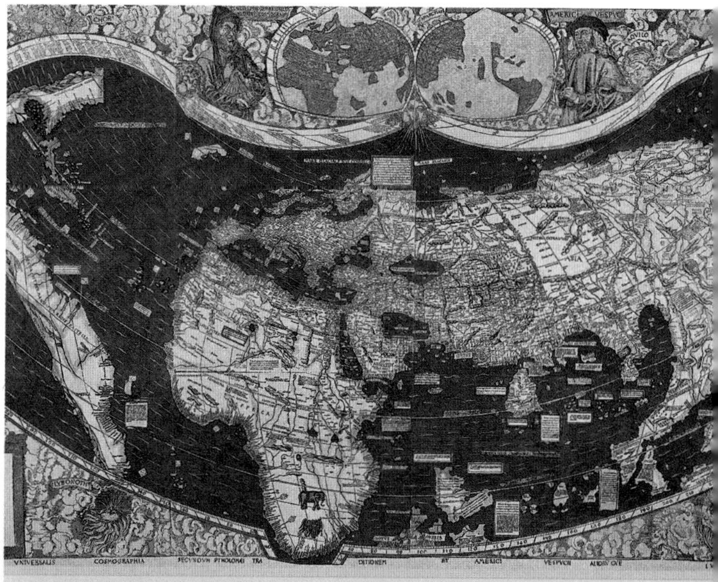

>> This 1507 map was the first to call the lands of the Western Hemisphere the "Americas." **Analyze Primary Sources** How accurate is the depiction of the Americas on this map?

CHECK UNDERSTANDING What was Columbus's purpose in sailing west across the Atlantic?

The Spanish Build an American Empire

Until his last breath, Columbus insisted that his discoveries lay close to the coast of China. Other explorers, however, demonstrated that he had reached the margins of two previously unknown continents. In 1497, **John Cabot**, a Genoese mariner employed by the English, sailed to Newfoundland. In tropical waters far to the south, a Portuguese fleet commanded by **Pedro Alvarez Cabral** discovered the coast of Brazil in 1500. A year later, **Amerigo Vespucci**, another Genoese mariner, explored enough of South America's coast to deem it a continent. European mapmakers began to call the newly discovered continents by a variant of Vespucci's first name—America. Between 1519 and 1522, a voyage begun by **Ferdinand Magellan** succeeded in encircling the entire globe, filling in even more of the increasingly detailed picture of Earth.

Cortés Conquers the Aztecs At the start of the 1500s, the Spanish learned of a spectacular Indian empire in central Mexico. Those soldiers who explored central Mexico and defeated the Indian civilizations there were called **conquistadors**. In 1519, the brilliant and ruthless **Hernán Cortés** led a group of about 600 volunteers from Cuba to the coast of Mexico. Born in 1485, Cortés had university training as a lawyer. An ambitious man, he left Spain in 1504 to try his luck in Cuba, where he became rich by acquiring plantations and gold mines. But he hungered for more.

Marching inland, Cortés reached the great central valley, home of the Aztec Empire. The approach of Cortés's army alarmed the Aztec ruler, **Moctezuma**. Hoping to intimidate them with his own power, Moctezuma invited the Spanish into his great city.

The largest and richest city in the Americas, Tenochtitlán occupied a cluster of islands in a large lake. The population of about 140,000 dwarfed Spain's largest city, Seville, which had about 70,000 inhabitants.

The Aztec city's central plaza of tall stone pyramid-temples dazzled with a combination of red, blue, and ochre stucco. Bernal Diaz, a soldier, recalled, "These great towns and pyramids and buildings arising from the water, all made of stone seemed like an enchanted vision. . . . Indeed, some of our soldiers asked whether it was not all a dream."

The city's gold and silver inflamed the Spanish desire to conquer and plunder. By seizing Moctezuma, the Spanish provoked a violent uprising during which Moctezuma died and the Spanish were driven from the city. Returning with reinforcements, including many revenge-seeking local groups who had themselves been brutalized by the Aztecs, Cortés captured Tenochtitlán. The cost, however, was high. Four months of fighting reduced the city to rubble.

The victors enslaved many American Indian captives. They also forced local Aztec people to work raising a Spanish capital, Mexico City, on the ruins of Tenochtitlán. They transformed the shell of Moctezuma's palace into a residence for Cortés. Grateful for the stunning conquest and a share in the immense plunder, the Spanish king appointed Cortés to govern Mexico.

The Conquistadors Expand Their Empire The Spanish extended their empire deep into North and South America. During the 1530s, Francisco Pizarro conquered the powerful Incas of Peru with just 180 soldiers.

In addition to their pursuit of wealth, conquistadors were motivated by their religious faith and by loyalty to their monarch. They reasoned that riches were wasted on the non-Christian American Indians. Those riches should belong to Christians who served the Spanish Crown—and who were willing to help convert the native people. These notions had been deeply ingrained in Spanish culture as a result of the centuries-long *reconquista.*

The conquistadors benefited from their superior weapons. These included steel-edged swords, pikes, and crossbows. Such weapons were far more durable and deadly than the stone-edged swords, axes, and arrows of the Indians. Because sixteenth-century guns were so heavy, inaccurate, and slow to reload, only a few conquistadors carried them. Yet these guns gave the Spanish a psychological advantage. Belching fire and smoke, they produced a thunderous roar that was terrifying and spread confusion.

Although most conquistadors fought on foot, the few with horses proved especially dreadful. The Indians had never experienced the shocking power and speed of mounted men. "The most essential thing in new lands is horses," observed a conquistador. "They instill the greatest fear in the enemy and make the Indians respect the leaders of the army." But the greatest advantage came from something the conquistadors did not even know they carried—disease.

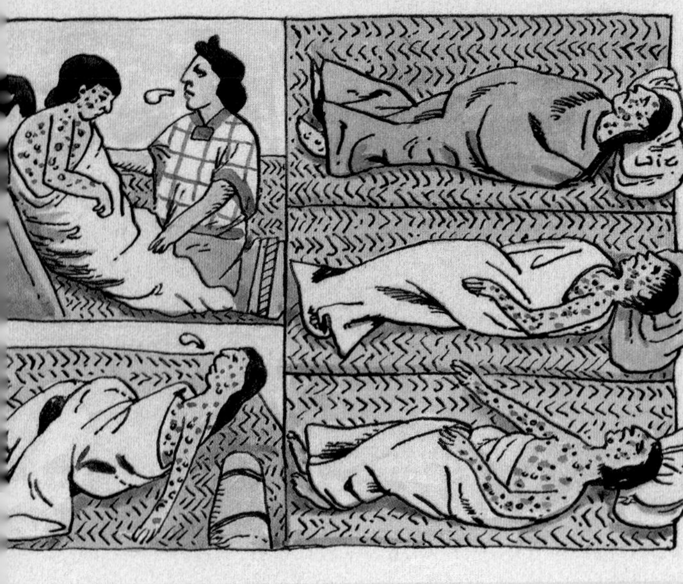

>> Aztecs fell victim to European diseases, such as smallpox.

Disease Devastates Native Peoples Brutal exploitation and disease combined to reduce the population of the Americas. When Columbus established a settlement on Hispaniola in 1492, the island's original population numbered about 300,000. By 1548, the island's population declined to a mere 500. The Spanish forced the natives, known as the Tainos, to labor in mines and on ranches and plantations. Those who resisted suffered deadly raids on their villages by colonial soldiers. Overworked and underfed, the native population was especially vulnerable to disease.

The ravages of these diseases were not confined to Hispaniola. In the century after the arrival of the Europeans in the Americas, experts believe that successive epidemics reduced the native population to about one-fifth of its pre-1492 numbers.

The great European killers included smallpox, typhus, diphtheria, bubonic plague, and cholera. These were diseases that had existed in Europe for centuries. As a result, the European population over the generations had developed some natural defenses against them. That is, among the population there was a percentage of people whose bodies were able to fight off the diseases before they became fatal. The native populations of the Americas had not built up such natural defenses. While Europeans also carried disease from the Americas back to Europe, American Indian populations were devastated by this exchange of infections. In some cases, entire villages simply disappeared.

For the Spanish, the reduction of the native population complicated their colonization plans. They had depended on American Indians to provide the labor for their new enterprises. Left with large tracts of fertile but depopulated lands, the colonists needed a new source of workers. They turned to

American Indian Population, 1492–1800

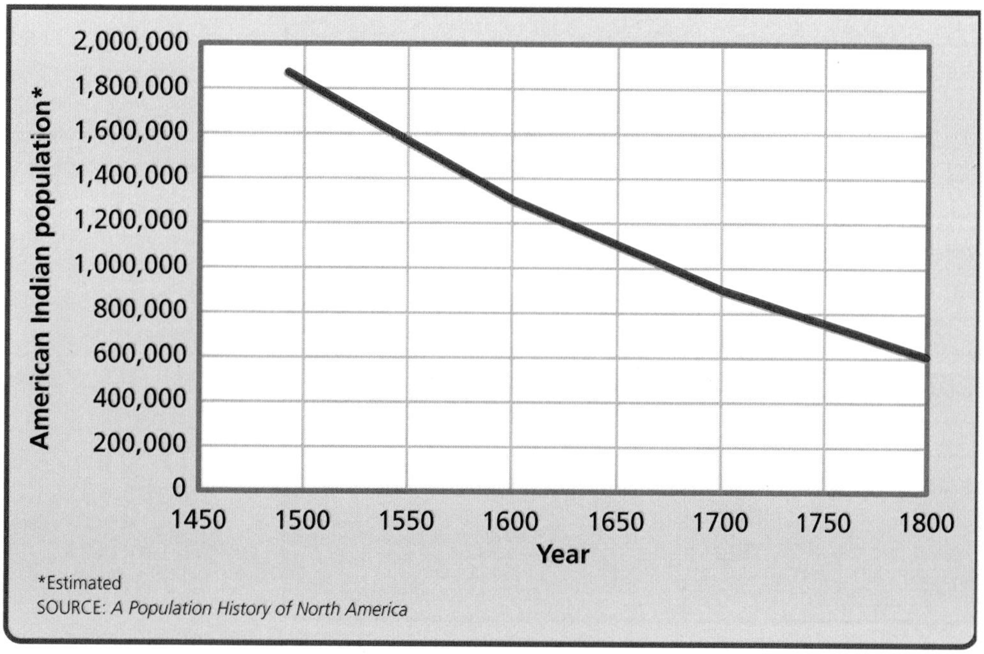

>> **Analyze Graphs** Based on this graph, how did the American Indian population change after the late 1400s?

importing enslaved Africans to work the new sugar plantations on the tropical coasts.

☑ **RECALL** How did the conquistadors justify their conquest of the Aztec and Inca empires?

The Columbian Exchange

The Europeans who began arriving in the Americas in the late 1400s brought more than weapons, diseases, and a thirst for wealth and power. The colonizers also brought plants and animals that were new to the Americas. Indeed, the European arrival brought about an ecological revolution. Never before in human history had so many of the world's plants, animals, and microorganisms been so thoroughly and so abruptly mixed and dispersed. We call this phenomenon the **Columbian Exchange**.

Exchange of Plants and Animals Determined to farm the American land in a European manner, the colonists introduced their domesticated livestock: pigs, horses, mules, sheep, and cattle. They also brought seeds for their domesticated plants. These included wheat, barley, rye, oats, grasses, and grapes.

In a land where large mammals such as cattle and horses did not exist, the new plants and animals brought drastic changes to the environment.

Roaming cattle and pigs consumed the wild plants and the shellfish that the Indians needed for their own diet. The livestock also invaded the Indians' fields to consume their maize, beans, and squashes.

The peoples of the Americas adapted to the newly introduced plants and animals. In time, they learned to raise and consume European cattle. On the Great Plains, the American Indians acquired runaway horses. This enabled them to hunt bison more efficiently and resist efforts to colonize their land.

While exporting domesticated plants and livestock to the Americas, the Europeans imported productive plants from their American colonies. Maize and potatoes from the Americas produced more food per acre than traditional European crops such as wheat. European farmers enjoyed larger harvests by adding, or switching to, the American plants. Europeans also adopted tomatoes, beans, peppers, and peanuts. This improvement in the European diet led to a European population explosion.

The Columbian Exchange and Global Population The Columbian Exchange helped trigger enormous population shifts around the world.

Larger harvests aided by new American crops fueled European population growth. From about 80 million in 1492, Europe's population grew to 180 million by 1800. That growth nearly doubled

Population of Europe, 1492–1800

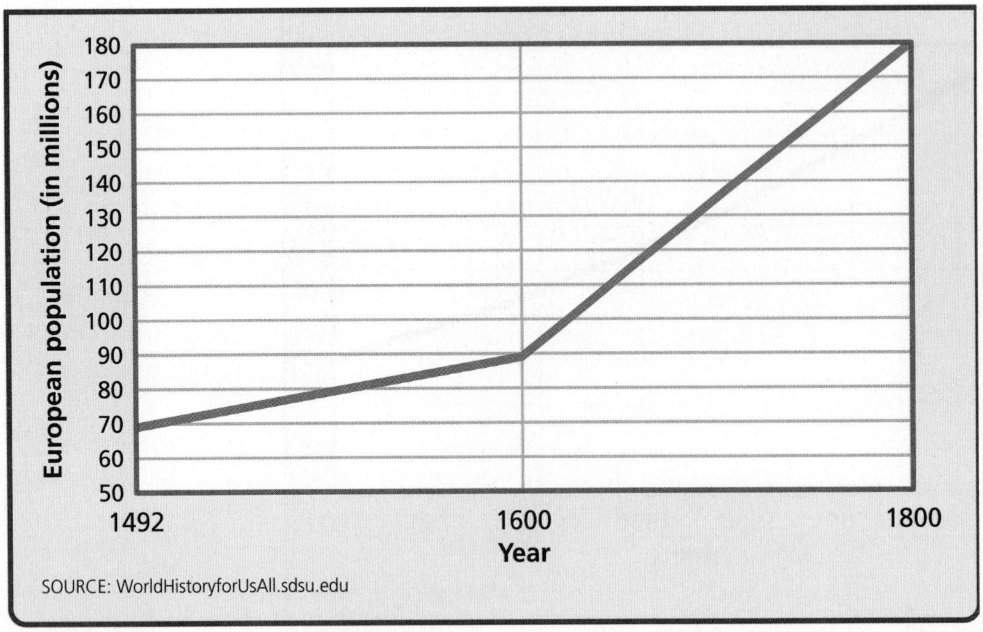

>> **Analyze Graphs** Why did the population changes shown on this graph spur emigration from Europe to the Americas?

Europe's share of the world's population from about 11 percent in 1492 to 20 percent in 1800. Meanwhile, the American Indian proportion of the global population collapsed from about 7 percent in 1492 to less than 1 percent in 1800.

The European surplus population flowed westward across the Atlantic to replace the depleted populations of the Americas. The colonizers imported millions of enslaved Africans. Never before had so many people moved so far with such a powerful impact. As a result, maritime trade and migration, both forced and voluntary, integrated four continents: Europe, Africa, South America, and North America.

☑ **IDENTIFY SUPPORTING DETAILS** How did the Columbian Exchange affect traditional diets in Europe and the Americas?

☑ ASSESSMENT

1. **Use Context Clues** What made Europe in the 1400s a "divided" society?
2. **Infer** What positive impact did the Crusades have on Europe?
3. **Support Ideas with Examples** Which new technologies expanded trade in the late 1400s?
4. **Distinguish** What was the result of Christopher Columbus's settlement on the island of Hispaniola?
5. **Apply Concepts** In spite of being outnumbered, how did the Spanish conquistadors defeat the native inhabitants of the Americas?
6. **Quest Connection** How did European leaders view Native Americans? How did these views affect native people?

1.4

Spanish explorers traveled through the South and Southwest hoping to find fabled cities of gold. This 1905 lithograph by artist Frederic Remington depicts one such group.

Spain and France in the Americas

During the sixteenth century, the Spanish created a great empire by conquering and colonizing the lands in the Caribbean as well as large portions of North and South America. This American empire was more than ten times larger than Spain and rich in gold and silver. The potential for great wealth motivated other European nations to join the quest for colonies in the Americas. Soon rivalries emerged in the Americas as European empires vied for territory.

BOUNCE to Activate Flipped Video

Objectives

Explain the religious rivalry among European nations.

Describe Spanish society in New Spain and Peru.

Evaluate the causes and effects of Spanish imperial policies in the American Southwest.

Explain how the fur trade affected both native peoples and the French in North America.

Describe French expansion into Louisiana.

Key Terms

missionaries
presidios
viceroy
mestizos
missions
Northwest Passage
Quebec
Samuel de Champlain
coureurs de bois
metis

European Rivalries Spread to the Americas

Enriched by conquests in the Americas, Spain financed an aggressive military policy in Europe. This aggression alarmed the Dutch, French, and English, who sought their own share of the riches in the Americas. These nations probed the coast of North America, seeking places where they might establish their own colonies. They also encouraged pirates to rob Spanish treasure ships.

Conflicts over acquiring lands in the Americas was just one issue that emerged in the 1500s. Religious divisions also added to the conflict among nations in Europe. In 1517, a movement called the Protestant Reformation began in Germany when a monk named Martin Luther challenged the authority of the Catholic Church. Luther and other dissenters became known as Protestants because they protested against the power of the pope and against the Church, which they viewed as corrupt and materialistic.

Protestants favored the individual's right to seek God by reading the Bible and by heeding ministers who delivered

GO ONLINE to access your digital course

evangelical sermons. Without the unifying power of the pope, Protestants soon divided into many different denominations, including Lutherans, Calvinists, Baptists, Anglicans, and Quakers.

The Protestant movement spread throughout northern Europe, including the Netherlands and England. The French divided into hostile Protestant and Catholic camps, but the Spanish remained Catholic. Indeed, Spanish monarchs led the Catholic effort to suppress Protestantism. Rival nations carried the conflict across the Atlantic to their new colonies in the Americas.

☑ **CHECK UNDERSTANDING** Against what key issues did Protestants rebel?

Governing the Spanish American Empire

Although the conquistadors were successful at conquering territory and establishing colonies for Spain, they were not effective at running the colonies. Under Spanish rule, Indians were enslaved and forced to labor on encomiendas, large Spanish-owned plantations. They were also forced to mine for silver and gold. They suffered harsh treatment and were often beaten or worked to death.

King Charles I of Spain became concerned about the management of his American territories. Rather than turning native people into a reliable labor force that could make money for the government, the conquistadors' brutality destabilized the region. The king heeded the advice of priests like Bartolomé de Las Casas, who urged the government to reform the treatment of American Indians. Spain sent out Catholic friars as **missionaries**—people who work to convert others to their religion. The friars wanted to spread Catholicism, while the Spanish government hoped to use the friars as a cheap way to build settlements and profit from American Indian labor.

Although less brutal than the conquistadors, the friars demanded that the Indians surrender their traditions in favor of Christian beliefs and Spanish ways. The missionaries also forced Indians to work for them. The friars relied on Spanish soldiers who set up **presidios**, or forts, near the missions.

Spain Establishes New Spain and Peru During the 1530s and 1540s, the Spanish Crown divided Spain's American empire into two immense regions, known as viceroyalties, each ruled by a **viceroy** appointed by the king. The viceroyalty of New Spain consisted of Mexico, Central America, and the Caribbean islands. The viceroyalty of Peru included all of South America except Portuguese Brazil. To control the viceroys, the Spanish Crown forced them

Viceroyalties of New Spain and Peru, c. 1545

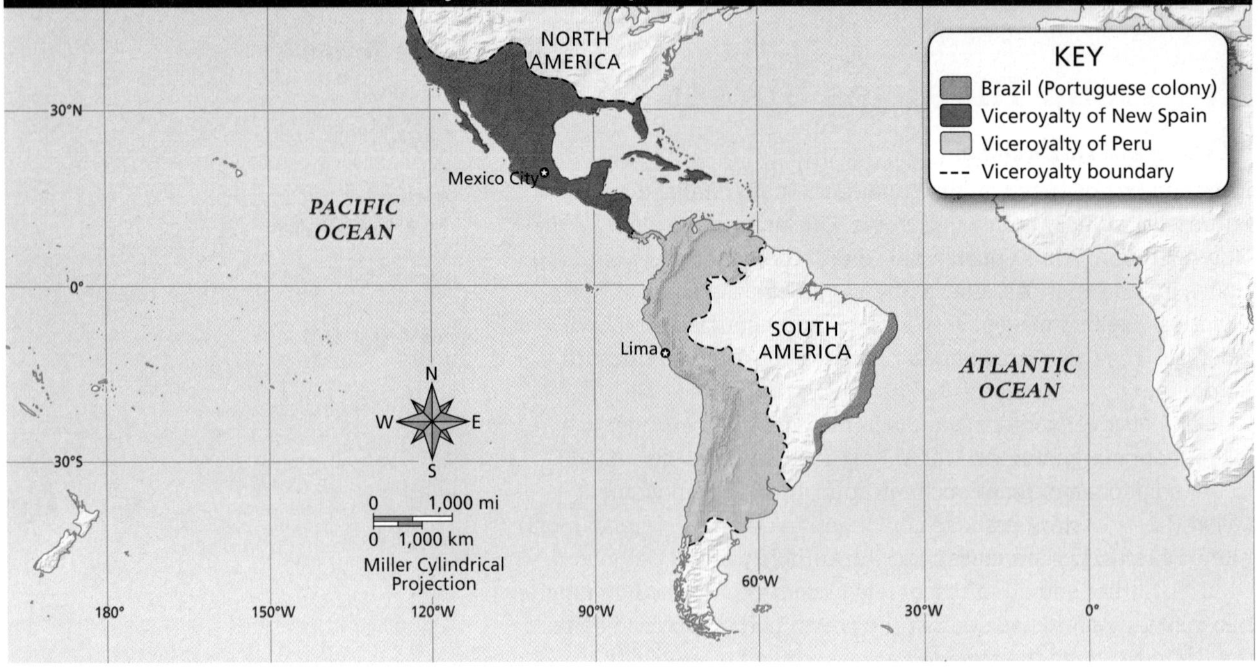

>> This map shows land claimed by Spain and Portugal. **Analyze Maps** How did the Viceroyalties of New Spain and Peru reflect the decisions made under the earlier Treaty of Tordesillas?

BOUNCE to Activate Gallery

to share power with a Crown-appointed council and an archbishop. The Spanish did not permit elected assemblies in their colonies.

Racial Hierarchy in Spain's American Colonies During the sixteenth century, about 250,000 Spanish people immigrated across the Atlantic to the American empire. These Spanish immigrants, most of whom were men, generally took Indian wives. Children of mixed Spanish and Indian ancestry became known as **mestizos**. As the American Indian population declined from diseases, the mestizos became the largest segment of Spain's colonial population by the eighteenth century. The next largest population group were enslaved Africans, especially in the Caribbean region.

To maintain their authority, colonial officials developed a complex system of racial hierarchy known as the *castas*. At the bottom lay Africans and Indians, while Spaniards were at the pinnacle. The higher *castas* enjoyed superior status and greater legal privileges at the expense of those of lower status.

In both New Spain and Peru, the Spanish developed an urban, cosmopolitan culture. Carefully planned towns had a spacious grid of streets, with the town hall and a church arranged around a central plaza. The wealthiest families resided near the central plaza. The common people lived in the outer districts of the towns.

DEFINE What was the *castas*?

>> According to the label here, *from a cambujo and an india, a tente en al aire is born.* These are a few of the many detailed terms the Spanish used to classify people based on their ancestry.

Spanish Explorers Seek Wealth in the North

Cortés' success in conquering and plundering Mexico inspired later conquistadors. Seeking their own golden empires, Hernando de Soto and Francisco Vásquez de Coronado led expeditions into the lands north of Mexico.

De Soto Explores Florida In 1539, de Soto's conquistadors crossed present-day Florida, Georgia,South Carolina, North Carolina, Tennessee, Alabama, Mississippi, and Arkansas. Frustrated in their search for riches, the conquistadors massacred Indian villages, ravaged fields, emptied storehouses, and burned towns. After de Soto died of disease in 1542, his men gave up and fled to Mexico in boats. They left behind deadly new diseases, which continued to spread among the Indians of the Southeast.

>> Construction on Mexico City's cathedral went on throughout the colonial period. Churches and cathedrals from these years can be found across Spain's former empire, from Chile to California.

Coronado Meets the Pueblos and Searches for Gold Coronado marched north from Mexico into the Rio Grande valley in 1540. Unable to defeat the Spanish, the Pueblo Indians in the region tried to get rid of them by appealing to their greed. The Pueblos told alluring stories of a golden kingdom named Quivira to the northeast, on the far side of a great, grassy plain.

In pursuit of Quivira, Coronado and his men crossed the Great Plains to what is now Kansas. They found only villages of grass-thatched lodges inhabited by Wichita Indians, who possessed neither gold nor silver. Returning to the Rio Grande in a rage, the Spanish took a bloody revenge on the Pueblos before retreating to Mexico in 1542.

Spain Attacks the French in Florida After the expensive failures of de Soto and Coronado, the Spanish Crown lost interest in the northern lands. Lacking tangible wealth, the northern frontier did not seem worth the effort to conquer and colonize. But attacks by French, Dutch, and English pirates began to change Spanish minds during the 1560s. By occupying Florida and the Rio Grande valley, the Spanish hoped to create a defensive zone, to keep hostile European rivals far from the precious mines and towns of Mexico. This plan became urgent when the Spanish learned that the French had built a small base on the Atlantic coast of Florida. Worse still, these French colonists were Protestants, whom the Spanish hated as heretics.

In 1565, Pedro Menendez de Avilés attacked and destroyed the French base, slaughtering the captured Protestants. He then founded the fortified town of St. Augustine, which became the first enduring colonial town within what would later become the United States. However, Florida failed to attract a large number of Spanish colonists, who numbered a mere 1,000 by the end of the century. Friars tried to convert Indians to Christianity by building **missions** in the native villages. By 1675, the friars had gathered 20,000 native converts in 36 mission churches spread across northern Florida.

IDENTIFY MAIN IDEAS Why did the Spanish explore and colonize Florida in the 1600s?

Colonization and Conflict in New Mexico

During the 1590s, a Spanish expedition led by Juan de Oñate returned to the lands explored by Coronado in the Rio Grande valley. There, Spain established the colony of New Mexico, with Santa Fe as the capital after 1607. The colony's isolation from Mexico, however, reduced the colonists' income and drove up the cost of their imported goods.

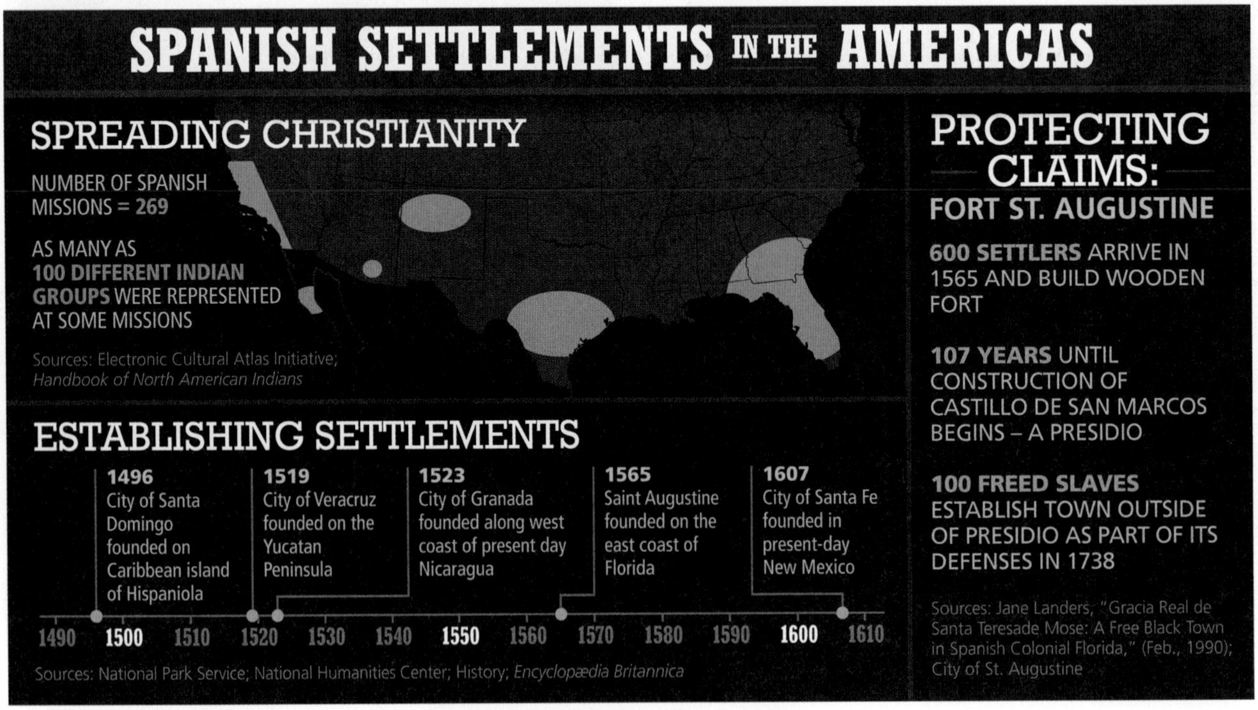

>> **Analyze Information** What factors likely explain the gradual spread of Spanish influence shown on this infographic?

Spanish Missions in New Mexico

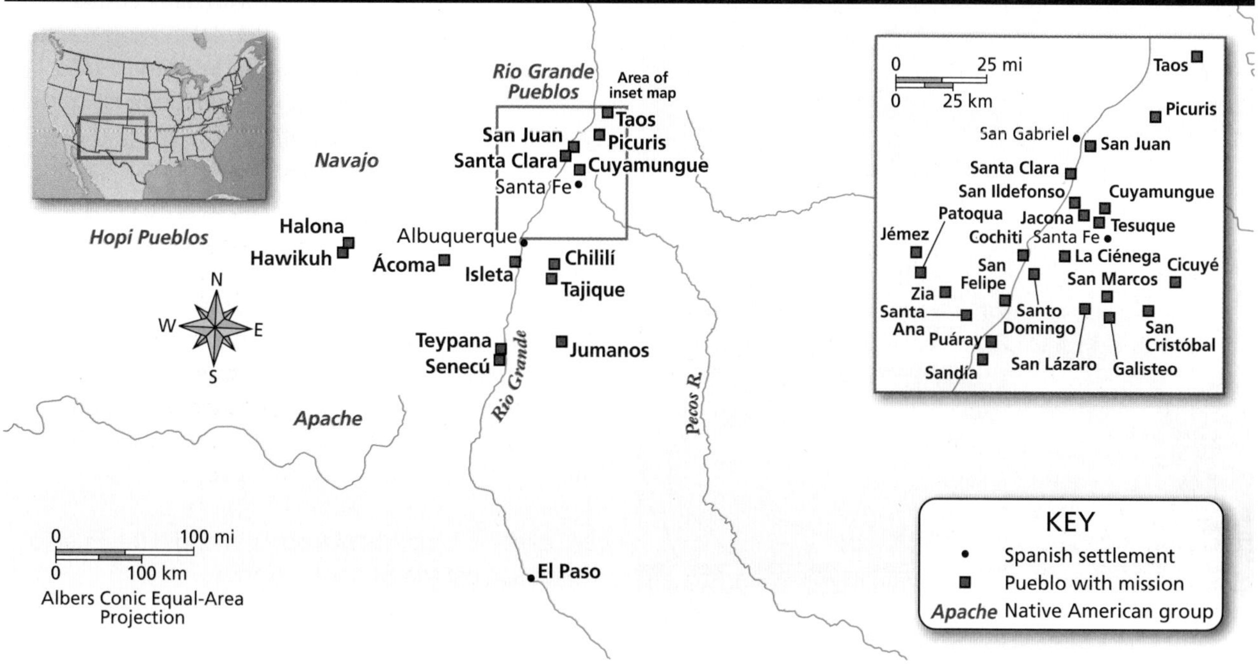

>> **Analyze Maps** How did New Mexico's physical geography influence the locations of Spanish missions there?

Missions in New Mexico Because few Spanish settlers wished to join such an isolated and poor colony, New Mexico's colonial population stagnated. In 1638, the 2,000 colonists were greatly outnumbered by the 40,000 Pueblo Indians. A soldier described New Mexico as "at the ends of the earth . . . remote beyond compare."

As in Florida, only the friars thrived in New Mexico. By 1628, they had founded 50 missions. The progress was remarkable because the friars demanded so much from their converts. Christian churches replaced the circular *kivas,* the sacred structures for religious dances and ceremonies.

The priests smashed or burned the *katsina* figures held sacred by the Indians. (*Katsinas* are wooden figures that represent ancestral spirits.) The friars also expected the Indians to dress, cook, eat, and speak like Spaniards.

Tensions Rise Between Friars and Pueblos For a couple of generations, the Pueblos did their best to adapt. In part, the Indians acted from fear of the Spanish soldiers, who backed up the friars with firearms and horses. The Pueblos were also interested in the domesticated animals and metal tools provided by the missions.

But the Pueblos would not give up all of their traditional beliefs. Instead, they considered Christianity a supplement to their own sacred practices. To please the priests, the Indians became public Christians, but they privately mixed Christianity with traditional ways, keeping in secret their *kivas* and *katsinas*. When the missionaries discovered these secrets, they felt the fury of betrayal. The harsh punishments inflicted by the friars angered the Pueblos.

Conditions worsened during the 1660s and 1670s. A prolonged drought undercut the harvests, reducing many Pueblos to starvation. Disease, famine, and violence cut their population from 40,000 in 1638 to 17,000 by 1680. The losses made it harder for the Pueblos to pay tribute in labor and crops to the missionaries and colonists.

Pueblo Revolt of 1680 Fed up, in 1680 the Pueblos revolted under the leadership of a shaman named Popé. Encouraging resistance to Spanish ways, Popé urged a return to the traditional Pueblo culture and religion. The rebels also drew support from the Apaches, who had their own scores to settle with the Spanish slave raiders. The Indians destroyed and plundered missions, farms, and ranches. Abandoning Santa Fe, the colonial survivors and Christian Indians fled to El Paso, which at the time was on the southern margin of New Mexico. The Pueblo Revolt was the greatest setback that the Indians ever inflicted on colonial expansion.

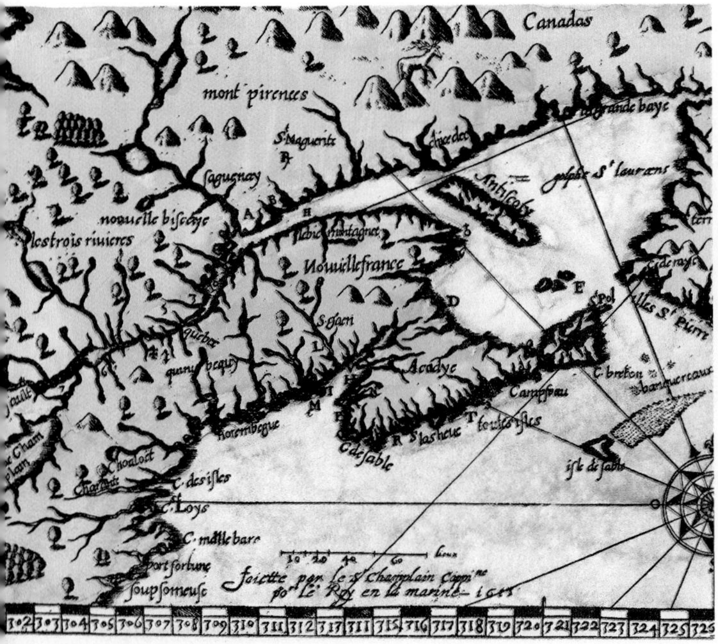

PART OF CHAMPLAIN'S 1613 MAP.[1]

>> French traders and explorers mapped parts of the Americas that became New France. This 1613 map shows part of the Great Lakes and northeastern Atlantic regions.

>> French fur traders like this man profited from capturing beavers and selling their valuable fur.

After victory deprived them of a common enemy, the Pueblos remained feuding with one another and with the Apaches. The renewed violence discredited Popé, who had promised that the rebellion would bring peace and prosperity. Losing influence, he died sometime before 1690. During the following three years, the Spanish reclaimed New Mexico.

The bloody revolt taught the Pueblos and the Spanish to compromise. The Pueblos accepted Spanish authority, while the Spanish colonists practiced greater restraint. The Pueblos once again became public Catholics while quietly maintaining traditional ceremonies in their *kivas*. The Spanish and the Pueblos increasingly needed one another for mutual protection against the Apaches of the surrounding plains and mountains.

☑ **CHECK UNDERSTANDING** Why did the Pueblo revolt against the Spanish colonists?

The French Settle in North America

Spain's success with its American colonies encouraged other European nations to establish colonies. French explorers led expeditions along the North American Atlantic seaboard during the 1500s. These explorers established a number of French settlements along the St. Lawrence River and began trading fish and animal furs with American Indians in the region. In time, these small settlements grew and became the nucleus of present-day Canada.

During the early 1500s, explorers who sailed for France, including Giovanni de Verrazano and Jacques Cartier, were less interested in establishing colonies and more interested in finding a **Northwest Passage**—a water route to Asia through the cold waters of present-day Canada. They probed the eastern coastline of North America, from present-day North Carolina to Newfoundland. During the 1530s and 1540s, Cartier investigated the St. Lawrence River.

France Establishes New France The French king claimed the region that Cartier explored as New France. At the mouth of the St. Lawrence River, French mariners fished for cod and hunted for whales and seals. The mariners met Indian hunters, who offered furs in trade. Rendered scarce in Europe by excessive hunting, furs, especially beaver furs, commanded high prices.

Indians eagerly traded fur for metal arrowheads, hoes, axes, knives, and hatchets, all useful both as tools and weapons, and for iron or brass kettles, which made it easier to boil their meals. A Montagnais Indian explained, "The Beaver does everything perfectly well, it makes kettles, hatchets, swords, knives, bread; in short, it makes everything." Increasingly, the Indians hunted for a foreign market rather than just for their own subsistence.

Killing the beaver faster than the animals could reproduce, the coastal Indians sought new stocks by invading the hunting territories of their neighbors. This provoked wars between Indian groups.

Those without metal weapons lost these wars, which also gave them a powerful incentive to trade with the French. Every American Indian nation tried to attract European traders and keep them away from rival Indian groups.

Just as American Indians fought one another over trade, the traders plundered and killed one another in competition for furs. To repel rivals, the French built a fortified trading post at **Quebec** on the St. Lawrence River in 1608. It was the first permanent European settlement in Canada.

>> Founded in 1608, Quebec was the first permanent European settlement in Canada. **Draw Conclusions** How did Quebec's location contribute to its defense and economic prosperity?

Relationships Between the French and Indians Unlike the Spanish in Mexico, the Canadian French could not afford to intimidate, dispossess, or enslave the Indians. The French needed them as hunters and suppliers of furs—roles that the Indians eagerly performed. Few in number, the French took little land, which lessened conflict with Canada's Indians. This distinguished the French from English colonists, who aimed to displace American Indians and control their land.

Samuel de Champlain, Quebec's founder, traded with the Montagnais, Algonquin, and Huron Indians. In return, they expected Champlain to help them against their foes, the Iroquois, who lived to the south in what is now New York.

In 1609, Champlain and nine French soldiers helped their allies attack an Iroquois camp beside the lake later named after Champlain. The Iroquois assembled their warriors in a mass formation. They counted on their wooden shields, helmets, and body armor for protection from arrows. They were shocked when Champlain and his soldiers fired their guns, instantly killing Iroquois chiefs and warriors. Bewildered, the Iroquois warriors retreated.

Champlain won the battle at a high long-term cost. He made enemies of the powerful Iroquois, who for decades thereafter raided the French settlements. The battle also revolutionized Indian warfare. The Iroquois abandoned wooden armor, and they avoided massed formations. Instead, they relied on trees for cover and shifted their tactics to hit-and-run raids. They also demanded guns as the price of trade. Obtaining guns from Dutch traders on the Hudson River, the Iroquois became better armed than their Algonquin, Montagnais, and Huron enemies.

Jesuit Missionaries in New France Like the Spanish, the French dispatched Catholic priests as missionaries to convert the Indians. Most French Catholic missionaries belonged to the Jesuit order. They enjoyed their greatest success among the Huron Indians of the Great Lakes region. But that success attracted Iroquois warriors, who destroyed the Huron villages between 1648 and 1649. Killing hundreds, including most of the priests, the raiders carried away thousands of Huron captives. Many were adopted by the Iroquois. The Jesuit missions survived only in the St. Lawrence Valley between the major towns of Montreal and Quebec.

DESCRIBE Describe the relationship between the French fur traders and the Montagnais, Algonquin, and Huron Indians.

Living in New France

New France's government resembled that of New Spain. Both were strictly controlled by powerful monarchs of the homeland. The French king appointed a military governor-general, a civil administrator known as the *intendant*, and a Catholic bishop. Like the Spanish, the French king did not permit an elected assembly in Canada.

Settling New France Attracting few immigrants, New France grew slowly. By 1700, the colony still had only 15,000 colonists. Potential colonists objected to the hard work of clearing dense forests to plant new farms. The long Canadian winter shocked newcomers from temperate France. Worst of all, immigrants dreaded the Iroquois raids.

Most French colonists were farmers who settled in the St. Lawrence Valley. To the west, American Indians dominated the vast hinterland of forests and lakes, where the colonists were few and scattered. In the Great Lakes and Illinois countries, the French established a handful of settlements, including Detroit. Settlers lived by a mix of farming and trade.

Establishing Peace Brings Benefits To survive and prosper in an Indian world, the French had to adopt some of the Indians' ways. Known as ***coureurs de bois*** (koo rer duh BWAH), many fur traders married Indian women. The children of these marriages become known as the ***metis***.

With the help of the *coureurs de bois* and the *metis,* the French allied with the Great Lakes Indians, who primarily spoke an Algonquian language. The allies defeated the Iroquois during the 1680s and 1690s, compelling them to make peace in 1701. At last, the fur traders of the Great Lakes and the grain farmers of the St. Lawrence Valley could work in safety from Iroquois raids.

The French Look South In 1682, the French explorer Robert de La Salle was hoping to find a Northwest Passage. Guided by American Indians, he made his way south on the Mississippi River toward what he hoped was an opening to the Pacific Ocean. Instead, he found the Gulf of Mexico. La Salle claimed the territory around the Mississippi River basin for France, naming it Louisiana, in honor of King Louis XIV.

In 1718, near the river's mouth, the French founded New Orleans, which became the colony's largest town and leading seaport.

Like Canada, Louisiana struggled to attract colonists. The economy provided few opportunities beyond trading with the Indians for deerskins or raising tobacco of poor quality. The hot climate and swampy landscape also promoted deadly diseases,

French Settlements and American Indians in New France

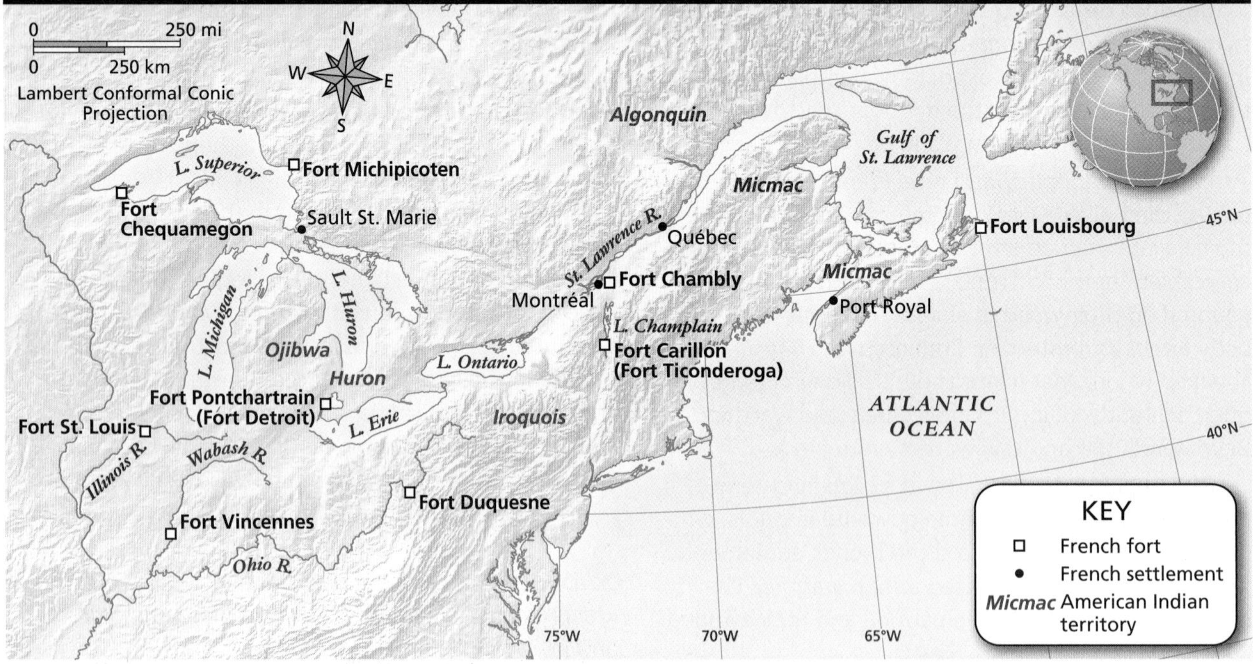

>> **Analyze Maps** How did the geography of northeastern North America influence the locations of French settlements?

BOUNCE to Activate Chart

especially dysentery and malaria. By 1731, Louisiana had lost two-thirds of its settlers. The colony had just 2,000 whites and 4,000 enslaved Africans.

The French primarily valued Louisiana as a military base to keep the English from taking control of the immense Mississippi watershed. As in the Great Lakes country, the French sought Indian allies to help them confine the English colonies that were growing to the east along the Atlantic coast.

IDENTIFY CENTRAL IDEAS Why was the control of New Orleans important to the French?

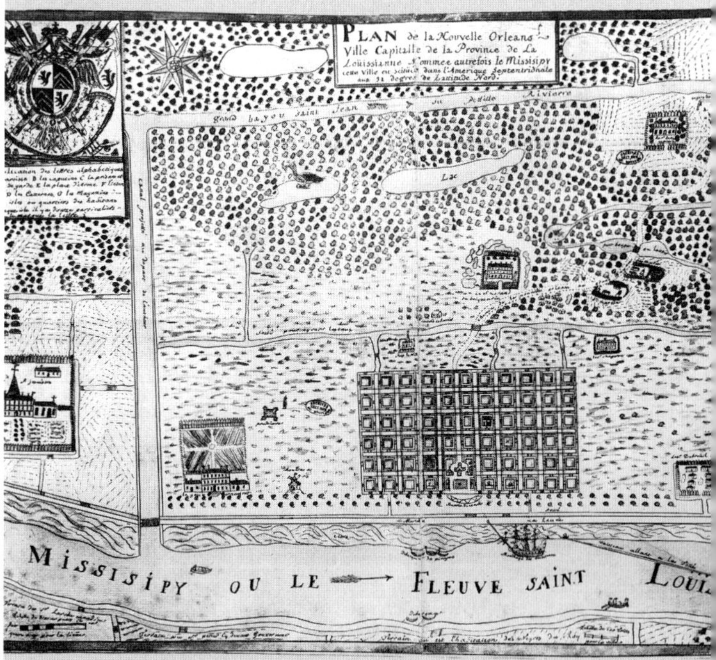

>> Despite a hot, humid climate and the danger of coastal storms, the French built a settlement at New Orleans.

ASSESSMENT

1. **Draw Conclusions** What effect did the Protestant Reformation have on cultural unity in Europe and on the European colonies in the New World?
2. **Paraphrase** Why was the *castas* developed in New Spain in the sixteenth century?
3. **Express Ideas Clearly** How did the Pueblo Indians attempt to rid the Southwest of the Spanish after Francisco Vásquez de Coronado's expedition?
4. **Infer** How and why did the Spanish and French differ in their treatment of the native inhabitants of the lands they colonized?
5. **Apply Concepts** Why did the French have problems attracting colonists to Louisiana, and why did they consider it a valuable colony in spite of this?
6. **Connections to Today** Roman Catholicism and the Spanish language spread across Latin America at this time without the help of modern technology. How can cultural and ideas spread farther and more quickly today?

Connections to Today

Like the Oglala Lakota, many American Indian nations maintain their own police departments.

Take Action to Inform People About Native American Governments

Today, more than 5 million Native Americans and Alaska Natives live across the country. About 20% live on tribal land, including reservations and trust areas.

1. **Choose** one of the following topics:
   - Native American governments: Identify a Native American government in your state or region and research its structure and powers.
   - Continuing conflicts: Research a recent controversy related to the rights of Native American groups, such as conflict over land use or government jurisdiction.
   - Native American languages: Research the most widely-spoken Native American languages, and the efforts underway to promote their use today.
2. **Ask Questions** Generate a list of questions you have about the topic.
3. **Learn** about the topic and major issues related to it. Make sure your research includes information directly from tribal governments and the native people they govern. Take notes as you conduct your research and continue to generate questions as you learn more.
4. **Inform the Public** Create a poster informing the general public about the topic you researched. Provide your audience with background on Native American life in the United States today. Summarize your key findings and include engaging imagery to grab viewers' attention.

GO ONLINE to www.SavvasRealize.com and access your digital course

Use the texts, quizzes, interactivities, Quest Inquiries, Flipped Videos, and other resources from this Topic to prepare for the Topic Test.

- Quest Inquiries
- Quizzes
- Interactivities
- Texts
- Flipped Videos

While online you can also check the progress you've made learning the topic and course content by viewing your grades, test scores, and assignment status.

SAVVAS realize™

Topic 1 Quick Study Guide

LESSON SUMMARIES

Use these Lesson Summaries, and the longer versions available online, to review the key ideas for each lesson in this Topic.

Lesson 1: The Peoples of the Americas

The first ancestors of today's American Indians migrated at least 15,000 years ago from Asia to North America, either by a land bridge or by sea. Over time, they developed cultures influenced by the climates and natural resources of different geographic regions. They developed agriculture and advanced societies. For American Indians, political power was dispersed, spirituality was tied to nature, and land was a common resource.

Lesson 2: The West Africans

The great West African kingdoms had large towns, advanced economies, and complex political structures. A thriving trade network linked the region with North Africa. Some West Africans practiced Islam; others held traditional beliefs. Although slavery was common in West Africa, European merchants expanded the practice to the Americas.

Lesson 3: Europeans Make Contact

Beginning in the 1400s, Europe experienced increased trade, economic growth, and a cultural awakening. As Europeans explored the wider world, they made contact with the peoples of the Americas. The Spanish built an American empire by conquering the Aztecs, Incas, and other native peoples. They brought new crops and ideas to the Americas, as well as diseases that killed millions of Indians.

Lesson 4: Spain and France in the Americas

Rivalries in Europe led to competition between European countries in the Americas. The Spanish imposed harsh rule on their American colonies, which extended into what are now the southern and southwestern United States. Meanwhile, the French founded colonies in what are now Canada, the Great Lakes, and Louisiana. The French were more interested in trade with American Indians than in conquest.

QUEST! FINDINGS

Write your Essay Refer to your responses to the Quest Connections to help you write your essay and present it to the class. Use the rubric and other Quest resources online to guide your work.

GO ONLINE to access lesson summaries

VISUAL REVIEW

Use these graphics to review some of the key terms, people, and ideas from this Topic.

Native American Culture Regions

WAYS OF LIFE IN CULTURE REGIONS	
Arctic/Subarctic	Hunting, fishing
Northwest Coast	Fishing, gathering, wooden houses
California/Great Basin/Plateau	Gathering, fishing
Southwest	Desert farming, adobe houses in villages
Great Plains	Hunting, farming villages along rivers
Eastern Woodland	Hunting, farming, wooden houses
Southeast	Farming, some hunting and fishing

Changes in Europe

West Africa

KINGDOMS AND SOCIETIES

Major Kingdoms	Society and Culture
• Ghana: about 700–1200 • Mali: about 1200–1468 • Songhai: 1468–1591	• Traditional beliefs, Islam • Kinship groups own land • Slavery was widespread • Slavery not based on race

French and Spanish Colonies in the Americas

EUROPEAN NATION	MAJOR ECONOMIC ACTIVITIES	GOVERNMENT
Spain	• gold and silver mining • trading • farming	• Crown-appointed viceroys or governors • no elected officials
France	• fur trading • some farming	• Crown-appointed governors • no elected officials

Topic 1 Assessment

KEY TERMS, PEOPLE, AND IDEAS

1. Why do many scholars believe that the first Americans **migrated** to North America during the last **ice age**?
2. Where in the Americas did agriculture originate, and to which regions of North America did it spread?
3. How was **Mali** connected to North Africa, and how was **Mansa Musa's** role in Mali a key to the spread of Islam from North Africa through West Africa?
4. What connection was there between the **Renaissance** and the work of **Prince Henry the Navigator**?
5. What did **Christopher Columbus** and **Amerigo Vespucci** have in common?
6. How are the stories of **Moctezuma** and **Hernán Cortés** connected?
7. What is the name for the exchange of plants, animals, and microorganisms after the European arrival in the Americas, and what effects did it have?
8. In Spanish colonization, what different roles were played by **viceroys** and **missionaries**?
9. What was the connection between **coureurs de bois** and **metis**?

CRITICAL THINKING

10. **Analyze Interactions** How did the environment help shape American Indian ways of life?
11. **Compare and Contrast** How did slavery as practiced in West Africa differ from that later practiced in the Americas?
12. **Draw Inferences** What effect do you think the printing press had on European exploration?
13. **Explain an Argument** How did the conquistadors justify their conquest of the Aztec and Inca empires?
14. **Summarize** How did colonists in Spanish America categorize members of society? Explain your answer.
15. **Identify Cause and Effect** How did the economy of the French colonies depend on a good relationship with American Indians?
16. **Analyze Visuals**

Look at this bronze sculpture made in the 1500s or 1600s to commemorate a queen mother of Benin, in West Africa. (a) What does this image suggest about the cultures of West Africa at the time when the trans-Atlantic trade in enslaved people was beginning? (b) How might this movement of millions of people have influenced the cultures of the Americas?

17. **Writing Activity: Write a Research Paper** The text below is taken from a memorandum from the governor of New France to a high official in France. It discusses the government program to recruit and pay French women—known as "the king's daughters"—to settle in New France. Use evidence from your text and the passage to answer the questions. (a) What seems to be the main purpose of this program? (b) Why do you think Talon requests young women who are "healthy and strong for farm work?" Conduct research to answer these questions: Why did France create this program? What was its long-term impact on New France? Write a research paper with your findings, citing reliable sources.

Memorandum from Jean Talon on Canada

All the girls who came this year are married, except for 15 whom I've placed with families I know, until the soldiers who want to marry them have set up households and a way to feed them. . . .

It would be good to strongly recommend that those who are sent to this country not be "disgraced by nature" [a reference to their moral quality], that they have nothing unappealing about their appearance, that they are healthy and strong for farm work or at least that they have some skill for manual labor. I've written along these lines to the directors.

Three or four girls of birth and distinguished for their quality [meaning born to aristocratic families] would serve to marry some officers . . .

—*Jean Talon, November 10, 1670, written to Jean-Baptiste Colbert*

18. **Connections to Today** The interaction between governments and native people is sometimes talked about as a one-way street: the government does something *to* a native group and that group simply deals with the consequences. But of course native people can act in their own interests and make their own decisions. Find an example in this topic of a Native American group acting decisively in the face of colonialism. What did they do? How did their actions work out? How can Native Americans act to defend their rights today?

DOCUMENT-BASED QUESTIONS

The Maya people of present-day Mexico and Guatemala had a rich civilization before the arrival of the Spanish in the early 1500s, as the images here show. The *Popol Vuh* includes myths of the Quiché (kee CHAY) Maya from the time when their civilization was at its peak, while the *Chilam Balam of Chumayel* offers a Mayan view of the Spanish conquest. Read or view these documents, then answer the questions that follow.

DOCUMENT A

Thus the grandeur and power of the sons of the Quiché grew, when they built the town of the ravines out of stone and mortar. Then the small tribes and the great tribes came before the king. The Quiché increased when their glory and majesty waxed, when they raised the house of their gods and the house of their lords. . . . The lords were really loved and great was their glory; and the sons and the vassals held the birthdays of the lords in great respect. . . .

—*From* Popol Vuh, *translated by Delia Goetz and Sylvanus Griswold Morley*

DOCUMENT B

This photo shows the elaborate architecture of Uxmal, a Mayan city.

DOCUMENT C

This Mayan codex, or book, deals with astronomy and religious ritual. It shows the complexity of the Mayan writing system.

DOCUMENT D

11 Ahau is the . . . [period] when the foreigners arrived. They came from the east when they arrived. . . . Then . . . came the beginning of our misery. It was the beginning of tribute, the beginning of church dues, the beginning of strife with purse-snatching, the beginning of strife with blow-guns, . . . the beginning of robbery with violence, . . . the beginning of debts enforced by false testimony . . . This was the origin of service to the Spaniards and priests, of service to the local chiefs . . . while the poor people were harassed.

—*From* The Book of Chilam Balam of Chumayel, *translated by Ralph L. Roys*

19. Which is the best description of the perspective of Document A on Maya civilization?

A. Regretful
B. Respectful
C. Proud
D. Defiant

20. Which of the following statements about Maya civilization does Document B best support?

A. Its thriving economy supported bustling cities.
B. It was sophisticated in technology and the arts.
C. It had a wide gap between rich and poor.
D. It suffered from environmental crises.

21. As one of the few surviving Maya codices, or books, Document C suggests that

A. a rich historical source on the Maya has been lost.
B. Mayan writing is too complex to understand.
C. the Maya relied more on pictures than on words.
D. Mayan and European cultures were very different.

22. Writing Tasks What thoughts might a Maya living at the time of the Spanish conquest have had about that conquest? Use specific evidence from all of the documents above, along with information from this Topic, to support your answer.

GO ONLINE to access more practice

Topic 2

England's American Colonies (1607–1754)

ESSENTIAL QUESTION Why Do People Move?

GO ONLINE to access the eText, videos, Interactive Primary Sources, Biographies, and other online resources.

An eighteenth-century view of Charleston, South Carolina

Connections to Today

Repressive governments around the world today carefully censor information. They operate state-owned media, criticizing or harassing independent media outlets in order to weaken their critics and erode the public's trust in objective reporting.

In this topic you'll read about how Americans established laws to protect a free press so that we, the people, would have the right to criticize our representative leaders without fear, thereby preventing government from hiding truth from us. What forces threaten press freedom today?

NBC LEARN

Learn about King Philip's War.

BOUNCE to Activate My Story Video

Topic 2 Overview

In this Topic, you'll learn about the establishment of England's North American colonies, immigration to these new colonies, and the development of their uniquely American identity. Look at the lesson outline and explore the timeline. As you study this Topic, you'll complete the Quest Inquiry.

LESSON OUTLINE

Key Events in England's American Colonies (1600–1750)

1607
Jamestown colony established

1619
First enslaved Africans brought to Virginia

1630
John Winthrop founds the Massachusetts Bay Colony

1682
William Penn establishes Philadelphia in the colony of Pennsylvania

1705
Virginia General Assembly passes law supporting permanent enslavement of Africans

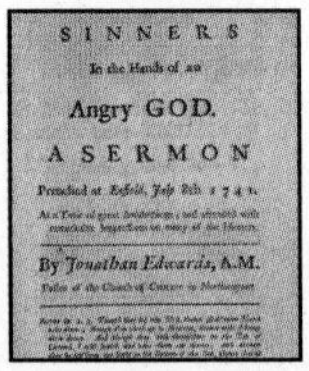

1741
Jonathan Edwards preaches sermon "Sinners in the Hands of an Angry God"

1600 1625 1650 1675 1700 1725 1750

QUEST! INQUIRY

Create a Museum of Colonial History

What was life really like for people who settled in England's American colonies? In this Quest, you will create a media presentation showing the social, political, or economic significance of several artifacts.

STEP 1
With your group, select six artifacts that represent some aspect of colonial life in your region. Consider the social, political, and economic significance of each in order to capture its "story."

STEP 2
Research the colonies in your assigned region. Gather images of artifacts from this region. Find information about the social, political, or economic significance of each artifact.

STEP 3
Use the information you have collected to write captions explaining two significant social, political, or economic aspects of life related to each artifact. Create your portfolio.

STEP 4
Present your trifold or digital portfolio to the class or another audience. Afterward, reflect on the experience and think about how you could improve your next project.

GO ONLINE to access complete Quest materials

2.1

Jamestown was built on a swampy island, separated from the mainland by a small winding river. Most of the area was wetland that was unsuitable for farming. In the foreground, the James River flows past the triangular fort and settlement.

BOUNCE to Activate Flipped Video

Objectives

Explain why England wanted colonies and how they were planned.

Describe how Jamestown was settled, why the colony struggled, and how it survived.

Explain the relationship between American Indians and settlers in the Southern Colonies.

Discuss how Maryland, the Carolinas, and Georgia were settled.

Key Terms

charter
joint-stock company
Powhatan
John Smith
House of Burgesses
royal colonies
proprietary colonies
Bacon's Rebellion
Lord Baltimore
James Oglethorpe

The Southern Colonies Take Root

Unclaimed by the Spanish and French, the Atlantic coast of North America attracted English attempts at colonization during the 1580s. England's first attempts to establish a colony in North America failed, but in 1607 they succeeded in founding Jamestown, which became part of the colony of Virginia. By 1732, four more Southern Colonies had been established: Maryland, North Carolina, South Carolina, and Georgia.

England Establishes Colonies in North America

The first promoters of English colonies were wealthy gentlemen from southwestern England. They included Sir Walter Raleigh, a special favorite of Queen Elizabeth I. English patriots and devout Protestants, these men wanted to advance their fortunes and increase the power of England.

They promised that an American colony would solve some of England's problems: a growing population and increased poverty due to a stagnant economy. The promoters proposed shipping poor people across the Atlantic to work in a new colony. By mining for gold and silver and by raising plantation crops, these workers would generate new wealth for England.

Difficulties at Roanoke After obtaining a **charter**, or certificate of permission, from the Crown, the group formed a **joint-stock company**. This was a business venture founded and run by a group of investors who were to share in the company's profits and losses. During the 1580s, Raleigh twice tried to colonize Roanoke, a small island on the North Carolina coast (then considered a part of Virginia). But English ships struggled to land supplies, and the

GO ONLINE to access your digital course

sandy, infertile soil produced scanty crops. Raleigh's first colonists returned home in despair. The second group of settlers mysteriously vanished.

The Virginia Company Sends More Colonists

The English tried again under the new leadership of the Virginia Company, a corporation of great merchants based in London. In 1607, the colonists proceeded to Chesapeake Bay, a superior location north of Roanoke. The Chesapeake offered fertile land, along with many good harbors and navigable waterways, like the James River, where the colonists founded the settlement of Jamestown. Although the site of their new settlement protected them from possible attack from passing Spanish ships, it left them vulnerable to attacks by local American Indians.

Although divided into 30 American Indian groups, the region's 24,000 Indians shared an Algonquian language. They were also united by the rule of an unusually powerful chief named **Powhatan**. In his sixties, Powhatan impressed the English colonists with his dignity, keen mind, and powerful build.

Rather than confront the colonists at risk of heavy causalities, Powhatan hoped to contain them and to use them against his own enemies, the American Indians of the interior. He especially wanted to trade with the colonists for their metal weapons.

The colonists, however, wanted Indian lands. They refused to recognize that the American Indians occupied, used, and had ancestral ties to these lands. Despite the many native villages and their large fields of maize, Captain **John Smith** described Virginia as "overgrowne with trees and weedes, being a plaine wilderness as God first made it." The English insisted on improving that "wilderness" into profitable farmland.

CHECK UNDERSTANDING How did Powhatan deal with the English colonists?

Early Challenges in Jamestown

The colonists founded a new settlement and named it Jamestown to honor King James I. The surrounding swamps defended the town from attack, but those swamps also bred mosquitoes that carried deadly diseases, especially malaria. The colonists also suffered from hunger, for they were often too weakened by disease to tend their crops. Between 1607 and 1622, the Virginia Company transported some 10,000 people to the colony, but only 20 percent of them were still alive in 1622.

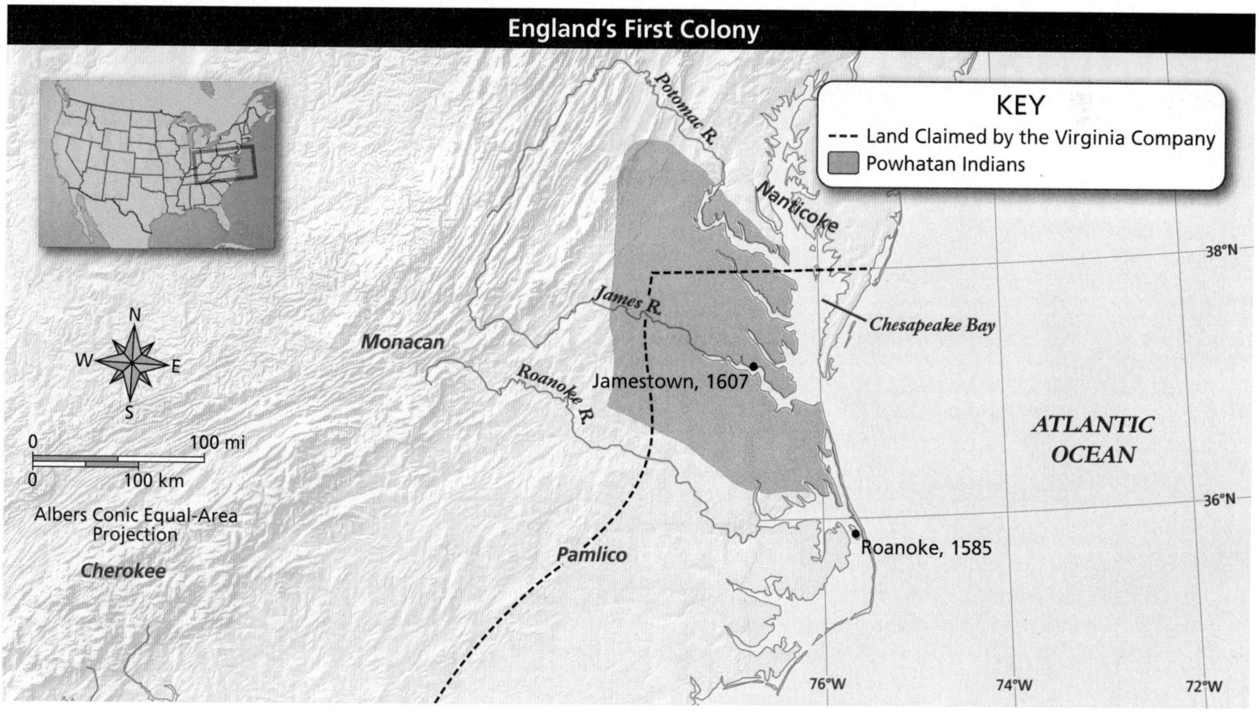

>> **Analyze Maps** Why do you think early settlements in the Americas were founded on or near bodies of water?

At War With American Indians In 1609, war broke out between the Indians and the starving colonists. In 1613, the English captured Powhatan's favorite daughter, Pocahontas. As an English captive, Pocahontas converted to Christianity and married a colonist named John Rolfe. Weary with war, Powhatan reluctantly made peace. When Powhatan died in 1618, power passed to his brother Opechancanough (oh PEHCH uhn kah noh), who hated the invaders from England.

The Tobacco Crop Saves Jamestown At first the colony was not profitable. By 1616, the Virginia Company had spent more than 50,000 English pounds—an immense sum for that time. Yet all it had to show for it was an unprofitable settlement of 350 diseased, hungry, and unhappy colonists. The company saved the colony by allowing the colonists to own and work land as their private property. As farmer-owners, rather than company employees, the colonists worked harder to grow the corn, squash, and beans that ensured their survival. But to make a profit, they still needed a commercial crop to market in England.

Led by John Rolfe, the colonists learned how to cultivate tobacco in 1616. West Indian tobacco had become extraordinarily popular for smoking in Europe. King James fought a losing battle when he denounced smoking as "a custom loathsome to the eye, hateful to the nose, harmful to the brain, [and] dangerous to the lungs." Eventually, though, he learned to love the revenue that the Crown reaped by taxing tobacco imports.

Because tobacco plants needed a long, hot, and humid growing season, the crop thrived in Virginia but not in England. That difference gave the colonial farmers an advantage. Their tobacco production surged from 200,000 pounds in 1624 to more than 1.5 million pounds in 1640. The Chesapeake region became the principal supplier of tobacco in Europe. The profits attracted more immigrants to Virginia.

Free Land Encourages Settlement Beginning in 1619, the Virginia Company offered free land. Under the headright system, anyone who paid for passage to Virginia or who paid for another person's passage received 50 acres of land. This enabled the wealthiest colonists to acquire large plantations. To work those plantations, landowners imported workers from England. The population of Virginia began to grow.

The House of Burgesses The Virginia Company also granted political reforms. In 1619, it allowed the planters to create the **House of Burgesses**, the first representative body in colonial America.

Male landowners could elect two leaders, known as Burgesses, to represent their settlement in the

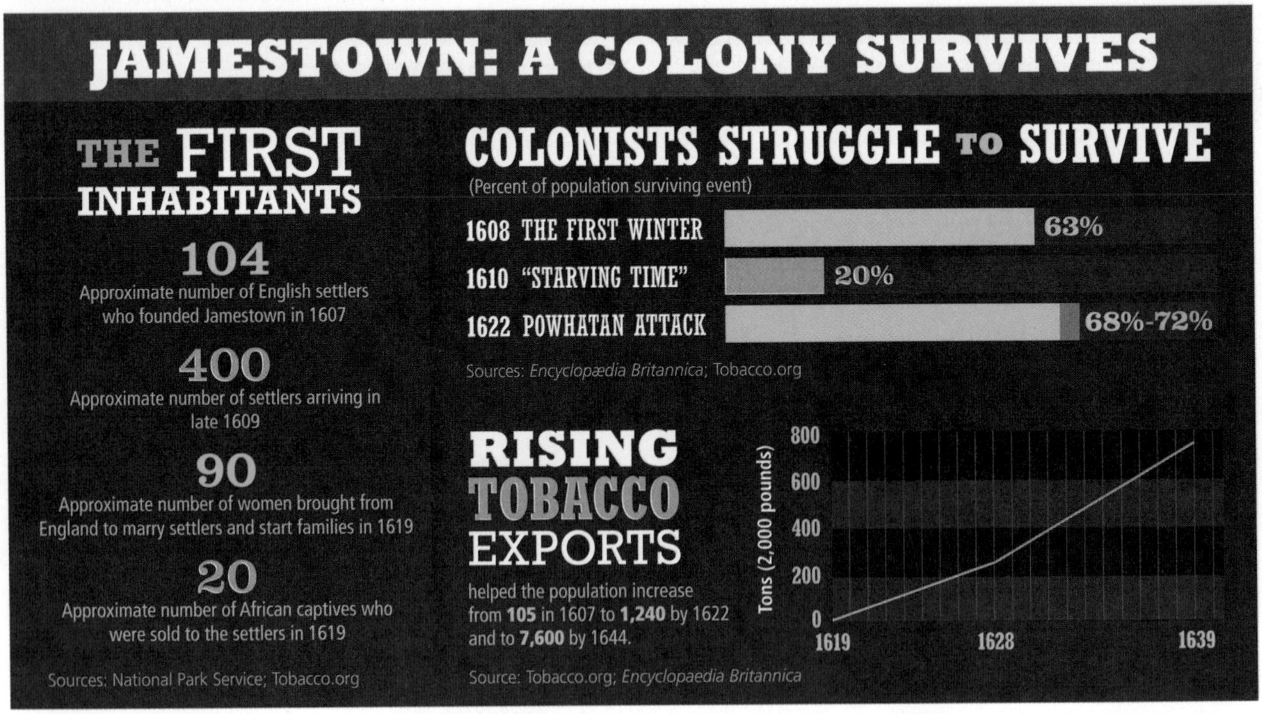

>> **Analyze Information** Which factors most challenged the settlers at Jamestown? Which factors most helped them succeed?

BOUNCE to Activate Gallery

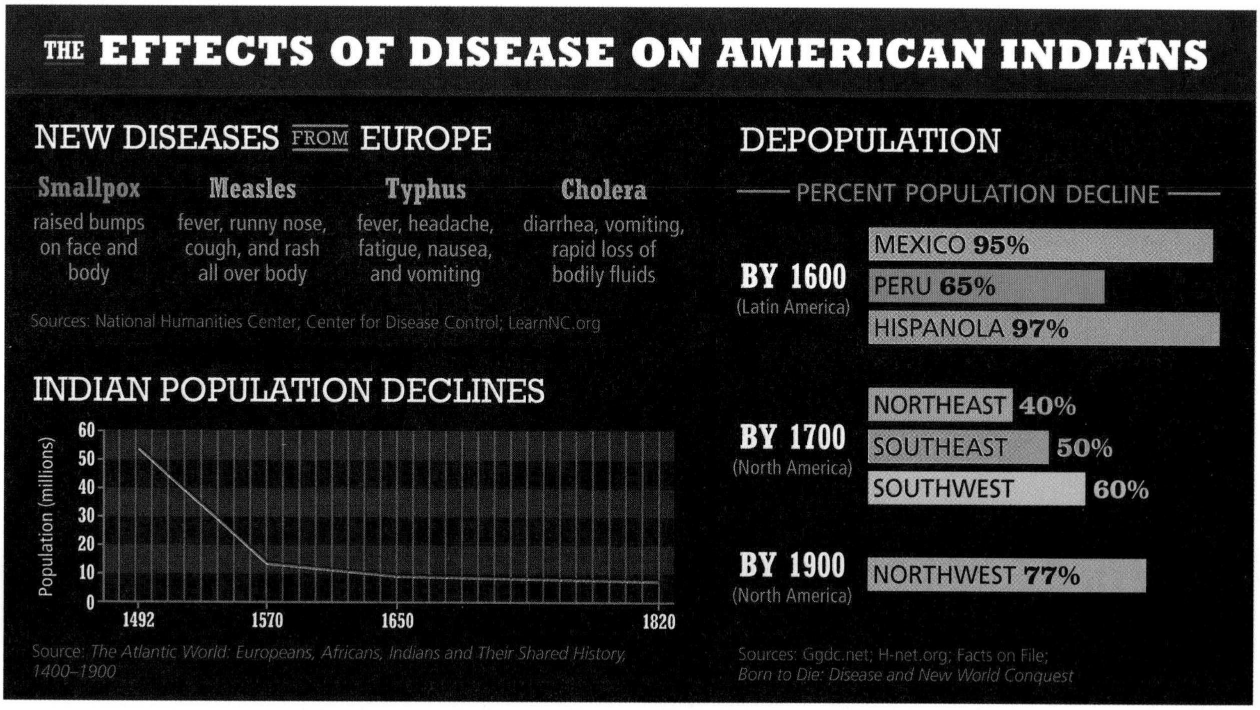

>> **Analyze Information** What explains the changes in the American Indian population over time?

colonial government. The House of Burgesses had the power to make laws and raise taxes. It began a strong tradition of representative government in the English colonies.

In 1624, the Crown took over Virginia, making it the first royal colony in the English empire. During the seventeenth century, the English developed two types of colonial governments: royal and proprietary. The **royal colonies** belonged to the Crown, while the **proprietary colonies** belonged to powerful individuals or companies.

☑ **IDENTIFY CENTRAL IDEAS** What was significant about the political structure of the House of Burgesses?

Expansion in Virginia Creates Conflict

As the colonists expanded their tobacco plantations, they took more land from the American Indians, who became enraged. In 1622, Opechancanough led a surprise attack that burned plantations and killed nearly a third of the colonists.

The Algonquin Indians Fight Back But counterattacks by the colonial survivors destroyed the Indian villages and their crops, reducing the Indians to starvation. Defeated, Opechancanough made peace in 1632. The victors took more land and spread their settlements northward to the Potomac River.

With English settlements expanding, yet another war broke out between the colonists and American Indians. In 1644, intense fighting killed hundreds of colonists and thousands of Indians, including Opechancanough. Disease and war reduced the Virginia Algonquins from 24,000 in 1607 to only 2,000 by 1670. The survivors became confined to small areas surrounded by colonial settlements. The number of settlers continued to surge, reaching 41,000 in 1670. The English had come to stay, to the alarm of Indians in the interior.

Bacon's Rebellion As the European and African populations of Virginia increased, settlers moved onto less fertile lands in the interior. They faced greater danger from American Indians angered by their intrusion.

The royal governor of Virginia, William Berkeley, worsened the growing crisis. Berkeley levied heavy taxes on the planters and used the proceeds to reward a few favorites from the wealthiest class, which dominated the House of Burgesses. He also expressed contempt for a free press and public education for common people.

In 1675, war erupted between the American Indians and the settlers in the Potomac Valley. The settlers wanted to exterminate all of the colony's Indians. When Berkeley balked, the settlers rebelled under the leadership of the ambitious and reckless Nathaniel Bacon.

To popular acclaim, Bacon's men slaughtered American Indians, peaceful as well as hostile. When Berkeley protested, Bacon marched his armed followers to Jamestown in a revolt called **Bacon's Rebellion**. Black people joined the rebels alongside poor whites, frightening wealthy planters. In September 1676, they drove out the governor and burned the town. A month later, however, Bacon died suddenly of disease, and his rebellion collapsed. Berkeley regained power, but the rebellion had undermined his credibility. In 1677, the king appointed a new governor, and Berkeley returned to England.

Bacon's Rebellion showed that poorer farmers would not tolerate a government that catered only to the wealthiest colonists. The colony's leaders reduced the taxes paid by the farmers and improved their access to frontier land. But that frontier policy provoked further wars with the American Indians of the interior.

RECALL Describe the causes of Bacon's Rebellion.

England Expands Its Southern Colonies

Virginia was the first of the Southern Colonies to be settled. During the seventeenth and eighteenth centuries, England established the Southern Colonies of Maryland, North Carolina, South Carolina, and Georgia.

Maryland Becomes a Colonial Refuge In 1632, at the northern head of Chesapeake Bay, the English king established a second Southern Colony, named Maryland. The name honored Mary, the queen of the new monarch, Charles I (son of James). Charles gave Maryland to a favorite aristocrat, **Lord Baltimore**, who owned and governed it as a proprietary colony. Lord Baltimore founded Maryland as a colonial refuge for his fellow Catholics, who were discriminated against in England by the Protestant majority. Contrary to Lord Baltimore's hopes, however, more Protestants than Catholics immigrated to Maryland. Relations between the two groups deteriorated into armed conflict later in the century.

England Settles in the Carolinas In 1670, the English established a new colony on the coast, north of Florida but south of Virginia. Called Carolina to honor King Charles II, the new colony included present-day North Carolina and South Carolina. The first settlement and capital was Charles Town, also named to honor the king. Carolina officially belonged to a group of English aristocrats—the Lords Proprietor—who remained in England, entrusting the colony's leadership to ambitious men from the West Indies.

In 1691, the Lords Proprietor set aside the northern half of their territory as the distinct

The Southern Colonies

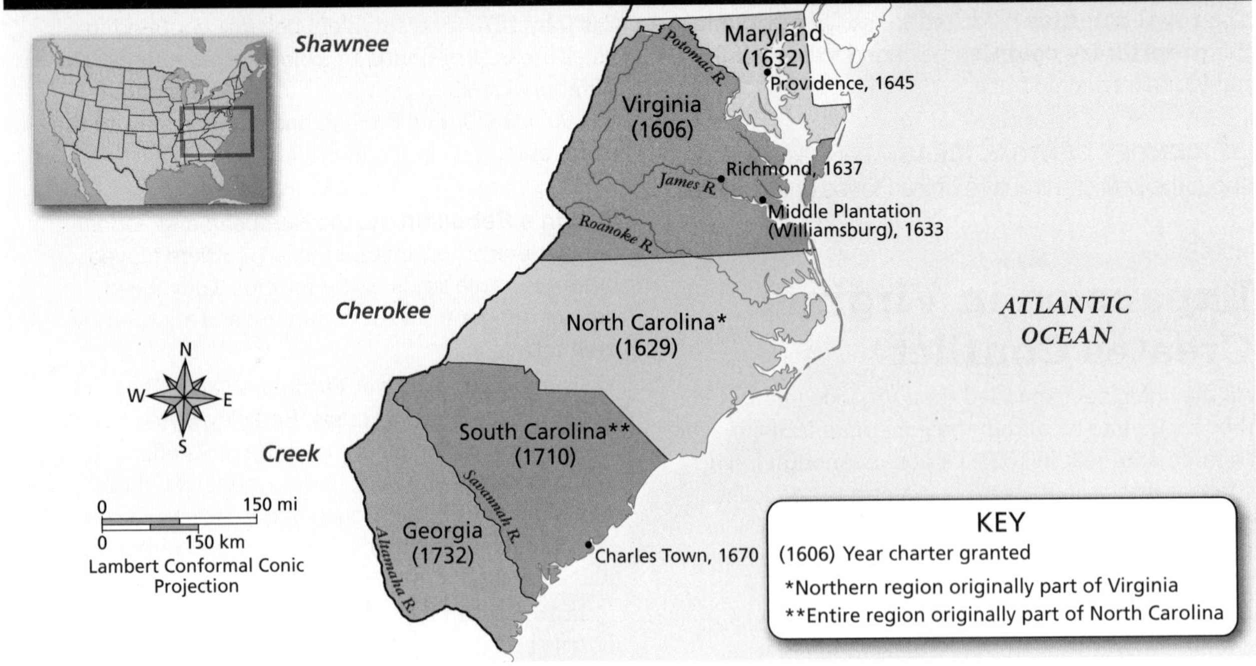

>> **Analyze Maps** Which features formed Georgia's borders?

colony of North Carolina. In 1729, the North and South Carolinians rejected the control by the Lords Proprietor. The Carolinians demanded and received a Crown takeover. Thereafter, the king appointed their governors, who had to cooperate with elected assemblies in each colony.

James Oglethorpe Establishes Georgia In 1732, Georgia began as a proprietary colony intended to protect South Carolina against Spanish Florida. Led by **James Oglethorpe**, the Georgia trustees designed their colony as a haven for English debtors, who had been jailed because they could not pay their debts. Yet, most of Georgia's first colonists were poor English traders and artisans, or religious refugees from Switzerland and Germany.

Oglethorpe set strict rules for colonists. They could not drink alcohol and could not own enslaved Africans. Georgia's colonists had to work their own land and could therefore not own large plantations. These restrictions angered the colonists, who protested until the trustees surrendered to the Crown. Georgia became a royal colony in 1752.

CHECK UNDERSTANDING How did James Oglethorpe make Georgia different from other Southern Colonies?

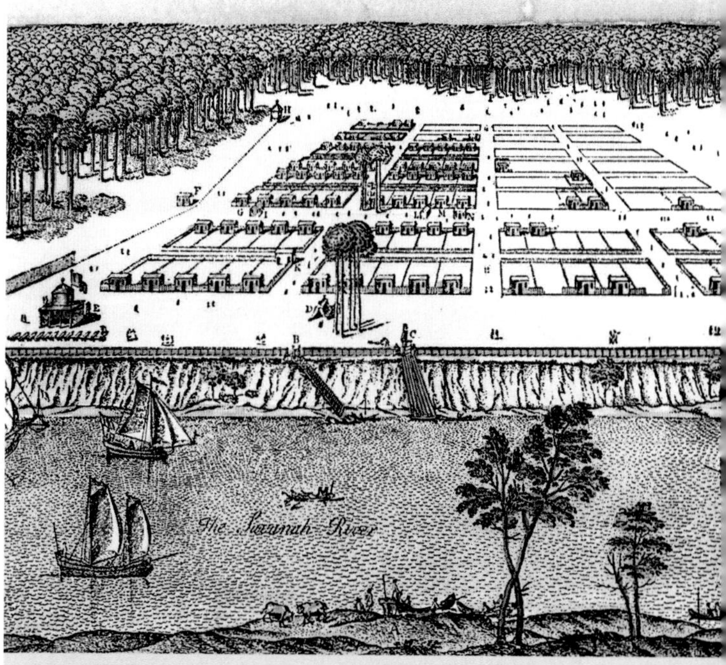

>> Savannah, Georgia, was first settled in 1733. It later served as Georgia's colonial capital.

BOUNCE to Activate Gallery

ASSESSMENT

1. **Cite Evidence** Why did many wealthy Englishmen favor the development of colonies in America?
2. **Distinguish** Discuss the Chesapeake Bay colonists' evolving relationship with Powhatan.
3. **Summarize** What were the results of the conflict between English settlers and the Algonquin Indians?
4. **Sequence Events** How was the colony originally known as Carolina governed, and how did it become divided into what we now know as North Carolina and South Carolina?
5. **Quest Connections** What caption would you write for a tobacco leaf in your Museum of Colonial History?

2.2

This portrait shows John Winthrop, Puritan leader and Governor of the Massachusetts Bay Colony.

BOUNCE to Activate Flipped Video

Objectives

Explain why some Puritans left England.

Describe the Puritan colony in Massachusetts and explain why Rhode Island, Connecticut, and New Hampshire were founded.

Analyze the relationship between New Englanders and American Indians.

Key Terms

Puritans
Separatists
Pilgrims
Mayflower Compact
John Winthrop
Roger Williams
Anne Hutchinson
Pequot War
King Philip's War
Metacom

GO ONLINE to access your digital course

New Lives in New England

Far to the north of the Southern Colonies, the English founded another set of colonies during the 1600s. New England was a land of dense forests, rolling hills, and a short growing season. New England demanded hard labor to farm, and offered little prospect of getting rich. Before long, however, trade and commerce would bring prosperity to New England.

Disagreement With the Church of England

Most of the New England colonists were religious dissenters who disagreed with the established church. Known as **Puritans**, they wanted to purify the Church of England, or Anglican Church, the only official and legal church in that kingdom. The Puritans believed that the Anglican Church, although Protestant, retained too many ceremonies from the Catholic Church. Puritans also wanted congregations to have more control over their own affairs. They did not like the organization of the Anglican church, in which a Catholic-style hierarchy of bishops controlled the local congregations. While some Puritans sought to reform the Anglican Church, others known as **Separatists** began their own churches.

Puritan Beliefs and Values The Puritans followed the teachings of the theologian John Calvin. They believed that they could prepare for God's saving grace by leading moral lives, praying devoutly, reading the Bible, and heeding their ministers' sermons. But not even the most devout could claim salvation as a right and a certainty, for they believed God alone determined who was saved. Salvation depended on the will of God rather than good behavior or adherence to church rules.

Puritans came from all ranks of English society, including aristocrats. Most belonged to "the middling sort"—a term used to describe small-property holders, farmers, shopkeepers, and skilled artisans. Their modest properties put them economically ahead of much of the English population.

Puritanism reinforced the values of thrift, diligence, and morality. Puritans insisted that men honored God by working hard in their occupations. One Puritan explained, "God sent you unto this world as unto a Workhouse, not a Playhouse."

Puritan Challenges Lead to Persecution By challenging England's official church, the Puritans troubled the English monarchs who led the Anglican Church. During the 1620s, King Charles I began to persecute the Puritans. His bishops dismissed Puritan ministers from their parishes and censored or destroyed Puritan books. Some Puritans sought a colonial refuge in North America, where they would be able to escape the supervision of Anglican bishops. In their own colony, the Puritans could worship in their own churches and make their own laws, which they derived from the Bible. By living morally and prospering, they hoped to inspire their countrymen in England to adopt Puritan reforms.

☑ **IDENTIFY MAIN IDEAS** Why did Puritans challenge the Anglican Church?

Puritans Arrive in North America

In 1620, the first Puritan Separatist emigrants, who were later called **Pilgrims**, crossed the Atlantic in the ship the *Mayflower* to found the Plymouth Colony on the south shore of Massachusetts Bay. Before they disembarked, the group of about 100 made an agreement called the **Mayflower Compact**. The settlers agreed to form a government and obey its laws. This idea of self-government would later become one of the founding principles of the United States.

Massachusetts Bay Colony In 1630, **John Winthrop** led a much larger group of Puritans to America. Winthrop exhorted his fellow Puritans to make their new colony "A City upon a Hill," an inspirational example for the people of England. Winthrop explained:

> For we must consider that we shall be as a City upon a hill. The eyes of all people are upon us. [So] that if we shall deal falsely with our God in this work we have undertaken, and so cause him to withdraw his present

The New England Colonies Around 1763

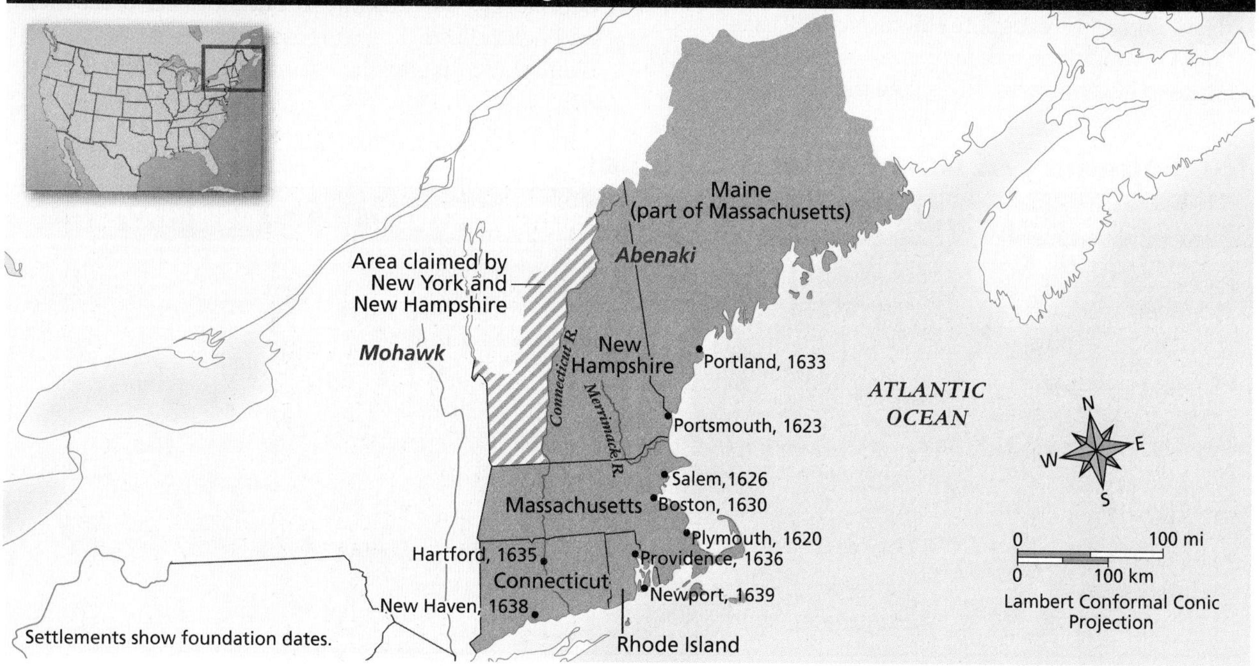

>> The color indicates land claims rather than areas of English settlement.
Analyze Maps How did New England's geography affect its economy?

BOUNCE to Activate 3D Model

> help from us, we shall be made a story and a byword throughout the world.
>
> —John Winthrop, 1630

Beginning with the town of Boston, these Puritans established the Massachusetts Bay Colony on the north shore of that broad bay. In Massachusetts, settlers established a republic, where the Puritan men elected their governor, deputy governor, and assembly. This was the most radical government in the colonies because it was the only one that elected its governor.

From the towns of Plymouth and Boston, colonists spread rapidly along the coast and into the interior. To the northeast, New Hampshire and Maine emerged, where Puritans settled uneasily in fishing communities that were Anglican. To the southeast, Rhode Island became a haven for especially radical Puritans. More conservative Puritans founded Connecticut along the Connecticut River and New Haven beside Long Island Sound. By the end of the seventeenth century, the Massachusetts Bay Colony included Maine and Plymouth, while Connecticut absorbed New Haven.

Religious Differences Lead to New Colonies Most of the Puritans immigrated to New England to realize their own ideal society—and certainly not to champion religious toleration. A leading New Englander denounced "the lawlessnesse of liberty of conscience" as an invitation to heresy and anarchy. No Catholics, Baptists, or Quakers need come to New England—except to Rhode Island. Dissenters were given, in the words of one Puritan, "free Liberty to keep away from us." To make that point, the Massachusetts government executed four Quakers and burned their books. The Puritans feared that God would punish any people who tolerated individual choice in religion.

The Puritans also purged their own people for expressing radical religious opinions. During the 1630s, **Roger Williams** and **Anne Hutchinson** angered the authorities by arguing that Massachusetts had not done enough to break with Anglican ways. Williams argued that settlers had no right to take land from the American Indians. He said they needed to purchase the land from the Indians.

As a woman, Hutchinson seemed doubly dangerous to Puritan leaders who insisted that only men should exercise public influence. Though she ably defended herself in a trial, John Winthrop banished Hutchinson from Massachusetts.

Prosecuted by the authorities, Williams fled to Rhode Island, where he founded Providence in 1636. Rhode Island was a rare haven for religious toleration in the colonial world. Hutchinson and her family moved to the colony after she was exiled from Massachusetts. Rhode Island attracted Baptists, Quakers, and Jews. Lacking a majority for any one faith, the Rhode Islanders agreed to separate church and state. They believed that mingling church and state corrupted religion.

Salem Witch Trials In addition to punishing religious dissenters, the New England Colonies prosecuted suspected witches. Whenever cattle and children sickened and died, the New Englanders suspected evil magic. For the safety of the community, witches had to be identified, prosecuted, and neutralized. The supposed victims of magic blamed neighbors who seemed to bear them ill will.

The Founding of New England Colonies

MASSACHUSETTS	RHODE ISLAND	CONNECTICUT	NEW HAVEN
• Plymouth Colony founded in 1620 by Puritan Separatists • Massachusetts Bay Colony established by John Winthrop, leader of a group of one thousand Puritans • Practiced a form of self-government	• Roger Williams banned from Massachusetts Bay Colony for his radical beliefs; founded Rhode Island in 1636 • Became a haven for radical Puritans and other dissenters • Settled by Irish Protestants, French Huguenots, and Jews	• Led by Thomas Hooker, conservative Puritans from Massachusetts Bay Colony founded Hartford in 1636 • Absorbed New Haven Colony in 1665 • Maintained good relations with American Indians	• Founded in 1638 by conservative Puritans led by John Davenport and Theophilus Eaton • Became part of Connecticut in 1665 • Originally named Quinnipiac, renamed Newhaven in 1640

SOURCE: *Encyclopædia Britannica*

>> **Analyze Information** Which issue mostly led to the founding of new colonies in New England during this time?

BOUNCE to Activate Gallery

THE SALEM WITCH TRIALS

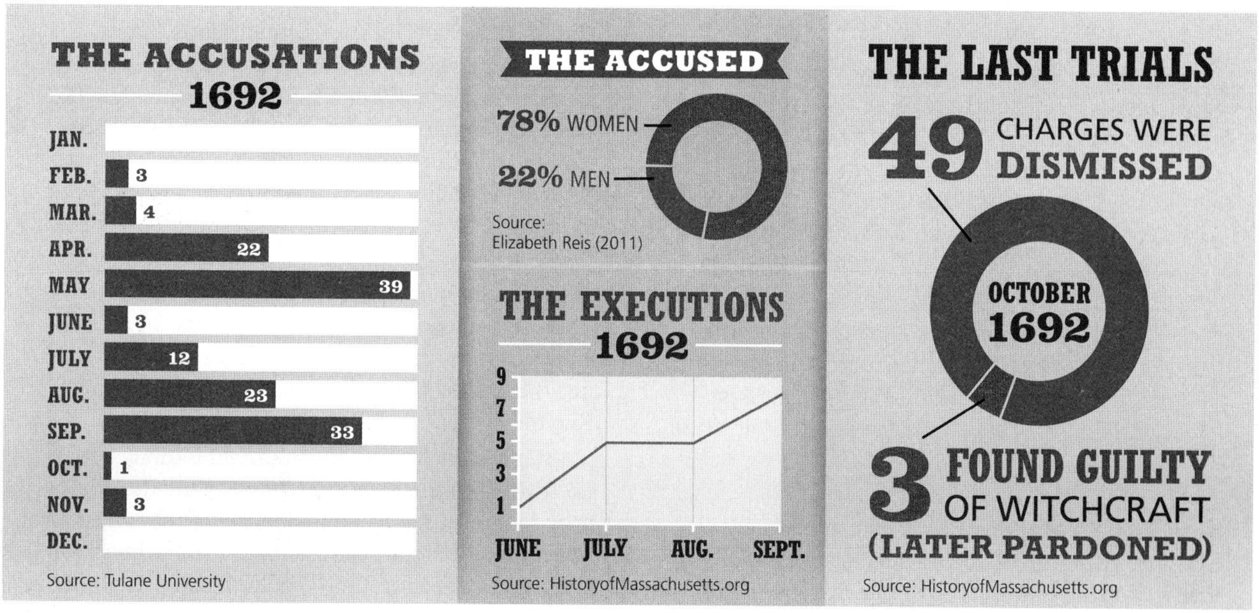

>> **Analyze Information** What dramatic changes took place in the Salem witch trials between June and November 1692?

The most spectacular accusations occurred in and around Salem, Massachusetts, in 1692. The authorities there tried, convicted, and executed 19 suspected witches. But when the accusations reached members of prominent families, including the governor's wife, the judges dropped any further trials. Reassessed as a fiasco, the Salem mania ended the prosecution of witches in New England.

IDENTIFY Identify the new colonies the Puritans established in New England.

English Relationships With American Indians

The Puritans saw American Indians as lazy savages who accepted life in the wild, instead of laboring to conquer nature. The colonists remade the land to resemble England by clearing and fencing fields for cultivation in the English fashion. They built English-style houses, barns, mills, and churches. They introduced domesticated cattle, sheep, horses, and pigs. Colonists also killed wild animals that preyed on livestock.

The Pequot War By the 1630s, the Puritans of New England were engaged in a brisk fur trade with the Pequots and several other American Indian nations. However, it was an uneasy relationship. Rivalry over control of the trade, coupled with Indian opposition to English territorial expansion, led to the outbreak of the **Pequot War**.

In 1636, Puritans accused the Pequots of murdering an English trader. But the Pequots denied the accusation. Allied with Narragansett and Mohegan Indians—enemies of the Pequots—the Puritans attacked several Pequot villages. In turn, the Pequots raided a Puritan village. Outraged, the Puritans burned a Pequot village filled with mostly women and children and killed most of its 600 to 700 inhabitants.

The carnage was so complete that even the Puritans' American Indian allies were shocked by the "manner of the Englishmen's fight . . . because it is too furious, and slays too many men." In 1638, by the Treaty of Hartford, the victorious English, Narragansetts, and Mohegans virtually eliminated the Pequot nation. The Pequots lost all their lands and surviving Pequots went to live among other American Indian peoples.

Attempts to Convert the Indians After the Pequot War, the Puritans worked to convert and transform the American Indians into versions of English Christians. They pressured the American Indians to move into special "praying towns," where they could be closely supervised by missionaries. By 1674, Massachusetts had 14 praying towns with 1,600 American Indian inhabitants. After restricting the American Indians to a few special towns, the Puritans claimed most of their lands for colonial settlement.

The missionaries forced the praying-town American Indians to abandon their traditional ways and to don English clothing. The missionaries insisted upon the English division of gender roles. They urged the American Indian men to forsake hunting and fishing in favor of farming. The American Indian women were supposed to withdraw from the cornfields to tend the home and to spin and weave cloth—just as English women did.

However, only a minority agreed to enter the praying towns. As the colonists continued to expand their settlements at the Indians' expense, most American Indians despaired of keeping their lands without a war.

King Philip's War In 1675, a massive Indian rebellion erupted. The colonists called it **King Philip's War**, after a chief of the Wampanoag Indians named **Metacom** who was known to the colonists as "King Philip." After Philip, or Metacom, led attacks against towns in the Plymouth colony, the war spread as a loose confederation of American Indians raided English settlements

With guns acquired from traders, the American Indians at first devastated the New England settlements, destroying 12 towns. But the tide of war turned in 1676, when the rebels began to starve because their crops were destroyed by colonial counterattacks. The American Indians also ran out of ammunition after losing their access to colonial traders. In August, Metacom died in battle, shot down by a praying-town American Indian who served with the colonists. The war killed at least 1,000 English colonists and about 3,000 American Indians.

The defeated American Indians lost most of their remaining lands in southern New England. They survived only as a small minority on limited lands within a region dominated by the newcomers. In 1700, the 92,000 colonists outnumbered New England's 9,000 American Indians.

Some of the defeated American Indians fled northward to the French colony of Canada, where they found refuge. Whenever the French waged war on the English, the refugee American Indians sought revenge by raiding the New England frontier. Those wars became frequent and bloody after 1689, as the English and the French escalated their struggle to dominate North America.

CHECK UNDERSTANDING How did King Philip's War affect the American Indians in New England?

King Philip's War, 1675–76

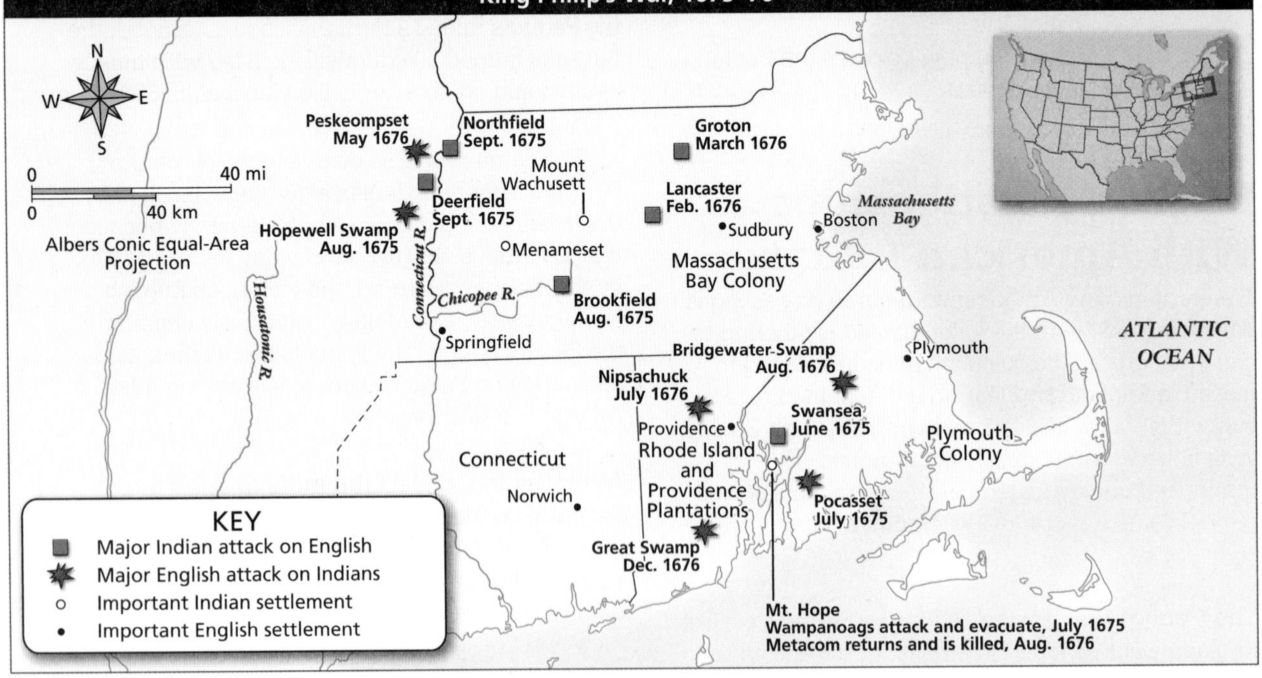

>> **Analyze Maps** Why did most confrontations take place far from Boston?

BOUNCE to Activate Chart

ASSESSMENT

1. **Generate Explanations** Explain how John Calvin influenced the social values of the New England Puritans.
2. **Identify Central Issues** Discuss the typical Puritan attitude toward dissenters and those of other religions.
3. **Identify Cause and Effect** Discuss the causes and effects of the Pequot War on the American Indian population in New England.
4. **Summarize** What was King Philip's War and what long-term effects did it have on southern New England?
5. **Connections to Today** Why would local authorities be unable to exile or persecute dissenters like Anne Hutchinson and Roger Williams today?

>> The Pilgrims meet Samaset.

Of Plymouth Plantation: William Bradford

Between 1630 and 1651, William Bradford, governor of the Plymouth Colony, kept a journal of the settlers' experience. This journal was published as *Of Plymouth Plantation*, an important source for understanding the colonists' motivations for settlement and the challenges they faced in crossing the ocean and colonizing an unfamiliar land.

Of Plymouth Plantation also describes the first contact between the English colonists and the local American Indians, some of whom knew much more about the English than the English knew about them! Sadly, the peace that Bradford describes between the two groups did not last, and in 1636 the English attacked local Indian peoples, setting off the tragic Pequot War.

Primary Source

All this while the Indians came skulking about them, and would sometimes show them selves [at a distance], but when any aproached near them, they would [run] away. And once they [stole] away their tools wher they had been at worke, & were gone to [dinner]. But about the 16. *of March* a certaine Indian came [boldly] amongst them, and spoke to them in broken English, which they could well understand, but marvelled at it. At length they understood by discourse with him, that he was not of these parts, but belonged to the [eastern] parts, wher some English-ships came to [fish], with whom he was aquainted, & could name [many] of them by their names, amongst whom he had [got] his language.

DETERMINE CENTRAL IDEAS How did the English-speaking American Indian man learn English?

He became [helpful] to them in aquainting them with many things concerning the state of the [country] in the east-parts wher he lived, which was afterwards profitable unto them; as also of the people hear, of their names, number, & strength; of their situation & distance from this place, and who was [chief] amongst them. His name was *Samaset*; he [told] them also of another Indian [whose] name was *Squanto*, a native of this place, who had been in England & could speake better English [than] him selfe. Being, after some time of entertainmente & gifts, [dismissed], a while after he came againe, & 5. more with him, & they brought [again] all the [tools] that were stolen away before, and made way for the coming of their great Sachem [chief], called *Massasoyt*; who, about *4. or 5. days after*, came with the [chief] of his [friends] & other attendance, with the aforesaid *Squanto*. With whom, after [friendly] entertainment, & some gifts given him, they made a peace with him (which hath now continued this 24. years) in these terms.

1. That neither he nor any of his, should injurie or doe hurte to any of their peopl.

2. That if any of his did any hurte to any of theirs, he should send the offender, that they might punish him.

3. That if any thing were taken away from any of theirs, he should cause it to be restored; and they should doe the like to his.

4. If any did unjustly warr against him, they would aide him; if any did warr against them, he should aide them.

5. He should send to his neighbours [associates], to [notify] them of this, that they might not wrong them, but might be likewise comprised in ye conditions of peace.

6. That when [their] men came to them, they should leave their bows & arrows behind them.

DRAW INFERENCES What problems are the peace terms meant to address?

After these things he returned to his place caled *Sowams*, some 40. mile from this place, but *Squanto* continued with them, and was their interpreter, and was a [special] instrument sent of God for their good beyond their expectation. He directed them how to set their [corn], [where] to take fish, and to procure other [commodities], and was also their pilott to bring them to unknowne places for their profitt, and never left them till he [died].

SUMMARIZE Why does Bradford describe Squanto as "sent of God for their good beyond their expectation"?

He was a *native of this place*, & scarce any left alive [besides] him selfe. He was caried away with [diverse] others by one *Hunt*, a [master] of a ship, who thought to sell them for slaves in Spaine; but he got away for England, and was entertained by a [merchant] in London, & [employed] to New-foundland & other parts, & lastly brought hither into these parts by one Mr. *Dermer*, a gentle-man [employed] by Sr. Ferdinando Gorges & others, for discovery, & other designes in these parts.

DETERMINE CENTRAL IDEAS Describe the route and reason for Squanto's journey from his homeland.

ASSESSMENT

1. **Draw Inferences** Why do you think Squanto and the other Indians brought back the tools they had taken from the English?
2. **Summarize** How would you describe relations between the local Indians and the English settlers of Plymouth in the first few decades?
3. **Determine Meaning** What does the passage suggest about what some Europeans are doing to the Indians?
4. **Draw Conclusions** What does the passage reveal about contact and interactions between Europeans and Native Americans in the years before English colonization?
5. **Draw Inferences** In what ways do you think the agreement described in item 4 of the peace treaty might have changed the relationship among Native American groups?

GO ONLINE to access primary sources

2.3

In this engraving, Swedish settlers arrive on the shores of the Delaware River.

BOUNCE to Activate Flipped Video

Objectives

Explain how Dutch New Netherland became English New York.

Describe William Penn's relationship with the American Indians in Pennsylvania.

Compare and contrast the Pennsylvania Colony with other colonies.

Analyze the importance of religious and ethnic diversity in the Middle Colonies.

Key Terms

push factor
pull factor
William Penn
Quakers

The Middle Colonies Thrive

During the early seventeenth century, the English developed two distinct clusters of settlements along the Atlantic coast: colonies around the Chesapeake Bay to the south and New England to the north. Along the mid-Atlantic coast, the Dutch and Swedes established their own small colonies. Growing English power threatened the Dutch and the Swedes. Soon, England would control most of the Atlantic seaboard.

New Netherland and Its Neighbors

Beginning in 1609, Dutch merchants sent ships across the Atlantic and up the Hudson River to trade for furs with American Indians. In 1614, they founded a permanent settlement at Fort Nassau (later called Fort Orange) on the upper river. To guard the mouth of the river, the Dutch built New Amsterdam at the tip of Manhattan Island in 1625. New Amsterdam became the largest town in the Dutch colony of New Netherland. With the finest harbor on the Atlantic coast, New Amsterdam was also a major seaport and the colony's government headquarters. Coming to trade or to farm, the Dutch—in contrast to the French, Spanish, and Puritan English—made virtually no missionary effort to convert American Indians.

Diversity in New Netherland Thrives The Dutch West India Company appointed the governor and an advisory council of leading colonists, but they did not permit an elected assembly. Although run by authoritarian governors, New Netherland tolerated various religious groups, including Jews. That toleration drew an especially diverse group of colonists not only from the Netherlands but also from France, Germany, and Norway. As in

GO ONLINE to access your digital course

New England, most of the colonists were of the middle class and poor. They came as families—unlike the unattached young men who predominated in the early Chesapeake Bay settlements.

Push-and-Pull Factors Despite an appealing location and religious toleration, the Dutch colony attracted few immigrants. In 1660, New Netherland had only 5,000 colonists—better than the 3,000 in New France, but far behind the 25,000 in the Chesapeake area and the 33,000 in New England. Why did the colonization of New Netherland falter?

In mobilizing migration to the colonies, push factors were stronger than pull factors. **Push factors** motivate people to leave their home countries. For example, religious persecution pushed the Puritans out of England. **Pull factors** attract people to a new location. For example, the promise of a better life and fertile soil may pull people to a new land. During the seventeenth century, push was stronger in England than in the Netherlands. With the Netherlands' booming economy and a high standard of living, the Dutch had less cause to leave home than did the English, who suffered from a stagnant economy. The Dutch did not have the masses of roaming poor who became servants in the Southern Colonies. And the tolerant Dutch lacked a disaffected religious minority, such as the Puritans who founded New England. The English succeeded as colonizers largely because their troubled society failed to satisfy their people at home.

Scandinavians Establish New Sweden In 1638, traders founded New Sweden on the lower Delaware River, within what is now the state of Delaware. Settlers built Fort Christina at the site of present-day Wilmington.

Like the Dutch colony of New Netherland, New Sweden had a dual economy: the fur trade with American Indians and grain farming by colonists. Some of the colonists were Swedes, but most came from Finland, then under Swedish rule. Skilled at pioneer farming in heavily forested Scandinavia, these colonists adapted quickly to the thick woodland of North America. They introduced many frontier techniques that eventually became adopted in many regions of North America, including the construction of log cabins.

Eventually, New Sweden extended to both sides of the Delaware River into present-day New Jersey, Pennsylvania, and Maryland. Although highly skilled, the approximately 500 New Sweden colonists were too few to hold the land after a violent confrontation with their Dutch neighbors. In September 1655, the Dutch governor, Peter Stuyvesant, appeared with seven warships, compelling the Swedish commander to surrender.

The Middle Colonies Around 1763

>> The colored areas indicate land claims rather than areas of European settlement. **Analyze Maps** Which rivers were important to settlers in the Middle Colonies? Explain.

BOUNCE to Activate Gallery

Tensions Between the Netherlands and England

The Dutch and English became violent rivals in global commerce during the 1650s and 1660s. The English leaders resented that the more efficient Dutch shippers captured most of the trade exporting Chesapeake tobacco and West Indian sugar.

In 1664, an English fleet forced Governor Stuyvesant to surrender his colony. The English renamed it New York, after the Duke of York, who received it as a proprietary colony. New Amsterdam became the city of New York, while Fort Orange became known as Albany. Victory secured the mid-Atlantic coast for the English, closing the gap between the Chesapeake Colonies to the south and the New England Colonies to the north. Under English rule, the conquered region became known as the Middle Colonies.

New Jersey Becomes a Colony In 1664, the Duke of York granted the lands between the Hudson and the Delaware rivers as a new colony called New Jersey. English Puritans and Scots settled the eastern half, while the west attracted English Quakers. Relatively small and poor, New Jersey was dominated by its larger and wealthier neighbors: New York to the north and Pennsylvania to the west. Settlers were allowed religious freedom, which helped attract a diverse population and fostered tolerance.

☑ **IDENTIFY MAIN IDEAS** Why did New Netherland have a diverse population?

Religious Toleration in Pennsylvania

Pennsylvania began as a debt paid to **William Penn** by King Charles II of England. Although the son of an admiral, Penn had embraced the Quaker faith, a radical form of Protestantism. As a wealthy gentleman, Penn was an unusual Quaker. Most Quakers were tradespeople, shopkeepers, and small farmers who distrusted rich and powerful men. In turn, the gentry of England generally despised the Quakers. William Penn envisioned an American colony where Quakers could live in peace and free from the persecution that they suffered in England.

Quaker Beliefs and Values In contrast to the Puritan emphasis on sacred scripture and sermons by ministers, the **Quakers** sought an "Inner Light" to understand the Bible. The Quakers did not have clergy, and considered women spiritually equal to men. Quakers welcomed both men's and women's contributions to their meetings. As pacifists, the Quakers refused to bear arms. They also tolerated other faiths. Unlike Puritan Massachusetts, Pennsylvania would have no privileged church with tax support.

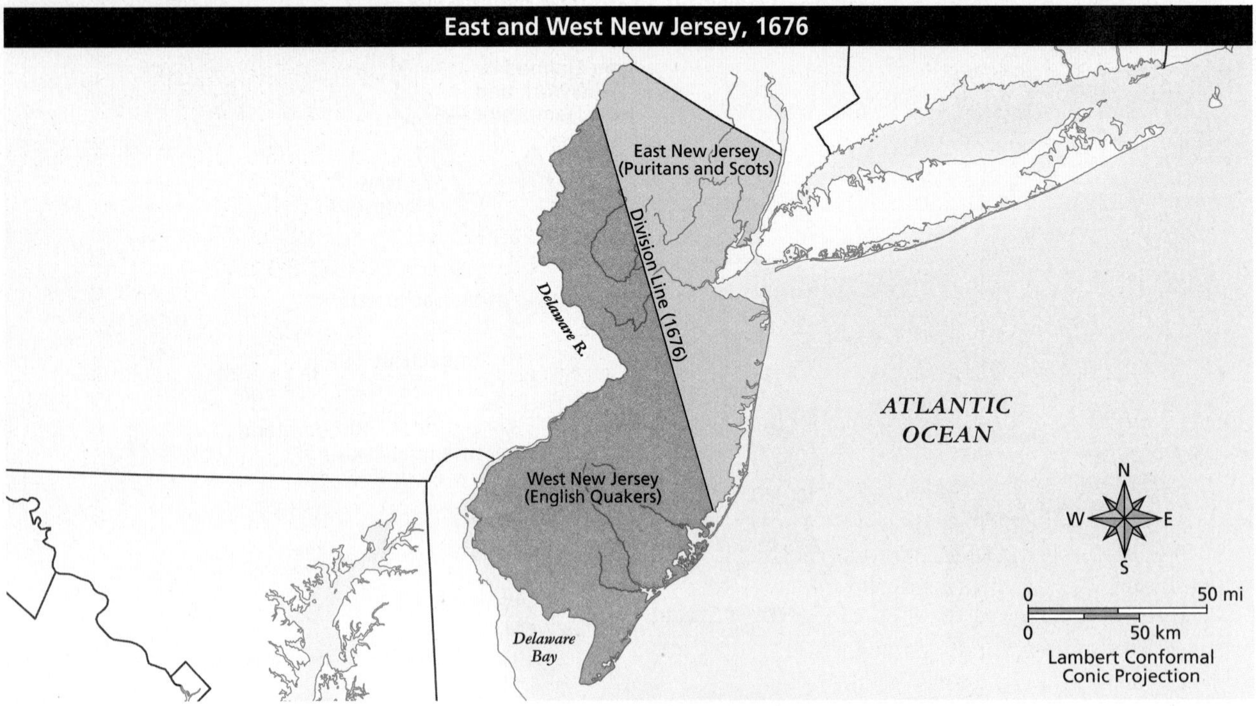

>> **Analyze Maps** Lands claimed by Europeans were already occupied by Native Americans. How did the division of New Jersey likely shape its development over time?

Pennsylvania Prospers and Grows In 1680, the king granted to Penn the land west of the Delaware River as the colony of Pennsylvania, which means "Penn's Woods." In 1682, Penn arrived with 23 ships bearing 2,000 colonists. For his capital, Penn established a city named Philadelphia, which means "City of Brotherly Love."

Thanks to a temperate climate, fertile soil, and a navigable river, the colonists prospered and multiplied, reaching 18,000 inhabitants by 1700. As with the New England Puritans—but unlike the Chesapeake colonists—most early Pennsylvanians came as families of middle-class means. Most were Quakers, but the colony also attracted Anglicans as well as German Baptists and Lutherans.

Cultivating peace with the local American Indians, the Pennsylvanians avoided the sort of rebellions that devastated Virginia, New England, and New Mexico. Called Delawares by the English, the local American Indians were Algonquian speakers. Unlike most other colonial leaders, Penn treated American Indians with respect and paid fair prices for their land.

>> William Penn sought to make his colony of Pennsylvania a tolerant place for Quakers and other religious groups.

The Middle Colonies Prove Welcoming for Many The Middle Colonies developed an ethnic and religious diversity greater than either the Chesapeake or New England areas, where almost all of the white colonists came from England. The Middle Colonies included Dutch, Swedes, Finns, French Protestants, Germans, Norwegians, and Scots—as well as English. By faith, they were Quakers, Baptists, Anglicans, Presbyterians, Lutherans, Dutch Reformed, German Reformed, and Jews. No single ethnic group or specific religious denomination possessed a majority in any Middle Colony. In 1644, a Jesuit priest described New Amsterdam.

> No religion is publicly exercised but the Calvinist, and orders are to admit none but Calvinists, but this is not observed, for there are, besides Calvinists, in the Colony Catholics, English Puritans, Lutherans, Anabaptists, [etc.]
>
> —Reverend Isaac Jogues, 1644

>> Although William Penn had been granted the land by the king of England, he purchased more land from American Indians in the region and maintained good relations with them.

The diversity of the Middle Colonies violated the traditional belief that political order depended on ethnic and religious uniformity. Thrown together in unexpected combinations, the various colonists had to learn how to tolerate their differences. In their ethnic and religious pluralism, the Middle Colonies anticipated the civic values of toleration and respect for diversity that would characterize the United States.

IDENTIFY MAIN IDEAS Why were the Middle Colonies more diverse than either the Southern or New England colonies?

ASSESSMENT

1. **Generate Explanations** Explain what push and pull factors are and how they relate to Dutch and English colonization in the Americas.
2. **Distinguish** In what ways did the Quakers differ from other religious groups in the Middle Colonies?
3. **Generate Explanations** Explain the circumstances behind the English takeover of Dutch New Netherland.
4. **Distinguish** How did the ethnic and religious makeup of the Middle Colonies differ from the Chesapeake and New England areas?
5. **Quest Connections** Look back through the lesson. What image would you choose to represent Pennsylvania in your Museum of Colonial History and why?

2.4

Olaudah Equiano was an enslaved African American who became free when he purchased his liberty. He later wrote an influential book about being enslaved and supported the British abolitionist movement.

Immigration and Slavery in the Colonies

BOUNCE to Activate Flipped Video

Objectives

Explain how European immigration to the colonies changed between the late 1600s and 1700s.

Analyze the development of slavery in the colonies.

Describe the experience of enslaved Africans in the colonies.

Key Terms

indentured servant
triangular trade
Middle Passage
Phillis Wheatley

As the colonies developed, Europeans began to arrive in greater numbers. At first, most immigrants were English, but during the 1700s larger numbers of Germans and Scots-Irish arrived. Africans who had been taken unwillingly from their homelands and enslaved also arrived. These newcomers would reshape American colonial society.

Immigrants Populate the Colonies

After a difficult start, England's American colonies grew steadily. By 1700, approximately 250,000 people of European background lived in the colonies. That number would rise tenfold during the next 75 years. Much of this growth came as a result of emigration from Europe.

Immigrants From England During the 1600s, about 90 percent of the migrants to the English colonies came from England. About half of these immigrants were **indentured servants**—poor immigrants who paid for passage to the colonies by agreeing to work for four to seven years.

Instead of receiving a wage, indentured servants received basic food, clothing, and shelter—generally just enough to keep them alive. Since indentured servants were only useful to their indenturers during their term of service, many were treated almost like enslaved people. Unlike enslaved Africans, however, they had a date when their term of service would be completed and they would be free. At the end of their term, they were supposed to receive clothes, tools, food, and sometimes land.

Developments in England caused the percentage of immigrants to drop dramatically. Prior to 1660, many English left their homeland

GO ONLINE to access your digital course

because of religious and political turmoil. High unemployment and low wages in England added to the troubles. After 1660, however, the English economy improved and political and religious conflicts diminished. Increasingly, English people chose to stay in England.

The Scots and Scots-Irish While English emigration shrank, Scottish emigration soared. Generally poorer than the English, the Scots had more reasons to seek their fortunes elsewhere. They also gained easier legal access to the colonies after 1707. In that year, Great Britain was formed by the union of England, Wales, and Scotland. After the formation of Great Britain, many Scots became colonial officials. Some became royal governors. Scottish merchants also captured a growing share of the colonial commerce, especially the tobacco trade from the Chesapeake Bay area.

The Scots emigrated to the 13 colonies in three waves. The first wave came from the Scottish lowlands. The second came from the Scottish highlands, and the third came from the province of Ulster in Northern Ireland. In the colonies, the Ulster Scots became known as the Scots-Irish or Scotch-Irish.

Many of the Scots-Irish were descendants of Protestant Scots, (the majority of whom were Presbyterian), who had settled in Northern Ireland. Nearly 250,000 Scots-Irish people came to the colonies in the 1700s in search of land. Many moved west to the mountainous "back country" that stretched from Pennsylvania to the Carolinas. There, they built farms on the frontier lands recently taken from the American Indians.

>> Many German immigrants settled on farms in Germantown, Pennsylvania, during the 1700s.

BOUNCE to Activate Map

Migration from Germany Germans were second only to the Scots-Irish as eighteenth-century emigrants from Europe to British America. Most of the 100,000 who immigrated to the colonies were Protestant. Almost all came from the Rhine Valley in southwestern Germany and northern Switzerland.

What factors explain the flood of German immigrants? They felt pushed by war, taxes, and religious persecution. During the 1700s, Germany was divided into many small principalities, frequently involved in wars. To build palaces and to wage war, German princes heavily taxed their people and forced young men to join the army. Most princes also demanded religious conformity. Germany also lacked enough farmland for its growing population.

In 1682, William Penn recruited a few Germans to settle in Pennsylvania, where they prospered. In letters to relatives and friends, immigrants reported that wages were high while land and food were cheap. In Pennsylvania, an immigrant could obtain a farm six times larger than a typical peasant holding in Germany. Pennsylvania demanded almost no taxes and did not force its young men to become soldiers.

Immigration Drives Change and Diversity Immigration brought changes to the colonies. In Pennsylvania, for instance, new waves of Scottish and German immigrants made the Quakers a minority in that colony. Although the different groups often distrusted one another at first, no group was large enough to impose its beliefs or to drive the others out of the colony. Instead, they all gradually accepted that a diverse society was an economic boon and the best guarantee for their own faith.

CHECK UNDERSTANDING Why did Scots and Germans emigrate from their homelands?

Enslaved Africans Provide Labor

During the 1600s, landowning colonists in the Chesapeake region needed workers to raise crops. Indentured servants filled this need, and most early indentured servants were English. Yet, as English

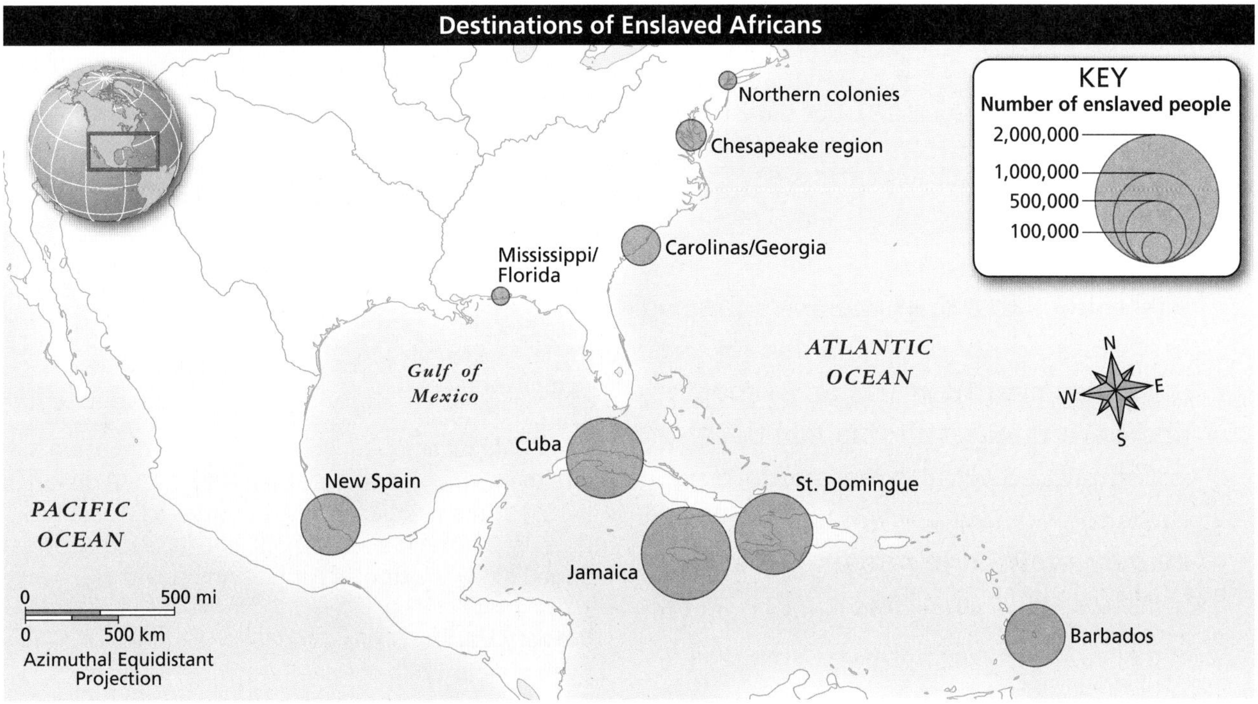

>> **Analyze Maps** Based on this map, was slavery more or less important to the economy of colonial North America than it was to other regional economies? What details support your evaluation?

immigration began to decline in the late 1600s, the demand for labor in the colonies grew. As a result, many colonists began to turn to another source of labor: enslaved Africans.

Slavery Emerges in the Colonies In the early colonial period there were bound laborers of European, African, and Native American descent. In some colonies, Native Americans were enslaved in higher numbers than people of African descent.

However, colonists increasingly turned to bound African laborers to meet their labor needs. By the mid-1600s, most colonies began passing laws that supported the permanent enslavement of Africans. In 1705, Virginia's General Assembly declared that "All servants imported . . . who were not Christians in their native Country . . . shall be accounted and be slaves."

Other laws stated that the children of enslaved African Americans were also enslaved. This change in legal status strengthened the racist idea that people of African origin were inferior to whites.

The Transatlantic Slave Trade Once established, slavery expanded rapidly. During the 1700s, the British colonies imported approximately 1,500,000 enslaved Africans. The great majority went to the West Indies, but at least 250,000 came to the 13 colonies to labor on plantations and in homes. The American colonists supported and grew rich from the slave trade, or trade in enslaved people. The Rhode Island economy revolved around this trade. The Rhode Island economy revolved around slave trading, while other New England colonies provided food and goods to the slave-based economies of the West Indies.

Traders purchased enslaved people from African merchants and chiefs in the coastal kingdoms of West Africa. Most of those enslaved Africans were kidnapped by armed men or taken in wars between kingdoms. Europeans sometimes directly seized captives themselves, and promoted the trade by offering high prices for enslaved people.

Enslaved Africans came to the Americas as part of a three-part voyage called the **triangular trade**. Traders in enslaved people sailed from Europe to Africa, where they traded manufactured goods for enslaved Africans. Then, in the **Middle Passage**, shippers carried the enslaved Africans across the Atlantic to the American colonies. After selling the enslaved people for colonial goods, the traders returned to the mother country.

The brutality of the Middle Passage was extreme. On a voyage that lasted two months or more, enslaved Africans suffered the psychological trauma of separation from their families and villages—as they sailed toward a strange land and an unknown future. Traders in enslaved people branded their victims with hot irons, placed them in shackles, and jammed them into dark holds so crowded that the African slaves could hardly move. The foul air promoted disease, and the ill might be thrown overboard to prevent the spread of disease. Some Africans, hoping for death, refused to eat.

One ship's surgeon witnessed a shocking scene.

> Upon the Negroes* refusing to take sustenance [food], I have seen coals of fire, glowing hot, put on a shovel and placed so near their lips as to scorch and burn them. And this has been accompanied with threats of forcing them to swallow the coals if they any longer persisted in refusing to eat.
>
> —Alexander Falconbridge, 1788

*Note that *Negroes* is an outdated term meaning Black people.

Traders in enslaved people had an interest in delivering as many healthy captives as possible. However, due to the conditions, at least 10 percent of those making the Middle Passage in the 1700s did not survive.

>> Enslaved African Americans in the Southern Colonies often worked at agricultural tasks, as shown in this 1725 illustration.

BOUNCE to Activate Gallery

IDENTIFY SUPPORTING DETAILS What were the effects of the new laws in the 1700s concerning enslaved Africans?

Africans in the American Colonies

Following the ordeal of the Middle Passage, enslaved Africans faced a bleak future in America. At slave auctions, colonial buyers often broke up families to make it more difficult to plot escape or rebellion. The newly enslaved Africans were ordered about in an unfamiliar language and put to work beside strangers who shared only their skin color. Arriving with distinct languages and identities as Ashantis, Fulanis, Ibos, and many others, the enslaved Africans forged a new culture as African Americans.

Slavery Varies Slavery varied considerably by region. In 1750, enslaved African Americans were small minorities in New England and the Middle Colonies. In those two regions, most enslaved African Americans labored as farmhands, dockworkers, sailors, and house servants.

Many more enslaved African Americans lived in the Southern Colonies, where they raised labor-intensive crops of tobacco, rice, indigo, or sugar. In the Chesapeake, they comprised 40 percent of the population. In coastal South Carolina, enslaved African Americans outnumbered the white population. To maximize their profits, masters demanded as much work as possible while minimizing the cost of feeding, clothing, and housing enslaved people. Most of the African slaves lived in crude huts with dirt floors, no windows, and few furnishings. Their work was long and hard: at least 12 hours a day, 6 days a week under the close supervision of an overseer, who whipped those who resisted.

A New Culture Emerges In the colonies, African Americans developed a rich culture based on African traditions and their circumstances in North America. These traditions represented a blend of African cultures, as plantations, farms, and cities contained Africans from many different ethnic groups. Most African Americans adopted the Christianity of their masters, blending it with some African religious traditions. They modified African instruments, crafting banjos, rattles, and drums to create a music that emphasized rhythm and percussion.

Enslaved Africans Resist Enslavers could never break enslaved African Americans' longing to be free. In the South and especially in the West Indies,

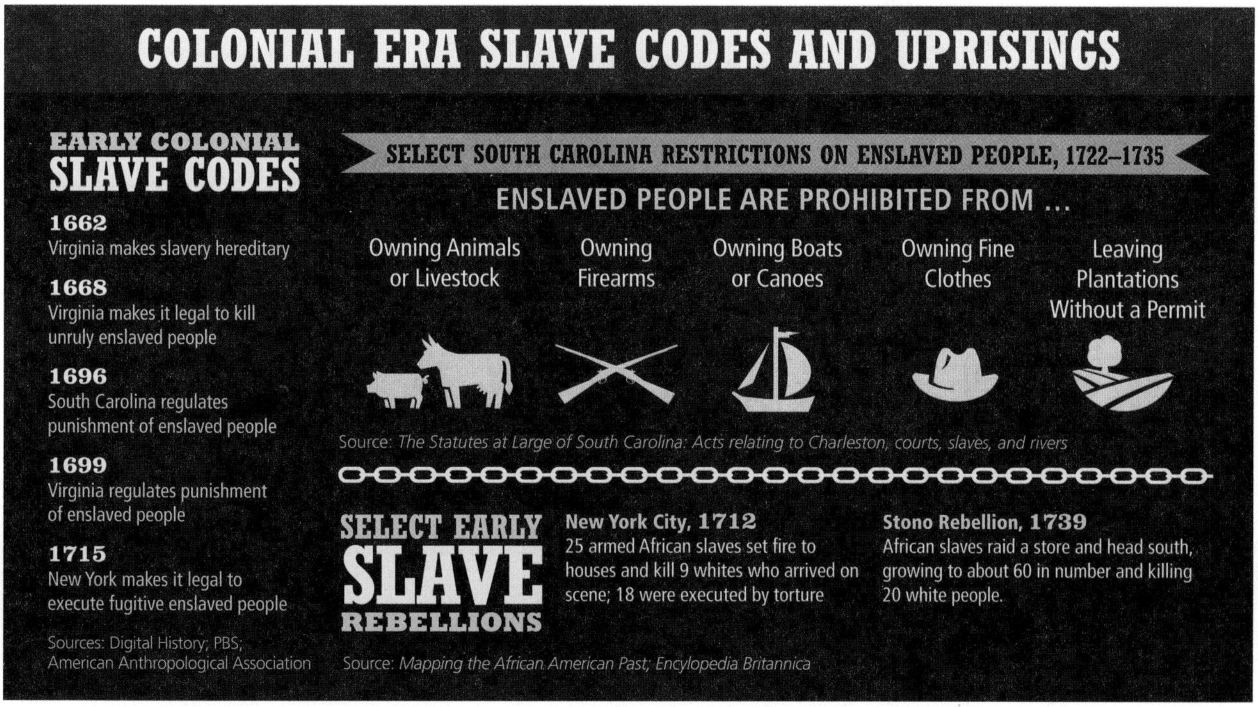

>> **Analyze Information** How did colonial governments attempt to prevent enslaved African Americans from rebelling?

some enslaved Africans rebelled. On the mainland, the largest uprising erupted in 1739 at Stono in South Carolina, where about 60 African slaves killed 20 whites before suffering defeat and execution.

Running away was more common. In the West Indies and Carolinas, enslaved Africans became *maroons*, a name for those who hid in forests or swamps. Other runaways fled to remote American Indian villages or Florida, where the Spanish welcomed them with food, land, and freedom. The Spanish sought to weaken the British colonies and to strengthen their own frontier militia with freed African Americans. In fact, Fort Mose near St. Augustine, became the first free Black settlement in what is now the United States. In the Chesapeake and northern colonies, runaways tried to fit into small free Black communities.

Many more of the enslaved Africans, however, opted for a more subtle form of rebellion. They stayed on the plantations, but they resisted by working slowly, feigning illness, pretending ignorance, or breaking tools.

Free African Americans Although most African Americans remained slaves for life, a few did obtain their freedom. For example, an enslaved African American might manage to earn money and purchase his or her freedom or might be set free by an enslaver.

Free African Americans tended to live in cities, where they faced discrimination. A rare few managed to overcome enormous obstacles to distinguish themselves. One example was **Phillis Wheatley** of Boston, who published a book of poems in 1773.

☑ **IDENTIFY MAIN IDEAS** In what ways did slavery differ in the North and the South?

☑ ASSESSMENT

1. **Identify Central Issues** What factors encouraged a diverse population of immigrants to settle in Pennsylvania?
2. **Summarize** What conditions were African slaves subjected to during the transatlantic voyage to the Americas?
3. **Summarize** Describe what life was like for an enslaved African American in the Southern Colonies during the mid-1700s.
4. **Support Ideas with Examples** Aside from open rebellion, what other methods of resistance were employed by African American slaves in the 1700s?
5. **Quest Connections** If you included an indenture contract in your Museum of Colonial History, what caption would you use to explain the difference between an indentured servant and an enslaved person?

2.5

Increased trade allowed some well off colonists to live comfortable lifestyles in spacious furnished homes filled with consumer goods.

BOUNCE to Activate Flipped Video

Objectives

Analyze the economic relationship between England and its colonies.

Explain the impact of geography on the economies of the New England, Middle, and Southern colonies.

Compare and contrast differences in the social structure of the three major colonial regions.

Key Terms

mercantilism
Parliament
Navigation Acts
staple crop
cash crop
dame school

Economic and Social Life in the Colonies

England's colonization of the Americas was driven in large part by financial concerns. The purpose of the English colonies was to increase the wealth and power of England—the mother country. The economic policy of mercantilism supported those ideas.

England and Its Colonial Economy

The British Economy and Mercantilism The policy of **mercantilism** holds that a nation or an empire could build wealth and power by developing its industries and exporting manufactured goods in exchange for gold and silver. This policy encouraged monarchs to minimize imports from rival empires and to drive those rivals out of colonial markets. By selling more than it purchased, the empire could build wealth in the form of gold or silver.

In general, the colonies fit into the mercantile system because of their unique economic strengths. In England, land was scarce whereas people were numerous, which meant that labor was cheap. Money for investment was abundant. This combination favored the development of industry.

In the colonies, however, there was more land but fewer people and less money for investment. That combination favored agriculture. As a result, more than 90 percent of the colonists lived and worked on farms or plantations. They exported their produce

GO ONLINE to access your digital course

in ships to buy tropical goods from Africa or the Caribbean or manufactured goods from England.

The Navigation Acts Increase Colonial Commerce The English regarded colonial commerce as the key to imperial power. By controlling colonial trade, they could collect more customs duties—taxes on imported goods. They used this money to build a stronger navy, which enabled them to defeat the Dutch and later the French. To obtain more sailors, ships, and trade, **Parliament** in the mid-1600s enacted a series of trade laws called the **Navigation Acts**.

The Navigation Acts stated that only English ships with English sailors could trade with English colonies. The acts also specified that especially valuable colonial goods, including tobacco and sugar, be shipped only to the mother country.

Colonial ships were free to take their other products elsewhere. For example, New Englanders could export fish to Portugal and Spain.

Finally, the colonies had to import all their European goods via an English port, where they paid customs duties. For example, if a Virginian wanted a bottle of French wine, the wine had to come to America by way of an English port, rather than directly from France. Violators risked the confiscation of their ships and cargoes.

The Navigation Acts promoted the dramatic growth of English colonial commerce and the nation's prosperity. During the 1600s, English merchant shipping doubled. The value of imports and exports increased at least sixfold. In 1600, England had been a relatively poor nation, trading primarily with nearby northern Europe. By 1700, England's commerce was global, and London had become Europe's leading seaport.

At first, the Navigation Acts hurt the colonists economically because they had depended upon Dutch ships and Dutch manufactured goods. That changed by 1700.

Protected by the Navigation Acts, British manufacturing and shipping improved in quality and quantity, outstripping the Dutch. The colonists could obtain better goods from British suppliers at lower costs. Thereafter, colonists often protested some particular feature of the Navigation Acts, but not the whole system.

A Consumer Revolution Most colonists lived on farms or plantations. There, they produced most of their own food, fuel, and homespun cloth. But no farm or plantation could produce everything that a family needed. The colonists wanted to purchase expensive imported goods, such as sugar from the West Indies, tea from India, and manufactured goods from Britain. To obtain those goods, every colonial farm and plantation needed to produce a surplus of produce that they could export.

The expanding transatlantic commerce produced a "consumer revolution" that brought more and cheaper goods to the colonies. Between 1720 and 1770, colonial imports per person increased by 50 percent.

An immigrant from Germany marveled that "it is really possible to obtain all the things one can get in Europe in Pennsylvania, since so many merchant ships arrive there every year."

British manufacturers increasingly needed the growing American market. In 1700, the American colonies consumed about 10 percent of British exports. The rate of consumption rose to 37 percent by 1772. Grateful for the prosperity and consumer goods, the British and the colonists felt greater pride in their shared empire.

Both the middle class and the poorer class, however, bought more than they could afford. Americans suffered from a chronic trade imbalance,

The Navigation Acts

1651	1660	1663	1733
Goods imported to England from Asia, Africa, and the Americas could be transported only in English ships.	The American colonies could export sugar, tobacco, cotton, and indigo only to England, Ireland, or another English colony.	Under the Staple Act, all foreign goods shipped to the colonies had to pass through English ports, where a duty was collected.	Duties were increased on sugar traded between the French Indies and the American colonies under the Molasses Act.

SOURCES: *Encyclopædia Britannica;* Archives.gov

>> **Analyze Information** In what ways did the Navigation Acts allow England to control the supply of goods to the colonies?

as they imported more than they exported. Most colonists bore mounting debts. The shortage of cash and the increasing debts fed a nagging unease at odds with the overall prosperity and general contentment with the empire.

Triangular Trade Between Three Continents

During the 1700s, a pattern of trade emerged that connected England, its colonies, and West Africa. Trade among the three continents had three main parts and formed a triangular shape. On the first leg of the journey, British ships loaded with manufactured goods sailed to Africa's west coast. There, they swapped British manufactures—such as guns and cloth—for enslaved Africans. On the second, or middle, leg, the traders then carried the enslaved Africans to the American colonies. After selling the African slaves for colonial raw material—such as sugar, timber, and tobacco—the traders returned to Europe.

☑ **IDENTIFY MAIN IDEAS** What was the purpose of the Navigation Acts?

Regional Economic Differences

By the early 1700s, the economic and social foundations of Britain's North American colonies were in place. As the colonies developed, three distinct regions emerged, each with its own economic and social structure: New England, the Middle Colonies, and the South. Despite their differences, the regions were part of Britain's North American empire. Later in the eighteenth century, events would lead the colonies to unite against a common cause: British rule.

The vast majority of people in the 13 colonies made their living as farmers. Other than shipbuilding and some ironworks, the colonies lacked industries. The few small cities were all seaports that focused on trade with England.

In spite of these broad similarities, the colonies had by the mid-1700s developed important regional distinctions. Variations in geography and climate helped explain the differences between life in New England, the Middle Colonies, and the South.

Climate Influences the New England Economy

New England is a region with cold winters, a short growing season, and a rugged landscape. For these reasons, New Englanders could not raise the crops most in demand by Europeans: tobacco, sugar, rice, and indigo. Instead, most New Englanders worked small farms where they raised livestock and grew wheat, rye, corn, and potatoes for their own use. None of these commodities could profitably be shipped to England, where a similar climate permitted production of the same crops.

The Triangular Trade

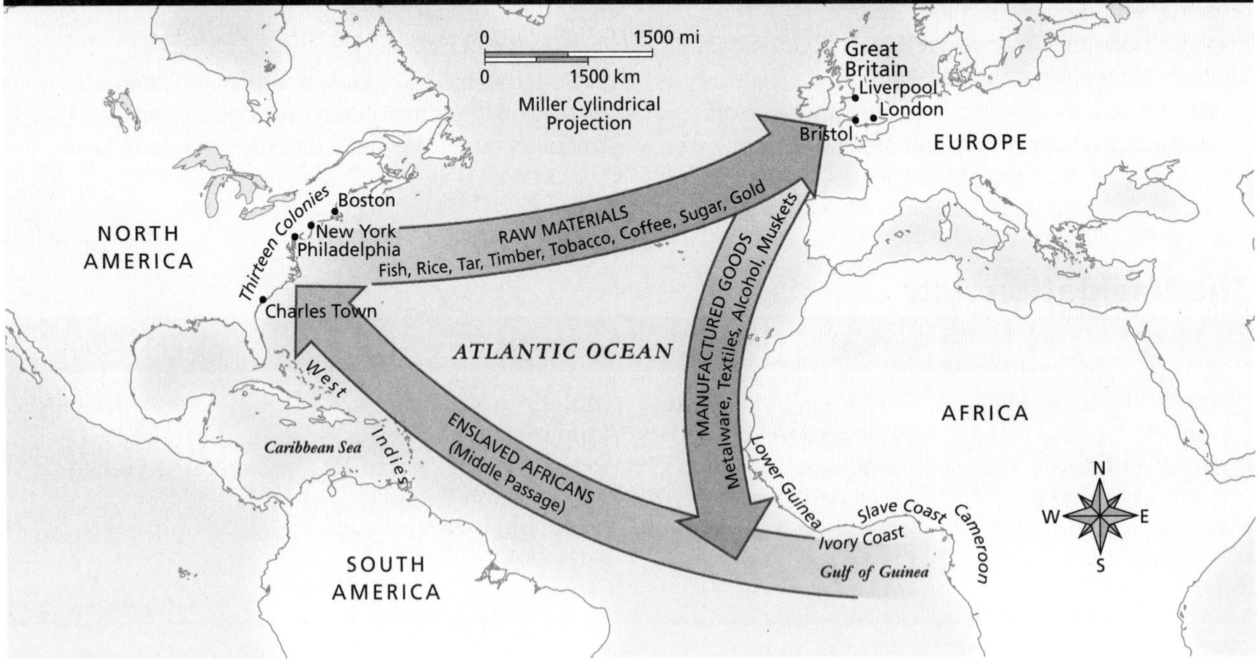

>> **Analyze Maps** What goods did England provide to West Africa? What did the colonies send to England?

New Englanders did ship some products from their shores. They exported lumber from their forests and fish—especially cod—from the sea. They salted and then shipped the fish to Europe or to the West Indies to feed enslaved Africans working on sugar plantations. New Englanders also used wood harvested from regional forests to build ships.

The principal seaport in the region was Boston, which had about 16,000 people in 1750. There, merchants did a lively business carrying out the busy trade between the colonies and Great Britain.

The Middle Colonies Depend on Farming As in New England, family farms prevailed in the Middle Colonies. But those farms were more prosperous than those in New England. With a more temperate climate, farmers in the Middle Colonies were able to produce more and better wheat than did the New Englanders.

Thanks to a growing export trade in wheat, the Middle Colonies boomed during the eighteenth century—while New England's economy stagnated. Philadelphia and New York became the two great seaports of the prospering Middle Colonies. Still, neither of these cities was large by today's standards. In 1760, Philadelphia had a population of only 25,000.

Profitable Crops Drive Southern Growth Because of an even warmer climate and longer growing season, the Southern Colonies could raise the most valuable and profitable colonial crops. In the Chesapeake colonies of Virginia and Maryland, planters raised staple crops of tobacco, though some in the 1700s were switching to wheat. **Staple crops** are crops that are in steady demand. These crops were also **cash crops**, crops grown for sale.

North Carolina produced cattle and lumber, while South Carolina and Georgia harvested rice and indigo. (Cotton would not become an important crop until the 1790s.) Charleston, South Carolina, was the region's largest port. Near the coast, most of the population consisted of enslaved Africans working on plantations. In the hillier areas inland from the coast, white settlers and family farms predominated.

DESCRIBE Describe the ways in which agriculture differed in the three colonial regions.

>> Most American colonists lived and worked on small farms like this one.

>> New Englanders took advantage of their long coastline to fish for cod and other seafood.

BOUNCE to Activate Map

Regional Social Differences

The three colonial regions also varied in the shape and form of the social life that developed there. Factors such as availability of education and patterns of settlement helped create distinct differences between the regions.

Differences in Population In New England and the Middle Colonies, there were relatively few African Americans. In parts of the South, they formed the majority of the population.

The three regions also attracted different types of free settlers. During the seventeenth century, most immigrants to the South were poor, young, single men. Seeking work for the short term and a farm for the long term, they worked as indentured servants. In contrast, most of the immigrants to seventeenth-century New England were of the middle class and could pay their own way. They immigrated to the colony as families, which meant a better balance between males and females. For example, in 1650, New England had six males for every four females, compared with four men for every woman in the Chesapeake area.

European immigrants seemed to prefer the Middle Colonies most of all. These colonies became the most ethnically and culturally diverse region in the entire British Empire. In addition to religious tolerance, the Middle Colonies offered immigrants greater economic opportunities.

Though a less desirable destination for immigrants than the other regions, New England provided a healthier environment. A hilly land with fast-flowing rivers and streams, New England was free of the malaria and dysentery that killed so many colonists elsewhere. In New England, people who survived childhood could expect to live to about 70 years, compared to 45 years in the Chesapeake region.

With a healthier environment and better balance between men and women, New England had rapid population growth. During the seventeenth century, New England received only 21,000 immigrants—a fraction of the 120,000 transported to the Chesapeake area. Yet in 1700, New England had 91,000 colonists, more than any other region.

Women Have Limited Rights By law and custom, there were few opportunities for women outside the home. Most women were legal dependents of men, and men held all the power in colonial households. Married women could not own property, could not vote, could not hold political office, and could not serve on a jury. Although women who were widowed could inherit a portion of their husband's property, they did not have any political rights.

Both men and women depended on one another to run farms, businesses, and households. Men generally did the work of planting, raising, and

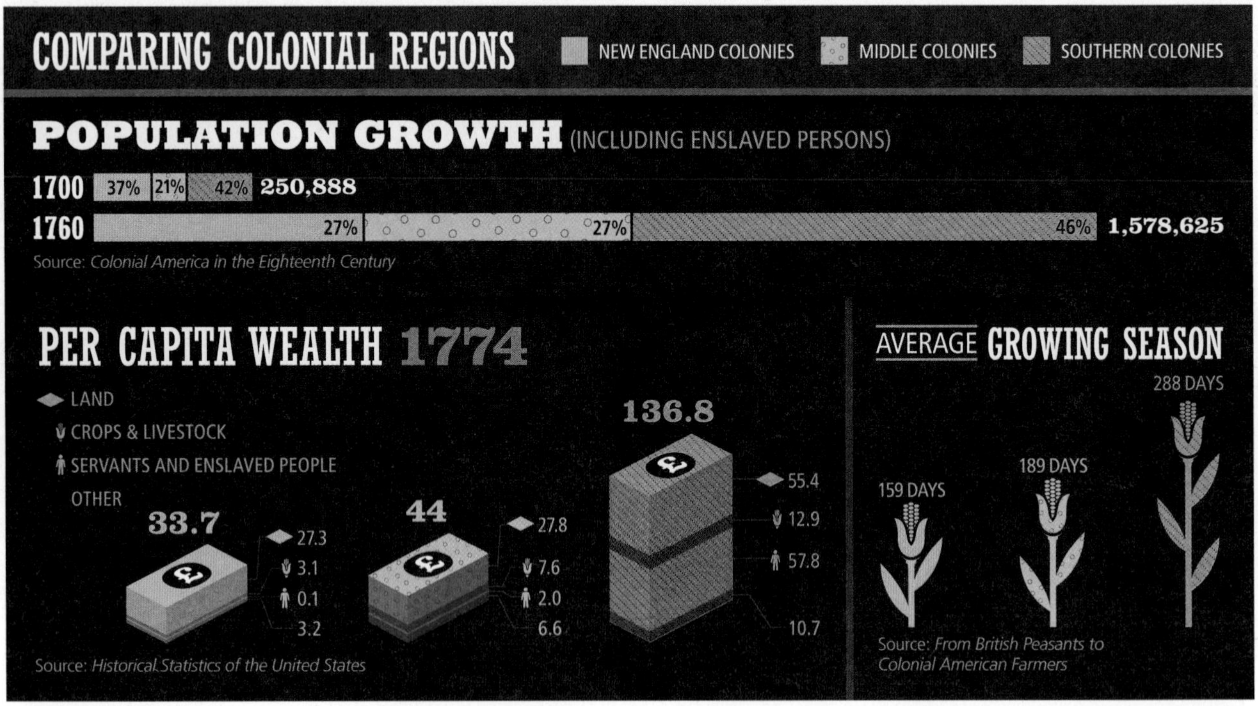

>> Analyze Information Which of the three main colonial regions was most unlike the other two? Explain your answer.

BOUNCE to Activate Gallery

harvesting crops. Women usually managed the household duties, such as cooking, gardening, sewing, and child care.

Differences in Community Life The New England Colonies granted land to men who banded together to establish a town. New England leaders favored compact settlement in towns to support public schools and to sustain a local church. As a result, more adults were literate in New England than in the other colonial regions.

In addition, while New England had fewer wealthy families than in the other regions, there was a greater degree of economic equality. Most men in New England owned their own farm, shop, or fishing boat.

In the Southern Colonies, the plantation economy based on slavery produced great profits. However, each large plantation was far from the next, and backcountry farmers were excluded from plantation society. With a population that was spread far and wide, Southern colonists found it harder to sustain churches and schools. Illiteracy was more common in the South. Slavery also promoted greater economic inequality. A few white landowners became rich planters, but most remained common farmers.

>> Throughout the colonies, women worked mostly on domestic chores such as spinning.

Public Education in the Colonies As you have read, schooling was more available in New England than elsewhere in the colonies. By the mid-1600s, Massachusetts law required towns to provide schools where students could learn the basics of reading and writing. The goal was to enable students to read the Bible.

Larger New England towns offered a more advanced "grammar school" education—generally to boys only. Some girls did receive a grammar school education in **dame schools**—private schools operated out of a woman's home.

Outside of New England, education was less widely available. Many colonists taught reading and mathematics to their own children. Wealthier families might hire a tutor to teach their children or send them to England to get an education.

Colleges were few, small, and very expensive. Most colonies had none, and only New Jersey had more than one—the College of New Jersey (Princeton) and Queens (Rutgers). Even the oldest and largest colleges—Harvard in Massachusetts, William and Mary in Virginia, and Yale in Connecticut—had fewer than 150 students. Only young men from prosperous families could attend. Most graduates became ministers.

During the colonial era, rules and regulations at colleges were quite strict. Students were expected to live moral and righteous lives, risking punishment or expulsion if they broke a rule.

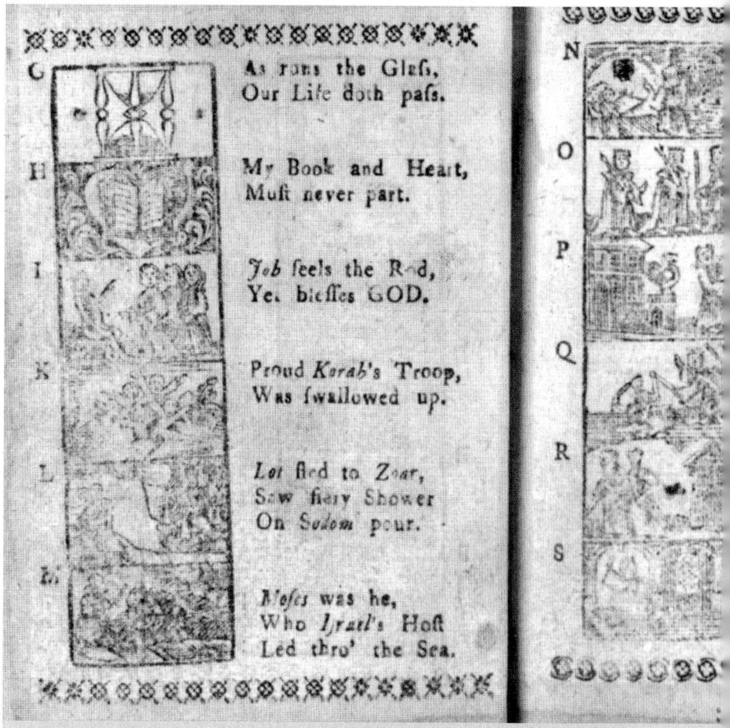
G As runs the Glaſs,
Our Life doth paſs.

H My Book and Heart,
Muſt never part.

I Job feels the Rod,
Yet bleſſes GOD.

K Proud Korah's Troop,
Was ſwallowed up.

L Lot fled to Zoar,
Saw fiery Shower
On Sodom pour.

M Moſes was he,
Who Iſrael's Hoſt
Led thro' the Sea.

N O P Q R S

>> Early textbooks called primers helped colonial students learn reading, writing, and other skills.

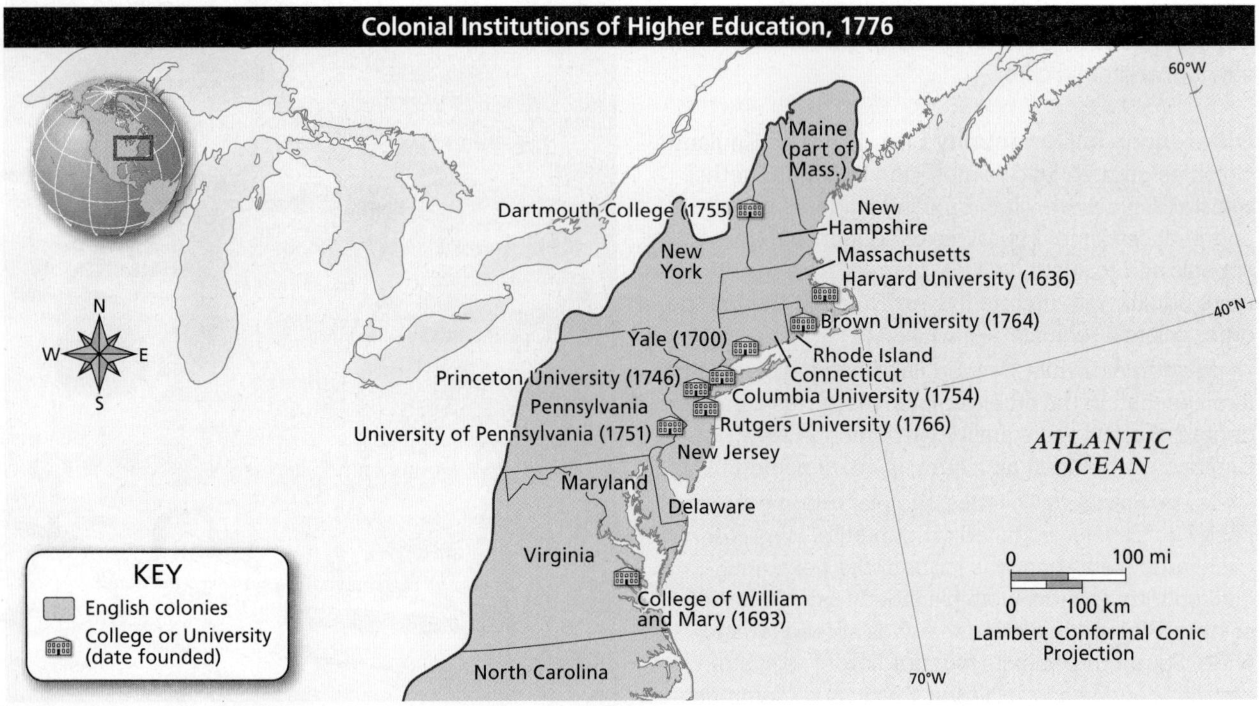

>> **Analyze Maps** Where did most of the college-educated population in colonial America likely live after completing their educations?

> If any scholar shall be guilty of profane swearing, cursing, vowing, any petty or implicit oath, profane . . . use of the [name of God], . . . fighting, striking, quarreling, challenging, turbulent words or behavior, . . . idleness, lying, defamation, talebearing, or any other suchlike immoralities, he shall be punished by fine, confession, . . . or expulsion, as the nature and circumstances of the case may require.
>
> —Regulations at Yale College, 1745

The highly educated minority were expected to lead the common people. Although most colonists attended only grammar schools, most were better educated than their counterparts in Europe.

CHECK UNDERSTANDING What factors pulled the majority of European immigrants to the Middle Colonies?

ASSESSMENT

1. **Generate Explanations** Explain the economic policy of mercantilism and how it related to England's relationship with the American colonies.
2. **Cite Evidence** What were the Navigation Acts and what effect did they have of the British economy in the 1600s?
3. **Compare and Contrast** the economies of New England and the Southern colonies during the 1700s.
4. **Summarize** What was the legal status of women in colonial America, and what was their position in a typical colonial household?
5. **Support Ideas With Examples** What educational opportunities existed in the colonies during the mid-1600s, and how did the opportunities offered to boys differ from those offered to girls?
6. **Quest Connections** In your Museum of Colonial History, how might a colonial textbook reveal the different approaches to education in the colonies?

2.6

In 1215, a group of barons forced the English king to sign the Magna Carta, a document guaranteeing certain individual liberties. Centuries later, American colonists drafted documents asserting these same rights.

Creating an American Identity

During the eighteenth century, the colonists looked to England as their model for literature, government, and their economy. Important English documents, such as the Magna Carta and the English Bill of Rights, were the basis of colonial government and law. In addition, the colonial economy was dependent on trade with England. Although the relationship between England and the colonies was a close one, during the 1700s, the distant American colonies began to form their own ideas about government and the economy.

BOUNCE to Activate Flipped Video

Objectives

Explore how English traditions influenced the development of colonial governments.

Explain how the ideas of the Enlightenment shaped the colonists' worldview.

Describe how the Great Awakening affected colonial society.

Key Terms

Magna Carta
English Bill of Rights
habeas corpus
salutary neglect
Enlightenment
Benjamin Franklin
Great Awakening

Early Government in the Colonies

England developed an empire of many disunited colonies during the 1600s. Lacking money, the English Crown granted charters to private companies or lords proprietors, individuals who supported the monarchy. Compared to the Spanish or French, the English monarch exercised little direct control over the colonists.

Foundations of English Government Also unlike the kings of France and Spain, the English monarchs were bound to uphold the provisions of the **Magna Carta**, a document English nobles forced King John to accept in 1215. The Magna Carta protected English nobles by limiting the king's ability to tax them and by guaranteeing due process, or the right to a trial. Before levying a tax, the king needed the consent of the nobles.

After the Magna Carta, a council of nobles continued to advise English monarchs. The nobles also maintained the right to approve taxes—one of their most important powers. During the 1300s, the council of nobles gained more power and evolved into the lawmaking body known as Parliament. The English Parliament became a bicameral, or two-house, legislature. Members of the House of Lords

GO ONLINE to access your digital course

were nobles, who inherited their positions, and church leaders. Commoners elected members of the House of Commons. However, only men with property could vote. Although this limited the number of eligible voters, England allowed more people to vote than any other European nation at the time.

Colonists Experiment With Self-Rule Although they were thousands of miles away from their homeland, most settlers in the North American English colonies asserted that they were entitled to the same rights as any other English subject. Nevertheless, the type of government in the American colonies varied from region to region.

In New England, the Puritans established republics with elected governors. Elsewhere, the distant Crown or lords proprietors appointed the governor of a colony. But that governor had to share power with the propertied colonists. Those colonists authorized their own elected representatives in a colonial assembly to debate the raising of taxes. Colonists also claimed they were protected by English common law, which emphasized individual liberties.

King James II Asserts Royal Power In 1685, James II became king of England and tried to rule without Parliament. An open Catholic, he alarmed the Protestant majority of England. The new king also tightened control over the New England Colonies by revoking their government charters.

Then, he combined them with New York and New Jersey into a larger colony known as the Dominion of New England. The Dominion replaced the colonies' elected assemblies with a Crown-appointed governor-general and council. The Dominion angered the colonists, who insisted upon their right to refuse to pay taxes unless approved by their own elected representatives.

Impact of the Glorious Revolution In 1689, the colonists learned that James II had been overthrown in England in a coup called the Glorious Revolution. The plotters replaced him with two Protestant monarchs, King William and Queen Mary. The new monarchs promised to cooperate with Parliament and to support the Anglican church. William and Mary also agreed to sign an **English Bill of Rights**, a document guaranteeing a number of freedoms and restating many of the rights granted in the Magna Carta. These rights included **habeas corpus**, the idea that no one could be held in prison without being charged with a specific crime.

The English Bill of Rights also stated that a monarch could not keep a standing army in times of peace without Parliament's approval. News of the English upheaval inspired rebellions among colonists in Massachusetts, New York, and Maryland. In

The Dominion of New England, 1686–1689

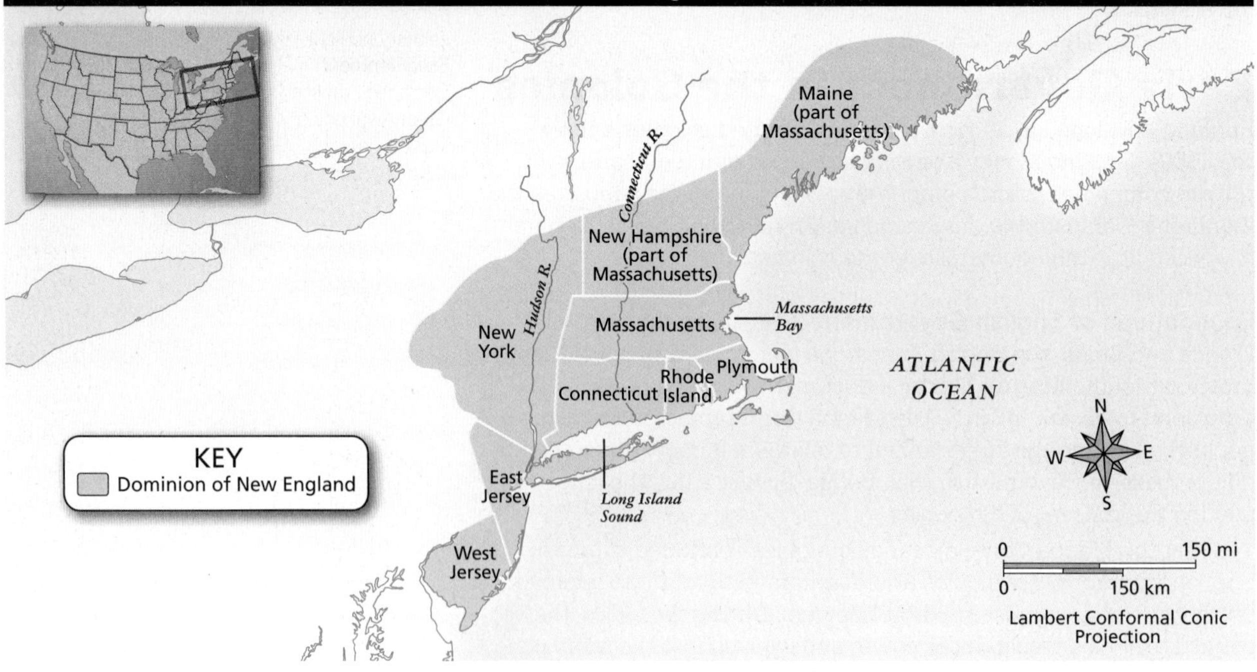

>> **Analyze Maps** How might the size of the Dominion of New England have affected England's ability to rule the supercolony?

Boston, colonial militia arrested the king's appointed governor-general, the hated Sir Edmond Andros.

All the rebels claimed loyalty to the new monarchs who brought about changes in the colonies. Protestant rebels in Maryland were delighted when William and Mary converted their colony into a royal colony. The new monarchs merged the Massachusetts and Plymouth colonies into a single royal colony, called Massachusetts. The new charter provided a royal governor assisted by an appointed council and an elected assembly. The assembly was permitted to choose council members, subject to the governor's approval. The king let Rhode Island and Connecticut keep their old charters, which allowed them to elect their governors as well as their assemblies.

Compromise was harder in New York. There, the leader of the rebellion, Jacob Liesler, had seized the position of governor. Liesler, however, made many political enemies. When England appointed a new governor, Liesler was forced to surrender. He was quickly tried, convicted, and executed in 1691. That hasty trial and execution left a bitter legacy. For the next generation, Liesler's supporters and enemies feuded, souring politics in New York.

The Glorious Revolution encouraged England to adopt a colonial policy that historians would later call **salutary neglect.** England allowed its colonies local self-rule. In return, the Crown expected colonial cooperation with its economic policies and assistance in the empire's wars against France and Spain.

Establishing Freedom of the Press About 50 years after the Glorious Revolution, conflict broke out between the English-appointed governor and colonists in New York City. In 1734, articles criticizing the governor appeared in the *New York Weekly Journal*, a newspaper printed by John Peter Zenger. Although Zenger did not write the articles, the governor had Zenger imprisoned for libel—printing falsehoods that are intended to damage a person's reputation. He sat in jail for eight long months awaiting trial. When Zenger came to trial, his lawyer argued that the articles were not libelous but truthful. The jury agreed and found Zenger not guilty. Today, Zenger's case is considered an early victory for freedom of the press.

CHECK UNDERSTANDING What was the impact of the Glorious Revolution on the 13 colonies?

>> After the Glorious Revolution ousted King James II, King William (left) and Queen Mary (right) took the throne.

BOUNCE to Activate Gallery

>> New York publisher John Peter Zenger won a 1730s court case that claimed he had published falsely damaging criticisms of the government.

BOUNCE to Activate Gallery

New Ideas Empower Individuals

During the 1600s and 1700s, Europe experienced an intellectual movement known as the **Enlightenment**—a movement headed by thinkers who believed that all problems could be solved using human reason. The Enlightenment challenged old ways of thinking about science, religion, and government in Europe. Enlightenment thinkers changed the way many American colonists viewed the world as well.

New Ideas About the Physical World

Enlightenment philosophers formulated new ideas and suggested radically new ways of thinking about the world. However, these thinkers were influenced by the work of scientists who were part of a movement now called the Scientific Revolution. During the 1500s, scientists began to use observation and experimentation to learn about the physical world. Scientists, such as Sir Isaac Newton, used reason and observation to formulate new ideas about mathematics and physics. Those ideas challenged the traditional power of religious leaders to explain the physical world.

Enlightenment thinkers, like Rousseau and Voltaire of France and John Locke of Great Britain, looked for natural laws that could be applied to government, society, and economics. Many Enlightenment philosophers focused on government. Some, like Locke, challenged the unlimited power of monarchs. Locke believed that people had natural rights that came from God, not from monarchs. Locke's ideas would have an enormous influence on American political leaders in the late 1700s.

Enlightenment thinkers like John Locke not only challenged the unlimited power of monarchs but the power of the Church as well. Locke suggested that self-knowledge is acquired through experience and reason and that individuals are able to discern God's existence and laws for themselves. This idea in turn challenged the authority of the Church as an intermediary between God and humanity.

>> John Locke was one of the leading thinkers of the Enlightenment.

The Enlightenment's Impact on the Colonies A number of colonists were inspired by Enlightenment ideas. One such person was **Benjamin Franklin**. A successful printer, Franklin's hunger for knowledge embodied Enlightenment ideals.

He conducted scientific experiments and invented a number of devices, including the lightning rod and bifocal eyeglasses. Franklin authored almanacs and books. Not many other colonists had the financial means to build their lives around the pursuit of knowledge. The majority knew little about Enlightenment philosophers.

Religion in the Colonies Many colonists came to America to freely practice their religions. However, most colonists were intolerant of religions other than their own. This was especially true in New England, where the church establishment was strongest. In contrast, the ethnic and religious diversity of the Middle Colonies allowed tolerance to thrive in that region.

Churches filled a key role in social life, especially in rural areas. Families who lived on widespread farms and plantations looked to the church as a place to gather with members of their community. Churches also served as a public space for reading government proclamations, for posting new laws, and for holding elections.

☑ **CHECK UNDERSTANDING** How did Enlightenment ideas affect traditional beliefs?

The Great Awakening

During the mid-eighteenth century, a religious movement swept through the colonies. Known as the **Great Awakening**, the movement was ignited by powerful evangelical preachers traveling from town to town giving emotional sermons that deeply touched listeners. Hundreds, sometimes thousands, of people would gather to be inspired by a preacher's words. In contrast to church worship, these sermons often took place in open fields.

Preachers stressed that personal religious experience was important in seeking God's salvation. Although the idea that individuals could determine God's law for themselves and find their own salvation remained popular, they rejected the Enlightenment view that everything in the world could be explained by natural law and reason. Jonathan Edwards of Massachusetts was a leading preacher during the period of the Great Awakening.

Edwards used the vivid images of an angry God dangling unbelievers like a spider over a roaring fire to inspire listeners to repent of their sins and experience the shock of conversion. In his well-known sermon "Sinners in the Hands of an Angry God," Edwards created this frightening metaphor in order to encourage his listeners to accept divine grace.

>> Jonathan Edwards was among the most influential preachers in the American colonies during the Great Awakening.

> O sinner! Consider the fearful danger you are in: it is a great furnace of wrath, a wide and bottomless pit, full of the fire of wrath, that you are held over in the hands that God, whose wrath is provoked and incensed as much against you, as against many of the damned in hell. You hang by a slender thread.
>
> —Jonathan Edwards, 1741

In Britain, a minister named George Whitefield was inspired by Edwards's sermons and began to travel through England, preaching in a similar manner. In 1739, Whitefield, now England's most celebrated preacher, came to tour the colonies. For two years, he attracted large and enthusiastic crowds. Like Edwards, he promoted an emotional style of worship.

Indeed, Whitefield urged common people to forsake ministers who favored a more subdued and rational style. Many other preachers copied Whitefield to spread the revivals. Indeed, the Great Awakening did much to inspire the American people with a sense of their own spiritual worth and value as individuals.

>> British preacher George Whitefield gave more than 18,000 sermons, sometimes speaking to crowds so large that the meetings had to be held outside.

The Great Awakening Fosters Tolerance and Equality The Great Awakening had a profound impact on the colonies. Preaching that individuals could find their own salvation, the movement challenged the authority of existing churches and led to the formation of new churches in the colonies. The

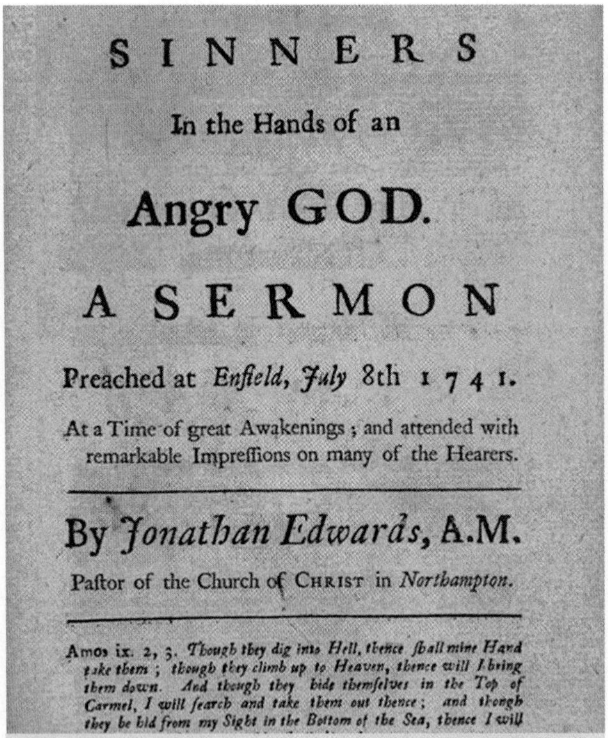

SINNERS
In the Hands of an
Angry GOD.
A SERMON
Preached at *Enfield, July* 8th 1741.
At a Time of great Awakenings; and attended with remarkable Impreſſions on many of the Hearers.

By *Jonathan Edwards*, A.M.
Paſtor of the Church of CHRIST in *Northampton.*

Amos ix. 2, 3. *Though they dig into Hell, thence ſhall mine Hand take them; though they climb up to Heaven, thence will I bring them down. And though they hide themſelves in the Top of Carmel, I will ſearch and take them out thence; and though they be hid from my Sight in the Bottom of the Sea, thence I will*

>> Jonathan Edwards's sermon "Sinners in the Hands of an Angry God" was reprinted many times. It warned readers to ask God's forgiveness.

movement also inspired ordinary people, including women, to begin preaching. To many ordained ministers and established churches, especially in colonies like Massachusetts where church and state were united, this was regarded as a political and social threat. Many Presbyterian, Dutch Reformed, and Congregationalist congregations were split between those who followed the preachers of the Great Awakening and those who did not. Eventually, the acceptance of the new churches contributed to an increase in tolerance of religious diversity.

The movement also encouraged the spread of democratic practices in the colonies. Evangelical preachers stressed that salvation and belief was open to everyone, not to just a privileged elite. Some of the more radical preachers even welcomed African Americans and women as spiritually equal and stressed that every person has the right to interpret Scripture. The Evangelical preachers of the Great Awakening argued that formal church rites were not as important as the act of experiencing God's spirit.

By challenging traditional religious beliefs and practices, the Great Awakening intensified colonists' sense of themselves as individuals, helped spread ideas of equality, and challenged ideas of hierarchy in religious organization. By the 1760s, the movement had helped prepare the ground for a political transformation as well. Many colonists began to believe that if they could choose their method of worship, they should have the right to choose their form of government.

☑ **IDENTIFY CENTRAL IDEAS** How did the Great Awakening lead to the growth of democratic ideas in the colonies?

☑ ASSESSMENT

1. **Generate Explanations** Discuss the effect of King James II's policies towards the American colonies.
2. **Compare and Contrast** the Enlightenment and the Great Awakening.
3. **Distinguish** How did John Locke's philosophy differ from the commonly held beliefs of his time?
4. **Support Ideas with Evidence** Discuss the importance of churches in colonial social life in the 1600s and 1700s.
5. **Connections to Today** Why is John Peter Zenger's trial relevant to today's conflict between government and the press?

GO ONLINE to access this biography:
John Locke

Connections to Today

Candlelight vigil in Pakistan on World Press Freedom Day

Take Action About Freedom of the Press

Today, freedom of the press is under attack worldwide. Americans are fortunate that the United States Constitution protects this freedom—an important liberty built on the foundations of the John Peter Zenger trial of 1734.

1. **Choose** one of the following freedom of the press-related topics:
    - **Libel laws:** Research the libel laws of foreign countries and the effects of these laws on freedom of the press.
    - **Government repression:** Investigate the increasing attacks on press freedom worldwide.
    - **Disinformation campaigns:** Research resources you can use to help identify "fake news"—false information that might include fictitious events, unproven conspiracy theories, and rumors.
2. **Ask Questions** Create a list of questions you have about the topic.
3. **Learn** about the topic and the major issues related to the topic. Are there any major debates related to the topic or issues? What are the strongest arguments on each side of the debate? Take notes as you conduct your research and continue to create questions as you learn more.
4. **Raise Awareness** In order to raise awareness of the growing threats to freedom of the press, the United Nations has declared May 3 to be World Press Freedom Day. Create a digital collage of images to show how citizens and newspapers acknowledge this day worldwide.

Topic 2 Quick Study Guide

LESSON SUMMARIES

Use these Lesson Summaries, and the longer versions available online, to review the key ideas for each lesson in this Topic.

Lesson 1: The Southern Colonies Take Root

In 1607, the first permanent English colony of Virginia was established in Jamestown. After years of hunger, disease, and conflict with American Indians, the colony found success by growing and exporting tobacco, and set up the first representative body in colonial America. The English established other southern colonies, starting with Maryland in 1632.

Lesson 2: New Lives in New England

Puritan communities, unhappy with the official Church of England, founded settlements in Massachusetts, the first of the New England colonies. Although Massachusetts Puritans sought religious freedom for themselves, they were intolerant of religious diversity, which led dissenters to found other colonies in New England. Throughout New England, the practice of self-governance shaped religious and political life. As the colonists gained control over the region, conflicts with American Indians increased.

Lesson 3: The Middle Colonies Thrive

The coastal lands between England's colonies in the South and New England became known as the Middle Colonies. Here the Dutch and others colonized the region, allowing anyone to buy land, regardless of nationality or religion. This helped create ethnic and religious diversity in the Middle Colonies, a diversity that increased even after Dutch lands fell under English control.

Lesson 4: Immigration and Slavery in the Colonies

Religious freedom and economic opportunity drew Europeans to the English colonies. However, most African immigrants were transported to the Americas against their will, to labor in slavery. Despite slavery's brutal conditions, a unique African American culture developed that blended the traditions of Africa and Europe.

Lesson 5: Economic and Social Life in the Colonies

Unique regional identities began developing almost as soon as the first colonists arrived in North America. Geography, economic activities and culture interacted to create distinct regional identities.

Lesson 6: Creating an American Identity

Although regional differences had emerged throughout the English colonies, colonists in all regions were united by British legal and political traditions, and by cultural movements such as the Enlightenment, which appealed to human reason, and the Great Awakening, which appealed to religious faith.

QUEST! FINDINGS

Create a Museum of Colonial History

Refer to your responses to the Quest Connections to help you create your museum to present to the class. Use the rubric and other Quest resources online to guide your work.

GO ONLINE to access lesson summaries

VISUAL REVIEW

Use these graphics to review some of the key terms, people, and ideas from this Topic.

13 English Colonies

COLONY	DATE OF SETTLEMENT
Southern Colonies	
Virginia	1607
Maryland	1632
Carolina (in 1691, the colony divides into:) North Carolina South Carolina	1670
Georgia	1632
New England Colonies	
Massachusetts	1620
New Hampshire	1623
Connecticut	1634
Rhode Island	1636
Middle Colonies	
New York	1624
New Jersey	1630
Delaware	1638
Pennsylvania	1644

New England Puritans

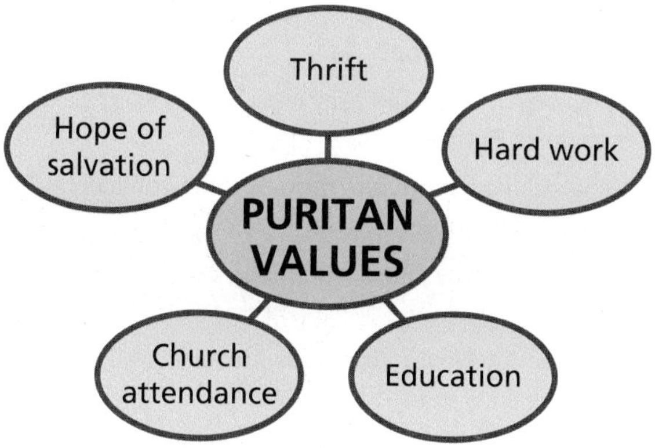

Regional Climates and Economies

REGION	CLIMATE	ECONOMY
New England	Cold, long winters	Exports of lumber and fish
Middle Colonies	Temperate climate	Exports of wheat
Southern Colonies	Warm; long growing season	Exports of tobacco, lumber, cattle, rice, indigo

Laws Reinforce Slavery

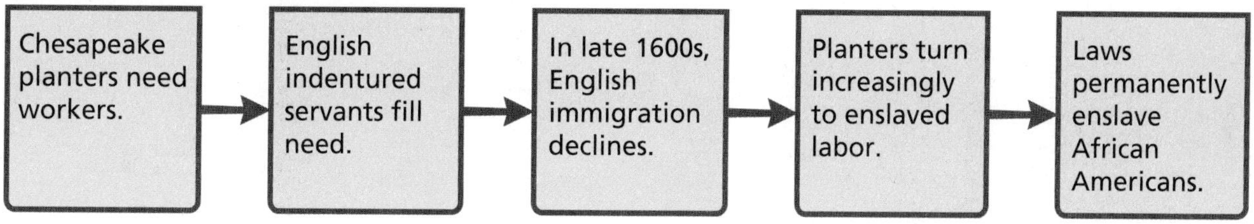

Topic 2 Assessment

KEY TERMS, PEOPLE, AND IDEAS

1. What was the significance of the Virginia **House of Burgesses**?
2. What was the difference between **royal colonies** and **proprietary colonies**?
3. Why did Georgia's colonists rebel against **James Oglethorpe**?
4. Why were most of the early New England colonists known as **Puritans**?
5. How did the **triangular trade** tie three continents together economically?
6. Under the policy of **mercantilism,** what was the relationship between an empire and its colonies?
7. How did the **Navigation Acts** help England control its colonies and increase its wealth?
8. How did the policy of **salutary neglect** benefit both England and its colonies?
9. What was the central idea behind the **Enlightenment**?

CRITICAL THINKING

10. **Determine Central Ideas** Why were the Massachusetts Puritans so intolerant of the religious beliefs of their fellow Protestants?
11. **Draw Inferences** In what ways was William Penn's colony of Pennsylvania unlike other English colonies?
12. **Draw Conclusions** How did slavery affect the economic life of the colonies?
13. **Compare and Contrast** What were the advantages and disadvantages of living in New England compared to the other colonies?
14. **Summarize** Why did distinct regional identities develop in the colonies?
15. **Identify Cause and Effect** How did the Great Awakening strengthen tolerance and equality?
16. **Use Visual Information** Study the map. What aspect of the triangular trade conformed to the theory of mercantilism?

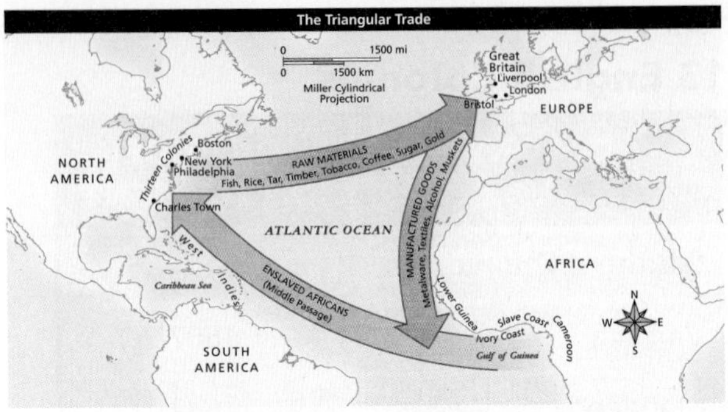

17. **Writing Activity: Write an Explanatory Essay** In 1644, a Jesuit priest described New Amsterdam:

> "No religion is publicly exercised but the Calvinist, and orders are to admit none but Calvinists, but this is not observed, for there are, besides Calvinists, in the Colony Catholics, English Puritans, Lutherans, Anabaptists, [etc.]"
> —Reverend Isaac Jogues

Write a two-paragraph essay based on the excerpt, explaining the relationship between religious diversity and tolerance in the Middle Colonies.

18. **Connections to Today** Opponents of press freedom often say that writers should be punished for libel—false claims intended to damage a person's reputation. Do you think libel should be taken into consideration when discussing press freedom? What sort of people do you think might have most to fear from reporters investigating their behavior?

DOCUMENT-BASED QUESTIONS

Settlers came to England's American colonies for many reasons. Read the documents below, then answer the questions that follow.

DOCUMENT A

In this excerpt from a sermon given aboard a ship bound for Massachusetts, John Winthrop, a leading Puritan, explained the purpose of settlement.

"For we must consider that we shall be as a City upon a hill. The eyes of all people are upon us. [So] that if we shall deal falsely with our God in this work we have undertaken, and so cause him to withdraw his present help from us, we shall be made a story and a byword throughout the world."

—John Winthrop, 1630

DOCUMENT B

In this excerpt from a pamphlet of 1609, the writer encourages investors and adventurers to help develop the Virginia colony.

"And as for the generall sort that shall goe to bee planters, bee they never so poore, so they be honest, and painefull, the place will make them rich: all kinde of Artificers wee must first imploy, are Carpenters, Ship-wrights, Masons, Sawyers, Brickemakers, Bricklayers, Plowmen, Sowers, Planters, Fishermen, Coopers, Smiths, Mettel-men, Taylors, Turners, and such like, to make and fitte all necessaries, for comfort and use of the Colony, and for such as are of no trades (if they bee industrious) they shall have there imployment enough, for there is a world of means to set many thousands a worke, partly in such things as I mentioned before, and many other profitable works, for no man must live idle there."

—Excerpt from *Nova Britannia: Offering Most Excellent fruites by Planting in Virginia*

DOCUMENT C

This image shows William Penn and his supporters meeting American Indians.

DOCUMENT D

This excerpt is from a letter from the Dutch West India Company to Peter Stuyvesant, the governor of New York.

"Your last letter informed us that you had banished from the province and sent hither by ship a certain Quaker, John Bowne by name; although we heartily desire, that these and other sectarians remained away from there, yet as they do not, we doubt very much, whether we can proceed against them rigorously without diminishing the population and stopping immigration, which must be favored at a so tender stage of the country's existence. You may therefore shut your eyes, at least not force people's consciences, but allow every one to have his own belief, as long as he behaves quietly and legally gives no offence to his neighbors and does not oppose the government."

—From a letter from the Dutch West India Company to Peter Stuyvesant, *1663*

19. In Document A, John Winthrop suggests that
- **A.** the colony might fail.
- **B.** God will withdraw His support for the colony.
- **C.** the Puritan colony must set an example of Godliness.
- **D.** the colony has been a success in the eyes of the world.

20. In Document B, the writer argues that the Virginia colony
- **A.** will provide plenty of jobs and make men rich.
- **B.** will welcome religious dissenters.
- **C.** will produce a large population.
- **D.** offers wealth from its tobacco plantations.

21. In Document C, the image seems to represent what aspect of Pennsylvania's policy toward American Indians?
- **A.** its policy of constant warfare
- **B.** its policy of removing American Indians from their lands
- **C.** its attempt to treat them with respect
- **D.** its attempt to enslave them

22. In Document D, the Dutch West India Company is
- **A.** opposing "sectarians" or members of radical religious sects.
- **B.** asking the governor to ban Quakers.
- **C.** warning against uncontrolled immigration.
- **D.** promoting religious tolerance.

23. Writing Tasks Write a paragraph describing the various reasons why settlers were attracted to England's colonies and the characteristics that came to define each region. Use the sources on this page and what you have learned in this topic to formulate your response.

GO ONLINE to access more practice

Topic 3

The American Revolution (1754–1783)

ESSENTIAL QUESTION When Is War Justified?

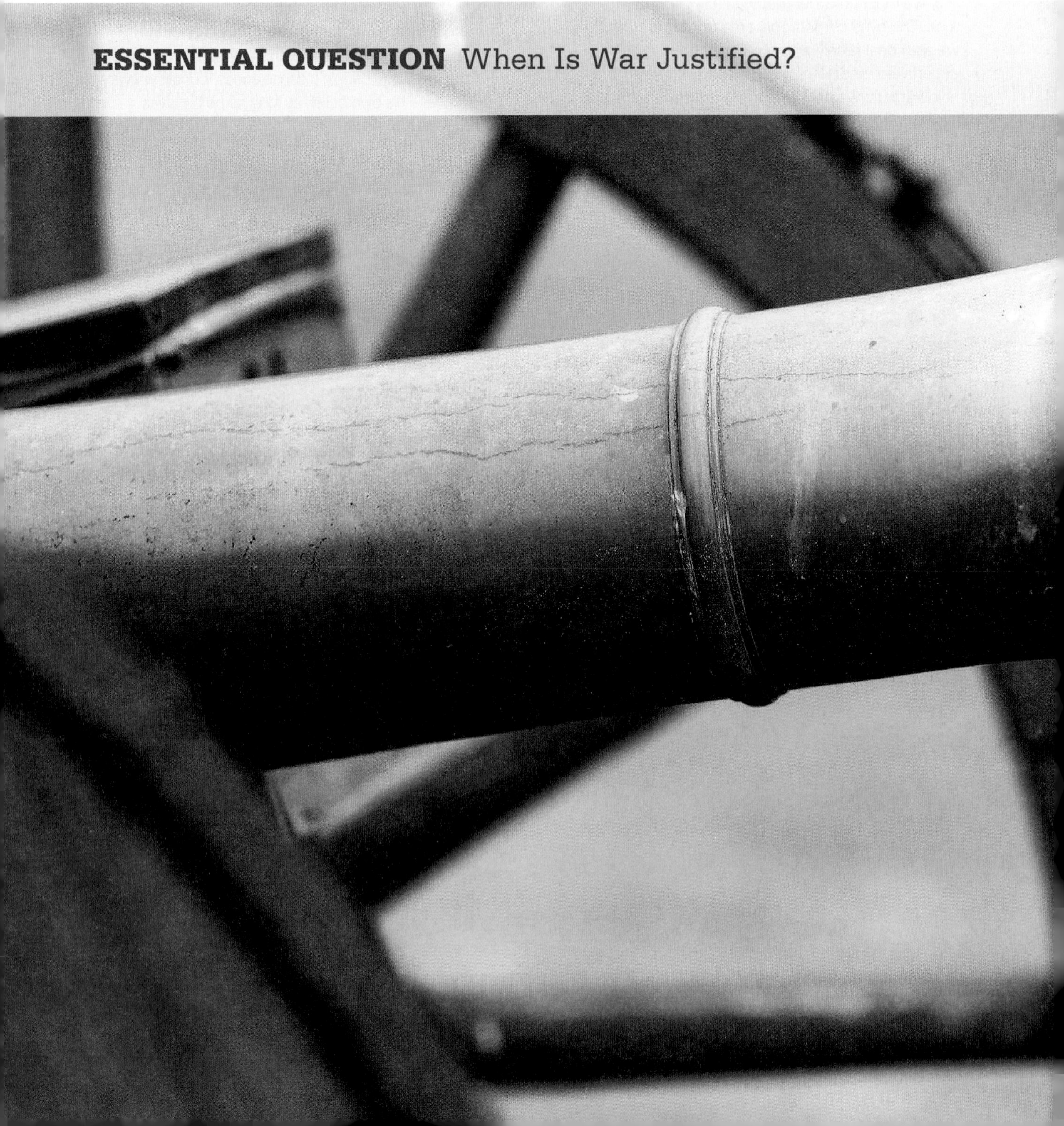

GO ONLINE to access the eText, videos, Interactive Primary Sources, Biographies, and other online resources.

The American Revolution began in 1775 after years of tension between Britain and several of its North American colonies.

Connections to Today

All over the world people gather in crowds to demand change. Sometimes they break the law to do so—especially where authoritarian governments declare protest illegal. Protest and civil disobedience were central to the story of American independence. Americans gathered around liberty poles, organized boycotts, threw tea into Boston Harbor, and even attacked officials. What issues do you think motivate protesters to take to the streets today?

NBC LEARN

Learn about George Washington's victories in war and peace.

BOUNCE to Activate My Story Video

Topic 3 Overview

In this Topic you'll learn about the era of the American Revolution, including the causes of the war, the growing Patriot movement, and the events and battles of the Revolution. Look at the lesson outline and explore the timeline. As you study this Topic, you'll complete the Quest team project.

LESSON OUTLINE

3.1 The French and Indian War

3.2 Causes of the Revolution

3.3 The Colonists Declare Independence

3.4 Americans Win the Revolution

The American Revolution

1754
French and Indian War begins

1763
Treaty of Paris is signed

1765
Parliament passes the Stamp Act

1773
Boston Tea Party takes place in Boston Harbor

1775
Battles of Lexington and Concord occur

1776
Declaration of Independence is signed

1781
British surrender at Yorktown

1750 | 1760 | 1770 | 1780 | 1790

QUEST! INQUIRY

Civic Discussion: British Tax Policy

Was the British tax policy in America following the French and Indian war justified? In this Quest, you'll analyze historical documents and varying points of view to prepare for an informed civic discussion about British tax policy.

STEP 1
Read the Discussion Launch. Then discuss the major points with the other team members in your group. Write the points your group agreed on in the Information Organizer.

STEP 2
Analyze several sources to understand different people's perspectives on the main question. As you read, analyze each source and fill in Step 2 of the Information Organizer.

STEP 3
After your group has been assigned a YES or NO position on the main issue, prepare the most compelling arguments in support of your position. Present your arguments and then switch sides.

STEP 4
Discuss the main question from your point of view. Reflect on what you learned and draw your own informed conclusion about the discussion question.

GO ONLINE to access complete Quest materials

3.1

Benjamin Franklin supported the idea of colonial unity and created the "Join, or Die" political cartoon. **Analyze Political Cartoons** How is the idea of unity expressed in the political cartoon?

BOUNCE to Activate Flipped Video

Objectives

Explain the relationship among the British colonists, the French, and the American Indians in the mid-eighteenth century.

Describe the causes and major events of the French and Indian War.

Analyze the causes and effects of Pontiac's Rebellion.

Summarize how the wars and their outcomes changed the relationship between Britain and the colonies.

Key Terms

Iroquois
George Washington
French and Indian War
Edward Braddock
Pontiac's Rebellion
Proclamation of 1763
Albany Plan of Union
Benjamin Franklin

The French and Indian War

Conflict between the great European empires spread to the American colonies throughout the late seventeenth and early eighteenth centuries. The British and the colonists fought a series of wars against the French and their American Indian allies. In the process, however, the relationship between the British and their colonies became strained.

Competition for North American Colonies

By the mid-eighteenth century, England, France, Spain, and the Netherlands were locked in a worldwide struggle for empire. In North America, Britain's greatest rival was France. While Britain controlled numerous colonies on the Atlantic seaboard, France controlled a vast territory that extended from the St. Lawrence River to the Gulf of Mexico. Between 1689 and 1748, the British and the French fought a series of wars. Most of the fighting took place in Europe, but some spilled over into North America. Before long, British colonists were drawn into the war.

Europeans Compete for American Indian Allies Each war between England and France was followed by a treaty that resolved nothing. Great Britain longed to drive the French from North America, and to accomplish this, the British needed to neutralize the great French advantage: French support from most of the American Indians in the region. American Indians dominated the forest passages between the frontiers of the rival empires.

GO ONLINE to access your digital course

The American Indians benefited from their middle position between the competing empires. The British and French both gave generous gifts, especially of arms and ammunition, to woo the American Indians. If one empire won a total victory, the American Indians would lose their leverage and receive harsher treatment from the victors. The **Iroquois** for example were also aware that the land that they lived on was at stake.

> We know our Lands are now become more valuable. The white People think we do not know their value; but we are sensible [aware] that the Land is everlasting, and the few Goods we receive for it are soon worn out and gone. . . . Besides, we are not well used [treated] with respect to the lands still unsold by us. Your people daily settle on these lands, and spoil our hunting. . . . Your horses and cows have eaten the grass our deer used to feed on.
>
> —Canasatego, Iroquois leader, July 7, 1742

Thus, the American Indians recognized the importance of preserving the balance of power between the French and the British.

The British Colonies Grow Stronger That balance began to tip as the British colonial population grew. In 1754, the 1.5 million British colonists greatly outnumbered the 70,000 French. The increasingly powerful British often treated the American Indians harshly and did little to stop settlers from taking Indian lands.

Compared to the British, the French were more restrained. Needing American Indian allies, the French treated most American Indians with respect and generosity. The outnumbered French worked with their American Indian allies to resist British colonial expansion. The French built a string of small forts and trading posts along the Great Lakes and down the Ohio and Mississippi rivers. Lightly built and thinly manned, the posts depended upon American Indians for protection. Most American Indians accepted these posts because, as one chief explained, "we can drive away the French when we please." That was not true of the British. Yet, while most Americans Indians supported the French, some fought for the British.

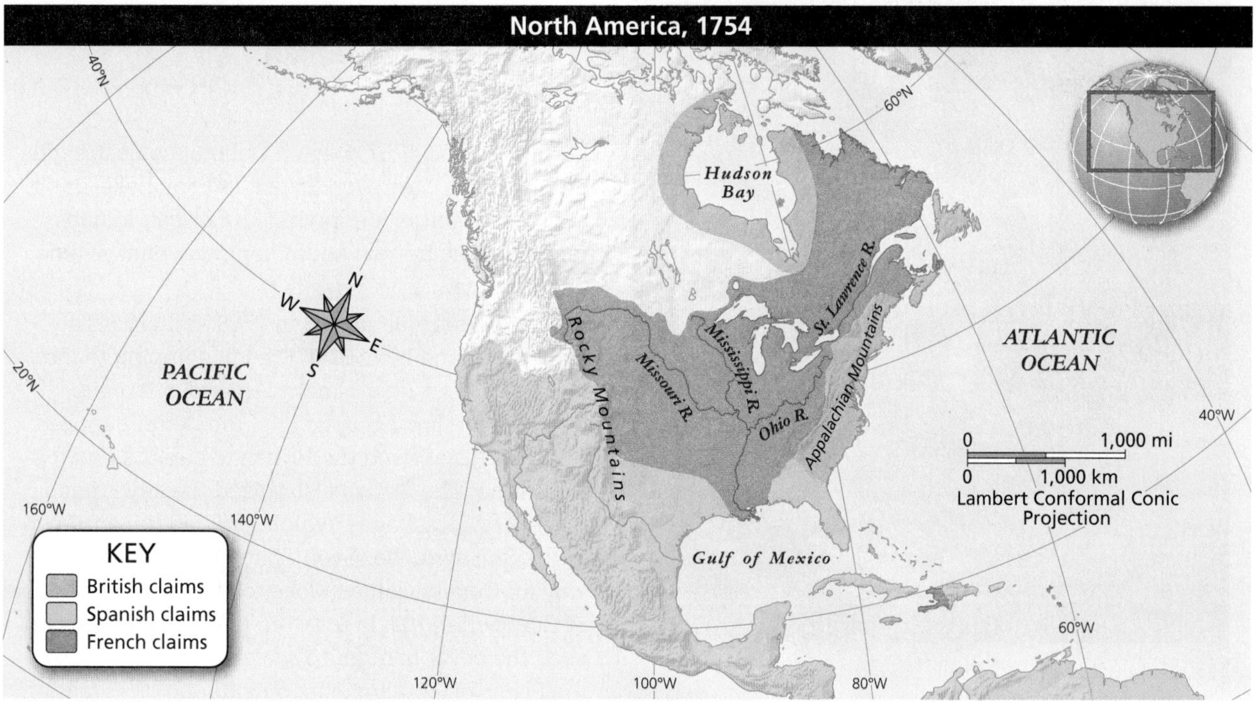

>> **Analyze Maps** Based on this map, is it surprising that Britain eventually took control of much of the land France claimed in North America? Explain your answer.

CHECK UNDERSTANDING How did American Indians affect the balance of power between the British and the French?

An Important British Victory

One point of conflict between France and Britain was the fertile Ohio River valley, claimed by both countries but largely unsettled by either. To discourage British colonists from moving into this area, known as the Ohio Country, the French built Fort Duquesne in what is now western Pennsylvania.

The new fort angered the British governor of Virginia, Robert Dinwiddie. In 1754, he sent colonial troops to evict the French. Dinwiddie entrusted the command to a young, ambitious Virginian named **George Washington**. Washington's troops attacked and defeated a small French force. But Washington had to surrender when the French counterattacked. This incident set off a conflict between the British and French in North America that the British colonists called the **French and Indian War**. In time, the North American conflict merged with the Seven Years War, a wider war fought around the world by Britain, France, and others.

>> General Edward Braddock, commander of British forces in North America, was ambushed and killed on his way to attack Fort Duquesne in 1755 during the French and Indian War.

BOUNCE to Activate Map

The British Struggle at First At first, the British fared poorly in North America. In 1755, a combined British and colonial force did overwhelm two French forts near Nova Scotia. Those troops evicted the French settlers, known as Acadians, and gave their farms to New Englanders. But the British army suffered a disastrous defeat when General **Edward Braddock** marched into a French and Indian ambush near Fort Duquesne. Braddock died, but Washington led a skillful retreat that saved half of that army. Later, Washington recalled the battle in a letter to his mother.

> . . . [We] were attacked by a body of French and Indians, whose number (I am certain) did not exceed 300 men. Ours consisted of about 1,300 well-armed troops, chiefly of the English soldiers, who were struck with such a panic that they behaved with more cowardice than it is possible to conceive. The officers behaved gallantly in order to encourage their men, for which they suffered greatly, there being near 60 killed and wounded—a large proportion out of the number we had!
>
> —George Washington, 1755

In 1756 and 1757, French General Louis-Joseph de Montcalm destroyed British forts on Lake Ontario and Lake George. Meanwhile, American Indians raided British frontier settlements in Pennsylvania and Virginia.

The tide of war shifted in 1758 and 1759. The British managed to cut off French shipping to the Americas. As a result, many American Indians deserted the French in favor of the better-supplied British. This allowed the British to capture Fort Duquesne. The British also seized the key French fortress of Louisbourg, which guarded the entrance to the St. Lawrence River. That victory cleared the way for General James Wolfe to attack the stronghold of Quebec in 1759. In a daring gamble, Wolfe's men used the cover of night to scale a cliff and occupy the Plains of Abraham just outside the city walls. Marching out to attack, Montcalm suffered defeat and death.

North America, 1763

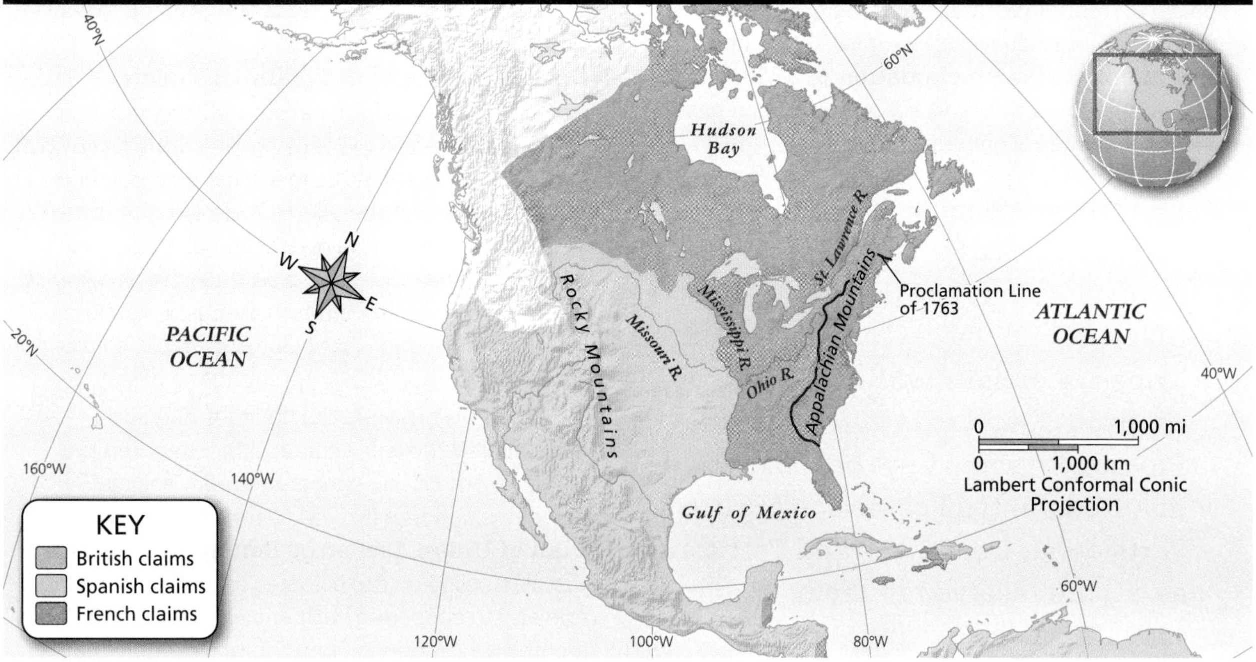

>> **Analyze Maps** Which nation was Britain's main rival in North America by 1763?

In 1760, the British captured Montreal and forced the French governor general to surrender the rest of Canada, including the forts around the Great Lakes. The British had succeeded in their major North American goal.

Treaty of Paris (1763) Fighting continued in other parts of the world. The British also won major victories in India, the Philippines, West Africa, and the West Indies. In 1763, the Treaty of Paris ended the war triumphantly for the British, who kept Canada, the Great Lakes region, the Ohio River valley, and Florida. They had driven the French from North America. Thereafter, the Mississippi River became the boundary between British and Spanish claims in North America.

IDENTIFY MAIN IDEAS How did the French and Indian War change the balance of power between the groups that claimed territory in North America?

Pontiac's Rebellion

The conquest of Canada was dreadful news to American Indians of the interior. No longer could they play the French and the British against each other. Indeed, the British military commander Lord Jeffrey Amherst quickly cut off delivery of goods to American Indians. British settlers flooded onto American Indian lands in western Pennsylvania and Virginia.

The American Indians affected included the Mississauga, Ottawa, Potawatomi, Ojibwa, Wyandot, Miami, Kickapoo, Mascouten, Delaware, Shawnee, and Seneca. During the spring of 1763, members of these groups surprised and captured most of the British forts in the Ohio River valley and along the Great Lakes. Through the summer and fall, they also raided settlements in western Pennsylvania, Maryland, and Virginia. The British called this uprising **Pontiac's Rebellion**, after an Ottawa chief named Pontiac who organized an attack on Detroit.

The goal of the American Indians was to weaken the British and lure the French back into North America. But they failed to capture the three largest and strongest British posts: Detroit, Niagara, and Fort Pitt (formerly Fort Duquesne).

During 1764, the American Indian attackers ran short of gunpowder, shot, and guns. Without a European supplier, their war fizzled. At the same time, the British government sought a quick end to the expensive war. The Crown blamed Amherst for the crisis, recalling him in disgrace. Thomas Gage, the new commander, recognized that respect for the American Indians would cost less than military expeditions against them.

The various American Indian nations made peace in return for British promises to restrain the settlers. The British rebuilt their forts, but they also tried to enforce the **Proclamation of 1763**. This document ordered colonial settlers to remain east of the Appalachian Mountains.

> And whereas it is just and reasonable, and essential to our Interest, and to the Security of our Colonies, . . . the several Nations or Tribes of Indians with whom We are connected, and who live under our Protection, should not be molested or disturbed in the Possession of such Parts of our Dominions and Territories as . . . are reserved to them, or any of them, as their Hunting Grounds.
>
> —Proclamation of 1763

The British troops, however, were too few to restrain the thousands of colonists who pushed westward. Troops burned a few log cabins, but the settlers simply rebuilt them. It was clear that the boundary set by the proclamation could not protect the American Indians. At the same time, it irritated the colonists, who resented efforts to limit their expansion.

Disagreements With the British Colonies The French and Indian War, as well as Pontiac's Rebellion, revealed the tensions between the British and their colonists. After investing so much blood and money to conquer North America, the British wanted greater control over their colonies. They also had a large war debt, plus the expensive job of guarding the vast territories taken from the French. The British thought that colonists should help pay these costs.

Bickering between the colonies had also complicated the war effort and had angered the British. With British encouragement, colonial delegates had met in 1754 to review the **Albany Plan of Union**. Drafted by **Benjamin Franklin**, the plan called on the colonies to unite under British rule and to cooperate with one another in war. It created an American continental assembly that would include delegates from each colony. However, none of the colonies would accept the plan for fear of losing some of their own autonomy.

The British also dropped the plan, fearing that creating greater unity among the colonies might make them more difficult to manage.

THE COLONIAL FRONTIER c.1760

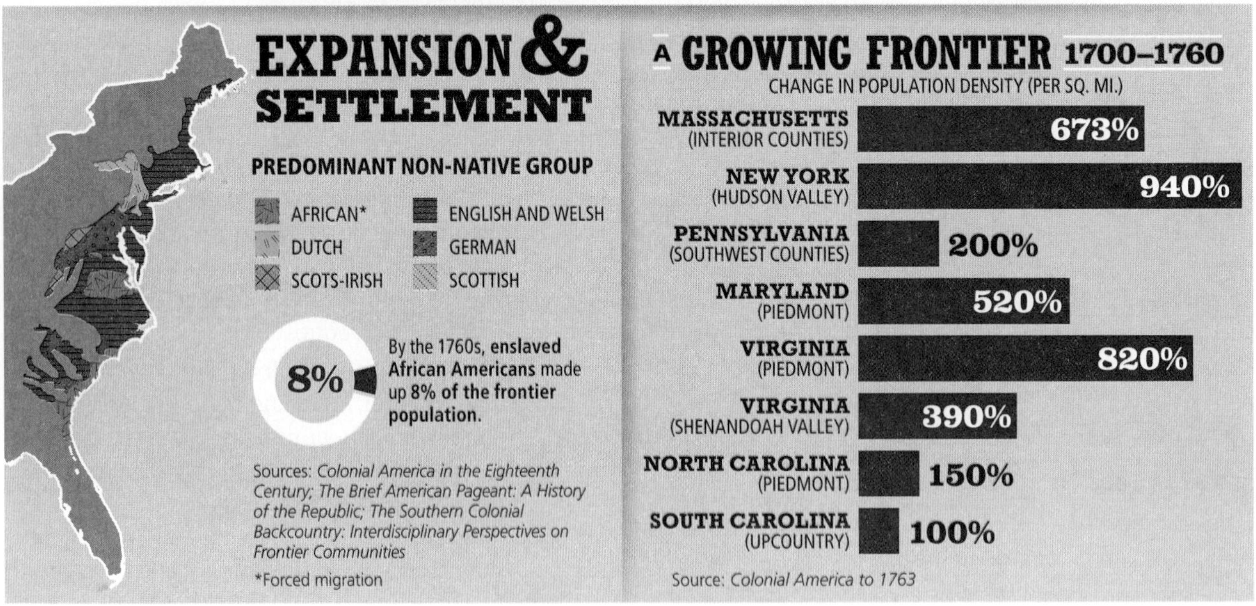

>> **Analyze Information** What factors may explain the steady westward growth of settlement during the early 1700s?

During the 1760s, the British acted on their own to impose new taxes and new regulations on colonial trade. Those changes angered colonists who wanted to preserve the sort of loose empire that had, for so long, produced so many benefits at so little cost to them.

DESCRIBE What circumstances led to Pontiac's Rebellion, and what was the outcome?

ASSESSMENT

1. **Summarize** How did the American Indians of the interior benefit from the early conflicts between the French and British?
2. **Generate Explanations** How did the French and Indian War turn in favor of the British?
3. **Distinguish** How was the Treaty of Paris different from previous treaties signed between the British and French in the Americas?
4. **Summarize** What was the Albany Plan of Union, and how was it received by the colonists?
5. **Quest Connection** How did the aftermath of the French and Indian War affect Britain's relations with its American colonists?

3.2

Paul Revere helped demonize the British by engraving this picture of the Boston Massacre. British troops were known as Redcoats because of their red jackets. **Analyze Primary Sources** How can you tell that Revere intended this engraving to be used as propaganda?

BOUNCE to Activate Flipped Video

Objectives

Describe the colonists' political heritage.

Explain the colonists' reaction to new taxes.

Describe the methods the colonists used to protest British taxes.

Summarize how the colonists reacted to the Townshend Acts.

Understand the significance of the First Continental Congress in 1774.

Key Terms

salutary neglect
Stamp Act
John Adams
Patrick Henry
Sons of Liberty
nonimportation agreements
Boston Massacre
committees of correspondence
Boston Tea Party
Intolerable Acts
First Continental Congress

GO ONLINE to access your digital course

Causes of the Revolution

The American colonists enjoyed Britain's protection during the French and Indian War while paying very little of the cost. Meanwhile, they profited from trade within the British Empire. Most importantly, they cherished the political rights that they enjoyed as British subjects. When Parliament began to tax the colonists to raise revenue, they protested. Eventually, the protests turned to rebellion, and rebellion turned to war.

The Foundations of Colonial Government

The colonists believed that Great Britain enjoyed the best government on Earth. British liberty included due process of common law, trial by jury, and freedom of the press from censorship. Above all, the colonists cherished the right to pay no tax unless it was levied by their representatives. Colonial governments followed the British model, but colonists' protests during the 1760s revealed that there were some important differences.

British Government Serves as an Example The British government had three branches. Executive power belonged to the monarch. Legislative power was divided between two houses of Parliament: the House of Lords and the House of Commons. Aristocrats inherited seats in the House of Lords. Only officials in the House of Commons were elected, and only a small percentage of the people could vote.

Similarly, each colony, except Pennsylvania, had a two-house legislature: an elected assembly and a council of prominent colonists appointed to life terms by the governor. Colonial governors were appointed by, represented, and served the king. Only Connecticut and Rhode Island elected their own governors, while Pennsylvania's entire assembly was elected. The colonists did not elect any members of British Parliament.

By modern standards, the British system was far from democratic. To those in power, democracy seemed dangerous in a society where people inherited wildly unequal property and status. In 1770, the British prime minister, Lord North, insisted, "I can never acquiesce in the absurd opinion that all men are equal."

Most Britons and colonists agreed, and wealthy men controlled government in the colonies as in Great Britain.

Different Ideas About Representation Despite similarities, colonial politics differed from the British model in several ways. The British constitution was not a formal document but a collection of laws and traditions accumulated over centuries. In contrast, the colonists' rights had traditionally been spelled out in formal legal documents such as the royal charters of Maryland or South Carolina, as well as informal written agreements like the Mayflower Compact.

In addition, two thirds of free colonial men owned enough property to qualify to vote, compared to less than a fourth of British men. By 1760, political upheaval in Great Britain and European wars had enabled the elected colonial assemblies to increase their powers at the expense of the royal governors. Since the colonies lacked aristocrats with inherited titles, most leaders in the assembly and council were wealthy planters and merchants related by blood or marriage. The assemblies often withheld salaries from unpopular governors.

British officials hoped to change the situation by taxing the colonists to provide salaries to royal governors and judges. Crown salaries would make them less responsive to the assemblies and councils. But that prospect alarmed the colonists, who began to recognize their deviations from Britain as important advantages. Members of Parliament believed that they "virtually represented" every British subject, including the colonists. While Parliament expected the colonists to obey, the colonists saw themselves as equal members of the British political body. Since the late 1600s, England had followed a policy of **salutary neglect**, allowing its colonies local self-rule. So when Parliament tried to levy taxes on the colonies, they objected. The colonists believed that only their own elected officials had that right.

☑ **IDENTIFY MAIN IDEAS** How did the colonists' views of political representation and rights differ from those of the British government?

Comparing British and Colonial Governments

GREAT BRITAIN	AMERICAN COLONIES
King	**Governor**
• Inherited executive power • Unable to veto laws passed by Parliament	• Appointed by and served the king but paid by the colonial legislature • Able to veto laws passed by council and assembly
Parliament	**Colonial Legislatures**
House of Lords • Aristocrats with inherited titles also inherited legislative power • Had power to veto laws **House of Commons** • Elected by men who held significant amounts of property • Less than 1/4 of British men qualified to vote • Had to approve all legislation	**Upper House or Council** • Appointed by governor • Prominent colonists but without inherited titles • Served as advisors to the governor **Lower House or Assembly** • Elected by men who held property • About 2/3 of colonial men qualified to vote • Represented citizens of towns and counties • Originated all tax and budget bills

Source: Digital History

>> **Analyze Information** How did colonists exercise direct control over their government?

New Taxes Create Conflict

The Seven Years' War—which came to include the French and Indian War in the colonies—nearly doubled Britain's national debt and greatly expanded its territories. Parliament needed to raise money, both to pay the debt and to protect the colonies. People in Britain paid far more taxes than the colonists did. This seemed unfair, for the war had been fought largely to protect the colonists. Parliament decided that the colonists could and should pay more to help the Empire.

The Sugar, Quartering, and Stamp Acts Colonial merchants had grown rich from trade, often smuggling or bribing officials to avoid duties, or taxes, on imports. In 1764, the new prime minister, George Grenville, proposed raising money by collecting duties already in effect. The law, known as the Sugar Act when put into effect, actually lowered the duty on foreign molasses. However, it also assigned customs officers and created courts to collect the duties and prosecute smugglers.

Grenville hoped that these measures would encourage colonists to pay the tax.

In early 1765, Parliament passed another unpopular law, the Quartering Act. This act required the colonies to provide housing and supplies for the British troops stationed there after the French and Indian War. Colonists complained, but most went along with the changes because they accepted Parliament's right to regulate trade and provide for defense.

In March 1765, Parliament passed a bill intended to raise money from the colonies. The **Stamp Act** required colonists to pay a tax on almost all printed materials, including newspapers, books, court documents, contracts, and land deeds. This was the first time that Parliament had imposed a direct tax within the colonies.

Taxation Without Representation The colonists angrily protested the Stamp Act, which was to take effect in November. They claimed that it threatened their prosperity and liberty. Colonial leaders questioned Parliament's right to tax the colonies directly.

They argued that the colonies had no representation in Parliament, so Parliament had no right to tax them. Some colonists believed that if they accepted this tax, Parliament would add even more taxes, stripping away their property and political rights. Many colonists thought that the stamp tax revealed a conspiracy by British officials to destroy American liberties.

The colonists' arguments puzzled the members of Parliament. After all, most Britons paid taxes although they could not vote. Many large British cities did not elect representatives to Parliament, which claimed to represent everyone in the Empire. Parliament dismissed the colonial opposition as

>> **Analyze Information** How successful were new British taxes at paying for the costs of the French and Indian War?

selfish and narrow-minded. The Empire needed money, and Parliament had the right to levy taxes anywhere in the Empire. Of course, Parliament's argument did not sway the colonists, who were appalled to discover that the British were denying their right to tax themselves.

CHECK UNDERSTANDING Why did the British feel justified in passing the Sugar and Stamp Acts, and why did colonists feel justified in objecting to these laws?

>> The British Parliament passed the Stamp Act of 1765 to impose a tax on printed materials in the colonies. **Interpret** What does this teapot suggest about the colonists' views of the Stamp Act?

Opposition to Taxes Strengthens

Tax resistance among the colonists took three forms: intellectual protest, economic boycotts, and violent intimidation. All three forms combined to force the British to back down. Colonial leaders wrote pamphlets, drafted resolutions, gave speeches, and delivered sermons to persuade colonists to defy the new taxes. The surge in political activity astonished **John Adams**, a prominent Massachusetts lawyer who observed "our presses have groaned, our pulpits have thundered, our legislatures have resolved, our towns have voted."

Enlightenment Ideas Colonial protests drew upon the liberalism of the Enlightenment. Europe's leading liberal writers included Baron de Montesquieu of France and John Locke of England. They argued that people had divinely granted natural rights, including life, liberty, and property. A good government protected these individual rights. Locke insisted that government existed for the good of the people.

Therefore, people had the right to protest any government that violated this "social contract" by failing to protect their rights.

Patrick Henry, a young Virginia representative, used these ideas to draft a radical document known as the Virginia Resolves. He argued that only the colonial assemblies had the right to tax the colonists.

> Resolved therefore, That the General Assembly of this colony, together with his majesty or his substitutes have, in their representatives capacity the only exclusive right and power to lay taxes and imposts upon the inhabitants of this colony; and that every attempt

The TIMES are Dreadful Doleful Dismal Dolorous, and DOLLAR-LESS.

of the STAMP
An Emblem of the Effects
Of the fatal Stamp

Adieu Adieu to the LIBERTY of the PRESS.

Thursday, October 31. 1765 — NUMB 1195

THE
PENNSYLVANIA JOURNAL;
AND
WEEKLY ADVERTISER.

EXPIRING: In Hopes of a Resurrection to LIFE again.

I am ſorry to be obliged to acquaint my readers that as the Stamp Act is feared to be obligatory upon us after the *firſt of November* ensuing (The Fatal To-morrow), The publiſher of this paper, unable to bear the Burthen, has thought it expedient to ſtop awhile, in order to deliberate, whether any methods can be found to elude the chains forged for us, and eſcape the inſupportable ſlavery, which it is hoped, from the laſt repreſentation now made againſt that act, may be effected. Mean while I muſt earneſtly Requeſt every individual of my Subſcribers, many of whom have been long behind Hand, that they would immediately diſcharge their reſpective Arrears, that I may be able, not only to ſupport myſelf during the Interval, but be better prepared to proceed again with this Paper whenever an opening for that purpoſe appears, which I hope will be ſoon.
WILLIAM BRADFORD.

>> This Pennsylvania Journal published in 1765 was printed using a skull in place of the royal tax stamp. Acts such as these illustrated the colonists' discontent with the British government.

>> Samuel Adams was an organizer of the colonial protest group the Sons of Liberty.

BOUNCE to Activate Gallery

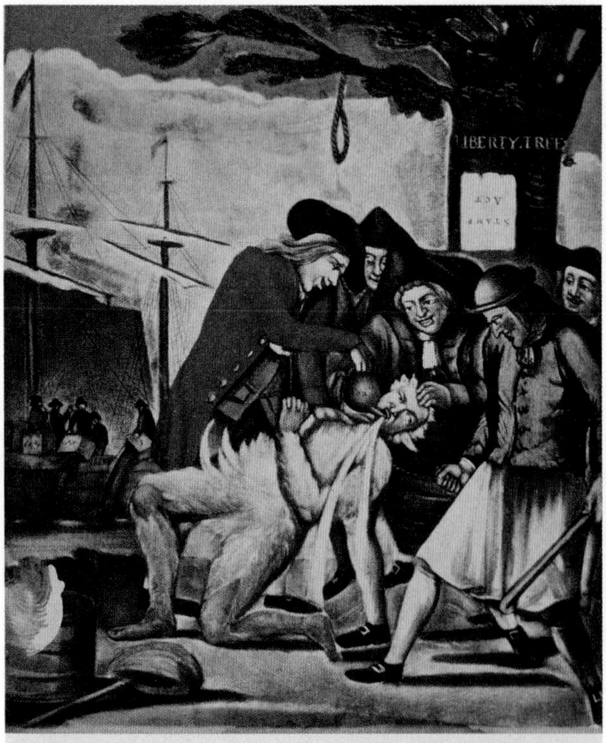

>> In this painting, Bostonians pour hot tea down the throat of a tax collector who has been tarred and feathered. **Speculate** How do you think this type of artwork affected colonists still loyal to the British Crown?

> to vest such power in any other person or persons whatever than the General Assembly aforesaid is illegal, unconstitutional, and unjust, and has a manifest tendency to destroy British as well as American liberty.
>
> —Patrick Henry, May 29, 1765

On May 30, 1765, the Virginia House of Burgesses accepted most of Henry's resolves, but rejected two—including the one above—because they were deemed too radical. Colonial newspapers, however, printed all six, believing that they had been accepted. Eight other colonies then adopted resolves similar to Henry's original proposal.

Patriot Leaders Emerge Colonists violently opposed the Stamp Act, which affected every colonist. In the months following the passage of the act, colonists began to work together to fight it, which led to a new, but still fragile, sense of American unity. Those who opposed the British taxes called themselves "Patriots." In the seaport streets, people showed a powerful new interest in politics. To lead the popular protests, some men formed associations known as the **Sons of Liberty**. Their most famous leader was Boston's Samuel Adams, a cousin of John Adams.

As the protests continued, angry crowds assaulted colonists who supported or helped to collect the taxes. The crowds were especially violent in Boston. In August 1765, a mob led by the Sons of Liberty tore down the office and damaged the house of the stamp tax collector.

The Massachusetts lieutenant governor, Thomas Hutchinson, denounced this riot. He insisted that the colonists had a legal duty to pay Parliament's taxes. Another mob destroyed Hutchinson's house. Thereafter, no one in Boston dared to voice support for the stamp tax. By the end of the year, every stamp collector in the colonies had resigned, leaving no one to collect the taxes.

Colonial Boycotts Threaten the British Economy Some colonial leaders opposed the tax but feared the violence of the crowds. To control and coordinate their protest activities, nine colonies sent delegates to a Stamp Act Congress held in New York City in October 1765. Members of this congress encouraged a consumer boycott of goods imported from Britain. Local committees enforced these **nonimportation agreements**, which threatened British merchants and manufacturers with economic ruin.

Women played an important economic role in the boycotts. When colonists stopped buying British goods, they needed "homespun" cloth to substitute for British-manufactured cloth. Colonial women organized to weave cloth. Their work was cheered by spectators and by Patriot newspapers.

Women also gave up certain comforts when they pledged not to buy any manufactured British goods. Known as "Daughters of Liberty," these women won respect for their efforts in the political struggle.

The combination of tactics worked. Under pressure from British merchants and manufacturers, Parliament repealed the Stamp Act in 1766. But the struggle was not over, for Parliament also passed an act declaring its right to levy taxes on the colonists.

☑ **DESCRIBE** How did the ideas of the Enlightenment influence colonial protests against British taxes?

>> British troops row to shore from their ships in Boston Harbor in this engraving by Paul Revere. **Infer** How might residents of other colonies have felt if they saw this engraving?

Protests Lead to Violence

The Stamp Act crisis showed that the colonists would not accept a direct tax. But the British government still needed to raise money to pay its debt and support troops in the colonies. Charles Townshend, the Crown's chief financial officer, thought that colonists would accept indirect taxes on commerce. After all, they had long accepted customs duties in principle, though evading them in practice. In 1767, Parliament passed the Townshend Acts, which levied new import duties on everyday items such as glass, lead, paint, paper, and tea.

To Townshend's surprise, the colonists insisted that they would pay no new taxes of any sort to Parliament. They also resented Townshend's plans to use the money to pay the salaries of colonial governors and judges, making them more independent of the colonial assemblies. That prospect alarmed the colonists, who valued their financial control of the governors.

The Boston Massacre In response to the Townshend Acts, the colonists revived their protests, boycotts, and street violence. Once again, the largest riots occurred in Boston, where many of the British customs officials abused their power. The Massachusetts legislature issued a circular letter denouncing the Townshend duties. Few other colonial legislatures paid attention to it until the governor dissolved the Massachusetts legislature in retaliation for their protest.

In an already tense situation, customs officers seized the merchant ship *Liberty* in June 1768 for smuggling. The ship belonged to John Hancock, a wealthy merchant and a prominent colonial politician. The seizure set off riots against the customs officers. To suppress the riots, the Crown sent 4,000 troops to occupy Boston, a city of only 16,000 people. For over a year, the presence of British troops inflamed popular anger, especially because the poorly-paid soldiers competed with unskilled workers for jobs.

One night in March 1770, a group of colonists hurled snowballs and rocks at British soldiers guarding the Customs House. The nervous soldiers fired into the crowd, killing five colonists. The dead included Crispus Attucks, a sailor of mixed American Indian and African ancestry, who, historians believe, may have escaped slavery in his twenties. Led by Samuel Adams, Patriots called the killings the **Boston Massacre**. Adams later organized local **committees of correspondence** throughout Massachusetts. The committees provided leadership and promoted cooperation. By 1773, several other colonies had created committees, which helped build colonial unity.

Once again, Parliament backed down. The British withdrew troops from Boston and dropped most of the Townshend duties. But to preserve the principle of Parliamentary supremacy, Parliament kept the tax on tea. Therefore, colonists continued to boycott British tea and to drink smuggled Dutch tea.

The Boston Tea Party The tea boycott worsened financial problems for the already struggling British East India Company. To help the company and encourage the colonists to pay the tax, Parliament passed a law allowing the company to sell directly to the colonists. This made their tea cheaper than the smuggled tea, even with the tax.

Instead of buying the cheaper tea, the colonists protested that the British were trying to trick them into paying the tax. If the East India Company sold tea directly, it would also hurt the wealthy colonists who smuggled tea. On the night of December 16, 1773, Boston Patriots took matters into their own hands. They boarded three British ships laden with tea and dumped the tea into the harbor. The event became known as the **Boston Tea Party**.

DEFINE What was the purpose of the Townshend Acts, and how did colonists respond?

The First Continental Congress

The Bostonians' actions outraged Parliament and the Crown. To punish Boston, Parliament passed the Coercive Acts. These laws closed the port of Boston to trade until inhabitants paid for the destroyed tea, including the tax on the tea. They also increased the power of the governor at the expense of the elected assembly and town meetings. To enforce these measures, the British sent warships and troops to Boston.

The Intolerable Acts The colonists were outraged. In addition to closing the port, the five laws that made up the Coercive Acts forced colonists to house British troops and allowed British officials to be tried in Britain for crimes committed in the colonies. One of the laws, the Quebec Act, extended Canada's southern border, cutting off lands claimed by several colonies. The horrified colonists called the new laws the **Intolerable Acts**. They rejected the idea that the British could shut down trade and change colonial governments at will.

In rural Massachusetts, people reacted to the British actions with violence. Armed with clubs and guns, they forced the courts of law to shut down. They also assaulted anyone who accepted an office under the governor or spoke in favor of obeying Parliament. They coated some victims in hot tar and feathers—a punishment both humiliating and painful.

A New Congress Convenes Fortunately for Massachusetts, the other colonies also opposed the Coercive Acts and viewed them as a threat to their freedom.

The Quebec Act, 1774

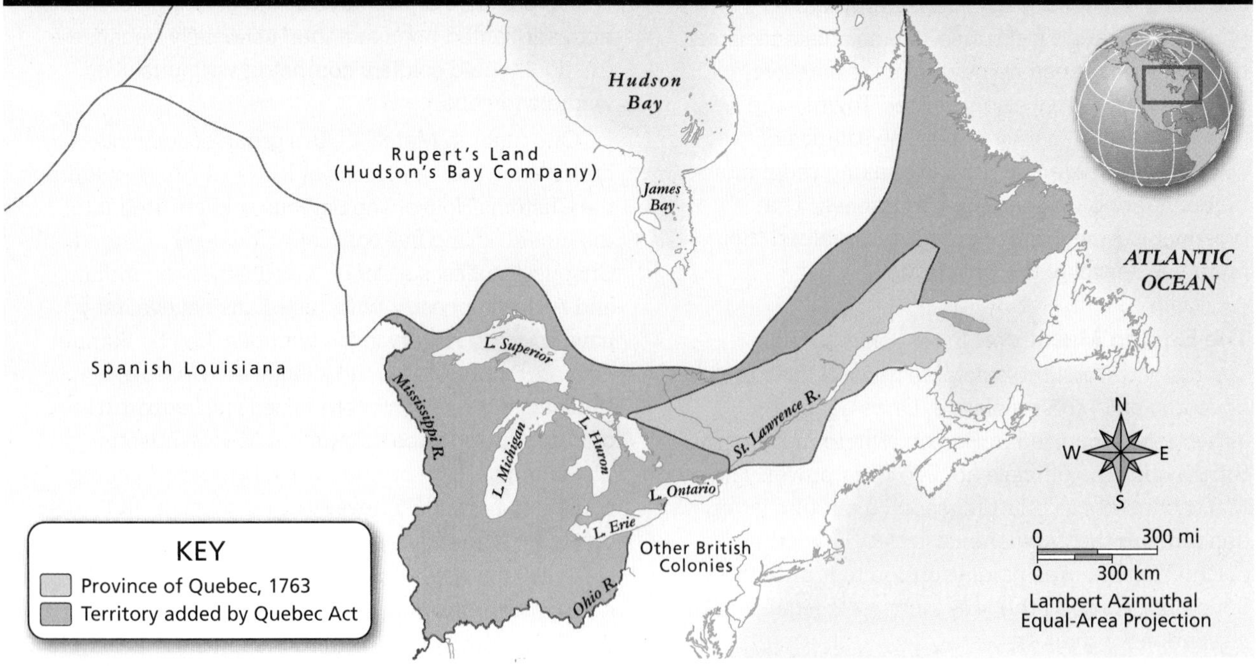

>> **Analyze Maps** In which regions of the frontier did the Quebec Act mostly block development?

British Acts

ACT	PURPOSE	COLONISTS' REACTION
Sugar Act (1764)	To compensate for the money spent on the war with the French	Protested and confiscated cargo held if duties went unpaid
Stamp Act (1765)	To raise revenue for the British Empire through taxation of colonial printed materials	Refused to use the stamps, harassed colonial stamp distributors, rioted
Quartering Act (1765)	To require colonists to provide lodging, food, and transportation to British forces	Residents of New York refused to comply, resorted to physical violence
Townshend Acts (1767)	To enforce the British Empire's authority over the colonies by suspending representative assemblies and imposing taxes	Hostility toward British agents, evasion of taxes, physical violence
Tea Act (1773)	To make British tea marketable in America and to help the British East India Company sell its surplus of tea	Patriots dumped chests full of tea into Boston Harbor
Intolerable Acts (1774)	To punish the colonies for their acts of defiance	Physical violence, prompted meeting of the First Continental Congress

Source: *Encyclopædia Britannica*

>> **Analyze Information** What colonial affairs did the British most try to control?

BOUNCE to Activate Cartoon

In the fall of 1774, delegates from every colony except Georgia met in Philadelphia, Pennsylvania, for the **First Continental Congress**. Virginia's delegates included the fiery Patrick Henry, who became famous for declaring, "Give me liberty, or give me death." Henry's passion for liberty did not extend to the enslaved people on his own estate. Still, he delighted the New England delegates by declaring, "The distinctions between Virginians, Pennsylvanians, New Yorkers, and New Englanders are no more. I am not a Virginian, but an American."

To pressure Parliament to withdraw the Coercive Acts, the delegates announced a boycott of all British imports. Throughout the colonies, the Patriots established local committees and provincial congresses to enforce the boycotts. In effect, the Patriots established new governments that bypassed Parliament and the Crown. By including common shopkeepers, artisans, and farmers, the committees expanded the ranks of the politically active. In the spring of 1775, a newly arrived immigrant marveled, "They are all liberty mad."

By 1774, Patriot John Adams had decided that he already lived in a new country named America. He also believed that Americans could unite to defeat the British. But Adams was ahead of most colonists, who still hoped to remain within the British Empire, provided that Parliament would revoke the Coercive Acts and stop trying to tax them. Far from blaming the king, most colonists still expected that he would side with them against Parliament. Within two years, however, events would prove Adams right.

IDENTIFY SUPPORTING DETAILS What made the Coercive Acts intolerable to the colonists?

ASSESSMENT

1. **Summarize** Describe the structure of the British government during the 1700s, and explain how these features were reflected in the colonies.
2. **Identify Central Issues** What arguments did the colonists make against taxation, and why did the British Parliament find these arguments difficult to understand?
3. **Summarize** What three tactics did colonists use to protest British taxes?
4. **Sequence Events** What events led to the Boston Tea Party?
5. **Summarize** What was the First Continental Congress, and what did it accomplish?
6. **Quest Connection** What was the justification for the Quartering Act? How did it relate to other British goals in their policy towards North America?

GO ONLINE to access these biographies: Samuel Adams and Crispus Attucks

Political Turmoil in Boston

Boston was at the center of political events in the years leading up to the American Revolution. Two contrasting views on the city's disorder were recorded by two very different women.

The first letter below was written by Anne Hulton, a British woman who accompanied her brother when he was sent to Boston as a tax officer. She wrote the letter to a friend at home in England after an attack on government officials by an angry mob.

The second letter comes from Abigail Adams, a committed opponent of British policies and wife of John Adams, a delegate to the Continental Congress. She wrote it just before the Boston Tea Party.

As you read, compare Adams' and Hulton's views of British rule and American resistance.

>> Many of Abigail Adams' letters have survived to the present day, giving historians a unique view into her life and experiences. Adams would go on to serve as the nation's second First Lady.

Primary Source 1

Letter from Anne Hulton to Elizabeth Lightbody, June 30, 1768

Dear Madam . . .
You will be surprised to hear how we were obliged to fly [escape] from the Place in six Days after [we arrived] and take Refuge on board the Romney Man of War lying in Boston Harbour. Mrs. Burch at whose house I was, had frequently been alarmed with the Sons of Liberty surrounding her house with the most hideous howlings . . . [and] many insults and outrages She has been exposed since her arrival, and threatened with greater voilences [violence]. She had had removed her most valuable Effects and held herself in readiness to depart at an hours notice . . .

These Sons of Voilence [Violence] after attacking Houses, breaking Window, beating, Stoning, and bruizing several Gentlemen belonging to the Customs [tax officials], the Collector mortally, and burning his boat, They consulted what was to be done next, and it was agreed to retire for the night, All was ended with a Speech from one of the Leaders, concluded thus, "We will defend our Liberties and property, by the Strength of our Arm and the help of our God, to your tents O Israel [go home]." This is a Specimen of the Sons of Liberty, of whom no doubt you have heard, and will hear more.

ANALYZE WORD CHOICE What does the leader of the Sons of Liberty say that is so threatening to Hulton?

The next Day the Commissioners [tax officials] had sufficient notice of their danger and the Plots against them, All their friends Advised em to retire to a more secure place, the Governor particularly telling em it was not in his power to protect em.

That evening Saturday We set off in a Barge under a Convoy of Man of War Boats with Marines, their bayonets fixed, to the Romney, a fifty Gun Ship of War, lying ready in the Harbour . . .

DRAW CONCLUSIONS How does Hulton get to the Romney? Does this show British strength or British weakness? Explain your answer.

Primary Source 2

Letter from Abigail Adams to Mercy Otis Warren, December 5, 1774

My Dear Mrs. Warren . . .
You Madam are so sincere a Lover of your Country, and so Hearty a mourner in all her misfortunes that it will greatly aggravate your anxiety to hear how much she is now oppressed and insulted. . . .

The Tea that bainfull [destructive] weed is arrived. Great and I hope Effectual opposition has been made to the landing of it. To the publick papers I must refer you for perticuliars. You will there find that the proceedings of our Citizens have been United, Spirited and firm. The flame is kindled and like Lightning it catches from Soul to Soul. Great will be the devastation if not timely quenched or allayed [relieved] by some more Lenient Measures.

Altho the mind is shocked at the Thought of shedding Humane Blood, more Especially the Blood of our Countrymen, and a civil War is of all Wars, the most dreadfull Such is the present Spirit that prevails, that if once they are made desperate Many, very Many of our Heroes will spend [give] their lives in the cause, With [a famous quote] in their Mouths, "What a pitty it is, that we can dye but once to save our Country. . . ."

CITE EVIDENCE How can you tell that Abigail Adams still considers herself British, sharing a nationality with the government's soldiers?

Such is the present Situation of affairs that I tremble when I think what may be the direfull concequences–and in this Town must the Scene of action lay. My Heart beats at every Whistle I hear, and I dare not openly express half my fears—Eternal Reproach and Ignominy be the portion of all those who have been instrumental in bringing these fears upon me. There was a Report prevaild that to morrow there will be an attempt to Land this weed of Slavery. I will then write further till then my worthy friend adieu.

USE CONTEXT CLUES What is the 'weed of slavery?' Why does Adams use that phrase to describe it?

ASSESSMENT

Be sure to cite specific evidence from the sources as you answer the following questions.

1. **Draw Inferences** Hulton says that the governor was unable to protect the commissioners. What does that reveal about the situation in Boston?
2. **Evaluate Arguments** What hostile phrase does Hulton use to mock the Sons of Liberty? Do you think her attitude is justified, given her experience?
3. **Predict** What does Adams believe is needed to stop the disorder? Do you think this is likely to be done?
4. **Compare and Contrast** How does Adams describe the "shedding of humane blood?" How is this different from the way Hulton describes violence against tax officials?
5. **Develop Empathy** How do you think Hulton would have reacted to Adams letter, had she seen it?

GO ONLINE to access primary sources

3.3

This painting depicts Benjamin Franklin, John Adams, and Thomas Jefferson working to draft the Declaration of Independence.

BOUNCE to Activate Flipped Video

Objectives

Explain why fighting broke out at Lexington and Concord and the response of the Second Continental Congress.

Describe the Loyalists' view of the Patriots.

Analyze the impact of Thomas Paine's *Common Sense.*

Assess why Congress declared independence, and the ideas underlying the Declaration of Independence.

Key Terms

Paul Revere
militia
minutemen
Loyalists
Second Continental Congress
Continental Army
Thomas Paine
republic
Declaration of Independence
Thomas Jefferson
natural rights

GO ONLINE to access your digital course

The Colonists Declare Independence

In 1776, the colonists of British America made three important decisions. First, they declared independence from Britain. Second, they chose a republican model for their new government. Third, they confederated the 13 states as the United States of America. These decisions were unprecedented and risky. The colonists gambled their lives and property but found a strength that surprised and changed the world.

The First Shots Are Fired

The dispute between the British government and the colonists had taken a drastic turn. Following the passage of the Coercive Acts, military commander General Thomas Gage had been named governor of Massachusetts. John Hancock, Samuel Adams, and other colonial leaders then convened a Provincial Congress to govern Massachusetts without Gage. They also began to stockpile arms and ammunition.

The Battles of Lexington and Concord On April 19, 1775, war erupted at Lexington and Concord, two country towns west of Boston. Gage provoked the battles by sending troops to arrest Hancock and Adams in Lexington and to seize Patriot weapons stockpiled in Concord.

Tipped off by Patriots, including **Paul Revere**, who had ridden into the countryside to warn of the approaching British troops, the local Patriots rallied to drive the troops back to Boston. The Patriot fighters were **militia**, full-time farmers and part-time soldiers.

By morning, about 70 Patriots had gathered on the Lexington Green. The British soldiers, called Redcoats, marched into town at dawn, and the British commander ordered the colonial militia to disperse. As they did, someone fired a shot. When the shooting stopped, eight Patriots were dead. The Redcoats marched on to Concord. What happened next stunned the British. Following a skirmish with Patriots in Concord, the British troops began their march back to Boston. However, hundreds of **minutemen**, or Patriot militia who responded quickly to calls for soldiers, lined the roads, firing at the British from behind trees and stone walls.

Stunned and exhausted, the British reached the safety of Boston in the late afternoon. The Patriots had killed or wounded more than 200 British soldiers, and the Patriots raced to take further action against the British. From throughout New England, thousands of Patriot militiamen rushed to confine the British troops in the city. Provincial assemblies of Patriots seized control of the New England colonies. **Loyalists**, or colonists who remained loyal to Britain, fled to take refuge in Boston. But would the rest of the colonies help New England fight the British?

The Second Continental Congress The answer came in May 1775, when delegates from all the colonies assembled in Philadelphia for the **Second Continental Congress**. To the relief of New Englanders, Congress assumed responsibility for the war. Armed volunteers from the Middle and Southern Colonies marched north to join the Patriot siege of Boston. Congress gave the command of the new **Continental Army** to George Washington. Washington had served as a colonial officer in the French and Indian War, and he came from Virginia, the largest and most powerful colony. New England needed Virginia's help to win the war.

Some radical members of the Continental Congress wanted to declare American independence from Britain, but they recognized that most of their constituents were not yet ready to do so. Most colonists still hoped to remain within the British Empire but without paying taxes to Parliament. In July 1775, after three months of bloodshed, Congress sent an "Olive Branch Petition" to King George III. The petition reaffirmed the colonists' allegiance to the king but not to Parliament. The king rejected the petition and sent more troops to Boston.

CHECK UNDERSTANDING How were the Battles of Lexington and Concord a turning point in relations between the colonies and Britain?

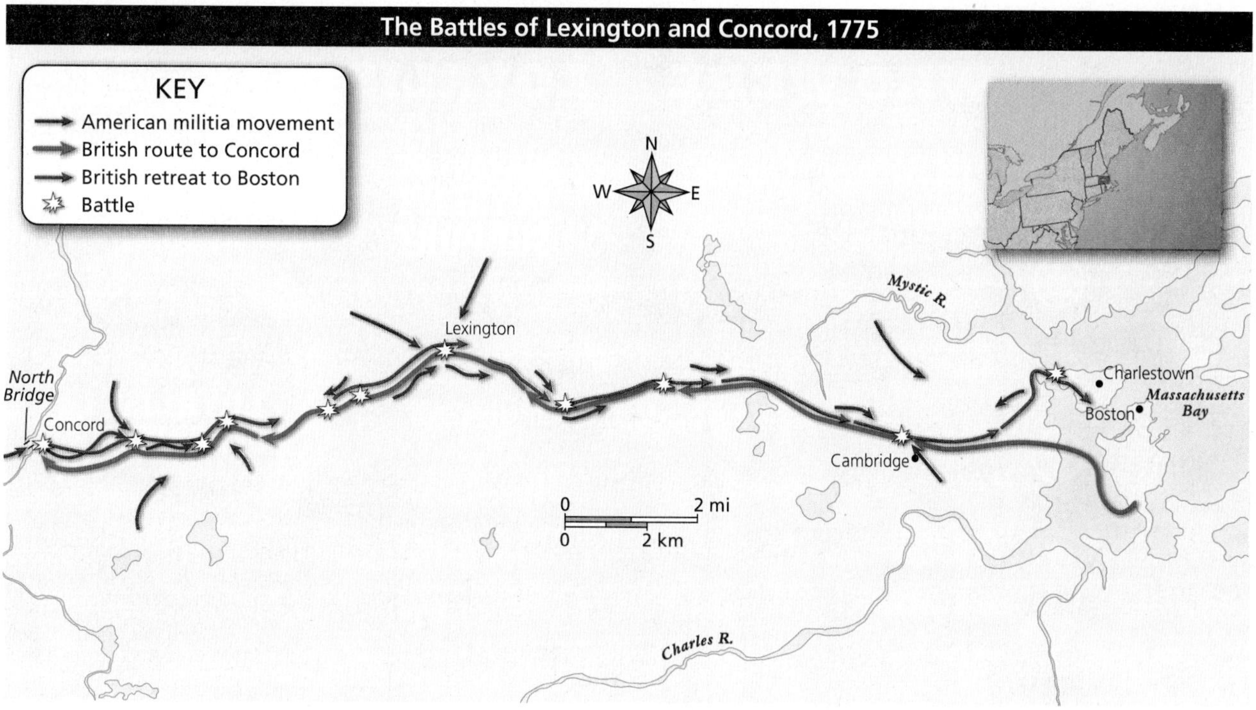

>> **Analyze Maps** Sequence the British troop movements in the series of conflicts shown on this map.

Colonists Disagree Over British Rule

Most colonists supported the Continental Congress and the boycott of British imports, but a large minority preferred British rule. These colonists became known as Loyalists. Champions of law and order, many Loyalists dreaded Patriot crowds and committees, viewing them as illegal and brutal. The conflicting viewpoints of the Loyalists and Patriots caused strife when it came to the idea of separating from Great Britain. Loyalists felt that the British throne would provide a more legitimate government than one that would result from any new and independent nation that could be developed by the Patriots. One Loyalist declared, "If I must be enslaved, let it be by a King at least, and not by a parcel of upstart, lawless committeemen. If I must be devoured, let me be devoured by the jaws of a lion, and not gnawed to death by rats and vermin."

Loyalists Fear Disorder Although many Loyalists opposed Britain's taxes, they felt that Parliament and the Crown must be obeyed as the legitimate government of the Empire. The Loyalists feared that the resistance would lead to a deadly and destructive war that Britain seemed certain to win. They doubted that the colonists could defeat an empire that had recently crushed the combined powers of France and Spain.

During the summer of 1774, two old friends and lawyers walked together to discuss the crisis: John Adams, a Patriot, and Jonathan Sewell, a Loyalist. During the conversation, Sewell warned Adams, "Great Britain is determined on her system. Her power is irresistible, and it will certainly be destructive to you, and all those who . . . persevere in opposition to her designs."

Adams boldly replied, "I know that Great Britain is determined in her system, and that . . . [has] determined me on mine. . . . Swim or sink, live or die, survive or perish with my country—that is my unalterable determination."

Loyalists Disagree with Patriots About a fifth of the colonists remained loyal, and many more wished to remain neutral. According to stereotype, Loyalists were wealthy elitists who sold out their fellow colonists to reap profitable offices in the British government. A few Loyalists did fit that description, but many more were ordinary farmers and artisans. Others belonged to cultural minorities who feared oppression by the Patriot majority.

Loyalists disliked the taxes, oaths of allegiance, and militia drafts demanded by the new Patriot authorities to support the Patriots' war. They also resented the Patriots for shutting down Loyalist newspapers and for punishing people who criticized the Patriots' actions. Loyalists concluded that the

>> **Analyze Information** How did the events of the war likely reshape the population distribution of the Americas?

Patriots demanded more in taxes and allowed less free speech than did the British.

Loyalism also appealed to American Indians and to enslaved people. American Indians wanted British help to keep out the settlers pressing westward. Because enslavers led the revolution in the Southern Colonies, the people they enslaved saw the British as the true champions of liberty. Thousands of enslaved people sought their freedom by running away to join the British forces.

IDENTIFY MAIN IDEAS What were some reasons Loyalists opposed the Patriots' cause?

The Decision to Declare Independence

In January 1776, a short but powerful book swung popular opinion in the colonies in favor of independence. Entitled *Common Sense*, the book was by **Thomas Paine**, a recent immigrant from England who had been both an artisan and a tax collector. In *Common Sense*, many Americans read what they longed to believe but had not known how to express. Similar ideas would soon appear in a declaration of the colonists' independence.

The Idea of a New Republic In simple but forceful and direct language, Paine proposed a radical course of action for the colonies: independence from Britain, republican state governments, and a union of the new states.

Paine denounced the king and aristocrats of Britain as frauds and parasites. He wanted the common people to elect all of their government, not just a third of it.

Paine depicted the king, rather than Parliament, as the greatest enemy of American liberty. He hated the rigid class structure of Britain for smothering the hopes of common people without a noble title or money. A **republic**, he argued, would provide opportunities to reward merit rather than inherited privilege. Freed from the empire, Americans could trade with the entire world.

By uniting to form a republic, Americans could establish a model that would inspire common people everywhere to reject kings and aristocrats. Paine concluded, "The cause of America is in a great measure the cause of all mankind." This view was new and powerful in 1776, when the revolution was a desperate gamble.

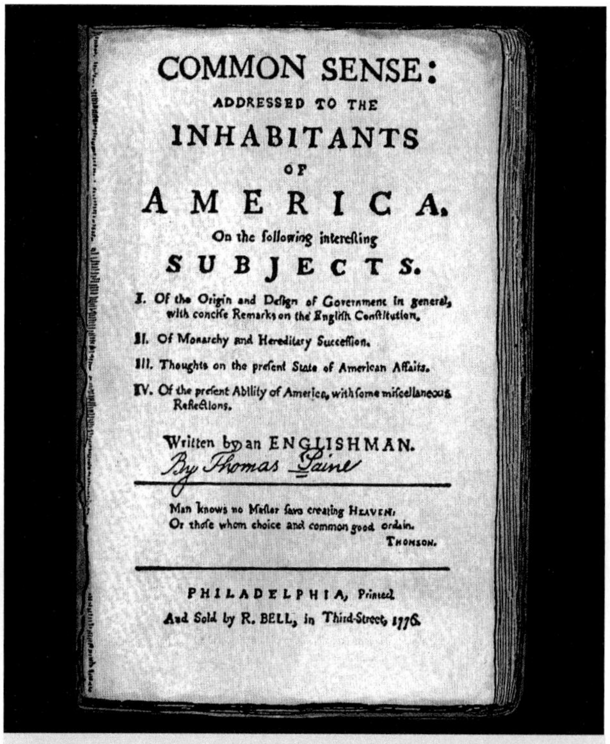
COMMON SENSE:
ADDRESSED TO THE
INHABITANTS
OF
AMERICA,
On the following interesting
SUBJECTS.
I. Of the Origin and Design of Government in general, with concise Remarks on the English Constitution.
II. Of Monarchy and Hereditary Succession.
III. Thoughts on the present State of American Affairs.
IV. Of the present Ability of America, with some miscellaneous Reflections.
Written by an ENGLISHMAN.
By Thomas Paine
Man knows no Master save creating HEAVEN,
Or those whom choice and common good ordain.
THOMSON.
PHILADELPHIA, Printed,
And Sold by R. BELL, in Third-Street, 1776.

>> *Common Sense*, written by Thomas Paine in 1776, had a profound influence on the American Revolution.

BOUNCE to Activate Gallery

A Declaration of Independence By the spring of 1776, Paine's ideas had built momentum for American independence. Noting the shift in public opinion, Congress selected a committee to draft a document declaring American independence and explaining the reasons for it. On July 2, Congress voted that America was free. Two days later, they approved the **Declaration of Independence**.

Drafted by **Thomas Jefferson**, the Declaration drew upon Paine's ideas to denounce the king as a tyrant who made American independence necessary. Although primarily a long list of colonial grievances, the Declaration also advanced the bold idea that "all men are created equal." Congress embraced the Enlightenment ideas that all men are born with **natural rights** that cannot be taken away by a government. Jefferson called them "unalienable rights."

This sweeping statement was far ahead of the social and economic reality in the new United States. For example, the phrase "all men are created equal" was not generally seen as including woman. And many of the signers of the Declaration forced enslaved people to work on their farms and plantations. But the idea of equality would inspire future generations of Americans, including women and enslaved people, to make a better, more equal society.

Declaring independence on paper was one thing. Achieving it was another. The colonists faced many challenges before they could become an independent nation. No colony in the Americas had yet won independence from a European empire. Fighting the British for independence would pit the poorly organized colonists against the greatest military power on Earth.

IDENTIFY CENTRAL IDEAS How did the Declaration of Independence draw on Enlightenment ideas to argue for colonial independence?

ASSESSMENT

1. **Describe** What important decisions were made by the colonists in 1776?
2. **Sequence Events** What Patriot actions provoked the Battles of Lexington and Concord?
3. **Compare and Contrast** How were the perspectives of Patriots and Loyalists different?
4. **Generate Explanations** Why did Thomas Paine encourage the development of a republic in the colonies?
5. **Cite Evidence** How did Enlightenment ideas influence the Declaration of Independence?
6. **Connections to Today** In the 1770s, Americans were deeply divided between Patriots and Loyalists. What are the country's deepest divisions today? How do they compare with divisions during this period?

GO ONLINE to access these biographies: George Washington and Thomas Jefferson

Primary Sources

Declaration of Independence

Introduction

By signing the Declaration of Independence, members of the Continental Congress sent a clear message to Britain that the American colonies were free and independent states. Starting with its preamble, the document spells out all the reasons the people of the United States have the right to break away from Britain.

>> Presenting the Declaration of Independence.

Primary Source

When in the Course of human events, it becomes necessary for one people to dissolve the political bands which have connected them with another, and to assume among the powers of the earth, the separate and equal station to which the Laws of Nature and of Nature's God entitle them, a decent respect to the opinions of mankind requires that they should declare the causes which impel [force] them to the separation.

We hold these truths to be self-evident, that all men are created equal, that they are endowed [gifted] by their Creator with certain unalienable [cannot be taken away] Rights, that among these are Life, Liberty and the pursuit of Happiness. That to secure these rights, Governments are instituted among Men, deriving their just powers from the consent of the governed. That whenever any Form of Government becomes destructive of these ends, it is the Right of the People to alter or to abolish it, and to institute new Government, laying its foundation on such principles and organizing its powers in such form, as to them shall seem most likely to effect their Safety and Happiness. Prudence [cautiousness], indeed, will dictate that Governments long established should not be changed for light and transient causes; and accordingly all experience hath shown that mankind are more disposed to suffer, while evils are sufferable, than to right themselves by abolishing the forms to which they are accustomed. But when a long train of abuses and usurpations [unjust uses of power], pursuing invariably the same Object evinces a design to reduce them under absolute Despotism [rule of absolute power], it is their right, it is their duty, to throw off such Government, and to provide new Guards for their future security. Such has been the patient sufferance of these Colonies; and such is now the necessity which constrains them to alter their former Systems of Government. The history of the present King of Great Britain is a history of repeated injuries and usurpations, all having in direct object the establishment of an absolute Tyranny over these States. To prove this, let Facts be submitted to a candid world.

He has refused his Assent to Laws, the most wholesome and necessary for the public good. He has forbidden his Governors to pass Laws of immediate and pressing importance, unless suspended in their operation till his Assent should be obtained; and when so suspended, he has utterly neglected to attend to them. He has refused to pass other Laws for the accommodation of large districts of people, unless those people would relinquish [give up] the right of Representation in the Legislature, a right inestimable [priceless] to them and formidable to tyrants only. He has called together legislative bodies at places unusual, uncomfortable, and distant from the depository of their public Records, for the sole purpose of fatiguing them into compliance with his measures. He has dissolved Representative Houses repeatedly, for opposing with manly firmness his invasions on the rights of the people. He has refused for a long time, after such dissolutions [closing down], to cause others to be elected; whereby the Legislative powers, incapable of Annihilation, have returned to the People at large for their exercise; the State remaining in the mean time exposed to all the dangers of invasion from without, and convulsions [riots] within.

He has kept among us, in times of peace, Standing Armies without the Consent of our legislatures. He has affected to render the Military independent of and superior to the Civil power. He has combined with others to subject us to a jurisdiction foreign to our constitution, and unacknowledged by our laws; giving his Assent to their Acts of pretended Legislation: For quartering [lodging] large bodies of armed troops among us: For protecting them, by a mock Trial, from punishment for any Murders which they should commit on the Inhabitants of these States: For cutting off our Trade with all parts of the world: For imposing Taxes on us without our Consent: For depriving us in many cases, of the benefits of Trial by Jury: For transporting us beyond Seas to be tried for pretended offences: For abolishing the free System of English Laws in a neighbouring Province, establishing therein an Arbitrary government, and enlarging its Boundaries so as to render it at once an example and fit instrument for introducing the same absolute rule into these Colonies:

. . . He has kept among us, etc. He has abdicated Government here, by declaring us out of his Protection and waging War against us. He has plundered our seas, ravaged our Coasts, burnt our towns, and destroyed the lives of our people . . .

In every stage of these Oppressions We have Petitioned for Redress [correction of wrongs] in the most humble terms: Our repeated Petitions have been answered only by repeated injury. A Prince, whose character is thus marked by every act which may define a Tyrant, is unfit to be the ruler of a free people.

Nor have We been wanting in attentions to our British brethren. We have warned them from time to time of attempts by their legislature to extend an unwarrantable jurisdiction over us. We have reminded them of the circumstances of our emigration and settlement here. We have appealed to their native justice and magnanimity [generosity], and we have conjured [begged] them by the ties of our common kindred, to disavow these usurpations, which would inevitably interrupt our connections and correspondence. They too have been deaf to the voice of justice and of consanguinity [relation by blood]. We must, therefore, acquiesce in the necessity, which denounces our Separation, and hold them, as we hold the rest of mankind, Enemies in War, in Peace Friends.

We, therefore, the Representatives of the United States of America, in General Congress, Assembled, appealing to the Supreme Judge of the world for the rectitude [justness] of our intentions, do, in the Name, and by Authority of the good People of these Colonies, solemnly publish and declare, That these United Colonies are, and of Right ought to be Free and Independent States; that they are Absolved from all Allegiance to the British Crown, and that all political connection between them and the State of Great Britain, is and ought to be totally dissolved; and that as Free and Independent States, they have full Power to levy War, conclude Peace, contract Alliances, establish Commerce, and to do all other Acts and Things which Independent States may of right do. And for the support of this Declaration, with a firm reliance on the protection of Divine Providence, we mutually pledge to each other our Lives, our Fortunes and our sacred Honor.

ASSESSMENT

1. **Identify Cause and Effect** How might the ideas about equality expressed in the Declaration of Independence have influenced later historical movements, such as the abolitionist movement and the women's suffrage movement?

2. **Identify Key Steps in a Process** Why was the Declaration of Independence a necessary document for the founding of the new nation?

3. **Draw Inferences** English philosopher John Locke wrote that government should protect "life, liberty, and estate." How do you think Locke's writing influenced ideas about government put forth in the Declaration of Independence?

4. **Analyze Structure** How does the declaration organize its key points from beginning to end?

GO ONLINE to access primary sources

3.4

On Christmas night, 1776, Washington and his troops crossed the icy Delaware River to attack British forces at Trenton. Despite enduring the harshest conditions, Washington's forces were victorious.

Americans Win the Revolution

BOUNCE to Activate Flipped Video

Objectives

Explain the advantages the British held at the start of the war and the mistakes they made by underestimating the Patriots.

Describe the war in the Middle States and along the frontier.

Assess why the British failed to win the war in the South.

Describe how the British were finally defeated and the terms of the Peace Treaty.

Analyze how the Revolution affected Americans and people worldwide.

Key Terms

William Howe
mercenary
Battle of Trenton
Charles Cornwallis
Battle of Princeton
Saratoga
Marquis de Lafayette
Benjamin Franklin
Valley Forge
Monmouth
Kings Mountain
Yorktown
Treaty of Paris
manumission

To make their independence a reality, the Patriots had to win a hard and bloody war against the world's most powerful empire. Britain's population was nearly four times larger than the 2.5 million people in the colonies. At least a fifth of the colonists were Loyalists. Another fifth were enslaved people, who were likely to join the British to escape their condition. Many others remained neutral for as long as possible.

The War Begins

At the beginning of the war, Britain seemed to have great advantages. A leader in manufacturing, Britain produced more ships and weapons than the colonists did. The British also had an established government, while the Americans were starting from scratch. Meanwhile, the Continental Congress struggled to pay for the war. Lacking the authority to collect taxes, Congress and the states printed paper money to pay their debts, producing inflation that damaged the economy. The Continental soldiers suffered from hunger and cold, while the British troops were well trained and had plenty of supplies. The odds seemed slight that the Patriots could win.

The British Underestimate Patriot Resistance In 1775, the British did not take the Patriots seriously as an enemy. Two months after the defeat at Concord, they repeated their mistake at the Battle of Bunker Hill. By fortifying hills overlooking Boston, the Patriots hoped to drive the British from that seaport. To retake the hills, the new British commander, Lord **William Howe**, ordered a frontal assault by soldiers in the middle of the day. Carrying heavy packs and wearing red uniforms, his men marched uphill

GO ONLINE to access your digital course

>> The Battle of Bunker Hill in Charlestown on June 17, 1775, was the first major battle of the American Revolution. Although the British won, the battle gave courage to the Patriots to face British troops.

>> In their fight against the Patriots, the British employed German professional soldiers called Hessians, shown here in distinctive helmets.

BOUNCE to Activate Chart

straight into a murderous fire from entrenched Patriots. Why did Howe put his soldiers in such a dangerous position?

Howe wanted to win the battle despite giving the Patriots every advantage. That would prove, in another general's words, "that trained troops are invincible against any numbers or any position of untrained rabble." Instead of proving Howe's point, the British suffered a bloodbath as two charges failed. A third charge captured the hills only because the Patriots ran out of ammunition. Technically, the British had won the battle, but they suffered more than twice the Patriot casualties. The Patriots had won a psychological victory.

In January 1776, six months after the Battle of Bunker Hill, Colonel Henry Knox arrived with cannons to reinforce the Patriots outside Boston. His men had hauled the cannons hundreds of miles from upstate New York, where Ethan Allen's militia men had captured them from Fort Ticonderoga. With Patriot cannons shelling both Boston and the British ships in the harbor, the British abandoned the city in March.

A Flawed Strategy Lord Howe continued to pursue a misguided strategy. The British thought that they were fighting a traditional European war. They believed that the Patriots would surrender if Howe could defeat the Continental Army and capture the major seaports, including Philadelphia, the Patriot capital. In fact, the British accomplished these goals but still lost the war.

The British never fully understood that they were fighting a different type of war, a revolutionary war. The Patriots understood that it was a struggle to win the hearts and minds of the civilian population. Instead of surrendering after setbacks, the Patriots kept on fighting.

Thomas Paine wrote an inspiring series of essays, *The American Crisis*, which George Washington read to encourage his troops. Meanwhile, the British further angered colonists when they hired German **mercenaries**, or soldiers who fought for hire. These "Hessians," as they were called, had a particularly brutal reputation.

The Patriots' Strengths Patriot persistence owed much to Washington's leadership. He realized that to preserve his Continental Army from destruction, he could not risk all on a major battle under unfavorable conditions. Outnumbered and often outmaneuvered, Washington lost most of the battles, but his skillful retreats saved his army to fight another day. By preserving and inspiring his soldiers, Washington sustained them through incredible hardships.

His small but committed army hung together despite the casualties and the soldiers' hunger and ragged clothing.

By preoccupying the British army, Washington's Continental Army freed local militias to suppress Loyalists in the countryside.

Civilian Support Proves Invaluable To succeed, the Continental Army needed aid and support from the civilian population. Throughout the war, women's work was crucial. Women freed their husbands and sons for military service by running farms and shops. They also made clothing, blankets, and shoes for the soldiers. Without these contributions, the Patriots could not have sustained their army.

However, the British navy also blockaded the ports, making many items scarce and expensive. A few colonists took advantage of the shortages by profiteering, or selling in-demand items at a very high price. Furthermore, the Patriots caused inflation by issuing paper money. As a result, the value of money decreased. If farmers sold their crops to the Patriots, they would be paid in "Continentals," paper money issued by the Continental Congress. It would be worth nothing if the Patriots lost. The British army, however, paid for their food in gold.

During the war, some women followed their husbands into the army. They received rations for maintaining the camps and washing clothing. A few women even helped fire cannons or served as soldiers by masquerading as men. For her service, Deborah Sampson later won a military pension from Congress. Another story says that Mary Hays became known as Molly Pitcher for delivering water to troops during the battle at Monmouth. Legend says that she even stepped in and took her husband's place at the cannon.

☑ **DESCRIBE** Identify the strengths of the Patriots.

The War in the Middle States and Frontier

After the British left Boston in early 1776, they decided to attack New York City and cut off New England from the rest of the colonies. After winning a series of battles, Howe captured the city on September 15. About 30,000 British and German troops nearly crushed the poorly trained Continentals. Forced to retreat across New Jersey, Washington saved his army and the Revolution by counterattacking on December 26. Crossing the Delaware River in the middle of Christmas night,

>> American women contributed to the war effort by managing farms and households while men were away fighting. Some women even served on the battlefield.

>> This 1779 woodcut shows a female Continental soldier.

he surprised a garrison of more than 1,000 German mercenaries at the **Battle of Trenton**. This modest victory raised the spirits of the troops and of Patriot supporters at a critical moment.

The Patriots See Military Success Washington began 1777 with another victory. Again moving his troops in the night, Washington inflicted heavy casualties on General **Charles Cornwallis**'s troops at the **Battle of Princeton**. During the remainder of 1777, however, Washington suffered more defeats. In the fall, he lost Philadelphia to Howe's army.

Led by General John Burgoyne, another British army marched from Canada to invade New York's Hudson Valley. Falling into a Patriot trap at **Saratoga**, Burgoyne surrendered in October. The greatest Patriot victory yet, Saratoga suggested that the United States might just win the war.

Allies Assist the Patriots' Cause The victory at Saratoga took on greater importance because it encouraged France to recognize American independence and to enter the war. France welcomed the opportunity to weaken an old enemy, Britain. During the early years of the war, however, the French had doubted that the Patriots could win. Unwilling to risk an open alliance, they had limited their assistance to secret shipments of arms and ammunition. But that covert aid kept the Patriot army alive and fighting. Some French volunteers, including the aristocrat and Patriot general **Marquis de Lafayette** also provided military expertise.

>> Baron Von Steuben drilled soldiers at Valley Forge during the winter of 1777 and 1778.

After Saratoga, the French risked an open alliance with the United States. Negotiated in February 1778, the alliance reflected the diplomatic genius of **Benjamin Franklin**, the leading American negotiator in Paris. A cunning gentleman, Franklin became popular in France by presenting himself in public as a simple American who loved the French. As the French army and navy began attacking the British, the war became more equal. Although the first joint operations failed miserably, the alliance would produce the biggest victory of the war in 1781.

The British suffered another blow in 1779 when Spain entered the war as a French ally. The Spanish also wanted to weaken the British, but they feared that American independence would inspire their own colonists to rebel against Spanish rule.

Spain was not an official American ally, but the Spanish governor of Louisiana, Bernando de Gálvez, provided money and supplies to the Patriots and prevented British ships from entering the Mississippi River at New Orleans.

The Continental Army Faces Struggles Back in Pennsylvania, Washington's army spent the harsh and hungry winter of 1777 to 1778 at **Valley Forge** outside of Philadelphia. The soldiers suffered from a lack of supplies and food. Washington reported to Congress that nearly a third of his 10,000 soldiers had no coats or shoes.

> Unless some great . . . change suddenly takes place . . . this Army must inevitably be reduced to one or other of these three things. Starve, dissolve, or disperse in order to obtain subsistence in the best manner they can.
>
> —George Washington, Valley Forge, December 23, 1777

Despite their hardships, the soldiers improved from careful drilling supervised by a German volunteer, Baron Von Steuben, who had come to help the Patriots. In June 1778, the British evacuated Philadelphia, retreating across New Jersey to New York City. On the way, they fought off Washington's pursuit at **Monmouth**, New Jersey. The Continental soldiers demonstrated their improved discipline under fire.

Key Battles of the American Revolution

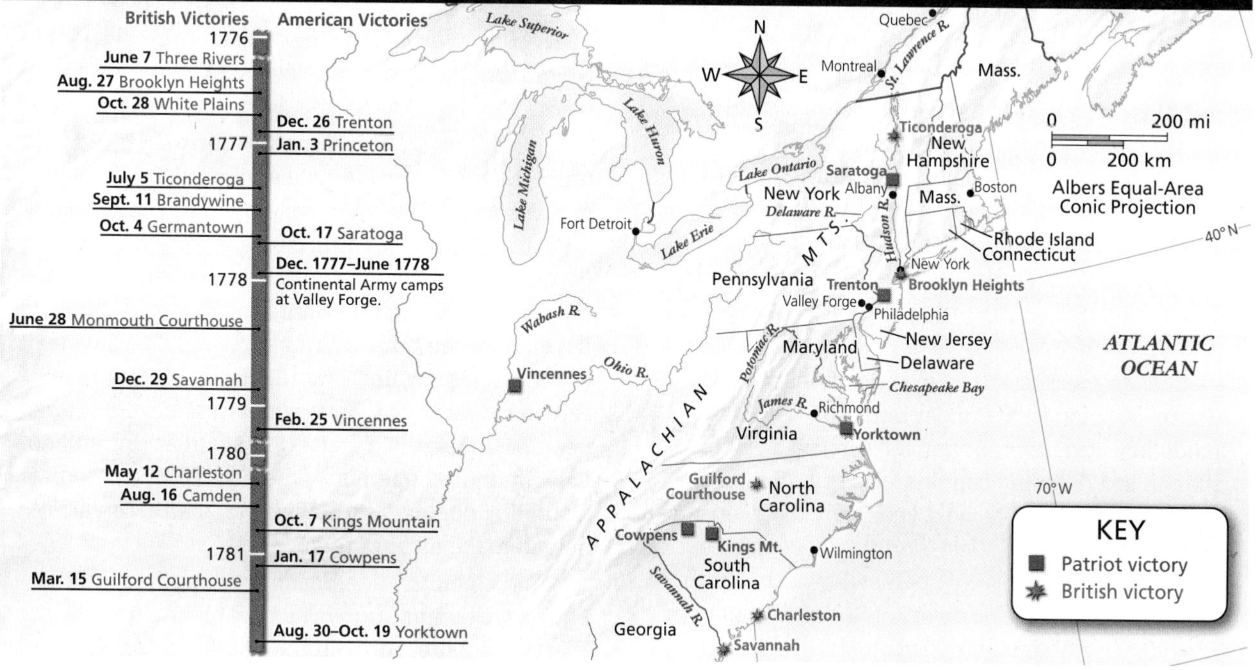

>> **Analyze Maps** In which region did most key battles take place? What geographic factors explain help explain this?

BOUNCE to Activate Timeline

Despite having won most of the battles, the British had little to show for it beyond their headquarters in New York City. Despairing of winning in the North, the British turned their attention elsewhere.

The Frontier War Defying the Proclamation of 1763, colonists had begun to settle west of the Appalachian Mountains in the early 1770s. The outbreak of war between the colonists and the British escalated the frequent skirmishes between settlers and American Indians, leading the settlers to claim more Indian lands.

The frontier war was especially destructive. Most American Indians sided with the British, who had promised to keep the colonists in the east. With British urging, American Indians increased attacks on colonial settlements in 1777. Meanwhile, white settlers increasingly attacked and killed neutral American Indians or disregarded truces, beginning a cycle of revenge that continued for years.

The War in the West In the Northwest, Colonel George Rogers Clark led the Patriot militia in the fight against the British. They took the settlements of Kaskaskia and Cahokia in the spring of 1778. By late summer, Clark's 175 soldiers and their French settler allies had captured all the British posts in the areas that would become Indiana and Illinois.

The British and their American Indian allies responded a few months later, recapturing a fort at Vincennes, Indiana. Clark's men—all unpaid volunteers—quickly rallied, marching from their winter quarters on the shores of the Mississippi River. In late February 1779, they reached Vincennes and convinced many American Indians to abandon their British allies, allowing the Patriots to recover the fort. At war's end, the Patriot outposts allowed Americans to lay claim to the Ohio River valley.

Meanwhile, in upstate New York, American Indian and British forces attacked several frontier outposts in 1779. In return, Patriot troops burned 40 Iroquois towns, destroying the power of the Iroquois Federation. But the American Indians continued to attack settlers with deadly effect, forcing many of them to return east.

CHECK UNDERSTANDING Why was the Battle of Saratoga a turning point in the American Revolution?

The War in the South

As the war continued, the British expected Loyalist support in the South, especially among the farmers of North Carolina, South Carolina, and Georgia. But the British wasted this support by continuing their misguided strategy. Instead of supporting Loyalist militias, the British continued to wage a conventional war.

Initial British Victories In the South, as in the North, the British won most of the battles and captured the leading seaports. In late 1778, they seized Savannah, Georgia. During the spring of 1780, they captured Charleston, South Carolina—along with 5,000 Patriot soldiers. That summer, the British crushed another Patriot army at Camden, South Carolina.

Just as the British began their offensive in the South, Spanish forces under Bernardo de Gálvez made key attacks on British forts in the Gulf Coast region. In 1780, they captured the British fort at Mobile, Alabama. The next year, they took Pensacola, the capital of British West Florida. These moves were intended to solidify Spanish power in North America, but they also diverted British troops from the offensive against the Patriots.

The Patriot Cause Gains Support Despite winning major battles, the British failed to control the southern countryside, where the Revolution became a brutal civil war between Patriot and Loyalist militias. Both sides plundered and killed civilians. A German officer in the British service observed, "This country is the scene of the most cruel events. Neighbors are on opposite sides, children are against their fathers."

In October 1780, at **Kings Mountain** in South Carolina, the Patriots crushed a Loyalist militia and executed many of the prisoners. As the Loyalists lost men and territory, neutral civilians swung over to the Patriot side. They increasingly blamed the British troops for bringing chaos into their lives. A disgusted Loyalist explained to a British officer, "The lower sort of People, who were . . . originally attached to the British Government, have suffered so severely, [and] been so frequently deceived, that Great Britain has now a hundred enemies, where it had one before." Instead of destroying the Patriots, the British army helped make more of them.

As the countryside became sympathetic to the Patriots, General Cornwallis became frustrated. The Continental Army in the South was small, but it was led by two superb new commanders, Nathanael Greene and Daniel Morgan. In early 1781, the Continental Army inflicted heavy losses on the British at the battles of Cowpens in South Carolina and Guilford Courthouse in North Carolina. Thwarted in his attempts to take the Carolinas, Cornwallis marched north into Virginia. He was leading his troops directly into a trap.

>> The Continental Army halted Lord Cornwallis' advance into North Carolina in the Battle of Cowpens on January 17, 1781. **Hypothesize** What effect did victories such as the Battle of Cowpens have on Patriot soldiers?

☑ **IDENTIFY SUPPORTING DETAILS** Identify reasons why the British fared so poorly in the South.

The War Comes to a Conclusion

Although it seemed unlikely at the start, the Patriots ultimately won the war. Four main factors contributed to their success. First, the British made tactical mistakes because they initially underestimated the Patriots. Second, the British misunderstood the political nature of the conflict. Third, the Patriots were highly motivated and benefited from Washington's shrewd leadership. Fourth, the Patriots received critical assistance from France.

The Surrender at Yorktown During the late summer of 1781, Washington boldly and rapidly marched most of his troops south. He planned to trap Cornwallis's army at **Yorktown**, Virginia. For the plan to work, however, Washington needed a French fleet to arrive at the right moment to prevent the British navy from evacuating their army by sea.

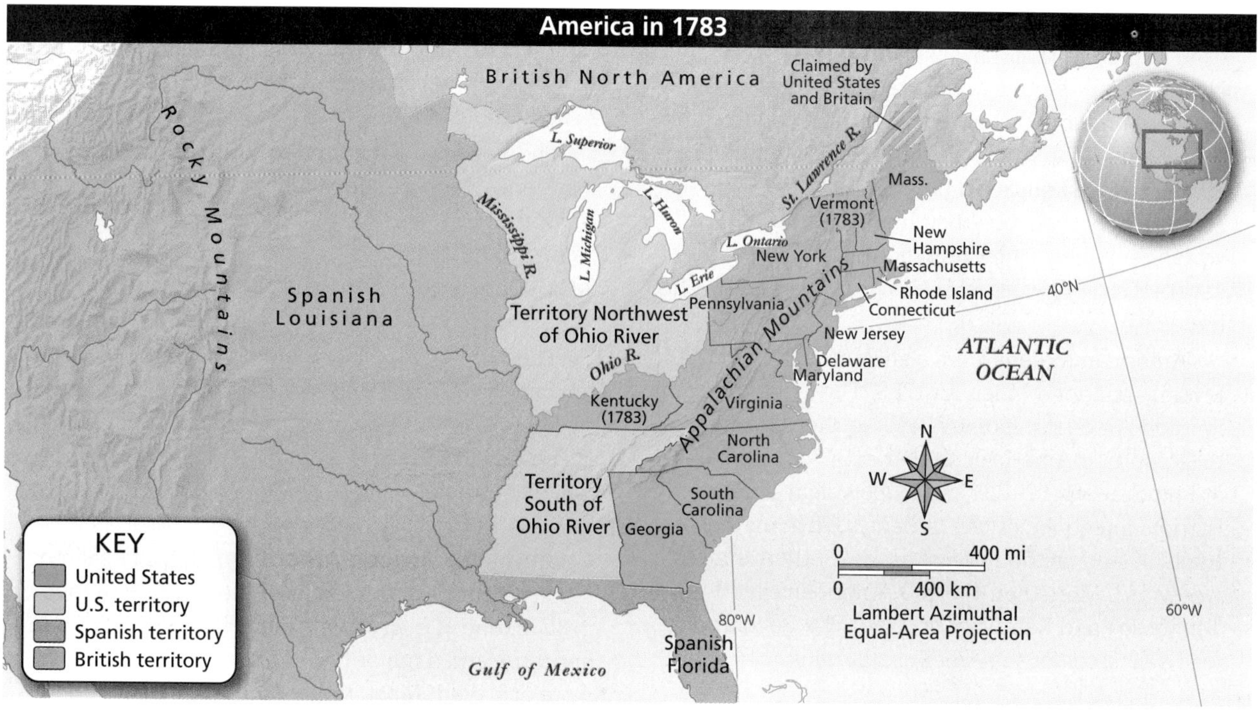

>> This map shows the United States after the Treaty of Paris. **Analyze Maps** Why might the Spanish have been upset about the new borders?

BOUNCE to Activate Map

Although Washington thought that a French fleet was on its way, he could not be certain when it would arrive.

The French fleet appeared at just the right moment to block the mouth of the Chesapeake Bay, trapping the British navy. Given the lack of efficient long-distance communication, this coordination was an incredible stroke of luck for the Patriots. Trapped by land and by sea, Cornwallis surrendered his army of 8,000 at Yorktown on October 19, 1781. The French had made the critical difference. At Yorktown, their soldiers and sailors outnumbered Washington's Americans.

The Treaty of Paris The loss of 8,000 soldiers was a crushing blow to the British war effort. After seven years of fighting, the British public was fed up with the casualties and the heavy taxes to pay for the war. In early 1782, a new administration came to power, determined to make peace. An American delegation, including Benjamin Franklin and John Adams, negotiated a favorable treaty with the British. In 1783, the **Treaty of Paris** recognized American independence and granted generous boundaries to the United States. At the negotiating table, Franklin secured far more territory than the Patriots had won in the war.

By making a separate peace with the British, the Americans strained their alliance with the French, who had expected to control the negotiations. France and Spain each negotiated their own treaties with Britain.

RECALL How did the Revolutionary War come to an end?

The Impact of the Revolution

By eighteenth-century standards, the American Revolution was very radical. For the first time, overseas colonies of a European empire had escaped control of their mother country to create a republican union—something long dismissed as a dangerous fantasy. By defying the conventional wisdom of their time, the Patriots began an enormous experiment aimed at creating a more open and equal society.

The Patriots promised liberty and opportunity, but some Americans won more than others. The greatest winners were Patriot men of at least modest prosperity. They secured political rights and the economic benefits of western expansion. The losers were Loyalists and American Indians who had sided with the British.

The Consequences for British Allies The British tried to protect their Loyalist allies by setting conditions in the treaty, but state laws and mob violence prevented most Loyalists from returning to their homes after the war. About 90,000—including 20,000 formerly enslaved people—became refugees. About half of them resettled in what is now Canada, which remained under British rule. Many who had escaped slavery were re-enslaved in the British West Indies.

American Indians were also stunned when the British abandoned them in 1783. The Treaty of Paris ignored American Indians, leaving them vulnerable to expanding American settlements. In treaties at Fort Stanwix in 1784 and Hopewell in 1785, the Patriots forced American Indians to give up massive tracts of land as the price of peace. Settlers surged westward. More than 100,000 Americans lived in Tennessee and Kentucky by 1790. The Revolution was a disaster for the American Indians.

Women's Public Voices Grow Stronger Women gained few political or legal rights as a result of the war, but they won respect based on the new conception of women as "republican mothers." Abigail Adams and Judith Sargent Murray noted that the Republic needed virtuous citizens, who learned their virtue from their mothers. This invited women to speak out on issues that affected their ability to raise virtuous children.

The Revolution inspired some women to seek a larger voice in public affairs. In a famous letter of 1776, Abigail Adams asked her husband, John, to "remember the Ladies" in drafting the new nation's laws. Although John Adams respected his wife, he dismissed her request.

The law reserved legal and political rights to husbands. Widows could vote in New Jersey but nowhere else. As was the norm in most of Europe at the time, wives could not own property or make contracts.

>> The American Revolution inspired American women like Judith Sargent Murray, shown in this portrait, to campaign for women's rights.

Changes for African Americans Slavery seemed inconsistent with the ideals of the Revolution, but in 1776, one of every five Americans was of African ancestry, and a majority of African Americans were enslaved. Most white Americans—including some Patriot leaders—accepted slavery as natural. British and Loyalist critics mocked Patriots, such as Washington and Jefferson, as hypocrites who spoke of liberty while practicing slavery. In 1778, the Patriot governor of New Jersey confessed that slavery was "utterly inconsistent with the principles of Christianity and humanity; and in Americans, who have idolized liberty, peculiarly odious and disgraceful."

The Revolution inspired many enslaved people to demand freedom. In the northern states, some petitioned legislatures for emancipation and sued their enslavers in the courts. About 5,000 African Americans joined Patriot militias, the Continental Army, or the small Continental Navy in return for a promise of freedom. However, the southern states feared armed Black troops as a threat to the slavery so at least 50,000 enslaved people escaped from the South to join the British.

The Revolution led to emancipation in the North, where slavery was not critical to the economy and enslaved people numbered only 5 percent of the population. While laws eventually banned slavery in the northern states, many northern enslavers sold people to the South before they could become free.

Emancipation failed in the South, where enslaved people amounted to about one third of the population and were essential to the plantation economy. In Maryland and Virginia, some planters voluntarily freed the enslaved people on their estates, a practice known as **manumission**. After 1800, however, southern states passed laws to discourage further manumissions.

After the American Revolution: New Revolutions Begin

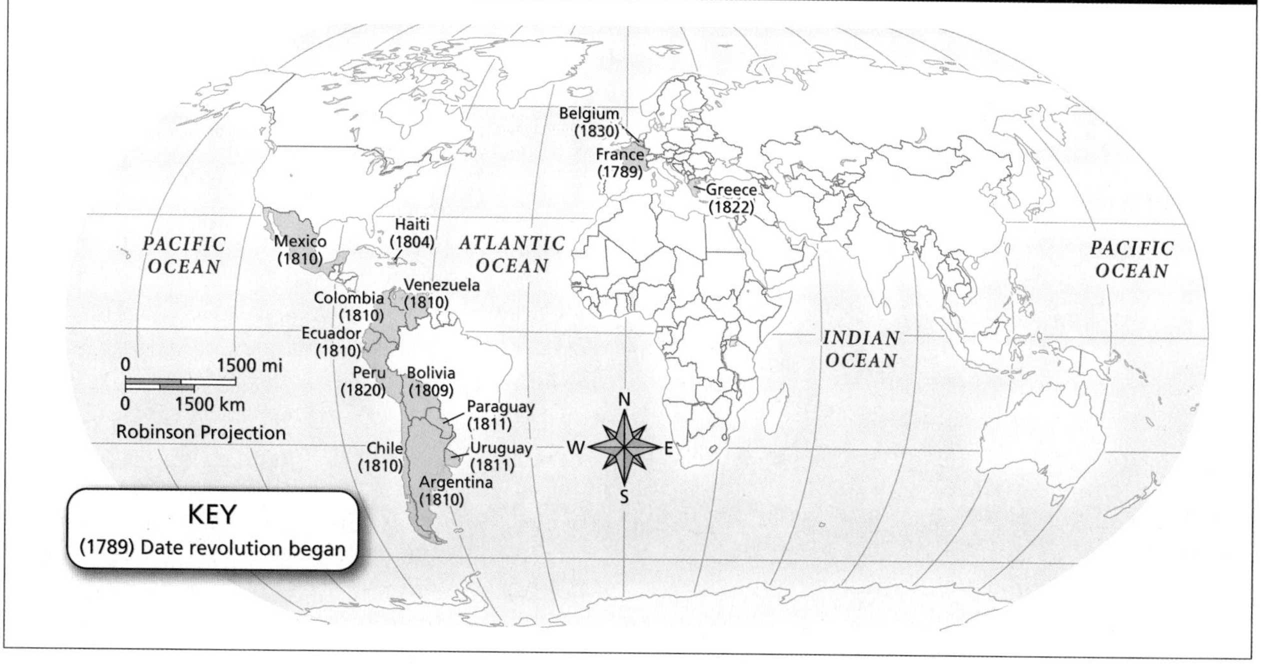

>> **Analyze Maps** Describe the spread of revolutionary movements worldwide during the late 1700s and early 1800s.

Southern whites feared that formerly enslaved people would seek revenge for past treatment. However, by 1810, about 20,000 southern enslaved African Americans had been freed.

Revolutionary Ideas Spread Perhaps the greatest effect of the Revolution was to spread the idea of liberty, both at home and abroad. The statement that "all men are created equal" was radical when Jefferson drafted the Declaration of Independence. Although Jefferson probably intended his statement to apply to white men, African Americans and women repeated those words to claim their rights.

Over the next three centuries, the Patriots' principles inspired revolutions around the world. Beginning with the French Revolution in 1789, European republicans cited the American precedent to overthrow kings and aristocrats. In the nineteenth century, independent republics emerged throughout Latin America. As Thomas Paine had predicted, the American Revolution changed the world.

DESCRIBE What impact did the Revolutionary War have on women?

GO ONLINE to access these biographies: Abigail Adams and Benjamin Franklin

ASSESSMENT

1. **Generate Explanations** How did the outcome of the Battle of Bunker Hill foreshadow the course of the Revolutionary War?
2. **Summarize** What role did Benjamin Franklin play during the Revolutionary War, and how was it important?
3. **Summarize** Why did the American Indians choose to ally themselves with the British, and what was the result of this alliance?
4. **Cite Evidence** Why might the American Revolution in the South be considered a civil war?
5. **Identify Central Issues** What effect did the Revolutionary War have on slavery in the new United States?
6. **Connections to Today** Many governments in the modern world have been in the same position as the British during the Revolutionary War, struggling to fight rebels who survive defeat after defeat because of civilian support. How can modern technologies help governments trying to fight rebels? How can they help rebel groups?

Connections to Today

A 2019 pro-democracy protest Hong Kong

Take Action to Inform People About Modern Protest Movements

Protests are part of political struggles around the world today. While some movements in recent years have been successful, forcing policy changes or overthrowing authoritarian governments, others have been brutally crushed. Many achieve mixed success.

1. **Choose** one of the following topics:
   - **Motivations:** Identify the goals of a recent protest movement.
   - **Strategies:** Investigate a recent protest movement and identify the key tactics used by its participants.
   - **Government responses:** Compare government responses to recent protests in one authoritarian country and one democratic country.
   - **Results:** Evaluate the effects of a recent protest movement.
2. **Ask Questions** Generate a list of questions you have about the topic.
3. **Learn** about the topic and major issues related to it. Take notes as you conduct your research and continue to generate questions as you learn more.
4. **Letter to the Editor** Write a letter to the editor of a local paper either supporting or critiquing a recent protest movement you studied. Explain why you agree or disagree with protesters' actions, goals, or tactics. Be sure to include evidence to support your views.

GO ONLINE to www.SavvasRealize.com and access your digital course

Use the texts, quizzes, interactivities, Quest Inquiries, Flipped Videos, and other resources from this Topic to prepare for the Topic Test.

- Quest Inquiries
- Quizzes
- Interactivities
- Texts
- Flipped Videos

While online you can also check the progress you've made learning the topic and course content by viewing your grades, test scores, and assignment status.

SAVVAS realize™

Topic 3 Quick Study Guide

LESSON SUMMARIES

Use these Lesson Summaries, and the longer versions available online, to review the key ideas for each lesson in this Topic.

Lesson 1: The French and Indian War

In the mid-1700s, France and Britain repeatedly fought for control of North America. Native American groups fought on both sides. During the French and Indian War, 1754–1763, the British and their Native American allies finally defeated the French and ended their influence on the continent.

Lesson 2: Causes of the Revolution

After the French and Indian War, tensions between the British government and American colonists increased. The British imposed new policies, including new taxes, and colonists organized to resist them. Violence broke out in 1770, when British troops in Boston opened fire on a crowd.

Lesson 3: The Colonists Declare Independence

In 1775, British troops tried to seize weapons stockpiled by the colonists near Boston. The colonists fought back and war began. Delegates from all 13 colonies met in Philadelphia. They issued a Declaration of Independence and established a Continental Army.

Lesson 4: Americans win the Revolution

At first the Continental Army struggled against better trained and equipped British forces. The newly-declared United States formed an alliance with France and Spain and eventually turned the tide of the war. The Americans and their allies defeated the British 1781 and signed a peace treaty in 1783.

QUEST! FINDINGS

Participate in Your Civic Discussion Refer to your responses to the Quest Connections to help you prepare for and conduct your discussion. Use the rubric and other Quest resources online to guide your work.

GO ONLINE to access lesson summaries

VISUAL REVIEW

Use these graphics to review some of the key terms, people, and ideas from this Topic.

The French and Indian War

The French and Indian War

Causes	Effects
• England and France compete for power in Europe • French and English make alliances with Native Americans • French and English fight over territory in North America and elsewhere	• France loses colonies in North America • Britain gains control of Canada • Proclamation of 1763 limits colonial settlement

The Boston Massacre

The Boston Massacre

↓

In **1767** Parliament passes the Townshend Acts, taxing everyday goods to pay colonial officials

↓

In **1768**, customs officials seize John Hancock's ship, leading to a riot in Boston

↓

The British send 4,000 troops to Boston, inflaming tensions

↓

In **1770** British troops open fire on crowd in Boston, killing five colonists

↓

Colonists form Committees of Correspondence to organize resistance; British withdraw troops from Boston

Key British Legislation, 1764–1774

ACT	EFFECT
Sugar Act (1764)	• Lowered tax on molasses, but made it easier to enforce
Stamp Act (1765)	• Added fee to printed materials • First direct tax on colonists • Provoked boycotts and rioting • Repealed in 1766
Quartering Act (1765)	• Required colonial assemblies to feed and house British troops in the colonies
Townshend Acts (1767)	• Applied new taxes to everyday goods, including tea • Led to protests and rioting • All taxes repealed except for tax on tea
Coercive Acts (1774)	• Punished Boston for the Boston Tea Party • Called the Intolerable Acts by colonists • Led to boycotts and resistance

Key Events of the Revolutionary War

DATE	MAJOR EVENT
1774	First Continental Congress meets
1775	Battles of Lexington and Concord
1776	British capture New York; Declaration of Independence
1778	United States allies with France
1781	Cornwallis surrenders at Yorktown
1783	Treaty of Paris signed

Topic 3 Assessment

KEY TERMS, PEOPLE, AND IDEAS

1. What was the **Albany Plan of Union** and why did it fail?
2. How did the **French and Indian War** lead to **Pontiac's Rebellion?**
3. What did the **Stamp Act** do? What was unique about it?
4. What was the purpose of **committees of correspondence**? What prompted colonists to organize them?
5. What was the purpose of the Coercive Acts, and why did colonists call them the **Intolerable Acts?**
6. How is a **militia** different from a professional army?
7. How did the **Second Continental Congress** react to the outbreak of fighting in Massachusetts?
8. Why was the **Battle of Trenton** so important to Continental troops and their supporters?
9. What role did the French play in the defeat of the British at **Yorktown?**

CRITICAL THINKING

10. **Compare and Contrast** The French and the British had different approaches and goals in colonizing North America. Compare the two, and explain how Britain's strategy helped lead to its victory over the French.
11. **Analyze Sequence** In general, how did the British govern their American colonies in the years before the French and Indian War? How did their approach change afterwards?
12. **Analyze Interactions** How did the "daughters of liberty" play a role in resisting British policy in the 1760s?
13. **Identify Key Steps in a Process** How did the Boston Tea Party eventually lead to the Battles of Lexington and Concord?
14. **Summarize** What was the key strategic mistake made by the British in their conduct of the war? How did they fail to understand the kind of war they were fighting?
15. **Draw Conclusions** How did the Battle of King's Mountain show how the war changed when it came to the South?
16. **Analyze Visuals** This engraving shows the Battle of Bunker Hill. The British are in control of Boston, on the left. Across the harbor on the right, the Americans are dug in on Bunker Hill. What are the British using to fight this battle? How does that show advantages that they will have throughout the war?

17. **Writing Activity: Write an Argument** In the resolution below, Patrick Henry makes a strong argument about Britain's right to tax the colonists. How might a British government official have responded to him? Make an argument from that point of view.

> Resolved therefore, That the General Assembly of this colony, together with his majesty or his substitutes have, in their representatives capacity the only exclusive right and power to lay taxes and imposts upon the inhabitants of this colony; and that every attempt to vest such power in any other person or persons whatever than the General Assembly aforesaid is illegal, unconstitutional, and unjust, and has a manifest tendency to destroy British as well as American liberty.
>
> —*Patrick Henry, May 29, 1765*

18. **Connections to Today** Protest movements can take on a life of their own. The first people to speak up against a government policy or organize a political event can't always see where their movement will end. Do you think the first Americans to write pamphlets or deliver sermons against the Sugar Act in the 1760s imagined their protests would lead to independence a decade later? Explain your answer with evidence from the Topic.

DOCUMENT-BASED QUESTIONS

While American revolutionary leaders took a strong stand for freedom, they left the issue of slavery unresolved. In fact, many were enslavers themselves. The British were not slow to notice this contradiction. Read the documents below, then answer the questions that follow.

DOCUMENT A

I wish most sincerely there was not a slave in the province—it allways appeard a most iniquitous [vicious] scheme to me. Fight ourselfs for what we are daily . . . plundering from those who have as good a right freedom as we have—you know my mind upon this subject.

—Abigail Adams, September 22, 1774

DOCUMENT B

[I]n every human Breast, God has implanted a Principle, which we call Love of Freedom; it is impatient of Oppression. . . . I will assert, that the same Principle lives in us. God grant Deliverance [rescue from] . . . all those whose Avarice [greediness] impels them to countenance [allow] . . . Calamities [affliction] of their fellow Creatures. This I desire not for their Hurt, but to convince them of the strange Absurdity of their Conduct whose Words and Actions are so . . . opposite.

—Phillis Wheatley, an African American poet, March 11, 1774

DOCUMENT C

I do hereby further declare all indentured Servants, Negroes, or others, (appertaining [belonging] to Rebels,) free that are able and willing to bear Arms, they joining His MAJESTY'S Troops as soon as may be, for the more speedily reducing this Colony to a proper Sense of their Duty . . . GOD save the KING

—Proclamation by Governor Dunmore of Virginia, November 7, 1775

DOCUMENT D

WHEREAS lord Dunmore, by his proclamation, dated on board the ship William, off Norfolk, the 7th day of November 1775, hath offered freedom to such able-bodied slaves as are willing to join him, and take up arms, against the good people of this colony . . . by an act of the General Assembly now in force in this colony, it is enacted, that all negro or other slaves, conspiring to rebel or make insurrection, shall suffer death, and be excluded all benefit of clergy

—Declaration by the Virginia General Convention, December 14, 1775

19. What do documents A and B have in common?
- **A.** Both argue that slavery is a neccessary evil.
- **B.** Both oppose slavery and hope for its end.
- **C.** Both argue that enslaved people can help win the war.
- **D.** Both believe that slavery is unrelated to the American Revolution.

20. In Document A, Abigail Adams critiques her own society. What does she criticize in particular?
- **A.** Greed
- **B.** Prejudice
- **C.** Hypocrisy
- **D.** Rebellion

21. How does Governor Dunmore hope to turn slavery into an advantage for his side in the war?
- **A.** Convincing enslaved people to join his cause
- **B.** Enslaving rebels as punishment for their actions
- **C.** Showing the British people the reality of slavery
- **D.** Freeing all enslaved people in the colonies

22. **Writing Task** Write a paragraph explaining how slavery complicated the American Revolution. What roles did the institution of slavery and enslaved people themselves play in the war for independence? Use the sources as well as additional information you have learned about slavery at the time.

GO ONLINE to access more practice

Topic 4

Establishing the New Nation (1781–1789)

ESSENTIAL QUESTION What Is the Role of Government?

GO ONLINE to access the eText, videos, Interactive Primary Sources, Biographies, and other online resources.

A copy of the Constitution

Connections to Today

Despite months of work by some of the nation's brightest minds, the fate of the new Constitution hung precariously in the balance. To convince some reluctant leaders to support the new plan, a promise was made to add a listing of the people's rights to the document. That promise was fulfilled by 1791. The first of those ten additions guarantees freedom of speech.

Since then, the definition of speech has evolved in ways the Framers could not have imagined. How does that fact affect the application of the First Amendment, written so long ago?

NBC LEARN

Learn about Alexander Hamilton and the shaping of the new nation.

BOUNCE to Activate My Story Video

Topic 4 Overview

In this Topic, you'll learn about the efforts that went into establishing the founding documents and the government of the new United States of America, including the Articles of Confederation, the Constitution, and the Bill of Rights. Look at the lesson outline and explore the timeline. As you study this Topic, you'll complete the Quest Inquiry.

LESSON OUTLINE

4.1 The Articles of Confederation

4.2 The Constitutional Convention

4.3 The Enduring Constitution

Key Events of the New Nation

1777 Articles of Confederation approved by Congress

1781 Articles of Confederation ratified by all of the states

1785 Land Ordinance sets up a system for managing lands in the Northwest Territory

1787 Daniel Shays leads farmers in western Massachusetts in what becomes known as Shays' Rebellion

1787 Constitutional Convention meets in Independence Hall in Philadelphia

1788 U.S. Constitution is ratified by the last key state and becomes the supreme law of the land

1789 Congress sends the B of Rights to the states

1775 1780 1785 1790

QUEST! INQUIRY

Analyzing Ideas that Influenced the Constitution

How did Enlightenment ideas influence the writing and ratification of the United States Constitution? In this Quest, you'll analyze the work of Enlightenment thinkers and write an essay about their influence on the founding ideas of the United States.

STEP 1
Watch a video about the Constitutional Convention and discuss it in class or with a partner. Generate questions about issues the delegates at the convention faced and their ideas about government.

STEP 2
Examine six sources related to Enlightenment ideas and their influence on the writing of the U.S. Constitution and answer the questions about each document.

STEP 3
Synthesize evidence from the sources to formulate conclusions, and then write an essay about how the Enlightenment influenced the writing and ratification of the Constitution.

STEP 4
Reflect on the process of analyzing the documents and writing the essay and think about how you can apply what you have learned in the future.

GO ONLINE to access complete Quest materials

4.1

An engraving made during Shays' march to Springfield, Massachusetts, depicts Shays and another leader of the rebellion, Job Shattuck. **Deduce** What was the significance of Shays' Rebellion?

BOUNCE to Activate Flipped Video

Objectives

Explain how the states' new constitutions reflected republican ideals.

Describe the structure and powers of the national government under the Articles of Confederation.

Summarize the Congress's plan for the settlement and governance of western lands.

Understand why tensions with foreign countries revealed the weakness of the U.S. government.

List the main weaknesses of the Articles.

Key Terms

republic
unicameral legislature
bicameral legislature
Articles of Confederation
John Dickinson
federal
Northwest Territory
Land Ordinance of 1785
Northwest Ordinance of 1787
Shays' Rebellion

The Articles of Confederation

After the Revolutionary War, the Patriots feared the creation of another tyrannical or abusive government, so they refused to entrust the new Union with much power. As a result, most authority remained with the states. Within a short time, the powerful states and weak national government faced severe problems.

The States Create Republics

Upon declaring independence in 1776, the Continental Congress invited each new state to write a constitution to establish its government. Although these documents varied, they all called for **republics**, or governments in which the people elect their representatives. But the Patriots disagreed over the proper design for those republics. Some Patriots, such as Thomas Paine, sought changes that would promote democracy by putting more power in the hands of the people—meaning, in those days, white men. In contrast, more conservative Patriots distrusted the ability of the average white man. They hoped instead to preserve many colonial institutions.

A Preference for Democracy The more democratic Patriots wanted to create state governments with strong legislatures and weak governors (or with no governor at all). Seeking greater rights for more people, these leaders preferred a **unicameral legislature**, or one with a single house, whose members were elected by the people. Pennsylvania and Georgia adopted these more democratic constitutions.

GO ONLINE to access your digital course

Maintaining Colonial Traditions Most states, however, including Massachusetts and New York, chose to create more conservative state constitutions. These state governments had a bicameral legislature and a strong governor. A **bicameral legislature** is a lawmaking body with two houses, such as a Senate and a House of Representatives. These constitutions set the qualifications for office in such a way as to balance the power of the less wealthy members of the House with that of the wealthy, well-educated members of the Senate.

Accountability Even the conservative constitutions, however, dramatically expanded the power of white men, most often those who owned property.

In contrast to the colonial era, voters chose the members of both houses of the new legislatures, rather than just the members of the lower house. Almost all states also enlarged their legislatures. Creating smaller districts and a greater number of representatives made representatives more accountable to their constituents, meaning the voters in their districts. In almost all states, the voters also elected the governor—something only two colonies had done previously.

Still, democratic and conservative Patriots disagreed about who would vote. The democratic Patriots wanted equal political rights for almost all free men, even those who had little or no property. Pennsylvania's state constitution opened voting to all men over the age of 21 who paid any taxes.

In most states, however, the conservatives preserved colonial property requirements to vote. John Adams warned that allowing poor men to vote would "confound and destroy all distinctions, and prostrate all ranks to the common level." He opposed political equality as foolish and unworkable. But even in the conservative states, most free men qualified to vote because owning farms was so widespread. In every state, both theory and practice excluded those who were enslaved and women from voting.

Over time, in most states, the most democratic institution—the House of Representatives—gained power at the expense of the Senate and the governor. By the mid-1780s, this concentration of legislative power troubled conservative Patriots who feared the "tyranny of the majority."

Religious Liberty Because the American Revolution promoted greater religious liberty, most states also guaranteed freedom of religion in their constitutions. Before this time, states collected taxes to support religious establishments. The freedom to choose among several faiths had been controversial. After the Revolution, however, religious liberty and pluralism became the norm. These principles were set out in the Virginia Statute for Religious Freedom, drafted by Thomas Jefferson and passed in 1786. Massachusetts and Connecticut, however, kept their Congregational established churches, which continued to draw fire from Baptists and Methodists.

☑ **DESCRIBE** Why did some states choose unicameral and some choose bicameral legislatures?

Bicameral Versus Unicameral Legislatures

BICAMERAL	UNICAMERAL
Features two chambers/houses	Features one chamber/house
Typical in large countries with federal systems of government (e.g., United States, Germany, Brazil)	Typical in small countries with unitary systems of government (e.g., Denmark, Finland, New Zealand)
Legislation is usually passed more slowly because both houses have to agree; may prevent impulsive legislation	Legislation is usually passed quickly because there is only one house to decide on a bill; may lead to impulsive legislation
Power is spread more evenly, but system is more costly to maintain	Power more concentrated, but system is cheaper to maintain
All but three colonies had bicameral systems in 1776; today, all states but one have bicameral legislatures	Three colonies had unicameral systems in 1776; today, Nebraska is only state with a unicameral legislature

Sources: *Encyclopædia Britannica*; Kentlaw.itt.edu

>> **Analyze Information** What main advantages does a bicameral legislature offer? What advantages does a unicameral legislature offer?

Union Under the Articles of Confederation

In 1777, the Continental Congress drafted the original constitution for the union of the states, known as the **Articles of Confederation**. A confederation is a league or alliance of states that agree to work together. Under the leadership of **John Dickinson** of Pennsylvania, the Congress designed a loose confederation of 13 states, rather than a strong and centralized nation. The Articles reflected the principles of the Declaration of Independence and rejected the centralized power of the British Empire as a threat to liberty. As Article II reads, "Each state retains its sovereignty, freedom, and independence, and every power, jurisdiction, and right, which is not by this Confederation expressly delegated to the United States, in Congress assembled."

A Federal Government The new **federal**, or national, government comprised a congress of delegates, chosen by state legislatures rather than by voters. Although states could choose to send as many as seven delegates, each state—no matter how large or small—had a single vote. Enormous Virginia had no more power than tiny Rhode Island. The powers to make, implement, and enforce the laws were all placed with the Congress. The national government included no President or executive branch. Instead, executive power was spread among several committees of congressmen.

Powers of the National Congress The Articles granted certain limited powers to Congress. These powers were mostly external: to declare and conduct war and to negotiate peace, to regulate foreign affairs, and to administer relations with American Indian nations. The Congress had no power to raise money through taxes. Therefore, it relied on contributions from the states, which were unreliable.

On some minor issues, a majority of seven states could pass a law. On major issues, including declaring war and making treaties, two thirds of the states (nine) had to approve. Amending the Articles was almost impossible because all 13 states had to approve any change. In 1781, all of the states finally ratified the Articles.

☑ **DESCRIBE** What was the structure of the new government under the Articles of Confederation?

The Northwest Territory

One of the most important accomplishments of the national Congress under the Articles of Confederation was establishing plans to settle and govern a vast territory over which they had authority. This territory, called the **Northwest Territory**, lay north of the Ohio River and west of Pennsylvania to the Mississippi River. By selling this land to speculators and farmers, the Congress hoped to raise revenue and extend America's republican society westward.

Land Ordinance of 1785 Western settlement, however, threatened to escape the government's control. By 1784, hundreds of settlers had already crossed the Ohio River to build their own farms. This provoked war with American Indians, who defended their land. Already strapped for cash, the federal

The Government Under the Articles of Confederation

STRUCTURE	FOREIGN POLICY	MILITARY	FINANCE
• Made Congress the governing body of the federal government; no executive or judicial branch • Gave each state one vote in Congress	• Gave Congress the power to sign treaties and make alliances with other nations • Gave Congress the power to manage relations with American Indians • Gave Congress the power to declare war	• Gave Congress the power to build a navy • Gave Congress the power to raise an army only by asking the states for troops	• Did not give Congress the power to tax • Gave Congress the power to borrow money. • Did not give Congress the power to create a single, national currency

Sources: *Encyclopædia Britannica;* Central Connecticut State University; OurDocuments.gov; USHistory.org

>> **Analyze Information** Did Congress or the states exercise more authority under the Articles? What details from the chart support your answer?

The Northwest Territory

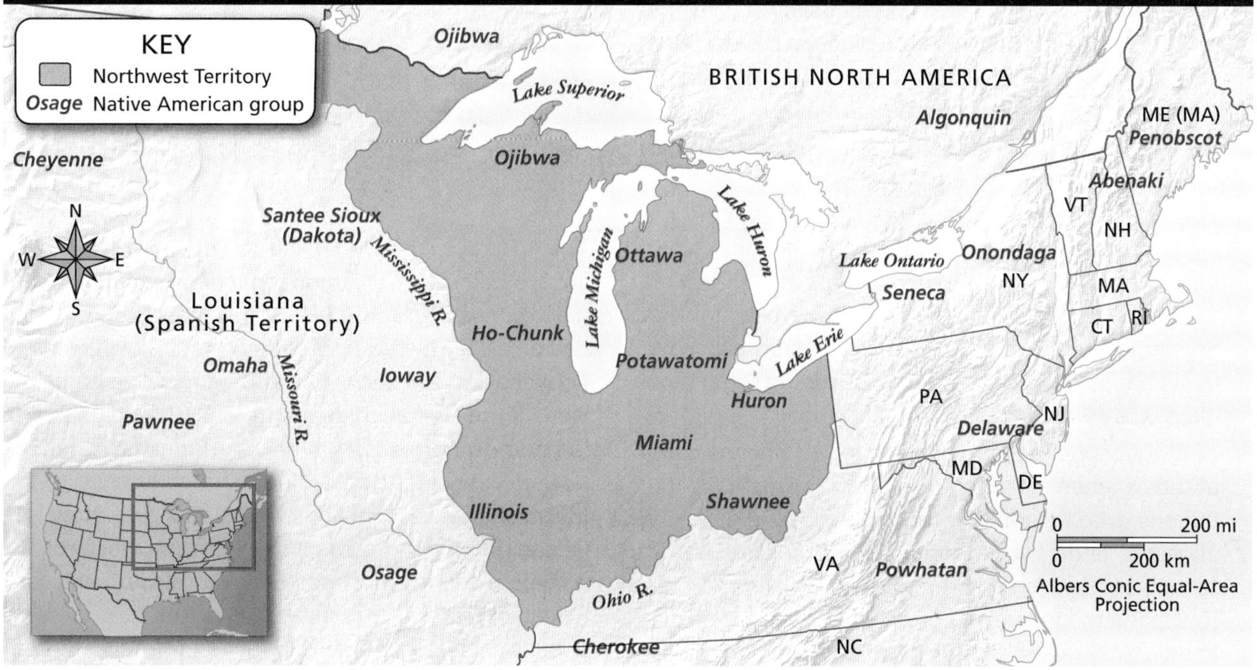

>> **Analyze Maps** How might the location of the Northwest Territory have made it difficult for the Confederation government to manage it?

BOUNCE to Activate Gallery

leaders could not afford to fight wars provoked by unregulated settlement.

Congressmen also feared that the settlers would secede from the Union, form their own states, and turn to the British or the Spanish empire for protection. If deprived of western lands, the federal government would be hard-pressed to pay its debts and would probably collapse. To save the Union, federal leaders needed to regulate frontier settlement.

In ordinances, or laws, adopted in 1785 and 1787, the Congress defined a program for managing the Northwest Territory. In the **Land Ordinance of 1785**, the Congress designed a system for dispensing, or distributing, public lands. By running a grid of lines north to south and east to west, federal surveyors divided the land into hundreds of townships, each six square miles. They then subdivided each township into 36 "sections" of one square mile (640 acres), to be sold for at least one dollar per acre.

Since ordinary farmers could not afford to pay $640, the price and size of the sections favored wealthy land speculators who had cash. To obtain land, ordinary settlers had to buy it from the speculators. The Congress sometimes broke its own rules to further benefit speculators.

For example, in 1787, the Congress sold 1.5 million acres for a mere 10 cents per acre to the Ohio Company, a politically powerful group of land speculators and army officers from New England.

Government under the Northwest Ordinance

The **Northwest Ordinance of 1787** provided a government for the western territory based on Thomas Jefferson's ideas. At first, the Congress would appoint a territorial government led by a governor, secretary, and three judges. The citizens would enjoy freedom of religion, trial by jury, and the rights of common law, including habeas corpus. Once a territory had 5,000 men, the territory could establish an elected assembly—but the governor retained an absolute veto over its laws. When the population of a territory reached 60,000, residents could request admission to the Union as a state on equal terms with the original 13 states, provided the new state adopted a republican constitution. The midwestern states of Ohio, Indiana, Illinois, Michigan, Wisconsin, and part of Minnesota were later formed out of the Northwest Territory.

The Northwest Ordinance of 1787 also barred slavery from the territory. However, the ordinance did not free those who were already enslaved and the ban was not enforced. Historical evidence shows that the practice of enslaving humans was widespread in the Northwest Territories. In fact, it was statehood that ended slavery in the region, from which five new states would enter the Union as free states rather than as states that allowed slavery. This federal restriction set a precedent that would later alarm people in southern states who wanted to expand slavery throughout the territories.

By adopting the Northwest Ordinances, Congress discarded the British model of organizing new territories into colonies that were kept permanently subordinated. Instead, Congress designed the territories to attract American settlers and to assure their acceptance of federal rule. In the wake of the Revolution, few Americans would settle where they could not enjoy basic freedoms, including the right to elect those who would set their taxes.

But freedom and opportunity for Americans came at the expense of the region's 100,000 American Indians, who the military tried to force off their ancestral lands. During the mid-1780s, American Indians refused to cede the territory west of the Ohio River, and the federal government lacked the means to defeat them and their English and Spanish allies. After the Revolution, Congress had insufficient funds to support the army, so it was reduced to only 350 men, who could barely defend themselves much less conquer the Northwest Territory.

IDENTIFY CENTRAL IDEAS What was the purpose of the Northwest Ordinance?

Relations With Foreign Powers

During the mid-1780s, the Spanish and the British did not take the United States seriously. To them, the republican Confederation seemed weak to the point of anarchy, or lawlessness.

The Closure of New Orleans The Spanish had always been wary of American independence, and they distrusted American expansion westward because they feared it threatened their colonies of Louisiana and Mexico. To discourage settlement west of the Appalachian Mountains, the Spanish forbade American trade with New Orleans. American settlers expected to ship their produce down the Mississippi River to market in Spanish-held New Orleans. The Congress lost support from western settlers when it almost accepted the closure of New Orleans in return for commercial agreements to benefit northeastern merchants. George Washington observed, "The Western settlers . . . stand, as it were, upon a pivot; the touch of a feather would turn them any way."

Disputes with Britain Relations with the British Empire were also strained. In the peace treaty that ended the American Revolution in 1783, the British had tried to cultivate American goodwill. A year later, the British abandoned that policy in favor of

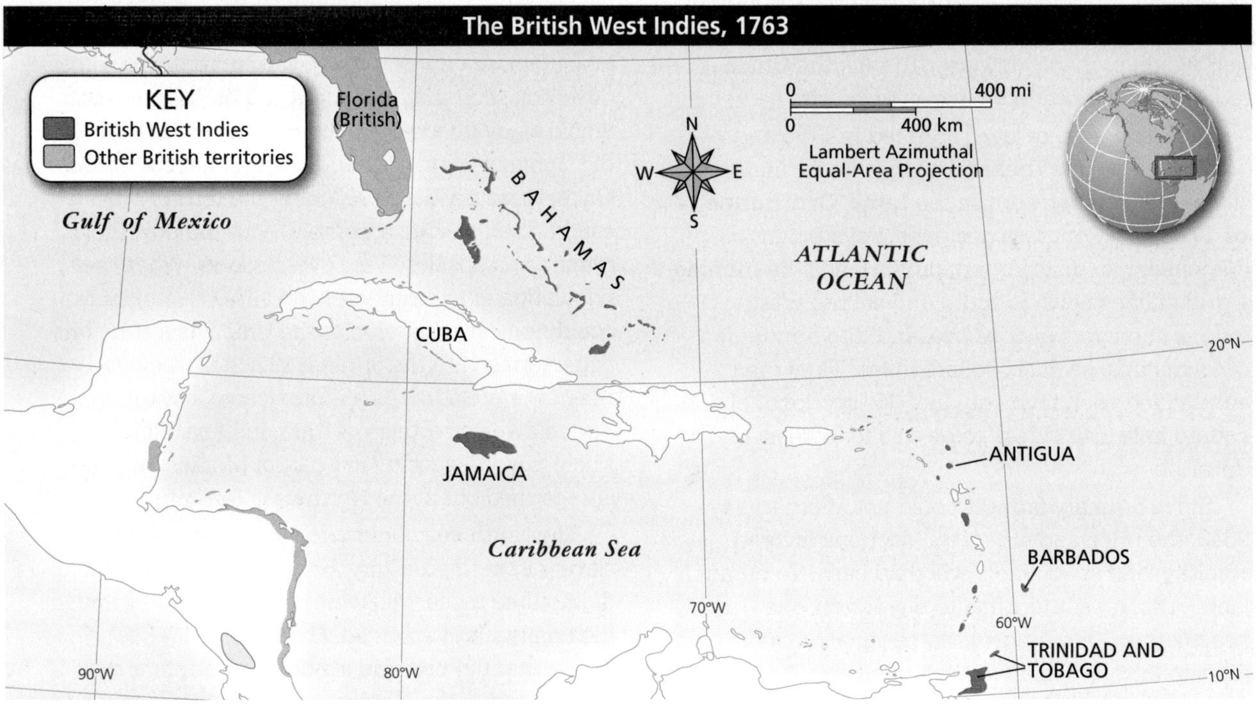

>> **Analyze Maps** What geographic factors likely made the British West Indies an important trade partner with the young United States?

BOUNCE to Activate Chart

making the Americans pay for their independence. Rejecting the new doctrine of free trade championed by Scottish economist Adam Smith, the British used the Navigation Acts to renew their commitment to mercantilism, a policy whereby a country tries to amass wealth through trade.

This meant that Americans could only trade with the British Empire under rules that favored British interests. They could certainly import all the British manufactures that they wanted, but they could no longer freely send their ships to trade with the British West Indies—the most important market for American fish, lumber, and grains, much of which was used to supply the huge enslaved population in the West Indies. During the 1780s, the British reserved this valuable trade for their ships to benefit their merchants.

This restriction especially hurt Massachusetts, which had more ships than any other state and a greater need for the West Indian market for its fish and lumber. In retaliation, Massachusetts prohibited British ships from transporting its exports. But this retaliation did not work because the other states did not support Massachusetts. In addition, the Congress was too weak to coordinate a common front against Britain's mercantile policy. American merchants began to call for a stronger national government.

The British Empire also embarrassed the Confederation by keeping frontier forts on the American side of the boundary set by the peace treaty. To please the American Indians, the British kept their forts at Niagara, Detroit, and Michilimackinac. For justification, the British cited American violations of the peace treaty. Contrary to the spirit of the treaty, some states had blocked attempts by British merchants to collect debts and attempts by Loyalists to reclaim their confiscated properties. The Congress could not make the states honor the treaty.

Britain's hold on the forts angered Americans, but they could do nothing because they could not afford to raise and keep an army. Like the merchants, many settlers wanted a national government strong enough to compel British respect on the frontier.

☑ **RECALL** Why were Americans unable to resist British control of frontier forts?

Weaknesses of the Articles of Confederation

The fledgling government under the Articles of Confederation found itself facing a host of difficulties. It soon became clear to many that the Articles themselves were part of the problem.

Weaknesses of the Articles of Confederation

- Congress could not levy or collect taxes.
- Congress was powerless to regulate interstate commerce and foreign trade.
- Each state had only one vote in Congress, regardless of its size.
- A two-thirds majority (9 out of 13 states) was required to pass laws.
- Articles could only be amended with the consent of all states.
- There was no separate executive branch to carry out acts of Congress.
- There was no system of federal courts.

>> **Analyze Information** Which weaknesses would likely cause the most problems for the nation over time?

Economic Weaknesses Under the Articles, the federal Congress could not establish a common currency, nor could it regulate interstate commerce or levy taxes. For financial support, the Congress relied solely on contributions from the states, which were unreliable. The Congress could do nothing to compel states to pay their share. Without money, the federal government could not pay its immense war debts. Between 1781 and 1786, the Congress received only one sixth of what it requested from the states. By 1786, it needed $2.5 million to pay the interest on its debts but had only $400,000 on hand. The states had bankrupted the nation.

To survive, the Congress sought a constitutional amendment to permit a federal 5 percent duty on imported goods. Twice that amendment failed when a single state balked: Rhode Island in 1782 and New York in 1786. If amending the Articles was so difficult, perhaps only a new constitution could save the Union.

Shays' Rebellion Meanwhile, a slowdown in the trading of goods increased unemployment in the seaports and reduced the prices paid to farmers for their produce. Without the West Indian market for their shipping, Americans could not pay for their imported manufactured goods. Their debts to British suppliers mounted. In 1785, those suppliers curtailed their credit and demanded payments from the American import merchants. These demands sent a shock wave through the weak American economy as the importers sought to collect from their own debtors in the countryside. Most Americans were

Events Leading to the Constitutional Convention

- Two efforts to allow Congress to tax imports fail
- Treaty of Paris demands that the United States repay its debts
- Britain refuses to vacate forts in American territory
- Shays' Rebellion begins
- The British flood U.S. markets with British goods
- States impose duties on goods from other states
- Spain bars American ships from the Mississippi River

→ Congress votes to hold a **Constitutional Convention** to revise the Articles of Confederation

SOURCE: Encyclopædia Britannica; U.S. State Department

>> **Draw Inferences** Some six years passed between the time when the last state ratified the Articles of Confederation and when Congress decided to hold a convention to revise them. Compare this to the time between the Constitutional Convention and today. What does this tell you?

farmers, and most farmers were in debt. They lacked the cash to pay their debts on short notice, especially when prices fell for their crops. Losing lawsuits for debt, they faced the loss of their crops, livestock, and even their farms to foreclosure.

In western Massachusetts in 1786, farmers took up arms to shut down the courts to block any foreclosure hearings. Farmers did not want to lose their property or go to prison, but they could not pay the higher taxes imposed by the Massachusetts government. Daniel Shays, a veteran of the Revolutionary War, became a leader among the farmers. In 1787, he led about 1,000 farmers to seize weapons from the Springfield Armory and attempted to shut down the courts. The elected leaders of Massachusetts insisted that the new republic could not survive if people violently interfered with the courts. In eastern Massachusetts, the state raised an army, which marched west to suppress what became known as **Shays' Rebellion**.

Most other states avoided rebellion by satisfying their debtors with relief measures. Some states suspended lawsuits for debt until the depression lifted. More common were state laws to flood the money supply with paper money. Paper money made it easier for debtors to pay, while reducing the value that creditors could collect. Naturally, what relieved the debtors infuriated their creditors, who felt cheated.

Creditors blamed the relief measures on excessive democracy. They saw the state governments as too responsive to the opinion of the public, which wanted debtor relief. James Madison agreed: "Liberty may be endangered by the abuses of liberty as well as [by] the abuses of power." Some thought of abandoning republicanism in favor of an American monarchy, but most hoped to save the republic by establishing a stronger national government. This stronger government would be capable of controlling the states whenever they threatened commercial property.

IDENTIFY MAIN IDEAS What did events in the 1780s show about the United States government under the Articles of Confederation?

ASSESSMENT

1. **Express Problems Clearly** What problem led to the development of the Articles of Confederation?
2. **Connect** What economic situation led to Shays' Rebellion and how did these economic problems demonstrate the weaknesses of the Articles of Confederation?
3. **Cite Evidence** What was the purpose of the Northwest Ordinance of 1787?
4. **Summarize** Describe the states' relationship with foreign countries like Britain and Spain under the Articles of Confederation.
5. **Compare and Contrast** How did the governments established in states with liberal-minded leaders differ from those with more conservative-minded leaders?
6. **Connections to Today** Like freedom of speech, freedom of religion is also guaranteed under the First Amendment. In what way were the seeds of this right sown during the confederation period?

GO ONLINE to access this biography: Adam Smith

Letter to Reverend William Gordon: George Washington

Just months before resigning his command of the Continental Army, General George Washington received a letter from Reverend William Gordon, a clergyman from Massachusetts who wished to write a history of the war. Reverend Gordon described the difficulty the Massachusetts legislature faced in collecting the taxes needed to satisfy the state's obligations from the war. In his reply, General Washington expresses his thoughts about the powers held by the Confederation Congress and about those who feared an increase in those powers.

>> George Washington resigned his commission as head of the Continental Army in December 1783.

Head Quarters Newburgh 8th July 1783

Dear Sir, . . .

. . . It now rests with the confederated Powers [the states], by the line of conduct they mean to adopt, to make this Country great, happy, & respectable; or to sink it into littleness—worse perhaps—into Anarchy and Confusion; for certain I am, that unless adequate Powers are given to Congress for the general purposes of the Federal Union that we shall soon moulder [decay] into dust and become contemptable [contemptible] in the Eyes of Europe, if we are not made the sport of their Politicks—to suppose that the general concerns of this Country can be directed by thirteen heads, or one head without competent powers, is a solecism [something improper], the bad effects of which every Man who has had the practical knowledge to judge from, that I have, is fully convinced of; tho' none perhaps has felt them in so forcible, & distressing a degree.

DRAW INFERENCES Why was General Washington in a unique position to judge the "bad effects" of a national Congress that lacked adequate powers?

The People at large, and at a distance from the theatre of Action, who only know that the Machine was kept in motion, and that they are at last arrived at the first object of their wishes are satisfied with the event, without investigating the causes of the slow progress to it, or of the Expenses which have accrued & which they now seem unwilling to pay—great part of which has arisen from the want of energy in the Federal Constitution which I am complaining of. . . .

SUMMARIZE Summarize what General Washington is talking about in this section of his letter.

. . . We are known by no other character among Nations than as the United States—Massachusetts or Virginia is no better defined, nor any more thought of by Foreign Powers than the County of Worcester in Massachusetts is by Virginia, or Gloucester County in Virginia is by Massachusetts (respectable as they are); and yet these Counties with as much propriety [appropriateness] might oppose themselves to the Laws of the State in which they are, as an Individual State can oppose itself to the Federal Government, by which it is, or ought to be bound. Each of these Counties has, no doubt, its local polity [political organization] & interests. These should be attended to, & brought before their respective legislatures with all the force their importance merits; but when they come in contact with the general Interest of the State—when superior considerations preponderate [exceed in importance] in favor of the whole—their Voices should be heard no more—so should it be with individual States when compared to the Union—

ASSESS AN ARGUMENT What argument is General Washington making in this section? Is it a valid argument?

Otherwise I think it may properly be asked for what purpose do we farcically [laughably] pretend to be United? Why do Congress spend Months together in deliberating upon, debating, & digesting plans, which are made as palatable [acceptable], & as wholesome to the Constitution of this Country as the nature of things will admit of, when some States will pay no attention to them, & others regard them but partially; . . . A hundred thousand men coming one after another cannot move a Ton weight—but the united strength of 50 would transport it with ease. So has it been with great part of the expense which has been incurred this War. In a Word, I think the blood & treasure, which has been spent in it has been lavished to little purpose, unless we can be better Cemented; and that is not to be effected while so little attention is paid to the Recommendations of the Sovereign Power.

To me it would seem not more absurd, to hear a traveler, who was setting out on a long journey, declare he would take no money in his pocket to defray the Expenses of it but rather depend upon chance & charity lest he should misapply it, [than are the expressions of so much fear of the powers and means of Congress.] —For Heavens sake who are Congress? —are they not the Creatures of the People, amenable [answerable] to them for their Conduct, and dependent from day to day on their bread? Where then can be the danger of giving them such Powers as are adequate to the great ends of Government. . . .

. . . I am Dr Sir—Yr Most Obedt & Most Hble Servt

Geo. Washington

UNDERSTAND MEANING What does General Washington mean when he says that Congress are "the Creatures of the People"?

ASSESSMENT

1. **Determine Author's Point of View** What is General Washington's position on the question of whether the federal Congress should be given more power?
2. **Understand Meaning** How does General Washington believe the United States will be viewed by European powers? What situation does he believe will bring this about?
3. **Analyze Word Choice** What is General Washington referring to when he mentions "thirteen heads"? Why does he think thirteen heads is a problem?
4. **Determine Author's Purpose** What is General Washington's meaning and purpose when he writes: "I think the blood & treasure, which has been spent in it has been lavished to little purpose, unless we can be better Cemented"?
5. **Analyze Style and Rhetoric** What analogies does General Washington use to help make his points?

GO ONLINE to access primary sources

4.2

In 1787, the Constitutional Convention met in this Assembly Room in Independence Hall in Philadelphia, Pennsylvania, to discuss amendments to the Articles of Confederation.

The Constitutional Convention

After Shays' Rebellion, many Americans agreed that they needed a stronger federal government to preserve the Union. The Congress called for a convention to meet in Philadelphia in 1787 "for the sole and express purpose of revising the Articles of Confederation." Instead of revising the Articles of Confederation, however, the delegates created an entirely new constitution.

BOUNCE to Activate Flipped Video

Objectives

Understand the reasons leaders called for the Constitutional Convention.

Summarize the rival plans of government proposed at the convention.

Describe the compromises made in order to reach agreement on the Constitution.

Key Terms

Alexander Hamilton
James Madison
Virginia Plan
New Jersey Plan
Great Compromise
federalism
Three-Fifths Compromise

Leaders Assemble at the Convention

By 1787, most Americans agreed that the Articles of Confederation were flawed and needed at least two major changes. First, almost everyone wanted Congress to have the power to regulate interstate and international commerce. Second, most Americans also supported granting Congress the power to levy taxes. To draft proposed amendments to the Articles, 12 of the 13 states sent delegates to a special convention in Philadelphia in May 1787. (Rhode Island refused to participate.) Once done, the plan was to submit the proposed amendments to the 13 state legislatures for ratification.

The Federal Convention was slated to begin on May 14. However, only the delegates from Pennsylvania and Virginia made it there on time. More than a week would pass before there were enough delegates to begin the meeting.

The Delegates Gather The Federal Convention opened in the Pennsylvania State House, now known as Independence Hall, on May 25, when 29 delegates had finally arrived. Other delegates

GO ONLINE to access your digital course

continued to arrive during the subsequent weeks and months. The proceedings of the convention were shrouded in secrecy so the delegates could speak freely. Because of this, the windows of the hall were often closed for privacy. It was an especially hot summer in 1787, so the delegates were frequently uncomfortable in their closed-off space.

Although Thomas Jefferson and John Adams were away in Europe serving as diplomats, the convention included most of the other leading statesmen of the day.

Several leaders emerged, including Alexander Hamilton of New York and James Madison of Virginia. The eldest delegate was Benjamin Franklin of Pennsylvania, who, along with George Washington, added great prestige to the proceedings. Other leaders in attendance were Roger Sherman, Gouverneur Morris, James Wilson, Elbridge Gerry, William Paterson, John Dickinson, Charles Pinckney, Edmund Randolph, and George Mason.

These delegates were not typical Americans. They were all white males, many were wealthy, nearly half held people in slavery, and more than half of them were lawyers. Many of the delegates had helped to write their state constitutions, seven had been governors, twenty-one had fought in the American Revolution, and eight had signed the Declaration of Independence. After reading the names of those in attendance, Jefferson remarked that it was "an assembly of demi-gods." The delegates unanimously elected George Washington as the president of the convention.

Hamilton and Madison Bring Different Viewpoints The convention's leading thinkers were Alexander Hamilton and James Madison. Bold in action, **Alexander Hamilton** was very conservative in principles.

Hamilton disliked the idea of democracy. He praised the British constitution, including its king and House of Lords, as "the best model the world has ever produced." He insisted that a balanced government should have elements of aristocracy and monarchy as well as of republicanism. Hamilton believed that such a government would have real power to command its citizens and impress foreign empires. Gouverneur Morris of Pennsylvania also advocated a strong central government at the convention. Morris thought that the President should hold office for life.

James Madison showed his eagerness to participate in the convention by arriving in Philadelphia 11 days early. He had also sent a letter to George Washington in April outlining his thoughts about what should be debated at the convention. Madison had concluded that only a strong nation

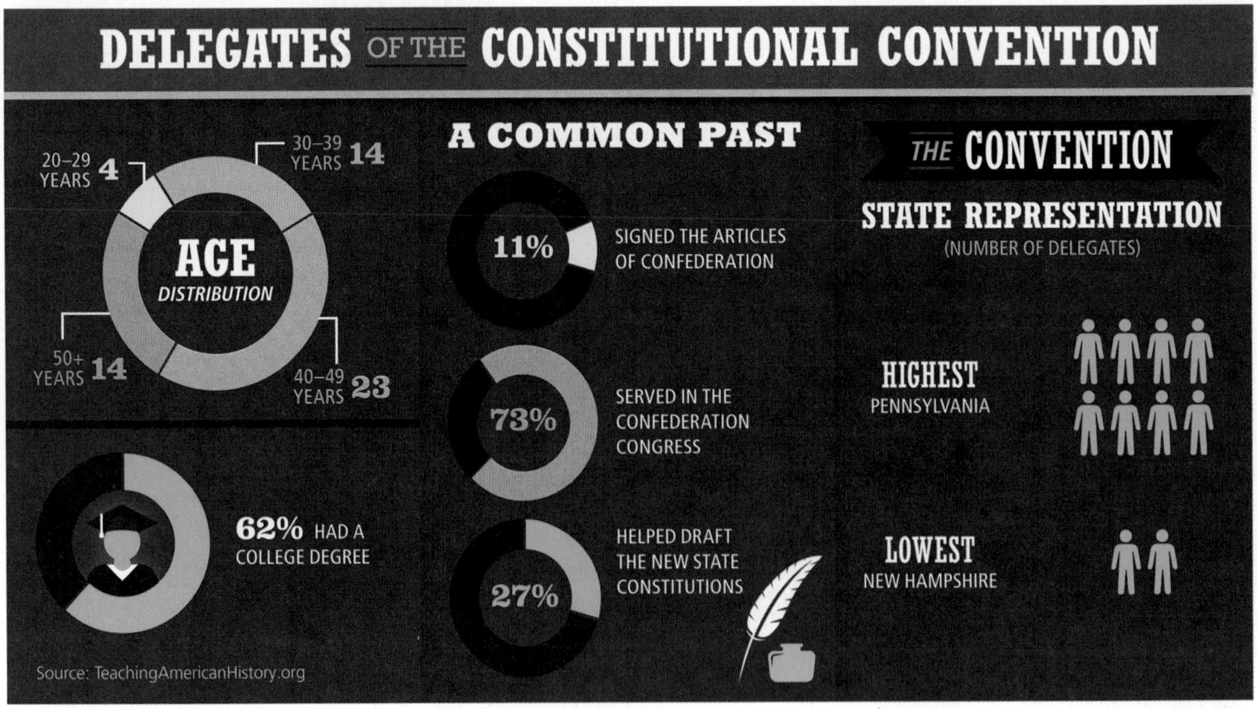

>> **Analyze Information** Based on this infographic, what experience did the framers of the Constitution draw on in developing the new plan for government?

BOUNCE to Activate Gallery

could rescue the states from their own democratic excesses. Although a critic of democracy, Madison favored republicanism rather than a constitution modeled after the British system. His challenge was to design a government that was both strong and republican.

Rejecting the old notion that a republic needed to be small and homogeneous, he insisted that a large republic with diverse interests would best preserve the common good. He reasoned that the numerous interests would "check" one another. Madison hoped that the nation's most learned men, rather than the many local political leaders he saw in the state legislatures, would govern the new national Republic. In addition to providing the basic blueprint for the Constitution, Madison kept the notes that are the best record of the convention.

DESCRIBE What ideas and goals did the delegates bring to the Constitutional Convention of 1787?

>> Alexander Hamilton represented the state of New York at the Constitutional Convention in 1787. The state's other two delegates opposed the new plan for the national government and left the convention early.

Constitutional Compromises

Before a constitution could be written and approved, the delegates needed to come to an agreement about what it should contain. To achieve this goal, they advanced and debated a number of proposals for several months.

The Virginia Plan Most of the delegates preferred an ambitious scheme proposed by Madison called the **Virginia Plan**. In addition to securing the power to tax and to regulate commerce, Madison proposed a government that divided power among three branches—the legislative, the executive, and the judicial. The plan proposed a bicameral legislature with a House of Representatives and a Senate. In both houses, the states with larger populations would have more members. Madison's plan also included a daring feature—the national Congress would have the power to veto any state law, just as Parliament had done with colonial laws.

The Virginia Plan also called for a strong President. The President would enjoy a relatively long term in office of seven years but could not be elected a second time. The President would command the armed forces and manage foreign relations. He would appoint all executive and judicial officers, subject only to approval by the Senate. A critic of the plan, Patrick Henry, worried that such a powerful President could "easily become a king."

>> James Madison, a Virginia delegate to the Constitutional Convention, is widely considered the "Father of the Constitution."

The New Jersey Plan Some of the delegates advocated only modest changes to the Articles of Confederation. Favored by the small states, their proposal, introduced by William Paterson of New Jersey, became known as the **New Jersey Plan**. This plan gave Congress the powers to regulate commerce and to tax, but it kept the three chief principles of the Articles of Confederation. First, it retained a unicameral legislature representing the states as equals, no matter how large or small. Second, it preserved an executive committee rather than adopting a singular President. Third, the states remained sovereign except for those few powers specifically granted to the national government. Under the New Jersey Plan, the United States would remain a loose confederation.

Need for Compromise Something had to be done in order to prevent the convention from ending in a stalemate. The delegates were far from a unanimous decision concerning the structure of the new government, and without the compromises laid out below, they may never have reached an agreement.

Led by Roger Sherman of Connecticut, the delegates reached a compromise between the Virginia and the New Jersey plans, known as the Connecticut Compromise, or the **Great Compromise**. John Dickinson of Delaware played a key role in crafting this compromise, which made a concession to the small states: The Senate would equally represent every state, regardless of size, by allowing two senators per state. In keeping with the Virginia Plan, the House of Representatives would represent population, granting more power to the larger states.

Compromising on Federalism In another concession, Madison abandoned his cherished national veto over state laws. Instead, the compromise simply forbade the states from enacting the sorts of laws that offended many during the 1780s.

For instance, the states could no longer issue their own money or provide debtor relief at creditors' expense. By compromising between the Virginia Plan and the New Jersey Plan, the delegates supported a system known as **federalism**, which divided government power between the federal government and state governments.

Compromising on Slavery The debates over the Constitution revealed that a great division pitted the southern against the northern delegates. The southerners feared future domination by the northern states, which had more free people. They worried that northern domination would threaten the system

Population Estimates Used at the Constitutional Convention

STATE	POPULATION ESTIMATES* White Population	Black Population	NUMBER OF REPRESENTATIVES
New Hampshire	102,000		3
Massachusetts	360,000		8
Rhode Island	58,000		1
Connecticut	202,000		5
New York	238,000		6
New Jersey	138,000		4
Pennsylvania	360,000		8
Delaware	37,000		1
Maryland	170,000	80,000	6
Virginia	252,000	280,000	10
North Carolina	164,000	60,000	5
South Carolina	102,000	80,000	5
Georgia	78,000	20,000	3

*States with no entries had Black populations of less than 100 people.
Source: *The Documentary History of the First Federal Elections, 1788–1790*

>> **Analyze Data** Use the data in this chart to explain why the southern States feared northern domination in Congress.

of enslaving people, which was essential to the southern economy and southern society. The delegates from South Carolina and Georgia threatened to walk out unless the Constitution protected the institution of slavery.

The subject tore at Madison. On the one hand, he wanted a powerful nation, and he despised slavery as "the most oppressive dominion ever exercised by man over man." On the other hand, he, like nearly half of the other delegates, was himself an enslaver.

He also knew that southern voters would reject a constitution that threatened slavery. So he assured his constituents in Virginia that the Constitution offered slavery "better security than any that now exists."

That security took three forms. First, the Constitution forbade Congress from blocking the importation of enslaved Africans for twenty years, and, in fact, Georgia and South Carolina alone would import another 100,000 enslaved people by 1808. Second, a compromise known as the **Three-Fifths Compromise** counted each enslaved person as three fifths of a person to be added to a state's free population in allocating representatives to the House of Representatives and electoral college votes. The three-fifths clause gave the southern states more seats in Congress and more power in presidential elections than they would have enjoyed had only free people been counted—as the northern delegates preferred.

Third, the Constitution required all states to return freedom seekers to their owners. In other words, escaping to a free state did not free an enslaved person. Northerners were required to help enforce the system of enslaving humans as the price of union.

Compromising on a Bill of Rights Most state constitutions had adopted bills of rights to protect civil liberties from the power of government. But the federal delegates declined to include a bill of rights in their constitution. A South Carolina delegate, Charles C. Pinckney, explained, "such bills generally begin with declaring that all men are by nature born free." Such a declaration would come "with a very bad grace when a large part of our property consists in men who are actually born slaves." Unlike the Declaration of Independence, the Constitution did not proclaim that all men were born free and equal.

On September 17, the Constitutional Convention concluded with 42 delegates still present. Many, including Madison, disliked the compromises, but Franklin appealed to all to unite in support of the "federal experiment." Hamilton reluctantly accepted the Constitution as the only alternative to "anarchy and Convulsion."

>> Roger Sherman's Great Compromise helped resolve a dispute between large and small states over the distribution of federal power.

BOUNCE to Activate Chart

>> Howard Chandler Christy's 1940 painting *Scene at Signing of the Constitution* commemorates the completion of the document. George Washington, president of the convention, stands at top right. **Describe** Which other delegates appear prominently in this painting?

In the end, 39 delegates signed the document, while three refused to sign out of protest. George Mason and Edmund Randolph of Virginia and Elbridge Gerry of Massachusetts considered the document to be flawed. Next came the greater challenge of winning approval from the states.

CHECK UNDERSTANDING Describe the government structure proposed by the New Jersey Plan. How did this differ from the structure proposed in the Virginia Plan?

ASSESSMENT

1. **Compare and Contrast** Compare how the views of Alexander Hamilton and James Madison regarding government were similar and different.
2. **Summarize** How did the Constitutional Convention address the concerns of southern delegates that northern states might try to end the system of enslaving humans?
3. **Summarize** What was the Connecticut Compromise, also known as the Great Compromise, and what issues was it meant to address?
4. **Identify Central Issues** What were the main flaws in the Articles of Confederation? How did the new Constitution address these issues?
5. **Quest Connection** How did the Three-Fifths Compromise and the decision not to include a bill of rights in the Constitution measure up to the ideals of the Enlightenment regarding natural rights? Explain.

GO ONLINE to access these biographies: James Madison, Roger Sherman

Primary Sources

Virginia Statute for Religious Freedom: Thomas Jefferson

In 1786, the Virginia legislature adopted the Statute for Religious Freedom, written by Thomas Jefferson. The law is still part of the Virginia state constitution. Other states followed Virginia's lead. The Statute for Religious Freedom later became the basis for the First Amendment to the United States Constitution, which guarantees freedom of religion.

>> Thomas Jefferson

I. Whereas Almighty God hath created the mind free . . . that to compel a man to furnish contributions of money for the propagation [spreading] of opinions which he disbelieves and abhors [hates], is sinful and tyrannical . . . that our civil rights have no dependence on our religious opinions, any more than our opinions in physics or geometry. . . .

II. Be it . . . enacted by the General Assembly, that no man shall be compelled to frequent or support any religious worship, place, or ministry whatsoever, nor shall be enforced, restrained, molested, or burdened in his body or goods, nor shall otherwise suffer, on account of his religious opinions or belief; but that all men shall be free to profess, and by argument to maintain, their opinions in matters of religion, and that the same shall in no wise diminish, enlarge, or affect their civil capacities.

DETERMINE MEANING What do you think Jefferson meant by "civil capacities" in the last sentence of Article II?

III. And although we well know that this Assembly, elected by the people for the ordinary purpose of legislation only, have no power to restrain the acts of succeeding assemblies, constituted with powers equal to our own, and that therefore to declare this act to be irrevocable [impossible to invalidate or take back] would be of no effect in law; yet we are free to declare, and do declare, that the rights hereby asserted are of the natural rights of mankind, and that if any act shall hereafter be passed to repeal the present, or to narrow its operation, such an act will be infringement of natural right.

SUMMARIZE What are the main points made in Article III?

ASSESSMENT

1. **Cite Evidence** What part of this excerpt could be cited as support for the idea that government funds, which come from sources such as taxes, should not be given to religious institutions?
2. **Analyze Structure** What is the purpose of each of the three articles in the Statute?
3. **Paraphrase** Restate Article II in your own words.

GO ONLINE to access primary sources

4.3

Published between 1787 and 1788, *The Federalist* is a series of essays that were written to persuade voters to support ratification of the new Constitution. **List** What are two methods used today to make voters aware of changes in government?

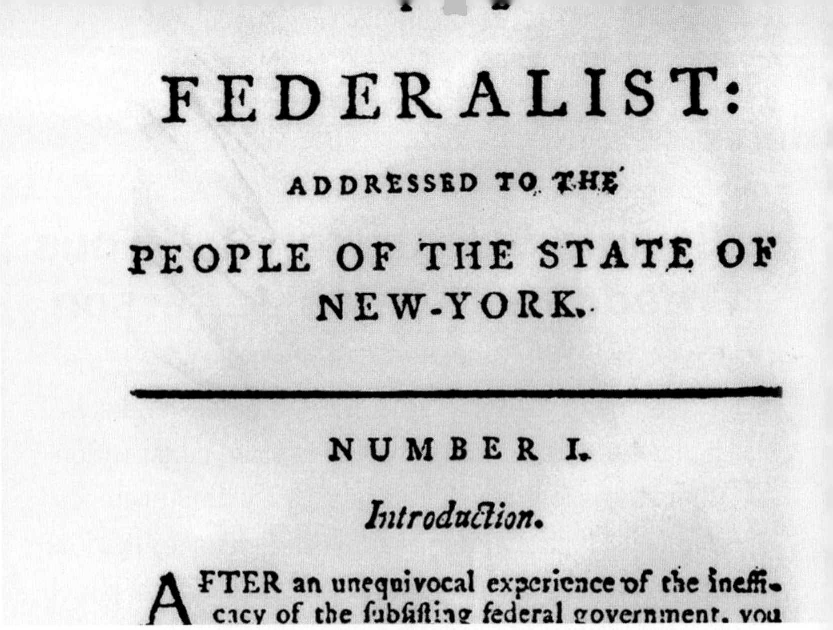
FEDERALIST:

ADDRESSED TO THE

PEOPLE OF THE STATE OF NEW-YORK.

NUMBER I.

Introduction.

AFTER an unequivocal experience of the ineffi-
cacy of the subsisting federal government, you

BOUNCE to Activate Flipped Video

Objectives

Summarize the arguments for and against ratification of the Constitution.

Describe how the Constitution was ratified.

Explain the principles of the Constitution.

Key Terms

ratification
Federalist
Antifederalist
The Federalist
John Jay
Bill of Rights
popular sovereignty
limited government
separation of powers
checks and balances
electoral college

The Enduring Constitution

The delegates to the Constitutional Convention had designed a strong federal government. All but three delegates endorsed the new Constitution, despite the fact that many felt it was imperfect. Today, we know that one of its flaws was that it failed to consider the viewpoints of women, African Americans, and Native Americans. In 1787, however, white men held all the power. So, after most of the delegates signed it, the proposed document was printed, circulated, and hotly debated. Would the states accept the plan? If not, what would become of the new nation?

The Debate Over Ratification

By drafting a new Constitution, the delegates had exceeded their mandate, which had only authorized them to propose amendments to the Articles of Confederation. Official approval, or **ratification**, of an entirely new constitution was doomed if all 13 states had to approve it as the Articles required. To improve the odds of ratification, the delegates arbitrarily decided to change the rules.

Under these new rules, delegates determined that approval by nine states would suffice. They also took the ratification decision away from the state legislatures, for they would most certainly oppose a new constitution that would deprive them of some power. Instead, specially elected conventions would determine a state's choice for or against the Constitution.

Federalists and Antifederalists Face Off Two groups soon emerged in the debate: the **Federalists**, who favored ratification of the Constitution, and the **Antifederalists**, who opposed it. The Federalists included George Washington, James Madison,

GO ONLINE to access your digital course

and Alexander Hamilton. They stressed the weaknesses of the Articles and argued that only a new government based on the proposed Constitution could overcome the difficulties facing the nation.

Antifederalists Argue Against a Strong Government Critics of the Constitution, known as Antifederalists, denounced it as a retreat from the liberty won by the Revolution. The Antifederalists especially disliked that the Constitution lacked a bill of rights to protect basic liberties from the powers of the government.

Antifederalists also noted that the Constitution greatly increased the powers of the central government and created a more elitist government by concentrating power in relatively few hands at a great distance from most voters. The Antifederalists believed that liberty could not survive unless the federal government remained weak, which meant that most power should belong to the state governments. One Antifederalist asked:

> What have you been contending for these ten years past? Liberty! What is Liberty? The power of governing yourselves. If you adopt this Constitution, have you this power? No: you give it into the hands of a set of men who live one thousand miles distant from you.
>
> —James Lincoln, South Carolina delegate

The Antifederalists included such leading Patriots as Samuel Adams and John Hancock of Massachusetts, George Clinton of New York, and Richard Henry Lee and Patrick Henry of Virginia. Successful state politicians, they distrusted the Federalist effort to subordinate the states to a stronger national Union.

The Federalists Win Support Most farmers recognized that the Constitution threatened the state debtor-relief laws that had rescued their farms from foreclosure. Common farmers also distrusted the lawyers, merchants, and other wealthy men who promoted the Constitution, viewing them as aristocrats hostile to the Republic. In South Carolina, farmers protested by staging a mock funeral around a coffin with the word *Liberty* painted on its side. Because most citizens were farmers, the proposed Constitution lacked majority support in 1787.

However, the Constitution had the support of two of the most popular and trusted men in the country—George Washington and Benjamin Franklin. Their support allayed the fears of many rural Americans. Some frontier farmers also endorsed the Constitution because they hoped that a stronger nation would

Federalists Versus Antifederalists

FEDERALISTS	ANTIFEDERALISTS
Supported the idea of a strong central government	Supported the idea of a weaker central government and stronger state governments
Made up mostly of people who owned property, including political leaders and wealthy merchants	Made up of well-known politicians such as Patrick Henry, as well as rural farmers
Endorsed the Constitution but thought the Articles of Confederation were weak	Endorsed the Articles of Confederation but not the Constitution
Believed that the checks and balances built into the Constitution were adequate to protect individual liberties	Convinced that the Constitution did not provide adequate separation of powers among the branches of government
Believed including a bill of rights in the Constitution was unnecessary, since state governments protected individual rights	Wanted to include a bill of rights in the Constitution

Source: *Encyclopædia Britannica*

>> **Analyze Information** What was the main issue over which Federalists and Antifederalists disagreed?

Ratification of the Constitution

STATE	DATE	VOTE	STATE	DATE	VOTE
Delaware	Dec. 7, 1787	30–0	South Carolina	May 23, 1788	149–73
Pennsylvania	Dec. 12, 1787	46–23	New Hampshire	June 21, 1788	57–46
New Jersey	Dec. 18, 1787	38–0	Virginia	June 25, 1788	89–79
Georgia	Jan. 2, 1788	26–0	New York	July 26, 1788	30–27
Connecticut	Jan. 9, 1788	128–40	North Carolina*	Nov. 21, 1789	195–77
Massachusetts	Feb. 6, 1788	187–168	Rhode Island	May 29, 1790	34–32
Maryland	April 28, 1788	63–11	* Second vote; ratification was originally defeated by a vote of 184–84		

>> **Analyze Charts** Why are New Hampshire, Virginia, and New York shown in a different color than the rest of the states?

defeat the American Indians and take control of the British forts along the Great Lakes.

The Federalists also enjoyed popular support in the seaports, which hosted most of the ratifying conventions. Unlike rural farmers, most urban artisans supported the Constitution. Hurt by the depression of the 1780s, these artisans hoped that a strong national government could expand American commerce. The seaports also had most of the nation's newspapers, the printers of which strongly endorsed the Constitution.

The Federalists were also better organized than the Antifederalists. Acting quickly after the Constitutional Convention, the Federalists built a nationwide network of support. Their national experience and connections gave them a great advantage in coordinating the first national political campaign. By contrast, the Antifederalists were state politicians who struggled to build alliances across state lines.

The Federalist Papers The Federalists' case for ratification of the Constitution appeared in ***The Federalist***, a series of 85 essays that came to be called the Federalist Papers. Three leading Federalists—Madison, Hamilton, and **John Jay**—wrote the essays, which were published in New York newspapers in 1787 and 1788, a time of heated debate in New York's ratifying convention.

The essays argued that the separation of powers in three branches of government would prevent the concentration of power dreaded by the Antifederalists. The authors were also eager for the United States to have a strong central government, as supported by Madison in *The Federalist,* No. 10. Federalist leaders feared that the United States would dissolve without a strong government. They argued, in *The Federalist,* No. 51, that the checks and balances in the Constitution prevented any of the three branches from gaining too much power. The authors insisted that the real threat to liberty came from the state legislatures, which lacked sufficient checks and balances. Hamilton also wrote of the importance of a judicial branch in *The Federalist,* No. 78. Today, these essays help scholars, judges, and lawyers understand the meaning of the Constitution.

☑ **CHECK UNDERSTANDING** How did Federalists respond to Antifederalist charges that the Constitution gave the federal government too much power?

Ratifying Conventions in the States

Exploiting their advantages, the Federalists pushed for quick ratifying conventions in five states. By mid-January 1788, the Federalists had won ratification in Delaware, Pennsylvania, New Jersey, Georgia, and Connecticut. These early victories generated momentum. To complete ratification, the Federalists needed only four of the remaining eight states. But the Antifederalists mounted a stronger fight in those states.

>> Delegates to the Massachusetts ratifying convention debated the proposed constitution at Boston's Old State House, shown here.

BOUNCE to Activate Chart

The States Ratify the Constitution In Massachusetts, the Federalists faced defeat until they made two key concessions to sway the moderate Antifederalists, led by Governor John Hancock. First, the Federalists appealed to Hancock's vanity. They hinted that he could become the nation's first Vice President by switching sides. Second, to make that switch easier, they promised to support key amendments to the Constitution. They would add a bill of rights, but only after ratification—not as a condition for it. In early February, following Hancock's lead, the Massachusetts convention ratified the Constitution.

The promise of a bill of rights helped the Federalists win most of the remaining states. Maryland ratified in April; South Carolina, in May; and New Hampshire, in early June. These states provided the winning nine, but the new nation would not last without the support of Virginia and New York. In late June, Virginia narrowly ratified, despite the forceful opposition of Patrick Henry, the greatest political orator of his generation. In July, New York also narrowly approved after Hamilton threatened New York City's secession from the state to join the Union if the state rejected the Constitution.

With the ratification of 11 states, the Congress of the Confederation made plans for the establishment of the new government and chose New York City as the temporary capital. The new Congress convened there on March 4, 1789, in Federal Hall. Plans for electing the nation's first President and Vice President were made. Within a short time, Rhode Island and North Carolina, which had previously rejected the Constitution, reconsidered and joined the Union.

The Bill of Rights If the Federalists deserve credit for the Constitution, the Antifederalists deserve credit for the **Bill of Rights**, the first ten amendments to the Constitution. Only the forceful resistance of the Antifederalists obliged the Federalists to add a listing of rights to the Constitution.

In the newly elected Congress, Madison drafted the Bill of Rights. Many of these amendments relied on the earlier Virginia Declaration of Rights. Madison limited the amendments to guarantees of individual rights, leaving the federal framework the same. He also avoided any sweeping preamble that declared all men equal in their creation and rights. That omission enabled enslavers to persist in denying rights to enslaved men and women. The protected rights included freedom of religion, speech, press, assembly, and petition; protection from unreasonable searches and seizures; and the right to a speedy and public trial.

Madison feared that any finite list of rights would later be abused in order to deny rights left unmentioned. So the Ninth Amendment stated: "The enumeration in the Constitution, of certain rights, shall not be construed to deny or disparage others retained by the people." That left open the subsequent development of additional rights. Congress passed the Bill of Rights in 1789.

DESCRIBE How did the inclusion of a bill of rights represent a victory for the Antifederalists?

Separation of Powers and Checks and Balances

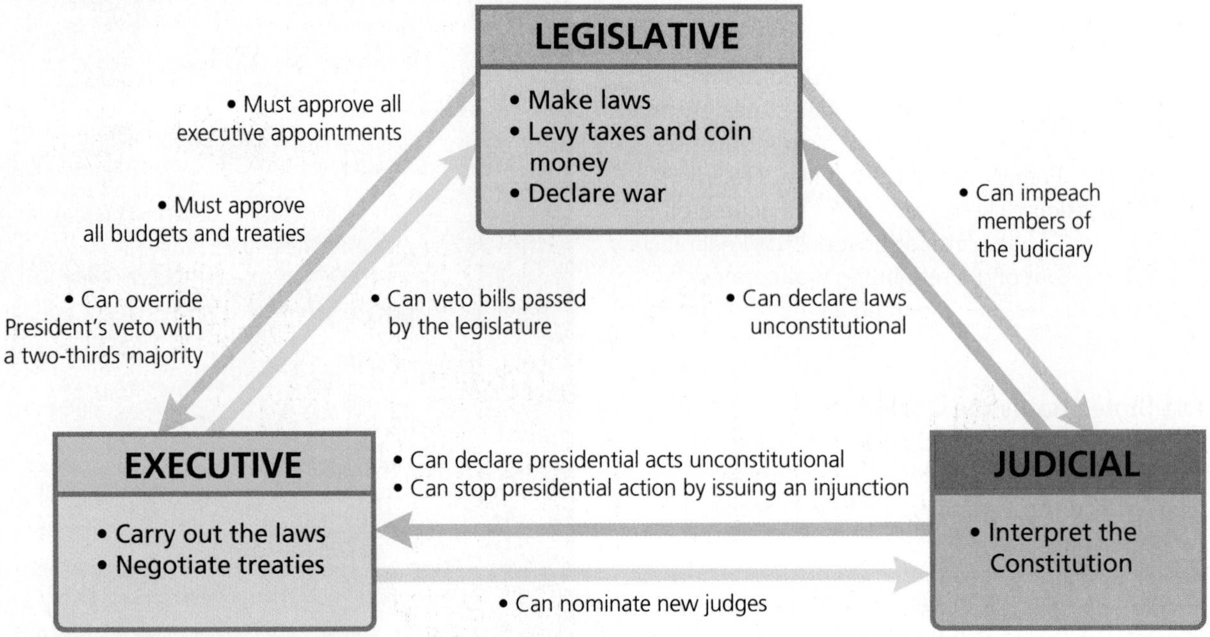

Sources: National Center for Constitutional Studies; Texas Tech University; *Encyclopædia Britannica*

>> **Analyze Diagrams** How did the powers granted to the new U.S. branches of government solve the problem of concentrating power in one body as was the case under the Articles of Confederation?

BOUNCE to Activate Chart

Constitutional Principles

The republic established by the Constitution of the United States became a symbol of freedom not only to Americans but also to countries in Europe and to republics in Latin America. The authors of the Constitution established a representative government based on these basic principles: popular sovereignty, limited government, separation of powers, federalism, checks and balances, and representative government.

Popular Sovereignty The Constitution abides by the principle of **popular sovereignty**, in which all government power comes from the people. In other words, the government derives its political authority from the people. In the early days of the nation, "the people" referred to white men only, however—and often only white men who owned property.

Limited Government Popular sovereignty ensures that a government's power is restricted, or limited. In a **limited government**, the Constitution specifically states what powers the government has. The principle of limited government also refers to the rule of law, which means that government leaders are not above the law.

Separation of Powers The Constitution mandates the **separation of powers** within the federal government into distinct legislative, executive, and judicial branches to prevent misuse of power by any of the three branches.

The Constitution assigns certain specific powers to each of these three branches of the federal government. The legislative branch, or Congress, enacts laws. The executive branch, headed by the President, carries out the laws, negotiates treaties, and commands the armed forces. The judicial branch interprets the Constitution and applies the law. The Constitution also establishes a Supreme Court and authorizes Congress to establish other courts as needed.

Federalism Just as the Constitution divides power among the three branches of the federal government, it also divides power between the states and the federal government, a division known as federalism. At the time, this meant that the states could no longer issue their own paper money or provide debtor relief at creditors' expense. These delegated powers belonged exclusively to the federal government.

Federalism also reserves some powers to the state governments. For example, states regulate all elections. The federal and state governments also hold some overlapping, or concurrent, powers, including the power to tax.

Checks and Balances The Constitution also limits the power of government by establishing a system of **checks and balances** designed to prevent one branch from seizing too much power. For example, only Congress has the power to enact laws, but the President may veto those laws. However, a two-thirds majority in both houses of Congress can override the President's veto. The President nominates judges, but the Senate must approve them.

Representative Government The writers of the Constitution had misgivings about the democratic rule of the majority. Many saw democracy as something that would lead to mob rule. Instead of forming a direct democracy in which all citizens vote on every matter, the writers provided for an indirect democracy in which voters elect representatives to be their voice in government. At this time, voters included only white males, and often only those who owned property.

For example, the Constitution stipulated that citizens would directly elect only the representatives to the House of Representatives. The state legislatures, rather than the voters, would choose the members of the Senate (who would serve for six years, rather than the two years representatives served). Similarly, an **electoral college**, or group of persons chosen from each state, would indirectly elect the President. Each state legislature would determine whether to choose those electors or let the citizens elect them.

In addition, the indirectly elected President and senators would choose the least democratic branch of all: the judiciary. By giving the federal judges (including the Supreme Court Justices) life terms, the delegates meant to insulate them from democratic politics.

The Constitution Endures The Constitution became the supreme law of the land in 1789. With amendments, it has endured for more than 200 years. At about 7,000 words, the Constitution is relatively brief and often ambiguous. Therefore, it invites debate.

Some politicians, including Thomas Jefferson, argued that the Constitution should be interpreted narrowly and literally to restrict federal power. Most Federalists, including George Washington, insisted that the Constitution be read broadly to allow for the expansion of federal power when necessary.

How is it that a Constitution written when the nation was a loose union of 13 states continues to guide the actions of the government today? The Framers knew that they could not anticipate future social, economic, and political events. They,

>> **Analyze Maps** Based on this map, how has the United States applied the rules of the Constitution to the structure of the U.S. Congress over time?

therefore, worded parts of the Constitution to permit some flexibility. The Constitution has survived and thrived in part because it provides a process for changes in its content. The Constitution makes amendment possible but difficult. Two thirds of both houses of Congress must approve an amendment, which becomes law only when ratified by three fourths of the states. Since the Bill of Rights, only 27 amendments have been added to the Constitution.

LIST What are four of the main political principles underlying the U.S. Constitution?

ASSESSMENT

1. **Determine Central Ideas** Why did the Federalists generally have more support for their ideas than the Antifederalists during the ratification period?
2. **Generate Explanations** Is the American system of government a direct democracy? Why or why not?
3. **Generate Explanations** How does a document written over two hundred years ago remain relevant and responsive to current social, economic, and political events?
4. **Apply Concepts** What is the principle of federalism and how is it reflected in the relationship between federal and state government?
5. **Quest Connections** Enlightenment thinker Baron de Montesquieu wrote that to prevent the abuse of power, "it is necessary . . . that power should be a check to power." What principle of the Constitution reflects this idea?

GO ONLINE to access these biographies: John Jay, Alexander Hamilton

Connections to Today

Thanks to the First Amendment, Americans are free to speak their minds at community meetings and elsewhere.

Take Action on Free Speech

A major step in establishing the new nation was creating the Bill of Rights, one part of which protects freedom of speech. That right is just as important today as it was in 1791.

1. **Choose** one of the following topics related to free speech:
   - **Social media:** Learn how the right to free speech relates to social media, including cyberbullying, hate speech, and private censorship.
   - **Student speech:** Explore the extent to which student speech is protected and whether the Internet has led to any changes in that area, such as school Internet filters.
   - **Controversial speech:** Some speech is controversial, such as professional football players kneeling during the national anthem. What is the purpose and effect of this type of speech?
2. **Ask Questions** Generate a list of questions about your topic, such as whether the Supreme Court has ruled on any social media cases.
3. **Learn** about the topic by conducting research using online sources, including news articles. What debates are related to this topic? What are the arguments on each side? Take notes as you conduct your research and continue to ask questions as you learn more.
4. **Simulate a Trial** Write a closing argument that might be given to a jury hearing a free speech case related to your topic. Be sure to summarize the main arguments in the case and be persuasive! Then share your closing argument with your classmates and community.

Topic 4 Quick Study Guide

LESSON SUMMARIES

Use these Lesson Summaries, and the longer versions available online, to review the key ideas for each lesson in this Topic.

Lesson 1: The Articles of Confederation

In 1777, the Continental Congress drafted the Articles of Confederation, which established a loose confederation of states. The new national government included no executive branch, and the powers to make, implement, and enforce the laws were given to a one-house Congress. The weaknesses of the Articles contributed to the troubles of the fledgling government.

Lesson 2: The Constitutional Convention

To fix the weaknesses of the Articles of Confederation, 12 states sent delegates to a convention in Philadelphia in 1787. Rather than amend the Articles, the delegates decided to create a new constitution for the country.

Lesson 3: The Enduring Constitution

The proposed Constitution was supported by the Federalists and opposed by the Antifederalists. Virginia and New York, whose support was essential, ratified it in 1788. The new government was a representative democracy based on popular sovereignty, limited government, separation of powers, federalism, checks and balances, and representative government.

QUEST! FINDINGS

Write Your Ideas That Influenced the Constitution Essay Refer to your responses to the Quest Connections to help you write your essay. Use the rubric and other Quest resources online to guide your work.

GO ONLINE to access lesson summaries

VISUAL REVIEW

Use these graphics to review some of the key terms, people, and ideas from this Topic.

Convention Compromises

VIRGINIA PLAN

- Bicameral Congress
- Number of members in both houses based on population

NORTHERN PLAN

Enslaved people not counted

THE GREAT COMPROMISE

- Bicameral Congress
- States equally represented in Senate and represented by population in House

THREE-FIFTHS COMPROMISE

Enslaved people counted as 3/5 of a person for representation in the House and the electoral college

NEW JERSEY PLAN

- Unicameral Congress
- Each state has the same number of representatives

SOUTHERN PLAN

Each enslaved person counted as one person

Principles of the Constitution

Popular sovereignty	The people are the only source of the government's power.
Limited government	The government has only the powers the Constitution gives it.
Separation of powers	The government's power is divided among three branches: legislative, executive, judicial.
Checks and balances	Each branch of government has the power to limit the actions of the other two.
Federalism	The federal and state governments share power.
Representative government	Citizens elect legislators to represent them.

The Government Under the Articles of Confederation

STRUCTURE	FOREIGN POLICY	MILITARY	FINANCE
• Made Congress the governing body of the federal government; no executive or judicial branch • Gave each state one vote in Congress	• Gave Congress the power to sign treaties, make alliances, and declare war • Gave Congress the power to manage relations with American Indians	• Gave Congress the power to build a navy • Gave Congress the power to raise an army only by asking the states for troops	• Did not give Congress the power to tax or to create a single, national currency • Gave Congress the power to borrow money

Topic 4 Assessment

KEY TERMS, PEOPLE, AND IDEAS

1. What is the difference between a **unicameral legislature** and a **bicameral legislature**? Which type of legislature did most of the early state governments have?
2. What was the purpose of the Land Ordinance of **1787** and how did it work?
3. What was the impact of **Shays' Rebellion**?
4. How did the **Great Compromise** resolve the conflict between supporters of the **Virginia Plan** and supporters of the **New Jersey Plan**?
5. Who wrote ***The Federalist*** and what was its goal?
6. How did the **Bill of Rights** try to meet the concerns of **Antifederalists**?
7. How is the President chosen under the **electoral college** system?
8. How are the principles of **separation of powers** and **checks and balances** related?

CRITICAL THINKING

9. **Assess an Argument** In 1776, John Adams argued against changing requirements for voting: "There will be no end of it. New claims will arise. Women will demand a vote. Lads from 12 to 21 will think their rights not enough attended to, and every man, who has not a farthing, will demand an equal voice with any other in all acts of state. It tends to confound and destroy all distinctions, and prostrate all ranks to one common level." Restate the main idea of this argument in your own words. What assumptions is this argument based on? How were Adams' views reflected in the early state constitutions?
10. **Evaluate Information** Describe the way the government worked under the Articles of Confederation. Then, explain two of the government's weaknesses.
11. **Draw Conclusions** How do you think the United States might have been different today if the Articles of Confederation had remained in place?
12. **Identify Key Steps in a Process** What do you think were the four most important steps that led to the establishment of our constitutional republic in the United States? Explain your reasons for choosing each step.
13. **Analyze Interactions** In what ways did Alexander Hamilton and James Madison work toward different goals? In what ways did they work toward the same goal?
14. **Use Visual Information** Look at the cartoon below. What was important about the particular moment that the cartoonist shows? Do you think the cartoonist was a Federalist or an Antifederalist?

From the Independent Chronicle and Universal Advertiser, Boston, Thursday June 26, 1788.

15. **Draw Inferences** The Constitution includes an amendment process so that it can be changed if necessary. Which compromises at the Constitutional Convention were later undone by amendment?
16. **Writing Activity: Write an Argument** The excerpt below is from *The Federalist*. Write an essay based on this excerpt and your own knowledge. First, identify which principles of the U.S. Constitution are reflected in this excerpt. Then, state whether you think the federal government and the state governments should have equal authority, or whether one should have more authority over the other. Give reasons for your opinion.

> [I]n a single republic, all the power surrendered by the people is submitted to the administration of a single government; and [illegal seizures of power] are guarded against by a division of the government into distinct and separate departments. In the compound republic of America, the power surrendered by the people is first divided between two distinct governments, and then the portion allotted to each subdivided among distinct and separate departments. Hence a double security arises to the rights of the people. The different governments will control each other, at the same time that each will be controlled by itself.
> —*Federalist* No. 51

17. **Connections to Today** Give one example showing how the definition of "speech" has changed since the First Congress wrote the First Amendment in the Bill of Rights. Is this new type of speech protected under the First Amendment? Explain.

DOCUMENT-BASED QUESTIONS

The decision to ratify the new Constitution was not an easy one. Americans disagreed strongly on the proposed new government. Read the documents below, then answer the questions that follow.

DOCUMENT A

The following excerpt is from a speech given at the Massachusetts ratifying convention.

> "We contended with Great Britain—some said for a three-penny duty on tea, but it was not that. It was because they claimed a right to tax us and bind us in all cases whatever. And does not this Constitution do the same? Does it not take away all we have—all our property? Does it not lay all taxes, duties, imposts, and excises? . . . These lawyers, and men of learning, and moneyed men, that talk so finely and gloss over matters so smoothly, to make us poor illiterate people swallow down the pill, expect to get into Congress themselves. They expect to be the managers of this Constitution, and get all the power and all the money into their own hands. And then they will swallow up all of us little folks. . . ."
>
> —*Amos Singletary, farmer, 1788*

DOCUMENT B

Another farmer also offered his viewpoint at the Massachusetts convention.

> "I have lived in a part of the country where I have known the worth of good government by the want of it. There was a black cloud [Shays' Rebellion] that rose in the east last winter, and spread over the west. . . . It brought on a state of anarchy and that led to tyranny. . . . Now, Mr. President, when I saw this Constitution, I found that it was a cure for these disorders. It was just such a thing as we wanted. I got a copy of it and read it over and over. I had been a member of the convention to form our own state constitution, and had learnt something of the checks and balances of power; and I found them all here."
>
> —*Jonathan Smith, farmer, 1788*

DOCUMENT C

This excerpt is from a letter by "Cato," believed by many scholars to be the governor of New York, George Clinton.

> ". . . that the number of representatives are too few . . . that the mode in which they are appointed and their duration, will lead to the establishment of an aristocracy, that the senate and President are improperly connected . . . these are some of the many evils that will attend the adoption of this government."
>
> —*Letter V by "Cato,"* The New York Journal, *November 22, 1787*

DOCUMENT D

This chart shows the order in which the states ratified the Constitution and the vote in each state ratifying convention.

Ratification

Delaware	30–0
Pennsylvania	46–23
New Jersey	38–0
Georgia	26–0
Connecticut	128–40
Massachusetts	187–168
Maryland	63–11
South Carolina	149–73
New Hampshire	57–46
Virginia	89–79
New York	30–27
North Carolina*	195–77
Rhode Island	34–32

*Second vote; ratification was originally defeated by a vote of 184–84

18. Which of these documents most clearly reflects the Federalist position?
A. Document A
B. Document B
C. Documents A and C
D. Documents B and C

19. The authors of Documents A and C both argue that the new Constitution would
A. create too weak a federal government.
B. support political stability in the new nation.
C. endanger the rights of ordinary citizens.
D. provide a workable system of checks and balances.

20. Based on Document D, which state had the highest percentage of delegates who opposed the new Constitution?
A. Pennsylvania
B. Massachusetts
C. New Hampshire
D. Rhode Island

21. Writing Task Summarize the hopes and fears people on each side of the ratification debate had about the new Constitution. Then use specific evidence from the documents above, along with information from this Topic, to answer this question: How close do you think the Constitution came to being rejected?

GO ONLINE to access more practice

The Early Republic (1789–1840)

ESSENTIAL QUESTION What makes a government successful?

GO ONLINE to access the eText, videos, Interactive Primary Sources, Biographies, and other online resources.

President George Washington

Connections to Today

The office of the U.S. President comes with great responsibility as outlined in Article II of the Constitution. In part, Article II states that the President commands the armed forces, makes treaties with foreign nations, and nominates Supreme Court justices. The executive power of the President is balanced by the powers of Congress and the Supreme Court.

In this topic you will learn about seven presidents each of whom exercised power in different ways. Do you think any single president can change or redefine the presidency?

NBC LEARN

Learn about Lucy Larcom and her weaving opportunity.

BOUNCE to Activate My Story Video

Topic 5 Overview

In this Topic you'll learn about the challenges faced by the new nation as it established its government, expanded its territory, and faced external enemies and internal division. Look at the lesson outline and explore the timeline. As you study this Topic, you'll complete the Quest Inquiry.

LESSON OUTLINE

5.1 The New Government Finds Its Way

5.2 Jefferson as President

5.3 The War of 1812

5.4 The Beginning of the Industrial Revolution

5.5 Differences Between North and South Grow

5.6 Nationalism Influences Policies

5.7 Jacksonian Democracy

Key Events of the Early Republic

1789
George Washington becomes the first President of the United States

1793
Samuel Slater builds the first water-powered textile mill

1801
Thomas Jefferson becomes president; John Marshall becomes Chief Justice of the Supreme Court

1813
Shawnee warrior Tecumseh is killed in battle

1815
British are defeated at the Battle of New Orleans

1823
President James Monroe issues the Monroe Doctrine

1832
South Carolina's legislature votes to nullify the protective tariff

1785 · 1795 · 1805 · 1815 · 1825 · 1835

QUEST! INQUIRY

Civic Discussion: The Death Penalty

Should the death penalty be repealed in the United States? The Eighth Amendment prohibits "cruel and unusual punishments." Is the death penalty a form of cruel and unusual punishment? In this Quest, you'll investigate the viewpoints for and against capital punishment in order to argue for and against each side.

STEP 1

With your group, read the arguments for and against the death penalty and write down major points from your reading. Discuss the major points with your group.

STEP 2

Research the issue by reading several sources. Carefully evaluate each source, and then analyze the evidence the sources provide for their perspectives.

STEP 3

Use the evidence to formulate arguments for the position assigned to you. After presenting your position, listen to the other side's arguments, and then switch sides.

STEP 4

Reach your own conclusion, and then share your point of view with your group. Listen carefully as others share their thoughts. Then think about what you have learned and answer the questions.

GO ONLINE to access complete Quest materials

5.1

In 1789, George Washington was inaugurated as the nation's first president under the new Constitution in New York City, then the U.S. capital.

BOUNCE to Activate Flipped Video

Objectives

Describe how Washington's administration built the federal government.

Analyze Hamilton's plans for the economy and the opposition to them.

Explain how a two-party system emerged in the new nation.

Explain how territorial expansion brought Americans into conflict with the British and with American Indians.

Describe American relations with Britain, France, and Spain.

Analyze how the political parties' debates over foreign policy further divided them.

Key Terms

administration
precedent
Cabinet
tariff
loose construction
strict construction
Whiskey Rebellion
political party
Democratic Republicans
Little Turtle
Battle of Fallen Timbers
French Revolution
John Jay
XYZ Affair
Alien and Sedition Acts
Virginia and Kentucky resolutions
Aaron Burr

GO ONLINE to access your digital course

The New Government Finds Its Way

In 1789, the leaders of the new federal government of the United States gathered in New York City. Besides ideals, they had very little to guide them. The newly ratified Constitution was clear on some points but vague on others. It was also entirely untested. Those who had written the Constitution, along with the new President, George Washington, knew full well that a good start would secure the daring experiment in republican union. But early mistakes could doom it.

Creating a New Government

The new government started out with huge problems. It had inherited a national debt of $52 million from the Confederation—a huge burden for a nation with a farm economy and only about 3 million people. With no navy and an army of only around 400 men, the United States was not respected by other countries. At New Orleans, the Spanish closed the Mississippi River to American trade. Along the Great Lakes, the British kept forts within American territory.

President Washington Fortunately, the new government enjoyed extraordinary leaders. In 1789, the new electoral college unanimously elected George Washington as President of the United States. As a revolutionary leader, Washington enjoyed widespread respect and popularity. Yet he took the difficult job reluctantly.

> About ten o'clock I bade farewell to Mount Vernon, to private life, and to domestic felicity, and with a mind oppressed with more anxious and painful sensations than I have words to express, set out for New York.
>
> —George Washington, April 16, 1789

Massachusetts patriot John Adams was elected Vice President. Washington's **administration**, or the officials in the executive branch of government, at first consisted of just himself, Adams, and about a dozen clerks. Besides the newly elected Congress, there were few other federal officers. There were also few set rules to guide the administration. Quickly after taking office, Washington began setting important **precedents**, or acts or statements that become traditions to be followed.

Building the Court System The Constitution called for one Supreme Court and several smaller ones, but intentionally left to Congress the responsibility of organizing a federal court system. Madison, who had been elected to the House of Representatives in the first Congress, helped to pass the Judiciary Act of 1789. This act established a judiciary, or a system of courts. The U.S. judiciary was made up of thirteen federal district courts, one for each state. Three circuit courts would hear appeals from the state courts and a six-member Supreme Court would decide contested cases. The Supreme Court also served as a trial court in certain cases involving states or foreign affairs. The act also established the office of Attorney General to prosecute and defend cases on behalf of the federal government. Washington appointed John Jay as the first Chief Justice of the Supreme Court.

Creating the President's Cabinet One of Washington's most important precedents was the formation of a **Cabinet**, or the group of federal leaders who headed the major departments of the executive branch and advised the President. The first four executive departments were the departments of State, Treasury, and War, and the Attorney General. The State Department, led by Thomas Jefferson, conducted foreign policy. The War Department supervised national defense. The Secretary of the Treasury, Alexander Hamilton, managed the nation's finances. Nominated by the President, the Cabinet members were approved by the Senate. In 1907, the Cabinet was officially recognized by law.

CHECK UNDERSTANDING Why was setting up the Cabinet an important precedent?

Addressing the Nation's Debt

Hamilton was tasked with organizing the young nation's immense debts and setting it on a course of economic security. A true Federalist, he believed that a strong, centralized government was necessary to preserve the Union. As he developed his plans, Hamilton faced fierce and vocal opposition from Antifederalists, who feared that a strong national government would threaten states' rights and people's freedoms. Their struggles and debates made clear that two very different views of government were emerging in the new nation.

Hamilton's Plan Hamilton despised the nation's agricultural economy as backward. He wanted to quickly develop a commercial and industrial economy that could support a large federal government along with a strong army and navy. He regarded the national debt of $52 million and the additional $25 million in debts owed by the individual states as assets.

>> Washington's Cabinet included some of the nation's most respected statesmen of the era. (from left) George Washington, Henry Knox, Alexander Hamilton, Thomas Jefferson, and Edmund Randolph.

Rather than pay down those debts using cash reserves, he meant to fund them by selling government bonds, which would pay annual interest to the holders. Such bonds delighted investors, who welcomed an opportunity to reap annual profits.

To pay the annual interest on the bonds, Hamilton proposed new excise taxes and high **tariffs**, or taxes on imported goods, to raise revenue for the federal government and protect struggling American manufacturers from foreign competition. He also asked Congress to charter a Bank of the United States that could regulate state banks, strengthen the national government, and ensure that business interests were closely aligned with those of the government.

Promoting Commerce and Industrial Growth

Hamilton saw three great benefits from his system. First, it would establish the nation's financial credibility, making it easier to borrow money in the future. Second, it would buy political support from the wealthiest Americans, which Hamilton believed was essential for the government's stability. Third, it would enrich investors, who could then build new ships, wharves, storehouses, and factories.

In other words, his plan would promote the accumulation of capital needed for commercial and industrial growth.

Hamilton's program was intended to redistribute wealth in two ways: from farmers to merchants and from the South to the North. About eighty percent of the nation's debt was owed to merchants in the seaport cities of the Northeast. During the 1780s, they had bought up notes issued by the Congress or by the states. Those notes had lost most of their value but the merchants had bought them anyway as an investment. Because they paid only a fraction of the original value of the notes, and because Hamilton proposed paying them at full value, the merchants would profit under Hamilton's plan. But to pay those debts, the federal government would tax the American people, who were mainly farmers.

Southern States Oppose Hamilton's Plan The southern states, which were overwhelmingly agricultural, had done a better job of paying their own debts. Why, southerners wondered, should they pay federal taxes to bail out the northern states? And why should their tax dollars flow into the pockets of creditors in the Northeast? Opposition to Hamilton's plans grew steadily in the South.

To justify his ambitious program, Hamilton interpreted the Constitution broadly, relying on its "implied powers" and its clause empowering Congress to enact laws for the "general welfare." His broad interpretation, or **loose construction**, appalled his critics, including Jefferson and Madison. They favored a **strict construction**, or limiting the federal government to powers explicitly granted by the Constitution. They opposed Hamilton's plans for assuming state debts. Fearing that a national bank would benefit the North at the expense of the South, they also argued that the Constitution did not authorize Congress to charter one.

THE DEBT PROBLEM 1789–1791

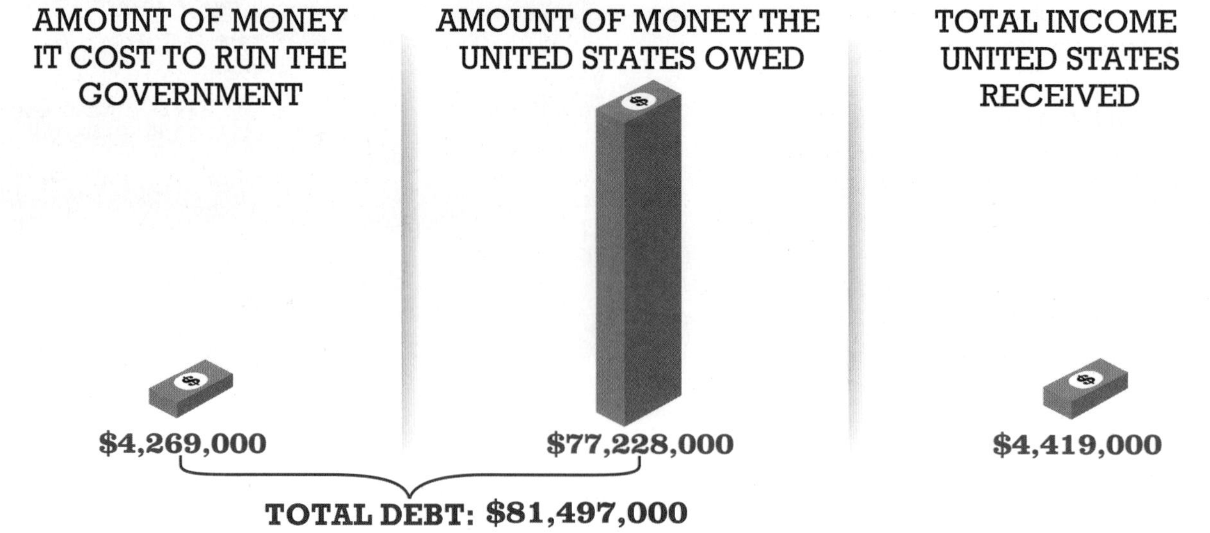

Source: *Historical Statistics of the United States*

>> **Analyze Data** How would you explain the debt problem facing the new government?

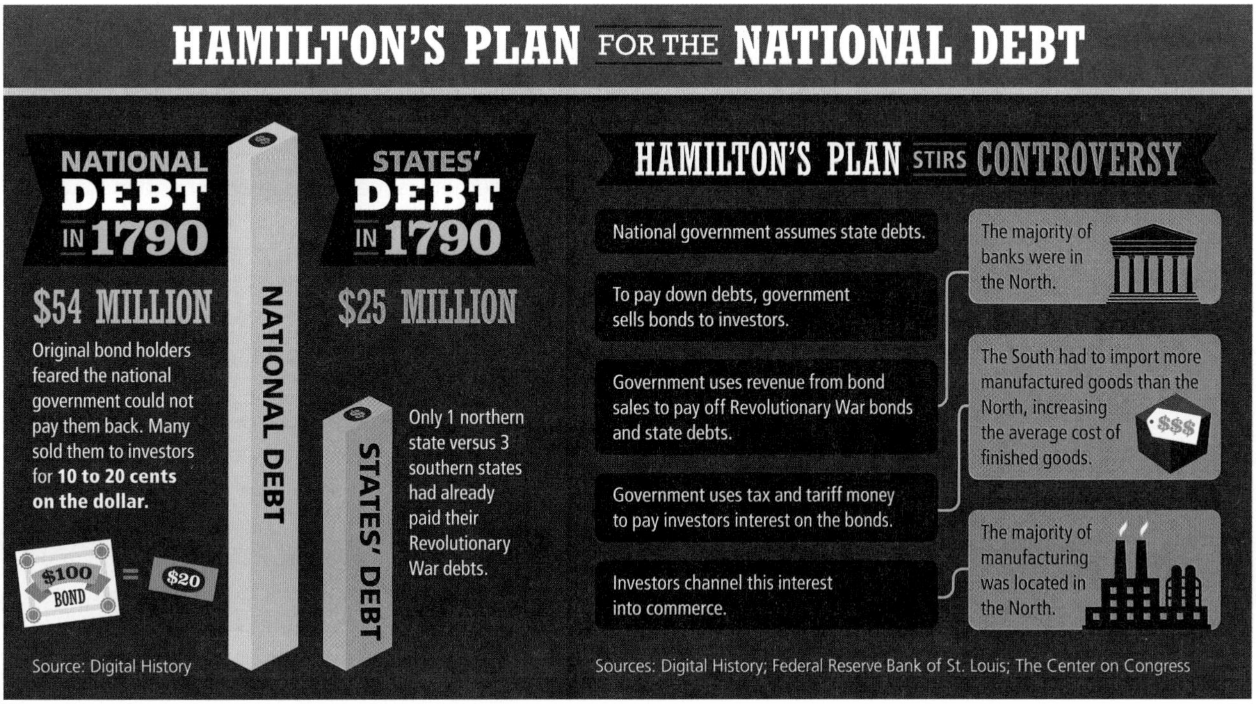

>> **Analyze Information** Which region of the United States mostly benefited from Hamilton's plan? Justify your response.

Hamilton Compromises As Americans aligned themselves either with Hamilton or with Madison and Jefferson, debate heated up. Jefferson declared that Hamilton's system "flowed from principles adverse to liberty and . . . calculated to undermine and demolish the republic." Jefferson and Madison insisted that Hamilton was betraying the American Revolution to establish a "kingly government."

They pointed to Great Britain, where factories made owners wealthy but kept most of the workers in poverty. Fearing that industrial development led to greater inequality, they concluded that America needed to keep a farm economy in order to sustain the Republic.

In 1791, by a narrow vote, Congress approved full funding of the federal debt, the implementation of new excise taxes, and the creation of a national bank. But in order to get southerners to agree to the assumption of state debts, Hamilton promised that in ten years the national capital would move southward to the banks of the Potomac River, between Maryland and Virginia. To honor the first President, who was reelected in 1792, the new capital became known as Washington, District of Columbia.

The Whiskey Rebellion In western Pennsylvania, mountains made it difficult to transport bulky bushels of grain to eastern markets. So people distilled their grain into whiskey, which was more compact and of higher value. Rural farmers hated the excise tax on whiskey, which reminded them of the British taxes that had led to the Revolution. In 1794, farmers resisted the tax by intimidating and attacking tax collectors.

Hamilton welcomed the opportunity to demonstrate the new power of the nation by suppressing the **Whiskey Rebellion**. Washington agreed, observing, "We had given no testimony to the world of being able or willing to support our government and laws." Under Hamilton's command, 12,000 militiamen marched west into the troubled region. The rebellion quickly dissolved. Rather than resist such overwhelming force, most rebels stayed home or ran away. Hamilton arrested twenty suspects, but only two were convicted. Jefferson mocked that "an insurrection was announced and proclaimed and armed against, but could never be found."

☑ **IDENTIFY CENTRAL IDEAS** What were the key components of Hamilton's plan?

Political Divisions Lead to Two Parties

The Whiskey Rebellion highlighted the growing division in American politics. The federal government, headed by Washington and Hamilton, sought to secure its power and authority. Meanwhile the opposition, led by Madison and Jefferson, grew stronger.

The Whiskey Rebellion Stirs Debate The Whiskey Rebellion, and its outcome, fueled disagreement. The Federalists blamed the rebellion in part on a set of political clubs known as the Democratic Societies. The clubs had formed to oppose the Federalists. Although these clubs were small and scattered, Washington denounced them as "the most diabolical attempt to destroy the best fabric of human government and happiness." Jefferson and Madison defended the societies, fearing that aristocracy would triumph if leaders were immune from constant public scrutiny and criticism. They were alarmed that the Federalists had sent so many troops to suppress popular dissent in western Pennsylvania. As debate over the rebellion continued, the two sides gradually emerged as distinct political groups.

Political Parties Emerge The authors of the Constitution wanted to avoid organized **political parties**, or groups of people who seek to win elections and hold public office in order to shape government policy. They deemed these groups to be "factions" that threatened the unity of a republic. Despite these intentions, politicians eventually formed two parties: the Federalists, led by Hamilton and John Adams, and the **Democratic Republicans**, led by Jefferson and Madison. This party was also know as the Republicans.

Northerners, especially merchants, tended to favor the Federalists, who promoted industry and trade. In contrast, southerners, especially farmers, voted mainly for the Democratic Republicans because they believed the country's economy should be based on agriculture. Despite these regional divisions, Federalists and Democratic Republicans could be found in every social class, in every type of community, in every region, and in every state. Political elections were closely contested most of the time.

The first two Presidents and most of the governors, state legislators, and congressmen were Federalists. Their early electoral success indicated that they were able to attract a majority of voters. Voters credited the Federalists with the new Constitution and with the nation's increased prosperity and stability during the 1790s.

But many common people continued to support the Democratic Republicans. They worried that the Federalists would concentrate wealth and power in the hands of the elite and that the federal government would hold too much power. Democratic

Political Parties in the Fourth Congress, 1795–1797

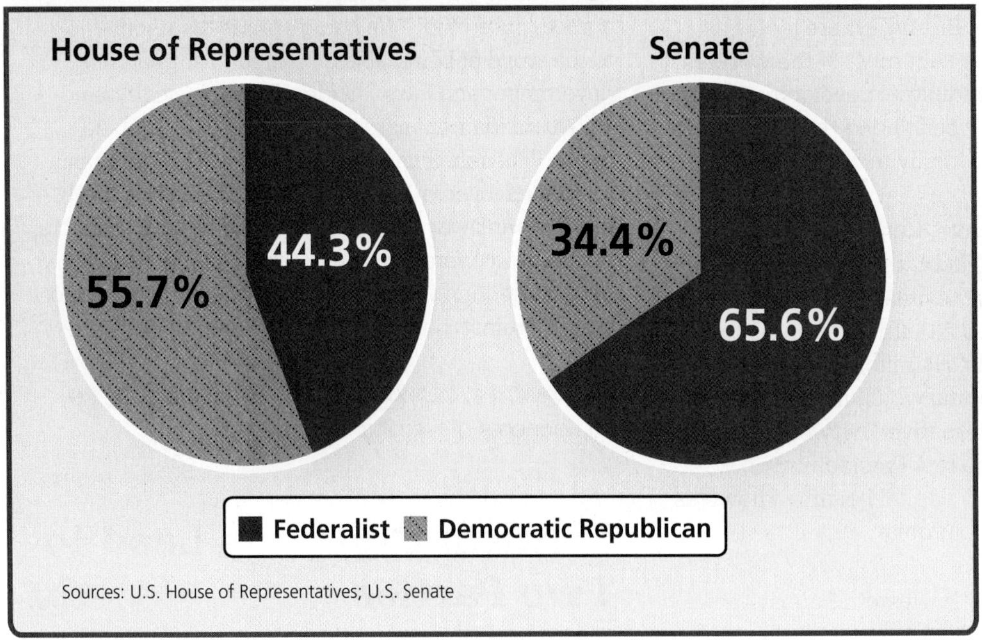

>> **Analyze Data** Based on what you know about the early republican government, were state legislatures likely controlled more by Democratic Republicans or by Federalists? How can you tell?

BOUNCE to Activate Chart

American Indians in the Northwest Territory, c. 1787

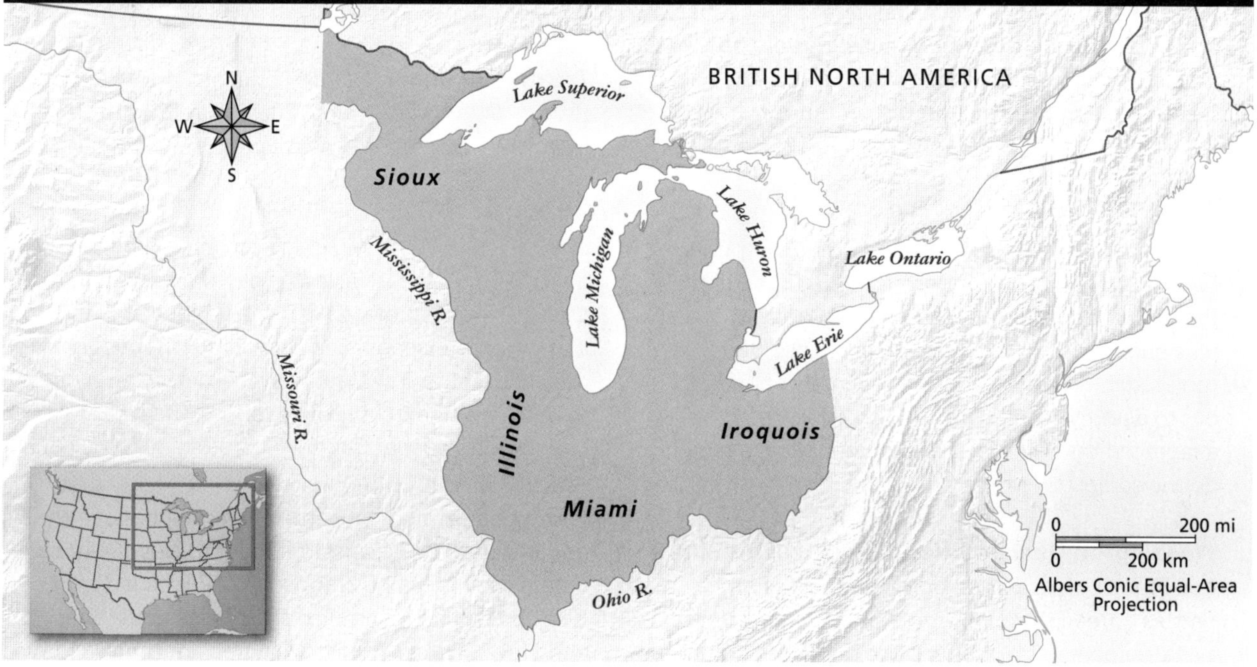

>> **Analyze Maps** Why was the Miami nation especially opposed to U.S. settlement on the Northwest Territory?

Republicans wanted the states to hold more power relative to the federal government. They and many voters also believed that the Democratic Republican Party offered more social mobility.

☑ **IDENTIFY** Identify the key differences between the Federalists and the Democratic Republicans.

Domestic and Foreign Affairs

In addition to building a government, making peace with American Indians, and maintaining control over expanded borders, the young United States had to establish itself in the international community during a volatile time. By 1793, Britain and France had resumed war, and it became difficult for the United States to stay neutral. Debate over America's response to a war and to a revolution in France affected the nation's foreign policy as well as its domestic structure.

Settlement in the Northwest Territory Although the Treaty of Paris had granted the United States a vast new territory west of the Appalachians, the British kept their forts on the American side of the Great Lakes. Hoping to limit American settlement in the Northwest Territory, the British provided arms and ammunition to the Miami Indians and their allies, who were actively resisting American expansion into their lands.

In 1790, American Indians led by the war chief **Little Turtle** defeated a small force sent by President Washington to stop attacks against settlers. In 1791 in the Ohio Valley, British guns helped a confederacy of many American Indian nations, again led by Little Turtle, to crush a larger American force commanded by General Arthur St. Clair.

But the tide turned in August 1794 when federal troops led by General Anthony Wayne defeated the American Indian confederacy at the **Battle of Fallen Timbers**, named for the fallen trees that covered the battle site. Wayne's decisive victory forced the American Indians to accept his peace terms. In the Treaty of Greenville, American Indian leaders ceded most of the present state of Ohio to the U.S. government. This also opened the Northwest Territory to settlement.

Americans and the French Revolution While the British were helping American Indians take a stand against the United States, the young nation struggled to chart a steady course in the area of foreign policy. In 1789, Americans welcomed news of the **French Revolution**, an uprising in France. Grateful for French help during the American Revolution, many Americans now saw the French as fellow republicans in a hostile world of aristocrats and kings. In 1793, however, leaders of the French Revolution began executing thousands of opponents, including the French king and his family. They also declared war on the monarchies of Europe, including Great Britain.

In response, Americans divided along party lines. The Democratic Republicans regretted the executions but still preferred the French Republic to its monarchist foes. Jefferson regarded the French Revolution as "the most sacred cause that ever man was engaged in." But the Federalists decided that the French revolutionaries were bloody anarchists out to destroy religion and social order. They suspected that the Democratic Republicans meant to do the same.

Washington Declares Neutrality By 1793, Britain and France were at war. Both American political parties agreed that the United States was too weak to participate in the war and too dependent on trade with Britain, which provided nearly 90 percent of American imports. That trade generated most of the federal revenue, which came primarily from tariffs and only secondarily from excise taxes.

If the United States entered the conflict, it could bankrupt the federal government. In 1793, President Washington, therefore, issued a proclamation of American neutrality, which became a foundation of American policy toward Europe until the twentieth century. The powerful British navy tested that neutrality by seizing American ships trading with the French colonies in the West Indies. Those seizures added to American outrage at the British policy along the new nation's western frontier.

Treaties Maintain Peace To avoid war with Britain, Washington sent Chief Justice **John Jay** to London to negotiate a compromise with the British. In the Jay Treaty of 1794, the British gave up their forts on American soil, but they kept most of their restrictions on American ships. The treaty also required Americans to repay prewar debts to the British. Washington and the Federalists favored this compromise, but the Democratic Republicans denounced the Jay Treaty as a sellout. After a heated debate, the Senate narrowly ratified the treaty, keeping the peace.

In 1795, the United States also signed a treaty with Spain. American settlers needed to move their goods down the Mississippi River to New Orleans, where they could be shipped to markets in the East. But, Spain controlled the Mississippi River and New Orleans. To ensure a free flow of trade, an American diplomat, Thomas Pinckney, negotiated a favorable treaty with the Spanish, who feared that an Anglo-American alliance might threaten their American possessions. Pinckney's Treaty guaranteed Americans free shipping rights on the Mississippi River and access to New Orleans. The treaty also established the northern boundary of Spanish Florida.

The removal of British forts, victories over American Indians, and secure access to New Orleans encouraged thousands of Americans to move westward. By 1800, nearly 400,000 Americans lived

Jay's Treaty & Pinckney's Treaty

JAY'S TREATY (U.S. & BRITAIN)	PINCKNEY'S TREATY (U.S. & SPAIN)
• Americans must settle pre-Revolutionary war debts to British merchants. • British must leave the Northwest Territory by June 1, 1796. • British must pay claims made against them by U.S. merchants. • United States given trading privileges with England and the British West Indies. • Mississippi River open to both countries. • Prohibited supplying food and weapons to privateers owned by British enemies in U.S. ports. • Joint commissions must settle territorial boundaries between both countries.	• Americans can temporarily store goods tax-free in New Orleans. • Americans can freely navigate the Mississippi River in Spanish territory. • Southern boundary of the United States set at 31° N latitude. • Each country must prevent Indians within its borders from attacking the other country. • Both countries can navigate the seas freely.

Source: *Encyclopædia Britannica*

>> **Analyze Information** What effect did these two treaties have on U.S. trade and commercial interests?

Election of 1796

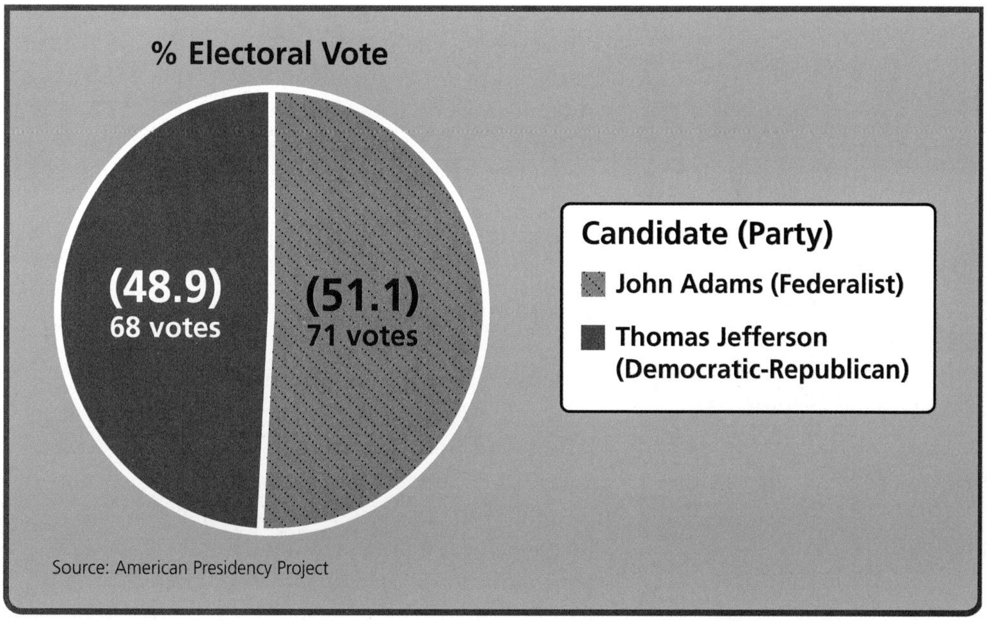

>> **Analyze Data** What do these election results suggest about the balance of political power in the United States in 1796?

beyond the Appalachian Mountains. By selling land to these settlers, the federal government gained revenue that helped to pay off the national debt.

Washington's Farewell In 1792, Washington had won reelection without opposition, but he declined to run again in 1796. In ailing health, he longed to escape the political turmoil by returning to his beloved plantation, Mount Vernon. He also recognized that the young nation needed him to set an example by walking away from power, proving that he was no king. His voluntary retirement after two terms set a precedent honored by all Presidents until the 1940s.

Washington retired with a record of astounding achievements. On the frontier, the American Indians had been defeated, the western lands opened to settlement, and the Whiskey rebels suppressed. He had kept the nation out of the war in Europe.

A booming foreign trade boosted tariffs, which funded the government and the national debt. Many historians have concluded that without Washington's skillful leadership, the nation may not have survived the harsh tests of the early 1790s. In a farewell address, Washington offered sound political advice for his successors, calling on them to temper their political strife in favor of national unity and to avoid "entangling alliances" that might lead to overseas wars.

☑ **IDENTIFY CENTRAL IDEAS** Why did the British support American Indian resistance to westward expansion in the United States?

Foreign Policy Affects Domestic Politics

The Federalist candidate, John Adams, narrowly defeated Thomas Jefferson in the 1796 presidential election. The nation voted along regional lines, with Jefferson winning most of the southern electoral votes and Adams carrying almost all of the northern states. Due to an awkward feature of the Constitution, Jefferson, as the second place finisher, became Adams's Vice President.

Adams Confronts France Although honest and dedicated, Adams could also be stubborn and pompous. Lacking tact, he made few friends and many enemies. Those foes included Hamilton, who had retired from public office but who tried to control the Federalist Party and the national government from behind the scenes. His meddling weakened the Adams administration.

A French crisis briefly unified the nation. The Jay Treaty of 1794 had offended the French as a betrayal of their 1778 treaty of alliance with the United States. To show their irritation, in 1796 the French began

>> A 1798 cartoon shows a fight that broke out in Congress between Federalist Roger Griswold (with cane) and Democratic Republican Matthew Lyon (with tongs). **Analyze Political Cartoons** What is the cartoon's view of Congress during the Adams administration? How can you tell?

>> A 1798 political cartoon depicts the outcome of the XYZ Affair. **Analyze Political Cartoons** What view does this cartoon suggest about the French treatment of the United States?

seizing American merchant ships. Adams sent envoys to Paris to negotiate peace. But three French officials—known in code as X, Y, and Z—demanded humiliating terms, including $250,000 in bribes. Adams broke off negotiations. Called the **XYZ Affair**, the insult roused public sentiment against France. In 1798, the Federalist majority in Congress expanded the army and authorized a small navy, which won some surprising victories over French warships. To pay for the expanded military, Congress imposed unpopular taxes on stamps and land.

The Alien and Sedition Acts The Federalists exploited the war fever by passing the controversial **Alien and Sedition Acts** in 1798. The Alien Act authorized the President to arrest and deport non-citizens who criticized the federal government. Because most non-citizen immigrants supported the Democratic Republicans, the Federalists made it difficult for them to become citizens. The Sedition Act made it a crime for citizens to publicly criticize the federal government. Arguing that criticism undermined trust in the government, the Federalists used this act to silence Democratic Republican opposition.

The Sedition Act did allow juries to acquit defendants who could prove the literal truth of their statements. But that still put the burden of proof on the defendants, reversing the tradition of presuming someone innocent until proven guilty. In the end, the federal government convicted ten men of sedition, including those in Massachusetts who erected a liberty pole comparing the Federalists to the Loyalists who had supported the British king.

Virginia and Kentucky Respond In two Democratic Republican states, the state legislatures passed controversial resolves in response to the acts. Written by Jefferson and Madison in 1798 and 1799, the **Virginia and Kentucky resolutions** declared the Sedition Act unconstitutional. The resolves even hinted that states had the power to nullify federal laws that were unconstitutional. Though this doctrine of nullification threatened to dissolve the union, no other state legislatures adopted it. Instead, the presidential election of 1800 would decide the balance of federal power and states' rights.

The Election of 1800 By 1800, the Sedition Act and the new federal taxes had become very unpopular. Sensing that trend, in 1799 Adams had suspended expansion of the army and sent new diplomats to France to seek peace. Those moves angered many Federalists, including Hamilton, who

Election of 1800

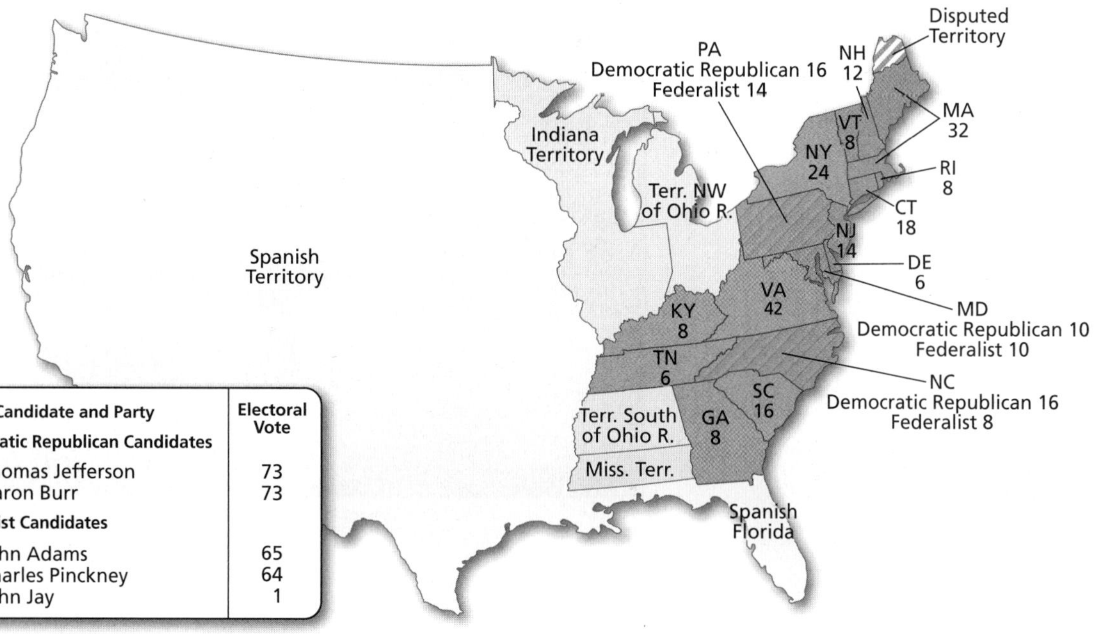

Candidate and Party	Electoral Vote
Democratic Republican Candidates	
Thomas Jefferson	73
Aaron Burr	73
Federalist Candidates	
John Adams	65
Charles Pinckney	64
John Jay	1

>> **Analyze Maps** Which regions mostly supported Federalists? Which regions preferred Democratic Republicans?

worked to undermine Adams's reelection. Adams lost the heated election to Jefferson.

Jefferson and his running mate, **Aaron Burr**, tied. The voters had meant for Jefferson to become President and Burr to become Vice President. But because the Constitution did not then allow a distinction between electoral votes, the House of Representatives had to decide between the two. Hamilton preferred Jefferson, so in early 1801 the Federalist congressmen allowed Jefferson to become President. This peaceful transfer of power from one party to another set a valuable precedent. To avoid another electoral crisis, in 1804 the Constitution was amended to require electors to vote separately for President and Vice President. Offended by Hamilton's criticism, Burr killed him in a duel in 1804.

CHECK UNDERSTANDING What was the doctrine of nullification?

ASSESSMENT

1. **Summarize** What was the Judiciary Act of 1789, and how did it help shape the federal government as we know it today?
2. **Summarize** What methods did Alexander Hamilton use to balance the national debt?
3. **Interpret** Why did southern states overwhelmingly oppose Hamilton's plan to balance the national debt?
4. **Identify Central Issues** What were the Democratic Societies, and how did American leaders respond to them?
5. **Analyze Information** What was the XYZ Affair and what were its implications for American foreign policy?
6. **Connections to Today** George Washington's Cabinet consisted of four leaders to head four executive departments. How has today's executive Cabinet changed from Washington's time? How has it remained the same?

GO ONLINE to access this biography: John Adams

5.2

Democratic Republican leader and author of the Declaration of Independence Thomas Jefferson assumed the presidency in 1801 following one of the most bitter presidential campaigns in American history.

BOUNCE to Activate Flipped Video

Objectives

Understand why some saw Jefferson's election as a "Democratic Republican revolution."

Explain the impact of John Marshall's tenure as Chief Justice of the United States.

Identify the importance of the Louisiana Purchase.

Analyze Jefferson's foreign policies.

Key Terms

bureaucracy
John Marshall
judicial review
Marbury v. *Madison*
Louisiana Purchase
Lewis and Clark Expedition
Barbary War
impressment
embargo

GO ONLINE to access your digital course

Jefferson as President

In addition to capturing the presidency in 1800, the Democratic Republicans won control of Congress and most of the state governments. The Federalists would never reclaim national power. Besides taking government in a new direction, the Jefferson administration left a profound legacy with its acquisition of new territory.

A New Direction for American Government

When the Democratic Republicans took power, they spoke of the election as a "revolution." Jefferson insisted that "the Revolution of 1800 was as real a Revolution in the principles of our government as that of 1776 was in its form." In that view, those in the Jefferson administration set out to do things quite differently from their predecessors, who had copied the style of the British monarchy.

Jefferson Streamlines Government Jefferson encouraged Congress to abandon the Alien and Sedition Acts, as well as the hated taxes on stamps, land, and alcoholic spirits. Unlike Hamilton, Jefferson wanted to retire the national debt by paying it down. Despite reducing taxes, he cut the national debt from $80 million when he took office to $57 million in 1809. To do this he made major cuts to the army and navy and streamlined the government's **bureaucracy**, or the departments and workers that make up the government. He also benefited when customs revenue from imports increased with a dramatic growth in foreign trade. In addition, the westward movement of American farming families increased the sale of federal lands. These two revenues drove down the federal debt.

A Change in Style The Federalists believed that expensive displays taught the public to respect their leaders. Without that respect, they did not think that the government could survive. In contrast, the Democratic Republicans hated the Federalist displays of wealth as an aristocratic threat to the republic.

Although Jefferson was wealthy, refined, and educated, he recognized the popularity of a common style. A friend described Jefferson in this way.

> If his dress was plain, unstudied, and sometimes old-fashioned in its form, it was always of the finest materials . . . and if in his manners he was simple, affable, and unceremonious, it was not because he was ignorant of but because he despised the conventional and artificial usages of courts and fashionable life.
>
> —Mrs. Samuel Harrison Smith, c. 1801

CHECK UNDERSTANDING Why was Jefferson's victory in the election of 1800 considered a "revolution"?

John Marshall Shapes the Supreme Court

When Thomas Jefferson became President in 1801, **John Marshall** became Chief Justice of the Supreme Court. Although the two men were cousins, they were political enemies. Marshall was a Federalist, a last-minute appointee by the outgoing President, John Adams. Marshall's appointment had a major impact on the Supreme Court and on its relationship with the rest of the federal government. Over 35 years, he participated in more than 1,000 court decisions, writing over half of them—more than any other Supreme Court Justice in U.S. history.

The Power of the Judicial Branch Marshall applied four of Hamilton's principles to interpret the Constitution. First, his Supreme Court claimed the power to review the acts of Congress and of the President to determine if they were constitutional. This power is known as **judicial review**.

U.S. National Debt, 1791–1811

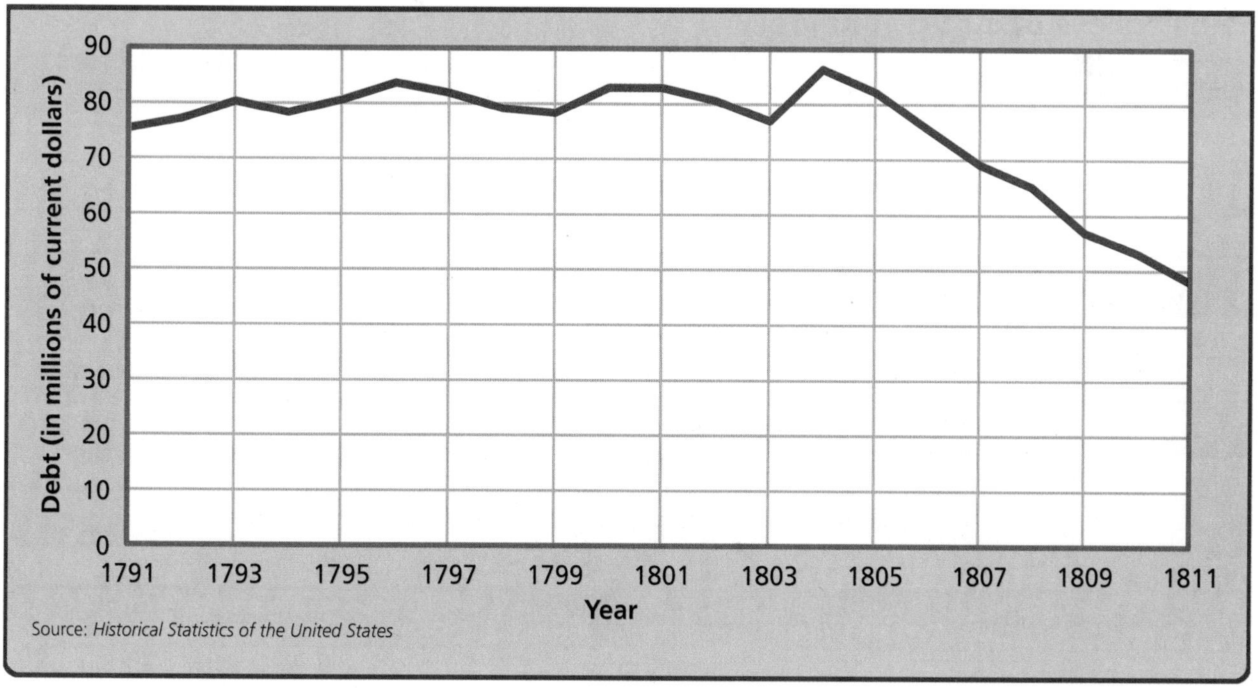

>> **Analyze Data** Based on this graph, what happened to the national debt during Jefferson's first term as President?

Second, he insisted that federal laws were superior to state laws. Third, like Hamilton, Marshall broadly interpreted the Constitution to find implied powers for the national government. Fourth, he insisted upon the "sanctity of contracts." This limited the power of state governments to interfere with business.

The Legacy of Judicial Review In 1803, Marshall first asserted the power of judicial review in the case of ***Marbury* v. *Madison***. In early 1801, outgoing President John Adams had appointed William Marbury, a Federalist, a justice for the District of Columbia. The incoming Secretary of State, James Madison, refused to deliver the official papers of appointment. When Marbury complained to the Supreme Court, Marshall ruled in favor of Madison by declaring unconstitutional part of the Judiciary Act of 1789.

This ruling was a stroke of genius. Marshall gave the Democratic Republicans what they wanted by denying Marbury his appointment. But in doing so, Marshall claimed a sweeping power for the Supreme Court that the Democratic Republicans did not want that Court to have.

After all, the Constitution was silent on what institution should judge the constitutionality of congressional actions. In the Kentucky and Virginia resolutions of 1798, Jefferson and Madison had claimed that power for the state legislatures. Because of Marshall, today we accept that the Supreme Court will review the constitutionality of federal laws.

The Marshall Court Sets Precedents After establishing the precedent of judicial review, Marshall never again ruled a federal law unconstitutional. Instead, most of his decisions overruled state laws, usually to defend businesses and interstate commerce from state interference, or strengthened judicial review.

These decisions set precedents critical to the development of the new nation's legal and economic systems. Like Hamilton, Marshall interpreted the Constitution broadly to find the implied powers needed for a strong national government.

☑ **IDENTIFY MAIN IDEAS** Why was *Marbury* v. *Madison* such an important decision?

A Growing Nation Looks Westward

Jefferson insisted that farm ownership—which freed citizens from dependence on a landlord or on an employer—was essential to the freedom of Americans. Yet without expansion there would not be enough farms for the rapidly growing population.

The Process of Judicial Review

1. A lower court ruling is appealed to the Supreme Court challenging the constitutionality of a law.
2. Supreme Court justices review the appeal and vote on whether to hear the case.
3. If 4 out of 9 justices agree to review the case, the Supreme Court orders the case records.
4. Petitioner submits a brief outlining the legal challenge to the constitutionality of related laws; respondent submits a brief outlining the legal argument for defense Supreme Court Justices listen to the oral arguments presented by both parties.
5. Supreme Court debates and votes on case during a Justices' Conference.
6. If a majority vote for the petitioner, the law or statute is held unconstitutional and is assumed void by the ruling.

Source: United States Courts

>> **Analyze Information** What happens to a case if fewer than four justices agree to review it?

U.S. Population, 1790–1810

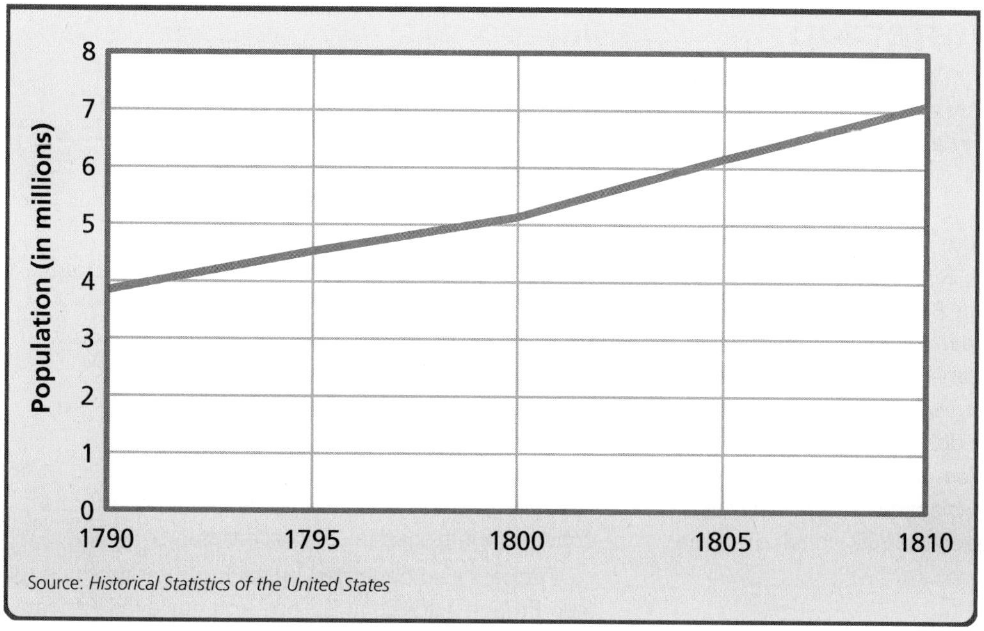

>> **Hypothesize** What may have been two challenges for the U.S. government presented by the population changes shown here?

BOUNCE to Activate Gallery

With the population doubling every 25 years, the nation needed twice as much land every generation to maintain farm ownership.

The Louisiana Territory To get more land, Jefferson wanted the United States to expand to the Pacific—despite the fact that much of the continent was already inhabited by American Indians or claimed by other nations. At first, Jefferson believed that Spain's vast Louisiana Territory west of the Mississippi River would be easy to conquer. He noted that the Spanish colonists were few, their empire was weak, and they were distracted by the war in Europe. Jefferson's plans went awry, however, when the United States got a new and far more dangerous neighbor to the west.

In 1801, France's military dictator, Napoleon Bonaparte, had forced Spain to give him the Louisiana Territory, including the strategic city of New Orleans. The French threatened to block American access to the market in New Orleans. An alarmed Jefferson considered joining the British in an alliance to fight France.

The Louisiana Purchase Jefferson reasoned that he could avoid war by offering to buy New Orleans from the French. When James Monroe and Robert Livingston, the American minister in France, approached Napoleon, they found him surprisingly receptive. Napoleon's imperial plans had been foiled by slave rebels in the Caribbean colony of Saint Domingue, which is now Haiti. Led by Toussaint L'Ouverture, the rebels defeated a French army sent to suppress them. Without that army to occupy Louisiana and needing money to fight the British, Napoleon decided to sell all of the Louisiana Territory.

In the **Louisiana Purchase** of 1803, Jefferson obtained a vast territory extending from the Mississippi River to the Rocky Mountains.

At about 828,000 square miles, the Louisiana Territory nearly doubled the size of the United States. For all of this, the United States paid only $15 million. Although a great bargain, the Louisiana Purchase was also something of an embarrassment, as it contradicted Jefferson's constitutional principles. He had long argued for a minimal federal government, and the Constitution did not authorize the federal government to buy territory from a foreign country. Jefferson confessed that he had "done an act beyond the Constitution."

In 1804, Jefferson sent Meriwether Lewis and William Clark to explore the new territory, in what became known as the **Lewis and Clark Expedition**. The men were guided much of the way by a Shoshone woman, named Sacajawea, and her husband.

IDENTIFY CENTRAL IDEAS What was Jefferson's main reason for purchasing the Louisiana Territory from France?

Foreign Difficulties Challenge Jefferson

While Jefferson succeeded in his plans to expand to the west, he faced a number of significant challenges to solidifying the stability and economy of the United States.

Conflict in North Africa The Barbary States of North Africa—Morocco, Algiers, Tunis, and Tripoli—were profiting by seizing American ships and sailors in the Mediterranean Sea. To buy immunity from that piracy, the Washington and Adams administrations had paid protection money to the Barbary States. Jefferson was willing to do the same until the ruler of Tripoli increased his price. In 1801, Jefferson sent the small American navy to blockade the port of Tripoli, winning a favorable peace in 1805, concluding the **Barbary War**.

The Re-Export Trade Fuels Conflict with Britain As the population grew and spread westward, the United States needed to expand overseas markets for the surplus produce raised on its new farms. From 1793 to 1807, war in Europe aided this goal.

The dominant British navy quickly captured most of France's merchant ships. To supply food to the French colonies in the West Indies and to export their sugar, the French turned to American ships. Because the British had banned direct American voyages between the French West Indies and France, American merchants picked up cargoes in the French colonies and took them to ports in the United States, where they unloaded them. Then the merchants reshipped the cargoes to France as if they were American products.

The value of this "re-export" trade soared from about $300,000 in 1790 to nearly $59 million in 1807, creating a boom for the American economy. To meet the new demand, American shipyards produced hundreds of new ships, tripling the size of the nation's merchant marine by 1807. Prosperous American merchants built new wharves, warehouses, and mansions, boosting the construction trades in seaport cities.

Farmers also benefited by selling their produce to feed French soldiers in Europe and enslaved Africans and plantation owners in the West Indies.

The British hated the re-export trade for two reasons. First, it helped the French economy, which sustained Napoleon's army. Second, the new trade helped the United States become Britain's greatest commercial competitor. In 1805, as British merchants lost markets and profits to American shippers, British

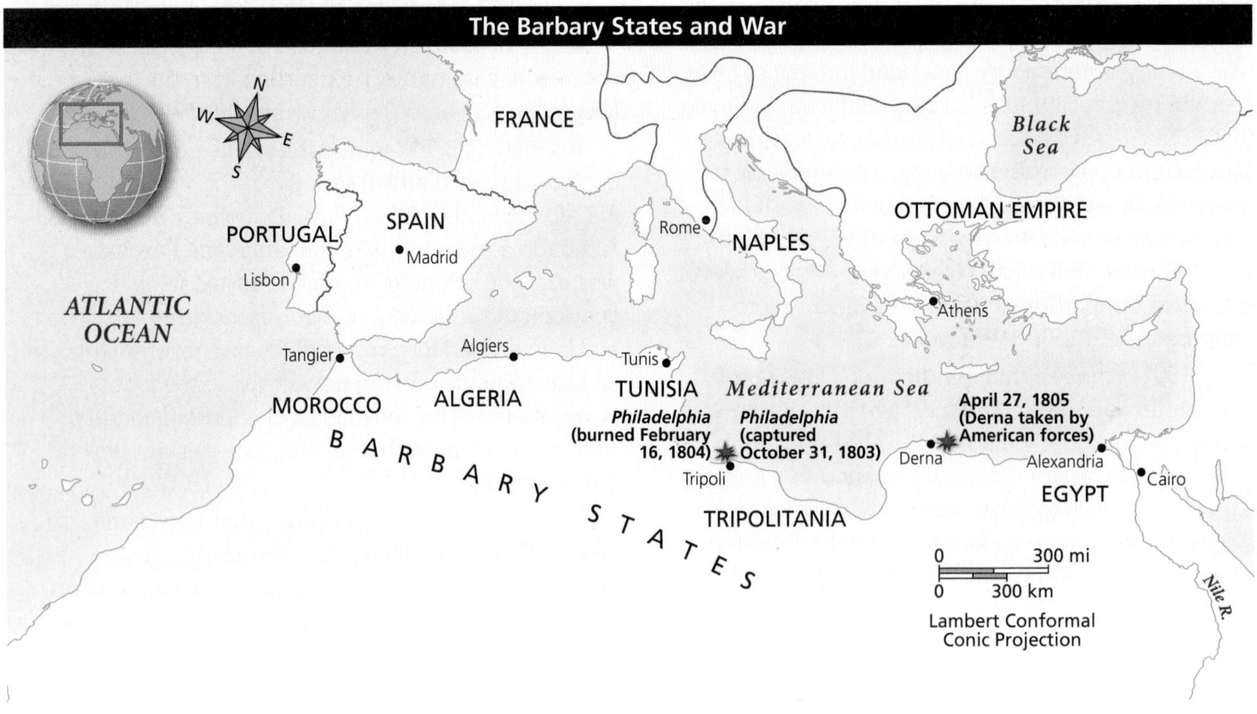

>> During the Barbary War, the USS *Philadelphia* was seized by the enemy. Rather than allowing the ship to be used by the Barbary States, the U.S. sent saboteurs to set it on fire.

U.S. Cotton Production, 1790–1810

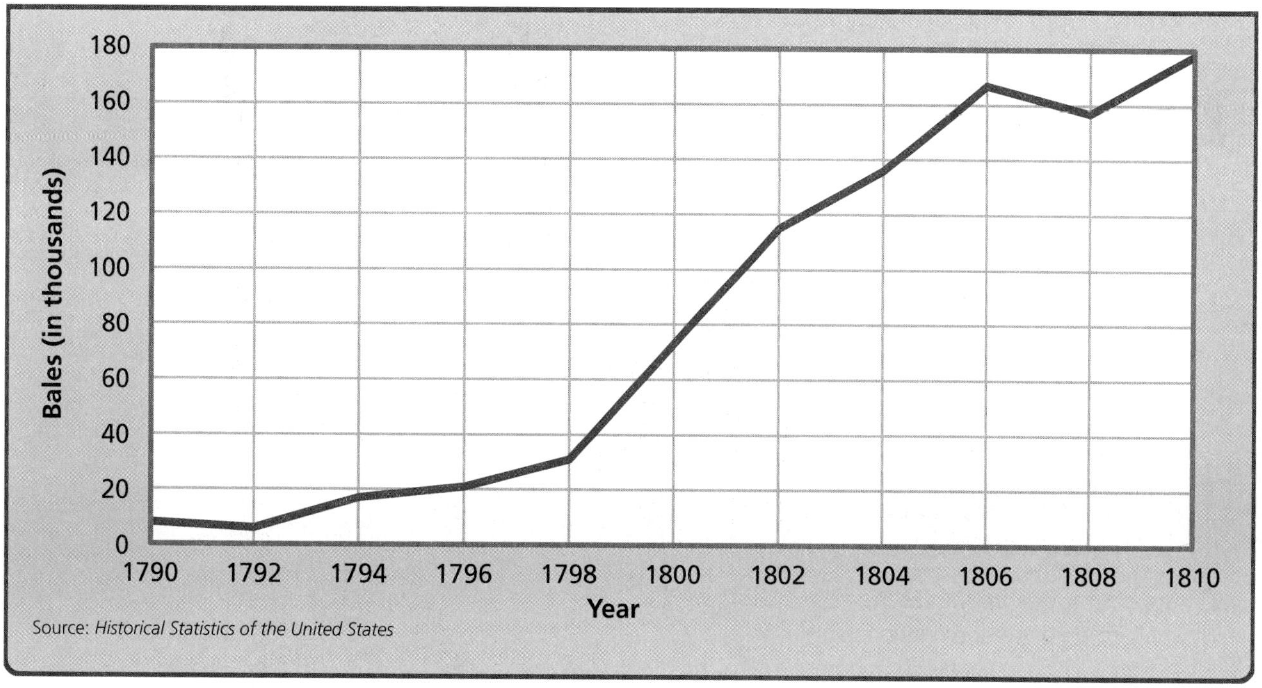

>> **Analyze Data** Despite international conflicts, American cotton continued to be shipped to overseas markets. During which years did cotton production soar?

BOUNCE to Activate Cartoon

warships began to stop and confiscate growing numbers of American merchant ships for trading with the French.

Britain Impresses American Sailors The British navy also angered the United States by relying on **impressment**, or taking American sailors from their ships and forcing them to serve in the British navy. Engaged in a tough war, the British desperately needed sailors for their huge fleet. Britain insisted that anyone born within its empire was a British subject for life. Yet British naval officers also took American-born sailors. By 1812, about 6,000 American citizens had been impressed for the harsh duty of serving on a British warship.

At first, Federalist merchants were willing to regard the British abuses as unfortunate costs of doing business on the high seas. They pointed out that the old trade with Great Britain remained even more valuable than the new re-export trade with France. But Democratic Republicans insisted that the British actions insulted the United States and threatened the country's economic growth. In 1807, when the British attacked an American warship, the *Chesapeake*, in order to take some of its sailors, many Americans—including many Federalists—were outraged.

Jefferson's Embargo Fails The United States lacked a navy large enough to challenge the British fleet. Jefferson balked at the high cost of building a bigger navy, which would undermine his policies of reducing the national debt and keeping taxes low. He also worried that a large military would become a threat to the Republic.

As an alternative to war, in 1807 Jefferson persuaded Congress to declare an **embargo**, suspending trade with the British by ordering American ships to stay in port. He expected the embargo to starve the British and close their factories, creating riots in the streets.

Instead, the British found other markets in South America. Meanwhile, the embargo bankrupted American merchants, threw American sailors out of work, and hurt farmers, who could no longer export their crops. Exploiting voter anger, the Federalists gained support in the northern states, especially in New England.

Even Jefferson had to admit failure, lifting the embargo just before he retired from the presidency in 1809. Despite having been easily reelected in 1804, the embargo had caused his popularity to lag. He was succeeded by his friend James Madison, who defeated a Federalist rival in the election of 1808.

DESCRIBE Describe Jefferson's foreign policy response to British impressment of American sailors.

ASSESSMENT

1. **Summarize** What accomplishments distinguished President Jefferson's administration from the previous two?
2. **Synthesize Evidence** How did Chief Justice John Marshall shape the Supreme Court?
3. **Summarize** Why did American merchant ships establish a reexport trade in the Atlantic?
4. **Distinguish** How did the Federalists and Democrat Republicans react to the British navy's use of impressment on American sailors?
5. **Support Ideas with Evidence** How did *Marbury v. Madison* affect the relationship between the legislative and executive branches?
6. **Connections to Today** During the early 1800s, both political parties—the Democrat Republicans and the Federalists—had support in particular geographic regions of the United States. Is there geographic regional support for the Democrats and Republicans today? Explain.

GO ONLINE to access this biography: John Marshall

5.3

The flag that flew over Fort McHenry inspired the composition of the "Star-Spangled Banner." **Analyze Primary Sources** What does the condition of this flag suggest about the fighting at Fort McHenry?

The War of 1812

Just a few decades after its founding, the United States found itself involved in a major war. The war tested not only the young nation's resources and strength but the solidarity of its people as well. Despite their political divisions, Americans managed both to fight a war and to get the country back on track in the war's aftermath.

BOUNCE to Activate Flipped Video

Objectives

Identify the events that led to the War Hawks' call for war.

Analyze the major battles and conflicts of the War of 1812.

Explain the significance of the War of 1812.

Key Terms

Tecumseh
Battle of Tippecanoe
War Hawks
War of 1812
Andrew Jackson
Francis Scott Key
"The Star-Spangled Banner"
Battle of New Orleans
Treaty of Ghent
Hartford Convention

The Road to War

Congress Deals with Britain and France Democratic Republicans felt humiliated by the failure of the 1807 embargo against Britain. With persistent British abuses on the oceans and American Indian resistance in the West, Americans increasingly blamed the British. In 1809, Congress replaced the embargo with the Nonintercourse Act. Aimed at Britain and France, the act stated that the United States would resume trade with whichever of those countries lifted their restrictions on American shipping.

The following year, Congress passed legislation that went a step further. Macon's Bill No. 2 restored trade with both Britain and France but also promised that if either country actively recognized American neutrality, then the United States would resume trading sanctions against the other country.

When France agreed to withdraw decrees against American shipping, President Madison ordered sanctions against the British. In the meantime, however, France continued to seize American ships.

American Indians Defend Their Lands On the western frontier, two Shawnee Indian brothers, the prophet Tenskwatawa and the warrior **Tecumseh**, wanted to preserve American Indian

GO ONLINE to access your digital course

>> South Carolina Congressman John C. Calhoun was among the "War Hawks" calling for a declaration of war in 1811.

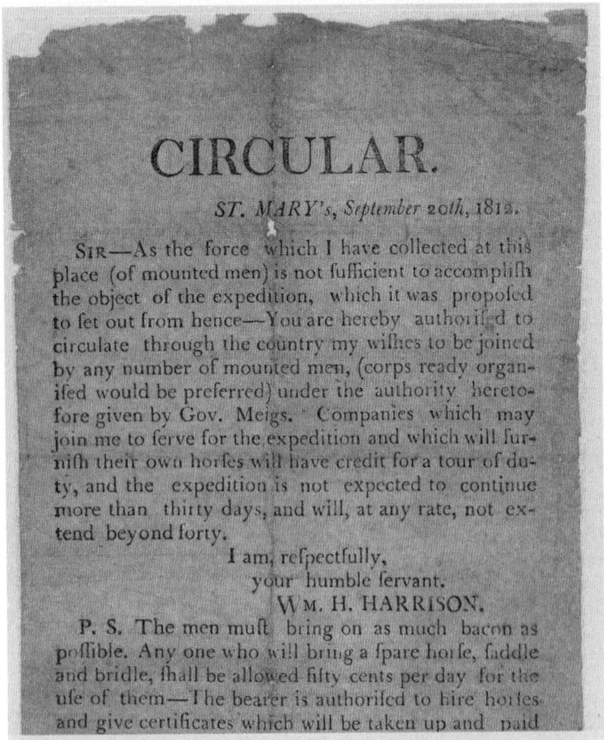

CIRCULAR.

ST. MARY's, September 20th, 1812.

SIR—As the force which I have collected at this place (of mounted men) is not fufficient to accomplifh the object of the expedition, which it was propofed to fet out from hence—You are hereby authorifed to circulate through the country my wifhes to be joined by any number of mounted men, (corps ready organifed would be preferred) under the authority heretofore given by Gov. Meigs. Companies which may join me to ferve for the expedition and which will furnifh their own horfes will have credit for a tour of duty, and the expedition is not expected to continue more than thirty days, and will, at any rate, not extend beyond forty.

I am, refpectfully,
your humble fervant.
WM. H. HARRISON.

P. S. The men muft bring on as much bacon as poffible. Any one who will bring a fpare horfe, faddle and bridle, fhall be allowed fifty cents per day for the ufe of them—The bearer is authorifed to hire horfes and give certificates which will be taken up and paid

>> An 1812 announcement of recruitment efforts

culture and unite the American Indian nations in armed resistance against American expansion. They were angered by the government's repeated use of dishonest treaties to take their lands. In late 1811, while Tecumseh was seeking allies in the South, Governor William Henry Harrison of the Indiana Territory led troops into the brothers' village of Prophetstown, along the Tippecanoe River. After the **Battle of Tippecanoe**, the Americans burned Prophetstown. The Amerian Indian movement lost some momentum, though most American Indians escaped to fight again.

The War Hawks Push for War In 1811, some aggressive young politicians, known as the **War Hawks**, took the lead in Congress. Representing farmers and settlers from the southern and western states, the War Hawks included John C. Calhoun of South Carolina and Henry Clay of Kentucky. Strongly nationalist, they denounced the impressment of American sailors and British support for American Indians. The War Hawks pushed for a war against Britain to restore national honor. They insisted that invading British-held Canada would deprive the American Indians of their main source of arms and drive the British out of North America. The War Hawks also believed that if the United States seized Canada, the British would make maritime concessions to get Canada back. However, the War Hawks underestimated how determined the British were to dominate world trade.

☑ **CHECK UNDERSTANDING** Why did the War Hawks call for war against Britain?

War With Britain

Humiliated by British interference with American trade, impressments, and support for American Indian attacks on settlers, President Madison urged Congress to declare war on Britain in June of 1812. Although the **War of 1812** deeply divided the nation, Madison narrowly won reelection later that year. Disunited, unprepared, and with only a small army and navy, the United States went to war once again with the world's greatest power.

American Troops Face Defeat Thomas Jefferson acted as adviser to Madison. He urged that with a population of 8 million, the United States could easily conquer Canada, which had only 250,000 people. Indeed, the prospects for a victory looked favorable. An overland invasion would save the cost of building a bigger navy to fight the British.

In addition, Jefferson argued that the United States did not even need a professional army. The citizen militia of the states could do the job quickly and with little expense. He called the conquest of Canada "a mere matter of marching."

Jefferson's assumptions proved to be wrong. In fact, the small British and American Indian forces in Canada repeatedly defeated the American invasion attempts in 1812 and 1813. Reliance on the state militias proved a disaster. Having had no professional training, many militiamen broke rank and fled when attacked. The American regular army performed almost as poorly. One blundering general, William Hull, surrendered Detroit to a much smaller British force commanded by Isaac Brock and assisted by American Indians led by Tecumseh. Instead of bolstering American pride, the attempted invasion of Canada only further embarrassed the nation.

Victory Against the American Indians To the surprise of many Americans—and to the shock of the British—the small American navy performed well, capturing four British ships during 1812. On Lake Erie, American ships led by Oliver Hazard Perry defeated a British flotilla in 1813, enabling an American army, commanded by William Henry Harrison, to retake Detroit.

The Americans made little progress in conquering Canada, but within the United States, they did defeat Britain's American Indian allies. In October 1813, Harrison's army killed Tecumseh and scattered his supporters. In 1814, **Andrew Jackson** of Tennessee crushed the Creek Indians of Alabama, who had allied with the British. To make peace, the survivors surrendered most of their lands. Jackson then invaded the Spanish colony of Florida, defeating the Seminole Indians and seizing the Spanish fort at Pensacola.

The British Army Attacks During 1812 and 1813, most of the British forces were in Europe fighting Napoleon. In early 1814, however, the French dictator's defeat freed up thousands of British troops to fight in North America. During the summer and fall, the British took the offensive. While the British navy blockaded the coast, British forces invaded the United States. One army occupied land that is now eastern Maine, easily brushing aside the weak defense by local militia. From Montreal, a second army invaded northern New York, while a third British force landed in Maryland and marched on Washington, D.C. In late 1814, a British fleet carried a fourth army into the Gulf of Mexico to attack New Orleans.

>> Shawnee warrior Tecumseh spearheaded a spiritual and military resistance movement among American Indians living near the Ohio Valley.

>> This 1814 poster shows some of the war's leading generals, including future presidents Andrew Jackson (top center) and William Henry Harrison (bottom center).

BOUNCE to Activate Map

On the defensive, the Americans fought better than they had when invading Canada. Except for the occupation of what is now Maine, the British attacks ended in defeat. The British did capture the national capital, easily accessible by ship via the Chesapeake Bay, and burned the White House and Capitol in revenge for the burning of government buildings in Canada. But the British suffered defeat when they moved on to attack Baltimore. Lawyer **Francis Scott Key**, who observed the British attack on Fort McHenry, celebrated the American victory by writing a poem that later became the national anthem known as **"The Star-Spangled Banner"**.

> O say, can you see, by the dawn's early light, What so proudly we hail'd at the twilight's last gleaming, Whose broad stripes and bright stars, thro' the perilous fight, O'er the ramparts we watch'd, were so gallantly streaming?
>
> —Francis Scott Key, 1814

Meanwhile, on Lake Champlain near Plattsburgh, New York, American ships defeated a British fleet, forcing British troops to retreat to Canada.

>> This engraving shows the defeat of the British at the Battle of New Orleans.

LIST Make a list of significant American successes and failures during the War of 1812.

The Impact of the War of 1812

The Americans won their greatest victory at the **Battle of New Orleans** in January 1815. From a strong and entrenched position, General Andrew Jackson routed the British attack. In this lopsided battle, the Americans suffered only 71 casualties, compared to 2,036 British casualties. The bloodshed at New Orleans was especially tragic because it came two weeks after the Americans and the British had signed a peace treaty at Ghent in Belgium. Unfortunately, notifying the soldiers in North America took over a month because of the slow pace of sailing ships.

The Treaty of Ghent The Americans had failed to conquer Canada, while the British had failed in their American invasions. Weary of war, both sides agreed to a peace treaty that restored prewar boundaries. They agreed to set up a commission to discuss any boundary disputes at a future time. The treaty did not address the issues of neutrality or impressments.

But after Napoleon's defeat, the British no longer needed to impress American sailors or to stop American trade with the French. The Americans interpreted the **Treaty of Ghent** as a triumph because they learned of it shortly after hearing of Jackson's great victory. That sequence of events created the illusion that Jackson had forced the British to make peace. Americans preferred to think of the conflict as a noble defense of the United States against British aggression.

Federalists Seek Power After the War of 1812 and Jackson's victory in New Orleans, Americans experienced a surge of nationalism and a new confidence in the strength of their republic. By weathering a difficult war, the nation seemed certain to endure, and most Americans were giddy with relief. The outcome discredited the Federalists, who looked weak for opposing a war that became popular once it was over. Strongest in New England, the Federalists had undermined the war effort there. In December 1814, Federalist delegates from the New England states had met at Hartford, Connecticut, to consider secession and making a separate peace with Britain.

Drawing back from the brink, the delegates instead demanded constitutional amendments designed to strengthen New England's political power.

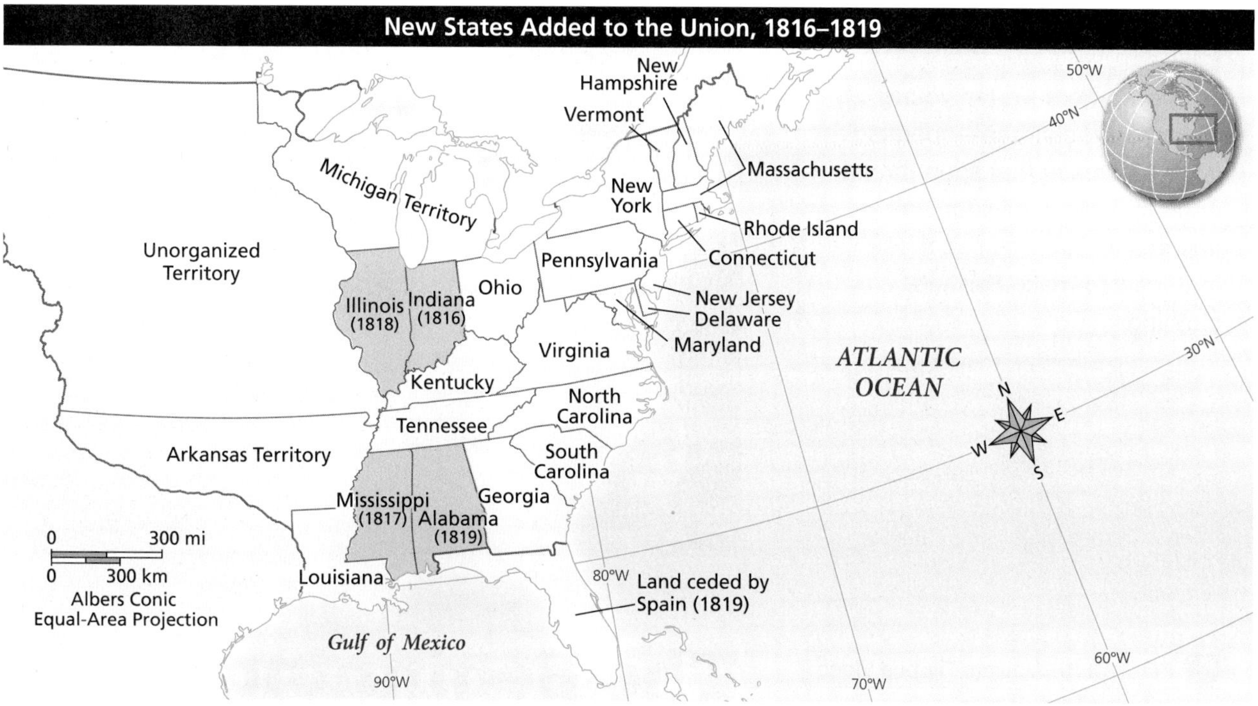

>> **Analyze Maps** What does this map suggest about the growth and spread of the U.S. population during the 1810s?

Unfortunately for the delegates of the **Hartford Convention**, their demands reached Washington, D.C., at the same time as news of the peace treaty and Jackson's victory. That bad timing embarrassed the Federalists, who were mocked as defeatists and traitors. Madison ignored their demands, and the voters punished the Federalists in the elections that followed. By 1820, the Federalist Party was dead—a sad fate for the party that had created the federal government only to lose faith in it during the War of 1812.

American Indian Lands Become New States

Events during the War of 1812 ended most American Indian resistance east of the Mississippi River for the time being. As a result of various defeats of American Indians in the South, millions of acres of southern land also opened up for settlement. Settlement in the South and West led to the establishment of the new states of Indiana (1816), Mississippi (1817), Illinois (1818), and Alabama (1819). The union grew bigger and stronger.

Meanwhile, American settlers had been pouring into Spanish Florida, creating cross-border conflict among the region's Seminole Indians, Americans, and the Spanish. Fugitive slaves from the United States, seeking sanctuary in Florida, added to the tensions. Over the next decade, the conflict would contribute to Spain's decision to cede Florida to the United States. In return, the United States renounced its claims to Texas, as part of the Adams-Onís Treaty signed in 1819.

IDENTIFY CENTRAL IDEAS Why did Federalists organize the Hartford Convention?

ASSESSMENT

1. **Support Ideas with Evidence** How did American Indians affect the United States' conflict with Britain?
2. **Infer** Discuss the role impressment played in the decision to go to war with Great Britain.
3. **Support Ideas with Evidence** How did the results of the War of 1812 affect American morale?
4. **Summarize** What was the Hartford Convention and what effect did it have on the Federalist Party?
5. **Connections to Today** What foreign policy challenges did Thomas Jefferson and James Madison face during their presidencies? What foreign policy issues does the U.S. President face today?

5.4

Textile workers—often young women and children—operated large machines that spun thread or cloth. Later, individual tailors and seamstresses used those materials to make finished clothing.

BOUNCE to Activate Flipped Video

Objectives

Summarize the key developments in the transportation revolution of the early 1800s.

Analyze the rise of industry in the United States in the early 1800s.

Describe some of the leading inventions and industrial developments in the early 1800s.

Key Terms

turnpike
National Road
Erie Canal
Industrial Revolution
Samuel Slater
Francis Cabot Lowell
"Lowell girls"
interchangeable parts
Eli Whitney
Samuel F.B. Morse

GO ONLINE to access your digital course

The Beginning of the Industrial Revolution

Developments in technology began to transform life in the United States in the early 1800s. New methods of transporting and manufacturing goods changed the way people lived and worked. The United States was set on a course of industrialization that would shape life in the nation for decades.

New Technology Revolutionizes Transportation

The original 13 states hugged the Atlantic Coast, and all major settlements in the United States had sprung up near a harbor or river because water provided the most efficient way to move people and goods. At the start of the nineteenth century, overland transportation consisted of carts, wagons, sleighs, and stagecoaches pulled by horses or oxen over dirt roads. Moving goods just a few dozen miles by road could cost as much as shipping the same cargo across the ocean.

Building Better Roads In an effort to improve overland transportation, some states chartered companies to operate **turnpikes**—roads for which users had to pay a toll. The term came from the turnpikes, or gates, that guarded entrances to the roads. Turnpike operators were supposed to use toll income to improve the roads and ease travel. But only a few turnpikes made a profit, and most failed to lower transportation costs or increase the speed of travel. The country's best route, which was made of crushed rock, was the **National Road**. Funded by the federal government, this roadway extended west from Maryland to the Ohio River (in present-day West Virginia) in 1818.

Steamboats Cut Travel Times The first major advance in transportation was the development of the steamboat. By burning wood or coal, the engine boiled the water to create steam. The force of the steam turned a large, rotating paddle, which pushed the boat through the water. American Robert Fulton designed the first commercially successful steamboat—the *Clermont*.

The steamboat made it much easier to travel upstream against the current. For example, before the steamboat, it took about four months to travel the 1,440 miles from New Orleans to Louisville, Kentucky, along the Mississippi and Ohio rivers. In 1820, a steamboat made the same journey in just 20 days. By 1838, it took a steamboat only six days. Steamboats unlocked the great potential of the Mississippi River Basin for moving people and goods. The number of steamboats plying the rivers of that system grew from 230 in 1834 to nearly 700 in 1843.

Steam-powered ships also revolutionized transatlantic travel. By 1850, a steamship could cross the Atlantic in 10 to 14 days, compared to the 25 to 50 days for a sailing ship.

Canals Connect Markets A second transportation advance of the early 1800s was the construction of canals. The nation's canal network grew from 100 miles in 1816 to 3,300 miles in 1840. Mostly built in the Northeast, canals provided efficient water transportation that linked farms to the expanding cities.

The best-known canal of the era was the **Erie Canal**. Completed in 1825, it ran 363 miles across New York State from Lake Erie to the Hudson River. Before this canal went into service, it could cost $100 or more to ship a ton of freight overland from the city of Buffalo on the shores of Lake Erie to New York City. The canal lowered that cost to just $4.

By funneling western produce to the Hudson River, the Erie Canal helped make New York City the nation's greatest commercial center. As a result, the city grew quickly. From a population of 124,000 in 1820, its population surged to 800,000 in 1860. The canal also enhanced the value of farmland in the Great Lakes region, because farmers there now had easier access to eastern markets for their goods.

The increase of commerce, and the growth of the country, have been very accurately measured by the growth of the business of the Canal. It has

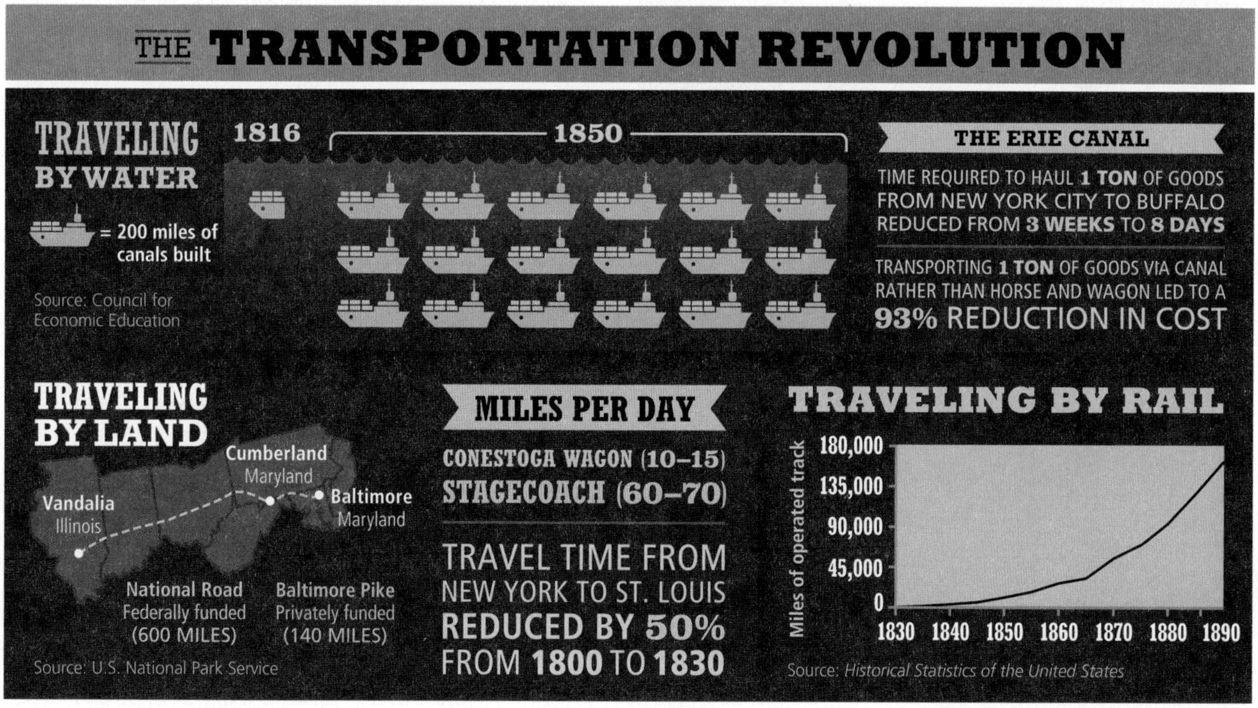

>> **Analyze Information** Which of the transportation advances shown here do you think was the most revolutionary? Justify your selection.

BOUNCE to Activate Map

been one great bond of strength, infusing life and vigor into the whole. Commercially and politically, it has secured and maintained to the United States the characteristics of a homogeneous [sharing common features] people.

—Report by the Secretary of the Treasury, 1853

Railroads Further Ease Transport The most dramatic advance in transportation in the 1800s was the arrival of a new mode of transportation—railroads. This technology, largely developed in Great Britain, began to appear in the United States in the 1820s. Horses pulled the first American trains. But clever inventors soon developed steam-powered engines, which could pull heavier loads of freight or passengers at higher speeds than horses could manage.

Compared to canals, railroads cost less to build and could more easily scale hills. Trains moved faster than ships and carried more weight. Their introduction put a quick end to the brief boom in canal building. Meanwhile, the American rail network expanded from 13 miles of track in 1830 to 31,000 miles by 1860. In 1800, a journey from New York City to Detroit, Michigan, took 28 days by boat. In 1857, the same trip took only two days by train.

>> Samuel Slater's textile mill in the 1790s

BOUNCE to Activate 3D Model

IDENTIFY What were the major developments in transportation between 1800 and 1860?

The Industrial Revolution

Developments in technology also transformed manufacturing. This transformation became known as the **Industrial Revolution**, which changed not only the nation's economy but also its culture, social life, and politics.

The Industrial Revolution began in Great Britain during the 1700s, with the development of machines, powered by steam or fast-flowing rivers, to perform work that had once been done by hand. The first machines spun thread and wove cloth more quickly and cheaply.

The Nation's First Textile Mills To protect its industrial advantage, the British banned the export of machinery, as well as the emigration of workers with knowledge of the technology. However, a skilled worker named **Samuel Slater** defied that law and moved to the United States.

Slater used his detailed knowledge of the textile machinery to build the nation's first water-powered textile mill in 1793 at Pawtucket, Rhode Island. The mill used the flowing Blackstone River to power its machinery, which produced one part of the textile: cotton thread. Slater and his business partners later built more factories along New England rivers. These factories used the so-called family system, in which entire families, including parents and children, were employed in the mills. Those families settled in villages owned by factory owners and located around the mills.

Lowell Transforms the Manufacture of Cloth Boston merchant **Francis Cabot Lowell** developed another industrial system in Massachusetts. In 1811, he toured England's factory towns to gather secret information. Returning home, Lowell organized a company called the Boston Associates. In 1813, the associates built their first mill at Waltham, Massachusetts, in which all operations in the manufacture of cloth occurred—instead of just the production of thread. During the 1820s, they built more factories on the Merrimack River and established a new town called Lowell.

Their system employed young, single women recruited from area farms. The company enforced strict rules of behavior and housed the **"Lowell girls"** in closely supervised boardinghouses. After a few years of work, most of the young women married and left the factories.

Factories Change Businesses and Workers' Lives The speed and volume of production were not the only things changed by the growth of factories. Factories also changed the working lives of thousands of people. Machines increased the pace of work and divided labor into many small tasks done by separate workers. This process reduced the amount of skill and training required for individual jobs. Factory owners benefited because untrained workers were more numerous and less costly to employ. In some trades, owners achieved those benefits without adopting new machines. The manufacture of clothing and shoes are two examples.

As you have read, America's first factories produced thread or cloth rather than finished clothing. During the 1820s, a garment trade developed primarily in New York City. Contractors provided cloth to poor women who made the clothes in their homes without the help of machines. They earned about $1 per week.

Shoemaking followed a similar model. Lynn, Massachusetts, led the nation in this industry. A few men performed the skilled and better-paying tasks of cutting and shaping leather for the tops of the shoes. For less pay (about 50 cents a week), women sewed the shoes together.

☑ **IDENTIFY MAIN IDEAS** What changes occurred in the United States with the rise of industry in the early 1800s?

>> U.S. textile production led to the growth of industrial cities such as Lowell, Massachusetts, established during the 1820s.

BOUNCE to Activate Illustration

Innovations in Industry and Agriculture

A number of key innovations paralleled the revolutions in transportation and industry in the early 1800s. These also dramatically affected the American economy and society.

New Methods of Production To improve efficiency in factories, manufacturers designed products with **interchangeable parts**, identical components that could be used in place of one another. Inventor **Eli Whitney** introduced this idea to the United States. Traditionally, items such as clocks and muskets were built one at a time by skilled artisans who made each part and assembled the device from start to finish by hand. As a result, a part that would work in one gun or clock might not work in any other. Whitney proposed making muskets in a new way—by manufacturing each part separately and precisely. Under Whitney's system, a part that would work in one musket would work in another musket. In other words, the parts would be interchangeable.

It took some years for American manufacturers to make interchangeable parts reliably. Yet the use of interchangeable parts eventually led to more efficient production of a wide range of manufactured goods. One of the products manufactured with interchangeable parts was the sewing machine. Invented by Elias Howe and improved by Isaac Singer, the sewing machine lowered the cost and increased the speed of making cloth into clothing.

Morse Improves Communication In 1837, American **Samuel F.B. Morse** invented the electric telegraph, which allowed electrical pulses to travel long distances along metal wires as coded signals. The code of dots and dashes is called Morse code after its inventor. Before the telegraph, a message could travel only as fast as a horse or a ship could carry a letter. By using Morse's invention, a message could be delivered almost instantly. By 1860, the nation had 50,000 miles of telegraph lines.

Agricultural Production Increases Despite the growing size and power of the nation's factories, agriculture remained the predominant activity in the United States. But change affected farming as well. American farms became more productive, raising larger crops for the market. In 1815, American farmers sold only about a third of their harvests. By 1860, that share had doubled. The gains came partly from the greater fertility of new farms in the Midwest. Farmers also adopted better methods for planting, tending, and harvesting crops and for raising livestock. After 1840, large farms also employed the steel plow invented by John Deere and the mechanical reaper developed by Cyrus McCormick.

IDENTIFY Identify the key innovations between 1820 and 1860 that transformed communications and agriculture in the United States.

ASSESSMENT

1. **Summarize** Discuss the impact the Erie Canal had on the farming industry.
2. **Identify Cause and Effect** How did the development of the steamboat affect American travel?
3. **Generate Explanations** In what ways did the advent of railroads affect canals?
4. **Infer** Discuss the Industrial Revolution and its effect on American manufacturing.
5. **Summarize** Discuss the role Francis Cabot Lowell played in the American Industrial Revolution.
6. **Connections to Today** In the 1800s, changes in technology changed the way in which people worked. How does technology change how people work today? Should the government help people transition from one type of work to another? Explain.

5.5

The vast majority of enslaved African Americans were forced to work as field hands. By the mid-1800s, about two thirds of all enslaved African Americans labored on cotton plantations.

Differences Between North and South Grow

BOUNCE to Activate Flipped Video

Objectives

Analyze why industrialization took root in the northern part of the United States.

Describe the impact of industrialization on northern life.

Analyze the reasons that agriculture and slavery became entrenched in the South.

Key Terms

Tariff of 1816
capital
labor union
nativist
cotton gin

Industrialization occurred mainly in the Northeast, where it changed the very structure of society. In the South, a boom in cotton production helped deepen the region's commitment to slavery. The two parts of the country developed in different ways—a fact that increasingly complicated politics in the United States.

Industrialization Takes Hold in the North

Thomas Jefferson had hoped to preserve the United States as a nation of farmers. Instead, between 1815 and 1860, the United States developed an industrial sector, or a distinct part of the economy or society dedicated to industry. Without intending to do so, Democratic Republican policies contributed to that industrial development.

The Origins of Industrialization The embargo of 1807 and the War of 1812 cut off access to British manufactured goods. Eager for substitutes, Americans built their own factories in the Northeast.

After the war, however, British goods once again flowed into the United States, threatening to overwhelm fledgling American manufacturers. Congress could have let those industries wither from the competition. Instead, Congress imposed the **Tariff of 1816**, a tariff on imports designed to protect American industry. This tariff increased the price of imported manufactured goods by an average of 20 to 25 percent. The inflated price for imports

GO ONLINE to access your digital course

encouraged Americans to buy products made in the United States. The tariff helped industry, but it hurt farmers, who had to pay higher prices for consumer goods.

Why the Northeast? Most of the new factories emerged in the Northeast. There were several reasons for this. One reason was greater access to **capital**, or the money needed to build factories or other productive assets. In the South, the land and the climate favored agriculture. Thus, people there invested capital in land and labor in the form of enslaved African Americans. The Northeast had more cheap labor to work in the factories. In addition, the Northeast had many swiftly flowing rivers to provide water power for the new factories.

CHECK UNDERSTANDING What factors contributed to the industrialization in the North in the early 1800s?

Industrialization Changes Northern Society

The arrival of industry changed the way many Americans worked by reducing the skill required for many jobs. This trend hurt highly skilled artisans, such as blacksmiths, shoemakers, and tailors, who could not compete with manufacturers working with many low-cost laborers. Most artisans suffered declining wages.

>> A middle-class American family of the 1820s

Workers Take Action Troubled workers responded by seeking political change. During the 1820s, some artisans organized the Workingmen's Party to compete in local and state elections. They sought free public education and laws to limit the working day to ten hours versus the standard twelve.

The party also supported the right of workers to organize **labor unions**—groups of workers who unite to seek better pay and conditions. Most early labor unions focused on helping skilled tradesmen, such as carpenters or printers. Unions went on strike to force employers to pay higher wages, reduce hours, or improve conditions.

In 1834 and 1836, for example, the Lowell mill girls held strikes when employers cut their wages and increased their charges for boarding. Singing "Oh! I cannot be a slave!" they left their jobs and temporarily shut down the factory. The Lowell strikes failed to achieve their goals, however. The women eventually returned to work and accepted the reduced pay.

Factory owners sometimes turned to the courts for protection. In 1835, a New York City court convicted 20 tailors of conspiracy for forming a union. Such convictions angered workers. But, neither the union movement nor the Workingmen's Party prospered in the early 1800s.

A Larger Middle Class While hurting some working Americans, industrialization helped others. The middle class expanded, as men worked as bankers, lawyers, accountants, clerks, auctioneers, brokers, and retailers. In the social scale, the middle class was ranked above the working class of common laborers but below the upper class of wealthy business owners.

Most middle-class men worked in offices outside of their homes. They also began to set up home in suburban areas away from the crowds, noise, and smells of the urban workshops and factories. Factory workers, however, could not afford to move into the new suburbs. Neighborhoods, therefore, became segregated by class as well as by race. This contrasted with colonial cities and towns, where people of all social classes lived close to one another.

For the middle class, work created distinct gender roles. In middle class families, wives and mothers stayed at home, which became havens from the bustle of the working world, while the men went off

Immigrant Populations of the 20 Largest U.S. Cities, 1850

>> **Analyze Maps** Which regions attracted the most immigrants during this time?

BOUNCE to Activate Chart

to work and returned with the money to support the household. Working-class and farm families could not afford such an arrangement. In those families, women and children also had to work.

Immigrants Arrive from Ireland and Germany

In the 1840s, most members of the new middle class and most of the nation's farmers had been born in the United States. Increasingly, however, the working class was comprised of immigrants. Prior to 1840, immigration consisted mainly of Protestants from England or Scotland. During the 1830s, about 600,000 immigrants arrived.

That number more than doubled to 1,500,000 during the 1840s and nearly doubled again to 2,800,000 in the 1850s.

This surge came primarily from Ireland and Germany, two lands suffering from political upheavals, economic depressions, and rural famines. In Ireland, mass starvation occurred in the 1840s as a result of a fungus that destroyed the potato crop. The potato had been the primary food source for the Irish poor. As hundreds of thousands of Irish were starving to death, huge amounts of livestock, corn, and other foods were being exported from Ireland to England. Because of this fact, a few historians suggest that the famine was an act of genocide. However, most historians dismiss this idea because there was no deliberate British policy to exterminate the Irish. In fact, the British government provided some relief with soup kitchens for the starving and work projects for the jobless.

Even so, it is estimated that more than a million Irish people died of starvation or famine-related diseases. Another million or more left Ireland, emigrating to Australia or North America. Those who came to America joined many other Irish and German immigrants. Germans had fled their homeland during the same period when their political revolution failed.

Unlike most of their predecessors, the new immigrants tended to be Catholic or Jewish. In search of work, they arrived in the seaports of the Northeast. A small minority, mostly German, could afford to set up shops or move to the West to buy farmland. But most immigrants had to find work on the docks, in factories, at construction sites, or in middle-class homes as domestic servants.

Immigration boosted the Northeast's share of the nation's population. It also promoted urban growth. In 1860, immigrants comprised more than 40 percent of the population of New York City. Some working-class immigrants moved on to new cities in the Midwest, including Cincinnati, Chicago, Cleveland, and Detroit. Very few went to the South, which lacked factory jobs for wage workers.

The rapid influx of so many newcomers created social and political strains. Poverty forced many immigrants to cluster in shabby neighborhoods. The newcomers competed against free African Americans for jobs and housing. Rioters attacked African Americans, killing some and burning others' homes.

Catholic immigrants also faced discrimination from American-born Protestants. Protestants distrusted the Catholic Church, thinking it to be hostile to republican government. Protestant workers also resented the competition from newcomers who were willing to work for lower wages. Riots between Protestants and Catholics occurred in Philadelphia in 1844 and in Baltimore in 1854.

Some politicians, particularly in the Whig Party, exploited ethnic tensions. Called **nativists**, they campaigned for laws to discourage immigration or to deny political rights to newcomers. To defend their interests, many immigrants became active in the Democratic Party.

☑ **IDENTIFY CENTRAL IDEAS** How did industrialization change the experience of working people?

Agriculture Drives Southern Society

During the 1780s, Thomas Jefferson, James Madison, and George Washington, who themselves were enslavers, hoped that slavery would gradually fade away. They thought that a shift from tobacco to wheat cultivation would slowly undermine the system of enslavement, making it less profitable. Indeed, they saw some evidence of such a trend in Virginia and Maryland, where many of the enslaved were freed during the 1780s.

That trend, however, did not affect the Deep South—the region to the south and southwest of Virginia. In fact, the trend did not last even in Virginia. Slavery became more profitable as cotton became the South's leading crop.

Cotton Production Surges In the Deep South, three developments worked together to boost cotton production: the cotton gin, western expansion, and industrialization. In 1793, Eli Whitney invented the **cotton gin** while working in Georgia. This machine reduced the amount of time and the cost of separating the cotton seeds from the valuable white fiber.

The cotton gin made cotton cultivation much more profitable. Previously a minor crop, cotton became the South's leading product. From 5 million

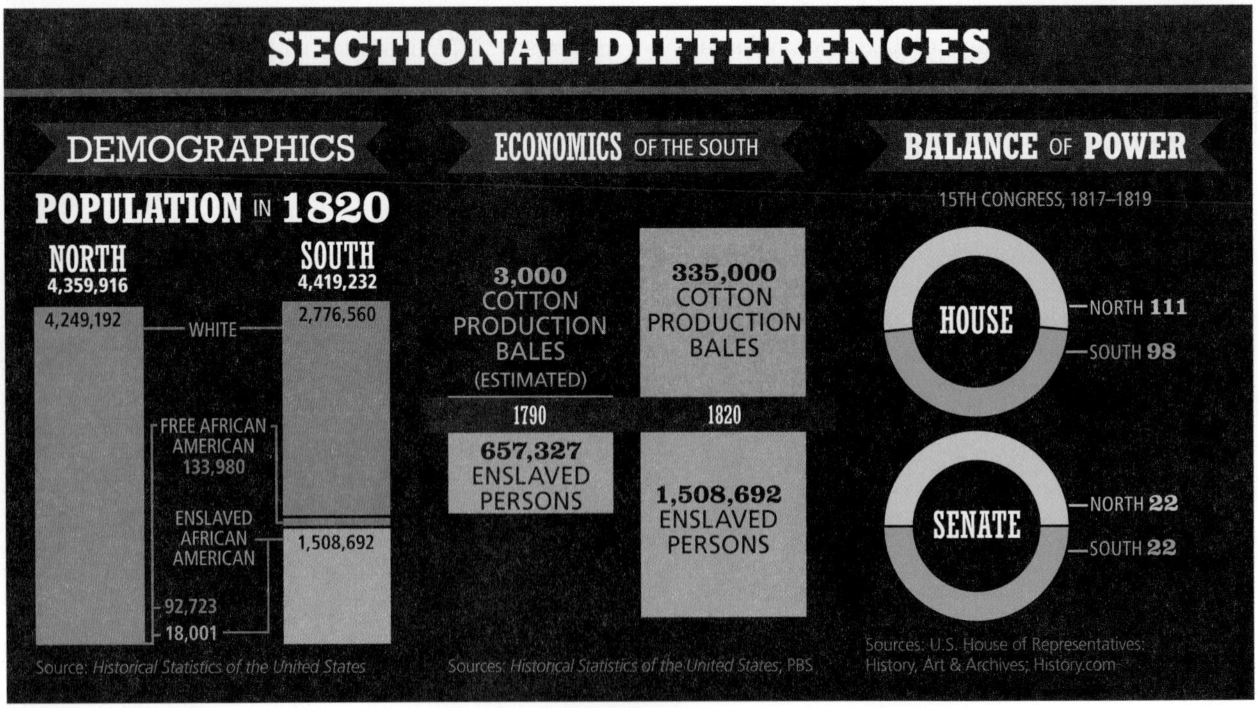

>> **Analyze Information** What was the main difference between the North and the South in 1820?

BOUNCE to Activate 3D Model

pounds in 1793, cotton production surged to 170 million pounds in 1820.

In part, that surge came as planters in older states—Georgia, South Carolina, and North Carolina—switched to growing cotton. But mostly it came as planters moved west or south to make new plantations in Florida, Tennessee, Alabama, Mississippi, Arkansas, Louisiana, and east Texas. These areas offered fertile soil and a warm climate well suited for growing cotton.

The increase in the cotton supply filled a growing demand from textile factories in the Northeast and in Europe. By 1840, southern plantations produced 60 percent of the cotton used by American and European factories. Cotton and cotton textiles accounted for over half the value of all American exports. With good reason, Americans spoke of "King Cotton" as the ruler of their economy.

Cotton Production and Slavery Increase

Growing cotton required workers as well as land. Southern planters met this need with enslaved African Americans. After federal law abolished the overseas trade in enslaved people in 1808, illegal trade and interstate trade filled the gap. Many of the enslaved African Americans came from the fading tobacco plantations of Virginia and Maryland, where planters who once grew crops now acquired their income from trading slaves.

Because cotton was so profitable, the demand for enslaved African Americans soared. The enslaved became more valuable to their owners. In 1802, an enslaved person could sell for $600. By 1860, that price had tripled to $1,800. The total number of slaves increased from 1.5 million in 1820 to 4 million in 1860. Far from withering, the trade in enslaved humans flourished and became more deeply entrenched in the southern economy.

Economic Consequences of the Cotton Boom

Although many plantation owners became rich, cotton production limited regional development. Most of the South became too dependent on one crop. That dependence paid off in most years, when cotton prices were high. But prices sometimes plummeted, forcing many planters into bankruptcy.

Another problem was that plantations dispersed the population. The South lost out on the urban growth needed for an industrial economy. Only one southern city, New Orleans, ranked among America's top fifteen cities in 1860. The South also lacked the commercial towns so common in the Northeast and Midwest. In 1860, a traveler in Alabama noted, "In fact the more fertile the land, the more destitute is the country of villages and towns."

>> The grand entryway of the Madewood Plantation House in Louisiana shows the opulence characteristic of large plantation homes. Plantations like Madewood relied on enslaved African Americans to maintain their lifestyles.

BOUNCE to Activate Gallery

The stunted commercial development in the South did not attract the immigrants who needed wage work. Consequently, the northern population grew much faster than the southern population. In 1850, the North had twice as many free people as did the South. That trend increased the political power of the North, especially in the House of Representatives. And that political trend alarmed southern whites who did not trust northerners to protect slavery.

The South also paid an economic price for keeping two fifths of its people in slavery. Though some enslavers allowed Black laborers to sell some of their time for wages—and some used those wages to purchase the freedom of family members—most enslaved African Americans owned little, and therefore contributed little to the consumer market. The South's limited consumer demand discouraged southern entrepreneurs from building factories. It was more profitable to buy a plantation.

Cultural Consequences of Slavery A dispersed population and the burden of slavery affected the culture of the South. Planters opposed education for the enslaved and cared little about providing it to poor whites. The rate of southern white illiteracy was

15 percent—three times higher than what it was in the North and West.

Although slavery was central to life in the South, enslavers were a minority. No more than one fourth of white men enslaved people in 1860. Three fourths of these enslaved fewer than 10 African Americans, and about 3,000 white men enslaved 100 or more. The typical enslaver lived in a farmhouse and enslaved about four or five African Americans.

Why, then, did southern whites so vigorously defend the slave system? Part of the answer lies in the aspirations of common farmers. They hoped some day to acquire their own enslaved African Americans and plantations. Common whites also dreaded freeing Blacks for fear they would seek bloody revenge. All classes of whites also believed that they shared a racial bond. Even the poorest whites felt a sense of racial superiority.

They also reasoned that southern whites enjoyed an equality of rights impossible in the North, where poor men depended on wage labor from rich mill owners. Southern farmers took pride in their independence. They credited that independence to a social structure that kept enslaved African Americans at the bottom.

By the 1850s, proslavery forces rejected the criticism of slavery once expressed by Jefferson, Madison, and Washington. They no longer defended the enslavement of African Americans as a necessary evil but touted the institution as a positive good. They also insisted that slavery was kinder to African Americans than industrial life was to white workers.

> The negro slaves of the South are the happiest, and, in some sense, the freest people in the world. . . . The free laborer must work or starve. He is more of a slave than the negro, because he works longer and harder for less allowance than the slave.
>
> — George Fitzhugh, *Cannibals All! or, Slaves Without Masters,* 1857

Despite these claims, no northern workers fled to the South to become slaves, while hundreds of slaves ran away to seek wage work in the North.

IDENTIFY CENTRAL ISSUES Why did slavery spread in the South, rather than fade away?

ASSESSMENT

1. **Summarize** What factors contributed to the Northeast's high concentration of factories?
2. **Generate Explanations** Explain how the emerging middle class affected the social structure of many cities.
3. **Generate Explanations** How did the cotton gin affect the growth of slavery in the South?
4. **Summarize** How did the nation respond to the goals of the Workingmen's Party and other labor unions?
5. **Identify Central Issues** How did the religious backgrounds of immigrants who settled in the United States in the 1800s differ from that of earlier immigrants? How did this affect people's perception of the new immigrants?

5.6

President James Monroe was the fifth president of the United States.

Nationalism Influences Policies

BOUNCE to Activate Flipped Video

Objectives

Analyze the causes and effects of nationalism on domestic policy during the years following the War of 1812.

Describe the impact of nationalism on the nation's foreign policy.

Summarize the struggle over the issue of slavery as the nation grew.

Key Terms

nationalism
Henry Clay
American System
John Quincy Adams
Adams-Onís Treaty
Monroe Doctrine
Missouri Compromise

Nationalism was a dominant political force in the years following the War of 1812. It affected economic and foreign policy and was supported by Supreme Court rulings. The building of the nation's pride and identity was an important development that shaped politics and the arts.

The Influence of Nationalism on Domestic Affairs

In 1817, a newspaper in Boston described politics as entering an "era of good feelings." The Democratic Republican Party operated almost without opposition. In the election of 1820, James Monroe won reelection as President by receiving almost all of the electoral votes cast. A spirit of **nationalism** swept the country.

Clay Promotes Nationalist Economic Policies The Tariff of 1816 was an example of an economic policy that promoted the growth of industry. By embracing a protective tariff, many Democratic Republicans betrayed their former principles. Once they had opposed federal power, supported agriculture, and favored trade unburdened by tariffs. Now they used federal power to help industrialists and their workers.

Henry Clay was one of the leading advocates of this new economic nationalism. He regarded the protective tariff as part of a larger, ambitious federal program he called the **American System**. Clay and his supporters wanted the federal government to build new roads and canals to link the Atlantic states with the Midwest. Clay insisted that the tariff and "internal improvements"

GO ONLINE to access your digital course

would work together to tie the different regions into a harmonious and prosperous whole.

Clay also favored reestablishment of a national bank. The charter for the first Bank of the United States, created during Washington's administration, expired in 1811. That freed private and state banks to print their own money, which caused widespread uncertainty about the value of money. A national bank, Clay argued, would provide federal control over the nation's money supply and banking practices. In 1816, Congress established the second Bank of the United States. But most congressmen opposed using federal funds for internal improvements.

The Marshall Court Increases Federal Power

Under John Marshall, who served as Chief Justice from 1801 to 1835, the Supreme Court favored a strong federal government and a national economy. Marshall applied several Federalist principles to interpret the Constitution. For example, the Marshall Court claimed the power to review the acts of Congress and of the President for their constitutionality. This was established in the landmark decision *Marbury* v. *Madison* (1803). Marshall also insisted upon the "sanctity of contracts." In *Dartmouth College* v. *Woodward* (1819) and *Fletcher* v. *Peck* (1810), the Marshall Court limited a state government's power to interfere in business contracts.

Further, the Marshall Court insisted that federal law was superior to state law. This point was famously established in *McCulloch* v. *Maryland* (1819). The case involved the renewed Bank of the United States. When it was reestablished in 1816, branches were placed in states across the country. In effect, the bank competed with and threatened many state and local banks. In Maryland, state officials tried to defend their banks by levying a tax on the operations of the Bank of the United States.

The Marshall Court struck down this Maryland law. Embracing a broad interpretation of the Constitution, Marshall insisted that Congress had the power to charter a national bank. Further, no state could destroy such a bank with taxes.

Finally, Marshall broadly interpreted the Constitution to give greater power to the national government. In the 1824 case *Gibbons* v. *Ogden*, Marshall rejected a steamboat monopoly granted by the state of New York. The monopoly threatened the business of a steamboat operator who had run a service between New Jersey and New York. Marshall ruled that steamboat traffic was "commerce" and that the power to regulate commerce involving more than one state—interstate commerce—belonged to the federal government. As in *McCulloch* v. *Maryland*, the ruling extended federal power by creating a broad definition of commerce and by asserting the supremacy of federal over state law.

In general, Marshall's Court encouraged the development of large, farflung business corporations by freeing them from meddling by the states. (Think, for example, how difficult it might have been to build a railroad company that covered several states if each state had the power to establish its own monopolies within its borders.)

Corporations took the place of the older, smaller, and simpler forms of business—single proprietorships and limited partnerships whose reach was confined to a small area. Due in part to

Select Supreme Court Cases Presided Over By John Marshall

YEAR	CASE	PRINCIPLES ESTABLISHED
1803	**Marbury v. Madison**	Established principle of judicial review – Supreme Court has the power to declare federal laws unconstitutional
1819	**McCulloch v. Maryland**	Established Congress's constitutional authority to create a national bank
1821	**Cohens v. Virginia**	Established the Supreme Court's right to review state cases involving constitutional questions
1824	**Gibbons v. Ogden**	Affirmed Congress's right to regulate interstate commerce

Source: Streetlaw

>> **Analyze Information** What effects did these decisions have on the various branches of government?

BOUNCE to Activate Chart

the Marshall Court, the United States increasingly became one large integrated market.

"Boom and Bust" Cycles Affect the Economy As the national market emerged and more enterprises became interconnected over greater distances, the economy became subject to periodic shocks, or panics. These panics were the result of "busts" in a "boom-and-bust" cycle that is common in capitalism. In capitalism, individuals own most productive property—factories and farms—and markets set prices. During the "boom" phase, high consumer demand encourages owners to expand production. But once the expanded supply of goods exceeds demand, a "bust" follows. Prices fall and producers cut back on production, closing factories and firing workers. Those jobless workers then have less to spend, hurting other businesses.

Between 1815 and 1860, there were three great panics that occurred: 1819, 1837, and 1857. Thousands of factory workers lost their jobs.

The panics also hurt farmers and planters as demand declined for their grain or cotton. When farm prices fell, many farmers and planters could not pay their debts. They, therefore, lost their properties to lawsuits and foreclosures.

Panics led many workers and farmers to doubt capitalism—or at least to blame the banks, especially the Bank of the United States. The panics lifted after a year or two, however, and "boom" times returned. These economic revivals quieted the doubts.

Nationalism Spurs a Renaissance Nationalism also influenced art and literature. Artists celebrated America's beautiful landscape, while novelists expressed pride in the nation's immense potential. A period known as the American Renaissance ensued, in which literature reflected the nationalistic spirit. James Fenimore Cooper of New York became the first American to make a career as a novelist. His most celebrated novels, a series known as *The Leatherstocking Tales*, created the genre of frontier adventure tales that persists to this day. There were also several regional voices in literature. For instance, Cooper influenced William Gilmore Simms, a southern writer who gave frontier stories a more southern voice.

☑ **IDENTIFY CENTRAL IDEAS** How did proponents of economic nationalism think it would benefit the country?

>> This illustration shows a dramatic scene from *Leatherstocking Tales*. **Draw Conclusions** How did nationalism inspire writers and artists to shape a uniquely American culture?

BOUNCE to Activate Gallery

Nationalism Leads to American Expansion

Nationalism also influenced the nation's foreign policy. A key figure in this development was **John Quincy Adams**, James Monroe's Secretary of State and the son of former President John Adams. Monroe and Adams hoped to reduce the nation's great regional tensions by promoting national expansion.

The United States Gains Spanish Territories In 1819, American pressure and Adams's diplomacy persuaded Spain to sell Florida to the United States. Spain had felt pressured to give up their claims by the First Seminole War that occurred in 1818. The Seminoles were an American Indian group from southern Georgia and northern Florida, an area that was governed by Spain. Seminoles clashed often with white settlers, who were upset with the Seminoles for providing safe havens for runaway slaves. American General Andrew Jackson led a force into Florida to fight the Seminoles and seize Spanish forts.

Though Jackson had not been told to act against the Spanish, the episode made it clear that Spanish control of Florida was very weak. Ratified in 1821, the

Adams-Onís Treaty also ended Spanish claims to the vast Pacific Coast territory of Oregon. The British also claimed Oregon, but in 1818, the United States and Great Britain agreed to share the contested territory. Following the Adams-Onís Treaty, Americans began to settle in Florida and pursue the fur trade in Oregon.

The Monroe Doctrine Adams also formulated the famous foreign policy doctrine named for President Monroe—the **Monroe Doctrine**. This policy responded to threats by European powers, including France, to help Spain recover Latin American colonies that had declared their independence. Monroe and Adams were eager to protect those new republics. The British shared that goal and proposed uniting with the United States to warn the other European powers to stay out of Latin America. Adams and Monroe, however, preferred to act without a British partner.

In 1823, Monroe issued a written doctrine declaring that European monarchies had no business meddling with American republics. In return, the United States promised to stay out of European affairs.

> . . . [T]he occasion has been judged proper for asserting, as a principle in which the rights and interests of the United States are involved, that the American continents, by the free and independent condition which they have assumed and maintain, are henceforth not to be considered as subjects for future colonization by any European powers. . . .
>
> —James Monroe, address to Congress, December 2, 1823

The Monroe Doctrine meant little in 1823 when the Americans lacked the army and navy to enforce it. The Latin American republics kept their independence with British, rather than American, help. The doctrine did, however, reveal the nation's growing desire for power. The doctrine became much more significant in the 1890s and in the twentieth century, when the United States increasingly sent armed forces into Latin American countries.

☑ **CHECK UNDERSTANDING** How was nationalism reflected in John Quincy Adams's foreign policy?

Slavery and the Missouri Compromise

The spirit of nationalism failed to suppress regional differences in the United States. Such differences made the nation more difficult to govern. In 1819, this difficulty became evident in a crisis over Missouri's admission to the Union as a new state. At that point, the Union had an equal number of slave and free states—which meant equal regional power in the United States Senate. If Missouri entered the Union as a slave state, or a state in which slavery was legal, it would tip the balance in favor of the South. This prospect alarmed northern congressmen. A New York congressman proposed banning slavery

The Monroe Doctrine Throughout American History

YEAR	PRESIDENT	DETAILS
1845	James K. Polk	European powers were warned not to interfere with development of Oregon, California, or Texas.
1867	Andrew Johnson	France withdrew its troops from Mexico when the United States sent troops to the Rio Grande.
1895	Grover Cleveland	United States called for arbitration in a border dispute between Venezuela and British Guiana.
1902	Theodore Roosevelt	United States sent naval support in response to German, Italian, and English ships attacking Venezuelan city.

Sources: *Encyclopædia Britannica*; Digital History; U.S. Department of State; National Park Service

>> **Analyze Information** How did the application of the Monroe Doctrine change over time?

The Missouri Compromise

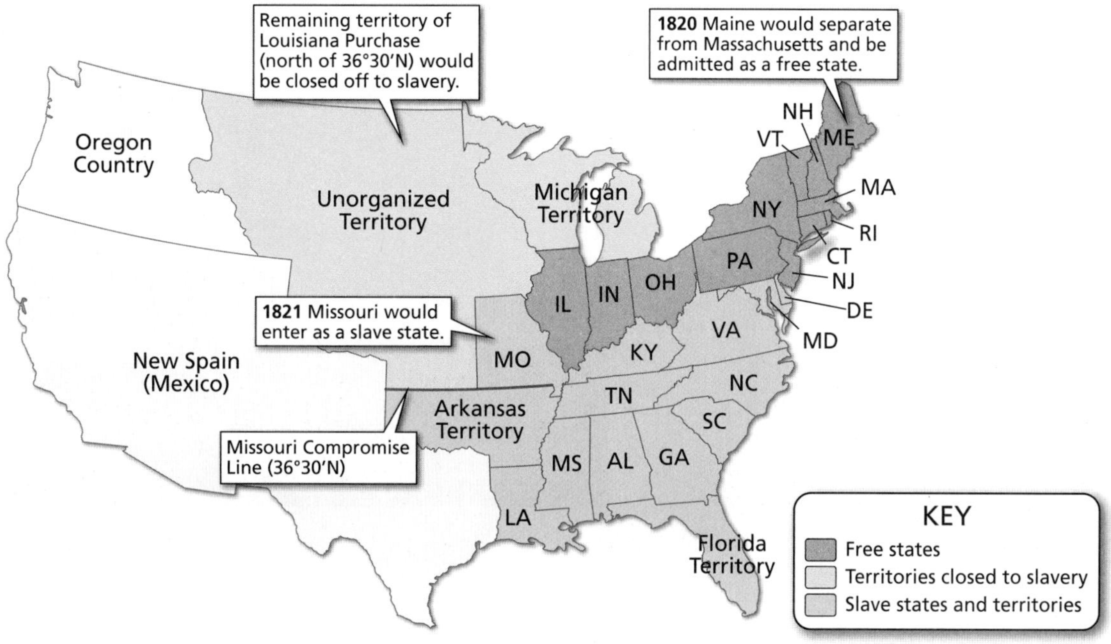

>> **Analyze Maps** What did the Missouri Compromise reveal about the state of the Union?

in Missouri as a price for joining the Union. The proposed ban outraged southern leaders, who claimed a right to expand slavery westward.

In 1820, after a long and bitter debate, Henry Clay crafted the **Missouri Compromise**. The northern district of Massachusetts would enter the Union as the free state of Maine to balance admission of Missouri as a slave state. To discourage future disputes over state admissions, the compromise also drew a line across the continent from the southwestern corner of Missouri to the nation's western boundary. Territories south of that line would enter as slave states. Those north of the line would become free states.

The compromise solved the short-term crisis. But that crisis had exposed the growing division between the North and the South over the expansion of slavery. Jefferson worried, "This momentous question, like a fire-bell in the night, awakened and filled me with terror. I considered it at once the [death] knell of the Union."

Southern whites felt insulted by the northern attacks on their region's reliance on slavery. They also felt threatened. In 1822, they blamed the Missouri debates for inspiring Denmark Vesey to plan a slave revolt. Vesey, a African American freedman, prepared slaves to seize control of Charleston, South Carolina. The revolt, however, never took place because Charleston officials learned of the plot. These officials arrested, tried, convicted, and hanged Vesey and 34 others. Shaken by their close call, southern politicians insisted that their safety required northern silence on slavery.

IDENTIFY CENTRAL IDEAS How did sectionalism threaten the expansion of the United States?

ASSESSMENT

1. **Describe** Henry Clay's plan for an ambitious federal program called the American System.
2. **Analyze Information** How did the Marshall Court increase federal power, and what were some far reaching effects of its rulings?
3. **Generate Explanations** What was the Monroe Doctrine and how did it affect U.S. foreign relations?
4. **Apply Concepts** What was the Missouri Compromise, and what problem was it intended to address?
5. **Connections to Today** Do you think it is important for recent Presidents to promote feelings of nationalism? What might be some positive and negative effects of nationalism?

GO ONLINE to access these biographies: John Quincy Adams, James Monroe

5.7

Jackson exercised such firm authority as President that his critics sometimes called him "King Andrew." **Analyze Political Cartoons** What details symbolize Jackson's abuse of power?

BOUNCE to Activate Flipped Video

Objectives

Analyze the movement toward greater democracy under Andrew Jackson.

Summarize the causes and effects of the removal of American Indians in the early 1800s.

Evaluate the significance of the debate over tariffs and the idea of nullification.

Summarize the key events of the conflict over the second Bank of the United States in the 1830s.

Analyze the political environment in the United States after Andrew Jackson.

Key Terms

Jacksonian Democracy
caucus
Andrew Jackson
Martin Van Buren
spoils system
Indian Removal Act
Trail of Tears
Tariff of Abominations
John C. Calhoun
nullification
Whigs

Jacksonian Democracy

During the mid-1820s, Andrew Jackson became the symbol of American democracy. Historians refer to the movement as **Jacksonian Democracy**. In his speeches and writings, Jackson celebrated majority rule and the dignity of the common people. He projected himself as a down-to-earth common man with humble roots, an image which was meant to contrast with the aristocratic leaders of the past.

Andrew Jackson Enters National Politics

Jackson's life embodied the nation's ideal of expanding opportunity. He was born in a log cabin, orphaned as a boy, and wounded during the American Revolution. Moving west to the then-frontier, he had become a wealthy lawyer and planter in Tennessee. Jackson won military fame in the War of 1812 and in the wars against the Creeks and Seminoles. Although he showed an interest in politics, serving short terms as both a member of the U.S. House and Senate, Jackson initially shrugged off suggestions of running for President. However, he decided to run in 1824.

The Election of 1824 The election of 1824 signaled a shift in American political and social life. As a new political party emerged, the nation expanded its concept of democracy in some ways and narrowed it in others. As the presidential election of 1824 approached, two-term President James Monroe announced that he would not seek a third term. His presidency was marked by what appeared to be general political harmony. There was only one major political party, and the nation seemed to be united

GO ONLINE to access your digital course

in its purpose and direction. Beneath this surface, however, disagreements were emerging. These would become obvious in the election of 1824.

Four Candidates Four leading Democratic Republicans hoped to replace Monroe in the White House. John Quincy Adams, Monroe's Secretary of State, offered great skill and experience. A caucus of Democratic Republicans in Congress preferred William Crawford of Georgia. A **caucus** is a closed meeting of party members for the purpose of choosing a candidate. War hero **Andrew Jackson** of Tennessee and Henry Clay of Kentucky provided greater competition for Adams.

The House Decides the Election The crowded race produced no clear winner. Jackson won more popular votes than did Adams, his next nearest competitor. Jackson did well in many southern states and in the western part of the country. Adams ran strongest in the Northeast. But neither won a majority of the electoral votes needed for election. As a result, for the second time in the nation's history (the first was in 1800), the House of Representatives had to determine the outcome of a presidential election. There, Clay threw his support to Adams, who became President. When Adams appointed Clay as Secretary of State, Jackson accused them of a "corrupt bargain," in which he thought Clay supported Adams in exchange for an appointment as Secretary of State.

Jackson's opposition weakened Adams's presidency. Taking a broad, nationalist view of the Constitution, Adams pushed for an aggressive program of federal spending for internal improvements and scientific exploration. Jackson and other critics denounced this program as "aristocratic" for allegedly favoring the wealthy over the common people. This would become a growing theme in national politics.

Jackson Looks Ahead to 1828 Much of the criticism of Adams's presidency came from Andrew Jackson. Indeed, Jackson and his supporters spent much of Adams's term preparing for the next election. Jackson especially relied upon New York's **Martin Van Buren**, who worked behind the scenes to build support for Jackson. Meanwhile, Jackson traveled the country drumming up support among the voters—a new practice.

Jackson hoped to exploit the increasingly democratic character of national politics. In the 1824 presidential election, a growing number of states had chosen their presidential electors based on popular vote. This was a shift from the method used in the first presidential elections, in which state legislatures chose electors. By 1836, every state but South Carolina was choosing electors based on the popular vote. Voters also had an increased role in choosing other state and local officials across the country. For example, the use of caucuses was replaced in many cases by more public conventions in which voters had a greater say in who became a candidate for office.

THE ELECTION OF 1824

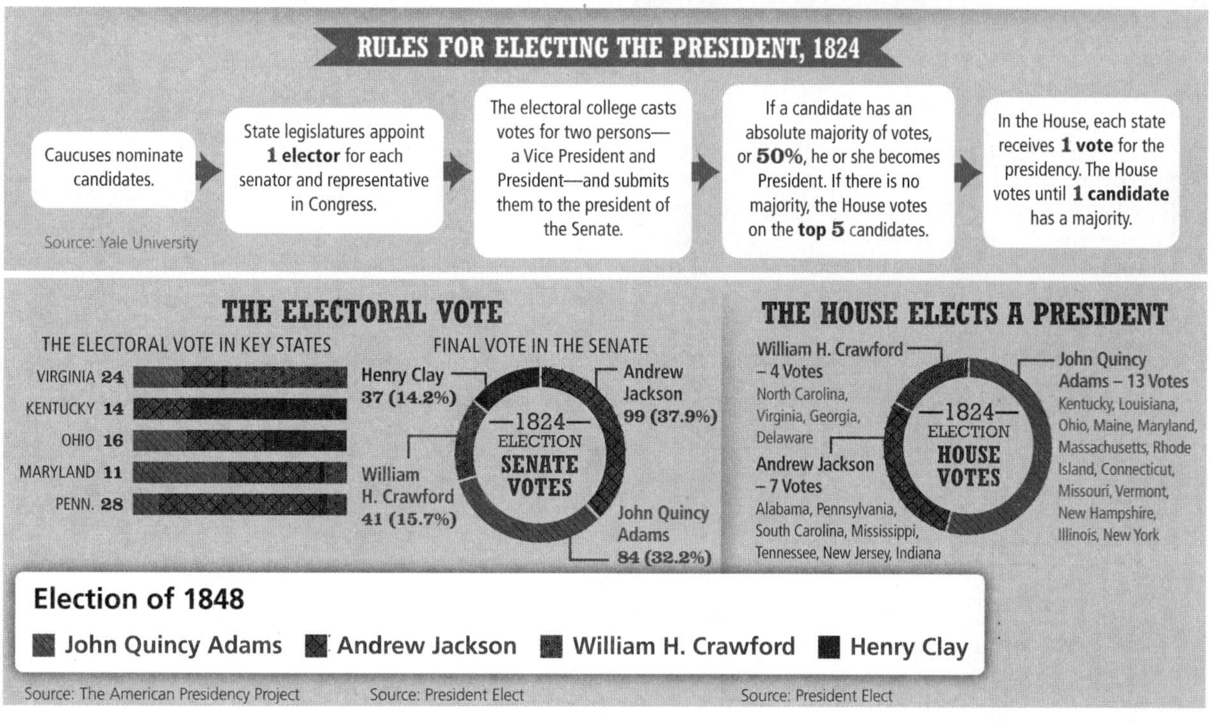

>> **Analyze Information** How did John Quincy Adams win the presidency?

During the 1810s and 1820s, many states rewrote their constitutions. Those documents had originally restricted the right to vote and hold office to men who owned property. In 1776, about three fourths of all free men could meet the property-ownership requirement because they owned a farm or a shop. But that qualified proportion slipped as more men worked for wages in the expanding industries. Without their own farm or shop, they could not vote. The economic losses caused by the Panic of 1819 had also removed many voters from the rolls.

The new state constitutions expanded the electorate by abolishing the property requirement. In most states, any white man who paid a tax could vote and hold office. These changes increased participation in elections. Male voter turnout that had been less than 30 percent in the elections of the early 1800s reached almost 80 percent in 1840.

Unfortunately, the expansion of democracy did not benefit all Americans. Most of the new constitutions also took the vote away from free African Americans—even those with property. Nor did the new constitutions allow women to vote. (With the exception of New Jersey, in which a loophole in the state constitution allowed property-owning women to vote until 1807, no state had ever allowed women to cast a ballot.) In addition, American Indians, who were not citizens of the United States, were denied the vote. Democracy was limited to white men.

>> Before 1824, presidential election results did not include a popular vote count. By 1840, the number of voters had skyrocketed. This painting, entitled *The County Election* by George Caleb Bingham, reflects this trend.

Jackson and the Democrats Win the Election of 1828 By the election of 1828, Jackson's supporters were calling themselves Democrats, not Democratic Republicans. Jacksonian Democracy triumphed in the presidential election of 1828. With 56 percent of the popular vote and two thirds of the electoral votes, Jackson defeated Adams. A rowdy crowd attended Jackson's inauguration in Washington, D.C. Their raucous conduct symbolized the triumph of the democratic style during the Jacksonian Era, which became known as "the age of the common man."

Jackson owed his victory to his campaign manager Martin Van Buren, who revived the Jeffersonian partnership of southern planters and northern common people. The party promised a return to Jeffersonian principles: strong states and a weak federal government that would not interfere in slavery. Only those principles, Van Buren argued, could keep sectional tensions from destroying the Union.

Democrats Change Politics While returning to old principles, the Democrats innovated in party structure. They developed a disciplined system of local and state committees and conventions. The party cast out anyone who broke with party discipline. While becoming more democratic in style, with carefully planned appeals to voters and great public rallies, elections also became the business of professional politicians and managers.

The new party rewarded the faithful with government jobs. Whereas Adams had displaced only a dozen government officials when he became President, Jackson replaced hundreds. He used the government jobs to reward Democratic activists. Van Buren's "reward" was appointment as Secretary of State, the coveted steppingstone to the presidency.

The Democrats defended the use of jobs as rewards for political loyalty. Senator William Learned Marcy of New York defended the Jacksonians.

> They boldly preach what they practice. When they are contending for victory, they avow [state] the intention of enjoying the fruits of it. If they are defeated, they expect to retire from office. If they are successful, they claim, as a matter of right, the advantages of success. They

> see nothing wrong in the rule, that to the victor belongs the spoils [loot] of the enemy.
>
> —Senator William Learned Marcy, speech before Congress, January 1832

Critics, however, denounced the use of political jobs as a reward for party loyalty, a practice they called the **spoils system**.

☑ **IDENTIFY CENTRAL IDEAS** How did Jackson's life embody his political beliefs?

American Indian Removal

Jackson's political base lay in the South, where he captured 80 percent of the vote. Those voters expected Jackson to help them remove the 60,000 American Indians living in the region. These Indians belonged to five nations: the Cherokee, Chickasaw, Creek, Choctaw, and Seminole.

Southern voters had good reason to expect Jackson's help with American Indian removal. Jackson's victory in the Creek War of 1814 had led to the acquisition of millions of Creek acres in Georgia and Alabama. His war with the Seminoles in 1818 paved the way for the Adams-Onís Treaty and American control of Florida.

However, many American Indians had remained in the South. In many cases, they had even adopted white American culture. For example, many practiced Christianity, established schools, owned private property, and formed constitutional, republican governments. A Cherokee named Sequoyah invented a writing system for the Cherokee language so they could print their own newspaper and books. These American Indians in the five southeastern tribes became known as the "five civilized tribes."

States Seize Indian Lands Many southern whites, however, denounced the "civilizing" of American Indian cultures as a sham. Indians could never be civilized, southerners insisted. President Jackson agreed that the American Indians should make way for white people. "What good man would prefer a country covered with forests and ranged by a few thousand savages to our extensive Republic?" he asked. Indeed, southern whites wanted the valuable lands held by the American Indians. Between 1827 and 1830, the states of Georgia, Mississippi, and Alabama dissolved the Indian governments and seized these lands.

>> This Thomas Nast political cartoon satirizes Andrew Jackson's support for the spoils system. **Analyze Political Cartoons** What is the meaning of the phrase printed on the pedestal's base?

BOUNCE to Activate Chart

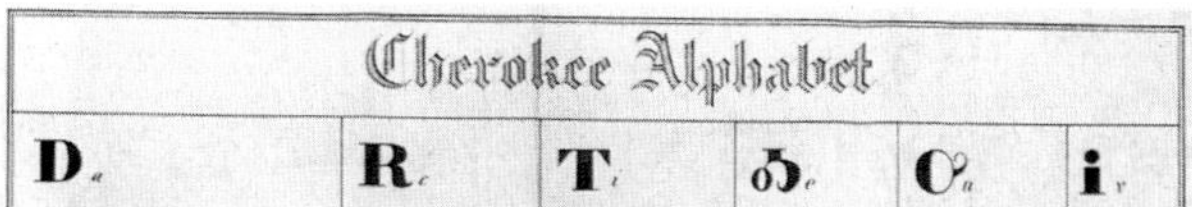

>> The Cherokee nation adopted some European and American practices such as the use of written language. **Compare** How did the Cherokee alphabet resemble the English alphabet?

In 1832, after the American Indians appealed their case to the federal courts, John Marshall's Supreme Court tried to help them. In *Worcester* v. *Georgia*, the Court ruled that Georgia's land seizure was unconstitutional. The federal government had treaty obligations to protect the American Indians, the Court held, and federal law was superior to state law. President Jackson, however, ignored the Court's decision. "John Marshall has made his decision, now let him enforce it," Jackson boldly declared. Although often a nationalist, Jackson favored states' rights in this case.

Even before this ruling, Jackson had urged Congress to pass the **Indian Removal Act** of 1830. This act sought to peacefully negotiate the exchange of American Indian lands in the South for new lands in the Indian Territory (modern-day Oklahoma).

> Rightly considered, the policy of the General Government toward the red man is not only liberal, but generous. He is unwilling to submit to the laws of the States and mingle with their population. To save him from this alternative, or perhaps utter annihilation, the General Government kindly offers him a new home. . . .
>
> — President Andrew Jackson, message to Congress, December 6, 1830

The Choctaws and Chickasaws reluctantly agreed to leave their southeastern homelands for new lands in the West. A few stayed behind, but they suffered violent mistreatment by whites.

The Trail of Tears and Armed Resistance The Jackson administration continued pressuring remaining American Indian groups to sell their lands and move west.

In 1835, a small group of Cherokees who did not represent their nation made an agreement with the government under which all Cherokees would leave the South for Oklahoma. Though the rest of the Cherokees protested, the federal government sought to enforce the treaty. In 1838, U.S. soldiers forced 16,000 Cherokees to walk from their lands in the Southeast to Oklahoma along what came to be called the **Trail of Tears**. At least 4,000 Cherokees died of disease, exposure, and hunger on their long, hard journey.

Some American Indians in the South resisted removal. In 1836, after a number of violent conflicts with white settlers, troops forcibly removed the

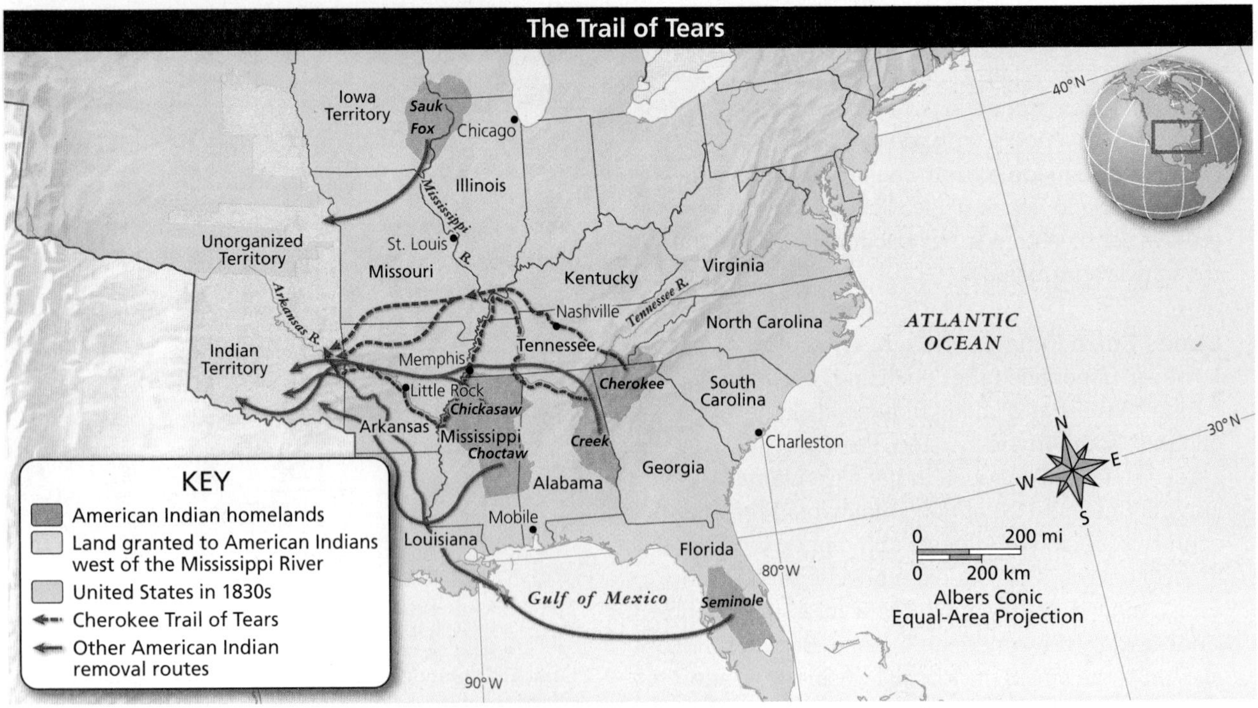

>> **Analyze Maps** Why were Americans willing to give up the Indian Territory to American Indians?

BOUNCE to Activate Timeline

The Nullification Crisis of 1833

In both 1828 and 1832, Congress passes tariffs on imported goods, which benefit northern manufacturers but hurt southern planters.

↓

South Carolina votes to nullify, or void, both the 1828 and 1832 tariffs within the state's borders and threatens to secede from the Union if force is used against the state.

↓

Force Bill gives Jackson authority to use troops to enforce federal law in South Carolina.

↓

Congress reduces the tariffs on imports.

↓

South Carolina suspends its nullification of the tariffs but nullifies the Force Bill.

>> **Analyze Information** How did the nullifcation crisis reveal tensions between state and federal authority?

Creeks from their southern lands. In Florida, the Seminoles fought the Second Seminole War between 1835 and 1842. In the end, American troops forced most Seminoles to leave Florida.

Removal also affected American Indians in the Midwest. In Illinois, a chief named Black Hawk led the resistance by the Sauk and Fox nations. In what became known as Black Hawk's War, they fought federal troops and local militia until crushed in 1832.

☑ **CHECK UNDERSTANDING** Why did many white Americans want American Indians removed from the southeastern United States?

The Debate Over Nullification

Jackson's presidency featured a number of conflicts and crises, and it helped bring about the formation of a rival political party. In spite of this, Jackson was able to secure the election of a handpicked successor. That administration was unable to survive its own crises and gave way to a Whig presidency.

The protective tariffs had long been a topic of debate and discord in the United States. In general, the industrial North favored them, but the agricultural South disliked them.

In 1828, Congress adopted an especially high tariff. Southerners called it the **Tariff of Abominations**. This tariff had been designed by members of Congress not only to promote American industry but to embarrass President Adams and ensure a Jackson victory in that year's presidential election. In fact, Adams did sign the tariff, though reluctantly, and it did help bring about his defeat in 1828.

Calhoun Promotes Nullification Jackson's Vice President, **John C. Calhoun** of South Carolina, violently opposed the tariff. During the War of 1812, he had been a strong nationalist. But his opinions changed after the Missouri controversy of 1819 and 1820. This episode convinced him that the future of slavery, which he supported, required a stronger defense of states' rights. Toward that end, he began to champion the concept of **nullification**, which meant that states could nullify, or void, any federal law deemed unconstitutional.

Calhoun and his supporters expected Jackson to reject a protective tariff. After all, Jackson was not a supporter of the tariff, and they hoped he might take action against it on his own. He did modify the tariff rates, but not enough to satisfy Calhoun.

South Carolina Threatens Secession In 1832, the South Carolina legislature nullified the protective tariff and prohibited the collection of federal tariff duties in South Carolina after February 1, 1833.

Further, the state threatened to secede from the Union if the federal government employed force against South Carolina. Calhoun resigned the vice presidency and instead became a senator.

Jackson generally supported states' rights, and he wanted a lower tariff. He drew the line at nullification and secession, however. "Disunion by armed force is treason," Jackson thundered. He felt the Union must be perpetual and states must honor federal law.

> I can have within the limits of South Carolina fifty thousand men, and in forty days more another fifty thousand. . . . The Union will be preserved. The safety of the republic, the supreme law, which will be promptly obeyed by me.
>
> —President Andrew Jackson, December 9, 1832

Other state legislatures around the country supported him by passing resolutions rejecting nullification.

Webster Defends the Union In Congress, Daniel Webster of Massachusetts became the great champion of nationalism. In an 1830 debate over nullification, he had blasted the notion in a fiery speech. "Liberty *and* Union, now and forever, one and inseparable," he declared. Webster defined the Union as the creation of the American people rather than of the states. In 1833, Webster led the way in pushing for passage of a Force Bill, giving Jackson authority to use troops to enforce federal law in South Carolina.

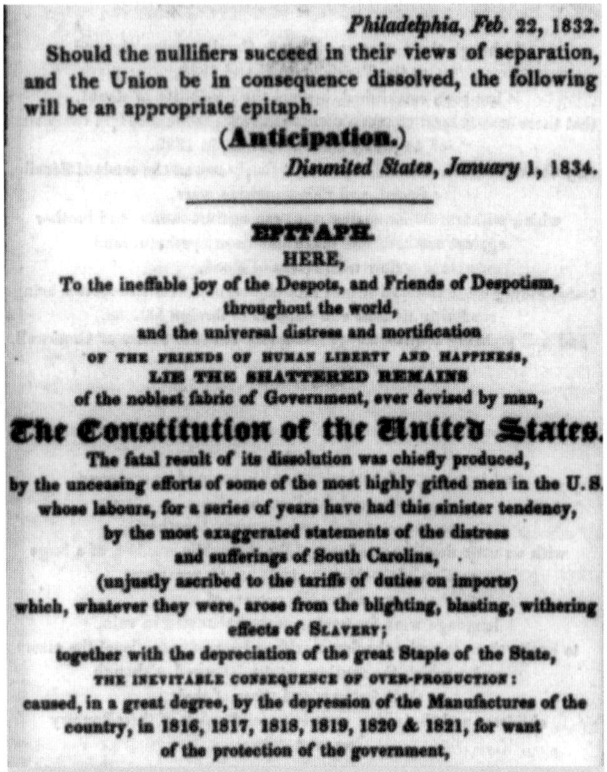

Philadelphia, Feb. 22, 1832.

Should the nullifiers succeed in their views of separation, and the Union be in consequence dissolved, the following will be an appropriate epitaph.

(Anticipation.)

***Disunited States, January* 1, 1834.**

EPITAPH.

HERE,
To the ineffable joy of the Despots, and Friends of Despotism,
throughout the world,
and the universal distress and mortification
OF THE FRIENDS OF HUMAN LIBERTY AND HAPPINESS,
LIE THE SHATTERED REMAINS
of the noblest fabric of Government, ever devised by man,
The Constitution of the United States.
The fatal result of its dissolution was chiefly produced,
by the unceasing efforts of some of the most highly gifted men in the U. S.
whose labours, for a series of years have had this sinister tendency,
by the most exaggerated statements of the distress
and sufferings of South Carolina,
(unjustly ascribed to the tariffs of duties on imports)
which, whatever they were, arose from the blighting, blasting, withering
effects of SLAVERY;
together with the depreciation of the great Staple of the State,
THE INEVITABLE CONSEQUENCE OF OVER-PRODUCTION:
caused, in a great degree, by the depression of the Manufactures of the
country, in 1816, 1817, 1818, 1819, 1820 & 1821, for want
of the protection of the government,

>> Opponents of the nullification theory published this notice announcing the death of the U.S. Constitution in a Philadelphia newspaper in 1832.

The Crisis Avoided At the same time, with Jackson's support, Congress also reduced the tariff. This reduced South Carolina's militancy. In March, a special convention suspended that state's ordinance of nullification. Still, the convention made a political statement by nullifying the now-unnecessary Force Bill. The crisis passed. Jackson and Webster could declare victory. The difficult questions of nullification and secession, however, had been postponed rather than resolved.

☑ **IDENTIFY CENTRAL IDEAS** How did the nullification crises threaten the Union?

Economic Change Leads to the Bank War

Notwithstanding his fight over nullification, Jackson was a supporter of the agricultural South. Indeed, he longed to revive Jefferson's ideal of an agrarian republic, in which almost all white men owned farms and enjoyed a rough equality. But industrialization worked against that vision. Increasing numbers of Americans worked in cities for wages instead of on their own farms. In the cities, a gap widened between rich owners and poor workers. Wealth became more abstract and fluid since it was measured in bank stock versus land. The changes troubled many Americans.

Jackson Fights the National Bank Jacksonian Democrats suspected that the new economy encouraged corruption and greed. They howled when industry sought special advantages, such as protective tariffs or federal subsidies for roads and canals. Industry claimed these advantages promoted economic growth. To Jackson and his followers, they seemed mainly to enrich wealthy people at the expense of everyone else.

Jacksonian Democrats promised to rescue the Republic from a new form of aristocracy they called the "Money Power."

Jacksonian Democrats especially disliked the second Bank of the United States, which had been chartered by Congress in 1816. They saw it as a dangerous, and perhaps even corrupt, special interest that favored rich investors. Many business leaders, on the other hand, valued the Bank. They believed it promoted economic growth by providing a stable currency—paper money—in which people could have confidence. They argued that a lack of confidence in the money supply could cause serious harm to the economy.

The Bank had many supporters in Congress. In 1832, they voted to renew thc Bank's charter. Jackson, however, vetoed the renewal. He denounced the Bank as "unauthorized by the Constitution, subversive of the rights of the states, and dangerous to the liberties of the people." He opposed government action that led to "the advancement of the few at the expense of the many." He regretted "that the rich and powerful too often bend the acts of government to their selfish purposes." Jackson posed as the defender of "the humble members of society—the farmers, mechanics, and laborers."

A New Political Party The Bank's supporters denounced Jackson as a power-hungry tyrant trampling on the rights of Congress. The veto shocked them because previous Presidents had so rarely used that power—only nine times in forty-two years.

Led by Henry Clay and Daniel Webster, in 1832 the Bank's friends formed a new political party known as the **Whigs**. (The name came from a British political party.) The Whigs were nationalists who wanted a strong federal government to manage the economy. Relying on a broad interpretation of the Constitution, they favored the American System of protective tariffs, internal improvements, and a national bank. Whigs also appealed to northern Protestants who wanted the government to promote moral reform.

The emergence of the Whigs renewed two-party politics in the United States. For the next twenty years, Whigs challenged Jackson's Democrats in local, state, and national elections. These close contests drew growing numbers of voters to the polls.

In the presidential election of 1832, the Whigs nominated Henry Clay. Voters, however, reelected the popular Jackson in a landslide. Longtime Jackson supporter Martin Van Buren became the new Vice President. Emboldened by the public support, Jackson completed his attack on the second Bank of the United States by withdrawing federal funds and placing them in state banks. Though its charter still had several years to run, Jackson's action weakened it severely. As Secretary of the Treasury, Roger B. Taney managed Jackson's plan to undermine the Bank of the United States. When John Marshall died in 1835, Jackson rewarded Taney by appointing him Chief Justice of the United States.

>> In a political cartoon published shortly after the U.S. Congress formally censured Jackson after he refused to turn over documents relating to his veto of the National Bank bill, Senator Henry Clay forcibly silences Jackson. **Analyze Political Cartoons** What does this cartoon suggest about Jackson's ability to resist the U.S. Congress?

RECALL What were the key arguments for and against the second Bank of the United States?

National Politics After Jackson

Jackson reveled in his victory, but the Bank's destruction weakened the economy. Relieved from federal regulation, state banks expanded, inflating prices with a flood of paper bank notes. The face value of bank notes exploded from $10 million in 1833 to $149 million in 1837. The inflation hurt the common people that Jackson had professed to help.

The Panic of 1837 Economic trouble was still in the future when Jackson retired from politics in 1836. In that year's election, voters chose Martin Van Buren, Jackson's favorite, to become President.

Soon after Van Buren took office in 1837, the economy suffered a severe panic. A key trigger was Jackson's decision, taken months earlier, to stop

>> An 1840 illustration depicts the theatrical presidential campaign of Benjamin Harrison and running mate John Tyler.

accepting paper money for the purchase of federal land. The effect was a sharp drop in land values and sales. As a result, hundreds of banks and businesses that had invested in land went bankrupt. Thousands of planters and farmers lost their land. One out of three urban workers lost his or her job.

Those who kept their jobs saw their wages drop by 30 percent. The Panic of 1837 was the worst depression suffered by Americans to that date.

The Whigs's Victory Is Undermined The depression in 1837 revived the Whigs. In 1840, they ran William Henry Harrison for President and John Tyler for Vice President. Harrison was known as "Old Tip" for his successes at the Battle of Tippecanoe against the Indians in 1811. The Whigs ran a campaign that was light on ideas but heavy on the sort of theatrics that would become common in American politics. For example, the Whigs organized big parades and coined a catchy slogan—"Tippecanoe and Tyler too"—to garner voters' attention. With more creativity than honesty, Whig campaign managers portrayed Harrison as a simple farmer who lived in a log cabin and drank hard cider instead of the expensive champagne favored by Van Buren. Turning the political tables, the Whigs persuaded voters that Van Buren was ineffective, corrupt, and an aristocrat who threatened the Republic. This helped Harrison win the presidency and meant that the Whigs had succeeded in capturing Congress.

The Whig victory proved brief, however. A month after assuming office, Harrison died of pneumonia. Vice President John Tyler of Virginia became the President. He surprised and horrified the Whigs by rejecting their policies. He vetoed Congress's legislation to restore the Bank of the United States and to enact Clay's American System. The Whigs would have to wait for a future election to exercise full control of the government.

☑ **IDENTIFY MAIN IDEAS** What happened following the 1840 election that crippled the Whigs' political agenda?

☑ ASSESSMENT

1. **Describe** How was the election of 1824 ultimately decided?
2. **Cite Evidence** Why did many states change qualifications for voting in the 1810s and 1820s?
3. **Analyze Information** What was the Trail of Tears and how did it affect the American Indian population in the Southeast?
4. **Analyze Data** What effect did the Panic of 1837 have on the American economy?
5. **Connections to Today** How did President Andrew Jackson's personality affect his campaign and his presidency? Do you think recent presidents' personalities affected their campaigns and their presidencies? Explain your reasoning.

GO ONLINE to access this biography: Andrew Jackson

Democracy in America: Alexis de Tocqueville

Alexis de Tocqueville, a young French writer, visited the United States in 1831. During his travels, he observed firsthand the impact of Jacksonian democracy. After returning to France, Tocqueville began writing *Democracy in America*, a detailed look at American politics, society, economics, religion, and law. In these excerpts from *Democracy in America,* Tocqueville discusses the role of the American people in their government and gives his view of the American character.

>> *The County Election* George Caleb Bingham

In America the principle of the sovereignty of the people is not either barren or concealed, as it is with some other nations; it is recognized by the customs and proclaimed by the laws; it spreads freely, and arrives without impediment at its most remote consequences. If there be a country in the world where the doctrine of the sovereignty of the people can be fairly appreciated, where it can be studied in its application to the affairs of society, and where its dangers and its advantages may be foreseen, that country is assuredly America.

I have already observed that, from their origin, the sovereignty of the people was the fundamental principle of the greater number of British colonies in America. It was far, however, from then exercising as much influence on the government of society as it now does. Two obstacles, the one external, the other internal, checked its invasive progress. It could not ostensibly disclose itself in the laws of colonies which were still constrained to obey the mother-country: it was therefore obliged to spread secretly, and to gain ground in the provincial assemblies, and especially in the townships.

SUMMARIZE According to Tocqueville, how did the principle of popular sovereignty spread throughout the British colonies?

. . . it is at least true that in the United States the county and the township are always based upon the same principle, namely, that everyone is the best judge of what concerns himself alone, and the most proper person to supply his private wants.

DETERMINE CENTRAL IDEAS Recall that laissez-faire is the economic principle that says business should be free from government interference. How is the principle of laissez-faire represented in this section of Tocqueville's text?

In America the people appoints the legislative and the executive power, and furnishes the jurors who punish all offences against the laws. The American institutions are democratic, not only in their principle but in all their consequences; and the people elects its representatives directly, and for the most part annually, in order to ensure their dependence. The people is therefore the real directing power; and although the form of government is representative, it is evident that the opinions, the prejudices, the interests, and even the passions of the community are hindered by no durable obstacles from exercising a perpetual influence on society. In the United States the majority governs in the name of the people, as is the case in all the countries in which the people is supreme. The majority is principally composed of peaceful citizens who, either by inclination or by interest, are sincerely desirous of the welfare of their country. But they are surrounded by the incessant agitation of parties, which attempt to gain their co-operation and to avail themselves of their support.

EXPLAIN AN ARGUMENT What does Tocqueville mean when he says that American institutions are "democratic" both in their "principle" and their "consequences"?

The inhabitants of the United States are never fettered by the axioms of their profession; they escape from all the prejudices of their present station; they are not more attached to one line of operation than to another; they are not more prone to employ an old method than a new one; they have no rooted habits, and they easily shake off the influence which the habits of other nations might exercise upon their minds from a conviction that their country is unlike any other, and that its situation is without a precedent in the world. America is a land of wonders, in which everything is in constant motion, and every movement seems an improvement. The idea of novelty is there indissolubly connected with the idea of amelioration. No natural boundary seems to be set to the efforts of man; and what is not yet done is only what he has not yet attempted to do.

This perpetual change which goes on in the United States, these frequent vicissitudes of fortune, accompanied by such unforeseen fluctuations in private and in public wealth, serve to keep the minds of the citizens in a perpetual state of feverish agitation, which admirably invigorates their exertions, and keeps them in a state of excitement above the ordinary level of mankind. The whole life of an American is passed like a game of chance, a revolutionary crisis, or a battle. As the same causes are continually in operation throughout the country, they ultimately impart an irresistible impulse to the national character. The American, taken as a chance specimen of his countrymen, must then be a man of singular warmth in his desires, enterprising, fond of adventure, and, above all, of innovation. The same bent is manifest in all that he does; he introduces it into his political laws, his religious doctrines, his theories of social economy, and his domestic occupations; he bears it with him in the depths of the backwoods, as well as in the business of the city. . .

DRAW CONCLUSIONS What explains the qualities of adaptability that Tocqueville perceives in the American character?

ASSESSMENT

1. **Explain an Argument** Explain why Tocqueville regards the principle of individualism as such a crucial social value.
2. **Summarize** What impressed Tocqueville during his time in America? Cite examples to support your answer.
3. **Draw Conclusions** In what way could Tocqueville's book be relevant today?

Primary Sources Comparing Viewpoints

A Trail of Tears

In May 1830, President Andrew Jackson convinced Congress to pass the Indian Removal Act. This act sought to move approximately 60,0000 people from five Indian nations from their homelands in the Southeast to "Indian Territory" in present-day Oklahoma. For the American Indians, this was a betrayal of treaties signed with earlier Presidents that guaranteed the right to their homelands.

The following sources provide two points of view on Indian removal. The first is a statement written by Lewis Ross, the brother of John Ross, the Cherokee Principle Chief. The second is from Andrew Jackson's Message to Congress on December 6, 1830.

As you read, look for contrasts in Ross's and Jackson's viewpoints on Indian rights.

>> This painting shows the Cherokee's forced migration to Indian Territory.

Primary Source 1

Address of the Committee and Council of the Cherokee Nation, in General Council Convened, to the People of the United States, Lewis Ross, January 20, 1830

We wish to remain on the land of our fathers. We have a perfect and original right to remain without interruption . . . The treaties with us, and laws of the United States made in pursuance [enactment] of treaties, guaranty our residence and our privileges, and secure us against intruders. Our only request is, that these treaties may be fulfilled, and these laws executed.

ASSESS AN ARGUMENT What reasons does Ross give for the Cherokee staying on their land?

But if we are compelled to leave our country, we see nothing but ruin before us. The country west of the Arkansas territory is unknown to us. From what we can learn of it, we have no prepossessions [impressions] in its favor. All the inviting parts of it, as we believe, are preoccupied by various Indian nations, to which it has been assigned. They would regard us as intruders . . . The far greater part of that region is, beyond all controversy, badly supplied with wood and water; and no Indian tribe can live as agriculturists [farmers] without these articles. All our neighbors, in case of our removal, though crowded into our near vicinity; would speak a language totally different from ours, and practice different customs. . . . Were the country to which we are urged much better than it is represented to be, and were it free from the objections which we have made to it, still it is not the land of our birth, nor of our affections. It contains neither the scenes of our childhood, nor the graves of our fathers. . .

DESCRIBE How does Ross describe the land the Cherokee will be assigned?

Primary Source 2

Andrew Jackson's Message to Congress, December 6, 1830

. . .It gives me pleasure to announce to Congress that the benevolent policy of the Government, steadily pursued for nearly thirty years, in relation to the removal of the Indians beyond the white settlements is approaching to a happy consummation [end]. . . .

The consequences of a speedy removal will be important to the United States, to individual States, and to the Indians themselves.... It puts an end to all possible danger of collision between the authorities of the General and State Governments on account of the Indians. It will place a dense and civilized population in large tracts of country now occupied by a few savage hunters. By opening the whole territory between Tennessee on the north and Louisiana on the south to the settlement of the whites it will incalculably strengthen the southwestern frontier and render the adjacent States strong enough to repel future invasions without remote aid. It will relieve the whole State of Mississippi and the western part of Alabama of Indian occupancy, and enable those States to advance rapidly in population, wealth, and power. . . .

ANALYZE WORD CHOICES What words does Jackson use to describe the American Indians? Why do you think he uses those words?

. . .What good man would prefer a country covered with forests and ranged by a few thousand savages to our extensive Republic, studded with cities, towns, and prosperous farms embellished with all the improvements which art can devise or industry execute, occupied by more than 12,000,000 happy people, and filled with all the blessings of liberty, civilization and religion?. . . .

DISTINGUISH AMONG FACT, OPINION, AND REASONED JUDGMENT How much of the information in the paragraph above is based on fact? How much is opinion or reasoned judgment? Explain.

Doubtless it will be painful [for American Indians] to leave the graves of their fathers; but what do they more than our ancestors did or than our children are now doing? To better their condition in an unknown land our forefathers left all that was dear in earthly objects. Our children by thousands yearly leave the land of their birth to seek new homes in distant regions. . . .

COMPARE Do you think comparing the reasons for Indians and white settlers leaving their homelands was a fair comparison for Jackson to make? Why or why not?

ASSESSMENT

1. **Determine Meaning** What were Lewis Ross's main arguments and concerns about the Cherokee leaving their homeland?
2. **Compare and Contrast** How did the descriptions of Indian Territory provided from Ross and Jackson differ? Who do you think gave a more accurate description? Explain.
3. **Explain** Why do you think Andrew Jackson did not mention treaties between American Indians and the U.S. government? Why did Lewis Ross mention treaties?
4. **Draw Inferences** What can you infer about the difference between the way in which white Americans viewed land and the way in which American Indians viewed land?

GO ONLINE to access primary sources

Connections to Today

Delegates from each state come to their political party's convention to support a candidate for president.

Take Action on Understanding the Role of the President

1. **Choose** one of the following topics about what the office of the President is like today:
    - **Electoral College:** Conduct research into the way in which presidential elections are won and leading ideas for altering or abolishing this system.
    - **Constitution:** Read Article II of the Constitution to find out the qualifications, role, and responsibilities of a president.
    - **The Imperial Presidency:** How has the role of the President changed over time? Has the President become more powerful? Why or why not?
2. **Ask Questions** Generate a list of questions about the topic you have selected. What might you want to know about your topic?
3. **Learn** about your topic by using a variety of sources. Use the Internet and your library to find newspaper and magazine articles. Interview people in your community what they think about the role of the President.
4. **Raise Awareness** Create a website or poster that shows what you have learned in your research and share it within your class as well as somewhere in your community.

Topic 5 Quick Study Guide

LESSON SUMMARIES

Use these Lesson Summaries, and the longer versions available online, to review the key ideas for each lesson in this Topic.

Lesson 1: The New Government Finds Its Way

President George Washington set many precedents and guided the nation through domestic and foreign crises. Two rival political parties emerged. Federalist John Adams won the presidency by a slim margin in 1797.

Lesson 2: Jefferson as President

President Thomas Jefferson reduced the national debt by making budget cuts and benefiting from an increase in revenue. In 1803, Jefferson doubled the size of the United States with the Louisiana Purchase. Judicial review increased the power of the Supreme Court.

Lesson 3: The War of 1812

British impressment of U.S. sailors and its support for American Indians led to the War of 1812. After several battles, the U.S. armed forces stopped the British invasion. The Treaty of Ghent ended the war in December 1814 establishing prewar boundaries.

Lesson 4: The Beginning of the Industrial Revolution

From 1800 to 1860, innovations in transportation transformed the way goods and people moved across the nation. The Industrial Revolution changed manufacturing methods, altering the way people lived and worked. New inventions made farmers more productive.

Lesson 5: Differences Between North and South Grow

Industry in the North grew due to protective tariffs and access to capital. During the 1840s and 1850s, immigration from Ireland and Germany swelled due to troubles in Europe. The South relied on cotton which became highly profitable after the invention of the cotton gin. As cotton plantations spread, plantation owners relied on enslaved African Americans for labor.

Lesson 6: Nationalism Influences Policies

During James Monroe's presidency, strong feelings of nationalism arose. Henry Clay's American System improved the infrastructure. John Marshall's Supreme Court made rulings supporting the power of the federal government and large corporations. The nation expanded acquiring Florida and Oregon Territory. The Monroe Doctrine warned European powers to stay out of Latin America. In the United States, sectional differences persisted between free and slave states and led to the Missouri Compromise.

Lesson 7: Jacksonian Democracy

In a close election, Andrew Jackson lost the 1824 presidential election to John Quincy Adams. Strategic campaigning and political maneuvering allowed Jackson to win in 1828. Jackson's presidency was marked by the Indian Removal Act of 1830 a nullification crisis, and closing the National Bank. Martin Van Buren was elected president in 1836. In 1840, Whig candidate William Henry Harrison was elected, but died in office. Vice President John Tyler became president but stunned Whigs by rejecting their policies.

QUEST! FINDINGS

Have a Civic Discussion Have students complete the Topic Quest by holding a civic discussion about the Eighth Amendment and the death penalty. Tell students to read the sources then direct them to the civic discussion rubric on Realize to make sure that they are prepared for their discussion.

GO ONLINE to access lesson summaries

VISUAL REVIEW

Use these graphics to review some of the key terms, people, and ideas from this Topic.

First Political Parties

FEDERALISTS	DEMOCRATIC REPUBLICANS
Led by Alexander Hamilton	Led by Thomas Jefferson
Favored a strong central government	Thought states should have more power
Wanted to base economy on industry and trade	Wanted to base economy on farming
Were pro-British	Were pro-French
Supported a loose construction of the Constitution	Supported a strict construction of the Constitution

Early Presidents: Events and Issues

PRESIDENT AND TERM		KEY EVENTS AND ISSUES
George Washington	1789–1797	Set many precedents: court system, Cabinet, and national bank
John Adams	1797–1801	XYZ Affair; Alien and Sedition Acts; increased taxes
Thomas Jefferson	1801–1809	Reduced the nation debt; Louisiana Purchase; unsuccessful embargo against Britain
James Madison	1809–1817	Battle of Tippecanoe; War of 1812
James Monroe	1817–1825	Nationalism led to an "era of good feelings"; acquired Florida and Oregon; Monroe Doctrine; Missouri Compromise
John Quincy Adams	1825–1829	Internal improvements and scientific exploration; appointed Henry Clay Secretary of State; tariffs
Andrew Jackson	1829–1837	Spoils system; Indian Removal Act; nullification crisis; closed national bank

Key Inventions and Innovations in the 1800s

INVENTIONS	EFFECTS
Turnpikes	Expanded transportation routes
Steamboats	Allowed faster travel, shipping, and upstream movement
Canals	Expanded transportation routes; linked farms to East; new regions settled
Railroads	Moved goods faster; connected East and West
Textile Mills	Provided jobs; increased the speed of producing textiles
Interchangeable Parts	Made efficient production of many manufactured goods
Cotton Gin	Rise in cotton production; expanded enslavement of African Americans

Topic 5 Assessment

KEY TERMS, PEOPLE, AND IDEAS

1. Define **tariff**. Who supported tariffs? Who opposed tariffs?
2. What do **loose construction** and **strict construction** mean? Explain which view Thomas Jefferson held, and why?
3. Explain why Shawnee Indian brothers **Tecumseh** and Tenskwatawa wanted to unite American Indian nations in the western frontier. Why did they fail?
4. Who was **Eli Whitney**? What were his main contributions?
5. What was the **Tariff of 1816**? Why did Congress pass the tariff?
6. Who formed early **labor unions** and what was the purpose?
7. What is a **caucus**? How did the use of caucuses change with the expansion of democracy and the changing economy?
8. What was the **spoils system** and was its purpose?
9. Who were the **Whigs**? What policies did they support?

CRITICAL THINKING

10. **Draw Inferences** Though George Washington supported most Federalist beliefs, he refused to declare himself a Federalist. Why do you think this was so?
11. **Identifying Supporting Details** How did John Marshall help establish the authority of the Supreme Court?
12. **Summarize** What effect did the War of 1812 have on political parties?
13. **Compare and Contrast** In what ways were the Virginia and Kentucky Resolutions of 1798 and 1799 and John C. Calhoun's support for nullification in the 1820s similar? How were they different? How were both of these issues resolved?
14. **Categorize** Categorize and explain the factors that led to less industrial growth in the South than in the North.
15. **Analyze Interactions** Was President Jackson's refusal to uphold the Supreme Court's decision in the debate over the Cherokees a legitimate use of the system of checks and balances? Explain.
16. **Cite Evidence** The Whigs supported a strong federal government to manage the economy. Could the same statement be said about Jacksonian Democracy?
17. **Use Visual Information** Study the graph below. Based on the information on the graph, describe and explain the reason for the trend in cotton production.

U.S. Cotton Production, 1790–1810

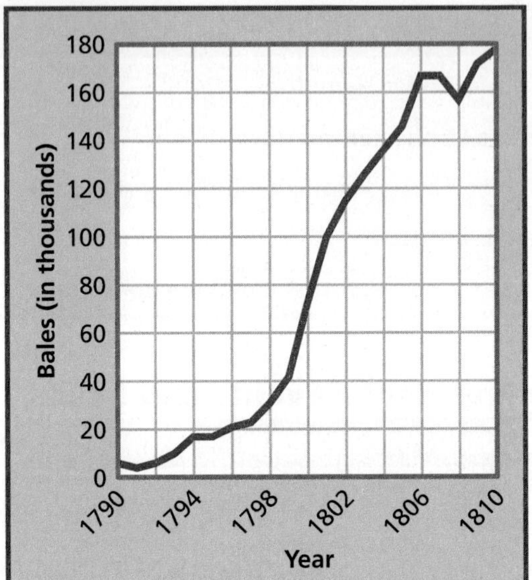

SOURCE: Historical Statistics of the United States

18. **Writing Activity: Research** Use the source below as well as other print and digital resources to write a research paper that answers the following questions in depth. (a) What advice is Washington giving in his Farewell Address? (b) To what extent did the following presidents follow Washington's advice: John Adams, Thomas Jefferson, James Madison and James Monroe. Remember to write a thesis statement that tells the main idea of your research report. In addition, write a strong introduction, at least three paragraphs, and a conclusion that support your ideas.

> . . . The great rule of conduct for us in regard to foreign nations is, in extending our commercial [relating to trade] relations, to have with them as little political connection as possible. So far as we have already formed engagements, let them be fulfilled with perfect good faith. Here let us stop. Europe has a set of primary interests which to us have none; or a very remote relation. . . .
> —George Washington's Farewell Address, 1796

19. **Connections to Today** Give an example of how one or two of the early U.S. presidents managed a domestic or foreign crisis. Have present-day presidents managed a similar or different crisis? Explain.

DOCUMENT-BASED QUESTIONS

The Monroe Doctrine guided U.S. foreign policy, to greater and lesser extents, throughout the nineteenth and into the twentieth centuries. Read the documents below, then answer the questions that follow.

DOCUMENT A

In the wars of the European powers in matters relating to themselves we have never taken any part, nor does it comport with our policy so to do. . . With the movement in this hemisphere we are of necessity more immediately connected.

. . . We owe it, there, to candor and to the amicable relations existing between the United States and those powers to declare that we should consider any attempt on their part to extend their system to any portion of this hemisphere as dangerous to our peace and safety.

—James Monroe, address to Congress, December 2, 1823

DOCUMENT B

The question presented by the letters you have sent me, is the most momentous which has ever been offered to my contemplation since that of Independence. . . . Our first and fundamental maxim should be, never to entangle ourselves in the broils of Europe. Our second, never to suffer Europe to intermeddle with [this side of the] Atlantic affairs. America, North and South, has a set of interests distinct from those of Europe, and peculiarly her own. She should therefore have a system of her own, separate and apart from that of Europe.

—Thomas Jefferson, letter to James Monroe, October 24, 1823

DOCUMENT C

This political cartoon shows European leaders viewing U.S. ships. A caption reads "Let it be written so it can be read."

LET IT BE WRITTEN SO IT CAN BE READ.—From the *Herald* (New York).

DOCUMENT D

Monroe essentially declared that the United States would not tolerate intervention in the Americas by European nations. Monroe also promised that the United States wouldn't interfere with already established colonies or with governments in Europe. In one sense, this declaration was an act of isolationism, with America withdrawing from the political tempests of Europe . . . On the positive side, the Doctrine marked what might be called the last step in America's march to independence, which had begun in the Revolution and moved through post-independence foreign treaties, the Louisiana Purchase, the War of 1812, and the postwar agreements.

—Kenneth Davis, historian

20. In Document A, Monroe describes European actions in the Americas as

A. dangerous.
B. unlawful.
C. necessary.
D. amicable.

21. Which of the following statements most accurately summarizes Thomas Jefferson's ideas as expressed in Document B?

A. He supported the principles of the Monroe Doctrine
B. He supported just one of the principles of the Monroe Doctrine.
C. He quietly opposed the principles of the Monroe Doctrine.
D. He vigorously opposed the principles of the Monroe Doctrine.

22. Which documents assert that the Monroe Doctrine had become a success?

A. Documents A and B
B. Documents B and C
C. Documents C and D
D. Documents D and A

23. **Writing Task** Did the Monroe Doctrine express a policy of isolationism? Use your knowledge of American history and specific evidence from the primary sources above to explain your answer.

GO ONLINE to access more practice

Topic 6

Reshaping America in the Early 1800s (1800–1860)

ESSENTIAL QUESTION How Should We Handle Conflict?

GO ONLINE to access the eText, videos, Interactive Primary Sources, Biographies, and other online resources.

A covered wagon

Connections to Today

In your final years of high school, your thoughts may be turning to what comes next. If you're thinking of continuing your studies, you may be wondering how to afford it, with the cost of higher education increasing.

In this topic you'll read about how Americans developed a publicly funded school system, so that all children, regardless of their family's wealth, would receive an education. Today the debate over public funding has shifted to higher education, but the question is much the same: Should education be free?

NBC LEARN

Learn about the Edmonson sisters and their audacious escape.

BOUNCE to Activate My Story Video

Topic 6 Overview

In this Topic, you'll learn about the dramatic changes the United States underwent as large numbers of Americans began moving west, religious revival swept the nation, and Americans put their religious ideals to practice by working toward reform. Look at the lesson outline and explore the timeline. As you study this Topic, you'll complete the Quest Inquiry.

LESSON OUTLINE

6.1 Moving West

6.2 Texas and the Mexican-American War

6.3 The Nation Expands to the Pacific

6.4 A Religious Awakening Sparks Reform

6.5 The Abolition Movement

6.6 Women Work for Change

Key Events of the Early 1800s

1820 · 1830 · 1840 · 1850

1821
Mexico wins independence

1826
Jedediah Smith blazes the California Trail

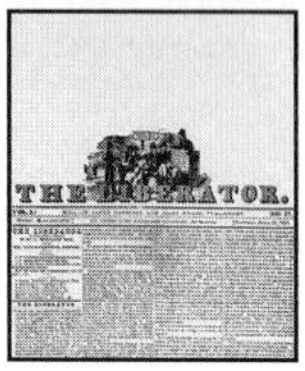

1831
William Lloyd Garrison begins publishing *The Liberator*

1836
Texas declares independence

1843
Dorothea Dix seeks better treatment of people with mental illness

1846
Mexican-American War begins

1848
Gold is discovered in California

1848
Women's rights convention is held in Seneca Falls, New York

QUEST! INQUIRY

Westward Movement and the Issue of Slavery

How did westward expansion affect the debate over slavery and abolition? In this Quest, you'll investigate documents related to this debate before writing an essay on this subject.

STEP 1
Watch a video about the slavery debate, and discuss questions about pro- and anti-slavery arguments. Then read two primary source excerpts about abolitionist strategies and discuss the excerpts with a partner or in class.

STEP 2
Examine six documents relating to slavery and abolition during westward expansion, and check your understanding of each document.

STEP 3
Consider all the evidence and viewpoints to formulate your own conclusions. Then write an essay answering the question: How did westward expansion affect the debate over slavery and abolition?

STEP 4
Use what you have learned from investigating this historical question as you continue to learn and read more about history.

GO ONLINE to access complete Quest materials

6.1

In the 1873 illustration "American Progress" by John Gast, figures representing progress sweep westward across the western landscape. **Analyze Primary Sources** What does this illustration suggest about westward expansion?

BOUNCE to Activate Flipped Video

Objectives

Summarize the settlement and development of the Spanish borderlands.

Explain the concept of Manifest Destiny and how it influenced westward expansion.

Analyze the causes and challenges of westward migration.

Key Terms

Junípero Serra
expansionist
Manifest Destiny
Santa Fe Trail
Mountain Men
Oregon Trail
Brigham Young
Treaty of Fort Laramie

Moving West

In 1830, what is now the American Southwest was part of Northern Mexico. Like the former British colonies in the East, this region had a long colonial history, one that dated back to the Spanish conquest of the Americas.

The Borderlands of Northern Mexico

Challenges in New Mexico Founded in 1598, New Mexico was the oldest colony along New Spain's northwestern frontier. Yet, by 1765, only about 9,600 colonists lived in New Mexico, half of them in the two major towns of El Paso and Santa Fe. The rest lived on farms and ranches scattered through the long Rio Grande valley.

One factor discouraging further settlement was the policy of the Hapsburg kings of Spain, who did not want to invest money in areas that seemed lacking in gold or silver. However, when the Bourbons took over the crown of Spain in 1700 they began investing in their colonies.

In the 1700s, European colonization and migrations among Native American groups began to affect Native Americans such as the Apaches. The Apaches lived by hunting vast herds of buffalo. These hunts became easier after 1680 when the Apaches acquired horses from the Spanish. On horseback, men could see farther, travel faster, and kill their prey more quickly and in greater safety. At the same time, local Indians began to acquire firearms from French traders.

GO ONLINE to access your digital course

Warfare Threatens the Colony In 1800, a trader on the Great Plains remarked, "This is a delightful country and, were it not for perpetual wars, the natives might be the happiest people on earth." The conflict stemmed largely from competition for the buffalo herds. Well-armed groups, such as the Comanches of the Rocky Mountains and the Lakotas of the Mississippi Valley, spread at the expense of Apaches and other long-time residents of the Great Plains.

The defeated Apaches fled west into New Mexico, where they raided Pueblo and Spanish settlements, taking horses, sheep, cattle, and captives. Some Apaches found a haven in the canyons of northwest New Mexico, where they became known as Navajos. The Pueblos taught their Navajo neighbors how to weave, make pottery, grow corn, and herd sheep. But most Apaches remained hunters.

Raids on Spanish settlements became more frequent and destructive, for the Apaches were now armed, mounted, and desperate. The Comanches began to attack New Mexico as well. In 1777, a governor sadly reported that American Indian raids had reduced his colony "to the most deplorable state and greatest poverty."

Spanish officials rescued New Mexico by building stronger frontier defenses and using more flexible diplomacy with Native Americans. By providing gifts and weapons, the new officials found it cheaper to form bonds with some Indians than to fight them all. In general, Spain paid Comanche and Navajo allies to attack the Apaches. For the most part, the strategy worked.

Although most Apache groups remained defiant, some accepted peace on Spain's terms. And the alliance program did reduce raids on New Mexico. As the colony became safer, its population grew and its economy developed. By 1821, the Hispanic population had grown to about 40,000.

Settlement is Limited in Texas New Mexico's growth and improved security did not extend to Texas, its sister colony to the east along the Gulf of Mexico. In Texas, Native Americans were more formidable and the colony remained weaker. The Spanish had founded Texas as a buffer zone to protect the valuable towns and mines of Mexico to the south. Like New Mexico, Texas was a mixture of ranches, missions, and military *presidios*.

But Texas stagnated because few settlers felt attracted to such a distant and poor region subject to raiders. In 1760, only about 1,200 colonists lived in Texas, primarily in and around San Antonio. Ranchers drove longhorn cattle southward for sale in Mexico.

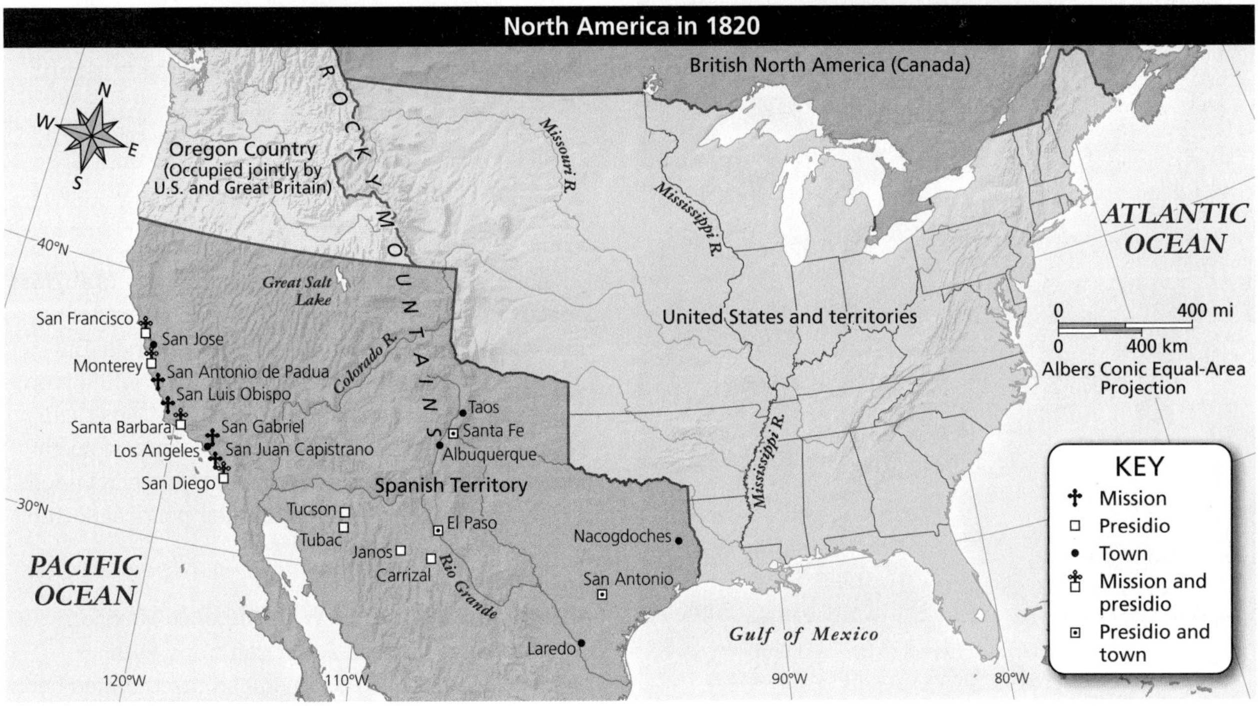

>> **Analyze Maps** In the West, Native American lands were slowly overrun. What geographic and political obstacles did Americans moving west face in the 1820s?

Missions Thrive in California In the 1760s, the Spanish extended their northern buffer zone to the west by colonizing the California coast. They were afraid of losing the region to Russian traders probing south from Alaska. As in Texas, Spain had trouble attracting settlers to California. Potential settlers were daunted by California's isolation from Mexico. The distance to market discouraged the export of California's livestock and grains. The limited economy depended on royal money sent to supply and pay the soldiers.

Lacking colonists, the Spanish leaders sought to convert American Indians to Christianity. Led by Father **Junípero Serra**, Franciscan priests set up a string of Catholic missions. The missions were more successful in California than in Texas or New Mexico. Because the local American Indians lacked guns and horses, California missions suffered few raids.

By the time of Father Serra's death in 1784, California had two agricultural towns (San Jose and Los Angeles), four *presidios*, and nine missions. In 1821, when Spanish rule ended, the system had grown to 20 missions housing more than 18,000 American Indian converts.

American Indians constructed buildings, dug irrigation ditches, erected fences, herded cattle, and cultivated grain. But large numbers died of diseases, and the Spanish had to round up more American Indians to replace them.

>> American Indians were forced to live and work on mission grounds, where Spanish priests taught about Christianity. **Predict Consequences** What were some likely consequences of Spanish influence on the Indian way of life?

BOUNCE to Activate Chart

CHECK UNDERSTANDING How did conflict develop between Spanish settlers and American Indians in the Southwest?

America Looks to the West

In 1821, a revolution toppled Spanish rule and established Mexico as an independent republic. The U.S. government officially recognized its fellow republic to the south. But American **expansionists**, people who favored territorial growth, soon began to covet New Mexico, Texas, and California. Thinly settled but rich in resources, the three provinces seemed ripe for American plucking.

Manifest Destiny Expansionists justified their views by pointing to the weakness of the Mexican government and economy. They argued that the Mexicans did not deserve to keep lands so badly needed for American settlement.

In 1845, journalist John L. O'Sullivan wrote an influential editorial in favor of expansion.

> The American claim is by the right of our manifest destiny to overspread and possess the whole of the continent which Providence has given us for the development of the great experiment of liberty and . . . self-government entrusted to us.
>
> —John L. O'Sullivan, *New York Morning News,* December 27, 1845

Expansionists were soon using the term **Manifest Destiny** to refer to the belief that God wanted the United States to own all of North America. But O'Sullivan envisioned liberty primarily for white men. Expansion would come at the expense of American Indians and Mexicans. And southern expansionists hoped to create more slave states, or states in which slavery was legal, to strengthen their political position in Congress.

American Commerce With Mexico Mexican independence spurred American trade with northern Mexico. The Spanish had discouraged such contacts, but Mexican officials welcomed them. Indeed, trade and migration promoted economic growth in the border provinces. Still, as the Spanish had feared, American traders and settlers would come to threaten the security of Mexico's border. Americans seeking economic opportunity and lands in the Mexican border state of Coahilla y Texas, for example, eventually challenged the authority of the Mexican government there and launched a rebellion.

Merchants from Missouri saw Mexican independence as an opportunity to open trade across the Great Plains with Santa Fe, the capital of New Mexico. Welcomed by the Mexican officials, the traders launched a growing commerce along what became known as the **Santa Fe Trail**. In exchange for American manufactured goods, the New Mexicans offered horses, mules, furs, and silver.

In the 1820s, mariners from the Northeast began sailing around South America to the California coast, where they traded manufactured goods for tallow and hides from California ranches. Like New Mexico, California became economically dependent on commerce with the United States.

>> Covered wagons arrive at the terminus of the Santa Fe Trail that began in Missouri. Merchants and migrants traveling the full length of the trail crossed some 800 miles of mainly undeveloped land.

BOUNCE to Activate 3D Model

Mountain Men Cross the Rockies Other traders ventured up the Missouri River and into the Rockies seeking valuable furs from the abundant beaver of the mountain streams. The daring young American trappers who hunted for beaver pelts in the Rockies were called **Mountain Men**. Most worked for two large fur companies, which provided their supplies.

Restless in pursuit of furs, the Mountain Men explored the Rockies, making important discoveries. They blazed the best route through the mountains, via South Pass in what is now Wyoming. Some Mountain Men then pressed westward to the Great Salt Lake in the arid Great Basin of Utah. In 1826, Jedediah Smith crossed the Great Basin and the Sierra Nevada to reach California. In addition to trapping, he traded with the Mexican residents. Smith's trade route became the California Trail, linking the United States with the Pacific coast.

>> In time, the Mountain Men undermined their own way of life, killing beaver faster than the beaver could reproduce. **Hypothesize** What sort of dangers did Mountain Men face? Why do you think they chose this way of life?

Missionaries Follow the Oregon Trail A branch of this trail turned northwest at South Pass to reach Oregon Country. In 1836, Marcus and Narcissa Whitman followed this route, which became known as the **Oregon Trail**, to found an Indian mission at Walla Walla.

The Whitman compound served as a magnet and way station for farm families bound farther west to the fertile Willamette Valley. In 1847, the Whitmans were killed by American Indians who blamed them for a deadly measles epidemic. But by then, the tide of migration to Oregon was unstoppable.

☑ **DESCRIBE** Describe the role the Mountain Men played in American westward expansion.

Settling New Lands in the West

In 1842, an official government expedition led by John C. Frémont set off across the western country, following trails blazed by the Mountain Men and people like the Whitmans. Although Frémont found little that was new, his vivid and romantic reports gave wider publicity to the fertility of the Far West. In the years that followed, the overland trails drew thousands of settlers west to California and Oregon.

A Long Journey West Commencing in springtime at the western edge of Missouri, the demanding journey covered nearly 2,000 miles and took about five months to complete. Oxen pulled the emigrants' wooden wagons covered with canvas. For security and mutual help, most emigrants traveled in trains of from 10 to 100 wagons and from 50 to 1,000 people. Eager to get to the fertile and humid Pacific, the emigrants bypassed the Great Plains, which they considered little better than a desert, and the Great Basin, which truly was a desert. They were also in a hurry to get across two cold and lofty mountain chains, the Rockies and the Sierra Nevada.

Most of the emigrants were farm people from the Midwest. Men relished the journey as an adventure, while many women more keenly felt the hardships and anxieties. "What had possessed my husband, anyway, that he should have thought of bringing us away out through this God-forsaken country?" wrote one woman in her diary. Other women, traveling with their families or on their own, relished the opportunities that lay ahead, and looked forward to opening boarding houses or other business ventures.

Indeed, the journey was a gamble that cost many their property and some their lives. Emigrants faced hunger, exposure, disease, poisoned streams—or worse. In 1846, the Donner Party got lost on the way to California. Trapped by snow in the Sierra Nevada, the starving survivors resorted to cannibalism.

Despite the dangers, the rewards of the journey could be great. Most of those who persevered gained bigger and better farms in Oregon or California than they had owned in the East or Midwest. Between 1840 and 1860, about 260,000 Americans crossed the continent to settle on the west coast.

Mormons Prosper in New Zion One group of people preferred to settle along the way. These were the Mormons. Mormon founder Joseph Smith was killed in 1844 by a mob in Illinois. The mob disapproved of Smith's religious beliefs.

Leadership passed to **Brigham Young**, a brilliant organizer with a powerful will. Convinced that the Mormons could not survive among hostile neighbors, Young organized an exodus. In 1847, he led Mormons across the Great Plains and the Rockies to establish

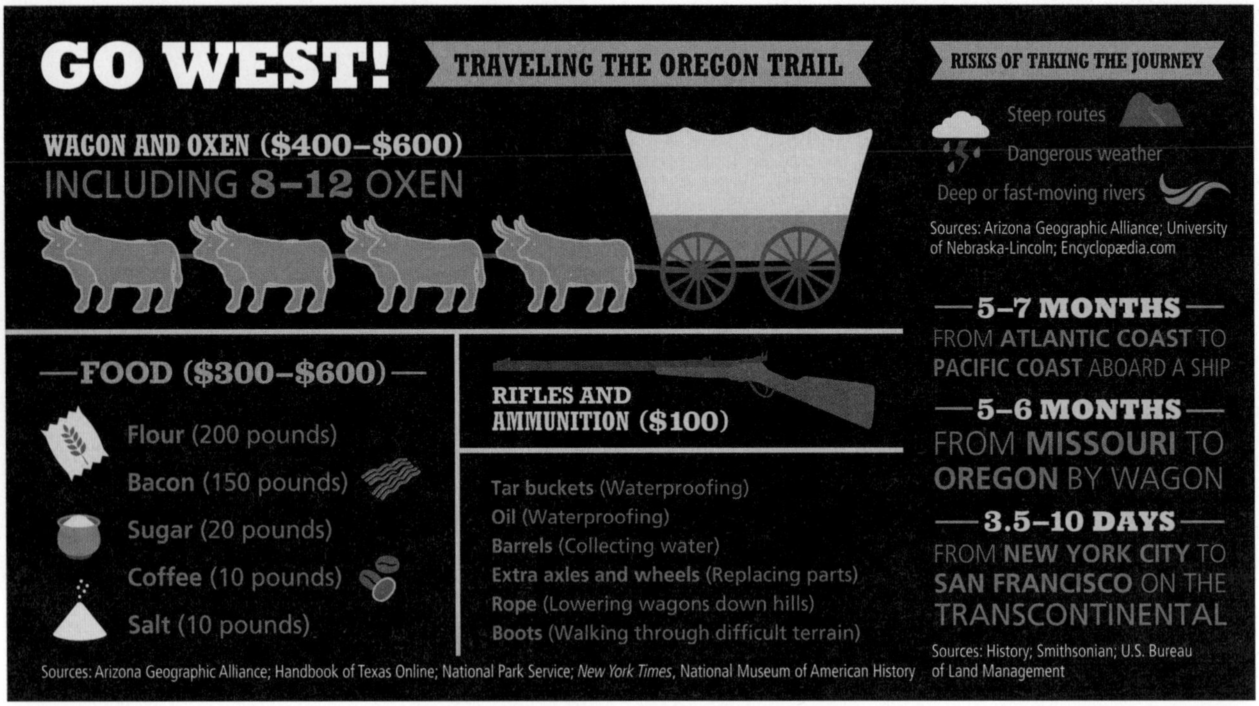

>> **Analyze Information** How did travelers prepare for the possible dangers of the trail?

the colony of New Zion on the eastern shore of the Great Salt Lake. Through hard work and cooperation, the Mormons made the arid land bloom by diverting water from mountain streams. By 1860, some 40,000 Mormons lived in the West.

Despite their achievements and their isolation, other Americans continued to distrust the Mormons. During the 1850s, after the territory had passed from Mexico to the United States, the government forced the Mormons to accept federal authority. New Zion became the federal territory of Utah.

Restricting the Plains Indians So long as wagons kept moving west, American Indians usually left the settlers alone. Nevertheless, the federal government sought to protect migrants by restricting the Plains Indians.

The 1851 **Treaty of Fort Laramie** bound the American Indians to territories away from the major trails. But the American Indians clung to their mobile way of life, pursuing buffalo across all artificial boundaries. As migration continued, the stage was set for future conflict.

LIST Create two lists—one identifying the difficulties and the other list identifying the opportunities that awaited migrants to the West.

>> The Oregon Trail, shown here in the 1850s, was originally used by fur traders and missionaries but quickly became the main route settlers took to reach the Northwest. **Infer** What geographic features presented challenges for travelers?

BOUNCE to Activate Map

ASSESSMENT

1. **Infer** What made the Mormons different from most other settlers heading West at the time?
2. **Interpret** Explain how the Spanish dealt with the issue of Apache raids in New Mexico during Spain's early settlement of northern New Mexico.
3. **Summarize** What was the initial purpose of the California missions? How did they achieve this purpose?
4. **Interpret** What did the advent of the Santa Fe Trail signify for American commerce with the republic of Mexico?
5. **Quest Connections** Discuss the contributions of the Mountain Men and the Whitmans to westward expansion in America.

6.2

Mexican forces lost the 1847 Battle of Buena Vista near Monterrey, Mexico, despite outnumbering U.S. troops by nearly three to one. **Speculate** How could such a small number of American troops defeat a much larger Mexican force?

BOUNCE to Activate Flipped Video

Objectives

Describe how Texas was settled and how it won independence from Mexico.

Explain the debate around the annexation of Texas.

Identify the causes and outcome of the Mexican-American War.

Key Terms

Stephen F. Austin
Antonio López de Santa Anna
autonomy
Lone Star Republic
Alamo
Sam Houston
James K. Polk
Zachary Taylor
Winfield Scott

Texas and the Mexican-American War

With American expansionists seeking new territory and Mexico in control of most of the land to the south and west, conflict between the two nations seemed almost inevitable. The flashpoint for conflict became Texas. In time, that conflict would lead to a war that would vastly increase the size of the United States.

Texas Fights for Independence

Of all the Mexican provinces, Texas was most vulnerable to U.S. expansion. Offering abundant, fertile land, Texas lay closest to the United States. And it had only a small Hispanic population, known as *Tejanos*(teh HAH nohs), to defend the province. In 1821, only about 4,000 Tejanos lived in Texas.

Americans Settle in Texas To develop and defend the province, Mexico adopted a risky strategy: It agreed to allow Americans to settle in Texas. In return for cheap land grants, Americans had to agree to become Mexican citizens, to worship as Roman Catholics, and to accept the Mexican constitution, which banned slavery.

Americans who were granted permission to settle the land and attract other colonists were known as empresarios. Mexico hoped this strategy would convert American settlers from a potential threat to an economic asset.

Led by **Stephen F. Austin**, American emigrants began to settle east of San Antonio, founding the town of Austin. Like

GO ONLINE to access your digital course

settlers on other frontiers, these newcomers sought the economic opportunity of good farmland in large portions. Mostly coming from the southern United States, they raised corn, pigs, cattle, and cotton. By 1835, Texas was home to about 30,000 American settlers, known as Anglo-Texans. They outnumbered Tejanos by about six to one.

Poor Relations with the Mexican Government

Relations between Anglo-Texans and the Mexican government soured by 1830. Despite their oaths of allegiance and their land grants, the settlers had not honored their part of the bargain. They remained Protestants and ignored Mexico's slavery ban by smuggling in enslaved African Americans to work their farms and plantations. In turn, the Anglo-Texans felt dismayed by the unstable Mexican government, which suffered from military coups.

In 1834, the charismatic but ruthless general **Antonio López de Santa Anna** seized power in Mexico City. Santa Anna favored a centralized, authoritarian government dominated by the military. His coup troubled those liberal Mexicans who preferred a decentralized federal system like that of the United States. Santa Anna's rule especially angered the people of Texas, both Anglo-Texans and Tejanos, who wanted greater **autonomy**, or independent control over their own affairs. One Anglo-Texan protested that Santa Anna would "give liberty to our slaves and make slaves of ourselves."

Texans Declare Independence In 1835, the Texans rebelled against Mexican rule. They seized the Mexican garrisons at Goliad and San Antonio. A year later, the Texans declared their independence and adopted a republican constitution. Their new nation became known as the **Lone Star Republic** because of the single star on its flag.

To crush the rebellion, Santa Anna led his army north into Texas. In March 1836, his forces attacked the small Texan garrison at the **Alamo**, a fortified former mission in San Antonio. After 12 days of cannon fire, Mexican troops overran the walls of the Alamo. Refusing to keep prisoners, Santa Anna ordered the defenders slaughtered. The victims included Anglo-Texans Jim Bowie and Davy Crockett, as well as a dozen Tejanos. A few weeks later, Santa Anna ordered a similar mass execution of Texan prisoners who had surrendered at Goliad.

Santa Anna expected the slaughter to frighten other Texans into surrendering. Instead, the fallen defenders of the Alamo became martyrs to the cause of Texan independence. The slogan "Remember the Alamo" rallied the Texans and attracted volunteers to their cause from the southern United States.

Led by **Sam Houston**, the Texans drew Santa Anna eastward into a trap. In April, they surprised and crushed the Mexican army at the Battle of San Jacinto. Houston's men killed 630 and captured 730 Mexicans, including Santa Anna himself, while suffering only 32 casualties.

Fearing execution, Santa Anna signed a treaty recognizing Texan independence. He conceded generous boundaries that stretched the new republic south and west to the Rio Grande. On paper, Texas even got half of New Mexico, including its capital of Santa Fe.

Of course, the government in Mexico City refused to honor a treaty forced on a captured and disgraced dictator. The Mexicans only would accept an independent Texas that remained within its traditional boundaries, which extended no farther

Timeline of the Texas Revolution

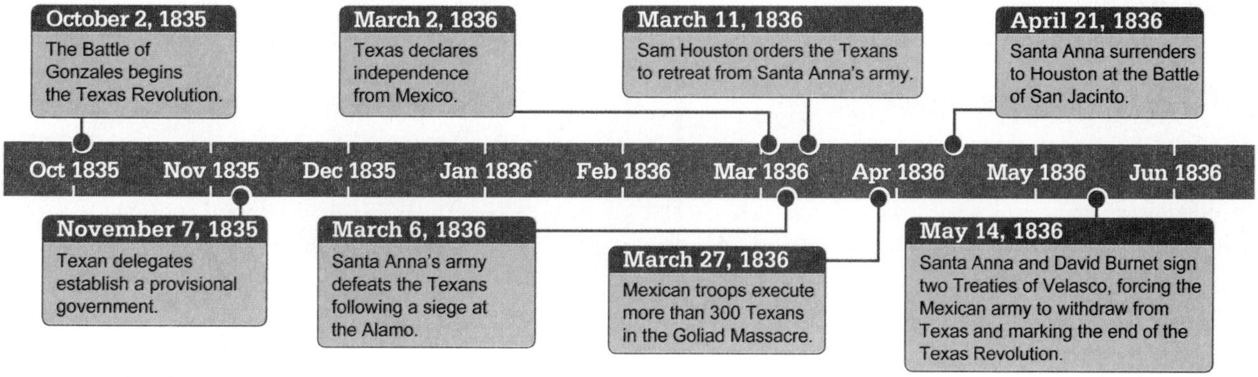

Source: *Encyclopædia Britannica;* Texas State Historical Association

>> **Analyze Information** What effect did the declaration of Texan independence likely have on the course of the revolution?

south than the Nueces River. For the next decade, a border war persisted between Texas and Mexico.

IDENTIFY CENTRAL ISSUES What issues led Anglo-Texans and Tejanos to seek independence from Mexico?

The Expansion Debate

Texans elected Sam Houston as their first president. He quickly asked the United States to annex Texas. President Jackson favored the request, but he could not overcome opposition in Congress. Northern representatives balked at adding another slave state, especially one so big and potentially powerful. For nearly a decade, Texas applied in vain for annexation. Houston tried to pressure Congress by pretending to consider joining the British Empire. At the time, Britain and the United States jointly occupied the Oregon Territory in the Pacific Northwest. The prospect alarmed expansionists.

The Expansion Debate Drives Election The annexation of Texas became a key issue in the 1844 presidential election. Southern expansionists supported **James K. Polk** of Tennessee. A Jacksonian Democrat and an enslaver, Polk devoutly believed in Manifest Destiny. Whig candidate Henry Clay opposed annexation.

Polk reasoned that northerners would accept the annexation of Texas if they got their own prize. He promised them the Oregon Territory. Polk threatened to go to war with Britain if it did not concede all of Oregon. Polk's vow to obtain both Texas and Oregon helped him win a decisive electoral victory.

Polk Compromises on Oregon However, northern Democrats soon felt betrayed by the new President. They had reluctantly supported annexing Texas because Polk had also vowed to grab all of Oregon. Instead, in June 1846 Polk compromised with the British, agreeing to split the Oregon Territory at the 49th parallel of latitude. The United States got the future states of Washington, Oregon, and Idaho. The British kept what became the Canadian province of British Columbia. An Ohio Democrat sputtered, "Our rights to Oregon have been shamefully compromised. The administration is Southern, Southern, Southern!"

Polk compromised because the nation could not afford two wars. He wanted to fight weak Mexico rather than powerful Britain. Indeed, by the time the Oregon compromise was completed, war with Mexico had already begun.

CHECK UNDERSTANDING Why did Northern members of Congress object to annexing Texas?

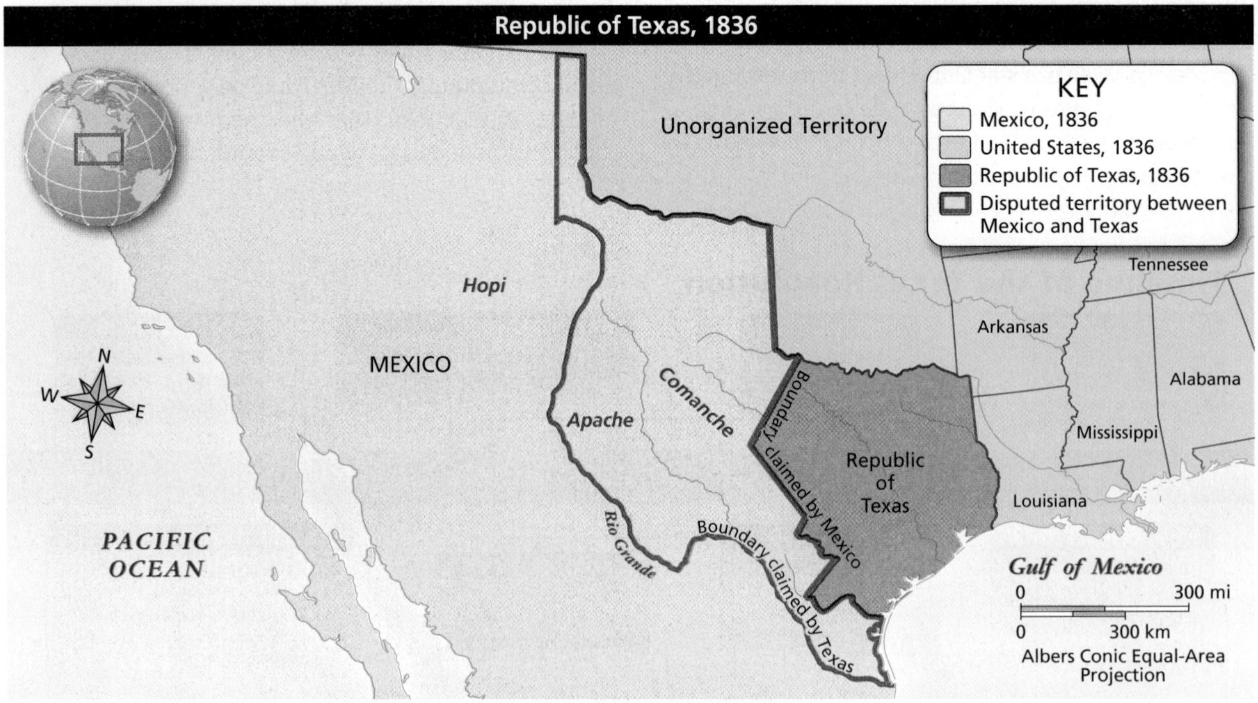

>> **Analyze Maps** How could the border disputes shown here have affected the United States?

BOUNCE to Activate Chart

The Oregon Treaty, 1846

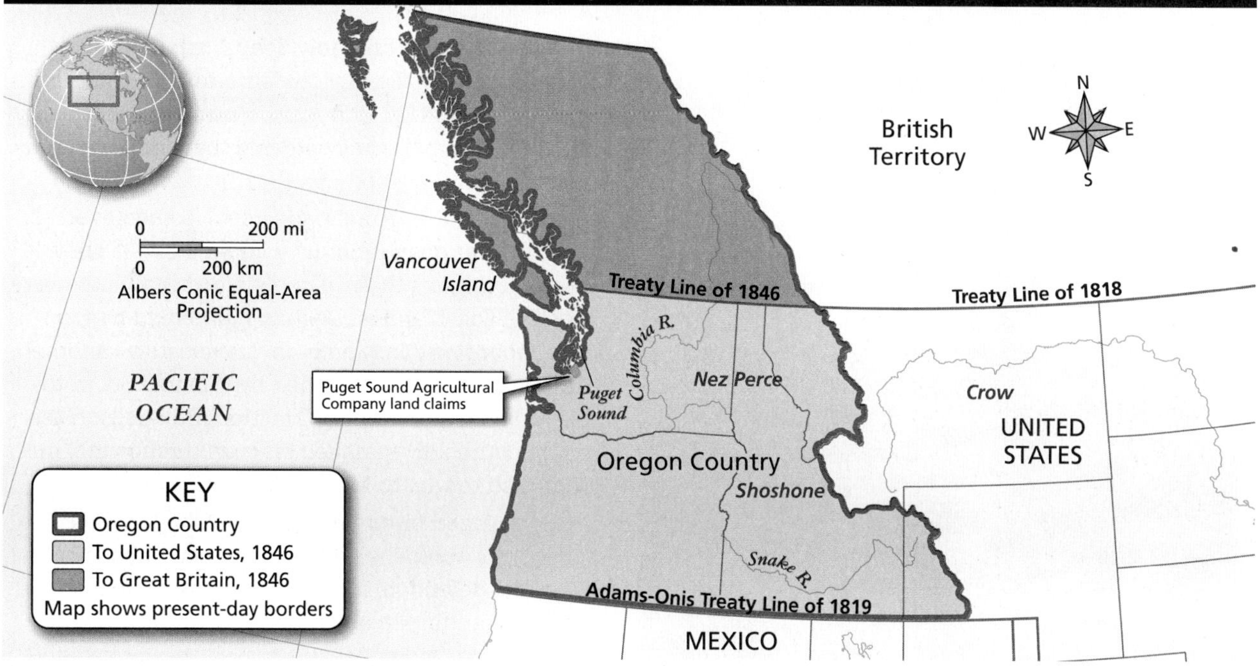

>> **Analyze Maps** What factors made the area shown on this map appealing to both the United States and Great Britain?

BOUNCE to Activate Map

The Mexican-American War

A month before Polk took office, Congress narrowly voted to annex Texas, which entered the Union as a slave state in December 1845. Annexation inflamed the long-standing border dispute between Texas and Mexico. Polk endorsed the Texan claim to the land south and west of the Nueces River as far as the Rio Grande. This claim tripled the traditional size of Texas. Outraged, the Mexicans refused to recognize the annexation.

U.S. Troops Occupy the Borderland Polk sent American troops led by General **Zachary Taylor** to occupy the contested borderland between the two rivers. While waiting for the inevitable conflict, Polk drafted a declaration of war. He did not have to wait long. In May 1846, a Mexican patrol clashed with American soldiers, killing eleven. Polk rushed his war message to Congress.

> We have tried every effort at reconciliation. . . .But now, after reiterated menaces, Mexico has passed the boundary of the United States, has invaded our territory and shed American blood upon the American soil.
>
> —James K. Polk, war message to Congress, May 11, 1846

Of course, the Mexicans saw the clash differently: To them it was an American invasion that shed Mexican blood on Mexican soil.

Democrats, especially those from the South, were enthusiastically in favor of war with Mexico. Most Whigs, especially those from the North, opposed war. They believed that Polk had deliberately provoked the war by sending troops to Texas. Whigs also feared that Polk would not settle for even the biggest version of Texas but planned to annex the adjacent northern Mexican provinces, including New Mexico and California. The conquered territories might then become slave states, increasing southern power in Congress.

Despite their suspicions, most Whigs did not dare block the declaration of war. They knew that the war had wide popular support—and they remembered the demise of the Federalist Party after it had opposed the War of 1812. On May 13, Congress voted overwhelmingly to declare war on Mexico.

A Decisive Victory for U.S. Forces In the war, the United States had great advantages. It was

>> U.S. Army officer General Winfield Scott secured a number of decisive victories that helped the United States triumph in the Mexican-American War.

much larger, wealthier, and more populous than Mexico. The Mexicans lacked the industries that so quickly and abundantly supplied the Americans with arms and ammunition. The Americans also had a larger and better navy and more advanced artillery. Above all, the United States enjoyed superb officers, well trained at the military academy at West Point. Generals Zachary Taylor and **Winfield Scott** received exceptional support from their junior officers, including Robert E. Lee, Ulysses S. Grant, and William T. Sherman. (All these men would later play key roles in the U.S. Civil War.) Meanwhile, Mexicans were bitterly divided because Santa Anna had resumed his dictatorship.

In this one-sided war, the United States won every major battle. During the summer of 1846, General Stephen W. Kearny quickly conquered New Mexico. Meanwhile, the U.S. Navy helped American settlers, led by explorer John C. Frémont, to seize control of California. Until they could legally join the United States, these rebels organized the short-lived Bear Flag Republic. Frémont joined forces with Kearny to bring all of California under American control.

Taylor led another army deeper into northern Mexico, seizing the city of Monterrey in September. In February 1847, Santa Anna tried to retake the city. But Taylor's small army defeated the more numerous Mexicans at the bloody Battle of Buena Vista.

By early 1847, American forces had achieved all of Polk's war goals—but he wanted more. A New England critic of the war complained that with every victory, "Our Manifest Destiny higher and higher kept mounting." In March, the navy carried another American army, commanded by Winfield Scott, to the Mexican port city of Veracruz. After seizing the port, Scott boldly marched his men through 200 miles of rugged terrain to Mexico City.

Scott faced bitter resistance at Chapultepec (chah POOL tuh pehk), a fortress above Mexico City. The defenders included six young Mexican cadets—ranging in age from 13 to 19—who fought to the death. Today, Mexico honors the cadets who fell at Chapultepec as *Los Niños Héroes*, or the Child Heroes.

In September 1847, Scott captured Mexico City. After little more than a year and a half of fighting, the Mexican-American War had ended in a thorough American victory.

IDENTIFY SUPPORTING DETAILS Identify the advantages the United States had in the Mexican-American War.

ASSESSMENT

1. **Identify Cause and Effect** What factors contributed to the large influx of American settlers in Texas in the early 1800s?
2. **Interpret** Why did the Mexican government refuse to honor the treaty granting Texas independence?
3. **Summarize** Why did President James K. Polk support the annexation of Texas, and how did he convince northerners to accept the annexation?
4. **Infer** What major advantages did the United States have in its war with Mexico?
5. **Quest Connections** Why did the Whigs fear that the U.S. would add new territories?

GO ONLINE to access this biography: Sam Houston

6.3

Placer mining used water to sort through gravel and other material in order to find valuable gold, which would sink as other material washed away. **Infer** What challenges made placer mining slow and difficult?

The Nation Expands to the Pacific

As a result of its quick victory in the Mexican-American War, the United States finally achieved the expansionists' goal of Manifest Destiny. Yet, the long-term effects of the war served to highlight growing differences between North and South and set the stage for future conflict.

BOUNCE to Activate Flipped Video

Objectives

Explain how the Mexican-American War helped the United States achieve the goal of Manifest Destiny.

Identify the causes and effects of the California Gold Rush.

Key Terms

Treaty of Guadalupe Hidalgo
Gadsden Purchase
Wilmot Proviso
California Gold Rush
forty-niner
placer mining
hydraulic mining

The U.S. Gains Territory

In February 1848, the defeated Mexicans made peace with the Americans. The **Treaty of Guadalupe Hidalgo** (gwah duh LOO pay ee THAHL goh) forced Mexico to give up the northern third of their country and added 1.2 million square miles of territory to the United States.

Territorial Expansion In return for leaving Mexico City and paying $15 million, the United States kept New Mexico and California. The nation also secured the Rio Grande as the southern boundary of Texas.

The treaty angered the Mexican people who bitterly resented the outcome of the war for decades. The treaty also dismayed Polk, but for a different reason. After Scott captured Mexico City, the President decided that he wanted to keep more of Mexico. He blamed his negotiator, Nicholas Trist, for settling for too little. But Polk had no choice but to submit the treaty to Congress because northern public opinion would not support a longer war.

In the **Gadsden Purchase** of 1853, the United States obtained from Mexico another 29,640 square miles in southern Arizona and New Mexico. The Americans bought this strip to facilitate the building of a railroad across the continent. Along with the

GO ONLINE to access your digital course

annexation of Texas, the Treaty of Guadalupe Hidalgo and the Gadsden Purchase increased the area of the United States by about one third. Only the Louisiana Purchase had added more territory. The new lands comprised present-day New Mexico, California, Nevada, Utah, Arizona, and half of Colorado.

The Wilmot Proviso Even before the war ended, the consequences of gaining land from Mexico stirred fierce debate. In 1846, Whig congressman David Wilmot of Pennsylvania had proposed a law, known as the **Wilmot Proviso**, that would ban slavery in any lands won from Mexico. The proposal broke party unity and instead divided Congress along sectional lines. Most northern Democrats joined all northern Whigs to support the Wilmot Proviso. Southern Democrats joined southern Whigs in opposition. The Proviso passed in the House of Representatives, but it failed narrowly in the Senate.

Over the next 15 years, the Wilmot Proviso passed in the House only to fail in the Senate. The Proviso brought the slavery issue to the forefront and weakened the two major parties, which had long tried to avoid discussing the issue in Congress. Thus, the lands won from Mexico increased tensions between North and South.

IDENTIFY CENTRAL IDEAS How did the Mexican-American War heighten tensions over slavery?

The California Gold Rush

To most Americans, the new lands in the West seemed too distant for rapid settlement. But in early 1848, workers at John Sutter's sawmill found flecks of gold in the American River east of Sacramento, California.

Gold Seekers Head to California By summer, news of the gold strike caused a sensation in the eastern United States. In a mass migration known as the **California Gold Rush**, some 80,000 fortune seekers headed for California in search of easy riches. This mass migration grew particularly strong in 1849. About half of these **forty-niners** traveled by land trails. Another half went by ship around South America or via a short land passage at the Isthmus of Panama. The ships' destination was San Francisco.

The golden news also attracted miners from around the Pacific Rim. Many fortune seekers came from South America, especially Peru and Chile. Another 25,000 laborers migrated from China to California during the 1850s. From a mere 14,000 in 1847, California's population of settlers surged to 225,000 in just five years.

Life As a Forty-Niner Forty-niners flocked to the gold fields with high hopes. One young man described the excitement of departing for California from Indiana.

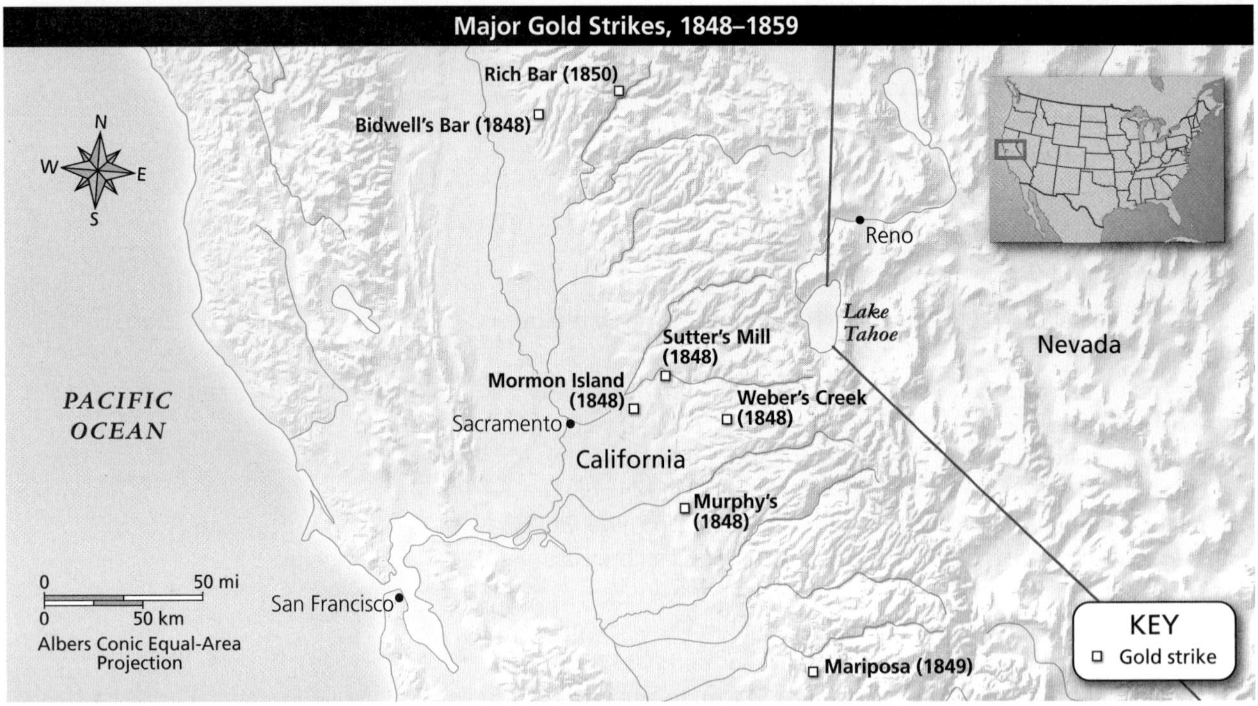

>> **Analyze Maps** In which regions of California were most gold strikes located?

>> **Analyze Information** What were the immediate economic effects of the Gold Rush in California cities and towns?

BOUNCE to Activate Gallery

> The diggings had been discovered but a twelvemonth before, and the glowing tales of their marvelous richness were on every tongue. Our enthusiasm was wrought up to the highest pitch, while the hardships and perils . . . were scarcely given a passing thought.
>
> —David Rohrer Leeper, "The Argonauts of '49"

At first, the miners used cheap metal pans, picks, and shovels to harvest gold flecks from the sand along the banks and bottoms of rivers and streams. This process was known as **placer mining**. A few miners got rich, but most worked hard for little gain. Because food and clothing were so expensive, shrewd traders made more money selling goods to the miners than the miners made by panning for gold.

Conditions were hard in the crowded mining camps. Poor sanitation promoted diseases, especially cholera and dysentery, killing hundreds. In addition, life was cheap and law was scarce in the camps. Almost all of the inhabitants were men, who felt frustrated by their failure to find much gold and by their lack of family life. Competition and fights became common. One forty-niner noted, "It is surprising how indifferent people become to the sight of violence and bloodshed in this country."

In search of order, the miners carried out their own rough justice. Without official legal authority, they acted as judges, juries, and executioners.

Mining Methods Improve Placer mining soon gave way to more efficient methods that required more money and equipment. One method was to dam and divert rivers to expose their beds. Another method, **hydraulic mining**, employed jets of water to erode gravel hills into long lines of sluices to catch the gold. Hydraulic mining damaged the environment by leveling hills and clogging rivers with sediment.

Those with the most money turned to "hard rock mining," searching in the mountains for veins of quartz that contained gold. Miners extracted gold by digging deep tunnels and shafts braced with posts and beams and drained by pumps. One California newspaper complained that the new type of large-scale mining operation "degrades the sturdy miner into a drudge . . . while [mine owners] reap the great profit of his endeavor." The democratic age of placer mining was over. With few exceptions, wealthy investors rather than common miners owned the mines and enjoyed the profits.

>> In hydraulic mining, miners used a water cannon to blast gravel hills and dislodge minerals. This technique was more efficient but more damaging to the environment than placer mining.

Indians and Mexicans Face Discrimination Newcomers from the eastern United States quickly asserted their dominance over California. To discourage the Chinese, they levied a heavy tax on foreign miners. White miners also terrorized and killed American Indians by the thousands. Losing their land, many surviving American Indians became workers on farms and ranches. The California government itself pursued a policy of racial extermination. California's first governor, Peter Burnett, declared to legislators in 1851 "That a war of extermination will continue to be waged between the two races until the Indian race becomes extinct, must be expected."

Mob violence drove most Mexican Americans away from the gold fields. Those who stayed had to pay the foreign miners' tax, even though Mexicans had been in California long before the new American majority.

Californios, or Californians descended from Spanish settlers, also lost most of their land. Contrary to the Treaty of Guadalupe Hidalgo, the courts ignored land titles created under Mexican law.

The Debate over California Statehood The new Californians wanted quickly to organize a state and enter the union. In October 1849, their leaders held a convention and drew up a state constitution. The new constitution excluded African Americans, both enslaved and free. Most of the new Californians were northerners who did not want to compete with southern enslavers who could use slave labor to seek gold. Nor did the miners want any free Blacks to live in California.

California's application for statehood stirred discord between North and South. At the time, the Union was comprised of 15 free states and 15 slave states. Admission of a new free state would thus tip the delicate regional balance in the Senate. Over the next decade, debate over the spread of slavery into the lands won from Mexico would grow increasingly bitter. Thus, westward expansion became a major source of the division that ultimately led to the tragic Civil War.

IDENTIFY SUPPORTING DETAILS What problems did forty-niners face in the California gold fields?

ASSESSMENT

1. **Summarize** What was the Treaty of Guadalupe Hidalgo, and why were neither the Mexican people or President Polk satisfied with it?
2. **Identify Cause and Effect** What was the Wilmot Proviso, and what effect did it have on Congress after the Mexican-American War?
3. **Compare and Contrast** How did hard rock mining differ from older methods such as placer mining? What were the economic implications of this type of mining during the Gold Rush?
4. **Analyze Information** What problems did Indians and Mexicans in California face as a result of the California Gold Rush?
5. **Quest Connections** How did the California constitution deal with slavery, and what long-term effects did this have on U.S. politics?

6.4

During the Second Great Awakening, religious revival meetings were held in open fields. This illustration depicts an 1850s camp meeting of the Duck Creek Methodist Episcopal church in Ohio.

A Religious Awakening Sparks Reform

By the early 1800s, the United States was well established as an independent, growing country. During this time of optimism, as settlers pushed westward and industry encouraged economic growth, American society was shaken by a religious movement that inspired Americans to change themselves and the world around them for the better.

BOUNCE to Activate Flipped Video

Objectives

Explain how the Second Great Awakening affected the United States.

Describe the discrimination that some religious groups suffered from in the mid-1800s.

Trace the emergence of the utopian and transcendentalism movements.

Analyze the goals and methods of the public school movement.

Evaluate the effectiveness of the prison reform and temperance movements.

Key Terms

Second Great Awakening
revivalist
Charles Grandison Finney
evangelical
Joseph Smith
Mormon
Unitarian
utopian community
Transcendentalist
Ralph Waldo Emerson
Henry David Thoreau
public school movement
Horace Mann
Dorothea Dix
penitentiary movement
temperance movement
Neal Dow

The Second Great Awakening

This was not the first religious movement to shape American society. In the early 1700s, Americans had experienced a burst of religious energy known as the Great Awakening. Another revival of religious feeling called the **Second Great Awakening** swept the country beginning in the early 1800s and lasted for nearly half the century. Protestant preachers started and led the Second Great Awakening. They preached that salvation was open to all, not just to an elite. These preachers were known as **revivalists**, because they wanted to revive, or reenergize, the role of religion in America. The preachers' emphasis on individual responsibility in gaining salvation encouraged the idea that people could improve themselves and their souls. This was a powerful and welcome message in a young country that valued individualism and self-reliance.

The Second Great Awakening profoundly influenced American life. Church membership skyrocketed, especially among Baptists and Methodists. Moreover, the movement's focus on spiritual

GO ONLINE to access your digital course

self-improvement encouraged Americans to improve society as well, by working for a wide variety of social reforms.

Evangelical Revivals Lead to Reform The Second Great Awakening began on the frontier in Kentucky and then spread north and south, reaching the cities of the Northeast in the 1820s.

Its religious fervor was spread through outdoor services known as "revivals" or "camp" meetings that lasted for as long as a week. Plentiful food and lively religious music added to the appeal of the gatherings, which were often held in isolated rural areas.

One of the most influential revivalists was former attorney **Charles Grandison Finney**. In passionate sermons, Finney dramatically proclaimed his own faith and urged his listeners to do the same. This **evangelical** style of worship, designed to elicit strong emotions and attract converts, proved highly successful. At Finney's revivals, hundreds of people at a time declared their faith. A great majority of these people were women, who now began to participate in the kind of public speaking that had traditionally been denied them.

Another leading preacher was Lyman Beecher, a Yale-educated minister. Like Finney, Beecher became known for his fiery sermons. Beecher also traveled widely, urging people to read the Bible, join a church, and embrace religion. In 1832, Beecher became president of the new Lane Theological Seminary in Cincinnati, Ohio, which trained more evangelical preachers to join the revival.

Many revivalists' sermons featured the idea that the United States was leading the world into the millennium, or the thousand years of glory following the Second Coming of Jesus. Called millennialism, the belief that the millennium was at hand inspired some reformers to try to ready their society by perfecting it through reform.

The Role of Religion in Public Life During the Second Great Awakening, some Americans wanted the government to encourage public morality by supporting religion. Others disagreed with this aim, holding that the government should protect public life from religious control. An example of the tension between the two groups is the defeat of the Sabbatarian reform movement.

The Sabbatarians wanted the federal government to uphold the Christian Sabbath (a special day of each week reserved for worship) as a day of rest by not allowing any business transactions or mail delivery on that day. Congress insisted it had no authority to interfere with trade and refused to ban commerce on the Sabbath. The debate over church and state continues to this day.

RELIGION IN THE UNITED STATES 1850

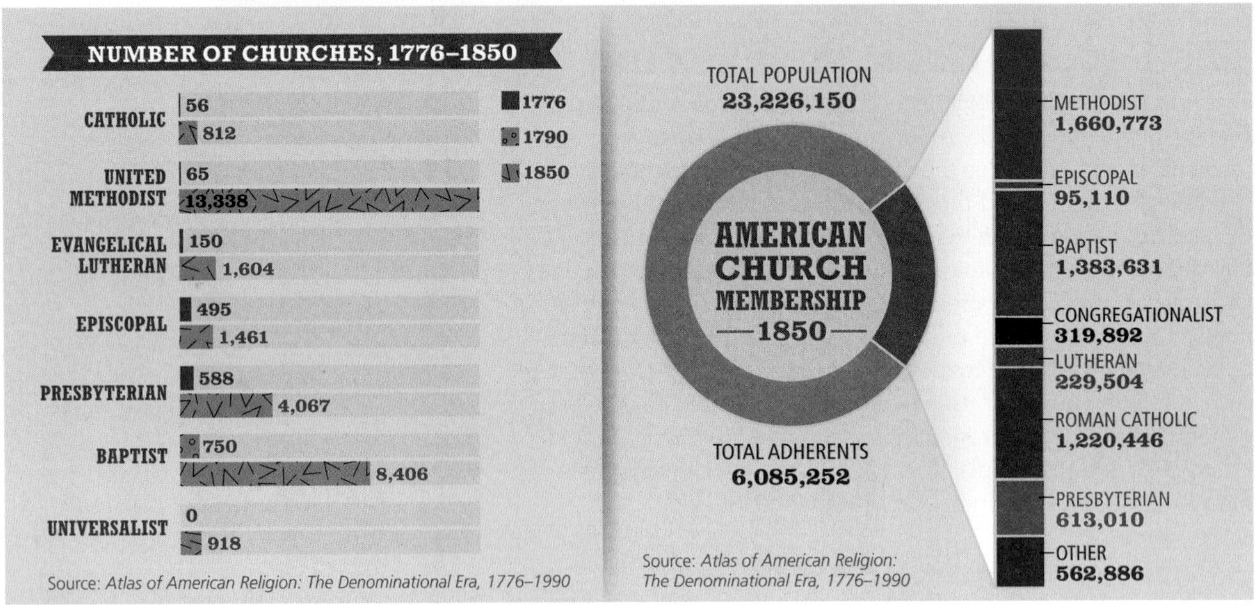

>> **Analyze Information** How did the Second Great Awakening affect church membership by the mid-1800s?

BOUNCE to Activate Gallery

Membership in the Church of Jesus Christ of the Latter-Day Saints, 1830–1900

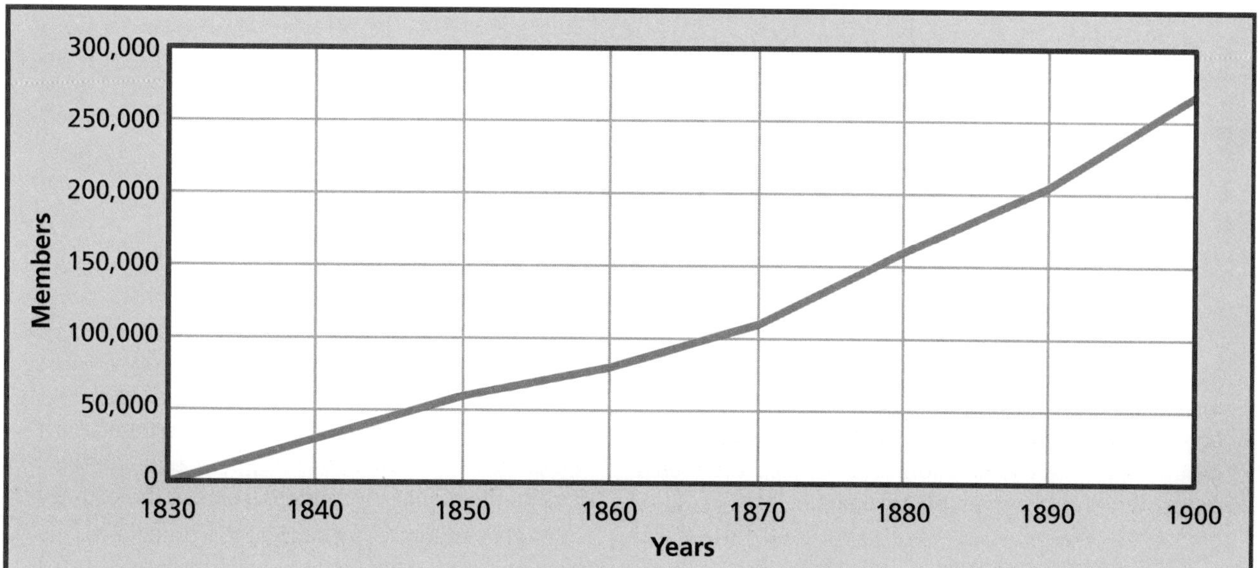

Source: Rodney Stark, "The Rise of a New World Faith"

>> **Analyze Data** Based on this graph, what prediction can you make about Mormon church membership in 1910?

African Americans Form Their Own Churches The Second Great Awakening helped spread ideas of spiritual equality. Many preachers of the Second Great Awakening welcomed African Americans at their revivals. However, some African Americans established their own, separate churches. Led by a former enslaved person named Richard Allen, a group of Philadelphians formed their own church in 1787. African Americans in several other cities did the same. In 1816, these churches united to become the African Methodist Episcopal (AME) Church. By 1826, the AME Church had nearly 8,000 members.

Religion had a special significance for enslaved African Americans, who regarded the Biblical accounts of the Israelites in bondage as a metaphor for their own captivity. Religion also offered the promise of eternal freedom after a lifetime of oppression. African American hymns, called spirituals, gave the enslaved people strength to deal with the difficulties of their lives.

For some, the tension between religious ideals and their cruel captivity inspired them to revolt against their oppressors. Indeed, many men who led slave revolts said they were called by God to lead enslaved people out of bondage.

New Religious Groups Heightened religious awareness also led to the formation of two new religious groups. In New York State, **Joseph Smith** spoke and wrote of visions he said directed him to found a new religious group. In 1830, Smith and a few followers organized the Church of Jesus Christ of Latter-day Saints, whose members are commonly called the **Mormons**. The church grew rapidly, attracting more than 1,000 members in just a few months. It would grow to become one of the most influential religious groups in the country.

In New England, members of several Puritan or Congregational churches began to argue that, instead of seeing God as a "Trinity," people should see God as a single divine being—a unity. They organized themselves into a separate religious group called the **Unitarians**, after their belief.

The Unitarians' views diverged from established religious creeds and a literal interpretation of the Bible. They reflected a growing Christian liberalism, which influenced many other religious groups in the nineteenth century.

CHECK UNDERSTANDING What was the Second Great Awakening?

Religious Discrimination and Intolerance

The preachers of the Second Great Awakening were Protestant. By the mid-1800s, well over half of all Americans were also Protestant. Non-Protestants were in the distinct minority and faced discrimination.

Mormons Are Pushed West Many Americans were wary of the new Mormon Church. Mormons isolated themselves in their own communities where they followed practices that were frowned upon by their neighbors, such as allowing men to have more than one wife. Further, the Mormons became economically powerful because they held land as a group rather than as individuals. They also voted as a group, which gave them political power.

The Mormons' power angered their neighbors. As a result, wherever they set up communities, their neighbors tried to chase them away, sometimes using violence. Mormons were chased out of Ohio and then Missouri.

They sought refuge in Illinois, founding the town of Nauvoo, which grew rapidly. In 1844, Joseph Smith declared his intention to run for President. Many non-Mormons were outraged. In the ensuing violent conflict, Smith was murdered.

Smith's successor, Brigham Young, led the Mormons far west to the Great Salt Lake valley in present-day Utah, then a part of Mexico. Here, Mormon communities thrived. They recruited new members from Europe and developed irrigation systems so they could farm the dry desert land.

Catholics and Jewish People Face Discrimination Members of the Roman Catholic Church faced particularly harsh discrimination in the early 1800s. Many Protestants viewed Catholicism as incompatible with American ideals of democracy. They believed that Catholics would choose loyalty to the Pope, the leader of the Roman Catholic Church, over loyalty to the United States. "Down with Popery," yelled Protestants in Philadelphia as they rioted against Catholic worshippers, echoing the sentiments of many Americans across the country.

Moreover, most Catholics of the time faced discrimination for another reason: their poverty. Many were poor immigrants from Ireland. Because they had little money, they would work for extremely low wages, which threatened other workers. Because Irish immigrants arrived in increasingly large numbers, many feared they were growing too powerful. Those who opposed Catholic immigrants were known as "nativists."

Mormon Migrations, 1830–1847

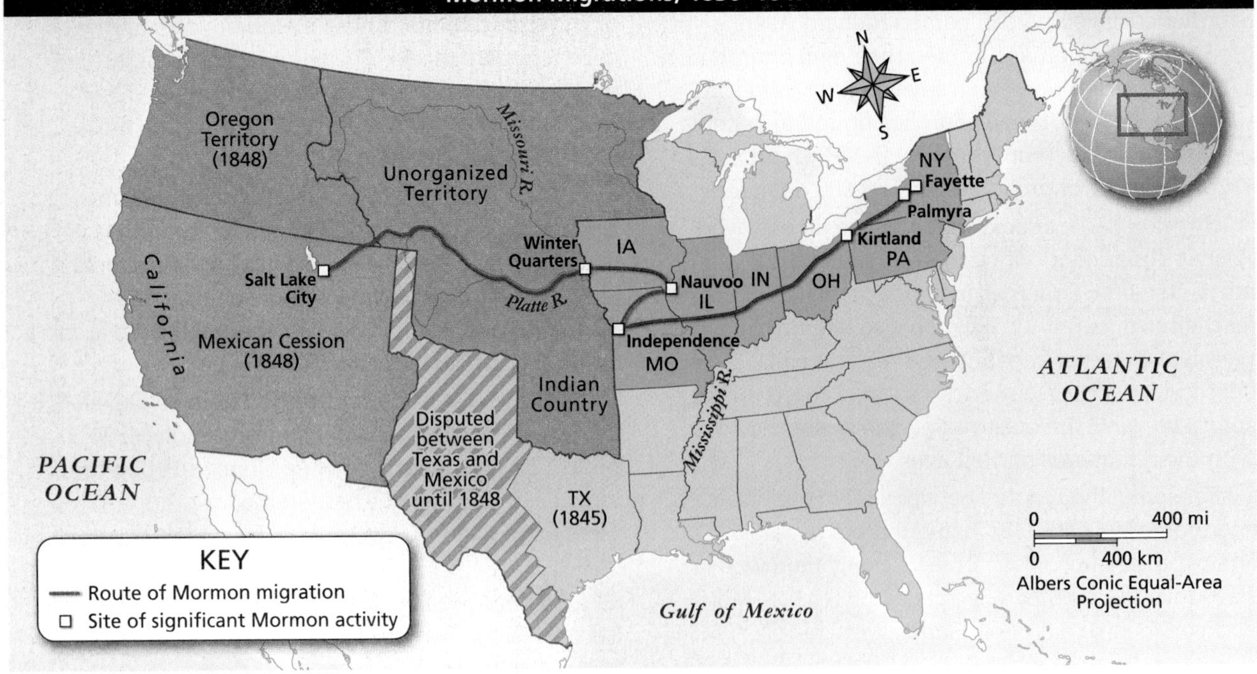

>> **Analyze Maps** New settlers continued to overrun Native American lands. Based on the map, why do you think the Mormons chose Salt Lake City for resettlement?

Jewish people also faced discrimination. Until late in the nineteenth century, state constitutions, from New England to the South, required public officials to be Christians, sometimes specifically Protestant. Jews were then barred from holding office. In the early 1800s, there were only about 2,000 Jewish people in America, mostly clustered in Rhode Island, New York, and Pennsylvania. In the 1840s, when Jewish people came to America in greater numbers to escape political unrest in Europe, Americans often ostracized them.

☑ **IDENTIFY SUPPORTING DETAILS** Why did many Protestants discriminate against Mormons, Catholics, and Jewish people?

>> Displaced Mormons settled in Nauvoo, Illinois, in 1839. Nauvoo remained the center of the Mormon religion until Brigham Young led the Mormons to Utah in 1848.

Utopias and Transcendentalism

In the early 1800s, many Americans turned to Protestant churches, while some formed new religious groups. Still others sought different routes to try to fashion a more perfect society.

Utopian Communities Aspire to Perfection

During the early 1800s, dozens of groups of Americans sought to improve their lives in a unique way. They chose to distance themselves from society by setting up communities based on unusual ways of sharing property, labor, and family life. These settlements came to be called **utopian communities**, or utopias, because they aspired to be perfect communities. Organizers of utopias hoped their settlements would both engender virtue in their members and inspire those outside their communities.

Two well-known utopian communities were New Harmony, in Indiana, and Brook Farm, near Boston. In 1825, Robert Owen, a British social reformer, sought to have people from different backgrounds work together in a cooperative society at New Harmony.

The society attracted some 1,000 people whom Owen described as "the industrious and well-disposed of all nations." At Brook Farm in 1841, George Ripley and 80 others sought to combine physical and intellectual labor. Brook Farm failed after only six years, while New Harmony lasted just two years. Most of the 50 or so other utopian communities were similarly short-lived.

>> Printed shortly after anti-Catholic riots in Philadelphia, this 1844 sheet music glorifies the ideals of the nativist movement. **Analyze Primary Sources** Why is the flag shown as torn and damaged?

The Shakers Another group that set up a chain of separate communal living societies was the United Society of Believers in Christ's Second Appearing, more commonly known as the Shakers. The

>> American author and leading Transcendentalist Ralph Waldo Emerson emphasized the sacredness of nature and the importance of the individual's inner life.

Shakers had organized during the middle 1700s but reached their peak during the 1840s. Shakers set up independent villages in New Hampshire, New York, Ohio, and Illinois. Men and women lived in separate housing and did not marry or have children. The communities grew only when adults joined or when the group took in orphans. The economy flourished because of the Shaker's careful attention to high-quality crafts and farm produce. Remnants of their settlements still exist today.

The New Philosophy of the Transcendentalists

In New England, a group known as the **Transcendentalists** developed a new way to look at humanity, nature, and God, and the relationship among them. They were called the Transcendentalists because they believed that people could *transcend,* or go beyond, logic or tradition in order to reach the deepest truths. They believed that individuals should listen to nature and to their own consciences—instead of religious doctrines—to learn the truth about the universe.

Ralph Waldo Emerson, a former Unitarian minister, was the leading Transcendentalist. He celebrated the interplay between the individual and the universe in sermons, essays, and poems. "Within man," Emerson wrote, "is the soul of the whole; the wise silence; the universal beauty." Emerson gathered a group of men and women who met regularly in his Concord, Massachusetts, home to read and talk about ways to develop a rich spiritual life for individuals and for society. They published their ideas in their magazine, *The Dial*, which was edited by Margaret Fuller.

One of Emerson's most important followers was **Henry David Thoreau**. In 1846, Thoreau was jailed after refusing to pay taxes to support the Mexican-American War, which he viewed as immoral. Thoreau explained his thinking in a landmark essay, "Civil Disobedience," in which he argues that a person must be true to his or her own conscience, even if it means breaking the law. "Civil Disobedience" provided inspiration to later leaders who fought for civil rights around the world and is still widely read and admired.

>> American writer Henry David Thoreau published *Walden*, an influential series of essays in 1854. The collection retold Thoreau's experiences during a roughly two-year experiment in living simply and in solitude near Walden Pond in Massachusetts.

IDENTIFY CENTRAL IDEAS How did the methods of people who created utopian societies differ from those of other reformers?

Public Education Reform

The spiritual self-improvement inspired by the Second Great Awakening encouraged campaigns to improve and perfect society as well. Soon, many Americans began to put their religious ideals into practice by working to reshape, or reform, parts of American life. Their efforts would affect several groups of the most disadvantaged Americans.

The leaders of the Second Great Awakening preached that their followers had a sacred responsibility to improve life on Earth through reform, especially for the disadvantaged. Not all reformers were motivated by religion. Many were simply moved by the suffering they saw. One of most popular reform movements was in the field of education.

Reformers Stress the Value of Education Since colonial times, most American children had been taught at home by their parents. Some communities established schools. *The American Spelling Book*, created by Noah Webster in the 1780s, remained the most popular schoolbook.

In order to emphasize America's cultural independence from England, Webster developed more rational spellings that he felt expressed American honesty and directness.

Still, reformers saw education in America as woefully inadequate. Because there were no public schools that children were required by law to attend, most children did not go to school. Reformers who led the **public school movement**, also called the common school movement, sought to establish such a system of tax-supported public schools. They argued that expanding education would give Americans the knowledge and intellectual tools they needed to make decisions as citizens of a democracy. Education would promote economic growth by supplying knowledgeable workers and help keep wealthy, educated people from oppressing the uneducated poor.

Horace Mann Shapes Public Education One of the greatest school reformers was **Horace Mann**. Mann grew up poor and had firsthand experience with inadequate schooling. He never forgot his humble beginnings, which inspired him to work to provide all children with a better education than he had received.

As a leader in the Massachusetts Senate, Mann championed the creation of a state board of education. He resigned from the Senate in 1837 to chair the first board. In this capacity, Mann advanced the idea of free public schools that all children were required by

>> Some young people, like these students, learned subjects such as reading and mathematics at local schools. But most young people were taught by their parents or not at all.

BOUNCE to Activate Gallery

>> Like modern educational materials, textbooks like this one from the mid-1800s used text and images to help students learn facts and concepts. **Analyze Primary Sources** How does this textbook math problem differ from its counterpart today?

law to attend. He argued for state oversight of local schools, standardized school calendars, and adequate school funding. Mann also led the fight to abolish corporal, or physical, punishment. Further, he worked to establish training to create a body of well-educated, professional teachers.

Mann's influence was felt nationwide. Because of his work and the work of other school reformers, state legislatures across the country set aside funds to support free public schools. The reformers faced resistance from reluctant taxpayers and those who believed that education should include specific religious teaching. Despite opposition, within the next few decades, government-supported public schools became the norm across the nation. The percentage of American children attending school doubled.

Many women played key roles in the school reform movement. They petitioned their local legislatures to support public education and became teachers in the new schools. Catharine Beecher, a daughter of evangelical preacher Lyman Beecher, and Emma Willard established schools for women in Connecticut, Ohio, and New York. Elizabeth Blackwell and Ann Preston helped to establish medical training for women by the 1850s.

☑ **DESCRIBE** Describe the accomplishments of the public school movement.

Social Reform Movements

Americans who had little or no voice in how they were treated were of special concern to many reformers. That was one reason why many reformers worked tirelessly to help Americans who were imprisoned or mentally ill. Women were at the forefront of these social campaigns. This in itself was an extraordinary change in American social history, as women had traditionally been discouraged from taking on public roles.

Dorothea Dix Fights for Change One reformer who turned her religious ideals into action was **Dorothea Dix**. In 1841, she began teaching Sunday school in a Massachusetts prison. When she discovered that people suffering from mental illnesses were housed along with hardened criminals, she decided to act to change things.

Dix spent two years visiting every prison, almshouse (place for housing the poor), and hospital in Massachusetts. Then she wrote to the state legislature, vividly describing the horrors she had seen and demanding action.

> I tell what I have seen—painful and shocking as the details often are—that from them you may feel more deeply the imperative obligation

U.S. Public School Enrollment, 1850–1920

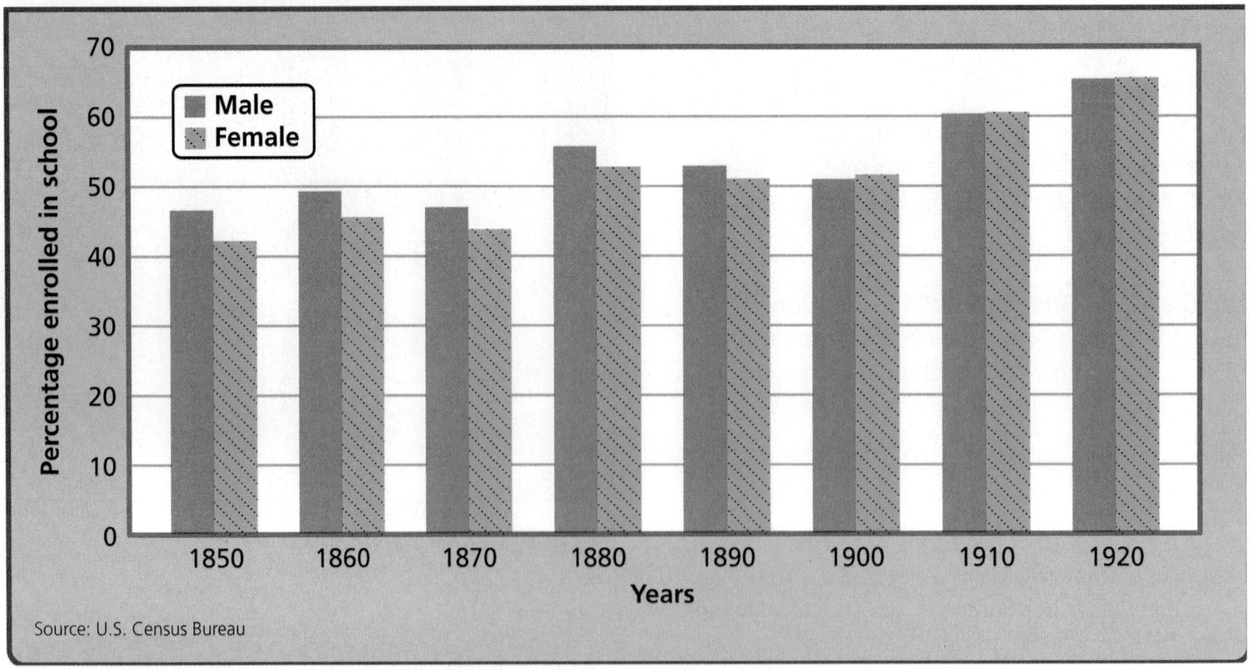

>> **Analyze Data** Why might school enrollment have varied over time?

which lies upon you to prevent the possibility of a repetition or continuance of such outrages upon humanity. . . . I come as the advocate of [the] helpless, forgotten, [and] insane. . . . Men of Massachusetts . . . raise up the fallen, succor the desolate, restore the outcast, defend the helpless.

—Dorothea Dix, petition to the Massachusetts Legislature, 1843

>> Dorothea Dix fought for social reform in prisons and hospitals throughout the state of Massachusetts. Her efforts contributed to the establishment of 32 state hospitals for the mentally ill.

Dix went on to campaign across the nation, encouraging other communities to build humane hospitals for people with mental illnesses. Her campaign was remarkably successful, leading directly to the creation of the first modern mental hospitals.

New Ideas for Prisons Dix and others also worked to reform American prisons. Until that time, most people viewed prisons as a place to punish criminals.

Prison reformers, however, thought that prisons should make criminals feel penitence, or sorrow for their crimes. The prison reform movement is thus sometimes called the **penitentiary movement**.

Two types of penitentiaries were proposed by reformers. The Pennsylvania System, advocated by the Philadelphia Society for Alleviating the Miseries of Public Prisons, was embodied in the Eastern State Penitentiary. In Eastern State, prisoners were urged to repent while they lived in complete solitary confinement, working alone in their cells and exercising in individual yards. The Pennsylvania System was expensive to run, and its complete isolation of prisoners came to be viewed as cruel. The second type of penitentiary was based on a system used in Auburn Prison, in Central New York, in the 1820s. In Auburn, prisoners worked with one another during the day in strict silence but slept in individual cells at night. Many American prisons followed the Auburn model.

>> A Massachusetts hospital for mentally ill people established during the 1800s

The Temperance Movement When reformers surveyed American society, they saw a country in desperate need of reform. Ongoing industrialization caused rapid and unsettling changes. Crime, sickness, poverty, and neglected families and children seemed rampant. Many reformers attributed these problems to the widespread use of alcohol.

In response, reformers launched the **temperance movement**, an effort to end alcohol abuse and the

>> Women who supported the temperance movement sometimes protested the sale and consumption of alcohol in taverns like this one.

problems created by it. Temperance means drinking alcoholic beverages in moderation. Some reformers believed in prohibition, or a complete ban, on alcohol consumption. Temperance reformers published pamphlets and posters warning that wasting money on liquor prevented people from buying food for their families. They argued that drinking alcohol led to violence and crime. Because alcohol abuse was directly related to domestic abuse, many women became involved in the campaign. The American Temperance Society, which had thousands of members in several states, held meetings where people were urged to pledge to refrain from drinking alcohol.

The Washington Temperance Society sought to help drinkers through dramatic public confessions, discussion, and counseling.

However, the temperance movement had real success only when the reformers won changes in the law. **Neal Dow**, who earned a worldwide reputation for his lectures on alcohol abuse, became mayor of Portland, Maine, in 1851. He succeeded in securing the passage of the so-called "Maine Law," which restricted the sale of alcohol. Within a few years, a dozen states had passed similar temperance laws. Temperance would remain an enduring issue for the next hundred years.

☑ **IDENTIFY MAIN IDEAS** What was the goal of the temperance movement?

☑ ASSESSMENT

1. **Hypothesize** What was the goal of the Sabbatarian reform movement? Why did it fail?
2. **Cite Evidence** How did the Mormon Church become such a powerful force by the mid-1800s? How did other Americans view the church?
3. **Express Ideas Clearly** Describe a typical Shaker living community during the early 1800s.
4. **Construct** Explain how Horace Mann worked to reform education in the 1800s.
5. **Connections to Today** Reformers claimed that public education would spur economic growth. What are the economic arguments for supporting publicly-funded higher education today?

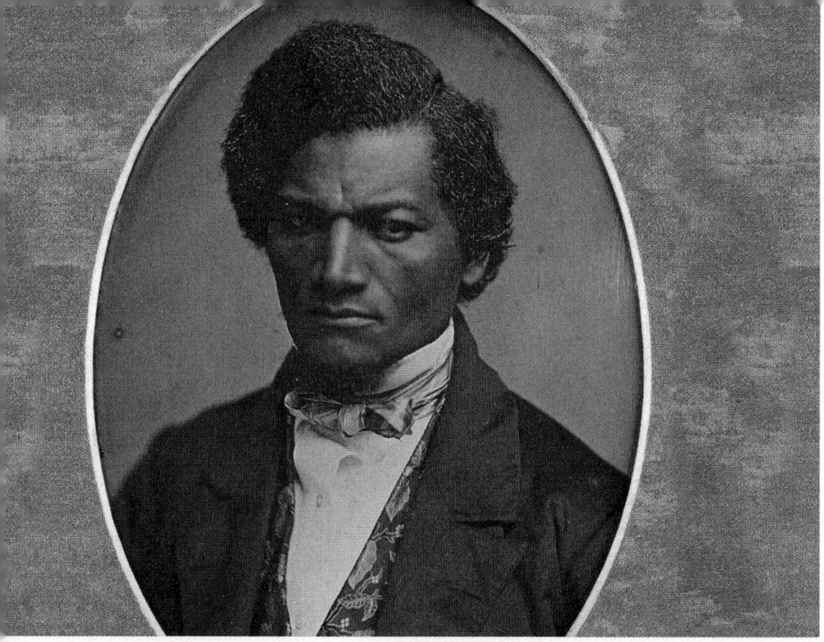

6.5

Frederick Douglass was one of the most brilliant orators of his day and a leader of the abolition movement. A former slave, Douglass used his experiences to speak out against the abuses of slavery to audiences across the country and abroad.

The Abolition Movement

During the period of reform that swept the United States in the early and middle 1800s, reformers tried to improve life through campaigns to help children, families, and disadvantaged adults. Soon, reformers also set out to help another group of exploited people: enslaved African Americans in the South.

BOUNCE to Activate Flipped Video

Objectives

Describe the hardships of the lives of enslaved African Americans and the ways in which they coped.

Explain the struggles and successes of free African Americans in the mid-1800s.

Identify the leaders and tactics of the abolition movement.

Summarize the positions and tactics of those opposed to abolition.

Key Terms

freedman
Nat Turner
abolition movement
William Lloyd Garrison
Frederick Douglass
Gag Rule

Life as an Enslaved African American

Slavery, an American institution since colonial times, expanded across the South in the early 1800s with the growth of cotton farming. By 1830, from Maryland to Texas, some 2 million Africans and African Americans were held as slaves in the United States. About one third of these people were children under ten years of age. All of them struggled in their captivity, knowing that they were at the mercy of enslavers who could sell them and break up their families at will.

Cruel Treatment Most of these unfortunate men, women, and children labored from dawn to dusk at backbreaking tasks—cultivating fields of cotton, loading freight onto ships, or preparing meals in scorching hot kitchens. Enslavers who held large numbers of people in bondage employed "overseers" to manage their enslaved workers. These overseers maintained brutal work routines by punishing people physically with beatings, whippings, and maimings, and mentally, through humiliation and the threat of being separated from family members. The basics of life—food, clothing, and shelter—were barely adequate for most enslaved people.

GO ONLINE to access your digital course

The conditions under which enslaved people lived can be difficult to imagine. One glimpse of the heartbreak that tormented so many is provided by a letter from an enslaved woman, apparently pregnant, to her mother, who had been sold. She wrote to say that now her husband had also been sold.

> A cloud has settled upon me and produced a change in my prospect, too great for words to express. My husband is torn from me, and carried away by his master. . . . I went to see him—tried to prevail on him not to carry my husband away . . . but mother—all my entreaties and tears did not soften his hard heart. . . . A time is fast approaching when I shalt want my husband and my mother, and both are gone!
>
> —Emily, an enslaved African American, 1836

Such anguish was commonplace. This woman was relatively lucky—she could read and write, and managed to get a letter to a distant family member. More often, enslaved people were not allowed to learn to read, and family members who were separated never heard from one another again.

Spirit and Strength The miserable conditions forced on enslaved people took their inevitable toll. Some, losing all hope, took their own lives. Others simply toiled through a lifetime of pain and sadness. But, in a remarkable triumph of spirit over hardship, many enslaved people maintained their hope and their dignity. They developed many ways of coping with their inhumane conditions. They worked to maintain networks of family and friends.

Parents kept family traditions alive by naming children for beloved aunts, uncles, or grandparents and by passing on family stories that their children could cherish wherever they might find themselves. Enslaved people took comfort in their religion, which shone the light of hope in the midst of their difficult lives.

Resistance Many enslaved people did whatever they could to fight back against their oppressors. Resistance took many forms, including sabotage, such as breaking tools or outwitting overseers, and the more direct method of escape. Tens of thousands of enslaved people fled to the North or to Mexico, where slavery was prohibited. A loose network of ever-changing escape routes called the Underground Railroad helped many reach freedom.

Some enslaved people decided not to run but to fight. Indeed, historians estimate that nearly 200 significant slave revolts took place in the first half of the 1800s. In 1811, Charles Deslondes led hundreds

Major Slave Revolts, Eighteenth and Nineteenth Centuries

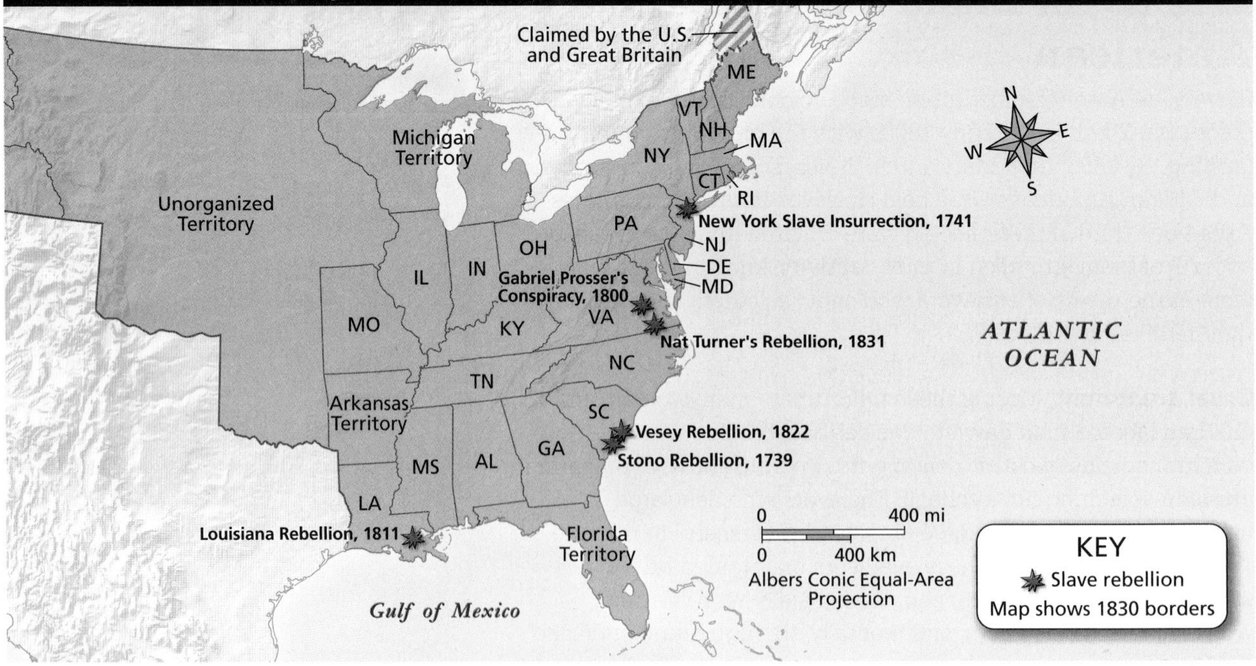

>> **Analyze Maps** Where did the earliest rebellion take place? Where did most rebellions take place?

BOUNCE to Activate Gallery

SLAVERY IN THE UNITED STATES, 1780–1850

Free African Americans Organize
Growing communities of free African Americans developed their own institutions, out of which new leadership would emerge in the fight for abolition.

1780
In Newport RI, the Free African Society is formed to care for the poor and sick.

1784
In Boston, African American Freemasons form a lodge.

1787
In Philadelphia, the Free African Society is formed to provide care and religious services.

1794
In Philadelphia, the Free African Society builds its own house of worship.

Legal Struggles over Slavery 1790–1850
On the national level, the struggle against slavery was marked by advances and setbacks.

1793
Fugitive Slave Act of 1793 authorizes local governments to seize and return freedom seeking enslaved people to their enslavers.

1794
Slave Trade Act of 1794 prohibits the use of U.S. ports for building slave ships.

1800
Slave Trade Act of 1794 is amended to authorize U.S. ships to seize vessels involved in the trade of enslaved people.

1808
1807 law banning the importation of enslaved people takes effect.

1850
Fugitive Slave Act of 1850 forces local population to assist in the capture of freedom seeking enslaved people.

Sources: New York Public Library; History; Politico; Many Thousands Gone by Ira Berlin

>> **Analyze Information** Why didn't laws against the trade in enslaved people end slavery itself?

of rebels toward New Orleans, attacking plantations along the Mississippi River before the rebellion was crushed. In 1822, Denmark Vesey planned what would have been the greatest slave revolt in American history in Charleston, South Carolina.

Vesey was a **freedman**, or former slave. Traveling to Haiti as a ship's carpenter, he was inspired by the successful slave rebellion that had taken place there in the 1790s. Vesey nurtured his dream of a revolt after becoming frustrated with his status as a second-class citizen in Charleston. When authorities shut down Vesey's church, Vesey plotted a slave uprising. The plan called for enslaved people in the city and on surrounding plantations to seize weapons from guardhouses and arsenals, destroy Charleston and free all of the enslaved people living nearby. His plan was thwarted, however, when news of it leaked. In the end, Vesey and dozens of his accomplices were hanged.

In 1831, a slave named **Nat Turner** was more successful in carrying out his plans for revolt. Turner had taught himself to read the Bible and believed that he had received a sign from God instructing him to lead his people to freedom.

In August of 1831, he led followers through the countryside near Richmond, Virginia, intending to capture a nearby armory and gain more weapons. On their journey, Turner's group killed nearly 60 people before the local militia stopped their march. During the manhunt that followed, the local militia killed dozens of African Americans. Turner was captured after six weeks. He and his associates were executed.

Terrified by the idea of a successful slave revolt, southerners reacted by passing much more stringent laws to control the enslaved African Americans. In some places, it became illegal to teach enslaved people to read. Often, they were forbidden to gather in groups unless an overseer was present. Yet, these restrictions did nothing to dampen the spirit of the enslaved people who were determined to resist their captivity—and they inspired free people in the North to work against slavery.

☑ **IDENTIFY SUPPORTING DETAILS** How did enslaved African Americans resist their captivity?

Free African Americans

Not all people of African descent in the United States were held as slaves. Beginning with Massachusetts and Pennsylvania in the 1780s, northern states had gradually outlawed slavery by the 1840s. In Maryland and Virginia, many enslavers were slowly manumitting, or officially freeing, their African American slaves. The net result was a large and growing population of free African Americans. Despite their freedom, however, they suffered from persistent racial discrimination.

Moreover, the very existence of free African Americans concerned many white Americans, especially enslavers. They felt that the large population of free African Americans made those still in bondage long all the more for freedom. In 1816, some of the South's most prominent enslavers established the American Colonization Society (ACS). The goal of the ACS was to encourage the migration of free African Americans to Africa.

The ACS established Liberia, a colony on the west coast of Africa, and by 1830 some 1,100 people from the United States had been relocated there.

Most free African Americans were wary of the motives of the ACS. Most had been born in America, and they considered the United States their home. Moreover, they feared that colonization was just a plan to strengthen slavery by exiling the most able African American leaders. Although several thousand free African Americans did eventually migrate to Liberia, most chose to stay in the country of their birth.

Many free African Americans worked together to establish churches and schools. Some acted to try to change and improve the lives of enslaved African Americans. In Boston, a free African American named David Walker published a pamphlet that used religion as the base for a blistering attack on slavery.

> You may do your best to keep us in wretchedness and misery, to enrich you and your children, but God will deliver us from under you. . . . Treat us then like men, and we will be your friends. And there is no doubt in my mind, but that the whole of the past will be sunk into oblivion, and we yet, under God, will become a united and happy people. The whites may say it is impossible, but remember that nothing is impossible with God.
>
> — David Walker, *Appeal to the Colored Citizens of the World,* 1829

Walker's pamphlet was outlawed in the South, where the economy depended on slave labor. Still, it reached a wide audience in the North, where more people were beginning to view slavery as fundamentally incompatible with the religious views they embraced during the Second Great Awakening.

☑ **DESCRIBE** Describe how free African Americans coped with discrimination and worked to end slavery in the mid-1800s.

Free African American Population, 1860

>> **Analyze Maps** Which regions of the nation had the most and fewest numbers of free African American residents? What factors likely explain these differences?

The Antislavery Movement Grows

Misgivings about slavery had been spreading across the nation since Revolutionary times. Many northerners objected to it on moral grounds. By 1804, all states north of Maryland had passed legislation to end slavery. In 1807, bringing new enslaved people to any part of the United States from Africa was banned, but even in the North, the process of ending slavery was uneven and slow. Slavery was an established institution in the South, where slave labor played an important role in the economy.

By the early 1800s, a growing number of Americans opposed to slavery became activists. Because these activists wanted slavery abolished, or ended, they became known as abolitionists. The great reform movement they led was the **abolition movement**.

>> Antislavery activists like these in Virginia faced violence from supporters of slavery.

BOUNCE to Activate Gallery

Abolitionists Demand Emancipation The first abolitionists were Quakers and other evangelical religious groups, along with free Black northerners and enslaved people themselves. In the early 1800s, a printer named **William Lloyd Garrison**, who lived in Boston, Massachusetts, became one of the leading abolitionists.

Garrison began his antislavery career by working for Benjamin Lundy, a Baltimore Quaker who published America's first antislavery newspaper. In 1831, Garrison began publishing his own antislavery newspaper, *The Liberator*. Garrison used dramatic language to attract readers and convince them that slavery was morally wrong. This technique of trying to effect change by persuading people through moral arguments is called moral suasion. It was a favorite technique of leaders of many reform movements.

Garrison was in favor of emancipation, or the freeing of enslaved people. At first he thought, like most abolitionists, that this should be accomplished gradually over time to minimize economic and social disruption. But Garrison soon took the radical step of advocating immediate emancipation and the extension of full political and social rights to African Americans.

In cities across the Northeast and the Midwest, abolitionist societies, made up of people who shared Garrison's views, sprang up. Founded by Garrison in 1833, the American Anti-Slavery Society had over 150,000 members nationally by 1840. However, membership was restricted to men. To allow women to participate in the cause, the Philadelphia Female Anti-Slavery Society was formed in 1833. This organization was the nation's first biracial organization of female abolitionists.

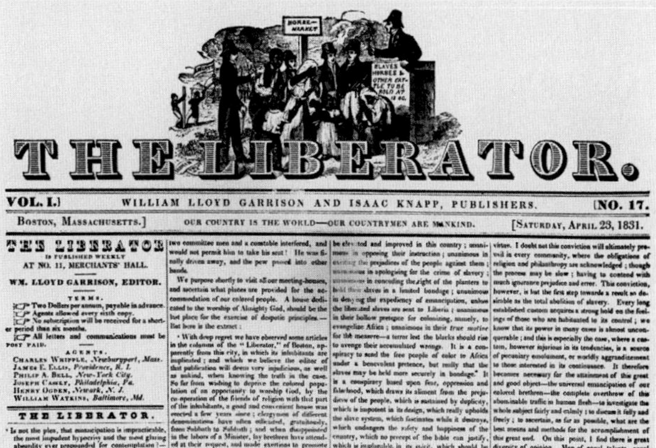

THE LIBERATOR.

VOL. I.] WILLIAM LLOYD GARRISON AND ISAAC KNAPP, PUBLISHERS. [NO. 17.

BOSTON, MASSACHUSETTS.] OUR COUNTRY IS THE WORLD—OUR COUNTRYMEN ARE MANKIND. [SATURDAY, APRIL 23, 1831.

THE LIBERATOR
IS PUBLISHED WEEKLY
AT NO. 11, MERCHANTS' HALL.

WM. LLOYD GARRISON, EDITOR.

TERMS.
☞ Two Dollars per annum, payable in advance.
☞ Agents allowed every sixth copy.
☞ No subscription will be received for a shorter period than six months.
☞ All letters and communications must be POST PAID.

AGENTS.
Charles Whipple, *Newburyport, Mass.*
James E. Ellis, *Providence, R. I.*
Philip A. Bell, *New-York City.*
Joseph Cassey, *Philadelphia, Pa.*
Henry Ogden, *Newark, N. J.*
William Watkins, *Baltimore, Md.*

THE LIBERATOR.

'Is not the plea, that emancipation is impracticable, the most impudent hypocrisy and the most glaring absurdity ever propounded for contemplation?—Can any suppositious expediency, any dread of political disorder, or any private advantage, justify the prolongation of corruption, the enormity of which is unequalled, or repel the holy claim to its extinction! The system is so entirely corrupt, that it admits of no cure but by a TOTAL and IMMEDIATE abolition. For a gradual emancipation is a virtual recognition of the right, and establishes the rectitude of the practice. If it be just for one moment, it is hallowed for ever; and if it be inequitable, not a day should it be tolerated.'
BOURNE.

two committee men and a constable interfered, and would not permit him to take his seat! He was finally driven away, and the pew passed into other hands.

We purpose shortly to visit all our meeting-houses, and ascertain what places are provided for the accommodation of our colored people. A house dedicated to the worship of Almighty God, should be the last place for the exercise of despotic principles.—But here is the extract:

'With deep regret we have observed some articles in the columns of the "Liberator," of Boston, apparently from this city, in which its inhabitants are implicated; and which we believe the editor of that publication will deem very injudicious, as well as unkind, when knowing the truth in the case. So far from wishing to deprive the colored population of an opportunity to worship God, by the co-operation of the friends of religion with that part of the inhabitants, a good and convenient house was erected a few years since; clergymen of different denominations have often officiated, gratuitously, from Sabbath to Sabbath; and when disappointed in the labors of a Minister, lay brethren have attended at their request, and made exertions to promote the prosperity of their congregation; for many years a Sabbath School has been taught, composed entirely of colored children and adults; in addition to this, if we mistake not, at their request the public school money is given them in proportion to the number of their children, and they thus have a day school of their own.

After such interest had been shown for that class of people, was it to be expected that an attack should be made upon the very persons who have shown such liberality? This is indeed gratifying to the enemies of benevolent exertions; and were the

be elevated and improved in this country; unanimous in opposing their instruction; unanimous in exciting the prejudices of the people against them; unanimous in apologising for the crime of slavery; unanimous in conceding the right of the planters to hold their slaves in a limited bondage; unanimous in denying the expediency of emancipation, unless the liberated slaves are sent to Liberia; unanimous in their hollow pretence for colonizing, namely, to evangelize Africa; unanimous in their *true motive* for the measure—a terror lest the blacks should rise to avenge their accumulated wrongs. It is a conspiracy to send the free people of color to Africa under a benevolent pretence, but really that the slaves may be held more securely in bondage." It is a conspiracy based upon fear, oppression and falsehood, which draws its aliment from the prejudices of the people, which is sustained by duplicity, which is impotent in its design, which really upholds the slave system, which fascinates while it destroys, which endangers the safety and happiness of the country, which no precept of the bible can justify, which is implacable in its *spirit*, which should be annihilated at a blow.

These are our accusations; and if we do not substantiate them, we are willing to be covered with reproach.

In attacking the principles, and exposing the evil tendency of the Society, we wish no one to understand us as saying, that all its friends are equally guilty, or actuated by the same motives. Nor let him suppose, that we exonerate any of them from

virtue. I doubt not this conviction will ultimately prevail in every community, where the obligations of religion and philanthropy are acknowledged; though the process may be slow; having to contend with much ignorance prejudice and error. This conviction, however, is but the first step towards a result so desirable as the total abolition of slavery. Every long established custom acquires a strong hold on the feelings of those who are habituated to its control; we know that its power in many cases is almost unconquerable; and this is especially the case, where a custom, however injurious in its tendencies, is a source of pecuniary emolument, or worldly aggrandizement to those interested in its continuance. It therefore becomes necessary for the attainment of this great and good object—the universal emancipation of our colored brethren—the complete overthrow of this abominable traffic in human flesh—to investigate the whole subject fairly and calmly; to discuss it fully and freely; to ascertain, as far as possible, what are the best means and methods for the accomplishment of this great end. On this point, I find there is great diversity of opinion. Men of equal talents, equal piety, and equal benevolence, take different and almost opposite views of the whole subject: my mind has been much perplexed, by hearing what seemed to me very strong arguments on both sides of the question.

With regard to the main subject, universal emancipation, as I before remarked, I have no doubt. I think it may, and it ought to be accomplished; but with regard to the means of its accomplishment, I do

>> Founded by Boston printer and abolitionist William Lloyd Garrison, *The Liberator* appealed to readers' sense of morality in the hopes of persuading them that slavery was wrong and must be ended immediately.

The American Anti-Slavery society implemented moral suasion by printing antislavery pamphlets and distributing them to churches and other community organizations. The American Anti-Slavery Society and similar groups also supported a team of hundreds of lecturers who spoke against slavery at camp meetings and other public gatherings. They insisted that enslaving human beings was counter to most Americans' religious ideals.

Other Abolitionist Leaders Theodore Weld, a student at the Lane Theological Seminary in Ohio, became another leading abolitionist. Weld shared Garrison's belief in the power of moral suasion. However, whereas Garrison resorted to public confrontation, Weld chose to work through the churches. Weld married Angelina Grimké, the daughter of a southern enslaver, who was so moved by the abolition movement that she went north to join it. She and her sister Sarah Grimké spoke and wrote against slavery. Another well-known abolitionist, and arguably the most eloquent, was **Frederick Douglass**, a former slave whose booming voice filled lecture halls with touching stories about the difficulty of his life as a slave.

>> Many southerners opposed abolitionism. This illustration shows the burning of abolitionist newspapers by South Carolina slavery supporters in 1835. **Infer** How did slavery create an atmosphere of violence even for those who were not enslaved?

David Ruggles was another important African American abolitionist leader who became involved in the anti-slavery movement in New York in the 1830s. Ruggles wrote for newspapers throughout the Northeast and established the first Black-owned bookstore, where he sold anti-slavery publications. He was also active on the Underground Railroad, helping hundreds of enslaved people find freedom, including Frederick Douglass.

CHECK UNDERSTANDING How did abolitionists attempt to bring about the end of slavery in the United States?

The Backlash Against Abolition

Despite the growing call of abolitionists, most Americans continued to support slavery. The voices against abolition came from both the slave states of the South and the free states of the North.

Southerners Defend Slavery As abolitionists were developing their arguments against slavery, southern enslavers intensified their arguments in support of it. They publicized their conviction that slavery was necessary because it formed the foundation of the South's agricultural economy. Moreover, they argued, slavery benefited the North, since the North's textile and shipping industries depended upon southern cotton.

They further maintained that a slave labor force was superior to the wage labor force of the North. They argued that northern employers and laborers would be inevitably at odds, since employers wanted workers to work more for less money while workers wanted to work less for more money.

Enslavers maintained that in contrast, such conflict was avoided in the South, where the well-being of enslaved people depended on their enslavers' fortunes and enslavers' fortunes depended on the well-being of their enslaved people.

But some southerners went even further, claiming that the Bible supported slavery, that enslaved people could not survive without enslavers, and that the enslavement of Africans was historically inevitable. Such assertions were clearly racist, but many people of the time believed them.

As abolitionist rhetoric grew more strident, southern support for gradual manumission, or freeing, of enslaved people decreased. Southern spokespeople stepped up their arguments about the value of slavery, and southern enslavers tried to prevent southerners from reading abolitionist publications. Post offices refused to deliver abolitionist newspapers. Southerners—even many of those who did not own enslaved people—embraced slavery as their preferred way of life, to be defended at all costs.

Resistance to Abolition in the North Southerners were not alone in their resistance to abolition. Most northerners agreed with them and many organized to oppose abolitionist aims. In Boston in 1835, Garrison was chased through the streets by an angry mob as a result of his antislavery views. In Philadelphia in 1838, the Grimké-Weld wedding, attended by both white and African American guests, so infuriated local residents that they burned down the antislavery meeting hall. In Alton, Illinois, irate crowds destroyed abolitionist newspaper editor Elijah Lovejoy's printing press several times, killing Lovejoy himself in November 1837.

In city after city, white workers, fearing African American competitors would take their jobs, launched stiff resistance to abolition. Wealthy industrialists resented the presence of African American entrepreneurs in their midst. They also worried that the end of slavery would cut off the supply of southern cotton for northern textile mills.

Many white northerners were biased against Southern politicians and institutions, but they did not want to wrestle with the problems of African Americans either. They wanted to stay out of the controversy about slavery.

When southern politicians pushed a **Gag Rule**, a law which prohibited debate and discussion in Congress on the subject of slavery, some northerners supported them. First passed in 1836, the Gag Rule was renewed annually for eight years.

Slavery Divides the Nation Although the abolition movement remained small and mostly confined to the North, it was vocal—and persistent. The debate over slavery divided Americans like no other issue. It widened regional cultural differences between the largely urban and industrialized North and the largely rural and agricultural South. Indeed, the divisive issue of slavery would soon prove to be a major factor as the country began to break apart.

IDENTIFY CENTRAL ISSUES Why did many Americans oppose abolishing slavery?

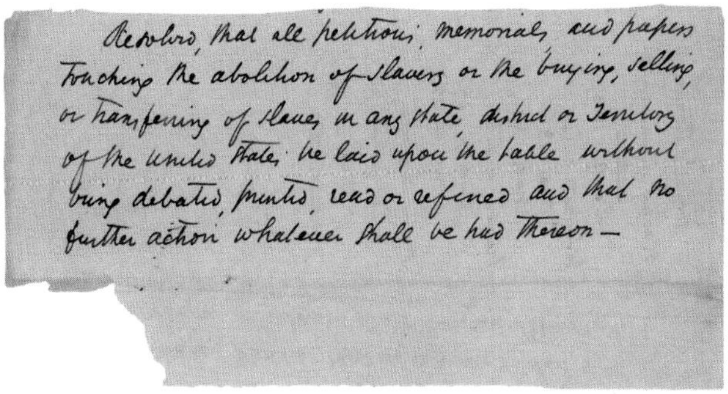
Resolved, that all petitions, memorials, and papers touching the abolition of slavery or the buying, selling, or transferring of slaves, in any State, district or Territory of the United States, be laid upon the table without being debated, printed, read or referred and that no further action whatever shall be had thereon —

>> Passed in 1836, the Gag Rule prevented all discussion of matters pertaining to slavery in the U.S. Congress.

ASSESSMENT

1. **Identify Cause and Effect** How did Nat Turner and Denmark Vesey lead slave revolts in the 1800s, and what effect did their efforts have on slavery in the South?
2. **Support Ideas with Evidence** What was the purpose of the American Colonization Society, and why were most free African Americans wary of the Society?
3. **Compare and Contrast** What did William Lloyd Garrison do to promote the abolition movement? How did his views differ from those of most abolitionists at the time?
4. **Generate Explanations** Discuss some of the reasons many northerners opposed abolition in the 1800s.
5. **Quest Connections** How did the institution of slavery expand in the South in the early 1800s, and what were living conditions like for enslaved people during that time?

GO ONLINE to access these biographies: Frederick Douglass; William Lloyd Garrison

Independence Day Speech: Frederick Douglass

Frederick Douglass was one of the leading figures of the movement to abolish slavery. As a former slave himself, he had first-hand knowledge of the brutality of slavery and traveled the world demanding its abolition. His eloquence and passion made him one of the most famous speakers of his day.

In 1852, Douglass accepted an invitation from the leading citizens of Rochester, New York, to speak at their Fourth of July celebration. Douglass delivered a scathing speech in which he attacked the hypocrisy of celebrating independence and freedom in a nation where millions of people were enslaved.

>> Photograph of Frederick Douglass taken around 1855

. . . Fellow-citizens, pardon me, allow me to ask, why am I called upon to speak here to-day? What have I, or those I represent, to do with your national independence? Are the great principles of political freedom and of natural justice, embodied in that Declaration of Independence, extended to us?. . .

DETERMINE AUTHOR'S POINT OF VIEW Which lines in the Declaration of Independence represent "the great principles of political freedom and natural justice"? Why would those lines ring hollow to an enslaved person or an abolitionist?

Your high independence only reveals the immeasurable distance between us. The blessings in which you, this day, rejoice, are not enjoyed in common. The rich inheritance of justice, liberty, prosperity and independence, bequeathed by your fathers, is shared by you, not by me. The sunlight that brought light and healing to you, has brought stripes and death to me. This Fourth July is yours, not mine. You may rejoice, I must mourn. To drag a man in fetters [chains] into the grand illuminated temple of liberty, and call upon him to join you in joyous anthems, were inhuman mockery and sacrilegious irony. Do you mean, citizens, to mock me, by asking me to speak to-day?. . .

Must I undertake to prove that the slave is a man? . . . The slaveholders themselves acknowledge it in the enactment of laws for their government. They acknowledge it when they punish disobedience on the part of the slave. There are seventy-two crimes in the State of Virginia which, if committed by a black man . . . subject him to the punishment of death; while only two of the same crimes will subject a white man to the like punishment. What is this but the acknowledgment that the slave is a moral, intellectual, and responsible being? . . . It is admitted in the fact that

Southern statute books are covered with enactments forbidding, under severe fines and penalties, the teaching of the slave to read or to write. . . .

EXPLAIN AN ARGUMENT How does Douglass prove that even slaveholders recognize that the enslaved person is a human being?

What, am I to argue that it is wrong to make men brutes, to rob them of their liberty, to work them without wages, to keep them ignorant of their relations to their fellow men, to beat them with sticks, to flay their flesh with the lash, to load their limbs with irons, to hunt them with dogs, to sell them at auction, to sunder their families, to knock out their teeth, to burn their flesh, to starve them into obedience and submission to their masters? Must I argue that a system thus marked with blood, and stained with pollution, is wrong?. . . .

ANALYZE WORD CHOICE Douglass asks questions beginning with "am I to argue" and "Must I argue". What is he trying to say here?

What, to the American slave, is your 4th of July? I answer; a day that reveals to him, more than all other days in the year, the gross injustice and cruelty to which he is the constant victim. To him, your celebration is a sham; your boasted liberty, an unholy license; your national greatness, swelling vanity; your sounds of rejoicing are empty and heartless; your denunciation of tyrants, brass fronted impudence; your shouts of liberty and equality, hollow mockery; your prayers and hymns, your sermons and thanksgivings, with all your religious parade and solemnity, are, to him, mere bombast, fraud, deception, impiety, and hypocrisy—a thin veil to cover up crimes which would disgrace a nation of savages. . . .

Allow me to say, in conclusion, notwithstanding the dark picture I have this day presented, of the state of the nation, I do not despair of this country. There are forces in operation which must inevitably work the downfall of slavery. "The arm of the Lord is not shortened," and the doom of slavery is certain. I, therefore, leave off where I began, with hope. While drawing encouragement from "the Declaration of Independence," the great principles it contains, and the genius of American Institutions, my spirit is also cheered by the obvious tendencies of the age.

DETERMINE CENTRAL IDEAS What are the "forces" that will bring about the downfall of slavery?

ASSESSMENT

1. **Determine Central Ideas** In the first two paragraphs above, Douglass addresses the audience as "fellow citizens" but then sets up a contrast between two separate groups of people. Which group does he represent? Which group is he addressing?
2. **Compare and Contrast** What contrast does Douglass draw between the lives of enslaved people and the lives of free citizens?
3. **Analyze Style and Rhetoric** How does Douglass use religion to give moral weight to his argument against slavery?
4. **Determine Meaning** What allows Douglass to end on a hopeful note? How will the principles of the Declaration of Independence help abolish slavery?

GO ONLINE to access primary sources

6.6

This cartoon depicts the Seneca Falls Convention in New York in 1848. **Interpret** Does this cartoon depict the event in a humorous or serious way? Explain the behavior of the spectators in the galleries.

BOUNCE to Activate Flipped Video

Objectives

Identify the limits faced by American women in the early 1800s.

Trace the development of the women's movement.

Describe the Seneca Falls Convention and its effects.

Key Terms

matrilineal
Sojourner Truth
women's movement
Lucretia Mott
Elizabeth Cady Stanton
Seneca Falls Convention
Amelia Bloomer
suffrage
Married Women's Property Act

Women Work for Change

A spirit of reform permeated American life in the early and middle 1800s. Women took active roles in the abolition movement and other reform movements. Soon, some of these reformers began to work to gain equality for women as well. Their efforts would lay the groundwork for women's struggle for equal rights over the next hundred years.

Women Fight for Reforms

In the 1800s, American women's freedoms and rights were sharply limited. Instead of taking a powerful role in public life, women were expected to make a difference privately, by influencing their husbands and raising their children to be good citizens. But this idealized role was too limiting for women. Largely as a result of the Second Great Awakening, women of the early 1800s began to take on more active roles in public life.

Women's Rights Are Limited In the early 1800s, American women lacked many basic legal and economic rights. Under the ancient legal traditions that dominated the United States, women usually could not hold property or hold office or vote, and they were discouraged from speaking at public gatherings. Formal educational opportunities for American women were virtually unheard of. In the rare instances of divorce, husbands generally gained custody of children.

Some of the groups living in America—certain American Indians, African Americans, and Mexican Americans—had a tradition of affording women a significant amount of power. In these cultures, women controlled or influenced work patterns and family structures. Some cultures were **matrilineal**, that is, the inheritance of family names and property followed the female line in the family. But for most American women, legal and economic rights lagged far, far behind those of American men.

Women Take Advantage of New Opportunities

The drive to reform American society created by the Second Great Awakening provided new opportunities for women. Many joined reform groups sponsored by their churches. Women played leading roles in all of the great reform movements of the day.

Catharine Beecher, Emma Willard, Elizabeth Blackwell, and Ann Preston advanced education during the public school movement. Dorothea Dix almost single-handedly launched reforms in the way the country treated prisoners and people who suffered from mental illness. Most community leaders of the temperance movement were women; after all, they and their children were the primary victims of alcohol abuse among men.

The abolition movement attracted some of the most thoughtful women of the day, including Angelina and Sarah Grimké. Many abolitionist groups, like the Philadelphia Female Anti-Slavery Society, were made up entirely of women. One of the most effective abolitionist lecturers was **Sojourner Truth**, a former slave from New York who held audiences spellbound with her powerful speeches.

Women Enter the Workplace In the 1820s and 1830s, the Northeast was rapidly industrializing. This provided the first real economic opportunity in the nation's history for women to work outside the home. Thousands of young women, who previously would have stayed in the family home, went to work in the new mills and factories.

This gave many women a small degree of economic independence (although their wages were typically sent to their husbands or fathers) and a larger degree of social independence as they developed networks of friendships with other factory workers. By 1830, a few women's labor unions had formed, and some groups had held strikes for better wages and working conditions.

☑ **CHECK UNDERSTANDING** What led to women becoming leaders of various reform movements?

Women Seek Expanded Rights

Although many women became leading reformers, and many others entered the workforce, there had still been virtually no progress in women's rights. Real progress began only when two historical trends coincided in the 1830s. First, many urban middle-class northern women began to hire servants to do their housework, allowing these middle-class women more time to think about the society in which they wanted to raise their children. Second, some abolitionist women began to notice some similarities between slavery and the restrictions placed on their own lives.

The Origins of the Women's Rights Movement

The similarities between the powerlessness of enslaved African Americans and the powerlessness

Political and Economic Status of Women in the Early 1800s

Women could not vote.
Women could not hold public office.
Women could not serve on juries.
Few women received any level of higher education.
Women could not work in most trades or professions.
When they did work, women were paid less than men doing the same jobs, and their fathers or husbands often took what money they did earn.
Married women lost legal control of any money or property they owned before marriage to their husbands. Married women could not testify against their husbands in court, sue for divorce, or gain custody of their children.

>> **Analyze Charts** Given the restrictions listed in this chart, how much freedom did women have in the early 1800s?

BOUNCE to Activate Chart

>> During the 1800s, middle-class women were seen as domestic caretakers and moral guardians of the home. **Analyze Primary Sources** What does this illustration suggest about women's work and status?

>> Elizabeth Cady Stanton and her daughter in 1856

of women were hard to ignore. In fact, many women argued that their lack of rights made them almost the same as enslaved people. These women, along with a handful of men in the abolition movement, began to work for women's rights.

They began the **women's movement**, a movement working for greater rights and opportunities for women, of the early and middle 1800s. This stage of the women's movement lasted throughout the 1800s and into the early 1900s.

Women's rights reformers began to publish their ideas in pamphlets and books. One of these reformers was the Transcendentalist writer Margaret Fuller, who believed that what women needed was not personal power but "as a nature to grow, as an intellect to discern, as a soul to live freely and unimpeded, to unfold such powers as were given her . . .". The Grimké sisters also published their ideas on women's rights. In *Letters on the Equality of the Sexes and the Condition of Women*, Sarah Grimké argued that God made men and women equal and that therefore men and women should be treated equally. Building on her sister's ideas, Angelina Grimké Weld defended the rights of both enslaved people and women on moral grounds.

> The investigation of the rights of the slave has led me to a better understanding of my own. . . . Human beings have *rights,* because they are *moral* beings. . . [I]f rights are founded on the nature of our moral being, then the *mere circumstance of sex* does not give to man higher rights and responsibilities, than to woman.
>
> —Angelina Grimké, *Letters to Catherine E. Beecher,* 1838

Disagreement Within the Women's Movement

The women who spoke up for full equality were a small minority, however. Even among abolitionists there was disagreement about how much public leadership women should take. When an international abolitionist convention met in London in 1840, the group fractured over whether women should be allowed to join in the men's business meetings. Some abolitionists thought that they should not. Two who thought they should were **Lucretia Mott** and **Elizabeth Cady Stanton**.

Both Mott and Stanton were active reformers, supporting particularly the temperance and abolitionist causes. Mott had helped found the

WOMEN IN THE 1800s

OPPORTUNITIES FOR SOCIAL MOBILITY

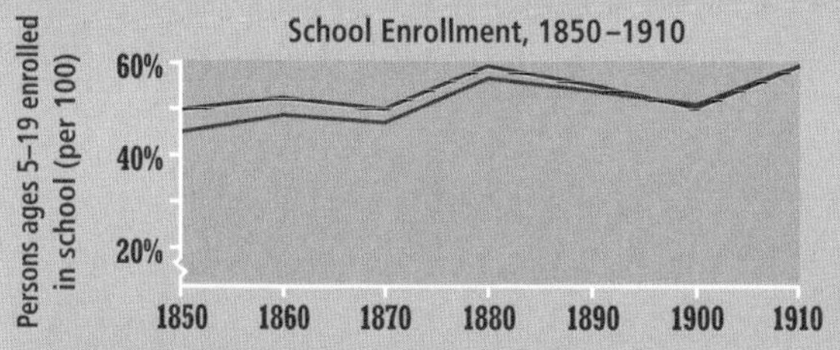

Source: *Historical Statistics of the United States*

"WE WOULD HAVE EVERY PATH LAID OPEN TO WOMAN AS FREELY AS TO MAN.

—Margaret Fuller, *Woman in the Nineteenth Century*

LITERACY RATES

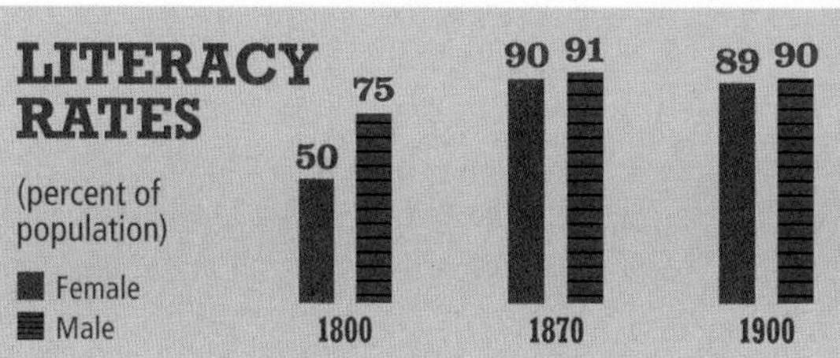

Sources: *Nineteenth-Century Women Learn to Write;* UNESCO

EXPANDED OPPORTUNITIES 1800–1920

PUBLIC PRIMARY AND SECONDARY SCHOOL TEACHERS

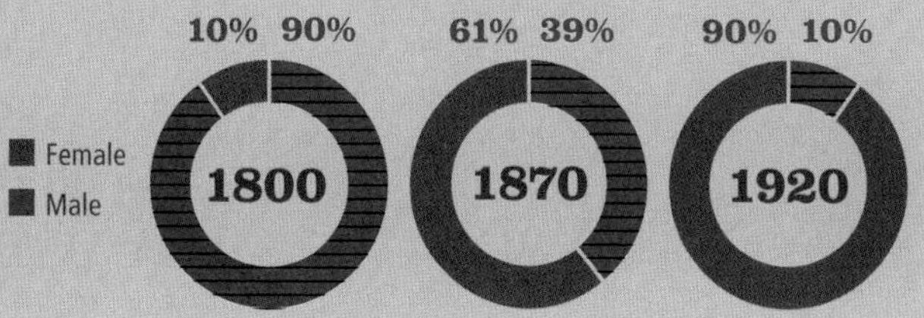

Sources: Binghamton University; *Historical Statistics of the United States*

>> **Analyze Information** Based on this infographic, how did educational opportunities for women change during the 1800s and early 1900s?

BOUNCE to Activate Timeline

American Anti-Slavery Society and the Philadelphia Female Anti-Slavery Society. Stanton was married to a leading abolitionist, Henry Stanton. (Both Elizabeth and Henry were already keenly interested in women's rights.) These two women, outraged that women were refused full participation at a meeting to discuss the promotion of human decency and equality, were inspired to take a dramatic step to advance women's rights.

IDENTIFY MAIN IDEAS What conditions led women to organize and push for equal rights?

The Seneca Falls Convention

In 1848, Mott and Stanton helped organize the nation's first Women's Rights Convention in Seneca Falls, New York. Often called the **Seneca Falls Convention**, the meeting attracted hundreds of men and women. One of the most illustrious participants was Frederick Douglass. The delegates to the convention adopted a "Declaration of Sentiments," modeled after the language of the Declaration of Independence. The Declaration of Sentiments was ridiculed, and the convention resulted in few concrete improvements in women's rights. It did, however, mark the beginning of the women's movement in the United States.

Inspiring Women The Seneca Falls Convention inspired generations of young women. One of these was **Amelia Bloomer**, who actually attended the convention. While she remained relatively quiet there, she would soon become a leading voice for women's rights. In the following years, Bloomer published a newspaper, *The Lily*, in which she advocated equality of women in all things—including the right to wear pants instead of dresses.

Another woman who drew inspiration from the convention was Susan B. Anthony, whose involvement in the temperance and abolition movements led her to work for greater rights for women as well. Anthony would help lead the charge to win a single, critical right for women: the right to vote. This quest for **suffrage** would prove to be a long, hard fight.

Women Gain Some Rights In 1848, the same year as the Seneca Falls Convention, the state of New York passed a law, the **Married Women's Property Act**, guaranteeing many property rights for women. Elizabeth Cady Stanton had worked hard for its passage. Twelve years later, the law was amended to make it more comprehensive. New York's efforts to advance property rights for women would become a model for similar laws in other states in the years to come.

By the middle 1800s, American women had laid the foundation for a future in which equality seemed a real possibility. They had become wage earners. They had become reformers. And they had started to voice their call for justice.

CHECK UNDERSTANDING What was the significance of the Seneca Falls Conference to the women's movement?

ASSESSMENT

1. **Support Ideas with Examples** What legal limitations did women face in the United States during the early 1800s? How did the rights of women in certain minority groups differ from the majority?
2. **Summarize** some of the ways in which women became involved with reform movements in the 1800s.
3. **Paraphrase** Briefly describe how the Women's Rights Movement began and summarize its main argument.
4. **Hypothesize** Why were most women barred from holding leadership positions in the abolition movement, and how did Lucretia Mott and Elizabeth Cady Stanton's involvement in the movement inspire them to take a dramatic step towards advancing women's rights?
5. **Connections to Today** Educational opportunities increased for women in the 1800s. Why does education remain the key to expanding rights for women today?

GO ONLINE to access this biography: Elizabeth Cady Stanton

Connections to Today

Young people protest in New York city against banks profiting from student loans.

Take Action About Public Funding of Higher Education

During the 1800s, Americans debated whether it was right for the government to fund public schools. Today, a similar debate is raging over the public funding of higher education.

1. **Choose** one of the following funding for higher education-related topics:
    - **State funding cuts:** Research the effects of state funding cuts on higher education after the Great Recession.
    - **Funding differences:** Investigate how private and public educational institutions are funded.
    - **Growing need:** Look into why demands for public funding of higher education are increasing.
2. **Ask Questions** Create a list of questions you have about the topic.
3. **Learn** about your topic, using a variety of sources, such as online sources, primary and/or secondary sources, data, or interviews. Are there any major debates related to the topic or issues? What are the strongest arguments on each side of the debate? Take roles as you conduct your research and continue to generate questions as you learn more.
4. **Have a Debate** Organize a debate with classmates, choosing sides to either support or oppose publicly funded education.

Topic 6 Quick Study Guide

LESSON SUMMARIES

Use these Lesson Summaries, and the longer versions available online, to review the key ideas for each lesson in this Topic.

Lesson 1: Moving West

After Mexico gained independence from Spain in 1821, American trade in Mexican territory increased and westward migration began. Although these lands were still occupied by American Indians, a belief in Manifest Destiny encouraged Americans to migrate west to California, Oregon, and Utah.

Lesson 2: Texas and the Mexican-American War

The annexation of Texas in 1845 further enflamed the border dispute between Texas and Mexico. Mexico refused to recognize the annexation. The dispute led to war between the U.S. and Mexico.

Lesson 3: The Nation Expands to the Pacific

After the Mexican-American War, the United States gained territory in what is now southern Arizona and New Mexico. These new lands, while fulfilling the goal of Manifest Destiny, intensified the fight over slavery.

Lesson 4: A Religious Awakening Sparks Reform

Starting in the 1800s, a strong revival of religious feeling, known as the Second Great Awakening, swept through the country. The movement inspired Americans to improve their lives and the lives of others.

Lesson 5: The Abolition Movement

The debate over slavery continued to intensify. Some Americans favored ending slavery gradually. A growing Abolition movement, however, strengthened efforts to end slavery immediately.

Lesson 6: Women Work for Change

Women were active in the rising reform movements in the early and middle 1800s. Soon, efforts turned toward seeking greater equality for women. That fight would continue for decades to come.

QUEST! FINDINGS

Westward Movement and the Issue of Slavery Refer to your responses to the Quest Connections to help you investigate documents and write your essay. Use the rubric and other Quest resources online to guide your work.

GO ONLINE to access lesson summaries

VISUAL REVIEW

Use these graphics to review some of the key terms, people, and ideas from this Topic.

Expansion of the United States, 1800–1850

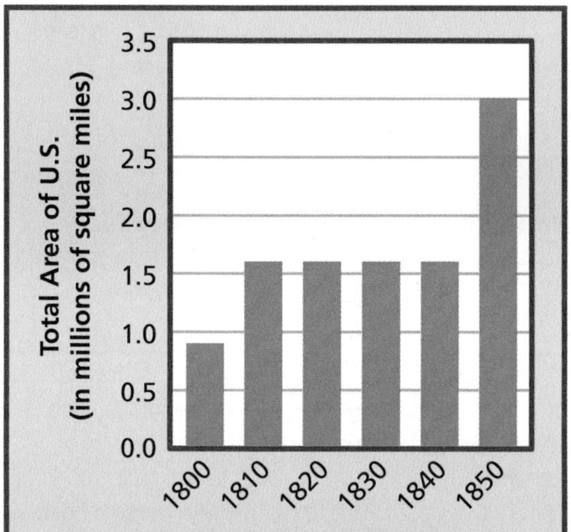

Source: Historical Standards of the United States: Colonial Times to 1970

Causes and Effects of Westward Movement

CAUSES

- Oregon has fertile land.
- Texas is ideal for raising cattle and growing cotton.
- Many Americans believe in Manifest Destiny.
- Mormons seek a safe home.
- Gold is discovered in California.

↓

WESTWARD MOVEMENT

↓

EFFECTS

- Texas wins war for independence.
- United States annexes Texas.
- Britain and United States divide Oregon.
- United States defeats Mexico in war.
- Cotton Kingdom spreads.

The Spirit of Reform

Reform Movements

Social Reform

- Humane treatment for mentally ill
- Prison reform
- Temperance movement against alcohol
- Improvements in education

Anti-Slavery Movement

- End of slavery in the North
- Establishment of Liberia
- Abolitionist speeches, books, and newspapers
- Underground railroad

Women's Rights Movement

- Seneca Falls Convention
- Schools for Women
- New legal rights in some states
- New work opportunities

Topic 6 Assessment

KEY TERMS, PEOPLE, AND IDEAS

1. How did American **expansionists** justify their interest in gaining new territories?
2. How did Texans force **Santa Anna** to grant them independence?
3. How did the **Treaty of Guadalupe Hidalgo** affect the American goal towards achieving Manifest Destiny?
4. Why did people seek to establish **utopian communities** between 1820 and 1850?
5. What was the purpose of the **Gag Rule**?
6. Why did slavery end earlier in the North than in the South?
7. How did laws discriminate against women in the early 1800s?
8. Explain how **transcendentalism** affected the reform movement.
9. What were some of the reforms **Horace Mann** sought for public education?

CRITICAL THINKING

10. **Summarize** Describe the events that led Texans to declare their independence from Mexico.
11. **Analyze Information** What problems would arise if California were added to the Union?
12. **Summarize** What sparked the rise of the reform movement in the mid-1800s?
13. **Explain an Argument** Why might some abolitionists have supported a gradual end to slavery? What position do you think Frederick Douglass or William Lloyd Garrison would have taken?
14. **Draw Conclusions** Discuss the positive and negative factors of Manifest Destiny.
15. **Draw Inferences** Why do you think some women were opposed to women's suffrage?
16. **Use Visual Information** Study the map. Why do you think most of the uprisings of enslaved people took place in the South?

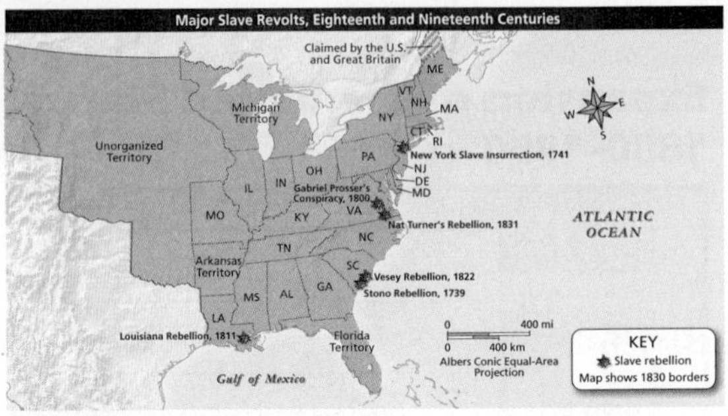

17. **Writing Activity: Write an Explanatory Essay** Frederick Douglass denounced the trade in enslaved people in this 1852 speech at the New York Abolitionist Society:

> "Fellow citizens, this murderous traffic is, today, in active operation in this boasted republic. I see the bleeding footsteps; I hear the doleful wail of [chained] humanity on the way to the slave markets where the victims are to be sold like horse, sheep, and swine. . . . My soul sickens at the sight."

(1) What words does Douglass use to stir up anger against the trade in enslaved people? (2) What does he mean when he refers to "this boasted republic"? (3) Why was he an effective speaker for the cause?

18. **Connections to Today** Today many argue that the rising costs of higher education is increasing income inequality because poorer students cannot afford to get a college degree. Others wonder why taxpayers should fund the education of those whose degrees will eventually enable them to earn higher wages than most taxpayers. What are some other arguments against publicly funded higher education?

DOCUMENT-BASED QUESTIONS

During and immediately after the American Revolution, northern states passed laws gradually ending slavery. In 1808, Congress prohibited bringing any more African slaves into the country. Yet, the institution persisted. The documents below provide different points of view on slavery. Read the documents, then answer the questions that follow.

DOCUMENT A

Design for a British anti-slavery medallion

DOCUMENT B

In this excerpt, an enslaver defends slavery by contrasting the suffering of wage laborers in the North with the food and lodging provided to enslaved people in the South.

"When the day's labor is ended, [the wage laborer] is free, but is overburdened with the cares of family and household, which makes the freedom an empty and delusive [deceptive] mockery. . .. The Negro slave is free, too, when the labors of the day are over and free in mind as well as body, for the master provides food, raiment [clothing], house, fuel, and everything else necessary to the physical well-being of himself and family."

—*From Cannibals All! Or Slaves Without Masters* by George Fitzhugh

DOCUMENT C

"Slavery is ruinous to whites—retards improvement—roots out industrious population, banishes the yeomanry [farmers] of the country—deprives the spinner, the weaver, the blacksmith, the shoemaker, the carpenter of employment and support. The evil admits no remedy—it will continue to increase, until the whole country will be inundated with one black wave. . . . Labor of every species is disreputable because [it is] performed mostly by slaves. . . and the general aspect of the countryside marks the curse of a wasteful, idle, reckless population who have no interest in the soil. . . ."

—*From the speech given by a delegate at the Virginia legislature, Niles' Weekly Register, vol. 43, Sept. 8, 1832*

DOCUMENT D

". . . we, (coloured people of these United States) are the most degraded, wretched, and abject set of beings that ever lived since the world began. . . . The Indians of North and South America—the Greeks—the Irish, subjected under the king of Great Britain—the Jews, that ancient people of the Lord—the inhabitants of the islands of the sea. . . all the inhabitants of the earth, (except, however, those sons of Africa) are called men, and of course are and ought to be free. But we, (coloured people) and our children are brutes! And of course are. . . Slaves to the American people and their children forever!! To dig their mines and work their farms; and thus go on enriching them; from one generation to another with our blood and our tears."

—*From Appeal to the Coloured Citizens of the World by David Walker*

19. Documents A and D both emphasize

A. the hope that all men will one day be treated as brothers

B. enslaved Africans in Britain were freed before enslaved people in America

C. the importance of being treated as fellow human beings

D. the need to constantly ask for an equal place in society

20. In Document B, the enslaver's argument

A. deliberately distorts the meaning of the word *free*.

B. supports the idea that only wage laborers enjoy true freedom.

C. suggests that wage laborers and enslaved people are equally free.

D. could be used to support abolition.

21. What conclusion does the speaker in Document C make about the effect of slavery on the economy?

A. Maintaining enslaved people is expensive but the owner does benefit.

B. The labor market is ruined because so many jobs were now performed by enslaved people.

C. Agricultural labor is responsible for an increase in market goods.

D. Slave labor is the answer to the crumbling economy in the South.

22. Writing Task What points of view did people have about slavery? Use information from the Topic, along with information from these documents to support your answer. Consider frames of reference, biases, and the ways people presented and justified their positions.

GO ONLINE to access more practice

Topic 7

Sectional Divisions and Civil War
(1846–1865)

ESSENTIAL QUESTION When is war justified?

GO ONLINE to access the eText, videos, Interactive Primary Sources, Biographies, and other online sources.

President Abraham Lincoln

Connections to Today

The Civil War revealed just how divided the nation could become. Today, more than 150 years later, our nation is still divided over many issues. This has been the case since the nation began, with active citizens voicing their concerns and debating important topics over time.

The North and South still exist today, and many new regions have formed since then. How do Americans still disagree today? Do views differ by region? How do we handle such differences? Consider these questions as you read about the Civil War.

NBC LEARN

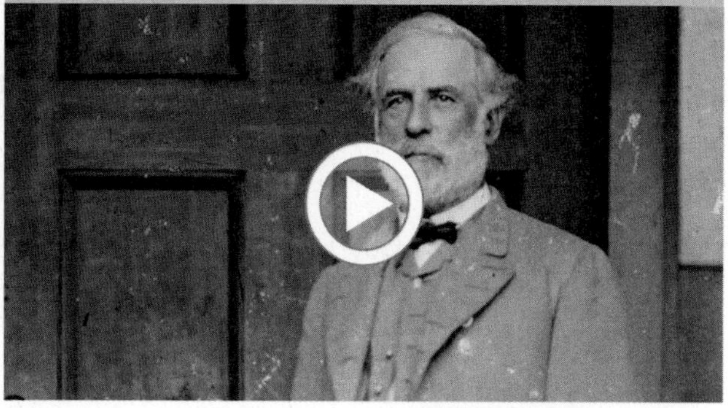

Learn about Robert E. Lee, "the marble man."

BOUNCE to Activate My Story Video

Topic 7 Overview

In this Topic, you'll learn more about the divisive issue of slavery, how conflict between the North and South led to the Civil War, and how the war impacted both sides in the conflict. Look at the lesson outline and explore the timeline. As you study this Topic, you'll complete the Quest Inquiry.

LESSON OUTLINE

7.1 Slavery Divides the Nation

7.2 Violence Escalates

7.3 The Civil War Begins

7.4 African Americans and the War

7.5 Everyday Life During the War

7.6 Key Civil War Battles

7.7 The Impact of the Civil War

Key Events of the Sectional Divisions and Civil War (1850–1865)

1850
Compromise of 1850

1857
Supreme Court rules in *Dred Scott* case

1859
John Brown's raid on Harpers Ferry, Virginia

1861
Civil War begins

1861
1st Battle of Bull Run near Manassas, Virginia

1863
Emancipation Proclamation

1865
Lee surrenders at Appomattox Court House, Virginia

1865
Lincoln assassinated by John Wilkes Booth

1850 1855 1860 1865

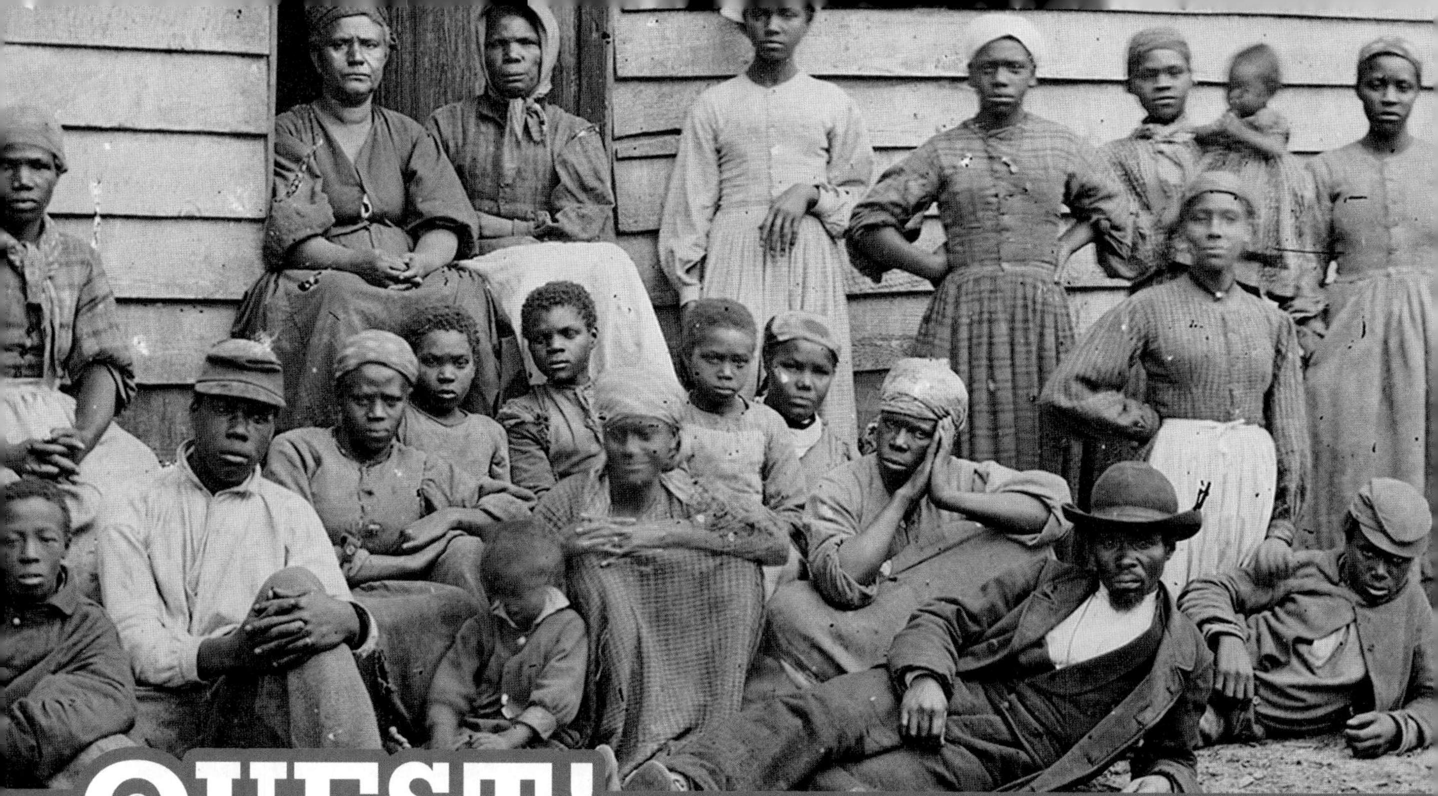

QUEST! INQUIRY

Project-Based Learning: Create a Civil War Documentary

How did ordinary citizens experience the Civil War and explain the justifications for war? In this Quest, you'll research and analyze letters, diaries, and other primary source writings of ordinary citizens to develop an understanding of how the war affected them. Then you will produce a documentary about the people you have researched.

STEP 1
Read the project launch and watch the documentary clip. With your team, generate questions about everyday life for various people during this period.

STEP 2
Research the lives of the group of Americans assigned to your team. Gather sources, such as maps, charts, and pictures, and then write an outline.

STEP 3
As a team, organize and plan your documentary, create a storyboard from your outline, and write a script. Then create and edit your documentary.

STEP 4
Present your documentary and then reflect on the experience of doing this project.

GO ONLINE to access complete Quest materials

7.1

Washington, D.C. was a hub of trade in enslaved people during the early 1800s.

BOUNCE to Activate Flipped Video

Objectives

Contrast the economies, societies, and political views of the North and the South.

Describe the role of the Free-Soil Party in the election of 1848.

Analyze why slavery in the territories was a divisive issue between North and South and how Congress tried to settle the issue in 1850.

Analyze why the Fugitive Slave Act increased tensions between the North and South.

Key Terms

Wilmot Proviso
Free-Soil Party
popular sovereignty
secede
Compromise of 1850
Fugitive Slave Act
personal liberty laws
Underground Railroad
Harriet Tubman
Harriet Beecher Stowe

GO ONLINE to access your digital course

Slavery Divides the Nation

From the nation's earliest days, the issue of slavery divided Americans. As the nation expanded, the problem became more pressing. Should slavery be allowed in the new western territories? Southerners said yes; many northerners said no.

Different Perspectives on the Issue of Slavery

After the American Revolution, the North and the South developed different ways of life. Most northerners still lived in rural areas, but the North also developed a number of busy cities, embraced technology and industry, and built factories staffed by paid workers. As immigrants arrived in northern ports, the North became an increasingly diverse society.

The South, on the other hand, remained an agrarian, or agricultural, society. The southern economy was based largely on a single crop: cotton. An organized plantation system and labor from enslaved African Americans made cotton one of the most important cash crops in the United States.

However, northern and southern economies also depended on one another. The North depended on southern cotton to make textile products, and the South depended on the North for manufactured goods.

By the mid-nineteenth century, cotton cultivation and slavery had spread across the Deep South—that is, through Florida and Alabama into Louisiana, Mississippi, and Texas. As the country continued to expand, Americans faced a crucial question: Should slavery be allowed to spread to new American territories west of the Mississippi River?

Wilmot Proviso Sparks Controversy Americans had long avoided the troubling issue of the expansion of slavery. But when the United States gained new territories as a result of the Mexican War in the late 1840s, the nation had to decide whether to admit these lands as slave territories or free territories. The delicate balance of power between North and South—free and slave—depended on this decision.

During the early days of the Mexican War, Pennsylvania congressman David Wilmot had predicted the dilemma. He proposed a law stating, "neither slavery nor involuntary servitude shall ever exist in any" lands won from Mexico. Southerners angrily denounced the **Wilmot Proviso**. The northern-dominated House of Representatives approved the law, but the Senate voted it down.

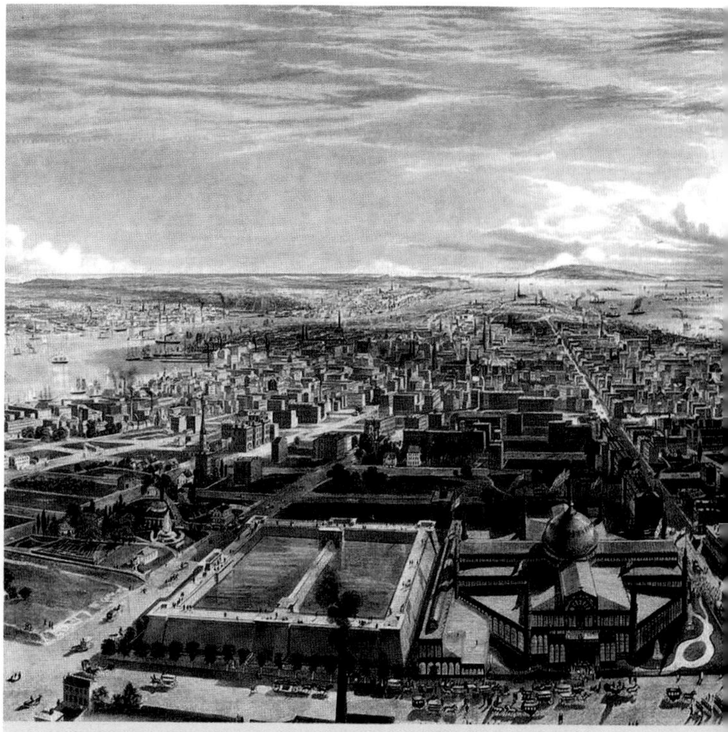

>> This image shows the northern city of New York in 1855. **Infer** What might everyday life have been like in New York during this time?

Northern Perspectives on Slavery Slavery ended early, but slowly, in the North. By 1800, there were about 50,000 enslaved people in the North, compared to nearly one million in the South. In 1860, there were still 18 enslaved people in New Jersey due to divides over slavery and complicated laws there, but none in other northern states. Still, most white northerners at the time viewed African Americans as inferior. African Americans could not vote, nor serve on juries or the militia. They also faced severe discrimination. Only some white northerners held strong opinions about slavery.

A vocal minority of northerners were abolitionists, or people who wanted to end slavery. They believed that slavery was morally wrong. Some abolitionists favored a gradual end, while others demanded that all slavery be outlawed at once.

Not all northerners wanted to end slavery. Some white northern bankers, mill owners, and merchants earned a lot of money on southern cotton and tobacco or by trading or transporting enslaved people. They were sympathetic to southern plantation owners and did not want to abolish slavery.

Some northern workers—especially those in unskilled, low-paying jobs—also opposed abolition, fearing that people who were freed from slavery might come north and compete with them for work.

>> This 1841 illustration shows an idealized vision of enslaved people interacting with their enslaver and his family. **Analyze Primary Sources** What illusions about slavery and southern society are reflected in this illustration?

Southern Perspectives on Slavery Slavery was an integral part of southern life. Many white southerners believed that God intended that African Americans should provide the labor for white "civilized" society. In a speech before Congress in 1837, planter John Calhoun of South Carolina firmly defended and even praised the virtues of slavery. "I hold it [slavery] to be a good . . . ," he said, " . . . and [it] will continue to prove so if not disturbed by the . . . spirit of abolition." Calhoun's words expressed the feelings of many white southerners.

By the 1850s, many southern politicians, journalists, and economists had begun to argue that the northern free labor system harmed society more than slavery did. White southerners claimed that enslaved people were healthier and happier than northern wage workers. A few white southerners, however, were outspoken in their belief that slavery actually harmed the southern economy. Kentuckian James G. Birney, North Carolinian Hinton Rowan Helper, and other southerners who spoke out against slavery were often ostracized by their neighbors.

CHECK UNDERSTANDING How did white northerners and southerners view slavery?

Slavery's Effect on the 1848 Election

The Wilmot Proviso had given the nation's political parties a new focus. In the 1848 presidential campaign, both Democrats and Whigs split over the question of whether to limit the expansion of slavery. New political factions emerged, with slavery at the center of debate.

>> Former President Martin Van Buren was the Free-Soil candidate for the presidency in 1848. **Interpret** What do the images on this poster tell you about the party?

The Free-Soil Party Several factions united in support of the Wilmot Proviso to form the new **Free-Soil Party**. Pledged to a "national platform of freedom" that would "resist the aggressions of the slave power," they nominated New Yorker Martin Van Buren as their candidate for President. The Free-Soil Party promised "free soil, free speech, free labor, and free men." Their main goal was to keep slavery out of the western territories.

Whigs and Democrats Put the Choice to Voters For decades, the major parties—the Whigs and Democrats—had avoided the slavery issue, thus managing to win support in both the North and the South.

In 1848, they hoped once again to attract voters from all sides of the slavery debate. But with the Free-Soilers calling for limits to slavery in the territories, the major parties were forced to take a stand.

Both Democrats and Whigs addressed the problem by embracing the idea of **popular sovereignty**, a policy stating that voters in a territory—not Congress—should decide whether or not to allow slavery there. This idea had wide appeal, since it seemed in keeping with the traditions of American democracy. Furthermore, it allowed Whigs and Democrats to sideline the issue of slavery and focus on the personal exploits and triumphs of their candidates.

The Whigs nominated Zachary Taylor, a general and a hero of the Mexican War. The Democrats put forward Governor Lewis Cass of Michigan. Cass opposed the Wilmot Proviso and supported popular sovereignty. Taylor, who was primarily a military man, revealed little of his political opinions. But Taylor was a slaveholding Louisiana planter, so many southern voters automatically assumed that he supported slavery.

When the votes were counted, Taylor won the election, with slim majorities in both northern and southern states. Van Buren did not carry any states, but he did draw sufficient votes to cost Cass the election. The Free-Soil Party, which had won 10 percent of the vote with its antislavery platform, had clearly captured Americans' attention.

EXPLAIN How did the Free-Soil Party affect the issues and the outcome of the presidential election of 1848?

The Election of 1848

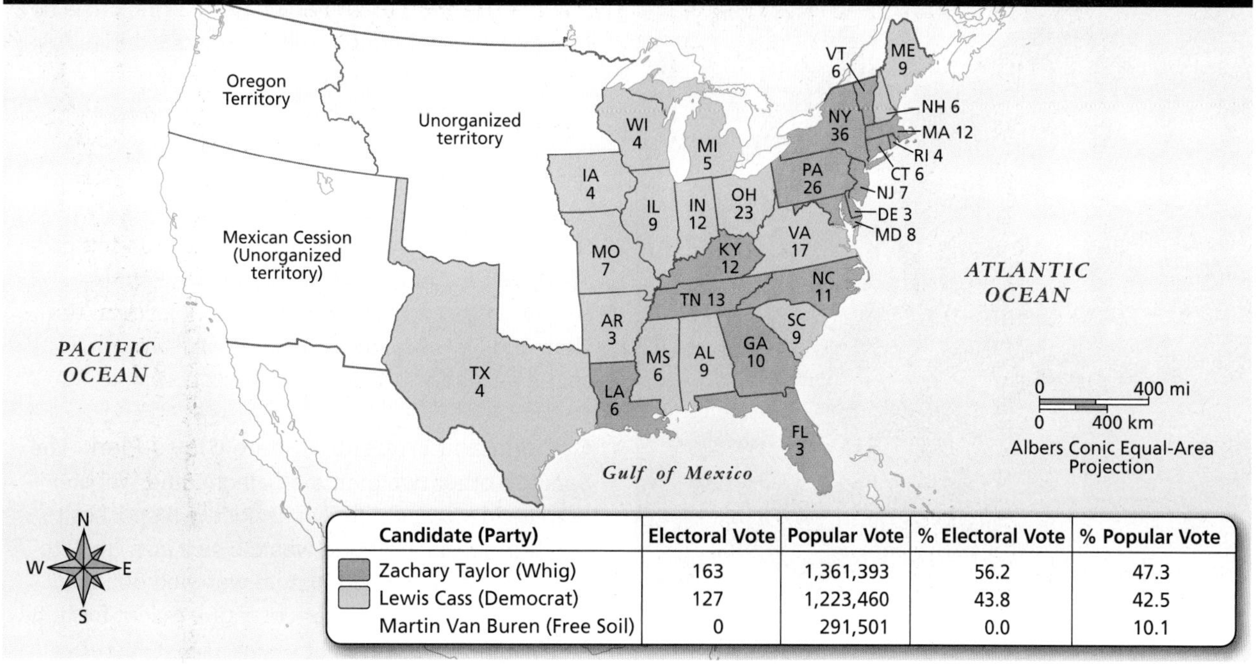

Candidate (Party)	Electoral Vote	Popular Vote	% Electoral Vote	% Popular Vote
Zachary Taylor (Whig)	163	1,361,393	56.2	47.3
Lewis Cass (Democrat)	127	1,223,460	43.8	42.5
Martin Van Buren (Free Soil)	0	291,501	0.0	10.1

>> **Analyze Maps** What does this map reveal about sectional political affiliations in the late 1840s?

The Compromise of 1850 Averts a Crisis

To expand slavery or restrict it—this dilemma came to haunt the rapidly growing nation. In 1848, gold was discovered in California, and soon thousands of adventurers were headed west to seek their fortune. Before long, the burgeoning western territories would petition for entry into the Union. Should these new states allow slavery? Who would decide?

California Starts a Crisis "Gold fever," as it came to be known, drew people from all over the world. They dug into the western foothills of California's Sierra Nevada, setting up towns with names that reflected their hopes and their origins: Gold Run, Eldorado (Spanish for "gilded one"), Dutch Flats, Chinese Camp, French Corral, Negro Bar, Iowa Hill.

Within a year, more than 80,000 people had journeyed to California. As the influx continued, California became a wild, lawless place. Californians recognized that they needed a government to bring order to the chaos. In 1849, they drafted a constitution and asked to be admitted to the Union as a free state (a state in which slavery was not allowed).

California's request caused an uproar in the nation. For years, the North and the South had accused each other of being "aggressors" on the issue of slavery. And for years, the two sides had maintained a delicate balance in Congress of slave states (states in which slavery was allowed) and free states. Now, southerners angrily noted that adding California as a free state would tip the balance toward free states.

Other concerns simmered around the edges of the slavery issue, threatening to come to an explosive boil. Texas, a slave state, and the federal government were locked in a dispute over Texas's northwestern border. New Mexico and Utah were organizing to become territories but seemed likely to someday join the Union as free states. In the North, abolitionists seemed to be gaining ground in their bid to ban slavery in Washington, D.C.

In the meantime, southerners demanded that the federal government enforce the weak and often-neglected Fugitive Slave Law of 1793. The law stated that enslaved people who were trying to escape must be returned to their enslavers, but it provided no government aid to do so. Many southerners wanted the law to be enforced.

Clay Proposes a Compromise Since the War of 1812, the Senate had benefited from the leadership of three extraordinary statesmen: Daniel Webster from the North, John Calhoun from the South, and Henry Clay from the West. Clay's ability to work out

>> Henry Clay urged the Senate to adopt a compromise on the slavery issue. It was one of his last major actions in the Senate.

>> Massachusetts Senator Daniel Webster was a strong nationalist.

compromises to the thorniest problems had earned him the title the "Great Pacificator." In the crisis now brewing, Clay, although in his seventies and ailing, once again came forward.

Clay urged the North and South to reach an agreement. He advanced a series of compromise resolutions, offering concessions to both the South and the North. The most significant proposed that Congress admit California as a free state but also enact a stricter fugitive slave law. Popular sovereignty would decide the slavery issue in the Utah and New Mexico territories. Clay's attempt at sectional justice garnered wide support.

Calhoun and Webster Debate Clay's Plan The Senate's other two giants—Calhoun and Webster—prepared long and deeply passionate responses to Clay's proposal. Calhoun was too sick and weak to deliver his own speech, but he watched defiantly from his seat as a younger colleague read it for him.

Calhoun's speech expressed his fear "that the agitation on the subject of slavery would, if not prevented by some timely and effective measure, end in disunion." But Calhoun did not believe that Clay's proposal gave the South enough protection. If the North would not submit to the South's demands, "let the states agree to separate and part in peace. If you are unwilling that we should part in peace, tell us so, and we shall know what to do." In other words, if the North did not agree, the South would **secede**, or break away, from the Union.

Daniel Webster, also ill and nearing the end of his life, tried to rally both northerners and southerners to the cause of unity. In an emotional speech, Webster urged senators to accept Clay's compromise. He suggested that the cotton and tobacco crops that flourished under slavery would not grow in California. Thus, he argued, popular sovereignty would allow the South to feel a measure of comfort but would not result in the spread of slavery to the West. (In fact, California eventually became a cotton-producing state—although a free one.)

Though some abolitionists felt betrayed by Webster's conciliatory three-hour speech, it persuaded many northerners to support the compromise.

The Senate Passes the Compromise of 1850 Over the years, Congress had adopted a variety of measures in order to preserve the Union. The Northwest Ordinance of 1787 had limited slavery. The Missouri Compromise of 1820 had maintained the balance between slave and free states. Now, in yet another effort to ward off division, the Senate adopted legislation based on Clay's proposals. It became known as the **Compromise of 1850**.

THE COMPROMISE OF 1850

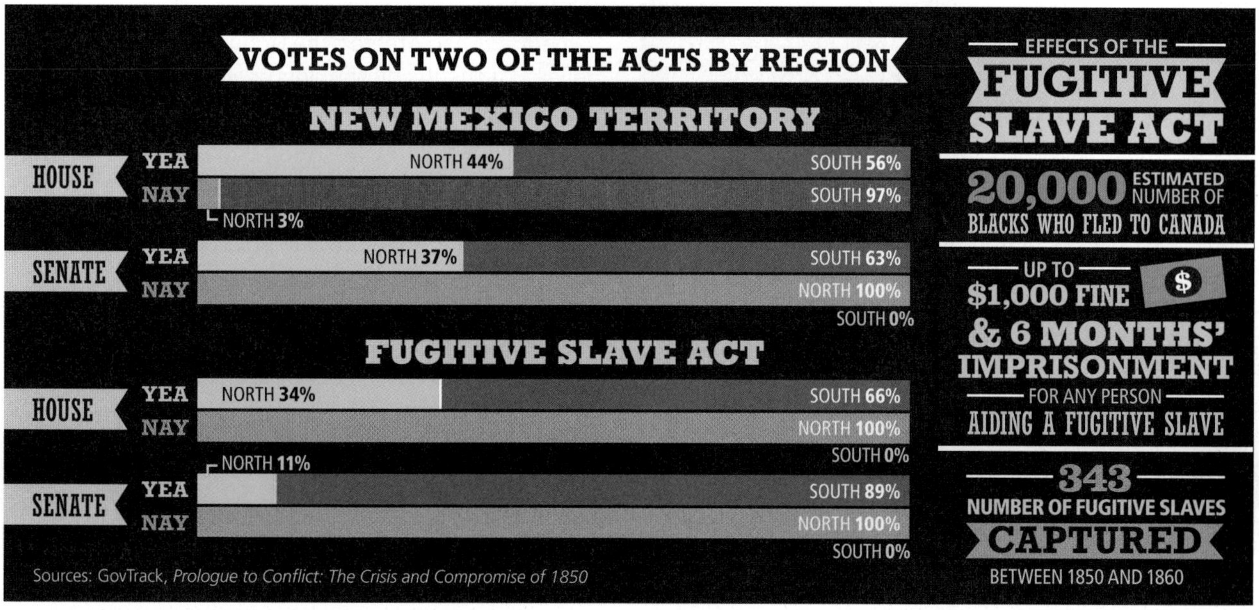

>> **Analyze Information** How were the votes on two of the Compromise's measures divided? How would you describe the impact of the Fugitive Slave Act?

BOUNCE to Activate Chart

The debate over ratification of the compromise raged for months. Young northern radicals, such as New York's William Seward, argued that the morality of God's "higher law" against slavery was more important than popular sovereignty or national unity. Equally radical southerners organized boycotts against northern goods, and a few even promoted separation from the Union.

The proceedings erupted into violence in the Senate when Senator Thomas Hart Benton of Missouri, who supported California's admission as a free state, denounced Mississippi senator Henry Foote, who opposed it. Furious, Foote rose from his seat and aimed a loaded revolver at Benton. The alarmed senators tried to restore order. But Benton was defiant, shouting "I am not armed! I have no pistols! I disdain to carry arms! Stand out of the way, and let the assassin fire!" At last, a senator from New York seized the revolver and locked it in a desk. Order was restored.

Still, debate dragged on. With dozens of speeches—one lasting two days—an exhausted Clay struggled to gain supporters for the compromise. But in the end, the young senator Stephen A. Douglas of Illinois took charge. Working tirelessly, Douglas steered each component of Clay's plan through the Congress, persuading the Senate to adopt each measure separately.

By September 1850, the obstacles to agreement had melted away: Both Calhoun and the slaveholding President Taylor were dead. Unlike Taylor, the new President, Millard Fillmore, supported the compromise. At last, the Senate passed the Compromise of 1850.

California was admitted as a free state, and the policy of popular sovereignty was applied to the territory acquired from Mexico. Texas relinquished its claims on New Mexico in return for $10 million from the federal government with which to settle its debts.

One by one, the other provisions passed. Slavery would remain undisturbed in Washington, D.C., but trade in enslaved people was prohibited. And a new **Fugitive Slave Act** amended the earlier law, including the requirement that private citizens assist with apprehending people trying to escape slavery. Also, those who assisted an enslaved person's escape attempt could be fined or imprisoned.

Most Americans, in both the North and South, breathed a sigh of relief that the crisis had been laid to rest. Though the Compromise of 1850 restored calm for the moment, it carried the seeds of new crises to come.

SUMMARIZE What were the provisions of the Compromise of 1850?

>> Some enslaved African Americans were caught trying to escape. Soldiers sometimes escorted them and their captors because crowds often tried to free the captured men and women.

>> Published in 1851, this cartoon satirizes the results of the Fugitive Slave Act. **Analyze Political Cartoons** Why does one abolitionist suggest that "this is all your fault, Webster"?

Northern Resistance to Slavery Increases

Americans had greeted the Compromise of 1850 with relief. But the ink on the document had barely dried before the issue of slavery resurfaced, this time with violent results.

The Compromise of 1850 was meant to calm the fears of Americans. But one provision, the new Fugitive Slave Act, had the opposite effect. The law, which required citizens to catch and return people trying to escape enslavement, enraged many northerners. It angered both the abolitionists and other northerners who felt forced to support the system of slavery.

Northerners also resented what they saw as increasing federal intervention in the affairs of the independent states. A few northern states struck back, passing **personal liberty laws**. These statutes nullified the Fugitive Slave Act and allowed the state to arrest as kidnappers those who apprehended fugitives. Many northerners agreed with abolitionist William Lloyd Garrison when he demanded "nothing less than . . . a Revolution in the Government of the country."

African Americans, of course, despised the law. Some of those caught trying to escape enslavement were really free people who had been kidnapped and sold into slavery. Although imprisoned African Americans could appeal to a judge for release, the law awarded $10 to judges who ruled in favor of enslavers but only $5 to those who ruled that the captive should be set free. Many free and enslaved African Americans who were subjected to this law plotted and carried out resistance. Through the succeeding decade, tempers flared and violence erupted as far north as Canada, as far west as Kansas, and as far south as Virginia.

Many Northerners Defy the Law In 1851, a small group of free African Americans gathered in a farmhouse in Christiana, Pennsylvania. Heavily armed, they had come to protect several fugitives from their Maryland enslaver, who had brought a federal official to reclaim them. In the scuffle that followed, the enslaver was killed. White bystanders refused to help the enslaver. Although more than 30 people were tried for conspiracy, none was found guilty, and no one was tried for the murder of the enslaver.

The "Christiana Riot" was a dramatic enactment of a scene that was played out in many northern communities. In Vermont and New Hampshire, in New York City, in Oberlin, Ohio, and in Baltimore, Maryland, African Americans and white bystanders

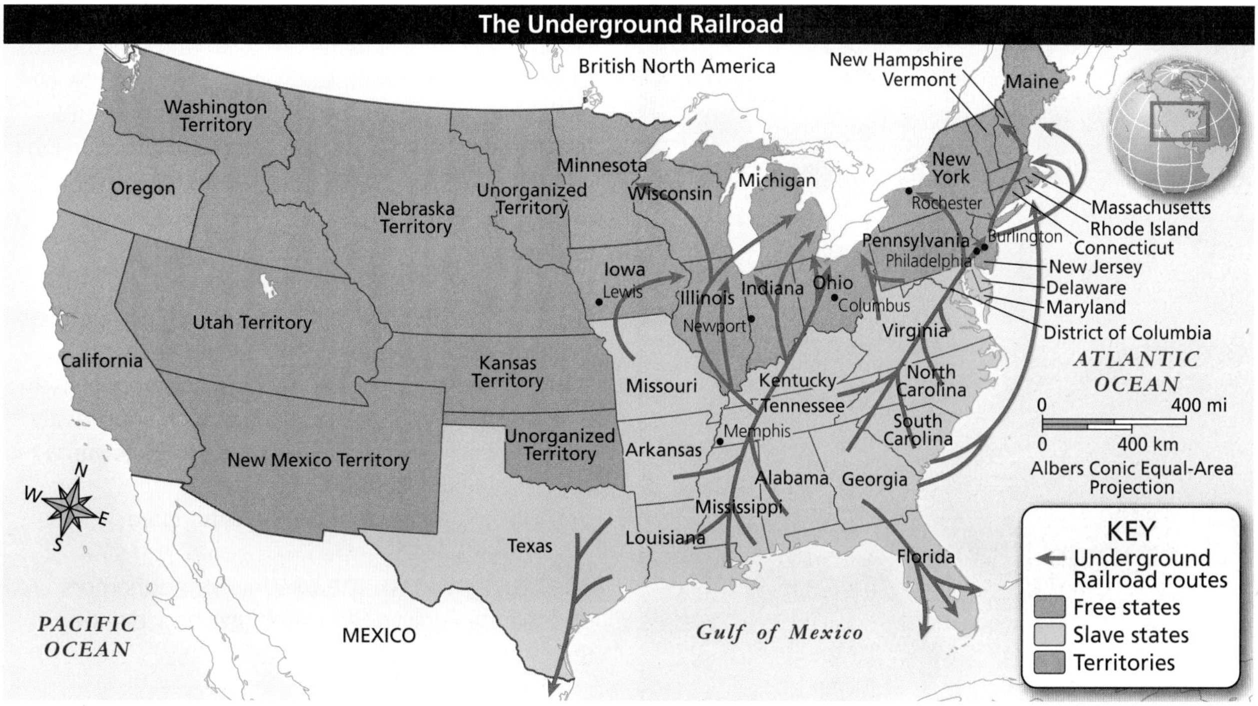

>> **Analyze Maps** Which sections of the Underground Railroad were likely the riskiest for fugitives to pass through?

BOUNCE to Activate Map

defied officials who tried to return fugitives to slavery.

The Underground Railroad Ferries People to Freedom Northern abolitionists and free African Americans risked their lives and safety to help enslaved people escape to freedom through a loosely organized network known as the **Underground Railroad**. Although it was not underground and had no tracks or cars, this escape system used railroad terminology to describe its actions. A secret network of "conductors" hid people trying to escape enslavement in farm wagons and on riverboats. They then moved them to destinations in the North or in British North America (Canada)—sometimes even as far as England. Using complex signals and hiding places, the Underground Railroad carried its passengers over hundreds of miles of dangerous terrain.

Underground Railroad conductors had to be resourceful and daring. One of the most courageous was **Harriet Tubman**, a formerly enslaved African American who escaped to freedom. She was known as "Black Moses" because, like Moses in the Bible, she led her people out of bondage. After her own escape in 1849, Tubman made almost two dozen trips into the South, guiding hundreds to freedom, including her own parents. Southern planters placed a large reward on her head, but she was never captured.

Several fugitives published dramatic escape stories that inspired African Americans and struck fear in the hearts of white southerners. In one account, six-foot-tall Henry "Box" Brown described how he had himself packed into a small crate and shipped from Richmond, Virginia, to the Underground Railroad agents in Philadelphia. Light-skinned Ellen Craft and her husband, William, made their escape by posing as an invalid gentleman and his loyal servant.

Abolitionist Authors Portray Life Under Slavery In 1852, **Harriet Beecher Stowe** published *Uncle Tom's Cabin,* a powerful condemnation of slavery. Stowe's sympathetic main character, Uncle Tom, gave slavery a face for those who had never witnessed it firsthand. Set in the South where slavery occurred, Stowe's story features the gentle and patient Uncle Tom, a frightened enslaved mother, and various enslavers. Selling 300,000 copies in its first year, the novel spread compassion for enslaved people in the North, but it infuriated people in the South.

African American abolitionist Martin Delany also wrote an antislavery novel, called *Blake.* It is the story of an African American who chooses to

>> This 1881 illustration shows a scene from *Uncle Tom's Cabin* in which a woman tries to escape slavery with her young daughter. **Contrast** How does this image differ from the depictions of enslaved life embraced by white southerners?

rebel violently rather than to submit like Uncle Tom. The protagonist, Blake, murders a white enslaver in order to make his escape, a scenario that terrified enslavers. In the following excerpt, Blake stands up to his enslaver's threat to whip him.

> I won't be treated like a dog. You sold my wife away from me, after always promising that she should be free. . . . And now you talk about whipping me. Shoot me, sell me, or do anything else you please, but don't lay your hands on me, as I will not suffer you to whip me!
>
> —Martin R. Delany, *Blake*

Formerly enslaved African Americans also wrote about the horrors of being enslaved and their escape to freedom. Two examples were *Narrative of the Life of Frederick Douglass* by Frederick Douglass and *Incidents in the Life of a Slave Girl* by Harriet Jacobs.

White southerners responded by writing their own versions of southern life. In these accounts, enslaved African Americans were portrayed as happy and carefree people, gently cared for, and taught Christianity by kind enslavers. They claimed that only mentally ill enslaved people ran away. A southern doctor even reported his discovery of a disease he called Drapetomania, which supposedly caused enslaved people to flee. "With the advantages of proper medical advice," he claimed "this troublesome practice" could be eliminated.

☑ **IDENTIFY MAIN IDEAS** Why did northerners oppose the Fugitive Slave Act, and how did they respond to the law?

☑ ASSESSMENT

1. **Compare and Contrast** Daniel Webster and John Calhoun's response to the Compromise of 1850.
2. **Check Understanding** How did southerners respond to northern objections to the Compromise of 1850?
3. **Cite Evidence** What impact did the publication of novels like Harriet Beecher Stowe's *Uncle Tom's Cabin* and Martin Delany's *Blake* have on the American public at the time?
4. **Discuss** Harriett Tubman's significance to the abolitionist movement.
5. **Connections to Today** Many people in the North and South objected to the various compromises prior to the Civil War. For what reasons might the population of a particular region object to a federal law today?

GO ONLINE to access these biographies: John C. Calhoun, Daniel Webster

7.2

Representative Brooks beat Senator Sumner with a cane meant to train dogs. **Analyze Political Cartoons** What does this depiction tell you about the event?

Violence Escalates

Although Congress meant well, its repeated attempts to resolve the question of slavery resulted in a jumble of contradictory, and often unenforceable, policies. The Missouri Compromise, the Wilmot Proviso, and the Compromise of 1850 each seemed to offer the solution. But, in reality, the issue lay beyond the ability of patchwork legislation to resolve.

BOUNCE to Activate Flipped Video

Objectives

Assess how the Kansas-Nebraska Act was seen differently in the North and South.

Explain why fighting broke out in Kansas and the effects of that conflict.

Analyze how deepening sectional distrust affected the nation's politics.

Compare the positions of Abraham Lincoln and Stephen Douglas on the issue of slavery.

Explain the effect of John Brown's raid on the slavery debate.

Key Terms

Kansas-Nebraska Act
John Brown
"Bleeding Kansas"
nativist
"Know-Nothings"
Republican Party
Dred Scott
Roger B. Taney
Abraham Lincoln
Stephen A. Douglas
Harpers Ferry

The Kansas-Nebraska Act and "Bleeding Kansas"

Popular Sovereignty in the Nebraska Territory It was Senator Stephen Douglas who forced the issue of slavery to the surface once again. In 1854, Douglas introduced a bill to set up a government in the Nebraska Territory. The area would be organized, Douglas proposed, according to the principle of popular sovereignty. That is, the people of the territory themselves would decide whether to allow slavery or to outlaw it when they applied for statehood. On the surface, Douglas's plan made sense. In fact, it seemed to be a democratic solution. But would it work in practice?

The Kansas-Nebraska Act Once again, Congress was gripped in bitter debate. After pressure from the South, which feared Nebraska might decide to enter as a free state, Douglas amended the bill to divide the region into two distinct territories, Kansas and Nebraska. The idea was that Kansas would become a slave state and Nebraska would organize as a free state, but those assumptions were not written into the bill. In the spring of 1854, Congress accepted this proposal and passed the **Kansas-Nebraska Act**. Some northerners pointed out that, in effect, the Kansas-Nebraska Act nullified the Missouri Compromise by

GO ONLINE to access your digital course

>> A figure represents the antislavery ideal "Liberty for Kansas." **Analyze Primary Sources** Why does the figure have broken chains around her feet?

BOUNCE to Activate Cartoon

>> Proslavery "Border Ruffians" crossed into Kansas from neighboring Missouri to agitate for proslavery policies

allowing slavery to spread to areas that had been free for more than 30 years.

Bitter Disputes in Kansas Most of the people who came to the newly opened territory of Kansas were farmers looking for land. But Kansas also attracted settlers—northern and southern—with political motives. Each group wanted to outnumber the other so that when it came time to vote, they could control the government. Their competition to settle the territory would have deadly consequences.

By 1855, proslavery settlers had set up a territorial government near the border of Missouri, a slave state. During the election, proslavery residents from Missouri, known as Border Ruffians, had swept into Kansas and coerced local voters into voting for proslavery candidates. They also cast their own illegal votes. The new legislature quickly passed proslavery laws, including penalties for antislavery agitation and a requirement that officeholders take a proslavery oath. Within two years, they had called a convention and developed a constitution that would have legalized slavery and punished those who spoke or wrote against it.

Northern abolitionists also rushed into Kansas. The New England Emigrant Aid Society raised money to help several thousand free-state supporters establish the town of Lawrence, a few miles east of the proslavery capital of Lecompton. These settlers joined other free-state advocates in establishing an antislavery government in Topeka. By early 1856, this Topeka government had petitioned Congress for statehood. Kansas now had two governments petitioning for statehood. It was a sure setup for disaster.

"Bleeding Kansas" On May 21, 1856, Border Ruffians raided the antislavery town of Lawrence, Kansas. They pillaged homes, burned down the Free State Hotel, and destroyed the presses of *The Kansas Free State* newspaper.

Swift retaliation came from **John Brown**, a New York abolitionist who had moved his family several times in pursuit of opportunities to confront slavery head-on and who now made his home near Lawrence. With his sons and a few friends, Brown carried out a midnight execution of five proslavery settlers near Pottawatomie Creek, about 20 miles south of Lawrence.

When stories of the incident reached the East, abolitionists were stunned. While they were outraged at the events that triggered it, they condemned Brown's massacre. In Kansas, both sides armed for battle. Throughout the fall of 1856, violent outbreaks

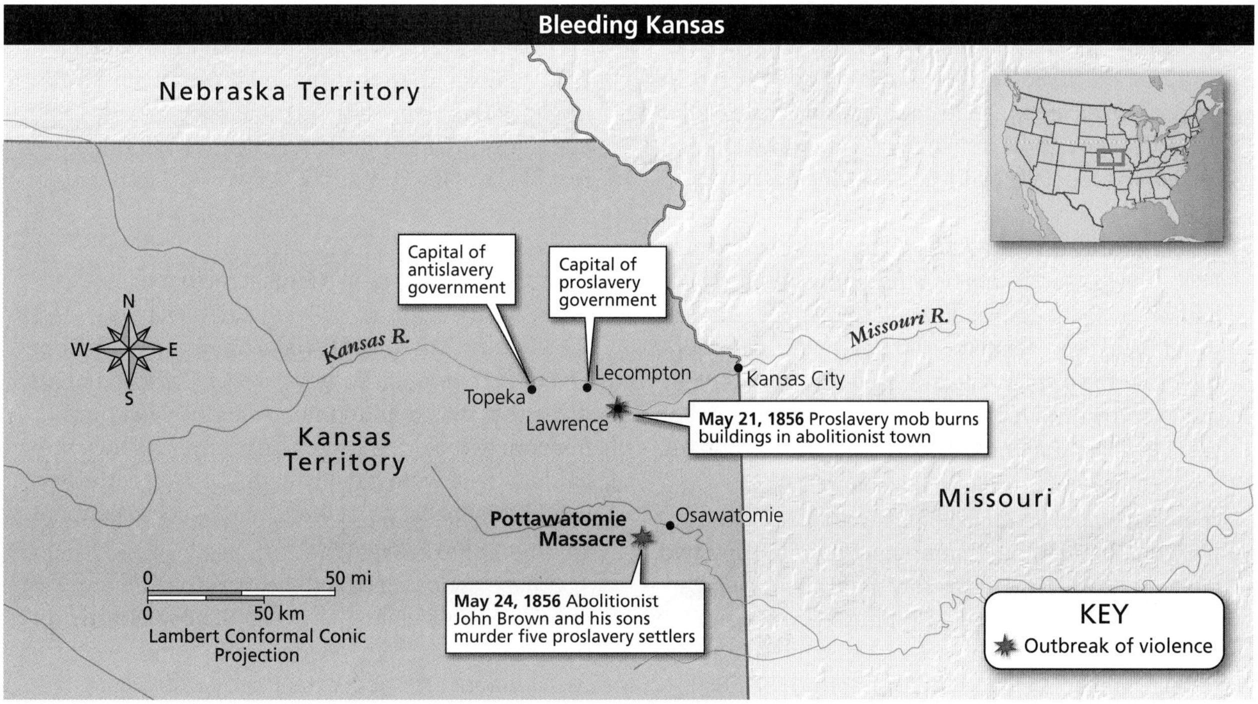

>> **Analyze Maps** Which region of Kansas experienced the most conflicts? What explains that pattern?

occurred in various locales around Lawrence. Reporters characterized the territory as **"Bleeding Kansas"**. By now, it was clear that popular sovereignty was not a solution to the slavery issue.

Over the next several years, the question of how to admit Kansas to the Union baffled local residents, political parties, the U.S. Congress, and the Supreme Court. Although the Border Ruffians had determined the outcome of the election, President Franklin Pierce urged Congress to admit Kansas as a slave state in 1858. However, Congress refused and Kansas submitted four constitutions before it finally entered as a free state in 1861, after the Civil War had already begun.

Violence in the Senate The violent battles over slavery were not limited to Kansas. Tempers ran high in Congress, and some members went to work armed not only with words but also with pistols and canes. In May 1856, just as fighting broke out in Kansas, Massachusetts senator Charles Sumner delivered a blistering speech on the Senate floor, which came to be known as "The Crime Against Kansas." He blasted southerners for their bullying and fraud in the Kansas elections, and he referred to the Border Ruffians from Missouri as "hirelings, picked from the drunken spew and vomit of an uneasy civilization—in the form of men."

Then, Sumner insulted South Carolina senator Andrew Butler, who was absent. But a few days later, Butler's nephew, South Carolina representative Preston Brooks, attacked Sumner in the Senate, beating him unconscious with a cane.

What happened next illustrates the division between pro and antislavery forces. Congress tried to punish Brooks by removing him from office. His constituency simply reelected him and sent him back. Sumner was so badly injured that he could not return to the Senate for three years. The Massachusetts voters reelected him anyway, using his empty seat as a public reminder of southern treachery. The divide between North and South grew ever wider and deeper.

☑ **EXPLAIN** Why did violence break out in Kansas?

Regional Tension Affects National Politics

Americans had always lived with sectional differences, but they temporarily resolved those differences through negotiation and compromise. By the mid-1850s, however, the battle over slavery threatened to tear the nation apart.

Traditionally, American political parties extended across sectional lines. Democrats and Whigs came from the North, South, and West. Presidents, too, had come from all areas of the country. But in the 1840s, American politics increasingly reflected regional tensions, especially over the issue of slavery.

Decline of the Whig Party The Compromise of 1850, as well as the policies that grew out of it, caused political upheaval. Millard Fillmore—the last Whig President—angered the South with his support for California's entry as a free state. Northerners inflamed by his support of the Fugitive Slave Act and popular sovereignty left the party in large numbers.

For the 1852 presidential election, Whigs searched unsuccessfully for a candidate and a platform to unite their members. But with their two visionary leaders—Henry Clay and Daniel Webster—dead, the party fell back on Winfield Scott, a military hero. Deeply divided over the issues, the Whigs lost to the Democrats, who solidly endorsed the 1850 Compromise that they hoped and believed would preserve the Union. The Whigs would never again achieve enough harmony to mount a presidential campaign.

>> A Know-Nothing party ribbon used in the campaign of 1844 **Analyze Primary Sources** According to the Know-Nothings, who were the "native Americans"?

The Know-Nothings By the mid-1800s, a growing immigrant population was changing the country. For example, up to that time, Protestantism—which includes Baptists, Methodists, Presbyterians, and many other groups—had been the dominant American religion. By 1850, however, Americans of Irish and German descent and Spanish-speaking natives of lands ceded by Mexico had made Catholicism the nation's largest religious group. Many native-born white Protestants were alarmed by the change. These "**nativists**" raised questions that reflected their point of view. Would Catholics bring ideas that would undermine America's religious freedom? Would the newcomers take jobs away from workers who were already here? Or, alternatively, would they be lazy, not work, and become paupers, weighing down society?

These concerns fueled the growth of an anti-immigrant movement. Dubbed **"Know-Nothings"** because members responded with "I know nothing" when questioned about their nativist organization, the group quickly gathered momentum. By 1855, the Know-Nothings had abandoned secrecy to form the American Party. Like the Whigs, however, the American Party soon divided over the issue of slavery in the western territories.

Birth of the Republican Party As the old parties broke up, antislavery zeal gave rise to the new **Republican Party** in 1854. Opposition to slavery was the center of the Republican philosophy. Attracting antislavery Democrats, Whigs, Free-Soilers, and Know-Nothings, the Republican Party grew rapidly in the North. It included a coalition of businessmen who believed that slavery stifled industry, as well as moral leaders who feared that slavery encouraged vice. By 1856, it was ready to challenge the older, established parties.

☑ **IDENTIFY CENTRAL ISSUES** How did deepening sectional differences impact national politics?

Sectional Divisions Split the Country

For many years, the North and South tried to ignore or patch over their differences. But by the mid-1850s, the dispute over slavery caused sectional differences to intensify.

The Election of 1856 Republicans, at their first national convention, nominated for President the abolitionist John C. Frémont, a colorful Mexican War

The Election of 1856

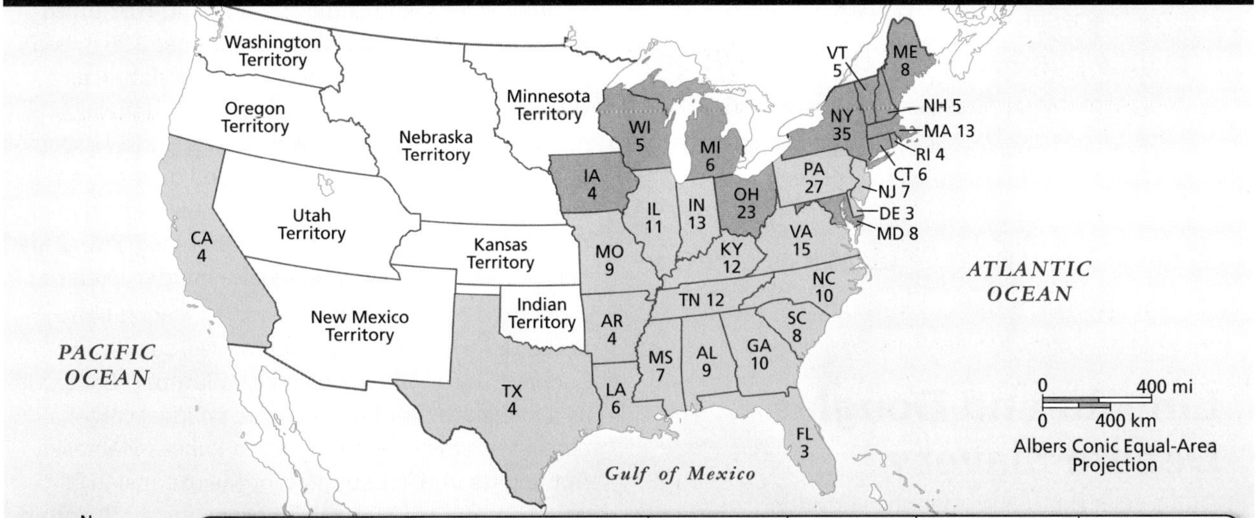

Candidate (Party)	Electoral Vote	Popular Vote	% Electoral Vote	% Popular Vote
James Buchanan (Democrat)	174	1,836,072	58.8	45.3
John C. Frémont (Republican)	114	1,342,345	38.5	33.1
Millard Fillmore (American/Know-Nothing)	8	873,053	2.7	21.6

>> **Analyze Maps** How closely did the election results of 1856 follow sectional lines?

BOUNCE to Activate Map

hero who had helped win California's independence. The Democrats nominated James Buchanan of Pennsylvania, while the Know-Nothings put up former President Millard Fillmore.

"Free Soil, Free Labor, Free Men, Frémont!" Under this slogan, the Republican Party tried to rally Americans to reject popular sovereignty and to insist that slavery be excluded from the western territories. They also campaigned to admit Kansas as a free state. But Buchanan, who promised that as President he would stop "the agitation of the slavery issue," won the election, supported by the large majority of southerners.

His running mate from the South, John C. Breckinridge, further bolstered his campaign. Still, the Republican Frémont, with his solid abolitionist platform, made a strong showing, winning one third of the popular vote and 11 northern states.

The *Dred Scott* Decision While passions still ran high from the 1856 election, another event fueled the flames of division. In 1857, the U.S. Supreme Court ruled in the case of **Dred Scott**, an enslaved African American from Missouri. Scott had sued for his freedom on the basis that his enslaver had taken him to the free state of Illinois and Wisconsin Territory, where slavery was outlawed by the Missouri Compromise. In other words, between 1834 and 1838, Scott had lived mostly on free soil while remaining enslaved.

With the help of abolitionists, Scott's case reached the Supreme Court under Chief Justice **Roger B. Taney**. In its decision handed down in March 1857, the Court ruled against Scott. In a controversial decision, the Court decided that enslaved people and their descendants were property, not citizens, and therefore were not entitled to sue in the courts.

It also said that the Missouri Compromise was unconstitutional because it was illegal for Congress to deprive an owner of property—in this case, an enslaved person—without due process of law.

Southerners celebrated the decision, but the North viewed it with alarm. Abolitionists labeled the ruling a southern conspiracy. Some suggested that the North should secede from the Union. Others insisted that the members of the Supreme Court should be impeached. Leading African American abolitionist Frederick Douglass predicted that the decision would actually hasten the end of slavery.

> The Supreme Court . . . [is] not the only power in the world. We, the abolitionists and colored* people, should meet this decision, unlooked for and monstrous as it appears, in a cheerful spirit. This very attempt to blot out forever the

hopes of an enslaved people may be one necessary link in the chain of events preparatory to the complete overthrow of the whole slave system.

—Frederick Douglass, 1857. *Note that *colored* is an outdated term describing Black people.

RECALL What were the main findings in the Dred Scott case?

Lincoln and Douglas Debate Slavery

Throughout the 1850s, American attention was riveted on westward expansion. But no discussion of expansion, or any aspect of the nation's future, could get beyond the issue of slavery. In 1858, Stephen Douglas and Abraham Lincoln held a series of seven debates while competing for a seat in the U.S. Senate. Thousands of Americans attended the Lincoln-Douglas debates and listened raptly as the two candidates presented opposing views of slavery and its role in America.

>> Abraham Lincoln photographed during his senatorial campaign in 1858

"Honest Abe" and "The Little Giant" Raised in rural poverty and largely self-taught, **Abraham Lincoln** began his political career at age 25, when he was elected to the Illinois state legislature as a Whig. By 1836, he had been admitted to the Illinois bar and was practicing law in Springfield. He soon gained a reputation for integrity and directness that earned him the title "Honest Abe." Lincoln seemed to be staunchly opposed to slavery, but his political life was marked by a desire to steer a middle course.

In the 1840s, Lincoln had served a short stint in the U.S. House of Representatives, supporting Zachary Taylor and his policy of admitting California as a free state. But Lincoln's real political career began with his opposition to the Kansas-Nebraska Act and its implicit support for the expansion of slavery promoted by rival Illinois politician **Stephen A. Douglas**.

Douglas was, in many ways, the opposite of Lincoln. Lincoln was tall, lanky, and slow of speech. Douglas was short, round, and filled with energy and a commanding voice. These qualities earned him the nickname the "Little Giant." His critics, however, questioned his motives and his sincerity. Unlike Lincoln, Douglas supported the annexation of Texas, and he promoted popular sovereignty as the solution to regional tensions. But many wondered if he promoted these policies because he believed in them or because he had a financial stake in the railroads that would profit from them.

Douglas's Position Douglas had supporters in both the North and the South. Though he was not an enslaver, his wife had inherited enslaved people, and he was somewhat sympathetic to slavery. Popular sovereignty, he insisted, was the implied intent of the Constitution. He expressed this sentiment in the seventh and last debate.

> This Union was established on the right of each State to do as it pleased on the question of slavery, and every other question.
>
> —Stephen A. Douglas, 1858

Douglas was seeking the support of both southern and northern Democrats. But while some southerners supported him, many northern Democrats distrusted what they believed were his self-serving motives.

Lincoln's Position When Lincoln stood before these same audiences, he spoke of the "eternal struggle between right and wrong." He repeatedly

Illinois Senate Election, 1858*

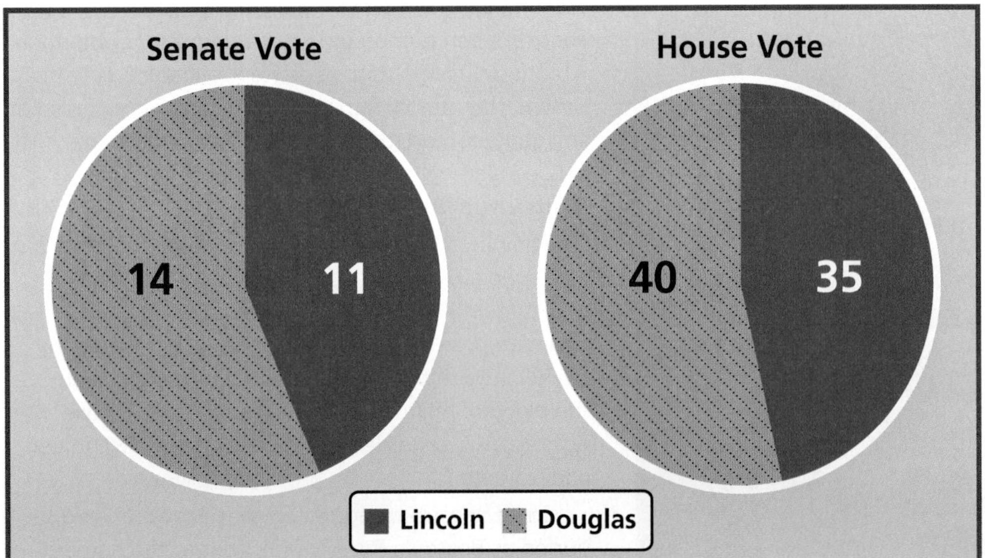

*Elected by Illinois General Assembly, which consisted of 25 State Senators and 75 State Representatives
Source: Northern Illinois University

>> **Analyze Data** How many votes separated Douglas and Lincoln?

referred to the *Dred Scott* decision as wrong. He attacked popular sovereignty as wrong.

He condemned slavery as a system whereby one person does the "work and toil to earn bread" and someone else does the eating. While Lincoln, like most white people of his day, ridiculed the idea of social and political equality with African Americans, he strongly affirmed the idea of their natural rights.

> There is no reason in the world why the negro is not entitled to all the natural rights enumerated in the Declaration of Independence—the right of life, liberty, and the pursuit of happiness. I hold that he is as much entitled to these as the white man. . . . In the right to eat the bread, without the leave of anybody else, which his own hand earns, he is my equal and the equal of Judge Douglas, and the equal of every living man.
>
> —Abraham Lincoln, 1858

The debates lasted for weeks. When they were over, Douglas won the election by a slim margin. But Lincoln had not really lost. As a result of the debates, Lincoln won a large following that would serve him well the next time he ran for national office.

☑ **CHECK UNDERSTANDING** What were Lincoln's views on slavery and popular sovereignty?

The Raid on Harpers Ferry

Both Lincoln and Douglas believed that the slavery crisis had to be resolved within the framework of the nation's laws. Abolitionist John Brown felt no such constraints. Brown viewed himself as an angel of God, avenging the evil of slavery. Even before one of his sons was killed in Bleeding Kansas, he had concluded that violence was the best way to reach his goal. By late 1857, Brown had begun planning his attack. For many months, he crisscrossed New England, the Midwest, and Canada, soliciting recruits and funds to mount an armed assault on slavery.

Capture at the Arsenal By the fall of 1859, Brown was ready. "Men, get your arms," he cried, "we will proceed to the Ferry." Gathering his following of 21 men—including 5 free African Americans—Brown set out to seize the federal arsenal in **Harpers Ferry**, Virginia (now in West Virginia). He hoped to

>> In this painting, John Brown pauses on his way to his execution to kiss an enslaved woman's baby. **Determine Point of View** Do you think the person who painted this image was pro or antislavery? Why?

inspire local enslaved African Americans to join a revolution that would destroy slavery in the South.

Brown had chosen Harpers Ferry because it was a hub of trains and canals, which would offer efficient escape routes. This locale was also near the borders of Pennsylvania, a free state, and Maryland, where there were many free African Americans. It seemed the ideal launching point.

But the effort failed. Few Americans—Black or white—were prepared to join a rebellion organized by this intense, fanatical white man. Frederick Douglass, a close friend, refused to join, warning Brown that his mission "would array the whole country against us." A few African American and white abolitionists sent money for guns, but in the end, Brown's revolution came to naught. Local residents surrounded Brown's men in the arsenal, and federal troops soon arrived to arrest them. Two more of Brown's sons were killed in the fray, but a few of the rebels escaped to Canada. Brown and several others, however, went to the gallows.

Brown's Execution Brown's attack increased the heat in already-boiling tempers. Similar to the *Dred Scott* decision, suspicion and rumors were widespread.

Stephen Douglas accused the Republicans of instigating Brown's attack, and southern congressmen demanded an investigation. But when Abraham Lincoln and other Republicans condemned Brown, the rumors subsided. Yet, many congressmen still came armed to the Capitol. The uncertainty caused a steep drop in cotton prices, and many southerners prepared for war.

Many northerners thought abolitionist activism had gone too far. But others now saw Brown as a courageous martyr. They were moved to tears when he proclaimed his willingness to "mingle my blood . . . with the blood of my children and with the blood of millions in this slave country whose rights are disregarded by wicked, cruel, and unjust enactments."

Some admirers suggested that Brown should be buried at Boston's Bunker Hill, next to the heroes of the American Revolution. A popular song later immortalized him, celebrating the fact that "his soul goes marching on." On the morning of his execution, Brown made the prophetic prediction that "the crimes [of slavery] of this guilty land will never be purged away, . . . without very much bloodshed." Many Americans agreed with him.

RECALL How did northerners respond to John Brown's raid and execution?

ASSESSMENT

1. **Check Understanding** What was the Kansas-Nebraska Act and what consequences did it have on the region?
2. **Compare and Contrast** the positions of Abraham Lincoln and Stephen A. Douglas on slavery in their Senate debates.
3. **Express Ideas Clearly** Who were the "Know-Nothings" and how were they an example of the changing political landscape in the 1850s?
4. **Draw Conclusions** How did John Brown differ from other antislavery politicians like Abraham Lincoln?
5. **Connections to Today** This lesson shows that northerners tended to support one political party, while southerners tended to support another. This trend has continued into modern elections. What does this say about the North and South today?

GO ONLINE to access this biography: John Brown

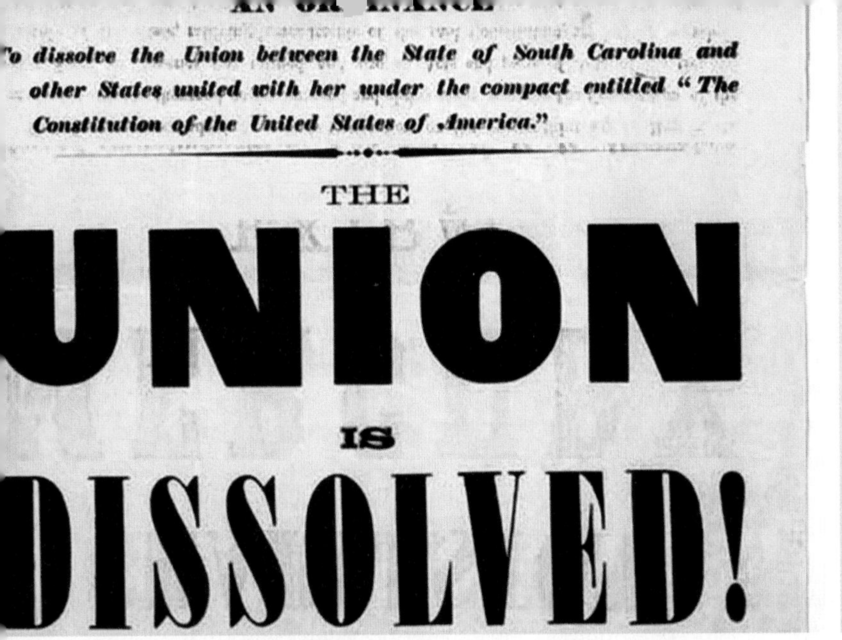
o dissolve the Union between the State of South Carolina and other States united with her under the compact entitled "The Constitution of the United States of America."

THE
UNION
IS
DISSOLVED!

7.3

A Charleston, South Carolina, newspaper announces secession in 1860.

The Civil War Begins

BOUNCE to Activate Flipped Video

Despite repeated attempts at compromise, disagreement between the North and the South over the issue of slavery continued to deepen. With the election of Republican President Abraham Lincoln in 1860, the crisis came to a head. The Union of states that had been formed less than a hundred years before was about to dissolve.

Objectives

Compare the candidates in the election of 1860, and analyze the results.

Analyze why southern states seceded from the Union.

Assess the events that led to the outbreak of war.

Contrast the resources and strategies of the North and South.

Describe the outcomes and effects of the early battles of the Civil War.

Key Terms

Jefferson Davis
John C. Breckinridge
border state
Confederate States of America
Crittenden Compromise
Fort Sumter
blockade
Robert E. Lee
Anaconda Plan
Stonewall Jackson
George B. McClellan
Ulysses S. Grant
Battle of Shiloh

Sectional Politics in the Election of 1860

John Brown's raid and execution were still fresh in the minds of Americans as the 1860 presidential election approached. Uncertainty about Kansas—would it be a slave state or a free state?—added to the anxiety. In the North, loss of confidence in the Supreme Court resulting from the *Dred Scott* decision and rage about the Fugitive Slave Act's intrusion into the states' independence further aggravated the situation.

The issue of states' rights was on southern minds as well. Would northern radicals conspire to eliminate slavery not only in the territories but also in the original southern states?

In the spring of 1860, Mississippi senator **Jefferson Davis** convinced Congress to adopt resolutions restricting federal control over slavery in the territories. The resolutions also asserted that the Constitution prohibited Congress or any state from interfering with slavery in the states where it already existed. Even southerners who did not own enslaved African Americans felt that their way of life and their honor were under attack.

GO ONLINE to access your digital course

With ill will running so deep, the upcoming elections posed a serious dilemma. It was hard to imagine that either northerners or southerners would accept a President from the other region. Could the Union survive?

Democrats Split Between Two Nominees The Democrats held their nominating convention in Charleston, South Carolina. For ten days, they argued about the issue that had plagued the nation for decades: slavery. The southern Democrats called for a platform supporting federal protection of slavery in the territories. The northern Democrats, who backed Stephen Douglas, supported the doctrine of popular sovereignty.

When the Douglas forces prevailed, the delegates from eight southern states walked out and formed a separate convention. The Democrats were now split into two parties. The northern Democrats nominated Stephen A. Douglas. The southern Democrats nominated the Vice President, **John C. Breckinridge** of Kentucky. Breckinridge was committed to expanding slavery into the territories.

The Constitutional Union Party In the meantime, the few remaining Whigs teamed up with the Know-Nothings to form the Constitutional Union Party. They hoped to heal the split between North and South. Their candidate was John Bell, a little-known moderate from Tennessee. Their platform condemned sectional parties and promised to uphold "the Constitution of the country, the Union of the States, and the enforcement of the laws."

The Republican Nominee The Republicans, who had gained great strength since their formation, held their nominating convention in Chicago. After several ballots, they nominated Abraham Lincoln as their candidate.

When the party convened, seasoned politician William H. Seward of New York had been the favorite to win the nomination. But when many delegates began to worry that Seward's antislavery views were too radical, the convention went with the more moderate Lincoln.

The Republican platform called for the end of slavery in the territories. At the same time, the Republicans defended the right of each state to control its own institutions and stipulated that there should be no interference with slavery in the states where it already existed. Abraham Lincoln—with his great debating skills, his moderate views, and his reputation for integrity—was seen as the ideal candidate to carry the Republican platform to victory.

Lincoln Wins Without the South Benefiting from the fracturing among the other political parties, Lincoln won the election handily, with 40 percent of the popular vote and almost 60 percent of the electoral vote. Still, he did not receive a single southern electoral vote. In fact, he was not even on the ballot in most southern states.

Breckinridge was the clear favorite among southern voters, carrying every cotton state, along with North Carolina, Delaware, and Maryland. The **border states** of Virginia, Kentucky, and Tennessee—whose economic interests were not as closely tied to slavery as the cotton states were—gave their votes to Bell. Stephen A. Douglas, although running second to Lincoln in the popular vote, won only in Missouri and New Jersey.

The election of 1860 demonstrated that Americans' worst fears had come to pass. There were no longer any national political parties. Bell and

The Candidates for President, 1860

ABRAHAM LINCOLN	STEPHEN DOUGLAS	JOHN BELL	JOHN BRECKINRIDGE
• Republican • Illinois • Platform: Slavery must not be allowed in the territories.	• Northern Democrat • Illinois • Platform: Popular sovereignty should decide the issue of slavery in the territories when they become states.	• Constitutional Unionist • Tennessee • Platform: The federal government should support slavery and also defend the Union.	• Southern Democrat • Kentucky • Platform: The federal government must protect slavery.

>> **Analyze Charts** On which main issue did the candidates in the 1860 election disagree?

The Election of 1860

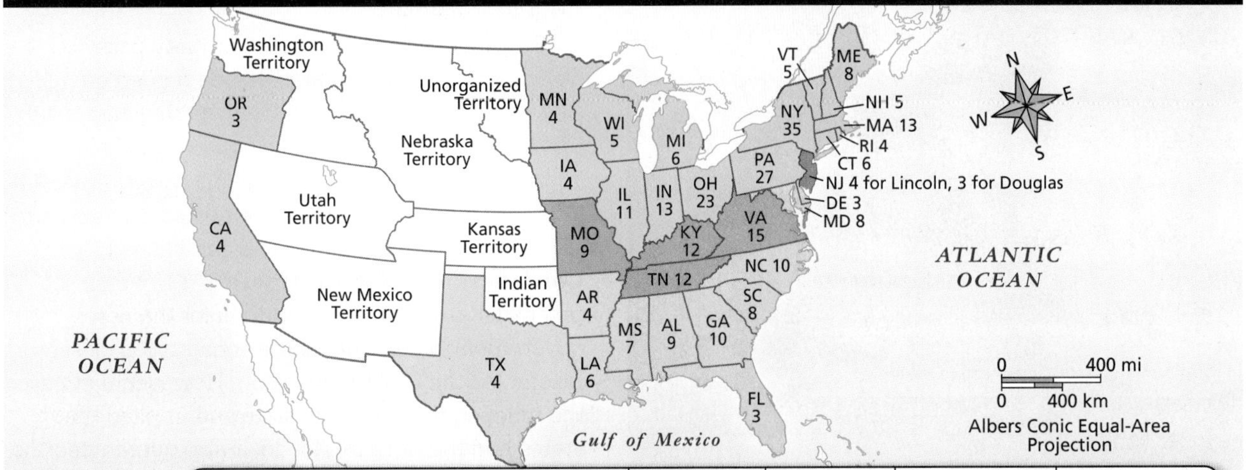

Candidate (Party)	Electoral Vote	Popular Vote	% Electoral Vote	% Popular Vote
Abraham Lincoln (Republican)	180	1,866,452	59	40
John C. Breckinridge (Southern Democrat)	72	847,953	24	18
Stephen A. Douglas (Democrat)	12	1,380,202	4	29
John Bell (Constitutional Union)	39	590,901	13	13
New Jersey Electoral Votes: 4 Lincoln, 3 Douglas				

>> **Analyze Maps** How was Lincoln able to win election as President without carrying any southern states?

Breckinridge competed for southern votes, while Douglas and Lincoln competed in the North and West. The North and South were now effectively two political entities, and there seemed no way to bridge the gap.

☑ **EXPLAIN** How did the election of 1860 reflect the break between the North and the South?

The Collapse of the Union

Southerners were outraged that a President could be elected without a single southern vote. In the southerners' perception, the South no longer had a voice in the national government. They decided to act.

Southern States Secede As soon as Lincoln's election was confirmed, the South Carolina legislature summoned a state convention. Meeting in Charleston on December 20, 1860, and without a dissenting vote, the convention declared that "the union now subsisting between South Carolina and the other States, under the name of the 'United States of America,' is hereby dissolved." They cited as their reason for seceding the election of a President "whose opinions and purposes are hostile to slavery."

> On the 4th of March next, [a new administration] will take possession of the Government. It has announced . . . that a war must be waged against slavery until it shall cease throughout the United States. . . . The Guarantees of the Constitution will then no longer exist; the equal rights of the States will be lost. The slaveholding States will no longer have the power of self-government, or self-protection, and the Federal Government will have become their enemy.
>
> —Declaration of the Immediate Causes Which Induce and Justify the Secession of South Carolina From the Federal Union, December 20, 1860

In the next few weeks, six other states of the Deep South seceded from the Union. Sentiments favoring secession were not always unanimous, with the gravest doubts surfacing in Georgia. State senator Alexander H. Stephens, though alarmed by Lincoln's election, was devoted to the Union of states under the Constitution: "This government of our fathers, with all its defects, comes nearer the objects

>> The Confederate cabinet included former U.S. Congressmen Alexander Stephens (seated center left) and John Reagan (seated center right), and U.S. Senators Judah P. Benjamin (seated far left), Stephen M. Mallory (seated left), and Robert Toombs (seated far right).

BOUNCE to Activate Chart

>> James Buchanan's failure to keep the nation together in late 1860 has led many historians to consider him the worst president in U.S. history.

of all good government than any other on the face of the Earth," he said.

But Georgia voted to secede anyway. Like delegates in the other states that depended on slavery to grow cotton, they believed they had to take this step to protect their property and way of life.

The Confederate States of America In February 1861, the seven seceding states established the **Confederate States of America**. They then proceeded to frame a constitution for the new government. The Confederate constitution closely resembled the U.S. Constitution. However, it stressed the independence of each state and implied that states had the right to secede. It also guaranteed the protection of slavery. To win the support of Britain and France, which adamantly opposed the trade in enslaved people, it prohibited importing new enslaved people from other countries.

Not all southerners backed the Confederacy. Some large planters with economic ties to the North still hoped for a compromise. So, too, did many small farmers with no vested interest in slavery. To gain the loyalty of such citizens, the Confederacy chose former Mississippi senator Jefferson Davis as their president.

Davis had supported the Compromise of 1850, but he had also insisted that the South should be left alone to manage its own culture and institutions—including slavery.

The Two Sides Fail to Compromise Some politicians sought a final compromise. Kentucky senator John Crittenden proposed a constitutional amendment allowing slavery in western territories south of the Missouri Compromise line. He also called for federal funds to reimburse enslavers for unreturned fugitives. Lincoln, now President-elect, warned that Crittenden's plan would "lose us everything we gained by the election." A narrow margin of senators voted down this **Crittenden Compromise**.

President Buchanan, in his last few weeks in office, told Congress that he had no authority to prevent secession. He lamented the breakup of the Union and sympathized with the South's concerns, but he made no serious effort to resolve the crisis. Other pacifying attempts also failed. A secret peace convention held in Washington, which drew delegates from the border states as well as the North and South, failed to reach a compromise that could save the Union.

Union Forts Seized by the Confederacy, January–April, 1861

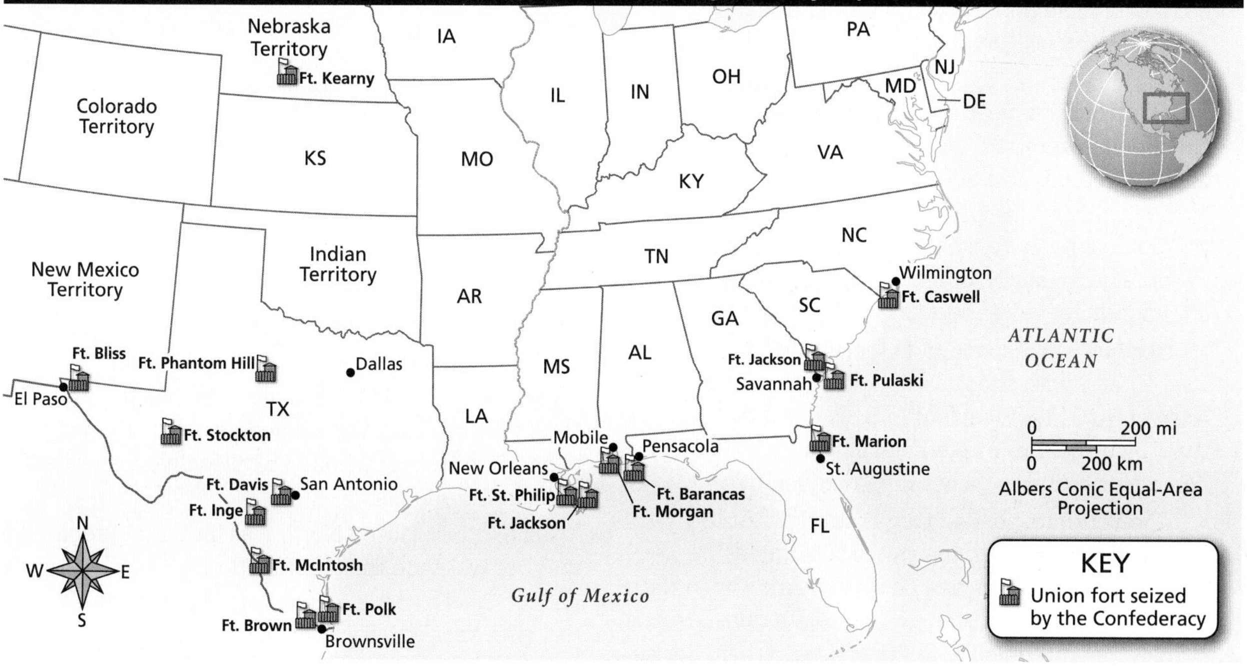

>> **Analyze Maps** What geographic factors made certain Union forts vulnerable to Confederate forces?

Lincoln Appeals to the South Amid this turmoil, the new President took office. Lincoln had no illusions about the challenge he faced. He confronted "a task," he feared, "greater than that which rested upon [President George] Washington."

Lincoln was sworn in as President on March 4, 1861. In his inaugural address, he took a firm but conciliatory tone toward the South. "I have no purpose, directly or indirectly, to interfere with the institution of slavery in the states where it exists," he began. But he did intend to preserve the Union. "No state, upon its own mere action, can lawfully get out of the Union," he said. Still, he would avoid violence. There would be no war, he pledged, unless the South started it. He concluded with an appeal to the South to live in peace.

> We are not enemies, but friends. We must not be enemies. Though passion may have strained, it must not break our bonds of affection. The mystic chords of memory, stretching from every battle-field, and patriot grave, to every living heart and hearthstone, all over this broad land, will yet swell the chorus of the Union, when again touched, as surely they will be, by the better angels of our nature.
>
> —Abraham Lincoln, March 4, 1861

Conflict Erupts over Federal Forts and Arsenals When the southern states seceded, they seized the federal forts and arsenals within their borders. Only four forts remained in Union hands. The most important of these was **Fort Sumter**, which guarded the harbor at Charleston, South Carolina. In January 1861, President Buchanan tried to send troops and supplies to the fort, but the unarmed supply ship sailed away when Confederate guns fired on it. Upon taking office, Lincoln had to decide whether to take the risk required to hold on to these forts or yield to Confederate demands that they be surrendered.

By April, the troops at the fort desperately needed food and supplies. Lincoln, who still hoped to bring back the South without bloodshed, faced a dilemma. Should he try to resupply the fort? Or should he let the Confederates take it? Lincoln struggled to make a decision. During his inaugural address, he had promised southerners that "the government will not assail you." But as President, he was sworn to defend the property of the United States. A wrong move could touch off a war. At last, trying to steer a middle course, Lincoln notified South Carolina that he was sending supplies—food only, no arms—to the fort.

The Confederacy Attacks Fort Sumter South Carolinians were suspicious of Lincoln's motives and ordered the Fort Sumter garrison to surrender to the Confederacy. When the Union troops refused, the Confederates fired on the fort. The Union troops eventually ran out of ammunition, forcing the commander to surrender.

Northerners responded to the attack on Fort Sumter with shock and anger. A few days later, on April 15, President Lincoln declared that "insurrection" existed and called for 75,000 volunteers to fight against the Confederacy.

The South responded just as strongly. At the outbreak of hostilities, the states of Virginia, Arkansas, Tennessee, and North Carolina joined the Confederacy. As in the North, the South raised troops quickly and struggled to equip and train them before sending them into battle.

Both sides predicted a short skirmish, with victory only a few days or months away. These predictions were unfounded. Americans faced years of terrible suffering before the fighting that had begun at Fort Sumter finally ended.

☑ **SUMMARIZE** What events led to the onset of the Civil War?

Resources and Strategies

In 1861, the long, bitter dispute over slavery erupted into war. The first shots at Fort Sumter set the stage for a long, costly struggle. At stake was the survival of the United States.

As the Civil War began, each side possessed significant strengths and notable weaknesses. At first glance, most advantages appeared to add up in favor of the Union.

The Union's Advantages The North enjoyed a tremendous advantage in population. Nearly 21 million people lived in the states that stayed in the Union. By contrast, the Confederacy had a population of only 9 million, of whom 3.5 million were enslaved African Americans.

The industrialized North was far better prepared to wage war than the agrarian South. Most of the nation's coal and iron came from Union mines, and the vast West was a source of gold, silver, and other resources.

The densely populated urban areas of the Northeast supported a wide variety of manufacturing. With mechanized factories and a steady flow of European immigrants seeking work, the Union could produce more ammunition, arms, uniforms, medical supplies, and railroad cars than the Confederacy could. In addition, the Union had a larger railroad network for moving troops and material.

The Union had a small but well-organized navy. By the spring of 1861, the Union had about 40

Timeline of Events Leading to the Civil War

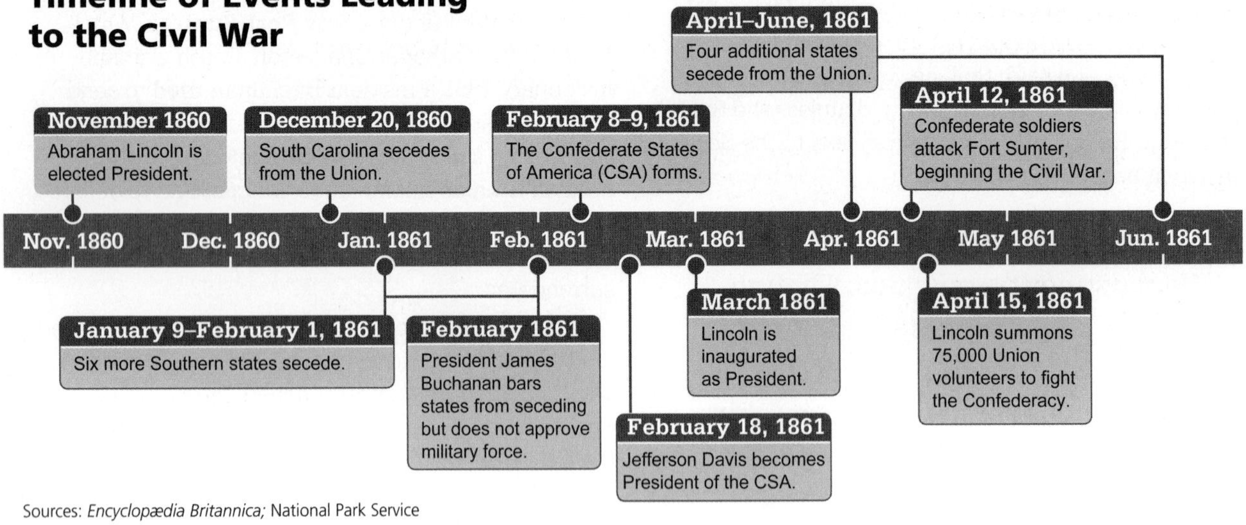

Sources: *Encyclopædia Britannica;* National Park Service

>> **Analyze Information** What do you think was the most significant turning point in the events leading to the war? Justify your response.

UNION AND CONFEDERATE RESOURCES, 1861

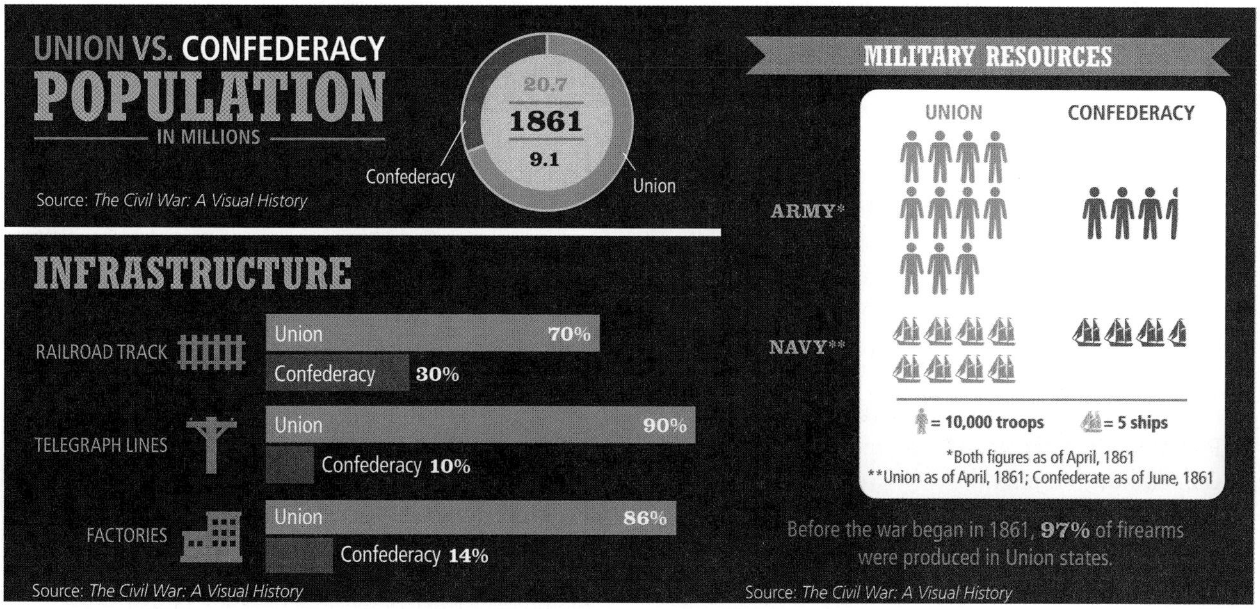

>> **Analyze Information** Based on this infographic, which side had the advantage in terms of resources at the beginning of the war? What strategies might the disadvantaged side use to resist the other side's superiority?

seaworthy vessels, with more under construction. By the end of 1861, the North had more than 250 vessels. The South had only about 20 ships when war broke out, leaving it vulnerable to a naval **blockade**, in which Union ships prevented merchant vessels from entering or leaving the South's few good ports, thereby crippling southern trade.

Finally, while the Confederate government was new and inexperienced, the North had an established government and an outstanding leader in Abraham Lincoln. Not everyone recognized this fact at the outset of the war, but Lincoln's leadership would prove invaluable to the Union cause.

The Confederacy's Advantages Still, the North did have some distinct weaknesses compared to the South. One of the Confederacy's advantages was psychological. Many northerners were willing to let the South go. To them, preserving the Union was not worth killing and dying for. But the Confederacy was fighting for survival. Although there were pockets of pro-Union feeling in places such as western Virginia, most southern whites believed passionately in the Confederate cause. Even those who were not enslavers resented what they saw as northern efforts to dominate them.

When the war began, the regular U.S. Army, consisting of professional soldiers, numbered only about 16,000 men, some of whom became Confederates. Lincoln called for 75,000 new recruits and received an enthusiastic response, with 100,000 men volunteering from the northern states. However, these new recruits signed on for three months of service, hardly long enough to form an efficient fighting team. The South faced similar challenges in assembling its armies, but it had a strong military tradition and fine leaders like Virginia's **Robert E. Lee**. Lee, who had an outstanding record in the United States Army, actually opposed secession and slavery. Yet he turned down an offer to command Union forces.

> With all my devotion to the Union, and the feeling of loyalty and duty of an American citizen, I have not been able to make up my mind to raise my hand against my relatives, my children, my home. I have therefore resigned my commission in the army, and save in defense of my native state... I hope I may never be called upon to draw my sword.
>
> —Robert E. Lee, letter to his sister, April 20, 1861

In fact, Lee did accept command of the Confederate Army and provided the South with inspiring military leadership throughout the war. The North struggled to find a commander of such caliber.

Finally, the Confederacy had a number of strategic advantages. It did not need to conquer the North; it simply had to avoid defeat, expecting that in time the North would give up the effort. By and large, southern forces would be fighting a defensive war on familiar, friendly ground while northern forces had to fight an offensive war in enemy territory. Union troops and supplies had to travel farther to reach the field of battle.

The North also had to devote precious military resources to defending Washington, D.C. Only the Potomac River separated the Union capital from Confederate Virginia.

The Confederacy Counts on Time and Foreign Aid As the two sides prepared for war, Union and Confederate leaders contemplated their goals and how they might go about meeting them. While northerners hoped for a quick victory, southern strategists planned for a prolonged war.

The strategy of the Confederacy had two main thrusts. Militarily, the South hoped to preserve its small armies while doing enough damage to erode the Union's will to fight. Politically, it hoped to win formal recognition from Britain and France. Trade with these nations was crucial to the South, since the supply of manufactured goods from the North was now cut off. By the same token, the European textile industry was dependent on southern cotton. Confederate leaders reasoned that if the war dragged on, French and British mills would run out of raw cotton. Therefore, these countries might be willing to provide military aid to the South.

>> Residents of border states had divided allegiances. Some, like this soldier of the 33rd Missouri, fought for the Union. Others crossed state lines to join the Confederate Army.

The Union Plans Its Attack The initial Union strategy was a two-part plan devised by General Winfield Scott, a Virginia-born hero of the Mexican-American War and the commander of all U.S. forces in 1861. First, the Union would blockade southern ports, starving the South of income and supplies. Then, Union forces would drive southward along the Mississippi River. Union control of the Mississippi would split the Confederacy in two, fatally weakening it. Scott's plan came to be known as the **Anaconda Plan**, after a type of snake that coils around its prey and squeezes it to death.

Some antislavery congressmen thought Scott's plan was too timid. They favored a massive military campaign that would quickly free enslaved people across the South. Lincoln also hoped that a decisive victory over rebel forces massed in northern Virginia and around Richmond might lead the Confederacy to negotiate an end to the crisis. Despite such criticism and concentration on winning quickly, the Anaconda Plan remained central to the Union war strategy.

Lincoln Appeases the Border States The Union also faced a tricky political question: how to prevent the secession of Missouri, Kentucky, Delaware, and Maryland. Although these border states allowed slavery, they had not joined the Confederacy. Lincoln knew that if they chose to secede, the Union could be lost. To reduce this threat, the President insisted that his only goal was to save the Union. In his First Inaugural Address, he announced, "I believe I have no lawful right to [interfere with slavery], and I have no inclination to do so." Although Lincoln's stand troubled abolitionists, he did succeed in keeping the border states loyal to the Union.

☑ **COMPARE AND CONTRAST** How did the Union and the Confederacy compare in strengths and weaknesses?

The Civil War, 1861–1862

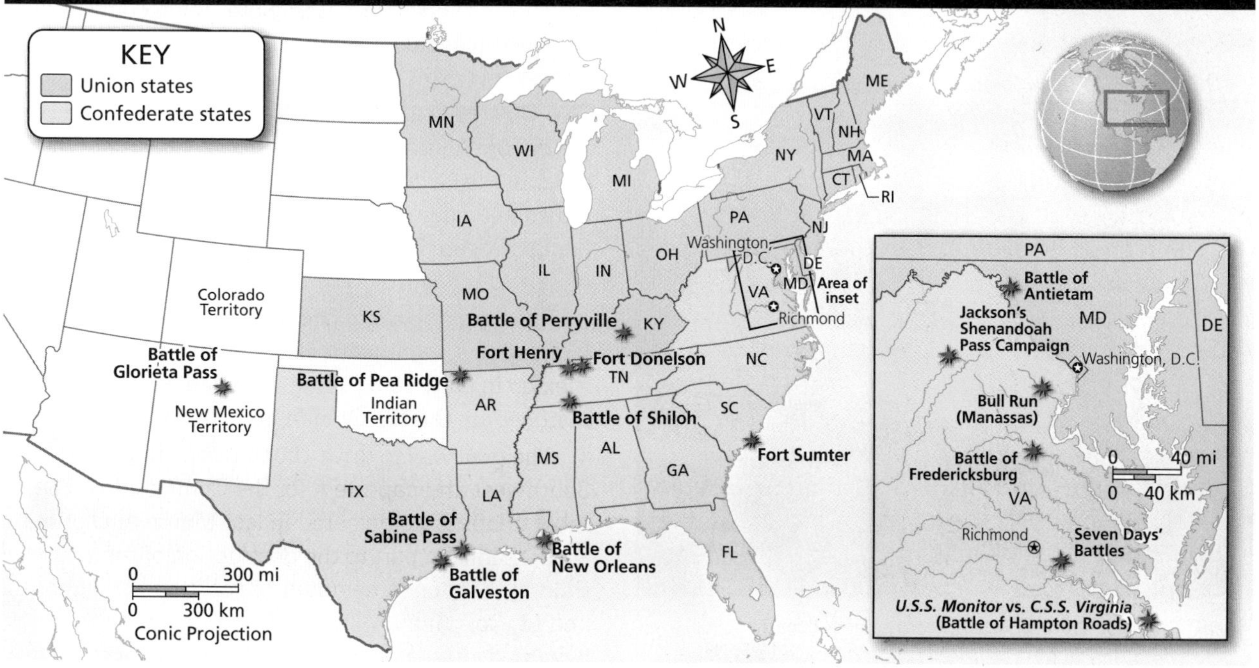

>> **Analyze Maps** Which regions of the country experienced the most significant fighting during 1861 and 1862?

BOUNCE to Activate Timeline

The First Year of the Civil War

The Civil War started slowly. The first large battle did not take place until three months after the firing on Fort Sumter. Ultimately, the conflict would span nearly four years and stretch across much of the continent.

Stonewall Jackson Rebuffs the Union In July 1861, General Scott sent General Irvin McDowell and more than 30,000 Union troops to do battle with Confederate forces waiting outside Washington. The two armies met at Bull Run, a creek near Manassas, Virginia. In the battle's first hours, Union troops gained the upper hand. But a determined stand led by Confederate General Thomas J. Jackson sent them scrambling back to Washington. Confederates nicknamed their hero **"Stonewall" Jackson** in honor of his refusal to yield to the Union armies.

The battle, known as the Battle of Bull Run in the North and the Battle of Manassas in the South, surprised those who had hoped the war would end quickly—and who were unprepared for the carnage modern warfare could produce. Lincoln responded by calling for additional troops and by replacing McDowell with **General George B. McClellan**.

The Battle of Shiloh Shocks Both Sides While McClellan began to organize his Army of the Potomac, **General Ulysses S. Grant** pursued the Mississippi Valley wing of the Anaconda Plan. In February 1862, he directed the attack and capture of two Confederate strongholds—Fort Henry on the Tennessee River and Fort Donelson on the Cumberland River. His bold action drove Confederate forces from western Kentucky and much of Tennessee and boosted northern morale. However, in April, Grant's troops fought a terrible battle in southwest Tennessee. In just two days of fighting, nearly 25,000 Union and Confederate soldiers were killed or wounded. The **Battle of Shiloh** horrified both the North and South and damaged Grant's rising reputation.

The Union Claims New Orleans While Shiloh shocked the public, it did not slow the course of the war. Just days later, Union ships under the command of David Farragut sailed through the Gulf of Mexico and seized the vital southern port of New Orleans at the mouth of the Mississippi. Emboldened by his success, Farragut continued to sail north, hoping to capture the Confederate stronghold of Vicksburg, Mississippi. The Confederates, however, stopped Farragut's fleet more than 50 miles from his goal. Meanwhile, pushing southward from Tennessee,

>> This 1862 illustration depicts the naval conflict between the Union *Monitor* and Confederate *Virginia*, formerly known as the *Merrimack*. **Contrast** How was the fighting between ironclads different from that of earlier naval wars?

>> The Confederate States of America established its capital at Richmond, Virginia, just over 100 miles from the Union capital at Washington, D.C.

Grant's land forces were also checked in their advance on Vicksburg. Complete Union control of the Mississippi would have to wait.

The Confederates Lose the Southwest The American Southwest held strategic value to both sides in the Civil War. The region held rich gold mines and offered access to California and the Pacific Ocean. Despite its importance, neither side stationed many troops in the region.

Fighting did take place as far west as Arizona. But the most significant action occurred in New Mexico in early 1862, when a Confederate force marched up the Rio Grande from Texas.

The goal was to drive Union troops from the Southwest and capture it for the Confederacy. The rebel troops were defeated in late March at Glorieta Pass, thanks in part to the destruction of their supply train by a Union force under Major John Chivington and Lt. Col. Manuel Chavez. The Confederates eventually retreated back into Texas, never to mount another threat to Union control of the Southwest.

The Union and Confederacy also vied for the loyalty of the Southwest's residents—many of whom in the past had been treated as outcasts. The Union got help from Mexican American militia in Texas, which worked to disrupt Confederate supply lines. Both sides also courted American Indian groups throughout the entire West. The Cheyennes were able to bargain with the Union government for land in return for their aid. The Confederates persuaded the Creeks and Choctaws to support their cause. They also sought support from the Cherokee nation. The Cherokees, however, split over the question of which side to support. Such conflict within American Indian groups was not uncommon as loyalties shifted during the course of the war.

Ironclad Ships Take to the Seas Few of the major battles of the Civil War took place at sea. However, one notable exception occurred in 1862 when the Union ship *Monitor* clashed with its Confederate opponent *Virginia* off the Virginia coast. The Union had hired a European engineer to design the *Monitor* as a model for a fleet of ships plated with iron armor. The Confederacy, meanwhile, had built the ironclad *Virginia* by refitting a Union ship previously known as the *Merrimack*. On March 9, the two ironclads met in battle. Though neither ship emerged the victor, the contest signaled the beginning of the end of wooden warships.

☑ **DESCRIBE** How did the early battles of the Civil War surprise both sides?

A Stalemate in the East

While Union and Confederate forces squared off in the Mississippi Valley and farther west, major fighting in the East focused on the state of Virginia. As elsewhere, the outcomes did not prove decisive for either side.

General McClellan Favors Caution Since taking command of Union forces after Bull Run, General McClellan had been planning what he hoped would be a decisive drive on the Confederate capital at Richmond, Virginia. A skilled leader beloved by his troops, McClellan was also very cautious. He did not want to execute his plan until he felt his troops were ready.

McClellan's caution caused friction with Lincoln, who was anxious for military victories. Yet, even as he pushed McClellan to act, the President was unwilling to give the general all the forces for which he asked. Lincoln insisted on holding a large force near the capital to protect it from Confederate attack. Stonewall Jackson's brilliant campaign in the spring of 1862 in the nearby Shenandoah Valley of Virginia increased Lincoln's concerns.

By midsummer, Lincoln insisted that McClellan take action. Reluctantly, McClellan sailed his army southward across Chesapeake Bay. The force landed on a peninsula southeast of Richmond and then began its march toward the capital. For this reason, the action was called the Peninsular Campaign.

General Lee's Leadership Holds Richmond McClellan's army was actually larger than the force defending Richmond. But Confederate General Robert E. Lee led his troops skillfully. In a series of battles known as the Seven Days (June 26–July 2), Lee took advantage of McClellan's cautious style. The Union advance stalled and McClellan retreated to Washington.

After the retreat, Lincoln replaced McClellan. This move proved to be a mistake. At the Second Battle of Bull Run in late August, Lee's Confederates handed the Union a crushing defeat. Stonewall Jackson was instrumental in outmanuevering a larger Union force and nearly destroying it before the Federals could retreat.

The victory, known in the South as the Second Battle of Manassas, led Lincoln to return McClellan to command. Lee and McClellan would soon face off in the single bloodiest day of the Civil War.

EXPLAIN Why did the Union advance into Confederate territory in the summer of 1962? What was the result of this campaign?

GO ONLINE to access these biographies: Abraham Lincoln, Jefferson Davis

>> Virginian Thomas "Stonewall" Jackson was one of the Confederate Army's finest generals. He led troops at key battles, including the First and Second Battles of Bull Run, Antietam, and Chancellorsville.

ASSESSMENT

1. **Discuss** What was the Republican Party's platform and what factors led to its nomination of Abraham Lincoln in the presidential campaign of 1860?
2. **Draw Conclusions** What were the main ideals of the Confederate States of America? Why was Jefferson Davis chosen as its president?
3. **Discuss** What were the Confederacy's military and political strategies to win the Civil War?
4. **Discuss** What was the role of warships in the Civil War?
5. **Identify Central Ideas** In what way did President Lincoln and General McClellen disagree on Union strategy?
6. **Connections to Today** How did the formation of the Confederate States of America demonstrate how regional differences can lead to political problems?

7.4

Soldiers of the 4th U.S. Colored Infantry at Fort Lincoln just outside Washington, D.C.

BOUNCE to Activate Flipped Video

Objectives

Analyze why Lincoln decided to issue the Emancipation Proclamation and what it achieved.

Assess the different roles that African Americans played in the Civil War.

Key Terms

contraband
Battle of Antietam
Emancipation Proclamation
Militia Act
54th Massachusetts Regiment

African Americans and the War

Despite Lincoln's efforts to downplay the issue of slavery, abolitionists kept up the pressure to end slavery. Soon, Lincoln himself recognized the need to include freedom for enslaved African Americans among the goals of the war. His actions helped bring about the beginning of the end of slavery in the United States. At the same time, African American soldiers joined the fight for freedom.

Emancipation and the Civil War

Pressures at home and abroad urged Lincoln to address slavery. Abolitionists, such as Frederick Douglass and William Lloyd Garrison, as well as the thousands who supported them, were impatient with Lincoln's policies. Another reason for Lincoln to act was that slavery was unpopular in Europe. Antislavery sentiment was one of the main reasons why Great Britain was reluctant to aid the Confederacy.

Union Troops Meet Enslaved African Americans On the battlefield, Union officers faced a dilemma: what to do with enslaved African Americans who came under their control. It was absurd, argued these officers, to return enslaved people to their enslavers. Early on, Union General Benjamin Butler had gathered hundreds of African American refugees into his camps and set them to manual labor. He declared the fugitives under his protection to be **contraband**, or captured war supplies. General John Frémont went a step further, declaring that enslaved people who came under his command in Missouri were free. Fearing retaliation from the border states, Lincoln reversed Frémont's order.

GO ONLINE to access your digital course

Lincoln Proposes a Plan for Emancipation

Lincoln realized he could not avoid the slavery issue for long. He secretly began working on a plan for the emancipation of enslaved African Americans living in Confederate states. In the summer of 1862, he shared his ideas with a surprised Cabinet. The members generally supported Lincoln's plan but agreed that its announcement should wait. After the Union failure at the Second Battle of Bull Run, such a proclamation might look like an act of desperation.

What was needed was a major Union victory. Several weeks later, Lincoln got his opportunity.

Victory at Antietam Provides an Opportunity

After his army's recent victories, General Lee was brimming with confidence. In early September 1862, he led his troops into Maryland, the border state where many favored the South. Lee hoped to inspire a pro-Confederate uprising. A victory on Union soil might also spur European recognition of the Confederacy. Lee also hoped to acquire an abundance of food supplies for his hungry army in an area unmolested by war.

Lee's invasion did not go according to plan. On September 8, the general issued a "Proclamation to the People of Maryland" that invited them to ally themselves with the South. But Marylanders responded to the invitation with far less enthusiasm than Lee had anticipated. A few days later, Union soldiers found a copy of Lee's battle plan wrapped around some cigars at an abandoned rebel campsite. As a result, Lee lost the crucial element of surprise. When McClellan reviewed the orders, he exclaimed, "Here is a paper with which if I cannot whip Bobbie Lee, I will be willing to go home."

The two armies converged at Sharpsburg, Maryland, and McClellan's troops fanned out near Antietam Creek. On September 17, Union troops attacked Lee's army in three phases, moving from one side of the Confederate line to the other. By the end of the day, more than 23,000 soldiers lay dead or wounded. The **Battle of Antietam** marked the bloodiest single day of the Civil War. With his army exhausted and Maryland still in the Union, Lee retreated to Virginia. Though Union losses exceeded Confederate losses, Lincoln had the victory he needed to move forward with emancipation.

EXPLAIN Why did Lincoln consider emancipation, and why did he wait to announce his plan?

>> Massachusetts newspaper publisher William Lloyd Garrison was one of the nation's leading abolitionists.

>> Enslaved people known as "contrabands" escaped from southern plantations to gather behind Union lines for protection. Before 1863, however, they could not legally claim freedom from enslavement.

The Emancipation Proclamation

>> This 1864 painting depicts Lincoln's presentation of the Emancipation Proclamation to members of his Cabinet. Secretary of War Edwin Stanton sits at the far left, and Secretary of State William Seward sits facing Lincoln.

BOUNCE to Activate Gallery

>> An abolitionist illustration contrasts the horrors faced by enslaved people with a vision of a better life under freedom. **Contrast** How does the artist suggest that life will change for African Americans after emancipation?

On September 22, 1862, Lincoln formally announced the **Emancipation Proclamation**. Issued as a military decree, it freed all enslaved people in states still in rebellion against the Union after January 1, 1863. It did not, however, apply to loyal border states or to places that were already under Union military control. Lincoln hoped that the proclamation might convince some southern states to surrender before the January 1 deadline.

Many northerners responded to the Emancipation Proclamation with great excitement. "We shout for joy that we live to record this righteous decree," rejoiced Frederick Douglass. Some who had once criticized Lincoln for inaction now praised his name and held rallies in honor of the proclamation, such as an African American minister in Philadelphia.

> The morning dawns! The long night of sorrow and gloom is past. . . . The Proclamation has gone forth, and God is saying . . . to this nation Man must be free. . . . Your destiny as white men and ours as black men are one and the same.
>
> —Jonathan C. Gibbs, January 1, 1863

Critics on Both Sides Respond Others were less enthusiastic. William Lloyd Garrison grumbled that "what is still needed is a proclamation distinctly announcing the total abolition of slavery." British abolitionists applauded the President's move—but also wondered about Lincoln's conviction, since he attacked slavery only in areas over which he had no control. Lincoln also received criticism in Congress. Many Republicans felt that the proclamation had not gone far enough, while many Democrats felt that it was too drastic a step. The Proclamation may have been one factor leading to Democratic gains in the fall congressional elections.

The Proclamation Changes the War Although the Emancipation Proclamation did not actually free a single enslaved African American, it was an important turning point in the war. For white southerners, the call to free enslaved people ended any desire for a negotiated end to the war. Confederate leaders now determined that they must fight to the end.

For African Americans in the North, the proclamation made them eager to join the Union army and fight against slavery. Even before Lincoln's decree, growing demands by African Americans—and a growing need for soldiers on the frontlines—had led the Union to reconsider its ban on African American soldiers. Just two months before the proclamation, Congress had passed the **Militia Act**, mandating that African American soldiers be accepted into the military.

☑ **SUMMARIZE** What impact did the Emancipation Proclamation have?

African Americans Join the Fight

With the Emancipation Proclamation, the Union moved from allowing African American troops to actively recruiting them. African American and abolitionist leaders were asked to seek volunteers. The abolitionist governor of Massachusetts enthusiastically supported the formation of the all African American **54th Massachusetts Regiment**. By war's end, more than 180,000 African American volunteers had served in the Union military. The Confederacy considered drafting enslaved and free African Americans in 1863 and 1864, but most white southerners opposed their enlistment.

Earning Respect and Honor Racist attitudes left many whites with low expectations for African American troops. But performance in battle proved these expectations to be false. In June 1863, accounts appeared of a battle in Port Hudson, Mississippi—the first major test for African American soldiers.

A Union officer declared that "my prejudices with regard to negro troops have been dispelled by the battle. . . . The brigade of negroes behaved magnificently."

A few weeks later, the 54th Massachusetts followed Robert Gould Shaw, their respected white officer, into battle at Fort Wagner in Charleston harbor. During the unsuccessful assault, Shaw and many of his men were killed. Nevertheless, the 54th had earned respect for its discipline and courage. One soldier received the Congressional Medal of Honor—the first of almost two dozen African American soldiers to be decorated for bravery.

Still, African American troops faced prejudice. They were usually assigned menial tasks, such as cooking, cleaning, and digging latrines. They often

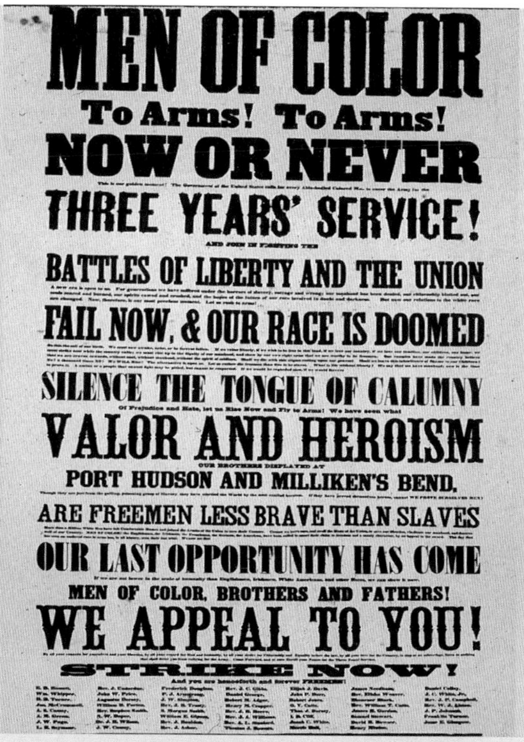

>> Posters like this one urged northern African American men to join the Union Army and fight in the Civil War. Famed abolitionist Frederick Douglass is one of the signers listed. **Generate Explanations** Why might abolitionists have supported African American enlistment?

BOUNCE to Activate Gallery

>> This drummer had been enslaved prior to his service in the 79th U.S. Colored Infantry.

>> Before the Emancipation Proclamation, "contraband" escapees from the South could not formally join the Union Army, but they often served unofficially in support roles. These men worked driving pack teams and moving supplies.

served the longest guard duty and were placed in exposed battle positions. It took a three-year effort to win equal pay. African American soldiers also knew that if captured, they would be killed. In one bloody incident, Confederates massacred nearly 200 African American soldiers who were trying to surrender at Fort Pillow, Tennessee. Nevertheless, African Americans supported the Union in hundreds of battles, and some 70,000 lost their lives.

Enslaved People Support the Union Enslaved African Americans in the South also played an important role in the war, finding a variety of ways to passively or actively help the Union forces. White enslavers often abandoned plantations for the safety of southern cities, leaving enslaved African Americans to manage the estate. Advancing Union forces often enlisted these African Americans to produce food for northern troops.

Other African Americans used their familiarity with the terrain to serve as spies or scouts for Union armies. Sometimes, emancipated African Americans organized their own military units. Regiments of freed African Americans appeared in such places as South Carolina, Kansas, and Missouri. Across the South, African Americans seized the opportunity to begin to shape their own civilian lives. Some demanded, and got, wages for their work. Others simply abandoned their enslavers, fleeing to Union camps or to the North or West. They turned Lincoln's promise of freedom into a reality. However, many enslaved African Americans in the South were forced to serve the Confederacy, most often as laborers.

EXPLAIN What effect did the Emancipation Proclamation have on African American soldiers?

ASSESSMENT

1. **Identify Cause and Effect** What effect did the Battle of Antietam have on the Union and Confederate armies?
2. **Cite Evidence** How did critics respond to the Emancipation Proclamation, and what impact did it have on American politics?
3. **Identify Cause and Effect** How did enslaved African Americans in the South help the Union war effort?
4. **Check Understanding** What was the Confederacy's policy regarding African American soldiers? What impact did this policy have on their war effort?
5. **Quest Connections** How do you think most members of the 54th Massachusetts Regiment justified fighting in the Civil War?

Emancipation Proclamation: Abraham Lincoln

Five days after the Union victory at Antietam, Abraham Lincoln issued the Emancipation Proclamation. The presidential decree freed all enslaved persons in states under Confederate control as of January 1, 1863. One of the most important documents in American history, it changed the nature of the Union cause and paved the way for the eventual abolition of slavery by the Thirteenth Amendment in 1865.

Primary Source

Whereas on the twenty-second day of September, in the year of our Lord one thousand eight hundred and sixty-two, a proclamation was issued by the President of the United States, containing, among other things, the following, to wit [namely]:

That on the first day of January, in the year of our Lord one thousand eight hundred and sixty-three, all persons held as slaves within any State or designated part of a State, the people whereof shall then be in rebellion against the United States, shall be then, thenceforward [from then on], and forever free; and the Executive Government of the United States, including the military and naval authority thereof, will recognize and maintain the freedom of such persons, and will do no act or acts to repress such persons, or any of them, in any efforts they may make for their actual freedom. . . .

And by virtue of the power, and for the purpose aforesaid, I do order and declare that all persons held as slaves within said designated States, and parts of States, are, and henceforward shall be free; and that the Executive government of the United States, including the military and naval authorities thereof, will recognize and maintain the freedom of said persons.

And I hereby enjoin [direct; order] upon the people so declared to be free to abstain from all violence, unless in necessary self-defence; and I recommend to them that, in all cases when allowed, they labor faithfully for reasonable wages.

And I further declare and make known, that such persons of suitable condition, will be received into the armed services of the United States to garrison [occupy with troops] forts, positions, stations, and other places, and to man vessels of all sorts in said service.

And upon this act, sincerely believed to be an act of justice, warranted [authorized; justified] by the Constitution, upon military necessity, I invoke the considerate judgment of mankind, and the gracious favor of Almighty God. . . .

ASSESSMENT

1. **Draw Conclusions** The number of enslaved people who were freed because of the Emancipation Proclamation increased gradually over time. Why do you think that was?
2. **Determine Author's Purpose** Why do you think President Lincoln issued the proclamation? Explain your answer.
3. **Explain an Argument** What justification does Lincoln give for issuing the proclamation?
4. **Assess an Argument** Do you agree with the justifications you cited in the previous answer? Why or why not?
5. **Integrate Information from Diverse Sources** How do the ideas expressed in the Emancipation Proclamation relate to the ideas expressed in both the Declaration of Independence and the U.S. Constitution? Is the proclamation an extension of these documents, a rebuttal to them, or something else? Explain your answer.

GO ONLINE to access primary sources

7.5

Civil War physician Mary Edwards Walker was the first woman to serve with the Army Medical Corps and the first woman to win the Congressional Medal of Honor.

BOUNCE to Activate Flipped Video

Objectives

Analyze how the war changed the economy and society in the North and the South.

Discuss how northern and southern soldiers experienced the war.

Explain the impact of the war on women.

Key Terms

income tax
bond
Homestead Act
conscription
Copperhead
habeas corpus
inflation
Clara Barton
Susie King Taylor

GO ONLINE to access your digital course

Everyday Life During the War

As African Americans rushed to join Union ranks, the war dragged on. The fighting brought hard times to the home fronts of both the North and South and helped transform many aspects of American life. Between 1861 and 1865, the economy and society of both regions underwent deep and lasting changes. These changes would help launch the North into the modern world, while the South suffered physical and social damage that persisted for decades.

Daily Life in the North

The war had a huge impact on northern industry. For example, the drop in southern cotton production severely damaged the large cotton textiles industry. At the same time, other industries boomed as demand for clothing, arms, and other supplies spiked. To meet the demand, industry became more mechanized.

Efforts to Support the War Paying to supply the military was a major economic challenge. To help meet the cost, the Union government introduced a tax based on an individual's earnings. At first, the **income tax** was 3 percent on all income over $800 a year. As the war continued, the tax was increased. The Union also raised tariffs, which brought in revenue and helped northern industry by raising the cost of imported goods.

The biggest source of wartime funds came from the sale of government **bonds**. In return for the purchase price, the buyer received a certificate promising to pay the holder a larger amount of money at a future date. The Union sold billions of dollars worth of bonds to banks and individuals. Citizens were encouraged to buy bonds as an act of patriotism.

To increase the amount of cash in circulation and to help people buy war bonds, Congress passed the Legal Tender Act in 1862. This law allowed the Treasury to issue paper money, called "greenbacks" because of the color of the paper used. For the first time, the United States had a single, common currency that its citizens could use to purchase goods.

The War Spurs Expansion The Civil War also helped bring about far-reaching changes in the use of public land in the West. For years, the question of how to use this land had been dominated by the slavery issue. In addition, northern and southern companies squabbled over the route for a proposed rail line linking California to the East. With secession, however, these issues disappeared. In 1862, Congress passed the **Homestead Act**, making western land available at very low cost to those who would farm it. The war also resolved the argument over the route of the intercontinental railroad. The Pacific Railroad Act granted land to companies to build rail lines through Union territory.

Some Northerners Resist the Draft In 1863, the Union instituted **conscription**, also called the draft, to meet the unending demand for fresh troops. Under this system, any white man between the ages of 20 and 45 might be called for required military service. However, a man could pay $300 to hire a replacement. Thus, at a time when laborers earned less than $2 per day, the burden of conscription fell mostly on recent immigrants and others who held low-paying jobs.

Many working men resented the fact that the rich could pay to avoid the draft. They also worried about losing their jobs to African Americans, who were not subject to conscription. Anger over the draft led to violence. In the New York Draft Riot of July 1863, a mob of poor white working men went on a four-day rampage, damaging factories that made war supplies and attacking African Americans. African Americans were also targeted in similar racist attacks in other northern cities.

Civil Liberties During the War Draft rioters were not the only northerners angered by the war effort. A faction calling themselves "Peace Democrats" opposed Lincoln's conduct of the war and demanded an end to the fighting. Their opponents dubbed them **Copperheads**, after a type of poisonous snake. While some Copperheads promoted violence against the Union, most remained loyal to it and wanted only to end the war.

The Homestead Act, 1862

President Lincoln signs the Homestead Act on May 20, 1862.

↓

The Homestead Act allows the government to make grants of public land of up to 160 acres.

↓

Homestead farmers must agree to cultivate the land for a period of five years.

↓

Daniel Freeman, a Scout in the Union Army from Nebraska, becomes the first homestead farmer on Jan. 1, 1863.

↓

Homestead farmers fill out an application, improve the land, and then file a patent to own the land.

↓

By 1934, ten percent of land in the United States has gone to homestead farmers and 1.6 million applications have been filed.

Sources: The National Archives and Records Administration; *Encyclopædia Britannica*

> **Analyze Information** How did the Civil War simplify westward expansion?

>> This cartoon criticizes the Union's efforts to enact a blockade against Southern ports early in the war. **Analyze Political Cartoons** What problems does the artist suggest initially kept the Union blockade from being effective?

The President, however, viewed any effort to undermine the war effort as a grave threat to the nation. To deal with this crisis, he suspended the constitutional right of **habeas corpus**, which protects a person from being held in jail without being charged with a specific crime. Lincoln also empowered the military to arrest people suspected of disloyalty to the Union, including some who had criticized the President and others who had participated in draft riots. The Supreme Court ruled that Lincoln did not have the right to suspend habeas corpus, but the President ignored the ruling. This violation of rights protected under the Constitution is an early example of the struggle to balance national security with prized individual rights in times of war.

☑ **SUMMARIZE** What economic impact did the Civil War have on the North?

Daily Life in the South

The Civil War made great economic demands on the South as well. But, unlike the North, the Confederacy lacked the resources to meet these demands. As the war dragged on, the South seemed in danger of collapse.

Blockades Stifle the South The most pressing threat was the Union blockade of southern ports. Small, swift ships known as "blockade runners" were initially effective at avoiding capture and delivering needed supplies to the South. However, by 1863, the Union blockade was about 80 percent effective. As a result, southerners were forced to depend almost entirely on their own farms and factories. This production was often complicated by nearby military operations. Even when farmers were able to harvest crops, they had difficulty getting the food to market or to the troops because rivers and rail lines were often blocked by Union forces.

>> Although the South was mostly rural and agricultural, it had some industrial development like this Richmond munitions factory.

Paying for the War Proves Difficult Much of the South's wealth was invested in land and in more than 3 million enslaved African Americans. Most of that enslaved labor was devoted to producing market crops, such as cotton, tobacco, and sugar. The war drastically reduced the value of these crops, leaving President Jefferson Davis with few sources of money with which to finance the Confederate military effort.

The South used every opportunity to ease its economic squeeze. When possible, Confederate soldiers seized Union weapons, food, and supplies—often from bodies on the battlefields. Union shoes and boots were especially prized. Although Britain remained officially neutral, British shipyards helped the Confederacy build blockade runners. Entrepreneurs built ironworks in several southern cities. Still, the costs of the war quickly outran the South's resources. Duties on the South's few imports were hard to collect, and many southerners resisted the 10 percent tax on farm produce.

Like the Union, the Confederacy issued paper money, backed only by the government's promise to pay. Many doubted the value of Confederate money.

Prices soared as those with items to sell demanded more and more Confederate cash. This **inflation**, combined with the shortage of food, led to riots in some parts of the South. In a note to North Carolina Governor Zebulon Vance, one woman reported on the dire conditions in that state.

> I have threatened for some time to write you a letter—a crowd of we poor women went to Greensborough yesterday for something to eat as we had not a mouthful [of] meat nor bread—what did they do but put us in jail—we women will write for our husbands to come home and help us.
>
> —Nancy Mangum, 1863

Wartime Challenges Threaten Unity Hardships quickly began to weaken southern unity. As early as August 1861, Mary Boykin Chesnut of South Carolina wrote in her diary of "the rapid growth of the party forming against Mr. Davis." Indeed, Jefferson Davis found that his attempts to build unity were often hampered by his stubborn personality and by the fierce spirit of independence that had led to secession in the first place.

Some states resisted sending troops outside their own borders or having their militia serve under commanders from other states.

As in the North, the Confederate government enacted conscription laws, seized private property in support of the war effort, and suspended habeas corpus. In response, some southerners called for Davis's impeachment. In Georgia, there was even talk of seceding from the Confederacy.

☑ **EXPLAIN** Why did the South face more severe economic challenges than the North?

>> This Confederate banknote promised to pay the bearer 500 Confederate dollars two years after the signing of a treaty to end the Civil War. **Hypothesize** Why might Confederate money have had little immediate value?

BOUNCE to Activate Gallery

A Soldier's Life

Just under half the eligible men in the Union and four out of five eligible men in the South served in the military during the Civil War. Their experiences mingled adventure, danger, comradeship, pride, and terrible hardship.

New Experiences Away From Home The Civil War gave many young men their first taste of travel. A typical regiment comprised recruits from the same town who had all joined together. For most soldiers, army life was months of tedious marching and drilling punctuated by brief periods of fierce and deadly combat. Soldiers were often homesick and bored. When not preparing for battle, they passed the time writing letters home, playing games, and attending religious revivals. One Confederate chaplain noted that many southern men "have come out of this war Christian soldiers."

In the border states especially, many families suffered divided loyalties, with brothers or sons fighting on different sides. Soldiers might find themselves far from home but camped across the battlefield from family.

It was not uncommon for soldiers to exchange greetings with the "enemy" between engagements.

Soldiers Face Death On and Off the Battlefield As you have read, new technology used in the Civil War resulted in killing on a scale never before seen in America. Tens of thousands of soldiers died on the battlefields and many more were injured. Powerful new weapons caused gaping wounds, and the most frequent treatment was the amputation of limbs—sometimes without anesthesia. Doctors lacked modern knowledge about infection, so even minor wounds could prove deadly.

>> An 1862 photo shows Union officer George Custer (right) with captured Confederate officer and former West Point classmate James B. Washington. The Civil War pitted many soldiers against peers, friends, and even family members.

BOUNCE to Activate Gallery

>> During the war, Clara Barton organized needed supplies, helped military families locate missing soldiers, and supported other relief efforts. Later, she founded the American Red Cross to spread those efforts globally.

For those who survived the fighting, life in camp had its own dangers. Poor drinking water and lack of sanitation led to a rapid spread of illness in the ranks. For every soldier killed in battle, two died of disease.

Worse yet were the prison camps. On both sides, prisoners of war faced overcrowding and filth while in captivity. African American prisoners in Confederate camps were usually killed outright.

The most notorious camp was the open-pen prison at Andersonville, Georgia. By the summer of 1864, some 33,000 Union prisoners had been crowded into its confines. With their own troops starving, Confederates had little incentive to find food for Union prisoners. During the 15 months that Andersonville remained in operation, more than 12,000 Union prisoners died of disease and malnutrition.

☑ **DESCRIBE** What dangers did soldiers face during the war?

Women's Roles in Wartime

Many women had long sought an active role in public life. The Civil War offered them new opportunities. Even women who did not choose new roles often were forced to assume unfamiliar responsibilities.

Women Replace Men at Work The vast majority of women did not get close to military action, but many took over family businesses, farms, or plantations. With so many men away at the front, women made inroads into professions that had previously been dominated by men. By war's end, for example, most teaching jobs had been taken over by women.

Hundreds of women from the North and the South masqueraded as men and marched into battle. At least four women are known to have fought in the bloody Battle of Antietam. More commonly, wives joined husbands in camps, cooking and doing laundry. Like their husbands and brothers, some African American women in the South served as spies and guides.

Nurses Follow Men into Battle In both the North and South, the most notable military role for women was nursing. The development of nursing as a profession began slowly, as small groups of women formed organizations to assist returning soldiers and their families. Beginning in 1861, **Clara Barton** took the effort one step further. After collecting medical supplies, she secured permission to travel with Union Army ambulances and assist in "distributing comforts for the sick and wounded of both sides."

President Lincoln approved the formation of the United States Sanitary Commission, which authorized women to oversee hospitals and sanitation in military installations. This systematic program of federal responsibility for public health would be yet another lasting effect of the Civil War.

Another nurse during the Civil War, **Susie King Taylor,** was born to enslaved African American parents, but was sent to live with her grandmother at age seven. During the Civil War, she joined other African Americans who traveled to Union occupied territory. Later she wrote a memoir describing her experiences as both a nurse and a teacher. *Reminiscences of My Life in Camp with the 33d United States Colored Troops, Late 1st S.C. Volunteers,* was the only memoir written by an African American Civil War nurse.

RECALL What was one achievement of Clara Barton?

>> Susie King Taylor gained a basic education in Georgia during the 1850s. She then used that knowledge to teach freed African Americans there. Later she became a Civil War nurse, serving for three years.

ASSESSMENT

1. **Discuss** how the role of women changed during the Civil War.
2. **Explain** How did the Union's system of conscription work? What were some criticisms of this system?
3. **Analyze Information** Discuss the steps the Union took to increase revenue for the war effort.
4. **Identify Cause and Effect** How did the war affect settlement in the West and the Intercontinental Railroad?
5. **Cite Evidence** Explain how foreign countries and entrepreneurs assisted the South's ailing economy.
6. **Quest Connections** In what ways might the experiences of female nurses during the Civil War have been unique?

7.6

Vicksburg cave shelters photographed in 1863

BOUNCE to Activate Flipped Video

Objectives

Explain what the Union gained by capturing Vicksburg.

Describe the importance of the Battle of Gettysburg.

Analyze how the Union pressed its military advantage after 1863.

Key Terms

siege
Vicksburg
Gettysburg
George Pickett
Gettysburg Address
total war
William Tecumseh Sherman

Key Civil War Battles

In the early stages of the war, the North had only limited success in achieving its military goals. But after months of difficult fighting and military setbacks, the Union enjoyed some stunning military successes in 1863. Though there was much bloodshed to come, that year marked the beginning of the end for the Confederacy.

The Siege at Vicksburg

Although Union General Grant's troops battled the Confederates in Kentucky and central Tennessee in late 1862, the major focus of the Union's western campaign remained the Mississippi River. The Anaconda Plan depended on gaining control of the river and cutting the South in half. Yet, after two years of war, the Confederacy still had strongholds at Port Hudson, Louisiana, and Vicksburg, Mississippi. "Vicksburg is the key!" Lincoln proclaimed. "The war can never be brought to a close until that key is in our pocket."

Vicksburg Stands Well Protected Grant made several attempts to fulfill Lincoln's goal, but it was a daunting task. The mighty Vicksburg fortress towered high above the waters of the Mississippi. Along the city's western edge, Confederate gunners could rain deadly fire on any gunboats that might approach. In May 1862, they thwarted one such assault under Union Admiral David Farragut. Grant even tried digging a canal so that Union ships could bypass the stretch of the river dominated by the Vicksburg batteries, but the attempt failed. Vicksburg's location also protected it from attack by land. A Union assault in late 1862 stalled out in the labyrinth of swamps, creeks, and woods guarding the northern approaches to the city.

GO ONLINE to access your digital course

Grant Surrounds the City and Fort In the spring of 1863, Grant devised a new plan to take the Confederate stronghold. First, he marched his troops southward through Louisiana to a point south of Vicksburg. At the same time, he ordered a cavalry attack on rail lines in central Mississippi to draw Confederate attention away from the city. On April 30, some 20,000 of Grant's men crossed the river and headed northeast to capture the Mississippi state capital at Jackson.

After sacking that city, the Federals turned west toward Vicksburg, gaining control of the main rail line leading into the city and fortress. Vicksburg was completely cut off.

Grant launched two frontal assaults against the Confederates but failed to break their defenses. So, on May 22, he placed Vicksburg under **siege**. A siege is a military tactic in which an army surrounds, bombards, and cuts off all supplies to an enemy position in order to force its surrender. For more than a month, Union guns kept up steady fire from land and river. One astonished resident noted "ladies walk[ing] quietly along the streets while the shells burst above them, their heads meanwhile protected by parasol." The constant fire and lack of supplies gradually weakened Vicksburg's defenders.

Finally, on July 4, 1863, the Confederate commander concluded that his position was hopeless and ordered his forces to surrender. The siege of **Vicksburg** was over. Days later, after it learned of Vicksburg's surrender, the Confederate garrison at Port Hudson, Louisiana, also surrendered to the Union. With its last strongholds on the Mississippi in Union hands, the Confederacy was split in two.

☑ **RECALL** What military strategy did Grant use at Vicksburg?

>> General Ulysses S. Grant (lower right with spyglass) led a weeks-long siege against the Confederate stronghold at Vicksburg.

Confederate Advances Are Met at Gettysburg

While Union troops advanced in the West, the situation was different in the East. Despite claiming victory at Antietam, Lincoln soon replaced General McClellan for failing to pursue the retreating Confederates. McClellan's successor, General Ambrose Burnside, headed south, hoping to win a decisive victory.

>> This 1862 photograph shows part of the battlefield at Fredericksburg. **Make Predictions** How did fighting on farm fields like this one probably affect the lands of the South over time?

Victories Embolden Lee to Go North The Army of the Potomac met General Lee's Army of Northern Virginia at Fredericksburg, Virginia,

>> Union foot soldiers training to master assault tactics, 1863

in December 1862. Burnside had 120,000 troops, while Lee had fewer than 80,000. But Lee, aided by Generals Stonewall Jackson and James Longstreet, soundly defeated the new Union commander. Union casualties were more than double those of the Confederacy.

Lincoln replaced Burnside with General Joseph Hooker, who launched his own offensive against Lee in the spring. The two armies clashed at Chancellorsville, just west of Fredericksburg. Once again, the Confederates overwhelmed the Federals.

The loss at the Battle of Chancellorsville was devastating to the Union. Upon hearing the news, President Lincoln paced the room, muttering "What will the country say? What will the country say?" Nevertheless, Lee paid dearly for his victory, losing the incomparable Stonewall Jackson during the fighting. After being accidentally shot by his own men, Jackson died a few days after the battle.

Though he was upset by the loss of Jackson, Lee sensed an opportunity to win international support for the Confederacy, demoralize the Union, and perhaps even force an end to the war. Once again, he decided to invade the North. In June 1863, Lee's army set off through Virginia's Shenandoah Valley and crossed into Union territory, eventually reaching Pennsylvania.

>> During the Battle of Gettysburg, Confederate troops unsuccessfully tried to break through Union lines during an assault at Little Round Top, shown here.

Union Troops Take the High Ground at Gettysburg Lee's invasion caused great concern throughout the Union. The Army of the Potomac, now under the leadership of General George Meade, set out to engage the Confederates. Meanwhile, a Confederate unit headed for the town of Gettysburg, hoping to seize footwear from the shoe factory there.

On the morning of July 1, Lee's men ran into several brigades of Union cavalry commanded by General John Buford. Buford's men spread out northwest of town and called for reinforcements. This was the start of the decisive Battle of **Gettysburg**, which would last for the next three days.

As the main bodies of both armies converged on Gettysburg, the first day of the fighting went to the Confederates. They pushed the smaller Union force back through the town and onto higher ground to the south. But nightfall halted the Confederate advance. This allowed General Meade to bring up the rest of his army and strengthen the Union position. Union troops dug in along a two-and-a-half mile defense line stretching from Culp's Hill and Cemetery Hill southward along Cemetery Ridge. The Federal line ended at two more rocky hills, Little Round Top and Big Round Top. Troubled that the Union now held the high ground, Confederate General James Longstreet regretted, "It would have been better had we not fought at all than to have left undone what we did."

Confederates Suffer a Stunning Blow As July 2 dawned, Lee's men prepared to assault both ends of the Union line. Lee ordered one force to move against the northern part of Meade's defenses while General Longstreet attacked the southern end of Cemetery Ridge. Late in the afternoon, Longstreet's troops charged against a large body of Union soldiers that had mistakenly abandoned Little Round Top and moved westward off Cemetery Ridge. The two sides hammered at each other for several hours in some of the fiercest fighting of the war. The rebels, however, failed to breach the Union line.

Meanwhile, Union troops had noticed the undefended position on Little Round Top. They hurried forward just in time to meet the gray tide of Confederates rushing uphill. Anchoring the Union defense of the hilltop was a Maine unit under Colonel Joshua L. Chamberlain. Chamberlain's men stood firm against numerous Confederate attacks, but their numbers and ammunition eventually dwindled. Chamberlain responded by ordering a bayonet charge that shocked and scattered his exhausted enemy. Hundreds of Confederates surrendered and the fighting drew to a close. Night fell and the Union still held the high ground.

Lee was not discouraged. Despite opposition from Longstreet—and believing that victory was still within reach—the Confederate commander attacked one more time. The result was disastrous. In the early afternoon of July 3, Lee commenced an artillery barrage aimed at the center of the Union line. He had hoped his cannon would break up the Union defenses in advance of an infantry attack on Cemetery Ridge.

When Lee's men, including a division under General **George Pickett**, marched toward the ridge, thousands of Confederates were mowed down by Union rifle and cannon fire. After the failure of Pickett's Charge, Lee ordered the general to reposition his division. "General Lee," replied Pickett, "I have no division now." The Battle of Gettysburg was over. On the battlefield lay more than 50,000 dead and wounded. About half of these were Confederates—nearly a third of Lee's fighting force. Lee abandoned his invasion of the North and led his limping army back into Virginia. The South had suffered a crushing defeat. It would never again attempt to fight on Union soil.

The Gettysburg Address In November 1863, Lincoln came to the Gettysburg battlefield to dedicate a cemetery for the fallen soldiers. There, he delivered his **Gettysburg Address**. He described

The Battle of Gettysburg, 1863

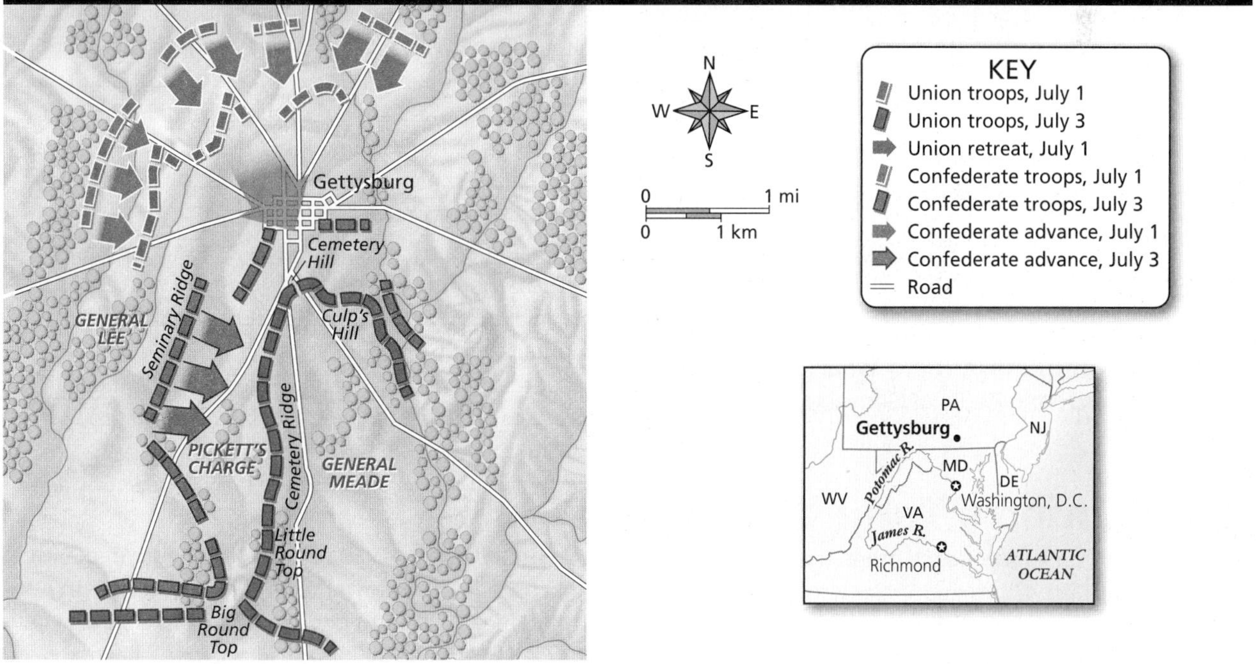

>> **Analyze Maps** Based on the map, which positions were the most heavily contested in the Battle of Gettysburg?

BOUNCE to Activate 3D Model

THE PROGRESSION OF THE CIVIL WAR

THEATERS OF THE CIVIL WAR

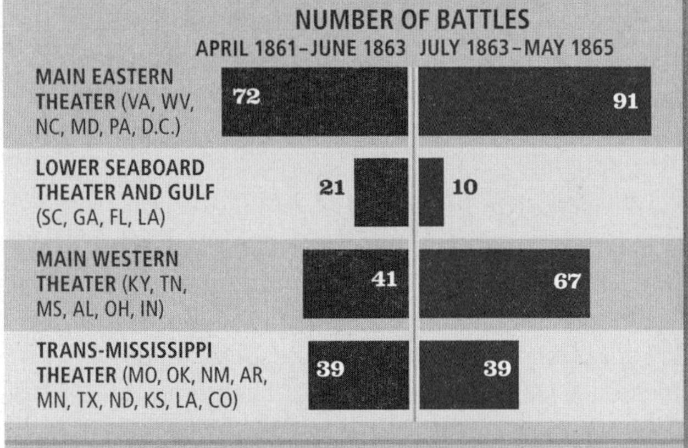

384 MAJOR BATTLES TOOK PLACE DURING THE CIVIL WAR

Source: U.S. National Park Service

OUTCOMES OF KEY BATTLES

BATTLE	YEAR	CASUALTIES	OUTCOME
First Battle of Bull Run	1861	U 2,950 C 1,750	Confederate victory
Battle of Shiloh	1862	U 13,047 C 10,694	Union victory
Battle of Gettysburg	1863	U 23,000 C 28,000	Union victory
Battle of Spotsylvania	1864	U 18,000 C 12,000	Confederate victory
Battles of Petersburg	1864–1865	U 42,000 C 28,000	Union victory

IN 1862 ALONE, THERE WERE **7 BATTLES** WITH AT LEAST **10,000 CASUALTIES**

Sources: History; PBS; Civilwar.org

>> **Analyze Information** Based on the infographic, who seemed to be winning the Civil War by the end 1863? Justify your answer.

BOUNCE to Activate Map

the Civil War as a struggle to fulfill the Declaration of Independence and to preserve a nation "dedicated to the proposition that all men are created equal." Today, the speech is recognized as an enduring statement of American values and goals.

> [W]e here highly resolve that these dead shall not have died in vain—that this nation under God, shall have a new birth of freedom—and that government of the people, by the people, for the people, shall not perish from the earth.
>
> —Abraham Lincoln, November 19, 1863

CHECK UNDERSTANDING What geographic significance did the Battle of Gettysburg have?

The Union's Total War

Coming within a day of each other, the Union victories at Gettysburg and Vicksburg dealt a severe blow to the Confederacy. Lee's troops were in retreat and the Mississippi River was in Union hands. Gone, too, was any hope for the Confederacy to win recognition from Britain or France. The war was not over—indeed, the Confederacy would still win some victories, such as that at Chickamauga, Georgia, in the fall of 1863. In general, however, the situation of the South was dire.

Grant Sets His Sights on Richmond Lincoln recalled General Grant from the Mississippi Valley in early 1864 to take charge of the entire Union military effort. The President knew that Grant would accept nothing less than victory. He was correct. Grant set his sights on the Confederate capital of Richmond. "I propose to fight it out," he declared, "if it takes all summer." Grant's campaign did last all summer and for months beyond.

He engaged Lee's army in a series of ferocious battles: the Wilderness, Spotsylvania Court House, and Cold Harbor. Grant's strategy was to inflict more losses on the Confederates than their limited resources could withstand. The cost of Grant's relentless advance was horrifying. Tens of thousands of Union and Confederate soldiers fell on the battlefields of Virginia. In the North, public outrage began to grow.

Grant's attack did not target the South's military forces alone. He followed a strategy of **total war**, which meant striking civilian as well as military targets. The purpose of total war is to weaken not just an enemy's armies but also the economy that supports the enemy and the overall will of the people to fight. The South was suffering serious losses that it could not hope to replace.

Sherman Presses East to the Sea The Union's total war strategy was also implemented by General **William Tecumseh Sherman**. In May 1864, he set out from the Tennessee-Georgia border with 60,000 troops on a 250-mile march to capture the port of Savannah, Georgia.

During his "March to the Sea," Sherman ordered his men to get supplies by looting along the way, then to destroy anything of potential value left behind. Cutting a 60-mile-wide swath through Georgia, Sherman's army tore up railroad tracks, destroyed buildings, and vandalized hundreds of private homes. With Union forces closing in on Atlanta, Confederate troops abandoned the city. Sherman's men occupied it on September 2 and forced the residents to leave. When the mayor asked Sherman to reconsider his order, the general responded with a letter.

> You might as well appeal against the thunder-storm as against these terrible hardships of war. They are inevitable, and the only way the people of Atlanta can hope once more to live in peace and quiet at home is to stop the war. . . . We don't want your negroes or your horses or your houses or your lands . . . but we do want, and will have, a just obedience to the laws of the United States. That we will have, and if it involves the destruction of your improvements, we cannot help it.
>
> —William T. Sherman, letter to James Calhoun, September 12, 1864

Once Atlanta was emptied, Union troops burned it to the ground. "Sherman the Brute," as southerners called him, continued eastward and captured Savannah in late December.

Lincoln Wins Reelection As 1864 drew to a close, Lincoln had much to celebrate. While his military commanders were winning victories on the battlefield, he had won reelection in November.

The campaign had been difficult. Lincoln had lost some support even in his own party. Some Republicans criticized the President for grasping too

>> Union General William Tecumseh Sherman surveys the area near Atlanta, Georgia, on his devastating March to the Sea.

BOUNCE to Activate Gallery

>> Democratic candidate George McClellan sought to balance his personal promise to win the war with the Democratic Party's desire to seek a negotiated peace with the Confederacy. **Analyze Political Cartoons** What point of view on the likelihood of peace does this cartoon support?

The Election of 1864

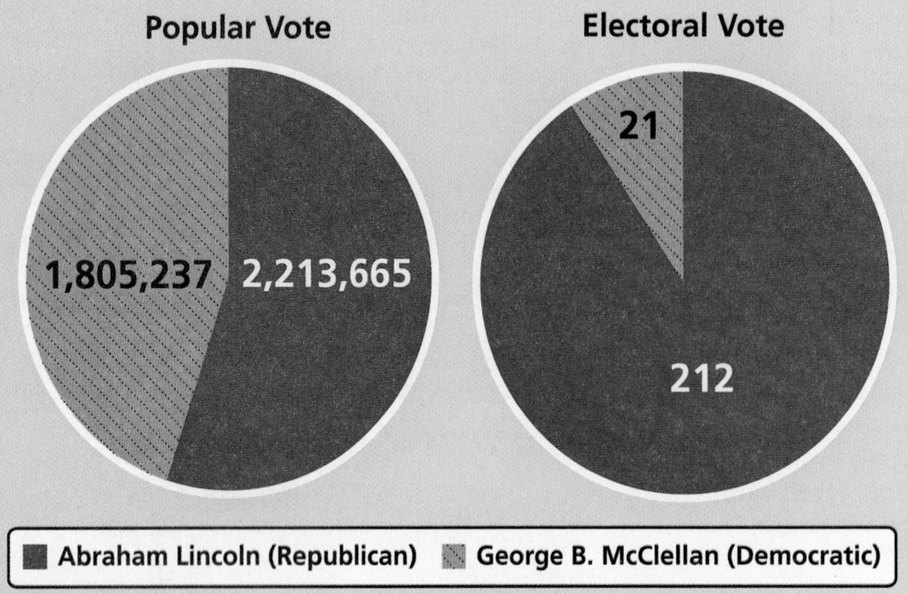

Source: *Encyclopædia Britannica*

>> **Analyze Graphs** How close was the popular vote in the election of 1864? The electoral vote? What may explain these differences?

much authority; others charged that he was not fully committed to ending slavery. Democrats, fractured into several factions, finally nominated George McClellan, the popular former Union commander.

Lincoln's presidency had seemed in jeopardy. However, Union victories boosted his popularity. Many Union soldiers, loyal to Lincoln, were allowed to go home to vote. When the ballots were in, McClellan won 45 percent of the popular vote, but Lincoln received 212 of the 233 electoral votes. The reelection of Abraham Lincoln destroyed any last Confederate hopes that the North would cave in and negotiate a peace.

☑ **LIST** What were the respective objectives of General Grant's and General Sherman's campaigns in 1864?

Assessment

1. **Apply Concepts** Discuss the significance of the Battle of Vicksburg.
2. **Draw Conclusions** What did General Lee hope to accomplish by invading the North?
3. **Identify Cause and Effect** What long-term consequences did the Battle of Gettysburg have on the Confederate war effort?
4. **Identify Central Ideas** What difficulties did Lincoln face during the 1864 presidential campaign? How did the Union war effort help him win reelection?
5. **Quest Connections** How did General Sherman justify the destruction that his army caused during his March to the Sea? Find evidence for your answer in the letter he wrote to Atlanta's mayor.

GO ONLINE to access these biographies: Robert E. Lee, Ulysses S. Grant

Gettysburg Address: Abraham Lincoln

At the Battle of Gettysburg, more than 51,000 Confederate and Union soldiers were listed as wounded, missing, or dead. President Lincoln gave this brief speech at the dedication of the Gettysburg National Cemetery on November 19, 1863. The five known manuscript copies of the speech differ slightly, and historians debate which version Lincoln actually delivered. But the address is considered one of the most eloquent and moving speeches in American history. As Lincoln described the significance of the war, he invoked the Declaration of Independence and its principles of liberty and equality, and he spoke of "a new birth of freedom."

Four score [a group of twenty] and seven years ago our fathers brought forth on this continent, a new nation, conceived [planned] in Liberty, and dedicated to the proposition [judgment or opinion] that all men are created equal.

Now we are engaged in a great civil war, testing whether that nation, or any nation so conceived and so dedicated, can long endure. We are met on a great battle-field of that war. We have come to dedicate a portion of that field, as a final resting place for those who here gave their lives that the nation might live. It is altogether fitting and proper that we should do this.

☑ **DETERMINE CENTRAL IDEAS** Why does Lincoln begin his speech by referencing the nation's founding?

But, in a larger sense, we can not dedicate—we can not consecrate [make sacred]—we can not hallow [honor as holy]—this ground. The brave men, living and dead, who struggled here, have consecrated it, far above our poor power to add or detract. The world will little note, nor long remember what we say here, but it can never forget what they did here. It is for us the living, rather, to be dedicated here to the unfinished work which they who fought here have thus far so nobly advanced. It is rather for us to be here dedicated to the great task remaining before us—that from these honored dead we take increased devotion to that cause for which they gave the last full measure of devotion—that we here highly resolve [decide] that these dead shall not have died in vain—that this nation, under God, shall have a new birth of freedom—and that government of the people, by the people, for the people, shall not perish from the earth.

☑ **DETERMINE MEANING** What is the "unfinished work" for which these soldiers have fought?

☑ ASSESSMENT

1. **Determine Author's Purpose** Why does Lincoln deliver this speech, and what effect does he hope it will have on the nation?
2. **Compare and Contrast** How might Northerners and Southerners have responded to this address by Lincoln?
3. **Draw Conclusions** What do you think makes this speech so powerful, and why is it considered so important to American history?

GO ONLINE to access primary sources

7.7

Under the terms of the surrender at Appomattox, Grant (sitting on the left side of the table) allowed Lee's soldiers to return to their homes as long as they swore not to fight against the Federal Army again. **Describe** How do the opposing generals appear to regard each other in this painting?

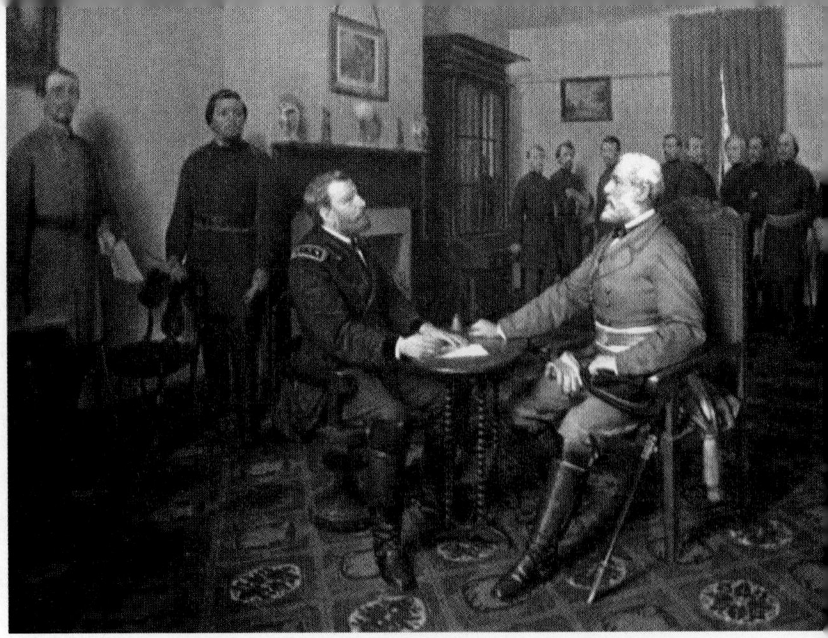

BOUNCE to Activate Flipped Video

Objectives

Analyze the final events of the Civil War.

Explain why the North won the war.

Assess the impact of the Civil War on the North and South.

Key Terms

Thirteenth Amendment
John Wilkes Booth
Mathew Brady
Land Grant College Act

Impact of the Civil War

After four years of bitter struggle and sacrifice, the Confederacy stood on the brink of defeat. As Lee prepared to surrender to Grant, Lincoln began to plan for the future. The Civil War had lasting effects on both the North and the South. With the fighting over, Americans faced the difficult challenge of rebuilding their nation.

The War's End

In the summer of 1864, Grant continued his bloody drive toward Richmond. But at Petersburg, about 20 miles south of Richmond, the Confederates made a desperate stand. Petersburg was a vital railroad center. If Grant captured it, he could cut all supply lines to Richmond.

Union Forces Lay Siege to Petersburg As he had at Vicksburg, Grant turned to siege tactics. Throughout the summer and fall and into the winter, his forces tightened their grip around Petersburg. Both sides dug trenches and threw up fortifications to guard against attack.

By March 1865, the two opposing lines of defense stretched for more than 30 miles around Petersburg.

Fighting was fierce. Union troops suffered more than 40,000 casualties. The Confederates lost 28,000 men. However, unlike Grant, Lee had no replacement troops in reserve. As the siege of Petersburg wore on, Union strength grew in comparison to the Confederate defenders.

Lincoln Plans to Heal the Nation With the Confederate position truly desperate, southerners began to talk of peace. In February

GO ONLINE to access your digital course

1865, a party led by Confederate Vice President Alexander Stephens met with Lincoln to discuss a feasible end to the war. However, these discussions produced no results. One reason for the failure was that the U.S. Congress, with Lincoln's support, had recently proposed the **Thirteenth Amendment** to the Constitution. If ratified, the amendment would outlaw slavery in the United States. The Confederate peace delegation was unwilling to accept a future without slavery. (The Thirteenth Amendment was ratified in December 1865.) Despite the failure of the February meeting, Lincoln was confident of an eventual victory.

>> Powerful artillery such as this cannon, known as the "Dictator," helped the Union secure a victory at Petersburg after months of siege.

He now began to turn his attention to the process of bringing the Confederate states back into the Union. This would be no easy task. Many northerners had a strong desire to punish the South harshly.

Lincoln had a different goal. While committed to the defeat of the Confederacy and an end to slavery, he believed that the Union should strike a more generous stance with the rebellious states. At the beginning of March, in his Second Inaugural Address, Lincoln declared his vision of a united and peaceful nation. "With malice toward none," Lincoln said, Americans should "do all which may achieve and cherish a just and lasting peace."

The Confederates Surrender at Appomattox

Several weeks later, the Confederates made a desperate attempt to break the siege. They failed. Recognizing that the situation was hopeless, Lee ordered a retreat from Petersburg on the night of April 2, 1865. Richmond, now defenseless, was evacuated and set aflame.

Lee's one hope was to join with Confederate forces in North Carolina. Setting out on the march, the men suffered from a lack of food and constant harassment by Union forces.

>> Actor John Wilkes Booth entered the President's box while Lincoln watched a play in Washington, D.C. Booth then shot Lincoln.

BOUNCE to Activate Gallery

Finally, Lee and his starving, exhausted soldiers were trapped at the town of Appomattox Court House, Virginia. On April 9, Lee formally surrendered to Grant. The Union general refused to allow his troops to gloat. "The war is over," he said, "the rebels are our countrymen again."

Lee's surrender did not officially end the war. The South still had some 170,000 soldiers under arms, and it took until June for other Confederate generals scattered around the South to complete similar surrenders. In Texas, African Americans celebrated June 19, 1865, as "Juneteenth," the day that Texas was forced to free enslaved African Americans there, ending slavery in the Confederacy. Juneteenth is still celebrated today.

The President Is Slain On April 14, just days after Lee's surrender, Lincoln decided to relax by attending a new comedy, *Our American Cousin,* at nearby Ford's Theatre in Washington, D.C. During the performance, actor and Confederate supporter **John Wilkes Booth** approached the President's private box. Booth fired a single shot into the back of Lincoln's head. Leaping to the stage, he was heard to call out *"Sic semper tyrannis!"* ("Thus ever to tyrants," the motto of Virginia) and "the South is avenged."

Mortally wounded, Lincoln died the next morning. Booth became the target of a massive manhunt. After several days, he was shot and killed while hiding in a barn in Virginia. Soon, it was discovered that Booth had been part of a plot to kill not only Lincoln but also the Vice President and the Secretary of State.

The plotters hoped to cause chaos and panic in the North, thereby giving the South time to regroup and continue the war. Although Secretary of State William Seward was attacked and seriously injured by one of Booth's accomplices, Booth was the only man to carry out his part of the plot. Four of his accomplices were later hanged as co-conspirators.

Lincoln's tragic death had a deep political impact. His murder united his northern supporters and critics, who now saw him as both a hero and a symbol of freedom. Gone was the strong, skilled leader who had guided the nation through its greatest crisis.

☑ **SUMMARIZE** How did the Civil War end?

Explaining the North's Victory

With hindsight, it is tempting to claim that the Union victory had been certain from the outset, but that is not the case. When the war began, the South had confidence, outstanding military leadership, and a strong determination to defend its land. By contrast, many northerners were far less committed to the fight.

But as northerners warmed to the conflict, they were able to marshal their greater technological prowess, larger population, and more abundant resources. Moreover, the Union was able to develop new advantages, particularly brilliant and fearless military leaders, such as Grant and Sherman, who were willing to do everything it took to win the war. Meanwhile, the South used up its resources, unable to call upon fresh troops and supplies. According to historian Richard Current, the Confederacy's inability to gain a European ally and the North's military superiority sealed the South's fate.

> [I]t seems to have become inevitable once two dangers for the Union had been passed. One of these was the threat of interference from abroad. The other was the possibility of military disaster resulting from the enemy's superior skill or luck on the battlefield. . . . Both dangers appear

Reasons for Union Victory

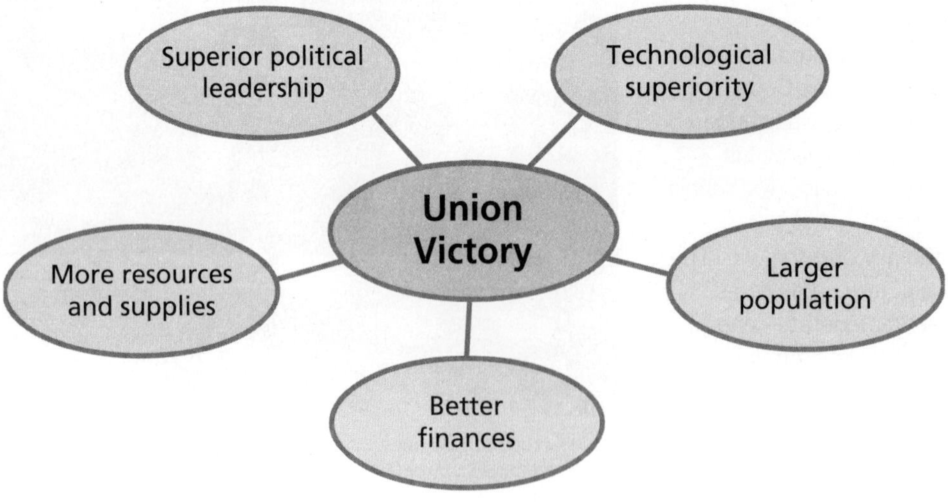

Source: HistoryToday.com

>> **Analyze Charts** Which of these reasons do you think was most significant in securing a Union victory? Explain your choice.

to have been over by midsummer, 1863. . . . Thereafter, month by month, the resources of the North began increasingly to tell, in what became more and more a war of attrition.

—Richard N. Current, in *Why the North Won the Civil War*

The North also enjoyed the steady leadership of President Lincoln. At a time when opinion in the North was bitterly divided, he applied uncommon skill to the difficult task of keeping the nation together.

Finally, Lincoln's decision to proclaim emancipation was a fateful step that changed the nature of the war. Lincoln's determination—and the determination of thousands of African Americans in the North and South—sustained northern spirits, even as the war sapped southern resolve.

☑ **EXPLAIN** Why did the North win the Civil War?

>> Historians generally acknowledge Lincoln as one of the finest U.S. presidents for his strong leadership during the Civil War.

The Costs of War

The United States had never experienced a war like the Civil War. Some individual battles produced casualties greater than the United States had previously sustained in entire wars. When the war was over, more than 600,000 Americans were dead. Hundreds of thousands more were maimed.

The Civil War ushered in the harsh reality of modern warfare. For the first time, ordinary citizens could see the carnage of the battlefield through the photographs of journalists such as **Mathew Brady**. His exhibition "The Dead at Antietam" provided graphic evidence of the terrible realities of war.

Economic Impact After the fighting ended, social and political disillusionment on both sides fed economic greed. The era following the war came to be known as the Gilded Age—a term that suggested a superficial glitter and beauty covering up an underlying decay. Nevertheless, in the North, the industrial boom that was fueled by the war continued.

In 1862, Congress passed both the **Land Grant College Act** and legislation authorizing a protective tariff. The Land Grant College Act was also called the Morrill Act after its sponsor Justin Morrill, a congressman from Vermont. It gave money from the sale of public lands to states for the establishment of universities that taught "agriculture and mechanical arts." The tariff protected northern industry from foreign competition and raised much-needed revenue for the Union war effort. It also led to a surge in manufacturing that lasted far beyond the end of the war. After 1865, northern factories, banks, and cities underwent sweeping industrialization, helping the United States emerge as a global economic power.

In contrast, rebuilding the South was slow and tortured. Southern cities, such as Richmond and Atlanta, lay in ruins, as did many of the region's factories and railroads. The South struggled to regain its economic footing after the war, often relying on northern investment and seeking ways to enter the modern cash economy. For many decades, agriculture would remain at the center of the southern economy. Northerners, forgetting Sherman's destruction of southern assets, would often blame the slow recovery on southerners' own shortcomings.

Societal Impact As a result of the war, the southern landscape was in shambles. Many Confederate soldiers returned to find their homes and farms destroyed. Millions of dislocated white southerners drifted aimlessly about the South in late 1865. Defeat had shaken them to the very core of their beliefs. Some felt that they were suffering a divine punishment, with one southerner mourning, "Oh, our God! What sins we must have been guilty of that we should be so humiliated by Thee now!" Others, however, came to view the Civil War as a

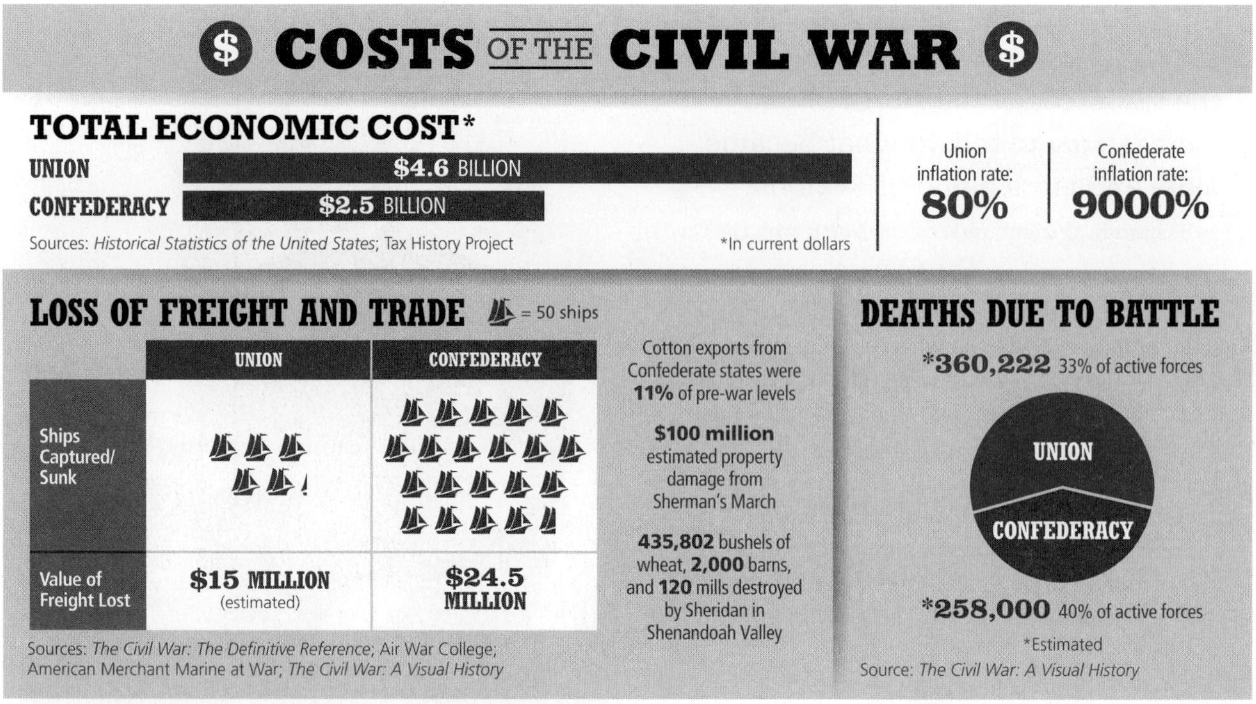

>> **Analyze Information** Based on this infographic, which side suffered more due to its involvement in the Civil War? Explain your answer.

BOUNCE to Activate Chart

lost, but noble, cause. These white southerners kept the memory of the struggle alive and believed that, eventually, the South would be redeemed.

African Americans of the South were equally disoriented. But they also had a new sense of hope. Freedom promised them a new life with new opportunities, including a chance to own land and to control their own lives. Some headed west to take advantage of the Homestead Act. African American southerners eagerly joined the migration that would mark American society for many years. However, as Reconstruction began, most African Americans in the South found that freedom was a promise not fully delivered.

Political Impact In many ways, the Civil War eased the history of disunity in American political life. While sectional differences remained strong, never again would such differences trigger threats of secession. Instead, over time, the economic, political, and social life of the nation's disparate regions would increasingly intertwine.

Debates over states' rights did not end with the Civil War. Still, the war helped cement federal authority. The government had fought a war to assert that individual states did not have the power to break the national bond forged by the Constitution. Increasingly, the federal government would come to play a larger role in Americans' lives. And more Americans would see themselves as citizens, not just of a state, but of a united nation.

☑ **COMPARE AND CONTRAST** What economic effects did the Civil War have on the North and the South?

☑ ASSESSMENT

1. **Analyze Information** What did John Wilkes Booth hope to accomplish with the assassination of President Lincoln? How did people in the North respond to the assassination?
2. **Describe** why the siege of Petersburg would prove to be one of the most significant conflicts of the Civil War.
3. **Identify Cause and Effect** How did President Lincoln's leadership affect the Union's Civil War victory?
4. **Explain** How did African Americans in the South respond to the end of the war?
5. **Connections to Today** Why might it take many years for a nation to recover from a war? Include in your answer some examples of issues that the South faced after the Civil War.

The Costs of War at Vicksburg

The siege of Vicksburg illustrates vividly the costs of the Civil War on soldiers, civilians, and property. During the siege, Vicksburg residents lived in caves for protection from Union bombardments. At times food was so scarce that people ate rats and mule meat to survive. When the siege ended on July 4, 1863, a battered Vicksburg fell into Union hands. Thousands of soldiers had been killed, wounded, or captured. Many civilians had also been injured or killed. Those who survived would never forget the terror of what they endured.

Mary Ann Webster Loughborough lived in Vicksburg during the siege. Her account that follows details some of her experiences. Conversely, William G. Christie wrote his observations as a Union artillery soldier during the siege.

As you read, think about how the sources make you feel about war. Then answer the questions to compare the two perspectives.

>> Citizens of Vicksburg endured 47 days of siege and union bombardments such as this.

Primary Source 1

My Cave Life in Vicksburg, Mary Ann Webster Loughborough, 1864

Our new habitation was an excavation made in the earth, and branching six feet from the entrance, forming a cave in the shape of a T. In one of the wings my bed fitted; the other I used as a kind of a dressing room; in this the earth had been cut down a foot or two below the floor of the main cave; I could stand erect here; and when tired of sitting in other portions of my residence, I bowed myself into it, and stood impassively resting at full height . . .

CITE EVIDENCE What evidence is there that living in a cave was uncomfortable?

Sitting in the cave, one evening, I heard the most heartrending screams and moans. I was told that a mother had taken a child into a cave about a hundred yards from us; and having laid it on its little bed, as the poor woman believed, in safety, she took her seat near the entrance of the cave. A mortar shell came rushing through the air, and fell with much force, entering the earth above the sleeping child . . . taking away the young innocent life without a look or word of passing love to be treasured in the mother's heart. . . .

How very sad this life in Vicksburg!—how little security can we feel, with so many around us seeing the morning light that will never more see the night! . . .

How blightingly [destructively] the hand of warfare lay upon the town! even in the softening light of the moon—the closed and desolate houses—the gardens, with gates half open, and cattle standing amid the loveliest flowers and verdure [plants]! This carelessness of appearance and evident haste of departure was visible everywhere—the inhabitants, in this perilous time, feeling only anxiety for personal safety and the strength of their cave homes. . . .

DETERMINE AUTHOR'S POINT OF VIEW How does the author feel about the situation in Vicksburg?

Primary Source 2

Letter from William G. Christie at Vicksburg, June 6, 1863

[S]o we are getting up towards the Head and it may be we will crush the life out of the Pesky varmint in a year or so. The law of compensation, and you might say of dispensation [taking away] make things about even in the long run. The Negro worked and the master [reaped]. Building fine houses, and laying out Beautiful gardens, making [granaries], riding round in fine carriages; and in short enjoying themselves in every sensual way you can possibly think of until they waxed Proud, and fat and so they Brought on [their] own Punishment, and tis full I assure you, there are large numbers of [their] fine houses gone up in smoke, [their] fields are [lying] Idle or are in the hands of the government, worked By and for the Negro. [Their] fine carriages are used for ambulances: and [their] People are slain.

DRAW CONCLUSIONS What is the author's attitude toward the southerners?

Sons and Brothers: Fathers and children are mangled on the same field of Death, and now since we have invested this city, even [their] women and children are slain, for let me tell you . . . shell[s] don't discriminate between combatants and those that are not. Let every one of you be thankful you are not in a Besieged city night and Day, night and day there is that loud roar from the [mortar] Boats, on the River up goes sixty or a hundred Pounds of iron into the air, some seven hundred feet, making what a man of science would call a Parabolic curve. But I think if you could see it you would say Diabolic: Down, Down, it falls, and [finally] bursts, and scatters Death to all, we hear some that don't Burst go [crashing] through a house, or with a chug, in the ground. The Batteries [cannons] on the land side are never Idle, all at once some of them are shooting, night and day so you see that there is But little rest for the wicked.

SUMMARIZE What details about the siege does the author describe?

ASSESSMENT

Be sure to cite specific evidence from the sources as you answer the following questions.

1. **Identify Central Ideas** What central ideas does Loughborough express?
2. **Analyze Style and Rhetoric** Describe Christie's writing style.
3. **Compare and Contrast** How are the attitudes toward the bombardments similar and different between the two authors?
4. **Assess an Argument** Do you think Christie's opinion toward southerners is fair? Explain.
5. **Draw Conclusions** How do the sources make you feel about the Civil War? Explain.

GO ONLINE to access primary sources

Connections to Today

Many Americans today use protests to express their views about societal issues.

Take Action to Find Common Ground

Looking back on the Civil War, you might conclude that Americans were never more divided than during that grim period of American history. However, as the nation has grown and changed since the 1860s, Americans continue to disagree about many important issues.

1. **Choose** one of the following organizations that promote ways in which citizens can discuss opposing views constructively.
    - **Living Room Conversations**
    - **Bridge the Divide**
    - **National Conversation Project**
2. **Ask Questions** Generate a list of questions about your organization. What are their goals? How and where do they operate?
3. **Learn** about the organization by conducting research. Use online sources and take notes. Continue to generate questions as you learn more.
4. **Raise Awareness** Does the work of your group inspire you? Create a poem, song, essay, or artwork to answer this question: *How do we unite when we are divided about so many issues?* Present your work to the class.

Topic 7 Quick Study Guide

LESSON SUMMARIES

Use these Lesson Summaries, and the longer versions available online, to review the key ideas for each lesson in this Topic.

Lesson 1: Slavery Divides the Nation

Despite compromises to allow slavery in some states and territories but not in others, the nation remained divided over slavery. The Fugitive Slave Act, a provision of the Compromise of 1850, required citizens to help return African Americans trying to escape enslavement. Outraged, many northerners defied the law. Some even helped enslaved people escape through the Underground Railroad.

Lesson 2: Violence Escalates

The Kansas-Nebraska Act called for settlers to vote on whether to allow slavery, leading to violence between pro- and antislavery settlers in Kansas. Politicians continued to debate slavery, which even led to violence in the Senate. Abolitionist John Brown led an uprising in Virginia in order to start a revolt of enslaved African Americans. Federal troops intervened, and Brown was executed.

Lesson 3: The Civil War Begins

After Abraham Lincoln was elected President in 1860, many southern states left the Union to form the Confederate States of America. The Civil War began when Confederates fired upon Union troops at Fort Sumter. Heavy fighting and bloodshed in 1861 halted the belief that the war would end quickly.

Lesson 4: African Americans and the War

Strong antislavery sentiment pressured President Lincoln to address slavery. After a strategic Union victory at Antietam in 1862, he issued the Emancipation Proclamation. It stated that enslaved people in states in rebellion against the Union were free. For many, this set the purpose of the war as a fight against slavery. Many African Americans joined the Union Army to fight.

Lesson 5: Everyday Life During the War

A Union blockade during the war caused financial hardships in the South. Both sides used conscription to draft soldiers to fight. Soldiers experienced the horrors of war, disease, and prison camps. Women filled roles vacated by men who left to fight. Some women were nurses.

Lesson 6: Key Civil War Battles

Union victories at Vicksburg and Gettysburg in 1863 turned the tide of the war. By 1864, Union generals began to wage total war against the South, striking both civilian and military targets. As President Lincoln won reelection, the war's end was near.

Lesson 7: Impact of the Civil War

The Civil War ended when the Confederates surrendered in 1865. The four-year war had cost a staggering amount of lives, money, and resources. Americans looked to the daunting task of rebuilding. However, it would have to be done without President Lincoln, who was assassinated by a Confederate sympathizer days after the war ended.

QUEST!

Create Your Documentary Have students complete the Quest Inquiry by creating their documentaries. Direct students to the documentaries rubric on Realize to make sure that their work meets the project requirements. You may wish to remind students to use the Information Organizer to organize their research.

GO ONLINE to access lesson summaries

VISUAL REVIEW

Use these graphics to review some of the key terms, people, and ideas from this Topic.

Key Government Actions Affecting Slavery

GOVERNMENT ACTION	EFFECT ON SLAVERY
Compromise of 1850	California was admitted as a free state. Territories acquired from Mexico (Utah and New Mexico) would use popular sovereignty to determine if slavery would be allowed. The trade in enslaved people ended in Washington, D.C. The Fugitive Slave Act was passed.
Fugitive Slave Act	Part of the Compromise of 1850, the law forced all Americans to help apprehend African Americans trying to escape enslavement. It also declared that anyone who assisted an enslaved person's escape attempt could be fined or imprisoned. The law angered many northerners.
Kansas-Nebraska Act	This 1854 law opened the Nebraska Territory to slavery by applying popular sovereignty (people in the territory would decide whether slavery would be allowed). Nebraska Territory became Kansas and Nebraska. Fighting erupted in Kansas between proslavery and antislavery forces.
Emancipation Proclamation	Issued by President Lincoln in 1862, the Proclamation stated that all enslaved people in states in rebellion against the Union were free. This did not immediately free any enslaved people, but it set the purpose of the Civil War as a struggle to end slavery.

Key Battles of the Civil War

Union Victories

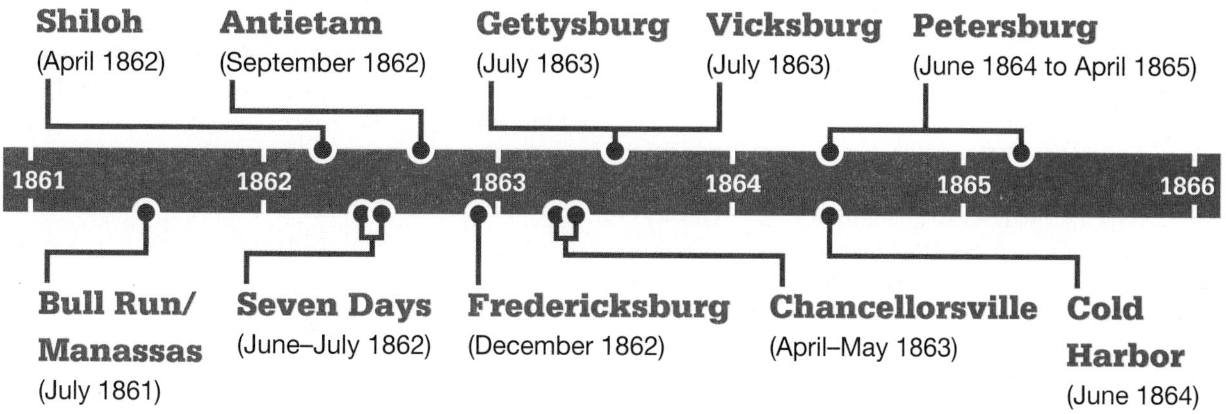

Confederate Victories

Topic 7 Assessment

KEY TERMS, PEOPLE, AND IDEAS

1. Under the **Fugitive Slave Act,** what would happen to people who assisted an enslaved person trying to escape?
2. What was the **Underground Railroad,** and how did it work?
3. Why did Kansas become a battleground for proslavery and antislavery forces?
4. Why did **John Brown** launch an attack at Harpers Ferry?
5. What was **Jefferson Davis's** point of view on the slavery issue?
6. How was **Ulysses S. Grant** important to the Union war effort?
7. What were the effects of the **Battle of Antietam**?
8. Who were the **Copperheads**?
9. How did the siege of **Vicksburg** and the **Battle of Gettysburg** change the course of the war?

CRITICAL THINKING

10. **Compare Points of View** How did Calhoun and Webster respond to Clay's proposed compromise? With which side did the majority of Congress agree?
11. **Recognize Bias** What attitudes did abolitionist writers and proslavery writers portray in their novels?
12. **Analyze Information** In what ways did the Kansas-Nebraska Act support the expansion of slavery?
13. **Identify Points of View** Why was the Crittenden Compromise unacceptable to Lincoln?
14. **Analyze Information** How did African American soldiers surpass the initial expectations that the Union had about them?
15. **Analyze Photographs** Study the image of Richmond, Virginia, in 1865. What does the photograph suggest about the needs of the postwar period?

16. **Make Comparisons** Which side suffered more from the Civil War, the North or the South? Explain your answer.
17. **Writing Activity: Write an Informative Essay** Write a three-paragraph essay describing how people in the Union and the Confederacy generally reacted to the Emancipation Proclamation. Include **(a)** evidence from the text and the source below and **(b)** supporting details to explain the wide variety of reactions to the Proclamation at the time.

> The morning dawns! The long night of sorrow and gloom is past . . . The Proclamation has gone forth, and God is saying . . . to this nation Man must be free. . . . Your destiny as white men and ours as black men are one and the same.
> *–Jonathan C. Gibbs, January 1, 1863*

18. **Connections to Today** What can Americans today learn from the mistakes and tragedies of the Civil War? What can the war teach us about resolving conflicts peacefully, standing up for personal rights, and uniting as a nation?

DOCUMENT-BASED QUESTIONS

Union General William Tecumseh Sherman implemented a strategy of total war during his "march to the sea" in 1864. The concept of total war called for expanding military targets to include civilian economic resources. Use your knowledge of the Civil War and Documents A, B, C, and D to answer questions 19–22.

DOCUMENT A

"Sherman's Atlanta campaign in May to September 1864 won the confederate prize that insured Lincoln's reelection that year. Sherman ordered a civilian evacuation of Atlanta, burned everything of any military value, and in November headed out of the city in his famous 'march to the sea.' More than any other Civil War commander, Sherman grasped the brutal logic of total war. In such a war, civilian morale and economic resources are as much military targets as the enemy's armies. For Sherman, war unleashed the fury of hell, and he refused to sentimentalize the killing and pillaging required for victory."

—William L. Barney, *The Reader's Companion to American History*

DOCUMENT B

"Citizens of Atlanta leaving the City in Compliance With General Sherman's Orders."

CITIZENS OF ATLANTA LEAVING THE CITY IN COMPLIANCE WITH GENERAL SHERMAN'S ORDER.

The faithful picture of war scenes have an interest beyond that which the war gives them. They present people and customs of a bygone generation. The customs of men and women, the strange shape of trunks, and the patterns of shawls and blankets are in strong contrast with those of to-day.

DOCUMENT C

"Many people on both sides believed that the war would be short—one or two battles and the cowardly Yankees or slovenly rebels would give up. . . . Responsible leaders on both sides did not share the popular faith in a short war. Yet even they could not foresee the kind of conflict this war would become—a total war, requiring total mobilization of men and resources, destroying these men and resources on a massive scale, and ending only with unconditional surrender. In the spring of 1861 most northern leaders thought in terms of a limited war. Their purpose was not to conquer the South but to suppress insurrection and win back the latent loyalty of the southern people. The faith in southern unionism lingered long."

—James M. McPherson, *Battle Cry of Freedom*

DOCUMENT D

"William Tecumseh Sherman was considered one of the ablest generals in the Federal army, but he was a cruel one. . . . His celebrated march through Georgia put a stain upon his name that will cling to it as it is found upon the pages of history. . . . With his grand army veterans, almost unopposed, he had overrun and desolated the fairest sections of the South, burning cities, towns, and country dwellings; had wantonly destroyed many millions of dollars worth of property, both public and private; had made thousands of women and children and aged men homeless and destitute by burning their homes and destroying their means of subsistence. And it was to glorify him for these deeds of barbarism that 'Marching through Georgia' was written, and it is for this that it is sung."

—Milford Overley, "What 'Marching Through Georgia' Means"

19. The authors of Documents A and C define total war as a

A. total mobilization of men and resources against both military and civilian targets.

B. diplomatic effort aimed at avoiding the outbreak of hostilities.

C. military effort concentrated entirely on civilian targets.

D. policy for controlling the civilian population of cities.

20. According to Document A, why might Sherman have refused to "sentimentalize" total war?

A. He wanted to protect Confederate government property.

B. He wanted captured Confederate soldiers to help rebuild war-torn areas.

C. He wanted more troops and supplies from Washington.

D. He wanted to overlook civilian suffering to win the war.

21. Analyze Information Why does the author of Document D dislike General Sherman?

22. Writing Task What impact did the military strategy of total war have on the people of the South during the Civil War? Use your knowledge of the war and specific evidence from the primary sources above to support your opinion.

GO ONLINE to access more practice

Topic 8

Reconstruction (1865–1877)

ESSENTIAL QUESTION How Can We Ensure Equality for All?

GO ONLINE to access the eText, videos, Interactive Primary Sources, Biographies, and other online resources.

The Freedmen's Bureau set up schools across the South after the Civil War.

Connections to Today

Reconstruction was a divisive period, and no issue was more explosive than the right to vote. Should former rebels have it? Can freed African Americans keep it? These issues led to serious violence. Modern voting rights issues seem tame by comparison, but they still have the power to divide us. Americans argue strenuously about voting rights for convicted criminals, for example, and about the security and fairness of our elections. Why do so many Americans continue to believe the right to vote is worth fighting for?

NBC LEARN

Learn about the Freedmen's Bureau.

BOUNCE to Activate My Story Video

Topic 8 Overview

In this Topic, you'll learn about the issues and events of Reconstruction. Look at the lesson outline and explore the timeline. As you study this Topic, you'll complete the Quest team project.

LESSON OUTLINE

8.1 Plans for Reconstruction Clash

8.2 Reconstruction Changes the South

8.3 Reconstruction's Impact

Key Events of Reconstruction

1866
President Johnson vetoes Civil Rights Act

1867
the Tenure of Office Act tries to limit president's power

1868
Florida rejoins Union

1869
Wyoming Territory grants women the vote

1871
Octavius Catto killed in anti-African American riot

1872
Freedmen's Bureau is dissolved

1877
Reconstruction ends

1865 1868 1871 1874 1877

QUEST! INQUIRY

Civic Discussion: Andrew Johnson's Impeachment

Was the impeachment of President Andrew Johnson justified? How did significant people or groups influence this event during Reconstruction? In this Quest you'll explore this question by examining the sources, the evidence and by holding a civic discussion.

STEP 1
Read the discussion launch and discuss the major points with your classmates.

STEP 2
Examine the sources to understand the various authors' perspectives on the main question. Assess the author's claims, reasoning and evidence.

STEP 3
Join either the YES or NO group to work on your answer to the question. As a group present your arguments and evidence before switching sides.

STEP 4
Present your own opinion and record your point of view on the Information Organizer. Reflect on what you've learned about the divisive issues of Reconstruction.

GO ONLINE to access complete Quest materials

8.1

Radical Republican leader Thaddeus Stevens

BOUNCE to Activate Flipped Video

Objectives

Explain the multiple reasons why a plan was needed for the reconstruction of the South.

Compare the strengths and weaknesses of the Reconstruction plans of Lincoln, Johnson, and Congress.

Discuss Johnson's political difficulties and impeachment.

Key Terms

Reconstruction
Radical Republicans
Wade-Davis Bill
Freedmen's Bureau
Andrew Johnson
Black Codes
Civil Rights Act of 1866
Fourteenth Amendment
impeach
Fifteenth Amendment

GO ONLINE to access your digital course

Plans for Reconstruction Clash

Even before the end of the Civil War, Congress and the President disagreed about how the seceded states would rejoin the Union. When the war ended, bitterness between the North and South was compounded by a power struggle between the executive and legislative branches of government. The issues that arose and how they were dealt with would have consequences for generations to come.

The Challenges of Reconstruction

When the Civil War ended, parts of the South lay in ruins—homes burned, businesses closed, many properties abandoned. African Americans, though emancipated, lacked full citizenship and the means to make a living. During the era of **Reconstruction** (1865–1877), the federal government struggled with how to return the eleven southern states to the Union, rebuild the South's ruined economy, and promote the rights of the formerly enslaved.

How to Reunite the Union To many Americans, the most important issue was deciding the political fate of Confederate states. Should Confederate leaders be tried for treason, or should they be pardoned so that national healing could proceed as quickly as possible? And what should be the process by which southern representatives could reclaim their seats in Congress?

The Constitution provided no guidance on secession or readmission of states. It was not clear whether Congress or the President should take the lead in forming Reconstruction policy. Some argued that states should be allowed to rejoin the Union quickly with few conditions. But many claimed that the defeated states should first swear loyalty to the federal government and adopt state constitutions that guaranteed freedmen's rights.

How to Rebuild the Southern Economy The Civil War devastated the South's economy. Between 1860 and 1870, the South's share of the nation's total wealth declined from more than 30 percent to 12 percent.

The Union army had destroyed factories, plantations, and railroads. Nearly half of the region's livestock and farm machinery were gone. About one fourth of southern white men between the ages of 20 and 40 had died in the war. In addition, more than 3 million newly freed African Americans were now without homes or jobs. After the war, the land was the South's most valuable asset, and arguments raged over who should control it.

During Reconstruction, some people proposed using the land to benefit freed people. General Sherman proposed that millions of acres abandoned by planters or confiscated by the federal government should be given to freed people. "Forty acres and a mule," he suggested, would be sufficient to support a family. Many Black southerners wanted a chance to buy land, as the African American Reverend Garrison Frazier expressed in early 1865: "We want to be placed on land until we are able to buy it and make it our own."

Southern landowners rejected the idea that the government could give away their land. Many white northerners worried that confiscating property violated the Constitution. In the face of opposition, the dream of "forty acres and a mule" never became a reality.

How to Extend Citizenship to African Americans The Thirteenth Amendment freed African Americans from slavery, but it did not grant them the rights of full citizenship. Freed people hoped that they would gain voting rights and access to education, benefits that most northern African Americans also did not have. Most leaders of the Republican Party, which at the time dominated the federal government, supported programs to extend full citizenship to African Americans. However, most white southerners opposed the idea. They feared it would undermine their own power and status in society.

☑ **SUMMARIZE** What three significant issues did the federal government have to address during Reconstruction?

>> Union troops celebrate their victory in a May 1865 parade in Washington, D.C.

>> Two men stand amidst the rubble of Charleston, South Carolina, in 1865. **Analyze Images** How does this photograph show both the destruction and strength of the South?

>> Lincoln meets with three of his top generals shortly before the end of the war in this 1868 painting by George P.A. Healy. **Interpret** Why might this painting be entitled *The Peacemakers*?

>> President Abraham Lincoln, shown here at his second inauguration in March of 1865, argued that Confederate states had never truly had the right to leave the Union.

Competing Reconstruction Plans

Even during the war, Union politicians had debated how to repair the nation's political structure and economy. For President Lincoln, one of the first major goals was to reunify the nation.

Lincoln's Ten Percent Plan Throughout the war, Lincoln had hoped that southern states might easily rejoin the Union after the war. To this end, in 1863 he issued a Proclamation of Amnesty and Reconstruction, known as the "Ten Percent Plan." According to its terms, as soon as ten percent of a state's voters took a loyalty oath to the Union, the state could set up a new government. If the state's constitution abolished slavery and provided education for African Americans, the state would regain representation in Congress.

Lincoln was willing to pardon former Confederates, and he considered compensating them for the labor of enslaved people who had been freed. In addition, he did not require a guarantee of social or political equality for African Americans. He recognized pro-Union governments in Arkansas, Louisiana, and Tennessee even though they denied African Americans the right to vote.

Lincoln took the position that the Union was unbreakable and therefore the southern states had never really left the Union. In his Second Inaugural Address, delivered a month before the war ended, Lincoln promised forgiveness.

> With malice toward none, and charity for all, with firmness in the right as God gives us to see the right, let us strive on to finish the work we are in, to bind up the nation's wounds . . . to do all which may achieve and cherish a just and a lasting peace among ourselves and with all nations.
>
> —Lincoln's Second Inaugural Address, March 1865

Radical Republicans and the Wade-Davis Bill Members of Lincoln's own party opposed his plan. Led by Representative Thaddeus Stevens and Senator Charles Sumner, these "**Radical Republicans**" in Congress insisted that the Confederates had committed crimes—by enslaving African Americans and by entangling the nation in war.

Plans for Reconstruction

LINCOLN	JOHNSON	RADICAL REPUBLICAN
• Required 10 percent of a state's voters to take an oath of loyalty to the Union in order to form a new government and rejoin the Union • Required states to accept emancipation • Offered full pardons to all former Confederates	• Required former Confederates with property worth $20,000 or more to obtain presidential pardon in order to vote or hold office; gave full pardon to others • Required ratification of the Thirteenth Amendment	• Required 50 percent of a state's voters to take an oath of loyalty to the Union in order to call a constitutional convention and elect a new government • Divided South into five military districts • Required state legislatures to adopt new constitutions guaranteeing African American suffrage • Required states to ratify the Fourteenth Amendment in order to seat representatives in Congress

Sources: *Encyclopædia Britannica*; Smithsonian; PBS

>> **Analyze Information** Which plan made it easiest for former Confederate states to rejoin the United States? Which treated those states the most harshly?

BOUNCE to Activate Chart

The Radical Republicans advocated full citizenship, including the right to vote, for African Americans. They favored punishment and harsh terms for the South, and they supported Sherman's plan to confiscate Confederates' land and give farms to freedmen.

Rejecting Lincoln's Ten Percent Plan, Congress passed the **Wade-Davis Bill** in 1864. It required that a majority of a state's prewar voters swear loyalty to the Union before the process of restoration could begin. The bill also demanded guarantees of African American equality. President Lincoln killed this plan by withholding his signature.

The Freedmen's Bureau One Radical Republican plan did receive the President's support. This was the Bureau of Refugees, Freedmen, and Abandoned Lands, known as the **Freedmen's Bureau**. Its goal was to provide food, clothing, health care, and education for both African American and white refugees in the South.

The Freedmen's Bureau helped reunite families that had been separated by slavery and war. It negotiated fair labor contracts between freed African Americans and white landowners. By representing African Americans in the courts, the Bureau also established a precedent that African American citizens had legal rights.

EXPLAIN How did Lincoln's and the Radical Republicans' plans for Reconstruction differ?

The Johnson Presidency and Reconstruction

Lincoln was assassinated in April 1865, just weeks after his second inauguration. Lincoln's death thrust his Vice President, **Andrew Johnson**, into the presidency.

Johnson's Plan for Reconstruction Like Lincoln, Johnson wanted to restore the political status of the southern states as quickly as possible. He offered pardons and the restoration of land to almost any Confederate who swore allegiance to the Union and the Constitution. His main requirement was that each state ratify the Thirteenth Amendment and draft a constitution that abolished slavery. However, Johnson resented wealthy planters and required that they and other Confederate leaders write to him personally to apply for a pardon.

Johnson's dislike of the planter class did not translate into a desire to elevate African Americans. Like many southerners, Johnson expected the United States to have a "government for white men." He did not want African Americans to have the vote. In fact, he had little sympathy for their plight.

Johnson supported states' rights, which would allow the laws and customs of the state to outweigh federal regulations. States would, therefore, be able to limit the freedoms of freed African Americans.

>> Civil rights supporters rejoiced at the passage of the Civil Rights Act of 1866, but President Andrew Johnson argued that the law violated the U.S. Constitution.

By the time Congress reconvened in December 1865, most Confederate states had met Johnson's requirements for readmission. Radical and moderate Republicans remained hopeful that African American political rights would soon follow.

Black Codes in the South That hope was soon dashed. Beginning with the state conventions required by Johnson, southern leaders proceeded to rebuild their prewar world. Many states limited the vote to white men, and some sent Confederate officials to the U.S. Congress. All the states instituted **Black Codes**—laws that sought to limit the rights of African Americans and keep them as landless workers.

The codes required African Americans to work in only a limited number of occupations, most often as servants or farm laborers. Some states prohibited African Americans from owning land, and all set up vagrancy laws. These laws stipulated that any African American person who did not have a job could be arrested and sent to work as prison labor. Even though the South remained under Union military occupation, white southerners openly used violence and intimidation to enforce the Black Codes.

Conflict Between Johnson and Congress

Both Radical and moderate Republicans were infuriated by the South's disregard of the spirit of Reconstruction. When southern representatives arrived in Washington, D.C., Congress refused them their seats. Congress also formed a committee to investigate the treatment of freed people.

Through the spring of 1866, the political situation grew worse. While the Radicals claimed that federal intervention was needed to advance African American political and civil rights, President Johnson accused them of trying "to Africanize the southern half of our country."

When Congress passed a bill to allow the Freedmen's Bureau to continue its work and to provide it with authority to punish state officials who failed to extend civil rights to African Americans, Johnson vetoed it. Undaunted, Congress sought to overturn the Black Codes by passing the **Civil Rights Act of 1866**. This measure created federal guarantees of civil rights and superseded any state laws that limited them. But once again, Johnson vetoed the law, because he thought Reconstruction measures were against constitutional principles. Johnson was now openly defying Congress.

>> In this political cartoon, Andrew Johnson betrays the interests of an African American veteran. **Analyze Political Cartoons** What symbolism does the cartoon use to influence viewers' opinions of Johnson and African American veterans?

IDENTIFY MAIN IDEAS Why did moderate and Radical Republicans in Congress oppose Johnson's plan for Reconstruction?

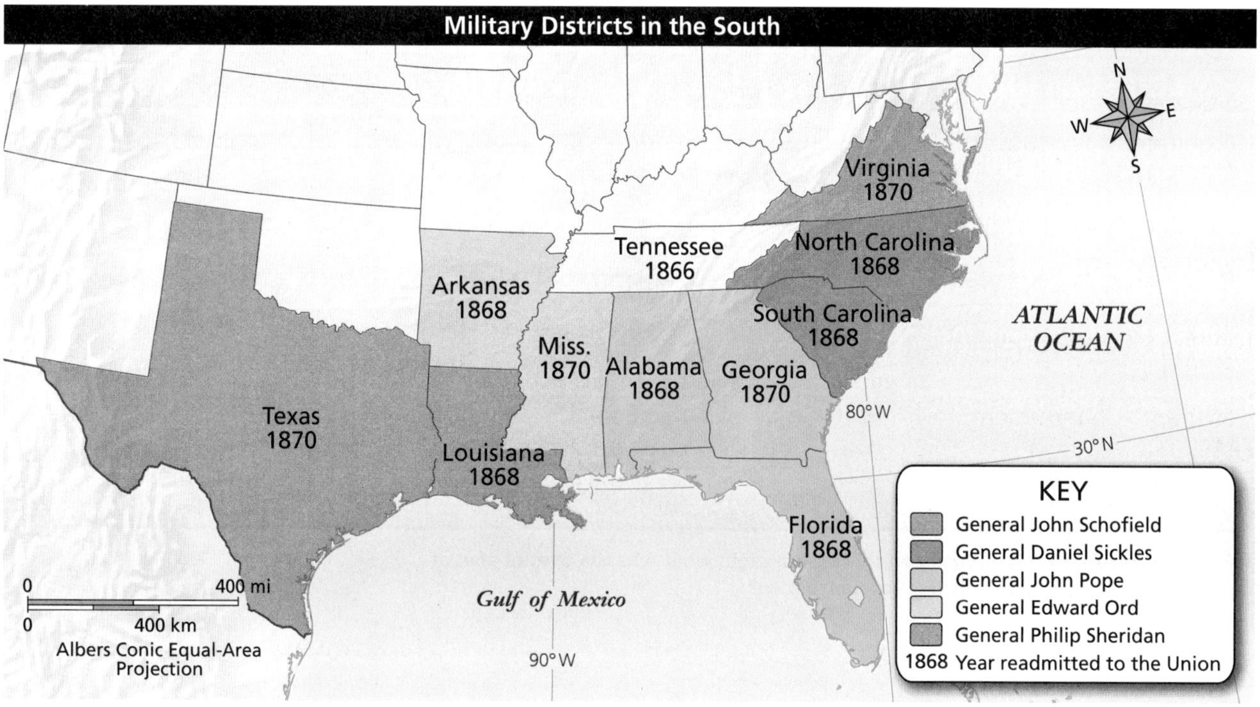

>> **Analyze Maps** How do you think southerners felt about miliary rule by northern generals?

Congress Passes a Plan for Reconstruction

As violence against African Americans in the South increased, moderate and Radical Republicans blamed the rising tide of lawlessness on Johnson's lenient policies. Congress then did something unprecedented. With the required two-thirds majority, for the first time ever, it passed major legislation over a President's veto. The Civil Rights Act of 1866 became law.

The Fourteenth Amendment Feeling their strength in Congress, a coalition of Radical and moderate Republicans spent nearly a year designing a sweeping Reconstruction program. To protect freedmen's rights from presidential vetoes, southern state legislatures, and federal court decisions, Congress passed the **Fourteenth Amendment** to the Constitution. It guaranteed equality under the law for all citizens.

Under the amendment, any state that refused to allow African American people to vote would risk losing the number of seats in the House of Representatives that were represented by its African American population. The amendment states that this representation was based on "counting the whole number of persons in each State," specifically referring to the Three-Fifths Compromise, which was nullified by the Thirteenth Amendment. The measure also counteracted the President's pardons by barring leading Confederate officials from holding federal or state offices.

Congress again passed legislation over Johnson's veto with the ratification of the Military Reconstruction Act of 1867. The act divided the 10 southern states that had yet to be readmitted into the Union into five military districts governed by former Union generals. The act also delineated how each state could form their new state government and receive congressional recognition. In each state, voters were to elect delegates to write a new constitution that guaranteed suffrage for African American men. Then, once the state ratified the Fourteenth Amendment, it could reenter the Union.

Johnson's Impeachment The power struggle between Congress and the President reached a crisis in 1867. To limit the President's power, Congress passed the Tenure of Office Act. Under its terms, the President needed Senate approval to remove certain officials from office. When Johnson tried to fire Secretary of War Edwin Stanton, the last Radical Republican in his Cabinet, Stanton barricaded himself in his office for about two months.

Angrily, the House of Representatives voted to **impeach** Johnson, that is, to charge him with wrongdoing in office, for trying to fire Stanton.

Major Reconstruction Legislation, 1865–1870

LEGISLATION	PROVISIONS
Freedmen's Bureau Acts (1865–1866)	Create a government agency to provide services to freed African Americans and war victims
Civil Rights Act of 1866	Grants citizenship to African Americans and outlaws Black Codes
Reconstruction Act of 1867	Divides former Confederacy into military districts
Fourteenth Amendment (1868)	Guarantees citizenship to African Americans and prohibits states from passing laws to take away a citizen's rights
Fifteenth Amendment (1870)	States that no citizen can be denied the right to vote because of "race, color, or previous condition of servitude"
Enforcement Act of 1870	Protects voting rights by making intimidation of voters a federal crime

>> **Analyze Information** Based on this information, what was the overall goal of new laws and amendments during Reconstruction?

The trial in the Senate lasted through the spring of 1868. In the end, the Radicals failed—by only one vote—to win the two-thirds majority necessary in the Senate to remove Johnson from office. Several moderate Republicans backed away from conviction. They felt that using impeachment to get rid of a President who disagreed with Congress would upset the balance of power in the government. During his impeachment trial, Johnson had promised to enforce the Reconstruction Acts. In his remaining time in office, he kept that promise.

The Fifteenth Amendment In 1868, the Republican candidate, former Union general Ulysses S. Grant was elected President. Although he won the electoral vote by a huge margin and had a significant lead in the popular vote, his opponent, Horatio Seymour, a Democrat from New York, received a majority of the white vote. Republican leaders now had another reason for securing a constitutional amendment that would guarantee African American suffrage throughout the nation.

In 1869, Congress passed the **Fifteenth Amendment** forbidding any state from denying suffrage on the grounds of race, color, or previous condition of servitude. Unlike previous measures, this guarantee applied to northern states as well as southern states. Both the Fourteenth and Fifteenth amendments were ratified by 1870, but both contained loopholes that left room for evasion. States could still impose voting restrictions based on literacy or property qualifications, which in effect would exclude most African Americans. Soon the southern states would do just that.

☑ **IDENTIFY CENTRAL ISSUES** What was the main goal of the Fifteenth Amendment?

☑ ASSESSMENT

1. **Interpret** What did Sherman think should be done with lands that had come under government control during the war? How did northern and southern whites react to his plan?
2. **Summarize** What political gains did African Americans hope to achieve after the passage of the Thirteenth Amendment, and how did white southerners respond to these ideas?
3. **Distinguish** How did Lincoln show generosity to white southerners at the expense of African Americans during Reconstruction?
4. **Support Ideas with Evidence** What were Black Codes, and how did they limit the rights of African Americans in the South?
5. **Summarize** Describe the efforts of Radical and moderate Republicans to grant additional rights to African Americans.
6. **Quest Connection** What was the central issue that divided Congress from President Johnson and led to his impeachment?

Primary Sources

Second Inaugural Address: Abraham Lincoln

Lincoln delivered his second inaugural address just over a month before his death. He spoke about the war, slavery, and the need "to bind up the nation's wounds." The speech's closing words of reconciliation and healing are today carved in the walls of the Lincoln Memorial.

Note: In this source, Lincoln uses the term *colored,* which is an outdated term describing Black people.

>> President Abraham Lincoln

At this second appearing to take the oath of the Presidential office there is less occasion for an extended address than there was at the first. Then a statement somewhat in detail of a course to be pursued seemed fitting and proper. Now, at the expiration of four years, during which public declarations have been constantly called forth on every point and phase of the great contest which still absorbs the attention and engrosses the energies of the nation, little that is new could be presented. The progress of our arms, upon which all else chiefly depends, is as well known to the public as to myself, and it is, I trust, reasonably satisfactory and encouraging to all. With high hope for the future, no prediction in regard to it is ventured.

DETERMINE MEANING Why does the President say this second inaugural address will be shorter than the first inaugural address?

. . . On the occasion corresponding to this four years ago all thoughts were anxiously directed to an impending civil war. All dreaded it, all sought to avert it. While the inaugural address was being delivered from this place, devoted altogether to saving the Union without war, insurgent [rebelling against authority or government] agents were in the city seeking to destroy it without war—seeking to dissolve the Union and divide effects by negotiation. Both parties deprecated [expressed disapproval of] war, but one of them would make war rather than let the nation survive, and the other would accept war rather than let it perish, and the war came.

COMPARE AND CONTRAST Whom does Lincoln blame for the outbreak of the war?

One-eighth of the whole population were colored slaves, not distributed generally over the Union, but localized in the southern part of it. These slaves constituted a peculiar [special] and powerful interest. All knew that this interest was somehow the cause of the war. To strengthen, perpetuate, and extend this interest was the object for which the insurgents would rend [tear apart] the Union even by war, while the Government claimed no right to do more than to restrict the territorial enlargement of it. Neither party expected for the war the magnitude or the duration which it has already attained. Neither anticipated that the cause of the conflict might cease with or even before the conflict itself should cease. Each looked for an easier triumph, and a result less fundamental and astounding. Both read the same Bible and pray to the same God, and each invokes His aid against the other.

DETERMINE CENTRAL IDEAS What, according to the President, was the cause of the Civil War?

Primary Sources

It may seem strange that any men should dare to ask a just God's assistance in wringing their bread from the sweat of other men's faces, but let us judge not, that we be not judged. The prayers of both could not be answered. That of neither has been answered fully. The Almighty has His own purposes. "Woe unto the world because of offenses; for it must needs be that offenses come, but woe to that man by whom the offense cometh." If we shall suppose that American slavery is one of those offenses which, in the providence of God, must needs come, but which, having continued through His appointed time, He now wills to remove, and that He gives to both North and South this terrible war as the woe due to those by whom the offense came, shall we discern therein any departure from those divine attributes which the believers in a living God always ascribe to Him?

DETERMINE MEANING What are the "offenses" discussed in this passage?

Fondly [with trust] do we hope, fervently [with strong emotion] do we pray, that this mighty scourge of war may speedily pass away. Yet, if God wills that it continue until all the wealth piled by the bondsman's two hundred and fifty years of unrequited [with nothing given in return] toil shall be sunk, and until every drop of blood drawn with the lash shall be paid by another drawn with the sword, as was said three thousand years ago, so still it must be said "the judgments of the Lord are true and righteous [morally correct] altogether."

DRAW INFERENCES Why might this passage have been particularly inspiring to Radical Republicans?

With malice toward none, with charity for all, with firmness in the right as God gives us to see the right, let us strive on to finish the work we are in, to bind up the nation's wounds, to care for him who shall have borne the battle and for his widow and his orphan, to do all which may achieve and cherish a just and lasting peace among ourselves and with all nations.

PARAPHRASE Rewrite this paragraph in your own words.

ASSESSMENT

1. **Analyze Structure** What examples can you find in Lincoln's address of organizing ideas into groups of three?
2. **Draw Conclusions** Based on this address, how do you think Lincoln would have dealt with Southern states returning to the Union if he had lived to complete his second term? Explain your answer.
3. **Make Inferences** How does this address reveal the mixed emotions that Lincoln and many Northerners had toward the South during the end of the war?

GO ONLINE to access primary sources

8.2

Radical Republican members of South Carolina's first legislature after the war

Reconstruction Changes the South

BOUNCE to Activate Flipped Video

Objectives

Explain how Republicans gained control of southern state governments.

Analyze the role of the Freedmen's Bureau and how freed people adjusted to freedom.

Evaluate the South's new economic system and its impact on poor farmers.

Summarize efforts to limit African Americans' rights and the federal government's response.

Key Terms

scalawag
carpetbagger
segregation
integration
sharecropping
share-tenancy
tenant farming
Ku Klux Klan
Enforcement Acts

Before the Civil War, a limited number of powerful white men had controlled the South. In the wake of the war, a very basic question needed to be resolved. Who would gain power and how would they use it? How this question was answered at the time would have both immediate and lasting consequences.

Republicans Dominate Government

By 1870, all of the former Confederate states had met the requirements under Radical Reconstruction and rejoined the Union. Republicans dominated their newly established state governments.

African Americans at the Polls Almost 1,500 African American men—some born free, some recently released from slavery—helped usher the Republican Party into the South by taking on roles in state and local governments. These new African American citizens served the South as school superintendents, sheriffs, mayors, coroners, police chiefs, and representatives in state legislatures. Six served as lieutenant governors.

Two state legislatures—in Mississippi and South Carolina—had African American Speakers of the House. Between 1870 and 1877, two African American senators and fourteen African American congressmen served in the U.S. Congress.

GO ONLINE to access your digital course

>> This cartoon appeared in a northern newspaper in the 1870s. **Analyze Political Cartoons** What do the weapons and soldiers in the cartoon represent?

BOUNCE to Activate Gallery

>> This illustration shows a meeting of southerners sympathetic to Reconstruction policies, or "scalawags" as they were called by former Confederates.

Most importantly, millions of southern African American men were now voters. Since the Radical Republicans required a loyalty oath, many white southerners were not eligible to vote, or chose to stay away from the constitutional conventions and from the elections that followed. African American men, however, quickly signed up to use their new right of suffrage. Thus, by 1868, many southern states had both African American-elected officials and a strong Republican Party. Ironically, South Carolina—the state that had ignited the Civil War—became the one state where an African American majority ruled the legislature, though only for a short time.

New Opportunities The Republican Party attracted not only African American southerners but also others who sought change and challenge.

Scalawags, as southern white critics called them, were white men who had been locked out of pre–Civil War politics by their wealthier neighbors. The new Republican Party invited them in.

They found allies in northern men, almost all white, who relocated to the South. These northerners came seeking to improve their economic or political situations, or to help make a better life for freedmen. Many southern white people resented what they felt was the invasion of opportunists, come to make their fortunes from the South's misfortune. Southerners labeled the newcomers "**carpetbaggers**," after the inexpensive carpet-cloth suitcases often carried by northerners.

Most carpetbaggers were young and literate. Since only the wealthy minority of white southerners could read, a northerner with even a basic education had a real advantage. For carpetbaggers, the opportunities in the new South were as abundant as those in the western frontier: new land to be bought, new careers to be shaped.

Many freed people, such Blanche K. Bruce, similarly moved to improve their situations. Born into slavery in Virginia, Bruce learned to read from his enslaver's son. When the war began, Bruce left the plantation and moved to Missouri, where he ran a school for African American children for a short time before moving on to Oberlin College in Ohio.

In 1866, Bruce—now 25 years old—went south to Mississippi, where he became a prosperous landowner and was elected to several local political positions. In 1874, in his mid-thirties, Bruce was elected to the U.S. Senate.

For African Americans like Bruce, the South was the only place to pursue a political career. Even though the Fifteenth Amendment established suffrage nationally, no African American congressman was elected from the North until the twentieth century.

Women and Reconstruction During Reconstruction, talk about voting rights was in the air. Still, the Republican Party did not support women's suffrage, arguing that they could not rally national support behind the essential goal of African American suffrage if they tried to include women, too. Even so, the Reconstruction South offered northern women—white and African American—opportunities that they could not pursue at home.

In medical facilities, orphanages, and other relief agencies, single women carved out new roles and envisioned new horizons. They also participated in what was the most enduring development of the new South—the shaping of a public school system.

A Public School System Takes Shapes Mandated by Reconstruction state constitutions, public schools grew slowly, drawing in only about half of southern children by the end of the 1870s. Establishing a new school system was expensive. This was especially so since southerners opted for **segregation**, or separation of the races. Operating two school systems—one white, one African American—severely strained the southern economy. A few of the most radical white Republicans suggested **integration**—combining the schools—but the idea was unpopular with most Republicans. Nevertheless, the beginning of a tax-supported public school system was a major Reconstruction success.

Despite these successes, the South still faced many challenges. Many southerners remained illiterate. The quality of medical care, housing, and economic production lagged far behind the North and, in some cases, behind the newly settled West.

Legal protection for African Americans was limited, and racial violence remained a problem throughout the twentieth century.

Corruption Hinders Reconstruction In the North and the South, political offices were more and more a route to wealth and power rather than an honor bestowed on an outstanding citizen. However, conditions in the South were not unlike the rest of the country in that respect. Ambitious people everywhere were willing to bribe politicians in order to gain access to attractive loans or contracts.

>> By the late 1800s, segregation had become widespread across the South in new public school systems and other places.

Some of the most attractive arenas for corruption involved the developing railroads. Republicans were the party of African American freedom, but they were also the party of aggressive economic development. Building railroads had two big advantages. First, the construction of tracks and rail cars created jobs. Second, the rail lines would provide the means to carry produce and industrial goods to expanded markets. Hence, in many states across the nation, legislatures gave public land or lent taxpayers' money to railroad speculators.

In some cases, the speculators delivered on their promises and repaid the loans. But southern leaders, who had fewer resources and less financial expertise than their northern peers, found that a good number of their loans were stolen or mismanaged. The actions of Republican speculators gave critics of Reconstruction an excuse to claim that African American politicians—also reliably Republican—were dishonest or incompetent.

☑ **DESCRIBE** How did politics in the South change during Reconstruction?

>> Before emancipation, few African Americans had been able to legally wed under Southern state laws. During Reconstruction, families could formalize their relationships.

>> Estey Hall was built in the 1870s to house female students at Shaw University, which was founded to educate freed African Americans in North Carolina.

Freed People Rebuild Their Lives

For newly freed African Americans, some of the most important priorities were trying to develop new social institutions and economic relationships. Some freedmen deliberately moved away from the plantation, even if the owner had been a generous person. As one minister put it, "As long as the shadow of the great house falls across you, you ain't going to feel like no free man and no free woman."

Jobs and Family For the first time, many African American men and women could legalize and celebrate their marriages, build homes for their families, and make choices about where they would reside (though these choices were restricted by Black Codes limiting what work they might do). Life presented new problems and opportunities.

> I stayed on [the plantation] 'cause I didn't have no place to go. . . . Den I starts to feeling like I ain't treated right. So one night I just put that new dress in a bundle and set foot right down the big road, a-walking west!
>
> —Mary Lindsey, age 19

Many African Americans headed for southern cities, where they could develop churches, schools, and other social institutions. They also hoped to find work. Skilled men might find work as carpenters, blacksmiths, cooks, or house servants; women took in laundry, or did child care or domestic work. However, most often, African American workers had to settle for what they had had under slavery: substandard housing and poor food in return for hard labor.

The majority of African American families remained in rural areas. There, they labored in such occupations as lumbering, railroad building, or farming land for landowners—white or African American—who themselves were often poor.

The Role of Public Institutions Freed people immediately realized the intrinsic value of learning to read and perform basic arithmetic. Only in this way could they vote wisely and protect themselves from being cheated. So the Freedmen's Bureau schools filled quickly. By 1866, there were as many as 150,000 African American students—adults and children—acquiring basic literacy. Three years later, that

African American Farm Ownership, 1870–1910

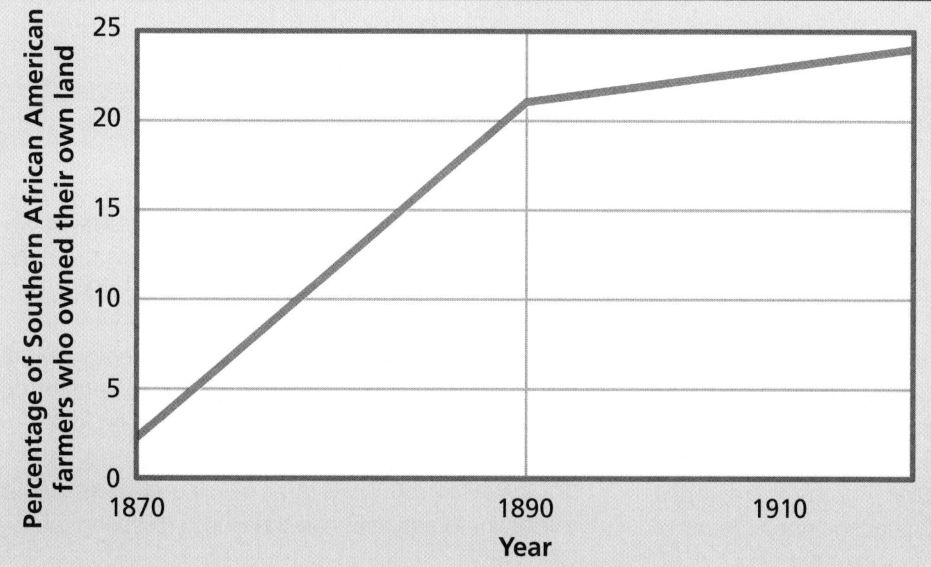

Source: Loren Schweninger, "A Vanishing Breed: Black Farm Owners in the South, 1651–1982," *Agricultural History* (Summer 1989)

>> **Analyze Data** Based on this graph, how did overall land ownership patterns in the South probably change during the time shown?

number had doubled. Tuition amounted to 10 percent of a laborer's wage, but attendance at Freedmen's schools represented a firm commitment to education.

In addition to establishing its own schools, the Freedmen's Bureau aided African American colleges. It also encouraged the many northern churches and charitable organizations that sent teachers, books, and supplies to support independent schools. Mostly these schools taught the basics of reading, writing, and math, but they also taught life skills, such as health and nutrition, or how to look for a job.

African American churches were an important component of Reconstruction education. Under slavery, many enslaved people had to attend white-run churches in which they had no say. Now, with freedom, African American churches were established throughout the South and often served as school sites, community centers, employment agencies, and political rallying points. By providing an arena for organizing, public speaking, and group planning, churches helped develop African American leaders. A considerable number of African American politicians began their careers as ministers.

☑ **SUMMARIZE** How did the Freedmen's Bureau and African American churches help African Americans build new lives in the South?

Land Distribution in the South

Many of the South's problems resulted from the uneven distribution of land. As an agricultural region, the South's wealth was defined by land ownership. Yet, in 1860, the wealthiest 5 percent of white southerners owned almost half the region's land. Relatively few people held the rest of the land. In fact, more than 90 percent of southern land was owned by only 50 percent of the people. This meant that even before the war, the South had a large number of white citizens with little or no land. After the war, millions of landless southern white people were competing with millions of landless African American people for work as farm laborers on the land of others.

The plan developed by General Sherman and the Radical Republicans to give or sell land to freed people did not provide a solution. Congress had no interest in Thaddeus Stevens's radical suggestion that large plantations be confiscated from once-wealthy planters and redistributed to freedmen. A few African American men, however, were able to gather together the means to buy land. By 1880, about 7 percent of the South's land was owned by African Americans.

Sharecropping and Share-Tenancy Even large land owners had no money to purchase supplies or pay workers. As a result, many southerners adopted one of three arrangements: sharecropping, share-tenancy, or tenant-farming.

The first two of these systems could be carried out without cash. Under the **sharecropping** system, which embraced most of the South's African American and white poor, a landowner dictated the crop and provided the sharecropper with a place to live, as well as seeds and tools, in return for a "share" of the harvested crop. The landowner often bought these supplies on credit, at very high interest, from a supplier. The landlord passed on these costs to the sharecropper. Hence, sharecroppers were perpetually in debt to the landowner, and the landowner was always in debt to the supplier. For the sharecropper, this created a kind of debt peonage or bondage.

One problem was that most landlords, remembering the huge profits from prewar cotton, chose to invest in this crop again. Dishonest landowners could lie about the cost of supplies, devaluing the sharecropper's harvest that now amounted to less than the season's expenses. Also, the price a farmer could get for cotton and other cash crops fluctuated, tending downward in the late 1800s. Thus the sharecropper could never move, because he always owed the owner the labor for next year's crop.

Share-tenancy was much like sharecropping, except that the farmworker chose what crop he would plant and bought his own supplies. Then, he gave a share of the crop to the landowner. In this system, the farmworker had a bit more control over the cost of supplies. Therefore, he might be able to grow a variety of crops or use some of the land to grow food for his family. With these choices, it became more possible to save money.

Tenant Farming The most independent arrangement for both farmer and landowner was a system known as **tenant farming**. In this case, the tenant paid cash rent to a landowner and then was free to choose and manage his own crop—and free to choose where he would live. This system was only viable for a farmer who had some cash to get started, good money-management skills—and good luck.

☑ **SUMMARIZE** What three farming systems came to dominate agriculture in the South following the Civil War?

Changes in the South Spark Violence

The struggle to make a living in a region devastated by war led to fierce economic competition. Economic uncertainty in turn fueled the fire of white southerners' outrage. Already resentful of the Republican takeover of local politics and of occupation by federal troops, white southerners from all economic classes were united in their insistence that African Americans not have full citizenship.

Agricultural Systems After the Civil War

SHARECROPPING	SHARE-TENANCY	TENANT FARMING
• Landowners supplied tenants with food, shelter, tools, and supplies. • Sharecroppers gave a portion of their crop to the landowner as payment and kept the rest. • Sharecroppers did not own the crops or land. • Sharecroppers often became indebted to landowners.	• Tenants purchased most of their own tools and supplies. • Tenants kept a share of the crop for themselves and gave one quarter or one third of their crop to the landowner. • Tenants owned the crops but not the land. • Tenants were able to save money to purchase their own tools and supplies.	• Tenants purchased and used their own farm tools and supplies. • Tenants paid the landowner in cash for rights to work the land. • Tenants owned the crops but not the land. • Tenants were able to save money to purchase their own land.

Sources: *Encyclopædia Britannica*; National Park Service; United States Department of Agriculture; Oklahoma State University; Texas State Historical Association

>> **Analyze Information** What was one challenge for farmers common to all three agricultural systems?

BOUNCE to Activate Chart

The Ku Klux Klan The more progress African Americans made, the more hostile white southerners became as they tried to keep freedmen in a subservient role. Many were committed to white supremacy, the belief that white people are superior to others, especially Black people, and should have control over them. During Reconstruction, dozens of loosely organized groups of white southerners emerged to terrorize African Americans. The best known of these was the **Ku Klux Klan**, formed in Tennessee in 1866. Klan members roamed the countryside, especially at night, burning homes, schools, and churches, and beating, maiming, or killing African Americans and their white allies. Dressed in white robes and hoods, mounted on horses, these gangs aimed to terrorize freed people and keep them from exercising their rights.

The Klan took special aim at the symbols of African American freedom: African American teachers and schools, churches and ministers, politicians, and anyone—white or African American—who encouraged African American people to vote. Unfortunately, often their tactics succeeded. In many rural counties, African American voters were too intimidated to go to the polls.

In Jackson County, Florida, random acts of racial violence against African Americans developed into organized attacks that became known as the Jackson County War. Between 1869 and 1871, dozens of African Americans and Republican party officials were murdered.

>> Members of the Ku Klux Klan and other white supremacists terrorized freed African Americans and their supporters during Reconstruction.

The Federal Response Racial violence grew even more widespread, in the North as well as in the South, after the Fifteenth Amendment guaranteed all American men the right to vote. In Arkansas, Republican legislators were murdered. In New Orleans, riots broke out. One freed woman from South Carolina reported that the Klan killed her husband, a sharecropper on the land of one Mr. Jones. The widow explained that Klan members were incensed because Mr. Jones had had "poor white folks on the land, and he [evicted them], and put all these blacks on the premises."

The U.S. Congress took action, passing **Enforcement Acts** (also known as Ku Klux Klan Acts) in 1870 and 1871. The acts made it a federal offense to interfere with a citizen's right to vote. Congress also held hearings inviting African American politicians and other observers to describe the situation in the South. George Ruby of Texas told how he had been dragged into the woods and beaten because he had opened a school in Louisiana. Emanuel Fortune, one of Florida's political organizers, reported that his "life was in danger at all times" because he was "a leading man in politics."

>> Slain Philadelphia teacher Octavius Catto

Racial violence at the polls was not limited to the South. In the 1870 election in Philadelphia, a company of marines was sent in to protect African American voters. When no such protection was supplied for the 1871 elections, an African American teacher, Octavius Catto, was killed in anti-African American political riots.

At a protest meeting that followed, one African American Philadelphian spoke out.

> The Ku Klux of the South are not by any means the lower classes of society. The same may be said of the Ku Klux of the North. . . . Let no man think that we ask for people's pity or commiseration. What we do ask is fairness and equal opportunities in the battle of life.
>
> —Isaiah Wears, 1871

Congress used the Ku Klux Klan Acts to indict hundreds of Klansmen throughout the South. After 1872, on account of the federal government's readiness to use legal action, there was a decline in violence against Republicans and African Americans. The hatred may have been contained, but it was far from extinguished. Smoldering beneath the surface, it would flare up in the coming decades.

EXPLAIN How did the federal government respond to the rise of racial violence in the South during Reconstruction?

ASSESSMENT

1. **Summarize** How did African American citizens take advantage of their newly granted political rights, and what affect did they have on American politics?
2. **Summarize** Who were the so-called "carpetbaggers" and what characteristics did they commonly share?
3. **Express Problems Clearly** What were some of the new social opportunities for African Americans in the South after the Civil War, and how were African Americans prevented from taking full advantage of these opportunities?
4. **Summarize** How was land distributed in the South both before and just after the Civil War?
5. **Identify Main Ideas** What were the Ku Klux Klan's main goals and what methods did they employ to achieve them?
6. **Connection to Today** After the Civil War, land distribution in the South was an important issue. Owning land made farmers independent and gave them a path to prosperity. Which economic issues are similarly important today? Explain your answer.

GO ONLINE to access this biography: Hiram Rhodes Revels

The Promises and Disappointments of Reconstruction

During Reconstruction, many rights won by African Africans were slowly eroded as government policy changed. The first speech below was delivered by Reverend E.J. Adams, a leader in South Carolina's African American community. He spoke in 1867 at a high point for Reconstruction, just after Congress had passed several laws protecting the rights of African Americans.

The second speech was delivered by Senator Hiram Revels in 1870, in a very different political atmosphere. Revels was the first African American to serve in the Senate. In his first speech in office, he objected to a bill readmitting Georgia to the Union despite its exclusion of African Americans from political office.

As you read, compare the views of these two men on Reconstruction.

>> Two African Americans served in the Senate during Reconstruction, Hiram Rhodes Revels, pictured here, and Blanche Bruce. After the end of Reconstruction, no African Americans served in the Senate for nearly a century.

Primary Source 1

Address by Reverend E.J. Adams, March 19, 1867

Fellow Citizens: These are revolutionary times. For many years a contest, terrible in its nature, has been waged between despotism and republican principles, between freedom and slavery . . . Russia hath given freedom to over thirty millions of serfs, and Germany hath recently extricated itself [escaped] from the despotism of Europe. We find today Canada struggling for liberty, and Ireland too is endeavoring to grasp the flag of liberty. So, too, with regard to our nation. The little leaven that was planted in this country when the government was founded has succeeded in permeating itself through every fiber of this great body politic, and now the flag that once floated over four millions of slaves, today waves in triumph over more than thirty millions of freemen. . . .

DRAW CONCLUSIONS What does "leaven", the yeast that causes bread to rise, refer to here?

Some are opposed to universal suffrage on the ground that a black man is not capable of exercising that right with judgment. But . . . men who are led instinctively to support the liberty of the country in the time of war[,] by placing the ballot box in their hands, will also be led to support the right in the time and hour of peace. Universal suffrage is the only reward that can be given for the long years of slavery and disfranchisement of the now colored citizens of the United States. . . .

Again, a perfect Union, justice, domestic tranquility, the common defense, the general welfare, and the blessings of liberty cannot be secured without universal suffrage. It is the only means of defense for the illiterate and the poor. . . .

ANALYZE STYLE AND RHETORIC What famous document is Adams paraphrasing here?

Primary Source 2

The State of Georgia, Speech by Hiram Revels, March 16, 1870

Mr. President, I rise at this particular juncture in the discussion of the Georgia bill with feelings which perhaps never before entered into the experience of any member of this body. . . .

And here let me say further, that the people of the North owe to the colored race a deep obligation which it is no easy matter to fulfill. When the federal armies were thinned by death and disaster... from what source did our nation in its seeming death throes gain additional and new-found power? It was the [African American] sons of the South that valiantly rushed to the rescue, and but for their intrepidity [bravery] and ardent daring many a northern fireside would miss today paternal counsels [a father's advice] or a brother's love. . . .

USE CONTEXT CLUES What do "paternal counsels" at northern firesides have to do with African Americans in the South?

[The Georgia legislature] which was elected under the constitution framed and supported by colored men declared that a man having more than an eighth of African blood in his veins was ineligible to office or a seat in the legislature of the state of Georgia. . . . In the month of September 1868, twenty-eight [African American] members of the legislature were expelled from that body. . .

The courts of law, at least so far as colored men were regarded, were a shameless mockery of justice. And here an illustration, perhaps, will the better give point to my last remark. A case in which was involved the question whether or not a colored man was eligible to one of the county offices was taken before the superior court, and the judge upon the bench rendered as his judicial opinion that a man of color was not entitled to hold office. I am told, sir, that the colored man in question is a graduate of Oberlin [College], Ohio, and served with honor as a commissioned officer in the Union army during the late war. Is any comment needed in this body upon such a condition of affairs in the state of Georgia? Sir, I trust not.

DRAW INFERENCES Why might the exclusion of African Americans from political offices lead to the courts becoming a "shameless mockery of justice?"

ASSESSMENT

Be sure to cite specific evidence from the sources as you answer the following questions.

1. **Determine Author's Purpose** Why do you think Adams listed examples of the contest between freedom and slavery around the world?
2. **Identify Supporting Details** What is Revels' key example of the way African Americans are being excluded from power in Georgia? What makes this example particularly effective?
3. **Evaluate Arguments** How do both Adams and Revels connect African Americans' military service to their political rights?
4. **Compare and Contrast** How was the tone of the two speakers different? What best explains this?
5. **Develop Empathy** What unique feelings do you think Hiram Revels is referring to in the first paragraph of his speech?

GO ONLINE to access primary sources

8.3

Although many African Americans cast ballots for the first time during Reconstruction, they found it increasingly difficult to vote as Reconstruction ended.

Reconstruction's Impact

In the end, most northerners came to realize what southerners already knew. The rebuilding of the political, economic, and social life of the South would not be easy, nor would it happen quickly. As reformers lost their resolve, old prejudices took new shapes. The end of Reconstruction did not come suddenly. However, ever since the Radical Republicans failed to convict President Johnson, their power and crusading zeal had faded.

BOUNCE to Activate Flipped Video

Objectives

Explain why Reconstruction ended.

Evaluate the successes and failures of Reconstruction.

Describe the experience of African Americans in the changing South.

Assess how whites created a segregated society in the South and how African Americans responded.

Key Terms

Civil Rights Act of 1875
Redeemer
Rutherford B. Hayes
Compromise of 1877
Jim Crow laws
poll tax
literacy test
grandfather clause
Booker T. Washington
W.E.B. Du Bois
Ida B. Wells

Reconstruction Comes to an End

Dwindling Support for Reform As the 1860s ended, voters and politicians outside the South increasingly turned their attention to other pressing issues—reforming politics and the economy, among other things. Also, the continued cost of military operations in the South worried many. Gradually and quietly, beginning in 1871, troops were withdrawn from the South. In 1872, the Freedmen's Bureau was dissolved.

At the same time, faith in the presidency of Ulysses S. Grant faded, and the Republican Party began to splinter. Republicans had high hopes for the Union general and war hero. Grant had promised a tough stance against ongoing southern oppression of African American citizens.

However, corruption plagued the Grant's administration, making it difficult for him to pursue Reconstruction policies and causing support for the President and his positions. The death of Radical Republican leader Charles Sumner in 1874 also symbolized an important transition. A generation of white

GO ONLINE to access your digital course

reformers, forged by abolitionist fervor and anxious to carry that passion into the national politics of Reconstruction, had passed away. Without such leaders to temper it, northern racial prejudice reemerged.

Civil Rights and the Supreme Court The Thirteenth, Fourteenth, and Fifteenth amendments guaranteed African Americans' rights, including the right to vote. Likewise, the **Civil Rights Act of 1875** guaranteed African American citizens the right to ride trains and use public facilities, such as hotels. Yet it was left to the courts to interpret how these new amendments and laws would be applied.

In the 1870s, in a series of landmark cases, the Supreme Court chipped away at African American freedoms. In what became known as the *Slaughterhouse Cases* (1873), the Court restricted the scope of the Fourteenth Amendment. In these cases, a group of small slaughterhouses in Louisiana contested a state action that granted a monopoly over the industry to one corporation.

They claimed that the monopoly violated their rights as citizens, under the Fourteenth Amendment, by depriving them of property without due process. The U.S. Supreme Court ruled against the smaller slaughterhouses. It concluded that though a citizen had certain national rights, the federal government had no control over how a state chose to define rights for its citizens.

Although this case dealt with a conflict among large and small businesses, the ruling itself set a dangerous precedent by weakening the protections of the Fourteenth Amendment. Southern states no longer felt bound by the amendment to protect the civil rights of their African American citizens.

Two years later, the Supreme Court heard the case of *United States* v. *Cruikshank*. This case involved a white militia that attacked Republican elected officials and their supporters at a courthouse in Louisiana, killing about 150 African Americans in what became known as the Colfax Massacre. The Court ruled that the due process and equal protection clauses of the Fourteenth Amendment protected citizens only from the action of the state and not from the action of other citizens. African Americans could not turn to the Federal government when states failed to protect them.

The Return of Southern Political Power While the Klan intimidated with violence and the courts with legal interpretation, some southern Democrats devised a more subtle strategy for suppressing African American rights. They put together a coalition to return the South to the rule of white men. To appeal to small farmers, they emphasized how

The Majority Party in State Legislatures, 1868 and 1876

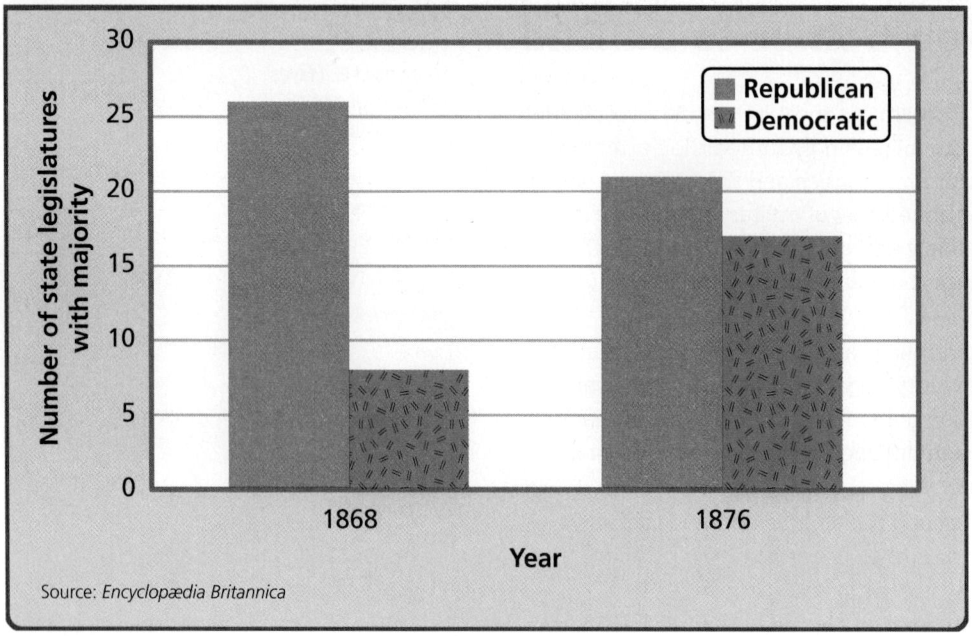

>> **Analyze Graphs** How did the representation of African Americans in these state legislatures likely change during the time period shown? Explain your answer.

BOUNCE to Activate Cartoon

★ THE ELECTION OF 1876 ★

BREAKING DOWN THE VOTE

55% States where Hayes won the popular vote

73% Southern states that voted for Tilden

Source: The American Presidency Project

THE BATTLE IN KEY STATES

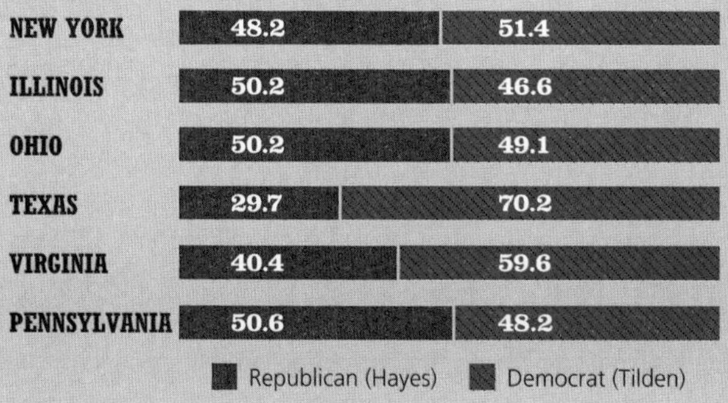

Source: The American Presidency Project

THE CONTROVERSY

1. Early election results showed Tilden had a **184-165** electoral vote lead
2. **20 remaining electoral votes** from Florida, Louisiana, South Carolina, and Oregon in dispute
3. Democrats used fraud and violence to win state elections (state legislatures directed electors) in **Florida, Louisiana, and South Carolina**
4. Republican-controlled electoral boards threw out enough Democratic votes in FL, LA, and SC to give Hayes **185 electoral votes**
5. Congress appointed Electoral Commission (8 Republicans, 7 Democrats); voted **8-7** to accept Hayes' electoral votes
6. Republicans and Democrats accused of brokering "deal" giving southern support in Congress for ratification of commission votes in exchange for ending **Reconstruction in the South**

Source: PBS

>> **Analyze Information** Why was the outcome of the election of 1876 so controversial?

Republican programs like schools and road-building resulted in higher taxes. They compromised with local Republicans by agreeing to African American suffrage.

In return, southern Republicans joined their Democratic neighbors in ostracizing white southerners who supported the Radical Republicans. Playing on the national sensitivity to corruption, the new coalition seized every opportunity to discredit African American politicians as being both self-serving and incompetent. These Democrats and Republicans agreed that racial segregation should be the rule of the new South.

The main focus of their strategy was compromise: finding common issues that would unite white southerners around the goal of regaining power in Congress. These compromisers have become known as **Redeemers**, politicians who aimed to repair or "redeem" the South in the eyes of Congress.

Sometimes their strategy is described as being designed to "redeem" or reclaim the South from northern domination. In either case, their plan brought some success. By 1870, Virginia, North Carolina, and Tennessee had reinstated wealthy white southern men as governors and had sent former Confederate leaders back to the U.S. Congress. Other former Confederate states soon followed their lead. In the congressional elections of 1874, the Republicans lost their control over the House of Representatives. The South had united behind a revitalized Democratic Party.

The Disputed Election of 1876 Ends Reconstruction With the Radical Republicans' loss of power, the stage was set to end northern domination of the South. The 1876 election pitted Ohio Republican **Rutherford B. Hayes** against New York Democrat Samuel Tilden. Hayes, a respected Union general, had served in the House of Representatives in 1866. He had resigned to become governor of Ohio, where he developed a reputation for honesty and reform-mindedness. Tilden had been active in fighting corruption in New York City. Both candidates, then, held appeal for voters who were tired of corrupt leadership.

Tilden received 51 percent of the popular vote and carried all of the southern states. However, Republicans claimed that the votes had been miscounted in three southern states, which happened to be states where Republicans controlled the reporting of ballots. Not surprisingly, in the recount, the Republicans found enough mistakes to swing the election to Hayes by one electoral vote.

When southern Democrats protested the results of this vote, Congress was charged with mediating the crisis. It formed a commission of five senators (chosen by the Republican-dominated Senate), five representatives (chosen by the Democratic House of Representatives), and five Supreme Court Justices.

In what became known as the **Compromise of 1877**, Hayes was elected President. In return, the remaining federal troops were withdrawn from the South, a southerner was appointed to a powerful cabinet position, and southern states were guaranteed federal subsidies to build railroads and improve their ports. Federal Reconstruction was over. The South and the millions of recently freed African Americans were left to negotiate their own fate.

☑ **EXPLAIN** Why did the presidential election of 1876 signal the end of Reconstruction?

Reconstruction Leaves a Mixed Legacy

Was Reconstruction a "success" or a "failure"? There have been many different answers from southerners and northerners, African American and white, then and now. All agree, however, that some things were forever changed when the victorious North tried to remake the vanquished South.

Among the enduring changes to the South were the introduction of a tax-supported school system and an infusion of federal money to modernize railroads and ports. In addition, the economy expanded from one crop—cotton—to a range of agricultural and industrial products. There was a gradual transition to a wage economy from a barter-and-credit system. But some historians say that these changes might have happened anyway, since southern planters were concerned about their debt-ridden society even before the war.

Reconstruction failed to heal the bitterness between North and South or to provide lasting protection for freed people. However, it did raise African Americans' expectations of their right to citizenship, and it placed before Americans the meaning and value of the right to vote.

A New Start for African Americans Before the Civil War, no African American in the South, and only a small number in the North, had the right to vote. Few African American southerners owned land. Most worked others' land, without pay, and without hope of improving their lot.

Reconstruction changed these things. By 1877, a few southern African Americans owned their own farms. That number would grow slowly through the next decades. Before the Civil War, most southern African Americans worked—involuntarily—in agriculture. Reconstruction began to give them choices. Perhaps most importantly, the Freedmen's Bureau helped reunite freed people with their families and promoted literacy within African American communities.

Though it fell far short of its ambitious goals, Reconstruction opened new vistas for African Americans, North and South. The Thirteenth, Fourteenth, and Fifteenth amendments provided hope for full inclusion in American society, though it would take later generations to use them to gain racial equality.

Division in the Women's Suffrage Movement One of the ironies of Reconstruction is that it gave the vote to African American men, while fragmenting the women's movement that had often been supportive of African American freedom. In the debate over the Fifteenth Amendment, there was disagreement about whether it should also include

Effects of Reconstruction

- Union is restored.
- African Americans gain citizenship and voting rights.
- South's economy and infrastructure are improved.
- Southern states establish public school system.
- Ku Klux Klan and other groups terrorize African Americans.
- Sharecropping system takes hold in the South.

>> **Analyze Information** From the perspective of an African American in the South, how was Reconstruction a success and how was it a failure?

Democrats Regain Control

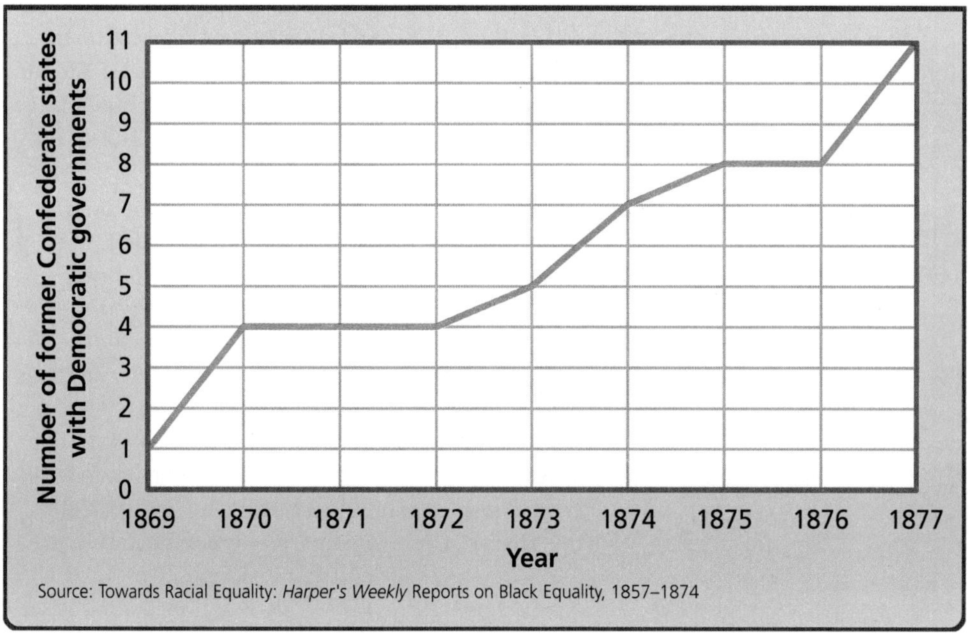

>> **Analyze Charts** Based on what you have learned about the South during Reconstruction, what reasons might explain the pattern shown here?

a clause giving women the right to vote. Some felt the Fifteenth Amendment could not be ratified if it included women's suffrage. Those who agreed with this position formed the American Woman Suffrage Association (AWSA) in 1869.

Others, like Elizabeth Cady Stanton, believed that women and African Americans should get the vote immediately. They formed the National Woman Suffrage Association (NWSA). This group scored its first victory in 1869, when the Wyoming Territory became the first political unit to extend the vote to women.

Both the NWSA and the AWSA included some African American women. However, a further division occurred when a group of African American women split off to form the Colored Women's Progressive Franchise association in 1880.

Party Allegiance in State and National Politics American politics were irrevocably shaped by the Civil War and Reconstruction. The Republican Party, born out of the controversy over slavery, continued to be seen by many as "the party of Lincoln, that ended slavery." As a result, white southerners shunned the party, while African Americans—in both the North and South—embraced it. Consequently, the Democratic Party came to dominate the white South.

Following Reconstruction, national Republicans became the party of big business—a reputation that continues to the present. The national Democratic Party, which identified with industrial laborers, differed from southern Democrats and had to maintain a delicate balance with its southern faction on this issue, as well as on the question of race.

Questions of State vs. Federal Power Which political unit has more power—the federal government or the individual states? In cases of disputes about public policy, which branch of the federal government has the last word? These questions have perplexed American lawmakers since the drafting of the Constitution. During Reconstruction, these questions acquired deeper meaning as the federal government asserted its authority not only over southern states but also over state laws in other regions.

In the end, American voters and their representatives in government opted for a balance of power, at the expense of protecting freed people in the South. With the demise of the Radical Republicans, most congressmen concluded that it was better to let the South attend to its own affairs than to leave a whole region under the control of federal military power and federal political control.

That choice would have far-reaching social, political, and economic implications.

EXPLAIN Why did Reconstruction policies split the women's suffrage movement?

The South Restricts African American Rights

During Reconstruction, the federal government had sought to secure equal rights for African Americans. Following the end of Reconstruction in 1877, however, African Americans and other minorities experienced a narrowing of their rights. This turn away from equality for all in the 1880s and 1890s had a lasting impact on society in the United States.

Jim Crow Laws Following the disputed presidential election of 1876, President Hayes removed federal troops from the South. This action allowed southern states to reassert their control over African Americans without concern about federal intervention. Southern governments enacted various measures aimed at disenfranchising, or taking away the voting rights of, African Americans and enacted **Jim Crow laws** that kept African Americans and whites segregated, or apart. Some laws separated whites from other minorities as well. During the late 1800s, the U.S. Supreme Court would continue to issue rulings that undermined civil rights for African Americans and other minorities. Not until the mid-1900s would many Jim Crow laws be overturned in the courts.

The Civil Rights Act of 1875 had guaranteed African American citizens the right to ride trains and use public facilities throughout the nation. However, in 1883, the Supreme Court issued decisions in five cases, which became known as the Civil Rights Cases, that overturned this law. In these cases, the Supreme Court ruled that decisions about who could use public accommodations was a local issue, to be governed by state and local, not federal, laws. Southern municipalities took advantage of this ruling to uphold segregation in many areas of public life and to further limit the rights of African Americans.

State Limitations on Voting Rights The Fifteenth Amendment, which became part of the United States Constitution in 1870, prohibited state governments from denying someone the right to vote because of "race, color, or previous condition of servitude." After Reconstruction, southern states

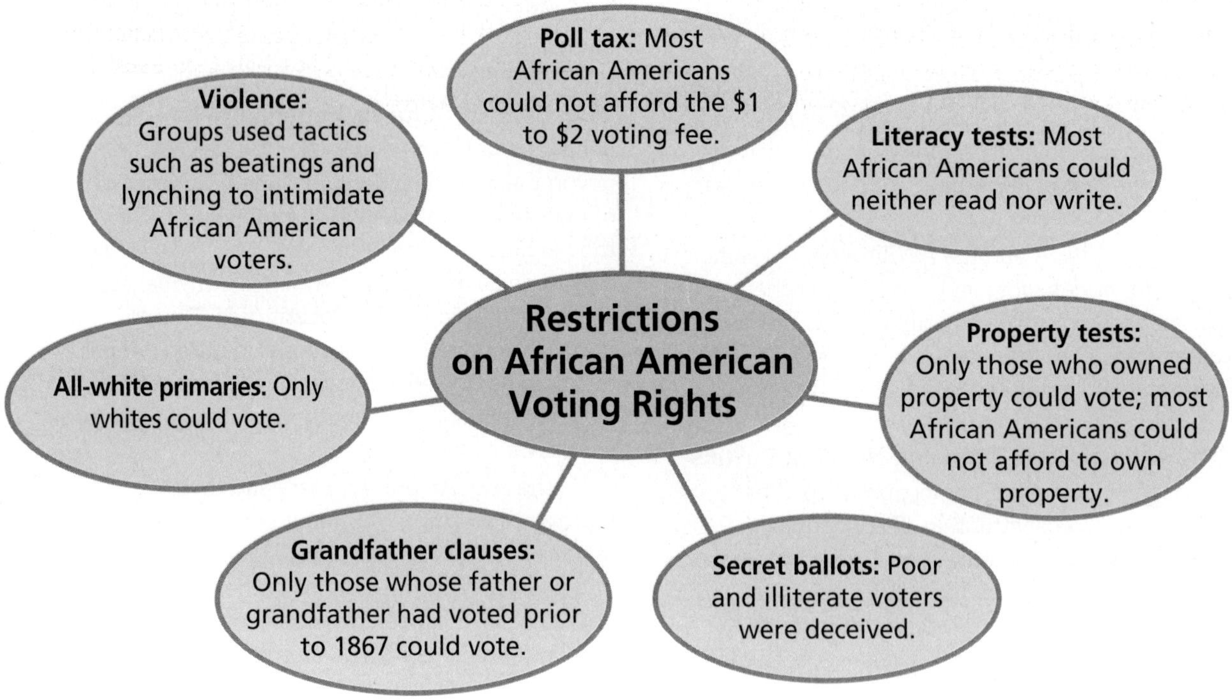

Sources: National Park Service; Tn.gov

>> **Analyze Information** How were many white southerners protected from voting restrictions like these?

BOUNCE to Activate Chart

Voter Turnout in South Carolina, 1876–1896

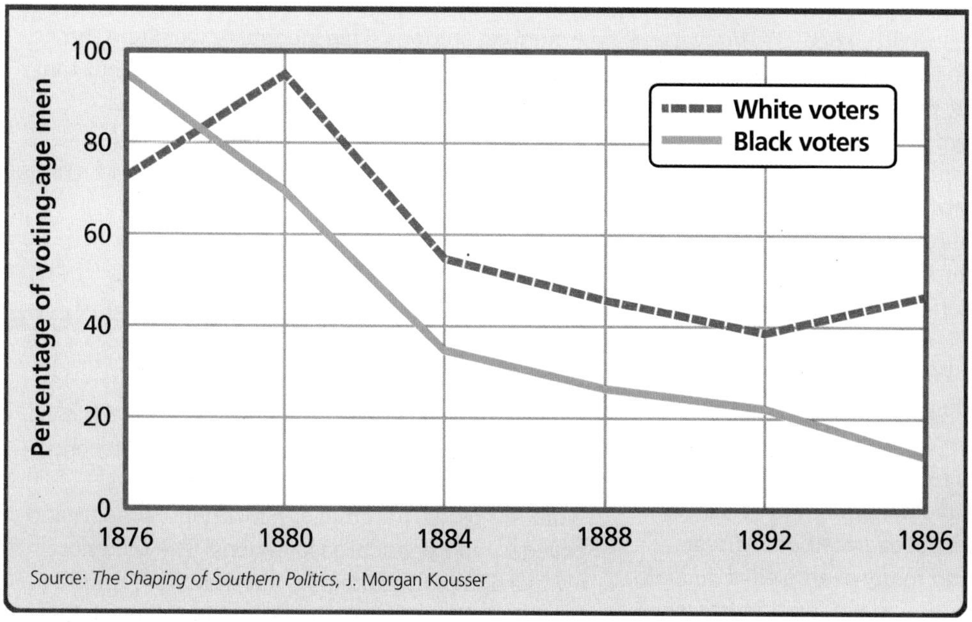

>> **Analyze Graphs** How were patterns of white and African American voter turnout similar and different during this time?

worked around this amendment by passing a number of restrictive measures.

They enacted a **poll tax**, which required voters to pay a tax to vote. The tax, which began in Georgia, cost voters $1 or $2 to vote. Poor African Americans could scarcely afford such a fee. The states also required voters to pass **literacy tests** and "understanding" tests. Because African Americans had been exploited economically and denied an education, these restrictions disqualified many of them as voters.

Southern states also enacted **grandfather clauses**, which allowed a person to vote as long as his ancestors had voted prior to 1866 or 1867. Of course, the ancestors of the African American freedmen did not vote prior to 1866 or 1867, but the ancestors of many whites did.

These grandfather clauses enabled poor and illiterate whites, but not African Americans, to vote. Some southern states also established all-white primaries, meaning that only whites had a voice in selecting who got to run in general elections. In addition, whites resorted to violence to keep African Americans from participating in the political process. As South Carolina senator Ben Tillman put it: "We have done our level best. We have scratched our heads to find out how we could eliminate the last one of them [Black voters]. We stuffed ballot boxes. We shot them."

As a result of these actions, throughout the Deep South, African American participation in politics fell dramatically. In Louisiana, for example, the number of African Americans registered to vote plummeted from 130,000 in 1894 to just more than 1,300 in 1904. In Florida, between 1885 and 1889, statutes were introduced to limit voting by African Americans. On the eve of World War II, in 1940, only 3 percent of all African Americans in the South could vote.

The Spread of Segregation As the nineteenth century drew to a close, Jim Crow laws became a way of life in the South. Initially, some white southerners opposed Jim Crow laws on the grounds that if some aspects of life were segregated, in time all aspects of life would become segregated, imposing an undue burden on society. "If there must be Jim Crow cars [railroad], there should be Jim Crow waiting saloons. And if there were Jim Crow saloons," stated a prominent Charleston newspaper writer, "then there would have to be Jim Crow jury boxes and a Jim Crow Bible for colored witnesses." The whole idea, he concluded, was "absurd."

Nevertheless, widespread segregation became a reality. In addition to Jim Crow railroad cars and waiting stations, southern states established Jim Crow jury boxes and Bibles, as well as cemeteries, restaurants, parks, beaches, and hospitals.

The Jim Crow system went beyond legal segregation, however. African Americans had to follow an elaborate, yet unwritten code that governed how they could speak to and interact with white people. Violations might include speaking to a white person in a manner deemed disrespectful, or simply arguing with a white person. Those seen by white people as breaking the rules of the racial hierarchy might be lynched, or murdered by a mob without any kind of due process. White people used lynchings to terrorize African Americans and to enforce white supremacy. Despite their extreme brutality, lynchings attracted large crowds. White people brought their children, and even made postcards showing the events as souvenirs.

Lynchings were more rare in Northern States, but African Americans still faced mistreatment there. Even in states without legal segregation, African American migrants found many examples of de facto segregation—or segregation in act if not in law, such as restrictions on where they were allowed to live and work.

Then, in *Plessy* v. *Ferguson* (1896), the Supreme Court upheld the constitutionality of Jim Crow laws. The majority opinion argued that as long as states maintained "separate but equal" facilities, they did not violate the Fourteenth Amendment. In reality, separate facilities were rarely equal. For instance, in 1915, South Carolina spent nearly 14 dollars for every white student but less than 3 dollars for every African American student. This inequality would be the premise that later overturned segregation, but that did not happen for many years to come.

DESCRIBE How did U.S. Supreme Court rulings allow for legal segregation?

African American Leaders Seek Reform

Even during the darkest days of Jim Crow, African Americans refused to accept the status of second-class citizens. They established newspapers, women's clubs, fraternal organizations, schools and colleges, and political associations. They did not always agree on strategies, but they were united in their determination to "never turn back" until they had equality.

Booker T. Washington The most famous African American leader at this time was **Booker T. Washington**. Born into slavery in 1856, he argued that African Americans needed to accommodate themselves to segregation, meaning that they should not focus their energies on seeking to overturn Jim Crow laws. Instead, he called for African Americans to "pull themselves up from their own bootstraps" by building up their prosperity and establishing their reputations as hardworking and honest citizens.

> The wisest among my race understand that the agitation of questions of social equality is the extremest folly, and that progress in the enjoyment of all the privileges that will come to us must be the result of severe and constant struggle rather than artificial forcing. . . . It is important and right that all privileges of the law be ours, but it is vastly more important that we be prepared for the exercises of these privileges.
>
> —Booker T. Washington, Atlanta Exposition address, 1895

>> African American leader Booker T. Washington

Washington led the Tuskegee Institute, a school in Macon County, Alabama. It became known for providing "industrial education," sometimes referred to as vocational education. Such an education, Washington hoped, would prepare African Americans to exercise the privileges of citizenship.

W.E.B. Du Bois A native of Great Barrington, Massachusetts, **W.E.B. Du Bois**, earned his Ph.D. from Harvard University in 1896, and went on to criticize Washington's willingness to accommodate southern whites. Echoing the spirit of the abolitionists, he argued that African Americans should demand full and immediate equality and not limit themselves to vocational education. Du Bois did not feel that the right to vote was a privilege that African Americans needed to earn. He also argued that Washington wrongly shifted the burden of achieving equality from the nation to the "Negro's shoulders" alone.

Ida B. Wells One African American woman who fought for justice was **Ida B. Wells**. Born into slavery in 1862, Wells grew up in Holly Springs, Mississippi.

Her father, James Wells, became a prominent local businessman and raised her to fight for the rights of African Americans. As a young adult, Wells moved to Memphis, Tennessee, where she worked as a schoolteacher and became active in her church. Wells bought a local newspaper, renamed it *Free Speech*, and wrote articles that condemned the mistreatment of African Americans.

In 1892, after a mob attack on close friends in Memphis, she wrote an editorial attacking the practice of lynching in the South. "Eight Negroes lynched since last issue of the 'Free Speech,'" Wells declared. "If Southern white men are not careful, they will over-reach themselves and public sentiment will have a reaction."

Local whites responded to Wells's editorial by running her out of town. In exile, Wells embarked on a lifelong crusade against lynching. She wrote three pamphlets aimed at awakening the nation to what she described as the "southern horrors" of legalized murder. She also toured Europe and helped organize women's clubs to fight for African American rights.

An Unfulfilled Promise Historians today refer to the late 1800s as the nadir, or lowest point, of race relations in U.S. history. Reconstruction had raised the hope of political and social integration. However, the everyday realities of segregation and discrimination challenged that promise. The legacy of slavery, the Civil War, and Reconstruction stretched on for decades to come.

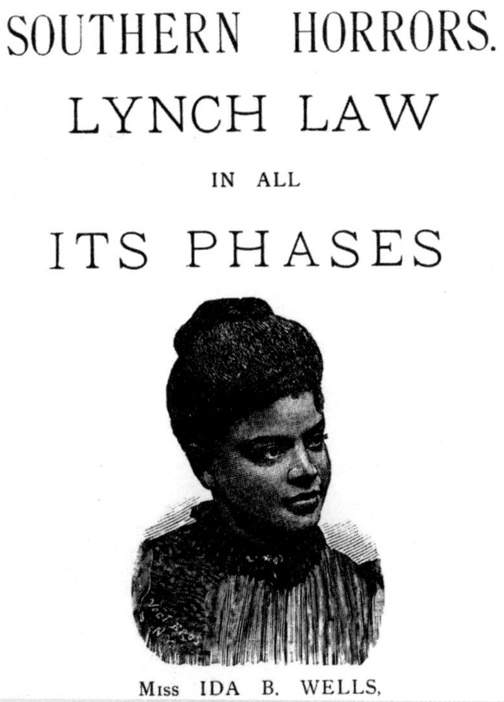
SOUTHERN HORRORS.

LYNCH LAW

IN ALL

ITS PHASES

MISS IDA B. WELLS,

>> Ida B. Wells wrote and spoke extensively in favor of a federal anti-lynching law.

COMPARE AND CONTRAST How did Washington, Du Bois, and Wells protest the ongoing mistreatment of African Americans?

ASSESSMENT

1. **Synthesize** Explain how Reconstruction changed the lives of African Americans in the South.
2. **Interpret** How did *Plessy* v. *Ferguson* affect segregation in United States?
3. **Summarize** Discuss Ida B. Wells' contributions to efforts to protect the rights of African Americans.
4. **Identify** What strategy did the politicians known as Redeemers employ to gain political power? What was the outcome?
5. **Connections to Today** Voting rights were hotly contested during Reconstruction. Today, Americans still debate their limits. Nearly all states restrict the voting rights of people convicted of serious crimes, with some taking that right away permanently. Some argue that this is unfair. Take a stand on the issue.

Connections to Today

A voter registration drive

Take Action about Voter Turnout

Securing the right to vote has long been a difficult issue. But convincing people to exercise that right is a different struggle. Voter turnout can be low in our country, but many organizations work hard to get voters to the polls.

1. **Choose** one of the following topics:
    - Voter turnout in your community
    - Obstacles to voting
    - Efforts to increase turnout
2. **Ask Questions** Generate a list of questions you have about the topic.
3. **Learn** about the topic and major issues related to it. Are there any major debates related to the topic or issues? What are the strongest arguments on each side? Take notes as you conduct your research and continue to generate questions as you learn more.
4. **Conduct a Community Service Project** Use what you've learned about voter participation to help boost voter turnout. Create a public service announcement or public notice informing people about the importance of voting and providing information on how to register to vote. Be sure to check with local authorities to ensure that the information you're sharing is accurate.

GO ONLINE to www.SavvasRealize.com and access your digital course

Use the texts, quizzes, interactivities, Quest Inquiries, Flipped Videos, and other resources from this Topic to prepare for the Topic Test.

- Quest Inquiries
- Quizzes
- Interactivities
- Texts
- Flipped Videos

While online you can also check the progress you've made learning the topic and course content by viewing your grades, test scores, and assignment status.

SAVVAS realize™

Topic 8 Quick Study Guide

LESSON SUMMARIES

Use these Lesson Summaries, and the longer versions available online, to review the key ideas for each lesson in this Topic.

Lesson 1: Plans for Reconstruction Clash

During the era of Reconstruction (1865–1877), the federal government debated how to return the southern states to the Union, rebuild the South's ruined economy, and promote the rights of freed people. After President Lincoln's assassination in 1865, Andrew Johnson became President, and struggled with "Radical Republicans" in Congress who wanted African Americans to have full citizenship, including the right to vote. As violence against African Americans in the South increased, Congress passed the Fourteenth Amendment, which guaranteed equality under the law for all citizens. It also passed the Fifteenth Amendment, which forbade any state from denying suffrage on the grounds of race or color.

Lesson 2: Reconstruction Changes the South

The millions of African American men who could now vote brought the Republican Party to power in the South. A new public school system was established, but Southerners ensured that schools remained segregated. With slavery now illegal, landowners set up a sharecropping system in which the landowner provided the sharecropper with a place to live in return for a "share" of the harvested crop. White southerners formed secret organizations like the Ku Klux Klan to terrorize African Americans. After Congress passed the Fifteenth Amendment, which guaranteed all American men the right to vote, racial violence increased.

Lesson 3: Reconstruction's Impact

In 1871 Federal troops were withdrawn from the South, ending Reconstruction. In the 1870s, the Supreme Court chipped away at African American freedom, as southern Democrats returned the South to rule by white men. Some white southerners tried to reverse the gains African Americans had achieved during the Reconstruction era. African American freedoms were curtailed, as whites passed Jim Crow laws that enforced segregation and laws that limited voting rights. Despite these setbacks, African Americans began organizing to defend their rights.

QUEST! FINDINGS

Hold Your Civic Discussion Refer to your responses to the Quest Connections to help you participate in a civic discussion. Use the rubric and other Quest resources online to guide your work.

GO ONLINE to access lesson summaries

VISUAL REVIEW

Use these graphics to review some of the key terms, people, and ideas from this Topic.

Political Beliefs of Radical Republicans

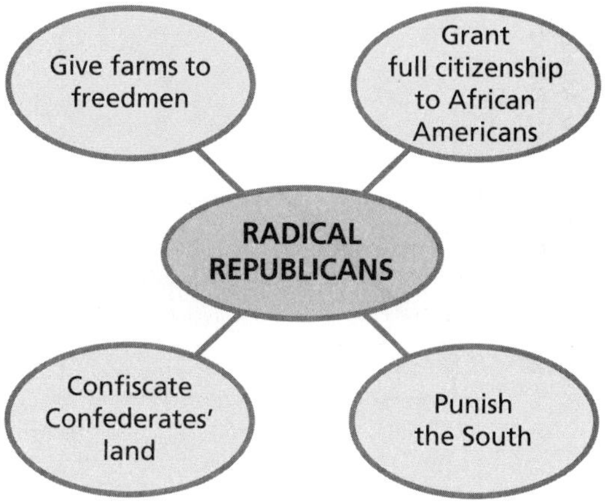

Limitations on Voting Rights Imposed by the States

RESTRICTIVE MEASURE	FUNCTION	EFFECT
Poll tax	Each person had to pay a tax to vote.	The poor could not afford to vote.
Literacy test	Each person had to be able to read in order to vote.	African Americans who had been denied education could not vote.
Grandfather clauses	Each person could vote only if his ancestors had voted before 1866 or 1867.	African Americans are disqualified from voting.

Reaction to Reconstruction

CONGRESSIONAL ACTION	REACTION
Fourteenth Amendment guarantees equality under the law for all citizens.	Supreme Court restricts scope of Fourteenth Amendment.
Fifteenth Amendment forbids any state from denying voting rights.	States pass measures to restrict voting rights.
Civil Rights Act of 1875 guarantees African American citizens the right to ride trains and use public facilities.	States pass Jim Crow laws to enforce segregation.

Long-term Effects of Reconstruction

- Political divisions deepen.
- Constitutional amendments lay foundations for civil rights.
- Reaction against African American civil rights sets in.
- Southern economy diversifies.
- Southern railroads and ports modernize.
- South gets tax-supported school system.
- Women's movement coalition fragments.

Topic 8 Assessment

KEY TERMS, PEOPLE, AND IDEAS

1. What was Lincoln's "Ten Percent Plan" for the South?
2. According to the **Radical Republicans**, how should former Confederates be punished?
3. Why did the former Confederate states adopt the **Black Codes**?
4. Why did the House of Representatives **impeach** President Johnson?
5. Why did **segregation** hurt the Southern economy?
6. Why did **sharecropping** and **share-tenancy** develop?
7. Describe the issues that divided Republicans during the early Reconstruction period.
8. Why are the late 1800s considered the "nadir" or lowest point of race relations?
9. What freedoms were guaranteed by the **Fourteenth** and **Fifteenth Amendments** to the Constitution?

CRITICAL THINKING

10. **Draw Inferences** Why did so many white southerners oppose extending full citizenship to African Americans?
11. **Make Generalizations** How did churches lay the foundation for the development of African American leaders?
12. **Identify Cause and Effect** How did inequalities in land ownership contribute to racial tensions during Reconstruction?
13. **Summarize** (a.) How did the Supreme Court help erode African Americans' freedom? (b.) How did it attempt to limit the federal government's power in its decision concerning the Fourteenth Amendment?
14. **Draw Conclusions** Why did Reconstruction help fragment the women's movement?
15. **Find the Main Idea** Why did African American political participation rise and then suddenly decrease?
16. **Analyze Graphs** The graph at the top of the next column shows the percentage of African American farmers who owned their own land between 1870 and 1890. What does the graph reveal?

African American Farm Ownership, 1870–1890

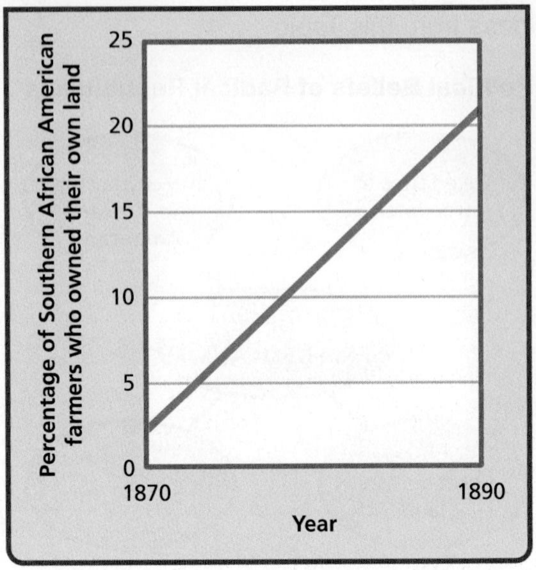

17. **Writing Activity: Compose a Historical Narrative** The Niagara Movement speech presented a list of demands. Write a narrative essay that describes what the demands reveal about the problems African Americans faced during and soon after Reconstruction. A historical narrative tells a story about real people, places, events.

> We want full manhood suffrage, and we want it now, henceforth and forever.
>
> Second. We want discrimination in public accommodation to cease. Separation in railway and street cars, based simply on race and color, is un-American, un-democratic, and silly. We protest against all such discrimination. . . .
>
> We are not more lawless than the white race, we are more often arrested, convicted, and mobbed. We want justice even for criminals and outlaws. We want the Constitution of the country enforced. . . .
>
> —*W.E.B Du Bois*

18. **Connections to Today** One voting rights issue that divides Americans today is whether to lower the voting age from 18 to 16. Supporters argue that young people should have a say in issues that affect them, while opponents say that people under 18 are not ready for the responsibility of voting. Take a stand on this issue and present three solid arguments to support your opinion.

DOCUMENT-BASED QUESTIONS

Read the documents below, then answer the questions that follow.

DOCUMENT A

President Lincoln made this speech a few days after the war ended.

> We all agree that the seceded States, so called are out of their proper relation with the Union; and that the sole object of the government, civil and military, in regard to those States is to again get them into that proper practical relation. I believe it is not only possible, but in fact, easier to do this, without deciding, or even considering, whether these States have ever been out of the Union, than with it. Finding themselves safely at home, it would be utterly immaterial whether they had ever been abroad. Let us all join in doing the acts necessary to restoring the proper practical relations between these States and the Union; and each forever after, innocently indulge his own opinion whether, in doing the acts, he brought the States from without, into the Union, or only gave them proper assistance, they never having been out of it.
>
> —*Abraham Lincoln, April 11, 1865*

DOCUMENT B

This cartoon of the 1870s shows a woman, representing the South, being crushed by a carpetbagger.

DOCUMENT C

In the secondary source at the top of the next column, a historian considers Reconstruction.

> A truly radical program would have called for the confiscation of land for the freedmen. Land was the principal form of Southern wealth, the only effective weapon with which the ex-slaves could have battled for economic competence and social equality. . . . . The dominant Radicalism of the day naively assumed that a people's salvation could be obtained through the ballot and the spelling book. . . .
>
> —*Francis Simkins, 1939*

DOCUMENT D

This excerpt is from a newspaper published in 1865.

> There is one, and only one, sure and safe policy for the immediate future: namely: the North must remain the absolute Dictator of the Republic until the spirit of the North shall become the spirit of the whole country. . . . . The South is still unpurged of her treason. Prostrate in the dust she is no less a traitor at this hour than when her head was erect. . . . . They cannot be trusted with authority over their former slaves. . . . . The only hope for the South is to give the ballot to the Negro and in denying it to the rebels.
>
> —*The Independent, May 5, 1865*

19. In Document A, Lincoln urges Congress to
- **A.** take vengeance and punish the South.
- **B.** not treat southern states as traitors.
- **C.** impose heavy taxation on southern states.
- **D.** ignore calls for states' rights.

20. Analyze Political Cartoons The Document B cartoon shows the South as
- **A.** triumphing over the Union.
- **B.** oppressed by Reconstruction.
- **C.** accepting the Union victory.
- **D.** ready to rejoin the Union.

21. In Document C, the writer believes that the Radical Republicans
- **A.** should have been more lenient with the South.
- **B.** solved the problems of racial inequality.
- **C.** should have been even more radical.
- **D.** helped destroy the South's economy.

22. In Document D, the writer clearly supports
- **A.** the Radical Republicans.
- **B.** the moderate Republicans.
- **C.** Southern Democrats.
- **D.** Lincoln's Ten Percent Plan.

23. Writing Activity: Primary Source Using these documents and what you have learned in this topic, write a paragraph discussing the conflicting perspectives on Reconstruction.

GO ONLINE to access more practice

Topic 9

Industry and Immigration (1865–1914)

ESSENTIAL QUESTION How do science and technology affect society?

GO ONLINE for immersive experiences designed to help you explore the lives of immigrants in the late 1800s and early 1900s through rich primary sources. Also access the eText, videos, Biographies, and other online resources.

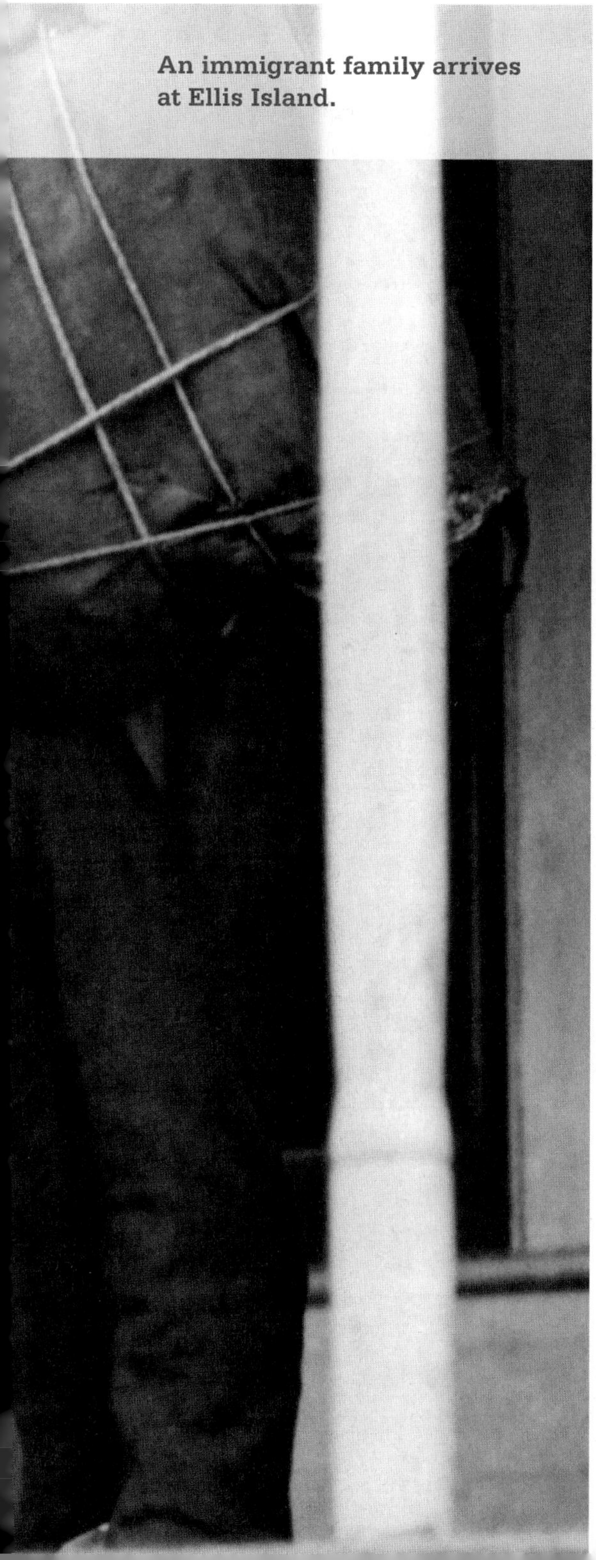

An immigrant family arrives at Ellis Island.

Connections to Today

The percentage of Americans who were born abroad hit a high mark in 1910, then declined for most of the 1900s. Today, however, that percentage has climbed back to near-historic levels. In 2017, more than 40 million immigrants lived in the United States, making up 13.7% of the population. But immigration today is remarkably different from a century ago. Today most immigrants come from Asia and Latin America, not from Europe. How do you think the changing origins of immigrants has affected American culture?

NBC LEARN

Hear the story of an immigrant entrepreneur.

BOUNCE to Activate My Story Video

Topic 9 Overview

In this Topic, you'll learn about industry and immigration in America between 1865 and 1914. Look at the lesson outline and explore the timeline. As you study this Topic, you'll complete the Quest team project.

LESSON OUTLINE

9.1 Innovation Boosts Growth

9.2 Big Business Rises

9.3 The Organized Labor Movement

9.4 The New Immigrants

9.5 A Nation of Cities

9.6 New Ways of Life

Industry and Immigration (1865–1914)

1871
Fire destroys Chicago

1872
Yellowstone Park established

1880
Edison invents the light bulb

1886
American Federation of Labor is founded

1894
Pullman strike halts railroad traffic

1910
Angel Island opens

1870 | 1880 | 1890 | 1900 | 1910

QUEST! INQUIRY

Civic Discussion: Andrew Carnegie

What do you think about the success of industrialists like Carnegie, who grew rich during the second Industrial Revolution? In this Quest you'll participate in a group discussion about Carnegie's influence on America.

STEP 1

Join a small group and read the discussion launch. Take notes as you read and discuss the major points with your group.

STEP 2

Read and analyze the sources that give different perspectives on the main question. As you analyze each source, fill in step 2 of the Information Organizer.

STEP 3

After your group has been assigned a YES or NO position on the main question, prepare the most compelling arguments in support of your position. Present your arguments and then switch sides.

STEP 4

Discuss the question from your own point of view. Think about what you have learned through the discussion and answer the questions in Step 4 of the Information Organizer.

GO ONLINE to access complete Quest materials

9.1

Thomas Edison, one of history's most prolific inventors, poses with one of his many creations. By the age of 22, Edison had already produced his first major invention, a machine to report stock prices.

BOUNCE to Activate Flipped Video

Objectives

Analyze the factors that encouraged industrialization in the United States in the late 1800s.

Explain how new inventions, scientific discoveries, and technological innovations fueled growth and improved the standard of living.

Explain the challenges faced by the South in industry and agriculture in the late 1800s.

Describe the impact of industrialization in the late 1800s.

Key Terms

entrepreneurs
free enterprise
laissez-faire
protective tariffs
patent
Thomas Edison
Bessemer process
suspension bridges
time zones
mass production
cash crop

Innovation Boosts Growth

The Industrial Revolution began in the British textile industry in the 1700s. Within a few decades, it spread to other European countries and the new country of the United States, which had the greatest number of resources to expand the revolution. The first Industrial Revolution was marked by the introduction of steam power and the factory system. Coal and iron became key resources. Around the 1850s, the Industrial Revolution entered a new phase, dominated by steel, oil, and a major new power source—electricity. These new energy sources significantly improved the standard of living throughout the country. This second Industrial Revolution also had a distinctly American character.

American Industry Grows

The Civil War challenged industries to make goods more quickly and efficiently, especially in the North, which already had an industrial base. Using new tools and methods, factories stepped up production of guns, ammunition, medical supplies, and uniforms. The food industry developed ways to process foods so they could be shipped long distances. Railroads expanded, and more efficient methods of creating power were developed. Meanwhile, the government encouraged immigration to meet the increasing demand for labor in the nation's factories.

Natural Resources Fuel Economic Development The country's growth was fueled, in part, by its vast supply of natural resources. Numerous coal mines along the eastern seaboard provided fuel to power steam locomotives and factories. Thick forests were cut into lumber for construction.

GO ONLINE to access your digital course

Iron ore was converted into iron and later into steel to build bridges, railroad tracks, and machines. The nation's many navigable riverways transported these and other resources to cities and factories.

Many technological innovations expanded the country's natural resource base even further. In 1859, Edwin Drake used a steam engine to drill the world's first successful oil well near Titusville, Pennsylvania. Before Drake's innovation, oil, which was used for light and fuel, was mainly obtained from boiling down whale blubber. But whale hunting was time-consuming, and whales were becoming scarce. Drilled oil was relatively cheap to produce and easy to transport. The oil industry grew quickly after 1859 and encouraged the growth of related industries such as kerosene and gasoline.

Another technological innovation of the 1850s made it easier to process iron ore into steel. Steel production soon skyrocketed as boatloads of iron ore moved across the Great Lakes from cities in Minnesota to Pittsburgh, Pennsylvania, and other cities that became steel-making centers. The steel rails produced by these new steel-making cities encouraged economic development by allowing railroads to bring distant natural resources to eastern cities and factories.

The Workforce Grows Population changes also promoted the growth of industry. After the Civil War, large numbers of Europeans, and some Asians, immigrated to the United States. They were pushed from their homelands by factors such as political upheaval, religious discrimination, and crop failures.

In 1881 alone, nearly three quarters of a million immigrants arrived in America. That number climbed steadily, reaching almost one million per year by 1905.

Immigrants were willing to work for low wages because competition for jobs was fierce. And they were prepared to move frequently in pursuit of economic opportunity. All of these factors meant that industries had a huge, and willing, workforce to fuel growth. The potential workforce grew even larger in the 1890s, when droughts and competition from foreign farmers drove American farmers in large numbers to seek jobs in the cities.

Free Enterprise Encourages the Rise of Entrepreneurship In 1868, Horatio Alger published his first novel, *Ragged Dick or Street Life in New York*. This wildly successful novel told the story of a poor boy who rose to wealth and fame by working hard. Alger's novels stressed the possibility that anyone could vault from poverty and obscurity to wealth and fame.

In this excerpt, he describes how Ragged Dick starts his climb to success.

Growth in Mineral Production, 1870–1910

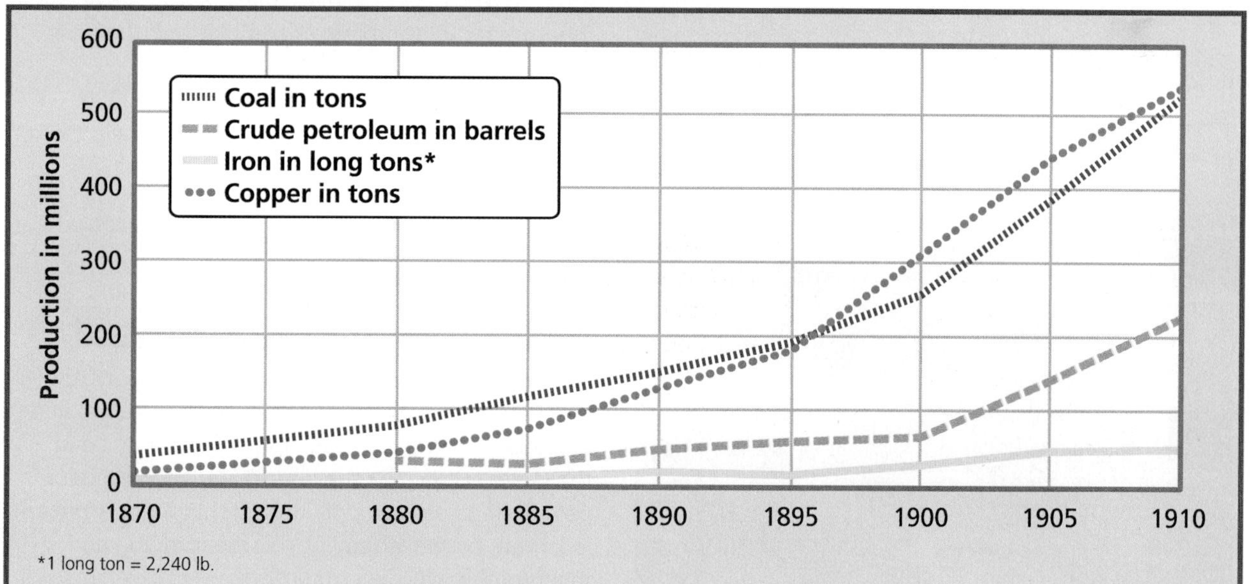

SOURCE: *Historical Statistics of the United States*

>> Technological innovation prompted the country's production of natural resources to increase significantly. **Analyze Graphs** What relationship do you see between natural resources and economic growth?

> Ten dollars a week was to him a fortune. . . . Indeed, he would have been glad, only the day before, to get a place at three dollars a week. . . . Then he was to be advanced if he deserved it. It was indeed a bright prospect for a boy who, only a year before, could neither read nor write. . . . Dick's great ambition to "grow up 'spectable'" seemed likely to be accomplished after all.
>
> —Horatio Alger, 1868

The "rags to riches" idea depended on the system of capitalism, in which individuals own most businesses.

The heroes of this system were **entrepreneurs**, or people who build and manage businesses or enterprises in order to make a profit. Entrepreneurs invest time, money, or both in a product or service, often risking their own livelihoods on the chance of success.

>> Andrew Carnegie was an entrepreneur who thrived in the American free enterprise system. He built successful businesses and contributed much of his wealth to philanthropic causes.

The rise of entrepreneurship fueled industrialization and economic growth in the late 1800s. Entrepreneurs thrived under the idea of **free enterprise**, or the freedom to run a business for profit with minimal regulation beyond what is necessary to protect the public interest. Entrepreneurs competed among themselves for consumers' dollars. If one business priced a certain product too high, consumers might buy a similar product from a competitor. So entrepreneurs found innovative ways to increase efficiency, cut costs, and lower prices, which enabled them to compete and survive in the free enterprise system. The factories, railroads, and mines they established created jobs and also attracted foreign investment.

Laissez-Faire Policies Encourage Growth The government encouraged **laissez-faire** policies, which allowed businesses to operate under minimal government regulation. Without government regulation, workplace conditions were sometimes challenging. However, laissez-faire policies, along with a strong legal system that enforced private property rights, provided the predictability and security that businesses and industries desired and encouraged investment and growth. These factors created an economic environment in which entrepreneurs could flourish.

To promote the buying of American goods, Congress enacted **protective tariffs**, or taxes that made imported goods cost more than those made in the United States. The government also gave innovative railroad builders millions of acres of land in return for their promise to quickly link the East and West coasts.

☑ **IDENTIFY MAIN IDEAS** What factors help explain the growth of industry in the late 1800s?

Innovation Drives Economic Development

Fueled by entrepreneurship, competition, and the free enterprise system, the drive for innovation and efficiency seemed to touch every sphere of life in the United States by the late 1800s. The number of patents increased rapidly during this time. A **patent** is a grant by the federal government giving an inventor the exclusive right to develop, use, and sell an invention for a set period of time. Business leaders invested heavily in these new scientific discoveries and innovations, hoping to create new industries and expand old ones. Eager consumers welcomed new

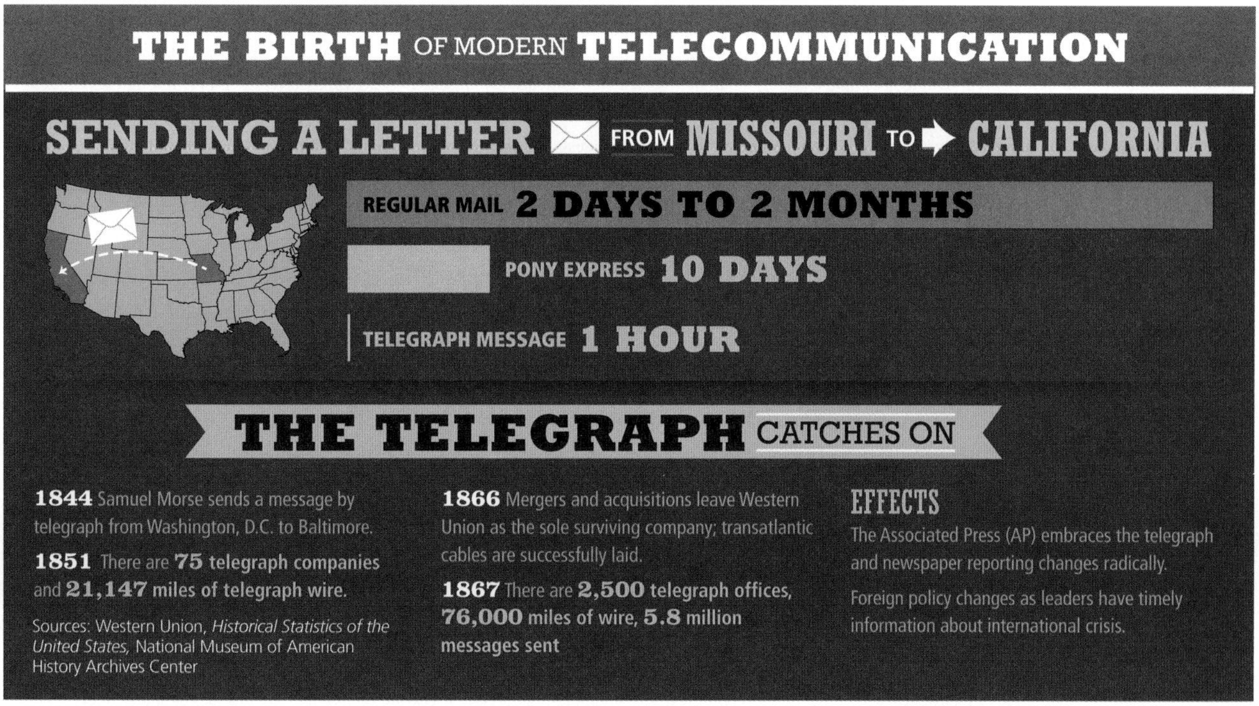

>> The telegraph could send a message exponentially faster than standard mail. **Infer** How did telecommunication innovations improve the standard of living in the United States?

BOUNCE to Activate Gallery

inventions to the market, helping to spur the nation's economic development.

Electricity Improves Standards of Living With support from wealthy industrialists like J.P. Morgan, inventor **Thomas Edison** established a research laboratory at Menlo Park, New Jersey in 1876. Edison, a creative genius who had only a few months of formal education, would receive more than 1,000 patents for new inventions and scientific discoveries. In 1880, for example, with the goal of developing affordable lighting for homes, Edison and his team invented the light bulb, experimenting with thousands of different types of materials to find one that worked. Within a few years, they had also developed plans for central power plants to light entire sections of cities. Other inventors, such as the African American Lewis Latimer, improved upon Edison's work, and other uses for electricity improved Americans' standard of living. George Westinghouse, for example, developed technology to send electricity over long distances. Electricity lit city streets and powered homes and factories, extending the number of hours in the day when Americans could work and play.

Innovation in Communications In 1844, inventor Samuel Morse perfected telegraph technology, or the process of sending messages over wire. In 1876, Alexander Graham Bell patented the telephone. The two inventions attracted investors. Within a few years, 148 telephone companies had strung more than 34,000 miles of wire, and long-distance lines linked several cities in the Northeast and Midwest. By 1900, there were more than one million telephones in the United States, and more than 100,000 miles of telegraph wire linked users across the land. In 1896, Guglielmo Marconi invented the wireless telegraph. Innovative entrepreneurs later built on Marconi's achievement and developed the radio. All of these inventions improved communication between Americans. Instead of waiting days for a letter to arrive, Americans could receive telegraphs in a matter of minutes or hear loved ones' voices immediately on the telephone. Improved communication also meant that news of public events spread quickly.

Steel, Innovation, and Economic Development In the 1850s in England, a man named Henry Bessemer developed a process for purifying iron to make strong, but lightweight, steel. American industries quickly adopted the **Bessemer process**, and by 1890 the United States was outproducing British steel manufacturers. Strong steel made possible a host of innovations, including skyscrapers and the elevators to service them. One of its most dramatic uses was in the construction of **suspension bridges**, bridges in which the roadway is suspended by steel cables. The first suspension bridge was the Brooklyn Bridge, spanning the East River in New York City. Completed in 1883, it was at the time of its construction the longest bridge in the world.

Technology Affects Travel As railroads expanded, they made other use of new technologies and also encouraged innovation. George Westinghouse patented air brakes for trains in 1869, while Granville Woods patented a telegraph system for trains in 1887.

Woods was one of many African Americans who developed and patented new inventions. Meanwhile, meatpacker Gustavus Swift developed refrigerated cars for transporting food. By 1883, there were three transcontinental railroad lines in the United States.

The expanding transportation network caused some problems, however. Throughout most of the 1800s, most towns set their clocks independently. When trains started regular passenger service between towns, time differences made it hard to set schedules. In 1884, delegates from 27 countries divided the globe into 24 **time zones**, one for each hour of the day. The railroads adopted this system, which is still used today.

Technology also affected how Americans traveled and where they lived. Electric streetcars, commuter trains, and subways appeared in major cities. As a result, Americans could live in neighborhoods outside the city and commute to work. Factory production of automobiles with gas-powered engines began in 1902. Experiments in manned flight in a heavier-than-air craft by Orville and Wilbur Wright, among others, in the early 1900s marked the birth of aeronautics, another new industry. Women, too, introduced new inventions. For example, Mary Anderson invented a windshield wiper for streetcars that was patented in 1903.

An Upward Spiral of Growth Railroads played a key role in transforming American industries and businesses. They could transport large amounts of goods long distances quickly, cheaply, and efficiently. Because they linked the nation, they allowed businesses to obtain raw materials easily and to sell finished goods to larger numbers of people. They encouraged new methods for management and administration, which were soon adopted by the rest of the business community. In addition, the expanding railroad network stimulated innovation in many other industries.

An abundance of natural resources and an efficient transportation system to carry raw materials and finished goods set up a spiral of related growth. For example, factories turned out plate glass for windows of passenger rail cars. The factories

Railroads and Time Zones, 1905

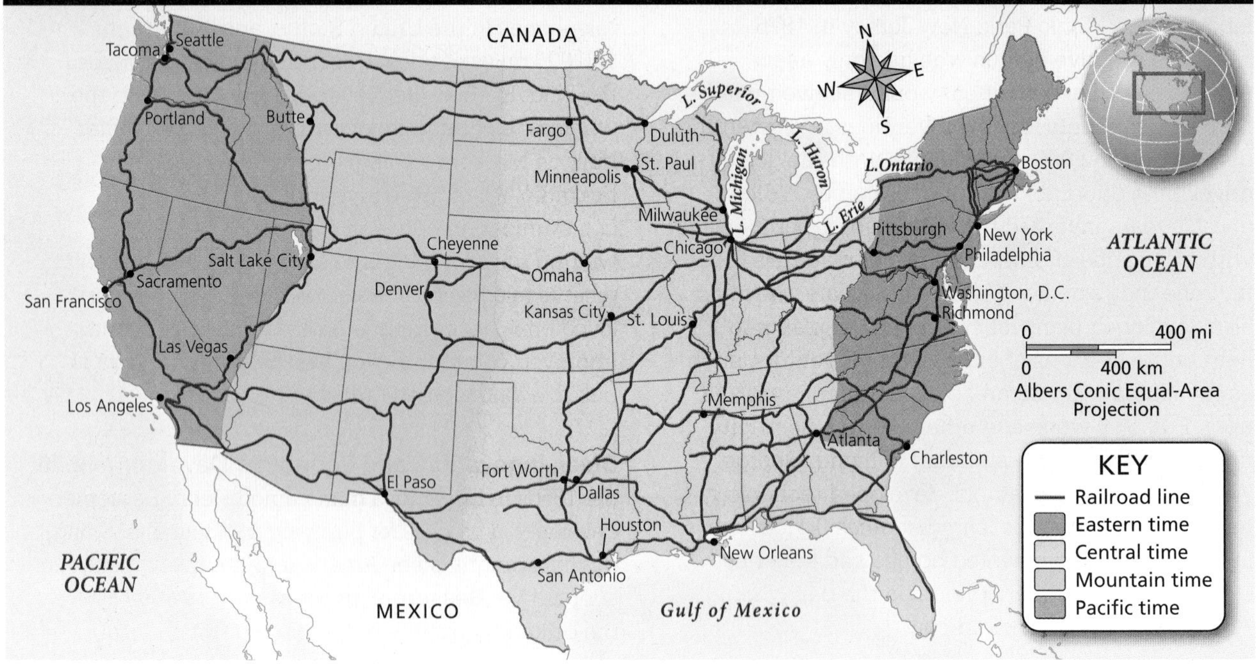

>> These four time zones are still in effect, though the boundaries have changed. **Analyze Maps** How might the creation of time zones have affected residents of Pittsburgh more than those of New York?

BOUNCE to Activate Map

needed freight cars to carry the windows to their destinations.

Those freight cars were created in factories that used railroads to transport fuel to supply the furnaces that turned out more railroad cars. In this way, factory production generated more factory production.

To meet the growing demand, factory owners and other innovators developed systems for turning out large numbers of products quickly and inexpensively. Known as **mass production**, these systems depended upon machinery to carry out tasks that were once done with hand tools. In addition, Frederick Taylor and others studied the flow of work and workers' places in it to develop a system of industrial management that found the most efficient ways for workers to use new machinery. These technological and management innovations improved the standard of living for some Americans by increasing the development of an economic middle class. Middle-class Americans, especially those that lived in the industrialized North, could afford less expensive products produced by companies utilizing new technology.

>> A worker does her job in a typical Alabama textile mill in the early 1900s. **Interpret** In what way is this worker a symbol of the "New South"?

☑ **CHECK UNDERSTANDING** How did new technologies influence industrialization?

Industrialization and the New South

While industry boomed in the North after the Civil War and Reconstruction, the South fell behind. The South struggled to develop its industry, and there were some pockets of success, especially in tobacco-processing, stone-quarrying, and furniture-making. In the 1890s, Atlanta, Georgia, for example, was one of the earliest cities to develop an electric trolley system. But even though cities like Atlanta and Knoxville, Tennessee, grew strongly, the South struggled to overcome economic and social obstacles to broad industrial and urban development. As a result, the South remained largely agricultural and developed a smaller middle class than the North.

However, some post-Reconstruction industrial growth was led by many southern white leaders who envisioned a modernized economy that included not only agriculture but also mills and factories. Atlanta newspaper editor Henry Grady was among those who called for a "New South." A gifted orator, Grady thought the South should use its resources to develop industry:

> There was a South of slavery and secession—that South is dead. There is a South of union and freedom—that South, thank God, is living, breathing, growing every hour. . . . The old South rested everything on slavery and agriculture, unconscious that these could neither give nor maintain healthy growth. The new South presents a perfect democracy . . . a social system compact and closely knitted, less splendid on the surface, but stronger at the core . . . and a diversified industry that meets the complex needs of this complex age.
>
> —Henry Grady, 1886

New Industries Develop Before the Civil War, the South had shipped its raw materials—including cotton, wood, and iron ore—abroad or to the North for processing into finished goods. In the 1880s, northern investors and entrepreneurs backed textile factories in North Carolina, South Carolina, and Georgia, as well as cigar and lumber production, especially in North Carolina and Virginia. In Florida, Vicente Martinez Ybor, an immigrant from Cuba, set up cigar manufacturing in Ybor City, which became part of Tampa. Other private investment in coal-, iron-, and steel-processing created urban centers in Nashville, Tennessee, and Birmingham, Alabama.

During this time, farming also became somewhat more diversified, with an increase in grain, tobacco, and fruit crops. Even the landscape of farming changed as smaller farms replaced large plantations.

Railroads Connect Cities and Towns The South needed reliable transportation to aid its industrial growth. To meet this need, southern rail lines expanded, joining rural areas with urban hubs such as Mobile and Montgomery in Alabama and the bustling ports of New Orleans, Louisiana, and Charleston, South Carolina. Yet, by the 1880s, only two rail lines—from Texas to Chicago and from Tennessee to Washington, D.C.—linked southern freight to northern markets.

To combat economic isolation, southerners lobbied the federal government for economic help and used prison labor to keep railroad construction costs down. Gradually, rail connections helped expand small hubs such as Meridian, Mississippi, and Americus, Georgia. The newer cities of Atlanta, Dallas, and Nashville developed rapidly and began rivaling older cities.

The Southern Economy Lags Behind Despite these changes, the southern economy continued to lag behind the rest of the country. While the North was able to build on its strong industrial base, the South first had to repair the damages of war. Moreover, industry rests on a three-legged stool: natural resources, labor, and capital investment, or money invested to start or improve the business. The South had plenty of the first but not enough of the second and third.

Sustained economic development also requires workers who are well trained and productive, but public education in the South was limited.

In fact, the South spent less than any other part of the country on education, and it lacked the technical and engineering schools that could have trained the people needed by industry. At the same time, low wages discouraged skilled workers from coming to the South, and the lure of higher wages or better conditions elsewhere siphoned off southern workers.

Additionally, very few southern banks had survived the war, and those that were functioning had fewer assets than their northern competitors. Most of the South's wealth was concentrated in the hands of a few people. Poor tenant farmers and factory workers did not have cash to deposit.

Wholesale Price of Cotton, 1865–1890

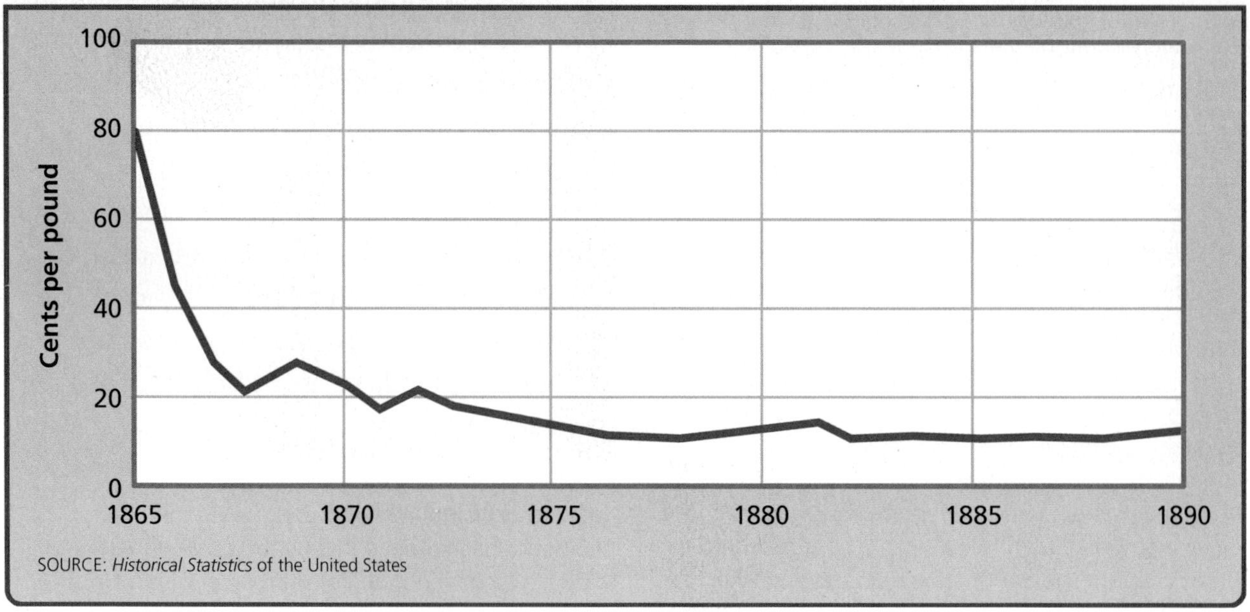

>> The price of cotton fell dramatically following the Civil War. **Analyze Graphs** What factors contributed to cotton's declining value?

With few strong banks, southern financiers were dependent on northern banks to start or expand businesses or farms. The southern economy suffered from this lack of labor and capital.

Farm Issues in the South Before the Civil War, most southern planters had concentrated on such crops as cotton and tobacco, which were grown not for their own use but to be sold for cash. The lure of the **cash crop** continued after the war, despite efforts to diversify. Cotton remained the centerpiece of the southern agricultural economy. However, during the war, many European textile factories had found suppliers outside the South, and the price of cotton had fallen. Now, the South's abundance of cotton simply depressed the price further.

Dependence on one major crop was extremely risky. In the case of southern cotton, it was the boll weevil that heralded disaster. The boll weevil, a beetle which could destroy an entire crop of cotton, appeared in Texas in the early 1890s. Over the next decade, the yield from cotton cultivation in some states dropped by more than 50 percent. Fortunately, the African American inventor George Washington Carver introduced crop rotation as a way to replenish soil that had been worn out by cotton production.

>> A manager on a late nineteenth-century cotton plantation weighs the amount of cotton picked by laborers.

☑ **IDENTIFY SUPPORTING DETAILS** What factors inhibited southern economic recovery?

The Effects of Industrialization

Free enterprise and industrialization touched every aspect of American life in the late 1800s, from the way businesses and farms operated to the kinds of products Americans used. They also affected the country's relationship with the world and with its own environment.

Dominating World Markets By the 1880s, American exports of grain, steel, and textiles dominated international markets. Although Britain was building railroads to access natural resources in Africa, Asia, and other places across the world, by 1900, the United States had almost as many miles of railroad track as the rest of the world combined. The United States could easily transport goods from where they were made or grown to ports where they could be shipped around the world. Exports of food and goods greatly expanded the American economy. As the United States grew as a world economic power, it often clashed with the economic policies of other countries.

>> From freight yards such as this massive complex in New York City, American industry transported food and other goods nationwide, greatly increasing Americans' access to consumer products.

>> Factories, with their multitude of smoke stacks, created a great deal of air pollution. Industrial waste was a byproduct of the Industrial Revolution.

Daily Life Changes Massive changes in industry altered how Americans lived and worked. As farms became mechanized, fewer farm laborers were needed to feed the nation. Out-of-work farmers and their families moved to urban areas to find work, especially in the increasingly industrial North. The mass production of goods meant that these new urban dwellers had easy access to clothing and supplies that they would have had to make by hand in the past. Yet they faced higher costs of living, were dependent upon cash wages to buy food, and performed repetitive work in factories.

Concerns About the Environment In the early 1800s, few worried about how industry might affect the environment. However, by the late 1800s, industrial waste had risen dramatically and mining had begun to damage the land. In the Midwest, increasing agricultural production had led to soil erosion and dust storms. People began to raise concerns about protecting natural resources. Congress responded by setting aside protected lands that would eventually become part of the National Park Service. Its creation of Yellowstone Park in 1872 was one of the first federal responses to concerns about the environment, and Yellowstone was the first such national park established anywhere in the world. Over the next decades, many more square miles of American land would be set aside to be protected.

IDENTIFY CENTRAL IDEAS Explain how industrialization impacted the lives of Americans.

ASSESSMENT

1. **Compare and Contrast** the risks and goals of entrepreneurs and inventors.
2. **Identify Central Issues** Why was the South slower to industrialize than the North?
3. **Cite Evidence** that there were some negative effects of industrialization.
4. **Infer** why the free enterprise system was so important to entrepreneurs and why entrepreneurs were crucial to the free enterprise system.
5. **Support Ideas with Evidence** What did the United States have that made it so successful during the second Industrial Revolution? Include as many factors as you can think of.
6. **Quest Connections** How did individual entrepreneurs and inventors contribute to increasing standards of living during this period? Identify three examples.

GO ONLINE to access this biography: Andrew Carnegie

Primary Sources Comparing Viewpoints

The Consequences of Industrialization

During the Industrial Revolution, Americans saw both the positive and negative sides of the enormous changes taking place around them. Below you will read two contrasting perspectives. Sadie Frowne, an immigrant from Europe who worked in a New York sweatshop talks about one of the major downsides, namely the danger and sheer unpleasantness of work in an industrial-era factory. Industrialist Andrew Carnegie, meanwhile, highlights the positive.

As you read, compare the viewpoints of Frowne and Carnegie on life in the industrial era.

>> Workers at a basket factory in Indiana in 1908

Primary Source 1

"The Story of a Sweatshop Girl: Sadie Frowne," 1902

At seven o'clock we all sit down to our machines and the boss brings to each one the pile of work that he or she is to finish during the day, what they call in English their "stint." This pile is put down beside the machine and as soon as a skirt is done it is laid on the other side of the machine. Sometimes the work is not all finished by six o'clock and then the one who is behind must work overtime. Sometimes one is finished ahead of time and gets away at four or five o'clock, but generally we are not done till six o'clock.

☑ **DESCRIBE** How long does Frowne typically work?

The machines go like mad all day, because the faster you work the more money you get. Sometimes in my haste I get my finger caught and the needle goes right through it. It goes so quick tho, that it does not hurt much. I bind the finger up with a piece of cotton and go on working. We all have accidents like that. Where the needle goes through the nail it makes a sore finger, or where it splinters a bone it does much harm. Sometimes a finger has to come off. Generally, tho, one can be cured by a salve.

All the time we are working the boss walks about examining the finished garments and making us do them over again if they are not just right. So we have to be careful as well as swift. But I am getting so good at the work that within a year I will be making $7 a week, and then I can save at least $3.50 a week. I have over $200 saved now.

The machines are all run by foot power, and at the end of the day one feels so weak that there is a great temptation to lie right down and sleep. But you must go out and get air, and have some pleasure.

☑ **EXPLAIN** What does it say about conditions in her workplace that Sadie feels the need to spend time outside after work?

Primary Source 2

"The Gospel of Wealth," Andrew Carnegie, 1889

The problem of our age is the proper administration of wealth, so that the ties of brotherhood may still bind together the rich and poor in harmonious relationship. The conditions of human life have not only been changed, but revolutionized, within the past few hundred years. In former days there was little difference between the dwelling, dress, food, and environment of the chief and those of his retainers [supporters]. ... The contrast between the palace of the millionaire and the cottage of the laborer with us today measures [shows] the change which has come with civilization. This change, however, is not to be deplored, but welcomed as highly beneficial.

SUMMARIZE What is the 'problem of our age?'

It is easy to see how the change has come. One illustration will serve for almost every phase of the cause. In the manufacture of products we have the whole story. It applies to all combinations of human industry, as stimulated and enlarged by the inventions of this scientific age. Formerly [in the past] articles were manufactured at the domestic hearth [at home] or in small shops which formed part of the household. The master and his apprentices worked side by side, the latter living with the master, and therefore subject to the same conditions. . . .

But the inevitable result of such a mode of manufacture was crude articles at high prices. Today the world obtains commodities [goods] of excellent quality at prices which even the generation preceding this would have deemed incredible. . . . The poor enjoy what the rich could not before afford. What were the luxuries have become the necessaries of life. . . .

The price we pay for this salutary [helpful] change is, no doubt, great. We assemble thousands of operatives [workers] in the factory, in the mine, and in the countinghouse, of whom the employer can know little or nothing, and to whom the employer is little better than a myth. All [contact] between them is at an end. Rigid Castes are formed, and, as usual, mutual ignorance breeds mutual distrust. Each Caste is without sympathy for the other, and ready to credit [believe] anything disparaging in regard to it.

EXPLAIN Why are employers so distant from their employees?

ASSESSMENT

Be sure to cite specific evidence from the sources as you answer the following questions.

1. **Analyze Word Choices** What is Sadie Frowne's attitude towards the injuries she and other workers endure at her factory? Does it surprise you? Why or why not?
2. **Determine Author's Point of View** Does Andrew Carnegie think that the Industrial Revolution is a good or a bad thing for society, on balance? Why?
3. **Analyze Sequence** Summarize the change in manufacturing that Andrew Carnegie describes. What are the effects of this change?
4. **Compare and Contrast** Looking at the two sources, which writer has the better first-hand knowledge of life in a factory? Who takes a broader view of the effects of the Industrial Revolution on society?
5. **Develop Empathy** How do you think Sadie Frowne might react to reading Andrew Carnegie's *Gospel of Wealth*? Explain your answer.

GO ONLINE to access primary sources

9.2

The Standard Oil Company continued to refine its production processes with new technologies in its many refineries.

Big Business Rises

The rapid industrial growth that occurred after the Civil War transformed American business and society. Yet it was only the beginning. The rise of big business, characterized by the investment of huge amounts of private financial resources, helped the United States push aside strong economies like Britain's, to become one of the most economically powerful countries in the modern world.

BOUNCE to Activate Flipped Video

Objectives

Analyze different management innovations that businesses used to increase their profits.

Describe the public debate over the pros and cons of big business.

Explain how the government took steps to block abuses of corporate power.

Key Terms

corporation
monopoly
cartel
John D. Rockefeller
horizontal integration
trust
Andrew Carnegie
vertical integration
Social Darwinism
Interstate Commerce Commission (ICC)
Sherman Antitrust Act

Corporations Find New Ways of Doing Business

Until the mid-nineteenth century, most businesses were run by one person or family. This meant that no business could grow bigger than one family's ability to invest in it or run it. Businesses were also local, buying and selling to customers who lived nearby. Industrialization changed all this. Railroads provided businesses with access to raw materials and customers from farther and farther away. Business leaders, desiring the profits offered by these larger markets, responded by combining funds and resources.

The Corporation Meets New Needs To take advantage of expanding markets, investors developed a form of group ownership known as a **corporation**. In a corporation, a number of people share the ownership of a business. If a corporation experiences economic problems, the investors lose no more than they had originally invested in the business. The corporation was the perfect solution to the challenge of expanding business, especially for risky industries such as railroads or mining. A corporation had the same rights as an individual: it could buy and sell property, and it could sue in the courts. If one person chose to leave the group, others could buy his interests.

GO ONLINE to access your digital course

Corporations were perfectly suited to expanding markets. They had access to huge amounts of capital, or invested money, allowing them to fund new technology, enter new industries, or run large plants across the country. Aided by railroads and the telegraph, corporations had the ability to operate in several different regions. After 1870, the number of corporations in America increased dramatically. They were an important part of industrial capitalism. The economic free-market system centered around industries.

Finding New Ways to Gain Advantage

Corporations worked to maximize profits in several ways. They advertised their products widely, which enabled them to reach more potential customers. They paid low wages to workers and tried to obtain raw materials as cheaply as possible. They adopted forms of business organization, such as horizontal or vertical integration, and applied other innovations in production management to seek out efficiencies that would in turn decrease their cost of producing goods or services. Like J. P. Morgan, the heads of some corporations supported research laboratories where inventors could experiment with new processes that could lower production costs or new products that could bring future profits.

Others thought of new ways to make their businesses profitable. Cornelius Vanderbilt, an entrepreneur in the railroad industry, got his start in the steamboat business. He succeeded in getting his competitors to pay him to relocate because his low fares were driving them out of business. Some corporations worked to eliminate competition by forming a **cartel**. In this arrangement, businesses making the same product agree to limit their production and thus keep prices high. **John D. Rockefeller**, an Ohio oil tycoon, made agreements with railroads that made it difficult for his competitors to ship their products:

> [Rockefeller's company] killed its rivals, in brief, by getting the great trunk lines to refuse to give them transportation. Vanderbilt is reported to have said that there was but one man—Rockefeller—who could dictate to him.
>
> —H. D. Lloyd, *The Atlantic*, 1881

Business Management Innovations Business leaders continued to develop ever more effective ways to decrease costs and increase profits. One way was to merge competing firms into a giant company whose size would lead to lower production costs. This system of consolidating many firms in the same business is called **horizontal integration**. Some corporations used horizontal integration to gain a **monopoly**, or complete control of a product

Economic Advantages of Being Big

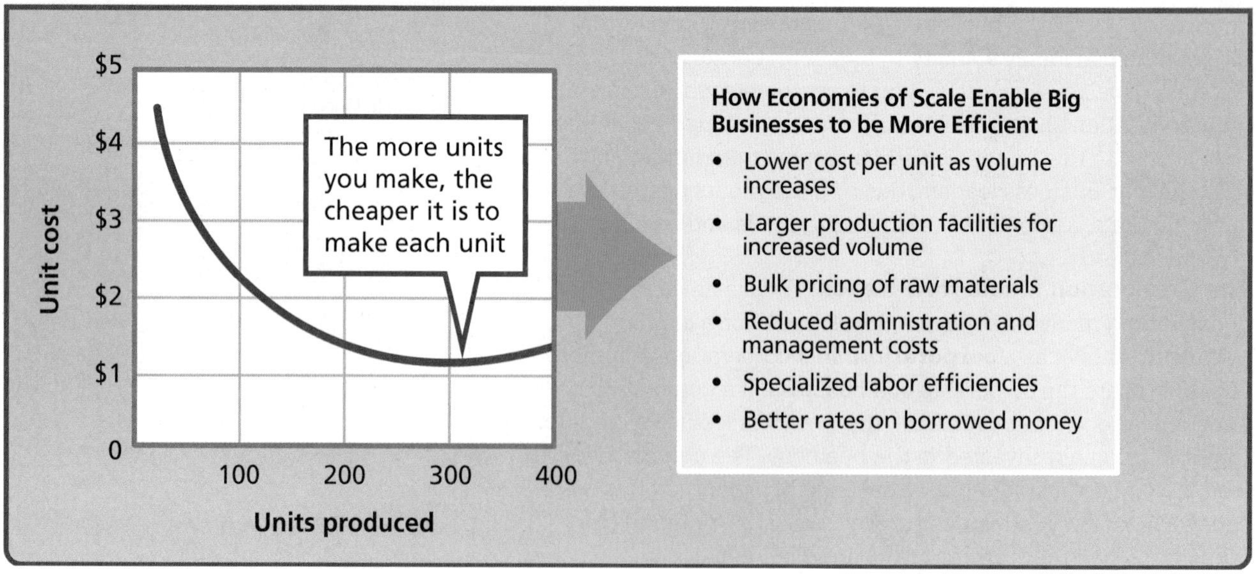

>> Production costs usually decrease as more goods are produced. **Analyze Graphs** What competitive advantages do larger businesses have over smaller ones?

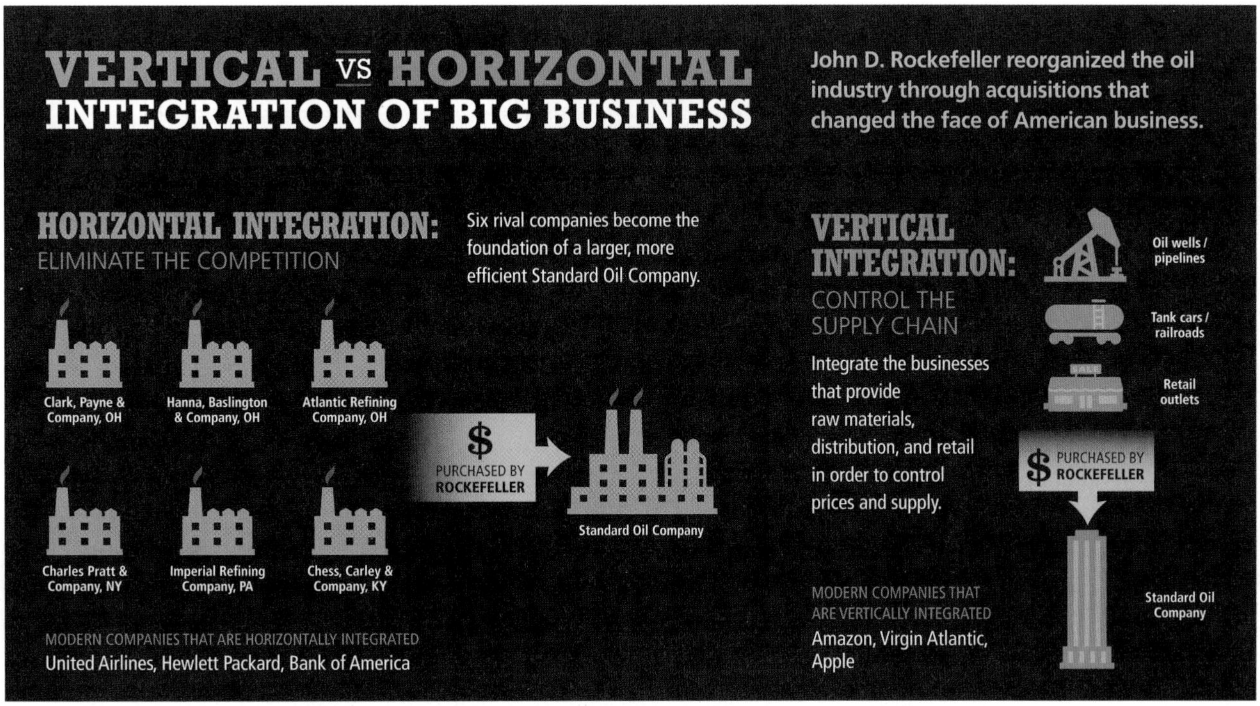

>> Management innovations such as horizontal and vertical integration allowed American businesses to remain competitive in the age of industrialization. **Contrast** What differences do you see between horizontal and vertical integration?

or service. To do this, a company either bought its competitors or drove them out of business. With no remaining competition and an efficient production process, the company was free to set its own prices based on demand for its products. This power did not always mean higher prices for consumers, but the potential for setting high prices was there. The management innovation of horizontal integration made business more efficient but occasionally had a negative impact on labor, because workers at smaller companies driven out of business would need to find employment elsewhere.

Production management, a management innovation designed to maximize the efficiency of a production process, also impacted labor. Business owners were understandably interested in controlling labor costs and continually looked for ways to improve worker productivity in conjunction with new machines. As a result, business owners could often meet production goals with fewer skilled workers. Those without the required skills to work with the new technologies and those unable to maintain the pace of a regimented workflow on factory floors oftentimes found themselves without work.

Rockefeller was one of the first businessmen to use horizontal integration. However, Ohio state law prevented one company from owning the stock of another. This meant that Rockefeller could not buy out his competitors. Instead he found a way to get around the law by forming a new type of business organization called a **trust**. In a trust, companies assigned their stock to a board of trustees, who combined them into a new organization that the trustees ran. By the early 1880s, Rockefeller and his Standard Oil trust controlled most of the oil refined in the United States.

In Ohio and elsewhere, trusts arose, in part, because state laws governing corporations were inadequate. In many states in the mid-1800s, corporations could only be chartered by the state legislature passing an act. Business leaders looked for more flexible ways to build their businesses. For some business leaders, trusts were also a way to bring efficiency and stability to a free market where competition could be fierce and unpredictable. As state laws changed, trusts were replaced by other types of business mergers. However, the public continued to apply the term "trust" to any form of monopolistic business association.

Rockefeller, steel tycoon **Andrew Carnegie**, and other business leaders also strengthened their companies and made the workplace more efficient by gaining control of the different businesses that were involved in all stages of manufacturing their products. Carnegie, for example, owned the coal mines and iron-ore fields that provided the raw materials for his steel, as well as the ships and railroads that brought them to his steel mills. This process, called **vertical integration**, allowed companies to reduce their costs of production.

☑ **IDENTIFY MAIN IDEAS** How were corporations able to decrease costs and increase profits?

The Pros and Cons of Big Business

Throughout the 1880s, business mergers created powerful empires for those who controlled steel, railroads, meat, farm equipment, sugar, lumber, and a number of other enterprises. However, many smaller companies and consumers began to question the goals and tactics of those who led these businesses.

"Robber Barons" or "Captains of Industry"?

Many small businesses were bought up or squeezed out of competition. Those that joined trusts often found that they received few profits. Some consumers were alarmed by the high prices that monopolies and cartels sometimes set on their products. Gradually, many consumers, workers, and the federal government came to believe that systems like trusts, cartels, and monopolies gave powerful business leaders unfair advantages. They believed that perhaps the government's laissez-faire policies had hurt workers and consumers. People who held these views began to refer to these leaders as "robber barons."

>> "The Protectors of Our Industries" shows Cornelius Vanderbilt II and other business leaders. **Analyze Political Cartoons** What point of view about these leaders does this cartoon express?

BOUNCE to Activate Gallery

At the same time, other people believed that these industrialists served the nation positively. They believed that laissez-faire policies had allowed business to flourish according to free enterprise principles. They recognized that the spread of factories, steel mills, and railroads provided jobs for an ever-growing labor force. Large, efficient corporations often lowered prices for consumers. Business supporters also noted that the industrialists' efficient business practices and support for developing technology benefited the nation's economy, stimulating innovation and shaping the United States into a strong international leader. Furthermore, many business leaders, like Carnegie, Rockefeller, and Vanderbilt, were important philanthropists. Andrew Carnegie wrote of his deep believe in philanthropy in "The Gospel of Wealth." He stated, that

> ...rich men.. have it in their power during their lives to busy themselves in organizing benefactions [donations] from which the masses of their fellows will derive [get] lasting advantage, and thus dignify their own lives.
>
> —Gospel of Wealth, *Andrew Carnegie,* 1889

They established universities, museums, and libraries, believing that such institutions made it possible for the disadvantaged to rise to wealth. For these reasons, people who took this point of view thought of business leaders as "captains of industry."

The Causes and Effects of Social Darwinism

In 1859, biologist Charles Darwin published *On the Origin of Species*, arguing that animals evolved by a process of "natural selection" and that only the fittest survived to reproduce. Yale professor William Graham Sumner soon applied this theory to the rough-and-tumble world of American capitalism, calling it **Social Darwinism**. He declared that wealth was a measure of one's inherent value and those who had it were the most "fit."

The theory of Social Darwinism, caused by this modification of Darwin's scientific findings, became a social issue when it was used to justify a wide variety of beliefs and conditions. Supporters of the laissez-faire economic system argued that the government should stay out of private business, because interference would disrupt natural selection.

Many Social Darwinists believed that the nation would grow strong by allowing its most vigorous members to rise to the top, and that it was wrong to use public funds to assist the poor. Social Darwinism was often used to fuel discrimination. Social Darwinists pointed to the poverty-stricken condition of many minorities as evidence of their unfitness.

☑ **CHECK UNDERSTANDING** How did people explain their support or opposition to big business?

The Changing Relationship Between Government and Business

The great industrialists' methods and their influence on the nation's economy worried some Americans. Competing railroads took part in practices such as fixing rates and pooling, or entering into secret agreements to divide up the nation's freight. Many Americans felt that price fixing and pooling drove up rates and were unfair to consumers. They also thought that unfair business practices and poor wages and working conditions for the labor force had made the costs of the government's laissez-faire policies too high. They wanted the federal government to take action.

Attempts to Regulate Business Finally, in 1887, Congress responded by creating the **Interstate Commerce Commission (ICC)** to monitor railroad shipping rates. However, it could only keep watch on railroads that crossed state lines. Also, it could not make laws or control the railroads' transactions. Although court rulings favoring states and railroads weakened even these few powers, the ICC was the first federal agency to monitor business practices. Over the next several decades, the government would create many other federal bodies to regulate American businesses.

Similarly, the federal government slowly became involved in regulating trusts. In 1890, the Senate passed the **Sherman Antitrust Act**, which outlawed any trust that operated "in restraint of trade or commerce among the several states." The government claimed that it had a constitutional right to regulate such commerce. But for more than a decade, the law was seldom enforced because court rulings generally favored business owners.

In fact, it was often used in businesses' favor because they successfully argued in court that labor unions restrained trade. However, the ICC and the Sherman Antitrust Act began a trend toward federal limitations on corporations' power.

>> In this cartoon, men labeled *Populist, Democrat, Republican*, and *Silverite* toss a Business Man around on a sheet. **Analyze Political Cartoons** According to this artist, who is in control of business?

>> Railroads all travel to one destination. **Analyze Political Cartoons** What does the "robber baron" in this cartoon represent?

Sherman Antitrust Act, 1890

ADVANTAGES	DISADVANTAGES
• Enabled Congress to regulate trade between states and end monopolistic practices • Tried to eliminate hidden monopolies (trusts) that affected trade • Enabled competitors to sue trustees of rival companies for loss of revenue • Levied fines against those forming trusts	• Difficult to enforce • Lacked clear definition of the practices that resulted in a restraint of trade • More often used successfully against labor unions than monopolies

>> The Sherman Antitrust Act tried to create a fair marketplace in which the needs of businesses, workers, and consumers were addressed. **Analyze Charts** Why might some businesses disagree with the Sherman Antitrust Act?

BOUNCE to Activate Chart

A Difficult Balance Between Business, Government, and Consumer These limits on corporations' power were made in an attempt to create a fair environment for competition. They sought to prevent any one company from undercutting market forces by driving its competition out of the market, which would allow the company rather than the market to determine the best price for its products. To this end, the federal government tried many kinds of legislation and regulation—with a mixture of costs and benefits. Often neither businesses nor consumers felt that their interests were well-served by government policies and actions.

The costs and benefits of anti-trust acts continued to be debated. Over the course of 50 years, corporations, federal regulatory agencies, consumers, unions, and the courts struggled to find an acceptable balance between fair prices and wages, as well as workers' safety and dignity and the corporations' legitimate quest for efficiencies that would provide a fair return on the investment and risk involved in doing business in a free-market system. Historians continue to assess the ways in which—and the degree to which—that attempt at balance was met. Historians and economists also debate the question of who should have the responsibility for developing the policies to achieve that balance. Indeed, these issues are still part of the relationship between business, government, and the consumer in our own time.

IDENTIFY SUPPORTING DETAILS How did the federal government attempt to regulate business?

ASSESSMENT

1. **Generate Explanations** Why did forming corporations allow big business to increase in power and profitability?
2. **Interpret** the effects of monopolies and cartels on the consumer.
3. **Summarize** what made John D. Rockefeller such a successful businessman.
4. **Compare Points of View** Why would one person use the term "robber baron" and another "captain of industry" to describe the same person?
5. **Support Ideas with Examples** Cite arguments for and against increased federal regulatory power of private business using specific examples to support your answer.
6. **Quest Connections** How did Andrew Carnegie believe wealthy industrialists like himself could make a contribution to society in areas outside of business?

GO ONLINE to access these biographies: John D. Rockefeller and William Graham Sumner

9.3

Members of the Industrial Workers of the World (IWW) rally in New York City's Union Square.

The Organized Labor Movement

As industrialization intensified, the success of the booming American economy relied heavily on its workers. But struggles between business owners and workers also intensified, as workers rebelled against low pay and unsafe working conditions. To keep the economy thriving, Americans had to find ways to ease the tensions between business owners and workers.

BOUNCE to Activate Flipped Video

Objectives

Assess the impact of business practices on workers in the late 1800s.

Compare the goals and strategies of the first labor unions.

Analyze the causes and effects of strikes in the late 1800s.

Key Terms

sweatshops
company towns
collective bargaining
socialism
Knights of Labor
Terence V. Powderly
Samuel Gompers
American Federation of Labor (AFL)
Haymarket Riot
Homestead Strike
Eugene V. Debs
Pullman Strike

Workers Endure Difficulties

The industrial expansion in the United States produced great wealth for the owners of factories, mines, railroads, and large farms. It also brought general improvements to American society in the form of a higher standard of living, wider availability of cheap goods, and increased access to public institutions like museums and schools. However, the economic growth of the late 1800s caused domestic issues. Many of the people who performed the work in the nation's great industries struggled to survive. In addition, workers—especially immigrants, women, and minorities—often faced ridicule and discrimination.

The Hardships of Factory Work In the 1880s and 1890s, factory owners, seeking to keep down production costs, employed people who would work for low wages. Immigrants made up a large percentage of the workforce. Far from home, lacking good English-speaking skills, and often very poor, immigrants would generally take almost any job. Factory workers toiled long hours—12 hours a day, 6 days a week. Countless thousands of others worked similar hours in small, hot, dark, and dirty workhouses known as

GO ONLINE to access your digital course

>> Work in the textile mills could be very dangerous, and it was not unheard of for an inexperienced, young worker (some as young as eight years old) to lose a finger in an accident.

>> A surplus of immigrant labor made it difficult for sweatshop workers, such as these women, to demand fair wages and safe working conditions.

sweatshops. Sweatshop workers, mainly women, labored long hours at machines making mass-produced items. Owners ensured productivity by strictly regulating workers' days. They clocked work and break hours and fined workers for breaking rules or working slowly.

Factory work was often dangerous. Workspaces were poorly lit, often overheated, and badly ventilated. Some workers lost their hearing from the noisy machines. Accidents were common, both from faulty equipment and from lack of proper training. Despite the harsh conditions, employers suffered no shortage of labor. There were always more people than jobs.

Children in the Workplace As industrialization advanced, more jobs opened up for women. They worked as laundresses, telegraph operators, and typists. But most women—and their families—worked in the factories. Since low wages meant that both parents needed jobs, bringing children to work kept them off the streets and close to their parents. It also meant that the children could earn a wage, which helped the family to survive.

By the end of the 1800s, nearly one in five children between the ages of 10 and 16 worked rather than attending school. Harsh conditions stunted their physical and mental growth. By the 1890s, social workers began to recognize the social issues caused by child labor. They lobbied to get children out of factories and into child care or schools. Eventually, the efforts of social workers and other reformers prompted states to pass legislation to stop child labor.

Company Towns and Wage Slavery As immigrants flooded into manufacturing centers, employers had to house them. In Florida, Vicente Martinez Ybor offered the workers in his cigar factories new houses that could be purchased over time. Elsewhere, however, workers were not so lucky. Many laborers, especially those who worked in mines, were forced to live in isolated communities near their workplaces. The housing in these communities, known as **company towns**, was owned by the business and rented out to employees. The employer also controlled the "company store," where workers were forced to buy goods. The company store sold goods on credit but charged high interest. As a result, by the time the worker was paid, most of the wages were owed back to the employer. Since workers could be arrested if they left their jobs before they completely repaid these debts, employers could hold onto workers through a system that workers' advocates called "wage slavery." Through management of their company towns, employers could also reinforce ethnic competition and distrust. For example, Mexican, African American, or Chinese workers could be segregated in separate towns.

IDENTIFY CENTRAL IDEAS In what ways did labor conditions affect families?

The Growth of Labor Unions

Industrialization and free enterprise lowered the prices of consumer goods but helped business investors gain large profits. Workers usually did not object to their employer making a profit from their work. After all, if the business was not profitable, it could close and leave workers jobless.

However, workers were understandably frustrated that their wages did not earn enough to buy many consumer goods, even at lower prices. They also resented working in unsafe conditions that in some cases ruined their health and therefore their ability to earn a living. Increasingly, workers organized to demand better wages and working conditions. Employers usually opposed the growing labor movement, which they saw as a threat to their businesses and profits. Employers tended to view efforts to improve wages or working conditions as a violation of their property rights—their right to run their businesses as they saw fit.

Early Labor Protests As early as the 1820s, factory workers tried to gain more power by using the technique of **collective bargaining**, or negotiating as a group with their employer for higher wages or better working conditions. A related tool to collective bargaining was the strike, in which workers refused to work until certain demands were met. Most strikes were local, but sometimes they involved workers in a whole industry across a state, a region, or the country.

The first national labor union, founded in 1834, was the National Trades Union, open to workers from all trades. It lasted only a few years. However, strikes succeeded in reducing the length of the workday in some regions. By the mid-1800s, a six-day work week with a 10-hour workday became the standard in most New England factories. Gradually, national unions began to reappear.

>> Many working-class families struggled to get by on low wages.

Socialism Influences Labor In the 1830s, a movement called **socialism** spread throughout Europe. Socialism is an economic and political philosophy that favors public, instead of private, control of property and income. Socialists believe that society, not just private individuals, should control a nation's wealth. That wealth, they argue, should be distributed equally to everyone.

In 1848, the German philosophers Karl Marx and Friedrich Engels expanded on the ideas of socialism in a treatise titled *The Communist Manifesto*. This pamphlet denounced capitalism and predicted that workers would overturn it. Most Americans rejected these ideas, believing that they threatened the American ideals of free enterprise, private property, and individual liberty. The wealthy in particular opposed socialism because it threatened their fortunes. But many labor activists borrowed ideas from socialism to demand social reform.

The Knights of Labor In 1869, Uriah Stephens founded a labor union called the **Knights of Labor**. Stephens, a tailor who had worked around the country, included all workers of any trade, skilled or unskilled, in his union. The Knights also recruited women and African Americans. Under Stephens, the union functioned largely as a secret society, devoted to broad social reform such as replacing capitalism

>> The Knights of Labor were sometimes portrayed in a comical fashion in the media.

BOUNCE to Activate Cartoon

>> Many laborers sought better working conditions and better pay through unionization.

with workers' cooperatives. The Preamble to the Knights' Constitution, written in 1878, read:

> The recent alarming development and aggression of aggregated wealth, which, unless checked, will inevitably lead to the pauperization and hopeless degradation of the toiling masses, render it imperative, if we desire to enjoy the blessings of life, that a check should be placed upon its power . . . and a system adopted which will secure to the laborer the fruits of his toil. . . .
>
> —Preamble to the Knights' Constitution, 1878

In 1879, **Terence V. Powderly** took on the leadership of the Knights. Powderly abandoned the secretive nature of the Knights. Under his leadership the union used collective bargaining, boycotts, and the threat of strikes to win gains for workers. But like Stephens, Powderly also pursued reforms intended to free workers from wage labor. He planned large-scale manufacturing cooperatives which members workers would operate and take a share in the profits. By 1885, the Knights had grown to include some 700,000 men and women nationwide, of every race and ethnicity. By the 1890s, however, after a series of failed strikes, the Knights had largely disappeared. Many Knights who worked in skilled crafts or trades abandoned the union for a new, rival labor organization, the American Federation of Labor.

A New Organization for Workers **Samuel Gompers** was a poor Jewish immigrant from England who had worked his way up to head the Cigarmakers' Union in New York. In 1886, Gompers helped found the **American Federation of Labor (AFL)** and served as its president for nearly 40 years. While the Knights of Labor was open to nearly all workers, the AFL was a loose organization of some 100 unions of skilled workers devoted to specific crafts. These trade unions retained their individuality but gained strength in bargaining through their affiliation with the AFL.

Gompers set high dues for membership in the AFL, pooling the money to create a strike and pension fund to assist workers in need. Unlike the Knights of Labor, the AFL did not aim for larger social gains for workers. Instead, it focused on specific workers' issues such as wages, working hours, and working conditions. In testimony before

Influential Labor Unions

NAME	DATE FOUNDED	SIGNIFICANCE
National Trades Union	1834	First national union; open to workers from all trades
Knights of Labor	1869	Sought general ideological reform; open to workers of all trades
American Federation of Labor	1886	Focused on specific workers' issues; organization of skilled workers from local craft unions
American Railway Union	1893	First industrial union; open to all railway workers

>> Different labor unions continued to advocate for worker's rights. **Analyze Tables** How were all of these labor unions similar? What were some ways in which they differed?

a government labor commission, Gompers argued in fact that unions and strikes were the only way workers' issues such as these could be addressed:

> We recognize that peaceful industry is necessary to successful civilized life, but the right to strike and the preparation to strike is the greatest preventive to strikes.
>
> If the workmen were to make up their minds tomorrow that they would under no circumstances strike, the employers would do all the striking for them in the way of lesser wages, and longer hours of labor.
>
> —Report on the (U.S.) Industrial Commission on Capital and Labor, 1890

The AFL also pressed for workplaces in which only union members could be hired. Because of its narrow focus on workers' issues, the AFL was often called a "bread and butter" union.

The AFL was not as successful as the Knights in rapidly gaining the widespread support of workers, partly because of its own policies. It opposed union membership for women because Gompers believed their presence in the workplace drove wages down. While it was theoretically open to African Americans, member unions usually found ways to exclude them. Nevertheless, by 1910 AFL membership had reached two million workers.

☑ **IDENTIFY** What similarities and differences existed in the goals of various labor unions?

Labor Unions Lead Protests

As membership in labor unions rose and labor activists became more skilled in organizing large-scale protests, a wave of bitter confrontations between labor and management hit the nation. The first major strike occurred in the railroad industry in 1877. Striking workers, responding to wage cuts, caused massive property destruction in several cities. State militias were called in to protect strikebreakers, or temporary workers hired to perform the jobs of striking workers. Finally, the federal government sent in troops to restore order. In the decades to follow, similar labor disputes would affect businesses, the government, and the organization of labor unions themselves.

Workers Protest in Chicago In May 1886, thousands of workers mounted a national demonstration for an eight-hour workday. Strikes erupted in several cities, and fights broke out between strikers and strikebreakers. Conflict then escalated between strikers and police who were brought in to halt the violence. On May 4, protesters gathered at Haymarket Square in Chicago. The diverse crowd included anarchists, or radicals opposed to all government. A protester threw a bomb, killing a policeman. In the subsequent frenzy, dozens of people, both protesters and policemen, were killed. Eight anarchists were tried for murder, and four were executed.

The **Haymarket Riot** left an unfortunate legacy. The Knights of Labor fizzled out as people shied away from radicalism. Employers and much of the American public became even more suspicious of union activities, associating them with violence.

Steelworkers Clash with the Pinkertons In the summer of 1892, a Carnegie Steel plant in Homestead, Pennsylvania, cut workers' wages. The union immediately called a strike. Andrew Carnegie's partner, Henry Frick, responded by bringing in the Pinkertons, a private police force known for their ability to break up strikes. The Pinkertons killed several strikers and wounded many others in a standoff that lasted some two weeks. Then, on July 23, an anarchist who had joined the protesters tried to assassinate Frick. The union had not backed his plan, but the public associated the two. Recognizing that public opinion was turning against unions, the union called off the strike in November. The **Homestead Strike** was part of an epidemic of steelworkers' and miners' strikes that took place as economic depression spread across America. In each case, troops and local militia were called in to suppress the unrest.

A Union Addresses Social Issues in a Pullman Town In 1893, inventor George Pullman, whose Pullman Palace Car Company produced luxury railroad passenger cars, laid off many of his workers and cut wages by 25 percent. Although the economic slowdown plaguing the nation at the time justified this action to some degree, Pullman did not reduce the rents in his company town near Chicago, where his workers lived. In May 1894, workers sent a delegation to discuss their situation with Pullman. He refused to negotiate and fired three workers. His other workers responded by going on strike.

When Pullman brought in strikebreakers, the workers turned to the newly organized American Railway Union (ARU) for help. Founded by former railroad worker **Eugene V. Debs,** the ARU was organized as an industrial union, grouping all railroad workers together rather than into separate trade unions according to the job they held. Debs believed

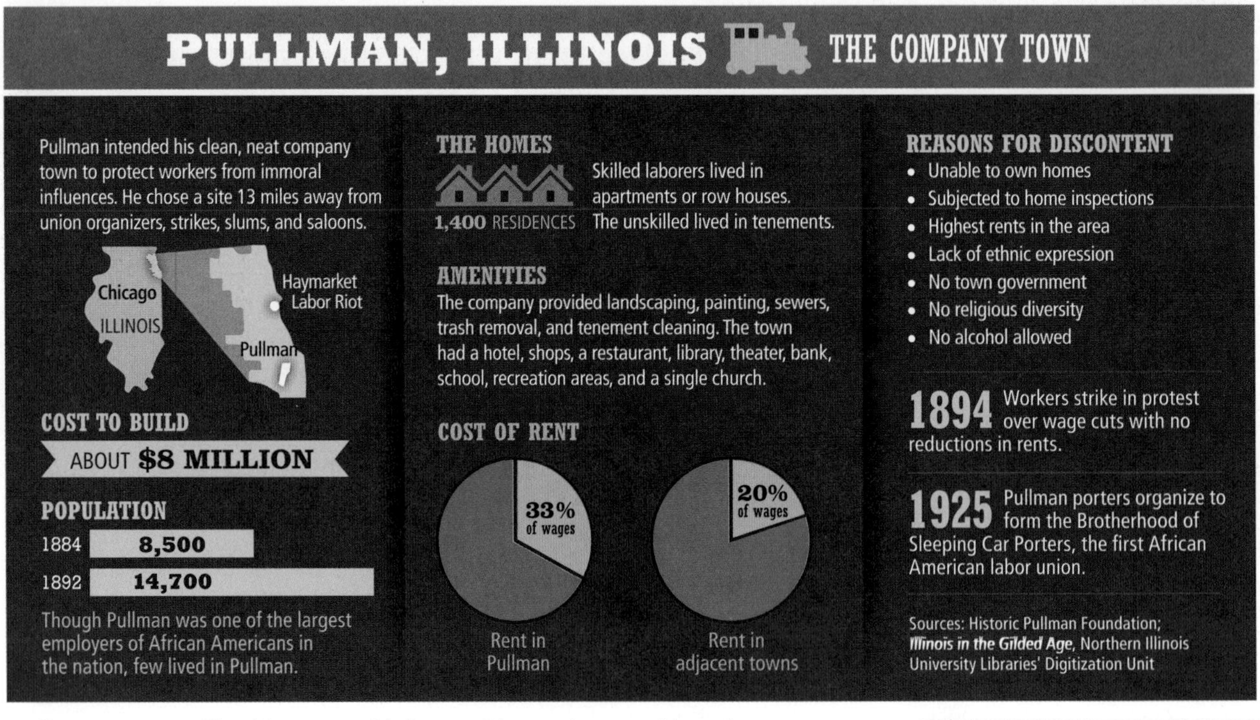

>> Company towns like this one provided everything workers would need, but at a significant cost. **Analyze Graphs** What reasons account for the workers' complaints about Pullman?

BOUNCE to Activate Chart

that industrial unions allowed workers to exert united pressure on employers.

The ARU ordered a nationwide strike against Pullman. By June 1894, nearly 300,000 railworkers were refusing to work on, handle, or move any trains that had Pullman cars on them. As the **Pullman Strike** escalated, the nation's railroad traffic came to a halt. Railroad owners cited the Sherman Antitrust Act to argue that the union was illegally disrupting free trade. Since the nation's mail moved by train, the federal government took action to end the strike. A federal court ordered a halt to the strike. When Debs defied the court order, President Grover Cleveland sent in federal troops to force the strikers back to work. Debs was jailed for conspiring against interstate commerce. Debs appealed his conviction, claiming that the government had no authority to halt the strike. However, the Supreme Court upheld Debs' conviction in the case *In re Debs* in 1895, ruling that protecting interstate commerce and the private property rights of the railroads was a lawful exercise of government power.

>> Eugene V. Debs, leader of the American Railroad Union, speaks to a crowd. Debs was known as a fiery and inspirational speaker.

The Impact of Labor Unions The outcome of the Pullman Strike set an important trend. Employers, hoping to maintain profitability and thus create more jobs, appealed frequently for court orders against unions, citing legislation like the Sherman Antitrust Act. The federal courts and other federal officials routinely supported these appeals, denying unions recognition as legally protected organizations and limiting union gains for more than 30 years. As the twentieth century opened, industrialists, workers, and government continued to battle over numerous labor issues. Collective bargaining, strikes, and legislation would become the way of life for American industry.

In the decades after Pullman, the labor movement split into different factions, some increasingly influenced by socialism. By the end of the 1800s, Debs had become a Socialist. He helped organize the American Socialist Party in 1897, running for President in 1900. In 1905, he helped found the Industrial Workers of the World (IWW), or Wobblies. The IWW was a radical union of unskilled workers with many Socialists among its leaders. In the first few decades of the 1900s, the IWW led a number of strikes, many of them violent.

CHECK UNDERSTANDING Why did workers turn to the strike as a tactic to win labor gains?

ASSESSMENT

1. **Determine Point of View** Why does the concept of child labor in factories seems so terrible to us today when it was a widely accepted practice in the 1800s?
2. **Compare** life in a company town with life today for a low-paid worker.
3. **Generate Explanations** Someone's "bread and butter" is his or her means of support, or livelihood. Why was the AFL called a "bread and butter" union while the Knights of Labor was not?
4. **Express Problems Clearly** Why did labor unions such as the Knights of Labor, the AFL, and the ARU have such a difficult time carrying out a successful strike?
5. **Quest Connections** How did Andrew Carnegie's company treat striking workers in Homestead, Pennsylvania? How does that affect your opinion of him?

GO ONLINE to access this biography: Karl Marx

9.4

GO ONLINE to **Project Imagine: Give Your Son a Better Life** to witness the choices made by immigrants coming to the United States.

BOUNCE to Activate Flipped Video

Objectives

Compare the "new immigrants" of the late 1800s to earlier immigrants.

Explain the push and pull factors leading immigrants to America.

Describe the challenges that immigrants faced establishing new lives in America.

Analyze how immigrants adapted to American life while contributing to American culture.

Key Terms

"new" immigrants
steerage
Ellis Island
Angel Island
Americanization
"melting pot"
nativism
Chinese Exclusion Act

The New Immigrants

Immigration has been a central theme in American history. However, when the foreign-born population of the United States nearly doubled between 1870 and 1900, some Americans feared that the newcomers would damage American culture. Instead, Americans adopted parts of immigrants' cultures, while immigrants adopted parts of American culture. The contributions of immigrants, combined with the existing culture, helped shape American culture into a diverse and unique whole.

New Immigrants Seek Better Lives

A Rush of "New" Immigrants Immigrants had always come to America for economic opportunity and religious freedom. Until the 1870s, the majority had been Protestants from northern and western Europe. They came as families to settle in the United States, often on farms with family or friends who had come previously. Many had saved some money for the journey, had a skill or trade, or had a formal education.

Many German and Irish Catholics had immigrated in the 1840s and 1850s, and more arrived after the Civil War. Some Americans had prejudices against Catholics, but the Irish spoke English and the German Catholics benefited from the good reputation of their Protestant countrymen. Although many lacked skills and money, the children of these immigrants were often able to blend into American society. Beginning in the 1870s, Irish and Germans were joined by **"new" immigrants** from southern and eastern Europe. They arrived in increasing numbers until the outbreak of World War I.

GO ONLINE to access your digital course

In contrast to "old" immigrants who had come before the Irish and Germans, "new" immigrants were often Catholic or Jewish, and likely to settle in cities rather than on farms. Many came alone, planning to save some money in the United States and return home to live. They came from Italy, Greece, Poland, Hungary, and Russia in large numbers. After 1900, immigrants from Southern and Eastern Europe made up more than 70 percent of all immigrants, up from about 1 percent in the mid-1800s. Many native-born Americans felt threatened by these newcomers with different cultures and languages.

Causes of Immigration The legal immigration of these immigrants changed demographic patterns in the United States. Two types of factors caused this immigration, as they have caused people to immigrate before and after the rush at the turn of the twentieth century. Push factors are those that compel people to leave their homes, such as famine, war, or persecution. For example, in the 1880s, farmers had a difficult time in many parts of the world. In Mexico, Poland, and China, land reform and low prices for crops forced many farmers off their land. Some chose to come to America to make a new start. Beginning in the 1840s, China and eastern Europe experienced repeated wars and political revolutions. These events disrupted economies and created political refugees. One of the largest groups to settle in America were Russian and eastern European Jews. Beginning in the 1880s, they fled religious persecution and came to the United States to live in safety, and hopefully, achieve a better life.

Another type of factor that leads to immigration is a pull factor. Pull factors are those that draw people *to* a new place, such as economic opportunity or religious freedom. In addition to a vague hope for opportunity, the United States offered special attractions, including plentiful land and employment. The 1862 Homestead Act and aid from railroad companies made western farmland inexpensive. The railroads even offered reduced fares to get there because they needed customers in the West for their own businesses to succeed. Until 1885, immigrants were recruited from their homelands to build railroads, dig in mines, work in oil fields, harvest produce, or toil in factories. Others hoped to strike it rich by finding gold in the West.

Many others were "chain immigrants," joining family or friends who had already settled in America. The immigrants who had arrived earlier promised to help the newcomers find work and housing, and sometimes they even sent them tickets for the journey. Immigrants may have lured their families and friends to America with the promise of religious

Immigration from Europe, 1870-1910

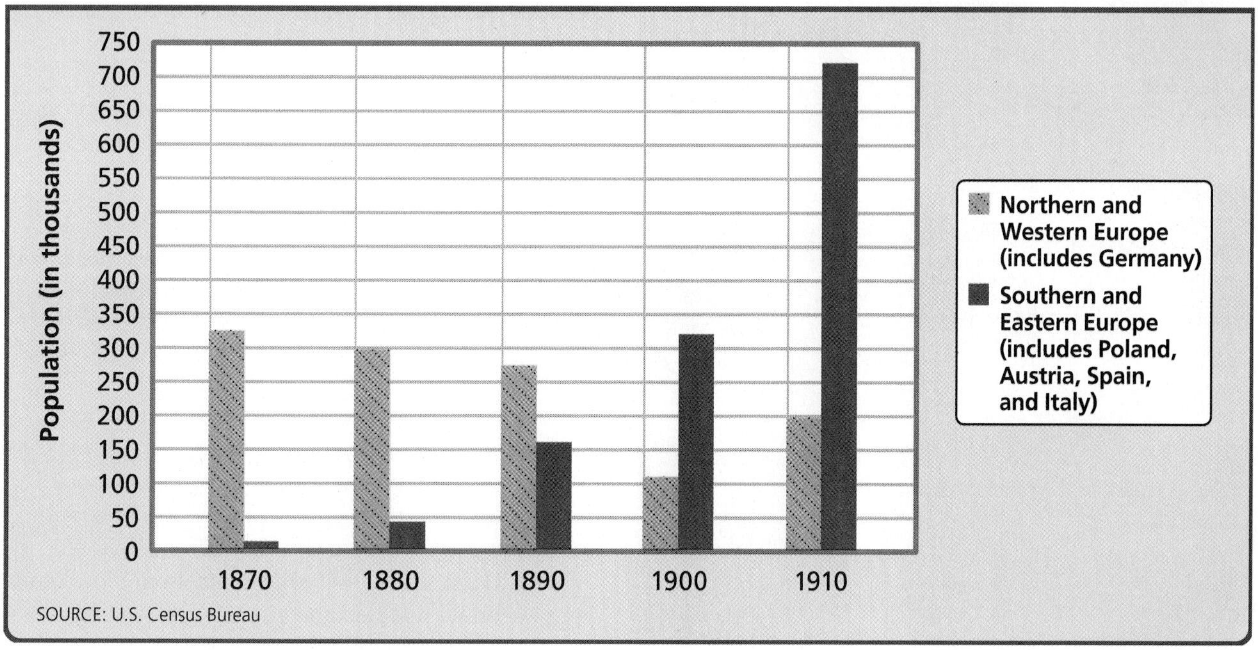

>> The number of immigrants increased at the turn of the twentieth century. **Analyze Graphs** Which region shows the greatest increase in immigration during the time period shown on the graph?

BOUNCE to Activate Chart

and political freedom. In America, one could worship and vote as one chose without fear of persecution by the government. Many immigrants in the late nineteenth century had both push and pull factors that helped them decide to leave the familiar for the unknown. For example, Cuban immigrants in Florida were both "pulled" by the attraction of work in industries like cigar manufacturing, and "pushed" out of Cuba by the political turbulence of the revolutionary struggle against Spain in the 1860s and 1870s.

☑ **IDENTIFY SUPPORTING DETAILS** What details from the reading help explain why immigrants came to America?

Optimism and the Immigrant Experience

Immigrant experiences varied greatly. However, there were common themes: a tough decision to leave home and family, a hard and costly journey with an uncertain end, and the difficulties of learning a new language and adjusting to a foreign culture. Nevertheless, many immigrants were optimistic that moving to America would lead to better lives. As one young Russian Jewish woman explained, "America means for an Immigrant a fairy promised land that came out true, a land that gives all they need for their work, a land which gives morality through her churches and education through her free schools and libraries." Millions of people decided that such possibilities outweighed the risks and set out for the United States.

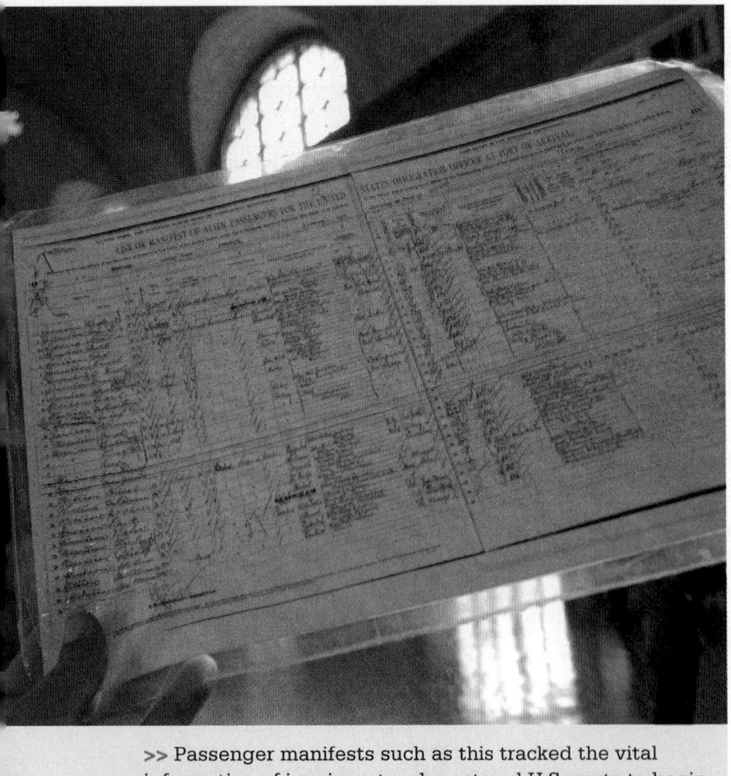

>> Passenger manifests such as this tracked the vital information of immigrants who entered U.S. ports to begin their lives as Americans.

The Long Journey to America Coming to America was a big task. Travelers needed money for passage and to make a new start, although some had only enough for a ticket. Usually, they brought only what they could carry. Reaching a port of departure was often difficult. In war-torn areas, just getting to the ship could be dangerous.

By the 1870s, steamships made the trip across the Atlantic safer and faster than ever before. However, it could be an awful voyage. Most immigrants traveled in **steerage**, the worst accommodations on the ship. Located on the lower decks with no private cabins, steerage was crowded and dirty. Illness spread quickly, while rough weather could force seasick passengers to stay in cramped quarters for days at a time. Under these conditions, even healthy immigrants fell ill, while frail passengers sometimes died. On other voyages, passengers were fortunate to have beautiful weather and no illness onboard.

Immigrants Arrive at Ellis and Angel Islands The first stop for ships at American ports was a processing station where immigration officials decided who could or could not stay in the United States. To enter, immigrants had to be healthy and show that they had money, a skill, or a sponsor to provide for them. Often the sponsor was an industrialist who needed workers. Most European immigrants arrived in New York Harbor. Beginning in 1892, they were processed at the busy, New York Harbor immigration station **Ellis Island**.

First and second-class passengers were inspected on the ship and released, unless they had obvious medical problems. All third-class, or steerage, passengers were sent to Ellis Island. There, immigration officers conducted legal and medical inspections. Since the shipowners did a preliminary screening before passengers boarded, only about 2 percent of immigrants were denied entry; the rest took a ferry to New York City. In 1907, 10-year-old Edward Corsi arrived with his family from Italy. Years later, when he had become an immigration official, he remembered his first impressions:

I realized that Ellis Island could inspire both hope and fear. Some of the passengers were afraid . . . ; others were impatient, anxious to get through the inspection and be off to their destinations.

—Edward Corsi, *In the Shadow of Liberty,* 1935

Chinese and other Asian immigrants crossed the Pacific Ocean, many arriving in San Francisco Bay. Chinese immigrants came in larger numbers in the 1850s to work in mines, on railroads, and on farms and fisheries. After 1882, Chinese immigrants were turned away unless they could prove that they were American citizens or had relatives living in America. **Angel Island**, a processing center for Chinese immigrants, opened in San Francisco Bay in 1910. If Ellis Island was welcoming to some, Angel Island was always formidable. It was designed to filter out Chinese immigrants. Officials often assumed that Chinese newcomers would misrepresent themselves in order to gain entry.

While most immigrants left Ellis Island within hours, Chinese immigrants at Angel Island were often held for weeks or even months in poor conditions waiting for permission to stay in the United States. To pass the time and express their frustrations, many carved poems into the walls at Angel Island. One detainee wrote:

Lin, upon arriving in America,

Was arrested, put in a wooden building,

And made a prisoner.

I was here for one autumn.

The Americans did not allow me to land.

I was ordered to be deported.

—*Taoist from the Town of Iron*

In addition to San Francisco and New York, thousands of immigrants arrived during this period through other ports on the East Coast such as Boston, Baltimore, and Philadelphia, southern ports such as New Orleans and Galveston, or western ports such as Los Angeles.

☑ **CHECK UNDERSTANDING** What factors made the trip to America difficult for many immigrants?

>> The experience of Asian immigrants like these ones on the West Coast was often less welcoming than that of European immigrants in the East.

Social Issues Affecting Immigrants

Passing immigration inspections was just the first step. Once in America, immigrants immediately faced tough decisions such as where to settle and how to find work. On top of that, most had to learn a new language and new customs. Sometimes immigrants worked with an agent who spoke their language for help finding work and housing, but many agents took advantage of the newcomers to make money. Lucky immigrants had contacts through family and friends who could help them navigate a new and strange world.

Americanization Movement Most new immigrants stayed in cities, close to industrial jobs in factories. There, they often lived in ethnic neighborhoods with people who shared their native language, religion, and culture. Neighbors might have come from the same country, region, or even village.

By 1890, many cities had huge immigrant populations. In San Francisco and Chicago, immigrants made up more than 40 percent of the population. Four out of five inhabitants of New York City were foreign born or had foreign-born parents. While exclusionist policies forced some people to live in ghettoes, these neighborhoods also provided familiarity. Specialty shops, grocers, and clothing stores provided a taste of the food and culture that immigrants had left behind.

In many cities, volunteer institutions known as settlement houses ran **Americanization** programs, helping newcomers learn English and adopt American dress and diet. At the same time, immigrants helped one another through fraternal associations, such as the Polish National Alliance and the Ancient Order of Hibernians (an Irish Catholic organization). These organizations, based on ethnic or religious identity, provided social services and financial assistance to encourage people to pursue economic opportunity while making them feel more at home in the United States. Many settlement workers and immigrants alike believed that American society was a **"melting pot"** in which white people of all different nationalities blended to create a single culture. The term came from the name of a play that opened in 1908. This model excluded Asian immigrants, who became targets of social and legal discrimination.

Despite the hopes of settlement workers, immigrants often held on to their traditions. Their children, however, became more Americanized, without memories of homes and families left behind. Some adults reported that they dreamed of returning to their homelands, but most immigrants did not return to their country of origin. Instead, they established fraternal lodges and religious institutions that made them feel more comfortable in their new surroundings.

Catholics, in particular, established churches and parochial schools. In many cities, Irish Catholic churches stood side by side with Italian Catholic churches—each built to serve the needs of its own community. The immigrants' churches, schools, and institutions reminded native-born Americans that new cultures were changing American society.

New Immigrants Face Hostility Accepting immigrants into American society was not always easy. Newcomers often faced **nativism**, which was a tendency towards preferring native-born, white Americans over "new" immigrants. During the economic recessions of the late nineteenth century, competition for jobs and housing fueled resentment. Many native-born workers worried that immigrants would work for lower pay. Nativist intellectuals backed up their beliefs with dubious scientific rhetoric that linked immigrants' physical characteristics to criminal tendencies or lesser intellectual abilities. Social Darwinism also played a role in nativism.

Religious and cultural differences sparked suspicion between native-born Americans and immigrants, as well as between different immigrant ethnic groups. Many Irish, German, Italian, and Polish immigrants practiced Roman Catholicism, and some Protestants feared that Catholics' first loyalty was to the Pope rather than to American ideals. Anti-semitism in the United States was nothing new—the U.S. Army had briefly expelled all Jews from Grant's military department in 1862—and the arrival of Jews fleeing persecution in Eastern Europe only complicated the issue. Some native-born Jews worried that these Eastern European immigrants, who were culturally quite different than American or German Jews, would fuel anti-Jewish attitudes and that the newcomers would not be able to Americanize. Some native-born white Protestants would not hire, vote for, or work with Catholics or Jews. Some Americans even signed restrictive

>> "Looking Backward" shows a man carrying his possessions being confronted by a group of well-dressed men. **Analyze Political Cartoons** What do the shadows behind the well-dressed men represent?

contracts agreeing not to rent or sell property to Catholics, Jews, African Americans, or other groups they considered "non-native."

Policies Restrict Some Immigration Extreme hostility toward Chinese laborers had led Congress to pass the **Chinese Exclusion Act** in 1882. The act prohibited immigration by Chinese laborers, limited the civil rights of Chinese immigrants already in the United States, and forbade the naturalization of Chinese residents. The act had unintended negative consequences on the economy, especially in states such as California that relied on cheap Chinese labor. Restricting the immigration of Chinese laborers made it difficult for large single-crop ranches to be profitable. The act also prevented many Chinese in the United States from visiting their families in China, fearing they would not be permitted to return. In 1898, a court case established that Chinese people born in America were United States citizens and could, therefore, come and go freely. However, many immigration officials ignored this ruling.

In the same year, Congress passed another act that prohibited the entry of anyone who was a criminal, immoral, a pauper, or likely to need public assistance. In practice, the law was used to bar many poor or handicapped immigrants. These acts marked the beginning of legislation restricting immigration in the United States. Until then, anti-immigrant activity had been episodic and often short-lived. Immigration became a constant topic of conversation throughout America.

IDENTIFY CENTRAL IDEAS Why did some Americans want to restrict immigration?

>> Immigrants arrive at Ellis Island. The labor provided by immigrants like these helped fuel the burgeoning U.S. economy.

BOUNCE to Activate Gallery

Immigrants Affect American Society

Despite anti-immigrant sentiment, immigrants of many racial and ethnic groups transformed American society. They fueled industrial growth, acquired citizenship, participated in the democratic process, and made their traditions part of American culture. Mexican Americans in the Southwest developed effective ranching techniques, while Chinese, Irish, and Mexican laborers built the railroads. Equally important, immigrants labored in coal mines, steel mills, textile mills, and factories. Immigrant women worked in factories, as seamstresses, as laundresses, and doing piecework. Others became domestic servants. Though the conditions were harsh and immigrants received few benefits, their labor helped the United States become an economic world power.

Immigrants' Contributions to American Culture Immigrants not only helped propel the American economic engine; they also helped shape the evolving American culture. Immigrants from around the world brought their languages, religions, and cuisines to the United States. New foods and the words to describe them quickly became part of the American vocabulary. European Jews introduced bagels; Italian immigrants popularized pasta dishes like spaghetti; German immigrants brought sausages called wieners and Frankfurters. The Chinese introduced a vast knowledge of how to use plants for medicinal purposes as well as foods such as chow mein.

Many individual immigrants made valuable contributions to American culture. Andrew Carnegie, a Scottish immigrant, turned to philanthropy following the sale of his steel empire. He donated some $288 million to social and educational causes in the United States. James Naismith, who moved from Canada to Massachusetts, invented the sport of basketball in the late 1800s. In addition, Alexander Graham Bell, also born in Scotland, revolutionized modern communications with his patent of the telephone in 1876. Belgian immigrant Leo Baekeland transformed technology with the development of modern plastics. Inventor Nikola Tesla, born in what is now Croatia, pioneered discoveries in the generation and transmission of electricity.

Immigrants Lead Labor and Social Movements

The lives of many immigrants in the 1800s were very hard. Many lived in overcrowded slums and unhealthy and unsafe tenement housing. Others took dangerous jobs in mines and factories. Increasingly, immigrants demanded a voice, becoming active in labor unions and politics. They lobbied for policies to protect the poor and powerless and used their votes to elect governments favorable to those goals. Some of the political leaders they supported became powerful.

Among these influential activists was Irish immigrant Mary Harris Jones, also known as Mother Jones. She fought for the union rights of coal miners. Samuel Gompers was a Jewish cigar maker from England who became an influential labor organizer and leader. Gompers' leadership of the American Federation of Labor, through which he organized national unions comprised of local chapters, became the model for unionism in the United States. Union leaders like Gompers and Mother Jones demanded reforms that helped immigrants as well as all laborers. Immigrants expanded the definition of *American*.

☑ **IDENTIFY** In what ways did immigrants assimilate to and change American culture?

☑ ASSESSMENT

1. **Summarize** What are the push and pull factors that motivate immigration? Give two examples of each.
2. **Infer** What was the most likely reason that healthy first and second-class passengers were admitted to the U.S. without being processed at Ellis Island, while those in steerage had to go through processing?
3. **Compare and Contrast** How were the roles of settlement houses and fraternal organizations the same? Different?
4. **Summarize** How were Chinese immigrants treated in the late 1800s?
5. **Identify Central Issues** How did immigrants help the United States become the country it is today?
6. **Connections to Today** In this period, one way that immigrants left a visible mark on their communities was by building their own houses of worship. Identify one way immigrants today make their mark on their communities?

Primary Sources

The Promised Land, Mary Antin

Mary Antin was a Jewish woman born in 1881 in Polotsk, a town in Belarus, then a part of the Russian Empire. As a girl, she sailed from Russia to Boston with her mother and siblings. Educated first in Russia and then in the United States, she was a gifted writer whose poems were published in local newspapers while she was still in school. In 1912, the *Atlantic Monthly* magazine began publishing her autobiography, *The Promised Land* in installments. It was a sensation and Antin became a well-known figure.

This selection from Antin's autobiography explains how she felt when she first learned about George Washington in school. She uses this episode to elaborate on her feelings about America, and how her new country compared to her birthplace.

>> Children play at Ellis Island while their parents wait or are detained.

Primary Source

For if I found that I was a person of small consequence, I discovered at the same time that I was more nobly related than I had ever supposed. I had relatives and friends who were notable people by the old standards, —I had never been ashamed of my family, —but this George Washington, who died long before I was born, was like a king in greatness, and he and I were Fellow Citizens.

There was a great deal about Fellow Citizens in the patriotic literature we read at this time; and I knew from my father how he was a Citizen, through the process of naturalization, and how I also was a citizen by virtue of my relation to him. Undoubtedly I was a Fellow Citizen, and George Washington was another. It thrilled me to realize what sudden greatness had fallen on me; and at the same time it sobered me, as with a sense of responsibility. I strove to conduct myself as befitted a Fellow Citizen. . . .

DETERMINE MEANING What did Antin and George Washington have in common? How does this make Antin feel?

What more could America give a child? Ah, much more! As I read how the patriots planned the [American] Revolution, and the women gave their sons to die in battle, and the heroes led to victory, and the rejoicing people set up the Republic, it dawned on me gradually what was meant by my country. The people all desiring noble things, and striving for them together, defying their oppressors, giving their lives for each other—all this it was that made my country.

SUMMARIZE What about the American Revolution "made" her country, according to Antin?

It was not a thing that I understood; I could not go home and tell Frieda about it, as I told her other things I learned at school. But I knew one could say "my country" and feel it, as one felt "God" or "myself." My teacher, my schoolmates, Miss Dillingham [her favorite teacher], George Washington himself could not mean more than I when they said "my country," after I had once felt it. For the Country was for all the Citizens, and I was a Citizen. And when we stood up to sing "America," I shouted the words with all my might. I was in very earnest proclaiming to the world my love for my new-found country.

DRAW CONCLUSIONS What sentiment does Antin find it impossible to share with Frieda?

"I love thy rocks and rills [streams],
Thy woods and templed hills."

Boston Harbor, Crescent Beach, Chelsea Square [places around Boston]—all was hallowed ground to me. As the day approached when the school was to hold exercises in honor of Washington's Birthday, the halls resounded at all hours with the strains of patriotic songs; and I, who was a model of the attentive pupil, more than once lost my place in the lesson as I strained to hear, through closed doors, some neighboring class rehearsing "The Star-Spangled Banner." If the doors happened to be open, and the chorus broke out unveiled—

"O! say, does that Star-Spangled Banner yet wave
O'er the land of the free, and the home of the brave?"—

delicious tremors ran up and down my spine, and I was faint with suppressed enthusiasm.

Where had been my country until now? What flag had I loved? What heroes had I worshipped? The very names of these things had been unknown to me. Well I knew that Polotzk was not my country. It was goluth—exile.

DETERMINE CENTRAL IDEAS How does what you know about Jewish life in Eastern Europe at this time help explain Antin's attitude in the last paragraph?

ASSESSMENT

1. **Cite Evidence** How did Antin become a citizen? What did she believe was her duty as a citizen?
2. **Determine Author's Purpose** What single word would you use to describe Antin's tone in this passage? Explain your answer.
3. **Predict** How might Antin have reacted to obstacles she faced in the United States, such as economic troubles or prejudice? Would the attitude she expresses here have helped or hurt her?
4. **Draw Conclusions** Why do you think Antin found the *Star Spangled Banner* so inspirational?

9.5

GO ONLINE to **Project Imagine: Explore Immigrant Life in New York City** to explore life for immigrants living and working in the nation's largest city.

A Nation of Cities

As one historian has noted, America was born on the farm and moved to the city. In 1860, most Americans lived in rural areas, with only 16 percent living in towns or cities with a population of 8,000 or more. By 1900, that percentage had doubled, and nearly 15 million Americans lived in cities with populations of more than 50,000. Migration to urban areas during this time changed the demographics, or statistical characteristics, of the population of the United States. This upsurge in urbanization both reflected and fueled massive changes in the way Americans lived.

BOUNCE to Activate Flipped Video

Objectives

Analyze urban growth in the late 1800s.

Explain how technology improved city life.

Evaluate the problems caused by rapid urban growth and ways that city dwellers tried to solve them.

Key Terms

urbanization
rural-to-urban migrants
skyscrapers
Elisha Otis
mass transit
suburbs
Frederick Law Olmsted
tenements
cholera

Americans Migrate to Cities

In the late nineteenth century, America experienced a period of **urbanization** in which the number of cities and people living in them increased dramatically. Still, numbers and statistics do not tell the whole story of how Americans became city folk. Urban people lived differently from rural people.

People in the country lived and worked on farms, either owned by their family or rented from a larger landowner. Their work was driven by the growing cycle. They did a lot of their work outside when weather permitted. In contrast, many people in cities worked for large companies inside factory buildings or sweatshops, rode trolley cars or walked to work, and lived in apartment buildings. Unlike farming, factory work was a year-round, daily grind, and workers had no control over their schedules. Over time, this structured scheduling, combined with the urban way of life, became part of American culture.

City Life Beckons to Immigrants and Migrants America's major cities were manufacturing and transportation centers clustered in the northeast, on the Pacific coast, and along the

GO ONLINE to access your digital course

waterways of the midwest. Connected by the new railroad lines, cities became magnets for immigrants and rural Americans. The newcomers were attracted by jobs in factories or the service industries. Those with a little money opened shops. The educated increasingly joined the new middle-class professions, working in offices.

Women's opportunities, in particular, were dramatically expanded in urban areas. In addition to factory work, they could take in boarders, do piecework, or become domestic servants. Educated women found work as teachers or in offices as secretaries and typists.

While many city jobs offered only hard work for little reward, cities offered variety, promise, and even a bit of glamour. By saving part of their wages, city workers might attain some comforts or perhaps even move into the growing middle class. At the least, they could increase their children's opportunities by sending them to school. While some laborers were trapped in an endless cycle of poverty, only the very poorest were unable to enjoy a somewhat higher standard of living in the late nineteenth century.

Life was hard in the city, but many still loved it. Horace Greeley, a politician and New York City newspaper editor, wrote in the 1860s, "We cannot all live in cities, yet nearly all seem determined to do so." City churches, theaters, social clubs, and museums offered companionship and entertainment.

>> City streets became crowded as more and more people of various incomes and classes sought their fortunes in big cities.

BOUNCE to Activate Gallery

Cities Attract Immigrants The demographics of many cities changed very quickly as legal immigrants arrived. By 1900, some urban populations were more than 40 percent foreign born. Some immigrants found their way to a city through happenstance, while others joined relatives or were recruited by companies needing labor. In this way, neighborhoods, cities, regions, and industries often acquired a majority of workers from a particular locale. For example, employees at the steel mills of western Pennsylvania were predominantly Polish, while the textile factories of New York became a center for eastern European Jewish people. Domestic servants in the Northeast were primarily Irish women, while Scandinavians worked in the fish-packing industry of the Pacific Northwest.

Farmers Migrate to Urban Areas Demographic patterns also changed in response to the many **rural-to-urban migrants** who moved to cities in the 1890s. For many rural Americans, making a living on a farm had become increasingly difficult. In addition to unpredictable weather conditions, isolation, and limited opportunities, farmers faced economic struggles that hindered their livelihoods. New technologies enabled farmers to produce more crops, but the greater supply caused prices to drop. These factors, combined with the excitement and variety of city life, sparked widespread rural-to-urban migration. However, the move from farm to factory could be wrenching. Former agricultural workers often found themselves working in dim light and narrow confines. The pace of work was controlled by rigid schedules, with no slow seasons. However, factory work paid wages in cash, which was sometimes scarce on family farms.

Midwestern cities such as Minneapolis–St. Paul and Chicago exploded in the decade between 1880 and 1890. Many of the newcomers were immigrants or migrants from the rural West.

African Americans moving out of the rural South were also part of the migration, although on a smaller scale. The majority of the migrating African Americans stayed in southern cities, but the few Black migrants to northern and western cities paved the way for a much larger migration after World War I.

Urban Subcultures Emerge The combination of massive migration from rural areas and immigration from abroad transformed life in urban areas. Many

Comparison of Rural and Urban Populations

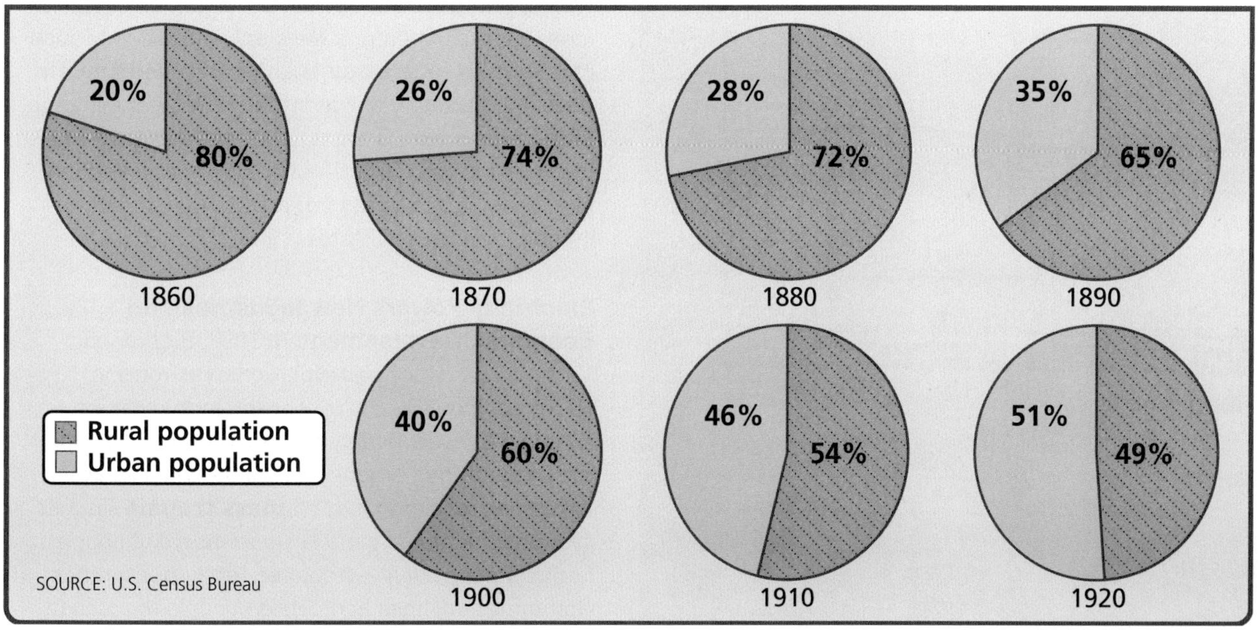

>> The percentage of the population living in urban areas increased relative to those living in rural areas over several decades. **Analyze Graphs** What factors account for the demographic shift from rural to urban areas over these decades?

new arrivals were young unmarried men and women free from the control of their families and communities. In their leisure time they flocked to amusement parks and dance halls to meet one another and date. The more anonymous environment of cities also made it easier for migrants to seek out same-sex partners. By the 1890s, certain urban neighborhoods had "gay" bars or meeting places. Not coincidentally, this was also the time when our modern concepts of lesbian and gay male sexual orientation and heterosexual orientation emerged as discrete categories of identity.

Meanwhile, some of the larger American cities developed so-called "bohemian" racially-mixed neighborhoods that attracted artists, writers, political radicals, gay men and lesbians, and others whose lives defied social conventions. The bohemian neighborhood of Greenwich Village in New York City was home to Emma Goldman, the feminist anarchist whose lecture tour of 1915 included speeches in favor of gay rights—a shocking demand at the time but a foretaste of things to come.

☑ **CHECK UNDERSTANDING** Why did many people choose to move to cities?

Technology Improves City Life

As cities swelled in size, politicians and workers struggled to keep up with the demands of growth to provide water, sewers, schools, and safety. American innovators stepped up to the task by developing new technologies to improve living conditions. The middle and upper classes benefited most from the innovations, but every city dweller was affected. Electric trolleys and subways, building codes, and other innovations increased the pace of urbanization and economic development in cities across the country.

Engineers Build Skyward with Steel The cities of the late nineteenth century began to take their modern form. For the first time, skylines became recognizable by their **skyscrapers**. Steel was first mass-produced to create railroad rails, but architects and engineers realized the possibilities of using this strong and resilient metal for the construction of buildings. Skyscrapers of ten stories and taller had steel frames and used artistic designs to magnify their imposing height. Inside, they provided office space in cities that had no room left on the ground. Increased office space in turn allowed more businesses to establish themselves and more people

>> Electric cable cars carried passengers all around the city.

BOUNCE to Activate Illustration

>> The "White City" was architect Daniel Burnham's version of the ideal city, designed for an exhibition in Chicago in 1893. It included buildings, parks, and electric streetlights.

to live in closer proximity to each other, which further stimulated economic development in urban areas. But tall buildings were only realistic because of other new technology. In the 1850s, **Elisha Otis** developed a safety elevator that would not fall if the lifting rope broke. Central heating systems were also improved in the 1870s. Technological innovations like these, dramatically improved the standard of living in the United States.

Electricity Powers New Industries and Economic Development In 1888, Richmond, Virginia, introduced a revolutionary invention: streetcars powered by overhead electric cables. Within a decade, every major city followed. It was the beginning of a transportation revolution. New industries revolving around **mass transit**—public systems that could carry large numbers of people fairly inexpensively—reshaped the nation's cities. Commuter rail lines had carried people to areas in and around cities since the 1870s. However, they were powered by coal-driven steam engines, making them slow, unreliable, and dirty. Some cities used trolleys pulled by horses, which were slower and left horse waste all over the streets. Electricity, on the other hand, was quiet, clean, and efficient.

Electric cars also ran on a reliable schedule and could carry many more people than horse-drawn carts. Electric cable cars were not practical in every city, however. Cables strung in narrow streets could block fire trucks, and traffic congestion often prevented streetcars from running on schedule. In 1897, Boston solved this problem by running the cars underground in the nation's first subway system. New York City followed in 1904. Electric cable cars and subways allowed urban economies to expand even faster. These new industries efficiently moved people in and around cities, making it possible for urban populations to grow at an increasingly rapid pace.

Middle and upper class people who could afford transit fares moved away from the noise and dirt of the industrial city. They built housing in the cleaner, quieter perimeter, known as streetcar **suburbs**. From there, they rode mass transit into the center of the city to work, shop, or be entertained, returning to their homes in the evening. Poorer people remained in city centers so that they could walk to work.

City Planners Lay Out Cities As cities grew larger and more complex, architectural firms expanded to offer city-planning services designed to make cities more functional and beautiful, even as their populations skyrocketed. Mass transit allowed city planners to separate parts of the city by zoning, or designating certain areas for particular functions. Through the 1890s, cities established separate zones for heavy industry, financial institutions, and residences. They also built public spaces, such as public libraries, government buildings, and universities.

Parks and recreational spaces were one of the most important aspects of city planning. Since the 1850s, cities had built parks as a solution to some of the problems of urban growth. Philadelphia purchased areas along the Schuylkill River to protect the city's water supply from industrial pollution. They hired landscape engineer **Frederick Law Olmsted** to design Fairmount Park. Olmsted had also designed New York City's Central Park and similar parks in other cities.

IDENTIFY CENTRAL IDEAS How did public transportation change urban areas?

Urban Living Creates Social Issues

Urbanization led to many social issues caused by overcrowding and poverty. In 1890, New York's Lower East Side had a population of more than 700 people per acre. As immigrants and rural migrants arrived, they crowded into neighborhoods that already seemed to be overflowing.

Housing Conditions Worsen As newcomers moved into urban areas, those who could not afford to ride mass transit had to live within walking distance of the industrial plants and factories where they worked. Housing in densely populated neighborhoods was often aging and usually overcrowded. Most urban workers lived in **tenements**: low-cost multifamily housing designed to squeeze in as many families as possible. Sometimes, several families lived in one apartment or even one room. They used the space for sewing clothes or doing other piecework to earn money. For those who had moved from rural areas, adapting to the lack of fresh air and open space could be challenging.

Tenement owners usually lived in the suburbs or in fashionable downtown areas, away from the industrial grime. However, they built apartments for desperate people who had little choice about where they lived. With few windows and little sanitation, tenements were unhealthy and dangerous. In 1890, journalist Jacob Riis drew attention to the plight of New York tenement dwellers:

>> Most immigrants and rural migrants could only afford to live in poorer urban neighborhoods. **Infer** Why would life in an urban setting be both a blessing and a curse for new arrivals?

BOUNCE to Activate 3D Model

> Go into any of the 'respectable' tenement neighborhoods . . . you shall come away agreeing [that] . . . life there does not seem worth living. . . . [T]he airshaft . . . seems always so busy letting out foul stenches . . . that it has no time to earn its name by bringing down fresh air.
>
> —Jacob Riis, *How the Other Half Lives*

Public Health Concerns Cities in the late 1800s were filthy. Unpaved streets were snarled with ruts and littered with trash and even dead horses that were left to rot. Alleys between tenements were clogged with food waste and trash. Only the newest urban dwellings had indoor toilets, and the shared toilets in tenements often overflowed.

These conditions were perfect for breeding diseases. For example, **cholera**, a particularly dangerous illness, reached epidemic proportions several times in the United States in the 1800s, killing thousands. Cholera spreads when people drink contaminated water. While fresh water supplies and

>> The Great Chicago Fire of 1871 killed 200–300 people and left more than 100,000 homeless.

less burdened sanitary systems in rural areas helped avoid epidemics, preventing them in urban areas required action.

During the 1880s, planners attempted to regulate housing, sanitation, sewers, and public health. They began to take water from reservoirs that were separate from the polluted rivers and lakes. In the next decade, urban standards of living improved as a new filtration system improved water quality even more. Private companies competed for lucrative contracts to manage water distribution.

Safety in Cities In addition to public health concerns, cities also faced the dangers of fire, crime, and conflict. Even one careless act could have devastating consequences in crowded housing. Open fireplaces and gas lighting could start fires that quickly swept through a city. As the nineteenth century drew to a close, many cities developed professional firefighting teams.

At night, the streets were dangerous, yet many factory workers had to travel to and from work in the dark. In response to this challenge, professional, uniformed city police forces replaced the lone constable and the decentralized neighborhood watch. The new officers were civil servants who took exams and regularly patrolled city neighborhoods. They were aided in their task of ensuring safety by new electric streetlights.

However, the police were unable to overcome the challenge of tension between urban groups. In every big city, communities clashed along ethnic and racial fault lines. Police allowed immigrants to sleep in the station houses to avoid the violence in the streets. Even very young boys joined neighborhood gangs for safety.

Race, class, and neighborhood loyalties and conflicts continued to define neighborhood life for many generations.

☑ **IDENTIFY SUPPORTING DETAILS** What issues created by urban living made life difficult for many city dwellers?

☑ ASSESSMENT

1. **Identify Central Ideas** What factors encouraged the rural-to-urban migration of farmers in the 1890s?
2. **Draw Conclusions** Why was it important for architecture to become a specialized, professional career in the late 1800s?
3. **Generate Explanations** Why was public health a major concern in large cities during the 1880s?
4. **Analyze Information** How did urban gangs that were such a source of tension in the late 1800s reflect wider social problems?
5. **Connections to Today** Do you think the availability of public entertainment is still a big draw for city life? Why or why not?

9.6

GO ONLINE to **Project Imagine: Define Your Identity as an American to see how immigrants became a part of the changing American culture.**

New Ways of Life

Novelist Mark Twain satirized American life in his 1873 novel, *The Gilded Age: A Tale of Today*. He depicted American society as gilded, or having a rotten core covered with gold paint. Most Americans were not as cynical. The dizzying array of things to do and buy convinced the growing middle class that modern America was in a true golden age.

BOUNCE to Activate Flipped Video

Objectives

Explain how technology, new types of stores, and marketing changed Americans' standard of living.

Analyze mass culture and education in the late 1800s.

Describe new popular cultural movements in the late 1800s.

Key Terms

Mark Twain
Gilded Age
conspicuous consumerism
mass culture
Joseph Pulitzer
William Randolph Hearst
Horatio Alger
Tin Pan Alley
vaudeville

Free Enterprise Improves Life

Still, Twain's label stuck, and historians refer to the last decades of the nineteenth century as "the **Gilded Age**." The new lifestyle that middle-class Americans adopted during this period—shopping, sports, and reading popular magazines and newspapers—contributed to the development of a commonly shared American culture that would persist for the next century.

Industrialization and urbanization changed the lives of American workers. The application of scientific discoveries and technological innovations by the free enterprise system improved the standard of living in the United States. Driven by entrepreneurs, American businesses were able to create products and services that made daily life easier and more fun for many people. Mass produced materials and products lowered the prices of many goods, enabling ordinary Americans to purchase items that previously had been out of reach.

In addition, more people began to work for wages—in offices, on public transportation systems, or in factories as laborers and foremen. Even some farmers found themselves with extra time and cash as machinery improved and they were easily able to grow and sell more crops. At the same time, more products were available than ever before and at lower prices. This led to a culture

GO ONLINE to access your digital course

of **conspicuous consumerism**, in which people wanted and bought the many new products on the market. All but the very poorest working-class laborers were able to do and buy more than they would have in the past.

New Ways of Shopping Expanding on a trend that was developing in Britain, France, Russia, and other countries, Rowland H. Macy opened what he called a department store in New York in 1858. It soon became the largest single store in America and served as a model for many more U.S. stores. Its sales methods—widespread advertising, a variety of goods organized into "departments," and high-quality items at fair prices—became the standard in large urban stores. By the 1870s, many big cities had department stores: Jordan Marsh in Boston, Marshall Field in Chicago, and Wanamaker's in Philadelphia.

John Wanamaker developed innovative ways to keep customers satisfied. He was the first to offer a money back guarantee. In addition, he placed large newspaper advertisements to attract customers. Later, Wanamaker became Postmaster General. In that position, he lowered the bulk shipping rates and began free delivery to rural areas, which led to a boom in the mail-order catalog business.

>> The carpet sweeper was a new invention of the Gilded Age and a status symbol among the middle class.

BOUNCE to Activate Illustration

While department stores pioneered new marketing and sales techniques, companies began to create trademarks with distinctive logos that consumers would recognize. For the first time, consumers began to notice and buy brand name goods. Long-distance shipping allowed consumers in Atlanta, Cincinnati, and San Francisco to purchase the same products.

Technology and Free Enterprise Lead to Higher Standards of Living After the Civil War, Americans began to measure success by what they could buy. Equating purchasing power with a higher social status, middle-class and some working-class consumers rushed to update their wardrobe with new clothing styles and to modernize their homes with new technologies, such as the carpet sweeper and the telephone. Technological innovations drove the development of new industries, which in turn created more jobs; wealth; and discretionary, or extra, income in consumers' hands. The cost of living decreased in part because factory-manufactured products often cost less than old-style handmade goods. Scientific discoveries, including better sanitation and medical care, contributed to better health, causing life expectancy to climb. The result was more middle-class Americans with more money to spend and greater opportunities to spend it on things they *chose* rather than just on things they *needed*.

The end of the nineteenth century is sometimes called the Victorian Era, after the queen of England. The rich were richer than ever before, and the middle class tried to imitate their lifestyle. Factory-produced clothing and prepackaged food gave homemakers a break from some activities, but rising expectations of cleanliness and more complicated meals meant that they spent more time on those tasks.

Other luxuries, like indoor plumbing, also became common. On the other hand, many women had to work outside their homes to achieve a middle-class lifestyle.

Life changed for men, as well. Innovations in public transportation allowed families to live at a distance from the dirt, noise, and bustle of industry. However, it often meant that men became commuters, leaving home early in the morning and returning late in the evening. Still, their culture taught them that hard work would bring the reward of more discretionary income with which to purchase the exciting products newly available on the market.

☑ **IDENTIFY MAIN IDEAS** How did consumption patterns change in the late nineteenth century?

A Mass Culture Develops

One of the effects of the spread of transportation, communication, and advertising was that Americans all across the country became more and more alike in their consumption patterns. Rich and poor could wear the same clothing styles, although the quality of that clothing varied. Household gadgets, toys, and food preferences were often the same from house to house. This phenomenon is known as **mass culture**.

The Newspaper Industry Expands The newspapers of the Gilded Age both reflected and helped create mass culture. Between 1870 and 1900, the number of newspapers increased from about 600 to more than 1,600. No one knew more about newspapers than **Joseph Pulitzer**, a Hungarian immigrant who had fought in the Civil War. Active in Missouri politics in the 1870s, Pulitzer moved to New York in the 1880s, where he started a morning paper, the *World*. It was so successful that Pulitzer soon started publishing the *Evening World*. The papers were inexpensive because they were supported in part by businesses that placed advertisements in their pages.

>> Joseph Pulitzer's *Evening World* enjoyed a large readership.

The job of a newspaper, Pulitzer believed, was to inform people and to stir up controversy. His newspapers were sensationalistic, filled with exposés of political corruption, comics, sports, and illustrations. They were designed to get the widest possible readership, rather than simply to report the news. Pulitzer soon found a competitor in **William Randolph Hearst**, whose *Morning Journal* employed the same tactics. Their sensational styles sold many papers.

At the same time, ethnic and special-interest publishers catered to the array of urban dwellers, especially immigrants. The *Philadelphia Tribune*, begun in the 1880s, targeted the African American market. In New York, there were six Italian-language papers by 1910. Each sold more than 10,000 copies daily. The Yiddish-language daily paper, *The Forward,* sold 120,000 copies.

The Arts Reflect the Characteristics and Issues of the Times Mark Twain was not the only author to take a critical look at society during the Gilded Age. Novels that explored harsh realities were popular. Stephen Crane exposed the slums of New York in his *Maggie: A Girl of the Streets* (1893). He later wrote *The Red Badge of Courage*, which explored the psychological aspects of war. Other novelists focused on moral issues. **Horatio Alger** wrote about characters who succeeded by hard work, while Henry James and Edith Wharton questioned a society based upon rigid rules of conduct. Playwrights such as John Augustin Daly mirrored Twain's disapproval of the Gilded Age.

Musicians and songwriters, who explored the realities of everyday life, also flourished in the Gilded Age. A section of New York City, which would eventually be named **Tin Pan Alley**, became the center of the music publishing industry and the name of the style of popular music developed there. These music publishers provided sheet music that Americans throughout the country could enjoy in their homes. Ragtime, a forerunner to jazz music, was also gaining popularity. Developed by African Americans, ragtime was upbeat and highly rhythmic, which some people found disturbing.

The vitality of city life also inspired graphic artists. Philadelphia's Thomas Eakins painted a larger-than-life illustration of a medical operation, complete with exposed flesh. Painter Robert Henri and his associates developed a style of painting known as the Ashcan School that dramatized the starkness and squalor of New York City slums and street life.

>> African American children had new opportunities as students in the Gilded Age. However, they were taught in segregated classrooms with resources that lagged behind those available to white children.

>> Amusement parks attracted large crowds. **Compare** How do you think today's amusement parks compare to those of the Gilded Age?

BOUNCE to Activate Gallery

The Growth of Public Schools Newspapers and literature flourished, in part, because more Americans could read. Public education expanded rapidly. Slowly in the South and rapidly in the North, grade-school education became compulsory. Many locales provided public high schools, although only a small percentage of young people attended. In 1870, the nation had only a few hundred high schools; in 1910, there were more than 5,000. Kindergartens also appeared as a way to help working-class mothers. As a result, the literacy rate climbed to nearly 90 percent by 1900.

Schools taught courses in science, woodworking, and drafting, providing skills that workers needed in budding industries. The curriculum also included civics and business training. Urban leaders counted on schools to help Americanize immigrants, teaching them English and shaping them into good citizens.

Teacher-training schools responded to the call. Not only did they grow in number, but they also developed more sophisticated ideas about teaching and learning. Reformer John Dewey sought to enhance student learning by introducing new teaching methods.

Institutions of higher education also began to provide specialized training for urban careers. Today's liberal arts curriculum was largely designed during this era. A few of the new careers—teaching, social work, and nursing—were open to middle-class women. This led to an upsurge in women's colleges, since women were barred from many men's colleges. However, many state universities began to accept women into their classes.

Limited access to white institutions led to a growth in schools and colleges for African Americans. Across the South, the number of normal schools, agricultural colleges, and industrial-training schools mushroomed as the children of newly freed slaves set out to prepare to compete as free people.

☑ **IDENTIFY SUPPORTING DETAILS** What details can you use to identify the changes in mass culture that occurred in the late nineteenth century?

A Boom in Popular Entertainment

Urban areas with thousands of people became centers for new types of entertainment in the Gilded Age. Clubs, music halls, and sports venues attracted large crowds with time and money to spend. The middle class began to take vacations at this time, while the working classes looked for opportunities to escape from the busy city, even if just for a day.

Amusement Parks Attract City Dwellers In 1884, Lamarcus Thompson opened the world's first roller coaster. At ten cents a ride, Thompson averaged more than $600 per day in income. The roller coaster was the first ride to open at Coney Island—the nation's best-known amusement park—at the edge of the Atlantic Ocean in New York City. Soon, Coney Island added a hotel and a horseracing track. Similar amusement parks, located within easy reach of a city, were built around the country.

While earlier generations had enjoyed a picnic in the park, the new urbanite—even those with limited means—willingly paid the entry fees for these new, more thrilling, entertainments. Urban residents of all ethnicities and races could be found at these amusement spots, though each group was usually relegated to a particular area of the parks. The parks represented a daylong vacation for city laborers who could not afford to take the long seaside vacations enjoyed by the wealthy.

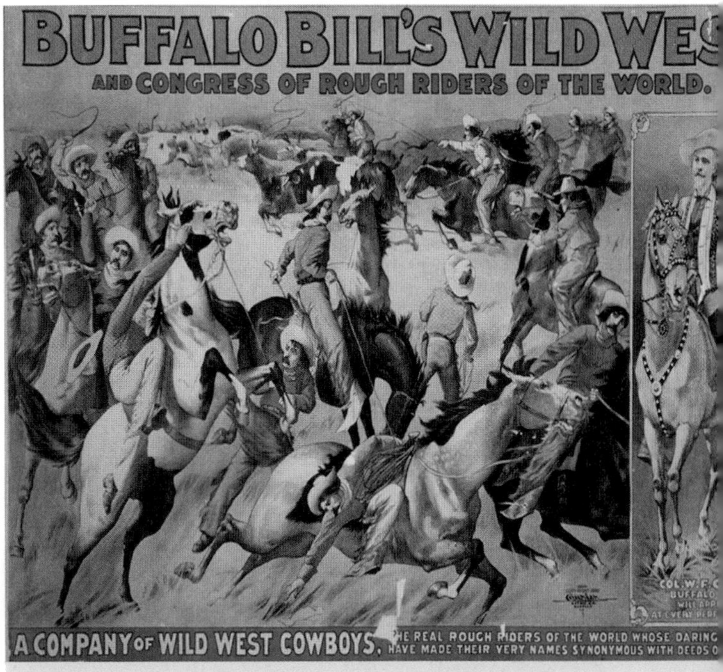

>> Buffalo Bill's Wild West Show was a popular outdoor show in the late nineteenth century.

Audiences Flock to Outdoor Events In 1883, "Buffalo Bill" Cody threw a Fourth of July celebration near his ranch in Nebraska. He offered prizes for competitions in riding, roping, and shooting. So many people attended that Cody took his show on the road, booking performances at points along railroad lines. Buffalo Bill's Wild West Show toured America and Europe, shaping the world's romantic notion of the American West. The show included markswoman Annie Oakley and the Sioux leader Sitting Bull, as well as displays of riding, roping, and horse-and-rider stunts.

Religious-inspired entertainment also grew in popularity. The Chautauqua Circuit, a kind of summer camp that opened in 1874, sponsored lectures and entertainment along New York's Chautauqua Lake. It began as a summer school for Methodist Sunday school teachers but soon became—and remains today—something of a cross between community college and a country fair, with lectures on intellectual subjects, music, exotic food, and crowd-pleasing special attractions. Soon, Chautauqua leaders were transporting their tents to small towns all across America to deliver comic storytelling, bands and singers, and lectures on politics or morals. A family might stay at a camp for as long as two weeks. Many people saw their first "moving pictures," or movies, in a Chautauqua tent. Theodore Roosevelt called Chautauqua "the most American thing in America."

New Forms of Urban Entertainment Cities, with their dense populations, offered many glitzy shows and various types of entertainment. At first, **vaudeville** shows were a medley of musical drama, songs, and off-color comedy. In 1881, an entrepreneur named Tony Pastor opened a theater in New York, aiming to provide families with a "straight, clean variety show." By 1900, a few companies owned chains of vaudeville theaters, stretching all across the country.

Performance theater was not the only option. Movie theaters, called nickelodeons, soon introduced motion pictures, charging a nickel for admission. Films such as *The Great Train Robbery* became wildly popular. In music halls, ragtime bands created a style of music that would later evolve into jazz.

Some cities—including Philadelphia, Chicago, Atlanta, Buffalo, and Omaha—hosted exhibitions of new technology and entertainment. These extravaganzas stretched Americans' imaginations to see a future filled with machines and gadgets and other technological innovations that would continue to improve their lives. Millions of visitors saw everything from steam engines to typewriters and telephones. In many ways, the new amusements mirrored urban life, filled with variety, drama, bright colors, and a very fast pace.

>> Pitcher Cy Young won 511 games over his career and helped the Boston Red Sox win the 1903 World Series.

Organized Sports Attract New Fans Baseball—America's national sport—had been around for a number of years before the National League organized it into a business in 1876. After that, baseball soon became a public show. Major cities built stadiums that seated thousands, like Boston's Fenway Park. Stadium billboards advertising everything from other sports to toothpaste and patent medicines helped pay for the extravaganza. There were even baseball songs. The most famous—*Take Me Out to the Ball Game*—was written in 1908. Until 1887, teams sometimes included African American players. After the Chicago White Stockings refused to play against a team that had a Black player, separate African American teams emerged by 1900.

Like baseball, horse racing, bicycle racing, boxing, and football became popular spectator sports. University football clubs formed on campuses around the country, but they faced a public outcry at the violence of the game. Rule changes made it into the sport we know today. Meanwhile, James Naismith invented basketball at the Springfield, Massachusetts, YMCA in 1891. Heroes emerged in major sports, particularly in boxing, as immigrants and ethnic Americans rooted for the boxers who shared their background.

☑ **CHECK UNDERSTANDING** Identify changes that redefined popular entertainment in the late nineteenth century.

☑ ASSESSMENT

1. **Infer** Why was Mark Twain so cynical about American society in the 1870s that he called this period "the Gilded Age?"
2. **Identify Central Issues** How did the middle-class life change during the Victorian Era?
3. **Cite Evidence** What evidence can you cite to support the idea that the growth of the newspaper industry is related to increasing public school attendance?
4. **Generate Explanations** What factors led to the increase in the number of colleges and universities during the Gilded Age?
5. **Identify Cause and Effect** Why were amusement parks so successful during the Gilded Age?
6. **Connections to Today** Urbanization led to changes in popular culture in the late 1800s and early 1900s. How has technology affected today's popular culture?

Connections to Today

San Francisco has been an important destination for Chinese and other Asian immigrants for more than a century. This photograph shows the city's famous Chinatown neighborhood.

Take Action by Learning About Immigration

You learned that immigration had an enormous impact on the nation during the late 1800s and early 1900s. Immigrants still come to the United States from all over the world today. Debates about immigration loom large in our political conversation.

1. **Choose** one of the following topics:
    - The origins of immigrants: Conduct research to identify the top three countries of origin for immigrants to the United States and to your state specifically.
    - Contributions of immigrants: Research an immigrant who has made an important contribution in a field that interests you, such as technology or the arts.
    - Numbers of immigrants: Use census data to find the number of immigrants who live in your community today, and to discover how that number has changed over time.
2. **Ask Questions** Generate a list of questions you have about the topic.
3. **Learn** about the topic and major issues related to it. Are there any major debates related to the topic or issues? What are the strongest arguments on each side?
4. **Present Information** Prepare a presentation informing viewers in your community about the topic you researched. Make sure to summarize your key findings in a clear way. Include photos, charts, or graphs with key data to engage your audience.

Topic 9 Quick Study Guide

LESSON SUMMARIES

Use these Lesson Summaries, and the longer versions available online, to review the key ideas for each lesson in this Topic.

Lesson 1: Innovation Boosts Growth

After the Civil War, industrialization transformed American life. Mass production helped the United States' economic growth, while the nation's factories attracted immigrant workers. Government encouraged the success of businesses and capitalism flourished. But while industry boomed in some parts of the United States, the South grew more slowly. In the North, workers began forming labor unions.

Lesson 2: Big Business Rises

Investors developed a form of group ownership known as a corporation. Corporations worked to maximize profits in several ways. Although many believed business leaders benefited the nation's economy, others persuaded the federal government to limit the power of big business with the Sherman Antitrust Act of 1890.

Lesson 3: The Organized Labor Movement

As industries grew, conflict developed between workers and employers. Many activists were influenced by socialism, which favors public, instead of private, control of property. Labor unions seeking better wages, working hours, and conditions began organizing massive protests and strikes, which often led to violence. After the Pullman Strike of 1894, the federal government supported businesses over labor.

Lesson 4: The New Immigrants

The 1870s saw a surge in immigration from southern and eastern Europe. Many of the new immigrants were fleeing famine, war and persecution and were drawn to America's economic opportunities and religious freedom. Although they helped fuel industrial growth, they faced hostility by native-born Americans and anti-immigrant laws passed by Congress.

Lesson 5: A Nation of Cities

In the late 1800s, American cities grew dramatically, due to migration from rural areas and immigration from abroad. New technologies introduced new means of transportation and taller buildings. Problems of overcrowding, poor sanitation and crime developed, forcing wealthier people to move to the suburbs and encouraging city planning.

Lesson 6: New Ways of Life

As Americans grew wealthier, consumerism increased. Department stores sold goods at fair prices. Advertising and communication helped create a mass culture of new products and entertainment. Public education expanded and helped raise literacy, while newspapers and magazines increased sales.

QUEST! FINDINGS

Hold your Civic Discussion Refer to your responses to the Quest Connections to help you participate in a civic discussion. Use the rubric and other Quest resources online to guide your work.

GO ONLINE to access lesson summaries

VISUAL REVIEW

Use these graphics to review some of the key terms, people, and ideas from this Topic.

Cities Change in the late 1800s

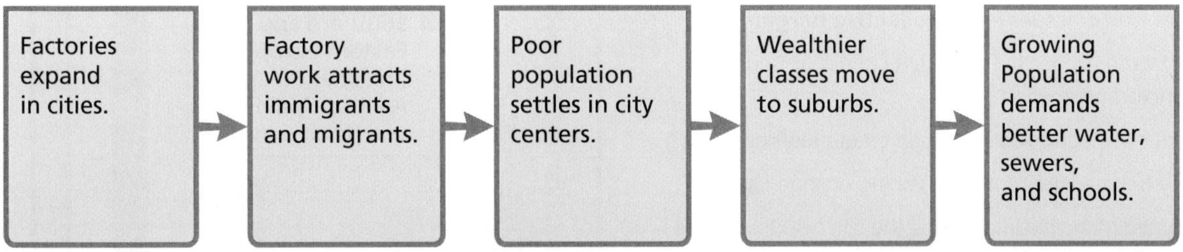

America's Second Industrial Revolution

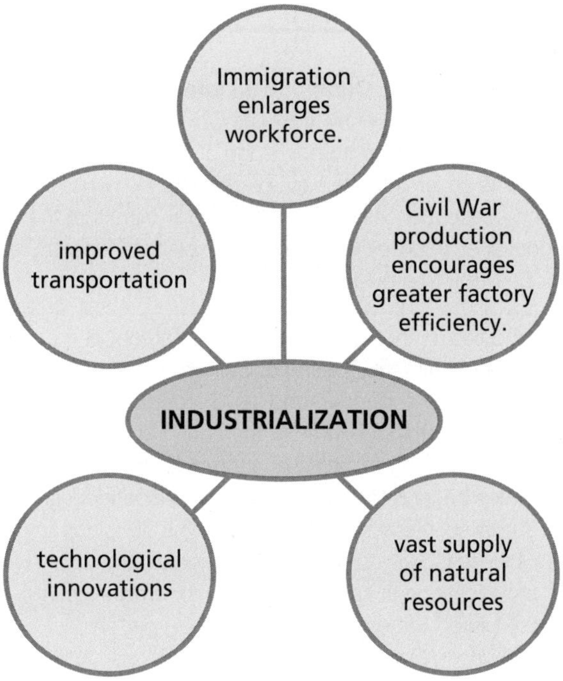

Causes of Increased Immigration in Late 1800s

PUSH FACTORS	PULL FACTORS
Famine, land reform, and low crop prices in Mexico, Poland, and China	Economic Opportunity; availability of cheap land
War and Political Conflict in China Eastern Europe, and Cuba	Peaceful, orderly and democratic political system in U.S.
Religious Persecution: Russian and Eastern European Jews flee homelands.	Religious freedom

Topic 9 Assessment

KEY TERMS, PEOPLE, AND IDEAS

1. How did **laissez-faire** government policies encourage growth?
2. How did **Thomas Edison** transform American life?
3. What are some features of a **corporation**?
4. What kind of issues led to **collective bargaining**?
5. Why were American Protestants afraid of increased Catholic immigration?
6. What new technologies helped create **skyscrapers**?
7. How did the introduction of zoning change cities?
8. Why did Mark Twain describe the late 1800s as **"the Gilded Age"**?
9. Which businessmen were responsible for the establishment of department stores?

CRITICAL THINKING

10. **Compare and Contrast** How did the experience of Asian immigrants in the West differ from that of European immigrants in the East?
11. **Cite Evidence** (a) Was the labor movement inevitable? (b) Explain your answer.
12. **Identify Cause and Effect** How did the United States change as it shifted from an agrarian to an industrial society?
13. **Compare and Contrast** (a) Compare the resources essential to the first and second Industrial Revolutions in the United States. (b) What effect did the second Industrial Revolution have on Americans' lives?
14. **Summarize** How did American farmers respond to new challenges in the mid to late 1800s?
15. **Draw Conclusions** How did the art of the Gilded Age reflect society?
16. **Analyze Graphs** Look at the bar graph that follows. What does the graph reveal? Then use a graphing calculator to help you change the bar graph into a line graph.

Immigration from Europe, 1890–1910

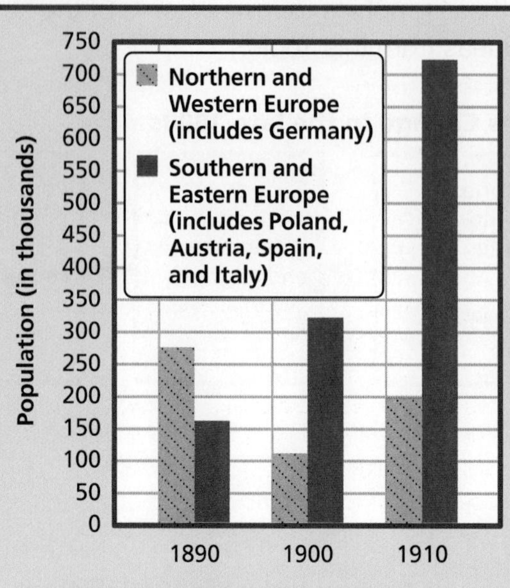

SOURCE: U.S. Census Bureau

17. **Writing Activity: Compose an Informative Essay** Use the excerpt below from The Chinese Exclusion Act of 1882 and your knowledge of immigration history to write an informative essay explaining the causes and consequences of this law. Keep in mind that the goal of an informative essay is to explain an idea or topic—not to provide an opinion

> Whereas, in the opinion of the Government of the United States the coming of Chinese laborers to this country endangers the good order of certain localities within the territory thereof: Therefore, . . . the coming of Chinese laborers to the United States be, and the same is hereby, suspended; and during such suspension it shall not be lawful for any Chinese laborer to come, or having so come after the expiration of said ninety days, to remain within the United States.
> —*Chinese Exclusion Act, 1882*

18. **Connections to Today** Immigration is a divisive political topic today. It can inspire passionate feelings on all sides. What issues related to immigration do you think are the most hotly debated? Do you think there is room for compromise? Explain your answer.

DOCUMENT-BASED QUESTIONS

Read the documents below, then answer the questions that follow.

DOCUMENT A

This excerpt is from a letter written by the president of the American Federation of Labor.

> There was a time when workmen were denied the right of leaving their employers, when they were part of the soil, owned by their employers. . . . Not many years ago, when workmen counseled with each other for the purpose of resisting a reduction in their wages or making an effort to secure an increase, it was held to be a conspiracy punishable by imprisonment. Through the effort of organized labor, an enlightened public sentiment changed all this until to-day the right to unite for material, moral, and social improvement on the part of workers is accepted by all.
>
> —*Samuel Gompers to Editor, Washington Evening Star, May 15, 1900*

DOCUMENT B

This political cartoon, titled "The Protectors of Our Industries" appeared in 1883.

DOCUMENT C

This excerpt from Andrew Carnegie's autobiography records a dispute between workers and management.

> Gentlemen of the Blast Furnace Committee, you have threatened our firm that you will break your agreement and that you will leave these blast furnaces . . . unless you get a favorable answer to your threat by four o'clock today. It is not three but your answer is ready. You may leave the blast furnaces. . . . The worst day that labor has ever seen in this world is that day in which it dishonors itself by breaking its agreement. You have your answer.
>
> —*The Autobiography of Andrew Carnegie August 1920*

DOCUMENT D

This article, condemning the actions of a miners' union, was published in 1902.

> I am not exaggerating when I say that since the concessions demanded in 1900 were granted the management of the vast industries centered in the anthracite districts has been hampered by a condition which can only be termed anarchy. An example of the course pursued by the labor agitators is the mandate issue by the United Mine Workers, that no member thereof should work with a non-union man. The United Mine Workers have been endeavoring to enforce that order on our property and the properties of all other coal operators whom I have seen. I know of workmen, on our own property and on others, who assert that they cannot possibly do an honest day's work if they comply with the existing regulations of the United Mine Workers.
>
> —*John Markle, Collier's Weekly 1902*

19. Document A suggests that by 1900,
- **A.** slow unions were weak and discredited.
- **B.** the courts had destroyed union power.
- **C.** labor had won the right to organize.
- **D.** collective bargaining was not working.

20. Analyze Political Cartoons Document B criticizes
- **A.** unions that interfere with productivity.
- **B.** business leaders who exploit their workers.
- **C.** government officials who oppose unions.
- **D.** the tension between unions and management.

21. In Document C, what is Carnegie's view of organized labor?
- **A.** Businesses should bargain with employees.
- **B.** Workers should be paid fair wages.
- **C.** Employees should honor work agreements.
- **D.** Labor should have the right to strike.

22. In Document D, the writer describes unions as
- **A.** anarchists and bullies.
- **B.** defenders of workers' interests.
- **C.** reasonable and moderate.
- **D.** effective and powerful.

23. Writing Tasks Write a paragraph explaining which side you would have supported in the labor conflicts of this time. Use the sources as well as additional information you have learned.

GO ONLINE to access more practice

Topic 10

Challenges in the Late 1800s (1865–1900)

ESSENTIAL QUESTION What are the challenges of diversity?

GO ONLINE to access the eText, videos, Interactive Primary Sources, Biographies, and other online resources.

A crowd watches the completion of the transcontinental railroad.

Connections to Today

Imagine future travelers in California boarding a clean energy high-speed rail and riding 380 miles between Los Angeles and San Francisco in under three hours, instead of the 12 hours it takes today. It's a challenging project and to succeed must surmount many social, political, and economic roadblocks.

In this topic, you will learn about another huge transportation project. In 1869, the transcontinental railroad achieved its goal and succeeded in making travel from the Atlantic to the Pacific coast faster than ever. How did it happen?

NBC LEARN

Learn about the Lakota Sioux in the late 1800s.

BOUNCE to Activate My Story Video

Topic 10 Overview

In this Topic, you'll learn about the challenges that Americans faced in the late 1800s. Look at the lesson outline and explore the timeline. As you study this Topic, you'll complete the Quest Inquiry.

LESSON OUTLINE

10.1 American Indians Under Pressure

10.2 The West is Transformed

10.3 Corruption Plagues the Nation

10.4 Farm Issues and Populism

Key Events of Challenges in the Late 1800s

1869
Transcontinental railroad connects East and West

1876
Sioux defeat U.S. troops in Battle of Little Bighorn

1883
Civil Service Commission is established

1887
Dawes Act breaks up Indian reservations

1892
The Populist Party forms

1893
Economic depression begins

1865 — 1875 — 1885 — 1895

QUEST! INQUIRY

Creating a Layered Map of the American West

What was life like in the American West of the late 1800s? In this Quest you'll investigate the political, social, and economic aspects of the West in this period and then create a layered map to display your findings.

STEP 1

With your group, research either a set of states or a group of layers in the Information Organizer. Prepare to investigate by breaking down the Guiding Question into smaller questions.

STEP 2

Identify which themes or human characteristics, your group will show on the map. Gather information and decide how to present this information on the map.

STEP 3

Create the map layers and review the final map. With your group, come up with a list of questions and answers on the information you can identify in the databases and map layers.

STEP 4

Present your layered map to an audience. Reflect on what you have learned and how your group worked together as a team.

GO ONLINE to access complete Quest materials

10.1

Two Ogala chiefs, American Horse (left) and Red Cloud (right) led the resistance against the government's plans to build a road through Sioux hunting grounds.

BOUNCE to Activate Flipped Video

Objectives

Compare the ways American Indians and white settlers viewed and used the land.

Describe the conflicts between white settlers and Indians.

Analyze the impact of the Indian Wars.

Evaluate the effectiveness of the government's Americanization and reservation policies towards American Indians.

Key Terms

reservations
Sand Creek Massacre
Sitting Bull
Battle of the Little Big Horn
Chief Joseph
Wounded Knee
assimilated
Dawes General Allotment Act

American Indians Under Pressure

In 1787, the Constitution granted sole power for regulating trade with the American Indians to Congress. Then, Congress made treaties with American Indian nations to force the nations from their homelands. During the 1830s, the federal government forced American Indians from the east to resettle west of the Mississippi River and promised them the land there forever. In the 1840s through the 1860s, pressure from white settlers weakened this promise. The conflicts between settlers and American Indians continued during and after the Civil War. The interaction changed both cultures, but irrevocably damaged American Indian cultures.

Cultures Forced to Adapt

By the end of the Civil War, most American Indians—about 250,000 of them—lived in the region west of the Mississippi River referred to as "The Great American Desert." Although they were lumped together in the minds of most Americans as "Indians," American Indians embraced many different belief systems, languages, and ways of life.

Cultural Similarities and Differences Geography influenced the cultural diversity of American Indians. In the Pacific Northwest, the Klamaths, Chinooks, and Shastas benefited from abundant supplies of fish and forest animals. Farther south, smaller bands of hunter-gatherers struggled to exist on diets of small game, insects, berries, acorns, and roots. In the arid lands of New Mexico and Arizona, the Pueblos irrigated the land to grow corn, beans, and squash. They built adobe homes high in the cliffs to protect themselves from aggressive neighbors. The more mobile Navajos lived in homes made of mud or in hogans that could be moved easily.

GO ONLINE to access your digital course

The most numerous American Indians were the Plains Indians, including the Sioux, Blackfeet, Crows, Cheyenne, and Comanches. Some of these groups included Indians from east of the Appalachians, who had blended into the Plains Indian groups. The Plains Indians were expert horsemen and hunters. The millions of buffalo that roamed the Plains provided a rich source for lodging, clothing, food, and tools.

In general, Indian cultures respected the natural world and the resources that the land provided. Many white people valued and respected the land, too. However, many whites also viewed the land as a resource that could be used to produce wealth. These differing views sowed the seeds of conflict.

American Settlers Move West In the early 1800s, the government carried out a policy of moving American Indians out of the way of white settlers.

President Jackson moved the Cherokees off their land in Georgia and onto the Great Plains. To white settlers, American Indians were welcome to what they called the Great American Desert as they thought it was uninhabitable. To limit conflict, an 1834 law regulated trade relations with Indians and strictly limited the access of white people to this Indian Territory. New European-American settlement generally paused at the eastern rim of the territory and resumed in the Far West.

By the 1850s, however, federal policy toward American Indians was again challenged: gold and silver had been discovered in Indian Territory as well as settled regions farther west. Americans also wanted a railroad that crossed the continent. In 1851, therefore, the federal government began to restrict Indians to smaller areas. By the late 1860s, many Indian peoples lived on **reservations**, specific areas set aside by the government for the Indians' use. This change in their demographic patterns, a direct result of being forced to migrate to reservations, made their previous ways of life difficult if not impossible to sustain. Indians often faced poverty and the loss of their traditional ways of life on reservations.

Two more developments also threatened American Indian civilizations: White settlers introduced diseases to which Indians had no immunity, and the vitally important buffalo herds were destroyed. In the 1870s, hunters would kill hundreds of buffaloes in a single day for their hides. They skinned the animals and left the meat to rot. In addition, trainloads of tourists arrived to kill buffaloes purely for sport. They left both the meat and the valuable hides behind.

☑ **IDENTIFY SUPPORTING DETAILS** How were American Indian cultures threatened in the 1800s?

American Indian Land Loss, Pre-1850–1890

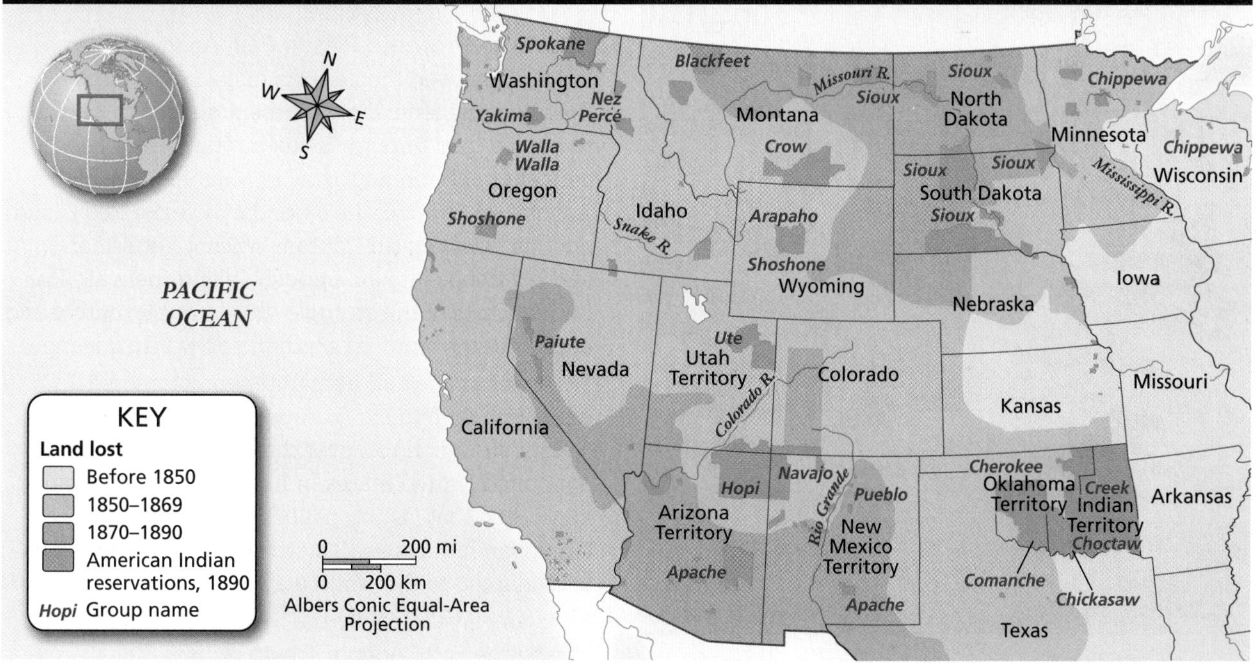

>> The U.S. government relocated many American Indian groups following the Civil War.
Analyze Maps Describe the process of how American Indians lost their land.

Settlers and American Indians Collide

The rapid industrial development and economic expansion that followed the Civil War set American Indians and white settlers on a path to conflict. Advances in communication and transportation that supported industrial growth also reinforced white Americans' faith in manifest destiny. Horace Greeley, editor of the New York Tribune, encouraged the poor to move west.

> If you strike off into the broad, free West, and make yourself a farm from Uncle Sam's generous domain, you will crowd nobody, starve nobody, and neither you nor your children need evermore beg. . . .
>
> —New York Tribune, February 5, 1867

Greeley, and many others, ignored the fact that American Indians inhabited half of the area of the United States. Indians often fought to retain or regain whatever they could.

>> The Cheyenne and Arapaho Indians gathered at Sand Creek on November 29, 1864. Many women and children died in the massacre.

Conflict Throughout the Plains In 1862, while the Civil War raged in the East, a group of Sioux Indians resisted threats to their land rights by attacking European-American settlements in eastern Minnesota. In several attacks, the Sioux killed more than 400 settlers, including many women and children. In response, the government waged a full-scale war against the Sioux, who then were pushed west into the Dakotas.

The Sioux rebellion sparked a series of attacks on settlements and stagecoach lines as other Plains Indians also saw their way of life slipping away. Each battle took its toll, raising the level of distrust on all sides. In the fall of 1864, a band of Colorado militia under commanding officer John Chivington came upon a camp of Cheyenne and Arapaho Indians near Fort Lyons at Sand Creek. The fort's commander had given the Cheyenne leader permission to stay there temporarily. Chivington's troops opened fire, killing between 150 to 200 Cheyenne and Arapaho men, women, and children.

The incident became known as the **Sand Creek Massacre**. It spawned another round of warfare as Plains Indians joined forces to repel white settlement.

Once the Civil War ended, regiments of Union troops—both white and African American—were sent to the West to bring peace to the Plains. Recruitment posters for volunteer cavalry promised that soldiers could claim any "horses or other plunder" taken from the Indians. The federal government asserted that the troops were needed to maintain order.

Efforts to Promote Peace Fail As the Plains Indians renewed their efforts to hold onto what they had, the federal government announced plans to build a road through Sioux hunting grounds to connect gold-mining towns in Montana. Hostilities intensified. In 1866, the legendary warrior Red Cloud and his followers led Captain William Fetterman and his troops into an ambush, killing them all. The human costs of the struggle drew a public outcry and called the government's Indian policy into question.

As reformers and humanitarians promoted education for Indians, European-American settlers sought strict controls over them. The government-appointed United States Indian Peace Commission concluded that lasting peace would come only if American Indians settled on farms and reservations and adapted to the white way of life.

In an effort to pacify the Sioux, the government offered the Fort Laramie Treaty of 1868. The government agreed not to build the road through Sioux territory and to abandon three forts. The treaty

American Indian Wars, 1860–1890

>> **Analyze Maps** What do the locations of the clashes between American Indians and the U.S. government suggest about westward expansion?

BOUNCE to Activate Map

included the Black Hills in the Sioux reservation, and it also promised a school and other communal buildings. The Sioux and other Indians who signed the treaty agreed to live on a reservation under federal supervision with support from the federal government.

This type of promise of government support to American Indians was part of many agreements between the government and American Indian groups who were going onto reservations in various parts of the West.

The Bureau of Indian Affairs, established in 1824, handled affairs between American Indians and the government. The agency appointed an agent who was responsible for distributing land and adequate supplies to anyone willing to farm as well as for maintaining peaceful relations between a reservation and its neighbors.

The government's plans and policies for peace did not always work out, however. Most American Indians were disappointed with the reservations on which they were living and had little trust that the government would keep its promises. Chief Piapot, an Indian leader in Canada facing a similar situation with the government there, offered his viewpoint:

> In order to become sole masters of our land they relegated us to small reservations as big as my hand and make us long promises, as long as my arm; but the next year the promises were shorter and got shorter every year until now they are the length of my finger, and they keep only half of that.
>
> —Chief Piapot, 1895

Unfortunately, in the United States, many Indian agents were unscrupulous and stole funds and resources that were supposed to be distributed to the Indians. Even the most well-meaning agents often lacked support from the federal government or the military to enforce the terms of the treaties that were beneficial to American Indians. Not unexpectedly, some Indians refused to live under such conditions.

CHECK UNDERSTANDING Why did tensions exist between settlers and American Indians?

The Indian Wars Conclude

The conditions facing American Indians had all the ingredients for tragedy. Indians were confined to isolated areas, which were regularly ravaged by poverty and disease. The government, intentionally or not, failed to live up to many of the promises made to various groups of American Indians. Frustration, particularly among young warriors, turned to violence. Guns replaced treaties as the government defeated American Indians who were openly rebelling.

>> These Navajo Indians were forced to relocate from the lands they knew and relegated to the Bosque Redondo reservation in present-day Arizona and eastern New Mexico.

The Long Walk of the Navajos In 1863 the government sent the famous frontiersman Kit Carson to subdue the Navajos, who were fighting to protect their southwestern homeland. After Carson's forces destroyed their homes, crops, and livestock, about two thirds of the 12,000 Navajos surrendered in 1864. Carson then sent them on a 300-mile forced march, known as the Long Walk, to a reservation in what is now eastern New Mexico.

The poor soil on the small reservation was not suited to the kinds of agriculture the Navajos practiced. In addition, they were forced to live alongside their Apache enemies. Finally, after four years of death, disease, and starvation, the government relented. The surviving Navajos were allowed to return to a new reservation in their homeland.

>> The Plains Indians fought the Red River War to protect their tradition of buffalo hunting. Here, braves leave camp to hunt buffalo.

The Southern Plains Indians Surrender The Red River War, a series of major and minor incidents, led to the final defeat of the powerful southern Plains Indians, including the Kiowas and Comanches. It marked the end of the southern buffalo herds and the opening of the western panhandle of Texas to white settlement. At the heart of the matter was the failure of the United States government to abide by and enforce the terms of the 1867 Treaty of Medicine Lodge. White buffalo hunters were not kept off Indian hunting grounds, food and supplies from the government were not delivered, and white lawlessness was not punished. Hostilities began with an attack by Indians led by Comanche Chief Quanah Parker on a group of Texans near the Red River in June 1874. Hostilities ended a year later, after the last Comanche holdouts surrendered to U.S. troops.

Battle of the Little Big Horn It was the lure of gold that led to the defeat of the Indians on the northern Plains. The Black Hills Gold Rush of 1875 drew prospectors onto Sioux hunting grounds in the

Dakotas and neighboring Montana. Some of this area was supposed to be protected by the 1868 Treaty of Fort Laramie. When the Sioux, led by chiefs Crazy Horse and **Sitting Bull**, assembled to drive them out, the U.S. Army sent its own troops against the American Indians.

In June 1876, a colonel named George Custer rushed ahead of the other columns of the U.S. cavalry and arrived a day ahead of the main force. Near the Little Bighorn River, in present-day Montana, Custer and his force of about 250 men unexpectedly came upon a group of at least 2,000 Indians. Crazy Horse led the charge at what became known as the **Battle of the Little Big Horn**, killing Custer and all of his men.

Cries for revenge motivated army forces to track down the Indians. Sitting Bull and a small group of followers escaped to Canada. Crazy Horse and his followers surrendered, beaten by weather and starvation. By then, their will and the means to wage major resistance had been crushed.

>> Sitting Bull was a famed fighter and Hunkpapa war chief. By the late 1860s, his reputation was so great that the Lakota Sioux chose him as the first-ever chief of all seven Lakota tribes.

The Fighting Concludes Further West Farther west, in Idaho, another powerful drama played out. In 1877, the federal government decided to move the Nez Percés to a smaller reservation to make room for white settlers. Many of the Nez Percés were Christians and had settled down and become successful horse and cattle breeders. They had a great deal to lose.

Trying to evade U.S. troops who had come to enforce their relocation, the Nez Percés's leader **Chief Joseph** led a group of refugees on a trek of more than 1,300 miles to Canada. Stopped just short of the border, Chief Joseph surrendered with deeply felt words: "I will fight no more forever." Banished with his group to a barren reservation in Oklahoma, he later traveled twice to Washington, D.C., to unsuccessfully appeal for his people's return to their homeland.

>> A group portrait of a Sioux group by the Cheyenne River. Nearly all these men were killed in the battle at Wounded Knee.

Indian Resistance Comes to an End With the loss of many leaders and the destruction of their economy, American Indians' ability to resist diminished.

In response, many Indians welcomed a religious revival based on the Ghost Dance. Practitioners preached that the ritual would banish white settlers and restore the buffalo to the Plains. As the popularity of the movement spread, government officials became concerned about where it might lead.

In 1890, in an effort to curtail these activities, the government ordered the arrest of Sitting Bull.

> There is not among these three hundred bands of Indians one which has not suffered cruelly at the hands either of the Government or of white settlers. The poorer, the more insignificant, the more helpless the band, the more certain the cruelty and outrage to which they have been subjected . . . . It makes little difference where one opens the record of the history of the Indians; every page and every year has its dark stain . . . .
>
> —Helen Hunt Jackson, 1881

>> An American Indian family poses unhappily at the Warm Springs Reservation in Oregon, visual evidence of the discontent created by the policy of relocating Indians to reservations.

In the confrontation, he and several others were killed. In response, a group of Sioux left their reservation, hoping to hide out in the Badlands region. Troops then set out after the group of Indians as they fled. The cavalry finally caught up with them at Wounded Knee, in present-day South Dakota. Having been partially disarmed by U.S. troops, the Sioux were badly outgunned in the fight that followed. In the end, more than 100 men, women, and children died. The end of the Ghost Dance War at **Wounded Knee** also marked the end of major Indian resistance to white expansion and large-scale resistance to the Indian policies of the United States government.

☑ **LIST** What conflicts ended major Indian resistance?

The Government Encourages Assimilation

The reservation policy was a failure. Making Indians live in confined areas as wards of the government was costly in human and economic terms. Policy makers hoped that as the buffalo became extinct, Indians would become farmers and be **assimilated** into national life by adopting the culture and civilization of whites.

Critics Disagree with Indian Policies A few outspoken critics defended the Indians' way of life. In *A Century of Dishonor*, Helen Hunt Jackson decried the government's treatment of American Indians. Susette La Flesche, the granddaughter of a French trader and an Omaha Indian woman, also used her writing and lecturing talents to fight for recognition of the Indians and Indian rights in the courts. Born on the Omaha reservation in Nebraska, she studied in the East and returned to the reservation to teach.

The Americanization Movement In 1871, Congress had passed a law stating that "no Indian nation or tribe within the United States would be recognized as an independent nation, tribe, or power with whom the United States may contract by treaty." Indians were now to be dealt with as individuals. One reason for this change was to weaken American Indians' tribal cultures.

Reformers believed that Indians had to give up tribal loyalties and behaviors before they could adopt mainstream American values and assimilate into American society. The Americanization movement aimed at American Indians was also aimed at new immigrants from other countries.

One way reformers thought assimilation and Americanization could be accomplished was with the passage of the **Dawes General Allotment Act** (sometimes known as the Dawes Severalty Act) by Congress in 1887, which encouraged Indians to become private property owners and farmers. The Dawes Act ended the reservations' tribal landholding system. Each Indian family was allotted, or assigned, 160-acres of the tribe's reservation to own as a farmstead. The size of these allotments was based on the eastern experience of how much land was needed to support a family. In the arid West, however, the allotment was often not big enough.

To protect Indian landowners from unscrupulous land speculators, the Dawes Act specified that the land could not be sold or transferred from its original family for 25 years. Congress hoped that by the end of that time, younger Indians would embrace the values of farming and individual land ownership.

Traditional tribal feasts, dances, and even funeral practices were outlawed, and American Indian religions were discouraged. To further speed assimilation, missionaries and other reformers established boarding schools, to which Indian parents were pressured to send their children. There Indian children were to learn and live by the rules, dress, customs, and culture of white America. Ultimately, the struggle to retain their homelands, freedom, and culture proved tragic. Although many Indian peoples faced these challenges with courage and determination, tens of thousands died in war or on poverty-stricken reservations. Only a small number were left to carry on their legacy.

IDENTIFY MAIN IDEAS What was the main idea of the Americanization movement, and how did the Dawes Act promote that idea?

>> As their old way of life was taken from them, many American Indians were forced to assimilate into contemporary American life.

BOUNCE to Activate Timeline

ASSESSMENT

1. **Summarize** the reasons American Indian culture was irrevocably changed by the end of the 1800s.
2. **Compare and Contrast** how white settlers and American Indians viewed nature.
3. **Support a Point of View with Evidence** Determine why Chief Piapot asserted that the Canadian government "keep[s] only half" of the promises made to American Indians.
4. **Compare and Contrast** the relocations and outcomes for the Navajo and Nez Percés.
5. **Quest Connections** What lasting effects did life on reservations have on American Indian nations, including the efforts of the U.S. government to abolish their practices and beliefs?

10.2

A large gathering celebrates the 1869 completion of the Transcontinental Railroad. **Analyze Information** Why was the completion of the Transcontinental Railroad seen as a turning point in the history of the United States?

BOUNCE to Activate Flipped Video

Objectives

Analyze the impact of mining and railroads on the settlement of the West.

Explain the impact of physical and human geographic factors on the settlement of the Great Plains.

Analyze treatment of Chinese immigrants and Mexican Americans in the West.

Discuss the ways various groups used land in the West and conflicts among them.

Key Terms

vigilantes
Transcontinental Railroad
land grants
open-range system
Homestead Act
Exodusters
Las Gorras Blancas

The West Is Transformed

The West was swept by enormous change after the Civil War. As railroads increased access, settlers, ranchers, and miners permanently transformed millions of acres of western land. Mining was the first great boom in the West. Gold and silver were the magnets that attracted a vast number of people. Prospectors from the East were just a part of a flood that included people from all around the world.

Mining and the Growth of Railroads

Mining Towns Expand Across the West From the Sierra Nevada to the Black Hills, there was a similar pattern and tempo to the development of mining regions. First came the discovery of gold or silver.

Then, as word spread, people began to pour into areas such as Pikes Peak in Colorado and the Yukon river near what is now Alaska. During the Klondike Gold Rush, mining camps sprang up quickly to house the thousands of people who flooded the region near the Yukon river. They were followed by more substantial communities. Miners dreamed of finding riches quickly and easily. Others saw an opportunity to make their fortune by supplying the needs of miners for food, clothing, and supplies.

The rough-and-tumble environment of these communities called out for order. To limit violence and administer justice in areas without judges or jails, miners set up rules of conduct and procedures for settling disputes. In extreme situations,

GO ONLINE to access your digital course

self-appointed law enforcers known as **vigilantes** punished lawbreakers. As towns developed, they hired marshals and sheriffs, like Wyatt Earp and Bat Masterson, to keep the peace. Churches set up committees to address social problems.

Some mining towns—like Leadville, Colorado, and Nevada City, Montana—were "boomtowns." They thrived only as long as the gold and silver held out.

Even if a town had developed churches and schools, it might become a ghost town, abandoned when the precious metal disappeared. In contrast, Denver, Colorado; Boise, Idaho; and Helena, Montana, were among the cities that diversified and grew.

Mining Becomes Big Business The first western mining was done by individuals, who extracted the minerals from the surface soil or a stream bed. By the 1870s, the remaining mineral wealth was located deep underground. Big companies with the capital to buy mining equipment took over the industry. Machines drilled deep mine shafts. Tracks lined miles of underground tunnels. Crews—often recruited from Mexico and China—worked in dangerous conditions underground.

The arrival of the big mining companies highlighted an issue that would relentlessly plague the West: water and its uses. Large-scale mining required lots of water pumped under high pressure to help separate the precious metals from silt. As the silt washed down the mountains, it fouled water being used by farmers and their livestock.

Despite these concerns, the federal government continued to support large mining companies by providing inexpensive land and approving patents for new inventions. Mining wealth helped fuel the nation's industrial development.

The Transcontinental Railroad Impacts the Frontier As industry in the West grew, the need for a railroad to transport goods increased as well. The idea of a **transcontinental railroad**, a rail link between the East and the West, was not new. Arguments over the route it should take, however, had delayed implementation. While the Civil War kept the South out of the running, Congress finally took action.

Unlike Europe, where railroads were built and owned by governments, in the United States, not all railroads were built with government support; they were built by private enterprise. However, Congress encouraged construction of the transcontinental railroad in two ways: It provided money in the form of loans and made **land grants**, giving builders wide stretches of land, alternating on each side of the track route.

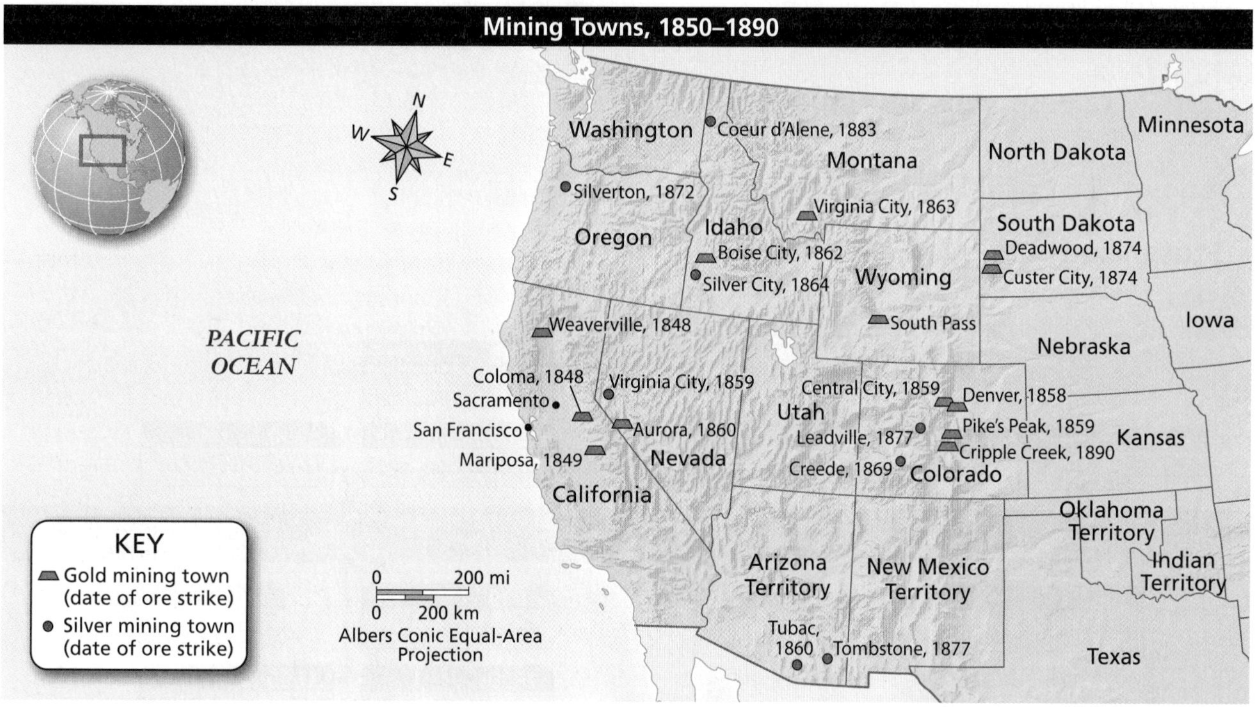

>> The hope of wealth from gold and silver drew many Americans west. **Analyze Maps** Where were the biggest gold mining regions? How do you think gold discoveries affected migration?

BOUNCE to Activate Chart

Simultaneously in 1863, the Central Pacific started laying track eastward from Sacramento, California, while the Union Pacific headed westward from Omaha, Nebraska. Construction proved to be both difficult and expensive.

The human cost of building the railroad was also high. Starved for labor, the Central Pacific Company brought recruits from China and set them to work under harsh contracts and with little regard for their safety. Inch by inch, they chipped and blasted their way through the granite-hard Sierra Nevada and Rockies. Meanwhile, working for the Union Pacific, crews of Irish immigrants crossed the level plains from the East. The two tracks eventually met at Promontory, Utah, in 1869, the same year that the Suez Canal was completed in Egypt. The continent and the world seemed to be shrinking in size.

Railroads Spur Settlement and Growth The completion of the Transcontinental Railroad inspired a flurry of similar railroad building. By 1883, the Northen Pacific Railroad had connected St. Paul, Minnesota, with Seattle in Washington Territory.

Ten years later, James J. Hill completed a competing railroad line between St. Paul and Everett, Washington. Hill and his business partners built the Great Northern Railway without any government support. His low fares drew thousands of immigrants and other Americans to migrate west and settle along his tracks. His success allowed him to eventually gain control of the Northern Pacific, too.

The effects of the railroads were far reaching. They tied the nation together, moved products and people, and spurred industrial development. They brought western meat and farm products to the tables of eastern consumers. In turn, goods manufactured in eastern factories moved west by train and improved the lives of settlers on the frontier. Once again, the application of technological innovation by the free enterprise system was clearly raising the standard of living in the United States.

The growth of railroads also stimulated the growth of towns and cities. Speculators vied for land in places where a new railroad might be built, and towns already in existence petitioned to become a stop on the western rail route. Railroads intensified the demand for Indians' land and brought white settlers who overwhelmed Mexican American communities in the Southwest. The economic impact of the transcontinental railroads helped lead to the closing of the frontier in the late nineteeth century. There was no turning back the tide as waves of pioneers moved west. The arrival of masses of new residents led to changes in political boundaries, as territories became states.

The addition of states to the Union exemplifies the West's growth. Requirements for statehood included a population of at least 60,000 inhabitants. Between 1864 and 1896, ten territories met those requirements and became states.

☑ **IDENTIFY SUPPORTING DETAILS** How did the railroads encourage economic growth in the West?

Statehood Achieved, 1864-1896

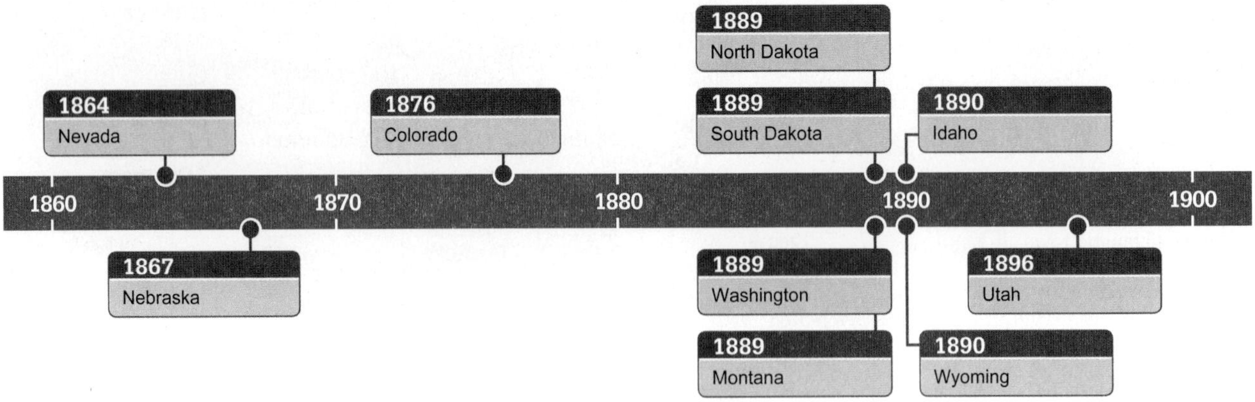

>> **Analyze Data** Based on the dates of admission in this timeline, during which decade did the most population growth in the West probably take place?

Land Use in the West

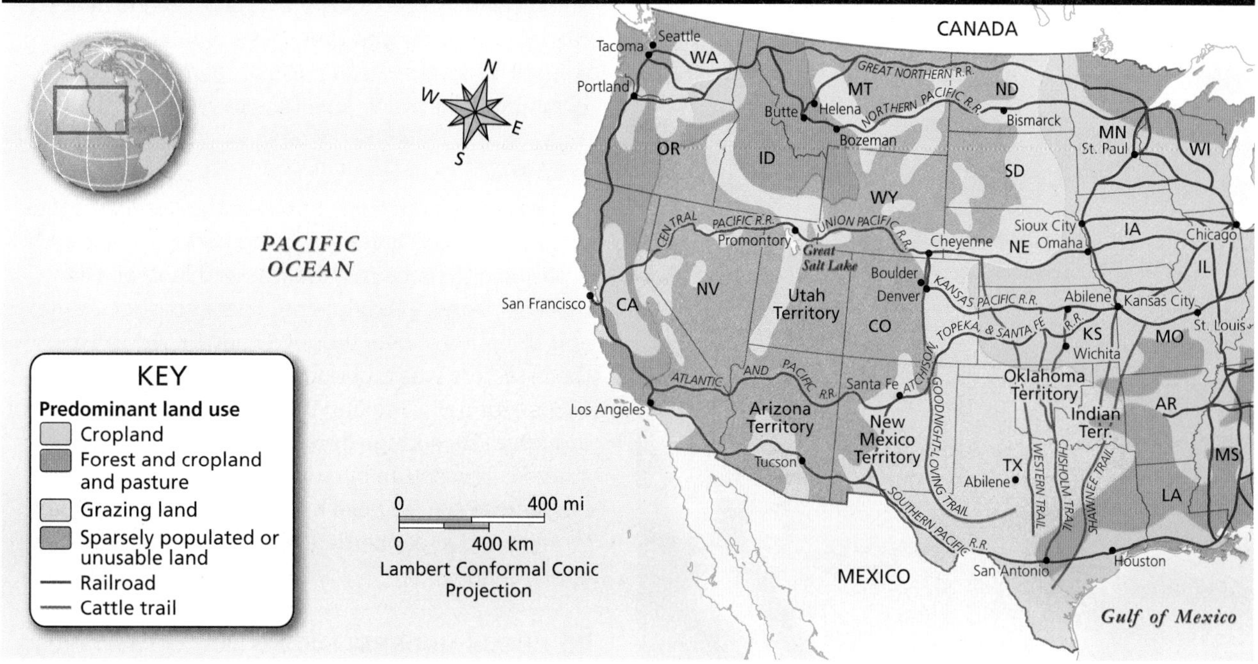

>> Ranching was an important economic activity throughout much of the West. **Analyze Maps** How might the physical geography of the West have affected where ranching most flourished?

The Cattle Industry Boom

Cattle ranching fueled another western boom. This was sparked by the vast acres of grass suitable for feeding herds of cattle. Once the railroad provided the means to move livestock to eastern markets, the race was on for land and water.

Longhorns and Vaqueros Long before the arrival of eastern settlers in the West, Mexicans in Texas had developed an efficient system for raising livestock. The Texas longhorn, which originated in Mexico, roamed freely and foraged for its own feed. Each owner marked—or "branded"—the cattle so they could be identified. Under this **open-range system**, property was not fenced in. Though ranchers claimed ownership and knew the boundaries of their property, cattle from any ranch grazed freely across those boundaries. When spring came, the ranchers would hire cowboys to comb thousands of acres of open range, "rounding up" cattle that had roamed all winter.

The culture of the cowboy owed its very existence to the Mexican vaqueros who had learned to train horses to work with cattle and had developed the roping skills, saddle, lariat, and chaps needed to do the job.

Cowboys and Cattle Drives Once the cattle were rounded up, cowboys began the long cattle drive to take the animals to a railroad that would transport them to eastern markets. The trek from Texas, Colorado, or Montana to the nearest junction on the transcontinental railroad could take weeks or even months.

The cowboys' work was hard, dangerous, low-paying, and lonely—often involving months of chasing cattle over the countryside. A band of cowboys often included a mix of white, Mexican, and African American men.

Cow Towns Cattle drives concluded in such railroad towns as Dodge City, Kansas, where the cattle were sold and the cowboys were paid. These "cow towns" gave rise to stories about colorful characters, often outlaws, such as Wild Bill Hickok, Doc Holliday, Wyatt Earp, and Jesse James. They were also the site of rodeos, competitions based on the cowboys' skills of riding, roping, and wrestling cattle. Bill Pickett, an African American cowboy, is credited with inventing bulldogging, in which a cowboy leaps from his horse onto a steer's horns and wrestles the steer to the ground.

>> Settlers on the relatively dry, treeless Great Plains used the available sod to build homes for their families.

BOUNCE to Activate 3D Model

>> African Americans welcome new migrants from the South to St. Louis. **Hypothesize** Why might the lands and opportunities of the Great Plains have been especially appealing to African Americans following the Civil War?

The Open Range Comes to a Close Open-range ranching flourished for more than a decade after the Civil War. During that time, several million cattle were driven from Texas north to railroad stops in Wyoming, Nebraska, and Kansas. However, by the mid-1880s, the heyday of open-range ranching came to an end.

Several factors contributed to the demise of the open range. The invention of barbed wire made it possible to fence in huge tracts of land on the treeless plains. The supply of beef exceeded demand, and the price of beef dropped sharply. Added to these factors was a period of extreme weather in the 1880s—brutally freezing winters followed by summer droughts. As springs dried up, herds of cattle starved. The nature of cattle ranching changed as ranchers began to raise hay to feed their stock, and farmers and sheepherders settled on what had been open range.

CHECK UNDERSTANDING How did the railroad affect the cattle industry?

Farmers Settle the Plains

The Great Plains were the last part of the country to be heavily settled by white people. The region was originally set aside for Indians because it was viewed as too dry for agriculture. Yet, with the coming of the transcontinental railroad, millions of farmers moved into the West in the last huge westward migration of European Americans in the mid to late 1800s.

The push-and-pull factors that encouraged settlement were varied. Like the miners and cattle ranchers, farmers were looking for a better life.

Railroads advertised land for sale, even sending agents to Europe to lure new immigrants, especially from Scandinavia. Other immigrants fled political upheavals in their native lands.

Westward Migration and Settlement Throughout its history, the nation's westward expansion had been marked by migrants settling on public land they did not own. These settlers, called "squatters," pressured the government to allow them to gain ownership of this land. In 1841, Congress passed the Preemption Act, giving squatters the right to buy up to 160 acres for $1.25 per acre before the land was offered for sale to other buyers. This law set the stage for the **Homestead Act**, passed in 1862. Under the Homestead Act, the government offered farm plots of 160 acres to anyone willing to live on the land for five years, dig a well, and build a road. These two laws

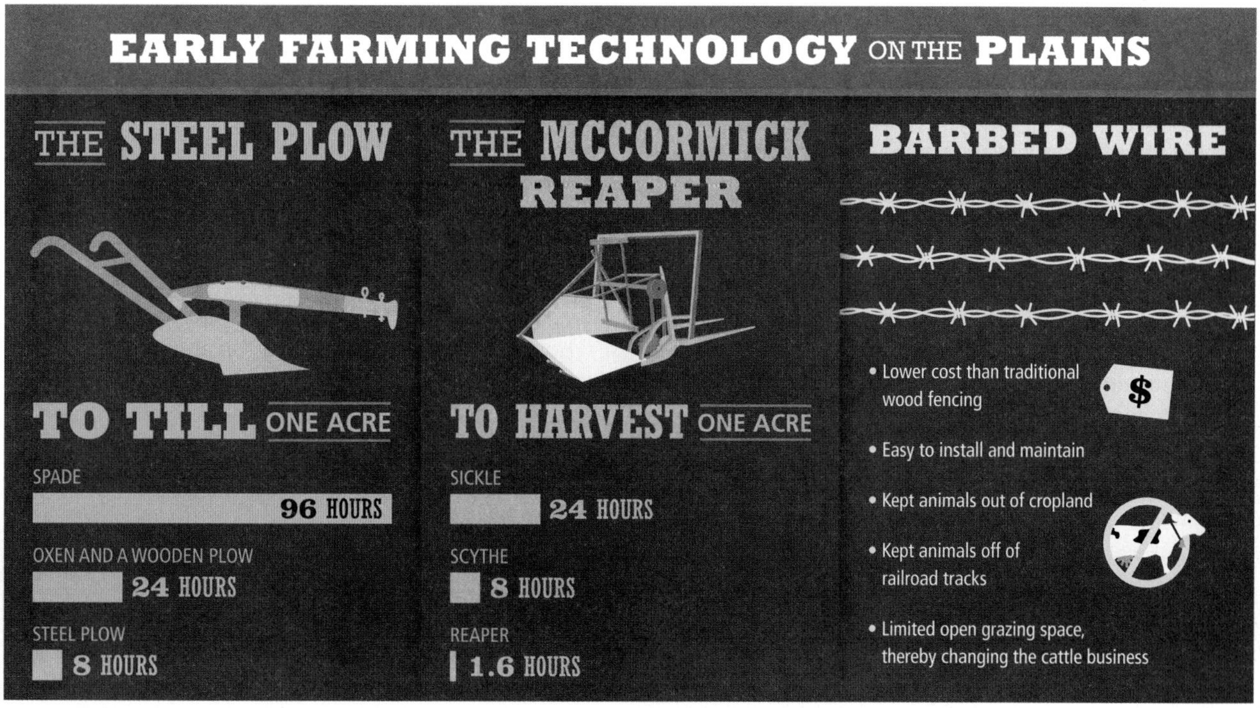

>> **Analyze Data** How did the growth of innovative technology allow the Great Plains to support a larger population and more profitable economic activities?

encouraged further settlement and farming in the West, eventually leading to the close of the frontier.

Opportunities in the West such as mining and cattle herding were generally male occupations, so much of the western migration was led by men. But as farming expanded, more women arrived, too. They all had a job to do, such as tending the family and farm or working as an entrepreneur running a boardinghouse, laundry, or bakery.

Some of the new settlers were former enslaved African Americans who fled the South after the end of Reconstruction. Benjamin Singleton, a Black businessman from Tennessee, helped organize a group of African Americans called the "**Exodusters**." They took their name from the biblical story of Moses leading the exodus of the Jews out of bondage and into a new life in the "Promised Land." The Exodusters' "promised land" was in Kansas and Oklahoma, where they planted crops and founded several enduring all-Black towns.

Homesteading the Plains Physical and human geographic factors made the lives of homesteaders on the Plains difficult. Windstorms, blizzards, droughts, plagues of locusts, and heart-rending loneliness tested their endurance. On the treeless plains, few new arrivals could afford to buy lumber to build a home. Instead, they cut 3-foot sections of sod and stacked them like bricks, leaving space for a door and one window. The resulting home was dark, dirty, and dingy.

Necessity is the mother of invention, and farmers on the Plains had many needs beyond housing. The development of barbed wire, a length of wire with twisted barbs, enabled a farmer to fence land cheaply to keep out wandering livestock. The development of a plow that could tackle the sod-covered land, the grain drill that opened furrows and planted seed, the windmill that tapped underground water, and dry-farming techniques were some of the innovations that enabled farmers to succeed. To spur development of better ways to farm, Congress passed the Morrill Act in 1862, which made land grants to states for the purpose of establishing agricultural colleges.

Nothing, however, prepared farmers for a series of blizzards and droughts in the 1880s and 1890s that killed animals and ruined harvests. Some of the discouraged and ill-prepared settlers headed back east. The farmers who remained became more commercial and depended more on scientific farming methods.

IDENTIFY MAIN IDEAS Why did farmers move to the Plains?

Minorities Encounter Difficulties

From the 1850s onward, the West had the widest diversity of people in the nation. With fewer than 20 percent of the nation's total population, it was home to more than 80 percent of the nation's Asian, Mexican and Mexican American, and American Indian residents. Almost all of the nation's 100,000 Chinese immigrants lived in the West.

Economic Issues Challenge Chinese Immigrants During the same time that Jim Crow arose in the South, Chinese immigrants faced racial prejudice on the West Coast. In 1879, California barred cities from employing people of Chinese ancestry. Several years later, San Francisco established a segregated "Oriental" school. Elsewhere, mobs of whites attacked Chinese workers, saying they had taken "white" jobs. Congress responded to these attacks by passing the Chinese Exclusion Act in 1882, which prohibited Chinese laborers from entering the country.

Brave Chinese immigrants challenged discrimination. Saum Song Bo questioned why he should support a fund-raising drive to build the Statue of Liberty. "That statue represents Liberty holding a torch which lights the passage of those of all nations who come into this country," Bo wrote in a letter published in *American Missionary* in 1898. "But are the Chinese allowed to come? As for the Chinese who are here, are they allowed to enjoy liberty as men of all other nationalities enjoy it?"

Chinese immigrants also turned to the federal courts to protect their rights but with mixed results. In 1886, in the case of *Yick Wo* v. *Hopkins*, the U.S. Supreme Court sided with a Chinese immigrant who challenged a California law that banned him and other Chinese from operating a laundry. In 1898, the Court ruled that individuals of Chinese descent, born in the United States, could not be stripped of their citizenship. Yet the Court upheld the Chinese Exclusion Act and several other discriminatory measures.

>> Surviving harsh conditions, these Mexican-American women in San Antonio, Texas, prepare a meal outside their dwelling.

BOUNCE to Activate Gallery

Land Ownership Proves Difficult for Mexican Americans Like African Americans and Asian Americans, Mexican Americans struggled against discrimination in the latter decades of the 1800s. One historian has described Mexican Americans as "foreigners in their own land." At the center of their struggle stood land. The Treaty of Guadalupe Hidalgo, signed at the end of the Mexican-American War, guaranteed the property rights of Mexicans who lived in the Southwest prior to the war. Still, four out of five Mexican Americans who lived in New Mexico lost their land, as did Mexican Americans in other southwestern states.

This land loss resulted from several factors. When Anglo Americans and Mexican Americans laid claim to the same land, U.S. courts put the burden of proof on Mexican Americans to show that they really owned the land. Differences in legal customs, and the fact that much of the land was held communally, not individually, made it difficult for many Mexican Americans to do so.

In addition, Anglo Americans used political connections to take land away from Mexican Americans. The "Sante Fe Ring," an association of prominent white businessmen and government officials, got the federal government to grant the group control of millions of acres of land in New Mexico. Thousands of Mexican Americans had lived on and farmed this land for many years. Since New Mexico was a territory, not a state, however, Mexican Americans, who comprised the majority of the population, had no representatives in Washington, D.C., to challenge this deal.

Mexican Americans Defend Property Rights Throughout the Southwest—in Texas, New Mexico,

Arizona, and California—Mexican Americans fought to maintain their rights. Many especially resented the loss of their land. One group, **Las Gorras Blancas**, targeted the property of large ranch owners by cutting holes in barbed-wire fences and burning houses. The group declared: "Our purpose is to protect the rights and interests of the people in general; especially those of the helpless classes." Supported by a national labor organization, the Knights of Labor, the group also had a newspaper to voice their grievances.

As anti-Mexican feelings increased, a group of Hispanic citizens in Tucson, Arizona, formed the Alianza Hispano-Americana in 1894 to protect the culture, interests, and legal rights of Mexican Americans. Within two years, new branches of the organization opened in other cities.

IDENTIFY SUPPORTING DETAILS During this period, what impact did the Supreme Court have on people of Chinese descent?

>> Miners used a great deal of water in their mining operations, often with negative consequences for farmers and ranchers.

Struggles and Change Across the West

There is a sharp contrast between the picture of the West depicted in novels and movies and the reality of life on the Plains. The West was a place of rugged beauty, but it was also a place of diversity and conflict.

Tension Over Economic Resources The various ways that settlers sought to use western land were sometimes at odds with one another. Conflicts between miners, ranchers, sheepherders, and farmers led to violence and acts of sabotage. Grazing cattle ruined farmers' crops, and sheep gnawed grass so close to the ground that cattle could not graze the same land. Although miners did not compete for vast stretches of grassland, runoff from large-scale mining polluted water that ran onto the Plains—and everyone needed water. And no matter who won, American Indians lost.

Early on, geologist John Wesley Powell recognized water as an important but limited resource. He promoted community control and distribution of water for the common good. Despite his efforts, water usage remained largely unregulated, a system that benefited some but disadvantaged others.

Prejudices and Discrimination Conflict came in many guises. For example, ranchers often belittled homesteaders, labeling them "sodbusters" to mock their work in the soil and their modest houses. Conflict also arose because the view of the ownership of natural resources varied. For many generations, Mexicans had mined salt from the salt beds of the El Paso valley. Mexicans viewed these areas as public property, open to all. However, when Americans arrived in the 1870s, they laid claim to the salt beds and aimed to sell the salt for profit. In 1877, in what became known as the El Paso Salt War, Americans and Mexicans clashed over access to this crucial commodity. When the battles ended, the salt beds were no longer communal property. Now, users would have to buy this natural product.

Ethnic tensions often lurked beneath the surface. Many foreign-born white people sought their fortunes on the American frontier, especially in the years following the mid-century revolutions in Europe. Their multiple languages joined the mix of several dozen American Indian language groups. Differences in food, religion, and cultural practices reinforced each group's fear and distrust of the others. But mostly it was in the larger cities or towns that discrimination was openly displayed. Chinese immigrants, Mexicans, and Mexican Americans were most often its targets.

Population Growth Ends the Frontier The last major land rush took place in 1889 when the federal government opened the Oklahoma Territory to homesteaders. On April 22, thousands of "boomers" gathered along the border. When the signal was given, they charged in to stake their claims. However, they found that much of the best land had already been taken by "sooners," who had sneaked into the territory and staked their claims before the official opening.

The following year, the 1890 national census revealed the extent of population growth in the West when it concluded that there was no longer a square mile of the United States that did not have at least a few white residents. The great American frontier was closed. This was in part due to completion of transcontinental railroads, which made it easier for people to migrate across the country. The country, the report said, no longer had a "frontier," which at the time was considered an uninhabited wilderness where no white person lived. The era of free western land had come to an end.

However, the challenges and tensions were far from over. Controversies over Indians' land rights were still to come. So, too, were more battles over water and over the mistreatment of minority citizens—especially Chinese and Mexican Americans. As African Americans migrated west and claimed places among the farmers, miners, railroad workers, entrepreneurs, inventors, and public servants, they indeed found new opportunities, but often these new opportunities were intertwined with discrimination.

☑ **IDENTIFY** What reasons can you identify to help explain prejudice and discrimination in the West?

☑ ASSESSMENT

1. **Support Ideas with Examples** Explain the ways mining shaped the West.
2. **Identify Cause and Effect** Describe the effects of large companies mining for minerals in the West.
3. **Summarize** the effects of the Transcontinental Railroad on the United States.
4. **Identify Patterns** in the effects of white settlers' westward expansion on other cultures.
5. **Hypothesize** Why did settlers expand westward despite the challenges of the physical environment there?
6. **Connections to Today** How do modern modes of transportation change the economy? How might they encourage new jobs and industries while ending others?

10.3

Former Civil War general Ulysses S. Grant proved unable to keep corruption and scandal from troubling his presidential administration.

Corruption Plagues the Nation

While Congress enacted many major reforms during Reconstruction, it passed very few measures between 1877 and 1900. Instead, inaction and corruption were serious political issues during the Gilded Age. This raised questions of whether or not democracy could succeed in a time dominated by large and powerful industrial corporations and men of great wealth.

BOUNCE to Activate Flipped Video

Objectives

Analyze the issues of weak leadership and corruption in national politics in the 1870s through 1890s.

Discuss civil service reform in the late 1800s.

Assess the importance of economic issues in the late 1800s.

Key Terms

spoils system
civil service
Pendleton Civil Service Act
gold standard
political machines
fiat money

Political Power Proves Difficult to Keep

Party loyalties were so evenly divided that no faction or group gained control for any period of time. After Grant left office, only twice between 1877 and 1897 did either the Republicans or Democrats gain control of the White House and both houses of Congress at the same time. Furthermore, neither held control for more than two years in a row. This made it very difficult to pass new laws. Most of the elections were very close as well, allowing those who lost to block new legislation until they got back in power.

Political Corruption Under President Grant Ulysses S. Grant was a popular war hero but a disappointing President. Allied with the Radical Republicans, he promised to take a strong stand against southern resistance to Reconstruction. But Grant's ability to lead was marred by scandal. He gave high-level advisory posts to untrustworthy friends and acquaintances who used their positions to line their own pockets. His own Vice President, Schuyler Colfax, was investigated and implicated in a scheme to steal profits from the Union Pacific Railroad. In addition, a plan by

GO ONLINE to access your digital course

railroad developer and financier Jay Gould to corner the gold market actually included President Grant's brother-in-law.

When Grant ran for reelection in 1872, some reform-minded Republicans withdrew their support and teamed up with some Democrats to create the Liberal Republican Party. The Liberal Republicans advocated civil service reform, removal of the army from the South, and an end to corruption in southern and national governments. Grant easily defeated their presidential candidate, the *New York Tribune* editor Horace Greeley.

Not long after the election, however, Americans sensed the aura of greed surrounding American politics. When scandal swirled around the members of his administration including his private secretary, the Secretary of War, and members of Congress, Grant seemed to look the other way. Even though he had stated, "Let no guilty man escape," he seemed to lack the will to root out this corruption. Confidence in public officials plummeted.

Across the nation, local scandals came to light. Many city officials sold lucrative public construction contracts to their friends or diverted money from city accounts. The most notorious of these scandals involved a band of New York City Democratic politicians led by state senator William "Boss" Tweed. The "Tweed Ring," as it came to be known, plundered millions of dollars from the city's treasury. By 1873, when Tweed was convicted and sentenced to prison, the public's confidence in its leaders was at a low ebb.

>> Scandals such as the secret deal that gave Republican Rutherford B. Hayes (on left) the presidency troubled Gilded Age politics. A number of administrations from this era suffered under weak or corrupt leadership.

BOUNCE to Activate Gallery

Corruption Continues in Subsequent Administrations In comparison to Lincoln, Grant and the other Presidents of the Gilded Age that followed him appeared particularly weak. Although they, like Lincoln, won by slim margins that reflected the nation's diversity of opinion on important issues, these presidents differed from Lincoln in that, once in office, they lacked integrity. Rutherford B. Hayes owed his election in 1876 to a secret deal to end Reconstruction. Benjamin Harrison became only the second President in history to lose the popular vote but win the electoral college vote. Chester Arthur, who took the helm following James Garfield's assassination, upset so many of his fellow Republicans that he failed to win his own party's presidential nomination in 1884.

The most noteworthy President of the era was Grover Cleveland. In an era known for its corruption, Cleveland maintained a reputation for integrity. He once observed, "A Democratic thief is as bad as a Republican thief." Cleveland enjoyed an extremely rapid rise to political prominence. In 1881, running as a reformer, he won the race for mayor in Buffalo, New York. A year later, he became the governor of New York, and in 1884, he became the first Democrat to win the White House in 24 years.

In 1888, even though he won the popular vote, Cleveland lost to Benjamin Harrison. But Cleveland came back to rewin the presidency in 1892.

IDENTIFY MAIN IDEAS Why did the public lose trust in the federal government?

Growth of Political Machines and Corruption

Grover Cleveland's reputation for honesty was the exception. Many government officials routinely accepted bribes. As Henry Adams, the great-grandson of John Adams, observed, "One might search the whole list of Congress, Judiciary, and Executive . . . [from] 1870 to 1895, and find little but damaged reputation."

Voter Turnout in Selected Presidential Elections, 1872-1916

YEAR	TOTAL TURNOUT	REPUBLICANS	DEMOCRATS	VOTER TURNOUT PERCENTAGE	RESULT
1872	6,460,000	3,597,000	2,843,000	71.3	Ulysses S. Grant, Republican
1876	8,422,000	4,037,000	4,284,000	81.8	Rutherford B. Hayes, Republican
1880	9,217,000	4,453,000	4,414,000	79.4	James A. Garfield, Republican
1884	10,053,000	4,850,000	4,880,000	77.5	Grover Cleveland, Democrat
1892	12,061,000	5,183,000	5,555,000	74.7	Grover Cleveland, Democrat
1900	13,968,000	7,218,000	6,357,000	73.2	Theodore Roosevelt, Republican
1908	14,884,000	7,675,000	6,412,000	65.4	William Howard Taft, Republican
1916	18,531,000	8,534,000	9,128,000	61.6	Woodrow Wilson, Democrat

SOURCE: *Historical Statistics of the United States*, U.S. Census Bureau

>> **Analyze Data** Is it probable that the presidents of the Gilded Age enjoyed strong popular support for their ideas? Why or why not?

BOUNCE to Activate Chart

Political Supporters Are Given Jobs Political parties and the spoils system were central components of politics during the Gilded Age.

Under the **spoils system**, which was first used by President Andrew Jackson as far back as the 1820s, politicians awarded government jobs to loyal party workers, with little regard for their qualifications. Parties held elaborate rallies and parades to get out the vote. However, candidates for the presidency did not take part in the campaign. They felt it lowered the reputation of the presidency.

Parties developed sophisticated **political machines** that reached virtually into every ward, in every precinct, in many cities in the nation. In large cities, political machines were often run by "bosses" or a small group of people. These groups, like Tammany Hall in New York City or the Pendergast machine in Kansas City, controlled cities for decades. The political machines worked by winning the loyalty of large immigrant groups by promising, and in some cases, delivering, solutions to problems like poor sanitation or transportation. The spoils system also played a role, with political machines rewarding loyal organizers with city jobs. With voter loyalty secured, the political machine was assured of its political power and often became very corrupt.

The spoils system served as the glue that helped make the parties so powerful. The Postmaster General, who headed the U.S. Postal Service, for example, could reward thousands of supporters with jobs. Likewise, other officials could and did use federal contracts to convince people to vote for their candidates. Ironically, political participation probably got a boost from the spoils system and the fierce partisanship of the era. About 75 to 80 percent of all those who could vote did vote in presidential elections during the Gilded Age.

Political Cartoons Alert the Public Though many Americans saw nothing wrong with politicians rewarding their friends, writers such as Mark Twain, political cartoonists, and others who thought about American politics expressed their concern about the damaging effects of corruption.

"The Bosses of the Senate," one of the most famous political cartoons of the time, drawn by Joseph Keppler, showed a cluster of businessmen representing various trusts, glaring down on the chambers of the Senate.

Thomas Nast created a series of cartoons which exposed the illegal activities of Boss Tweed and the Tammany Hall political machine in New York City. Eventually, Tweed was arrested. He escaped and fled to Spain. While there, Tweed was identified through one of Nast's cartoons. The Tammany Hall machine, however, lived on.

Civil Service Reform Efforts The feeling that the spoils system corrupted government, or at least made it terribly inefficient, prompted a number of prominent figures to promote civil service reform. The **civil service** is a system that includes federal jobs in the executive branch. In a reformed system, most government workers would get their jobs due to their expertise and maintain them regardless of which political party won the election.

Reforming the spoils system did cause controversy. Without the spoils system, politicians felt they would not attract the people needed to run their parties. Independent attempts by politicians to change the system failed. For example, when Rutherford B. Hayes became President in 1877, he worked for civil service reform. He even placed well-known reformers in high offices. However, the Republican Party did not support his reform efforts. It took the 1881 assassination of President James Garfield by Charles J. Guiteau to make civil service reform a reality. Guiteau shot Garfield because he believed that the Republican Party had not fulfilled its promise to give him a government job.

The Pendleton Civil Service Act Chester A. Arthur became President after the assassination of Garfield. While Arthur defended the spoils system, he supported the movement for civil service reform, which had been strengthened because of public indignation over Garfield's assassination. Arthur signed the **Pendleton Civil Service Act** in 1883. This act established a Civil Service Commission, which wrote a civil service exam. Individuals who wanted to work for the government had to take the exam, and getting a job depended on doing well on the exam, not on manipulating one's political connections. Initially, the act covered only a small percentage of federal employees, but its reach grew over time, reducing the power of the spoils system.

>> Charles J. Guiteau, an unstable individual who felt he was owed a government position, assassinated President Garfield in 1881. **Infer** What effect did Garfield's assassination have on civil service reform?

CHECK UNDERSTANDING How did the spoils system encourage government corruption and, eventually, government reform?

Economic Policy Challenges Continue

The public's discontent was worsened by economic turmoil and uncertainty. In the fall of 1873, one of the nation's most influential banks failed, apparently as a result of overextended loans to the expanding railroad industry. A wave of fear known as the Panic of 1873 spread through the financial industry and across the nation. Bank failures, job losses, and the uncertain economy added to the array of the nation's concerns. Events such as this prompted political leaders to debate the best ways to keep the economy moving forward.

The tariff and monetary policy were critical economic issues during this time. Leaders looked to these two areas for ways to stabilize the economy, but both issues were divisive. The tariff issue sharply split the Democrats and Republicans.

Monetary policy gave rise to independent political parties or movements that disagreed with the major parties' commitment to the **gold standard**. Using the gold standard meant that the government would use gold as the basis of the nation's currency. Paper money was backed by the government's gold reserves, and could, in theory, be redeemed for actual gold.

Americans Continue to Discuss Tariffs The debate over the tariff had deep roots in American history. The tariff, or the tax on imports of manufactured goods and some agricultural products, was created as early as 1810 to protect newly developed industries. Since then, the debate to lower or increase tariffs continued. Differences over the tariff had divided the Federalists and Jeffersonians and the Democrats and Whigs. During the Gilded Age, it divided the Republicans and Democrats. The tariff question became a major issue during the presidential election of 1888. The Republicans favored a high tariff, arguing that it would allow American industries to grow and promote jobs in manufacturing. Democrats countered that high tariffs increased the costs of goods to consumers and made it harder for American farmers to sell their goods abroad.

Different Ideas About Monetary Policy Two related factors turned monetary policy into a bitter issue during the Gilded Age. During the Civil War, the federal government issued paper money, known as greenbacks. The greenbacks were **fiat money,** or currency not backed by gold or silver. After the war, because the fiat money had contributed to wartime inflation (a rise in prices), the government retired, or got rid of, the greenbacks. Over the next century, the United States and other major world economies would edge towards going off a metallic standard and onto fiat money gradually, making the final move in the 1970s. However, in the 1870s, the debate centered on whether to use gold or gold *and* silver to back the paper money.

In 1873, Congress passed the Coinage Act of 1873. This law reversed the government policy of backing money with both gold and silver. Using only gold meant that the money supply was smaller and each dollar would be worth more. Bankers and others involved in international trade favored the gold standard because it discouraged inflation and made dollars worth more overseas. In contrast, most farmers favored keeping silver to create inflation. Already struggling, they hoped the rise in prices would increase their income. Those who favored the minting of silver—in other words, considering silver as money—protested against what they termed the "Crime of 1873" and prompted Congress to mint silver dollars. The Bland-Allison Act, passed in 1878, specified that the U.S. Treasury make a certain amount of silver-backed dollars each month, but not as many as the Free Silver advocates would have liked. The debate over whether to consider silver as money alongside gold continued until the passage of the Gold Standard Act in 1900, which set gold as the only metal backing paper dollars.

☑ **CHECK UNDERSTANDING** Why did Republicans and Democrats differ in their view of the tariff issue?

☑ ASSESSMENT

1. **Summarize** the reasons why President Cleveland's reputation was considered the exception to the rule for presidents from the 1870s through the 1890s.
2. **Interpret** Why do you think that party loyalties were so evenly divided after the end of the Civil War?
3. **Cite Evidence** of the corruption of the spoils system.
4. **Compare Points of View** Describe the debate pertaining to tariffs during the Gilded Age.
5. **Draw Conclusions** Why were political cartoons such an effective weapon against corruption?
6. **Connections to Today** The Panic of 1873 was in part caused by a bank extending large loans to the railroad industry. What risks or benefits do public or private investors take when financing new transportation innovations today?

10.4

Life was difficult for prairie farmers, who faced the difficulties of nature as well as unpredictable prices and rising debts. **Hypothesize** Why were farmers willing to put up with the hardships that came with their way of living?

BOUNCE to Activate Flipped Video

Objectives

Analyze the economic issues farmers faced in the late 1800s.

Describe the groups farmers formed to address their problems and what they accomplished.

Evaluate the impact of the Populist Party, and explain why the party did not last.

Key Terms

Oliver H. Kelley
Grange
Farmers' Alliance
Populist Party
William Jennings Bryan
William McKinley

Farm Issues and Populism

Following the Civil War, millions of men and women migrated west in search of the American dream. However, in the late 1880s and early 1890s, their dream began to turn into a nightmare, which, in turn, sparked a social and political movement known as populism. This movement displayed the dissatisfaction of millions of ordinary Americans—poor farmers, small landholders, and urban workers—and produced one of the largest third-party movements in American history.

Farmers Face Economic Difficulty

The farmers of the West and the South were willing to accept the difficulties of farm life. Yet farmers discovered that other enormous obstacles stood in the way of realizing their dreams.

They received low prices for their crops, but they had to pay high costs for transportation. Debts mounted while their influence on the political system declined.

Farm Issues Result in Rising Debt Between 1870 and 1895, farm prices plummeted. Cotton, which sold for about 15 cents a pound in the early 1870s, sold for only about 6 cents a pound in the mid-1890s. Corn and wheat prices declined nearly as rapidly. One study estimated that by the early 1890s, it was costing farmers more to produce corn than they could get by selling it, so they burned it to use as fuel. Planting more crops did not help. On the contrary, the more crops farmers produced, the more prices declined.

During the same time period, the cost of doing business rose. To pay for new machinery, seed, livestock, and other needs, farmers went into debt. An increasing number of farmers

GO ONLINE to access your digital course

mortgaged their farms to raise funds to survive and became tenant farmers—meaning they no longer owned the farm where they worked.

Big Business Practices Affect Farmers Farmers blamed big business, especially the railroads and the banks, for their difficulties. They protested that railroads, as monopolies, charged whatever rates they wanted. Likewise, they complained that banks set interest rates at unfairly high levels. Southern farmers, especially Black sharecroppers, faced the added problem of having to deal with dishonest merchants and landlords who paid less for crops and charged more for supplies than promised.

In addition, farmers grew angry because they felt the nation had turned its back on them. The United States had a long tradition of electing leaders from farm states with agricultural backgrounds, like Thomas Jefferson. Yet it now appeared that most of the nation's leaders came from urban industrial states. Moreover, farmers felt that they performed honest labor and produced necessary goods, while bankers and businessmen were the ones who got rich. One editor for a farmers' newspaper explained:

> There are three great crops raised in Nebraska. One is the crop of corn, one a crop of freight rates, and one a crop of interest. One is produced by farmers who sweat and toil to farm the land. The other two are produced by men who sit in their offices and behind their bank counters and farm the farmers.
>
> —*Farmers' Alliance*, 1890

Farmers, however, refused to accept these circumstances. They took action.

DESCRIBE What concerns did many farmers share about their businesses?

Farmers Seek Change Through Alliances

Farmers created a network of organizations, first in the Midwest and then in the South and West, to address their problems. The Granger movement, also known as the "Patrons of Husbandry," was the first.

The Courts Have Their Say Organized in 1867 by **Oliver H. Kelley**—a Minnesota farmer, businessman, journalist, and government clerk—the organization popularly known as the **Grange** attracted about a million members. The goals of the Grange included providing education on new farming techniques and calling for the regulation of railroad and grain elevator rates.

In the mid-1870s, the states of Illinois, Wisconsin, and Minnesota enacted laws that set maximum

Falling Prices of Farm Crops

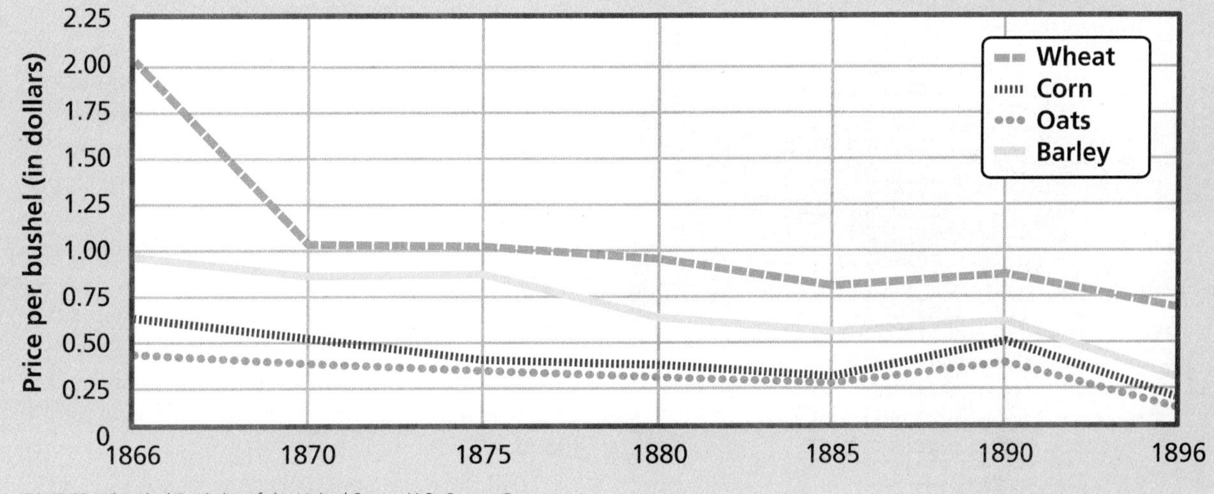

SOURCE: *Historical Statistics of the United States;* U.S. Census Bureau

>> Over this 30-year period, falling commodity prices hit American farmers hard.
Analyze Graphs What trend does the graph show? What might explain that trend?

>> The Granger movement, which promoted the rights and interests of farmers, inspired this illustration. **Determine Point of View** How does the illustrator view the importance of American farmers?

rates for shipping freight and for grain storage. The railroad companies challenged these "Grange Laws" in the courts. The Supreme Court upheld some decisions and overturned others, depending on the context of individual cases. In one of the significant "Granger Cases," *Munn* v. *Illinois*, the Court ruled against a Chicago grain-storage facility that challenged the constitutionality of an 1871 Illinois law setting maximum rates for shipping freight. This decision upheld the right of states to regulate private industries in some circumstances. However, in *Wabash* v. *Illinois* (1886) the Court ruled against state regulation. In this decision, the Court overturned an Illinois law by declaring that individual states did not have the power to regulate interstate commerce. Eventually, the Grangers helped to prompt the federal government to establish the Interstate Commerce Commission (ICC) to oversee interstate transportation.

Farmers and the Railroads Disagree Although the Grange declined in the late 1870s, farm protest remained strong. Faced with serious difficulties, Texas farmers in the 1870s began to organize and to negotiate as a group for lower prices for supplies.

The idea spread. Local organizations linked together in what became known as the **Farmers' Alliance**. These organizations soon connected farmers not only in the South but also in the West, and for a brief period farmers of all races and ethnicities banded together for their common cause. Because of regularly rising rates, the Alliances wanted the government to regulate the interest that banks could charge for loans. Farmers' Alliance members also tried to convince the government to force railroads to lower freight prices so members could get their crops to markets outside the South at reduced rates.

The railroads, however, argued that their prices were justified by the expense of building the railroads to begin with and by intense competition between rail companies. They had to charge high prices to earn profits and create more jobs. Often railroads would offer rebates or other incentives to larger shippers who used their rails. In addition, they would charge more to ship freight short distances than they would for long trips because they had competitors for long hauls, but not for short hauls. This was known as the "short haul and long haul" practice.

The Interstate Commerce Act, passed in 1887, prohibited several of these practices, although it proved hard to enforce.

>> Farmers plowed through difficult soil, often with no family members or hired workers to help them, just one of the many hardships they faced.

Alliances Encourage Reform Farmers' Alliances, such as the Southern Farmers' Alliance, became important reform organizations. They formed cooperatives to collectively sell their crops, and they called on the federal government to establish "sub-treasuries," or postal banks, to provide farmers with low-interest loans. They hoped the cooperatives would push the costs of doing business down and the prices for crops up. Some of the cooperative efforts succeeded. The Georgia Alliance led a boycott against manufacturers who raised the price of the special cord that farmers used to wrap bundles of cotton.

Farmers' alliances organized across racial lines were short-lived. Soon, the Southern Farmers' Alliance organized only white farmers.

There was also an Alliance network for African American farmers. R. M. Humphrey, a white Baptist minister, headed the Colored Farmers' Alliance, which had been organized by African American and white farmers.

Nearly one million African American farmers joined the group by 1891. The Colored Farmers' Alliance recognized that both white and African American farmers shared the same difficulties, but racial tensions prevented any effective cooperation between the groups.

>> Many African American farmers joined the Colored Farmers' Alliance.

☑ **IDENTIFY SUPPORTING DETAILS** What reforms did the farmers' organizations introduce?

The Beginnings of Populism

The spread of the Farmers' Alliances culminated with the formation of the **Populist Party**, or People's Party, in 1892. These Populists sought to build a new political party from the grassroots up. They ran entire slates of candidates for local, state, and national positions. Like a prairie fire, the Populist Party spread rapidly, putting pressure on the two major political parties to consider their demands.

>> The Populists, or People's Party, fielded candidates for office in local, state, and national elections in 1892. **Interpret** What Populist political goals does the slogan shown here suggest?

Populist Goals The Populist Party spelled out their views in their platform, which they adopted in Omaha, Nebraska, in July 1892. The platform warned about the dangers of political corruption, an inadequate monetary supply, and an unresponsive government. The Populist Party proposed specific remedies to these political issues. To fight low prices, they called for the coinage of silver, or "free silver." To combat high costs, they demanded government ownership of the railroads. Mary Elizabeth Lease, a fiery Populist Party spokesperson, also advanced the cause of women's suffrage.

The Populist Party nominated James B. Weaver of Iowa as their presidential candidate and James Field of Virginia as his running mate. Both had risen to the rank of general in the United States and Confederate armies, respectively, and their nominations represented the party's attempt to overcome the regional divisions that had kept farmers apart since the end of the Civil War. (Southern white voters had supported the Democrats; northerners, the Republicans.) The Populist Party also sought to reach out to urban workers, to convince them that they faced the same enemy: the industrial elite.

Early Impacts of the Populist Party For a new political party, the Populists did quite well in 1892. Weaver won more than one million votes for the presidency, and the Populists elected three governors, five senators, and ten congressmen. In 1894, the Populist Party continued to expand its base, gaining seats in the state legislatures and prompting the major political parties to consider endorsing its ideas.

In the South, the Populist Party had to unite Black and white voters if it hoped to succeed politically. Tom Watson, Georgia's most famous Populist Party leader, made a strong case for casting aside racial prejudice in favor of a political alliance between the races. However, the Democratic Party successfully used racist tactics, such as warning that a Populist victory would lead to "Negro supremacy," to diminish the appeal of the Populist Party.

IDENTIFY What did the Populist Party hope to accomplish?

Populism's Declining Influence

In 1893, a four-year-long depression began that worsened conditions not only for already-suffering farmers but for other Americans as well. Labor unrest and violence engulfed the nation. The major parties failed to satisfactorily respond to the nation's distress.

In the midst of national discontent, the Populist Party's dream of forging a broad coalition with urban workers grew. The Populists' relative success at the polls in 1892 and 1894 raised their hopes further. The decision of the Democratic Party to nominate **William Jennings Bryan** as their presidential candidate put the election for the Populists on an

The Populist Party, 1890–1900

>> Around the turn of the century, the Populist Party became a viable alternative to the two established political parties. **Analyze Maps** What does the map show about the popularity of the Populist Party?

BOUNCE to Activate Chart

entirely different plane, leading some to believe they could win the White House that year.

The Impact of William Jennings Bryan Born in Salem, Illinois, William Jennings Bryan moved to Lincoln, Nebraska, where he set up a law practice in 1887. He earned the nickname the "boy orator," in part by displaying his strong debating skills during his successful run for the United States Congress in 1890. In 1896, Bryan addressed the national Democratic convention on the subject of the gold standard, attacking Grover Cleveland and others in the party who opposed coining silver. The audience listened and cheered as Bryan spoke for "the plain people of this country," for "our farms," and declared "we beg no longer." The speech became known as the "Cross of Gold" speech because it ended with the following line: "You shall not press down upon the brow of labor this crown of thorns, you shall not crucify mankind upon a cross of gold."

The speech so moved the Democratic delegates that they nominated Bryan as their party's presidential candidate. He was just 36 years old and had not been a contender for the nomination until then. Bryan's advocacy of "free silver," or the coinage of silver as well as gold, and his support of a number of other Populist Party proposals, placed the Populists in a difficult situation.

Holding their convention after the Democrats, the Populists had to decide whether to nominate their own presidential candidate and continue to focus on building a broad-based movement from the bottom up or to endorse Bryan with the hope that they could capture the White House in 1896. They chose the latter course.

Bryan's campaign was like none other before. For the first time, a presidential candidate toured the nation, speaking directly to the people. In contrast, **William McKinley**, the Republican candidate, accumulated approximately $15 million, 30 times the amount Bryan had, and allowed party regulars to do the campaigning for him. Marcus Hanna, the political powerhouse who orchestrated McKinley's run, cast Bryan and his Populist Party supporters as a potential dictator and a threat to the Republic. For instance, one cartoon published in the pro-Republican *Los Angeles Times* depicted the Democratic-Populist coalition as a collection of evil witches, who fed the fires of sectionalism, discontent, and prejudice in order to win the election.

Populism's Long-Term Impact McKinley won the election of 1896 and went on to win reelection, again over Bryan, in 1900. Bryan's emphasis on

>> William Jennings Bryan, a gifted orator and Populist Party stalwart, gives a speech to his supporters.

BOUNCE to Activate Gallery

>> This cartoon depicts William Jennings Bryan as a large snake swallowing the Democratic donkey. **Analyze Cartoons** Was this cartoon's creator a Populist supporter? How can you tell?

The Presidential Election of 1896

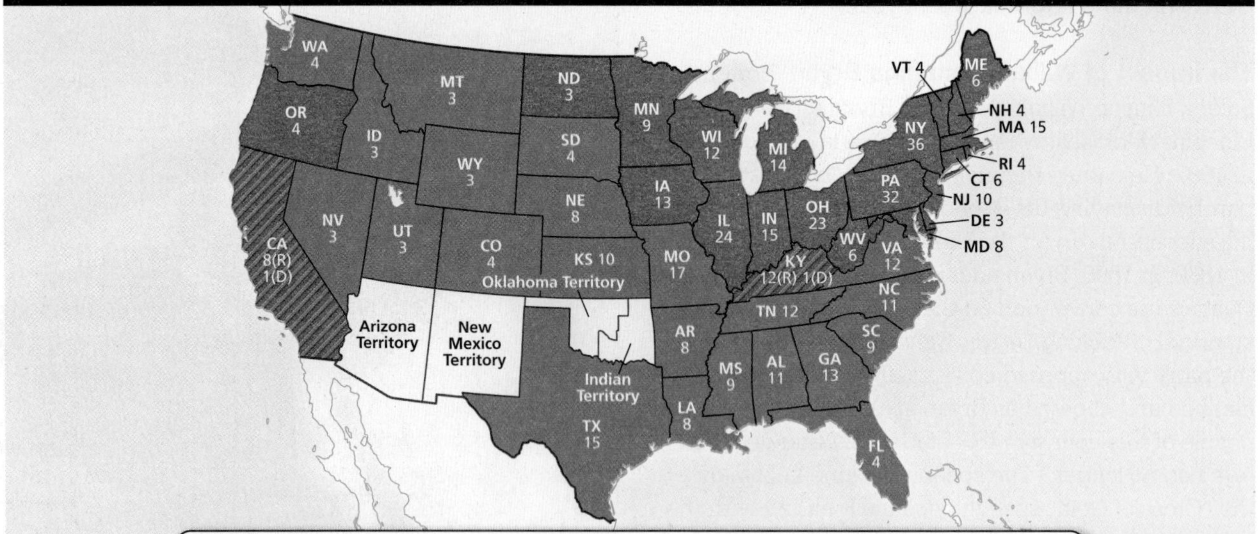

Candidate (Party)	Electoral Vote	Popular Vote	% Electoral Vote	% Popular Vote
William McKinley (Republican; R)	271	7,104,779	60.6	51.0
William Jennings Bryan (Democrat; D)	176	6,502,925	39.4	46.7
States with Split Electoral Votes				

>> In the presidential election of 1896, William Jennings Bryan won more states but fewer electoral votes than the victorious William McKinley. **Analyze Maps** In which regions was Bryan the most popular?

monetary reform, especially free silver, did not appeal to urban workers, and the Populist Party failed to win a state outside of the South and West. Moreover, the decision to endorse Bryan weakened the Populists at the local and state levels, and the party never recovered from its defeat in 1896. The Populist Party lingered for nearly a decade. By the early 1900s, it had disappeared as a feasible alternative to the two major political parties. Most of the voters who supported the Populist Party returned to the Democratic Party in 1896.

Even though the Populist Party fell apart, its impact as a third party inspired other third parties, notably the Progressive Party in the early 1900s. Many of the specific reforms that it advocated became a reality in the early decades of the 1900s. The Progressives supported a graduated income tax, regulation of the railroads, and a more flexible monetary system. Moreover, populism had a lasting effect on the style of politics in the United States. For a brief time, there was even a coalition of whites and Blacks in Texas. They were able to find a common political ground.

Increasingly, candidates campaigned directly to the people, and, like Bryan, they emphasized their association with ordinary Americans.

RECALL How did some of the ideas of the Populist Party influence twentieth century politics?

ASSESSMENT

1. **Generate Explanations** Why did farmers blame big business for their hardships?
2. **Summarize** the strategies by which farmers sought economic change at the end of the nineteenth century.
3. **Draw Conclusions** Determine the reasoning behind the Democratic Party's decision to nominate William Jennings Bryan as their presidential candidate.
4. **Compare and Contrast** the positions of the Democratic Party and the Populist Party with regard to racial equality.
5. **Connections to Today** Explain how the Populist Party influenced twentieth-century politics, even after its decline. Do you think the Populist Party influences politics today? Why or why not?

Preamble to the Platform of the Populist Party

The People's, or Populist, Party adopted its party platform in 1892 at its national convention in Omaha, Nebraska. The movement, which emerged from the Farmer's Alliance in the 1880s, sought political reforms and a redistribution of political and economic power.

>> Farmers on the prairie

The conditions which surround us best justify our co-operation; we meet in the midst of a nation brought to the verge of moral, political, and material [financial] ruin. Corruption dominates the ballot-box, the Legislatures, the Congress, and touches even the ermine of the bench.

The people are demoralized; most of the States have been compelled to isolate the voters at the polling places to prevent universal intimidation and bribery. The newspapers are largely subsidized or muzzled, public opinion silenced, business prostrated, homes covered with mortgages, labor impoverished, and the land concentrating in the hands of capitalists. The urban workmen are denied the right to organize for self-protection, imported pauperized labor beats down their wages, a hireling standing army, unrecognized by our laws, is established to shoot them down, and they are rapidly degenerating into European conditions.

DETERMINE CENTRAL IDEAS What is the party's view of democracy in America?

The fruits of the toil [labor] of millions are boldly stolen to build up colossal fortunes for a few, unprecedented [never having happened or existed before] in the history of mankind; and the possessors of these, in turn, despise the Republic and endanger liberty. From the same prolific [producing a lot of something] womb of governmental injustice we breed the two great classes—tramps and millionaires. . . .

. . . Silver, which has been accepted as coin since the dawn of history, has been demonetized to add to the purchasing power of gold by decreasing the value of all forms of property as well as human labor, and the supply of currency is purposely abridged to fatten usurers, bankrupt enterprise, and enslave industry. A vast conspiracy against mankind has been organized on two continents, and it is rapidly taking possession of the world. If not met and overthrown at once it forebodes terrible social convulsions, the destruction of civilization, or the establishment of an absolute despotism.

We have witnessed for more than a quarter of a century the struggles of the two great political parties for power and plunder [loot], while grievous [causing grief or suffering] wrongs have been inflicted upon the suffering people. We charge that the controlling influences dominating both these parties have permitted the existing dreadful conditions to develop without serious effort to prevent or restrain them.

DETERMINE MEANING To which two parties does "the two great political parties" refer?

Neither do they now promise us any substantial reform. They have agreed together to ignore, in the coming campaign, every issue but one. They propose to drown the outcries of a plundered people with the uproar of a sham battle over the tariff, so that capitalists, corporations, national banks, rings, trusts, watered stock, the demonetization of silver and the oppressions of the usurers may all be lost sight of. They propose to sacrifice our homes, lives, and children on the altar of mammon; to destroy the multitude in order to secure corruption funds from the millionaires.

Assembled on the anniversary of the birthday of the nation, and filled with the spirit of the grand general and chief who established our independence, we seek to restore the government of the Republic to the hands of "the plain people," with which class it originated. We assert our purposes to be identical with the purposes of the National Constitution; to form a more perfect union and establish justice, insure domestic tranquility, provide for the common defence, promote the general welfare, and secure the blessings of liberty for ourselves and our posterity.

We declare that this Republic can only endure as a free government while built upon the love of the whole people for each other and for the nation; that it cannot be pinned together by bayonets; that the civil war is over, and that every passion and resentment which grew out of it must die with it, and that we must be in fact, as we are in name, one united brotherhood of free men.

Our country finds itself confronted by conditions for which there is no precedent in the history of the world; our annual agricultural productions amount to billions of dollars in value, which must, within a few weeks or months, be exchanged for billions of dollars' worth of commodities consumed in their production; the existing currency supply is wholly inadequate to make this exchange; the results are falling prices, the formation of combines and rings, the impoverishment of the producing class. We pledge ourselves that if given power we will labor to correct these evils by wise and reasonable legislation, in accordance with the terms of our platform.

We believe that the power of government—in other words, of the people—should be expanded . . . to the end [result] that oppression, injustice, and poverty shall eventually cease in the land. . . .

DETERMINE MEANING According to the preamble, who controls power in the nation?

ASSESSMENT

1. **Paraphrase** In your own words, describe what the Populist Party views as the failings of the two major parties.
2. **Identify Supporting Details** List three details from the platform that support the Populist Party's position.
3. **Draw Conclusions** What types of laws do you think the Populist Party might support? Give specific examples.

GO ONLINE to access primary sources

Connections to Today

Many communities offer bicycle rentals as an easy way to get around.

Take Action by Learning About Transportation Today

1. **Choose** one of the following topics about transportation today:
    - **Environmental concerns:** Conduct research about the popularity of rental bicycles, rental e-scooters, or e-bicycles in many urban centers and small towns.
    - **Safety:** Conduct research into the safety of new and established travel technologies, for example, trucks, airplanes, self-driving cars, electric cars, or e-scooters.
    - **Public transportation:** Conduct research into how public transportation could be improved in your community.
2. **Ask Questions** Generate a list of questions about the topic you have selected. What might you want to know about your topic?
3. **Learn** about your topic by using a variety of sources. Use the Internet and your library to find newspaper and magazine articles. Interview people in your community about transportation.
4. **Raise Awareness** Create a poster that shows what you have learned in your research and discuss your findings with your class. Share your poster with the community by posting it at a local library or community center.

LESSON SUMMARIES

Use these Lesson Summaries, and the longer versions available online, to review the key ideas for each lesson in this Topic.

Lesson 1: American Indians Under Pressure

As white settlers moved west in the late 1800s, pressure mounted on American Indians, who resisted the seizure of their lands. In 1887, Congress granted farmsteads to Indian families while reformers established schools to help Indian children to assimilate into white society.

Lesson 2: The West is Transformed

The transcontinental railroad, completed in 1869, linked the East and West, moving products and people while spurring industrial and urban growth in the West. Cattle ranching and mining boomed. The government offered farm plots to homesteaders on the Great Plains. Meanwhile, both Chinese immigrants and Mexican Americans faced racial prejudice and discrimination.

Lesson 3: Corruption Plagues the Nation

During the late 1800s, inaction and political corruption plagued political life. Politicians gave government jobs to loyal party workers. However, in 1883 Congress established a civil service commission that based employment on qualifications rather than on party loyalty. During this period, Democrats and Republicans argued over the tariff and monetary policy

Lesson 4: Farm Issues and Populism

Between 1870 and 1895 crop prices fell and the cost of doing business rose, plunging farmers into debt. Farmers blamed the railroad and the banks, and formed Farmers' Alliances, which in turn led to the creation of the Populist Party in 1892. The Populists endorsed Williams Jennings Bryan in the 1896 presidential election. After the defeat of Bryan by Republican William McKinley, the party never recovered.

QUEST! FINDINGS

Create Your Layered Map of the American West Refer to your responses to the Quest Connections to help you create your layered map to present to an audience. Use the rubric and other Quest resources online to guide your work.

GO ONLINE to access lesson summaries

VISUAL REVIEW

Use these graphics to review some of the key terms, people, and ideas from this Topic.

American Indian Experience in the West

CONFLICT	OUTCOME
1862 Sioux Rebellion in Minnesota	U.S. pushes Sioux into the Dakotas.
1864 Sand Creek Massacre in Colorado	Plains Indians unite to resist white settlement.
1874 Red River War	Comanches and Kiowas surrender.
1876 Custer and his men killed at Battle of the Little Big Horn.	U.S. takes revenge on Sioux.
1877 Nez Percés try to flee to Canada.	Nez Percés sent to reservation in Oklahoma.
1890 Ghost Dance War	Sioux crushed at Wounded Knee in South Dakota.

Railroads Transform the West

RAILROADS

- tied the nation together.
- encouraged cattle ranching.
- moved products and people.
- stimulated growth of towns.
- increased demands for Indian lands.
- spurred industrial development.

The Tariff Question

Republicans	supported a high tariff	to encourage industries to grow and increase manufacturing jobs.
Democrats	opposed a high tariff	believing it would increase cost of goods and make it harder for farmers to sell goods abroad.

Economic Challenges to Farmers

Crop prices fall as more crops are produced. → Farmers go into debt and become tenant farmers. → Farmers blame railroads and banks for overcharging. → Farmers form Farmers' Alliance and Populist Party.

Topic 10 Assessment

KEY TERMS, PEOPLE, AND IDEAS

1. What was the purpose of the **Dawes General Allotment Act**?
2. For what reasons were American Indians forced from their lands?
3. Why did the **open-range system** come to an end?
4. What factors helped create ethnic diversity in the West?
5. How did the **Pendleton Civil Service Act** undermine the **spoils system**?
6. How did **political machines** contribute to corruption in the late 1800s?
7. Why did farmers support backing money with silver?
8. What were the goals of the **Populist Party**?
9. Why did farmers blame the banks and railroads for their economic problems?

CRITICAL THINKING

10. **Draw Conclusions** What were the consequences of the 1871 law banning recognition of Indian nations or tribes?
11. **Compare and Contrast** Why was the Americanization movement aimed at both immigrants and Indians?
12. **Identify Cause and Effect** (a.) How did railroads change the West? (b.) How did these railroads affect the economy?
13. **Summarize** What kinds of discrimination did ethnic minorities face in the West?
14. **Cite Evidence** Why was it so difficult to pass laws in the late 1800s?
15. **Identify Cause and Effect** Why did farmers suffer economically as the U.S. became more industrialized?
16. **Analyze Graphs** Study the graph. Which crop suffered the sharpest decline after 1866?

Falling Prices of Farm Crops

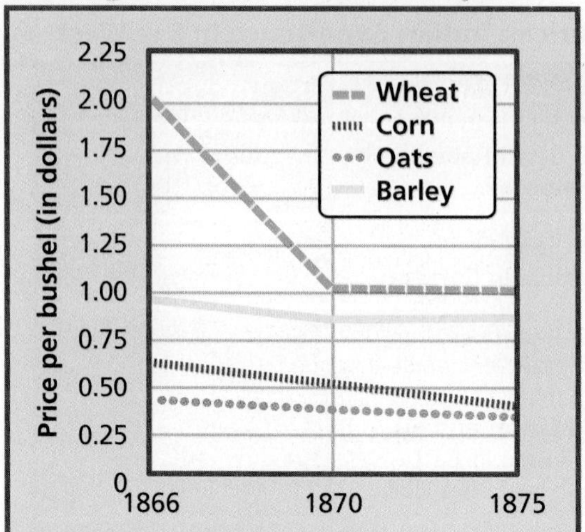

SOURCE: *Historical Statistics of the United States;* U.S. Census Bureau

17. **Writing Activity: Write an Argument** Evaluate how Chief Joseph's argument reflects the experience of American Indians and the clash of cultures in the West during the late 1800s.

> All men were made by the same Great Spirit Chief. They are all brothers. The earth is the mother of all people, and all people should have equal rights upon it. You might as well expect all rivers to run backward as that any man who was born a free man should be contented penned up and denied liberty to go where he pleases. If you tie a horse to a stake, do you expect he will grow fat? If you pen an Indian up on a small spot of earth and compel him to stay there, he will not be contented nor will he grow and prosper. I have asked some of the Great White Chiefs where they get their authority to say to the Indian that he shall stay in one place, while he sees white men going where they please. They cannot tell me.
>
> —*Chief Joseph of the Nez Percés*

18. **Connections to Today** What types of transportation tie the nation and the world together today?

DOCUMENT-BASED QUESTIONS

The Populist Movement emerged as America was rapidly moving from an agrarian to an ever more industrialized society. Read the documents below, then answer the questions that follow.

DOCUMENT A

This excerpt is from a speech by the Populist campaigner Mary Elizabeth Lease.

> This is a nation of inconsistencies. The Puritans fleeing from oppression became oppressors. We fought England for our liberty and put chains on four millions of blacks. We wiped out slavery and our tariff laws and national banks began a system of white wage slavery worse than the first. . .. Wall Street owns the country. . .. The West and South are bound and prostrate before the manufacturing East. . .. We will stand by our homes and stay by our fireside by force if necessary, and we will not pay our debts to the loan-shark companies until the government pays its debts to us.
>
> —*Mary Elizabeth Lease*

DOCUMENT B

This illustration was produced by the Grange, an organization formed to support farmers.

DOCUMENT C

This excerpt is from a speech by William Jennings Bryan.

> The man who is employed for wages is as much a businessman as his employer; . . . the merchant at the crossroads store is as much a business man as the merchant of New York; the farmer who goes forth in the morning and toils all day, . . . is as much a business man as the man who goes upon the board of Trade and bets upon the price of grain; the miners who go down a thousand feet into the earth, or climb two thousand feet upon the cliffs, and bring forth from their hiding places the precious metals. . . are as much business men as the few financial magnates who, in a back room, corner the money of the world. We come to speak of this broader class of business men.
>
> —*William Jennings Bryan, Democratic National Convention, 1896*

DOCUMENT D

This excerpt is from a secondary source about Populism.

> As the People's party died, many of the disillusioned dropped out of politics. This is part of the reason the percent of eligible voters to cast ballots in presidential races dropped thirty percent between 1896 and 1924. Others continued the egalitarian struggle by joining Eugene V. Debs in the Socialist party. Many, however, returned to the reform wings of their own parties. Several farmer demands [later] became law, . . .
> namely monopoly regulation, banking/currency reform, and the graduated income tax. Populists had also advocated direct democracy with reforms such as the initiative and referendum. . .. America, however, adopted Populist reforms selectively and piecemeal. The result was hardly the egalitarian vision of Populism in its heyday.
>
> —*Worth Robert Miller, The Gilded Age: Essays on the Origin of Modern America*

19. In Document A, the country is suffering because of
A. the government.
B. the people of the South and West.
C. tariffs and the banks.
D. the two-party system.

20. Analyze Images What do you think is the political message of the Document B image?

21. In Document C, Bryan's use of repetition is to emphasize that people who are not in business
A. should be valued as much as businessmen.
B. should not have the power of businessmen.
C. control the political system.
D. should be running the country.

22. Writing Activity Write a paragraph explaining whether you think Populism was a product of its time or was addressing issues relevant to other periods of American history.

Topic 11

America Comes of Age (1890–1920)

ESSENTIAL QUESTION What can individuals do to affect society?

GO ONLINE to access the eText, videos, Interactive Primary Sources, Biographies, and other online resources.

Theodore Roosevelt

Connections to Today

Today, the United States is a global powerhouse that has between 500 and 800 military bases in more than 70 nations. From these bases the United States defends its allies and interests.

As you will learn, in the late 1800s the United States began to emerge as a world power. Through war or other means, the United States began to acquire overseas territories. In fact, some of today's U.S. military bases abroad have their roots in the period of U.S. expansion that began more than 100 years ago.

NBC LEARN

Learn about the life of Jane Addams, an important reformer.

BOUNCE to Activate My Story Video

Topic 11 Overview

In this Topic, you'll learn about the decades when America emerged as a world power. Look at the lesson outline and explore the timeline. As you study this Topic, you'll complete the Quest Inquiry.

LESSON OUTLINE

11.1 Progressives Drive Reform

11.2 Women Gain Rights

11.3 Striving for Equality

11.4 Reformers in the White House

11.5 American Influence Grows

11.6 The Spanish-American War

11.7 The United States Emerges as a World Power

Key Events of America Comes of Age

1893
United States overthrows Queen Liliuokalani in Hawaii

1898
United States annexes Hawaii; Spanish-American War

1909
NAACP is formed

1911
Triangle Shirtwaist factory fire

1914
Clayton Antitru
Act is passed

1920
19th Amendme
is ratified, gra
women the rig
to vote

1890 1900 1910

QUEST! INQUIRY

Analyzing Historians' Viewpoints on the Spanish-American War

How does historiography influence our view of an event? In this Quest you'll investigate historians' views of the causes, course, and consequences of the Spanish-American War before writing an essay on this subject.

STEP 1
With your team, watch a video about the Spanish-American War and discuss it with a partner.

STEP 2
Examine the six sources relating to the U.S. Intervention in Cuba and answer the questions that follow each document.

STEP 3
Write an essay comparing the historians' viewpoints. Use evidence from the documents and support your argument with facts.

STEP 4
Reflect on the process of analyzing the documents and writing the essay and then complete the Self-Assessment.

GO ONLINE to access complete Quest materials

11.1

Some child laborers such as these young coal miners endured difficult and dangerous working conditions during the early 1900s.

BOUNCE to Activate Flipped Video

Objectives

Identify the causes of Progressivism and compare it to Populism.

Analyze the role that journalists and novelists played in the Progressive Movement.

Evaluate some of the social reforms that Progressives tackled.

Explain what Progressives hoped to achieve through political reforms.

Key Terms

Progressivism
muckraker
Lincoln Steffens
Jacob Riis
Upton Sinclair
Social Gospel
settlement house
Jane Addams
direct primary
initiative
referendum
recall
Seventeenth Amendment

Progressives Drive Reform

Industrialization, urbanization, and immigration brought many benefits to America, but they also produced challenging social problems. In response, a movement called **Progressivism** emerged in the 1890s. Progressives believed that new ideas and honest, efficient government could bring about social justice. Progressive ideas brought lasting reforms that still affect society today.

The Progressive Era Begins

The people who made up the Progressive Movement came from many walks of life. They came from all political parties, social classes, ethnic groups, and religions. Many Progressive leaders emerged from the growing middle class, whose power and influence was rapidly spreading. Dissatisfied industrial workers also joined the Progressive Movement. So did wealthy Americans driven by a desire to act for the good of society.

Progressive Beliefs and Influences What the Progressives shared in common was a belief that industrialization and urbanization had created troubling social and political problems. Progressives wanted to bring about reforms that would correct what they saw as problems and injustices. They encouraged their state legislatures and the federal government to enact laws to address the issues faced by the poor. Progressives wanted to use logic and reason to make society work in a more efficient and orderly way. Many, motivated by religious faith, sought social justice.

GO ONLINE to access your digital course

Progressivism was similar to the Populist Movement of the late 1800s. Both were reform movements that wanted to get rid of corrupt government officials and make government more responsive to people's needs. Both sought to eliminate the perceived abuses of big business. Despite these similarities, the two movements differed. At the forefront of Progressivism were middle-class people. They believed that highly educated leaders should use modern ideas and scientific techniques to improve society. Leaders of the Populist Movement, on the other hand, consisted mostly of farmers and workers.

Progressive Goals Some Progressives thought that political reform was the most urgent need. For many women, the number one goal was winning the right to vote. Other Progressives considered honest government to be the most important goal.

Reformers targeted city officials who built corrupt organizations, called political machines. The bosses of these political machines used bribery and violence to influence voters and win elections. They counted on the loyalty of city workers who looked the other way when they took public money for themselves. Bosses also helped people solve personal problems, which often kept voters loyal.

Corrupt and ineffective government combined with the booming growth of cities produced other problems. The people living in America's crowded cities needed paved streets, safe drinking water, decent housing, and adequate municipal services. The lack of adequate services led to wretched living conditions for the urban poor. Too often, dishonest business owners and politicians controlled municipal services. Bribes and shady deals made them rich while conditions for urban residents remained unsafe and little changed.

While some Progressives focused on government, others were worried about big business. As you have learned, wealthy industrialists built huge companies that limited competition and sometimes raised prices. Middle-class Progressives wanted the government to "bust the trusts" and so create more economic opportunities for smaller businesses. Progressives complained that the Sherman Antitrust Act of 1890 was inadequate and ineffective in limiting the abuses of big business. Business leaders, in contrast, argued that big companies produced goods more efficiently and therefore consumers could buy them at lower prices, which benefited everyone. They feared that government regulation would hurt these efficiencies and the economy as a whole.

>> During the Progressive Era, volunteers like this one from the Salvation Army helped those less fortunate in many ways.

>> **Analyze Political Cartoons** According to the artist, what is the effect of the street railroad monopoly on the taxpayer?

>> Progressives worried about the unhealthy conditions facing children who lived in urban slums. These children are playing near a dead horse.

BOUNCE to Activate Illustration

>> Muckrakers such as Nelly Bly wrote news articles that stirred public opinion in favor of Progressive causes.

Other Progressive reformers focused on the class system. Often motivated by religious faith, they sought to reduce the gap between the rich and the poor. They attacked the harsh conditions endured by miners, factory workers, children forced to work, and other laborers. They wanted to improve conditions in city slums. They wanted social welfare laws to help children, workers, and consumers.

LIST Which areas of society did Progressive reformers wish to change?

The Impact of Muckrakers

Socially conscious journalists and other writers dramatized the need for reform. Their sensational investigative reports uncovered a wide range of ills afflicting America in the early 1900s. Even though Theodore Roosevelt agreed with much of what they said, he called these writers **muckrakers** because he thought them too fascinated with the ugliest side of things. (A muckrake is a tool used to clean manure and hay out of animals' stables.) The writers were angry at first but in time took up Roosevelt's taunting name as a badge of honor.

The muckrakers' articles appeared in magazines and newspapers that entered millions of American homes. People across the nation were horrified by the conditions that muckrakers revealed. Muckrakers' accounts prompted Americans to push for reforms to correct these ills.

Journalists Uncover Injustices One leading muckraker was **Lincoln Steffens**. He was the managing editor at *McClure's*, a magazine known for uncovering social problems. In 1903, Steffens published *The Shame of the Cities*, a collection of articles on political corruption in the nation's cities. His reports exposed how the government of Philadelphia let utility companies charge their customers excessively high fees. He showed how corrupt politicians won elections by bribing and threatening voters, and revealed how political corruption affected all aspects of life in a city.

> The visitor [to St. Louis] is told of the wealth of the residents, of the financial strength of the banks, and of the growing importance of the industries; yet he sees poorly paved, refuse-burdened streets, and dusty or mud-covered alleys; he passes a ramshackle firetrap crowded with

the sick and learns that it is the City Hospital. . . . Finally, he turns a tap in the hotel to see liquid mud flow into [the] wash basin or bathtub.

—Lincoln Steffens and Claude Wetmore, "Corruption and Reform in St. Louis," *McClure's Magazine*, October 1902

Another influential muckraker was **Jacob Riis**, a photographer for the *New York Evening Sun*. Riis turned his camera on the crowded, unsafe, rat-infested tenement buildings where the urban poor lived. Between 1890 and 1903, he published several works, including *How the Other Half Lives*, that shocked the nation's conscience and led to reforms.

Other outraged writers joined Riis and Steffens. In *The History of Standard Oil,* Ida Tarbell reported that John D. Rockefeller used ruthless methods to ruin his competitors, charge higher prices, and thereby reap huge profits. Some writers proclaimed the need to improve schools or warned of the breakdown of family life because mothers had to work long hours in factories. John Spargo focused attention on the dangerous and difficult lives of child workers.

>> Walter Rauschenbusch became the leading proponent of the Social Gospel movement with the publication of his 1907 work *Christianity and the Social Crisis*.

Novelists Highlight Social Issues Fiction writers put a human face on social problems. They developed a new genre — the naturalist novel — that portrayed human misery and the struggles of common people. Theodore Dreiser, a midwesterner raised in poverty, published *Sister Carrie* in 1900. His provocative novel traces the fate of a small-town girl drawn into the brutal urban worlds of Chicago and New York.

Naturalist novels became very popular. Frank Norris's *The Octopus* fascinated readers by dramatizing the Southern Pacific Railroad's stranglehold on struggling California farmers.

In *The Jungle*, **Upton Sinclair** related the despair of immigrants working in Chicago's stockyards and revealed the unsanitary conditions in the industry. Sinclair's account eventually prompted regulations to protect food safety. African American author Frances Ellen Watkins portrayed the struggles of Black Americans in her 1892 novel *Iola Leroy*.

RECALL Who were the muckrakers and what did they accomplish?

Reformers Impact Society

The work of the muckrakers increased popular support for Progressivism. Progressive activists promoted laws to improve living conditions, public health, and schools. They urged government to regulate businesses. They worked as volunteers living among the people they sought to help. They believed that careful social planning would make American life better.

Issues Affecting the Social Gospel Many reformers, like Walter Rauschenbusch, thought that Christianity should be the basis of social reform. A child of German immigrants, Rauschenbusch had become a Baptist minister. He blended ideas from German socialism and American Progressivism to form what he called the **Social Gospel**. By following Bible teachings about charity and justice, he explained, people could make society "the kingdom of God;" that is, make life on earth closer to the promised paradise of heaven by helping others and making the world more just. However, Social Darwinists like William Graham Sumner believed that society was governed by the "survival of the fittest," and opposed the Social Gospel movement.

Many Protestant leaders followed Rauschenbusch's program. Many churches already provided community support and help. Issues such as child labor and long working hours led social Gospel adherents to call for the end of child labor and a shorter workweek. They also urged the government to limit the power of corporations and trusts.

Jane Addams Contributes to the Settlement House Movement An important goal of many Progressives, including those influenced by religious ideals, was to improve the lives of poor people in the cities. One approach was the **settlement house**, a community center that provided social services to the urban poor. Most settlement houses were privately funded and run by volunteers, many of whom were women. Settlement house workers gave mothers classes in child care and taught English to immigrants. They ran nursery schools and kindergartens. They also provided theater, art, and dance programs for adults.

A woman named **Jane Addams** became a leading figure in the settlement house movement. While visiting Europe, she was inspired by the work at Toynbee Hall, a settlement house in London. In 1889, Addams opened Hull House, a settlement house in Chicago. Over the years, Hull House grew to include 13 buildings. Through Hull House's programs, Addams made significant social and economic contributions to the lives of the local poor. By educating children and adults, these programs increased their earning power.

Furthermore, the success of Hull House inspired other college-educated, middle-class women to become social workers. By 1911, the country had more than 400 settlement houses. Addams was also politically active. She supported the Progressive party candidacy of Theodore Roosevelt in 1912 and later helped found the American Civil Liberties Union. She worked closely with labor and other reform groups seeking to use political means to improve working conditions for the urban poor.

Using Hull House as a base, Addams also worked for laws regulating labor and tenement houses. In addition, she worked for women's suffrage and world peace, sharing the Nobel Peace Prize in 1931.

Religious organizations such as the Young Men's Christian Association (YMCA) also provided services to the urban poor. In addition to its goal of promoting Christian values, the YMCA offered classes, dances, and sports. Christian missionaries like Dwight L. Moody were very active in the YMCA.

Progressive-Era Issues Affecting Children

Progressives also tried to help children. A lawyer named Florence Kelley helped ban child labor in the state of Illinois, and other states soon passed similar laws. In 1902, Kelley helped form the National Child Labor Committee, which successfully lobbied the federal government to create the U.S. Children's Bureau in 1912. This new agency examined any issue that affected the health and welfare of children. The agency still works to protect children today.

Improvements for Children in the Progressive Era

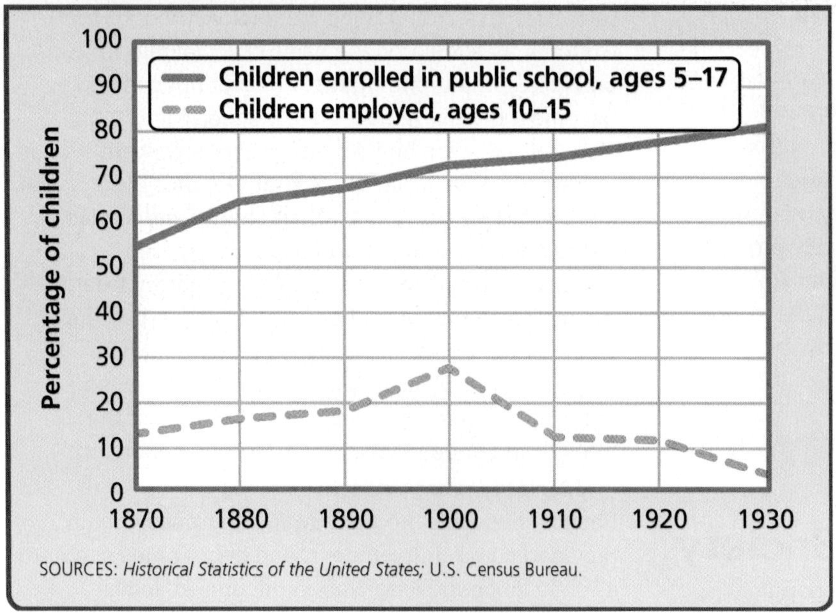

>> **Analyze Information** How did child labor laws affect children's employment levels during the Progressive Era?

But progress in children's rights had a long way to go. In 1916, Congress passed the Keating-Owens Act, which banned child labor in all states. However, two years later, the Supreme Court ruled the law unconstitutional. It was not until 1938 that Congress would end child labor for good.

Progressives also tried to better children's lives by improving education. A number of states passed laws that required children to attend school until a certain age. However, there were heated debates about what children should learn and how they should learn. Some argued that they should be taught only work skills. Others said they should learn to appreciate literature and music. Most educators agreed that girls should learn different things from boys.

Educator John Dewey criticized American schools for teaching children to memorize facts but not to think creatively. Dewey wanted schools to teach new subjects such as history and geography, as well as practical skills like cooking and carpentry. His ideas were not adopted at once, but in later years, many states put them into effect.

Reforms in the Workplace In the early 1900s, the United States had the highest rate of industrial accidents in the world. Long hours, poor ventilation, hazardous fumes, and unsafe machinery threatened not only workers' health but also their lives. Each year some thirty thousand workers died on the job, while another half a million were injured.

In March 1911, a fire at the Triangle Shirtwaist Factory in New York City shocked Americans and focused attention on the need to protect workers. Workers in the factory had little chance to escape the raging fire because managers had locked most of the exits. The fire killed 146 workers, most of them young Jewish women. Many jumped from the windows in desperation. Inside the smoldering ruins, firefighters found many more victims, "skeletons bending over sewing machines."

After the blaze, outraged Progressives intensified their calls for reform. New York passed laws to make workplaces safer, and other cities and states followed suit. Many states also adopted workers' compensation laws, which set up funds to pay workers who were hurt on the job.

Progressives also persuaded some states to pass laws limiting the workday to ten hours. However, their efforts suffered a blow in 1905 when the Supreme Court ruled in *Lochner* v. *New York* that such laws were unconstitutional. Until the 1930s, the court ruled against many labor laws, but Progressives continued to work towards the goal of protecting workers.

>> Jane Addams founded one of the nation's first settlement houses, Hull House, in 1889. Here, she sits with a group of children visiting Hull House in 1935.

>> Firefighters fought to extinguish the catastrophic Triangle Shirtwaist Fire. **Draw Conclusions** How did accidents like this fire at the Triangle Shirtwaist Factory in 1911 lead to improvements in working conditions?

BOUNCE to Activate Gallery

RECALL How did Progressives work to help the urban poor?

Progressive Reforms Impact Government

Progressive reformers sought to reform the political process in order to reform society. They wanted to free government from the control of political bosses and powerful business interests. They wanted to give people more control over their government and make government more effective and efficient in serving the public.

Reformers Change City Government Just as the Triangle Shirtwaist Factory fire spurred reformers to action, so did another disaster. In 1900, a massive hurricane left the city of Galveston, Texas, in ruins. One of the greatest national calamities in American history, the hurricane killed more than 8,000 people. As an emergency measure, Galveston replaced its mayor and board of aldermen with a five-person commission. Each commissioner was an expert in a different area of city affairs, such as public safety or streets and sewers, and headed the departments responsible for that area.

>> The Galveston Hurricane of 1900 destroyed countless structures, such as this public school.

The commission form of government proved very efficient as the city carried out a tremendous rebuilding effort. The following year, Galveston decided to permanently adopt the commission form of government.

Known as the Galveston plan, many other cities decided to take up the commission form of government. By 1918, nearly 500 cities had adopted some form of the Galveston plan. Dayton, Ohio, and other cities modified the plan by empowering the city council or commission to hire a professional city manager to oversee all of city government. The new city governments curbed the power of bosses and their political machines. The reform governments purchased public utilities so that electric, gas, and water companies could not charge city residents unfairly high rates.

Progressive Reforms Impact Political Process Progressives also pushed for election reforms, taking up some Populist ideas. Traditionally, party leaders picked candidates for state and local offices.

But in Wisconsin, reform governor Robert M. La Follette established a **direct primary,** an election in which citizens themselves vote to select nominees for upcoming elections. By 1916, all but four states had direct primaries.

Progressives also wanted to make sure that elected officials would follow citizens' wishes. To achieve this goal, they worked for three other political reforms: the initiative, the referendum, and the recall. The **initiative** gave people the power to put a proposed new law directly on the ballot in the next election by collecting citizens' signatures on a petition. This meant that voters themselves could suggest laws instead of waiting for elected officials to act. The **referendum** allowed citizens to approve or reject laws passed by a legislature. The **recall** gave voters the power to remove public servants from office before their terms ended.

Progressives won yet another political reform: They adopted the Populist call for the direct election of senators by voters, not state legislators.

Progressives believed that Americans should choose their own senators rather than allowing state legislatures to do so. Several states already held elections in which voters advised their legislature about which person to name, although states formally retained this decision under the U.S. Constitution. However, the proposed reform was not universally popular. Some members of Congress argued that direct election would weaken the states' power to block actions of the federal government, an important constitutional check. With the support

PROGRESSIVES AND ELECTION REFORMS

THE SEVENTEENTH AMENDMENT

BEFORE U.S. senators were elected by state legislatures.

AFTER Senators were chosen by the voters in the states by direct election.

STATE ELECTION REFORMS

STARTED IN THE PROGRESSIVE ERA

Initiative Voters can petition to place constitutional amendments on the ballot.

Referendum Voters can petition to repeal an existing law.

Recall Voters can remove elected representatives without waiting for the next election.

ATTEMPTED RECALLS OF PUBLIC OFFICIALS

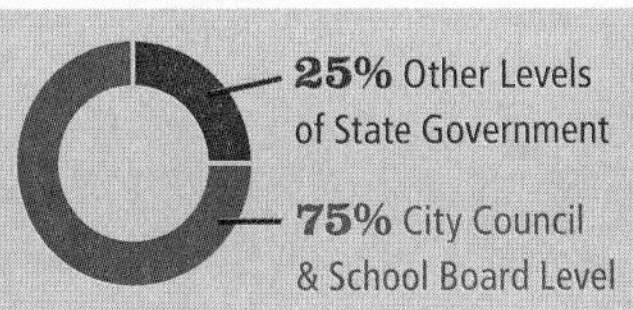

Source: Eagleton Institute of Politics

USE OF INITIATIVES ON STATE BALLOTS

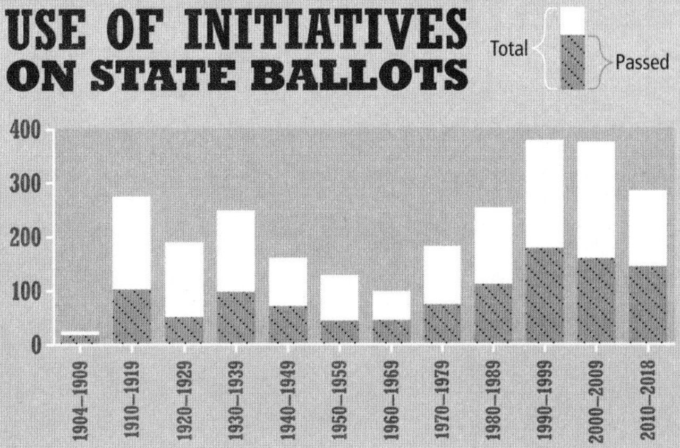

Source: Initiative and Referendum Institute

>> **Analyze Information** What was the most significant Progressive election reform? Cite two pieces of information to support your answer.

of 31 state legislatures, however, Congress passed a constitutional amendment to enact this change in 1911. The states ratified the **Seventeenth Amendment** two years later.

States Lead the Progressive Movement

Dynamic Progressives became the leaders of several states, and chief among them was Robert La Follette of Wisconsin. Elected governor in 1900, "Fighting Bob" won the passage of many reform laws. Under his leadership, the Wisconsin state government forced railroads to charge lower fees and pay higher taxes. La Follette helped his state to improve education, make factories safer, and adopt the direct primary. Progressives called Wisconsin the "laboratory of democracy."

Hiram Johnson, governor of California, shattered the Southern Pacific Railroad's stranglehold on state government. He put in place the direct primary, initiative, referendum, and recall. He also pushed for another goal of some Progressives—planning for the careful use of natural resources such as water, forests, and wildlife.

Other Progressive governors included Theodore Roosevelt of New York and Woodrow Wilson of New Jersey. Roosevelt worked to develop a fair system for hiring state workers and made some corporations pay taxes. Wilson reduced the railroads' power and pushed for a direct primary law. Both Roosevelt and Wilson later became President and brought reforms to the White House.

CHECK UNDERSTANDING How did Progressive reformers change local and state governments?

ASSESSMENT

1. **Compare and Contrast** the Populist and Progressive movements.
2. **Summarize** the ways in which Progressives tried to help children.
3. **Generate Explanations** How did the development of settlement houses affect urban American society?
4. **Identify Cause and Effect** Explain how the Triangle Shirtwaist Factory fire affected workers' rights.
5. **Draw Conclusions** How did muckrakers influence efforts to enact social reform?

GO ONLINE to access this biography: Dwight Moody

Primary Sources

How the Other Half Lives: Jacob Riis

Jacob Riis immigrated to the United States from Denmark in 1870. After living for several years in extreme poverty, he found a job as a police reporter for the *New York Tribune*. He became one of the leading muckrakers of the Progressive Era. Riis's writing and photographs helped expose the harsh living conditions in the crowded tenements of New York City. This excerpt is from Riis's 1890 book, *How the Other Half Lives*.

>> A tenement of the late 1800s

The problem of the children becomes, in these swarms, to the last degree perplexing. Their very number make one stand aghast [horrified]. I have already given instances of the packing of the child population in East Side tenements. They might be continued indefinitely until the array [orderly arrangement] would be enough to startle any community. For, be it remembered, these children with the training they receive—or do not receive—with the instincts they inherit and absorb in their growing up, are to be our future rulers, if our theory of government is worth anything. More than a working majority of our voters now register from the tenements.

DETERMINE CENTRAL IDEAS According to Riis, why should all Americans be concerned about tenement children?

I counted the other day the little ones, up to ten years or so, in a Bayard Street tenement that for a yard has a triangular space in the center with sides fourteen or fifteen feet long, just room enough for a row of ill-smelling closets [toilets] at the base of the triangle and a hydrant at the apex [highest point]. There was about as much light in this "yard" as in the average cellar. I gave up my self-imposed task in despair when I had counted one hundred and twenty-eight in forty families.

SUMMARIZE What is the tenement like on Bayard Street that Riis describes?

Bodies of drowned children turn up in the rivers right along since summer whom no one seems to know anything about. When last spring some workmen, while moving a pile of lumber on a North River pier, found under the last plank the body of a little lad crushed to death, no one had missed a boy, though his parents afterward turned up. The truant [a pupil who misses school without permission] officer assuredly does not know, though he spends his life trying to find out, somewhat illogically, perhaps, since the department that employs him admits that thousands of poor children are crowded out of the schools year by year for want of room.

SUMMARIZE What is Riis's complaint about the education received by tenement children?

The law has done what it could. That was not always a great deal, seldom more than barely sufficient for the moment. An aroused municipal conscience endowed the Health Department with almost autocratic powers in dealing with this subject, but the desire to educate rather than force the community into a better way dictated their exercise with a slow conservatism that did not always seem wise to the impatient reformer. . Tenements quite as bad as the worst are too numerous yet; but one tremendous factor for evil in the lives of the poor has been taken by the throat, and something has unquestionably been done, where that was possible, to lift those lives out of the rut where they were equally beyond the reach of hope and of ambition. It is no longer lawful to construct barracks to cover the whole of a lot. Air and sunlight have a legal claim, and the day of rear tenements is past. Two years ago a hundred thousand people burrowed in these inhuman dens; but some have been torn down since. Their number will decrease steadily until they shall have become a bad tradition of a heedless past. The dark, unventilated bedroom is going with them, and the open sewer. The day is at hand when the greatest of all evils that now curse life in the tenements—the dearth of water in the hot summer days—will also have been remedied, and a long step taken toward the moral and physical redemption of their tenants.

SUMMARIZE Why has the problem of overcrowded tenements begun to change?

The sea of a mighty population, held in galling fetters, heaves uneasily in the tenements. Once already our city, to which have come the duties and responsibilities of metropolitan greatness before it was able to fairly measure its task, has felt the swell of its resistless flood. If it rise once more, no human power may avail to check it. The gap between the classes in which it surges, unseen, unsuspected by the thoughtless, is widening day by day. No tardy enactment of law, no political expedient, can close it. Against all other dangers our system of government may offer defence and shelter; against this not. I know of but one bridge that will carry us over safe, a bridge founded upon justice and built of human hearts. I believe that the danger of such conditions as are fast growing up around us is greater for the very freedom which they mock. The words of the poet, with whose lines I prefaced this book, are truer to-day, have far deeper meaning to us, than when they were penned forty years ago:

"—Think ye that building shall endure
Which shelters the noble and crushes the poor?"

ASSESSMENT

1. **Identify Supporting Details** What details in this excerpt may have shocked readers of the time? Why do you think muckrakers sought to shock their audience?
2. **Determine Meaning** To whom does the "Other Half" in the title refer? Why do you think Riis uses this phrase?
3. **Identify Cause and Effect** How do you think Riis's account might have contributed to social reforms for tenement housing?

GO ONLINE to access primary sources

11.2

Women often used protests to demand suffrage. Draw Conclusions Why did activities in the woman's suffrage movement draw criticism from some groups of American women?

BOUNCE to Activate Flipped Video

Objectives

Analyze actions taken by women to address social issues affecting workers and families.

Explain actions taken during the Progressive era to expand opportunities for women, including the right to vote.

Evaluate the tactics reform leaders used to win passage of the Nineteenth Amendment.

Key Terms

Florence Kelley
National Consumers League (NCL)
temperance movement
Margaret Sanger
Frances Willard
suffrage
Ida B. Wells
Susan B. Anthony
Carrie Chapman Catt
National American Woman Suffrage Association (NAWSA)
Alice Paul
Nineteenth Amendment

Women Gain Rights

In the early 1900s, a growing number of women were no longer content to have a limited role in society. Women activists helped bring about Progressive reforms and won the right to vote. In the years ahead, women would continue the struggle to expand their roles and rights.

Expanding Opportunities for Women

In the early 1900s, more middle-class women wanted to do more than fulfill their roles as wives and mothers. They were ready to do other tasks besides the important ones of raising children, cooking meals, cleaning the home, and caring for family members. They wanted to expand their role in the community.

Education helped many women achieve their goals. By the 1890s, a rising number of women's colleges prepared them for careers as teachers or nurses. Some, such as Bryn Mawr College in Pennsylvania and the School of Social Work in New York, trained them to lead the new organizations working for social reform. The number of women attending college jumped. By 1900, one third of all college students, nationwide, were women. By attending college, women expanded their own economic opportunities. Armed with education and modern ideas, many middle-class white women began to tackle problems they saw in society.

Economic and Social Issues for Women Working-class women had worked outside of the home for decades, taking difficult jobs with long hours and dangerous conditions. They were usually expected to hand over their wages to their husbands, fathers, or brothers. Many women labored in factories that made cigars or clothing. Others toiled as laundresses or servants.

GO ONLINE to access your digital course

Immigrants, African Americans, and women from rural areas filled these jobs, and most of them had little or no education.

As a result, they could easily be cheated or bullied by their employers. Without being able to vote, women had little influence on the politicians who could look after their interests.

Addressing Economic Issues A key goal of women reformers was to limit the number of work hours. They succeeded in several states. For example, a 1903 Oregon law capped women's workdays at ten hours. Five years later, in *Muller v. Oregon*, the Supreme Court reviewed that law. Lawyer Louis D. Brandeis argued that long working hours harmed working women and their families.

The Supreme Court agreed with Brandeis. Based on their role as mothers, it said, women could be "properly placed in a class" by themselves. As a result, laws could limit their work hours, even if similar laws would not be allowed for men. At the time, Progressives viewed this decision as a victory for women workers. In later years, however, this ruling was used to justify paying women less than men for the same job.

Florence Kelley believed that women were hurt by unfair prices for goods they had to buy to run their homes. In 1899, she helped found the **National Consumers League (NCL),** which is still active today. The NCL gave special labels to "goods produced under fair, safe, and healthy working conditions" and urged women to buy them and avoid products that did not have these labels. The NCL pushed for other reforms as well. It backed laws calling for the government to inspect meatpacking plants, to make workplaces safer, and to make payments to the unemployed.

Florence Kelley also helped form the Women's Trade Union League (WTUL), another group that tried to improve conditions for female factory workers. It was one of the few groups in which upper-class and working-class women served together as leaders. The WTUL pushed for federal laws that set a minimum wage and an eight-hour workday. It also created the first workers' strike fund, which could be used to help support families who refused to work in unsafe or unfair conditions.

Women Address Social Issues A main goal of Progressive women was to improve family life. They pushed for laws that could help mothers keep families healthy and safe. One focus of this effort was the **temperance movement** led by the Women's Christian Temperance Union (WCTU). The WCTU,

>> Like their male counterparts, women workers, like these women in a cigar factory near Pittsburgh, Pennsylvania, struggled with unpleasant and sometimes unhealthy working conditions.

>> Women protested the production and sale of alcohol to generate support for the Eighteenth Amendment.

along with other groups such as the Anti-Saloon League promoted temperance, the practice of never drinking alcohol. Members felt that alcohol often led men to squander their earnings on liquor and neglect or abuse their families. Formed in the 1870s, the WCTU gained strength during the Progressive Era. The WCTU was led by the influential speaker **Frances Willard** from 1879 until her death in 1898. Her work contributed to the passage of the Eighteenth Amendment in 1919, which outlawed the production and sale of alcohol.

Temperance was Willard's primary goal, but she also supported women's **suffrage**—the right to vote. She argued that women needed the vote to prohibit the sale of alcohol. Like many WCTU members, Willard also promoted other social causes, such as public health and welfare reform.

Nurse **Margaret Sanger** thought that family life and women's health would improve if mothers had fewer children. In 1916, Sanger, herself one of 11 children, opened the country's first birth-control clinic. Very controversial at the time, Sanger was jailed several times as a "public nuisance" for distributing information about birth control. But federal courts eventually said doctors could give out information about family planning. In 1921, Sanger founded the American Birth Control League to make this information available to more women.

African American women also worked for social change. In 1896, **Ida B. Wells**, an African American teacher and journalist, helped form the National Association of Colored Women (NACW). Wells was well-known for leading an anti-lynching campaign through her writing and speaking tours. The NACW's goal was to help families strive for success and to assist those who were less fortunate. With money raised from educated Black women, the NACW set up daycare centers to protect and educate Black children while their parents went to work.

>> Ida B. Wells, who was born into slavery, became a prominent Progressive activist promoting freedom from violence and equal opportunities for African Americans.

BOUNCE to Activate Gallery

RECALL What steps did women take to win workers' rights?

Women Seek Equal Political Rights

One of the boldest goals of Progressive women was suffrage. They argued that women participating in the democratic process through voting was the only way to make sure that the government would protect children, foster education, and support family life. As Jane Addams explained, women needed the vote because political issues reached inside people's homes.

> If the street is not cleaned by the city authorities no amount of private sweeping will keep the tenement free from grime; if the garbage is not properly collected and destroyed a tenement-house mother may see her children sicken and die of diseases from which she alone is powerless to shield them, although her tenderness and devotion are unbounded.
>
> She cannot even secure untainted meat for her household, . . . unless the meat has been inspected by city officials.
>
> —Jane Addams, *Ladies Home Journal*, 1910

Major Organizations of the Progressive Era With High Female Participation

NCL	National Consumers League	The nation's oldest consumer advocacy organization; it represents consumers on marketplace and workplace issues.
WTUL	Women's Trade Union League	The WTUL strove to reform working conditions by supporting women in labor unions and strikes.
WCTU	Women's Christian Temperance Union	The WCTU conducted "Women's Crusades" to "agitate, educate, and legislate" against the destructive power of alcohol.
NACW	National Association of Colored Women	The NACW promoted the moral, mental, and material progress by women of color, through women's suffrage and education.
NAWSA	National American Woman Suffrage Association	The NAWSA lobbied for state suffrage amendments that would lead to a federal amendment.
NAOWS	National Association Opposed to Woman Suffrage	Until passage of the 19th Amendment, the NAOWS argued that woman suffrage would impede women from making social changes.
NWP	National Woman's Party	Grown out of the NAWSA, the NWP used more militant methods to enfranchise women nationally.
NAACP	National Association for the Advancement of Colored People	The NAACP aims to educate citizens on civil rights, eliminate race prejudice, and ensure political, educational, social, and economic equality.

>> **Hypothesize** Why would an organization such as NAOWS oppose woman suffrage?

The Early Fight for a Constitutional Amendment

Since the 1850s, reformers such as **Susan B. Anthony** and Elizabeth Cady Stanton had tirelessly struggled for the right for women to have a voice in political issues. Although Anthony and other women's right activists had favored ending slavery, they felt betrayed when Radical Republicans did not include women in the Fourteenth and Fifteenth amendments.

In 1869, Anthony and Stanton formed the National Woman Suffrage Association to fight for a constitutional amendment that would grant women the right to vote. They argued that just as the Constitution had been amended to extend the vote to African Americans, it should be amended to extend the vote to women.

In 1872, Anthony voted in an election in Rochester, New York, an illegal act for which she was tried and ultimately convicted in federal court. While awaiting trial, she toured the nation, delivering a speech titled "Is It a Crime for a Citizen of the United States to Vote?" Anthony declared, "Our . . . government is based on . . . the natural right of every individual member . . . to a voice and a vote in making and executing the laws." However, her speech failed to convince the nation to enact a women's suffrage amendment. An amendment was introduced in Congress and rejected in 1887. By the time of Anthony's death in 1906, only four western states—Wyoming, Utah, Colorado, and Idaho—had granted women the right to vote.

Women Lobby for Expanded Rights

In the 1890s, the national suffrage effort was reenergized by **Carrie Chapman Catt**. Catt had studied law and worked as one of the country's first female school superintendents.

A captivating speaker, Catt traveled around the country urging women to join the **National American Woman Suffrage Association (NAWSA)**, created in 1890 by the merger of Anthony's organization and a rival women's suffrage group. In 1900, Catt became the president of the NAWSA. She promoted what became known as her "winning plan," which called for action on two fronts to expand women's right to participate in the democratic process. Some teams of women lobbied Congress to pass a constitutional amendment giving women the right to vote. Meanwhile, other teams used the new referendum process to try to pass state suffrage laws. The strategy at the state level eventually helped women win the right to vote in New York, Michigan, and Oklahoma.

Catt introduced a "society plan" to recruit wealthy, well-educated women. She and her army of workers signed on women from all levels of society, including African Americans, Mexican Americans, and Jewish immigrants. All these women, called "suffragists," helped promote suffrage in their own areas.

Activists Use Nonviolent Protests By 1910, as Progressivism was nearing its height, the women's suffrage movement was growing stronger too. A new generation of leaders had emerged. Besides Catt, they included Jane Addams and Harriet Stanton Blatch, the daughter of Elizabeth Cady Stanton. The movement's new leaders expanded its goals to include calls for improvements in education, reforms of corrupt government, and labor reforms such as the passage of child labor laws. These activists presented suffrage as not only an expansion of the democratic process but also as a way to help solve many of society's other ills.This strategy linked the women's suffrage movement with the powerful wave of Progressive reform.

The suffrage movement's new goals also helped it grow by making it more appealing to working women. The rising number of college-educated women flooded into the movement as well. Some women, known as social activists, took to the streets, organizing mass parades and rallies. Catt, while cautious about these new methods, added them to her tactics at the NAWSA. Some women social activists grew even more daring in their strategies to win the vote.

Alice Paul, their best known leader, was raised in a Quaker home where she was encouraged to be independent. Paul attended a Quaker college and the New York School of Social Work before earning a Ph.D. from the University of Pennsylvania in 1912. She believed that drastic steps were needed to win the vote. By 1913, she was organizing women to recruit others across the nation. They drew in women of many backgrounds, from Maud Younger, known as the "millionaire waitress" because she organized California's first waitresses' union, to Nina Otero-Warren, a Hispanic woman who headed New Mexico's State Board of Health.

By 1917, Paul had formed the National Woman's Party (NWP), which used public protest marches. The NWP became the first group to march with picket signs outside the White House. Hundreds of women were arrested in these protests. Some went on hunger strikes, stating that they would not eat until they could vote. While in jail, some women, including Paul, were force-fed to end their hunger strikes. The NWP methods angered many people, including women in other suffrage groups. Nevertheless, they did help women the right to vote because the NWP's actions drew attention to their cause and made less-radical groups like the NAWSA look tame by comparison.

The Nineteenth Amendment Expands Political Rights In the 1916 presidential election, both the Democratic and the Republican parties called

Passage of Women's Suffrage

>> **Analyze Maps** In which region of the United States did the majority of states achieve full suffrage for women before the passage of the Nineteenth Amendment?

for extending the right to vote to women. As the movement gained support, however, opposition to it also increased. The liquor industry strongly opposed women's suffrage because of women's support for temperance. The textile industry also opposed suffrage because it feared women would favor laws limiting child labor. Even some women worked against the movement. The National Association Opposed to Woman Suffrage (NAOWS) believed that the effort to win the vote would take women's attention away from family and volunteer work that benefited society in many ways. But as pressure for women's suffrage grew, the NAOWS faded away.

When the United States entered World War I in April 1917, President Woodrow Wilson proclaimed that "the world must be made safe for democracy." Suffragists were astounded.

How could America be a democracy, they wondered, if women could not vote? Nevertheless, Carrie Catt and Florence Kelley led the NAWSA to support the war effort. Their actions and those of the NWP convinced a growing number of legislators to support a women's suffrage amendment.

In June 1917, envoys from Russia visited President Wilson. Alice Paul and her activists saw a golden opportunity. The Russians had just overthrown their czar, established a republic, and granted women the right to vote. As the envoys neared the White House, the suffragists stunned an embarrassed Wilson by unveiling a banner that proclaimed America was not a democracy. In 1918, an amendment to extend the vote to women was once again considered by Congress. It passed in the House of Representatives but was narrowly rejected in the Senate.

The following year, the amendment was offered in Congress once again. In June 1919, Congress finally approved the **Nineteenth Amendment,** which stated that the right to vote "shall not be denied or abridged on account of sex."

On August 18, 1920, the Tennessee State House of Representatives passed the amendment by one vote. With Tennessee's ratification, enough states had passed the amendment that it became official. Alice Paul and Carrie Catt both claimed responsibility for the victory. In fact, according to historian Nancy Cott, "neither the shocking militancy of the National Women's Party nor the ladylike moderation of NAWSA was so solely responsible for victory as each group publicly claimed." The rival groups both contributed to the triumph of the women's suffrage movement, which also gave a boost to the budding civil rights movement of the twentieth century. The impact of the Nineteenth

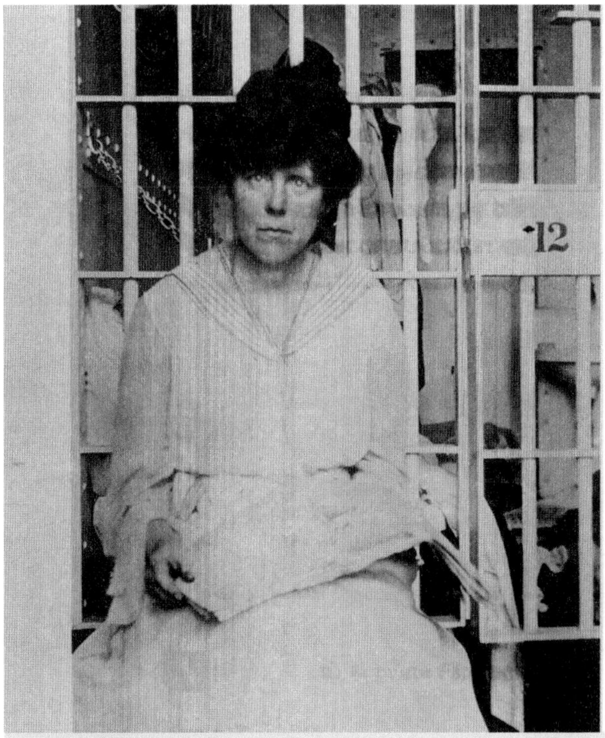

>> Women who protested their lack of suffrage often landed in jail, where they continued to protest despite their confinement.

BOUNCE to Activate Timeline

>> Millions of women voted for the first time after the passage of the Nineteenth Amendment prohibited states from denying the right to vote based on sex.

Amendment was felt immediately. On November 2, 1920, Catt, Paul, and millions of other American women voted for the first time in a U.S. presidential election.

CHECK UNDERSTANDING How did the Nineteenth Amendment expand participation in the democratic process?

ASSESSMENT

1. **Generate Explanations** Explain how *Muller* v. *Oregon* represented a victory for women reformers during the Progressive Era but presented a setback for them in later years.
2. **Determine Point of View** Explain why some women's rights activists were angry when the rights of African Americans were expanded after the Civil War.
3. **Summarize** Discuss the strategies of Carrie Chapman Catt's "winning plan."
4. **Generate Explanations** Explain how the women's suffrage movement changed with the rise of Progressivism.
5. **Compare and Contrast** the strategies of the National American Woman Suffrage Association and the National Woman's Party.

GO ONLINE to access these biographies: Elizabeth Cady Stanton, Susan B. Anthony

11.3

Segregation remained common throughout the Progressive Era. This one-room school in Anthoston, Kentucky, was for African Americans only. Many students are absent to harvest tobacco.

Striving for Equality

BOUNCE to Activate Flipped Video

Objectives

Analyze Progressives' attitudes toward minority rights.

Describe the political organizations formed by African Americans to promote civil rights.

Examine the actions taken by other minority groups to expand their rights.

Key Terms

Americanization
Booker T. Washington
W.E.B. Du Bois
Niagara Movement
National Association for the Advancement of Colored People (NAACP)
Urban League
Anti-Defamation League
mutualistas
American Indian Citizenship Act of 1924

Prejudice and discrimination against minorities continued even as the Progressive Movement got underway. But in the spirit of Progressivism, African Americans, Latinos, Catholics, Jews, and new immigrant groups worked to help themselves. Their efforts paved the way for the era of civil rights that would follow decades later.

Minorities Face Challenges in the Progressive Era

The Progressive Era was not so progressive for nonwhite and immigrant Americans. Most Progressives were white Anglo-Saxon Protestant reformers who were indifferent or actively hostile to minorities. They tried to make the United States a model society by encouraging everyone to follow white, middle-class ways of life.

The Americanization Movement Settlement houses and other civic groups played a prominent role in the **Americanization** efforts of many Progressives. While they taught immigrants English, their programs also tried to change how immigrants lived and change what they believed were radical politics. They advised immigrants how to dress like white middle-class Americans and pushed them to replace the foods and customs of their homelands with Protestant practices and values. These reformers believed that assimilating immigrants into American society would make them more loyal and moral citizens.

Many Progressives found the immigrants' use of alcohol especially alarming. In many European countries, it was customary for families to serve wine or beer with meals. Many reformers, however, believed that these practices showed moral faults. As a result, prejudice against immigrants was one of the forces behind the temperance movement.

GO ONLINE to access your digital course

Effects of Racism and *Plessy* v. *Ferguson* Many Progressives shared the same prejudice against nonwhites held by other white Americans of the time. They believed that some people were more fit than others to play a leading role in society. They agreed with invalid scientific theories that said that dark-skinned peoples had less intelligence than whites. In the late 1800s, southern Progressives used these misguided theories to justify the passage of laws that kept African Americans from voting.

Some southern Progressives urged an end to the violence and terrorism waged against African Americans but still did not advocate equal rights. Edgar Gardner Murphy, an Episcopal minister and a leading Alabama Progressive, advised that African Americans "will accept in the white man's country the place assigned him by the white man, . . . not by stress of rivalry, but by genial cooperation with the white man's interests."

After the Supreme Court issued its *Plessy* v. *Ferguson* (1896) decision, which upheld Jim Crow laws, states across the North and the South had passed even more restrictive segregation laws. By 1910, segregation was the norm across the nation. After 1914, even the offices of the federal government in Washington, D.C., were segregated as a result of policies approved by President Woodrow Wilson, a Progressive.

CHECK UNDERSTANDING What attitudes did most Progressives hold about minorities and immigrant groups?

African Americans Promote Civil Rights

In the face of these injustices, the nation's most visible African American leader urged patience. **Booker T. Washington** told Blacks to move slowly toward racial progress. By working hard and waiting patiently, he believed, African Americans would gradually win white Americans' respect and eventually would be able to exercise their full voting and citizenship rights.

Other African Americans rejected this view. The most outspoken among them were **W.E.B. Du Bois** and William Monroe Trotter. Both men had been raised in New England and educated at Harvard University. Both urged African Americans to demand immediately all the rights guaranteed by the Constitution.

A New Civil Rights Organization Du Bois and Trotter were especially concerned that all across the South, Black men were being denied the right to vote. In the summer of 1905, they and other leading African American thinkers met at Niagara Falls. They had to meet in Canada because no hotel on the New York side of the border would give them rooms.

The **Niagara Movement,** as the group called itself, denounced the idea of gradual progress. Washington, they said, was too willing to compromise African Americans' basic rights. They also condemned his notion of teaching only trade skills. This kind of education, Du Bois said, "can create workers, but it cannot make *men*." Talented Blacks should be taught history, literature, and philosophy, so they could think for themselves. Du Bois had a significant impact on the ways African Americans and concerned white people thought about equality.

Two Views on Civil Rights

BOOKER T. WASHINGTON 1856–1915	W.E.B. DU BOIS 1868–1963
"[The Negro must] live peaceably with his white neighbors ... the Negro [must] deport himself modestly ... depending upon the slow but sure influences that proceed from the possessions of property, intelligence, and high character for the full recognition of his political rights."	"We claim for ourselves every single right that belongs to a freeborn American ... and until we get these rights we will never cease to protest ... How shall we get them? By voting where we may vote, by persistent, unceasing agitation, by hammering at the truth, by sacrifice and work."
Washington believed that African Americans had to achieve economic independence before civil rights. Black people must tolerate discrimination while they proved themselves equal to white people. Slowly, civil rights would come.	Du Bois believed that Black Americans had to demand their social and civil rights or else become permanent victims of racism. African Americans must fight every day for the rights given to them in the Constitution.

>> **Analyze Information** How did the views of these two leaders on the ways in which African Americans should secure civil rights differ?

BOUNCE to Activate Timeline

NAACP Promotes Civil Rights In the summer of 1908, a white mob in Springfield, Illinois, attempted to lynch two African American prisoners in the city jail. Upon learning that the prisoners had been removed to safety, the rioters turned their anger against the city's Black residents, killing two people and burning 40 homes.

The Springfield riot also got the attention of a number of white reformers. They now joined with African Americans who were fighting to protect their lives and securing their civil rights. Even before the Springfield riot, there were incidents in Wilmington, North Carolina, and in Atlanta, Georgia. In Wilmington in 1898, whites attacked African Americans killing as many as 300. In Atlanta in 1906, 100 were killed.

In 1909, several white reformers joined with leaders of the Niagara Movement to form the **National Association for the Advancement of Colored People (NAACP).** The NAACP was a political organization that aimed to help African Americans be "physically free from peonage [forced, low-paid labor], mentally free from ignorance, politically free from disfranchisement, and socially free from insult."

NAACP leaders included white and Black Progressives who had worked in other areas of social reform. Among them were Jane Addams, Ray Stannard Baker, and Florence Kelley. Ida B. Wells, owner of a Tennessee newspaper, used her publication to make clear the horror of lynching at great risk to her own safety. She and the others planned the group's strategy—to use litigation in the courts to challenge unfair laws and expand the right to participate in the democratic process. In the early 1900s, the NAACP focused on the battle for equal access to decent housing and professional careers like teaching. It drew strength from members like W.E.B. Du Bois, who edited the NAACP's magazine, *The Crisis*, and the lawyer, teacher, and former diplomat James Weldon Johnson.

Urban League Seeks to Expand Economic Opportunities Across the country, African Americans were migrating from rural to urban areas during this period. Local Black clubs and churches set up employment agencies and relief efforts to help African Americans get settled and find work.

In 1911, more than 100 of these groups in many cities joined into a network called the **Urban League.** While the NAACP helped middle-class Blacks struggle for political and social justice, the Urban League focused on poorer workers. It helped families buy clothes and books and send children to school. It also helped factory workers and domestic servants find jobs. Both the NAACP and the Urban League still aid African Americans today.

>> W.E.B. Du Bois (center) and other founding members of the Niagara Movement attended the Niagara Conference in 1905.

BOUNCE to Activate Gallery

RECALL Why did African Americans and others decide it was time to organize against discrimination?

Protecting Rights for Ethnic and Religious Minorities

African Americans were not alone in seeking rights. Individuals and organizations of diverse ethnic and religious groups spoke out against unfair treatment and took action by creating self-help agencies. For example, in northern cities, Catholic parishes offered a variety of social services to immigrants. In Chicago, a network of Polish Catholic groups grew so strong that it earned the nickname American Warsaw.

Expanding Rights and Opportunities for Jews Jews in New York had formed the B'nai B'rith in 1843 to provide religious education and to help Jewish families. In response to growing anti-Semitism, the group founded the **Anti-Defamation League** in

1913. Its goal was— and still is—to defend Jews and others against physical and verbal attacks, false statements, and "to secure justice and fair treatment to all citizens alike. . . ." In this way, the group expanded political rights for Jews and others. During the late 1800s and early 1900s, some business refused to hire or serve Jewish people. The Anti-Defamation League led efforts to expand economic opportunities for Jews and other minorities by fighting this form of discrimination.

Expanding Rights and Opportunities for Mexican Americans Mexican Americans also organized to help themselves. Those living in Arizona formed the Partido Liberal Mexicano (PLM), which offered Mexican Americans many of the same services that the Urban League gave to African Americans. In several states, Mexican Americans formed **mutualistas,** groups that made loans and provided legal assistance. The mutualistas also had insurance programs to help members if they were too sick to work.

Many Mexican Americans were forced to sign unfair labor contracts that kept them in debt to people whose land they worked. In 1911, the Supreme Court struck down a law that enforced that system.

>> Asian Americans faced widespread discrimination. California state laws placed barriers to the property rights of Japanese immigrant farmers, for example.

American Indians Gain Citizenship Progressives did little to help American Indians. The Dawes General Allotment Act, passed in 1887, had divided reservations into plots for individuals to farm. But the law also said that lands not given to individual Indians could be sold to the general public. By 1932, nearly two thirds of the lands held by tribes in 1887 were in the hands of whites.

Carlos Montezuma, an American Indian from Arizona, helped establish the Society of American Indians in 1911, the first organization formed to promote Indian rights and protest federal Indian policy. A doctor, Montezuma treated American Indians living on reservations. He urged American Indians to preserve their cultures and avoid being dependent on the government.

The Mission Indian Federation, founded by California Indians in 1919, called for civil rights and self-determination for Indians. Both the Society of American Indians and the Mission Indian Federation are just two examples of how Indians organized and asserted their own rights. Many reformers, who hoped that Indians could be assimilated into American society like immigrants, found this position troubling.

The Dawes Act barred American Indians from selling their plots of land for 25 years. The law provided that they would then get the title to the land and become citizens. This policy was intended to speed American Indians' assimilation into white society, abolish Indian tribes' cultures, and end attempts at self-government. By the 1920s, however, it was clear that the policy was not achieving this goal. So Congress tried another approach. The congressional act **American Indian Citizenship Act of 1924** made all American Indians citizens of the United States, with full voting rights. For American Indians, this law was an important step toward political equality with other Americans.

The official reason for granting citizenship and voting rights was to reward American Indians for their service in World War I. However, supporters also hoped that the reform would help the Americanization process.

Fighting for Rights and Opportunities for Asian Americans Asian Americans also had to protect themselves and struggled to expand their political rights. In 1907, in an informal agreement between the United States and Japan—known as the "Gentlemen's Agreement"—the United States promised not to impose restrictions on Japanese immigration and Japan promised not to allow further emigration to the U.S. Of course, many

Japanese immigrants were already in California, where they were forced to send their children to segregated schools. A 1913 California law said that only American citizens could own land. Because Japanese immigrants could not become citizens, the law forced them to sell their land. Japanese Americans found a way around this, however, by putting the land in their children's names. Because their children had been born in the United States, they were American citizens. The law also affected immigrants from China and India, who were also not allowed to become citizens.

Japanese immigrant Takao Ozawa fought the law in court that blocked Asian Americans from becoming citizens. In 1922, however, the Supreme Court ruled against him. A newspaper read by Japanese Americans commented, "The slim hope that we had entertained . . . has been shattered completely."

☑ **IDENTIFY** What strategies did other minority groups use to defend their rights?

☑ ASSESSMENT

1. **Generate Explanations** Discuss the contradictions of the Progressive Movement.
2. **Compare and Contrast** the ideologies of Booker T. Washington and W.E.B. Du Bois.
3. **Draw Conclusions** Discuss both the positive and negative implications of the American Indian Citizenship Act of 1924.
4. **Summarize** What were the goals of the National Association for the Advancement of Colored People (NAACP)?
5. **Compare** the efforts of Mexican Americans, American Indians, Asian Americans, and Jews to fight against discrimination during the Progressive Era.

Atlanta Exposition Address: Booker T. Washington

In 1895, African American leader Booker T. Washington addressed a predominantly white audience in Atlanta. He urged fellow Blacks to build friendly relations with whites and to start "at the bottom" by working at "the common occupations of life." Other Black leaders rejected Washington's plan and called it the "Atlanta Compromise."

>> Booker T. Washington

One-third of the population of the South is of the Negro race. No enterprise seeking the material, civil, or moral welfare of this section can disregard this element of our population and reach the highest success. I but convey to you, Mr. President and Directors, the sentiment of the masses of my race when I say that in no way have the value and manhood of the American Negro been more fittingly and generously recognized than by the managers of this magnificent Exposition at every stage of its progress. It is a recognition that will do more to cement the friendship of the two races than any occurrence since the dawn of our freedom.

Not only this, but the opportunity here afforded will awaken among us a new era of industrial progress. Ignorant and inexperienced, it is not strange that in the first years of our new life we began at the top instead of at the bottom; that a seat in Congress or the state legislature was more sought than real estate or industrial skill; that the political convention or stump [political] speaking had more attractions than starting a dairy farm or truck garden [garden where vegetables are grown to be sold]. . . .

☑ **DRAW INFERENCES** What do you think Washington meant by "the first years in our new life"?

Our greatest danger is that in the great leap from slavery to freedom we may overlook the fact that the masses of us are to live by the productions of our hands, and fail to keep in mind that we shall prosper in proportion as we learn to dignify and glorify common labour, and put brains and skill into the common occupations of life; shall prosper in proportion as we learn to draw the line between the superficial and the substantial, the ornamental gewgaws of life and the useful. No race can prosper till it learns that there is as much dignity in tilling a field as in writing a poem. It is at the bottom of life we must begin, and not at the top. Nor should we permit our grievances to overshadow our opportunities.

☑ **EXPLAIN AN ARGUMENT** What does Washington mean by beginning "at the bottom of life"?

To those of my race who depend on bettering their condition in a foreign land or who underestimate the importance of cultivating [developing] friendly relations with the Southern white man, who is their next-door neighbor, I would say: "Cast down your bucket where you are" [make use of the resources that you don't realize are all around you]— cast it down in making friends in every manly way of the people of all races by whom we are surrounded.

UNDERSTAND MEANING What was Washington calling a "foreign land"? Why was it foreign?

Cast it down in agriculture, mechanics, in commerce, in domestic service [working as a servant in the employer's home], and in the professions [occupations that require special education, such as medicine or law]. And in this connection it is well to bear in mind that whatever other sins the South may be called to bear, when it comes to business, pure and simple, it is in the South that the Negro is given a man's chance in the commercial world. . . . Our greatest danger is that in the great leap from slavery to freedom we may overlook the fact that the masses of us are to live by the productions of our hands, and fail to keep in mind that we shall prosper in proportion as we learn to dignify and glorify common labour, and put brains and skill into the common occupations of life. . . . No race can prosper till it learns that there is as much dignity in tilling [plowing] a field as in writing a poem. It is at the bottom of life we must begin, and not at the top. Nor should we permit our grievances to overshadow our opportunities. . . .

ANALYZE STYLE AND RHETORIC How did Washington make use of repetition in this paragraph and the previous one? What purpose does the repetition serve?

. . . While we take pride in what we exhibit as a result of our independent efforts, we do not for a moment forget that our part in this exhibition would fall far short of your expectations but for the constant help that has come to our educational life, not only from the Southern states, but especially from Northern philanthropists, who have made their gifts a constant stream of blessing and encouragement.

The wisest among my race understand that the agitation of questions of social equality is the extremest folly, and that progress in the enjoyment of all the privileges that will come to us must be the result of severe and constant struggle rather than of artificial forcing. No race that has anything to contribute to the markets of the world is long in any degree ostracized. It is important and right that all privileges of the law be ours, but it is vastly more important that we be prepared for the exercise of these privileges. The opportunity to earn a dollar in a factory just now is worth infinitely more than the opportunity to spend a dollar in an opera-house.

DRAW INFERENCES In the final paragraph what idea or political position is Washington arguing against?

ASSESSMENT

1. **Determine Central Ideas** What is the main idea of the speech as excerpted here?
2. **Draw Conclusions** Do you agree with the central idea expressed in the address? Cite examples to support your answer.
3. **Analyze Interactions** Why do you think some Black leaders rejected the ideas Washington expressed in this address?

GO ONLINE to access primary sources

11.4

President Theodore Roosevelt dedicated his considerable energy and abilities to achieving Progressive reforms.

BOUNCE to Activate Flipped Video

Objectives

Analyze how Theodore Roosevelt influenced the changing relationship between the federal government and private business.

Explain the impact of Roosevelt's actions towards managing the environment.

Compare and contrast Roosevelt's policies with Taft's and Wilson's policies.

Describe Wilson's efforts to regulate the economy.

Assess the legacy of the Progressive Era.

Key Terms

Theodore Roosevelt
Square Deal
Hepburn Act
Meat Inspection Act
Pure Food and Drug Act
John Muir
Gifford Pinchot
National Reclamation Act
New Nationalism
Progressive Party
Woodrow Wilson
New Freedom
Sixteenth Amendment
monetary policy
Federal Reserve Act
Clayton Antitrust Act

Reformers in the White House

In the late 1800s, the United States had several weak and ineffective Presidents. The arrival of Theodore Roosevelt, a charismatic figure who embraced Progressive ideals, ushered in a new era. Roosevelt pushed for many Progressive reforms and expanded the powers of the presidency. He changed the way Americans viewed the roles of the President and the government.

Roosevelt Changes the Relationship Between Government and Business

In 1901, when **Theodore Roosevelt** became President of the United States, he was only 43 years old.

However, he had packed quite a lot into those years, gaining a reputation for being smart, energetic, and opinionated. The sickly child of wealthy parents, he had used his family's resources to develop both his strength and his mind. Observers said Theodore Roosevelt generated so much energy that if you met him, you left the event with bits of his personality "stuck to your clothes."

Roosevelt's Path to the Presidency Roosevelt had graduated with honors from Harvard University in 1880. He spent only a few months studying law at Columbia University before being elected to the New York State Assembly. After three years' service there, and after the deaths of both his mother and his wife, Alice, Roosevelt retired to a ranch in the West. There he developed a love of the wilderness.

GO ONLINE to access your digital course

Theodore Roosevelt could not remain long out of the spotlight, however. By 1889, he had returned to politics. As president of New York City's Board of Police Commissioners, he gained fame by fighting corruption. President William McKinley noticed him and named him Assistant Secretary of the Navy. When the Spanish-American War broke out in 1898, Roosevelt resigned the post to form the Rough Riders, a volunteer cavalry unit that became famous during the war.

After the end of the conflict, the young war hero was elected governor of New York, where he pushed for Progressive reforms. His reform efforts annoyed Republican leaders in the state, however. They convinced McKinley to choose Roosevelt as his running mate so Roosevelt would leave New York—and them—alone. McKinley was reelected President in 1900, but within a few months he was assassinated, and Roosevelt became President. He soon dominated public attention. Journalists vied for interviews with him and children begged their parents for a teddy bear, the new stuffed animal named for him.

Progressive reformers were pleased to see the benefits of the ICC spreading, namely that the powerful railroads were finally under control. This pleased farmers as well, who had long sought such regulation. But the Elkins Act and the ICC in general had costs.

He called his program the **Square Deal**. Its goals were to keep the wealthy and powerful from taking advantage of small business owners and the poor. Roosevelt's idea of fair government did not mean that everyone would get rich or that the government should take care of the lazy. He compared his Square Deal to a hand of cards.

> When I say I believe in a square deal, I do not mean to give every man the best hand. If good cards do not come to any man, or if they do come, and he has not got the power to play them, that is his affair. All I mean is that there shall be no crookedness in the dealing.
>
> —Theodore Roosevelt, 1905

Intervening Between Owners and Workers

Roosevelt often stepped in to labor disputes with the authority and power of the federal government. One example was in 1902, when Pennsylvania coal miners went on strike. The miners wanted a pay raise and a shorter workday. Roosevelt sympathized with the overworked miners, but he knew that a steady supply of coal was needed to keep factories running and homes warm. He wanted the strike ended quickly.

First, Roosevelt tried to get mine owners to listen to workers' concerns. When this failed, he threatened to send federal troops to take control of the mines and to run them with federal employees. His threat forced the mine owners to give the miners a small pay raise and a nine-hour workday. For the first time, the federal government had stepped in to help workers in a labor dispute.

This coal strike intervention was one of many steps Roosevelt took to control the power of corporations. Within a year, Roosevelt convinced Congress to establish the Department of Commerce and Labor to monitor businesses engaged in interstate commerce.

The ICC Takes on the Railroads The cost of shipping freight on railroads had been an issue since the 1870s. Railroad companies often could charge whatever they wanted. The railroads' power was especially troublesome for western farmers. They had no other way to move their products to eastern markets.

>> People seize coal from a stalled train during the 1902 coal strike. **Analyze Images** How does this image reinforce Roosevelt's belief that it was important for the coal strike to end quickly?

In 1887, Congress had created the Interstate Commerce Commission (ICC) to oversee rail charges for shipments that passed through more than one state. The ICC was supposed to make sure that all shippers were charged the same amounts. By 1900, though, the Supreme Court had stripped away most of the ICC's power. So Roosevelt pushed Congress to pass the Elkins Act in 1903, which imposed fines on railroads that gave special rates to favored shippers. In 1906, he got Congress to pass the **Hepburn Act**, which gave the ICC even greater powers. This law allowed ICC for the first time to set maximum shipping rates. The act also set maximum rates for ferries, toll bridges, and oil pipelines. Finally, it gave any ruling by the ICC the legal force of a court order.

Progressive reformers were pleased to see the powerful railroads finally brought under control. Farmers who had long sought such regulation especially felts its benefits. But the Elkins Act and the ICC in general had costs, as its critics pointed out. The ICC's five commissioners were not elected to their positions. Once appointed by the President and approved by the Senate, they could not be removed during their term.

Some Americans found the ICC's independence from the public will and from all three branches of government to be troubling. In addition, when the ICC exercised its new power and limited railroad rates, its action harmed the economy. The value of railroad stocks plummeted, which helped to bring on the financial panic that swept the nation in 1907.

A Trustbuster Enforces Legislation It did not take long for the President and his administration to earn a reputation as "trustbusters." In response to an antitrust suit filed by Roosevelt's attorney general, the Supreme Court ruled in 1904 that the Northern Securities Company—a big railroad company—was an illegal trust. The decision forced the company to split into smaller companies. The next year, the Court found that a beef trust and several powerful agricultural companies had broken antitrust laws.

Roosevelt was not interested in bringing down all large companies. He saw a difference between "good trusts" and "bad trusts." Big businesses could often be more efficient than small ones, he believed. Big business was bad, he said, only if it bullied smaller companies or cheated consumers.

So he supported powerful corporations as long as they did business fairly. His supporters called him a "trust-tamer," but some wealthy Progressives criticized his trustbusting. Other critics claimed that his good trust-bad trust distinction meant that antitrust laws were being applied unevenly and thus unfairly. This practice may even have been unconstitutional—a violation of the private property protections in the Fifth and Fourteenth Amendments.

Despite such criticisms, most Americans were pleased with the antitrust prosecutions. However, they were also conflicted. They deeply distrusted and feared the big corporations' huge concentrations of wealth and power. But at the same time, they

Early Progressive Legislation

LEGISLATION	EFFECT
Sherman Antitrust Act (1890)	Outlawed monopolies and practices that restrained trade, such as price fixing
National Reclamation Act (1902)	Provided for federal irrigation projects by using money from the sale of public lands
Elkins Act (1903)	Imposed fines on railroads that gave special rates to favored shippers
Hepburn Act (1906)	Authorized the federal government to regulate railroad rates and set maximum prices for ferries, bridge tolls, and oil pipelines
Meat Inspection Act (1906)	Allowed the federal government to inspect meat sold across state lines and required inspections of meat-processing plants
Pure Food and Drug Act (1906)	Allowed federal inspection of food and medicine and banned the shipment and sale of impure food and the mislabeling of food and medicine

>> **Analyze Charts** Which of these acts do you believe was the most important? Why?

treasured the consumer benefits the companies' size often provided.

Regulating the Food and Drug Industries In 1906, muckraker Upton Sinclair published his novel *The Jungle*. His descriptions of the filthy, unhealthy conditions in meatpacking plants revolted the public and infuriated the President, having an immediate impact. Roosevelt urged Congress to pass the **Meat Inspection Act** that same year.

It provided federal agents with the power to inspect any meat sold across state lines and required federal inspection of meat-processing plants. Today, when we eat lunchmeat or grilled chicken, we trust that federal inspectors have monitored the plant where it is produced. If there is a serious problem, the government can force the meatpacker to pull the product off the shelves before many people become sick. This regulation is one lasting result of Progressives' insistence that the government take responsibility for food safety.

The **Pure Food and Drug Act** benefited the public by placing the same controls on other foods and on medicines. Although there was some concern that here again the federal government was taking on too much of the states' constitutional police power, most Americans felt like the benefits outweighed the costs. The act also banned the interstate shipment of impure food and the mislabeling of food and drugs. Today, the Food and Drug Administration (FDA) still enforces this law and others. The FDA monitors companies to make sure people are not hurt by dangerous substances or dishonest labels. For example, before a drug can be sold, it must be tested and approved by the FDA.

☑ **RECALL** What was the purpose of such legislation as the Hepburn Act and the Meat Inspection Act?

Managing the Environment

Roosevelt's deep reverence for nature also shaped his policies. The books he published on hunting and the rugged West reflected his fascination with the competition between humans and the wilderness. He was pleased that the federal government had established Yellowstone National Park in 1872 to protect wildlife, and he admired California naturalist **John Muir**, whose efforts had led Congress to create Yosemite National Park in 1890.

>> **Analyze Political Cartoons** What does this cartoon suggest about Roosevelt's differing approaches to regulating trusts?

>> President Roosevelt met with John Muir in Yosemite National Park, California, in 1903. **Contrast** How did Roosevelt's views on preserving wilderness areas differ from Muir's?

BOUNCE to Activate Gallery

Conservation or Preservation? In 1891, Congress had given the President the power to protect timberlands by setting aside land as federal forests. Following Muir's advice, Roosevelt closed off more than 100 million acres of forestland. However, the President did not agree with Muir that all wild areas should be preserved, or left untouched. Some wild lands held valuable resources, and Roosevelt thought those resources were meant to be used. This view became clear in his forest policy. In typical Progressive style, he called on experts to draw up plans for both conserving and using the forests.

Roosevelt drew on the "rational use" ideas of **Gifford Pinchot**, who led the Division of Forestry in the U.S. Department of Agriculture. Pinchot recommended a different approach—that forests be preserved for public use. By this, he meant that forests should be protected so that trees would have time to mature into good lumber. Then the protected areas should be logged for wood to build houses and new areas placed under protection. "The object of our forest policy," explained Pinchot, "is not to preserve the forests because they are refuges for the wild creatures of the wilderness, but rather they are the making of prosperous homes."

Pinchot's views came to dominate American policies toward natural resources. Conservation, or the planned management of natural resources, became government policy for managing public lands. But private ownership inspired conservation, too. In some cases, private ownership gave people the incentive to handle the natural resources on their land wisely so they would not damage the long-term value of their property.

In all, Roosevelt worked with Congress to establish five national parks and established 18 national monuments or historical landmarks under the Antiquities Act of 1906. Together, these unique places formed the core of the National Park Service, which was established in 1916 and still works today to conserve and share many natural and historic landmarks in the United States.

Roosevelt's views on land use went beyond the belief that public lands should, in some cases, be preserved or put to use for wider societal benefit. In 1908, the Supreme Court of the State of Maine handed down a decision saying, essentially, that the government could restrict the cutting of trees on private land in order to prevent erosion. Roosevelt backed up this governmental action, publicly stating his view that the needs of the community outweighed the private property rights of individuals or industries.

This was a controversial stance. The idea that private property, whether a person's own personal property or that of his or her business, is protected

>> **Analyze Maps** Why might larger national parks be located in the West?

by the Fifth Amendment to the Constitution is one of the bedrock ideals of American society and industry. The Fifth Amendment states that no "private property [shall] be taken for public use, without just compensation." Many individuals and business owners felt that restrictions on the use of their property, such as those imposed by antitrust regulation or environmental protection regulation, violated this right. This tension between private property rights and public use for the good of the community is still present today.

Changes in Population Affect Water Policy

Another highly controversial natural resource issue was water. Over centuries, American Indians had used various irrigation methods to bring water to the arid Southwest. The situation changed in the late 1800s, when newcomers began mining and farming in Utah, New Mexico, Colorado, Nevada, and California. Mining machinery required a great deal of water, and water-sharing systems long used by those states' Mexican American residents were challenged by the new people and businesses who arrived. Private irrigation companies came to the area, staked claims to sections of riverbeds, and redirected the water so farmers could revive—or "reclaim"—dried-up fields. As increases in population strained environmental resources, bitter fights developed over who should own water rights and how the water should be shared.

Roosevelt sprang into action on this issue. He listened to Nevada representative Francis Newlands, who wanted the federal government to help western states build huge reservoirs to hold and to conserve water. Roosevelt pushed Congress for a law that would allow it.

In 1902, Congress passed the **National Reclamation Act**, which gave the federal government the power to decide where and how water would be distributed. The government would build and manage dams that would create reservoirs, generate power, and direct water flow. This would make water from one state's rivers and streams available to farmers in other states. The full effect of the Reclamation Act was felt over the next few decades, as water management projects created huge reservoirs and lakes where there had been dry canyons. Examples include the Salt Valley Project in Arizona and the Roosevelt Dam and Hoover Dam on the Colorado River.

RECALL What was the purpose of the National Reclamation Act?

>> **Analyze Political Cartoons** What clues in this cartoon reveal what type of policies the author believes Taft will enact as president?

A New Direction In Presidential Politics

Roosevelt left the presidency after two terms in office, saying he wished to enjoy private life. He was still a powerful force in the Republican Party, however, and he used that power to help his Secretary of War William Howard Taft win the presidency in 1908. Roosevelt expected Taft to continue his programs of managing business and natural resources. Political cartoonists made caricatures of Roosevelt handing over what he called "my policies" to Taft, who seemed to have no ideas of his own.

Taft's Agenda Differs But Taft soon set his own agenda. He approved the Payne-Aldrich Act (1909), which did not lower tariffs as much as Roosevelt had wanted. He also pushed Congress to pass the Mann-Elkins Act (1910), which gave the government control over telephone and telegraph rates. He encouraged Congress to propose an income tax. Perhaps most importantly, he dropped Roosevelt's distinction between good trusts and bad trusts.

Taft's Justice Department brought lawsuits against twice as many corporations as Roosevelt's had done. One result was that in 1911, the Supreme Court "busted" the trust built by the Standard Oil Company. But Taft also supported what the Court called its "rule of reason," which relaxed the hard line set by the Sherman Antitrust Act. The rule of reason allowed big monopolies so long as they did not "unreasonably" squeeze out smaller companies. Roosevelt publicly criticized these decisions. Then Taft's attorney general sued to force U.S. Steel to sell a coal company it had bought. Roosevelt, who had earlier approved the purchase of the company, fumed.

Taft further infuriated Roosevelt and other Progressives in the Republican Party when he fired Gifford Pinchot for publicly criticizing Secretary of the Interior Richard Ballinger. Pinchot charged that Ballinger, who opposed Roosevelt's conservation policies, had worked with business interests to sell federal land rich in coal deposits in Alaska. Although a congressional investigation later cleared Ballinger of these charges, the damage had been done.

Roosevelt's Response Roosevelt began traveling the country speaking about what he called the **New Nationalism**—a program to restore the government's trustbusting power. Declaring himself as "strong as a bull moose," Roosevelt vowed to tackle the trusts in a third presidential term. The Taft-Roosevelt battle split the Republican Party as an election neared: progressives bolted from the party and set up the **Progressive Party**. Reformer Jane Addams nominated Roosevelt as the Progressive Party's candidate for the 1912 presidential election.

The Republicans nominated Taft. The question was whether a third party like the Progressive Party could have an impact in a national election. In addition, Eugene V. Debs was the Socialist Party's candidate. A bitter election loomed.

Wilson Takes Advantage of Republican Discord The split created an opportunity for the Democrats and their candidate, **Woodrow Wilson**, to win the White House. Wilson's ideas had caught the attention of William Jennings Bryan, who helped Wilson win the Democratic nomination. As a student and later as a professor, Wilson had thought a great deal about good government. His doctoral thesis, *Congressional Government,* had launched him on a career teaching in college before he became the reforming governor of New Jersey.

Wilson shaped his ideas into a program he called the **New Freedom**. His plan looked much like Roosevelt's New Nationalism. It, too, would place strict government controls on corporations. In a speech on the New Freedom, Wilson outlined his aim to provide more opportunities—more freedom—for small businesses.

> The man with only a little capital is finding it harder and harder to get into the field, more and more impossible to compete with the big

Taft and Roosevelt

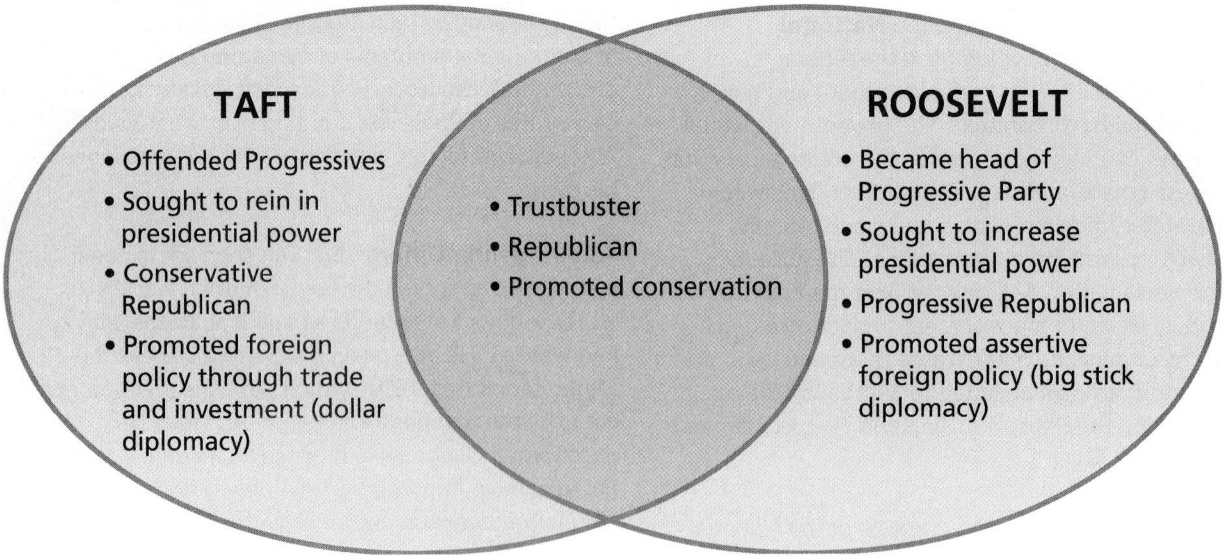

>> **Analyze Information** How did Taft's and Roosevelt's views on government and politics differ?

BOUNCE to Activate Chart

Presidential Election of 1912

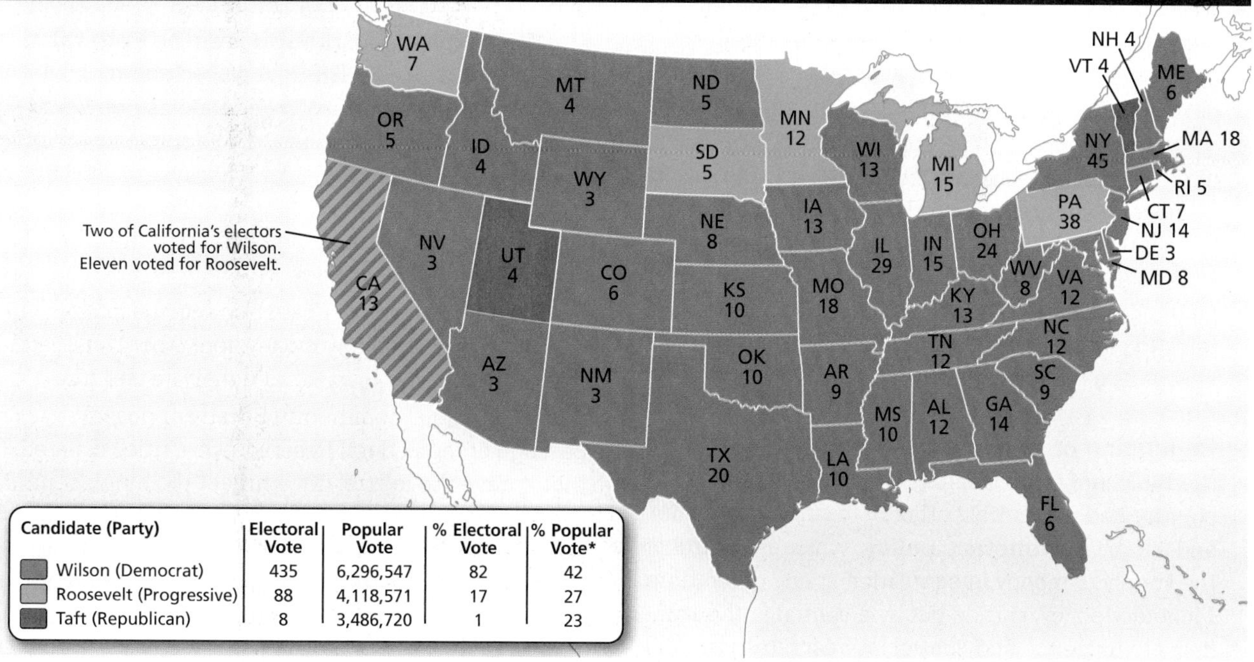

Candidate (Party)	Electoral Vote	Popular Vote	% Electoral Vote	% Popular Vote*
Wilson (Democrat)	435	6,296,547	82	42
Roosevelt (Progressive)	88	4,118,571	17	27
Taft (Republican)	8	3,486,720	1	23

>> **Analyze Maps** What evidence shown on the map supports the conclusion that divisions within the Republican party made the Democrats more likely to win the 1912 election?

fellow. Why? Because the laws of this country do not prevent the strong from crushing the weak.

— Woodrow Wilson, "The New Freedom," 1913

Though he did not win the majority of the popular vote, Wilson received more than four times the number of Electoral College votes that went to Roosevelt or to Taft. The Progressive Party had indeed had an impact on the election. By splitting the Republican vote, the Progressive Party helped the Democrat Wilson to win the White House. The pious and intellectual son of a Virginia minister, Wilson was the first man born in the South to win the presidency in almost 60 years.

CHECK UNDERSTANDING How did President Taft influence Roosevelt's decision to run for a third term?

Wilson Endorses Further Regulation

Republicans Theodore Roosevelt and William Howard Taft introduced the country to forceful Progressive Presidents. Democrat Woodrow Wilson used the expanded power of the presidency to promote a far-reaching reform agenda. Some of Wilson's economic and antitrust measures are still important in American life today.

President Wilson attacked what he called the "triple wall of privilege"—the tariffs, the banks, and the trusts—that blocked businesses from being free. Early in his first term, he pushed for new laws that would bring down those three walls and give the government more control over the economy.

A New Tax on Income First, Wilson aimed to prevent big manufacturers from possibly charging unfairly high prices to their customers. One way to do this was to lower the tariffs on goods imported from foreign countries so consumers could buy foreign goods if American companies' prices were too high. Wilson called a special session of Congress and convinced its members to pass the Underwood Tariff Bill, which cut tariffs.

Tariffs had been one of the main sources of revenue, or money coming in, for the federal government. To make up for the loss of tariff revenue, the Underwood Tariff Act of 1913 included a provision to create a graduated income tax. The recently passed **Sixteenth Amendment** gave Congress the power to collect an income tax without restrictions. A graduated income tax means that wealthy people pay a higher percentage of their income than do poor people. The revenue from the income tax more than made up for the money the government lost by lowering tariffs on imports.

Taxing incomes proved to be a very controversial reform. Both Republicans and conservative Democrats strongly opposed ratification of the Sixteenth Amendment, as did prominent business leaders. The graduated tax became and continues to be the battleground between those who favor lower rates to stimulate economic growth and those who view it as a means to further public investment.

Regulation of Commercial Banks Next, Wilson tried to change the banking system. At the time, the country had no central authority to supervise banks and establish **monetary policy**, which is control of the supply of money in circulation at any given time. Monetary policy, carried out by a central authority, helps to influence and control interest rates with the goal of promoting economic growth and stability and controlling inflation and deflation. Without such a central authority, interest rates for loans could fluctuate wildly, and a few wealthy bankers had a great deal of control over national, state and local banks' reserve funds. This meant that a bank might not have full access to its reserves when customers needed to withdraw or borrow money.

Wilson pushed Congress to pass the **Federal Reserve Act** (1913). This law placed commercial banks under the control of a Federal Reserve Board, which set up regional banks to hold the reserve funds from those commercial banks. This system, still in place today, helps protect the American economy from having too much money end up in the hands of one person, bank, or region.

The Federal Reserve Board also sets the interest rate that banks pay to borrow money from other banks, and it supervises banks to make sure they are well run.

The financial community bitterly opposed passage of the Federal Reserve Act. Critics claimed that it gave the federal government too much control over the nation's economy and banking system, a point of view that some Americans still hold today. However, some historians have called the Federal Reserve Act the most important piece of economic legislation before the 1930s.

Wilson and Congress Strengthen Antitrust Regulation Like Presidents before him, Wilson focused on trusts. He agreed with Roosevelt that trusts were not dangerous as long as they did not engage in unfair practices.

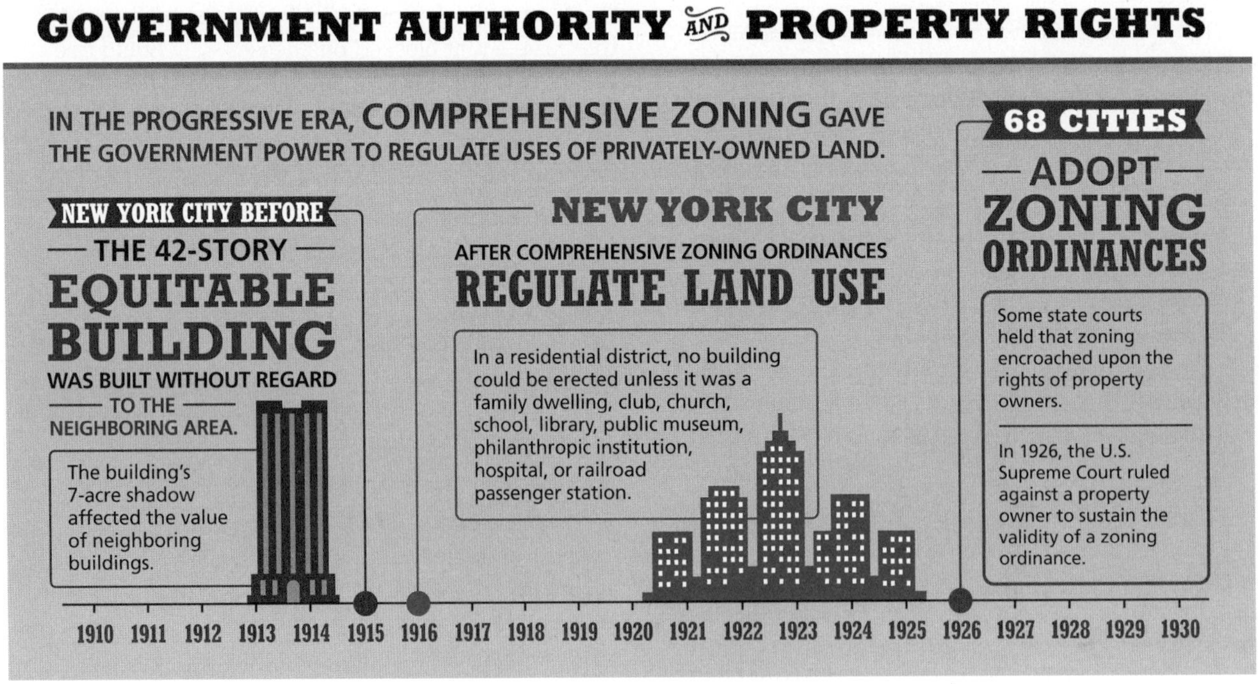

>> **Analyze Information** How did comprehensive zoning both protect and possibly violate property rights?

Progressive Legislation During Wilson's Presidency

LEGISLATION	EFFECT
Underwood Tariff Act (1913)	Lowered tariffs on imported goods and established a graduated income tax
Federal Reserve Act (1913)	Created the Federal Reserve Board to oversee banks and manage reserve funds
Federal Trade Commission Act (1914)	Established the Federal Trade Commission to monitor business practices, false advertising, and dishonest labeling
Clayton Antitrust Act (1914)	Strengthened the Sherman Antitrust Act by spelling out specific activities businesses could not do

>> **Analyze Charts** Which of these pieces of legislation do you think is the most important?

In 1914, Wilson persuaded Congress to create the **Federal Trade Commission (FTC)**. Members of this group were named by the President to monitor business practices that might lead to monopoly. The FTC was also charged with watching out for false advertising or dishonest labeling. Congress also passed the **Clayton Antitrust Act** (1914), which strengthened earlier antitrust laws by spelling out those activities in which businesses could not engage.

These laws are still in effect today, protecting both businesses and consumers from abusive business activities. In recent years, the FTC has prosecuted companies that traded stocks dishonestly and fined companies that published false ads. The FTC also regulates buying on the Internet. Some Americans argue, however, that such government regulation interferes with the workings of a free enterprise system and sometimes hurts competition.

Workers Gain Rights The Clayton Antitrust Act also ushered in a new era for workers by protecting labor unions from being attacked as trusts. Now, workers could organize more freely. Samuel Gompers of the American Federation of Labor (AFL) praised the new law as the "Magna Carta" of labor.

On the heels of these protections came the Workingman's Compensation Act (1916), which gave wages to temporarily disabled civil service employees. That same year, Wilson pushed for the Adamson Act to prevent a nationwide railroad strike, which would have stopped the movement of coal and food, leaving millions of Americans cold and hungry. Railroad union leaders insisted on the eight-hour day, but railroad managers would not accept it. Wilson called many company leaders to the White House, pleading with them to change their minds and avert a strike. When those efforts failed, he worked with Congress to pass the Adamson Act, which limited railroad employees' workdays to eight hours.

However, Wilson did not always support organized labor, as a tragic incident known as the Ludlow Massacre showed. In the fall of 1913, coal miners in Ludlow, Colorado, demanded safer conditions, higher pay, and the right to form a union. When the coal company refused, they walked off the job. Evicted from company housing, the miners and their families set up in a tent city near the mines. The strike continued through the winter. Then, on April 20, 1914, the Colorado National Guard opened fire on the tent city and set fire to the tents, killing some 26 men, women, and children. In the end, Wilson sent federal troops to restore order and break up the strike. The miners' attempt to form a union had failed.

☑ **IDENTIFY SUPPORTING DETAILS** How did the government regulate commercial banks?

The Progressives' Legacy

The political reforms of the Progressives had a lasting effect on the American political system. The initiative, referendum, and recall and the Seventeenth and Nineteenth amendments expanded voters' influence. Progressive reforms also paved the way for future trends. Starting in this period, the federal government grew to offer more protection to Americans, but at the same time gaining more control over people's lives.

The American economy today showcases the Progressives' legacy. Antitrust laws, the Federal Reserve Board, and the other federal agencies watch closely over the economy. Controls that Roosevelt and Wilson put in place continue to provide consumer protections. In later years, the government, for better or worse, built on those actions to extend regulation over other aspects of business.

The Progressive years also greatly expanded the government's role in managing natural resources. However, federal action on dams, national parks, and resource use remain major areas of debate, especially in the West. Those debates and decisions affect people in other regions as well. For example, while farmers in California, Arizona, or New Mexico worry about getting enough water to grow crops, the rest of the nation awaits the delivery of the food they grow.

It is true that many of the problems identified by the Progressives still plague us today. There are still dishonest sellers, unfair employment practices, and problems in schools, cities, the environment, and public health. However, the Progressive reformers passed on the idea that government can take action to help people and private enterprise fix those problems.

GO ONLINE to access this biography: Theodore Roosevelt

IDENTIFY MAIN IDEAS What is the essential legacy of Progressive political reform movements?

ASSESSMENT

1. **Compare and Contrast** the domestic policies of President Roosevelt and President Taft.
2. **Compare Points of View** Explain why some people supported President Wilson's graduated income tax and why others opposed it.
3. **Generate Explanations** Explain the purpose of the Federal Trade Commission and discuss the criticism it has received.
4. **Contrast** Explain how President Roosevelt disagreed with John Muir about environmental preservation.
5. **Generate Explanations** Explain how President Wilson affected workers' rights.

The Jungle: Upton Sinclair

When Upton Sinclair published *The Jungle* in 1906, he meant to open America's eyes to the plight of workers in the filthy, dangerous Chicago stockyards. Instead, popular outrage focused on the wider-reaching threat of spoiled meat. Congress quickly passed the nation's first legislation regulating the meat, food, and drug industries. Sinclair, disappointed by his failure to provoke more sympathy for the overworked, underpaid workers, noted "I aimed at the public's heart, and by accident I hit it in the stomach."

>> A slaughterhouse in the late 1800s

There was never the least attention paid to what was cut up for sausage. . . . There would be meat that had tumbled out on the floor, in the dirt and sawdust, where the workers had tramped [walked heavily] and spit uncounted billions of consumption [tuberculosis] germs. There would be meat stored in great piles in rooms; and the water from leaky roofs would drip over it, and thousands of rats would race about on it. It was too dark in these storage places to see well, but a man could run his hand over these piles of meat and sweep off handfuls of the dried dung of rats. These rats were nuisances, and the packers would put poisoned bread out for them; they would die, and then rats, bread, and meat would go into the hoppers [containers] together.

DETERMINE AUTHOR'S POINT OF VIEW What does Sinclair describe in this passage, and what is his viewpoint on the subject?

This is no fairy story and no joke; the meat would be shoveled into carts, and the man who did the shoveling would not trouble to lift out a rat even when he saw one—there were things that went into the sausage in comparison with which a poisoned rat was a tidbit [small piece of food]. There was no place for the men to wash their hands before they ate their dinner, and so they made a practice of washing them in the water that was to be ladled into the sausage. There were the butt-ends of smoked meat, and the scraps of corned beef, and all the odds and ends of the waste of the plants, that would be dumped into old barrels in the cellar and left there. Under the system of rigid economy which the packers enforced, there were some jobs that it only paid to do once in a long time, and among these was the cleaning out of the waste barrels.

Every spring they did it; and in the barrels would be dirt and rust and old nails and stale water—and cartload after cartload of it would be taken up and dumped into the hoppers with fresh meat, and sent out to the public's breakfast.

EXPLAIN AN ARGUMENT According to Sinclair, why are the waste barrels not cleaned more often?

Primary Sources

The winter was coming on again, more menacing and cruel than ever. It was October, and the holiday rush had begun. It was necessary for the packing machines to grind till late at night to provide food that would be eaten at Christmas breakfasts; and Marija and Elzbieta and Ona, as part of the machine, began working fifteen or sixteen hours a day. There was no choice about this—whatever work there was to be done they had to do, if they wished to keep their places; besides that, it added another pittance to their incomes. So they staggered on with the awful load. They would start work every morning at seven, and eat their dinners at noon, and then work until ten or eleven at night without another mouthful of food. Jurgis wanted to wait for them, to help them home at night, but they would not think of this; the fertilizer mill was not running overtime, and there was no place for him to wait save in a saloon. Each would stagger out into the darkness, and make her way to the corner, where they met; or if the others had already gone, would get into a car, and begin a painful struggle to keep awake. When they got home they were always too tired either to eat or to undress; they would crawl into bed with their shoes on, and lie like logs. If they should fail, they would certainly be lost; if they held out, they might have enough coal for the winter. . . .

. . . He crossed a long bridge over a river frozen solid and covered with slush. Not even on the river bank was the snow white—the rain which fell was a diluted solution of smoke, and Jurgis' hands and face were streaked with black. Then he came into the business part of the city, where the streets were sewers of inky blackness, with horses sleeping and plunging, and women and children flying across in panic-stricken droves. These streets were huge canyons formed by towering black buildings, echoing with the clang of car gongs and the shouts of drivers; the people who swarmed in them were as busy as ants—all hurrying breathlessly, never stopping to look at anything nor at each other. The solitary trampish-looking foreigner, with water-soaked clothing and haggard face and anxious eyes, was as much alone as he hurried past them, as much unheeded and as lost, as if he had been a thousand miles deep in a wilderness.

A policeman gave him his direction and told him that he had five miles to go. He came again to the slum districts, to avenues of saloons and cheap stores, with long dingy red factory buildings, and coal-yards and railroad tracks; and then Jurgis lifted up his head and began to sniff the air like a startled animal—scenting the far-off odor of home. It was late afternoon then, and he was hungry, but the dinner invitations hung out of the saloons were not for him. . . .

ANALYZE STYLE AND RHETORIC In a few words, how would you describe the world that Sinclair has represented in these paragraphs?

ASSESSMENT

1. **Draw Conclusions** What reforms is the author calling for by describing these scenes?
2. **Draw Conclusions** What do you think it would have been like to work in this factory?
3. **Identify Cause and Effect** What effect do you think reading this selection from *The Jungle* would have had on Americans during this time period?
4. **Analyze Style and Rhetoric** How would you describe Sinclair's writing style, and how does it make his writing more convincing?

GO ONLINE to access primary sources

11.5

A Japanese print shows Commodore Matthew Perry meeting Japanese officials. By opening access to Japanese markets, Perry helped expand U.S. power abroad.

American Influence Grows

For most of its early history, America played a small role in world affairs, mostly by choice. But in the late 1800s, this began to change. With leading spokesmen calling for the United States to join the ranks of the world's major powers, the United States began to acquire influence and territories outside its continental borders. The United States was abandoning isolationism and emerging as a new power on the global stage.

BOUNCE to Activate Flipped Video

Objectives

Identify the key factors that caused Americans to want to take a greater role overseas.

Explain how the United States took its first steps toward the position of a world power.

Evaluate the acquisition of Hawaii by the United States.

Key Terms

imperialism
extractive economies
Alfred T. Mahan
Social Darwinism
Frederick Jackson Turner
Matthew Perry
Queen Liluokalani
Sanford B. Dole

America on the World Stage

During the Age of Imperialism, from the mid-1800s through the early 1900s, powerful nations engaged in a mad dash to extend their influence across much of the world. European nations added to colonies they had established during the Age of Exploration by acquiring new colonies in Africa and Asia.

Following European success, Japan and the United States also began to consider the benefits of **imperialism**, the policy by which strong nations extend their political, military, and economic control over weaker territories. Although imperialism would prove an awkward fit for the United States, the nation's desire to take its place on the world stage spurred some territorial expansion and a larger increase in influence.

Economic Causes of Imperialism One reason why European nations and Japan rushed to grab colonies was the desire for raw materials and natural resources. They sought colonies to provide tea, rubber, iron, petroleum, and other materials for their industries at home. These colonial economies were examples of **extractive economies**. The imperial country extracted, or removed, raw

GO ONLINE to access your digital course

materials from the colony and shipped them to the home country. Possession of colonies gave nations an edge in the competition for global resources. In contrast to those other world powers, however, the resource-rich United States had fewer concerns about shortages of raw materials in the nineteenth century.

For Americans, the problem was not a shortage of materials, but a surplus of goods. The booming U.S. economy of the late 1800s was producing more goods than Americans could consume. Farmers complained that excess production resulted in declining crop prices and profits. Industrialists urged expanding trade into new overseas markets where American commodities could be sold. Otherwise, they warned, American factories would close and unemployment would rise. Senator Albert J. Beveridge, a Progressive and friend of Theodore Roosevelt, explained why the United States needed to become a world power:

> Today we are raising more [crops] than we can consume. Today we are making more than we can use. . . . Therefore we must find new markets for our produce, new occupation for our capital, new work for our labor.
>
> —Senator Albert J. Beveridge, "The March of the Flag," 1898

>> The USS *Brooklyn* played a substantial role in American naval operations in the Caribbean Sea and in Asia. U.S. leaders believed in the value of a strong military during the late 1800s.

BOUNCE to Activate Chart

Alfred T. Mahan Stresses U.S. Military Strength

To expand and protect their interests around the world, nations built up their military strength. **Alfred T. Mahan**, a military historian and an officer in the United States Navy, played a key role in transforming America into a naval power. In *The Influence of Sea Power Upon History*, Mahan asserted that since ancient times, many great nations had owed their greatness to powerful navies. Mahan believed strongly that control of the seas during wartime was crucial to a nation's success. He called upon America to build a modern fleet. Mahan also argued that the United States would need to acquire foreign bases where American ships could refuel and gather fresh supplies.

Influenced by the ideas of Mahan and others, the United States expanded and modernized its navy by building new steel-plated, steampowered battleships such as the USS *Maine*. By 1900, the United States had the third-largest navy in the world. Leaders such as U.S. Senator Henry Cabot Lodge, a strong supporter of American expansionism, continued to encourage a naval build-up into the early twentieth century. Lodge and others believed that a strong navy was vital to the protection of U.S. interests both at home and abroad.

Social Darwinism, Missionaries, and National Superiority European and Japanese imperialists used ideas of racial, national, and cultural superiority to justify taking over colonies. One of these ideas was **Social Darwinism,** the belief that life consists of competitive struggles in which only the fittest survive. Social Darwinists felt that certain nations and races were superior to others and therefore were destined to rule over inferior peoples and cultures. Some prominent Americans embraced these ideas and began to worry that if the United States remained isolated while European nations gobbled up the rest of the world, America would not survive.

One reason that these Americans embraced Social Darwinism was that they had long believed that God had granted them the right and responsibility to settle the frontier. They spoke of America's "Manifest Destiny" to expand all the way to the Pacific Ocean. In a best-selling work titled *Our Country,* Josiah Strong picked up on this theme. A religious missionary, Strong argued that Americans had a responsibility to spread their Western values. "God is training the Anglo-Saxon race," he asserted, "for its mission [to civilize] weaker races." Influenced by Strong, many American missionaries journeyed to foreign lands to gain converts to Christianity. Although missionaries were often motivated by a sincere desire to spread their faith, the linking of missionary work to the concept of U.S. expansionism strengthened American presence in these territories.

In *The Significance of the Frontier in American History,* historian **Frederick Jackson Turner** noted that the frontier had been closed by gradual settlement in the nineteenth century. Throughout American history, he continued, the frontier had traditionally supplied an arena where ambitious Americans could pursue their fortunes and secure a fresh start. It had thus served as a "safety valve," siphoning off potential discontent.

Now that America had spanned the continent, advocates of Turner's thesis urged overseas expansion as a way to keep the "safety valve" open and avoid internal conflict.

IDENTIFY What factors influenced Americans to play a more active role in the world?

>> **Draw Conclusions** What part of the Salvation Army's mission do the blue-jacketed people seem to be carrying out in this illustration?

America Begins to Expand

Beginning in the mid-1800s, with little fanfare, America focused more and more on expanding its trade and acquiring new territories. One of America's first moves toward world power came before the Civil War.

American Expansionism in the Pacific Begins

In 1853, Commodore **Matthew Perry** sailed a fleet of American warships into present-day Tokyo Bay, Japan. Prior to Perry's arrival, Japan had denied the rest of the world access to its ports. In fact, because most Japanese people had never seen steamships before, they thought the ships in Perry's fleet were "giant dragons puffing smoke." Perry cleverly won the Japanese emperor's favor by showering him with lavish gifts. Japanese leaders also realized that by closing off their nation to the outside world, they had fallen behind in military technology. Within a year, Perry negotiated a treaty that opened Japan to trade with America.

Perry's journey set a precedent for further expansion across the Pacific Ocean. In 1867, the United States took possession of the Midway Islands. Treaties in 1875 and 1887 increased trade with the Hawaiian Islands and gave the United States the right to build a naval base at Pearl Harbor.

The Klondike Gold Rush In 1867, Secretary of State William Seward bought Alaska from Russia for $7.2 million. Journalists scoffed at the purchase and referred to Alaska as "Seward's Folly" and "Seward's Icebox." They wondered why the United States would want a vast tundra of snow and ice 1,000 miles north of its border. But Seward's purchase almost doubled the country's size, and the "icebox" turned out to be rich in timber, oil, and other natural resources. Alaska also greatly expanded America's reach across the Pacific. Scholars today see Seward's purchase as a key milestone on America's road to power.

By the mid-1880s, gold had been discovered in several locations near Alaska, sparking the Klondike Gold Rush. The stampede to the Klondike goldfields in British Columbia and Yukon territory led to the development of new towns in Alaska. However, the human geography challenges of sparse settlement and lack of transportation routes and the physical geography challenges caused by nearby mountains and a frigid climate ended the rush by 1899.

>> In Hawaii, American owners of sugar plantations, such as this one, exerted broad and increasing influence over local affairs.

BOUNCE to Activate Gallery

>> Hawaiian Queen Liluokalani unsuccessfully resisted U.S. influence in Hawaii.

American Expansionism in Latin America U.S. business leaders saw Latin America as a natural place to expand their trade and investments. Secretary of State James Blaine helped them by sponsoring the First International Pan-American Conference in 1889. Blaine preached the benefits of economic cooperation to delegates of 17 Latin American countries. The conference also paved the way for the construction of the Pan-American Highway system, which linked the United States to Central and South America.

In 1895, tensions rose between America and Great Britain because of a border dispute between British Guiana and Venezuela. Claiming that Britain was violating the Monroe Doctrine, President Cleveland threatened U.S. intervention. After some international saber-rattling, the British accepted a growing U.S. sphere of influence in Latin America. Relations between Britain and the United States soon improved.

☑ **RECALL** Why did journalists criticize Seward for his purchase of Alaska?

The Acquisition of Hawaii

By the 1890s, the Hawaiian Islands had been economically linked to the United States for almost a century. Since the 1790s, American merchant ships had stopped at Hawaii on their way to East Asia. Missionaries had established Christian churches and schools on the islands. Americans had also established sugar cane plantations there. In 1887, American planters convinced King Kalakaua (kah LAH kah oo ah) to amend Hawaii's constitution so that voting rights were limited to only wealthy landowners, who were, of course, the white planters.

Influence of Dole and Other Americans in Hawaii In the early 1890s, American planters in Hawaii faced two crises. First, a new U.S. tariff law imposed duties on previously duty-free Hawaiian sugar. This made Hawaiian sugar more expensive than sugar produced in the United States. The sugar growers in Hawaii therefore feared that they would suffer decreasing sales and profits.

The other problem was that in 1891, Kalakaua died and his sister Liliuokalani (lih lee oo oh kah LAH nee) was his successor. A determined Hawaiian nationalist, **Queen Liluokalani** resented the increasing power of the white planters, who owned much of Hawaiian land. She abolished the constitution that had given political power to the white minority.

With the backing of U.S. officials, the American planters responded quickly and forcefully. In 1893, they overthrew the queen. John Stevens, U.S. minister to Hawaii, ordered United States Marines to help the rebels seize power. The new government, led by influential lawyer **Sanford B. Dole**, asked President Benjamin Harrison to annex Hawaii to the United States.

Dole, born in Hawaii of missionary parents, was a well-respected lawyer and jurist who was connected to Hawaii's planter elite. His cousin, James Dole, moved to Hawaii in 1899 and helped build a pineapple company that still exists today.

The United States Annexes Hawaii After Liluokalani's overthrow, President Harrison signed the treaty of annexation but could not get the required Senate approval before Grover Cleveland became President. Cleveland ordered a full investigation, which revealed that the majority of the Hawaiian people did not approve of the treaty. Cleveland refused to sign the agreement and apologized for the "flagrant wrong" done by the "reprehensible conduct of the American minister."

However, American sentiment for annexation remained strong, especially on the West Coast, where California business interests had close ties with the planters in Hawaii. In 1897, a new President entered the White House. William McKinley's administration favored annexation, and in 1898, after the outbreak of the Spanish-American War, Congress proclaimed Hawaii an official U.S. territory with Sanford B. Dole as its first governor.

CHECK UNDERSTANDING How did American planters react to Queen Liluokalani's actions when she gained power?

ASSESSMENT

1. **Generate Explanations** Explain why many world powers developed extractive economies during the 1800s, and why this was less important for the United States.
2. **Draw Conclusions** Explain why the United States needed to expand its trade into new markets.
3. **Evaluate Arguments** Explain how some used Social Darwinism to justify imperialism.
4. **Summarize** the concept of Manifest Destiny.
5. **Generate Explanations** Explain how the United States gained influence in Latin America.
6. **Connections to Today** Do you think Frederick Jackson Turner's ideas about the frontier being important as a safety valve apply to the United States today? Why or why not?

GO ONLINE to access this biography: Queen Liluokalani

11.6

African Americans made up approximately 10 percent of U.S. forces during the Spanish-American War. **Infer** What do you think motivated African Americans to join the armed forces during the Spanish-American War?

BOUNCE to Activate Flipped Video

Objectives

Explain the causes of the Spanish-American War.

Identify the major battles of the Spanish-American War.

Describe the consequences of the war, including the debate over imperialism.

Examine the causes and consequences of the Philippine insurrection.

Key Terms

José Martí
William Randolph Hearst
Yellow Press
jingoism
George Dewey
Emilio Aguinaldo
Rough Riders
Treaty of Paris
insurrection
guerrilla warfare
William Howard Taft

The Spanish-American War

American power and economic interests around the world were growing. Still, the United States remained reluctant to risk war with other powers to acquire colonies. That changed, however, in 1898, when America went to war against Spain. The United States acquired colonies and became a world power.

Causes of the Spanish-American War

U.S. Sympathies for Cuban Rebels At the end of the nineteenth century, Spain was an imperial nation in decline. Its formerly vast empire had dwindled to a small number of possessions, including the Philippine Islands in the Pacific and the Caribbean islands of Puerto Rico and Cuba.

By 1897, American entrepreneurs had invested $50 million in sugar cane plantations and other ventures in Cuba, which lay just 90 miles off the Florida coast. These businessmen saw Cuba as a growing market for American products. However, the island was very unstable. Yearning for freedom, the Cubans repeatedly rebelled against Spanish rule.

In 1895, Cuban patriot **José Martí** launched a war for independence from Spain. With cries of *"Cuba Libre!"* ("Free Cuba!"), rebel fighters used guerrilla tactics of hit-and-run raids against Spanish forces. In response, Spanish General Valeriano Weyler devised a plan to deprive the rebels of food and recruits. He herded the rural population into reconcentration camps, where tens of thousands died from disease and starvation. Meanwhile,

GO ONLINE to access your digital course

the Cubans and Spanish destroyed American property.

Many Americans favored the Cubans, whose struggle for freedom and democracy reminded Americans of their own revolutionary heritage. José Martí had also been campaigning through the Cuban immigrant communities of Florida to raise money for the rebellion. The brutality of Spanish tactics intensified American affection and sympathy for the rebels. But other Americans, especially business people, were worried about U.S. economic interests in Cuba and hoped that Spain would quickly put down the rebellion.

Influence of Mass Media Rival newspaper publishers Joseph Pulitzer and **William Randolph Hearst** heightened the public's dislike of the Spanish government. Their publications were called the **Yellow Press** because they featured a popular comic-strip character called The Yellow Kid. To boost readership, Pulitzer's *New York World,* Hearst's *New York Journal,* and similar newspapers posted sensational headlines and pictures on their front pages. Their stories exaggerated Spanish atrocities and compared Cuban rebels to the patriots of the American Revolution.

President William McKinley warned the Spanish to quickly establish peace, or the United States would take whatever steps it "should deem necessary to procure this result." Spain recalled General Weyler and offered the Cuban rebels some reforms. But the rebels insisted on independence, which Spain refused to grant. McKinley ordered the battleship *Maine* to Havana harbor to protect American citizens in Cuba.

Then, in February 1898, the *Journal* published a private letter written by Enrique Dupuy de Lôme, Spain's ambassador to Washington, D.C. The letter, stolen by Cuban rebels and leaked to Hearst, called McKinley a weak and stupid politician. Hearst published the letter under the sensational headline, "Worst Insult to the United States in Its History." The letter fueled American **jingoism,** or aggressive nationalism, and inflamed relations with Spain.

The Explosion of the *Maine* Soon after the *Journal* published de Lôme's letter, the *Maine* exploded in Havana harbor. Of the 350 officers and crew on board at the time, 266 died. The Yellow Press promptly accused Spain of blowing up the battleship. One *Journal* headline even declared: "War? Sure!"

President McKinley ordered a special naval board of inquiry to investigate the cause of the explosion. On March 28, 1898, the board concluded that a mine

>> A group of Cuban rebels attacked a Spanish plantation overseer.

>> Graphic illustrations such as this one depicting the explosion of the USS *Maine* had a profound influence on attitudes in the United States.

BOUNCE to Activate Gallery

had destroyed the battleship. Years later, follow-up investigations raised doubts about the naval board's findings, but, at the time, most people blamed Spain.

The Spanish-American War Begins War fever gripped the nation. In newspapers, speeches, and songs, patriotic Americans implored their fellow citizens to "Remember the *Maine*!" In response to American demands, Spain agreed to abolish the reconcentration camps and make other concessions, but it was too little too late. On April 11, 1898, McKinley asked Congress for the authority to use force against Spain to end the fighting in Cuba "in the name of humanity, in the name of civilization, in behalf of endangered American interests."

Eight days later, Congress enacted four resolutions that amounted to a declaration of war on Spain. The fourth resolution—the Teller Amendment—stipulated that the United States had no intention of annexing Cuba. The navy quickly blockaded Cuban ports, and McKinley called for more than 100,000 volunteers to join the army. In response, Spain declared war on the United States.

RECALL Why did Americans object to Spanish actions in Cuba?

American Forces Defeat the Spanish

Americans responded enthusiastically to the war. About 200,000 men enlisted in the army, up from the 25,000 that enlisted at the beginning of 1898. In early May, as the United States Army prepared to attack, Americans heard news of a great naval victory over Spain. But, surprisingly, the victory was not in Cuba. Rather, it was in the Pacific Ocean, on the opposite side of the world.

Acquiring the Philippines On May 1, 1898, Commodore **George Dewey** steamed his squadron of vessels into Manila Bay, in the Spanish-held Philippines. The Americans completely surprised the Spanish fleet that was stationed in the bay.

Upon issuing the order to "fire when ready," Dewey watched his ships quickly destroy the Spanish force. While no Americans died during the naval battle, nearly 400 Spanish sailors lost their lives. Americans gleefully received news of the victory and proclaimed Dewey a hero.

While Dewey was winning an astounding victory over the Spanish navy, Filipino nationalists led by **Emilio Aguinaldo** (ahg ee NAHL doh) were defeating the Spanish army. Like the Cubans, the Filipinos were fighting for freedom from Spain. In

Spanish-American War: Securing the Philippines

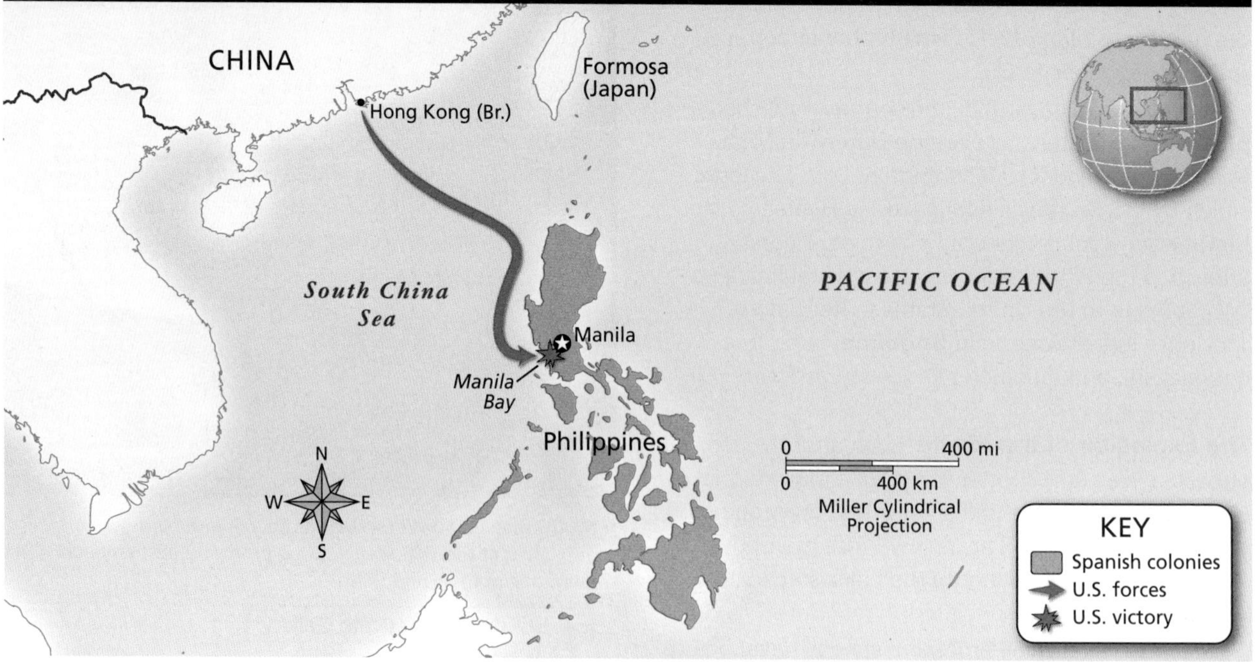

>> **Analyze Maps** Why did American forces likely launch their attack on the Philippines from the British port city of Hong Kong?

Spanish-American War: Securing Cuba

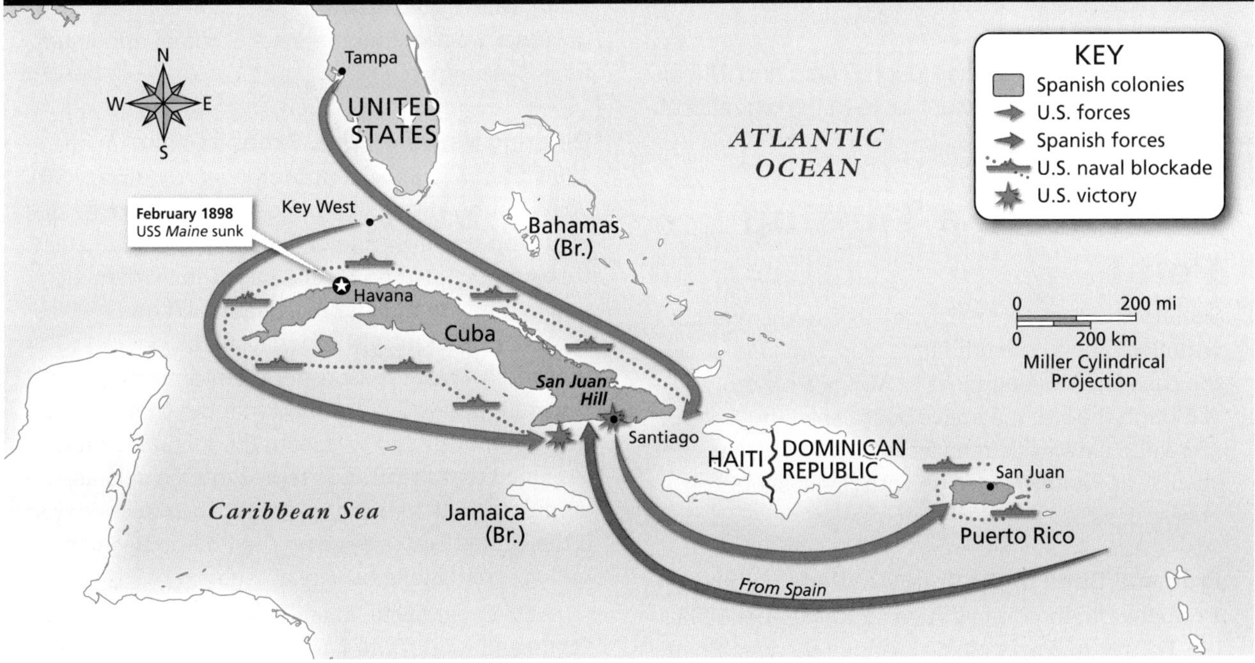

>> **Analyze Maps** How do you think the U.S. naval blockade affected Spain's troop shipments to Cuba during the Spanish-American War?

August, after some 15,000 U.S. soldiers had landed on the islands, Spanish troops surrendered to the United States.

Victory in Cuba Meanwhile, American troops landed in Cuba in June 1898. U.S. Marines captured Guantánamo Bay, and a force of 17,000 soldiers under U.S. Army General William Shafter stormed ashore east of Santiago.

In spite of their excitement for the war, the troops faced deplorable conditions. They were poorly trained and supplied.

As they assembled for duty around Tampa, Florida, the soldiers were issued obsolete weapons and heavy wool uniforms that were unsuitable for Cuba's tropical climate. Corrupt and inefficient officials provided the men with rotting and contaminated food.

General Shafter's army consisted of state National Guard units and regular army units, including the African American Ninth and Tenth Cavalry regiments from the western frontier. Another cavalry unit was organized and commanded by the future President Theodore Roosevelt. His **Rough Riders** consisted of rugged westerners and upper-class easterners who relished what Roosevelt called the "strenuous life."

The Rough Riders and Roosevelt gained fame for the role they played in the battles for Kettle and San Juan hills outside Santiago, Cuba. Joined by African American soldiers from the Ninth and Tenth Cavalries, the Riders stormed up those hills to secure high ground surrounding Santiago. One war correspondent described a charge of the African American soldiers:

> [T]hey followed their leader up the terrible hill from whose crest the desperate Spaniards poured down a deadly fire of shell and musketry. They never faltered. . . . [T]heir aim was splendid, their coolness was superb. . . . The war had not shown greater heroism.
>
> —War correspondent, 1898

Two days after the battle of San Juan Hill, the Spanish navy made a desperate attempt to escape from Santiago's harbor. U.S. forces, which had blockaded the harbor, destroyed the Spanish fleet as it tried to break out. Surrounded, outnumbered, and dispirited, Spanish forces in Santiago surrendered. Although a few battles followed when U.S. forces occupied the island of Puerto Rico, another Spanish possession, the fighting had come to an end. Although almost 3,000 Americans died during the war, only around 380 died in combat. Disease, especially malaria and yellow fever, caused most of the deaths.

RECALL How did the Rough Riders and African American cavalry units contribute to the war effort?

The War as a Turning Point

Secretary of State John Hay referred to the conflict with Spain as a "splendid little war" because of the ease and thoroughness of America's victory. Although the war may have been "splendid," it created a new dilemma for Americans: What should the United States do with Spain's former possessions?

Pros and Cons of the Treaty of Paris Signed by Spain and the United States in December 1898, the **Treaty of Paris** officially ended the war. Spain gave up control of Cuba, Puerto Rico, and the Pacific island of Guam. It also sold the Philippines to the United States for $20 million.

The Teller Amendment, passed by Congress when it declared war on Spain, prevented the United States from taking possession of Cuba. The amendment did not, however, apply to the Philippines. Americans disagreed over whether to grant the Philippines independence or take full control of the Pacific nation.

Guam, with its excellent harbor and mid-Pacific location, was desired as a coaling station to fuel U.S. Navy and merchant ships traveling to the Far East. Between 1898 and 1950 (aside from the period of its occupation by Japan during World War II), Guam's governor was an American naval officer appointed from Washington, D.C.

Differing Views on U.S. Expansionism In an 1899 interview, President McKinley explained, "We could not give [the Philippines] back to Spain—that would be cowardly and dishonorable." He believed that America had no choice but to "take them all, and to educate the Filipinos, and uplift and civilize . . . them." McKinley's imperialist supporters presented similar reasons for maintaining control of the Philippines. They argued that the United States had a responsibility to govern the Filipinos. They reasoned that the islands represented a valuable stepping stone to trade in China. They warned that if the United States gave up the Philippines, other nations would take control of them.

Anti-imperialists, including William Jennings Bryan and Mark Twain, rejected these arguments. In 1899, a large group of anti-imperialists formed the American Anti-Imperialist League. The league condemned imperialism as a crime and attacked it as "open disloyalty to the distinctive principles of our government."

The debate reached its climax in the U.S. Senate, where senators had to consider ratifying the Treaty of Paris. In February 1899, the Senate voted 57 to 27 in favor of the treaty. By a single "yes" ballot, the vote met the two-thirds majority necessary to ratify the treaty.

Although the military conflict had been expensive, its economic effects on the United States were mainly positive. There was much more

Effects of the Treaty of Paris, 1898

AMERICAN EXPANSION	NEW CHALLENGES
• U.S. acquires the Philippines • Treaty benefits U.S. much more than Spain • Guam and Puerto Rico become part of U.S. territory • U.S. expands influence and becomes new player in world politics	• Guerrilla fighting against U.S. troops in the Philippines lasts three years • U.S. loses ten times more troops in the Philippines than in the Spanish-American War • Public opinion in U.S. divided over the issue of imperialism in Philippines • Because of its rising global influence, U.S. clashes with China and Japan

>> **Analyze Information** How did the Spanish-American War contribute to the rise of the United States as a world power?

agreement about the war's effects among the U.S. business community than in Congress.

The acquisition of Puerto Rico, Guam, and the Philippines gave the U.S. Navy secure bases and coaling stations for its ships. The westward move of American power and influence was desired by farmers and industrialists who saw Asia, and China especially, as an untapped market for their goods.

After the war, tropical agriculture, mostly in sugar, became big business for U.S. companies in Puerto Rico and Cuba. By 1895, U.S. interests already had more than $50 million invested in Cuba, and trade with the island, mostly in sugar, was worth twice that. These interests certainly welcomed the increased American intervention and control after the Spanish-American War. In 1901, U.S. legislation known as the Platt Amendment put the internal, external, and economic affairs of Cuba under the control of the United States. It also established the U.S. naval base at Guantánamo Bay. The amendment was mostly repealed in 1934, but the naval base remains even today.

CHECK UNDERSTANDING Why did American leaders think it was important to keep the Philippines?

>> **Analyze Political Cartoons** What does the portrayal of the territories on the wall poster imply about American involvement in those regions?

BOUNCE to Activate Chart

>> Emilio Aguinaldo fought first as an American ally against the Spanish, then led an insurrection against America in favor of Filipino self-rule.

Effects of U.S. Expansionism in the Philippines

America's decision to keep the Philippines reflected a desire to expand its influence, compete with European colonial powers, and gain new trade in Asia.

The Filipino nationalist leader Emilio Aguinaldo had thought that the United States was an ally in the Filipino struggle for independence. His forces had fought side by side with the Americans against the Spanish. However, after the United States decided to maintain possession of the Philippines, Aguinaldo grew disillusioned with America. He helped organize an **insurrection**, or rebellion, against U.S. rule. The rebels believed they were fighting for the same principle of self-rule that had inspired America's colonial patriots during the American Revolution.

Guerrilla War Erupts in the Philippines

Outgunned by American troops, Filipino insurgents relied on **guerrilla warfare,** a form of nontraditional warfare generally involving small bands of fighters attacking behind enemy lines. In turn, the American military used extraordinary measures to crush the rebellion. Like the Spanish in Cuba, U.S. soldiers gathered civilians into overcrowded concentration camps. General Jacob Smith ordered his soldiers not to take prisoners. "I wish you to kill and burn, the more you kill and burn the better you will please me," he commented. A California newspaper defended such actions:

> Let us all be frank. WE DO NOT WANT THE FILIPINOS. WE WANT THE PHILIPPINES. All of our troubles in this annexation matter have been caused by the presence in the Philippine Islands of the Filipinos. . . . The more of them killed the better. It seems harsh. But they must yield before the superior race.
>
> —San Francisco *Argonaut,* 1902

In the spring of 1901, the Americans captured Aguinaldo. Although the fighting did not end immediately, his capture marked the beginning of the end of the insurrection. The war in the Philippines took more lives than the Spanish-American War. Nearly 5,000 Americans and 200,000 Filipinos died in the fighting. The U.S. government sent more than 100,000 troops to fight in the war and spent upwards of $400 million to defeat the insurgency. The conflict highlighted the rigors of fighting against guerrilla insurgents.

The Philippines Begin Limited Self-Rule In 1901, **William Howard Taft**—a future President of the United States—became governor of the Philippines. Taft had large ambitions for helping the islands recover from the rebellion. He censored the press and placed dissidents in jail to maintain order and to win the support of the Filipino people. At the same time, he began several policies to improve the situation of the Filipinos. He extended limited self-rule, with the Philippine Assembly convening in Manila in 1907. He also ordered the construction of roads, bridges, and schools. He established a public health system to care for Filipinos.

In 1916, Congress passed the Jones Act, which pledged that the Philippines would ultimately gain their independence. Thirty years later, after U.S. forces liberated the islands from Japanese occupation at the end of World War II, the Philippines finally became an independent nation.

Growing U.S. Position as a World Power In 1900, William Jennings Bryan ran against William

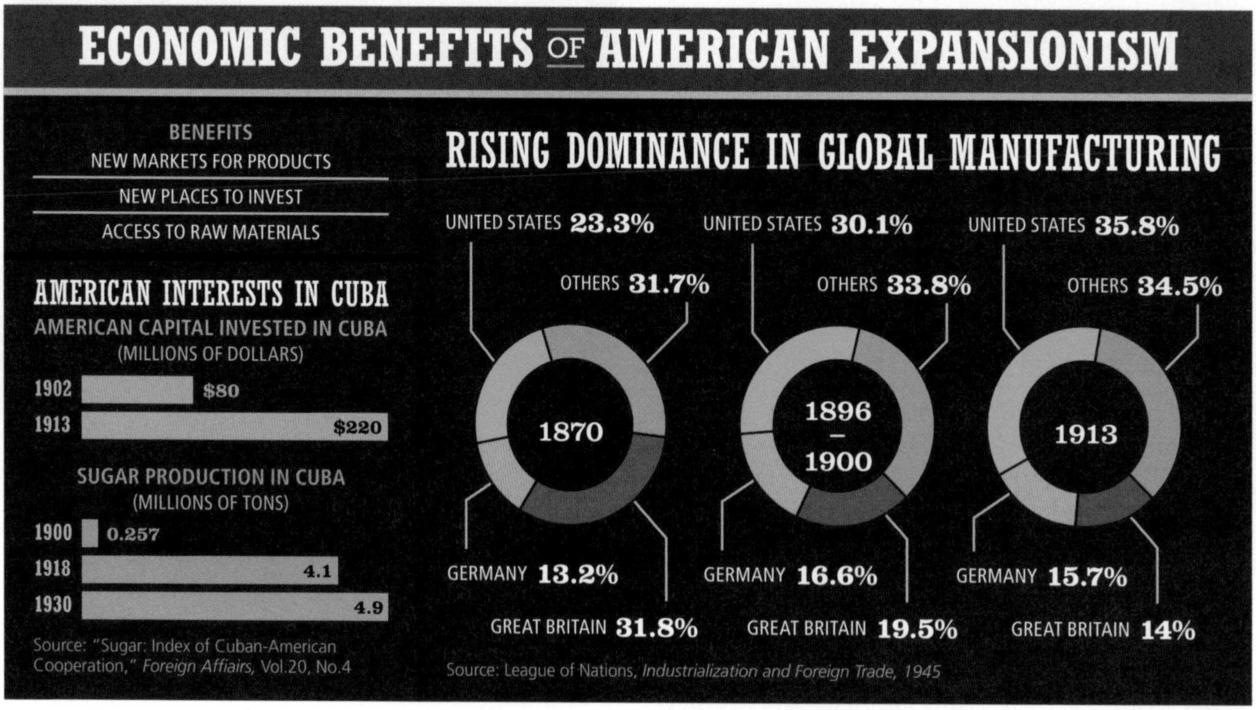

>> **Analyze Information** How did American investment in Cuba in the early 1900s affect the level of sugar production in Cuba?

McKinley for the presidency. To bolster his chances of winning reelection, the Republican McKinley named Theodore Roosevelt, the "hero of San Juan Hill," as his vice-presidential running mate. Emphasizing the overwhelming U.S. victory over Spain, McKinley soundly defeated Bryan. The President's reelection signaled America's continuing faith in his expansionist policies.

The Spanish-American War was a significant event in the emergence of the United States as a world power. As a result of the war, the United States had an empire and a new stature in world affairs. The war marked a turning point in the history of American foreign policy.

RECALL Why did hostilities erupt in the Philippines after the Spanish-American War?

ASSESSMENT

1. **Identify Cause and Effect** Explain how the Yellow Press affected relations between the United States and Spain.
2. **Compare Points of View** Discuss how Emilio Aguinaldo's opinion of the United States changed after the Spanish-American War.
3. **Summarize** the results of the Treaty of Paris and the Teller Amendment, and explain why these proved to be complicated for the United States.
4. **Draw Conclusions** Discuss the role of the Spanish-American War in determining the winner of the 1900 U.S. presidential election.
5. **Make Generalizations** Describe the conditions that U.S. troops faced during the Spanish-American War, and how they affected the war's outcome.
6. **Connections to Today** Newspapers, called the "Yellow Press," influenced U.S. opinion and gained support for the Spanish-American War. Do you think the press or media plays the same role today? Explain.

11.7

These U.S. troops in Beijing China, were part of a multinational force deployed to put down the Boxer Rebellion in 1900.

BOUNCE to Activate Flipped Video

Objectives

Analyze how economic concerns influenced the Open Door Policy and U.S. relations with Japan.

Examine what happened to Puerto Rico and Cuba after the Spanish-American War.

Analyze the effects of Roosevelt's "big stick" diplomacy and Taft's "dollar diplomacy."

Compare Wilson's "moral diplomacy" with the foreign policies of his predecessors.

Key Terms

spheres of influence
John Hay
Boxer Rebellion
Open Door Policy
Russo-Japanese War
"Gentlemen's Agreement"
Great White Fleet
Foraker Act
Platt Amendment
"big stick" diplomacy
Panama Canal
Roosevelt Corollary
"dollar diplomacy"
"moral diplomacy"
Francisco "Pancho" Villa

The United States Emerges as a World Power

As the United States emerged as a world power following the Spanish-American War, American leaders looked to strengthen economic and military interests in Latin America and East Asia. In East Asia, American leaders devised policies to open China and other Asian markets to U.S. producers. Meanwhile, Americans called for a more substantial role in Latin America, viewing the region as the nation's backyard. Increasing influence in both regions brought economic benefits, but also increased international tensions.

U.S. Trade and Intervention in China

By 1899, once-mighty China had fallen into political, economic, and military disarray. Its huge population, however, was a tempting target for other nations' imported goods. Rather than compete for Chinese trade, Britain, France, Germany, and Russia carved China into distinct **spheres of influence**. Within its zone, each power had privileged access to Chinese ports and markets. Japan also expanded its regional influence, grabbing territory in China and Korea. Since the United States did not have a zone, this system of "special privileges" threatened to limit American trade in China.

A Call for Equality in Commerce In order to overcome these barriers, U.S. Secretary of State **John Hay** issued the first of

GO ONLINE to access your digital course

a series of notes to foreign diplomats in 1899. He notified the leaders of imperialist nations that the United States expected "perfect equality of treatment for commerce" in China. Hay's note had little immediate impact on the actions of European nations or Japan. However, it served as a guiding principle of American foreign policy in Asia for years to come.

The U.S. Intervenes in the Boxer Rebellion In response to the growing influence of outsiders in their country, some Chinese joined secret societies. One such society, the Righteous and Harmonious Fists, won the nickname "Boxers" from Europeans because its members trained in martial arts. The secret societies celebrated traditional Chinese customs and criticized Western ways. They also condemned Chinese converts to Christianity. Over time, simmering anger exploded into an outright rebellion against the "foreign devils."

In May 1900, the Boxers killed foreign missionaries and besieged the foreign diplomats' district in Beijing. A multinational force of European, American, and Japanese troops was sent to the Chinese capital to quash the **Boxer Rebellion**. An initial force of 2,100 soldiers grew to more than 20,000, including 2,000 Americans. After putting down the rebellion, European powers compelled China's imperial government to pay an indemnity, or money to repair damage caused by the rebellion. This poured more fuel onto the nationalist fire. Chinese nationalists would eventually revolt and overthrow the emperor in 1911.

The Open Door Policy As the Boxer Rebellion engulfed China, Secretary of State Hay reasserted America's **Open Door Policy**, which argued for equal privileges among countries trading with China. In a second note to European powers, Hay stated that the United States wanted to "preserve Chinese territorial and administrative entity." In other words, America did not want colonies in China; it just wanted free trade there. As an act of goodwill, the United States used some of the indemnity money it received from China to fund scholarships for Chinese students to study in America. Hay and others strongly believed that access to the markets in China was crucial to rebounding from an economic depression in the 1890s. The goal of the Open Door Policy was to bring American businesses the new foreign markets they needed.

IDENTIFY What was the purpose of the Open Door Policy?

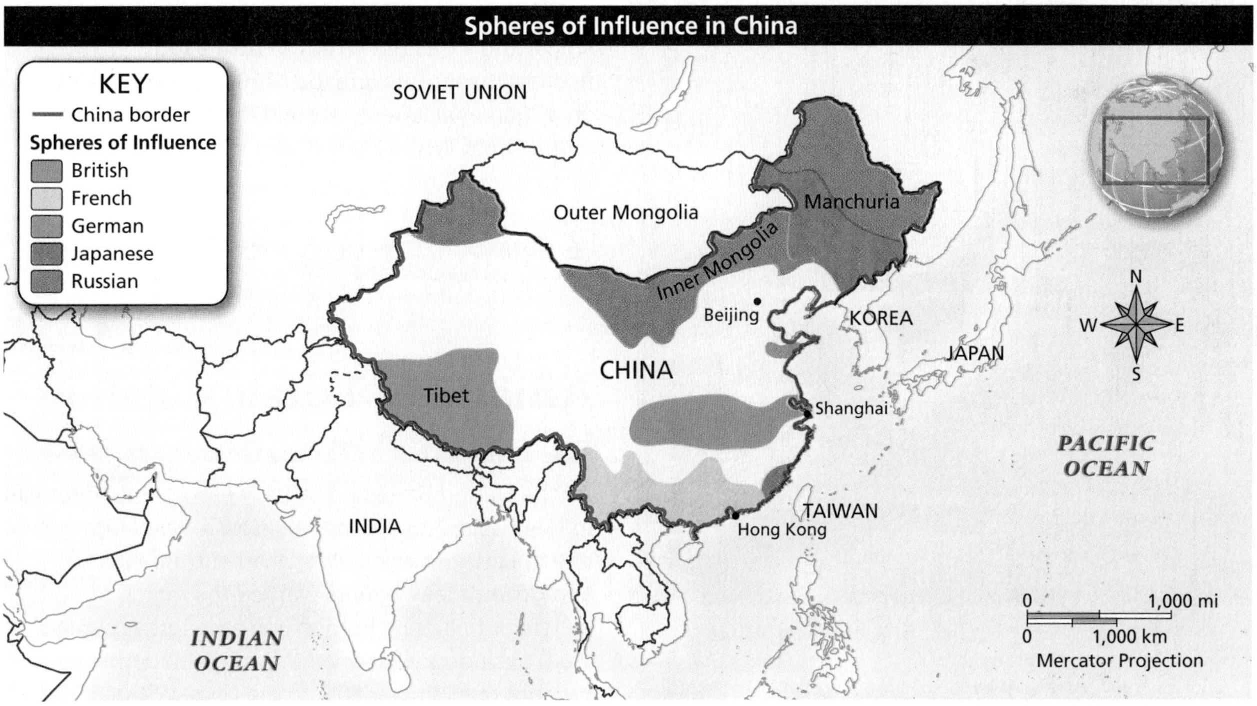

>> **Analyze Maps** What can you conclude about the influence of the United States in China during the early twentieth century?

Roosevelt Works With Japan

Like the United States, Japan wanted to expand its influence in China. Japan also disapproved of the European "carve-up" of the region. Furthermore, the Japanese took offense of the presence of Russian troops in Manchuria, a region of China that bordered Russia. In February 1904, without a declaration of war, Japan attacked and bottled up Russia's Pacific fleet stationed at Port Arthur, China. The Japanese followed up on this victory with a series of major land engagements in Manchuria that caused more than 100,000 Russian casualties. However, Japan also suffered heavy losses in the fighting.

Resolving the Russo-Japanese War In 1905, representatives from Russia and Japan met in Portsmouth, New Hampshire, to negotiate an end to the **Russo-Japanese War**. When the talks stalled, Theodore Roosevelt, now President, intervened and convinced the two sides to sign a peace treaty. For his efforts, Roosevelt won the Nobel Peace Prize. The President's intervention—and his receipt of the famous award—prominently displayed America's growing role in world affairs.

>> The Great White Fleet, part of Roosevelt's plan to protect American interests in Asia, departs from a U.S. port in 1907. **Analyze Information** Explain why Asian nations might have not have believed that the voyage of the fleet was a "good will cruise."

Racial Prejudice Affects Foreign Relations

Despite Roosevelt's achievement, America entered troubled waters in its relations with Japan. A root cause of this trouble was anti-Asian sentiment on the West Coast of the United States. In the fall of 1906, the San Francisco School Board banned Japanese, Chinese, and Korean children from attending public schools with white children. The incident drew Japan's immediate wrath. One Tokyo journal demanded that Japan retaliate. "Stand up Japanese nation! Our countrymen have been HUMILIATED on the other side of the Pacific," the newspaper cried out.

Roosevelt disapproved of the decision to segregate Asian children in the San Francisco schools. He understood Japan's anger with America. To calm tensions, he negotiated a **"Gentlemen's Agreement"** with Japan. According to the pact, the school board pledged to end its segregation policy. In return, Japan agreed to limit the emigration of its citizens to the United States.

The Great White Fleet Shows Naval Power

While Roosevelt used diplomacy to ease tensions with Japan, he also promoted military preparedness to protect U.S. interests in Asia. Expressing rising concerns about Japan's territorial expansion at the expense of China, Korea, and Russia—the President won congressional support for a new force of navy ships, known as the **Great White Fleet**. In 1907, Roosevelt sent this armada of 16 white battleships on a "good will cruise" around the world. The voyage of the Great White Fleet demonstrated America's increased military power to the world.

☑ **SUMMARIZE** What conditions led to the Russo-Japanese War?

American Foreign Policy in Latin America

As the United States tentatively asserted its interests in East Asia, Americans called for a more aggressive role in Latin America. American entrepreneurs and government leaders wanted the region to be a sphere of influence from which other great powers were excluded. American influence in Latin America brought obvious benefits to the United States, but it also contributed to anti-American hostility and instability in the region.

U.S. Interventions in Latin America

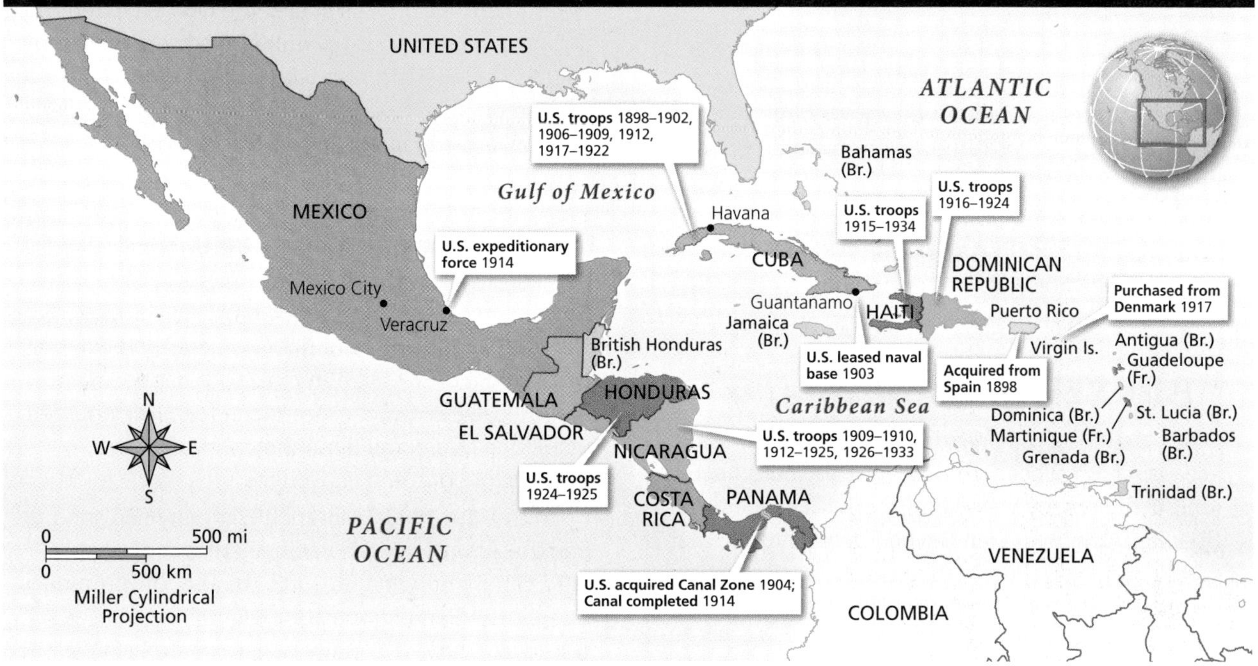

>> **Analyze Maps** Describe U.S. foreign policy towards Latin America in the early 1900s.

BOUNCE to Activate Map

America's victory over Spain liberated the Puerto Rican and Cuban people from Spanish rule. But victory left the fates of these islands unresolved. Would Puerto Rico and Cuba become independent nations? Or would they become colonies of the United States? As questions lingered in the aftermath of war, the United States assumed control in Puerto Rico and Cuba.

Foreign Policy Decisions in Puerto Rico As the smoke from the Spanish-American War cleared, America's new acquisition of Puerto Rico remained under direct U.S. military rule. In 1900, Congress passed the **Foraker Act**, which established a civil government in Puerto Rico. The act authorized the President of the United States to appoint a governor and part of the Puerto Rican legislature. Puerto Ricans could fill the rest of the legislature in a general election.

Whether Puerto Ricans could enjoy citizenship rights in the United States, however, remained unclear. This unusual situation led to a series of court cases, known as Insular Cases, in which the Supreme Court determined the rights of Puerto Ricans. One case examined whether the U.S. government could assess taxes on Puerto Rican goods sold in the United States. The Supreme Court ruled the taxes legal and determined that Puerto Ricans did not enjoy the same rights as U.S. citizens.

In 1917, President Woodrow Wilson signed the Jones-Shafroth Act. It granted Puerto Ricans more citizenship rights and gave the islanders greater control over their own legislature. Still, many Puerto Ricans expressed their discontent because they did not enjoy all of the same rights as Americans.

Relations with Cuba Although the Treaty of Paris granted Cuban independence, the United States Army did not withdraw from the island until 1902. But before the U.S. military left, Congress obliged Cuba to add to its constitution the **Platt Amendment**. The amendment restricted the rights of newly independent Cubans and effectively brought the island within the U.S. sphere. It prevented Cuba from signing a treaty with another nation without American approval. It also required Cuba to lease naval stations to the United States. Additionally, the Platt Amendment granted the United States the "right to intervene" to preserve order in Cuba.

Many Cubans strongly disliked the Platt Amendment but soon realized that America would not otherwise end its military government of the island. The United States, for its part, was unwilling to risk Cuba's becoming a base for a potentially hostile great power.

Cuba thus added the Platt Amendment to its constitution as part of a treaty with the United States. The treaty made Cuba a protectorate of the United States and governed their relationship for decades.

GENERATE EXPLANATIONS Why did Cuba add the Platt Amendment to its constitution?

"Big Stick" Diplomacy

Upon assuming the presidency after McKinley's assassination, Theodore Roosevelt promoted a new kind of diplomacy based on America's success in the Spanish-American War. Beyond determining what would happen to Puerto Rico and Cuba, Roosevelt developed a broader policy for U.S. action in Latin America. Historians have called this Roosevelt's **"big stick" diplomacy** since it depended on a strong military to achieve America's goals. "Big stick" stemmed from the President's admiration for an old African saying, "Speak softly and carry a big stick; you will go far."

Roosevelt's view that America needed to carry a big stick during the Age of Imperialism flowed from his adherence to balance-of-power principles and from his view of the United States as a special nation with a moral responsibility to "civilize," or uplift, weaker nations. In this sense, the new President held beliefs similar to those of imperial powers in Europe and Asia. Roosevelt also felt that America's elite—its statesmen and captains of industry—had to accept the challenge of international leadership.

Physical and Human Geographic Factors Impact the Panama Canal One of Roosevelt's biggest dreams was to create a passage from the Caribbean Ocean to the Pacific Ocean through Central America. He did not originate the plan, but he played a crucial role in making it happen. But first, Roosevelt and the American team of engineers worked to overcome a number of human and physical geographic challenges.

In the late 1800s, a French company had tried to link the Atlantic to the Pacific across the Isthmus of Panama but failed. In 1903, the U.S. government bought the Panama route for $40 million. The canal would allow the U.S. navy to gain control of both the Atlantic and the Pacific Oceans. It would increase America's military security and protect its new territories, while helping its shipping trade reach overseas markets more easily and cheaply.

Before it could build a canal through Panama, however, the United States needed the consent of the Colombian government. At the time, Panama was part of independent Colombia. American efforts

The Panama Canal

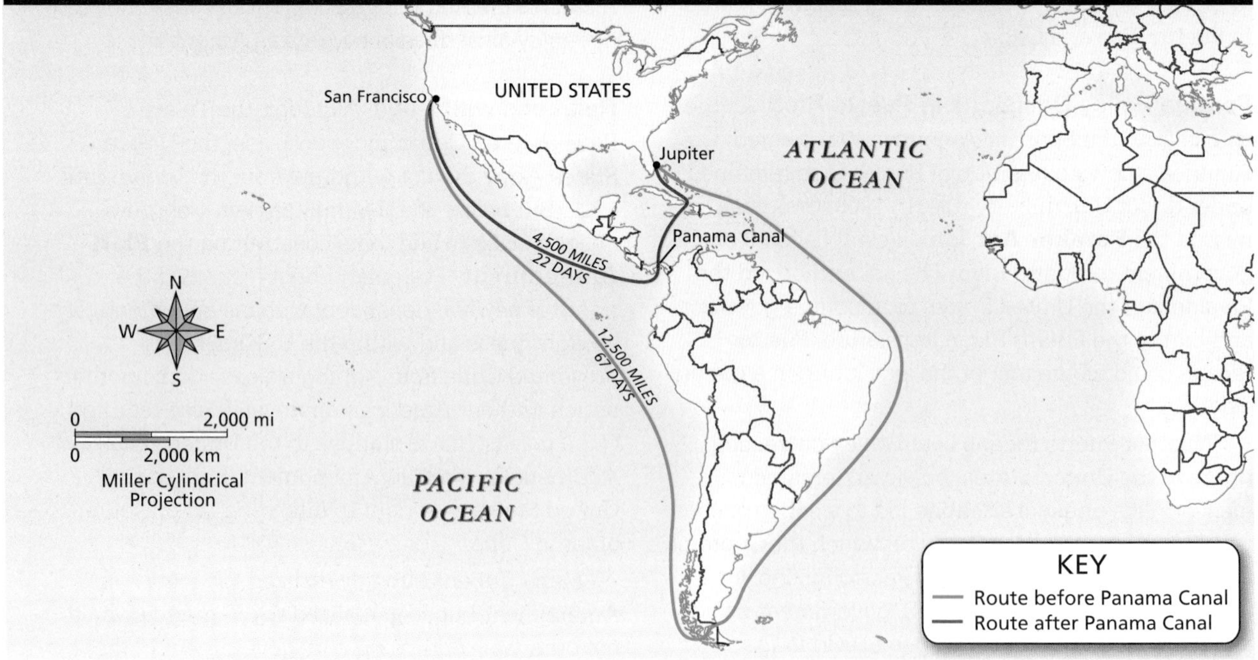

>> **Analyze Maps** How did the construction of the Panama Canal benefit long-distance shippers?

BOUNCE to Activate Gallery

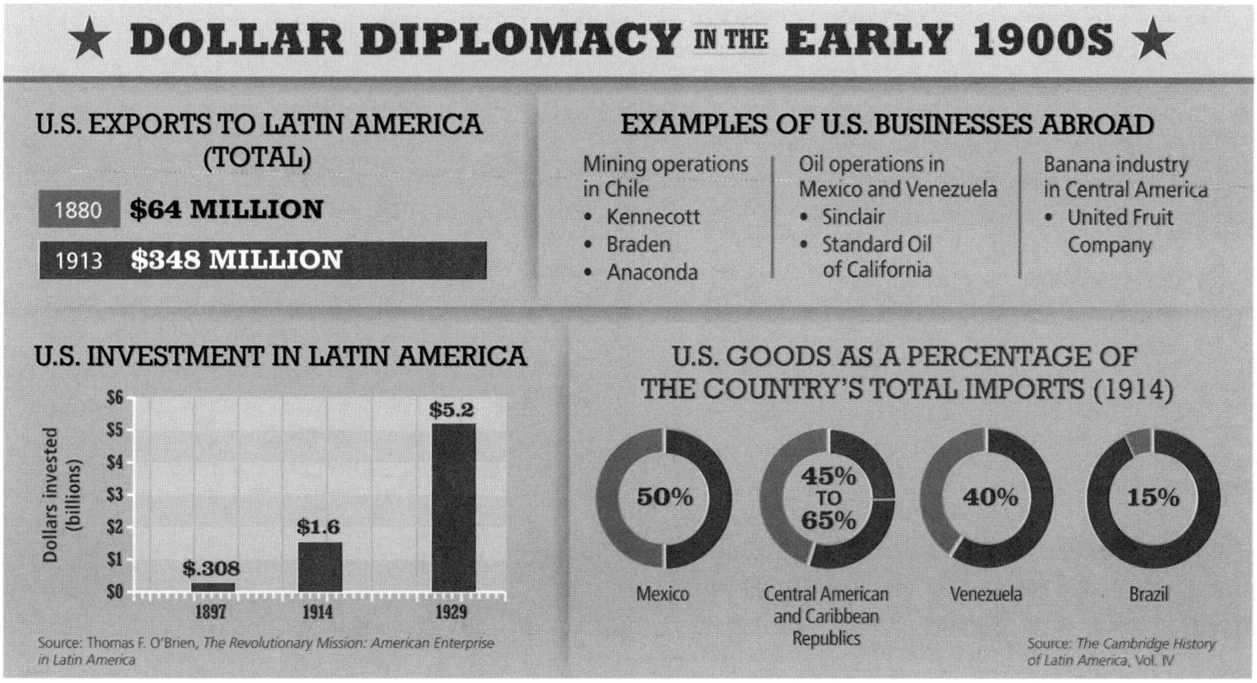

>> **Analyze Information** How did U.S. involvement in Latin American economies illustrate "dollar diplomacy"?

to negotiate a purchase of land across the isthmus stalled when Colombia demanded more than the United States was willing to provide.

So Roosevelt stepped in. The President dispatched U.S. warships to the water off Panama to support a Panamanian rebellion against Colombia. The appearance of the United States Navy convinced the Colombians not to suppress the uprising. Panama soon declared its independence from Colombia. The new nation immediately granted America control over the "Canal Zone." To secure this land for its vital trade link, America agreed to pay Panama $10 million and an annual rent of $250,000.

More than 35,000 workers helped dig the **Panama Canal**. The physical geography and climate of the region were both factors that impacted the enormous project. Workers built a series of locks to raise ships to the level of Gatún Lake, 85 feet above sea level, to cross the isthmus. Completion of the canal depended on scientific breakthroughs by doctors as they learned how to combat tropical diseases. Still, more than 5,000 canal workers died from disease or accidents while building the canal. When the finished waterway opened in 1914, it cut some 8,000 nautical miles off the trip from the west coast to the east coast of the United States.

American Expansionism Requires an Updated Monroe Doctrine In the early 1900s, the inability of Latin American nations to pay their debts to foreign investors raised the possibility of European intervention. In 1903, for example, Germany and Britain blockaded Venezuelan ports to ensure that debts to European bankers were repaid. Roosevelt concluded: "If we intend to say hands off to the powers of Europe, then sooner or later we must keep order ourselves." So in a 1904 message to Congress, he announced a new Latin American policy.

The President's **Roosevelt Corollary** updated the Monroe Doctrine for an age of expansionism and economic influence. In the case of "chronic wrongdoing" by a Latin American nation—the kind that Europeans might use to justify military intervention—the United States would assume the role of police power, restoring order and depriving other creditors of the excuse to intervene. This change, Roosevelt argued, merely reasserted America's long-standing policy of keeping the Western Hemisphere free from European intervention.

The Latin American Response Many Latin Americans resented America's role as the hemisphere's police force. They disagreed with Roosevelt's belief that Latin Americans could not police themselves. Francisco García Calderón, a Peruvian diplomat, contended that the Monroe Doctrine had taken on an "aggressive form with Mr. Roosevelt." Like Calderón, Nicaraguan spokesman Augusto Sandino felt that the United States threatened the "sovereignty and liberty" of his people. Sandino eventually led an army of guerrillas against U.S. Marines in Nicaragua in the 1920s.

Taft's Foreign Policies Lead to "Dollar Diplomacy" Roosevelt handpicked William Howard Taft to succeed him as the Republican candidate for President in 1908. Taft shared Roosevelt's basic foreign policy objectives. After defeating William Jennings Bryan in the general election, Taft wanted to maintain the Open Door Policy in Asia and ensure ongoing stability in Latin America. The new President pursued both goals with the aim of affecting economic issues such as expanding American trade through foreign policy.

Taft hoped to achieve these ends by relying less on the "big stick" and more on **"dollar diplomacy."** As Taft commented in 1912, he looked to substitute "dollars for bullets." The policy aimed to increase American investments in businesses and banks throughout Central America and the Caribbean. Americans busily invested in plantations, mines, oil wells, railways, and other ventures in those regions. Of course, "dollar diplomacy" sometimes required a return to the "big stick" and military intervention. Such was the case when President Taft dispatched troops to Nicaragua in 1909—and again in 1912—to protect the formation of a pro-American government there.

IDENTIFY MAIN IDEAS How did "dollar diplomacy" affect American foreign policy?

Wilson's "Moral Diplomacy"

During the 1912 presidential election campaign, Democratic candidate Woodrow Wilson criticized the foreign policies of his Republican predecessors Theodore Roosevelt and William Howard Taft. After his election victory, Wilson appointed the anti-imperialist William Jennings Bryan as Secretary of State, which sent a strong message to the American people.

A New Emphasis on Foreign Policy Wilson intended to take U.S. foreign policy in a different direction. He promised that the nation would "never again seek one additional foot of territory by conquest" but would instead work to promote "human rights, national integrity, and opportunity." Wilson spelled out his new **"moral diplomacy,"** or "missionary diplomacy," in a message to the American people:

DIFFERENT APPROACHES TO FOREIGN POLICY

Roosevelt	Taft	Wilson
Big stick diplomacy • Believed American military should be used to achieve goals • Wanted to "civilize" other countries • Did not believe nations should be self-governing • Supported rebellion in Panama • Opposed European intervention in the Western Hemisphere (Roosevelt Corollary)	Dollar diplomacy • Believed U.S. should invest in foreign economies to increase American influence • Continued Roosevelt's foreign policy but with less aggression • Worked for stability in Latin America • Worked to expand economic opportunities in China	Moral diplomacy • Believed U.S. should spread peace and democracy rather than colonize foreign countries • Believed other nations should be self-governing • Continued to use American military in Latin America • Wished to cultivate a friendship with Latin America

>> **Contrast** How did Roosevelt and Wilson differ in their approach to governing colonial territories?

We must prove ourselves [Latin America's] friends and champions upon terms of equality and honor. . . .

We must show ourselves friends by comprehending their interest, whether it squares with our own interest or not. . . . Comprehension must be the soil in which shall grow all the fruits of friendship. . . . I mean the development of constitutional liberty in the world.

—Woodrow Wilson, October 27, 1913

In spite of his stated preference for "moral diplomacy" over "big stick" or "dollar diplomacy," Wilson used the military on a number of occasions to guide Latin Americans in the directions that he thought proper. In 1915, Wilson sent marines to Haiti to protect American investments and to guard against the potential of German or French aggression in the nation. Wilson prodded the government of Haiti to sign an agreement that essentially gave the United States the right to control its financial and foreign affairs. The marines did not leave until 1934. Under Wilson, U.S. soldiers and sailors also intervened in the Dominican Republic and in Mexico.

Revolution Grips Mexico For decades, Mexican dictator Porfirio Díaz had followed policies that benefited his country's small upper class of wealthy landowners, clerics, and military men. With Díaz's encouragement, foreign investments in Mexico grew. As a result, American business leaders owned large portions of Mexico's industries. While foreign investors and Mexico's aristocracy grew rich, Mexico's large population of farmers struggled in poverty.

In 1911, Francisco Madero led the Mexican Revolution that toppled Díaz. Madero was committed to reforms but was a weak administrator. In 1913, General Victoriano Huerta seized power and executed Madero. Under "dollar diplomacy," Taft likely would have recognized Huerta as the leader of Mexico because Huerta pledged to protect American investments. But under "moral diplomacy," or "missionary diplomacy," Wilson refused to do so, declaring that he would not accept a "government of butchers." Instead, Wilson favored Venustiano Carranza, another reformer, who had organized anti-Huerta forces.

>> The United States supported Mexican rebel leader Pancho Villa's insurrection against the Mexican government until his forces conducted an attack in the United States in 1916.

Intervention in Mexico In 1914, the President used the Mexican arrest of American sailors as an opportunity to help Carranza attain power. Wilson sent marines to occupy the Mexican port of Veracruz. The action caused Huerta's government to collapse, and Carranza assumed the presidency.

Huerta's fall from power cheered many Mexicans and appeared to validate Wilson's "moral diplomacy." However, Wilson soon discovered that he faced more trouble in Mexico. The new Carranza government was slow in bringing about reforms, and rebels again rose up, this time under the leadership of **Francisco "Pancho" Villa**. For a while, Wilson courted Villa. After American support disappeared in 1916, Villa's forces crossed into New Mexico and raided the town of Columbus, leaving 18 Americans dead. President Wilson responded by sending General John J. Pershing and more than 10,000 troops on a "punitive expedition" to Mexico.

Pershing's forces chased Villa for several months but failed to capture the rebel leader. Wilson eventually withdrew American troops from Mexico in 1917, mostly because of his concerns about World War I raging in Europe.

Not long afterward, the United States declared war on Germany. Free from hunting Villa, Pershing took command of the American Expeditionary Force in France.

A generation earlier, few would have believed it possible that more than one million American troops would engage in a large-scale war in Europe. But the triumph over Spain and U.S. actions in Asia and Latin America demonstrated that America had emerged as a world power. Now, World War I would test that new global strength.

IDENTIFY CENTRAL IDEAS What effect would "moral diplomacy" have on American foreign policy decisions?

ASSESSMENT

1. **Summarize** What was the impact of the Platt Amendment?
2. **Sequence Events** Discuss the events that led to the Boxer Rebellion.
3. **Identify Cause and Effect** What events contributed to a hostile relationship between Japan and the United States?
4. **Draw Conclusions** How did Puerto Rico pose a problem for the United States after the Spanish-American War?
5. **Generate Explanations** Explain the purpose of the Roosevelt Corollary.
6. **Connections to Today** The Great White Fleet was a way for the U.S. armed forces to show its power in 1907. How does the United States show its power today?

Connections to Today

U.S. Marines deliver USAID supplies to the Philippines after a typhoon hit the nation.

Take Action by Learning About U.S. Global Presence

The United States remains a world power and shows its influence in the world not only through its strong military but also through a diplomatic corps and ordinary citizens working to assist people around the world in numerous ways.

1. **Choose** one of the following topics about U.S. worldwide strength:
    - **Life on a Military Base:** Investigate what life is like on an overseas military base for soldiers, sailors, or airmen and their families.
    - **Life at an Embassy or Consulate:** Investigate what life is like at an overseas embassy or consulate. What work do the people of the U.S. diplomatic corps do?
    - **Civilian Aid:** Investigate the work of USAID. How does it contribute to U.S. National security?
2. **Ask Questions** Generate a list of questions about the topic you have selected. What might you want to know about your topic?
3. **Learn** about your topic by using a variety of sources. Use the Internet or your library to find newspaper or magazine articles, data, or interviews with people involved in the work.
4. **Raise Awareness** Create an annotated map of the world or a region of the world that shows the location or locations of the group you studied. Include information about the mission of your group/organization.

Topic 11 Quick Study Guide

LESSON SUMMARIES

Use these Lesson Summaries, and the longer versions available online, to review the key ideas for each lesson in this Topic.

Lesson 1: Progressives Drive Reform

Progressivism rose in the 1890s to tackle problems brought by industrialization, urbanization, and immigration. Journalists helped pass laws ending child labor and ensuring worker safety. New laws also targeted political corruption and limited the power of business interests. Political practices such as the ballot initiative, the referendum and the recall were introduced.

Lesson 2: Women Gain Rights

In the early 1900s, the number of women attending college increased. Women fought for the right to vote and to own property. Some women campaigned against the consumption of alcohol, while others established charitable organizations. In several states, women's groups used the referendum process to gain the right to vote. In 1920 the Nineteenth Amendment extended the vote to women.

Lesson 3: Striving for Equality

The Progressive Era did not bring much progress for minorities and immigrants. However, African Americans continued to oppose segregation and discrimination, founding the National Association for the Advancement of Colored People, which fought for civil rights and the right to vote. Meanwhile, Jews formed the Anti-Defamation League to fight verbal attacks and false statements.

Lesson 4: Reformers in the White House

Progressive reforms marked the presidencies of both Theodore Roosevelt and Woodrow Wilson. Roosevelt took on big business and extended federal protection of natural resources. The 1912 presidential election was won by Wilson, who believed the government should play an active role in the economy.

Lesson 5: American Influence Grows

During the late 1800s, the United States was emerging as a new power on the global stage, extending its economic, political, and military influence over weaker nations. A large naval force opened up Japan to American trade. The United States purchased Alaska and annexed Hawaii.

Lesson 6: The Spanish-American War

Cuban patriot José Martí launched a war for independence from Spain. After the American battleship *USS Maine* exploded in Havana Harbor, Congress declared war on Spain. Spanish troops in the Philippines and Cuba surrendered to the United States. However, in the Philippines, nationalists rebelled against U.S. rule.

Lesson 7: The United States Emerges as a World Power

By 1900, the United States was becoming more active internationally. The U.S. helped put down an uprising in China and negotiated and end to the Russo-Japanese War. In 1907, America sent a fleet of ships around the world as a display of power. The U.S. also built the Panama Canal.

QUEST! FINDINGS

Write Your Essay Refer to your responses to the Quest Connections to help you write your essay comparing historians' viewpoints on the Spanish-American War. Use the rubric and other Quest resources online to guide your work.

GO ONLINE to access lesson summaries

VISUAL REVIEW

Use these graphics to review some of the key terms, people, and ideas from this Topic.

The Spanish-American War Begins

1868–1878 First struggle for Cuban independence; Cubans flee to Florida.

↓

José Martí travels through Florida, raising money for Cuban rebels.

↓

1895 Martí launches Cuban war for independence.

↓

U.S. sympathy for Cuban rebels grows.

↓

1898 USS *Maine* explodes in Havana harbor; U.S. declares war on Spain.

Municipal Reforms

GOVERNMENT REFORMS	ELECTION REFORMS
• Commission form of government • City managers • Trained administrators • City-owned public utilities	• Direct primary • Initiative • Referendum • Recall

Minorities Organize

African Americans	1905 Niagara Movement formed 1909 NAACP organized 1911 Urban League founded
Jews	1913 Anti-Defamation League formed
Mexican Americans	PLM formed in Arizona Mutualistas formed in several states
American Indians	1911 Society of American Indians formed
Asian Americans	Takao Ozawa fights law that blocks Asian Americans from becoming citizens.

Topic 11 Assessment

KEY TERMS, PEOPLE, AND IDEAS

1. How did the **Social Gospel** movement contribute to reform?
2. How did the **settlement house** improve the lives of the poor?
3. How did Progressives shape public policy?
4. Describe ways that women fought to gain the right to vote.
5. What role did **Americanization** play in the Progressive Movement?
6. Why was the **Sixteenth Amendment** introduced?
7. How did **Alfred T. Mahan** influence American expansionism?
8. How did the Jones Act affect the Philippines?
9. Why did the United States acquire territories?

CRITICAL THINKING

10. **Compare and Contrast** (a.) What were the similarities and differences between the goals of the Populist and the Progressive movements? (b.) Compare and contrast the kinds of voters who supported these parties.
11. **Cite Evidence** Cite evidence of women's increasing confidence and freedom in the Progressive Era.
12. **Draw Conclusions** Why did so many Progressives ignore the plight of racial and ethnic minorities?
13. **Make Generalizations** (a.) Why were Theodore Roosevelt's views on land use so controversial? (b.) How did these views reflect his Progressive politics?
14. **Identify Cause and Effect** Analyze the major factors that drove United States imperialism.
15. **Draw Inferences** What were the economic, military, and security motivations behind the building of the Panama Canal?
16. **Analyze Maps** Look at the map. Why was Florida so strategically important during the Spanish-American War? (Use an appropriate tool to judge distances.)

Spanish-American War: Securing Cuba

17. **Writing Activity: Write an Informative Essay** Analyze this excerpt from an editorial written during the Filipino insurrection and what you learned about the United States and the Philippines in this Topic. What does it reveal about the attitudes and goals behind U.S. expansionism? Use your answers to the question and primary and secondary sources to write an informative essay. Remember to write a thesis and site evidence from the sources.

> Let us all be frank. WE DO NOT WANT THE FILIPINOS. WE WANT THE PHILIPPINES. . . . The islands are enormously rich; they abound in dense forests of valuable hardwood timber; they contain mines of the precious metals; their fertile lands will produce immense crops of sugar cane, rice and tobacco. Touched by the wands of American enterprise, fertilized with American capital, these islands would speedily become richer than Golconda was of old.
>
> But unfortunately, they are infested by Filipinos. There are many millions of them there, and it is to be feared that their extinction will be slow.
>
> —*San Francisco Argonaut, 1902*

18. **Connections to Today** In the early 1900s, several U.S. presidents used terms that described their foreign policies. What terms would you use to describe U.S. foreign policy today?

DOCUMENT-BASED QUESTIONS

The economic policies of progressive presidents such as Theodore Roosevelt and Woodrow Wilson were controversial. Read the documents below, then answer the questions that follow.

DOCUMENT A

In this document, Woodrow Wilson discusses the nature and formation of trusts.

> I take my stand absolutely, where every progressive ought to take his stand, on the proposition that private monopoly is indefensible and intolerable. And there I will fight my battle. And I know how to fight it. Everybody who has even read the newspapers knows the means by which these men built up their power and created these monopolies. Any decently equipped lawyer can suggest to you statutes by which the whole business can be stopped. . . . I know they can be stopped by law.
>
> *—Woodrow Wilson, 1913*

DOCUMENT B

This political cartoon shows President Theodore Roosevelt with the good and bad trusts.

DOCUMENT C

This excerpt is from the Progressive Party platform.

> This country belongs to the people who inhabit it. Its resources, its businesses, its institutions, and its laws should be utilized, maintained, or altered in whatever manner will best promote the general interest. It is time to set the public welfare in the first place. . . .
>
> We demand . . . that those who profit by control of business affairs shall justify that profit and that control by sharing with the public the fruits thereof. We therefore demand a strong national regulation of interstate corporations. . . .
>
> *—Progressive "Bull Moose" Party Platform, 1912*

DOCUMENT D

This excerpt is from a speech against government regulation.

> What effect is what you may do here going to have upon the future welfare, productiveness, and value of the greatest single industrial interest in the country? . . . . Gentlemen, you may pass an act that will so compromise the value of the property and the prosperity of the communities of this country that it will bring widespread disaster. . . .
>
> What I say, gentlemen, is that [it] is a very, very serious moment when an Anglo-Saxon government undertakes the charge of the people's money and says how much they shall earn by the exercise of their constitutional rights of liberty and property.
>
> *—David Wilcox, President of Delaware and Hudson Railroad, testimony to Congress, 1905*

19. In Document A, Woodrow Wilson promises that he will
A. defend big business against regulation.
B. introduce government regulation.
C. not interfere with the economy.
D. create a fairer tax system.

20. Analyze Images In Document B, what issue does this political cartoon illustrate?

21. In Document C, the Progressive Party is calling for
A. increased taxation of the rich.
B. forced distribution of wealth.
C. the lifting of all economic regulation.
D. a fairer balance of public and private interests.

22. In Document D, the speaker is saying that government regulation of earnings is
A. dangerous to prosperity and productivity.
B. completely justified.
C. guaranteed by the constitution.
D. consistent with rights of liberty and property.

23. Writing Activity: Primary Source Write a paragraph explaining whether or not you think the progressive movement's calls for government regulation of business was justified. Use the sources as well as additional information you have learned.

GO ONLINE to access more practice

Topic 12

World War I and the 1920s (1914–1929)

ESSENTIAL QUESTION How should we handle conflict?

project Imagine

GO ONLINE for immersive experiences designed to help you explore the highs and lows of the 1920s through rich primary sources. Also access the eText, videos, Biographies, and other online resources.

Dancers on the cover of a 1926 *Life* magazine

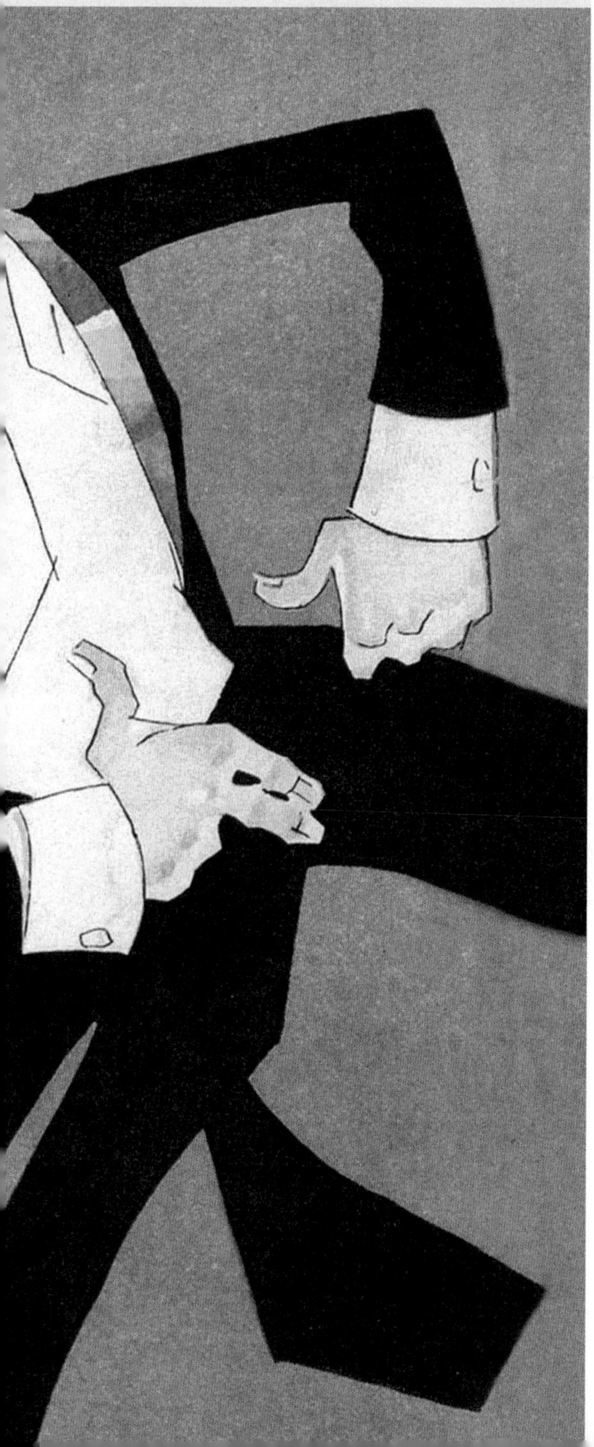

Connections to Today

Do you follow "influencers" on social media? Are you a fan of singers who first gained fame by uploading videos to the internet? In this topic you'll read about how motion pictures and the radio turned movie actors, singers, and sports figures into celebrities. As all the world becomes a stage, modern technology is giving everyone the means to perform and become famous. What are the positive and negative effects of this democratization of fame?

NBC LEARN

Learn about the life of film star Louise Brooks.

BOUNCE to Activate My Story Video

Topic 12 Overview

In this Topic, you'll learn about World War I and the 1920s. Look at the lesson outline and explore the timeline. As you study this Topic, you'll complete the Quest Inquiry.

LESSON OUTLINE

Key Events of World War I and the 1920s

1914 Assassination of Austrian archduke triggers World War I

1915 Sinking of the *Lusitania*

1916 Battles of Verdun and Somme cause more than 2 million casualties

1917 United States declares war on Germany

1918 Armistice with Germany ends war

1919 Prohibition begins

1927 Charles Lindbergh flies solo across Atlantic

1910 · 1915 · 1920 · 1925 · 19

QUEST! INQUIRY

The League of Nations

Should the United States have joined the League of Nations or would that organization have undermined American sovereignty? In this Quest you'll explore the refusal of the United States to support the League of Nations.

STEP 1

Read the Discussion Launch and take notes. Then discuss the major points with the other members of your group. Write the points that your group agreed with in the Information Organizer.

STEP 2

Study several sources to understand different people's perspectives on the main question. As you read and analyze each source, fill in Step 2 of the Information Organizer.

STEP 3

After your group has been assigned a YES or NO position on the main question, prepare the most compelling arguments in support of your position. Present your arguments and then switch sides.

STEP 4

Discuss the main question from your own point of view. Reflect on what you've read and heard about the question and how different perspectives have broadened your understanding.

GO ONLINE to access complete Quest materials

12.1

This poster highlights the fact that even though Belgium declared its neutrality, Germany still invaded.

BOUNCE to Activate Flipped Video

Objectives

Identify the causes of World War I.

Analyze the impact of technological innovations in weaponry that resulted in stalemate on the Western Front.

Analyze reasons behind isolationism and neutrality in the United States before 1917.

Explain why the United States entered the conflict on the side of the Allies.

Key Terms

Alsace-Lorraine
militarism
Franz Ferdinand
William II
Western Front
casualty
contraband
U-boats
Lusitania
Zimmermann note

GO ONLINE to access your digital course

America Enters World War I

In 1914, nationalism, militarism, imperialism, and entangling alliances combined with other factors to lead the nations of Europe into a brutal war. The war quickly spread around the globe. The United States remained neutral at first but ended up abandoning its long tradition of staying out of European conflicts.

The Causes of World War I

Until 1914, there had not been a large-scale European conflict for nearly one hundred years. However, bitter, deep-rooted problems simmered beneath the surface of polite diplomacy. Europe was sitting on a powder keg of nationalism, regional tensions, economic rivalries, imperial ambitions, and militarism.

Nationalism Escalates Tension in Europe Nationalism, or devotion to one's nation, kick-started international and domestic tension. In the late 1800s, many Europeans began to reject the earlier idea of a nation as a collection of different ethnic groups. Instead, they believed that a nation should express the nationalism of a single ethnic group.

This belief evolved into an intense form of nationalism that heightened international rivalries. For example, France longed to avenge its humiliating defeat by a collection of German states in 1871 and regain **Alsace-Lorraine**, the territory it lost during that conflict. Nationalism also threatened minority groups within nation states. If a country existed as the expression of "its people," the majority ethnic group, where did ethnic minorities fit in?

The spread of the theory of Social Darwinism did not help soothe the competitive instinct. Social Darwinism applied biologist Charles Darwin's ideas of natural selection and "survival of the fittest" to human society. Social Darwinists believed that the fittest nation would come out ahead in the constant competition among countries.

Nationalism also destabilized old multinational empires such as Austria-Hungary and the Ottoman Empire. This was particularly true in the Balkan region of southeastern Europe.

For example, when Serbia emerged as an independent nation in 1878, it challenged the nearby empire of Austria-Hungary in two ways: by trying to gain territory controlled by the empire, where Serbs lived, and by the example it offered to Austria-Hungary's diverse peoples.

The nationalist sentiments of the period sometimes spilled over into the economic goals of each nation. Industrial output, trade, and the possession of an overseas empire were the yardsticks of wealth and greatness. The leading industrial nations competed for lands rich in raw materials as well as for places to build military bases to protect their empires. Britain already had a large empire, and France commanded a smaller one. But Germany, Italy, Belgium, Japan, and the United States also rushed to join the race to expand. Together, industrialized nations jostled among themselves as they carved colonies out of Africa, claimed islands in the Pacific, and began to nibble away at China.

Militarism Increases Arms Production For some European leaders, the question was not so much *if* a great war would start but *when.* To prepare, leaders increased the size of their armies and stockpiles of weapons. No nation readied its war machinery more than Germany. By 1914, it had a huge standing army and the largest, deadliest collection of guns in the world. It also built up its navy enough to rival Britain's, the world's strongest at that time. To keep up, Britain, too, increased the size of its navy. A spirit of **militarism**, or glorification of the military, grew in the competing countries and fueled this arms race even more.

The contest between Germany and Britain at sea and between Germany, France, and Russia on land guaranteed one important thing: The next major war would involve more troops and more technologically advanced weapons than ever before. Machine guns, mobile artillery, tanks, submarines, and airplanes would change the nature of warfare.

Alliances Between Nations Increase the Potential for War European leaders also prepared for war by forming alliances. Before 1914, two major ones emerged.

>> **Analyze Maps** Based on the map, describe one possible disadvantage the Central Powers of Germany and Austria-Hungary face.

Germany, Austria-Hungary, and Italy joined together in the Triple Alliance (although Italy never fought with it). Opposed to the Triple Alliance was the Triple Entente, made up of France, Russia, and Great Britain. Alliances emboldened leaders to act recklessly. They knew that if they did declare war, powerful allies were obligated to fight along with them. No country wanted to be seen as an unreliable partner. European leaders thought less of the advantages of peace and more of the possible benefits of war. Some also hoped that a foreign war would help to smooth over domestic problems.

A Significant Assassination On June 28, 1914, Archduke **Franz Ferdinand**, heir to the throne of Austria-Hungary, and his wife Sophie left for a routine visit to Sarajevo (sar uh YAY voh), the capital city of the Austro-Hungarian province of Bosnia. But a handful of young Bosnians had other plans for the archduke and his wife. These men were ethnic Serbs who believed that Bosnia rightfully belonged to Serbia, and they saw Franz Ferdinand as a tyrant.

After the archduke's driver made a wrong turn, Gavrilo Princip, one of the conspirators, noticed the couple in the car, pulled a pistol from his pocket, and fired it twice. First Sophie and then Franz Ferdinand died. People around the world were shocked by the murders. But no one expected that they would lead to a great world war.

☑ **RECALL** What countries formed the Triple Entente?

The Great War Begins

Everything was in place for a great conflict—nationalist ambitions, large armies, stockpiles of weapons, alliances, and military plans. The nations of Europe were hurtling like giant trains toward a great collision. Archduke Franz Ferdinand's assassination was the incident that triggered this conflict.

Alliances Cause a Chain Reaction Soon after the assassination, Kaiser **William II**, the German emperor, assured Austria-Hungary that Germany would stand by its ally if war came. Confident in Germany's support, Austria-Hungary then sent a harsh ultimatum to Serbia demanding Serbia's total cooperation in an investigation into the assassination. When Serbia did not agree to all of the demands, Austria-Hungary declared war on July 28, 1914.

Because of the alliance system, what otherwise might have been a localized quarrel quickly spread. In early August, Russia mobilized for war to help its ally Serbia against Austria. This caused Germany, Austria's ally, to declare war against Russia. Very quickly, other European nations found themselves being dragged into the conflict, forced to declare war because of their commitments to their respective alliances.

Major Players in World War I

ALLIED POWERS	NEUTRAL POWERS	CENTRAL POWERS
France	Switzerland	Germany
Britain	Spain	Austria-Hungary
Russia	The Netherlands	Ottoman Empire
Serbia	Denmark	
Italy	Sweden	
Japan	Norway	
United States	Albania	

SOURCE: *Britannica Encyclopedia*

>> **Analyze Charts** Why was one alliance called "The Central Powers"? (Consulting a map may help you answer.)

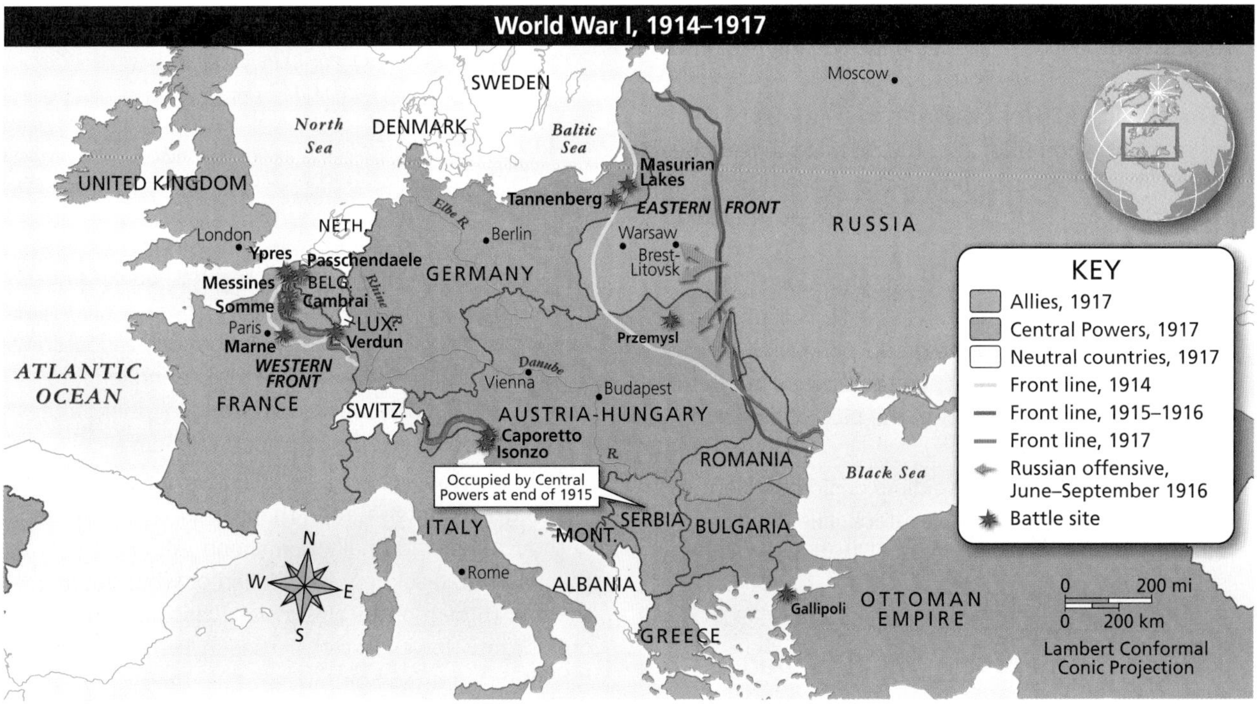

>> **Analyze Maps** What challenge did Germany's location present to its pursuit of victory in the war?

France, Russia's ally, promptly declared war against Germany. The very next day, Germany declared war against neutral Belgium, so that it could launch an invasion of France through that small country. Great Britain, which had treaties with France and Belgium, immediately declared war against Germany. In less than one week, the Central Powers of Germany, Austria-Hungary, and Bulgaria were at war against the Allied Powers of Britain, France, Russia, and Serbia. The Ottoman Empire later joined the Central Powers.

German soldiers fought through Belgium and moved southwest into France, toward Paris. Then in September, with the German advance only 30 miles from Paris, the French and the British counterattacked and stopped the German forces near the Marne River.

Technological Innovations Lead to Stalemate

After the Battle of the Marne, the Germans settled onto high ground, dug trenches, and fortified their position. When the French and British attacked, the German troops used machine guns and artillery to kill thousands of them. The French and British then dug their own trenches and used the same weapons to kill thousands of counterattacking Germans.

Soon, 450 miles of trenches stretched like a huge scar from the coast of Belgium to the border of Switzerland. Although fighting went on in Eastern Europe, the Middle East, and in other parts of the world, this **Western Front** in France became the critical battle front. The side that won there would win the war.

The war dragged on for years, and it was hideously deadly—much more so than anyone had expected. The primary reason for the length of the war and its deadly nature was the simple fact that the defensive weapons of the time were better and more devastating than the offensive ones. Generals on each side threw their soldiers into assaults against the enemy without fully considering the new technology. Charging toward trenches that were defended by artillery, machine guns, and rifles was futile. In virtually every battle on the Western Front, the attacking force suffered terribly.

Even the use of poison gas did nothing to benefit the offense, despite its horrifying effects. Airplanes and tanks were both first used during World War I, but neither broke the stalemate.

Airplanes were mostly used for reconnaissance, or observing an area for military purposes. The torn-up ground caused by endless shelling created a need for a new military technology—the tank. Military leaders hoped tanks could plow through devastated battlefield areas, but the first tanks weren't able to ride over such uneven terrain and often broke down during crucial battles. Ineffective offensives and effective defenses produced only a deadly stalemate.

The Reality of Trench Warfare The stalemate led to gruesome conditions for the men in the trenches of the Western Front. The soldiers battled the harsh conditions of life often as fiercely as they attacked the enemy. They developed "trench foot" from standing for hours in wet, muddy trenches. They contracted lice from the millions of rats that infested the trenches. Dug into the ground, the soldiers lived in constant fear, afraid to pop their heads out of their holes and always aware that the next offensive might be their last.

Even on a quiet day, soldiers could be killed by snipers or a surprise gas attack, like the one described by French officer Paul Truffaut at Verdun:

> The special shells the men call "shells on wheels" [shells filled with poison gas] are whizzing by continuously. They explode silently and have no smell but can be deadly. They killed several men yesterday. One of my men refused to put his mask on because he couldn't smell anything. All of a sudden, he was dizzy, foaming at the mouth and his skin went black, then he went rigid and died.
>
> —Paul Truffaut, March 5, 1917

In between enemy lines was an area known as "no man's land." Artillery barrages had blasted no man's land until any fields, trees, or homes, that had once existed there, were charred beyond recognition. Soldiers went "over the top" of their trenches into this muddy, nearly impassable wasteland when they attempted to attack the entrenched enemy.

Casualties—or soldiers killed, wounded, or missing—mounted first in thousands, then hundreds of thousands, and finally in millions. Almost one million French soldiers were killed or wounded in just the first three months of the war. The Germans lost only slightly fewer. In two battles in 1916—Verdun (ver DUHN) and the Somme (suhm)—the British, French, and Germans sustained more than 2 million casualties. The British suffered 60,000 casualties on the first day alone at the Somme and achieved virtually nothing. And still the stalemate dragged on.

☑ **IDENTIFY SUPPORTING DETAILS** What technologies encouraged a stalemate between opposing armies?

Deadly Technology of World War I

TECHNOLOGY	APPLICATION
POISON GAS	Gases such as chlorine, phosgene, and mustard gas could kill, blind, or burn their victims.
MACHINE GUNS	Improved machine guns could fire 600 bullets per minute.
FLAMETHROWER	A new technology, flamethrowers consisted of a backpack and a gun that could shoot flames as far as 60 feet.
ARTILLERY FIELD GUNS	These long-range cannons caused more casualties than any other type of weapon.
TANKS AND ARMORED CARS	Both sides tried to develop vehicles that could go over rough ground and barbed-wire, with limited success.
AIRPLANES	Planes were used for reconnaissance, bombing, and fighting but did not prove decisive.
SUBMARINES	German U-boats, or submarines, used torpedoes as well as on-deck guns to sink ships.

>> **Analyze Charts** Based on the types of weapons listed in the chart, what can you conclude about either side's ability to inflict casualties on the other side?

The United States Remains Neutral

As the war spread in Europe, President Woodrow Wilson called for Americans to be "impartial in thought as well as action." In a "melting pot" nation that tried to make Americans of peoples from diverse origins, Wilson did not want to see the war set Americans against one another. At first, most Americans viewed the conflict as a distant European quarrel for land and influence. Unless the nation's interests were directly threatened, Americans wanted no part of it. They preferred to maintain what they viewed as traditional American isolation from European disputes. Still, many Americans felt the war's effects and few were truly impartial in thought. Most held a preference for one or another combatant, and many businesses benefited from the increased demand by warring nations for American goods.

Many Americans Choose Sides In 1914, one third of Americans were foreign-born. Many still thought of themselves in terms of their former homelands—as German Americans, Irish Americans, Polish Americans, and so on. With relatives in Europe, many people supported the nation in which they were born.

Some German Americans in the Midwest and some Irish Americans along the East Coast felt strongly that the Central Powers were justified in their actions. Many Americans had emigrated from Germany or Austria-Hungary. Millions of Irish Americans harbored intense grudges over the centuries of Great Britain's domination of their homeland. They hoped that Ireland would gain its independence as Britain became entangled in the war. Many Jewish Americans who had fled Russia to escape the Czarist regimes' murderous pogroms against Jews hoped for Russia's defeat.

Most Americans, however, sided with Britain and France, both of which had strong historic ties with the United States. America's national language was English, its cultural heritage was largely British, and its leading trading partner was Britain. France had aided the American cause during the Revolutionary War.

U.S. Opinion Solidifies No event at the beginning of the war swayed American opinion more than the vicious German invasion of neutral Belgium. German soldiers marching through Belgium committed numerous atrocities, killing unarmed civilians, and destroying entire towns. British journalists and propagandists stressed, and sometimes exaggerated,

>> Soldiers took cover in trenches during gas attacks. **Hypothesize** Why do you think many people consider poisonous gas attacks to be morally wrong while accepting attacks by machines guns, artillery, and tanks?

BOUNCE to Activate 3D Model

>> **Analyze Political Cartoons** Based on the cartoon, what can you infer about President Wilson's attitude toward the war?

BOUNCE to Activate Chart

the brutality of the Germans' actions. Americans might have only dimly understood the causes of the war, but they clearly perceived the human cost of the war for Belgium.

Eventually, three distinct positions on the war crystallized among Americans. One group, the isolationists, believed that the war was none of America's business and that the nation should isolate itself from the hostilities. A second group, the interventionists, felt that the war did affect American interests and that the United States should intervene in the conflict on the side of the Allies. A third group, the internationalists, occupied the middle ground. Internationalists believed that the United States should play an active role in world affairs and work toward achieving a just peace but not enter the war.

CHECK UNDERSTANDING Into what three positions did U.S. opinion generally fall?

>> The British Navy was the strongest in the world. **Draw Conclusions** Why was naval superiority so important to Great Britain's war effort?

>> After German U-boats sank the British passenger ship *Lusitania* near the Irish coast, it became clear to many Americans that even ships carrying civilians were potential targets.

Reasons for U.S. Entry into the War

An internationalist, President Wilson sincerely desired peace in his country and around the world. Between the start of the war in 1914 and America's entry into it in 1917, Wilson attempted to use his influence to end the conflict among the warring countries. He failed in this great effort. Ultimately, he also failed to keep the United States out of the war.

Britain Blockades German Ports Early in the war, British leaders decided to use their navy to blockade Germany to keep essential goods from reaching the other country. International law generally allowed **contraband** goods, usually defined as weapons and other articles used to fight a war, to be confiscated legally by any belligerent nation. Noncontraband goods, such as food, medical supplies, and other nonmilitary items, could not be confiscated. Britain, however, contested the definition of noncontraband articles. As the war continued, Britain expanded its definition of contraband until it encompassed virtually every product, including gasoline, cotton, and even food—in spite of international law.

Passenger Ships Fall Victim to the War at Sea Germany responded by attempting to blockade Britain—even though it lacked the conventional naval forces to do so. Instead, in February 1915, Germany began sinking Allied ships using its

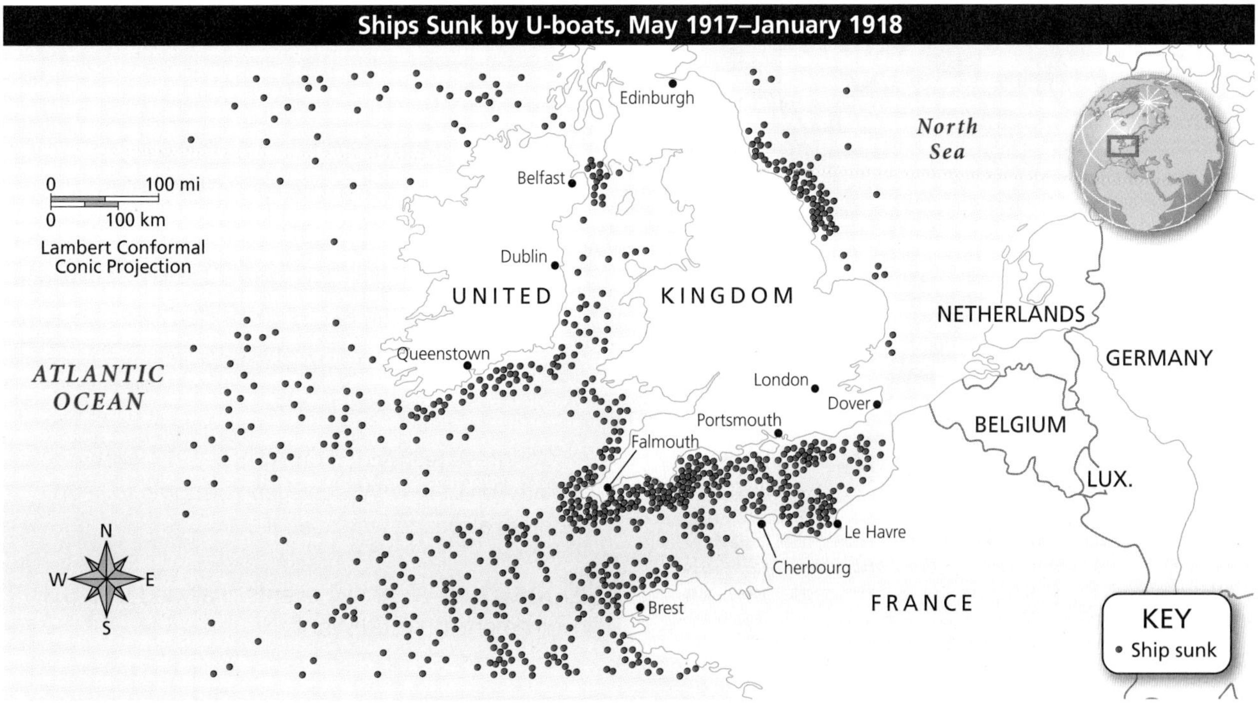

>> German U-boats destroyed more than 11 million tons of Allied shipping and killed nearly 14,000 people. **Analyze Maps** Why were U-boat attacks clustered in particular areas?

U-boats, or submarines. The reality of the German blockade struck America on May 7, 1915, when a German U-boat sank the British passenger liner ***Lusitania*** off the coast of Ireland.

Nearly 1,200 people perished. German officials correctly claimed that the ship was carrying ammunition and other contraband. Americans protested that an unarmed and unresisting ship should not be sunk without first being warned and provided with safety for its passengers. President Wilson was stunned but still wanted peace. "There is such a thing as a man being too proud to fight," he told his fellow citizens. "There is such a thing as a nation being so right that it does not need to convince others by force that it is right."

Germany helped to keep the United States out of the war by eventually promising not to sink any more passenger ships. But in 1916, Germany violated that promise by sinking the unarmed French passenger ship *Sussex*. Another storm of protest erupted in America. Again, Germany pledged not to sink unarmed ships. This promise, called the Sussex Pledge, would not last long.

Preparations for War President Wilson wanted to remain at peace, but even he must have realized the futility of that hope. At the end of 1915, Wilson began to prepare the nation for war.

Many believed that "preparedness" was a dangerous course that could actually provoke war. Even so, Congress passed two pieces of legislation in 1916 to prepare for the possibility of U.S. involvement. The National Defense Act expanded the size of the army, and the Naval Construction Act ordered the building of more warships.

Still, Wilson hoped to avoid conflict. In 1916, he ran for reelection with the slogan "He kept us out of war." It was a close election, but Wilson won a narrow victory over Republican Charles Evans Hughes.

The United States Is Neutral No Longer Wilson did not have much time to enjoy his victory. In early 1917, two events occurred that helped to push the United States into the war. Both events showed Germany's increasing aggression, the main reason why the United States ultimately entered the war.

American trade with the Allies had sustained Britain and France in the war, while the British blockade of Germany had stopped the flow of American goods to the Central Powers. As far as Germany was concerned, desperate times demanded desperate measures.

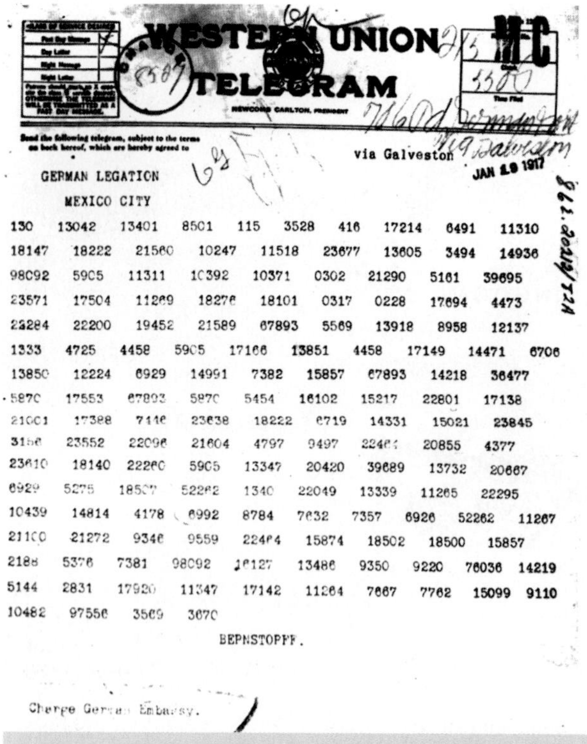

WESTERN UNION TELEGRAM

NEWCOMB CARLTON, PRESIDENT

Send the following telegram, subject to the terms on back hereof, which are hereby agreed to

via Galveston

JAN 19 1917

GERMAN LEGATION

MEXICO CITY

130 13042 13401 8501 115 3528 416 17214 6491 11310
18147 18222 21560 10247 11518 23677 13605 3494 14936
98092 5905 11311 10392 10371 0302 21290 5161 39695
23571 17504 11269 18276 18101 0317 0228 17694 4473
22284 22200 19452 21589 67893 5569 13918 8958 12137
1333 4725 4458 5905 17166 13851 4458 17149 14471 6706
13850 12224 6929 14991 7382 15857 67893 14218 36477
5870 17553 67893 5870 5454 16102 15217 22801 17138
21001 17388 7446 23638 18222 6719 14331 15021 23845
3156 23552 22096 21604 4797 9497 22464 20855 4377
23610 18140 22260 5905 13347 20420 39689 13732 20667
6929 5275 18507 52262 1340 22049 13339 11265 22295
10439 14814 4178 6992 8784 7632 7357 6926 52262 11267
21100 21272 9346 9559 22464 15874 18502 18500 15857
2188 5376 7381 98092 16127 13486 9350 9220 76036 14219
5144 2831 17920 11347 17142 11264 7667 7762 15099 9110
10482 97556 3569 3670

BEPNSTOPFF.

Charge German Embassy.

>> Discovery of the Zimmermann note (a coded telegram) along with unrestricted submarine warfare by Germany led Wilson to ask Congress for a declaration of war.

BOUNCE to Activate Timeline

In January 1917, suffering severe supply shortages due to the blockade, Germany took action. First, German Foreign Minister Arthur Zimmermann sent a telegram to Mexico. The **Zimmermann note** proposed an alliance with Mexico, stating that if the United States declared war on Germany, Mexico should declare war on the United States. In return, after a German victory, Mexico would get back the states of Texas, New Mexico, and Arizona, which it had lost in 1848 after its defeat in the Mexico-American War. The telegram was intercepted by the British, who gave it to American authorities. Next, Germany once again announced unrestricted submarine warfare against Britain.

Although most leaders knew Mexico had no intention of attacking the United States, Americans were shocked by the publication of the Zimmermann note. Even Wilson no longer called for peace. On April 2, 1917, he asked Congress for a declaration of war against Germany:

> The world must be made safe for democracy. Its peace must be planted upon the tested foundations of political liberty. . . . We are but one of the champions of the rights of mankind. We shall be satisfied when those rights have been made as secure as the faith and the freedom of nations can make them.
>
> —Woodrow Wilson, April 2, 1917

Congress responded on April 6, 1917, with a declaration of war. Wilson's long struggle to keep America at peace was over.

☑ **IDENTIFY** What two events finally led to U.S. involvement in World War I?

☑ ASSESSMENT

1. **Analyze Information** Discuss the form of nationalism that prevailed in Europe before World War I, and explain how it contributed to the start of the war.
2. **Identify Cause and Effect** Explain why the assassination of Franz Ferdinand led to more than a localized quarrel.
3. **Generate Explanations** Explain why President Wilson initially opposed U.S. involvement in World War I, and why he later changed his mind.
4. **Make Decisions** World War I is generally considered to be the first instance of total war, where every of-age citizen and all possible resources are mobilized in the war effort. In light of this, do you believe Britain's blockade of Germany—which eventually extended to all goods, thereby violating international law—was justified? Explain your opinion.
5. **Compare and Contrast** Discuss the ways in which World War I differed from previous wars.
6. **Quest Connections** Discuss what might have happened if the League of Nations had existed in 1914.

GO ONLINE to access this biography: Woodrow Wilson

12.2

As the United States went to war, many women joined the workforce. This defense worker is welding the shell casing of a depth charge—an antisubmarine explosive.

The Home Front During World War I

Before the war, the federal government played a minor role in the daily lives of most Americans. But during World War I, the government assumed new powers. It regulated industrial and agricultural production, worked to shape public opinion, and established a new military draft. While war required sacrifice, it also brought new economic opportunities, and many Americans migrated to other parts of the country in search of these opportunities. The war permanently changed Americans' relationship with their government.

BOUNCE to Activate Flipped Video

Objectives

Analyze how the U.S. government mobilized the public to support the war effort.

Describe opposition to World War I and how the federal government responded to it.

Analyze the causes and effects of migration and social changes that occurred during World War I.

Key Terms

Selective Service Act
Bernard Baruch
Committee on Public Information (CPI)
George Creel
conscientious objector
Espionage Act
Great Migration

Mobilizing for War

War affects many things, but its greatest impact is on the lives of ordinary people. People fight, sacrifice, and sometimes die in war. People work to produce the food that soldiers eat and the guns that soldiers fire. People shape the information that others receive about the war. War may be the result of conflicts between nations, but it touches the lives of millions of individuals.

Expanding the Army When the United States entered World War I, the U.S. Army was only a small fraction of the size of European armies. To build the army, President Wilson encouraged Americans to volunteer for service and pushed Congress to pass the **Selective Service Act**. The act, which Congress passed in May 1917, authorized a draft of young men for military service in Europe. On the first day of its enactment, June 5, 1917, more than 9.6 million Americans registered for the draft and were assigned a number. The government held a "great national lottery" in July to decide the order in which the first draftees would be called into service. Blindfolded, Secretary of War Newton D. Baker pulled

GO ONLINE to access your digital course.

number 258 out of a jar. The group of men assigned that number became the very first draftees.

Over the course of the war, more than 24 million Americans registered for the draft. Of these, about 2.8 million were actually drafted into the armed forces. Including volunteers, the total number of American men in uniform during World War I reached nearly 4.8 million. More than 4 million of these were sent to help the Allies in France.

Managing Economic Effects The economic effects of the international military conflict of World War I on the United States were significant. While the Selective Service Commission raised an army, President Wilson worked to shift the national economy from peacetime to wartime production. This process proved slow and frustrating. First, the Council of National Defense, which was formed in August 1916, created an array of new federal administrative agencies to oversee different phases of the war effort. Individual agencies regulated food production, coal and petroleum distribution, and railway use. The government determined what crops farmers grew, what products industries produced, and how supplies moved around on the nation's trains.

Problems and administrative overlap soon led to the creation of the War Industries Board (WIB). The WIB eventually became independent of the Council of National Defense. Headed by **Bernard Baruch** (buh ROOK), an influential Wall Street investment broker who reported directly to the President, the WIB regulated all industries engaged in the war effort. Baruch's agency determined what products industries would make and how much they would cost. The system of free enterprise was curtailed to fulfill the nation's acute need for war materials. Americans decided to cooperate rather than compete in order to defeat the Central Powers. They also bought war bonds to help the war effort.

What Baruch did for industry, future U.S. president Herbert Hoover achieved for agriculture. As head of the Food Administration, he set prices high for wheat and other foodstuffs to encourage farmers to increase production. He also asked Americans to conserve food as a patriotic gesture. If the American people ate less, then more food could be shipped to American and other Allied soldiers. To this end, Hoover instituted wheatless Mondays and Wednesdays, meatless Tuesdays, and porkless Thursdays and Saturdays.

Convincing the American People Hoover's efforts would have been fruitless if the American people did not believe in supporting the war. Most Americans did not understand the reasons for the war in 1914, and many questioned why the United States became

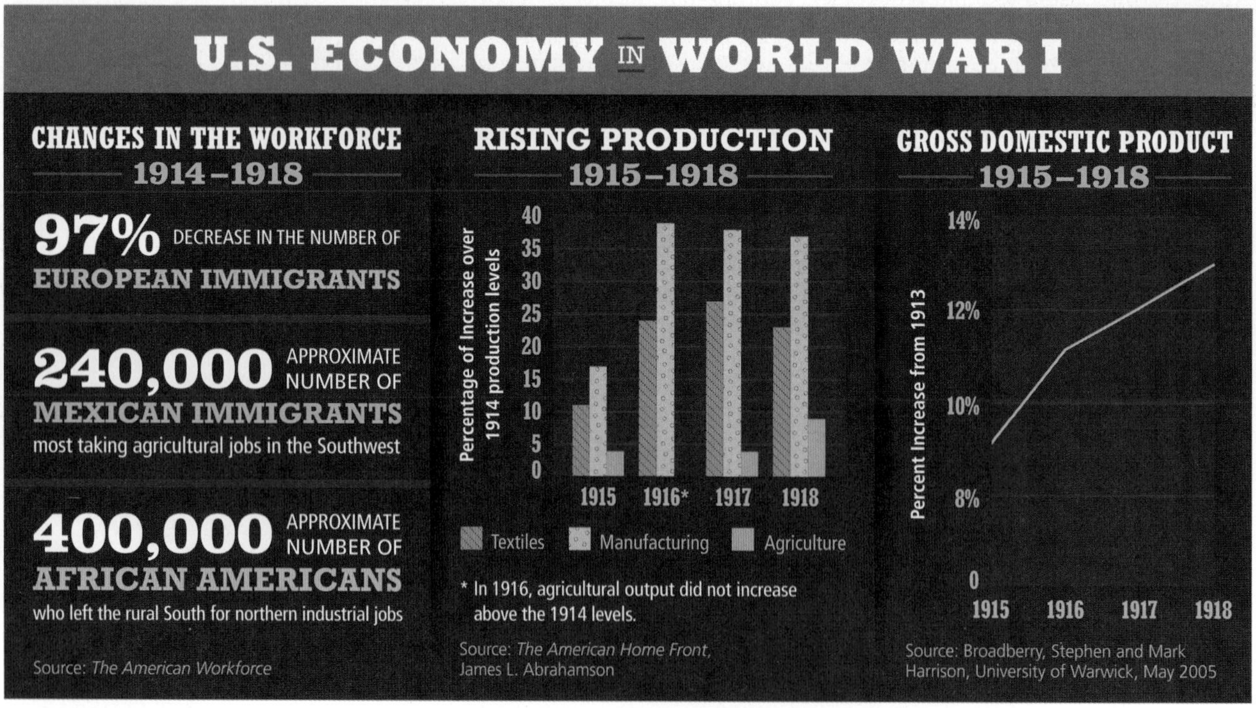

>> **Analyze Charts** Which segment of the U.S. economy was strongest from 1914–1918? Why?

involved in 1917. It was the job of the **Committee on Public Information (CPI)** to educate the public about the causes and nature of the war. The CPI had to convince Americans that the war effort was a just cause.

Wilson appointed **George Creel** as the director of the CPI. A former journalist and a passionate admirer of American institutions, Creel combined education and a widespread advertising campaign to "sell America." The CPI distributed 75 million pamphlets and 6,000 press releases, and it assembled an army of 75,000 speakers who gave lectures and brief speeches on America's war aims and the nature of the enemy. In addition, the CPI designed, printed, and distributed millions of posters that dramatized the needs of America and its allies. The CPI also stressed the cruelty and wickedness of the enemy, particularly Germany, which in some cases aggravated resentment toward German Americans. Still, using these methods, Creel and the CPI earned widespread support for the American war effort.

RECALL What cornerstone of U.S. business philosophy was partially abandoned to aid the war effort?

>> Some citizens showed their opposition to the war and the draft by staging protests.

Opposition to the War

The CPI's work was important because Americans did not always peacefully agree with one another about the war. Members of two large ethnic groups, German Americans and Irish Americans, tended to oppose the Allies for different reasons. Swept up in patriotic fervor, some people treated German Americans with prejudice, or intolerance. Other Americans were pacifists who opposed war for any reason. One major issue raised by U.S. involvement in World War I was that the government acted in ways that sometimes trespassed on individual liberties to quiet dissent, or differing opinions.

Opposition to the Draft Without a doubt, the draft created controversy. Some Americans believed it was an illegal intrusion of the federal government into their private lives. Some men refused to cooperate with the Selective Service process.

They were often court-martialed and imprisoned. Others simply tried to avoid the draft. Perhaps as many as 12 percent of men who received draft notices never responded to them.

Many Americans were **conscientious objectors**, people whose moral or religious beliefs forbid them to fight in wars. In theory, the Selective Service Act exempted from combat service members of "any well recognized religious sect or organization . . . whose existing creed or principles forbid its members to participate in war." In practice, this policy was widely ignored. This was a constitutional issue, because the First Amendment guarantees freedom of religion. In addition, some conscientious objectors were treated badly by their local draft boards, and others were humiliated in training camps. As America's participation in the war increased, however, the government improved its treatment of conscientious objectors.

Women Oppose the War Some American women also opposed the war. Before the war, a number of leading American feminists, including reformer Jane Addams, formed the Women's Peace Party and, with pacifist women from other countries, the Women's International League for Peace and Freedom. Jeannette Rankin, the first woman to serve in the U.S. House of Representatives, voted against the declaration of war. After America joined the Allies, some women continued to oppose the war, but most supported American war efforts. For example, the influential National American Woman Suffrage Association (NAWSA) dropped its initial peace initiatives and supported America's war objectives. After adopting this new policy, NAWSA doubled in size.

The Federal Government Stifles Dissent

Constitutional issues raised by federal government policy during World War I also centered on the First Amendment rights of free speech. The work of the CPI created a mood in America that did not welcome open debate. Some felt the CPI stifled the free expression of controversial opinions and worried about the impact of a rigorous military campaign on democracy. They did not want the freedoms that Americans held most dear to become victims of the conflict. Americans treasured their Constitution and the Bill of Rights. And were not U.S. soldiers fighting for freedom?

At the same time, since so much depended on individuals doing their part in the military or on the home front, retaining national unity was vital to America's success in the war. As in previous and future wars, the government navigated a difficult path between respecting and restricting individual rights. Authorities tended to treat harshly individuals who worked against U.S. participation in the war.

In June 1917, Congress passed the **Espionage Act**, allowing postal authorities to ban treasonable or seditious newspapers, magazines, or printed materials from the mail. Thus, another First Amendment freedom, the freedom of the press, was compromised. It also enacted severe penalties for anyone engaged in disloyal or treasonable activities. Anyone found obstructing army recruiters, aiding the enemy, or generally interfering with the war effort could be punished with up to a $10,000 fine and 20 years of imprisonment.

In 1918, Congress limited freedom of speech even further with the passage of the Sedition Act. The act made it unlawful to use "disloyal, profane, scurrilous, or abusive language" about the American form of government, the Constitution, or the military forces. The government employed the Sedition Act to prosecute socialists, political radicals, and pacifists. Eugene V. Debs, the leader of the Socialist Party in America, was imprisoned under the act. For his crime—giving a mildly antiwar speech to a convention of socialists in Canton, Ohio—he was sentenced to a 10-year term in a federal prison.

The Supreme Court upheld the constitutionality of the Sedition Act in the case of *Schenck* v. *United States* (1919). The Court ruled that there are times when the need for public order is so pressing that First Amendment protections of speech do not apply. The Debs case and others like it show that the war did lead the federal government to follow policies that raised important constitutional issues about the suppression of personal freedoms and individual rights.

Espionage and Sedition Court Cases During World War I

DEFENDANT	ACCUSATIONS	ARGUMENT
KATE RICHARDS O'HARE	Claimed U.S. involvement in World War I was only to protect U.S. corporate interests and criticized soldiers; accused of violating the Espionage Act of 1917 and the Sedition Act of 1918	First Amendment (freedom of speech)
EUGENE V. DEBS	Criticized U.S. government for prosecuting those who violated the Espionage Act of 1917 and made a speech opposing the war; accused of violating the Espionage Act of 1917 and the Sedition Act of 1918	First Amendment (freedom of speech); led to the Supreme Court case *Debs* v. *United States* in 1919
CHARLES T. SCHENCK	Opposed military draft; accused of violating the Espionage Act of 1917 and Sedition Act of 1918	First Amendment (freedom of speech); led to the Supreme Court case *Schenck* v. *United States* in 1919
EMMA GOLDMAN	Opposed U.S. involvement in the war; accused of conspiring against the draft law in 1917	First Amendment (freedom of speech)

>> **Analyze Charts** Do you think Eugene V. Debs should have been arrested during World War I? Why or why not?

BOUNCE to Activate Gallery

Prejudice Against German Americans

Sometimes, the war enthusiasm created by the CPI and other groups took an ugly turn. Some German Americans were treated harshly during the war. Largely because of CPI efforts, Americans regarded Germany's kaiser as arrogant, its generals as ruthless, and its soldiers as spike-helmeted brutes. Germany was seen as the primary foe among the Central Powers. Popular movies, such as *The Kaiser, the Beast of Berlin*, as well as some CPI posters and speeches intensified this feeling by portraying Germany as a cruel enemy. Some Americans wrongly generalized that if Germany was cruel, then all German people were cruel.

As a result, Americans stopped teaching German in public schools and discontinued playing the music of Beethoven and Brahms. They renamed German measles "liberty measles," cooked "liberty steaks" instead of hamburgers, and walked their "liberty pups" instead of dachshunds.

German Americans were pressured to prove their loyalty to America by condemning the German government, giving up speaking German and reading German-language newspapers, and participating enthusiastically in any patriotic drive. Occasionally, hatred of the German enemy boiled over into violence against German Americans. Some German Americans were harassed, others were beaten, and a few were killed for no other reason than they were born in Germany or spoke with a German accent.

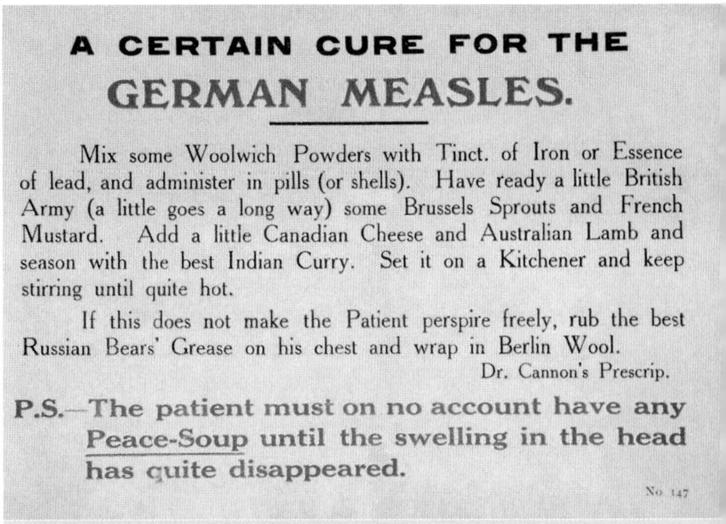
A CERTAIN CURE FOR THE
GERMAN MEASLES.

Mix some Woolwich Powders with Tinct. of Iron or Essence of lead, and administer in pills (or shells). Have ready a little British Army (a little goes a long way) some Brussels Sprouts and French Mustard. Add a little Canadian Cheese and Australian Lamb and season with the best Indian Curry. Set it on a Kitchener and keep stirring until quite hot.

If this does not make the Patient perspire freely, rub the best Russian Bears' Grease on his chest and wrap in Berlin Wool.

Dr. Cannon's Prescrip.

P.S.—The patient must on no account have any Peace-Soup until the swelling in the head has quite disappeared.

No 147

>> Unlike this humorous postcard with a "cure" for German measles, other anti-German sentiment was often more strident.

GENERATE EXPLANATIONS Why was the status of conscientious objectors a constitutional issue?

The War Changes American Society

The war was not only a turning point in the economic and political lives of Americans, but it also brought substantial social changes. New opportunities opened up for women, African Americans, and Mexican Americans. Some left their homes to seek new ones where they could take advantage of these opportunities. Asian-Americans were also drafted, and some fought in Europe.

Women Welcome New Opportunities Before the war, some American women campaigned for women's suffrage. They won the vote in several western states and still hoped to gain the franchise nationally. Many feared that the war would draw attention away from their efforts. In fact, the war gave women new chances and won them more support for the right to vote.

As men entered the armed forces, many women moved into the workforce for the first time. Women filled jobs that were vacated by men who had gone to fight. They worked in munitions factories, on the railroads, as telegraph operators and trolley conductors, and in other jobs that were previously open only to men. Others labored on farms. Some joined the Red Cross or the American Women's Hospital Service and went overseas. They worked as doctors, nurses, ambulance drivers, and clerks. Thousands enlisted when the Army Corps of Nurses was created in 1918. Women proved that they could succeed in any type of job, regardless of difficulty or risk.

By their efforts and sacrifices during the war, women convinced President Wilson to support their suffrage demands. He contended that granting the vote to women was "vital to winning the war." If women could do the work of men, they certainly deserved the same voting privileges as men. Finally, in 1919, Congress passed the Nineteenth Amendment giving the vote to women. The required two thirds of states ratified the amendment in the summer of 1920, a victory more than 70 years in the making.

African Americans and the Great Migration The war similarly presented new opportunities to African Americans. From the outset, most African American leaders supported the war. "If this is our country, then this is our war," wrote African American leader W.E.B. Du Bois. He viewed the struggle as an excellent opportunity to show all Americans the loyalty and patriotism of African Americans. Thousands of them enlisted or were drafted into the army and sailed for the battlefields of France. On the battlefield, they fought in segregated units under the command of white officers. Altogether, 367,000 African Americans served in the military. Hundreds died for their country.

Despite their sacrifice, many African American soldiers in Europe suffered the same racism and disrespect that they had at home. White soldiers refused to salute Black officers; African American soldiers often received substandard clothing.

Meanwhile, a great movement of African Americans from the rural South to the industrial North was taking place. This movement to the "Land of Hope," as many African Americans referred to the North at that time, is called the **Great Migration**. A migration is a movement of a group of people to a new place. Migrations are often described as being caused by "push-pull" factors: people migrate because some factors "push" them away from where they have been living while other factors "pull" them toward their destination.

For African Americans during the Great Migration, factors that "pushed" them out of the South included Jim Crow segregation laws, lynching and other racial violence, and few economic opportunities other than as servants, sharecroppers, or tenant farmers. Many raised cotton, and the arrival in 1910 of an insect pest called the boll weevil ruined their crops, providing yet another push out of the South.

At the same time, the North "pulled" them with the lure of economic opportunities in prosperous cities and wartime factories. As more African Americans moved North, they themselves became pull factors for family and friends back in the South. Newspapers in the North, such as the Chicago *Defender*, an African American newspaper that was widely read in the South, encouraged the migration:

> I beg you, my brother, to leave the benighted land. . . . Get out of the South. . . . Come north then, all you folks, both good and bad. . . . The *Defender* says come.
>
> —*Chicago Defender*

The Great Migration

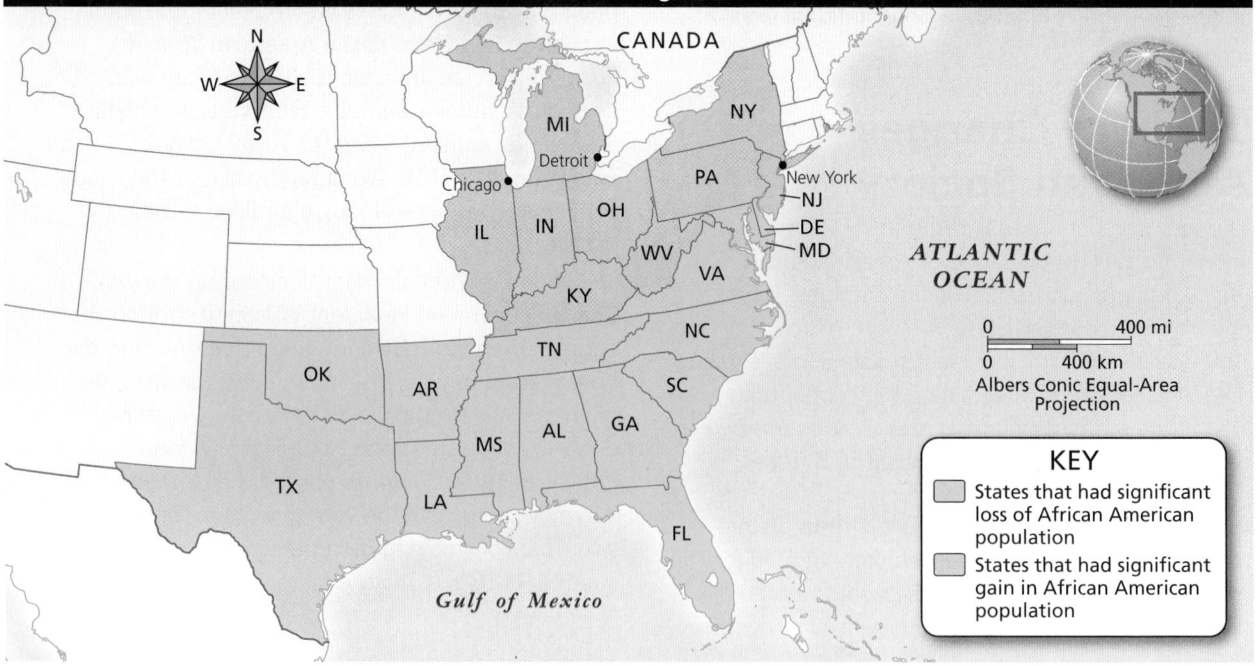

>> **Analyze Maps** How did World War I help create this demographic shift?

BOUNCE to Activate Chart

African Americans moved to Chicago, as the *Defender* encouraged, where they found work in meatpacking plants. They migrated to Detroit, where they obtained jobs in auto factories. They traveled to smaller industrial towns in the Midwest and to the giant cities of the Northeast. Between 1910 and 1930, more than 1.2 million African Americans moved to the North. Millions more eventually made the journey. Although they did not entirely escape discrimination in the North, many did find more opportunity. The Great Migration was one of the most dramatic demographic, or population, shifts in American history.

The effects of this change in demographic pattern are still with us today. For example, in 1910, about one percent of Detroit's population was African American. In 2010, 83 percent of the residents were African American. Similarly, other large cities across the North—Chicago, Philadelphia, New York—have high concentrations of African Americans as a direct result of the Great Migration.

Mexicans Move North Some of the same factors that pushed African Americans out of the South and pulled them to the North caused Mexicans to cross the border into the United States. Because of the ongoing Mexican Revolution, many Mexicans faced violence and desperate poverty. They also wanted better economic opportunities. Most immigrated to the American West, where they sought work on large ranches and farms in Texas and along the Pacific Coast. Increased wartime demands for food and a decrease in American farmworkers (since many were serving in the army) created jobs that Mexican migrants filled.

Some of the Mexican migration was seasonal. Many workers crossed the border to harvest fruits or grains or to pick cotton while each crop was in season, then crossed back into Mexico. But others stayed and made the United States their home. Some Mexican workers migrated first to the Southwest and then to the northern states in search of factory jobs, but a large population stayed in California. They formed *barrios* (BAHR ee ohz), or Hispanic neighborhoods, in Los Angeles and in smaller cities in California's Imperial Valley, a farming region just north of the Mexican border. California had always had a rich Hispanic heritage, but these new immigrants added an important economic dimension to that heritage.

>> As Mexican immigrants came to the United States they sought to create new economic opportunities for themselves and their children in the American West.

☑ **DRAW CONCLUSIONS** What do you think was the most significant motivation behind the Great Migration?

☑ ASSESSMENT

1. **Generate Explanations** Explain how the role of the federal government changed during World War I.
2. **Draw Conclusions** Discuss the purposes and effects of the Committee on Public Information.
3. **Evaluate Arguments** Discuss the constitutional issues raised by the government's response to antiwar sentiments.
4. **Make Generalizations** How did wartime patriotism affect German Americans?
5. **Identify Cause and Effect** Discuss women's roles in the war effort, and explain how the war influenced the women's suffrage movement.
6. **Quest Connections** How did the war create opportunities for Mexican migrant workers?

12.3

The energy and enthusiasm that American forces brought to the battlefield gave a tremendous boost to the Allied war effort.

BOUNCE to Activate Flipped Video

Objectives

Understand the contributions of the American Expeditionary Force to the Allied victory in World War I.

Describe the issues raised by President Wilson's Fourteen Points.

Analyze the decisions made at the Paris Peace Conference and included in the Treaty of Versailles.

Evaluate the pros and cons of U.S. participation in the League of Nations.

Explain why the U.S. Senate did not ratify the Treaty of Versailles.

Key Terms

convoy
Vladimir Lenin
John J. Pershing
American Expeditionary Forces (AEF)
Fourteen Points
self-determination
League of Nations
Henry Cabot Lodge
reparations
influenza
irreconcilables
reservationists

The End of World War I

When the United States entered World War I in the spring of 1917, the conflict had become a deadly, bloody stalemate. The war would be won or lost on the Western Front in France. Since 1914, both sides had tried desperately to break the stalemate there—and failed. The American entry into the war would play a key role in the Allied victory.

America Joins the Fighting

To European leaders, the United States was a great unknown. Ethnic divisions in the United States raised questions about how committed American troops would be in combat. Some doubted that the United States could raise, train, equip, and transport an army fast enough to influence the outcome of the war. Desperate German military leaders renewed unrestricted submarine warfare, hoping to end the conflict before the Americans could make a difference.

The Convoy System The Allies immediately felt the impact of the renewed unrestricted submarine warfare. German U-boats sank merchant ships in alarming numbers, faster than replacements could be built. As one merchant ship after another sank to the bottom of the sea, the Allies lost crucial supplies.

Together, the Allies addressed the problem of submarine warfare by adopting an old naval tactic: convoying. In a **convoy**, groups of merchant ships sailed together, protected by warships. The arrangement was designed to provide mutual safety at sea. Convoys made up of British and American ships proved to be an instant success. Shipping losses from U-boat attacks fell sharply as they had risen. Germany's gamble had failed.

GO ONLINE to access your digital course

The War Ends on the Eastern Front Meanwhile, the situation on land began to swing in favor of the Central Powers. The Allies were exhausted by years of combat. Russia was torn by revolutions. In March 1917, a moderate, democratic revolution overthrew Czar Nicholas II but kept Russia in the war. In November 1917, radical communists led by **Vladimir Lenin** (LEHN ihn) staged a revolution and gained control of Russia.

Russia stopped fighting in mid-December, and on March 3, 1918, the Treaty of Brest-Litovsk ended the war between Russia (soon to become the Soviet Union) and Germany. The end of the war on the Eastern Front allowed Germany to send more soldiers to the Western Front.

General John J. Pershing and the AEF In the spring of 1918, Germany launched an all-out offensive on the Western Front. A series of five offensives threatened to break through Allied defenses and open a path to Paris. The hard-pressed Allies organized a joint command under French General Ferdinand Foch (fawsh).

General **John J. Pershing**, the commander of U.S. forces in Europe, arrived in France with a small force in mid-1917. However, it was not until early 1918 that U.S. troops began arriving in larger numbers. The forces under Pershing's command were called the **American Expeditionary Forces (AEF)**. By the end of the war, more than two million men would serve overseas in the AEF. Although the Allies wanted to use U.S. soldiers to replenish their armies, Pershing was adamant about keeping U.S. forces independent.

At about the time of Pershing's arrival, the first German offensive began to stall. By the end of March 1918, Allied counterattacks and German exhaustion ended the first great German offensive. Germany had gained miles rather than yards of land but failed to end the war before American troops could arrive in force. Both sides lost hundreds of thousands of men, but the Allied forces were being bolstered by American troops.

More fighting followed, and with each passing week, American troops made more and more contributions on the battlefield, driven forward by Pershing's leadership. Germany launched several more offensives. Allied defenses buckled and stretched but did not break. Each failed offensive weakened Germany more and raised Allied hopes. A British volunteer nurse working near the front described the arrival of new American troops:

> I pressed forward with the others to watch the United States physically

>> A church in Ypres (EE-pruh), Belgium, lies in ruins. The use of powerful new military technologies by both the Allied and Central powers left many parts of Europe devastated.

>> American vessels crossed the Atlantic Ocean in convoys to help defend themselves against German U-boat attacks. **Identify Cause and Effect** Why was it so important to find a solution to the U-boat threat?

entering the War, so god-like, so magnificent, so splendidly unimpaired in comparison with the tired, nerve-wracked men of the British Army. So these were our deliverers at last, marching up the road to Camiers in the spring sunshine!

—Vera Brittain, *Testament of Youth*

American Troops in Battle American troops, called "doughboys," saw significant action in the late spring and summer of 1918. Americans fought on the defensive along with the French at the Second Battle of the Marne and on the offensive at the Battle of Cantigny (kahn tee NYEE), where they dislodged a large German force from fortified positions. They battled valiantly at Château-Thierry (sha TOH tir EE) and Belleau (beh LOH) Wood, Meuse-Argonne (myooz ahr GAHN) and Saint-Mihiel (mee YEHL). Although it took some time, American troops learned quickly and fought bravely.

One of America's greatest war heroes was Alvin York of Tennessee. On October 8, 1918, York was one of thousands of Americans fighting in the Meuse-Argonne region of northeastern France. Trapped behind enemy lines, York and 16 other Americans took cover from blistering machine-gun fire. As half of the American force fell to German bullets, York took aim with his rifle and silenced a nearby German machine-gun nest. He then dodged a flurry of bullets to attack several other machine gunners and even charged one German position with only a pistol! When the firefight died down, York and the surviving Americans had taken the German position against amazing odds. York's battlefield heroics earned him a Congressional Medal of Honor.

Alvin York was only one of thousands of heroes, many of whom died and most of whom were never recognized for their deeds. They followed orders, fought bravely, and made great sacrifices. Although African American soldiers often faced discrimination in the United States Army, they demonstrated their patriotism in dozens of engagements. For example, an entire African American unit, the 369th Infantry Regiment, received the *Croix de Guerre*, a French award for bravery, for its members' actions in the Meuse-Argonne region.

The fighting in the Meuse-Argonne region is also called the Meuse-Argonne campaign. The campaign was a widespread attack along the Western Front launched in September of 1918. The AEF under General Pershing were tasked with advancing through the thick, tangled Argonne Forest. The dense trees and rocky ridges gave the advantage to the German defenses, but the Americans persisted. After weeks of heavy fighting, they had driven the Germans from the forest. The American victory in

Key Battles Involving Americans in World War I

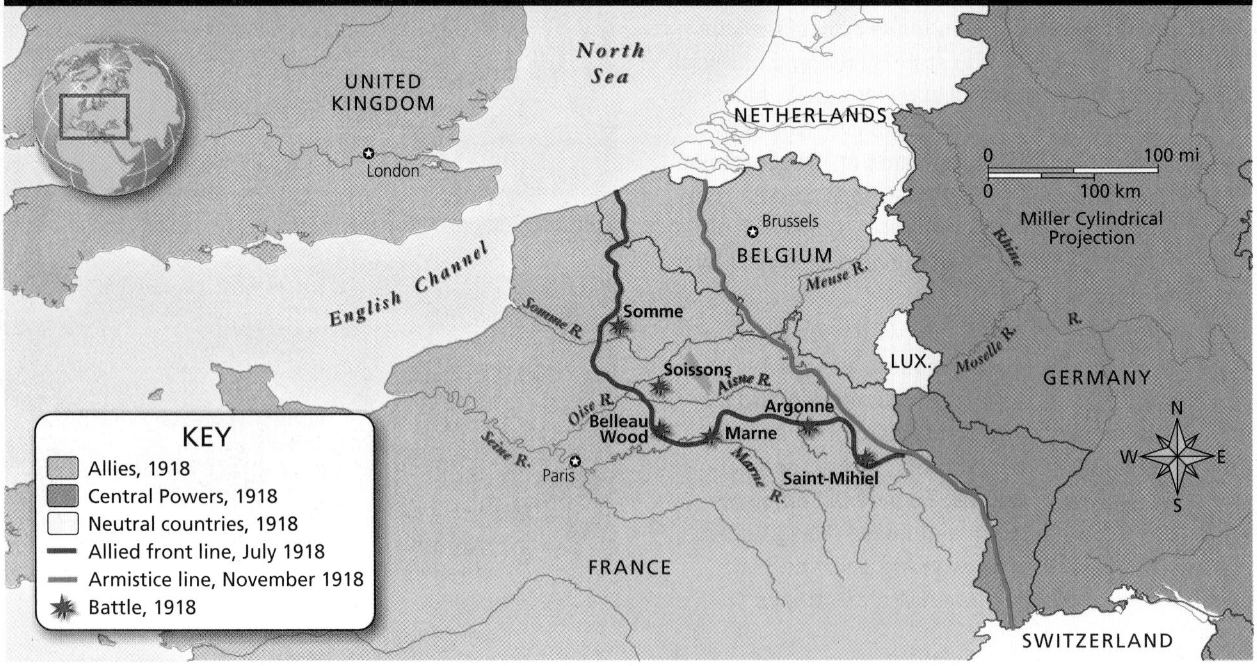

>> **Analyze Maps** Why did Germany ask for peace while they still controlled most of Belgium and northeast France?

BOUNCE to Activate Map

the Battle of the Argonne Forest was a devastating defeat for Germany that hastened the end of the war.

Germany Surrenders The American troops, added to those of France, Britain, and Italy, gave the Allies a military advantage. By the fall of 1918, the German front was collapsing. Both the German and Austro-Hungarian armies had had enough. Some men deserted, others mutinied, and many refused to fight. Their leaders faced little choice but to surrender. On November 11, 1918, Germany surrendered to the Allies in a railway car in Compiegne (kohn PYEHN), France. The war was over.

Of the millions of soldiers who mobilized to fight, almost 5 million Allied and 8 million Central Power troops were dead. Nearly 6.5 million civilians were also dead, victims of the terrible conflict. Of the 2 million U.S. soldiers sent to Europe, about 1.4 million served on the front. More than 50,000 lost their lives, and about 230,000 were wounded. It was left to the peacemakers to determine whether the results would justify the costs.

GENERATE EXPLANATIONS What contributions did the U.S. military make to World War I?

>> Alvin York, a conscientious objector before the war, earned the Medal of Honor after helping Allied forces defeat the Germans at the Battle of Argonne Forest.

Wilson Wants "Peace Without Victory"

Vladimir Lenin, leader of the communist revolution in Russia, maintained that the entire war was nothing more than an imperialistic land-grab. Once in power, he exposed secret treaties that Russia had made with the other Allies in which they agreed to divide among themselves the empires of their enemies. These revelations undercut the morality of the Allied cause in the war.

For President Woodrow Wilson, however, the war was not about acquisitions and imperialism—it was about peace and freedom. In January 1917, Wilson had introduced the idea of a "peace without victory" in an address to Congress:

> Only a tranquil Europe can be a stable Europe. . . .[There] must be a peace without victory . . . .Victory would mean peace forced upon the loser, a victor's terms imposed upon the vanquished. It would be accepted in humiliation...and would leave a sting, a resentment, a bitter memory

>> President Wilson asks Congress to declare war in April, 1917.

upon which terms of peace would rest, not permanently, but only as upon quicksand.

—Woodrow Wilson, "Peace Without Victory" speech, January 22, 1917

The Fourteen Points In another address to Congress in January 1918, Wilson answered Lenin's charges about the nature of the conflict by outlining America's war aims in what became known as the **Fourteen Points**. At the heart of the Fourteen Points was his idea of "peace without victory." Wilson proposed a peace inspired by noble ideals, not greed and vengeance.

The Fourteen Points raised some major issues. They sought to fundamentally change the world by promoting openness, encouraging independence, and supporting freedom. Critical of all secret treaties, Wilson called for open diplomacy. He insisted on freedom of the seas, free trade, a move toward ending colonialism, and a general reduction of armaments.

Wilson championed national **self-determination**, or the right of people to choose their own form of government. This would lead to the creation of several new, independent states but also raised many questions of which populations would achieve statehood and under what circumstances. Finally, he asked for a **League of Nations** to secure "mutual guarantees of political independence and territorial integrity to great and small states alike."

Wilson Travels to Paris In early 1919, the victorious Allies held a peace conference in Versailles (ver sī), a suburb of Paris, in the former palace of Louis XIV. President Wilson believed that the peace conference was too important to be left to career diplomats and lesser politicians, so he crossed the Atlantic Ocean himself to represent the United States at the conference, something no president had ever done.

Wilson did not invite any leading Republicans to join him in his peace delegation. Wilson's decision angered Republicans,who had won control of Congress in the 1918 elections.

Senator **Henry Cabot Lodge**, a leading Republican foreign policy expert, was especially angry. Wilson left Lodge behind because Wilson disliked him intensely, but the feeling was mutual. Lodge and Wilson had fundamentally different views about America's place on the world stage. Lodge was suspicious of Wilson's progressivism and idealism, which he viewed as dangerously naive. Whereas Wilson spoke of "peace without victory" and "mutual guarantees," Lodge, keen to move the United States into the position of a world power, spoke unabashedly about putting American interests first:

Wilson's Fourteen Points, 1918

1. Make no secret diplomatic agreements.	**6.** Evacuate and restore Russian territories seized during the war.	**11.** Redraw boundaries of Balkan states based on nationalities and historical allegiances.
2. Allow freedom of the seas in peace and war.	**7.** Restore and protect Belgium's sovereignty.	**12.** Separate the Ottoman Empire into independent countries according to nationality; guarantee all nations access to the Dardanelles.
3. Remove as many economic trade barriers as possible between countries.	**8.** Restore French territory and settle the debate over Alsace-Lorraine.	
4. Reduce stockpiles of military armaments to lowest point needed for domestic safety.	**9.** Adjust Italy's boundaries according to the nationalities of populations living there.	**13.** Restore and protect Poland as a sovereign state with access to the sea.
5. Adjust colonial claims, giving more weight to the views of the colonized peoples.	**10.** Allow the peoples of the former Austro-Hungarian Empire to choose their own governments.	**14.** Establish an association of nations to provide collective security and to ensure peace.

>> **Analyze Charts** How did Wilson's Fourteen Points aim to reduce the potential for future wars to develop?

"I can never be anything else but an American, and I must think of the United States first, and when I think of the United States first . . . I am thinking of what is best for the world, for if the United States fails, the best hopes of mankind fail with it."

—Henry Cabot Lodge, letter to President Woodrow Wilson, 1919

The decision to leave Lodge behind would come back to haunt Wilson.

However, when the American president arrived in France, adoring crowds greeted him. "Never has a king, never has an emperor received such a welcome," wrote one journalist.

IDENTIFY CENTRAL IDEAS What was the central idea behind Wilson's "peace without victory" proposal?

>> Woodrow Wilson joined French Prime Minister Georges Clemenceau on the left, and British Prime Minister David Lloyd George, on the right, at Versailles in 1919.

The Paris Peace Conference

Wilson's idealism did not inspire the other Allied leaders at the peace conference. They blamed Germany for starting the war, reminded Wilson that they had suffered more in the war than the United States, and insisted that Germany make **reparations,** or payment for war damages. They wanted to weaken Germany so that it would never threaten Europe again.

Allied Leaders Reject Wilson's Ideas British prime minister David Lloyd-George and French premier Georges Clemenceau (klay mahn SOH) knew that the citizens of their countries expected both peace and victory. Lloyd-George insisted on protecting the existing colonial status quo and punishing Germany. Clemenceau wanted to make Germany pay dearly for what it had done to France. In addition to reparations, he demanded the return of Alsace-Lorraine and several key German colonies. Besides Britain and France, other Allies also had goals of their own and were skeptical of Wilson's grand vision.

Once the Versailles conference began, Clemenceau, Lloyd-George, Italian Premier Vittorio Orlando, and other Allied leaders started to chip away at Wilson's Fourteen Points. Onto the scrap heap of failed proposals they piled freedom of the seas, free trade, the liberation of colonial empires, a general disarmament, and several other ideas.

>> Senator Henry Cabot Lodge disagreed with Wilson over the proposed League of Nations, arguing that entangling the United States in European affairs would weaken U.S. sovereignty.

>> The League of Nations' first session took place in Geneva, Switzerland, in November 1920.

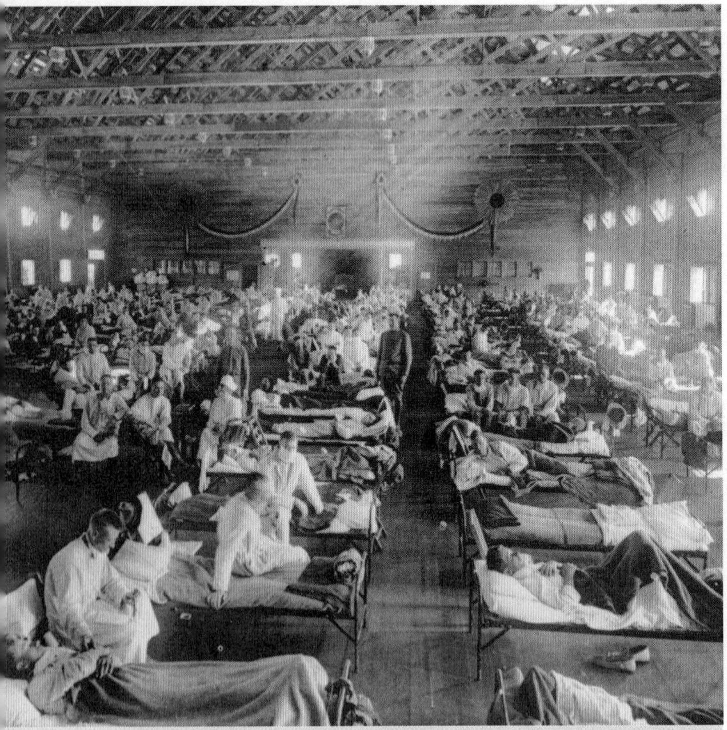

>> The spread of the influenza pandemic from 1918 to 1919 left millions dead worldwide, creating a sense of dread among peoples of all nations. Pictured are soldiers at an army hospital in Kansas.

The League of Nations Wilson lost a number of battles but kept fighting to salvage a League of Nations, a world organization where countries could gather and peacefully resolve their quarrels. On this point, Wilson refused to compromise. The other delegates finally voted to make the League of Nations part of the treaty.

Problems With the Peace In the end, the various peace treaties created almost as many major issues as they solved. The changes in political boundaries that resulted from the international conflict were not always driven by self-determination or the best interests of the people living there. In the new map that emerged from the Paris Peace Conference, national self-determination was violated almost as often as it was confirmed. In Europe, several populations of Germans found themselves attached to non-German nations. The same was true of several Austrian populations.

Furthermore, in the Middle East, the breakup of the Ottoman Empire led to new political boundaries in which ethnic groups were clustered together randomly. To form Iraq, for example, the Versailles peacemakers threw together three provinces of the defeated Ottoman Empire—Basra, Baghdad, and Mosul. But Basra had natural links to the Persian Gulf and India, Baghdad to Persia, and Mosul to Turkey and Syria. The various regions had no sense of Iraqi nationalism. In addition, Iraq, like other holdings in the Middle East, Asia, and Africa, was not allowed to practice self-determination. It was attached to Britain as a mandate, or territory overseen by another nation.

☑ **DRAW CONCLUSIONS** Why did the Allies reject Wilson's ideas for peace?

America Rejects the Treaty of Versailles

When Wilson left Versailles to return to the United States, he knew the treaty was not perfect. But he believed that over time the League could correct its problems. He still thought that a lasting peace could emerge.

The Flu Pandemic The movement from war to peace would have been difficult even in the best of times. But the end of 1918 and 1919 were not the best of times. In September 1918, an unusually deadly form of the **influenza**, or flu, virus appeared. Research in recent years shows that the 1918

Comparing Irreconcilables, Reservationists, and Wilson Democrats

IRRECONCILABLES	RESERVATIONISTS	WILSON DEMOCRATS
• Opposed the treaty in any form • Convinced that the idea of a League of Nations was idealistic and unrealistic • Suspicious of the actions and intents of the other countries in the League of Nations • Wished to maintain American isolationism	• Would accept the treaty if it were modified • Believed the League of Nations removed congressional power to declare war, making it unconstitutional • Opposed Article 10 of the League Covenant, which required the U.S. to defend other members of the League under certain circumstances	• Most supported the treaty • Believed no changes to the treaty were necessary • Wanted U.S. to be part of the League of Nations

>> **Analyze Charts** What was the primary difference between reservationists and irreconcilables?

influenza virus was originally a bird flu that mutated to spread to humans. Many historians now believe that the virus originated in the United States, then traveled around the world, thus becoming a pandemic.

As many as 50 million people died—among them, about 675,000 Americans. The Great Influenza pandemic, also called the Great Pandemic or the Flu Pandemic of 1918, coming on the heels of the Great War, gave a sense of doom and dread to people around the globe.

The pandemic may have even reached Wilson at the Paris Peace Conference. He fell seriously ill, and his temperature reached 103 degrees. Wilson's physician diagnosed the president as suffering from the flu. Although there is some doubt that it was actually the flu, there is no doubt that Wilson's sickness kept him from participating in many meetings. His illness may have been a factor in Wilson not achieving all he had hoped to.

Wilson Faces Opposition at Home Much as Wilson faced opposition to his ideas at the Paris Peace Conference, he faced opposition in the United States to the Treaty of Versailles he had negotiated—but for different reasons. German Americans thought the treaty was too harsh toward Germany, especially the "war guilt clause" that suggested that Germany had caused the war. Irish Americans criticized the failure to create an independent Ireland.

Most important, however, the treaty would need to be submitted to the Republican-controlled Senate Foreign Relations Committee and then ratified, or approved, by the Republic-controlled Senate. In both bodies, as well as in his own Democratic Party, Wilson faced stiff opposition.

A handful of senators believed that the United States should not get entangled in world politics or involved in world organizations at all. Known as **"irreconcilables,"** these isolationist senators opposed any treaty that had a League of Nations folded into it. They particularly disliked Article 10 of the League covenant. Article 10 called for mutual defense by the signers of the treaty, a pledge that each nation would "respect and preserve . . . the territorial integrity and existing political independence of all the Members of the League."

A larger group of senators, led by Henry Cabot Lodge and known as **"reservationists,"** were opposed to the treaty as it was written. Some wanted only small changes, while others demanded larger ones.

For example, many felt Article 10 could lead the United States into a war without the consent of Congress, which was unconstitutional. Reservationists believed that the language of the article was too vague and demanded that it not contradict the power of Congress to declare war. But with some changes, the reservationists were prepared to vote for the Treaty of Versailles. They knew that polls indicated that the American people favored the League of Nations.

Wilson had compromised in Versailles, but he was not ready to compromise in Washington, D.C. When the Senate delayed its ratification vote, Wilson took his case directly to the people. The

>> As part of his speaking tour to promote the League of Nations, President Wilson makes a stop in St. Louis, Missouri.

BOUNCE to Activate Chart

League of Nations had become his personal crusade, and convincing the American people of its worth would test his leadership. The qualities of effective leadership, for a president of the United States, include the ability to appeal to a wide variety of people and persuade them that certain ideas are in the best interest of the country. Even though he was ill and weak, he set himself the grueling task of crossing the country and giving 32 addresses in 33 days. But his health failed on September 25, 1919, in Pueblo, Colorado. He was rushed back to Washington, D.C., but suffered a debilitating stroke a few days later. As the Senate prepared to vote on the treaty, Wilson lay close to death, barely able to speak.

The United States Fails to Approve Treaty of Versailles In November 1919, one year after the war ended, a treaty revised to eliminate the complaints of the reservationists reached the Senate for a vote. Wilson would not compromise and told his Democratic supporters to vote with the irreconcilables against it. They did, and it was defeated. Next, the Senate voted on the treaty without any changes. The Democrats voted for it, but the combined strength of the irreconcilables and reservationists defeated it. Once more it was voted on, this time with only modest changes. Again, Wilson told his followers to vote against it. Although some Democrats voted for it, the combination of Wilson Democrats and irreconcilables defeated the treaty.

The problem was not that most of the Senate was isolationist. Except for the irreconcilables, most senators wanted the United States to participate in world affairs. They differed slightly on what form that participation would take.

However, at a moment that demanded compromise, Wilson and his opponents refused to put aside personal and political differences for the good of the country. The tragedy of the failed votes was that without full American support, the League of Nations would prove unable to maintain peace among nations.

It was the League of Nations that U.S. opponents of the Treaty of Versailles most objected to. In evaluating the pros and cons of U.S. participation in the international organization and treaty, opponents judged that the cons outweighed the pros. They were especially concerned that the League would entangle the United States in conflicts that would not advance U.S. interests. Supporters, in contrast, thought the pros outweighed the cons. They thought the United States would benefit by being part of an international organization in which other countries could come to the aid of the United States. They also wanted the United States to have a voice in international politics—before a huge conflict broke out.

DRAW CONCLUSIONS What was the principal argument of the irreconcilables against the Treaty of Versailles?

ASSESSMENT

1. **Evaluate Arguments** Explain the reasoning behind President Wilson's concept of "peace without victory." Do you think it was a viable idea? Explain why or why not.
2. **Apply Concepts** What opposition did President Wilson's ideas face among Allied nations as well as within the United States?
3. **Generate Explanations** Explain how European and Middle Eastern nations adjusted to peace after the Paris Peace Conference.
4. **Describe** the impact of the Great Influenza pandemic after World War I.
5. **Quest Connections** Explain why the United States failed to approve the Treaty of Versailles, and discuss how this impacted the future of world relations.

GO ONLINE to access this biography: John J. Pershing

Primary Sources

The Fourteen Points: Woodrow Wilson

In a speech to Congress on January 8, 1918, President Wilson laid out America's war aims and his vision for peace after the war. His speech included fourteen key points upon which he believed the peace following the war must be based. However, not all of Wilson's ideas were adopted at the Paris Peace Conference.

>> Woodrow Wilson (center foreground) in Paris

We entered this war because violations of right had occurred which touched us to the quick and made the life of our own people impossible unless they were corrected and the world secure once for all against their recurrence. What we demand in this war, therefore, is nothing peculiar [unique] to ourselves. It is that the world be made fit and safe to live in; and particularly that it be made safe for every peace-loving nation which, like our own, wishes to live its own life, [and] determine its own institutions, [choose its own government] be assured of justice and fair dealing by the other peoples of the world as against force and selfish aggression. All the peoples of the world are in effect partners in this interest, and for our own part we see very clearly that unless justice be done to others it will not be done to us. The program of the world's peace, therefore, is our only program; and that program, the only possible program as we see it, is this:

DISTINGUISH AMONG FACT, OPINION, AND REASONED JUDGMENT When Wilson says, "The program of the world's peace, therefore, is our only program, the only possible program as we see it, is this," is this a fact, an opinion, or a reasoned judgment? Explain your answer.

1. Open covenants [formal agreements] of peace, openly arrived at, after which there shall be no private international understandings of any kind but [instead] diplomacy shall proceed always frankly [openly and honestly] and in the public view.

EXPLAIN AN ARGUMENT Why might Wilson think that prohibiting secret agreements between nations is necessary in order to avoid war?

2. Absolute freedom of navigation upon the seas, outside territorial waters, alike in peace and in war, except as the seas may be closed in whole or in part by international action for the enforcement of international covenants.

PARAPHRASE Restate Point 2 in your own words.

3. The removal, so far as possible, of all economic barriers and the establishment of an equality of trade conditions among all the nations consenting to the peace and associating themselves for its maintenance.

4. Adequate guarantees given and taken that national armaments will be reduced to the lowest point consistent with domestic safety.

ANALYZE WORD CHOICES What two things does Wilson leave unspecified in Point 4?

5. A free, open-minded, and absolutely impartial adjustment of all colonial claims, based upon a strict observance of the principle that in determining all such questions of sovereignty the interests of the populations concerned must have equal weight with the equitable claims of the government whose title is to be determined. . . .

8. All French territory should be freed and the invaded portions restored, and the wrong done to France by Prussia in 1871 in the matter of Alsace-Lorraine, which has unsettled the peace of the world for nearly fifty years, should be righted, in order that peace may once more be made secure in the interest of all.

9. A readjustment of the frontiers of Italy should be effected along clearly recognizable lines of nationality.

10. The peoples of Austria-Hungary, whose place among the nations we wish to see safeguarded and assured, should be accorded the freest opportunity to autonomous development.

11. Rumania, Serbia, and Montenegro should be evacuated; occupied territories restored; Serbia accorded free and secure access to the sea; and the relations of the several Balkan states to one another determined by friendly counsel along historically established lines of allegiance and nationality; and international guarantees of the political and economic independence and territorial integrity of the several Balkan states should be entered into.

12. The Turkish portion of the present Ottoman Empire should be assured a secure sovereignty, but the other nationalities which are now under Turkish rule should be assured an undoubted security of life and an absolutely unmolested opportunity of autonomous development, and the Dardanelles should be permanently opened as a free passage to the ships and commerce of all nations under international guarantees.

13. An independent Polish state should be erected which should include the territories inhabited by indisputably Polish populations, which should be assured a free and secure access to the sea, and whose political and economic independence and territorial integrity should be guaranteed by international covenant.

14. A general association [organization] of nations must be formed under specific covenants for the purpose of affording mutual guarantees of political independence and territorial integrity to great and small states alike.

INTEGRATE INFORMATION FROM DIVERSE SOURCES Does an association of nations as mentioned in point 14 exist today? If so, what is it?

ASSESSMENT

1. **Compare and Contrast** Points 8–13 deal with specific territorial issues, such as breaking up the Ottoman and Austro-Hungarian Empires and restoring sovereignty to Belgium and Poland. To an American in 1918, how would those points be different from points 1–5 and 14?
2. **Draw Conclusions** Preventing war seems like an admirable goal. Why might a country reject some or all of Wilson's points?
3. **Integrate Information From Diverse Sources** Why might isolationists oppose some or all of Wilson's Fourteen Points?
4. **Draw Inferences** What political impact do you think Wilson's Fourteen Points had?

12.4

GO ONLINE to **Project Imagine: Enjoy the Roaring Twenties** to explore the exciting new choices, such as buying a car, that were available to some Americans.

The Postwar Economy Booms

November 11, 1918, was a day celebrated around the world. World War I—known then as the Great War—had ended with the armistice. The greatest war in human history to date had ended. Every year, the United States celebrates Veteran's Day on November 11 to commemorate the service of Americans in the armed forces in any war. With the war's end, the United States faced a painful adjustment period, then a decade of amazing economic growth and prosperity.

BOUNCE to Activate Flipped Video

Objectives

Describe the economic problems America faced after World War I.

Explain the economic growth and prosperity of the 1920s, including how Henry Ford and the automobile industry helped spark the boom.

Analyze the consumer revolution and the bull market of the 1920s.

Compare the different effects of the economic boom on urban, suburban, and rural America.

Key Terms

inflation
creditor nation
Henry Ford
mass production
Model T
scientific management
assembly lines
consumer revolution
installment buying
bull market
buying on margin

Postwar Issues

But in 1918, the victory was bittersweet. The flu pandemic still raged, and it would end up killing far more Americans than had died in the war.

> [The Year] 1918 has gone: a year momentous as the termination of the most cruel war in the annals of the human race; a year which marked the end, at least for a time, of man's destruction of man; unfortunately a year in which developed a most fatal infectious disease causing the death of hundreds of thousands of human beings.
>
> —Journal of the American Medical Association, December 28, 1918

The flu faded out in 1919. The next year, an American public tired of world affairs and problems at home, elected a new president. Republican Warren G. Harding easily defeated the Democratic nominee, Governor James M. Cox of Ohio. Harding's campaign

GO ONLINE to access your digital course

slogan captured perfectly the national mood: "Return to Normalcy," meaning a return to normal life as it was in prewar times. Yet the election itself was not "normal." For the first time, women voted in a presidential election. For the first time, election returns were reported by radio. A return to "normalcy" in a rapidly changing world would prove elusive.

Women and African Americans Confront New Realities Women and African Americans had made significant advances during the war. However, the end of the war also spelled the end of wartime economic opportunities for both groups. A postwar recession, or economic slowdown, created a competitive job market. By 1920, there were fewer women in the workforce than there had been in 1910.

In northern industrial cities, tense race relations erupted into violence as white veterans competed with African American workers for jobs and housing. During 1919, race riots erupted in cities throughout the country. The worst, in Chicago, went on for 13 days. In 1921, violence erupted in Tulsa, Oklahoma. A group of armed African American men—many of them returning veterans—tried to protect a young African American man from lynching when shots were fired and a riot broke out. Over the next 18 hours, a mob of white racists attacked the city's African American residents, who defended themselves and their communities despite being outnumbered. By the time what many people now refer to as the Tulsa race massacre was over, at least 10 whites and more than 30 African Americans were dead, with credible evidence that mass graves containing many more African American victims exist. In the African American neighborhood of Greenwood, white rioters burned 35 city blocks to the ground.

>> Rioters burned the homes of African Americans in Tulsa, Oklahoma, during race riots in 1921.

Inflation and Labor Unrest During the war, **inflation**, or rising prices, had been held in check. After the conflict, Americans rushed to buy consumer goods rather than war bonds. The scarcity of these goods, coupled with widespread demand, caused inflation. On the other hand, during the war, the price of agricultural goods had risen. After the war, prices fell sharply, making it difficult for farmers to pay their mortgages or buy what they needed for the next growing season. This began a long period of tough times for farmers.

Another effect of postwar inflation was felt by workers when their wages did not buy as much as they had during the war. In 1919, more than 4 million workers, or 20 percent of the workforce, went on strike. Demanding rewards for their wartime patriotism, workers struck for higher wages and shorter workdays. The workers won some of the strikes, but they lost far more. When some strikes turned violent, the pro-management press blamed the presence of radicals among the strike leaders.

The United States Grows as a World Power Despite Harding's election and some Americans' desire to return to what life was like before the war, the United States could not totally withdraw from world affairs. By 1920, even with postwar economic problems, the United States was an economic giant. It was the richest, most industrialized country in the world. After the war, British and French demands for American goods created an immense trade imbalance. Europeans had to borrow money from American bankers and obtain lines of credit with American business firms to pay for the goods.

The United States was now the largest **creditor nation** in the world, meaning that other countries owed the United States more money than the United States owed them. World War I shifted the economic center of the world from London to New York City. A world without America playing a major economic role had become simply impossible to conceive.

RECALL What was a significant cause of inflation after the war?

The Impact of Henry Ford and the Automobile

In the decade after World War I, the American economy experienced tremendous growth. Using revolutionary mass production techniques, American workers produced more goods in less time than ever before. The boom fundamentally changed the lives of millions of people and helped create the modern consumer economy.

The decade got off to a rocky start, however. There was a mild recession in 1918 to 1919 and a more serious one in 1920 to 1921. These were partly due to converting wartime production back to domestic production and the return of soldiers into the workforce. Once the economy did take off, the prosperity was not shared by everyone. Still, there is no doubt that the U.S. economy in the 1920s roared.

Rarely, if ever, has the nation enjoyed such an economic boom as it did during this decade. The recession that had followed World War I quickly ended. All signs pointed to economic growth. Stock prices rose rapidly. Factories produced more and more goods and, with wages on the rise, more and more people could afford to buy them.

Much of this explosive growth was sparked by a single business: the automobile industry. Carmaker **Henry Ford** introduced a series of technological and management innovations to his fledgling automobile business. Ford's methods and ideas revolutionized production, wages, working conditions, and daily life.

>> Entrepreneurs like Henry Ford, pictured with his son Edsel, ushered in the age of the automobile and helped create an economic boom after the war.

BOUNCE to Activate Illustration

Ford, Mass Production, and the Model T Ford did not originate the idea of **mass production**, the rapid manufacture of large numbers of identical products. It had been used, for example, to make sewing machines and typewriters. But such products involved only hundreds of parts—not the thousands that go into the production of cars. Ford brought mass production to new heights.

Early in the century, only wealthy city dwellers could afford cars. The automobile was often seen as a symbol of the class divisions in the country. City drivers who ventured out onto country roads frightened horses and cows, coated crops with dust, and rutted dirt roads. "To the countryman," said Woodrow Wilson in 1906, cars "are a picture of the arrogance of wealth."

Ransom Olds had introduced a less expensive car, the Oldsmobile, in 1901. But it was Henry Ford who truly brought the automobile to the people. In 1908, he introduced the **Model T**, a reliable car the average American could afford. The first Model T sold for $850. Soon after, Ford opened a new plant on the Detroit River. The Detroit location gave Ford easy access to steel, glass, oil, and rubber manufactured in Pennsylvania, Ohio, Indiana, and Illinois.

Ford hired **scientific management** experts to improve his mass-production techniques. Scientific management was a relatively new method of improving efficiency, in which experts looked at every step of a manufacturing process to find ways to reduce time, effort, and expense. Studying a process to minimize the time it takes to do a task is called time-study analysis. Studying a process to minimize the motion it takes to do a task is called motion-study analysis. Together, they are often known as "time and motion study." The idea was pioneered by Frederick Winslow Taylor in his book, *The Principles of Scientific Management*. Scientific management is sometimes called Taylorism.

Ford also studied the techniques of Chicago meatpacking houses, where beef carcasses were moved on chains past a series of meat cutters, each of whom cut off a specific part of the carcass. Ford reversed the process. He put his cars on moving **assembly lines**. At each step, a worker added something to construct the automobile. In two years, the application of assembly line techniques showed huge productivity enhancements, reducing the time it took to manufacture a Model T from more than 12 hours to just 90 minutes.

The efficiency of the assembly line allowed Ford to keep dropping the sale price. The cost of a Model T fell to $350 by 1916 and to $290 by 1927. It was slow, dull, and available only in black. But the Model T was the first car that ordinary people could afford. In 1919, only 10 percent of American families owned an automobile. By 1927, 56 percent did.

When it came to managing the men who made up his labor force, Ford also proved that he was not afraid of innovation. In 1914, he more than doubled the wages of a large number of his workers, from $2.35 to $5 a day. He also reduced their workday from 9 hours to 8 hours. In 1926, he became the first major industrialist to give his workers Saturday and Sunday off. Before Ford, the idea of a "weekend" hardly existed. Ford shrewdly realized that if workers made more money and had more leisure time, they would become potential customers for his automobiles. The combination of the Model T and the "five-dollar day, forty-hour week" made Ford not only a very rich man but also one of the shapers of the modern world.

The Automobile Changes America The boom in the automotive industry, caused in part by Ford's production efficiencies, caused economic growth in other industries related to car manufacture or use. The steel, glass, rubber, asphalt, wood, petroleum, insurance, and road-construction industries all benefited. For example, one seventh of all steel output was used to make automobiles. The need for gasoline prompted a nationwide search for petroleum deposits. Oil discoveries in California, Texas, New Mexico, and Oklahoma brought vast numbers of workers and money to the Southwest. Petroleum-based industries boomed, increasing employment and tax revenues. Thus, energy in the form of gasoline had a major impact on the American way of life.

Road construction also boomed, especially when the federal government introduced the system of numbered highways in 1926. The millions of cars on American roads led to the rapid appearance of thousands of service stations, diners, and motor hotels (a term later shortened to *motels*). The growth in all these industries created new and often better-paying jobs, spurring national prosperity.

The automobile caused additional economic effects. Other forms of ground transportation, such as railroads and trolleys, suffered a decline in use. With cars, people could go where they wanted, when they

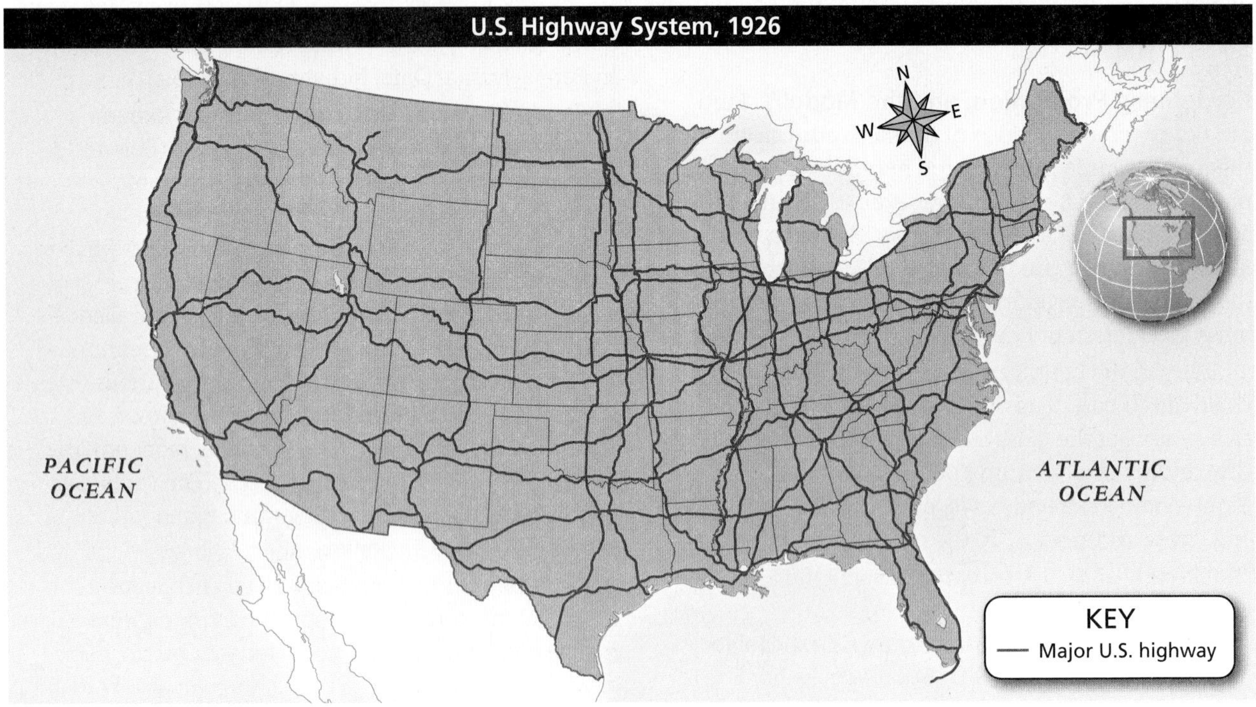

>> Analyze Maps How did the creation of an affordable car affect the development of roads in the United States?

wanted. They did not have to travel along set tracks on set schedules.

The automobile prompted a new sense of freedom and prosperity. Never had Americans been so mobile. Entire families crowded into their cars for cross-country vacations or Sunday drives. Ownership of an automobile came to symbolize participation in the American dream of success and high standard of living.

Finally, automobiles altered residential patterns. The ability to drive to work permitted people to live farther from their places of employment. This led to the development of suburban communities linked to cities by arteries of highways and roads. Los Angeles, one of the first cities whose growth was influenced by the automobile, developed in a sprawling, haphazard fashion. It became, according to one observer, "a series of suburbs in search of a city."

☑ **IDENTIFY SUPPORTING DETAILS** What effect did increased automobile production have on other industries?

>> With the U.S. economy growing again, companies began to use advertisements to target consumers based on their desires rather than their needs.

Economic Growth in the 1920s

The 1920s saw what has been called a **consumer revolution**, in which a flood of new, affordable goods became available to the public. The widespread availability of electrical power supported the consumer revolution. Electric washing machines, vacuum cleaners, and irons made housekeeping easier and less time-consuming. Accessible electricity also contributed to radio and refrigerator sales.

Advertising and Installment Buying The growing advertising industry also played its part. Using new "scientific" techniques and psychological research, advertisers were able to sell more products to more Americans than ever before. Magazine and newspaper ads often focused on the desires and fears of Americans more than on what people really needed.

Finally, new ways of buying fueled the consumer revolution. People who did not have enough ready cash could buy what they wanted on credit. **Installment buying**, in which a consumer would make a small down payment and then pay off the rest of the debt in regular monthly payments, allowed Americans to own products they might otherwise have had to save up for years in order to buy.

The Bull Market Consumers were not the only Americans buying and selling in a big way. During the 1920s, the stock market enjoyed a dizzying **bull market**, a period of rising stock prices. More and more Americans put their money into stocks in an effort to get rich quick. By 1929, around 4 million Americans owned stocks.

The desire to strike it rich often led investors to ignore financial risks. As the market soared, people began **buying on margin**—another form of buying on credit. By purchasing stock on margin, a buyer paid as little as 10 percent of the stock price upfront to a broker. The buyer then paid the broker for the rest of the stock over a period of months. The stock served as collateral, or security, for the broker's loan. As long as the price of the stock rose, the buyer had no trouble paying off the loan and making a profit. But if the price fell, the buyer still had to pay off the loan. Buyers gambled that they would be able to sell the stock at a profit long before the loan came due. Buying stocks on the hope that their price will rise is called stock market speculation.

>> The economic prosperity Americans experienced during the 1920s prompted large investments in urban construction. Here riveters worked on New York City's Empire State Building in 1931.

>> Rapidly rising stock prices created a daily frenzy of activity in the New York Stock Exchange, where the majority of U.S. stocks were traded.

In truth, this big bull market stood on very shaky ground. But most people ignored the dangers. By the middle of 1929, economic authorities proclaimed that America and the stock market had entered a "new era." Stock prices would continue their march upward, they said, while boom-and-bust economics would become a thing of the past.

Science, Technology, and the Free Enterprise System Science, technology, and the free enterprise system combined to boost the economic development of the United States in the 1920s. The science was not just in scientific management, but in the growing knowledge of many aspects of the world. Scientists conducted research on everything from rubber plants to electronics. This scientific knowledge enabled engineers to create the technologies—automobiles, for example, or radios—that were useful to people.

These new technologies would not have been widespread without the free enterprise system. The profit motive gave business owners a reason to turn technology into products to sell. Competitive markets encouraged innovation. The free enterprise system also created the jobs that provided workers with the money to purchase the many new products that came to market. Thus, the prosperity of the 1920s was boosted by a mix of scientific advances, inventive technologies, and the free enterprise system.

☑ **DEFINE** How would you define *installment buying*?

Urban, Suburban, and Rural Areas

The economic boom did not affect all parts of the nation equally. While urban and suburban areas prospered, rural Americans faced hardships.

People Migrate to Cities In the 1920s, the movement of people was toward cities. Immigrants settled in cities. Farmers left their fields for cities. The direction of the African American Great Migration was toward northern cities. Many Mexicans crossing the border relocated to southwestern cities.

As in the late nineteenth century, cities grew and changed shape. In addition, the adoption of skyscraper technology caused cities to stretch skyward. Steel-framed skyscrapers with light coverings of masonry and glass began to dominate the skylines of the nation's cities. New York's Empire State Building, finished in 1931, symbolized the power and majesty of the United States.

Suburbs Expand Improved mass transportation and the widespread use of automobiles caused cities to expand outward. More urban workers moved to the suburbs. Western and southern cities, developed after the automobile revolution, encompassed suburban areas as well as inner cities. Suburbs mushroomed, growing much faster than inner cities.

Slowly at first, but more rapidly as the century progressed, suburbs drained people and resources from the cities, causing the demographic patterns of both types of places to change. Catering to middle- and upper-class residents, suburbs tended to be more conservative and Republican. Meanwhile, one effect of this migration was that the inner cities at the heart of older urban areas began a slow but steady decline.

Many Americans Face Challenges In the cities and suburbs, Americans enjoyed prosperity and the fruits of growth. They participated in the consumer economy and in the joys of automobile ownership. The wealthiest urban residents—owners and managers of businesses—reaped fabulous rewards, which they often pumped back into the bull market. But there were problems looming ahead. America's wealth was poorly distributed. Industrial wages rose at a much slower rate than corporate salaries.

Even worse, farm incomes declined during the decade. Many people living in the country did not participate in the consumer benefits and economic gains of the decade. They formed part of another America—poorer and outside the economic boom. In particular, farmers suffered from growing debt and falling farm prices. A protest song of 1928 expressed their frustration:

> 'Leven-cent cotton, forty-cent meat,
> How in the world can a poor man eat?
> Mule's in the barn, no crop's laid by,
> Corncrib empty and the cow's gone dry.
>
> —Bob Miller and Emma Dermer, "Eleven Cent Cotton"

If the wealthy believed that the country had entered an age of permanent prosperity, the "other Americans" saw things differently.

>> As more families could afford automobiles, they moved away from the city to nearby suburbs. **Hypothesize** Why would many Americans want to move from cities to suburbs?

BOUNCE to Activate Gallery

IDENTIFY SUPPORTING DETAILS What general migration patterns existed in the 1920s?

ASSESSMENT

1. **Identify Cause and Effect** Explain how women and African Americans were affected by the postwar economy.
2. **Identify Central Issues** Discuss the innovations and techniques that Henry Ford used in order to make automobiles more affordable.
3. **Identify Patterns** Discuss the impact of the automobile industry on residential patterns.
4. **Draw Conclusions** Describe important changes that affected the consumer experience during the 1920s, and discuss their impact.
5. **Quest Connections** Explain how the U.S. position as a world power changed after World War I.

12.5

Calvin Coolidge, shown here on the left en route to his inauguration, promised to enact policies that promoted business. He believed that the creation of wealth benefited the entire society.

BOUNCE to Activate Flipped Video

Objectives

Analyze how the policies of Presidents Harding and Coolidge encouraged economic growth and prosperity in the 1920s.

Discuss the effects of political scandals, including Teapot Dome, on Harding's presidency.

Explain the role that the United States played in the world during the 1920s.

Key Terms

Warren G. Harding
Andrew Mellon
Herbert Hoover
Teapot Dome scandal
Calvin Coolidge
Washington Naval Disarmament Conference
Kellogg-Briand Pact
Dawes Plan

Government in the 1920s

Woodrow Wilson hoped that the presidential election of 1920 would prove that Americans supported both the League of Nations and his vision of the role the United States should play in the world. He suggested that electing Democratic presidential candidate James M. Cox of Ohio would show support for the League. However, the election of Republican candidate **Warren G. Harding** of Ohio would serve as a final rejection of U.S. support for the League.

The Harding Administration

Harding had a different view of the presidential race. He knew that national elections seldom turned on a single issue. Harding campaigned for a rejection of Wilsonian idealism. He was tired of Progressive reforms and foreign crusades, and he was betting the American public was, too. Harding won in a landslide, and Republicans won control of Congress, as well. Americans had decisively rejected Wilson's ideas.

What exactly did Harding's election signal? Some interpret it as Americans' desire to retreat from involvement in world affairs, others as a rejection of Progressive reform efforts or a swing back to laissez-faire economics. No matter how it was interpreted, however, it was clear that Harding and his successor, Calvin Coolidge, favored conservative policies that aided the growth of business rather than pursuing reform as the Progressives had done. This pattern—a period of activism followed by a more laissez-faire approach—would repeat itself in the 1950s and 1980s.

Harding's Economic Policies Encourage Growth Harding signaled the economic direction of his administration by naming

GO ONLINE to access your digital course

wealthy banker **Andrew Mellon** Secretary of the Treasury. Mellon believed that prudent economic policy meant supporting legislation that advanced business interests. He disliked the relatively new income tax, favoring instead low taxes on individuals and corporations. Mellon also cut the fat from the budget. By 1925, Congress had reduced spending from a wartime high of $18 billion to $3 billion. Instead of sinking deeper into debt, the Treasury actually showed a surplus.

Harding signed a bill raising protective tariff rates by about 25 percent. The tax on imports made it easier for American producers to sell goods at home. However, in retaliation, European nations also hiked tariffs, making American goods harder to sell overseas. This tariff war weakened the world economy and would have ramifications in the 1930s.

Under the Progressive leadership of Roosevelt and Wilson, the federal government had passed laws to break up monopolies, protect workers, and restrict the absolute freedom of business leaders. By contrast, Harding favored a return to a more traditional laissez-faire approach. He and Mellon worked to reduce government regulation of business. Harding's Return to Normalcy, including reducing taxes and reducing government regulation, helped to cause the economic growth and prosperity of the 1920s.

Still, the Harding administration did not abandon social goals. Harding's thoughtful and energetic Secretary of Commerce, **Herbert Hoover** worked with business and labor leaders to achieve voluntary advancements.

What the Progressives hoped to achieve through legislation, Hoover attempted to attain with the cooperation of interest groups. He enjoyed great successes at getting people to work together instead of battling one another.

Some Officials Betray the Public Trust Harding was a kind, likable man, but he was not especially intelligent. Perhaps no President was friendlier, and few had less sense of what was expected of a President. Faced with a tax issue, Harding lamented, "I listen to one side and they seem right . . . I talk to the other side, and they seem just as right, and here I am where I started. . . . What a job!"

Rather than struggle to master the complexities of the job, Harding trusted others to make decisions. Many were his close friends, men he enjoyed relaxing and gambling with at late-night poker games. Known as the Ohio Gang, they were not honest public servants like Mellon and Hoover. They were mostly greedy, small-minded men who saw government service as a chance to get rich at the expense of the very citizens they were supposed to serve.

Charles Forbes, head of the Veterans' Bureau, practiced graft on an immense scale and wasted hundreds of millions of taxpayers' dollars. For example, his department bought $70,000 worth of floor cleaner—enough to last 100 years—at more than 24 times the fair price. Another Harding pal,

Leaders of Business Deregulation

PRESIDENT WARREN G. HARDING AND VICE PRESIDENT CALVIN COOLIDGE	SECRETARY OF THE TREASURY ANDREW MELLON
• Wanted a conservative government that benefited business • Promoted the policy of laissez faire for business • Named commissioners who favored government deregulation of business • Assigned business leaders to government positions • Turned the Federal Reserve Board and Interstate Commerce Commission into pro-business agencies	• Wanted a conservative government that benefited business • Promoted the policy of laissez faire for business • Sponsored the Mellon Plan, which reduced taxes for businesses • Lowered taxes for the wealthy (often business owners)

>> **Analyze Charts** How were Harding and Coolidge's plans to stimulate economic production similar to Mellon's plans? How were they different?

Attorney General Harry Daugherty, used his position to accept money from criminals.

The Teapot Dome Scandal Comes to Light The worst scandal involved Secretary of the Interior Albert Fall. In 1921, Fall arranged to transfer oil reserves in Elk Hills, California, and Teapot Dome, Wyoming, from the Navy Department to the Interior Department. The oil reserves were intended for the navy's use in times of emergency. Harding signed the transfer.

Once Fall had control of the oil, he forgot about the needs of the navy. He leased the properties to private oilmen in return for "loans"—which were actually bribes. Rumors of the deal led to a Senate investigation, and, by 1924, the entire sordid affair was revealed to the public. Later, the oil reserves were returned to the government. Fall was sentenced to a year in prison, but those accused of bribing him were acquitted.

Harding himself never saw the full extent of the **Teapot Dome scandal**. In fact, he only had a growing suspicion that his friends were up to no good. But that was enough, as he said, to keep him "walking the floor nights." In July 1923, he visited Alaska during a speaking tour. On his return voyage, he suffered a heart attack and died on August 2. Americans mourned Harding as they had mourned no other President since Lincoln. When the full extent of the scandals emerged, however, the public formed a different opinion of him. The Teapot Dome scandal hurt U.S. citizens' trust in the federal government and its leaders, especially the Executive Branch. But the calm and assured manner in which Harding's successor, Calvin Coolidge, eliminated corrupt elements from the government restored most Americans' faith. Coolidge was reelected in a landslide the next year.

>> Secretary of the Interior, Albert Fall, sits on a rock, sipping tea. **Analyze Political Cartoons** What does this cartoon suggest about Fall's role during the Teapot Dome scandal?

BOUNCE to Activate Cartoon

RECALL What policies did Andrew Mellon pursue when he became Secretary of the Treasury?

Economic Prosperity Under Coolidge

News of Harding's death reached Vice President **Calvin Coolidge** during a visit to his father's Vermont farm. Almost immediately, the elder Coolidge, a justice of the peace, used the family Bible to swear in his son as President.

In personality, Coolidge was far different from the outgoing, back-slapping Harding. Known as Silent Cal, he was quiet, honest, and frugal—a man who measured his words carefully. He placed his trust in business and put his administration in the hands of men who held to the simple virtues of an older America. Political sharpies out to make a quick buck had no place in the Coolidge administration. Neither did Progressives who believed in an activist government bent on sweeping reforms.

Business Leaders Have the Support of the White House Coolidge admired productive business leaders. "The man who builds a factory," Coolidge once said, "builds a temple." He believed that the creation of wealth benefited the nation as a whole. In 1925, he expressed this view in his best-known speech:

> The chief business of the American people is business. They are profoundly concerned with producing, buying, selling, investing, and prospering in the world. . . .We make no concealment of the fact that we want wealth, but there are many other things that we want very much

INCOME TAX RATES IN THE 1920s

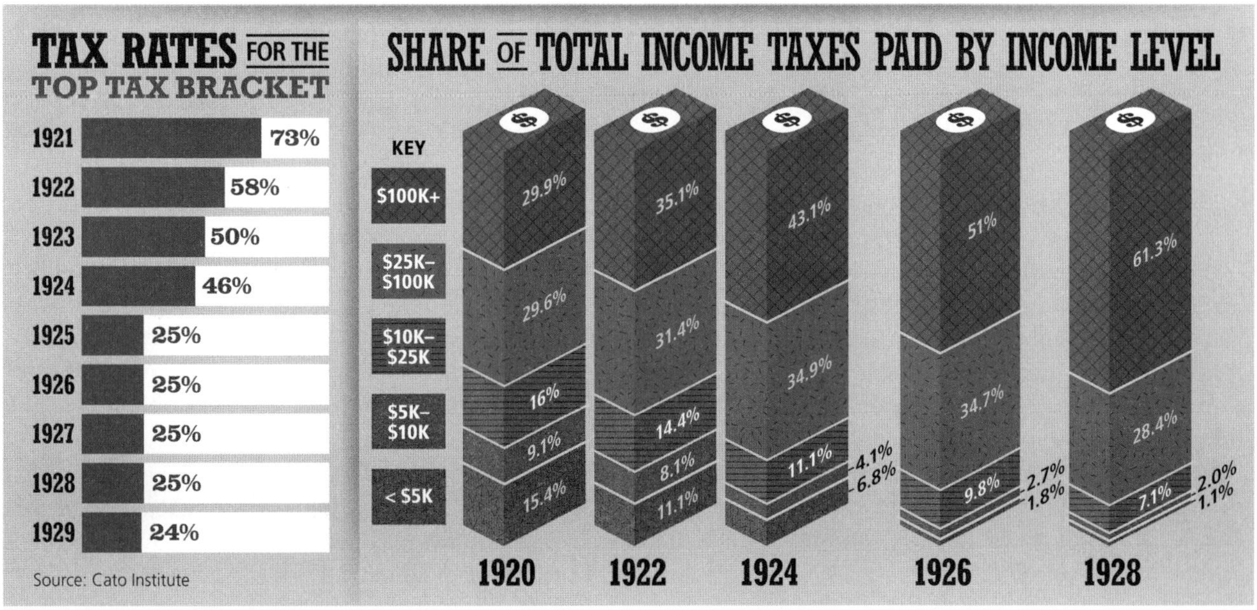

>> **Analyze Charts** How did tax rates change for top earners in the 1920s? How did the share of taxes paid by the top income earners change?

> more. We want peace and honor, and that charity which is so strong an element of all civilization. The chief ideal of the American people is idealism.
>
> —Calvin Coolidge, speech to the American Society of Newspaper Editors

Coolidge's statement of values and principles has often been oversimplified as "the business of America is business." However, in his approach to the economy, Coolidge continued to follow the goals of Secretary of the Treasury Mellon by reducing the national debt, trimming the federal budget, and lowering taxes to give incentives for businesses. Collectively referred to as the "Mellon Income Tax Cuts," the Revenue Acts of 1921, 1924, and 1926 successively lowered marginal tax rates on individuals and corporations. Although tax rates on high-income earners were significantly reduced, the total amount paid by those earners increased as incomes rose. In response to the Revenue Acts as well as other factors, the unemployment rate fell from over 6 percent to approximately 3 percent between 1922 and 1929, benefiting workers in all income brackets.

Coolidge thus oversaw increasing tax revenues and a spectacular boom in the national economy. For almost six years, the economy soared, generating industrial profits, spectacular growth in the stock market, and general prosperity, especially for urban Americans.

Some Problems Remain Yet, there were grave problems breeding in the nation. Farmers struggled to keep their land as the prices of their goods fell.

Labor unions demanded higher wages and better working conditions. African Americans faced severe discrimination, especially in the South, where Jim Crow laws made enforced segregation a way of life. African American leaders urged Congress to pass an anti-lynching law. In the Southwest, Mexican Americans confronted shamefully low wages and efforts to force them to return to Mexico.

To all of these concerns, Silent Cal remained silent. Like Harding, he mistrusted the use of legislation to achieve social change. Unlike Progressive Presidents, he believed that it was beyond the federal government's role to help create an ideal nation.

☑ **DESCRIBE** What was the purpose of the Revenue Acts of 1921, 1924, and 1926?

America's Place in a Changed World

World War I had caused sweeping changes around the globe. An old order five hundred years in the making had collapsed in just a few years. It was as if the world's compass was out of whack and no one knew where to turn for directions. German and Russian monarchies toppled, and new forms of government were created. The Austro-Hungarian and Ottoman empires ceased to exist. Britain and France emerged from the war victorious but economically and politically weakened. In contrast, the victorious United States came out of the war strong, confident, and prosperous.

Seeking Stability After World War I While World War I was a turning point for the United States in the realm of foreign affairs, the nation was still unsure of the requirements of its new status. Could America retreat from the political affairs of other countries yet continue to expand its economic reach across the globe? Under both Harding and Coolidge, America continued to play an increasingly important role in world business and trade. Beyond economic interests, U.S. foreign policy was largely shaped by reaction to World War I. No previous war had been as deadly. Citizens of all nations agreed: It must never happen again. But how could this goal be achieved?

One solution was to avoid another arms race, such as the naval rivalry between Germany and Britain that had contributed to the outbreak of the war. In 1921 and 1922, diplomats gathered in Washington, D.C., to halt another naval arms race before it got out of control. World leaders agreed to limit construction of large warships and hammered out a settlement on several problems between Japan and the West. This **Washington Naval Disarmament Conference** did not end the world's naval problems, but it raised hopes that nations could solve disagreements without resorting to war.

A later attempt to prevent war was the **Kellogg-Briand Pact** of 1928. Secretary of State Frank B. Kellogg and French Foreign Minister Aristide Briand (bree AHN) drew up a treaty to "outlaw" war "as an instrument of national policy." Eventually, 62 nations ratified the pact. But, in reality, the pact was unenforceable. Kellogg knew it, Briand knew it, and so did the rest of the diplomats. No sooner was the ink dry than everyone involved forgot about it.

Although Congress applauded the useless Kellogg-Briand Pact, it refused to join the World Court, an international body which at least promised to help mediate international disputes. As much as possible, most American leaders in the 1920s hoped to avoid another war by keeping the rest of the world at arm's length.

Collecting Reparations After the War Money issues were another matter. The United States insisted that Britain and France repay their huge war debts to the United States. For this to happen, though, Germany had to make the reparation payments to Britain and France imposed by the Treaty of Versailles. The complex financial issue threatened to undermine the international economy. Some statesmen suggested reducing or even canceling both war debts and reparations. But the frugal Coolidge insisted that a debt was a debt and had to be paid.

Washington Naval Disarmament Conference, 1921

FOUR-POWER PACT	FIVE-POWER NAVAL LIMITATION TREATY	NINE-POWER PACT
United States, Britain, France, and Japan Any disagreement between two countries regarding territorial possessions in the Pacific would be discussed by all four countries before any action was to be taken.	**United States, Britain, France, Japan, and Italy** These countries hoped to reduce the number of warships in their possession by placing tonnage limits on ships.	**United States, China, Britain, France, Japan, Italy, Belgium, the Netherlands, and Portugal** China was to open its doors equally to all countries wishing to do business there, and all other countries were to recognize China's independence and territorial integrity.

>> **Analyze Charts** How did the Washington Naval Disarmament Conference try to reduce the potential for major wars?

The United States in International Affairs, 1920–1929

DEVELOPMENT	GOAL	U.S. ACTION
League of Nations, 1920	To prevent war and settle disputes between nations	U.S. membership favored by Wilson; rejected by Senate
World Court, 1920	To make judgments in international disputes	U.S. participation favored by Harding; rejected by Senate
Dawes Plan, 1924	To arrange Germany's reparations payments following World War I	U.S. headed a committee to oversee the collection of war debts.
Kellogg-Briand Pact, 1928	To "outlaw war . . . as an instrument of national policy"	U.S. agreed with many other nations to renounce war as a means of settling international disputes.
Policy of Non-Recognition, 1917–1933	To undermine the growing power of the Soviet Union	U.S. refused to recognize the Soviet government.
Nicaragua, 1927–1932	To restore peace and protect American citizens	U.S. sent marines to Nicaragua to crush the rebellion.

>> **Analyze Charts** What international organizations or agreements did the United States take part in? Which did it pass on? Why do you think U.S. leaders chose not to take part in those organizations or agreements?

In 1924, an agreement known as the **Dawes Plan** arranged U.S. loans to Germany. By enabling Germany to make reparation payments to Britain and France, the Dawes Plan helped Britain and France to repay their debts to the United States. Of course, the entire scheme was financed by U.S. money.

After the stock market crash of 1929, however, the well of U.S. money went dry. Germany stopped reparation payments, and Britain and France ended war-debt payments to the United States.

In the end, the war-debt situation damaged America's reputation in the eyes of the world. People from Britain and France thought that it was heartless for American bankers and politicians to insist on repayment of debts and not to take into account the human costs of the war. In the next war, the United States would take a more flexible approach to war loans.

CHECK UNDERSTANDING What was the purpose of the Dawes Plan?

ASSESSMENT

1. **Generate Explanations** Discuss the corruption that existed within the Harding administration, and explain how it impacted the American public.
2. **Identify Central Issues** Summarize the main components of President Coolidge's economic philosophy.
3. **Describe** the social and economic problems that existed during the Coolidge administration, and explain why President Coolidge did not address them.
4. **Draw Conclusions** Discuss the international attempts that were made to prevent another world war, and consider why they were unsuccessful.
5. **Quest Connections** Explain the importance of the United States' role in the international collection of reparations after World War I.

GO ONLINE to access this biography: Warren Harding

12.6

GO ONLINE to Project Imagine: Should Prohibition Be Repealed? to give your opinion on one of the issues that divided Americans in the 1920s—Prohibition.

BOUNCE to Activate Flipped Video

Objectives

Compare economic and cultural life in rural America to that in urban America.

Analyze how foreign events after World War I and nativism contributed to the first Red Scare.

Analyze the causes and effects of changes in U.S. immigration policy in the 1920s.

Describe the goals and motives of the Ku Klux Klan in the 1920s.

Analyze the intended and unintended effects of Prohibition.

Key Terms

modernism
fundamentalism
Scopes Trial
Clarence Darrow
Williams Jennings Bryan
Red Scare
Palmer Raids
Nicola Sacco
Bartolomeo Vanzetti
eugenics
quota system
Ku Klux Klan
Prohibition
Eighteenth Amendment
Volstead Act
Bootleggers

GO ONLINE to access your digital course

An Unsettled Society

In the 1920s, while many city dwellers enjoyed a rising standard of living, most farmers suffered through hard times. Conflicting visions of what the nation should be heightened the urban-rural division. Some of these issues, such as immigration policy and teaching the theory of evolution, still divide Americans today.

Americans Debate New Ideas and Values

The 1920 census reported that, for the first time in American history, more people lived in urban areas than in rural regions. This simple fact had profound consequences. The nation had been divided before, but usually along north-south or east-west lines. In the 1920s, however, the split was between urban America and rural America. On virtually every important social and cultural issue, the two groups differed.

Urban Americans enjoyed new consumer products and a wide array of leisure activities. They generally showed an openness toward social change and the new discoveries of science. The growing trend to emphasize science and secular values over traditional religious beliefs became known as **modernism**.

By contrast, rural Americans did not participate fully in the consumer bonanzas, and they missed out on many of the new forms of leisure. People in the country generally embraced a more traditional view of religion, science, and culture.

An Evolving Job Market Emphasizes Education

Rural and urban Americans differed in their attitudes toward formal education. In rural America, prolonged formal education had not seemed vital. Farmers expected their children to master the "Three R's"—reading, writing, and arithmetic. But beyond that, having a formal education was not vital to the many farm tasks that needed to be done. Muscle, endurance, and knowledge of crops and animals seemed more important to farmers than abstract knowledge learned from books.

Formal education took on more importance in urban America. Mental ability, not muscular fitness, was seen as the essential ingredient for success. Mastery of mathematics and language could spell the difference between a low-paying, unskilled job and a higher-paying position as an office worker. By 1930, more American teens were graduating from high school, and more Americans than ever before went to college.

>> The rise of modernism, with its emphasis on urbanism, intellectualism, and individualism, threatened traditionalists who believed America's social foundations were deteriorating.

Some Embrace Religious Fundamentalism

In the 1920s, many devout Americans believed that Christianity was under siege throughout the world. They pointed to Soviet communist attacks on the Orthodox Church in Russia and to revolutionary assaults on the Roman Catholic Church in Mexico.

At home, a growing number of Christians were upset by what they saw as secular trends in religion and culture. They reaffirmed their belief in the fundamental, or basic, truths of their religion. This approach, often called **fundamentalism** emphasized Protestant teachings and the belief that every word in the Christian Bible was literal truth. Fundamentalists believed that the answer to every moral and scientific question could be found in the Bible. Their ideas took root all over the country but were especially strong in rural America, where revivalists like Billy Sunday inspired the faithful.

>> Clarence Darrow (left) and William Jennings Bryan have a conversation during the Scopes Trial.

Bryan and Darrow Clash Over Evolution

Fundamentalism and modernism clashed head-on in the **Scopes Trial** of 1925. At issue was the theory of evolution, developed by English scientist Charles Darwin. Darwin believed that complex forms of life, such as human beings, had developed gradually from simpler forms of life. According to fundamentalists, this theory clashed with the description of creation in their Bible.

In 1925, Tennessee passed a law making it illegal to teach Darwin's theory in the state's public schools. The American Civil Liberties Union convinced John Scopes, a high school biology teacher in Dayton, Tennessee, to challenge the law.

When Scopes taught evolution in his classroom, he was promptly arrested.

The Scopes Trial drew nationwide attention. Journalists flocked to Dayton to cover the emotionally charged event, which many dubbed the "Monkey Trial" because of the mistaken belief that Darwin claimed that human beings descended from monkeys.

Clarence Darrow, the most celebrated defense attorney in America, traveled from his home in Chicago to defend Scopes. Darrow was well-known for defending labor union leaders like Eugene V. Debs and William Haywood, in addition to other famous cases. A talented speaker, he did not always win his cases, but he often revealed key issues to the public during the well-publicized trials. Three-time presidential candidate **William Jennings Bryan**, a long-time defender of rural values, served as an expert for the prosecution. Bryan, considered one of the greatest orators of his day, was charged with defending what many fundamentalists thought of as the literal truth of divine creation found in their Bible.

Both men had a significant impact on the trial by drawing national attention to it. The highlight of the trial came when Darrow called Bryan to the stand as an expert on the Bible. Bryan said that the Bible stated the literal truth. He testified that he believed that God created Adam and Eve and that Joshua made the sun stand still. Darrow tried to use science to cast doubt on such beliefs, but Bryan firmly stated, "I accept the Bible absolutely."

Scopes was found guilty of breaking the law—a fact that was never in question—and fined $100. The public, however, was paying closer attention to a more essential issue. The trial was a public confrontation between fundamentalism and modernity, between a literal and a liberal interpretation of scripture. While the Scopes Trial showcased a major cultural and religious division, it did not heal the conflict or answer its central questions. When the trial was over, each side still believed in the truth of its position. The conflict over evolution continues today.

☑ **RECALL** How does modernism contrast with more traditional ideas about religion?

The Red Scare

As Americans continued to grapple with the ideas of modernity, the emergence of the Soviet Union as a communist nation challenged other essential U.S ideals. In contrast to capitalism and the free enterprise systems, which emphasized the right to own private property, communist ideology called for public ownership of property and an international workers' revolution as a prelude to the death of capitalism. To this end, Soviet leader Vladimir Lenin encouraged and supported revolutions outside of his country. In Central and Eastern Europe, a series of communist revolts did break out, making it seem like the worldwide revolution was starting.

Fear of a Potential Revolution This revolutionary activity abroad, coupled with labor strikes across the United States following the end of World War I, caused the first American **Red Scare**, a wave of widespread fear of suspected communists and radicals thought to be plotting revolution within the United States. Real revolutionary activity inside

The Scopes Trial: How Did They Differ?

THE PROSECUTION: WILLIAM JENNINGS BRYAN	THE DEFENSE: DUDLEY FIELD MALONE (WITNESS CALLED BY DEFENSE ATTORNEY, CLARENCE DARROW)
"It is high time for the people who believe in religion to make their protest against the teaching of irreligion in the public schools under the guise of science and philosophy."	"We are ready to tell the truth as we understand it and we do not fear all the truth that they can present as facts."

>> **Analyze Charts** Based on the quotes given in the chart, how did the Scopes trial reveal divisions within U.S. society?

America gave substance to the scare. Authorities discovered bombs mailed to important industrialists and government officials, including Attorney General A. Mitchell Palmer. Suspected anarchists, members of a radical political movement, exploded bombs in cities across America, including one that killed about 40 people on Wall Street in 1920.

As the leading law-enforcement official, Palmer mounted a broad offensive against radicals in the United States in 1919 and 1920. In a series of raids in early 1920, known as the **Palmer Raids**, police arrested thousands of people, some who were radicals and some who were simply immigrants from southern or Eastern Europe. Most were never charged or tried for a crime. The government then deported hundreds of radicals or suspected radicals.

To many, these actions seemed to have the effect of attacking the liberties that Americans held most dear. A group of people in New York City formed the American Civil Liberties Union (ACLU) in 1920 to protect these liberties. The ACLU tried to do this by becoming involved in important court cases.

In 1925, ACLU lawyers defended Benjamin Gitlow in the Supreme Court case *Gitlow* v. *New York*. Gitlow was convicted under a state law on criminal anarchy for distributing a "left-wing manifesto." The Court did not overturn the New York conviction, but did establish the "incorporation" doctrine that holds that provisions of the First Amendment were "incorporated" by the Fourteenth Amendment, thus applying to State as well as Federal laws.

>> Lenin's support for revolutions of working class people everywhere against the system of capitalism led leaders to fear just such an uprising within the United States.

A Questionable Conviction **Nicola Sacco** (SAH koh) and **Bartolomeo Vanzetti**(van ZEHT ee) were Italian immigrants and known anarchists. They were charged with shooting and killing two men during a holdup at a shoe factory in a town near Boston. Eyewitnesses of the event said the robbers "looked Italian." Sacco and Vanzetti were arrested and charged with the crime. Even though the ACLU provided defense counsel, the two men were found guilty in a swift and decisive trial, despite the fact that there was little hard evidence against them. Some prominent legal scholars, intellectuals, and liberal politicians charged that the convictions were based more on Sacco and Vanzetti's ethnicity and political beliefs than on the facts of the crime. Nevertheless, on August 23, 1927, the two men were put to death in the electric chair.

>> In New York City, thousands of people protested against the verdict in the Sacco and Vanzetti trial. Many felt government prosecutors were unjustly targeting immigrants without sufficient evidence.

At its worst, hysteria accompanied by violence characterized the Red Scare. By the summer of 1920, the height of the Red Scare had ended. Americans saw that democracy and capitalism were more powerful in the United States than Lenin's call for worldwide revolution. But, as shown by the Sacco and Vanzetti trial, the effects of the great fear would linger throughout the 1920s in negative feelings towards immigrants, labor unions, and, to some extent, the reforms pushed by Progressives before World War I.

☑ **RECALL** What was the Red Scare?

Immigration in the 1920s

As the trial of Sacco and Vanzetti came to a close, another social issue involved the ongoing boom in immigration continued. As in the past, nativists, or those who preferred native-born Americans to immigrants, argued that the new arrivals took jobs away from native-born workers and threatened American religious, political, and cultural traditions.

Eugenics and Social Darwinism Influence the Perception of Immigrants Although nativist politicians had been able to restrict immigration from China in 1882, they had failed to push through laws to restrict immigration from southern and eastern Europe. On the eve of U.S. entry into World War I, however, Congress did pass a law requiring immigrants to take a literacy test.

>> The rise of nativism within the United States led to increased restrictions on immigration, such as the rejection of immigrants who could not read and write in their own language.

Immigrants who could not read or write their own language were prohibited from entering the United States. President Wilson vetoed the law, but Congress overrode Wilson's veto. Immigration dropped during the war, worsening labor shortage problems during the war.

During the postwar Red Scare, fear that communists and socialists from eastern Europe were traveling to the United States with their revolutionary doctrines caused the debate to heat up once again. On one side were nativists who disagreed with traditional immigration policy. On the other side were many Americans who viewed the immigration experience as part of what made an American an American. Nearly all Americans who could trace their ancestry back far enough discovered foreign origins.

Nativists were concerned that immigrants would diminish America's political and economic power. They believed that many immigrants had undesirable physical and social traits and would therefore be unproductive members of society.

These views were partly based on **eugenics**, the since-discredited idea that intelligence and other favorable social traits were inheritable characteristics passed on by one's parents and more frequently found in some races than others. Eugenics was related to Social Darwinism, the idea that life was a competition in which only the fittest survive. The rise of both Social Darwinism and eugenics was caused in part by Charles Darwin's theory of natural selection. Both were also motivated by ethnic or racial prejudice to some degree. Those who believed in both theories wanted the United States to be that fittest nation that survived, and to ensure that it was, sought to exclude those they thought of as weaker and undesirable.

Many nativists who believed in eugenics thought the human race could be improved by controlling which people had children. Therefore, they thought it best to restrict immigration to those whom they deemed to have desirable traits that would in turn be passed on to future generations of Americans.

Congressional Legislation Restricts Immigration In addition to eugenics and Social Darwinism, other events such as World War I, the Russian Revolution, and the Red Scare strengthened the nativist position and affected congressional legislation. Two subsequent laws— the Emergency Quota Act of 1921 and the National Origins Act of 1924— established a **quota system** to govern immigration from specific countries.

Effects of Quotas on Immigration

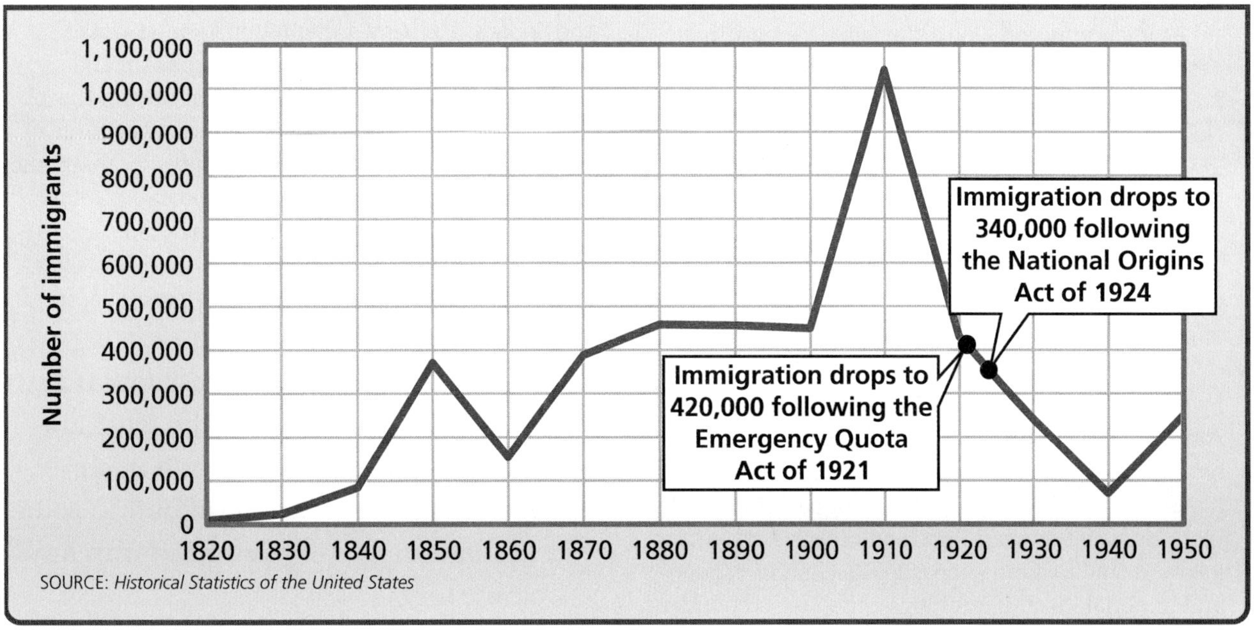

>> **Analyze Charts** What effect did the Emergency Quota Act of 1921 and the National Origins Act of 1924 have on immigration to the United States?

BOUNCE to Activate Timeline

The National Origins Act, also known as the Immigration Act of 1924, set up a simple formula: The number of immigrants of a given nationality each year could not exceed 2 percent of the number of people of that nationality living in the United States in 1890. The year 1890 was chosen because it was before the great wave of immigration from southern and eastern Europe. For example, the act permitted about 65,721 immigrants from England and Northern Ireland to come to America every year, but it allowed only about 5,802 immigrants from Italy. The act also continued to exclude most Asian immigrants. The effect of eugenics, Social Darwinism, and nativist sentiment in general was that America closed its "golden door" to many of the people trying to enter.

More Mexicans Arrive for Economic Opportunity The quota system did not apply to Mexico, which was still reeling from the 1910 revolution. Settling in sparsely populated regions of the Southwest, Mexican immigrants made significant contributions to local economies. Many found work harvesting crops in California and Texas. A smaller number sought jobs in the factories and farms of the North or Midwest.

Many Mexican immigrants faced discrimination and hostility in their new homes. They often competed with native-born Americans for jobs and were frequently subjected to brutality and violence.

RECALL What was the purpose of the National Origins Act?

The Ku Klux Klan in the Early 1900s

Immigration restriction was an attempt to turn back the clock to what many saw as a simpler, better time. Many lashed out against symbols of change. Some even turned to organizations that supported doctrines of hate and employed violence and terror to achieve their ends.

The Klan Reorganizes In 1915, on Stone Mountain in Georgia, a revived **Ku Klux Klan** was formally organized. The original Klan had been formed in the South during Reconstruction largely to terrorize African Americans who sought to vote. Although the new Klan continued to promote hatred of African Americans, it was also aimed at the new America taking shape in the cities. It targeted Jews, Catholics, and immigrants. In the wake of postwar labor unrest, the Klan opposed labor unions—especially because many union members were immigrants or political radicals. The Klan also claimed to stand against lawbreaking and immorality.

At its height, the Klan's "Invisible Empire" had perhaps 4 to 5 million members. Most were in the South, but there were also branches in the Midwest, Northeast, and West—in both rural areas and in small industrial cities. One center of Klan strength was Indiana, where Klan leader David Stephenson ruled with an iron fist and controlled numerous politicians. There were special women's branches of the Klan as well. However, some male Klan leaders were strongly opposed to women taking an active role in politics.

Klan members boycotted businesses owned by anyone who was Jewish, Catholic, or African American. The Klan terrorized citizens in the night, often by burning crosses outside their homes. Klansmen usually wore masks to conceal their identities, met to wave flags and preach hate, and followed leaders with such titles as Grand Dragon and Imperial Wizard. But behind the Klan's confident facade were Americans fearful of change.

Many Americans Oppose the Klan's Values

Organizations such as the NAACP and the Jewish Anti-Defamation League, battled against the Klan and its values. The NAACP continued its anti-lynching crusade, supporting legislation in 1922 that passed in the House of Representatives but not in the Senate. The Anti-Defamation League worked to reduce anti-Semitic slurs in newspapers and break down barriers in higher education and the job market. Individuals also embraced the idea of racial, ethnic, religious, and cultural diversity. For them, the notion of the "melting pot" was as old as America itself. Journalist William Allen White noted:

> To make a case against a birthplace, a religion, or a race is wickedly un-American and cowardly. The whole trouble with the Ku Klux Klan is that it is based upon such deep foolishness that it is bound to be a menace to good government in any community.
>
> —William Allen White, letter to the editor of the *New York World*, 1921

The Klan itself became thoroughly corrupt. Its leaders bribed politicians, stole from its members' dues, and lied to its members. Stephenson ended up going to prison for assault and second-degree murder. By the late 1920s, the Klan stood exposed. Although the organization never disappeared, it became less significant.

>> A group photo of the twentieth annual session of the NAACP in Cleveland, Ohio in 1929.

☑ What actions did Klan members take to accomplish their goals?

Prohibition Divides Americans

Another divisive issue was **Prohibition**, the banning of alcohol use. Since the early 1800s, temperance reformers had crusaded against alcohol. Temperance was a cause held dear by many Progressives. By 1917, some 75 percent of Americans lived in "dry" counties that had banned liquor. World War I increased support for temperance. It seemed unpatriotic to use corn, wheat, and barley to make alcohol when soldiers overseas needed bread.

The Eighteenth Amendment Bans Alcohol

In 1919, the states ratified the **Eighteenth Amendment** to the Constitution. It forbade the manufacture, distribution, and sale of alcohol anywhere in the United States. The amendment had been passed largely on the strength of rural votes. Many Progressives felt that its passage was one of

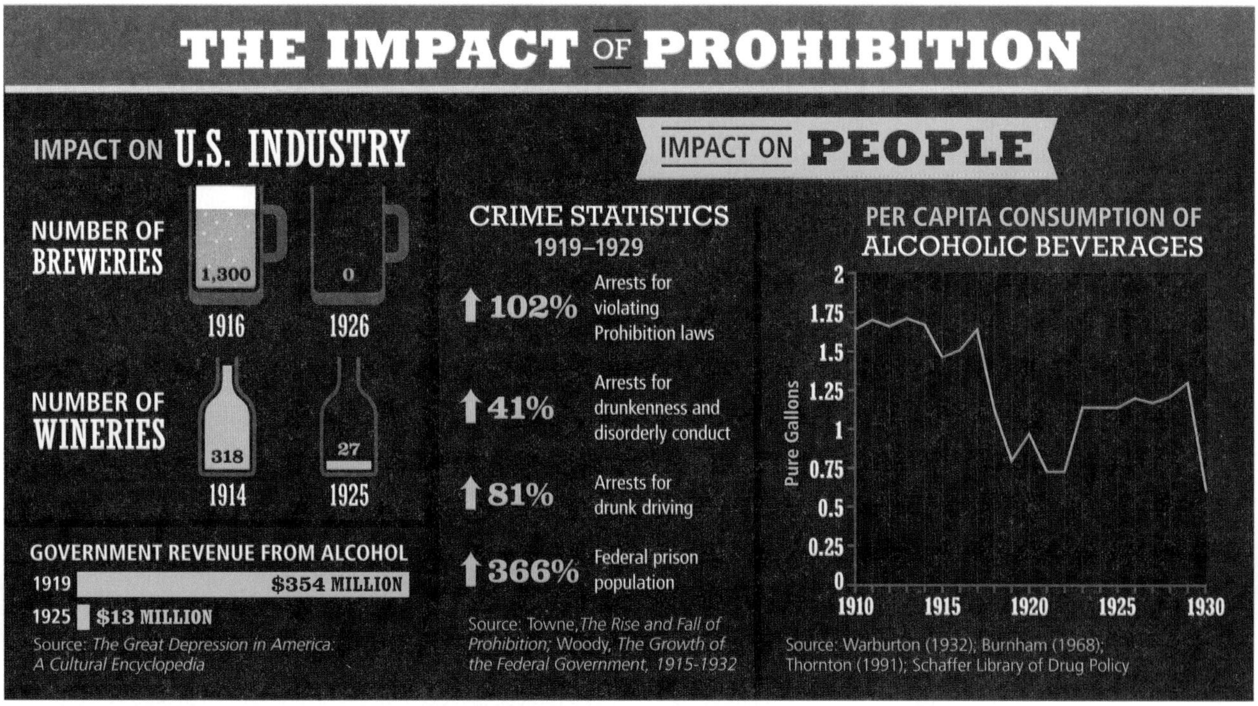

>> **Analyze Charts** Summarize the effects of Prohibition on American society.

BOUNCE to Activate Gallery

the greatest impacts of the whole Progressive reform movement. Congress then passed the **Volstead Act**, a law that officially enforced the amendment.

Advocates of Prohibition, known as "drys," called it a "noble experiment." They argued that the impact of Prohibition would be improved individuals, strengthened families, and better societies. In fact, drinking—as well as alcoholism and liver disease caused by drinking—did decline during the first years of Prohibition but soon rose again to near pre-Prohibition levels.

Opponents of Prohibition, dubbed "wets," countered that the ban on alcohol did not stop people from drinking. Instead, they argued, Prohibition's impact was to help create an atmosphere of hypocrisy and increased organized crime.

Many Americans Ignore the Volstead Act As the wets noted, the Volstead Act did not stop Americans from drinking, but it did prevent them from purchasing drinks legally. The gap between the law and individual desires was filled by a large illegal network. People made alcohol in homemade stills or smuggled it in from other countries.

Bootleggers sold illegal alcohol to consumers. In cities, secret drinking establishments, known as speakeasies, attracted eager customers. In South Florida, "rum-runners" smuggled in rum and other spirits from across the Florida Straits.

Government agents worked tirelessly to stop the flow of illegal liquor. However, they were short-handed, and the demand for alcohol was too great. There were millions of dollars to be made by both organized and unorganized criminals. Particularly in cities, policemen and politicians tended to look the other way when liquor was involved. They rationalized their actions by saying that if people wanted to drink, they would drink.

Al Capone, a Chicago gang leader, was the most famous criminal of the Prohibition era. He defended his illegal actions:

> I make my money from supplying a public demand. If I break the law, my customers, who number hundreds of the best people in Chicago, are as guilty as I am. The only difference between us is that I sell and they buy. Everybody calls me a racketeer. I call myself a businessman.
>
> —Al Capone, quoted in *Era of Excess* (Sinclair)

The problem was that under the guise of providing a glass of beer or scotch, organized crime spread into other areas of society. Capone's other "businesses" included prostitution, drugs, robbery,

>> Protesters in 1932 were led by New York City Mayor Jimmy Walker. **Draw Conclusions** Looking at the banners, what reason were the marchers using to advocate the repeal of Prohibition?

and murder. Thus, one effect of Prohibition was to contribute to the growth of organized crime in America.

The Constitution Is Amended Again By the mid-1920s, most city politicians clamored for the repeal of the Eighteenth Amendment. But to many rural Americans, liquor and crime were tied to other divisive cultural issues of the day. Thus, like immigration and evolution, the debate over Prohibition became part of a battle over the future of America.

In the culturally divided 1920s, Americans could not reach a satisfactory settlement on the issue. However, illegal economies that thrived on the production and distribution of alcohol continued to thrive and legal enforcement of Prohibition was oftentimes lax. As popular dissatisfaction with the Eighteenth Amendment grew, Congress finally repealed Prohibition with the passage of the Twenty-First Amendment in 1933. It was ratified by the states later that same year.

IDENTIFY MAIN IDEAS Why was the Volstead Act passed?

GO ONLINE to access this biography: Billy Sunday

ASSESSMENT

1. **Make Generalizations** Explain how the lifestyles of urban and rural Americans differed during the 1920s.
2. **Generate Explanations** Explain how the Scopes Trial illustrated the conflict between modernism and fundamentalism.
3. **Apply Concepts** Identify the flaws of the trial of Nicola Sacco and Bartolomeo Vanzetti.
4. **Distinguish Between Fact and Opinion** Discuss the main ideas of eugenics, and explain why it is no longer a prominent belief in the United States.
5. **Identify Cause and Effect** Explain how Prohibition contributed to the growth of organized crime in the United States.
6. **Quest Connections** What connections do you see between U.S. immigration policies and the refusal to join the League of Nations?

12.7

GO ONLINE to Project Imagine: Adjust to Changing Times for Women to see how the lives of women, like these college students, changed during the decade.

The Roaring Twenties

The automobile reshaped American culture, creating new forms of recreation and making it easier for people to travel. Other factors also contributed to changing ways of daily life. Americans listened to the radio, went to the movies, and followed the exploits of sports heroes. In the process, a new mass culture emerged—one whose shape and character closely resemble our own.

BOUNCE to Activate Flipped Video

Objectives

Describe how increased leisure time and technological innovations led to a widespread shared popular culture in the 1920s.

Analyze the changing role of women in the 1920s.

Describe how the concept of modernism shown in art and literature reflected postwar disillusionment.

Key Terms

Charlie Chaplin
The Jazz Singer
Babe Ruth
Charles Lindbergh
flapper
Sigmund Freud
"Lost Generation"
F. Scott Fitzgerald
Ernest Hemingway

Popular American Culture in the 1920s

The 1920s was in many respects the first decade of our modern era. Even as cultural issues divided Americans from different regions or economic levels, technology was beginning to break down other barriers. Nowhere is this more evident than in the leisure interests of the American people.

Americans Enjoy More Leisure Time The growth of cities changed leisure patterns. On farms, people worked from dawn to dusk, with little time to spare. In the evenings, a farm family might play games, read, or sing together around the piano. Occasionally, they joined other farm families and townsfolk for picnics or a game of baseball. They did not have the time or the money for more extensive leisure pursuits.

City life was different. The average workweek in all industries fell from 70 hours in 1850 to 55 in 1910 to 45 by 1930. The workweek itself also changed from seven days a week to six and at last to five. At the same time, salaries and wages were on the rise.

GO ONLINE to access your digital course

Innovation in the Motion Picture Industry With more free time and disposable income, urban and suburban Americans looked to new sources of entertainment. Motion pictures helped supply that demand.

The technology to make motion pictures had been around for a generation, but the movie industry rose to new heights in the 1920s. A handful of huge studios in Hollywood, California, established monopolies that controlled the production, distribution, and exhibition of movies. During the 1920s, from 60 to 100 million Americans went to the movies each week. Ornate movie palaces or small local theaters became America's cultural classrooms.

For most of the decade, the studios made silent pictures. They were an ideal entertainment at a time when millions of immigrants spoke little English. Motion pictures transcended languages and even literacy, treating universal themes in familiar ways that allowed any viewer to follow the stories. Motion pictures became America's democratic art. Unlike theatrical productions or classical concerts, movies were available to anyone with a few cents to spare. In addition, the fact that movies were silent made it easier for them to cut across geographical boundaries. Hollywood's biggest movies and stars became nearly as popular in far corners of the globe as they were at home. By 1926, Hollywood movies accounted for a majority of the British and French film markets. Film was one of the first mediums to diffuse popular American culture to the rest of the world.

Many stars of the silent era portrayed ordinary folks, and films often portrayed the social issues and characteristics of the time in which they were made. Comedian **Charlie Chaplin**, the most popular silent film star, played the Little Tramp in many films. In *The Immigrant*, Chaplin played a penniless immigrant on a voyage across the Atlantic to the United States. Although the film belonged to the genre of comedy, it depicted some of the challenges and uncertainties that many immigrants of the time faced as they made their own way to America's shores. Chaplin's character was equal parts hobo, dreamer, and poet but an eternal optimist in his ability to charm his audience and continually reinvent himself. Other stars played more romantic types. Adorable Mary Pickford was known as "America's Sweetheart" for her girlish roles in light romances. Douglas Fairbanks played handsome, athletic adventurers. In the western genre, William S. Hart was a steely-eyed cowboy who came into town to restore law and order.

In 1927, film history changed, suddenly and forever, with the release of ***The Jazz Singer***, the first movie with sound synchronized to the action. Audiences were amazed when Al Jolson said—not pantomimed—"You ain't heard nothin' yet" and then

INNOVATIONS CHANGE HOW PEOPLE LIVE

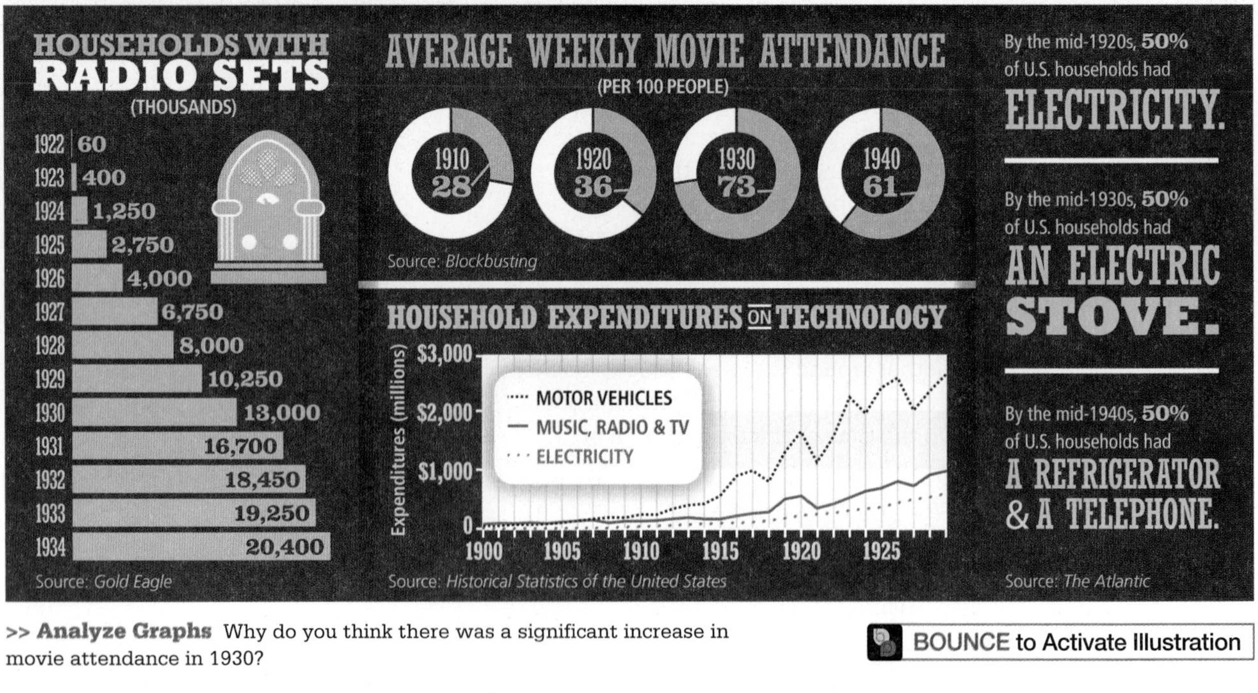

>> **Analyze Graphs** Why do you think there was a significant increase in movie attendance in 1930?

BOUNCE to Activate Illustration

launched into a song. Silent pictures quickly faded out, replaced by "talkies." But whether silent or with sound, movies spoke directly to the desires, needs, fears, and fantasies of millions of people in the United States and around the world.

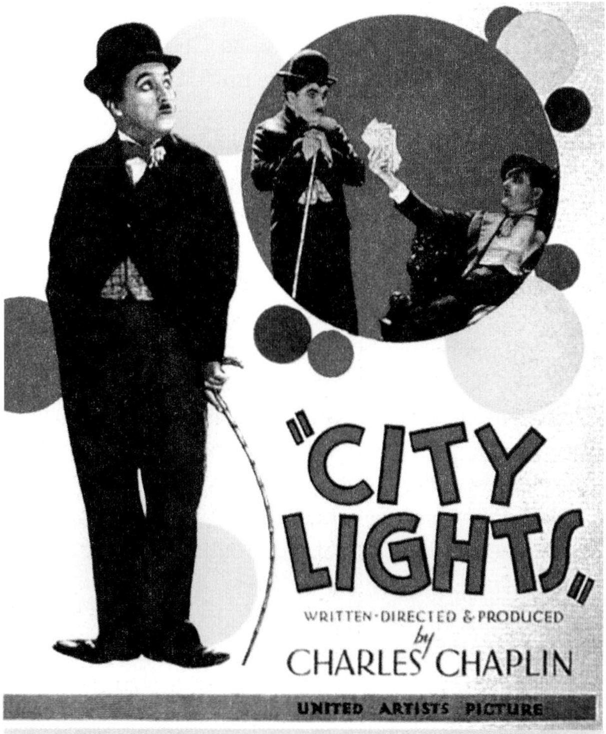

>> Before "talkies," or movies with synchronized sound, Americans went to the movies to see silent pictures. Charlie Chaplin was perhaps the most famous of all silent film actors.

The Radio Impacts American Society Like the movies, the phonograph and the radio also became powerful instruments of mass popular culture. Each was the result of both technological advances and business enterprise. Millions of radios and phonographs (as well as phonograph records) were marketed in the 1920s. On a deeper level, the phonograph and radio helped produce a standardized culture. Americans in the East and West and North and South listened to the same songs, learned the same dances, and shared the same popular culture as they never had before.

The radio, or wireless, was developed in the 1890s by Italian inventor Guglielmo Marconi. Before the 1920s, the radio was an innovation used by a small group of military technicians, telephone operators, and amateur "wireless" operators. Then, in 1920, an executive of the Westinghouse company started radio station KDKA in Pittsburgh, Pennsylvania. It was an immediate success. Within three years, there were almost 600 licensed stations broadcasting to more than 600,000 radio sets. Americans listened to music, educational lectures and religious sermons, and news and weather reports. They also heard commercials for a wide variety of consumer products.

Radios brought distant events into millions of homes in a way unmatched by newspapers or magazines. In 1927, much of America listened to a championship boxing match between Gene Tunney and Jack Dempsey. That night, theaters and movie houses played to empty seats as Americans huddled next to their sets. Even the men on death row at Sing Sing prison listened to the broadcast. Before the 1920s, such coverage of an event had been impossible. Although radio programs and music occasionally broadcast racial or cultural stereotypes as well, such as the radio show *Amos 'n Andy* in the 1920s, the radio allowed Americans to keep up with current events around the country as they occurred.

Americans Share Music With the Phonograph The phonograph allowed people to listen to the same music they heard on the radio, but whenever they wanted. Early phonographs employed difficult-to-use wax cylinders and suffered from poor sound quality. In the 1920s, grooved disc recordings and superior sound reproduction improved the sound of the earlier machines, and production of phonographs rose to

>> The invention of the phonograph and grooved disc record stimulated the growth of the music industry. By the 1920s, records had one song on each side and rotated at 78 revolutions per minute (rpm).

approximately five million in 1929. There was also a corresponding rise in record sales. The first country-western album to sell over one million copies was produced in 1924.

As the popularity of country-western music rose, one positive impact was that the uniquely American symbol of the cowboy and life on the the western frontier was mythologized throughout the country. A negative impact was that stereotypes of westerners and country-dwellers sometimes also spread. Recordings helped bring country and western music from the South and West to the North and East, while pop tunes from New York City's Tin Pan Alley traveled in the other direction, creating national markets for different genres of music. As they listened to the same songs, Americans also learned the same fashionable dances, from the fox trot to the Charleston.

☑ **IDENTIFY MAIN IDEAS** How did films like *The Immigrant* reflect the social issues of the time?

>> With the help of increased newspaper readership and radio coverage, sports figures like Babe Ruth became national heroes and symbols of American culture.

American Role Models

Hollywood's chief rivals for the creation of heroes were the nation's baseball parks, football fields, and boxing rings. Before the 1920s, there were relatively few nationally famous athletes, such as boxer John L. Sullivan and all-around athlete Jim Thorpe. Most sports stars were local heroes. This changed by the 1920s, often called the Golden Age of Sports.

Media Coverage Creates Sports Heroes Thanks to increased newspaper readership and the rise of radio coverage, every major sport boasted nationally famous performers. Perhaps the leading sports hero was baseball home-run king **Babe Ruth**. Others included Red Grange in football, Jack Dempsey in boxing, Bobby Jones in golf, and Bill Tilden in tennis. Women athletes, too, contributed to the hero culture, from tennis player Helen Wills to Gertrude Ederle, the first woman to swim the English Channel.

Why did athletes reach such heights of popularity? Part of the answer is that the Golden Age of Sports was also the Golden Age of the Sportswriter. Such journalists as Damon Runyon and Grantland Rice captured the excitement of sports events in their colorful prose. Turning the finest athletes into seemingly immortal gods, the sportswriters nicknamed Babe Ruth the Sultan of Swat and dubbed Notre Dame's football backfield the Four Horsemen.

The other part of the answer is that the decade needed heroes. World War I had shattered many Americans' faith in progress, making the world seem cheap and flawed. Athletic heroes reassured Americans that people were capable of great feats and lofty dreams. If in our heroes we see our idealized selves, the sports heroes of the 1920s gave Americans a sense of hope.

A Transatlantic Flight Even the biggest sports stars could not match the adoration given to aviators. In the 1920s, the airline industry was in its infancy. Flying aces had played a role in World War I, and a few small domestic airlines carried mail and passengers. But airplanes were still a novel sight to most Americans. The pilot became a new breed of hero, a romantic daredevil who risked death with every flight.

As aviation technology improved by leaps and bounds in the early twentieth century, many dreamed of flying across the Atlantic Ocean. These dreams were made possible by innovators such as Glenn Curtiss, who designed an aircraft engine capable of just such a flight. As flight crews were successfully flying longer distances across the

Atlantic, daring aviators wondered if they could accomplish the same feat alone.

Then aviator **Charles Lindbergh** attempted the long journey alone. In May 1927, he took off from Long Island, New York, in his tiny single-engine plane, the *Spirit of St. Louis*, and headed east— to Paris, France. Other pilots had flown across the Atlantic Ocean before, but Lindbergh was the first to do it solo and non-stop. The flight took more than 33 hours, and the lone pilot had to stay awake the entire time. He also recalled, "In the daytime I knew where I was going, but in the evening and at night it was largely a matter of guesswork."

When Lindbergh landed in Paris, he became an instant media celebrity, dubbed Lucky Lindy and the Lone Eagle. The radio reported on his landing, and movie newsreels showed his triumphant return home. The modest young man from the Midwest made an impact as the greatest hero of his time.

☑ **IDENTIFY** For what accomplishment was Charles Lindbergh known?

>> The individualism and modernism of the early 1920s prompted many women to see themselves as equals to men, deserving the same political and social rights.

The Role of Women Changes

In a 1931 book, *Only Yesterday*, journalist Frederick Lewis Allen attempted to make sense of the fads, heroes, and problems of the 1920s. Featured prominently was the New Woman. During the decade, many women challenged political, economic, social, and educational boundaries to prove that their role was as vital outside the home as inside it. Women's roles began to change in many ways, caused by the overall changes that society was undergoing, as well as the passage of the Nineteeth Amendment in 1920. The effect of these changes was that women made more and more contributions to shape American culture.

Flappers Push Back Against Expectations

During the Victorian Age of the late 1800s and early 1900s, middle-class women had been expected to center their lives on the home and family. The New Woman of the 1920s, noted Allen, was more liberated. She wore dresses with shorter hemlines, put on more makeup, danced to the latest crazes, and generally assumed that she had the same political and social rights as any man.

Popular magazines, sociological studies, novels, and movies all echoed Allen's observations. The rejection of Victorian morality seemed so total and the New Woman so novel that the change amounted to a "revolution in manners and morals." The symbol of all these changes was the **flapper**, a young woman with short skirts and rouged cheeks who had her hair cropped close in a style known as a bob.

There was only a germ of truth in the various observations. The Victorian code of separate spheres for men and women was disappearing but not as rapidly or as completely as Allen indicated. The flapper was undoubtedly more publicized than imitated. Still, the image of the flapper underscores an important aspect of the decade. Not all women aspired to be flappers, but many wanted more control over their lives—and got it.

Women's Political Rights The great fight for suffrage had been won with the passage of the Nineteenth Amendment. Soon women looked for a way to use their political rights to make an impact. But what was the next step? Some groups, such as the National American Woman Suffrage Association, called on women to work in reform movements, run for office, or fight for laws to protect women and children in the workplace. Some women had success in public life. In 1925, Nellie Tayloe Ross of Wyoming and Miriam Ferguson of Texas became the first women to take office as elected state governors.

The National Women's Party took a more militant position, demanding complete economic, social, and political equality with men. Their primary goal was the passage of an Equal Rights Amendment. Many women, though, believed that a new constitutional amendment was premature. They set more achievable goals and made significant strides in employment. The efforts of these political organizations and women elected to public office redefined the role of women in American culture and opened doors through which others would walk in the decades to come. Although most working women continued to toil in domestic service and manufacturing, others moved into clerical, sales, and management positions. Women also won jobs in journalism, aviation, banking, and the legal and medical professions.

Life at Home Changes Perhaps the most widespread revolution taking place in women's lives was a quiet one. During the decade, women tended to live longer, marry later, and have fewer children, freeing their time to pursue other interests. Some entered the workforce, others devoted more time to charitable work, and still others joined clubs that discussed books and ideas. All these pursuits enlarged the intellectual world of women.

The consumer economy of the 1920s benefited women. Electric vacuum cleaners and irons took some of the labor and drudgery out of household chores. Of course, not all women shared in the blessings of technology. Many homes in rural America had no access to electricity. For women in these regions, household labor continued to involve intense, even painful, work. They drew and carried water from wells, heated irons on stoves, and washed clothes by hand. Here again, the split between urban and rural Americans was distinct.

RECALL Why would many who advocated for women's political equality have thought 1925 was a significant year?

>> Modernist painters like Edward Hopper expressed their reservations about the progress of civilization. **Evaluate Sources** What themes does Hopper's 1927 painting "Automat" express?

BOUNCE to Activate Chart

Social Issues Are Reflected in Art and Literature

No area of American life, however, reflected the impact of World War I more than literature and the arts. The war altered the way writers and artists viewed the world, changed the way they approached their craft, and inspired them to experiment with new forms and fresh ideas.

Postwar Uncertainty During the Victorian era, most poets and novelists had expressed a belief in progress, placing boundless faith in human potential. But World War I called the notion of progress into question.

How could a society ruled by the idea of progress embark on a war that killed millions of people, destroyed monuments of civilization, and left survivors hungry, homeless, and hopeless? This was not an action of a rational people, a new generation of writers argued, but the irrational exploits of civilization without a sense of direction.

This pessimistic, skeptical worldview sparked an artistic movement known as modernism. Modernism in both art and literature to some extent also reflected some of the issues and characteristics of American society in the 1920s, from the renewed interest in new technology to the uncertainty of many in a rapidly changing world.

The theories of Jewish-Austrian psychologist **Sigmund Freud** (SIHG muhnd froid) also contributed to literary and artistic modernism. Freud argued that much of human behavior is driven not by rational thought but by unconscious desires. To live in society, people learn to suppress these desires. But the tension between outward behavior and the subconscious, said Freud, could lead to mental and even physical illness. Freud's theories led writers and artists to explore the subconscious mind.

Modern Art Moves in New Directions

Modernism clashed head-on with traditionalism most dramatically in the field of modern art. Since the late 1800s, European painters had led the way in seeking a fresh visual idiom, or language. They moved away from art that copied reality and experimented with more abstract styles.

Most Americans got their first real glimpse of the new European approach at a major art show at New York's 69th Infantry Regimental Armory in 1913. Traditionalists were outraged by the Armory Show, and Theodore Roosevelt said that most of it represented the "lunatic fringe" of the art world. But many American painters and sculptors were inspired by the bold new styles. They began their own search for artistic honesty in abstract patterns. In the 1920s, paintings by Edward Hopper, Man Ray, Joseph Stella, and Georgia O'Keeffe demonstrated the richness and varied styles of American artists. At the same time, the works of artists such as Archibald Motley and William H. Johnson portrayed African American perspectives on modern life.

Postwar American Literature Flowers American writers of the 1920s are often referred to as the **"Lost Generation"** because they no longer had faith in the cultural guideposts of the Victorian era. But many were inspired by their "lost" condition to search for new truths and fresh ways of expressing those truths. Never in American history had one decade seen the emergence of so many great literary talents. A list of writers who rose to distinction in the 1920s includes F. Scott Fitzgerald, Ernest Hemingway, Edith Wharton, Sinclair Lewis, William Faulkner, Gertrude Stein, Eugene O'Neill, and T. S. Eliot. Each of these writers remains today on any list of distinguished American authors.

Novelist **F. Scott Fitzgerald** explored the reality of the American dream of wealth, success, and emotional fulfillment. In *This Side of Paradise*, he wrote that his generation had "grown up to find all Gods dead, all wars fought, and all faiths in man shaken." In *The Great Gatsby* (1925), his most accomplished work, Fitzgerald showed the American dream ending in nightmare.

In the novel, through hard work and careful planning, James Gatz re-creates himself as Jay Gatsby, a successful tycoon. Gatsby fills his home with wild parties, dancing, and bootleg liquor:

>> American writers F. Scott Fitzgerald and his wife Zelda, visited the French Riviera often in the 1920s. In many ways, their turbulent life together mirrored Fitzgerald's stories of striving and tragedy.

> In the main hall a bar with a real brass rail was set up, and stocked with gins and liquors and with cordials so long forgotten that most of his female guests were too young to know one from another. By seven o'clock the orchestra had arrived, no thin five-piece affair, but a whole pitful of oboes and trombones and saxophones. . . . People were not invited—they went there. They got into automobiles which bore them out to Long Island, and somehow they ended up at Gatsby's door.
>
> —F. Scott Fitzgerald, *The Great Gatsby*

But in the end, Gatsby is destroyed by the very things he hoped to achieve. His lofty dreams end in a violent, meaningless death.

Ernest Hemingway explored similar themes but in a new idiom. Hemingway felt betrayed, not only by the American dream, but also by literary language itself. In *A Farewell to Arms*, his 1929 novel about World War I, Hemingway's narrator says:

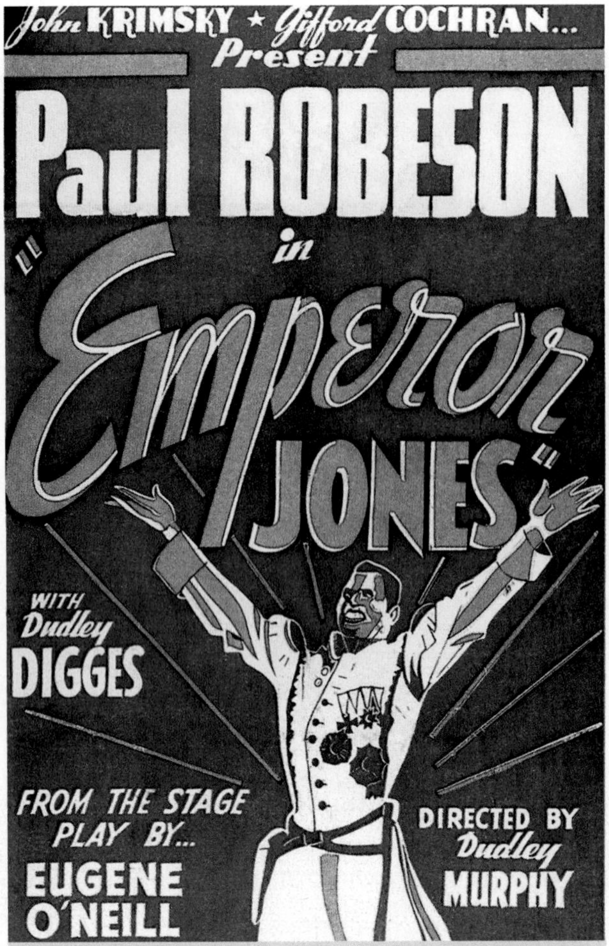

>> *The Emperor Jones* was Eugene O'Neill's initial attempt at expressionism. Starring Paul Robeson, it was the first play on Broadway with a racially integrated cast.

> I was always embarrassed by the words sacred, glorious, and sacrifice. . . .I had seen nothing sacred, and the things that were glorious had no glory and the sacrifices were like the stockyards at Chicago if nothing was done with the meat except to bury it. . . .Abstract words such as glory, honor, courage, or hallow were obscene beside the concrete names of villages, the numbers of roads, the names of rivers, the numbers of regiments and the dates.
>
> —Ernest Hemingway, *A Farewell to Arms*

Influenced by Freud, other writers explored the subconscious mind. Playwright Eugene O'Neill experimented with techniques that put the subconscious right on stage. In *The Emperor Jones*, the title character gets lost in a jungle and is attacked by imaginary beings called Little Formless Fears. In *Strange Interlude*, characters turn away from their conversations with other people on stage and speak their thoughts directly to the audience.

Certainly many poets and novelists of the decade were disillusioned. Like Hemingway and Fitzgerald, they wrestled with the meaning of the war and life itself. But in the end, their efforts resulted in the creation of literary masterpieces, not worthless products of aimless despair.

Gay Subculture Becomes More Visible

Prohibition criminalized alcohol-based nightlife, forcing many people to break the law. In the illegal activities of the speakeasies many "straight" Americans came into contact with openly gay men and lesbians, whose meeting places had been subject to police raids for decades. During the social experimentation of the 1920s, increasing numbers of films, books, and popular songs referenced lesbian and gay male sexual orientation, while in the cities gay men and lesbians also became bolder and more visible. In this rebellious decade, some defied laws against cross-dressing, and in New York City drag balls began attracting thousands, growing larger every year. Yet despite this greater visibility, gay men and lesbians still lived in fear of anti-gay laws. They were still subject to arrest, imprisonment, blackmail, the loss of jobs and rejection by family for behavior that society considered immoral and criminal.

CHECK UNDERSTANDING What themes did F. Scott Fitzgerald include in many of his stories?

ASSESSMENT

1. **Draw Conclusions** Explain why silent pictures were an ideal form of entertainment during the 1920s.
2. **Make Generalizations** Explain why sports heroes became popular during the 1920s.
3. **Identify Central Issues** Explain how modernist literature related to the prominent issues and ideas of the 1920s.
4. **Identify Cause and Effect** Explain how World War I led to the rise of modernism.
5. **Draw Conclusions** Explain how the flapper related to the lives of most American women.
6. **Connections to Today** Do you think that greater visibility of minorities in popular culture helps advance the cause of civil rights?

Women's Lives

During the 1920s, social and cultural change deepened divisions in American society, especially between urban areas, where the rate of change was quickening, and rural areas, where change came more slowly. For many women in urban areas these changes were liberating, while for many rural women, life remained a struggle against economic hardship.

The following sources about two very different women show contrasting perspectives. The first is a magazine article that describes a fashionable young woman, or "flapper", living in an area and social setting where modern styles and attitudes were gaining ground. The second is a letter from a young rural woman to her senator, describing her hardships and requesting a loan.

As you read, think about how the lives of these two women may have shaped their viewpoints. Then answer the questions to compare their perspectives.

>> In the 1920s, the behavior and dress of many young women shocked their elders.

Primary Source 1

"Flapper Jane," Bruce Bliven, *New Republic,* September 9, 1925

Jane's a flapper.

Let us take a look at the young person as she strolls across the lawn of her parents' suburban home, having just put the car away after driving sixty miles in two hours. She is, for one thing, a very pretty girl. Beauty is the fashion in 1925. . . .

Her dress, as you can't possibly help knowing if you have even one good eye, and get around at all outside the Old People's Home, is also brief. It is cut low where it might be high, and vice versa. The skirt comes just an inch below her knees, overlapping by a faint fraction her rolled and twisted stockings.

ANALYZE STYLE AND RHETORIC How does the writer introduce the idea of a generation gap between the young and old?

The idea is that when she walks in a bit of a breeze, you shall now and then observe the knee (which is not rouged that's just newspaper talk) but always in an accidental, Venus-surprised-at-the-bath sort of way. This is a bit of coyness which hardly fits in with Jane's general character. Jane's haircut is also abbreviated. She wears of course the very newest thing in bobs, even closer than last year's shingle. It leaves her just about no hair at all in the back, and 20 percent more than that in the front. . . . Because of this new style, one can confirm a rumor heard last year: Jane has ears. . . .

"Jane," say I, "I am a reporter representing American inquisitiveness. Why do all of you dress the way you do?"

"In a way," says Jane, "'it's just honesty. Women have come down off the pedestal lately. They are tired of this mysterious-feminine-charm stuff. Maybe it goes with independence, earning your own living and voting and all that. . . .

"Of course, not so many girls are looking for a life meal-ticket nowadays. Lots of them prefer to earn their own living and omit the home-and-baby act. Well, anyhow, postpone it years and years. They think a bachelor girl can and should do everything a bachelor man does."

DETERMINE AUTHOR'S POINT OF VIEW What connection does Jane draw between social changes and women's fashion?

Primary Source 2

Letter from Mollie Bostic to Senator W.E. Borah, Boise (Idaho), March 25, 1922

My dear Senator Borah,

I understand that the Federal Farm Loan Association is for the benefit of farmers, and especially so in cases of emergency and extreme and urgent need.

Two years ago, we bought 25.2 acres of land about 3½ miles west of Nampa in the Deer Flat Section, price $3600, terms $600 down and $500 annually, interest at 7% to be paid semi-annually. . . .

I want to get a Federal loan of $2500 on the place on any reasonable terms. . . .

Senator Borah, mamma is even selling her cows and chickens, all she has to live on, and even what little furniture she has in the house to try to raise money to make this payment. We need help and we need it bad, and that is the real purpose for which the Federal Farmers Loan Association was established, but we can't wait three months to get it. It is all well and good for those men in office holding salaried positions, perfectly safe and secure to sit back and say we must abide by rules and regulations, but this does not lift the burden from the farmer's shoulders who is making the terrific struggle to keep his head above water. . . .

SUMMARIZE What is the writer, Ms. Bostic, asking for and why does she need it?

This is not an appeal for sympathy. All I ask is just a chance, just an opportunity, hence this urgent appeal for help in case of extreme need and I sincerely trust that you will do something for us. Should fortune ever favor us with an opportunity to render you assistance in any way, you can rest assured that a favor of this kind will never be forgotten.

Thanking you most cordially for any assistance which you may be able to render, and sincerely hoping and waiting for some favorable results, I am,

Most respectfully yours,

Miss Mollie Bostic

DRAW INFERENCES What kind of help might Ms. Bostic be able to offer the senator?

ASSESSMENT

Be sure to cite specific evidence from the sources as you answer the following questions.

1. **Determine Central Ideas** In the first source, how does the young woman explain the changes in women's lives?
2. **Summarize** How would you describe Ms. Bostic's attitude toward government?
3. **Draw Inferences** How might the two women's views on the economy differ?
4. **Draw Conclusions** Why might the young woman who lives on the farm be less concerned about fashion than the flapper?
5. **Analyze Interactions** What do you think Ms. Bostic might point out to the flapper if they were to meet?

GO ONLINE to access primary sources

12.8

GO ONLINE to Project Imagine: Explore African American Life to learn about the struggles, music, and culture of Africans Americans like artist and poet Gwendolyn Bennett, pictured here.

The Harlem Renaissance

As a result of World War I and the Great Migration, millions of African Americans relocated from the rural South to the urban North. This mass migration continued through the 1920s and contributed to a flowering of music and literature. Jazz and the Harlem Renaissance made a lasting impact, not only on African Americans but on the culture all Americans share.

BOUNCE to Activate Flipped Video

Objectives

Analyze how the Great Migration and the philosophies of Marcus Garvey affected African Americans in the 1920s.

Trace the development of jazz and its impact on American society and the rest of the world.

Discuss the themes explored by writers and artists of the Harlem Renaissance.

Key Terms

Marcus Garvey
jazz
Louis Armstrong
Bessie Smith
Harlem Renaissance
Claude McKay
Langston Hughes
Zora Neale Hurston

Support for Black Nationalism in Urban Areas

Like the immigrants who traveled from Europe and Asia, African Americans who left the South dreamed of a better future. They had heard stories of economic opportunity, social advancement, and greater political rights. The South, they reasoned, was a dead end. Locked into low-paying rural jobs, barred from decent schools, faced with the reality of Jim Crow oppression and the threat of lynching, they pointed their compasses north.

Migration Creates Opportunities and Challenges Migration was not easy. Many white southerners tried to keep Black laborers in the South by force. However, African Americans hoped for a better life in the North. Wages in a Detroit auto plant or a Pittsburgh steel mill were far better than what a sharecropper earned in the South. In such cities as New York, Chicago, Pittsburgh, and Cleveland, African Americans had a growing political voice. In those towns, there also existed Black middle and upper classes. African American ministers, physicians, lawyers, teachers, and journalists practiced their professions and served as role models to the younger generation.

GO ONLINE to access your digital course

>> Marcus Garvey, an African American nationalist, promoted the idea that African Americans should separate themselves from whites and support their own communities.

BOUNCE to Activate Timeline

>> The African American population of Harlem, New York continued to grow after World War I and in the 1920s.

But in coming North, African Americans had not escaped racism and oppression. On average, they were forced to live in the worst housing and labor in the lowest paying jobs. In addition, as the race riots of the summer of 1919 demonstrated, violence was a threat to African Americans north as well as south of the Mason-Dixon line. After World War I, African Americans increased their demand for a real solution to the country's racial problems.

New York City's Harlem became the focal point for the aspirations of hundreds of thousands of African Americans. Some 200,000 Blacks settled in Harlem. Migrants from the South mixed with recently arrived immigrants from Caribbean islands, such as Jamaica. This dynamic blend of different cultures and traditions bred new ideas.

The Impact of Marcus Garvey The most prominent new African American leader to emerge in the 1920s was **Marcus Garvey**. Born in Jamaica, Garvey traveled widely before immigrating to Harlem in 1916. From his travels, Garvey drew one important conclusion: Blacks were exploited everywhere. Like the Black nationalists of the 1800s before him, he promoted the idea of universal Black nationalism and organized a "Back to Africa" movement. Unlike Booker T. Washington or W.E.B. Du Bois, Garvey did not call for Black people and white people to work together but advocated the separation of the races.

Garvey's message found willing converts in American cities. By the mid-1920s, his Universal Negro Improvement Association boasted almost 2.5 million members and sympathizers. His advocacy of Black pride and Black support of Black-run businesses won considerable support.

Garvey's movement fell apart in the second half of the decade. The federal government sent him to prison for mail fraud and then deported him to Jamaica. Without his powerful leadership, the Universal Negro Improvement Association lost its focus and appeal.

Although Garvey's movement died, his ideas did not fade. The nationalist and separatist aspects of the Nation of Islam and the Black Power movement in the 1960s borrowed from Garvey's ideas. So, too, did later appeals to Black pride, self-reliance, and cultural ties to Africa. Harlem's major newspaper, the *Amsterdam News*, later wrote, "In a world where black is despised, he taught [African Americans] to admire and praise black things and black people."

DESCRIBE What challenges did many African American migrants face as they moved north?

The Evolution of Jazz

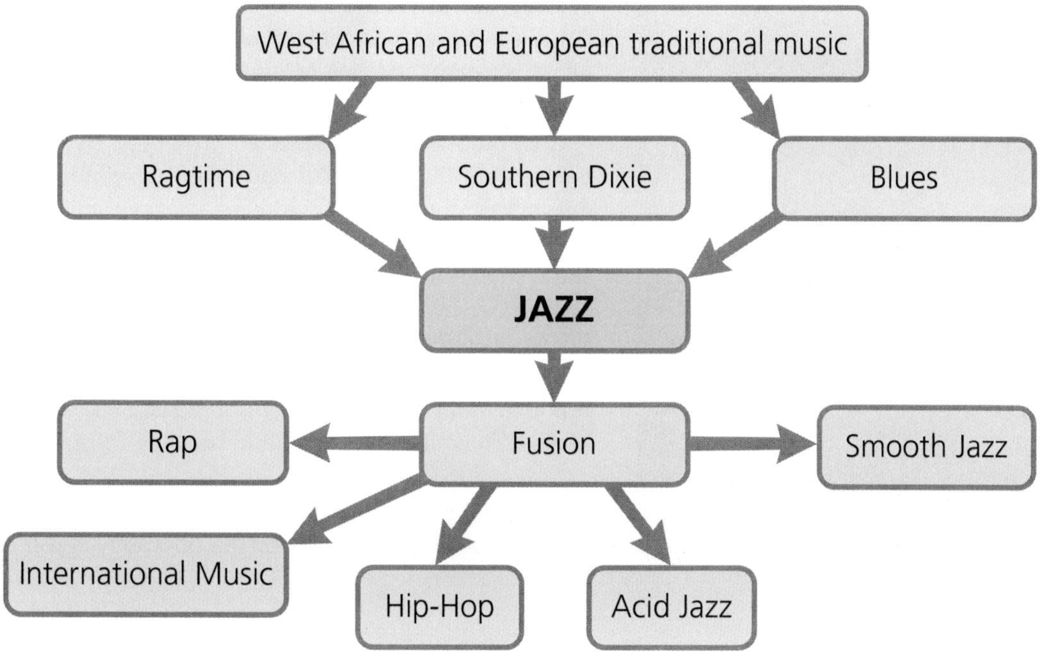

SOURCE: ALLYOURJAZZ.com

>> **Analyze Charts** How is the development of jazz related to modern musical genres such as hip-hop and rap?

The Jazz Age

It was F. Scott Fitzgerald who called the 1920s the "Jazz Age." However, it was African Americans who contributed the jazz. A truly indigenous American musical form, **jazz** is based on improvisation. Jazz musicians creatively recombine different forms of music, including African American blues and ragtime, and European-based popular music. Jazz music was fast, free, loud, rebellious, and fun—a perfect soundtrack for the 1920s.

A Unique Musical Style Jazz emerged in the South and Midwest, particularly New Orleans, where different cultures and traditions fused. Early jazz artists won fame playing in Storyville, a section of New Orleans known for its night life. From the South, it spread north with the Great Migration of African Americans.

Trumpet player **Louis Armstrong** became the unofficial ambassador of jazz. After playing with King Oliver's band in New Orleans and Chicago and with Fletcher Henderson's orchestra in New York, Armstrong began to organize his own groups. His ability to play the trumpet and his subtle sense of improvisation made him a legend and influenced the development of jazz. After Armstrong, all jazz bands featured soloists. Many also began to feature vocal soloists, such as **Bessie Smith**, the "Empress of the Blues."

Jazz Wins Worldwide Popularity Jazz was more than a musical style. It was also a symbol of the Roaring Twenties.

It was part of the Prohibition era, played in speakeasies and nightspots in New York, Chicago, St. Louis, and Los Angeles. It was the sound of the Cotton Club, one of Harlem's most famous attractions, where African Americans played African American music to all-white audiences. Phonograph records and radio spread the influence of jazz across the country and beyond. By the end of the decade, the popularity of jazz had spread to Europe as well.

But jazz was still more. It was a demonstration of the depth and richness of African American culture. Many musicians, such as Armstrong, introduced rhythms and themes with clear African roots into their music to better convey the African American cultural experience. Gerald Early, a modern scholar of English and African American studies, predicted that, in the future, America will be best remembered for three great contributions—the Constitution, baseball, and jazz. All three enriched lives, opened windows to new possibilities, and lifted the human spirit. Jazz announced that the United States was a land of shared cultures and traditions.

>> Duke Ellington's music integrated "big-band" and jazz sounds and increased the popularity of jazz orchestras.

The jazz movement was then a reflection of an evolving African American identity born of shared historical experience, including the contemporary experiences of the Great Migration and continuing troubled race relations.

Jazz quickly bridged the races. Trumpeter Bix Beiderbecke (Bì der behk) became the first white musician to contribute to the styles and popularity of jazz. Jazz sounds influenced such white songwriters and composers as Cole Porter, Irving Berlin, and George Gershwin, whose jazz-inspired orchestral work *Rhapsody in Blue* premiered in 1924. The title of a song by African American bandleader Duke Ellington best captures how jazz changed popular music: "It Don't Mean a Thing If It Ain't Got That Swing."

☑ **IDENTIFY SUPPORTING DETAILS** What effect did the Great Migration have on the popularity of jazz?

The Harlem Renaissance

Jazz and blues were expressions of the African American experience. The pain of the African American experience can be heard in the blues, and the joy of that experience in the soaring notes of jazz. The range of such African American musicians as Duke Ellington and Cab Calloway speaks to the varieties of African American life. But in the 1920s, there were other expressions of African American culture. Novelists, poets, and artists celebrated their culture and explored questions of race in America. This flowering of African American culture became known as the **Harlem Renaissance**. The Harlem Renaissance helped give a new vocabulary and dynamic to race relations in the United States.

>> African American music legends, including Duke Ellington and Cab Calloway, played regularly at Harlem's many nightclubs.

Cultural Movements in Literature and Art

In the 1920s, the term the "New Negro" entered the American vocabulary. At the time, the term *Negro* was preferred by many Black Americans. The "New Negro" suggested a radical break with the past. No longer would African Americans silently endure the old ways of exploitation and discrimination. The new mood was most vividly expressed in Harlem, which attracted African American artists and writers from all over the country and beyond. In their work, these artists and writers explored the pains and joys of being Black in America, leaving a legacy that spoke to all Americans of all times.

Artists such as Aaron Douglas created paintings with stylized art that reflected African Americans' racial pride and collective historical experience, while other artists such as Jacob Lawrence and Archibald J. Motley, Jr., expressed similar sentiment in their colorful paintings of urban life.

Many writers communicated the same themes. Jean Toomer's *Cane* (1923) set the literary tone for the Harlem Renaissance. A collection of short stories, poems, and sketches, *Cane* presented African American life and folk culture in all its richness.

Soon, other African American writers joined Toomer at the forefront of the Harlem Renaissance. Jamaican immigrant **Claude McKay** was the most militant of these writers. In his novels and poems, McKay showed ordinary African Americans struggling for dignity and advancement in the face of discrimination and economic hardships. After white racists unleashed a wave of violence against African Americans in Chicago, McKay wrote a poem that expressed his sense of anger and militancy:

> If we must die—let it not be like hogs,
>
> hunted and penned in an inglorious spot.
>
> While round us bark the mad and hungry dogs,
>
> Making their mock at our accursed lot.
>
> What though before us lies the open grave?
>
> Like men we will face the murderous, cowardly pack,
>
> Pressed to the wall, dying but fighting back!
>
> —Claude McKay, "If We Must Die"

McKay represented the political and ideological left wing of the Harlem Renaissance. More in the center was **Langston Hughes**, probably the most powerful African American literary voice of his time. For Hughes, the force of the movement was a celebration of African culture and life. In more than 50 works of fiction, poetry, journalism, and criticism, he captured the remarkable diversity of everyday African American life. In the last line of his autobiography *The Big Sea,* Hughes wrote, "Literature is a big sea full of many fish. I let down my nets and pulled. I'm still pulling."

>> The writer Jean Toomer's works appealed to African Americans to remember their pasts. **Infer** Why would Toomer emphasize this theme in his works?

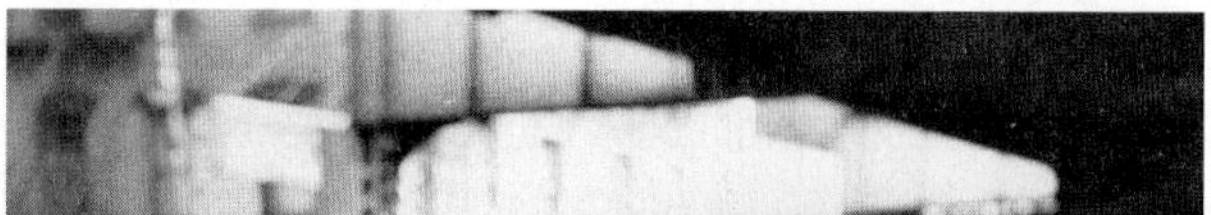

>> Langston Hughes, shown here in the 1950s, emphasized the celebration of the unique aspects of African American culture and history and promoted his vision of a racially integrated, but just, society.

BOUNCE to Activate Gallery

>> In her work, writer Zora Neale Hurston gave voice to the desire of many women, both African American and white, for greater independence. Hurston's work also explored the rich cultural heritage of African Americans.

Another powerful voice was **Zora Neale Hurston**. Hurston traveled the rural back roads of her native Florida, collecting folk tales in books such as *Mules and Men*. But Hurston also looked to the future. Her 1937 novel *Their Eyes Were Watching God* expressed the new longing for independence felt by many women, Black and white.

The Lasting Impact of the Harlem Renaissance The Harlem Renaissance gave a new public voice to African American culture. It altered the way many white Americans viewed African American culture and even the way some African Americans viewed themselves. James Weldon Johnson, poet and secretary of the NAACP, noted:

> A great deal has been accomplished in this decade of 'renaissance'. . . .Today, one may see undesirable stories, but one may also read stories about Negro singers, Negro actors, Negro authors, Negro poets. The connotations of the very word *Negro* have changed. A generation ago many Negroes were half or wholly ashamed of the term.
>
> Today, they have every reason to be proud of it.
>
> —James Weldon Johnson, article in *Harper's Magazine*, 1928

The movement was not, however, without its critics. Some, such as Langston Hughes, expressed a degree of disillusionment with the movement's inability to improve the political status and economic opportunities of African Americans. However, the artistic forms and cultural debates associated with the Harlem Renaissance continue even today.

Although the Harlem Renaissance came to a close as the nation fell into economic difficulty in the late 1920s, the sense of group identity and African American solidarity that it created would become part of the bedrock on which the later civil rights movement would be constructed.

☑ **IDENTIFY** What themes did Langston Hughes and Zora Neale Hurston explore?

☑ ASSESSMENT

1. **Compare** Describe how the ways in which African Americans migrated during the Great Migration were similar to the immigrants who arrived from other countries in the early 1900s.
2. **Summarize** Discuss the benefits and the pitfalls of African American life in the North.
3. **Draw Conclusions** Discuss the collapse of the Universal Negro Improvement Association and describe its lasting legacy in American culture.
4. **Generate Explanations** Explain why the "Jazz Age" represented an important transition for American society.
5. **Apply Concepts** Analyze the importance of Langston Hughes's writing during the Harlem Renaissance.
6. **Connections to Today** In the 1920s, movie stars and sports figures became role models for many people. Are modern celebrities admired in the same way or has the nature of celebrity changed? Explain your reasoning.

Primary Sources

Poems: Langston Hughes

Langston Hughes wrote about how it felt to be African American, describing a range of emotions from the pain of racial prejudice to his deep pride in his culture and heritage. The poems below are among his most famous.

>> Langston Hughes stands at the front of this photo of writers and intellectuals taken in 1924.

Primary Source 1

The Negro Speaks of Rivers

I've known rivers:
I've known rivers ancient as the world and older than the flow of human blood in human veins.

My soul has grown deep like the rivers.

I bathed in the Euphrates [river in the Middle East] when dawns were young.

I built my hut near the Congo [river in Central Africa] and it lulled me to sleep.
I looked upon the Nile [river in Egypt] and raised the pyramids above it.

I heard the singing of the Mississippi when Abe Lincoln went down to New Orleans, and I've seen its muddy bosom turn all golden in the sunset.

I've known rivers:
Ancient, dusky [dark] rivers.

My soul has grown deep like the rivers.

☑ **DETERMINE CENTRAL IDEAS** What point do you think Hughes is making when he names four different rivers around the world, at four different periods in history?

Primary Source 2

My People

The night is beautiful,
So the faces of my people.

The stars are beautiful,
So the eyes of my people.

Beautiful, also, is the sun.
Beautiful, also, are the souls of my people.

☑ **COMPARE AND CONTRAST** Why does this poem compare "his people" to the night, the stars, and the sun?

Primary Source 3

The Negro Mother

Children, I come back today
To tell you a story of the long dark way
That I had to climb, that I had to know
In order that the race might live and grow.
Look at my face—dark as the night—
Yet shining like the sun with love's true light.
I am the child they stole from the sand
Three hundred years ago in Africa's land.
I am the dark girl who crossed the wide sea

Carrying in my body the seed of the free.
I am the woman who worked in the field
Bringing the cotton and the corn to yield.
I am the one who labored as a slave,
Beaten and mistreated for the work that I gave—
Children sold away from me, husband sold, too.
No safety, no love, no respect was I due.
Three hundred years in the deepest South:
But God put a song and a prayer in my mouth.
God put a dream like steel in my soul.
Now, through my children, I'm reaching the goal.
Now, through my children, young and free,
I realize the blessings denied to me.
I couldn't read then. I couldn't write.
I had nothing, back there in the night.
Sometimes, the valley was filled with tears,
But I kept trudging on through the lonely years.
Sometimes, the road was hot with sun,
But I had to keep on till my work was done:
I had to keep on! No stopping for me—
I was the seed of the coming Free.
I nourished the dream that nothing could smother
Deep in my breast—the Negro mother.
I had only hope then, but now through you,
Dark ones of today, my dreams must come true:
All you dark children in the world out there,
Remember my sweat, my pain, my despair.
Remember my years, heavy with sorrow—
And make of those years a torch for tomorrow.
Make of my past a road to the light
Out of the darkness, the ignorance, the night.
Lift high my banner out of the dust.
Stand like free men supporting my trust.
Believe in the right, let none push you back.
Remember the whip and the slaver's track.
Remember how the strong in struggle and strife
Still bar you the way, and deny you life—
But march ever forward, breaking down bars.
Look ever upward at the sun and the stars.
Oh, my dark children, may my dreams and my prayers
Impel you forever up the great stairs—
For I will be with you till no white brother
Dares keep down the children of the Negro mother.

SUMMARIZE How would you summarize the message of this poem?

Primary Source 4

Harlem

What happens to a dream deferred?
Does it dry up
like a raisin in the sun?
Or fester like a sore—
And then run?
Does it stink like rotten meat?
Or crust and sugar over—
like a syrupy sweet?

Maybe it just sags
like a heavy load.

Or does it explode?

DETERMINE MEANING What is the meaning of the phrase "a dream deferred"?

ASSESSMENT

1. **Analyze Style and Rhetoric** In the first two poems, Hughes repeats words and sentence structures. What effect does this technique create?
2. **Identify Author's Point of View** What is the speaker's attitude toward his identity as an African American?
3. **Identify Cause and Effect** Hughes was one of the important writers of the Harlem Renaissance, a 1920s creative movement of African American artists and writers. What effect you think Hughes's poems might have had on other African Americans at this time?
4. **Determine Meaning** What is the political message of "Harlem"?
5. **Draw Inferences** Many of Hughes's poems reference women or mothers. How does this connect these poems to the social changes unfolding in the 1920s?

Connections to Today

A vlogger recording a broadcast from a local restaurant

Take Action About Celebrity and Mass Culture

In the 1920s, the new media of motion pictures and radio helped create a mass culture of celebrity that unified the country. Today, technology has created new kinds of media and celebrities who are just as influential.

1. **Choose** one of the following celebrity-culture topics:
   - **The End of Merit-based Fame:** Research how celebrity became based on media exposure and image rather than on merit, talent, or achievement.
   - **Privacy vs. Scrutiny:** Investigate stories of celebrities whose lives have been negatively affected by constant scrutiny and online abuse. Do celebrities automatically forfeit their privacy in exchange for fame?
   - **Unity or Division?:** Does mass media provide Americans with a common frame of reference that brings them together to share a unified national identity? Or does mass media intensify individual and group differences, making Americans less unified?
2. **Ask Questions** Create a list of questions you have about the topic.
3. **Learn** about your topic, using a variety of sources, such as online sources, primary and/or secondary sources, data, or interviews.
4. **Write a Blog Entry** Write a blog entry on the theme of celebrity or mass culture. Share your views on the aspect of celebrity or mass culture that you studied.

Topic 12 Quick Study Guide

LESSON SUMMARIES

Use these Lesson Summaries, and the longer versions available online, to review the key ideas for each lesson in this Topic.

Lesson 1: America Enters World War I

In Europe a political assassination, an arms race, nationalism, and a system of alliances helped set off World War I in 1914. The United States tried to remain neutral but entered the war on the side of the Allies in 1917.

Lesson 2: The Home Front During World War I

The United States quickly enlarged its army and increased food production. Congress banned certain publications and limited freedom of speech. The war brought social change as jobs opened up for women and African Americans.

Lesson 3: The End of World War I

America's involvement in the war reduced submarine attacks and helped force Germany's surrender. President Wilson promoted the League of Nations but opposition in Congress stopped U.S. participation in that organization.

Lesson 4: The Postwar Economy Booms

By 1920, the United States was the richest, most industrialized country in the world. Mass production, especially of automobiles, brought an economic boom. During the consumer revolution, Americans bought goods and stocks on credit. The suburbs grew as more people used their cars to commute.

Lesson 5: Government in the 1920s

President Warren Harding, elected in 1920, reduced regulations on business. His administration was rocked by bribery scandals. After Harding's death, President Calvin Coolidge established a more honest administration that also favored big business.

Lesson 6: An Unsettled Society

After World War I, tensions and conflicts increased across America. The conservatism and fundamentalism of rural society clashed with the modernist values of the cities. Fears of communism provoked a Red Scare, while racism and anxieties over immigration helped revive the Ku Klux Klan. The banning of alcohol led to organized crime.

Lesson 7: The Roaring Twenties

As urban Americans' wages rose in the 1920s, they enjoyed the new entertainment technology of movies, phonographs, and radios. Women ran for political office and more joined the workforce. Modernism in clothing, psychology and the arts took hold.

Lesson 8: The Harlem Renaissance

Millions of African Americans left the South to find jobs in northern cities, where they developed middle class communities and a growing political voice. Harlem in New York City became the center of a creative community producing influential music, literature and art.

QUEST! FINDINGS

Discuss the League of Nations Refer to your responses to the Quest Connections to help you discuss the League of Nations. Use the rubric and other Quest resources to guide your work.

GO ONLINE to access lesson summaries

VISUAL REVIEW

Use these graphics to review some of the key terms, people, and ideas from this Topic.

Causes and Effects of America's Entry into World War I

CAUSES	EVENT	EFFECTS
• Many Americans have cultural ties with Britain and France. • Reports of German atrocities outrage Americans. • Germany's submarine attacks on shipping. • The Zimmerman note reveals proposed deal between Germany and Mexico.	• America Enters World War I	• The Allies defeat the Central Powers. • The Government's role in daily life increases. • African Americans and Mexican Americans migrate north. • More women enter the workforce. • The U.S. adopts isolationism in foreign policy. • The U.S. becomes a world economic power.

New Cultural Trends

Mass Culture	Radio and movies influence people of different regions.
Prohibition	Crime rises as Americans defy the ban on alcohol.
Modernism	The arts reflect the rapid changes in attitudes and values underway in industrial societies.
Fundamentalism	Many Christians promote a literal interpretation of the Bible and return to "traditional values".
Jazz	New musical genre blends African American and European styles.
Harlem Renaissance	Literature and art express pride and aspirations of African Americans.

Postwar Economic Boom

U.S. ECONOMY IN THE 1920S

- Bull market in the stock market
- Growth of the advertising industry
- Newly available technology
- Buying on credit and installment buying

Topic 12 Assessment

KEY TERMS, PEOPLE, AND IDEAS

1. Why did the **Zimmermann note** outrage American public opinion?
2. What measures did the U.S. government take to prepare Americans for war?
3. How did World War I change the lives of minorities and women?
4. Why didn't the United States support the **League of Nations**?
5. Why did **inflation** and other economic problems follow demobilization?
6. How did Ford's system of **mass production** and **assembly lines** affect the economy?
7. What was the issue behind the **Scopes Trial** of 1925?
8. What caused the **Red Scare**?
9. What social changes led to the resurgence of the **Ku Klux Klan**?

CRITICAL THINKING

10. **Make Generalizations** What long-term trends led to the outbreak of World War I?
11. **Make Inferences** How did the technologies of the second Industrial Revolution shape the strategies and course of World War I?
12. **Identify Cause and Effect** (a.) Evaluate how the economic boom of the 1920s changed consumers, businesses, manufacturing, and marketing practices. (b.) How might some of these practices have led to economic problems?
13. **Summarize** How did the war affect America's international economic standing?
14. **Draw Conclusions** What was the relationship between modernism and the Fundamentalist movement?
15. **Compare and Contrast** How did Marcus Garvey's views differ from the views of Booker T. Washington and W.E.B. Du Bois?
16. **Analyze Maps** Study the map below. What does the map illustrate? What is the significance of the different colored blocks of states?

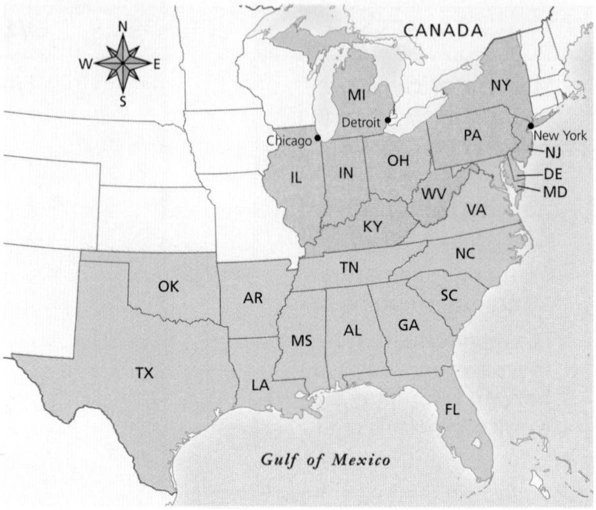

17. **Writing Activity: Write an Argument** Analyze this excerpt from a letter from Henry Cabot Lodge to President Woodrow Wilson. Consider how Lodge's view of America's place in the world differs from Wilson's. Write one or two paragraphs that use logical reasoning to point out the differences between Lodge's and Cabot's points of view. Make sure your writing lays out your ideas clearly, provides evidence, and has a clear conclusion.

> I can never be anything else but an American, and I must think of the United States first, and when I think of the United States first . . . I am thinking of what is best for the world, for if the United States fails, the best hopes of mankind fail with it.
> —*Henry Cabot Lodge, letter to President Woodrow Wilson, 1919*

18. **Connections to Today** The democratization of fame is one of the ways in which technology is changing our lives. But is "going viral" a worthy goal? Is celebrity culture reinforcing false values, fantasies, and illusions? Consider the positive and negative effects of this trend on society and on celebrities themselves.

DOCUMENT-BASED QUESTIONS

During World War I, open debate and political dissent were discouraged and sometimes punished. Read the documents below, then answer the questions that follow.

DOCUMENT A

These excerpts are from laws that Congress passed to support America's war effort during World War I.

> . . . and whoever, when the United States is at war, shall willfully cause or attempt to cause insubordination, disloyalty, mutiny, refusal of duty, in the military or naval forces of the United States, or shall willfully obstruct the recruiting or enlistment service of the United States, to the injury of the service of the United States, shall be punished by a fine of not more than $10,000 or imprisonment for not more than twenty years, or both.
>
> —*Espionage Act, 1917*

> Whoever, when the United States is at war . . . shall willfully utter, print, write, or publish any disloyal, profane, scurrilous, or abusive language about the form of government of the United States, or the Constitution of the United States. . . shall be punished by a fine of not more than $10,000 or imprisonment for not more than 20 years, or both. . .
>
> —*Sedition Act, 1918*

DOCUMENT B

DOCUMENT C

This excerpt is from the trial of Eugene Debs.

> If the law under which I have been convicted is a good law, then there is no reason why sentence should not be pronounced upon me. I listened to all that was said in this court in support and justification of this prosecution, but my mind remains unchanged. I look upon the Espionage Law as a despotic enactment in flagrant conflict with democratic principles and with the spirit of free institutions. . . .
>
> —*Eugene V. Debs, Statement to the Court, 1918*

DOCUMENT D

This is an excerpt from the Supreme Court's decision in *Schenck v. United States,* which tested the constitutionality of the 1917 Espionage Act.

> . . . The question in every case is whether the words used are used in such circumstances and are of such a nature as to create a clear and present danger that they will bring about the substantive evils that Congress has a right to prevent. It is a question of proximity and degree. When a nation is at war many things that might be said in time of peace are such a hindrance to its effort that their utterance will not be endured so long as men fight and that no Court could regard them as protected by any constitutional right.
>
> —*Schenck v. United States, 1919*

19. The laws appearing in Document A had the effect of

A. restricting religious freedom.
B. ending the right to bear arms.
C. suspending the right to jury trial.
D. restricting freedom of speech.

20. Analyze Images What point of view is represented by the demonstrators shown in Document B?

21. In Document C, the person being tried clearly believes that the Espionage Act

A. protects freedom of expression.
B. is an attack on democratic freedoms.
C. undermines religious freedom.
D. would end freedom of assembly.

22. In Document D, the Supreme Court confirms that in times of "clear and present danger" the government may

A. institute a draft to enlarge the army.
B. imprison all dissenters.
C. take control of industrial output.
D. determine what speech is dangerous.

23. Writing Task Write a paragraph explaining whether you think the government was justified in curtailing freedom of speech after the U.S. entered World War I. Use the sources as well as additional information you have learned about this issue.

Topic 13

The Great Depression and the New Deal (1928–1941)

ESSENTIAL QUESTION What should governments do?

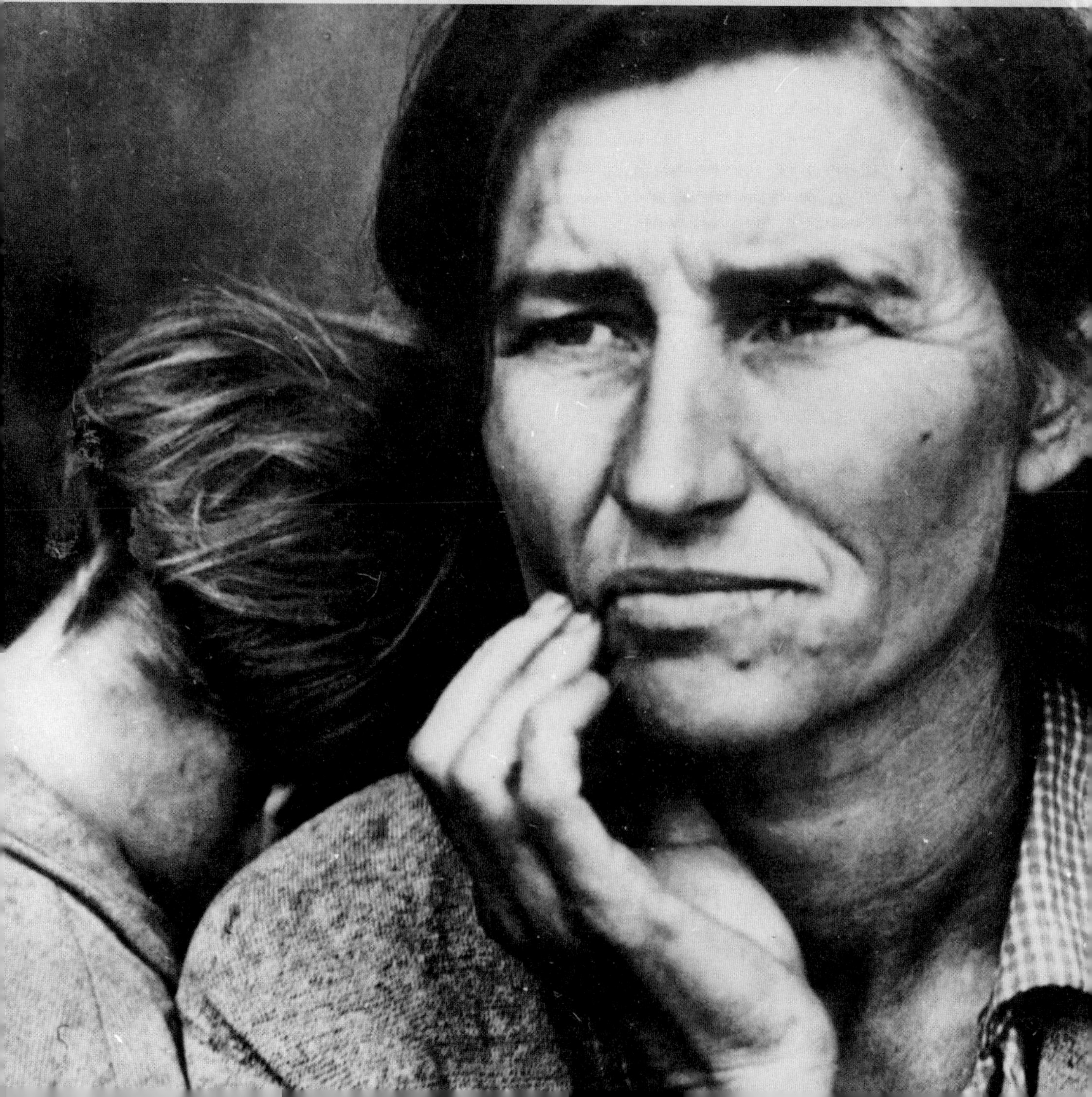

project Imagine

GO ONLINE for immersive experiences designed to help you experience the struggles of Americans during the Great Depression through rich primary sources. Also access the eText, videos, Biographies, and other online resources.

Dorothea Lange's famous photograph, "Migrant Mother"

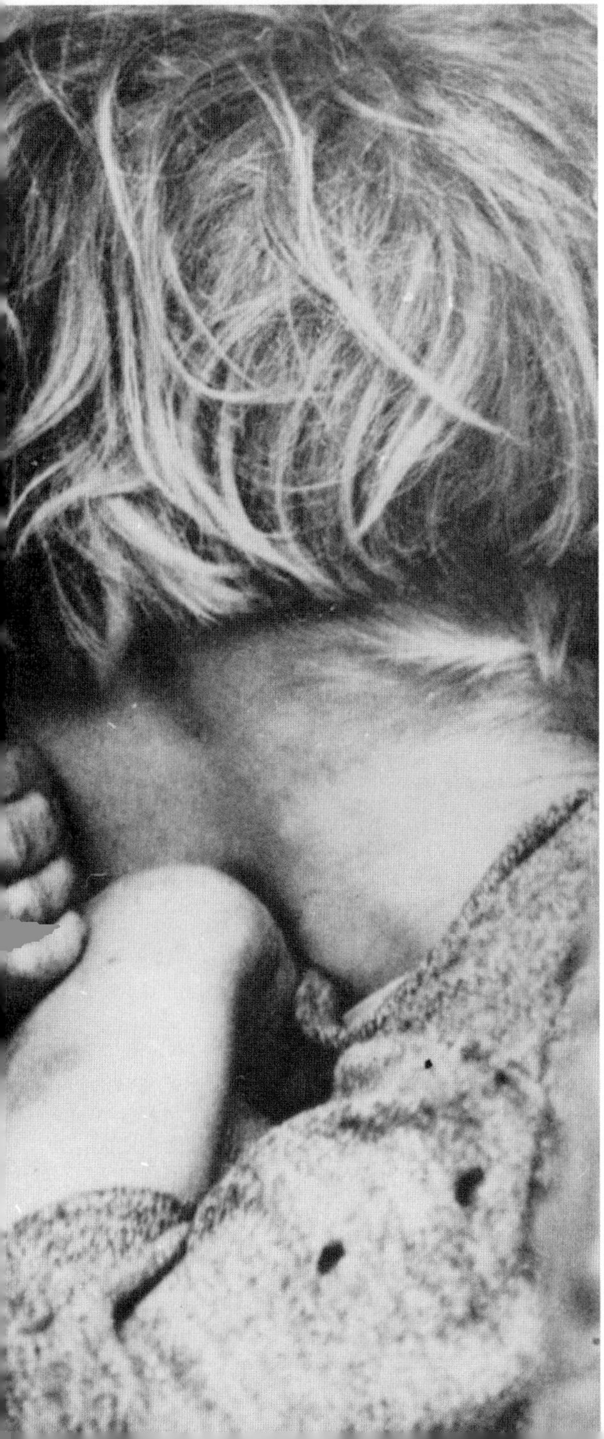

Connections to Today

You awaken one morning to a black sky lit with an eerie orange glow. Ash is raining down and winds roar in the distance. This sort of experience is all too familiar to Californians, where wildfires have become larger, more common, and more destructive over the last decade.

Compare this to the scene on the Great Plains during the 1930s: Black skies created by mile-high dust clouds that blocked out the sun, covered cars, and seeped into homes. What role have humans played in helping to bring about these environmental disasters?

NBC LEARN

Learn about the impact of Dorothea Lange's photography

BOUNCE to Activate My Story Video

Topic 13 Overview

In this Topic you'll learn about the events of the Great Depression and the New Deal. Look at the lesson outline and explore the timeline. As you study this Topic, you'll complete the Quest Inquiry.

LESSON OUTLINE

13.1 Causes of the Depression
13.2 Americans Suffer
13.3 Two Presidents Respond
13.4 The New Deal Expands
13.5 Effects of the New Deal
13.6 Culture During the Depression

Key Events of the Great Depression and the New Deal

1929
Stock market crashes; Great Depression begins

1935
Social Security Act is passed

1939
The movie *Gone With the Wind* is released

1925 1930 1935 1940

1932
Franklin D. Roosevelt elected President

1938
Fair Labor Standards Act allows workers more rights

1940
Roosevelt wins third term as President

QUEST! INQUIRY

Opposition to the New Deal

As the government took drastic measures to deal with the Great Depression, why did so many oppose these "New Deal" programs? In this Quest you'll investigate this question and then write an essay explaining the reasons for this opposition.

STEP 1
Watch a video about a New Deal public works project. Then discuss it in class or with a partner.

STEP 2
Examine six sources related to New Deal programs and answer the questions attached to each. Prepare to write an essay in which you explain why some Americans opposed the New Deal.

STEP 3
In your essay, explain the problems caused by the Depression and the solutions discussed in the documents. Consider the advantages and disadvantages of each solution.

STEP 4
Reflect on the process of analyzing the documents and writing the essay. Then complete the Self-Assessment.

GO ONLINE to access complete Quest materials

13.1

When depositors went to the Union Bank in New York City in 1931, they could not withdraw their money. **Predict Consequences** How do you think the American public reacted to bank failures?

BOUNCE to Activate Flipped Video

Objectives

Identify how weaknesses in the economy in the 1920s caused the Great Depression.

Explain why the stock market crashed in 1929 and the crash's effect on the economy.

Describe how the Great Depression deepened in the United States and spread overseas.

Identify the causes of the Great Depression and discuss how historians differ about them.

Key Terms

business cycle
gross national product
Herbert Hoover
speculation
Black Tuesday
Great Depression
Hawley-Smoot Tariff

GO ONLINE to access your digital course

Causes of the Depression

During the Roaring Twenties, many Americans enjoyed what seemed like limitless prosperity. Then, in October 1929, the mighty bull market crashed. As production fell and unemployment rose, the U.S. economy lurched into a period of dramatic decline.

Hidden Economic Problems in the Roaring Twenties

At first, some Americans saw this contraction as a regular contraction of the nation's **business cycle**, which explains the periodic growth and contraction of the economy. It most certainly was not regular. Production, employment, and income will normally expand, contract, and expand again over time in a cyclical way. However, a number of factors combined in the 1920s to turn the normal, cyclical expansions and contractions of the nation's economy into an economic collapse in the 1930s.

For most of the 1920s, however, Republican leaders exuded confidence about both their party and their country. The Roaring Twenties had been a Republican decade. In 1920, Americans sent Warren G. Harding to the White House, and four years after that, they sent Calvin Coolidge. Neither election had been close.

Once in office, both Presidents watched the country grow increasingly prosperous. Consumption and the stock market both went up. So did the **gross national product**, which is the total value of the goods and services produced by a country.

No matter what index an economist chose to consult, the conclusion was always the same: Times were good in America—and they were getting better. Republicans took credit for the bullish economy, and most Americans heartily agreed.

Hoover Sweeps to Victory When the Republicans met at their 1928 nominating convention, they chose **Herbert Hoover**—an accomplished public servant—to run for the White House. Born in Iowa, Hoover was orphaned as a child. But he overcame this personal tragedy and eventually graduated from Stanford University with a degree in geology. He became a mining engineer and worked all over the world. By 1914, after amassing a vast fortune, he retired from engineering and devoted himself to public service.

Herbert Hoover came to the attention of Americans during World War I, first as the brilliant coordinator of the Belgium relief program and then as head of the Food Administration. During the Harding and Coolidge administrations, Hoover served as Secretary of Commerce. His philosophy was simple but effective.

He stressed the importance of competition, but he also believed in voluntary cooperation between labor and management. American greatness showed itself, Hoover maintained, when owners, workers, and government officials converged on common goals.

With a solid record of accomplishments behind him and seemingly endless prosperity in front of him, Hoover was a formidable presidential candidate in 1928. While his campaign ads noted how Republicans had "put the proverbial 'chicken in every pot,'" Hoover spoke glowingly of ending poverty in America:

> By adherence to the principles of decentralized self-government, ordered liberty, equal opportunity, and freedom to the individual, our American experiment in human welfare has yielded a degree of well-being unparalleled in all the world. It has come nearer to the abolition of poverty, to the abolition of fear of want, than humanity has ever reached before.
>
> —Herbert Hoover, campaign speech, 1928

>> An affluent middle-class family poses for a portrait in 1924. Many families bought their first automobile and radio during the 1920s as mass-produced consumer products became more affordable.

>> During his 1928 campaign, Herbert Hoover emphasized his belief that competition was vital to ensure robust economic growth.

>> Mechanized farm equipment became more common during the 1920s, but many farmers still used basic equipment such as this horse-drawn plow.

>> The gap between rich and poor widened in the 1920s; the wealthy built large homes and began to fill them with lavish furnishings.

Hoover's contest with Democratic nominee Alfred E. Smith of New York was, in the end, no contest at all. Americans voted overwhelmingly for Hoover, prosperity, and the continuation of Republican government. When the new President took office in March 1929, America was awash in a sea of confidence. Few imagined that an economic disaster lay just seven months in the future.

But even as Hoover delivered his victory speeches, economic troubles were beginning to worry some Americans. The prosperity of the 1920s was not as deep or as sturdy as Hoover claimed. Throughout the U.S. economy, there were troubling signs.

Farmers Face Challenges After World War I

American farmers faced difficult times during the 1920s. Farmers made up one fourth of the American workforce during the decade.

To meet the unprecedented crop demands created by World War I, they had increased harvest yields and bought more land to put under the plow. They also bought costly tractors and other mechanized farm equipment to help them meet demand. Farmers amassed huge debts doing this, and the additional mortgage payments followed them into the 1920s.

After the war, the demand for American crops fell sharply. Despite this drop, postwar production remained high because of increasingly mechanized farm equipment and more intensive farming methods. Farms were getting bigger and yielding bumper crops at harvest. However, farmers were failing to sell off their huge crop surpluses and to pay the debts they owed banks and other institutions.

The result was a rural depression that affected millions of Americans. Hard-pressed to pay their debts, forced to sell their goods in a glutted and competitive world market, and confronted by several natural disasters, farmers did not share in the boom times of the 1920s. They did not have the cash to buy the new consumer goods produced by American industries.

They lived largely on credit from month to month, often teetering on the brink of financial ruin. Any downward slide in the economy was likely to hit America's struggling farmers first and hardest.

A Significant Gap Between the Rich and the Poor Unlike farmers, industrial workers participated in the great national success story. During the 1920s, their wages rose steadily, as did their disposable income. Many purchased Model T Fords along with a variety of other consumer products. Though they were certainly not wealthy, industrial laborers were

Income Distribution, 1929

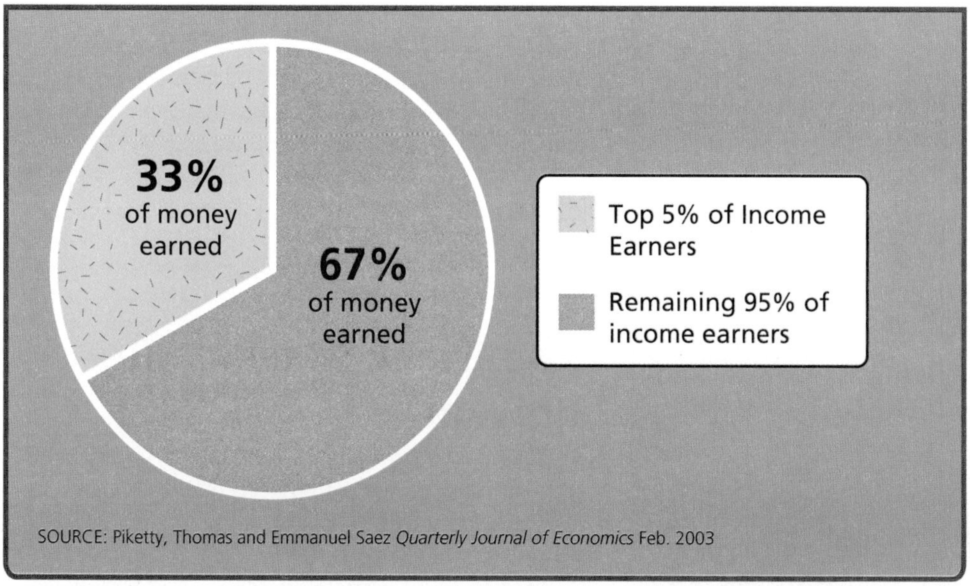

>> **Analyze Graphs** Based on the information in the pie chart, what share of total income earned in 1929 did the top 5 percent of income earners account for?

in a better financial position than their fathers had been a generation before.

But the problem was that while wages rose gradually, worker productivity increased astronomically. Between 1923 and 1929, output per person-hour jumped 32 percent, but workers' wages inched up only 8 percent. During that same period, corporate profits from worker output skyrocketed 65 percent. All these figures pointed to the fact that during the 1920s, the rich became much, much richer, while industrial workers simply became less poor.

In few periods of the country's history have so small a number of rich Americans dominated such a large percentage of the country's total wealth. In 1929, for example, the wealthiest 1 percent of the population earned about the same amount of money as the bottom 42 percent.

Uneven Distribution of Wealth Creates Problems This uneven distribution of the nation's wealth created economic problems. More than 60 percent of all American families had yearly incomes of less than $2,000 per year. In contrast, 24,000 of the country's wealthiest families enjoyed annual incomes of more than $100,000, which was 50 times more than what most families were earning. But these wealthy families did not eat 50 times more food than lower-income families. The wealthiest households did not purchase 50 times more automobiles or radios or ovens. The rich undoubtedly spent a lot on consumer products. The problem was that the wealthiest few could not buy enough to keep the economy booming.

A healthy economy needs more people to buy more products, which in turn creates even more wealth. In this way, a healthy economy avoids underconsumption that can limit economic growth. The uneven distribution of wealth in the 1920s pointed to an uncertain future for the American economy.

From the overproduction of the struggling farmer to the underconsumption of the lower-income industrial worker, deep-seated problems created economic instability. Too many Americans did not have enough money to buy what they needed or wanted.

Americans Rely on Credit For a time, the expansion of credit partially hid this problem. Americans bought automobiles, appliances, radios, and other goods on credit. Using the installment plan, they paid a small percentage down and the rest over a period of months or years. By the end of the decade, 80 percent of radios and 60 percent of cars were purchased on installment credit. Americans even bought stock on credit, making such stock purchases on margin. Every year, Americans accumulated more debt. In the past, they had feared

>> Dazed investors gathered outside the New York Stock Exchange as the stock market crashed on October 29, 1929.

>> Despair gripped many Americans following the stock market crash. Some people who were hardest hit by the crash had to sell their belongings just to pay their bills.

debt and put off buying goods until they had all of the cash to pay for those items.

Easy credit changed this behavior during the 1920s. But the growing credit burden could mask the problem of Americans living beyond their means for only so long before the economy imploded.

RECALL What problem did farmers face following World War I?

The Stock Market Hits Bottom

By 1929, some economists were observing that soaring stock prices were based on little more than confidence. The prices had no basis in reality. Although other experts disagreed, it became clear that too much money was being poured into stock **speculation**, as investors gambled (often with money they did not even have) on high-risk stocks in hopes of turning a quick profit. If the market's upward climb suddenly reversed course, many investors would face economic devastation.

On September 3, 1929, the stock market began to sputter and fall. Prices peaked and then slid downward in an uneven way. At the end of October, however, the slide gave way to a free fall.

After the Dow Jones average dropped 21 points in one hour on October 23, many investors concluded that the boom was over. They had lost confidence—the very thing that had kept the market up for so long.

The next day, October 24, came to be known as Black Thursday. With confidence in the stock market failing, nervous investors started to sell. Stock in General Electric that once sold at $400 a share plunged to $283. Across the United States, investors raced to pull their money out of the stock market. On October 29, **Black Tuesday**, the bottom fell out. More than 16 million shares were sold as the stock market collapsed in the Great Crash. Billions of dollars were lost. Whole fortunes were wiped out in hours. Many speculators who had bought stock on margin lost everything they had. President Hoover tried to soothe Americans by insisting that the "business of the country is on a sound and prosperous basis." But by November 13, the Dow Jones average had dropped like a brick from its September high of 381 to 198.7. The Great Crash represented a rare extreme in the nation's business cycle and a turning point for the American economy.

IDENTIFY What is stock speculation?

ECONOMIC TRENDS & THE GREAT DEPRESSION

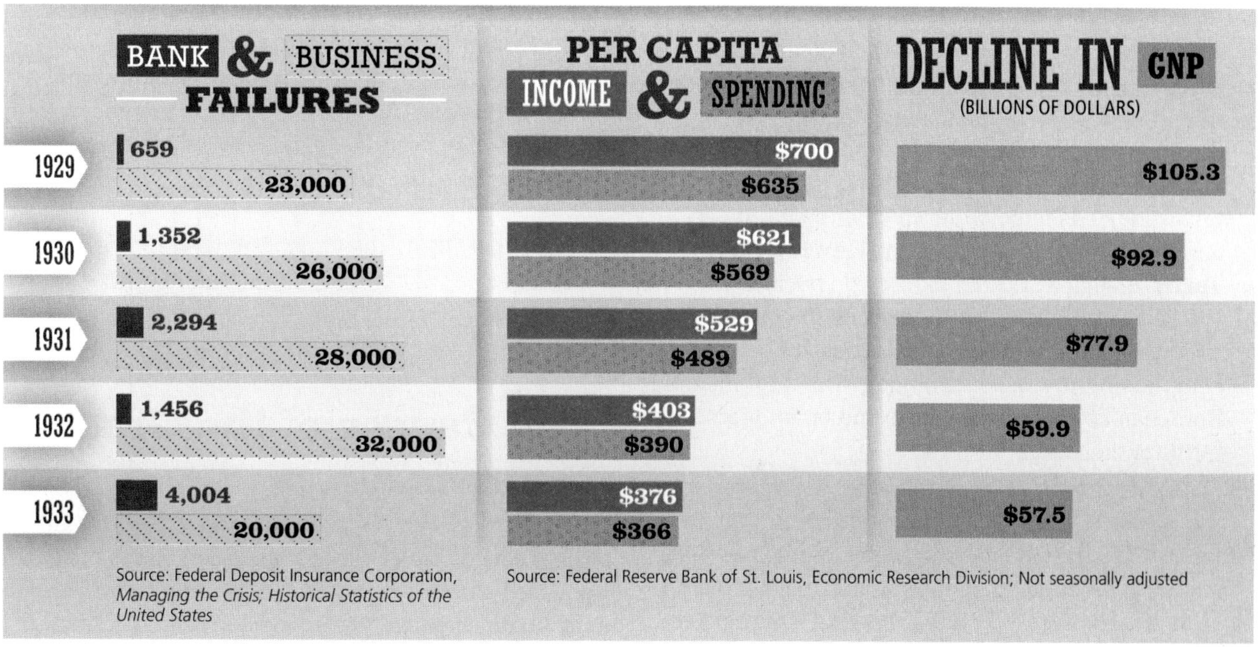

>> **Analyze Graphs** According to the Per Capita Income and Spending graph, were Americans as a whole going into debt during the depression, or were they "just getting by"?

BOUNCE to Activate Chart

The Great Depression Begins

The stock market crash marked the beginning of the **Great Depression**, a period lasting from 1929 to 1941 in which the economy faltered and unemployment soared. Though it did not start the depression by itself, the crash sparked a chain of events that quickened the collapse of the U.S. economy.

Bank Failures Occur Across the Nation One of the first institutions to feel the effects of the stock market crash was the country's banking system. The crisis in confidence continued as frightened depositors feared for their money and tried to withdraw it from their banks. Few banks could survive a sustained "run" of requests by depositors for their money. In 1929, some 650 commercial banks failed. A year later, 1,350 failed. And a year after that, nearly 2,300 went under. By 1932, many Americans feared that no banks would be left standing.

Another cause of many bank failures was misguided monetary policy by the Federal Reserve. During the 1920s, the Federal Reserve, which regulates the amount of money in circulation, cut interest rates to stimulate economic growth. But in 1929, worried about investors speculating too much with borrowed money, the "Fed" limited the money supply to discourage lending. As a result, there was too little money in circulation to help the economy after the stock market crash. When plummeting stock prices sent investors to the banks to secure whatever hard money they had left, the banks were cleaned out of currency and forced to close.

Decreasing Demand Proves Challenging for Businesses Banks were not the only institutions to face the harsh financial realities of the depression. The collapse of stock prices, combined with reduced consumer spending, spelled trouble for American business. Business leaders believed that the survival of their companies depended on production cutbacks to maintain price levels and layoffs to reduce payroll. While their stocks were still falling, companies began closing plants and forcing workers into the growing ranks of the unemployed. In August 1931, Henry Ford closed several of his Detroit automobile factories, putting nearly 75,000 people out of work.

Like a snowball rolling downhill, the problem of production cuts kept getting bigger and bigger. As businesses closed plants and fired workers to save money, consumers spent less. So businesses cut production even more, closing more plants and firing more workers. By 1933, nearly 25 percent of all American workers had lost their jobs.

The Impact of Tariffs New tariffs compounded the nation's woes and helped to spread the depression. Intending to reverse the downward slide, the government moved to protect American products from foreign competition by raising tariffs, the taxes on goods imported from other countries. In June 1930, Congress passed the **Hawley-Smoot Tariff**. President Hoover signed the bill into law. The Hawley-Smoot Tariff raised taxes on foreign imports to such a level that the foreign goods could not compete in the American market. The tariff inspired European countries to retaliate and enact protective tariffs of their own.

Far from solving the problems of the depression, the Hawley-Smoot Tariff added to them. At a time when American manufacturers and farms had a glut of unsold products, the international move toward high protective tariffs closed markets. This closure was not just harmful to American producers. It was equally disastrous to the global economy. The ripple effect caused by the Hawley-Smoot Tariff helped to damage international trade.

Other Nations Endure Economic Hardship The Hawley-Smoot Tariff was one of the causes of a depression spreading across the globe. As we saw earlier, the European problems of reparation payments, war debt payments, and international imbalance of trade had already created a shaky economic structure. In the early 1930s, the structure collapsed. Germany ceased their reparation payments, and the United States agreed to suspend France and Britain's war debt payments. The international economy had largely been funded by American loans to Europe, but the crisis in the United States drastically curtailed those loans. As a result, European nations experienced the same cycle of business failures, bank collapses, and high unemployment as the United States. The depression had become a global nightmare.

BROOKLYN DAILY EAGLE
And Complete Long Island News
LATE NEWS
WALL STREET 1:15 PRICES ★★
NEW YORK CITY, THURSDAY, OCTOBER 24, 1929. 32 PAGES THREE CENTS
WALL ST. IN PANIC AS STOCKS CRASH
Attempt Made to Kill Italy's Crown Prince
STOCKS CRASH IN RUSH TO SELL; BILLIONS LOST
ASSASSIN CAUGHT IN BRUSSELS MOB; PRINCE UNHURT
Hollywood Fire Destroys Films Worth Millions
FEAR 52 PERISHED IN LAKE MICHIGAN; FERRY IS MISSING
PIECE OF PLANE LIKE DITEMAN'S IS FOUND AT SEA
High Duty Group Gave $700,000 to Coolidge Drive
CARNEGIE CHARGE OF PAID ATHLETES ROUSES COLLEGES
HOOVER'S TRAIN HALTED BY AUTO PLACED ON RAILS
WARDER SOUGHT TO KEEP SEA TRIP SECRET, AID SAYS
SOMERS NAMED AS HEAD OF NEW EXCHANGE BANK

>> The *Brooklyn Daily Eagle* ran a front-page headline that described the fear and panic that spread immediately after the stock market crashed in late 1929.

BOUNCE to Activate Chart

☑ **DESCRIBE** As the Great Depression progressed, how did one wave of job losses lead to further job losses?

The Causes of the Great Depression

Historians and economists struggle to identify the exact causes of the Great Depression. Some have stressed a single root cause in their explanations of the financial crisis. The economist Milton Friedman believed that the depression resulted from the contraction in the money supply. The twin events of the stock market crash in 1929 and the run of bank failures in 1930, added to the Federal Reserve's monetary policy decisions, left too little money in circulation for the nation's economic needs.

John Maynard Keynes was one of the most influential economists of the depression. He argued that the lack of government interference in the economy led to the depression. Critical problems in money supply, distribution of wealth, stock speculation, consumer spending, productivity, and employment could have been controlled, he said, by proactive government policies.

Keynes's work points to a fundamental difference between many economists regarding the depression. While Keynes recommended that governments spend more money to keep people employed when the economy slows, other noted economists like Ludwig von Mises and Friedrich von Hayek criticized centralized economic planning and management.

There will never be a fully accepted answer to the question of what caused the Great Depression. But clearly, problems in consumption contributed heavily to it. Economic hardships before 1929 in Europe and rural America, coupled with an uneven distribution of wealth and over-speculation in the stock market, created dangerous economic conditions. When this was combined with poor or misinformed economic decisions by Congress and President Hoover, the Great Depression resulted.

CHECK UNDERSTANDING What factors contributed to the Great Depression?

ASSESSMENT

1. **Summarize** the philosophies that led Herbert Hoover to a presidential victory in 1928.
2. **Contrast** the experiences of farmers with those of urban workers during the economic boom of the 1920s.
3. **Generate Explanations** Explain how an uneven distribution of wealth weakened the U.S. economy.
4. **Check Understanding** Explain how the Great Depression extended beyond the United States and became an international problem.
5. **Connections to Today** Over recent decades, Californians have built homes in or near forests and other "wildland" areas, which makes them vulnerable to wildfires. How does this situation compare with that of farmers in the years following World War I?

GO ONLINE to access these biographies: Milton Friedman, Friedrich Hayek

13.2

GO ONLINE to **Project Imagine: Survive the Great Depression** for first-person perspectives on how the Great Depression affected many groups of Americans.

BOUNCE to Activate Flipped Video

Objectives

Examine the spread of unemployment in America's cities.

Analyze the effects of the Great Depression on farmers.

Analyze the impact of human and geographical factors that created the Dust Bowl.

Describe how the Great Depression affected family life and the lives of African Americans and Mexican Americans.

Key Terms

bread line
Hooverville
tenant farmer
Dust Bowl
Okies
repatriation

GO ONLINE to access your digital course

Americans Suffer

The stock market crash signaled the end of boom times and the beginning of hard times. As investors mourned their losses, Americans watched the economy stagger into the Great Depression. In the cities and on the farms, desperate poverty gripped the nation. Even after prosperity returned, those who had lived through the crisis would remember the pain and worries of the depression. Tested by extreme hardship, this generation of Americans forged a character and will strong enough to overcome economic ruin and restore prosperity.

Economic Hardship Shakes the Cities

The Great Depression had a deep and lasting impact on the lives of the people who lived through it.

Few Americans grasped the underlying problems of the 1920s economy or the subtle reasons for the stock market crash. Fewer still comprehended how the crash led to the Great Depression. But they did understand the *effects* of the economic crisis. Workers understood having a job one day and being unemployed the next. Whole families knew the fear and shame of losing their homes.

The Great Depression touched most Americans because many Americans either experienced or knew someone who experienced the hardships and loss caused by the economic catastrophe. For many, their lives were never the same again.

Unemployment Leaves Families Struggling The threat of widespread unemployment and destitution affected workers in cities and towns across the United States. Between 1921 and 1929, annual average unemployment rates had never risen above 3.7 percent. But then the depression hit, and the rate shot up. By 1933, it had climbed to a shocking 24.9 percent.

Despite this high rate, millions of workers were able to keep their jobs. However, most had their wages or hours cut. Many workers brought home paychecks that were 10, 20, sometimes 30 percent less than their pre-depression checks.

Yet statistics tell only part of the story. The human drama of unemployment unfolded over and over again, in city after city across the nation. For a man employed as a factory worker, the 1920s had promised a chance at upward economic mobility. He had been able to provide for his family, enjoy a decent standard of living, and save something for retirement. Then the depression hit. The man saw his hours cut and his workweek shortened. Eventually, he was laid off. Looking for another job, he trudged from one factory to the next. "No help wanted here" or "We don't need nobody" greeted him at every turn. The man's clothes began to look worn. His collars and cuffs became frayed, and his pants became shiny at the knees. He said less, stared more, and moved slower.

Maybe his wife was able to find work washing and ironing clothes or laboring as a maid. But those jobs were hard to find, too. At home, children ate smaller meals. Water replaced milk. Meat disappeared from the table.

Hunger lurked about the home like an unwanted guest. Sometimes the parents and children received free meals in public soup kitchens. Often the only place for the family to get a free scrap of food was in a **bread line**, where people lined up for handouts from charities or public agencies.

Poverty Becomes a Reality for Many Men like the factory worker just described moved from unemployed to unemployable. Whole families descended into hunger and homelessness. Their dreams of success and prosperity turned into nightmares of failure and poverty.

The Challenges of Homelessness As Americans lost their jobs and ran through their savings, they had to scrounge wherever they could to keep from going hungry. They sold furniture, pawned jewelry, and moved to cheaper lodgings—anything to keep their pantries stocked and rents paid. In many cities, they ran out of money, were evicted from their homes, and ended up on the streets.

Homeless people slept on park benches, in empty railway cars, or in cardboard boxes. Many grouped together in **Hoovervilles**, makeshift shantytowns of tents and shacks built on public land or vacant lots. Homeless people, some of whom had worked as skilled carpenters before the crisis, cobbled houses

>> Unemployed men gathered outside a busy New York City unemployment office during the 1930s. New York police officers stood guard. **Draw Conclusions** Why do you think this unemployment office required guarding?

>> Struggling Americans built temporary shelters called "Hoovervilles" like this in one Washington, D.C. This encampment was home to war veterans, who were lobbying the government for help.

together out of lumber scraps, tar paper, tin, and glass. One of the largest Hoovervilles in the country sprang up in the middle of Central Park in New York City. There, the homeless covered themselves with newspapers, called Hoover blankets, to stay warm at night. They walked around looking for jobs with their empty pants pockets turned inside out, a sign of poverty known as Hoover flags.

Despite the difficulties of life during the depression, many Americans did what they could to boost morale and help their neighbors. During a New York City newspaper strike, Mayor Fiorello LaGuardia read comic strips to children over the radio. In Reading, Pennsylvania, members of the Taxpayers Protection League staged nonviolent protests to thwart evictions. Nevertheless, thousands of other Americans found no such escapes from their misery.

☑ **IDENTIFY** What was a Hooverville?

Rural America Struggles with Poverty

In cities and towns across the nation, Americans faced a terrible plight. The numbers of the unemployed, homeless, and hopeless increased like a casualty list in some great war. In rural areas, people fared no better. In fact, sometimes their condition was even worse. Farmers had been suffering even before the Great Depression. Falling commodity prices and accumulating debt had made it a struggle for farmers to keep their heads above water. Many failed to stay afloat and sank so deep that they lost their farms.

Crop Prices Fall Then the bottom fell out of the economy and the depression added more woes. Crop prices fell even further, and new debts were added to old debts. In 1919, a bushel of wheat sold for $2.16; in 1932, it sold for 38 cents. A pound of cotton fetched 35.34 cents in 1919; the same pound fetched 6.52 cents in 1932. The same was true of other farm products, as well—corn and beans, cattle and hogs. The income farmers generated was not enough to allow them to continue farming. They could not pay their debts, purchase more seed, repair equipment, and buy what their families needed to survive. Overburdened by the diminishing returns for their labor, some farmers buckled under the stress.

To make matters even worse, the Great Plains was suffering through a choking drought, an ecological disaster that lasted for years. As a result, many more farmers lost their farms and moved. They traveled about the country, looking for work and fighting for survival.

Commodity Price Levels, 1919-1932

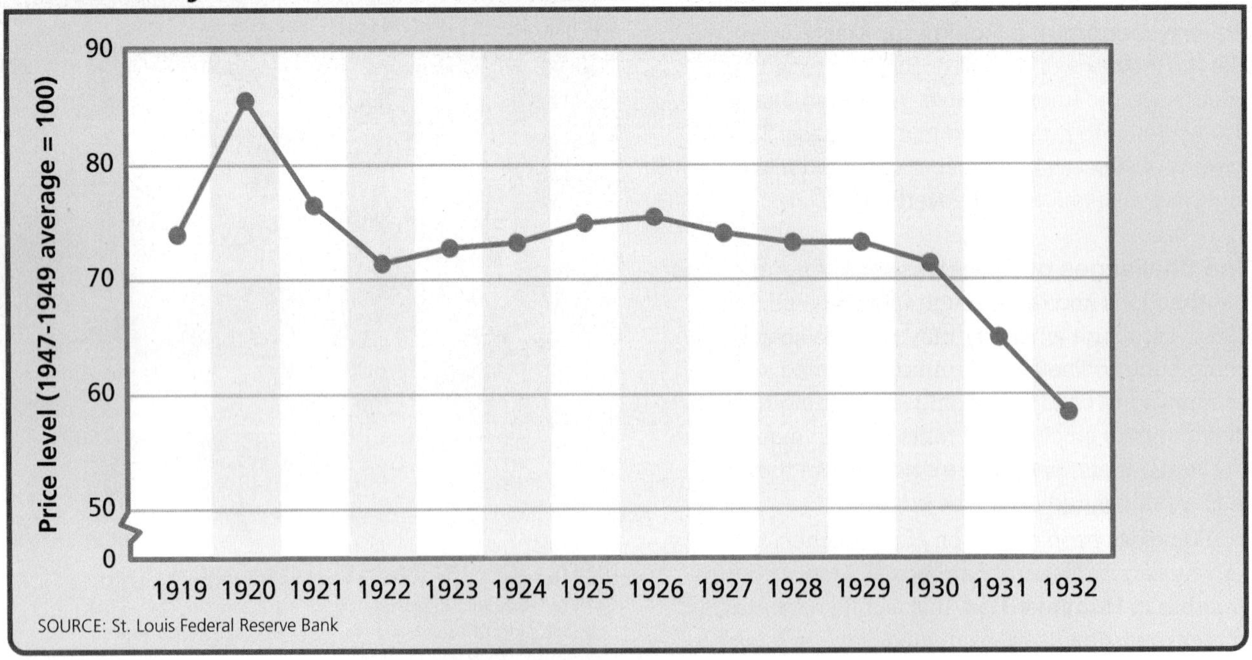

>> **Draw Conclusions** A commodity is any product that can be bought or sold, including farm products. Why did commodity prices fall after 1920, even though the Great Depression was years away?

In Sioux City, Iowa, in 1932, the Sioux City Milk Producers Association threatened to strike if its members did not see higher profits for their milk. When the association's threats were ignored by local storeowners, farmers dumped 1,000 gallons of milk on a road outside the city. Despite such a drastic—and for many Americans unthinkable—action, farmers everywhere feared losing everything.

Losing the Family Farm Between 1930 and 1934, nearly one million farmers failed to pay their mortgages and lost their farms. Banks foreclosed on their lands and houses and repossessed their farming equipment. The bankers sold what they could at public auctions. Some farmers remained on the land as **tenant farmers**, working for bigger landowners rather than for themselves. But another effect was that many people drifted away from their rural communities, and migrated to cities to look for some other kind of work.

Cesar Chavez, who later became a well-known labor organizer, recalled the troubles his proud father had during the depression. A California bank repossessed his father's small ranch, and the family was evicted from their house. Chavez remembered how it felt to lose his home:

> We had been poor, but we knew every night there was a bed *there*, and *this* was our room. . . . But that all of a sudden changed. When you're small, you can't figure these things out. You know something's not right and you don't like it, but you don't . . . let that get you down.
>
> You sort of just continue to move.
>
> —Cesar Chavez

Like the Chavez family, other farmers moved on after their losses. But for those who remained, Mother Nature dealt a cruel blow to already cruel times.

The Dust Bowl Farmers who survived the tumble in prices were still not safe. Through the mid-1930s, a drought in the Great Plains added to their problems. Water was a constant problem in the region. Normal rainfall seldom exceeded the 20 inches a year that traditional American agricultural practices demanded. As a result, droughts on the Great Plains were often more devastating than those

>> Dairy farmers poured out their milk as part of a 1932 protest. **Infer** What can you infer about the price farmers received for milk in 1932?

>> Many American farmers struggled to keep their farms during the Great Depression. In time, falling prices and rising debt forced many, like this Oregon farmer, to sell or abandon their farms.

in the East and Midwest. In the years before the nation's western rivers were dammed and irrigation practices became widespread, there were few answers to the drought threat.

New farming methods made drought conditions worse. Intensive farming came to prominence throughout the region in the late nineteenth and early twentieth centuries.

Farmers then had moved onto the Plains and plowed under much of the natural grasses in order to plant oceans of winter wheat. And after 1909, there were many more farmers, too. In that year, the federal government expanded the acreage allotted in the Homestead Act to 320 acres per settler. So a new wave of transplants decided to try farming on the often marginal lands that were still available on the Great Plains.

All this intensive farming reduced the amount of grassland available to graze livestock, causing overgrazing on what was left. In addition, new tractor-pulled disk plows pulverized the soil, making it more vulnerable to wind erosion. Population growth and shifts in population distribution, along with new methods of farming, tipped the ecological balance of the region. In the past, plains grasses prevented the topsoil from blowing away during periods of drought. By the early 1930s, that dwindling grassy safety net could no longer do the job.

In 1932, this human interaction with the environment led to loose topsoil caused by overfarming and overgrazing. This, combined with the physical geographic factors of drought and high winds, led to disaster on the Great Plains. The winds kicked up towering dust storms that began to blow east.

These gigantic clouds of dust and dirt could rise from ground level to a height of 8,000 feet. The dust storms moved as fast as 100 miles per hour and blotted out the sun, plunging daylight into darkness.

Most of the dust storms started in the southern Great Plains, especially in the High Plains regions of Texas, Oklahoma, Kansas, New Mexico, and Colorado. This swath of parched earth became known as the **Dust Bowl**. For people living in these hardest hit regions, depression and dust storms defined the misery of the "dirty thirties."

Those unfortunate enough to be caught in a dust storm were temporarily choked and blinded by the swirling dirt. The storms killed cattle and birds, blanketed rivers, and suffocated fish. Dirt seeped into houses, covering everything with a thick coat of grime. Some dust clouds blew east as far as the Atlantic coast, dumping acres of dirt on Boston, New York, and Washington, D.C. Altogether, dust storms displaced twice as much dirt as Americans had scooped out to build the Panama Canal.

The Dust Bowl

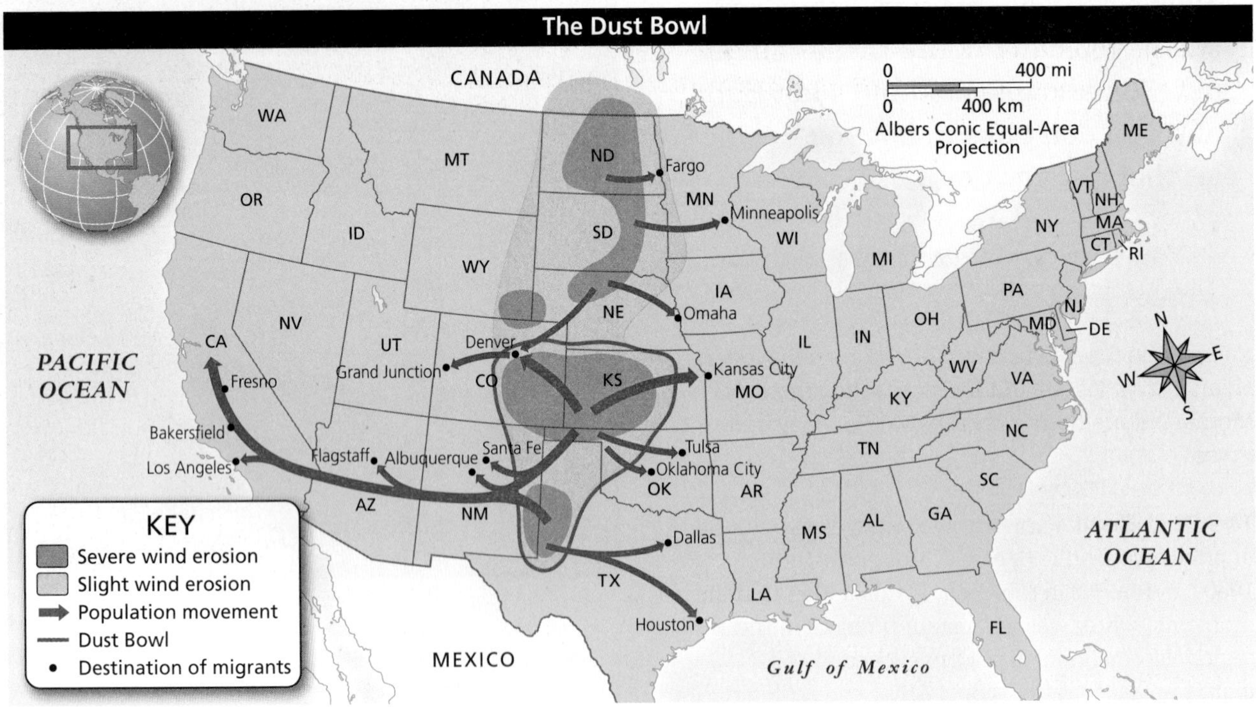

>> **Analyze Maps** Which two states appear to have been hardest hit by erosion? What is unusual about California's location compared to other destinations?

BOUNCE to Activate Gallery

Moving Wherever Work Can Be Found Many farm families trapped in the Dust Bowl had little choice but to leave the region. They had lost their farms to the banks and had nowhere to live. Dust storms had destroyed most remaining opportunities in their locale. Although only some came from Oklahoma, Dust Bowl refugees were generally referred to as **Okies**, regardless of their states of origin.

Okie families packed onto rickety trucks and headed toward California or Oregon or Washington, any place where a job might be found. Before the pace slowed, 800,000 people migrated out of Missouri, Arkansas, Oklahoma, and Texas alone.

The collapse of agriculture and the Great Plains Dust Bowl caused millions of other Americans to leave the midwestern and southern regions where they were born. Many migrated to California, lured by the promise of jobs, but were crushed when that promise too often proved empty. In reality, the migrants faced fierce competition from Mexican American, Filipino, and other farm laborers who were also seeking work. Many of them gave up farming and headed for nearby cities such as Los Angeles, San Francisco, and San Diego, hoping to find factory work or to join the military.

In California, the social and economic impact of these migrants was immense. The increased numbers of workers drove wages down. Migrants had to move constantly to follow harvests and formed huge camps that created public health problems.

Other farm families headed north or east to the cities of the Northeast and Midwest, again looking for jobs, shelter, and relief. One of the irreversible effects of this massive migration—some 2.5 million people left the Plains states alone—was that rural states lost population while states with large cities gained population. It was one of the largest migrations in the nation's history, once again changing the nation's demographic patterns.

The Dust Bowl had other effects as well. The farmers best able to survive the Great Depression were the ones with the biggest operations. They often bought repossessed land at rock-bottom prices and expanded their holdings into large commercial farms. The Dust Bowl also motivated the government to help Great Plains farmers. After the initial crisis, immense federal projects dammed western rivers. Dams eventually provided irrigation that made farm profits possible on the Great Plains.

☑ **CHECK UNDERSTANDING** How did some farmers become tenant farmers?

>> Large clouds of dust engulfed farmhouses like these in Stratford, Texas, in 1935. The intensity of Dust Bowl storms caused many to lose their farms to the banks and forced families to migrate.

>> A Missouri family headed west to look for work in 1937. **Make Predictions** What types of opportunities were available to farmers forced to migrate westward?

Hard Times Hit Most Americans

One of the ironies of the depression was the word itself. In the nineteenth and early twentieth centuries, an economic slump was called a "panic" or a "crisis." President Hoover used the word *depression* to describe the state of affairs because he thought it sounded less severe than the other terms. But before long, Hoover's "depression" gave way to the "Depression" and then the "Great Depression." The term described not only a state of mind, but also an economic reality. It showed a despondent America, filled with people overwhelmed by seemingly inescapable poverty. Not only did the depression make victims of the men and women who lost jobs, it also was an economic and emotional crisis that profoundly affected U.S. society.

Families Suffer During the Depression For millions of Americans, the depression was an intensely personal affair. Men who lost their jobs and could not find other work often felt that they had betrayed their families. They had been the "breadwinners," the providers, the ones whose paychecks fed and clothed the family and kept a roof over everyone's head. The loss of a job meant a reduction in status. Different men reacted differently to unemployment. Many labored tirelessly to find a new job, while others sank into shame and despair. Some even deserted their families.

The unemployed were not the only ones who suffered. Men lucky enough to have jobs lived in constant fear that the next paycheck would be their last. They often felt guilty for being employed while so many of their relatives and friends were suffering. Few Americans were spared from the crisis.

Wives and children experienced the pain of their husbands and fathers. Birthrates plummeted to the lowest levels in American history—a sure sign of family distress. Mothers worked constantly to stretch meager family incomes.

They sewed clothes, searched for odd jobs, and valiantly tried to meet their families' needs. With both parents preoccupied with making something out of nothing, family discipline often declined. Some children quit school. Others ran away from home. Families coped with the depression as best they could. Some huddled together, working to survive the hard times. Others broke apart, making those times even harder and lonelier.

>> Mothers like this one struggled during the Great Depression to find ways to earn additional income, while trying to ensure their children had enough to eat.

BOUNCE to Activate Gallery

Poor Minorities Suffer Disproportionately The depression affected everyone, but it did not affect them equally. Americans on the bottom rung of the economic ladder—the poorest of the poor, often minorities with no financial resources—felt the sting of the depression the keenest. A Howard University sociologist noted early in the crisis that African Americans were "the last to be hired and the first to be fired." In the South, landowners threw African American sharecroppers off the plots they had been farming. Many of these workers migrated to northern cities, but there were no jobs waiting there. Only more poverty greeted them. In 1932, unemployment among African Americans hovered around 50 percent, nearly double the national rate.

However, African Americans had long stood firm against the challenges of poverty. They relied on the emotional resources of family and religion to cope with grim times. During his interview with a depression historian, an African American man explained what the depression meant to African Americans:

> The Negro was born in depression. It didn't mean too much to him, The Great American Depression, as you call it. There was no such thing.

> The best he could be was a janitor or a porter or shoeshine boy. It only became official when it hit the white man.
>
> —Clifford Burke, quoted in *Hard Times*, 1970

Hard times came upon Mexican Americans and others as well. As more Okies headed west out of the Dust Bowl, the competition for jobs between those migrants and Mexican American and Asian American farmworkers in states like California heated up. A flood tide of workers struggled to find and keep farm jobs. Often, Mexican Americans and Asian Americans faced the additional burden of discrimination when competing with white farmhands for those jobs.

In the Southwest, many white Americans clamored for Asian American and Mexican American **repatriation**. Repatriation involved efforts by local, state, and federal governments to encourage or coerce immigrants and their naturalized children to return to their country of origin. Hundreds of thousands of people of Mexican ancestry—many of them U.S. citizens—were pushed out of the United States. Some were deported, others pressured to leave voluntarily. Even so, many more remained. By the end of the 1930s, Mexican Americans were working in most economic sectors of the Southwest, including farming, ranching, and industry.

Compared to the exit of Mexican Americans, the number of Europeans departing was small. Still, nearly 200,000 European immigrants left the United States between 1931 and 1934, the peak years of repatriation. How many of these departures were involuntary is impossible to know.

What is known, however, is that the United States severely restricted all immigration during the depression. Tragically, this policy included denying entrance to thousands of German Jews who were fleeing Nazi persecution in their homeland.

CHECK UNDERSTANDING Why did the Great Depression affect minority groups more severely?

ASSESSMENT

1. **Generate Explanations** Explain how urban society changed as a result of job loss during the Great Depression.
2. **Describe** the ways in which farmers dealt with the hardships of the Great Depression.
3. **Identify Cause and Effect** Explain how the invention of new farming methods contributed to the Dust Bowl.
4. **Compare and Contrast** Compare the experiences of African Americans with those of white Americans during the Great Depression.
5. **Connections to Today** Hundreds of thousands of people migrated out of the Great Plains due to drought and dust storms. Do you think wildfires have caused people to leave California? Why or why not?

"The Story of Seattle's Hooverville": Jesse Jackson

In 1931 in Seattle, Washington, a former lumberjack named Jesse Jackson helped start a shantytown for people who had lost their homes and jobs to the depression. Mr. Jackson became Hooverville's unofficial mayor and represented it in meetings with city officials. In 1938, he wrote this account describing how the Hooverville got started and what it was like to live there.

>> The Seattle Hooverville grew to include 600 shacks and 1,200 inhabitants.

. . . We immediately took possession of the nine-acre tract of vacant property of the Seattle Port Commission and proceeded to settle down. We set in with the resources we found strewn over this property to construct relief shelters of our own. We were among the first to face and taste the bitter realities of a social system that would not provide employment for willing workers to enable them to care for themselves, or a humane relief system to relieve their sufferings in a time like this.

DRAW CONCLUSIONS Why might the location of the Hooverville on property owned by the Seattle Port Commission be advantageous for the shantytown's residents?

It seemed but a few short days until more than fifty shacks were set up, and then our troubles began. Business houses in this district did not know us. They considered us a bunch of ne'er-do-well undesirables and wanted to be rid of us. Seattle health officials decided our shacks were unfit for human habitation and a menace to health conditions in the city, and posted official notices on our doors, informing us of the fact and giving us seven days in which to vacate them. We had no other place to go and thought that the authorities were bluffing, so we paid no attention to the notices. The authorities were not bluffing; at the expiration of the seven-day notice, at five a.m., just as daylight was breaking, in one of the heaviest downpours of rain that fell in Seattle that fall, a regiment of uniformed officers of law and order swooped down upon us, with cans of kerosene and applied the torch. Amidst the confusion that followed, we salvaged our few belongings, and just as soon as the officers were out of sight, we returned and rebuilt our burned shanties. . . .

By this time a heated city election was on, and, one of the issues was the destruction of the shacks of Seattle's unemployed. The result was a new city administration. . . .

In June, 1932, the new administration was inaugurated, and a committee of different city departments . . . called us together. The spokesman for the party told us that we were going to be tolerated until conditions improved, that they were going to lay down a few simple rules and regulations for us to follow and for us to select a board of commissioners from the ranks to enforce these regulations. . . .

The melting pot of races and nations we had here called for a commission of several races and nations. Two whites, two negroes [a term for African American people no longer favored today, but considered appropriate in the 1930s], and two Filipinos were selected. . . .

USE CONTEXT CLUES What does this selection tell you about the effect the depression might have had on race relations? Explain.

The shacks in Hooverville are built out of every sort of material, and all sorts of architecture is followed, as it suits the taste of the builder and the material he had to build it from. Some are no bigger than piano boxes and some have five rooms. There is no gas, electricity, or running water. Kerosene lamps are used for lighting and wood stoves are used to cook and heat with. We have no modern house furnishings. The furnishings are either castoffs or hand made. Bunks are made of wood; boxes are used for tables and chairs. We discovered that gas tanks from automobiles made good stoves to cook and heat with when set upon legs and a pipe was fitted to take care of the smoke. The writer's stove is made from an ice tank once used by an ice company to freeze a cake of ice in. An end is fitted with a door, and a hole is cut to take care of the stovepipe, which is made from a discarded gutter pipe. The ingenuity of the men in working over discards and castoffs, leads many people to remark that "you fellows have gone back to pioneering." We apply the hobo term and call it plain, downright "jungling [finding new uses for old items and making do while living in a community of hobos]." . . .

ANALYZE WORD CHOICES Why might the men in the Hooverville prefer the term "jungling" to "pioneering"?

Hooverville is the abode of the forgotten man. Seattle city authorities have decreed that no women or children would be permitted to live here, so no more than a dozen women live here.

The men are past middle age in life. Seldom is anyone living here under thirty years of age. . . .

Pretty near every day brings something new. This is just another shanty town, nine and a half acres of ground, but be it ever so humble, it's home sweet home. . . .

ANALYZE STYLE AND RHETORIC What emotions does the author evoke when he uses the phrase "it's home sweet home"?

These last few days I have had a lot of foreign-born making application for their first papers [citizenship papers]. . . . Down here in this settlement, I find that they are standing pretty solidly behind Mr. Roosevelt and the present administration. They have tried to hand out a little something to everybody, after a fashion, as they say. The foreign-born is taking out his papers so that he can get on the W.P.A. If you haven't got your papers; they'll look at you and say "You're a nice fellow, but we can't do anything for you." The boys down here don't blame Mr. Hoover for this mess. It is just one of those things that happen.

ASSESSMENT

1. **Draw Inferences** Based on this account, why do you think Jesse Jackson was chosen to be the "mayor" of the Seattle Hooverville?
2. **Daw Conclusions** What is Mr. Jackson's opinion of the other men who live in the shantytown?
3. **Distinguish Among Fact, Opinion, and Reasoned Judgment** Find one sentence in the excerpt that is a statement of fact and one sentence that is an opinion.
4. **Determine Meaning** Mr. Jackson writes that "Hooverville is the abode of the forgotten man." What is the meaning of the word *abode* and what does Mr. Jackson mean by this sentence?
5. **Analyze Sequence** How does Mr. Jackson's account of interactions with city officials reflect the progression of the depression throughout the nation?

GO ONLINE to access primary sources

13.3

GO ONLINE to **Project Imagine: Work to End the Depression** to see how people tried to solve the problem of unemployment.

BOUNCE to Activate Flipped Video

Objectives

Evaluate Hoover's approaches to resolving the Great Depression and how Americans reacted to them.

Contrast Hoover's approach to the economic crisis with Franklin D. Roosevelt's approach.

Describe the programs that were part of the first New Deal and their immediate effect on Americans' lives.

Identify the New Deal's opponents and their major criticisms.

Key Terms

localism
Reconstruction Finance Corporation (RFC)
trickle-down economics
Hoover Dam
Bonus Army
Douglas MacArthur
Franklin D. Roosevelt
Eleanor Roosevelt
New Deal
fireside chats
Federal Deposit Insurance Corporation (FDIC)
Tennessee Valley Authority (TVA)
Civilian Conservation Corps (CCC)
National Recovery Administration (NRA)
Public Works Administration (PWA)
Charles Coughlin
Huey Long

Two Presidents Respond

From big cities to farms and small towns, the Great Depression spread misery far and wide across the United States. The unemployed and the homeless crowded into shantytowns. Giant dust storms swallowed the Great Plains. As the crisis deepened, Herbert Hoover struggled to respond to the nation's problems. In 1932, as a result of President Hoover's cautious and failed response, Americans turned to a new leader who called for increased government intervention to try to stop the depression.

Hoover's Response Fails

President Hoover did not cause the Great Depression. But Americans looked to him as their President to solve the crisis. He tried. Hoover was an intelligent man, familiar with business methods and economic theory. He labored long hours, consulted a wide range of experts, and tried to marshal the resources of the country to solve the problems of the depression. As the effects of the Great Depression on the U.S. economy worsened, he tried several different approaches. In the end, although he failed to discover the right formula, it was not because of a lack of effort.

At the start of the economic downturn, Hoover followed a hands-off policy. Like most economists of the day, the President viewed the upswings and downswings of business cycles as natural occurrences. He felt that government should not interfere with such events. Periodic depressions were like storms. They could not be avoided, but strong businesses could weather them without the support of the government.

Relying on Volunteerism A policy of doing nothing, however, was no policy at all. Hoover soon recognized this fact and turned

GO ONLINE to access your digital course

to a policy he had used in the past. As Secretary of Commerce during the 1920s, Hoover had encouraged business and labor to work voluntarily toward common goals. To address the current crisis, he asked business and industrial leaders to keep employment, wages, and prices at current levels. He simultaneously called for the government to reduce taxes, lower interest rates, and create public-works programs. The plan was to put more money into the hands of businesses and individuals to encourage more production and consumption. This, President Hoover said, would reverse the cycle that had led to the depression.

Lastly, the President requested that wealthier individuals give more money to charity. Millions of Americans did give money, clothing, and food to private and religious charities, which then distributed the goods to those in need. The idea was for all Americans to join forces voluntarily to combat the depression.

>> Two young residents of a shantytown in Washington, D.C. **Determine Point of View** What do the signs in the photo tell you about how the poor perceived the government's role in the economic crisis?

Voluntary Cooperation Fails Although the plan was well-intentioned, Hoover's program relied too much on voluntary cooperation. The President believed he could persuade Americans to act in the best interests of the country as a whole, rather than in their own best interests. He took care to encourage, not legislate, the nation's recovery. But volunteerism did not work. Businesses cut wages and laid off workers because business owners thought they had to do so to keep their businesses afloat. Farmers boosted production because they thought that producing more crops would help them keep their family farms. Most Americans followed individual, not cooperative, courses.

President Hoover had also asked state and local governments to provide more jobs and relief measures. He had faith in **localism**, the policy whereby problems could best be solved at local and state levels. However, in this severe situation, towns and states simply did not have the financial or human resources to combat the crisis successfully. Making matters worse, the President strongly resisted using federal resources to provide direct relief to individuals. Believing it to be unconstitutional, President Hoover opposed public assistance and instead favored "rugged individualism" which allowed people to better themselves through their own efforts. Yet as the months wore on, unemployment increased, charities ran low on money, and local and state governments could no longer plug the leaks in the economy. Some critics began to argue that the crisis demanded decisive federal action.

>> **Analyze Political Cartoons** What does this cartoon say about the difference between President Hoover's perception of the depression and the reality many Americans faced?

Hoover Reverses Course With Hoovervilles and homelessness on the rise, it became evident that the President's policies were not working. Poor Americans called trucks pulled by horse or mule "Hoover wagons," campfires "Hoover heaters," and cardboard boxes "Hoover houses." The association of the President's name with suffering and want indicated Americans' negative feelings about their leader and his failed policies.

Faced with growing and increasingly harsh criticism, President Hoover finally decided to reverse course and use federal resources to battle the depression. Believing the economy suffered from a lack of credit, he urged Congress to create the **Reconstruction Finance Corporation (RFC)**. Created by Congress in early 1932, the RFC gave more than a billion dollars of government loans to railroads and large businesses. The agency also lent money to banks so that they could extend more loans to struggling businesses. Hoover believed that if the government lent money to bankers, they would lend it in turn to businesses. Companies would then hire workers, production and consumption would increase, and the depression would end. This theory, known as **trickle-down economics**, held that money poured into the top of the economic pyramid will trickle down to the base.

Although the RFC put the federal government at the center of economic life, it did not work well under the President's guidance. The RFC lent out billions, but all too often bankers did not increase their loans to businesses. Additionally, businesses often did not use the loans they received to hire more workers. In the end, the money did not trickle down to the people who needed it the most.

Despite the failings of the RFC, Hoover succeeded with one project that made a difference. During the 1920s while secretary of commerce, Hoover had called for the construction of a dam on the Colorado River. By the time Hoover became President in 1929, Congress had approved the project as part of a massive public-works program. Workers broke ground on Boulder Dam (later renamed **Hoover Dam**) in 1930. Construction brought much-needed employment to the Southwest during the early 1930s.

CHECK UNDERSTANDING Why was Hoover's faith in localism as a response to the depression misplaced?

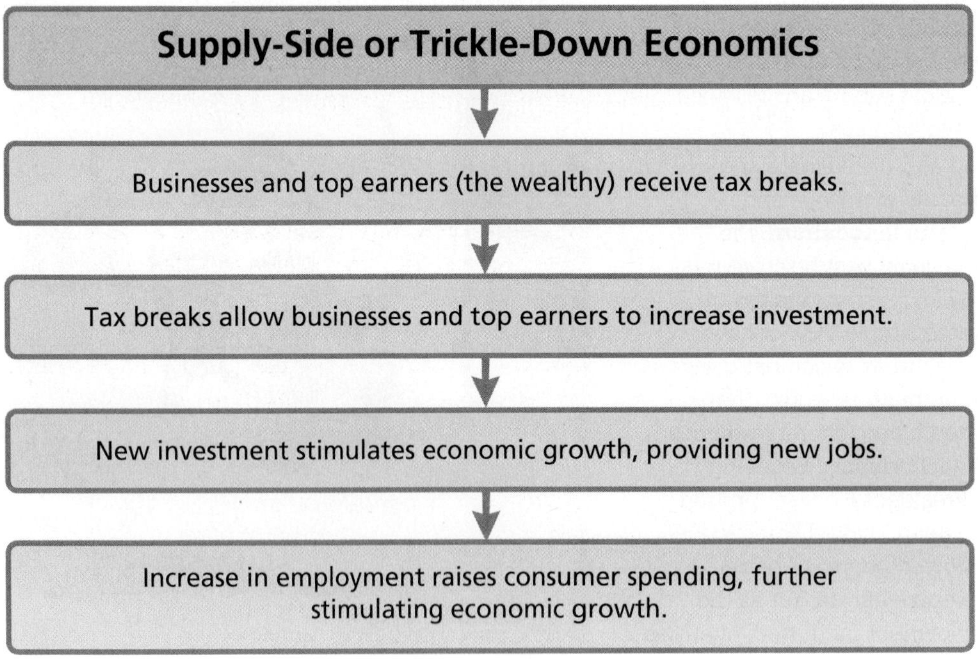

SOURCE: Harvard Kennedy School

>> **Analyze Charts** Supply-side or trickle-down economics is a theory that plays out differently based on economic circumstances. In theory, how does trickle-down economics generate economic growth?

Challenging Economic Times Lead to Protest

From the Oval Office, Hoover worked hard to end the depression. But to many out-of-work Americans, the President became a symbol of failure. Some people blamed capitalism, while others questioned the responsiveness of democracy. Many believed the American system was due for an overhaul.

Calls for Radical Change Some Americans thought the answer to the country's problems was the rejection of capitalism and the acceptance of socialism or communism. They argued that capitalism created great inequities of wealth and an unhealthy atmosphere of competition in society. In fact, they saw the depression as a sign that capitalism was about to collapse. Looking at the Soviet Union, they maintained that a state-run economy was the only avenue out of the depression. However, even during the worst of the crisis, most Americans were unmoved by communist calls for revolution. Communism's appeal proved no match for Americans' guarantees of individual freedom and dreams of progress and opportunity.

Fascist appeals from the political right also failed to hold any attraction. Economic troubles in Europe contributed to the rise to power of fascist leaders like Benito Mussolini in Italy and Adolf Hitler in Germany. Despite this political shift abroad, fascists failed to gain power in the United States. Although some questioned the ability of America's capitalistic and democratic institutions to overcome the crisis, most Americans never lost faith in their country.

The Bonus Army Marches on Washington Although most Americans did not want a revolution, many did desire substantial changes. In 1932, thousands of World War I veterans marched on Washington, D.C., demanding a solution to their particular problem. They became known as the **Bonus Army**.

In 1924, Congress had passed the Adjusted Compensation Act, which provided for a lump-sum payment to veterans of World War I in 1945. But in 1931, many veteran groups began to call for an early payment of the bonus, arguing that out-of-work vets needed the money to support their families. In May and June of 1932, almost twenty thousand veterans arrived in the capital, setting up camps and occupying empty government buildings. The House of Representatives agreed with their aims and passed a bill to provide early payment of the bonuses. However, the bill was defeated in the Senate in mid-June.

>> Over 2,000 veterans held a vigil on the U.S. Capitol lawn after Congress failed to approve a bill to provide veterans with early bonus pay for their past services.

Some of the Bonus Army marchers left, discouraged. Others stayed to continue to lobby for the bill. A riot broke out in July when police tried to evict the marchers from government buildings.

The Protests End Badly Although President Hoover sympathized with the marchers, he called for General **Douglas MacArthur** and federal troops to "[s]urround the affected area and clear it without delay." MacArthur exceeded his order, deciding to move the marchers out of the city altogether. He ordered his troops to ready tear gas and fix bayonets.

The Army force that pushed the marchers out included not only MacArthur but also the future World War II generals Dwight Eisenhower and George Patton. While Eisenhower regretted the use of the Army to solve a political problem, Patton ordered his troops to brandish their sabers in a show of force. Force was exactly what MacArthur used. More than one thousand marchers were tear-gassed, and many were injured, some very badly.

After the removal, MacArthur said that the marchers were a gang of revolutionaries bent on taking over the government:

They had come to the conclusion, beyond a shadow of a doubt, that they were about to take over . . . direct control of the government. . . . It is my opinion that had the President let it go on another week the institutions of our government would have been very severely threatened.

—Douglas MacArthur, 1932

Hoover had not ordered the use of such force against the veterans. Nevertheless, photographs of American troops marching with fixed bayonets against ragged veterans shocked the nation. Evalyn McLean, a Washington, D.C., resident, remembered the army's actions:

I saw in a news reel the tanks, the cavalry, and the gas-bomb throwers running those wretched Americans out of our capital. I was so raging mad. . . .

—Evalyn McLean, Washington, D.C., resident in the summer of 1932

>> General Douglas MacArthur (left) confers with Colonel Dwight Eisenhower (far right) as they prepare to clear out the Bonus Army marchers in Washington, D.C.

Any chance that Hoover had for winning reelection in November ended after the summer of 1932.

RECALL What argument was made by some in favor of turning to socialism or communism in the face of the depression?

Americans Turn to Roosevelt

In 1928, Herbert Hoover had almost no chance of losing his bid for the presidency. In 1932 however, he had almost no chance of winning reelection. With unemployment nearing 25 percent, people's savings wiped out by bank failures, long lines at soup kitchens, stomachs grumbling from hunger, and the number of homeless increasing every day, the depression had taken its toll. Most Americans felt that their President had failed completely, and they were ready for a change. In July of 1932, the governor of New York, **Franklin D. Roosevelt** (FDR) accepted the Democratic Party's nomination for President.

Political Success and Personal Challenge

Strangely enough, Democrats had chosen a presidential candidate who had never known economic hardship. As a child, Franklin Delano Roosevelt had enjoyed all the privileges of an upper-class upbringing, including education at elite schools and colleges. From his parents and teachers, FDR gained a great deal of self-confidence and a belief that public service was a noble calling.

In 1905, Franklin married his distant cousin **Eleanor Roosevelt**. President Theodore Roosevelt, Eleanor's uncle and Franklin's fifth cousin gave the bride away. In time, Eleanor would also become deeply involved in public affairs.

Like Teddy Roosevelt, Franklin rose quickly through the political ranks. After election to the New York State Senate, he served as Woodrow Wilson's Assistant Secretary of the Navy. In 1920, Roosevelt was the Democratic Party's vice presidential candidate. Although the Democrats lost the election, many considered him the rising star of the party. Then, in the summer of 1921, tragedy struck.

While vacationing, FDR slipped off his boat into the chilly waters of the North Atlantic. That evening, he awoke with a high fever and severe pains in his back and legs. Two weeks later, Roosevelt was diagnosed with polio, a dreaded disease that at the time had no treatment. He never fully recovered the use of his legs.

1932 Presidential Election

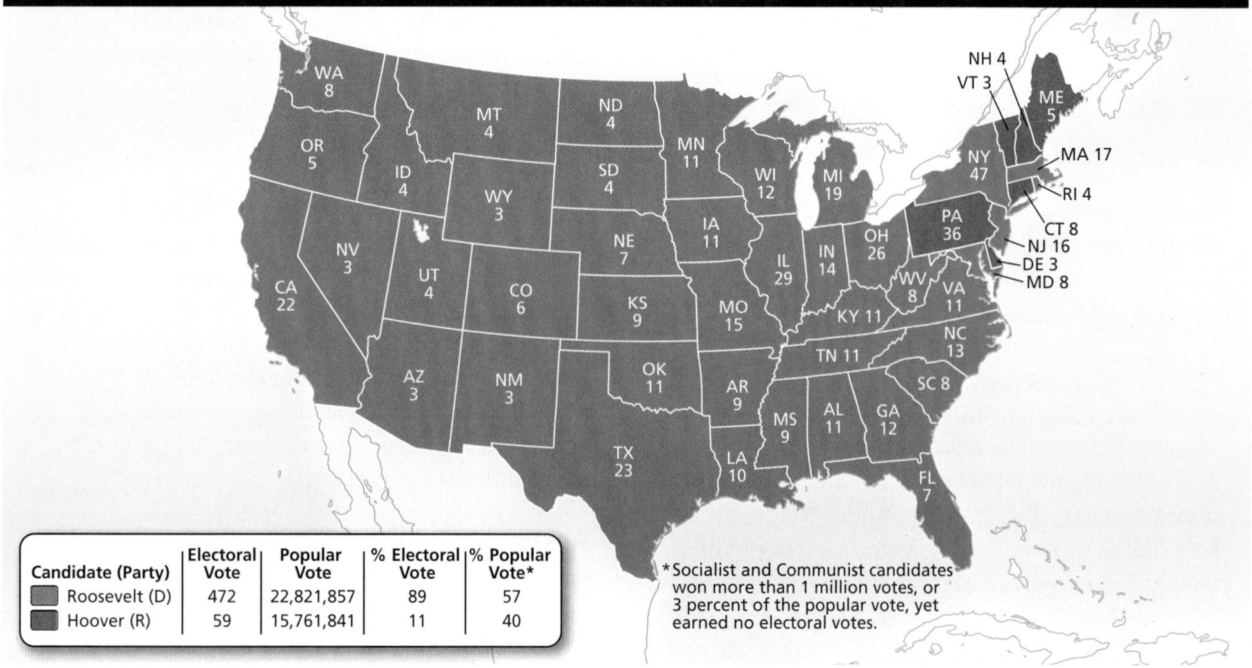

Candidate (Party)	Electoral Vote	Popular Vote	% Electoral Vote	% Popular Vote*
Roosevelt (D)	472	22,821,857	89	57
Hoover (R)	59	15,761,841	11	40

*Socialist and Communist candidates won more than 1 million votes, or 3 percent of the popular vote, yet earned no electoral votes.

>> **Analyze Maps** Why is an election such as the 1932 Presidential election referred to as a "landslide victory"?

FDR did not allow his physical disability to break his spirit. With Eleanor's encouragement, he made a political comeback. In 1928, he was elected governor of New York and earned a reputation as a reformer. In 1932, he became the Democrats' presidential candidate, pledging "a new deal for the American people."

Roosevelt Becomes President When FDR pledged a **"New Deal,"** he had only a vague idea of how he intended to combat the depression. Believing that the federal government needed to play an active role in promoting recovery and providing relief to Americans, he experimented with different approaches to see which ones worked best.

> The country needs, and, unless I mistake its temper, the country demands, bold, persistent experimentation. It is common sense to take a method and to try it. If it fails, admit it frankly and try another. But above all, try something!
>
> —Franklin D. Roosevelt, speech at Oglethorpe University, May 22, 1932

The 1932 election campaign pitted Roosevelt and his running mate, John Nance Garner, against President Hoover. The two men advocated very different approaches to the problems of the Great Depression. Hoover believed that relief should come from state and local governments and private agencies. Roosevelt believed that the depression required strong action and leadership by the federal government. As President Hoover correctly noted, "This campaign is more than a contest between two men. . . . It is a contest between two philosophies of government."

President Hoover's popularity declined as the Great Depression worsened. Even longtime Republicans deserted him. FDR—with the support of those who embraced his ideas as well as those who opposed Hoover's approach—won a landslide victory, winning the electoral votes of all but six states.

Americans had to wait four long months between Roosevelt's election, in November 1932, and his inauguration, in March 1933. Meanwhile, they watched helplessly as thousands of banks collapsed and unemployment soared. In Roosevelt's First Inaugural Address, he calmed listeners, stating" . . . let me assert my firm belief that the only thing we have to fear is fear itself. . . ." He went on to explain that the government would use its resources to put people to work and help farmers keep their land.

Forming the Brain Trust To help him plan the New Deal, FDR sought the advice of a diverse group of men and women. Among the most influential was a group of professionals and academics whom the press nicknamed the "Brain Trust." Roosevelt, a Democrat, displayed his bipartisan openness by nominating two Republicans, Henry Wallace and Harold Ickes (IHK uhs), to serve as his Secretary of Agriculture and Secretary of Interior. Roosevelt also nominated Frances Perkins, a social worker, to serve as his Secretary of Labor. She became the first female Cabinet member in U.S. history.

Throughout his presidency, FDR depended heavily on his wife, Eleanor. She traveled widely, interacting with the American people and serving as FDR's "eyes and ears." For example, in 1933, the Bonus Army, which had marched on Washington, D.C., in 1932, returned to the capital. The veterans once again sought early payment of their bonus for World War I service. Like President Hoover, FDR informed the marchers that the government could not afford to pay them their bonus. But unlike Hoover, who had sent the army to evict the Bonus Army, FDR sent Eleanor. She sang songs with the veterans and made them feel that the government cared.

>> President Roosevelt talked directly to the American public through his "fireside" radio broadcasts. He used these broadcasts as an opportunity to calm the fears of the American people.

CHECK UNDERSTANDING In your own words, explain what Hoover meant when he said the 1932 presidential election was "a contest between two philosophies of government."

The New Deal Begins

During his first weeks in office, which became known as the Hundred Days, Roosevelt proposed and Congress passed 15 major bills. These measures had three goals: relief, recovery, and reform. Roosevelt wanted to provide relief from the immediate hardships of the depression and achieve a long-term economic recovery. He also instituted reforms to prevent future depressions.

Restoring the Nation's Confidence President Roosevelt wasted no time dealing with the nation's number one crisis. Late in 1932, banks had begun to fail in great numbers. A banking panic gripped the nation as frightened depositors lined up outside banks, trying to withdraw their savings.

The day after his inauguration, President Roosevelt called Congress into a special session and convinced them to pass laws to shore up the nation's banking system. The Emergency Banking Bill gave the President broad powers—including the power to declare a four-day bank "holiday." Banks all over the country were ordered to close. The closings gave banks time to get their accounts in order before they reopened for business.

Eight days after becoming President, Roosevelt delivered an informal radio speech to the American people. This was the first of many presidential **fireside chats**. They became an important way for Roosevelt to communicate with the American people. In the first fireside chat, FDR explained the measures he had taken to stem the run on banks. His calming words reassured the American people. When the bank holiday ended, Americans did not rush to their banks to withdraw their funds. Roosevelt had convinced them that the banks were a safe place to keep their money.

Reforming the Financial System A number of Roosevelt's proposals sought to reform the nation's financial institutions.

One act created the **Federal Deposit Insurance Corporation (FDIC)**, which insured bank deposits up to $5,000. In the following year, Congress established the Securities and Exchange Commission (SEC) to regulate the stock market and make it a safer place for investments.

The Tennessee Valley Authority

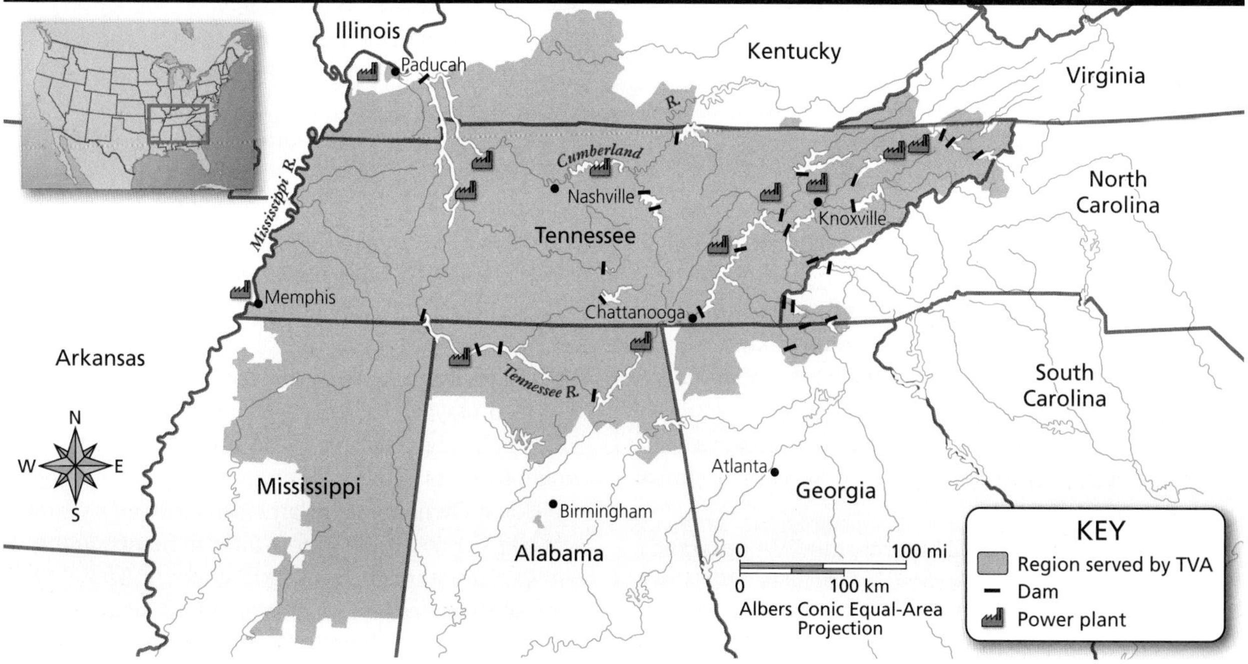

>> **Analyze Maps** Use the map and the text to describe specifically the number of TVA projects, what states benefited, and how they benefited.

BOUNCE to Activate Gallery

These financial reforms helped restore confidence in the economy. Runs on banks ended, largely because Americans now had confidence that they would not lose their lifetime savings if a bank failed. Therefore, more Americans trusted their money to a bank, where it could be lent out to individuals and businesses, helping to ensure an adequate money supply. The stock markets also stabilized as regulated trading practices reassured investors. Today, both organizations continue to affect the lives of U.S. citizens. The FDIC continues to insure bank deposits so Americans can trust their money to banks. The SEC continues to regulate trading practices so Americans feel comfortable investing in the stock market.

To further solve the banking crisis, FDR took action to combat the currency shortage. In April 1933, Roosevelt ordered individuals and businesses to turn in any gold they owned worth more than $100 to the Federal Reserve and stopped U.S. banks from exporting and redeeming gold. The Federal Reserve began to accumulate and hold on to gold reserves, which it pegged to a certain value. Then in June 1933, a joint resolution of Congress cut the tie between gold and paper money. Americans could no longer redeem their paper money for its value in gold. With these actions, FDR's administration took another step in the shifting trend from a gold standard to fiat money, or money that is not backed by gold or silver, only a government decree. The move had the advantage of making the money supply more flexible and controllable. However, many experts, even some of Roosevelt's advisers, believed that devaluing the dollar was risky and dangerous and would have long-term negative effects.

Reforming Agriculture A number of New Deal programs were aimed at easing the desperate plight of American farmers. For years, the supply of crops grown by American farmers had far exceeded demand. Prices dropped to the point where it was no longer profitable to grow some crops. To counter this, Congress passed the Agricultural Adjustment Act (AAA), which sought to end overproduction and raise crop prices. To accomplish these goals, the AAA provided financial aid, paying farmers subsidies to cut production and forego planting on some of their land. Some farmers plowed under crops and killed off excess livestock. Many Americans believed it was immoral to kill livestock or destroy crops while people went hungry. By 1934, however, farm prices began to rise.

These governmental actions to help farmers proved a mixed blessing for the nation, however. Some farmers didn't qualify for the program.

The increase in farm prices also raised the price of food. In addition, the AAA left many tenant farmers unemployed when large landowners took the land they were farming out of production.

Creating the TVA Americans living in the Tennessee River valley of the rural South were among the poorest in the nation. Few had electricity, running water, or proper sewage systems. In 1933, Congress responded by creating a government agency called the **Tennessee Valley Authority (TVA)**. The TVA built a series of dams in the Tennessee River valley to control floods and to generate electric power. The agency also replanted forests and built fertilizer plants. These projects created jobs and attracted industry with the promise of cheap power.

Despite its accomplishments, the TVA attracted a host of critics. Some labeled it "socialist," because it gave government direct control of an industry. Private power companies complained that they could not compete with the TVA, because the agency paid no taxes. However, the TVA's successes in improving life in the Tennessee Valley have ensured its survival to the present.

Relief and Recovery During the Hundred Days, Roosevelt proposed and Congress enacted numerous other relief measures. To counter the depression's devastating impact on young men, FDR created the **Civilian Conservation Corps (CCC)**. The CCC provided jobs for more than 2 million young men. They replanted forests, built trails, dug irrigation ditches, and fought forest fires. As time went on, programs such as the CCC became more inclusive, extending work and training to Mexican American and other minority youth, as well as to whites. FDR called the CCC his favorite New Deal program.

Congress passed a number of other relief acts. The Federal Emergency Relief Act (FERA) granted federal funds to state and local agencies to help the unemployed. The short-lived Civil Works Administration (CWA) provided jobs on public-works projects. On another front, Congress created the Home Owners Loan Corporation (HOLC), which loaned money at low interest rates to homeowners who could not meet mortgage payments. The Federal Housing Administration (FHA) insured bank loans used for building and repairing homes.

These New Deal measures marked a clear break from the policies of the Hoover administration, which had avoided direct relief to individuals. The $500 million appropriated for FERA represented the largest peacetime expenditure by the federal government to that time.

The centerpiece of the early New Deal's recovery program was the National Industrial Recovery Act, which established the **National Recovery Administration (NRA)**. Roosevelt called the NRA "the most important and far-reaching legislation ever enacted by the American Congress." Working with business and labor leaders, the NRA developed codes of fair competition to govern whole industries. These codes established minimum wages for workers and minimum prices for the goods that businesses sold. The idea behind these codes was to increase the wages of workers so they could buy more goods and raise prices so companies could make a profit.

Another major piece of New Deal legislation was the **Public Works Administration (PWA)**, which built bridges, dams, power plants, and government buildings. The PWA was responsible for building many important structures that are still in use today, such as New York City's Triborough Bridge, the Overseas Highway linking Miami and Key West, Florida, and the Bonneville Dam on the Columbia River in the Pacific Northwest. These public-works projects improved the nation's infrastructure and created millions of new jobs for workers.

☑ **RECALL** What was the purpose of FDR's fireside chats?

>> Analyze Political Cartoons Cite evidence from the cartoon that supports the conclusion that New Deal programs had negative effects on the American public.

Critics of the New Deal

While Roosevelt had little difficulty gaining support from Congress for his proposals, a minority of Americans expressed their opposition to the New Deal. Critics on the political right thought the changes the New Deal brought were too radical. Critics on the left thought that they were not radical enough. Several of FDR's critics attracted mass followings and made plans to challenge him for the presidency in 1936.

Too Much or Not Enough? The chief complaint of conservatives against the New Deal was that it made the federal government too powerful. Critics contended that the government was telling business how to operate, spending large sums of money, and piling up a huge national debt.

To many conservatives, the New Deal was destroying free enterprise and undermining individualism. In a 1934 book entitled *The Challenge to Liberty*, former President Herbert Hoover described the New Deal as "the most stupendous invasion of the whole spirit of liberty" in the nation's history. Robert Taft, the son of former President William Howard Taft and a leading Republican in Congress, believed that Roosevelt's programs threatened individual freedom.

In 1934, these critics formed the American Liberty League. Supporters included prominent business leaders, such as Alfred Sloan and William Knudsen of General Motors. Leading Democrats, such as John W. Davis, the Democrats' presidential nominee in 1924, and Al Smith, the nominee in 1928, joined the Liberty League because they felt Roosevelt had deserted the Democratic Party's principles of a limited federal government.

While conservatives accused FDR of supporting socialism, some leading socialists charged that the New Deal did not do enough to end the depression. Norman Thomas, the Socialist Party's presidential candidate, claimed that FDR's only concern was saving the banking system and ensuring profits for big business. The American Communist Party described the New Deal as a "capitalist ruse."

Populist Critics Gain a Following The most significant criticism of FDR came from a cluster of figures whose roots were in the Populist movement. They saw themselves as spokesmen for poor Americans, challenging the power of the elite. Roosevelt's strongest and most popular critics were Francis Townsend, Father Charles Coughlin, and Huey Long.

>> Louisiana Senator Huey Long drew attention for his sharp criticism of New Deal programs and his belief that income should be redistributed from the wealthy to the poor through taxes.

Townsend, a doctor from California, had a simple approach to resolving the economic effects of the Great Depression. It called for the federal government to provide $200 a month to all citizens over the age of 60. These funds, he argued, would filter out to the rest of society and produce an economic recovery. To promote this plan, he established "Townsend Clubs" and held meetings that resembled old-time church revivals.

Father **Charles Coughlin** presented an even bigger challenge to FDR. Coughlin, a Roman Catholic priest, had attracted millions of listeners to his weekly radio show.

At first, Coughlin supported the New Deal, but in time he broke with FDR, accusing him of not doing enough to fight the depression. Coughlin said that Roosevelt had "out-Hoovered Hoover" and called the New Deal "the raw deal."

Coughlin mixed calls for the nationalization of industry with anti-Semitic remarks and attacks on "communists" who, he charged, were running the country. By the early 1940s, Coughlin's views became so extreme that Roman Catholic officials forced him to end his broadcasts.

Canadian by birth, Coughlin could not run against FDR in the 1936 election. However, he threatened to throw his support behind an even more popular New Deal critic, Senator **Huey Long** of Louisiana. Long was an expert performer whose folksy speeches delighted audiences. Long's approach to solving the depression was his "Share Our Wealth" program that proposed high taxes on the wealthy and large corporations, and the redistribution of their income to poor Americans.

> God invited us all to come and eat and drink all we wanted. He smiled on our land and we grew crops of plenty to eat and wear. . . . [But then] Rockefeller, Morgan, and their crowd stepped up and took enough for 120,000,000 people and left only enough for 5,000,000 for all the other 125,000,000 to eat. And so the millions must go hungry and without those good things God gave us unless we call on them to put some of it back.
>
> —Huey Long radio broadcast, 1934

Roosevelt viewed Long as a serious political threat. Indeed, a poll taken in 1935 estimated that, under the right circumstances, Long could have attracted up to 4 million votes in the 1936 presidential election. Although not enough votes to win the election, his candidacy could have drawn votes from Roosevelt, damaging the President's chances. But Long never got that opportunity.

For years he had ruled Louisiana as if he owned the state, wresting control of nearly every facet of governance from local and other state officials. On his way to achieving this dominance, he made many enemies. In 1935, a political enemy assassinated Long, ending the most serious threat to Roosevelt's presidency.

☑ **IDENTIFY MAIN IDEAS** Why were many conservatives opposed to New Deal programs?

☑ ASSESSMENT

1. **Compare and Contrast** the political philosophies of Herbert Hoover and Franklin D. Roosevelt regarding economic relief during the Great Depression.
2. **Draw Conclusions** Explain how changing power structures in Europe influenced U.S. politics during the Great Depression.
3. **Compare Points of View** Explain why the Tennessee Valley Authority received support from some Americans and criticism from others.
4. **Identify Central Ideas** Discuss the significance of the Hundred Days.
5. **Connections to Today** What did the government do to ease the plight of farmers as part of the New Deal? Is this approach applicable to the wildfire situation in California? If so, how? If not, what other approach might the government take to deal with this crisis?

GO ONLINE to access these biographies:
Franklin D. Roosevelt, John Nance Garner

13.4

GO ONLINE to **Project Imagine: See the New Deal in Action** to explore projects that provided employment during the depression

The New Deal Expands

FDR's goals for the first phases of the New Deal were relief, recovery, and reform. Progress had been made, but there still was a long way to go. Beginning in early 1935, Roosevelt launched an aggressive campaign to find solutions to the ongoing problems caused by the Great Depression. This campaign, sometimes known as the Second New Deal, created Social Security and other programs that continue to have a profound impact on the everyday lives of Americans.

BOUNCE to Activate Flipped Video

Objectives

Analyze ways that the New Deal promoted social and economic reform and its long-term effects.

Explain how New Deal legislation affected the growth of organized labor.

Evaluate the impact of Roosevelt's plan to increase the number of U.S. Supreme Court justices on the course of the New Deal.

Key Terms

- Works Progress Administration (WPA)
- John Maynard Keynes
- pump priming
- Social Security Act
- Wagner Act
- collective bargaining
- Fair Labor Standards Act
- Congress of Industrial Organizations (CIO)
- sit-down strike
- court packing

Expanding New Deal Programs

In his fireside chats, press conferences, and major addresses, Roosevelt explained the challenges facing the nation. He said that the complexities of the modern world compelled the federal government to "promote the general welfare" and to intervene to protect citizens' rights. Roosevelt used legislation passed during the second phase of the New Deal to try to accomplish these goals. This second wave of legislation addressed the problems of the elderly, the poor, and the unemployed; created new public-works projects; helped farmers; and enacted measures to protect workers' rights. It still focused on relief, recovery, and reform, but it now had a more long-term focus. It was during this period that the first serious challenges to the New Deal emerged.

New Jobs Programs In the spring of 1935, Congress appropriated $5 billion for new jobs and created the **Works Progress Administration (WPA)** to administer the program. President Roosevelt placed his longtime associate, Harry Hopkins, in charge. The WPA built or improved a good part of the nation's highways,

GO ONLINE to access your digital course

dredged rivers and harbors, and promoted soil and water conservation.

The WPA even provided programs in the arts for displaced artists, writers, and actors. As Hopkins explained, artists "have to eat just like other people."

By 1943, the WPA had employed more than 8 million people and spent about $11 billion. Its workers built more than 650,000 miles of highways and 125,000 public buildings. Among the most famous projects funded by the WPA were the San Antonio River Walk and parts of the Appalachian Trail.

Critics argued that FDR was using the WPA to build voter loyalty to the Democratic Party. In addition, these programs were expensive, and the government paid for them by spending money it did not have. The federal deficit—$461 million in 1932—grew to $4.4 billion in 1936. The enormous expenditures and growing debt led many to criticize the government's public-works projects as wasteful. Some economists disagreed. British economist **John Maynard Keynes** argued that deficit spending was needed to end the depression. According to Keynes, putting people to work on public projects put money into the hands of consumers who would buy more goods, stimulating the economy. Keynes called this theory **pump priming**.

>> Social Security was established to help retirees. Retired bookkeeper Ida Fuller of Ludlow, Vermont, displayed her monthly check here. It was for $41.30.

Aiding Older Americans The United States was one of the few industrialized nations in the world that did not have some form of pension system for the elderly. During the depression, many elderly people had lost their homes and their life savings and were living in poverty. On January 17, 1935, President Roosevelt unveiled his plans for Social Security.

The **Social Security Act**, passed by Congress in 1935, established a pension system for retirees. It also established unemployment insurance for workers who lost their jobs. In addition, the law created insurance for victims of work-related accidents and provided aid for poverty-stricken mothers and children, the blind, and the disabled. It was funded by a payroll tax on employers and workers.

The Social Security Act had many flaws. At first, it did not apply to domestic workers or farmworkers. Since African Americans were disproportionately employed in these fields, they were not eligible for many of the benefits of Social Security. Widows received smaller benefits than widowers, because people presumed that elderly women could manage on less money than elderly men. Despite these shortcomings, Social Security proved the most popular and significant of the New Deal programs.

Social Security continues today to provide basic economic security to millions of Americans. Its programs act as a safety net for senior citizens, the poor, and others in financial need. Popular support for Social Security continues, although concern mounts over the program's long-term funding and ability to keep making payments.

Supporting American Farms Another New Deal program that passed in 1935 included further help for farmers. When the depression began, only 10 percent of all farms had electricity, largely because utility companies did not find it profitable to run electric lines to communities with small populations. To bring farmers into the light, Congress established the Rural Electrification Administration (REA). The REA loaned money to electric utilities to build power lines, bringing electricity to isolated rural areas. This program had a tremendous, beneficial effect on rural communities. The REA was so successful that by 1950, about 80 percent of American farms had electricity.

New Deal programs changed the relationship of the federal government to the American farmer. The government was now committed to providing price supports, or subsidies, for agriculture. Critics attacked price supports for undermining the free market. Others observed that large farms, not small

AGRICULTURE & THE NEW DEAL

AGRICULTURAL ADJUSTMENT ACT 1933

- Congress set price supports to offset falling prices by controlling the supply and demand for farm products.
- Farmers were paid to reduce acreage farmed.
- Taxes were levied against food processors to pay for subsidies.
- The Supreme Court later declared the Act unconstitutional and it was amended.

Source: U.S. Department of Agriculture

COTTON ACREAGE TAKEN OUT OF PRODUCTION & FARMER AGREEMENTS SIGNED 1933

Cotton Acreage Taken Out of Production		Farmer Agreements Signed
927,812	ARKANSAS	99,808
454,230	LOUISIANA	108,533
931,813	MISSISSIPPI	62,130
10,487,991	U.S.	1,031,549

Source: *The Second Great Emancipation;* National Bureau of Economic Research

FARM FORECLOSURES IN THE COTTON BELT STATES (PER 1,000 FARMS)

	1925–1930	1931–1933
ARKANSAS	17.3	31.7
LOUISIANA	15.8	26.4
MISSISSIPPI	16.1	41.1
U.S.	17.1	31.7

Source: National Bureau of Economic Research

DAIRY PRICES	GRAINS PRICES	COTTON AND COTTONSEED PRICES	MEAT PRICES	WHEAT PRICES
↑ 44%	↑ 200%	↑ 100%	↑ 50%	↑ 120%

Source: *The Agricultural Outlook for 1935*

>> **Analyze Data** How do the data on farm foreclosures point to a need for the Agricultural Adjustment Act of 1933? Did the reduction of cotton acreage have its desired effect on prices?

farmers, benefited most from federal farm programs. Even during the 1930s, many noticed that tenant farmers and sharecroppers, often African Americans, did not fully share in the federal programs. Yet farm prices stabilized, and agriculture remained a productive sector of the economy.

Water for an Expanding West Many of the New Deal public-works water projects had an enormous impact on the development of the American West. The government funded the complex Central Valley irrigation system in California. The massive Bonneville Dam in the Pacific Northwest controlled flooding and provided electricity to a vast number of citizens.

☑ **DESCRIBE** Why was it necessary to establish the Rural Electrification Administration in order to bring electricity to farmers?

Labor Unions Thrive

Even before the Great Depression, most industrial workers labored long hours for little pay. Few belonged to labor unions. During the Great Depression, however, there was an upsurge in union activity. New unions enlisted millions of workers from the mining and automobile industries.

A New Relationship Between Workers and Business Owners Roosevelt believed that the success of the New Deal depended on raising the standard of living for American industrial workers. This, he believed, would improve the entire economy. The National Labor Relations Act of 1935 was the most important piece of New Deal labor legislation.

Also called the **Wagner Act**, it recognized the right of employees to join labor unions and gave workers the right to **collective bargaining**. Collective bargaining meant that employers had to negotiate with unions about hours, wages, and other working conditions. The law created the National Labor Relations Board (NLRB) to look into workers' complaints.

The **Fair Labor Standards Act** of 1938 provided workers with additional rights. It established a minimum wage, initially at 25 cents per hour, and a maximum workweek of 44 hours. It also outlawed child labor. The minimum wage remains one of the New Deal's most controversial legacies. In the years ahead, the minimum wage would be gradually raised. Today, whenever a raise in the minimum wage is proposed, economists and political leaders debate the wisdom of such an increase. Supporters say such raises are necessary for low-paid workers to keep pace with the rising cost of living. Opponents counter that some producers will pass the wage increases on to consumers in the form of higher prices. They also fear that minimum wage increases will increase unemployment if some employers cut jobs to keep their labor costs the same.

Workers Organize for Gains The upsurge in union activity came at the same time as a bitter feud within the major labor federation, the American Federation of Labor (AFL). The AFL represented skilled workers—such as plumbers, carpenters, and electricians—who joined trade or craft unions. Few workers in the major industries belonged to the AFL, and the AFL made little effort to organize them.

Fed up with the AFL's reluctance to organize these workers, John L. Lewis, the president of the United Mine Workers, and a number of other labor leaders established the **Congress of Industrial Organizations (CIO)**. The workers targeted by the CIO-organizing campaigns tended to be lower paid and ethnically more diverse than those workers represented by the AFL.

In December 1936, members of the CIO's newly formed United Automobile Workers (UAW) union staged a **sit-down strike**, occupying one of General Motors's most important plants in Flint, Michigan. In a sit-down strike, workers refuse to leave the workplace until a settlement is reached. When the police and state militia threatened to remove them by force, the workers informed Michigan governor Frank Murphy that they would not leave.

> We fully expect that if a violent effort is made to oust us many of us will be killed and we take this means of making it known to our wives, to our children, to the people of the State of Michigan and the country, that if this result follows from the attempt to eject us, you are the one who must be held responsible for our deaths!
>
> —Auto workers sit-down committee, Flint, Michigan, January 1936

The strike lasted for 44 days until General Motors, then the largest company in the world, agreed to recognize the UAW. This union success led to others.

By 1940, 9 million workers belonged to unions, twice the number of members in 1930. Just as important, union members gained better wages and working conditions.

CHECK UNDERSTANDING Why did workers such as miners and automobile workers feel the need to split away from the AFL and start the CIO?

Federal Minimum Wage, 1938–2020

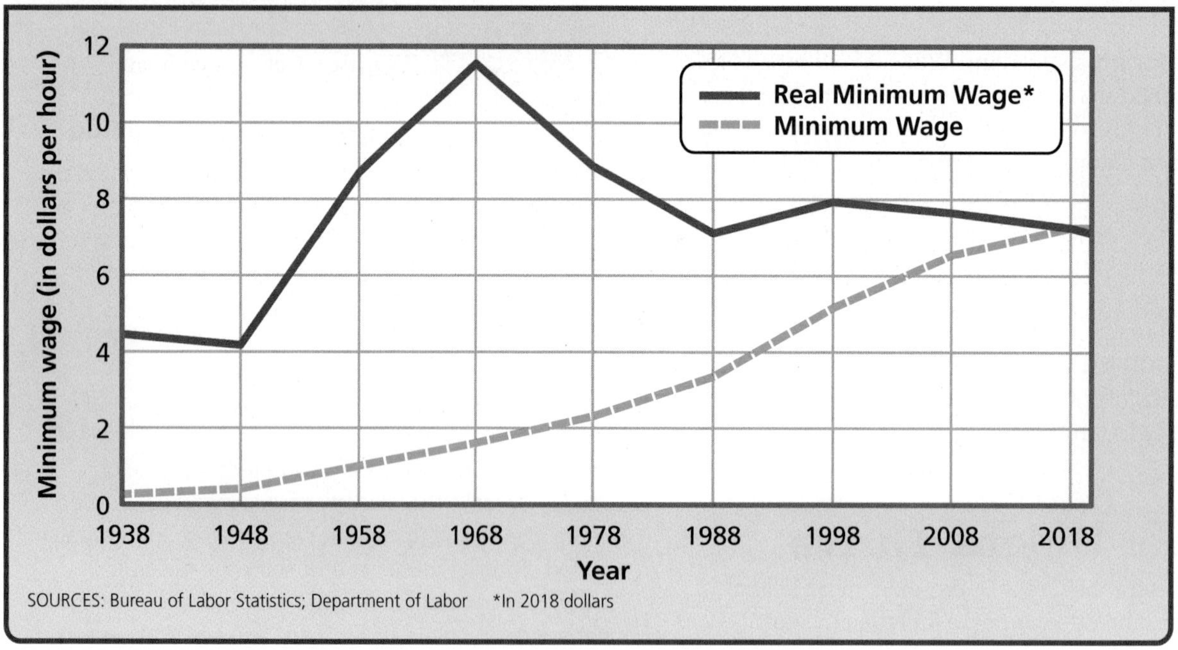

>> **Analyze Data** The real minimum wage is the constant dollar value of the minimum wage, adjusted for inflation. Using the graph, describe how the real minimum wage has changed since 1938.

Labor Union Membership, 1920–1960

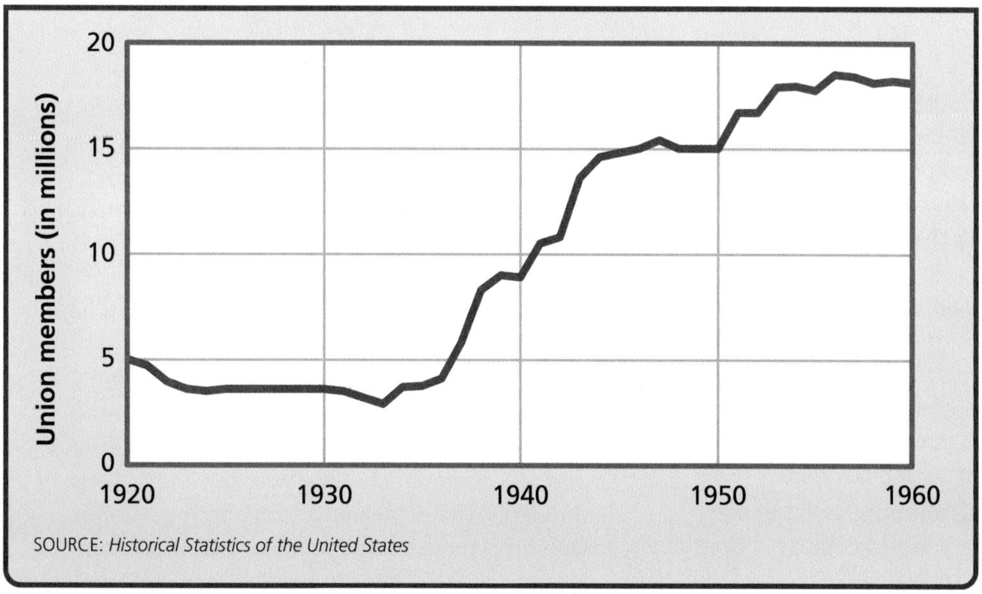

>> **Analyze Graphs** What factors explain the increase in union membership after the mid 1930s?

Opposition to the New Deal

Franklin Roosevelt won an overwhelming victory in the presidential election of 1936. He received 61 percent of the vote, compared to just 37 percent for his Republican challenger, Alfred M. Landon. Roosevelt carried every state but Maine and Vermont. FDR entered his second term determined to challenge the group that he considered the main enemy of the New Deal—a Supreme Court that had struck down many of his programs.

Some New Deal Policies Face Judicial Scrutiny A year before the 1936 election, the Supreme Court had overturned one of the key laws of Roosevelt's first hundred days. In the case of *Schechter Poultry* v. *United States*, the Supreme Court unanimously ruled that since the President has no power to regulate interstate commerce, the National Industrial Recovery Act was unconstitutional. The power to regulate interstate commerce rests with Congress and cannot be delegated to the executive branch.

One pro-New Deal newspaper captured the mood of many Democrats: "AMERICA STUNNED; ROOSEVELT'S TWO YEARS' WORK KILLED IN TWENTY MINUTES."

Not long afterward, the Court ruled a key part of the Agricultural Adjustment Act unconstitutional. Roosevelt charged that the Court had taken the nation back to "horse-and-buggy" days. He expected the Court to strike down other New Deal measures, limiting his ability to enact new reforms.

Roosevelt's Court-Packing Scheme On February 5, 1937, in a special address to Congress, FDR unveiled a plan that would dilute the power of the sitting Justices of the Supreme Court. He called for adding up to six new Justices to the nine-member Court. He justified his proposal by noting that the Constitution did not specify the number of judges on the Court. He added that many of the Justices were elderly and overworked. Critics, recognizing that Roosevelt's new appointees would most likely be New Deal supporters, called his plan **court packing**. They accused him of trying to increase presidential power and upsetting the delicate balance between the three branches of the federal government.

Some critics urged Americans to speak out.

> If the American people accept this last audacity of the President without letting out a yell to high heaven, they have ceased to be jealous of their liberties and are ripe for ruin.
>
> —Dorothy Thompson, newspaper columnist, 1937

Given Roosevelt's enormous popularity, he might have convinced Congress to enact his plan. In the end there was no need, however, because the Court began to turn his way. On March 29, 1937, the Court ruled 5 to 4 in favor of a minimum wage law. Two weeks later, again by a vote of 5 to 4, the Supreme Court upheld the constitutionality of the Wagner Act. In both cases, Justice Owen J. Roberts provided the deciding vote. Pundits called it the "switch in time to save nine," because Roberts had previously voted against several New Deal programs. Roberts's two votes in support of the New Deal removed FDR's main reason for packing the Court.

Shortly after this switch, Judge Willis Van Devanter, who had helped strike down several New Deal programs, resigned from the Court. This enabled FDR to nominate a Justice friendlier to the New Deal. With more retirements, Roosevelt nominated a number of other new Justices, including Felix Frankfurter, one of his top advisers.

Indeed, 1937 marked a turning point in the history of the Court. For years to come, the Court more willingly accepted a larger role for the federal government. Yet the court-packing incident had the impact of weakening FDR politically. Before the court-packing plan, FDR's popularity prevented critics from challenging him. FDR's attempt to force a change to the relationship among the executive and judicial branches of government was off-putting to many Americans, even those who had supported him since 1932. Now that Roosevelt had lost momentum, critics felt free to take him on. And even though after 1937 the Court did not strike down any more laws, Roosevelt found the public much less willing to support further New Deal legislation.

Economic Setbacks Help Conservative Candidates The turmoil over the Supreme Court had barely faded when the Roosevelt administration faced another crisis.

During 1935 and 1936, economic conditions had begun to improve. Unemployment had fallen 10 percent in four years. With the economy doing better, FDR cut back on federal spending in order to reduce the rising deficit. But he miscalculated.

While Roosevelt reduced federal spending, the Federal Reserve Board raised interest rates, making it more difficult for businesses to expand and for consumers to borrow to buy new goods. Suddenly, the economy was in another tailspin. Unemployment soared to more than 20 percent. Nearly all of the gains in employment and production were wiped out.

Largely because of the downturn, the Democrats suffered a setback in the 1938 congressional elections. Republicans picked up 7 Senate and 75 House seats. Although Democrats still maintained a majority in both houses of Congress, Roosevelt's power base was seriously weakened because many southern Democrats already were only lukewarm supporters of the New Deal. Needing their support for his foreign policies, FDR chose not to try to force any more reforms through Congress. In addition,

Unemployment, 1929–1943

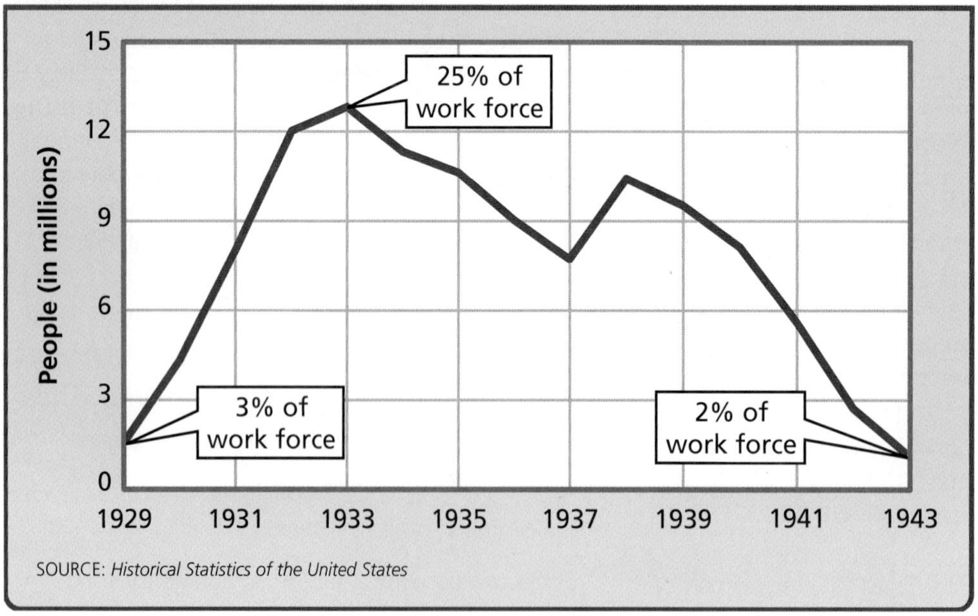

>> **Analyze Graphs** How did Roosevelt's cutback on federal spending in 1937 affect the unemployment rate?

BOUNCE to Activate Timeline

the President's attention was increasingly drawn to events in Europe and Asia that would in 1939 lead to the outbreak of World War II.

CHECK UNDERSTANDING Why did President Roosevelt's critics see his attempt to expand the Supreme Court as a challenge to the balance of power in the U.S. government?

ASSESSMENT

1. **Compare and Contrast** Discuss the similarities and differences between the first phase of the New Deal and the second phase.
2. **Identify Cause and Effect** Explain how the second phase of the New Deal affected farmers and changed their relationship with the federal government.
3. **Describe** the New Deal's impact on the American West.
4. **Evaluate Arguments** Discuss the effectiveness of strategies used by the United Automobile Workers' Union to protest General Motors.
5. **Connections to Today** One way that wildfires start is due to sparks from electrical lines. How were power lines also an issue for farmers during the depression? Compare and contrast the two situations.

>> **Analyze Political Cartoons** In this cartoon, what does the artist suggest is the relationship of the new Supreme Court Justices to President Roosevelt? What does Uncle Sam's reaction suggest?

BOUNCE to Activate Chart

GO ONLINE to access this biography: John Maynard Keynes

13.5

GO ONLINE to **Project Imagine: Does FDR Deserve a Third Term?** to give your opinion about the changes that FDR brought to the presidency, including his radio fireside chats.

BOUNCE to Activate Flipped Video

Objectives

Identify the social and political contributions of Eleanor Roosevelt, Frances Perkins, and other women involved in New Deal programs.

Explain how the New Deal expanded economic opportunities for racial and ethnic minorities.

Analyze how the New Deal changed the shape of American party politics and lessened ethnic and social divisions within American society.

Evaluate the effect of the New Deal on the historical role of the federal government and Franklin D. Roosevelt on the presidency.

Key Terms

Black Cabinet
Mary McLeod Bethune
Indian New Deal
New Deal coalition
welfare state

Effects of the New Deal

The New Deal provided desperately needed relief from the depression and enacted reforms that guarded against economic catastrophe. It did not end the depression, however. World War II, with its massive military spending, would do that. Yet, the New Deal mattered enormously because it brought fundamental changes to the nation. It changed the role of the federal government in the economy, the power of the presidency, and the relationship of the American people to their government.

Women Play Increasingly Significant Political Roles

The New Deal provided some women with the opportunity to increase their political influence and to promote women's rights. Foremost among them was Eleanor Roosevelt, who transformed the office of First Lady from a largely ceremonial role to a position of active involvement in the political process. In fact, her more prominent role would set a precedent of increasing involvement in social and political affairs that many subsequent First Ladies would follow. Eleanor Roosevelt made numerous political, social, and economic contributions to American society. Representing the President, she toured the nation. She visited farms and Indian reservations and traveled deep into a coal mine. She helped FDR on his campaigns and offered advice on policy issues. In her newspaper column, "My Day," she called on Americans to live up to the ideal of equal justice for all.

"Eleanor Roosevelt is the First Lady of Main Street," explained magazine writer Margaret Marshall. "She occupies the highest social position in the land. Yet she makes friends on a plane or

GO ONLINE to access your digital course

a train even as you and I." Mrs. Roosevelt's causes included advancing public health and education, promoting the arts in rural areas, and even addressing flood control. She exhibited boundless energy, traveling more than 60,000 miles in two years.

Molly Dewson, head of the Women's Division of the Democratic Party, observed that Eleanor Roosevelt provided women with an unprecedented access to the President. "When I wanted help on some definite point, Mrs. Roosevelt gave [me] the opportunity to sit by the President at dinner and the matter was settled before we finished our soup."

The Roosevelt Administration included the first female Cabinet member, Secretary of Labor Frances Perkins. She played a leading role in establishing Social Security. Perkins also helped win approval of the Fair Labor Standards Act, which ended child labor and established a minimum wage.

However, the New Deal did not fight to end gender discrimination in the workplace. Indeed, some historians have argued that a number of New Deal programs reinforced traditional gender differences. The WPA and other relief programs employed women but made a much greater effort to provide work to men first. For example, women were not eligible to work for the CCC. Domestic workers, a category of jobs held primarily by women, were exempted from Social Security and the Fair Labor Standards Act.

☑ **DESCRIBE** What role did Eleanor Roosevelt play during her husband's presidency?

A Stronger Political Voice for African Americans

When the depression hit, African American workers were often the first to lose their jobs. By 1934, the unemployment rate for African Americans was almost 50 percent, more than twice the national average. Eleanor Roosevelt and others urged the President to improve the situation of African Americans.

As the New Deal progressed, Eleanor Roosevelt increasingly used her position to protest against racial discrimination. At a meeting held by the Southern Conference on Human Welfare, a biracial group that sought to promote racial reforms, the First Lady sat with the Black delegates—a daring move in segregated Birmingham, Alabama. When a white police officer told her that she was violating local segregation laws, Mrs. Roosevelt moved her chair to

>> Eleanor Roosevelt visited an Ohio coal mine in one of her many trips around the country. Her outreach changed the role of First Lady, After Eleanor, First Ladies were often expected to be deeply involved in the nation's affairs.

>> Secretary of Labor Frances Perkins, here shaking hands with steel workers, helped secure the passage of key programs that ended child labor and established a minimum wage.

the space between where the Black delegates and the white delegates were required to sit. She then delivered a rousing and provocative keynote address in favor of racial reform.

> We are the leading democracy of the world and as such must prove to the world that democracy is possible and capable of living up to the principles upon which it was founded. The eyes of the world are upon us, and often we find they are not too friendly eyes.
>
> —Eleanor Roosevelt, November 22, 1938

The President invited many African American leaders to advise him. These unofficial advisers became known as the **Black Cabinet**. They included Robert Weaver and William Hastie, Harvard University graduates who rose to high positions within the Department of the Interior. Hastie later served as a federal judge, and Weaver became the first African American Cabinet member in the 1960s.

Mary McLeod Bethune was another member of the Black Cabinet. The founder of what came to be known as Bethune Cookman College in Florida, she was a powerful champion of racial equality. In her view, the New Deal had created a "new day" for African Americans. She noted that African Americans gained unprecedented access to the White House and positions within the government during Roosevelt's presidency.

Nevertheless, Roosevelt did not always follow the advice of his Black Cabinet. Racial discrimination and injustice continued to plague African Americans. When the NAACP launched an energetic campaign in favor of a federal anti-lynching law, the President refused to support it. FDR told Black leaders that he could not support an anti-lynching law, because if he did, southern Democrats "would block every bill I ask Congress to pass." Hence, no civil rights reforms became law during the 1930s.

Several New Deal measures also unintentionally hurt African Americans. Federal payments to farmers to produce fewer crops led white landowners to evict Black sharecroppers whose labor was no longer necessary from their farms. Even though they benefited from the WPA and other relief measures, African Americans often did not receive equal wages. Social Security and the Fair Labor Standards Act exempted domestic workers and farm laborers, two occupations in which African Americans were employed in great numbers.

RECALL What role did the Black Cabinet play in the Roosevelt Administration?

>> The New Deal benefited American Indians as well as other minority groups. It provided funds for the Navajo to open a new hospital in Fort Defiance, Arizona in 1938.

New Deal Legislation for American Indians

Attempting to improve the lives of American Indians, the Roosevelt administration made major changes in long-standing policies. The 1887 Dawes Act had divided tribal lands into smaller plots. By the early 1930s, it was clear that the act had worsened the condition of the people it was designed to help. Of the original 138 million acres American Indians had owned in 1887, only 48 million remained in American Indian hands, and much of it was too arid to farm. John Collier, the New Deal's Commissioner of Indian Affairs, warned that the Dawes Act was resulting in "total landlessness for the Indians."

To prevent further loss of land and improve living conditions for American Indians, Collier developed the **Indian New Deal**, a program that gave Indians economic assistance and greater control over their own affairs. Collier got funding from New Deal agencies for the construction of new schools and hospitals and to create an Indian Civilian Conservation Corps. In addition, the Bureau of Indian

The African American Vote by Party Affiliation, Selected Elections

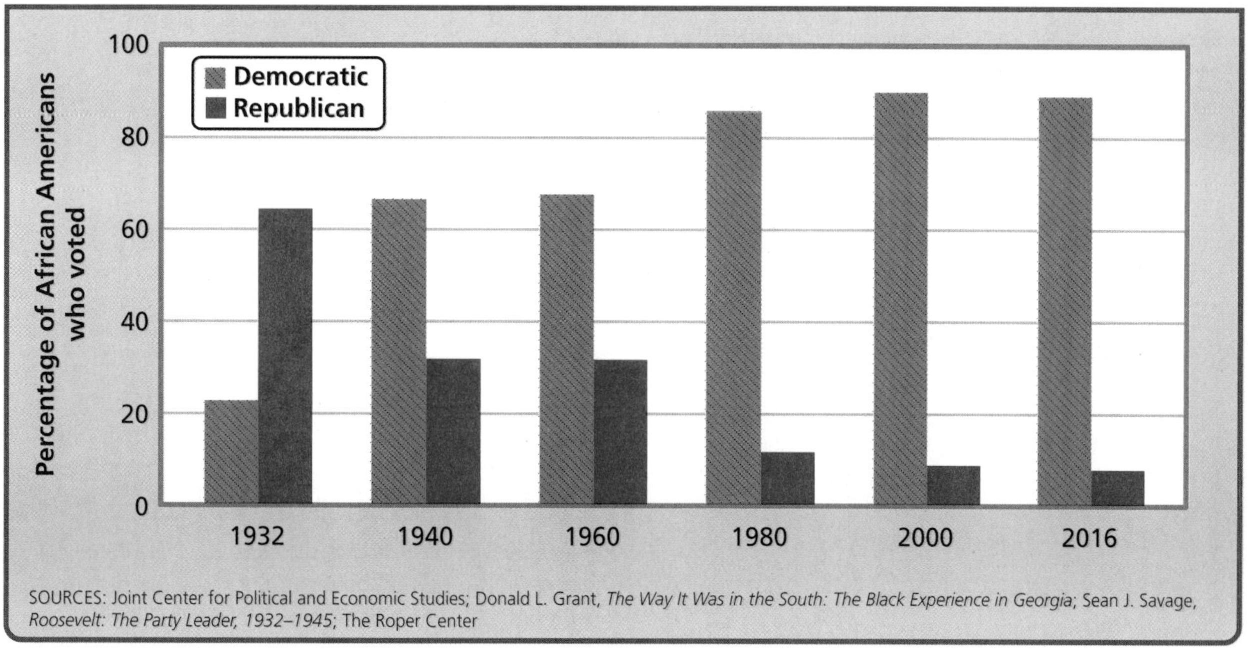

>> **Analyze Graphs** How would you describe the changes in African American voting behavior from 1932 to 2016?

Affairs, in a reversal of previous policies, encouraged the practice of Indian religions, native languages, and traditional customs. Collier also convinced Congress to pass the Indian Reorganization Act of 1934, considered the centerpiece of the Indian New Deal. This law restored tribal control over American Indian land.

Although it did not immediately improve their standard of living, the Indian Reorganization Act gave American Indians greater control over their destiny. But some New Deal measures actually hurt American Indians. For example, federal authorities determined that large herds of sheep tended by the Navajos were causing soil erosion on the Colorado Plateau.

As a result, the federal government enacted a Navajo Livestock Reduction program, which mandated that the Navajo sell or kill thousands of sheep. The Navajo deeply resented this act. They did not believe that their sheep threatened the soil and they did not trust the motives of government agents.

☑ **IDENTIFY SUPPORTING DETAILS** What was the purpose of the Indian Reorganization Act of 1934?

A New Political Coalition Emerges

By the time he died in 1945, Roosevelt had been elected to four terms as President. His legendary political skills had united an unlikely alliance of Americans into a strong political force called the **New Deal coalition**. This coalition brought together southern whites, northern blue-collar workers—especially those with immigrant roots—poor midwestern farmers, and African Americans.

African American voting patterns show the importance of the New Deal coalition. Before the New Deal, most African Americans voted Republican, the party of Abraham Lincoln. Responding to the efforts of Franklin and Eleanor Roosevelt, African Americans began to vote Democratic during the 1930s. This trend was strongest in the West and the North. For example, in 1934, Arthur W. Mitchell, an African American Democrat, defeated Oscar De Priest, an African American Republican, to represent the largely Black south side of Chicago. Mitchell became the first African American Democrat elected to Congress.

The New Deal coalition gave the Democratic Party a sizable majority in both houses of Congress. Before FDR's election, the Democrats had been the minority party in the House of Representatives for all but eight years since 1895. But from 1932 to 1995, the Democrats controlled the majority of seats in the House of Representatives for all but four years. The coalition that elected Roosevelt in 1932 went on to secure the White House for the Democrats in six of the next eight presidential elections.

Besides forging a powerful political coalition, Roosevelt and the New Deal helped to unify the nation. Social and ethnic divisions, so much a part of the 1920s, diminished significantly during the 1930s. Immigrant communities, in particular, gained a greater sense of belonging to the mainstream. Programs such as the CCC and WPA allowed individuals of varied backgrounds to get to know one another, breaking down regional and ethnic prejudices. As one CCC worker observed:

> The Civilian Conservation Corps is a smaller melting pot within the big one. We are thrown together in such a way that we have to get acquainted whether or not we want to. . . . Different races and nationalities look each other in the face, work and eat together for the first time. And it is a safe bet, we think, that this process many times results in the elimination of traditional prejudices based on ignorance and misinformation.
>
> —C. W. Kirkpatrick, CCC worker

☑ **CHECK UNDERSTANDING** How did the New Deal coalition affect the balance of power in the House of Representatives and the executive branch?

New Deal Legislation Expands the Historical Role of Government

New Deal programs greatly increased the size and scope of the federal government. "For the first time for many Americans," writes historian William Leuchtenburg, "the federal government became an institution that was directly experienced. More than the state and local governments, it came to be *the* government." Moreover, the government began to do things it had never done before, from withdrawing taxes directly from workers' paychecks to distributing benefits to the elderly.

Major New Deal Legislation, 1935–1938

PROGRAM	EFFECTS
Social Security Act (SSA) 1935	Created a "safety net" in the form of a pension system and unemployment insurance; provided payments to workers injured on the job, the poor, the elderly, and people with disabilities
Works Progress Administration (WPA) 1935	Employed millions of people on government projects ranging from highway construction to arts programs
Rural Electrification Administration (REA) 1935	Provided loans to electric companies to build power lines, bringing electricity to isolated rural areas
National Labor Relations Act (Wagner Act) 1935	Outlawed unfair labor practices; granted workers the right to organize unions and to bargain collectively; created the National Labor Relations Board (NLRB)
National Youth Administration (NYA) 1935	Provided young Americans between 16 and 25 with jobs and counseling; tied to the WPA
Banking Act of 1935	Finalized the creation of the FDIC and made insurance for bank deposits permanent; created a board to regulate the nation's money supply and interest rates on loans
United States Housing Authority (USHA) 1937	Provided housing for lower income families; led to the 1937 passing of the United States Housing Act, which subsidized construction of low-cost public housing by providing federal loans
Fair Labor Standards Act 1938	Established nationwide compulsory regulation of wages and hours; banned child labor, established a minimum wage of 25 cents per hour, and set the workweek at 44 hours
Food, Drug, and Cosmetic Act 1938	Prohibited the mislabeling of food, drugs, and cosmetics, and ensured their safety and purity

>> **Analyze Charts** The New Deal is considered by some to be a reform movement. Formulate an opinion about whether or not this view can be justified, using specific examples from the chart.

Though the New Deal did not end the depression, it did help restore the American economy. It created the foundation for sustained and stable growth. According to Pulitzer Prize-winning historian David Kennedy, "the unparalleled economic vitality of the post-1940 decades was attributable to many factors. But the [economic expansion] . . . owed much to the New Deal."

The Federal Government Plays an Increasingly Significant Role During the New Deal, the federal government broke from the tradition of laissez-faire, or leaving the economy alone, which had characterized most of American history. This changed the relationship between government and private business. Instead of being hands-off, now the federal government accepted responsibility for spurring economic growth, or pump priming. For the first time, the government had acted as an employer of the unemployed and a sponsor of work projects. FDR accepted the idea that the federal government had to do something to get the economy going again, and Democrats and many Republicans agreed.

FDR's rejection of laissez-faire policies led a number of New Deal critics to accuse him of promoting socialism. However, many New Deal measures actually strengthened capitalism and helped make possible the economic boom of the post-World War II era.

The FDIC and SEC restored Americans' trust in banks and the stock market, and the significant gap between the rich and the poor remained relatively lower for several decades. The Federal Housing Authority (FHA) provided low-interest loans, increasing home ownership.

The New Deal affected millions of individual workers and their families. The Wagner Act boosted union membership, which continued to grow after World War II. Minimum wage increases improved the purchasing power of minorities and those at the bottom rung of the economic ladder. New Deal legislation created child labor laws, workers' compensation laws, and unemployment insurance, programs that had important and enduring effects on the U.S. economy.

The New Deal also had a major impact on rural Americans. Regional public-works projects, such as the TVA and Bonneville Dam, reduced flooding and provided water for irrigation. Along with the Rural Electrification Administration, these dams brought electricity to farmers in the Southeast and the Northwest. Rose Dudley Scearce of Shelby, Kentucky, recalled what the REA meant to her farm family:

>> These men are working on the Arkansas River flood control project funded by the Works Progress Administration (WPA).

BOUNCE to Activate Map

> The first benefit we received from the REA was light, and aren't lights grand? My little boy expressed my sentiments when he said, 'Mother, I didn't realize how dark our house was until we got electric lights.' . . . Like the rest of the people, we changed our storage-battery radio into an electric radio. . . . Next we bought an electric refrigerator. . . . The next benefit we received from the current was our electric stove. . . . Now with a vacuum cleaner, I can even dust the furniture before I clean the carpet, the carpet gets clean, and I stay in good humor.
>
> —Rose Dudley Scearce, "What the REA Service Means to Our Farm House"

In California, the Central Valley Project provided irrigation for the Central Valley by transporting water from reservoirs in the wetter, northern region of the state. The system also produced electricity.

A Federal Safety Net for Those in Need "We are going to make a country in which no one is left out," Franklin Roosevelt once told Frances Perkins. The many programs he enacted to realize this goal led to the rise of a **welfare state** in the United States, a governmental system that assumes responsibility for providing for the welfare of children and the elderly, as well as the poor, sick, disabled, and unemployed.

The creation of the American welfare state was a major change in government policy. With the exception of military veterans, most Americans had never received any direct benefits from the federal government. State and local governments, private charities, and families had long served as the safety net for needy Americans. However, New Deal legislation changed the historical roles of state and federal governments. It established the principle that the federal government, not state or local government, was responsible for the welfare of all Americans. In the latter half of the twentieth century, the reach of federal government programs would grow greatly.

New Deal reforms sparked debate over the proper role of the federal government in the private lives of Americans and in the economic life of the nation. It energized liberals who would push for an even greater role for the federal government. But it troubled conservatives who argued that the expansion of the federal government limited American rights. For example, many argued that New Deal legislation increasing the strength of unions and raising the minimum wage infringed on the rights of business owners and limited job creation and economic growth. Many also did not support federal welfare programs, because they felt that the federal government was assuming responsibilities that were otherwise granted to the states by the Tenth Amendment. Indeed, this very debate over the role of the federal government in the lives of its citizens divides liberals and conservatives to this day.

Conservation Efforts Produce Mixed Results Reared in New York State's beautiful Hudson River valley, Franklin Roosevelt had a great love of nature. As a child, FDR also loved outdoor sports and became an expert swimmer and sailor. A number of his New Deal programs, such as the CCC, aimed at restoring forests and preserving the environment.

Other federal agencies started soil conservation efforts. Perhaps most visibly, New Dealers worked hard to end the Dust Bowl, a symbol of the degraded state of the land at the beginning of the depression.

Franklin Roosevelt also continued the conservation work of his cousin, President Theodore Roosevelt. The government set aside about 12 million acres of land for new national parks, including Shenandoah National Park in Virginia, Kings Canyon National Park in California, and Olympic National Park in Washington State.

However, not all New Deal programs helped the environment. Several of the large public-works projects, such as the Central Valley Project, the TVA and the string of dams along the Columbia River, had a mixed impact. The dams controlled floods, generated electric power, and provided irrigation, but they also upset the natural habitats of some

FDR'S EFFECT ON THE PRESIDENCY
• Increased power of the President and the executive branch
• Made mass media, such as radio, an essential tool for promoting administration policies
• Expanded role of the President in managing the economy
• Expanded role of the President in developing social policy
• Won third and fourth terms, leading to passage of Twenty-second Amendment, which limited Presidents to two consecutive terms
• Expanded White House staff to include experts and advisers on domestic and foreign policy
• Shaped the President's image as caretaker of the American people
• Increased the power and involvement of the federal government in American life

>> **Analyze Charts** How did FDR's policies affect the role of the executive branch?

aquatic life. Massive reservoirs created by these projects also displaced some people and destroyed some traditional Native American burial, hunting, and fishing grounds.

An Expansion of Executive Power In no area did FDR have a greater impact than on the office of the President itself. The expanding role of the government, including the creation of many new federal agencies, gave the executive branch much more power. New Deal administrators, such as Harry Hopkins, head of the WPA, commanded large bureaucracies with massive budgets and little supervision by Congress. Their authority increased Roosevelt's influence. Indeed, some commentators even began to speak of the rise of an imperial presidency, an unflattering comparison to the power exercised in the past by rulers of great empires.

FDR also affected the style of the presidency. His mastery of the radio captivated Americans. His close relations with the press assured a generally popular response to his projects from the major media. Because he served for such a long time and was such an outstanding communicator, FDR set a standard that future Presidents had a hard time fulfilling.

Later, during World War II, FDR's presidential power grew even greater. As commander in chief of the nation's armed forces, he exercised enormous authority over many aspects of life.

Most Americans accepted the President's increased authority as a necessary condition of wartime. But after the war, they sought to protect the delicate balance between the different branches of government and between the federal and state governments. The debate over the increasing power of the executive branch relative to other branches is another New Deal legacy that lives on today.

One way that Americans sought to guard against the growing power of the President was by amending the Constitution. When Roosevelt ran for an unprecedented third term in 1940, he knew that he had broken an unwritten rule, established by George Washington, that Presidents should serve only two terms. He won that election and then ran and won a fourth term in 1944. But after Roosevelt's death in 1945, there was a growing call for limiting a President's term in office. In 1951, the Twenty-second Amendment was ratified, limiting the President to two consecutive terms.

>> President Roosevelt, here having lunch with CCC recruits, set the standard for all future presidential hopefuls with his ability to relate to and communicate with the American public and press.

BOUNCE to Activate Chart

DEFINE How would you define a welfare state?

ASSESSMENT

1. **Support a Point of View with Evidence** Explain why some people argue that the New Deal reinforced traditional gender differences.
2. **Identify Central Issues** Explain how Franklin and Eleanor Roosevelt affected the civil rights of African Americans.
3. **Generate Explanations** Explain how the New Deal helped to unify people within United States.
4. **Identify Cause and Effect** Discuss the environmental impact of New Deal programs.
5. **Quest Connections** How did Franklin Roosevelt's time in office affect the power of the presidency?

Discrimination in the CCC?

The Civilian Conservation Corps (CCC) was a New Deal program created to relieve the unemployment and poverty that the depression had unleashed. The CCC put men—but not women—to work, and some men in the CCC were treated differently than others. White CCC director Robert Fechner defended CCC policies in a letter to a civil rights organization, excerpted below. In the second excerpt, Luther Wandall describes how the policy translated into real life for African Americans.

As you read, look for specific details that reveal the position each man takes on the issue of discrimination in the CCC.

>> At this Texas CCC camp, African American workers were not allowed to stand with white workers for this group photograph.

Primary Source 1

Letter from CCC director Robert Fechner to the president of the National Association for the Advancement of Colored People (NAACP), September 1935

Dear Mr. Griffith,
The President has called my attention to the letter you addressed to him on September 14, 1935, in which you ask for information relating to the policy of segregation in CCC camps.

The law enacted by Congress setting up the Emergency Conservation Work specifically indicated that there should be no discrimination because of color. I have faithfully endeavored to obey the spirit and the letter of . . . the law. . . .

At the very beginning of this work, I consulted with many representative individuals and groups who were interested in the work, and the decision to segregate white enrollees, negro enrollees, and war veterans, was generally approved. I believe that the record of the past thirty months will sustain the wisdom of our decision.

While segregation has been the general policy, it has not been inflexible, and we have a number of companies containing a small number of negro enrollees. I am satisfied that the negro enrollees themselves prefer to be in companies composed exclusively of their own race.

This segregation is not discrimination and cannot be so construed. The negro companies are assigned to the same types of work, have identical equipment, are served the same food, and have the same quarters as white enrollees. I have personally visited many negro CCC companies and have talked with the enrollees and have never received one single complaint. I want to assure you that I am just as sincerely interested as anyone in making this work of the greatest possible value to all who have a part in it.
Sincerely yours,
Robert Fechner
Director

ANALYZE ARGUMENTS What evidence does Director Fechner offer to support his argument that "[t]his segregation is not discrimination"?

Primary Source 2

"A Negro in the CCC," Luther Wandall, *The Crisis*, August 1935

. . . We reached Camp Dix about 7:30 that evening. As we rolled up in front of headquarters an officer came out to the bus and told us: "You will double-time as you leave this bus, remove your hat when you hit the door, and when you are asked questions, answer 'Yes, sir,' and 'No, sir.'"

And here it was that Mr. James Crow [a reference to laws that enforced segregation throughout much of the country beginning in the 1870s, known as "Jim Crow" laws] first definitely put in his appearance. When my record was taken at Pier 1, a "C" was placed on it. When the busloads were made up at Whitehall street an officer reported as follows: "35, 8 colored." But until now there had been no distinction made.

USE CONTEXT CLUES What is the meaning of the "C" on Mr. Wandall's record? Did it bother him? How can you tell? Why might he have been bothered by this?

But before we left the bus the officer shouted emphatically: "Colored boys fall out in the rear." The colored from several buses were herded together, and stood in line until after the white boys had been registered and taken to their tents. This seemed to be the established order of procedure at Camp Dix.

This separation of the colored from the whites was complete and rigidly maintained at this camp. . . .

We were finally led away to our tents. And such tents! They were the worst in Camp Dix. Old, patched, without floors or electric lights. . . .

COMPARE AND CONTRAST How does Luther Wandall's description of the living quarters for African Americans compare to Robert Fechner's?

ASSESSMENT

Be sure to cite specific evidence from the sources as you answer the following questions.

1. **Determine Author's Purpose** Judging by the person to whom Mr. Fechner's letter was addressed, as well as its tone, what do you think was his purpose in writing his letter?
2. **Summarize** Does Luther Wandall experience discrimination in the CCC? Explain.
3. **Compare and Contrast** How do Robert Fechner and Luther Wandall's viewpoints differ related to segregation in the CCC?
4. **Cite Evidence** Compare the dates on each source. Is it possible that one source influenced the other? Which one?
5. **Infer** Mr. Fechner notes that he has "never received one single complaint" about the discrimination in the CCC from the African American CCC companies he has visited. Why might this have been the case?
6. **Develop Empathy** How would you have felt if you had had the same experiences as Luther Wandall in the CCC? What might you have written in response to Mr. Fechner's letter?

GO ONLINE to access primary sources

13.6

Photographer Dorothea Lange's "Migrant Mother" (right) was in fact Florence Owens Thompson, who settled in California where she raised her ten children and passed away in 1983.

BOUNCE to Activate Flipped Video

Objectives

Trace the growth of radio and the movies in the 1930s and how both media reflected the characteristics and issues of their time.

Explain the relationship between the New Deal and the arts.

Describe the major themes of literature in the Depression era.

Key Terms

Frank Capra
Federal Art Project
mural
Dorothea Lange
John Steinbeck
Lillian Hellman

Culture During the Depression

Mass entertainment flourished during the New Deal years as Americans sought escape from the worries of the depression. And, for the first time, the government played an active role in the arts, creating programs that put artists to work. It was a golden age for entertainment, and the movies, music, and works of literature produced during this era hold a unique place in American culture.

A New Age in American Entertainment

Entertainment became big business during the 1930s. Large radio networks, such as NBC and CBS, were broadcasting giants, while a cluster of film companies—including MGM, Warner Brothers, Twentieth Century Fox, and Paramount—dominated the silver screen. By 1935, two in three homes owned a radio; by the end of the decade, about nine in ten did. In 1939, nearly two thirds of all Americans attended at least one movie a week. Stars in both industries made fortunes and attracted loyal followings. Glossy fan magazines tracked the stars' personal and professional lives.

Temporary Relief From the Challenges of the Depression

Above all, when Americans went to the movies during the Great Depression, they did so as a means of escapism. They sought relief from their concerns through a good laugh, a good cry, a lyrical song, or by seeing good triumph over evil. *The Wizard of Oz*, one of the most memorable depression-era films, delivered all four. It promised weary audiences that their dreams really would come true.

GO ONLINE to access your digital course

The big movie studios churned out the popular genres of musicals, romantic comedies, and gangster films. Children marveled at the colorful animation of Walt Disney's *Snow White and the Seven Dwarfs*. For a good scare, teens and young adults flocked to *Frankenstein*. Adults watched dancers Fred Astaire and Ginger Rogers glide effortlessly across the ballroom floor in *Top Hat*. And millions wept as they watched the stormy love affair between characters played by Clark Gable and Vivien Leigh in the Civil War epic *Gone With the Wind*.

>> Even as the depression continued, Americans flocked to the movies. Adjusted for inflation, the 1939 epic *Gone With the Wind* is the largest grossing movie of all time.

BOUNCE to Activate Gallery

Depression-Era Films Reflect Social Issues In the early 1930s, many films reflected the public's distrust of big business and government. Gangster movies, such as *Public Enemy* starring James Cagney, were very popular. These films showed a declining faith in government and law enforcement, with characters turning to crime to survive the depression. But as the New Deal restored confidence, the government regained its glow, and movies began portraying government officials as heroes. In 1935, Cagney portrayed an FBI agent who captured the bad guys in *G-Men*.

Other films reflected the struggle against hardship that many Americans were waging by focusing on the strength of average Americans. Director **Frank Capra** was a leader of this genre. The characters in his films were everyday people struggling with the hardships of the time. In Capra's *Mr. Smith Goes to Washington*, actor James Stewart plays a junior senator who fights against the greed and corruption he finds in the nation's capital. Depression-era audiences cheered Capra's films, which celebrate American idealism and the triumph of the common man over the forces of adversity.

Radio's Increasing Popularity The success of the movie industry was matched by that of radio. The national radio networks broadcast popular shows starring comedians such as Bob Hope and Jack Benny. Americans avidly followed soap operas, variety shows, and humorists, such as Will Rogers. Dramatic shows were also popular. *The Lone Ranger* started its run in 1933 and ran for more than 20 years. The detective serial *The Shadow* began each thrilling episode with the haunting line, "Who knows what evil lurks in the hearts of men?"

In addition to providing entertainment, the family radio provided information. FDR used his fireside chats to explain and promote his New Deal programs. Newscasters delivered the daily news and political commentary.

>> Radio was not just a way for Americans to listen to music. As the film industry exploded, so did radio shows, such as comedian Bob Hope's variety show (above).

On at least one occasion, radio listeners had a hard time recognizing the difference between news and entertainment. It happened on the night of October 30, 1938, when millions of Americans tuned in to a drama called *War of the Worlds*, directed by Orson Welles. The Mercury Theatre broadcast was so realistic that many people believed that Martians were actually invading. Panic gripped areas of the country until announcers insisted that it was all make-believe.

The Sounds of an Era Like films and radio shows, various genres of music provided a diversion from hard times. Whether listening to the radio at home or dancing in nightclubs, Americans enjoyed the popular music of the day. "Swing" music played by "big bands" topped the charts. Duke Ellington, Benny Goodman, Artie Shaw, Glenn Miller, and Jimmy and Tommy Dorsey were some of the top swing musicians, a term probably derived from Ellington's tune "It Don't Mean a Thing If It Ain't Got That Swing." The most popular vocalist of the era was Bing Crosby.

Latin music was very popular. The rhythms of the rumba and the samba had a special appeal for dancers, and Latin bands were prominently featured in films and on the radio.

>> Not all popular music in the 1930s described happier days. American blues musician Huddie Ledbetter, better known as "Leadbelly," played music that reflected the harsh experiences of African Americans.

Some genres of music were more somber, reflecting the issues of the time, including folk and ethnic music. Black singers focused on the harsh conditions faced by African Americans.

Huddie Ledbetter, a folk singer known as "Leadbelly," described experiences of African Americans with the songs "Cotton Fields" and "The Midnight Special." Folk singer Woody Guthrie wrote ballads about the Okies, farmers who fled Dust Bowl states and headed to California. Guthrie's song "Dust Bowl Refugee" helped listeners understand the Okies's plight.

☑ **CHECK UNDERSTANDING** Why were many of Frank Capra's films so popular with many Americans?

Increased Funding for the Arts

During the New Deal, the federal government provided funding for the arts for the first time in American history. Recognizing that many artists and writers faced dire circumstances, WPA administrator Harry Hopkins established a special branch of the WPA to provide artists with work. Programs such as the **Federal Art Project**, the Federal Writers' Project, and the Federal Theatre Project offered a variety of job opportunities to artists.

In federally funded theaters, musicians and actors staged performances that were often free to the public. In a series of new state guidebooks, WPA writers recorded the history and folklore of the nation.

Artists painted huge, dramatic **murals** on public buildings across the nation. These paintings celebrated the accomplishments of the workers who helped build the nation. Many of the murals can still be seen in public buildings today.

Photographers also benefited from federal arts programs. The Resettlement and Farm Security Administration (FSA) sought to document the plight of America's farmers. Roosevelt's top aide, Rexford Tugwell, told the head of the FSA, "Show the city people what it's like to live on the farm." Walker Evans and **Dorothea Lange** were among the FSA photographers who created powerful images of impoverished farmers and migrant workers, including Lange's famous photo "Migrant Mother."

When Dorothea took that picture that was the ultimate. She never surpassed it. . . . She has all the suffering of mankind in her but all the perseverance too. A restraint and a strange courage.

—Roy Stryker, FSA, on Dorothea Lange's "Migrant Mother"

Some members of Congress warned of negative impacts of the Federal Art, Writers' and Theatre programs, fearing that they promoted radical values. Congressman J. Parnell Thomas described the Federal Writers' and Theatre projects as "a hotbed for Communists." Eleanor Roosevelt and others defended the programs on the grounds that they did not "believe in censoring anything." Nonetheless, congressional support for the programs declined. Although the Federal Art, Writers' and Theatre programs ceased to exist in the late 1930s and early 1940s, they set a precedent for further federal funding of the arts and humanities in the 1960s.

☑ **DESCRIBE** What was the purpose of the Federal Art Project?

>> The Federal Art Project employed artists to create colorful murals—such as this one in the Allegheny County Courthouse in Pittsburgh, Pennsylvania—in buildings throughout the nation.

BOUNCE to Activate Gallery

The Depression Era Reflected in Literature

The literature of the 1920s, from authors such as F. Scott Fitzgerald and Ernest Hemingway, sometimes overshadows the literature of the 1930s. Still, the depression era produced some memorable works in multiple genres of literature that reflected some of the issues and characteristics of their unique time.

American Society Under the Microscope

During the depression, many writers drifted to the left and crafted novels featuring working-class heroes. They believed that the American economic system no longer worked and they blamed this failure on political and business leaders. Many artists of the 1930s saw "ordinary Americans" as the best hope for a better day.

The most famous novel of the 1930s was **John Steinbeck's** *The Grapes of Wrath*. Steinbeck follows the fictional Joad family from their home in Oklahoma, which has been ravaged by Dust Bowl conditions, to California, where they hope to build a better life. But instead of the Promised Land, the Joads encounter exploitation, disease, hunger, and political corruption.

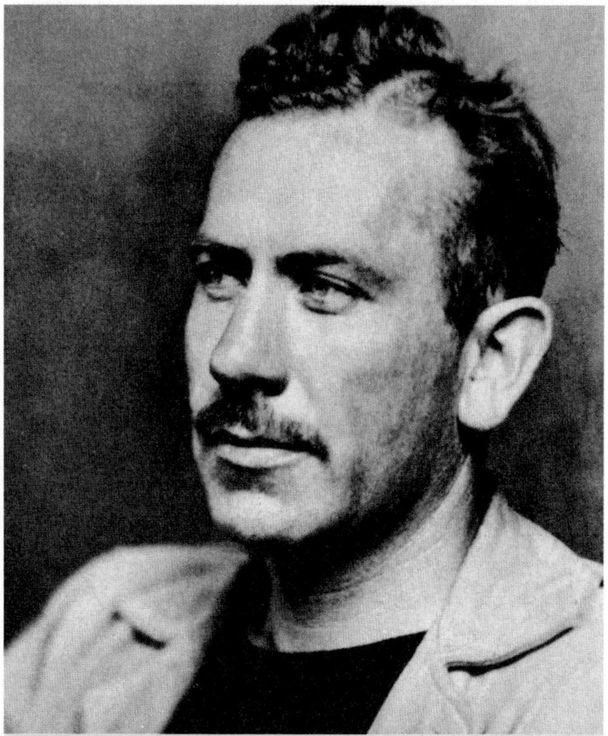

>> Like many other authors of the 1930s, John Steinbeck, author of *The Grapes of Wrath* and *Of Mice and Men,* wrote works that focused on the struggles of America's poor and working class.

>> Although comic books were not new, the 1930s saw the birth of the "superhero" comic. The exploits of Superman thrilled comic-book fans in the 1930s.

African American writers captured the special plight of Black people, facing both the depression and continuing prejudice. Richard Wright's *Native Son* explored racial prejudice in a northern urban setting. Wright was an outspoken critic of racial discrimination.

Playwrights Champion Women and the Working Class In New York, some important playwrights had their first successes during the New Deal period. **Lillian Hellman**, a New Orleans native, wrote several plays featuring strong roles for women. Hellman's plays *The Children's Hour, The Little Foxes*, and *Watch on the Rhine* are also notable for their socially conscious subject matter that reflected some controversial issues of the time.

Clifford Odets was another dramatist who achieved prominence in the 1930s. His plays *Waiting for Lefty* and *Awake and Sing!* chronicle the struggles of the working class during the Great Depression.

Comics Entertain and Inspire On a lighter note, many Americans devoured comic strips and comic books during the 1930s. Among the most popular comic strips were *Flash Gordon*, a science-fiction saga; *Dick Tracy*, a detective story; and *Superman*, the first great "superhero" comic. The success of *Superman*, which began in 1938, quickly led to a radio show and later to a popular television series and several feature films. *Superman* reassured Americans that ordinary citizens, like mild-mannered Clark Kent, could overcome evil.

☑ **RECALL** What were some themes common to depression-era literature?

☑ ASSESSMENT

1. **Generate Explanations** Explain how music helped unify people during the Great Depression.
2. **Apply Concepts** Discuss the relationship between escapism and American entertainment during the 1930s.
3. **Draw Conclusions** Explain how the U.S. entertainment industry changed during the 1930s.
4. **Make Generalizations** Explain why John Steinbeck's novel *The Grapes of Wrath* achieved so much success during the 1930s.
5. **Quest Connections** Why did some people criticize the New Deal's art, theater, and writing programs?

Connections to Today

A firefighter battles a wildfire near a freeway in Simi Valley, California.

Take Action to Protect the Environment

During the 1930s, human interaction with the environment led to a major catastrophe known as the Dust Bowl. Today, the nation faces other threats.

1. **Choose** one of the following topics related to human interaction with the environment:
   - **Wildfires:** Explore the causes and consequences of wildfires and investigate efforts to prevent wildfires, as well as reactions to those efforts.
   - **Floods:** Research the types of floods and the role that climate change is playing in flooding in the United States.
   - **Wetlands:** Learn about the importance of wetlands and the threats they face, including those caused by human activity and natural events.
2. **Ask Questions** Generate a list of questions about your topic. Perhaps you want to know what percentage of wildfires are caused by human interaction with the environment, for example.
3. **Learn** about the topic by conducting research. Use online sources, magazines, interviews, and government sources. Are there any controversies related to this topic? What are the arguments on each side? Take notes as you conduct your research and continue to generate questions as you learn more.
4. **Take Action** Create a series of short social media posts to educate the public about your topic. Use bold graphics and short statements to give information about causes, cautions, and solutions.

Topic 13 Quick Study Guide

LESSON SUMMARIES

Use these Lesson Summaries, and the longer versions available online, to review the key ideas for each lesson in this Topic.

Lesson 1: Causes of the Depression

The prosperity of the 1920s masked deep economic problems. Although some people had become very rich, they could not buy enough goods to keep the economy strong. In addition, too much money was poured into buying stocks. The stock market crash of 1929 marked the beginning of the Great Depression, which lasted until 1941.

Lesson 2: Americans Suffer

Unemployment rose dramatically during the Great Depression. Americans lost their homes and were forced to migrate in search of work. Drought, overfarming, and overgrazing caused a Dust Bowl on the Great Plains, adding to the economic woes that had already devastated farmers. Many African Americans in the South moved north. For many, the Great Depression was a time of despair.

Lesson 3: Two Presidents Respond

President Hoover's policies in response to the Great Depression were deeply unpopular. As a result, Franklin D. Roosevelt was elected President in 1932. President Roosevelt introduced the first New Deal, which put millions back to work building bridges, dams, and government buildings, providing electricity, and planting forests.

Lesson 4: The New Deal Expands

Roosevelt expanded the New Deal by providing jobs and introducing Social Security. New laws expanded workers' rights, established a minimum wage, and outlawed child labor. The Supreme Court resisted some key laws of the New Deal, but began to accept a larger role for the federal government.

Lesson 5: Effects of the New Deal

The New Deal brought more women and African Americans to positions of political influence. American Indians gained new schools and hospitals as well as control over their lands. New Deal programs increased the size of the government and introduced elements of a welfare state by providing for the poor, elderly, sick, and unemployed.

Lesson 6: Culture During the Depression

Entertainment became big business during the 1930s. Americans went to the movies to escape their worries, while radios brought entertainment and President Roosevelt's broadcasts into the home. Swing music and the blues flourished. The federal government funded the arts. Photographers and writers drew attention to social problems.

QUEST! FINDINGS

Write Your New Deal Essay Refer to your responses to the Quest Connections to help you write your essay. Then share it with the class. Use the rubric and other Quest resources online to guide your work.

GO ONLINE to access lesson summaries

VISUAL REVIEW

Use these graphics to review some of the key terms, people, and ideas from this Topic.

Major Causes of the Great Depression

Opposition to the New Deal

CRITICISM FROM THE LEFT	CRITICISM FROM THE RIGHT
• New Deal does not do enough to end the Great Depression. • FDR's only concern is saving banks and big business. • New Deal does not address redistribution of wealth.	• New Deal makes government too powerful. • Increased government role in economy equals socialism. • New Deal destroys free enterprise and individual freedom. • New Deal creates huge national debt.

Effects of the New Deal

Immediate Effects

- Banking system is stabilized.
- Federal payments help farmers.
- Work-relief programs provide jobs.
- Social Security provides safety net.
- New Deal helps unify the nation.

Long-term Effects

- Power of the presidency increases.
- Government takes active role in economy.
- New Deal coalition is a powerful political force.
- Wagner Act protects workers and raises standard of living.
- Minorities and women gain positions in government.

Topic 13 Assessment

KEY TERMS, PEOPLE, AND IDEAS

1. How did the stock market crash contribute to the **Great Depression**?
2. What created the Dust Bowl?
3. Why did President Hoover believe in **trickle-down economics**?
4. What policies were adopted during the **"New Deal"**?
5. What is the economic theory behind **pump priming**?
6. How did **Mary McLeod Bethune** help advance the rights of African Americans?
7. What groups made up the **New Deal coalition**?
8. What characterizes a **welfare state**?
9. Why did some members of Congress oppose the **Federal Art Project**?

CRITICAL THINKING

10. **Identify Cause and Effect** What economic problems were developing in the 1920s?
11. **Cite Evidence** (a.) Why were farmers hit so badly during the depression? (b.) How did they cope with the situation?
12. **Explain an Argument** Why was the establishment of a minimum wage so controversial?
13. **Draw Conclusions** In what ways did the New Deal change the relationship between the federal government and state governments?
14. **Summarize** (a.) How did the arts of the 1930s reflect the social and political realities of the time? (b.) What sort of subject matter attracted artists and writers in the 1930s?
15. **Make Inferences** Why were conservatives so troubled by the policies of the New Deal?
16. **Analyze Graphs** The graph at the top of the next column shows the parties that African Americans voted for in 1932 and 1940. (a.) What change does the graph show? (b.) Why do you think there was such a dramatic shift in 8 years?

The African American Vote by Party Affiliation, 1932 and 1940

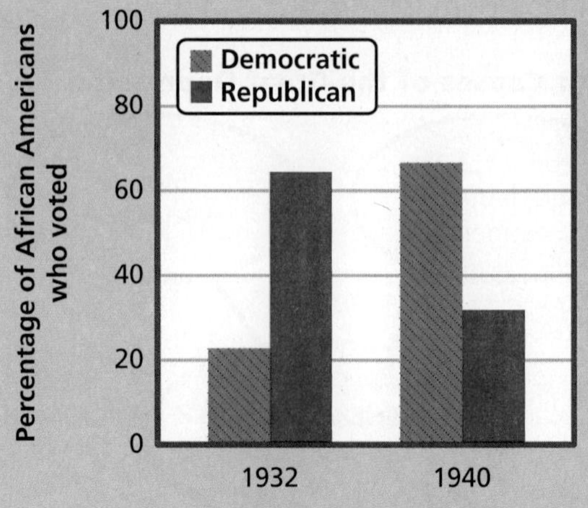

SOURCES: Joint Center for Political and Economic Studies; Donald L. Grant, *The Way It Was in the South: The Black Experience in Georgia*; Sean J. Savage, *Roosevelt: The Party Leader, 1932–1945*

17. **Writing Activity: Write a Narrative** Evaluate how labor relations changed during the New Deal using the excerpt below, your text, and your knowledge of the period. Write a brief historical narrative in one or more paragraphs describing a labor strike from two points of view: labor leaders and factory owners. Recall that a historical narrative is a fictional account based on real people, places, events.

> We feel it proper to recall to you the assurances that you have given many times publicly that you would not permit force or violence to be used in ousting us from the plants. . . . Governor, we have decided to stay in the plant. We have no illusions about the sacrifices which this will entail. We fully expect that if a violent effort is made to oust us many of us will be killed and we take this means of making it known to our wives, to our children, to the people of the State of Michigan and the country, that if this result follows from the attempt to eject us, you are the one who must be held responsible for our deaths.
> *—Auto workers sit-down committee; Flint, Michigan, January 1936*

18. **Connections to Today** The United States faces wildfires and other threats to the environment. What should be the role of the government in addressing these matters? Should the government step in as it did during the 1930s? Or should the government avoid getting involved? Write a one-page response to this question, using evidence from this lesson and the information you gathered in your Take Action project.

DOCUMENT-BASED QUESTIONS

New Deal programs attracted critics and supporters from across the political spectrum. Read the documents below, then answer the questions that follow.

DOCUMENT A

This excerpt is from a radio speech by the New Deal critic, Senator Huey Long of Louisiana.

> . . . So now, ladies and gentlemen, we come to that plan of mine for which I have been so roundly denounced and condemned by . . . spellers and speakers and spoilers of the Roosevelt administration. It is for the redistribution of wealth and for guaranteeing comforts and conveniences to all humanity out of this abundance in our country. I hope none will be horror-stricken when they hear me say that we must limit the size of the big man's fortune in order to guarantee a minimum of fortune, life and comfort to the little man; . . .
>
> —*Senator Huey Long, Radio Speech, 1935*

DOCUMENT B

This political cartoon was inspired by the economic term "pump priming".

DOCUMENT C

This excerpt is from a speech by former president Herbert Hoover.

> But their illegal invasions of the Constitution are but the minor artillery with which this New Deal philosophy of government is being forced upon us. They are now using a more subtle and far more effective method of substituting personal power and centralized government for the institutions of free men. It is not by violation of the Constitution that they are making headway today. It is through taking vast sums of the people's money and then manipulating its spending to build up personal power. By this route relief has been centralized in their hands. . . . By this route government has entered into business in competition with the citizen. In this way a score of new instruments of public power have been created.
>
> — *Former president Herbert Hoover, 1936*

DOCUMENT D

This excerpt is from an interview with Claude Pepper, a Florida senator during the New Deal.

> So, I guess that I came probably under the spell of Roosevelt more than anything else. . . . well, my first speech in the Senate, June 17, 1937 . . . was a liberal speech. One of the things that I pointed out was that in every period of the past, whenever there were problems to be met, there was somebody raising the red flag of danger and saying, "you can't afford to do that." Or, "we mustn't do that." And I said, "But the progress of humanity has been achieved by those who have said, 'let's go ahead."
>
> —*Claude Pepper, 1974*

19. In Document A, Huey Long criticizes the New Deal for
A. its socialist elements.
B. being too ambitious.
C. favoring right-wing programs.
D. not addressing economic injustice.

20. Analyze Political Cartoons Based on Document B, what were some arguments against the New Deal?

21. In Document C, former president Herbert Hoover is criticizing the New Deal for
A. increasing government power.
B. undermining religious freedom.
C. tampering with the Supreme Court.
D. using the arts to promote its propaganda.

22. Document D describes Florida senator Pepper's
A. opposition to the New Deal.
B. support for the New Deal.
C. fear of new social programs.
D. warning against government expansion.

23. Writing Task Write a paragraph explaining whether you think the arguments posed by the opponents or the supporters of the New Deal are more persuasive. Give reasons for your opinion, supported by these documents and your text.

GO ONLINE to access more practice

Topic 14

World War II (1931–1945)

ESSENTIAL QUESTION When is war justified?

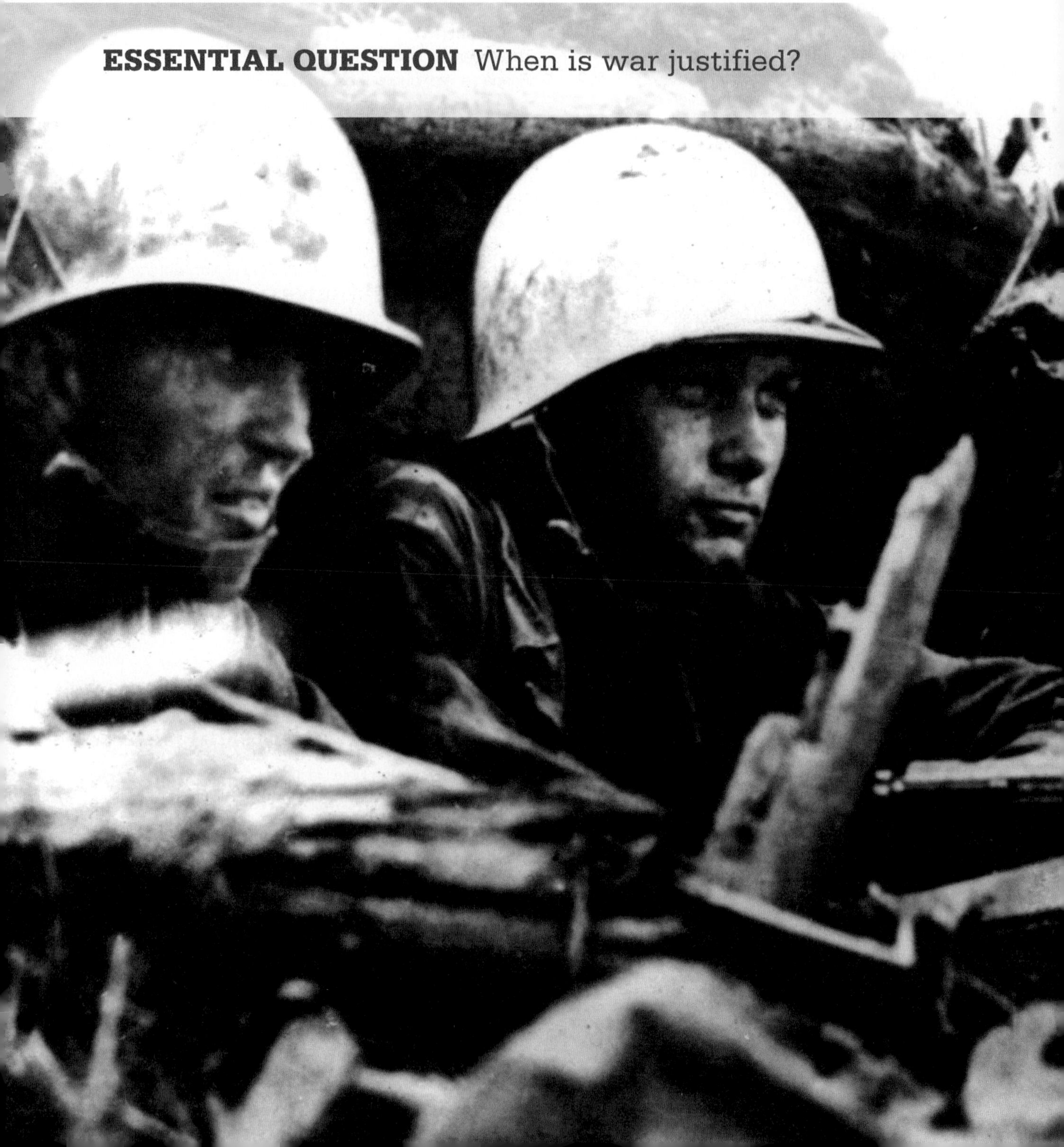

project Imagine

GO ONLINE for immersive experiences designed to help you feel the tragic drama of World War II through rich primary sources. Also access the eText, videos, Biographies, and other online resources.

American troops in Burma, 1944

Connections to Today

Water bottles, food wrap, earbuds—these everyday items all contain synthetic plastic and many of them eventually end up in the world's oceans. Scientists predict that by the year 2050, the oceans could contain more plastic waste than fish.

How did we get here? The plastics industry boomed during World War II, when plastics were used in parachutes, ropes, and tires. Their use quickly spread to non-military applications after the war. In this topic, you'll read about other technologies developed during the war.

NBC LEARN

Hear about one American's experience in World War II.

BOUNCE to Activate My Story Video

Topic 14 Overview

In this Topic, you will learn about the events of World War II. Look at the lesson outline and explore the timeline. As you study this Topic, you'll complete the Quest Inquiry.

LESSON OUTLINE

14.1 Rise of Aggressive Dictators

14.2 America Debates Involvement

14.3 The United States Enters World War II

14.4 A War on Two Fronts

14.5 The Home Front

14.6 The Allies Win World War II

14.7 The Holocaust

14.8 Impact of World War II

Key Events of World War II

1933 Hitler becomes chancellor of Germany.

1939 Germany invades Poland, beginning World War II.

1940 Roosevelt wins third term.

June 1941 Germany invades the Soviet Union.

December 1941 Japan attacks Pearl Harbor; United States enters World War II.

1942 Nazi leaders plan mass murder of Europe's Jews.

1944 D-Day landing in France.

1945 World War II ends.

1930 | 1935 | 1940 | 1945

QUEST! INQUIRY

Building a "Memories of World War II" Website

What was it like to hear about the bombing of Pearl Harbor, to serve in the Army in Europe or the Navy in the Pacific? In this Quest you'll explore life during World War II and document three people's experiences on a website that you'll create.

STEP 1

With your team, make a list of questions you want to answer about how the war affected people, then identify three individuals whose lives were deeply affected by the war.

STEP 2

Research those three people to learn more about their experiences during the war.

STEP 3

Tell the stories of these three people on your website as a tribute to the sacrifices they made during the war.

STEP 4

Share your website with your classmates and community! Reflect on what you've learned about war, human resilience, and teamwork.

GO ONLINE to access complete Quest materials

14.1

Hitler was a powerful speaker who attracted masses of people with promises of "Germany Over All." **Infer** Why do you think dictators hold rallies and marches?

BOUNCE to Activate Flipped Video

Objectives

Explain the rise of dictatorships in the Soviet Union, Italy, Germany, and Japan in the 1930s.

Summarize acts of aggression by Italy, Germany, and Japan.

Analyze the responses of Britain, France, and the United States to the aggressive regimes.

Key Terms

aggression
totalitarianism
Joseph Stalin
Benito Mussolini
fascism
Adolf Hitler
anti-Semitic
Spanish Civil War
General Francisco Franco
appeasement
Franklin D. Roosevelt
Anschluss
Neville Chamberlain
Munich Pact

GO ONLINE to access your digital course

Rise of Aggressive Dictators

The effects of World War I and the Great Depression touched almost every corner of the world. In some countries, these upheavals led to the rise of a new kind of brutal dictatorship—the totalitarian state. These states were led by absolute dictators, leaders willing to use acts of **aggression** to invade other nations in order to enhance their own power. Their actions would destroy the peace established after World War I and spark a new, even deadlier, global conflict.

Peace Dissolves

In November 1918, World War I ended when Germany surrendered to the Allies. In 1919, delegates from 27 nations met in Versailles to hammer out a peace agreement, but only Britain, France, and the United States had a real say in most of the important decisions. Germany and Russia were not even present. From the first, many Germans resented the resulting Treaty of Versailles. Other nations also grumbled over the peace settlements.

Italy and Japan, both part of the Allied powers in World War I, had expected to gain far more territory for their sacrifices. The war that President Woodrow Wilson had called "a war to end all wars" had left behind a mountain of bitterness, anger, frustration, and despair, often capped by a burning desire for revenge.

During the 1920s many nations, new and old, moved steadily toward democracy and freedom. Others, however, took the opposite direction, embracing repressive dictatorships and **totalitarianism**, a government in which a single party or leader controls the economic, social, and cultural lives of its people. Throughout history there have been dictatorships, countries ruled by one person or small groups of people. But totalitarianism, emerging as a twentieth-century phenomenon, controls all aspects of life. It is more extreme than a simple dictatorship. At the head of the government is a strong, charismatic leader who uses terror, spies, and police force to impose the will of the state upon the citizens. Unlike democracies, people living in totalitarian states have no individual rights. The government controls the media and uses propaganda to indoctrinate people. Schools and youth organizations foster the state ideology. The government crushes opposition and censors any political rivals or divergent ideas.

Why did totalitarian regimes take hold in the years leading up to World War II? Historians lay much of the blame on the destruction and bitterness left behind by World War I and the desperation caused by the Great Depression.

PREDICT CONSEQUENCES How do you think totalitarian regimes will affect the peace following World War I?

>> The Paris Peace Conference met at the Palace of Versailles and lasted a year. The crowds of delegates from participating nations wrote a series of treaties.

Strict Regimes in the Soviet Union and Italy

The 1917 communist revolution in Russia inaugurated the first totalitarian state. The communist leader Vladimir Lenin created the beginnings of a totalitarian system of control to maintain power. His programs resulted in civil war, starvation, famine, and the death of millions of Russians.

Stalin Rules the Soviet Union After Lenin's death in 1924, **Joseph Stalin** took the reins as the head of the Communist Party. In Russian, Stalin means "man of steel," and it is an apt description of the dictator's personality. Stalin was suspicious, cruel, ruthless, and tyrannical. He did not think twice about killing rivals or sentencing innocent people to death. His efforts to transform the Soviet Union into an industrial power and form state-run collective farms resulted in the deaths of at least 10 million people.

In what became known as the Great Terror, Stalin purged the Communist Party of real or suspected traitors in the 1930s, ordering the deaths or imprisonment of up to a million people. The purge also included most of the higher officers of the Red Army, among many others. Political prisoners and criminals were sent to dreaded forced labor camps, known as the Gulag.

>> Displaying the totalitarian traits of discipline and militarism, Japanese students march past representatives of Japan, Germany, and Italy.

BOUNCE to Activate Gallery

>> In this staged photo, a fatherly Stalin poses with a young girl. Years later, his government sent her to the Gulag. **Apply Concepts** How is this photo an example of propaganda?

>> Shown in a typical pose, Mussolini often spoke of restoring Italian pride. His arrogant stance matched his message.

A combination of fear and massive propaganda kept Stalin in power. Publicity about Stalin was designed to create an idol, encouraging a cult of personality in which he was credited for all good things. In newspapers, billboards, and schools, the public was fed a constant diet of communist success. Soviet art was censored; only positive images of Stalin and Soviet life were permitted. Images showing Stalin as a kindly father figure masked the reality of labor camps and the consequences of any resistance to his rule.

Mussolini Establishes an Italian Dictatorship

Italian totalitarianism was in many ways a direct result of World War I and the peace treaties that ended it.

Although Italy was on the winning side, it did not get the land along the Adriatic coast it had hoped to obtain from the division of Austria-Hungary. Added to this frustration, a postwar economic depression made it difficult for returning veterans to find jobs. The country began to tumble into chaos. The communist movement grew. Peasants began seizing land and workers went on strike or took over control of factories. Trade declined and taxes increased. New American immigration laws limited immigration to the United States. Law and order broke down as competing groups fought each other in the streets. The government, weak and inept, was unable to restore stability.

It was during this period that **Benito Mussolini** entered the world stage. In 1919, Mussolini founded the Fasci di Combattimento (FAH shee dee kohm ba tee MEHN toh), or Fascist Party, a right-wing organization that promised to restore efficiency and order and make Italy great again. **Fascism** appealed to many looking for strong leadership and restored national pride. Followers of Mussolini, known as Black Shirts, fought in the streets against socialists and communists.

Fearing revolution, in 1922 Italian King Victor Emmanuel III asked Mussolini to form a government. Calling himself Il Duce (ihl DOO chay), or "the leader," Mussolini consolidated his control over the government and the army within a few years. He outlawed political parties, took over the press, created a secret police, organized youth groups to indoctrinate the young, and suppressed strikes. He opposed liberalism and socialism. Still, his hold over Italy was never as powerful as Stalin's grip on the Soviet Union.

☑ **COMPARE AND CONTRAST** What did Stalin and Mussolini have in common? In what ways did they differ?

Germany and Japan Change Leadership

After World War I, Germany became a democracy. The Weimar (vī mahr) Republic (named after the town of Weimar where the government was created) struggled throughout the 1920s to establish a functional democracy. However, Germany was beset by severe economic troubles in the 1920s, including runaway inflation. Anger over the Treaty of Versailles and internal disunity also plagued the young government. The Weimar Republic's ship of state was slowly sinking.

The Nazi Party In the early 1930s, the worldwide Great Depression hit the Weimar Republic hard, worsening already existing problems. Increasingly, antidemocratic parties on the right, especially the National Socialist German Workers' Party, or Nazi (NAHT see) Party, threatened the republic.

Regardless of the party's name, Nazis were not socialists. They bitterly opposed socialism, communism, or any other *-ism* that promoted class interests or workers' rights above German ethnic solidarity. **Adolf Hitler** led the Nazi Party. The son of a minor Austrian civil servant, Hitler was a failed artist, a wounded and decorated World War I soldier, and a person who teetered on the brink of madness.

Hitler joined the small Nazi Party after the war and soon gained control of it. While in prison after the party attempted a rebellion, Hitler dictated the book *Mein Kampf* ("My Struggle"), in which he gave his explanations for the problems facing Germany. He criticized many people, political programs, and ideologies, but his sharpest assaults were against communists and Jews. Hitler was violently **anti-Semitic**, or prejudiced against Jewish people.

Anti-Semitism had troubled Europe for centuries, mainly motivated by religious intolerance and economic resentment. In the late nineteenth century, new pseudo-scientific theories—meaning theories falsely claiming to be based on science—arose about Jews as a race. These theories, along with the rise of nationalism, caused Jews to be treated as ethnic outsiders. Hitler spread this type of thinking. He preached that the greatest threat confronting Germany was the Jewish people who lived there. In *Mein Kampf*, which quickly became a national bestseller, Hitler presented a blueprint of his hatreds and plans for world domination.

>> Inflation ruined the Weimar Republic. By the end of 1923, one dollar was equal to four trillion marks (German dollars). Here, children play with stacks of worthless money.

>> Both civilians and military personnel welcomed Hitler to a rally in Nuremberg in 1933. Rallies were held yearly as grand propaganda events lasting several days.

BOUNCE to Activate Gallery

Hitler Rules a German Dictatorship The shattered German economy—with its widespread unemployment, homelessness, and hunger—played into the Nazis' hands as they promised that Germany would rise again from the quagmire of reparations and the economic depression. Recognizing the power of Hitler's party, in January 1933 the president of the Weimar Republic appointed Hitler chancellor of Germany. Over the next two years, Hitler became president as well as chancellor, consolidated his power, and ruled unchecked by the Reichstag (RĪKS tahg), or the German parliament.

By 1935, the democratic institutions of the Weimar Republic were silenced, and Hitler spoke alone as the voice of Germany. Like Stalin and Mussolini, Hitler was the symbol of his totalitarian regime. Aided by a secret police that crushed all opposition, a state-controlled press that praised his accomplishments, and a state-controlled educational system that indoctrinated the young, Hitler assumed a godlike aura.

By the late 1930s, Hitler's economic policies, including rearmament and massive public-works projects, had ended the depression in Germany. Many Germans became his followers and cheered for him at Nazi rallies. In their eyes, he had made his promises a reality. "Once Hitler came to power, it was wonderful. Everybody had a job and there weren't any more unemployed people," remembered one German citizen.

However, Hitler's leadership had dark undertones of oppression, based on extreme anti-Semitism and the rejection of democracy. Hitler maintained his power by alternately brainwashing the public with lies and propaganda or by terrifying them into silence through ruthless violence.

He rejected freedom for the people and openly attacked Jewish people, communists, and socialists. Describing his rule in a speech in 1937, he said:

> For everyone has to obey orders. We have obeyed orders. . . . And I must demand this of every German: You, too, must be able to obey orders, . . . We shall educate our People to do this and ignore the obstinacy or stupidity of individuals. Bend or break—one or the other. We cannot permit this authority, the authority of the German People, to be challenged...
>
> —Adolf Hitler, May 1, 1937

>> In Japan, girls experienced military life by marching in formation. Students were taught obedience and self-sacrifice for the good of the nation.

Militarism Gains Support in Japan In Japan, the 1920s was a period of increased democracy and peaceful change. The Japanese government reduced the power of the military, passed laws to give all men the right to vote, legalized trade unions, and allowed several diverse political parties to be established. This period ended when the Great Depression discredited Japan's civilian leaders in the 1930s.

Reasserting their traditional powers, military leaders argued that expansion throughout Asia would allow Japan to gain natural resources and new markets for its goods. They promised that expansion would solve Japan's economic troubles and guarantee future security. Throughout the 1930s, the military played a significant role in shaping Japanese foreign and domestic policy. Japan, however, did not become a true totalitarian dictatorship. No charismatic leader like Stalin or Hitler emerged. Instead, Japan continued as a nominal constitutional monarchy headed by a mainly aloof emperor, but with the military assuming dictatorship-like powers over the masses. As with Germany and Italy, Japanese military leaders had strong control over the life of the people and ended many democratic freedoms. Opposition

Aggression and Appeasement

AGGRESSIVE ACTION	DATE	WORLD REACTION
Japan invades Manchuria.	1931	League of Nations condemns the action; Japan withdraws from League.
Italy invades Ethiopia.	1935	League of Nations endorses sanctions against Italy but does not enforce them.
Germany sends troops into Rhineland.	1936	League of Nations denounces the move as a violation of the Treaty of Versailles, but takes no action.
Germany and Italy support fascists in Spanish Civil War.	1936–1939	France, Great Britain, and United States refuse to get involved or to provide weapons to democratic Republican forces. League of Nations remains neutral.
Japan invades China.	1937	Japan is criticized for violating peace treaty, but no action taken to stop aggression.
Germany annexes Austria.	1938	World powers take no action to stop violation of the Treaty of Versailles.
Germany demands Sudetenland.	1938	Munich Pact is signed and Germany gains the Czech territory.

>> **Analyze Charts** What was the world reaction to these aggressive actions? What was the effect of this reaction on the aggressors?

BOUNCE to Activate Map

was suppressed, media was censored, and schools instilled obedience to the nation.

The Japanese Empire Expands As the power shifted toward military control, Japan started on a course of aggressive military expansion. Extreme nationalists urged Japanese domination of the region. In 1931, Japan attacked Manchuria (man CHUR ee uh), a region in northeastern China, and established a puppet state. The new nation was named Manchukuo (man choo kwoh). Japan controlled its domestic and foreign policies, as well as its abundant natural resources. In 1937, Japan moved against China, gaining control over major Chinese railroad lines and coastal areas. In the then capital city of Nanjing, Japanese soldiers murdered more than 200,000 people and burned a large area of the city. Their brutality earned the incident the name "the Rape of Nanjing."

IDENTIFY CAUSE AND EFFECT How did the Great Depression affect Germany and Japan?

Dictators Move to Gain Territory

In the 1930s, the Italian and German dictatorships resorted to acts of aggression similar to those of Japan in Asia. Throughout the decade, neither the League of Nations nor democratic nations succeeded in stopping the aggression. It was a time that recalled a line from Irish poet William Butler Yeats: "The best lack all conviction and the worst are full of passionate intensity."

Weakness of the League of Nations In many ways, the League of Nations never recovered after the United States refused to join it. The League was also handicapped by its own charter.

It had no standing army and no real power to enforce its decrees. It was only as strong as its members' resolve, and during the worldwide depression of the 1930s, those members lacked resolve. When aggressive nations began to test the League, they discovered that the organization was long on words and short on action.

Hitler and Mussolini Challenge the Peace From the first, Hitler focused on restoring Germany's strength and nullifying the provisions of the Treaty of Versailles. From 1933 to 1936, he rebuilt the German economy and dramatically enlarged the army, navy, and air force in direct defiance of the treaty. In the mid-1930s, Hitler began to move toward his goal of reunifying all Germanic people into one Reich, or state. He spoke often of the need for Germany to expand to gain *Lebensraum* (LAY buhns rowm), or

>> Spanish government troops fought fascist-supported rebels.

>> **Analyze Political Cartoon** Who do the small men represent? What point do you think the cartoon was making with this image?

living space, for its people. In 1935, he reclaimed the Saar (sahr) region from French control when Saarlanders voted to rejoin Germany.

In 1936, in another direct challenge to the League, Hitler sent German troops into the Rhineland. This region was part of western Germany and under German political control.

However, under the terms of the Treaty of Versailles, it was demilitarized; Germany was forbidden to have troops in the region. Reoccupation was a test. Would France or the League defend the terms of the Treaty? The answer was no. To all these actions, the League failed to respond.

Meanwhile, Mussolini commenced his own imperial plans. In 1935, Italy invaded Ethiopia, an independent country in east Africa. Its emperor, Haile Selassie (Hì luh suh lah SEE), appealed to the League of Nations for support. The organization did almost nothing, and Ethiopia fell.

Dictators Support War in Spain Fascists were also victorious in a bloody conflict that raged from 1936 until 1939, know as the **Spanish Civil War**. The Nationalists, who had fascist tendencies, rebelled against Spain's democratic Republican government.

Both Hitler and Mussolini sent military and economic aid to the Nationalist leader, **General Francisco Franco**, using the conflict to test some of their new military technology. Though the Soviet Union provided some support for the Republican side, France, Britain, and the United States remained largely on the sidelines, deploring the bloodshed but refusing to provide weapons to the Republican forces.

☑ **EXPRESS PROBLEMS CLEARLY** Why did the League of Nations fail to halt German and Italian aggression?

Aggression Meets Appeasement

The policy that France and Britain pursued against aggressive nations during the 1930s is known as **appeasement**. It is a policy of granting concessions to a potential enemy in the hope that peace can be maintained. Unfortunately, appeasement only spurred the fascist leaders to become more bold, adventurous, and aggressive.

Why did France and Britain appease the fascist powers? There were a number of reasons. World War I was so horrible that some leaders vowed never to allow another such war to break out. Other leaders believed that the Soviet Union posed a greater threat than Nazi Germany. They maintained that a strong Germany would provide a buffer against the Soviet menace. Still other leaders questioned the resolve of their own people and their allies—particularly the United States.

The United States played an important role in this appeasement policy. Worried about the rise of dictatorships in Europe and Asia, **Franklin D. Roosevelt** wanted to mend fences with nearby countries. In the 1930s, he pursued a Good Neighbor policy with Latin American nations. The program emphasized trade and cooperation, not military force, as the basis for a stable relationship with these countries. In fact, the United States withdrew troops from several nations. It agreed not to intervene in Latin America and to consult with other nations if faced with danger. Roosevelt also improved relations with the Soviet Union by restoring diplomatic relations with the Soviet government, although he remained wary about allying too closely with the communist nation. However, he did not take a forceful line against German aggression. Instead, the country concerned itself with its own economic troubles and embraced a policy of isolationism.

Hitler took advantage of the lack of commitment and unity among France, Britain, and the United States. In the spring of 1938, he brought Austria into his Reich.

Austria was given little choice but to accept this union, called the **Anschluss** (AHN shloos). In the fall, Hitler turned toward the Sudetenland, a portion of western Czechoslovakia that was largely populated by ethnic Germans.

Many people expected the conflict over the Sudetenland to lead to a general war. But once again, Britain and France appeased Germany. At the Munich Conference with Hitler, British prime minister **Neville Chamberlain** and French premier Edouard Daladier sacrificed the Sudetenland to preserve the peace. On his return to London, Chamberlain told a cheering crowd that the **Munich Pact** (MYOO nihk), the agreement reached at the conference, had preserved "peace for our time." He was wrong. It merely postponed the war for 11 months.

IDENTIFY EFFECTS Did the appeasement policy of Britain, France, and the United States have the intended effect? Explain your answer.

>> Returning with the signed Munich Pact, Chamberlain announced confidently that it would maintain peace. Instead it was a turning point in the path to war and later became a symbol of failure.

ASSESSMENT

1. **Identify Central Issues** What economic conditions led to the rise of totalitarianism in Europe and Asia?
2. **Generate Explanations** How did Hitler and Mussolini use the Spanish Civil war to their advantage?
3. **Support Ideas with Examples** Was the policy of appeasement successful against Hitler and Germany? Explain your answer.
4. **Identify Central Issues** In what way did the Anschluss present a challenge to the United States and its allies?
5. **Quest Connections** Since the United States was in the midst of the depression, how concerned do you think young married couples, small business owners, and political leaders were about events in Europe at this time? Why?

GO ONLINE to access these biographies: Joseph Stalin, Benito Mussolini

14.2

Many interventionists wanted to repeal the early Neutrality Acts of 1935 to 1937. This rally, organized by labor unions, was held to urge stronger U.S. involvement in the European conflict.

BOUNCE to Activate Flipped Video

Objectives

Understand the course of the early years of World War II in Europe.

Describe Franklin Roosevelt's foreign policy in the mid-1930s and the great debate between interventionists and isolationists.

Explain how the United States became more involved in the conflict.

Key Terms

blitzkrieg
Axis Powers
Allies
Winston Churchill
Neutrality Act of 1939
Charles Lindbergh
Tripartite Pact
Lend-Lease Act
Atlantic Charter

America Debates Involvement

While Britain and France appeased the dictator in Germany at Munich, American President Franklin Roosevelt condemned aggression in Asia but did little to stop it. As war exploded in Europe, it became increasingly difficult for the United States to maintain its neutrality. Once again, Americans would have to decide what role they were willing to play in shaping world events.

Roosevelt Criticizes Acts of War

The unrestrained violence of the 1937 Japanese attack on China shocked Americans, even before the notorious Rape of Nanjing in December 1937. Japan attacked without a declaration of war. Its planes rained terror on Chinese cities, especially Shanghai and Nanjing. The Japanese had even killed three American sailors when Japanese warplanes sank the United States gunboat *Panay* on the Chang River.

In the midst of these bloody events, President Franklin Roosevelt criticized Japan's aggression in a speech in Chicago on October 5,1937. He lamented the "reign of terror and international lawlessness," the bombing of civilian populations, and the horrible acts of cruelty. Speaking in a city where American isolationist sentiments were strong, Roosevelt suggested that no part of the world was truly isolated from the rest of the world. He warned:

> When an epidemic of physical disease starts to spread, the community approves and joins in a quarantine of the patients in order to

GO ONLINE to access your digital course

protect the health of the community against the spread of the disease. . . . War is a contagion, whether it be declared or undeclared. It can engulf states and peoples remote from the original scene of hostilities. We are determined to keep out of war, yet we cannot insure ourselves against the disastrous effects of war and the dangers of involvement.

—President Franklin Roosevelt, Quarantine speech, October 5, 1937

>> Japanese planes frequently bombed China during the invasion in 1937. The Chinese army lacked the equipment and training needed to defend the country.

Roosevelt's solution for stopping aggression involved an informal alliance of the peace-loving nations, but he did not suggest what steps the peaceful nations should take in quarantining the aggressive ones. Americans, unhappy with the failure of World War I to make the "world safe for democracy," were not ready for another attempt at peacekeeping in Europe.

Roosevelt's speech was widely criticized, and for a time, the President backed away from his more interventionist stance. "It's a terrible thing to look over your shoulder when you are trying to lead—and find no one there." Roosevelt remarked to a speechwriter. The speech did, however, alert some Americans to the threat Japan posed to the United States.

☑ **INTERPRET** Why do you think Roosevelt compared war to a disease in his Quarantine speech?

>> President Roosevelt addressed the nation about the world political situation, which he said had "been growing progressively worse." He did not specifically mention the aggressor states, but they were known to be Germany, Italy, and Japan.

War Breaks Out in Europe

Roosevelt's words failed to prevent Japan from extending its control over much of China. Similarly, France and Britain's efforts to appease Hitler in Europe failed to limit the dictator's expansionist plans. By the end of 1938, even the leaders of France and Britain realized that Hitler's armed aggression could only be halted by a firm, armed defense. The urgency of the situation grew in the spring of 1939 when Hitler violated the Munich Pact by absorbing the remainder of Czechoslovakia into his German Reich.

Hitler was open about his view of war and conquest. He believed that there was no morality in war, only victory and defeat. Just one month before the attack on Poland, he instructed his generals to be ruthless and merciless. "When starting and waging a war it is not right that matters, but victory. Close your hearts to pity. Act brutally. Eighty million people [Germans] must obtain what is their right. . . . The stronger man is right."

Poland Falls to German Blitzkrieg Finally, British and French leaders saw the need to take action. They vowed not to let Hitler take over another country without consequences. Poland seemed the next likely target for Hitler, so Britain and France signed an alliance with Poland, guaranteeing aid to the Poles if Hitler attacked.

Hitler, however, was more concerned about war with the Soviet Union than with Britain and France. Not wanting to fight a war on two fronts, Germany signed the Nazi-Soviet Nonaggression Pact with the Soviets on August 23, 1939. The two former rivals publicly promised not to attack one another. Secretly, they agreed to invade and divide Poland and recognize each other's territorial ambitions. The public agreement shocked the West and guaranteed a German offensive against Poland.

A new world war that would be a turning point in world history came to Europe in the early hours of September 1, 1939, when a massive German **blitzkrieg** (BLIHTS kreeg), or sudden attack, hit Poland by surprise from three directions. Blitzkrieg means "lightning war."

It was a relatively new style of warfare that emphasized the use of speed and firepower to penetrate deep into the enemy's territory. The newest military technologies made it devastatingly effective. Using a coordinated assault by tanks and planes, followed by motorized vehicles and infantry, Germany broke through Poland's defenses and destroyed its air force.

The situation became even more hopeless on September 17 when the Soviet Union invaded Poland from the east, taking control of the Baltic nations of Estonia, Latvia, and Lithuania soon after. Although France and Britain declared war against Germany, they did nothing to help save Poland. By the end of the month, a devastated Poland fell in defeat.

Axis Powers Overwhelm Western Europe Europe was at war, just as it had been 21 years earlier. The **Axis Powers** eventually included Germany, Italy, Japan, and several other nations. The **Allies** included Britain, France, and eventually many other nations, including the Soviet Union, the United States, and China.

But after the Polish campaign, the war entered an eight-month period of relative quiet, known in Britain as the "phony war." Things would not remain quiet for long, however.

The next storm erupted with raging fury in the spring of 1940. Germany's nonaggression pact with

Military Expenditures

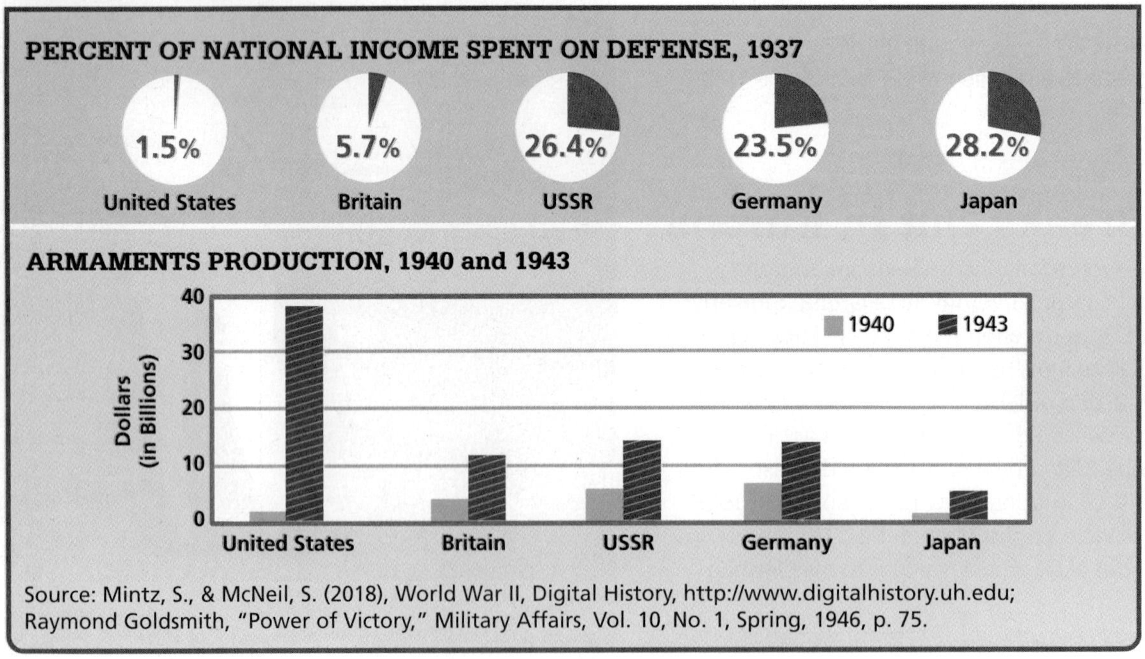

Source: Mintz, S., & McNeil, S. (2018), World War II, Digital History, http://www.digitalhistory.uh.edu; Raymond Goldsmith, "Power of Victory," Military Affairs, Vol. 10, No. 1, Spring, 1946, p. 75.

>> In the 1930s, dictators built their power on nationalism and militarism. **Analyze Charts** Which nations were most likely preparing for war in 1937? Why did armaments production for the United States increase so much more than it did for the other countries between 1940 and 1943? Use all the information provided to answer.

the Soviet Union freed Hitler to send his army west. On April 9, 1940, Germany attacked Denmark and Norway. The two countries fell almost immediately. On May 10, he sent his blitzkrieg forces into the Netherlands, Belgium, and Luxembourg. The small nations fell like tumbling dominoes. Hitler seemed invincible; his army unstoppable.

France Falls Hitler next set his sights on France. France had prepared for Germany's invasion by constructing an interconnected series of fortresses, known as the Maginot Line, along its border with Germany. Additionally, France had stationed its finest armies along its border with Belgium—the route that Germany had used to attack France in 1914. In between the Maginot Line and Belgium lay the Ardennes, a hilly, forested area that military experts considered invasion proof.

But once again the military experts were wrong. In early May 1940, German tanks rolled through the Ardennes, ripped a hole in the thin French line there, and raced north toward the English Channel. The German plan involved attacking the French and British forces from the front and the rear and trapping them against the channel. It almost worked. Only a few tactical German mistakes gave Britain enough time to evacuate its forces from the French port of Dunkirk. While tanks, artillery, and heavy equipment had to be abandoned, some 338,000 British and French troops had to escape to Britain. Had the evacuation failed, it is doubtful if Britain, with 70 percent of its troops at Dunkirk, could have remained in the war.

The Miracle of Dunkirk was a proud moment for Britain, but as the new prime minister **Winston Churchill** cautioned Parliament, "wars are not won by evacuations." Although the British army escaped, the Germans took Paris and forced the French to surrender in the same railway car that the French had used for the German surrender in 1918. France was then divided into two sections: a larger northern section controlled by the Germans and known as Occupied France, and a smaller southern section administered by the French and known as Unoccupied France, or Vichy France, after its capital city. Although Vichy France was officially neutral, it collaborated with the Nazis.

Air Forces Fight Battle of Britain France had fallen to Hitler in just 35 days. Hitler next turned his fury on Britain. After the evacuation at Dunkirk, Churchill made it clear that he had no intention of continuing the policy of appeasement. He told his nation:

>> Speed and massive power contributed to the success of the blitzkrieg.

BOUNCE to Activate Map

>> Private citizens who owned fishing boats, pleasure craft, and anything that floated helped evacuate troops from Dunkirk. The rescue was a triumph, not only of naval and air forces, but also of the discipline of the troops and the heroism of ordinary citizens.

>> Winston Churchill succeeded Neville Chamberlain as prime minister in May 1940. He toured London even during intense bombings, inspiring the British to continue the fight.

>> German bombers attacked Britain nightly for months, hoping to break British morale. The planes first attacked airfields and military factories, but then switched to bombing cities and civilians. Londoners took refuge in the city's subways, which were used as air raid shelters.

BOUNCE to Activate Gallery

> We shall go on to the end. We shall fight in France, we shall fight on the seas and oceans, we shall fight with growing confidence and growing strength in the air, we shall defend our island, whatever the cost may be, we shall fight on the beaches, we shall fight on the landing grounds, we shall fight in the fields and in the streets, we shall fight in the hills; we shall never surrender.
>
> —Winston Churchill, June 4, 1940

Churchill's words stirred his nation as the British readied themselves for battle.

Hitler's plan to invade Britain, codenamed Operation Sea Lion, depended upon Germany's Luftwaffe, or air force, destroying the British Royal Air Force and gaining control over the skies above the English Channel. The Battle of Britain, then, was an air battle, fought over the English Channel and Great Britain. It began in July 1940. The British lost nearly 1,000 planes, the Germans more than 1,700. Germany bombed civilian as well as military targets, destroying houses, factories, and churches and conducted a months-long bombing campaign against London itself, known as "the blitz." But the British held on and, sensing failure, Hitler made a tactical decision to postpone the invasion of Britain indefinitely.

SUMMARIZE Which side seemed to be winning the war at the end of 1940?

American Reaction Is Divided

Winston Churchill referred to the United States in many of his speeches during the crisis in France and the Battle of Britain. The fight against Hitler, Churchill implied, was more than simply a European struggle. Nazi aggression threatened the freedoms and rights cherished by democratic nations everywhere. The contest was between ideologies as well as nations.

Public Opinion Supports Isolation President Roosevelt shared Churchill's concerns, but at the beginning of the war in Europe he understood that the majority of Americans opposed U.S. intervention.

The severe economic crisis of the Great Depression had served to pin the nation's attention firmly on domestic affairs throughout the 1930s. In addition, many believed that U.S. involvement in World War I had been a deadly, expensive mistake. The rise of fascism in Europe made the sacrifices of World War I seem even more pointless.

In the 1930s, numerous books and articles presented a new theory about why the United States had become involved in World War I that disturbed many Americans. The theory held that big business had conspired to enter the war in order to make huge fortunes selling weapons. In 1934, a senate committee chaired by Gerald Nye of South Dakota looked into the question. Although the Nye Committee discovered little hard evidence, its findings suggested that "merchants of death"—American bankers and arms manufacturers—had indeed pulled the United States into World War I. The committee's findings further reinforced isolationist sentiments.

In order to avoid making the "mistakes" that had led to U.S. involvement in World War I, Congress passed the Neutrality Acts of 1935, 1936, and 1937. The acts imposed certain restrictions on Americans during times of war. For example, Americans were prohibited from sailing on ships owned by belligerents or nations at war. The acts also prevented Americans from making loans to belligerents or selling them arms and munitions. The acts did not distinguish between aggressors like Germany and Italy and victims like Poland, or their allies, France and Britain.

Interventionists Press for Aid to Allies Once war began in Europe, Roosevelt felt confined by the limitations of the Neutrality Acts. Though he issued a proclamation of American neutrality, he was firmly anti-Nazi and wanted to aid the democracies of Europe. In the end, Congress agreed and passed the **Neutrality Act of 1939**, which included a cash-and-carry provision. This provision allowed belligerent nations to buy goods and arms in the United States if they paid cash and carried the merchandise on their own ships. Since the British navy controlled the seas, cash-and-carry in effect aided the Allies.

Many Americans disagreed with the President's open support for the Allies. They argued that FDR's policies violated American neutrality and threatened to push the United States into the war. Between early 1940 and late 1941, a great debate raged in America between isolationists and interventionists. The debate became particularly heated after the fall of France left Britain standing alone against Germany. Interventionist organizations, such as the Committee to Defend America by Aiding the Allies, claimed that Britain was fighting for free countries everywhere. Sending aid to Britain was a way for America to stay out of the conflict.

THE TUG OF WAR

>> **Analyze Political Cartoons** Do you think this cartoon is arguing for a policy of isolation or intervention? Explain your answer.

Isolationists Plead to Remain Neutral Isolationists countered by claiming that giving aid to the Allies was automatically harming the Axis and would culminate with the United States entering the conflict. They argued that the only way to keep America safe was to follow a policy of complete neutrality. The America First Committee, an isolationist group, held rallies and sponsored speeches that criticized the President's openly pro-British policies. American aviator **Charles Lindbergh** became the leading isolationist voice.

Lindbergh believed that the real threats to America were the Soviet Union and Japan, and he did not want to see his country weaken itself fighting in Western Europe to save Britain. "We must band together to prevent the loss of more American lives in these internal struggles of Europe. . . . Our safety does not lie in fighting European wars. It lies in our own internal strength, in the character of the

>> With the fall of France, more Americans began to accept the inevitability of U.S. involvement in the war. There was little public resistance to the first peacetime draft.

>> Inspired by Roosevelt's Four Freedoms speech, the illustrator Norman Rockwell created four paintings, each illustrating one of the freedoms. In *Freedom of Speech*, Rockwell shows a man speaking at a town meeting.

BOUNCE to Activate Gallery

American people and of American institutions." Lindbergh's addresses were measured and clear. He appealed to Americans' minds but not their hearts.

Roosevelt Shifts Closer to Involvement Events in Europe shocked Americans out of strict neutrality. Reports by Edward R. Murrow, a CBS reporter stationed in London, during the blitz brought the war into American living rooms. His frequent live radio reports, which began with the words "This is London," emphasized that the Germans were bombing not armies or military sites but civilians—grandparents, parents, and children.

These reports and the turn of events in Europe against the Allies convinced many Americans that the United States needed to at least prepare to defend itself.

Shortly after the fall of France in September 1940, Germany, Italy, and Japan signed the **Tripartite Pact** and became allies. In that same month, after a heated debate between isolationists and interventionists, Congress passed a Selective Service Act—a peacetime draft—providing for the military training of 1.2 million troops and 800,000 reserve troops each year.

At the same time, President Roosevelt took an additional step to strengthen Britain. He gave Britain fifty World War I-era destroyers in exchange for eight British defense bases. Britain needed the ships to convoy goods across the Atlantic. Believing the act to be an emergency measure, the President made the transfer without the consent of Congress.

The American people evaluated FDR's leadership the next month in the presidential election. Roosevelt ran for an unprecedented third term against Republican nominee Wendell L. Willkie of Indiana. Willkie was critical of FDR's handling of both the economy and foreign affairs but not of the President's basic positions on either. Since the differences between the candidates were minor, Americans voted overwhelmingly not to change leaders in the middle of a crisis.

☑ **IDENTIFY CENTRAL ISSUES** What were the main arguments in the debate between isolationists and interventionists?

America Moves Closer Toward War

Once safely reelected, President Roosevelt increased his support of Britain. When Britain began to run short on funds to purchase cash-and-carry goods

Lend-Lease Aid Given by the United States

YEAR	TO BRITISH EMPIRE	TO SOVIET UNION
1941 (March-December)	$ 1.1 billion	$20.0 million
1942	$ 4.8 billion	$ 1.4 billion
1943	$ 9.0 billion	$ 2.4 billion
1944	$10.8 billion	$ 4.1 billion
1945 (January-August)	$ 4.4 billion	$ 2.8 billion
TOTAL	$30.1 billion	$10.7 billion

Source: *British War Economy,* W.K. Hancock and M.M. Gowing

>> **Analyze Charts** How much Lend-Lease aid did the United States give the Allies by the end of 1941? Why did the United States give more aid to the British Empire than to the Soviet Union?

in the United States, FDR took the opportunity to address Congress. On January 6, 1941, he spoke about "four freedoms"—freedom of speech, freedom of worship, freedom from want, and freedom from fear—that were threatened by Nazi and Japanese militarism. The President also said that he believed that the best way to stay out of the conflict with Germany was to aid Britain.

The United States Helps the Allies With the Lend-Lease Act Roosevelt compared America's situation to the scenario of a fire in a neighbor's home. If a neighbor asked to borrow your fire hose to put out the fire, you would not debate the issue or try to sell the hose. Extending help was both being a good neighbor and acting to keep the fire from spreading to your own home.

Britain, Roosevelt said, needed American aid, and it had run out of money to pay for it. The President called for the United States to become "the great arsenal for democracy." Once again, Americans answered Britain's plea for help. In March 1941, Congress approved the **Lend-Lease Act**, symbolically numbered 1776, after another heated debate between isolationists and interventionists.

The act authorized Roosevelt to "sell, transfer title to, exchange, lease, lend, or otherwise dispose of, to any such government any defense article" whenever he thought it was "necessary in the interests of the defense of the United States." By 1945, the United States had sent more than $40 billion of Lend-Lease aid to the Allies, including the Soviet Union. The Lend-Lease Act was nothing less than an economic declaration of war against Germany and the Axis Powers.

The Atlantic Charter Outlines Mutual Goals In August 1941, President Roosevelt and Prime Minister Churchill met secretly on a warship off the misty coast of Newfoundland.

They discussed their mutual war aims, the first being strategy: Their priority was the defeat of Germany, then Japan. They talked not only about Britain's problems in the war but also about their hopes for the world after Hitler's defeat. There would be no conquests made in subjugated territories. On board the ship they signed the **Atlantic Charter**, a document that endorsed national self-determination and an international system of "general security."

The signing of the Atlantic Charter signaled the deepening alliance between the two nations, made it clear that Britain had the full moral support of the United States, and demonstrated Roosevelt's international leadership as he shaped the relationship between the U.S. and its allies. The charter also cast the conflict in moral terms: The Allies were dedicated to freedom and opposed to domination by totalitarian dictatorships.

>> In this photo, German Admiral Doenitz reviews sailors standing aboard passing U-boats. The U-boats attacked merchant ships, preventing supplies from reaching Britain. By 1940, they were traveling in "wolf packs."

U.S. Navy Battles German U-Boats Hitler was not blind to U.S. actions in support of the Allies. Nor did he fail to notice the fact that the United States had begun to escort arms shipments to Iceland, where the British picked them up and transported them to England.

In the fall of 1941, he ordered his German U-boats, or submarines, to attack American ships. The U-boats shot at the USS *Greer*, hit the USS *Kearny*, and sunk the USS *Reuben James*, killing more than a hundred sailors. The attacks shocked and angered Americans, moving them closer to declaring war on Germany. Though the United States was still officially a neutral nation, President Roosevelt gave orders to the Navy to attack German U-boats on sight. By June 1941, Germany had gone to war against its former ally, the Soviet Union. By November, war against the United States seemed inevitable.

CATEGORIZE Would you categorize President Roosevelt as an isolationist or an interventionist? Give two reasons for your answer.

ASSESSMENT

1. **Draw Conclusions** Did most Americans support President Roosevelt when he condemned Japanese aggression in Asia?
2. **Generate Explanations** Why did Germany sign a non-aggression pact with the Soviet Union?
3. **Describe** Describe Germany's successes at the beginning of World War II.
4. **Support Ideas with Examples** After war began in Europe, did President Roosevelt follow an interventionist or isolationist policy? Support your answer with examples.
5. **Connections to Today** In what way might the altercations at sea between Germany and the United States have affected American spending on technology research? What events in the present-day might result in the same thing? Explain.

GO ONLINE to access these biographies: Winston Churchill, Adolf Hitler

Four Freedoms: Franklin D. Roosevelt

In his State of the Union address to Congress on January 6, 1941, President Franklin D. Roosevelt stressed the danger that aggressive dictatorships presented to the United States. He urged the American people to support "those who are resisting aggression and are thereby keeping war away from our Hemisphere"—namely the Allies. At the end of his speech, Roosevelt set out the ideals that he believed Americans should fight for: the Four Freedoms.

>> Poster showing *Freedom of Speech* by Norman Rockwell

I address you, the Members of the Seventy-seventh Congress, at a moment unprecedented in the history of the Union. I use the word "unprecedented," because at no previous time has American security been as seriously threatened from without as it is today. . . .

. . . I suppose that every realist knows that the democratic way of life is at this moment being directly assailed in every part of the world–assailed either by arms, or by secret spreading of poisonous propaganda by those who seek to destroy unity and promote discord in nations that are still at peace.

During sixteen long months this assault has blotted out the whole pattern of democratic life in an appalling number of independent nations, great and small. And the assailants are still on the march, threatening other nations, great and small.

DETERMINE MEANING Who was threatening democracy when Roosevelt gave this speech?

Therefore, as your President, performing my constitutional duty to "give to the Congress information of the state of the Union," I find it, unhappily, necessary to report that the future and the safety of our country and of our democracy are overwhelmingly involved in events far beyond our borders. . . .

. . . In the future days, which we seek to make secure, we look forward to a world founded upon four essential human freedoms.

DETERMINE MEANING Roosevelt explains that he is describing "essential human freedoms." How do the words *essential* and *human* help define his meaning of freedom?

The first is freedom of speech and expression—everywhere in the world.

The second is freedom of every person to worship God in his own way—everywhere in the world.

ASSESS AN ARGUMENT Roosevelt's description of the first and second freedoms reflects the First Amendment of the Constitution, which guarantees freedom of speech and religion. **a.** Why do you think Roosevelt echoes the Constitution? **b.** Do you think that the reference strengthens or weakens his argument? Explain.

Primary Sources

The third is freedom from want—which, translated into world terms, means economic understandings which will secure to every nation a healthy peacetime life for its inhabitants—everywhere in the world.

DRAW INFERENCES The third freedom is not mentioned in the First Amendment. Roosevelt introduces it here. The word *want* as it is used here means lacking things that are necessary to survive, such as food and shelter. Recall that this speech was given in early 1941. Think about what happened in the United States in the 1930s. What reaction do you think the idea of "freedom from want" would have caused in Roosevelt's listeners?

The fourth is freedom from fear—which, translated into world terms, means a world-wide reduction of armaments [weapons] to such a point and in such a thorough fashion that no nation will be in a position to commit an act of physical aggression against any neighbor—anywhere in the world. . . .

DETERMINE AUTHOR'S POINT OF VIEW The fourth freedom is "freedom from fear." What is Roosevelt's interpretation of "freedom from fear"?

That is no vision of a distant millennium [thousand years]. It is a definite basis for a kind of world attainable in our own time and generation. That kind of world is the very antithesis of the so-called new order of tyranny which the dictators seek to create with the crash of a bomb.

To that new order we oppose the greater conception—the moral order. A good society is able to face schemes of world domination and foreign revolutions alike without fear.

USE CONTEXT CLUES After outlining the four freedoms, Roosevelt speaks about his vision and what is happening in Axis-controlled countries. **a.** Use context clues to determine the meaning of *antithesis*. **b.** Find a word in the text that is the antithesis of Roosevelt's vision of freedom.

Since the beginning of our American history, we have been engaged in change—in a perpetual [continuous, lasting] peaceful revolution—a revolution which goes on steadily, quietly adjusting itself to changing conditions—without the concentration camp or the quick-lime in the ditch. The world order which we seek is the cooperation of free countries, working together in a friendly, civilized society.

DETERMINE CENTRAL IDEAS Explain what President Roosevelt means by a "revolution."

This nation has placed its destiny in the hands and heads and hearts of its millions of free men and women; and its faith in freedom under the guidance of God. Freedom means the supremacy of human rights everywhere. Our support goes to those who struggle to gain those rights or keep them. Our strength is our unity of purpose. To that high concept there can be no end save victory.

DETERMINE MEANING What victory is Roosevelt referring to?

ASSESSMENT

1. **Draw Inferences** What does Roosevelt believe America's role in the world should be?
2. **Analyze Style and Rhetoric** Why do you think the President repeats the phrase "everywhere in the world"?
3. **Compare Points of View** How do you think an isolationist would respond to Roosevelt's speech?
4. **Determine Author's Purpose** Do you think Roosevelt highlighted the "Four Freedoms" during his 1941 State of the Union address to prepare the nation for war? Why or why not? Cite specific passages from his speech to support your answer.

GO ONLINE to access primary sources

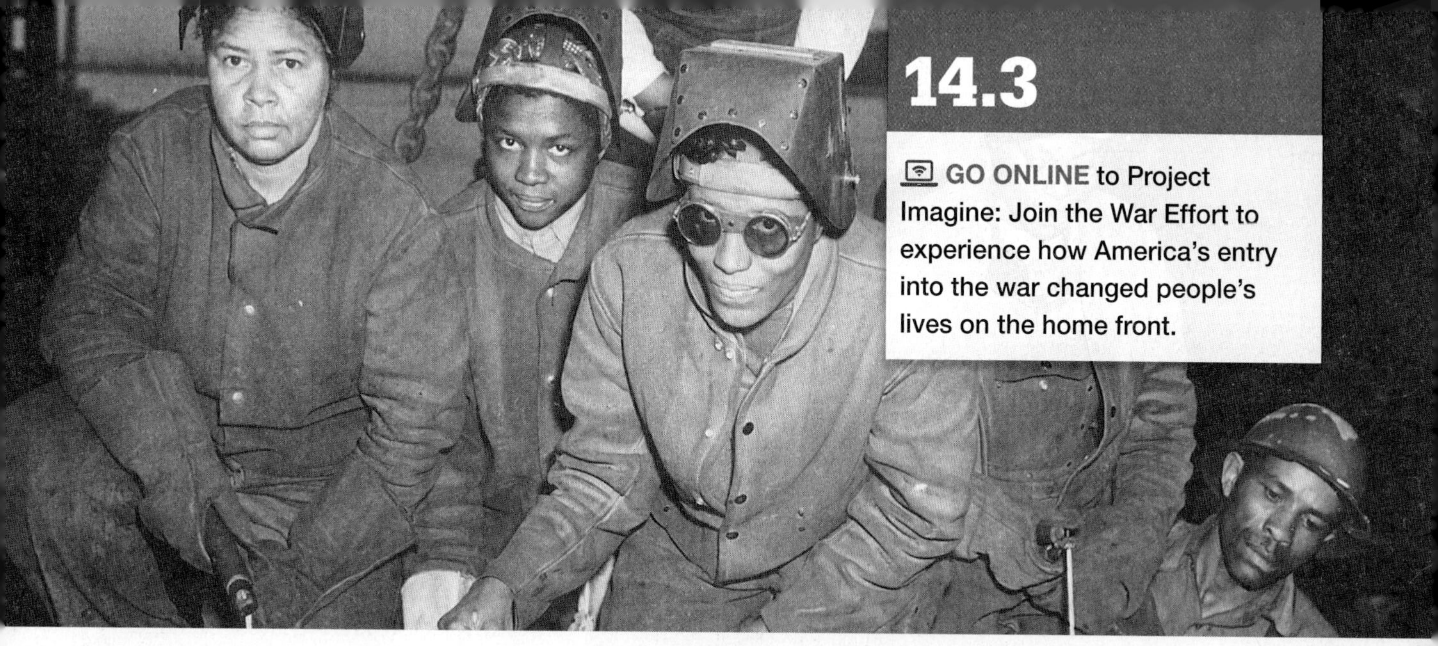

14.3

GO ONLINE to Project Imagine: Join the War Effort to experience how America's entry into the war changed people's lives on the home front.

The United States Enters World War II

BOUNCE to Activate Flipped Video

Objectives

Explain why Japan decided to attack Pearl Harbor and describe the attack itself.

Outline how the United States mobilized for war after the attack on Pearl Harbor.

Summarize the course of the war in the Pacific through the summer of 1942.

Key Terms

Hideki Tojo
Pearl Harbor
George Marshall
Women's Army Corps (WAC)
Douglas MacArthur
Bataan Death March
Battle of Coral Sea

In the beginning of December 1941, the United States had engaged in warlike activity but had yet to commit itself to the fighting. A surprise attack on Pearl Harbor, an American naval base in Hawaii, ended all debate and brought the United States into the war. The participation of the United States in this war, as in World War I, would be a decisive factor in the deadly struggle.

Japan Attacks the United States

Although Japan and the United States had been allies in World War I, conflict over power in Asia and the Pacific had been brewing between the two nations for decades prior to 1941. Japan, as the area's industrial and economic leader, resented any threats to its authority in the region. The presence of the United States in Guam and the Philippines posed such a threat. The United States also supported China in its ongoing struggle with Japan by sending aid and providing military advice. At the same time, Japan relied on trade with the United States to supply much-needed natural resources.

U.S. Involvement in the Pacific Grows As war broke out in Europe, the power of the Japanese Empire continued to grow in China and its influence began to be felt in Indochina. In July of 1940, President Roosevelt tried to stop this expansion by placing an embargo on important naval and aviation supplies to Japan, such as oil, iron ore, fuel, steel, and rubber.

After Japan signed the Tripartite Pact in September of 1940 with Germany and Italy, FDR instituted a more extensive embargo. The embargo slowed, but did not stop, Japanese expansion as

GO ONLINE to access your digital course

I saw more planes coming in, passing over Battleship Row dropping bombs. I remember very clearly what looked like a dive-bomber coming in over the *Arizona* and dropping a bomb. I saw that bomb go down through what looked like a stack, and almost instantly it cracked the bottom of the *Arizona*, blowing the whole bow loose. It rose out of the water and settled. I could see flames, fire, and smoke coming out of that ship, and I saw two men flying through the air and the fire, screaming as they went.

—Corpsman James F. Anderson, aboard the hospital ship USS *Solace* in Pearl Harbor

>> The USS *Arizona* sank during the attack. Nearly 1,200 sailors and marines died aboard this ship, which still lies at the bottom of the harbor.

BOUNCE to Activate Map

the Japanese were able to secure the resources they needed within their new possessions.

In 1941, General **Hideki Tojo** (hì DEHK ee TOH joh) became the Japanese prime minister. Known as "the Razor" for his sharp mind, he focused intently on military expansion but sought to keep the United States neutral. Throughout the summer of 1941, Japan and the United States attempted to negotiate an end to their disagreement, but with little success. Japan was bent on further expansion, and the United States was firmly against it. Finally, in late November 1941, Cordell Hull, the U.S. Secretary of State, rejected Japan's latest demands.

Diplomatic relations continued for the next week, but Tojo had given up on peace. By early December he had made the decision to deliver a decisive first blow against the United States.

The Attack on Pearl Harbor As Japanese diplomats wrangled in the U.S. capital, Japan's navy sailed for **Pearl Harbor**, Hawaii, the site of the United States Navy's main Pacific base. The forces that Tojo sent from Japan under the command of Vice Admiral Chuichi Nagumo (joo EE chee nah GOO moh) included 6 aircraft carriers, 360 airplanes, an assortment of battleships and cruisers, and a number of submarines. Their mission was to eradicate the American naval and air presence in the Pacific with a surprise attack. Such a blow would prevent Americans from mounting a strong resistance to Japanese expansion.

On December 7, 1941, the attackers struck with devastating power, taking the American forces completely by surprise.

The Aftermath of the Attack The Americans suffered heavy losses: nearly 2,500 people killed, 8 battleships severely damaged, 3 destroyers left unusable, 3 light cruisers damaged, and 160 aircraft destroyed and 128 more damaged. The U.S. battle fleet was out of commission for nearly six months, allowing the Japanese to access the raw materials of their newly conquered territories, just as they had planned.

Despite these losses, the situation was not as bad as it could have been. The most important ships—aircraft carriers—were out at sea at the time of the attack and survived untouched. In addition, seven heavy cruisers were also out at sea. Of the battleships in Pearl Harbor, only three—the USS *Arizona*, the USS *Oklahoma*, and the USS *Utah* —suffered irreparable damage. American submarine bases also survived the morning, as did important fuel supplies and maintenance facilities.

In the final analysis, Nagumo proved too conservative. He canceled a third wave of bombers and refused to seek out the aircraft carriers. The American Pacific Fleet survived.

Congress Declares War The attack on Pearl Harbor was a turning point for the United States. The Japanese dictatorship's aggression, culminating in the attack on Pearl Harbor, was a compelling reason for the United States to enter the war.

As the news spread across the nation and FDR prepared to address Congress, Americans rallied together. Many did not know what to expect, but they anticipated monumental changes. Journalist Marquis Child recalled thinking, "Nothing will ever be the same," and added, "it never was the same."

The smoke rising from Pearl Harbor left little doubt in anyone's mind about the necessity of declaring war on Japan. Earlier in 1941, further qualms about supporting the Allies had risen when Stalin's Soviet Union joined their ranks. The Soviet Union became one of the Allies when Germany went back on the Nazi-Soviet Nonaggression Pact and invaded the Soviet Union in June 1941. Although the alliance with the Soviet Union would continue to be an uneasy one, Pearl Harbor finally ended the political divisions between isolationists and interventionists.

On December 8, President Roosevelt gave a speech to Congress asking for a declaration of war:

> Yesterday, December 7, 1941—a date which will live in infamy—the United States of America was suddenly and deliberately attacked by naval and air forces of the Empire of Japan. . . . The facts of yesterday speak for themselves. The people of the United States have already formed their opinions and well understand the implications to the very life and

>> In late 1941, the prime minister of Japan, Hideki Tojo, planned a surprise attack on American forces.

>> Japanese planes are readied for the attack aboard the Japanese aircraft carrier *Hiryu*. **Determine Point of View** Who do you think took this picture? Why would that person have wanted to document this event?

>> To inspire the war effort, this poster shows a battered American flag and a quote from Lincoln's Gettysburg Address. **Connect** Why did the poster's creator recall the Gettysburg Address?

>> Young men waited in line to volunteer for the United States Navy on December 8, 1941. The draft was already in place, but many young men volunteered before being drafted.

BOUNCE to Activate Gallery

safety of our nation. . . . No matter how long it may take us to overcome this premeditated invasion, the American people in their righteous might will win through to absolute victory.

—President Franklin Roosevelt, Message Asking for War Against Japan, December 8, 1941

After President Roosevelt's speech, the House voted 388 to 1 to declare war against Japan, and the Senate joined them unanimously. True to their military commitments with Japan, Germany and Italy declared war on the United States. Congress in turn declared war on Germany and Italy.

The United States became a full ally with Britain, France, and the Soviet Union against the Axis Powers. Democrats and Republicans put aside their political differences to unify the nation as it faced the task of winning a war on multiple fronts.

IDENTIFY CAUSE AND EFFECT How did Pearl Harbor change American opinion about the war?

Patriotism Inspires Rapid Mobilization

Following the Japanese attack, a spirit of patriotism and service swept across the country. Americans joined the military, volunteered with the Red Cross and other organizations, and moved into new jobs to help the war effort.

High Levels of Enlistment in the Military The military draft was already in place under the Selective Training and Service Act of 1940. After Pearl Harbor, however, men rushed to volunteer for the various branches of the armed forces. In all, 38.8 percent of those who served in the military volunteered, with the remaining 61.2 percent responding to the draft.

Organizing and supplying the military was a massive job. As army chief of staff, General **George Marshall** directed the military buildup, from coordinating and training troops to overseeing the manufacturing and delivery of all necessary supplies.

During the course of the war, more than 16 million Americans served in the military. From 1941 to 1942 alone, the army grew from about 1.4 million to more than 3 million, the navy increased from under 300,000 to more than 600,000, and the marines expanded from about 54,000 to almost 150,000.

Americans from all ethnic and racial backgrounds joined the fight. Approximately 300,000 Mexican Americans and 25,000 American Indians served in integrated units. More than 250,000 Filipinos joined up as U.S. citizens, since the Philippines were under U.S. control at the time.

Nearly one million African Americans also joined the military. At first, they were limited to supporting roles. However, about 50,000 African Americans eventually served in combat units. In addition, many of those in service and support units played vital, dangerous roles in military operations such as the D-Day invasion and the Battle of the Bulge. A small number of African Americans eventually served in integrated units, but the military was not officially desegregated until after the war. Despite the obstacles facing them, African Americans served patriotically and with distinction.

>> Mexican Americans served in integrated units during World War II. Some units, like this one, were largely made up of Mexican Americans because they were recruited from Mexican American communities.

Gay Men and Lesbians Face Official Hostility Gay men and lesbians faced a unique kind of hostility as they signed up, as the military made an unprecedented effort to reject them from participating in the armed forces. During the 1930s, psychiatrists defined gay male and lesbian sexual orientation as a mental illness, a diagnosis that influenced U.S. military policies. Although gay men and lesbians served in the armed forces in significant numbers, they were forced to conceal their identity, risking imprisonment or dishonorable discharge if their sexual orientation was revealed. However, the mass enlistment of the war drew gay men and lesbians out of small towns and into the larger cities and bases, where they began meeting one another. Ironically, wartime persecution helped forge a sense of gay identity and set the stage for the beginnings of the gay rights movement.

>> This poster shows (left to right) women in the United States Marines, Navy, Army, and Coast Guard. **Interpret** What strikes you about the appearance of these women? Why did the artist portray them in this way?

Women Join the Fight Over 350,000 women also responded to the call. In 1941, Representative Edith Nourse Rogers introduced a bill to establish a Women's Army Auxiliary Corps. This group became the **Women's Army Corps (WAC)** in 1943. The WAC was part of the regular army, not an auxiliary attachment, and women who served in it received the same benefits as men. More than 150,000 women volunteered for the service.

The WACs fulfilled important functions as clerical workers, truck drivers, instructors, and lab technicians for the United States Army. Over the course of the war, 15,000 WACs served abroad and over 600 received medals for their service. Around 100,000 American women joined the

>> The Liberty Ship *Robert E. Peary* was built in four days. Kaiser's shipyards welded rather than riveted prefabricated parts, cutting the time it took to make these cargo ships by one third.

>> Workers at Chrysler's Detroit Tank Arsenal assemble M-3 Medium tanks. Nicknamed the "General Grant," these tanks arrived just in time to help the British hold North Africa.

United States Navy's female corps and tens of thousands more joined similar groups in the United States Marine Corps and Coast Guard. More than 57,000 nurses served in the Army Nurse Corps, putting themselves in danger to care for the wounded.

FDR Leads Domestic Industry's Rapid Mobilization From the start, Roosevelt and the other Allied leaders knew that American production would play a key role in helping the Allies win the war. Although America's industry had started to mobilize in response to the Lend-Lease Act, American production still needed to churn out war materials faster. In January 1942, FDR created the War Production Board (WPB) to oversee the conversion of peacetime industry to war industry.

The WPB called for factories to convert to airplane, tank, or bomb production. Conversions started immediately, although the competing demands of different industries and agencies for scarce resources caused much confusion.

Next, FDR and Congress created a host of other agencies that worked together to organize the production effort. Together, the agencies allocated scarce materials to the proper industries, regulated the production of civilian goods, established production contracts, negotiated with organized labor, and controlled inflation. The Office of War Mobilization (OWM) supervised all of these efforts.

FDR also reached out to business leaders, who had often opposed his New Deal programs, to ask them to lend their expertise as leaders or advisers to several of these agencies. Called "Dollar-a-Year-Men," many executives were paid little or nothing to come to Washington to help in the war effort.

The Production Miracle Under government direction, Americans created a "production miracle." The massive defense spending finally ended the Great Depression. The unemployment rate fell from 19 percent in 1938 to just 1.2 percent in 1944. For the first time in more than a decade there was a job for almost every worker. Each year of the war, the United States raised and met its production goals for military materials.

The Ford Motor Company poured its resources into war production, building over 8,000 B-24 Liberator bombers. Using an innovative assembly process, Henry J. Kaiser's shipyards produced large merchant "Liberty Ships" in as little as three and a half days. In 1944, American production levels were double those of all the Axis nations put together.

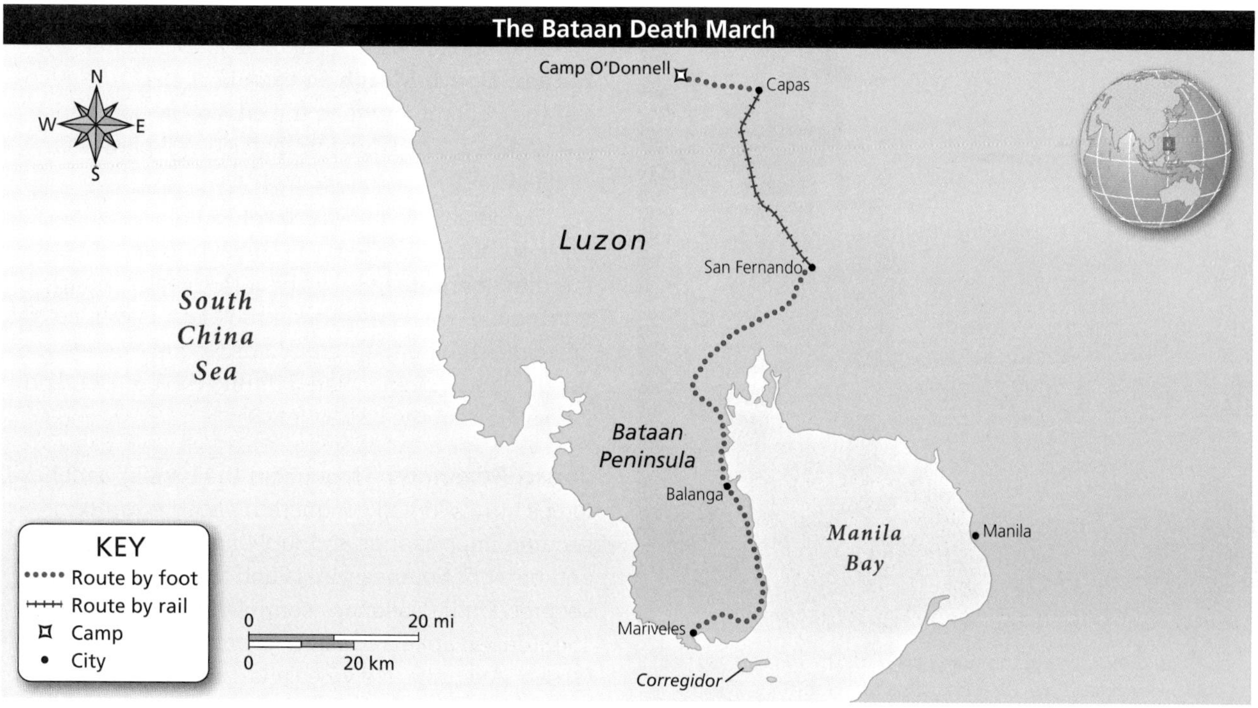

>> The march from Bataan is notorious for the inhumane way the Allied prisoners of war were treated. **Analyze Maps** Which parts of the march were by foot? Which parts were by rail?

The success of American domestic industry's rapid mobilization gave the Allies a crucial advantage. In a toast at a wartime conference, Allied leader Joseph Stalin praised American production: "To American production, without which the war would have been lost."

California played a huge role in America's war effort as the number of military bases in the state increased from 16 to 41. By the end of the war, California would be the nation's fastest growing state, and the experience of war would transform the state demographically, economically, socially, and politically.

CLASSIFY Which was more important, military or industrial mobilization?

The Early War in the Pacific

After Pearl Harbor, the Japanese knew they had to move fast to gain footholds in Asia and the Pacific. Although Japan's population was smaller than that of the United States, the Japanese did have military advantages, including advanced weapons and a well-trained and highly motivated military. At the start of the Pacific war, the outlook was grim for the United States.

Losses in the Philippines In December 1941, General **Douglas MacArthur**, commander of United States Army forces in East Asia, struggled to hold the U.S. positions in the Philippines with little support. The task grew even more daunting when the Japanese destroyed half of the army's fighter planes in the region and rapidly took Guam (gwahm), Wake Island, and Hong Kong. The main land attack came on December 22.

With Japanese forces advancing on two sides, MacArthur and his troops fell back from Manila to the Bataan (buh TAN) Peninsula and a fortification on Corregidor (kuh REHG uh dor) Island, where they dug in for a long siege. Trapped, the Allies suffered greatly, lacking necessary supplies and rations.

Realizing that it was only a matter of time before the Allies were forced to surrender, Roosevelt ordered MacArthur to leave to take command of the army in the Southwest Pacific. After MacArthur left on March 11, the remaining Allied forces held out on the Bataan Peninsula until early April, when about 70,000 troops surrendered.

Japanese troops forced the sick and malnourished prisoners of war to march more than 60 miles inland.

>> A B-25 bomber plane takes off from the aircraft carrier USS *Hornet* on April 18, 1942. This plane and its five crewmembers, along with 15 other planes, made a daring raid on Tokyo.

>> Pilots from the famous Flying Tigers flew planes painted with their trademark tiger shark faces.

More than 7,000 American and Filipino troops died on the grueling journey, which is known as the **Bataan Death March**. In early May 1942, the Allies lost the Philippines when the citadel on Corregidor surrendered. The long fight had slowed part of the Japanese advance for five months.

The Bataan Death March was against the rules set out in the Geneva Convention and other international agreements about the treatment of prisoners of war and wounded soldiers. It was not the first time that humane standards for the treatment of prisoners had been violated during the conflict, and it was far from the last.

Japan Advances Throughout the Pacific, Japanese forces attacked and conquered. These advances secured important oil and rubber supplies for Japan and brought Southeast Asia and the western Pacific securely under Japanese control. By the summer of 1942, Japan appeared ready to dominate the Indian Ocean, Australia, New Zealand, and the central Pacific. Japan's strategy was to take over so much of the Pacific region that the Allies would be too discouraged to fight back. In May 1942, the Allies needed to regroup quickly to have any hope of victory in the Pacific.

The United States Strikes Back After Pearl Harbor, FDR wanted the United States to retaliate against Japan. American military leaders devised a plan for a nighttime bombing raid from the deck of the aircraft carrier USS *Hornet*, led by Colonel James Doolittle. While still 800 miles away from mainland Japan, the *Hornet* was detected, so rather than wait for night, Doolittle led a force of 16 B-25 bombers against Tokyo. They delivered their payload on the Japanese capital just after noon.

The raid killed 50 Japanese people and damaged 100 buildings. The pilots then flew to China, where they crash-landed. Doolittle's Raid proved a minimal military gain, but it bolstered American morale for the long fight ahead.

Another group that contributed bravely to the American cause was the American Volunteer Group, known as the Flying Tigers. Led by retired army captain Claire Chennault, the pilots volunteered to fight the Japanese in the Pacific in 1941, flying their missions out of Burma. Between December 1941 and July 1942, the Flying Tigers destroyed 296 Japanese aircraft in China and Burma.

The Battle of Coral Sea Halts the Advance The **Battle of Coral Sea** also helped to kindle hope for the American military in the Pacific. In early May 1942, the Japanese moved to take Port Moresby in

Japanese Aggression, December 1941–June 1942

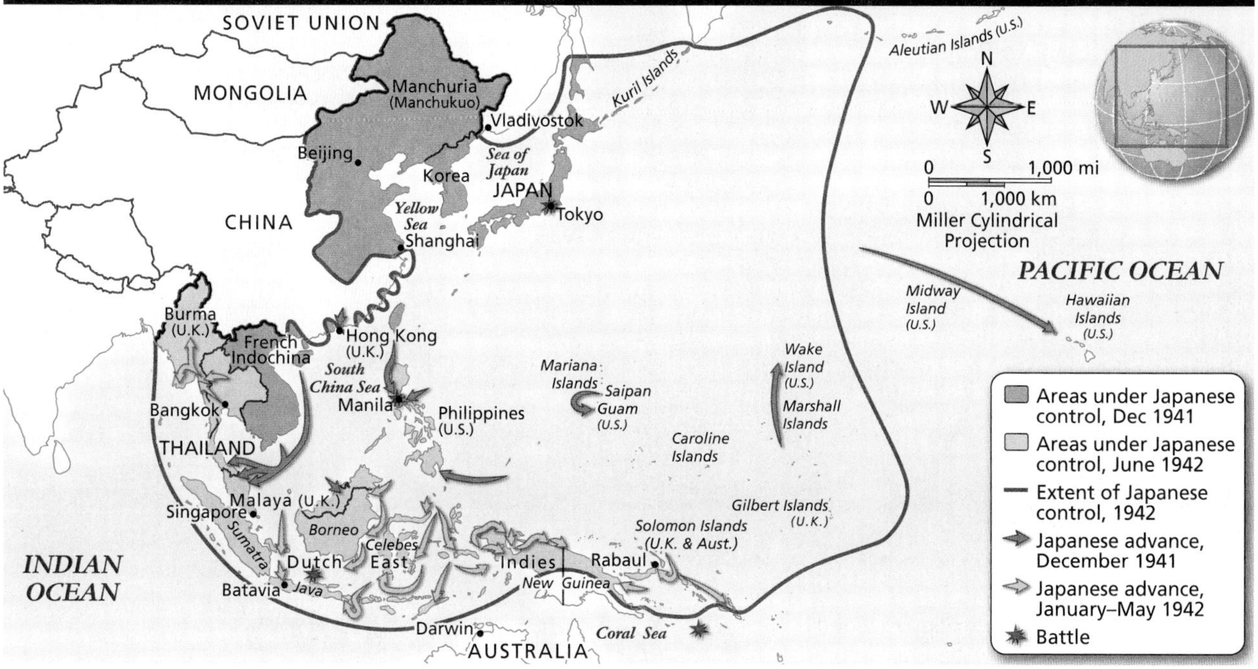

>> By mid-1942, the Japanese controlled much of Southeast Asia and the Pacific. **Analyze Maps** Summarize the position of the Allies in the Pacific in June 1942.

BOUNCE to Activate Map

New Guinea. From that position they could threaten Australia and protect their important military bases at Rabaul (also in New Guinea). To counter Japan's move, the United States sent two aircraft carriers, the USS *Lexington* and USS *Yorktown*, along with support vessels. On May 7 and 8, in the middle of a Pacific storm, Japanese and U.S. aircraft carriers engaged in battle. It was the first sea fight in which enemy warships never sighted one another. Instead, U.S. airplanes attacked Japanese ships and vice versa.

Although technically the Battle of Coral Sea proved a draw, strategically it was a victory for the United States because it forced the Japanese to call off their attack on New Guinea. It marked a shift in momentum toward the Americans. From that day on, the Pacific theater of battle would be won or lost on the strength of aircraft carriers and planes. Here the productive capacity of the United States gave Americans a marked advantage over their adversaries. The war would last three more years, but the dark days of early 1942 were over.

SEQUENCE EVENTS What happened in the Pacific theater from December 1941 through May 1942?

ASSESSMENT

1. **Identify Central Issues** Why did having the Soviet Union as an ally contradict one of the reasons for United States involvement in the war?
2. **Compare and Contrast** Compare and contrast the contributions of Generals George Marshall and Douglas MacArthur during the first months of the war.
3. **Support Ideas with Examples** What actions did Americans take to show their patriotism after Pearl Harbor?
4. **Make Predictions** What did the Bataan Death March foreshadow about the war in the Pacific?
5. **Connections to Today** Do you think it is necessary for a country to spend large amounts on defense during peacetime? Explain, referencing spending before and during World War II in your answer.

GO ONLINE to access these biographies: Oveta Culp Hobby, George Marshall

14.4

GO ONLINE to Project Imagine: Follow News from the Battle Front for first-person perspectives on key battles.

BOUNCE to Activate Flipped Video

Objectives

Analyze the reasons for and impact of the Allies' "Europe First" strategy.

Explain why the battles of Stalingrad and Midway were major turning points in the war.

Discuss how the Allies put increasing pressure on the Axis in North Africa and Europe.

Key Terms

Dwight Eisenhower
George S. Patton, Jr.
Omar Bradley
unconditional surrender
saturation bombing
strategic bombing
Tuskegee Airmen
Chester Nimitz
Battle of Midway

A War on Two Fronts

The attack on Pearl Harbor brought the United States into World War II on the Allied side. By June 1942, the Allies were battered but still fighting. British pilots had fought off a Nazi invasion of their island, while at the Battle of Coral Sea, the U.S. Navy had frustrated Japanese plans to extend their domination in the Pacific. Though years of fighting lay ahead, the Allies spied signs of hope.

Allied Strategy

The Axis Powers never had a coordinated strategy to defeat the Allies. Germany, Italy, and Japan shared common enemies but had strategies that reflected their individual political and military goals. Hitler wanted to dominate Europe and eliminate "inferior" peoples. Mussolini had dreams of an Italian empire stretching from the eastern Adriatic to East Africa. Tojo sought Japanese control of the Western Pacific and Asia.

The Allies shared more unified goals, although they did not completely trust one another. Roosevelt and Churchill feared that Stalin wanted to dominate Europe.

Stalin believed that the West wanted to destroy communism. None of the Allies wanted to risk a breakdown in their alliance, however. Roosevelt worked closely with Churchill to manage the relationship with their powerful but problematic ally, Stalin.

Roosevelt, Churchill, and Stalin considered Germany the most dangerous enemy. None felt Japan or Italy posed a serious long-term threat. Only Germany had the resources to simultaneously bomb Britain, fight U.S. and British navies on the Atlantic, and invade the Soviet Union across a 1,200-mile front. Thus, although their ultimate goal was to fight and win a two-front war, Roosevelt

GO ONLINE to access your digital course

and the other Allied leaders agreed to pursue a "Europe First" strategy. They would focus on finishing the war in Europe before trying to end the war in Asia.

INFER Why do you think Churchill and Stalin favored a Europe First strategy?

The European Front

The first blow America struck against the Axis was by fulfilling Roosevelt's promise to be the "arsenal of democracy." American factories turned out millions of tons of guns, tanks, and other supplies—enough to keep the Soviets and British battling Germany for years. The problem was delivering the weapons, food, and medical supplies that fueled the Allied war machine.

War in the Atlantic Hitler was determined to cut the supply lines between the United States and Europe before American aid could make a difference. German U-boats patrolled the Atlantic and Caribbean, sinking more than 3,500 merchant ships and killing tens of thousands of Allied seamen. "The only thing that ever really frightened me during the war was the U-boat peril," Churchill wrote.

Finally, in mid-1943, the Allies began to win the war in the North Atlantic. As in World War I, convoys of escort carriers protected Allied shipping.

A new invention, radar, helped Allied vessels locate U-boats on the surface at night. Bombers and underwater depth charges allowed Allied forces to sink U-boats faster than Germany could manufacture them.

Soviets and Nazis Battle for Stalingrad Germany had attacked the Soviet Union in June 1941, sending one army north toward Leningrad, a second east toward Moscow, and a third south toward Stalingrad. Although Hitler's forces pushed deep into Soviet territory, killing or capturing millions of soldiers and civilians, they did not achieve their main objective of conquering the Soviet Union. Soviet resistance and brutal winter weather stopped the German advance.

In 1942, Hitler narrowed his sights and concentrated his armies in the southern Soviet Union. His goal this time was to control the rich Caucasus oil fields. To achieve this objective, he would have to capture the city of Stalingrad.

The struggle for Stalingrad was especially ferocious. German troops advanced slowly, fighting

>> German troops march through Berlin, Germany, to mark the surrender of France in 1940. **Interpret** What does this photo suggest about the power of the Axis armies during the early years of the war?

>> American sailors watch as Allied bombers attack a German U-boat, 1944. A few minutes after this photo was taken, the U-boat was sunk.

BOUNCE to Activate Gallery

>> Soviet troops fought in the ruins of buildings in Stalingrad in 1942.

>> Airplanes played a key role during the war in North Africa, bombing enemy troops and carrying supplies to war zones. Here, a U.S. cargo plane flies over pyramids in Egypt.

BOUNCE to Activate Gallery

bitter block-by-block, house-by-house battles in the bombed-out buildings and rubble.

Soviet troops then counterattacked, trapping the German forces. Yet Hitler refused to allow his army to retreat. Starving, sick, and suffering from frostbite, the surviving German troops finally surrendered on January 31, 1943.

The Battle of Stalingrad was the true turning point of the war in Europe, ending any realistic plans Hitler had of dominating the entire continent. Nazi armies were forced to retreat westward back toward Germany. Instead, it was the Soviet Union that now went on the offensive.

War in North Africa Meanwhile, another important campaign was taking place in the deserts and mountains of North Africa, where the British had been fighting the Germans and Italians since 1940. Several goals motivated the Allied campaign in North Africa. Stalin had wanted America and Britain to open a second front against Germany in Western Europe, which would help relieve German pressure on the Soviet Union.

Roosevelt and Churchill felt they did not have the resources to prepare for an invasion of mainland Europe. An invasion of North Africa, however, required less planning and fewer supplies. In addition, forcing Germany out of North Africa would pave the way for an Allied invasion of Italy.

Allied soldiers had to fight in many different types of terrain during the war. But the Sahara of North Africa—the world's largest desert—presented special challenges. In hot, dry weather, sandstorms choked and blinded troops. Tanks kicked up enormous dust clouds that were visible miles away, making it difficult for troops to move without being seen. Furthermore, most supplies for Allied troops in North Africa had to be brought in by sea, where transport ships faced German attacks.

In November 1942, the British won a major victory at El Alamein (ehl al uh MAYN) in Egypt and began to push westward. The victory prevented Germany from gaining access to the Suez Canal and oil fields in the Middle East.

About the same time, Allied troops landed in Morocco and Algeria and began to move east toward key German positions. An energetic American officer, General **Dwight Eisenhower** —known as Ike—commanded the Allied invasion of North Africa.

In February 1943, German general Erwin Rommel (known as the Desert Fox) led his Afrika Korps against the Americans at the Kasserine Pass in Tunisia. Rommel broke through the American lines in an attempt to reach the Allied supply base at Tebessa in Algeria. Finally, American soldiers stopped the assault. Lack of supplies then forced Rommel to retreat.

Allies Take Over North Africa The fighting at the Kasserine Pass taught American leaders valuable lessons. They needed aggressive officers and troops better trained for desert fighting. To that end, Eisenhower put American forces in North Africa under the command of **George S. Patton, Jr.**, an innovative tank commander.

A single-minded general known as Blood and Guts, Patton told his junior officers:

> You usually will know where the front is by the sound of gunfire, and that's the direction you should proceed. Now, suppose you lose a hand or an ear is shot off, or perhaps a piece of your nose, and you think you should walk back to get first aid. If I see you, it will be the last . . . walk you'll ever take.
>
> —George S. Patton, Jr., 1943

>> General George Patton was one of the most famous American military leaders during World War II. He led American troops to victory in North Africa.

Serving under Patton was another able general, **Omar Bradley,** who took command of Patton's group in March 1943 when Patton moved on to help plan the next Allied move. American forces advanced east toward Tunisia with increasing confidence. Simultaneously, the British pressed westward from Egypt, trapping Axis forces in a continually shrinking pocket in Tunisia. Rommel escaped, but his army did not. In May 1943, the remaining German and Italian forces in North Africa—some 240,000 troops—surrendered.

IDENTIFY CAUSE AND EFFECT How did geographic factors affect the war on the North Atlantic, at Stalingrad, and in North Africa?

Axis Powers on the Defensive

Germany was now on the defensive, and the Allies planned to keep it that way. In January 1943, Roosevelt and Churchill met in Casablanca, Morocco, to plan their next move. The conference resulted in two important decisions. First, the Allies decided to increase bombing of Germany and invade Italy. Second, Roosevelt announced that the Allies would accept only **unconditional surrender**, or giving up completely without any concessions. Hitler, Mussolini, and Tojo could not hope to stay in power through a peace agreement.

Italy Surrenders The Allies next eyed Italy. The island of Sicily was the obvious target for an invasion, as it was situated across the Mediterranean from Tunisia and only two miles from the Italian mainland. The Allies could invade Sicily without great risk from U-boats and under the protection of Allied aircraft. In July 1943, British and American armies made separate landings in Sicily and began to advance across the island before joining forces in the north. Once again, Eisenhower commanded the joint American-British forces, with Patton and Bradley both leading significant American forces.

Eisenhower hoped to trap Axis forces on Sicily, but they escaped to the Italian mainland. Still, the 38-day campaign achieved important results: It gave the Allies complete control of the western Mediterranean, paved the way for an invasion of Italy, and ended the rule of Benito Mussolini. On September 3, 1943, Italy surrendered to the Allies and five weeks later declared war on Germany.

But Hitler was not through with Italy. After a small German airborne force rescued Mussolini from a mountaintop fortress, Hitler installed him as head of a puppet state in northern Italy. In the south, German military forces continued the fight against the Allies.

The invasion of Italy was a slow, grinding slog. Italy was crisscrossed with mountains and rivers. Heavy rains and mountain snows made combat difficult. Soldiers fought in ankle-deep mud. In the mountains, where tanks and heavy artillery were useless, Allied forces depended on mules to haul supplies up slippery and steep roads. To make matters worse, the Germans occupied the best defensive positions. Fighting continued into 1945. The Allies won battles, but none were important enough to end the war in Italy.

Allied Bombers Attack Germany Stalin continued his demand that Roosevelt and Churchill open a second front in France. While the Allies did not launch a massive invasion of France until 1944, they did open a second front of another kind in early 1942. From bases in England, Allied bombers launched nonstop attacks against Germany.

Flying by night in order to avoid being shot down in large numbers, British planes dropped massive amounts of bombs on German cities, including civilian targets. The goal of this **saturation bombing** was to inflict maximum damage.

By day, American bombers targeted Germany's key political and industrial centers. The goal of this campaign of **strategic bombing** was to destroy Germany's capacity to make war. A Nazi official later commented that "the fleets of bombers might appear at any time over any large German city or important factory."

The bravery and contributions of an African American fighter squadron known as the **Tuskegee Airmen** played a key role in the campaign, escorting bombers and protecting them from enemy fighter pilots. In more than 1,500 missions over enemy territory in Europe, the Tuskegee Airmen did not lose a single bomber.

Overall, though, the bombing missions cost the Allies dearly. Bomber crews suffered an incredibly high 20 percent casualty rate. But they successfully carried the war into Germany, day after day and night after night. This second front in the sky did indeed relieve some of the pressure on the Soviet armies on the Eastern Front and helped pave the way for an all-out Allied offensive.

☑ **PARAPHRASE** What was the situation in Italy after September 1943?

>> The B-24 *Liberator*, shown here in a cross-section, was the king of American bombers during the war, faster than previous planes and able to fly on longer missions while carrying more bombs.

BOUNCE to Activate 3D Model

Battle of Midway

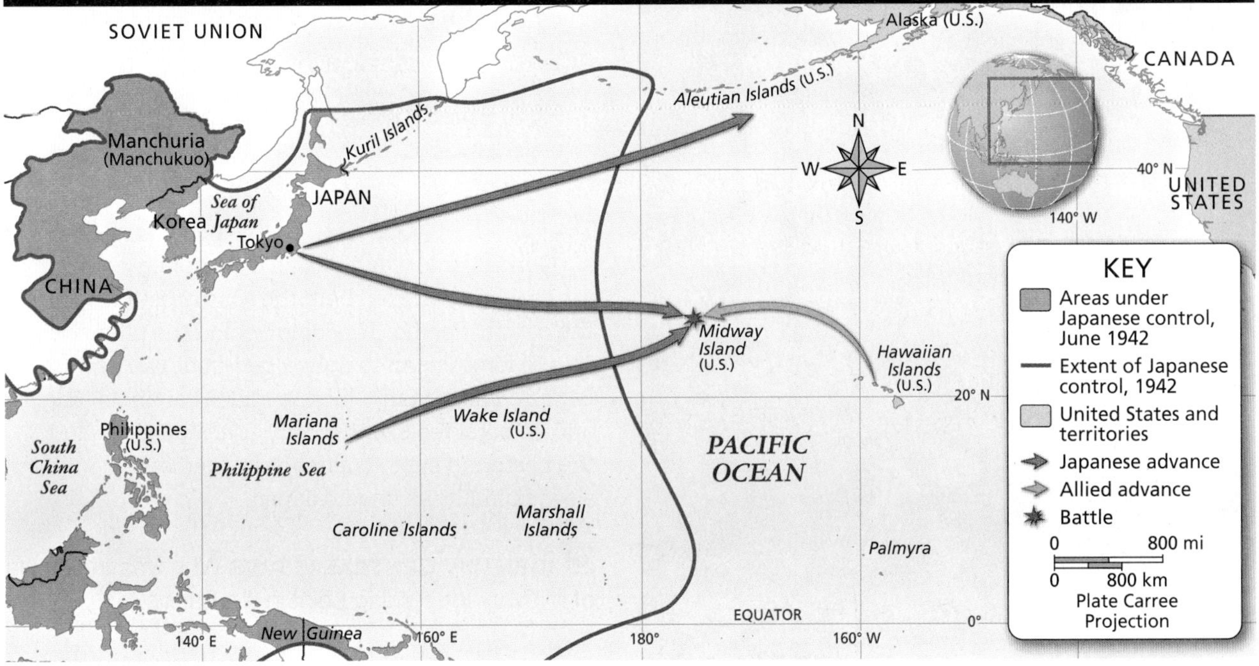

>> **Analyze Maps** Why was the location of Midway Island so significant? **Make Predictions** What impact would a Japanese victory at Midway have on the war in the Pacific?

Turning Points in the Pacific

While the Allies pursued their "Europe First" strategy, they did not ignore the Pacific. Through May 1942, Japanese forces continued to advance with seemingly unstoppable momentum. They had attacked American, British, and Dutch colonies, winning control of the Philippines, Malaya, Dutch East Indies, Hong Kong, Wake Island, Guam, and Burma. Then, the United States struck back. The American success at the Battle of Coral Sea in May 1942 served as a warning that the war in the Pacific was about to change.

Americans Triumph at Midway Admiral Yamamoto, commander of Japanese forces in the Pacific, knew that the United States Navy was a powerful threat. Before the Americans could retaliate for Pearl Harbor, Yamamoto sought to destroy American aircraft carriers in the Pacific. He turned his attention to Midway, an American naval base in the Central Pacific that was vital to the defense of Hawaii. Losing Midway would force American defenses back to the California coast. Yamamoto's ambitious plan entailed taking Midway and establishing a military presence in the Aleutians, a string of islands off the coast of Alaska.

What Yamamoto did not realize was that Admiral **Chester Nimitz**, commander of the United States Navy in the Pacific, knew the Japanese plans. U.S. Navy code breakers had intercepted Japanese messages. To meet the expected assault, Nimitz sent his only available aircraft carriers to Midway. The Japanese navy was stretched out across more than a thousand miles, from the Aleutians to well west of Midway. American forces were all concentrated near Midway.

The Japanese began their attack on June 4, 1942. In the **Battle of Midway**, the most important naval battle of World War II, the United States dealt Japan a decisive defeat. American torpedo planes and dive bombers sank four Japanese aircraft carriers, along with all 250 aircraft on board and many of Japan's most experienced pilots. The United States lost only one aircraft carrier.

Midway was the turning point of the war in the Pacific, ending the seemingly unstoppable Japanese advance. Japan still had a powerful navy, committed troops, and fortified positions. But Japanese forces would never again threaten Hawaii or dominate the Pacific. Japan was now on the defensive.

Americans Take the Offensive The first American offensive in the Pacific took place in August 1942,

>> U.S. soldiers in the jungles of Guadalcanal, 1942. **Express Problems Clearly** How might conditions like this affect the U.S. advance through the Pacific toward Japan?

with an assault on the island of Guadalcanal. After six months of fierce combat, Japanese forces withdrew. One marine described the fighting on Guadalcanal in these words:

> It was beautiful, but beneath the loveliness . . . Guadalcanal was a mass of slops and stinks and pestilence; of scum-crusted lagoons and vile swamps inhabited by giant crocodiles . . . of ants that bite like fire, of tree leeches that fall, fasten and suck; of scorpions, of centipedes whose foul scurrying across human skin leaves a track of inflamed flesh, of snakes and land crabs, rats and bats and carrion birds and of a myriad of stinging insects.
>
> —Robert Leckie, *Delivered From Evil: The Saga of World War II*

Guadalcanal was part of a U.S. strategy to approach Japan from both the southwest Pacific and the central Pacific. The logic behind the offensives was to force Japan to fight a two-front war and to capture bases from which to attack Japan. In jungles and on coral reefs, under torrential monsoons and the blistering sun, American servicemen began their slow, painful trek toward Japan.

IDENTIFY CENTRAL ISSUES Why was the Battle of Midway the turning point in the Pacific?

ASSESSMENT

1. **Identify Central Issues** Why did Roosevelt support a "Europe First" strategy even though it had been Japan that had first attacked the United States?
2. **Draw Conclusions** Why was the Battle of Stalingrad a turning point in the European war?
3. **Compare and Contrast** How did British and American bombing strategies in Europe differ? How were they the same?
4. **Apply Concepts** How does the Battle of Midway illustrate the importance of intelligence gathering and espionage in modern warfare?
5. **Connections to Today** What technology developed during World War II helped Allied ships evade German U-boats? What connection(s) to today does this technology have? Describe any benefits of this modern-day connection.

GO ONLINE to access these biographies: Omar Bradley, George Patton

14.5

GO ONLINE to Project Imagine: Do Your Part on the Home Front to see how Americans supported the troops in many ways, including growing food in victory gardens, collecting scrap metal, and buying war bonds.

The Home Front

While the men and women of the armed forces served overseas, their families served on the home front. Every American, regardless of age or background, was expected to help boost morale and make sacrifices to shoulder the cost of the war. The war effort stirred patriotism and caused ordinary citizens to take exceptional actions.

BOUNCE to Activate Flipped Video

Objectives

Examine how the need to support the war effort changed American lives.

Analyze the effects of the war on civil liberties for Japanese Americans and others.

Explain how World War II increased opportunities for women and minorities.

Describe how World War II caused migration within the United States and the effects of that migration.

Key Terms

war bond
rationing
Office of War Information (OWI)
internment
442nd Regimental Combat Team
A. Philip Randolph
Executive Order 8802
demographics
bracero program

Patriotism on the Home Front

The war also promoted economic recovery and spurred a massive movement of people around the country. And, while wartime fears and tensions tested civil liberties, new opportunities for women and minorities would spur stronger efforts to ensure equal rights after the war was over.

The Financial Cost of the War The war eventually cost Americans $330 billion, which was double the total amount of federal expenditures since the founding of the nation. In six years, the national debt skyrocketed from $42 billion to $269 billion. To help raise funds, Congress levied a 5 percent tax on all working Americans.

In addition, millions of Americans bought war bonds. By buying **war bonds**, citizens lent the government money in order to help fund the war. They bought the bonds at face value, say $25, and then received a certain amount of interest after ten years. The bonds allowed Americans both to save income and invest in the war effort. The government reminded Americans that every dollar spent on war bonds meant another bullet or bomb and another step closer to victory.

GO ONLINE to access your digital course

Controlling Shortages With factories converting to make goods needed for the war, consumer products soon became scarce. As shortages led to price increases, many feared that inflation would run wild. To manage this problem, FDR created the Office of Price Administration, which had the authority to control wages and set maximum prices.

Another form of economic control was **rationing**. Americans were issued coupon books that limited the amount of certain goods that they could buy. Rationing ensured that raw materials such as rubber and gasoline found their way into war production. Also, rationing of food items ensured that fighting troops would have enough food.

Rationing of food and raw materials created shortages. To help with these shortages, people carpooled to work, recycled tires, and grew their own food in "victory gardens" planted in vacant lots or in their backyards. By 1943, more than 20 million victory gardens had been planted, from tiny household plots to public areas like Copley Square in Boston. Although most Americans accepted the need for wartime controls, others resented the restrictions. Unscrupulous profiteers manipulated the ration coupon system to create a "black market," an illegal underground network for the sale of restricted goods.

>> In this poster, people on the home front are urged to grow vegetables for victory. **Determine Point of View** Why would the idea of a victory garden have appealed to Americans?

Labor Unrest The government also restricted job mobility to ensure constant production. In some places, wages lagged behind rising prices and profits, and working conditions were less than ideal. Some workers also opposed sharing the workplace with women and African Americans. In 1940 and 1941, strikes were common throughout the country. The nation's labor unions worked with the National War Labor Board to resolve most issues, however, and the strikes never seriously impacted production.

Raising Morale The federal **Office of War Information (OWI)** worked closely with the media to encourage support of the war effort. The OWI tried to spotlight common needs, minimize racial and economic divisions, and downplay problems of poverty and crime. Under the OWI's guidance, the radio, print, and film industries reminded Americans that they were in a struggle between dictatorship and democracy.

Hollywood proved a capable and willing ally in this cause. Documentaries like Frank Capra's *Why We Fight* series highlighted the need to defeat fascism. Fiction films showed patriotic Americans pitching in overseas or on the home front. Movie stars and popular singers volunteered their time to sell war bonds and entertain the troops. Through the United Service Organizations (USO), volunteers boosted the morale of those who were fighting the war.

Encouraged by government and media, Americans voluntarily contributed to the war effort in dozens of large and small ways. They took new jobs and worked overtime at them. Retired citizens went back to work to help out. Americans bought war bonds and paid higher taxes. They volunteered for the Red Cross, manning blood banks, rolling bandages, and sending millions of care packages to soldiers overseas. They collected paper, scrap metal, and cooking fat to recycle for the effort. Instead of buying new, many people followed the motto "Use it up, wear it out, make it do, or do without."

☑ **SUMMARIZE** How did the federal government control resources needed for the war effort?

Japanese Incarceration

Not all Americans were included in the spirit of unity. The attack on Pearl Harbor also spread fear across the United States. The federal government began drafting policies aimed toward immigrants and citizens from the Axis nations living in the United States. All of these resident "enemy aliens" were required to register with the government, submit to fingerprinting, and list their organizational affiliations.

Executive Order 9066 Originally, laws made no distinction among nationalities. German, Italian, and Japanese immigrants living in the United States were subject to arrest or deportation if deemed dangerous to national security. Some 11,000 German immigrants and hundreds of Italian immigrants were held in camps; others faced curfews or travel restrictions. Federal orders also forced all three groups to vacate the West Coast temporarily in the winter of 1942. Once public fears subsided, FDR removed Germans and Italians from the enemy aliens list.

People of Japanese ancestry living in the United States—whether citizens or not—received no such respite. Believing people of Japanese ancestry to be inherently disloyal, West Coast leaders pressed FDR to address the "threat." In February 1942, the President issued Executive Order 9066, designating certain areas as war zones from which anyone might be removed for any reason.

By September, the government had forcibly removed more than 100,000 people from their homes on the West Coast. Those removed included both *Issei,* Japanese immigrants, and *Nisei,* native-born American citizens of Japanese descent. The incarcerees were forced to sell their property at a loss and allowed to take only necessary items.

Why did Japanese Americans generally face harsher treatment than Italian or German Americans? Several factors help explain the difference: racism, the smaller numbers of Japanese Americans, their lack of political clout, and their relative isolation from other Americans. In Hawaii, where Japanese Americans comprised one third of a multiracial society, no incarcerations took place.

Incarceration The first orders stipulated only that Japanese Americans must leave designated military zones, but leaders in interior states objected. The governor of Arizona insisted his state did not want to become a "dumping ground for enemy

UNITED STATES DEPARTMENT OF JUSTICE

★

NOTICE

TO ALIENS OF ENEMY NATIONALITIES

★ The United States Government requires all aliens of German, Italian, or Japanese nationality to apply at post offices nearest to their place of residence for a Certificate of Identification. Applications must be filed between the period February 9 through February 28, 1942. *Go to your postmaster today for printed directions.*

FRANCIS BIDDLE,
Attorney General.

EARL G. HARRISON,
Special Assistant to the Attorney General.

AVVISO

Il Governo degli Stati Uniti ordina a tutti gli stranieri di nazionalità Tedesca, Italiana e Giapponese di fare richiesta all' Ufficio Postale più prossimo al loro luogo di residenza per ottenere un Certificato d'Identità. Le richieste devono essere fatte entro il periodo che decorre tra il 9 Febbraio e il 28 Febbraio, 1942.

Andate oggi dal vostro Capo d'Ufficio Postale (Postmaster) per ricevere le istruzioni scritte.

敵國外人注

日獨伊諸國ノ國籍ヲ

二月九日ヨリ二十八日マデ

近イ郵便局デ自分證

今日モ早速郵便局ヘ行キ

>> All German, Italian, and Japanese immigrants living in the United States had to register with the U.S. government. **Identify Supporting Details** Why was this notice printed in four languages?

>> This family from Washington state was sent to an incarceration camp in California. **Express Problems Clearly** What constitutional issues were raised by these forced removals?

BOUNCE to Activate Gallery

>> The Japanese American owner of this store had to sell his goods quickly and at a loss due to incarceration. Few Japanese Americans were able to recover their property after the war.

>> Veterans of the 442nd Regimental Combat Team gather in Honolulu for the seventieth anniversary of Pearl Harbor. The group had been awarded the Congressional Gold Medal the month before.

aliens." The War Department then initiated a policy of **internment**, or temporary imprisonment of members of a specific group. Today, we say these people were *incarcerated*. Japanese American men, women, and children were transported to camps in isolated locations such as Poston, Arizona, and Jerome, Arkansas. With few exceptions, Nisei and Issei remained in the camps for the duration of the war.

Families huddled into stark one-room shacks, while single people were herded into drafty bunkhouses. Camp schools were hopelessly underfunded. Incarcerees often suffered from food shortages and substandard medical care. The psychological effects could be just as severe.

> The resettlement center is actually a jail—armed guards in towers with spotlights and deadly tommy guns, fifteen feet of barbed-wire fences, everyone confined to quarters at nine. . . .
>
> What really hurts [is being called] 'Japs.' 'Japs' are the guys we are fighting.
>
> —Ted Nakashima, *The New Republic*, June 5, 1942

Japanese Americans Fight for Rights Since many of those incarcerated in the camps were American citizens, the federal government's policy raised constitutional issues. Some Japanese Americans went to court to fight for their rights. In two cases, *Hirabayashi* v. *United States* (1943) and *Korematsu* v. *United States* (1944), the Supreme Court upheld the government's wartime policy. Not until 1988 did the government offer an apology and $20,000 payments to surviving incarcerees.

Japanese Americans also faced another form of discrimination. At first, they were not accepted into the armed forces. But after the government lifted the ban in early 1943, many eagerly enlisted. The **442nd Regimental Combat Team** was one of the most highly decorated Army regiments in the history of the U.S. Army, and is one of the most historic military units in American military history.

The contributions of the 442nd provided an eloquent answer to the notion that Japanese Americans were not loyal citizens.

☑ **CONSTRUCT** Why were Japanese Americans incarcerated during World War II?

Increased Opportunities in Employment

All over the United States, American industry quickly converted to war production to meet the nation's military needs. As the economic effects of World War II brought the Great Depression to an end, the millions of unemployed men who had been such a common sight during the 1930s seemed to vanish overnight. They either joined the military, worked to produce food for the world on the nation's rich farms, or labored in factories producing war materiel. Soon, factories needed to hire workers outside of their usual pool of mostly white men. To keep production going, more women and more African Americans found opportunity in defense industries, although they still faced significant obstacles to gaining and succeeding in those jobs.

>> Posters like this one sought to motivate women to take jobs in the defense industry. **Evaluate Sources** How does the artist convey the message that women should work for the war effort?

Women Work in Defense Industries Government and industry launched an all-out publicity campaign urging women to do their part to meet wartime production quotas. The image of a strong, determined female worker, hair tucked under a kerchief, graced countless magazines and posters. The name "Rosie the Riveter" was first used in a 1942 song, and several real-life Rosies won national publicity. But "Rosie" was really a symbol for an army of women who made artillery shells, sewed uniforms, and welded planes.

Years later, one of them spoke about the contribution that women had made:

> Our war effort . . . it was a good success and a good thing that we did it. It's a good thing that the women went in. It's a good thing that they showed the world that they can do things too. 'Oh, it's dirty work.' Well, making a pie can be dirty work.
>
> —Meda Montana Hallyburton Brendall, Veterans History Project, Library of Congress

Despite the government's encouragement, there were still obstacles to women working in war industry. They were generally paid less than men for the same or similar work. Some new workers also faced hostility in their new workplaces. Still, by the end of the war, women made up more than one third of the wartime workforce.

A woman working outside the home was nothing new, but wartime pressures created two sharp breaks from the past. Many women found jobs, especially in heavy industry, that fell outside the traditional realm of women's work. The need for labor also weakened the common practice that a woman quit her job once she married. Three fourths of women working in war industries were married, and 60 percent were older than 35 years.

Wartime Work Changes Women's Lives Although the image of Rosie the Riveter working in a factory was widespread, women labored in both blue-collar and white-collar jobs. Most factory owners expected women to step aside once men returned home at war's end. In white-collar settings, however, the war accelerated long-term trends toward increased employment. During the 1940s, the number of women employed in secretarial and clerical work increased fivefold.

With fathers in the military and mothers in the workplace, children's lives began to change. The federal government spent $50 million building day-care centers for children of working mothers. Still, only about 130,000 kids ended up in day-care centers and most were not filled to capacity. Many parents preferred to leave their children in the care of neighbors or relatives.

>> A. Philip Randolph was a leader in the campaign for civil rights for African Americans for decades. Twenty years after World War II, he was one of the key voices behind the influential March on Washington in 1963.

>> This cartoon is from 1943, two years after Executive Order 8802. **Analyze Political Cartoons** Who is the figure in the middle? Why do you think this cartoon was necessary in 1943?

Wartime work helped women move closer to achieving the American Dream, gaining success through hard work and initiative. They benefited from the experience in several ways. They earned paychecks—some for the first time. They formed new and different relationships and gained organizational experience. "I decided that if I could learn to weld like a man," noted one laborer, "I could do anything it took to make a living." The confidence and knowledge women developed enriched their postwar experiences and helped create opportunities for their daughters in the years ahead.

African Americans Seek Employment Opportunities Many African American leaders hoped that the war might provide jobs and alleviate the dismal economic situations that faced African Americans. However, few found meaningful employment with national defense employers before Pearl Harbor. Out of 100,000 Americans working in the aircraft industry in 1940, for example, only 240 were African Americans. Even jobs provided by the government and military remained segregated.

African American leaders stressed the need for a "Double V" campaign—victory against fascism abroad and victory against discrimination at home. The charismatic and savvy labor leader **A. Philip Randolph** asserted that African Americans would no longer accept second-class citizenship. "We loyal Negro American citizens demand the right to work and fight for our country," he proclaimed.

In June 1941, Randolph presented President Roosevelt with a list of demands, including the end of discriminatory practices in the federal government and in industries with federal contracts. He also took steps to organize a massive protest march on Washington, D.C.

Roosevelt Issues Executive Order 8802 FDR had hoped to put civil rights reform on the back burner while war raged in Europe and Asia. But Randolph persisted in his plans. With the United States nearing involvement in the war, the President feared that the sight of a huge protest march on the nation's capital would undermine unity and fuel enemy propaganda. So, under pressure, he issued **Executive Order 8802**. This measure assured fair hiring practices in any job funded with government money and established the Fair Employment Practices Committee to enforce these requirements. By 1944, nearly 2 million African Americans worked in defense industries, although racist practices were still common.

Such victories encouraged African Americans to join organizations dedicated to promoting equal rights. The National Association for the Advancement of Colored People (NAACP) grew to 500,000 members. In 1942, civil rights leaders founded the Congress of Racial Equality (CORE), an organization that sought to apply nonviolent protest to fight segregation. Although segregation still prevailed in the military, the South, and other parts of the nation, wartime developments helped set the agenda for the civil rights struggles of the coming decades.

COMPARE AND CONTRAST How were the employment experiences for women and African Americans the same? How did they differ?

>> In this photo, a group protests segregation in the military in early 1948. **Identify Cause and Effect** How might wartime experiences have strengthened the will to fight a Jim Crow military?

BOUNCE to Activate Gallery

Migration During World War II

Wartime needs encouraged migration. People from rural areas, both whites and African Americans, moved north to industrial cities and west to California. They sought jobs in wartime industries or near military bases. Farmers looked for creative ways to keep their farms producing necessary food. The moving population and new jobs invigorated Americans but the effects of changing demographics also led to strain and unrest in some areas.

Workers on the Move During World War II, the movement of people within the country fostered long-term changes in demographic patterns. **Demographics** are statistics that show human characteristics of a population, such as age or race.

California alone gained two million new residents seeking work in shipyards and other industries related to the war. The South lost residents in its rural areas, but grew by a million people overall. In fact, after receiving billions of dollars to fund industry and build military bases, the South and the Southwest together became a growing economic and political force. Older industrial cities in the North, such as Detroit and Chicago, also boomed.

Population shifts affected Native Americans, too. As they left reservations to work in defense industries, Native Americans had the opportunity to learn new skills. Many of these workers, as well as Native American veterans, never returned to reservations after the war.

>> This Mexican family heads to the United States to help fill jobs under the Bracero Program, which continued into the 1960s.

Migration Changes Farming Meanwhile, American farmers faced a challenge. They needed to produce more food than ever before, both to power

>> Los Angeles police arrest a group of young Mexican Americans in 1943. Some of them, like the second prisoner from the right, wear the flashy zoot suits that gave the incident its name.

the American war effort and to send to Allies abroad. However, more and more people left farms for the military or jobs in the cities. As a result, farmers had to develop new farming methods, including more efficient machinery and better fertilizers, to improve yields with fewer workers.

Farmers also found several solutions to alleviate the rural population drain. First, teenagers too young to enlist helped out more. Also, tens of thousands of Axis prisoners of war were paid to work on farms, which was allowed under the Geneva Convention. Finally, the United States partnered with Mexico to operate the **Bracero Program**, bringing laborers from Mexico to work on American farms, especially in the West. During the war years, several hundred thousand Mexican workers embraced this opportunity and migrated to the United States. In the long term, the bracero program initiated decades of migratory labor in the West.

Conflict Springs From Migration In the summer of 1943, migration led to racial violence in some cities. The worst occurred in Detroit, where conflict arose over the construction of housing for Black workers in an all-white neighborhood. Some 100,000 white and African Americans broke into scattered fights at a city park. By the next morning, full-scale riots erupted in which 25 African Americans and 9 whites were killed. Federal troops ended the violence, but the city's problems were never resolved.

Like African Americans, Mexican Americans had dealt with racism and violence for years. Few had mastered the English language, and many languished in slums while struggling to find work. A violent incident in 1943 highlighted these problems. In the Los Angeles area, many Mexican and Mexican American youths dressed in stylish "zoot suits," which featured baggy pants and long jackets. That June, mobs of off-duty sailors roamed through the Mexican sections of Los Angeles, attacking "zooters." When the so-called "Zoot Suit Riots" ended, police arrested the zoot-suited victims instead of their attackers.

After the riots, an indignant Governor Earl Warren formed a committee to investigate the causes of the outbreak and demanded that the guilty parties be punished. Although the committee blamed the lack of sufficient recreation for the violence, long-brewing racial tensions acted as the true spark.

DEFINE What was the Bracero Program?

ASSESSMENT

1. **Identify Central Issues** What were some positive effects of the war on the U.S. economy?
2. **Predict Consequences** Predict two possible consequences for wartime women factory workers when men began to return from overseas after the war.
3. **Synthesize** How did the war affect American farming?
4. **Compare** How were the causes of the Detroit race riots and the Los Angeles Zoot Suit Riots similar?
5. **Check Understanding** How did the U.S. government deal with Japanese Americans during the war? How did they respond?
6. **Quest Connections** How do you think the attack on Pearl Harbor affected the attitude of Americans on the home front toward higher taxes, rationing, and other wartime sacrifices?

GO ONLINE to access this biography: Lulu Belle Madison White

Home Front Experiences

As Americans died on battlefields thousands of miles from home, people on the home front desperately searched for ways to help the war effort. The first excerpt below is from an essay written for a magazine contest by an African American woman who gave up a modeling career to work in a war factory. The other is a letter to First Lady Eleanor Roosevelt from an African American mother who answered the call to give blood, only to be turned away by the Red Cross. **As you read, compare the experiences of these women as they sought to contribute to the home front war effort.**

>> The American Red Cross handed out these pamphlets to encourage people to give blood during the war.

Primary Source 1

"What My Job Means to Me," Leotha Hackshaw, *Opportunity*, 1943

In order to make eight o'clock time at the plant in Long Island I had to get up at five-thirty in the morning. Before going to work I had to bathe and dress my two-year old son, prepare his breakfast and then get myself ready to leave my home in the Bronx. The girl who cared for the baby during the day was due to arrive at seven but she rarely put in an appearance before seven-thirty. As a result . . . I always arrived at the time clock gasping for breath and would remain a bundle of nerves for the rest of the day. . . .

ANALYZE INFORMATION Did Ms. Hackshaw's family situation make it easier or more difficult to take a job in a war factory? Why?

. . . I went to work for the Army Ordnance inspecting finished binoculars. I was one of eight inspectors in the plant and the only Negro. I remember the morning I reported to the plant. Everyone was too surprised and curious to say much. Many of them had never worked with a Negro before. With them as with me it was a question of adjusting to each other. . . If anyone had expected a riot between the white girls (mostly Irish-American) and the incoming Negro girls they must have been disappointed. No interest was shown whatever. The company workers were very friendly to me.

DRAW INFERENCES On Ms. Hackshaw's first day, how did the reaction of her coworkers seem to make her feel?

. . . [I]t never fails to stir me with the thrill of knowing that I am doing something worthwhile in the winning of the war. Every binocular becomes a symbol to me; a symbol of the freedom and liberty the world possessed so recently and which it would possess again. It means something else besides. It is the "open sesame" [magic words used in stories that allow a door to open] which takes me back to the historical beginning of the Negro in these United States. Before my eyes the first slave-ship landed in Jamestown in 1619. I see them sold on the block. I see the whip fall and hear the lash amid the cries of families torn apart forever. . . . I see a black man, a slave, go down in death and in history to be known as the first American to fall in the American Revolution. . . . And soon I hear a great man proclaim the black man FREE! And as a result of being free these men feel free and do the things that free men should. . . . On and on they pass before my eyes, achieving and proving their worth. Until today I see over one million black men in the armed forces of the country.

ANALYZE STYLE AND RHETORIC When Ms. Hackshaw talks about "the first American to fall in the American Revolution," she is referring to Crispus Attucks, who was killed during the Boston Massacre in 1770. What is Ms. Hackshaw's purpose in mentioning Attucks?

Primary Source 2

Letter to Eleanor Roosevelt from Sylvia Tucker, Detroit, Michigan, 1941

[Dear Mrs. Roosevelt,]
I was shocked . . . and grieved to learn that the "eternal color question" was paramount [of greatest importance] to the grave war situation. After explaining . . . that both my loyalty to my country and to my young son, who will be eligible for Military Service in two months, prompted my offer, . . . [I] challenged . . . [the doctor] to accept my blood and place it in a container and label it "Negro Blood" and after due process make it available for some Negro mother's son, who, like his white American brothers-in-arms, must face shot and shell and death as these things know no "color line." I begged him to do this—I would have paid for the processing, if need be. . . . I fear that the time may come when all blood—white or black—may be needed—so many, many lives depend upon it! . . .

This is not a letter of hate, despite the disappointment and bitterness and humiliation I suffered at the Red Cross on last Thursday—rather, it is an appeal for immediate mutual understanding and goodwill and the exercise of "the brotherhood of God and the fellowship of Man." The American Red Cross holds the destiny of thousands of human being[s], white and black,—make them understand that "We are Americans, too," and we want to make the blood sacrifice [donate blood to save the lives of those wounded in battle]—we must make the blood sacrifice not only for the present "5%" [the percentage of the armed forces that, in December 1941, was made up of African American soldiers] but for the vast percentage of soldiers that must be called and must face the Hell of War before this conflict is over.

IDENTIFY AUTHOR'S POINT OF VIEW What is Sylvia Tucker's point of view regarding African Americans giving blood?

ASSESSMENT

Be sure to cite specific evidence from the sources as you answer the following questions.

1. **Draw Inferences** What does Ms. Hackshaw's comment about Irish and African American girls at the plant reveal about prevailing attitudes related to race at the time?
2. **Understand Meaning** What does Sylvia Tucker mean when she says "these things know no 'color line'"?
3. **Analyze Arguments** What argument(s) does Sylvia Tucker make to convince Mrs. Roosevelt that African Americans should be allowed to give blood?
4. **Compare and Contrast** How were Leotha Hackshaw and Sylvia Tucker's experiences the same? How did they differ?
5. **Predict** How might Sylvia Tucker have reacted to the last paragraph of the excerpt from Leotha Hackshaw's essay? Explain your answer.

GO ONLINE to access primary sources

14.6

GO ONLINE to Project Imagine: Advise Truman on the Atomic Bomb to consider the decision that helped bring the war to an end.

The Allies Win the War

In 1942 and 1943, the Allies turned back the Axis advances. In the last two years of the war, 1944 and 1945, they delivered the final, crushing blow. They attacked Germany from the west and east, and the United States advanced across the Pacific to the doorstep of Japan. In the process, Americans created a new weapon that would change both warfare and global politics.

BOUNCE to Activate Flipped Video

Objectives

Analyze the planning and impact of the invasion of Normandy.

Understand how the Allies achieved final victory in Europe.

Explore the reasons President Truman decided to use the atomic bomb against Japan.

Key Terms

Battle of the Bulge
Harry S. Truman
island-hopping
kamikaze
Albert Einstein
Manhattan Project
J. Robert Oppenheimer

Planning Germany's Defeat

Opening a Second Front Throughout 1943, Franklin Roosevelt, Winston Churchill, and Joseph Stalin argued over when they would start a second front in France. Up to that point, Soviet troops had done most of the fighting in Europe. Stalin insisted that Britain and the United States carry more of the military burden by attacking Germany in the west, thereby forcing Germany to divide its troops.

Roosevelt sympathized with Stalin's position, but Churchill hesitated and delayed. Recalling the slaughter of British troops on the Western Front in World War I, he was not anxious to see history repeat itself. He argued that the German U-boat presence was too great in the English Channel and that the Allies needed more equipment, more landing craft, and better-trained soldiers.

The Big Three Meet In November 1943, Roosevelt and Churchill traveled to Teheran, Iran, for their first face-to-face meeting with Stalin. Churchill continued to voice concerns about an invasion of France, but Roosevelt sided with Stalin. Reluctantly, Churchill

GO ONLINE to access your digital course

>> Joseph Stalin, Franklin Roosevelt, and Winston Churchill (left to right) at the Teheran Conference, November 1943

>> General Dwight Eisenhower (left) and British General Bernard Montgomery (right) led the Allied invasion of Normandy.

agreed. After years of war, Allied soldiers would invade France and begin their march toward Germany. At the end of the Teheran Conference, the Big Three issued a joint statement that gave no hint of their earlier disagreements:

> We have reached complete agreement as to the scope and timing of the operations to be undertaken from the east, west and south. The common understanding which we have here reached guarantees that victory will be ours. . . . No power on earth can prevent our destroying the German armies by land, their U Boats by sea, and their war planes from the air.
>
> —Declaration of the Three Powers, December 1, 1943

Six months after the Teheran Conference, the plan to open a second front in France became reality. The massive Allied invasion of France was given the code name Operation Overlord.

☑ **IDENTIFY SUPPORTING DETAILS** Why did Roosevelt and Churchill not agree to open a second front in France until late 1943?

The Invasion of Normandy

Operation Overlord involved the most experienced Allied officers in Europe. American General Dwight D. Eisenhower again served as Supreme Commander. British General Bernard Montgomery served as commander of the ground forces, while General Omar Bradley led the American troops who would participate in the invasion.

Eisenhower Plans the Invasion U.S. Army chief of staff George Marshall had long pushed for an Allied invasion of France, believing that the British strategy of invading North Africa and Italy would not contribute to Germany's defeat. Although he was the obvious choice to lead the invasion of Normandy once the Allies had finally agreed to do so, Roosevelt decided that he was too valuable to remove from his current position. Instead, Roosevelt looked to Eisenhower.

Eisenhower had been given command of all American forces in Europe in 1942—even though

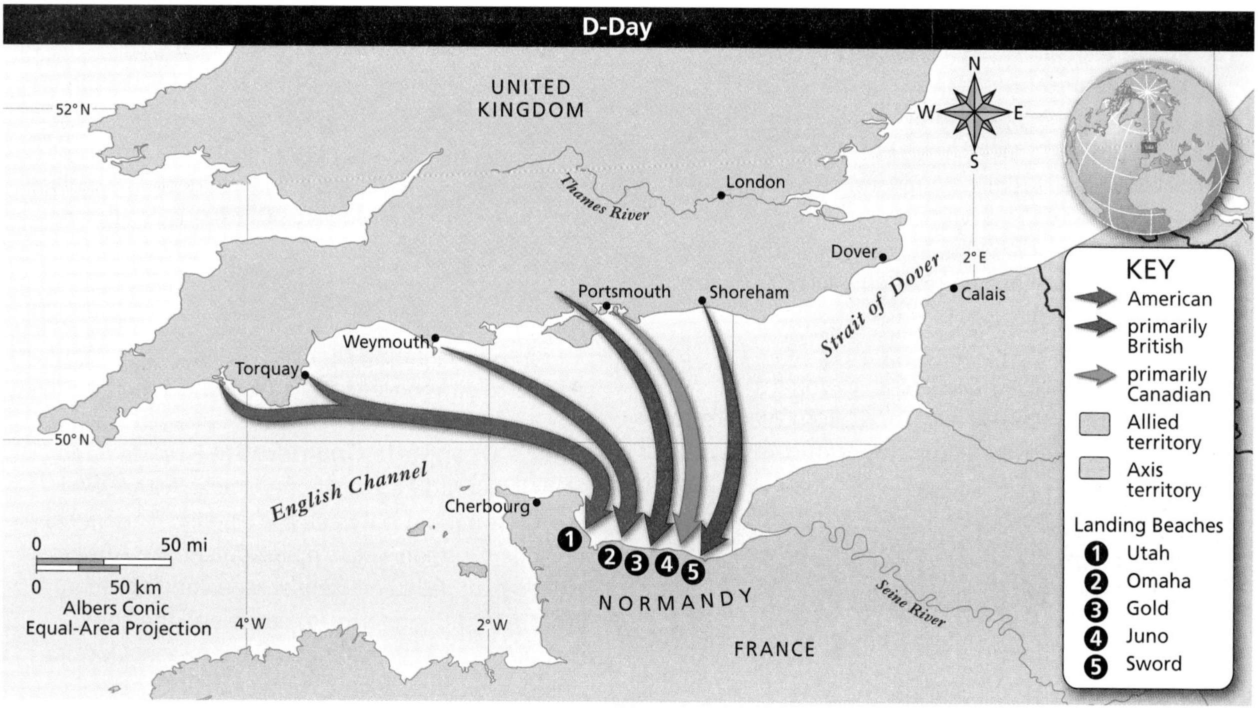

>> **Analyze Maps** Summarize the Allied invasion of Normandy. Support your answer with evidence from the map.

BOUNCE to Activate Gallery

more than 350 other generals had more seniority. After strong performances in North Africa and Italy, he was made Supreme Commander of Allied Forces. In this role, he planned Operation Overlord.

Overlord involved 21 American divisions and 26 primarily British and Canadian divisions. Some ten other countries also contributed troops. The fleet landed on a 50-mile stretch of beach in Normandy and was the largest ever assembled, comprising more than 4,400 ships and landing crafts.

The plan involved striking five Normandy beaches (code-named Utah, Omaha, Gold, Juno, and Sword), but it also included an elaborate deception: the creation of a fictional Allied army under American General George S. Patton. The Allies set up fake headquarters in southeast England across the English Channel from Calais, France, equipped with wood and cardboard tanks, useless ships, and radio messages. The Allies hoped to convince the Germans that the Allied attack would come at Calais, not farther west in Normandy. In the end, the deception worked. Hitler ordered his top tank division to Calais.

Allies Storm the Beaches On June 6, 1944—known as D-Day—the Allies launched the invasion. More than 11,000 planes prepared the way, attempting to destroy German communication and transportation networks and weaken Nazi beach defenses. At 6:30 A.M., after a rough crossing of the English Channel, the first Allied troops landed.

On four beaches, the landings were lightly opposed and casualties were low. But at Omaha, one of the two beaches assigned to American forces, the Germans offered strong opposition.

Germans Defend Normandy On the cliffs overlooking the beach, the Germans had dug trenches and built small concrete pillbox structures from which heavy artillery could be fired. They had the beach covered with a wide variety of deadly guns. They had also heavily mined the beaches. When the first American soldiers arrived, they stepped out of their landing crafts into a rainstorm of German bullets and shells. Out on the water, some crafts dumped their occupants too far from the beach; those soldiers, weighed down by heavy packs and weapons, drowned.

One writer called D-Day "the longest day." For many American soldiers, it was a very short day—and their last day on Earth. Some fought bravely and died. Others fought bravely and survived. By the end of the day, the Allies had gained a toehold in France. Within a month, more than one million Allied troops had landed at Normandy—but there they were held by German defenses.

In mid-July, under General Bradley—the commander of all American forces in France—Allied bombers launched an enormous assault on the German lines, opening up a gap that American armored divisions raced through. General Patton took charge of the U.S. Third Army and began an all-out drive across France, advancing rapidly toward Paris. Berlin, the capital of Germany, was still a long road ahead, but the Allies had taken the first, and most important, step on that road.

DRAW CONCLUSIONS Why do you think it was so important to the Allies for Operation Overlord to succeed? Use evidence from the text to support your answer.

Defeat of Germany

After D-Day, Germany faced a hopeless two-front war. Soviet soldiers were advancing steadily from the east, forcing German armies out of Latvia, Romania, Slovakia, and Hungary. Mile by mile, Germany lost the lands it had once dominated and the natural resources it had once plundered.

Allies on the Move Allied armies were also on the move in the west. British and Canadian troops had finally broken through the German lines in northern France and moved south to join Patton's American forces. In August 1944, the Allies liberated Paris.

>> An American soldier waves from his tank as the Allies enter Paris in August 1944.

Hitler had ordered his generals to destroy the French capital, but they disobeyed him, leaving the "City of Lights" as beautiful as ever. As Parisians celebrated, Allied troops kept advancing.

As a mood of hopelessness fell over Germany, Rommel and other leading German generals plotted to overthrow Hitler. On July 20, 1944, a German officer planted a bomb at Hitler's headquarters.

The explosion killed or wounded 20 people, but Hitler survived. Rommel took poison to escape being put on trial. Claiming that fate was on his side, Hitler refused to surrender to the advancing Allied troops.

Hitler's Desperate Counterattack In December 1944, Hitler ordered a counterattack. With Allied troops strung out between the English Channel and the Alps, German forces massed near the Ardennes. Hitler's plan called for English-speaking German soldiers in U.S. uniforms to cut telephone lines, change road signs, and spread confusion. German tanks would then secure communication and transportation hubs.

The counterattack, known as the **Battle of the Bulge**, almost succeeded. The Germans caught the Allies by surprise, created a bulge in the American line, and captured several key towns. Snowy, cloudy skies prevented the Allies from exploiting their air superiority. But at the Belgian town of Bastogne (bas TOHN), American forces led by Eisenhower and Patton held despite frostbite and brutal German assaults. Then, on December 23, the skies cleared and Allied bombers attacked German positions.

After reinforcements arrived, the Allies went back on the offensive, steadily pushing the Germans out of France. The Battle of the Bulge was a desperate attempt to drive a wedge between American and British forces. Instead, the battle crippled Germany by forcing it to use its reserve troops and supplies. Ultimately, it shortened the time Hitler had left.

Winston Churchill gave U.S. forces full credit for the Allied victory at the Battle of the Bulge:

> The United States troops have done almost all the fighting and have suffered almost all the losses. They have suffered losses almost equal to those of both sides at the Battle of Gettysburg. . . . [The Battle of the Bulge] will, I believe, be regarded as an ever-famous American victory.
>
> —Winston Churchill, Address to the House of Commons, January 18, 1945

World War II in Europe, 1942–1945

>> **Analyze Maps** Use the information on the map to summarize the course of World War II in Europe from 1942 through 1945. Support your answer with evidence from the map.

BOUNCE to Activate Map

Courage Under Fire The sacrifices made by American troops in battles such as the Battle of the Bulge were significant—as was the courage these young soldiers showed in combat. In fact, some 40 percent of the Congressional Medals of Honor—the highest military award given by the United States—awarded since 1900 were given for service in World War II. Of the 464 Medals of Honor awarded for World War II, 266 were given posthumously.

Audie Murphy was one recipient of the Medal of Honor. In fact, he received more medals than any other American in World War II. In January 1945, his squad was set upon by German troops. Ordering his men to withdraw, Murphy climbed atop a burning tank that was in danger of exploding. For an hour, he used the tank's machine gun to hold off the enemy:

> Germans reached as close as 10 yards, only to be mowed down by his fire. He received a leg wound, but ignored it and continued the single-handed fight until his ammunition was exhausted. He then made his way to his company, refused medical attention, and organized the company in a counterattack.
>
> —Medal of Honor Citation for Audie Murphy

Germany Surrenders By January 1945, the Soviet Army had reached the Oder River outside Berlin. The Allies also advanced northward in Italy. In April, Benito Mussolini tried to flee but was captured and executed. By this time, American and British troops had crossed the Rhine River into Germany, and a U.S. force soon reached the Elbe River, 50 miles west of Berlin. Allied forces were now in position for an all-out assault against Hitler's capital.

Hitler was by now a physical wreck: shaken by tremors, paranoid from drugs, and kept alive by mad dreams of a final victory. He gave orders that no one followed and planned campaigns that no one would ever fight. Finally, on April 30, he and a few of his closest associates committed suicide. His "Thousand Year Reich" had lasted only a dozen years.

On May 7, in a little French schoolhouse that had served as Eisenhower's headquarters, Germany surrendered. Americans celebrated V-E (Victory in Europe) Day. Sadly, President Roosevelt did not see the momentous day. He had died a few weeks earlier.

It would be up to the new President, **Harry S. Truman**, to see the nation through to final victory.

☑ **IDENTIFY SUPPORTING DETAILS** Why do you think the authors write that "Germany faced a hopeless two-front war" after D-Day? Use evidence from the text to support your answer.

Americans Advance Toward Japan

While war still raged in Europe, American forces in the Pacific had been advancing in giant leaps. Under the leadership of General Douglas MacArthur, they followed an **island-hopping** strategy, capturing some Japanese-held islands and ignoring others in a steady path toward Japan.

Navajo troops played a vital role in the Pacific island-hopping campaign. The Navajo language has no written alphabet, and at the start of the war only a small number of non-Navajo people could understand it—none of them Japanese. Navajo radio operators, known as code talkers, developed and memorized a secret code using the language, and they used it to send critical messages from island to island. The code was never broken by the Japanese.

Struggle in the Pacific From Tarawa and Makin in the Gilbert Islands, American forces jumped ahead to Eniwetok and Kwajalein in the Marshall Islands. Then, they took another leap to Saipan, Tinian, and Guam in the Mariana Islands. By 1944, the United States Navy, under Admiral Nimitz, was blockading Japan, and in October General MacArthur began the fight to retake the Philippines.

American forces took each island only after a difficult struggle. Time and again, Japanese defenders fought virtually to the last man. Rather than surrender, many Japanese troops readily killed themselves. At the same time, Japanese **kamikaze** (kah muh KAH zee) pilots deliberately crashed their planes into American ships. By the end of the war, more than 3,000 Japanese pilots had died in kamikaze missions. Their deaths, however, did not prevent MacArthur from retaking the Philippines—as he had promised when he left the islands in 1942—or the U.S. Navy from sinking Japanese ships.

American Forces Near Japan One of the fiercest battles in the island-hopping campaign took place in February and March 1945.

On Iwo Jima (EE woh JEE muh), a 5-mile-long island 650 miles southeast of Tokyo, the capital of Japan, United States Marines faced a dug-in,

World War II in the Pacific, 1942–1945

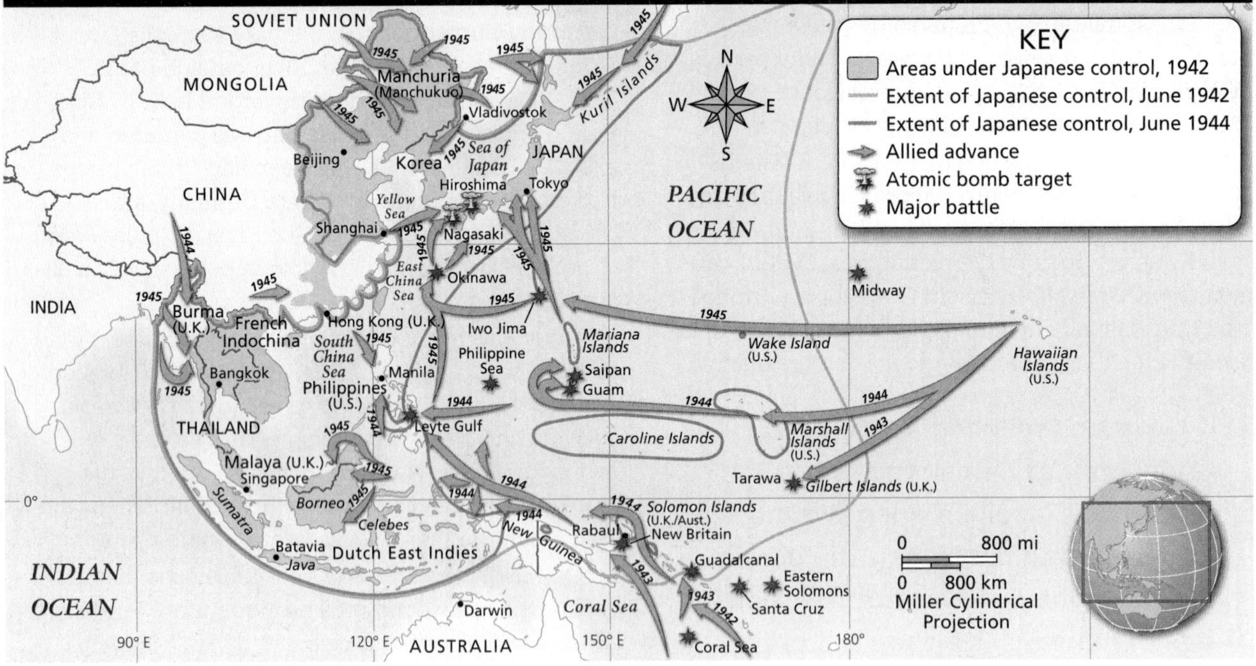

>> **Analyze Maps** Use the information on the map to summarize the course of World War II in the Pacific from 1942 through 1945. Support your answer with evidence from the map.

BOUNCE to Activate Map

determined enemy. In 36 days of fighting, more than 23,000 marines became casualties. But in the end, the Allies took the island.

The fight for Okinawa (oh kuh NAH wuh) in April 1945 was even deadlier than Iwo Jima. Only 340 miles from Japan, Okinawa contained a vital air base, necessary for the planned invasion of Japan. Taking Okinawa was the most complex and costly operation in the Pacific campaign, involving half a million troops and 1,213 warships. U.S. forces finally took Okinawa but at a cost of roughly 50,000 casualties.

American Bombers Attack Japan From Okinawa and other Pacific bases, American pilots could bomb the Japanese home islands. Short on pilots and aircraft, low on fuel and ammunition, Japan was virtually defenseless. American bombers hit factories, military bases, and cities. In a single night in March 1945, B-29 bombers destroyed 16 square miles of Tokyo. The raid killed over 83,000 Japanese—more than either of the later atomic bombs—and injured 100,000 more.

>> A two-man team of Navajo code talkers transmit secret orders over their radio. **Summarize** How did code talkers contribute to the American war effort?

USE VISUAL INFORMATION Look at the image of destruction in Tokyo. How might American bombing like this affect the war in the Pacific?

The War Comes to an End

Advances in technology helped determine the outcome of World War II. Allied and Axis scientists labored to make planes faster, bombs deadlier, and weapons more accurate. As always in warfare, specific military needs resulted in scientific discoveries and technological innovations.

Science and Technology Help Win the War

Scientists and engineers on both sides of the war worked on the development of conventional weapons at a rapid pace, creating and improving many wartime technologies. They developed fast and powerful aircraft, ships, and weapons, as well as radar and sonar to detect enemy aircraft and ships. To treat sick and wounded soldiers, they developed a way to mass-produce penicillin, an antibiotic, and to more easily transport and store blood plasma.

To supply military needs, they invented synthetic materials such as nylon, used to make parachutes and vehicle tires. But the most crucial scientific development of all was the atomic bomb.

>> In 1945, U.S. bombers launched devastating attacks on Tokyo, killing tens of thousands of people and destroying large areas of the city.

BOUNCE to Activate Gallery

Scientists Develop the Atomic Bomb In the early 1930s, scientists learned how to split the nuclei of certain elements. They also discovered that this

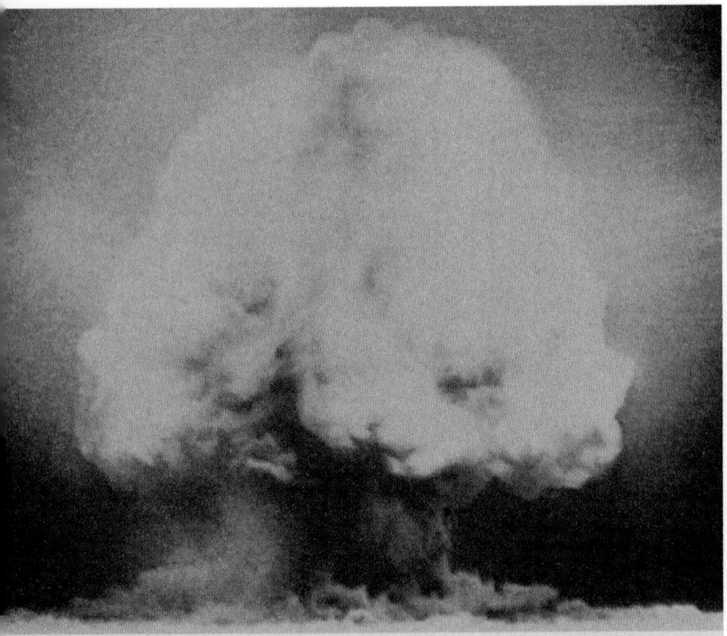

>> The world's first atomic bomb, code-named Trinity, was detonated in the New Mexico desert on July 16, 1945. **Hypothesize** Why do you think it was important to the Allies that they successfully develop an atomic bomb before the Axis?

>> President Harry Truman decided to use the atomic bomb against Japan in an effort to end the war and limit American casualties.

process of nuclear fission released tremendous energy. Over the next decade, they learned more about the nature of the atom, the effect of a chain reaction, and the military uses of uranium.

Early in the war, **Albert Einstein**, the world's most famous scientist, signed a letter that alerted President Roosevelt about the need to proceed with development of atomic weapons. In 1942, Roosevelt gave the highest national priority to the development of an atomic bomb. The program, code-named the **Manhattan Project**, cost several billion dollars and employed tens of thousands of people.

The two primary leaders of the project were General Leslie Groves and physicist **J. Robert Oppenheimer**. Groves was responsible for building facilities, acquiring materials, recruiting scientists, and providing security. Oppenheimer ran the scientific aspect of the project from Los Alamos, New Mexico. Scientists working on the top-secret project included many refugees from Europe, including Enrico Fermi, developer of the first atomic reactor.

On the morning of July 16, 1945, in a barren area outside of Alamogordo, New Mexico, the first atomic bomb was tested. The flash of light was clearly visible 180 miles away, and the sound was heard at a distance of 100 miles. Watching the blast, Oppenheimer recalled the following line from a Hindu poem: "Now I am become Death, the destroyer of Worlds."

The general's thoughts were less poetic. Turning to an aide, Groves said, "The war's over. One or two of those things and Japan will be finished."

Truman Decides to Use the Bomb The decision to use the bomb fell directly on the shoulders of Harry Truman.

The new President fully understood the ethical issues presented by using the bomb, especially against civilians. At the same time, he also knew that the Axis Powers had nuclear scientists, and there was no way to tell how close they were to developing their own bomb. Ultimately, Truman's chief priority was to save American lives. His military advisers predicted that, in light of the ferocious defense waged by Japanese soldiers during the island-hopping campaign, an invasion of Japan might cost as many as 1,000,000 American casualties.

In truth, Truman did not agonize over the decision to use the atomic bomb against Japan. For the President, abstract ethical issues did not outweigh very real American lives and an opportunity to end the war. Later, some critics would condemn

Truman's decision. But in the late summer of 1945, no one close to him did so.

Hiroshima and Nagasaki Are Destroyed On August 6, 1945, U.S. pilots dropped an atomic bomb on Hiroshima. It exploded at 8:15 A.M. One survivor of the blast later recalled the first moments:

> After I noticed the flash, white clouds spread over the blue sky. It was amazing. It was as if blue morning-glories had suddenly bloomed up in the sky. . . . Then came the heat wave. It was very, very hot. Even though there was a window glass in front of me, I felt really hot. It was as if I was looking directly into a kitchen oven.
>
> —Isao Kita, Hiroshima Witness

Within two minutes, more than 60,000 of Hiroshima's 344,000 residents were dead or missing.

Over the next three days, Japanese leaders debated whether to surrender or continue to fight. Then, on August 9, two events rocked Japan. First, the Soviet Union declared war against Japan and invaded Japanese-held Manchuria. Next, the United States dropped a second atomic bomb on Nagasaki, killing 35,000 residents.

Japan Surrenders Debate continued at the highest levels of Japanese government. Finally, Emperor Hirohito made the decision to surrender.

On August 15, the Allies celebrated V-J (Victory in Japan) Day. Japan officially surrendered on September 2 aboard the USS *Missouri*.

But even as the Allies celebrated victory, the horrifying costs of the war began to become clear. As many as 60 million people, mostly civilians, had died in the conflict. Cities, factories, farms, and roads lay in ruins in large parts of Europe and Asia, and millions of refugees were homeless. More than 400,000 Americans had lost their lives. Winning the war had been an enormous effort for the Allies. Peace would bring new challenges.

SUMMARIZE How did scientific discoveries and technological innovations affect the war?

>> Americans celebrate the surrender of Japan in August 1945, New York City. At long last, World War II was over.

ASSESSMENT

1. **Draw Conclusions** Which Ally bore the brunt of Germany's assault during the first years of the war?
2. **Draw Conclusions** On what issues did Stalin, Roosevelt, and Churchill disagree?
3. **Draw Conclusions** Where and when did the Allies open a second front in Europe? What was the result?
4. **Synthesize** How did the Allies go about pushing the Japanese back in the Pacific?
5. **Identify Central Issues** What were the consequences of the decision to bomb Hiroshima and Nagasaki?
6. **Connections to Today** Today, the countries of the world have tried to limit which countries are allowed to produce nuclear weapons. Why do you think this is the case?

GO ONLINE to access these biographies: Dwight Eisenhower, Chester Nimitz

14.7

In this famous image associated with the Holocaust, Nazi troops remove Jewish residents from the Warsaw ghetto after a failed uprising in 1943.

BOUNCE to Activate Flipped Video

Objectives

Trace the roots and progress of Hitler's campaign against the Jews.

Explain the goals of Hitler's "final solution" and the nature of Nazi death camps.

Examine how the United States responded to the Holocaust.

Key Terms

Holocaust
anti-Semitism
Nazism
Kristallnacht
genocide
concentration camps
death camps
War Refugee Board

The Holocaust

From the time he came to power, Adolf Hitler had targeted Jews for persecution. By the end of the war, the Nazis had murdered 6 million Jews and 5 million other people they considered inferior. In 1945, there was no word for Hitler's murderous plan of extermination. Today, it is called the Holocaust. We continue to remember this tragedy and seek ways to prevent anything like it from ever happening again.

Roots of the Holocaust

The mass murders of Jews, as well as other "undesirables," were a direct result of a racist Nazi ideology that considered "Aryans" superior to other people. "Aryan" was a Nazi term for white people who were not Jewish, especially those with Germanic, Nordic, and Anglo-Saxon blood. Among the groups that the Nazis considered inferior were the Slavic peoples of Russia and Eastern Europe.

From the start, the Nazi movement trafficked in **anti-Semitism**. Hitler blamed Jews for all the ills of Germany, from communism to inflation to abstract painting—and, especially, for the defeat of Germany in World War I. Other extremists influenced Hitler's ideas and shared his prejudices. In the 1920s, his was just another angry voice in the Weimar Republic, advancing simplistic answers for the nation's grave economic, political, and social troubles. In 1933, however, Hitler became chancellor of Germany.

Hitler's Campaign Against the Jews Hitler's persecution of the Jews began as soon as he came to power. At first, his focus was economic. He urged Germans to boycott Jewish-owned businesses, and he barred Jews from jobs in civil service, banking, the stock exchange, law, journalism, and medicine. In 1935, Hitler moved to a broader legal persecution—the Nuremberg Laws,

GO ONLINE to access your digital course

named for the city that served as the spiritual center of **Nazism**. They denied German citizenship to Jews, banned marriage between Jews and non-Jews, and segregated Jews at every level of society. Yet even these measures were not enough for Hitler. He hinted that, in the future, there might be what he called the "Final Solution to the Jewish question."

Hitler employed the full power of the state in his anti-Semitic campaigns. Newspapers printed scandalous attacks against Jews. Children in schools and the Hitler Youth movement were taught that Jews were "polluting" German society and culture. Comic books contained vile caricatures of Jews.

The Violence of Kristallnacht Acts of violence against Jews were common. The most serious attack on German Jews took place on November 9, 1938. It became known as **Kristallnacht** (KRIHS tahl nahkt), or the "Night of the Broken Glass." After a Jewish refugee killed a German diplomat in Paris, Nazi officials ordered attacks on Jews in Germany, Austria, and the Sudetenland. Secret police and military units destroyed more than 1,500 synagogues and 7,500 Jewish-owned businesses, killed more than 200 Jews, injured more than 600 others, and arrested thousands.

Refugees Try to Escape Between 1933 and 1937, about 129,000 Jews fled Germany and Nazi-controlled Austria. They included some of the most notable figures in the scientific and artistic world, including physicist Albert Einstein.

More Jews would have left, but they were not generally welcomed into other countries. During the Great Depression, with jobs scarce, the United States and other countries barred their doors to many Jews. In 1939, the ocean liner *St. Louis* departed Germany for Cuba with more than 900 Jewish refugees on board. Only 22 of the Jewish passengers received permission to stay in Cuba and U.S. officials also refused to accept any of the refugees. The ship returned to Germany. More than a quarter of the Jews aboard the *St. Louis* later died in the Holocaust.

☑ **IDENTIFY STEPS IN A PROCESS** How did the Nazis deprive Jewish people of their rights?

>> This propaganda poster from 1935 glorifies the image of what the Nazis saw as the ideal "Aryan" youth. At the same time, posters and comic books viciously caricatured people the Nazis considered "inferior."

>> Hitler is greeted by children in Poland. The white shirts and ties worn by the girls were part of the uniform of the female branch of the Hitler Youth movement.

Hitler's "Final Solution"

Since 1933, the Nazis had denied Jews the rights of citizenship and committed acts of brutality against them. These acts of persecution were steps toward Hitler's "Final Solution to the Jewish question": the systematic extermination of all Jews living in the regions controlled by the Third Reich. Today, we use the word **genocide** to describe this type of willful annihilation of a racial, political, or cultural group.

The First Concentration Camps In 1933, the year he became chancellor, Hitler opened the first Nazi **concentration camps**, areas where members of specially designated groups were confined. The earliest camps included Dachau, Sachsenhausen, and Buchenwald. Later, Ravensbruck, not far from Berlin, was opened for female prisoners.

In theory, the camps were designed not to kill prisoners, but to turn them into "useful members" of the Third Reich. The Third Reich was the Nazi name for the regime that controlled Germany from 1933 to 1945. The Nazis imprisoned political opponents such as labor leaders, socialists, and communists, as well as anyone—journalists or novelists, ministers or priests—who spoke out against Hitler. Many Jews as well as "Aryans" who had intimate relations with Jews were sent to camps. Other groups targeted as "undesirable" included Sinti and Roma ("Gypsies"), Jehovah's Witnesses, gay men, the poor, alcoholics, conscientious objectors, the physically disabled, and people with mental illness.

Camp administrators assigned serial numbers to prisoners and dressed them in vertically striped uniforms with triangular insignias. For example, political prisoners wore red insignias, gay men pink, Jews yellow, and Jehovah's Witnesses purple. Inside the walls of the concentration camps, there were no real restraints on sadistic guards. They tortured and even killed prisoners with no fear of reprisals from their superiors.

Death by starvation and disease was common. In addition, doctors at camps such as Dachau conducted horrible medical experiments that killed inmates or left them deformed. Prisoners were made subjects of bogus experiments on oxygen deprivation, hypothermia, and the effects of altitude. Bodies were mutilated without anesthesia. Thousands of prisoners died in agonizing pain, including some 5,000 mentally or physically disabled children.

The Nazis Build Death Camps When Germany invaded Poland and the Soviet Union, the Nazis gained control of large territories that were home to millions of Jews. Under Nazi rule, Jews in Warsaw, Lodz, and other Polish cities were forced to live in crowded, walled ghettos. Nazis also constructed additional concentration camps in Poland and Eastern Europe.

At first, the murder of Jews and other prisoners tended to be more arbitrary than systematic. But at the Wannsee Conference in January 1942, Nazi

Concentration Camps in Europe

>> **Analyze Maps** How did the locations of death camps differ from the location of concentration camps?

BOUNCE to Activate Gallery

leaders made the decision to move toward Hitler's "Final Solution." Reinhard Heydrich, an SS leader known as "the man with an iron heart," outlined a plan to exterminate about 11,000,000 Jews. Although the minutes of the meeting do not use the word "kill," everyone there understood that killing was their goal.

Many concentration camps, especially in Poland, were designated as **death camps**, camps where prisoners were systematically exterminated. The largest death camp was Auschwitz in southern Poland. Others included Treblinka, Maidenek, Sobibor, Belsec, and Chelmno. Prisoners from various parts of the Reich were transported by trains to the death camps and murdered. Nazis forced prisoners into death chambers and pumped in carbon monoxide or crammed the prisoners into shower-like facilities and released the insecticide Zyklon B.

Some concentration camps that the Nazis converted into death camps did not have gassing equipment. In these camps, Nazi guards shot hundreds of thousands of prisoners. Nazi "Action Groups" that followed the army into Eastern Europe also shot several million Jews and buried them in ditches.

In fully functioning death camps, the bodies of murdered prisoners were further desecrated. Human fat was turned into soap; human hair was woven into wigs, slippers, and mattresses; cash, gold fillings, wedding rings, and other valuables were stripped off the victims. After the Nazis had taken what they wanted, they burned the bodies in crematoriums.

By 1945, about 6 million European Jews had been murdered. But Jews were not the only victims. As many as 5 million others lay dead, including nearly 2 million non-Jewish Poles. While many survivors lived with constant nightmares of the experience, or with the sorrow and guilt of being the last members of their families, many others determined to rebuild their lives and families in the United States, Israel, or elsewhere and continue to be productive citizens.

SUMMARIZE What actions did the Nazis take to carry out Hitler's "Final Solution?"

Allied Response to the Holocaust

Could the Holocaust have been prevented? Could western democracies—especially Britain, France, and the United States—have intervened to stop the slaughter of millions of innocent people? There are no simple answers. However, many people today believe that the West could have done more than it did.

>> Jewish prisoners were shipped in cattle cars with no food or water to death camps across Europe. The yellow star that the Nazis forced Jews to wear can be seen on one women's coat in this photograph.

>> These concentration camp survivors were photographed shortly after their camp was liberated by the Allies. Prisoners were starving, ill-clad, and crammed into bare wooden bunks.

Early Inaction Before the war, the United States and other countries could have accepted more Jewish refugees from Germany and Austria. However, the U.S. State Department at first made a conscious effort to block Jewish immigration. Later commentators have blamed this failure on several factors: anti-Semitism, apathy, preoccupation with the Great Depression, and a tendency to underestimate Hitler's genocidal plans.

The United States Takes Limited Action Once the war started, news of the mass killings filtered to the West.

By the end of 1942, the Allies acknowledged that Jews were being taken to Poland and killed. In April 1943, British and American officials hosted the Bermuda Conference to discuss rescuing surviving Jewish refugees from Europe. However, no concrete action was taken.

By early 1944, however, FDR began to respond to the reports. He established the **War Refugee Board**, a government agency that worked with the Red Cross to save thousands of Eastern European Jews, especially in Romania and Hungary.

Tragically, too few were saved. Of the Allies, the Soviet Union was closest to the death camps, but Stalin showed no concern. Britain and the United States expressed sympathy, but their resources and strategy were focused on defeating Hitler not on stopping his genocidal campaign. They might have bombed railway lines to the death camps, but the camps were not military targets.

>> These Jewish children from Austria were among those who eventually found homes with adoptive families in the United States.

A War Department official told the Refugee Board that bombing the railway lines "could be executed only by the diversion of considerable air support essential to the success of our forces now engaged in decisive operations elsewhere." The Allies also refused to pressure countries within the Nazi sphere of influence to stop the transportation of Jews to Germany.

The Liberation of the Concentration Camps As they pushed toward Germany from the east and west, Soviet and American troops liberated the camps one by one. For most Americans, the enormity of the Nazi crime became real only when the camp liberators began to report back on what they found. When they saw it all—the piles of dead bodies, the warehouses full of human hair and jewelry, the ashes in crematoriums, the half-dead emaciated survivors—they realized as never before that evil was more than an abstraction.

Hardened by war, accustomed to the sight and smell of death, the liberators were nevertheless unprepared for what they saw. Major Richard Winters was stunned almost beyond belief:

> The memory of starved, dazed men, who dropped their eyes and heads when we looked at them through the chain-link fence, in the same manner that a beaten, mistreated dog would cringe, leaves feelings that cannot be described and will never be forgotten. The impact of seeing those people behind that fence left me saying, only to myself, 'Now I know why I'm here.'
>
> —Richard Winters, quoted in *Band of Brothers* (Ambrose)

The liberation of the camps led to an outpouring of American sympathy and sincere longing to aid the victims. Many survivors found temporary or permanent homes in the United States.

The revelation of the Holocaust also increased demand and support for an independent Jewish homeland. In 1948, when the Jewish community in the Palestine Mandate proclaimed the State of Israel,

President Truman immediately recognized the new nation. Since then, the United States has continued to offer strong support to Israel.

Today, people in the United States and around the world are working to make sure that the Holocaust is not forgotten. In 1993, the United States Holocaust Memorial Museum opened in Washington, D.C. Holocaust memorials can also be found in many states across the nation. In 1994, movie director Steven Spielberg founded an institute that recorded nearly 52,000 interviews with survivors and witnesses of the Holocaust.

DEMONSTRATE REASONED JUDGMENT Do you think the U.S. military made the right decision or the wrong decision when they decided not to bomb railway lines leading to the death camps? Explain your reasoning.

>> In April 1945, former prisoners of Dachau gather as their American liberators raise the American flag over the camp.

BOUNCE to Activate Chart

ASSESSMENT

1. **Generate Explanations** How were Hitler's racial ideas and policies connected to his concept of extreme nationalism?
2. **Describe** How did Hitler put his anti-Semitic ideas into practice as chancellor of Germany?
3. **Define** What was the "Final Solution"?
4. **Connect** How are the Holocaust and the creation of Israel connected?
5. **Quest Connections** How did the United States government respond to the German campaign against the Jews?

Primary Sources

The Diary of a Young Girl: Anne Frank

In 1933, Adolf Hitler was elected Chancellor of Germany. During World War II, his Nazi Party rounded up European Jews, many of whom were transported to death camps. Anne Frank was a young Jewish girl who hid with her family in small, concealed rooms in her father's office. Frank kept a diary from June 12, 1942 to August 1, 1944, when her family's hiding place was discovered. She died in a concentration camp in 1945. Frank's father survived and published her diary to share Anne's story with the world.

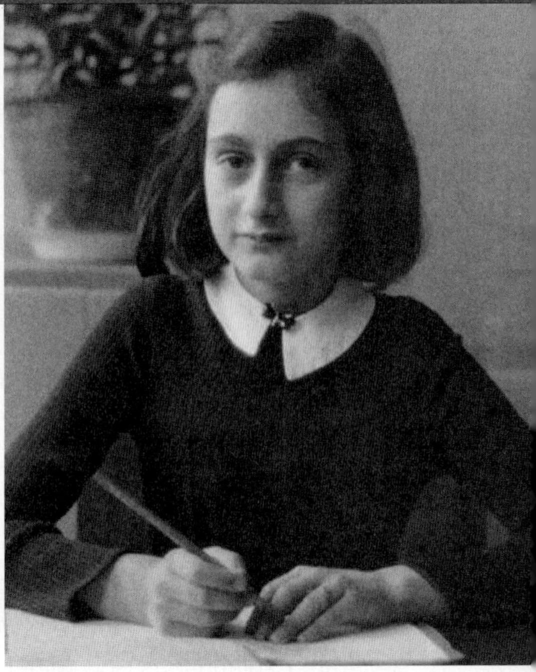

>> Anne Frank

Saturday, June 20, 1942

. . . My father . . . didn't marry my mother until he was thirty-six and she was twenty-five. My sister Margot was born in Frankfort am Main in Germany in 1926. I was born on June 12, 1929. . . . Because we're Jewish, my father immigrated to Holland in 1933, when he became the Managing Director of the Dutch Opekta Company. . . .

Our lives were not without anxiety, since our relatives in Germany were suffering under Hitler's anti-Jewish laws. After the pogroms [organized killing and other persecution of Jews] in 1938 my two uncles (my mother's brothers) fled Germany, finding safe refuge in North America. . . .

☑ **IDENTIFY SUPPORTING DETAILS** What details from the passage above show that Frank and her family were concerned about the Nazis?

After May 1940 the good times were few and far between: first there was the war, then the capitulation [surrender] and then the arrival of the Germans, which is when the trouble started for the Jews. Our freedom was severely restricted by a series of anti-Jewish decrees: Jews were required to wear a yellow star; Jews were required to turn in their bicycles; Jews were forbidden to use streetcars; Jews were forbidden to ride in cars, even their own; Jews were required to do their shopping between 3 and 5 P.M.; Jews were required to frequent only Jewish-owned barbershops and beauty parlors; Jews were forbidden to be out on the streets between 8 P.M. and 6 A.M.; Jews were forbidden to go to theaters, movies, or any other forms of entertainment; Jews were forbidden to use swimming pools, tennis courts, hockey fields or any other athletic fields; . . . Jews were forbidden to sit in their gardens or those of their friends after 8 P.M.; Jews were forbidden to visit Christians in their homes; Jews were required to attend Jewish schools, etc. You couldn't do this and you couldn't do that, but life went on. Jacque [Anne's best friend] always said to me, "I don't dare do anything anymore, 'cause I'm afraid it's not allowed." . . .

DETERMINE MEANING What does Jacque mean when she says, "I don't dare do anything anymore, 'cause I'm afraid it's not allowed"?

Thursday, November 19, 1942

. . . Countless friends and acquaintances have been taken off to a dreadful fate. Night after night, green and gray military vehicles cruise the streets. They [the Germans] knock on every door, asking whether any Jews live there. If so, the whole family is immediately taken away. If not, they proceed to the next house. It's impossible to escape their clutches unless you go into hiding. They often go around with lists, knocking only on those doors where they know there's a big haul to be made. They frequently offer a bounty, so much per head. It's like the slave hunts of the olden days. I don't mean to make light of this; it's much too tragic for that. In the evenings when it's dark, I often see long lines of good, innocent people accompanied by crying children, walking on and on, ordered about by a handful of men who bully and beat them until they nearly drop. No one is spared. The sick, the elderly, children, babies and pregnant women—all are marched to their death.

We're so fortunate here, away from the turmoil. We wouldn't have to give a moment's thought to all this suffering if it weren't for the fact that we're so worried about those we hold dear, whom we can no longer help. I feel wicked sleeping in a warm bed, while somewhere out there my dearest friends are dropping from exhaustion or being knocked to the ground.

I get frightened myself when I think of close friends who are now at the mercy of the cruelest monsters ever to stalk the earth.

And all because they're Jews. . . .

ASSESS AN ARGUMENT Why does Frank say she is "fortunate" to have a hiding place? Do you agree? Explain and support your response.

GO ONLINE to access primary sources

Wednesday, May 3, 1944

. . . we often say in despair, ". . . Why all this destruction?"

The question is understandable, but up to now no one has come up with a satisfactory answer. Why is England manufacturing bigger and better airplanes and bombs and at the same time churning out new houses for reconstruction? Why are millions spent on the war each day, while not a penny is available for medical science, artists or the poor? Why do people have to starve when mountains of food are rotting away in other parts of the world? Oh, why are people so crazy? . . .

Saturday, July 15, 1944

. . . I still believe, in spite of everything, that people are truly good at heart.

It's utterly impossible for me to build my life on a foundation of chaos, suffering, and death. I see the world being slowly transformed into a wilderness, I hear the approaching thunder that, one day, will destroy us too, I feel the sufferings of millions. And yet, when I look up at the sky, I somehow feel that everything will change for the better, that this cruelty too will end, that peace and tranquility [calm] will return once more. . . .

EXPLAIN AN ARGUMENT Why does Frank describe people as "crazy"? What problems does she observe?

ASSESSMENT

1. **Draw Inferences** What was the purpose of the restrictions the Nazis imposed on Jews? What were the effects of these laws?
2. **Analyze Style and Rhetoric** How would you describe the tone of Frank's diary? How does she relate to her subject matter?
3. **Determine Central Ideas** How does reading Frank's diary differ from reading a secondary source about the Holocaust? What might her diary teach readers today that other sources cannot?

14.8

The Potsdam Conference was the only time Harry Truman and Joseph Stalin met face to face. Though they seem friendly here, their mutual distrust helped shape the postwar world.

BOUNCE to Activate Flipped Video

Objectives

Evaluate the goals that Allied leaders set for the postwar world.

Describe the steps that the United States and other nations took toward international cooperation.

Explain the impact of World War II on the postwar United States.

Key Terms

Yalta Conference
superpowers
General Agreement on Tariffs and Trade (GATT)
United Nations (UN)
Universal Declaration of Human Rights
Geneva Convention
Nuremberg Trials

Impact of World War II

World War II (1939-1945) was a turning point that changed the nation and the world in profound ways. Many Americans came home determined to extend the ideals of democracy and freedom at home as well as abroad. In addition, the United States emerged from the war prepared to take on the complex and vital role in world affairs that it still holds today.

Planning the Postwar World

World War II differed from World War I in several ways. One major difference was that it was fought to the bitter end.

In 1918, the Kaiser surrendered before the Allies could invade Germany. By contrast, in World War II, Japan and Germany kept fighting long after their defeat was certain. In the last year of the war, they lost battle after battle, retreated from the lands they had conquered, and saw the slow destruction of their military forces. Allied bombing devastated their cities and industries. Yet Germany fought on until Hitler committed suicide, and Japan refused to surrender until after the bombing of Hiroshima and Nagasaki.

The Yalta Conference The protracted fighting gave the Allies time to make plans for a postwar world. Roosevelt, Churchill, and Stalin met at Yalta on the Black Sea in February 1945 to discuss final strategy and crucial questions concerning postwar Germany, Eastern Europe, and Asia. At the **Yalta Conference**, the Big Three agreed that Poland, Bulgaria, and Romania would hold free elections. However, Stalin later reneged on this promise.

GO ONLINE to access your digital course

Roosevelt and Churchill were not in a good position to press Stalin too hard. The Red Army already occupied much of Eastern Europe, and Roosevelt wanted Soviet help in the war against Japan. Vague promises were about as much as Stalin would give.

The Potsdam Conference A dramatically altered Big Three met in July 1945 in the Berlin suburb of Potsdam. Although Stalin remained in power in the Soviet Union, Harry S. Truman had become U.S. President in April upon the death of FDR. After the start of the conference, Clement Attlee replaced Churchill as prime minister of Britain.

At Potsdam, Truman took the reins of international leadership and began to reshape the relationship of the United States with its Allies. While in Potsdam, Truman learned of the successful test of the atomic bomb. But he was more focused on Europe and the Soviet Union than on Asia. Truman was more distrustful of Stalin than Roosevelt had been. Fearing Soviet domination of Eastern Europe, Truman continued to press for free elections after the war.

At the meeting, the Big Three formalized the decision to divide Germany into four zones of occupation: Soviet, American, British, and French. They agreed to new borders and free elections for Poland, and they recognized the Soviets' right to claim reparations for war damages from the German sector they controlled. Stalin also reaffirmed his Yalta pledge to enter the war against Japan.

☑ **COMPARE AND CONTRAST** How did the leaders and decisions made at the Potsdam Conference differ from those at the Yalta Conference?

International Impact of the War

After the war ended in August 1945, plans for the postwar world had to be turned into realities. However, the changes that took place were often not what the Allies had envisioned at Yalta and Potsdam.

Worldwide Political Changes World War II changed political boundaries in many parts of the world. The borders of Poland, for example, shifted slightly to the west. In time, as you will learn, differences between the Soviet Union and its former Allies led to the division of Germany into two countries: communist East Germany and noncommunist West Germany. Nearly all the nations of Eastern Europe became communist states under Soviet control.

Other countries experienced profound political changes. Communist and noncommunist interests clashed in Eastern Europe. In China, a long-standing civil war between Nationalists and communists resumed.

In Japan, General Douglas MacArthur headed an American military occupation and supervised the writing of a new constitution. It abolished the armed forces except for purposes of defense, gave women the right to vote, enacted democratic reforms, and established the groundwork for full economic recovery. In 1951, Japan and the United States signed a peace treaty that formally ended World War II and disbanded what was left of Japan's colonial empire.

The War Weakens Imperialism The war also marked the end of Western European domination of the world. Since the 1500s, nations such as Britain, France, and Spain had exerted paramount influence on global developments. They colonized much of Africa, the Middle East, Asia, and the Americas. They controlled world trade and finance, led the

>> This photograph shows (left to right) Churchill, Roosevelt, and Stalin at the Yalta Conference. Roosevelt died only a few months after this picture was taken.

BOUNCE to Activate Map

Industrial Revolution, and stood at the forefront of world military power.

The aggressive acquisition of territories by Japan and Germany underscored the abuses of imperialism. After World War II, colonial peoples renewed their drive for independence from European powers. Freed from Japanese domination, the East Indies had no interest in returning to Dutch colonial status.

Nor did Indochina want to see the return of French rule. India, Burma, colonies in the Middle East and Africa—all had their sights set on independence.

By the end of the war, it was clear that the Age of Imperialism was in the twilight of its existence. The British Empire, the predominant power of the nineteenth century, came out of the war suffering severe economic shortages and, within decades, would see the loss of most of its colonies.

New Superpowers Emerge Into the power vacuum stepped the United States and the Soviet Union. They had played the most decisive roles in defeating the Axis Powers, and they emerged from the war confident and strong. Indeed, they so dominated the postwar world that they became known as **superpowers**.

>> Red Army troops proudly parade through Prague, Czechoslovakia, in 1945. **Connect** How does this photograph illustrate two advantages the Soviet Union enjoyed in the postwar world?

Of the two superpowers, the United States was clearly the stronger. Except for the attack on Pearl Harbor, no major battle had been fought on U.S. soil. In addition, American industry had boomed during the war. By 1945, America was wealthy, militarily powerful, and confident. By contrast, much of the war had been fought on Soviet soil. Its industries, cities, and peoples had suffered terribly.

Still, the Red Army controlled most of Eastern Europe and threatened to move farther west. Militarily, although the Americans had the atomic bomb, the Soviets had the Red Army, the world's largest military force.

☑ **IDENTIFY EFFECTS** What impact did World War II have on the relative roles of the United States and Britain in the world?

International Organizations and Treaties

Americans were quick to recognize that their nation had taken on a new position in the world. After World War I, the Senate had rejected the Treaty of Versailles and refused to join the League of Nations. Many Americans now viewed these decisions as mistakes that contributed to the rise of fascism and the outbreak of another war. As World War II drew to a close, Americans were ready to embrace the idea of world organizations.

Economic Effects of World War II World War II paved the way for a restructuring of the world economy. The United States took on major responsibilities in shaping the postwar world economy.

After meeting in 1944 with the Allies in Bretton Woods, New Hampshire, the U.S. government pushed for establishment of the International Monetary Fund and the World Bank. The United States provided most of the working capital for these new organizations, which worked to foster global economic and financial stability. The agreements made at Bretton Woods also represented another step in the shifting trend from the gold standard to fiat money, or money that is not redeemable in gold or silver. The international currency system was pegged to the U.S. dollar, with the United States agreeing to keep the price of gold at a certain level, effectively making the dollar the new standard.

In 1947, the United States signed the **General Agreement on Tariffs and Trade (GATT)**, a treaty designed to expand world trade by reducing tariffs. It went into effect on January 1, 1948. Between its signing and 1993, average tarrifs dropped from 40 percent to 5 percent. Losing protective tariffs has caused some industries in the United States to suffer from competition with foreign goods but the lower tariffs encouraged world trade in general. GATT was replaced by the World Trade Organization (WTO) in 1995.

The United Nations Even more importantly, the United States led the charge for the establishment of the **United Nations (UN)**, an organization that many hoped would succeed where the League of Nations had failed. In April 1945, delegates from 50 nations met in San Francisco to write the charter for the UN. The Senate overwhelmingly ratified the charter, and the UN later set up its permanent home in New York City. A major goal of the UN was to prevent further world wars or events such as the Holocaust.

The United Nations was organized on the basis of cooperation between the Great Powers, not on the absolute equality of all nations. All member nations sat on the General Assembly. However, the five major World War II Allies—the United States, the Soviet Union, Britain, France, and China—were assigned permanent seats on the most powerful arm of the UN, the Security Council.

President Truman named former First Lady Eleanor Roosevelt to represent the United States at the UN. Mary McLeod Bethune was appointed consultant on interracial affairs at the UN's charter conference.

As elected chair of the Commission on Human Rights, the former First Lady guided the drafting of the **Universal Declaration of Human Rights**, a 1948 document that defined rights that belonged to all people in the world. It states:

> Recognition of the inherent dignity and of the equal and inalienable rights of all members of the human family is the foundation of freedom, justice and peace in the world. . . . All human beings are born free and equal in dignity and rights. They are endowed with reason and conscience

>> American, British, and Soviet delegates vote at a United Nations meeting. The three Allies held permanent seats on the Security Council, but wartime cooperation soon turned to conflict.

>> This statue of Eleanor Roosevelt stands at the Franklin D. Roosevelt Memorial in Washington, D.C. Behind her is the insignia of the UN.

and should act toward one another in a spirit of brotherhood.

—Universal Declaration of Human Rights

The Declaration condemns slavery and torture, upholds freedom of speech and religion, and affirms that "everyone has the right to a standard of living adequate for the health and well-being of himself and his family." Though the document sets lofty goals it has proved difficult to enforce.

Over the next decades, the UN set up a refugee agency to help people displaced by the war.

It also aided the move away from colonialism, helped to create the Jewish state of Israel, mediated regional conflicts, and provided food and other aid to much of the world.

Not all Americans support participation in the United Nations and other international bodies. Some argue that giving decision-making authority to global organizations undermines U.S. sovereignty.

War Crimes Trials In the effort to create a better world, the Allies did not forget to punish the people who had caused so much destruction and death.

>> A 1948 war crimes tribunal found Tojo (right) guilty of waging wars of aggression and allowing inhumane treatment of prisoners of war. Tojo accepted full responsibility and was condemned to death.

BOUNCE to Activate Gallery

During the war, the Axis Powers had repeatedly violated the **Geneva Convention**, an international agreement governing the humane treatment of wounded soldiers and prisoners of war.

The Allies tried more than a thousand Japanese citizens for committing atrocities in China, Korea, and Southeast Asia and brutally mistreating prisoners of war. Hundreds were condemned to death, including Prime Minister Hideki Tojo and the general responsible for the Bataan Death March.

Americans more closely followed the **Nuremberg Trials**, in which the Allies prosecuted Nazis for war crimes. The trials turned a glaring spotlight on the evils of the Third Reich. The first of the Nuremberg Trials involved key leaders of Nazi Germany, such as Hermann Göring. Day by day, prosecutors described their crimes, detailing especially the horrors of the Holocaust. Most of the defendants pleaded that they were just following orders, that Hitler was the source of all the crimes. But Robert Jackson, the American prosecutor, pointed out the importance of holding former Nazi officials responsible for their actions:

> No half-century ever witnessed slaughter on such a scale, such cruelties and inhumanities. . . . If we cannot eliminate the causes and prevent the repetition of these barbaric events, it is not an irresponsible prophecy to say that this twentieth century may yet succeed in bringing the doom of civilization.
>
> —Robert Jackson, closing speech, Nuremberg War Crimes Trials, 1946

Some of the Nazis were hanged; others received long prison terms. The evidence presented at the trials increased world support for the establishment of Israel as a Jewish homeland.

In the following decades, Allied or Israeli authorities captured and tried such other Nazis as Adolf Eichmann, a leading architect of the "Final Solution," and Klaus Barbie, a Gestapo officer convicted of torturing and murdering Jews and resistance fighters in Lyon, France. The periodic trials kept alive the memory of the Nazi crimes against humanity.

IDENTIFY STEPS IN A PROCESS What steps did the United States take to increase its role in the postwar world?

Domestic Impact of the War

A new American identity rose from World War II. Americans regarded the Nazis as totalitarian, racist, and warlike. During the war, U.S. leaders and American popular culture had emphasized that the Allies were fighting a "people's war" for tolerance, freedom, democracy, and peace. Although many Americans felt that their country had not always lived up to that ideal, they hoped that the postwar period would usher in significant changes.

A Leader on the Global Stage Millions of Americans had spent several years closely following the war. They had attached world maps to their walls and traced the paths of U.S. troops in the deserts of North Africa, the forests of Europe, and the coral islands of the Pacific. For this generation of Americans, the world had somehow become a smaller, more interconnected place. They had learned to think in global terms.

Few Americans called for a return to a policy of isolationism or retreat from their global responsibilities. They recognized that what happened in the far reaches of the globe affected them, that America's national security was linked to world security.

>> This 1943 poster emphasizes America as a defender of liberty. After the war, the United States continued to take on the role of leader of the Free World in opposition to the Soviet Union.

BOUNCE to Activate Gallery

Impact on the Economy and Government World War II ended the Great Depression and ushered in decades of economic growth. Expansion in world trade, spurred by GATT and other treaties, also contributed to postwar economic prosperity.

The war also redistributed wealth across the country. Defense industries and military bases in the South and West spurred people to move to these regions, which in turn created more wealth and encouraged further migration. Wartime factory work also created new and higher-paying job opportunities for women, African Americans, and other minorities, raising their expectations of what they should be able to achieve.

Like other wars, World War II led to a greater governmental influence in economic affairs. From the collection of raw materials to attempts to control inflation, the government had made the important decisions to guide the economy. In the process, it established the expanded economic role that government would play in postwar America.

The war also increased the power of the U.S. presidency. The War Powers Acts of 1941 and 1942 gave the President broad powers to conduct the war. Backed by these laws, FDR issued Executive Orders to take actions he felt necessary to win the war. These included orders that established a Censorship Board and banned hiring discrimination in government-funded defense industries. The War Powers Acts raised constitutional issues in that some felt that the greater powers of the Executive branch threatened the traditional separation of powers laid out in the Constitution.The increased use of Executive Orders as a presidential tool remains controversial today.

Demanding Equal Rights African American soldiers in World War II had clearly believed they were fighting two foes: dictatorship overseas and racism in the United States. Less than two months after Pearl Harbor, one of the nation's leading Black newspapers published a letter from a young man in Wichita, Kansas:

> Being an American of dark complexion and some 26 years, these questions flash through my mind: 'Should I sacrifice my life to live half American?' 'Will things be better for the next generation in the peace to follow?' . . .

> I suggest that while we keep defense and victory in the forefront that we don't lose sight of our fight for true democracy at home.
>
> —James G. Thompson, letter to the *Pittsburgh Courier*, January 31, 1942

World War II gave renewed vigor to the fight for civil rights. In this battle, African Americans were not alone. A growing number of white Americans also called for the nation to live up to its promise to be a beacon of freedom, democracy, and justice.

MAKE PREDICTIONS How do you think World War II will change the way Americans view the role of the United States in the world in the following decades?

ASSESSMENT

1. **Predict** Based on the information in this lesson, predict at least one postwar issue about which the former Allies will disagree.
2. **Compare** In what way were the Universal Declaration of Human Rights and the postwar push for civil rights both reactions to the war?
3. **Analyze Context** Why did Americans agree to participate in the UN after World War II when many had rejected participation in the League of Nations after World War I?
4. **Identify Patterns** How did World War II impact the American economy? Did the war have the same impact on the British economy?
5. **Recognize Cause and Effect** In your opinion, what was the most important effect of World War II on the United States? Support your answer with evidence.
6. **Quest Connections** How might the changes brought by World War II to the South and West have affected the lives of both new migrants and native residents?

GO ONLINE to access this biography: Hideki Tojo

Primary Sources

Charter of the United Nations

In 1945, representatives of 50 countries met in San Francisco to sign a charter creating the United Nations, a new peacekeeping organization. Here are the preamble and first two articles of that charter.

>> Delegates vote at UN meeting

We The Peoples Of The United Nations Determined

- to save succeeding [later] generations from the scourge of war, which twice in our lifetime has brought untold sorrow to mankind, and
- to reaffirm faith in fundamental human rights, in the dignity and worth of the human person, in the equal rights of men and women and of nations large and small, and
- to establish conditions under which justice and respect for the obligations arising from treaties and other sources of international law can be maintained, and
- to promote social progress and better standards of life in larger freedom,

And For These Ends

- to practice tolerance and live together in peace with one another as good neighbours, and
- to unite our strength to maintain international peace and security, and
- to ensure, by the acceptance of principles and the institution of methods, that armed force shall not be used, save in the common interest, and
- to employ international machinery for the promotion of the economic and social advancement of all peoples,

Have Resolved To Combine Our Efforts To Accomplish These Aims

Accordingly, our respective Governments, through representatives assembled in the city of San Francisco, who have exhibited their full powers found to be in good and due form, have agreed to the present Charter of the United Nations and do hereby establish an international organization to be known as the United Nations.

DRAW INFERENCES The preamble mentions "the scourge of war, which twice in our lifetime has brought untold sorrow to mankind." To what events is the preamble referring in this excerpt?

Chapter I: Purposes And Principles

Article 1

The Purposes of the United Nations are:
1. To maintain international peace and security, and to that end: to take effective collective measures for the prevention and removal of threats to the peace, and for the suppression of acts of aggression or other breaches of the peace, and to bring about by peaceful means, and in conformity with the principles of justice and international law, adjustment or settlement of international disputes or situations which might lead to a breach of the peace;

2. To develop friendly relations among nations based on respect for the principle of equal rights and self-determination of peoples, and to take other appropriate measures to strengthen universal peace;
3. To achieve international co-operation in solving international problems of an economic, social, cultural, or humanitarian character, and in promoting and encouraging respect for human rights and for fundamental freedoms for all without distinction as to race, sex, language, or religion; and
4. To be a centre for harmonizing the actions of nations in the attainment of these common ends.

Article 2

The Organization and its Members, in pursuit of the Purposes stated in Article 1, shall act in accordance with the following Principles.
1. The Organization is based on the principle of the sovereign equality of all its Members.
2. All Members, in order to ensure to all of them the rights and benefits resulting from membership, shall fulfill in good faith the obligations assumed by them in accordance with the present Charter.
3. All Members shall settle their international disputes by peaceful means in such a manner that international peace and security, and justice, are not endangered.
4. All Members shall refrain in their international relations from the threat or use of force against the territorial integrity or political independence of any state, or in any other manner inconsistent with the Purposes of the United Nations.
5. All Members shall give the United Nations every assistance in any action it takes in accordance with the present Charter, and shall refrain from giving assistance to any state against which the United Nations is taking preventive or enforcement action.
6. The Organization shall ensure that states which are not Members of the United Nations act in accordance with these Principles so far as may be necessary for the maintenance of international peace and security.
7. Nothing contained in the present Charter shall authorize the United Nations to intervene in matters which are essentially within the domestic jurisdiction of any state or shall require the Members to submit such matters to settlement under the present Charter; but this principle shall not prejudice the application of enforcement measures under Chapter Vll.

DETERMINE MEANING In Article 2, Principle 1, what does *sovereign* mean?

ASSESSMENT

1. **Cite Evidence** If one country's governing party is inflicting terrible human rights abuses on members of the opposition party, can the United Nations intervene? Cite the part(s) of the charter that support your opinion.
2. **Explain an Argument** Consider this scenario: several years of drought in western Asia have led to widespread famine. The UN arranges to bring convoys of food to starving people. One country, a member of the UN, does not want to let relief workers cross its borders. Does any part of the charter cited here support or rebut the country's position? Explain your answer.
3. **Draw Conclusions** Has the United Nations been successful in its mission "to save succeeding generations from the scourge of war"? Explain your answer.

Connections to Today

An activist dresses in plastic bags to raise awareness about their impact on the environment.

Take Action to Learn About Plastics

The crisis of war often spurs researchers to develop new technologies and innovations. These advances, born of necessity in a time of peril, often transfer into use in civilian life.

1. **Choose** one of the following technology-related topics:
   - **Medical Field:** Explore how single-use plastic medical devices impact health care and the environment.
   - **Recycling:** Research what happens to recycled plastic and the challenges and opportunities presented by recycling.
   - **Innovation:** Research new products that are emerging to replace common plastic products we use in everyday life.
2. **Ask Questions** Generate a list of questions about your topic. Perhaps you want to know more about how plastic is made or recycled, for example.
3. **Learn** about the topic by conducting research. Use online sources, magazines, interviews, government sources, and so on. Are there any major debates related to this topic? What are the arguments on each side? Take notes as you conduct your research and continue to generate questions as you learn more.
4. **Create a PSA** Create a radio Public Service Announcement (PSA). Your PSA should inform the public about the impact of plastics on people's lives and on the environment.

Topic 14 Quick Study Guide

LESSON SUMMARIES

Use these Lesson Summaries, and the longer versions available online, to review the key ideas for each lesson in this Topic.

Lesson 1: Rise of Aggressive Dictators

Throughout the 1930s, the rise of dictatorships in the Soviet Union, Germany, Italy, and Japan challenged world peace. Seeking to preserve the peace, Western democracies responded to acts of aggression with appeasement policies.

Lesson 2: America Debates Involvement

As the war raged in Europe, the United States maintained an isolationist position, which became increasingly difficult as its allies fell under German occupation.

Lesson 3: The United States Enters World War II

American neutrality ended when Japan carried out a surprise attack on Pearl Harbor in 1941. The United States declared war on Japan. Germany and Italy declared war on the United States.

Lesson 4: A War on Two Fronts

In June 1942, American forces won the Battle of Midway, ending Japanese expansion in the Pacific. The following year, the Russians turned back the German invasion of the Soviet Union, while American forces defeated German and Italian troops in North Africa before invading and defeating Italy. By the end of 1943, both Germany and Japan were on the defensive.

Lesson 5: The Home Front

In the United States, the war changed life in various ways: jobs opened up for women and minorities, people moved to work in defense industries, and the government brought Mexican laborers to work on farms. After the attack on Pearl Harbor, the government moved Japanese Americans on the west coast to isolated camps, where they were held for the duration of the war.

Lesson 6: The Allies Win World War II

On June 6, 1944, known as D-Day, British and American forces invaded France. In 1945, the advance of the Soviet Army from the east, and the United States Army from the west forced Germany to surrender on May 7. In the Pacific, American forces slowly advanced on Japan. In August 1945, U.S. pilots dropped atomic bombs on Hiroshima and Nagasaki, forcing Japan to surrender.

Lesson 7: The Holocaust

When Allied soldiers began to liberate Nazi concentration camps, they uncovered the horrors of the Holocaust. After the war, President Truman immediately recognized the new nation of Israel when it was established by Jews in Palestine.

Lesson 8: Impact of World War II

As World War II ended, Allied leaders met to discuss the postwar world and divided Germany into four zones. After the war, the United States led the move to establish the United Nations and the U.S. and Soviet Union became world superpowers.

QUEST! FINDINGS

Create Your "Memories of World War II" Website Refer to your responses to the Quest Connections to help you create your website. Then share it with the class. Use the rubric and other Quest resources online to guide your work.

GO ONLINE to access lesson summaries

VISUAL REVIEW

Use these graphics to review some of the key terms, people, and ideas from this Topic.

Allied Leaders, World War II

WORLD POLITICAL	U.S. MILITARY
• Winston Churchill, Britain • Joseph Stalin, Soviet Union • Franklin D. Roosevelt, United States • Harry S. Truman, United States	**In Europe** • Dwight Eisenhower • George S. Patton • Omar Bradley **In the Pacific** • Douglas MacArthur • Chester Nimitz

Five Turning Points of World War II

1942	**Battle of Midway** halts Japanese expansion in the Pacific.
1942	**Battle of El Alamein** begins Allied offensive against Axis Powers in North Africa.
1942–1943	**Battle of Stalingrad** ends Nazi advances in Europe.
1944	**D-Day** invasion opens second front in Europe, paving way for final defeat of Germany.
1945	**Manhattan Project** develops atomic bomb, used to end war in the Pacific.

World War II Home Front

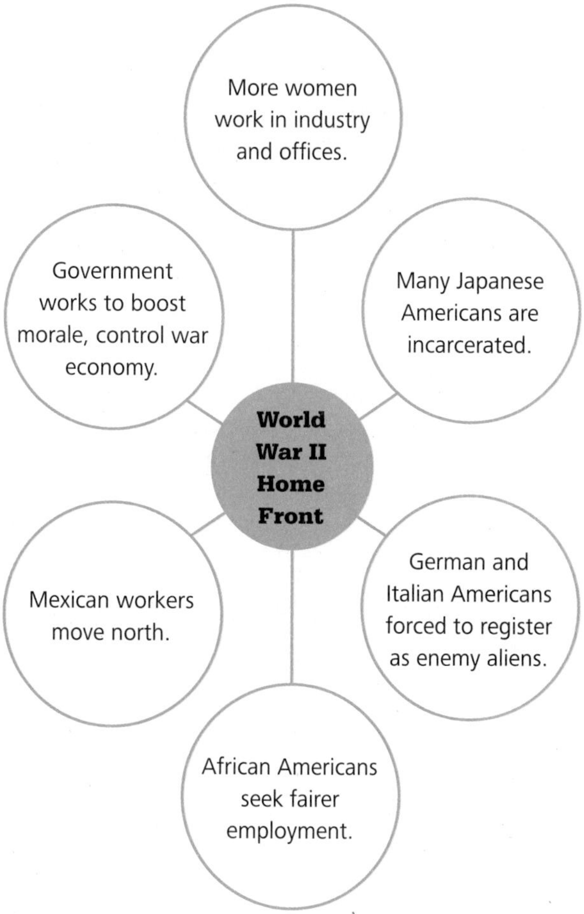

World War II Deaths, Selected Nations

COUNTRY	MILITARY DEATHS	CIVILIAN DEATHS
AXIS		
Germany	3,500,000	780,000
Italy	242,000	153,000
Japan	1,300,000	672,000
ALLIES		
France	213,000	350,000
Britain	264,000	93,000
China	1,310,000	1,000,000
Soviet Union	7,500,000	15,000,000
United States	292,000	6,000

Topic 14 Assessment

KEY TERMS, PEOPLE, AND IDEAS

1. How did **Adolf Hitler** contribute to the outbreak of World War II?
2. How did the Allies turn the tide against the Axis?
3. What was the **bracero program** and what were its long-term effects?
4. How did the Allies defeat the Axis powers?
5. How did **anti-Semitism** lead to the **Holocaust**?
6. Why did **Franklin D. Roosevelt** sponsor the **Lend-Lease Act**?
7. How did the war change life on the American home front?
8. What were the effects of the Holocaust?
9. What were the major immediate and long-term effects of World War II internationally?

CRITICAL THINKING

10. **Find the Main Idea** Identify three key events in the U.S. transition from isolationism to involvement in the early years of World War II.
11. **Summarize** (a) What was the chief goal of Allied leaders during World War II? (b) What strategy did they design to meet this goal?
12. **Make Generalizations** Make a generalization about how American women contributed to the war effort, both on the home front and in combat. Give two examples to support your generalization.
13. **Evaluate Information** (a) Why did Stalin want Roosevelt and Churchill to open a second front in Europe? (b) What action did the Allies take to accomplish this goal? (c) Evaluate its success.
14. **Draw Conclusions** Explain the significance of World War II as a turning point in history. Consider the following as you frame your answer: the roles of the United States and the Soviet Union in the postwar years and the introduction of nuclear warfare as a result of the war.
15. **Make Generalizations** Describe how American involvement in World War II had economic effects on the home front.
16. **Analyze Maps** Look at the map at the top of the next column. (a) What event does the map illustrate? (b) Describe this event. (c) Why do you think the people responsible for this incident were tried as war criminals after the war?

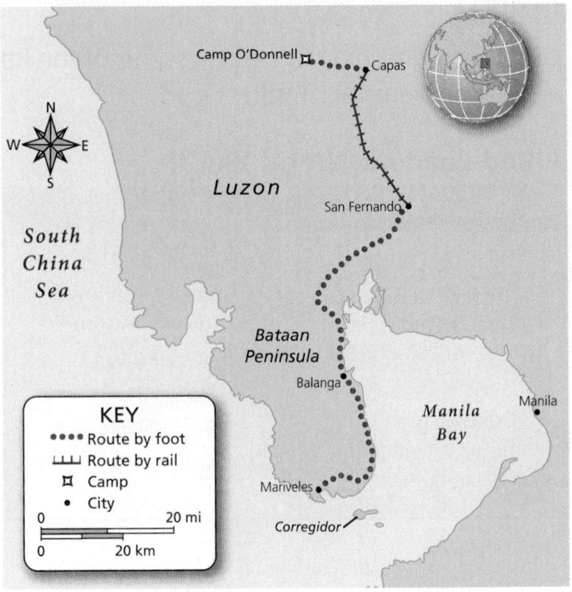

17. **Writing Activity: Write a Research Paper** In 1941, before the United States entered World War II, President Roosevelt addressed Congress to talk about "four freedoms":

> . . . we look forward to a world founded upon four essential human freedoms.
>
> The first is freedom of speech and expression—everywhere in the world.
>
> The second is freedom of every person to worship God in his own way—everywhere in the world.
>
> The third is freedom from want—which, translated into world terms, means economic understandings which will secure to every nation a healthy peace time life for its inhabitants—everywhere in the world.
>
> The fourth is freedom from fear—which, translated into world terms means a worldwide reduction of armaments to such a point and in such a thorough fashion that no nation will be in a position to commit an act of physical aggression against any neighbor—anywhere in the world. . . .

What was the President's purpose in giving this speech? Research the circumstances surrounding it and how it was received by Britain and Germany. Write a research paper in which you answer these questions.

18. **Connections to Today** Developments in technology and science can be used for both good and bad purposes. What is the role of government when new scientific advancements or technologies are developed?

DOCUMENT-BASED QUESTIONS

President Truman's decision to use the atomic bomb against Japan continues to stir controversy. Read the documents below, then answer the questions that follow.

DOCUMENT A

This excerpt is from a petition signed by 154 of the scientists who developed the atomic bomb.

> The war has to be brought speedily to a successful conclusion and attacks by atomic bombs may very well be an effective method of warfare. We feel, however, that such attacks on Japan could not be justified, at least not unless the terms which will be imposed after the war on Japan were made public in detail and Japan were given an opportunity to surrender. ...
>
> The development of atomic power will provide the nations with new means of destruction. The atomic bombs at our disposal represent only the first step in this direction, and there is almost no limit to the destructive power which will become available in the course of their future development.
>
> —*Leó Szilárd, Petition to the President of the United States, July 17, 1945*

DOCUMENT B

This photograph shows Hiroshima after the bombing on August 6, 1945. The single bomb destroyed 4.7 square miles of Hiroshima and some 68% of its buildings. Between 70,000 and 80,000 people were killed by the explosion or its aftereffects.

DOCUMENT C

This excerpt is from a letter written by Truman.

> When the message came to Potsdam that a successful atomic explosion had taken place in New Mexico, there was much excitement and conversation about the effect on the war then in progress with Japan. ... I asked Gen. Marshall what it would cost in lives to land on the Tokyo plain and other places in Japan. It was his opinion that 1/4 million casualties would be the minimum cost as well as an equal number of the enemy.
>
> We sent an ultimatum to Japan. It was ignored. ...
>
> Dropping the bombs ended the war, saved lives and gave the free nations a chance to face the facts.
>
> —*Harry Truman, January 12, 1953*

DOCUMENT D

This excerpt is from a book written by a onetime historian for the Nuclear Regulatory Commission.

> The use of atomic bombs was decisive in ending the war. After Hiroshima, the emperor for the first time came out unequivocally for surrender, and he soon intervened directly to persuade the cabinet to accept the Potsdam Declaration. ...
>
> Even without use of the atomic bombs, the war would probably have ended before an American invasion of Kyushu [one of Japan's main islands] became necessary. Conditions in Japan were steadily deteriorating before the atomic attacks and would have continued to worsen as the war dragged on. The destruction of cities from B-29 raids, diminishing food supplies, and decreasing public morale fostered enough discontent to worry the emperor and his advisers. ...
>
> —*J. Samuel Walker, Prompt and Utter Destruction, 1997*

19. The scientists who signed the petition believed that atomic weapons

A. would not help bring the war to a quick end.
B. should be used immediately to end the war.
C. might be used if there was no other option.
D. were too dangerous to use for any reason.

20. Analyze Photographs Based on Document B, what effect do you think the bombing might have had on those who witnessed it?

21. According to President Truman, his main goal in deciding to use the atomic bomb was to

A. save American and Japanese lives.
B. punish Japan for carrying on the war.
C. demonstrate the power of nuclear weapons.
D. destroy the nation of Japan.

22. Writing Task Write a paragraph explaining whether you think Truman's decision to use the atomic bomb on Hiroshima and Nagasaki was justified. Use the sources as well as additional information you have learned about the bombings.

GO ONLINE to access more practice

Topic 15

Postwar America (1945–1960)

ESSENTIAL QUESTION What is America's role in the world?

GO ONLINE to access the eText, videos, Interactive Primary Sources, Biographies, and other online resources.

A school air-raid drill in 1952

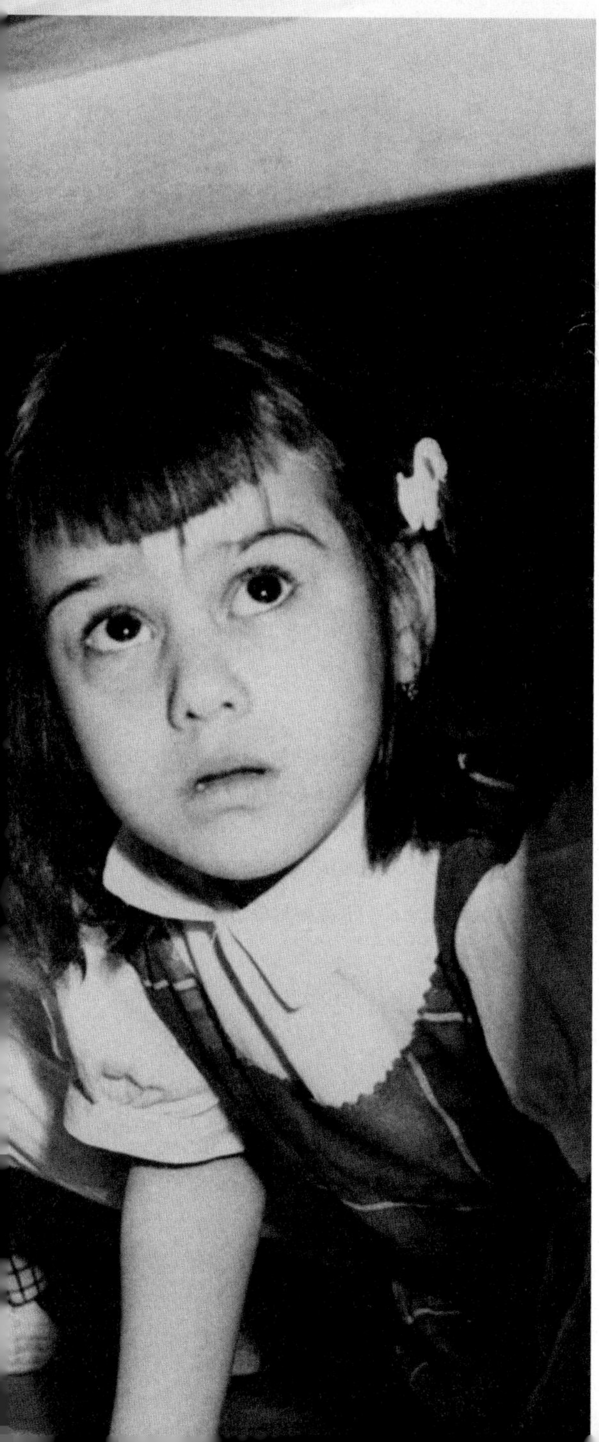

Connections to Today

Who do you generally hang out with: Musicians? Gamers? Skaters? Athletes?

People tend to be friends with other people who have similar interests and values. Another way people group together is by age. People born during a certain period of time tend to have similar experiences growing up and certain shared characteristics. In this topic, you will learn about the first postwar generation to get an identity label, the baby boomers. What is the name for your generation and how are generational identities formed?

NBC LEARN

Learn how Senator Margaret Chase Smith responded to events in the postwar United States.

BOUNCE to Activate My Story Video

Topic 15 Overview

In this Topic, you'll learn about the United States in the years after World War II. Look at the lesson outline and explore the timeline. As you study this Topic, you'll complete the Quest Inquiry.

LESSON OUTLINE

Key Events of the Postwar United States

1945
World War II ends; Soviets occupy Eastern Europe

1948
Congress approves Marshall Plan

1949
NATO is formed

1950
Korean War begins; McCarthy begins anti-communist campaign

1951
Levittown, NY, suburb is built

1953
Convicted spies Ethel and Julius Rosenberg are executed

1956
Interstate Highway Act expands highway construction

1945 | 1950 | 1955 | 1960

QUEST! INQUIRY

Understanding McCarthyism in the 1950s

How did Senator Joseph McCarthy become so powerful during the Red Scare of the 1950s? Why did McCarthyism have such an impact on domestic United States policy? In this Quest you'll explore this question before writing an essay to present your answer.

STEP 1
Watch the video and discuss it in class or with a partner. Consider the questions it raises about the Red Scare and McCarthyism.

STEP 2
Examine the source documents relating to McCarthyism and answer the questions attached to each document. Then review the relevant skills tutorials.

STEP 3
Consider all the evidence and draw your own conclusions. Write an essay to answer the question: Why did McCarthyism have such a powerful effect on American life in the 1950s?

STEP 4
Reflect on the process of analyzing the documents and writing the essay and then complete the Self-Assessment.

GO ONLINE to access complete Quest materials

15.1

The United States and Great Britain supplied goods to West Berlin by plane during the Berlin Airlift.

BOUNCE to Activate Flipped Video

Objectives

Trace the reasons that the wartime alliance between the United States and the Soviet Union unraveled.

Explain how President Truman responded to Soviet aggression in Eastern Europe.

Describe the causes and results of Stalin's blockade of Berlin.

Key Terms

satellite state
Cold War
iron curtain
Truman Doctrine
George F. Kennan
containment
Marshall Plan
Berlin airlift
North Atlantic Treaty Organization (NATO)
Warsaw Pact

The Beginning of the Cold War

In the 1930s, the policies of isolationism and appeasement did nothing to stop the rise of dictatorships and the outbreak of global war. After World War II, U.S. leaders viewed these past policies as mistakes. They sought new ways to keep the United States safe and to protect its interests around the world.

Background of the Cold War

When Franklin Roosevelt died in April 1945, the nation was at a critical point. The United States was still at war. In addition, relations with the Soviet Union—one of the most important wartime allies—were beginning to break down.

Soviet Aggression Against Its Citizens The United States and the Soviet Union had been united only in their opposition to Nazi Germany. Beyond that, they had little in common. The United States was a capitalist democracy. Its citizens believed in free elections, economic and religious freedom, private property, and respect for individual differences. The Soviet Union was a dictatorship.

Under Joseph Stalin, the Communist Party made all key economic, political, and military decisions. The Soviet people could not worship as they pleased, own private property, or express their views freely. Those who opposed or questioned Stalin risked imprisonment and death.

GO ONLINE to access your digital course

Soviets Control Eastern Europe By the time Roosevelt, Stalin, and Churchill met at Yalta in February 1945, it was clear that the Allies would defeat Germany. But it was unclear how Germany and the nations of Eastern Europe would be governed after the war. Soviet troops occupied much of Eastern Europe and parts of Germany.

Stalin wanted to keep Germany weak and divided. He also wanted Eastern Europe to remain under the control of the Soviet Union. The United States and Great Britain sought a stronger, united Germany and independent nations in Eastern Europe. At the conference, Stalin agreed to establish "broadly representative" governments and free elections in Eastern Europe and to divide Germany only temporarily into zones of occupation.

Despite Stalin's promises, nearly all of the lands occupied by the Soviet Red Army in the spring of 1945 remained under Soviet control after the war. The Eastern European countries of Poland, Czechoslovakia, Hungary, Romania, and Bulgaria, as well as the eastern portion of Germany, became **satellite states**, or countries falling within the Soviet sphere of influence.

>> A Soviet soldier raises the Soviet flag over Berlin, Germany, in April 1945.

Wartime Alliance Unravels By the time Soviet, British, and U.S. leaders met at Potsdam in the summer of 1945, Harry Truman had succeeded Franklin Roosevelt as President. Truman and Clement Attlee, the new British prime minister, hoped that Stalin would confirm the decisions made at Yalta. However, Stalin refused to commit to allowing free elections in Eastern Europe.

Truman left Potsdam believing that the Soviet Union was "planning world conquest" and that the alliance with the Soviet Union was falling apart. With the Soviet Red Army at his command, Stalin seemed to present a real threat. Thus, the stage was set for a worldwide rivalry between the United States and the Soviet Union. The 46-year struggle became known as the **Cold War** because the two superpowers never faced each other directly in a "hot" military conflict.

☑ **CONTRAST** How did the goals of U.S. and Soviet foreign policy differ after World War II?

Responding to the Soviet Challenge

President Truman was not the only world leader who believed that Stalin had aspirations toward world domination. Winston Churchill also spoke out

>> Winston Churchill delivers his "Iron Curtain" speech. This descriptive phrase became a lasting symbol of the brutal division that communism had created in Western Europe.

BOUNCE to Activate Timeline

forcefully against the Soviet Union. On March 5, 1946, he gave an important speech at Fulton College in Missouri, Truman's home state. Referring to a map of Europe, Churchill noted that "an **iron curtain** has descended across the Continent."

East of that iron curtain, the Soviet Union was gaining more control by installing communist governments and police states and by crushing political and religious dissent. In addition, Churchill feared, the Soviets were attempting to spread communism to Western Europe and East Asia. The only solution, Churchill said, was for the United States and other democratic countries to stand firm.

Truman Faces Soviet Aggression in Eastern Europe Truman shared Churchill's beliefs. Born in a small town in Missouri, Truman had been too poor to attend college. He is the only President since 1901 without a college education. Instead, he worked the family farm, fought in France during World War I, and eventually began a political career. His life was a testament to honesty, integrity, hard work, and a willingness to make difficult decisions. "The buck stops here" was his motto as President. It meant that the person sitting in the Oval Office had the obligation to face problems head on and make hard decisions.

In 1947, no issue was more weighty than the growing crisis between the United States and the Soviet Union. After World War II, a number of European and Asian countries were struggling against communist movements supported by the Soviets. In particular, the governments of Greece and Turkey were battling communist forces seeking to gain control. Greece and Turkey needed aid, and in 1947 the United States was the only country with the resources to help them.

The Truman Doctrine Opposes Soviet Aggression On March 12, 1947, President Truman addressed both houses of Congress. With emotion in his voice, Truman described the plight of the Greek and Turkish people. The fight they were waging, he said, was the fight that all free people had to confront. Truman requested money from Congress "to support free peoples who are resisting attempted subjugation [conquest] by armed minorities or by outside pressures." If the United States retreated into isolationism, he warned, the peace of the world and the welfare of the nation would be in danger. The fall of a nation to communism, Truman argued, could lead its neighbors into communism as well.

>> Greek soldiers bring in possible guerrilla operatives for questioning. The anticommunist struggle in Greece and Turkey led President Truman to formulate the Truman Doctrine.

> I believe that it must be the policy of the United States to support free peoples who are resisting attempted subjugation by armed minorities or by outside pressures. I believe that we must assist free peoples to work out their own destinies in their own way. I believe that our help should be primarily through economic and financial aid which is essential to economic stability and orderly political processes.
>
> —President Harry S. Truman, Address Before a Joint Session of Congress, March 12, 1947

Congress responded by voting to give $400 million in aid to Greece and Turkey. President Truman's promise to aid nations struggling against communist movements became known as the **Truman Doctrine**, and it set a new course for American foreign policy.

IDENTIFY CAUSE AND EFFECT What events caused President Truman to propose what became known as the Truman Doctrine?

The United States Contains Soviet Expansion

In the July 1947 issue of the magazine *Foreign Affairs,* a writer who called himself "X" published an article titled "The Sources of Soviet Conduct." The author was really **George F. Kennan**, an American diplomat and a leading authority on the Soviet Union. His article presented a blueprint for the American policy that became known as **containment** because its goal was to keep communism contained within its existing borders.

Kennan Urges a Policy of Containment Kennan contended that while Stalin was determined to expand the Soviet empire, he would not risk the security of the Soviet Union for expansion. In Kennan's view, the Soviet Union would only expand when it could do so without serious risks. Stalin would certainly not chance war with the United States—a war that might destroy his power in the Soviet Union—just to spread communism.

Kennan cautioned his readers that there would be no quick, easy solution to the Soviet threat. Containment would require a full commitment of American economic, political, and military power:

> We are going to continue for a long time to find the Russians difficult to deal with. It does not mean that they should be considered as embarked upon a do-or-die program to overthrow our society by a given date. . . . In these circumstances, it is clear that the main element of any United States policy toward the Soviet Union must be that of long-term, patient but firm and vigilant containment of Russian expansive tendencies.
>
> —George Kennan, "The Sources of Soviet Conduct"

>> George Kennan, an expert on Russian history and culture, was the driving force behind American policy toward the Soviet Union in the early years of the Cold War.

>> German workers reconstruct a Berlin concert hall. The Marshall Plan helped Germany rebuild all aspects of its society, improving Germans' quality of life in the difficult postwar years.

The United States Responds with the Marshall Plan The containment policy's first great success was in Western Europe. After World War II, people there confronted severe shortages of food, fuel, and medical supplies, as well as brutally cold winters.

In this environment of desperate need, Secretary of State George C. Marshall unveiled a recovery plan for Europe. In a speech at Harvard University, he warned that without economic health, "there can be no political stability and no assured peace."

In early 1948, Congress approved the **Marshall Plan**. Over the next four years, the United States gave about $13 billion in grants and loans to nations in Western Europe. The program provided food to reduce famine, fuel to heat houses and factories, and money to jump-start economic growth. Aid was also offered to the Soviet satellite states in Eastern Europe, but Stalin refused to let them accept it.

The Marshall Plan provided a vivid example of how U.S. aid could serve the ends of both economic and foreign policy. The aid helped countries that desperately needed assistance. The prosperity it stimulated then helped the American economy by increasing trade. Finally, the good relationships that the aid created worked against the expansion of communism.

Shipments Financed by the Marshall Plan, 1948–1951

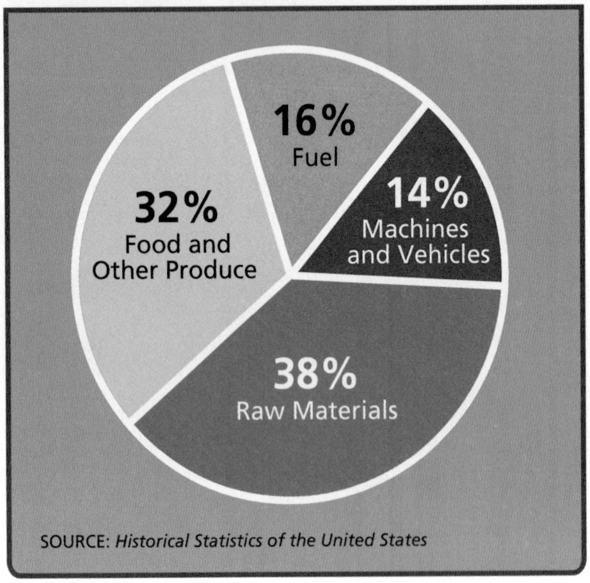

>> **Analyze Graphs** Which American industries would have benefited from the shipments shown in this graph?

BOUNCE to Activate Gallery

☑ **IDENTIFY MAIN IDEAS** Why did George Kennan think that containment would prevent Soviet expansion?

Soviet Aggression Drives the Cold War

The front lines of the Cold War were located in Germany. The zones that were controlled by France, Britain, and the United States combined to form West Germany. West Germany was bordered on the east by the Soviet-controlled East Germany. The Allies also controlled the western part of Berlin, a city tucked deep inside communist East Germany.

United States and Britain Launch the Berlin Airlift West Berlin was, as one Soviet leader later described it, "a bone in the throat" of the Soviet Union. Its relative prosperity and freedom stood in contrast to the bleak life of East Berliners. Stalin was determined to capture West Berlin or win other concessions from the Western allies. In June 1948, he stopped all highway, railway, and waterway traffic into West Berlin. Without any means of receiving aid, West Berlin would fall to the communists.

Stalin was able to close roads, stop barges, and block railways, but he could not blockade the sky. As a result, the United States and Britain supplied West Berlin through a massive airlift that lasted nearly one year. Food, fuel, medical supplies, clothing, toys—everything the residents of West Berlin needed was flown into the city.

Even through rain and snow, goods arrived regularly. The **Berlin airlift** demonstrated to West Berlin, the Soviet Union, and the world how far the United States and its allies would go to protect the noncommunist parts of Europe and contain communism.

The North Atlantic Treaty Organization In May 1949, Stalin was forced to acknowledge that his attempt to blockade West Berlin had failed. The Berlin airlift was a proud moment for Americans and Berliners and a major success for the policy of containment. One Berlin resident later recalled her feelings when the blockade was finally lifted:

> Sheer joy—nothing else. Nothing else. Joy, and [the feeling that], 'We have done it!' . . . That was so very important. The West has won! I say

Cold War Alliances, 1955

NATO		WARSAW PACT
Belgium	Netherlands	Albania
Canada	Norway	Bulgaria
Denmark	Portugal	Czechoslovakia
France	Turkey	East Germany
Greece	United Kingdom	Hungary
Iceland	United States	Poland
Italy	West Germany	Romania
Luxembourg		Soviet Union

>> Greece and Turkey joined NATO in 1952, and West Germany in 1955. The other countries were original members of the organization formed in 1949. **Analyze Tables** Which NATO countries were not located in Europe?

> this quite deliberately in such a crass way because you wanted to know how I felt emotionally. The West— well, we have succeeded. And the West has won and the others have not!
>
> —Ella Barowsky, CNN interview, 1996

The Berlin airlift demonstrated that Stalin could be contained if Western nations were prepared to take forceful action. The **North Atlantic Treaty Organization (NATO)**, formed in 1949, provided the military alliance to counter Soviet expansion. Twelve Western European and North American nations agreed to act together in the defense of Western Europe. Member nations agreed that "an armed attack against one or more of them . . . shall be considered an attack against all of them." This principle of mutual military assistance is called collective security.

In 1955, West Germany became a member of NATO. In response, the Soviet Union and its satellite states formed a rival military alliance, called the **Warsaw Pact**. All the communist states of Eastern Europe except Yugoslavia were members.

Like members of NATO, nations of the Warsaw Pact pledged to defend one another if attacked. Although members agreed on paper not to interfere in one another's internal affairs, the Soviet Union continued to exert firm control over its Warsaw Pact allies.

GO ONLINE to access this biography: Harry S. Truman

EXPLAIN How did the United States and its allies respond to Soviet aggression in Europe?

ASSESSMENT

1. **Identify Cause and Effect** Describe the factors that led to the creation of the Truman Doctrine, as well as how the doctrine affected U.S. foreign policy.
2. **Evaluate Arguments** Describe George F. Kennan's argument in favor of the containment policy and explain why he thought it would be successful.
3. **Generate Explanations** How did the concept of collective security lead to the creation of the North Atlantic Treaty Organization (NATO)?
4. **Summarize** the effects of the Marshall Plan on the United States and Western European countries.
5. **Connections to Today** Compare life under the communist government in the Soviet Union in the 1950s to life in the United States today. How might the communist government have affected Soviet culture? How does that culture differ from American culture today?

Primary Sources

"The Sinews of Peace": Winston Churchill

In 1946, former Prime Minister Winston Churchill was invited to speak at a college in a small town in Missouri. Surprisingly, Churchill accepted the invitation, prompted in part by his desire to give voice to his views and in part by a note from President Truman reading "Hope you can do it. I'll introduce you."

Churchill used the podium at Westminster College to issue a warning about the Soviet Union's expanding influence in postwar Europe. In his address, he described the political and ideological division between the East and West as an "iron curtain." Extensive press coverage soon catapulted the term onto the world stage and into general usage. Churchill's iconic speech became a defining moment in the Cold War.

>> Churchill received an honorary degree from Westminster College before giving his now-famous address.

Primary Source

The United States stands at this time at the pinnacle [height] of world power. It is a solemn moment for the American Democracy. For with primacy [being first] in power is also joined an awe-inspiring accountability to the future. . . .

DETERMINE AUTHOR'S PURPOSE Why do you think Churchill believes the United States has "accountability to the future"?

A shadow has fallen upon the scenes so lately lighted by the Allied victory. Nobody knows what Soviet Russia and its Communist international organization intends to do in the immediate future, or what are the limits, if any, to their expansive and proselytizing [persuading] tendencies. I have a strong admiration and regard for the valiant Russian people and for my wartime comrade, Marshal Stalin. . . . It is my duty however, for I am sure you would wish me to state the facts as I see them to you, to place before you certain facts about the present position in Europe.

From Stettin in the Baltic to Trieste in the Adriatic, an iron curtain has descended across the Continent. Behind that line lie all the capitals of the ancient states of Central and Eastern Europe. Warsaw, Berlin, Prague, Vienna, Budapest, Belgrade, Bucharest and Sofia, all these famous cities and the populations around them lie in what I must call the Soviet sphere, and all are subject in one form or another, not only to Soviet influence but to a very high and, in many cases, increasing measure of control from Moscow. . . . The Communist parties, which were very small in all these Eastern States of Europe, have been raised to preeminence and power far beyond their numbers and are seeking everywhere to obtain totalitarian control. . . .

. . . An attempt is being made by the Russians in Berlin to build up a quasi-Communist party in their zone of Occupied Germany by showing special favors to groups of left-wing German leaders. At the end of the fighting last June, the American and British Armies withdrew westwards, in accordance with an earlier agreement . . . in order to allow our Russian allies to occupy this vast expanse of territory which the Western Democracies had conquered.

If now the Soviet Government tries, by separate action, to build up a pro-Communist Germany in their areas, this will cause new serious difficulties in the British and American zones, and will give the defeated Germans the power of putting themselves up to auction between the Soviets and the Western Democracies. Whatever conclusions may be drawn from these facts—and facts they are—this is certainly not the Liberated Europe we fought to build up. Nor is it one which contains the essentials of permanent peace.

DETERMINE MEANING What does Churchill mean when he says the Germans will have the "power of putting themselves up to auction"?

. . . I do not believe that Soviet Russia desires war. What they desire is the fruits of war and the indefinite expansion of their power and doctrines. But what we have to consider here today while time remains, is the permanent prevention of war and the establishment of conditions of freedom and democracy as rapidly as possible in all countries. Our difficulties and dangers will not be removed by closing our eyes to them. They will not be removed by mere waiting to see what happens; nor will they be removed by a policy of appeasement. . . .

EXPLAIN AN ARGUMENT Why do you think Churchill believes appeasement will not be effective in dealing with the Soviet threat?

Last time I saw it all coming and cried aloud to my own fellow-countrymen and to the world, but no one paid any attention. Up till the year 1933 or even 1935, Germany might have been saved from the awful fate which has overtaken her and we might all have been spared the miseries Hitler let loose upon mankind. . . .

. . . If the population of the English-speaking Commonwealths be added to that of the United States with all that such cooperation implies in the air, on the sea, all over the globe and in science and in industry, and in moral force, there will be no quivering, precarious [unstable] balance of power to offer its temptation to ambition or adventure. On the contrary, there will be an overwhelming assurance of security. If . . . all British moral and material forces and convictions are joined with your own in fraternal [brotherly] association, the high-roads of the future will be clear, not only for us but for all, not only for our time, but for a century to come.

MAKE INFERENCES What is Churchill implying by proposing that the Commonwealths "be added to" and "joined with" the United States?

ASSESSMENT

1. **Draw Conclusions** Why might Churchill use the term *democracy* so frequently in this speech?
2. **Predict** Based on the content of this speech, what nations do you think are likely to join the effort against Soviet expansion?
3. **Determine Author's Point of View** How does Churchill express a sense of urgency in addressing the expansion of Soviet controlled nations? Cite specific passages from the source.
4. **Hypothesize** How do you think the leader of the Soviet Union, Joseph Stalin, would have reacted to this speech?

GO ONLINE to access primary sources

15.2

A U.S. soldier aims a missile while his fellow soldiers take cover during a Korean War battle. For President Truman, supporting South Korea in the Korean War was about stopping the spread of communism.

BOUNCE to Activate Flipped Video

Objectives

Explain how Mao Zedong and the communists gained power in China.

Describe the causes and the reasons for U.S. involvement in the Korean War.

Identify the long-term effects and outcomes of the Korean War.

Key Terms

Jiang Jieshi
Mao Zedong
38th parallel
Douglas MacArthur
limited war
Southeast Asia Treaty Organization (SEATO)

The Korean War

Europe had been the first focus of the Cold War. But in the early 1950s, U.S. involvement in the Korean War made East Asia the prime battleground in the long, hard Cold War struggle. The division between North and South Korea remains a source of international tension today.

China Turns Communist

Since the time of the Russian Revolution in 1917, the Soviets had hoped to spread communism to every corner of the world, training foreigners in Marxist theory and revolutionary strategy. The Soviets were confident that communism would attain worldwide influence. In 1949, events in China seemed to justify their confidence.

U.S. Policy During China's Civil War Before Japan invaded China in 1937, Nationalist leader **Jiang Jieshi** (zhee AHNG zhì SHEE), known in the United States as Chiang Kai-shek, had been fighting a civil war against communists led by **Mao Zedong** (mow zeh DUHNG). Although Jiang and Mao temporarily joined forces in an uneasy alliance to fight Japan, the civil war resumed with a new fury after the war ended.

The Soviet Union supported Mao, while the United States sent several billion dollars in aid to Jiang. American leaders feared that Jiang's defeat would create a communist superpower spanning most of Asia.

Jiang's regime proved unequal to the task. Nationalist generals were reluctant to fight. And, while masses of Chinese people faced starvation, corrupt officials diverted U.S. aid dollars into their own

GO ONLINE to access your digital course

pockets. By promising to feed the people, Mao won increased support.

China Falls to Communism In 1948, Mao's forces dominated the war. Jiang appealed to President Truman, asking for American military intervention. However, the U.S. government had no intention of sending American troops to support Jiang's corrupt government. In 1949, Jiang fled the Chinese mainland, taking control of the large offshore island of Taiwan. Mao's communists then took control of the world's most populous country, renaming it the People's Republic of China.

Mao's victory was an immense shock to Americans. Not only was China under the control of sworn enemies of the United States, but communist regimes now controlled about one fourth of the world's landmass and one third of its population. "Who lost China?" Americans asked. Many critics blamed the Truman administration, saying that the United States had failed to give enough support to Jiang. But Secretary of State Dean Acheson argued:

> The unfortunate but inescapable fact is that the ominous result of the civil war in China was beyond the control of the government of the United States. Nothing that this country did or could have done within the reasonable limits of its capabilities could have changed the result.
>
> —Secretary of State Dean Acheson, "White Paper on China," August 1949

☑ **CHECK UNDERSTANDING** Why were the communists able to win the Chinese Civil War?

U.S. Involvement in Korea

The focus of attention turned to the peninsula of Korea, separated from northeast China by the Yalu River. Once controlled by Japan, Korea had been divided into two independent countries by the United States and the Soviet Union after World War II. The dividing line was set at the **38th parallel**. The Soviets installed a communist government and equipped the North Korean armed forces. The United States provided smaller amounts of aid to noncommunist South Korea.

>> Jiang Jieshi, shown with his U.S.-educated wife Soong May-ling, led an anti-communist Chinese government that attracted Western support.

>> Portraits of Mao Zedong (right), Chairman of the People's Government, and Zhu De (left), leader of the People's Liberation Army, adorn a truck during a celebration of the founding of the People's Republic of China.

North Korea Invades South Korea American occupation troops remained in South Korea until June 1949. Their departure coincided with the communist victory in China. Soon after, North Korea began a major military buildup.

On June 25, 1950, North Korean forces attacked across the 38th parallel. The 90,000 North Korean troops were armed with powerful tanks and other Soviet weapons. Within days, the northerners overtook the South Korean capital city of Seoul and set out in pursuit of the retreating South Korean army.

Reasons for U.S. Involvement President Truman remembered how the policy of appeasement had failed to check the German aggression that sparked World War II. This knowledge, coupled with the U.S. policy of containment, caused Truman to announce that the United States would aid South Korea.

Within days, the UN Security Council unanimously voted to follow Truman's lead, recommending that "the Members of the United Nations furnish such assistance to the Republic of Korea as may be necessary to repel the armed attack and to restore international peace and security in the area." Undoubtedly, the Soviet Union would have used its veto power to block the UN resolution if it had been present for the vote. However, it had been boycotting Security Council sessions because the UN had refused to seat Mao's People's Republic of China.

Truman did not ask Congress for a formal declaration of war, as required by the Constitution. However, supported by the UN resolution, Truman ordered American troops who were stationed in Japan to move to South Korea. The soldiers were mainly occupation troops who had not been trained for forced marches in monsoon rains or heavy combat in rice paddies, nor did they have the military equipment needed to stop the invasion. Soon, they joined their South Korean allies in retreating to the southeast corner of the peninsula near the city of Pusan. There, the allies held fast. As fresh supplies and troops arrived from Japan, soldiers from other UN countries joined the American and South Korean forces.

>> President Truman pins a medal on General Douglas MacArthur, who commanded the coalition of American-led United Nations forces in Korea.

The U.S. and Its Allies Counterattack By September 1950, the UN forces were ready to counterattack. General **Douglas MacArthur**, the World War II hero, had a bold plan to drive the invaders from South Korea. He suspected that the rapid advance of North Korean troops had left North Korea with limited supply lines. He decided to strike at this weakness by launching a surprise attack on the port city of Incheon well behind enemy lines. Because Incheon was such a poor landing site, with swift currents and treacherous tides, MacArthur knew that the enemy would not expect an attack there.

MacArthur's bold gamble paid off. On the morning of September 15, 1950, U.S. Marines landed at In'chŏn and launched an attack on the rear guard of the North Koreans. Communist forces in South Korea began fleeing back to North Korea. By October 1950, the North Koreans had been driven north of the 38th parallel.

With the retreat of North Korean forces, U.S. officials had to decide what to do next. Should they declare their UN mandate accomplished and end the war? Or should they send their forces north of the 38th parallel and punish the communists for the invasion? Truman was concerned about the action China would take if the United States carried the war into North Korea. Chinese leaders publicly warned the Americans not to advance near its borders. But MacArthur did not take this warning seriously. He assured Truman that China would not intervene in the war. Based on this advice, the United States pushed a resolution through the UN,

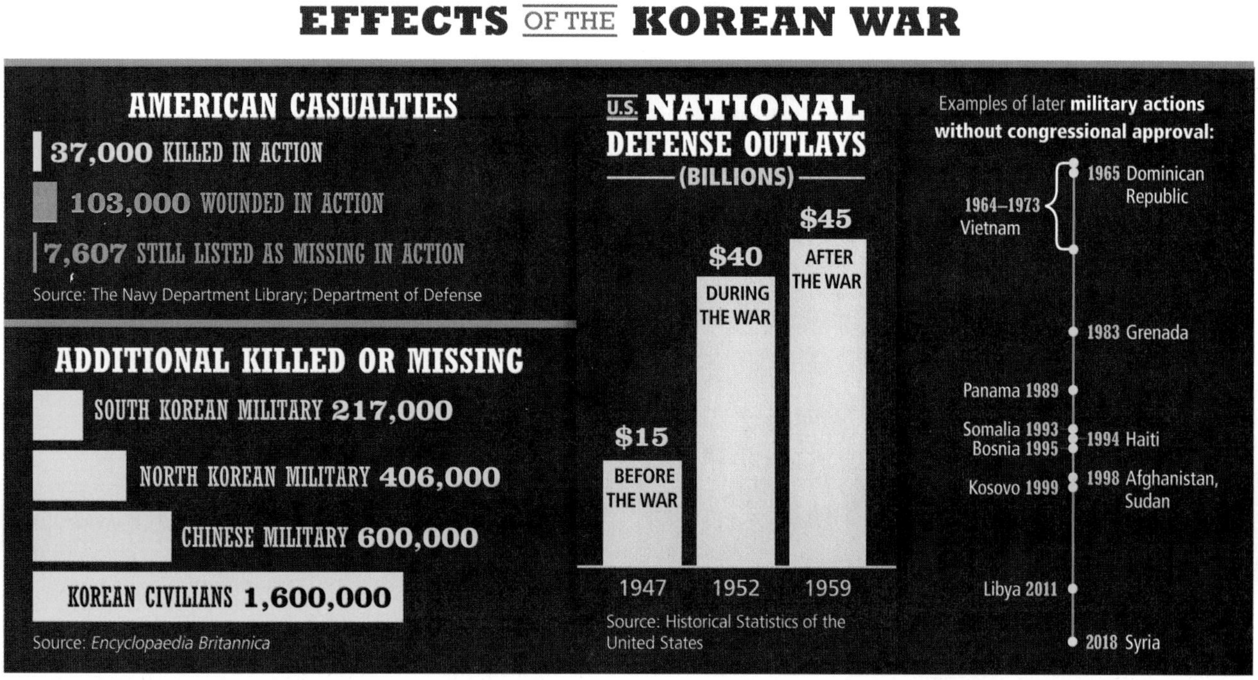

>> **Analyze Data** After the Korean War, how much more did the U.S spend on defense than it had before the war?

BOUNCE to Activate Map

calling for a "unified, independent, and democratic" Korea.

Truman and MacArthur Disagree on Military Goals Highly confident, MacArthur attacked north of the 38th parallel. Despite mountainous terrain and freezing temperatures, by Thanksgiving the Allied advance had reached the Chinese border at the Yalu River. Then, on November 25, 1950, some 300,000 Chinese soldiers attacked South Korean and U.S. positions. Badly outnumbered, the UN troops were forced back.

With China now in the war, the United States confronted a major land war in Asia. It was possible that this war could not be won without huge commitments of troops and even atomic weapons. Truman steadfastly ruled out both of these options. MacArthur, who favored an invasion of China, was enraged. He distrusted Truman's policy of a **limited war** fought to achieve only specific goals. As a soldier, MacArthur favored total victory.

Unable to sway Truman, the general sent a letter to the House Republican leader attacking the President's policies. After the letter became public, Truman fired MacArthur for insubordination. There was a huge outcry in the United States, and MacArthur returned home a national hero.

RECALL How did President Truman react to the North Korean invasion of South Korea?

Outcomes of the Korean War

By the spring of 1951, Allied forces had regrouped and stabilized their position near the 38th parallel. The stalemate lasted until 1953. During that time, the two sides fought small, bloody battles with limited results. At the same time, diplomats tried to devise an acceptable peace agreement.

Short-Term Outcomes of the Korean War The stalemate was a key issue in the presidential election of 1952. Republican candidate Dwight D. Eisenhower promised that if elected he would end the war. Upon his election, he visited South Korea, spoke with the troops, and studied the enemy's fortifications.

Eisenhower became President in January 1953. The former general was convinced that only strong action would break the stalemate. When peace talks threatened to fail, he hinted that he might introduce nuclear weapons into the conflict. That warning, along with the death of Joseph Stalin, convinced the communists to settle the conflict. On July 27, 1953, after slightly more than three years of fighting, the

>> Ongoing military exercises between U.S. and South Korean forces, such as these on the Namhan River, emphasize the U.S. commitment to the safety and security of the South Korean people.

two sides signed a cease-fire. That cease-fire is still in effect today.

Long-Term Outcomes of the Korean War There was no victory in the Korean War. North Korea remained a communist country allied to China and the Soviet Union, and South Korea stayed a noncommunist country allied to the United States and the major democracies. The two Koreas remained divided at about the 38th parallel.

Yet the war had important long-term outcomes. Truman had committed U.S. troops to battle without a congressional declaration of war. This set a precedent that future Presidents would follow. The Korean War also seemed to support the growing belief among policymakers that the fall of one nation to communism could have a ripple effect throughout the region. The Korean War also led to increased military spending. By 1960, military spending accounted for nearly half of the federal budget. More than a million U.S. soldiers were stationed around the world.

A new alliance underscored U.S. interest in Asia. Like NATO, the **Southeast Asia Treaty Organization (SEATO)** was a defensive alliance aimed at preventing the spread of communism. Its members included Pakistan, Thailand, the Philippines, Australia, New Zealand, France, Britain, and the United States.

IDENTIFY CAUSE AND EFFECT What were the most important outcomes of U.S. participation in the Korean War?

ASSESSMENT

1. **Generate Explanations** Why did the United States send financial aid to Jiang Jieshi at the beginning of the Chinese civil war, but later refuse his request for military aid?
2. **Identify Patterns** Explain how President Truman's knowledge of previous historical events influenced him to initiate U.S. involvement in Korea.
3. **Contrast** the opinions of President Truman and General MacArthur regarding U.S. military action in Korea after China became involved.
4. **Identify Cause and Effect** What long-term impact did the result of the Korean War have on the United States' foreign and military policy?
5. **Quest Connections** How do you think the actions of communist North Korea in the 1950s affected public opinion in the United States related to communism?

GO ONLINE to access this biography: Mao Zedong

15.3

Analyze Political Cartoons A vise squeezes the world between the two superpowers' weapons. What does this cartoon have to say about efforts to build up nuclear arms?

The Cold War Intensifies

By 1950, the United States and the Soviet Union were, by far, the two most powerful nations in the world. The conflicting ideologies and goals of these rival nations led to a worldwide struggle for influence. The policies followed by the two superpowers would help shape the history of the twentieth century for much of the world, from Latin America to the Middle East.

BOUNCE to Activate Flipped Video

Objectives

Describe how Cold War tensions were intensified by the arms race between the United States and the Soviet Union.

Explain how Eisenhower's response to communism differed from that of Truman.

Analyze the impact on the United States of significant international Cold War conflicts.

Describe how Cold War tensions were intensified by the space race.

Key Terms

mutually assured destruction
John Foster Dulles
massive retaliation
brinkmanship
Nikita Khrushchev
nationalize
Suez crisis
Eisenhower Doctrine
Central Intelligence Agency (CIA)
National Aeronautics and Space Administration (NASA)

The Arms Race Intensifies Tensions

A change in the balance of world power is usually gradual, taking place over decades or even centuries. But sometimes, the shift happens in the blink of an eye. Such a major shift in the balance of power in the Cold War took place on September 2, 1949. Instruments in an American B-29 aircraft flying over Alaska detected unusual atmospheric radiation. The radiation cloud was drifting eastward from the direction of Siberia.

American nuclear scientists analyzed the data that the aircraft had gathered. They then reached an inescapable conclusion: The Soviet Union had set off an atomic bomb.

Cold War Worries Rise The news shook U.S. leaders. They had believed that the Soviet Union was years away from developing an atomic bomb. Now, the Americans no longer had a monopoly on atomic weaponry.

The news that the Soviets had the bomb was followed the next month by news of the communist takeover of China. In a very

GO ONLINE to access your digital course

short time, Americans sensed that the world was a much more dangerous and threatening place.

The Arms Race Speeds Up During the Cold War, specific needs resulted in scientific discoveries and technological innovations in the military. Three months after news that the Soviets had developed an atomic bomb, President Truman directed the Atomic Energy Commission to continue its work on atomic weapons, including the hydrogen bomb. Developers predicted that the H-Bomb would be 1,000 times as powerful as an atomic bomb. They hoped it would restore the United States' military advantage over the Soviets.

Some scientists, such as J. Robert Oppenheimer and Albert Einstein, opposed developing the H-Bomb, claiming it would only lead to a perpetual arms race. Others argued that Stalin would continue to develop more powerful weapons no matter what the United States did.

In 1952, the United States tested the first hydrogen bomb. The next year, the Soviets tested one of their own. More bombs and tests followed. Most of these tests were conducted above ground, spewing radioactive waste into the atmosphere. Atomic testing in the American West, such as in the Nevada desert, led to increased atmospheric radiation and long-range health problems for people living downwind of the test sites.

During the next four decades, the United States and the Soviet Union developed and stockpiled increasingly powerful nuclear weapons. They armed planes, submarines, and missiles with nuclear warheads powerful enough to destroy each country many times over. Both sides hoped that this program of **mutually assured destruction** would prevent either country from actually using a nuclear device against the other. Still, the threat of nuclear destruction seemed to hang over the world like a dark cloud.

☑ **RECALL** Why did the United States government decide to build a hydrogen bomb?

Eisenhower's Response to Soviet Aggression

President Dwight Eisenhower knew firsthand the horrors of war and the need to defend democracy. He had led the World War II Allied invasions of North Africa, Italy, and Normandy. Having worked with top military and political leaders during the war, he was capable of speaking the language of both.

President Eisenhower accepted much of Truman's foreign policy. He believed strongly in a policy to actively contain communist aggression. The President's secretary of state, **John Foster Dulles**, was an experienced diplomat who had helped organize the United Nations after World War II. Dulles endorsed the President's vision of the role the United States should play in the world and had stood firmly behind U.S. efforts to contain communism through involvement in Korea. Containment, Dulles believed, could prevent the possibility of a "domino effect" throughout Southeast Asia, with one country after another falling under communist rule.

In their approach toward foreign policy, President Eisenhower and Dulles differed significantly from both Truman and his Secretary of State, Dean Acheson. Both teams of men considered the spread of communism the greatest threat to the free world. But President Eisenhower believed that Truman's approach to foreign policy had dragged the United States into an endless series of conflicts begun by the Soviet Union. These limited, regional conflicts threatened to drain the country's resources.

>> Like President Truman, President Eisenhower (left) and his Secretary of State, John Foster Dulles (right), believed that the containment of communism was essential to U.S. foreign policy.

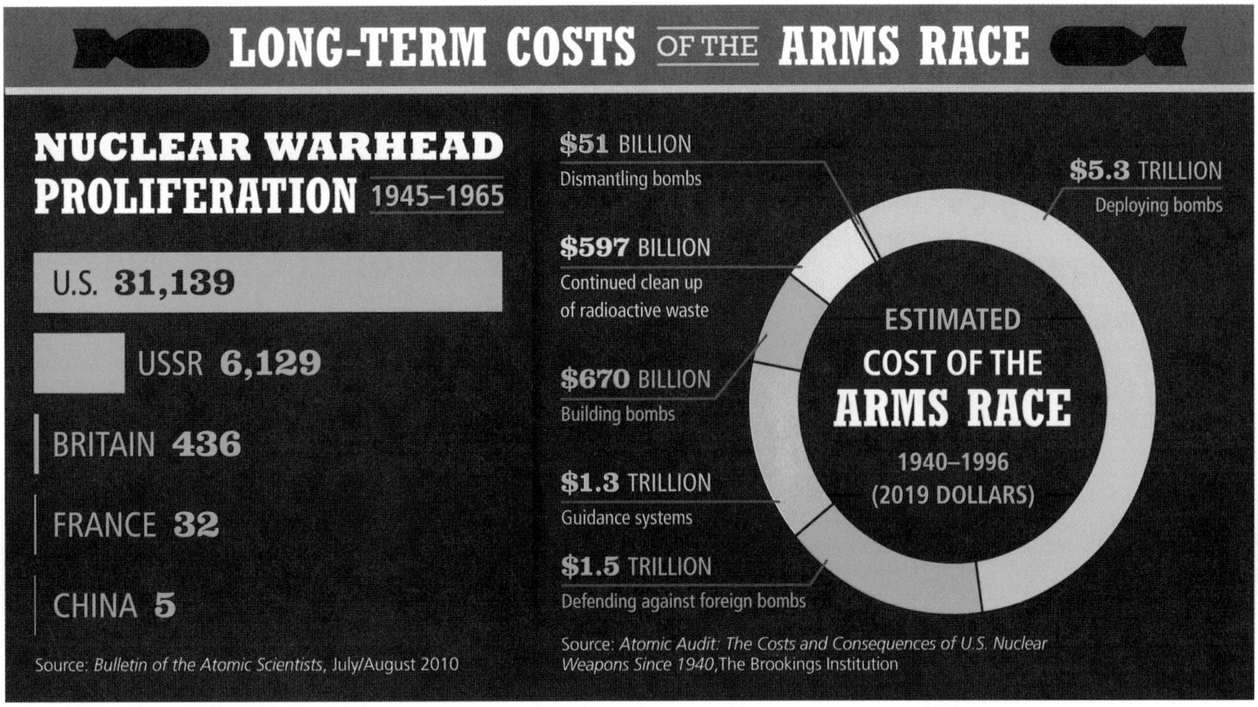

>> **Analyze Data** How does the data shown in the infographic illustrate Eisenhower's approach to defense spending?

BOUNCE to Activate Chart

Eisenhower's Policies toward Communism

President Eisenhower opposed spending billions of dollars on conventional forces, such as troops, ships, tanks, and artillery. Instead, he focused on stockpiling nuclear weapons and building the planes, missiles, and submarines needed to deliver them. He assumed that if there were a major war, it would be nuclear.

Eisenhower's new policy drew some criticism: conservatives felt that downgrading conventional forces would weaken American defense, while liberals feared that preparing for nuclear war made such a war more likely. Still, Eisenhower's approach did save money by providing a "bigger bang for the buck." In 1953, the defense department spent more than $47.6 billion; in 1955, that figure dropped to $35.5 billion.

In 1954, Dulles announced the policy of **massive retaliation**. The United States would respond to communist threats to its allies by threatening to use crushing, overwhelming force, perhaps even nuclear weapons.

> A potential aggressor must know that he cannot always prescribe battle conditions to suit him. . . . The way to deter aggression is for the free community to be willing and able to respond vigorously at places and with means of his choosing.
>
> —John Foster Dulles, 1954

Dulles further believed that only by going to the brink of war could the United States protect its allies, discourage communist aggression, and prevent war. "You have to take some chances for peace, just as you must take chances in war," he said in 1956. Dulles's approach became known as **brinkmanship**.

Stalin's Death Eases Tensions On March 5, 1953, Soviet dictator Joseph Stalin died, setting off a short power struggle. **Nikita Khrushchev** soon emerged as the new head of the Soviet Union. Although a communist and a determined opponent of the United States, Khrushchev was not as suspicious or as cruel as Stalin. He condemned the excesses of the Stalin regime and inched toward more peaceful relations with the democratic West.

In July 1955, Khrushchev met with Eisenhower at a conference in Geneva, Switzerland. Although the meeting yielded few significant results, it did seem

>> In 1956, Poland revolted against Soviet rule. Here, the crowd carries a Polish flag during an anti-communist demonstration.

>> Hungarian nationalists in 1956 burn a portrait of Hungarian communist party leader Matyas Rakosi. Unlike the protests in Poland, the uprising in Hungary was violently put down by the Soviet military.

to be a small move toward the "peaceful coexistence" of the two powers.

☑ **CONTRAST** How was Eisenhower's approach to foreign affairs different from Truman's?

International Cold War Conflicts

Peaceful coexistence was easier to imagine than it was to practice. The United States and the Soviet Union remained deeply divided. The Soviet Union would not allow free elections in the areas it controlled, and it continued to attempt to spread communism around the world. Dulles talked about "rolling back" communism and liberating the countries under Soviet rule.

Uprisings Behind the Iron Curtain: Poland and Hungary American talk of "rolling back" communist borders and Khrushchev's talk of "peaceful co-existence" were taken seriously by people in Soviet-dominated countries behind the iron curtain. People in Poland, Hungary, and Czechoslovakia resented the control exerted by the Soviet Union. Many hungered for more political and economic freedom.

In 1956, two uprisings shook Eastern Europe. First, workers in Poland rioted against Soviet rule and won greater control of their government. Since the Polish government did not attempt to leave the Warsaw Pact, Soviet leaders permitted the changes.

Then, encouraged by Khrushchev's words and Poland's example, Hungarian students and workers organized huge demonstrations. They demanded that pro-Soviet Hungarian officials be replaced, that Soviet troops be withdrawn, and that noncommunist political parties be organized. Khrushchev responded brutally, sending Soviet soldiers and tanks to crush the Hungarian revolution. The Soviets executed many of the revolution's leaders, killed hundreds of other Hungarians, and restored hard-line communists to power.

Americans watched these events with horror. Eisenhower's massive retaliation approach had failed. In reality, the Soviet Union knew that the United States would not use nuclear weapons—or any other weapons—to guarantee Hungarian independence from the Soviet Union.

The Hungarian revolt added a new level of hostility to international relations. At the 1956 Olympic Games, held that November in Melbourne, Australia, the bitter feelings surfaced. A water-polo match between the Soviet Union and Hungary

Suez Canal Region

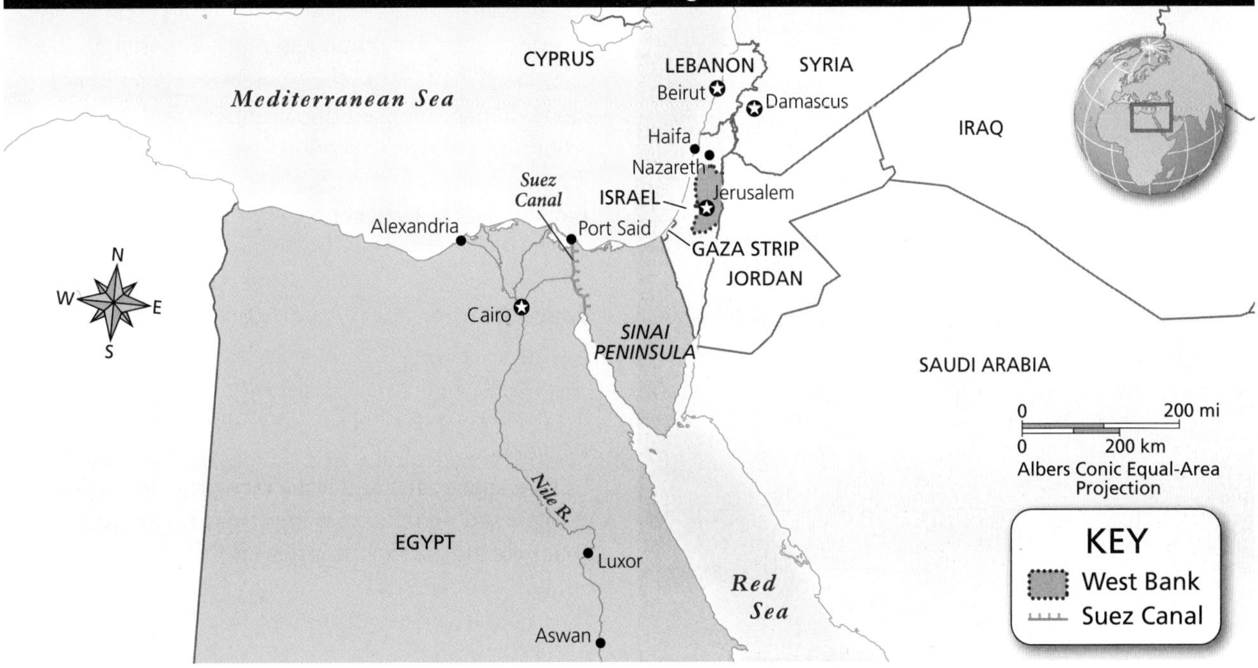

>> **Analyze Maps** The Suez Canal connects the Mediterranean Sea and the Red Sea. Why was the canal so strategically important?

BOUNCE to Activate Map

turned violent. Sportswriters called it the "blood in the water" match.

The Suez Crisis That same year, the United States found itself involved in another Cold War conflict, this time in the Middle East. As Cold War tensions intensified, Egypt's president Gamal Abdel Nasser tried to use the U.S.–Soviet rivalry to his advantage.

Nasser wanted to construct a dam on the Nile River at Aswan. The United States and Britain initially offered to fund the project, but when Nasser recognized the communist People's Republic of China and opened talks with the Soviet Union, the Eisenhower administration withdrew its offer. In response, Nasser **nationalized** the Suez Canal, placing it under government control. The canal, which connects the Mediterranean Sea and the Red Sea, had originally been managed by a British-French company and was protected by British armed forces.

Nasser's action threatened the flow of Middle Eastern oil to Europe. Without consulting President Eisenhower, Britain and France plotted to get the canal back into Western hands. They joined forces with Israel, a young nation that had long suffered from raids along its border with Egypt. Britain and France used the **Suez crisis** as an excuse to seize control of the Suez Canal. Israel viewed Egypt's nationalization of the canal as a violation of international law and wanted to preserve freedom for Israeli shipping.

President Eisenhower was outraged by these actions. Rather than support his Western allies, Eisenhower criticized them and refused to supply them with U.S. oil. The three nations had counted on Eisenhower's support. When it did not come, they were forced to withdraw their troops from Egypt.

The Eisenhower Doctrine Eisenhower's response to the attempted seizure of the Suez Canal did not mean that he was unconcerned with communist influence in the Middle East. In response to Soviet influence there and elsewhere, the President made a statement in January 1957 that became known as the **Eisenhower Doctrine**. Eisenhower announced that the United States would use force to help any Middle Eastern nation threatened by communism. Eisenhower used his doctrine in 1958 to justify sending troops to Lebanon to put down a revolt against its pro-American government.

The Eisenhower administration also used the **Central Intelligence Agency (CIA)** in its struggle against communism. Congress had created the CIA in 1947 as an intelligence-gathering organization. Eisenhower gave it a new task. He approved covert,

>> In the years immediately following the Soviets' launch of *Sputnik 1*, the United States responded by developing many of its own satellites. This one was launched in 1960.

BOUNCE to Activate Gallery

or secret, CIA operations to protect American interests. In 1953, the CIA aided a coup that installed a new government in Iran. In 1954, it accomplished a similar mission in Guatemala. While both operations helped to place anticommunist leaders in power, they also created long-term resentment against the United States.

The Space Race Increases Tensions Although the United States successfully contained the spread of communism on the ground, it did suffer a setback in space. On October 4, 1957, the Soviet Union launched a 184-pound steel ball containing a small transmitter into an orbit of Earth. The Soviets named the tiny satellite *Sputnik 1*. The following month they launched a much larger satellite. It carried a dog, named Laika, to see how a living creature would react to space travel. Since there was no way to return the satellite to Earth, Laika died in orbit.

The launches shocked many Americans, who had long believed that superior technology would keep the United States ahead of the Soviet Union. Would Soviet space technology give them the rocket power to launch missiles that could reach American cities?

In a state of crisis, Congress quickly approved the National Defense Education Act, a $1 billion program intended to produce more scientists and science teachers. The act authorized money for loans to enable high school and college graduates to continue their education in science. In addition, Congress created the **National Aeronautics and Space Administration (NASA)** to coordinate the space-related efforts of American scientists and the military. Eventually, these actions by Congress led to the Apollo space program and human exploration of the moon.

The space race and arms race provided some unexpected benefits that improved Americans' quality of life, as technologies originally intended for military or space use, such as the microwave and the internet, eventually became available among the wider population.

IDENTIFY CENTRAL ISSUES How did the Hungarian and Suez crises of 1956 intensify Cold War tensions?

ASSESSMENT

1. **Generate Explanations** Explain how the concept of mutually assured destruction influenced the course of the Cold War.
2. **Compare and Contrast** the foreign policies of Presidents Eisenhower and Truman.
3. **Generate Explanations** Explain the logic behind John Foster Dulles' strategy of brinkmanship.
4. **Identify Cause and Effect** Discuss how Stalin's death affected tensions between the Soviet Union and the United States.
5. **Connections to Today** Many world events in the 1950s worried Americans and made them fearful of the future, including the Korean War, the communist takeover of China, the ability of the Soviets to create an atomic bomb, and the launching of *Sputnik 1*. What events and issues make Americans anxious today?

15.4

Senator Joseph McCarthy's accusations that communist sympathizers worked in the U.S. government led to controversial televised Senate hearings.

Cold War Fears at Home

BOUNCE to Activate Flipped Video

Objectives

Describe the efforts of President Truman and the House Un-American Activities Committee to fight communism at home.

Explain how domestic spy cases intensified fears of communist influence in the U.S. government.

Analyze the rise and fall of Senator Joseph McCarthy and the methods of McCarthyism.

Key Terms

Red Scare
Smith Act
House Un-American Activities Committee (HUAC)
Hollywood Ten
blacklist
Alger Hiss
Julius and Ethel Rosenberg
Venona Papers
Joseph R. McCarthy
McCarthyism

Americans have often faced the difficult task of balancing the need to provide national security with the need to protect people's rights and freedoms. In times of crisis, rights have sometimes been limited. Beginning in the late 1940s, the Cold War dominated American life. For some of those years, the nation was in the grip of a new Red Scare. The hunt for communists netted some spies, but it also disrupted the lives of thousands of innocent Americans.

Cold War Tensions Rise at Home

The Cold War influenced many aspects of American life. American soldiers fought and died in Korea. Industries hummed with activity, turning out weapons and supplies. Americans read newspaper articles about who "lost" China or who was winning the "space race." Popular culture reflected an "us-versus-them" attitude—proponents of democracy versus totalitarians, capitalists versus communists, the West versus the East. In the end, the Cold War was turning out to be every bit as global and as encompassing as World War II had been.

The Second Red Scare The fear that communists both outside and inside the United States were working to destroy American life created a reaction known as a **Red Scare**. The 1917 Russian Revolution and the communists' call for worldwide revolution had led to a similar Red Scare in 1919 and 1920. However, the Red Scare that followed World War II went deeper and wider—and lasted far longer—than the earlier one. President Truman's Attorney General, J. Howard McGrath, expressed the widespread fear of communist influence when he warned that communists

GO ONLINE to access your digital course

>> Civil Defense posters warned Americans to remain on high alert for a nuclear attack.

>> Playwright and screenwriter Lillian Hellman was blacklisted after telling HUAC, "I am not willing...to bring bad trouble to people who, in my past association with them, were completely innocent of any talk or any action that was disloyal or subversive."

"are everywhere—in factories, offices, butcher stores, on street corners, and private businesses. And each carries in himself the death of our society."

The spread of communism into Eastern Europe and Asia raised concerns that American communists, some in influential government positions, were working for the enemy. In truth, some American communists were agents of the Soviet Union, and a handful of them held high-ranking positions in government. However, overwhelmingly, government officials were loyal to the United States.

Recognizing public concern about domestic communism, President Truman used an executive order to create a Federal Employee Loyalty Program in March 1947. The order permitted the FBI and other government security agencies to screen federal employees for signs of political disloyalty. About 3,000 federal employees either were dismissed or resigned after the investigation.

The order also empowered the Attorney General to compile a list of "totalitarian, fascist, or subversive organizations" in the United States. Americans who belonged to or supported organizations on the Attorney General's list were singled out for more intense scrutiny. Many were labeled "security risks" and dismissed from their jobs.

The Truman administration also used the 1940 **Smith Act** to cripple the Communist Party in the United States. This act made it unlawful to teach or advocate the violent overthrow of the U.S. government. In 1949, a New York jury found 11 communists guilty of violating the Smith Act and sent them to prison.

The House Un-American Activities Committee

Congress joined in the search for communists. In 1938, the House of Representatives had created the **House Un-American Activities Committee (HUAC)** to investigate possible subversive activities by fascists, Nazis, or communists. After the war, the committee conducted several highly publicized hearings on communist activities in the United States. Cold War fears were intensified by HUAC investigators, who probed the government, armed forces, unions, education, science, newspapers, and other aspects of American life.

The best-known HUAC hearings targeted the movie industry in 1947. The HUAC investigations uncovered people who were, or had been, communists during the 1930s and 1940s. A group of left-wing writers, directors, and producers known as the **Hollywood Ten** refused to answer questions, asserting their Fifth Amendment rights against self-incrimination. The hearings turned into a war of attacks and counterattacks as committee members and witnesses yelled at each other and pointed accusatory fingers.

After the hearings, the Hollywood Ten were cited for contempt of Congress and were tried, convicted, and sent to prison. Movie executives circulated a **blacklist** of entertainment figures who should not be hired because of their suspected communist ties. The careers of those on the list were shattered. Not until the case of *Watkins* v. *United States* (1957) did the Supreme Court decide that witnesses before HUAC could not be forced to name radicals they knew.

The HUAC investigation had a powerful impact on filmmaking. In the past, Hollywood had been willing to make movies about controversial subjects such as racism and anti-Semitism. Now, most producers concentrated only on entertainment and avoided addressing sensitive social issues.

Red Scare Intensifies Cold War Fears The case of the Hollywood Ten demonstrated that in the mood of fear created by Soviet aggression, freedom of speech was not guaranteed. Americans lost their jobs because they had belonged to or contributed to an organization on the Attorney General's list. Others were fired for associating with people who were known communists or for making remarks that were considered disloyal. Teachers and librarians, mail carriers and longshoremen, electricians and construction workers—people from all walks of life—might be accused and dismissed from their jobs.

The effort to root out communist influence from American life cut across many levels of society. Communists were exposed and blacklisted in the country's academic institutions, labor unions, scientific laboratories, and city halls. No one was above suspicion. The case of J. Robert Oppenheimer illustrates the difficulty of distinguishing loyalty from disloyalty. During World War II, Oppenheimer had led the Manhattan Project, which developed the atomic bomb. After the war, he became chairman of the General Advisory Committee of the U.S. Atomic Energy Commission (AEC). However, Oppenheimer had ties to people who belonged to the Communist Party, including his wife and brother.

In 1954, the AEC denied Oppenheimer access to classified information. Although the AEC had no evidence that Oppenheimer himself had ever been disloyal to the United States, it questioned whether his communist ties disqualified him from holding this position.

SUMMARIZE What steps did Truman and Congress take to investigate communist influence in the United States?

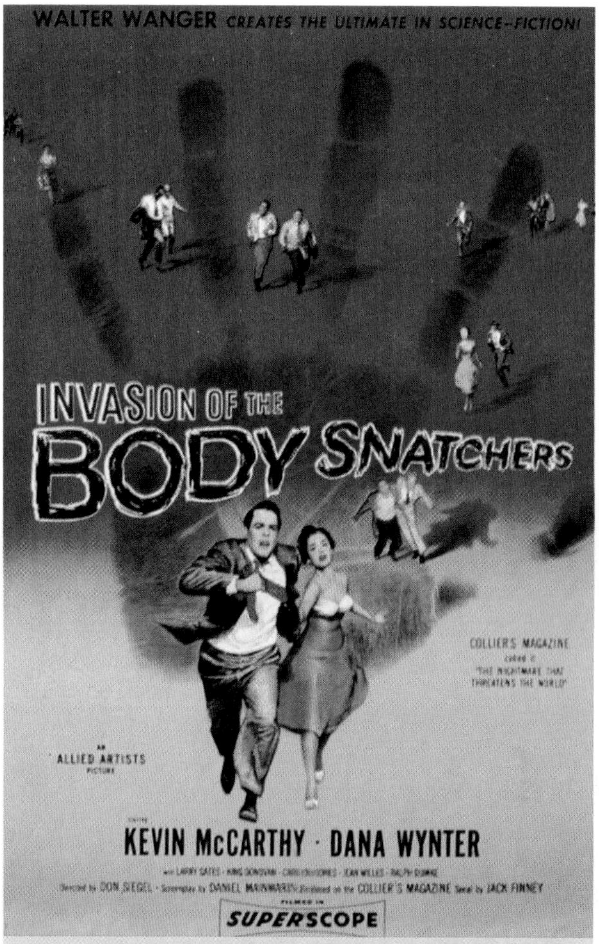

>> The 1956 film *Invasion of the Body Snatchers* expressed Americans' fears of invasion and infiltration during the era of the Red Scare.

BOUNCE to Activate Gallery

Domestic Spy Cases Increase Fears

Two sensational spy trials drew the nation's attention to the threat posed by communist agents working to subvert the United States. The accused in the two cases could not have been more different. **Alger Hiss** had been educated at Johns Hopkins University and Harvard Law School. **Julius and Ethel Rosenberg** were from the poor, lower east side of Manhattan. Although Hiss and the Rosenbergs never met, their crimes and their trials have linked them in the public's imagination.

HUAC Investigates Alger Hiss Until 1948, Alger Hiss's career seemed flawless. A seemingly dedicated government servant, Hiss had worked on several important New Deal agencies and helped to organize the United Nations. But a man named Whittaker Chambers disputed Hiss's image. As a young man, Chambers had become a communist espionage agent. But Chambers later turned against communism because of the brutality of Stalin's rule. Chambers began writing compellingly about the evils of communism. In 1948, he testified before HUAC about his communist past and named Alger Hiss as one of his contacts in the government.

Hiss soon appeared before HUAC. He denied that he was a communist and an espionage agent, and he denied that he even knew Whittaker Chambers. But Richard Nixon, a young member of Congress from California, convinced the other committee members to press the case. Slowly, Hiss's story began to unravel. Chambers proved that he did know Hiss and that Hiss had given him confidential government documents. Chambers had even kept a microfilm copy of some of those documents, storing them in a hollowed-out pumpkin on his Maryland farm.

Hiss was tried for perjury. The first trial ended in a hung jury, meaning a jury that cannot agree on a verdict. At his second trial, he was found guilty and sentenced to five years in prison. Even after his conviction, many Americans continued to believe that Hiss was innocent. However, as years passed, the evidence grew overwhelmingly against him.

FINAL DAILY NEWS 3¢

NEW YORK'S PICTURE NEWSPAPER

Vol. 32. No. 245 New York 17, Friday, April 6, 1951 88 Main+4 Manhattan Pages 3 Cents

A-SPY COUPLE DOOMED TO DIE

Story on Page 3

Use Chiang's Army, Mac Asks

Story on Page 2

On Way to Chair. Gloved hands folded, Mrs. Ethel Rosenberg, 35, rides in rear of prison van on way to Women's House of Detention. Julius Rosenberg, 32, is separated from his wife by wire screen in van outside U. S. Courthouse. They were sentenced to death for passing A-bomb secrets to Reds, enabling Russia to perfect bomb ahead of schedule. —Story p. 3

>> A jury found Julius and Ethel Rosenberg guilty of passing atomic secrets to the Soviet Union and sentenced them to death for espionage.

BOUNCE to Activate Timeline

The fact that someone as influential as Hiss was a communist agent raised serious concerns.

The Hiss case had another unexpected effect. The congressional hearings thrust Richard Nixon into the national spotlight. In 1952, he was named Eisenhower's running mate and would later become President.

The Rosenbergs and the Venona Papers

Nothing created more concern about internal security than the charge that some Americans had helped the Soviets build an atomic bomb. The case began when a scientist named Klaus Fuchs was charged with sending atomic secrets to the Soviet Union. The investigation against Fuchs ultimately led to the arrest of Ethel and Julius Rosenberg in 1950. The Rosenbergs were charged with conspiring to pass secret information about nuclear science to Soviet agents.

The trial of the Rosenbergs generated intense controversy in the United States and around the world. The case against them was based largely on the word of one confessed spy. Pleading innocent, the Rosenbergs claimed that they were being persecuted for being Jewish and for holding unpopular beliefs. In the end, both were found guilty and sentenced to death. Many believed that the harsh sentence was intended as a lever to force them to identify other members of the alleged spy ring. But the Rosenbergs claimed they had no such information. After 26 months on death row, the Rosenbergs were electrocuted in 1953.

Years of debate followed the executions. Some insisted that anti-Semitic sentiment led to the Rosenbergs' conviction and death. However, in 1995, the U.S. National Security Agency released secret Soviet messages that the United States had intercepted in the 1940s, known as the **Venona Papers**. The papers revealed the names of many Americans who spied for the Soviet Union. These documents confirmed the guilt of some of those investigated by HUAC, including the Rosenbergs and Alger Hiss.

EXPLAIN Why did the Rosenberg case attract nationwide attention and controversy?

McCarthyism

The early Cold War years saw one ominous event after another. The fall of China, Soviet nuclear bombs, and the exposure of Soviet agents in the United States all undermined American confidence. At that time, as Americans worried about the nation's security, a clever and unscrupulous man began to take advantage of this sense of fear and helplessness. He suggested that these setbacks were really caused by the work of traitors inside the United States.

The Rise of Senator Joe McCarthy In February 1950, a little-known senator from Wisconsin made a speech in Wheeling, West Virginia. The senator, **Joseph R. McCarthy**, charged that the State Department was infested with communist agents. He waved a piece of paper, which, he said, contained the names of State Department employees who were secretly communists.

> The reason why we find ourselves in a position of [weakness] is not because the enemy has sent men to invade our shores, but rather because of the traitorous actions of those who have had all the benefits that the wealthiest nation on earth has had to offer—the finest homes, the finest college educations, and the finest jobs in Government we can give. . . . I have here in my hand a list of 205 [individuals] that were known to the Secretary of State as being members of the Communist Party and who nevertheless are still working and shaping the policy of the State Department.
>
> —Joseph McCarthy, February 9, 1950

The charge provoked a furor. When challenged to give specific names, McCarthy said he had meant that there were "205 bad security risks" in the department. Then he claimed that 57 employees were communists. Over the next months, the numbers on his list changed. McCarthy never did produce the list of communists. Still, with the outbreak of the Korean War in June 1950, McCarthy's accusations grabbed the attention of the American public.

At the time of the above speech, McCarthy was finishing his first term in the Senate. He had accomplished very little in that term and was looking for a popular issue on which to focus his 1952 reelection campaign. Anticommunism seemed to be just the issue. McCarthy was easily reelected to a second term.

>> The charges from McCarthy and others that communists were working from within to overthrow the American government helped spread panic through popular culture.

The Methods of McCarthyism In the following four years, McCarthy put forward his own brand of anticommunism—so much so that the term **McCarthyism** became a catchword for extreme, reckless charges. By making irresponsible allegations, McCarthy did more to discredit legitimate concerns about domestic communism than any other single American. Between 1950 and 1954, McCarthy was perhaps the most powerful politician in the United States. Piling baseless accusations on top of charges that could not be proved, McCarthy became chairman of an investigations subcommittee. Merely being accused by McCarthy caused people to lose their jobs and destroyed their reputations. He attacked ruthlessly. When caught in a lie, he told another.

When one case faded, he introduced a new one. Confident because of his increasing power, McCarthy took on larger targets. He attacked former Secretary of State George Marshall, a national hero and author of the Marshall Plan. Even other senators came to fear McCarthy. They worried that he would brand them as communist sympathizers.

The "Lavender Scare" Hysteria over national security also targeted gay men and lesbians, who were considered vulnerable to blackmail and thus likely to reveal national secrets. The Red Scare of the 1950s overlapped with an anti-gay Lavender Scare. Congress held closed-door as well as open public hearings on the threat posed by gay men and lesbians in sensitive government positions. The systematic investigation, interrogation, and firing of thousands of suspected gay men and lesbians from federal government positions soon extended further—into surveillance and persecution of suspected lesbians and gay men in state and local government, education, and private industry.

McCarthy Loses Support In 1954, McCarthy went after the United States Army, claiming that it, too, was full of communists. Army leaders responded that McCarthy's attacks were personally motivated.

Finally, the Senate decided to hold televised hearings to sort out the allegations. For weeks, Americans were riveted to their television sets. Most were horrified by McCarthy's bullying tactics. For the first time, the public saw McCarthy badger witnesses, twist the truth, and snicker at the suffering of others. It was an upsetting sight for many Americans.

By the time the hearings ended in mid-June, the senator had lost many of his strongest supporters. The Senate formally censured him for his reckless accusations, which means it issued a condemnation or formal statement of disapproval. Although McCarthy continued to serve in the Senate, he had lost virtually all of his power and influence.

McCarthy's downfall in 1954 signaled the decline of the Red Scare, although in some places, McCarthy-style investigations continued. The nation had been damaged by the suppression of free speech and by the lack of open, honest debate. At the same time, however, the threat to the nation's democratic institutions had caused Americans to realize how important those institutions were and how critical it was to preserve them.

☑ **IDENTIFY CAUSE AND EFFECT** What events led to Senator McCarthy being censured by the U.S. Senate?

☑ ASSESSMENT

1. **Summarize** Explain the purpose of the House Un-American Activities Committee, or HUAC, and the effect the committee had on the American public.
2. **Cite Evidence** What tactics did Joseph McCarthy use to remain powerful and influential?
3. **Generate Explanations** Why did the televising of the Senate hearings help end McCarthyism?
4. **Compare Points of View** Explain the debate on the convictions of Julius and Ethel Rosenberg, and how this debate changed when the Venona Papers were revealed.
5. **Connections to Today** What effect did postwar suspicions about possible communist influence in the United States have on American culture in the 1950s? Do you think we have similar cultural influences today? Explain.

GO ONLINE to access this biography: Joseph McCarthy

15.5

President Dwight D. Eisenhower led the United States during a time of exuberant growth and prosperity.

Postwar Prosperity

After World War II, many Americans worried that the war's end would bring renewed economic depression. Numerous economists shared this pessimistic view of the future, predicting that the American economy could not produce enough jobs to employ all those who were returning from the military. Yet instead of a depression, Americans experienced the longest period of economic growth in American history, a boom that enabled millions of Americans to enter the middle class. This era of sustained growth fostered a widespread sense of optimism about the nation's future.

BOUNCE to Activate Flipped Video

Objectives

Describe how the United States made the transformation to a booming peacetime economy.

Discuss the growth of the Sunbelt and the effects of migration.

Describe changes in the U.S. economy in the postwar period.

Discuss the accomplishments and leadership qualities of Presidents Harry Truman and Dwight Eisenhower.

Key Terms

demobilization
GI Bill of Rights
baby boom
productivity
Sunbelt
service sector
information industry
franchise business
Sam Walton
Estée Lauder
multinational corporation
AFL-CIO
Taft-Hartley Act
Fair Deal

Causes and Effects of Prosperity in the 1950s

At the end of the war in August 1945, more than 12 million Americans were in the military. Thousands of American factories were churning out ships, planes, tanks, and all the materials required to help fight the war in the Pacific. Virtually overnight, both the need for such a huge military machine and the focus on war production came to an end. Orders went out from Washington, D.C., canceling defense contracts, causing millions of defense workers to lose their jobs. Wartime industries had to be converted to meet peacetime needs.

As Americans set about enjoying the fruits of peace, President Harry Truman responded to calls to "bring the boys home for Christmas" by starting **demobilization**, meaning the dismissal of members of the military from service. By July 1946, only 3 million remained in the military.

Americans were happy that the war was over, but they retained some sense of unease about the future. One poll taken in the fall of 1945 showed that 60 percent of Americans expected their earnings to fall with the return of a peacetime economy. "The

GO ONLINE to access your digital course

American soldier is . . . worried sick about postwar joblessness," *Fortune* magazine observed.

Impact of the GI Bill To help veterans, the federal government enacted the Servicemen's Readjustment Act of 1944, also known as the **GI Bill of Rights**. The GI bill had an enormous impact on American society. The bill provided a year of unemployment payments to veterans who were unable to find work. Those who attended college after the war received financial aid. The act also entitled veterans to government loans for building homes and starting businesses, which fueled an upsurge in home construction. This, in turn, led to explosive growth in suburban areas.

But perhaps the greatest contribution of the GI bill came in education. The average soldier was inducted into the armed forces at the time when he or she would have been finishing high school. The bill encouraged veterans to enter or return to college. Each veteran was eligible to receive $500 a year for college tuition—enough to cover the cost of most colleges. The bill also provided $50 a month for living expenses and $75 a month for married veterans. Eight million veterans eventually took advantage of these education benefits.

Despite the many provisions of the GI Bill, African American veterans found that its benefits often did not extend to them. Most banks would not give loans to Black applicants, and suburban America met them with hostility. However, some Black GIs were able to attend historically Black colleges on the GI Bill, and a few even attended previously all-white universities.

A Baby Boom Increases Consumption Upon their return, soldiers quickly made up for lost time by marrying and having children. Americans had put off having children because of the depression and war. Now, confident that the bad times were behind them, many married couples started families. This led to what population experts termed a **baby boom**. In 1957, at the peak of the baby boom, one American baby was born every 7 seconds, a grand total of 4.3 million for the year. One newspaper columnist commented, "Just imagine how much these extra people . . . will absorb—in food, in clothing, in gadgets, in housing, in services. . . ."

Postwar Inflation Fortunately, unemployment did not materialize, nor did a depression return. However, Americans experienced some serious economic problems. The most painful was skyrocketing prices. With war's end, the federal government ended rationing and price controls, both of which had helped keep inflation in check during the war. A postwar rush to buy goods created severe inflationary pressures. There was just too much money to spend on too few goods. Overall, prices rose about 18 percent in 1946. The price of some products, such as beef, nearly doubled within a year.

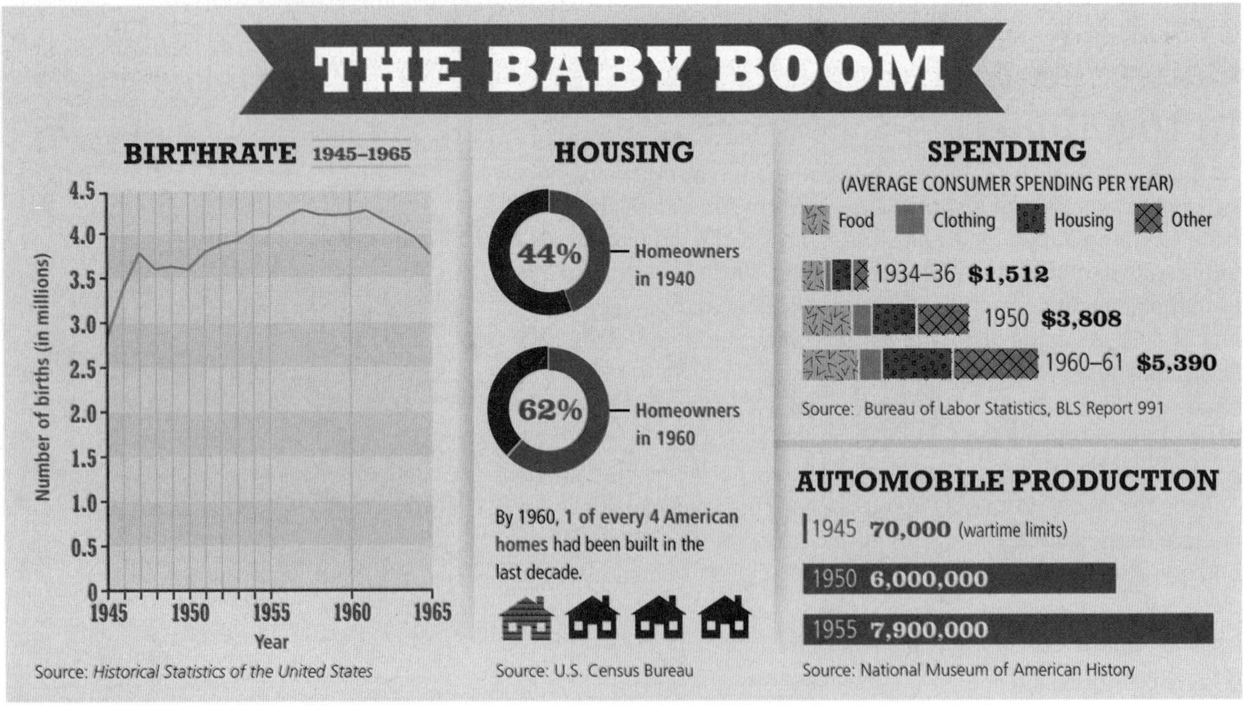

>> **Analyze Data** In your opinion, which is more important to the U.S. economy, home ownership or automobile ownership? Why?

Free Enterprise Improves U.S. Standard of Living During the depression, Americans could not buy the goods they desired. The economy improved during the war, but wartime restrictions kept spending down and limited economic growth. The end of wartime restrictions finally opened the floodgates to consumer purchases. As demand soared, businesses employed more people to produce goods. This created a cycle in which people were able to buy new goods, leading businesses to hire more workers, who in turn bought more goods.

At the end of World War II, the United States was the only developed nation largely untouched by the devastation. Although it had only 6 percent of the world's population, the United States produced about 50 percent of the world's total output. Americans at this time enjoyed a higher standard of living than any other nation in the world.

Technological Progress Enhances Productivity The American economy benefited from numerous technological advances during the postwar period. Some developments, such as the use of atomic energy, were the result of war research. The use of computers increased, and businesses gradually began to depend on them. Farms benefited from improved machinery and chemicals, allowing farmers to grow more crops with fewer laborers. Worker **productivity**—the rate at which goods are produced or services performed—continued to improve, largely because of new technology.

Military Spending Supports Growth Increased government spending boosted the economy, too. The Cold War had a number of economic effects. With the outbreak of the Korean War and the escalating Cold War with communist nations in Europe and Asia, the United States once again committed a significant part of its budget to defense spending. This was an expense that led President Eisenhower to warn about the rise of a "military-industrial complex" that, if left unchecked, could endanger democracy. Military spending led to new technologies and new materials, such as plastics and new light metal alloys, that found widespread use outside the military. Other large federal spending programs, such as the Marshall Plan, stimulated foreign demand for goods made in the United States.

IDENTIFY CAUSE AND EFFECT How did the baby boom contribute to increased economic prosperity during the 1950s?

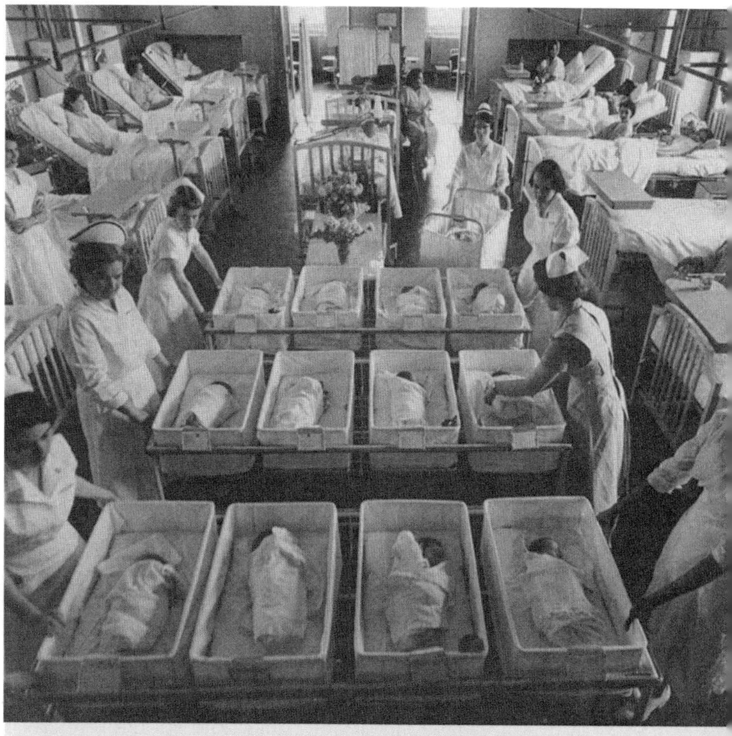

>> The end of the war and the nation's newfound prosperity prompted many young Americans to start families. The result was a "baby boom" that increased the population by 27 percent.

>> Postwar American prosperity led to widespread depictions in the media of an idealized suburban society.

Americans Migrate to the Sunbelt

Another crucial trend of the postwar era was the growth of the **Sunbelt**, the name given to the southern and western states. By the mid-1960s, California passed New York as the state with the largest population. The migration to Sunbelt cities, such as Houston, Texas, and Los Angeles, California, continued for the rest of the twentieth century.

Causes of Migration Many factors played a role in attracting people to the Sunbelt. A warm, sunny climate drew some Americans. A booming industrial economy and rapidly growing cities attracted people to Texas, which added more than 3 million new residents in the 1940s and 1950s. The explosive growth of the aerospace and electronics industries also attracted newcomers to the Sunbelt.

The development of air conditioning also played a major role. Invented in 1902, air conditioners were at first used only in public buildings, such as movie theaters and courthouses. But after World War II, the development of window units made it possible to cool homes. Northerners who had visited states like Florida, Texas, or Arizona only in winter could now live in hotter climates all year round.

Latinos contributed to the growth of the Sunbelt and Sunbelt cities. In the late 1950s and early 1960s, many Cubans, who were escaping the new regime of Fidel Castro, made Miami, Florida, their new home. Prior to World War II, most Mexican Americans had lived in rural areas. However, by the 1960s, the majority of them migrated to urban areas, such as Los Angeles; El Paso, Texas; and Phoenix, Arizona.

Effects of Migration on Society and the Environment As people moved to the suburbs and the Sunbelt, their political power went with them. Thus, suburbs and the Sunbelt gained representation. Urbanites in the Northeast and Midwest lost political power.

Urban and suburban growth created environmental concerns, ranging from traffic jams and smog to water shortages. To meet growing populations, communities utilized valuable open lands for housing, schools, roads, new businesses, and parking lots. In the 1960s and 1970s, environmental groups would begin to grapple with some of the byproducts of this growth.

CHECK UNDERSTANDING What motivated so many Americans to migrate to the Sunbelt?

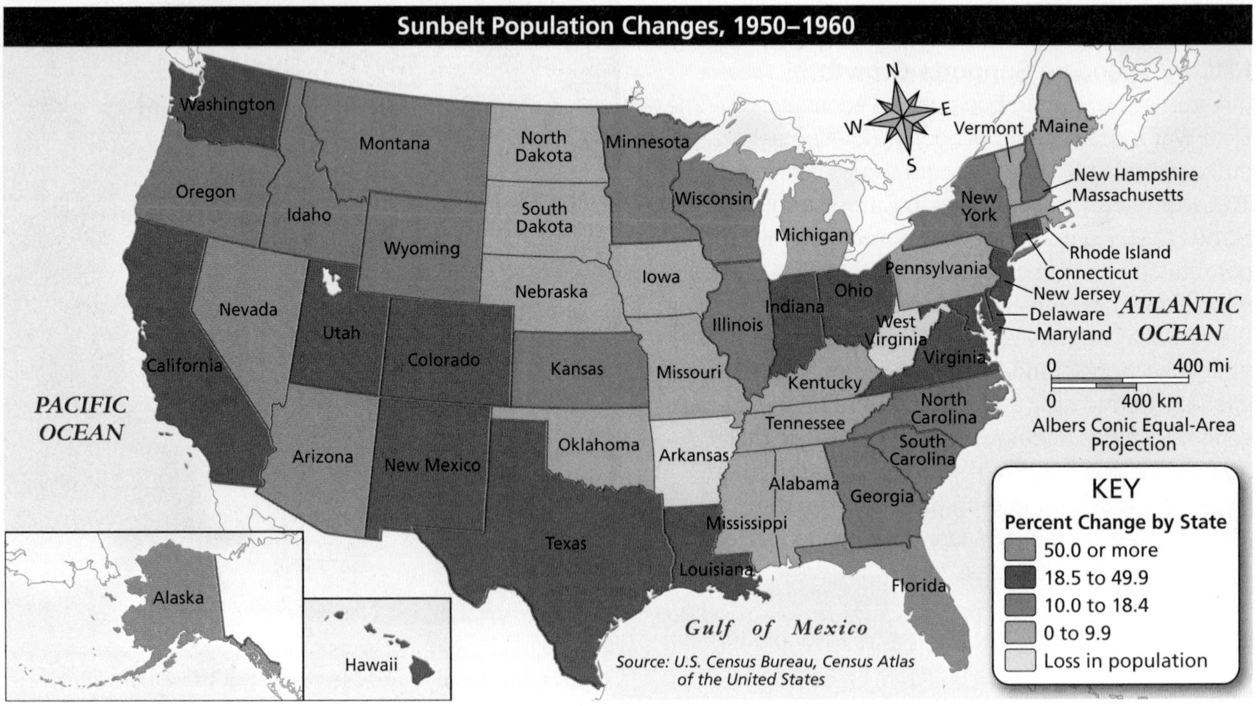

>> **Analyze Maps** Several states in the Sunbelt saw significant growth in their populations. Based on the map, which states had the most growth? Which states lost population?

Innovations and Economic Development

The important postwar population shifts were matched by equally groundbreaking structural changes in the American economy. For the first time in American history, more people found employment in the **service sector**—businesses that provide services, such as healthcare, law, retail, banking, or insurance—than in the manufacturing sector. These shifts led some to describe the United States as a postindustrial society.

>> During the 1950s, many Americans moved to the warm and sunny South and West, the so-called "Sunbelt." Huge developments, like Lakeland Park in California, met their need for housing.

Innovative Computers Drive Economic Growth

Between 1947 and 1957, the percentage of the American workforce employed in industrial or blue-collar jobs declined 4 percent. During the same time period, employment in the service sector, or white-collar jobs, rapidly grew.

The new workforce included many who worked in **information industries**, including those who built or operated the first computers. These computers were enormous. One of the first, named ENIAC, short for Electronic Numerical Integrator and Computer, took up roughly 18,000 square feet, or the size of three basketball courts! Despite its size, it was less powerful than today's desktop computer.

Still, ENIAC was a remarkable advance. Computers gradually shrank in size, and by the 1960s, the government and private industry had found many uses for this new technology. Hotels used computers to help make reservations, and banks used them to keep track of accounts. Industries started using computers to automate work or perform jobs once done by people. Technological innovations such as these improved the standard of living in the United States. They were spurred on by competition, profit, individual initiative, and the private ownership of goods and capital—key components of the free enterprise system.

Changes in the Labor Force Meanwhile, the number of women in the labor force continued to grow, doubling between 1940 and 1960. Many of these women worked part time. Few pursued long-term careers and most remained underpaid. Yet without their paychecks, their families would have found it difficult to remain in the middle class.

While the service sector grew rapidly, both the number and the percentage of Americans who made a living by farming continued to decline. In 1935, one fourth of the nation's families lived on farms. By 1960, fewer than one in ten families did. At the same time, improvements in technology, ranging from mechanical cotton pickers to chemical pesticides, made agriculture much more productive. This allowed fewer workers to grow even more food. New irrigation systems helped transform much of the land in the Southwest from arid to fertile fields.

The Role of Entrepreneurs At home, the postwar era saw the rise of **franchise businesses**. A franchise business allows a company to distribute its products or services through retail outlets owned by independent operators.

Franchises were attractive to consumers because they stressed quality and sameness, no matter where one was in the United States. The Holiday Inn franchise came into existence following a trip that home builder Kemmons Wilson took to Washington, D.C., with his family of five children. Wilson became frustrated when he found hotels difficult to locate, overpriced, and lacking adequate parking facilities. As he traveled, according to author David Halberstam, "Wilson became more irritated until he turned to his wife and announced that he was going into the hotel business. Everyone in this country, he thought, had a car and a family, and sooner or later everyone had to go somewhere." Today, there are tens of thousands of Holiday Inn hotels all over the world.

Many postwar critics lamented the growth of franchise businesses. For them, the franchises represented a growing lack of originality, evidence that the United States was becoming a "bland" nation in which people ate bland food, lived in bland look-a-like houses, and watched bland television shows that followed the same plot line.

Entrepreneurs Lead Management Innovations The transition from an industry-based to a service-based economy created opportunities for entrepreneurs. For example, Californians Richard and Maurice McDonald opened their new restaurant in 1948. The brothers emphasized efficiency, low prices, high volume, and quick service. They did away with anything that slowed down the process, including plates, glasses, dishwashing, and tipping. In 1955, Ray Kroc began to franchise McDonald's system and name. By the end of the century, McDonald's had become the most successful food service organization in history, and the name McDonald's came to stand for low-priced, standardized-quality food.

>> The original McDonald's restaurant in San Benardino, California featured 15 cent hamburgers.

BOUNCE to Activate Gallery

Other entrepreneurs' names also came to represent their businesses. For example, Wal-Mart, a discount merchandising business founded by **Sam Walton**, became one of the most successful businesses in the late twentieth century. Another entrepreneur, **Estée Lauder**, founded a cosmetics company that specialized in skin care and protection products.

Lauder's focus on selling her products only in high-end department stores created a $100 million dollar business by the 1970s. Walton and Lauder are just two of the millions of small business entrepreneurs whose businesses grew, allowing them to achieve the American dream.

American Corporations Go Multinational As the postwar economy expanded, so did **multinational corporations**, companies that produced and sold their goods and services all over the world and established branches abroad. General Motors, General Electric, and IBM produced a larger and larger share of all of the goods sold. Changing business strategies and management innovations allowed many of these corporations to earn large portions of their profits abroad. Coca Cola, for instance, sold its soft drinks all over the globe. Hollywood movies found eager audiences in Tokyo, Mexico City, and Germany.

Effects of Prosperity on Labor The prosperity of the 1950s was reflected in generally good times for the labor movement. In 1955, the AFL and the CIO, which had split in the mid-1930s, united to form the **AFL-CIO**. The new organization enjoyed a good deal of political clout, especially within the Democratic Party. Yet trade unions also lost some momentum during the late 1940s and early 1950s. Most of the new white-collar workers did not join unions, and labor's image was tarnished by a corruption scandal involving the Teamsters Union. Government investigators accused the Teamsters, who represented truck drivers, of illegally using their members' funds.

☑ **EXPLAIN** In what ways did American business change during the postwar period?

Truman's Postwar Leadership

As the postwar economy evolved and new demographic patterns changed society, American leaders faced rapidly shifting domestic and foreign political landscapes. On April 12, 1945, when Franklin Roosevelt died, Harry S. Truman had been Vice President for only 4 months. When Eleanor Roosevelt told him that her husband had died, Truman responded, "Is there anything I can do for you?" She replied, "Is there anything we can do for you? For you are the one in trouble now."

Eleanor Roosevelt's remark captured Harry Truman's predicament. He had to preside over one of the more difficult times in American history. The postwar years saw the beginning of the Cold War and communist takeovers in Europe and Asia. At home, inflation, labor unrest, and communist advances created a sense of deep unrest in the American public during the Truman years.

>> Unmet demands for pay raises in the face of inflation led to labor unrest, such as this strike at a Pittsburgh steel mill, during the Truman administration.

Relationships with Congress and Labor From the first days of his presidency, President Truman faced a double-barreled challenge: a restless labor movement and a combative Republican Party. Trade unionists demanded pay increases to keep up with inflation. When employers refused to meet labor's demands, millions of steel, coal, railroad, and automotive workers went on strike.

The wave of strikes was one of the largest in American history. It prompted Congress to enact the **Taft-Hartley Act**, a law that outlawed the closed shop—a workplace in which only union members can be hired. Taft-Hartley rolled back some of the rights that labor unions had gained during the New Deal. Although President Truman vetoed the Taft-Hartley Act, Congress overrode his veto.

Support for Civil Rights Unlike FDR, who avoided challenging the power of white southern senators and representatives, President Truman refused to remain passive, insisting that "we must correct the remaining imperfections in our practice of democracy." He established a special committee on civil rights to investigate race relations. Although the committee made several recommendations for civil rights reforms, Congress did not pass any meaningful civil rights legislation until the late 1950s.

Truman took matters into his own hands in one area when he issued an executive order desegregating the military. This was more successful. By 1951, most units had been integrated.

Truman Defeats Dewey By the spring of 1948, Truman's standing had sunk so low that he faced challenges from both the right and the left in his own Democratic Party. Southern Democrats, angry at Truman's support for civil rights, left the party and established the States' Rights Party. They named South Carolina governor Strom Thurmond as their candidate for President. At the other end of the political spectrum, Henry Wallace, who had been Vice President during FDR's third term, broke with Truman over foreign policy issues. Wallace became the candidate of a new Progressive Party.

The breakaway of two large blocs of Democrats was accompanied by the Republican Party's nomination of Thomas Dewey, the governor of New York, for President. Few people thought that Truman had any chance of winning the 1948 election. Truman, however, did not see it that way.

He staged an energetic "whistle stop" train tour of the nation, delivering over 300 speeches and traveling 31,000 miles in a matter of weeks. At train stops in small towns, Truman attacked the current Congress as "do nothing" and the worst in history. "Give 'em hell, Harry!" some in the crowd would cry out during his speeches.

Although every political poll predicted that Dewey would win easily, Truman won by a narrow margin. He had managed the political upset of the century.

Consequences of Truman's Presidency Shortly after the election, Truman announced a far-ranging legislative program, which he called the **Fair Deal**. The Fair Deal, he explained, would strengthen existing New Deal reforms and establish new programs, such as national health insurance. But

>> Americans enjoyed peace and prosperity under the Eisenhower administration. For many, it was a time for new homes, new cars, and family vacations.

BOUNCE to Activate Chart

Congress was not in a reforming mood, and Truman failed to win approval for most of his Fair Deal proposals.

Legislative failure and a stalled war in Korea contributed to Truman's loss of popularity. He chose not to seek the 1952 Democratic nomination. His reputation, however, has improved through the years. Today, many historians applaud him for his common-sense approach, as the first President to challenge public discrimination and as a determined opponent of communist expansion.

RECALL Why was Truman's victory in 1948 so surprising?

Eisenhower Leads a Thriving Nation

The 1952 election was hardly a contest. The Republican candidate, Dwight Eisenhower, was so popular that both the Democratic and Republican parties had wanted him as their presidential candidate. Eisenhower, whose nickname was Ike, charmed the public with his friendly smile, reassuring personality, and record of service and honesty. The Democratic candidate, Adlai Stevenson, a senator from Illinois, failed to catch the popular imagination the way Eisenhower did.

Dwight Eisenhower had spent nearly his entire adult life in the military and had never held a political office before 1952. Thus, Americans could not know for certain which way he would guide the nation upon taking office. However, most Americans believed that Eisenhower's calm personality mirrored his political views and that he would keep to the "middle road," achieving a balance between liberal and conservative positions.

Eisenhower did chart a middle course as President. While he shared the conservative view that the federal government had grown too strong, he did not support the repeal of existing New Deal programs, such as Social Security and the minimum wage. Federal spending actually increased during his presidency. Eisenhower even introduced several large new programs. For example, he created an interstate highway system and began to spend federal dollars for education, specifically to train more scientists.

One reason for Eisenhower's popularity was the strength of the American economy during the 1950s. His presidency was one of the most prosperous, peaceful, and politically tranquil in the twentieth century.

IDENTIFY SUPPORTING DETAILS Why did federal spending increase during Eisenhower's presidency?

ASSESSMENT

1. **Summarize** the reasons for American prosperity at the end of World War II.
2. **Infer** Why did so many veterans choose to enter or return to college after the war?
3. **Support Ideas with Examples** What effects did technology have on the agricultural sector in the postwar years?
4. **Generate Explanations** What effects did the baby boom have on the economy between 1940 and 1955?
5. **Quest Connections** Many Americans believed that the strong postwar economy and technological innovations were proof of the success of the American free enterprise system. How would this have made these Americans feel about the spread of communism? Why?

15.6

Americans' yearning for a better life after World War II, coupled with innovations in home building, led to explosive growth in suburban areas.

Mass Culture in the 1950s

The 1950s marked a period of changing national population distribution. Between 1940 and 1960, more than 40 million Americans moved to the suburbs, one of the largest mass migrations in history. Rural regions suffered the most dramatic decline in population, but people also came by the thousands from older industrial cities. They sought, as one father put it, a place where "a kid could grow up with grass stains on his pants."

BOUNCE to Activate Flipped Video

Objectives

Examine the rise of the suburbs and the growth of the interstate highway system.

Explain the causes and effects of prosperity in the 1950s on consumers.

Discuss postwar changes in family life.

Describe changes in education in the postwar period.

Describe the rise of new forms of mass culture.

Key Terms

Interstate Highway Act
consumerism
median family income
nuclear family
Dr. Benjamin Spock
Billy Graham
California Master Plan

Suburban Migration

Causes and Effects of Suburban Growth People flocked to the suburbs in part because the nation suffered from a severe shortage of urban housing. During the depression and World War II, new housing construction had come to a near standstill. At war's end, as Americans married and formed families, they went in search of a place they could call their own.

Fortunately, at this time of peak demand, developers figured out how to build affordable housing in a hurry. William Levitt became a leader in the mass production of suburban homes. Rows of houses in Levittown, a suburb of New York City on Long Island, were built using the same plan. This method enabled workers to build houses in weeks rather than months. On the installment plan, buyers could pay $58 a month toward the cost of a home. Demand for the homes was so great that Levitt built two other Levittowns—one outside Philadelphia, Pennsylvania, and the other in New Jersey. These houses were ideal for young couples starting out because they were affordable and comfortable. Other

GO ONLINE to access your digital course

developers adopted Levitt's innovative techniques, and suburbs were soon springing up across the country.

Suburban development benefited from investment by the government. State and federal governments constructed thousands of miles of highways that linked the suburbs to cities. New home buyers also benefited from the GI bill and the Federal Housing Administration (FHA), which provided low-interest loans. FHA-backed loans allowed home buyers to pay as little as 5 to 10 percent of the purchase price and to pay off their mortgages over 30 years. However, these suburban communities remained predominantly white, because of discriminatory practices by real estate agents, landlords, and property owners.

Residents of new suburbs faced the challenge of establishing new towns with churches, synagogues, schools, and police and fire departments. Through these institutions, the suburbanites forged a sense of community. During the 1950s, the suburbs became increasingly self-contained. While suburban residents of earlier generations had depended on the city for entertainment and shopping, the postwar suburban dweller could find a vast array of goods and services in nearby shopping centers.

>> President Eisenhower authorized funding of the massive new interstate highway system. One outcome was that new suburbanites could more easily commute by car to jobs in major cities.

BOUNCE to Activate Illustration

Interstates Support Migration and Prosperity
Free enterprise combined with government action to improve the quality of life in suburban communities. Committed to the idea of easing automobile travel, President Eisenhower authorized the first funding of the interstate system in 1953. Further legislation passed by Congress in 1956 resulted in the **Interstate Highway Act**, which authorized funds to build 41,000 miles of highway consisting of multilane expressways that would connect the nation's major cities.

Such expressways, Eisenhower argued, would safely carry the nation's growing automobile traffic, boost economic prosperity, and provide a valuable transportation network to strengthen national defense. This represented the biggest expenditure on public works in history, bigger by far than any project undertaken during the New Deal. In 1990, further recognition of President Eisenhower's role in establishing the massive highway system led to a renaming of the system. It became the Dwight D. Eisenhower System of Interstate and Defense Highways.

Besides easing commutes from suburbs to cities, highways boosted the travel and vacation industries. Vacationers drove to national parks, to beaches, and to new destinations, such as Las Vegas. With more money and more children, families sought leisure activity. Walt Disney met this demand by building an extraordinary amusement park in California. Disneyland excited the imagination with visions of the future, including make-believe rides in space.

Technological Innovations Lead to the "Car Culture" During the 1920s, automobile ownership had soared in the United States. With the explosion of suburban growth in the 1950s, Americans grew even more dependent upon their cars. The number of registered automobiles jumped from 26 million in 1945 to 60 million in 1960.

These new automobiles tended to have big engines and enormous horsepower. They came with the newest technology, such as power steering and brakes and automatic transmissions. Harley Earl of the Ford Motor Company captured the mood of the 1950s by designing cars with lots of chrome that reminded people of jet airplanes.

While some suburbanites rode the train or other forms of mass transportation, Americans increasingly depended upon their cars to commute to work. Suburbanites also needed their cars to shop at suburban shopping malls. Entrepreneurs opened fast-food restaurants and drive-in movie theaters, both of which catered to the car culture. While

Distribution of Families by Income, 1947 and 1970

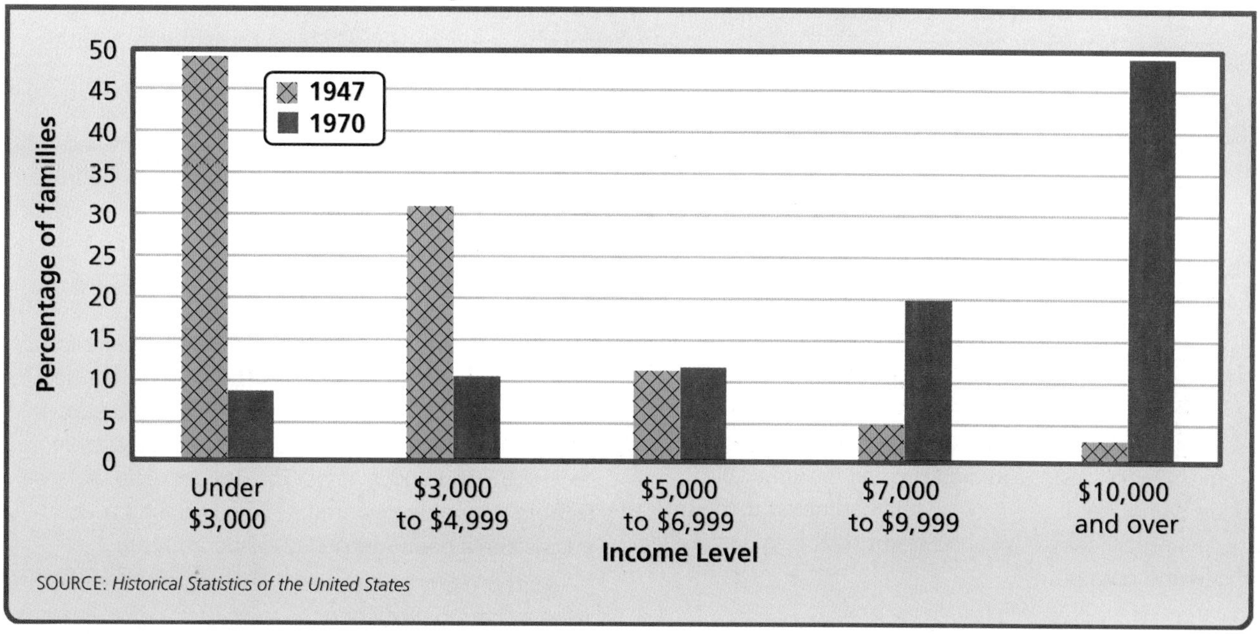

>> **Analyze Data** Look at the top two income brackets shown in this graph. How did the change in income in these brackets from 1947 to 1970 affect U.S. consumer culture?

these businesses flourished, many older businesses, often located in older city neighborhoods, struggled to survive.

CHECK UNDERSTANDING How did suburban businesses benefit from the "car culture"?

Increased Consumption and Consumerism

For much of our history, Americans were taught to save their money. "A penny saved is a penny earned," advised Benjamin Franklin. However, as the U.S. economy began to boom in the postwar era, Americans were caught up in a wave of **consumerism**, buying as much as they could, much of it on credit. What accounted for this spending spree?

Free Enterprise System Improves Standards of Living One reason Americans spent more was that they had more money to spend. During the 1950s, **median family income** rose from $3,319 to $5,417. The median is that number where half the numbers are lower and half the numbers are higher.

This rise in income meant that the average American family had twice as much real income in the 1950s as it had had during the prosperous years of the 1920s. Consumer-oriented companies found new and innovative ways to encourage buying on credit. For example, General Motors advertised its cars with the slogan "Buy Now, Pay Later." The Diner's Club introduced the first credit card.

Technological Innovations Drive New Conveniences Embracing the free-enterprise system, American businesses developed technological and purchasing innovations that improved the standard of living. Home appliances topped the list of the goods that Americans bought. Families purchased electric washing machines and dryers, refrigerators and ranges. These labor-saving appliances helped transform housework, lessening the physical demands of everything from washing clothes to preserving foods.

With money to spend, easy credit, and new goods to buy, shopping became a new pastime for Americans. Supermarkets, where customers could buy everything from milk to mops, appeared. Shopping centers sprouted all over suburbia and Americans bought one product in particular in record numbers: Televisions. In 1946, manufacturers produced fewer than 6,000 TV sets. Seven years later, Americans purchased 7 million sets, and by the end of the decade, 90 percent of all households owned a television.

IDENTIFY CAUSE AND EFFECT What were some reasons why consumption skyrocketed in the postwar era?

Families and Communities in the Fifties

American society had been shaken to its core by the mass mobilizations and disruption brought about by World War II. As Americans readjusted to life in peacetime, they embraced traditional ideals of family life and community.

The "Ideal" American Family During World War II, many women—including married women with children — had gone off to work in factories. In 1943, women made up 25 percent of the workers in the wartime auto industry. With the war's end, however, most of the women who had entered the workforce returned to being homemakers. Now, a more traditional image of the family took hold, one in which women stayed home and men served as "breadwinners." Women who wanted a career outside the home faced social pressures to rethink their decisions.

>> Women in the 1950s were encouraged to return to traditional family roles by staying home to raise families.

During the 1950s, the ideal family was one in which men worked and supported their families and women stayed home and reared their children. In the popular magazines of the postwar era, social scientists and other opinion makers described the **nuclear family**, or a household consisting of a mother and father and their children, as the backbone of American society. For the nuclear family to function smoothly, experts claimed, women had to accept their role as homemakers. Television shows and movies made similar assertions. For example, in the 1955 Hollywood movie *The Tender Trap*, actress Debbie Reynolds declared, "A woman isn't a woman unless she's been married and had children."

As the 1950s progressed, however, more women were willing to challenge the view that a woman could not have a career outside the home. By 1960, women held one third of the nation's jobs. Approximately half of these women workers were married.

Challenges to the Postwar Ideal As television and movies were reinforcing the postwar ideal of heterosexual family life and rigid gender roles, a series of highly publicized events seemed to challenge those very ideals. In 1948 and 1953 Alfred Kinsey, a biologist and zoologist, along with his team of researchers, published reports on male and female sexuality. The reports were highly controversial due to their startling conclusions and their discussion of taboo subjects, including lesbian and gay male sexual orientation. Despite the fact that some criticized Kinsey's research methods, his work had enormous influence, including his findings challenging the assumption that being a lesbian, gay man, or bisexual was somehow sick or pathological. Around the same time, a former U.S. soldier underwent sex reassignment surgery (currently referred to as "gender confirmation surgery") to become a woman—Christine Jorgensen. In the early 1950s, the media turned Jorgensen into a celebrity, and she used her fame and wit to speak out in defense of transgender people (at that time referred to as "transsexuals").

Baby Boom Increases Focus on Children More so than in the past, family life revolved around children. Not surprisingly, the best-selling book of the era was **Dr. Benjamin Spock's** *Common Sense Book of Baby and Child Care*. Parents bought and read his book because they wanted expert advice on how to raise their children. Spock emphasized the importance of nurturing children, from their earliest days as infants through their teen years. Mothers, Spock suggested, should not worry about spoiling their children because children could not get too much comfort and love. Some criticized Spock for promoting what they called "a permissive culture." Nevertheless, Spock's book remained extremely popular for several decades.

Another sign of the degree to which family life revolved around children was the amount of money parents spent on their children. Some parents defended their spending by arguing that it would help prevent another depression. Others saw no need to defend their decisions; they believed that spending was simply a part of nurturing and caring for their children.

As baby boomers became teens, their impact on the economy and American culture became even more noticeable. While as children they received toys, such as Davy Crockett caps and Barbie dolls, as teens they purchased much more expensive items. As *LIFE* magazine observed:

> The time is past when a boy's chief possession was his bike and a girl's party wardrobe consisted of a fancy dress worn with a string of dime-store pearls. . . . Today's teenagers surround themselves with a fantastic array of garish and often expensive baubles and amusements. They own 10 million phonographs, over a million TV sets, 13 million cameras.
>
> —*LIFE*, August 31, 1959

Billy Graham Contributes to a Religious Revival

The 1950s also witnessed a revival of religion in the United States. Organized religious groups became more powerful and more houses of worship were built. Regular church attendance rose from about 50 million in 1940 to about 80 million in 1958. The evangelist **Billy Graham** attracted millions to religious revivals that he held around the nation.

Roman Catholic bishop Fulton Sheen effectively used television to reach audiences estimated at 10 million a week. During the 1950s, Congress added the words "In God We Trust" to the dollar bill and "under God," to the Pledge of Allegiance. These additions were aimed at making clear the contrast between the centrality of religion in American society and the atheism, or nonbelief in God, of communist societies.

>> In 1954, Dr. Jonas Salk created a polio vaccine. The vaccine was ordered for all American children and was eventually used around the globe to virtually eradicate polio.

BOUNCE to Activate Gallery

Specific Needs Lead to Medical Innovations

During the 1950s, American families benefited from numerous advances in medicine. By 1952, Dr. Jonas Salk was refining a vaccine against polio, the disease that had struck down Franklin Roosevelt and that, in 1952 alone, had crippled tens of thousands and killed 1,400 people, mostly children. By 1960, the widespread distribution of Salk's new vaccine and an oral vaccine developed by Albert Sabin had nearly eliminated the disease.

At the same time, antibiotics, such as penicillin, came into widespread use. The antibiotics helped control numerous infectious diseases caused by bacteria, such as whooping cough and tuberculosis. As a result of these medical advances and a better understanding of the importance of diet, children born after 1946 had a longer life expectancy than those born before 1946.

The year 1946 also saw the founding of the Communicable Disease Center (CDC), in order to influence health promotion and prevent disease. This agency later became the Centers for Disease Control and Prevention.

CONNECT How did the focus on children and teenagers contribute to prosperity during the 1950s?

Educational Opportunities and Priorities

As the economy grew, so too did opportunities for Americans to attain higher education. A more educated work force boosted economic productivity. In 1940, only about 15 percent of college-age Americans attended college. By the early 1960s, however, close to 40 percent did. The percentage of Americans who completed high school also rose sharply. "The astonishing growth of education in the late 1940s (and thereafter)," wrote historian James Patterson, "seemed yet another sign that the American Dream was well and alive."

Defense Spending Shapes Education Priorities New priorities meant that students had expanded opportunities. In Texas, for example, the state legislature passed laws guaranteeing young people the chance to attend public school through the twelfth grade. Large sums of money were needed to meet the education needs of the baby-boom generation. Most of the funding for education came from local and state governments, but after the Soviet Union launched *Sputnik 1* in 1957, many Americans called for more federal funds for education.

In a mood of crisis, Congress quickly approved the National Defense Education Act. Its $1 billion program was aimed at producing more scientists and science teachers. The act authorized money for loans to high school and college graduates to continue their scientific education.

Education Becomes More Accessible The postwar era saw the stirrings of a movement to make education more accessible. Many states poured funds into their public universities, making it easier for ordinary Americans to attend college. California, for example, established a **California Master Plan**, which called for three tiers of higher education: research universities, state colleges, and community colleges. All of them were to be accessible to all of the state's citizens. Other states also built or expanded their college systems.

On another front, in 1954, the Supreme Court ruled in *Brown* v. *Board of Education of Topeka* that segregated schools were unconstitutional. However, it would be years before many schools were actually integrated.

EXPLAIN How did American educational priorities change in the years following World War II?

>> Television gained such popularity during the 1950s that many families got into the habit of watching their favorite shows even while eating dinner.

Television Shapes American Culture

In 1938, when television was still just a curiosity, E. B. White, author of *Charlotte's Web*, wrote that it "is going to be the test of the modern world. . . . We shall stand or fall by the television." While White's view may have been exaggerated, clearly television has had an enormous impact on American society.

Between 1945 and 1960, Americans purchased television sets at a faster pace than they had bought either radios or cars during the 1920s. The popularity of this new technology threatened the movie industry because families stayed home to watch TV rather than go out to watch movies at the theater.

Although television attracted viewers of all ages, it had a special influence on children. Baby-boom children rushed home from school to watch the *Howdy Doody Show* or the *Mickey Mouse Club*. Children also watched hours of cartoons and shows featuring their favorite superheroes, such as the Lone Ranger. Westerns were especially popular during the 1950s and early 1960s.

Among the most memorable shows were sitcoms about families. Fifty million Americans tuned in each week to watch the *I Love Lucy* show, starring the comedic actress Lucille Ball. Other popular family sitcoms included *Leave It to Beaver*, *The Adventures of Ozzie and Harriet*, and *Father Knows Best*.

These shows reflected and reinforced the ideal of the 1950s family. None of the family sitcoms had important African American characters. None of the major characters got divorced. Major real-life problems, such as mental illness, alcoholism, and personal depression, rarely, if ever, appeared. As journalist and historian David Halberstam noted, "No family problem was so great that it could not be cleared up within the allotted twenty-two minutes."

Even before television emerged in the 1950s, a mass national culture had begun to develop in the United States. Nationally broadcast radio programs, Hollywood films, and other forms of popular culture had helped erode distinct regional and ethnic cultures. Television sped up and reinforced this process. Americans in every region of the country watched the same shows and bought the same goods they saw advertised.

Television changed political campaigns. During the 1952 presidential campaign, Americans could see the candidates in action. Usually, candidates with more money could buy more advertising time. The impact of television on elections continues today.

SUMMARIZE How did television reflect and reinforce the ideal of the nuclear family in the postwar period?

ASSESSMENT

1. **Identify Cause and Effect** Discuss how the religious revival during the 1950s was linked to Americans' response to communism.
2. **Support Ideas with Evidence** Describe the role television played for children during the 1950s.
3. **Support a Point of View with Evidence** "The astonishing growth of education in the late 1940s (and thereafter) seemed yet another sign that the American Dream was well and alive."
   —Historian James Patterson
   What caused the growth of education that Patterson references? Why was this a sign that the American Dream was "well and alive"?
4. **Generate Explanations** Explain the effect that the car culture had on businesses in older inner-city neighborhoods.
5. **Connections to Today** During the postwar period, American culture underwent many changes. Which cultural characteristics that arose during the 1950s are still present in American society today? Which characteristics have faded from American culture?

15.7

Not everyone experienced prosperity during the 1950s. Stubborn areas of long-term poverty, such as this part of rural West Virginia, saw little benefit from the boom times.

BOUNCE to Activate Flipped Video

Objectives

Summarize the arguments made by critics who rejected the culture of the fifties.

Describe the causes and effects of urban and rural poverty.

Explain the problems that many minority groups faced in the postwar era.

Key Terms

beatniks
rock-and-roll
Elvis Presley
urban renewal
termination policy

Social Issues of the 1950s

Despite the prosperity of the 1950s, not all people benefited. Some groups were left out of the era's prosperity. Others, who had obtained more wealth, wondered whether all of the material things they acquired had actually led to a better life. The discontent of the 1950s would manifest the first signs of the dissent that would dominate the 1960s.

Critics and Rebels Emerge

The failure to provide equal opportunities to minorities was one source of discontent during the postwar era. Another was the belief that while material conditions were better in the 1950s, the *quality* of life had not improved. Many intellectuals and artists did not consider suburban homes, shopping centers, and an unending supply of new products as representing a better life.

Cultural Movements Against Conformity Many social critics complained about an emphasis on conformity. In a book called *The Lonely Crowd*, sociologists David Riesman and Nathan Glazer lamented that Americans had sacrificed their individualism in order to fit into the larger community. They also criticized the power of advertising to mold public tastes. The theme of alienation, or not fitting in, dominated a number of popular novels of the era. The bestseller *The Man in the Gray Flannel Suit*, by Sloan Wilson, followed a World War II veteran who could not find

GO ONLINE to access your digital course

real meaning in life after the war. Holden Caulfield, the main character in J. D. Salinger's *Catcher in the Rye*, a favorite among many teens, mocked the phoniness of adult society.

Although not published until 1963, Betty Friedan's *The Feminine Mystique* described the plight of the suburban housewife during the 1950s. By the 1960s, Friedan would be at the forefront of a movement to change the social and political status of women in American society.

The Impact of the Beat Generation on American Society An additional critique of American society came from a small group of writers and artists called **beatniks**, or the beats. The beats refused to conform to accepted ways of behavior. Conformity, they insisted, stifled individualism. They displayed their dislike of American society by careless dress and colorful jargon.

In their poems, such as Allen Ginsberg's "Howl," and novels, such as Jack Kerouac's *On the Road*, the beats lambasted what they saw as the crass materialism and conformity of the American middle class. Many Americans, in turn, were outraged by their behavior and believed that beatnik values would have a negative impact on society.

Hollywood captured this rebellious spirit and youthful defiance in several influential films in the 1950s. In *Rebel Without a Cause*, James Dean portrayed a tormented teenager who rejects the values of the establishment while trying to fit in with his peers.

Actor Marlon Brando became a symbol of rebellion for his role as the leader of a motorcycle gang in the film *The Wild One*. These characters—and ultimately, Dean and Brando themselves—became role models for disenchanted youth.

A New Style of Music In the summer of 1951, a relatively unknown white disc jockey named Alan Freed began broadcasting what commonly had been called "race" music to listeners across the Midwest. Renaming the music **rock-and-roll**, Freed planted the seed for a cultural revolution that would blossom in the mid-1950s.

Rock music originated in the rhythm-and-blues traditions of African Americans. As African Americans began to move north, they brought their musical traditions with them. Independent recording companies began recording rhythm-and-blues (R&B) music. Rock-and-roll borrowed heavily from rhythm and blues. As Chuck Berry, known as the pioneer

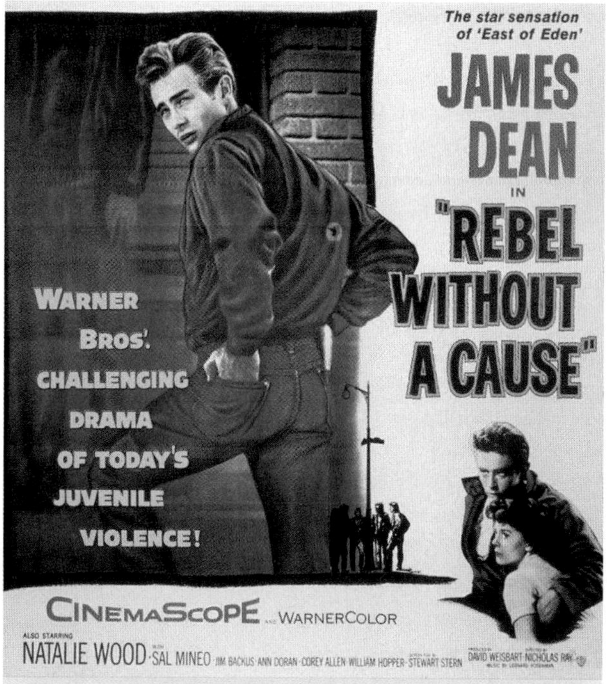

>> Some popular entertainment of the 1950s, including movies such as *Rebel Without a Cause*, questioned the values of the middle class.

>> Chuck Berry was one of the most popular musicians of early rock-and-roll. This new musical genre blurred the racial divisions of 1950s society.

of rock-and-roll, put it, "It used to be called boogie-woogie, it used to be called blues, used to be called rhythm and blues. . . . It's called rock now."

In the past, whites had not heard live performances of rhythm-and-blues music due to Jim Crow laws in the South or more subtle forms of segregation in the North. In the postwar era, however, the radio allowed this music to attract a wider white audience. For example, a young **Elvis Presley** listened to a Memphis radio station that played African American gospel tunes. He began to integrate those tunes into the music he played. Meanwhile, in the early 1950s, Sam Phillips set up a recording studio in Memphis to record and play the music of some of Memphis's best African American blues performers, such as B. B. King. One day Phillips heard Presley and almost immediately recognized that he had found the person he had been looking for.

Presley's arrival set off the new rock craze. His first hit, "Heartbreak Hotel," sold in the millions, and his success sparked a new popularity for rock music. Presley, along with African American performers such as Chuck Berry, Fats Domino, Little Richard, and Ray Charles, had a profound influence on popular music throughout the world.

>> Rock-and-roll singer Elvis Presley became extremely popular with young people, but some Americans worried that his performances were subversive or immoral.

BOUNCE to Activate Gallery

Yet at first, not everyone liked Elvis or the new rock craze, which many saw as having a very negative impact on culture. When Ed Sullivan, the host of a famous TV variety show, invited Elvis to sing on his show, he directed cameramen to show Elvis only from the waist up, because many parents objected to Elvis's gyrating hips and tight pants. Ministers complained about the passions that rock music seemed to unleash among so many youngsters. Congress held hearings on the subversive nature of rock music.

INFER Why was Elvis Presley able to popularize rock-and-roll more easily than African American musicians in the 1950s?

Poverty in the Cities and Rural Areas

Behind the new household appliances, the spreading suburbs, the burgeoning shopping malls, and the ribbons of highways was a very different United States. It was a nation of urban slums, desperate rural poverty, and discrimination. People who were poor and dispossessed were well hidden.

In an influential 1962 book entitled *The Other America*, Michael Harrington shocked many Americans by arguing that poverty was widespread in the United States. Harrington claimed that 50 million Americans—one fourth of the nation—lived in poverty. Despite American affluence, Harrington said, poverty plagued African Americans in the inner cities, rural whites in areas such as Appalachia, and Hispanics in migrant farm labor camps and urban barrios. Harrington argued that Americans could not afford to ignore the existence of the poor:

> The poor live in a culture of poverty. [They] get sick more than anyone else in the society. . . . Because they are sick more often and longer than anyone else, they lose wages and work and find it difficult to hold a steady job. And because of this, . . . their prospect is to move to an even lower level . . . toward even more suffering.
>
> —Michael Harrington, *The Other America*, 1962

>> **Analyze Data** What push and pull factors might have affected Americans in the South during this period?

Effects of Migration on Cities During the decades that followed World War II, African Americans and other nonwhite minorities moved in great numbers from rural areas to cities in search of better economic opportunities. In the same period, however, American cities were suffering a severe decline as middle-class white families moved to the suburbs.

The loss of the middle class hurt cities economically because the middle class paid a large share of the taxes. It hurt them politically, as well, because as the suburbs gained population, they also gained representation in state legislatures and the national government. This combination of declining economic and political power put a serious strain on cities, leading to a deterioration of services, such as garbage removal and street repair. In turn, as the conditions worsened and crime increased in what was now called the inner city, more of the middle class decided to move to the suburbs.

Federal, state, and local governments tried to reverse the downward trend in American cities by developing **urban renewal** projects. With these projects, the government cleared large tracts of older housing and built freeways and developments that, it was hoped, would "revitalize" downtown areas. Unfortunately, the projects often backfired. Urban renewal drove people from their homes to make room for the new projects and highways. The poor were forced to seek housing in neighborhoods that were already overcrowded and overburdened. One resident of East Harlem, New York, who lost his home to an urban renewal project, observed:

Middle-class flight only worsened inner-city problems, such as inadequate services and schools.

> Nobody cared what we wanted when they built this place. They threw our houses down and pushed us there and pushed our friends somewhere else. We don't have a place around here to get a cup of coffee or a newspaper even, or borrow fifty cents.
>
> —*America's History Since 1865*

The federal government tried to ease the shortage of affordable housing by constructing public housing. At the time, these housing projects seemed a godsend to those who lived there. Rent was cheap and the residents often enjoyed certain services, like hot running water, for the first time in their lives. Yet, since the public housing was often built in poor neighborhoods, the projects led to an even greater concentration of poverty. This, in turn led to other problems, such as crime.

Migration from Rural Areas The plight of the rural poor was just as bad if not worse than that of the urban poor. Mississippi Delta sharecroppers, coal miners in Appalachia, and farmers in remote areas were left behind as others prospered, and often their economic situation got worse as time passed. A major transformation in farming was taking place. Corporations and large-farm owners came to dominate farm production. Many independent small-farm owners found it difficult to compete with the large farms and slipped into poverty.

Many farmers responded by leaving their rural communities behind, joining the waves of the poor who relocated to the city. Others remained behind, wondering if they would ever get to enjoy the benefits of the new economy.

☑ **RECALL** How did the federal government respond to the decline of American cities?

Struggles of Minorities

During the postwar years, the battle for civil rights in the South began to gain headlines. Yet, in the same time period, African Americans and other minorities also fought for equality in the urban north and west. Central to their struggles were efforts to overcome housing and employment discrimination.

Discrimination against Puerto Ricans Latinos from Puerto Rico and Mexico and American Indians faced many of the same problems that African Americans encountered in the years following World War II. Puerto Rican migrants to New York City, for example, often found themselves clustered together in many of the poorest inner city neighborhoods with employment opportunities limited by both formal and informal forms of discrimination. As newcomers whose native language was not English, they enjoyed little political power. Thus, they received little help from city governments in getting better services, education, or an end to discriminatory practices.

Labor Conditions and Mexicans Both Mexicans and Mexican Americans faced a similar situation in the United States. During World War II, the U.S. government had established the Bracero Program as a means of addressing the shortage of agricultural workers. *Braceros* was a term for Mexican migrant farmworkers in the United States. The program gave temporary visas to Mexican immigrants. By

Poverty in the United States, 1955–2018

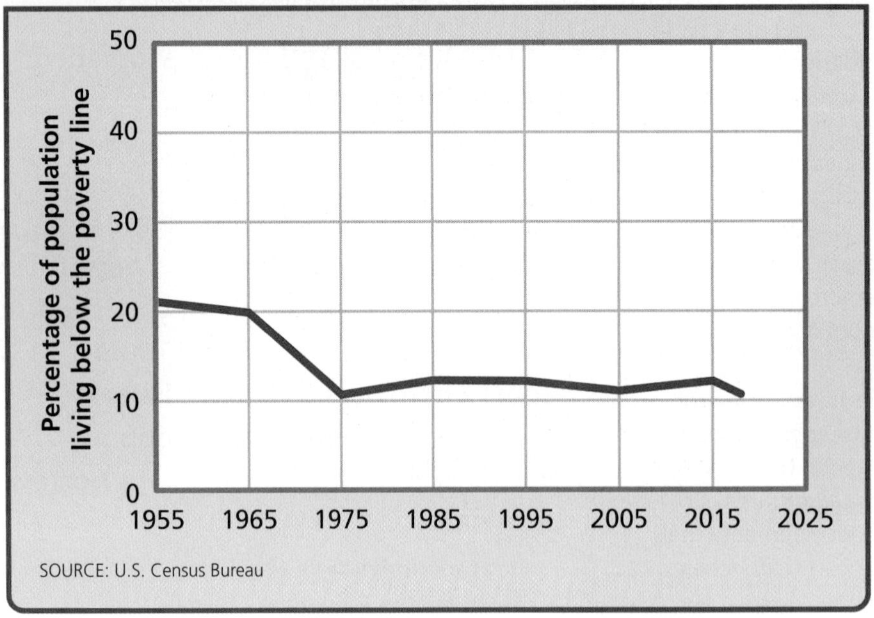

>> **Analyze Graphs** This graph shows how poverty levels changed from 1955–2018. Overall, what was the poverty trend during this period?

1964, 3 million Mexicans had worked in the United States under the program, most of them as farm laborers. Many were exploited and cheated by their employers. Mexican workers followed crops from state to state. Often, children worked alongside their parents. The migrants had little power to oppose the exploitation, for if they complained about conditions, employers threatened to deport them back to Mexico. One U.S. Department of Labor official called the program "legalized slavery."

One champion of the rights of Mexican migrant workers, Ernesto Galarza, joined the effort to organize unions for Mexican farm laborers.

American Indians In 1953, the federal government enacted the **termination policy**, a major change in the rules governing American Indians. The law sought to end tribal government and to relocate American Indians to the nation's cities. It also terminated federal responsibility for the health and welfare of American Indians. Proponents of the policy argued that it would free American Indians to assimilate, or merge, into American society. While some American Indians praised the intent of the program, most came to agree with Senator Mark Hatfield of Oregon who argued that it made things worse. "[T]he social and economic devastation which these policies have wrought upon many groups has been tremendous. . . . While these problems were already severe among Indian societies generally, they have become epidemic among terminated Indians."

EXPLAIN What were some of the problems that minorities had to overcome in the postwar era?

ASSESSMENT

1. **Make Generalizations** Describe the impact beatniks had on society and culture in the 1950s.
2. **Support Ideas with Evidence** Describe the struggles and discrimination minorities faced in the post-World War II United States.
3. **Draw Conclusions** Explain the significance of Alan Freed renaming "race" music as rock-and-roll music.
4. **Identify Central Issues** Describe the impact that the migration of middle-class families to suburbs had on the economic stability of the nation's cities.
5. **Quest Connections** How might McCarthyism have contributed to Americans' desire to conform during the 1950s?

>> Puerto Ricans, like previous waves of immigrants, formed communities in specific urban neighborhoods.

BOUNCE to Activate Map

>> The sheer difficulty of the work undertaken by migrant farmworkers, coupled with the low wages, led to activism and, eventually, positive changes.

Connections to Today

How many generations can you identify in this family photograph?

Take Action to Understand Generational Identities

Every generation has its own unique culture, shaped by the experiences and events of the era. This was true of the postwar generation; it is true today.

1. **Choose** one of the following cultural topics:
    - **Defining a Generation:** Research how and why each post–World War II generation got its name.
    - **Conflicting Generations:** Describe the meaning of the term "generation gap" and how different generations are portrayed in the media.
    - **Determining Public Policy:** Explore how the expectations and goals of different generations affect public policy.
2. **Ask Questions** Generate a list of questions you have about the topic.
3. **Learn** about the topic and the major issues and debates related to it. Take notes as you conduct your research and continue to generate questions as you learn more.
4. **Take Action** Choose a generation from the baby boomers to the present and create a visual collage illustrating its characteristics, contributions, and/or values. Include short captions explaining the characteristics of the group you chose and how your collage is meant to represent the group. Then create a second collage showing the same information for your own generation.

GO ONLINE to www.SavvasRealize.com and access your digital course

Use the texts, quizzes, interactivities, Quest Inquiries, Flipped Videos, and other resources from this Topic to prepare for the Topic Test.

- Quest Inquiries
- Quizzes
- Interactivities
- Texts
- Flipped Videos

While online you can also check the progress you've made learning the topic and course content by viewing your grades, test scores, and assignment status.

SAVVAS realize™

Topic 15 Quick Study Guide

LESSON SUMMARIES

Use these Lesson Summaries, and the longer versions available online, to review the key ideas for each lesson in this Topic.

Lesson 1: The Beginning of the Cold War

After the defeat of Nazi Germany, the Soviet Union set up communist governments in Eastern Europe. The U.S. resisted Soviet power through a policy of containment and by providing economic aid to Europe. Stalin's blockade of West Berlin ended with a humanitarian victory for the West.

Lesson 2: The Korean War

In 1950, a year after the communist Mao Zedong took control of China, troops from communist North Korea invaded South Korea. American and United Nations forces won back South Korea and battled North Korea until a cease-fire was declared in 1953.

Lesson 3: The Cold War Intensifies

An arms race between the United States and the Soviet Union began in 1949. During the 1950s, a series of world crises threatened to bring the superpowers into direct confrontation. As tensions grew, President Eisenhower declared that the U.S. would use force to help any nation threatened by communism.

Lesson 4: Cold War Fears at Home

During the Red Scare of the late 1940s, an anti-communist panic spread in the United States. 3000 federal employees lost their jobs, and a blacklist destroyed the careers of some entertainers. Spy trials took place in the early 1950s while Senator McCarthy led a campaign of accusations against suspected communists.

Lesson 5: Postwar Prosperity

After World War II, the GI Bill of Rights helped veterans start careers. Veterans also started families and a baby boom followed. The nation was now in the longest period of economic growth in its history. Populations shifted, the service sector grew, and President Eisenhower helped create the highway system.

Lesson 6: Mass Culture in the 1950s

American culture was transformed in the 1950s, as millions moved to the suburbs. Family income rose as did consumer spending. Women were encouraged to stay at home rather than start careers. Televisions became widely available, and educational opportunities expanded.

Lesson 7: Social Issues of the 1950s

Discontent with postwar American suburban life soon emerged among artists, writers, and the young. Many began calling attention to urban slums, rural poverty, and racial discrimination. A youth culture of revolt found expression in the new musical genre of rock-and-roll.

QUEST! FINDINGS

Write Your McCarthyism Essay Refer to your responses to the Quest Connections to help you write your essay. Then share it with the class. Use the rubric and other Quest resources online to guide your work.

GO ONLINE to access lesson summaries

VISUAL REVIEW

Use these graphics to review some of the key terms, people, and ideas from this Topic.

The Postwar Boom

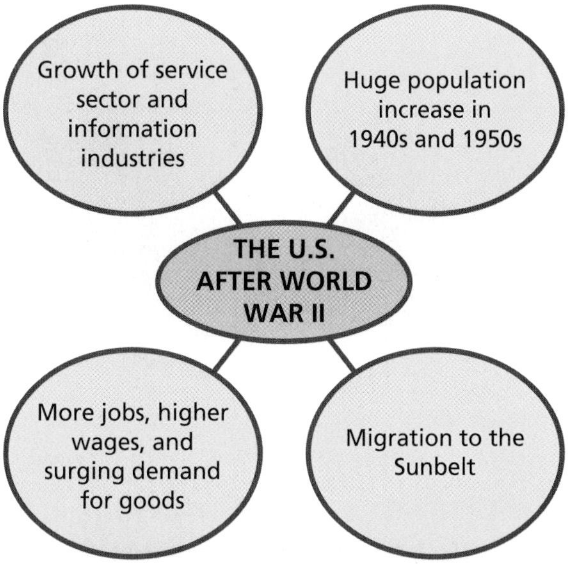

Early Cold War Flashpoints

FLASHPOINT	ACTION AND REACTION
Poland	• U.S. urges democratic elections. • USSR installs communist government.
Turkey	• USSR demands territory from Turkey; communist rebels threaten Greece. • U.S. adopts Truman Doctrine to aid Turkey, Greece, and other states resisting communism
Berlin	• USSR blockades West Berlin. • U.S. and Britain airlift supplies to the city.
Korea	• North Korea invades South Korea. • U.S. and UN enter war on South Korean side. • China enters war on North Korean side.
Europe	• NATO is formed for mutual defense. • USSR forms Warsaw Pact for mutual defense.

Cold War Alliances, 1955

NATO	WARSAW PACT
Belgium, Netherlands, Canada, Norway, Denmark, Portugal, France, Turkey, Greece, United Kingdom, Iceland, United States, Italy, West Germany, Luxembourg	Albania, Bulgaria, Czechoslovakia, East Germany, Hungary, Poland, Romania, Soviet Union

The Cold War at Home

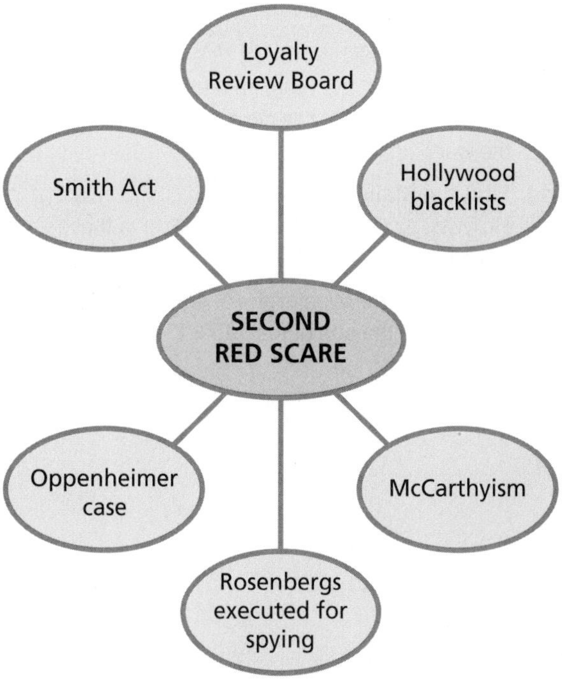

Topic 15 Assessment

KEY TERMS, PEOPLE, AND IDEAS

1. What political developments led to the beginning of the **Cold War**?
2. How did the **Marshall Plan** serve both economic and foreign policy goals?
3. Why were **NATO** and the **Warsaw Pact** formed?
4. How did the **Truman Doctrine** shape U.S. foreign policy?
5. How did the U.S. policy of containment shape the Korean War?
6. How did President Eisenhower and **John Foster Dulles** change the tone of the arms race?
7. Why was the postwar United States described as a postindustrial society?
8. How did the **Interstate Highway Act** transform American communities?
9. How did the **baby boom** affect the U.S. economy?

CRITICAL THINKING

10. **Determine Central Ideas** (a) Why was the Berlin airlift considered to be a moral victory for the West? (b) How was the airlift related to the policy of containment?
11. **Identify Cause and Effect** What factors contributed to American postwar prosperity?
12. **Draw Inferences** (a) How did postwar prosperity increase social divisions? (b) How did this prosperity increase ethnic divisions?
13. **Make Generalizations** (a) How did women's roles change in the years immediately following World War II? (b) How did this contrast with their roles during the war?
14. **Find the Main Idea** (a) Why did HUAC investigate Hollywood? (b) What were the effects of these investigations on filmmaking and scriptwriting?
15. **Cite Evidence** What signs of rebellion and discontent emerged in the arts of the 1950s?
16. **Analyze Maps** Look at the map below. (a) Where is the 38th parallel located relative to the Korean peninsula? (b) How is China's location important relative to North Korea and the Korean War?

North Korea and South Korea, 1950

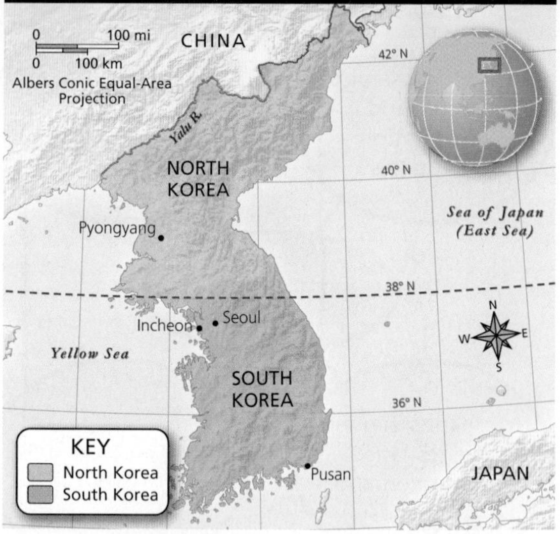

17. **Writing Activity: Write an Argument** Use your knowledge of foreign policy events and the excerpt below from George Kennan to agree or disagree with Kennan's advice. Write an essay that makes precise claims and organizes your argument logically. Remember to use credible evidence to back up your argument.

> We are going to continue for a long time to find the Russians difficult to deal with. It does not mean that they should be considered as embarked upon a do-or-die program to overthrow our society by a given date. . . . In these circumstances, it is clear that the main element of any United States policy toward the Soviet Union must be that of long-term, patient but firm and vigilant containment of Russian expansive tendencies.
>
> —*George Kennan, "The Sources of Soviet Conduct"*

18. **Connections to Today** The baby boom generation of the 1950s shared in a national mass culture based on consumerism, economic growth, and other mutual experiences and values. What shared experiences and values define your generation?

DOCUMENT-BASED QUESTIONS

The Cold War helped create a Red Scare. Read the documents below, then answer the questions that follow.

DOCUMENT A

This excerpt is from a famous speech by Senator Joseph McCarthy.

> In my opinion the State Department, which is one of the most important government departments, is thoroughly infested with communists. I have in my hand 57 cases of individuals who would appear to be either card-carrying members or certainly loyal to the Communist Party, but who nevertheless are still helping to shape our foreign policy. One thing to remember in discussing the communists in our government is that we are not dealing with spies who get 30 pieces of silver to steal the blueprints of new weapons. We are dealing with a far more sinister type of activity because it permits the enemy to guide and shape our policy.
>
> —*Senator Joseph McCarthy, February 1950*

DOCUMENT B

This cover is from a propaganda comic book published in 1947.

DOCUMENT C

This excerpt is from a secondary source on Joseph McCarthy.

> [He] was in many ways the most gifted demagogue ever bred on these shores. No bolder seditionist ever moved among us—nor any politician with a surer, swifter access to the dark places of the American mind. The major phase of McCarthy's career was mercifully short. It began in 1950, three years after he had taken his seat in the Senate, where he had seemed a dim and inconsiderable figure. . . . If he was anything at all in the realm of ideas, principles, doctrines, he was a species of nihilist; he was an essentially destructive force, a revolutionist without any revolutionary vision, a rebel without a cause.
>
> —*Richard H. Rovere,* Senator Joe McCarthy

DOCUMENT D

This excerpt is from a secondary source.

> Emotions ran very, very high about how to conduct the Cold War, about how to deal with the threat of Stalinism, both abroad but also at home. You had American soldiers dying in Korea. The Korean War formed the vivid backdrop for all of McCarthy's career. There was a bitter, bitter partisan battle in which people were prepared to say almost anything to blacken the reputations and to smear their political opponents. McCarthy did it, and his Republican allies did it. You also have to remember that the Democrats were quite prepared to do the same thing, and often did against McCarthy, calling him a Nazi sympathizer, talking about his investigations as posing a threat to American democracy and so on, charges which really don't, in the light of historical evidence and historical perspective, hold any kind of water.
>
> —*Arthur Herman,* The Rise and Fall of Joseph McCarthy

19. In Document A, McCarthy's accusation is that
- **A.** foreign spies are stealing documents.
- **B.** communists are shaping government policy.
- **C.** communists are working in state governments.
- **D.** the military is full of communist sympathizers.

20. Analyze Images How do you think images like the one in Document B prepared the ground for the Red Scare?

21. In Document C, the author depicts McCarthy as
- **A.** bold and perceptive.
- **B.** unworthy of notice.
- **C.** sinister and powerful.
- **D.** principled and honorable.

22. In Document D, the historian's view of McCarthy is that
- **A.** his tactics posed no threat to democracy.
- **B.** he nearly destroyed democracy in the 1950s.
- **C.** his campaign was completely unjustified.
- **D.** he was out of touch with world events.

23. Writing Task Write a paragraph explaining what effects the Red Scare had on domestic policy and politics. Use the sources as well as additional information you have learned.

GO ONLINE to access more practice

Topic 16

Civil Rights and Reform in the 1960s (1945–1968)

ESSENTIAL QUESTION How can we ensure equality for all?

project
Imagine

GO ONLINE to access immersive experiences designed to help you feel the drama of the civil rights movement through rich primary sources. Also access the eText, videos, Biographies, and other online resources.

Dr. Martin Luther King, Jr. during the March on Washington in 1963.

Connections to Today

The Movement for Black Lives was founded in 2016 in response to violence against African Americans. The Movement is actually a loose coalition of several groups, including Black Lives Matter. Its platform echoes arguments made by civil rights and Black Power activists of the 1960s. Like the Black Power movement, it, too, has generated controversy. While its opponents see only rage, anger, and anti-police sentiments, its supporters consider it to be an important civil rights movement.

In this topic, you'll explore how African Americans fought for their civil rights in the 1960s. What strategies did they use to gain civil rights?

NBC LEARN

Learn more about how teenager Minnijean Brown-Trickey helped advance the cause of civil rights.

BOUNCE to Activate My Story Video

Topic 16 Overview

In this Topic, you'll learn about the civil rights movement and the reforms of the 1960s. Look at the lesson outline and explore the timeline. As you study this Topic, you'll complete the Quest Inquiry.

LESSON OUTLINE

16.1 The Civil Rights Movement Strengthens

16.2 The Movement Surges Forward

16.3 Successes and Setbacks

16.4 Kennedy's Reforms

16.5 Reform Under Johnson

Key Events of Civil Rights and Reform

1945 | 1955 | 1965

1948 President Truman desegregates the military

1954 *Brown v. Board of Education*

1957 Desegregation of Central High in Little Rock, Arkansas

1962 James Meredith enrolls at the University of Mississippi

1963 March on Washington

1964 Civil Rights Act is passed

1968 Dr. Martin Luther King is assassinated

QUEST! INQUIRY

Creating an Interactive Timeline on Civil Rights

How much have the lives of African Americans changed since the Civil Rights movement of the 1960s? Has the nation achieved the promise of full equality for its people? In this Quest you'll explore these questions and then create a timeline that displays your findings.

STEP 1

With your team, discuss questions you have about how the lives of African Americans have changed and what you might show on your timeline.

STEP 2

Identify 10 events of the civil rights movement and choose charts, maps, and other graphics that might appear on your timeline

STEP 3

Create the timeline and chart your progress in the Project Tracker. Publish your timeline on the web.

STEP 4

Present your timeline to a live audience and explain your conclusions. Allow your audience to react and discuss their observations. Reflect on what you have learned.

GO ONLINE to access complete Quest materials

16.1

GO ONLINE to Project Imagine: Witness Milestones in the Civil Rights Movement for a firsthand view of key moments in the movement's history.

BOUNCE to Activate Flipped Video

Objectives

Describe efforts to end segregation in the 1940s and 1950s.

Explain the importance of the landmark case of *Brown* v. *Board of Education.*

Describe the controversy over school desegregation in Little Rock, Arkansas.

Discuss the Montgomery bus boycott and its impact.

Key Terms

de jure segregation
de facto segregation
Thurgood Marshall
Earl Warren
Orval Faubus
Civil Rights Act of 1957
Rosa Parks
Martin Luther King, Jr.

The Civil Rights Movement Strengthens

The postwar period brought prosperity to many, but most African Americans were still treated as second-class citizens. The civil rights movement, a broad and diverse effort to attain racial equality, challenged the nation to live up to its ideal that all are created equal. The movement also demonstrated that ordinary men and women could perform extraordinary acts of courage and sacrifice to achieve social justice, a lesson that continues to inspire people around the world today.

Segregation Limits Equality

African Americans had a long history of fighting for their rights. After World War II, the struggle intensified, as African Americans grew increasingly dissatisfied with their second-class status.

Separate but Not Equal In the South, Jim Crow laws enforced strict separation of the races. Segregation that is imposed by law is known as **de jure segregation**. In 1896, in *Plessy* v. *Ferguson*, the Supreme Court had ruled that such segregation was constitutional as long as the facilities for Blacks and whites were "separate but equal." But this was seldom the case. The facilities for African Americans were rarely, if ever, equal.

In the South and elsewhere, segregation extended to most areas of public life. Officials enforced segregation of schools, hospitals, transportation, restaurants, cemeteries, and beaches. One city even forbade Blacks and whites from playing checkers together.

GO ONLINE to access your digital course

Discrimination Throughout the Country In the North, too, African Americans faced segregation and discrimination. Even where there were no explicit laws, **de facto segregation**, or segregation by unwritten custom or tradition, was a fact of life. African Americans in the North were denied housing in many neighborhoods. They faced discrimination in employment and often could get only low-paying jobs.

Jim Crow laws and more subtle forms of discrimination had a widespread and severe impact on African Americans. Black Americans occupied the bottom rungs of the economic ladder. Compared to white Americans, they had significantly higher rates of poverty and illiteracy, as well as lower rates of homeownership and life expectancy. Although African Americans living in the North could vote, most who lived in the South could not. Very few African Americans held public office.

In the West and Southwest, Asian Americans and Mexican Americans, too, faced de facto segregation and, in some cases, legal restrictions.

>> Segregated drinking fountains in the South were a stark reminder that the ideals of equality described in the Declaration of Independence had yet to be attained.

BOUNCE to Activate Gallery

Civil Rights Advance Slowly in the 1940s In many ways, World War II set the stage for the rise of the modern civil rights movement. President Roosevelt banned discrimination in defense industries in 1941. Gunnar Myrdal's publication in 1944 of *An American Dilemma* brought the issue of American prejudice to the forefront of public consciousness. Lastly, after risking their lives defending freedom abroad, African Americans were unwilling to accept discrimination at home.

In the 1940s, new organizations arose to try to bring an end to racial injustice and expand participation in the democratic process. James Farmer and several others founded the Congress of Racial Equality (CORE) with the goal of ending discriminatory policies and improving relations between races. Its members were deeply influenced by the teachings of Henry David Thoreau and Mohandas Gandhi about the use of nonviolent protest to confront injustice. They became convinced that African Americans could apply similar nonviolent methods to gain civil rights. CORE organized nonviolent protests such as sit-ins against segregation in public facilities in Chicago, Detroit, Denver, and other northern cities.

Success was limited, but one highly visible break in the wall of segregation did take place in 1947. Jackie Robinson joined the Brooklyn Dodgers, becoming the first African American to play major league baseball. Robinson braved death threats and rough treatment, but throughout his career he won the hearts of millions and paved the way for integration of other sports.

>> On February 26, 1946, racial tensions led to mass arrests of African Americans in Columbia, Tennessee. A young attorney named Thurgood Marshall helped with their legal defense.

BOUNCE to Activate Gallery

Nevertheless, African Americans continued to face discrimination and felt that racial equality was long overdue. However, the vast majority of white Americans took the opposite view. Racial violence erupted in the South, sometimes against African American veterans who were just trying to register to vote.

In the wake of this violence, President Truman appointed a Committee on Civil Rights to investigate race relations. In its report, the committee recommended a number of measures to ensure equal opportunity for all Americans, including an antilynching law and federal protection of voting rights. Unfortunately, Truman was unable to win congressional support for these initiatives. However, in 1948, he did use his executive power to order the desegregation of the military. Integration was a slow process, but over time, the U.S. armed forces would become one of the most integrated institutions in the United States.

☑ **IDENTIFY SUPPORTING DETAILS** What tactics did some civil rights organizations use during the 1940s?

A Landmark Supreme Court Decision

Although the civil rights movement had made some gains in the 1940s, it stalled in the early 1950s. One of its greatest disappointments was the NAACP's failure, after decades of lobbying Congress, to make the lynching of African Americans a federal crime. The NAACP decided to turn to litigation in the federal courts to attain its political goals.

The NAACP Turns to Litigation in the Courts

Thurgood Marshall was a lawyer for the NAACP. In 1950, the NAACP won a number of key court cases. In *Sweatt* v. *Painter,* the Supreme Court ruled that the state of Texas had violated the Fourteenth Amendment by establishing a separate, but unequal, all-Black law school. Similarly, in the *cases of Sipuel* v. *Board of Regents of the University of Oklahoma* and *McLaurin* v. *Oklahoma State Regents*, the Court ruled that the state of Oklahoma had violated Ada Lois Sipuel Fisher's and George McLaurin's constitutional rights. Even though Sipeul Fisher had been admitted to the University of Oklahoma College of Law and McLaurin had been admitted to the graduate school of the University of Oklahoma, they were denied equal access to the library, dining hall, and classrooms. According to the Supreme Court, a truly equal education involved more than simply admitting African Americans to previously all-white universities.

The Supreme Court Issues a Broad Decision

Not long after it won these cases, the NAACP mounted a much broader challenge to segregated public education at all grade levels. This challenge became known as *Brown* v. *Board of Education*. In the *Sweatt, Sipuel,* and *McLaurin* cases, the NAACP

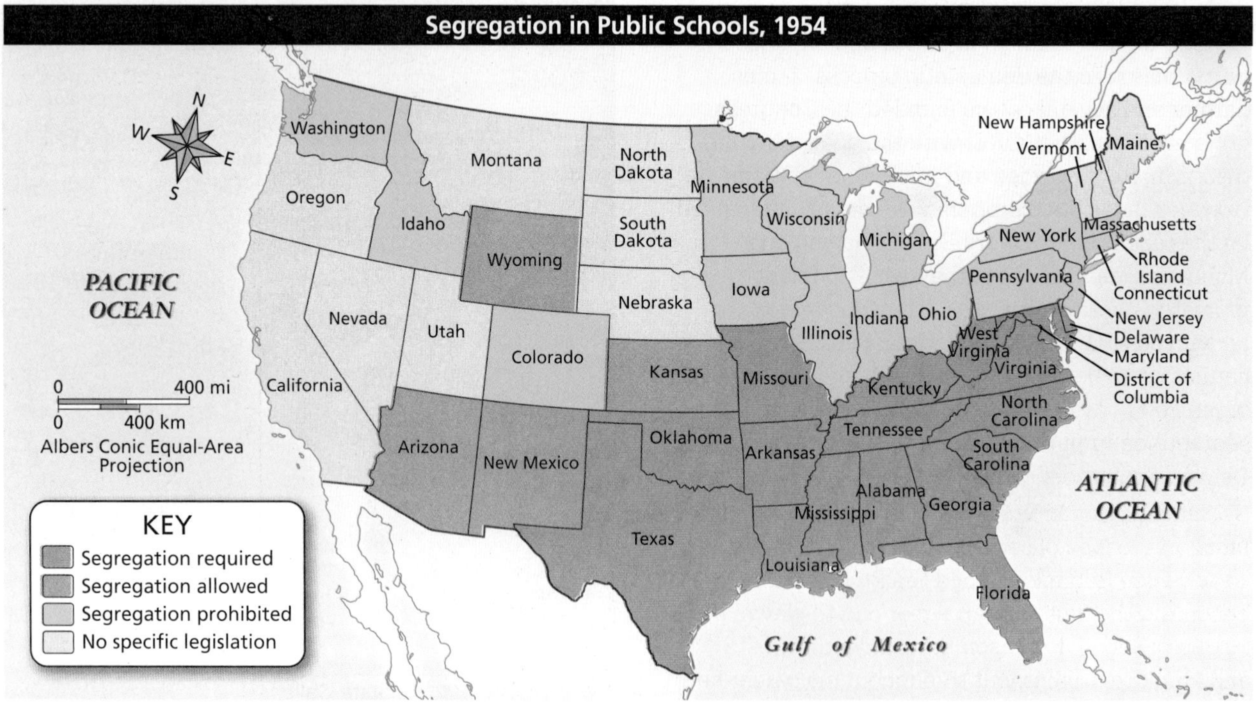

>> In 1954, each state had its own laws governing segregation in public schools.
Analyze Maps What states required segregation in 1954?

EFFECTS OF BROWN v. BOARD OF EDUCATION

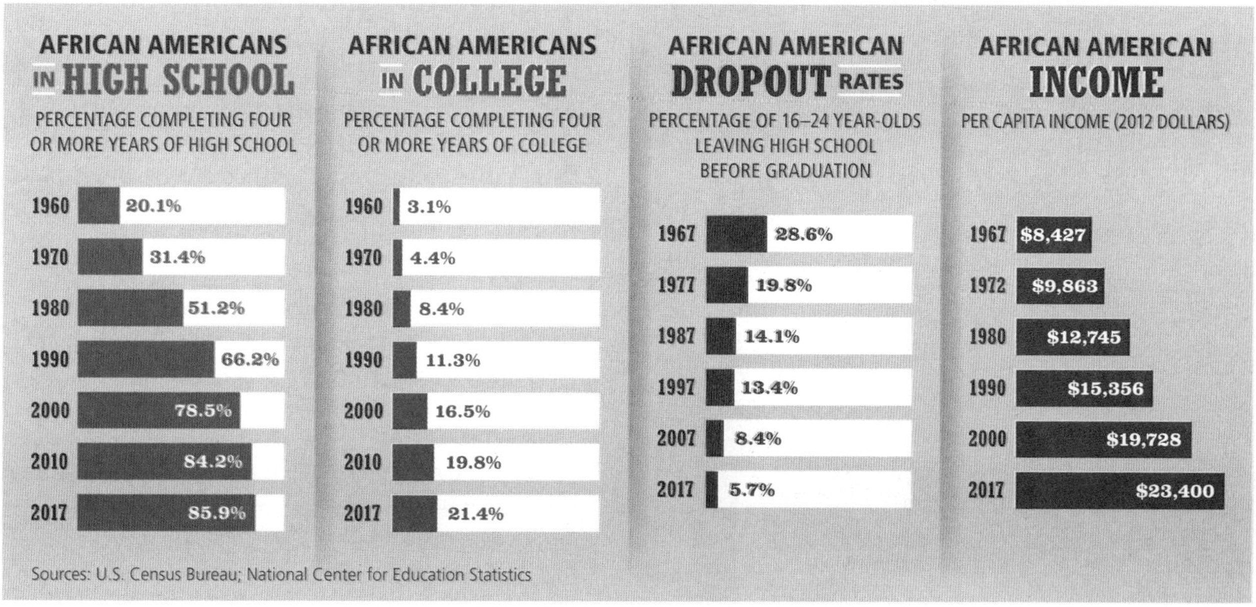

>> In what ways are these graphs related? **Analyze Data** Cite evidence to support the claim that school desegregation improved the lives of minorities living in the United States.

asserted that Texas and Oklahoma had failed to provide equal educational experiences. In the *Brown* case, however, the NAACP challenged the "separate but equal" principle itself, which had been established in the 1896 *Plessy* v. *Ferguson* case.

The Supreme Court agreed with the NAACP's argument that segregated public education violated the U.S. Constitution. All nine of the Court's Justices supported the *Brown* decision, which was written by newly appointed Chief Justice **Earl Warren**. "Does segregation of children in public schools solely on the basis of race . . . deprive the children of the minority group equal education opportunities?" Warren asked in his decision. "We believe that it does." The Chief Justice and the Court declared, "in the field of public education the doctrine of 'separate but equal' has no place."

In the same month as the *Brown* decision, the Supreme Court decided another civil rights case, this time involving Mexican Americans. In *Hernandez* v. *Texas*, the Court ended the exclusion of Mexican Americans from trial juries. The *Hernandez* decision was the first Supreme Court ruling against discrimination targeting a group other than African Americans.

The Public Response The *Brown* decision was one of the most significant and controversial in American history. Because public education touched so many Americans, it had a much greater impact than cases involving only professional and graduate schools. Moreover, by overturning the principle of "separate but equal," the Court lent its support to the views of many civil rights advocates that all forms of segregation are wrong.

In a separate ruling, known as *Brown II*, the Court called for the implementation of its decision "with all deliberate speed" across the nation. However, most white southerners had no intention of desegregating their schools without a fight. In 1956, about 100 southern members of Congress endorsed "The Southern Manifesto." They pledged to oppose the *Brown* ruling through all "lawful means," on the grounds that the Court had misinterpreted the Constitution.

More ominously, the Ku Klux Klan, a white supremacist hate group, staged a revival. Many prominent white southerners and businessmen organized "White Citizens Councils" that declared that the South would not be integrated. The Citizens Councils imposed economic and political pressure against those who favored compliance with the Supreme Court's decision.

✓ **CHECK UNDERSTANDING** How did earlier legal decisions differ from *Brown* v. *Board of Education*?

>> Elizabeth Eckford, one of nine students chosen to integrate Little Rock High School in Little Rock, Arkansas, walked past an angry crowd as officers from the National Guard stood by.

>> President Eisenhower ordered troops from the National Guard to protect African American students as they entered Little Rock High School in Little Rock, Arkansas.

Conflict Between Federal and State Power

Historically, education had been a state matter. States and local school boards ran the schools, and the federal government had little involvement. Local and state officials resisted the *Brown* decision's order to desegregate, and clashes with the federal government resulted. The most famous battle took place in 1957 in Little Rock, Arkansas.

Soldiers Arrive at a High School in Little Rock

The Little Rock school board had established a plan to gradually desegregate its schools, beginning with Central High School. Nine young African American students were chosen from many who volunteered to enroll. But Arkansas Governor **Orval Faubus** announced his opposition to integration and called out the Arkansas state National Guard. When the nine students arrived at Central High, the soldiers blocked their way.

One of the nine, Elizabeth Eckford, has described the scene. An angry white mob began to approach her, with some screaming, "Lynch her! Lynch her!" Eckford sought out a friendly face, someone who might help. "I looked into the face of an old woman and it seemed a kind face," she recalled, "but when I looked at her again she spat on me." Fortunately, another white woman whisked Eckford away on a public bus before the mob could have its way. None of the Little Rock Nine gained entrance to the school that day.

Up until the Little Rock crisis, President Eisenhower had provided little leadership on the civil rights front. Following the *Brown* decision, he did not urge the nation to rapidly desegregate its schools. Privately, he expressed his misgivings about the ruling. But when Governor Faubus resisted the will of the federal courts, Eisenhower realized he had to act. He sent federal troops to Little Rock to protect the students and to enforce the Court's decision. Eisenhower explained this action in a nationally televised address:

> It is important that the reasons for my action be understood by all our citizens. . . . A foundation of our American way of life is our national respect for law. . . .
>
> If resistance to the federal court orders ceases at once, the further presence of federal troops will be unnecessary and the City of Little

Rock will return to its normal habits of peace and order and a blot upon the fair name and high honor of our nation in the world will be removed.

—President Dwight D. Eisenhower, "Address on Little Rock," 1957

For the entire school year, federal troops stayed in Little Rock, escorting the nine students to and from Central High and guarding them on the school grounds. On the last day of class, Ernest Green, the one senior of the nine, became the first African American to graduate from Central High School. The showdown demonstrated that the President would not tolerate open defiance of the law. Still, most southern states found ways to resist full compliance with the Court's decision. Many years would pass before Black and white children went to school together.

Political Lobbying Leads to a New Civil Rights Act While organizations like CORE continued to nonviolently protest discrimination in public places in the North, the political lobbying efforts of civil rights forces yielded a small victory when Congress voted to pass the **Civil Rights Act of 1957**. President Eisenhower signed the bill into law, which established the United States Civil Rights Commission and gave it the power to investigate violations of civil rights. It empowered the U.S. Attorney General to bring lawsuits to address civil rights violations. The law also gave the Attorney General greater power to protect the voting rights of African Americans. But overall, it lacked teeth. CORE leader Bayard Rustin noted, however, that it had symbolic importance as the first civil rights law passed by Congress since Reconstruction.

☑ **IDENTIFY MAIN IDEAS** How did the crisis in Little Rock spark a conflict between state and federal government?

The Montgomery Bus Boycott

In addition to legal efforts during this era, some civil rights activists took direct action to end segregation. On December 1, 1955, **Rosa Parks** did just that. She boarded a bus in Montgomery, Alabama, and sat down in an empty seat. Several stops later, the bus driver requested that she give up her seat to a white passenger. Montgomery law required African American passengers to give up their seats to whites. After Rosa Parks refused to obey the law, she was arrested. "The [policemen] asked if the driver had asked me to stand up, and I said yes, and they wanted to know why I didn't," Parks later recalled. "I told them I didn't think I should have to stand up. After I had paid my fare and occupied a seat, I didn't think I should have to give it up."

>> For years, public buses in many states segregated riders along racial lines.

Rosa Parks's Act Transforms a Movement
Parks's action set in motion a chain of events that transformed the civil rights movement. Over the next few days, a core of civil rights activists led by the Women's Political Council in Montgomery organized a one-day bus boycott. They called upon the Black community to refuse to ride the buses as a way to express their opposition to Parks's arrest, in particular, and segregation, in general. Meanwhile, during the Montgomery bus boycott, the NAACP began preparing a legal challenge.

For a long while, many people thought that Parks had refused to give up her seat simply because she was tired after a long day of work. In reality, Parks had a record of fighting for civil rights. She had been active in the Montgomery chapter of the NAACP for years. This does not mean that she set out to get arrested and spark a movement. However, her choice to not give up her seat was an effective form of nonviolent protest and an influential moment in the civil rights movement's struggle for the equality.

>> Dr. Martin Luther King, Jr., became known for his powerful speeches calling for desegregation and racial equality.

BOUNCE to Activate Gallery

Martin Luther King Calls for Nonviolent Protest On the evening following the boycott, the Montgomery Improvement Association (MIA), which was made up of religious and community leaders, held a meeting. Dr. **Martin Luther King, Jr.**, a Baptist minister, addressed the group. Though he had little time to prepare, King delivered an inspirational speech that brought the audience to its feet. Noting that African Americans were tired of segregation and oppression, King declared that there was no alternative but to protest. However, he called for the protest to be nonviolent. He urged them not to become resentful, which would lead to hatred toward whites, but rather to follow Christian doctrine and love them.

After King spoke, the MIA vowed to continue the boycott and chose King as its leader. For more than a year, African Americans in Montgomery maintained their boycott of the buses. They did so despite economic pressures from their employers and threats of violence by the Ku Klux Klan. King himself survived a bombing of his house. Fortunately, his wife and baby daughter were not home at the time.

Finally, in 1956, the Supreme Court ruled that the Montgomery city law that segregated buses was unconstitutional. After more than a year, the MIA ended its boycott, and African Americans began to ride the buses again.

Ministers Inspire the Movement The bus boycott represented a tremendous victory for African Americans in Montgomery and across the nation. The boycott revealed the power that African Americans could have if they joined together. The protest also elevated King and his philosophy of nonviolence into a prominent position within the civil rights movement.

After the boycott, King and another Montgomery minister, Ralph Abernathy, established the Southern Christian Leadership Conference (SCLC) to continue the struggle for civil rights. Made up largely of southern African American ministers, the SCLC advocated nonviolent resistance to fight injustice. The SCLC went on to organize a series of protests, including a Prayer Pilgrimage in Washington, D.C., in 1957, which helped convince Congress to pass civil rights legislation. Still, discrimination and segregation remained widespread.

CHECK UNDERSTANDING Why did the Montgomery Improvement Association ask African Americans to boycott Montgomery's bus system?

ASSESSMENT

1. **Generate Explanations** Explain how events during World War II set the stage for the rise of the modern civil rights movement.
2. **Compare Points of View** Explain how President Eisenhower's position on civil rights changed after Governor Orval Faubus brought the Arkansas National Guard to Little Rock.
3. **Summarize** the effect that Dr. Martin Luther King, Jr. had on the Montgomery bus boycott.
4. **Contrast** Explain how the *Brown* v. *Board of Education* case differed from previous Supreme Court cases.
5. **Distinguish** between de jure segregation and de facto segregation.
6. **Connections to Today** African Americans used some very effective methods to protest against inequality, including broadcasts on radio and television and newspaper editorials. How do you think social media and technology might have changed the way minorities fight against inequality today?

GO ONLINE to access these biographies: Rosa Parks, Martin Luther King, Jr.

School Desegregation in Little Rock, Arkansas

>>After the 1954 *Brown* ruling, the first school to be integrated was Little Rock High School in Little Rock, Arkansas, in 1957. Federal troops escort the nine African American students to the high school.

The 1896 Supreme Court ruling in *Plessy* v. *Ferguson* stated that separate facilities for whites and African Americans did not violate the Constitution as long as those facilities were equal. In the South, schools, restaurants, and all public places were segregated by race, but in reality, the facilities for African Americans were always inferior to those of whites.

In Primary Source 1, you will read an excerpt from the 1954 Supreme Court case *Brown* v. *Board of Education*, which ordered schools to desegregate. Primary Source 2 is a letter Daisy Bates, a leader in Arkansas' NAACP, wrote to Roy Wilkins, an NAACP official, describing how the "Little Rock Nine" were treated by the school and white classmates.

As you read, look for the difference between the Court ruling and the application of that ruling.

Primary Source 1

From *Brown* v. *Board of Education* (1954)

Today, education is perhaps the most important function of state and local governments. Compulsory [mandatory] school attendance laws and the great expenditures [costs] for education both demonstrate our recognition of the importance of education to our democratic society. It is required in the performance of our most basic public responsibilities, even service in the armed forces. It is the very foundation of good citizenship. Today it is a principal instrument in awakening the child to cultural values, in preparing him for later professional training, and in helping him to adjust normally to his environment. In these days, it is doubtful that any child may reasonably be expected to succeed in life if he is denied the opportunity of an education. Such an opportunity, where the state has undertaken to provide it, is a right which must be made available to all on equal terms.

DRAW CONCLUSIONS Explain why the justices believe an education is important. Which of the Court's reasons do you consider most important? Explain.

We come then to the question presented: does segregation of children in public schools solely on the basis of race, even though the physical facilities and other "tangible" [concrete, real] factors may be equal, deprive the children of the minority group of equal educational opportunities? We believe that it does. . . .

IDENTIFY THE CENTRAL IDEA What is the Court's opinion of segregation in education?

To separate [children] from others of similar age and qualifications solely because of their race generates a feeling of inferiority as to their status in the community that may affect their hearts and minds in a way unlikely ever to be undone. . . .
We conclude that, in the field of public education, the doctrine of "separate but equal" has no place. Separate educational facilities are inherently [naturally] unequal. Therefore, we hold that the plaintiffs [those who sued in court] and others similarly situated for whom the actions have been brought are, by reason of the segregation complained of, deprived of the equal protection of the laws guaranteed by the Fourteenth Amendment....

ANALYZE WORD CHOICES Why does the Court refer to "hearts and minds"? What do the justices mean by these terms?

Primary Source 2

From Daisy Bates' Letter to Roy Wilkins, December 17, 1957

Dear Mr. Wilkins,

Conditions are yet pretty rough in the school for the children. Last week Minnie Jean's mother, Mrs. W.B. Brown, asked me to go over to the school with her for a conference with the principal. . . . Subject of Conference: "Firmer disciplinary measures, and the removal of Minnie Jean from the glee club's Christmas Program." The principal had informed Minnie Jean in withdrawing her from the program that "When it is definitely decided that Negroes will go to school here with the whites, and the troops are removed, then you will be able to participate in all activities." We strongly challenged this statement, which he denied making in that fashion.

CITE EVIDENCE What reason did the principal give for taking Minnie Jean out of the Christmas Program? How did Bates react to that reasoning?

We also pointed out that the treatment of the children had been getting steadily worse for the last two weeks in the form of kicking, spitting, and general abuse. As a result of our visit, stronger measures are being taken against the white students who are guilty of committing these offenses. For instance, a boy who had been suspended for two weeks, flunked both six-weeks tests, and on his return to school, the first day he knocked Gloria Ray into her locker. As a result of our visit, he was given an indefinite suspension. . . .

DESCRIBE How did the school discipline one white student for his behavior?

ASSESSMENT

1. **Compare and Contrast** Based on the primary sources and your reading of the text, how did the Supreme Court's interpretation of the Constitution differ between *Brown* v. *Board of Education* (1954) and *Plessy* v. *Ferguson* (1896)?
2. **Summarize** How does Daisy Bates describe the treatment toward the African American students in Little Rock High School by the administration? By the white students?
3. **Identify Effects** What effects do you think the Supreme Court ruling in *Brown* v. *Board of Education* had on the nation?
4. **Drawing Conclusions** How do these primary source excerpts help you understand how Supreme Court rulings are applied?
5. **Empathy** How do you think Minnie Jean felt about the principal's decision to remove her from the glee club's Christmas Program?

GO ONLINE to access primary sources

16.2

GO ONLINE to Project Imagine: Travel to Civil Rights Landmarks to see the sites of two historic protests for change.

The Movement Surges Forward

Despite the *Brown* decision and other civil rights victories, little changed in the everyday lives of most African Americans. Nonetheless, activists continued to struggle for civil rights. In the early 1960s, the movement experienced a groundswell of support. This surge produced a dramatic shift in race relations, led to the passage of landmark civil rights legislation in 1964, and set the stage for future reforms.

BOUNCE to Activate Flipped Video

Objectives

Describe the sit-ins, freedom rides, and the actions of James Meredith in the early 1960s.

Explain how the protests at Birmingham and the March on Washington were linked to the Civil Rights Act of 1964.

Describe how the Civil Rights Act of 1964 addressed minority rights in the United States.

Key Terms

sit-in
Student Nonviolent Coordinating Committee
"freedom ride"
James Meredith
Medgar Evers
George Wallace
March on Washington
filibuster
Civil Rights Act of 1964

Student Activists Promote Civil Rights

After the *Brown* decision, many Black youths expected that their schools would integrate quickly and that other racial reforms would follow. Change was not quick to come, however. Disappointed by the lack of progress, young African Americans began to challenge segregation with new vigor and determination.

Nonviolent Protests Challenge Segregation On February 1, 1960, four African American college students ordered doughnuts and coffee at a Woolworth's lunch counter in Greensboro, North Carolina. As they expected, the white waitress refused to serve them. In the South, nearly all restaurants that served whites refused to serve Blacks. To protest this discrimination, the four students sat down on the stools at the lunch counter, where they stayed until closing time.

Word of the Greensboro **sit-in** spread rapidly, sparking a wave of similar protests across the nation. In Oklahoma City, Oklahoma, for instance, students led by Clara Shepard Luper staged sit-ins and, later, marches to protest racial inequality.

GO ONLINE to access your digital course

Elsewhere, protesters held "wade-ins" at public beaches and "read-ins" at public libraries, refusing to leave beaches or libraries reserved for whites only. African Americans boycotted buses. Groups of demonstrators knelt in prayer. Other activists carried picket signs in demonstrations and wrote letters to newspapers and government officials to express their support of the protests in the South.

Political Organizations Encourage Nonviolent Protest The sit-ins marked the birth of a new activism, especially among young African Americans. To build on the momentum they had gained, about 175 students from 30 states met at Shaw University, in Raleigh, North Carolina. There, on Easter weekend in 1960, they listened to James Lawson deliver an inspiring address:

> We who are demonstrators are trying to raise what we call the 'moral issue.' That is, we are pointing to the viciousness of racial segregation and prejudice and calling it evil or sin. . . . [We are also] asserting, 'get moving.' The pace of change is too slow. At this rate it will be another generation before the major forms of segregation disappear. . . . Most of us will be grandparents before we can live normal human lives.
>
> —James Lawson, "From a Lunch Counter Stool," 1960

>> In 1960, students at the University of Michigan joined the call for civil rights and equality for all Americans.

BOUNCE to Activate Gallery

Ella Baker, a veteran of the struggle for civil rights, had organized the meeting. The granddaughter of enslaved African Americans, Baker had been active in the National Association for the Advancement of Colored People (NAACP) and the Southern Christian Leadership Conference (SCLC). She helped the young activists to establish a new civil rights organization, the **Student Nonviolent Coordinating Committee**, or SNCC. Its goal was to create a grass-roots movement that involved all classes of African Americans in the struggle to defeat white racism and to obtain equality.

RECALL How did students and other young people energize the civil rights movement in the 1960s?

Freedom Rides Begin Throughout the South

The next battleground was interstate transportation. Political activists targeted this industry because they knew that travel between states was subject to federal rather than state regulation. In fact, the Supreme Court had recently ruled in *Boynton* v. *Virginia* (1960) that segregation on interstate buses and in waiting rooms was illegal. Civil rights activists were now going to test the federal government's willingness to enforce the law.

Freedom Riders Risk Physical Harm In the spring of 1961, CORE staged a **"freedom ride"** through the Deep South. Riders set off in two separate buses from Washington, D.C., bound for New Orleans. En route, they defied segregationist codes. African Americans sat in the front of the bus and used "white" restrooms in bus stations.

In Alabama, the trip took a dangerous turn. After departing from Anniston, segregationists firebombed one of the buses. When the second bus arrived in Birmingham, a white mob attacked the riders.

The President Intervenes

The President Intervenes Photographs of the bombed-out bus and the injured riders appeared in newspapers and on television screens around the world, prodding President John F. Kennedy to intervene. Kennedy had intervened before. The previous year, when he was running for the presidency, Kennedy had helped to win Martin Luther King's release from a Georgia prison after state officials had sentenced King to six months in jail for a traffic violation. King was freed and Kennedy, with the help of African American voters, went on to win the presidential election of 1960.

Kennedy now took action to stem the violence against the freedom riders. His administration worked out a deal with Mississippi's leaders. Police and state troopers agreed to protect the riders. The Federal Transportation Commission also issued an order mandating the desegregation of interstate transportation.

In exchange, the Kennedy administration agreed not to intervene when Mississippi authorities arrested the activists and sentenced them to jail for disturbing the peace. African Americans were disappointed with the deal Kennedy made and freedom riders suffered violence in jail.

The freedom riders achieved their immediate goal. They compelled a reluctant federal government to act. By refusing to allow violent mobs to deter them, the riders also displayed that intimidation would not defeat the movement.

>> Senator John F. Kennedy campaigns in 1960. Martin Luther King's endorsement of Kennedy helped Kennedy win the African American vote.

BOUNCE to Activate Gallery

DESCRIBE What did the freedom rides accomplish?

Public Institutions Open Doors to Minorities

In the fall of 1962 and spring of 1963, protests against racial discrimination intensified. The protesters put pressure on the federal government to help break down legal, or *de jure*, segregation. Meanwhile, violent resistance against the civil rights movement continued to grow, with many white Southerners opposing what they regarded as an overly-intrusive federal government interfering with race relations.

>> James Meredith, shown here with a federal escort, became the first African American student to integrate the University of Mississippi after winning a federal case guaranteeing his right to do so in 1962.

Litigation Against the University of Mississippi One struggle that gained international attention involved **James Meredith**. Meredith was an Air Force veteran who sought to enroll at the all-white University of Mississippi, known as "Ole Miss." He was aided by the NAACP, a political organization that had been using litigation to challenge the legality of segregation in the courts. In September

1962, with the support of the NAACP, Meredith won a federal court case that ordered the university to desegregate. Civil rights activist **Medgar Evers** was instrumental in this effort.

Mississippi governor Ross Barnett was determined to prevent the integration of the university. The issue became a standoff between the governor and the federal government.

On September 30, rumors of Meredith's arrival on the university's campus began to spread. Federal marshals had been assigned to protect him. Over the course of the night, a full-scale riot erupted, with federal marshals battling white protesters intent on scaring Meredith away.

As the rioting took place, President Kennedy addressed the nation on television. "Americans are free . . . to disagree with the law but not to disobey it," he declared. "For any government of laws . . . , no man, however prominent and powerful . . . is entitled to defy a court of law." The rioting went on throughout the night. By the time it ended, 160 people had been injured and 2 men had been killed.

The following morning, Meredith registered as a student and took his first class. He graduated from Ole Miss in 1963 and went on to obtain his law degree from Columbia University in New York City. Tragically, Medgar Evers was assassinated, on his front doorstep, in June 1963. Three years later, Meredith was shot and nearly killed. Both shootings stand as historical reminders of the high costs of fighting racial discrimination.

>> Scenes of young protesters being attacked with high-pressure hoses and dogs shocked Americans, prompting a cry for federal action.

A Letter from Birmingham Jail In the spring of 1963, Martin Luther King, Jr., and the SCLC targeted Birmingham, Alabama, for a major civil rights campaign. They chose Birmingham because of its reputation as the most segregated city in the South.

The campaign began nonviolently at first with protest marches and sit-ins. City officials got a court order prohibiting the demonstrations. On Good Friday, April 12, 1963, King decided to violate the order and join the demonstration personally, even though he knew it would lead to his arrest.

From his jail cell, King wrote a letter explaining why he and other civil rights activists were tired of waiting for reform: "For years now I have heard the word 'wait!' It rings in the ear of every Negro with piercing familiarity. This 'Wait!' has almost always meant 'Never.'"

One of the most poignant passages of the letter describes King's concern about the impact of discrimination on his children:

> Perhaps it is easy for those who have never felt the stinging darts of segregation to say, 'Wait.' But . . . when you suddenly find your tongue twisted and your speech stammering as you seek to explain to your six-year-old daughter why she can't go to the public amusement park that has just been advertised on television, and see tears welling up in her eyes when she is told that Funtown is closed to colored children. . . . Then you will understand why we find it difficult to wait.
>
> —Martin Luther King, Jr., "Letter from Birmingham Jail," 1963

The SCLC gave King's letter to the press, and it soon appeared in newspapers across the nation. The letter provided Americans with a clear explanation of King's philosophy of nonviolence and his use of direct action. Its powerful message and eloquence also stirred many white moderates to support the civil rights movement.

After King was released from jail, the SCLC increased the frequency of the demonstrations. For the first time, schoolchildren joined the "freedom marches." Eventually, Birmingham's Public Safety Commissioner, T. Eugene "Bull" Connor used police dogs and fire hoses on the protesters. Many Americans were shocked by media coverage of nonviolent protesters set upon by dogs and overwhelmed by the powerful jets of water. They sent telegrams and letters by the thousands to the White House, calling on the President to act.

Kennedy Addresses Minority Rights In Alabama, Governor **George Wallace** made it clear where he stood on civil rights: "I say segregation now! Segregation tomorrow! Segregation forever!" In response to the impending entrance of two African American students, Vivian Malone and James Hood, to the University of Alabama, Wallace vowed to stand "in the schoolhouse door" and personally block any attempt to integrate Alabama schools. Faced with this showdown, President Kennedy became convinced that he had to take a more active role in promoting civil rights.

On June 11, 1963, in order to facilitate the registration of Malone and Hood, Kennedy ordered the secretary of defense to call up the Alabama National Guard. Faced with the authority of the federal government, Governor George Wallace backed down.

He stepped aside and allowed the two students to enter the University of Alabama—only after proclaiming the rights of states to control their own schools. Later, reflecting on the showdown with Wallace, Vivian Moore stated, "I didn't feel I should sneak in. I didn't feel I should go around the back door. If [Wallace] were standing in the door, I had every right to face him and go to school."

That evening, as a result of the events in Alabama, President Kennedy delivered a moving televised address. Calling civil rights a "moral issue," he declared that the nation had an obligation to "fulfill its promise" of giving all Americans "equal rights and equal opportunities." President Kennedy sent to Congress a proposal for sweeping civil rights legislation. His brother, Attorney General Robert F. Kennedy, led the charge for passage of the bill. The president also helped form a group of African American and white lawyers who would collaborate to fight segregation.

☑ **EXPLAIN** How did James Meredith and Martin Luther King, Jr. prompt President Kennedy to promote civil rights?

>> Alabama Governor George Wallace, a staunch advocate of segregationist policies, attempted to block the integration of the University of Alabama in 1963.

Thousands Gather in the Nation's Capital

To put pressure on Congress to pass the new civil rights bill and to improve economic opportunities for Blacks, supporters made plans for a massive nonviolent protest in Washington, D.C. The event brought together the major political organizations promoting civil rights—including the NAACP, SCLC, and SNCC—as well as labor unions and religious groups.

The **March on Washington** took place on August 28, 1963. Organizers had hoped for 100,000 demonstrators. More than double that number showed up. They were a diverse group—young and old and from many different classes and religious backgrounds. More than a quarter of the marchers were white. Yet at the time, more than half of all whites disapproved of the march.

Before the march, there had been some concern about maintaining order at such a huge demonstration. Yet despite the massive numbers, the day was peaceful and even festive. Famous celebrities and entertainers were on hand to perform for the crowd.

The Washington Monument was the starting point for the day's events. Prominent singers performed songs, including the civil rights movement's unofficial anthem, "We Shall Overcome." Then the throng marched to the Lincoln Memorial. The main rally took place in front of the Lincoln Memorial, where a distinguished roster of speakers addressed the crowd. A. Philip Randolph, the elder statesman of the civil rights movement, gave the opening remarks. He was followed by representatives of various religious and labor groups.

The highlight of the day came when the final speaker, Martin Luther King, Jr., took the podium. King held the audience spellbound as he described his dream of a colorblind society "when all of God's children" would be free and equal. Millions more watched King's address live on television. This powerful and eloquent speech has come to be known as the "I Have a Dream" speech.

Behind the scenes, there was some tension between the organizations that had planned the March. SNCC, in particular, had wanted to stage a more militant protest to show its dissatisfaction with the pace of change. Yet for the public at large and for most who took part, the March on Washington represented a magical moment in American history.

>> A plaque outside the Sixteenth Street Baptist Church in Birmingham, Alabama, honors the four girls who died there. Three local Ku Klux Klansmen were eventually convicted of this crime.

The March on Washington was one of the largest political demonstrations in U.S. history. Widely covered in the media, the March increased awareness of the movement and built momentum for the passage of civil rights legislation.

Despite the huge numbers and the emotional intensity of the day, the March remained orderly and is considered a model for peaceful protest. The March on Washington has come to symbolize the civil rights movement.

IDENTIFY Why did Martin Luther King, Jr.'s speech during the March on Washington have such a profound effect on the nation?

A Significant Congressional Vote Addresses Minority Rights

On September 15, 1963, less than three weeks after the march, a bomb exploded in the Sixteenth Street Baptist Church in Birmingham. The church had been the SCLC's headquarters earlier that spring. Four young African American girls, all dressed in their Sunday best, were killed in the bombing.

Two months later, on November 22, 1963, President John F. Kennedy was assassinated in Dallas, Texas. Vice President Lyndon B. Johnson assumed the presidency.

Johnson was a southerner with racist views of African Americans and a long history of using racially abusive language in private. However, he surprised many Americans by immediately throwing his support behind the cause of civil rights. "No eulogy could more eloquently honor President Kennedy's memory," Johnson told Congress and the nation, "[than the] earliest passage of the civil rights bill for which he fought so long."

The civil rights bill faced strong opposition in Congress, but Johnson put his considerable political skills to work for its passage. The bill passed in the House of Representatives, but it faced a more difficult fight in the Senate, where a group of southern Democratic senators attempted to block it by means of a **filibuster**. This is a tactic by which senators give long speeches to hold up legislative business. The filibuster went on for more than 80 days until supporters finally put together enough votes to overcome it. In the end, the measure passed in the Senate, and President Johnson signed the **Civil Rights Act of 1964** into law in July.

The act banned segregation in public accommodations and gave the federal government the ability to compel state and local school boards to desegregate their schools. The act also allowed the Justice Department to prosecute individuals who violated people's civil rights and outlawed discrimination in employment on account of race, color, sex, or national origin. It also established the Equal Employment Opportunity Commission (EEOC), which is responsible for enforcing these provisions and investigating charges of job discrimination.

IDENTIFY SUPPORTING DETAILS How did the Civil Rights Act of 1964 try to end discrimination?

ASSESSMENT

1. **Draw Conclusions** What link do you see between the mass protests of the early 1960s and the Montgomery bus boycott of 1955?
2. **Contrast** Explain how the Student Nonviolent Coordinating Committee differed from other civil rights organizations.
3. **Analyze Information** What were some outcomes of the freedom rides?
4. **Summarize** the main points of Martin Luther King Jr.'s argument in "Letter from Birmingham Jail."
5. **Generate Explanations** Explain why the Student Nonviolent Coordinating Committee was dissatisfied after the March on Washington.
6. **Quest Connections** What was the effect of the Supreme Court ruling in *Boynton* v. *Virginia* (1960) on the civil rights movement? How might you depict this on your civil rights timeline?

Letter from Birmingham Jail: Martin Luther King, Jr.

These two excerpts are both from Dr. Martin Luther King, Jr. The first excerpt, "Letter from Birmingham Jail" was written in 1963, when King was jailed for disobeying a court order to stop leading a campaign of nonviolent protest against segregation and discrimination in Birmingham, Alabama. The letter was written in response to white Alabama clergymen who opposed the tactics of the protesters. The second excerpt is from King's closing address at the March on Washington—one of the most powerful speeches ever made.

>> Dr. Martin Luther King, Jr. during the March on Washington

Primary Source 1

My Dear Fellow Clergymen, While confined here in the Birmingham City Jail, I came across your recent statement calling our present activities "unwise and untimely." . . .

We have waited for more than 340 years for our constitutional and God-given rights. The nations of Asia and Africa are moving with jetlike speed toward the goal of political independence, and we still creep at horse and buggy pace toward the gaining of a cup of coffee at a lunch counter.

☑ **COMPARE AND CONTRAST** What point is King making when he compares America's civil rights progress with that of nations in Asia and Africa?

I guess it is easy for those who have never felt the stinging darts of segregation to say wait. But when you have seen vicious mobs lynch your mothers and fathers at will and drown your sisters and brothers at whim; when you have seen hate-filled policemen curse, kick, brutalize, and even kill your black brothers and sisters with impunity [without punishment]; when you see the vast majority of your 20 million Negro brothers smothering in an airtight cage of poverty in the midst of an affluent society; when you suddenly find your tongue twisted and your speech stammering as you seek to explain to your six-year-old daughter why she can't go to the public amusement park that has just been advertised on television, and see the tears welling up in her little eyes when she is told that Funtown is closed to colored children, . . . then you will understand why we find it difficult to wait. . . .

☑ **ANALYZE STYLE AND RHETORIC** In this passage, how does King's imagery discredit the arguments of those urging civil rights activists to be patient and wait for change?

You express a great deal of anxiety over our willingness to break laws. . . . The answer is found in the fact that there are two types of laws: There are just and there are unjust laws. I would agree with Saint Augustine that "An unjust law is no law at all." . . .

All segregation statutes are unjust because segregation distorts the soul and damages the personality. It gives the segregator a false sense of superiority, and the segregated a false sense of inferiority. . . .

☑ **IDENTIFY CAUSE AND EFFECT** What does King say are the effects of segregation?

Let us all hope that the dark clouds of racial prejudice will soon pass away and the deep fog of misunderstanding will be lifted from our fear-drenched communities and in some not too distant tomorrow the radiant stars of love and brotherhood will shine over our great nation with all their scintillating beauty.

Yours for the cause of Peace and Brotherhood, Martin Luther King, Jr.

Primary Source 2

"I Have a Dream": Martin Luther King, Jr.

. . . And so even though we face the difficulties of today and tomorrow, I still have a dream. It is a dream deeply rooted in the American dream.

I have a dream that one day this nation will rise up and live out the true meaning of its creed [set of fundamental beliefs or principles]: "We hold these truths to be self-evident; that all men are created equal."

I have a dream that one day on the red hills of Georgia, the sons of former slaves and the sons of former slave owners will be able to sit down together at the table of brotherhood.

I have a dream that one day even the state of Mississippi . . . will be transformed into an oasis of freedom and justice.

I have a dream that my four little children will one day live in a nation where they will not be judged by the color of their skin but by the content of their character.

I have a *dream* today.

I have a dream that one day, down in Alabama, . . . one day right there in Alabama little black boys and black girls will be able to join hands with little white boys and white girls as sisters and brothers.

This is our hope and this is the faith with which I return to the South.

With this faith we will be able to hew [chop, cut, shape] out of the mountain of despair a stone of hope. With this faith we will be able to transform the jangling discords of our nation into a beautiful symphony of brotherhood . . . .

–this will be the day when all of God's children will be able to sing with new meaning:

"My country 'tis of thee, sweet land of liberty, of thee I sing.

Land where my father died, land of the Pilgrims' pride,

From every mountainside, let freedom ring.". . .

When we allow freedom to ring—when we let it ring from every village and every hamlet [small village], from every state and every city, we will be able to speed up that day when *all* of God's children, black men and white men, Jews and Gentiles [non-Jews], Protestants and Catholics, will be able to join hands and sing in the words of the old Negro spiritual: "Free at last! Free at last!

Thank God Almighty, we are free at last!"

☑ **ANALYZE WORD CHOICES** Why does King envision people of all races and religions to one day be "free at last"? What would they be free from?

☑ ASSESSMENT

1. **Analyze Style and Rhetoric** In his letter from Birmingham Jail, how does King use rhetorical devices to support his argument against racial segregation? Cite specific examples from the text.
2. **Identify Supporting Details** In the letter, what details does King offer to support his main point that racial segregation is unjust?
3. **Analyze Style and Rhetoric** Cite three metaphors in King's speech.
4. **Draw Inferences** Why do you think King singles out three states in his speech? What effect does this have on his overall purpose?
5. **Analyze Style and Rhetoric** Like many powerful phrases, "the American dream" is open to interpretation. Why did King construct his speech around this well-known phrase?

GO ONLINE to access primary sources

16.3

GO ONLINE to Project Imagine: Choose Your Path During Freedom Summer to see how civil rights activists worked to gain equal rights.

BOUNCE to Activate Flipped Video

Objectives

Explain the significance of Freedom Summer, the march on Selma, and why violence erupted in some American cities in the 1960s.

Compare and contrast the goals and approaches taken by African American leaders to expand political rights and economic opportunities.

Describe the social and economic situation of African Americans by 1975.

Key Terms

Freedom Summer
Voting Rights Act
Twenty-fourth Amendment
Kerner Commission
Malcolm X
Nation of Islam
Black Power
Black Panthers
Lester Maddox
affirmative action

Successes and Setbacks

During the 1950s and 1960s, the civil rights movement made great strides forward. Yet racial injustice was not fully eradicated. Frustration with this situation led some African Americans to turn to more radical methods. Although the civil rights and Black Power movements were linked, their methods differed. African Americans achieved further successes, but for some the radicalism of the times left a bitter legacy.

Increasing Participation in the Political Process

None of the federal court decisions or civil rights measures passed through 1964 fundamentally affected the right to vote. The problem was a southern political system that used literacy tests, poll taxes, and intimidation to keep Black people from voting.

In Mississippi, in 1964, for instance, not a single African American person was registered to vote in five counties that had African American majorities. All of the major civil rights organizations sought to overcome these political injustices.

SNCC and Political Rights SNCC had spent several years organizing voter education projects in Mississippi. It met with little success and a great deal of violent opposition. But in 1964, it decided to get more directly involved in the political process. It called for a major campaign, known as **Freedom Summer**. About 1,000 volunteers, mostly Black and white students, were to flood Mississippi to register African Americans to vote. They also formed the Mississippi Freedom Democratic Party (MFDP),

GO ONLINE to access your digital course

an alternative to Mississippi's all-white regular Democratic Party, to give African Americans a voice in state politics. Fannie Lou Hamer, who had helped organize the Freedom Summer campaign, was elected vice chair of the party.

Even before most of the Freedom Summer volunteers had arrived, three civil rights workers—Michael Schwerner, James Chaney, and Andrew Goodman—disappeared. SNCC claimed that they were murdered; state authorities denied these charges.

President Johnson ordered a massive search for the three, which ended when their bodies were found buried in an earthen dam. All had been shot at point-blank range. Yet, despite the danger, almost all of the other volunteers remained in the state.

Work of Political Organizations After Freedom Summer ended in August 1964, an MFDP delegation traveled to the Democratic Convention in New Jersey, seeking to be recognized as Mississippi's only Democratic Party. At the convention, Fannie Lou Hamer, one of the MFDP's leaders, gave powerful testimony. She described how she and other activists had been beaten, fired from their jobs, and displaced from their homes all because, as she put it, they wanted "to register" and "live as decent human beings."

Despite Hamer's testimony, the Democrats refused to seat the MFDP. Instead, party officials offered a compromise: they would seat two MFDP members as "at-large delegates" and reform the nomination rules to guarantee greater minority representation in the future. The MFDP rejected this offer because it trivialized the sacrifices the MFDP members had endured to participate in a democracy they so cherished. Ironically, Mississippi's regular Democratic delegation left the convention in protest because the national party had made the offer to the MFDP.

Martin Luther King, Jr., Leads the March on Selma Early in 1965, Martin Luther King, Jr., and the SCLC organized a major campaign in Selma, Alabama, to pressure the federal government to enact voting rights legislation. The protests climaxed in a series of confrontations on the Edmund Pettus Bridge, on the main route from Selma to Montgomery. The first of these confrontations took place on March 7, 1965, a day that became known as "Bloody Sunday." Heavily armed state troopers and other authorities attacked the marchers as they tried to cross the bridge. Sheyann Webb, a six-year-old girl at the time, recalled the scene:

> I heard all of this screaming and . . . somebody yelled, 'Oh God, they're killing us!' . . . And I looked and I saw the troopers charging us . . . swinging their arms and throwing canisters of tear gas. . . . Some of them had clubs

Civil Rights Organizations

ORGANIZATION AND DATE FOUNDED	KEY PEOPLE	KEY FEATURES
National Association for the Advancement of Colored People (NAACP) 1909	Thurgood Marshall	Focused on legal cases to end segregation and gain legal equality
Nation of Islam 1930	Elijah Muhammad Malcolm X	Advocated separation of the races
Congress of Racial Equality (CORE) 1942	James Farmer	Organized peaceful protests to gain civil rights
Southern Christian Leadership Conference (SCLC) 1957	Martin Luther King, Jr. Ralph Abernathy	Church-based group dedicated to nonviolent resistance; organized demonstrations and protest campaigns
Student Nonviolent Coordinating Committee (SNCC) 1960	James Lawson Ella Baker Stokely Carmichael	Grass-roots movement of young activists; organized voter education projects in the South
Black Panther Party 1966	Huey Newton Bobby Seale	Militant group advocating armed confrontation; organized antipoverty campaigns

>> **Analyze Charts** What do you think are the strengths and weaknesses of each organization's approach to gaining civil rights for African Americans?

> and others had ropes and whips. . . . It was like a nightmare. . . . I just knew then that I was going to die.
>
> —Sheyann Webb, *Selma, Lord, Selma*, 1980

Webb survived, but the rampage continued. Television coverage of the violence outraged the nation. On March 15, President Johnson went on national television and called for a strong federal voting rights law. Historically, regulation of voting rights had been left to the states, but Johnson argued that "it is wrong to deny any of your fellow citizens the right to vote." He added, "Their cause is our cause too, because it is not just Negroes, but really it is all of us, who must overcome the crippling legacy of bigotry and injustice. And *we shall overcome*."

Voting Rights Act of 1965 Spurred by the actions of protesters, lobbying by the Washington bureau of the NAACP, and the words of the President, Congress passed the **Voting Rights Act** of 1965. The act banned literacy tests and empowered the federal government to oversee voting registration and elections in states that had discriminated against minorities. In 1975, Congress extended coverage to Hispanic voters in the Southwest.

Some legislation laid the groundwork for the Voting Rights Act. One such legal landmark was the **Twenty-fourth Amendment** to the Constitution, ratified in 1964. It banned the poll tax, which had been used to keep poor African Americans from voting. Also, in response to litigation, the federal courts handed down several important decisions that expanded the right to participate in the democratic process. *Baker* v. *Carr* and *Reynolds* v. *Sims* limited racial gerrymandering, the practice of drawing election districts in such a way as to dilute the African American vote, and established the legal principle of "one man, one vote." In 1973, the Supreme Court further challenged racial gerrymandering in *White* v. *Regester*.

These laws and decisions had a profound impact. Particularly in the Deep South, African American participation in politics skyrocketed. In Mississippi, the percentage of African Americans registered to vote jumped from just under 7 percent in 1964 to about 70 percent in 1986. Nationwide, the number of African American elected officials rose from fewer than 100 to more than 6,000 by the mid-1980s.

☑ **IDENTIFY CAUSE AND EFFECT** What impact did the protests in Selma, Alabama, have on the nation?

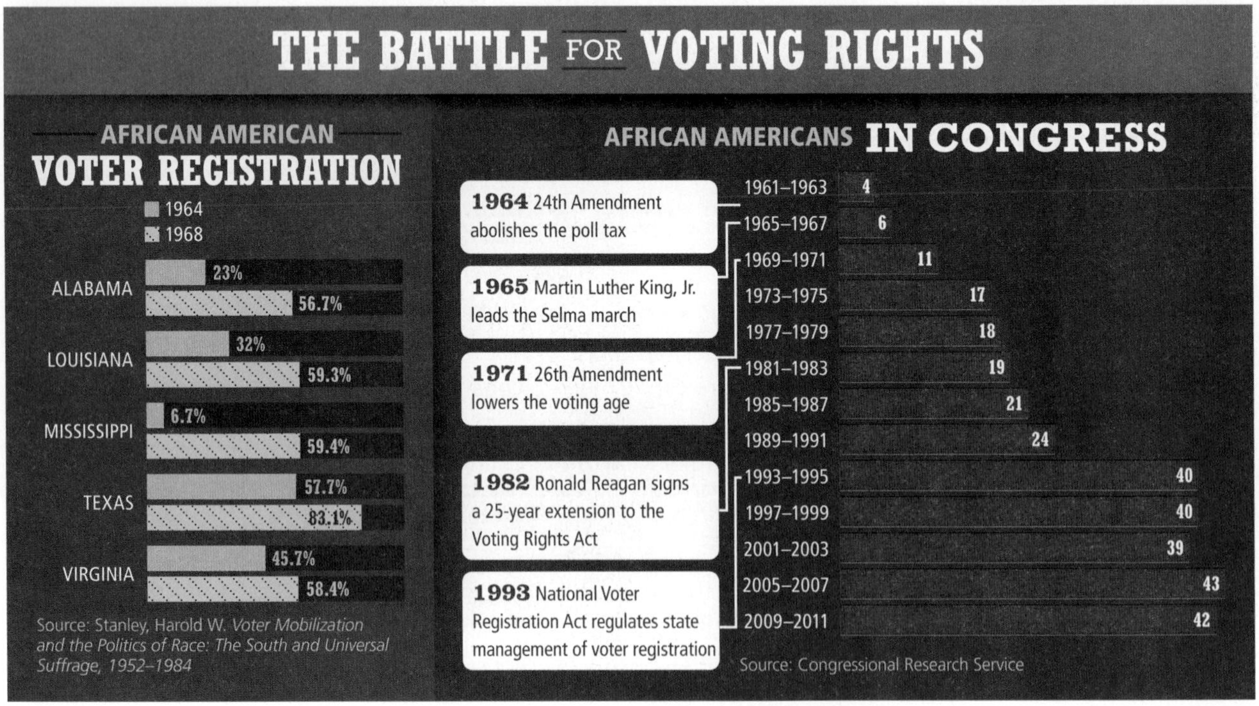

>> **Analyze Data** In which state did African Americans make the most gains in voter registration? Do you believe it's more important for African Americans to increase their representation in Congress, or in state government?

Violence Troubles Civil Rights Efforts

Many celebrated the passage of the Voting Rights Act of 1965. Yet for some African Americans, things had not changed much. In many urban areas, there was anger and frustration over systematic poverty, segregation, inadequate schools, lack of economic opportunities, and police brutality. That anger exploded into violence in several cities.

Disorder in the Cities Less than a week after Johnson signed the Voting Rights Act, one of the worst race riots in American history erupted in the predominantly African American neighborhood of Watts in Los Angeles. Violence, looting, and arson spread for several days before National Guard troops restored order.

Watts was one of many race riots that erupted in the 1960s. The worst violence occurred in Newark, New Jersey, and Detroit, Michigan, in the summer of 1967. In Detroit, 43 people died, and property damage reached $50 million. The outbursts frightened many Americans.

In most previous race riots, whites had used violence to keep African Americans "in their place." But now, some Blacks were using violence against police and white business owners in Black neighborhoods.

>> During the 1960s, race riots, like this one in Detroit, often left significant parts of largely African American neighborhoods burned out or otherwise destroyed.

BOUNCE to Activate Map

Investigating the Race Riots To determine the causes of the riots, President Johnson established the National Advisory Commission on Civil Disorders, known as the **Kerner Commission**. It concluded that long-term racial discrimination stood as the single most important cause of violence. The commission also recommended establishing and expanding federal programs aimed at overcoming the problems of America's urban ghettos.

> Our nation is moving toward two societies, one black, one white, separate and unequal. . . . Segregation and poverty have created the racial ghetto and a destructive environment totally unknown to most Americans.
>
> —National Advisory Commission on Civil Disorders, *Report*, 1967

The Kerner Commission's findings proved highly controversial. A number of conservative commentators argued against expanding federal spending.

>> Conservative critics argued that the Kerner Commission did not satisfactorily explain why the riots occurred.

They said that this amounted to rewarding the rioters. Others noted that the Black-white split that the report described ignored other minorities.

President Johnson did not follow up on the commission's recommendations, largely because the Vietnam War was consuming enormous sums of federal money. The riots also fueled a white backlash. Many whites opposed further reforms. However, the private sector stepped in to create economic opportunities for citizens. In 1967, the life insurance industry formed an Urban Problems Committee of CEOs who created a "Billion Dollar Urban Investment Program" to provide investments for low- and moderate- income housing and job-creating enterprises in poor urban areas.

☑ **RECALL** Why was the Kerner Commission formed?

New Civil Rights Groups

The racial rioting of the mid-1960s coincided with the radicalization of many African Americans, particularly young urban African Americans. Rather than advocating nonviolence and integration, they called for another approach.

Malcolm X Offers a Different Vision The most well-known African American radical was **Malcolm X**, who was born Malcolm Little in Omaha, Nebraska, in 1925. He adopted the X to represent his lost African name. Little, he argued, was his slave name. Malcolm had a difficult childhood. In his teens, he moved to Boston and then to New York City, where he became involved in drugs and crime and landed in prison on burglary charges at age 21.

While in prison, Malcolm became a convert to the **Nation of Islam**, a religious sect headed by Elijah Muhammad. The group prescribed strict rules of behavior, including no drugs or alcohol, and demanded a separation of the races.

After his release from prison, Malcolm became the Nation of Islam's most prominent minister. Working in high-poverty inner city neighborhoods, he preached a message of self-reliance and self-protection. He called for Black pride and spread the idea of Black nationalism, a belief in the separate identity and racial unity of the African American community. Malcolm was a "charismatic speaker who could play an audience as great musicians play instruments." His dynamic speeches won many adherents to his cause.

In 1964, Malcolm X broke away from the Nation of Islam and formed his own organization. He then made

>> At the 1968 Summer Olympic Games, U.S. athletes Tommie Smith, center, and John Carlos, right, raise their gloved fists to show their support for the Black Power movement.

a pilgrimage to Mecca, the holy city of Islam, afterward adopting the religious name el-Hajj Malik el-Shabazz. Returning to the United States, he suggested that it might be possible for Blacks and antiracist whites to cooperate. In February 1965, however, Malcolm X was shot and killed. Three members of the Nation of Islam were convicted of the murder.

The "Black Power" Movement Many young African Americans saw themselves as heirs of the radical Malcolm X. They began to move away from the principle of nonviolence and toward self-defense. They also began to question the goal of integration. As SNCC leader Stokely Carmichael put it:

> Integration . . . has been based on complete acceptance of the fact that in order to have a decent house or education, blacks must move into a white neighborhood or send their children to a white school. This reinforces the notion . . . that 'white' is automatically better and 'black' is by definition inferior.
>
> —Stokely Carmichael, "What We Want," 1966

>> At the University of California at Berkeley, Stokely Carmichael advocated combining the economic, social, and political power of African Americans to achieve civil rights.

Carmichael first used the term **"Black Power"** in 1966. In that year, James Meredith had set off on a "March Against Fear" across the state of Mississippi to encourage African Americans to register and vote. Meredith traveled only 20 miles before he was shot and left for dead by a white supremacist. SNCC, CORE, and SCLC members vowed to continue the march.

When they reached Greenwood, Mississippi, Carmichael and some other marchers were arrested. After his release, Carmichael told a crowd that African Americans needed "Black Power."

He later said that Black Power meant African Americans should collectively use their economic and political muscle to gain equality. Yet many white Americans felt threatened. They believed that Black Power meant Black violence.

The Black Panthers' Approach Not long after Carmichael's "Black Power" speech, Huey Newton and Bobby Seale formed the Black Panther Party in Oakland, California. Almost overnight, the **Black Panthers** became the symbol of young militant and proud African Americans. The Black Panthers organized armed patrols of urban neighborhoods to protect people from police abuse. They also created antipoverty programs, such as free breakfasts for

>> Members and sympathizers demonstrate their support for Black Panther leader Huey Newton as he stands trial for the murder of an Oakland police officer in Alameda County, California.

>> Poor People's Campaign members march through Atlanta on May 10, 1968, to promote economic justice. **Draw Conclusions** How did the goal of this march differ from previous civil rights demonstrations?

>> Civil rights activists at the Lorraine Motel in Memphis point toward the sniper's position moments after Dr. Martin Luther King, Jr., was shot by an assassin.

poor African American children. The Black Panthers gained national attention when they entered the state capitol in Sacramento carrying shotguns and wearing black leather jackets and berets to protest attempts to restrict their right to bear arms.

The Panthers' style appealed to many young African Americans, who began to wear their hair in "Afros" and to refer to themselves as "Black" rather than "Negro" or "colored."

Some, following the lead of Malcolm X, changed their name and celebrated their African heritage. At the same time, the Panthers' militancy often led to violent confrontations with police. Each side accused the other of instigating the violence.

☑ **EXPLAIN** What effect did Malcom X have on the civil rights movement?

King Expands His Dream

Martin Luther King understood the anger and frustration of many urban African Americans whose lives had changed little despite the civil rights reforms of the 1960s. However, he disagreed with the call for "Black Power" and sought a nonviolent alternative to combat economic injustice.

After spending about a year in Chicago's slums to protest conditions there, King made plans for a massive "Poor People's Campaign." The campaign's goal was to broaden civil rights' goals to address economic inequality in America.

King's Assassination: A Turning Point As part of this effort, King journeyed to Memphis, Tennessee, in early April 1968. There, he offered his assistance to sanitation workers who were striking for better wages and working conditions.

On April 3, King addressed his followers. He referred to threats that had been made against his life. "Like anybody, I would like to live a long life," King declared. "But I'm not concerned about that now. I just want to do God's will."

The following day, as King stood on the balcony outside his motel room, he was struck by a shot from a high-powered rifle. He died at a hospital shortly afterward, at the age of 39. James Earl Ray, a white ex-convict, was later charged with King's murder.

King's assassination marked an important turning point. His efforts had increased minority participation in the political process and encouraged racial integration. Yet much racist hostility persisted. For example, **Lester Maddox**, a restaurant owner in Atlanta, Georgia, gained national attention when

Civil Rights Legislation

Civil Rights Act of 1964	• Banned segregation in public accommodations • Increased federal authority to enforce school desegregation • Outlawed discrimination in employment on basis of race, color, and sex
Twenty-fourth Amendment (1964)	• Eliminated poll tax as voting requirement
Voting Rights Act of 1965	• Banned literacy tests as voting requirement • Empowered the federal government to supervise voter registration and elections
Fair Housing Act of 1968	• Banned discrimination in housing

>> **Analyze Information** Based on the information in the chart, which legislation dealt specifically with voting rights?

BOUNCE to Activate Chart

he closed his business rather than comply with the provisions of the 1964 Civil Rights Act that banned discrimination against African Americans in all public places. Hoping to maintain the status quo, Maddox then ran for and was elected governor of Georgia. After King's assassination, Governor Maddox would not even allow the civil rights leader's body to lie in state in the Georgia state capitol building.

The protests for Black freedom and racial equality that began in the mid-1950s crested in the late 1960s around the time of King's death. By then, the civil rights movement had made significant gains. Yet the impact of King's legacy would continue to grow. His messages of political equality and economic opportunity for all continue to define political discourse to this day.

Robert F. Kennedy Responds Robert F. Kennedy was campaigning for the presidency in Indianapolis when he heard of King's death. RFK stopped his campaign speech to give the audience the sad news. He reminded them that he had lost his own brother to an assassin's bullet. Kennedy asked those assembled to honor King's memory by replacing their anger and desire for revenge "with an effort to understand with compassion and love." Despite Kennedy's plea, riots broke out in hundreds of cities after King's assassination. Two months later, Robert Kennedy's life, too, was cut short by an assassin.

☑ **CHECK UNDERSTANDING** Why did King go to Memphis in 1968?

Results of the Civil Rights Movement

The civil rights movement of the 1950s and 1960s succeeded in eliminating legal, or de jure, segregation and knocking down some barriers to African American voting and participation in the political process. During the same period, African American poverty rates fell and the median income of African American men and women rose rapidly, as did the number of African Americans who graduated from high school. But African Americans still suffered the effects of decades of oppression and inequality and were poorer than white Americans by almost every measure.

One symbol of the progress that had been made was the appointment of Thurgood Marshall as the first African American Supreme Court Justice in 1967. The following year, in the wake of King's murder, Congress passed one final civil rights measure, the Fair Housing Act, which banned discrimination in housing. Still, the social and economic gap between many Blacks and whites remained. New measures aimed at closing this gap tended to provoke more controversy than consensus in America.

Controversies over Busing and Affirmative Action Attempts to increase economic opportunities for African Americans and to integrate neighborhoods and schools encountered great difficulties. To achieve desegregated schools, the federal courts had ordered the use of busing. Richard Nixon, who succeeded Lyndon Johnson as president,

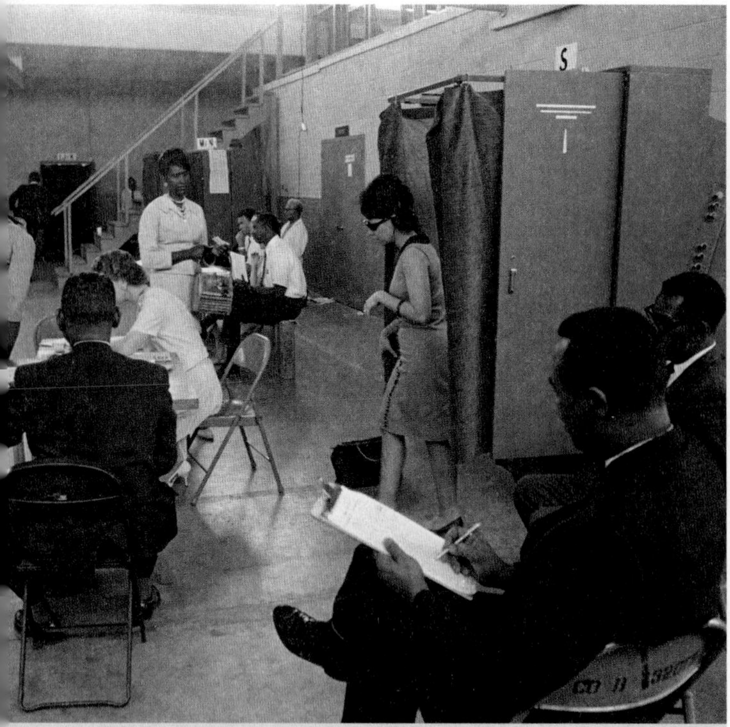

>> African American poll watchers observe voters in Tuskegee, Alabama, on May 31, 1966. **Hypothesize** Why were poll watchers present during voting?

criticized busing as a means of attaining racial balance.

At the same time, the Nixon administration formally established **affirmative action** as a means of closing the economic gap between Blacks and whites. In a short period of time, colleges and universities, businesses, and local and state governments followed the federal government's lead and implemented their own affirmative action plans to increase African American representation in schools and the workforce. In 1978, the Supreme Court, in its *University of California* v. *Bakke* decision, ruled that race could be taken into account when admitting students to college. However, the court also ruled that specific racial quotas were not allowed.

Affirmative action proved controversial almost from the start. Some whites argued that it constituted reverse discrimination and violated the goal of creating a colorblind society. Justice Thurgood Marshall disagreed. "Three hundred and fifty years ago, the Negro was dragged to this country in chains to be sold into slavery," Marshall wrote. "The position of the Negro today in America is the tragic but inevitable consequence of centuries of unequal treatment." Until the nation addressed the legacy of this unequal treatment, Marshall asserted, it would not fulfill its promise of providing equal rights and opportunities to all.

Affirmative action remains divisive. Critics—and even some supporters—contend that the practice has had unintended consequences, sometimes hurting the very people it is intended to help. For example, some studies show that minority students accepted through affirmative action at the nation's most selective universities do not have as high a graduation rate as minority students accepted through the regular admissions process at less selective institutions.

Changes to the Voting Rights Act The Voting Rights Act of 1965 continues to encourage minority participation in the democratic process. Congress has renewed the law four times. Recently, however, the Supreme Court has redefined the scope of the Act's provisions. In 1993, the Court ruled that the first district in North Carolina to elect an African American to Congress was shaped in a way that violated the rights of white voters. In 2013, the Court severely weakened the heart of the act, Section 5, which empowered the federal government to oversee election practices in states where voting rights are at risk. In a 5-4 decision, the Court released nine states, seven of them in the South, from federal supervision. The ruling cited the gains those states had made since 1965 in Black voter registration as rationale for the decision.

LIST What gains had the civil rights movement made by the early 1970s?

ASSESSMENT

1. **Generate Explanations** Explain how Martin Luther King, Jr.'s assassination marked a turning point for the civil rights movement.
2. **Sequence Events** Describe the events that led to President Johnson's call for federal voting legislation in 1965.
3. **Compare and Contrast** the efforts of Martin Luther King, Jr., and the Black Panthers to end economic injustice.
4. **Draw Conclusions** Discuss the conclusions of the Kerner Commission, and explain why many people found it controversial.
5. **Connections to Today** What civil rights issues does society struggle with today? What methods do you think are most effective to fight for civil rights?

16.4

President Kennedy and First Lady Jacqueline Kennedy brought youthful energy and glamour to the White House.

Kennedy's Reforms

The civil rights movement had begun gaining momentum in the 1950s, when President Dwight Eisenhower was presiding over a time of peace and prosperity. But even during this optimistic Eisenhower era, there were a number of issues that caused Americans grave concern. The launch of *Sputnik 1* showed that the rivalry between the United States and the Soviet Union was still intense. The U-2 spy plane incident demonstrated that the Cold War might heat up at a moment's notice. Deep, unsettled problems remained—problems for a new decade and a new generation of political leadership.

BOUNCE to Activate Flipped Video

Objectives

Discuss the election of 1960.

Evaluate Kennedy's domestic policies.

Assess the impact of Kennedy's assassination.

Key Terms

John F. Kennedy
Richard M. Nixon
New Frontier
Equal Pay Act
deficit spending
space race
Warren Commission

The Torch is Passed to a New Generation

Kennedy Versus Nixon In the presidential election of 1960, Democrat **John F. Kennedy** and Republican **Richard M. Nixon** were quite similar in a variety of ways. For the first time in U.S. history, both candidates had been born in the twentieth century, Nixon in 1913 and Kennedy in 1917. Both had served in the navy during World War II. Both had been elected to Congress in 1946 and to the Senate in the early 1950s. Both were passionate about foreign affairs and supported the Cold War fight against communism. Young and energetic, intelligent and hardworking, both wanted to be the first of their generation to lead the country.

Their differences, however, were as significant as their similarities. Kennedy was the son of a wealthy Boston businessman. His grandfather had been a state senator, and his father had served as the ambassador to Great Britain. Kennedy attended Harvard University. Although he was a Catholic and his religion was an issue in the election, he insisted that what church he attended should not be a factor.

GO ONLINE to access your digital course

Nixon, born in California, did not enjoy the advantages of a wealthy upbringing. His father struggled to make a living. As a young man, Nixon had to balance his time between his school studies and work to help support the family. Many voters respected him for these experiences and for those he'd gained as Vice President under Eisenhower.

Television Influences Voter Opinion The 1960 election highlighted the growing power and influence of television. The candidates agreed to four televised debates. During the campaign, Nixon was hospitalized with a knee infection. After getting out of the hospital, he committed himself to a grueling schedule of public appearances.

By the time of the first debate, held in late September in Chicago and watched by about 70 million people, Nixon looked pale and exhausted. He arrived at the television studio an hour early, but he refused the offer to have makeup applied to hide his newly growing beard. By contrast, Kennedy, tanned from open-air campaigning in California, looked healthy and confident. His relaxed manner, easy charm, and quick sense of humor added to his appeal.

In many ways, the debate boiled down to how the candidates looked and spoke, rather than what they said. Most Americans who listened to the debate on radio believed that Nixon had won. But the larger audience who watched the debate on television concluded that Kennedy was the clear victor. Although Nixon tried to change his image in the later debates, he was unable to significantly alter the country's initial impression of him. Kennedy's "victory" in Chicago proved crucial in the election.

Kennedy Wins a Close Election Kennedy not only looked better on television, but he also demonstrated an ability to react more quickly to unexpected events. For example, several weeks before the election, civil rights leader Martin Luther King. Jr., and a group of African American students were jailed during a protest in Atlanta, Georgia. Nixon said nothing publicly about the episode. Kennedy, however, telephoned King's wife, Coretta Scott King, to voice his concern. He also worked behind the scenes to obtain King's release on bail. Kennedy's actions attracted the strong support of African Americans in the election.

The election of 1960 was the tightest presidential election since 1888. In an election that witnessed the largest voter turnout in the country's history, Kennedy won by less than 120,000 of the 68 million votes cast. His electoral victory was more convincing. He carried enough states to give him 303 electoral votes to Nixon's 219. However, had a few thousand people voted differently in Illinois and Texas, the electoral vote and the election would have gone to Nixon.

☑ **RECALL** How did Kennedy attract strong support among African American voters?

A President's Unique Charisma

Kennedy's determination to change life at home resulted in his domestic agenda, called the New Frontier. Faced with a conservative Congress, Kennedy met with opposition as he fought to turn his vision into a reality. Still, he had some success in making changes in Social Security benefits, dealing with poverty and racial discrimination, and spurring new interest and expectations for the space program.

As John Kennedy showed in his 1960 campaign and in his Inaugural Address, he had a special charm—or charisma—that separated him from other politicians. With his exquisitely tailored clothes, quick smile, and sense of humor, he seemed closer

The Presidential Election of 1960

CANDIDATE	POPULAR VOTE	% POPULAR VOTE	ELECTORAL VOTE	% ELECTORAL VOTE
John Kennedy (Democrat)	34,227,096	49.7	303	56.4
Richard Nixon (Republican)	34,107,646	49.6	219	40.8

>> **Analyze Data** How do the percentages of the electoral vote compare to those of the popular vote?

BOUNCE to Activate Gallery

to a movie star than to a run-of-the-mill politician. Although he suffered many health problems, he projected youthful health and energy.

He surrounded himself with other distinguished men. Reporters dubbed them "the best and the brightest." They came from some of the country's most prestigious businesses and universities. Robert McNamara, president of Ford Motor Company, agreed to serve as Secretary of Defense. Dean Rusk, president of the Rockefeller Foundation, signed on as Secretary of State. Arthur Schlesinger, Jr., a Pulitzer Prize-winning historian, worked at the White House as a spokesperson for liberal causes and was a source of ideas for the President.

President Kennedy promised Americans that his administration would blaze a "**New Frontier**." The term described Kennedy's proposals to improve the economy, education, healthcare, and civil rights. He also hoped to jump-start the space program. In his nomination acceptance speech on July 15, 1960, in Los Angeles, California, Kennedy said,

> I stand tonight facing west on what was once the last frontier. . . . From the lands that stretch three thousand miles behind me, the pioneers of old gave up their safety, their comforts and sometimes their lives to build a new world here in the West. . . .
>
> But the problems are not all solved and the battles are not all won, and we stand today on the edge of a new frontier—the frontier of the 1960s—the frontier of unknown opportunities and perils—a frontier of unfulfilled hopes and threats.
>
> —John F. Kennedy, July 15, 1960

IDENTIFY CENTRAL IDEAS Why did many feel that Kennedy was a different kind of politician?

Domestic Priorities

Early in his presidency, occupied by events in Cuba and Berlin, Kennedy devoted most of his attention to foreign affairs. But by 1963 he had become more concerned about pressing problems at home.

>> President John F. Kennedy discusses the upcoming disarmament talks at Geneva with his top cabinet-level advisers in the White House on March 9, 1962.

>> During the early 1960s, studies found that millions of women working in skilled and technical jobs across the country received lower pay than men doing the same work.

Kennedy was troubled by the high levels of poverty in the United States. *The Other America*, Michael Harrington's bestselling and influential 1962 exposé of poverty in America, shocked Kennedy and many other Americans.

While Kennedy failed to get Congress to accept his more ambitious social programs, he did push through an increase in the minimum wage, an extension in Social Security benefits, and improvements in the welfare system.

In addition, in 1962 Kennedy established the President's Commission on the Status of Women, a blue-ribbon panel that studied how poverty and discrimination affected women. The difference in wages received by men and women for the same work was an especially glaring problem. And as Kennedy pointed out, working women with children "bear the heaviest burden of any group in our Nation." The **Equal Pay Act** (1963) required equal wages for "equal work" in industries engaged in commerce or producing goods for commerce. Although it contained various loopholes, the law was a crucial step on the road to fair and equal employment practices. The next year Congress would prohibit discrimination by employers on the basis of race, color, religion, national origin, or sex.

One Approach to Economic Stimulus Kennedy believed that increased prosperity would help to eliminate some of the nation's social problems. When he became President, the country was suffering from a high unemployment rate and a sluggish economy. To help the economy, Kennedy proposed tax credits to spur business investment in new factory equipment. At the same time, increased military spending created new jobs and boosted the economy.

In addition, Kennedy accepted the "new economics" of theorist John Maynard Keynes that advocated **deficit spending** to stimulate the economy. Deficit spending is the government practice of borrowing money in order to spend more than is received from taxes. In 1963, Kennedy called for dramatic tax cuts for middle-class Americans as a way to put more money in the pockets of more people. At the same time, he increased the tax burden on wealthier citizens. Kennedy's economic initiatives jump-started the tremendous economic growth of the late 1960s.

Cautious Steps toward Civil Rights Kennedy pursued a timid approach toward civil rights. He had narrowly won the 1960 election, and he had little real influence in Congress or even complete partisan support. He did not want to anger conservative, white southern members of Congress in his own party. They stood ready to block any civil rights legislation.

While Kennedy remained largely passive on civil rights issues, African Americans and their white allies challenged segregation in the South. In 1961,

Wage Disparity by Gender, 1960–2015

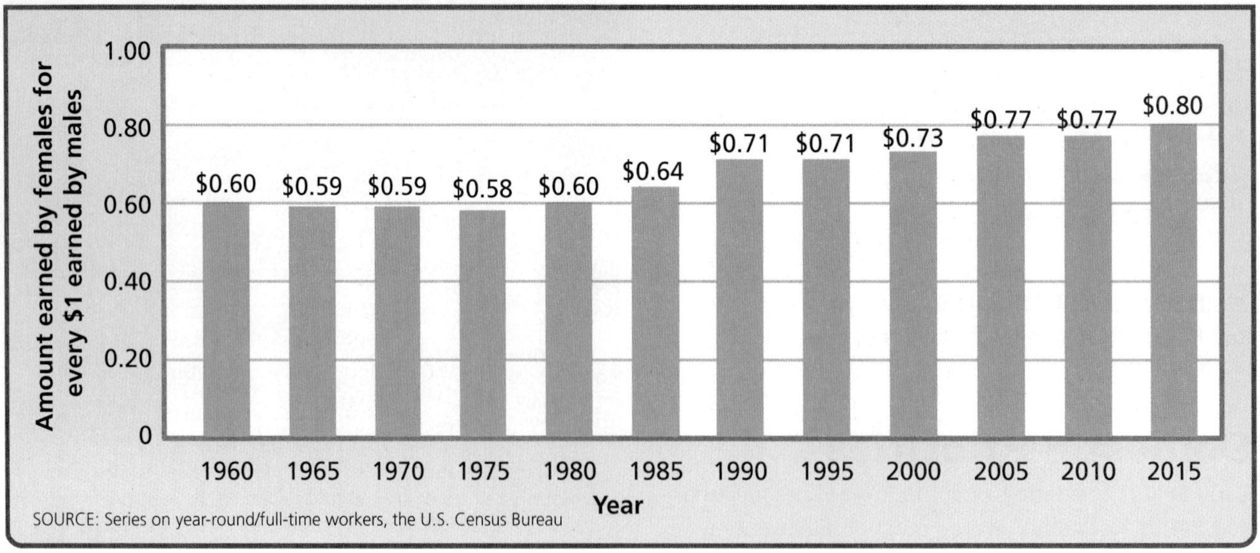

>> **Analyze Data** Based on the data in the graph, how many years did it take for the Equal Pay Act of 1963 to make a significant impact on women's rate of pay as compared to men's?

Key Events in the American Space Program

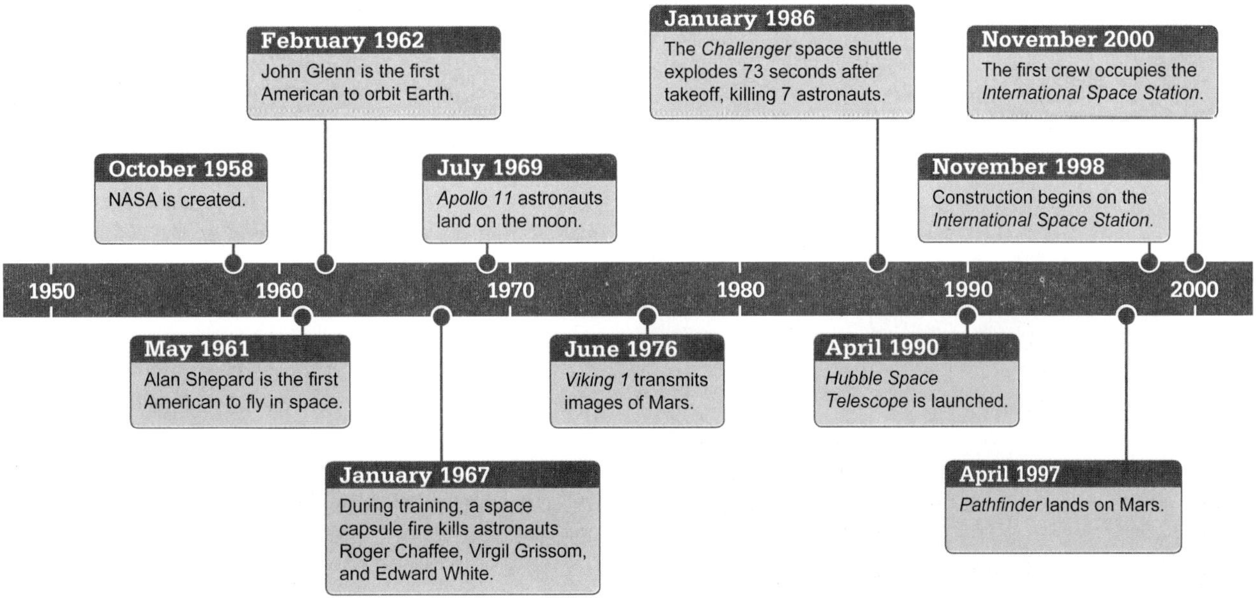

>> **Analyze Information** Based on the events in the timeline, how did the goals of the space program change over time?

they took "freedom rides" to desegregate interstate bus travel.

In 1963, Martin Luther King, Jr., took the civil rights struggle to Birmingham, Alabama. Such actions took courage and were met by angry, oftentimes violent, responses by white southerners.

In early 1963, Kennedy introduced a civil rights bill that demanded prosecution for voting-rights violations and federal money to aid school desegregation. Further violence in the South prompted Kennedy to introduce stronger civil rights legislation.

First to the Moon The launching of the satellite *Sputnik 1* by the Soviet Union in 1957 called into question American technological superiority. Although Congress created the National Aeronautics and Space Administration (NASA) in 1958, the Soviets' space program remained several steps ahead of the American program. In April 1961, for example, the Soviet cosmonaut Yuri Gagarin became the first human to orbit Earth.

Kennedy recognized that the United States and the Soviet Union were locked in a "**space race**," a competition between the Soviet Union and the United States to develop technology to land on the moon. In May 1961, NASA put astronaut Alan Shepard into a suborbital space flight aboard the Project Mercury space capsule Freedom 7. Encouraged by the success of Project Mercury, Kennedy committed the United States to landing a man on the moon by 1970.

America's quest to reach the moon was punctuated by enormous successes and heartbreaking failures. Astronaut John Glenn became the first American to orbit Earth in February 1962. But astronauts Virgil Grissom, Edward White, and Roger Chaffee burned to death when their docked capsule exploded in fire during a routine test. Finally, in July 1969, astronaut Neil Armstrong left his spacecraft *Columbia's* landing vehicle and became the first man to step on the moon. The mission was a successful completion of Kennedy's bold dream.

The moon landing in 1969 was a turning point in the space race. Never again would the Soviet Union rival the United States for supremacy in space. In addition, the space program's many innovations improved Americans' quality of life. For example, materials developed for the visors on the moon astronauts' helmets allowed eyeglass manufacturers to replace glass lenses with lighter, scratch-resistant ones. Today's cordless tools use the same technology that astronauts used on the moon. Manufacturers of athletic shoes applied high-tech features found in the astronauts' boots. Memory foam, enriched baby food, and freeze-drying technology are also among the hundreds of ways that space exploration has benefited society and improved the quality of life.

>> President Kennedy and his wife ride with Texas Governor John Connally and his wife in the presidential motorcade through Dallas, Texas, just prior to the President's assassination on November 22, 1963.

☑ **CHECK UNDERSTANDING** Why did Kennedy change his approach to civil rights issues?

Kennedy Is Assassinated

During his first two and a half years in office, Kennedy made the transition from politician to national leader. In foreign affairs he confronted Soviet challenges, made hard decisions, and won the respect of Soviet leaders and American citizens. He also spoke eloquently about the need to move toward a peaceful future. In domestic affairs he finally came to the conclusion that the federal government had to lead the struggle for civil rights. Added to his new maturity was his ability to inspire Americans to dream noble dreams and work toward lofty ends.

In November 1963, Kennedy traveled to Dallas, Texas, to mend political fences for his 1964 reelection bid. He never lived to see 1964. While his motorcade moved through the city, assassin Lee Harvey Oswald, perched by a window on the sixth floor of the Texas School Book Depository, fired three shots at the President. The third shot hit Kennedy in the back of his head. A half hour later, doctors at Parkland Memorial Hospital pronounced him dead.

Texan Lyndon B. Johnson, Kennedy's Vice President, was sworn in as the new President. Although many people would later question whether Oswald acted alone, the **Warren Commission**, which conducted the official investigation of the assassination, described Oswald as the "lone killer."

The senseless murder deeply saddened Americans across the nation. Millions of people watched Kennedy's funeral procession on television, and many reacted as if they had lost a family member. It seemed as if part of America's innocence had died with him.

☑ **DESCRIBE** What was the purpose of the Warren Commission?

GO ONLINE to access this biography: John F. Kennedy

☑ ASSESSMENT

1. **Compare and Contrast** the backgrounds and political beliefs of John F. Kennedy and Richard M. Nixon.
2. **Generate Explanations** Explain how television influenced the presidential election of 1960.
3. **Summarize** Discuss the accomplishments of the "New Frontier," President Kennedy's domestic policy plan.
4. **Identify Cause and Effect** Discuss the impact that the moon landing of 1969 had on American standards of living and on American foreign relations.
5. **Draw Conclusions** Explain how the United States' economy changed during President Kennedy's term.
6. **Connections to Today** Read the following quote from Thomas Jefferson's first Inaugural Address in 1801: "All . . . will bear in mind this sacred principle, that though the will of the majority is in all cases to prevail, that will to be rightful must be reasonable; that the minority possess their equal rights, which equal law must protect and to violate would be oppression." Do you think President Jefferson's words are relevant to our nation today? Explain why or why not.

Inaugural Address: John F. Kennedy

On January 20, 1961, President John F. Kennedy delivered his inaugural address. Kennedy projected youth and determination in his address. The speech was a call to action for all Americans

>> President Kennedy and First Lady Jacqueline Kennedy

. . . Let the word go forth from this time and place, to friend and foe alike, that the torch has been passed to a new generation of Americans—born in this century, tempered [toughened; strengthened] by war, disciplined by a hard and bitter peace, proud of our ancient heritage—and unwilling to witness or permit the slow undoing of those human rights to which this Nation has always been committed, and to which we are committed today at home and around the world.

DETERMINE MEANING Why does Kennedy characterize the post-war period as "a hard and bitter peace"?

Let every nation know, whether it wishes us well or ill, that we shall pay any price, bear any burden, meet any hardship, support any friend, oppose any foe, in order to assure the survival and the success of liberty. . . .

To that world assembly of sovereign states, the United Nations, our last best hope in an age where the instruments of war have far outpaced the instruments of peace, we renew our pledge of support—to prevent it from becoming merely a forum for invective—to strengthen its shield of the new and the weak—and to enlarge the area in which its writ may run.

Finally, to those nations who would make themselves our adversary, we offer not a pledge but a request: that both sides begin anew the quest for peace, before the dark powers of destruction unleashed by science engulf all humanity in planned or accidental self-destruction.

We dare not tempt them with weakness. For only when our arms are sufficient beyond doubt can we be certain beyond doubt that they will never be employed.

But neither can two great and powerful groups of nations take comfort from our present course--both sides overburdened by the cost of modern weapons, both rightly alarmed by the steady spread of the deadly atom, yet both racing to alter that uncertain balance of terror that stays the hand of mankind's final war.

DETERMINE CENTRAL IDEAS To what "two great and powerful groups of nations" is Kennedy referring?

Primary Sources

So let us begin anew—remembering on both sides that civility is not a sign of weakness, and sincerity is always subject to proof. Let us never negotiate out of fear. But let us never fear to negotiate.

Let both sides explore what problems unite us instead of belaboring those problems which divide us.

Let both sides, for the first time, formulate serious and precise proposals for the inspection and control of arms—and bring the absolute power to destroy other nations under the absolute control of all nations.

Let both sides seek to invoke the wonders of science instead of its terrors. Together let us explore the stars, conquer the deserts, eradicate disease, tap the ocean depths and encourage the arts and commerce.

Let both sides unite to heed in all corners of the earth the command of Isaiah—to "undo the heavy burdens . . . (and) let the oppressed go free."

And if a beach-head of cooperation may push back the jungle of suspicion, let both sides join in creating a new endeavor, not a new balance of power, but a new world of law, where the strong are just and the weak secure and the peace preserved.

All this will not be finished in the first one hundred days. Nor will it be finished in the first one thousand days, nor in the life of this Administration, nor even perhaps in our lifetime on this planet. But let us begin.

In your hands, my fellow citizens, more than mine, will rest the final success or failure of our course. Since this country was founded, each generation of Americans has been summoned to give testimony to its national loyalty. The graves of young Americans who answered the call to service surround the globe.

Now the trumpet summons us again—not as a call to bear arms, though arms we need; not as a call to battle, though embattled we are—but a call to bear the burden of a long twilight struggle, year in and year out, "rejoicing in hope, patient in tribulation [an experience that causes distress or suffering]"—a struggle against the common enemies of man: tyranny, poverty, disease, and war itself. . . .

CITE EVIDENCE One phrase in this passage of the speech is quoted from the Bible. Identify the phrase. Why do you think Kennedy included it?

In the long history of the world, only a few generations have been granted the role of defending freedom in its hour of maximum danger. I do not shrink from this responsibility—I welcome it. . . .

And so, my fellow Americans: ask not what your country can do for you—ask what you can do for your country.

My fellow citizens of the world: ask not what America will do for you, but what together we can do for the freedom of man. . . .

DETERMINE MEANING What does *shrink* mean in the sense that Kennedy uses it? What is he saying in that sentence?

Finally, whether you are citizens of America or citizens of the world, ask of us here the same high standards of strength and sacrifice which we ask of you. With a good conscience our only sure reward, with history the final judge of our deeds, let us go forth to lead the land we love, asking His blessing and His help, but knowing that here on earth God's work must truly be our own.

ASSESSMENT

1. **Compare and Contrast** How does Kennedy address America's allies as compared to America's enemies? Cite examples from the speech to support your answer.

2. **Analyze Style and Rhetoric** What phrases from this address have you heard before? Why are they so memorable?

GO ONLINE to access primary sources

16.5

President Johnson talks with an impoverished man about the challenges facing his Kentucky community.

Reform Under Johnson

Lyndon B. Johnson, who became President after Kennedy's assassination, shared the same goals as his predecessor. These goals shaped the purpose of Johnson's Great Society program. A seasoned politician, Johnson successfully pushed through significant domestic legislation that he hoped would become the first step to achieving the quality of life he thought all Americans should enjoy.

BOUNCE to Activate Flipped Video

Objectives

Evaluate Johnson's policies up to his victory in the 1964 presidential election.

Analyze Johnson's goals and actions as seen in his Great Society programs.

Assess the achievements of the Great Society in creating economic opportunities for citizens.

Analyze the effects of U.S. Supreme Court decisions.

Key Terms

Civil Rights Act
War on Poverty
Economic Opportunity Act
Great Society
Medicare
Medicaid
Immigration and Nationality Act of 1965
Warren Court
Barry Goldwater
Tinker v. Des Moines School District
judicial interpretation

Johnson's Path to the Presidency

Born in Stonewall, Texas, Lyndon B. Johnson was raised in the Hill Country town of Johnson City. He attended Southwest Texas State College and then taught for several years in Cotulla, Texas. There, at a tiny segregated school for Mexican Americans, he confronted firsthand the challenges faced by poverty-stricken minority students, and the lessons he learned remained with him for the rest of his life.

An Influential Legislator After teaching for several years, Johnson entered politics—first as a Texas congressman's secretary and then as the head of the Texas National Youth Administration.

In 1937, Johnson was elected to Congress, and during the next several decades he became the most powerful person on Capitol Hill. Elected to the Senate in 1948, Johnson proved himself a master of party politics and rose to the position of Senate majority leader in 1955. In the Senate, he was adept at avoiding conflict, building political coalitions, and working out compromises. His skill was instrumental in pushing the 1957 Civil Rights Act through Congress.

GO ONLINE to access your digital course

In 1960, he hoped to be chosen by the Democratic Party to run for President, but when Kennedy got the nomination Johnson agreed to join him on the ticket as the vice presidential nominee. A New Englander and a Catholic, Kennedy needed Johnson to help carry the heavily Protestant South. Johnson was also popular both with Mexican American voters and in the Southwest. He was an important part of Kennedy's victory in 1960.

Continuing Kennedy's Civil Rights Policies On becoming President after Kennedy's assassination, Johnson radiated reassurance and strength. His every action indicated that he was ready for the job and that the government was in good hands. Less than a week after the assassination, Johnson addressed a joint session of Congress.

> . . . [N]o memorial oration or eulogy could more eloquently honor President Kennedy's memory than the earliest possible passage of the Civil Rights Bill for which he fought so long.
>
> —President Johnson, Speech before a Joint Session of Congress, 1963

With Johnson's ability to build consensus, or agreement on an issue by a group, the **Civil Rights Act** became law in the summer of 1964. It outlawed discrimination in voting, education, and public accommodations. The act demanded an end to discrimination in hospitals, restaurants, theaters, and other places open to the public. It also created the Equal Employment Opportunity Commission to fight discrimination in hiring.

African Americans and Mexican Americans who faced almost daily discrimination benefited immeasurably from the legislation. Finally, Title VII of the 1964 Civil Rights Act prohibited discrimination on the basis of sex.

The Fight to Expand Economic Opportunity Johnson made his intentions clear in his first State of the Union address when he said it was time to "declare an unconditional war on poverty." The new President planned to fuse his own dreams for America onto Kennedy's legislative agenda. Although Kennedy had failed to get Congress to approve his tax bill calling for dramatic tax cuts for middle-class Americans, Johnson was able to maneuver it through. In addition, he had added a billion-dollar **War on Poverty** to the bill.

Johnson's War on Poverty introduced measures to train the jobless, educate the uneducated, and

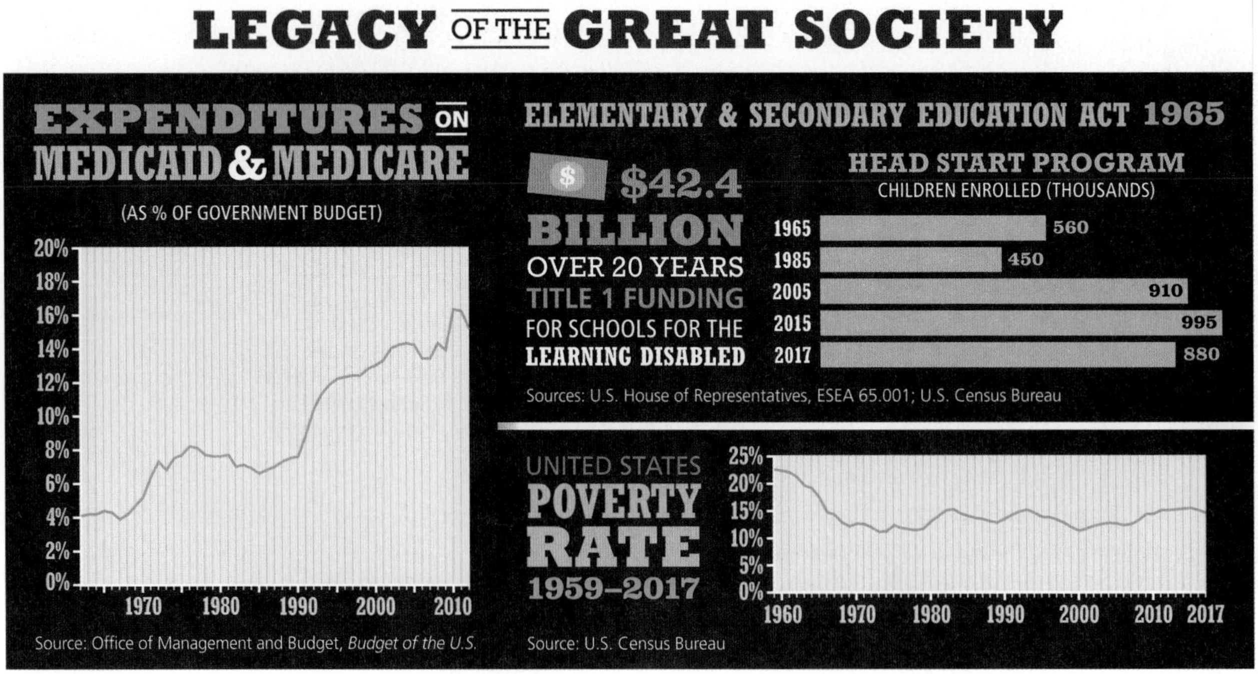

>> **Analyze Information** Use information from the chart to evaluate the effects of the Great Society on U.S. poverty levels over time. Do you think the programs were a success? Why or why not?

BOUNCE to Activate Chart

provide healthcare for those in need. The 1964 **Economic Opportunity Act** created the Job Corps to train young men and women between the ages of 16 and 21 in the work skills they needed to acquire better jobs and move out of poverty.

The act also established Volunteers in Service to America, or VISTA, patterned after Kennedy's Peace Corps, which sent American volunteers into poverty-stricken American communities in an effort to solve the country's pressing economic, educational, and medical problems. The volunteers served in inner city schools and on Indian reservations. They worked in rural health clinics and urban hospitals.

Perhaps the most successful element of the Economic Opportunity Act was the Head Start program. Funds were provided for play groups, day care, and activities designed to help underprivileged children get ready for elementary school. Head Start enjoyed bipartisan support for decades.

Johnson Defeats a Conservative Challenger If Johnson was to continue his War on Poverty and other social goals, he needed to win the 1964 presidential election. In that year, the Republicans nominated Arizona senator **Barry Goldwater**, whose economic and social views were directly opposed to Johnson's.

Whereas Johnson believed the federal government could best regulate the economy and promote social justice, Goldwater maintained that the federal government was the problem, not the solution. According to Goldwater, social and economic issues, such as racism and poverty, should not be addressed by the federal government.

Goldwater promised to rein in the federal government by reducing its size and restricting its activities. He favored significant tax cuts and right-to-work laws, and he opposed social welfare legislation and government spending on educational, public housing, and urban renewal programs.

In 1964, most Americans were not ready for Goldwater's conservative message. In addition, Johnson's campaign portrayed Goldwater as an extremist, suggesting that his election would ensure the repeal of civil rights legislation and economic ruin.

Johnson had prosperity on his side, as well as his own impressive legislative record and the legacy of Kennedy. In the November election, he won a landslide victory, capturing more than 60 percent of the popular vote and carrying all but six states.

Goldwater carried only Arizona and five southern states— Louisiana, Mississippi, Alabama, Georgia, and South Carolina. Furthermore, the outcome of the election was significant. The South was no longer solidly Democratic. Not only had Johnson won a ringing victory, but Democrats had captured both houses of Congress.

>> Barry Goldwater, the Republican nominee for President in 1964, strongly opposed the use of federal resources to address social issues.

Although Goldwater suffered a crushing political defeat in 1964, his conservative ideas resonated with many. Support for Goldwater's message remained strong in parts of California, propelling Ronald Reagan to the governor's office in 1966. When a conservative tide swept Reagan into the White House in 1981, Goldwater regained some influence and continued to be a strong voice on behalf of modern American conservatives.

RECALL How did Johnson continue Kennedy's plan to eliminate poverty in the United States?

Creating the Great Society

In the spring of 1964, in a speech at the University of Michigan, Johnson outlined his vision for America, calling it the **Great Society**. He said that during the past hundred years, Americans had spread across the continent, developed industrially, and created great wealth. But the work of America was not complete. He added,

> The challenge of the next half century is whether we have the wisdom to use that wealth to enrich and elevate our national life, and to advance the quality of our American civilization. . . .
>
> [W]e have the opportunity to move not only toward the rich society and the powerful society, but upward to the Great Society.
>
> —President Johnson, University of Michigan, May 22, 1964

For Johnson, the Great Society demanded "an end to poverty and racial injustice" and opportunity for every child.

Increasing Access to Healthcare In the first half of 1965, Congress passed parts of Johnson's Great Society legislation. Kennedy had supported similar legislation that failed to win congressional support.

>> President Johnson gave healthcare special attention. With Medicare and Medicaid, more Americans would be able to receive basic healthcare.

Johnson's agenda amended the Social Security Act by adding the Medical Care for the Aged Program, or **Medicare**, as it was more popularly called. Medicare provided basic health insurance for Americans in the Social Security system who were age 65 and older. It was funded by a new tax on workers' earnings and by payments from the Social Security benefits of retirees.

The new law also included a **Medicaid** feature that provided basic medical services to poor and disabled Americans who were not part of the Social Security system. Johnson signed the bill into law in Independence, Missouri, home of former President Harry Truman, who had called for a national health insurance program almost 20 years earlier.

When the Social Security Act was amended, few questions were raised about how programs like Medicare and Medicaid would be paid for in the years to come. Medicare has become increasingly expensive as medical costs have risen, the percent of retirees in the population relative to workers has increased, and because people live longer now than they did in 1965.

Investing in Public Education Along with health, education was one of the centerpieces of the Great Society program. Improved healthcare and education were necessary steps toward the goal of ending poverty.

The 1965 Elementary and Secondary Education Act was designed to aid schools in poorer communities. It provided federal funds to improve school libraries, learning centers, language laboratories, and services in impoverished school districts. The act dramatically increased funding for Indian, inner city, and Mexican American schools.

Environmental and Consumer Protection The Great Society program extended to improving the overall quality of American life. In the early 1960s, several best-selling books raised Americans' awareness about environmental and consumer problems. Rachel Carson's *Silent Spring* (1962) detailed how chemical fertilizers and pesticides were damaging the fragile ecosystem. Ralph Nader's *Unsafe at Any Speed* (1965) attacked the automotive industry for its lack of concern for passenger safety.

Both these books helped to foster environmental and consumer activity and led to several important pieces of legislation. The National Traffic and Motor Vehicle Safety Act (1966) established safety standards for automotive vehicles and created the National Highway Traffic Safety Administration to administer them. The Water Quality Act (1965),

U.S. Immigration and the Immigration and Nationality Act of 1965

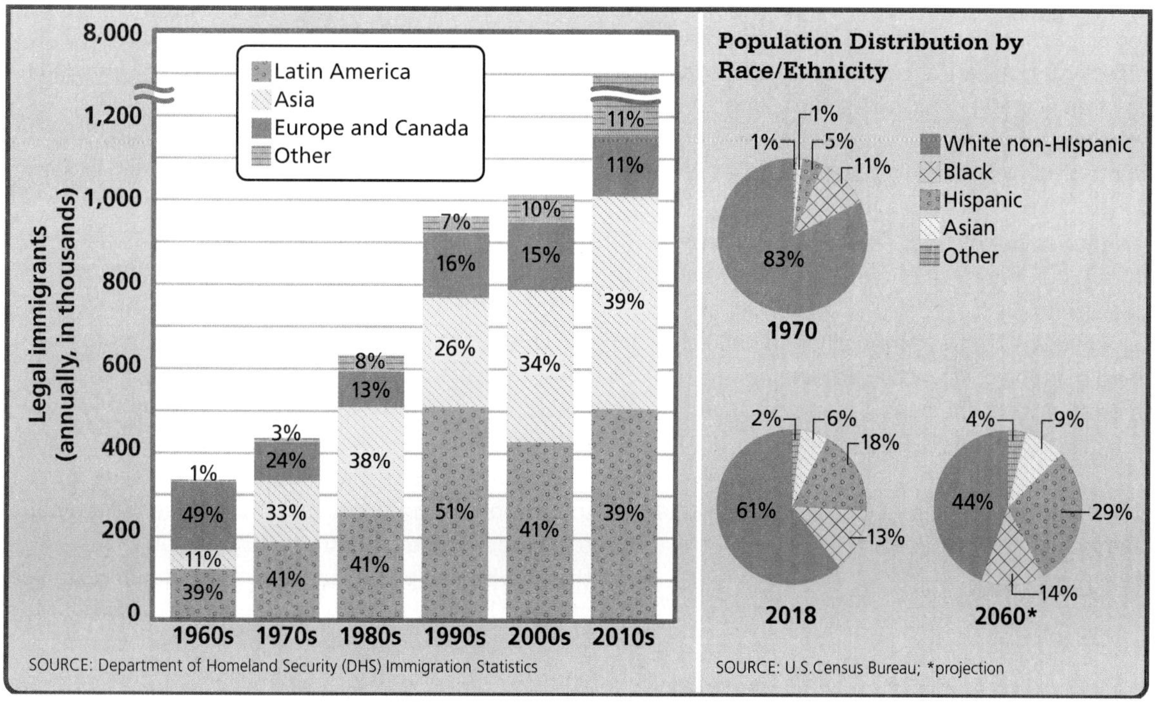

>> **Analyze Charts** Based on the data in the pie charts, which ethnic group is projected to grow the most by 2060?

the Clean Water Restoration Act (1966), and the Air Quality Act (1967) aimed at improving water and air standards in the country. The U.S. Public Health Service was empowered to enforce air quality standards, but dealing with water pollution was largely left to the states. Not until the Environmental Protection Agency was created in 1970 did the federal government gain significant regulatory power to protect the environment.

Less Restrictive Immigration Policies

Meanwhile, the civil rights movement was raising questions about America's long-standing immigration policy. The National Origins Acts of 1921 and 1924 had established a quota system that favored Western European immigrants and limited immigrants from other parts of the world. Such a discriminatory policy was clearly out of touch with the mood of the country in the early 1960s.

The **Immigration and Nationality Act of 1965** altered the quota system. Nearly 170,000 immigrants from the Eastern Hemisphere were allowed into the country. Nearly 120,000 immigrants from the Western Hemisphere were welcomed. Although family reunification was emphasized, same-sex partners of U.S. citizens were rejected. Immigrants from Latin America, Central America, the Caribbean, and Asia soon began to pour into the United States, providing the country with a pool of ideas, talent, and skills.

The doors of America were once again open to immigrants from around the world. During the 1960s and 1970s, millions of immigrants would arrive on American shores. Like earlier immigrants, many came seeking economic opportunity. Others were fleeing war or social unrest or were in search of political or religious freedom. As in the late nineteenth and early twentieth centuries, New York and the urban East and West coasts attracted many of the country's newest immigrants.

The Legacy of the Great Society Although critics said that Great Society programs did not work, many point out that these programs have improved the lives of millions of individual Americans. Poverty and infant mortality rates declined. Medicare and Medicaid delivered needed healthcare to millions of elderly and poor Americans. Head Start and other antipoverty programs provided the educational tools many underprivileged Americans needed to escape poverty. Congress also provided artists and scholars with assistance through the National Endowment for the Arts and Humanities, created in 1965.

The better future that the Great Society envisioned inspired many Americans, including women and minorities, to take action to expand their economic opportunities. Latino farm workers formed a union and organized national boycotts of farm products to win better wages. Latino students boycotted their schools to demand better education. Meanwhile, Asian Americans made economic gains unmatched by any other minority group. Women, too, made great advances during this time. By 1970 the percentage of women with college degrees was nearly double what it had been in 1950.

The Great Society victories may not have been as grandiose as Johnson predicted, but they were victories. The simple fact that 22.2 percent of all Americans lived below the poverty line in 1960 and 12.6 percent lived below the poverty line in 1970 says something about the triumphs of the Great Society.

IDENTIFY Which immigrant groups were affected by the Immigration and Nationality Reform Act of 1965?

The Impact of the Warren Court

During the 1960s, the Supreme Court demonstrated a willingness to take the lead on controversial social, religious, and political issues. Led by Chief Justice Earl Warren, the Supreme Court at this time—often called the **Warren Court**—became the most liberal in American history. Its decisions supported civil rights, civil liberties, voting rights, and personal privacy.

>> The Warren Court issued many landmark rulings in the areas of civil rights, criminal justice, the First Amendment, and legislative districting.

BOUNCE to Activate Gallery

A Principle of Voting Rights In several decisions the Supreme Court ruled in favor of the "one man, one vote" principle. The problem was one of apportionment of seats in state legislatures. During the twentieth century, large numbers of voters moved from rural to urban areas, but many state governments had not changed, or reapportioned, electoral districts to reflect the new conditions.

This led to an electoral imbalance. In many states, rural areas had more power and urban areas had less power than their populations actually mandated.

In *Baker* v. *Carr* (1962), the Supreme Court ruled in favor of reapportionment on the basis of "one man, one vote." Electoral districts, it said, had to reflect the numbers of people in those districts. In *Reynolds* v. *Sims* (1964), the Court reaffirmed its decision, adding that any arrangement other than "one man, one vote" violated the equal protection clause of the Fourteenth Amendment.

Redefining Civil Rights and Liberties In several decisions, the Warren Court expanded the definition of what constitutes free speech. For example, in ***Tinker* v. *Des Moines School District*** (1969), the Court ruled that wearing black armbands in school to protest the Vietnam War was protected as "symbolic" speech. The decision also made it clear that students do not give up all of their rights to free speech while in school.

In the *Tinker* decision, critics complained that the Court interpreted the Constitution too loosely, applying what critics have called **judicial interpretation** to the cases that came before them. That is, the Justices expanded the Constitution's meaning beyond the framers' original intent. In this case, the Court expanded the definition of free speech to include more than the spoken word. A narrow, or strict, construction of the First Amendment would have protected only actual speech.

The Warren Court also showed a heightened concern for the constitutional rights of accused lawbreakers. In four landmark cases, the Court broadened the individual rights of accused criminals and narrowed those of federal, state, and local government officials. In *Mapp* v. *Ohio* (1961), the Court ruled that evidence obtained illegally violated the Fourth Amendment and had to be excluded from federal and state trials. This ruling is part of the "incorporation doctrine" which is the doctrine through which the Court, over time, has incorporated into the Fourteenth Amendment's "due process" clause . By so doing, the Court has said that individuals have these rights at both the federal and state levels. In *Gideon* v. *Wainwright* (1963), the Court decided that all accused criminals had the right to a lawyer whether or not they could pay for one.

In *Escobedo* v. *Illinois* (1964), the Warren Court expanded on *Gideon* v. *Wainwright* by adding that every accused lawbreaker had to be offered access to a lawyer before questioning, and all evidence obtained from a suspect who had not been informed of his or her right to a lawyer could not be used in court. Finally, in *Miranda* v. *Arizona* (1966), the Court ruled that an accused criminal had to be informed of his or her Fifth and Sixth Amendment rights before being questioned.

Critics of these decisions argued that the Warren Court had tipped the balance of justice in favor of the rights of accused criminals. Today, many conservative justices still side with this opinion. The majority of the members of the Warren Court, however, countered that the rights of individuals had to be protected, especially when freedom hung in the balance.

Expanding Marriage Rights In 1967, the Warren Court ruled against laws forbidding interracial marriages. In *Loving* v. *Virginia*, the court ruled in favor of Mildred Loving, a Black woman, and Richard Loving, a white man, who had both been sentenced to prison for violating Virginia's anti-miscegenation laws by marrying each other. The ruling led to an increase in interracial marriages.

Church and State in the Public Sphere The Warren Court addressed the separation of church and state in the case of *Engel* v. *Vitale* (1962). The case involved whether or not a public school could require students to recite a state-sanctioned prayer. The Court ruled that school prayer was a violation of the First Amendment and an attempt by a governmental body to promote religion. The next year, the Court ruled in *Abington* v. *Schempp* that Bible reading in public schools also violated the First Amendment. The two decisions divided religious groups and the American people. Some welcomed the rulings, saying the government should have no say in personal religious matters. Others insisted the decisions were hostile to religion. The two decisions ignited, and continue to ignite, controversy. For more than 40 years, various religious groups have railed against these decisions.

IDENTIFY What major court ruling gave a person accused of a crime the right to have a lawyer?

GO ONLINE to access this biography: Lyndon B. Johnson

>> In the years following the *Miranda* v. *Arizona* decision, the reading of a suspect's "Miranda rights" became part of standard police procedure.

ASSESSMENT

1. **Define** What is a strict construction of the Constitution?
2. **Summarize** the policies that President Johnson implemented in order to "declare an unconditional war on poverty."
3. **Compare** President Johnson's success in the civil rights movement with President Kennedy's civil rights achievements.
4. **Generate Explanations** Explain why Lyndon B. Johnson defeated Barry Goldwater in the 1964 presidential election.
5. **Draw Conclusions** Describe the impact that the Warren Court had on the separation of church and state in the United States.
6. **Connections to Today** Presidents Kennedy, Johnson, and Nixon supported and signed pieces of civil rights legislation. What is the president's role today in getting legislation passed through Congress? How is it different and how is it the same?

Connections to Today

Marchers protest about a civil rights issue.

Take Action by Learning About Civil Rights Actions Today

1. **Choose** one of the following topics about the continuing fight for civil rights today:
   - **Racism:** Conduct research to find out what is being done to fight racism today.
   - **Bullying:** Conduct research to find out what is being done to protect the rights of those who are bullied online or in person.
   - **Mental Health:** Conduct research to find out what is being done to protect the rights of those who need support for mental health issues.
2. **Ask Questions** Generate a list of questions about the topic you have selected. What might you want to know about your topic?
3. **Learn** about your topic by using a variety of sources. Use the Internet or your library to find newspaper or magazine articles, data, or interviews with people involved in a civil rights issue of your choice.
4. **Raise Awareness** Create a photo gallery or poster aimed at raising awareness about the civil rights issue you researched. Share your gallery or poster with members of the community by posting it at a community center, library, or public space.

GO ONLINE to www.SavvasRealize.com and access your digital course

Use the texts, quizzes, interactivities, Quest Inquiries, Flipped Videos, and other resources from this Topic to prepare for the Topic Test.

- Quest Inquiries
- Quizzes
- Interactivities
- Texts
- Flipped Videos

While online you can also check the progress you've made learning the topic and course content by viewing your grades, test scores, and assignment status.

SAVVAS realize™

Topic 16 Quick Study Guide

LESSON SUMMARIES

Use these Lesson Summaries, and the longer versions available online, to review the key ideas for each lesson in this Topic.

Lesson 1: The Civil Rights Movement Strengthens

Civil Rights activism strengthened in the 1950s. In Montgomery, Alabama during a bus boycott against segregation, Dr. Martin Luther King called for nonviolent resistance. In Little Rock, Arkansas, federal troops arrived to protect African American students and enforce a Supreme Court decision ending segregated public education.

Lesson 2: The Movement Surges Forward

Young people launched a surge of civil rights protest in the early 1960s. Sit-ins, freedom rides, and other nonviolent protests swept the nation. A lawsuit helped desegregate the University of Mississippi. In Birmingham Alabama, the police attacked demonstrators. A massive demonstration in Washington D.C. helped pass the Civil Rights Act of 1964.

Lesson 3: Successes and Setbacks

With African Americans prevented from voting in the South, a massive campaign to register voters took place in 1964. In Selma, Alabama, marchers were attacked by state troopers. The nonviolence of the early civil rights movement gave way to more violent protests. Martin Luther King was assassinated, and Congress banned discrimination in housing.

Lesson 4: Kennedy's Reforms

The 1960 presidential election was won by John F. Kennedy, who increased the minimum wage and tried to gain equal pay for women. Kennedy also helped aid school desegregation and strengthened the space program. President Kennedy was assassinated in 1963.

Lesson 5: Reform Under Johnson

Lyndon Johnson, who became President after Kennedy's assassination, continued Kennedy's policies. The Civil Rights Act was passed along with other "Great Society" legislation designed to end poverty and racial injustice. Medicare and Medicaid were created, and the Supreme Court became more liberal in its decisions.

QUEST! FINDINGS

Create Your Interactive Timeline on Civil Rights Refer to your responses to the Quest Connections to help you create your timeline to present to the audience. Use the rubric and other Quest resources online to guide your work.

GO ONLINE to access lesson summaries

VISUAL REVIEW

Use these graphics to review some of the key terms, people, and ideas from this Topic.

Key Civil Rights Dates

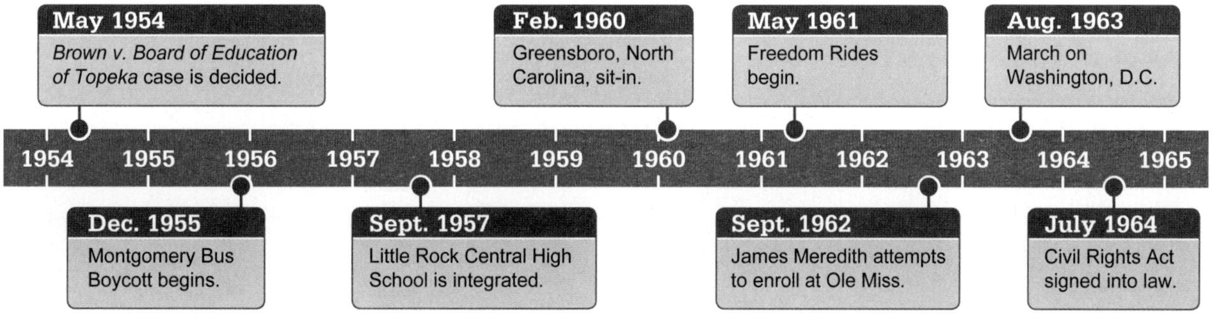

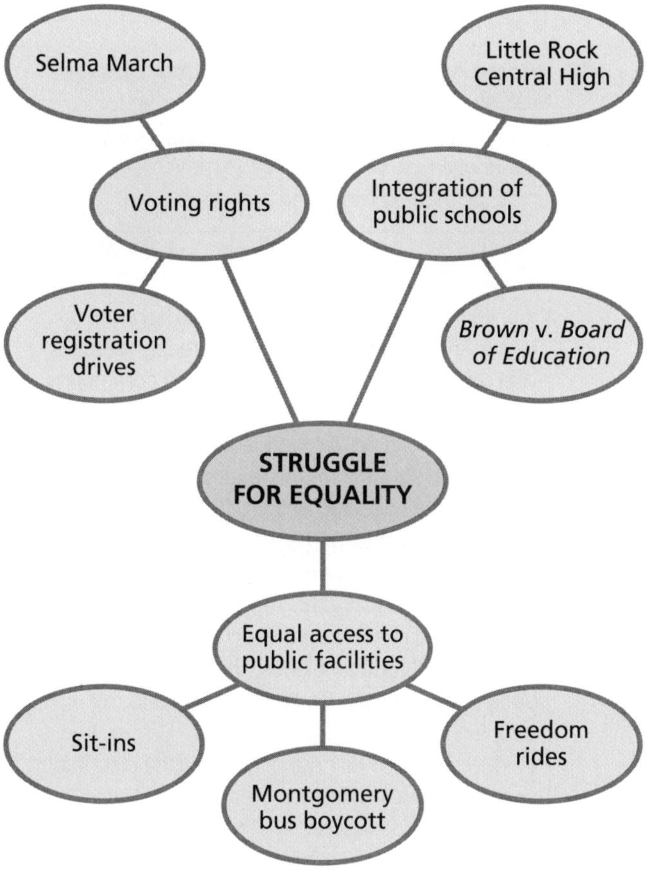

Civil Rights Legislation

Civil Rights Act of 1964	• banned segregation in public accommodations. • increased federal authority to enforce school desegregation. • outlawed discrimination in employment on basis of race, color, and sex.
Twenty-fourth Amendment (1964)	• eliminated poll tax as voting requirement.
Voting Rights Act of 1965	• banned literacy tests as voting requirement. • empowered the federal government to supervise voter registration and elections.
Fair Housing Act of 1968	• banned discrimination in housing.

Topic 16 Assessment

KEY TERMS, PEOPLE, AND IDEAS

1. What is the difference between **de jure** and **de facto segregation**?
2. What role did **Rosa Parks** play in the civil rights movement?
3. What was the relationship between the **freedom rides** and *Boynton* v. *Virginia*?
4. What recent changes have been made to the **Voting Rights Act** of 1965?
5. What was President Nixon's position on busing and **affirmative action**?
6. How did *Miranda* v. *Arizona* affect the rights of the accused?
7. What measures did President Kennedy take to improve women's rights?
8. What immigration policies were changed in the 1960s?
9. How did President Johnson fund **Medicare**?

CRITICAL THINKING

10. **Draw Inferences** (a.) Why were the nonviolent tactics of Dr. Martin Luther King and the SCLC so effective in influencing public opinion? (b.) What role might television have played in gaining support for the movement?
11. **Draw Conclusions** (a.) Why were young people of all races so active in the protests of the civil rights movement? (b.) Evaluate the success of this kind of coalition.
12. **Find the Main Idea** Why was school desegregation such an important goal for the civil rights movement?
13. **Evaluate Information** (a.) What was the purpose of the Civil Rights Act of 1964? (b.) In what ways did the Act strengthen *Brown* v. *Board of Education*?
14. **Compare and Contrast** How did the Black Panther movement differ from the earlier civil rights movement?
15. **Summarize** What was the relationship between the Great Society and the New Deal?
16. **Analyze Graphs** Study the graphs. How do they relate to *Brown* v. *Board of Education*?

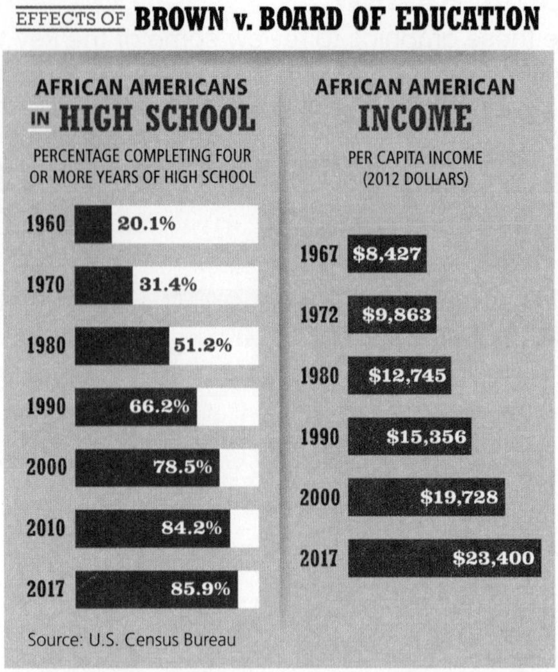

17. **Writing Activity: Write an Explanatory Essay** Evaluate why Dr. Martin Luther King called for nonviolent direct action. Use the excerpt below and your knowledge of the civil rights movement to write an essay that explains King's ideas.

> Oppressed people cannot remain oppressed forever. The yearning for freedom eventually manifests itself, and that is what has happened to the American Negro. . . . If one recognizes this vital urge that has engulfed the Negro community, one should readily understand why public demonstrations are taking place. The Negro has many pent-up resentments and latent frustrations, and he must release them. So let him march; let him make prayer pilgrimages to the city hall; let him go on freedom rides—and try to understand why he must do so. If his repressed emotions are not released in nonviolent ways, they will seek expression through violence; this is not a threat but a fact of history. So I have not said to my people: "Get rid of your discontent." Rather, I have tried to say that this normal and healthy discontent can be channeled into the creative outlet of nonviolent direct action.
>
> —*Dr. Martin Luther King, Jr., "Letter From Birmingham Jail," 1963*

18. **Connections to Today** Why is it important for U.S. citizens to learn about civil rights today?

DOCUMENT-BASED QUESTIONS

Great Society programs were as controversial as the New Deal had been in the 1930s. Read the documents below, then answer the questions that follow.

DOCUMENT A

In this excerpt from a speech, President Johnson describes the "Great Society" he hopes to create.

> The Great Society rests on abundance and liberty for all. It demands an end to poverty and racial injustice, to which we are totally committed in our time. But that is just the beginning.
>
> The Great Society is a place where every child can find knowledge to enrich his mind and to enlarge his talents. It is a place where leisure is a welcome chance to build and reflect, not a feared cause of boredom and restlessness. It is a place where the city of man serves not only the needs of the body and the demands of commerce but the desire for beauty and the hunger for community.
>
> *—President Lyndon Johnson, 1964*

DOCUMENT B

Study the photograph and answer the related question in the assessment section.

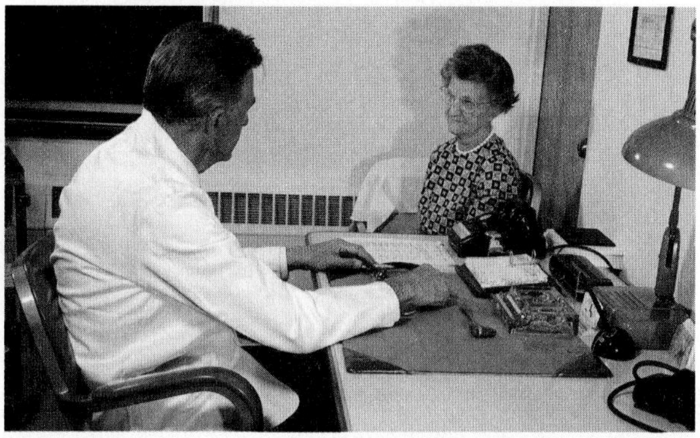

DOCUMENT C

This excerpt is from an article in the *Washington Post.*

> The backlash against the Great Society has been as enduring as its successes.
>
> Virtually every political battle that rages today has roots in the federal expansion and experimentation that began in the 1960s. It set terms of engagement for ideological warfare over how to grapple with income inequality, whether to encourage a common curriculum in schools, affirmative action, immigration. . .
>
> Many Great Society programs are now so popular it is hard to imagine the country as we know it without them. Others—including some of its more grandiose urban renewal efforts—are generally regarded as failures. Poverty remains with us, with the two parties in deep disagreement over whether government has alleviated it or made it harder to escape.
>
> *—Karen Tumulty, The Washington Post, May 17, 2014*

DOCUMENT D

This is an excerpt from the introduction to the memoir of Senator Everett Dirksen.

> On many domestic issues, Dirksen continued the balancing act so central to his effectiveness. . . . He took issue with Medicare, for example: "I would be eligible," he said indignantly. "Why should I be allowed to use dollars the government is taking from some young factory worker in Cleveland in the promise of providing for his old age?" The accumulation of Great Society spending programs appalled Dirksen. The taxpayers would have to come up with nearly $160 billion to fund them. Moreover, the programs brought with them an expanding federal bureaucracy and increasing centralization. To Dirksen, the Great Society was a misguided attempt at creating an immediate, utopian "blueprint for paradise."
>
> *—The Education of a Senator, Frank H. Mackaman, 1998*

19. In Document A, Johnson imagines the Great Society
A. as an unattainable and unrealistic goal.
B. as a society that undervalues commerce.
C. as a place of self-gratification.
D. as a society without poverty or injustice.

20. Analyze Photographs Based on Document B, what Great Society programs might relate to this scene.

21. In Document C, the writer argues that the Great Society programs
A. are no longer relevant.
B. were destructive and useless.
C. ended in the 1970s.
D. have shaped modern America.

22. In Document D, the writer describes Senator Dirksen as
A. supportive of Johnson's programs.
B. an opponent of the Great Society.
C. in favor of Medicare.
D. idealistic and visionary.

23. Writing Task Write a paragraph discussing the successes and failures of Johnson's Great Society programs in promoting social and economic stability. Use the sources as well as additional information you have learned.

Topic 17

The Vietnam War Era (1954–1975)

ESSENTIAL QUESTION What is America's role in the world?

GO ONLINE for immersive experiences designed to help you explore the experience of Americans during the Vietnam War through rich primary sources. Also access the eText, videos, Biographies, and other online resources.

U.S. soldiers near their base in Vietnam, 1966.

Connections to Today

Several million Americans served in the military during the Vietnam War. Millions more have since fought in conflicts all over the world. When soldiers come home, they face the challenge of rejoining civilian life. The government, in turn, faces the challenge of how best to help returning veterans. What does the government owe the men and women it has ordered into battle? And what do Americans owe those who have fought and sacrificed in their name?

NBC LEARN

Learn more about the experiences of Edie Meeks, a Vietnam War nurse

BOUNCE to Activate My Story Video

Topic 17 Overview

In this Topic, you'll learn about the events of the Vietnam War era. Look at the lesson outline and explore the timeline. As you study this Topic, you'll complete the Quest Inquiry.

LESSON OUTLINE	
17.1 The Cold War and Vietnam	**17.3** The Antiwar Movement
17.2 America's Role Escalates	**17.4** The War's End and Effects

Key Events of the Vietnam War Era

1954
Vietnam is divided into two countries.

1959
Fidel Castro takes power in Cuba.

1962
Cuban missile crisis

1963
Kennedy is assassinated; Johnson becomes president.

1964
Gulf of Tonkin Resolution

1965
Heavy U.S. bombing of Vietnam begins.

1968
Riots outside the Chicago Democratic Convention

1973
Paris Peace Accords

1975
Saigon falls to the North Vietnamese.

1950 · 1960 · 1970 · 1980

QUEST! INQUIRY

Document-Based Question: Reasons Behind the Antiwar Movement

Why did so many Americans oppose the Vietnam War? What were the anti-war movement's causes and consequences? In this Quest you'll explore the reasons why so many Americans were against the war and then write an essay explaining your findings.

STEP 1
Watch the video and discuss it in class or with a partner. Think about how and why the movement against the war gained momentum as the war progressed.

STEP 2
Examine sources relating to the Vietnam War and opposition to it. Answer the questions attached to each document.

STEP 3
Use the documents and your knowledge of history to write an essay that answers the question "Why did an antiwar movement develop in response to the Vietnam War?"

STEP 4
Reflect on the process of analyzing the documents and writing the essay and then complete the Self-Assessment.

GO ONLINE GO ONLINE to access complete Quest materials

17.1

GO ONLINE to **Project Imagine: Explore America's Road to War in Vietnam** to learn how the United States was slowly drawn into the unfolding conflict in Southeast Asia.

BOUNCE to Activate Flipped Video

Objectives

Explain the steps Kennedy took to change American foreign policy.

Analyze the causes and effects of the Bay of Pigs invasion and the Cuban Missile Crisis.

Assess the outcome of the Berlin Crisis and other foreign-policy events of the 1960s.

Describe the reasons that the United States helped the French fight Vietnamese nationalists.

Identify ways in which the United States opposed communism in Southeast Asia.

Analyze how the United States increased its involvement in Vietnam.

Key Terms

flexible response
Peace Corps
Alliance for Progress
Bay of Pigs Invasion
Cuban Missile Crisis
Nikita Khrushchev
hot line
Nuclear Test Ban Treaty
Berlin Wall
Ho Chi Minh
domino theory
Southeast Asia Treaty Organization (SEATO)
Vietcong
Gulf of Tonkin Resolution

GO ONLINE to access your digital course

The Cold War and Vietnam

John Kennedy's 1960 campaign stressed the need for the United States to move forward with vigor and determination. Kennedy argued that during the Eisenhower years America had lost ground in the Cold War struggle against communism. He pointed to the new communist regime under Fidel Castro in Cuba and charged that there was now a "missile gap" that left the U.S. nuclear missile force inferior to that of the Soviet Union. The first goal of the Kennedy administration would be to build up the nation's armed forces.

Kennedy Strives to Win the Cold War

Nowhere was the difference between Eisenhower and Kennedy more evident than in two important 1961 addresses. In his farewell address, Eisenhower counseled caution in foreign affairs. "The potential for the disastrous rise of misplaced power exists and will persist," he said.

As the first President born in the twentieth century, Kennedy proclaimed that a "new generation of Americans" was ready to meet any challenge. In his inaugural address, Kennedy warned his country's enemies:

> Let every nation know, whether it wishes us well or ill, that we shall pay any price, bear any burden, meet any hardship, support any friend, oppose any foe, in order to assure the survival and the success of liberty.
>
> —John F. Kennedy, Inaugural Address, January 20, 1961

As the Cold War continued into the 1960s, Kennedy took office facing the spread of communism abroad and the threat of nuclear war. Determined to succeed where he felt Eisenhower had failed, Kennedy's enthusiasm and commitment to change offered the hope that with hard work and persistence the United States could win the Cold War. Kennedy issued a challenge to Americans: "Ask not what your country can do for you; ask what you can do for your country."

>> President-elect Kennedy meets President Eisenhower at the White House in December, 1960. After he took office, Kennedy increased defense spending by $6 billion.

Significant National Decisions Impact the Cold War Eisenhower's defense policy of "massive retaliation" had emphasized the construction of nuclear weapons. Although Kennedy did not ignore the possibility of a nuclear war, he wanted to make sure that the United States was prepared to fight both conventional wars and conflicts against guerrilla forces. Kennedy therefore gave increased funding to conventional U.S. Army and Navy forces as well as to Army Special Forces, such as the Green Berets. He wanted a "**flexible response**" defense policy, one that prepared the United States to fight any type of conflict.

Important International Decisions Shape the Cold War The "Third World," as it was known at the time, was made up of the developing nations in Africa, Asia, and Latin America that did not align themselves with the United States or the Soviet Union. According to Soviet propaganda, Western capitalism created poverty and inequalities in the Third World, whereas communism promoted equality.

Like previous American leaders, Kennedy believed that democracy combined with prosperity would contain or limit the spread of communism. Therefore, he initiated programs to economically and politically strengthen the nations of the Third World. The **Peace Corps**, created in 1961, sent American volunteers around the world on "missions of freedom" to assist developing countries. They worked to provide technical, educational, and health services. The first Peace Corps volunteers arrived in Ghana, Africa, in 1961, to work as teachers. By the end of the year, the Peace Corps had volunteers working in two other countries in Africa—Nigeria and Tanzania. The program continues today and typically has thousands of volunteers in dozens of countries around the world.

>> By 1963, the Peace Corps had over 7,300 volunteers serving in over 40 countries, including Togo. President Kennedy appointed his brother-in-law, Sargent Shriver, as the Peace Corps's first director.

Other programs stressed purely economic development. One such project, the **Alliance for Progress** promised to resurrect America's Good Neighbor policy toward Latin America. During the 1950s, many Latin Americans had grown increasingly resentful of the United States, claiming that it had too much influence in their region. Kennedy hoped the Alliance for Progress would change that view.

At its start in 1961, the program pledged $20 billion to help 22 Latin American nations raise their per capita income, distribute income more equitably, and improve industry, agriculture, health, and welfare. Unlike the Peace Corps, however, the Alliance for Progress was not successful.

☑ **CONTRAST** How did the message of Kennedy's inaugural address differ from that of Eisenhower's farewell address?

Kennedy Responds to Communism in Cuba

In 1959, Cuban revolutionary Fidel Castro succeeded in overthrowing the regime of Fulgencio Batista. Initially, the United States attempted to cultivate good relations with Castro. However, it soon became clear that the Cuban leader was determined to nationalize land held by U.S. citizens, enforce radical reform measures, and accept Soviet economic and military aid. Thousands of wealthy and middle-class Cubans fled their country, many settling in Miami and southern Florida. Proud of their heritage and deeply anticommunist, they made new lives for themselves and their families in the United States.

Bay of Pigs Invasion After breaking diplomatic relations with Cuba in 1961, the Eisenhower administration authorized the Central Intelligence Agency (CIA) to plan an invasion of Cuba to overthrow Castro. The CIA recruited Cuban exiles and trained them in Guatemala. But when Eisenhower left office, the invasion plan was still that—an unexecuted plan.

Pressured by members of the CIA and his own aides, Kennedy decided to implement the plan. On April 17, 1961, a CIA-led force of Cuban exiles attacked Cuba in the **Bay of Pigs invasion**. The invasion was greatly mismanaged. The poorly equipped forces landed at the site with no protective cover. All but 300 of the 1,400 invaders were killed or captured. Not only did the Bay of Pigs invasion fail, it probably strengthened Castro's position in Cuba. It also turned many Cuban Americans against Kennedy.

Kennedy took personal responsibility for the failed invasion. He emphasized, however, that the United States would continue to resist "communist penetration" in the Western Hemisphere.

Cuba and the Bay of Pigs

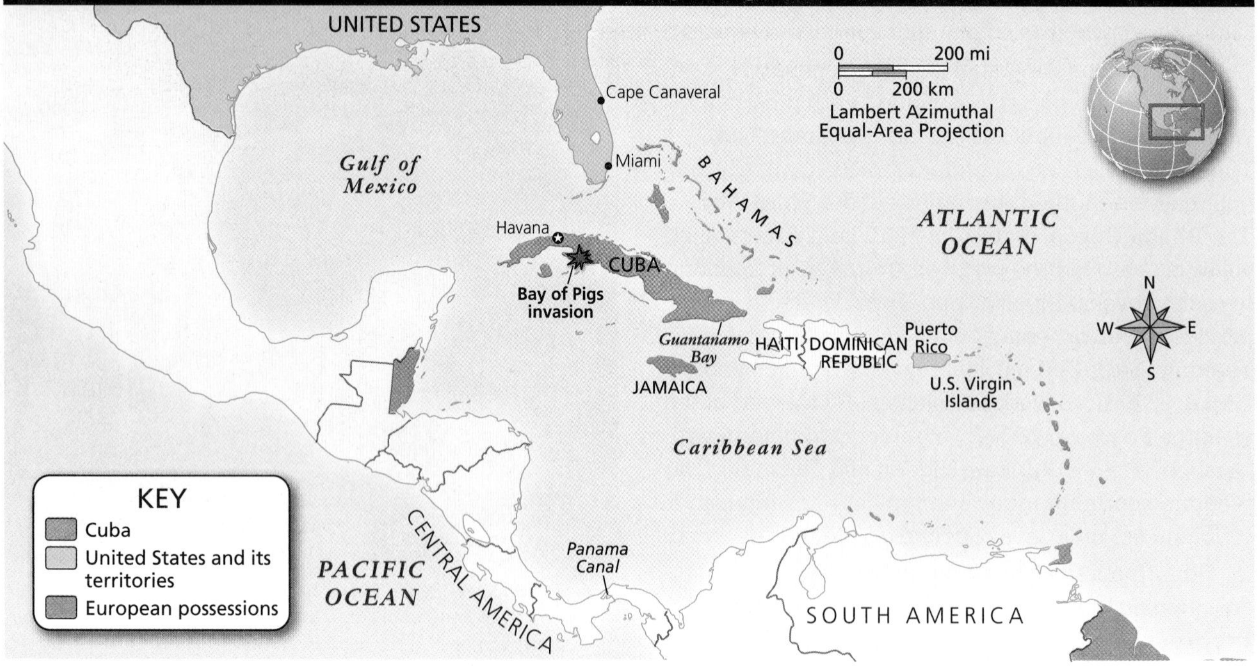

>> **Analyze Maps** Based on the information in the map, what factors might have influenced President Kennedy's decision to launch the Bay of Pigs invasion of Cuba, in 1961?

BOUNCE to Activate Timeline

Kennedy's Role in the Cuban Missile Crisis

Kennedy's efforts to contain communism were severely threatened during the **Cuban missile crisis**. In August and September of 1962 U.S. intelligence discovered that the Soviets were building nuclear missile sites in Cuba, apparently to protect Castro from another American invasion. When the sites were completed, major East Coast cities and the Panama Canal would be in range of the missiles.

In response to the perceived threat of Soviet aggression, Kennedy demanded the removal of the missiles. In a dramatic television address on October 22, 1962, he blamed **Nikita Khrushchev**, the Soviet premier, for causing a "reckless and provocative threat to world peace." He also announced that he had approved a naval quarantine (blockade) of Cuba to prevent the Soviets from completing the bases. Behind the scenes, however, Kennedy worked toward a diplomatic settlement. He indicated that he would remove U.S. missiles in Turkey and Italy if the Soviets removed their missiles in Cuba.

After six tense days during which nuclear war seemed a real possibility, Khrushchev agreed to honor the blockade and remove the missiles. As Secretary of State Dean Rusk later told a reporter, "Remember, when you report this, that, eyeball to eyeball, they blinked first."

>> Kennedy and Khrushchev smile for the cameras, but their June 1961 summit in Vienna, less than 2 months after the Bay of Pigs, was tense and combative.

The Impact of the Crisis During the Cuban missile crisis, Kennedy and Khrushchev stood on the edge of a nuclear war and then slowly backed away. In the Soviet Union, Khrushchev lost prestige and more hard-line leaders chipped away at his power. In the United States, Kennedy emerged as a more mature and thoughtful leader, one who had faced a frightening test and had remained calm and resolute. The crisis prompted both leaders to move toward détente—a relaxing of tension between rivals. They installed a "**hot line**" telephone system between Moscow and Washington, D.C., to improve communication. In 1963, the year after the crisis, the United States, Great Britain, and the Soviet Union signed the **Nuclear Test Ban Treaty**, the first nuclear-weapons agreement, which ended aboveground nuclear tests. Thirty-six other nations soon signed the agreement.

>> In 1961, workers build part of the Berlin Wall. The ninety-six-mile-long wall would divide Soviet controlled East Berlin from democratic West Berlin.

☑ **IDENTIFY SUPPORTING DETAILS** What diplomatic enticement did Kennedy offer the Soviets to help solve the Cuban Missile Crisis?

The Causes and Outcomes of the Berlin Crisis

Since 1958, Khrushchev wanted to sign a peace treaty that would put the western zones of Berlin under control of East Germany. His actions were motivated by the steady flow of skilled East German workers into West Berlin. Desiring to show his strength, Kennedy stood firm on America's commitment to defending the rights of West Berliners and West Germans. At a conference in Vienna in June 1961, Kennedy and Khrushchev focused on Berlin as the key issue. Khrushchev called the present situation "intolerable."

He demanded that the United States recognize the formal division of Germany and end its military presence in West Berlin. Kennedy refused. He did not want to give up occupation rights he considered critical to defending Western Europe. In a tense atmosphere, Khrushchev said, "I want peace, but if you want war, that is your problem." Kennedy answered, "It is you, not I who wants to force a change." The meeting ended abruptly. The conference, meant to relax Cold War tensions, only increased them.

After returning home, both world leaders made moves that threatened the peace. Kennedy asked Congress to dramatically increase military spending. Khrushchev ordered the construction of a wall between East and West Berlin. The **Berlin Wall** became a visible symbol of the reality of the two Germanys and the gulf between the communist East and the democratic West. Kennedy responded by sending 1,500 U.S. troops to West Berlin. For a time, Russian and American tanks moved within sight of each other. Yet, neither side could fully claim a victory.

☑ **HYPOTHESIZE** For what reason might the Soviets have wanted to gain control of West Berlin?

Reasons for U.S. Involvement in Indochina

Presidents Kennedy and Johnson shared a vision for a better America in the 1960s. They also shared a vision for a better world in which America would emerge victorious from its Cold War struggle against global communism. As part of this strategic and ideological battle, the United States established a new line of defense against communism in Vietnam. The conflict in Southeast Asia would grow to be one of the most costly wars in American history.

Situated far away in Southeast Asia, Vietnam did not attract significant American attention until the 1960s. Television news shows rarely mentioned it, and many Americans could not locate it on a

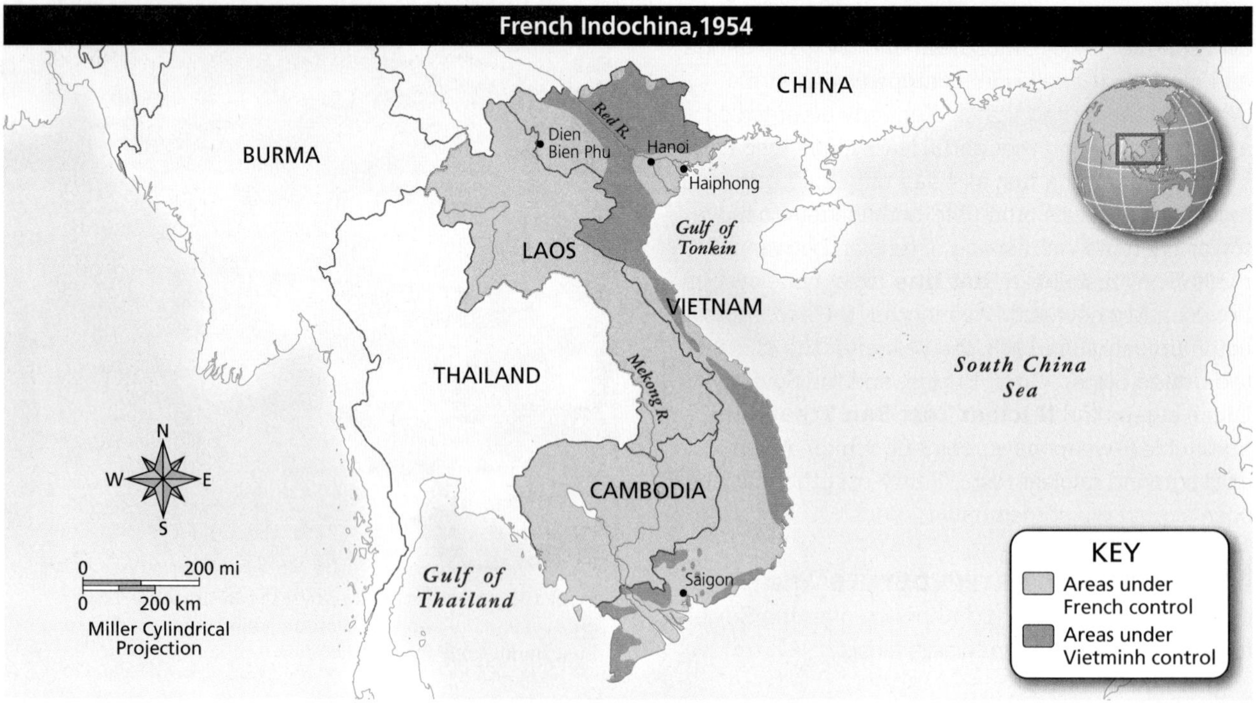

>> **Analyze Maps** Based on the information in this map, which regions of present-day Vietnam were particularly dangerous for French forces?

map. But over a span of more than ten years, the United States sent several million soldiers to fight in Vietnam. America's involvement in Vietnam had roots in European colonialism, Cold War politics, and Vietnamese calls for national independence.

French Control of Indochina in Southeast Asia

French Control of Indochina in Southeast Asia In the 1800s, French military forces established control over Indochina, a peninsula in Southeast Asia that includes the modern countries of Vietnam, Cambodia, and Laos. Slightly larger than the state of Texas, Indochina included almost 27 million people by the end of World War II. French colonial officials ruled Vietnam with an iron fist. They transplanted French laws into Vietnam and imposed high taxes. French business people acquired large rice and rubber plantations and controlled the mineral wealth of the country. Some Vietnamese, especially wealthier members of society, benefited from western culture and technology. Many others, however, were impoverished by colonialism.

Some Vietnamese rebelled against France's exploitative rule. **Ho Chi Minh** became the most important voice demanding independence for Vietnam. Born in 1890, Ho became involved in anti-French organizations as a young man and fled Vietnam in 1912.

He traveled the world, visiting American ports and living periodically in London, Paris, and Moscow. During his 30-year absence, Ho constantly thought and wrote about Vietnam, and he searched for westerners who would support his plans for Vietnamese independence. Ho embraced communism, and eventually Soviet communists rallied to his cause.

The French Fight Nationalism and Communism

During World War II, Japan had undermined French control over Vietnam. But when the conflict ended, France reasserted its colonial claims there. France's problem, however, was that colonialism was a dying institution. World War II had strengthened nationalist movements while weakening the economic and military positions of traditional European powers. In Vietnam, Ho Chi Minh clamored for independence as France struggled to maintain its dwindling global power.

Meanwhile, the United States faced a difficult decision. On the one hand, it supported decolonization. On the other hand, America wanted France as an ally in its Cold War effort to contain the Soviet Union.

President Harry S. Truman believed that if he supported Vietnamese independence, he would

>> Ho Chi Minh was a revolutionary leader who fought against French occupation. Later, he became the prime minister, then president of the Democratic Republic of Vietnam (North Vietnam).

weaken anticommunist forces in France. So, to ensure a strong, anticommunist Western Europe, Truman sacrificed his own anticolonial sentiments.

Vietnam thus became a pawn in Cold War politics. To ensure French support in the Cold War, Truman agreed to aid France's efforts to regain control over Vietnam. After communist forces won the civil war in China in 1949, America increased its aid to the French in Vietnam. Truman did not want to see another communist victory in Asia. Between 1950 and 1954, the United States contributed $2.6 billion to France's war efforts. Containing Ho Chi Minh's communist Vietminh—an abbreviation of the League for the Independence of Vietnam— became a national priority.

The Domino Theory Spurs U.S. Involvement in Vietnam

When President Dwight D. Eisenhower took office in early 1953, he continued Truman's policies toward Vietnam. He sent monetary aid to the French, arguing that by battling Ho Chi Minh, they were containing the spread of communism.

Eisenhower told a journalist that the fight in Vietnam involved more than the future of just one country:

> You have a row of dominoes set up, you knock over the first one, and what will happen to the last one is the certainty that it will go over very quickly. So you could have a beginning of a disintegration that would have the most profound influences.
>
> —Dwight D. Eisenhower, Arpil 7, 1954

The **domino theory** was the idea that if Vietnam fell to communism, its closest neighbors would follow. This in turn would threaten Japan, the Philippines, and Australia. In short, stopping the communists in Vietnam was important to the protection of the entire region.

In 1954, however, the French lost their eight-year struggle to regain Vietnam. The Vietminh trapped a large French garrison at Dien Bien Phu, a military base in northwest Vietnam, and laid siege to it for 55 days. During the siege, which one Frenchman described as "hell in a very small place," Vietminh troops destroyed the French airstrip, cut French supply lines, and dug trenches to attack key French positions. Finally, on May 7, 1954, after suffering some 15,000 casualties, the French surrendered.

The very next day at an international peace conference in Geneva, Switzerland, France sued for peace. According to the Geneva Accords, France granted independence to Vietnam, Laos, and Cambodia. The accords also divided Vietnam at the seventeenth parallel into two countries, North Vietnam and South Vietnam. Ho Chi Minh's communist forces ruled in North Vietnam, and an anticommunist government, supported by the United States, assumed power in South Vietnam. The accords also called for free elections in 1956 to unify Vietnam.

CHECK UNDERSTANDING Why was supporting the French in Indochina problematic for President Truman?

The United States Responds to Communism in Vietnam

During the Battle of Dien Bien Phu, France appealed to the United States for military support. President Eisenhower was willing to supply money but not soldiers. Ike would not commit American troops to defend colonialism in Asia. Nevertheless, the President firmly supported the new anticommunist government of South Vietnam.

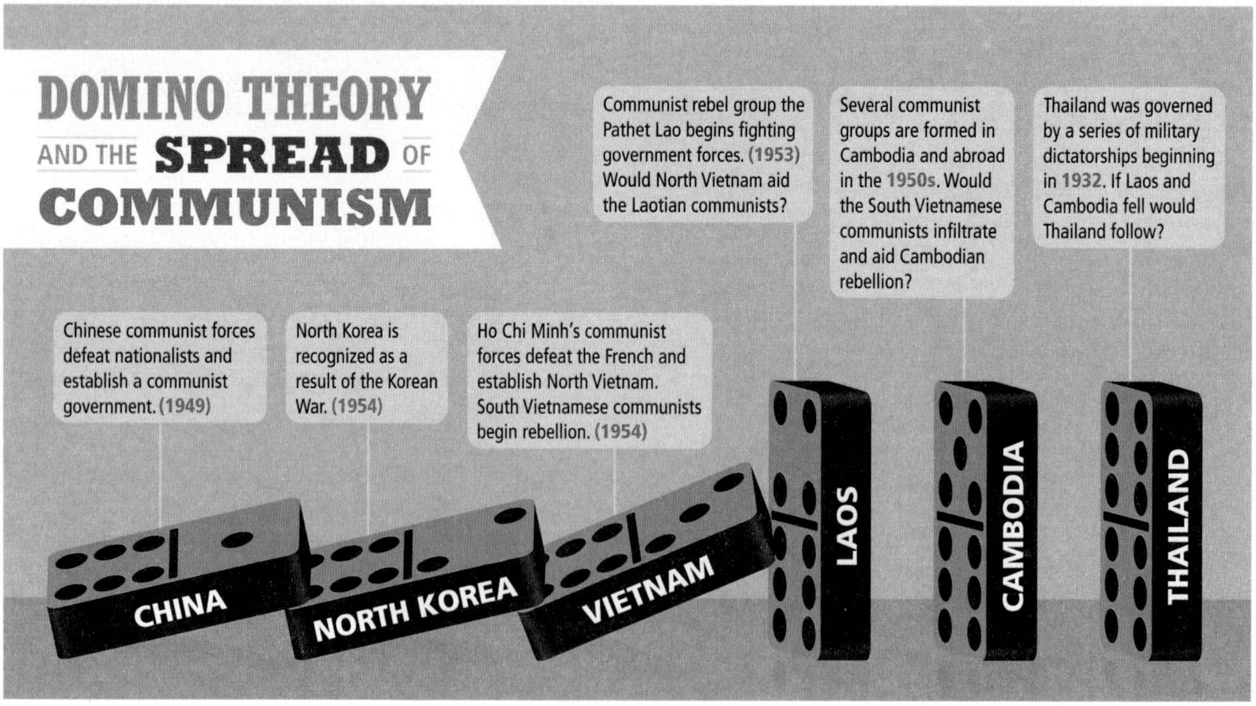

>> **Support a Point of View with Evidence** The graphic shows the international chain reaction that American strategists of the 1950s most feared. Were these strategists justified in their concern about the spread of communism? Explain.

BOUNCE to Activate Gallery

The U.S. Escalates Involvement in South Vietnam America channeled aid to South Vietnam in different ways. In 1954, the United States and seven other countries formed the **Southeast Asia Treaty Organization (SEATO)**. Similar to NATO's goal in Europe, SEATO's goal was to contain the spread of communism in Southeast Asia.

The United States provided economic and military aid to the South Vietnamese government led by Ngo Dinh Diem. Diem was an ardent nationalist and anticommunist. Although he lacked popular appeal, his anticommunism guaranteed American support. When it came time for the 1956 unification elections, American intelligence analysts predicted that Diem would lose to the more popular Ho Chi Minh. Rather than risk losing, Diem refused to participate in the elections, a move made with the support of the U.S. government.

>> French soldiers march Vietminh prisoners captured during fighting near Dien Bien Phu.

Impact of the Communist Insurgency By 1957, a communist rebel group in the South, known as the National Liberation Front (NLF), had committed itself to undermining the Diem government and uniting Vietnam under a communist flag. NLF guerrilla fighters, called **Vietcong**, launched an insurgency in which they assassinated government officials and destroyed roads and bridges. Supplied by communists in North Vietnam, the Vietcong employed surprise hit-and-run tactics to weaken Diem's hold on South Vietnam.

Diem's own policies also weakened his position in South Vietnam. A devout Roman Catholic in an overwhelmingly Buddhist nation, Diem did little to build a broad political base. Instead, he signed anti-Buddhist legislation and refused to enact significant land reforms. His lack of popular support hurt him in the civil war against North Vietnam. Only the support of the United States kept the unpopular leader in power.

>> Vietcong guerillas patrol the Saigon River in South Vietnam.

Kennedy Sends U.S. Troops to Vietnam After his election in 1960, President John F. Kennedy took a more aggressive stand against the communists in Vietnam. Beginning in 1961, he sent Special Forces troops to South Vietnam to advise the Army of the Republic of Vietnam (ARVN) on more effective ways to fight the communist forces. By 1963, more than 15,000 American military personnel were fighting in Vietnam.

Although U.S. military personnel fought bravely and achieved some success, Diem continued to alienate South Vietnamese citizens. By late 1963, his regime was in shambles. Buddhists protested his restrictive policies, occasionally by setting

>> President Johnson meets with his cabinet to discuss the Gulf of Tonkin incident. **Predict Consequences** How might the Gulf of Tonkin incident affect U.S. policy in Vietnam?

themselves on fire. The Kennedy administration eventually concluded that South Vietnam needed new leadership. Working behind the scenes, Americans plotted with anti-Diem generals to overthrow Diem's government. On November 1, 1963, Diem was removed from power; he was assassinated the following day.

Johnson Leads the Nation into the Vietnam War

Three weeks after Diem's fall, an assassin's bullet struck down President Kennedy. Vice President Lyndon B. Johnson was sworn in as the new President. Johnson was a Cold War traditionalist who held a monolithic view of communism. For this "Cold Warrior," communism in the Soviet Union, China, and Vietnam were all the same. He did not recognize subtle differences. He also knew that the American people expected victory in Vietnam.

Reasons for Escalating Conflict In 1964, President Johnson faced his first crisis in Vietnam. On August 2, the destroyer USS *Maddox* was patrolling the Gulf of Tonkin off the coast of North Vietnam. It fired warning shots at approaching North Vietnamese torpedo boats. The boats shot torpedoes at the *Maddox,* but missed. The *Maddox* then returned fire. Johnson promptly responded to the attack and to other North Vietnamese provocations. He announced that "aggression by terror against peaceful villages of South Vietnam has now been joined by open aggression on the high seas against the United States of America." Troubled by increasing strikes against an American ally, Johnson ordered an airstrike against North Vietnam.

Congress Gives Johnson Broad Military Powers The President next asked Congress to authorize the use of force to defend American troops. With little debate and only two senators voting against it, Congress agreed to Johnson's request and passed the **Gulf of Tonkin Resolution**. The resolution authorized the President "to take all necessary measures to repel any armed attack against the forces of the United States and to prevent further aggression." The resolution gave Johnson tremendous war powers. It allowed him to commit U.S. troops to South Vietnam and fight a war against North Vietnam without ever going back to Congress to ask for a declaration of war. By authorizing the resolution, Congress had handed its war powers as expressed in the Constitution to the executive branch. This raised questions about the relationship between the legislative and executive branches of government. Presidents Johnson and Nixon used the resolution as the legal basis for their military policies in Vietnam.

☑ **DESCRIBE** What role did religious issues play in Diem's troubles as leader of South Vietnam?

☑ ASSESSMENT

1. **Contrast** the foreign policies of Eisenhower and Kennedy during the Cold War.
2. **Identify Cause and Effect** Explain how World War II affected French colonial power in Vietnam.
3. **Draw Conclusions** Discuss reasons why the United States supported Ngo Dinh Diem, and explain how this changed in later years.
4. **Determine Point of View** Discuss President Truman's decision to support French efforts in Vietnam during the Cold War.
5. **Connections to Today** The Gulf of Tonkin Resolution gave President Johnson the authority to expand American involvement in Vietnam. How much control do you think Congress should have over the decision to send American troops abroad? Explain your answer.

Primary Sources

Letters Between Bobbie Lou Pendergrass and President Kennedy

Introduction

Starting in 1961, President John F. Kennedy sent American troops to Vietnam as advisors to the South Vietnamese military. By 1963, 15,000 Americans were serving in the country. Even at this early date, the death toll began to mount.

One of those killed during President Kennedy's term in office was Specialist James Delmas McAndrew. His sister Bobbie Lou Pendergrass wrote the President a powerful letter asking, in short, why her brother had to die. What cause was worth his sacrifice? Kennedy, clearly moved, responded with a concise explanation for American involvement in the war.

>> President Kennedy meets with General Maxwell Taylor and Secretary of Defense Robert McNamara on October 2, 1963.

Primary Source 1

February 18, 1963

Dear President Kennedy,

My brother, Specialist James Delmas McAndrew, was one of the seven crew members killed on January 11 in a Viet Nam [Vietnam] helicopter crash. . . .

My two older brothers entered the Navy and the Marine Corps in 1941 immediately after the war started—they served all during the war . . . then Jim went into the Marines as soon as he was old enough. . . . During those war years and even all during the Korean conflict we worried about all of them—but that was all very different. They were wars that our country [was] fighting, and everyone here knew that our sons and brothers were giving their lives for their country.

ANALYZE INTERACTIONS In which war did Pendergrass' two older brothers fight? What happened in 1941 that likely prompted them to join the navy?

I can't help but feel that giving one's life for one's country is one thing, but being sent to a country where half our country never even heard of and being shot at without even a chance to shoot back is another thing altogether!

Please, I'm only a housewife who doesn't even claim to know all about the international situation, but we have felt so bitter over this—can the small number of our boys over in Viet Nam possibly be doing enough good to justify the awful number of casualties? It seems that if we are going to have boys over there, that we should send enough to have a chance—or else stay home. Those fellows are just sitting ducks in those darn helicopters. If a war is worth fighting—isn't it worth fighting to win?

Please answer this and help me . . . to feel that even though Jim died in Viet Nam—and it isn't our war—it wasn't in vain. . . .

Very sincerely,
Bobbie Lou Pendergrass
Santa Ana
California

Primary Source 2

Mar 6 1963

Dear Mrs. Pendergrass:

I would like to express to you my deep and sincere sympathy in the loss of your brother. I can, of course, well understand your bereavement and the feelings which prompted you to write.

ANALYZE STYLE AND RHETORIC What tone is Kennedy aiming for in the paragraph above?

The questions which you posed in your letter can . . . . best be answered by realizing why your brother—and other American men—went to Viet Nam in the first place . . . . Americans are in Viet Nam because we have determined that this country must not fall under Communist domination. Ever since Viet Nam was divided, the Viet Namese have fought valiantly to maintain their independence in the face of the continuing threat from the North. Shortly after the division eight years ago it became apparent that they could not be successful . . . . without extensive assistance from other nations of the Free World . . . .

ANALYZE SEQUENCE What happened eight years ago that was so important? What followed this event, and why does that concern the United States?

Even with this help, the situation grew steadily worse under the pressure of the Viet Cong. By 1961 it became apparent that the troubles in Laos and. . . . in Viet Nam could easily expand. It is also apparent that the Communist attempt to take over Viet Nam, is only part of a larger plan for bringing the entire area of Southeast Asia under their domination. Though it is only a small part of the area geographically, Viet Nam is now the most crucial.

If Viet Nam should fall, it will indicate to the people of Southeast Asia that complete Communist domination of their part of the world is almost inevitable. Your brother was in Viet Nam because the threat to the Viet Namese people is, in the long run, a threat to the Free World community, and ultimately a threat to us also. For when freedom is destroyed in one country, it is threatened throughout the world. . . .

DESCRIBE Which foreign policy theory is Kennedy describing in this section?

James McAndrew must have foreseen that his service could take him into a war like this; a war in which he took part not as a combatant but as an advisor. . . . I know that as a soldier, he knew full scale war in Viet Nam is at the moment unthinkable.

I believe if you can see this as he must have seen it, you will believe as he must have believed, that he did not die in vain. . . .

Again, I would like to express to you. . . . my deepest personal sympathy.

Sincerely,
John F. Kennedy

ASSESSMENT

1. **Compare and Contrast** What makes the Vietnam War different from the Korean War and other conflicts, according to Pendergrass?
2. **Determine Author's Purpose** What does Pendergrass want Kennedy to do differently in his conduct of the war? Does this surprise you? Why or why not?
3. **Analyze Word Choice** What language does Kennedy use to justify the American presence in Vietnam? Do you find his wording as persuasive as he intended? Explain your answer.
4. **Determine Central Ideas** Why does President Kennedy believe Vietnam is so crucial?

17.2

GO ONLINE to **Project Imagine: Witness the Fighting in Vietnam** to discover what it was like to fight far from home in a challenging environment.

America's Role Escalates

After the Gulf of Tonkin Resolution, President Johnson began to shift U.S. military efforts in Vietnam into high gear. But America's leaders and soldiers soon found themselves stuck in a deadly quagmire with no quick victory in sight. The war began to weaken the economy, divide the American people, and erode the nation's morale.

BOUNCE to Activate Flipped Video

Objectives

Analyze the major issues and events that caused President Johnson to increase American troop strength in Vietnam.

Assess the nature of the war in Vietnam and the difficulties faced by each side.

Evaluate the effects of low morale on American troops and on the home front.

Key Terms

William Westmoreland
napalm
hawk
dove

Escalation of Forces in Vietnam

In February 1965, President Johnson dramatically altered the U.S. role in the Vietnam War. In response to a Vietcong attack that killed American troops at Pleiku, Johnson ordered the start of Operation Rolling Thunder, the first sustained bombing campaign against North Vietnam. Johnson hoped that this new strategy of intensive bombing would convince North Vietnam to stop reinforcing the Vietcong in South Vietnam.

The bombs caused widespread destruction, but they failed to convince North Vietnam to make peace. As the communist forces continued to fight, the United States committed more troops to battle them on the ground. American soldiers moved beyond their advisory roles and assumed greater combat responsibilities, while South Vietnamese troops accepted a secondary, more limited role in the war. U.S. military and civilian leaders hoped that American airstrikes, along with the troops on the ground, would eventually force the communists to the peace table.

Johnson Changes Strategies Johnson's change in strategy in 1965 stemmed primarily from the counsel of Secretary of

GO ONLINE to access your digital course

Defense Robert McNamara and General **William Westmoreland**, the American commander in South Vietnam. These two advisors believed that the United States needed to increase its military presence in Vietnam and do more of the fighting in order to win the war. Operation Rolling Thunder and increased troop commitments fulfilled this need to "Americanize" the war effort.

Beginning in March 1965, U.S. airstrikes hammered North Vietnam and Vietcong strong points in South Vietnam. Meanwhile, a secret bombing campaign against communist forces was also underway in Laos. Between 1965 and 1973, American pilots dropped more than 6 million tons of bombs on enemy positions—almost three times the tonnage dropped by all the combatants during World War II. In addition to conventional bombs, American pilots dropped napalm and sprayed Agent Orange. **Napalm** is a jellied gasoline which was dropped in large canisters that exploded on impact, covering large areas in flames. It clung to anything it touched and was difficult to extinguish. Agent Orange is an herbicide meant to kill plant life. U.S. forces used it to defoliate forest areas that might conceal enemy fighters and to disrupt the enemy's food supply. Almost half of South Vietnam's forested areas were sprayed at least once, and the ecological impact was devastating. There also may have been a hidden human cost, as many scientists believe that Agent Orange causes cancers and other physical problems.

As airstrikes intensified, American ground troops landed in South Vietnam. On March 8, 1965, U.S. Marines arrived to defend the airbase at Da Nang. They were soon followed by other troops. The soldiers accepted a wide range of missions. Some guarded bases. Others conducted search-and-destroy missions to kill as many Vietcong guerrillas as they could. Helicopters ferried commandos to and from remote locations for quick strikes against enemy positions.

Vietcong Tactics and Strategies Large-scale battles against Vietcong or North Vietnamese Army units were not typical of America's strategy in Vietnam. American soldiers generally fought lightly armed Vietcong guerrillas in small engagements.

Ho Chi Minh's military doctrine hinged on fighting only when victory was assured, which meant never fighting on his opponents' terms. He compared his troops to a tiger, while the Americans were like an elephant. If the tiger stands still, the elephant will crush it. But if the tiger keeps moving and occasionally jumps on the elephant to take a bite out of it, the elephant will slowly bleed to death.

During the war, the Vietcong behaved like Ho's tiger. They traveled light, often carrying just a rifle and a few handfuls of rice. They hid in tunnels during the day and emerged at night to ambush American patrols. They infiltrated American bases and set off explosives. They set booby traps that maimed and

Vietnam War, 1963–1967

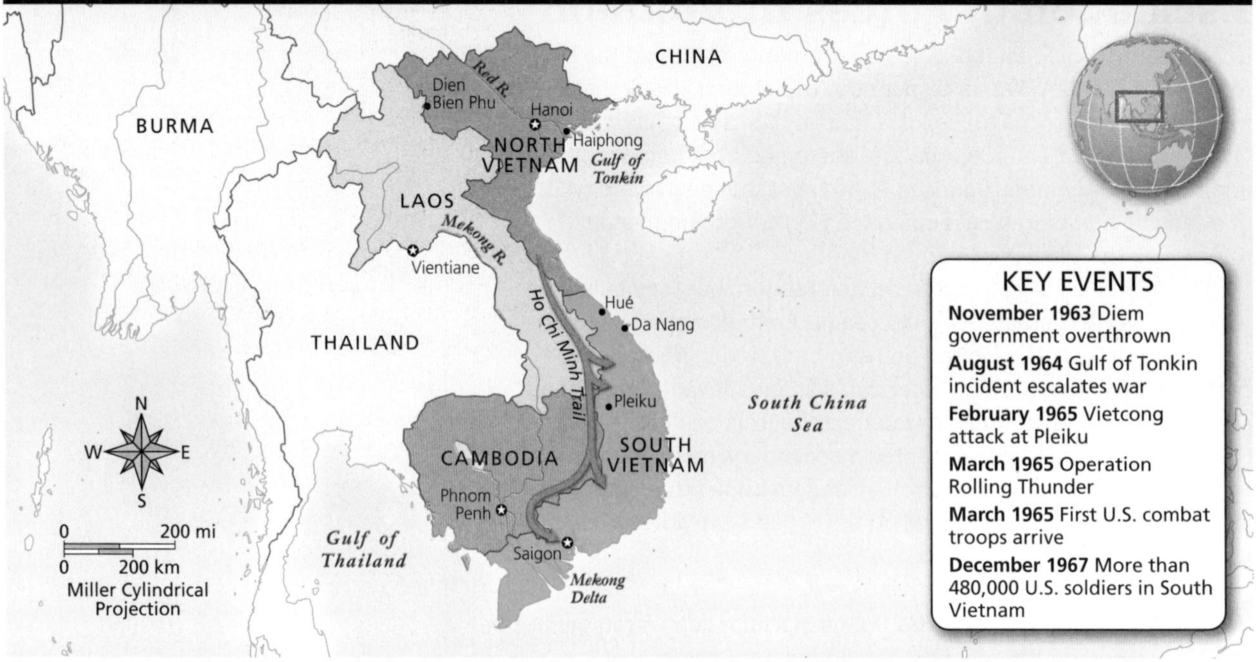

>> **Analyze Maps** Based on the information in the map, what advantage did the Ho Chi Minh Trail give the Vietcong?

BOUNCE to Activate Chart

VIETNAM EFFECTS OF ESCALATION

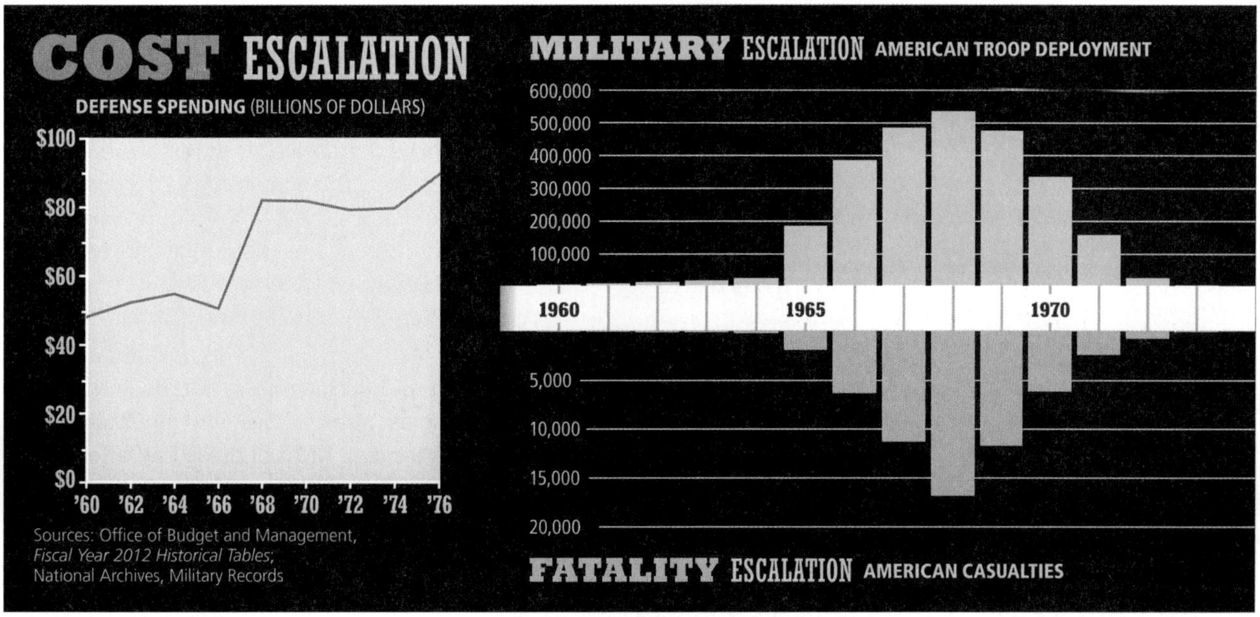

>> **Analyze Data** What does the data reveal about the war during the years 1965 to 1968?

maimed and crippled American troops. They covertly sent troops and supplies into South Vietnam using the Ho Chi Minh Trail, a route that passed through the mountains of neighboring Laos and Cambodia. Their strategy was to wear the Americans down. The leaders of North Vietnam and the Vietcong remained convinced that if they could just avoid losing the war, the Americans would eventually leave.

American Casualties Escalate American strategy during this stage of the war yielded limited results. U.S. bombers did disrupt North Vietnamese industry and slow the movement of supplies to the Vietcong. But when the communists did not sue for peace, American troop commitments and battlefield deaths escalated rapidly. By the end of 1965, there were 184,300 U.S. troops in Vietnam, and only 636 American soldiers had died in the war. Three years later, there were more than 500,000 U.S. troops in Vietnam, and the number of American dead had risen to more than 30,000.

Each year, the war claimed more American lives and cost more American dollars. But at the end of each year, the United States seemed no closer to success. America's mission was to help South Vietnam build a stable noncommunist nation and thereby win the "hearts and minds" of its citizens. But corruption plagued the South Vietnamese administrative structure. Outside of the major cities, the government enjoyed little support. Although American forces won most of the larger battles, they did not achieve a successful end to the war. By 1967, the war had devolved into a stalemate. Some U.S. critics of the war compared it to a quagmire—muddy terrain that sinks underfoot and is difficult to exit.

☑ **INFER** Why did General Westmoreland and Secretary of Defense McNamara want to "Americanize" the war?

Patriotism, Heroism, and Sinking Morale

For American soldiers in the field, the Vietnam War presented difficult challenges that demanded courage and patience. Unlike World War II, the Vietnam War did not emphasize territorial acquisition. The United States and its allies did not invade North Vietnam, march on Ho Chi Minh's capital of Hanoi, or attempt to destroy the communist regime. As in the Korean War, the United States was wary of triggering both Chinese and Soviet entry into the conflict. Instead, U.S. forces supported the survival and development of South Vietnam, which was besieged by the Vietcong and their North Vietnamese allies. In this fight, U.S. troops could never fully tell their friends from their enemies. Yet from the outset, they faced the dangers of Vietnam's battlefields with dedication and bravery.

I volunteered. . . . Ever since the American Revolution my family had people in all the different wars, and that was always the thing—when your country needs you, you go. You don't ask a lot of questions. . . .

—David Ross, United States Army medic

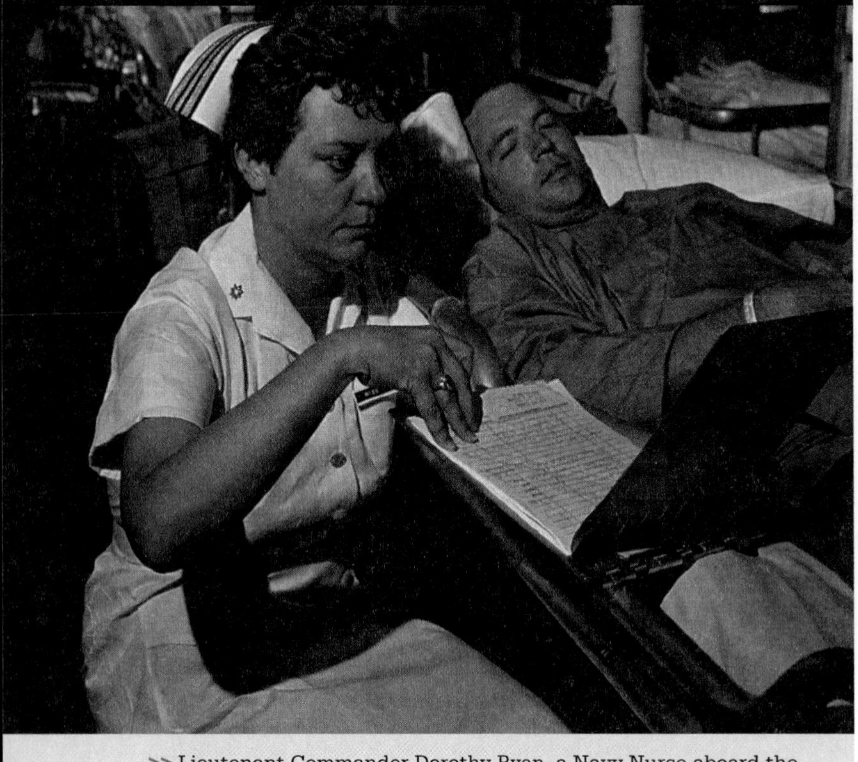

>> Lieutenant Commander Dorothy Ryan, a Navy Nurse aboard the hospital ship USS *Repose,* was one of about 10,000 American women who bravely served in Vietnam.

New Battlefield Dangers and Guerrilla Warfare Although American troops won numerous battles, they could not win the war outright. The problem was that the Vietcong and North Vietnamese avoided significant engagements. Rather than expose themselves to superior American firepower, the communists employed guerrilla warfare tactics, fighting smaller skirmishes where their small-unit abilities and their knowledge of the landscape bettered their chances for victory.

U.S. forces often had no alternative but to fight indecisive battles in the jungles, rice paddies, and mountains of Vietnam. Most of these battlefields abounded with natural cover. Clad in black clothing, Vietcong gunmen would spring out of the dense foliage, attack with automatic rifles and grenades, and disappear back into the landscape. Much of this fighting took place at night, which reduced the effectiveness of American planes, artillery, and troop tactics.

American Soldiers Fulfill Their Duty Despite the trials of war, American soldiers adapted to adverse conditions in Vietnam and fought with the same intensity that U.S. forces had shown in World Wars I and II. Many fought to prevent the spread of communism. Some fought to protect villagers in South Vietnam and win their trust and respect. Others fought because their country was at war, and they felt it was their duty. A medic in the First Infantry Division explained his reason for going to Vietnam:

> I volunteered. . . . Ever since the American Revolution my family had people in all the different wars, and that was always the thing—when your country needs you, you go. You don't ask a lot of questions. . . .
>
> —David Ross, United States Army medic

Later, many did ask questions about America's involvement in the war, but overwhelmingly while they were in Vietnam, the soldiers met their duties with courage. More than 58,000 of them gave their lives for their country.

Impact of the War on the U.S. Economy, 1968

INFLATION	Reached 4%
TAXES	Income tax increased by 10%
GDP (GROSS DOMESTIC PRODUCT)	Reached a high of 9.5% devoted to the war effort
GREAT SOCIETY INITIATIVES	President Lyndon B. Johnson's reform programs weakened by rising costs of the war: $94.3 billion spent on the war, $14.9 billion spent on welfare
EDUCATION	Out of the $277 billion spent by federal, state, and local governments,16% was directed toward education, 34% toward the military

>> **Analyze Data** In your opinion, which two effects had the most negative impact and why?

Women also displayed courage and valor. About 10,000 American military women served in Vietnam during the war. Most female military personnel were nurses.

Not only did they face danger working close to the front, but they also had to cope with the emotional toll of constantly working with injured and dying soldiers and civilians.

Lynda Van Devanter volunteered to go to Vietnam and spent a year there as a nurse. Like other nurses, she confronted war and death on a daily basis. However, on one occasion she had to deliver a baby. She later recalled:

> It was creation of life in the midst of all that destruction. And creation of life restored your sanity. . . . Those were the things that kept you going. That there was life coming. There was still hope.
>
> —Lynda Van Devanter, United States Army nurse

Questioning the Cause As the war lengthened, many Americans began to question U.S. involvement. The earliest soldiers in Vietnam had been volunteers, men committed to the fight against communism. But by the end of 1965, most American soldiers in Vietnam had been drafted into military service, and they were not as certain that preserving the government in South Vietnam was crucial to American interests. They sensed that many South Vietnamese people were indifferent—if not openly hostile—to their own government. Increasingly, it seemed that Americans were dying to defend a government that the South Vietnamese people were unwilling to defend themselves.

☑ **DESCRIBE** What relatively successful tactic did North Vietnamese and Vietcong fighters employ against U.S. forces?

Doubt Grows on the Home Front

The lack of progress toward victory in Vietnam also led to doubt in the United States. When President Johnson had begun to send troops to war, Americans had expected a relatively quick victory. After all, the United States was a militarily powerful, technologically advanced country, and North Vietnam was a poor country with comparatively little technology. Over the next few years, the Johnson administration kept asserting that an American victory was close at hand. But when that did not come, many began to question the President's foreign policy.

Impact of Defense Spending on the Economy The war strained government finances. President Johnson's Great Society plan called for enormous domestic spending to eliminate poverty, improve education and medical care, and fight racial discrimination. The costs of fighting a war on the other side of the world were just as mammoth. Although massive government spending lowered the unemployment rate, it also led to rising prices and inflation. The combination of heavy government spending, rising prices, and inflation forced Johnson to raise taxes. Ultimately, Johnson had to cut back on his Great Society reform initiatives to help pay for the war.

An Antiwar Movement Emerges As long as America's involvement in Vietnam had been small and relatively inexpensive, few politicians voiced serious opposition. Congress offered bipartisan support for the Vietnam policies of Johnson's predecessors. Soon after the Gulf of Tonkin Resolution, however, Congressional support began to waver over the President's escalation of the war.

Beginning in 1967, Congress—and eventually most of the nation—divided into two camps: hawks and doves. The mostly conservative **hawks** supported Johnson's war policy. Believing strongly in the containment of communism and the domino theory, they accepted rising troop levels, escalating costs, and increasing numbers of battlefield deaths. For the hawks, Vietnam was a crucial front in the Cold War. **Doves**, however, broke with Johnson's war policy. A diverse group that included liberal politicians, pacifists, student radicals, and civil rights leaders, doves questioned the war on both moral and strategic grounds. For them, the conflict was a localized civil war, not a vital Cold War battleground.

Senator J. William Fulbright, chairman of the Senate Foreign Relations Committee, emerged as the early leader of the doves in Congress. A Democrat who had supported the Gulf of Tonkin Resolution, Fulbright soon came to believe that the war in Vietnam was a national civil war, not a Cold War conflict directed from Moscow or Beijing. In 1967 and 1968, Fulbright held public hearings on the war, providing a platform for critics of the conflict.

RECALL How did the growing belief that the Vietnam War was not a vital, Cold War conflict affect American society?

ASSESSMENT

1. **Distinguish** Discuss the relationship between U.S. troops and South Vietnamese troops during the Vietnam War.
2. **Identify Cause and Effect** Explain how Operation Rolling Thunder represented a change in the U.S. war strategy.
3. **Compare and Contrast** Explain the advantages that North Vietnamese and Vietcong soldiers had over U.S. soldiers during the war.
4. **Generate Explanations** Explain the respective goals of the United States and North Vietnam during the Vietnam War.
5. **Determine Point of View** Discuss reasons that some Americans opposed the Vietnam War.
6. **Quest Connections** A large antiwar movement developed during the Vietnam War, but not during World War II. Compare these two conflicts. What made the Vietnam War different?

GO ONLINE to access this biography:
Lyndon B. Johnson

Life on the Front Lines

The United States faced a challenging opponent during the Vietnam War. Vietcong guerrillas fought an unconventional war. They used booby-traps and landmines, hid among civilians, and staged ambushes. The way the Vietcong fought made it hard for the United States to use its military advantages. What good was overwhelming air power if your enemy was hiding in a tunnel you couldn't find? American soldiers faced the uncertainty of never knowing where an enemy was or when an attack might come.

The primary sources quoted here show both sides of this story. The first comes from Vietcong fighter Tran Thi Gung. She recounts her experiences fighting the Americans. The second excerpt is taken from the diary of American soldier Peter Swisher, who faced off against guerrilla fighters in difficult circumstances.

As you read, compare the very different viewpoints of these two combatants.

>> Like Tran Thi Gung, many Vietnamese women served in the Vietcong. In addition to fighting on the front lines, some performed backbreaking labor hauling supplies over the mountains.

Primary Source 1

Account of Vietcong Guerrilla Fighter Tran Thi Gung

When the Americans pulled back we knew they would call in artillery fire, maybe even air strikes. So we grabbed their rifles and ran for the tunnels. There we took a short break and reloaded. As soon as it was quiet we returned to the trenches. The second time they advanced they took more casualties. They were such big targets, so easy to hit, I was no longer scared. They retreated again and once more the shelling began. They did this all day, from six in the morning till six at night. Every time they pulled back I crawled out of my hole to seize more weapons. . . .

DRAW INFERENCES How were the Vietcong fighters getting new weapons?

I think the Americans lost many people because they were applying conventional [traditional] tactics against our ambushes and tunnels. Their shells and bombs were extremely powerful and sometimes they killed people in the tunnels, but it didn't happen as often as you might think. . . .

When GIs [American soldiers] discovered tunnel openings they dynamited them, but the tunnels were so deep and had so many twists and turns, they couldn't do too much damage. It was like an underground maze. Most of the tunnels were just wide enough to crawl through and so cramped. There were only some places where you could sit up, never mind stand. Most of the time we lived in the dark. We used kerosene lamps for meetings but never candles. There wasn't enough oxygen so they went out very easily.

Usually we didn't have to stay underground for more than a few hours at a time. After all, we had to be aboveground to fight, right? But one time I was stuck in a tunnel for seven days and seven nights while the Americans were constantly bombing us. After several days our food supply ran short, so even though we were terribly hungry and thirsty, we just ate a few specks of dried rice and drank a few drops of water. When the bombing ended, American tanks rumbled through the area and accidentally buried the tunnel exits. Lots of times the Americans were able to block one or two exits, but there was always some way out. This time every single one was closed. Luckily we had American bayonets taken from the battlefield and we used them to dig ourselves out.

In addition to laying ambushes we guerrillas attacked enemy outposts. I always volunteered to sneak onto the bases at night to reconnoiter [observe] and draw maps so we could plan our attacks.

DESCRIBE What hardships did Tran Thi Gung experience?

Primary Source 2

Diary of Peter Swisher, April 9, 1970

Any war tries to run on a schedule—some form of an organized plan that will replace chaos with stability, and further the mission of actually winning the war.

EXPLAIN Does the idea of fighting a war on a schedule sound realistic? Why or why not?

However, this schedule also depends on the enemy—and in a war like Vietnam, with elusive guerrilla tactics, there are few, if any permanent schedules. The conventional American and South Vietnamese Army is resupplied periodically with food, ammunition, and material. And then it waits. It waits to be attacked.

We do send out "search and destroy" missions, but it is the enemy that chooses whether or not to fight us—and when the enemy does fight, he usually has the upper hand. This is the classic rule of guerrilla warfare.

It means that the front line in Vietnam can be anywhere—fighting in the jungle, slogging through the Delta [a swampy region], or getting hit by rockets and mortars in the supposedly "safe" military compound or a civilian community. Getting blown up by a booby-trap, a mine or a grenade thrown by a 65-year-old mama-san [older Vietnamese woman]. Anytime, anywhere anything can happen. The fighting starts and ends abruptly—sometimes in minutes, but seldom longer than hours. The rest of the time you wait.

COMPARE AND CONTRAST What hardships did Peter Swisher live through? How are they different from Tran Thi Gung's?

ASSESSMENT

Be sure to cite specific evidence from the sources as you answer the following questions.

1. **Draw Conclusions** What made the Vietcong's network of tunnels so effective against the Americans?
2. **Identify Cause and Effect** Why did the Vietcong refuse to fight on a 'schedule' determined by the Americans? How did this work to their advantage?
3. **Cite Evidence** Both Peter Swisher and Tran Thi Gung refer to their supplies. How is the supply situation different in the two armies?
4. **Synthesize** Why did the Vietcong fight in such a different way from the Americans?
5. **Develop Empathy** Why did the Vietcong's tactic of mixing with civilians make life so difficult for soldiers like Peter Swisher? How might American troops have reacted to the Vietcong's use of women as soldiers?

GO ONLINE to access primary sources

17.3

GO ONLINE to **Project Imagine: Investigate how the War Divided Americans** to see how Americans were split between supporters and opponents of the Vietnam War.

The Antiwar Movement

BOUNCE to Activate Flipped Video

Objectives

Describe the divisions within American society over the Vietnam War.

Analyze the Tet Offensive and the American reaction to it.

Summarize the factors that influenced the outcome of the 1968 presidential election.

Key Terms

draftee
Students for a Democratic Society (SDS)
"credibility gap"
Tet Offensive
Eugene McCarthy
Robert Kennedy

President Johnson sent more American troops to Vietnam in order to win the war. But with each passing year, casualty lists got longer and victory seemed further away. As soldiers died abroad and hawks and doves argued at home, the Vietnam War opened up a deep emotional rift in American society. After the war ended, it would take years for the country to heal itself.

Antiwar Sentiment Grows

The war in Vietnam divided Americans more deeply than any conflict since the Civil War. Although most Americans initially supported President Johnson's bombings and troop deployments, by 1966 critics began speaking out. Senator Fulbright's opposition to the war hurt Johnson in Congress, and the senator was soon joined by like-minded activists who believed that American soldiers were dying in a war that had little to do with American interests.

Protesting the Draft By 1965, most of the troops sent to Vietnam were no longer volunteers who had enlisted in the army. Instead, they were **draftees**—young men drafted into military service—who had been assigned a tour in Vietnam. In accordance with the Selective Service Act of 1948, the government drafted more than 1.5 million men into military service during the Vietnam War. All males had to register for the draft when they turned 18, and the Selective Service System called up draftees based on projected military needs.

Critics of the Selective Service System argued that the draft was not fair. The system gave local draft boards considerable

GO ONLINE to access your digital course

>> Frank E. Petersen, who later became the first African American Marine Corps general, prepares for combat in Vietnam.

>> Over 4,000 protestors marched near the Armed Forces Induction Center in New York City to voice their opposition to the draft during Stop-the-Draft week in October 1967.

BOUNCE to Activate Chart

influence in selecting men for service, and it also granted deferments to college students and men who worked in certain designated occupations. Most of the 2.5 million men who served in Vietnam came from working-class and poor backgrounds.

During the Johnson presidency, the number of African American troops fighting and dying in Vietnam was also disproportionately high. At the beginning of the war, African Americans suffered more than 20 percent of the total combat deaths, though they only made up around 10 percent of the U.S. population. Additionally, African American soldiers were more likely to serve in combat positions and less likely to become commissioned officers.

Civil rights leader Martin Luther King Jr., spoke out against the added war burden shouldered by African American soldiers. Speaking at a New York church in 1967, King said that the war was hurting the poor, both Black and white. Vietnam was drawing human and economic resources away from America's other wars on poverty and discrimination. He added that it hindered poor Americans in other more direct ways:

> It was sending their sons and their brothers and their husbands to fight and to die in extraordinary high proportions relative to the rest of the population. . . . [W]e have been repeatedly faced with the cruel irony of watching Negro and white boys on TV screens as they kill and die together for a nation that has been unable to seat them together in the same schools.
>
> —Martin Luther King, Jr., 1967

Perceived inequities in the draft led to widespread resistance. Antiwar advocates sponsored Stop the Draft Week in October 1967, and some draft-eligible males burned their draft cards in protest. Finally, in 1969, the Selective Service System adopted a lottery that was designed to eliminate deferment abuses and create a more diverse army of draftees.

Protests on College Campuses Across America, college campuses became centers of antiwar sentiment. Professors and students criticized the war for a variety of reasons, ranging from pacifism and the war's effects on the economy to a personal desire to avoid military service. Antiwar activity on college campuses did not, however, reflect the attitudes of all Americans.

In fact, many professors remained vocal in their defense of the war effort during lectures and at protest rallies. For the most part, though, colleges and universities were focal points of the strongest antiwar opinion.

Antiwar activities were part of more significant changes taking place on college campuses. Never before the 1960s had so many Americans entered colleges and universities. Between 1946 and 1970, the number of students enrolled in institutions of higher education increased from 2 million to 8 million. Many college students became a class unto themselves—segregated from the workforce, free from many adult responsibilities, and encouraged by their professors to think critically. Many of the students who embraced the antiwar cause came from middle-class families. Students from working-class families were less likely to protest against the war.

The University of Michigan and the University of California at Berkeley became important hubs of the antiwar movement. The **Students for a Democratic Society (SDS)** was founded in 1960 at the University of Michigan. Originally formed to campaign against racism and poverty, the SDS soon began campaigning to end the war in Vietnam. By 1964, SDS had organized campus "teach-ins" and demonstrations against the war and encouraged draft-age males to sign "We Won't Go" petitions.

The 26th Amendment Although today people take for granted that 18- to 20-year-olds can vote, this was not the case until 1971. The drive to gain voting rights for young adults was yet another instance of people during this era demanding equality of political rights. In addition, since the issue concerned rights for young people, student activism played a key role in getting out the movement's key message: "old enough to fight, old enough to vote."

This idea was not exactly new. President Eisenhower, the former Supreme Commander of Allied Forces in WWII, backed the idea in his 1954 State of the Union message. In it, he said that since 18- to-20-year-old citizens were again and again summoned to risk their lives for our nation, "they should participate in the political process that produces this fateful summons."

But it was not until the issue was pressed by young people whose lives might soon be on the line in Vietnam that support for this area of voting rights gained steam. Once the proposed constitutional amendment won congressional support on March 23, 1971, it was quickly ratified by the states. By July 7, 1971, once the ratification was certified, the 26th Amendment was in place.

>> Journalist Mike Wallace reports from the front lines. New broadcast technology meant that television viewers in the U.S. got an intimate glimpse of events in the war zone.

BOUNCE to Activate Gallery

The Role of the Media and the "Credibility Gap" Outside college campuses, other Americans soon enlisted in the antiwar cause. Hawks and doves drifted farther apart. More groups organized against the war, their names corresponding with whom they represented—Vietnam Veterans Against the War, Catholic Peace Fellowship, Another Mother for Peace, and so on.

Antiwar sentiment was to some degree the result of the news media's extensive coverage of the war. A large majority of American households now had television sets. Most Americans learned the news of the war by watching TV news reports. Thus, the war in Vietnam became the first "living-room war." Americans watched its progress—or lack of it—in their living rooms on nightly newscasts.

For the first time, the brutal reality of war was broadcast into Americans' homes. They saw what the TV cameramen saw: death, destruction, horrible injuries, civilian casualties, and chaos. Horrific images also filled newspapers and news magazines.

War correspondents issued reports, not of a string of great American victories leading to a clear goal, but of a messy conflict that seemed to lack a clear objective. As early as 1962, they printed the following gloomy forecast: "The United States seems inextricably committed to a long, inconclusive war."

Yet television and print journalists also broadcast and reported on government officials issuing optimistic statement after optimistic statement. Soon, a **"credibility gap"** emerged between what the Johnson administration said about the war and what many journalists reported about it. This gap referred to the American public's growing distrust of the statements made by the government.

☑ **ANALYZE INFORMATION** Before changes were made in 1969, why was the Selective Service System the subject of criticism?

The Tet Offensive

In November 1967, President Johnson brought General Westmoreland home from Vietnam to address the nation's concerns about the war. Westmoreland said that the Vietcong were declining in strength and could no longer mount a major offensive. As Westmoreland made his claims, however, the North Vietnamese and Vietcong were planning just such an attack.

Widespread Attacks In early 1968, U.S. officials anticipated a communist offensive. As expected, on January 21, the North Vietnamese Army hit Khe Sanh in northwest South Vietnam. However, ten days later, the communists expanded their attack by hitting U.S. and ARVN positions throughout South Vietnam. The **Tet Offensive**—named after the Vietnamese lunar new year—was a coordinated assault on 36 provincial capitals and 5 major cities, as well as the U.S. embassy in Saigon.

The communists planned to take and hold the cities until the urban population took up arms in their support. They thought the Tet Offensive had a good chance of ending the war.

The fighting was fierce, but in the end, American and South Vietnamese forces repelled the offensive, and there was no popular uprising against the government of South Vietnam. Although U.S. forces won a tactical victory by preventing the Vietcong and North Vietnamese Army from achieving their primary objectives, the Tet Offensive was a strategic blow to the Americans. It demonstrated that the communists had not lost the will or the ability to fight on.

Shifting Policy from Victory to Peace After the Tet Offensive, American military leaders seemed less confident of a quick end to the war. When Westmoreland requested more troops, President

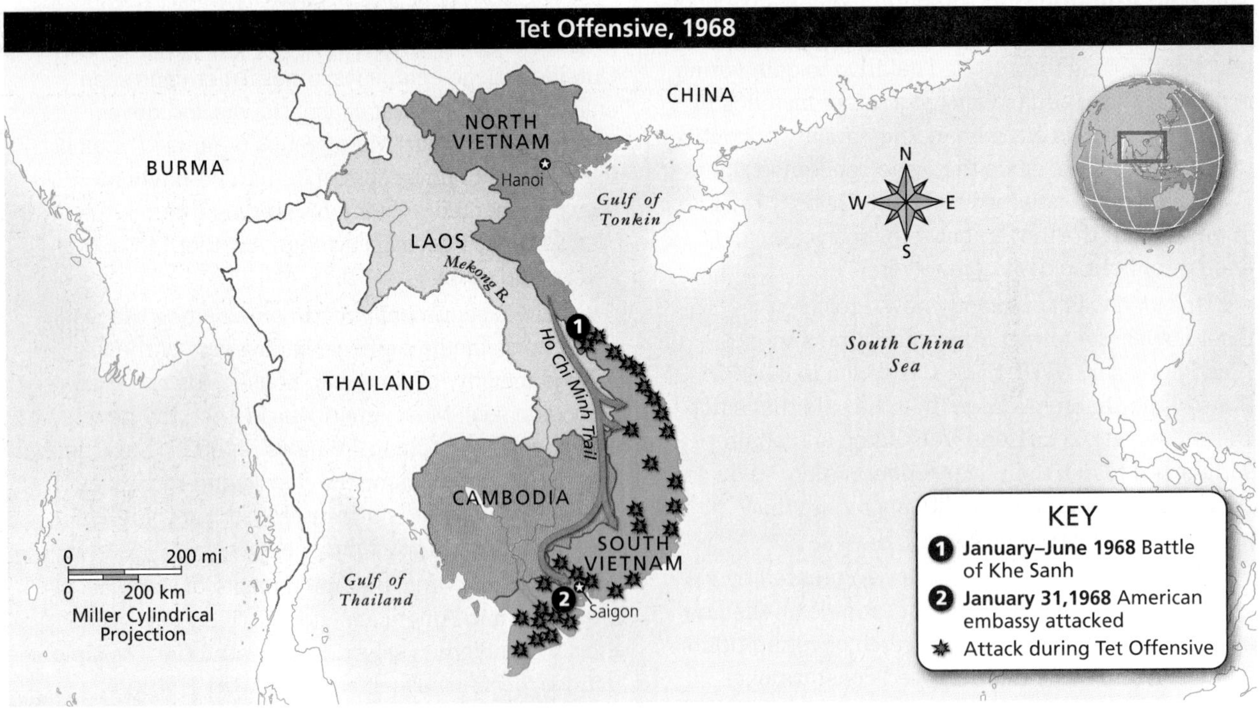

>> **Analyze Maps** Identify two regions of South Vietnam that were hard-hit by the Tet Offensive.

Johnson asked his new Secretary of Defense, Clark Clifford, to take an objective look at the military and political situation in Vietnam. The deeper Clifford delved into the matter, the more pessimistic he became. Sending more troops would inevitably require raising taxes, increasing draft rolls, and calling up reserves. It would lead to increased casualties in the field and dissent at home. And it still might not lead to victory. Clifford, calling the war "a bottomless pit," concluded that the President should radically shift U.S. policy from one that pursued victory to one that pursued a negotiated peace.

>> An American tank patrols among the ruins in Saigon following the Tet Offensive in 1968. American forces were unprepared due to a cease-fire supposedly in effect during the celebration of Tet.

Johnson Refuses to Seek Reelection While Clifford deliberated, many Americans began to turn dramatically against the war. Some marched in protest and engaged in antiwar activities. Others registered their disapproval at the polls. In early 1968, Minnesota senator **Eugene McCarthy**, the antiwar candidate for the Democratic Party nomination, made a surprisingly strong showing in the New Hampshire primary. Sensing that Johnson was in a politically weakened position, New York's Democratic senator **Robert Kennedy** announced his candidacy for the presidency. Both McCarthy and Kennedy believed that the war had divided America and drained resources away from the fights against poverty and discrimination. What Johnson feared most was happening: The war was undermining his presidency.

On March 31, 1968, two months after the Tet Offensive, the President addressed the nation on television. He announced that America would limit its bombing of North Vietnam and seek a negotiated settlement to the war. Johnson then shocked the nation by announcing that he would not run for another term as President. The speech marked another turning point in the war. The fight for victory was over. Peace was now the official government policy.

FINAL

DAILY NEWS

NEW YORK'S PICTURE NEWSPAPER ®

8¢

Vol. 49. No. 298 — New York N.Y. 10017, Thursday, June 6, 1968* — WEATHER: Sunny and warm.

RFK DEAD

Robert Francis Kennedy (1925-1968) — An assassin's bullet interrupted his moment of triumph.

>> The assassination of presidential candidate Robert Kennedy in June 1968 shocked the nation and the world.

☑ **DETERMINE RELEVANCE** What was the relevance of the Tet Offensive for U.S. policy makers?

The 1968 Presidential Race

Johnson's decision not to seek reelection in 1968 threw the presidential race wide open. Many Americans believed it provided an opportunity to enact fundamental political and social changes.

They argued that the future of the country was at stake. It was a time of new ideas and new plans. But the optimism and high hopes of the early campaign would soon die amidst political infighting, violence, and assassination.

King and Kennedy Assassinated In the spring and summer of the campaign season, bullets struck down two Americans who spoke out eloquently for peace in Vietnam and peaceful change in American society. Martin Luther King, Jr., the most prominent leader of the civil rights movement, had publicly turned against the war in 1967. He contributed compelling social and moral reasons to the argument for peace. But his voice was tragically silenced on April 4, 1968, when a racist assassin shot and killed him in Memphis, Tennessee.

Robert Kennedy was the next leader to fall. He had based his campaign for the presidency on compassion and idealism, and millions of Americans rallied to his camp. On June 5, 1968, at a rally celebrating his victory in the California primary, Kennedy asserted that "we are a great country, an unselfish country, a compassionate country," and that he intended "to make that the basis of my running." Minutes later, a Palestinian immigrant named Sirhan Sirhan shot Kennedy in the head, killing him instantly. Sirhan may have wanted revenge for America's support for Israel in that country's war with Egypt the year before.

>> Chaos ensued as police clashed with protestors outside the 1968 Democratic National Convention, held in Chicago.

The Chicago Democratic Convention The murders of King and Kennedy cast a dark shadow over the election campaigns. In August 1968, the Democrats convened in Chicago to choose a presidential candidate to represent their party in the November election. As the delegates arrived, so too did antiwar protesters. Chicago's mayor deployed police and members of the National Guard to prevent any outbreaks of violence.

Inside the convention, the Democrats angrily debated placing an antiwar plank in the party platform. They chose Hubert Humphrey, Johnson's Vice President, over Eugene McCarthy, who had garnered support from many antiwar groups. As the delegates cast their votes, violence between police and protesters erupted outside the convention. After police beat activists with nightsticks, some protesters retaliated by throwing rocks and bottles at the onrushing tide of police.

The television coverage of the fierce fighting in the streets and the bitter arguments on the convention floor shocked Americans. Chaos and civil disorder appeared to have replaced civil debate in the political arena. The divisions and violence in Chicago mirrored the deep divisions in American politics and the heartbreaking violence on the front lines in Vietnam.

Richard Nixon Wins the Presidency At a much more peaceful convention in Miami, Republicans nominated Richard M. Nixon, who promised if elected he would deliver "peace with honor." He wanted the United States out of Vietnam, but he also demanded honorable peace terms.

He promised to listen to "the great, quiet forgotten majority—the nonshouters and the nondemonstrators." This large group of Americans, described by one commentator as "the unyoung, the unblack, and the unpoor," was dubbed the "silent majority." Throughout his campaign, Nixon used a "southern strategy." This meant courting conservative white Southern voters who opposed integration and who had traditionally supported the Democratic party. Nixon did not directly appeal to racist views, but voiced his support for states' rights and law and order policies.

Alabama governor George Wallace also ran for the presidency on a third-party ticket. A lifelong Democrat prior to his entry into the race, Wallace said that neither of the traditional political parties represented white Southern voters who opposed integration and other social changes.

He had no sympathy for the demands of antiwar radicals, counterculture hippies, or African American militants. He represented the "white backlash" against the civil rights movement and the desire to press forward to victory in Vietnam.

The combination of Nixon's "southern strategy" and Wallace's third-party candidacy siphoned traditionally Democratic votes away from Humphrey. In a close election, Nixon captured victory by winning 43.6 percent of the popular vote and 301 electoral votes. Humphrey received 42.5 percent of the popular vote and Wallace 13.6 percent. The election marked the end of the Democratic "Solid South" and signaled significant changes in the nation's political landscape. Richard Nixon's ascendancy marked a new Republican domination of the American presidency.

EXPRESS IDEAS CLEARLY In your own words, who were the so-called "Silent Majority" and why did Nixon call them that?

ASSESSMENT

1. **Determine Point of View** Discuss the reasons that many Americans criticized the draft system during the Vietnam War.
2. **Generate Explanations** Explain why the Vietnam War became known as the first "living-room war."
3. **Apply Concepts** Discuss the factors that influenced Richard Nixon's victory in the 1968 presidential election.
4. **Analyze Information** Explain how the Tet Offensive affected U.S. confidence in the Vietnam War.
5. **Quest Connections** Discuss the role of college students in the antiwar movement.

17.4

GO ONLINE to **Project Imagine: Experience the Legacy of the Vietnam War** to learn how the effects of the war lingered for years to come, especially for veterans.

BOUNCE to Activate Flipped Video

Objectives

Assess Nixon's new approach to the war, and explain why protests continued.

Explain what led to the Paris Peace Accords and why South Vietnam eventually fell to the communists.

Evaluate the impact of the Vietnam War on the United States.

Key Terms

Vietnamization
My Lai
Pentagon Papers
Paris Peace Accords
Roy P. Benavidez
War Powers Act

The War's End and Effects

As a presidential candidate, Richard Nixon promised "peace with honor" and an end to a war that had fractured American society. Nixon did eventually withdraw American troops, and the Vietnam War finally ended. But the impact of the war endured. As the nation recovered from war, Americans reexamined the struggle against communism, the power of the presidency, and America's role in the world.

Attempts to Withdraw from Vietnam

Nixon's defenders argued that he was a hard-working patriot with a new vision for America. His critics charged that he was a deceitful politician bent on acquiring power and punishing his enemies. There were elements of truth to both views. But defenders and critics alike agreed that Richard Nixon was a determined man with abundant political talent. From his first day in office, the new President realized that ending the Vietnam War was the key to everything else he hoped to achieve.

Peace Talks Stall Though formal peace talks between the warring parties had begun in May 1968, the talks bogged down from the outset due to disagreements and a lack of compromise. When Richard Nixon took office in January 1969, his peace delegation firmly believed they could break the impasse. The Americans and South Vietnamese wanted all communist troops out of South Vietnam. They also wanted prisoners of war (POWs) returned.

Meanwhile, the North Vietnamese demanded an immediate American withdrawal from Vietnam and the formation of a

GO ONLINE to access your digital course

coalition government in South Vietnam that would include representatives from the Vietcong. Still hoping to win the war in the field, North Vietnam refused to budge from its initial position. And South Vietnam refused to sign any agreement that compromised its security.

Vietnamization President Nixon refused to accept the North Vietnamese peace terms. He was committed to a policy of "peace with honor" and believed that there were still military options.

He continued a gradual pullout of American troops, and expressed faith in the ability of the Army of the Republic of Vietnam (ARVN) to assume the burden of war. He called his approach **Vietnamization**—U.S. forces would withdraw as ARVN troops assumed more combat duties. The hope was that with continued American aid behind the front lines, the ARVN would fight its own battles to secure South Vietnam.

To reduce the flow of communist supplies to the Vietcong, Nixon ordered the secret bombing of the Ho Chi Minh Trail in Cambodia. This was a controversial move because it widened the scope of the war and helped to undermine the neutral government in Cambodia. In the end, neither Vietnamization nor secret bombings dramatically improved South Vietnam's chances of winning a war against the communists.

GENERATE EXPLANATIONS Explain why you think the bombings in Cambodia were kept secret.

>> President Nixon meets with his defense team in January 1971.

BOUNCE to Activate Timeline

Events Intensify the Antiwar Movement

Nixon inherited two things from Lyndon Johnson: an unpopular war and a vocal American opposition to it. The new President wanted "peace with honor," security for America's ally South Vietnam, and international respect for U.S. foreign policy. Antiwar activists wanted the war ended and American troops out of Vietnam—on any terms. Nixon found it increasingly difficult to achieve his goals and satisfy the snowballing antiwar movement.

The War Widens into Cambodia More than a year into office, Nixon had grown impatient with the snail's pace of the peace negotiations. In 1970, he attempted to break the stalemate by ordering a ground attack on North Vietnamese Army and Vietcong bases in Cambodia. Nixon also hoped to aid the pro-American Cambodian government in its fight

>> **Analyze Political Cartoons** What is the cartoon saying about the consequences of Nixon's lack of follow-through on a 1968 campaign promise?

against the Khmer Rouge, a communist movement supported by North Vietnam.

On the evening of April 30, Nixon addressed the American people, informing them of his decision to carry the war into Cambodia. He stressed that the war had become a measure of how committed the United States was to preserving freedom around the world:

> If, when the chips are down, the world's most powerful nation, the United States of America, acts like a pitiful, helpless giant, the forces of totalitarianism and anarchy will threaten free nations . . . throughout the world.
>
> —President Richard Nixon, 1970

The next morning, U.S. and ARVN forces crossed the border into Cambodia. These soldiers captured large stockpiles of weapons and supplies, but they did not break the stalemate. North Vietnam remained determined to have peace on its terms or no peace at all.

>> Fourteen-year-old Mary Ann Vecchio kneels over the body of Kent State student Jeffrey Miller, age 20.

The Kent and Jackson State Killings The Cambodian incursion had a profound impact on the peace movement at home. It stirred antiwar activists, who argued that Nixon had widened the war and made the world a more dangerous place. Throughout the country, college campuses erupted with protests. Several demonstrations prompted the police and National Guard to step in to preserve order.

On two campuses, confrontations between students and armed authorities led to deaths. Four days after Nixon's speech, demonstrators at Kent State University in Ohio threw rocks and bottles at members of the National Guard. In the confusion, the guardsmen fired into the crowd, killing four youths.

The Kent State killings led to demonstrations on other campuses. Tensions between local police and the students at Jackson State, a Historically Black College and University (HBCU) in Mississippi, had long been an issue. Students protested on the night of May 15th, inspired both by the killings at Kent State and by local civil rights issues. Police officers fired more than 150 rounds into the crowd, killing two young African Americans.

College demonstrations against the war sometimes prompted counterprotests by Americans who supported the President. In response to a May 8, 1970, antiwar rally in downtown New York City, construction workers staged a counter-demonstration, carrying American flags and chanting "All the Way USA."

Believing that some anti-war demonstrators had spit on the American flag, they pushed into the crowd and started hitting the antiwar protesters. The clash drew national attention. Days later, thousands of construction workers, businesspeople, secretaries, and housewives marched peacefully through Manhattan's streets in support of Nixon and the war effort. One man expressed his feelings about the march:

> I'm very proud to be an American, and I know my boy that was killed in Vietnam would be here today if he was alive, marching with us. . . . I know he died for the right cause, because in his letters he wrote to me he knew what he was fighting for: to keep America free. . . .
>
> —Robert Geary, May 20, 1970

As the fighting continued in Vietnam, the American home front became its own physical and emotional battlefield.

The My Lai Massacre In 1971, two events increased the pressure on Nixon to pull U.S. troops out of Vietnam. The first event had roots in a U.S. action in South Vietnam three years earlier.

On March 16, 1968, American forces searching for enemy troops in an area with a strong Vietcong presence came upon the village of **My Lai**. By this point in the war, many American troops had been injured and killed by Vietcong fighters posing as civilians. It was a recipe for disaster at My Lai, where Lieutenant William Calley's unit began shooting and killing unarmed civilians. During the assault, U.S. soldiers killed between four and five hundred Vietnamese.

Lt. Calley later maintained that he was following orders, but many of the soldiers present did not participate in the massacre. At least one risked his own life to stop it. The tragedy was made even worse by an inadequate military investigation of the incident. *Life* magazine eventually published disturbing photos taken during the event, and in March 1971, a military court convicted Lt. Calley of his participation in the attack. News of the My Lai massacre, the coverup, and Calley's trial shocked many Americans and added fuel to the burning antiwar fire.

>> A photographer captured the terrible scene in the village of My Lai where American troops killed civilians.

The Pentagon Papers On the heels of My Lai came the 1971 publication of the **Pentagon Papers** in *The New York Times*. The papers were a classified government history of U.S. involvement in Vietnam from 1945 to 1967. The study was leaked by one of its coauthors, Daniel Ellsberg. Nixon tried to block the full publication, but in *New York Times* v. *United States*, the Supreme Court ruled against the administration. The study revealed that American leaders involved the United States in Vietnam without fully informing the public and that President Johnson had even lied to Congress. Along with the invasion of Cambodia, the killings on college campuses, and the My Lai Massacre, the Pentagon Papers turned even more Americans against the war.

☑ **CHECK UNDERSTANDING** Why did the Nixon administration try to stop publication of the Pentagon Papers?

>> U.S. troops wait to return home after completing their tours in Vietnam. **Hypothesize** What difficulties might be faced by soldiers returning from duty?

BOUNCE to Activate Gallery

The Vietnam War Ends

The failings of Vietnamization and growing dissent at home forced President Nixon to search for some final way out of the conflict. A 1971 public-opinion poll revealed that two thirds of Americans favored withdrawing American troops, even if it meant a communist takeover of South Vietnam. Sensitive to the public mood, Congress pressed Nixon to bring the troops home. Many believed that to win reelection in 1972, he had to end the war.

American Troops Withdraw from Vietnam In October 1972, the United States and North Vietnam came to terms on a peace settlement. One month later, with lasting peace almost at hand, Nixon easily defeated the antiwar Democrat George McGovern for reelection. But Nixon's triumph was short-lived. The Vietnamese peace fell apart when North Vietnam refused to sign the agreement. Talks broke off, but renewed American bombing in North Vietnam finally induced the North Vietnamese to resume negotiations.

At last, in January 1973, the United States, South Vietnam, North Vietnam, and the Vietcong signed the **Paris Peace Accords.** The parties agreed to a cease-fire and a U.S. troop withdrawal from South Vietnam. POWs would be exchanged, but North Vietnamese troops would remain in South Vietnam. The National Liberation Front (Vietcong) would become a legitimate political party in South Vietnam, and South Vietnam's noncommunist government would remain in power pending a political settlement. With the Accords signed, the last American troops came home in March. Among the returning soldiers were more than 550 POWs, most of whom were pilots shot down during the war.

The Fall of Saigon For the United States, the war in Vietnam was over. For the Vietnamese, however, it continued. Neither North nor South Vietnam honored the cease-fire or worked toward a diplomatic settlement of their differences. In the spring of 1975, minor fighting escalated when North Vietnam launched an offensive against the South.

Without American aid and ground support, the ARVN was no match for the Soviet-supplied North Vietnamese Army. By the end of April, the communists had taken Saigon. After decades of fighting and millions of deaths, Vietnam was unified under one flag.

RECALL Did the Paris Peace Accords bring an end to fighting in Vietnam? Explain.

Effects of the Vietnam War

More than 58,000 American soldiers gave their lives serving their country in Vietnam; another 300,000 were wounded. Although figures are not exact, the Vietnamese death toll most likely exceeded 2 million.

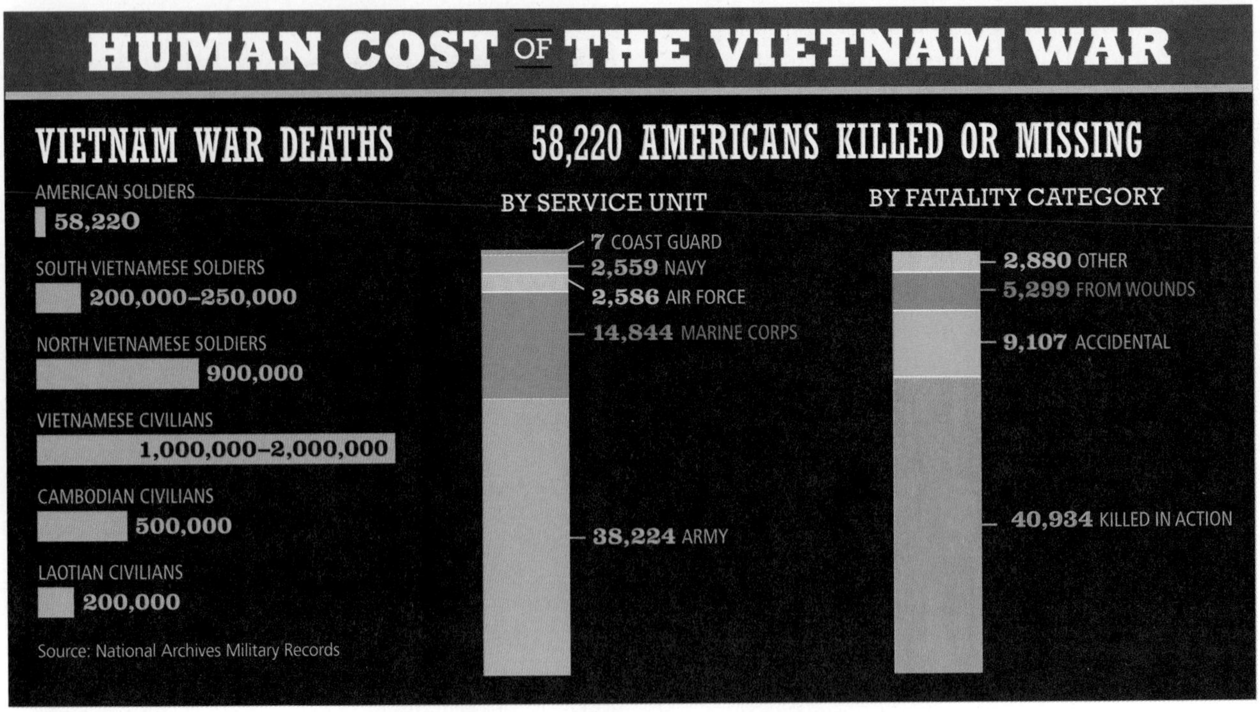

>> **Analyze Data** Compare the total number of civilian casualties to the number of military casualties. What do the totals tell you about the effects of modern warfare on civilian populations?

Peace, however, did not mean the end of pain and hardship. The end of the war created other problems in Southeast Asia. The war also affected American attitudes toward world affairs.

Southeast Asia After the War Many foreign-policy experts in the United States had predicted that if North Vietnam won the Vietnamese civil war, communism would spread to other nations in Southeast Asia. In a limited sense, they were right. Communist regimes eventually came to power in both Laos and Cambodia. In Cambodia, the ruling Khmer Rouge unleashed a genocide on the populace, killing everyone who had ties to the West or previous Cambodian governments. Between 1975 and 1979, upwards of 2 million Cambodians were executed or died in labor camps.

In an expanded sense, however, many American foreign-policy strategists misjudged the spread of communism. They concluded it was a monolithic global movement controlled by Moscow and Beijing. However, as the war's aftermath would attest, communist movements in Southeast Asia were nationalistic and intolerant of outside influences. In 1978, Vietnam invaded Cambodia and installed a pro-Vietnamese government. China supported the ousted Khmer Rouge. For more than ten years that followed, the U.S. supported a coalition of anti-communist Cambodian opposition groups that included the Khmer Rouge.

American Veterans Return Home The war and the peace divided Americans. Some argued that the United States should never have entered the war and that their leaders had lied to them. Others countered that the war was part of an ongoing struggle against communism and that in the end, the United States betrayed South Vietnam. An unfortunate result of the controversy was that the nation never fully expressed its appreciation to the returning veterans.

Overwhelmingly, the 2.5 million enlisted men who served in Vietnam did so with honor and distinction. Yet, unlike the soldiers that returned to the United States after World Wars I and II—the famed Doughboys and G.I. Joes—few Vietnam vets enjoyed the warmth and adulation of victory parades. In addition to the indifference that some veterans encountered, some also suffered from physical and psychological ailments for years when they returned home.

Not until almost a decade after the end of the war did Americans begin to fully honor the courage and sacrifice of these veterans. The Vietnam Veterans Memorial, dedicated in Washington, D.C., in 1982, stands as an eloquent testament to the men and women who served and died in Vietnam.

>> A veteran and his son visit the Vietnam Memorial in Washington, D.C. On this wall are the names of all military personnel who lost their lives in the war. The memorial was designed by Maya Lin, a 21 year-old architecture student.

Individuals of all races and genders served their country during the Vietnam War. There were countless actions of heroism and sacrifice, some of which were singled out for the Congressional Medal of Honor. For example, Army Sergeant Peter C. Lemon fought off numerous enemy assaults even after being seriously wounded three times. Marine Sergeant Rodney M. Davis was one of an astounding number of soldiers who gave his life to save the lives of others by diving on a live grenade and absorbing the explosion. Green Beret Sergeant **Roy P. Benavidez** was also decorated for his bravery in combat. Despite terrible injuries, he rescued the lives of at least eight men. For his outstanding gallantry, he was awarded the nation's highest military award: the Congressional Medal of Honor.

Sergeant Benavidez' gallant choice to join voluntarily his comrades who were in critical straits, to expose himself constantly to withering enemy fire, and his refusal to be stopped despite numerous severe wounds, saved the lives of at least eight men. His fearless personal leadership, tenacious devotion to duty, and extremely valorous actions in the face of overwhelming odds were in keeping with the highest traditions of the military service, and reflect the utmost credit on him and the United States Army.

—Citation, Congressional Medal of Honor, Sergeant Roy P. Benavidez

The Impact on U.S. Domestic and Foreign Policies The war was costly both monetarily and in the human toll of shattered lives. The war also altered American domestic and foreign policies. Lyndon Johnson's Great Society campaign against poverty and racism fell victim to the conflict. Increasingly, between 1964 and 1968, Johnson could not pay for both the Vietnam War and the Great Society. Paying for more guns left less money to pay for textbooks, school lunches, and prenatal care.

Additionally, the war undermined Americans' trust in their leaders and fragmented the Cold War consensus on foreign affairs. In 1973, Congress passed the **War Powers Act**. The act restricted the President's war-making powers by requiring him to consult with Congress within 48 hours of committing American forces to a foreign conflict. The act was a congressional attempt to check the unilateral formation of American foreign policy and stop the growth of the "imperial presidency."

>> The voting age was reduced from 21 to 18 in 1971. **Draw Conclusions** Why did the war focus attention on the voting age?

Thus, the Vietnam War had an important impact on the relationship between the legislative and executive branches of government. With the Gulf of Tonkin Resolution, Congress had years earlier granted the President a great deal of power to conduct war using "all necessary measures" without further legislative approval.

The War Powers Act was an attempt to regain some of that power from the executive branch and return it to the legislative branch. Ultimately, the question of where war-making power lies is a constitutional issue. On one hand, the Constitution gives the power to declare war to Congress. On the other, it makes the President commander in chief of the armed forces.

The Vietnam War had an impact on America foreign policy, as well. The deaths and costs and ultimate failure of the war left many Americans with "war fatigue." Even those who had not been personally touched by the war had grown weary of the conflict. This weariness of war became a social factor that would be reflected in the U.S. role in the world from the 1970s through 1990. Throughout this time, American citizens would cite the Vietnam War as a cautionary tale whenever the country considered using force abroad. Many Americans would view conflicts in Central America, Africa, the Balkans, and the Middle East through a lens tinted by the fear of "another Vietnam."

The Impact on the American Economy The United States spent about $738 billion (in 2011 dollars) to fight the Vietnam War. Since that time, the government has spent an additional $270 billion on benefits for veterans and their families. These payments continue, costing the federal government more than $20 billion every year. Therefore, the Vietnam War can be said to have cost the country more than $1 trillion—and the price keeps going up.

This is a staggering amount of money, and it has had an enormous impact on the American economy. Many economists view the spending on the Vietnam War as marking the end of the prosperity of post–World War II America. War spending meant war production, and so American factories made military goods instead of consumer goods, warping American

Economic Problems of the mid-1970s

UNEMPLOYMENT	Unemployment in the U.S. rose from 4 percent in 1970 to 9.5 percent by 1975.
INFLATION	Inflation reached 10 percent in the mid-1970s, the highest it had been in the twentieth century up to that point.
ENERGY CRISIS	An oil embargo in 1973 caused a severe shortage of gas, and prices soared from 40 cents per gallon in 1973 to $1.20 by 1980.
GOVERNMENT SPENDING	In 1970, total government spending was $321.8 billion; by 1975, spending had risen to $550.5 billion.

>> **Analyze Information** What economic problems affected the greatest number of Americans? Explain.

industry. Although the relationships are complex, war spending was a factor in federal budget deficits, inflation, higher interest rates, and a weaker dollar.

Interestingly, this greatly increased amount of defense spending did not cut into the amount of money the nation spent on education. By one estimate, public school expenditures actually increased by 58 percent in the 1960s and 27 percent in the 1970s. Federal aid outlays to college students also increased between 1965 and 1975. All in all, however, the American economy in the 1970s was marked by crises, which many attribute to the economic effects of the Vietnam War.

ANALYZE INFORMATION What effect did the quagmire in Vietnam have on U.S. foreign policy through 1990?

ASSESSMENT

1. **Identify Central Issues** Discuss the measures that President Nixon took in order to withdraw U.S. troops from the Vietnam War.
2. **Sequence Events** Explain the events leading up to the Kent State and Jackson State killings.
3. **Identify Cause and Effect** Discuss the economic effects of the Vietnam War, and explain how its costs are still affecting the United States today.
4. **Generate Explanations** Discuss the "war fatigue" that many Americans felt after the Vietnam War, and explain how it affected U.S. foreign policy.
5. **Generate Explanations** Explain how the spread of communism after the Vietnam War differed from U.S. strategists' expectations.
6. **Connections to Today** The Vietnam Veterans Memorial in Washington, D.C. is highly regarded and attracts millions of visitors each year. Some come to pay respects to loved ones who died in the conflict, leaving flowers or special objects. How does this memorial compare to monuments to conflicts in your area?

Connections to Today

Veterans Day is marked each November with parades and ceremonies across the country. These members of the United States Air Force are marching in New York City's parade.

Take Action About Veterans' Issues

After every American war, the Federal government has provided some support for its veterans. Private organizations and dedicated volunteers have assisted in these efforts. Governments and private organizations have also worked to honor veterans with memorials in many communities.

1. **Choose** one of the following topics:
    - The Department of Veteran's Affairs (VA)
    - Local veteran's services
    - Local war memorials
2. **Ask Questions** Generate a list of questions you have about the topic.
3. **Learn** about the topic and major issues related to it. Are there any major debates related to the topic or issues? What are the strongest arguments on each side? Take notes as you conduct your research and continue to generate questions as you learn more.
4. **Raise Awareness** Use what you have learned to create a Public Service Announcement video about services available to veterans in your area, or to inform the public about a local memorial.

GO ONLINE to www.SavvasRealize.com and access your digital course

Use the texts, quizzes, interactivities, Quest Inquiries, Flipped Videos, and other resources from this Topic to prepare for the Topic Test.

- Quest Inquiries
- Quizzes
- Interactivities
- Texts
- Flipped Videos

While online you can also check the progress you've made learning the topic and course content by viewing your grades, test scores, and assignment status.

SAVVAS realize™

Topic 17 Quick Study Guide

LESSON SUMMARIES

Use these Lesson Summaries, and the longer versions available online, to review the key ideas for each lesson in this Topic.

Lesson 1: The Cold War and Vietnam

A failed U.S. invasion of Cuba was followed by another crisis as President Kennedy forced the Soviets to remove nuclear missiles from that island. The Soviets build a wall between communist East Berlin and free West Berlin. The U.S. helped the French as they lost control of Vietnam, then committed more troops to that country.

Lesson 2: America's Role Escalates

In 1965, President Johnson launched a bombing campaign in Vietnam but was unable to gain a military advantage against the guerrilla tactics of the Vietcong. By 1968 the war had become a stalemate, with tens of thousands of Americans dead. Meanwhile, the financial costs of the war deepened political division at home.

Lesson 3: The Antiwar Movement

Optimistic U.S. government reports about the progress of the war were contradicted by events on the ground and led many Americans to doubt official statements. A communist offensive in 1968 showed that the enemy was strong enough to fight a long war. Opposition to the war and the draft grew, leading to violent disorder at home.

Lesson 4: The War's End and Effects

Although President Nixon began withdrawing U.S. troops from Vietnam, his decision to launch attacks in Cambodia revived the antiwar movement. In 1973 an agreement allowed U.S. troops to withdraw, but fighting continued until South Vietnam was defeated by the communists.

QUEST! FINDINGS

Complete your Document-Based Question Refer to your responses to the Quest Connections to help you write your essay. Use the rubric and other Quest resources online to guide your work.

GO ONLINE to access lesson summaries

VISUAL REVIEW

Use these graphics to review some of the key terms, people, and ideas from this Topic.

Kennedy's Foreign Policy

FOREIGN POLICY EVENT	OUTCOME
1959 Castro takes control of Cuba; thousands flee to Miami and southern Florida.	1961 In Bay of Pigs invasion of Cuba, Kennedy launches Eisenhower's plan to overthrow Castro but fails.
1961 Soviets build Berlin Wall.	Kennedy sends troops to West Berlin.
1962 Cuban missile crisis	Kennedy forces Soviets to withdraw missiles from Cuba.

Roots of U.S. Involvement in Vietnam

FRANCE LOSES CONTROL OF VIETNAM	
BEFORE	**AFTER**
French-Indochina War: French forces battle Vietnamese communists under Ho Chi Minh.	**Geneva Accords:** France grants independence to former colonies; Vietnam divided.
Cold War: Truman helps France in order to maintain Cold War alliance against the Soviets.	**SEATO:** U.S. assembles coalition to oppose spread of communism in Southeast Asia.
Domino Theory: Eisenhower continues aid to French to prevent communist victory.	**U.S. Intervention:** U.S. supports anticommunist Diem regime and sends troops to Vietnam.

The Antiwar Movement

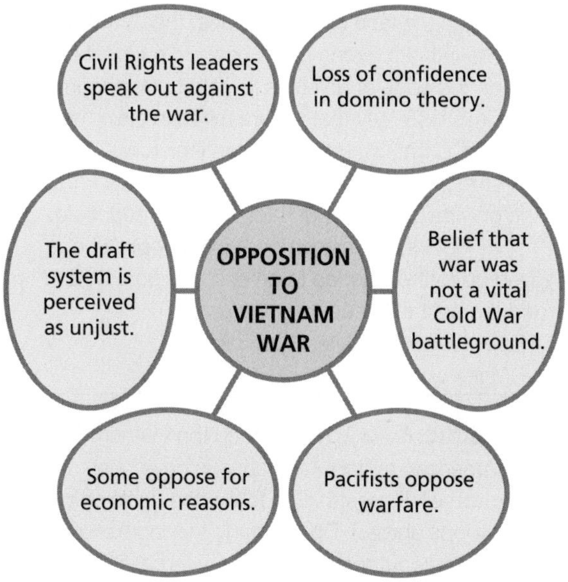

Long-term Consequences of Vietnam War

U.S. Foreign Policy	• Congress passes War Powers Act to restrict President's war powers. • Post-World War II consensus on foreign affairs fragments. • U.S. grows wary of involvement in foreign conflicts.
U.S. Domestic Policy	• Trust in government is undermined. • Costs of war weaken Great Society programs. • Veterans' benefits continue to rise.

Topic 17 Assessment

KEY TERMS, PEOPLE, AND IDEAS

1. What was the philosophy behind Kennedy's creation of the **Peace Corps** and the **Alliance for Progress**?
2. What role did **Nikita Khrushchev** play in the **Cuban missile crisis**?
3. How did Castro's revolution affect the United States?
4. How did the **domino theory** shape U.S. policy in Vietnam?
5. How did the Tet Offensive affect U.S. policy and public support for the war?
6. Why did Nixon expand the war into Cambodia?
7. How did the **Pentagon Papers** increase Americans' opposition to the war?
8. Why did Congress pass the **War Powers Act**?
9. What happened in Vietnam in the years after the **Paris Peace Accords** were signed?

CRITICAL THINKING

10. **Compare and Contrast** (a.) What was Kennedy's flexible response defense policy? (b) How did it differ from Eisenhower's policy?
11. **Cite Evidence** What were some successes and failures of Kennedy's foreign policy?
12. **Identify Cause and Effect** What factors caused the American involvement in the Vietnam War?
13. **Draw Inferences** (a.) How did the Gulf of Tonkin Resolution expand the President's power? (b.) How did the resolution affect the relationship between the legislative and executive branches of government?
14. **Draw Conclusions** (a.) What military advantages did the communist forces have in Vietnam? (b.) How did these advantages undermine the strength of U.S. forces?
15. **Make Generalizations** What were the consequences of the Vietnam War?
16. **Analyze Maps** Look at the map below. Why did the United States feel increasingly threatened by Castro's regime after the failed Bay of Pigs invasion?

Cuba and the Bay of Pigs

17. **Writing Activity: Compose an Informative Essay** Walter Cronkite was the most influential broadcast journalist of the 1960s. Use the excerpt below and your knowledge of the Vietnam War to write an informative essay evaluating how the media shaped public opinion about the war.

> To say that we are closer to victory today is to believe, in the face of the evidence, the optimists who have been wrong in the past. To suggest we are on the edge of defeat is to yield to unreasonable pessimism. To say that we are mired in stalemate seems the only realistic, yet unsatisfactory, conclusion. . . . But it is increasingly clear . . . that the only rational way out then will be to negotiate, not as victors, but as an honorable people who lived up to their pledge to defend democracy, and did the best they could.
> This is Walter Cronkite. Good night.
> —*Walter Cronkite, February 27, 1968*

18. **Connections to Today** Since the Vietnam War, American military interventions have been controversial. Protests often follow the decision to send troops abroad. Do you think this increased skepticism about the use of military force is a positive or negative impact of the Vietnam War?

DOCUMENT-BASED QUESTIONS

The Vietnam War transformed American politics, especially in the 1968 presidential race. Read the documents below, then answer the questions that follow.

DOCUMENT A

This excerpt is from a secondary source about Lyndon Johnson and Robert Kennedy.

> The feud that helped define the public lives of LBJ and RFK also helped shape the two greatest national undertakings of their times—the war on poverty and the war in Vietnam. Consumed by contempt for Ksennedy, Johnson transformed a potential ally into an archenemy. . . . As Johnson and Kennedy became ever more bitter enemies, they divided constituencies they once shared, weakening their party by forcing its members to choose between them. They exposed and exacerbated the growing divide within the Democratic Party and American politics in general.
>
> —*Jeff Shesol, Mutual Contempt*

DOCUMENT B

DOCUMENT C

This excerpt is from President Johnson's announcement on March 31, 1968.

> It is true that a house divided against itself by the spirit of faction, of party, of region, of religion, of race, is a house that cannot stand. There is division in the American house now. . . . I should not permit the Presidency to become involved in the partisan divisions that are developing in this political year. With America's sons in the fields far away, with America's future under challenge right here at home, with our hopes and the world's hopes for peace in the balance every day, I do not believe that I should devote an hour or a day of my time to any personal partisan causes or to any duties other than the awesome duties of this office—the Presidency of your country. Accordingly, I shall not seek, and I will not accept, the nomination of my party for another term as your President.
>
> —*President Lyndon B. Johnson, March 31, 1968*

DOCUMENT D

This excerpt is from a speech by Richard Nixon.

> For four years America's fighting men have set a record for courage and sacrifice unsurpassed in our history. . . . Never has so much military and economic and diplomatic power been used so ineffectively. . . . I say the time has come for the American people to turn to new leadership not tied to the mistakes and policies of the past. That is what we offer to America. And I pledge to you tonight that the first priority foreign policy objective of our next Administration will be to bring an honorable end to the war in Vietnam.
>
> —*Republican Presidential Nominee Richard M. Nixon, August 8, 1968*

19. In Document A, the relationship between President Johnson and Robert Kennedy is described as
A. strengthening the Democratic Party.
B. dividing the Republicans from the Democrats.
C. a feud destroying the Democrats from within.
D. caused by disagreement over Vietnam.

20. Analyze Photographs What does Document B reveal about the Democratic National Convention of 1968?

21. In Document C, Johnson explains that he will not run for a second term as president because
A. he is afraid of losing the election.
B. his Democratic support would be too weak.
C. he fears splitting the Democratic Party.
D. the Vietnam conflict is consuming his attention.

22. In Document D, Nixon is implying that
A. the war has been mismanaged.
B. the war is dividing the nation.
C. his administration would seek peace immediately.
D. the domino theory was bad foreign policy.

23. Writing Activity: Primary Source Write a paragraph explaining the political divisions that split the nation and the Democratic Party in 1968. Use the sources as well as additional information you have learned.

Topic 18

An Era of Change
(1960–1980)

ESSENTIAL QUESTION What are the challenges of diversity?

GO ONLINE to access the eText, videos, Interactive Primary Sources, Biographies, and other online resources.

1969 Poster for the famous music festival at Woodstock, New York

Connections to Today

Discrimination consists of biased practices based on age, race, sexual orientation, disability, or gender. One example of gender discrimination is that working women earn less than men and are often passed over for promotion. In this Topic, you'll learn how the women's movement of the 1960s and '70s drew attention to issues like workplace discrimination against women. Today, there are still very few women in upper management, raising the question: What can be done to achieve full gender equality in the workplace?

NBC LEARN

Learn more about Betty Friedan, the feminist activist.

BOUNCE to Activate My Story Video

Topic 18 Overview

In this Topic, you'll learn about events during an era of great change that began in 1960. Look at the lesson outline and explore the timeline. As you study this Topic, you'll complete the Quest Inquiry.

LESSON OUTLINE

18.1 The Counterculture of the 1960s

18.2 The Women's Rights Movement

18.3 Expanding the Push for Equality

18.4 The Environmental Movement

18.5 The Two Sides of the Nixon Presidency

18.6 Ford and Carter Struggle

An Era of Change (1960–1980)

1962
Rachel Carson's *Silent Spring* is published

1966
United Farm Workers union is formed

1967
Hippies converge on San Francisco

1969
Huge countercultural festival held at Woodstock, NY

1973
Oil embargo causes U.S. energy prices to soar

1974
Nixon resigns; Ford becomes president

1979
Protesters seize U.S. embassy hostages in Tehran, Iran

1960 · 1965 · 1970 · 1975 · 1980

QUEST! INQUIRY

Analyzing the Leadership Qualities of Nixon, Ford, and Carter

What effects did the leadership styles of Nixon, Ford and Carter have on the nation? How can we evaluate the success of these presidents' foreign and domestic policies? In this Quest you'll learn about presidential leadership and write an essay on the subject.

STEP 1
Watch a video about Watergate. Then discuss the video in class or with a partner. Write down questions you might have about Nixon's leadership.

STEP 2
Examine six sources relating to the leadership styles of Nixon, Ford, and Carter. Answer the questions attached to each document.

STEP 3
Draw your own conclusions based on all the evidence and viewpoints. Remember to read and revise your essay before submitting it to your teacher.

STEP 4
Reflect on what you have learned about the subject and about the process of writing your essay.

GO ONLINE to access complete Quest materials

18.1

In the later 1960s, "love-ins"—events celebrating love as a kind of social activism—showcased the countercultural desire to reject norms of behavior and dress.

BOUNCE to Activate Flipped Video

Objectives

Describe the rise of the counterculture.

List the major characteristics of the counterculture.

Evaluate the positive and negative impacts of the counterculture movement on American society.

Key Terms

counterculture
generation gap
Beatles
communes

The Counterculture of the 1960s

Many of the generation born after the challenging times of the Great Depression and World War II embraced a different worldview than that of their parents—a worldview that found dramatic expression in the counterculture movement that arose in the 1960s. Members of the counterculture adopted values that ran counter to mainstream culture. They rebelled against long-standing customs in dress, music, and personal behavior. The counterculture both challenged the values of mainstream American society and provoked a countermovement to reassert traditional values.

A Counterculture Emerges

Countercultural Values The counterculture was rooted in the events of the preceding decade. In the 1950s, the Beat movement had rejected materialism and emphasized the importance of personal experience. The civil rights movement introduced the idea of social and political protest, which intensified the Vietnam antiwar movement. Both movements prompted many to challenge a range of traditional social behavior, from restrictions on rights to cultural norms in dress or hairstyles. The counterculture also heightened distrust of authority, leading some young people to warn their peers, "Don't trust anyone over 30."

Members of the counterculture valued youth, spontaneity, and freedom of expression. In the mid-1960s a subculture known as the hippies emerged. These young people claimed to value peace, love, and freedom. They experimented with new styles of dress and music, freer sexual relationships, and the recreational use of drugs. Their values were so different from traditional ones that many social analysts described America as experiencing

GO ONLINE to access your digital course

a **generation gap**, in which there was a lack of understanding and communication between the old and young. Jerry Rubin, a political activist, described how young people's fashion for long hair divided parents from their children:

> Young kids identify short hair with authority, discipline. . . . Wherever we go, our hair tells people where we stand on Vietnam, Wallace, campus disruption, dope. . . . Yesterday I was walking down the street. A car passed by, parents in the front seat and a young kid, about eight, in the back seat. The kid flashed me the clenched fist sign. [Meaning: He identified with Rubin's long hair.]
>
> —Jerry Rubin, *America in the Sixties*

The baby boom that followed World War II resulted in a huge student population in the 1960s. Through their numbers alone, the baby boomers became a force for social change. The music industry rushed to produce the music they liked; clothing designers copied the styles they introduced; universities were forced to change college courses and rules to accommodate them.

>> The generation gap in dress: Ed Sullivan, the reserved TV host born in 1901, thanks the Rolling Stones' Mick Jagger after the Stones' performance on Sullivan's show in 1969.

BOUNCE to Activate Gallery

>> Members of the counterculture movement came together to promote what they felt was missing from mainstream culture; an emphasis on personal experience, love, and freedom.

The Generation Gap The large population of baby boomers and their emerging influence emphasized the growing divide between the younger and older generations. In the 1960s and 1970s, many parents and their children had little in common apart from their genes. Parents of boomer children were heavily influenced by the two major events of their own childhoods, the Depression and World War II. Boomers' parents had learned to live frugally through years of rationing during the Depression and war.

As teens, they had listened to big-band music. They generally valued loyalty and authority, and respected the military and veterans. Many also married at a young age, choosing to take on the responsibilties of a family. As a result, many in this so-called "silent generation," sought stability by conforming.

Their baby-boomer children on the other hand rejected tradition and authority in favor of individuality. "Do your own thing!" became the catchphrase of the young. Boomers did not want to fit in; they wanted to stand out. With the economic difficulties of the 1930s and 40s a distant memory, boomers grew up in a time of prosperity for much of the nation. Many embraced political activism and

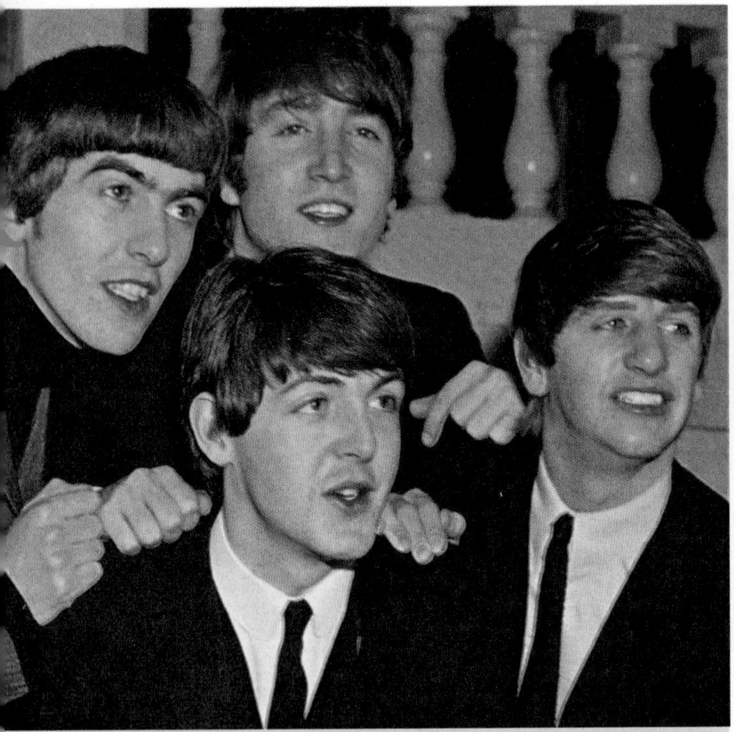

>> The Beatles, a rock band that emerged from the British counterculture, transformed American popular music and fashion in the 1960s.

>> This concert poster for the rock band The Grateful Dead shows the kind of "psychedelic" art that emerged from San Francisco in the 1960s.

opposed the Vietnam War. The boomer generation also expressed a distrust of tradition and authority, which was expressed in popular magazines like *MAD*. Rock-and-roll music shaped their worldview and set them apart from their parents, who had grown up in a very different world.

☑ **IDENTIFY SUPPORTING DETAILS** What accounts for the generational differences between baby boomers and their parents?

The Counterculture Shapes a Generation

Many people have used the so-called trinity of the counterculture—sex, drugs, and rock-and-roll—to define the youth generation. But the counterculture was also marked by an interest in spirituality.

A Cultural Revolution in the Arts By the 1960s, rock-and-roll had become a defining characteristic of the baby-boom generation. When the **Beatles** made a triumphant visit to the United States in 1964, more than 70 million Americans watched the English rock band perform on Ed Sullivan's television show. The Beatles also had an impact on folk musicians like Bob Dylan, whose protest songs highlighted the civil rights and peace movements.

As radical poet and activist John Sinclair put it, rock became "a weapon of cultural revolution," that urged listeners to reject conventions and, in many cases, the political policies of the government. Even after the counterculture had declined in significance, rock music remained popular among baby-boomers as well as their children.

The art and literature of the 1960s and 1970s also displayed a rebellious side. Andy Warhol's realistic paintings of ordinary grocery items, such as Campbell's soup cans, questioned traditional ideas of art and mocked the values of consumerism. In literature, the novels of Tom Wolfe and Hunter S. Thompson blurred the lines between reporting and political activism.

Experiments in Living and the Sexual Revolution Members of the counterculture rejected many traditional restrictions on sexual behavior in what became known as the "sexual revolution." They called for the enjoyment of sex for its own sake and often advocated new living patterns. For example, many hippies lived together in **communes**, or small communities in which the people have common interests and share resources.

The sexual revolution was one of the strongest indicators of the generation gap. One poll showed that nearly two-thirds of all Americans over the age of 30 opposed premarital sex, whereas a majority of those under age 29 did not. Eventually, however, the sexual revolution led to a more open discussion of sex in the mainstream media.

Impact of the Hippie Culture in San Francisco In 1967, as many as 2,000 people flocked to the Haight-Ashbury district of San Francisco, a center of the counterculture. Hippies there experimented with drugs, wore unconventional clothing, and listened to rock music and speeches by political radicals such as Timothy Leary, a one-time Harvard researcher. He preached that drugs could free the mind, and he encouraged American youths to "tune in," "turn on" to drugs, and "drop out" of mainstream society. The hippies of San Francisco attracted a great deal of media attention, much of it critical of the lifestyles they advocated. Life in Haight-Ashbury did lead to negative consequences. As in other enclaves of hippie culture, it experienced high rates of drug abuse that led to increased crime.

Seeking New Forms of Spirituality Some members of the counterculture sought spiritual enlightenment outside of the Judeo-Christian traditions in which they had been raised. Many explored Buddhism and other Eastern religions, while others sought spirituality by living in harmony with nature. Particularly in the late 1960s and early 1970s, some hippies established rural communes, seeking to live off the land as American Indians had in the past. These beliefs had a lasting impact on the budding environmental movement.

Positive and Negative Effects of the Counterculture By the end of the 1960s, many people, even those within the counterculture, had become disillusioned with some of its excesses. The utopian urge to discover a more authentic way of living had an unfortunate underside. Drug addictions and deaths from overdoses rose. The hedonism and violence of rock-and-roll seemed to be having a negative effect, as a number of rock musicians, most famously Jimi Hendrix and Janis Joplin, died of drug overdoses while only in their twenties. The downward spiral continued in 1969 with a tragedy at a music festival in Altamont, California.

While the Rolling Stones played, members of the Hells Angels, a motorcycle gang that had been hired to provide security, stabbed to death a Black man who had approached the stage. The ugly violence contradicted the values of "peace and love" that many hippies embraced.

At the same time, the movement's values were becoming increasingly shallow and self-centered. When the counterculture fell apart, most hippies abandoned their social experiments and melted right back into the mainstream. Still, the seeds of protest they had planted would influence the growing "rights revolution."

>> Members of the Hog Farm commune gather to prepare a meal. Living off the land, they created a community of like-minded people.

BOUNCE to Activate Gallery

IDENTIFY SUPPORTING DETAILS In what ways was the music of artists like Bob Dylan relevant to the time?

ASSESSMENT

1. **Describe** the defining characteristics of the counterculture movement.
2. **Generate Explanations** Explain how earlier social and political movements influenced the counterculture movement of the 1960s.
3. **Identify Cause and Effect** Discuss significant events that led to the decline of the counterculture movement.
4. **Draw Conclusions** Discuss the lasting effects of the counterculture movement.
5. **Quest Connections** Contrast the values of the baby boomers with those of the "silent generation."

18.2

Coretta Scott King, widow of Martin Luther King Jr., addresses a group of feminists at a National Women's Conference in support of minority women's rights.

BOUNCE to Activate Flipped Video

Objectives

Analyze why a movement to expand women's political rights arose in the 1960s.

Identify the goals and methods that political organizations used to promote women's rights.

Assess the impact of the women's movement on American society.

Key Terms

feminism
Betty Friedan
National Organization for Women (NOW)
Equal Rights Amendment (ERA)
Gloria Steinem
Phyllis Schlafly

The Women's Rights Movement

In the 1960s and 1970s, American women launched a broad-based movement to expand economic opportunities and attain equal rights. The women's movement fundamentally changed many aspects of American life—from family and education to careers and political issues. Today, the contributions of people of various gender groups continue to shape American culture.

A New Feminist Movement Pushes for Equality

Historians often refer to the women's movement of the 1960s and 1970s as the second wave of **feminism**, or the theory of political, social, and economic equality of men and women. The struggle for women's rights in the United States has had a long history, going back at least to the 1840s, when women drafted the Declaration of Sentiments at Seneca Falls, New York.

The phrase *second wave of feminism* also reminds us that the first wave, which culminated with women winning the right to vote in 1920, ended well before the nation addressed the call for full equality. In the decades that followed, women made little legal or social headway in the battle for equal rights. In fact, after World War II, most women gave up their jobs to returning servicemen and went back to their homes to take care of their families. During the 1950s, social analysts and popular culture portrayed women, especially suburban housewives, as the personification of America's achievement of the good life. By the 1960s, attitudes like these had begun to change.

GO ONLINE to access your digital course

Seeking to Redefine Traditional Roles Several factors influenced the rebirth of the women's movement in the 1960s and 1970s. The civil rights struggle prompted women to look at the ways in which society judged and discriminated against them as a group. As Casey Hayden and Mary King, two veterans of that movement, put it: "Sex and caste. There seem to be many parallels that can be drawn between the treatment of Negroes and the treatment of women in society as a whole." Hayden and King used the phrase "Jane Crow" to emphasize a link between racial and gender discrimination.

The civil rights movement both inspired women to demand gender equality and taught them how to achieve it. It also brought Black and white women together, strengthening their shared cause.

Women also wanted to redefine how they were viewed. Many women objected to the inaccuracy of the housewife stereotype. Some needed to work to support themselves or their families. Others wanted more opportunities outside the home. **Betty Friedan** powerfully articulated this message in her groundbreaking book *The Feminine Mystique*.

> The problem lay buried, unspoken, for many years in the minds of American women. It was a strange stirring, a sense of dissatisfaction. . . . Each suburban wife struggled with it alone. As she made the beds, shopped for groceries, matched slipcover material, ate peanut butter sandwiches with her children, chauffeured Cub Scouts and Brownies, lay beside her husband at night—she was afraid to ask even of herself the silent question—'Is this all?'
>
> —Betty Friedan, ***The Feminine Mystique,*** 1963

>> The 1960s and 1970s witnessed a broad-based struggle for equal rights among women in the United States.

>> Betty Friedan, president of the National Organization for Women (NOW), claimed that it was not simply men, but society in general, that kept women unequal.

Fighting Workplace Discrimination Despite the stereotypes, the number of women in the workforce grew throughout the 1950s and 1960s. Yet working women often found themselves in dead-end jobs. Regardless of the quality of their work, women found it difficult to advance or even retain their positions. Pregnancy, for example, was all too often seen as grounds for dismissal or demotion. In many cases, pregnant women were routinely denied leave or forced to take unpaid leave.

Even women with advanced training and education had their access to careers or advancement blocked, in many cases, by blatantly discriminatory employers. Sandra Day O'Connor, who ultimately became the first female Supreme

Court Justice, graduated near the top of her class at Stanford Law School in the early 1950s.

Yet while she found few employment opportunities upon graduation, her male counterparts won job offers at prestigious law firms. Facing such restrictions, women increasingly demanded equal treatment in the workplace.

IDENTIFY MAIN IDEAS What was an essential goal of the feminist movement?

The Role of Women's Civil Rights Organizations

Several years after she wrote *The Feminine Mystique,* Betty Friedan helped establish the **National Organization for Women (NOW)**. The organization—which dedicated itself to winning "true equality for all women" and to attaining a "full and equal partnership of the sexes"—galvanized the women's movement.

NOW Works to Expand Rights Through Lobbying NOW was formed to compel the federal government to enforce the part of the Civil Rights Act of 1964 that outlawed sex discrimination in employment. The organization set out to break down barriers of discrimination in the workplace and in education. It attacked stereotypes of women in the media and called for more balance in roles in marriages. Its major goal in the 1970s was to bring about passage of the **Equal Rights Amendment (ERA)**, an amendment to the Constitution that would guarantee gender equality under the law. The ERA initially had been proposed in the early 1920s but had never passed. NOW also wanted to protect reproductive rights, especially the right to an abortion. NOW worked within the existing political system, lobbying for political reforms and readying court cases to compel the government to enforce existing legislation that banned discrimination. For some women, NOW seemed too extreme; for others, it was not extreme enough. Still, NOW served as a rallying point to promote equality for all women.

>> In 1978, over 100,000 women marched in Washington, D.C., to demand that Congress extend the deadline for ratification of the Equal Rights Amendment.

BOUNCE to Activate Timeline

Feminists Raise Society's Awareness Through Different Methods Finding NOW too tame, radical feminists sought a more fundamental restructuring of society. Rather than seeking legislative change, these protesters sought to show the way society trapped women into adopting restrictive roles. Like the civil rights campaigners, they adopted a variety of nonviolent methods. In addition to public protests of the Miss America Pageant, radical feminists engaged in small-scale consciousness-raising efforts. Other feminists sought to raise public awareness by making personal issues political. Charlotte Bunch, for example, wrote that "there is no private domain of a person's life that is not political and there is no political issue that is not ultimately personal."

Some feminists, like **Gloria Steinem**, tried to change awareness through the mass media. After graduating from college, Steinem worked as a freelance writer, including a stint of undercover work at a club run by *Playboy* magazine. While society tended to view Playboy bunnies in glamorous terms, Steinem revealed how much humiliation they had to endure to make a living. In 1972, she helped co-found *Ms.*, a feminist magazine. Its title was meant to protest the social custom of identifying women by their marital status rather than as individuals.

Phyllis Schlafly and Conservatives Oppose the Women's Movement Some Americans—both men and women—openly challenged the women's movement. **Phyllis Schlafly**, for example, was a conservative political activist who denounced women's liberation as "a total assault on the family, on marriage, and on children." She worked hard to defeat the ERA, arguing that the act would compel women to fight in the military, end sex-segregated bathrooms, and hurt the family. Her argument resonated with many conservatives. Due to conservative opposition, the ERA fell three states short of becoming a constitutional amendment.

RECALL What was the purpose of the proposed Equal Rights Amendment?

The Impact of the Women's Movement

The women's movement affected all aspects of American society. Women's roles and opportunities expanded. Women gained legal rights that had been denied them. And feminists sparked an important debate about equality that continues today. Yet the issues they raised continue to divide Americans. Some say that women haven't made enough gains. Others fear that the movement has actually harmed society.

Achieving Equality of Political Rights Through Litigation Before the 1960s, there were no federal laws prohibiting gender discrimination. The Civil Rights Act of 1964, however, gave feminists a legal tool. It included a clause, called Title VII, that outlawed discrimination on the basis of sex. The clause was actually inserted by civil rights opponents, who thought it was so outlandish that it would make the entire bill look ridiculous.

When the bill actually passed, however, women used Title VII to challenge discrimination. The bill also set up the Equal Employment Opportunity Commission (EEOC) to enforce the federal prohibition on job discrimination.

Enforcing Title VII, even with the EEOC, was often difficult. Still, NOW and other feminist organizations tirelessly filed suits against employers who refused to hire women or to pay them fairly, compelling the federal government to act. President Kennedy established the Commission on the Status of Women in 1961 to examine workplace discrimination. Title IX of the Higher Education Act of 1972 banned discrimination in education. The Equal Credit Opportunity Act, passed in 1974, made it illegal to deny credit to a woman just because of her gender.

Title IX applied to many facets of educational opportunities but had an especially profound impact on collegiate athletics. In effect, Title IX said that

>> The battle for women's rights took place in many venues. In 1973, tennis player Billie Jean King demonstrated women's equality with men by defeating Bobby Riggs in The Battle of the Sexes.

>> As a result of Title IX, women's athletics increased dramatically in the 1980s. Many, like the Women's USA Basketball Team, now dominate international competitions.

the ratio of women to men participating in collegiate athletics had to mirror the ratio of women to men enrolled in the school.

Participation by women in college athletics has increased dramatically since 1972. Since then, however, the number of women coaches has decreased significantly. As women's sports gained in popularity and became revenue-generating sports, male coaches were drawn to these higher-profile positions. In 1972, the number of women coaching collegiate women's sports was over 90 percent. By 2010, that number was down to approximately 42 percent. This is one of the ways in which Title IX created unintended consequences that have been difficult to counteract.

Some feminists considered their most important legal victory to be the 1973 Supreme Court decision in *Roe* v. *Wade*, which assured women the right to legal abortions. Prior to *Roe*, most states outlawed or severely restricted abortion. Some women turned to illegal and often dangerous ways to end their pregnancies. The case and its decision were highly controversial at the time and still are today.

Expanding Economic and Employment Opportunities The women's movement fostered a shift in attitudes among both men and women, and the American workplace today reflects this change. The percentage of women in the workforce has grown, from about 30 percent in 1950 to more than 60 percent in 2000. So, too, has the number of married female workers. Fields long closed or severely limited to women—such as medicine, law, and accounting—have opened up as well. The general shift in attitudes symbolized by these changes has created a world of possibilities for many young women who never knew a time when women were not allowed to do these things.

Despite these gains, the average woman still earns less than the average man, partly because many women continue to work in fields that pay less. Some people have referred to this situation as a "pink-collar ghetto." Whether this is because of discrimination, or because women who shoulder family responsibilities often have limited job choices, remains a matter of debate. Many studies suggest that a "glass ceiling" exists, limiting the advancement of even the most highly educated and skilled women workers.

Most troubling, the United States has witnessed a feminization of poverty over the past 30 years. This means that the majority of the nation's poor people are single women. These are the women in the lowest-paying jobs, with the fewest benefits. Many of these poor women are single mothers, who must bear the costs and responsibilities of raising children alone while also working.

IDENTIFY What was the purpose of Title IX of the Higher Education Act of 1972?

>> **Analyze Data** What data support the conclusion that the women's rights reform movement affected women's opportunities outside the home environment?

BOUNCE to Activate Chart

ASSESSMENT

1. **Compare and Contrast** Identify similarities and differences between the first and second waves of feminism.
2. **Generate Explanations** Explain how the civil rights movement influenced the women's rights movement of the 1960s.
3. **Compare Points of View** Discuss both the support and criticism that the National Organization for Women received in the 1960s.
4. **Identify Central Issues** Discuss the achievements of Title IX, as well as its unintended consequences.
5. **Describe** the feminization of poverty that has occurred in recent decades.
6. **Connections to Today** The Equal Rights Amendment failed to be ratified in the 1970s. Do you think it would pass today? Explain your reasoning.

GO ONLINE to access this biography: Betty Friedan; Phyllis Schlafly

18.3

Cesar Chavez, leader of United Farm Workers, helped to improve working conditions that migrants faced on the fruit and vegetable farms where they worked.

BOUNCE to Activate Flipped Video

Objectives

Analyze the causes of the growth of the Latino population after World War II.

Evaluate significant leaders and the methods they used to achieve equality in political rights for Latinos and others.

Evaluate the means by which American Indians sought to expand their rights.

Describe the expansion of rights for consumers and the disabled.

Key Terms

Hector P. Garcia
Cesar Chavez
migrant farmworker
Dolores Huerta
United Farm Workers (UFW)
Chicano movement
American Indian Movement (AIM)
Japanese American Citizens League
Ralph Nader

GO ONLINE to access your digital course

Expanding the Push for Equality

Successes in the civil rights and women's movements signaled a growing rights revolution in the United States. Latinos, American Indians, and Asian Americans engaged in their own struggles for equality during the 1960s and 1970s, fighting to influence laws and government. Meanwhile, activists worked to expand rights for two broad groups: consumers and people with disabilities.

Latino Immigration Surges

After World War I, the United States passed legislation limiting European immigration. Yet during and after World War II, the country faced a growing demand for cheap labor. At the same time, the populations of Mexico and other Latin American nations grew steadily while job opportunities there declined. The combination of these factors created a steady stream of new immigrants to the United States. Some immigrants came legally, but others crossed the border illegally.

Latinos in the United States People whose family origins are in Spanish-speaking Latin America are called Latinos or Hispanics. They come from many different places, but they share the same language and some elements of culture. Spanish-speaking people lived in many parts of western North America before settlers from the United States arrived, and their numbers have grown steadily. Mexican Americans, known as Chicanos, have always made up the largest group of U.S. Latinos.

Legal and Illegal Immigration Beginning in 1942, Mexican immigrants came to the United States under the *bracero*, or farmhand, program. This program granted Mexican migrants temporary guest worker status, and over a period of 25 years, more than 4 million entered the United States. The *braceros* played a crucial role in sustaining agriculture during and after World War II.

Along with Mexicans who had migrated to the United States illegally in search of work, *braceros* who had outstayed their permits were targeted for deportation in the 1950s. In 1965, however, the government passed the Immigration and Nationality Act Amendments, eliminating national-origin quotas for immigrants. In the decades that followed, the number of legal Mexican and Asian immigrants surged. More than 400,000 Mexicans arrived during the 1960s, another 630,000 in the 1970s, and more than 1.5 million in the 1980s.

Latino Communities on the East Coast After World War II, large numbers of Puerto Ricans, Dominicans, and Cubans migrated to the United States. As citizens of a United States territory, Puerto Ricans came legally, leaving their homeland in search of better-paying jobs. In contrast, most Cuban and Dominican immigrants came to America as political refugees, fleeing their countries to escape the harsh rule of dictators. Most Puerto Rican, Cuban, and Dominican immigrants settled in urban areas, especially in New York City and Miami, Florida, which had notable effects on the demographic patterns in these cities.

DESCRIBE How did the farmhand program encourage Mexicans to legally migrate to the United States?

Latino Organizations Fight for Rights

Like other minorities, Latinos had long faced discrimination. After World War II, Latino veterans began agitating for equal treatment. Veteran **Hector P. Garcia**, for example, formed the American G.I. Forum to battle discrimination. In the 1960s and 1970s, influenced by the growing civil rights movement, Latinos increasingly fought for equal rights. They demanded better working conditions, salaries, and educational opportunities. Like African Americans, they sought federal protection of their right to vote and campaigned to elect politicians who represented their interests.

United States Latino Population

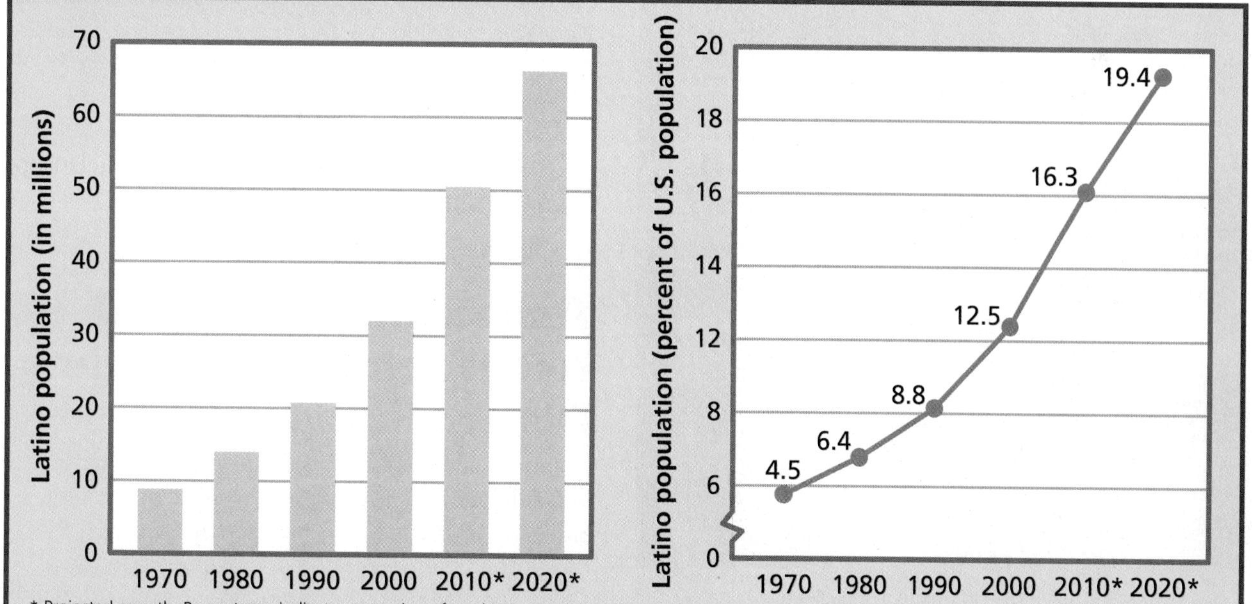

* Projected growth. Percentages indicate proportion of total U.S. population that is Latino.
SOURCE: U.S. Census Bureau

>> **Analyze Data** Based on the information in the chart, how much did the Latino population increase in the United States between 1970 and 2010?

The Role of Cesar Chavez in Organizing Farmworkers Immigrants, including Latino Americans and Filipino Americans, played a central role in the farm labor movement. The most influential Latino activist was **Cesar Chavez**. Chavez fought for rights for farm laborers, who were among the most exploited workers in the nation. Because they migrated from farm to farm—and often from state to state—to pick fruits and vegetables, they were known as **migrant farmworkers**. They labored for long hours in deplorable conditions, with no benefits.

Dolores Huerta was another activist who shared Cesar Chavez's concerns about migrant farmworkers. Huerta worked as a leader of a community service organization in Stockton, California. She founded the Agricultural Workers Association, which organized voter registration drives and worked to improve Hispanic neighborhoods. In 1962, Chavez and Huerta organized a farmworkers' union in Delano, California. In the late 1960s, Chavez and Huerta merged the union with a union of Filipino farm laborers to form what became the **United Farm Workers (UFW)**.

Committed to nonviolent tactics, the UFW implemented a workers' strike and consumer boycott of table grapes. With the help of Huerta, Chavez's top aide, the UFW urged people across the nation to boycott California grapes in order to win recognition from the growers. In 1975, California passed a law requiring collective bargaining between growers and union representatives. Farmworkers finally had a legal basis to ask for better working conditions.

>> To celebrate aspects of Mexican-American culture, Chicano artists painted colorful murals on the walls of city buildings, churches, housing projects, and schools throughout the Southwest.

BOUNCE to Activate Gallery

Actions Taken to Improve Opportunities While Chavez focused on farmworkers' rights, a broader Mexican American social and political effort grew, which came to be known as the **Chicano movement**. Part of it was dedicated to increasing Latinos' awareness of their history and culture. The Chicano Mural Movement, in which Mexican-American culture was celebrated in large, outdoor paintings, sprang up at this time. At California colleges and high schools, and in other states with a Mexican American population, Chicano students demanded that educators teach more about their heritage. Others in the movement focused on quality-of-life issues. For example, the National Council of La Raza was founded in 1968 with the goal of reducing poverty and discrimination and providing better opportunities for Latinos.

Much of the movement's energy was concentrated on attaining political strength for Latinos, or what some called "brown power." In Texas, José Angel Gutiérrez organized the political party La Raza Unida. The party worked for better housing and jobs, and it successfully supported Latino political candidates. In Florida, the Hispanic community's campaign for equal rights brought dramatic results. In 1979, Robert Martinez became Mayor of Tampa and in 1987 he became Forida's first Hispanic governor. By 1980, six Hispanics sat in Congress, representing districts from New York to California. Moreover, Hispanics gained greater representation in state, county, and city governments.

☑ **IDENTIFY CENTRAL IDEAS** Why was the United Farm Workers (UFW) formed in the 1960s?

American Indians and Asian Americans Battle Discrimination

American Indians had long suffered discrimination and suffered high rates of poverty, unemployment, and suicide. Inspired by the struggle for civil rights, they forged their own protest movements in the 1960s and 1970s. At the same time, Asian Americans fought long-standing discrimination.

American Indian Civil Rights Organizations Emerge As with the civil rights movement, the movement demanding change for American Indians was led by young people. In 1961, the National Indian Youth Council (NIYC) formed, with the goal of preserving native fishing rights in the Northwest. Over time, the group expanded its aims to include broad civil rights and sovereignty (self-government) for American Indians.

In 1968, the Chippewa activists Dennis Banks and George Mitchell helped found the **American Indian Movement (AIM)**. At first, AIM focused on helping Indians living in urban ghettos. Before long, however, AIM was addressing all civil rights issues, particularly the securing of land, legal rights, and self-government for American Indians.

Activism Leads to Confrontation In late 1969, a group of American Indians occupied the island of Alcatraz, the site of a federal prison in San Francisco Bay that had closed in 1963. Members of the Sioux tribe asserted that the island belonged to them under a treaty provision granting them unused federal land. About 100 American Indians representing 50 tribes joined the occupation. In spite of efforts by the Coast Guard and other federal authorities to evict them, the Indians maintained control of the island until mid-1971.

The 1970s saw another series of confrontations. In 1972, led by Dennis Banks and Russell Means, AIM orchestrated a "long march" from San Francisco to Washington, D.C. Upon arriving in the capital, they took control of the Bureau of Indian Affairs building. They temporarily renamed it the Native American Embassy, suggesting that American Indians are treated as foreigners.

Tragedy Returns to Wounded Knee In 1970, Dee Brown published *Bury My Heart at Wounded Knee*, which includes a chapter about the 1890 massacre of Sioux at Wounded Knee, South Dakota. Brown noted that in all the history of the American West,

> Only occasionally was the voice of an Indian heard, and then more often than not it was recorded by the pen of a white man. The Indian was the dark menace of the myths, and even if he had known how to write in English, where would he have found a printer or a publisher?

>> Russell Means (center), and Dennis Banks (right), early leaders of the American Indian Movement (AIM), brought the struggle for American Indians' rights to the public's attention.

BOUNCE to Activate Gallery

The best-selling book raised public consciousness about the historic mistreatment of American Indians. Building on this momentum, AIM planned a dramatic confrontation at Wounded Knee.

In late February of 1973, AIM took over the village and refused to leave until the government agreed to investigate the condition of reservation Indians. Federal authorities put Wounded Knee under siege, and two AIM members died in the resulting gunfire. The standoff ended in May when the government pledged to reexamine native treaty rights.

Fighting Discrimination Through Litigation Several landmark cases in the 1940s paved the way for American Indians to fight discrimination through litigation. In 1947, the Ninth Circuit Court of Appeals upheld the decision in *Mendez* v. *Westminster*, ruling that the segregation of Mexican American students in schools in California was unconstitutional. The 1948 decision in *Delgado* v. *Bastrop I.S.D.* ended segregation in the Texas public school system. The ruling stated that the segregation of children of Mexican descent in Texas was illegal.

American Indians activism spurred the passage of several laws in the 1970s. The Indian Self-Determination Act of 1975, for instance, fulfilled one of the main demands of the American Indian movement by granting tribes greater control over resources and education on reservations. American Indians also continued to win legal battles to regain land, mineral, and water rights. While politicians debated how the government should treat American Indians, the Indians themselves continued to suffer from disproportionately high rates of unemployment and other social ills.

Asian Americans Fight Discrimination Prejudice against people of Japanese and Chinese ancestry had long been a problem. The **Japanese American Citizens League**, founded in 1929 to protect Japanese Americans' civil rights, worked for decades to receive compensation for property lost by Japanese Americans interned in camps during World War II.

During the expanding rights revolution of the 1960s and 1970s, many other groups formed to combat discrimination against Asian Americans and to protect their rights. Asian American students joined together in opposition to the Vietnam War, helping to spur the Asian American movement.

This movement also worked to obtain Asian American courses in colleges and fair treatment when applying for a job, purchasing a home, or receiving medical treatment. In 1965, the Immigration and Nationality Act Amendments aided Asian immigrants by ending the nation's long-standing quota system established in 1924.

☑ **DESCRIBE** What was the significance of the *Mendez* v. *Westminster* court decision?

Rights for Consumers and the Disabled

During these years of reform many worked to protect the rights of consumers and Americans with disabilities.

A New Movement for Consumer Rights During the Progressive Era, reformers had pushed for measures to protect consumers, ranging from the Pure Food and Drug Act to the Meat Inspection Act. The consumer rights movement reemerged during the 1960s and 1970s. It was led by **Ralph Nader**, a lawyer who began to investigate whether flawed car designs led to increased traffic accidents. His book, *Unsafe at Any Speed* (1965), attacked automakers whose thirst for profits produced unsafe vehicles that endangered the public.

Nader's best-selling book stirred the nation and prompted Congress to pass the National Traffic and Motor Vehicle Safety Act in 1966. The act made safety belts standard equipment in all cars. Nader went on to form several consumer advocacy groups. Under his influence, consumer advocacy adopted many of the practices that shape it today, including research and government lobbying. Advocacy for workers began to gain more prominence as well. The Nixon administration proposed the idea for the Occupational Safety and Health Administration (OSHA), which mandated workplace safety regulations.

Rights-Expanding Legislation

LEGISLATION OR PANEL	PLANNED OR ACTUAL EFFECT
Equal Rights Amendment (ERA) (First proposed 1921; never passed)	Proposed constitutional amendment to guarantee gender equality
Panel on Mental Retardation (1961)	Explored ways the government could help people with disabilities
Title VII of the Civil Rights Act (1964)	Outlawed sex-based discrimination
Immigration and Nationality Act (1965)	Eased restrictions, making immigration easier for Latinos and Asians
National Traffic and Motor Vehicle Safety Act (1966)	Mandated safety equipment in cars
Indian Self-Determination Act (1975)	Gave Native Americans control over resources on reservations

>> **Analyze Charts** How did legislation enacted during the 1960s lead to the expansion of rights for minorities?

Historically, the nation had treated people with disabilities as defective. FDR hid the fact that he could not walk because he did not want society to assume he was incapable of serving as President. Yet by the 1970s, Americans with disabilities were expanding their rights. Disabled veterans from the Korean and Vietnam wars took part in this activism. The Kennedy administration called for change by establishing the Panel on Mental Retardation in 1961 to explore ways for the government to help people with intellectual disabilities.

The next year, Eunice Shriver, President Kennedy's sister, began an athletic camp for young people with disabilities that eventually became the Special Olympics. Over the next few years, the government passed a number of acts guaranteeing equal access to education for people with disabilities.

IDENTIFY SUPPORTING DETAILS What effects did the publication of the book *Unsafe at Any Speed* have on public safety?

>> Disabled athletes carry the torch during the opening ceremony of the 2013 Special Olympics Winter Games. The first Special Olympics was held in Chicago in 1968.

The Gay Rights Movement Advances

The civil rights movement also inspired the lesbian, gay, bisexual, and transgender (LGBT) community to become politically active. In the 1950s and 1960s, anti-gay laws continued to criminalize lesbian and gay male sexual orientation. Government purges, bar raids, and police entrapments sent thousands to prison or mental institutions every year. Faced with this repression, members of the LGBT community began organizing to defend their rights.

Activists Organize In San Francisco in 1961, José Sarria became the first openly gay person to run for public office. In San Francisco, Washington D.C., and New York City, protests against anti-gay laws and policies began to increase.

The Stonewall Riots In New York City, protests over entrapment and police raids on gay bars had been intensifying in the late 1960s. Then, in the early morning of June 28, 1969, young patrons of the Stonewall Inn in Greenwich Village rioted in response to a routine police raid. The riots continued for several days as news of the event attracted more LGBT supporters. The Stonewall Riots ignited a new militant phase in the gay-rights movement. Almost overnight, new organizations sprang up, calling on all LGBT people to "come out" of hiding and declare their sexual identity to their friends, families, and co-workers. Adopting this tactic, LGBT people worldwide began organizing annual Gay Pride marches, to commemorate the Stonewall Inn uprising of 1969, to increase visibility, and to agitate for change in attitudes and laws.

RECALL How did the LGBT rights movement change after Stonewall?

GO ONLINE to access these biographies: César Chávez; Hector P. Garcia

ASSESSMENT

1. **Generate Explanations** Explain why the United States experienced a new wave of immigration after World War II.
2. **Summarize** Discuss the role of the United Farm Workers in securing civil rights for Mexican Americans.
3. **Identify Steps in a Process** Discuss changes that altered the treatment of disabled people during the 1960s and 1970s.
4. **Describe** Ralph Nader's contributions to the consumer rights movement.
5. **Quest Connections** Describe the American Indian activism that occurred under Presidents Nixon and Ford, and explain why this activism often led to confrontations with the U.S. government.

18.4

Many people hoped nuclear energy would provide a safe alternative to fossil fuels, but the accident at Three Mile Island, in 1979, created resistance to nuclear energy production.

BOUNCE to Activate Flipped Video

Objectives

Assess the causes and effects of the environmental movement.

Analyze why environmental protection became a controversial issue.

Key Terms

Rachel Carson
toxic waste
Earth Day
Environmental Protection Agency (EPA)
Clean Air Act
Clean Water Act
Endangered Species Act

The Environmental Movement

The "rights revolution" of the 1960s and 1970s eventually influenced all aspects of American life—including people's right to a clean and safe environment. In 1962 a book called *Silent Spring* by biologist Rachel Carson pointed out that human actions were harming not only the environment but people themselves. Public awareness of environmental issues prompted an important debate about the government's role in environmental regulations.

Environmental Activists Sound the Alarm

In the 1920s, Progressives had worked to conserve public lands and parks. But few worried much about the ill effects of industrialization. In 1952, however, a blanket of deadly smog, caused by coal fires, engulfed the city of London, killing some 12,000 people. Ten years after London's Great Smog, a book sparked the modern environmental movement.

***Silent Spring* Launches a Movement** Coal smog is just one kind of **toxic waste**, or poisonous byproduct of human activity. Another is acid rain, or moisture in the air caused by the mixing of water with chemicals produced by the burning of fossil fuels. Toxic wastes are also produced when nuclear power is generated. Throughout the 1960s and 1970s, scientists learned more about toxic wastes and other environmental threats.

Rachel Carson's book *Silent Spring* described the deadly impact that pesticides were having on birds and other animals. Her book caused a sensation. Though the chemical industry

GO ONLINE to access your digital course

fought back, the public was convinced by her argument. Carson did more than point to the dangers of chemicals and toxic waste. She also insisted that human activity drastically altered the environment and that humans had a responsibility to protect it. Her work eventually compelled Congress to restrict the use of the pesticide DDT. It also spurred widespread environmental activism among Americans.

When a fire erupted on the Cuyahoga River in Cleveland, Ohio, in 1969, activists instantly spoke out. The fire occurred when a spark ignited floating oil and debris—byproducts of industrialization—on the river's surface. *Time* magazine reported that the river "oozes, rather than flows." Even more luridly, the magazine remarked that in the Cuyahoga, a person "does not drown but decays."

A Grassroots Movement Creates Earth Day

Events like the Cuyahoga River fire seemed to confirm the dire predictions of *Silent Spring*. One response to growing environmental concerns was a nationwide protest called **Earth Day**. Wisconsin senator Gaylord Nelson, who played the leading role in organizing the protest, wanted "to shake up the political establishment and force this issue [the environment] onto the national agenda." On April 22, 1970, close to 20 million Americans took part in Earth Day events across the nation. The yearly event attracted the support of many of the same people who had advocated civil and women's rights. It was also backed by a number of grassroots groups, including the Sierra Club, founded by John Muir in 1892, and the Wilderness Society, established in 1935. Historically, these groups had focused on conservation. With the rise of the environmental movement, however, they called for broader environmental protections.

Nixon Creates Government Entities to Manage the Environment In 1969, President Nixon declared that the 1970s "must be the years when America pays its debts to the past by reclaiming the purity of its air, its water and our living environment." Nixon had not come into office as an environmental activist. But the public's increasing concern with protecting the environment convinced him to support environmental reforms.

Under Nixon's leadership, Congress created the **Environmental Protection Agency (EPA)** in 1970. This federal agency's mission was to protect the "entire ecological chain." In addition to cleaning up and protecting the environment, the EPA sought to limit or to eliminate pollutants that posed a risk to the public's health, such as toxic substances that cause cancer. Nixon also signed a number of environmental laws.

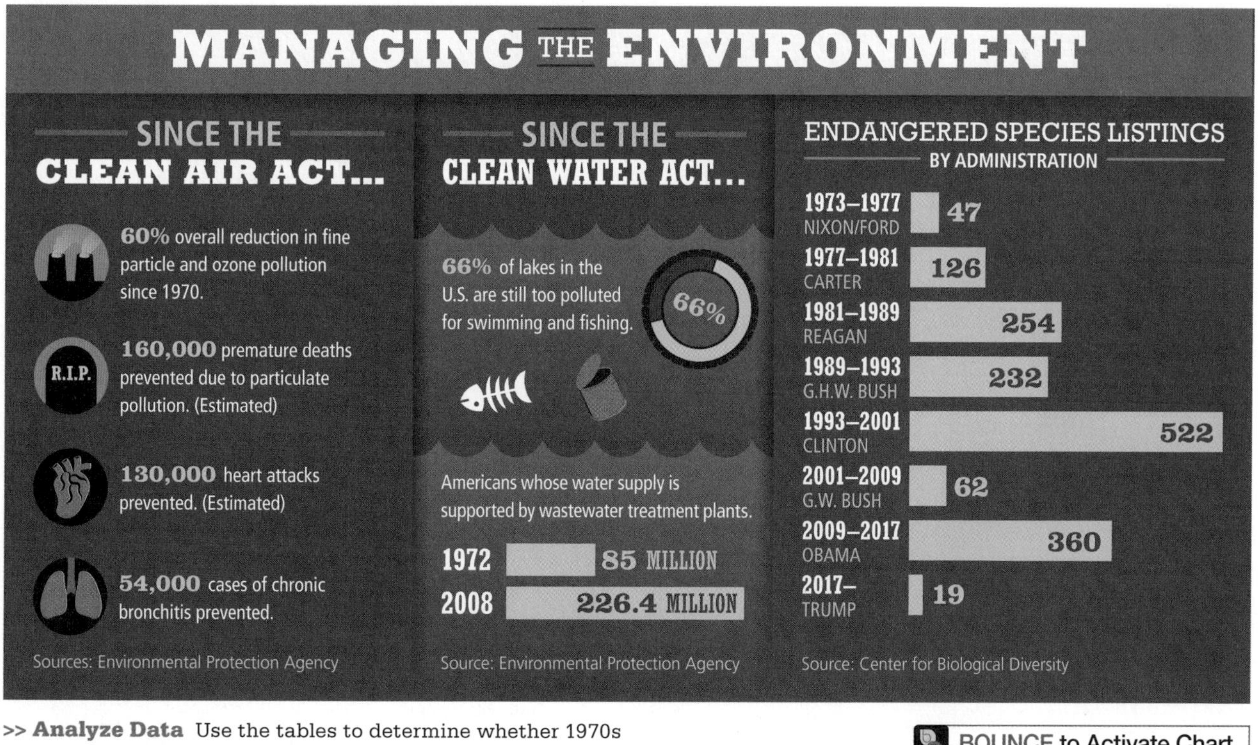

>> **Analyze Data** Use the tables to determine whether 1970s environmental legislation had a positive, neutral, or negative effect on the environment and the American public.

BOUNCE to Activate Chart

The **Clean Air Act** (1970) combated air pollution by, among other things, limiting the emissions from factories and automobiles. The **Clean Water Act** (1973) sought to limit the pollution of water by industry and agriculture. This law built on the Water Quality Act enacted by President Johnson. The **Endangered Species Act** (1973) promoted the protection of endangered plants and animals.

President Gerald Ford continued in Nixon's footsteps. In 1974, he created the Nuclear Regulatory Commission to make sure nuclear materials would be handled safely without harmful impacts on people or the environment.

☑ **EXPLAIN** How did the modern environmental movement develop?

Impact of Environmental Regulations

As the 1970s drew to a close, a series of environmental crises made the headlines. They reinforced the public's concern about the environment and produced calls for even more far-reaching actions. Yet, at the same time, a number of people began to wonder if the government had enacted too many regulations and was threatening property rights. Rather than calling for more federal actions, they tried to limit the government's role in environmental protection.

The EPA Investigates Love Canal In 1978, a resident of Love Canal, a community near Niagara Falls in upstate New York, hung a sign from his home that read: "Give me Liberty. I've Already Got Death."

This sign referred to the fact that residents of the community had exceptionally high rates of birth defects and cancer. Newspaper reporters and EPA investigators determined that these illnesses were caused by thousands of tons of toxic chemicals, which industries had been dumping in the ground for decades. One EPA administrator recalled the scene he witnessed following a heavy rain that sent toxic chemicals percolating up through the ground.

> I visited the canal area at that time. Corroding waste disposal drums could be seen breaking up through the grounds of backyards. Trees and gardens were turning black and dying. . . . Puddles of noxious substances were pointed out to me by the residents. Some of these puddles were in their yards, some were in their basements, others yet were

Superfund Sites

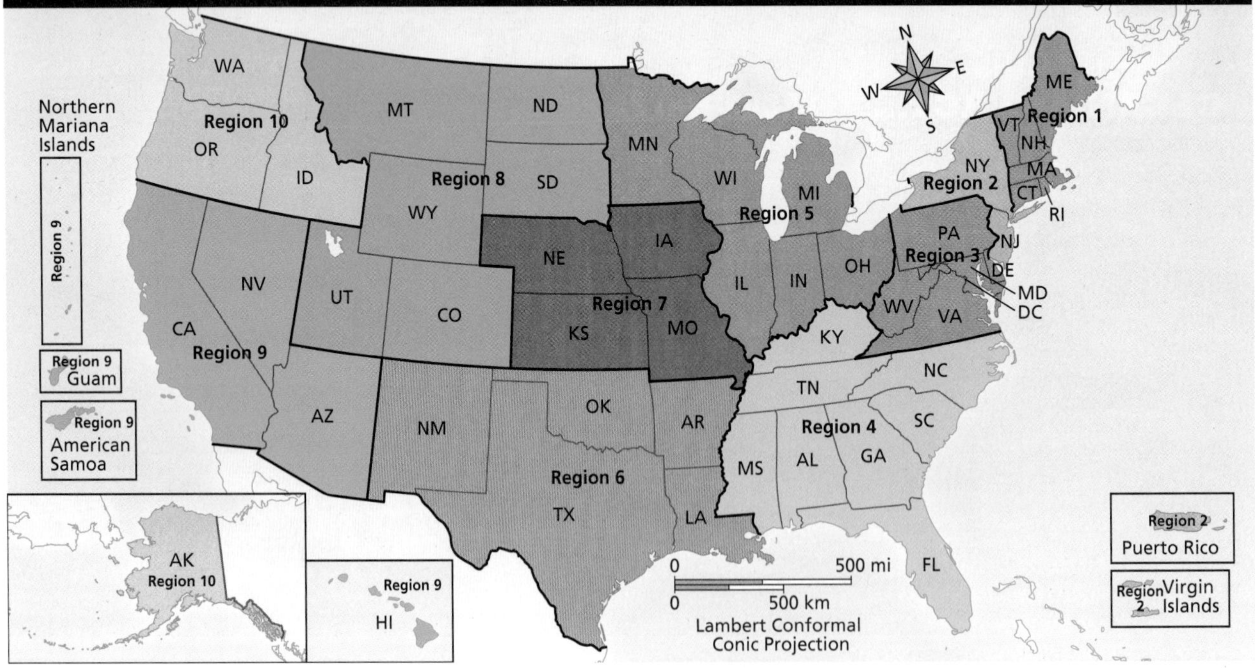

>> **Analyze Maps** This is how the EPA organizes its work by region. In what ways might hazardous waste vary by region?

BOUNCE to Activate Map

on the school grounds. Everywhere the air had a faint, choking smell. Children returned from play with burns on their hands and faces.

—Eckhardt Beck, *EPA Journal*, 1979

The Love Canal contamination, along with other events involving hazardous waste, prompted Congress to establish Superfund in 1980.

Meltdown at Three Mile Island Alters Public Opinion Shortly after the investigation at Love Canal, an accident occurred in the nuclear energy industry. On March 28, 1979, the core of the nuclear reactor at Three Mile Island outside Harrisburg, Pennsylvania, began to melt after the reactor malfunctioned. When the plant threatened to release radioactive gas, the governor declared a state of emergency and shut it down. To reassure the public that plant managers had contained the accident, President Jimmy Carter and his wife traveled to Three Mile Island and toured the reactor.

Even though the incident was contained and there proved to be no health risks, it had profound effects on America's energy policy. In the wake of the accident, public opinion shifted against nuclear energy, as Americans became fearful of possible disasters. The government temporarily stopped building new nuclear power plants. Even though it later lifted the ban, no new American nuclear plants were ordered for more than a quarter of a century. In the 2000s, with the nation threatened by energy shortages, many Americans began to call for building new nuclear plants.

Governmental Actions Challenge Fifth Amendment Rights As more environmental regulations were passed, opposition to them grew. Based on an understanding of the Fifth Amendment, which holds that citizens shall not be deprived of property without due process of law, many complained that environmental regulations stripped individuals, the businesses they owned, and the communities they lived in of their property rights by restricting what they could or could not do with their land. Some argued that private property owners would do a better job of protecting the environment than the government because the owners had an interest in preserving the profitability of their land. Many people—and especially industry leaders—also worried that too much environmental regulation would hamper business and jobs by diverting funds to cleaning up the air and water. Therefore, as the 1970s came to a close—and, indeed, to this day—Americans remained divided about what role the government should play in regulating industry and protecting the environment.

>> **Analyze Political Cartoons** What do you think the palm trees on the island suggest about the release of radiation at Three Mile Island?

EXPLAIN What arguments were raised against the environmental movement?

ASSESSMENT

1. **Describe** the environmental disasters of the 1960s and 1970s that strengthened environmental activism in the United States.
2. **Identify Patterns** Explain how the written word helped the environmental movement to gain momentum during the 1960s and 1970s.
3. **Compare and Contrast** Discuss the relationship between the environmental movement and other campaigns such as civil and women's rights movements.
4. **Identify Cause and Effect** Determine the causes of the Love Canal contamination, and explain its effects on the American public.
5. **Quest Connections** How did Presidents Nixon and Ford protect the environment?

Silent Spring: Rachel Carson

Rachel Carson was a marine biologist and conservationist who wrote extensively about ocean life. *Silent Spring*, published in 1962, examined how synthetic pesticides used by farmers and landowners were poisoning people and wildlife alike. The book issued a pointed critique against the ways human activities harmed the natural world. *Silent Spring* help launched a movement of concerned consumers, which led to the creation of the Environmental Protection Agency and a ban on a number of pollutants.

>> Rachel Carson

There once was a town in the heart of America where all life seemed to live in harmony with its surroundings. The town lay in the midst of a checkerboard of prosperous farms, with fields of grain and hillsides of orchards, where, in spring, white clouds of bloom drifted above the green fields. In autumn, oak and maple and birch set up a blaze of color that flamed and flickered across a backdrop of pines. Then foxes barked in the hills and deer silently crossed the fields, half hidden in the mists of the fall mornings.

Along the roads, laurel, viburnum and alder, great ferns and wildflowers delighted the traveler's eye through much of the year. Even in winter the roadsides were places of beauty, where countless birds came to feed on the berries and on the seed heads of the dried weeds rising above the snow. The countryside was, in fact, famous for the abundance and variety of its bird life, and when the flood of migrants was pouring through in spring and fall people traveled from great distances to observe them. Others came to fish the streams, which flowed clear and cold out of the hills and contained shady pools where trout lay. So it had been from the days many years ago when the first settlers raised their houses, sank their wells, and built their barns.

ANALYZE STYLE AND RHETORIC What phrases help create an image of life lived "in harmony with its surroundings"?

Then a strange blight [plant disease] crept over the area and everything began to change. Some evil spell had settled on the community: mysterious maladies [illnesses] swept the flocks of chickens; the cattle and sheep sickened and died. Everywhere was a shadow of death. The farmers spoke of much illness among their families. In the town the doctors had become more and more puzzled by new kinds of sickness appearing among their patients. There had been several sudden and unexplained deaths, not only among adults but even among children, who would be stricken suddenly while at play and die within a few hours.

There was a strange stillness. The birds, for example—where had they gone? Many people spoke of them, puzzled and disturbed. The feeding stations in the backyards were deserted. The few birds seen anywhere were moribund; they trembled violently and could not fly. It was a spring without voices. On the mornings that had once throbbed with the dawn chorus of robins, catbirds, doves, jays, wrens, and scores of other bird voices there was now no sound; only silence lay over the fields and woods and marsh.

On the farms the hens brooded, but no chicks hatched. The farmers complained that they were unable to raise any pigs—the litters were small and the young survived only a few days. The apple trees were coming into bloom but no bees droned among the blossoms, so there was no pollination and there would be no fruit. The roadsides, once so attractive, were now lined with browned and withered vegetation as though swept by fire. These, too were silent, deserted by all living things. Even the streams were now lifeless. Anglers no longer visited them, for all the fish had died.

COMPARE AND CONTRAST How do the events and the imagery of these paragraphs compare to the descriptions in the first paragraphs?

. . . No witchcraft, no enemy action had silenced the rebirth of new life in this stricken [distressed] world. The people had done it to themselves.

. . . This town does not actually exist, but it might easily have a thousands counterparts in America or elsewhere in the world. I know of no community that has experienced all the misfortunes I describe. Yet every one of these disasters has actually happened somewhere, and many real communities have already suffered a substantial number of them. A grim specter has crept upon us almost unnoticed, and this imagined tragedy may easily become a stark reality we all shall know. What has already silenced the voices of spring in countless towns in America? This book is an attempt to explain.

SUMMARIZE What is the world like that Carson describes in this passage, and why does she begin her book with this description?

. . . Only within the moment of time represented by the present century has one species—man—acquired significant power to alter the nature of his world.

During the past quarter century this power has not only increased to one of disturbing magnitude [great size] but it has changed in character. The most alarming of all man's assaults upon the environment is the contamination of air, earth, rivers, and sea with dangerous and even lethal [enough to cause death] materials. This pollution is for the most part irrecoverable [unable to be recovered]; the chain of evil it initiates not only in the world that must support life but in living tissues is for the most part irreversible. In this now universal contamination of the environment, chemicals . . . [are] changing the very nature of the world—the very nature of its life.

IDENTIFY CAUSE AND EFFECT According to Carson, why has nature begun to noticeably change in recent times?

ASSESSMENT

1. **Identify Cause and Effect** According to Carson, how are chemicals affecting life on Earth?
2. **Draw Inferences** Why do you think Carson chose to write this book? What changes do you think she hoped to instigate?
3. **Analyze Style and Rhetoric** How would you describe Carson's writing style in this passage, and how do you think this style advances her argument?
4. **Make Connections** Rachel Carson warned against chemical contamination of the Earth. What other threats to the environment have emerged since the publication of *Silent Spring*?

GO ONLINE to access primary sources.

18.5

President Richard Nixon meets with Chairman Mao Zedong in Beijing in 1972. Summarize How did Nixon's meeting with Mao Zedong reflect a shift in the foreign policy of the United States?

BOUNCE to Activate Flipped Video

Objectives

Describe Richard Nixon's leadership in foreign policy.

Define Nixon's foreign policy toward China and the Soviet Union.

Describe Richard Nixon's attitude toward "big" government.

Analyze Nixon's southern strategy.

Describe the effects of the Watergate political scandal.

Key Terms

Henry Kissinger
realpolitik
Zhou Enlai
Strategic Arms Limitation Treaty (SALT I)
détente
silent majority
stagflation
Organization of Petroleum Exporting Countries (OPEC)
southern strategy
affirmative action
Watergate
Twenty-fifth Amendment
executive privilege

The Two Sides of the Nixon Presidency

In the 1970s, President Nixon introduced many environmental reforms. Along with his leadership on environmental issues, Nixon took the nation in a new direction in foreign affairs. As a presidential candidate, Nixon had promised to end U.S. military involvement in the Vietnam War. Recognizing the potency of Soviet power and the increasing unwillingness of many Americans to pay the costs of containing communism everywhere, Nixon developed a new approach to the Cold War. His bold program redefined America's relations with the two titans of global communism, China and the Soviet Union.

Nixon's New Approach to Foreign Policy

Nixon's Cold War Foreign Policy During his years in office, Richard Nixon fundamentally reshaped the way the United States approached the world. Before Nixon took office, most American leaders shared a common Cold War ideology.

They stressed that a basic conflict existed between democratic, capitalist countries and totalitarian, communist ones. They divided the world into "us" and "them," and they established policies based on an assumption commonly held that "the enemy of my enemy is my friend." Therefore, a country opposed to communism was, by this definition, a friend of the United States. In a number of ways, Nixon and **Henry Kissinger**, his leading advisor on national security and international affairs, altered this Cold War policy approach.

GO ONLINE to access your digital course

At first glance, Richard Nixon's partnership with Henry Kissinger seemed improbable. Nixon was a conservative California Republican, suspicious of the more liberal East Coast Republicans and exhausted with the political and strategic theories of Ivy League intellectuals. Kissinger was a Harvard-educated Jewish émigré from Germany and a prominent figure in East Coast intellectual circles. In several prior presidential campaigns, Kissinger had actually worked against Nixon. However, both men were outsiders, equipped with an outsider's readiness to question accepted orthodoxy.

>> As head of the National Security Council (1969–1975) and as secretary of state (1973–1977), Henry Kissinger had a massive influence on American foreign policy.

BOUNCE to Activate Map

Kissinger and Realpolitik In foreign affairs, Nixon and Kissinger embraced the idea of **realpolitik**, a German word meaning "real politics." According to realpolitik, political goals should be defined by concrete national interests instead of abstract ideologies. The two statesmen argued that if Americans would put aside their Cold War biases and look at the world with fresh eyes, U.S. global interests could be surveyed not in black and white but in shades of gray. For example, China and the Soviet Union—America's ideological enemies—had the potential to become excellent trading partners. At the same time, West Germany and Japan—America's ideological friends—were fast developing into economic rivals.

Nixon and Kissinger also questioned some lingering Cold War assumptions. For instance, they concluded that there was no united worldwide communist movement, as Lyndon Johnson and other Presidents had believed. There were important differences between the unique ideologies of the Soviet Union and China and other communist countries, such as Yugoslavia, North Korea, and North Vietnam, which often behaved quite independently. As President, Nixon insisted on a flexible, pragmatic foreign policy that avoided ideological absolutes.

EXPLAIN How did Nixon and Kissinger reshape America's approach to foreign affairs?

>> In 1969, a parade in Beijing's Tiananmen Square celebrated the 20th anniversary of the founding of the People's Republic of China.

Opening Relations With China

From his first days in office, Nixon seemed determined to leave his mark on the nation's international affairs. Lyndon Johnson focused primarily on domestic affairs—the nuts and bolts of legislation and political deal-making. Nixon was more a man of the world, fascinated by global politics and shifting alliances. Johnson believed his Great Society would solidify his reputation as a great President. In stark contrast, Nixon thought his reorientation of American foreign policy would cement his legacy in the annals of U.S. history.

Reaching Out to China "You're not going to believe this," a Nixon aide told a journalist in 1969, "but Nixon wants to recognize China." It was an odd, almost unbelievable, statement. At the time, the communist People's Republic of China was the most populous country in the world, but it was not officially recognized by the United States. Nor had it been admitted to the United Nations. The China that the United States recognized as the official representative body of the Chinese people was the Nationalist Chinese government exiled on the island of Taiwan. Nixon built his impressive career as a hard-line "Cold Warrior," a vigilant opponent of communism. He was the last politician Americans could imagine to extend the olive branch of recognition—and thus peace—to the communists.

Ever the political realist, however, Nixon knew that the People's Republic of China could not be ignored forever. He recognized that establishing diplomatic relations with the Chinese communists would benefit the United States. From an economic standpoint, improved relations would bring significant trade agreements, especially benefiting California and the Pacific Coast. Politically, U.S. normalization would drive a wedge between China and the Soviet Union, who had strayed from their traditional alliance and become rivals for territory and diplomatic influence. Finally, if the United States forged stronger relations with the Chinese, they might pressure North Vietnam to accept a negotiated peace to end the conflict still raging at the time.

Normalizing U.S.-China Relations With so much to gain and so little to lose, Nixon quietly pushed ahead with his plans. In public, the Chinese made symbolic overtures toward a meeting. In April 1971, China invited an American table-tennis team to play against its athletes. This small action demonstrated China's willingness to talk. Henry Kissinger worked behind the scenes, talking with Chinese leaders and ironing out sensitive issues with Premier **Zhou Enlai**. Then, in July 1971, Nixon announced that he would make an official state visit to China.

In February 1972, the President made the trip and toured the Great Wall, the Imperial Palace, and other historic sites. Nixon sat down for lengthy talks with Zhou Enlai and Communist Party Chairman Mao Zedong. He even learned enough Chinese to make a toast in the language of his host country. The visit was a great success and an important step toward normalizing diplomatic relations with China.

The following year, American tourists started visiting and American companies set up a thriving trade with China. Nixon's China trip was the high point of his presidency. It bridged, as Zhou Enlai said, "the vastest ocean in the world, twenty-five years of no communication." In 1979, the United States and China established full diplomatic relations.

☑ **LIST** Why did Nixon reach out to China?

Establishing a Relationship with China

Pros	Cons
• Created a stronger front against the Soviet threat • Strengthened economic ties between both countries • Lifted the 22-year ban on travel to China • Formed stronger bond between East and West and greater cultural exchange	• Upset anti-communist American allies • Increased tensions temporarily between the United States and the Soviet Union • Eventually created a rift between the United States and China over the political status of Taiwan

>> **Analyze Charts** Based on the information in the chart, why was Nixon's policy toward China likely to be supported by American businesses?

Key Points of the SALT I Treaty, 1972

OFFENSIVE WEAPONS	DEFENSIVE WEAPONS
• Froze the number of intercontinental ballistic missiles (ICBMs) • Limited nuclear warheads to 5,700 each • Limited nuclear submarines to 42 each	• Prevented further development of antiballistic missiles (ABMs) • Limited ABMs to 200 each • Limited the ABM deployment area to 1 each • Limited the sites protected by ABMs to 2 each

>> **Analyze Charts** Based on the information in the chart, what was the purpose of the SALT I treaty?

Nixon's Policy of Détente

Nixon's trip to the People's Republic of China prompted an immediate reaction from the Soviet Union, which had strained relations with both countries. Soviet leader Leonid Brezhnev feared that improved U.S.-Chinese relations would isolate Russia. Therefore, he invited Nixon to visit Moscow. Nixon made the trip in May 1972. Afterward, the President reported to Congress that he and Brezhnev had reached agreements in a wide variety of areas:

> Recognizing the responsibility of the advanced industrial nations to set an example in combating mankind's common enemies, the United States and the Soviet Union have agreed to cooperate in efforts to reduce pollution and enhance environmental quality. We have agreed to work together in the . . . conquest of cancer and heart disease.
>
> —Richard Nixon, speech to Congress, June 1, 1972

Nixon also announced plans to conduct a joint U.S.-Soviet space mission. However, by far the high point of the summit was the signing of the first **Strategic Arms Limitation Treaty**. Otherwise known as SALT I, the treaty froze the deployment of intercontinental ballistic missiles (ICBMs) and placed limits on antiballistic missiles (ABMs), but it did not alter the stockpiling of the more dangerous multiple independent reentry vehicles (MIRVs). SALT I did not end the arms race between the United States and the Soviet Union. But it was a giant step in the right direction.

The importance of SALT I stemmed first and foremost from U.S. and Soviet efforts to reduce tensions between them. A policy aimed at easing Cold War tensions, **détente**, had replaced previous diplomatic efforts based on suspicion and distrust. With his visits to China and the Soviet Union coming within six months of each other, Richard Nixon dramatically altered America's global strategy. He relaxed the nation's inflexible stance toward communism and applied a more pragmatic approach to foreign policy. In the short term, the new relationships he forged helped the United States to end the Vietnam War. In the long term, Nixon's foreign-policy breakthroughs moved the world a step closer to the end of the Cold War.

☑ **EXPLAIN** How did SALT I support Nixon's new policy for dealing with the Soviet Union?

Nixon's Domestic Policy

Having eased tensions with the nation's two great Cold War adversaries, Richard Nixon stood at the summit of his long government career when he was reelected President in a landslide in November 1972. Yet, less than two years later, Nixon left office in disgrace—the first time a President of the United States had resigned. The Watergate scandal gripped the nation and shaped the values and attitudes toward government that many Americans hold today.

Nixon's Long Political Career Richard Nixon's political career had more ups and downs than a roller coaster ride. Brought up in hard times, he worked his way through college and law school. After service in the navy during World War II, Nixon was elected to the House of Representatives in 1946 and then to the Senate in 1950. As Dwight Eisenhower's running mate in 1952, he became Vice President with Eisenhower's victory. Nixon was not yet 40 years old.

>> A 1972 re-election campaign poster of President Nixon suggests that the country urgently needs his leadership.

>> Richard Nixon displays his signature victory signal to supporters during a 1968 rally. After he took office, he proposed to establish "new federalism," that would restructure American government.

Then came the defeats. In 1960, Nixon narrowly lost to John F. Kennedy in the race for the White House. Two years later, Nixon's career hit bottom when he lost an election to become governor of California. In 1968, however, Nixon made a dramatic comeback. Calling himself "the new Nixon," he narrowly defeated Democrat Hubert Humphrey to win the presidency.

Nixon's "New Federalism" During the campaign for President, Nixon cast himself as the spokesperson for those he called Middle Americans, or the **silent majority**. As Nixon put it at the 1968 Republican convention, he sought to speak for the "non-shouters, the non-demonstrators," the men and women who "work in America's factories . . . run America's businesses . . . serve in the Government . . . provide most of the soldiers . . . [and] give life to the American dream."

Winning the support of Middle America proved a tricky task. Nixon believed that Americans had tired of the "big" government of Lyndon Johnson's Great Society. However, he also believed that the American people still wanted the government to address various social ills, ranging from crime to pollution.

Nixon's solution was to call for the establishment of a "new federalism." As he explained in his 1971 State of the Union address, the nation needed "to reverse the flow of power and resources from the States and communities to Washington and start power and resources flowing back from Washington to the States and communities." Nixon proposed revenue sharing with the states. Under revenue sharing, the federal government gave the states the money to fund social programs. The states then controlled the operations of these programs.

Increasing the Size and Role of Government However, while returning power and money to the states, Nixon also sponsored many programs that increased the size and role of the federal government. During his presidency, a number of powerful new federal agencies and laws came into existence. The Occupational Safety and Health Administration (OSHA) regulates workplaces to make them safer for workers. The DEA, or Drug Enforcement Administration, administers the federal war against illegal drugs. The Environmental Protection Agency (EPA) enforces federal environmental standards. The Clean Air Act, signed into law in 1970, gives the EPA the power to set air quality standards.

Nixon's welfare policies also reflected his complicated domestic strategy. To decrease the power of the federal government, Nixon began

Federal Agencies Established Under Nixon

AGENCY	PURPOSE
Minority Business Development Agency (1969)	The MBDA fosters minority business enterprise. In 2012, the MBDA helped create and maintain 16,730 jobs.
Environmental Protection Agency (1970)	The EPA establishes federal standards to protect the environment. Today, the EPA continues working toward reducing water and air pollution and promoting human health. In 2009, the EPA made the first official finding regarding greenhouse gases and their detrimental effects on human health and the environment.
Occupational Safety and Health Administration (1971)	OSHA's goal is to protect citizens from death, illness, and injury sustained on the job. Between 1970 and 2013, employment in the United States has doubled; meanwhile, workplace fatalities have fallen more than 65 percent and on-the-job injuries and illnesses have been reduced by 67 percent.
Drug Enforcement Administration (1973)	The DEA provides a unified front against the global war on drugs. At its inception, the DEA had a budget of $75 million with 1,470 special agents. Today, these figures have risen to $2.02 billion and 5,000 special agents.

>> **Analyze Charts** Based on the information in the table, how did the creation of OSHA affect American workers?

to dismantle the Office of Economic Opportunity, the cornerstone of Lyndon Johnson's "war on poverty." Yet, Nixon also proposed creating a Family Assistance Plan (FAP), which called for providing a guaranteed or minimum income to every American family. Although the FAP did not become law, federal spending on other social programs, such as Social Security, Medicare, and public housing, grew steadily.

A 1970 reform added yearly cost-of-living increases to the checks of Social Security recipients. In 1972, Nixon signed legislation that increased the Social Security benefits of widows and widowers of retirees. He also signed the largest expansion of Medicare in the program's history. The legislation extended Medicare coverage to nearly 2 million Americans under age 65 who were receiving Social Security disability payments. The costs of these programs continues to rise, prompting many to voice their concerns about the long-term solvency of Social Security and Medicare.

The Struggling Economy As his presidency progressed, Nixon grappled with an increasingly troublesome economy. After decades of strong growth and low inflation, the U.S. economy experienced both recession and inflation at the same time. These symptoms began during the Johnson administration, but they grew stronger during the Nixon years, thanks partly to Vietnam War defense spending under both administrations. The combination of recession and inflation baffled economists and led them to coin a new term, **stagflation**, to describe the dual conditions of a stagnating economy and inflationary pressures.

Stagflation had several causes. Expanding federal budget deficits caused by spending for the Vietnam War produced inflation. Another cause was rising foreign competition, which cost thousands of Americans their jobs. Heavy industries such as steel and auto production, which had enjoyed a dominant position since World War II, proved especially vulnerable to foreign competition. Yet the factor that caused most Americans pain was the rapid increase in the price of oil.

In 1973, the **Organization of Petroleum Exporting Countries (OPEC)**, a multinational organization that sells oil to other nations and cooperates to regulate the price and supply of oil, raised oil prices by 70 percent. Then, in October, in response to the United States' support of Israel during the 1973 Arab war against Israel, OPEC's Arab members, who had formed OAPEC (Organization of Arab Petroleum Exporting Countries), placed an embargo on Israel's allies, including the United States. Dependent on imports for nearly one third of their energy, Americans soon felt the sting of this embargo as oil prices skyrocketed 400 percent in a single year. The embargo lasted until the spring of 1974 and resulted in gas lines at the pumps that stretched for blocks. With the end of the embargo, gas prices remained high.

Nixon fought stagflation in a variety of ways. In August 1971, he ended the Bretton Woods system of monetary management, in which other countries' currencies were pegged to the U.S. dollar, which in turn was pegged to a set amount of gold. Because this system was increasingly difficult to maintain and was unbalancing the U.S. economy, Nixon ended the convertibility between dollars and gold, meaning that dollars were no longer tied to gold prices. To fight stagflation, Nixon also placed a 90-day freeze on all wages and prices. The controls worked for a short time, causing a spurt of economic growth. However, price controls do not work well in a free economy, and the economy went into a tailspin in the mid-1970s.

☑ **IDENTIFY** What was the goal of President Nixon's "new federalism"?

Nixon's "Southern Strategy"

Having narrowly won the presidency in 1968, Richard Nixon set out to expand his base of support. He targeted blue-collar workers and southern whites, both of whom had traditionally voted for Democrats. Even before the election, he nominated Spiro Agnew, a relatively unknown Governor from Maryland, to serve as his running mate, in order to attract southern voters. By winning the support of southern whites, Nixon hoped to make the Republican Party a powerful force in the South. Commentators called this Nixon's **southern strategy**.

As part of his southern strategy, Nixon tried to place a number of conservative southerners as judges in federal courts. Most prominently, he nominated Clement Haynsworth and G. Harrold Carswell to serve on the U.S. Supreme Court. Both men failed to win Senate confirmation, in part because both had supported segregation in the past.

The School Busing Controversy Criticizing court-ordered busing of children to schools outside their neighborhood was another way Nixon reached out to southern whites and urban blue-collar workers. For years, many school districts in both the South and the North had resisted desegregation. In 1971, federal courts ordered school districts to bus students to achieve greater racial balance. Recognizing the unpopularity of busing, Nixon made a nationally televised address in which he called for a moratorium, or freeze, on court-ordered busing. By speaking forcefully, Nixon won the support of many busing opponents.

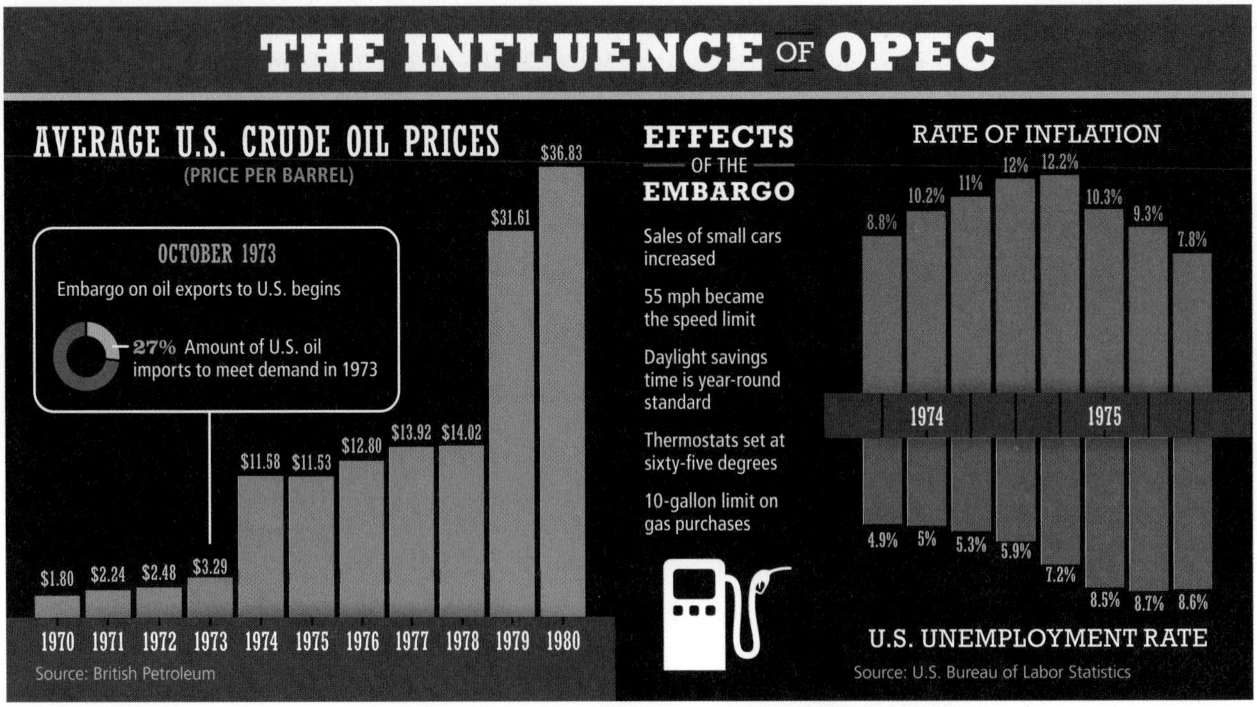

>> **Analyze Graphs** How did the 1973 oil embargo affect the price of gasoline in the United States?

Presidential Election of 1972

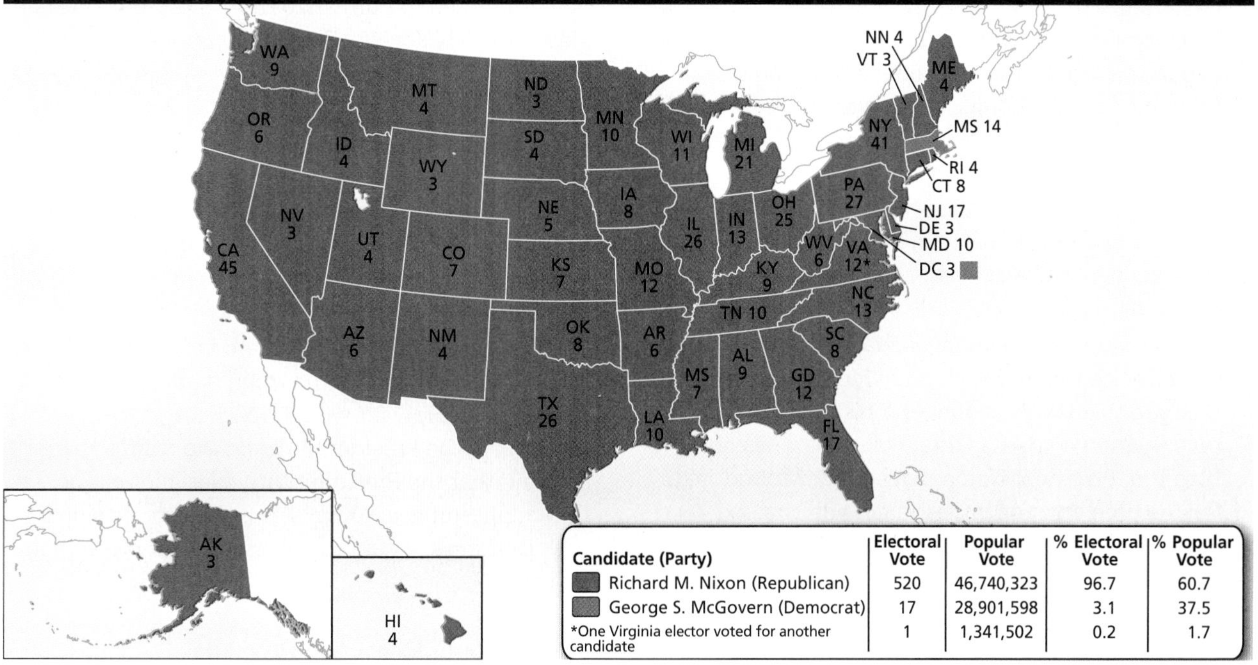

Candidate (Party)	Electoral Vote	Popular Vote	% Electoral Vote	% Popular Vote
Richard M. Nixon (Republican)	520	46,740,323	96.7	60.7
George S. McGovern (Democrat)	17	28,901,598	3.1	37.5
*One Virginia elector voted for another candidate	1	1,341,502	0.2	1.7

>> In 1972, a majority of voters in the American South were Democrats. **Analyze Maps** Based on the information in the map, what was significant about the presidential election of 1972?

New Civil Rights Initiatives Yet, as with much else that he did, Nixon's stance on civil rights was mixed. In 1969, the Nixon administration initiated the Philadelphia Plan, a program that required labor unions and federal contractors to submit goals and timetables for the hiring of minorities. It was a type of **affirmative action**, a policy that gives special consideration to women and minorities in the fields of education and employment, in order to make up for past discrimination.

Nixon's Assistant Secretary of Labor, Arthur Fletcher, who designed the Philadelphia Plan, argued:

> The Federal Government has an obligation to see that every citizen has an equal chance at the most basic freedom of all—the right to succeed. . . . Segregation didn't occur naturally—it was imposed. . . . The gap . . . between black and white . . . was growing wider and wider. . . . Visible, measurable goals to correct [these] imbalances are essential.
>
> —Arthur Fletcher, Assistant Secretary of Labor, speech on affirmative action, 1969

Nixon's Strategy Succeeds By the 1972 election, Nixon enjoyed high approval ratings. Some of this popularity was based on his trips to the Soviet Union and China. Some was based on his domestic policies.

Nixon ran a masterful political campaign in 1972, positioning himself as a moderate. He portrayed his opponents—George McGovern, an antiwar senator from South Dakota, and Alabama governor George Wallace—as extremists. (Wallace's campaign was cut short when he was shot and left paralyzed by a would-be assassin.)

Nixon and his Vice President, Spiro Agnew, successfully cast themselves as spokespersons for the silent majority. On election day, Nixon won almost 61 percent of the popular vote and nearly all of the electoral votes. He became the first Republican presidential candidate to sweep the entire South.

EXPLAIN In what ways did Nixon appear to send mixed messages about civil rights?

The Watergate Scandal Brings Nixon Down

As a triumphant Richard Nixon stood before the cameras on election night 1972, he had no idea that the seeds of his downfall had already begun to sprout. The botched burglary of Democratic Party headquarters at the Watergate complex in June 1972 received little attention at first. But as investigators began to unravel the connections between the burglars and the White House, **Watergate**, as the scandal become known, came to dominate the national news.

The Watergate burglars were tried in 1973. After the trial, one of them, James McCord, charged that administration officials had been involved in the break-in.

This led to a Senate investigation and to televised hearings, where numerous witnesses charged that the President and his top aides had taken part in a coverup. From the first news of the break-in, President Nixon denied any wrongdoing. Yet, as time went on, investigators discovered important links between the burglars and top Nixon administration officials.

The Watergate Break-in Goes Public Two young *Washington Post* journalists, Bob Woodward and Carl Bernstein, played a crucial role in lifting the veil of secrecy from the Watergate scandal. The two reporters followed tips provided by a secret government informant known as "Deep Throat," who was later revealed to be a top official of the FBI.

>> Watergate Committee Chair Senator Sam Ervin sits with other members of the committee as they listen to testimony at the 1973 Watergate hearings.

BOUNCE to Activate Chart

Woodward and Bernstein reported that the men who had attempted to burglarize the Watergate hotel had close ties to Nixon's reelection committee.

Nixon repeatedly proclaimed his innocence. For example, in November 1973, long after evidence had implicated his top aides and forced them to resign, Nixon declared, "I am not a crook." Yet the polls indicated that the public disagreed. One poll, taken the next month, showed that fewer than one in five Americans believed that he was being honest about the Watergate affair.

The Watergate scandal created a crisis in the relationship among the three branches of government. How far would Congress go to investigate the President? Would the courts demand that the President turn over information that might implicate him? And if the courts sided with Congress, would the President comply with its decisions?

The Limits of Executive Privilege The Watergate scandal came to a climax with a dizzying array of developments. In the fall of 1973, Vice President Spiro Agnew resigned in the face of an unrelated corruption scandal. According to the procedures established by the **Twenty-fifth Amendment**, which deals with presidential succession, Nixon nominated Gerald Ford to become his new Vice President.

Nixon's troubles multiplied when, in the summer of 1973, it was revealed that he had been secretly taping Oval Office conversations for many years. Many commentators speculated that these tapes would show that the President had played a leading role in trying to cover up the break-in.

Nixon refused to turn over these tapes to the special prosecutor investigating the scandal. The President justified withholding the tapes by claiming **executive privilege**. Executive privilege is the principle that the President has the right to keep certain information confidential. It took almost a year for the courts to sort out the matter. On July 24, 1974, in the case of *United States* v. *Nixon,* the Supreme Court disagreed that the tapes fell under the principle of executive privilege and ordered Nixon to turn them over. Chief Justice Warren Burger made it clear that the Court rejected Nixon's claim of executive privilege in this instance:

> The expectation of a President to the confidentiality of his conversations and correspondence . . . has all the values to which we

accord deference for the privacy of all citizens. . . . But this presumptive privilege must be considered in light of our historic commitment to the rule of law [the principle that all citizens are bound by the same laws]. . . .

The very integrity of the judicial system and public confidence in the system depend on full disclosure of all the facts, within the framework of the rules of evidence.

—U.S. Supreme Court, *United States* v. *Nixon*, 1974

>> On August 9, 1974, Richard Nixon waved farewell as he prepared to leave the grounds of the White House, after resigning as President of the United States.

Nixon Resigns When investigators listened to the tapes, they found that crucial parts of the conversations were missing. Nixon claimed his secretary had mistakenly erased them. Still, the tapes provided enough evidence of Nixon's involvement in the coverup to lead the Judiciary Committee of the House of Representatives to vote to impeach the President. The committee charged Nixon with obstructing justice in the coverup of the Watergate break-in, misuse of power, and refusing to comply with House subpoenas. A number of Republican committee members joined the Democrats in voting for impeachment.

Recognizing that the full House of Representatives would vote in favor of impeachment and that many Republicans would vote to convict him in a trial in the Senate, Nixon decided to resign. In a speech to the American public on August 8, 1974, Nixon informed the nation that he would step down the following day in the hope that he "will have hastened the start of that process of healing which is so desperately needed in America." The long ordeal of Watergate had finally come to an end. With it, Nixon became the first and only President to resign the presidency.

Historians disagree about whether Nixon knew beforehand of the decision to burglarize Democratic Party headquarters. Few doubt, however that he took part in the coverup. Testimony by his top aides, the Watergate tapes, and evidence gathered in the prosecution of the burglars all show that Nixon sought to quash the investigation.

Moreover, investigations revealed that Nixon had committed other abuses of presidential power. His reelection team had engaged in dirty tricks to secure his election. He had developed an "enemies list" and used federal agencies to go after his enemies. The President had ordered the FBI to place wiretaps on the telephones of those government employees and reporters he suspected of leaking information unfavorable to the administration.

Watergate's Lasting Impact In pursuit of personal power, Richard Nixon damaged the reputation of the presidency and shook the public's confidence in government. One conservative commentator, formerly a supporter of Nixon, echoed the disillusionment of many Americans:

The lies, the lies, the lies! . . . What a pity, what a pity! Here was a President who got us out of Vietnam, ended the draft . . . and by his bold overtures to Red China opened new avenues toward world peace. Now the good vanishes in the wreckage of the bad. The swearing-in of Gerald Ford can't come one hour too soon.

—James J. Kilpatrick, *National Review*, August 30, 1974

Polls revealed that from the late 1950s to the mid-1970s, the percentage of Americans who believed in the truth of government statements plummeted from 80 percent to 33 percent.

In the wake of Watergate, Congress enacted numerous reforms to try to restore the public's confidence in government and to prevent abuses of power in the future. It established a procedure for naming an independent counsel to investigate charges against the White House. The Federal Election Campaign Act of 1974 sought to limit the amount of money that individuals could give candidates, in order to prevent the corruption of the political process.

Yet, the Watergate affair also demonstrated that the nation could weather such a crisis. It showed the strength of the system of checks and balances. Both Congress and the Supreme Court had successfully checked the power of the President. According to *Time* magazine, Nixon's resignation represented an "extraordinary triumph of the American system." Watergate demonstrated that no person, not even a President, is above the law. As Gerald Ford said when he became President: "Our great republic is a government of laws and not of men."

DESCRIBE What role did Richard Nixon and his top aides play in the Watergate scandal?

ASSESSMENT

1. **Compare and Contrast** the backgrounds and beliefs of Richard Nixon and Henry Kissinger.
2. **Generate Explanations** Explain why President Nixon decided to recognize China.
3. **Identify Cause and Effect** Explain why gas prices skyrocketed during Nixon's presidency.
4. **Describe** President Nixon's position on civil rights.
5. **Quest Connections** Discuss the lasting effects of the Watergate scandal.

18.6

Despite repeated efforts to reach an agreement, President Carter failed to secure the release of American hostages in Iran, who were taken prisoner during the Iranian Revolution.

Ford and Carter Struggle

The Watergate scandal of the early 1970s took place during a decade that witnessed significant social, economic, and cultural changes. These changes contributed to a growing sense among Americans that something had gone wrong, that the nation had gotten off the right track. This sense of disquiet is even now a part of the nation's political dialogue.

BOUNCE to Activate Flipped Video

Objectives

Evaluate the presidency of Gerald Ford.

Evaluate Ford's foreign policies.

Assess the domestic policies of Jimmy Carter.

Discuss changing U.S. foreign policy in the developing world.

Analyze how American society changed in the 1970s.

Key Terms

Gerald Ford
pardon
Helsinki Accords
human rights
SALT II
boat people
Jimmy Carter
Christian fundamentalists
amnesty
Community Reinvestment Act
sanctions
developing world
Camp David Accords
Wisconsin v. Yoder

Ford Governs Through Difficult Times

Gerald Ford had been Nixon's Vice President and became President when Nixon resigned. Although only recently appointed as Vice President following the resignation of Nixon's two-term Vice President, Spiro Agnew, Ford brought a long record of public service to the presidency. A star football player at the University of Michigan, Ford enlisted in the United States Navy and fought in World War II. Following the war, Ford successfully ran for a seat in the U.S. Congress, where he served for 25 years, rising to the position of House Minority Leader in 1965. Democrats as well as Republicans supported Ford's nomination for Vice President because he had a reputation for hard work, integrity, and dependability.

Ford stepped into a delicate situation when he became President after Richard Nixon's resignation. Watergate had scarred the public's faith in government. Furthermore, the nation struggled with the most severe economic problems it had faced since the Depression. Ford wrestled with these problems but not very successfully. He left office with the economy still suffering and the public's distrust of government still high.

GO ONLINE to access your digital course

>> President Ford pardoned Richard Nixon on September 8, 1974. **Identify Cause and Effect** Why did this act reduce public support for Ford as President?

>> President Ford's "WIN," or Whip Inflation Now, strategy called for a combination of personal saving and discipline coupled with government action to stabilize the economy.

Pardoning Nixon Ford moved quickly to try to restore confidence in government. He selected Nelson Rockefeller, a former governor of New York State, to serve as his Vice President. He also promised to continue the foreign policy approaches of the Nixon administration.

Whatever support he gained from these steps was lost when Ford announced that he had **pardoned**, or officially forgiven, Richard Nixon for any crimes he may have committed as President. Though the pardon was meant to heal the nation's wounds, in some ways it achieved just the opposite. Ford's critics accused him of having made a secret deal, promising Nixon the pardon in exchange for the vice presidential nomination. Though Ford strongly denied this, his popularity declined dramatically.

The congressional election results of 1974 indicated the public's disapproval of the pardon and the impact of Watergate in general. The Republicans lost 48 seats in the House of Representatives, including Ford's longtime district in Grand Rapids, Michigan.

Stagflation Continues President Ford might have overcome this backlash if not for the troubled economy. The stagflation that plagued the nation during Nixon's presidency continued under Ford. Inflation hit double digits in 1974 and early 1975. To fight skyrocketing prices, Ford promoted a mostly voluntary plan known as WIN, or Whip Inflation Now. Unfortunately, WIN was a clear failure. Instead of improving, the economy took a turn for the worse. Factories closed down, consumer demand for goods dropped sharply, and the rate of unemployment rose steadily. Ford's popularity plummeted.

☑ **EXPLAIN** How did President Ford's WIN program try to address inflation?

Ford Continues Nixon's Foreign Policies

The ordeal of the Vietnam War led many to question the direction of American foreign policy. They asked: Why was the United States so concerned with fighting communism that it ended up supporting oppressive anticommunist governments? Should the United States continue to pursue détente with the Soviets? Or should it instead demand that the Soviet government grant its people more freedoms? Although the Soviet Union no longer exists, similar debates over the relationship between foreign policy and human rights continue to be heard today.

Relations with the Soviet Union remained central to U.S. foreign policy during the Ford administration. Upon assuming the presidency, Gerald Ford made clear that his foreign policy would differ little from that of Richard Nixon's. He retained Henry Kissinger as his Secretary of State and continued to pursue détente with the Soviet Union and China.

Continuing to Pursue Détente Ford and Soviet leader Leonid Brezhnev met in late 1974 and again the next year, when the two leaders endorsed the **Helsinki Accords**. This document put the nations of Europe on record in favor of **human rights**, or the basic rights that every human being is entitled to have. Some thought that President Ford would try to compel the Soviet Union to allow more political freedoms, but Ford decided to put arms control ahead of human rights. At his direction, the United States continued disarmament talks with the Soviets. These talks eventually led to an agreement known as **SALT II**, in which the two nations pledged to limit nuclear arms production. However, the U.S. Senate never ratified the treaty.

>> The Soviet Union continued to limit its people's freedoms. Alexander Solzhenitsyn was expelled from the Soviet Union in 1974 for writing novels that exposed the harsh conditions in Soviet labor camps.

Trouble in Southeast Asia Under Ford, the United States sought to forget turmoil of the Vietnam War. When the communist Khmer Rouge government of Cambodia began a genocidal slaughter of civilians, killing about 1.5 million people between 1975 and 1979, the United States did not intervene.

The main exception to this policy of noninvolvement came in May 1975, when the Khmer Rouge seized an American merchant ship, the *Mayaguez*, which had been steaming just outside Cambodian waters. Ford responded by sending in some United States Marines, who freed the ship.

South Vietnam fell to North Vietnam during Ford's presidency. As the communists took over, hundreds of thousands of Vietnamese, many of whom had worked with the United States, tried to escape. Many refugees took to the seas in rickety, unseaworthy boats. These **boat people** represented the largest mass migration of humanity by sea in modern history. Over a 20-year period, more than one million men, women, and children braved storms, pirates, and starvation in search of refuge abroad. Their immediate destinations were in other nations of Southeast Asia, but many eventually found refuge in the United States and Canada.

>> Hundreds of Vietnamese refugees were stranded for months on the freighter Tung An, waiting for a country to give them permission to disembark.

☑ **DESCRIBE** How did Ford deal with foreign policy challenges during his presidency?

A New President Faces Challenges

Prior to the mid-1970s, few Americans outside Georgia had ever heard of **Jimmy Carter**, a one-time governor of that state. But on election day 1976, Americans elected Carter President of the United States. He won a slim popular majority, receiving slightly more than 50 percent of the vote to Ford's 48 percent. In the electoral college, Carter won 297 votes compared to 240 for Ford.

Carter's rise was the result of several factors. Most important was the turmoil of the 1960s and Watergate, which created a backlash against professional politicians. Carter seized this opportunity by casting himself as a fresh face, a "Washington outsider" with no ties to Washington, D.C. A born-again Christian who taught Sunday school, Carter won the support of many **Christian fundamentalists**, people who believe in a strict, literal interpretation of the Bible as the foundation of the Christian faith. This group became increasingly involved in politics in the 1970s.

The Cost of Inexperience From the beginning of his presidency, Jimmy Carter sought to portray himself as a "citizens' President." He became the first President since William Henry Harrison to walk all the way from the Capitol to the White House during the inaugural parade. He held town meetings, wore casual clothes, and carried his own suitcase.

However, Carter's inexperience, which helped him get elected, hurt him during the early days of his presidency. As an outsider, he did not have close ties with the Democratic leadership in Congress. He also surrounded himself with aides whose experience in Washington was limited. Carter submitted numerous bills to Congress, but few of them passed without major changes by his own party.

Just one day after his inauguration, Carter fulfilled one of his campaign pledges by granting **amnesty**, or political pardons, to Americans who had evaded the draft during the Vietnam War. Carter hoped this act would help the nation move beyond the divisions caused by that war.

Yet the war remained an emotional issue, and many criticized the President for forgiving those who had refused to fight. Republican senator Barry Goldwater called the amnesty "the most disgraceful thing that a President has ever done."

>> Both during and after his presidency, Jimmy Carter, shown here with his mother, portrayed himself as an average American and political "outsider" who could help "clean up" Washington.

Economic Problems Sap Confidence Like Ford, Carter contended with the energy crisis and severe inflation. Inflation ate away at people's savings, raised prices, and made American goods more costly abroad. The U.S. automobile industry, long a symbol of the nation's economic power, became a symbol of its ills. Japanese car companies vastly expanded their sales in the United States by selling better-built and more fuel-efficient cars at reasonable prices. The situation grew so bad that Chrysler, one of the three major American automobile companies, needed a federal loan to survive.

At the center of the nation's economic ills lay the ongoing energy crisis. In 1973, a gallon of gas cost about 40 cents. By the end of the decade, it cost close to $1.20. To make matters worse, the winter of 1976– 1977 was an especially bitter one in parts of the United States, increasing the need for heating oil. Fuel shortages caused factory closings and business losses. The 1979 Oil Crisis caused another spike in gas prices and inflation.

Carter responded to the oil crisis by calling on Americans to conserve and by asking Congress to raise taxes on crude oil, which he hoped would encourage conservation. However, the bill that finally passed in the Senate had few of the President's ideas in it. Critics saw this as one more example of Carter's poor leadership skills.

Carter's Sanctions Against the Soviet Union, 1979–1980

RESPONSES TO THE SOVIET INVASION OF AFGHANISTAN
Asked the U.S. Senate not to ratify SALT II
Imposed a grain embargo on the Soviet Union in 1980
Called for a boycott of the 1980 Summer Olympics in Moscow
Revoked export licenses for high-technology items
Recalled the U.S. ambassador to the Soviet Union
Increased aid to Afghan resistance fighters

>> **Analyze Charts** What can you infer about the United States' relationship with the Soviet Union during the Carter administration?

To fight inflation, Carter nominated Paul Volcker to head the Federal Reserve Board. Under Volcker's lead, the Federal Reserve began raising interest rates. In the long term, this policy helped to end the inflation that had plagued the nation for so long.

The **Community Reinvestment Act** which Congress passed and Carter signed into law in 1977, also helped address the nation's economic woes. In order to create economic opportunity for citizens, this law required banks to make loans in the same neighborhoods where they took deposits. This requirement enabled many low- to moderate-income Americans, especially ethnic minorities, to become homeowners. The law remains in effect today. Whether it has had unintended consequences, possibly contributing to the mortgage crisis that triggered the Great Recession of 2007 to 2011 is an issue hotly debated in the business community.

LGBT Politicians Are Elected The growth of the lesbian, gay, bisexual, and transgender rights movement led to the pioneering role of gay politicians such as Elaine Noble, who was elected to the Massachusetts House of Representatives in 1974, and Harvey Milk, elected in 1977 to the San Francisco Board of Supervisors. Tragically, Harvey Milk was assassinated a year later. His death was deeply mourned by the LGBT community who regarded him as a martyr to the cause of gay rights. In 2009, thirty-one years after his assassination, he was awarded the Presidential Medal of Freedom.

☑ **LIST** What challenges did President Carter face?

Foreign Policy Changes Under Carter

Early in his presidency, Jimmy Carter proclaimed that, American foreign policy would be guided by a concern for human rights. Carter hoped to end acts of political repression such as torture, murder, and imprisonment without trial. This policy helped reaffirm the position of the United States as a nation of freedom and justice. However, it undercut the goal of better relations with the Soviet Union.

Soviet-American Relations Cool At first, Carter continued Nixon's and Ford's policies toward the Soviet Union. He continued efforts at arms control, meeting with Leonid Brezhnev in June 1979 and signing the SALT II treaty.

However, relations between the two superpowers soon took a decidedly frosty turn. The SALT II treaty was bitterly debated in the United States Senate, where its opponents argued that it put the national security of the United States in jeopardy. Then, in December 1979, the Soviet Union invaded Afghanistan to prop up a tottering communist government. Carter responded by withdrawing the SALT II treaty from Senate consideration and by imposing **sanctions**, or penalties, on the Soviets. The sanctions included a U.S. boycott of the 1980 Summer Olympic Games held in Moscow as well as a suspension of grain sales to the Soviet Union.

Attempts to Protect Human Rights Since the end of World War II, American Presidents had tended to see the **developing world**—the less developed nations of Asia, Africa, and Latin America—as another stage for the Cold War. Carter broke with

>> Sandinistas celebrate on the streets of Managua, Nicaragua's capital, after their defeat of the dictator Anastasio Somoza and his troops in July 1979.

>> President Carter helped to ease tensions in the Middle East by inviting Israeli Prime Minister Menachem Begin and Egyptian President Anwar Sadat to Camp David for peace talks in 1978.

that approach and insisted that U.S. relations with foreign countries should be determined by how a country treated its citizens.

Carter's emphasis on human rights led him to alter the U.S. relationship with a number of dictators. In Nicaragua, the Somoza family had ruled the country with an iron grip since the mid-1930s, most of the time with the support of the United States. In 1978, a leftist group known as the Sandinistas began a rebellion against the country's ruler, General Anastasio Somoza. His brutal response to the rebellion helped convince Carter to withdraw U.S. support. Without U.S. aid, General Somoza had to flee Nicaragua, and the Sandinistas came to power.

Other Foreign Policy Initiatives in Latin America

The Carter administration briefly sought to improve relations with communist Cuba, ruled by Fidel Castro since 1959. U.S.-Cuban relations soured in 1980, however, when Castro announced that any Cuban could leave the island from the port of Mariel for the United States. However, Castro insisted that any boats headed to the United States would also have to take criminals from Cuba's prisons.

Because of this requirement, the Mariel boatlift developed a bad reputation in the eyes of many Americans. Fewer than 20 percent of the people transported had spent time in prison, and many of those were political prisoners. Still, Americans were repelled by Castro's lack of concern for the welfare of the emigrants and by the idea that he would send criminals to the United States.

Carter's most controversial foreign policy move involved his decision to return the Panama Canal Zone to Panama. You will recall that in 1903, Panama had given the United States control of a wide strip of land across the middle of the country that later became the site of the Panama Canal. In 1977, Carter negotiated a set of treaties to return the Canal Zone to Panama by 1999. The United States Senate narrowly ratified the treaties in 1978, and all control of the canal was ultimately turned over to Panama.

☑ **IDENTIFY** In what way did President Carter's policies differ from those of Ford?

Success and Setback in the Middle East

Carter's greatest achievement in foreign policy came in the region that also saw his greatest setback. He helped negotiate a historic peace agreement between

Israel and Egypt, but failed to win the release of Americans held hostage by Iranian radicals.

The Camp David Accords Egypt had opposed Israel's existence since Israel's founding in 1948. As recently as 1973, Egypt and Syria had attacked Israel. By 1977, eager to improve relations, Egyptian President Anwar el-Sadat and Israeli Prime Minister Menachem Begin met in Jerusalem to negotiate a peace agreement.

To help continue the negotiations, Carter invited the two leaders to Camp David, the presidential retreat. For nearly two weeks, the three leaders carried on the difficult negotiations that produced what is known as the **Camp David Accords**. These agreements provided the framework for a peace treaty in which Egypt formally recognized the nation of Israel, becoming the first Arab nation to do so. In return, Israel withdrew its troops from the Sinai Peninsula, which it had controlled since the 1967 war. The preamble to the Accords states:

> After four wars during 30 years, despite intensive human efforts, the Middle East, which is the cradle of civilization and the birthplace of three great religions, does not enjoy the blessings of peace. . . . [Israel and Egypt] recognize that for peace to endure, it must involve all those who have been most deeply affected by the conflict. They therefore agree that this framework, as appropriate, is intended by them to constitute a basis for peace not only between Egypt and Israel, but also between Israel and each of its other neighbors. . . .
>
> —Camp David Accords, September 19, 1978

The Iran Hostage Crisis Carter hoped that the Camp David Accords would usher in a new era of cooperation in the Middle East. Yet, events in Iran showed that troubles in the region were far from over. Since the 1950s, the United States had supported the anticommunist rule of the Shah, or emperor, of Iran. In the 1970s, however, opposition to the Shah began to grow within Iran. Anger toward the nation that had long propped up the Shah's repressive regime—the United States—would soon boil over as well.

>> Ayatollah Khomeini is shown here in exile in France in 1978. A leader of the Iranian Revolution, he became the Supreme Ruler of Iran after the Shah was overthrown.

BOUNCE to Activate Timeline

Dying of cancer, the Shah fled Iran in January 1979. Fundamentalist Islamic clerics, led by the Ayatollah Khomeini (i yuh TOH luh koh MAYN ee), took power. Carter allowed the Shah to enter the United States to seek medical treatment. Enraged radical Iranian students invaded the U.S. Embassy and took 66 Americans as hostages. The Khomeini government took control of both the embassy and the hostages to defy the United States.

The hostage crisis consumed Carter's attention during the last year of his presidency. To many Americans, his failure to win the hostages' release was evidence of American weakness. As Peter Bourne put it in his biography of Jimmy Carter, "Because people felt that Carter had not been tough enough in foreign policy . . . some bunch of students could seize American diplomatic officials and hold them prisoner and thumb their nose at the United States."

The hostage crisis began to change the way Americans viewed the world outside their borders. Nuclear war between the two superpowers was no longer the only threat to the United States. Although the Cold War still concerned Americans, the threats posed by conflicts in the Middle East threatened to become the greatest foreign policy challenge of the United States.

DESCRIBE How did the seizure of the U.S. Embassy by Iranian students affect Americans' view of the world?

Unease Over Changing Values

Social and cultural changes that had begun in the 1950s and 1960s continued unabated in the 1970s. As a result, by the end of the decade, the United States was a very different society from the one it had been a generation earlier. These differences gave rise to an ongoing debate about the nation's values.

Migration, Immigration, and Politics After World War II, there had been a demographic shift as Americans moved to the southern and western states, in search of jobs and a better climate. The migration of Americans to the Sunbelt and the continued growth of the suburbs, both of which had begun in the post–World War II years, continued during the 1970s. As northern industries suffered, many blue-collar workers and their families moved from the Rust Belt states of the Northeast and Midwest to the Sunbelt of the South and West.

They sought work in the oil fields of Texas and Oklahoma and in the defense plants of southern California, the Southwest, and the Northwest. These changing demographic patterns changed the face of the United States.

The elections of Richard Nixon and Jimmy Carter demonstrated the growing political power of the Sunbelt. Earlier in the century, Presidents tended to come from the large northern industrial states, such as New York and Ohio. In the latter decades of the twentieth century, Presidents tended to come from the Sunbelt.

The influx of immigrants from Latin America and Asia represented a different kind of demographic change. Even before the 1970s, hundreds of thousands of Cubans, Puerto Ricans, and Mexicans had migrated to the United States in search of work and a better life. This migration, both legal and illegal, especially from Mexico and other Latin American countries, showed continued strength in the 1970s. The growing power of the Latino vote did not escape the notice of politicians. Richard Nixon was the first presidential candidate to seriously court the Spanish-speaking vote.

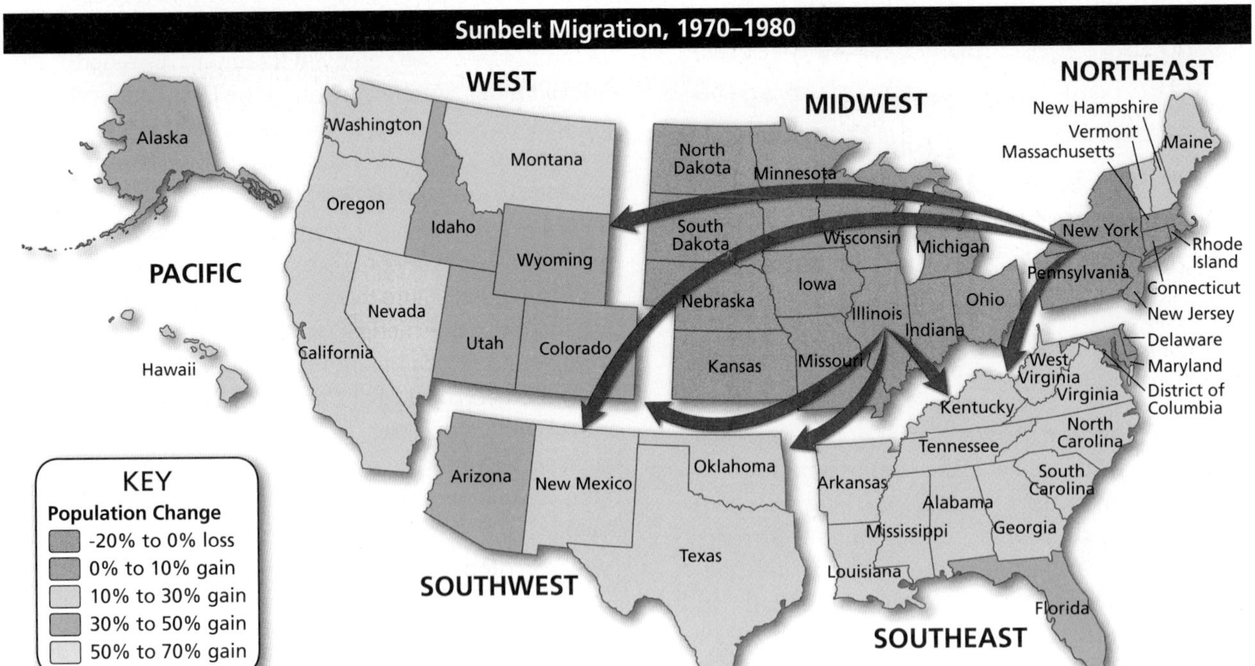

>> **Analyze Maps** Which regions of the United States most likely suffered economically as a result of population loss during the 1970s and 1980s?

Countercultural Styles Spread in the "Me Decade" During the 1960s, radicals had challenged many of society's traditional values. They questioned restrictions on premarital sex and drug use. They sported casual clothing and long hairstyles that many of their parents' generation found improper. Yet the counterculture remained a relatively isolated phenomenon during the 1960s. By the end of the 1970s, in contrast, these behaviors had become more widespread. Nationwide, the divorce rate had more than doubled between 1965 and 1979, and twice as many children were born out of wedlock. To some Americans, the new ways were a sign of troubled times.

Some critics called the 1970s the "me decade" because many Americans appeared to be absorbed with improving themselves. This trend was reflected in the rise of movements like Transcendental Meditation (TM), a practice based in Eastern religious ideas. Those who practiced TM sought to find inner relaxation and vitality by chanting their personal mantras for about half an hour twice a day.

The seventies also witnessed an increasing interest in personal fitness and health. Millions began to jog for exercise and to eat natural, or less processed, foods. In 1970, just over 100 men and women ran in the New York City Marathon. Ten years later, more than 14,000 ran in the race. Body building took off, too, largely due to the influence of Arnold Schwarzenegger. A charismatic personality, Schwarzenegger went on to become one of Hollywood's most popular actors and, later, governor of California.

Conservatives Call for a Return to Traditional Values The 1970s witnessed a resurgence of fundamentalist Christianity, partly as a response to the shift in values. To some commentators, it seemed as if the nation was experiencing another Great Awakening, like the great religious movements of the eighteenth and nineteenth centuries. Although the total number of Americans who attended church on a regular basis did not change much, the number of men and women who belonged to evangelical churches rose rapidly. One in five Americans considered himself or herself a religious fundamentalist by 1980.

Religious conservatives firmly opposed many of the social changes begun in the 1960s that had gone mainstream in the 1970s. They opposed the Supreme Court's rulings that legalized abortion and restricted prayer in school. Religious conservatives saw the latter as an unfair curtailment of religious freedom. In 1972, however, the Court upheld religious freedom

>> Televangelists, such as Reverend Jerry Falwell, were opposed to social changes that began in the 1960s and took root in the 1970s. They felt America was deviating from its moral path.

BOUNCE to Activate Chart

in ***Wisconsin* v. *Yoder*** when it ruled that the state could not compel Amish children to attend school beyond the eighth grade because doing so violated Amish religious principles.

In opposing some Supreme Court rulings and what they believed were the negative effects of social change, evangelical ministers used the media to gain a broader following. Those who preached on television, such as Jerry Falwell, Oral Roberts, and Marion "Pat" Robertson, became known as **televangelists**. These preachers reached millions of television viewers. Falwell's weekly television show, for example, was broadcast to 1.5 million viewers.

In 1979, Falwell formed a prominent Christian conservative organization known as the Moral Majority. He voiced the concerns of many fundamentalists:

> We must reverse the trend America finds herself in today. Young people . . . have been born and reared in a different world than Americans of past worlds. . . . They have learned to disrespect the family as God has

> established it. . . . They have been taught that the Bible is just another book of literature. . . . They have been introduced to the drug culture.
>
> —Reverend Jerry Falwell, *Listen America*, 1980

During the 1970s, religious conservatives began forming alliances with other conservatives. They worked with economic conservatives, who sought to cut taxes and government spending, as well as with supporters of a stronger foreign policy, who favored increasing defense spending. Together, they began forging a new political majority. By 1980, Ronald Reagan, another political outsider, would use this alliance to win election to the White House.

LIST In what ways did the United States change socially and culturally during the 1970s?

ASSESSMENT

1. **Generate Explanations** Explain why President Ford faced significant disapproval from the American public.
2. **Summarize** Discuss President Ford's efforts to pursue détente with the Soviet Union.
3. **Describe** the crises that occurred in Southeast Asia during Ford's presidency, and discuss the role of United States in these events.
4. **Identify Cause and Effect** Discuss some of the factors that influenced a resurgence of Christian fundamentalism during the 1970s.
5. **Quest Connections** Explain how President Carter's support for human rights influenced his foreign policy.

GO ONLINE to access this biography: Alexander Solzhenitsyn

Connections to Today

Artificial barriers prevent many women from workplace advancement.

Take Action About the Glass Ceiling

In the 1960s and '70s, women began speaking out against discriminatory practices that prevented qualified women from advancing into management-level positions. Although some things have changed, today women still face a "glass ceiling" that hinders advancement.

1. **Choose** one of the following glass-ceiling related topics:
    - **The Number of Women in Upper Management:** Research statistics that highlight the number of women in upper management, comparing those figures to the number of men who are running businesses. Investigate to determine if these figures have changed since the 1970s.
    - **Compare Earnings:** Investigate the difference in what women and men make while working the same jobs. Have these numbers changed over time?
    - **Federal Laws:** Research the laws passed in the 1960s and later, that were designed to prevent discrimination against women in the workplace.
2. **Ask Questions** Create a list of questions you have about the topic.
3. **Learn** about your topic, using a variety of sources, such as online sources, primary and/or secondary sources, data, and interviews.
4. **Raise Awareness** Interview older female relatives or neighbors to assess how much the working lives of women have changed since the 1970s. Then create a digital or print poster highlighting your findings. Share your poster with classmates and the broader community.

Topic 18 Quick Study Guide

LESSON SUMMARIES

Use these Lesson Summaries, and the longer versions available online, to review the key ideas for each lesson in this Topic.

Lesson 1: The Counterculture of the 1960s

During the 1960s, the generation born after World War II created a rebellious counterculture that brought about dramatic changes in fashion, music, and sexual behavior.

Lesson 2: The Women's Rights Movement

Inspired by the success of the civil rights movement, the women's rights movement gained strength in the 1960s. Although women won new legal rights, the Equal Rights Amendment was defeated.

Lesson 3: Expanding the Push for Equality

The civil rights movement also inspired other minorities such as Latinos, American Indians, Americans with disabilities, and the LGBT community to fight for their rights. A consumer rights movement prompted Congress to pass laws protecting the public.

Lesson 4: The Environmental Movement

The political activism of the 1960s also helped start the environmental movement. Public outcry over industrial pollution persuaded Congress to create the Environmental Protection Agency. New laws were passed to clean and protect the environment, although many feared that such laws would harm business.

Lesson 5: The Two Sides of the Nixon Presidency

President Nixon refocused American foreign policy toward economic benefits rather than ideology and reestablished a relationship with China. Negotiations were also opened with the Soviets. At home, however, Nixon faced economic problems and a political scandal that forced him to resign as President.

Lesson 6: Ford and Carter Struggle

Economic problems troubled Presidents Ford and Carter. Both Ford and Carter continued arms control negotiations with the Soviet Union, but Carter's foreign policy emphasized human rights. Although Carter succeeded in brokering peace between Egypt and Israel, he faced a crisis when Americans were taken hostage in the U.S. embassy in Iran. Meanwhile, fundamentalist Christians became more politically active.

QUEST! FINDINGS

Analyzing the Leadership Qualities of Nixon, Ford, and Carter Refer to your responses to the Quest Connections to help you discuss these presidents. Use the rubric and other Quest resources to guide your work.

GO ONLINE to access lesson summaries

VISUAL REVIEW

Use these graphics to review some of the key terms, people, and ideas from this Topic.

Values and Interests of the Counterculture

Influence of the Civil Rights Movement

THE CIVIL RIGHTS MOVEMENT

- African Americans push for legal and social equality.
- Groups use different tactics, including protesting, litigation, and working for political and legal change.
- Important legislation is passed, including the Civil Rights Act of 1964.

→

THE CIVIL RIGHTS MOVEMENT INFLUENCES OTHER GROUPS

- Women, Latinos, American Indians, and people with disabilities push for legal and social equality.
- Environmental and consumer groups demand legal changes.
- Women, Latinos, American Indians, and environmentalists use civil rights protest tactics to advance their own causes.

America's Foreign Policy Before and After Vietnam

PRESIDENTS	POLICIES
Truman **Eisenhower** **Kennedy** **Johnson**	Cold War Consensus: Belief that the U.S. faced a unified worldwide communist movement.
Vietnam War and its aftermath raise doubts about the worldwide unity of communism.	
Nixon	More pragmatic approach Opens dialogue with China and détente with USSR
Ford	Continues Nixon's policies
Carter	Emphasis on human rights

Topic 18 Assessment

KEY TERMS, PEOPLE, AND IDEAS

1. Why did a **generation gap** develop in the 1960s?
2. Why is the decision in *Roe* v. *Wade* so controversial?
3. What was the **Equal Rights Amendment (ERA)** intended to achieve?
4. By 1980, what were some signs that Latinos were gaining political power across the nation?
5. How did the **American Indian Movement (AIM)** effectively address problems?
6. Why was the **Environmental Protection Agency (EPA)** founded?
7. In what ways did **Henry Kissinger** and **Richard Nixon** change U.S. foreign policy?
8. How did Nixon's **southern strategy** change the political landscape?
9. How did the Iran Hostage Crisis affect Carter's presidency?

CRITICAL THINKING

10. **Compare and Contrast** What features did the social movements of the 1960s and 1970s have in common?
11. **Cite Evidence** (a.) What impact did Watergate have on the government and people of the United States? (b.) How did Watergate reinforce public attitudes toward the government that had been developing during the Vietnam War?
12. **Draw Conclusions** How did the Civil Rights movement help build coalitions among various groups fighting for rights?
13. **Draw Inferences** (a.) How did Nixon's domestic programs reflect his complex attitude to government power? (b.) Give example of some of Nixon's domestic programs.
14. **Evaluate** How successfully did government health policies and regulations promote public health and disease prevention in the 1970s?
15. **Identify Cause and Effect** How did President Carter's concern for human rights guide his foreign policy?
16. **Analyze Graphs** Study the graph below. Describe the impact of the oil embargo on the United States.

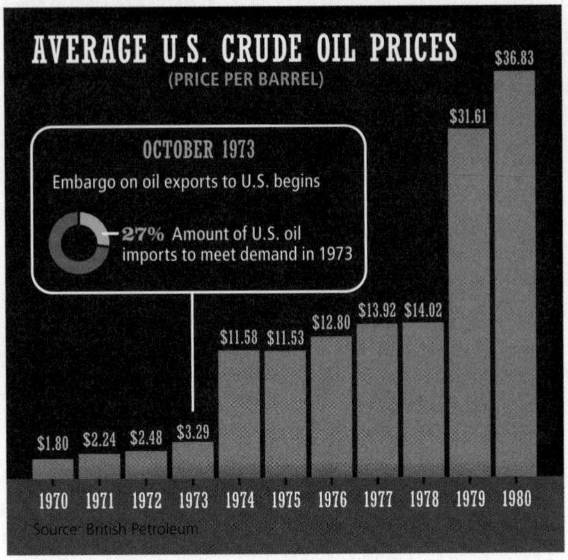

17. **Writing Activity: Explanatory** Evaluate the impact that passages like this from Rachel Carson's *Silent Spring* had on environmental legislation. Use the excerpt below and your knowledge of this issue.

> Only in the moment of the time represented by the present century has one species—man—acquired significant power to alter the nature of his world.
>
> During the past quarter century this power has not only increased to one of disturbing magnitude but it has changed in character. The most alarming of all man's assaults upon the environment is the contamination of air, earth, rivers, and sea with dangerous and even lethal materials. This pollution is for the most part irrecoverable; the chain of evil it initiates not only in the world that must support life but in living tissues is for the most part irreversible. In this now universal contamination of the environment, chemicals . . . [are] changing the very nature of the world—the very nature of its life.
>
> —Rachel Carson, *Silent Spring*

18. **Connections to Today** Practices that hold women back from promotion are often based on gender stereotypes. What kind of stereotypes prevent women's workplace advancement? Do such stereotypes have a negative impact on men as well? What kinds of jobs might men be prevented from doing because of gender stereotypes?

DOCUMENT-BASED QUESTIONS

The Watergate scandal has had a long-lasting impact on Americans' attitude to government. Read the documents below, then answer the questions that follow.

DOCUMENT A

This excerpt is from a famous television interview with President Nixon.

> If the president, for example, approves something because of the national security, or in this case because of a threat to internal peace and order of significant magnitude, then the president's decision in that instance is one that enable those who carry it out, to carry it out without violating a law. . . . in war time, a president does have certain extraordinary powers which would make acts that would otherwise be unlawful, lawful if undertaken for the purpose of preserving the nation and the Constitution, which is essential for the rights we're all talking about.
>
> —*President Nixon, from an interview with British TV host, David Frost, May 19, 1977*

DOCUMENT B

This photograph, taken on August 9, 1974, shows Richard Nixon after resigning as president.

DOCUMENT C

This excerpt is from a speech made by Barbara Jordan in Congress during the impeachment of Richard Nixon.

> . . . the president has counseled his aides to commit perjury, willfully disregard the secrecy of grand jury proceedings, conceal surreptitious entry, attempt to compromise a federal judge, while publicly displaying his cooperation with the processes of criminal justice. . . . Has the president committed offenses, and planned and directed, and acquiesced in a course of conduct which the Constitution will not tolerate? That's the question.
>
> —*Barbara Jordan, statement at the U.S. House Judiciary Committee Impeachment Hearings, Washington, D.C., July 25, 1974*

DOCUMENT D

This excerpt is from the website of the *Washington Post*, the newspaper that investigated the Watergate break-in.

> The Watergate affair was over, but its influence was not. The interlinked scandals generated a new and enduring skepticism about the federal government in American public opinion. The lingo of the scandal—"to cover-up," to "stonewall," and "to leak"—became part of the American political vocabulary. The newly assertive Congress passed campaign finance reform legislation and probed abuses of power at the CIA and other national security agencies. . . . Before long, the appointment of special prosecutors to investigate allegations of presidential wrongdoing became the norm in Washington. Watergate had changed American politics permanently and profoundly.
>
> —*The Washington Post Website*

19. In Document A, Nixon appears to be arguing that
- **A.** only war time justifies certain acts.
- **B.** everyone is equal in a court of law.
- **C.** violating the law is never acceptable.
- **D.** the President is above the law.

20. Analyze Photographs What does Document B reveal about Nixon's attitude as he left office?

21. In Document C, Barbara Jordan is
- **A.** defending the actions of the President.
- **B.** establishing the grounds for impeachment.
- **C.** clarifying Congress's role in the Watergate scandal.
- **D.** explaining that the Constitution allows the President's conduct.

22. Document D, the writer points out that Watergate
- **A.** shaped public attitudes and legislation.
- **B.** led to greater public trust in government.
- **C.** polarized the American public.
- **D.** destroyed political careers.

23. Writing Activity: Primary Source Write a paragraph explaining whether you think the Watergate scandal revealed strengths or weaknesses in the political system. Use the sources as well as additional information you have learned.

GO ONLINE to access more practice

Topic 19

America in the 1980s and 1990s (1980–1999)

ESSENTIAL QUESTION What makes a government successful?

GO ONLINE to access the eText, videos, Interactive Primary Sources, Biographies, and other online resources.

President Ronald Reagan at a reelection campaign rally

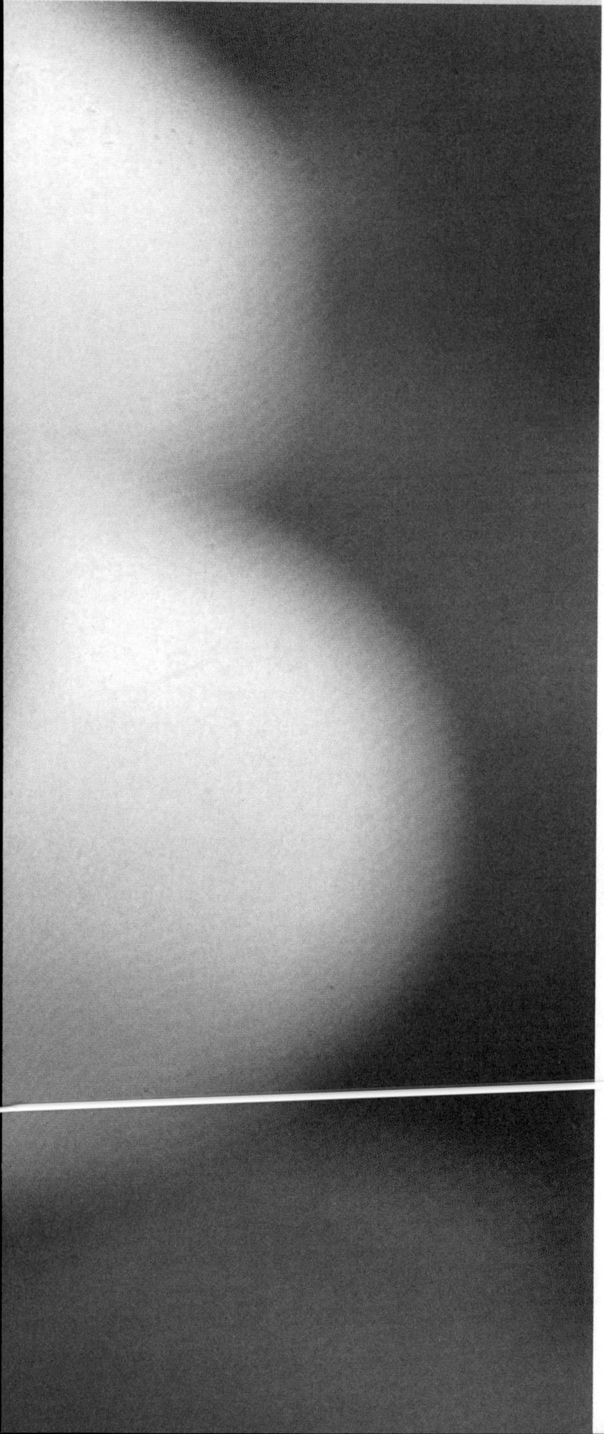

Connections to Today

Imagine a businesswoman having to wait for the newspaper to be delivered before she can check daily stock prices; or a scientist waiting weeks for a colleague in France to mail data so he can continue his research; or having to go to the library to find out how fast a cheetah runs. This was the world before the Internet.

While it was first developed in the 1970s, the Internet only reached the general public in the 1990s. Since then, its use has exploded. But is there a downside to this revolutionary technology?

NBC LEARN

Learn more about the experiences of Irene Zoppi, a Gulf War veteran.

BOUNCE to Activate My Story Video

Topic 19 Overview

In this Topic, you'll learn about the United States in the 1980s and 1990s. Look at the lesson outline and explore the timeline. As you study this Topic, you'll complete the Quest Inquiry.

LESSON OUTLINE

Key Events of the 1980s and 1990s

1980
Ronald Reagan wins the presidency

1983
Economy starts to recover from recession

1986
Space shuttle *Challenger* explodes after launch

1989
Berlin Wall falls

1991
Soviet Union breaks up; Cold War ends; Persian Gulf War ends

1993
President Clinton signs Family Medical Leave Act

1998
President Clinton is impeached

1980 1985 1990 1995 2000

QUEST! INQUIRY

Laissez-Faire?

Should government intervene to help the economy, or is it better for government not to interfere with the economy at all? In this Quest you'll discuss the question: Would laissez faire be the best economic policy for the United States?

STEP 1
Read the Discussion Launch and take notes about the major points. Discuss the points with the other members of your group.

STEP 2
Examine several sources that will provide different perspectives on the main question. As you read and analyze each source, fill in Step 2 of the Information Organizer.

STEP 3
After your group has been assigned a YES or NO position on the main question, prepare the most compelling arguments in support of your position. Present your arguments and then switch sides.

STEP 4
Discuss the main question from your own point of view. Reflect on what you've read and heard about the question and how different perspectives have broadened your understanding of the issues involved.

GO ONLINE to access complete Quest materials

19.1

At the 1980 Republican National Convention, presidential candidate Ronald Reagan and running mate George H. W. Bush emphasized the need for tax cuts, a balanced budget, and increased defense spending.

BOUNCE to Activate Flipped Video

Objectives

Describe the differences between liberal and conservative viewpoints.

Analyze the causes behind the conservative resurgence in the early 1980s.

Explain why Ronald Reagan won the presidency in 1980.

Key Terms

liberal
conservative
New Right
unfunded mandate
Moral Majority
Ronald Reagan

The Conservative Movement Surges

The two major political parties in the United States in the late twentieth century were the Democratic Party, many of whose members were **"liberals,"** and the Republican Party, whose members were often labeled **"conservatives."** Liberals generally favored government intervention to help the needy, whereas conservatives generally favored allowing the free market, private organizations, and individuals to do that. Although the two parties did agree on many basic issues, including core American values such as freedom and equality, they diverged on many others. In addition, individual members within both parties did not always conform to the views of their party's majority.

Liberals and Conservatives Diverge

In order to understand the Republican Party of the late twentieth century, one has to revisit the 1964 election, which marked a low point for conservatives. Republican Barry Goldwater, a favorite of the conservative movement, lost the election in a landslide to liberal Democrat Lyndon Johnson. Nonetheless, conservatives were not discouraged by this loss at the polls. On the contrary, they set out to build an organization and to put forth a clear vision of their goals and values that would enable them to win in the future.

Meanwhile, Goldwater returned to the Senate, where he continued to be the voice of conservatism and to forcefully advocate for conservative views. Goldwater found a supporter in California governor Ronald Reagan, who was emerging as a conservative leader. By 1980, the conservatives' efforts had paid off. Their new standard bearer, Ronald Reagan, was elected President. The modern

GO ONLINE to access your digital course

conservative movement that Reagan spearheaded shaped the nation's policies for decades to come.

Liberalism's Ideas and Goals In the late 1970s, liberals tended to believe that the federal government should play a significant role in improving the lives of all Americans. They valued social programs that helped the poor, unemployed, elderly, and others. They also sponsored laws that protected the rights of minorities and women, especially in the post–World War II period. They supported greater government regulation of industry. In the foreign policy realm, liberals tended to favor cooperating with international organizations like the United Nations.

Conservatism's Ideas and Goals In contrast, some conservatives felt that a large central government endangered economic growth and individual choice. They felt the liberal policies of the 1960s and 1970s had left a legacy of rising inflation and enormous waste. Furthermore, some conservatives criticized the liberal solution of "throwing money" at social problems. They sought to reduce taxes and limit government regulation of industry in order to promote economic growth. Conservative economist Milton Friedman and his wife Rose Friedman wrote in their book *Free to Choose*, "The story of the United States is the story of an economic miracle. . . . What produced this miracle? Clearly not central direction by government."

Other conservatives, neoconservatives, and traditionalists warned about the dangers posed to society by abandoning traditional values in favor of the new freedoms exemplified by the counterculture and advertised by the mass media. This concern with social issues, such as the perceived degeneration of modern youth, dovetailed with many conservatives' religious beliefs.

Anticommunism formed the third leg of modern conservatism. Most anticommunists focused on the dangers posed to the United States by the Soviet Union. They questioned the wisdom of the détente policy followed by Republican presidents Nixon and Ford, and by Democrat Jimmy Carter. They also fought against the SALT II treaty with the Soviet Union being debated in the Senate in 1979.

☑ **IDENTIFY** According to conservatives, what is the best way to promote economic growth?

The Increasing Popularity of the New Right

During the 1940s and 1950s, the lines separating Republicans and Democrats had blurred. The two parties had developed a bipartisan foreign policy aimed at containing communism. Both favored a relatively significant role for the government in domestic affairs. However, during the 1960s and 1970s, many Republicans became increasingly critical of the liberal policies of the Democrats. They advanced a new conservative agenda. The differences between the two major parties grew more pronounced. The **New Right**, as the resurgent conservative movement was called, grew rapidly

Liberal Viewpoints in the 1980s

ISSUE	VIEWPOINT
Role of government in the economy	Favored more government involvement to lessen extreme economic inequalities through • social programs • regulation of industry to protect safety and the environment
Foreign policy	Favored the use of diplomacy to combat communism
Healthcare	Favored regulation of healthcare industry to ensure that everyone had affordable healthcare
Energy	Favored exploring alternatives to oil and believed the government should regulate the gas and electric industries

SOURCE: *The road from here: Liberalism and realities in the 1980s*

>> **Analyze Information** Based on this chart, what might a liberal in the 1980s have believed about the minimum wage?

BOUNCE to Activate Chart

and was a coalition of several different groups with varying ideas and goals. This movement built part of its base through evangelical churches, televangelism, and other media outlets. Its leaders formed their ideology through organizations like the Young Americans for Freedom and went on to found a variety of think tanks and lobbying organizations.

The Decline of Liberalism One reason for the revival of the Republican Party was the unraveling of the Democratic Party. The Vietnam War and urban riots of the 1960s divided the same people who had rallied around President Johnson's vision of the Great Society.

The rise of the counterculture alienated many midwestern Americans and white conservative Christians in the South. Feminist advances were opposed by social leaders like Phyllis Schlafly. Watergate, the oil crises of the 1970s, and the Iran hostage crisis further weakened the public's faith in the federal government.

Just as importantly, the shifts in the economy of the 1970s, including the decline in northern industries, dampened America's optimism about the future. America had supported the Great Society, in part, because Johnson had suggested that the war on poverty and other new programs would not demand higher taxes. When the economy stagnated, liberal ideas lost their pull and conservative beliefs became more attractive.

Criticizing Liberal Programs Many conservatives believed that liberal policies were responsible for stagflation and other economic problems of the late 1970s. They believed that the government taxed citizens and businesses too heavily and spent too much on the wrong programs. They complained about **unfunded mandates**, programs required but not paid for by the federal government.

Some conservatives also criticized federal welfare programs, arguing that they rewarded lack of effort. Furthermore, they thought that Great Society programs did not work and that these programs had made the problem of poverty worse, not better. They pointed to other unintended consequences of such programs. For example, they charged that welfare contributed to the rise in the number of children born out of wedlock and therefore encouraged the decline of the traditional family—consisting of a married father and mother and their children. They also felt that affirmative action programs went too far and contributed to reverse discrimination.

Another group that supported the conservative platform was the "sagebrush rebels." Sagebrush rebels were activists who believed that the federal government controlled too much land in Western states. They thought the federal government should give control of this land to the states, to be used to their best economic advantage. Most environmentalists opposed the movement, because they did not want to expose preserved lands to possible development.

U.S. Inflation, 1978–1980

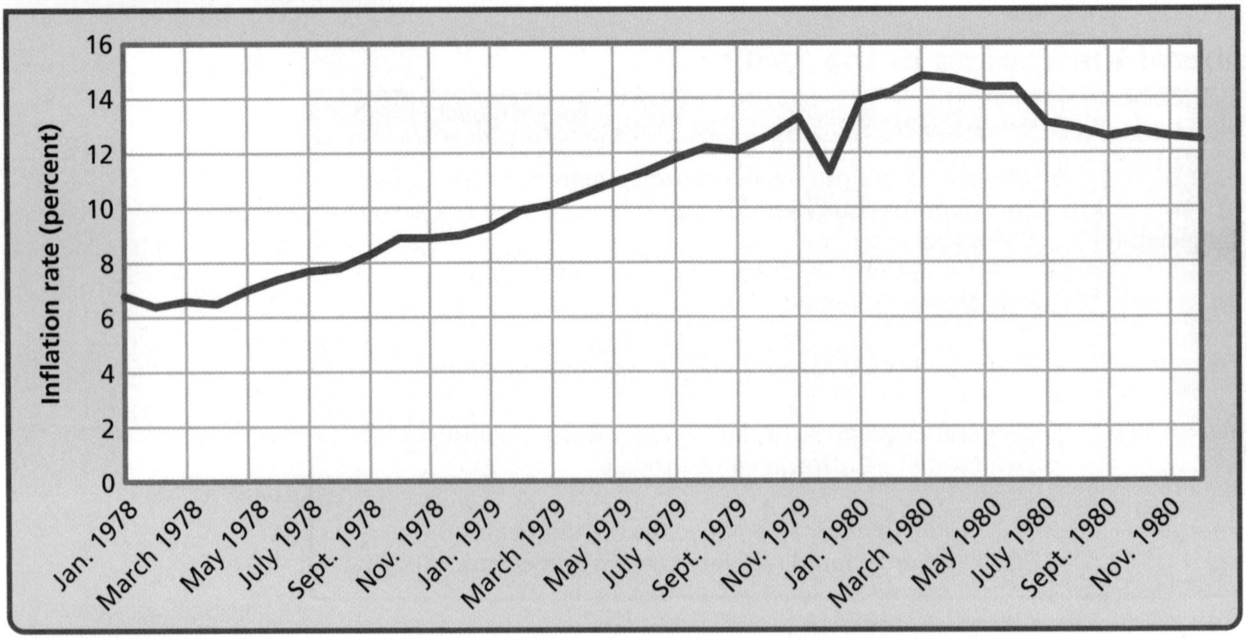

SOURCE: Bureau of Labor Statistics

>> **Analyze Data** During which years did the inflation rate rise steadily?

The Religious Right Emerges At the same time, concern with cultural change caused more religious groups to become actively involved in politics, such as the **Moral Majority**, founded by Reverend Jerry Falwell in 1979. It also worried about the decline of the traditional family. The Moral Majority opposed the 1962 Supreme Court decision *Engel* v. *Vitale*, which forbade government-written prayers in public schools, as well as the historic 1973 *Roe* v. *Wade* decision, which legalized abortion. It also condemned the Equal Rights Amendment and the gay rights movement. This movement had begun to suffer defeats nationally after singer and activist Anita Bryant launched her successful 1977 campaign to repeal a local anti-discrimination ordinance in Dade County, Florida.

The Moral Majority boosted the Republican Party's chances of winning the presidency by reaching out to Americans who had traditionally not participated in the political process. With other groups like it, the Moral Majority registered at least 2 million new voters before the 1980 presidential election. One of their tactics was to distribute Moral Majority "report cards" on candidates, which almost always favored Republicans.

>> Ronald Reagan, shown here in a 1951 Hollywood studio shot, originally supported New Deal policies. He later became a conservative, believing that Americans should oppose the expansion of the federal government.

Race, Demographics, and Conservatism

Demographic, or population, trends also strengthened the conservative movement. Historically, northern cities stood as strongholds of liberal Democrats. When an increasing number of Americans moved to the suburbs, their attachment to liberalism waned as they struggled financially during the tough economic days of the late 1970s. At the same time, Republicans emphasized issues that they believed would convince moderate liberals to switch their party allegiance. For instance, Republicans attacked school busing as a form of social engineering that threatened the long-cherished ideal of neighborhood schools.

Republicans benefited from the migration of Americans from the Rust Belt of the Northeast and Midwest to the Sunbelt of the South and West. This demographic shift, which began in the 1950s and continued through the 1970s, had many causes, including the sunny climate and opportunities for jobs in aerospace, technology, and other growing industries.

Republicans also benefited from a historical realignment of white voters in the Deep South. Since the Civil War, most white southerners had voted for the Democratic Party. So strong was southern support, in fact, that the region earned the nickname "the Solid South." When the Democratic Party embraced civil rights legislation in the 1950s and 1960s, however, a seismic shift began. Because many white southerners opposed this legislation, they moved their party allegiance to the Republicans, which at the same time picked up the banner of states' rights.

Ronald Reagan supported this notion of greater autonomy for the states and so was an integral part of the transformation of the American South from a Democratic Party stronghold throughout the first half of the century to a Republican Party stronghold by the 1980s. Many consider this change to be one of the most significant developments of 20th century American politics. Beyond the regional shift that occurred, civil rights became a core issue for the Democratic Party on a national level, while reducing the size of government and states' rights became central tenets of the Republican Party.

☑ **RECALL** Why did the Moral Majority oppose the Supreme Court's decision in *Engel* v. *Vitale*, 1962?

A Conservative Wins the White House

The growing conservative movement swept the Republican presidential candidate, **Ronald Reagan**, to victory in the 1980 election. Much more charismatic and polished than Goldwater, Reagan made clear his opposition to big government, his support for a strong military, and his faith in traditional values. Just as importantly, he radiated optimism, convincing Americans that he would usher in a new era of prosperity and patriotism.

Reagan's Path to the Presidency Born in Tampico, Illinois, in 1911, Reagan suffered the hardships of the Great Depression as a young adult before landing a job in Hollywood as a movie actor. Never a big star, Reagan appeared in many "B" or low-budget films. His most famous starring role was in *Knute Rockne*, a film based on the life of Notre Dame's legendary football coach.

When his acting career began to wane, Reagan became a spokesperson for General Electric and toured the nation giving speeches. Although once a staunch New Dealer, Reagan had become a Goldwater conservative. In these speeches, he began to criticize big government and high taxes and warned of the dangers of communism. In 1964, near the end of Goldwater's presidential campaign, Reagan delivered a nationally televised address in which he spelled out these views:

> "This is the issue of this election, whether we believe in our capacity for self-government or whether we abandon the American Revolution and confess that a little intellectual elite in a far-distant capital can plan our lives for us better than we can plan them ourselves."
>
> —Ronald Reagan, "A Time for Choosing," 1964

While the speech failed to bolster Goldwater's campaign, it won the admiration of many conservatives. Two years later, Reagan won the governorship of California. He served for two terms as governor and nearly won the Republican presidential nomination in 1976. In 1980, he won the nomination by a landslide. His opponent was Jimmy Carter, the Democratic incumbent.

The 1980 Election As the 1980 presidential election approached, Carter looked like a lame duck. Persistent inflation, the Iran hostage crisis, and the

1980 Presidential Election

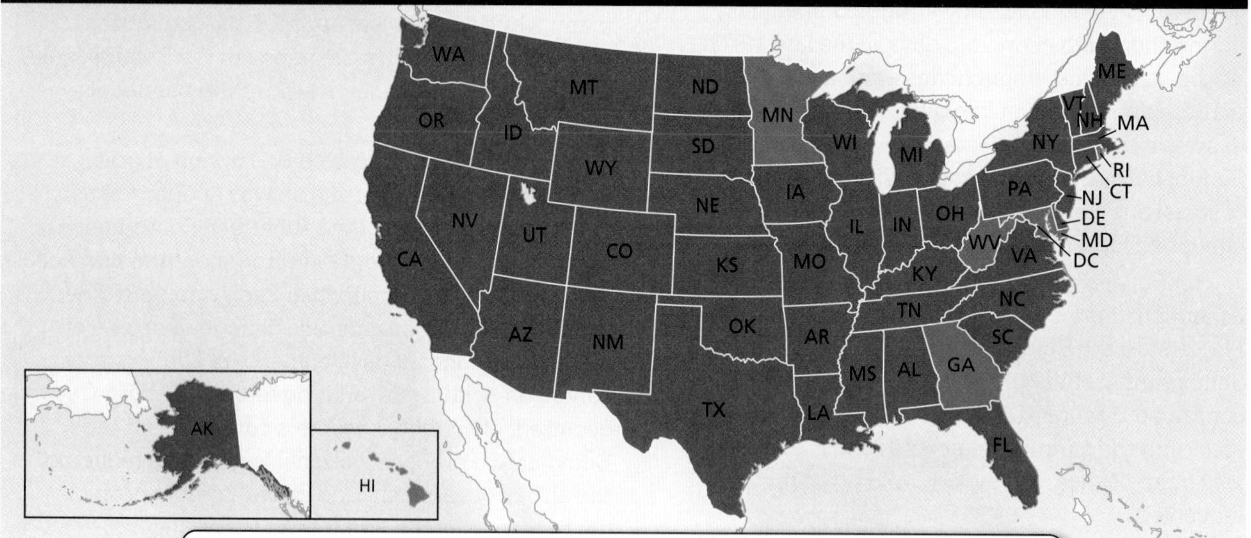

Candidate (Party)	Electoral Vote	% Electoral Vote	Popular Vote	% Popular Vote
Ronald Reagan (Republican)	489	90.9	43,904,153	50.7
Jimmy Carter (Democrat)	49	9.1	35,483,883	41.0
John Anderson (National Union)	0	0	5,720,060	6.6

>> **Analyze Information** Some describe the 1980 presidential election as a close contest. In what way was this true? In what way was it not true?

BOUNCE to Activate Timeline

Soviet invasion of Afghanistan made it easy for Reagan to cast the Carter presidency in a negative light. "Are you better off than you were four years ago?" Reagan asked audiences on the campaign trail, knowing that most Americans would answer, "No."

The race remained relatively close until about one week before the election, when Reagan and Carter held their only presidential debate. In this debate, Reagan's gifts as a communicator shone. He appeared friendly and even-tempered and calmed fears that he did not have enough experience to serve as President. On Election Day, Reagan won 50.7 percent of the popular vote. Because most states award electoral votes on a "winner-takes-all" basis, Reagan won an overwhelming majority of electoral college votes despite the narrow margin by which he won the popular vote. Even though the Democrats maintained control of the House of Representatives, Republicans captured the U.S. Senate for the first time since 1955. The conservatives were back.

IDENTIFY CENTRAL IDEAS What policies made Ronald Reagan attractive to conservative voters?

ASSESSMENT

1. **Describe** the factors that contributed to the decline of liberalism in the late 1970s.
2. **Apply Concepts** Discuss the emergence of the Moral Majority and explain its connection to the Republican Party.
3. **Generate Explanations** Explain how Ronald Reagan rose to prominence within the Republican Party.
4. **Identify Patterns** Explain how changing demographics contributed to the rise of conservatism in the 1970s.
5. **Quest Connections** Compare the viewpoints of liberals and conservatives in the 1980s with regard to government intervention in the economy.

GO ONLINE to access this biography: Ronald Reagan

19.2

President Reagan and First Lady Nancy Reagan celebrate his reelection at an inaugural ball in January 1985. A rebounding economy helped Reagan win election to his second term.

BOUNCE to Activate Flipped Video

Objectives

Analyze Reagan's economic policies as President.

Examine Reagan's leadership and how he strengthened the conservative movement.

Evaluate the steps taken to address various issues in the 1980s and early 1990s.

Key Terms

supply-side economics
deregulation
budget deficit
national debt
Savings and Loan crisis
Sandra Day O'Connor
voucher
Acquired Immunodeficiency Syndrome (AIDS)

The Reagan Era

Conservatives celebrated Ronald Reagan's election as the fulfillment of their dreams. Some even referred to his coming to power as the "Reagan Revolution." The Reagan Revolution would bring a significant shift in the political direction of the nation.

A New Direction for the American Economy

Tax Cuts and Deregulation Reagan and his advisors based their economic policies on the theory of "supply-side economics," sometimes called "Reaganomics." The theory of **supply-side economics** rests on the assumption that if taxes are reduced, the wealthy will invest more and thus create jobs.

The new jobs should give people more money to spend, causing the economy to grow. The government will then collect more in taxes. To cut taxes while still balancing the federal budget, however, Reagan also needed to reduce federal spending on programs favored by both Democrats and Republicans.

Congress approved most of Reagan's plan by passing the Economic Recovery Act of 1981, which reduced taxes by 23 percent over three years. The richest Americans received the largest tax cuts. Reagan justified this move by saying that the wealthy would use the money they saved to invest in new businesses. Reagan also convinced Congress to cut about $40 billion from the federal budget, mostly by cutting spending for social programs.

In addition to cutting taxes, Reagan also reduced the government's role in the economy by calling for **deregulation**, or the reduction or removal of government control over industry. Supporters believed that regulations had become too burdensome and that they restricted economic growth. Opponents argued

GO ONLINE to access your digital course

that the regulations prevented fraud and protected consumers and the environment. By the mid-1980s, Congress had deregulated the airline, telecommunications, and banking industries.

Social and Economic Issues Shortly after Reagan took office, the economy experienced a severe recession from 1980 to 1982. Unemployment rose to more than 10 percent in 1982. The recession hit blue-collar workers particularly hard. Many farmers, facing overseas competition, lost their farms. The policies that Paul Volcker, as head of the Federal Reserve Board, had introduced to tame the great inflation of the 1970s contributed to the recession in the early 1980s. Beginning in early 1983, however, the economy began to turn around. Inflation fell dramatically. The Gross National Product, or the annual income earned by Americans and American businesses, expanded at a healthy pace. The American economy seemed revitalized.

Despite this, the number of poor people, including the working poor, actually increased. In addition, immigrants from Latin America and Asia, attracted by employment prospects and political freedom, continued to pour into the United States. In the 1980s, more than 7.3 million legal immigrants and hundreds of thousands of unauthorized immigrants entered the country, many from Mexico. Many of these newcomers worked in low-paying jobs and struggled to make ends meet. Meanwhile, the richest Americans grew richer.

In Texas, tensions from this economic disparity reached a head in 1984 when a poor, largely Mexican American school system sued the state commissioner of education over inequalities in the education of minorities. After a nearly 10-year struggle, the case, *Edgewood I.S.D.* v. *Kirby*, led to a school funding system in Texas in which some tax money from more affluent, largely white school districts was transferred to less affluent, largely minority districts.

In 1986, President Reagan signed a sweeping immigration reform bill into law. It increased security at the Mexican border, imposed strict penalties on employers for hiring undocumented workers, and granted amnesty to any immigrant who had entered the country before 1982.

Problems With Deficits Reagan increased defense spending but failed to win the huge cuts in government spending that he wanted in other areas. These were some of the factors, along with a recession, that caused the federal **budget deficit**, or the shortfall between the amount of money spent and the amount taken in by the government, to

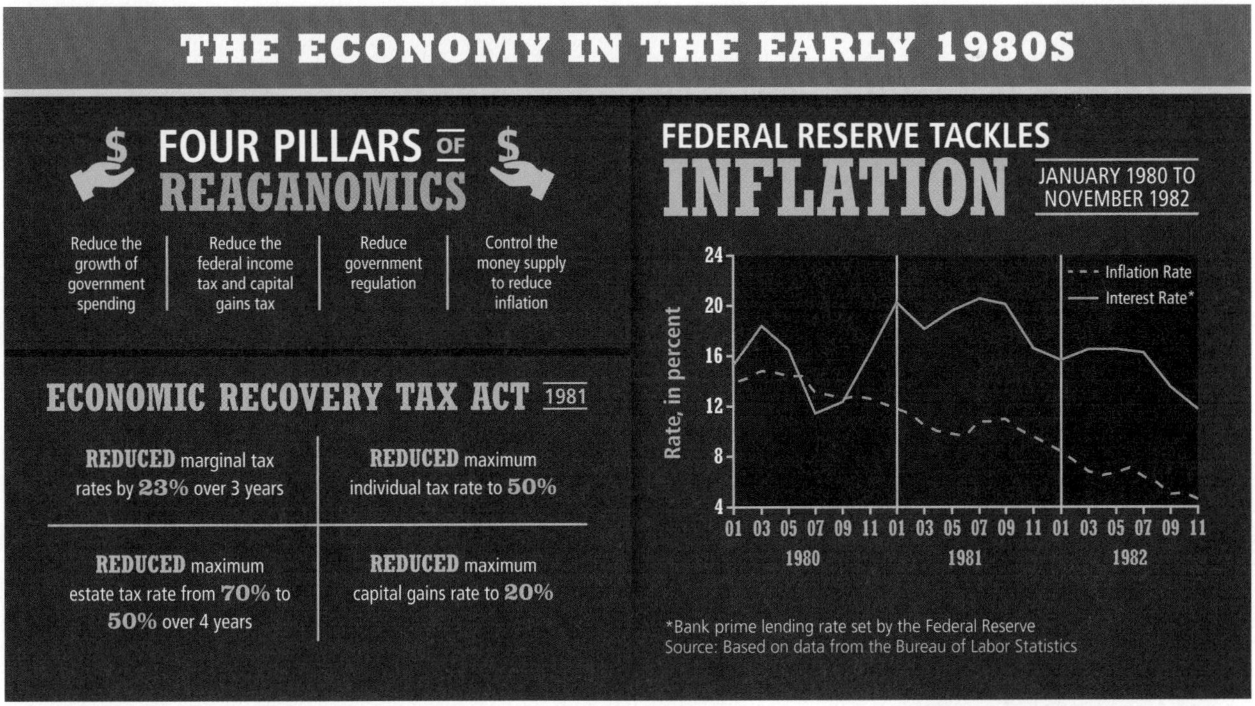

>> By raising interest rates to make it more expensive to borrow, the Federal Reserve reduced the growth of the money supply through new loans, thereby slowing inflation. **Analyze Data** What was the inflation rate in January 1980? What was it by November 1982?

BOUNCE to Activate Chart

skyrocket from about $79 billion in 1981 to more than $221 billion in 1986. The **national debt**, the amount of money the federal government owes to owners of government bonds, rose to $2.5 trillion.

In response to persistent budget deficits, Congress passed the Gramm Rudman-Hollings Act in 1985. The act sought to balance the budget by 1990 by requiring automatic cuts in federal spending if the deficit exceeded a certain amount. The federal budget deficit set new records, however, into the early 1990s.

The **Savings and Loan crisis** (also called the S&L crisis) in 1989 exacerbated deficit problems. In the late 1980s, about 1,000 Savings and Loan banks failed, some because of fraudulent behavior and others because they made too many risky loans. Critics blamed Reagan's deregulation policies for encouraging the banks to invest in riskier propositions. To prevent a broader panic, the federal government spent upwards of $200 billion to bail out depositors at the failed banks.

In the 1980s, the rising cost of Social Security also caused concern. As the number of elderly people in the country grew, the Social Security system began to collect less money than it paid out. In 1983, Reagan signed the Social Security Reform Act, which raised the minimum retirement age and increased payroll taxes for Social Security. It provided a temporary fix but did not solve the long-term problems of Social Security.

Trade Imbalance With Japan Another deficit that alarmed Americans was the nation's growing imbalance in world trade. American exports had been falling steadily since the 1970s due to a decline in domestic automobile, electronics, and other manufacturing industries.

Japan began to dominate the American market in televisions, automobiles, and other consumer products. At the same time, Japan's markets remained closed to many American-made goods.

When Japan refused to ease its restrictions on American imports, Reagan placed a tariff on Japanese electronics that doubled their price in American stores. Japanese trade restrictions eased in a deal to get this tariff removed. However, the United States continued to import many more Japanese products than American companies were able to sell in Japan.

Reagan and Organized Labor In 1981, when thousands of federally employed air-traffic controllers went on strike, Reagan refused to negotiate with the Professional Air Traffic Controllers Organization (PATCO). Instead, he fired the striking workers because they were violating a law forbidding federal employees from striking. Many Americans admired Reagan's strong, decisive stance. Some union supporters, however, claimed that Reagan's action represented an assault on the labor movement.

U.S. Trade Deficit with Japan, 1980–1990

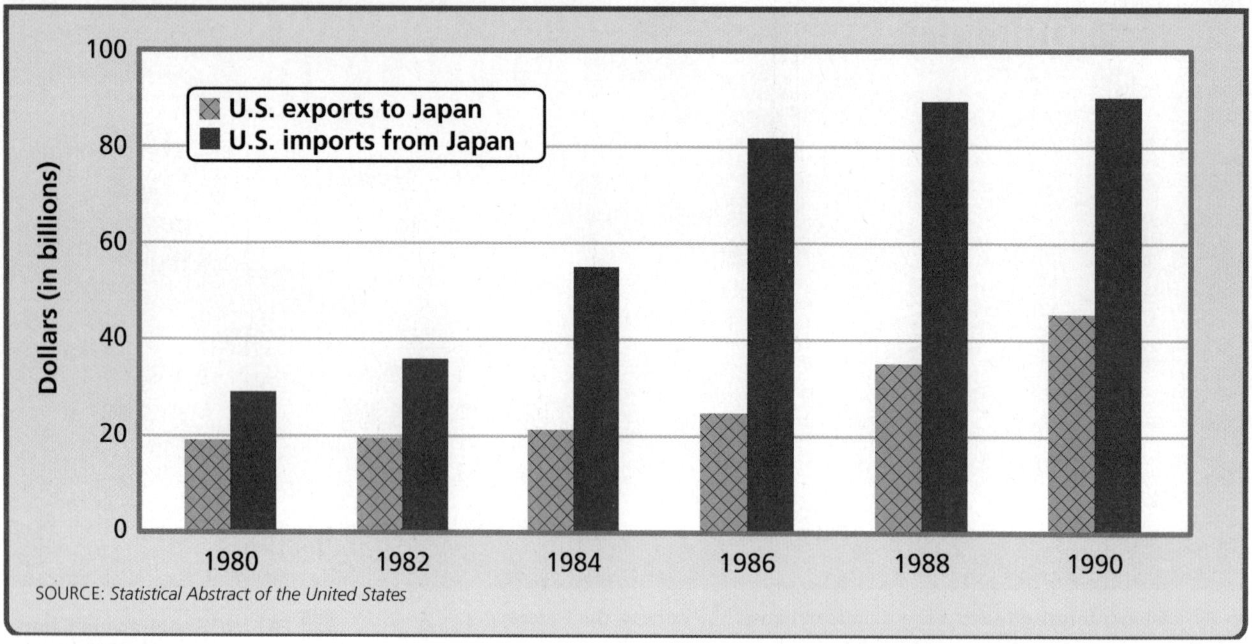

>> **Analyze Data** What happened to the trade deficit with Japan between 1980 and 1990?

The PATCO strike marked a turning point for organized labor. As the nation became more conservative, anti-union feelings grew. By 1980, the labor movement was already shrinking from its high levels of memberhip in the 1950s and 1960s. After the PATCO strike's highly visible failure, however, the decline became more rapid. Reagan's actions also signaled that it was acceptable for businesses to get tough with unions.

The Private Sector Creates Economic Opportunities Reagan believed that volunteerism and private initiative could create economic opportunities for citizens. In 1981, he praised an organization called the Clearinghouse on Corporate Social Responsibility for their work in improving Americans' quality of life. The Clearinghouse had evolved from the committee of insurance company CEOs who had first met in response to the urban riots of the late 1960s. One of the unintended consequences of this meeting was that by 1981, the organization had expanded to include life and health insurance trade associations. It actively supported community projects, employment of women and minorities, environment and energy conservation, and socially responsible investments. In 1982 it changed its name to the Center for Corporate Public Involvement.

☑ **IDENTIFY MAIN IDEAS** What is the central theory of Reaganomics, or supply-side economics?

>> Members of the air traffic controllers union, PATCO, picket at New York's LaGuardia Airport in August 1981.

Conservative Momentum Continues

Despite budget and debt problems, the economic recovery improved the national mood and helped Ronald Reagan's popularity. Reagan used his time in office to strengthen the conservative cause. Private conservative educational and research groups, such as Washington D.C.'s Heritage Foundation, supported Reagan and lobbied Congress on behalf of his programs.

Winning a Second Term During his 1984 campaign for reelection, President Reagan used the phrase "It is morning in America" as a campaign slogan:

> "It's morning again in America. In a town not too far from where you live, a young family has just moved into a new home. . . . Right down the street, one of the neighbors has just bought himself a new car with all the options. The factory down the river is working again. . . . Life is better, America is back. And people have a sense of pride they never felt they'd feel again."
>
> —Campaign commercial for the reelection of Ronald Reagan, 1984

This theme dovetailed nicely with Reagan's upbeat spirit, which he displayed even in his darkest moments. On March 30, 1981, for example, a disturbed man named John Hinckley, Jr., tried to assassinate the President. One bullet from Hinckley's gun lodged in Reagan's chest. According to one account, Reagan joked with the trauma team treating him, saying, "I hope you're all Republicans."

Americans voted overwhelmingly to reelect Reagan in 1984. He easily defeated Walter Mondale, the Democratic presidential nominee, and his running mate, Geraldine Ferraro, the first woman to be nominated for vice president by a major political party. However, Reagan's momentum did not lead to a total triumph for conservatives, as Democrats retained control of the House of Representatives.

>> In 1981, Sandra Day O'Connor became the first woman on the Supreme Court. To offset what he saw as liberal bias, President Reagan appointed three conservative judges to the Court during his presidency.

Creating Conservative Courts During his two terms, Reagan appointed judges who he hoped would reverse the liberal drift of the federal courts. He appointed three new Justices — Sandra Day O'Connor, Antonin Scalia, and Anthony Kennedy—to the Supreme Court and elevated William Rehnquist, a well-known conservative, to the position of Chief Justice in 1986. **Sandra Day O'Connor**, nominated in 1981, was the first female Justice and a moderate conservative. Although she voted with other conservatives on many issues, she consistently voted to uphold *Roe* v. *Wade*, which Reagan opposed.

Near the end of Reagan's first term, Congress passed the Equal Access Act. This act required public secondary schools to allow any group equal access to school facilities. Conservative Christian groups supported the act's passage because many public schools did not allow religious groups to meet on school property. The Supreme Court confirmed the constitutionality of the Equal Access Act in 1990 in *Board of Education of Westside Community Schools* v. *Mergens*.

George H.W. Bush Becomes President Reagan used his personal popularity to promote George H.W. Bush, his Vice President for eight years, as Bush campaigned for the presidency against Massachusetts governor Michael Dukakis in 1988. Bush had enjoyed a long and distinguished political career. He had served the nation in many ways: as a member of Congress from Texas, ambassador to the United Nations under Nixon, American envoy to China under Ford, and head of the Central Intelligence Agency (CIA). Despite these impressive credentials, Bush lacked the support of conservatives in the Republican Party, who questioned his commitment to their cause.

Although Bush called for a "kinder, gentler nation" in his campaign, both candidates attacked each other in negative campaign ads. Bush cemented his support among conservatives by promising not to raise taxes and by casting himself as a defender of traditional values. Although Bush defeated Dukakis in the presidential election, Democrats won a majority of seats in both houses of Congress.

>> In 1988, after serving for eight years as Vice President, George H.W. Bush ran for President against Democrat Michael Dukakis.

President Bush sought to control federal spending by encouraging Americans to volunteer. Government, he asserted, could take a smaller role in daily life if, "like a thousand points of light," community organizations and volunteers provided more help to the disabled, illiterate, and poor.

When Congress passed the Americans With Disabilities Act (ADA) in July 1990, Bush signed it into law. The act ensured that persons with disabilities would receive the same opportunities in employment as well as access to public places and transportation that other Americans took for granted. It benefited more than 43 million people and represented another step in the quest to protect the rights of all Americans.

CHECK UNDERSTANDING Did President Reagan's appointees to the Supreme Court follow his conservative agenda in full? Explain.

Culture, Challenge, and Change

Despite Reagan's vision of "morning in America" and Bush's "thousand points of light," in truth a great cultural and economic divide existed in 1980s society—a division partially defined by race, ethnicity, and gender. The economic recovery of the mid-1980s did not affect all segments of society equally. As the number of poor increased, so did violence and drug use in the nation's inner cities. At the same time, a culture of acquisition intensified among Americans.

Material Culture in the 1980s "I am a material girl," sang Madonna in her 1985 hit. For many Americans, her anthem to acquiring things characterized the decade.

Material acquisition especially defined a segment of society that came to be known as young urban professionals, or "yuppies"—Americans born in the baby boom that followed World War II and who made $40,000 a year or more in the 1980s. Because there were so many people in this demographic, their spending habits were noticed and often criticized by the media. Yuppies were characterized by their attachment to flashy cars and other possessions and for their obsession with making and spending money.

Another trend of the 1980s was a new obsession with physical fitness. Being "fit," however, meant more than just being healthy. It also meant looking good. Americans spent more than ever before on diet drinks and vitamins, sportswear, health club memberships, and home fitness videos and equipment. Some large companies, recognizing that healthy employees were more productive, opened in-house fitness facilities. They also sponsored programs and provided other incentives to help their employees get healthier. By the mid-1980s, nearly half of Americans exercised daily, compared to just 24 percent 20 years earlier. Critics observed that

>> President Bush signs the Americans With Disabilities Act on the South Lawn of the White House in 1990. Signing ceremonies often include key participants involved with the legislation.

>> A young urban professional, or yuppie, speaks on an early model of a cell phone in 1983.

these trends embodied the materialistic values of the 1980s. They complained that instead of trying to improve society, Americans were focused on improving themselves both physically and financially.

The Space Program in the 1980s The National Aeronautics and Space Administration (NASA) added a new type of spacecraft to its fleet in 1981. Unlike rockets that fell to earth and were discarded after a single use, the new space shuttle looked and landed like an airplane. It could take off again and again to complete multiple missions.

The promising shuttle program suffered a disastrous setback in January 1986, however, when the space shuttle *Challenger* exploded in midair less than 2 minutes after takeoff from Cape Canaveral in Florida. Its entire crew of seven astronauts was killed. The crew included New Hampshire schoolteacher Christa McAuliffe, the first private citizen to go into space. The explosion halted NASA's shuttle program for two years while scientists worked to eliminate technical problems. Nevertheless, space program technology continued to inspire many products—such as improved radial tires, the portable cordless vacuum cleaner, and better firefighting gear—that improved Americans' quality of life.

>> On January 28, 1986, millions of Americans watched on television as the space shuttle *Challenger* exploded minutes after takeoff. The tragedy shocked the nation, but the U.S. space program continued.

BOUNCE to Activate 3D Model

Cold War Culture in the 1980s The ongoing Cold War also shaped 1980s culture in the United States. The Olympic Games were held in Los Angeles in 1984. It was the first time the summer Olympics had come to this country in nearly 50 years. The festive opening ceremonies typified the Reagan era's emphasis on the renewal of America's greatness and patriotism.

The Olympics became a tool in the nation's Cold War rivalry with the Soviet Union. Along with most other communist countries, the Soviet Union boycotted the Los Angeles games. The Soviet-led boycott was in retaliation for President Carter's boycott of the 1980 games in Moscow to protest the Soviet invasion of Afghanistan. The United States won an unusually high number of medals at the Los Angeles games, an outcome that contributed to many Americans' impression that the Reagan era had brought about a revival of American strength and patriotism.

Confronting Challenging Issues at Home One of the most troubling problems the nation faced in the 1980s was a dramatic increase in the use of illegal drugs, especially cocaine. Once a problem largely confined to crime-infested areas of the nation's inner cities, cocaine use became much more widespread among other classes of American society during this time.

Reformers called for stopping the seemingly unrestricted flow of drugs into the United States and for harsher penalties for drug dealers. President Reagan responded by enlisting the Army and Navy to help stop the cocaine smuggling route into south Florida. The effort was successful. But by 1985, drug smugglers had shifted their operations to the U.S. border with Mexico. In 1986, Congress made the possession of drugs for sale an offense punishable by a minimum of 10 years in prison.

Many Americans also worried about the state of the nation's public education system. In 1983, the Department of Education issued *A Nation at Risk*. This study showed that students were consistently scoring lower on standardized tests as time passed. The report argued that American schools failed to prepare students adequately to compete with students around the globe.

Even before the report appeared, conservatives called for providing **vouchers**, or government checks, that could be used by parents to pay tuition at private schools. Conservatives argued that vouchers would force public schools to improve in order to attract and retain students. Liberals in Congress argued that vouchers would take much-needed money away from public schools.

In addition, the nation faced the threat of a new disease, **Acquired Immunodeficiency Syndrome (AIDS)**, which first came to doctors' attention in 1981. AIDS is the last stage of the Human Immunodeficiency Virus (HIV), which attacks the immune system of its victims. There is no known cure. When AIDS first reached the United States, it spread mainly among gay men and intravenous drug users. Later, the virus began infecting various other groups of people. By 1994, AIDS had killed more than 250,000 Americans.

President Reagan was criticized for the government's lack of response to the AIDS epidemic. Congress consistently felt that Reagan's requests for funds to battle the epidemic were too low and nearly doubled the money earmarked for AIDS research and education.

Meanwhile, AIDS activist groups such as ACT UP (AIDS Coalition to Unleash Power) demonstrated throughout the country, protesting governmental and societal indifference to the epidemic. ACT UP demanded a coordinated government policy to fight the disease and protested the high cost of AIDS treatments. In Washington, D.C., activists unveiled a memorial quilt, conceived by the LGBT activist Cleve Jones, containing the names of some 2000 people who had died of AIDS. It was not until George H.W. Bush's presidency, however, that funding for research on the disease rose substantially.

The attempt on Reagan's life in a 1981 shooting and the serious wounding of his aide, James Brady, renewed calls for stronger controls on handguns. These efforts were opposed by the National Rifle Association (NRA), led by Harlon Carter, which casted itself as the defender of Americans' Second Amendment right to keep and bear arms. In spite of the efforts of this powerful conservative group, attempts in the 1980s to ban armor-piercing bullets and plastic handguns that could get by airport metal detectors were eventually passed by Congress.

DESCRIBE How did the 1984 summer Olympics in Los Angeles help to bolster confidence during the Reagan era?

>> The AIDS Memorial Quilt, shown here as it was displayed in Washington, D.C., in 1987, has grown to 50,000 panels commemorating the lives of more than 105,000 people who lost their lives to AIDS or related illnesses.

ASSESSMENT

1. **Describe** the significant cultural changes that emerged during the 1980s.
2. **Draw Conclusions** Discuss the significance of President Reagan's use of the phrase "It is morning in America."
3. **Identify Central Issues** Discuss the significance of the 1984 summer Olympics in relation to the Cold War.
4. **Generate Explanations** Explain why President Reagan received criticism for his administration's response to the AIDS epidemic.
5. **Quest Connections** In what ways did the Reagan and Bush administrations attempt to reduce government intervention in the economy? What were the results of those efforts?

GO ONLINE to access this biography: Sandra Day O'Connor

19.3

This famous handshake between President Reagan and General Secretary Gorbachev at the 1988 Moscow Summit Conference symbolized the growing cooperation between the United States and the Soviet Union.

BOUNCE to Activate Flipped Video

Objectives

Analyze the ways that Ronald Reagan challenged communism and the Soviet Union.

Explain the events leading to the end of the Cold War.

Describe other foreign policy challenges that faced the United States in the 1980s.

Key Terms

Strategic Defense Initiative (SDI)
Contras
Mikhail Gorbachev
glasnost
perestroika
Iran-Contra affair

The Cold War Ends

President Ronald Reagan believed that the United States had lost its way in the wake of the Vietnam War. Rather than détente, he felt the United States should seek to roll back Soviet rule in Eastern Europe and elsewhere. Reagan believed that peace would come through strength. Although Reagan's foreign policies initially increased tension between the two superpowers, they contributed to the end of the Cold War.

Reagan Leads with "Peace Through Strength"

President Reagan believed that the United States needed to weaken communism by challenging it as much as possible without provoking war. To this end, he devised policies aimed at toppling communist nations, ranging from building new nuclear missile systems to funding covert operations against Soviet troops and allies around the globe.

Reagan Decides on U.S. Military Buildup Under Reagan, the United States committed itself to the largest peacetime military buildup in its history. Congress dedicated billions of dollars to the development and production of B-1 and B-2 bombers, MX missile systems, and other projects. In spite of massive protests by the nuclear freeze movement in the United States and abroad, the Reagan administration placed a new generation of nuclear missiles in Europe.

Reagan supported this massive military buildup, in part, because he did not believe that the Soviet Union could afford to spend as much on defense as the United States could. Reagan felt this applied particularly to the **Strategic Defense Initiative (SDI)**, a proposed program in which land and space-based lasers

GO ONLINE to access your digital course

would destroy any missiles aimed at the United States before they could reach their targets. Some dubbed the missile program "Star Wars," after the popular science-fiction movie trilogy, and claimed that it was unrealistic.

Reagan Involves the U.S. Abroad Reagan also sought to weaken the Soviet Union by supporting anticommunist rebellions around the globe. To this end, the United States funded and trained the mujahadeen (moo jah huh DEEN), anti-Soviet rebels in Afghanistan. Reagan's advisors believed that with U.S. help, these guerrillas could drive the Soviets out of Afghanistan. In 1988, Soviet forces finally began to withdraw after years of fierce Afghan resistance.

Closer to home, Secretary of State Alexander Haig feared that the newly formed Sandinista government in Nicaragua provided the Soviets with a "safe house" in America's backyard. To counter this threat, the administration backed a group of anticommunist counterrevolutionaries, known as the **Contras**. At the same time, the United States supported a right-wing government in El Salvador that was battling leftist rebels.

Many human rights activists strongly objected to this policy; even U.S. Ambassador Robert White described the legal system in El Salvador as "rotten" and called for the United States to suspend aid to the nation. Instead, Congress made funding for El Salvador's government dependent on the nation making progress on human rights.

In 1983, Reagan acted to counter another perceived threat in the Western Hemisphere. Members of a radical leftist movement, with some help from Cuba, had violently ousted the Grenadian prime minister. On October 25, 1983, U.S. troops invaded Grenada to prevent the island nation from becoming a communist outpost and to protect the lives of American medical students. Even though the legal grounds for this invasion proved questionable, most Americans approved of Reagan's decision.

Economic Pressures Force Gorbachev to Pursue Reforms In 1985, **Mikhail Gorbachev** (mee kah EEL GOR buh chawf) became the general secretary of the Soviet Union. Gorbachev ushered in a new Soviet era by pursuing the twin policies of *glasnost* and *perestroika*. ***Glasnost*** means "a new openness," and ***perestroika*** refers to reforming the Soviet system—for instance, by moving away from a socialist, or state-controlled, economy. Gorbachev's reforms created an opening for a shift in relations between the two superpowers. Gorbachev started these reforms mostly because the Soviet Union's economy had fundamentally failed. The nation

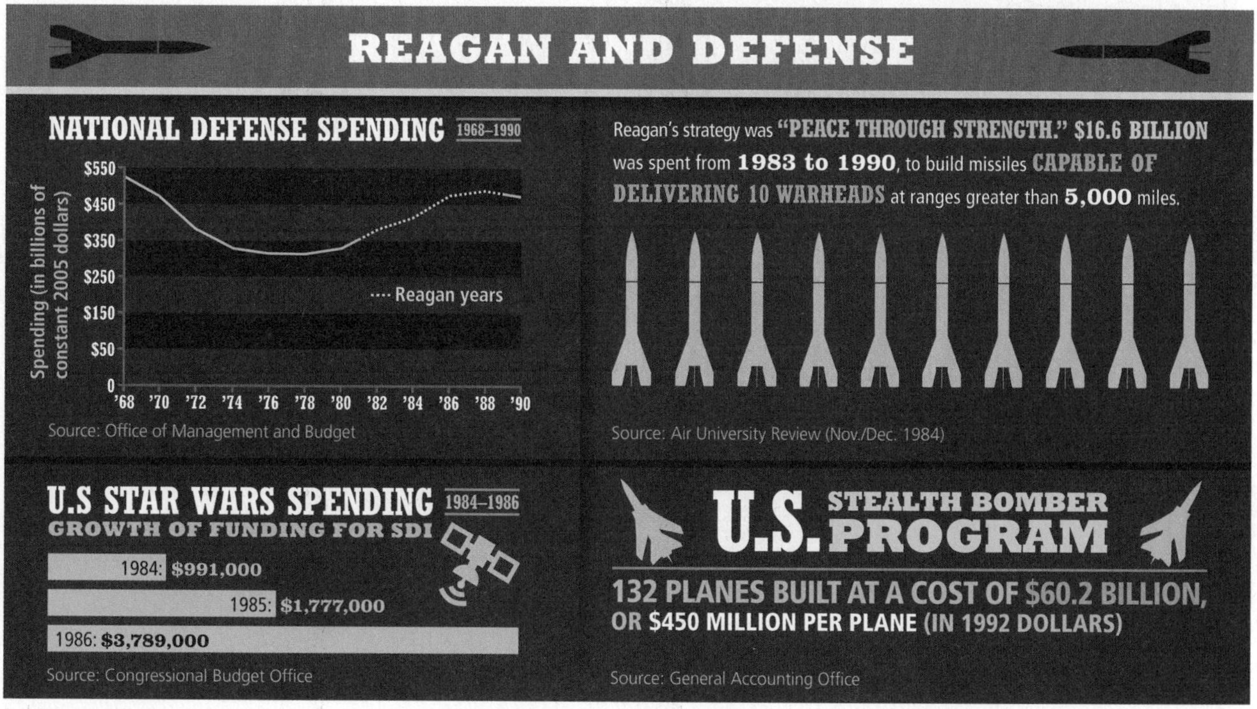

>> **Analyze Data** Based on the information in the graphic, summarize Reagan's "peace through strength" approach to national defense.

faced regular shortages of food. Its factories and workers could not compete with their Western counterparts. A huge chunk of the Soviet economy's money went toward paying for the military. The war in Afghanistan had drained Soviet resources. Gorbachev realized that his nation could not match the military buildup initiated by the Reagan administration.

Reagan and Gorbachev Reevaluate Their Positions Gorbachev's policies and personality helped soften the Soviet Union's international image. Reagan welcomed the change; he had finally found a Soviet leader with whom he could work to lessen the threat of nuclear war. While the two nations had held no summits during Reagan's first four years in office, their leaders met four times between 1985 and 1989.

During their final meeting in Moscow, Reagan and Gorbachev toasted each other at a state dinner, toured the sights like old friends, and held a joint press conference. At the press conference, a reporter asked Reagan about his description of the Soviet Union as an "evil empire." Reagan responded, "I was talking about another era." Then, Gorbachev allowed President Reagan to address students at Moscow State University on the benefits of the free-enterprise system and democracy:

> "Your generation is living in one of the most exciting times in Soviet history. It is a time when the first breath of freedom stirs the air and the heart beats to the accelerated rhythm of hope, when the accumulated spiritual energies of a long silence yearn to break free. . . . We do not know what the conclusion of this journey will be, but we're hopeful that the promise of reform will be fulfilled . . . leading to a new world of reconciliation, friendship, and peace."
>
> —Ronald Reagan, May 31, 1988

Even before this summit, the two nations had signed the Intermediate-Range Nuclear Forces (INF) Treaty in 1987, in which they had agreed—for the first time in the nuclear era—to dismantle an entire class of nuclear weapons. They had also begun negotiations on the START I Treaty, which would reduce the number of nuclear weapons in the world.

CHECK UNDERSTANDING Aside from his idea of "peace through strength," what other reason did Reagan have for massive military spending?

>> President Reagan meets for the first time with Soviet leader Mikhail Gorbachev in Geneva, Switzerland, in 1985.

BOUNCE to Activate Chart

Impact of the End of the Cold War

1991 was a turning point in American and world history. In a little over three years' time after Reagan's speech in Moscow, the Cold War had come to an end. The Berlin Wall came down; Poland, Czechoslovakia, and Hungary held democratic elections; and the Soviet Union disintegrated into numerous separate republics. *Time* magazine observed: "It was one of those rare times when the tectonic plates of history shift beneath men's feet, and nothing after is quite the same."

Communist Governments Fall in Eastern Europe More so than any other event, the fall of the Berlin Wall symbolized the end of communism in Europe. For decades, the wall had blocked travel from communist East Berlin to democratic West Berlin. Guards shot those who attempted to escape over the wall to West Berlin. Then, in November 1989, following the fall of East Germany's communist government, East German authorities opened the wall's gates.

The Fall of Communism in Eastern Europe and the Soviet Union

>> **Analyze Maps** Compare this map to a current map of Eastern Europe. What has happened to these former communist countries since 1991?

BOUNCE to Activate Gallery

Thousands climbed atop the wall; some even took sledgehammers and chipped away at the barricade. Within a year, East and West Germany would reunite as one single nation. Communists also lost power in Poland, Hungary, Czechoslovakia, Bulgaria, and Romania in 1989; in Albania in 1990; and in Yugoslavia in 1991.

The Soviet Union Disintegrates In August 1991, hard-liners in the Soviet Union attempted to stage a coup in a last-gasp attempt to maintain communist rule. But when millions of Russians, led by Boris Yeltsin, rallied in the streets of Moscow in support of Gorbachev, the coup fell apart. Not long afterward, the Communist Party lost power, and the Soviet Union separated into 15 independent republics. Boris Yeltsin became the new leader of the largest new republic, the Russian Federation.

Historians do not totally agree on what caused the Soviet Union to collapse. Most acknowledge that Gorbachev's policy of *glasnost* opened the floodgates to rebellions against Soviet domination of Eastern Europe. Likewise, they note that his policy of *perestroika* fostered a challenge to communist rule within the Soviet Union, and that the Soviet economy was in shambles.

Yet, a number of scholars give Reagan credit for bringing an end to the Cold War. By dedicating the United States to a massive arms buildup, they argue, he hastened the collapse of the Soviet economy as it strove to keep up. In turn, this compelled Gorbachev to promote reform at home and relinquish control of Eastern Europe.

The key rival and enemy of the United States for so many years had suddenly disappeared. President George H.W. Bush met and signed agreements with first Gorbachev and then Yeltsin to scale down and even eliminate certain types of nuclear weapons. Bush and Yeltsin issued a joint statement in 1992 pledging friendship and cooperation. The long Cold War, which had absorbed so much of the energy and resources of the Soviet Union and the United States since 1945, was finally over.

DESCRIBE What happened to the Soviet Union in the immediate aftermath of its breakup?

U.S. Involvement in the Middle East and the Iran-Contra Affair

Conflicts in the Middle East in the 1980s tested political relationships throughout the world. The Iran-Iraq War from 1980–1988 and increasing incidents of terrorism brought the United States into direct confrontation with several countries in the region.

>> The terrorist bombing of the U.S. Marine barracks in Beirut, Lebanon, in 1983 resulted in more than 240 deaths, including over 200 marines—the most killed in a single day since the Battle of Iwo Jima in 1945.

>> Colonel Oliver North testifies to Congress about the Iran-Contra affair in 1987. He was responding to allegations that the Reagan administration had illegally funded anticommunist Nicaraguan rebels.

The U.S. Retaliates Against Libya During the 1980s, the United States often clashed with Libya. The countries had once had a mutually beneficial trading relationship. Libya was ruled by Muammar al-Qaddafi (MOO uh mahr al kuh DAH fee), whom Reagan described as the "mad dog of the Middle East."

U.S.-Libya relations fell apart as American leaders became increasingly frustrated with Qaddafi's support of terrorist groups. In response, the United States placed economic sanctions on Libya.

In April 1986, following a terrorist attack on a Berlin nightclub, which Reagan blamed on Qaddafi, U.S. warplanes bombed Libya. Although Qaddafi survived unharmed, the air raid killed one of his family members. In the period following the attack, Qaddafi's criticism of the United States dwindled. Tensions between the countries continued through the early 1990s, though, as U.S. leaders suspected the Qaddafi regime of producing chemical weapons.

Reagan Sends Marines Into Lebanon Even as the Soviet Union collapsed and conflicts with Libya ignited, the United States faced additional problems in the Middle East. In 1982, Reagan sent a group of 800 United States Marines to Lebanon as part of an international peacekeeping force. The Marines' initial mission was to oversee the Palestinian withdrawal from Lebanon, which was torn by a civil war between Palestinian and Christian Maronite forces. The Palestinian forces were part of the Palestine Liberation Organization (PLO). Two weeks after the successful completion of that task, American soldiers returned to Lebanon following the massacre of Palestinian refugees by a Christian Lebanese faction in the civil war.

On October 23, 1983, a truck loaded with thousands of pounds of explosives smashed through barriers at the headquarters of the United States Marines in Beirut (bay ROOT), Lebanon's capital, and into a four-story building that housed hundreds of American military personnel. The explosion killed 241 service members. The United States government holds Hezbollah, an Iranian-backed Lebanese militant group, responsible. Reagan withdrew the remaining marines in February 1984. The incident illustrated, once again, the complicated and dangerous nature of Middle Eastern politics.

The Iran-Contra Affair Shakes the Presidency Reagan's presidency started with a breakthrough in the Middle East. Twenty minutes after he took the oath of office on January 20, 1981, Iran released all 52 Americans it had held hostage since 1979. But during his second term, the Iran-Contra affair tarnished Reagan's reputation.

The **Iran-Contra affair** began when the United States sold weapons to Iran in 1985 in exchange for Iran's promise to pressure terrorist groups in Lebanon to release some American hostages. The plan didn't work, and it contradicted the administration's policy of refusing to negotiate with terrorists.

Then, the administration used the money from the sale to fund the Contras in Nicaragua, despite the fact that in 1983 Congress had banned sending funds to the Contras. News of these deals became public in 1986. Although President Reagan accepted responsibility for the actions of his administration, he never admitted to ordering his aides to support the Contras. Ultimately, several leading administration officials and a top aide, Oliver North, were convicted on charges stemming from the scandal, although many of the convictions were later overturned on technical grounds. In spite of this, Reagan left office with high approval ratings.

RECALL Why did the Iran-Contra affair threaten the credibility of the Reagan administration?

ASSESSMENT

1. **Identify Cause and Effect** Discuss the components of President Reagan's "peace through strength" policy, and identify its effects.
2. **Identify Central Issues** Describe reasons for and responses to U.S. involvement in Central America during the 1980s.
3. **Generate Explanations** Explain how economic hardships and changing political relationships gave rise to a new era for the Soviet Union during the 1980s.
4. **Describe** the events that altered the relationship between Libya and the United States during the 1980s.
5. **Connections to Today** If social media had been available during the late 1980s, how do you think it might have affected events in Eastern Europe once the Soviet Union began having serious economic difficulties and President Gorbachev instituted his policies of *glasnost* and *perestroika*?

GO ONLINE to access these biographies: Mikhail Gorbachev, Lech Walesa

"Tear Down This Wall": Ronald Reagan

On June 12, 1987, President Reagan spoke in West Berlin, in front of the Brandenburg Gate at the Berlin Wall. His speech acknowledged the new Soviet leader Mikhail Gorbachev's efforts at reform in the Soviet Union. However, Reagan was not satisfied with Gorbachev's limited measures. He challenged the Soviet leader to show a real commitment to reform by tearing down the Berlin Wall that had stood between East and West Berlin since 1961. This wall symbolized the division between communism and democracy.

>> President Reagan in Berlin

Thank you very much. Chancellor Kohl, Governing Mayor Diepgen, ladies and gentlemen: Twenty-four years ago, President John F. Kennedy visited Berlin, speaking to the people of this city and the world at the City Hall. Well, since then two other presidents have come, each in his turn, to Berlin. And today I, myself, make my second visit to your city.

We come to Berlin, we American presidents, because it's our duty to speak, in this place, of freedom. But I must confess, we're drawn here by other things as well: by the feeling of history in this city, more than 500 years older than our own nation; by the beauty of the Grunewald and the Tiergarten; most of all, by your courage and determination. . . .

Our gathering today is being broadcast throughout Western Europe and North America. I understand that it is being seen and heard as well in the East. To those listening throughout Eastern Europe, a special word: Although I cannot be with you, I address my remarks to you just as surely as to those standing here before me. For I join you, as I join your fellow countrymen in the West, in this firm, this unalterable belief: Es gibt nur ein Berlin. [There is only one Berlin.]

DETERMINE AUTHOR'S PURPOSE Was this speech meant for one or multiple audiences? What was the intent behind this speech?

Behind me stands a wall that encircles the free sectors of this city, part of a vast system of barriers that divides the entire continent of Europe. From the Baltic, south, those barriers cut across Germany in a gash of barbed wire, concrete, dog runs, and guard towers. Farther south, there may be no visible, no obvious wall. But there remain armed guards and checkpoints all the same—still a restriction on the right to travel, still an instrument to impose upon ordinary men and women the will of a totalitarian state. Yet it is here in Berlin where the wall emerges most clearly; here, cutting across your city, where the news photo and the television screen have imprinted this brutal division of a continent upon the mind of the world. Standing before the Brandenburg Gate, every man is a German, separated from his fellow men. Every man is a Berliner, forced to look upon a scar.

DETERMINE CENTRAL IDEAS What was the significance of the Berlin Wall during the Cold War?

President von Weizsacker has said, "The German question is open as long as the Brandenburg Gate is closed." Today I say: As long as this gate is closed, as long as this scar of a wall is permitted to stand, it is not the German question alone that remains open, but the question of freedom for all mankind. Yet I do not come here to lament. For I find in Berlin a message of hope, even in the shadow of this wall, a message of triumph. . . .

In the 1950s, Khrushchev predicted: "We will bury you." But in the West today, we see a free world that has achieved a level of prosperity and well-being unprecedented [never having happened or existed before] in all human history. In the Communist world, we see failure, technological backwardness, declining standards of health, even want of the most basic kind—too little food. Even today, the Soviet Union still cannot feed itself. After these four decades, then, there stands before the entire world one great and inescapable conclusion: Freedom leads to prosperity. Freedom replaces the ancient hatreds among the nations with comity [courtesy] and peace. Freedom is the victor [winner].

CITE EVIDENCE What do you think Reagan thought about Khrushchev's prediction? Cite evidence from the speech to support your answer.

And now the Soviets themselves may, in a limited way, be coming to understand the importance of freedom. We hear much from Moscow about a new policy of reform and openness. Some political prisoners have been released. Certain foreign news broadcasts are no longer being jammed. Some economic enterprises have been permitted to operate with greater freedom from state control.

IDENTIFY SUPPORTING DETAILS What evidence does Reagan give that the Soviet Union may be becoming freer?

Are these the beginnings of profound changes in the Soviet state? Or are they token gestures, intended to raise false hopes in the West, or to strengthen the Soviet system without changing it? We welcome change and openness; for we believe that freedom and security go together, that the advance of human liberty can only strengthen the cause of world peace.

There is one sign the Soviets can make that would be unmistakable, that would advance dramatically the cause of freedom and peace. General Secretary Gorbachev, if you seek peace, if you seek prosperity for the Soviet Union and Eastern Europe, if you seek liberalization: Come here to this gate! Mr. Gorbachev, open this gate! Mr. Gorbachev, tear down this wall!

DETERMINE CENTRAL IDEAS According to Reagan, why should the tearing down of the Berlin Wall be a logical outcome of Gorbachev's policies?

ASSESSMENT

1. **Distinguish Among Fact, Opinion, and Reasoned Judgment** When Reagan says, "freedom is the victor," is that a fact, an opinion, or a reasoned judgment? Cite evidence from the speech to support your answer.
2. **Draw Conclusions** Why was Reagan's speech at the Berlin Wall such an important moment in his presidency?
3. **Analyze Style and Rhetoric** The greatest speeches rely on simple imagery that inspires strong emotions. What is so powerful about the image of a wall and its destruction?

GO ONLINE to access primary sources

19.4

Democratic presidential candidate Bill Clinton and his wife Hillary speak to supporters during the 1992 presidential campaign.

BOUNCE to Activate Flipped Video

Objectives

Analyze why George H.W. Bush decided to use force in some foreign disputes and not in others.

Summarize the cause and conduct of the Persian Gulf War and its results.

Explain why Bill Clinton won the presidency in 1992.

Assess the foreign policy goals and actions of the Clinton administration.

Describe U.S. relations with various Middle Eastern countries and groups.

Understand how the United States is affected by emerging economic issues such as changes in the global economy.

Key Terms

Manuel Noriega.
Tiananmen Square
apartheid
Nelson Mandela
divest
Operation Desert Storm
William Jefferson Clinton
H. Ross Perot
ethnic cleansing
al Qaeda
European Union (EU)
The North American Free Trade Agreement (NAFTA)
General Agreement on Tariffs and Trade (GATT)
World Trade Organization (WTO)

A New Era in Foreign Policy

When the Cold War came to an end, many Americans hoped that a new era of peace would dawn. Yet, events on the world stage during the Bush years demonstrated that the end of the Cold War would not lead to peace, but instead to a dangerous era of regional conflicts.

Bush Forges a New Role in the World

When the Soviet Union collapsed, the United States became an unopposed superpower—poised to take a leading role in world affairs under the leadership of President George H.W. Bush. Few leaders entered the White House with as much foreign policy experience as Bush. A graduate of Yale and a veteran of World War II, Bush had served as the U.S. Ambassador to the United Nations, as director of the CIA, and as Ronald Reagan's vice president. His experience would be put to the test as the United States faced a series of international crises during the late 1980s and early 1990s.

Political Changes and the War on Drugs in Latin America In the late 1980s and early 1990s, Latin America experienced a wave of democracy. In Central America, a peace plan devised by Costa Rican leader Oscar Arias (AH ree uhs) brought free elections in Nicaragua and the end of a long civil war in El Salvador. In Chile, the notorious military dictator Augusto Pinochet (ah GOO stoh pee noh SHAY) gave up power.

GO ONLINE to access your digital course

Not all developments in Latin America, however, pleased the Bush administration. Since the Nixon administration, the government had been waging a "war on drugs," or an attempt to stop illegal drug use by going after both sellers and users. Groups of racketeers in Latin America supplied a significant amount of the illegal drugs in the United States. The Bush administration arrested and tried several international drug figures, including Eduardo Martinez Romero, the reputed financier of a Colombian drug cartel. Even more spectacularly, in December 1989, Bush sent more than 12,000 U.S. troops to invade Panama and arrest Panama's military strongman **Manuel Noriega**.

Brought to the United States for trial, Noriega was convicted of several charges of drug trafficking and sentenced to 40 years in prison.

>> President Bush and First Lady Barbara Bush visit American troops in Saudi Arabia in 1990.

BOUNCE to Activate Map

China Resists Calls for Democracy Meanwhile, in the spring of 1989, Chinese students captured the world's attention by staging pro-democracy protests in **Tiananmen Square** in the heart of Beijing. Many Americans hoped that these protests might result in the fall of communism in China. Instead, on June 4, Chinese tanks rolled into Beijing, killed hundreds of protesters, crushed the demonstrations, and imprisoned many pro-democracy activists.

The Bush administration condemned this action and suspended arms sales to China. However, Bush did not believe that stiffer penalties would influence Chinese leaders. He made the pragmatic choice to remain engaged with China economically and diplomatically, rather than cut off ties with the country.

Pressures Force Changes in South Africa While China resisted changes, long overdue ones were taking place in South Africa. For years, the South African government, controlled by whites, had maintained an oppressive system of rigid segregation known as **apartheid**. The leader of the antiapartheid movement, **Nelson Mandela** (man DEHL uh), had been imprisoned since 1962. In the late 1980s, protests against apartheid within South Africa and around the globe grew. In the United States, many private firms **divested**, or withdrew investments, from South Africa. In the hope that sanctions would be less likely to destabilize the nation than divestiture, Congress overrode President Reagan's veto in 1986 and applied sanctions to South Africa that carried over into the Bush years. In 1990, President Bush met with Mandela after his release from jail and endorsed the drive to bring democracy to South Africa. Soon after, apartheid began to be

>> In 1990, President Bush welcomed Nelson Mandela to the White House to discuss ways to bring an end to apartheid in South Africa.

dismantled, and in 1994, South Africans elected Mandela as their leader in their first free elections.

U.S. Works for Peace and Human Rights With the fall of communism in 1991, the nation of Yugoslavia disintegrated into a bloody civil war. During this new crisis in the Balkans, Bush chose not to send troops because he feared that the conflict could embroil the United States in another Vietnam. It was not until 1992 that he supported a modest UN plan to restore peace in Bosnia, one of the new republics carved out of Yugoslavia. By then, more than 150,000 civilians had died.

The Bush administration acted more swiftly to protect human rights in Somalia. As part of "Operation Restore Hope," United States Marines landed in this East African nation in December 1992 to help establish a cease-fire between rival warlords and to deliver food to hundreds of thousands of starving people. Bush's humanitarian effort in Somalia was applauded by even his most persistent critics. First under the Bush administration and then under his successor's, however, the operation evolved into an attempt to restore a government to the African nation and ultimately led to the loss of American lives as U.S. troops attempted to quell the conflict.

>> Saddam Hussein (shown here) imprisoned, tortured, or executed anyone he believed to oppose his rule. **Hypothesize** Why was Iraq's invasion of Kuwait in 1990 considered such a threat by so many nations?

☑ **EXPRESS IDEAS CLEARLY** Explain the Bush administration's reaction to the Chinese government's crackdown on prodemocracy protests in Tiananmen Square.

The Persian Gulf War

The most important foreign-policy challenge faced by the Bush administration took place in the Persian Gulf. On August 2, 1990, Iraq invaded its tiny neighbor, Kuwait. Nearly 150,000 Iraqi troops quickly overran Kuwaiti forces.

A Dictator's Thirst for Power Leads to War Saddam Hussein, Iraq's ruthless dictator, had run the Middle Eastern nation with an iron fist since 1979. By invading Kuwait, Hussein sought to take over Kuwait's rich oil deposits. With Kuwait in his power, Hussein would control nearly 20 percent of the oil produced around the world. The United States feared how Hussein would use the influence that controlling such a large amount of oil would give him. In addition, nearby Saudi Arabia possessed even greater oil reserves. The United States did not want Hussein to seek to gain control of those reserves next. Oil drove many of the world's economies, including that of the United States. In 1970, the United States consumed around 14 million barrels of oil each day. By 1990, that number had increased to 17 million barrels a day.

President Bush made it clear that he would not tolerate Iraq's aggression against its neighbor and that he believed a "new world order" could emerge from the crisis, in which nations could "prosper and live in harmony." He worked to build an international coalition and backed a UN resolution demanding that Iraqi troops withdraw.

U.S. Spearheads Operation Desert Storm By late fall, about 700,000 troops had assembled in Saudi Arabia, including nearly 500,000 American forces. Britain and France sent troops, as did nine Arab states, including Egypt and Saudi Arabia. Other nations, for example Japan, agreed to help pay for the costs of the operation. Initially, Bush hoped that the presence of these troops, along with the economic sanctions against Iraq, would convince Hussein to withdraw his soldiers. At the same time, the President asked for and received from Congress the authority to use force, if necessary, to back up the UN's resolution that Iraq leave Kuwait.

The Persian Gulf War, 1991

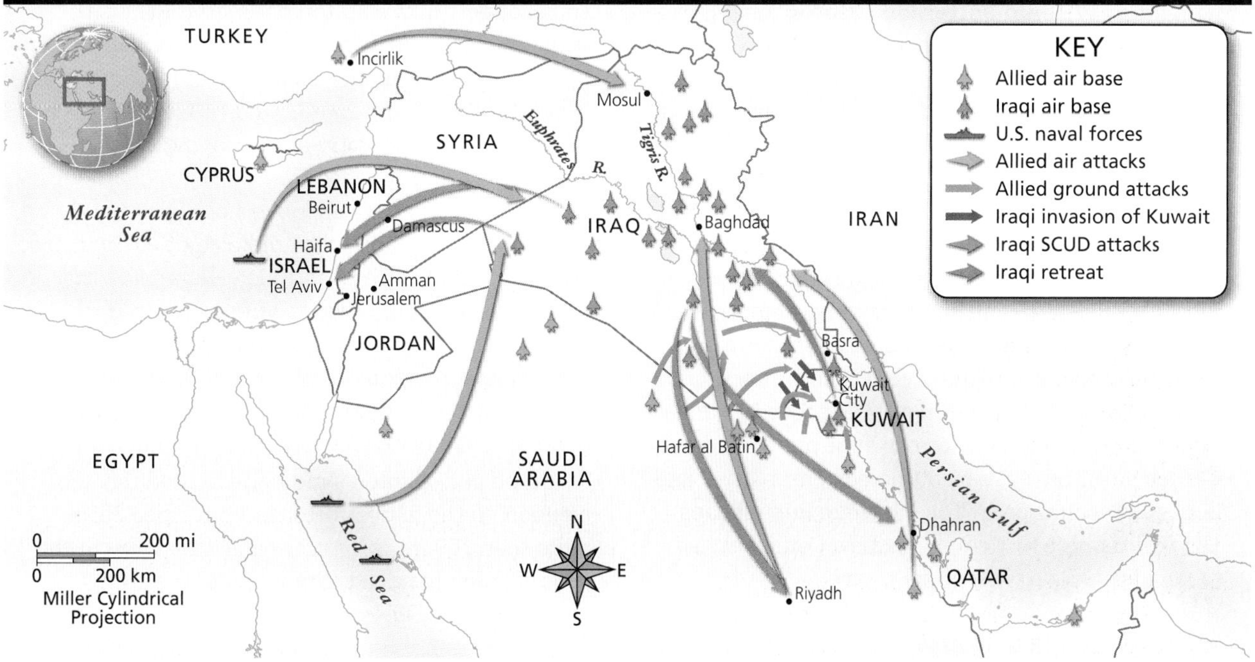

>> **Analyze Maps** What nations did Saddam Hussein retaliate against during the Persian Gulf War?

BOUNCE to Activate Gallery

Operation Desert Storm, the name given to the American-led attack on Iraqi forces, began on January 16, 1991. General Colin Powell, the Chairman of the Joint Chiefs of Staff, and General Norman Schwarzkopf devised and executed a strategy that began with five weeks of devastating aerial bombardment on Iraqi forces. Iraq countered by launching Scud missiles against coalition forces and Israel. Although these missiles did little serious damage, they struck terror in the hearts of many who feared they were armed with chemical warheads.

Lasting Effects of the War On February 24, coalition troops stormed into Kuwait. Completely overwhelmed, Iraqi troops surrendered or fled, setting fire to Kuwaiti oil rigs along the way. Less than five days after the ground war began, Iraq agreed to a UN-brokered cease-fire. It had lost an estimated 25,000 soldiers. American deaths totaled 148. "We've kicked the Vietnam syndrome once and for all," proclaimed Bush. He then chose to limit American actions to enforcing the UN resolution. The coalition's forces would compel Iraq to leave Kuwait but would not continue on to Baghdad, Iraq's capital, to topple Saddam Hussein. As a result, Hussein and his regime survived the war. Bush's public approval rating skyrocketed.

The United States remained in the region to help Iraqi refugees, establishing no-fly zones over northern and southern Iraq. However, Saddam Hussein and his supporters resented the U.S. presence. During Operation Desert Storm, similar resentment toward U.S. forces also grew in Saudi Arabia, where many troops were stationed. This resentment may have helped the terrorist organization al Qaeda attract new recruits, aided by their own anti-American propaganda.

☑ **DRAW CONCLUSIONS** Why did Saddam Hussein's regime survive the war?

Clinton Wins the 1992 Election

After the 1991 Persian Gulf War ended, President George H.W. Bush's approval rating reached 91 percent. In less than one year, however, public opinion had changed. Saddam Hussein had stayed in power, continuing to threaten peace in the Middle East. The American economy had gone into recession and the federal deficit had risen. People were angered by Bush's betrayal of his 1988 campaign pledge not to raise taxes. Bush's sinking popularity opened up the way for a Democratic challenge in the 1992 election.

"New Democrats" Emerge The Democrats nominated **William Jefferson Clinton**, governor of Arkansas, as their presidential candidate. Clinton was born in 1946 into a humble home and had worked his way through college and law school before being elected governor of Arkansas in 1978. To widen his appeal and distance himself from the stereotype of "tax and spend" liberals, Clinton promoted himself as a "New Democrat." New Democrats were centrists who sought to reconcile liberal and conservative ideals. They believed in strong national defense, tough stands on crime, free trade, and welfare reform, and they were more sympathetic to business concerns. They believed that government was necessary and important but that it had grown large and inefficient. Clinton's centrist position attracted conservative and liberal Democrats as well as moderate Republicans. His position as a moderate, practical Democrat had broad appeal for a wide range of voters.

Winning the White House By 1992, Clinton was poised to capitalize on Bush's political problems. He entered the presidential race along with Texas billionaire **H. Ross Perot**, who ran as an independent and promised to govern by sound business principles. A self-made billionaire, Perot built his campaign on economic populism and an appeal to Americans dissatisfied with the traditional two-party political system.

Clinton's campaign focused on economic and social opportunity. Clinton charged that Bush's economic policies had made the rich richer. He also pointed out that, unlike Bush, he came from a family that had struggled through hard times and knew what it was like to worry about paying bills. Bush responded by attacking Clinton's character. Republicans accused the governor of draft-dodging, marital infidelity, and other moral laxities. Bush also suggested that Clinton and his vice presidential candidate, Al Gore, were too inexperienced to lead the nation. Unlike his opponents, Perot opposed free-trade agreements with Mexico and Canada and stressed the importance of eliminating the U.S. government's budget deficit and national debt.

In the end, Clinton's message carried the election. In the largest voter turnout since 1960, more than 100 million Americans turned out at the polls. Clinton received 43 percent of the popular vote to Bush's 37 percent and Perot's 19 percent. Democrats also retained control of the House of Representatives and the Senate. Although Perot and his third party did not win any electoral votes, he garnered nearly 20 million votes. Some historians think Perot's presence on the ballot may have cost Bush the election by attracting voters who otherwise would have voted for the Republican candidate.

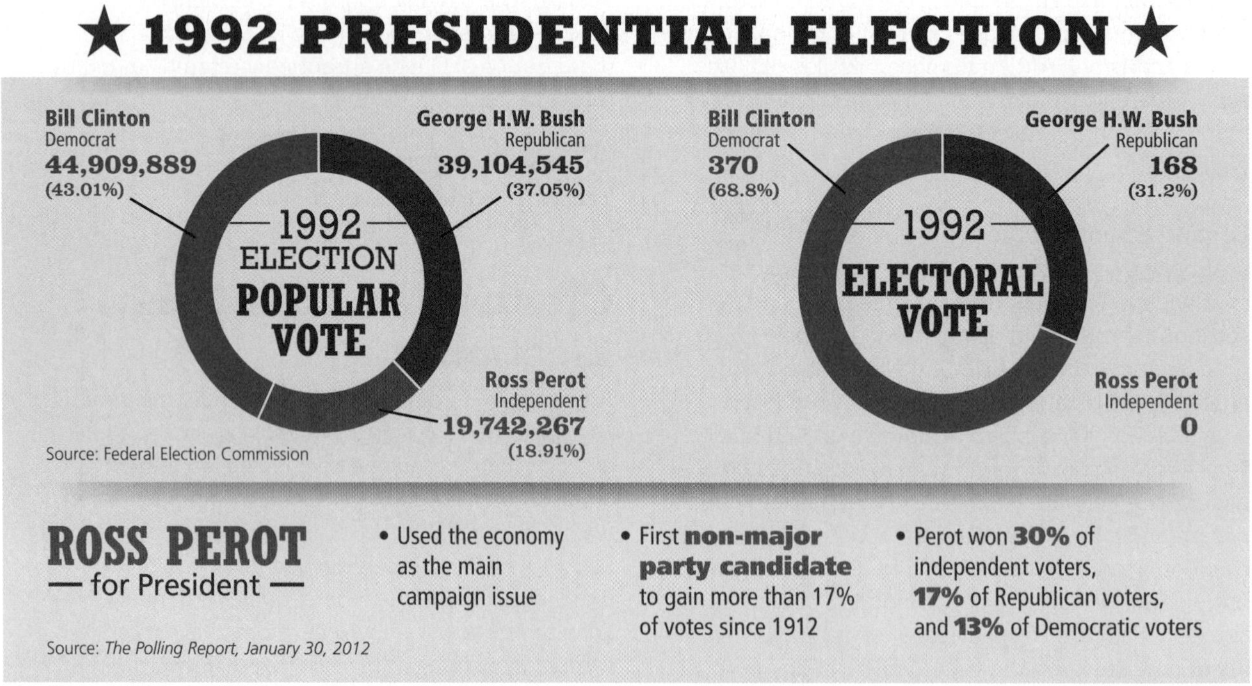

>> **Analyze Information** How is it that Bill Clinton won 43 percent of the popular vote but 69 percent of the electoral vote?

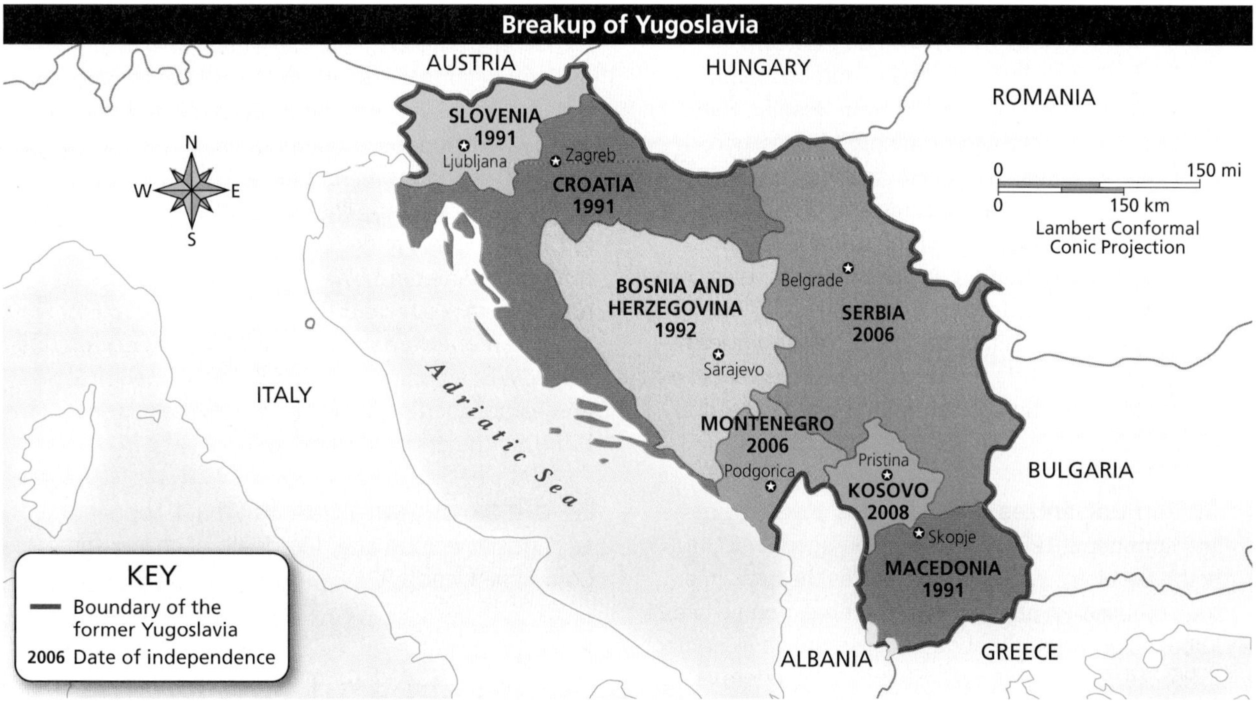

>> **Analyze Maps** From the map, which republic appears to have the potential to be the strongest? Consider not only size, but location of the former capital of Yugoslavia.

IDENTIFY According to some, what was the effect of a third party candidate on the 1992 presidential election?

Clinton Intervenes With Mixed Success

When Bill Clinton became president, the more than 40-year-old American foreign policy of fighting communism had just ended. The United States needed to develop a role for itself in the post–Cold War world. Americans were willing to provide economic aid, as they did to nations of the former Soviet Union. But many of them questioned military intervention abroad, fearing a costly commitment like the Vietnam War. With violence surging in regional conflicts throughout the world, however, Clinton found it necessary to intervene. He did so with mixed success.

U.S. Intervention in Somalia and Haiti In the late 1980s, civil war broke out in Somalia. By 1991, the government had disintegrated and the fighting had caused widespread famine. In 1992, the United States led a multinational force, later joined by the UN, to bring about peace and distribute food.

The coalition fell apart in 1994 when several countries, including the United States, suffered steep casualty rates and withdrew their troops. Eventually, the UN also withdrew, and civil war dragged on for several more years in the devastated country.

Meanwhile, conflict was simmering in Haiti. In 1990, Haitians brought Jean Bertrand Aristide to the presidency, in the nation's first free elections. Less than a year later, a military coup overthrew Aristide, plunging the country into turmoil. Thousands of Haitians left the country by boat to immigrate to the United States as political refugees. Many were sent back by American immigration officials, causing a public outcry. In 1994, Clinton sent American troops to Haiti to restore Aristide to power. Although American action improved the situation, within a decade Haiti faced a sinking economy and rising rates of disease and crime.

U.S. Involvement in the Balkans Crisis In the Balkans, the collapse of communism broke up the country of Yugoslavia. For decades, the communist leader Josip Broz Tito had contained ethnic and religious strife.

But his death in 1980, and the collapse of communism in 1989, left the country with no unifying forces. Soon, four of Yugoslavia's six major republics broke away and became independent nations, and long-suppressed ethnic and religious hostilities came boiling to the surface.

In newly independent Bosnia and Herzegovina, ethnic and religious rivalries among Eastern Orthodox Serbs, Catholic Croats, and Bosnian Muslims eventually led to civil war. Bosnian Serbs, with the help of Serbian-dominated Yugoslavia, attacked Bosnians and Croats. In many cases, they forcibly removed Bosnians and Croats from their homes and later murdered them. This state-sanctioned mass murder, violence, and rape, known as **ethnic cleansing**, shocked the world. The UN intervened with humanitarian aid. Yet atrocities continued on all sides of the struggle, and years went by before the world community intervened to stop the slaughter.

Clinton Galvanizes NATO Forces Finally in the late summer of 1995, Clinton encouraged NATO to bomb Serbian strongholds. This was the first time the organization had gone into combat, and its use of force quickly brought about a cease-fire. In December 1995, the Dayton Accords established a federated, multinational Bosnia. Although the ethnic cleansing had ended, the problems of the region continued. In 1998, violence flared up anew—this time in Kosovo, a province in southern Serbia that borders Albania. The fighting once again involved ethnic cleansing and also spread to the neighboring countries of Macedonia and Albania. A NATO bombing campaign forced Serbs to withdraw from Kosovo.

The Rwanda Genocide As ethnic hatred led to atrocities in the Balkans, mass murder was also underway far to the south in the African nation of Rwanda. Between April and July of 1994, Rwanda's majority Hutu population committed genocide as they exterminated more than 800,000 members of the Tutsi population. The bloodbath in turn forced 2,000,000 people to flee Rwanda, creating a major humanitarian crisis. The UN was unable to bring about a cease-fire, and President Clinton and other world leaders were criticized for their silence on this tragedy. Eventually, Tutsi-led forces gained ground and established a government of national unity, bringing the genocide to an end.

☑ **CHECK UNDERSTANDING** What happened to Yugoslavia soon after the death of its long-time communist leader?

America and the Middle East in the 1990s

In the 1990s, Israel's military responded to attacks by Palestinians. The level of violence grew increasingly fierce. Meanwhile, instability had increased in the region as a whole. As Clinton worked to address it, violence originating in the region spread outward, with the United States increasingly a target.

Israel, the West Bank, and the Gaza Strip, 2005

>> **Analyze Maps** What city is located on the border between Israeli and Palestinian territory?

Small Steps Toward Peace in Israel In 1993, Palestinians and Israelis conducted secret negotiations in Oslo, Norway. The resulting Declaration of Principles promised Palestinian self-rule in Jericho and the Gaza Strip, as well as security for the Israelis. The PLO formally recognized Israel and Israel recognized the PLO as the representative of the Palestinian people. The PLO renounced terrorism and violence and publicly expressed the goal of peaceful coexistence with Israel.

The declaration did not fully address the issues of Israeli settlements in the West Bank or all of Israel's security concerns, however, nor did it placate extremists on either side, who were suspicious of each other's intentions. It was an interim agreement meant to lead to a permanent two-state solution.

Chronic violence continued even though Israel withdrew from much of the West Bank, and later from Gaza. Israeli Prime Minister Yitzhak Rabin, who had agreed to the declaration, was assassinated in 1995 by an Israeli who opposed the Oslo Accords.

In 2000, Clinton invited Palestinian leader Yasir Arafat and Israeli prime minister Ehud Barak to Camp David to work on a peace agreement. Despite nearly two weeks of negotiations, the summit failed to meet its goal of two states living side by side in peace. Back in Israel, Barak was replaced as prime minister by Ariel Sharon, a "hawk" who once opposed any concessions to the Palestinians. In 2005, however, Sharon withdrew all Israeli settlers from Gaza. Nonetheless, Palestinian suicide bombings increased, and with them so did crackdowns by the Israeli military.

Terrorists Hit U.S. Targets In 1993, a terrorist group exploded a truck bomb in the parking garage beneath the World Trade Center in New York City, killing six people and injuring more than one thousand others. The plot was masterminded by a Kuwaiti-born militant whose objective was revenge against the United States for its aid to Israel.

Five years after the 1993 bombing at the World Trade Center, an Islamist terrorist group called **al Qaeda** set off car bombs within minutes of each other at American embassies in Nairobi, Kenya, and Dar es Salaam, Tanzania. The blasts killed 225 people and injured more than 5,500 others. Al Qaeda was led by a wealthy man from Saudi Arabia named Osama bin Laden. Bin Laden had fought in Afghanistan in the 1980s on the side of Islamists who sought to expel the Soviet Union. By the late 1990s, he had formed al Qaeda with the purpose of ending American involvement in Muslim countries.

>> Workers at a Philippine manufacturing plant make Blu-ray components, many of which will end up in products imported into the United States.

In 2000, al Qaeda bombed the USS *Cole*, an American warship anchored off the coast of Yemen, killing 17 American sailors. In spite of these attacks, most Americans remained much more focused on domestic issues than on the threat of international terrorism. No one fully understood the threat that al Qaeda posed to American interests and world peace.

RECALL Where did Osama bin Laden establish his credentials as an Islamic fundamentalist fighter in the 1980s?

Free Trade and Treaties

In the 1990s, the United States was both an important promoter of global trade and an example for newly industrializing nations. As more nations participated in economic globalization, the United States adjusted its own policies to ensure it would remain an economic powerhouse.

U.S. International Trade Policies and the Role of Free Trade As an economic leader and champion of the free enterprise system, America has had a major role in globalization. Free trade—the guiding

The European Union

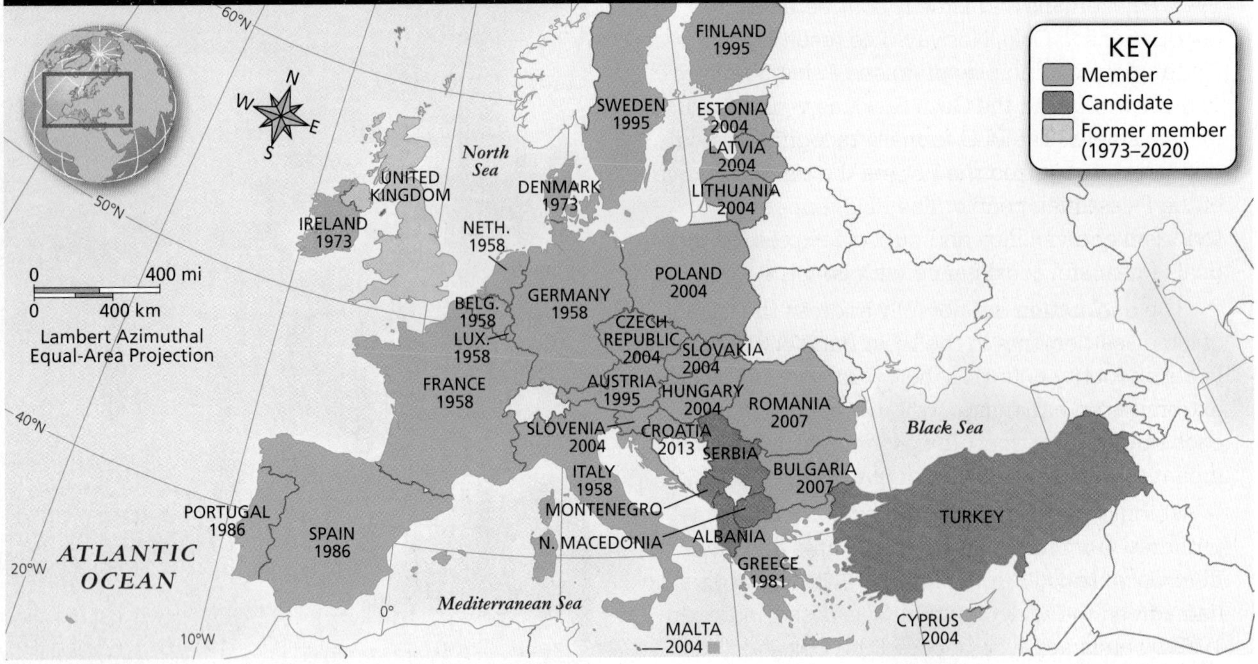

>> **Analyze Maps** In which part of Europe has EU membership expanded in the 21st century?

BOUNCE to Activate Gallery

principle of globalization—has been hotly debated in American politics. In the 1990s, Americans wanted the lower costs that free trade creates but worried about the loss of American jobs to other countries. Generally, Republicans supported the interests of business and free trade agreements. Democrats were more sympathetic to labor interests and often opposed legislation that might cost American jobs. Depending on which party was in power, free trade was either encouraged or opposed by social and political advocacy organizations across the political spectrum.

Bill Clinton challenged the traditional Democratic thinking by supporting free trade blocs, which in theory would increase the economic prosperity of particular regions. Europe is an example of a region in which such a bloc was set up. In 1958, a number of European nations established the European Economic Community, which became the **European Union (EU)** in 1993. The purpose of the union was to coordinate monetary and economic policies. By the end of the century, the EU had adopted a single currency, the euro, to promote economic efficiency. The EU's combined resources both encouraged trade among its members and challenged the economic leadership of the United States. North American free trade proponents believed a similar bloc would stimulate their own region.

The United States Joins NAFTA **The North American Free Trade Agreement (NAFTA),** a direct response to the EU, was originally proposed during the Bush administration. President Bush and leaders of the other nations signed the agreement in 1992, but Congress blocked it. It called for a gradual removal of trade restrictions among the United States, Canada, and Mexico. NAFTA's supporters maintained that creating a free trade zone in North America would promote economic growth, reduce prices, increase exports, and encourage economic investment. Most labor leaders, environmentalists, and liberal Democrats argued that NAFTA would force American manufacturers to relocate to Mexico, where wages were lower and environmental controls were less rigid. They feared that hundreds of thousands of American jobs would be lost.

President Clinton embraced NAFTA and pushed it through Congress. It went into effect in 1994, and afterward the three countries also signed agreements covering environmental protection, safety standards, and workers' rights. Fourteen years later, with the removal of remaining trade restrictions between the United States and Mexico, the final provisions of NAFTA went into effect in January 2008. The agreement continued to generate controversy, however, and it was replaced by a new trade agreement in 2020: the United States-Mexico-Canada Agreement (USMCA).

Expanding Global Trade Through the Free Enterprise System President Clinton signed a total of 270 free trade agreements, including the revision of the **General Agreement on Tariffs and Trade (GATT)** in 1994 and the accords of the **World Trade Organization (WTO)** in 1995. GATT's goal was to reduce tariffs to promote free trade. The WTO replaced GATT, expanding the organization's authority to negotiate trade agreements, settle disputes, and enforce compliance with them. Clinton also continued the strong U.S. support of the World Bank.

Critics complained that the WTO and World Bank favored business interests over environmental concerns and workers' rights. At the 1999 WTO meeting in Seattle, protesters filled the streets, disrupting the proceedings.

Yet most people agreed that economic globalization had a number of positive effects, such as exposing people to new ideas, technologies, and communications. In addition, nations involved in free trade often became more democratic. Normalizing trade—engaging in free trade with countries rather than imposing sanctions based on disagreements—also tended to strengthen economic ties. For example, normalizing trade with China encouraged that country to adopt free market reforms.

☑ **EXPLAIN** Why did some leaders support NAFTA while others opposed it?

☑ ASSESSMENT

1. **Describe** the political changes that occurred in Latin American during the 1980s and 1990s.
2. **Generate Explanations** Explain how U.S. policies influenced the fall of apartheid in South Africa.
3. **Identify Cause and Effect** Describe the events that led to Operation Desert Storm and discuss the campaign's lasting effects.
4. **Describe** President Clinton's position on free trade and explain how this challenged traditional expectations.
5. **Express Problems Clearly** Describe the problems that occurred as a result of the collapse of Yugoslavia after the Cold War.
6. **Connections to Today** How might dictators such as Saddam Hussein see the Internet as both a threat and a useful tool?

GO ONLINE to access this biography: James A. Baker III

Primary Sources

"Glory and Hope": Nelson Mandela

Nelson Mandela delivered this speech after having been elected president in South Africa's first multiracial election in 1994. Knowing that the injustices of apartheid would be hard to overcome, Mandela asked the people to work together for peace and justice.

>> Nelson Mandela and President George H.W. Bush

Your majesties, your royal highnesses, distinguished guests, comrades and friends:

Today, all of us do, by our presence here, and by our celebrations in other parts of our country and the world, confer [give] glory and hope to newborn liberty.

Out of the experience of an extraordinary human disaster that lasted too long must be born a society of which all humanity will be proud.

Our daily deeds as ordinary South Africans must produce an actual South African reality that will reinforce humanity's belief in justice, strengthen its confidence in the nobility of the human soul and sustain all our hopes for a glorious life for all. . . .

DETERMINE MEANING What does Mandela mean by "an actual South African reality"?

To my compatriots, I have no hesitation in saying that each one of us is as intimately attached to the soil of this beautiful country as are the famous jacaranda trees of Pretoria and the mimosa trees of the bushveld.

Each time one of us touches the soil of this land, we feel a sense of personal renewal. The national mood changes as the seasons change.

We are moved by a sense of joy and exhilaration when the grass turns green and the flowers bloom.

That spiritual and physical oneness we all share with this common homeland explains the depth of the pain we all carried in our hearts as we saw our country tear itself apart in terrible conflict, and as we saw it spurned, outlawed and isolated by the peoples of the world, precisely because it has become the universal base of the pernicious [highly destructive] ideology and practice of racism and racial oppression. . . .

We, the people of South Africa, feel fulfilled that humanity has taken us back into its bosom, that we, who were outlaws not so long ago, have today been given the rare privilege to be host to the nations of the world on our own soil.

We thank all our distinguished international guests for having come to take possession with the people of our country of what is, after all, a common victory for justice, for peace, for human dignity.

We trust that you will continue to stand by us as we tackle the challenges of building peace, prosperity, nonsexism, nonracialism and democracy. . . .

The time for the healing of the wounds has come.

The moment to bridge the chasms that divide us has come.

The time to build is upon us.

We have, at last, achieved our political emancipation [freedom from bondage or control by others]. We pledge ourselves to liberate all our people from the continuing bondage [slavery] of poverty, deprivation [lack of materials necessary for survival], suffering, gender and other discrimination. . . .

We have triumphed in the effort to implant [insert] hope in the breasts of the millions of our people. We enter into a covenant [binding agreement] that we shall build the society in which all South Africans, both black and white, will be able to walk tall, without any fear in their hearts, assured of their inalienable right to human dignity—a rainbow nation at peace with itself and the world.

SUMMARIZE What freedoms does Mandela call for in this passage?

As a token of its commitment to the renewal of our country, the new Interim Government of National Unity will, as a matter of urgency, address the issue of amnesty for various categories of our people who are currently serving terms of imprisonment.

We dedicate this day to all the heroes and heroines in this country and the rest of the world who sacrificed in many ways and surrendered their lives so that we could be free.

Their dreams have become reality. Freedom is their reward.

We are both humbled and elevated by the honor and privilege that you, the people of South Africa, have bestowed on us, as the first President of a united, democratic, nonracial and nonsexist South Africa, to lead our country out of the valley of darkness.

DETERMINE CENTRAL IDEAS What are the civic ideals of the new South Africa?

We understand it still that there is no easy road to freedom.

We know it well that none of us acting alone can achieve success.

We must therefore act together as a united people, for national reconciliation [a settling of differences that results in harmony], for nation building, for the birth of a new world.

Let there be justice for all. Let there be peace for all. Let there be work, bread, water, and salt for all.

Let each know that for each the body, the mind and the soul have been freed to fulfill themselves.

Never, never, and never again shall it be that this beautiful land will again experience the oppression of one by another and suffer the indignity of being the skunk of the world.

The sun shall never set on so glorious a human achievement!

Let freedom reign. God bless Africa!

PARAPHRASE In one or two sentences, write in your own words how Mandela concludes his speech.

ASSESSMENT

1. **Explain an Argument** When apartheid ended, there was a danger of a backlash by Black South Africans against white South Africans who had supported apartheid. How does Mandela's speech respond to that danger?
2. **Determine Author's Point of View** How would you describe the tone of Mandela's speech? How does this tone reflect Mandela's view of his country and its future?
3. **Determine Author's Purpose** Why do you think Mandela talks about building a new world, not just a new South Africa?

GO ONLINE to access primary sources

19.5

Computers revolutionized industry and the workplace in the last half of the twentieth century. Workers around the globe were required to learn new skills to remain competitive.

BOUNCE to Activate Flipped Video

Objectives

Assess the success of Clinton's domestic policies.

Describe the Contract With America and its impact.

Analyze the Clinton impeachment.

Evaluate the changes that new technological innovations brought to the economy and daily life in the 1990s.

Key Terms

Family Medical Leave Act
Brady Bill
Newt Gingrich
Contract With America
Kenneth Starr
impeachment
personal computer
biotechnology
satellite
Robert Johnson
Internet

Clinton and the 1990s

When Bill Clinton took the presidential oath of office on January 20, 1993, he faced a great challenge. Since 1968, Americans had chosen Republican presidents in five out of six elections. The Republican argument that government needed to be smaller and less intrusive resonated with many Americans. Clinton therefore needed to chart a middle course between the limited role for government advocated by Republicans and the traditional Democratic reliance on government programs to address social problems.

Clinton Enacts New Domestic Policies

Family Medical Leave Act Becomes Law Early in his presidency, Clinton signed the **Family Medical Leave Act**, which had been vetoed by President Bush. The act guaranteed most full-time employees 12 workweeks of unpaid leave each year for the birth and care of a newborn child, to recover from a serious illness, or to care for a close family member. The Clinton administration also raised the minimum wage, increased access to college loans, and expanded tax credits for higher education.

An Uphill Battle on Healthcare Reform Healthcare reform headed Clinton's list of priorities. The United States was the only developed country without national healthcare. Though Clinton did not advocate socialized medicine, he wanted a program that would guarantee care for all Americans. His wife, Hillary Clinton, was appointed to head a healthcare task force to investigate the issue. The task force conducted highly publicized hearings and

GO ONLINE to access your digital course

produced a long, detailed proposal that attracted immediate criticism from diverse interest groups. The bill never won congressional support and was ultimately dropped after about a year of debate.

Clinton had overestimated Americans' faith in the federal government's ability to solve the country's social problems. Many Americans did not feel that enlarging the federal bureaucracy and allowing the government to run healthcare was a good idea.

Fighting Crime and Violence Clinton also tried to address the issue of violence in American society. In 1993, he signed the **Brady Bill**, a gun-control act named for presidential aide James Brady, who had been wounded in the 1981 assassination attempt on President Reagan. Under Clinton, Congress also passed an anti-crime bill that increased funding for police and banned several kinds of assault weapons.

Still, violence continued to haunt the nation. In 1995, Americans were horrified by the bombing of a government building in Oklahoma City that killed 168 people and injured more than 800 others. The mass murder was not committed by foreign terrorists, but rather by homegrown anti-government extremists.

To ward off similar terrorist attacks, federal buildings in major cities were surrounded with barriers. New laws were passed to deter terrorism and impose stiffer penalties.

In 1999, yet another act of senseless violence stirred nationwide debate. At Colorado's Columbine High School, two heavily armed students killed 12 fellow students and a teacher, as well as wounding 24 others, before taking their own lives. In the aftermath of this tragedy, many schools across the nation installed metal detectors and other security measures. Still other schools instituted new anti-bully policies and "zero tolerance" approaches to school violence.

DESCRIBE Describe what the Clintons' healthcare reform package sought to supply for Americans.

Republicans Lead a Conservative Resurgence

After two years in office, Clinton had achieved a few lasting legislative victories. Yet the failure of his healthcare initiative signaled that his popularity, and his control of Congress, was waning. With the 1994 midterm elections approaching, congressional Republicans seized the opportunity to advance their own ideas.

>> In April 1995, domestic terrorist Timothy McVeigh detonated a bomb in front of the Alfred P. Murrah Federal Building in Oklahoma City. The attack killed more than 160 people and injured several hundred others.

>> In 1994, Congressman Newt Gingrich organized Republican opposition to Democratic policies around his Contract With America campaign.

BOUNCE to Activate Gallery

government should play a central role in the life of the nation."

Gingrich's Contract With America Georgia congressman **Newt Gingrich** led the opposition to Clinton. Gingrich was bold and aggressive and not interested in compromising with the Democrats: "We will cooperate, but we won't compromise." Many people thought that Gingrich's goal of the Republicans gaining control of the House of Representatives in 1994 was a nearly impossible task. After all, the Democrats had controlled the House for 58 of the previous 62 years.

Gingrich, however, galvanized Republicans around his **Contract With America**, a plan that attacked big government and emphasized patriotism and traditional values. The Contract With America called for congressional term limits, reduction of the federal bureaucracy, a balanced budget amendment to the Constitution, and large tax cuts, as well as increased defense spending, significant welfare reform, and tough anti-crime legislation. The idea was to capture the votes of Americans who felt the federal government was too big, too wasteful, and too liberal.

Republicans Sweep the 1994 Elections

Although most eligible voters did not vote in 1994, there was a strong turnout among Republicans. For the first time in 40 years, the Republicans won control of the House. They also captured the Senate and most of the governorships.

Newsweek magazine observed:

> "Last week in one of the most profound electoral routs in American history, Republicans won the right to occupy the Capitol and mount what their . . . commanders think of as a counterrevolution: a full-scale attack on the notion that a central government should play a central role in the life of the nation."

Once in office, Republicans in the House passed most of Gingrich's program. Getting the program through the Senate and signed by Clinton was not as successful, with only a handful of contract points becoming law. In addition, Republican attempts to slash Medicare and other government programs proved unpopular. Many Americans were also upset when the government shut down in 1995 because Congress would not pass Clinton's budget. Meanwhile, Clinton incorporated some of the conservative agenda into his own 1996 reelection bid. He signed a bill to reform welfare, passed legislation that appropriated more money for law enforcement, and called for stiffer sentencing for criminals. Finally, he made balancing the budget and reducing the federal deficit a priority.

A Strong Economy Lifts Clinton to Reelection

Beginning in the mid-1990s, the American economy broke out of recession and began to soar, starting the longest period of sustained growth in the country's history. Americans benefited from low unemployment, low inflation levels, and the government's efforts to balance the budget and reduce the deficit. In 1994, Clinton's disapproval rating had exceeded 60 percent, and few expected him to win a second term. As the 1996 election approached, however, the booming economy meant that few Americans had a compelling reason to change leadership.

The Republicans nominated Senate Majority Leader Robert Dole, a World War II hero and a moderate Republican. H. Ross Perot entered the race as the Reform Party candidate. Clinton skillfully captured the middle ground, labeling Dole as out-of-touch and Perot as a political quack. On election

"Republican Revolution" of 1994

PARTY AFFILIATION	HOUSE OF REPRESENTATIVES	CHANGE	SENATE	CHANGE
REPUBLICANS	230	+54	52	+9
DEMOCRATS	204	–54	48	–9

SOURCES: U.S. House of Representatives; U.S. Senate

>> **Analyze Charts** How did the Republican Revolution affect the balance of power between Democrats and Republicans in the federal government?

BOUNCE to Activate Chart

Federal Budget, 1990–2000

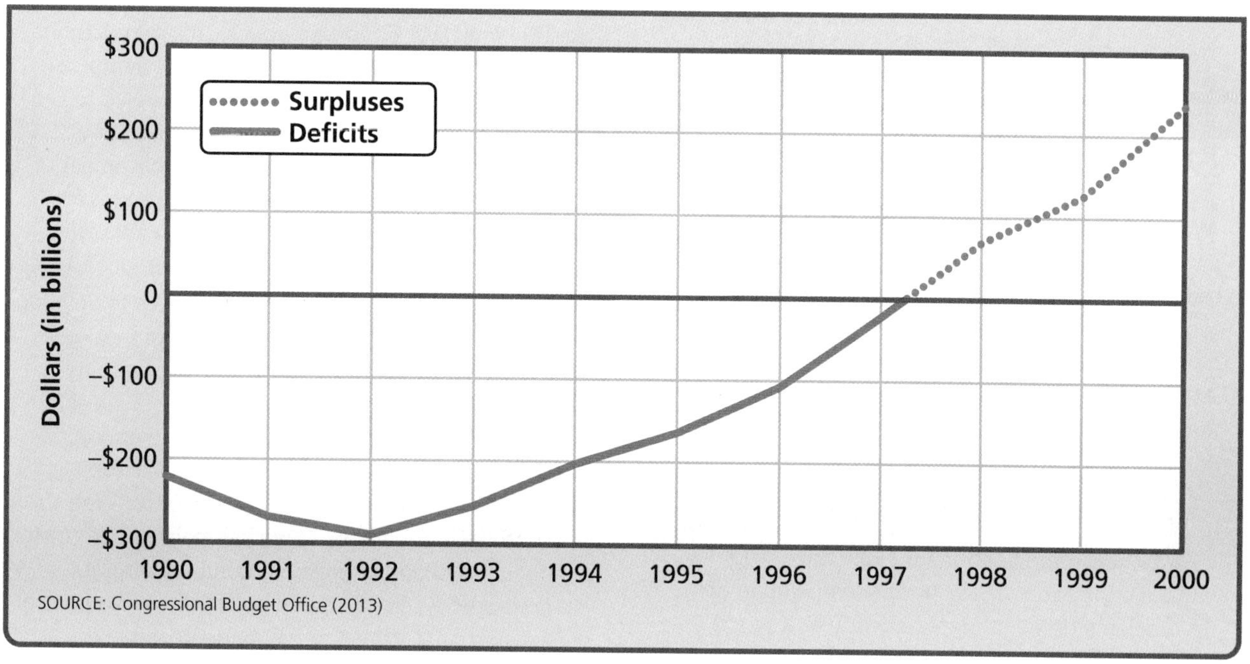

>> **Analyze Charts** What effect did President Clinton's economic policies have on the federal budget between 1993 and 2000?

day, Americans chose Clinton by a wide margin. The House of Representatives and Senate, however, retained their Republican majorities.

☑ **RECALL** Why did large numbers of Americans vote for Republican congressional candidates who supported the Contract With America?

Scandals, Impeachment, and Trial

President Clinton had dodged scandals from his first days in office. One, a sexual harassment suit, had stemmed from his years as governor of Arkansas. Another concerned investments that Bill and Hillary Clinton had made in the Whitewater Development Corporation, an Arkansas real estate company, in the 1970s and 1980s.

Investigating Clinton Leads to New Scandal A special prosecutor appointed by Attorney General Janet Reno investigated the Whitewater investment case and recommended that no criminal charges be filed. However, in July, Congress passed a new law requiring that special prosecutors be selected by a three-judge panel from the U.S. Court of Appeals. As a result, in August of 1994, special prosecutor **Kenneth Starr** was appointed to investigate the case again. In seven years of investigation, Starr failed to uncover any conclusive evidence of the Clintons' guilt, though some of their associates were convicted.

In the process of prosecuting Whitewater, Starr began investigating Clinton's relationship with a White House intern. Clinton had denied under oath that the two had had an affair. Eventually, Clinton admitted that he had lied. In 1998, Starr recommended **impeachment** proceedings on a number of counts, all related to the intern scandal rather than to Whitewater.

Impeaching and Acquitting the President Most Americans condemned Clinton's actions but opposed impeachment. Congressional Democrats, similarly, did not believe his behavior met the standard of "Treason, Bribery, or other high Crimes and Misdemeanors" required by the Constitution for the impeachment and removal of a president. Nevertheless, the House of Representatives, led by the Republican majority, impeached Clinton on charges of perjury and obstruction of justice.

In January 1999, the Senate tried the President. The removal of a president requires a two-thirds majority of senators, but Clinton's opposition did not have the necessary votes. The President was acquitted on both counts on February 12. However, the political scandal undermined confidence in the federal government and its leaders.

IDENTIFY What led to the appointment of Kenneth Starr as a special prosecutor to investigate the Whitewater case?

Digital Technology Changes American Life

During the twentieth century, the rate of technological change sped up dramatically. New technology touched every aspect of life, including how Americans worked, played, and communicated. At the same time, globalization transformed the American economy, bringing both new challenges and new opportunities.

The 1900s was a century of unparalleled change. In 1903, Orville Wright flew the first airplane. Less than 70 years later, astronaut Neil Armstrong walked on the moon. During that same span of time, television went from a novelty at a World's Fair to a standard household possession, and sophisticated microscopes and telescopes unveiled previously hidden worlds. One of the most important innovations was the development of the computer.

>> Popular computers of the 1980s and early 1990s were produced by Commodore, Texas Instruments, and Coleco.

Microchips and Microprocessors Lead to the Modern Computer Intense rivalry between enemies during World War II brought about a life-and-death race to develop new technologies, such as the computer. The U.S. government funded research that led to the creation of the first modern computer in 1946. This huge machine occupied the entire basement of the research lab. It calculated artillery ranges and performed computations for the atomic bomb.

Soon after World War II, universities and corporations joined government agencies to develop smaller, faster, more powerful computers that could perform a range of functions. The IBM company developed one of the first commercially successful computers in 1954. In the 1960s, a few companies located south of San Francisco, California, focused on developing improved technology for running the computer. Their efforts led to the microchip, a tiny fragment of silicon containing complex circuits, and the microprocessor, a silicon chip that held a central processing unit. These chips made possible the development of small computers, called **personal computers**.

Transforming Business and Industry At first, personal computers were a novelty item, used mainly by hobbyists. But by the 1980s, computers were transforming industries, research labs, and businesses. Personal computers could perform many different tasks but were small and simple enough for the average person to use. The technology that created them eventually spread to many other industries. Video games, cellular telephones, and other electronics all depended on microchips and microprocessors. Entrepreneurs played a large role in accelerating the use of personal computers. Steve Jobs's Apple Computers and Bill Gates's Microsoft made computers and software affordable for millions of Americans. Jeff Bezos's Amazon.com ushered in buying and selling products by computer. Like Andrew Carnegie and John D. Rockefeller a century before, these entrepreneurs amassed great fortunes by pioneering new technologies.

The great demand for newer, faster, and more versatile digital devices—coupled with the potential fortunes awaiting those who successfully delivered them—motivated a new breed of inventors and entrepreneurs. Improvements in technology and manufacturing helped develop faster-working and smaller components that drove down costs, allowing a great number of people to use these new technologies.

The Rise of Technology

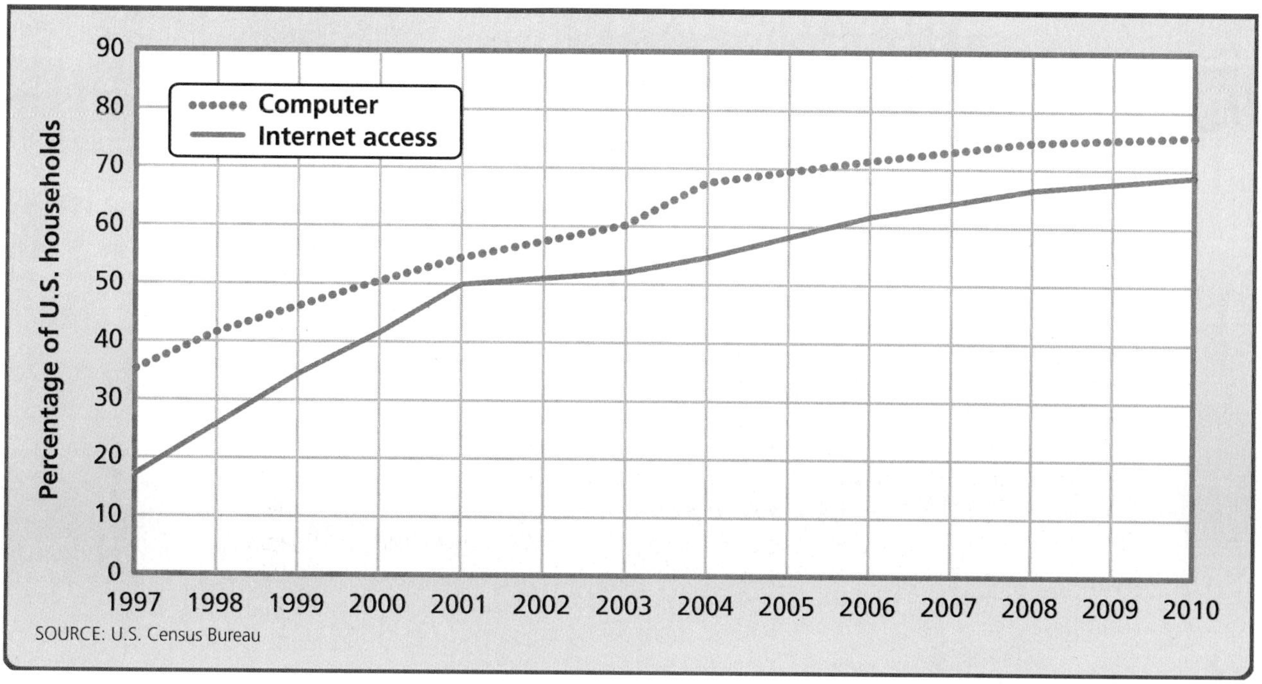

>> **Analyze Data** How did the difference between the percentage of homes with computers and those with Internet access change between 1997 and 2010?

BOUNCE to Activate Chart

Science and Agriculture Innovations Medical science also moved ahead by gigantic leaps in the late twentieth century, often aided by computer technology. Scientists developed drugs that extended patients' lives, reduced pain, and battled a huge number of diseases. They made artificial hearts and learned how to successfully transplant body organs. Such advancements, along with **biotechnology**, or the use of living organisms in the development of new products, produced a level of healthcare far above that known to any previous generation. Many of the advances in the biological sciences were spurred by federal research grants, such as those from the National Institute of Health and the National Science Foundation.

Advances in agricultural technology, including improved machinery, irrigation techniques, and growing methods, have brought profound changes to American society. While farms have grown larger and more productive, fewer people are needed to work them. In 1900, 50 percent of the labor force worked on farms. At the end of the century, only 2 percent did.

Satellite Technology Transforms Communication and Navigation Satellite technology increased the speed of global communications. **Satellites** are mechanical devices that orbit Earth in space, receiving and sending information-filled signals that are then relayed to televisions, telephones, and computers. Originally developed for military purposes during the Cold War, satellite technology was used in the 1970s by businessman Ted Turner to run the first "superstation." In 1980, **Robert Johnson** launched BET (Black Entertainment Television) using technology to broadcast into cable-equipped households across the country. Also in 1980, Turner began the 24-hour-per-day, all-news Cable News Network (CNN). Cellular telephones used similar satellite technology, allowing people to communicate away from their homes.

Scientists and engineers in the U.S. Department of Defense also applied satellite technology to develop the first Global Positioning System (GPS). They developed the system for use in the American military, but nonmilitary use later became widespread.

In GPS, a receiver on Earth measures how long radio signals from multiple satellites take to arrive at its location. Using this information, the receiver performs the necessary calculations to determine the user's latitude, longitude, or even altitude. Since its inception, the accuracy of GPS (and the fact that its signals are available for free) has caused a massive change in navigation for industrial and everyday users.

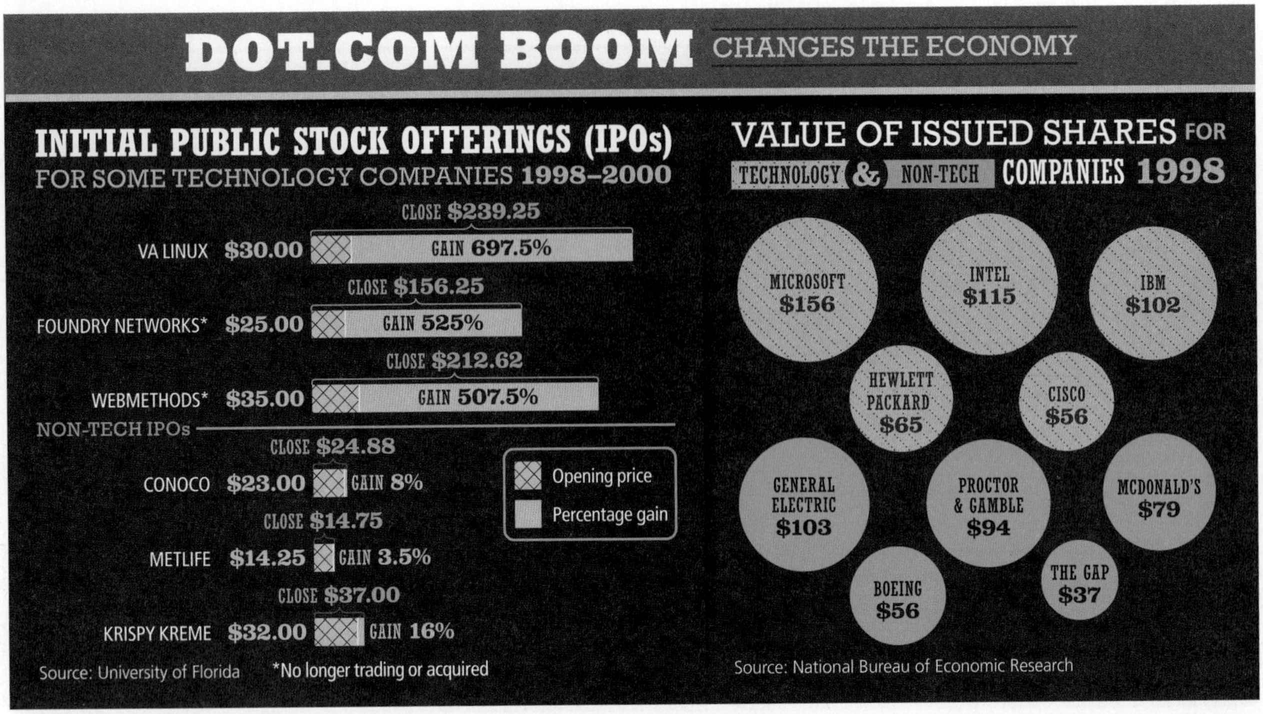

>> **Analyze Data** What does this data suggest about the value of technology companies in the late 1990s?

Creating the Internet In the 1970s, various branches of the U.S. government along with groups in several American universities led efforts to link computer systems together via cables and satellites. By the 1980s, the **Internet**, or World Wide Web, had been born, reaching the general public in the 1990s.

The Web made communication and access to information almost instantaneous. This breakthrough completely and profoundly transformed commerce, education, research, and entertainment. Email provided great advantages over the delays of postal mail and the expense of telephones. The impact has been especially great on people living in rural areas. The Internet's immense storage capacity also changed the world of research. In the 1980s, scientists and scholars primarily used the Internet to share information. By the early 1990s, they were using it as a research tool and an online database.

The Tech Boom Fuels Economic Growth In many ways, the free enterprise system drives technological innovation and has filled the marketplace with inexpensive personal computers, global positioning products, and cell phones. Fueled in part by the high-tech boom, the U.S. economy in the 1990s flourished. The strong economy produced the lowest unemployment rate in 30 years and high home-ownership rates. In addition, the federal government operated on the first balanced budget since the late 1960s and the largest budget surplus in U.S. history.

DESCRIBE What was the original inspiration for the development of the Internet?

ASSESSMENT

1. **Generate Explanations** Explain how the passage of new legislation reformed employment and education during Bill Clinton's presidency.
2. **Describe** the major steps that were taken to address crime and violence in the United States in the 1990s.
3. **Draw Conclusions** Discuss the impact of the conservative resurgence and determine its effect on the 1996 presidential election.
4. **Generate Explanations** Explain how changes in technology affected the U.S. economy during the twentieth century.
5. **Connections to Today** The Internet began as a tool for sharing information. Today, it is used for this purpose, but also as an online database. How do these two uses combine to pose a potential threat to privacy?

GO ONLINE to access this biography: Bill Clinton

1998 State of the Union Address: President Bill Clinton

Article II, Section 3 of the Constitution says, in part, that the President "shall from time to time give to the Congress Information of the State of the Union, and recommend to their Consideration such Measures as he shall judge necessary and expedient." In 1947, a title that had been used informally for this speech, the State of the Union Address, became its official name. President Bill Clinton gave the following State of the Union Address on January 27, 1998, midway through his second term.

>> President Bill Clinton speaks during a State of the Union address.

. . . We have moved past the sterile debate between those who say government is the enemy and those who say government is the answer. My fellow Americans, we have found a third way. We have the smallest government in 35 years, but a more progressive one. We have a smaller government, but a stronger nation.

DRAW INFERENCES To whom is the President referring when he speaks of "those who say government is the enemy and those who say government is the answer"?

We are moving steadily toward an even stronger America in the 21st century, an economy that offers opportunity, a society rooted in responsibility, and a nation that lives as a community.

First, Americans in this chamber and across our nation have pursued a new strategy for prosperity: Fiscal discipline to cut interest rates and spur growth. Investments in education and skills and science and technology and transportation to prepare our people for the new economy. New markets for American products and American workers.

When I took office, the deficit for 1998 was projected to be $357 billion and heading higher. This year, our deficit is projected to be $10 billion and heading lower.

For three decades, six presidents have come before you to warn of the damage deficits pose to our nation. Tonight I come before you to announce that the federal deficit, once so incomprehensibly large that it had 11 zeros, will be simply zero.

I will submit to Congress for 1999 the first balanced budget in 30 years. And, if we hold fast to fiscal discipline, we may balance the budget this year, four years ahead of schedule.

You can all be proud of that because turning a sea of red ink into black is no miracle. It is the product of hard work by the American people and of two visionary actions in Congress—the courageous vote in 1993 that led to a cut in the deficit of 90 percent.

DRAW CONCLUSIONS Why would members of Congress have needed courage to vote for a budget that cut the deficit?

And the truly historic bipartisan balanced budget agreement passed by this Congress.

. . . Last year, from this podium, I said that education has to be our highest priority. I laid out a ten-point plan to move us forward and urged all of us to let politics stop at the schoolhouse door. . . .

Last year, I proposed and you passed 220,000 new Pell grant scholarships [money for college that does not have to be repaid] for deserving students.

Student loans—student loans, already less expensive and easier to repay, now you get to deduct the interest.

Families all over America now can put their savings into new tax-free education IRAs. And this year, for the first two years of college, families will get a $1,500 tax credit—a Hope scholarship that will cover the cost of most community college tuition.

And for junior and senior year, graduate school, and job training, there is a lifetime learning credit. You did that and you should be very proud of it.

And because of these actions, I have something to say to every family listening to us tonight. Your children can go on to college. If you know a child from a poor family, tell her not to give up. She can go on to college. If you know a young couple struggling with bills, worried they won't be able to send their children to college, tell them not to give up—their children can go on to college.

If you know somebody who's caught in a dead-end job and afraid he can't afford the classes necessary to get better jobs for the rest of his life, tell him not to give up—he can go on to college.

Because of the things that have been done, we can make college as universal in the 21st century as high school is today.

And my friends, that will change the face and future of America. . . .

PARAPHRASE What are the main points the President is making about higher education?

As we enter the 21st century, the global economy requires us to seek opportunity not just at home but in all the markets of the world. We must shape this global economy, not shrink from it.

In the last five years we have led the way in opening new markets with 240 trade agreements that remove foreign barriers to products bearing the proud stamp, Made in the USA.

Today, record-high exports account for fully one-third of our economic growth. I want to keep them going because that's the way to keep America growing and to advance a safer, more stable world.

ASSESS AN ARGUMENT Why is the President making these points about the global economy? How effective is his argument?

Now, all of you know, whatever your views are, that I think this is a great opportunity for America. I know there is opposition to more comprehensive trade agreements.

I have listened carefully, and I believe that the opposition is rooted in two fears. First, that our trading partners will have lower environmental and labor standards, which will give them an unfair advantage in our market and do their own people no favors, even if there's more business.

And second, that if we have more trade, more of our workers will lose their jobs and have to start over. I think we should seek to advance worker and environmental standards around the world. I have made it abundantly clear that it should be a part of our trade agenda, but we cannot influence other countries' decisions if we send them a message that we're backing away from trade with them. . . .

ASSESSMENT

1. **Determine Author's Point of View** What is President Clinton's point of view on trade agreements?
2. **Explain an Argument** What argument does the President make in response to those who are concerned about environmental and labor issues in the countries with which we sign trade agreements?
3. **Develop Empathy** How does President Clinton help his audience to empathize with those struggling to pay for college?
4. **Analyze Style and Rhetoric** What words or approach does the President use to tout his accomplishments with regard to the budget?

GO ONLINE to access primary sources

Connections to Today

These cyberwarfare operators serving with the Maryland Air National Guard are monitoring cyberattacks on the operations floor of the 275th Cyber Operations Squadron, known as the Hunter's Den.

Take Action to Learn About Technology Safety

The Internet, cell phones, Global Positioning Systems (GPS)—these technologies are so tightly woven into the fabric of our days that we reach for them without thinking, the same way we reach for a toothbrush or a pen. But while using them, we must be aware of their potential risks.

1. **Choose** one of the following technology-related topics:
    - **Privacy:** Advertisers use "cookies" to track consumers' online activities and collect personal information. How can we protect our right to privacy?
    - **Identity Theft:** The Internet has led to a rise in identity theft. What can be done to help fight this crime?
    - **Cyberattacks:** What steps has the government taken to prevent attacks on infrastructure, elections, and businesses?
2. **Ask Questions** Generate a list of questions about your topic.
3. **Learn** about the topic by conducting research. Use online sources, including interviews and newspaper articles. Are there any major debates related to this topic? What are the arguments on each side?
4. **Organize a School Assembly** Organize an assembly to educate your classmates about the topic you researched. Invite a local tech company representative to speak to the group. Create visuals to show during the assembly that highlight key statistics, risks, and ways to protect against those risks.

Topic 19 Quick Study Guide

LESSON SUMMARIES

Use these Lesson Summaries, and the longer versions available online, to review the key ideas for each lesson in this Topic.

Lesson 1: The Conservative Movement Surges

In the 1970s the conservative movement of the New Right grew rapidly. Conservatives opposed the counterculture and blamed liberal policies for economic problems. They believed that the government taxed citizens and businesses too heavily and spent too much on the wrong programs. Concern with cultural change caused more religious groups to become actively involved in politics, such as the Reverend Jerry Falwell's Moral Majority. The conservative movement helped Ronald Reagan defeat Jimmy Carter in the 1980 presidential election.

Lesson 2: The Reagan Era

President Reagan reduced taxes and removed government control over industries. He also appointed conservative judges to federal courts and increased defense spending. While some grew rich, the number of poor increased and the national debt rose. Reagan remained popular and was reelected overwhelmingly in 1984.

Lesson 3: The Cold War Ends

Under President Reagan, the United States worked to weaken communism. Relations between the superpowers improved. The Cold War ended as communists lost power across Eastern Europe, and the Soviet Union fragmented. However, Reagan's second term was tarnished by a scandal involving weapons sales to Iran.

Lesson 4: A New Era in Foreign Policy

Under President George H. W. Bush, U.S. troops invaded Panama and arrested its dictator for drug trafficking. In the Middle East, U.S. forces went to war against Iraq after Iraq invaded Kuwait. In 1992, William Jefferson Clinton was elected President. Clinton intervened in conflicts in Somalia and Haiti and persuaded NATO to act militarily in the former Yugoslavia. The terrorist group al Qaeda attacked targets around the world, including a United States warship.

Lesson 5: Clinton and the 1990s

President Clinton was opposed by Newt Gingrich, who helped Republicans win sweeping victories in the 1994 midterm election. A scandal over Clinton's relationship with a young intern brought the President to trial, during which he was impeached by the House and acquitted by the Senate. The 1980s and 1990s also saw rapid technological change that began transforming modern life.

QUEST! FINDINGS

Hold Your Civic Discussion Refer to your responses to the Quest Connections to help you prepare for and hold a civic discussion about government's role in the economy. Use the rubric and other Quest resources online to guide your work.

GO ONLINE to access lesson summaries

VISUAL REVIEW

Use these graphics to review some of the key terms, people, and ideas from this Topic.

Key Dates in the Conservative Resurgence

1964	President Johnson signs Civil Rights Act; Southern Democrats begin defecting to Republican Party.
1968	In this presidential election year, disagreement over the Vietnam War splits and weakens the Democratic Party.
1973	The Court finds that the Constitution recognizes a woman's right to terminate her pregnancy through the first trimester.
1977	In Dade County, Florida, Anita Bryant launches anti-gay campaign, focusing conservative attention on the growing gay-rights movement.
1979	Reverend Jerry Falwell founds the Moral Majority; opposes *Engel* v. *Vitale, Roe* v. *Wade*, the ERA, and gay rights.
1980	Moral Majority mobilizes millions of voters to help elect Ronald Reagan.
1983	In Orlando, Florida, President Ronald Reagan denounces the Soviet Union as an "Evil Empire."

Liberal and Conservative Positions in the 1980s

LIBERAL POSITION	CONSERVATIVE POSITION
• Federal Government can improve lives through social programs. • The law should protect rights of minorities and women. • Industry should be regulated. • Encourage international diplomacy to combat communism; support détente	• Large federal government endangers economic growth and personal freedom • Policies of 1960s and 1970s are wasteful. • Reduce taxes to spur growth • Limit regulation of industry • Strengthen traditional values; oppose the counterculture • Confront communism abroad

President Reagan's Foreign Policy

Middle East	• Helps Anti-Soviet rebels in Afghanistan • Sends U.S. Marines to Lebanon but withdraws them after a terrorist bombing there
Latin America	• In Nicaragua, helps anticommunist Contras fight the Sandanista government • In El Salvador, supports the right-wing government against leftist rebels
The Caribbean	• U.S. troops invade Grenada to oppose communist forces.
Africa	• U.S. planes bomb Libya in retaliation for a terrorist attack in Berlin.

Highlights of the Late Twentieth Century

CLINTON PRESIDENCY
• 1992: NAFTA; troops to Somalia • 1993: Brady Bill; Declaration of Principles • 1994: Troops to Haiti • 1995: Forces into Bosnia as part of NATO • 1996: Welfare reform bill • 1999: Impeached by House; acquitted by Senate
TECHNOLOGICAL ADVANCES
• The Internet • Global communications • GPS navigation • Artificial hearts; new drugs and procedures • Improved farm machinery and techniques; larger farms

Topic 19 Assessment

KEY TERMS, PEOPLE, AND IDEAS

1. What kinds of groups made up the coalition of the **New Right**?
2. What policies did **Ronald Reagan** promote during the 1980 election?
3. What is the theory behind **supply-side economics**?
4. What was the goal of the Gramm Rudman-Hollings Act?
5. What events ended the Cold War in 1991?
6. What contradiction in the Reagan administration's foreign policy came to light in the **Iran-Contra affair**?
7. What events led to **Operation Desert Storm**?
8. How did schools across the country react to the tragedy at Columbine High School in Colorado?
9. What changes did the **Internet** bring about?

CRITICAL THINKING

10. **Identify Cause and Effect** (a.) What economic developments contributed to the conservative resurgence? (b.) What solutions to America's economic problems did conservatives support?
11. **Make Inferences** What caused the realignment of white voters in the Deep South?
12. **Cite Evidence** What effect did Reagan have on the labor movement?
13. **Determine Central Ideas** What two main events led to the break up of Yugoslavia?
14. **Draw Conclusions** What elements of the Conservative agenda did President Clinton incorporate into his 1996 election bid?
15. **Summarize** What industries helped power economic growth in the 1990s?
16. **Analyze Maps** Study the map at the top of the next column. (a.) What former communist nation broke up into the new nations shown here? (b.) Why did this event lead to an international crisis?

17. **Writing Activity: Write an Explanatory Essay** Use the excerpt below and your knowledge of history to write an essay explaining how the debate over federal spending influenced the politics of the 1990s.

> Borrowing, in lieu of higher taxes or lower government spending, may be viewed as appropriate during times of economic recessions, war, and other temporary challenges. . . . Federal borrowing might also be viewed as appropriate for federal investment, such as building roads, training workers, and conducting scientific research, contributing to the nation's capital stock and productivity. . . . In concept, federal spending that is well chosen . . . could ultimately contribute to producing a larger economy from which to pay the interest and principal on the borrowed funds. However, in practice, [the Congressional Budget Office] concluded that many federal investments might not significantly increase economic growth because some are selected for political or other noneconomic reasons. . . .
> *—from Federal Debt: Answers to Frequently Asked Questions, U.S. Government Accountability Office, 2004*

18. **Connections to Today** The Internet, developed in the 1970s, has led to many questions about protecting people's privacy. What should government, corporations, and individuals do to address this issue? Write a proposal focusing on the area you researched that outlines one specific action for each entity.

DOCUMENT-BASED QUESTIONS

In the early 1980s, President Reagan's foreign policy was highly controversial. Read the documents below, then answer the questions that follow.

DOCUMENT A

This excerpt is from President Ronald Reagan's famous "Evil Empire" speech in Orlando, Florida, in 1983.

> The truth is that a [nuclear] freeze now would be a very dangerous fraud, for that is merely the illusion of peace. The reality is that we must find peace through strength.
>
> I would agree to a freeze if only we could freeze the Soviets' global desires. A freeze at current levels of weapons would remove any incentive for the Soviets to negotiate seriously in Geneva. . . .
>
> So, in your discussions of the nuclear freeze proposals, I urge you to beware the temptation of pride—the temptation of blithely declaring yourselves above it all and label both sides equally at fault, to ignore the facts of history and the aggressive impulses of an evil empire, to simply call the arms race a giant misunderstanding and thereby remove yourself from the struggle between right and wrong and good and evil.
>
> *—Ronald Reagan, address to the National Association of Evangelicals in Orlando, Florida*

DOCUMENT B

This photograph shows Soviet leader Mikhail Gorbachev and President Ronald Reagan at the 1988 Moscow Summit Conference.

DOCUMENT C

This excerpt concerning U.S.-Soviet relations is from the State Department's website.

> Although formal nuclear arms control talks resumed, the relationship between Washington and Moscow remained tense throughout Reagan's first term. The President spoke of leaving "Marxism-Leninism on the ash-heap of history;" labeled the Soviet Union an "evil empire;" and introduced the Strategic Defense Initiative ("Star Wars"), which Soviet leaders found highly threatening.
>
> *—U.S. Department of State Office of the Historian*

DOCUMENT D

This excerpt is from a *Washington Post* article about Ronald Reagan and the Cold War.

> Less than a year after Reagan left office, the Berlin Wall fell, and the Cold War ended in 1991. The Soviet collapse was the result of many things, including shocks such as the Chernobyl disaster, rebellion in the Baltic republics and the rising expectations of consumers in a socialist system that could not produce a decent pair of jeans.
>
> But one of the major shocks was Reagan.
>
> *—David E. Hoffman, "Hastening an End to the Cold War,"* The Washington Post, *June 6, 2004*

19. In Document A, Reagan argues that a freeze would
A. allow the forces of good to triumph.
B. limit U.S. bargaining power.
C. force the Soviets to disarm.
D. end religious liberty.

20. Analyze Photographs Based on Document B, what progress was made in nuclear negotiations with the Soviets under Reagan?

21. Document C describes Reagan's foreign policy speeches as
A. alarming the Soviets.
B. highly religious in tone.
C. reassuring to the Soviets.
D. cautious and calculating.

22. In Document D, the writer says that the Soviet Union collapsed
A. despite Reagan's efforts.
B. because Reagan forced the Soviets to compete.
C. because its economy was weak.
D. for many reasons, including Reagan's policies.

23. Writing Task Write a paragraph explaining the role that Ronald Reagan played in the end of the Cold War. Use these sources as well as additional information you have learned.

GO ONLINE to access more practice

Topic 20

America in the Twenty-First Century (2000–Today)

ESSENTIAL QUESTION What are the benefits and costs of technology?

GO ONLINE to access the eText, videos, Interactive Primary Sources, Biographies, and other online resources.

Woman using Google Earth application on a tablet computer

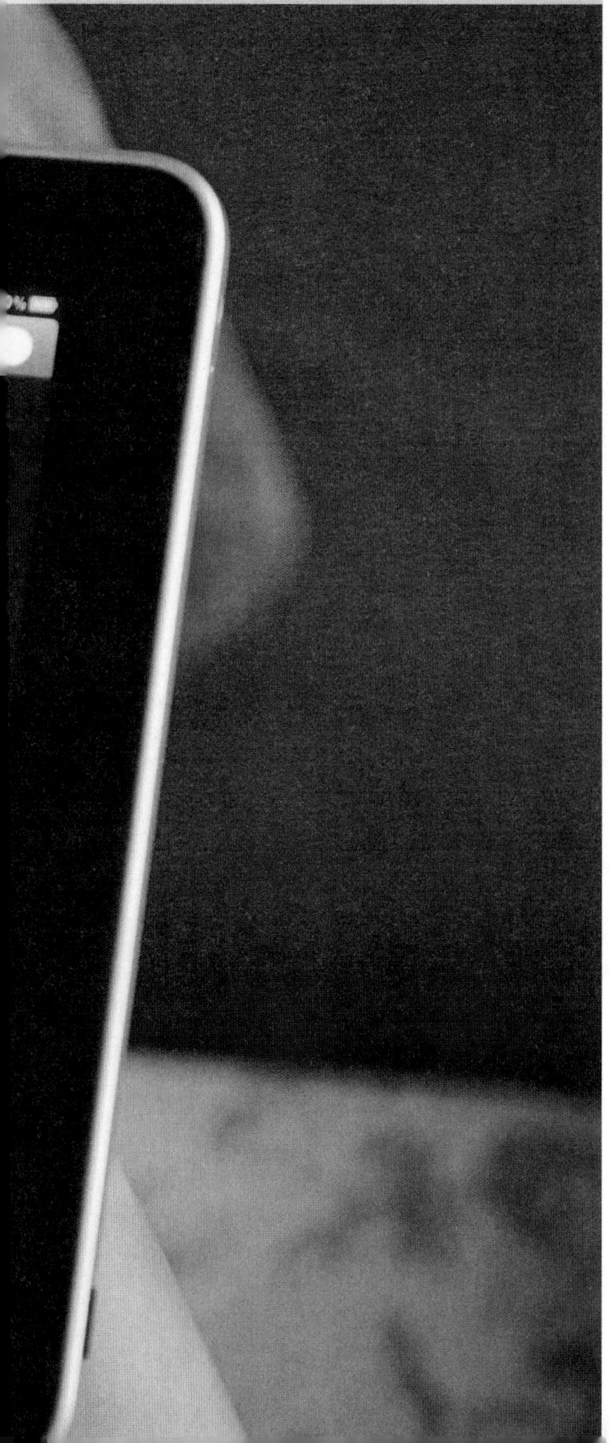

Connections to Today

Social media uses technology to connect people and ideas. People use social media to inform their friends and other citizens to take action on important issues. They post videos, write blogs, and display information in new ways to inspire others. Yet, it's important to think critically about what you see on social media platforms. Some of it may not be accurate or could contain negative messages.

In this topic, you will read about technology. Have you ever seen a video, blog, or post that inspired you in a positive way?

NBC LEARN

Learn more about Leslie Bradshaw, a technology entrepreneur.

BOUNCE to Activate My Story Video

Topic 20 Overview

In this Topic, you'll learn about America in the twenty-first century. Look at the lesson outline and explore the timeline. As you study this Topic, you'll complete the Quest Inquiry.

LESSON OUTLINE	
20.1 The George W. Bush Presidency	**20.3** The Donald Trump Presidency
20.2 The Barack Obama Presidency	**20.4** Americans Look to the Future

Key Events of America in the Twenty-First Century

2000
Florida vote recount in presidential election; George W. Bush elected

2001
Terrorists attack the United States; U.S. invades Afghanistan

2003
War in Iraq begins

2008
Great Recession begins; Barack Obama elected President

2009
American Recovery and Reinvestment enacted

2010
U.S. combat mission in Iraq ends; Affordable Care Act enacted

2016
Donald Trump elected President

2019
Trump impeached

2020
COVID-19 spreads to the United States; Joe Biden elected President

2000 | 2005 | 2010 | 2015 | 2020

QUEST! INQUIRY

Creating a U.S. Citizenship Course

What is your definition of a good citizen? What are some things that all U.S. citizens should know? In this Quest you'll learn more about American values and the duties and responsibilities of citizenship as you create a course for prospective U.S. citizens.

STEP 1
Read the project launch and select quotes from the recommended source to include on your timeline.

STEP 2
Divide American history into distinct historical eras and write test questions relating to each of these eras.

STEP 3
With your team, create a multimedia course using maps, charts, and other graphics to show how certain American values developed over time.

STEP 4
Present your course to an audience of your classmates or to a group of prospective citizens. Hold a team meeting to reflect on what you have learned.

GO ONLINE to access complete Quest materials

20.1

On October 17, 2000, Republican candidate George W. Bush (left) and Democratic candidate Al Gore (right) appeared in their third and final debate of the presidential campaign.

BOUNCE to Activate Flipped Video

Objectives

Assess the outcome of the 2000 presidential election.

Explain the goals and achievements of George W. Bush's domestic policy.

Explain the significance of terrorist attacks on the United States and U.S. involvement in world affairs.

Summarize the important issues of Bush's second term.

Understand the causes and effects of the 2008 financial crisis and economic recession.

Key Terms

George W. Bush
No Child Left Behind Act
Taliban
USA PATRIOT Act
Department of Homeland Security
weapons of mass destruction (WMD)
habeas corpus
Lionel Sosa

The George W. Bush Presidency

The year 2000 saw the Clinton presidency drawing to a close. Voters and candidates geared up for the 2000 presidential race, which promised to be a close election.

Controversy in the 2000 Election

Clinton's Vice President, Al Gore, Jr., of Tennessee, ran for the Democrats. Gore selected Connecticut Senator Joseph Lieberman as his Vice President. Lieberman was the first Jewish candidate on the ticket of a major party.

The Republicans chose **George W. Bush** as their candidate. A son of George H.W. Bush and a former governor of Texas, Bush was popular with conservatives. As governor, Bush had worked with Democrats as well as Republicans. He struck many Americans as sincere.

Ralph Nader, a third-party candidate from the left-of-center Green Party, also joined the presidential race in 2000. Many Democrats urged Nader to withdraw from the race, pointing out that any vote for him would likely be a vote taken away from Gore. Nader's candidacy would end up having a profound impact on the election.

A Close Vote On election night, Americans watched as the results came in. The vote margin in the Electoral College was razor thin. Although Gore received a half million more votes than Bush, both fell short of winning the 270 electoral votes needed to capture the presidency. The issue was Florida's 25 electoral votes. The popular vote in Florida was so close that a state law mandated

GO ONLINE to access your digital course

an automatic statewide recount. Bush led by a margin of 537 popular votes. He was awarded 271 electoral votes, one more than was needed to win the election. Nader received more than 97,000 votes in Florida. If, as many Democrats believe, the vast majority of votes for Nader would have otherwise gone to Gore, then Gore would have garnered Florida's 25 electoral votes and won the presidency.

The Supreme Court Steps In Given the extreme closeness of the votes, Democrats demanded a hand recount in several Florida counties. Republicans countered by suing in a Miami court to prevent the recount.

For more than a month, confusion reigned. The election was now affecting the relationships among the legislative, executive, and judicial branches of government.

Finally, the Supreme Court ruled on the issue. In the case of *Bush* v. *Gore*, the court ended the re-recounting by a 5-to-4 decision. On December 12, 2000, Gore conceded defeat, and Bush delivered a conciliatory victory speech.

CHECK UNDERSTANDING How did the Supreme Court end up deciding the winner of the 2000 election?

The Bush Domestic and International Agenda

Once in office, Bush turned his attention to domestic issues. Like most Republicans, Bush believed that tax cuts would stimulate the economy and create new jobs. In 2001, Bush pushed a highly controversial $1.3 trillion tax cut through Congress. The tax cut put more money in the hands of consumers. Critics pointed out that most of the benefits of the tax cut went to the wealthiest Americans. The tax cut also increased the federal budget deficit.

Focus on Education Bush's other domestic priority was education. He supported legislation that tied the federal funding of schools to academic achievement. The 2002 **No Child Left Behind Act** penalized schools that did not reach federal performance standards. It also called for improving teacher quality and other reforms.

Bush also addressed the concerns of older Americans who faced rising costs for prescription drugs. In 2003, Congress extended Medicare to cover prescription drugs for senior citizens. The measure was controversial. It was expensive and many seniors found its provisions confusing and its coverage inadequate.

Presidential Election of 2000

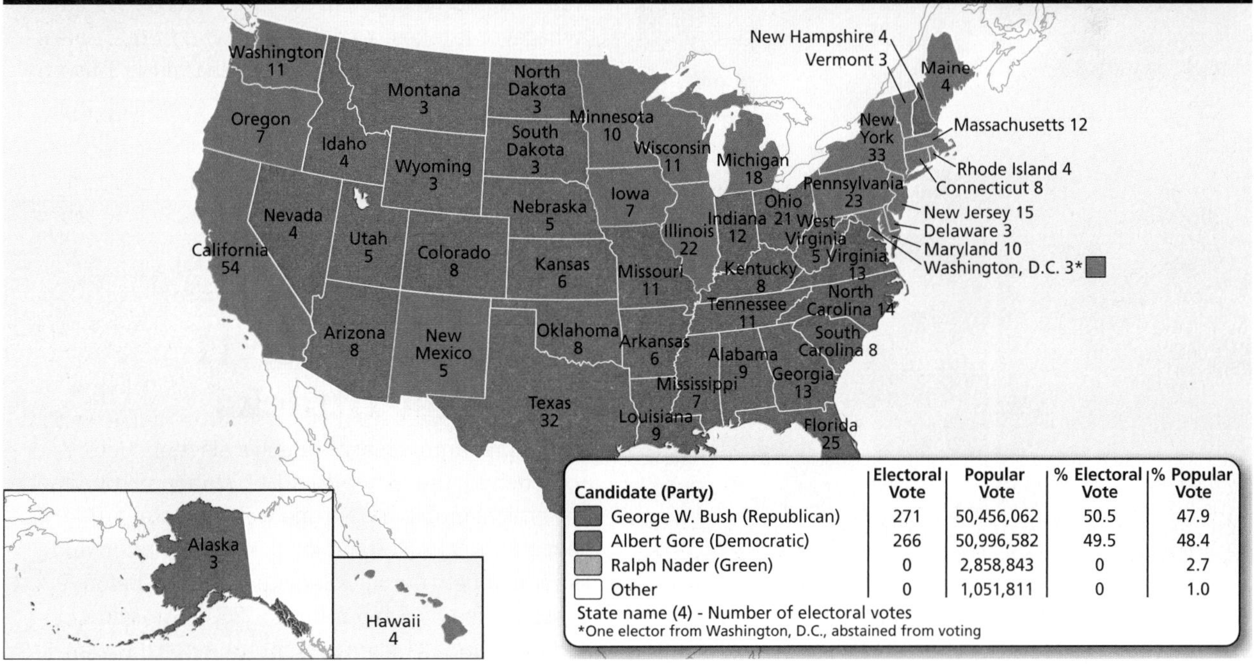

Candidate (Party)	Electoral Vote	Popular Vote	% Electoral Vote	% Popular Vote
George W. Bush (Republican)	271	50,456,062	50.5	47.9
Albert Gore (Democratic)	266	50,996,582	49.5	48.4
Ralph Nader (Green)	0	2,858,843	0	2.7
Other	0	1,051,811	0	1.0

State name (4) - Number of electoral votes
*One elector from Washington, D.C., abstained from voting

>> **Analyze Maps** In general, which regions of the United States voted for Bush? Which voted for Gore?

>> In 2002, President Bush signed the No Child Left Behind Act, fulfilling his campaign promise to pursue a domestic agenda that improved educational opportunities for America's children.

>> On September 11, 2001, the north tower of the World Trade Center (left) was already on fire when a second airliner crashed into the south tower (right).

Reforming Entitlements In his inaugural address, Bush promised to reform Social Security and Medicare, the government-run health plan for senior citizens. Together these programs account for about one third of the federal budget. Bush was concerned that because of a rapidly aging U.S. population and the rising cost of Medicare, these government programs would eventually become insolvent unless changes were made. Bush was able to make some progress on Medicare with the Medicare Act of 2003. But Democratic opposition to Social Security reform blocked Bush's efforts.

Bush's Foreign Policy In February 2005, the Kyoto Protocol went into effect around the world. The treaty signed by 140 nations is aimed at controlling global warming linked to carbon dioxide and other greenhouse gases. Negotiations took place in Kyoto, Japan, in 1997, with the help of the United States. Just months after assuming the presidency in 2001, George W. Bush announced that the United States would not abide by the treaty. The Bush administration argued that the treaty did not place emission limits on developing countries and that it could harm the U.S. economy. Many considered the Kyoto Protocol as an example of an international treaty undermining U.S. sovereignty.

In Asia, President Bush was faced with a number of challenges. North Korea admitted that it was developing nuclear weapons and threatened to unleash the deadly weapons if provoked by the United States. The nation's relationship with China was strained when Bush declared that he would do "whatever it takes" to defend Taiwan from China's aggression and then offered to sell arms to Taiwan. China considers Taiwan a defector province, but Taiwan considers itself independent from China.

☑ **RECALL** Why did the Bush administration decide to pull out of the Kyoto Protocol?

The September 11 Terrorist Attacks

As the first anniversary of Bush's election victory approached, the nation faced a number of important but typical problems. No one was expecting a devastating attack that would stun the nation and usher in a new era in U.S. history. Shortly before 9 A.M. Eastern time on September 11, 2001, American Airlines Flight 11 slammed into the north tower of the World Trade Center in New York City. Soon another hijacked plane hit the World Trade Center.

Just over an hour after the first crash, the World Trade Center towers began to collapse, spewing dust and debris over the city, and trapping the hundreds of firefighters and police who had gone into the towers to rescue people. As panicked people fled the area around the site, stunned Americans watched the horrific scenes unfold on their televisions. These two crashes were not accidents, but part of a carefully planned assault on the United States.

At 9:40 A.M. a third airliner that had been hijacked after leaving Washington, D.C., crashed into the Pentagon. Meanwhile, passengers on a fourth hijacked plane learned of the earlier crashes on their cellphones. They bravely stormed the cockpit, refusing to allow the hijackers to target another building. At 10:03 A.M., this fourth airliner crashed in a field near Pittsburgh. Soon after the attacks, it was confirmed that the al Qaeda Islamist terrorist group had spearheaded the attacks. In time, Americans also learned that nearly 3,000 people had died as a result of the attacks on 9/11.

>> In addition to the September 11 attacks in New York City, hijackers crashed a plane into the Pentagon in northern Virginia, taking the lives of more than one hundred government employees.

Al Qaeda's Campaign of Terrorism The suddenness, surprise, and cruelty of the 9/11 attacks against thousands of defenseless people was unprecedented in American history. However, Americans soon began to realize that the 9/11 attacks were the most destructive in a series of attacks that al Qaeda had launched against the United States. Al Qaeda, led by Osama bin Laden, the son of a wealthy businessman from Saudi Arabia, was an Islamist terrorist group. One of its goals was to end all American involvement in Muslim countries.

Throughout the 1990s, al Qaeda had been targeting Americans at home and abroad, and in fact, it had attempted to blow up the World Trade Center once before. In 1993 it exploded a bomb at the site, killing six people and injuring more than a thousand. In 1998, the organization set off car bombs at American embassies in Nairobi, Kenya, and Dar es Salaam, Tanzania, killing 225 people and injuring more than 5,500. In 2000, al Qaeda bombed the U.S.S. *Cole*, an American ship anchored off the coast of Yemen, killing 17 American sailors. In 2001, al Qaeda chose to attack the World Trade Center and the Pentagon because these buildings represented American economic and military power.

>> Osama bin Laden was a member of a wealthy Saudi Arabian family and a founder of the al Qaeda terrorist network.

BOUNCE to Activate Gallery

Americans responded to the 9/11 attacks as a unified, determined people. On the day of the attacks, President Bush addressed the nation:

"Today, our fellow citizens, our way of life, and our very freedom came under attack in a series of deliberate and deadly terrorist acts. . . . Thousands of lives were suddenly ended by evil, despicable acts of terror. . . . These acts of mass murder were intended to frighten our nation into chaos and retreat. But they have failed. . . . Terrorist attacks can shake the foundations of our biggest buildings, but they cannot touch the foundation of America. These acts shatter steel, but they cannot dent the steel of American resolve."

—President George W. Bush, September 11, 2001

Americans Unite in Troubling Times Americans were shocked by the 9/11 attacks, but they rallied to defend their nation. Millions of Americans rushed to donate money, supplies, services, and their own blood. Throughout the country, Americans put up flags to show their patriotism and determination.

>> Flags lined a freeway overpass in California on September 11, 2006, the fifth anniversary of the attacks. **Identify Cause and Effect** How does this photograph express the continuing impact of the September 11 attacks on American society?

Many held candlelight vigils and prayer services for the dead and bereaved. Continued fears of more terrorist attacks, however, kept the nation on edge. In October 2001, a newspaper editor in Florida died from an anthrax infection. Anthrax is a type of bacteria that has been used by several countries to create biological weapons. Traces of anthrax then appeared in news offices in New York City and in the office of a U.S. senator in Washington. Two postal workers who had handled materials containing anthrax died. The FBI investigation focused on a U.S. citizen with no known links to Al Qaeda, but he was never formally charged.

The Legacy of 9/11 September 11, 2001, became a watershed in modern American history, when Americans' confidence in their nation's security was deeply shaken. Americans came together to grieve, rebuild, and decide how to deal with the threat of terrorism. The name "9/11" quickly entered the national lexicon, with people viewing historical events and even ideas as "before 9/11" or "after 9/11."

The 9/11 attacks also had great impact on the nation's economy. Despite increased airport security, some Americans remained wary of air travel, which hurt the airline and travel industries. Businesses and households entered a period of uncertainty during which spending decreased. Estimates indicate that the attacks cost the economy one million jobs and reduced the country's output by three percent.

In the years since 9/11, travel increased, but airport security remained at a heightened level. Today, most domestic and international travelers must remove their shoes at security checkpoints so they can be scanned, have all carry-on and checked luggage scanned, and submit to a full-body scan machine. In addition, some people may be physically patted down or examined with a hand-held scanner. These security measures have become routine and travelers leave extra time before their flights to get through security.

The War on Terror and the Invasion of Afghanistan President Bush had been in office less than a year when these attacks occurred. The al Qaeda terrorist attack against the nation challenged the new President in unforeseen ways and led to a major shift in American foreign policy. In the wake of September 11, Bush and his advisers agreed that the most important priority should be finding and prosecuting the people behind 9/11. This would be just the first step in what Bush called the "war on terror." American government officials had determined that Osama bin Laden's al Qaeda network had been behind the attacks. Bin

Laden opposed the presence of American troops in Saudi Arabia, the U.S. economic boycott against Iraq, and U.S. support for Israel. Bin Laden and other al Qaeda leaders were in Afghanistan, where the Islamist **Taliban** government allowed them to operate training camps for terrorists.

Bush believed that any government that sponsored terrorism should be held accountable. He demanded that the Taliban turn bin Laden over to U.S. custody. When the Taliban refused, American forces, joined by Great Britain, invaded Afghanistan. Allied forces quickly overthrew the Taliban. Although American troops captured several of al Qaeda's leaders, Osama bin Laden escaped.

Ensuring National Security Bush moved quickly to prevent future terrorist attacks. Soon after September 11, Congress passed the **USA PATRIOT Act** to give law enforcement broader powers to monitor suspected terrorists. Critics claimed that the USA PATRIOT Act violated civil liberties. But many Americans were willing to give up some freedoms in return for improved security. Congress also approved calls for the creation of a new Cabinet-level **Department of Homeland Security** to coordinate security matters among federal, state, and local agencies.

The Bush administration exercised broad powers fighting the war on terror. The U.S. operations in Afghanistan led to the capture of alleged members of the Taliban and others fighting against the United States. These prisoners were sent to a U.S. base located at Guantanamo Bay, Cuba. Many of these prisoners were held for years without formal charges brought against them.

Controversy surrounded the holding of the prisoners, mostly on the grounds that their detentions violated the writ of **habeas corpus**. Because of the constitutional issues raised by federal government policy changes, the Supreme Court heard a series of cases dealing with this issue and the Bush administration's use of military tribunals rather than civilian courts to prosecute enemy combatants. In *Hamdan* v. *Rumsfeld*, the Court ruled that the Bush administration's use of military courts violated the Geneva Conventions and U.S. federal law, including the U.S. Uniform Code of Military Justice.

War on Terror Moves to Iraq Bush next contemplated invading Iraq as part of his wider war on terrorism. Bush and his advisors argued that Iraqi president Saddam Hussein was building nuclear, biological, and chemical **weapons of mass destruction (WMD)**. Despite many Americans' belief that UN weapons inspectors should be allowed to continue their search for Iraqi WMD, Congress authorized Bush to use military force against Iraq. On March 19, 2003, American and British military forces invaded Iraq in Operation Iraqi Freedom.

>> In Baghdad, Iraq's capital city, Saddam Hussein's statue was torn down following the U.S. invasion in 2003.

Saddam's forces collapsed almost immediately. As the Iraqi capital of Baghdad fell, Hussein and other Iraqi leaders went into hiding. A hunt for the fallen leader followed. After nine months in hiding, Saddam Hussein was captured in December 2003. U.S. troops found him in a deep hole outside of his hometown of Tikrit.

☑ **RECALL** Why did the fourth hijacked plane not reach its target on 9/11?

Bush's Second Term

The Iraq war, terrorism, and the federal budget deficit weighed heavily on Americans' minds as they voted in the 2004 presidential election. Bush campaigned as a "war president," saying he had proved his competency as commander-in-chief. Bush defeated the Democratic candidate for president, Massachusetts Senator John Kerry.

Among those casting ballots for Bush in 2004 were the nation's Latino voters. The Bush campaign turned to a Texas advertising agency run by

Lionel Sosa. With Sosa's help, Bush captured an estimated 40 percent of Latino voters in 2004.

Problems Surface in Iraq Iraq remained a major focus of Bush's second term as the war raged on. However, by late 2005, Iraq had a new constitution and the beginnings of a democracy. The following year, Saddam Hussein was tried and executed. Saddam's brutal rule had kept fighting in check among Iraq's three major groups: Sunnis, Shi'a, and Kurds. Now these groups fought bitterly for power. The year 2007 emerged as the deadliest in Iraq for U.S. soldiers, prompting Bush to authorize a troop surge that year. The surge lessened the violence, however, Iraq's democracy remained fragile.

In 2008, a Senate Intelligence Committee report determined that there was no credible evidence to support claims that Iraq was developing WMD or had ties to terrorist groups. Some accused the Bush administration of deliberately misleading Congress and the American people to win support for the war.

Troubles at Home Meanwhile, Bush faced domestic challenges. In August 2005, Hurricane Katrina hit the Gulf Coast. The storm had been brewing in the Gulf and before it hit land, evacuation orders were issued in New Orleans. Tens of thousands left the city but more than 100,000 had no way to get out, including the elderly and those in poor neighborhoods. Katrina caused much destruction in New Orleans and more than 1,800 people perished. It was also one of the nation's costliest storms and property damage topped more than $100 billion.

As fierce as the winds and rains of Katrina had been, New Orleans suffered even more after the storm passed. Rising waters soon breached levees protecting the low-lying city. Flooding, which rose to 15 feet, eventually covered about 80 percent of the city. Citizens were forced onto rooftops to await rescue and thousands of others sought shelter at the Superdome stadium.

The government's slow response to the damage was widely criticized. National discontent was reflected in the 2006 elections. For the first time in 12 years, Democrats won control of the House and the Senate.

☑ **EXPLAIN** How was discontent with the government's response to Hurricane Katrina reflected in the 2006 elections?

Digital Technology Impacts 21st Century Life

In the beginning of the 21st century, technological changes had a dramatic effect on the American economy. New technology influenced how and where people did their jobs.

Technology Transforms Workplaces Computer technology changed the nature of the American economy. Many workers found that they needed computer skills to get jobs. Banking, stockbroking, programming, and the many other occupations dependent on information and computers added millions of jobs to the service economy.

Many white-collar workers in the information economy saw their jobs radically changed. Professional workers were linked by a network of computers, servers, and cellphones. They used technology to hold meetings that involved participants sitting in offices around the world, to work in remote locations, or to work from home.

Computers had a huge impact on American industry. Computer-driven industrial robots performed tasks such as welding, loading, packaging, and assembling cars and electronics. Because robots could deliver high quality work around the clock, they enhanced productivity and allowed many businesses to become more competitive. Computers also allowed managers to accurately forecast demand for their goods. Applying just-in-time inventory strategies, producers received goods as they were needed, and increased efficiency by reducing their inventory costs and waste.

Americans Enjoy New Personal Technology Many of the innovations that people enjoy today were created during the first decade of the 21st century. Cell phones with touchscreen glass and increased memory were developed and earned the name "smartphones." Improved broadband Internet access turned phones that were primarily used to call family and friends into one used to text friends, check email, make appointments, take pictures, listen to music, and watch television shows and movies. Tablet computers allowed users to read books, magazines, and newspapers on a digital device. Some people even used tablets on the job.

Some early social media platforms also developed during this time, but with the emergence of Facebook and Twitter social media became widespread. E-commerce expanded, allowing shoppers to purchase products on their computers or smartphones 24/7—meaning all day and night.

Search engines, such as Google, were developed early in the century and have allowed people to find information at the click of a button. Sophisticated algorithms track your previous "clicks" on a website and suggest what you might want to search for, watch or listen to on streaming services, or what you might want to purchase on your favorite e-commerce sites.

☑ **EXPLAIN** How has technology changed the workplace?

The Financial Crisis of 2008

During the autumn of 2008, Americans faced a potentially disastrous economic crisis centered on the financial industry. The crisis stemmed in part from "subprime" home mortgage loans that banks had made to less-qualified, low-income borrowers. The higher interest rates on these loans made them more profitable for banks. The loans were then sold as mortgage-backed securities to investors.

The U.S. Slides into Recession The U.S. economy slid into the Great Recession in late 2007. Economic hardships included unemployment, which rose more than nine percent by 2009. Unemployed Americans could no longer pay their mortgages. Foreclosures—seizures of property from borrowers who are unable to repay their loans—increased. More than 7 million homes were foreclosed between 2007 and 2016.

As a result, housing prices fell more than 30 percent and mortgage-related investments lost their value. Several large banking and investment firms collapsed or were sold.

Too Big to Fail—The Financial Industry Bailout In September 2008, the stock market plunged. The country faced its worst economic crisis since the Great Depression. Treasury Secretary Henry Paulson and Federal Reserve chairman Ben Bernanke proposed a $700 billion bailout of the banks that had engaged in risky lending practices. The Bush administration told the public that some of these banks were "too big to fail." This meant that if they collapsed, the economy was likely to get even worse. The Troubled Asset Relief Program (TARP) was supported by Bush and approved by Congress.

TARP funds were used to make multibillion-dollar loans to at-risk banks, insurance companies, and other financial institutions that had made bad loans. TARP also bailed out three large automobile companies that faced bankruptcy, or financial collapse, so that 1 million workers would not lose

Housing Bubble Collapse, 2004–2010

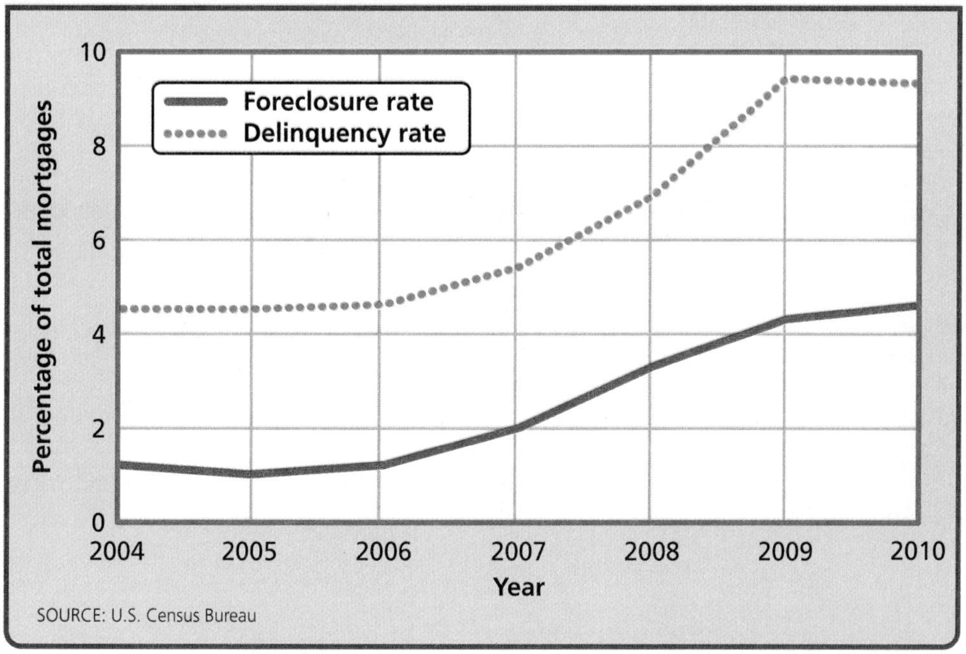

>> **Analyze Data** The graph shows shows the relationship between the foreclosure rate and the delinquency rate. In what year did trouble begin in the housing market?

The First Years of Recession, 2007–2008

2007	2008
• **January 25** – Home sales reach their lowest point since the late 1980s. • **February 21** – The rising default rate hits the subprime mortgage industry. • **August 10** – The Federal Reserve pumps $38 billion into the banking system. • **November 12** – A $75 billion superfund is approved to help build confidence in the credit markets. • **November 15** – The House passes the Mortgage Reform and Anti-Predatory Act of 2007. • **December 12** – The Federal Reserve pumps $40 billion into the U.S. financial system.	• **January 21–22** – Global stock markets collapse. • **June 26** – Crude oil hits a peak of $140 per barrel. • **September 7** – The federal government takes over Fannie Mae and Freddie Mac. • **October 6** – The federal government lends banks $900 billion. • **November 4** – Barack Obama wins the presidential election.

SOURCE: California Department of Finance

>> **Analyze Information** Based on the timeline, how did the federal government respond to the initial rise in default rates on home mortgages?

BOUNCE to Activate Chart

their jobs. In addition, TARP used some money to help homeowners refinance, or redo their loans so they would cost less, and encouraged banks to lower monthly mortgage payments to those who faced foreclosure. The program helped many, but not all homeowners as the banks now refused to refinance loans for people with bad credit or who owed too much on their mortgage. Even with TARP, the economy did not improve much.

Public outrage over the taxpayer-funded bailout grew after executives at some of these companies received multimillion-dollar bonuses. However, many credit the bailout with preventing a financial meltdown.

RECALL What was the source of public outrage at the taxpayer-funded bailout of the financial industry?

ASSESSMENT

1. **Describe** the key components of President Bush's domestic agenda, and explain why some of these initiatives were controversial.
2. **Support a Point of View with Evidence** Explain why the United States opposed the Taliban.
3. **Compare Points of View** Describe the purpose of Operation Iraqi Freedom, and explain why it was controversial among Americans.
4. **Generate Explanations** Discuss the intentions of the Kyoto Protocol, and explain why President Bush refused to abide by the treaty.
5. **Connections to Today** How do people use personal technology today?

20.2

Barack Obama takes the oath of office as his wife Michelle holds the Bible and daughters Malia (left) and Sasha (right) look on.

The Barack Obama Presidency

BOUNCE to Activate Flipped Video

Objectives

Assess the outcome of the 2008 presidential election.

Explain the goals of Barack Obama's economic and healthcare policies.

Describe Barack Obama's involvement in world affairs.

Summarize Obama's second term, including calls for social change.

Discuss how climate change is affecting the Earth.

Key Terms

Barack Obama
Tea Party Movement
Hillary Clinton

The 2008 election broke new ground in American politics. Democratic senator Barack Obama of Illinois became the first Black American to be nominated for President by a major party. Obama's running mate was Delaware senator Joe Biden. Arizona senator John McCain, the Republican nominee for President, chose Governor Sarah Palin of Alaska to be his running mate. The two presidential candidates differed in experience.

The 2008 Election

John McCain, the son and grandson of navy admirals, served as a pilot in the Vietnam War. He endured six years as a prisoner of war after his plane was shot down. McCain won election to the House of Representatives in 1982 and was elected to the United States Senate in 1986.

A graduate of Columbia University and Harvard Law School, Barack Obama had been a community organizer in Chicago. Obama served in the Illinois state legislature before being elected to the United States Senate in 2004.

The 2008 election drew a large voter turnout, with 62 percent of voters citing the economy as their main concern. Bush's low approval ratings, combined with McCain's campaign missteps, made a Republican victory seem almost impossible. In the election of 2008, Obama defeated McCain by a wide margin.

On January 20, 2009, Barack Obama became the 44th U.S. President and the first African American to hold the office. At a huge victory rally in Chicago in November, his words captured the historic moment: "If there is anyone out there who still doubts

GO ONLINE to access your digital course

that America is a place where all things are possible, who still wonders if the dream of our founders is alive in our time, who still questions the power of our democracy, tonight is your answer." In Congress, Democrats expanded their majority.

☑ **RECALL** Describe Barack Obama's background before he assumed the presidency in 2008.

President Obama Takes Action

Before taking office, President Obama had developed an economic stimulus package to pump money into the sinking economy. The $787 billion bill, the American Recovery and Reinvestment Act, was approved by Congress in February 2009. The stimulus package included tax cuts, aid to state and local governments, and funds for infrastructure projects.

Obama's Appointments Elected with the help of a coalition of minority voters, women, and young voters, President Obama sought to reflect the country's diversity in his cabinet appointments. Perhaps his most prominent appointment was that of **Hillary Clinton**, his former Democratic primary opponent. Clinton, the wife of President Bill Clinton and a senator from New York, served as Secretary of State during Obama's first term in office.

President Obama's first Supreme Court nomination added diversity to the Court. He nominated Sonia Sotomayor, the daughter of Puerto Rican parents. Sotomayor grew up in a public housing project in the Bronx and had overcome a difficult childhood. A federal judge since 1992, Sotomayor was confirmed in 2009, becoming the first Latina to serve as a Supreme Court justice. In 2010, Obama nominated Jewish American Elena Kagan to fill a vacancy in the Court. Kagan was known for working with both conservatives and liberals and had built a reputation as a passionate advocate of civil rights, including gay rights.

Healthcare Reform In 2008, more than 46 million Americans had no health insurance. During the campaign, Obama had pledged to create a national health plan to provide affordable coverage. He assigned Congress the job of fixing the healthcare system.

In November 2009, the House approved an overhaul of the nation's healthcare system. The Senate passed its own healthcare bill in December. However, after Democrats lost their filibuster-proof majority in the Senate, healthcare reform was in jeopardy. President Obama campaigned for the bill and won the support of wavering Democrats. In March 2010, in a dramatic vote, the House approved the Senate's healthcare bill. Despite unanimous Republican opposition in the House and Senate,

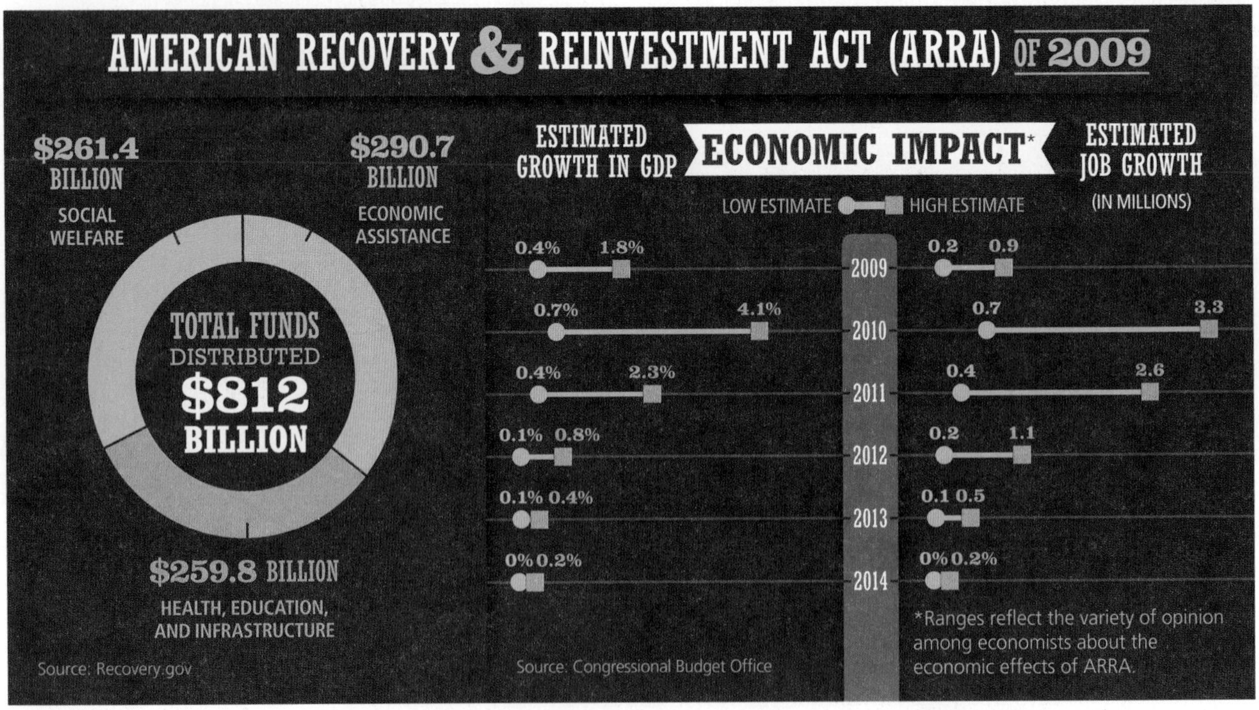

>> Unemployment benefits are classified as social welfare. **Analyze Data** Based on the information in the pie chart, what inference can you make about the unemployment rate in 2009?

BOUNCE to Activate Chart

it was the most significant federal healthcare legislation since Medicare was passed in 1965.

The bill, the Patient Protection and Affordable Care Act (ACA), quickly became known as "Obamacare." It was intended to provide coverage to the uninsured, prevent insurance companies from denying coverage to patients with pre-existing medical conditions, and provide subsidies to help low-income earners buy insurance. Still, many Americans opposed the new plan. They argued that it cost too much, put too great a burden on small businesses, and gave the federal government too much power.

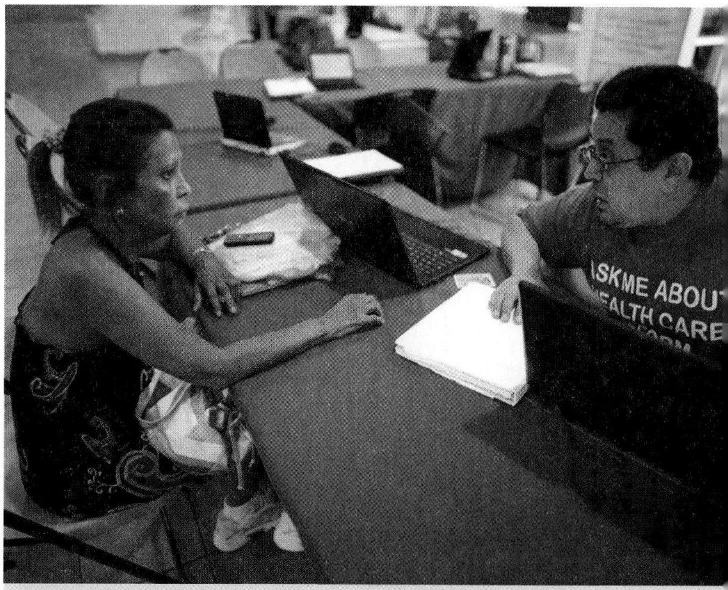

>> Thousands of Americans were able to sign up for health care under the Patient Protection and Affordable Care Act (ACA).

BOUNCE to Activate Chart

Iraq, Afghanistan, and the Arab Spring In August 2010, Obama announced, "The American combat mission in Iraq has ended." When the final pull-out took place in late 2011, more than 4,000 Americans had been killed and more than 31,000 wounded. During the American troop surge, Iraq was significantly more stable, although acts of terrorism continued. About 50,000 American troops remained behind in support roles.

At the same time, Obama increased the American military presence in Afghanistan. American and allied troops had gone into Afghanistan shortly after the 9/11 terrorist attacks, but they had never rid the country of the Taliban forces that had protected Osama bin Laden. Now, Obama asserted, American forces would focus on the Taliban in Afghanistan and their allies in Pakistan.

In May 2011, President Obama announced the death of al Qaeda leader Osama bin Laden. In a secret operation lasting less than an hour, Navy SEALS raided a compound in Pakistan and killed bin Laden, the mastermind behind the 9/11 terrorist attacks. However, Americans were well aware that the death of bin Laden did not end the threat of terrorism. Intelligence officers examined computer files and other evidence seized at bin Laden's compound in the hopes that such materials would aid the continuing war on terrorism.

In December 2010, a protest movement began in the North African nation of Tunisia. Tunisians flooded the streets protesting their autocratic government and demanding political and economic reform. On social media, images and videos of Tunisia's demonstrations spread like wildfire through the Arabic-speaking world. During early 2011, in what became known as the "Arab Spring," similar protests broke out in a number of nations including Bahrain, Libya, Jordan, Egypt, Syria, and Yemen. In some nations the protestors succeeded in overthrowing dictators. The North African nation of Libya was one such example.

In 2011, the United States participated in an international coalition aiding the rebels who were fighting to overthrow the Libyan dictator Muammar al-Qaddafi. Qaddafi had long supported terrorist groups, and was finally overthrown and executed by rebel fighters. In a similar fashion, rulers of a few nations were removed from office while other rulers made compromises and concessions to protestors. In nations, such as Bahrain and Syria, violence was used to suppress protestors. In Egypt, one dictator was replaced by another.

Economic Issues and Reforms America's economic problems continued. Unemployment had risen throughout 2009, peaking at 9.4 percent. By the summer of 2009, the Great Recession was largely over and by spring of 2010, the economy had stabilized. Yet, sluggish economic growth and a high unemployment rate left many Americans fearful about the future.

In July 2010, Obama signed into law a sweeping financial reform bill called the Dodd Frank Wall Street Reform and Consumer Protection Act. It aimed to change the Wall Street practices that had contributed to the 2008 financial crisis. The new law increased federal oversight of banks, hedge funds, and other financial institutions. It also created a

House of Representatives, 112th Congress

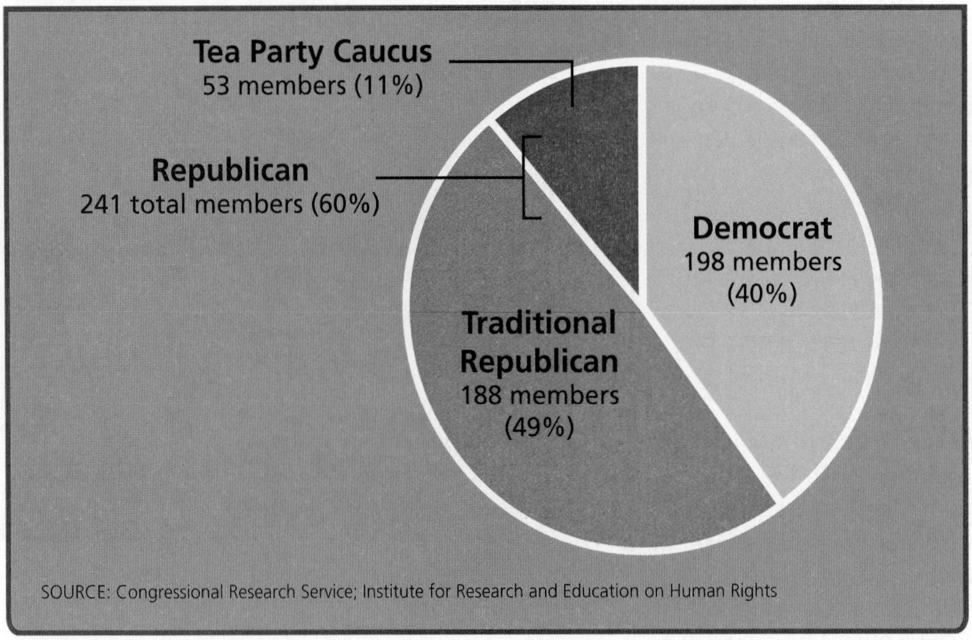

>> **Infer** Based on the pie chart, what can you infer about the political power of the Tea Party?

consumer protection agency to oversee credit card rates, bank fees, mortgages, and car loans. Critics argued, however, that the 2,300-page bill was too complex and too confusing to yield significant results. They said it would tighten credit and lead to further economic woes.

The 2010 Congressional Elections As the 2010 congressional elections approached, the nation seemed increasingly divided. While many Americans supported President Obama, others were angered by his actions. The strongest challenge came from the **Tea Party Movement** which emerged during Obama's first year in office. The movement took its name from the Boston Tea Party, a colonial protest against British taxes. The Tea Party Movement was made up of many local groups, united by a common desire to reduce the size and scope of the federal government.

Although they ran as Republicans, they were not traditional party candidates. They criticized many other Republicans as big spenders and urged a phase-out of programs such as Social Security and Medicare. In the 2010 elections, more than 40 candidates endorsed by the Tea Party were elected to the House and Senate.

Republicans won back control of the House of Representatives in the 2010 mid-term elections. Leaders of the new Republican-controlled House announced that their first priority would be to repeal Obama's healthcare bill. Meanwhile, in the final months of 2010, Congress passed a number of important measures, including extensions of the Bush tax cuts and an arms-control treaty with Russia.

☑ **IDENTIFY** What did the different Tea Party groups across the country have in common?

Obama's Second Term

As the 2012 presidential election approached, the nation's economy remained a major concern. Continued economic worries led to political polarization, and the established political parties were criticized by activists on the left and right. On the right, the Tea Party Movement urged Republicans to reduce taxation and the power of the federal government. On the left, critics from the Occupy Movement claimed that democracy was threatened by the accumulation of wealth and power in the hands of 1 percent of the population. For several months in late 2011 and early 2012, the mainly young people of the Occupy Movement set up tented encampments in American cities to draw attention to their cause.

Although the economic situation did not seem to be improving, the Obama administration received support on another front. In June 2012, the Supreme Court, in *National Federation of Independent Business* v. *Sebelius*, granted Obama a judicial victory by ruling that it was within Congress's power to introduce most provisions of the Affordable Care Act. The ruling surprised many observers who were convinced that the Act was unconstitutional.

The Election of 2012 The Democrats used the issue of income inequality in President Obama's 2012 election campaign against the Republican candidate Mitt Romney, whom they portrayed as out of touch with ordinary people. After a deeply divisive campaign, Romney was defeated by Obama, who received 51.1 percent of the popular vote and 332 electoral votes. Exit polls offered an insight into America's changing demographics: Obama's victory rested partly on a coalition of minority voters and the young. With surveys showing a shrinking white population, some suggested that the Republican party would have to broaden its appeal to minority voters and young people in order to win future elections.

Obama began his second term amidst a continuing economic recession at home and lingering military problems abroad, his power weakened by a divided electorate. Many conservative voters still questioned the wisdom of his universal healthcare act and leadership in the war against terrorism.

Continuing Economic Problems With an unemployment rate of just under eight percent, and job creation lagging behind presidential expectations, Obama faced a difficult task. The problems were significant. America imported more than it exported, creating an unfavorable balance of trade. In addition there were charges, and some evidence, that the country's economic competitors were guilty of unfavorable trade practices. Slow economic growth and failure to significantly reduce spending added to the woes.

Although the stock market moved steadily upward, so did gas prices, home prices, and overall consumer debt. Yet Democrats and Republicans in Congress showed little incentive to negotiate in order to pass effective legislation. In the autumn of 2013, negotiations to raise the borrowing limit for the government stalled as Republicans demanded a number of political concessions that Democrats refused to give. Among these Republican demands were a postponement of the Affordable Care Act, tax reform, and energy deregulation. As the parties could not agree on a budget bill to fund the government, certain government services were forced to shut down temporarily.

Foreign Policy During Obama's Second Term Revolutions and civil wars in the Middle East continued to challenge American policy. The scheduled pull-out of American troops from Iraq was completed in 2011. The hope was for democracy to flourish once U.S. troops left Iraq. However, the nation became politically unstable and wracked by sectarian violence.

By 2013, instability in Iraq took a bad turn when an Islamic terrorist militant group, sometimes known as the Islamic State in Iraq and Syria (ISIS), claimed territory in northern Iraq. As ISIS's influence spread, they began terrorizing Iraq's minority groups, and kidnapping and killing foreigners. U.S. troops were sent into Iraq to protect Iraqis. The United States began bombing ISIS's positions in 2014.

ISIS began to recruit young people online and encouraged them to kill civilians in Western countries that opposed them militarily. In the United States, a series of ISIS-inspired attacks included the murder of forty-nine people at a gay nightclub in Orlando, Florida in June 2016, by a shooter who declared allegiance to ISIS. It was the worst terror attack on U.S. soil since 9/11.

As civil war raged in Syria, the Obama administration found itself in a difficult position, wary of sending arms that might find their way into the hands of terrorists and reluctant to become involved in another war in the Middle East. Tensions also remained high over Iran's nuclear program, which many observers believe is intended to produce weapons rather than domestic energy. In November 2013, President Obama and other Western leaders persuaded Iran to accept an interim agreement to halt elements of its nuclear program and agree to weapons inspections in exchange for Western nations lifting some sanctions against that country.

Globalization and the Rustbelt Decades of free trade and globalization had moved manufacturing into poorer nations as corporations cut production costs. Both Republican and Democratic administrations encouraged this trend, which had helped create "rustbelts"—once prosperous manufacturing areas that now suffered from unemployment and depopulation. In most of the rustbelt and rural areas, the post-2008 economic recovery under President Obama never took hold. The lack of jobs increased resentment of unauthorized immigrants and led to calls for greater border controls.

IDENTIFY SUPPORTING DETAILS What foreign policy challenges did President Obama face in his second term?

>> Activists supporting the Black Lives Matter movement marched in Atlanta in 2016 to protest killings of Black men and boys by police.

A New Movement for Social Justice

Although Barack Obama's election as president showed that real racial progress had been made, other events during his presidency suggested that racism remained a problem in the country.

The Killing of Trayvon Martin On the evening of February 26, 2012, Trayvon Martin, a 17-year-old Black American, was visiting the neighborhood where his father's fiancée lived in Sanford, Florida. George Zimmerman, a volunteer neighborhood watchman for the gated community, confronted Martin. The confrontation ended with Zimmerman shooting the unarmed Martin. Charged with Martin's murder, Zimmerman claimed that he had shot in self-defense. At Zimmerman's trial, a Florida jury declared him not guilty.

Both the shooting and the not-guilty verdict stirred the nation. Many Americans believed that Martin had been shot because he was Black and wearing a hoodie. In response, many Americans put on hoodies as a sign of respect and solidarity. Celebrities and professional athletes such as LeBron James and Dwyane Wade were among those wearing hoodies as a statement.

GO ONLINE to access this biography: Barack Obama

The killing of Trayvon Martin and the acquittal of George Zimmerman touched a nerve that ran deep in American history. Black American men and teenagers had long lived in fear of being shot by police officers and other security personnel. What happened to Martin, many felt, could have happened to them.

Obama's Response President Obama said as much in a speech. "Trayvon Martin could have been me, 35 years ago," he said. Like other Black Americans he had experienced racial profiling. "There are very few African American men in this country who haven't had the experience of being followed when they were shopping in a department store. That includes me. There are very few African American men who haven't had the experience of walking across the street and hearing the locks click on the doors of cars. That happens to me—at least before I was a senator. There are very few African Americans who haven't had the experience of getting on an elevator and a woman clutching her purse nervously and holding her breath until she had a chance to get off. That happens often." Obama's brief statement personalized this American problem.

The Black Lives Matter Movement During the trial for Trayvon Martin's murder, the hashtag #BlackLivesMatter (BLM) began to appear in social media. This hashtag focused attention on the threat posed to Black people by racism and the idea that Black people's lives did not matter.

Although it was not yet a fully formed movement with a specific, agreed-upon agenda, Americans backing BLM argued that police were more likely to target Black males, stopping them on the street and pulling them over when they were driving. Too often, they argued, these events led to unjustified arrests and even police shootings. As the BLM movement gained strength and attracted followers, it used some of the same methods of peaceful protest and nonviolent civil disobedience employed by Martin Luther King, Jr., during the Civil Rights Movement. They organized marches, blocked streets, disrupted traffic, and used other methods to draw attention to their cause.

Supporters of the police rejected the criticisms by BLM activists. They argued that unjustified police violence toward Black people was rare, and they criticized lawless behavior that sometimes accompanied BLM protests.

The BLM Movement Grows Nothing, however, drew more attention to the concerns of BLM activists than the deaths of more Black men and women at the hands of the police. During 2014, several high-profile killings led to unrest. In July 2014, New York City police suffocated Eric Garner while arresting him for allegedly selling cigarettes illegally. While police had him in a chokehold, he said "I can't breathe," before he lost consciousness.

In August 2014, in the St. Louis suburb of Ferguson, Missouri, a police officer shot and killed Michael Brown, Jr. Witnesses disagreed on details of Brown's interaction with police, but what was not in doubt was that the police officer shot the unarmed Brown six times. One eyewitness claimed that, before being shot, Brown had raised his hands and said, "Don't shoot!" Protests began the day after the shooting. During the daytime, mostly peaceful BLM marchers chanted "Hands up, don't shoot!" At night, angry mobs looted and burned buildings.

Other deaths followed Michael Brown's. In November 2014, Tamir Rice, a 12-year-old Black American, was shot by a Cleveland police officer. Still other deaths followed during the mid- to late 2010s. BLM groups staged protests and marches after the Rice killing. They protested not only police shootings, but also their concerns about inadequate housing, health care, job opportunities, and other obstacles faced by millions of other Black Americans.

Taking a Knee In 2016, the most visible symbol of the BLM movement was Colin Kaepernick, the quarterback for the San Francisco 49ers football team. He condemned what he saw as police violence and sought attention for discrimination against Black Americans by refusing to stand when the National Anthem was played before games. At first, he sat on the bench during the anthem. After a conversation with a former NFL player who was a veteran of the Iraq and Afghanistan wars, Kaepernick decided that, out of respect for the flag, he should kneel rather than sit, and he began to take a knee during the anthem.

Soon other players from a range of backgrounds followed his example. Kaepernick's actions drew a range of reactions. Some praised his stand against racism, while others condemned him for a lack of patriotism or for unfair criticism of the police.

☑ **MAKE COMPARISONS** In what ways was the Black Lives Matter movement similar to the earlier Civil Rights Movement?

The Environment

On June 25, 2013, President Obama addressed an audience at Georgetown University on the subject of the environment. Briefly mentioning that the twelve warmest years in recorded history had occurred over the course of the previous fifteen years, he focused on the problems of climate change:

> Last year, temperatures in some areas of the ocean reached record highs, and ice in the Arctic shrank to its smallest size on record—faster than most models had predicted it would. These are facts.
>
> —President Obama, Georgetown University, June 25, 2013

President Obama's Climate Action Plan

EPA REGULATORY GOALS	
• Speed up the process of implementing regulations on greenhouse gas emissions • Issue flexible regulations to individual states to help reduce emissions • Replace use of hydrofluorcarbons (HFCs) in the United States with alternatives • Promote scientific research and development	• Work with foreign, state, and local governments to solve issues • Improve the EPA's internal management and workforce • Empower communities to advance the cause of environmental protection • Support the Presidential Council for an Advanced Energy Economy

SOURCE: Presidential Climate Action Project

>> **Analyze Information** How would President Obama's Climate Action Plan lower carbon-based emissions?

>> On November 30, 2015, at the Paris climate conference, President Obama said that the United States would take action to limit damage from climate change.

BOUNCE to Activate Map

Threats Due to Climate Change Coastal areas of the United States will be under threat if, as many scientists predict, the warming of the atmosphere leads to a rise in sea levels. In low-lying areas of Florida, high tides had already led to periodic flooding, especially in cities such as Miami. With Florida heavily dependent on tourism, an increase in sea levels could seriously affect the state's economy. In Hawaii, there was concern that a rise in sea levels, which had been underway for more than 100 years, might accelerate, threatening urban areas.

But climate change had implications far beyond rising seas. The Environmental Protection Agency reported in 2015 that in Alaska, where the increase in warming temperatures was more than twice the warming in the rest of the United States, forest wildfires were increasing, while sea ice was decreasing. Lakes were changing size, and permafrost was thawing. This melting permafrost, which might lead to ground subsidence or sinking, was a direct threat to transportation networks and buildings.

Taking Action on Climate Change Even before taking office, President Obama expressed a desire to limit greenhouse gas emissions. Climate scientists agreed that emissions of these gases, mainly from the burning of fossil fuels, were warming the climate. Under Obama, the United States attended an international climate conference in South Africa in 2011. The United States agreed to work with other countries on a framework to limit greenhouse gases. After a series of talks, negotiating teams from around the world met in Paris, France, in 2015 and signed the Paris Agreement. The agreement committed countries to reducing greenhouse gases in order to limit climate change. Nearly every country in the world accepted the Paris Agreement. Obama's Secretary of State, John Kerry, signed the agreement for the United States.

That same year, Obama announced implementation of the Clean Power Plan, requiring states to set goals for reducing greenhouse gas emissions. Both the Clean Power Plan and the Paris Agreement were met with mixed reactions. Critics charged that they would hurt economic growth. Supporters applauded the plan's concrete steps to bring about an eventual reduction in greenhouse gases.

EXPLAIN What are some effects of climate change?

ASSESSMENT

1. **Check Understanding** Discuss the goals and beliefs of the Tea Party Movement.
2. **Generate Explanations** Explain how changing demographics led to President Obama's reelection in 2012.
3. **Draw Conclusions** How did the emergence of ISIS change U.S. foreign policy in the Middle East?
4. **Identify Cause and Effect** What were the main causes and effects of the Black Lives Matter movement?
5. **Connections to Today** Protestors in Tunisia used social media to broadcast information across the Arab-speaking world. Which U.S. or world events today are transmitted through social media?

20.3

In 2017, Donald Trump was sworn in as the 45th President.

The Donald Trump Presidency

BOUNCE to Activate Flipped Video

Objectives

Discuss the outcome of the 2016 election.

Explain President Trump's national agenda.

Understand the causes and effects of U.S. foreign policy decisions.

Discuss President Trump's impeachment and his communication style.

Summarize the results of the 2020 election.

Key Terms

Donald Trump
Deferred Action for Childhood Arrivals (DACA)
trade protectionism
pandemic
Joe Biden

The 2016 election season brought significant changes to the American political landscape. During an unpredictable campaign, the Republican nominee **Donald Trump,** a property tycoon and television celebrity, gained the Republican nomination for president after running against seasoned Republican politicians in the primary. He was the first presidential nominee since Eisenhower without political experience.

The Democrats nominated Hillary Clinton, a former senator, secretary of state, and first lady. Clinton was the first female presidential nominee of a major party.

The 2016 Presidential Election

The political balance of power began to shift in the last two years of the Obama presidency. In the election of 2014, Republicans won control of both houses of Congress for the first time since 2005. Republicans won other offices, for example of the governors up for election in 2014, Republicans won 31, while the Democrats won 17. A Republican-controlled Congress would be likely to set a more conservative course.

During a chaotic Republican National Convention, Trump was nominated as the party's presidential candidate. Republican speakers began to rally against the Democratic candidate Hillary Clinton.

GO ONLINE to access your digital course

Trump's call to "Make America Great Again" reflected some Americans' fears of economic decline and anxiety over jobs, trade, terrorism, and immigration. At the Democratic National Convention, Clinton stressed how her political experience better qualified her for the presidency.

During the campaign, outrage over Trump's negative comments about immigrants, Muslims, women, and minorities provoked angry protests outside of Trump rallies. Trump's supporters were angered by Clinton's use of a private email server instead of an official server while she was secretary of state.

Close to the election, Trump held rallies during which his supporters responded positively to Trump's calls to "drain the swamp," meaning to rid government of what he considered corruption. Clinton campaigned just as hard as Trump, but many in the nation considered her an insider in Washington at a time when Trump's outsider status seemed to be resonating with voters.

Although Clinton won the popular vote by almost 3 million votes, Trump won the Electoral College, in a victory that surprised all those following the polls and the press. He became President and had a Republican majority in both houses of Congress.

☑ **IDENTIFY** What do you think Donald Trump meant by the term "drain the swamp"?

President Trump's National Agenda

During the campaign, Donald Trump promised dramatic changes to government policies and presidential style. From domestic issues to foreign policy, Trump challenged conventional wisdom and upended long-standing practices.

President Trump's Leadership Style Trump came into office telling his supporters that he would run the nation using his business and management skills. He promised to rescue the states in the Rustbelt by bringing manufacturing back to the United States. He signed into law business-friendly tax legislation and tax cuts. In 2017, Trump signed the Tax Cuts and Job Act into law.

Trump's use of social media was a unique part of his style. On the morning of his inauguration in January 2017, Trump used Twitter to tweet: "It all begins today! I will see you at 11:00 A.M. for the swearing-in. The MOVEMENT CONTINUES – THE WORK BEGINS!" It was just the beginning of many more tweets. President Trump opened a Twitter account in 2009 and started tweeting during his campaign. During his presidency, Trump used the social media platform to announce domestic and foreign policy decisions. Occasionally, Trump announced staff changes using Twitter.

2016 Presidential Election

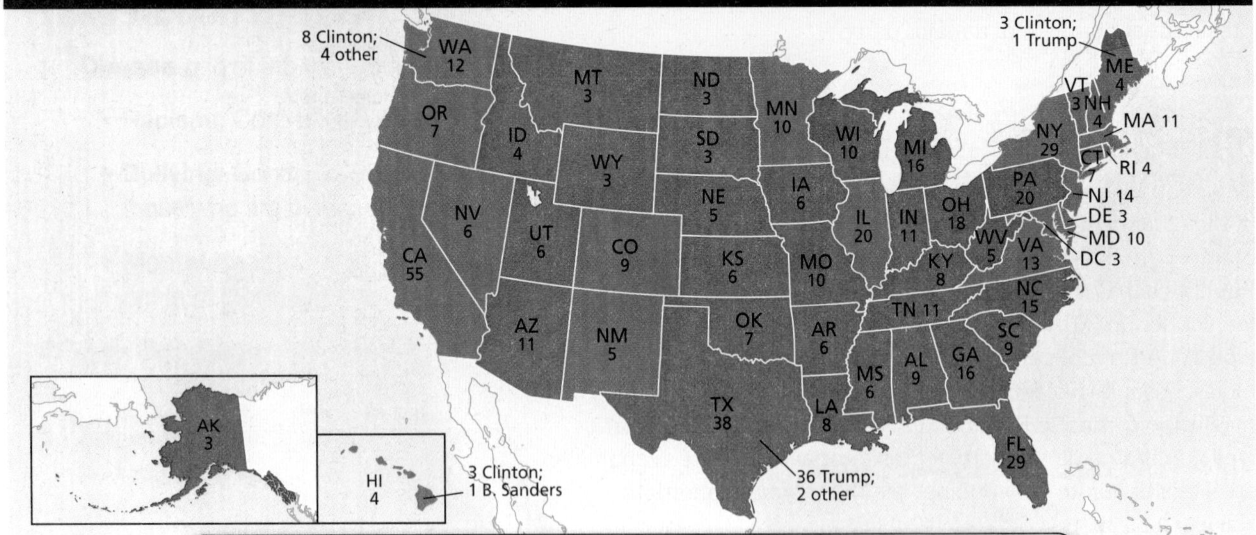

Candidate (Party)	Electoral Vote	Popular Vote	% Electoral Vote	% Popular Vote*
D. Trump (Republican)	304	62,984,825	56.5%	46.09%
H. Clinton (Democrat)	227	65,853,516	42.2%	48.18%

**Percentage does not reflect 5.73% of popular vote won by other candidates.*

>> **Analyze Maps** How is this map similar to and different from the election map of 2000?

Trump's Approach to Immigration The topic of immigration had long been debated in the United States. Much of the debate about immigration concerned unauthorized immigrants. A large number of immigrants to the United States were unauthorized, either because they entered the country without the proper documents or because they overstayed their visas. Unauthorized immigrants often worked in low-paying jobs, such as migrant farm work. The Immigration Reform and Control Act of 1986 tried to stop the flow of unauthorized immigrants by penalizing employers who hired them and by granting resident status to those living in the United States since 1982. Still, unauthorized persons continued to enter the United States.

In 2012, President Obama issued an Executive Order called **Deferred Action for Childhood Arrivals (DACA).** The executive order allowed some undocumented immigrants who had entered the country before their 16th birthday and before June 2007 to be exempted from deportation and to obtain renewable two-year work permits. In 2017, as promised, the Trump administration tried to end the program, but the Supreme Court rejected the government's action in 2020. The program's future remained uncertain.

President Trump also acted to limit immigration. In 2017, he ordered increased detention of unauthorized immigrants, including separating parents from their children. More than 2,600 children were separated from their parents, and many children were housed in substandard facilities. After a public outcry, the policy was rescinded in August 2018, and officials tried to reunite these children with their parents. Trump also limited legal access for asylum seekers, increased enforcement along the U.S.-Mexico border, and authorized the building of a wall along that border. All this reduced the flow of unauthorized immigrants to the United States, and it made it more difficult for refugees to find refuge in the nation.

Trump also tried to block the entry of nationals from several Muslim-majority countries, as well as North Korea and Venezuela. Courts across the country forced adjustments to this "travel ban."

Trump's Supreme Court Appointments Trump filled dozens of vacant judicial positions in federal courts with judges who had conservative records. Despite resistance from Democrats, Neil Gorsuch, President Trump's nominee to the Supreme Court, took over the seat vacated by the late conservative justice Antonin Scalia. The seat had been vacated early in 2016, but Senate Republicans refused to fill it until after that year's election. After a controversial Senate confirmation hearing, Brett Kavanaugh, another Trump nominee, gained a seat on the Supreme Court. The confirmation of Kavanaugh gave the Supreme Court in 2018.

>> Supreme Court decisions had approved limited policies favoring the admission of underrepresented minorities to universities such as the University of Texas (shown here), but the Trump administration opposed such policies.

When liberal justice Ruth Bader Ginsburg died in late 2020, Republicans abandoned their pledge in 2016 not to confirm a justice in an election year and hurried to fill the seat. Just a week before the 2020 election, they confirmed Amy Coney Barrett for the seat. This gave the Supreme Court a majority of conservative justices who would shape the nation's laws for many years to come.

Healthcare Policy Although President Obama's healthcare program expanded healthcare to 20 million more Americans, rising costs and the penalties for not buying insurance drew criticism. When he came into office, President Trump promised to lower prescription drug costs to consumers and to repeal the Affordable Care Act (ACA) and replace it with something better. Although Trump was not able to accomplish these goals, he took actions to overturn the ACA. The first day Trump was sworn into office, he signed an executive order instructing his administration to delay, defer, and exempt parts of the ACA.

In late 2017, led by Trump, the Republican Congress passed laws that revised the ACA. They eliminated the penalty for not having insurance and ended reimbursements to insurers for low-income Americans. These changes caused the price of insurance to go up 20 percent the following year. A group of Republican-led states, later joined by the Trump administration, filed a lawsuit against the ACA. The case made its way to the Supreme Court. The fate of the law depended on the Court's decision and on possible new legislation.

☑ **DESCRIBE** President Trump's position on immigration.

International Issues

President Trump's foreign policy was less about international cooperation and more about asserting U.S. interests in trade and economic issues. Trump policies tended toward **trade protectionism** to shield U.S. industries from foreign competition.

Economic Issues In his inaugural address, Trump promised to put "America first" in matters of foreign policy and trade. In practice, this meant imposing tariffs on U.S. trade partners and pressuring allies to spend more on defense. Trump shifted from collective trade deals to deals negotiated separately with each nation.

In 2017, President Trump ended U.S. participation in the Trans-Pacific Partnership (TPP). He negotiated a new trade deal to replace NAFTA, the free trade deal with Canada and Mexico. The new deal with Canada and Mexico is called the United States–Mexico–Canada Agreement (USMCA). The agreement required among other things that automobiles must have 75 percent of their components manufactured in one of the three nations to qualify for zero tariffs. Mexico agreed to new labor laws to give workers greater protection and the right to organize unions.

The Rise of China Beginning in the 1990s, there was friction between the United States and China over issues such as patents and intellectual property rights. The friction increased as China's economy grew to rival that of the United States in size. Despite evidence of industrial spying and computer hacking, the two nations were able to forge mutually profitable trade relations in the early part of the century.

The U.S. relationship with China changed in 2018. President Trump wanted to reduce the trade deficit with China. To that end, the Trump administration imposed tariffs on a number of imports from China including steel and aluminum. China then retaliated with tariffs on goods from the United States. These tariffs raised costs for U.S. consumers and manufacturers. U.S. tariffs hurt sales to China, reducing many farmers' incomes. While tariffs helped some manufacturers who produced goods also made in China, they hurt others due to higher costs and a

China's GDP, 2000–2018

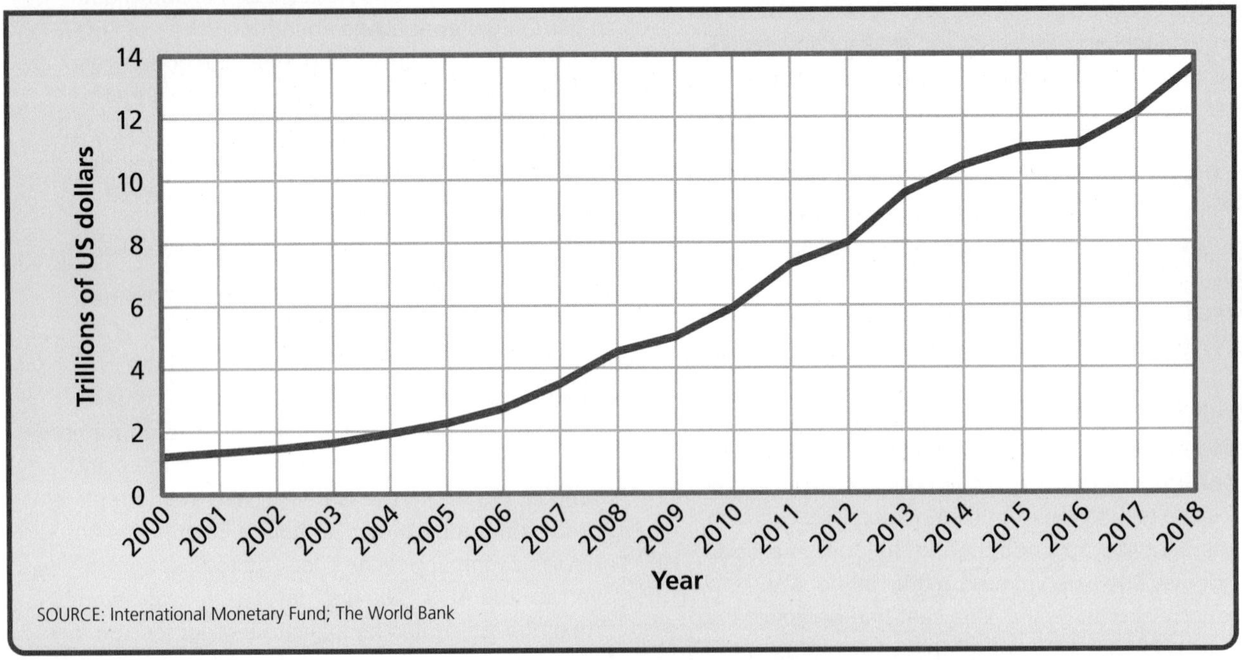

>> The U.S. GDP increased from $9.9 trillion in 2000 to $19 trillion in 2019. **Analyze Data** Predict China's GDP relative to the U.S. GDP in 25 years.

BOUNCE to Activate Before and After

loss of sales to China. As trade talks between the two nations faltered, each nation levied more tariffs on goods.

Foreign Policy Trump's "America First" policy and hesitancy toward international cooperation and global treaties determined his foreign policy. He reduced funding for the UN, scorned U.S.-led alliances such as NATO, and withdrew from international agreements such as the Iran nuclear deal.

Turmoil in the Middle East continued to draw U.S. military involvement. During Syria's civil war, the use of chemical weapons by Syria's ruler, Bashar al-Assad, prompted the United States and its allies to attack chemical weapons facilities and airbases in 2017 and 2018. Then, U.S. troops helped rebel forces trying to defeat ISIS. When Trump abruptly withdrew troops from Syria in 2019, the Syrian Kurds, U.S. allies in the war against Syria, faced assault by Turkey. In Iraq, although American involvement was reduced, some U.S. troops remained to help train the Iraqi military. In October 2019, Trump announced that Abu Bakr al Baghdadi, the leader of ISIS, had been killed by U.S. forces.

Meanwhile, civil war raged in Yemen. The United States supported the Saudi-led coalition in its struggle against Yemeni rebels. Yet many in Congress called for a resolution to the conflict. In October 2019, Trump vetoed bills that would have ended U.S. involvement in the war and blocked U.S. arms sales to Saudi Arabia.

Iran was a source of concern for the Trump administration. In January of 2020, a U.S. drone strike killed Qasem Soleimani, a high-level commander responsible for the deaths of U.S. and allied troops in the region. Iran retaliated by firing missiles at U.S. soldiers at Iraqi bases. The administration imposed new sanctions on Iran.

The Trump administration developed a close relationship with Israel's Prime Minister Benjamin Netanyahu. In 2018, the administration recognized Jerusalem as Israel's capital and moved the U.S. embassy from Tel Aviv to Jerusalem. Early in 2020, Trump and Netanyahu announced a plan to end the Israeli-Palestinian conflict. The Palestinians said they could not accept a deal that did not include their representatives and that they believed favored Israel.

In East Asia, tensions over North Korea's testing of nuclear weapons continued. In June 2018, Trump met the North Korean leader Kim Jong-un. But North Korea did not keep its promise to begin dismantling its nuclear weapons program. Trump met with Kim again in Hanoi in 2020, but a deal was not reached. North Korea continued to test its missiles.

New Environmental Policies Claiming that environmental regulations stifled economic growth, President Trump issued an executive order that allowed coal mining on federal lands and revoked Obama-era orders meant to curb climate change. In 2017, Trump announced that the United States would withdraw from the Paris climate agreement. The Trump administration also announced plans to open up the Arctic National Wildlife Refuge to oil and gas drilling.

☑ **SUMMARIZE** President Trump's foreign policy.

A Polarized Nation

President Trump's unique style both worked for and against him. Americans had never experienced a President who spoke to them so directly through social media.

A Divided Nation President Trump's policies and unconventional habits polarized voters. He used social media to make statements that delighted his supporters and angered his opponents. Controversies raged over the President's frequent attacks on the media and his comments about events, such as the August 2017 violent confrontation between right-wing, white supremacy extremists and anti-fascist groups in Charlottesville, Virginia.

Disputes over gun control also divided the nation. In 2017, a shooter opened fire on a huge crowd of concertgoers from a hotel room in Las Vegas, Nevada, leaving 58 dead and hundreds wounded. In 2018, deadly shootings occured at a high school in Parkland, Florida, and in a synagogue in Pittsburgh, Pennsylvania. Another, at a Walmart in El Paso, Texas, was aimed at the Latino community. These and other acts of violence, reignited debates over gun control and safety in schools, places of worship, and public places.

Starting in mid-2017, an investigation called by the U.S. Justice Department into possible cooperation between the Trump campaign and Russia during the 2016 presidential elections cast a long shadow over Trump's presidency. For two years, a team led by Robert Mueller investigated Trump for possible collusion and obstruction of justice and indicted more than 30 people involved in illegal activities such as money laundering or lying to the FBI. Some of these people worked for Trump before and after the election. In reporting his findings to the Congressional Intelligence Committee and the American public, Mueller was careful not to offer his opinion. Still, he said that the President had not been cleared of obstructing justice and had not been completely exonerated. Trump maintained that he had been fully cleared.

During the investigations, the President continued to stage campaign-style rallies across the country, to stay connected with his voting base and to raise support for his policies. Trump also turned to Twitter to criticize the investigation, Mueller, and the Democrats, calling them "angry thugs," and declaring himself the victim of a "witch hunt" among other things. He also blasted his own team, including his Attorney General Jeff Sessions, who ultimately resigned his position. The rate of turnover in President Trump's senior staff and Cabinet was unprecedented. By mid-2020, the turnover of his most senior staff in the executive office, not including his Cabinet, was more than 80 percent.

Meanwhile Trump's opponents also remained energized. In the 2018 mid-term elections, the Democrats gained control of the House of Representatives, but lost seats in the Senate. The winners in the House included over 35 women, bringing the total number of women in that chamber to 105—the largest number in U.S. history.

Impeachment Investigation After the Mueller investigation, some Democrats in Congress wanted to impeach Donald Trump. In 2019, a whistleblower raised concerns about Trump's phone calls to the President of Ukraine, Volodymyr Zelensky.

Based on the whistleblower's report, the House of Representatives started a formal impeachment inquiry. The House looked into allegations that Trump had withheld military aid to the nation of Ukraine to pressure its president to investigate the son of his political rival, former Vice President Joe Biden. As Representatives investigated, they called for witnesses and documents, but the White House refused to cooperate. Nevertheless, the House formally impeached Trump on charges that he had abused the power of his office for domestic political advantage and obstructed the House's ability to hold him accountable. It was only the third time that a U.S. President had been impeached.

Trump denied the allegations. He appeared before cheering supporters in Michigan and said, "It doesn't really feel like we're being impeached." The House Democrats sent the articles of impeachment to the Senate. This signaled the start of a trial. However, with a Republican majority in the Senate, removal of the President seemed unlikely. On February 5, 2020 the Senate voted to acquit the President, meaning it cleared Trump of all charges.

House of Representatives, 116th Congress

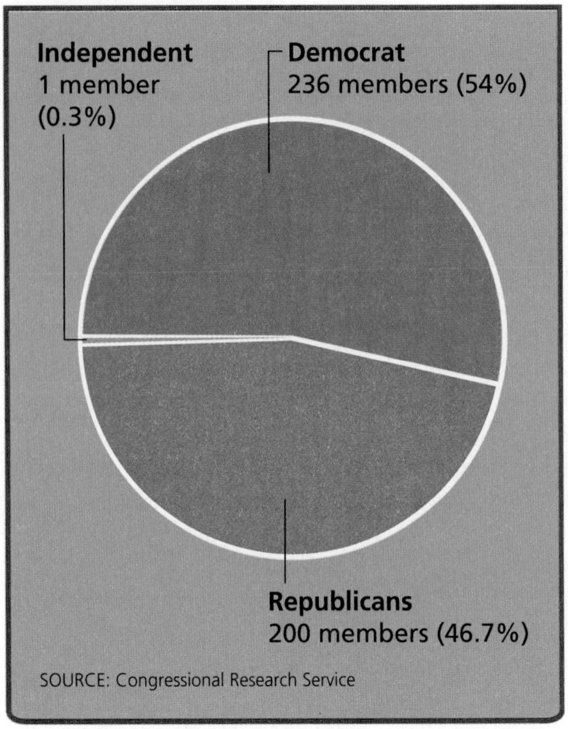

>> **Analyze Data** The 116th Congress began in 2019, after the 2018 elections. The previous House of Representatives was under Republican control. How would the relationship between President Trump and the House change under this Congress?

A Global Pandemic Strikes the Nation Toward the end of 2019, a deadly new virus began infecting people in Wuhan, China. Scientists named the disease caused by the virus *COVID-19*. The virus was highly contagious and soon spread out of China. By late January 2020, cases of the virus had appeared in the United States. COVID-19 soon become a worldwide **pandemic**, or widespread disease, with millions of cases around the world.

Although President Trump quickly suspended travel from China and Europe, many experts believed he was slow to declare a national emergency. By the time he did in mid-March, the nation faced a crisis as case numbers soared. There was a lack of effective masks and other protective gear, respirators, and tests for the virus, as well as a fear that some hospitals, especially those in large cities, would run short of hospital beds. The stock market plunged dramatically.

Many Americans were confronted with a highly contagious and serious disease for the first time in their lives. As non-essential businesses closed, many were furloughed or lost their jobs. Those who could worked from home. People limited their social circles and met with friends and family members virtually online. They faced shortages in grocery stores, including toilet paper and cleaning products.

Impact on Trump's Election Campaign The pandemic was terrible news for Trump, who had consistently boasted that his presidency had created a strong economy. Running for reelection, he faced two alternatives, both of them politically risky. If he listened to public health experts, he would have to impose stringent national guidelines requiring mask wearing, social distancing, and closing non-essential businesses. This could disrupt the economy and involve unpopular restrictions on people's activity. But if he did not adopt the advice of the experts, the country would face higher rates of infection and death.

The swift spread of the virus and the lack of effective remedies frightened millions of Americans. Medical experts counseled people to stay at home, wear masks, and practice social distancing. President Trump contradicted the medical experts, battled with Democratic mayors and governors, even questioned the necessity of masks and social distancing. Without supporting evidence, he promised that the virus would not last long.

Instead of one federal policy, state level officials followed their own paths in managing the pandemic based on local conditions. Some state officials imposed strict limits on business, travel, and gatherings while others allowed individuals to take their own precautions. Several times, Trump falsely declared victory over COVID-19 and called for a return to business as usual.

The stock market gradually recovered its losses, and government stimulus spending helped millions. Still, unemployment remained high, and infection rates and death tolls continued to climb across the country. Increasingly, during the presidential race, Trump struggled to defend his handling of the virus.

Tragic Killings Raise Issues of Social Justice While Americans were reeling from the impact of COVID-19, several police killings caused the nation to grapple with the systemic racism that pervaded the culture.

On May 2, 2020, police in Minneapolis arrested George Floyd, a Black man, for allegedly using counterfeit money. Several officers restrained Floyd, one of them by placing his knee on Floyd's neck. A bystander made a video recording of the incident on a cell phone. Several times Floyd complained "I can't

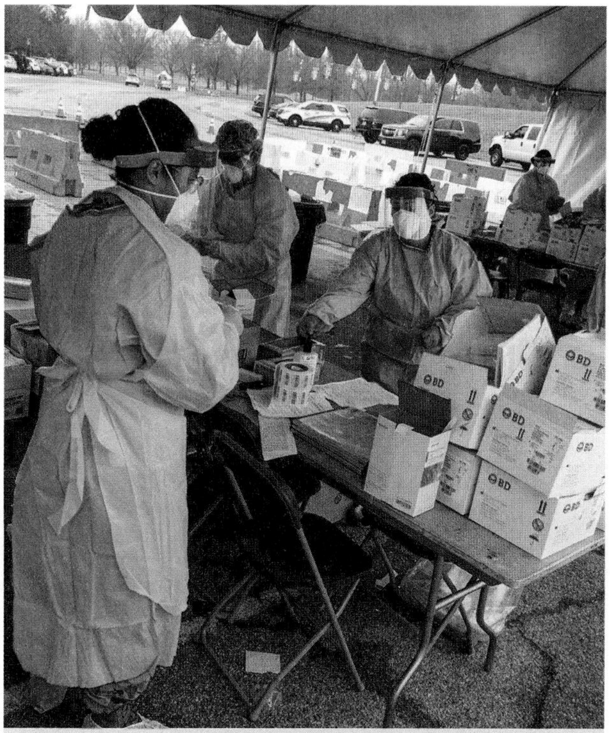

>> These healthcare workers were organizing test kits for COVID-19 at a drive-through testing site in 2020.

breathe." Still, the officer kept his knee on Floyd's neck until he lost consciousness and died.

Floyd's killing set off a series of protests across America. Participants included millions of Americans of all races outraged at the treatment of Black Americans by the police. The killing of Breonna Taylor in March 2020 contributed to the outrage. Taylor was a black woman guilty of no crime who was shot to death in her home by police officers executing a no-knock search warrant.

Black Lives Matter activists and many others argued that these separate events, as well as the deaths of many Black people in earlier years, were the result of institutional racism. Statisticians noted that Black men were more than twice as likely as white men to be killed by the police, and that men between the ages of 20 and 40 were at the most risk.

Protests and Riots Protests in response to the killings followed a pattern. During the day and early evening, protest marches were generally peaceful. But at night, often after an announced curfew, protests turned into destructive riots. During nighttime rioting, angry people burned buildings, looted stores, and clashed with the police. In a section of downtown Portland, Oregon, for instance, nighttime rioting became a regular occurrence.

>> At a rally in 2019, Donald Trump addressed his supporters in Louisiana.

At one point, President Trump sent armed federal agents to Portland to protect federal property.

Millions of Americans sympathized with the peaceful protestors and recognized the injustice of the killings while rejecting the rioting and respecting the work of most police. President Trump and other Americans denounced the protestors, focusing on the destructive rioting, and called for "law and order."

☑ **IDENTIFY** What was the result of the impeachment of President Trump?

The 2020 Election

The 2020 presidential election unfolded against this backdrop of a deadly pandemic and political polarization and unrest. Many commentators on both sides agreed that the election was one of the most important in recent history. Many argued that it would determine the fate of the country.

Choosing a Democratic Candidate A crowded field of almost 30 Democrats announced their candidacy for their party's nomination for the presidential race. The field was the most diverse in history, including four Black Americans, an openly gay man, two Latinos, an Asian American, and a Pacific Islander. By the end of the primary season, though, the former Vice President, **Joe Biden,** held the lead. Due to the coronavirus pandemic, the Democratic convention was held mostly online. The party nominated Biden as its candidate in August 2020.

Biden chose Kamala Harris as his running mate. Harris made history as the first Black woman and the first Asian-American woman to be nominated by a major political party as Vice President.

A Unique Election At the beginning of 2020, Trump was in a strong position, with a flourishing economy and a record of having fulfilled several of his 2016 campaign promises. As promised, he had imposed limits on "Obama Care," nominated conservative Supreme Court justices, deregulated different aspects of the economy, and reduced troop levels in foreign conflicts. In a normal election year, these achievements might have won Trump a second term. However, the COVID-19 pandemic, political polarization, and Trump's defiance of historical norms made this election different in many ways.

Biden largely avoided large election rallies out of concern that they might spread COVID-19. President Trump, in his campaign for re-election, did hold several large rallies despite recommendations against large gatherings by the Centers for Disease Control and Prevention. President Trump himself was diagnosed with the viral disease and was briefly hospitalized during the campaign.

Because of the pandemic, many voters chose to vote early or to vote by mail. During the campaign, Trump questioned the reliability of mail-in ballots, although they had been used in many states for years without concern. Trump discouraged the use of mail-in ballots, so a majority of the mail-in ballots came from Democrats.

Because so many people had voted early or by mail, the counting of ballots took longer than usual in many states. Although many votes—especially disproportionately Democratic mail-in votes—remained to be counted on the night after Election Day, Tuesday, November 3, Trump declared victory in the early morning hours of November 4, while he still led in the vote count.

As the week went on, however, the outcome of the election remained in flux. As early and mail-in ballots were counted, Biden's vote total overtook Trump's in several states. By Saturday, November 7, it was clear that Biden had won the vote in enough states for a majority of votes in the Electoral College. All of the major news networks announced that

Biden had won the election. That evening, Biden and Harris held a victory rally.

Voter turnout in the 2020 election was the highest ever recorded. Biden won more popular votes than any presidential candidate in U.S. history. He beat President Trump by more than 7 million votes. Biden beat Trump in the Electoral College as well, with 306 electoral votes for Biden and 232 for Trump. Biden won the vote in most large cities and their suburbs, while Trump won the vote in most rural areas and in some smaller cities.

Trump, meanwhile, asserted, without substantial evidence, that he had won the election and that his apparent loss was the result of electoral fraud. Attorneys for Trump's campaign filed a series of lawsuits alleging electoral fraud or irregularities in a number of states. However, they presented little evidence to support these charges, and courts rejected nearly all of the campaign's lawsuits as unfounded.

In addition, for weeks following Biden's victory, a large number of Republican politicians at the state and federal level refused to acknowledge Biden's victory or to congratulate Biden on his win, citing the President's right to contest the results. Together with the President's baseless claims of electoral fraud, these actions led a large percentage of the American people to continue to question Biden's victory and eroded trust in the country's democratic electoral system.

Convinced that the election had been stolen, thousands of Trump's followers gathered for a rally in Washington, D.C., on January 6, 2021, the same day Congress was meeting to certify the electoral votes. During a speech in front of the White House, Trump asked his supporters to march to the Capitol to stop the certification process. After arriving at the Capitol, their actions turned violent. Rioters stormed the building and smashed their way into halls of Congress. Lawmakers and aides had to be evacuated, and the certification process was halted. Rioters destroyed property and killed a police officer. One rioter was killed, and three others died. Once the building was cleared later that evening, lawmakers returned and succeeded in certifying the electoral votes. The event shocked the nation.

Congress quickly took action in response to the attack on the government and impeached President Trump for incitement of insurrection, making him the first president to be twice impeached. President Biden's inauguration took place as scheduled on January 20. In his inaugural address, Biden called for unity to meet the challenges of COVID-19, an economic crisis, climate change, and systemic racism. He promised to be a President for all Americans. But restoring unity would prove to be a difficult task.

>> Joe Biden (right) and Kamala Harris (left) appear at a victory rally on November 7, 2020, in Wilmington, Delaware, after winning election as President and Vice-President.

☑ **IDENTIFY** What were some unusual features of the 2020 election?

☑ ASSESSMENT

1. **Generate Explanations** How was having a majority in Congress in 2016 an advantage for President Trump?
2. **Check Understanding** Explain President Trump's position on the Affordable Care Act.
3. **Identify** Give one example of how President Trump implemented his "America First" policy.
4. **Connections to Today** Provide some examples of how politicians might effectively communicate through social media today.

I Tested Positive for Coronavirus. Here's What I Would Like You to Know: Tamar Weinberg

In this firsthand account, Tamar Weinberg, a young mother living in a New York suburb, recounts her experience of COVID-19, or coronavirus. She describes how the disease affected her and how the disease shows importance of protecting others.

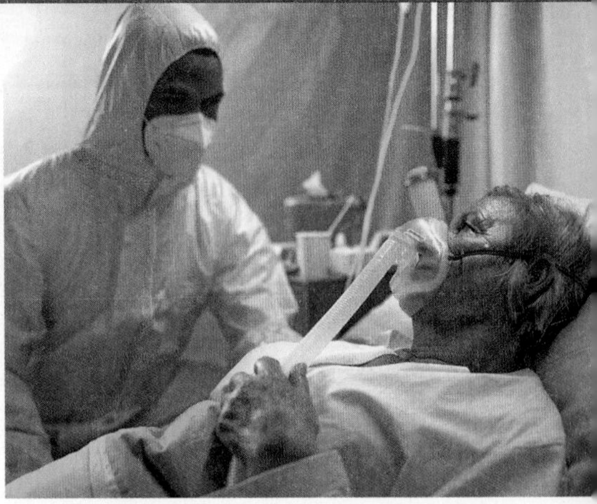

>> A patient being treated for COVID-19

. . .I had just put on my sneakers when I received the text:

School will be closed today, March 3. Please check your email for more information. Thank you. . . .

The full email explained that a member of the community tested positive for COVID-19. . . . little did we know the domino effect that already impacted dozens of us. . . .

ANALYZE STRUCTURE Why does the author write "little did we know" near the beginning of her account? How do these words spark the reader's curiosity?

Many who took the coronavirus test reported that they lost their sense of smell and taste right after testing. As someone who is looking to launch a personal fragrance brand, I was not willing to take a test if that were a possible outcome!

But then I lost my sense of smell and taste anyway—without the test. And I realized everyone who complained about losing these two senses was actually sick. . . . [S]everal days into my confinement and when my quarantine was actually supposed to be over, we drove as a family to the testing site to get our test. The date was March 15. . . .

On Wednesday, March 18, a website with test results was shared with my community. . .I log in.

Positive. And the results were posted the day before. I was happy to get exactly what I was looking for, that I had confirmation that these odd symptoms could only be attributed to the coronavirus. . . .I isolate now the best I can. . . .

CITE EVIDENCE Why was the author happy to get a positive test result?

If I hadn't known about that website, I would have found out about my positive COVID-19 culture only on March 20 when the Department of Health finally called me. My quarantine ended on March 15. That gave me five days I could've gone out and infected the world.

. . . I would have gone to the gym. I would have picked up a book I had on hold at the library from the very kind but old librarian behind the desk. I would have bought groceries. I would have gone for a run with a friend, if not by myself. I would have carried on with normal things.

ANALYZE STYLE AND RHETORIC Why do you think the author repeats the words "I would have" at the beginning of several sentences in a row? What point is she trying to make?

But I knew on March 15 that I would go test and do absolutely nothing else. . . . I knew that I wouldn't be going to the gym on the 16th, which was something I had once looked forward to. I knew deep in my heart that it is imperative to be socially responsible, and so before I found out anything about my test results, I would extend my self-quarantine even though I technically didn't have to.

I knew better, and I was lucky to have enough knowledge into the devastation I could have introduced to the world by leaving. So I didn't.

How many other people test, don't get their results in time and thus go out and carry out their normal things while carrying the virus on their person? I would imagine a fair number. How many other people living in the same dwelling as that person may be doing the same thing? I would imagine another fair amount. And how many people are carrying around the virus and have absolutely no symptoms at all, yet are spreading it to the world unknowingly? That's the scariest number of all.

DETERMINE MEANING What does the author mean by "the scariest number"? How can a number be scary?

We all need to quarantine because if we don't, we could be killing people. It's as simple as that. . . .

I have the coronavirus. And while ignorant people say this is no big deal, it is a huge deal. . . .

I have the coronavirus. And I'm okay. But I am going to do my part to make sure everyone else is too.

SUMMARIZE What lesson does the author draw from her experience?

ASSESSMENT

1. **Draw Inferences** How does the author view people's responsibility to one another in society?
2. **Identify Supporting Details** What evidence from the piece demonstrates the author's view of people's responsibility to one another?
3. **Draw Conclusions** How might the lessons learned from COVID-19 help society respond to new challenges, whether related to public health, the environment, or other areas?

GO ONLINE to access primary sources

20.4

America's civic traditions and ethnic diversity continue to be a source of strength as young Americans look to the future.

BOUNCE to Activate Flipped Video

Objectives

Analyze the causes of immigration and its effects on American society.

Summarize the causes and effects of changing demographics.

Discuss the environmental issues facing Americans.

Explain the effects of communications technology on the economy.

Understand the issues Americans face in the 21st century.

Key Terms

globalization
multinational corporations
Immigration Act of 1990
Violence Against Women Act
privatizing

GO ONLINE to access your digital course

Americans Look to the Future

By the early 21st century, American society had undergone many important changes since the previous century. It also faced different challenges. As the century progressed, America sought ways to preserve its heritage while at the same time adapting to rapid social, political, and technological change.

The American Economy Today

As the 21st century was beginning, new communications infrastructures—especially fiber-optic cables and computers—made it easier for companies to do global business. This increased **globalization,** or the process by which national economies, politics, cultures, and societies became integrated with those of other nations around the world.

The Impact of Multinational Corporations **Multinational corporations** are one example of a globalized business. Such a corporation might have its financial headquarters in one country and offices or factories in several others. The company then sells the products it makes to a worldwide market. Using the most cost-effective location for each activity can increase productivity.

Globalization has made more products and services available to greater numbers of people, often at lower prices. It has hastened the development of some nations. But it has also had some drawbacks. Industrial nations have seen their manufacturing jobs flow out to less developed nations. Steel that was once manufactured in Pittsburgh, for example, might now be made in China. In less developed nations, workers often lack the protections that workers have in industrial nations. Finally, linking world economies almost guarantees that economic problems in one region will affect others.

The Service Sector Expands With the production of services increasing faster than the production of goods, some economists say that America now has a service economy. Jobs in the service sector vary widely. Lawyers, teachers, doctors, research analysts, police officers, professional athletes, and movie stars are all service workers, as are salespeople and the people behind fast-food counters. Service workers are among the lowest-paid and the highest-paid people in the United States.

One of the fastest-growing parts of the service sector has been digital services, including software, website development, and data management. As the role of the Internet in our economy has grown, this area has been crucial to America's economic success.

The Rise of the Tech Giants Increasingly, American business has moved online. Companies advertise, market, and sell products online. They also coordinate activity among different locations online and store vital business data in what is known as "the cloud." This is really a network of "server farms" storing thousands of computers, which workers go online to access.

The rapid growth of business activity online has fueled the growth of companies that own the biggest online platforms. The most important of these are Amazon, the world's largest online retailer and a provider of cloud services; Microsoft, a seller of software and cloud services; Alphabet, which owns Google, the world's most-used search engine and popular content sources; and Facebook, the leading social media platform. Alphabet, Facebook, and Amazon earn large amounts of advertising revenue. Another tech giant, Apple, mainly sells devices and online services.

Consumers enjoyed the services tech giants delivered, often free of charge, though consumers boosted firms' advertising revenue by giving the firms free access to their data. The founders and early investors in these firms became rich through their success. Still, the ability of these few firms to capture much of online business and to control what people see online became increasingly controversial in the 2010s. Some critics called for their regulation.

The Decline of Organized Labor The rise of the service economy and the decline in American mining and manufacturing have had a strong impact on organized labor. When union membership was at its peak in 1945, about 35 percent of all American workers belonged to unions. By 2019, just 10.3 percent of workers were members of unions. By 2019, just 10.3 percent of workers were members of unions. As a result, the political power of labor unions has fallen. At the same time, workers' average wages—especially those of nonprofessional workers—have fallen when adjusted for inflation.

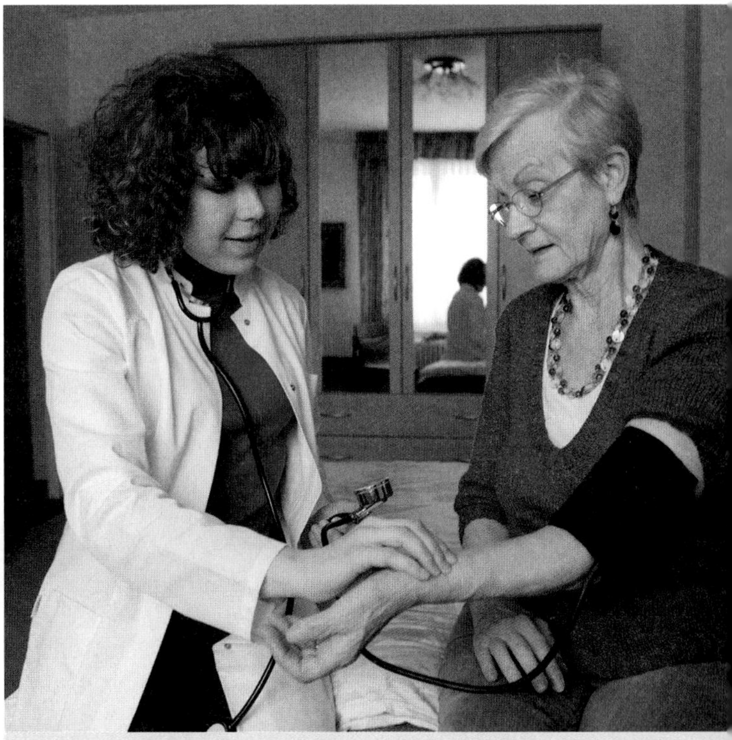

>> In the 2020s, an increasing number of jobs were available in the service industries such as healthcare, education, and technology.

Lower wages have led to a decrease in the wealth of working- and middle-class Americans. Higher costs for education, healthcare, childcare, and housing have put additional pressure on families.

☑ **IDENTIFY** What are two different service jobs that are available today?

Immigration Changes American Society

It is often said that the United States is a nation of immigrants. America has long attracted millions of immigrants seeking greater freedom and economic opportunity. Over time, however, the nature of immigration has changed.

Expanding Immigration For years, the government limited immigration to mainly northern and western

Europeans. In the 1960s, however, laws began to relax immigration limitations. The **Immigration Act of 1990** increased quotas by 40 percent and eased most remaining restrictions. As a result, the period from the 1990s to the 2000s saw the largest numbers of immigrants in the country's history. During that time, almost one million immigrants arrived in America each year from all over the globe, representing a wide variety of cultures and religions. Today, immigrants account for more than 13 percent of the total American population. This large-scale immigration has expanded religious pluralism in the United States.

Latinos Exert Their Influence Most of the new immigrants were Latinos. In 2018, 25 percent of the total immigrant population were Mexicans, with people from the Caribbean and Central America making up nearly 17 percent. Mexicans and Central Americans settled largely in the South and Southwest. Caribbean immigrants, many of them Cubans, settled in Florida. By 2017, a third or more of the residents of Texas, New Mexico, Arizona, and California were Latinos. Latinos are the fastest-growing ethnic group in the United States.

Like all immigrants, Latinos have varying educational and employment backgrounds. Often they take lower-paying jobs with no benefits. However, Latino immigrants have had a profound social, cultural, and political impact. By 2021, Latinos held several thousand political offices and 9 percent of the seats in Congress, primarily as Democrats. Cuban Americans in Florida, generally Republican, have had an enormous influence on American political policy concerning Cuba.

The Growing Asian Population Asians make up the second-largest source of the new immigrants. In 2018, they were more than 30 percent of the total immigrant population, with the largest numbers coming from China, the Philippines, and India. The largest numbers of Asian immigrants have settled in California, giving that state a large Asian minority.

Overall, Asian immigrants have the highest level of education. Some came to America with college degrees and marketable skills and found professional jobs. Others came from war-torn countries, with very little education.

CAUSE AND EFFECT How did the Immigration Act of 1990 affect immigration?

Sources of Immigration, 2000–2014

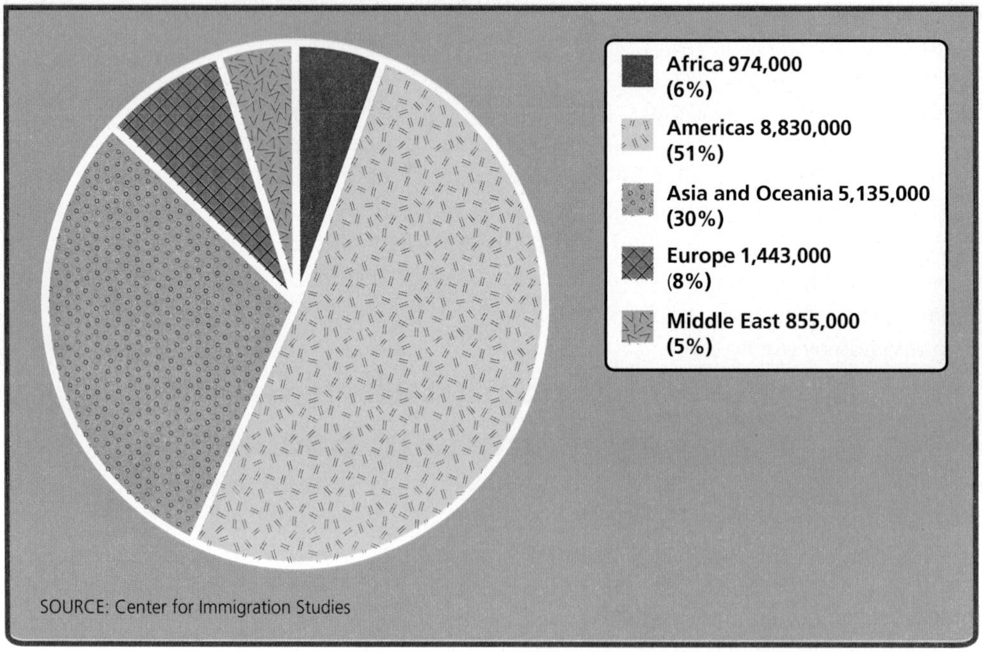

>> **Analyze Graphs** Given what you've learned about immigration during the early 20th century, how have the sources of immigration to the U.S. changed over the last 100 years?

American Demographics in Transition

During the 2010s, America's population shifted. Coastal cities as well as the Sunbelt, or the region of warm southern and southwestern states, saw rapid population and economic growth as people left the cold Northeast and the Rustbelt. Meanwhile, the family itself was changing.

New and Diverse Families In 1960, more than 70 percent of American households were headed by a working father and a nonworking mother, neither of whom had ever been divorced. By 2018, fewer than 15 percent of households fit this model.

In 2018, one out of every three marriages ended in divorce, and in a high percentage of households both parents worked outside the home. Single-parent households were far more common, with a quarter of all children growing up in a single-parent household. The number of children born to unmarried mothers also rose. In 1960, only 5 percent of children were born out of wedlock. In 2011, one out of every four white babies, one out of every three Latino babies, and two out of every three Black babies were born to unmarried mothers.

Combating Discrimination In theory, civil-rights legislation from the 1960s banned discrimination against Americans on the basis of "race, color, religion, or national origin." Still, inequality persisted for Black Americans, Hispanic or Latino Americans, Native Americans, and Asian Americans.

People from these groups reported facing discrimination frequently, in many different settings, whether being targeted for questioning, unjustified arrest, or violence by police, facing extra hurdles in applying for work, or encountering obstacles while shopping or doing business. Parents from these groups often feel a need to teach their children about the systemic discrimination they are likely to face due to their skin color or appearance. American Indians and Asian, Latino, and Black Americans have taken action to combat these kinds of discrimination, forming movements such as Black Lives Matter.

Women have won greater protection both inside and outside the workplace. Working women benefited from legislation to enforce equal pay for equal work, address child-care needs for working women, and end sexual harassment in the workplace. Issues such as spouse abuse and date rape are now widely discussed. Incidents of violence against women are more often reported and more often punished than ever before. The 1994 **Violence Against Women Act** increased federal resources to apprehend and prosecute men guilty of violent acts against women.

In recent years, women used social media to focus society's attention on violence against women with the slogan "Me Too." The "Me Too" movement gave many women the courage to accuse and prosecute men who assaulted them.

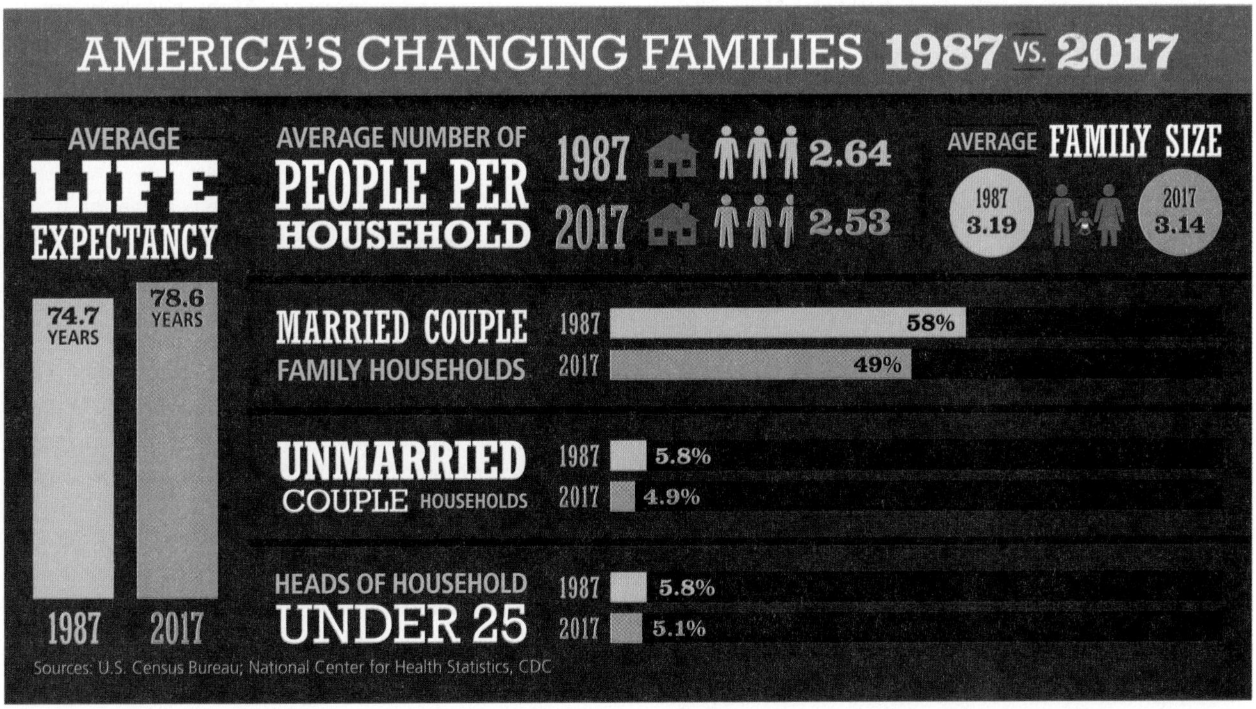

>> **Analyze Data** Using the information in the graphs, describe how the American family has changed over the past several decades.

>> Wind farms, like this one near Palm Springs, California, can produce electricity without releasing harmful carbon-based emissions, although some claim such farms are dangerous to wildlife. **Check Understanding** Are there any negative aspects of wind power?

BOUNCE to Activate Gallery

Civil rights also expanded for lesbian, gay, bisexual, transgender, and questioning (LGBTQ) people. In 2011, a ban against openly gay service members in the U.S. military was lifted. A growing number of states banned anti-gay discrimination.

In 2013, in the *United States* v. *Windsor*, the Supreme Court struck down part of a law that banned federal recognition of same-sex marriages. Soon after this, another Supreme Court ruling (*Obergefell* v. *Hodges*) made same-sex marriage legal throughout the nation. These rulings meant that married same-sex couples were entitled to the same rights enjoyed by heterosexual married couples. These rights included Social Security benefits, hospital visitation rights, healthcare benefits, and military family benefits. However, despite these advances, LGBTQ people still had no federal law to protect them from discrimination in housing or employment.

An Aging Population While the life expectancy of an American born in 1900 was less than 50 years, an American born in 2020 can expect to live to age 79. By 2019, older Americans tended to retire earlier, live longer, and exert more political influence. These factors have strained the country's social welfare system, especially Social Security and Medicare. In 1960, the federal government spent less than $100 billion on social welfare. By 2020, the amount had increased to $1.9 trillion.

With the large baby-boom generation mostly having reached retirement age, the issue of elder care has become critical. Falling birthrates have meant that as the baby boomers have retired, there have not been sufficient workers to cover their Social Security benefits. Politicians have been debating this reality.

In his second term, President George W. Bush called for **privatizing** Social Security by letting younger workers redirect Social Security deductions to private investments. Critics defeated the measure, saying that it would put younger workers at the mercy of fluctuating stock market returns without addressing the shortfall of funds. Today the debate continues.

DESCRIBE why politicians have been debating the issue of Social Security.

Environmental Concerns Continue

Our environment is constantly changing due to natural changes and human-made changes. The United States has suffered from many severe storms and wildfires in recent years. Many people worry that these events may be related to climate change. Concerned citizens and scientists worry that if we do not change our behaviors, the impact of climate change will continue to grow.

Climate Change Climate change is a change in the average weather over a long period of time. Our economy uses fossil fuels, such as oil and natural gas, to power industry, for transportation, and for heating and cooling. Carbon dioxide and other gases released when these fuels are burned collect in the atmosphere and create a "greenhouse effect." That is, the gases absorb sunlight and increase the surface temperature of the Earth. Too much warming has melted glaciers and ice caps at the North and South Poles causing water levels to rise. Low-lying islands and coastal cities are at risk. Climate change has been blamed for more frequent hurricanes, desertification (increase in the area of deserts), drought and wildfires. There is a risk of failed harvests that could cause famines. Climate scientists agree that we need to take action to reduce fossil fuel use to avoid serious consequences.

The Environment and Local Economies Environmental issues have become controversial largely because the environment is closely tied to local economies. The continental United States can be divided into four main environmental regions: the West, the South, the Northeast, and the Midwest. In the West, water is an important environmental and economic issue because it is often scarce. Population growth and drought put pressure on this important resource, which must be shared by private homes and businesses. Recent periods of drought in California, which supplies produce to the nation, have had a dramatic effect on the state's farming economy. The dry conditions led to terrible wild fires in California in 2019 that raged from Los Angeles in the south to Sonoma Valley in the north.

The West is also a region with vast tracts of land owned by the federal government. The government's management of this land touches issues of mining, logging, grazing and other development. In recent years the opening up of oil and gas development on public land has become a controversial issue.

Other regions face different environmental issues. The 2010 Deepwater Horizon spill in the Gulf of Mexico created environmental problems along the coast of many Southern states. In the Midwest, the Keystone XL pipeline project attracted protesters and litigation to stop it. This pipeline, which would transport crude oil from Canada to the oil refineries of the Gulf of Mexico, was opposed by President Obama but approved by President Trump. Critics condemned this project for its possible damage to the environment, while the project's supporters promised that it would bring jobs and a reliable oil supply.

Recycling and Green Architecture The environmental movement achieved victories at a local level. These often focused on the strategy of "reduce, reuse, recycle" to conserve resources and decrease the amount of waste going into landfills. State and local governments drove recycling efforts. Several states created a deposit policy on recyclable cans and glass bottles to encourage recycling.

The 2000s also saw increased interest in "green architecture," or architecture that integrates technology with environmental concerns to lessen the human impact on the environment. Green buildings might feature recycled materials, increased insulation to reduce heating and cooling energy use, and alternative sources of energy, such as solar or wind power.

>> Crops are grown on the top of this "green" building in the Brooklyn Navy Yards in New York City. The produce is sold to local restaurants and grocers and at farmers' markets.

BOUNCE to Activate 3D Model

As buildings became more energy-efficient, environmental groups worked to make cities healthier places to live. After decades of urban decline, American cities became safer and more prosperous, attracting new residents and businesses. Higher population densities meant less use of cars and more commuters walking or using public transportation. Parks were restored and waterways cleaned. In many places, urban agriculture took off, providing local residents with fresh produce.

EXPLAIN What is "green architecture"?

Technology Transforms Life

Digital technology—including smartphones, laptops, and tablet devices—shaped new ways of life and improved standards of living. The microchips that were developed for computers became essential components of "smart" televisions, drones, self-driving cars, and wearable technology. Dishwashers, refrigerators, washing machines, and hundreds of other appliances became part of what is often called a "smart" home. A smart home is one where the residents can control their appliances and lights from their phone, tablet, or computer. This technology helped to regulate traffic, entertain millions of people, and facilitate shopping through home shopping sites.

Computers, telephones, and global communications shaped the economic development of the United States. Technological innovation also created new industries and employment opportunities at home, while increasing the competitiveness of American products in world markets. Various technological and management innovations such as robotics and computer management allowed American companies to produce high-tech exports including computers, pharmaceuticals, electrical machinery, and scientific instruments, as well as products for the aerospace industry. The United States profited from its solar, wind, and smart-grid technology exports.

Mobile Technology Connects America and the World A revolution in information technology also transformed the ways Americans obtained information. More and more people got their news online rather than through traditional print media. This led to major disruptions and transformations in the media industry. The information revolution was not only limited to world news. Americans also used social media sites for information about friends or celebrities. Never in human history was so much information so easily obtained.

Technology also changed the way Americans consumed entertainment. Music, movies, and television shows could be retrieved in seconds on a personal computer linked to the Internet or with a smartphone. Some wondered whether streaming videos and podcasts might allow the Internet to replace television as the main entertainment medium. But the Internet also spread that entertainment wider than television ever could, by making American culture accessible to much of the world's population. Through films and videos, American freedoms and economic opportunities were broadcast to a growing audience worldwide. This trend proved risky, as it provoked violent reactions from radical groups who feared that local culture and traditions were being overwhelmed by American political and social ideals.

While the Internet had many positive effects on Americans' lives, it also exhibited a darker side. Social media platforms, which were designed to grab and hold users' attention, created a kind of technological addiction, with users unable to detach their attention from their screens. Privacy dissolved as advertisers and others tracked users' interests, personal information, and online habits. Ironically, while the Internet helped connect users, it

Internet Access at Home, 1997–2017

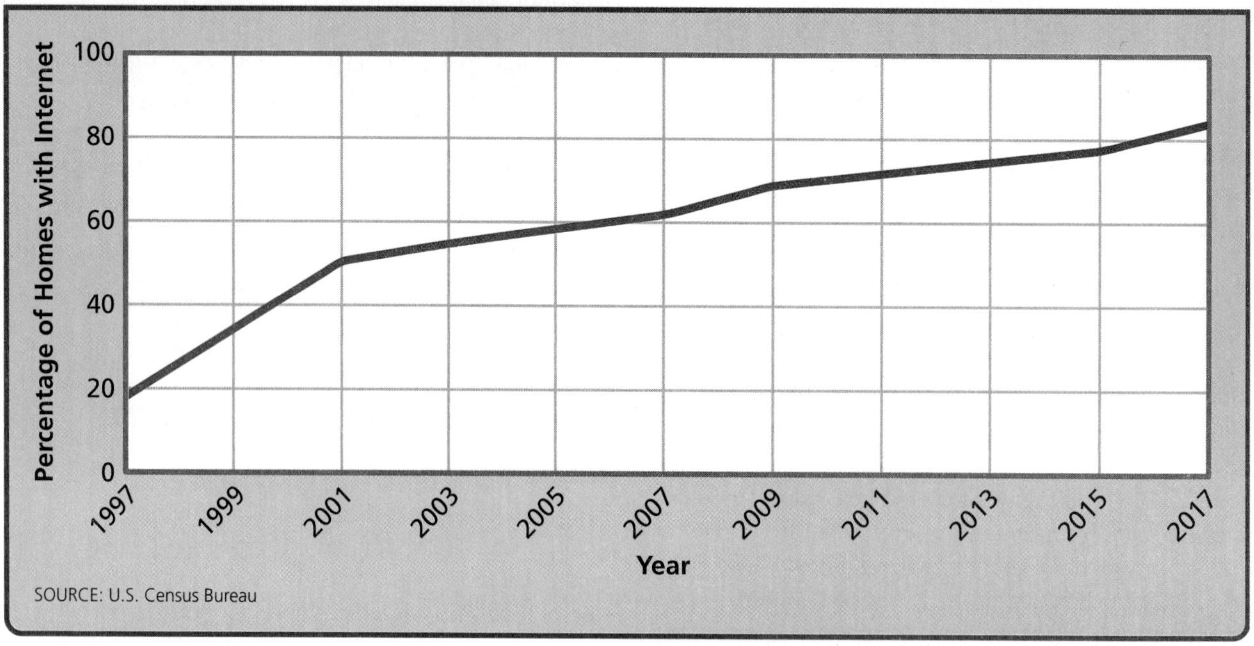

>> **Analyze Graphs** Describe the trend shown on the graph. In which years was the greatest increase in Internet access?

also became a divisive force, unleashing an epidemic of cyber-bullying and "trolling"—writing cruel comments to upset others.

The Internet also became a breeding ground for conspiracy theories and helped political extremists connect and organize. At the same time, social media fueled the spread of "fake news" and propaganda, undermined faith in institutions of government, and weakened confidence in the democratic process. The threat that the Internet posed to democracy became apparent as U.S. intelligence agencies and congressional committees confirmed that Russian operatives had manipulated social media platforms in favor of Donald Trump during the 2016 presidential election. In October 2017 Congress began questioning the leaders of Facebook, Google, and Twitter over the role that social media played in allowing Russian disinformation campaigns during the election.

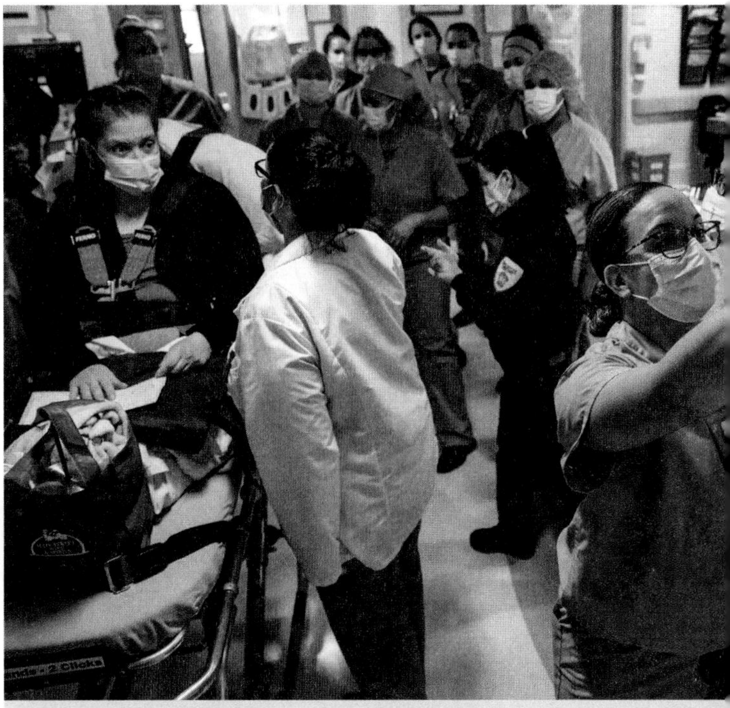

>> A woman who has recovered from the COVID-19 virus is getting ready to leave the hospital.

Advances in Science Just as American high-tech research made the country the leader in computer and other digital technology, American research and development laboratories ensured that the country remained on the cutting edge of medical and scientific innovation. No country spent more on medical research, and none introduced more advances in the field. In particular, new research in genetics opened up promising new possibilities for the treatment of cancer and other ailments. Genetic research promised to deliver safer pharmaceutical drugs.

By the 2020s, there was a wider range of medical options than ever before. From heart, kidney, and other organ transplants to microsurgery using video and fiber-optic cameras, American hospitals offered some of the most advanced medical treatments in the world. In addition, such American companies as Johnson & Johnson, Merck, Eli Lilly, and Pfizer helped the United States lead the world in pharmaceutical innovation.

Fighting COVID-19 As COVID-19 spread across the United States in 2020, the case numbers and death toll rose steadily. By the end of the year, more than 300,000 Americans had died of the disease.

Based on recommendations from scientists, some state governments took steps to try to control the spread of the virus. During temporary lockdowns, most businesses, places of worship, schools, colleges, and other places where large numbers of people congregate were closed. Others operated at a reduced level, and people who could, worked from home. People were asked to practice "social distancing," keeping a safe distance of six feet from one another when they had to go out. Many people wore masks to cover their noses and mouths when they went out in public, and some cities and states required masks in public. Travel out of or into the nation was stopped or severely restricted. The disease had widespread economic effects, as businesses laid off workers. Some businesses failed to survive the downturn.

Throughout 2020, scientists and healthcare workers made heroic efforts to control the disease. Doctors and other healthcare workers developed treatments through research and through efforts in hospitals. Treatments included new ways of using existing drugs and devices.

Meanwhile, researchers worked to develop new vaccines and treatments using genetic engineering. Genetic engineering is a form of biotechnology—the application of technology to biological processes—that involves altering genetic material to achieve a desired result. Genetic engineering can turn existing cells or microscopic organisms into factories that produce large quantities of vaccines, antibodies, or drugs. By late 2020, scientists using genetic engineering had developed several vaccines or treatments for COVID-19.

EXPLAIN What are some of the positive and negative influences of technology today?

Concerns and Hopes for the Future

Americans today are concerned about jobs and the solvency of long-term entitlement programs such as Social Security and Medicare. In addition, the nation is passing through a confusing time of rapid technological change. The revolution in digital and information technologies is comparable to the earlier industrial revolutions of the 1700s and 1800s. These eras of change were characterized by disruption, anxiety, and fears, but also by hopes and opportunities. Americans today are worried about changing patterns of employment and the growing strength of economic competitors. They worry about domestic terrorism, gun control, and school safety. Social injustice and systemic racism remain serious concerns.

But the shifting ground is also providing new perspectives and opportunities for innovation and entrepreneurship, activities that have always stood the nation in good stead. Throughout the country's history, America's resourcefulness and initiative have been among its greatest strengths.

The American ethos, or character, is made up of many other strengths that will continue to offer advantages. U.S. citizens, whatever their origins or ancestry, hold a common bond in standing for certain self-evident truths. In a world torn apart by sectarian strife, America's great strength lies in its religious and ethnic diversity and tolerance, and in its concept of a nation based not on a single, monolithic religious or ethnic identity, but on civic virtues and ideals. These virtues and ideals are the foundation of the republic.

In contrast to many other countries, whose governments retain power through brutal political repression, the American political system provides a strong advantage. American representative democracy allows great flexibility—to decide what policies to adopt or when to change political course. Unlike more authoritarian political systems, where only one party or group remains in control, America is open to diversity of thought and action and to peaceful political change. "We, the people" have the civic and patriotic responsibility to participate in this democratic process. The commitment to political education and voting are a reflection of this patriotism. In a very real sense, Americans work together to make a "more perfect union." These are the civic ideals that offer a path to success in a changing world.

☑ **SUMMARIZE** What advantages does the American political system offer?

☑ ASSESSMENT

1. **Generate Explanations** Explain how immigration has affected American society in recent decades.
2. **Describe** how the American family has changed.
3. **Identify Central Issues** Discuss new civil rights initiatives that have affected the United States.
4. **Compare Points of View** Compare and contrast opinions about large technology companies.
5. **Connections to Today** Explain how changes in technology have affected American culture.

Connections to Today

Teens use their phones to send and receive text and social media messages.

Take Action About Online Communication

Social media is part of many people's lives today. It has become our way of interacting with the world around us. How has social media influenced your life?

1. **Choose** one of the following topics related to social media:
    - **Community Issues:** What is an important issue in your community? Investigate how social media is used to inform people about the issue and how it might be better used.
    - **Political Campaigns:** Investigate the role social media platforms have played in recent elections and whether their use should be regulated.
    - **Reality check:** Research social media influencers and the debates that surround sharing a great deal about one's interests or hobbies on social media.
2. **Ask Questions** Generate a list of questions you have about the topic.
3. **Learn** about the topic and the major issues related to the topic. Are there any major debates related to the topic or issue?
4. **Raise Awareness** Write a blog or post about what you have learned in your research and share it with your school and your community.

Topic 20 Quick Study Guide

LESSON SUMMARIES

Use these Lesson Summaries, and the longer versions available online, to review the key ideas for each lesson in this Topic.

Lesson 1: The George W. Bush Presidency

The results of the 2000 presidential election were disputed. In Florida the vote was very close. The Supreme Court intervened and George W. Bush won. Bush attempted to improve education but Democrats resisted his attempts to reform Social Security. On September 11, 2001, terrorists from the group al Qaeda attacked the United States. Bush declared a war on terrorism, and the U.S. invaded first Afghanistan and then Iraq. In 2008 a major financial crisis began.

Lesson 2: The Barack Obama Presidency

In 2008, Barack Obama was elected as the first African American President. Obama ended the U.S. military mission in Iraq and introduced national health care reform. Although the American economy remained sluggish, Obama won reelection in 2012. During Obama's second term, the U.S. economy improved dramatically, and Americans launched a new movement for racial justice. Obama took action to protect the environment, including agreeing to the 2015 Paris climate accord.

Lesson 3: The Donald Trump Presidency

In 2016, Donald Trump defeated Hillary Clinton for the presidency. Trump had a unique style that included his use of social media to communicate with his followers. His domestic and foreign policy theme was "America First." Trump's policies decreased unauthorized immigration. He also appointed Supreme Court justices. Trump was defeated by Democrat Joe Biden in the 2020 election.

Lesson 4: Americans Look to the Future

At the beginning of the twenty-first century, the global economy and immigration continue to change the American economy and society. Civil rights have contined to expand for many Americans. Environmental concerns remain an important political issue, while technology continues its transformation of all aspects of life. Technological advances continue to improve standards of living and offer the prospect of controlling diseases such as COVID-19. America's diversity and democratic ideals remain a source of strength.

QUEST! FINDINGS

Creating a U.S. Citizenship Course Create your U.S. history timeline and citizenship course by reading parts of Alexis de Tocqueville's *Democracy in America.* Then work with your team to identify eras of history and develop your course. Use the rubric and other Quest online resources to guide your work.

GO ONLINE to access lesson summaries

VISUAL REVIEW

Use these graphics to review some of the key terms, people, and ideas from this Topic.

Major Policies of Three Presidents

PRESIDENT	MAJOR DOMESTIC POLICIES	FOREIGN POLICY EVENTS
George W. Bush	• No Child Left Behind • Tax Cuts • Hurricane Katrina • Troubled Asset Relief Program (TARP)	• Withdrew from Kyoto Protocol • After 9/11 invaded Afghanistan to find terrorists responsible for the attack • Imprisoned accused terrorists in the U.S. base in Guantanamo Bay, Cuba • Invaded Iraq to find WMDs; overthrew Iraqi dictator Saddam Hussein
Barack Obama	• American Recovery and Reinvestment Act • Patient Protection and Affordable Health Care Act • Dodd Frank Wall Street Reform Act and Consumer Protection Act • Deferred Action for Childhood Arrivals (DACA)	• Pulled most troops out of Iraq • Commanded Navy SEALS to capture and kill Osama bin Laden • Led coalition to overthrow Libya's dictator Muammar al-Qaddafi • Began withdrawing combat troops from Afghanistan • Began fighting ISIS
Donald Trump	• Worked toward ending unauthorized immigration and reducing the number of asylum seekers and refugees allowed into the U.S. • Tax Cuts and Jobs Act • Keystone Pipeline	• Renegotiated a trade agreement with Canada and Mexico • Began building a wall along the U.S.-Mexican border • Withdrew from Paris climate agreement • Increased tariffs on China and other nations • Met with North Korea's leader Kim Jong-un • Withdrew troops from Syria; continued to fight ISIS

Twenty-First Century Technology

- Broadband became widely available
- Cell phones converted into more powerful "Smartphones"
- Social media becomes widespread
- E-commerce allows for 24/7 shopping
- Search engines improved algorithms
- News, magazines, books, movies, and music were available online
- Small, but powerful microchips made wearable technology and "smart" devices for the home available

Topic 20 Assessment

KEY TERMS, PEOPLE, AND IDEAS

1. Why did the Supreme Court intervene to determine the outcome of the 2000 Presidential election?
2. What effect did the al Qaeda attacks of September 11, 2001 have on the American people and economy?
3. Why did American forces overthrow the **Taliban** in Afghanistan?
4. Why did the Bush administration invade Iraq?
5. What were the goals of the **Tea Party Movement**?
6. How has technology increased **globalization**?
7. What role do **multinational corporations** play in the global economy?
8. How did the **Immigration Act of 1990** change U.S. demographics?
9. Why are there concerns about Social Security benefits?

CRITICAL THINKING

10. **Identify Cause and Effect** (a.) How has the nature of the American economy changed? (b.) What kinds of jobs are available to American workers?
11. **Cite Evidence** How did the response to terrorism under President Bush affect domestic security?
12. **Summarize** (a.) What issues were addressed by *Hamdan* v. *Rumsfeld*? (b.) How did the Supreme Court rule in this case?
13. **Evaluate Information** (a.) Why did President Obama introduce the Patient Protection and Affordable Care Act? (b.) Why did many oppose it?
14. **Draw Inferences** What areas of the United States are most threatened by climate change?
15. **Make Generalizations** What did President Trump's promise to "put America first" mean in practice?
16. **Analyze Graphs** Study the graph. (a.) Identify the largest source of immigration. (b.) Explain why so many have come from this region.

Sources of Immigration, 2000–2014

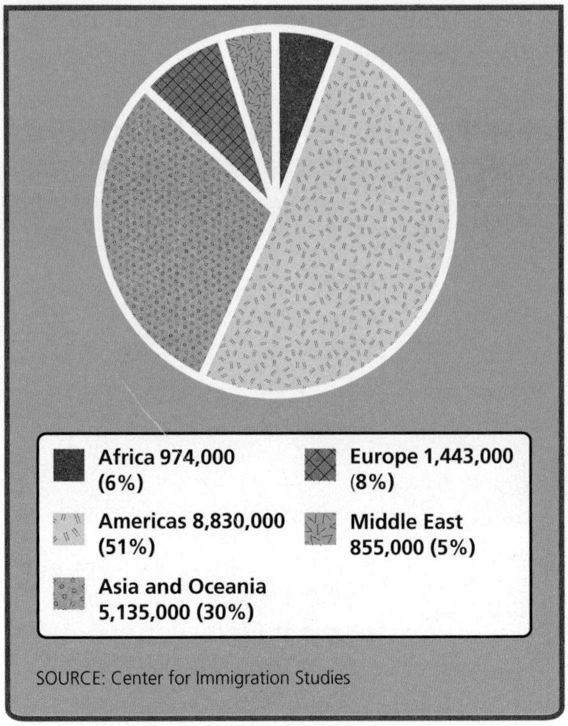

SOURCE: Center for Immigration Studies

17. **Writing Activity: Compose an Informative Essay** Evaluate how this excerpt from President Barack Obama's second inaugural address outlines his political views. Use your knowledge of Obama's programs and policies to write an informative essay. Remember to write a thesis, cite evidence, and maintain an organized, formal structure.

> But we have always understood that when times change, so must we; that fidelity to our founding principles requires new responses to new challenges; that preserving our individual freedoms ultimately requires collective action. For the American people can no more meet the demands of today's world by acting alone than American soldiers could have met the forces of fascism or communism with muskets and militias. No single person can train all the math and science teachers we'll need to equip our children for the future, or build the roads and networks and research labs that will bring new jobs and businesses to our shores. Now, more than ever, we must do these things together, as one nation and one people.
> —*Barack Obama, January 21, 2013*

18. **Connections to Today** What are some pros and cons regarding the use of social media by high school students?

DOCUMENT-BASED QUESTIONS

The War in Iraq was a controversial event both nationally and internationally. Read the documents below, then answer the questions that follow.

DOCUMENT A

This excerpt is from a contemporary newspaper editorial.

> Mr. Bush's "Plan for Victory" speech was, of course, the usual unadulterated nonsense. Its overarching theme—"We will never accept anything less than complete victory"—was being contradicted even as he spoke by rampant reports of Pentagon plans for stepped-up troop withdrawals. . . . The specifics were phony, too. Once again inflating the readiness of Iraqi troops, Mr. Bush claimed that the recent assault on Tal Afar "was primarily led by Iraqi security forces"—a fairy tale immediately unmasked by Michael Ware, a Time reporter embedded in the battle's front lines, as "completely wrong."
>
> *—Frank Rich, The New York Times, December 11, 2005*

DOCUMENT B

The photograph shows a toppled statue in Iraq after the U.S.-led invasion.

DOCUMENT C

This excerpt is from an address by Donald Rumsfeld, Secretary of Defense under Bush.

> It's a strange time:
>
> - . . . when a senior editor at Newsweek, disparagingly refers to the brave volunteers in our armed forces . . . as a "mercenary army;"
> - When the former head of CNN accuses the American military of deliberately targeting journalists. . . .
>
> Those who know the truth need to speak out against these kinds of myths and distortions that are being told about our troops and about our country. America is not what's wrong with the world.
>
> *—Donald Rumsfeld, Address at the American Legion National Convention, August 29, 2006*

DOCUMENT D

In this excerpt from a lecture, Amy Goodman, a journalist, examines media coverage of the war.

> Fairness and Accuracy in Reporting did a study. In the week leading up to General Colin Powell going to the Security Council to make his case for the invasions and the week afterwards—this was the period where more than half of the people in this country were opposed to an invasion—they did a study of . . . the four major newscasts. Two weeks. Three hundred and ninety-three interviews on war. Three were anti-war voices. Three of almost four hundred, and that included PBS. . . . [T]hey have to provide the diversity of opinion that fully expresses the debate and the anguish and the discussions that are going on all over this country. That is media serving a democratic society.
>
> *—Amy Goodman, "Independent Media in a Time of War," April 21, 2003*

19. In Document A, the writer claims that Bush's statements about the Iraq War are
A. too optimistic to be true.
B. the result of misinformation.
C. a reliable source of information about the war.
D. not revealing the truth about the situation.

20. Discuss the significance of the photograph shown in Document B.

21. In Document C, the media is characterized as
A. biased in favor of the war.
B. biased against the military.
C. supportive of the enemy.
D. influenced by foreign media.

22. In Document D, the speaker believes the media
A. was too supportive of the administration.
B. should have been supporting the war effort.
C. was gagged by the Bush administration.
D. was too favorable to the enemy.

23. **Writing Activity** Write a paragraph explaining why you think the Iraq War remains so controversial. Use the sources as well as additional information you have learned about this conflict.

GO ONLINE to access more practice

Constitution Quick Study Guide

Preamble

Articles

Article I. Legislative Department

Section 1.	Legislative Power, the Congress
Section 2.	House of Representatives
Section 3.	Senate
Section 4.	Elections and Meetings
Section 5.	Legislative Proceedings
Section 6.	Compensation, Immunities, and Disabilities of Members
Section 7.	Revenue Bills; President's Veto
Section 8.	Powers of Congress
Section 9.	Powers Denied to Congress
Section 10.	Powers Denied to the States

Article II. Executive Department

Section 1.	Executive Power; The President; Term; Election; Qualifications; Compensation; Oath of Office
Section 2.	President's Powers and Duties
Section 3.	President's Powers and Duties
Section 4.	Impeachment

Article III. Judicial Department

Section 1.	Judicial Power; Courts; Terms of Office
Section 2.	Jurisdiction
Section 3.	Treason

Article IV. Relations Among the States

Section 1.	Full Faith and Credit
Section 2.	Privileges and Immunities of Citizens
Section 3.	New States, Territories
Section 4.	Protection Afforded to States by the Nation

Article V. Provisions for Amendment

Article VI. Public Debts; Supremacy of National Law; Oath

Section 1.	Validity of Debts
Section 2.	Supremacy of National Law
Section 3.	Oaths of Office

Article VII. Ratification of Constitution

Amendments

1st Amendment:	**Freedom of Religion, Speech, Press, Assembly, and Petition**
2nd Amendment:	**Right to Keep, Bear Arms**
3rd Amendment:	**Lodging Troops in Private Homes**
4th Amendment:	**Search, Seizures, Proper Warrants**
5th Amendment:	**Criminal Proceedings, Due Process, Eminent Domain**
6th Amendment:	**Criminal Proceedings**
7th Amendment:	**Jury Trials in Civil Cases**
8th Amendment:	**Bail; Cruel, Unusual Punishment**
9th Amendment:	**Unenumerated Rights**
10th Amendment:	**Powers Reserved to the States**
11th Amendment:	**Suits Against the States**
12th Amendment:	**Election of President and Vice President**
13th Amendment:	**Slavery and Involuntary Servitude**
Section 1.	Slavery and Involuntary Servitude Prohibited
Section 2.	Power of Congress
14th Amendment:	**Rights of Citizens**
Section 1.	Citizenship; Privileges and Immunities; Due Process; Equal Protection
Section 2.	Apportionment of Representation
Section 3.	Disqualification of Officers
Section 4.	Public Debt
Section 5.	Powers of Congress
15th Amendment:	**Right to Vote—Race, Color, Servitude**
Section 1.	Suffrage Not to Be Abridged
Section 2.	Power of Congress
16th Amendment:	**Income Tax**
17th Amendment:	**Popular Election of Senators**
Section 1.	Popular Election of Senators
Section 2.	Senate Vacancies
Section 3.	Inapplicable to Senators Previously Chosen
18th Amendment:	**Prohibition of Intoxicating Liquors**
Section 1.	Intoxicating Liquors Prohibited
Section 2.	Concurrent Power to Enforce
Section 3.	Time Limit on Ratification
19th Amendment:	**Equal Suffrage—Sex**
Section 1.	Suffrage Not to Be Abridged
Section 2.	Power of Congress
20th Amendment:	**Commencement of Terms; Sessions of Congress; Death or Disqualification of President-Elect**
Section 1.	Terms of President, Vice President, members of Congress
Section 2.	Sessions of Congress
Section 3.	Death or Disqualification of President-Elect
Section 4.	Congress to Provide for Certain Successors
Section 5.	Effective Date
Section 6.	Time Limit on Ratification
21st Amendment:	**Repeal of 18th Amendment**
Section 1.	Repeal of Prohibition
Section 2.	Transportation, Importation of Intoxicating Liquors
Section 3.	Time Limit on Ratification
22nd Amendment:	**Presidential Tenure**
Section 1.	Restriction on Number of Terms
Section 2.	Time Limit on Ratification
23rd Amendment:	**Inclusion of District of Columbia in Presidential Election Systems**
Section 1.	Presidential Electors for District
Section 2.	Power of Congress
24th Amendment:	**Right to Vote in Federal Elections—Tax Payment**
Section 1.	Suffrage Not to Be Abridged
Section 2.	Power of Congress
25th Amendment:	**Presidential Succession; Vice Presidential Vacancy; Presidential Inability**
Section 1.	Presidential Succession
Section 2.	Vice Presidential Vacancy
Section 3.	Presidential Inability
26th Amendment:	**Right to Vote—Age**
Section 1.	Suffrage Not to Be Abridged
Section 2.	Power of Congress
27th Amendment:	**Congressional Pay**

The Preamble states the broad purposes the Constitution is intended to serve—to establish a government that provides for greater cooperation among the States, ensures justice and peace, provides for defense against foreign enemies, promotes the general well-being of the people, and secures liberty now and in the future. The phrase We the People emphasizes the twin concepts of popular sovereignty and of representative government.

PREAMBLE

We the People of the United States, in Order to form a more perfect Union, establish Justice, insure domestic Tranquility, provide for the common defence, promote the general Welfare, and secure the Blessings of Liberty to ourselves and our Posterity, do ordain and establish this Constitution for the United States of America.

Legislative Department

Section 1. Legislative power; Congress

Congress, the nation's lawmaking body, is bicameral in form; that is, it is composed of two houses: the Senate and the House of Representatives. The Framers of the Constitution purposely separated the lawmaking power from the power to enforce the laws (Article II, the Executive Branch) and the power to interpret them (Article III, the Judicial Branch). This system of separation of powers is supplemented by a system of checks and balances; that is, in several provisions the Constitution gives to each of the three branches various powers with which it may restrain the actions of the other two branches.

Article I.

Section 1.

All legislative Powers herein granted shall be vested in a Congress of the United States, which shall consist of a Senate and House of Representatives.

Section 2. House of Representatives

▶ **Clause 1. Election** Electors means voters. Members of the House of Representatives are elected every two years. Each State must permit the same persons to vote for United States representatives as it permits to vote for the members of the larger house of its own legislature. The 17th Amendment (1913) extends this requirement to the qualification of voters for United States senators.

▶ **Clause 2. Qualifications** A member of the House of Representatives must be at least 25 years old, an American citizen for seven years, and a resident of the State he or she represents. In addition, political custom requires that a representative also reside in the district from which he or she is elected.

▶ **Clause 3. Apportionment** The number of representatives each State is entitled to is based on its population, which is counted every 10 years in the census. Congress reapportions the seats among the States after each census. In the Reapportionment Act of 1929, Congress fixed the permanent size of the House at 435 members with each State having at least one representative. Today there is one House seat for approximately every 700,000 persons in the population.

The words "three-fifths of all other persons" referred to slaves and reflected the Three-Fifths Compromise reached by the Framers at Philadelphia in 1787; the phrase was made obsolete, was in effect repealed, by the 13th Amendment in 1865.

▶ **Clause 4. Vacancies** The executive authority refers to the governor of a State. If a member leaves office or dies before the expiration of his or her term, the governor is to call a special election to fill the vacancy.

Section 2.

▶ 1. The House of Representatives shall be composed of Members chosen every second Year by the People of the several States, and the Electors in each State shall have the Qualifications requisite for Electors of the most numerous Branch of the State Legislature.

▶ 2. No Person shall be a Representative who shall not have attained to the age of twenty-five Years, and been seven Years a Citizen of the United States, and who shall not, when elected, be an Inhabitant of that State in which he shall be chosen.

▶ 3. Representatives and direct Taxes* shall be apportioned among the several States which may be included within this Union, according to their respective Numbers, which shall be determined by adding to the whole Number of free Persons, including those bound to Service for a Term of Years and excluding Indians not taxed, three fifths of all other Persons. The actual Enumeration shall be made within three Years after the first Meeting of the Congress of the United States, and within every subsequent term of ten Years, in such Manner as they shall by Law direct. The Number of Representatives shall not exceed one for every thirty Thousand, but each State shall have at Least one Representative; and, until such enumeration shall be made, the State of New Hampshire shall be entitled to choose three, Massachusetts eight, Rhode Island and Providence Plantations one, Connecticut five, New York six, New Jersey four, Pennsylvania eight, Delaware one, Maryland six, Virginia ten, North Carolina five, South Carolina five, and Georgia three.

▶ 4. When vacancies happen in the Representation from any State, the Executive Authority thereof shall issue Writs of Election to fill such Vacancies.

---

* The gray words indicate portions of the Constitution altered by subsequent amendments to the document.

▶5. The House of Representatives shall choose their Speaker and other Officers; and shall have the sole Power of Impeachment.

▶ **Clause 5. Officers; impeachment** The House elects a Speaker, customarily chosen from the majority party in the House. Impeachment means accusation. The House has the exclusive power to impeach, or accuse, civil officers; the Senate (Article I, Section 3, Clause 6) has the exclusive power to try those impeached by the House.

Section 3.

▶1. The Senate of the United States shall be composed of two Senators from each State chosen by the Legislature thereof for six Years; and each Senator shall have one Vote.

▶2. Immediately after they shall be assembled in Consequences of the first Election, they shall be divided, as equally as may be, into three Classes. The Seats of the Senators of the first Class shall be vacated at the Expiration of the second Year; of the second Class, at the Expiration of the fourth Year; and of the third Class, at the Expiration of the sixth Year; so that one-third may be chosen every second Year; and if Vacancies happen by Resignation, or otherwise, during the Recess of the Legislature of any State, the Executive thereof may make temporary Appointments until the next Meeting of the Legislature, which shall then fill such Vacancies.

▶3. No Person shall be a Senator who shall not have attained to the Age of thirty Years, and been nine Years a Citizen of the United States, and who shall not, when elected, be an Inhabitant of that State for which he shall be chosen.

▶4. The Vice President of the United States shall be President of the Senate but shall have no Vote, unless they be equally divided.

▶5. The Senate shall choose their other Officers, and also a President pro tempore, in the Absence of the Vice President, or when he shall exercise the Office of President of the United States.

▶6. The Senate shall have the sole Power to try all Impeachments. When sitting for that Purpose, they shall be on Oath or Affirmation. When the President of the United States is tried, the Chief Justice shall preside: And no Person shall be convicted without the Concurrence of two thirds of the Members present.

▶7. Judgment in Cases of Impeachment shall not extend further than to removal from Office, and disqualification to hold and enjoy any Office of honor, Trust, or Profit under the United States: but the Party convicted shall nevertheless be liable and subject to Indictment, Trial, Judgment and Punishment, according to Law.

Section 3. Senate

▶ **Clause 1. Composition, election, term** Each State has two senators. Each serves for six years and has one vote. Originally, senators were not elected directly by the people, but by each State's legislature. The 17th Amendment, added in 1913, provides for the popular election of senators.

▶ **Clause 2. Classification** The senators elected in 1788 were divided into three groups so that the Senate could become a "continuing body." One-third of the Senate's seats are up for election every two years.

The 17th Amendment provides that a Senate vacancy is to be filled at a special election called by the governor; State law may also permit the governor to appoint a successor to serve until that election is held.

▶ **Clause 3. Qualifications** A senator must be at least 30 years old, a citizen for at least nine years, and must live in the State from which elected.

▶ **Clause 4. Presiding officer** The Vice President presides over the Senate, but may vote only to break a tie.

▶ **Clause 5. Other officers** The Senate chooses its own officers, including a president pro tempore to preside when the Vice President is not there.

▶ **Clause 6. Impeachment trials** The Senate conducts the trials of those officials impeached by the House. The Vice President presides unless the President is on trial, in which case the Chief Justice of the United States does so. A conviction requires the votes of two-thirds of the senators present.

No President has ever been convicted. In 1868 the House voted eleven articles of impeachment against President Andrew Johnson, but the Senate fell one vote short of convicting him. In 1974 President Richard M. Nixon resigned the presidency in the face of almost certain impeachment by the House. The House brought two articles of impeachment against President Bill Clinton in late 1998. Neither charge was supported by even a simple majority vote in the Senate, on February 12, 1999.

▶ **Clause 7. Penalty on conviction** The punishment of an official convicted in an impeachment case has always been removal from office. The Senate can also bar a convicted person from ever holding any federal office, but it is not required to do so. A convicted person can also be tried and punished in a regular court for any crime involved in the impeachment case.

Section 4. Elections and Meetings

▶ **Clause 1. Election** In 1842 Congress required that representatives be elected from districts within each State with more than one seat in the House. The districts in each State are drawn by that State's legislature. Seven States now have only one seat in the House: Alaska, Delaware, Montana, North Dakota, South Dakota, Vermont, and Wyoming. The 1842 law also directed that representatives be elected in each State on the same day: the Tuesday after the first Monday in November of every even-numbered year. In 1914 Congress also set that same date for the election of senators.

▶ **Clause 2. Sessions** Congress must meet at least once a year. The 20th Amendment (1933) changed the opening date to January 3.

Section 5. Legislative Proceedings

▶ **Clause 1. Admission of members; quorum** In 1969 the Supreme Court held that the House cannot exclude any member-elect who satisfies the qualifications set out in Article I, Section 2, Clause 2.

A majority in the House (218 members) or Senate (51) constitutes a quorum. In practice, both houses often proceed with less than a quorum present. However, any member may raise a point of order (demand a "quorum call"). If a roll call then reveals less than a majority of the members present, that chamber must either adjourn or the sergeant at arms must be ordered to round up absent members.

▶ **Clause 2. Rules** Each house has adopted detailed rules to guide its proceedings. Each house may discipline members for unacceptable conduct; expulsion requires a two-thirds vote.

▶ **Clause 3. Record** Each house must keep and publish a record of its meetings. The Congressional Record is published for every day that either house of Congress is in session, and provides a written record of all that is said and done on the floor of each house each session.

▶ **Clause 4. Adjournment** Once in session, neither house may suspend (recess) its work for more than three days without the approval of the other house. Both houses must always meet in the same location.

Section 4.

▶1. The Times, Places and Manner of holding Elections for Senators and Representatives, shall be prescribed in each State by the Legislature thereof; but the Congress may at any time by law make or alter such Regulations, except as to the Places of choosing Senators.

▶2. The Congress shall assemble at least once in every Year, and such Meeting shall be on the first Monday in December, unless they shall by Law appoint a different Day.

Section 5.

▶1. Each House shall be the Judge of the Elections, Returns and Qualifications of its own Members, and a Majority of each shall constitute a Quorum to do Business; but a smaller Number may adjourn from day to day, and may be authorized to compel the Attendance of absent Members, in such Manner, and under such Penalties, as each House may provide.

▶2. Each House may determine the Rules of its Proceedings, punish its Members for disorderly Behavior, and, with the Concurrence of two thirds, expel a Member.

▶3. Each House shall keep a Journal of its Proceedings, and from time to time publish the same, excepting such Parts as may in their Judgment require Secrecy; and the Yeas and Nays of the Members of either House on any question shall, at the Desire of one fifth of those Present, be entered on the Journal.

▶4. Neither House, during the Session of Congress, shall, without the Consent of the other, adjourn for more than three days, nor to any other Place than that in which the two Houses shall be sitting.

Section 6.

▶ 1. The Senators and Representatives shall receive a Compensation for their Services, to be ascertained by Law, and paid out of the Treasury of the United States. They shall in all Cases, except Treason, Felony, and Breach of the Peace, be privileged from Arrest during their Attendance at the Session of their respective Houses, and in going to and returning from the same; and for any Speech or Debate in either House, they shall not be questioned in any other Place.

Section 6. Compensation, Immunities, and Disabilities of Members

▶ **Clause 1. Salaries; immunities** Each house sets its members' salaries, paid by the United States; the 27th Amendment (1992) modified this pay-setting power. This provision establishes "legislative immunity." The purpose of this immunity is to allow members to speak and debate freely in Congress itself. Treason is strictly defined in Article III, Section 3. A felony is any serious crime. A breach of the peace is any indictable offense less than treason or a felony; this exemption from arrest is of little real importance today.

▶ 2. No Senator or Representative shall, during the Time for which he was elected, be appointed to any civil Office under the Authority of the United States, which shall have been created, or the Emoluments whereof shall have been increased during such time; and no Person holding any Office under the United States, shall be a Member of either House during his Continuance in Office.

▶ **Clause 2. Restrictions on office holding** No sitting member of either house may be appointed to an office in the executive or in the judicial branch if that position was created or its salary was increased during that member's current elected term. The second part of this clause—forbidding any person serving in either the executive or the judicial branch from also serving in Congress—reinforces the principle of separation of powers.

Section 7.

▶ 1. All Bills for raising Revenue shall originate in the House of Representatives; but the Senate may propose or concur with amendments as on other Bills.

Section 7. Revenue Bills, President's Veto

▶ **Clause 1. Revenue bills** All bills that raise money must originate in the House. However, the Senate has the power to amend any revenue bill sent to it from the lower house.

▶ 2. Every Bill which shall have passed the House of Representatives and the Senate, shall, before it become a law, be presented to the President of the United States: If he approve, he shall sign it, but if not he shall return it, with his Objections to that House in which it shall have originated, who shall enter the Objections at large on their Journal, and proceed to reconsider it. If after such Reconsideration two thirds of the House shall agree to pass the Bill, it shall be sent, together with the Objections, to the other House, by which it shall likewise be reconsidered, and if approved by two thirds of that House, it shall become a Law. But in all such Cases the Votes of both Houses shall be determined by Yeas and Nays, and the Names of the Persons voting for and against the Bill shall be entered on the Journal of each House respectively. If any Bill shall not be returned by the President within ten Days (Sunday excepted) after it shall have been presented to him, the Same shall be a law, in like Manner as if he had signed it, unless the Congress by their Adjournment, prevent its Return, in which Case it shall not be a Law.

▶ **Clause 2. Enactment of laws; veto** Once both houses have passed a bill, it must be sent to the President. The President may (1) sign the bill, thus making it law; (2) veto the bill, whereupon it must be returned to the house in which it originated; or (3) allow the bill to become law without signature, by not acting upon it within 10 days of its receipt from Congress, not counting Sundays. The President has a fourth option at the end of a congressional session: If he does not act on a measure within 10 days, and Congress adjourns during that period, the bill dies; the "pocket veto" has been applied to it. A presidential veto may be overridden by a two-thirds vote in each house.

▶ 3. Every Order, Resolution, or Vote to which the Concurrence of the Senate and House of Representatives may be necessary (except on a question of adjournment) shall be presented to the President of the United States; and before the Same shall take Effect, shall be approved by him, or, being disapproved by him, shall be repassed by two thirds of the Senate and House of Representatives, according to the Rules and Limitations prescribed in the Case of a Bill.

▶ **Clause 3. Other measures** This clause refers to joint resolutions, measures Congress often passes to deal with unusual, temporary, or ceremonial matters. A joint resolution passed by Congress and signed by the President has the force of law, just as a bill does. As a matter of custom, a joint resolution proposing an amendment to the Constitution is not submitted to the President for signature or veto. Concurrent and simple resolutions do not have the force of law and, therefore, are not submitted to the President.

Section 8. Powers of Congress

▶ **Clause 1.** The 18 separate clauses in this section set out 27 of the many expressed powers the Constitution grants to Congress. In this clause Congress is given the power to levy and provide for the collection of various kinds of taxes, in order to finance the operations of the government. All federal taxes must be levied at the same rates throughout the country.

▶ **Clause 2.** Congress has power to borrow money to help finance the government. Federal borrowing is most often done through the sale of bonds on which interest is paid. The Constitution does not limit the amount the government may borrow.

▶ **Clause 3.** This clause, the Commerce Clause, gives Congress the power to regulate both foreign and interstate trade. Much of what Congress does, it does on the basis of its commerce power.

▶ **Clause 4.** Congress has the exclusive power to determine how aliens may become citizens of the United States. Congress may also pass laws relating to bankruptcy.

▶ **Clause 5.** has the power to establish and require the use of uniform gauges of time, distance, weight, volume, area, and the like.

▶ **Clause 6.** Congress has the power to make it a federal crime to falsify the coins, paper money, bonds, stamps, and the like of the United States.

▶ **Clause 7.** Congress has the power to provide for and regulate the transportation and delivery of mail; "post offices" are those buildings and other places where mail is deposited for dispatch; "post roads" include all routes over or upon which mail is carried.

▶ **Clause 8.** Congress has the power to provide for copyrights and patents. A copyright gives an author or composer the exclusive right to control the reproduction, publication, and sale of literary, musical, or other creative work. A patent gives a person the exclusive right to control the manufacture or sale of his or her invention.

▶ **Clause 9.** Congress has the power to create the lower federal courts, all of the several federal courts that function beneath the Supreme Court.

▶ **Clause 10.** Congress has the power to prohibit, as a federal crime: (1) certain acts committed outside the territorial jurisdiction of the United States, and (2) the commission within the United States of any wrong against any nation with which we are at peace.

Section 8.

The Congress shall have Power

▶1. To lay and collect Taxes, Duties, Imposts and Excises to pay the Debts and provide for the common Defence and general Welfare of the United States; but all Duties, Imposts and Excises, shall be uniform throughout the United States;

▶2. To borrow Money on the credit of the United States;

▶3. To regulate Commerce with foreign Nations, and among the several States, and with the Indian Tribes;

▶4. To establish an uniform Rule of Naturalization, and uniform Laws on the subject of Bankruptcies throughout the United States;

▶5. To coin Money, regulate the Value thereof, and of foreign Coin, and fix the Standard of Weights and Measures;

▶6. To provide for the Punishment of counterfeiting the Securities and current Coin of the United States;

▶7. To establish Post Offices and post Roads;

▶8. To promote the Progress of Science and useful Arts, by securing, for limited Times to Authors and Inventors the exclusive Right to their respective Writings and Discoveries;

▶9. To constitute Tribunals inferior to the supreme Court;

▶10. To define and punish Piracies and Felonies committed on the high Seas, and Offences against the Law of nations;

▶11. To declare War, grant Letters of Marque and Reprisal, and make Rules concerning Captures on Land and Water;

▶ **Clause 11.** Only Congress can declare war. However, the President, as commander in chief of the armed forces (Article II, Section 2, Clause 1), can make war without such a formal declaration. Letters of marque and reprisal are commissions authorizing private persons to outfit vessels (privateers) to capture and destroy enemy ships in time of war; they were forbidden in international law by the Declaration of Paris of 1856, and the United States has honored the ban since the Civil War.

▶12. To raise and support Armies; but no Appropriation of Money to that Use shall be for a longer Term than two Years;

▶13. To provide and maintain a Navy;

▶ **Clauses 12 and 13.** Congress has the power to provide for and maintain the nation's armed forces. It established the air force as an independent element of the armed forces in 1947, an exercise of its inherent powers in foreign relations and national defense. The two-year limit on spending for the army insures civilian control of the military.

▶14. To make Rules for the Government and Regulation of the land and naval Forces;

▶ **Clause 14.** Today these rules are set out in three principle statutes: the Uniform Code of Military Justice, passed by Congress in 1950, and the Military Justice Acts of 1958 and 1983.

▶15. To provide for calling forth the Militia to execute the Laws of the Union, suppress Insurrections and repel Invasions;

▶16. To provide for organizing, arming, and disciplining the Militia, and for governing such Part of them as may be employed in the Service of the United States, reserving to the States respectively the Appointment of the Officers, and the Authority of training the Militia according to the discipline prescribed by Congress;

▶ **Clauses 15 and 16.** In the National Defense Act of 1916, Congress made each State's militia (volunteer army) a part of the National Guard. Today, Congress and the States cooperate in its maintenance. Ordinarily, each State's National Guard is under the command of that State's governor; but Congress has given the President the power to call any or all of those units into federal service when necessary.

▶17. To exercise exclusive Legislation in all Cases whatsoever, over such District (not exceeding ten Miles square) as may, by Cession of Particular States, and the Acceptance of Congress, become the Seat of the Government of the United States, and to exercise like Authority over all Places purchased by the Consent of the Legislature of the State in which the Same shall be, for the Erection of Forts, Magazines, Arsenals, Dockyards and other needful Buildings;—And

▶ **Clause 17.** In 1791 Congress accepted land grants from Maryland and Virginia and established the District of Columbia for the nation's capital. Assuming Virginia's grant would never be needed, Congress returned it in 1846. Today, the elected government of the District's 69 square miles operates under the authority of Congress. Congress also has the power to acquire other lands from the States for various federal purposes.

▶18. To make all Laws which shall be necessary and proper for carrying into Execution the foregoing Powers and all other Powers vested by this Constitution in the Government of the United States, or in any Department or Officer thereof.

▶ **Clause 18.** This is the Necessary and Proper Clause, also often called the Elastic Clause. It is the constitutional basis for the many and far-reaching implied powers of the Federal Government.

Section 9.

▶1. The Migration or Importation of such Persons as any of the States now existing shall think proper to admit, shall not be prohibited by the Congress prior to the Year one thousand eight hundred and eight, but a Tax or duty may be imposed on such Importation, not exceeding ten dollars for each Person.

Section 9. Powers Denied to Congress

▶ **Clause 1.** The phrase "such persons" referred to slaves. This provision was part of the Commerce Compromise, one of the bargains struck in the writing of the Constitution. Congress outlawed the slave trade in 1808.

▶ **Clause 2.** A writ of habeas corpus, the "great writ of liberty," is a court order directing a sheriff, warden, or other public officer, or a private person, who is detaining another to "produce the body" of the one being held in order that the legality of the detention may be determined by the court.

▶2. The Privilege of the Writ of Habeas Corpus shall not be suspended, unless when in Cases of Rebellion or Invasion the public safety may require it.

▶ **Clause 3.** A bill of attainder is a legislative act that inflicts punishment without a judicial trial. See Article I, Section 10, and Article III, Section 3, Clause 2. An ex post facto law is any criminal law that operates retroactively to the disadvantage of the accused. See Article I, Section 10.

▶3. No Bill of Attainder or ex post facto Law shall be passed.

▶ **Clause 4.** A capitation tax is literally a "head tax," a tax levied on each person in the population. A direct tax is one paid directly to the government by the taxpayer—for example, an income or a property tax; an indirect tax is one paid to another private party who then pays it to the government—for example, a sales tax. This provision was modified by the 16th Amendment (1913), giving Congress the power to levy "taxes on incomes, from whatever source derived."

▶4. No Capitation, or other direct, Tax shall be laid, unless in Proportion to the Census of Enumeration hereinbefore directed to be taken.

▶ **Clause 5.** This provision was a part of the Commerce Compromise made by the Framers in 1787. Congress has the power to tax imported goods, however.

▶5. No Tax or Duty shall be laid on Articles exported from any State.

▶ **Clause 6.** All ports within the United States must be treated alike by Congress as it exercises its taxing and commerce powers. Congress cannot tax goods sent by water from one State to another, nor may it give the ports of one State any legal advantage over those of another.

▶6. No Preference shall be given by any Regulation of Commerce or Revenue to the Ports of one State over those of another: nor shall Vessels bound to, or from, one State, be obliged to enter, clear or pay Duties in another.

▶ **Clause 7.** This clause gives Congress its vastly important "power of the purse," a major check on presidential power. Federal money can be spent only in those amounts and for those purposes expressly authorized by an act of Congress. All federal income and spending must be accounted for, regularly and publicly.

▶7. No Money shall be drawn from the Treasury, but in Consequence of Appropriations made by Law; and a regular Statement and Account of the Receipts and Expenditures of all public Money shall be published from time to time.

▶ **Clause 8.** This provision, preventing the establishment of a nobility, reflects the principle that "all men are created equal." It was also intended to discourage foreign attempts to bribe or otherwise corrupt officers of the government.

▶8. No Title of Nobility shall be granted by the United States: And no Person holding any Office of Profit or Trust under them, shall, without the Consent of the Congress, accept of any present, Emolument, Office, or Title, of any kind whatever, from any King, Prince, or foreign State.

Section 10. Powers Denied to the States

▶ **Clause 1.** The States are not sovereign governments and so cannot make agreements or otherwise negotiate with foreign states; the power to conduct foreign relations is an exclusive power of the National Government. The power to coin money is also an exclusive power of the National Government. Several powers forbidden to the National Government are here also forbidden to the States.

Section 10.

▶1. No State shall enter into any Treaty, Alliance, or Confederation; grant Letters of Marque and Reprisal; coin Money; emit Bills of Credit; make any Thing but gold and silver Coin a Tender in Payment of Debts; pass any Bill of Attainder, ex post facto Law, or Law impairing the Obligation of Contracts, or grant any Title of Nobility.

▶ **Clause 2.** This provision relates to foreign, not interstate, commerce. Only Congress, not the States, can tax imports; and the States are, like Congress, forbidden the power to tax exports.

▶2. No State shall, without the Consent of the Congress, lay any Imposts or Duties on Imports or Exports, except what may be absolutely necessary for executing its inspection Laws; and the net Produce of all Duties and Imposts, laid by any State on Imports or Exports, shall be for the Use of the Treasury of the United States; and all such Laws shall be subject to the Revision and Control of the Congress.

▶3. No State shall, without the Consent of Congress, lay any Duty of Tonnage, keep Troops, or Ships of War in time of Peace, enter into any Agreement or Compact with another State, or with a foreign Power, or engage in War, unless actually invaded, or in such imminent Danger as will not admit of delay.

▶ **Clause 3.** A duty of tonnage is a tax laid on ships according to their cargo capacity. Each State has a constitutional right to provide for and maintain a militia; but no State may keep a standing army or navy. The several restrictions here prevent the States from assuming powers that the Constitution elsewhere grants to the National Government.

Article II

Section 1.

▶1. The executive Power shall be vested in a President of the United States of America. He shall hold his Office during the Term of four Years, and, together with the Vice President, chosen for the same Term, be elected as follows:

▶2. Each State shall appoint, in such Manner as the Legislature thereof may direct, a Number of Electors, equal to the whole Number of Senators and Representatives to which the State may be entitled in the Congress: but no Senator or Representative, or Person holding an Office of Trust or Profit, under the United States, shall be appointed an Elector.

▶3. The Electors shall meet in their respective States, and vote by Ballot for two Persons, of whom one at least shall not be an Inhabitant of the same State with themselves. And they shall make a List of all the Persons voted for, and of the Number of Votes for each; which List they shall sign and certify, and transmit sealed to the Seat of the Government of the United States, directed to the President of the Senate. The President of the Senate shall, in the Presence of the Senate and House of Representatives, open all the Certificates, and the Votes shall then be counted. The Person having the greatest Number of Votes shall be the President, if such Number be a majority of the whole Number of Electors appointed; and if there be more than one who have such Majority, and have an equal Number of Votes, then, the House of Representatives shall immediately choose by Ballot one of them for President; and if no Person have a Majority, then from the five highest on the List the said House shall in like Manner choose the President. But in choosing the President, the Votes shall be taken by States, the Representatives from each State having one Vote; a quorum for this Purpose shall consist of a Member or Members from two thirds of the States, and a Majority of all the States shall be necessary to a Choice. In every Case, after the Choice of the President, the Person having the greatest Number of Votes of the Electors shall be the Vice President. But if there should remain two or more who have equal Votes, the Senate shall choose from them by Ballot the Vice President.

Executive Department

Section 1. President and Vice President

▶ **Clause 1. Executive power, term** This clause gives to the President the very broad "executive power," the power to enforce the laws and otherwise administer the public policies of the United States. It also sets the length of the presidential (and vice-presidential) term of office; see the 22nd Amendment (1951), which places a limit on presidential (but not vice-presidential) tenure.

▶ **Clause 2. Electoral college** This clause establishes the "electoral college," although the Constitution does not use that term. It is a body of presidential electors chosen in each State, and it selects the President and Vice President every four years. The number of electors chosen in each State equals the number of senators and representatives that State has in Congress.

▶ **Clause 3. Election of President and Vice President** This clause was replaced by the 12th Amendment in 1804.

▶ **Clause 4. Date** Congress has set the date for the choosing of electors as the Tuesday after the first Monday in November every fourth year, and for the casting of electoral votes as the Monday after the second Wednesday in December of that year.

▶4. The Congress may determine the Time of choosing the Electors, and the Day on which they shall give their Votes; which Day shall be the same throughout the United States.

▶ **Clause 5. Qualifications** The President must have been born a citizen of the United States, be at least 35 years old, and have been a resident of the United States for at least 14 years.

▶5. No Person except a natural born Citizen, or a Citizen of the United States, at the time of the Adoption of this Constitution, shall be eligible to the Office of President; neither shall any person be eligible to that Office who shall not have attained to the Age of thirty-five Years, and been fourteen Years a Resident within the United States.

▶ **Clause 6. Vacancy** This clause was modified by the 25th Amendment (1967), which provides expressly for the succession of the Vice President, for the filling of a vacancy in the Vice Presidency, and for the determination of presidential inability.

▶6. In Case of the Removal of the President from Office, or of his Death, Resignation, or Inability to discharge the Powers and Duties of the said Office, the Same shall devolve on the Vice President, and the Congress may by Law provide for the Case of Removal, Death, Resignation or Inability, both of the President and Vice President, declaring what Officer shall then act as President, and such Officer shall act accordingly, until the Disability be removed, or a President shall be elected.

▶ **Clause 7. Compensation** The President now receives a salary of $400,000 and a taxable expense account of $50,000 a year. Those amounts cannot be changed during a presidential term; thus, Congress cannot use the President's compensation as a bargaining tool to influence executive decisions. The phrase "any other emolument" means, in effect, any valuable gift; it does not mean that the President cannot be provided with such benefits of office as the White House, extensive staff assistance, and much else.

▶7. The President shall, at stated Times, receive for his Services, a Compensation, which shall neither be increased nor diminished during the Period for which he shall have been elected, and he shall not receive within that Period any other Emolument from the United States, or any of them.

▶ **Clause 8. Oath of office** The Chief Justice of the United States regularly administers this oath or affirmation, but any judicial officer may do so. Thus, Calvin Coolidge was sworn into office in 1923 by his father, a justice of the peace in Vermont.

▶8. Before he enter on the Execution of his Office, he shall take the following Oath or Affirmation:
"I do solemnly swear (or affirm) that I will faithfully execute the Office of President of the United States, and will to the best of my Ability, preserve, protect and defend the Constitution of the United States."

Section 2. President's Powers and Duties

▶ **Clause 1. Military, civil powers** The President, a civilian, heads the nation's armed forces, a key element in the Constitution's insistence on civilian control of the military. The President's power to "require the opinion, in writing" provides the constitutional basis for the Cabinet. The President's power to grant reprieves and pardons, the power of clemency, extends only to federal cases.

Section 2.

▶1. The President shall be Commander in Chief of the Army and Navy of the United States, and of the Militia of the several States, when called into the actual Service of the United States; he may require the Opinion, in writing, of the principal Officer in each of the executive Departments, upon any Subject relating to the Duties of their respective Offices, and he shall have Power to Grant Reprieves and Pardons for Offences against the United States, except in Cases of Impeachment.

▶ 2. He shall have Power, by and with the Advice and Consent of the Senate, to make Treaties, provided two thirds of the Senators present concur; and he shall nominate, and by and with the Advice and Consent of the Senate, shall appoint Ambassadors, other public Ministers and Consuls, Judges of the supreme Court, and all other Officers of the United States, whose Appointments are not herein otherwise provided for, and which shall be established by Law: but the Congress may by Law vest the Appointment of such inferior Officers, as they think proper, in the President alone, in the Courts of Law, or in the Heads of Departments.

▶ **Clause 2. Treaties, appointments** The President has the sole power to make treaties; to become effective, a treaty must be approved by a two-thirds vote in the Senate. In practice, the President can also make executive agreements with foreign governments; these pacts, which are frequently made and usually deal with routine matters, do not require Senate consent. The President appoints the principal officers of the executive branch and all federal judges; the "inferior officers" are those who hold lesser posts.

▶ 3. The President shall have Power to fill up all Vacancies that may happen during the Recess of the Senate, by granting Commissions which shall expire at the End of their next Session.

▶ **Clause 3. Recess appointments** When the Senate is not in session, appointments that require Senate consent can be made by the President on a temporary basis, as "recess appointments." Recess appointments are valid only to the end of the congressional term in which they are made.

Section 3.

He shall from time to time give to the Congress Information of the State of the Union, and recommend to their Consideration such Measures as he shall judge necessary and expedient; he may, on extraordinary Occasions, convene both Houses, or either of them, and in Case of Disagreement between them, with Respect to the Time of Adjournment, he may adjourn them to such Time as he shall think proper; he shall receive Ambassadors and other public Ministers; he shall take Care that the Laws be faithfully executed, and shall Commission all the Officers of the United States.

Section 3. President's Powers and Duties

The President delivers a State of the Union Message to Congress soon after that body convenes each year. That message is delivered to the nation's lawmakers and, importantly, to the American people, as well. It is shortly followed by the proposed federal budget and an economic report; and the President may send special messages to Congress at any time. In all of these communications, Congress is urged to take those actions the Chief Executive finds to be in the national interest. The President also has the power: to call special sessions of Congress; to adjourn Congress if its two houses cannot agree for that purpose; to receive the diplomatic representatives of other governments; to insure the proper execution of all federal laws; and to empower federal officers to hold their posts and perform their duties.

Section 4.

The President, Vice President and all Civil Officers of the United States, shall be removed from Office on Impeachment for and Conviction of, Treason, Bribery, or other high Crimes and Misdemeanors.

Section 4. Impeachment

The Constitution outlines the impeachment process in Article I, Section 2, Clause 5 and in Section 3, Clauses 6 and 7.

Article III

Section 1.

The judicial Power of the United States, shall be vested in one supreme Court, and in such inferior Courts as the Congress may from time to time ordain and establish. The Judges, both of the supreme and inferior Courts, shall hold their Offices during good Behaviour, and shall, at stated Times, receive for their Services, a Compensation, which shall not be diminished during their Continuance in Office.

Judicial Department

Section 1. Judicial Power, Courts, Terms of Office

The judicial power conferred here is the power of federal courts to hear and decide cases, disputes between the government and individuals and between private persons (parties). The Constitution creates only the Supreme Court of the United States; it gives to Congress the power to establish other, lower federal courts (Article I, Section 8, Clause 9) and to fix the size of the Supreme Court. The words "during good Behaviour" mean, in effect, for life.

Section 2. Jurisdiction

▶ **Clause 1. Cases to be heard** This clause sets out the jurisdiction of the federal courts; that is, it identifies those cases that may be tried in those courts. The federal courts can hear and decide—have jurisdiction over—a case depending on either the subject matter or the parties involved in that case. The jurisdiction of the federal courts in cases involving States was substantially restricted by the 11th Amendment in 1795.

▶ **Clause 2. Supreme Court jurisdiction** Original jurisdiction refers to the power of a court to hear a case in the first instance, not on appeal from a lower court. Appellate jurisdiction refers to a court's power to hear a case on appeal from a lower court, from the court in which the case was originally tried. This clause gives the Supreme Court both original and appellate jurisdiction. However, nearly all of the cases the High Court hears are brought to it on appeal from the lower federal courts and the highest State courts.

▶ **Clause 3. Jury trial in criminal cases** A person accused of a federal crime is guaranteed the right to trial by jury in a federal court in the State where the crime was committed; see the 5th and 6th amendments. The right to trial by jury in serious criminal cases in the State courts is guaranteed by the 6th and 14th amendments.

Section 2.

▶1. The judicial Power shall extend to all Cases, in Law and Equity, arising under this Constitution, the Laws of the United States, and Treaties made, or which shall be made, under their Authority;— to all Cases affecting Ambassadors, other public ministers, and Consuls;— to all Cases of Admiralty and maritime Jurisdiction;— to Controversies to which the United States shall be a Party;— to Controversies between two or more States;— between a State and Citizens of another State;— between Citizens of different States;— between Citizens of the same State claiming Lands under Grants of different States, and between a State, or the Citizens thereof, and foreign States, Citizens, or Subjects.

▶2. In all Cases affecting Ambassadors, other public Ministers and Consuls, and those in which a State shall be a Party, the supreme Court shall have original Jurisdiction. In all the other Cases before mentioned, the supreme Court shall have appellate Jurisdiction, both as to Law and Fact, with such Exceptions, and under such Regulations as the Congress shall make.

▶3. The trial of all Crimes, except in Cases of Impeachment, shall be by Jury; and such Trial shall be held in the State where the said Crimes shall have been committed; but when not committed within any State, the Trial shall be at such Place or Places as the Congress may by Law have directed.

Section 3. Treason

▶ **Clause 1. Definition** Treason is the only crime defined in the Constitution. The Framers intended the very specific definition here to prevent the loose use of the charge of treason—for example, against persons who criticize the government. Treason can be committed only in time of war and only by a citizen or a resident alien.

▶ **Clause 2. Punishment** Congress has provided that the punishment that a federal court may impose on a convicted traitor may range from a minimum of five years in prison and/or a $10,000 fine to a maximum of death; no person convicted of treason has ever been executed by the United States. No legal punishment can be imposed on the family or descendants of a convicted traitor. Congress has also made it a crime for any person (in either peace or wartime) to commit espionage or sabotage, to attempt to overthrow the government by force, or to conspire to do any of these things.

Section 3.

▶1. Treason against the United States shall consist only in levying War against them, or in adhering to their Enemies, giving them Aid and Comfort. No Person shall be convicted of Treason unless on the Testimony of two Witnesses to the same overt Act, or on Confession in open Court.

▶2. The Congress shall have Power to declare the Punishment of Treason, but no Attainder of Treason shall work Corruption of Blood, or Forfeiture except during the Life of the Person attainted.

Article IV

Section 1.

Full Faith and Credit shall be given in each State to the public Acts, Records, and judicial Proceedings of every other State. And the Congress may by general Laws prescribe the Manner in which such Acts, Records and Proceedings shall be proved, and the Effect thereof.

Section 2.

▶1. The Citizens of each State shall be entitled to all Privileges and Immunities of Citizens in the several States.

▶2. A Person charged in any State with Treason, Felony, or other Crime, who shall flee from justice, and be found in another State, shall on Demand of the executive Authority of the State from which he fled, be delivered up, to be removed to the State having Jurisdiction of the Crime.

▶3. No Person held to Service or Labor in one State, under the Laws thereof, escaping into another, shall, in Consequence of any Law or Regulation therein, be discharged from Service or Labor, but shall be delivered up on Claim of the Party to whom such Service or Labor may be due.

Section 3.

▶1. New States may be admitted by the Congress into this Union; but no new State shall be formed or erected within the Jurisdiction of any other State; nor any State be formed by the Junction of two or more States, or Parts of States, without the Consent of the Legislatures of the States concerned as well as of the Congress.

▶2. The Congress shall have Power to dispose of and make all needful Rules and Regulations respecting the Territory or other Property belonging to the United States; and nothing in this Constitution shall be so construed as to Prejudice any Claims of the United States, or of any particular State.

Section 4.

The United States shall guarantee to every State in this Union a Republican Form of Government, and shall protect each of them against Invasion; and on Application of the Legislature, or of the Executive (when the Legislature cannot be convened) against domestic Violence.

Relations Among States

Section 1. Full Faith and Credit

Each State must recognize the validity of the laws, public records, and court decisions of every other State.

Section 2. Privileges and Immunities of Citizens

▶ **Clause 1. Residents of other States** In effect, this clause means that no State may discriminate against the residents of other States; that is, a State's laws cannot draw unreasonable distinctions between its own residents and those of any of the other States. See Section 1 of the 14th Amendment.

▶ **Clause 2. Extradition** The process of returning a fugitive to another State is known as "interstate rendition" or, more commonly, "extradition." Usually, that process works routinely; some extradition requests are contested however—especially in cases with racial or political overtones. A governor may refuse to extradite a fugitive; but the federal courts can compel an unwilling governor to obey this constitutional command.

▶ **Clause 3. African Americans seeking freedom from enslavement** This clause was nullified by the 13th Amendment, which abolished slavery in 1865.

Section 3. New States; Territories

▶ **Clause 1. New States** Only Congress can admit new States to the Union. A new State may not be created by taking territory from an existing State without the consent of that State's legislature. Congress has admitted 37 States since the original 13 formed the Union. Five States—Vermont, Kentucky, Tennessee, Maine, and West Virginia—were created from parts of existing States. Texas was an independent republic before admission. California was admitted after being ceded to the United States by Mexico. Each of the other 30 States entered the Union only after a period of time as an organized territory of the United States.

▶ **Clause 2. Territory, property** Congress has the power to make laws concerning the territories, other public lands, and all other property of the United States.

Section 4. Protection Afforded to States by the Nation

The Constitution does not define "a republican form of government," but the phrase is generally understood to mean a representative government. The Federal Government must also defend each State against attacks from outside its border and, at the request of a State's legislature or its governor, aid its efforts to put down internal disorders.

Provisions for Amendment

This section provides for the methods by which formal changes can be made in the Constitution. An amendment may be proposed in one of two ways: by a two-thirds vote in each house of Congress, or by a national convention called by Congress at the request of two-thirds of the State legislatures. A proposed amendment may be ratified in one of two ways: by three-fourths of the State legislatures, or by three-fourths of the States in conventions called for that purpose. Congress has the power to determine the method by which a proposed amendment may be ratified. The amendment process cannot be used to deny any State its equal representation in the United States Senate. To this point, 27 amendments have been adopted. To date, all of the amendments except the 21st Amendment were proposed by Congress and ratified by the State legislatures. Only the 21st Amendment was ratified by the convention method.

Article V

The Congress, whenever two thirds of both Houses shall deem it necessary, shall propose Amendments to this Constitution, or, on the Application of the Legislatures of two thirds of the several States, shall call a Convention for proposing Amendments, which, in either Case, shall be valid to all Intents and Purposes, as Part of this Constitution, when ratified by the Legislatures of three fourths of the several States, or by Conventions in three fourths thereof, as the one or the other Mode of Ratification may be proposed by the Congress; Provided that no Amendment which may be made prior to the Year One thousand eight hundred and eight shall in any Manner affect the first and fourth Clauses in the Ninth section of the first Article; and that no State, without its Consent, shall be deprived of its equal Suffrage in the Senate.

National Debts, Supremacy of National Law, Oath

Section 1. Validity of Debts

Congress had borrowed large sums of money during the Revolution and later during the Critical Period of the 1780s. This provision, a pledge that the new government would honor those debts, did much to create confidence in that government.

Section 2. Supremacy of National Law

This section sets out the Supremacy Clause, a specific declaration of the supremacy of federal law over any and all forms of State law. No State, including its local governments, may make or enforce any law that conflicts with any provision in the Constitution, an act of Congress, a treaty, or an order, rule, or regulation properly issued by the President or his subordinates in the executive branch.

Section 3. Oaths of Office

This provision reinforces the Supremacy Clause; all public officers, at every level in the United States, owe their first allegiance to the Constitution of the United States. No religious qualification can be imposed as a condition for holding any public office.

Article VI

Section 1.

All Debts contracted and Engagements entered into, before the Adoption of this Constitution, shall be as valid against the United States under this Constitution, as under the Confederation.

Section 2.

This Constitution, and the Laws of the United States which shall be made in Pursuance thereof; and all Treaties made, or which shall be made, under the Authority of the United States, shall be the supreme Law of the Land; and the Judges in every State shall be bound thereby, anything in the constitution or Laws of any State to the Contrary notwithstanding.

Section 3.

The Senators and Representatives before mentioned, and the Members of the several State legislatures, and all executive and judicial Officers, both of the United States and of the several States, shall be bound by Oath or Affirmation, to support this Constitution; but no religious Test shall ever be required as a Qualification to any Office or public Trust under the United States.

Ratification of Constitution

The proposed Constitution was signed by George Washington and 37 of his fellow Framers on September 17, 1787. (George Read of Delaware signed for himself and also for his absent colleague, John Dickinson.)

Article VII

The ratification of the Conventions of nine States, shall be sufficient for the Establishment of this Constitution between the States so ratifying the same.

Done in Convention by the Unanimous Consent of the States present the Seventeenth Day of September in the Year of our Lord one thousand seven hundred and Eighty-seven and of the Independence of the United States of America the twelfth. In witness whereof We have hereunto subscribed our Names.

Attest:
William Jackson,
Secretary
George Washington,
President and Deputy from Virginia

New Hampshire
John Langdon
Nicholas Gilman

Massachusetts
Nathaniel Gorham
Rufus King

Connecticut
William Samuel Johnson
Roger Sherman

New York
Alexander Hamilton

New Jersey
William Livingston
David Brearley
William Paterson
Jonathan Dayton

Pennsylvania
Benjamin Franklin
Thomas Mifflin
Robert Morris
George Clymer
Thomas Fitzsimons
Jared Ingersoll
James Wilson
Gouverneur Morris

Delaware
George Read
Gunning Bedford, Jr.
John Dickinson
Richard Bassett
Jacob Broom

Maryland
James McHenry
Daniel of St. Thomas Jenifer
Daniel Carroll

Virginia
John Blair
James Madison, Jr.

North Carolina
William Blount
Richard Dobbs Spaight
Hugh Williamson

South Carolina
John Rutledge
Charles Cotesworth Pinckney
Charles Pinckney
Pierce Butler

Georgia
William Few
Abraham Baldwin

Amendments

The first 10 amendments, the Bill of Rights, were each proposed by Congress on September 25, 1789, and ratified by the necessary three-fourths of the States on December 15, 1791. These amendments were originally intended to restrict the National Government—not the States. However, the Supreme Court has several times held that most of their provisions also apply to the States, through the 14th Amendment's Due Process Clause.

1st Amendment. Freedom of Religion, Speech, Press, Assembly, and Petition

The 1st Amendment sets out five basic liberties: The guarantee of freedom of religion is both a protection of religious thought and practice and a command of separation of church and state. The guarantees of freedom of speech and press assure to all persons a right to speak, publish, and otherwise express their views. The guarantees of the rights of assembly and petition protect the right to join with others in public meetings, political parties, interest groups, and other associations to discuss public affairs and influence public policy. None of these rights is guaranteed in absolute terms, however; like all other civil rights guarantees, each of them may be exercised only with regard to the rights of all other persons.

2nd Amendment. Bearing Arms

The right of the people to keep and bear arms was insured by the 2nd Amendment.

3rd Amendment. Quartering of Troops

This amendment was intended to prevent what had been common British practice in the colonial period; see the Declaration of Independence. This provision is of virtually no importance today.

4th Amendment. Searches and Seizures

The basic rule laid down by the 4th Amendment is this: Police officers have no general right to search for or seize evidence or seize (arrest) persons. Except in particular circumstances, they must have a proper warrant (a court order) obtained with probable cause (on reasonable grounds). This guarantee is reinforced by the exclusionary rule, developed by the Supreme Court: Evidence gained as the result of an unlawful search or seizure cannot be used at the court trial of the person from whom it was seized.

5th Amendment. Criminal Proceedings; Due Process; Eminent Domain

A person can be tried for a serious federal crime only if he or she has been indicted (charged, accused of that crime) by a grand jury. No one may be subjected to double jeopardy—that is, tried twice for the same crime. All persons are protected against self-incrimination; no person can be legally compelled to answer any question in any governmental proceeding if that answer could lead to that person's prosecution. The 5th Amendment's Due Process Clause prohibits unfair, arbitrary actions by the Federal Government; a like prohibition is set out against the States in the 14th Amendment. Government may take private property for a legitimate public purpose; but when it exercises that power of eminent domain, it must pay a fair price for the property seized.

1st Amendment

Congress shall make no law respecting an establishment of religion, or prohibiting the free exercise thereof, or abridging the freedom of speech, or of the press; or the right of the people peaceably to assemble, and to petition the Government for a redress of grievances.

2nd Amendment

A well-regulated Militia being necessary to the security of a free State, the right of the people to keep and bear Arms, shall not be infringed.

3rd Amendment.

No Soldier shall, in time of peace be quartered in any house, without the consent of the Owner, nor, in time of war, but in a manner to be prescribed by law.

4th Amendment.

The right of the people to be secure in their persons, houses, papers, and effects, against unreasonable searches and seizures, shall not be violated, and no Warrants shall issue, but upon probable cause, supported by Oath or affirmation, and particularly describing the place to be searched, and the persons or things to be seized.

5th Amendment.

No person shall be held to answer for a capital, or otherwise infamous crime, unless on a presentment or indictment of a Grand Jury, except in cases arising in the land or naval forces, or in the Militia, when in actual service in time of War, or public danger; nor shall any person be subject for the same offence to be twice put in jeopardy of life or limb; nor shall be compelled in any criminal case to be a witness against himself, nor be deprived of life, liberty, or property, without due process of law; nor shall private property be taken for public use, without just compensation.

6th Amendment

In all criminal prosecutions, the accused shall enjoy the right to a speedy and public trial, by an impartial jury of the State and district wherein the crime shall have been committed, which district shall have been previously ascertained by law, and to be informed of the nature and cause of the accusation; to be confronted with the witnesses against him; to have compulsory process for obtaining witnesses in his favor, and to have the Assistance of Counsel for his defence.

6th Amendment. Criminal Proceedings

A person accused of crime has the right to be tried in court without undue delay and by an impartial jury; see Article III, Section 2, Clause 3. The defendant must be informed of the charge upon which he or she is to be tried, has the right to cross-examine hostile witnesses, and has the right to require the testimony of favorable witnesses. The defendant also has the right to be represented by an attorney at every stage in the criminal process.

7th Amendment

In Suits at common law, where the value in controversy shall exceed twenty dollars, the right of trial by jury shall be preserved, and no fact tried by a jury, shall be otherwise re-examined in any Court of the United States, than according to the rules of the common law.

7th Amendment. Civil Trials

This amendment applies only to civil cases heard in federal courts. A civil case does not involve criminal matters; it is a dispute between private parties or between the government and a private party. The right to trial by jury is guaranteed in any civil case in a federal court if the amount of money involved in that case exceeds $20 (most cases today involve a much larger sum); that right may be waived (relinquished, put aside) if both parties agree to a bench trial (a trial by a judge, without a jury).

8th Amendment

Excessive bail shall not be required, nor excessive fines imposed, nor cruel and unusual punishment inflicted.

8th Amendment. Punishment for Crimes

Bail is the sum of money that a person accused of crime may be required to post (deposit with the court) as a guarantee that he or she will appear in court at the proper time. The amount of bail required and/or a fine imposed as punishment must bear a reasonable relationship to the seriousness of the crime involved in the case. The prohibition of cruel and unusual punishment forbids any punishment judged to be too harsh, too severe for the crime for which it is imposed.

9th Amendment

The enumeration in the Constitution, of certain rights, shall not be construed to deny or disparage others retained by the people.

9th Amendment. Unenumerated Rights

The fact that the Constitution sets out many civil rights guarantees, expressly provides for many protections against government, does not mean that there are not other rights also held by the people.

10th Amendment

The powers not delegated to the United States by the Constitution, nor prohibited by it to the States, are reserved to the States respectively, or to the people.

10th Amendment. Powers Reserved to the States

This amendment identifies the area of power that may be exercised by the States. All of those powers the Constitution does not grant to the National Government, and at the same time does not forbid to the States, belong to each of the States, or to the people of each State.

11th Amendment. Suits Against States

Proposed by Congress March 4, 1794; ratified February 7, 1795, but official announcement of the ratification was delayed until January 8, 1798. This amendment repealed part of Article III, Section 2, Clause 1. No State may be sued in a federal court by a resident of another State or of a foreign country; the Supreme Court has long held that this provision also means that a State cannot be sued in a federal court by a foreign country or, more importantly, even by one of its own residents.

11th Amendment

The Judicial power of the United States shall not be construed to extend to any suit in law or equity, commenced or prosecuted against one of the United States by Citizens of another State, or by Citizens or Subjects of any Foreign State.

12th Amendment. Election of President and Vice President

Proposed by Congress December 9, 1803; ratified June 15, 1804. This amendment replaced Article II, Section 1, Clause 3. Originally, each elector cast two ballots, each for a different person for President. The person with the largest number of electoral votes, provided that number was a majority of the electors, was to become President; the person with the second highest number was to become Vice President. This arrangement produced an electoral vote tie between Thomas Jefferson and Aaron Burr in 1800; the House finally chose Jefferson as President in 1801. The 12th Amendment separated the balloting for President and Vice President; each elector now casts one ballot for someone as President and a second ballot for another person as Vice President. Note that the 20th Amendment changed the date set here (March 4) to January 20, and that the 23rd Amendment (1961) provides for electors from the District of Columbia. This amendment also provides that the Vice President must meet the same qualifications as those set out for the President in Article II, Section 1, Clause 5.

12th Amendment

The Electors shall meet in their respective States and vote by ballot for President and Vice President, one of whom, at least, shall not be an inhabitant of the same State with themselves; they shall name in their ballots the person voted for as President, and in distinct ballots the person voted for as Vice President, and they shall make distinct lists of all persons voted for as President, and of all persons voted for as Vice President, and of the number of votes for each, which lists they shall sign and certify, and transmit sealed to the seat of the government of the United States, directed to the President of the Senate;— The President of the Senate shall, in the presence of the Senate and the House of Representatives, open all the certificates and the votes shall then be counted;— the person having the greatest Number of votes for President shall be the President, if such number be a majority of the whole number of Electors appointed; and if no person have such a majority, then, from the persons having the highest numbers not exceeding three on the list of those voted for as President, the House of Representatives shall choose immediately, by ballot, the President. But in choosing the President, the votes shall be taken by States, the representation from each State having one vote; a quorum for this purpose shall consist of a member or members from two thirds of the States, and a majority of all the States shall be necessary to a choice. And if the House of Representatives shall not choose a President whenever the right of choice shall devolve upon them, before the fourth day of March next following, then the Vice President shall act as President, as in case of death or other constitutional disability of the President. The person having the greatest number of votes as Vice President, shall be the Vice President, if such number be a majority of the whole number of Electors appointed, and if no person have a majority, then from the two highest numbers on the list, the Senate shall choose the Vice President; a quorum for the purpose shall consist of two thirds of the whole number of Senators, a majority of the whole number shall be necessary to a choice. But no person constitutionally ineligible to the office of President shall be eligible to that of Vice-President of the United States.

13th Amendment. Slavery and Involuntary Servitude

Proposed by Congress January 31, 1865; ratified December 6, 1865. This amendment forbids slavery in the United States and in any area under its control. It also forbids other forms of forced labor, except punishments for crime; but some forms of compulsory service are not prohibited—for example, service on juries or in the armed forces. Section 2 gives to Congress the power to carry out the provisions of Section 1 of this amendment.

13th Amendment

Section 1. Neither slavery nor involuntary servitude, except as a punishment for crime whereof the party shall have been duly convicted, shall exist within the United States, or any place subject to their jurisdiction.

Section 2. Congress shall have power to enforce this article by appropriate legislation.

14th Amendment

Section 1. All persons born or naturalized in the United States and subject to the jurisdiction thereof, are citizens of the United States and of the State wherein they reside. No State shall make or enforce any law which shall abridge the privileges or immunities of citizens of the United States; nor shall any State deprive any person of life, liberty, or property, without due process of law; nor deny to any person within its jurisdiction the equal protection of the laws.

14th Amendment. Rights of Citizens

Proposed by Congress June 13, 1866; ratified July 9, 1868. Section 1 defines citizenship. It provides for the acquisition of United States citizenship by birth or by naturalization. Citizenship at birth is determined according to the principle of jus soli—"the law of the soil," where born; naturalization is the legal process by which one acquires a new citizenship at some time after birth. Under certain circumstances, citizenship can also be gained at birth abroad, according to the principle of jus sanguinis—"the law of the blood," to whom born. This section also contains two major civil rights provisions: the Due Process Clause forbids a State (and its local governments) to act in any unfair or arbitrary way; the Equal Protection Clause forbids a State (and its local governments) to discriminate against, draw unreasonable distinctions between, persons.

Most of the rights set out against the National Government in the first eight amendments have been extended against the States (and their local governments) through Supreme Court decisions involving the 14th Amendment's Due Process Clause.

Section 2. Representatives shall be apportioned among the several States according to their respective numbers, counting the whole number of persons in each State, excluding Indians not taxed. But when the right to vote at any election for the choice of electors for President and Vice President of the United States, Representatives in Congress, the Executive and Judicial officers of a State, or the members of the Legislature thereof, is denied to any of the male inhabitants of such State, being twenty-one years of age and citizens of the United States, or in any way abridged, except for participation in rebellion, or other crime, the basis of representation therein shall be reduced in the proportion which the number of such male citizens shall bear to the whole number of male citizens twenty-one years of age in such State.

The first sentence here replaced Article I, Section 2, Clause 3, the Three-Fifths Compromise provision. Essentially, all persons in the United States are counted in each decennial census, the basis for the distribution of House seats. The balance of this section has never been enforced and is generally thought to be obsolete.

Section 3. No person shall be a Senator or Representative in Congress, or elector of President and Vice President, or hold any office, civil or military, under the United States, or under any State, who, having previously taken an oath, as a member of Congress, or as an officer of the United States, or as a member of any State legislature, or as an executive or judicial officer of any State, to support the Constitution of the United States, shall have engaged in insurrection or rebellion against the same, or given aid or comfort to the enemies thereof. But Congress may, by a vote of two thirds of each House, remove such disability.

This section limited the President's power to pardon those persons who had led the Confederacy during the Civil War. Congress finally removed this disability in 1898.

Section 4. The validity of the public debt of the United States, authorized by law, including debts incurred for payment of pensions and bounties for services in suppressing insurrection or rebellion, shall not be questioned. But neither the United States nor any State shall assume or pay any debt or obligation incurred in aid of insurrection or rebellion against the United States, or any claim for the loss or emancipation of any slave; but all such debts, obligations and claims shall be held illegal and void.

Section 4 also dealt with matters directly related to the Civil War. It reaffirmed the public debt of the United States; but it invalidated, prohibited payment of, any debt contracted by the Confederate States and also prohibited any compensation of former slave owners.

Section 5. The Congress shall have power to enforce, by appropriate legislation, the provisions of this article.

15th Amendment. Right to Vote—Race, Color, Servitude

Proposed by Congress February 26, 1869; ratified February 3, 1870. The phrase "previous condition of servitude" refers to slavery. Note that this amendment does not guarantee the right to vote to African Americans, or to anyone else. Instead, it forbids the States from discriminating against any person on the grounds of his "race, color, or previous condition of servitude" in the setting of suffrage qualifications.

15th Amendment

Section 1. The right of citizens of the United States to vote shall not be denied or abridged by the United States or by any State on account of race, color, or previous condition of servitude.

Section 2. The Congress shall have power to enforce this article by appropriate legislation.

16th Amendment. Income Tax

Proposed by Congress July 12, 1909; ratified February 3, 1913. This amendment modified two provisions in Article I, Section 2, Clause 3, and Section 9, Clause 4. It gives to Congress the power to levy an income tax, a direct tax, without regard to the populations of any of the States.

16th Amendment

The Congress shall have power to lay and collect taxes on incomes, from whatever source derived, without apportionment among the several States, and without regard to any census or enumeration.

17th Amendment. Popular Election of Senators

Proposed by Congress May 13, 1912; ratified April 8, 1913. This amendment repealed those portions of Article I, Section 3, Clauses 1 and 2 relating to the election of senators. Senators are now elected by the voters in each State. If a vacancy occurs, the governor of the State involved must call an election to fill the seat; the governor may appoint a senator to serve until the next election, if the State's legislature has authorized that step.

17th Amendment

The Senate of the United States shall be composed of two Senators from each State, elected by the people thereof, for six years; and each Senator shall have one vote. The electors in each State shall have the qualifications requisite for electors of the most numerous branch of the State legislatures.

When vacancies happen in the representation of any State in the Senate, the executive authority of such State shall issue writs of election to fill such vacancies: Provided, That the legislature of any State may empower the executive thereof to make temporary appointments until the people fill the vacancies by election as the legislature may direct.

This amendment shall not be so construed as to affect the election or term of any Senator chosen before it becomes valid as part of the Constitution.

18th Amendment. Prohibition of Intoxicating Liquors

Proposed by Congress December 18, 1917; ratified January 16, 1919. This amendment outlawed the making, selling, transporting, importing, or exporting of alcoholic beverages in the United States. It was repealed in its entirety by the 21st Amendment in 1933.

18th Amendment.

Section 1. After one year from the ratification of this article the manufacture, sale, or transportation of intoxicating liquors within, the importation thereof into, or the exportation thereof from the United States and all territory subject to the jurisdiction thereof for beverage purposes is hereby prohibited.

Section 2. The Congress and the several States shall have concurrent power to enforce this article by appropriate legislation.

Section 3. This article shall be inoperative unless it shall have been ratified as an amendment to the Constitution by the legislatures of the several States, as provided in the Constitution, within seven years of the date of the submission hereof to the States by Congress.

19th Amendment. Equal Suffrage—Sex

Proposed by Congress June 4, 1919; ratified August 18, 1920. No person can be denied the right to vote in any election in the United States on account of his or her sex.

19th Amendment

The right of citizens of the United States to vote shall not be denied or abridged by the United States or by any State on account of sex.

Congress shall have power to enforce this article by appropriate legislation.

20th Amendment

Section 1. The terms of the President and Vice President shall end at noon on the 20th day of January, and the terms of Senators and Representatives at noon on the 3d day of January, of the years in which such terms would have ended if this article had not been ratified; and the terms of their successors shall then begin.

Section 2. The Congress shall assemble at least once in every year, and such meeting shall begin at noon on the 3d day of January, unless they shall by law appoint a different day.

Section 3. If, at the time fixed for the beginning of the term of the President, the President elect shall have died, the Vice President elect shall become President. If a President shall not have been chosen before the time fixed for the beginning of his term, or if the President-elect shall have failed to qualify, then the Vice President elect shall act as President until a President shall have qualified; and the Congress may by law provide for the case wherein neither a President elect nor a Vice President elect shall have qualified, declaring who shall then act as President, or the manner in which one who is to act shall be selected, and such person shall act accordingly until a President or Vice President shall have qualified.

Section 4. The Congress may by law provide for the case of the death of any of the persons from whom the House of Representatives may choose a President whenever the right of choice shall have devolved upon them, and for the case of the death of any of the persons from whom the Senate may choose a Vice President whenever the right of choice shall have devolved upon them.

Section 5. Sections 1 and 2 shall take effect on the 15th day of October following the ratification of this article.

Section 6. This article shall be inoperative unless it shall have been ratified as an amendment to the Constitution by the legislatures of three fourths of the several States within seven years from the date of its submission.

20th Amendment. Commencement of Terms; Sessions of Congress; Death or Disqualification of President-Elect

Proposed by Congress March 2, 1932; ratified January 23, 1933. The provisions of Sections 1 and 2 relating to Congress modified Article I, Section 4, Clause 2, and those provisions relating to the President, the 12th Amendment. The date on which the President and Vice President now take office was moved from March 4 to January 20. Similarly, the members of Congress now begin their terms on January 3. The 20th Amendment is sometimes called the "Lame Duck Amendment" because it shortened the period of time a member of Congress who was defeated for reelection (a "lame duck") remains in office.

This section deals with certain possibilities that were not covered by the presidential selection provisions of either Article II or the 12th Amendment. To this point, none of these situations has occurred. Note that there is neither a President-elect nor a Vice President-elect until the electoral votes have been counted by Congress, or, if the electoral college cannot decide the matter, the House has chosen a President or the Senate has chosen a Vice President.

Congress has not in fact ever passed such a law. See Section 2 of the 25th Amendment, regarding a vacancy in the vice presidency; that provision could some day have an impact here.

Section 5 set the date on which this amendment came into force.

Section 6 placed a time limit on the ratification process; note that a similar provision was written into the 18th, 21st, and 22nd amendments.

21st Amendment

Section 1. The eighteenth article of amendment to the Constitution of the United States is hereby repealed.

Section 2. The transportation or importation into any State, Territory, or possession of the United States for delivery or use therein of intoxicating liquors, in violation of the laws thereof, is hereby prohibited.

Section 3. This article shall be inoperative unless it shall have been ratified as an amendment to the Constitution by conventions in the several States, as provided in the Constitution, within seven years from the date of the submission hereof to the States by the Congress.

21st Amendment. Repeal of 18th Amendment

Proposed by Congress February 20, 1933; ratified December 5, 1933. This amendment repealed all of the 18th Amendment. Section 2 modifies the scope of the Federal Government's commerce power set out in Article I, Section 8, Clause 3; it gives to each State the power to regulate the transportation or importation and the distribution or use of intoxicating liquors in ways that would be unconstitutional in the case of any other commodity. The 21st Amendment is the only amendment Congress has thus far submitted to the States for ratification by conventions.

22nd Amendment. Presidential Tenure

Proposed by Congress March 21, 1947; ratified February 27, 1951. This amendment modified Article II, Section I, Clause 1. It stipulates that no President may serve more than two elected terms. But a President who has succeeded to the office beyond the midpoint in a term to which another President was originally elected may serve for more than eight years. In any case, however, a President may not serve more than 10 years. Prior to Franklin Roosevelt, who was elected to four terms, no President had served more than two full terms in office.

22nd Amendment

Section 1. No person shall be elected to the office of the President more than twice, and no person who has held the office of President, or acted as President, for more than two years of a term to which some other person was elected President shall be elected to the office of the President more than once. But this Article shall not apply to any person holding the office of President, when this Article was proposed by the Congress, and shall not prevent any person who may be holding the office of President, or acting as President, during the term within which this Article becomes operative from holding the office of President or acting as President during the remainder of such term.

Section 2. This article shall be inoperative unless it shall have been ratified as an amendment to the Constitution by the legislatures of three fourths of the several states within seven years from the date of its submission to the States by the Congress.

23rd Amendment. Presidential Electors for the District of Columbia

Proposed by Congress June 16, 1960; ratified March 29, 1961. This amendment modified Article II, Section I, Clause 2 and the 12th Amendment. It included the voters of the District of Columbia in the presidential electorate; and provides that the District is to have the same number of electors as the least populous State—three electors—but no more than that number.

23rd Amendment.

Section 1. The District constituting the seat of Government of the United States shall appoint in such manner as the Congress may direct:

A number of electors of President and Vice President equal to the whole number of Senators and Representatives in Congress to which the District would be entitled if it were a State, but in no event more than the least populous State; they shall be in addition to those appointed by the States, they shall be considered, for the purposes of the election of President and Vice President, to be electors appointed by a State; and they shall meet in the District and perform such duties as provided by the twelfth article of amendment.

24th Amendment. Right to Vote in Federal Elections—Tax Payment

Proposed by Congress August 27, 1962; ratified January 23, 1964. This amendment outlawed the payment of any tax as a condition for taking part in the nomination or election of any federal officeholder.

24th Amendment.

Section 1. The right of citizens of the United States to vote in any primary or other election for President or Vice President, for electors for President or Vice President, or for Senator or Representative in Congress, shall not be denied or abridged by the United States or any State by reason of failure to pay any poll tax or other tax.

Section 2. The Congress shall have power to enforce this article by appropriate legislation.

25th Amendment. Presidential Succession, Vice Presidential Vacancy, Presidential Inability

Proposed by Congress July 6, 1965; ratified February 10, 1967. Section 1 revised the imprecise provision on presidential succession in Article II, Section 1, Clause 6. It affirmed the precedent set by Vice President John Tyler, who became President on the death of William Henry Harrison in 1841. Section 2 provides for the filling of a vacancy in the office of Vice President. The office had been vacant on 16 occasions and remained unfilled for the rest of each term involved. When Spiro Agnew resigned the office in 1973, President Nixon selected Gerald Ford per this provision; and, when President Nixon resigned in 1974, Gerald Ford became President and chose Nelson Rockefeller as Vice President.

25th Amendment.

Section 1. In case of the removal of the President from office or of his death or resignation, the Vice President shall become President.

Section 2. Whenever there is a vacancy in the office of the Vice President, the President shall nominate a Vice President who shall take office upon confirmation by a majority vote of both Houses of Congress.

Section 3. Whenever the President transmits to the President pro tempore of the Senate and the Speaker of the House of Representatives his written declaration that he is unable to discharge the powers and duties of his office, and until he transmits to them a written declaration to the contrary, such powers and duties shall be discharged by the Vice President as Acting President.

This section created a procedure for determining if a President is so incapacitated that he cannot perform the powers and duties of his office.

Section 4. Whenever the Vice President and a majority of either the principal officers of the executive departments or of such other body as Congress may by law provide, transmit to the President pro tempore of the Senate and the Speaker of the House of Representatives their written declaration that the President is unable to discharge the powers and duties of his office, the Vice President shall immediately assume the powers and duties of the office as Acting President.

Thereafter, when the President transmits to the President pro tempore of the Senate and the Speaker of the House of Representatives his written declaration that no inability exists, he shall resume the powers and duties of his office unless the Vice President and a majority of either the principal officers of the executive department or of such other body as Congress may by law provide, transmit within four days to the President pro tempore of the Senate and the Speaker of the House of Representatives their written declaration that the President is unable to discharge the powers and duties of his office. Thereupon Congress shall decide the issue, assembling within forty-eight hours for that purpose if not in session. If the Congress, within twenty-one days after receipt of the latter written declaration, or, if Congress is not in session, within twenty-one days after Congress is required to assemble, determines by two-thirds vote of both Houses that the President is unable to discharge the powers and duties of his office, the Vice President shall continue to discharge the same as Acting President; otherwise, the President shall resume the powers and duties of his office.

Section 4 deals with the circumstance in which a President will not be able to determine the fact of incapacity. To this point, Congress has not established the "such other body" referred to here. This section contains the only typographical error in the Constitution; in its second paragraph, the word "department" should in fact read "departments."

26th Amendment.

Section 1. The right of citizens of the United States, who are eighteen years of age or older, to vote shall not be denied or abridged by the United States or by any State on account of age.

Section 2. The Congress shall have the power to enforce this article by appropriate legislation.

26th Amendment. Right to Vote—Age

Proposed by Congress March 23, 1971; ratified July 1, 1971. This amendment provides that the minimum age for voting in any election in the United States cannot be more than 18 years. (A State may set a minimum voting age of less than 18, however.)

27th Amendment.

No law varying the compensation for the services of the Senators and Representatives, shall take effect, until an election of Representatives shall have intervened.

27th Amendment. Congressional Pay

Proposed by Congress September 25, 1789; ratified May 7, 1992. This amendment modified Article I, Section 6, Clause 1. It limits Congress's power to fix the salaries of its members—by delaying the effectiveness of any increase in that pay until after the next regular congressional election.

Name	Party	State [a]	Entered Office	Age On Taking Office	Vice President(s)
George Washington (1732–1799)	Federalist	Virginia	1789	57	John Adams
John Adams (1735–1826)	Federalist	Massachusetts	1797	61	Thomas Jefferson
Thomas Jefferson (1743–1826)	Dem-Rep[b]	Virginia	1801	57	Aaron Burr/George Clinton
James Madison (1751–1836)	Dem-Rep	Virginia	1809	57	George Clinton/Elbridge Gerry
James Monroe (1758–1831)	Dem-Rep	Virginia	1817	58	Daniel D. Tompkins
John Q. Adams (1767–1848)	Dem-Rep	Massachusetts	1825	57	John C. Calhoun
Andrew Jackson (1767–1845)	Democrat	Tennessee (SC)	1829	61	John C. Calhoun/Martin Van Buren
Martin Van Buren (1782–1862)	Democrat	New York	1837	54	Richard M. Johnson
William H. Harrison (1773–1841)	Whig	Ohio (VA)	1841	68	John Tyler
John Tyler (1790–1862)	Democrat	Virginia	1841	51	none
James K. Polk (1795–1849)	Democrat	Tennessee (NC)	1845	49	George M. Dallas
Zachary Taylor (1784–1850)	Whig	Louisiana (VA)	1849	64	Millard Fillmore
Millard Fillmore (1800–1874)	Whig	New York	1850	50	none
Franklin Pierce (1804–1869)	Democrat	New Hampshire	1853	48	William R. King
James Buchanan (1791–1868)	Democrat	Pennsylvania	1857	65	John C. Breckinridge
Abraham Lincoln (1809–1865)	Republican	Illinois (KY)	1861	52	Hannibal Hamlin/Andrew Johnson[c]
Andrew Johnson (1808–1875)	Democrat	Tennessee (NC)	1865	56	none
Ulysses S. Grant (1822–1885)	Republican	Illinois (OH)	1869	46	Schuyler Colfax/Henry Wilson
Rutherford B. Hayes (1822–1893)	Republican	Ohio	1877	54	William A. Wheeler
James A. Garfield (1831–1881)	Republican	Ohio	1881	49	Chester A. Arthur
Chester A. Arthur (1829–1896)	Republican	New York (VT)	1881	51	none
Grover Cleveland (1837–1908)	Democrat	New York (NJ)	1885	47	Thomas A. Hendricks
Benjamin Harrison (1833–1901)	Republican	Indiana (OH)	1889	55	Levi P. Morton
Grover Cleveland (1837–1908)	Democrat	New York (NJ)	1893	55	Adlai E. Stevenson

Name	Party	State [a]	Entered Office	Age On Taking Office	Vice President(s)
William McKinley (1843–1901)	Republican	Ohio	1897	54	Garret A. Hobart/ Theodore Roosevelt
Theodore Roosevelt (1858–1919)	Republican	New York	1901	42	Charles W. Fairbanks
William H. Taft (1857–1930)	Republican	Ohio	1909	51	James S. Sherman
Woodrow Wilson (1856–1924)	Democrat	New Jersey (VA)	1913	56	Thomas R. Marshall
Warren G. Harding (1865–1923)	Republican	Ohio	1921	55	Calvin Coolidge
Calvin Coolidge (1872–1933)	Republican	Massachusetts (VT)	1923	51	Charles G. Dawes
Herbert Hoover (1874–1964)	Republican	California (IA)	1929	54	Charles Curtis
Franklin Roosevelt (1882–1945)	Democrat	New York	1933	51	John N. Garner/ Henry A. Wallace/Harry S Truman
Harry S Truman (1884–1972)	Democrat	Missouri	1945	60	Alben W. Barkley
Dwight D. Eisenhower (1890–1969)	Republican	New York (TX)	1953	62	Richard M. Nixon
John F. Kennedy (1917–1963)	Democrat	Massachusetts	1961	43	Lyndon B. Johnson
Lyndon B. Johnson (1908–1973)	Democrat	Texas	1963	55	Hubert H. Humphrey
Richard M. Nixon (1913–1994)	Republican	New York (CA)	1969	56	Spiro T. Agnew [d]/Gerald R. Ford [e]
Gerald R. Ford (1913–2006)	Republican	Michigan (NE)	1974	61	Nelson A. Rockefeller [f]
James E. Carter (1924–)	Democrat	Georgia	1977	52	Walter F. Mondale
Ronald W. Reagan (1911–2004)	Republican	California (IL)	1981	69	George H. W. Bush
George H.W. Bush (1924–2018)	Republican	Texas (MA)	1989	64	J. Danforth Quayle
William J. Clinton (1946–)	Democrat	Arkansas	1993	46	Albert Gore, Jr.
George W. Bush (1946–)	Republican	Texas	2001	54	Richard B. Cheney
Barack Obama (1961–)	Democrat	Illinois (HI)	2009	47	Joseph R. Biden
Donald J. Trump (1946–)	Republican	New York	2017	70	Michael R. Pence
Joseph R. Biden (1942–)	Democrat	Delaware (PA)	2021	78	Kamala Harris

[a] State of residence when elected; if born in another State, that State in parentheses.
[b] Democratic-Republican
[c] Johnson, a War Democrat, was elected Vice President on the coalition Union Party ticket.
[d] Resigned October 10, 1973.
[e] Nominated by Nixon, confirmed by Congress on December 6, 1973.
[f] Nominated by Ford, confirmed by Congress on December 19, 1974.

Declaration of Independence

Introduction

By signing the Declaration of Independence, members of the Continental Congress sent a clear message to Britain that the American colonies were free and independent states. Starting with its preamble, the document spells out all the reasons the people of the United States have the right to break away from Britain.

Primary Source

The Unanimous Declaration of the Thirteen United States of America

When in the Course of human events, it becomes necessary for one people to dissolve the political bands which have connected them with another, and to assume among the powers of the earth, the separate and equal station to which the Laws of Nature and of Nature's God entitle them, a decent respect to the opinions of mankind requires that they should declare the causes which impel [force] them to the separation. We hold these truths to be self-evident, that all men are created equal, that they are endowed [gifted] by their Creator with certain unalienable [cannot be taken away] Rights, that among these are Life, Liberty and the pursuit of Happiness. That to secure these rights, Governments are instituted among Men, deriving their just powers from the consent of the governed. That whenever any Form of Government becomes destructive of these ends, it is the Right of the People to alter or to abolish it, and to institute new Government, laying its foundation on such principles and organizing its powers in such form, as to them shall seem most likely to effect their Safety and Happiness. Prudence [cautiousness], indeed, will dictate that Governments long established should not be changed for light and transient causes; and accordingly all experience hath shown that mankind are more disposed to suffer, while evils are sufferable, than to right themselves by abolishing the forms to which they are accustomed. But when a long train of abuses and usurpations [unjust uses of power], pursuing invariably the same Object evinces a design to reduce them under absolute Despotism [rule of absolute power], it is their right, it is their duty, to throw off such Government, and to provide new Guards for their future security.

Such has been the patient sufferance of these Colonies; and such is now the necessity which constrains them to alter their former Systems of Government. The history of the present King of Great Britain is a history of repeated injuries and usurpations, all having in direct object the establishment of an absolute Tyranny over these States. To prove this, let Facts be submitted to a candid world.

He has refused his Assent to Laws, the most wholesome and necessary for the public good.

He has forbidden his Governors to pass Laws of immediate and pressing importance, unless suspended in their operation till his Assent should be obtained; and when so suspended, he has utterly neglected to attend to them.

He has refused to pass other Laws for the accommodation of large districts of people, unless those people would relinquish [give up] the right of Representation in the Legislature, a right inestimable [priceless] to them and formidable to tyrants only.

He has called together legislative bodies at places unusual, uncomfortable, and distant from the depository of their public Records, for the sole purpose of fatiguing them into compliance with his measures.

He has dissolved Representative Houses repeatedly, for opposing with manly firmness his invasions on the rights of the people.

He has refused for a long time, after such dissolutions [closing down], to cause others to be elected; whereby the Legislative powers, incapable of Annihilation, have returned to the People at large for their exercise; the State remaining in the mean time exposed to all the dangers of invasion from without, and convulsions [riots] within.

He has endeavoured to prevent the population of these States; for that purpose obstructing the Laws for Naturalization of Foreigners; refusing to pass others to encourage their migrations hither, and raising the conditions of new Appropriations of Lands.

He has obstructed the Administration of Justice by refusing his Assent to Laws for establishing Judiciary powers.

He has made Judges dependent on his Will alone, for the tenure [term] of their offices, and the amount and payment of their salaries.

He has erected a multitude of New Offices, and sent hither swarms of Officers to harass our people, and eat out their substance.

He has kept among us, in times of peace, Standing Armies without the Consent of our legislatures.

He has affected to render the Military independent of and superior to the Civil power.

He has combined with others to subject us to a jurisdiction foreign to our constitution, and unacknowledged by our laws; giving his Assent to their Acts of pretended Legislation:

For quartering [lodging] large bodies of armed troops among us:

For protecting them, by a mock Trial, from punishment for any Murders which they should commit on the Inhabitants of these States:

For cutting off our Trade with all parts of the world:

For imposing Taxes on us without our Consent:

For depriving us in many cases, of the benefits of Trial by Jury: For transporting us beyond Seas to be tried for pretended offences:

For abolishing the free System of English Laws in a neighbouring Province, establishing therein an Arbitrary government, and enlarging its Boundaries so as to render it at once an example and fit instrument for introducing the same absolute rule into these Colonies:

For taking away our Charters, abolishing our most valuable Laws, and altering fundamentally the Forms of our Governments:

For suspending our own Legislatures, and declaring themselves invested with power to legislate for us in all cases whatsoever.

He has abdicated Government here, by declaring us out of his Protection and waging War against us.

He has plundered our seas, ravaged our Coasts, burnt our towns, and destroyed the lives of our people.

He is at this time transporting large Armies of foreign Mercenaries [soldiers] to complete the works of death, desolation, and tyranny, already begun with circumstances of Cruelty and perfidy [dishonesty] scarcely paralleled in the most barbarous ages, and totally unworthy the Head of a civilized nation.

He has constrained our fellow Citizens taken Captive on the high Seas to bear Arms against their Country, to become the executioners of their friends and Brethren, or to fall themselves by their Hands.

He has excited domestic insurrections amongst us, and has endeavoured to bring on the inhabitants of our frontiers, the merciless Indian Savages whose known rule of warfare, is an undistinguished destruction of all ages, sexes and conditions.

In every stage of these Oppressions We have Petitioned for Redress [correction of wrongs] in the most humble terms: Our repeated Petitions have been answered only by repeated injury. A Prince, whose character is thus marked by every act which may define a Tyrant, is unfit to be the ruler of a free people.

Nor have We been wanting in attentions to our British brethren. We have warned them from time to time of attempts by their legislature to extend an unwarrantable jurisdiction over us. We have reminded them of the circumstances of our emigration and settlement here. We have appealed to their native justice and magnanimity [generosity], and we have conjured [begged] them by the ties of our common kindred, to disavow these usurpations, which would inevitably interrupt our connections and correspondence. They too have been deaf to the voice of justice and of consanguinity [relation by blood]. We must, therefore, acquiesce in the necessity, which denounces our Separation, and hold them, as we hold the rest of mankind, Enemies in War, in Peace Friends.

We, therefore, the Representatives of the United States of America, in General Congress, Assembled, appealing to the Supreme Judge of the world for the rectitude [justness] of our intentions, do, in the Name, and by Authority of the good People of these Colonies, solemnly publish and declare, That these United Colonies are, and of Right ought to be Free and Independent States; that they are Absolved from all Allegiance to the British Crown, and that all political connection between them and the State of Great Britain, is and ought to be totally dissolved; and that as Free and Independent States, they have full Power to levy War, conclude Peace, contract Alliances, establish Commerce, and to do all other Acts and Things which Independent States may of right do. And for the support of this Declaration, with a firm reliance on the protection of Divine Providence, we mutually pledge to each other our Lives, our Fortunes and our sacred Honor.

☑ ASSESSMENT

1. **Identify Cause and Effect** How might the ideas about equality expressed in the Declaration of Independence have influenced later historical movements, such as the abolitionist movement and the women's suffrage movement?
2. **Identify Key Steps in a Process** Why was the Declaration of Independence a necessary document for the founding of the new nation?

3. **Draw Inferences** English philosopher John Locke wrote that government should protect "life, liberty, and estate." How do you think Locke's writing influenced ideas about government put forth in the Declaration of Independence?
4. **Analyze Structure** How does the Declaration organize its key points from beginning to end?

The Pledge of Allegiance

Introduction

The Pledge of Allegiance was first written in 1892. It was revised twice before 1954, when the words "under God" were added, and it became the version that is still recited today.

Primary Source

I pledge allegiance [loyalty] to the Flag of the United States of America, and to the Republic for which it stands, one Nation under God, indivisible, with liberty and justice for all.

ASSESSMENT

1. **Determine Central Ideas** What is the main idea of the Pledge of Allegiance?
2. **Determine Author's Point of View** How do you think the author of the Pledge felt about the United States? Cite evidence from the pledge to support your answer.
3. **Analyze Style and Rhetoric** Why do you think the Pledge involves loyalty to the American flag as well as to the United States?
4. **Draw Conclusions** Why do you think we have a national pledge of loyalty to the country? What purpose does it serve?

GO ONLINE to access the 21st Century Skill Tutorials.

Sequence

Sequence means "order," and placing things in the correct order is very important. What would happen if you tried to put toppings on a pizza before you put down the dough for the crust? When studying history, you need to analyze the information by sequencing significant events, individuals, and time periods in order to understand them. Practice this skill by using the reading on this page.

> Richard Nixon was elected to the House of Representatives in 1946 and then to the Senate four years later. In 1952, with Dwight Eisenhower's election as President, Nixon became Vice President. However, Nixon lost to John F. Kennedy in the 1960 presidential election, and two years later lost an election for governor of California. However, in 1968, Nixon defeated Hubert Humphrey to win the presidency.

[1.] Identify the topic and the main events that relate to the topic. Quickly skim titles and headings to determine the topic of the passage. As you read the passage, write a list of significant events, individuals, or time periods related to the topic.

[2.] Note any dates and time words such as "before" and "after" that indicate the chronological order of events. Look through your list of events, individuals, or time periods and write down the date for each. This will give you information to apply absolute chronology by sequencing the events, individuals, or time periods. Remember that some events may have taken place over a number of months or years. Is your date the time when the event started or ended? Make sure to note enough details that you can remember the importance of the information. If no date is given, look for words such as "before" or "after" that can tell you where to place this event, time period, or individual compared to others on your list. This will allow you to apply relative chronology by sequencing the events, individuals, or time periods.

[3.] Determine the time range of the events. Place the events in chronological order on a timeline. Look for the earliest and latest events, individuals, or time periods on your list. The span of time between the first and last entries gives you the time range. To apply absolute chronology, sequence the entries by writing the date of the first event on the left side of a piece of paper and the date of the last event on the right side. Draw a line connecting the two events. This will be your timeline. Once you have drawn your timeline, put the events in order by date along the line. Label their dates. To apply relative chronology, sequence the significant individuals, events, or time periods on an undated timeline, in the order that they happened. You now have a clear image of the important events related to this topic. You can organize and interpret information from visuals by analyzing the information and applying absolute or relative chronology to the events. This will help you understand the topic better when you can see how events caused or led to other events. You will also be able to analyze information by developing connections between historical events over time.

Categorize

When you analyze information by categorizing, you create a system that helps you sort items into categories, or groups with shared characteristics, so that you can understand the information. Categorizing helps you see what groups of items have in common. Practice this skill as you study the map on this page.

The Presidential Election of 1896

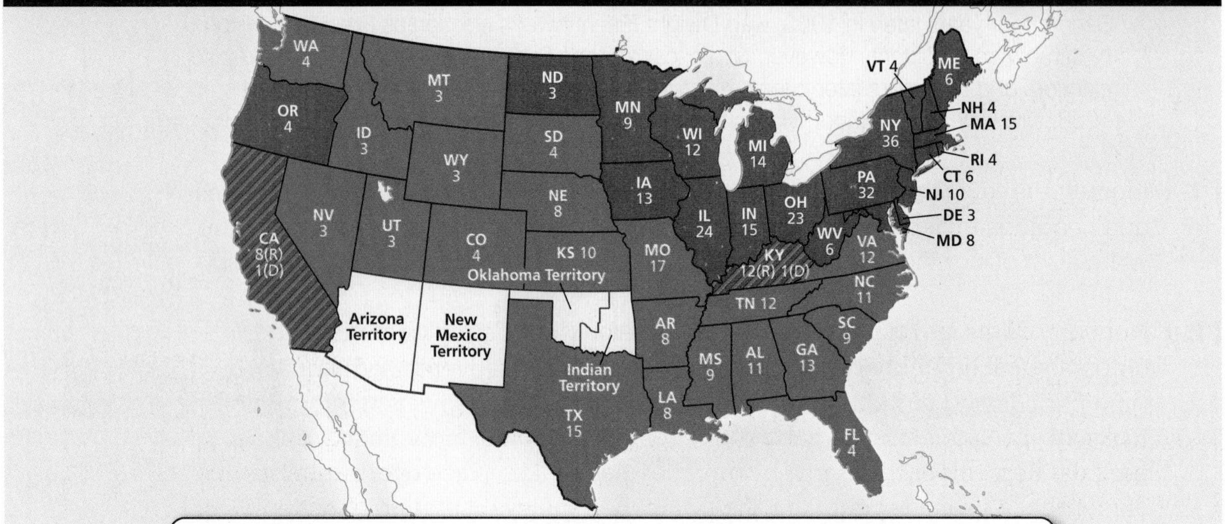

Candidate (Party)	Electoral Vote	Popular Vote	% Electoral Vote	% Popular Vote
William McKinley (Republican; R)	271	7,104,779	60.6	51.0
William Jennings Bryan (Democrat; D)	176	6,502,925	39.4	46.7
States with Split Electoral Votes				

[1.] Identify similarities and differences among items you need to understand. You need to pay careful attention and sometimes do research to find the similarities and differences among the facts, topics, or objects that you need to understand. Scientists find groups, or categories, of related animals by analyzing the details of the animals' bodies. For example, insects with similar wings, legs, and mouthparts probably belong in the same category. Gather similar information about all the things you need to understand. For example, if you know the location of one thing, try to find the locations of all the things you are studying. If you have different types of information about your topics, you will not be able to group them easily.

[2.] Create a system to group items with common characteristics. Once you have gathered similar kinds of information on the items you need to understand, look for items that share characteristics or features. Create categories based on a feature shared by all of the facts, topics, or objects you need to understand. For example, if you have gathered information on the population and political systems of several countries, you could categorize them by the size of their population or their type of political system.

[3.] Form the groupings. Put each of the items that you are studying into one of the categories that you have created. If some items do not fit, you may need to make a new category or modify your categories. Label each category for the characteristic shared by its members. Examples of labels for categories might include "Countries with more than 100 million people," "Countries with fewer than 1 million people," "Democracies," or "Dictatorships."

Analyze Cause and Effect

When you analyze information by identifying cause-and-effect relationships, you find how one event leads to the next. It is important to find evidence that one event caused another. If one event happened earlier than another, it did not necessarily cause the later event. Understanding causes and effects can help you solve problems. Practice this skill as you study the cause-and-effect chart on this page.

Causes and Effects of America's Entry into World War I

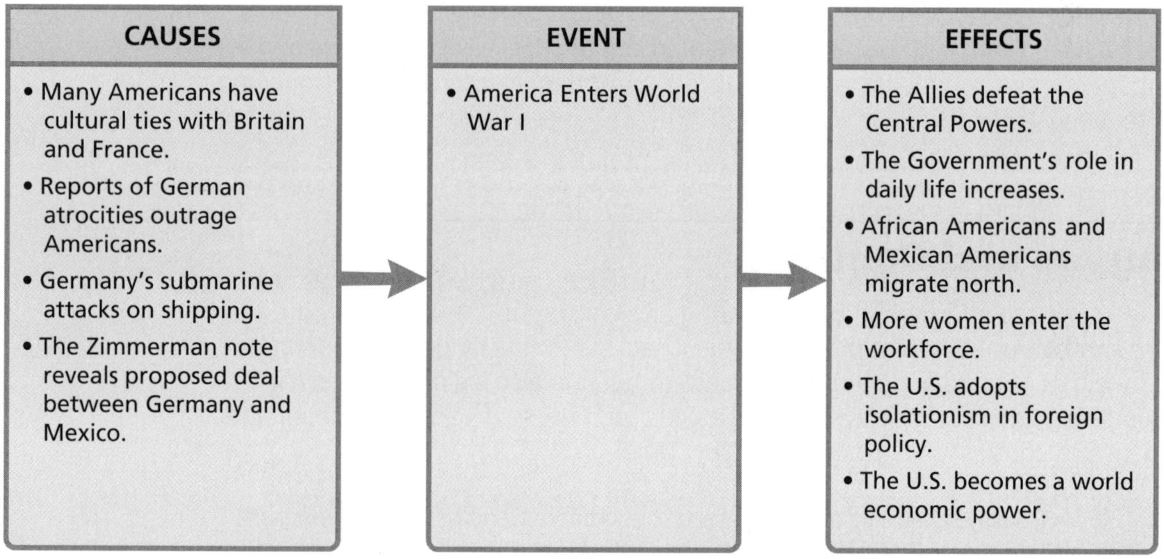

[1.] Choose a starting point of observation. When trying to understand a historical event, choose the time of that event. If you are trying to understand a current event, you can work backward from a starting point in the present.

[2.] Consider earlier events to try to find connections to your starting point, including any language that signals causes. Put the evidence together to identify true causes. When reading, look for events that come before your starting point. Analyze whether these earlier events caused later events. Identify words that signal cause, such as "reason," "because," and "led to." Analyze the information by developing connections between historical events. Make sure that there is evidence showing that the earlier events caused the later events and did not just happen earlier.

[3.] Consider later events to try to find connections to your starting point, including any language that signals effects. Put the evidence together to determine true effects. Look for events that come after your starting point. Analyze the information in order to determine whether these later events are effects of earlier events. Identify words that signal effect, such as "led to," "so," and "therefore." Make sure that there is evidence showing that these later events were caused by earlier events and did not just happen later.

[4.] Summarize the cause-and-effect relationship and draw conclusions. Once you have identified the cause-and-effect relationships between different events, describe these relationships. Draw a diagram that develops the connections between the two historical events. Draw conclusions about any relationships that you see.

Compare and Contrast

When you analyze information by comparing and contrasting two or more things, you look for similarities and differences between them. This skill helps you understand the things that you are comparing and contrasting. It is also a skill that you can use in making choices. Practice this skill as you read the text excerpt on this page. Compare and contrast the critics of the New Deal.

> While Roosevelt had little difficulty gaining support from Congress for his proposals, a minority of Americans expressed their opposition to the New Deal. Critics on the political right thought the changes the New Deal brought were too radical. Critics on the left thought that they were not radical enough. Several of FDR's critics attracted mass followings and made plans to challenge him for the presidency in 1936.

[1.] Look for related topics and characteristics that describe them. When you are looking for similarities and differences between two things, it can help to start by identifying relationships between them. What do the two things have in common? If two things have nothing in common, such as a dog and a piece of pie, it will be difficult to find similarities or differences. On the other hand, you can compare and contrast two countries or political systems. Look through the information you have on the things or topics you want to compare and contrast, and identify the characteristics, or features, that describe those things or topics.

[**2.**] Look for words that signal comparison ("both," "similar to," "also") or contrast ("unlike," "different," "instead"). Look for words that show comparison, or similarity, and those that show contrast, or difference. Take notes on these similarities and differences. This will make it possible to analyze information more quickly.

[**3.**] Identify similarities and differences in the topics, and draw conclusions about them. Look through your notes and analyze the ways in which your topics are similar and different. Usually, topics have both similarities and differences. Try to find patterns in these similarities and differences. For example, all the similarities between two countries might be related to climate, and all the differences might be related to economics. Draw conclusions based on these patterns. In this example, you might conclude that a country's economy does not depend on its climate. Identifying similarities and differences by comparing and contrasting two topics lets you draw conclusions that help you analyze both topics as well as other topics like them.

Identify Main Ideas and Details

You can analyze information in a selection by finding the main idea. A main idea is the most important point in a selection. Identifying the main idea will help you remember details, such as names, dates, and events, which should support the main idea. Practice this skill by reading the paragraph on this page. Find the main idea of this paragraph and the supporting details.

> During his first hundred days in office, which became known as the Hundred Days, Roosevelt proposed and Congress passed 15 major bills. These measures had three goals: relief, recovery, and reform. Roosevelt wanted to provide relief from the immediate hardships of the depression and achieve a long-term economic recovery. He also instituted reforms to prevent future depressions.

[**1.**] Scan titles, headings, and visuals before reading to see what the selection is about. Often, important ideas are included in titles, headings, and other special text. Special text may be primary sources, words that are highlighted, or ideas listed with bullet points. Also, take a look at visuals and captions. By analyzing these parts of the text, you should quickly get a sense of the main idea of the article.

[**2.**] Read the selection and then identify the main point of the selection, the point that the rest of the selection supports: this is the main idea. Read through the selection to identify the main idea. Sometimes, the main idea will be the first or second sentence of one of the first few paragraphs. Sometimes, it will be the last sentence of the first paragraph. Other times, no single sentence will tell you the main idea. You will have to come up with your own sentence answering the question, "What is the main point of this selection?"

[3.] Find details or statements within the selection that support or build on the main idea. Once you have identified the main idea, look for details that support the main idea. Many or most of the details should be related to the main idea. If you find that many of the details are not related to what you think is the main idea, you may not have identified the main idea correctly. Identify the main idea that the details in the selection support. Analyze the information in the text by finding the main idea and supporting details.

Summarize

When you analyze information by summarizing, you restate the main points of a passage in your own words. Using your own words helps you understand the information. Summarizing will help you understand a text and prepare for tests or assignments based on the text. Practice this skill by follow the steps to summarize the excerpt on this page.

> One of the most terrifying aspects of the Cold War was the arms race that began right after World War II. At first, the United States was the only nuclear power. By 1949, however, the Soviet Union had also developed nuclear weapons.
>
> Critics argued that a nuclear war would destroy both sides. Yet each superpower wanted to be able to deter the other from launching its nuclear weapons. Both sides engaged in a race to match each other's new weapons. The result was a "balance of terror." Mutually assured destruction—in which each side knew that the other side would itself be destroyed if it launched its weapons—discouraged nuclear war. Still, people around the world lived in constant fear of nuclear doom.

[1.] Identify and write down the main point of each paragraph in your own words. You may identify the main idea right at the beginning of each paragraph. In other cases, you will have to figure out the main idea. As you read each paragraph, ask yourself, "What is the point this paragraph makes?" The point the paragraph makes is the main idea. Write this idea down in your own words.

[2.] Use these main points to write a general statement of the overall main idea of the passage in your own words. Once you have written down the main idea for each paragraph, write down the main idea of the passage. Write the main idea in your own words. If you have trouble identifying the main idea of the passage, review the titles and headings in the passage. Often, titles and headings relate to the main idea. Also, the writer may state the main idea in the first paragraph of the passage. The main idea of a passage should answer the question, "What is the point this passage makes?"

[3.] Use this general statement as a topic sentence for your summary. Then, write a paragraph tying together the main points of the passage. Leave out unimportant details. Analyze the information in the passage by summarizing. Use the main idea of the passage as a topic sentence for your summary paragraph. Use the main ideas that you identified for each paragraph of the passage to write sentences supporting the main idea of the passage. Leave out details that are not needed to understand the main idea of the passage. Your summary should be in your own words, and it should be much shorter than the original passage. Once your summary is written, review it to make sure that it contains all the main points of the passage. If any are missing, revise your summary to include them. If the summary includes unimportant details, remove them.

Generalize

One good way to analyze materials about a particular subject is to make generalizations and predictions. What are the patterns and connections that link the different materials? What can you say about the different materials that is true of all them? Practice this skill by reading the following descriptions about the population of California in the 1850s. What generalization can you make about the people who went to California during the Gold Rush?

- Free African Americans ran churches and a newspaper, worked in the mines, and owned businesses that supplied miners.
- The work of Chinese immigrants in construction and services helped build the booming state. They also helped build the railroads that linked California with the rest of the country.
- Women played an important role in the California Gold Rush. Women ran stores, hotels, and provided food for the miners.

[1.] Make a list. Listing all of the specific details and facts about a subject will help you find patterns and connections.

[2.] Generate a statement. From your list of facts and specific details, decide what most of the items listed have in common. Analyze your information by making generalizations and predictions.

[3.] Ensure your generalization is logical and well supported by facts. Generalizations can be valid or invalid. A generalization that is not logical or supported by facts is invalid.

Make Predictions

You can analyze information by making generalizations and predictions. Predictions are educated guesses about the future, based on clues you find in written material and information you already have. When you analyze information by making generalizations and predictions, you are thinking critically about the material you read. Practice this skill by analyzing the definition of spoils system and predicting the possible negative effects of the spoils system if used in a corporation or sports team.

spoils system practice of the political party or group in power giving jobs and appointments to its supporters, rather than to people based on their qualifications.

[1.] Review the content. Read your material carefully and research any terms or concepts that are new to you. It's important to understand the material before analyzing the information to make a prediction.

[2.] Look for clues. Gathering evidence is an important part of making predictions. Look for important words, statements, and evidence that seem to support the writer's point of view. Ask questions about what you are reading, including who, what, where, when, why, and how. Look for and analyze clues to help you generalize and predict.

[3.] Consider what you already know. Use related prior knowledge and/or connect to your own experiences to help you make an informed prediction. If you have experience with the subject matter, you have a much better chance of making an accurate prediction.

[4.] Generate a list of predictions. After studying the content, list the clues you've found. Then use these clues, plus your prior knowledge, to form your predictions. List as many possible outcomes as you can based on clues in the material and the questions you have considered.

Draw Inferences

What is the author trying to tell you? To make a determination about the author's message, you analyze information by drawing inferences and conclusions. You consider details and descriptions included in the text, compare and contrast the text to prior knowledge you have about the subject, and then form a conclusion about the author's intent. Practice this skill by analyzing the chart and drawing inferences about the effectiveness of antitrust laws during the 1890s.

Sherman Antitrust Act, 1890

ADVANTAGES	DISADVANTAGES
• Enabled Congress to regulate trade between states and end monopolistic practices • Tried to eliminate hidden monopolies (trusts) that affected trade • Enabled competitors to sue trustees of rival companies for loss of revenue • Levied fines against those forming trusts	• Difficult to enforce • Lacked clear definition of the practices that resulted in a restraint of trade • More often used successfully against labor unions than monopolies

[1.] Study the image or text. Consider all of the details and descriptions included. What is the author trying to tell you? Look for context clues that hint at the topic and subject matter.

[2.] Make a connection. Use related prior knowledge to connect to the text or image. Analyze information by asking questions such as who, what, where, when, and how. Look for cause-and-effect relationships; compare and contrast. This strategy will help you think beyond the available surface details to understand what the author is suggesting or implying.

[3.] Form a conclusion. When you draw an inference, you combine your own ideas with evidence and details you found within the text or image to form a new conclusion. This action leads you to a new understanding of the material.

Draw Conclusions

When you analyze information by drawing inferences and conclusions, you connect the ideas in a text with what you already know in order to understand a topic better. Using this skill, you can "fill in the blanks" to see the implications or larger meaning of the information in a text. Practice this skill by reading the excerpt of text on this page. What conclusions can you draw based on the information in the paragraphs?

Challenging Economic Times

From the Oval Office, Hoover worked hard to end the depression. But to many out-of-work Americans, the President became a symbol of failure. Some people blamed capitalism, while others questioned the responsiveness of democracy. Many believed the American system was due for an overhaul.

Although some questioned the ability of America's capitalistic and democratic institutions to overcome the crisis, most Americans never lost faith in their country.

[1.] Identify the topic, main idea, and supporting details. Before reading, look at the titles and headings within a reading. This should give you a good idea of the topic, or the general subject, of a text. After reading, identify the main idea. The main idea falls within the topic and answers the question, "What is the main point of this text?" Find the details that the author presents to support the main idea.

[2.] Use what you know to make a judgment about the information. Think about what you know about this topic or a similar topic. For example, you may read that the English settlers of Jamestown suffered from starvation because many of them were not farmers and did not know how to grow food. Analyzing the information about their situation and what you know about people, you could draw the conclusion that these settlers must have had little idea, or the wrong idea, about the conditions that they would find in America.

[3.] Check and adjust your judgment until you can draw a well-supported conclusion. Look for details within the reading that support your judgment. Reading a little further, you find that these settlers thought that they would become rich after discovering gold or silver, or through trading with American Indians for furs. You can use this information to support your conclusion that the settlers were mistaken about the conditions that they would find in America. By analyzing the information further, you might infer that the settlers had inaccurate information about America. To support your conclusions, you could look for reliable sources on what these settlers knew before they left England.

Interpret Sources

Outlines and reports are good sources of information. In order to interpret these sources, though, you'll need to identify the type of document you're reading, identify the main idea, organize the details of information, and evaluate the source for point of view and bias. Practice this skill by finding a newspaper or online report on a bill recently passed by Congress or a decision recently decided by the Supreme Court. What steps will you take to interpret this report?

[1.] Identify the type of document. Is the document a primary or secondary source? Determine when, where, and why it was written.

[2.] Examine the source to identify the main idea. After identifying the main idea, identify details or sections of text that support the main idea. If the source is an outline or report, identify the topic and subtopics; review the supporting details under each subtopic. Organize the information from the outline or report and think about how it connects back to the overall topic listed at the top of the outline or report.

[3.] Evaluate the source for point of view and bias. Primary sources often have a strong point of view or bias; it is important to analyze primary sources critically to determine their validity. Evaluating each source will help you interpret the information they contain.

Create Databases

Databases are organized collections of information which can be analyzed and interpreted. You decide on a topic, organize data, use a spreadsheet, and then pose questions which will help you to analyze and interpret your data. Practice this skill as you create a database of changes in your state's population since 1960. You can find many kinds of state data in the U.S. Census. (census.gov)

[1.] Decide on a topic. Identify the information that you will convert into a table. This information may come from various sources, including textbooks, reference works, and Internet sites.

[2.] Organize the data. Study the information and decide what to include in your table. Only include data that is pertinent and available. Based on the data you choose, organize your information. Identify how many columns there will be and what the column headings will be. Decide the order in which you are going to list the data in the rows.

[3.] Use a spreadsheet. A spreadsheet is a computer software tool that allows you to organize data so that it can be analyzed. Spreadsheets allow you to make calculations as well as input data. Use a spreadsheet to help you create summaries of your data. For instance, you can compute the sum, average, minimum, and maximum values of the data. Use the graphing features of your spreadsheet program to show the data visually.

[4.] Analyze the data. Once all of your data is entered and you have made any calculations you need, you are ready to pose questions to analyze and interpret your data. Organize the information from the database and use it to form conclusions. Be sure to draw conclusions that can be supported by the data available.

Analyze Data and Models

Data and models can provide useful information about geographic distributions and patterns. To make sense of that information, though, you need to pose and answer questions about data and models. What does the data say? What does it mean? What patterns can you find? Practice this skill as you study the graph below.

Immigration from Europe, 1870-1910

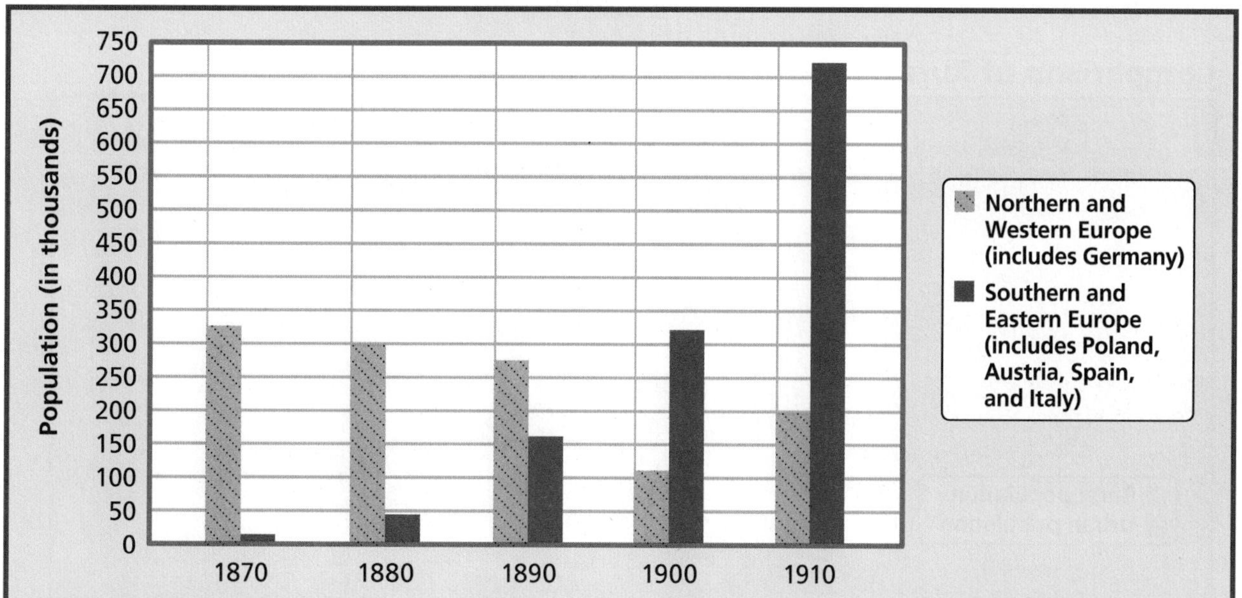

SOURCE: U.S. Census Bureau

[**1.**] Read the title to learn the geographic distributions represented by the data set, graph, or model.

[**2.**] Read the data given. When reviewing a graph, read the labels and the key to help you comprehend the data provided. Pose and answer questions to further understand the material. For example, you might ask "Who could use this data?" or "How could this data be used?" or even "Why is this data presented in this particular format?" Thinking critically about the data presented will help you make predictions and comprehend the data.

[**3.**] Study the numbers, lines, and/or colors to find out what the graphs or data represent. Next, find similarities and differences between multiple models of the same data. Do any additional research to find out more about why the information in the models differs.

[**4.**] Interpret the graph, data set, or model. Look for interesting geographic distributions and patterns in the data. Look at changes over time or compare information from different categories. Draw conclusions.

Read Charts, Graphs, and Tables

If you pose and answer questions about charts, graphs, or tables you find in books or online, you can find out all sorts of information, such as how many calories are in your favorite foods or what the value of a used car is. If you are trying to solve a math problem that includes a chart, graph, or table, you may need to also use a tool such as a concrete model, a ruler, a protractor, a calculator, a spreadsheet, a computer algebra system, a statistical package, or dynamic geometry software. Analyzing and interpreting the information you find in thematic charts, graphs, and tables can help you make decisions in your life. Practice this skill as you study the graph below.

Comparison of Rural and Urban Populations

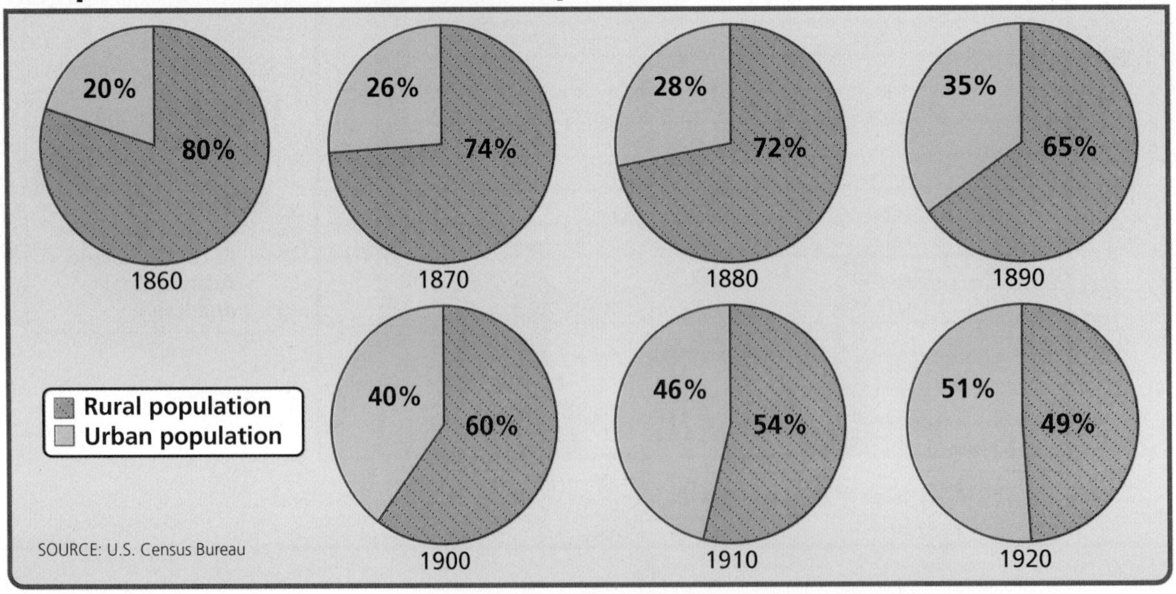

[1.] Identify the title and labels of a chart, graph, or table, and read the key, if there is one, to understand the information presented. The title often tells you the topic of the chart, graph, or table, or the type of information you will find. Make sure you understand how the graph shows information. A key or legend often appears in a small box near the edge of the graph or chart. The key will tell you the meaning of lines, colors, or symbols used on the chart or graph. Notice also the column and row headings, and use your reading skills to figure out the meanings of any words you don't know.

[2.] Determine consistencies and inconsistencies, to see whether there is a trend in a graph, chart, or table. Organize information from visuals such as charts and graphs and decide whether or not there is a trend or pattern in the information that you see. Evaluate the data and determine whether the trend is consistent, or steady. Remember that there could be some inconsistencies, or exceptions to the pattern. Try not to miss the overall pattern because of a couple of exceptions.

[3.] Draw conclusions about the data in a chart, graph, or table. Once you understand the information, try to analyze and interpret the information and draw conclusions. If you see a pattern, does the pattern help you to understand the topic or predict future events?

[4.] Create a chart or graph to make the data more understandable or to view the data in a different way. Does the data in the chart or graph help you answer questions you have about the topic or see any causes or effects? For example, you could use your mathematical skills to create circle graphs or bar graphs that visually organize the data in a different way that allows you to interpret the data differently.

[5.] Use the data or information in charts and graphs to understand an issue or make decisions. Use your social studies skills to make inferences, draw conclusions, and take a stand on the issue.

Create Charts and Maps

Thematic charts, graphs, and maps are visual tools for representing information. When you create a thematic chart, graph, or map you will start by selecting the type of data you want to represent. Then you will find appropriate data to include, organize your data, and then create symbols and a key to help others understand your chart, graph, or map. Practice this skill by creating a map of the presidential election of 1952. Use computer software to show how each state voted by party.

[1.] To create a chart or map, first select a region or set of data. Use a map to represent data pertaining to a specific region or location; use a chart to represent trends reflected in a set of data.

[2.] Research and find the data you would like to present in the chart or map. Your choice of data will be based on the theme you wish to explore. For example, a chart or map that explores the theme of changing demographics in New York might include data about the location of different ethnic groups in New York in the nineteenth, twentieth, and twenty-first centuries.

[3.] Organize the data according to the specific format of your chart or map.

[4.] Create symbols, a key (as needed), and a title. Create symbols to represent each piece of data you would like to highlight. Keep each symbol simple and easy to understand. After you have created the symbols, place them in a key. Add a title to your map or chart that summarizes the information presented. Your symbols and key will make it easier for others to interpret your charts and maps.

Analyze Political Cartoons

Political cartoons are visual commentaries about events or people. As you learn to analyze political cartoons, you will learn to identify bias in cartoons and interpret their meaning. You can start by carefully examining the cartoon and considering its possible meanings. Then you can draw conclusions based on your analysis. Practice this skill as you study the political cartoon below.

GO ONLINE to access the 21st Century Skill Tutorials.

[1.] Fully examine the cartoon. Identify any symbols in the cartoon, read the text and title, and identify the main character or characters. Analyze the cartoon to identify bias and determine what each image or symbol represents. Conduct research if you need more information to decipher the cartoon.

[2.] Consider the meaning. Think about how the cartoonist uses the images and symbols in the cartoon to express his or her opinion about a subject. Try to interpret the artist's purpose in creating the image.

[3.] Draw conclusions. Use what you have gleaned from the image itself, plus any prior knowledge or research, to analyze, interpret, and form a conclusion about the artist's intentions.

Read Physical Maps

What mountain range is closest to where you live? What major rivers are closest to you? To find out, you would look at a physical map. You can use appropriate reading skills to interpret social studies information such as that found on different kinds of maps. Physical maps show physical features, such as elevation, mountains, valleys, oceans, rivers, deserts, and plains. Practice this skill as you study the map on this page.

America in 1783

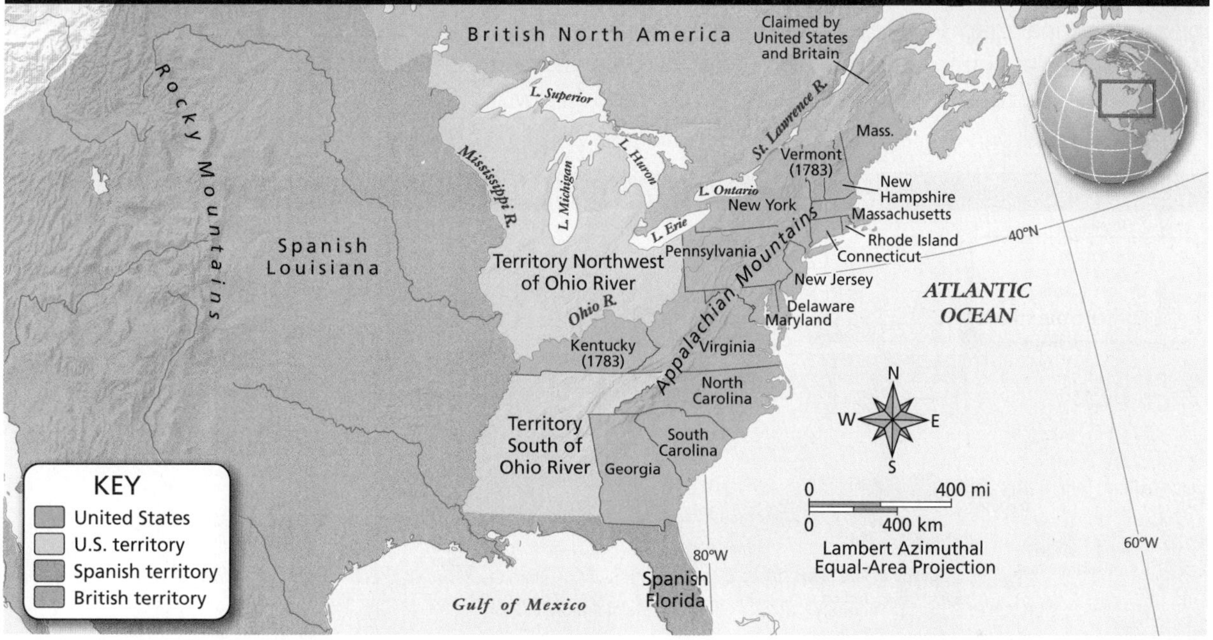

[1.] Identify the title and region shown on a map. A map's title can help you to identify the region covered by the map. The title may also tell you the type of information you will find on the map. If the map has no title, you can identify the region by reading the labels on the map.

[2.] Use the map key to interpret symbols and colors on a map. A key or legend often appears in a small box near the edge of the map. The legend will tell you the meaning of colors, symbols, or other patterns on the map. On a physical map, colors from the key often show elevation, or height above sea level, on the map.

[3.] Identify physical features, such as mountains, valleys, oceans, and rivers. Using labels on the map and colors and symbols from the key, identify the physical features on the map. The information in the key allows you to interpret the information from visuals such as a map. Rivers, oceans, lakes, and other bodies of water are usually colored blue. Colors from the key may indicate higher and lower elevation, or there may be shading on the map that shows mountains.

[4.] Draw conclusions about the region based on natural resources and physical features. Once you understand all the symbols and colors on the map, try to interpret the information from the map. Is it very mountainous or mostly flat? Does it have a coastline? Does the region have lots of lakes and rivers that suggest a good water supply? Pose and answer questions about geographic distributions and patterns shown on the map. Physical maps can give you an idea of lifestyle and economic activities of people in the region.

Read Political Maps

What is the capital of your state? What countries border China? To find out, you could look at a political map. Political maps are colorful maps that show borders, or lines dividing states or countries. They also show capitals and sometimes major cities. Practice reading political maps by studying the map below.

The Civil War, 1861–1862

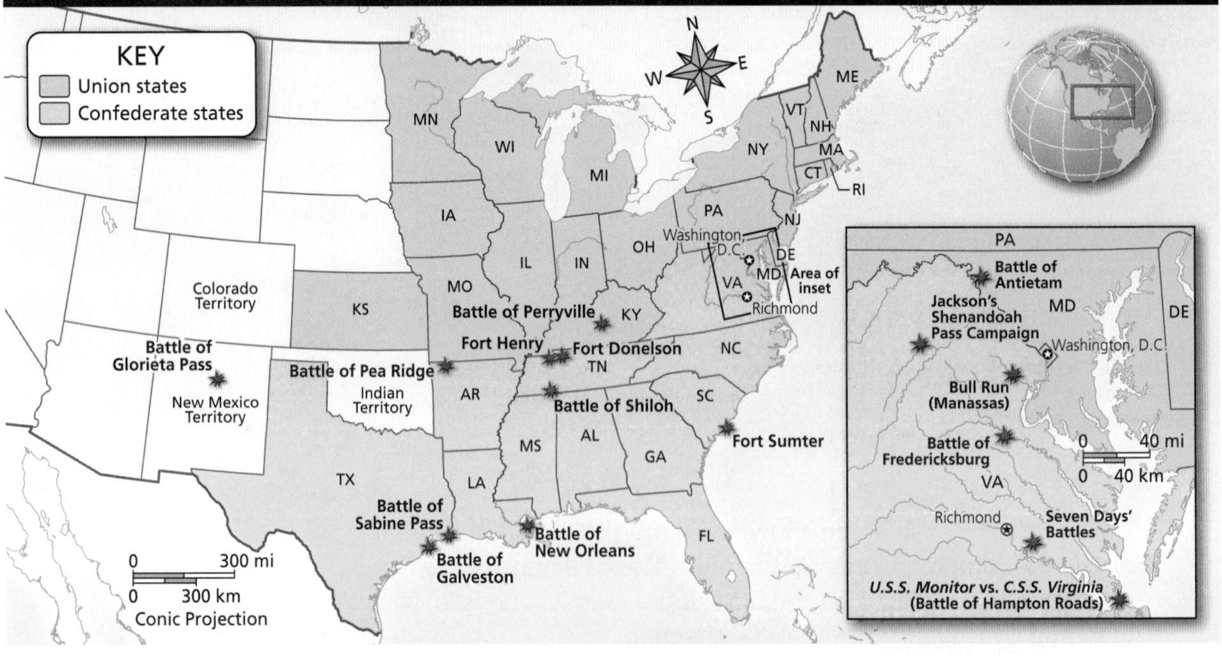

[1.] Identify the title of the political map and the region shown. A map's title can help you identify the region covered by the map. The title may also tell you the type of information you will find on the map. If the map has no title, you can identify the region by reading the labels on the map.

[2.] Use the map key to interpret symbols and colors on the map. A key or legend often appears in a small box near the edge of the map. The key will help you interpret information from visuals, including maps, by telling you the meaning of colors, symbols, or other patterns on the visual.

[3.] Identify boundaries between nations or states. Evaluate government data, such as borders, using the map. It is often easy to see borders, because each state or country will be a different color. If you cannot find the borders, check the key to find the lines used to mark borders on the map.

[4.] Locate capital cities. Look at the key to see how capital cities are shown on the map. They are often marked with a special symbol, such as a star.

[5.] Draw conclusions about the region based on the map. Once you understand all the symbols and colors on the map, use appropriate reading and mathematical skills to interpret social studies information, such as that shown on the map, in order to draw conclusions about the region. For example, are some countries very large with many cities? These countries are likely to be powerful and influential.

Read Special-Purpose Maps

Some maps show specific kinds of information. These special-purpose maps may show features such as climate zones, ancient trade routes, economic and government data, geographic patterns, or population. Locating and interpreting information from visuals, including special-purpose maps, is an important research skill. Practice this skill as you study the map on this page.

The Election of 1860

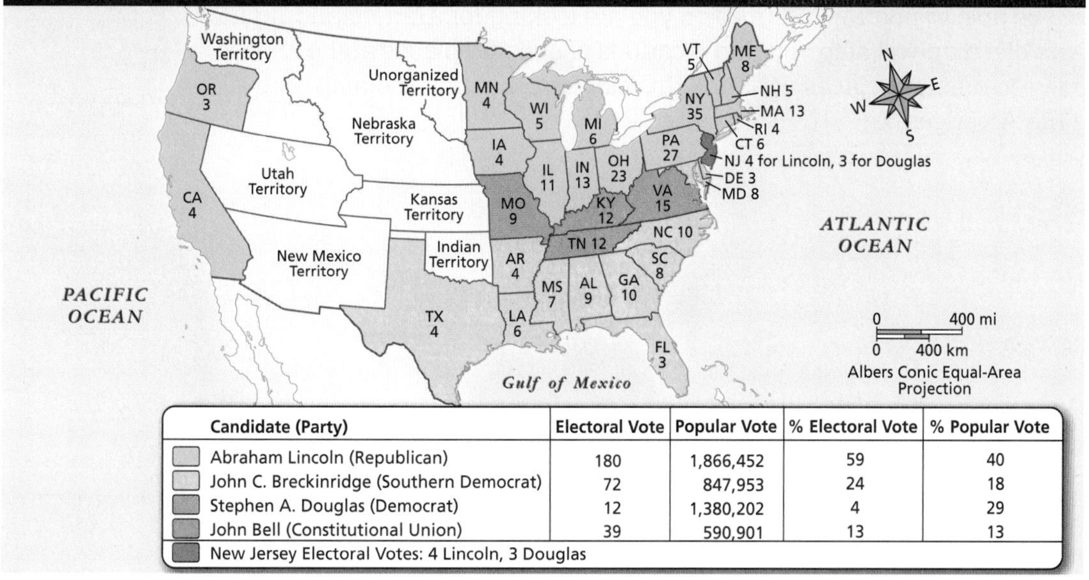

Candidate (Party)	Electoral Vote	Popular Vote	% Electoral Vote	% Popular Vote
Abraham Lincoln (Republican)	180	1,866,452	59	40
John C. Breckinridge (Southern Democrat)	72	847,953	24	18
Stephen A. Douglas (Democrat)	12	1,380,202	4	29
John Bell (Constitutional Union)	39	590,901	13	13
New Jersey Electoral Votes: 4 Lincoln, 3 Douglas				

[**1.**] Identify the title and determine the purpose of a map. A map's title can help you identify the region covered by the map. The title may also tell you the purpose of the map. If the map has no title, see what information the map shows to determine its purpose.

[**2.**] Use the map key to make sense of symbols and colors on a map. A key or legend often appears in a small box near the edge of the map. The key will tell you the meaning of colors, symbols, or other patterns on the map. Special-purpose maps use these colors and symbols to present information.

[**3.**] Draw conclusions about the region shown on a map. Once you understand all the symbols and colors on the map, you can use appropriate skills, including reading and mathematical skills, to analyze and interpret social studies information such as maps. You can pose and answer questions about geographic patterns and distributions that are shown on maps. For example, a precipitation or climate map will show you which areas get lots of rainfall and which are very dry. You can evaluate government and economic data using maps. For example, a population map will show you which regions have lots of people and which have small, scattered populations. A historical map will show you the locations of ancient empires or trade routes. Thematic maps focus on a single theme or topic about a region. For example, you can interpret information from a thematic map representing various aspects of Texas during the nineteenth or twentieth century by studying the Great Military Map, which shows forts established in Texas during the nineteenth century, or by studying a map covering Texas during the Great Depression and World War II. By mapping this kind of detailed information, special-purpose maps can help you understand a region's history or geography.

Use Parts of a Map

If you understand how to organize and interpret information from visuals, including maps, you will be able to find the information you are looking for. Understanding how to use the parts of a map will help you find locations of specific places and estimate distances between different places. Practice this skill as you study the map on the Migration to the Americas.

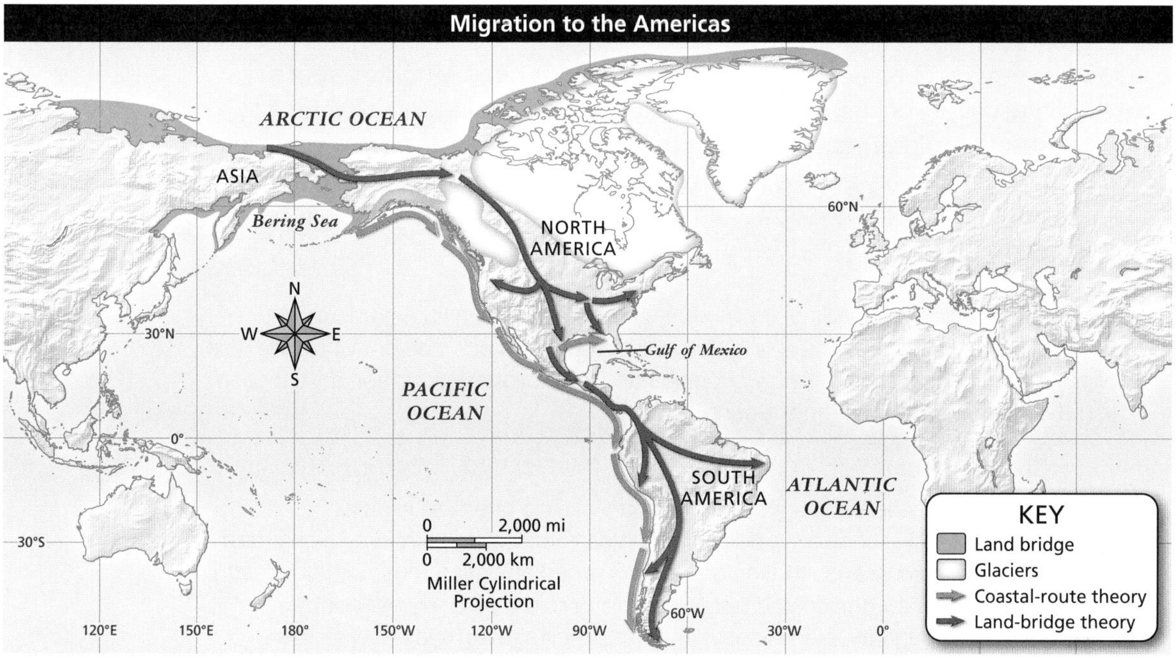

[1.] Identify the title and region of a map. Use appropriate reading skills to interpret social studies information such as map labels. A map's title can help you to identify the region covered by the map. The title may also tell you the type of information you will find on the map. If the map has no title, you can identify the region by reading the labels on the map.

[2.] Use the compass rose to determine direction. Although on most maps north is at the top of the map, you should always double check the compass rose. Often, on the compass rose, the first letter of each direction represents that direction. For example, "N" represents the direction "north." Some compass roses are as simple as an arrow pointing north.

[3.] Use the scale to estimate the distance between places. Use appropriate mathematical skills to interpret social studies information such as a map scale. The scale on a map shows how a measurement on the map compares to the distance on the ground. For example, if one inch on the map represents a mile, the number of inches between two places on the map is the distance in miles.

[4.] Use the key or legend on a map to find information about colors or symbols on a map. A key or legend often appears in a small box near the edge of the map. The legend will tell you the meaning of colors, symbols, or other patterns on the map.

[5.] Use the latitude and longitude grid to determine absolute locations. An absolute location is an exact description of a location on Earth's surface based on latitude and longitude. You can use the latitude and longitude lines on a map to find the absolute location of a place.

Analyze Primary and Secondary Sources

Primary sources are firsthand accounts of events. By contrast, secondary sources are secondhand accounts of events. Both sources are useful, but it is important to differentiate between valid primary and secondary sources. In this lesson, you'll learn how to locate and use primary and secondary sources to acquire information about the United States. Practice this skill by analyzing the two selections below about the Vietnam War and distinguishing between the primary and secondary source.

> "You carried 50 to 70 pounds of equipment, and it was tough going, particularly in forested areas. Often you'd have to pull yourself along from one tree branch to the next, or we'd have to help each other by gripping hands. And you couldn't see anything, so you didn't know what was there around you."
>
> —Sergeant William Ehrhart, United States Marines

> American soldiers generally fought lightly armed Vietcong guerrillas in small engagements. The Vietcong traveled light, often carrying just a rifle and a few handfuls of rice. They hid in tunnels during the day and emerged at night to ambush American patrols. They infiltrated American bases and set off explosives. They set booby traps that maimed and crippled American troops. Their strategy was to wear the Americans down.

[1.] Determine who created the source as well as when and why it was created. Determine whether it is a primary or secondary source. Identify the author of the document. Next, look for the date the document was written or the date when the document was first published. Most primary sources are written close to the date of the events described. Secondary sources are often written well after the events described. Firsthand observers or participants in an event create primary sources. People who did not witness an event create secondary sources. Primary sources record an event. Secondary sources analyze or draw conclusions about events. Secondary sources rely on both primary and secondary sources. Good research requires you to analyze and evaluate the validity of information, arguments, and counterarguments from a primary or secondary source for frame of reference.

[2.] Identify the main idea and supporting details, and determine whether they are facts or opinions. Read the text carefully and ask yourself, "What point is this text making?" This point is the main idea. Then reread the text and list details that support this main idea. Decide whether these details are facts or opinions. If the details are facts, it should be possible to confirm them in other sources. If the author uses emotional language that shows feelings, the supporting details are probably opinions. Carefully analyze and evaluate the validity of information, arguments, and counterarguments from primary and secondary sources for point of view.

[3.] Decide whether the source's information is biased or if it is accurate and credible. Check statements in the text against reliable sources, such as encyclopedias or books written by experts on the topic. If reliable sources agree with the text, it is probably fairly accurate. If most of the text seems to be opinions rather than facts, it is not an accurate source of information. Still, these opinions can teach you about the author's world. A writer who observed an exciting or scary event may use emotional language to describe the event, but the source may still be a reliable account. An important part of research is analyzing and evaluating the validity of the information, arguments, and counterarguments from primary and secondary sources for bias or propaganda.

Compare Viewpoints

When people disagree about a topic, they have different viewpoints. Knowing how to analyze and evaluate the validity of information, arguments, and counterarguments from both primary and secondary sources for point of view can help you to learn more about a topic. Practice this skill by reading the following quotations and comparing the viewpoints on dictatorship.

> "Dictatorship...involves costs which the American people will never pay: The cost of having our children brought up, not as free and dignified human beings, but as pawns..."
>
> –Franklin Roosevelt, State of the Union Address, January 4, 1939

> "The [Nazi Party] has laid down the directive...we must insist that all organs of education...have to [fulfill] their duty towards the community..."
>
> –Adolf Hitler, Speech delivered in German Reichstag on January 30, 1937

[1.] Identify the authors of texts presenting different points of view and identify each author's frame of reference. Frame of reference is a term that describes the experiences, values, and ideas that influence a person's opinions and actions. It can also be referred to as *point of view*. First, identify the group or individual that wrote each text. Determine if the source is primary or secondary. As you read, take note of any information about the author's experiences or background. Also, look for any signs of what the author thinks is important. These types of statements can help you analyze and evaluate the validity of information, arguments, and counterarguments from both primary and secondary sources for point of view.

[2.] Recognize any similarities and differences between the authors' frames of reference and identify the opinion of each author. Pay attention to any similarities and differences between the two authors' experiences, values, and ideas. Read carefully to identify the opinion of each author. In an article about a rock band, an author who played guitar in a band for ten years argues that Band A is the best band today because of its great guitarist. In a second article, another author who sang for many years argues that Band B is the best because of its lead singer. Notice how authors' arguments and counterarguments are shaped by their frame of reference, or point of view.

[3.] Draw conclusions about similarities and differences between authors' points of view. With some information about the point of view of each author, you can understand why they have different opinions. This helps you to analyze and evaluate the validity of the information, arguments, and counterarguments. In the example of the two authors writing about rock bands, each author stresses his or her own areas of expertise. You might decide to listen to the band recommended by the singer if you share an interest in vocals. If you are more interested in instrumentals, you might choose the band recommended by the guitarist.

Identify Bias

Being able to analyze and evaluate the validity of information, arguments, and counterarguments for bias helps you to determine whether primary or secondary sources you find online, in books, or in the media are reliable. When you are able to identify bias in written, oral, and visual material, you can see when someone is presenting only one side of an issue or basing an argument on emotion instead of facts. Practice this skill by applying the steps below whenever you read an editorial or an op-ed piece in the news media.

[1.] Identify the author of a source and the author's purpose. First, identify the author of the source. The author may be a group or an organization rather than a single person. The author may state his or her purpose very clearly in the source. If not, the type of source may give you an idea of the purpose. For example, the writer of an encyclopedia aims to summarize information about a subject. The author of a political Web site may want you to vote for a candidate.

[2.] Identify the main idea, and check whether the main idea is supported with facts or opinions. Read the document carefully and ask yourself, "What is the main point of this selection?" Your answer to this question is the main idea. Reread the document and list details that support this main idea. Decide whether these details are facts or opinions. To find out whether they are facts, check whether other reliable sources include the same information. If your source uses statements that shows feelings, those statements are probably opinions.

[3.] Look for the use of emotional language or one-sided opinions. Look for words that can show opinions such as "good" and "bad." Be aware of statements that make you feel angry, scared, or excited. Also, watch out for statements that only express one side of an issue. These are all signs of bias.

[4.] Draw conclusions about the author's bias, if any. Is the author using mostly emotional language with few facts to support his or her ideas? Are there insults or other very negative language in the source? If so, the source is probably biased. Similarly, if you notice that the author is presenting only one side of an issue, the source is probably not reliable. It is important to analyze and evaluate the information, arguments, and counterarguments in both primary and secondary sources for bias.

GO ONLINE to access the 21st Century Skill Tutorials.

Evaluate Existing Arguments

When you evaluate existing arguments, you must evaluate and analyze the point of view and biases of your sources and their authors. Who is the author and what is he or she trying to accomplish? How valid are the arguments in your primary and secondary sources? If you master these skills, you will be able to analyze and interpret social studies information such as speeches. Practice this skill as you read and evaluate the excerpt on this page.

> We hold these truths to be self-evident: that all men and women are created equal; that they are endowed by their Creator with certain inalienable rights; that among these are life, liberty, and the pursuit of happiness. . . .
>
> The history of mankind is a history of repeated injuries and usurpations [seizures] on the part of man toward woman, having in direct object the establishment of an absolute tyranny over her. To prove this, let facts be submitted to a candid [fair] world.
>
> He has never permitted her to exercise her inalienable right to the elective franchise.
>
> He has compelled her to submit to law in the formation of which she had no voice. . . .
>
> He has made her, if married, in the eye of the law, civilly dead. He has taken from her all right in property, even to the wages she earns. . . .
>
> Now, in view of this entire disfranchisement of one-half the people of this country, their social and religious degradation, in view of the unjust laws above mentioned, and because women do feel themselves aggrieved, oppressed, and fraudulently deprived of their most sacred rights, we insist that they have immediate admission to all the rights and privileges which belong to them as citizens of the United States.
>
> —*Declaration of Sentiments and Resolutions*, 1848

[1.] Identify the claim or thesis. What is the author or source claiming? The claim or thesis is usually found in the introduction and/or conclusion of a written or spoken argument.

[2.] Identify the reasons (claims to truth or facts) the author offers in support of his or her claim. What evidence does the author or source provide to support their claims? Make a list of the evidence provided to support each claim.

[3.] Evaluate the argument. Analyze and evaluate the validity of the evidence presented to support each claim. Use the appropriate skills to analyze and interpret social studies information, such as speeches. Research each claim to be sure that the author's statements are accurate. Carefully check for evidence of bias or propaganda. Be sure you understand the author's point of view and his or her frame of reference. Finally, check to be sure that the author's conclusions follow logically from the evidence presented. If the evidence is accurate, the author is free from bias, and conclusions follow logically from the evidence, the claims are probably valid.

Consider and Counter Opposing Arguments

Before you can effectively counter opposing arguments, you'll need to analyze possible counterarguments for frame of reference, bias, point of view, and propaganda. You'll plan your response ahead of time, collecting research and data. Then, you'll make a point of acknowledging the opposing view before presenting your counterarguments. To practice this skill, suppose you are preparing for a debate about raising the minimum wage in your state. Choose a side of the debate to support. What arguments will you use to support your side of the debate? What counterarguments will you anticipate the other side using? Why is it useful to anticipate the other side's arguments?

[1.] Fully understand your argument and the potential counter points. Do research as needed to find out more about other opposing views. Analyze and evaluate the validity of possible counterarguments from primary and secondary sources for frame of reference, bias, point of view, and propaganda.

[2.] Make predictions and outline a response to several of the opposing views. Continue researching as needed. Researching, analyzing, and evaluating the validity of opposing arguments will help you support and strengthen your own. Opposing arguments can consist of any reasons, conclusions, or claims that oppose yours. Outline your response to each opposing reason, conclusion, or claim.

[3.] To counter an opposing argument, first acknowledge the opposing view. This strategy shows that you have heard the opposing argument and are responding accordingly. Consider using statements such as "I understand your point, but you should also consider the following..." You can also respond by refuting facts, logic, etc. Be sure to respond to each opposing argument. Ignoring or dismissing a counterargument shows that your response is weak and unsupported.

Participate in a Discussion or Debate

When you participate effectively in a collaborative discussion or debate, your goal is to explain, analyze, and defend a point of view–often related to a current political or economic issue. To be a successful debater, you'll do your research, present your position, and defend your point of view in a courteous manner. You'll build on others' ideas and express your own clearly and persuasively. Use the steps below to prepare for a discussion on this question: Do you think the United States should act as a "global policeman?" Why or why not?

[1.] Research. Before participating in a discussion or debate, come to discussions prepared. Do research to gain knowledge of your subject so that you may be an informed and prepared participant. Take notes as needed to help you prepare. Jot down main points and any questions you may have. As you research, decide where you might stand on the issue. Be sure to gather research and sources that will allow you to explain, analyze, and defend your point of view.

[2.] Present your position. After you have organized your thoughts and decided where you stand, explain and defend your point of view. Explicitly draw on your preparation by referring to evidence from texts and other research on the topic to stimulate a thoughtful, well-reasoned exchange of ideas. Be sure to stay focused on the topic and your line of argument. Ask questions that challenge the accuracy, logic, or relevance of opposing views.

[3.] During the discussion or debate, be patient and courteous. Work with your classmates to promote civil, democratic discussions. Listen attentively, be respectful and supportive of peers, and speak only when instructed to do so by the moderator. Be sure to allow others to express their views; do not monopolize the debate or discussion. Speak clearly and slowly. Propel conversations by posing and responding to questions that may probe your reasoning and evidence.

Give an Effective Presentation

When you create a written, visual, and oral presentation, you teach, convince, or share information with an audience. Effective presentations use both words and visuals to engage audiences. Delivery is also important. For example, you can use the way you move, speak, and look at the audience to keep people interested. Use the steps below to prepare and deliver a presentation on U.S. President Richard Nixon's visit to China in 1972.

[1.] Identify the purpose of your presentation and your audience. Think about the purpose of your written, visual, and oral presentation. If this is a research report, you will need facts and data to support your points. If you are trying to persuade your audience, look for powerful photos. Keep your audience in mind. Consider their interests and present your topic in a way that will engage them.

[2.] Write the text and find visual aids for your presentation. Look online and in books and magazines for information and images for your presentation. Organize the information and write it up carefully so that it is easy for your audience to understand. Diagrams can show complicated information in a clear way. Visuals also get people interested in the presentation. So choose large, colorful images that people in the back of the audience will be able to see.

[3.] Practice and work to improve your presentation. Keep practicing your oral presentation until you know the material well. Then, practice some more, focusing on improving your delivery.

[4.] Use body language, tone of voice, and eye contact to deliver an effective presentation. Answer questions if the audience has them. At the beginning of your oral presentation, take a breath, smile, and stand up tall. Speak more loudly and more clearly than you would in normal conversation. Also, try not to rush through the presentation. Glance at your notes but speak naturally, rather than reading. Look at people in the audience. If people are confused, pause to clarify. Finally, leave time for people in the audience to ask questions.

Write an Essay

There are four steps to writing an essay. You'll start by selecting a topic and research sources, then you'll write an outline and develop a thesis or point of view. After drafting your essay, you'll carefully proofread it to be sure you've used standard grammar, spelling, sentence structure, and punctuation. Finally, you'll revise and polish your work. To practice this skill, select a topic that interests you about the modern U.S. presidency and develop a thesis. Then explain to a partner the steps you will take to write your essay.

[1.] Choose your topic and research sources. Check which types of sources you will need. Gather different types of reliable sources that support the argument you will be making.

[2.] Write an outline and generate a thesis. First write your topic at the top of the page then list all the points or arguments you want to make about the topic; also list the facts and examples that support these points. Your thesis statement will inform the reader of the point you are making and what question you will be answering about the topic. When writing your thesis, be as specific as possible and address one main idea.

[3.] Draft your essay. After finishing your research and outline, begin writing the body of your essay; start with the introduction then write a paragraph for each of your supporting points, followed by a conclusion. As you write, do your best to use standard grammar, spelling, sentence structure, and punctuation. Be sure any terminology is used correctly.

[4.] Revise. An important part of the writing process involves checking for areas in which information should be added, removed, or rewritten. Try to imagine that this paper belongs to someone else. Does the paper have a clear thesis? Do all of the ideas relate back to the thesis? Read your paper out loud and listen for awkward pauses and unclear ideas. Lastly, check for mistakes in standard grammar, spelling, sentence structure, punctuation, and usage.

Avoid Plagiarism

When you don't attribute ideas and information to source materials and authors, you are plagiarizing. Plagiarizing–claiming others' ideas and information as your own–is considered unethical. You can avoid plagiarizing by carefully noting down which authors and sources you'll be using, citing those authors and sources in your paper, and listing them in a bibliography. The issue of plagiarism in mass media and digital sources has become an important issue in recent years. As Internet users gain wider access to copyright information, the legal dangers of reusing someone else's work have grown. Practice this skill by following these steps.

[1.] Keep a careful log of your notes. As you read sources to gain background information on your topic, keep track of ideas and information and the sources and authors they come from. Write down the name of each source next to your notes from that particular source so you can remember to cite it later on. Create a separate section in your notes where you keep your own thoughts and ideas so you know which ideas are your own. Using someone else's words or paraphrasing their ideas does not make them yours.

[2.] Cite sources in your paper. You must identify the source materials and authors you use to support your ideas. Whenever you use statistics, facts, direct quotations, or paraphrases of others' views, you need to attribute them to your source. Cite your sources within the body of your paper. Check your assignment to find out how they should be formatted.

[3.] List your sources in a bibliography at the end of your paper. List your source materials and authors cited in alphabetical order by author, using accepted formats. As you work, be sure to check your list of sources from your notes so that none are left out of the bibliography.

Solve Problems

Problem solving is a skill that you use every day. It is a process that requires an open mind, clear thinking, and action. Practice this skill by considering the lack of volunteers for a local project such as a food bank or park clean up and using these steps to solve the problem.

[1.] Understand the problem. Before trying to solve a problem, make sure that you gather as much information as possible in order to identify the problem. What are the causes and effects of the problem? Who is involved? You will want to make sure that you understand different perspectives on the problem. Try not to jump to conclusions or make assumptions. You might end up misunderstanding the problem. If the problem is mathematical, you should start by explaining to yourself the meaning of a problem and look for entry points to its solution.

[2.] Consider possible solutions and choose the best one. Once you have identified the problem and gathered some information, list and consider a number of possible options. Right away, one solution might seem like the right one, but try to think of other solutions. Be sure to consider carefully the advantages and disadvantages of each option. It can help to take notes listing benefits and drawbacks. Look for the solution whose benefits outweigh its drawbacks. After considering each option, choose the solution you think is best. You should analyze givens, constraints, relationships, and goals, making conjectures about the form and meaning of the solution and planning a solution pathway rather than simply jumping into a solution attempt.

[3.] Make and implement a plan. Choose and implement a solution. Make a detailed, step-by-step plan to implement the solution that you choose. Write your plan down and assign yourself a deadline for each step. That will help you to stay on track toward completing your plan. Try to think of any problems that might come up and what you will do to address those problems. Of course, there are many things that you cannot predict. Stay flexible. Evaluate the effectiveness of the solution and adjust your plan as necessary.

Make Decisions

Everyone makes decisions. The trick is to learn how to make good decisions. How can you make good decisions? First, identify a situation that requires a decision and gather information. Then, identify possible options and predict the consequences of each option. Finally, choose the best option and take action to implement a decision. Practice this skill by considering the steps you should take when making a decision about which candidate you should vote for in a local, state, or national election.

[1.] Determine the options between which you must decide. In some cases, like ordering from a menu at a restaurant, your options may be clear. In other cases, you will need to identify a situation that requires a decision, gather information, and identify the options that are available to you. Spend some time thinking about the situation and brainstorm a number of options. If necessary, do a little research to find more options. Make a list of options that you might choose.

[2.] Review the costs and benefits of each option. Carefully predict the consequences of each option. You may want to make a cost-benefit list for each option. To do this, write down the option and then draw two columns underneath it. One column will be the "pro" or benefit list. The other column will be the "con" or cost list. Note the pros and cons for each of your options. Try not to rush through this process. For a very important decision, you may even want to show your list to someone you trust. This person can help you think of costs and benefits that you had not considered.

[3.] Determine the best option and act on it. Look through your cost-benefit lists. Note any especially serious costs. If an option has the possibility of an extremely negative consequence, you might want to cross it off your list right away. Look closely at the options with the most benefits and the fewest costs, and choose the one that you think is best. Once you have made a choice, take action to implement a decision. If necessary, make a detailed plan with clear steps. Set a deadline to complete the steps to keep yourself moving toward your goal.

Being an Informed Citizen

Informed citizens understand the responsibilities, duties, and obligations of citizenship. They are well informed about civic affairs, involved with their communities, and politically active. When it comes to issues they personally care about, they take a stand and reach out to others.

[1.] Learn the issues. A great way to begin to understand the responsibilities of citizenship is to first find topics of interest to you. Next, become well informed about civic affairs in your town, city, or country. Read newspapers, magazines, and articles you find online about events happening in your area or around the world. Analyze the information you read to come to your own conclusions. Radio programs, podcasts, and social media are also great ways to keep up with current events and interact with others about issues.

[2.] Get involved. Attend community events to speak with others who know the issues. Become well informed about how policies are made and changed. Find out who to speak to if you would like to take part in civic affairs and policy creation. There are government websites that can help direct you to the right person. These websites will also provide his or her contact details.

[3.] Take a stand and reach out. Write, call, or meet with your elected officials to become a better informed, more responsible citizen. Do research about candidates who are running for office to be an informed voter. Start your own blog or website to explore issues, interact with others, and be part of the community or national dialogue.

Political Participation

Political participation starts with an understanding of the responsibilities, duties and obligations of citizenship, such as serving the public good. When you understand your role as a political participant, you can get involved through volunteering for a political campaign, running for office, or interacting with others in person or online.

[1.] Volunteer for a political campaign. Political campaigns offer a wide variety of opportunities to help you become involved in the political process and become a responsible citizen by serving the public good. As a political campaign volunteer you may have the opportunity to attend events, make calls to voters, and explore your community while getting to know how other voters think about the responsibilities, duties, and obligations of citizenship.

[2.] Run for office in your school or community. A good way to become involved in your school or community is to run for office. Student council or community positions offer a great opportunity for you to become familiar with the campaign and election process.

[3.] Reach out to others. Start or join an interest group. Interest groups enable people to work together on common goals related to the political process. Write a letter or email a public official. By contacting an elected official from your area, you can either support or oppose laws or policies. You can also ask for help or support regarding certain issues.

[4.] Interact online. Social networking sites and blogs offer a great way for people of all ages to interact and write about political issues. As you connect with others, you'll become more confident in your role as a citizen working for the public good.

Voting

Voting is not only a right. It is also one of the primary responsibilities, duties, and obligations of citizenship. Before you can legally vote, however, you must understand the voter registration process and the criteria for voting in elections. You should also understand the issues and know where different candidates stand on those issues.

[1.] Check eligibility and residency requirements. In order to vote in the United States, you must be a United States citizen who is 18 years or older, and you must be a resident of the place where you plan to vote.

[2.] Register to vote. You cannot vote until you understand the voter registration process. You can register at city or town election offices, or when you get a driver's license. You can also register by mail or online. You may also have the option of registering at the polls on Election Day, but this does not apply in all states. Make sure to find out what you need to do to register in your state, as well as the deadline for registering. You may have the option of declaring a political party when registering.

[3.] Learn the issues. As the election approaches, research the candidates and issues in order to be an informed voter. Watch televised debates, if there are any. You can also review the candidates' websites. By doing these things and thinking critically about what you learn, you will be prepared to exercise your responsibility, duty and obligation as a United States citizen.

[**4.**] Vote. Make sure to arrive at the correct polling place on Election Day to cast your ballot. Research to find out when the polls will be open. Advance voting, absentee voting, and voting by mail are also options in certain states for those who qualify.

Serving on a Jury

As an American, you need to understand the duties, obligations and responsibilities of citizenship; among these is the expectation that you may be required to serve on a jury. You will receive a written notice when you are summoned to jury duty and you'll receive instruction on the special duties and obligations of a juror. You'll follow the American code of justice which assumes that a person is innocent until proven guilty, and you'll follow instructions about keeping trial information confidential.

[**1.**] Wait to receive notification. If you are summoned to serve as a juror, you will be first notified by mail. If you are chosen to move on to the jury selection phase, lawyers from both sides will ask you questions as they select the final jury members. It is an honor to serve as a juror, as it is a responsibility offered only to American citizens.

[**2.**] Follow the law and remain impartial. Your job is to determine whether or not someone broke the law. You may also be asked to sit on the jury for civil cases (as opposed to criminal cases); these cases involve lawsuits filed against individuals or businesses for any perceived wrong doing (such as broken contracts, trespassing, discrimination, etc.). Be sure to follow the law as it is explained to you, regardless of whether you approve of the law or not. Your decision about the trial should not be influenced by any personal bias or views you may have.

[**3.**] Remember that the defendant is presumed innocent. In a criminal trial, the defendant must be proven guilty "beyond a reasonable doubt" for the verdict to be guilty. If the trial team fails to prove the defendant to be guilty beyond a reasonable doubt, the jury verdict must be "not guilty."

[**4.**] During the trial, respect the court's right to privacy. As a juror, you have specific duties, obligations, and responsibilities under the law. Do not permit anyone to talk about the case with you or in your presence, except with the court's permission. Avoid media coverage once the trial has begun so as to prevent bias. Keep an open mind and do not form or state any opinions about the case until you have heard all of the evidence, the closing arguments from the lawyers, and the judge's instructions on the applicable law.

Paying Taxes

Paying taxes is one of the responsibilities of citizenship. How do you go about figuring out how much you've already paid in taxes and how much you still owe? It's your duty and obligation to find out, by determining how much has been deducted from your pay and filing your tax return.

[1.] Find out how taxes are deducted from your pay. In the United States, payroll taxes are imposed on employers and employees, and they are collected and paid by the employers. Check your pay stub to find out how much money was deducted for taxes. Be sure to also save the W-2 tax form your employer sends to you. You will need this form later on when filing your tax paperwork. Also save any interest income statements. All this information will help you fulfill your obligation as an American taxpayer.

[2.] Check the sales taxes in your state. All but five states impose sales and use taxes on retail sale, lease, and rental of many goods, as well as some services. Sales tax is calculated as the purchase price times the appropriate tax rate. Tax rates vary widely from less than one percent to over ten percent. Sales tax is collected by the seller at the time of sale.

[3.] File your tax return. Filing your tax return is more than an obligation: it's also a duty and responsibility of citizenship. You may receive tax forms in the mail, or pick them up at the local Post Office or library. Fill the forms in and then mail or electronically send completed tax forms and any necessary payments to the Internal Revenue Service (IRS) and your state's department of revenue. The IRS provides free resources to help people prepare and electronically file their tax returns; go to IRS.gov to learn more. Note: certain things such as charitable donations and business expenses are tax deductible.

Analyze Images

When analyzing an image, it's important to go beyond your first impressions. Look closely to determine the content of the image, make careful note of details in the image, and consider the context in which the image appears. Using clues you collect through this process, you can identify the purpose of the image shown.

[1.] Identify the content. When reviewing an image, look closely at the features and text, and determine which information is important. Consider the overall message of the image.

[2.] Note the details. When analyzing images of people, study facial expressions and body positions. Consider the emotions these expressions or positions suggest. Also consider the arrangement (how the objects or people are placed in an image). When considering the arrangement, examine the location (where something is placed) and the scale (the size of the visual components). For example, is one individual placed front and center while another is set far to the side? If so, the central figure is probably the most important.

[3.] Consider context. Where does the image appear? Is it on a billboard? In a textbook? In a magazine? Read all of the captions and credits. If possible, gather information about who created or paid for the image. Understanding the context of an image will help you to better understand its message.

[4.] Identify the purpose. Why did the artist create this image? Images can help illustrate a point, persuade an audience, or sell a product. If it is in an advertisement, chances are its purpose is to sell a product. If it's a political cartoon, it is probably offering commentary on a political situation or event. If it's in a newspaper, it is most likely intended to provide information to support a news story.

Use Context Clues

Using context clues can help you figure out the meaning of an unknown word. You look for context clues in the text surrounding an unfamiliar word. Once you find enough clues to predict a word's meaning, then you can check it by using a dictionary. Sometimes an author will define an unfamiliar word. Notice how James Madison defines the term "faction" in this excerpt from the *Federalist*, No. 10:

> AMONG the numerous advantages promised by a well constructed Union, none deserves to be more accurately developed than its tendency to break and control the violence of faction. . . . By a faction, I understand a number of citizens, whether amounting to a majority or a minority of the whole, who are united and actuated by some common impulse of passion, or of interest, adversed to the rights of other citizens, or to the permanent and aggregate interests of the community. . . .

[1.] Stop and reread the sentence when you find a word you do not know. When you find a word that you do not know, take a minute to reread the sentence. Do your best to understand the general meaning of the sentence even though there is a word that you do not know.

[2.] Identify the topic of the sentence and see if this helps you figure out the unknown word's meaning. After you have reread the sentence, determine its topic. The word that you do not know may be related to the topic of the sentence. This can help you get a sense of the meaning of the word.

[**3.**] Check around the unknown word for phrases or other words that describe it or link to ideas that are familiar to you. If the unknown word is not related to the topic of the sentence, check for other words and phrases that you know. Look to see how the unknown word is related to other words and phrases in the sentence.

[**4.**] Predict the word's meaning and then look up its definition in a dictionary. Try to predict the meaning of the word based on its connection to the topic or to other words in the sentence. Then, check your guess in a dictionary.

Develop a Clear Thesis

A thesis is a statement of your position or perspective on a topic. In order to define and express your thesis, you'll need to review the assignment, research and narrow down your topic, and then determine your position or point of view on the topic.

[**1.**] Review the assignment. First determine what kind of paper you are being asked to write (some examples are persuasive, analytical, narrative, or expository).

[**2.**] Research and narrow your topic. After selecting your topic, do research to find out what others have written about it. Familiarize yourself with the topic and be sure to explore sources that present varying viewpoints. Narrow the topic by focusing on one or two specific areas of interest.

[**3.**] Take a position on the topic. Form your own conclusion about the topic. Be specific and avoid general statements; this conclusion will serve as the thesis you address in your paper. Make sure you can support your thesis with evidence; you may need to make revisions as you move forward in the researching and drafting process. Your thesis statement should answer a specific question. A clear thesis will express one main idea and show your conclusions about a subject.

Distinguish Between Fact and Opinion

When you distinguish between fact and opinion, you separate information that is true from statements showing a person's beliefs or feelings. Separating fact from opinion will help you decide whether to trust the information in a source.

[1.] Identify the author of a source and his or her purpose for writing. Consider that purpose as you look for facts and opinions. First, find the author of the source. The author may be a group or an organization rather than a single person. The author may state his or her purpose very clearly in the source. If not, the type of source may give you an idea of the purpose. For example, the writer of an encyclopedia aims to summarize information about a subject. The author of a political Web site may want you to vote for a candidate.

[2.] Identify possible facts by looking for information that can be proven true. Do research to find out if the information is actually true. Read through the source and write down statements made by the author. Check other sources on this subject to see if they agree. Try to find reliable sources, such as encyclopedias, your textbook, and books written by experts on the topic. If you discover that reliable sources do not confirm statements in your source, it is not reliable. The statements you have identified are probably not true facts.

[3.] Decide if the author is expressing an opinion by looking for language that signals opinions and by looking for statements that are personal beliefs or judgments. Look for words that can show opinions, such as "good," "bad," "should," and "must." Statements such as "I think" and "I believe" also indicate opinions. Be aware of statements that make you feel angry, scared, or excited. The author may be using emotion rather than facts to support his or her ideas. Consider the evidence that the author gives to support his or her ideas and opinions. Sources that are full of opinions with few facts to support them are not reliable. Even if the source contains some facts, be careful if those facts all support the author's opinion. Check other reliable sources to see if the author has left out facts that do not support his or her opinion.

Evaluate Web Sites

Knowing how to evaluate Web sites will help you to understand how reliable a Web site is. Some Web sites are biased toward one point of view. Others may contain inaccurate information. The Internet is full of a confusing variety of sources and content that ranges from the reliable and accurate to the biased and false. Digital sources may also be full of slander and libel, so always check who has produced the content found on the Internet. Finally, many Web sites are out of date.

[1.] Identify the author or sponsor of the Web site, assess the reliability of the author, and identify any bias to find out whether the Web site is objective. Finding the author or sponsor of a Web site is not always easy. Check the bottom of the home page or look for a link that says "About Us." Then, try to learn about the author or sponsor. What is the goal of the Web site? Do you see emotional language or other language that suggests that the Web site is biased? Avoid Web sites with a clear bias, as they may not present both sides of a topic.

[**2.**] Identify when the Web site was last updated and determine whether the information is current. The copyright date or date that the Web site was created or updated can often be found at the bottom of the home page. For online encyclopedias, blogs, and other sites that frequently add new content, be sure to check the date of each entry. Some content may be much more recent than the date when the site was created. Think about your topic and then decide if the site in current. Are you researching something for a history class? In that case, even if the Web site is a number of years old, it may be a good source. On the other hand, if you are looking for information about an ongoing current event, information from a month ago might already be out of date.

[**3.**] Compare the content of the Web site to other Web sites and sources on the same topic. Once you have decided that a Web site seems reliable and up-to-date, be sure to check the site against other sources. Even the best sites may have mistakes. Read other reliable Web sites or do some more research at the library. Having at least two reliable sources for each piece of information will help to make sure that you have accurate information.

Analyze Media Content

When you analyze media content, you think carefully about who produced the content and why they produced it. You think critically about all aspects of the content. When you think carefully about content in this way, you can draw conclusions about the message and its intended impact. This is particularly important when analyzing content on the Internet, with its confusing variety of sources and content that ranges from the reliable and accurate to the biased and false. Digital sources may also be full of slander and libel, so always check who has produced the content found on the Internet. To practice this skill, research a controversial political topic on the Internet. Take note of the viewpoint of each source and identify the author. Explain how the bias of the author shapes the information that you have found.

[**1.**] Identify the media source and important information about the author. The source of a piece of media content may be a single writer or a whole organization. The name of the author may appear at the beginning of a book or article. However, for Web sites and some documents, you may need to look carefully for the person or organization that created the content. Try to learn all you can about the source. What experience does the author have? If the source is an organization, who gives money to the organization?

[**2.**] Determine the economic, social, and political context of the message. The context is the background that helps shape the message. Is the writer responding to a certain problem or situation? Is there an event, such as an upcoming election, that might be important to the writer? These factors may help you figure out the purpose of the writer and whether or not the writer is biased.

[**3.**] Identify the message, noting what is missing, and determine whether the message relies on stereotypes. Try to figure out the meaning of the message. Is the source leaving out important information? Is the message based on stereotypes or other inaccurate information? If you are not certain, you may want to read more about the topic to understand it better.

[**4.**] Draw conclusions about the intended impact of the message. Once you have thought about the context and content of the message, try to draw a conclusion about the purpose of the message. What does the writer hope that you will think or do after reading the message?

Organize Your Ideas

Before writing a paper or planning a speech, it's important to organize your ideas. You'll start by thinking about the task for which you're preparing. Next, you'll brainstorm organizational ideas and create an outline.

[**1.**] Consider the task. Before organizing your ideas, review the project you're working on. Why are you organizing your ideas? Who will be using your organized ideas? Are you planning a project, writing a paper, or getting ready to give a speech?

[**2.**] Brainstorm. Drawing a brainstorming map might help you see how your thoughts connect to one another, which will help you when you begin organizing your writing. Alternatively, brainstorm by simply listing your ideas. Another strategy is to explain your thinking out loud to someone else; this may help you organize your ideas in a more logical way.

[**3.**] Create an outline. Outline your main points and jot down the supporting details under each section.

Publish Your Work

Using the Internet, you can share your work by publishing it on Web sites, blogs, or wikis. Blogs are like online personal journals, and wikis are Web sites that many people can write and maintain.

[1.] Choose a topic that interests you and write about it in a classroom wiki or blog. Before picking a topic, think about the purpose or theme of the classroom wiki or blog. Choose a topic that fits that purpose. Read reliable sources to learn about your topic. Think about the best way to organize your ideas. After organizing your ideas, write your entry. Be sure to check for spelling and grammar errors before posting to the site. If possible, list your sources on the site.

[2.] Upload digital images to your entry in order to enhance the information. Search online for images related to your topic. Be careful to pick images that you have permission to use. In some cases, the person who made a photo or owns a photo does not want the photo to be used by other people. You may be able to find more information about a photo by clicking on it. In addition to photos, you can use maps, charts, graphs, and illustrations.

[3.] Ask classmates to build upon your ideas and post their comments. Engage in an online discussion forum with classmates and respond to one another's comments. In a wiki, your classmates may be able to edit your work. If you write a blog post, your classmates can make comments on your work. Try to respond to the comments of your classmates. If a classmate makes a good suggestion, edit your entry to improve it. If you think that your classmate's suggestion might not be correct, write a comment to explain this respectfully to your classmate. It is easy to feel self-conscious if a lot of people are reading your work. Focus on learning from your classmates and seeing your work from a fresh perspective.

Search for Information on the Internet

You can use the Internet for answers to all kinds of questions. The trick is to make sure you are finding reliable sources that provide accurate information. This is particularly important when analyzing content on the Internet, with its confusing variety of sources and content that ranges from the reliable and accurate to the biased and false. Digital sources may also be full of slander and libel, so always check who has produced the content found on the Internet. To practice this skill, research a topic on the Internet by first going to the website of a governmental or educational organization. Then find a website of a private individual and compare the information to the content found on a more reliable source.

[1.] Identify the topic and information you need, and enter key words or phrases about the topic into a search engine. Make a list of key words or phrases related to your topic. These could be names, dates, or other details about the topic. Enter your key words into a search engine. Read the titles of the first 10–20 results. If these results are too general, try adding more specific key words until you get results related to your topic.

[2.] Analyze headings and URLs to find reliable sources. Look for URLs that end in .edu or .gov, or Web sites of well-known newspapers, news magazines, and news broadcasters. Avoid sites that show bias, and try to find sites that give reliable sources for their information. You may get many results from the search engine. Look at the URLs, or Web addresses, to get clues about the source of the Web site. Within the URL, you may see the name of a newspaper, government office, or other reliable source. URLs that end in .edu are usually university Web sites. URLs that end in .gov are government offices. Writers at universities and government offices are often experts in their field and will try to present the facts without bias. Focus on the sites that seem the most reliable.

[3.] Use information from a variety of sites and check the online information against other sources, such as other reliable Web sites, encyclopedias, and newspapers. Be careful not to base your research on a single Web site. Even the best sites may have mistakes. Read other reliable Web sites or do some additional research at the library. Reading multiple sources will give you a better understanding of your topic.

Set a Purpose for Reading

When you set a purpose for reading, you decide what you want to learn from a text and make a plan for getting what you want. First, you get familiar with the text. Next, you identify exactly what you want to learn. Then, you can analyze the information by finding the main idea as you read.

[1.] Preview the text and scan titles, headings, special text, and images to identify the main ideas covered in the topic. Often, main ideas are included in titles, headings, and other special text. Special text may be primary sources, words that are highlighted, or ideas listed with bullet points. Also, take a look at visuals and captions. By previewing these pieces of information, you should quickly get a sense of the main idea of a text.

[2.] Think about the topic and decide *why* you are reading— your purpose, or what you want to learn. Before reading the text in more detail, make sure that you know why you are reading the text. What do you want to learn from this text? What information do you need? Having a clear purpose for your reading will help you to analyze the text, identify the main idea, and find the information that you need more quickly.

[3.] Analyze the text to find information that serves your purpose or tells you what you want to know. Take notes if needed. Read actively with your purpose in mind. Analyze the information in the text by finding the main idea. If the main idea of a paragraph does not seem related to your purpose, read through the paragraph quickly. In a long passage, you may even be able to skip some sections. Spend more time analyzing the sections that are related to your purpose. Make sure that you understand these sections. Take notes as you find the information that you need.

Support Ideas with Evidence

Without supporting evidence, your writing is just a statement of opinion. With evidence, however, it becomes a statement of fact. When you support ideas with evidence, you start by checking your assignment to be sure you know what kind of evidence you need. Next, you'll examine your sources to be sure they are appropriate for your topic. Finally, you'll correctly incorporate your evidence into your essay. If you are using the Internet to find evidence to support your opinion, remember to carefully avoid unreliable websites that might be full of inaccuracies and bias.

[1.] Review the assignment. Before you gather sources, make sure you understand the type of evidence you need to include to support your ideas.

[2.] Examine your sources. Ensure your evidence is related to your overall argument. Ask yourself the following: Why is this information important? Why does it matter? Does this evidence support my thesis? If so, how?

[3.] Incorporate your evidence. There are several different ways to present your evidence in writing. You can use quotes from your sources or include a summary; make sure to cite all of your sources so they can be identified. Other options include graphs, charts, or tables; excerpts from an interview; or photographs or illustrations. Make sure to cite evidence to back up each supporting point.

Write a Journal Entry

Journals are a great place to brainstorm and get creative. The process is simple: just think of a topic, express your ideas, and then review what you wrote. A Journal will allow you to write routinely over a period of time, whether it is months or days.

GO ONLINE to access the 21st Century Skill Tutorials.

[1.] Think of a topic that interests you.

[2.] Be open minded and express your ideas. Use your journal as a forum to explore your own unique thoughts. Journals are great for experimenting with creative writing, problem solving, and brainstorming.

[3.] Reread what you have written. Reviewing your journal will help you to remember some of the great ideas you've come up with and may help you in your creative or essay writing. What's more, revisiting past material will help you see how your writing has developed and give you a chance to think of new ideas to explore.

The United States: Political

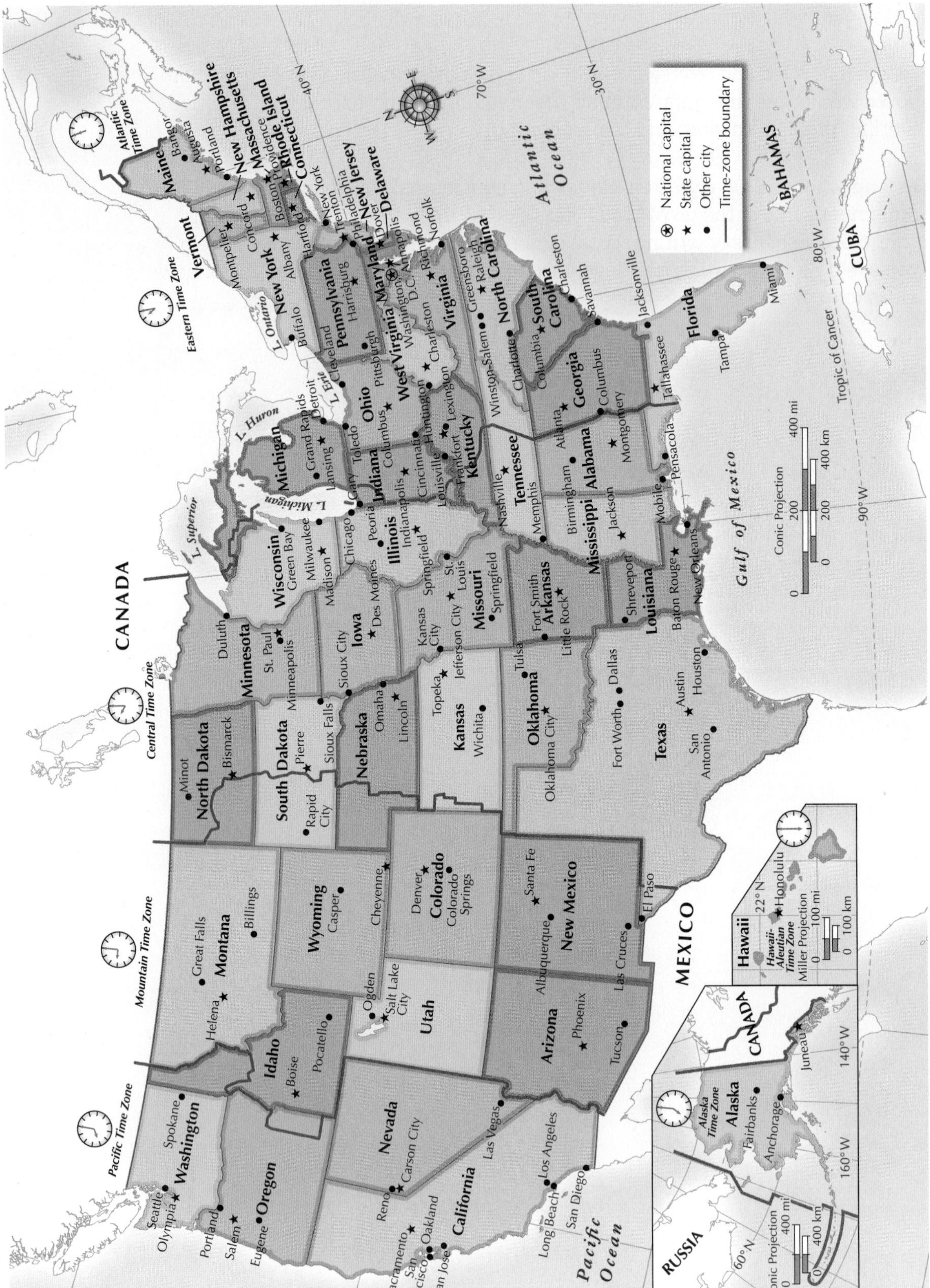

The United States: Physical

The World: Political

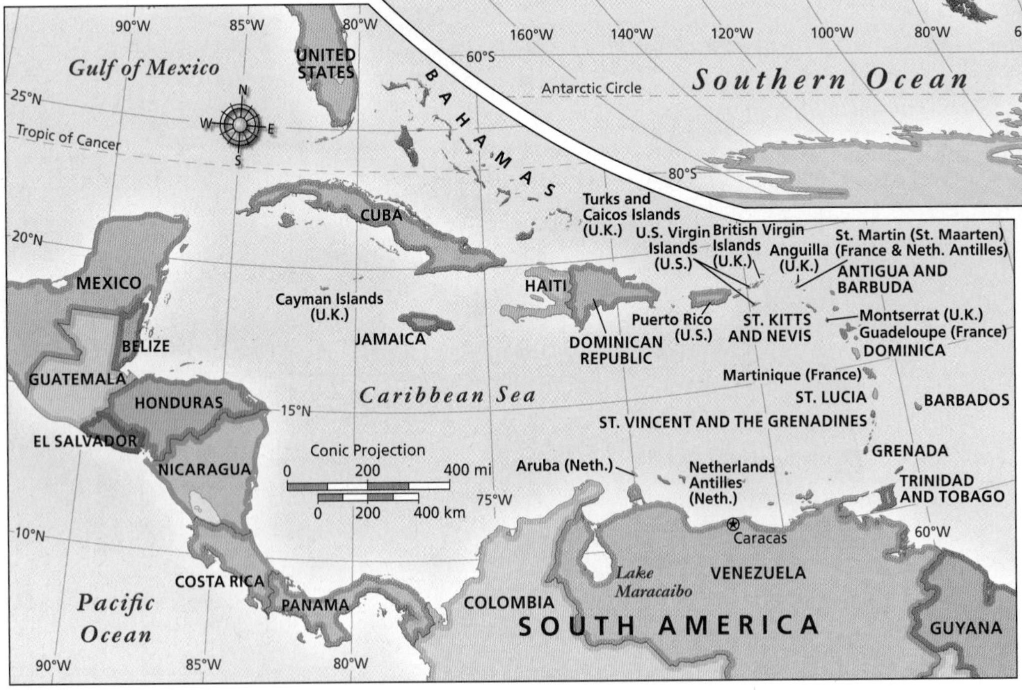

Arctic Ocean
Arctic Circle
ICELAND
see inset below
EUROPE
RUSSIA
ASIA
KAZAKHSTAN
MONGOLIA
GEORGIA
AZER.
ARMENIA
UZBEK.
TURKMEN.
KYRGYZSTAN
TAJIKISTAN
Tehran
Beijing
NORTH KOREA
SOUTH KOREA
Seoul
JAPAN
Tokyo
CHINA
MOROCCO
ALGERIA
LIBYA
ISRAEL
Cairo
EGYPT
IRAQ
JORDAN
KUWAIT
IRAN
AFGHAN.
BAHRAIN
QATAR
PAKISTAN
NEPAL
BHUTAN
New Delhi
Shanghai
Pacific Ocean
SAUDI ARABIA
Karachi
U.A.E.
OMAN
INDIA
MYANMAR (BURMA)
TAIWAN
BANGLADESH
LAOS
Hong Kong
Mumbai
AFRICA
ERITREA
CHAD
SUDAN
YEMEN
THAILAND
VIETNAM
Bangkok
CAMBODIA
MARSHALL ISLANDS
DJIBOUTI
CEN. AFR. REP.
SOUTH SUDAN
Addis Ababa
ETHIOPIA
SRI LANKA
PHILIPPINES
CAMEROON
SOMALIA
DEM. REP. OF THE CONGO
UGANDA
KENYA
MALDIVES
BRUNEI
MALAYSIA
FEDERATED STATES OF MICRONESIA
KIRIBATI
inset below
SÃO TOMÉ AND PRÍNCIPE
GABON
CONGO
RWANDA
BURUNDI
SINGAPORE
INDONESIA
NAURU
PAPUA NEW GUINEA
SOLOMON ISLANDS
TUVALU
TANZANIA
SEYCHELLES
Jakarta
TIMOR-LESTE
ANGOLA
MALAWI
COMOROS
Indian Ocean
Atlantic Ocean
ZAMBIA
MOZAMBIQUE
OCEANIA
FIJI ISLANDS
VANUATU
MADAGASCAR
ZIMBABWE
BOTSWANA
MAURITIUS
NAMIBIA
AUSTRALIA
New Caledonia (France)
ESWATINI
SOUTH AFRICA
LESOTHO
Cape Town
Sydney
NEW ZEALAND
N
W
E
S
Robinson Projection
0 1,000 2,000 mi
0 1,000 2,000 km
Southern Ocean
ANTARCTICA
20°W 0° 20°E 40°E 60°E 80°E 100°E 120°E 140°E 160°E
80°N
60°N
40°N
20°N
0°
20°S
40°S
60°S

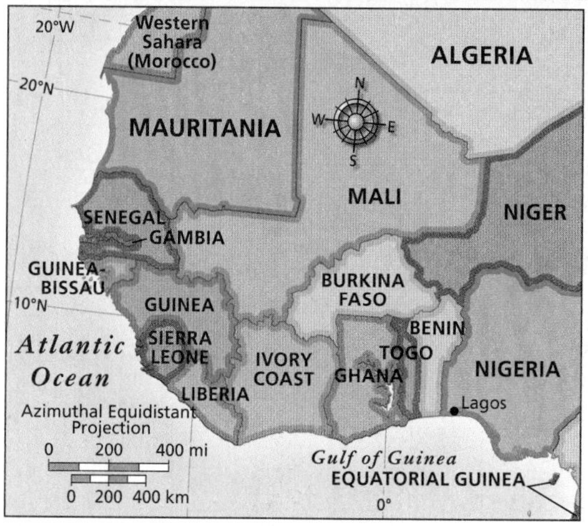
Western Sahara (Morocco)
ALGERIA
MAURITANIA
N
W
E
S
MALI
NIGER
SENEGAL
GAMBIA
GUINEA-BISSAU
GUINEA
BURKINA FASO
BENIN
SIERRA LEONE
TOGO
Atlantic Ocean
IVORY COAST
GHANA
NIGERIA
LIBERIA
Lagos
Azimuthal Equidistant Projection
0 200 400 mi
0 200 400 km
Gulf of Guinea
EQUATORIAL GUINEA
20°W
20°N
10°N
0°

Barents Sea
N
W
E
S
SWEDEN
FINLAND
Conic Projection
0 200 400 mi
0 200 400 km
NORWAY
ESTONIA
North Sea
DENMARK
LATVIA
Moscow
IRELAND
UNITED KINGDOM
Baltic Sea
LITHUANIA
RUSSIA
NETHERLANDS
London
BELARUS
Berlin
RUSSIA
POLAND
Atlantic Ocean
GERMANY
BELGIUM
LUX.
Kiev
Paris
CZECHIA
UKRAINE
Bay of Biscay
LIECH.
SLOVAKIA
FRANCE
SWITZ.
AUSTRIA
MOLDOVA
HUNGARY
SLOVENIA
CROATIA
ROMANIA
ANDORRA
MONACO
ITALY
SAN MARINO
BOS. AND HERZ.
SERBIA
PORTUGAL
Madrid
Corsica (France)
MONT.
KOS.
BULGARIA
Black Sea
SPAIN
Rome
N. MAC.
Istanbul
Gibraltar (U.K.)
Sardinia (Italy)
VATICAN CITY
ALBANIA
Ceuta (Spain)
Melilla (Spain)
Balearic Isands (Spain)
Sicily (Italy)
GREECE
TURKEY
MALTA
Mediterranean Sea
CYPRUS
SYRIA
MOROCCO
ALGERIA
TUNISIA
Crete (Greece)
LEBANON
20°W
10°W
0°
10°E
30°E
40°E
50°E
70°N
60°N
50°N

Africa: Political

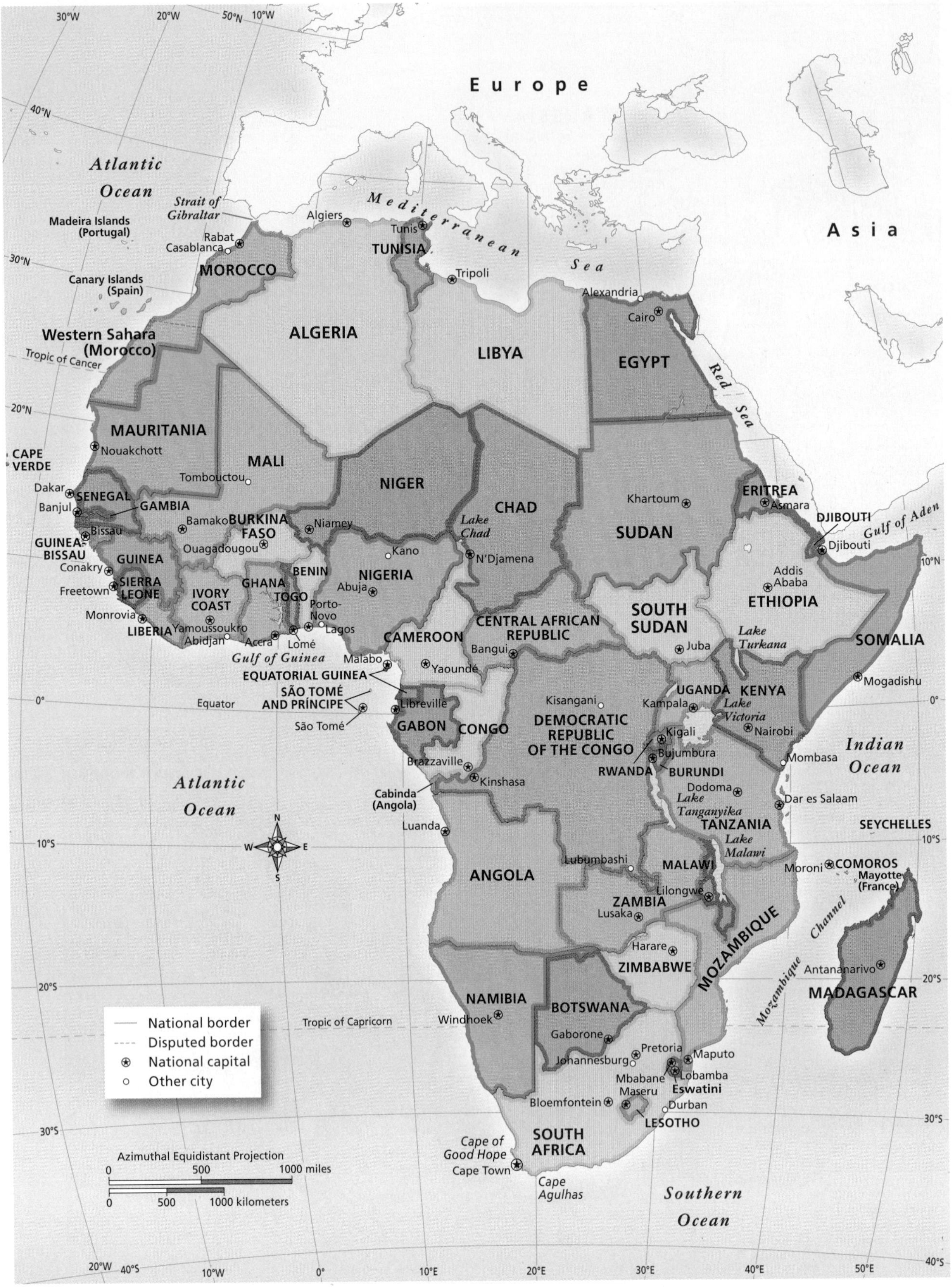

Africa: Physical

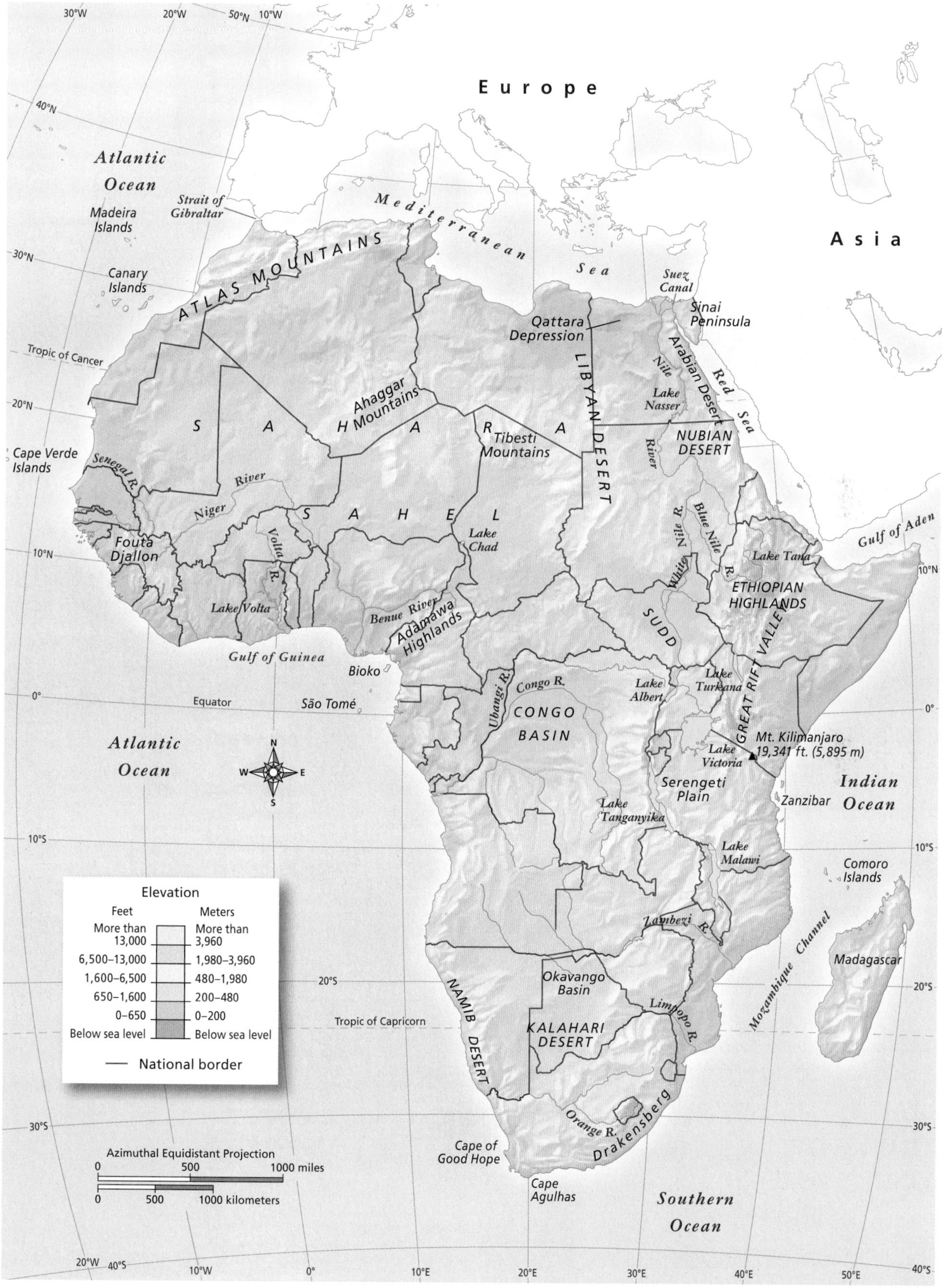

Asia: Political

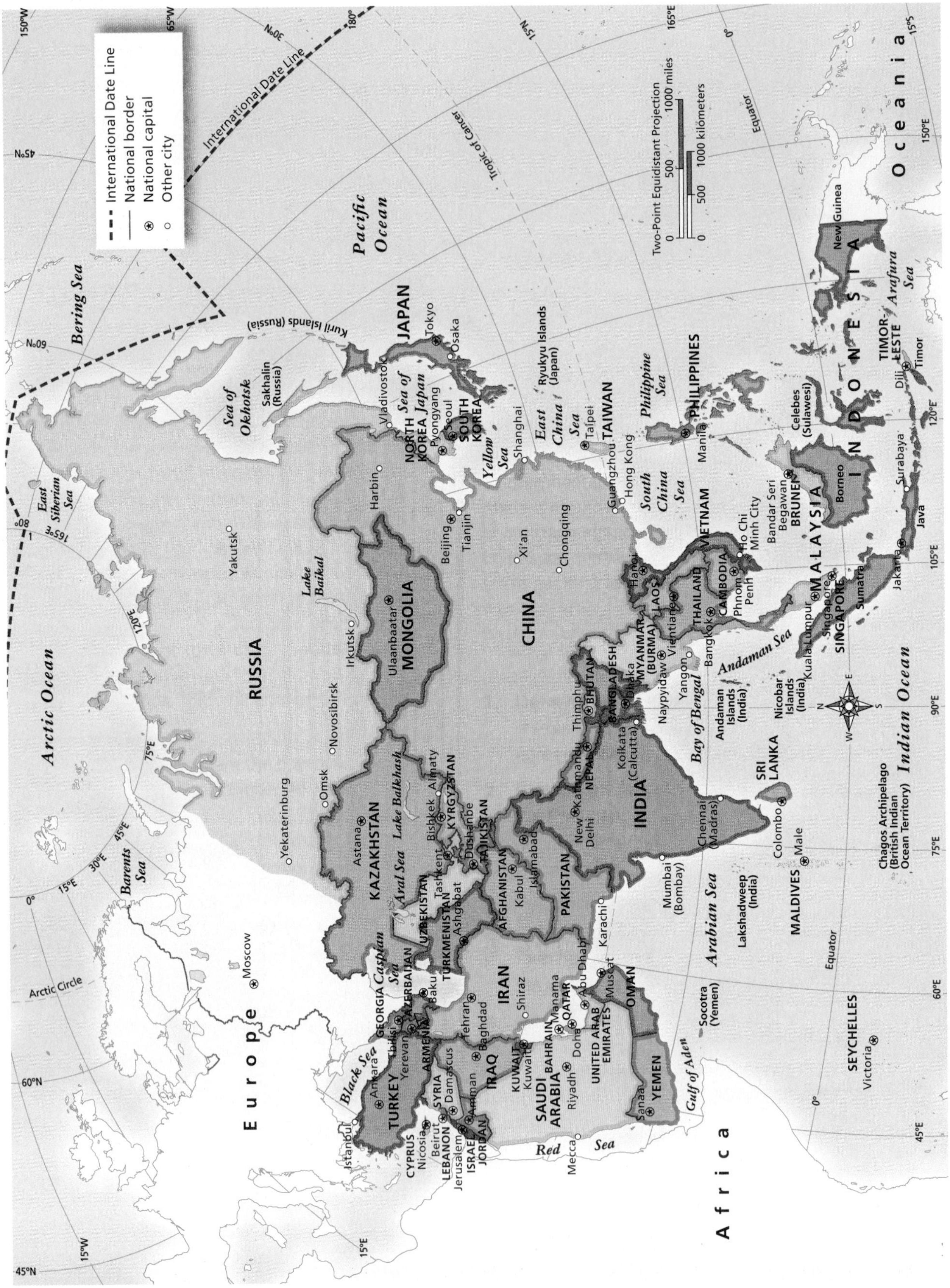

Asia: Physical

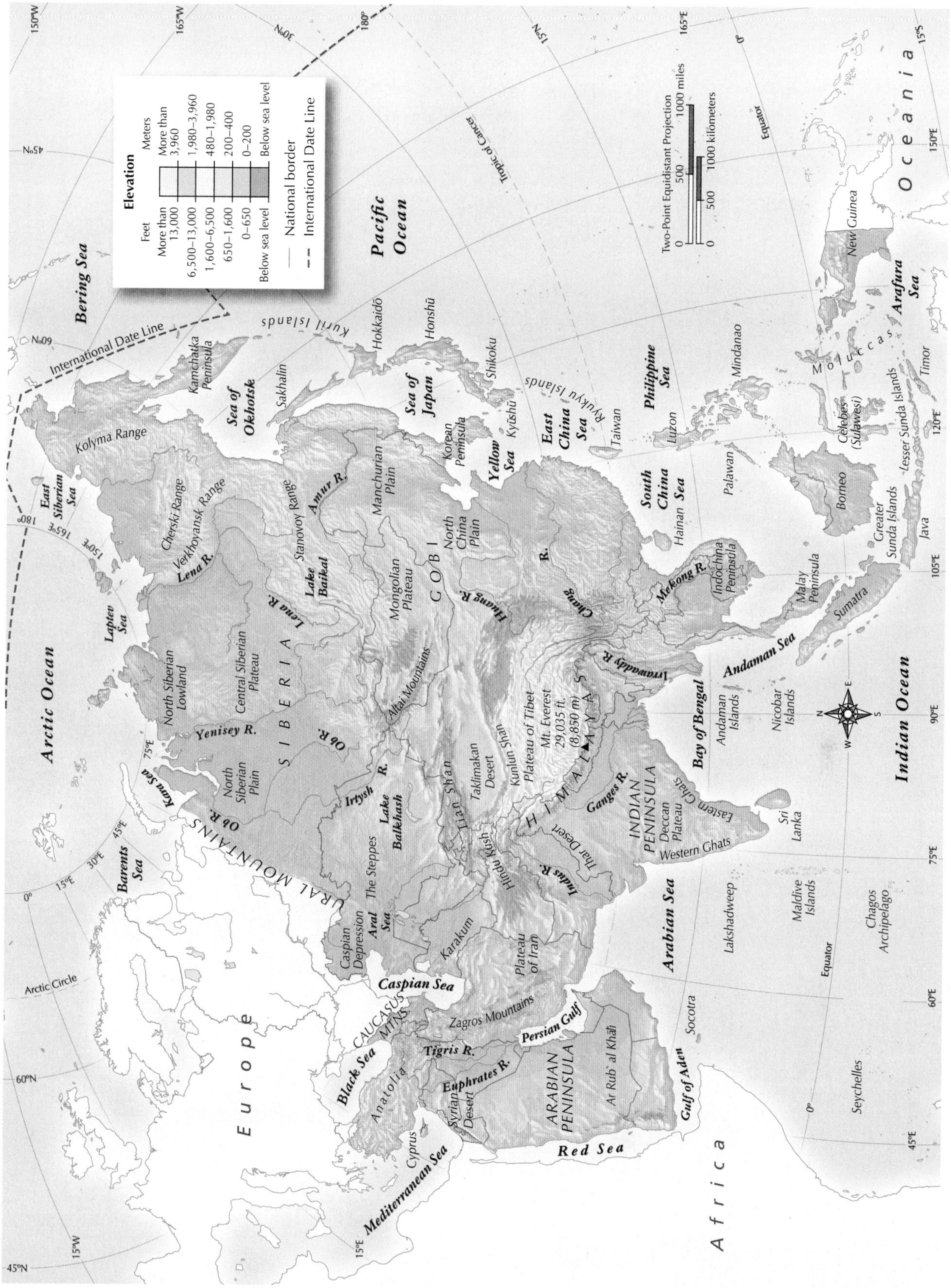

Europe: Political

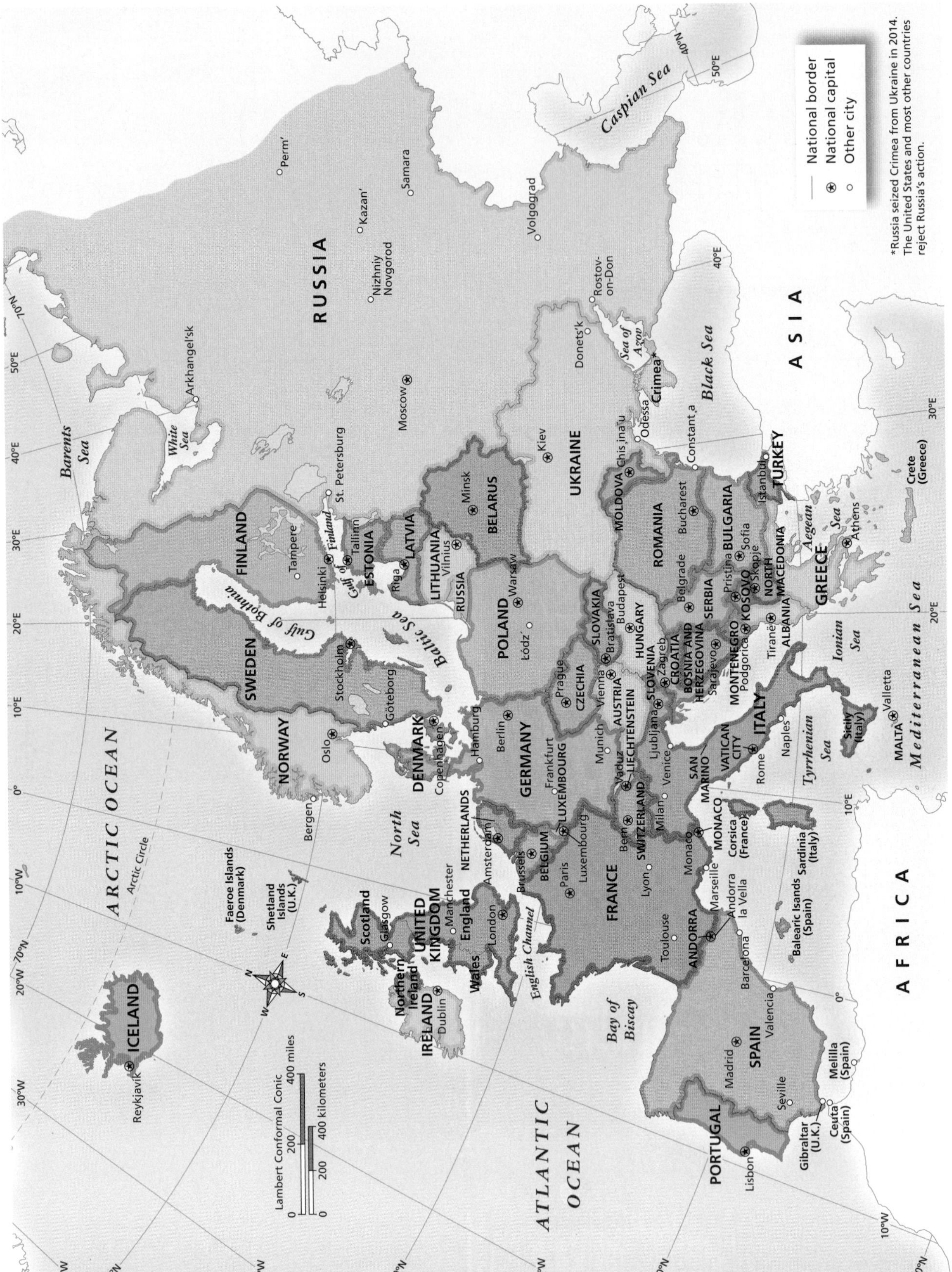

Europe: Physical

North and South America: Political

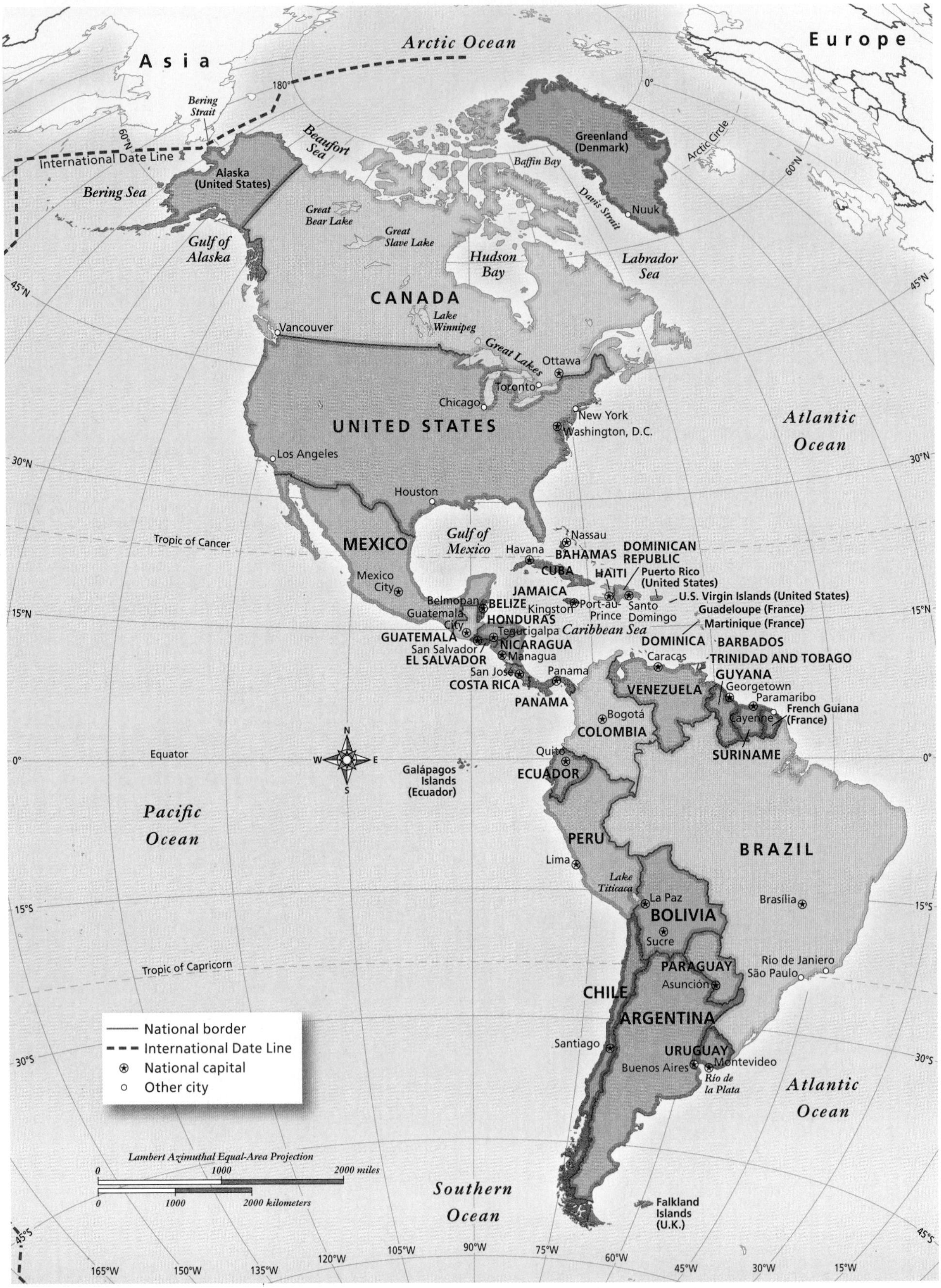

North and South America: Physical

Australia, New Zealand, and Oceania: Political-Physical

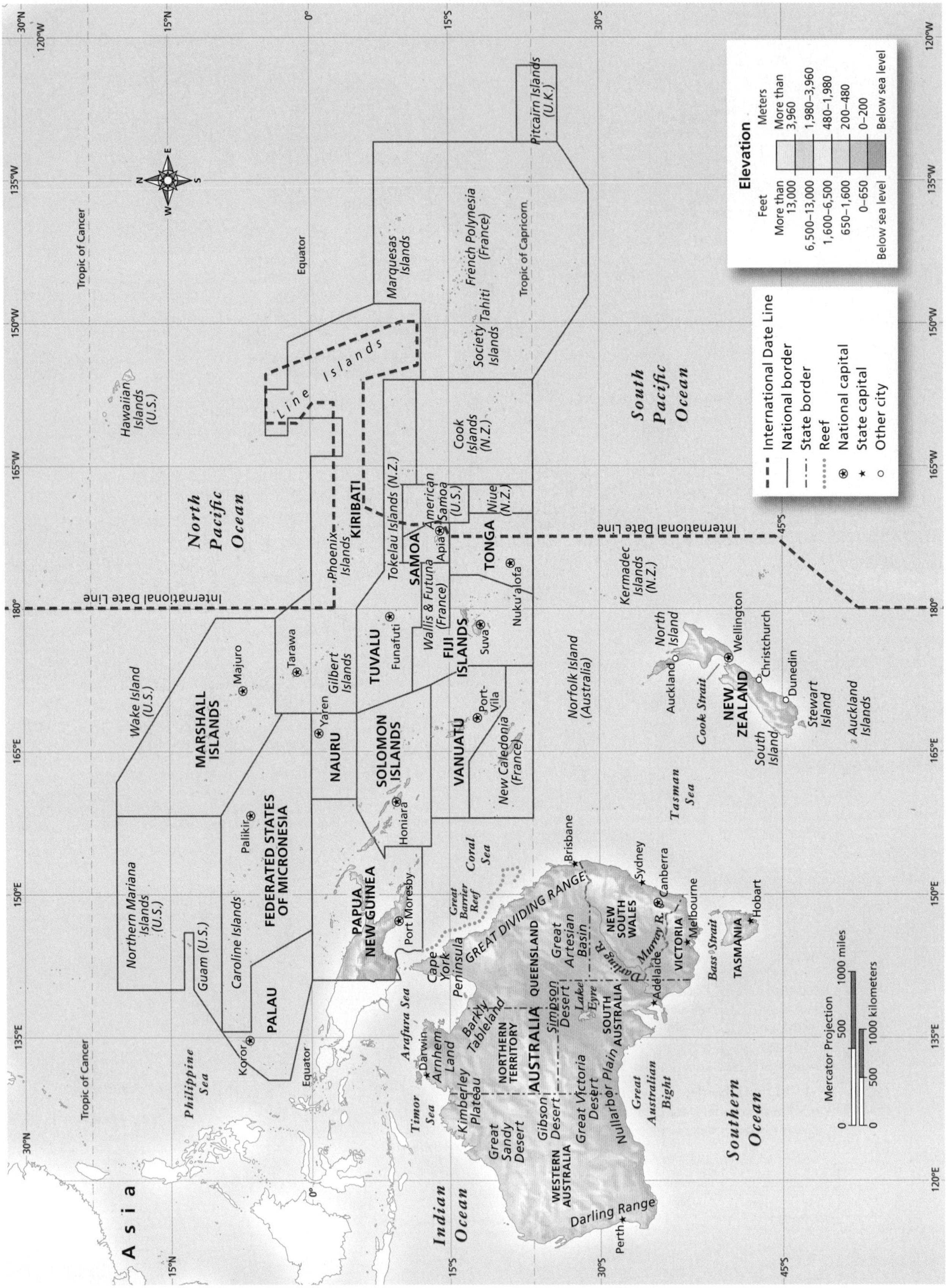

The Arctic: Physical

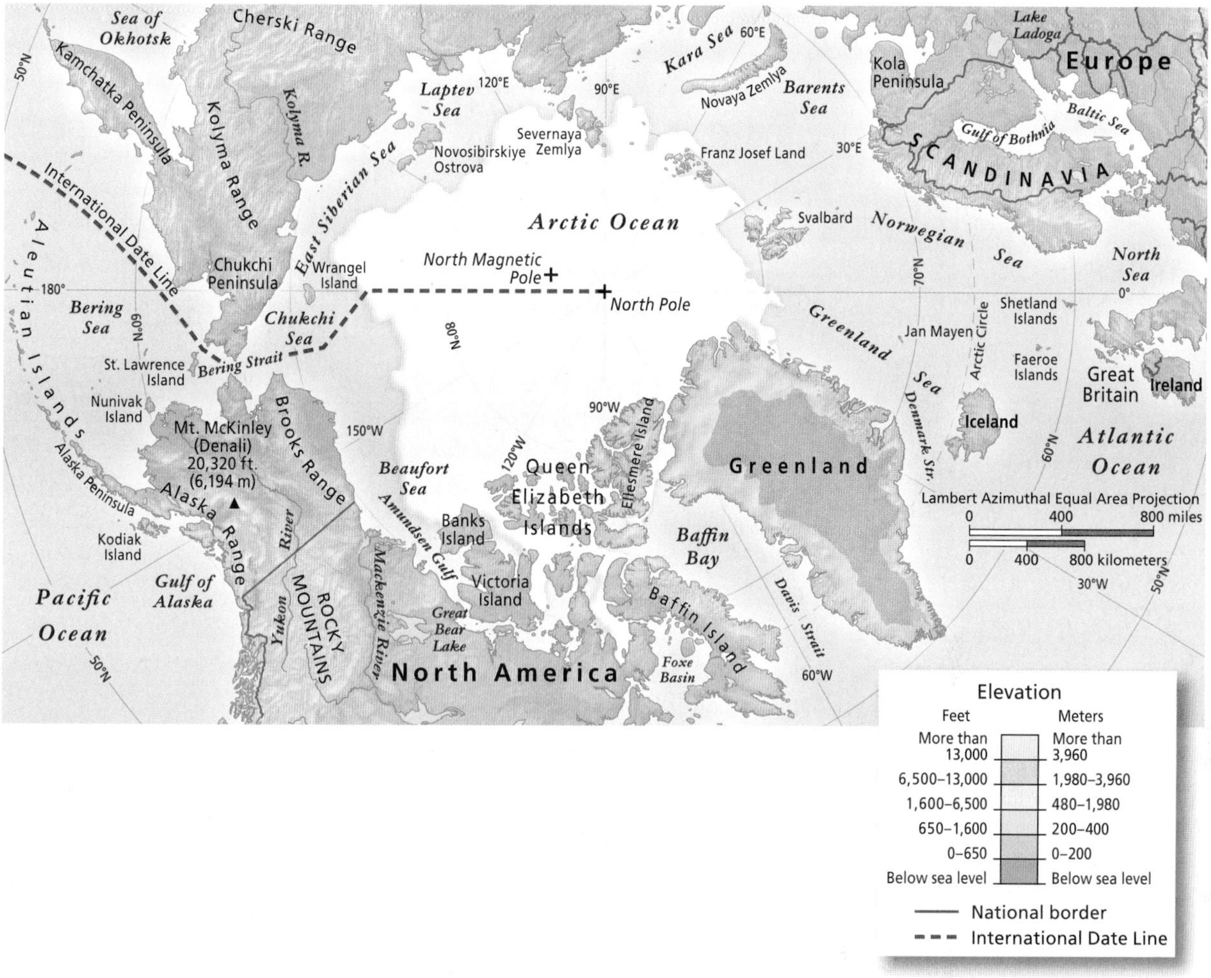

Antarctica: Physical

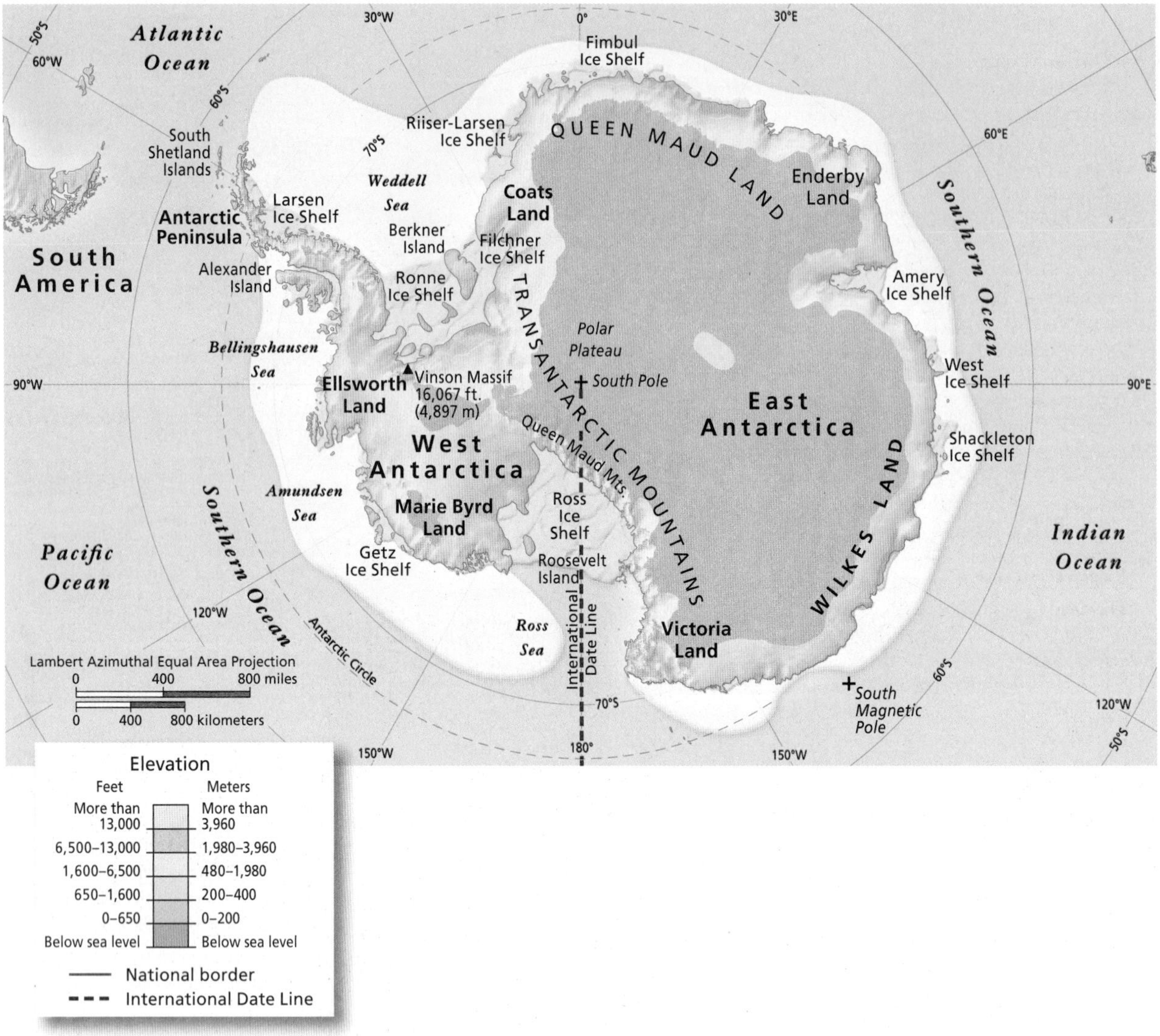

A

abolition movement a nineteenth-century movement that sought an end to slavery

Acquired Immunodeficiency Syndrome (AIDS) disease that attacks the immune system and has no known cure; it began spreading in the early 1980s and remains a serious global health crisis today

Adams-Onís Treaty an 1819 treaty in which Spain ceded Florida to the United States

Adams, John John Adams (1735–1826) was an American colonial lawyer and writer who became one of the foremost thinkers and activists among American patriots. He spoke out against British tax laws and served as a delegate from Massachusetts to the First Continental Congress. He went on to become the first Vice President and the second President of the United States.

Adams, John Quincy John Quincy Adams (1767–1848) was the sixth President of the United States. Prior to his presidency, Adams helped negotiate the Treaty of Ghent in 1814, which ended the War of 1812. As President Monroe's Secretary of State, Adams was the chief architect of the Monroe Doctrine. Adams returned to Congress after his presidency, where he fought for the abolition of slavery and the improvement of the arts and sciences.

Addams, Jane Jane Addams (1860–1935) cofounded Hull House, a settlement house in Chicago, in 1889. She lived and worked out of Hull House for the rest of her life. A pacifist and determined advocate for women's suffrage, Addams wrote many books and lectured widely. In 1931, she shared the Nobel Peace Prize.

administration staff of the executive branch

adobe sun-dried brick made from earth, water, and straw

affirmative action policy that gives special consideration to women and minorities to make up for past discrimination

AFL-CIO in 1955, the American Federation of Labor (AFL) and the Congress of Industrial Organization (CIO) labor unions united

aggression hostile actions or unprovoked attacks

Aguinaldo, Emilio Emilio Aguinaldo (1869–1964) was the leader of the Filipino forces that fought for independence against Spain in the 1890s. Disillusioned with the U.S. presence in the Philippines following the war, Aguinaldo helped organize an insurrection against U.S. rule. He was captured by U.S. forces in 1901, effectively ending the Filipino's fight for independence.

al Qaeda terrorist group established by Osama bin Laden to rid Muslim countries of Western influence

Alamo the fortified former mission in San Antonio that was the site of the 1836 defeat and slaughter of Texans by Mexican troops

Albany Plan of Union Benjamin Franklin's 1754 proposal to form one government for a group of Britain's colonies in North America

Alger, Horatio Horatio Alger (1832–1899) was an American author who sold more than 20 million copies of novels that explored the rags-to-riches theme. Alger created characters who rose to fame and wealth through hard work and determination.

Alien and Sedition Acts 1798 laws that allowed the government to imprison or deport non-citizen immigrants, known as aliens, and to prosecute those who criticized the government

Alliance for Progress President Kennedy's program that gave economic aid to Latin America

Allies group of countries led by Britain, France, the United States, and the Soviet Union that fought the Axis Powers in World War II

Alsace-Lorraine territory lost to Germany by France in 1871

American Expeditionary Forces (AEF) American forces in Europe during World War I

American Federation of Labor (AFL) labor union that organized skilled workers in a specific trade and made specific demands rather than seeking broad changes

American Indian Citizenship Act of 1924 granted citizenship to all Native Americans born within the territorial limits of the United States

American Indian Movement (AIM) group that focused on helping Indians, including the securing of legal rights, land, and self-government for Native Americans

American System Henry Clay's federal program designed to stimulate the economy with internal improvements and to create a self-sufficient nation

Americanization belief that assimilating immigrants into American society would make them more loyal citizens

amnesty general pardon for certain crimes

Anaconda Plan a northern Civil War strategy to starve the South by blockading seaports and controlling the Mississippi River

Angel Island immigrant processing station that opened in San Francisco Bay in 1910

Anschluss union of Germany and Austria in 1933

Anthony, Susan B. Susan B. Anthony (1820–1906) was a campaigner for reforms and civil rights throughout her life. At different times she took up the cause of abolition, temperance, and working women's rights. But it is for the cause of woman suffrage that Anthony is best known. In 1869, she and her friend, Elizabeth Cady Stanton, formed the National Woman Suffrage Association (NWSA), which led to over 30 years of relentless lecture tours, lobbying, and civil disobedience geared toward gaining the vote for women.

Anti-Defamation League organization formed in 1913 to defend Jews against physical and verbal attacks and false statements

anti-Semitic displaying prejudice and discrimination against Jewish people

anti-Semitism hatred of and discrimination against Jews

Antifederalists one who opposed ratification of the Constitution

apartheid political system of strict segregation by race in South Africa

appeasement policy of granting concessions in order to keep peace

Armstrong, Louis Louis Armstrong (1901–1971) was a jazz trumpeter and one of the most influential artists in the jazz history. He was also a bandleader, singer and comedian during his career.

Articles of Confederation the original federal constitution drafted by the Continental Congress in 1777

assembly lines arrangement of equipment and workers in which work passes from operation to operation in direct line until the product is assembled

assimilated absorbed into the main culture of a society

Atlantic Charter pact signed by Great Britain and the United States that endorsed certain principles for building a lasting peace and establishing free governments in the world

Austin, Stephen F. Stephen F. Austin (1793–1836) inherited his father's land grant from the Mexican government and eventually helped found key American settlements in Texas when that territory was still part of Mexico. Austin was an influential figure as Mexico and the United States fought for control of Texas. He also worked to protect the interests of American slaveholders in Texas.

autonomy the independent control over one's own affairs

Axis Powers group of countries led by Germany, Italy, and Japan that fought the Allies in World War II

Aztecs American Indian people dominant in Mexico before the Spanish conquest of the 16th century

B

baby boom increase in births between 1945 and 1964

Bacon's Rebellion an armed rebellion in 1676 by Virginia colonists led by Nathaniel Bacon against the rule of Governor William Berkeley

Baltimore, Lord Lord Baltimore (c.1580–1632) was the title bestowed upon English Roman Catholic politician George Calvert. After failing to establish colonies in present-day Newfoundland, Calvert successfully obtained a grant of land for the colony that later became Maryland. Lord Baltimore died in 1632, just before the Maryland charter passed. His sons, however, contributed to the founding of the Maryland colony.

Barbary War a war between the Barbary States and the United States

Barton, Clara Clara Barton (1821–1912) trained as a teacher but went on to serve as a nurse during the Civil War. Barton changed the role of women nurses by following men into battle and tending the wounded. In 1864, she was appointed the superintendent of nurses for the Army of the James. In 1865, she set up a bureau to help locate soldiers missing in action. In 1881, she organized the American Association of the Red Cross, which later became the American Red Cross.

Baruch, Bernard Bernard Baruch (1870–1965) was chairman of the War Industries Board during World War I. Baruch was a financier turned statesman who advised seven American presidents.

Bataan Death March during World War II, the forced march of American and Filipino prisoners of war under brutal conditions led by the Japanese military

Battle of Antietam a 1862 Civil War battle in which 23,000 troops were killed or wounded in one day, won by the Union

Battle of Coral Sea World War II battle that took place between Japanese and American aircraft carriers in May 1942, halting the Japanese advance in the Pacific

Battle of Fallen Timbers a 1794 battle in which federal troops defeated the Miami Confederacy of American Indians

Battle of Midway turning point of World War II in the Pacific, in which the Japanese advance was stopped

Battle of New Orleans War of 1812 battle when the United States defeated the British in January of 1815

Battle of Princeton 1777 Revolutionary War battle in New Jersey, won by the Continental Army

Battle of the Bulge last major German offensive on the Western Front during World War II; it was an unsuccessful attempt to push back the Allies that crippled Germany by forcing it to use more resources than it could afford

Battle of the Little Big Horn 1876 battle in which the Sioux defeated U.S. Army troops

Battle of Tippecanoe an 1811 battle in the Indiana Territory between American Indians and United States troops in which the American Indians were defeated

Battle of Trenton 1776 Revolutionary War battle in New Jersey, won by the Continental Army

Bay of Pigs invasion failed 1961 invasion of Cuba by a CIA-led force of Cuban exiles

Beatles The Beatles were an English rock-and-roll group featuring John Lennon, Paul McCartney, George Harrison, and Ringo Starr. From 1962 to 1970, the Beatles' songwriting and musical experimentation greatly expanded the scope of rock music.

beatniks small group of writers and artists, in the 1950s and early 1960s, who were critical of American society

Benavidez, Roy P. Roy P. Benavidez (1935–1998) was born in Cuero, Texas, but grew up in El Campo, where he was raised by his aunt and uncle after his parents died. He joined the army at the age of 19 and eventually went to Vietnam in 1965. For his bravery while wounded during a rescue mission in Cambodia in 1968, Benavidez was awarded the Medal of Honor (in 1981).

Berlin airlift program in which U.S. and British pilots flew supplies to West Berlin during a Soviet blockade

Berlin Wall dividing wall built by East Germany in 1961 to isolate West Berlin from communist-controlled East Berlin

Bessemer process method developed in the mid-nineteenth century for making steel more efficiently

Bethune, Mary McLeod Mary McLeod Bethune (1875–1955) was an American educator who served as a special adviser on minority affairs to President Franklin D. Roosevelt, as well as being active in several other reform organizations.

bicameral legislature a lawmaking body made up of two houses

Biden, Joseph R. Joe Biden (1942–) became the 46th president of the United States in 2021. At age 77, he was the oldest president to be elected to the office. Before becoming president, he served as vice president during the Barack Obama administration from 2009 to 2017. He was also a United States Senator for Delaware for 36 years.

"big stick" diplomacy Theodore Roosevelt's policy of creating and using, when necessary, a strong military to achieve America's goals

bilingual education system in which students are taught in their native languages as well as in English

Bill of Rights the first ten amendments to the Constitution, protecting freedoms guaranteed to citizens by the government

biotechnology application of technology to solving problems affecting living organisms

Black Cabinet group of African-American leaders who served as unofficial advisers to Franklin D. Roosevelt

Black Codes laws that restricted African Americans' rights and opportunities

Black Panthers organization of militant African Americans founded in 1966

Black Power movement in the 1960s that urged African Americans to use their collective political and economic power to gain equality

Black Tuesday October 29, 1929, when stock prices fell sharply in the Great Crash

blacklist list of persons who were not hired because of suspected communist ties

Bleeding Kansas a term used to describe the violence between proslavery and antislavery supporters in Kansas from 1854 to 1856

blitzkrieg "lightning war" that emphasized the use of speed and firepower to penetrate deep into the enemy's territory

blockade a military tactic in which a navy prevents vessels from entering or leaving its enemy's ports

Bloomer, Amelia Amelia Bloomer (1818–1894) was an American reformer who became influential in the temperance and women's rights movements. She founded *The Lily: A Ladies Journal Devoted to Temperance and Literature* in 1849, which she used to promote her positions on women's rights and temperance reforms. Bloomer is also known for promoting the right of women to wear pants instead of dresses. The pantaloons that she wore in public became known as "bloomers."

boat people refugees who fled nations of Southeast Asia by boat beginning in the 1970s

bond a certificate bought from the government that promises to pay the holder back the purchase amount plus interest at a future date

Bonus Army group of World War I veterans who marched on Washington, D.C., in 1932 to demand early payment of a bonus promised them by Congress

Booth, John Wilkes John Wilkes Booth (1838–1865) was an American actor and Confederate sympathizer who shot and killed President Abraham Lincoln on April 14, 1865. Eleven days after he assassinated Lincoln, Booth was killed at a farm in Virginia.

Bootlegger one who sells illegal alcohol

border state during the Civil War, a state that allowed slavery but remained in the Union: Delaware, Kentucky, Maryland, and Missouri

Boston Massacre incident on March 5, 1770, in which British soldiers killed five colonists in Boston

Boston Tea Party protest against British taxes in which Bostonian protestors dumped tea into the harbor on December 16, 1773

Boxer Rebellion violence started by members of a secret society in China, which prompted the governments of Europe and America to send troops to squash the rebellion

Bracero Program plan that brought laborers from Mexico to work on American farms

Braddock, General Edward General Edward Braddock (1695–1755) served as a British commander in North America during the French and Indian War. In 1754, he came to Virginia to lead the British forces on the continent. During an attempted assault on Fort Duquesne, Braddock's forces were defeated, and the general was killed.

Bradley, Omar Omar Bradley (1893–1981) was a U.S. Army officer who in World War II commanded Allied troops in North Africa, leading them to victory in the campaign. He then led his forces in the invasion of Sicily and helped plan the invasion of Normandy. From the Normandy invasion to the end of the war, Bradley commanded the massive U.S. ground forces attacking Germany from the west, over 1 million troops in all. After World War II, he served as chief of staff of the Army and as the first chairman of the U.S. Joint Chiefs of Staff.

Brady Bill law passed in 1993 requiring a waiting period on sales of handguns, along with a criminal background check on the buyer

Brady, Mathew Mathew Brady (c.1823–1896) was an American photographer and journalist best known for his photographic documentation of the Civil War.

bread line line of people waiting for food handouts from charities or public agencies

Breckinridge, John C. John C. Breckinridge (1821–1875) was a Kentucky lawyer who served as the 14th vice president of the United States under President James Buchanan. In the election of 1860, he was the nominee of the Southern Democrats in a divided Democratic Party. Breckinridge served as a Confederate officer during the Civil War, and later, as the Confederate secretary of war.

brinkmanship belief that only by going to the brink of war could the United States protect itself against Soviet aggression

Brown, John John Brown (1800–1859) was an American abolitionist best known for leading a raid on the federal arsenal at Harpers Ferry in 1859. During that raid, he and his co-conspirators were captured and later executed. Brown is remembered by some as a militant extremist and by others as a martyr in the cause against slavery.

Bryan, William Jennings William Jennings Bryan (1860–1925) was a Democratic and Populist leader who ran unsuccessfully three times for the U.S. presidency. During his career as a lawyer, politician, and speaker, he fought for reforms such as the income tax, Prohibition, and women's suffrage.

budget deficit shortfall between the amount of money spent and the amount of money taken in by the federal government

bull market period of rising stock prices

bureaucracy a group of departments and officials that make up an organization, such as a government

Burr, Aaron Aaron Burr (1756–1836) was the third Vice President of the United States. Angered by comments made by Alexander Hamilton, Burr challenged Hamilton to a duel in 1804, during which Hamilton was killed.

Bush, George W. George W. Bush (1946–) was a businessman and governor of Texas from 1995 to 2000 before being elected the 43rd president of the United States. Bush, a son of President George H.W. Bush, led the United States during the September 11 terrorist attacks in 2001 and the initial years of the wars in Afghanistan and Iraq. Bush was elected to a second term in 2004, finishing his presidency as the world's financial industry was on the verge of collapse in late 2008.

business cycle periodic growth and contraction of the economy

buying on margin system of buying stocks in which a buyer pays a small percentage of the purchase price while the broker advances the rest

C

Cabinet heads of the executive departments who meet as a group in order to advise the President

Cabot, John John Cabot (1450?–1499?) was an Italian explorer who was hired by Henry VII of England to explore the unknown lands of the Americas. In 1497, Cabot sailed west, crossing the North Atlantic, landing in Newfoundland, in present-day Canada. Cabot's voyages contributed to the eventual establishment of British colonies in North America.

Cabral, Pedro Alvarez Pedro Alvarez Cabral (1467?–1520) was a Portuguese navigator who is generally credited as the first European to land in present-day Brazil in 1500.

Calhoun, John C. John C. Calhoun (1782–1850) was a major American politician who served as U.S. Vice President, secretary of war, secretary of state, and in both houses of Congress. He was noted as a champion of states' rights and of slavery. His support for and work in establishing the second Bank of the United States, a permanent road system, and a standing army and modern navy made him one of the most influential supporters of American nationalism.
California Gold Rush the mass migration to California after the discovery of gold in 1848
California Master Plan a plan that called for three tiers of higher education: research universities, state colleges, and community colleges, all of which were to be accessible to all of the state's citizens
Camp David Accords 1978 agreement brokered by President Jimmy Carter between Egyptian and Israeli leaders that made a peace treaty between the two nations possible
capital money or wealth used to invest in business or enterprise
Capra, Frank Frank Capra (1897–1991) was an American motion picture director best known for his work during the 1930s and 1940s, for which he won three Academy Awards.
Carnegie, Andrew Andrew Carnegie (1835–1919) was an American industrialist and philanthropist who began Carnegie Steel, a corporation that dominated the American steel industry. He created charitable trust foundations and provided money for cultural and educational institutions.
carpetbagger a negative term for Northerners who moved to the South after the Civil War
Carson, Rachel Rachel Carson (1907–1964) was an American biologist most famous for writing *Silent Spring* and a number of other works on environmental pollution and the history of the oceans. Carson worked as a scientist and writer for the U.S. government before turning to writing full time.
cartel association of producers of a good or service that prices and controls stocks in order to monopolize the market
Carter, Jimmy Jimmy Carter (1924–) was the governor of Georgia from 1970 to 1974. In 1976, he defeated Gerald R. Ford to become President. After losing the presidency to Ronald Reagan in 1980, Carter devoted himself to national and international social concerns, advancing democracy, and human rights.
cash crop a crop grown for sale
Castro, Fidel Fidel Castro (1926–2016) helped to overthrow the Cuban government in 1959, and led the country from then until 2008. His communist government and ties to the Soviet Union were a source of conflict between Cuba and the United States.
casualty a soldier killed, wounded, or missing
Catt, Carrie Chapman Carrie Chapman Catt (1859–1947) was an educator before becoming involved in the women's suffrage movement in 1887. In 1890, she joined the National American Woman Suffrage Association (NAWSA). She became its president in 1900, and headed the organization almost without interruption until her death.
caucus a closed meeting of party members for the purpose of choosing a candidate
Central Intelligence Agency (CIA) U.S. intelligence-gathering organization
Chamberlain, Neville Neville Chamberlain (1869–1940) was prime minister of Great Britain from 1937–1940. To avoid war, he signed the Munich Pact with Germany, giving Hitler part of Czechoslovakia. The agreement became an infamous symbol for the failure of appeasement.
Champlain, Samuel de Samuel de Champlain (1567–1635) was a French explorer and the founder of the city of Quebec. He discovered the lake that bears his name. Champlain also explored down the Atlantic coast southward to Massachusetts Bay and beyond.
Chaplin, Charlie Charlie Chaplin (1889–1977) was a British comedian who produced, wrote, and directed many films throughout his career. Many consider him the greatest comic artist in motion picture history.
charter a legal document giving certain rights to a person or company
Chávez, César César Chávez (1927–1993) spent his childhood toiling, like his parents, as a migrant farmworker. As an adult, he established the National Farm Workers Association (NFWA) in 1962. Chávez led several high-profile non-violent protests that generally ended with better conditions for workers.
checks and balances a system in which each branch of the government has the power to monitor and limit the actions of the other two
Chicano movement movement to promote Mexican American social and political issues and culture
Chinese Exclusion Act 1882 law that prohibited the immigration of Chinese laborers
cholera a severe bacterial infection of the small intestine that causes dehydration, usually caused by drinking contaminated water
Christian fundamentalist a Christian who believes in a strict, literal interpretation of the Bible as the foundation of the Christian faith
Churchill, Winston Winston Churchill (1874–1965) was Prime Minister of Great Britain from 1940 to 1945, Churchill inspired the British during World War II. After the war, he was not re-elected. However, he resumed office again between 1951 to 1955. He strongly opposed the expansion of Soviet communism, referring to nations under communism as being behind the "Iron Curtain."
Civil Rights Act of 1866 a law that established federal guarantees of civil rights for all citizens
Civil Rights Act of 1875 a law that banned discrimination in public facilities and transportation
Civil Rights Act of 1957 law that established a federal Civil Rights Commission to investigate violations of civil rights
Civil Rights Act of 1964 outlawed discrimination in public places and employment based on race, religion, or national origin
civil service government departments and their non-elected employees
Civilian Conservation Corps (CCC) New Deal program that provided young men with relief jobs on environmental conservation projects, including reforestation and flood control
Clay, Henry Henry Clay (1777–1852) was an American politician who was elected to the U.S. House of Representatives and the U.S. Senate from the state of Kentucky. Clay was a leading proponent of economic nationalism, promoting federal support of internal improvements, a protective tariff, and a national bank. In 1820, Clay helped craft the Missouri Compromise to try to balance the rights of free and slave states.
Clayton Antitrust Act 1914 law that strengthened the Sherman Antitrust Act

Clean Air Act act passed in 1970 that sought to lessen air pollution by limiting the emissions from factories and automobiles

Clean Water Act 1973 law designed to restrict the pollution of water by industry and agriculture

Clinton, Hillary Hillary Clinton (1947–) was a successful and influential lawyer and advocate for children and families before becoming First Lady of the United States in 1992. She took an active role in Bill Clinton's administration, heading up the Task Force on National Health Care. In 2000, won a U.S. Senate seat for the State of New York. She sought, but failed to win, the Democratic presidential nomination in 2008, but was appointed Secretary of State by President Obama later that year. She resigned from that post in 2013.

Clinton, William Jefferson Bill Clinton (1946–) became the 42nd president of the United States in 1993 at the age of 46, the first "boomer" President. He was reelected to a second term in 1996. Two years later he was impeached by the House of Representatives but was acquitted by the Senate in 1999. Clinton presided over the longest period of peace-time economic expansion in American history, which included a balanced budget and a federal surplus.

Cold War worldwide rivalry between the United States and the Soviet Union

collective bargaining process in which employers negotiate with labor unions about hours, wages, and other working conditions

Columbian Exchange the global exchange of goods and ideas between Europe, Africa, and the Americas after Columbus made his first transatlantic voyage in 1492

Columbus, Christopher Christopher Columbus (1451–1506) was born in the seaport city of Genoa, Italy. Columbus began his seafaring life at age 14. He went to Portugal for navigator's training and settled there with his brother John. Columbus gained the support of Ferdinand II and Isabella I, the monarchs of Spain, and eventually made four voyages across the Atlantic Ocean to the Americas. Columbus's expeditions led Europeans to become aware of the existence of the American continents and launched the Spanish colonization of the Americas.

Committee on Public Information (CPI) federal government agency created during World War I to encourage Americans to support the war

committees of correspondence network of local groups that informed colonists of British measures and the opposition to them in the years before the Revolutionary War

communes small communities where people with common interests live and share resources

Community Reinvestment Act 1977 law that requires banks, and especially those that operate in low- to middle-income minority neighborhoods, to loan a portion of their deposits to the residents of those neighborhoods

company towns communities in which residents rely upon one company for jobs, housing, and buying goods

Compromise of 1850 a political agreement that admitted California to the Union as a free state while permitting popular sovereignty in the territories and enacting a stricter fugitive slave law

Compromise of 1877 an agreement by which Rutherford B. Hayes won the 1876 presidential election and in exchange agreed to remove all remaining federal troops from the South

concentration camps camps used by the Nazis to imprison "undesirable" members of society

Confederate States of America the government of 11 southern states that seceded from the United States and fought against the Union in the Civil War

Congress of Industrial Organizations (CIO) labor organization founded in the 1930s that was composed of industrial unions which represented all workers in an industry regardless of their job or skill

conquistadors Spanish conquerors

conscientious objector person whose moral or religious beliefs forbid him or her to fight in wars

conscription the drafting of citizens into military service

conservative person who tends to support limited government involvement in the economy, community help for the needy, and traditional values

conspicuous consumerism purchasing of goods and services with the purpose of impressing others

consumer revolution flood of new, affordable goods in the decades after World War I

consumerism large-scale buying, much of it on credit

containment policy of keeping communism contained within its existing borders

Continental Army army that represented the colonies during Revolutionary War

contraband supplies captured from an enemy during wartime

Contract With America Republican plan headed by Newt Gingrich that focused on scaling back the government, balancing the budget, and cutting taxes

Contras anticommunist counterrevolutionaries who opposed the Sandinista government in Nicaragua in the 1980s

convoy group of merchant ships sailing together, protected by warships

Coolidge, Calvin Calvin Coolidge (1872–1933) was President of the United States from 1923 to 1929. He acceded to office after the death of Warren Harding and continued many of the pro-business policies of his predecessor.

Copperhead a negative, or derogatory, term given to antiwar northern Democrats during the Civil War

Cornwallis, Charles General Charles Cornwallis (1738–1805) fought in the Seven Years' War in Europe before being sent to combat the Continental Army during the Revolutionary War. He won key victories in New Jersey and South Carolina, but he was trapped with his forces at Yorktown in 1781, where he surrendered to General Washington.

corporation company recognized as a legal unit that has rights and liabilities separate from each of its members

Cortés, Hernán Hernán Cortés (1485–1547) commanded the force of Spanish conquistadors that overthrew the Aztec empire and brought Mexico under the control of Spain. Trained as a lawyer, Cortés left Spain in 1504 to settle in Cuba, where he became rich by acquiring plantations and gold mines. Military skills, crafty diplomacy, and ruthlessness enabled Cortés to topple the Aztec government in its capital of Tenochtitlán despite being heavily outnumbered.

cotton gin a machine invented in 1793 to separate the cotton fiber from its hard shell

Coughlin, Charles Charles Coughlin (1891–1979) served as pastor of a Catholic Church in Michigan from 1926 to 1966. He won a huge audience in the 1930s for his radio broadcasts, first supporting President Roosevelt's New Deal and later opposing it as he adopted ultraconservative views. Coughlin vocally opposed U.S. entrance into World War II and after he began making anti-Semitic remarks, Catholic officials ordered him to stop broadcasting in 1942.

counterculture movement that upheld values different from those of mainstream culture
coureurs de bois from the French for "runner of the woods," French colonists who live in the woods as fur traders
court packing President Franklin D. Roosevelt's plan to add six new justices to the nine-member Supreme Court after the Court had ruled some New Deal laws to be unconstitutional
credibility gap American public's growing distrust of statements made by the government during the Vietnam War
creditor nation country which is owed more money by other countries than it owes other countries
Creel, George George Creel (1876–1953) was a journalist who served as chairman of the Committee on Public Information during World War I. He went on to hold other positions in the federal government. Creel was also an author. One of his books was *How We Advertised America*.
Crittenden Compromise an 1861 proposed constitutional amendment that attempted to prevent secession of the southern states by allowing slavery in all territories south of the Missouri Compromise line
Cuban missile crisis 1962 conflict between the United States and the Soviet Union resulting from the Soviet installation of nuclear missiles in Cuba

D

Da Gama, Vasco Vasco da Gama (1460?–1524) was a Portuguese navigator whose three voyages to India around the Cape of Good Hope opened up the sea route from western Europe to the East. He died in India upon arriving following his third voyage.
dame school an elementary school during colonial times, often operated out of a woman's home
Darrow, Clarence Clarence Darrow (1857–1938) was a lawyer whose work as defense council in many trials secured his place in legal history. He is best known for his defense of John Scopes in 1925.
Davis, Jefferson Jefferson Davis (1808–1889) was a southern planter who became the President of the Confederate States of America. Born in Kentucky, he grew up on a plantation in Mississippi. He attended the U.S. Military Academy at West Point and went on to serve in the Black Hawk War and the Mexican War. Though he opposed secession, he resigned his seat in the U.S. Senate when Mississippi seceded. He was elected President of the Confederacy at the Confederate Convention and was inaugurated on February 18, 1861.
Dawes General Allotment Act 1887 law that divided reservation land into private family plots
Dawes Plan agreement in which the United States loaned money to Germany, allowing Germany to make reparation payments to Britain and France
de facto segregation segregation by unwritten custom or tradition
de jure segregation segregation imposed by law
death camps Nazi camp designed for the extermination of prisoners
Debs, Eugene V. Eugene V. Debs (1855–1926) was a labor organizer and social leader who advocated for the rights of railway workers. He ran for president five times between 1900 and 1920 as a candidate for the Socialist Party.
Declaration of Independence document drawn up by the Second Continental Congress, and approved in 1776, that announced American independence and explained the reasons for it
Deferred Action for Childhood Arrivals (DACA) executive order by President Obama that allowed some undocumented immigrants who had entered the country before their 16th birthday and before June 2007 to be exempted from deportation and to obtain renewable two-year work permits
deficit spending practice of a nation paying out more money than it is receiving in revenues
demobilization sending home members of the army
Democratic Republicans led by Jefferson and Madison, one of the first political parties in the United States and also known as the Republicans
Demographics statistics that show human characteristics of a population
Department of Homeland Security department created by President Bush to coordinate domestic security efforts
deregulation reduction or removal of government controls over an industry, based on the belief that more freedom leads to greater success and profitability
détente flexible diplomacy adopted by President Richard Nixon to ease tensions between the United States, the Soviet Union, and the People's Republic of China
developing world countries that are less economically advanced than developed countries such as the United States and those of Western Europe
Dewey, George George Dewey (1837–1917) was an American naval officer who commanded the U.S. fleet that defeated the Spanish at the Battle of Manila Bay during the Spanish-American War. In 1899, Congress promoted Dewey to the rank of admiral of the navy, the highest rank ever held by a U.S. naval officer.
Dias, Bartolomeu Bartolomeu Dias (1450?–1500) was a Portuguese explorer who commanded the first European expedition to sail around the Cape of Good Hope at the southern tip of Africa in 1488. Dias accomplished this feat by learning how to use the counterclockwise winds and currents of the South Atlantic to get around southern Africa. Dias' success opened the sea route to Asia via the Atlantic and Indian oceans. Dias died in 1500 after his ship was lost at sea near the Cape of Good Hope.
Dickinson, John John Dickinson (1732–1808) worked as an attorney in Philadelphia before becoming involved in politics and devoting himself to the Patriot cause. In 1765, he served as Pennsylvania's representative to the Stamp Act Congress and wrote its declaration of rights and grievances. Later, he served as a delegate to the Continental Congress. In 1776–1777, he helped draft the Articles of Confederation. In 1787, he served as a delegate from Delaware to the Constitutional Convention to revise the Articles.
direct primary election in which citizens themselves vote to select nominees for upcoming elections
divest to take away or rid oneself of
Dix, Dorothea Dorothea Dix (1802–1887) was an American reformer who campaigned for 40 years to win better, more humane treatment for people with mental illness. She helped to establish state mental hospitals in 15 states and Canada, and even spread her ideas in Europe. She also worked to improve prisons, favoring the Pennsylvania System of penitentiaries.

Dole, Sanford B. Sanford B. Dole (1844–1926) played an important role in the overthrow of the Hawaiian monarchy. After the overthrow, Dole was elected president of the Provisional Government. He petitioned the American government to annex the Hawaiian Islands. In 1898, Hawaii became a United States territory with Dole as its first governor.

dollar diplomacy President Taft's policy of expanding American investments abroad

domino theory idea that if a nation falls to communism, its closest neighbors will also fall under communist control

Douglas, Stephen A. Stephen A. Douglas (1813–1861) was a U.S. Senator. Douglas was an ardent supporter of westward expansion and an advocate for popular sovereignty on the question of slavery in new states and territories. He helped win passage of the Compromise of 1850 and proposed the Kansas-Nebraska Act in 1854. Douglas gained national acclaim for his role in the Senate campaign debates with Abraham Lincoln in 1858.

Douglass, Frederick Frederick Douglass (1818?–1895) was born into slavery in Maryland and escaped to the North in 1838. In 1841, he spontaneously shared his experiences of enslavement at an antislavery convention, and he soon became a speaker for the abolitionist cause. His autobiography, *Narrative of the Life of Frederick Douglass,* first published in 1845, reached still more people. During the Civil War, Douglass worked as an adviser to President Lincoln. Douglass also lent strong support to the women's movement.

dove person who opposed U.S. involvement in the Vietnam War

Dow, Neal Neal Dow (1804–1897) became a politician and influential advocate of the temperance movement. As mayor of Portland, Mann worked to secure passage of the Maine Law, which restricted the sale of alcohol.

draftee a young American man drafted into military service

Du Bois, W.E.B. W.E.B. Du Bois (1868–1963) was an American educator, reformer, and champion of civil rights. He is best known for his book *The Souls of Black Folk* in which he criticizes the more accommodating approach of Booker T. Washington and advocates for full civil rights for African Americans. Du Bois went on to help found the National Association for the Advancement of Colored People (NAACP).

Dulles, John Foster John Foster Dulles (1888–1959) was a diplomat and political thinker. A strong anti-communist, he helped organize the United Nations after World War II and later served as Secretary of State under President Dwight Eisenhower. In this role, he helped formulate the Cold War policies of brinkmanship and "massive retaliation".

Dust Bowl term used for the central and southern Great Plains during the 1930s, when the region suffered from drought and dust storms

E

Earth Day annual event of environmental activism and protest, begun in 1970

Economic Opportunity Act law passed in 1964 creating antipoverty programs

Edison, Thomas Thomas Edison (1847–1931) was an American inventor. He held over 1,000 patents for inventions, including the light bulb, an early movie camera, and an alkaline battery.

Eighteenth Amendment constitutional amendment banning the manufacture, distribution, and sale of alcohol in the United States

Einstein, Albert German-born physicist Albert Einstein (1879–1955) developed the general theory of relativity, which describes the effects of gravity on the universe, and won the Nobel Prize for Physics in 1921. Einstein left Germany in the early 1930s after Nazi attacks on his work and settled in the United States, where he continued to pioneer new developments in the theory of general relativity. He is generally considered to be the most influential physicist of the 20th century.

Eisenhower Doctrine policy of President Eisenhower that stated that the United States would use force to help any nation threatened by communism

Eisenhower, Dwight Dwight D. Eisenhower (1890–1969) was given command of all American forces in Europe in 1942. After strong performances in North Africa and Italy, he was made Supreme Commander of Allied Forces. His skillful handling of the D-Day invasion and the drive to Germany won wide respect. Eisenhower went on to serve two terms as President before retiring.

electoral college a group of persons chosen from each state to indirectly elect the president and the vice president

Ellis Island island in New York Harbor that served as an immigration station for millions of immigrants arriving to the United States

Emancipation Proclamation a decree by President Lincoln that declared free all enslaved people living in Confederate states and territories still in rebellion against the Union on January 1, 1863

embargo an official ban or restriction on trade

Emerson, Ralph Waldo Ralph Waldo Emerson (1803–1882) is considered the founder of Transcendentalism. Emerson came from a long line of ministers and became a Unitarian minister himself in 1829. His essay "Nature" was a statement of the movement's beliefs. He came to believe that people could get closer to God by transcending the material world and appreciating the beauties of nature rather than through following organized religion.

Endangered Species Act law passed in 1973 with the goal of protecting endangered plants and animals

Enforcement Acts 1870 and 1871 laws, also known as the Ku Klux Klan Acts, that made it a federal offense to interfere with a citizen's right to vote

English Bill of Rights a document signed in 1689 that guaranteed the rights of English citizens

Enlightenment an eighteenth-century movement inspired by European philosophers who believed that society's problems could be solved by reason and science

entrepreneur a person who builds and manages a business or enterprise in order to make a profit, often risking his or her own money or livelihoods

Environmental Protection Agency (EPA) government agency committed to cleaning up and protecting the environment

Equal Pay Act 1963 law requiring men and women to receive equal pay for equal work

Equal Rights Amendment (ERA) proposed amendment to the Constitution to guarantee gender equality

Erie Canal a canal completed in 1825 that connected Lake Erie to the Hudson River

Espionage Act act passed by Congress in 1917 enacting severe penalties for anyone engaged in disloyal or treasonable activities

ethnic cleansing systematic effort to purge a society of an ethnic group through murder or deportation

eugenics the idea that the human race can be improved by controlling which people have children

European Union (EU) economic and political union of European nations established in 1993

evangelical a style of worship meant to elicit powerful emotions to gain converts

Evers, Medgar Medgar Evers (1925–1963) became the NAACP's first field secretary in Mississippi in 1954. He traveled the state recruiting members and organized voter-registration drives, demonstrations, and boycotts of companies that practiced discrimination. In 1963, he was assassinated outside of his home in Jackson, Mississippi.

Executive Order 8802 World War II measure that assured fair hiring practices in any job funded by the government

executive privilege principle that the President has the right to keep private certain communications between himself and other members of the executive branch

Exodusters African Americans who migrated from the South to the West after the Civil War

expansionist a person who favors expanding the territory or influence of a country

extractive economies economy in a colony where the colonizing country removed raw materials and shipped them back home to benefit its own economy

F

Fair Deal President Truman's program to expand New Deal reforms

Fair Labor Standards Act 1938 law that set a minimum wage, a maximum work week of 44 hours, and outlawed child labor

Family Medical Leave Act law guaranteeing most full-time employees 12 workweeks of unpaid leave each year for personal or family health reasons

Farmers' Alliance network of farmers' organizations that worked for political and economic reforms in the late 1800s

fascism a political movement that stressed extreme nationalism and autocratic rule

Faubus, Orval Orval Faubus (1910–1994) was the governor of Arkansas from 1954 to 1967. He is best known for ordering the Arkansas National Guard to block nine African American students from entering Little Rock Central High School in 1957, in defiance of a federal court order that mandated the end of racial segregation in schools. His efforts failed when President Eisenhower sent federal troops to usher the students into the school.

federal national

Federal Art Project division of the Works Progress Administration that hired unemployed artists to create artworks for public buildings and sponsored art-education programs and exhibitions

Federal Deposit Insurance Corporation (FDIC) government agency created during the New Deal that insures bank deposits, guaranteeing that depositors' money will be safe

Federal Reserve Act 1913 law that placed national banks under the control of a Federal Reserve Board, which operates regional banks that hold the reserve funds from commercial banks, sets interest rates, and supervises commercial banks

Federal Trade Commission (FTC). government agency established in 1914 to identify monopolistic business practices, false advertising, and dishonest labeling

federalism a political system in which power is shared between the national government and state governments

Federalist one who favored ratification of the Constitution

Federalist, The a series of 85 essays, written by James Madison, Alexander Hamilton, and John Jay, that explained and defended the Constitution

feminism theory that women and men should have political, social, and economic equality

Ferdinand, Franz Franz Ferdinand (1863–1914) was an archduke and heir to the throne of Austria-Hungary. His assassination in Sarajevo was an immediate cause of World War I.

fiat money currency not backed by gold or silver

Fifteenth Amendment an 1870 constitutional amendment that guaranteed voting rights regardless of race or previous condition of servitude

54th Massachusetts Regiment an all African American unit led by Union Colonel Robert Gould Shaw during the Civil War

filibuster tactic by which senators give long speeches to hold up legislative business

Finney, Charles Grandison Charles Grandison Finney (1792–1875) was an American lawyer, president of Oberlin College, and a central figure in the religious revival movement of the early 1800s. He held highly successful revivals in large cities such as New York and eventually moved to became a professor of theology in a newly formed theological school in Oberlin, Ohio.

fireside chats informal radio broadcasts in which President Franklin D. Roosevelt explained his view of issues at hand (including the Great Depression, New Deal programs, and World War II) to average Americans

First Continental Congress group of delegates representing all the American colonies, except Georgia, that met in 1774

Fitzgerald, F. Scott F. Scott Fitzgerald (1896–1940) was an American writer known for his depictions of American life in the 1920s, especially *The Great Gatsby*, published in 1925.

flapper young woman from the 1920s who defied traditional rules of conduct and dress

flexible response defense policy allowing for the appropriate action in any type of conflict

Foraker Act law establishing a civil government in Puerto Rico

Ford, Gerald Gerald Ford (1913–2006) was elected to Congress in 1949 and was named Vice President after Spiro T. Agnew resigned in 1973. Ford became President the next year when Nixon resigned. After losing the 1976 election to Jimmy Carter, Ford retired from politics.

Ford, Henry Henry Ford (1863–1947) was the founder of the Ford Motor Company. Ford revolutionized the automobile industry with his assembly line and treatment of workers. Ford's Model T ushered in the age of the automobile in the United States.

Fort Sumter a federal fort located in Charleston, South Carolina, where the first shots of the Civil War were fired

forty-niner a miner who went to California after the discovery of gold in 1848

442nd Regimental Combat Team World War II unit made up of Japanese American volunteers

Fourteen Points list of terms for resolving World War I and future wars outlined by American President Woodrow Wilson

Fourteenth Amendment an 1868 constitutional amendment that defined citizenship and guaranteed citizens equal protections under the law

franchise business to allow a company to distribute its products or services through retail outlets owned by independent operators

Franco, General Francisco General Francisco Franco (1892–1975) led a successful military revolt against the Spanish democratic government in the Spanish Civil War (1936–1939). He continued to rule Spain as a dictator until his death in 1975.

Franklin, Benjamin Benjamin Franklin (1706–1790) was an influential American statesman, inventor, and scientist. Trained as a printer, Franklin settled in Philadelphia, where he printed and published newspapers, his own writings, and the popular *Poor Richard's Almanac*. Franklin's contribution to the founding of the United States was significant. He was the only individual to sign all three principal documents of the new nation: the Declaration of Independence, the treaty with Great Britain that ended the American Revolution, and the U.S. Constitution. His scientific achievements include the formulation of a theory of electricity.

free enterprise freedom of private business to organize and operate for profit in a competitive system without interference by government beyond regulation necessary to protect public interest and keep the national economy in balance

Free-Soil Party an antislavery political party in the mid-1800s

freedman a person who has been freed from slavery

Freedmen's Bureau a federal agency designed to aid freed African Americans and poor white farmers in the South after the Civil War

freedom ride 1961 protest by activists who rode buses through southern states to test their compliance with laws banning segregation on interstate buses

Freedom Summer 1964 effort to register African American voters in Mississippi

French and Indian War war fought from 1754 to 1763 in which Britain and its colonies defeated France and its American Indian allies, gaining control of eastern North America

French Revolution an uprising against the French monarchy that began in 1789

Freud, Sigmund Sigmund Freud (1856–1939) developed psychological theories of the human psyche and therapies known as psychoanalysis.

Friedan, Betty Betty Friedan (1921–2006) was an American feminist who wrote the influential book *The Feminine Mystique* in 1963 and co-founded the National Organization for Women (NOW) in 1966.

Fugitive Slave Act a law that required all citizens to aid in apprehending people trying to escape slavery; a part of the Compromise of 1850

fundamentalism movement or attitude stressing strict and literal adherence to a set of basic religious principles

G

Gadsden Purchase the 1853 purchase of land (present-day Arizona and New Mexico) from Mexico

Gag Rule a rule lasting from 1836 to 1844 that banned debate about slavery in Congress

García, Héctor P. Héctor P. García (1914–1996) was an army doctor who served with distinction in World War II, earning the Bronze Star for his service in North Africa and Italy. He was born in Mexico but grew up in Mercedes, Texas. After leaving the army as a major in 1945, García returned to Texas to practice medicine, but he also began his lifelong work as a community leader, civil rights advocate, and political activist. In 1948, he helped to found the American G.I. Forum, an organization that supports Hispanic veterans and their families.

Garrison, William Lloyd William Lloyd Garrison (1805–1879) was an American journalist who significantly influenced the abolition movement. Garrison gave his first speech against slavery in 1829 and by 1831 he began publishing *The Liberator*, a strong antislavery newspaper. In addition, Garrison helped found the Anti-Slavery Society and was its president for 23 years.

Garvey, Marcus Marcus Garvey (1887–1940) was a charismatic leader who organized a Black nationalist movement in Harlem during the 1920s. Garvey promoted economic and cultural independence for African Americans.

General Agreement on Tariffs and Trade (GATT) international agreement first signed in 1947 aimed at lowering trade barriers

generation gap lack of understanding and communication between older and younger members of society

Geneva Convention international agreement governing the humane treatment of wounded soldiers and prisoners of war

genocide willful annihilation of a racial, political, or cultural group

"Gentlemen's Agreement" pact between the United States and Japan to end segregation of Asian children in San Francisco public schools; in return, Japan agreed to limit the emigration of its citizens to the United States

Gettysburg the site of a Civil War battle fought on Union territory, July 1–3, 1863 resulting in a Union victory that forced Confederate forces to retreat to the South

Gettysburg Address a speech by President Lincoln in which he dedicated a national cemetery at Gettysburg, Pennsylvania, and reaffirmed the ideas for which the Union was fighting the Civil War; delivered November 19, 1863

Ghana prominent kingdom in West Africa, known for its wealth and trade in gold, lasting from A.D. 800 to A.D. 1200

GI Bill of Rights legislation that eased the return of World War II veterans by providing education and employment aid

Gilded Age term coined by Mark Twain to describe the post-Reconstruction era as a facade of prosperity

Gingrich, Newt Newt Gingrich (1943–) is an American politician, author, and television commentator best known for serving as speaker of the U.S. House of Representatives from 1995 to 1998. Gingrich led the Republican takeover of the House in the 1994 midterm elections by helping to write the influential Contract With America platform.

glasnost Russian term for "new openness," a policy in the Soviet Union in the 1980s calling for open discussion of national problems

globalization process by which national economies, politics, cultures, and societies mix with those of other nations around the world

gold standard policy of designating monetary units in terms of their value in gold

Goldwater, Barry Barry Goldwater (1909–1998) served nearly 25 years in the U.S. Senate. In 1964, he ran for president and was soundly defeated by Lyndon Johnson. In 1974, Goldwater was instrumental in persuading President Nixon to resign in the aftermath of the Watergate scandal.

Gompers, Samuel Samuel Gompers (1850–1924) was an American labor leader and the first president of the American Federation of Labor. He advocated organized strikes and boycotts to achieve the organization's goals.

Gorbachev, Mikhail Mikhail Gorbachev (1931–) is a Soviet politician who served as the leader of the Soviet Union from 1985 to 1991. Gorbachev is best known for supporting the policies of *glasnost* and *perestroika,* which led to the collapse of the Soviet Union. Gorbachev's role in the rise of democratic government in Eastern Europe earned him the Nobel Peace Prize in 1990.

Graham, Billy Billy Graham (1918–2018) was an American evangelist who rose to prominence during the religious revival of the 1950s in the United States.

grandfather clause a law to disqualify African American voters by allowing the vote only to men whose fathers and grandfathers had voted before 1866 or 1867

Grange farmers' organization formed after the Civil War

Grant, Ulysses S. Ulysses S. Grant (1822–1885) was a Union general who later became the 18th president of the United States from 1869–1877. Grant won key victories along the Mississippi River, including at the Battle of Shiloh and the Battle of Vicksburg. He was appointed commander of all Union armies in March 1864, and led them to victory at Appomattox Court House, where he accepted General Lee's surrender on April 9, 1865.

Great Awakening a religious movement in the English colonies during the 1730s and 1740s that was heavily inspired by evangelical preachers

Great Compromise a compromise between the Virginia and New Jersey plans for a bicameral legislature; each state would have equal representation in the Senate and varied representation, based on the state's population, in the House of Representatives

Great Depression period lasting from 1929 to 1941 in which the U.S. economy faltered and unemployment soared

Great Migration movement of African Americans in the twentieth century from the South to the North

Great Society President Lyndon Johnson's goals in the areas of health care, education, the environment, discrimination, and poverty

Great White Fleet battleships sent by President Theodore Roosevelt in 1907 on a "good will cruise" around the world

gross national product the total value of the goods and services produced by a country

guerrilla warfare nontraditional combat methods

Gulf of Tonkin Resolution 1964 congressional resolution that authorized President Johnson to commit U.S. troops to South Vietnam to fight a war against North Vietnam

H

habeas corpus a constitutional guarantee that no one can be held in prison without charges being filed

Hamilton, Alexander Alexander Hamilton (1755/57–1804) was born in the British West Indies and went to New York to pursue his studies. There, he became involved in the Patriot cause and wrote three pamphlets supporting the Continental Congress's position on British trade policies. Hamilton fought during the American Revolution and served with George Washington. After the war, he studied law and went on to serve as a Pennsylvania delegate to the Constitutional Convention. Later, he became the first Secretary of the Treasury of the United States.

Harding, Warren G. Warren G Harding (1865–1923) served as president of the United States from 1921 to 1923. He promoted a "return to normalcy" following U.S. involvement in World War I. Harding died during his first term in office in 1923.

Harlem Renaissance period during the 1920s in which African American novelists, poets, and artists celebrated their culture

Harpers Ferry a town in Virginia (now in West Virginia) where abolitionist John Brown raided a federal arsenal in 1859

Hartford Convention an 1814 meeting of Federalists from New England who opposed the War of 1812 and demanded constitutional amendments to empower the region

hawk person who supported U.S. involvement in the Vietnam War

Hawley-Smoot Tariff protective tax on imports enacted by Congress in 1930 in an effort to counter the nation's slide into the Great Depression

Hay, John John Hay (1838–1905) served as U.S. secretary of state from 1895 to 1905, guiding U.S. diplomacy as the country emerged as a world power. He was instrumental in crafting the Open Door policy toward China.

Hayes, Rutherford B. Rutherford B. Hayes (1822–1893) was the nineteenth president of the United States. His election in 1876 was disputed, and his victory was secured by a Congressional commission and the Compromise of 1877. Hayes oversaw the withdrawal of the remaining federal troops from the South, signaling the end of Reconstruction.

Haymarket Riot 1886 labor-related protest in Chicago which ended in deadly violence

Hearst, William Randolph William Randolph Hearst (1863–1951) was an American newspaper publisher who created the nation's largest newspaper chain. Hearst, along with Joseph Pulitzer, helped popularize investigative reporting and sensationalist journalism.

Hellman, Lillian Lillian Hellman (1905–1984) was an American playwright and screenwriter known for her dramas that focused on social injustice and exploitation.

Helsinki Accords agreement made in 1975 among the nations of Europe, the Soviet Union, the United States, and Canada to respect and support human rights

Hemingway, Ernest Ernest Hemingway (1899–1961) was an American writer who won the Nobel Prize for Literature in 1954. He is known for his adventurous life and novels such as *The Sun Also Rises* and For *Whom the Bell Tolls.*

Henry the Navigator, Prince Prince Henry the Navigator (1394–1460) was the third son of King John I of Portugal and Philippa of Lancaster, an English noblewoman. Prince Henry established a school for Portuguese mariners where they learned about navigation, map making, and ship design. The nickname "The Navigator" was given to him by English writers incorrectly, since Henry never took part in any exploratory voyages.

Henry, Patrick Patrick Henry (1736–1799) was an American patriot, lawyer, and author. He is best known for a speech he gave before the Virginia Convention in 1775, during which he stated, "Give me liberty or give me death!" Henry served in the Virginia committee of correspondence and served as a Virginia delegate to the First Continental Congress. He fought during the Revolutionary War and went on to serve Virginia as state governor and state legislator.

Hepburn Act 1906 law that gave the Interstate Commerce Commission the authority to set maximum shipping rates for railroads and for ferries, toll bridges, and oil pipelines

Hiss, Alger Alger Hiss (1904–1996) was a former high-ranking State Department official investigated by HUAC as a communist spy and later convicted of perjury, but not espionage. Documents released in the 1990s supported the accusations against him.

Hitler, Adolf Adolf Hitler (1889–1945) was the leader of the National Socialist (Nazi) party and dictator of Germany from 1933–1945. He rose to power by promoting racist and nationalist views. In 1939, he invaded Poland, which began World War II. He established a system of concentration camps, leading to the Holocaust, a systematic and brutal murder of millions of Jews and others.

Ho Chi Minh Ho Chi Minh (1890–1969) was one of the most influential anticolonial leaders in Asia. Ho led North Vietnam's fight to reunify North and South Vietnam, serving as president of the Democratic Republic of Vietnam (North Vietnam) from 1945 to 1969.

Hollywood Ten group of movie writers, directors, and producers who refused to answer HUAC questions about communist ties

Holocaust the Nazi attempt to kill all Jews under their control

Homestead Act a 1862 law that gave 160 acres of land to citizens willing to live on and cultivate it for five years

Homestead Strike 1892 strike against Carnegie's steelworks in Homestead, Pennsylvania

Hoover Dam dam on the Colorado River that was built during the Great Depression

Hoover, Herbert Herbert Hoover (1874–1964) served as secretary of Commerce and later as the President of the United States from 1929 to 1933, during the Great Depression. His administration's response to the Great Depression was widely criticized for its ineffectiveness.

Hooverville term used to describe makeshift shantytowns set up by homeless people during the Great Depression

horizontal integration system of consolidating many firms in the same business

hot line direct telephone line between the White House and the Kremlin set up after the Cuban Missile Crisis

House of Burgesses colonial Virginia's representative assembly formed in 1619

House Un-American Activities Committee (HUAC) congressional committee that investigated possible subversive activities within the United States

Houston, Sam Sam Houston (1793–1863) was the only American to serve as governor of two different states—first Tennessee, then Texas. In between, he was commander of the Texan army, president of the Republic of Texas, and U.S. senator from Texas. Although an enslaver, Houston opposed the spread of slavery into the West. He was removed from the governorship of Texas after speaking out against Texas seceding from the Union.

Howe, William General William Howe (1729–1814) served as commander-in-chief of the British army from 1776 to 1778, during the Revolutionary War. Although he led British troops to victory in engagements including Bunker Hill, Brandywine, and Germantown, he resigned his command after failing to defeat General Washington's forces at Valley Forge.

Huerta, Dolores Dolores Huerta (1930–) grew up in Stockton, California, eventually becoming an elementary school teacher. After seeing the poverty of her students, many of whom were children of farm workers, she got involved in advocacy work for the workers and their families. In 1962 with César Chávez, Huerta cofounded the farm workers union that would become the United Farm Workers (UFW). While Chávez was the face of the organization, it was Huerta who used her organizational and negotiating skills to help the UFW succeed on behalf of its members.

Hughes, Langston Langston Hughes (1902–1967) was an influential poet and writer who thought of his work as a means to communicate the Black experience in the United States.

human rights basic rights held by every human being, including religious freedom, education, and equality

Hurston, Zora Neale Zora Neale Hurston (1891–1960) was a writer associated with the Harlem Renaissance who was trained as an anthropologist and went on to teach for a number of years. One of her more influential works was *Their Eyes Were Watching God,* published in 1935.

Hutchinson, Anne Anne Hutchinson (1591–1643) was an American religious leader. She arrived in Massachusetts in 1634, where she held meetings in her home to boldly promote her idea that God's grace alone was the key to salvation. But the colony's leaders opposed preaching by a woman and considered many of her beliefs to be dangerous. In 1637, she was banished and later moved to Rhode Island and still later to Long Island Sound in present-day New York. In 1643, she and most of her family were killed by American Indians.

hydraulic mining the use of water to erode gravel hills into long sluices to catch any gold

I

ice age period in Earth's history with low global temperatures and glaciers covering large areas

Immigration Act of 1990 law that increased the number of immigrants allowed in the U.S. per year

Immigration and Nationality Act of 1965 law that changed the national quota system to limits of 170,000 immigrants per year from the Eastern Hemisphere and 120,000 per year from the Western Hemisphere

Immigration Reform and Control Act of 1986 legislation that granted resident status to illegal immigrants residing in the United States since 1982 and penalized employers who hired illegal immigrants

impeach to accuse a public official of wrongdoing in office

impeachment accusation against a public official of wrongdoing in office

imperialism political, military, and economic domination of strong nations over weaker territories

impressment a policy of seizing people or property for military or public service

income tax a tax that must be paid by individuals and corporations based on money earned

indentured servant an individual who agrees to work without wages for a period of time in exchange for transportation to the colonies

Indian New Deal 1930s legislation that gave Indians greater control over their affairs and provided funding for schools and hospitals

Indian Removal Act an act passed by Congress in 1830 that allowed the federal government to negotiate land exchanges with the American Indians in the Southeast

Industrial Revolution a shift from manual labor to mechanized work that began in Great Britain during the 1700s and spread to the United States around 1800
inflation rising prices
influenza flu virus
information industry business that provide informational services
initiative process in which citizens put a proposed new law directly on the ballot
installment buying method of purchase in which buyer makes a small down payment and then pays off the rest of the debt in regular monthly payments
insurrection rebellion
integration the process of bringing together people of different races, religions, and social classes
interchangeable parts identical components that can be used in place of one another
Internet computer network that links people around the world, also called World Wide Web
internment temporary imprisonment of members of a specific group
Interstate Commerce Commission (ICC) first federal agency monitoring business operations, created in 1887 to oversee interstate railroad procedures
Interstate Highway Act the 1956 law that authorized the spending of $32 billion to build 41,000 miles of highway
Intolerable Acts American name for the Coercive Acts, which Parliament passed in 1774 to control the colonies
Iran-Contra affair political scandal under President Reagan involving the use of money from secret arms sales to Iran to illegally support the Contras of Nicaragua
iron curtain term coined by Winston Churchill to describe the border between the Soviet satellite states and Western Europe
Iroquois Also known as the Haudenosaunee, the Iroquois were a group of American Indian peoples who lived in upstate New York and neighboring lands. They included the Cayuga, Cherokee, Huron, Mohawk, Oneida, Onondaga, Seneca, and Tuscacora, who shared a language family and certain ways of life.
Iroquois League confederation made up of five Iroquois peoples: the Mohawks, Oneidas, Onondagas, Cayugas, and Senecas
irreconcilables isolationist senators who oppose any treaty ending World War I that had a League of Nations folded into it
island-hopping World War II strategy that involved seizing selected Japanese-held islands in the Pacific while bypassing others

J

Jackson, Andrew Andrew Jackson (1767–1845) was an American military officer before serving in the U.S. House of Representatives and Senate, and finally as the seventh U.S. President from 1829 to 1837. As a general in the U.S. Army during the War of 1812, Jackson successfully defended New Orleans. As President, he vetoed the renewal of the charter of the Bank of the United States, opposed the nullification issue in South Carolina, and initiated the spoils system.
Jackson, Stonewall Thomas Jonathan Jackson, also known as Stonewall Jackson (1824–1863), was one of the most renowned Confederate generals of the Civil War. He led his troops to a stunning victory at the Battle of Bull Run in 1861, surprising the Union with his leadership and the strength of southern resistance. He died of pneumonia after being accidentally shot by his own men near Chancellorsville, Virginia.
Jacksonian Democracy Andrew Jackson and his followers' political philosophy concerned with the interests of the common people and limiting the role of the federal government
Japanese American Citizens League organization that worked to protect the civil rights of Japanese Americans
Jay, John John Jay (1745–1829), a New York attorney, joined the Patriot cause during the American Revolution and served in the Continental Congress. He went on to serve as president of the Continental Congress and as a diplomat to Spain and France. Jay helped win favorable terms for the new nation in the Treaty of Paris. After the war, Jay continued in public service, and advocated ardently for ratification of the Constitution. As a Federalist, he wrote five of the essays included in *The Federalist,* under the pen name Publius. He was appointed the first Chief Justice of the U.S. Supreme Court by George Washington.
jazz American musical form developed by African Americans, based on improvisation and blending blues, ragtime, and European-based popular music
Jazz Singer, The an American musical released in 1927 that was the first feature-length movie with synchronized dialogue
Jefferson, Thomas Thomas Jefferson (1743–1826) was an American farmer, landholder, author, architect, lawyer, and statesman. He joined the Virginia House of Burgesses in 1768 and began advocating for American independence in the 1770s. Jefferson represented Virginia in the Second Continental Congress, during which time he drafted and revised the Declaration of Independence. He went on to serve as a diplomat to France and as the nation's first secretary of state, second vice president, and third president. Jefferson also founded the University of Virginia.
Jiang Jieshi Jiang Jieshi (1887–1975), also known as Chiang Kai-shek, was a Chinese Nationalist leader who opposed Mao Zedong's communist forces during the Chinese civil war. After the fall of mainland China, Jiang became the leader of a Nationalist government on the island of Taiwan.
Jim Crow laws segregation laws enacted in the South after Reconstruction
jingoism aggressive nationalism; support for warlike foreign policy
Johnson, Andrew Andrew Johnson (1808–1875) was a Tennessee tailor who rose to become the seventeenth President of the United States. In 1864, Johnson became Vice President under President Lincoln. Less than a year later, he became President following Lincoln's assassination. His disputes with Radical Republicans over Reconstruction led to his impeachment in 1868. After his presidency, Johnson returned to Tennessee. He served as a U.S. Senator until his death.
Johnson, Lyndon B. Lyndon Johnson (1908–1973) served in the House of Representatives and the Senate before being elected Vice President with President John Kennedy. On November 22, 1963, he was sworn in as the 36th President immediately following President Kennedy's assassination. He served from 1963 to 1969. In 1964, he signed the Civil Rights Act into law. He also championed the Great Society social program and worked without success to end the Vietnam War.

Johnson, Robert Beginning in the mid-1970s, Robert Johnson (1946–) worked in Washington, D.C., for the Corporation for Public Broadcasting and as a lobbyist for the new and growing cable industry. In 1980, he used his experience and connections to start BET, a cable network aimed at the largely underserved African American viewing audience. After many years of growth and success, Johnson and his investment partners sold BET in 1998, for $3 billion. The deal made Johnson the nation's first African American billionaire.

joint-stock company a company run by a group of investors who share the company's profits and losses

Joseph, Chief Chief Joseph (1840–1904) succeeded his father as chief of the Nez Percé in 1871. Six years later he led his followers on an unsuccessful flight to escape confinement on a reservation. First sent to Oklahoma, they were eventually returned to a new reservation in Washington state. However, Joseph was unable to secure their return to their tribal homeland.

judicial interpretation practice by which the courts expand and apply the Constitution's intent beyond the meaning of its written words

judicial review the power of the Supreme Court to decide whether acts of a president or laws passed by Congress are constitutional

K

kamikaze Japanese pilots who deliberately crashed planes into American ships during World War II

Kansas-Nebraska Act a 1854 law that divided the Nebraska Territory into Kansas and Nebraska, giving each territory the right to decide whether or not to allow slavery

Kelley, Florence Florence Kelley (1859–1932) played a major role at Hull House in calling attention to the working conditions of women and children. In 1899, she headed the newly founded National Consumers League. In 1909 Kelley helped found the NAACP.

Kelley, Oliver H. Kelley Oliver H. Kelley (1826–1913) was an employee in the U.S. Department of Agriculture who worked to improve the lives of farmers and the agricultural industry. He recognized the need to bring farmers together to protect their livelihoods. Kelly served as the first secretary of the Grange from 1867 until 1878.

Kellogg-Briand Pact 1928 agreement in which many nations agreed to outlaw war

Kennan, George F. George F. Kennan (1904–2005) was an American diplomat who spent several years serving in Eastern Europe and the Soviet Union. His observations about Soviet political attitudes and actions contributed to the formation of the U.S. policy of containment.

Kennedy, John F. John F. Kennedy (1917–1963) served in both the House of Representatives and the Senate before becoming the 35th President in 1961. He faced a number of foreign crises, especially in Cuba and Berlin, and managed to secure such achievements as the Nuclear Test-Ban Treaty and the Alliance for Progress. He was assassinated in Dallas, Texas.

Kennedy, Robert Robert Kennedy (1925–1968) was an assassinated antiwar candidate for the 1968 Democratic Party presidential nomination

Kerner Commission group set up to investigate the causes of race riots in American cities in the 1960s

Key, Francis Scott Francis Scott Key (1779–1843) was an American lawyer and amateur poet who is best known as the author of the "The Star-Spangled Banner," which became the U.S. national anthem in 1931.

Keynes, John Maynard John Maynard Keynes (1883–1946) was a British economist best known for his advocacy of government intervention to protect the economy from the negative effects of recessions, depressions, and booms. He outlined his ideas in *The General Theory of Employment, Interest, and Money,* published in 1936.

Khomeini, Ayatollah Ruhollah Ayatollah Ruhollah Khomeini (1902–1989) was an influential Iranian scholar and cleric. After leading an unsuccessful rebellion against the Shah of Iran in 1963, he fled to France, where his religious and political ideas became more extreme. After the Shah's overthrow in 1979, Khomeini returned to Iran and, supported by revolutionary forces, seized power, holding it until his death in 1989.

Khrushchev, Nikita Nikita Khrushchev (1894–1971) was a Communist Party leader who served as premier of the Soviet Union from 1958 to 1964. Khrushchev led the Soviet Union during the Cuban Missile Crisis, but lost power soon afterwards.

King Philip's War a conflict between English colonists and American Indians in New England

King, Martin Luther, Jr. Martin Luther King, Jr. (1929–1968) advocated nonviolent methods of protest while becoming perhaps the most influential leader of the civil right movement. He led the March on Washington in 1963, where he delivered his famous "I Have a Dream" speech. He was assassinated in 1968.

Kings Mountain a 1780 Revolutionary War battle in South Carolina in which Patriots defeated a Loyalist militia

Kissinger, Henry Henry Kissinger (1923–) served as a foreign policy advisor to Presidents Kennedy and Johnson. In 1969, President Nixon appointed him National Security Advisor, and Secretary of State in 1973. Kissinger received the Nobel Peace Prize in 1973 for his role in ending the Vietnam War.

Knights of Labor labor union that sought to organize all workers and focused on broad social reforms

Know-Nothings a political party of the 1850s, officially known as the American Party, that was anti-Catholic and anti-immigrant

Kristallnacht "Night of the Broken Glass," organized attacks on Jewish communities in Germany on November 9, 1938

Ku Klux Klan an organization that promotes hatred and discrimination against specific ethnic, racial, and religious groups

L

labor union an organization of workers

Lafayette, Marquis de The Marquis de Lafayette (1757–1834) was a French aristocrat who joined the American Patriot cause in 1777. He fought under General Washington, and returned to France in 1779 to persuade the king to send French forces to help the Americans. In 1780, he returned to command Patriot forces in Virginia. In 1781, he helped trap the British under General Cornwallis at Yorktown.

laissez-faire a theory advocating minimal government interference in the economy

Land Grant College Act a 1862 law that made money available to states to establish universities that taught agriculture and mechanical engineering

land grants land designated by the federal government for building schools, roads, or railroads

Land Ordinance of 1785 a law which designed a system for managing and settling lands in the Northwest Territory

Lange, Dorothea Dorothea Lange (1895–1965) was an American documentary photographer known for her portraits of displaced farmers and others suffering economic hardship during the Great Depression.

Las Gorras Blancas (the White Caps) group of Mexican Americans living in New Mexico who attempted to protect their land and way of life from encroachment by white landowners

Lauder, Estee Estee Lauder (1908?–2004) was an American businesswoman and philanthropist who founded a fragrance and cosmetics' empire.

League of Nations world organization established after World War I to promote peaceful cooperation among countries

Lee, Robert E. Robert E. Lee (1807–1870) was a Virginia military general who became the commander of the Confederate forces during the Civil War. On April 9, 1865, Lee surrendered his forces to Union General Grant at Appomattox Court House. After the war, he became the president of Washington College, now known as Washington and Lee University, in Lexington, Virginia.

Lend-Lease Act act passed in 1941 that allowed President Roosevelt to sell or lend war supplies to any country whose defense he considered vital to the safety of the United States

Lenin, Vladimir Vladimir Lenin (1870–1924) founded the Communist Party in Russia and led the Russian Revolution. He became dictator of Soviet Russia and promoted communism wherever he could. Lenin believed that a dedicated party of revolutionaries, as opposed to the population generally, was necessary for successful communist revolutions.

Lewis and Clark Expedition the 1804 expedition sent by President Jefferson to explore the newly-acquired Louisiana Territory

liberal person who tends to support government intervention to help the needy and favors laws protecting the rights of women and minorities

Liluokalani, Queen Queen Liluokalani (1838–1917) succeeded her brother King Kalakaua in 1891 as the leader of the Hawaiian people. She was the first and only reigning Hawaiian queen and the last Hawaiian sovereign to govern the islands. Although Liluokalani tried to regain control of lands owned by white plantation owners, she was overthrown in 1893, and the U.S. annexed Hawaii in 1898.

limited government a principle stating that the government has only as much authority as the people give it and, therefore, its power is limited

limited war war fought to achieve only specific goals

Lincoln, Abraham Abraham Lincoln (1809–1865) was born on a Kentucky farm. He was self-educated and became an attorney. He joined the Whig Party and was elected to serve in the Illinois state legislature. He ran an unsuccessful campaign against Stephen A. Douglas for a seat in the U.S. Senate in 1858, during which he gained national acclaim for his performance in a series of debates and for his strong stance against the expansion of slavery. Though he lost the Senate race, he went on to become president in 1861. He led the country during the Civil War and was assassinated in April 1865.

Lindbergh, Charles Charles Lindbergh (1902–1974) was an American aviator who completed the first non-stop, solo flight across the Atlantic Ocean.

literacy test a reading and writing test formerly used in some southern states to prevent African Americans from voting

Little Turtle Little Turtle (c. 1752–1812) was an American Indian leader of the Miami people. Resisting American expansion into the Northwest Territory, Little Turtle's forces won several victories against U.S. troops in 1790 and 1791. Little Turtle signed the Treaty of Greenville in 1795, ceding much of Ohio and parts of Illinois, Indiana, and Michigan to the United States.

localism policy relied on by President Hoover in the early years of the Great Depression, whereby local and state governments act as primary agents of economic relief

Lodge, Henry Cabot Henry Cabot Lodge (1850–1924) was a leading Republican senator who led the successful fight to keep the United States from joining the League of Nations after World War I. Before becoming a senator, he had served in the House. Earlier, he worked as a magazine editor and historian.

Lone Star Republic the nation formed in 1835 by Texans who declared independence from Mexico

Long, Huey Huey Long (1893–1935) was elected governor of Louisiana in 1928, where he won a wide following by providing reforms to help the poor during the depression. While serving in U.S. Senate (1932–1935), he became a vocal critic of Roosevelt's New Deal and called for a redistribution of the nation's wealth. In 1935, he announced his plan to run for President but was assassinated that same year.

loose construction a belief that the government has any power not forbidden by the Constitution

Lost Generation term for American writers of the 1920s marked by disillusion with World War I and a search for a new sense of meaning

Louisiana Purchase the 1803 purchase from France by the United States of the territory between the Mississippi River and the Rocky Mountains

Lowell girls young women who worked in the textile mills in Lowell, Massachusetts, in the early 1800s

Lowell, Francis Cabot Francis Cabot Lowell (1775–1817) was an American businessman who developed the world's first textile mill in which all operations in converting raw cotton into finished cloth were performed within one facility.

Loyalists colonists who remained loyal to Britain during the Revolutionary War

Lusitania British passenger liner sunk by a German U-boat during World War I

M

MacArthur, Douglas Douglas MacArthur (1880–1964) commanded American troops in World War I, where he developed a reputation for bravery. As supreme commander of Allied forces in the Pacific (1942–1945) he accepted Japan's surrender to end World War II. In 1950, he became commander of UN forces in the Korean War. He retired after his controversial removal from command in 1951, following a dispute with President Harry Truman.

Maddox, Lester Lester Maddox (1915–2003) was born in Atlanta, Georgia. A high school dropout, he ran a restaurant in the city from 1947 to 1964, when he closed it because he refused to serve African Americans. Elected governor (1967–1971), he fought against school desegregation.

Madison, James James Madison (1751–1836) was a Patriot who represented Virginia in the Continental Congress. In 1787, he participated in the Constitutional Convention and was a leading voice in replacing the Articles of Confederation with a new plan for government. For his part in winning passage of the 1787 Constitution, he became known as the Father of the Constitution. Madison went on to serve as Thomas Jefferson's secretary of state and then to become the fourth president of the United States.

Magellan, Ferdinand Ferdinand Magellan (1480–1521) was the son of Portuguese nobility who eventually became a navigator and explorer. In 1519, Magellan and his fleet of 5 vessels and about 270 men left Spain and sailed west. Sailing around South America, Magellan discovered the Strait of Magellan and then set out across the Pacific. After Magellan was killed in the Philippine Islands, only one of his ships and only 17 of the original sailors continued westward to Spain, making the first circumnavigation of the Earth.

Magna Carta an English document from 1215 that limited the power of the king and provided basic rights

Mahan, Alfred T. Alfred T. Mahan (1840–1914) was an American naval officer and historian who urged American leaders to build a stronger navy and to obtain naval bases in Cuba, Hawaii, and the Philippines. Mahan was also an early proponent of building a canal through Central America to allow U.S. naval vessels to move quickly between the Atlantic and Pacific oceans.

Malcolm X Malcolm X (1925–1965) served as a spokesman and minister for the Nation of Islam. His work helped the Nation of Islam, which had only 400 members when he was released from prison in 1952, grow to 40,000 members by 1960. He broke with the group shortly before his assassination in 1965.

Mali West African empire lasting from about A.D. 1200 to A.D. 1450 that prospered from the gold trade

Mandela, Nelson Nelson Mandela (1918–2013), the son of a chief of the African Tembu people, became the first Black president of South Africa in 1994. As a lawyer, Mandela began his fight against apartheid in 1952. In 1964 he was sentenced to life imprisonment for his anti-apartheid activism. He was released in 1990. Working with South African President F.W. de Klerk, Mandela helped end the country's apartheid system of racial segregation. He shared the Nobel Prize for Peace in 1993.

Manhattan Project code name of the U.S. government research project that developed the atomic bomb

Manifest Destiny the 19th century doctrine that westward expansion of the United States was not only inevitable but a God-given right

Mann, Horace Horace Mann (1796–1859) grew up in poverty but through hard work graduated from Brown University and later became a lawyer. He eventually served in the Massachusetts House of Representatives and as the president of the state Senate. Mann resigned his seat in the Senate to become the first chairman of the state board of education. Mann worked to establish free public schools that all children were required by law to attend.

Mansa Musa Mansa Musa (?–1332?) was the emperor of the West African empire of Mali from approximately 1307. At the time, the Mali empire was one of the largest in the world. Known for his generosity and religious devotion, Musa set out on a historic pilgrimage to Cairo and then to Mecca accompanied by a caravan of 60,000 men. Musa's pilgrimage displayed to the world the enormous wealth of Mali.

manumission the act of freeing someone from slavery

Mao Zedong Mao Zedong (1893–1976) was a Chinese leader who successfully led a communist revolution in mainland China. He was chairman of the communist People's Republic of China from 1949 to 1959, and chairman of the country's Communist Party until 1976.

Marbury* v. *Madison the 1803 Supreme Court case that established the principle of judicial review

March on Washington 1963 demonstration in which more than 200,000 people rallied for economic equality and civil rights

Married Women's Property Act a 1848 New York State law that guaranteed greater property rights for women; used as a model in other states

Marshall Plan foreign policy that offered economic aid to Western Europe after World War II

Marshall, George George C. Marshall (1880–1959) became the army's chief of staff in 1939. Marshall used his quiet strength, negotiating skills, and planning genius to build a fighting force as quickly as possible. As Secretary of State after the war, he devised a plan of aid, called the Marshall Plan, to help Western Europe recover. In 1950, he returned as Secretary of Defense at the start of the Korean War and helped to prepare the army one more time.

Marshall, John John Marshall (1755–1835) was the fourth Chief Justice of the United States. After serving under George Washington in the Revolutionary War, including the winter at Valley Forge, Marshall held various law and political positions. As chief justice, Marshall participated in more than 1,000 decisions, writing more than 500 of them himself, often advancing and defending judicial power and the principles of American federalism.

Marshall, Thurgood Thurgood Marshall (1908–1993) became counsel for the NAACP in 1938 and won 29 of the 32 major civil rights cases he argued over the next 23 years. In 1967, he became the first African American to sit on the Supreme Court and held the post until poor health caused him to retire in 1991.

Martí, José José Martí (1853–1895) was an exiled Cuban writer who became the symbol of Cuba's struggle for independence from Spain. Mart' helped establish the Cuban Revolutionary Party and was elected its leader in 1892. In 1895 Martí helped launched a war of independence against Spain. He died a month later in battle on the plains of Dos Ríos.

mass culture similar cultural patterns throughout a society as a result of the spread of transportation, communication, and advertising

mass production production of goods in large numbers through the use of machinery and assembly lines

mass transit public transportation systems that carry large numbers of people

massive retaliation policy of threatening to use massive force in response to aggression

matrilineal when inheritance is passed down through the female side of the family

Maya American Indian people of the Yucatán area of southern Mexico, Guatemala, and Belize whose civilization reached its height between A.D. 300–900

Mayflower Compact a framework for self-government of the Plymouth Colony signed on the ship *Mayflower* in 1620

McCarthy, Eugene Eugene McCarthy (1916–2005) was an antiwar candidate for the 1968 Democratic Party presidential nomination

McCarthy, Joseph R. Joseph R. McCarthy (1908–1957) was a U.S. Senator who led a series of high-profile investigations into Americans whom he accused of being disloyal to the United States. His tactics, known as McCarthyism, helped define the Red Scare of the 1950s.

McCarthyism negative catchword for extreme, reckless changes of disloyalty

McClellan, George B. George B. McClellan (1826–1885) was a Pennsylvania soldier who attended the U.S. Military Academy at West Point and served in the Mexican War before returning to West Point to teach. During the Civil War, he first served in Ohio and then was appointed commander of the Army of the Potomac. His caution led to conflicts with President Lincoln, and several key defeats at Richmond and Antietam resulted in his removal from command.

McKay, Claude Claude McKay (1890–1948) was a Jamaican-born poet and novelist whose influential work during and after the Harlem Renaissance sought to define a distinctive Black identity.

McKinley, William William McKinley (1843–1901) was the 25th president of the United States, serving from 1897 to 1901. McKinley led the United States during the Spanish-American War in 1898. McKinley's second term as president was cut short by an assassin in 1901.

Meat Inspection Act 1906 law that empowered the federal government to inspect meat sold across state lines and required federal inspection of meat processing plants

median family income a measure of average family income

Medicaid federal program created in 1965 to provide low-cost health insurance to poor Americans of any age

Medicare federal program created in 1965 to provide basic hospital insurance to most Americans over the age of sixty-five

Mellon, Andrew Andrew Mellon (1835–1937) served as secretary of the Treasury from 1921 to 1932. He played a significant role in reforming the U.S. tax structure by lowering marginal tax rates for individuals and businesses.

melting pot society in which people of different nationalities assimilate to form one culture

mercantilism an economic policy under which a nation accumulates wealth by exporting more goods than it imports

mercenary professional soldier who is paid to fight in a foreign army

Meredith, James James Meredith (1933–) attended an all-Black college before becoming the first Black student at the University of Mississippi in 1962. After he graduated, he earned a law degree and became involved in Republican Party politics. He was shot in Mississippi while on a protest march in 1966. After he recovered, he continued to be active in the civil rights movement.

mestizos people in Spanish colonial America who were of European and American Indian descent

Metacom Metacom (c.1638–1676), whom the English called King Philip, was a Wampanoag leader who launched the initial Indian attacks that began King Philip's War of 1675–1676.

metis person in French colonial America who was of French and American Indian descent

Middle Ages period in European history from the 5th century through the 14th century

Middle Passage the forced transport of enslaved Africans from West Africa to the Americas

migrant farmworker person who travels from farm to farm to pick fruits and vegetables

migrated to move from one region or habitat to another

militarism glorification of the military

militia trained citizens who serve as soldiers during an emergency

Militia Act a 1862 law that allowed African American soldiers to serve in the Union military

minutemen members of armed Patriot groups who would take the field at a moment's notice in the days leading up to and during the Revolutionary War

missionaries people sent to a foreign country in order to convert others to their religion

missions religious settlements usually run by Catholic priests and friars in colonial Spanish America

Missouri Compromise an 1820 agreement calling for the admission of Missouri as a state in which slavery was legal and Maine as a free state, and banning slavery in the Louisiana Purchase north of the 36° 30' N latitude

Moctezuma Moctezuma (1466–1520), the ninth Aztec emperor, became leader of the Aztec Empire in 1502, when it was at the height of its power. When Hernán Cortés and his troops arrived in Tenochtitlán in 1519, Moctezuma welcomed him. Moctezuma, however, was taken prisoner and Cortés established the city as headquarters for the Spanish invaders. Moctezuma's people eventually lost respect for him, wounding him as he tried to stop an uprising against the Spanish. He died shortly after and in 1521 the Aztec Empire came to an end.

Model T automobile manufactured by Henry Ford to be affordable on the mass market

modernism artistic and literary movement sparked by a break with past conventions

monetary policy control of the money supply by a central authority, including influencing interest rates to promote economic growth and stability

Monmouth 1778 Revolutionary War battle site in New Jersey where neither side won a clear victory

monopoly exclusive control by one company over an entire industry

Monroe Doctrine a foreign policy doctrine set forth by President Monroe in 1823 that discouraged European intervention in the Western Hemisphere

"moral diplomacy" Woodrow Wilson's statement that the U.S. would not use force to assert influence in the world, but would instead work to promote human rights

Moral Majority political organization established by Reverend Jerry Falwell in 1979 to advance religious goals

Mormon a member of the Church of Jesus Christ of Latter-Day Saints, which was organized in 1830 by Joseph Smith

Morse, Samuel F.B. Samuel F.B. Morse (1791–1872) was originally an art student who developed the idea of the electric telegraph. By 1838, he had developed the system of dots and dashes that became known throughout the world as the Morse Code. Later in life, Morse became a prominent philanthropist, donating to charities and helping to establish Vassar College.

Mott, Lucretia Lucretia Mott (1793–1880) was deeply committed to the ideal of reform. Known for her effective public speaking, she travelled the country promoting abolition. Frustrated by attempts to limit women's involvement in reform, Mott turned her attention to women's rights in the 1840s. She worked with Elizabeth Cady Stanton to organize the Seneca Falls Convention.

Mountain Men American trappers who explored the Rocky Mountains area in the early 1800s

muckraker writer who uncovers and exposes misconduct in government or business

Muir, John John Muir (1838–1914) emigrated with his family from Scotland in 1849. In 1876 he urged the federal government to adopt a forest conservation policy and was later instrumental in the establishment of California's Yosemite and Sequoia national parks. In 1892, Muir founded the Sierra Club, one of today's leading conservationist organizations.

multinational corporation company that produces and sells its goods and services all over the world

Munich Pact agreement made between Germany, Italy, Great Britain, and France in 1938 that sacrificed the Sudetenland to preserve peace

mural large painting applied directly to a wall or a ceiling

Mussolini, Benito Benito Mussolini (1883–1945) was a fascist leader and dictator of Italy between 1922–1945. He was called Il Duce ("the leader") and established a totalitarian dictatorship that promoted extreme nationalism. During his dictatorship, Italy invaded Ethiopia and partnered with Germany during World War II.

mutualistas organized groups of Mexican Americans that make loans and provide legal assistance to other members of their community

mutually assured destruction policy in which the United States and the Soviet Union hoped to deter nuclear war by building up enough weapons to destroy one another

My Lai village in South Vietnam where in 1968 American forces opened fire on unarmed civilians; U.S. soldiers killed between 400 and 500 Vietnamese

N

Nader, Ralph Ralph Nader (1934–) is an American lawyer and consumer advocate who has been involved in a variety of issues, including car safety, land use, insecticide regulation, and safe meat processing.

napalm jellied gasoline dropped in canisters that explode on impact and cover large areas in flame; dropped by U.S. planes during the Vietnam War

Nation of Islam African American religious organization founded in 1930 that advocated separation of the races

National Aeronautics and Space Administration (NASA) government agency that coordinates U.S. efforts in space

National American Woman Suffrage Association (NAWSA) group founded in 1890 that worked on both the state and national levels to gain women the right to vote

National Association for the Advancement of Colored People (NAACP) interracial organization founded in 1909 to abolish segregation and discrimination and to achieve political and civil rights for African Americans

National Consumers League (NCL) group organized in 1899 to investigate the conditions under which goods were made and sold and to promote safe working conditions and a minimum wage

national debt total amount of money that the federal government owes to the holders of government bonds

National Organization for Women (NOW) organization established by Betty Friedan to combat discrimination against women

National Reclamation Act 1902 law that gave the federal government the power to decide where and how water would be distributed through the building and management of dams and irrigation projects

National Recovery Administration (NRA) New Deal agency that promoted economic recovery by regulating production, prices, and wages

National Road a road built by the federal government in the early 1800s that extended from Maryland to Illinois

nationalism loyalty and devotion to one's nation

nationalize to place a private resource under government control

nativism inclination to favor native inhabitants as opposed to immigrants

nativist a person who favors native-born inhabitants over immigrants

natural rights universal rights, such as life and liberty, that derive from nature rather than from government, according to philosophers

Navigation Acts British trade laws enacted by Parliament during the mid-1700s that regulated colonial commerce

Nazism totalitarian movement led by Adolf Hitler's Nazi Party in Germany that instituted legal discrimination and atrocities against Jews

Neutrality Act of 1939 act that allowed nations at war to buy goods and arms in the United States if they paid cash and carried the merchandise on their own ships

New Deal programs and legislation pushed by President Franklin D. Roosevelt during the Great Depression to promote economic recovery and social reform

New Deal coalition political force formed by diverse groups who united to support Franklin D. Roosevelt and his New Deal

New Freedom Woodrow Wilson's program to place government controls on corporations in order to benefit small businesses

New Frontier President Kennedy's plan to improve the economy, fight racial discrimination, and explore space

"new" immigrants Southern and Eastern European immigrants who arrived in the United States in a great wave between 1880 and 1920

New Jersey Plan William Paterson's proposal for a unicameral legislature with each state having one vote

New Nationalism President Theodore Roosevelt's plan to restore the government's trustbusting power

New Right political movement supported by reinvigorated conservative groups in the latter half of the twentieth century

Niagara Movement group of African American thinkers founded in 1905 that pushed for immediate racial reforms, particularly in education and voting practices

Nimitz, Chester Chester Nimitz (1885–1966) took command of the U.S. Pacific Fleet shortly after the attack on Pearl Harbor in 1941. Under his leadership, the U.S. forces won victories at Midway, Tarawa, Marianas, and Iwo Jima, among other places. Nimitz's quiet leadership was key to the American victory in the Pacific during World War II.

Nineteenth Amendment 1920 constitutional amendment that gave women the right to vote

Nixon, Richard M. Richard M. Nixon (1913–1994) served as a Republican member of Congress and of the Senate as well as Vice President under Dwight D. Eisenhower. He ran for President in 1960 and lost to John F. Kennedy but won the office in 1968. His presidency was marked by significant accomplishments in foreign relations. In 1974, he resigned rather than be impeached for covering up illegal activities in the Watergate affair.

No Child Left Behind Act 2002 law aimed at improving the performance of primary and secondary schools particularly through mandated sanctions against schools not reaching federal performance standards

nonimportation agreements colonial consumer boycotts of British exports in response to taxes passed by Parliament

Noriega, Manuel Manuel Noriega (1938–2017) was a Panamanian military officer who gained control of the army in 1983, becoming the dominate leader in Panama. Allegations of election fraud, drug trafficking, money laundering, and espionage against the United States led to his capture by U.S. forces. He was found guilty in 1992 and sentenced to 40 years imprisonment.

North American Free Trade Agreement (NAFTA) agreement signed in 1993 calling for the removal of trade restrictions among Canada, Mexico, and the United States

North Atlantic Treaty Organization (NATO) military alliance formed to counter Soviet aggression

Northwest Ordinance of 1787 a law which provided a basis for governing the Northwest Territory

Northwest Passage a water route to Asia that many believed could be found through the cold waters of present-day Canada

Northwest Territory a vast territory north of the Ohio River and west of Pennsylvania as far as the Mississippi River

nuclear family an ideal or typical household with a father, mother, and children

Nuclear Test Ban Treaty 1963 nuclear-weapons agreement that banned aboveground nuclear tests

nullification a theory that states could nullify, or void, any federal law they deemed unconstitutional

Nuremberg Trials trials in which Nazi leaders were charged with war crimes

O

Obama, Barack Barack Obama (1961–) was elected the 44th president of the United States in 2008, becoming the first African American to hold the office. Obama served in the Illinois state legislature and the U.S. Senate prior to becoming President. Obama faced the wars in Afghanistan and Iraq, as well as a financial recession upon assuming the presidency. In 2009, Obama was awarded the Nobel Peace Prize.

O'Connor, Sandra Day Sandra Day O'Connor (1930–) received her undergraduate and law degrees from Stanford University, but because she was a woman, could not find work at a law firm. Instead, she found employment as a deputy district attorney in Northern California. After distinguishing herself for years in a number of fields—as an assistant attorney general, a senator, a Superior Court judge, and a judge for the Court of Appeals (all in the state of Arizona)—she became the first female U.S. Supreme Court Justice in 1981.

Office of War Information (OWI) government agency that encouraged support of the war effort during World War II

Oglethorpe, James James Oglethorpe (1696–1785) was an English army officer, politician, and founder of the British colony of Georgia in America. Oglethorpe served as a member of Parliament from 1722 to 1754. A noted philanthropist, Oglethorpe opposed the practice of imprisoning English debtors. He also believed that people of all religions deserved to live in a place that allowed religious freedom. In 1732, he received the charter for the colony of Georgia as a haven for English debtors.

Okies general term used to describe Dust Bowl refugees

Olmsted, Frederick Law Frederick Law Olmsted (1822–1903) was an influential American landscape architect best known for designing Central Park in New York City. Olmsted also contributed to the preservation of the Yosemite park in California, the park spaces around Niagara Falls, and a large system of public parks in Boston.

Open Door Policy an American statement that the government did not want colonies in China, but favored free trade there

open-range system method of ranching in which the rancher allowed his or her livestock to roam and graze over a vast area of grassland

Operation Desert Storm 1991 American-led attack on Iraqi forces after Iraq refused to withdraw its troops from Kuwait

Oppenheimer, J. Robert American physicist J. Robert Oppenheimer (1904–1967) was the director of the Manhattan Project, the U.S. government research project during World War II that produced the first atomic bombs. After the war, he became head of the Institute for Advanced Study in New Jersey, a center for theoretical research.

Oregon Trail a trail from Independence, Missouri, to Oregon that was used by pioneers in the mid-1800s

Organization of Petroleum Exporting Countries (OPEC) group of countries that sell oil to other nations and cooperate to regulate the price and supply of oil

Otis, Elisha Elisha Otis (1811–1861) was an American who invented the safety elevator in 1852. Otis's "safety hoist" was first designed for freight but was soon adapted for passenger services. The first elevator for passengers was installed in a store in New York City in 1857. Otis also developed a steam-powered elevator that became the basis for the Otis Elevator Company.

P

Paine, Thomas Thomas Paine (1737–1809) was an English-American author and political thinker who moved to Philadelphia in 1774, following a meeting with Benjamin Franklin. He is best known for his highly influential pamphlet, *Common Sense,* which helped bring support to the Patriot cause.

Palmer Raids the series of raids in the early 1920s initiated by Attorney General A. Mitchell Palmer, against suspected radicals and communists

Panama Canal human-made waterway linking the Atlantic to the Pacific across the Isthmus of Panama

pandemic a disease that has spread over a wide geographic area, usually across continents or the entire world

pardon official forgiveness of a crime and its punishment

Paris Peace Accords 1973 Peace agreement between the United States, South Vietnam, North Vietnam, and the Vietcong that effectively ended the Vietnam War

Parks, Rosa Rosa Parks (1913–2005) began the Montgomery bus protest in 1955 when she refused to give up her seat to a white passenger. She continued to be active in the civil rights movement while working for a member of Congress and starting a nonprofit organization to help young people.

Parliament the legislative body of the British government

patent official rights given by the government to an inventor for the exclusive right to develop, use, and sell an invention for a set period of time

Patton, George S., Jr. A colorful personality and a forceful leader greatly admired by troops under his command, George S. Patton (1885–1945) commanded U.S. tanks during World War I and quickly demonstrated his skill at leading mobile fighting units. During World War II, he led U.S. troops in North Africa and Europe, sweeping rapidly across France and Germany in the closing months of the war.

Paul, Alice Alice Paul (1885–1977) joined the leadership of the National American Woman Suffrage Association in 1912 but soon left to found a more militant organization, which became the National Woman's Party in 1917. After the passage of the 19th Amendment, Paul expanded her work for women's rights. In 1923 she introduced the first equal rights amendment into Congress.

Peace Corps American government organization that sends volunteers to provide technical, educational, and medical services to developing countries

Pearl Harbor American military base attacked by the Japanese on December 7, 1941

Pendleton Civil Service Act 1883 law that created a civil service system for the federal government in an attempt to hire employees on a merit system rather than on a spoils system

penitentiary movement a movement aimed at structuring prisons so that prisoners would feel penitent for their crimes

Penn, William William Penn (1644–1718) was an English Quaker, who after growing disillusioned with prospects of religious freedom in England, founded the colony of Pennsylvania as a refuge for Quakers and other religious minorities of Europe.

Pentagon Papers classified U.S. government study that revealed American leaders involved the United States in Vietnam without fully informing the American people; leaked to the *New York Times* in 1971

Pequot War a short outbreak of violence between English colonists and the Pequot Indians in 1636, during which a Pequot village was set afire, killing between 600 to 700 inhabitants

perestroika policy in the Soviet Union in the late 1980s calling for restructuring of the stagnant Soviet economy

Perot, H. Ross Ross Perot (1930–2019) was a self-made billionaire who founded Electronic Data Systems in 1962. Perot ran as an independent candidate for U.S. President in 1992, capturing 19 percent of the vote. In 1995 he founded the Reform Party and ran in the presidential election of 1996, but he did not win.

Perry, Matthew Matthew Perry (1794–1858) was a U.S. naval officer who led an American naval fleet in 1853 to 1854 that forced Japan into trade and diplomatic relations with the West after more than two centuries of isolation. Perry's journey opened further American expansion across the Pacific Ocean.

Pershing, John J. John J. Pershing (1860–1948) commanded the American Expeditionary Forces (AEF) in Europe during World War I. Earlier, he had served in the Philippines and in Mexico. After World War I, he served as chief of staff of the U.S. Army.

personal computer small computer intended for individual use

personal liberty laws the laws enacted by northern states to counteract the Fugitive Slave Act by granting rights to free African Americans and those seeking freedom

Pickett, George George Picket (1825–1875) was a soldier from Virginia who became a Confederate general during the Civil War. He is best known for leading a large contingent in what came to be known as Pickett's Charge at the Battle of Gettysburg on July 3, 1863.

Pilgrims English Separatists who sought religious freedom and founded Plymouth Colony in 1620

Pinchot, Gifford Gifford Pinchot (1865–1946) was appointed to head the U.S. Forest Service, but was fired in 1910 after a dispute with President Taft's Secretary of the Interior. In 1912, he helped form the Progressive Party that nominated Theodore Roosevelt to run for President. Pinchot continued his conservation work in Pennsylvania, where he was elected governor in 1922.

placer mining the use of metal pans, picks, and shovels to harvest gold from the banks and beds of rivers and streams

Platt Amendment set of conditions under which Cuba was granted independence in 1902, including restrictions on rights of Cubans and granting the U.S. the "right to intervene" to preserve order in Cuba

political machines a political party's organization that wins voter loyalty and guarantees power to a small group of leaders, who often abuse it for their own gain

political party an organization of people who seek to win elections and hold public office in order to shape government policy

Polk, James K. James K. Polk (1795–1849) was a lawyer and politician who served as the 11th president of the United States from 1845 to 1849. Before being elected President, Polk served in the Tennessee legislature and as Speaker of the U.S. House of Representatives. As President, Polk led the United States through the Mexican-American War, resulting in the United States gaining large territories along the Pacific coast and in the Southwest.

poll tax a sum of money to be paid before a person could vote

Pontiac's Rebellion uprising in 1763 by American Indians in the Great Lakes region

popular sovereignty a principle in which the people are the only source of government power

Populist Party People's Party; political party formed in 1891 to advocate a larger money supply and other economic reforms

Powderly, Terence V. Terence V. Powderly (1849–1924) was an American labor leader who led the Knights of Labor for several years in the late nineteenth century with the goal of leading American workers out of what he saw as the bondage of wage labor.

Powhatan Powhatan (?–1618) was the leader of the Powhatan empire when the English established the Jamestown Colony in 1607. Powhatan ruled over 30 Indian groups and between 13,000 and 34,000 people. Relations between the Powhatan people and the English colonists were mixed. Following the marriage of his daughter Pocahontas to the English planter John Rolfe, relations were generally peaceful, until Powhatan's death in 1618.

precedent an act or statement that becomes an example, rule, or tradition to be followed

presidios forts built by the Spanish in colonial America, usually in what is today the Southwest United States and California

Presley, Elvis Elvis Presley (1935–1977) was an American musician who became known as the "King of Rock-and-Roll." Presley's music combined elements of African American blues, gospel, country songs, and Tin Pan Alley ballads. His flamboyant personality and nonconformist image made Presley a teen idol and an inspiration to future rock-and-roll artists throughout the world.

privatizing to transfer from governmental ownership or control to private interests

Proclamation of 1763 declaration by the British king ordering all colonists to remain east of the Appalachian Mountains

productivity the rate at which goods are produced or services performed

Progressive Party political party that emerged from the Taft-Roosevelt battle that split the Republican Party in 1912

Progressivism movement that responded to the pressures of industrialization and urbanization by promoting reforms

Prohibition the forbidding by law of the manufacture, transport, and sale of alcohol

proprietary colonies English colonies granted to an individual or group by the Crown

protective tariffs taxes on imported goods making the price high enough to protect domestic goods from foreign competition

public school movement a movement aimed at providing greater educational opportunities through the establishment of tax-supported public schools

Public Works Administration (PWA) New Deal agency that provided millions of jobs constructing public buildings as well as airports, dams, and bridges

Pulitzer, Joseph Joseph Pulitzer (1847–1911) was an influential American newspaper editor and publisher. Pulitzer helped format the modern newspaper and included investigative reporting, sports and fashion coverage, comics, and illustrations in his papers.

Pull factor a factor that attracts people to a new location

Pullman Strike violent 1894 railway workers' strike which began outside of Chicago and spread nationwide

pump priming economic theory that favored public works projects because they put money into the hands of consumers who would buy more goods, stimulating the economy

Pure Food and Drug Act 1906 law that allowed federal inspection of food and medicine and banned the interstate shipment and sale of impure food and the mislabeling of food and drugs

Puritans English Protestants who believed in strict religious discipline and the simplification of worship in an effort to purify the Anglican church; settlers of the Massachusetts Bay Colony in 1630

Push factor a factor that motivates people to leave their home countries

Q

Quakers Members of the Religious Society of Friends, a Christian movement devoted to peaceful principles. The Quakers do not believe in having ministers, and instead rely on the doctrine of the "Inner Light," or sense of Christ's direct working in the soul. Quakers are pacifists and refuse to bear arms.

Quebec a fortified trading post built on the St. Lawrence River in 1608 that was the first permanent European settlement in Canada

quota system arrangement that limited the number of immigrants who could enter the United States from specific countries

R

Radical Republicans congressmen who advocated full citizenship rights for African Americans along with a harsh Reconstruction policy toward the South

Randolph, A. Philip A. Philip Randolph (1889–1979) was a strong labor leader and leader of the civil rights movement for decades. In 1925, he became head of the Brotherhood of Sleeping Car Porters. After more than a decade of battling, he got the Pullman Corporation to sign the first contract in history between a major company and a predominantly African American labor union. Next Randolph turned his attention to discrimination in war industries, convincing President Roosevelt to issue Executive Order 8802 in 1941. After the war, he persuaded President Truman to pass another executive order banning discrimination in the military. Randolph was a driving force behind the 1963 March on Washington.

ratification an official approval

rationing government-controlled limits on the amount of certain goods that civilians could buy during wartime

Reagan, Ronald Ronald Reagan (1911–2004) got his famous easy communication style from his background as a radio sports announcer, a host for TV shows, and most famously, an actor in movies. Although he was a Democrat as a young man, his views became more conservative, and he switched to the Republican Party. He was elected governor of California in 1966 where he carried out a conservative agenda during his two terms. In 1980, Reagan was elected to the first of his two terms as President.

realpolitik a foreign policy based on concrete national interests instead of abstract ideologies; promoted by Henry Kissinger during the Nixon administration

recall process by which voters can remove elected officials from office before their term ends

reconquista campaign, ending in 1492, that reestablished Spanish Christian rule on the Iberian Peninsula after 700 years of Muslim dominance

Reconstruction a program implemented by the federal government between 1865 and 1877 to repair damage to the South caused by the Civil War and to restore the southern states to the Union

Reconstruction Finance Corporation (RFC) federal agency set up by Congress in 1932 to provide emergency government credit to banks, railroads, and other large businesses

Red Scare fear that communists were working to destroy the American way of life

Redeemer a term for white southern Democrats who returned to political power after 1870

referendum process that allows citizens to approve or reject a law passed by a legislature

Renaissance period in European history lasting from the fourteenth to the sixteenth century, which ushered in a more secular outlook and encouraged freedom of thought, the importance of the individual, and renewed interest in classical learning

reparations payment for war damages
repatriation process by which government officials return persons to their country of origin
republic form of government in which officials are elected by the people
Republican Party a political party established around an antislavery platform in 1854
reservationists group of U.S. senators who were prepared to vote for the Treaty of Versailles as long as some changes were made to it
reservations public lands where Native Americans were required to live by the federal government
Revere, Paul Paul Revere (1735–1818) was an American silversmith who lived and worked in Boston. When the British approached Boston Harbor on April 16, 1775, Revere rode through the countryside to Concord warning the colonists and calling Patriots to arms. His adventures that night were recorded years later by Henry Wadsworth Longfellow in the poem "Paul Revere's Ride."
revivalist a preacher who works to renew the importance of religion in American life
Riis, Jacob Jacob Riis (1849–1914) was a Danish immigrant who became a New York City newspaper reporter in 1873. In 1888, as the crime reporter for the *New York Evening Sun,* he took photos of night life in the slums. Published in his 1890 book, *How the Other Half Lives,* the photos moved New York Police Commissioner Theodore Roosevelt to take up the cause of urban reform.
rock-and-roll popular music that grew out of the gospel and blues traditions of African Americans
Rockefeller, John D. John D. Rockefeller (1839–1937) was an American industrialist and philanthropist. He began the Standard Oil Company and dominated the oil industry with innovative, aggressive business practices. He also contributed money to different causes through the Rockefeller Foundation.
Roosevelt Corollary President Theodore Roosevelt's reassertion of the Monroe Doctrine to keep the Western Hemisphere free from intervention by European powers
Roosevelt, Eleanor Eleanor Roosevelt (1884–1962) was the wife of President Franklin D. Roosevelt. With FDR's election as President in 1932, Eleanor Roosevelt became a public figure in her own right, traveling the country promoting the causes of helping women, children, and the poor. After her husband's death, she served as a U.S. delegate to the United Nations (1945–1951), focusing on human rights and women's issues.
Roosevelt, Franklin D. Franklin D. Roosevelt (1882–1945) served as assistant secretary of the Navy (1913–1920), before running unsuccessfully for Vice President on the Democratic ticket in 1920. Stricken with polio the following year, Roosevelt recovered to resume his political career as governor of New York (1929–1933). Elected President in 1932, he lead the nation through the Great Depression and World War II before dying in office in 1945.
Roosevelt, Theodore Theodore Roosevelt (1858–1919) was governor of New York before becoming Vice President in 1901. Roosevelt became the youngest man to assume the presidency soon after. He was known for his anti-monopoly and conservation policies. He made an unsuccessful bid for another term in 1912 as the candidate of the Progressive Party.
Rosenberg, Julius and Ethel Julius (1918–1953) and Ethel Rosenberg (1915–1953) were two American civilians controversially convicted and executed for espionage during the Red Scare of the 1950s. Later evidence from the Venona Papers confirmed that both did have ties to Soviet espionage.
Rough Riders group of men, consisting of rugged westerners and upper-class easterners who fought during the Spanish-American War
royal colonies English colonies that were under direct control of the Crown
rural-to-urban migrants people who move from an agricultural area to a city
Russo-Japanese War a war between Japan and Russia in 1904 over the presence of Russian troops in Manchuria
Ruth, Babe Babe Ruth (1895–1948) was a professional baseball player known for his showmanship and ability to hit homeruns. He is a member of the Baseball Hall of Fame.

S

Sacco, Nicola Nicola Sacco (1891–1927) was an Italian immigrant convicted of murder and executed in 1927.
SALT II proposed agreement between the United States and the Soviet Union to limit certain types of nuclear arms production; also known as the Strategic Arms Limitation Treaty II, it was never ratified by the United States Senate
salutary neglect a British policy in the early 1700s that allowed the colonies virtual self-rule as long as Great Britain profited economically
sanctions penalties intended to make people obey laws and rules, especially measures taken to force a country to obey international law
Sand Creek Massacre 1864 incident in which Colorado militia attacked a camp of Cheyenne and Arapaho Indians, some of who were under U.S. Army protection
Sanger, Margaret Margaret Sanger (1879–1966) first coined the term "birth control" in a pamphlet she published in 1914. A medical organization she founded, the Birth Control Research Bureau, evolved into Planned Parenthood in 1942.
Santa Anna, Antonio López de Antonio López de Santa Anna (1794–1876) was a Mexican army officer and politician who played major roles in the political and military conflicts in Mexico in the mid-1800s, including the Texas revolt in 1836 and the Mexican-American War. Santa Anna ruled eleven times during the turbulent decades following Mexican independence.
Santa Fe Trail a trail developed by traders in the mid-1800s, connecting Independence, Missouri, to Santa Fe, New Mexico
Saratoga 1777 Revolutionary War battle considered to be the turning point in the war because the Patriot win convinced the French to ally officially with the United States
satellite mechanical device that orbits Earth, receiving and sending communication signals or transmitting scientific data
satellite state independent nation under the control of a more powerful nation
saturation bombing tactic of dropping massive amounts of bombs in order to inflict maximum damage
Savings and Loan crisis 1989 failure of about 1000 savings and loan banks, also known as S&Ls, as a result of risky and sometimes fraudulent business practices
scalawag a negative term for a southern white who supported the Republican Party after the Civil War

Schlafly, Phyllis Phyllis Schlafly (1924–2016) was an American writer and political activist, and was a well-known and outspoken defender of the traditional family. She was most famous for opposing the Equal Rights Amendment.

scientific management approach to improving efficiency, in which experts looked at every step of a manufacturing process, trying to find ways to reduce time, effort, and expense

Scopes Trial 1925 trial of a Tennessee school teacher for breaking a law that forbade teaching Darwin's theory of evolution

Scott, Dred Dred Scott (c.1800–1857) was an African American man born into slavery who sued for freedom on the grounds that he had lived for a time in a state where slavery was prohibited. In *Dred Scott v. Sandford*, the Supreme Court ruled against Scott, stating that his time in a free state did not nullify his status as an enslaved person, and that as such he was property and could not sue in the courts. Following the ruling, the sons of Scott's original enslaver purchased Scott and his wife and freed them both.

Scott, Winfield Winfield Scott (1786–1866) was a career U.S. Army officer who was one of the most influential American military figures of the first half of the 19th century. Scott held the rank of general in three wars and was the commanding general of the U.S. Army from 1841 to 1861. Scott was nominated as the Whig Party presidential candidate in 1852 but lost the election to Franklin Pierce.

secede to withdraw formally from a membership in a group or an organization

Second Continental Congress assembly of delegates representing every colony that met in 1775 in Philadelphia following the Battles of Lexington and Concord

Second Great Awakening a religious revival movement in the first half of the 1800s

segregation a forced separation, often by race

Selective Service Act act passed by Congress in 1917 authorizing a draft of men for military service

self-determination the right of people to choose their own form of government

Seneca Falls Convention held in New York in 1848, the first women's rights convention in the United States

separation of powers a principle that divides power among the executive, legislative, and judicial branches of government

Separatists English Protestants who wished to separate from the Anglican church

Serra, Junípero Junípero Serra (1713–1784) was a Spanish Franciscan priest who helped establish 9 missions in the present-day state of California. Born in Spain, Serra arrived in Mexico City in 1750 to begin missionary work among the American Indians. Serra's work in establishing the missions helped strengthen Spain's control of its California territory.

service economy economic system focused on the buying and selling of services

service sector businesses that provide services rather than manufactured goods

settlement house community center organized at the turn of the twentieth century to provide social services to the urban poor

Seventeenth Amendment 1913 constitutional amendment that allowed for the direct election of U.S. senators by citizens

share-tenancy much like sharecropping, except that the farmer chooses what crop to plant and buys the supplies

sharecropping a system in which a farmer tends to a portion of a planter's land in return for a share of the crop

Shays' Rebellion a farmers' rebellion, led by Daniel Shays, against higher taxes in Massachusetts

Sherman Antitrust Act 1890 law banning any trust that restrained interstate trade or commerce

Sherman, William Tecumseh William Tecumseh Sherman (1820–1891) was a judge's son from Ohio who became a renowned Union general during the Civil War. He fought in the Battles of Bull Run and Shiloh before joining forces with General Grant to lay siege to Vicksburg in 1863. Following their victory, Sherman led his "March to the Sea" 250 miles east to capture Savannah, Georgia.

Shiloh a 1862 Civil War battle in southwestern Tennessee where the Union won a victory but nearly 25,000 Union and Confederate troops were killed or wounded

siege a military tactic in which an enemy is surrounded and all supplies are cut off in an attempt to force a surrender

silent majority phrase introduced by President Richard Nixon to refer to a significant number of Americans who supported his policies but chose to not express their views

Sinclair, Upton Upton Sinclair (1878–1968) began writing for newspapers and completed several successful novels soon after he graduated college in 1897. His most famous work, *The Jungle,* was published in 1906. Sinclair continued to write muckraking pieces and in time became active in California politics, running unsuccessfully for governor in 1934. In 1942, he won a Pulitzer Prize for his novel *Dragon's Teeth.*

sit-down strike organized labor action in which workers stop working and occupy the workplace until their demands are met

sit-in form of protest during which participants sit and refuse to move

Sitting Bull Sitting Bull (1831?–1890) was a war chief and important spiritual leader who became the first-ever chief of all the Lakota Sioux bands in the 1860s. After surrendering to the Army in 1881, he lived on a reservation where he was killed by Indian police sent to arrest him.

Sixteenth Amendment 1913 constitutional amendment that gave Congress the authority to levy an income tax

skyscrapers very tall buildings

Slater, Samuel Samuel Slater (1768–1835) was an English-born industrialist who used his knowledge of cotton manufacturing and textile machinery to build the nation's first water-powered textile mill in 1793 at Pawtucket, Rhode Island.

Smith Act law that made it unlawful to teach or advocate the violent overthrow of the United States government

Smith, Bessie Bessie Smith (1898?–1937) was a blues vocalist widely known as the "Empress of the Blues." Smith sang with some of the great jazz musicians of the time, including Louis Armstrong.

Smith, John John Smith (c.1580–1631) was an English explorer and one of the leading promoters of English colonization in America. Smith helped to found the colony of Jamestown in 1607 and served as its leader from 1608 to 1609. His contributions also included creating detailed maps and descriptions of Virginia and New England.

Smith, Joseph Joseph Smith (1805–1844) was the founder of the Church of Jesus Christ of Latter-day Saints. After claiming to have had several revelations, Smith published the *Book of Mormon* in 1830. Smith and his Mormon followers built settlements in Ohio, Missouri, and Illinois. Settling in Nauvoo, Illinois, anti-Mormon citizens jailed Smith and his brother, who were eventually shot and killed by a mob in 1844.

Social Darwinism the belief held by some in the late nineteenth century that certain nations and races were superior to others and therefore destined to rule over them

Social Gospel reform movement that emerged in the late nineteenth century that sought to improve society by applying Christian principles

Social Security Act 1935 law that set up a pension system for retirees, established unemployment insurance, created insurance for victims of work-related accidents, and provided aid for poverty-stricken mothers and children, the blind, and the disabled

socialism system or theory under which the means of production are publicly controlled and regulated rather than owned by individuals

Songhai large West African empire lasting from around A.D. 1460 to A.D. 1600

Sons of Liberty organization of colonists formed in opposition to the Stamp Act and other British laws and taxes

Sosa, Lionel Lionel Sosa (1939–) is an advertising executive who gained success by helping companies market their products to Latino consumers. But he may be most famous for helping Republican candidates reach out to Latino voters. In the 2004 election with Sosa's help, George W. Bush was able to garner an estimated 40% of Latino votes, a huge increase over previous Republican presidential candidates.

Southeast Asia Treaty Organization (SEATO) defensive alliance aimed at preventing communist aggression in Asia

southern strategy tactic of the Republican Party to win presidential elections by securing the electoral vote of southern states

space race competition between the United States and the Soviet Union to successfully land on the moon

Spanish Civil War War in which Nationalist forces led by General Francisco Franco rebelled against the democratic Republican government of Spain

speculation practice of making high-risk investments in hopes of obtaining large profits

spheres of influence a region dominated and controlled by an outside power

Spock, Benjamin Benjamin Spock (1903–1998) was an American pediatrician and author whose 1946 book *Common Sense Book of Baby and Child Care* was one of the most influential books on parenting in the twentieth century. Spock broke from tradition by advising parents to show affection, understanding, and flexibility, and to promote and appreciate each child's individuality.

spoils system the practice of the political party in power giving jobs and appointments to its supporters, rather than to people based on their qualifications

Square Deal President Theodore Roosevelt's program of reforms to keep the wealthy and powerful from taking advantage of small business owners and the poor

stagflation term for the economic condition created in the late 1960s and 1970s by high inflation combined with stagnant economic growth and high unemployment

Stalin, Joseph Joseph Stalin (1878–1953) was a leader of communist Union of Soviet Socialist Republics (U.S.S.R.) from 1924–1953. His efforts to transform the Soviet Union into an industrial power and form state-run collective farms caused extreme hardship and millions of deaths. A partner with Germany in 1939, Stalin later joined the Allies in World War II. After the war, Stalin became an aggressive participant in the Cold War.

Stamp Act 1765 law passed by Parliament that required colonists to pay taxes on printed materials

Stanton, Elizabeth Cady Elizabeth Cady Stanton (1815–1902) was a lively and often fiery crusader for women's rights. While raising a growing family, she worked with Lucretia Mott and others to organize the Seneca Falls Convention. From the beginning, she pushed for women to fight for the right to vote, helping shape the direction of the movement for years to come.

Staple crop a crop that is in steady demand

"Star-Spangled Banner, The" a poem written by Francis Scott Key in 1814 that became the national anthem in 1931

Starr, Kenneth Kenneth Starr (1946–) is an American lawyer who served as the independent counsel in charge of the investigation that led to the impeachment of President Bill Clinton in 1998.

steerage third-class accommodations on a steamship

Steffens, Lincoln Lincoln Steffens (1866–1936) was a reporter and editor for the *New York Post* and, later, the muckraking *McClure's* magazine. Steffens wrote articles and books exposing government corruption at the state and municipal levels.

Steinbeck, John John Steinbeck (1902–1968) was an American novelist who frequently wrote about migratory farmworkers and other laborers during the Great Depression.

Steinem, Gloria Gloria Steinem (1934–) is an American feminist, political activist, and writer-editor, who played an influential role in the Women's Movement in the late twentieth century. In 2013, Steinem was awarded the Presidential Medal of Freedom.

Stowe, Harriet Beecher Harriet Beecher Stowe (1811–1896) was an American writer and abolitionist best known for her antislavery novel *Uncle Tom's Cabin,* published in 1852. She began writing her novel as a series of stories, which first appeared in the abolitionist newspaper *National Era* in 1851–1852.

Strategic Arms Limitation Treaty (SALT I) 1972 treaty between the United States and the Soviet Union that froze the deployment of intercontinental ballistic missiles and placed limits on antiballistic missiles

strategic bombing tactic of dropping bombs on key political and industrial targets

Strategic Defense Initiative (SDI) nicknamed "Star Wars," President Reagan's plan to develop innovative defenses to guard the United States against nuclear missile attacks

strict construction a belief that the government is limited to powers clearly stated in the Constitution

Student Nonviolent Coordinating Committee grass-roots movement founded in 1960 by young civil rights activists

Students for a Democratic Society (SDS) organization founded in 1960 at the University of Michigan to fight racism and poverty

suburbs residential areas surrounding a city

Suez crisis attempt by France and Great Britain to seize control of the Suez Canal in 1956

suffrage the right to vote

Sunbelt name given to the region of states in the South and the Southwest

superpowers strong nations that dominated the postwar world

supply-side economics economic theory which says that reducing tax rates stimulates economic growth

suspension bridges bridges that have a roadway suspended by cables

sweatshops small factories where employees have to work long hours under poor conditions for little pay

T

Taft-Hartley Act a law that restricted the power of labor unions

Taft, William Howard William Howard Taft (1857–1930) was the 27th president of the United States from 1909 to 1913. In 1901, Taft became the first civilian governor of the Philippines. In that post, Taft worked to rebuild the economy and reestablish order. In 1921, President Harding appointed Taft the 10th chief justice of the United States, where he served for 9 years.

Taliban Islamist faction that controlled most of Afghanistan from 1996–2001

Taney, Roger B. Roger B. Taney (1777–1864) served as the fifth Chief Justice of the U.S. Supreme Court. He is best known for his decision in *Dred Scott* v. *Sandford,* in which he wrote that enslaved persons were not entitled to the rights guaranteed by the Constitution and that Congress had no authority to ban slavery in the territories, as such laws would deprive slave owners of their property.

tariff a tax on imported goods

Tariff of 1816 a protective tariff established by Congress to encourage Americans to buy goods made in the United States

Tariff of Abominations an 1828 protective tariff, so-named by its southern opponents

Taylor, Susie King Susie King Taylor (1848–1912) was a Civil War nurse who was born to enslaved African American parents, but was sent to live with her grandmother at age seven. During the Civil War, she joined other African Americans who traveled to Union occupied territory. Later she wrote a memoir describing her experiences as both a nurse and a teacher.

Taylor, Zachary Zachary Taylor (1784–1850) grew up on the Kentucky frontier and enlisted in the army in 1806. Taylor served in the War of 1812, the Black Hawk War, and the Seminole Wars in Florida. He became a hero for his command of U.S. forces in the Mexican-American War. He was elected the 12th president of the United States in 1848 but died 16 months after taking office.

Tea Party Movement informal movement made up of local groups who want to reduce the size and scope of the federal government

Teapot Dome scandal Harding administration scandal in which the Interior Secretary leased government oil reserves to private oilmen for bribes

Tecumseh Tecumseh (1768–1813) was a Shawnee warrior from the Ohio Valley who spearheaded a spiritual and military resistance movement among American Indians in the early 1800s. Tecumseh actively resisted the United States, fighting in battles, rejecting treaties, and traveling widely to convince American Indian groups that they were all one people and that no one group had the right to make a treaty.

televangelist minister who uses the television to preach

temperance movement a movement aimed at stopping alcohol abuse and the problems created by it

tenant farmer farmer who pays rent to a landowner for the use of the land

tenant farming a system in which a farmer paid rent to a landowner for the use of the land

tenements multistory buildings divided into apartments to house as many residents as possible

Tennessee Valley Authority (TVA) government agency created during the New Deal to build dams in the Tennessee River valley to control flooding and generate electric power

termination policy a policy ending all programs monitored by the Bureau of Indian Affairs. It also ended federal responsibility for the health and welfare of Native Americans.

Tet Offensive communist assault on a large number of South Vietnamese cities in early 1968

Thirteenth Amendment the 1865 constitutional amendment that abolished slavery in the United States

38th parallel dividing line between North and South Korea

Thoreau, Henry David Henry David Thoreau (1817–1862) was an American essayist, poet, and philosopher and a leading figure in the Transcendentalist movement. Thoreau's most influential works include *Walden* a series of 18 essays describing his experiment in simple living, and the essay "Civil Disobedience," in which he argues that a person must be true to his or her own conscience, even if it means breaking the law.

Three-Fifths Compromise a compromise in which each enslaved person in a state would be counted as three fifths of a person for the purposes of legislative representation

Tiananmen Square site in Beijing where Chinese students' prodemocracy protests were put down by the Chinese government in 1989

time zones any of the 24 longitudinal areas of the world within which the same time is used

Tin Pan Alley section on 28th Street in New York City that became the center of the music publishing industry in the late 1800s; genre of popular American music

Tinker* v. *Des Moines School District 1969 Supreme Court case in which the Court ruled that the right to free speech extended to other types of expression besides the spoken word

Tojo, Hideki Hideki Tojo (1884–1948) became Japan's prime minister in October of 1941 when plans were already underway to attack the United States Navy at Pearl Harbor. He led Japan until July 1944. After the war, he was tried for war crimes and hanged in December 1948.

total war a military strategy in which an army attacks not only enemy troops but also the economic and civilian resources that support them

totalitarianism a theory of government in which a single party or leader controls the economic, social, and cultural lives of its people

toxic waste poisonous byproducts of human activity

trade protectionism a policy that protects domestic industries from unfair competition from foreign ones, usually using methods such as tariffs or quotas on the importation of certain goods

Trail of Tears a forced march of the Cherokee Indians to move west of the Mississippi in the 1830s

Transcendentalist a person who follows the literary and philosophical movement based on finding spiritual reality through nature and consciousness of self

Transcontinental Railroad rail link between the eastern and the western United States

Treaty of Fort Laramie the 1851 treaty that restricted American Indians to specific areas away from the major trails

Treaty of Ghent an 1814 agreement that ended the War of 1812

Treaty of Guadalupe Hidalgo the 1848 treaty ending the Mexican-American War

Treaty of Paris 1783 peace treaty that ended the Revolutionary War and affirmed American independence

triangular trade the three-way pattern of trade that involved England, English colonies in the Americas, and West Africa

trickle-down economics economic theory that holds that financial benefits given to banks and large businesses will trickle down to smaller businesses and consumers

Tripartite Pact agreement that created an alliance between Germany, Italy, and Japan during World War II

Truman Doctrine President Truman's promise to help nations struggling against communist movements

Truman, Harry S. Harry S. Truman (1884–1972) was President of the United States from 1945–1953. Truman took office after Franklin Roosevelt's death and led the nation during the final months of World War II, making the decision to use atomic weapons against Japan. In the early years of the Cold War, Truman worked to rebuild Europe and to oppose the spread of communism. When communist North Korea invaded South Korea in 1950, beginning the Korean War, Truman sent American troops into the conflict.

Trump, Donald J. Donald J. Trump (1946-) was elected the 45th president of the United States in 2016. Born in Queens New York, Trump was a businessman and television personality before he entered politics. As president, Trump renegotiated trade deals with foreign nations and changed the nation's relationships with foreign allies and foes. In 2019, Trump was the third president to be impeached by the House of Representatives. The Senate acquitted him in 2020.

trust group of separate companies that are placed under the control of a single managing board in order to form a monopoly

Truth, Sojourner Sojourner Truth (1797?–1883) was born into slavery with the name Isabella Van Wagener. She gained her freedom in 1827 and went on to become a leading African American evangelist and reformer in the abolition and women's rights movements. Her life story is retold in her book, *The Narrative of Sojourner Truth*.

Tubman, Harriet Harriet Tubman (c.1820–1913) was born into slavery in Maryland. In 1849, she escaped and traveled to Philadelphia. She then became a "conductor" on the Underground Railroad, leading hundreds of enslaved people, including her parents and siblings, to freedom in the North.

Turner, Frederick Jackson Frederick Jackson Turner (1861–1932) was an American historian whose works greatly influenced future writings about American history. Turner promoted using social sciences in historical writings and stressed the use of concepts such as immigration, urbanization, economic development, and social and cultural history when trying to understand historical events.

Turner, Nat Nat Turner (1800–1831) was born into slavery on a small plantation in Virginia. As an adult, Turner claimed to have been called upon by God to help lead the enslaved African Americans out of bondage. In 1831, Turner organized and led the only sustained armed uprising by enslaved people in American history, for which he was tried and hanged.

turnpike a road that requires users to pay a toll

Tuskegee Airmen African American squadron that escorted bombers in the air war over Europe during World War II

Twain, Mark Mark Twain (1835–1910) was the pen name for Samuel Langhorne Clemons, an American novelist and humorist who wrote famous works such as *Life on the Mississippi, The Adventures of Tom Sawyer,* and *The Adventures of Huckleberry Finn.* Twain's stories reflected the American experience as he saw it.

Twenty-fifth Amendment constitutional amendment ratified in 1967 that deals with presidential succession, vice presidential vacancy, and presidential disability

Twenty-fourth Amendment constitutional amendment that banned the poll tax as a voting requirement

U

U-boats German submarine

unconditional surrender giving up completely without any concessions

Underground Railroad a system that existed before the Civil War in which African American and white abolitionists helped people trying to escape enslavement travel to safe areas in the North and in Canada

unfunded mandate program or action required but not paid for by the federal government

unicameral legislature a lawmaking body made up of a single house

Unitarian a member of the Unitarian religion, which believes that God is a single divine being rather than a trinity

United Farm Workers (UFW) labor union of farm workers that used nonviolent tactics, including a workers' strike and consumer boycott of table grapes

United Nations (UN) organization founded in 1945 to promote peace

Universal Declaration of Human Rights document issued by the UN to promote basic human rights and freedoms

Urban League network of churches and clubs that set up employment agencies and relief efforts to help African Americans get settled and find work in cities

urban renewal government programs for redevelopment of urban areas

urbanization expansion of cities and/or an increase in the number of people living in them

USA PATRIOT Act law passed following September 11, 2001, giving law enforcement broader powers in monitoring possible terrorist activities

utopian community an isolated settlement established to achieve the goal of moral perfection

V

Valley Forge location in Pennsylvania where General Washington's army spent a difficult winter in 1777–1778

Van Buren, Martin Martin Van Buren (1782–1862) was the eighth president of the United States, serving from 1837 to 1841. He faced a national financial panic brought about in part by the transfer of federal funds from the Bank of the United States to state banks. He also was president during the Second Seminole War, a costly war that eventually led to the removal of most of the Seminole people from parts of Florida.

Vanzetti, Bartolomeo Bartolomeo Vanzetti (1888–1927) was an Italian immigrant convicted of murder and executed in 1927.

vaudeville type of show that included dancing, singing, and comedy sketches and became popular in the late nineteenth century

Venona Papers a series of Cold War-era secret Soviet documents intercepted and later released by U.S. intelligence officials

vertical integration system of consolidating firms involved in all steps of a product's manufacture

Vespucci, Amerigo Amerigo Vespucci (1454?–1512) was an Italian explorer and merchant who made early voyages to the Americas in 1499 and 1501. Vespucci explored enough of South America's coast to deem it a continent. The name for the Americas is derived from his first name.

viceroy in colonial Spanish America, king-appointed official who governed a province, colony, or country

Vicksburg a Confederate stronghold along the Mississippi River, the site of a siege by Union forces that lasted more than a month in 1863 and ended in a Union victory, splitting the Confederacy

Vietcong South Vietnamese communist rebels who waged a guerrilla war against the government of South Vietnam throughout the Vietnam War

Vietnamization President Nixon's plan for gradual withdrawal of U.S. forces as South Vietnamese troops assumed more combat duties

vigilantes self-appointed law enforcers

Villa, Francisco "Pancho" Francisco "Pancho" Villa (1878–1923) was a Mexican revolutionary and guerrilla leader. In 1916 Villa's forces killed 18 Americans in New Mexico, which resulted in U.S. General John J. Pershing's unsuccessful expedition into Mexico with 10,000 troops to capture and punish Villa.

Violence Against Women Act law passed in 1994 that increased federal resources to apprehend and prosecute men guilty of violent acts against women

Virginia and Kentucky resolutions state resolutions passed in 1798 declaring the Alien and Sedition Acts unconstitutional

Virginia Plan James Madison's proposal for a bicameral legislature with representation based on population

Volstead Act law enacted by Congress to enforce the Eighteenth Amendment

Voting Rights Act law that banned literacy tests and empowered the federal government to oversee voter registration

voucher certificate or other document that can be used in place of money

W

Wade-Davis Bill a law that required a majority of prewar voters in Confederate states to swear loyalty to the Union before restoration could begin

Wagner Act New Deal law that abolished unfair labor practices, recognized the right of employees to organize labor unions, and gave workers the right to collective bargaining

Wallace, George George Wallace (1919–1998) served as governor of Alabama from 1963 to 1967. He ran for president in 1968 on the American Independent Party ticket, championing states rights and winning five southern states in the election. Serving three more terms as governor (1971–1979, 1983–1987), he eventually renounced his segregationist beliefs.

Walton, Sam Sam Walton (1918–1992) was an American retail pioneer who founded Wal-Mart Stores, Inc., which became the largest retail sales chain in the United States.

war bond a bond bought to fund a war effort, redeemable for interest after a certain period of time

War Hawks members of Congress who pushed for war against Great Britain in the years leading up to the War of 1812

War of 1812 a war between the United States and Great Britain that lasted from 1812 to 1815

War on Poverty President Lyndon Johnson's programs aimed at aiding the country's poor through education, job training, proper health care, and nutrition

War Powers Act 1973 law passed by Congress restricting the President's war-making powers; the law requires the President to consult with Congress before committing American forces to a foreign conflict

War Refugee Board U.S. government agency founded in 1944 to save Eastern European Jews

Warren Commission committee that investigated the assassination of President Kennedy

Warren Court Supreme Court of the 1960s under Chief Justice Earl Warren, whose decisions supported civil rights

Warren, Earl Earl Warren (1891–1974) served three terms as governor of California before serving as Chief Justice of the Supreme Court from 1953 to 1969. Under his leadership, the Court decided several landmark cases that affected civil rights, criminal procedures, voting rights, and separation of church and state.

Warsaw Pact military alliance of the Soviet Union and its satellite states

Washington Naval Disarmament Conference meeting held in 1921 and 1922 where world leaders agreed to limit construction of warships

Washington, Booker T. Booker T. Washington (1856–1915) was born into slavery and grew up in poverty following emancipation. In 1881, Washington was chosen to head the Tuskegee Normal and Industrial Institution, where he promoted vocational education for African American students. He encouraged African American citizens to accept segregation and to instead focus on improving themselves through education and economic opportunities.

Washington, George George Washington (1732–1799) worked early on as a surveyor of the Virginia colony. Washington became interested in western expansion in the Ohio Country and invested in the Ohio Company. In 1752, he accepted an appointment to the military as an officer. Two years later, he led a company to drive out the French from Fort Duquesne. Later, he went on to serve as the commander-in-chief of the colonies' Continental Army and to become the first President of the United States.

Watergate political scandal involving illegal activities that led to the resignation of President Richard Nixon in 1974

weapons of mass destruction (WMD) nuclear, biological, and chemical weapons intended to kill or harm on a large scale

welfare state government that assumes responsibility for providing for the welfare of the poor, elderly, sick, and unemployed

Wells, Ida B. Ida B. Wells (1862–1931) was an African American journalist who worked throughout her life to end the practice of lynching in the South. She contributed to several newspapers, including the *Memphis Free Speech,* the *New York Age,* and the *Chicago Conservator.* In 1895, she published a detailed inquiry into lynching, entitled *A Red Record.*

Western Front battle front between the Allies and Central Powers in western Europe during World War I

Westmoreland, William From 1964 to 1968, General William Westmorland (1914–2005) was the commander of U.S. forces in the Vietnam War. Westmorland had previously served in World War II and the Korean War.

Wheatley, Phillis Phillis Wheatley (1753?–1784) was the first African American to publish a book of poems. As a servant for John Wheatley and his family, Phillis learned to read, write, and study. Phillis and the Wheatleys found a London publisher to print her volume of poetry, *Poems on Various Subjects, Religious and Moral,* in 1773.

Whigs members of the nationalist political party formed in 1832 in opposition to the Democrats

Whiskey Rebellion a 1794 uprising in western Pennsylvania that opposed the federal excise tax on whiskey

Whitney, Eli Eli Whitney (1765–1825) was an American inventor best known for his invention of the cotton gin, which he patented in 1794, to automate the removal of seeds from raw cotton. Whitney's greatest contribution, however, was developing the idea of mass-producing interchangeable parts. He did this in 1797 in order to fulfill a contract to supply muskets for the government.

Willard, Frances Frances Willard (1839–1898) was a professor who grew interested in the temperance movement in 1874. She joined the Women's Christian Temperance Union (WCTU), where she clashed with other members by insisting on linking its goals with women's suffrage. By 1879, she had gained enough support to be elected president of the WCTU, a position she held the rest of her life.

William II William II (1859–1941) was the German emperor and king of Prussia until the end of World War I in 1918.

Williams, Roger Roger Williams (1603–1683) was an English colonist in New England who founded the colony of Rhode Island. Williams believed that the English colonists had no right to take land that belonged to American Indians. Banished from Massachusetts with his followers, Williams founded Providence, Rhode Island, in 1636, on land purchased from American Indians. Williams' new colony established religious freedom and separation of church and state.

Wilmot Proviso the proposed, but rejected, 1846 bill that would have banned slavery in the territory won from Mexico in the Mexican War

Wilson, Woodrow Woodrow Wilson (1856–1924) entered politics in 1910 when he was elected governor of New Jersey. His reforms there brought him national attention and the Democratic presidential nomination in 1912. As President he guided the nation through World War I and negotiated the Versailles Treaty.

Winfrey, Oprah Ophrah Winfrey (1954–) worked as a television news reporter and anchor person before working as a morning talk show host. Her Chicago show, *The Oprah Winfrey Show,* began in 1985 and was syndicated nationally the next year. The show was a huge hit and spawned her media and entertainment empire, which includes a magazine and a cable television channel. Winfrey is a mainstay of *Forbes* magazine's list of riches people in America. Her net worth in 2013 was estimated at $2.9 billion.

Winthrop, John John Winthrop (1588–1649) was a Puritan lawyer who was the first governor of the Massachusetts Bay Colony after its founding in 1630. Winthrop's goal was to establish a pious Puritan state. Emphasizing group discipline and individual responsibility, Winthrop's colony thrived but his intolerance of new ideas led to discontent.

Wisconsin* v. *Yoder 1972 Supreme Court decision that extended freedom of religion to allow Amish parents, on religious grounds, to withdraw their children from public school after the eighth grade

Women's Army Corps (WAC) United States Army group established during World War II so that women could serve in non-combat roles

women's movement a movement beginning in the mid-1800s in the United States that sought greater rights and opportunities for women

Works Progress Administration (WPA) key New Deal agency that provided work relief through various public works projects

World Trade Organization (WTO) international organization formed in 1995 to encourage the expansion of world trade

Wounded Knee 1890 confrontation between U.S. cavalry and Sioux that marked the end of Indian resistance

X

XYZ Affair a diplomatic controversy in 1798 in which French officials demanded bribes of American negotiators

Y

Yalta Conference 1945 strategy meeting between Roosevelt, Churchill, and Stalin

Yellow Press newspapers that used sensational headlines and exaggerated stories in order to promote readership

Yorktown site in Virginia where, in 1781, General Cornwallis's British forces surrendered to General Washington

Young, Brigham Brigham Young (1801–1877) was an American religious leader who served as the second president of the Mormon church. After Mormon leader Joseph Smith's murder in June 1844, Young took command of the church and led the Mormons westward out of Illinois. He also served as the first governor of the new U.S territory of Utah.

Z

Zhou Enlai Zhou Enlai (1898–1976) lived abroad as a young man before returning to his native China in 1924 to help Mao Zedong lead a communist revolution there. When Mao established People's Republic of China in 1949, Zhou became its prime minister and foreign minister and was later the main architect of China's policy of détente with the United States in 1972.

Zimmermann note telegram written by German Foreign Minister Zimmermann proposing an alliance between Germany and Mexico against the United States during World War I

A

abolition movement > movimiento abolicionista Movimiento del siglo XIX que buscaba suprimir la esclavitud.

Acquired Immunodeficiency Syndrome (AIDS) > Síndrome de Inmunodeficiencia Adquirida (SIDA) Enfermedad que ataca el sistema inmunitario de sus víctimas; empezó a extenderse a principios de la década de 1980 y aún hoy sigue representando una seria crisis de salud mundial puesto que no se conoce cura.

Adams-Onís Treaty > Tratado de Adams-Onís Tratado de 1819 en el que España cedió Florida a los Estados Unidos.

Adams, John > Adams, John (1735–1826) Escritor y líder colonial estadounidense que se convirtió en uno de los más destacados pensadores y activistas de los patriotas estadounidenses. Se pronunció en contra de las leyes de impuestos forzadas por Gran Bretaña y sirvió como delegado de Massachusetts en el Primer Congreso Continental. Fue el primer vicepresidente y el segundo presidente de los Estados Unidos.

Adams, John Quincy > Adams, John Quincy (1767–1848) Sexto presidente de los Estados Unidos. Antes de su presidencia, ayudó a negociar el Tratado de Ghent en 1814, el cual terminó la Guerra de 1812. Como secretario de estado del presidente Monroe, Adams fue el principal arquitecto de la Doctrina Monroe. Regresó al Congreso después de su presidencia, donde luchó por la abolición de la esclavitud y la mejora de las ciencias y las artes.

Addams, Jane > Addams, Jane (1860–1935) Cofundadora de Hull House, una casa de asistencia en Chicago, en 1889. Vivió y trabajó en Hull House por el resto de su vida. Pacifista y determinada defensora del sufragio femenino, Addams escribió numerosos libros e impartió conferencias. En 1931 compartió el Premio Nobel de la Paz.

administration > administración Personal del poder ejecutivo.

adobe > adobe Ladrillos hechos de tierra, agua y paja, secados al sol.

affirmative action > acción afirmativa Política que da trato especial a las mujeres y minorías para resarcirlas de la discriminación del pasado.

AFL-CIO > Federación Estadounidense del Trabajo-Congreso de Organización Industrial En 1955 dos sindicatos de trabajadores (la Federación Estadounidense del Trabajo y el Congreso de Organización Industrial) se unieron.

aggression > agresión Acción hostil o ataque no provocado.

Aguinaldo, Emilio > Aguinaldo, Emilio (1869–1964) Líder del ejército filipino que luchó por su independencia contra España en la década de 1890. Desilusionado con la presencia de los Estados Unidos en Filipinas después de la guerra, Aguinaldo ayudó a organizar una insurrección en contra del gobierno estadounidense. En 1901 fue capturado por el ejército de los Estados Unidos, terminando así la lucha filipina por su independencia.

al Qaeda > al Qaeda Grupo terrorista establecido por Osama bin Laden para eliminar la influencia occidental en los países musulmanes.

Alamo > El Álamo Antigua misión fortificada en San Antonio que fue el sitio de la derrota de 1836 y la matanza de tejanos a manos de tropas mexicanas.

Albany Plan of Union > Plan de Unión de Albany Propuesta de Benjamin Franklin en 1754 de crear un gobierno para un grupo de las colonias inglesas de América del Norte.

Alger, Horatio > Alger, Horatio (1832–1899) Escritor estadounidense que vendió más de 20 millones de ejemplares de novelas que exploraban el tema de harapos a riquezas. Alger creó personajes que lograban fama y riqueza mediante el trabajo duro y la determinación.

Alien and Sedition Acts > Leyes de Extranjeros y de Sedición Leyes de 1798 que permitieron al gobierno arrestar o deportar a inmigrantes no naturalizados, conocidos como extranjeros, así como perseguir a aquellos ciudadanos que criticaran al gobierno.

Alliance for Progress > Alianza para el Progreso Programa del presidente Kennedy que daba asistencia económica a América Latina.

Allies > Aliados Grupo de países encabezado por Gran Bretaña, Francia, los Estados Unidos y la Unión Soviética, que peleó contra los Poderes del Eje en la Segunda Guerra Mundial.

Alsace-Lorraine > Alsacia-Lorena Territorio de Francia perdido ante Alemania en 1871.

American Expeditionary Forces (AEF) > Fuerzas Expedicionarias Estadounidenses Ejército estadounidense durante la Primera Guerra Mundial.

American Federation of Labor (AFL) > Federación Estadounidense del Trabajo Sindicato que organizó a los trabajadores calificados en oficios específicos e hizo pequeñas demandas en lugar de buscar cambios amplios.

American Indian Citizenship Act of 1924 > Ley de Ciudadanía Indígena de 1924 Ciudadanía otorgada a todos los nativos americanos nacidos dentro de los límites territoriales de los Estados Unidos.

American Indian Movement (AIM) > Movimiento de Indígenas Estadounidenses Grupo que se concentró en ayudar a los indígenas, incluyendo velar por sus derechos legales, su tierra y sus derechos de autodeterminación.

American System > sistema americano Programa federal de Henry Clay diseñado para estimular la economía con mejoras internas y para crear una nación autosuficiente.

Americanization > americanización Creencia que sostenía que la asimilación de los inmigrantes por la sociedad estadounidense los haría ciudadanos más leales.

amnesty > amnistía Perdón general a ciertos delitos.

Anaconda Plan > Plan Anaconda Estrategia del Norte durante la Guerra Civil con la que se pretendía causar la hambruna en el Sur, bloqueando los puertos marítimos y controlando el río Mississippi.

Angel Island > Isla Ángel Estación de procesamiento de inmigrantes que abrió sus puertas en la bahía de San Francisco en 1910.

Anschluss > Anschluss Unión de Alemania y Austria en 1933.

Anthony, Susan B. > Anthony, Susan B. (1820–1906) Activista de los derechos de la mujer que trabajó para ganar el derecho al voto de las mujeres.

Anti-Defamation League > Liga Antidifamación Organización formada en 1913 para defender a los judíos contra los ataques físicos y verbales así como las falsas declaraciones.

anti-Semitic > antisemítico Mostrar prejuicio y discriminación contra las personas judías.

anti-Semitism > antisemitismo Odio y discriminación contra las personas judías.

Antifederalists > antifederalistas Aquellos que se oponían a la ratificación de la Constitución.

apartheid > *apartheid* Sistema político de segregación intransigente basada en la raza, en Sudáfrica.

appeasement > apaciguamiento Política de otorgar concesiones a fin de mantener la paz.

Armstrong, Louis > Armstrong, Louis (1901–1971) Trompetista y uno de los artistas más influyentes en la historia del jazz. También fue el director de una banda, cantante y comediante.

Articles of Confederation > Artículos de la Confederación Constitución federal original preparada por el Congreso Continental en 1777.

assembly lines > línea de montaje Organización de equipos y trabajadores en la que el trabajo pasa de una operación a otra en una línea directa hasta que el producto queda ensamblado.

assimilated > asimilado Ser absorbido por la cultura dominante de una sociedad.

Atlantic Charter > Carta del Atlántico Acuerdo firmado por Gran Bretaña y los Estados Unidos que respaldaba determinados principios para construir una paz duradera y establecer gobiernos libres en el mundo.

Austin, Stephen F. > Austin, Stephen F. (1793–1836) Heredó la tierra que el gobierno mexicano otorgó a su padre y eventualmente ayudó a fundar asentamientos estadounidenses clave en Texas, cuando ese territorio aún formaba parte de México. Fue una figura influyente cuando México y los Estados Unidos lucharon por el control de Texas. También trabajó para proteger los intereses de los propietarios de esclavos en Texas.

autonomy > autonomía Control independiente de los propios.

Axis Powers > Poderes del Eje Grupo de países encabezado por Alemania, Italia y Japón que peleó contra los Aliados en la Segunda Guerra Mundial.

Aztecs > aztecas Pueblo indígena americano predominante en México antes de la conquista española en el siglo XVI.

B

baby boom > *baby boom* Aumento de nacimientos entre 1945 y 1964.

Bacon's Rebellion > Rebelión de Bacon Rebelión armada de 1676 que los colonos de Virginia liderados por Nathaniel Bacon llevaron a cabo contra el gobernador William Berkeley.

Baltimore, Lord > Baltimore, Barón de Título otorgado al político inglés católico romano George Calvert (c.1580–1632). Después de no poder establecer ninguna colonia en lo que actualmente es Newfoundland, Calvert logró obtener la concesión de tierras para la colonia que más tarde se convertiría en Maryland. Murió en 1632, poco antes de que se aprobara la carta de fundación de Maryland. Sin embargo, sus hijos contribuyeron a la fundación de la colonia de Maryland.

Barbary War > Guerra Berberisca Guerra entre los Estados de Berbería y los Estados Unidos.

Barton, Clara > Barton, Clara (1821–1912) Estudió para profesora pero sirvió como enfermera durante la Guerra Civil. Cambió el papel de las mujeres enfermeras al seguir a los hombres a la batalla y atender a los heridos. En 1864 fue nombrada superintendente de las enfermeras para el Ejército del James. En 1865 estableció una oficina para ayudar a localizar a los soldados perdidos en acción. En 1881 organizó la Asociación Estadounidense de la Cruz Roja, que más tarde sería la Cruz Roja Americana.

Baruch, Bernard > Baruch, Bernard (1870–1965) Director de la Junta de Industrias Bélicas durante la Primera Guerra Mundial. Fue un financiero convertido en estadista que asesoró a siete presidentes estadounidenses.

Bataan Death March > Jornada de la Muerte desde Baatan Durante la Segunda Guerra Mundial, la marcha forzada de prisioneros de guerra estadounidenses y filipinos en condiciones brutales impuestas por los militares japoneses.

Battle of Antietam > Batalla de Antietam Batalla de la Guerra Civil que ganó la Unión. Ocurrió en 1862 y en ella murieron o resultaron heridos 23,000 soldados en un día.

Battle of Coral Sea > Batalla del Mar del Coral Batalla entre aviones japoneses y estadounidenses, durante la Segunda Guerra Mundial, ocurrida en mayo de 1942 en el escenario del Pacífico.

Battle of Fallen Timbers > Batalla de Fallen Timbers Batalla ocurrida en 1794 en que tropas federales derrotaron a la Confederación Miami de indígenas norteamericanos.

Battle of Midway > Batalla de Midway Momento decisivo de la Segunda Guerra Mundial en el Pacífico, en que se detuvo el avance de los japoneses.

Battle of New Orleans > Batalla de Nueva Orleans Batalla de la Guerra de 1812 en la que los Estados Unidos derrotaron a los británicos en enero de 1815.

Battle of Princeton > Batalla de Princeton Batalla de la Guerra de Independencia ocurrida en Nueva Jersey en 1777 que ganó el Ejército Continental.

Battle of the Bulge > Campaña de las Ardenas Última ofensiva alemana en el frente occidental durante la Seguda Guerra Mundial; fue un intento infructuoso de hacer retroceder a los Aliados que dañó a Alemania al obligarla a usar más recursos de los que se podía permitir.

Battle of the Little Big Horn > Batalla del Little Big Horn Batalla de 1876 durante la cual los sioux derrotaron a las tropas del Ejército de los Estados Unidos.

Battle of Tippecanoe > Batalla de Tippecanoe Batalla de 1811 en el Territorio de Indiana entre los indígenas norteamericanos y las tropas de los Estados Unidos en la que los indígenas resultaron derrotados.

Battle of Trenton > Batalla de Trenton Batalla de la Guerra de Independencia ocurrida en Nueva Jersey en 1776 que ganó el Ejército Continental.

Bay of Pigs invasion > Invasión de la Bahía de Cochinos Invasión de 1961 por exilados cubanos encabezados por la CIA que fracasaron al tratar de invadir Cuba.

Beatles > los Beatles Grupo inglés de rock and roll formado por John Lennon, Paul McCartney, George Harrison y Ringo Starr. De 1962 a 1970, la composición y la experimentación musical de los Beatles ampliaron considerablemente el ámbito de la música rock.

beatniks > beatniks Pequeño grupo de escritores y artistas, en la década de 1950 y principios de los 1960, que criticaban a la sociedad estadounidense.

Benavidez, Roy P. > Benavidez, Roy P. (1935–1998) Nació en Cuero, Texas, pero creció en El Campo, donde fue criado por sus tíos después de la muerte de sus padres. Se unió al ejército a los 19 años de edad y finalmente fue a Vietnam en 1965. Benavidez fue recompensado con la Medalla de Honor (en 1981) por su valor estando herido durante una misión de rescate en Camboya en 1968.

Berlin airlift > puente aéreo de Berlín Programa en el que pilotos estadounidenses y británicos volaban llevando suministros a Berlín Occidental durante un bloqueo soviético.

Berlin Wall > Muro de Berlín Pared divisoria construida por Alemania Oriental en 1961 para aislar a Berlín Occidental de Berlín Oriental, que era controlado por los comunistas.

Bessemer process > proceso Bessemer Método desarrollado a mediados del siglo XIX para fabricar más eficientemente el acero.

Bethune, Mary McLeod > Bethune, Mary McLeod (1875–1955) Educadora estadounidense que sirvió como asesora especial para asuntos de las minorías para el presidente Franklin D. Roosevelt, además de ser activa en otras organizaciones de reformas.

bicameral legislature > legislatura bicameral Cuerpo legislativo formado por dos cámaras.

Biden, Joseph R. > Biden, Joseph R. (1942–) Joe Biden se convirtió en el 46to. presidente de los Estados Unidos en 2021. A los 77 años, fue el presidente de más edad en ser elegido para el cargo. Antes de ser presidente, fue vicepresidente durante el gobierno de Barack Obama de 2009 a 2017. También fue senador de los Estados Unidos por Delaware durante 36 años.

"big stick" diplomacy > "diplomacia del garrote" Política seguida por Theodore Roosevelt según la cual se organizaría y usaría, cuando fuera necesario, una fuerza militar poderosa para lograr los objetivos de los Estados Unidos.

bilingual education > educación bilingüe Sistema en el que se enseña a los estudiantes en su idioma nativo así como en inglés.

Bill of Rights > Carta de Derechos Primeras diez enmiendas de la Constitución, las cuales protegen las libertades que el gobierno garantiza a los ciudadanos.

biotechnology > biotecnología Aplicación de la tecnología para resolver problemas que afectan a los organismos vivos.

Black Cabinet > Gabinete Negro Grupo de líderes afroamericanos que fungieron como consejeros extraoficiales de Franklin D. Roosevelt.

Black Codes > códigos negros Leyes que limitaron los derechos y oportunidades de los afroamericanos.

Black Panthers > Panteras Negras Organización de militantes afroamericanos fundada en 1966.

Black Power > poder negro Movimiento de la década de 1960 que exhortó a los afroamericanos a usar su poder político y económico colectivo para lograr la igualdad.

Black Tuesday > Martes Negro El 29 de octubre de 1929, los precios de las acciones cayeron precipitadamente en la Gran Caída de la Bolsa.

blacklist > lista negra Lista de personas que no fueron contratadas por ser sospechosas de tener vínculos comunistas.

Bleeding Kansas > *Bleeding Kansas* Término usado para describir la violencia entre partidarios en favor y en contra de la esclavitud en Kansas de 1854 a 1856.

blitzkrieg > blitzkrieg "Guerra relámpago" que enfatizaba el uso de la velocidad y la capacidad bélica para penetrar muy adentro en el territorio enemigo.

blockade > bloqueo Táctica militar en la que una fuerza naval evita que los buques entren o salgan de los puertos enemigos.

Bloomer, Amelia > Bloomer, Amelia (1818–1894) Influyente reformista estadounidense de los movimientos por la templanza y los derechos de las mujeres. En 1849 fundó *The Lily: A Ladies Journal Devoted to Temperance and Literature,* la cual usó para promover sus posturas sobre las reformas a la templanza y a los derechos de las mujeres. También es conocida por promover el derecho de las mujeres a llevar pantalones en lugar de vestidos. Los pantalones que usaba en público se conocieron como *bloomers*.

boat people > balseros Refugiados que huían de sus naciones del sureste de Asia en botes durante la década de 1970

bond > bono Certificado comprado al gobierno que promete al titular pagar con intereses el monto de la compra en una fecha posterior.

Bonus Army > Ejército del Bono Grupo de veteranos de la Primera Guerra Mundial que marcharon en Washington, D.C. en 1932, para exigir el pago anticipado de un bono que les prometiera el Congreso por sus servicios militares.

Booth, John Wilkes > Booth, John Wilkes (1838–1865) Actor estadounidense y simpatizante confederado que disparó y mató al presidente Abraham Lincoln el 14 de abril de 1865. Once días después de asesinar a Lincoln, Booth murió en una granja de Virginia.

Bootlegger > contrabandista Quien vende alcohol ilegalmente.

border state > estado fronterizo Durante la Guerra Civil, estados donde se toleraba la esclavitud pero siguieron formando parte de la Unión: Delaware, Kentucky, Maryland y Missouri.

Boston Massacre > Masacre de Boston Incidente del 5 de marzo de 1770, durante el cual soldados británicos mataron a cinco colonos en Boston.

Boston Tea Party > Motín del Té de Boston Protesta del 16 de diciembre de 1773 contra los impuestos británicos en la cual los manifestantes de Boston lanzaron té en el puerto.

Boxer Rebellion > Rebelión Bóxer Actos de violencia iniciados por miembros de una sociedad secreta en China, que provocó que los gobiernos de Europa y los Estados Unidos enviaran tropas para sofocar la rebelión.

bracero program > programa de braceros Plan que trajo trabajadores de México a trabajar en granjas estadounidenses.

Braddock, General Edward > Braddock, General Edward (1695–1755) General que sirvió como comandante británico en Norteamérica durante la Guerra contra la Alianza Franco-Indígena. En 1754, llegó a Virginia para liderar el ejército británico en el continente. Murió durante un intento de asalto al Fuerte Duquesne, donde su ejército fue derrotado.

Bradley, Omar > Bradley, Omar (1893–1981) Oficial del ejército de los Estados Unidos que en la Primera Guerra Mundial dirigió las tropas aliadas en el norte de África, llevándolas a la victoria en la campaña. Luego dirigió a sus ejércitos a la invasión de Sicilia y ayudó a planear la invasión de Normandía. Desde la invasión de Normandía hasta el fin de la guerra, Bradley dirigió a las numerosas fuerzas terrestres de los Estados Unidos en el ataque a Alemania desde el oeste, más de un millón de hombres en total. Después de la Segunda Guerra Mundial, fue jefe de Estado Mayor de las Fuerzas Armadas y el primer presidente del Estado Mayor Conjunto de los Estados Unidos.

Brady Bill > Ley Brady Ley aprobada en 1993 que exige un período de espera para la venta de revólveres, junto con una verificación de los antecedentes delictivos del comprador.

Brady, Mathew > Brady, Mathew (c.1823–1896) Fotógrafo y periodista estadounidense conocido por su documentación fotográfica de la Guerra Civil.

bread line > cola de alimentación Fila de personas que esperan alimentos gratuitos de obras caritativas o agencias públicas.

Breckinridge, John C. > Breckinridge, John C. (1821–1875) Estadista de Kentucky que sirvió como Vicepresidente bajo el presidente James Buchanan; ganó la nominación presidencial del Partido Demócrata del sur en 1860.

brinkmanship > brinkmanship Creencia según la cual sólo estando al borde de la guerra los Estados Unidos podían protegerse contra la agresión comunista.

Brown, John > Brown, John (1800–1859) Abolicionista que atacó el arsenal federal en Harpers Ferry con la esperanza de comenzar una rebelión de los esclavos.

Bryan, William Jennings > Bryan, William Jennings (1860–1925) Líder demócrata y populista que se postuló sin éxito tres veces para la presidencia de los Estados Unidos. Durante su carrera profesional como abogado, político y orador, luchó a favor de las reformas como el impuesto sobre la renta, la prohibición y el sufragio femenino.

budget deficit > déficit presupuestario Faltante entre la cantidad de dinero gastado y la cantidad de dinero captado por el gobierno federal.

bull market > mercado alcista Período durante el cual suben los precios de las acciones.

bureaucracy > burocracia Grupo de departamentos y funcionarios que conforman una organización, como por ejemplo, un gobierno.

Burr, Aaron > Burr, Aaron (1756–1836) Tercer vicepresidente de los Estados Unidos. Molesto por los comentarios de Alexander Hamilton, Burr lo retó a un duelo en 1804, durante el cual Hamilton murió.

Bush, George W. > Bush, George W. (1946–) Hombre de negocios y gobernador de Texas de 1995 a 2000 antes de ser electo el 43° Presidente de los Estados Unidos. Bush, hijo del presidente George H.W. Bush, dirigió a los Estados Unidos durante los ataques terroristas del 11 de septiembre de 2001 y los primeros años de las guerras en Afganistán e Irak. Bush fue electo para un segundo periodo en 2004, terminando su presidencia cuando la industria financiera mundial estaba al borde del colapso a finales de 2008.

business cycle > ciclo económico Crecimiento y contracción periódicos de la economía.

buying on margin > comprar por margen Sistema de compra de acciones en el que el comprador paga un pequeño porcentaje del precio de compra mientras que el corredor anticipa el resto.

C

Cabinet > gabinete Jefes de los departamentos ejecutivos que se reúnen en grupo para aconsejar al presidente.

Cabot, John > Cabot, John (1450?–1499?) Explorador italiano que fue contratado por Enrique VII de Inglaterra para explorar territorios desconocidos de las Américas. En 1497 navegó hacia el oeste, cruzando el océano Atlántico, y llegando a Newfoundland, lo que actualmente es Canadá. Sus viajes contribuyeron al eventual establecimiento de las colonias británicas en Norteamérica.

Cabral, Pedro Alvarez > Cabral, Pedro Alvarez (1467?–1520) Navegante portugués a quien por lo general se le acredita ser el primer europeo que en 1500 llegó a lo que actualmente es Brasil.

Calhoun, John C. > Calhoun, John C. (1782–1850) Importante político estadounidense que ocupó el cargo de vicepresidente de los Estados Unidos, secretario de la Guerra, secretario de Estado y también ocupó un puesto en ambas cámaras del Congreso. Fue un destacado defensor de los derechos de los estados y partidario de la esclavitud. Su apoyo y esfuerzo a favor de establecer el segundo Banco de los Estados Unidos, un sistema permanente de carreteras, un ejército destacado y una marina moderna hicieron de él uno de los partidarios más influyentes del nacionalismo estadounidense.

California Gold Rush > fiebre del oro de California Migración masiva a California después que se descubriera oro en 1848.

California Master Plan > Plan Maestro de California Plan que llamaba a la creación de tres niveles de educación superior: universidades de investigación, universidades estatales y centros educacionales comunitarios, los cuales deberían ser accesibles para todos los ciudadanos del estado.

Camp David Accords > Acuerdos de Camp David Acuerdo de 1978 negociado por el presidente Jimmy Carter entre los lideres de Egipto e Israel, el cual hizo posible un tratado de paz entre ambas naciones.

capital > capital Dinero o bienes que se usan para invertir en negocios o empresas.

Capra, Frank > Capra, Frank (1897–1991) Director de cine estadounidense mejor conocido por su trabajo durante las décadas de 1930 y 1940, el cual le valió tres Premios de la Academia.

Carnegie, Andrew > Carnegie, Andrew (1835–1919) Industrial y filántropo estadounidense que comenzó la Carnegie Steel, una corporación que dominó la industria acerera de los Estados Unidos. Creó organizaciones de beneficiencia y dio dinero a instituciones culturales y educativas.

carpetbagger > *carpetbagger* Sobrenombre despectivo dado a los norteños que se mudaron al Sur después de la Guerra Civil.

Carson, Rachel > Carson, Rachel (1907–1964) Bióloga estadounidense mejor conocida por escribir *Silent Spring* y una serie de obras sobre la contaminación ambiental y la historia de los océanos. Carson trabajó como científica y escritora para el gobierno de los Estados Unidos antes de dedicarse todo el tiempo a escribir.

cartel > cártel Asociación de productores de un bien o servicio que coordina los precios y la producción.

Carter, Jimmy > Carter, Jimmy (1924–) Gobernador de Georgia de 1970 a 1974. En 1976, derrotó a Gerald R. Ford en la lucha por la presidencia. Después de perder la presidencia ante Ronald Reagan en 1980, Carter se dedicó a cuestiones nacionales e internacionales y a la defensa de la democracia y los derechos humanos.

cash crop > cultivo comercial Cosecha cultivada para la venta.

Castro, Fidel > Castro, Fidel (1926–2016) Ayudó a derrocar al gobierno cubano en 1959 y dirigió al país desde entonces hasta 2008. Su gobierno y sus alianzas comunistas con la Unión Soviética fueron una fuente de conflicto entre Cuba y los Estados Unidos.

casualty > baja Soldado muerto, herido o desaparecido.

Catt, Carrie Chapman > Catt, Carrie Chapman (1859–1947) Educadora antes de involucrarse en el movimiento sufragista femenino en 1887. En 1890, se unió a la Asociación Nacional Americana para el Sufragio Femenino (NAWSA, por sus siglas en inglés). Llegó a ser su presidenta en 1900 y dirigió la organización casi sin interrupciones hasta su muerte.

caucus > asamblea partidaria Reunión cerrada de los miembros de un partido con el propósito de elegir un candidato.

Central Intelligence Agency (CIA) > Agencia Central de Inteligencia Organización estadounidense para la recolección de inteligencia.

Chamberlain, Neville > Chamberlain, Neville Primer ministro de Gran Bretaña de 1937 a 1940. En un esfuerzo por evitar la guerra, firmó el Pacto de Munich con Alemania, dando a Hitler el control de los Sudetes, una parte de Checoslovaquia. El acuerdo se convirtió en un símbolo infame del fracaso del apaciguamiento.

Champlain, Samuel de > Champlain, Samuel de (1567–1635) Explorador francés y fundador de la ciudad de Quebec. Descubrió el lago que lleva su nombre. También exploró la costa sur del océano Atlántico hacia la bahía de Massachusetts y más allá.

Chaplin, Charlie > Chaplin, Charlie (1889–1977) Comediante británico que produjo, escribió y dirigió muchas películas durante su carrera. Muchos le consideran el mejor artista cómico en la historia del cine.

charter > carta Documento legal que confiere determinados derechos a una persona o compañía.

Chávez, César > Chávez, César (1927–1993) Pasó su niñez trabajando duro como obrero agrícola, igual que sus padres. Ya de adulto, estableció la Asociación Nacional de los Trabajadores Agrícolas (NFWA, por sus siglas en inglés) en 1962. Chávez lideró varias manifestaciones no violentas de alto perfil que generalmente terminaron con mejores condiciones para los trabajadores.

checks and balances > sistema de controles y equilibrios Sistema en que cada poder del gobierno tiene la facultad para vigilar y limitar las acciones de los otros dos.

Chicano movement > Movimiento Chicano Movimiento para promover la cultura y los problemas políticos de los mexicoamericanos.

Chinese Exclusion Act > Ley de Exclusión China Ley de 1882 que prohibía la inmigración de trabajadores chinos.

cholera > cólera Grave infección bacteriana del intestino delgado que causa deshidratación, provocada generalmente por beber agua contaminada.

Christian fundamentalist > fundamentalista cristiano Persona cristiana que cree en la interpretación estricta y literal de la Biblia como el fundamento de la fe cristiana.

Churchill, Winston > Churchill, Winston (1874–1965) Primer ministro de Gran Bretaña de 1940 a 1945, Churchill inspiró a los británicos durante la Segunda Guerra Mundial. Después de la guerra no fue reelegido. Sin embargo, reasumió el cargo entre 1951 y 1955. Se opuso enérgicamente a la expansión del comunismo soviético, argumentando que todas las naciones bajo el comunismo se encontraban detrás de la "Cortina de Hierro".

Civil Rights Act of 1866 > Ley de los Derechos Civiles de 1866 Ley que estableció las garantías federales a los derechos civiles de todos los ciudadanos.

Civil Rights Act of 1875 > Ley de los Derechos Civiles de 1875 Ley que prohibió la discriminación en lugares y transporte públicos.

Civil Rights Act of 1957 > Ley de los Derechos Civiles de 1957 Ley que estableció una Comisión Federal de Derechos Civiles.

Civil Rights Act of 1964 > Ley de los Derechos Civiles de 1964 Ley que prohibió la discriminación en lugares y empleos públicos con base en la raza, religión o nacionalidad.

civil service > servicio civil Departamentos gubernamentales y sus empleados que no son de elección popular.

Civilian Conservation Corps (CCC) > Cuerpo Civil de Conservación (CCC) Programa del Nuevo Trato que proporcionaba ayuda a los jóvenes con trabajo en proyectos de conservación del medio ambiente, incluyendo reforestación y control de inundaciones.

Clay, Henry > Clay, Henry (1777–1852) Político estadounidense electo para la Cámara de Representantes y el Senado de los Estados Unidos por el estado de Kentucky. Fue un líder partidario del nacionalismo económico, promoviendo el apoyo federal para mejoras internas, un arancel proteccionista y un banco nacional. En 1820 ayudó a llevar a cabo el Acuerdo de Missouri para tratar de equilibrar los derechos de los estados libres y esclavistas.

Clayton Antitrust Act > Ley Clayton Antimonopolio Ley de 1914 que fortalecía la Ley Sherman Antimonopolio.

Clean Air Act > Ley para el Aire Puro Ley aprobada en 1970 que buscaba disminuir la contaminación del aire al limitar las emisiones de fábricas y automóviles.

Clean Water Act > Ley para el Agua Limpia Ley aprobada en 1973 que buscaba restringir la contaminación industrial y agrícola del agua.

Clinton, Hillary > Clinton, Hillary (1947–) Exitosa e influyente abogada y defensora de los niños y las familias antes de convertirse en Primera Dama de los Estados Unidos en 1992. Desempeñó un papel activo en la administración de Bill Clinton, liderando un grupo de trabajo para investigar cómo garantizar servicios médicos a todos los estadounidenses. En 2000, ganó un escaño en el Senado para el Estado de Nueva York. Trató de ganar la nominación presidencial demócrata en 2008, pero no lo logró; fue nombrada secretaria de Estado por el presidente Obama ese año. Dimitió del cargo en 2013.

Clinton, William Jefferson > Clinton, William Jefferson (1946–) El 42° Presidente de los Estados Unidos en 1993 a la edad de 46 años, el primer presidente *boomer*. Fue reelecto para un segundo mandato en 1996. Dos años más tarde fue enjuiciado políticamente por la Cámara de Representantes pero fue absuelto por el Senado en 1999. Clinton presidió el periodo más largo de expansión económica en tiempos de paz en la historia de los Estados Unidos, lo que incluía un presupuesto equilibrado y un excedente federal.

Cold War > Guerra Fría Rivalidad mundial entre los Estados Unidos y la Unión Soviética.

collective bargaining > negociación colectiva Proceso en el que los patronos negocian con los sindicatos sobre los horarios, salarios y otras condiciones de trabajo.

Columbian Exchange > intercambio colombino Intercambio global de bienes e ideas entre Europa, África y las Américas posterior al primer viaje transatlántico de Colón en 1492.

Columbus, Christopher > Colón, Cristóbal (1451–1506) Nació en la ciudad portuaria de Génova, Italia. Comenzó su vida de marinero a la edad de 14 años. Fue a Portugal para aprender a navegar y se instaló allí con su hermano Juan. Colón consiguió el apoyo de los reyes de España, Fernando II e Isabel I, y realizó cuatro viajes a través del océano Atlántico hacia las Américas. Sus expediciones hicieron que los europeos conocieran la existencia del continente americano e inició la colonización española de las Américas.

Committee on Public Information (CPI) > Comité de Información Pública Organización creada por el gobierno durante la Primera Guerra Mundial para animar al público estadounidense a apoyar la guerra.

committees of correspondence > comités de correspondencia Redes de grupos locales que informaban a los colonos de las medidas británicas y de la oposición a ellas durante los años anteriores a la Guerra de Independencia.

communes > comunas Pequeñas comunidades donde personas con intereses comunes viven y comparten los recursos.

Community Reinvestment Act > Ley de Reinversión en la Comunidad Ley de 1977 que requiere que los bancos, y especialmente aquellos que operan en barrios de bajos y medios ingresos, presten una parte de sus depósitos a los residentes de esos barrios.

company towns > pueblos de compañía Comunidades cuyos residentes dependen de una compañía para obtener empleo, vivienda y compras.

Compromise of 1850 > Acuerdo de 1850 Acuerdo político que permitió la admisión de California a la Unión como estado libre al permitir la soberanía popular en los territorios y aplicar una ley más estricta a los esclavos fugitivos.

Compromise of 1877 > Acuerdo de 1877 Acuerdo por el cual Rutherford B. Hayes ganó las elecciones presidenciales de 1876 y a cambio aceptó retirar las tropas federales que permanecían en el Sur.

concentration camps > campos de concentración Campos usados por los nazis para encarcelar a miembros "indeseables" de la sociedad.

Confederate States of America > Estados Confederados de América Gobierno de 11 estados sureños que se separó de los Estados Unidos y peleó contra la Unión en la Guerra Civil.

Congress of Industrial Organizations (CIO) > Congreso de Organización Industrial Organización de trabajadores fundada en la década de 1930 que representó a sindicatos industriales de mano de obra no especializada.

conquistadors > conquistador Explorador español que se apropiaba de territorios en las Américas para España.

conscientious objector > objetor de conciencia Persona que rehúsa pelear en una guerra por convicciones morales o religiosas.

conscription > conscripción Llamado a filas de ciudadanos para cumplir el servicio militar.

conservative > conservador Que tiende a apoyar una participación gubernamental limitada en la economía, ayuda comunitaria para los necesitados, y mantiene los valores tradicionales.

conspicuous consumerism > consumismo desenfrenado Compra de bienes y servicios para efectos de impresionar a los demás.

consumer revolution > revolución consumista Flujo de bienes nuevos y asequibles durante las decadas posteriores a la Primera Guerra Mundial.

consumerism > consumismo Compras a gran escala, la mayoría de éstas a crédito.

containment > contención Política de mantener el comunismo contenido dentro de sus fronteras existentes.

Continental Army > Ejército Continental Ejército de las colonias durante la Guerra de Independencia.

contraband > contrabando Mercancías prohibidas por ley o tratado para ser importadas o exportadas; durante la Guerra Civil, el término fue utilizado para referirse a los esclavos afroamericanos que escaparon tras las líneas del Norte antes de la Proclamación de Emancipación.

Contract With America > Contrato con los Estados Unidos Plan republicano encabezado por Newt Gingrich enfocado en la reducción del gobierno, el equilibrio del presupuesto y la reducción de los impuestos.

Contras > Contras Contrarrevolucionarios anticomunistas opuestos al gobierno Sandinista de Nicaragua en la década de 1980.

convoy > convoy Grupo de buques mercantes que navegan juntos bajo la protección de buques de guerra.

Coolidge, Calvin > Coolidge, Calvin (1872–1933) Presidente de los Estados Unidos de 1923 a 1929. Accedió al cargo después de la muerte de Warren Harding y continuó muchas de las políticas a favor de las empresas de su predecesor.

Copperhead > cabeza de cobre Término negativo o despectivo con el que se denominaba a los demócratas del Norte que tenían una postura antibélica durante la Guerra Civil.

Cornwallis, Charles > Cornwallis, Charles (1738–1805) General que luchó en la Guerra de los Siete Años en Europa antes de ser enviado a combatir al Ejército Continental durante la Guerra de Independencia. Obtuvo victorias clave en Nueva Jersey y Carolina del Sur, pero en 1781 fue atrapado con su ejército en Yorktown, donde se rindió al general Washington.

corporation > corporación Compañía reconocida como entidad legal con derechos y responsabilidades separados de los de cada uno de sus miembros.

Cortés, Hernán > Cortés, Hernán (1485–1547) Dirigió el ejército de conquistadores españoles que derrocó al Imperio Azteca y puso a México bajo el control de España. Abogado de formación, Cortés dejó España en 1504 para establecerse en Cuba, donde se enriqueció al adquirir plantaciones y minas de oro. Hábil militar, diplomático astuto y cruel, pudo derrocar al gobierno azteca en su capital de Tenochtitlán a pesar de ser superados en números.

cotton gin > desmotadora de algodón Máquina inventada en 1793 para separar la fibra del algodón de la cáscara.

Coughlin, Charles > Coughlin, Charles (1891–1979) Sirvió como pastor de la Iglesia católica en Michigan de 1926 a 1966. Ganó una enorme audiencia en la década de 1930 por sus programas de radio, primero apoyando el Nuevo Trato del presidente Roosevelt y más tarde oponiéndose a él cuando adoptó puntos de vista ultraconservadores. Coughlin se opuso con ímpetu a la entrada de los Estados Unidos en la Segunda Guerra Mundial y en 1942, después de que comenzara a hacer observaciones antisemitas, las autoridades católicas le ordenaron detener sus emisiones.

counterculture > contracultura Movimiento que mantuvo valores diferentes a los de la cultura tradicional.

coureurs de bois > *coureur de bois* Término francés para "corredor de los bosques" que designa a los colonos franceses habitantes de los bosques que comerciaban con pieles.

court packing > reorganización de la Corte Plan del presidente Franklin D. Roosevelt para agregar seis nuevos magistrados a los nueve miembros de la Corte Suprema luego de que la Corte dictaminó que algunas leyes del Nuevo Trato eran inconstitucionales.

credibility gap > brecha de credibilidad Creciente desconfianza del público estadounidense ante declaraciones del gobierno durante la Guerra de Vietnam.

creditor nation > país acreedor País al que otros países le deben más dinero del que éste les debe.

Creel, George > Creel, George (1876–1953) Periodista que sirvió como jefe del Comité de Información Pública durante la Primera Guerra Mundial. Ocupó otros cargos en el gobierno federal. También fue escritor. Uno de sus libros fue *How We Advertised America*.

Crittenden Compromise > Resolución de Crittenden Enmienda constitucional propuesta en 1861 para intentar evitar la secesión de los estados del Sur al proponer que se permitiera la esclavitud en todos los territorios al sur de la línea del Acuerdo de Missouri.

Cuban missile crisis > crisis de los misiles de Cuba Conflicto entre los Estados Unidos y la Unión Soviética en 1962 como resultado de la instalación de misiles nucleares en Cuba por parte de los soviéticos.

D

Da Gama, Vasco > Da Gama, Vasco (1460?–1524) Navegante portugués cuyos tres viajes a la India alrededor del cabo de Buena Esperanza abrieron la ruta marítima desde Europa occidental hasta el Este. Murió en la India poco después de llegar allí en su tercer viaje.

dame school > escuela de dama Escuela primaria en la época colonial, a menudo con sede en la casa de una mujer.

Darrow, Clarence > Darrow, Clarence (1857–1938) Abogado cuyo trabajo como consejero de defensa en muchos juicios le aseguraron su lugar en la historia del derecho. Es muy conocido por su defensa de John Scopes en 1925.

Davis, Jefferson > Davis, Jefferson (1808–1889) Hacendado sureño que llegó a ser el presidente de los Estados Confederados de América. Nació en Kentucky y creció en una plantación en Mississippi. Asistió a la Academia Militar de West Point y también sirvió en la Guerra de Halcón Negro y en la Guerra México-Estadounidense. Aunque se oponía a la secesión, renunció a su cargo en el Senado de los Estados Unidos cuando Mississippi se separó. Fue elegido presidente de la Confederación en la Convención Confederada, e inaugurado en el cargo el 18 de febrero de 1861.

Dawes General Allotment Act > Ley de Asignación General Dawes Ley de 1887 que dividió las tierras de las reservaciones en parcelas familiares privadas.

Dawes Plan > Plan Dawes Acuerdo en el que los Estados Unidos prestó dinero a Alemania, permitiéndole a ésta hacer pagos de reparación a Gran Bretaña y Francia.

de facto segregation > segregación de facto Segregación basada en la costumbre o la tradición no escrita.

de jure segregation > segregación de iure Segregación impuesta por la ley.

death camps > campos de la muerte Campos diseñados por los nazis para el exterminio de prisioneros.

Debs, Eugene V. > Debs, Eugene V. (1855–1926) Líder organizador y social que defendió los derechos de los trabajadores de los ferrocarriles. Se postuló cinco veces entre 1900 y 1920 como candidato por el Partido Socialista.

Declaration of Independence > Declaración de Independencia Documento redactado por el Segundo Congreso Continental y aprobado en 1776, que anunció la independencia de los Estados Unidos y explicaba las razones para la misma.

Deferred Action for Childhood Arrivals (DACA) > Acción diferida para los llegados en la infancia Orden ejecutiva del presidente Obama que permitía estar exentos de ser deportados y obtener permisos de trabajo renovables cada dos años a algunos inmigrantes indocumentados que habían entrado al país antes de cumplir 16 años y antes de junio de 2007.

deficit spending > déficit de gastos Práctica gubernamental de gastar más de lo que se recibe a través de los impuestos recaudados.

demobilization > desmovilización Enviar a los miembros del ejército de vuelta a casa.

Democratic Republicans > Republicanos democráticos Miembros del Partido Republicano Democrático, uno de los primeros partidos políticos de los Estados Unidos, dirigido por Jefferson y Madison. También eran conocidos como los republicanos.

Demographics > Demografía Estadísticas que muestran las características humanas de una población.

Department of Homeland Security > Departamento de Seguridad Nacional Departamento a nivel de gabinete creado por el presidente Bush para coordinar los esfuerzos de seguridad interior.

deregulation > desregulación Reducción o eliminación de los controles gubernamentales en una industria, basada en la creencia de que más libertad conduce a mayor éxito y rentabilidad.

détente > distensión Diplomacia flexible adoptada por el presidente Richard Nixon para aliviar las tensiones entre los Estados Unidos, la Unión Soviética y la República Popular China.

developing world > mundo en vías de desarrollo Países con menor avance económico que los países desarrollados, como los Estados Unidos o los de Europa occidental.

Dewey, George > Dewey, George (1837–1917) Oficial de la Marina estadounidense que dirigió la flota que derrotó a los españoles en la batalla de la Bahía de Manila durante la Guerra Hispano-Estadounidense. En 1899, el Congreso promovió a Dewey al rango de admirante de la Marina, el mayor rango al que puede aspirar un oficial de la Marina de los Estados Unidos.

Dias, Bartolomeu > Dias, Bartolomeu (1450?–1500) Explorador portugués que en 1488 dirigió la primera expedición marítima alrededor del cabo de Buena Esperanza en el extremo sur de África. Dias logró esta hazaña aprendiendo cómo usar los vientos y las corrientes que soplan en dirección contraria a las agujas del reloj del Atlántico Sur para rodear el sur de África. Su éxito abrió la ruta marítima a Asia a través de los océanos Atlántico e Índico. Murió en 1500 cuando su barco se perdió en el mar cerca del cabo de Buena Esperanza.

Dickinson, John > Dickinson, John (1732–1808) Trabajó como abogado en Filadelfia antes de participar en política y dedicarse a la causa patriota. En 1765 sirvió como representante de Pennsylvania en el Congreso de la Ley del Timbre y escribió su declaración de derechos y reclamaciones. Más tarde, ocupó el cargo de delegado en el Congreso Continental. Entre 1776 y 1777 ayudó a redactar los Artículos de la Confederación. En 1787 sirvió como delegado de Delaware en la convención constitucional para revisar los artículos.

direct primary > elección primaria Elecciones en las que los ciudadanos votan directamente para elegir los candidatos para las siguientes elecciones.

divest > desposeer Quitarse o librarse de algo.

Dix, Dorothea > Dix, Dorothea (1802–1887) Reformadora estadounidense que hizo campaña durante 40 años para lograr un tratamiento mejor y más humano para las personas con enfermedades mentales. Ayudó a establecer hospitales mentales estatales en 15 estados y Canadá, e incluso difundió sus ideas en Europa. También trabajó para mejorar las prisiones, favoreciendo el Sistema de Penitenciarías de Pennsylvania.

Dole, Sanford B. > Dole, Sanford B. (1844–1926) Desempeñó un papel importante en el derrocamiento de la monarquía hawaiana. Después del derrocamiento, Dole fue electo presidente del Gobierno Provisional. Pidió al gobierno estadounidense que se anexaran las islas de Hawái. En 1898, Hawái pasó a ser territorio de los Estados Unidos siendo Dole su primer gobernador.

dollar diplomacy > diplomacia del dólar Política del presidente Taft de expandir las inversiones estadounidenses en el exterior.

domino theory > efecto dominó Idea de que si una nación cae en el comunismo, sus vecinos más cercanos también caerán bajo el control comunista.

Douglas, Stephen A. > Douglas, Stephen A. (1813–1861) Senador de los Estados Unidos. Apoyó con energía la expansión hacia el oeste y fue partidario de la soberanía popular sobre la cuestión de la esclavitud en los estados y territorios nuevos. Ayudó a ganar la aprobación del Acuerdo de 1850 y propuso la Ley Kansas-Nebraska en 1854. Ganó el reconocimiento nacional por su papel en los debates con Abraham Lincoln en la campaña al Senado de 1858.

Douglass, Frederick > Douglass, Frederick (1818?–1895) Nació en condición de esclavo en Maryland y escapó al Norte en 1838. En 1841, compartió de manera espontánea sus experiencias como esclavo en una convención contra la esclavitud y pronto se convirtió en orador por la causa abolicionista. Su autobiografía, *Narrative of the Life of Frederick Douglass,* fue publicada por primera vez en 1845, lo que llegó todavía a más personas. Durante la Guerra Civil, Douglass trabajó como asesor del presidente Lincoln. También prestó un fuerte apoyo al movimiento de las mujeres.

dove > paloma Persona opuesta a la participación estadounidense en la Guerra de Vietnam.

Dow, Neal > Dow, Neal (1804–1897) Llegó a ser un político y defensor influyente del movimiento por la templanza. Como alcalde de Portland, Dow trabajó para asegurar la aprobación de la Ley Maine, que restringía la venta de alcohol.

draftee > proyecto de ley Ley del Congreso que daba al gobierno la autoridad de alistar a los hombres en el ejército sin su consentimiento.

Du Bois, W.E.B. > Du Bois, W.E.B. (1868–1963) Educador reformador y defensor estadounidense de los derechos civiles. Es más conocido por su libro *The Souls of Black Folk* en el cual critica el enfoque más condescendiente de Booker T. Washington y aboga por los plenos derechos civiles para los afroamericanos. Du Bois también fundó la Asociación Nacional para el Progreso de la Gente de Color (NAACP, por sus siglas en inglés).

Dulles, John Foster > Dulles, John Foster (1888–1959) Diplomático y pensador político. Convencido anticomunista, ayudó a organizar las Naciones Unidas después de la Segunda Guerra Mundial y más tarde sirvió como secretario de Estado bajo el presidente Dwight Eisenhower. En este cargo, ayudó a formular las políticas arriesgadas y de "represalia masiva" de la Guerra Fría.

Dust Bowl > Dust Bowl Término usado para describir las Grandes Llanuras, durante la década de 1930 cuando la región quedó desolada por la sequía y las tormentas de polvo.

E

Earth Day > Día de la Tierra Evento anual de activismo y protesta ambiental, iniciado en 1970.

Economic Opportunity Act > Ley de Igualdad de Oportunidades Ley aprobada en 1964 que creó programas contra la pobreza.

Edison, Thomas > Edison, Thomas (1847–1931) Inventor estadounidense. Registró más de 1,000 patentes por inventos, entre ellos la bombilla eléctrica, una primera cámara de cine y una batería alcalina.

Eighteenth Amendment > Decimoctava Enmienda Enmienda constitucional que prohibió la fabricación, distribución y venta de alcohol en los Estados Unidos.

Einstein, Albert > Einstein, Albert (1879–1955) Físico de origen alemán, desarrolló la teoría general de la relatividad que describe los efectos de la gravedad en el universo y ganó el Premio Nobel de Física en 1921. Einstein abandonó Alemania a principios de la década de 1930, después de que los nazis atacaran su trabajo, y se estableció en los Estados Unidos, donde continuó siendo un pionero en el desarrollo de la teoría general de la relatividad. Por lo general es considerado el físico más influyente del siglo XX.

Eisenhower Doctrine > Doctrina Eisenhower Política del presidente Eisenhower que indicaba que los Estados Unidos usarían la fuerza para ayudar a cualquier nación amenazada por el comunismo.

Eisenhower, Dwight > Eisenhower, Dwight (1890–1969) Recibió el mando de todos los ejércitos estadounidenses en Europa en 1942. Después de sus rotundos éxitos en el norte de África e Italia, fue nombrado comandante supremo de las Fuerzas Aliadas. Su hábil manejo de la invasión del Día D y el avance hacia Alemania le hicieron ganar un amplio respeto. Antes de retirarse, Eisenhower fue Presidente durante dos periodos.

electoral college > colegio electoral Grupo de personas escogidas de todos los estados a fin de elegir indirectamente al presidente y vicepresidente.

Ellis Island > Isla Ellis Isla en el puerto de Nueva York que se usó como puesto de migración para millones de inmigrantes que llegaron a los Estados Unidos.

Emancipation Proclamation > Proclamación de Emancipación Decreto del 1 de enero de 1863 en el que el presidente Lincoln declaraba libres a los esclavos que vivían en los estados y en los territorios confederados aún en rebelión en contra de la Unión.

embargo > embargo Prohibición o restricción oficial del comercio.

Emerson, Ralph Waldo > Emerson, Ralph Waldo (1803–1882) Es considerado el fundador del trascendentalismo. Provenía de una larga línea de ministros y él mismo llegó a ser ministro unitario en 1829. Su ensayo "Nature" fue una declaración de las creencias del movimiento. Creía que las personas podían acercarse a Dios si trascendían del mundo material y apreciaban las bellezas de la naturaleza en lugar de seguir una religión organizada.

Endangered Species Act > Ley de Especies en Peligro de Extinción Ley aprobada en 1973 con el propósito de proteger las plantas y animales en peligro de extinción.

Enforcement Acts > Leyes de Aplicación Leyes de 1870 y 1871, también conocidas como Leyes del Ku Kux Klan, que definían como delito federal la interferencia con el derecho de un ciudadano de emitir su voto.

English Bill of Rights > Declaración de Derechos inglesa Documento firmado en 1689 que garantizaba los derechos de los ciudadanos ingleses.

Enlightenment > Ilustración Movimiento del siglo XVIII inspirado por filósofos europeos que creían que los problemas de la sociedad se podían resolver mediante la razón y la ciencia.

entrepreneur > empresario Persona que construye y administra negocios o empresas para obtener una ganancia, arriesgando a menudo su propio dinero o subsistencia.

Environmental Protection Agency (EPA) > Agencia de Protección Ambiental Agencia gubernamental comprometida con la limpieza y protección del ambiente.

Equal Pay Act > Ley de Pago Equitativo Ley aprobada en 1963 que exigía que hombres y mujeres recibieran paga igual por un trabajo igual.

Equal Rights Amendment (ERA) > Enmienda de Igualdad de Derechos Enmienda propuesta a la Constitución para garantizar la igualdad entre los sexos.

Erie Canal > Canal del Erie Canal terminado en 1825 que conectó el lago Erie con el río Hudson.

Espionage Act > Ley de Espionaje Ley aprobada por el Congreso en 1917 que establecía penas severas para cualquiera que participara en actividades desleales o de traición.

ethnic cleansing > limpieza étnica Esfuerzo sistemático para purgar una zona o sociedad de un grupo étnico mediante el asesinato o la deportación.

eugenics > eugenesia La idea de que la raza humana se puede mejorar controlando qué personas tienen hijos.

European Union (EU) > Unión Europea Unión económica y política de las naciones europeas establecida en 1993.

evangelical > evangélico Estilo de culto cuyo fin es suscitar emociones fuertes para atraer conversos.

Evers, Medgar > Evers, Medgar (1925–1963) Se convirtió en el primer secretario de campo de la Asociación Nacional para el Progreso de la Gente de Color (NAACP, por sus siglas en inglés) en Mississippi en 1954. Viajó por el estado reclutando miembros y organizó campañas de registro de votantes, manifestaciones y boicots a las compañías que practicaban la discriminación. En 1963, fue asesinado fuera de su casa en Jackson, Mississippi.

Executive Order 8802 > Orden Ejecutiva 8802 Medida durante la Segunda Guerra Mundial que garantizaba prácticas justas de empleo en cualquier puesto financiado por el gobierno.

executive privilege > privilegio ejecutivo Principio que indica que el Presidente tiene derecho a mantener en privado ciertas comunicaciones con otros miembros del poder ejecutivo.

Exodusters > Exodusters Grupo de afroamericanos que emigraron del Sur al Oeste después de la Guerra Civil.

expansionist > expansionista Persona que favorece la expansión del territorio o influencia de un país.

extractive economies > economía de extracción Economía de una colonia donde el país colonizador extraía materias primas y las enviaba a la madre patria para beneficiar su propia economía.

F

Fair Deal > Trato Justo Programa del presidente Truman para expandir las reformas del Nuevo Trato.

Fair Labor Standards Act > Ley de Normas Laborales Justas Ley de 1938 que estableció el salario mínimo, una semana laboral de un máximo de 44 horas, y prohibió el trabajo infantil.

Family Medical Leave Act > Ley de Permiso Médico Familiar Ley que garantiza a la mayoría de los empleados de tiempo completo 12 semanas laborales de permiso sin goce de sueldo cada año por razones personales o de salud familiar.

Farmers' Alliance > Alianza de Granjeros Red de organizaciones agrícolas que luchó por alcanzar reformas políticas y económicas a finales del siglo XIX.

fascism > fascismo Movimiento político que hace hincapié en el nacionalismo extremo y el gobierno autocrático.

Faubus, Orval > Faubus, Orval (1910–1994) Gobernador de Arkansas de 1954 a 1967. Es mejor conocido por ordenar a la Guardia Nacional de Arkansas que impidieran el paso de nueve estudiantes afroamericanos a la Escuela Secundaria Little Rock Central en 1957, desafiando la sentencia de una corte federal que ordenó el fin de la segregación racial en las escuelas. Sus esfuerzos fallaron cuando el presidente Eisenhower envió tropas federales para escoltar la entrada de los estudiantes a la escuela.

federal > federal nacional

Federal Art Project > Proyecto Federal de Arte División de la Administración de Progreso de Obras que contrató artistas desempleados para crear obras de arte en edificios públicos y patrocinó programas educativos y exhibiciones artísticas.

Federal Deposit Insurance Corporation (FDIC) > Corporación Federal de Seguro de Depósitos Agencia gubernamental creada durante el Nuevo Trato que asegura los depósitos bancarios, garantizando que el dinero de los depositantes estará seguro.

Federal Reserve Act > Ley de Reserva Federal Ley de 1913 que sometió a todos los bancos del país bajo el control de una Junta de Reserva Federal, que opera los bancos regionales que mantienen un fondo de reserva de los bancos comerciales, fija tasa de intereses y supervisa a los bancos comerciales.

Federal Trade Commission (FTC). > Comisión Federal de Comercio Agencia de gobierno establecida en 1914 para identificar las prácticas comerciales monopolistas, falsa propaganda y rótulos deshonestos.

federalism > federalismo Sistema político en el cual el poder se comparte entre el gobierno nacional y los gobiernos estatales.

Federalist > federalista Partidario de la ratificación de la Constitución.

Federalist, The > *Federalist, The* Serie de 85 ensayos escritos por James Madison, Alexander Hamilton y John Jay que explicaban y defendían la Constitución.

feminism > feminismo Teoría que las mujeres y los hombres deben tener igualdad política, social y económica.

Ferdinand, Franz > Fernando, Francisco (1863–1914) Archiduque y heredero al trono de Austria-Hungría. Su asesinato en Sarajevo fue una causa inmediata de la Primera Guerra Mundial.

fiat money > dinero fiduciario Moneda no respaldada por el oro y la plata.

Fifteenth Amendment > Decimoquinta Enmienda Enmienda constitucional de 1870 que garantizó el derecho al sufragio, independientemente de la raza o condición previa de servitud.

54th Massachusetts Regiment > 54.° Regimiento de Massachusetts Escuadrón de la Unión dirigido por el coronel Robert Gould Shaw durante la Guerra Civil, compuesto totalmente por soldados afroamericanos.

filibuster > discurso obstruccionista Táctica empleada por los senadores que consistió en hacer prolongados discursos para detener los asuntos legislativos.

Finney, Charles Grandison > Finney, Charles Grandison (1792–1875) Abogado estadounidense, presidente de Oberlin College y figura central del movimiento de renovación religiosa de principios del siglo XIX. Fue muy exitoso en las renovaciones en las grandes ciudades como Nueva York, y finalmente llegó a ser catedrático de teología en una escuela teológica recién abierta en Oberlin, Ohio.

fireside chats > charlas junto a la chimenea Transmisión informal de radio en la que el presidente Franklin D. Roosevelt explicaba su visión de los asuntos y programas del momento (incluyendo la Gran Depresión, los programas del Nuevo Trato y las cuestiones de la Segunda Guerra Mundial) a los estadounidenses promedio.

First Continental Congress > Primer Congreso Continental Grupo de delegados que se reunió en 1774 y representaba a todas las colonias norteamericanas, excepto a Georgia.

Fitzgerald, F. Scott > Fitzgerald, F. Scott (1896–1940) Escritor estadounidense conocido por sus representaciones de la vida de los Estados Unidos en la década de 1920, especialmente *El gran Gatsby,* publicada en 1925.

flapper > *flapper* Mujer joven de la década de 1920 que desafiaba las reglas tradicionales de conducta y atuendo.

flexible response > respuesta flexible Política de defensa que permite acciones apropiadas en conflictos de cualquier tamaño o tipo.

Foraker Act > Ley Foraker Ley que estableció un gobierno civil en Puerto Rico.

Ford, Gerald > Ford, Gerald (1913–2006) Elegido para el Congreso en 1949 y nombrado Vicepresidente después de que Spiro T. Agnew renunciara en 1973. Ford fue Presidente al año siguiente de la renuncia de Nixon. Después de perder las elecciones de 1976 ante Jimmy Carter, Ford se retiró de la política.

Ford, Henry > Ford, Henry (1863–1947) Fundador de la Ford Motor Company. Revolucionó la industria automotriz con su línea de montaje y el trato a los trabajadores. Su Modelo T dio lugar a la era del automóvil en los Estados Unidos.

Fort Sumter > Fuerte Sumter Fuerte federal ubicado en Charleston, Carolina del Sur, donde se dispararon las primeras balas de la Guerra Civil.

forty-niner > *Forty-Niners (los del 49)* Mineros que se dirigieron a California después del descubrimiento de oro en 1848.

442nd Regimental Combat Team > Equipo de Combate del Regimiento 442 Unidad de la Segunda Guerra Mundial compuesta por voluntarios estadounidenses de origen japonés.

Fourteen Points > Catorce Puntos Lista de condiciones planteada por el presidente estadounidense Woodrow Wilson para resolver la Primera Guerra Mundial y guerras futuras.

Fourteenth Amendment > Decimocuarta Enmienda Enmienda constitucional ratificada en julio de 1868, que garantizaba la plena ciudadanía y derechos a toda persona nacida en los Estados Unidos, protegía el debido proceso y garantizaba la protección igual por la ley.

franchise business > franquicia comercial Permiso para que una compañía distribuya sus productos o servicios por medio de establecimientos minoristas e independientes.

Franco, General Francisco > Franco, General Francisco (1892–1975) Dirigió con éxito un alzamiento militar en contra del gobierno democrático español en la Guerra Civil Española (1936–1939). Gobernó España como dictador hasta su muerte en 1975.

Franklin, Benjamin > Franklin, Benjamin (1706–1790) Influyente estadista, inventor y científico estadounidense. Aprendió el oficio de impresor y se estableció en Filadelfia, donde imprimía y publicaba periódicos, sus propios artículos y el popular *Poor Richard's Almanac.* Su contribución a la fundación de los Estados Unidos fue importante. Fue el único que firmó los tres documentos principales de la nueva nación: la Declaración de Independencia, el tratado con Gran Bretaña que finalizaba la Guerra de Independencia y la Constitución de los Estados Unidos. Sus logros científicos incluyen la formulación de una teoría de la electricidad.

free enterprise > libre empresa Libertad de las empresas privadas para organizar y operar con el fin de lograr beneficios en un sistema competitivo sin interferencia del gobierno más allá de la regulación necesaria para proteger el interés público y mantener en equilibrio la economía nacional.

Free-Soil Party > Partido "Free-Soil" Partido político antiesclavista de mitad del siglo XIX que promulgaba la libertad de suelo.

freedman > liberto Esclavo que ha obtenido la libertad.

Freedmen's Bureau > Oficina de Libertos Agencia federal creada para ayudar a los afroamericanos liberados y a los granjeros blancos pobres del Sur después de la Guerra Civil.

freedom ride > viaje por la libertad Protesta de activistas que en 1961 viajaron en autobús a través de los estados sureños para probar si acataban la prohibición contra la segregación en los autobuses interestatales.

Freedom Summer > Verano de Libertad Esfuerzo de 1964 por empadronar a votantes afroamericanos en Mississippi.

French and Indian War > Guerra contra la Alianza Franco-Indígena Guerra de 1754 a 1763 en la cual Gran Bretaña y sus colonias derrotaron a Francia y a sus aliados indígenas estadounidenses, ganando el control del este de América del Norte.

French Revolution > Revolución Francesa Levantamiento contra la monarquía francesa que empezó en 1789.

Freud, Sigmund > Freud, Sigmund (1856–1939) Desarrolló teorías psicológicas de la mente humana y terapias conocidas como psicoanálisis.

Friedan, Betty > Friedan, Betty (1921–2006) Feminista estadounidense que escribió el influyente libro *The Feminine Mystique* en 1963 y fue cofundadora de la Organización Nacional para Mujeres (NOW, por sus siglas en inglés) en 1966.

Fugitive Slave Act > Ley de Esclavos Fugitivos Ley que obligaba a todos los ciudadanos a apoyar la captura de las personas que trataban de escapar de la esclavitud; parte del Acuerdo de 1850.

fundamentalism > fundamentalismo Movimiento o actitud que enfatiza un cumplimiento estricto y literal de un conjunto de principios básicos.

G

Gadsden Purchase > Venta de la Mesilla Compra que hicieron los Estados Unidos a México en 1853 de tierras que son actualmente Arizona y Nuevo México.

Gag Rule > Ley de la Mordaza Reglamento que prohibía debatir el tema de la esclavitud en el Congreso entre 1836 y 1844.

García, Héctor P. > García, Héctor P. (1914–1996) Médico del ejército que sirvió con honores en la Segunda Guerra Mundial, ganando la Estrella de Bronce por sus servicios en el norte de África e Italia. Nació en México pero creció en Mercedes, Texas. Después de dejar el ejército como mayor en 1945, García regresó a Texas para practicar medicina, pero también comenzó su trabajo de toda una vida como líder de la comunidad, defensor de los derechos civiles y activista político. En 1948, ayudó a fundar la American G.I. Forum, una organización que apoya a los veteranos hispanos y sus familias.

Garrison, William Lloyd > Garrison, William Lloyd (1805–1879) Periodista estadounidense que influyó de manera importante en el movimiento abolicionista. Dio su primer discurso contra la esclavitud en 1829 y para 1831 comenzó a publicar *The Liberator,* un poderoso periódico antiesclavista. Además, Garrison ayudó a fundar la Sociedad Antiesclavista y fue su presidente durante 23 años.

Garvey, Marcus > Garvey, Marcus (1887–1940) Carismático líder que organizó un movimiento nacionalista de las personas de raza negra en Harlem durante la década de 1920. Garvey promovía la independencia cultural y económica para los afroamericanos.

General Agreement on Tariffs and Trade (GATT) > Acuerdo General sobre Aranceles y Comercio Tratado internacional firmado originalmente en 1947 diseñado para disminuir las barreras comerciales.

generation gap > brecha generacional Falta de entendimiento y comunicación entre los miembros más viejos y más jóvenes de la sociedad.

Geneva Convention > Convención de Ginebra Acuerdo internacional que regula el tratamiento humanitario de soldados heridos y prisioneros de guerra.

genocide > genocidio Aniquilación intencional de un grupo racial, político o cultural.

"Gentlemen's Agreement" > "Pacto entre Caballeros" Acuerdo entre los Estados Unidos y Japón para terminar la segregación de niños asiáticos en las escuelas públicas de San Francisco. A cambio, Japón aceptó limitar la migración de sus ciudadanos hacia los Estados Unidos.

Gettysburg > Gettysburg Lugar de una batalla de la Guerra Civil que tuvo lugar en territorio de la Unión del 1 al 3 de julio de 1863, la cual dio como resultado la victoria de la Unión y obligó a las fuerzas confederadas a retirarse al Sur.

Gettysburg Address > Discurso de Gettysburg Discurso del presidente Lincoln durante la inauguración del cementerio nacional en Gettysburg, Pennsylvania, en el que reafirmó las ideas por las que la Unión estaba peleando la Guerra Civil; lo pronunció el 19 de noviembre de 1863.

Ghana > Ghana Importante reino en África occidental, conocido por sus riquezas y comercio en oro, existente desde el siglo IX d. C. hasta el siglo XIII d. C.

GI Bill of Rights > Declaración de Derechos del Soldado Legislación que facilitaba el retorno de los veteranos de la Segunda Guerra Mundial ofreciendo ayuda para obtener educación y empleo.

Gilded Age > Edad Dorada Término usado para describir la era posterior a la Reconstrucción, que se caracterizó por una fachada de prosperidad para el país.

Gingrich, Newt > Gingrich, Newt (1943–) Político, autor y comentarista de televisión estadounidense, mejor conocido por servir como presidente de la Cámara de Representantes de los Estados Unidos de 1995 a 1998. Gingrich lideró la toma de poder republicana de la Cámara en las elecciones de medio término de la Cámara de 1994 al ayudar a redactar la influyente plataforma Contrato con América.

glasnost > glásnost Palabra rusa que significa "nueva apertura", política de la Unión Soviética de finales de la década de 1980 que hacía un llamado a la apertura y discusión de los problemas nacionales.

globalization > globalización Proceso mediante el cual las economías, políticas, culturas y sociedades de naciones se mezclan con las de las otras naciones de todo el mundo.

gold standard > patrón oro Política de designar las unidades monetarias en términos de su valor en oro.

Goldwater, Barry > Goldwater, Barry (1909–1998) Sirvió casi 25 años en el Senado de los Estados Unidos. En 1964, se presentó como candidato a la presidencia pero fue derrotado por mayoría por Lyndon Johnson. En 1974, Goldwater fue un elemento clave para convencer al presidente Nixon de que renunciara como consecuencia del escándalo Watergate.

Gompers, Samuel > Gompers, Samuel (1850–1924) Líder laborista estadounidense y el primer presidente de la Federación Estadounidense del Trabajo. Defendía las huelgas organizadas y los boicots para lograr los objetivos de la organización.

Gorbachev, Mikhail > Gorbachov, Mijail (1931–) Político soviético líder de la Unión Soviética de 1985 a 1991. Gorbachov es más conocido por apoyar las políticas de *glásnost* y *perestroika,* que llevaron al colapso de la Unión Soviética. Por su papel en el surgimiento de gobiernos democráticos en Europa Oriental, le fue otorgado el Premio Nobel de la Paz en 1990.

Graham, Billy > Graham, Billy (1918–2018) Evangelista estadounidense que se destacó durante el renacimiento religioso de la década de 1950 en los Estados Unidos.

grandfather clause > cláusula del abuelo Ley para descalificar a los votantes afroamericanos que permitía votar sólo a los hombres cuyos padres y abuelos habían votado antes de 1867.

Grange > Grange Organización de granjeros formada después de la Guerra Civil.

Grant, Ulysses S. > Grant, Ulysses S. (1822–1885) General de la Unión que más tarde llegó a ser el 18° presidente de los Estados Unidos de 1869 a 1877. Ganó victorias clave en el río Mississippi, entre ellas la Batalla de Shiloh y la Batalla de Vicksburg. En marzo de 1864 fue nombrado comandante de todos los ejércitos de la Unión, y los llevó a la victoria en Appomattox Court House, donde aceptó la derrota del general Lee el 9 de abril de 1865.

Great Awakening > Gran Despertar Movimiento religioso en las colonias inglesas durante las décadas de 1730 y 1740, fuertemente inspirado por los predicadores evangélicos.

Great Compromise > Gran Concertación Acuerdo mutuo entre los planes de Virginia y Nueva Jersey para una legislatura bicameral: cada estado tendría una representación equitativa en el Senado y una representación variada en la Cámara de Representantes con base en la población del estado.

Great Depression > Gran Depresión Período entre 1929 y 1941 durante el cual la economía de los Estados Unidos falló y el desempleo creció.

Great Migration > Gran Migración Desplazamiento de afroamericanos durante el siglo XX del Sur al Norte.

Great Society > Gran Sociedad Objetivos del presidente Johnson en las áreas de salud, educación, ambiente, discriminación y pobreza.

gross national product > producto nacional bruto Valor total de los bienes y servicios producidos por un país.

Great White Fleet > Gran Flota Blanca Barcos de guerra enviados por el presidente Theodore Roosevelt en 1907 en una "misión de buena voluntad" alrededor del mundo.

guerrilla warfare > guerra de guerrillas Métodos de combate no tradicional.

Gulf of Tonkin Resolution > Resolución del Golfo de Tonkin Resolución del Congreso de 1964 que autorizó al presidente Johnson a enviar tropas estadounidenses a Vietnam del Sur y entrar en guerra contra Vietnam del Norte.

H

habeas corpus > hábeas corpus Garantía constitucional para que nadie permanezca en prisión sin que se hayan presentado cargos en su contra.

Hamilton, Alexander > Hamilton, Alexander (1755/57–1804) Nació en las Antillas británicas y fue a Nueva York a continuar sus estudios. Allí participó en la causa patriota y escribió tres panfletos que apoyaban la postura del Congreso Continental sobre la política comercial británica. Hamilton luchó durante la Guerra de Independencia y sirvió con George Washington. Después de la guerra, estudió leyes y luego ocupó el cargo de delegado de Pennsylvania en la Convención Constitucional. Más tarde fue el primer secretario del Tesoro de los Estados Unidos.

Harding, Warren G. > Harding, Warren G. (1865–1923) Sirvió como Presidente de los Estados Unidos de 1921 a 1923. Promovió el "regreso a la normalidad" que continuó con la participación de los Estados Unidos en la Primera Guerra Mundial. Harding murió durante su primer mandato en el cargo en 1923.

Harlem Renaissance > Renacimiento de Harlem Período durante la década de 1920 en el que los novelistas, poetas, y artistas afroamericanos celebraron su cultura.

Harpers Ferry > Harpers Ferry Pueblo de Virginia (ahora Virginia Occidental) donde el abolicionista John Brown atacó un arsenal federal en 1859.

Hartford Convention > Convención de Hartford Reunión de 1814 de los federalistas de Nueva Inglaterra opuestos a la Guerra de 1812 y que exigió enmiendas constitucionales que daban poder a su región.

hawk > halcón Persona que apoyó la participación estadounidense en la Guerra de Vietnam.

Hawley-Smoot Tariff > Arancel Hawley-Smoot Impuesto de importaciones protector aprobado por el Congreso en 1930 en un esfuerzo por contrarrestar la caída de la nación a la Gran Depresión.

Hay, John > Hay, John (1838–1905) Secretario de Estado de 1895 a 1905, guiando la diplomacia de los Estados Unidos cuando el país emergía como una potencia mundial. Fue un elemento clave en la organización de la política de puertas abiertas hacia China.

Hayes, Rutherford B. > Hayes, Rutherford B. (1822–1893) El 19° presidente de los Estados Unidos. Su elección en 1876 fue disputada y su victoria fue asegurada por la comisión del Congreso y el Acuerdo de 1877. Supervisó la retirada de las tropas federales que quedaban en el Sur, firmando el fin de la Reconstrucción.

Haymarket Riot > Revuelta de Haymarket Protesta de 1886 de origen laboral ocurrida en Chicago que terminó con muertes violentas.

Hearst, William Randolph > Hearst, William Randolph (1863–1951) Editor de periódico que creó la cadena de periódicos más grande de la nación. Hearst, junto con Joseph Pulitzer, ayudó a popularizar el reporte de investigación y la prensa amarillista.

Hellman, Lillian > Hellman, Lillian (1905–1984) Autora teatral y guionista conocida por sus dramas que se enfocaban en la injusticia social y la explotación.

Helsinki Accords > Acuerdos de Helsinki Acuerdo realizado en 1975 entre los Estados Unidos, Canadá y las naciones de Europa, incluyendo la Unión Soviética, en la que todos los países acordaron apoyar los derechos humanos.

Hemingway, Ernest > Hemingway, Ernest (1899–1961) Escritor estadounidense que ganó el Premio Nobel de Literatura en 1954. Es conocido por su vida aventurera y novelas como *Fiesta* y *Por quién tocan las campanas.*

Henry the Navigator, Prince > Enrique el Navegante, príncipe (1394–1460) Tercer hijo del rey Juan I de Portugal y Felipa de Lancaster, una aristócrata inglesa. Estableció una escuela para marineros portugueses donde aprendían navegación, cartografía y diseño de barcos. El apodo de "el Navegante" se lo dieron de manera incorrecta los autores ingleses, dado que Enrique nunca formó parte de ningún viaje de exploración.

Henry, Patrick > Henry, Patrick (1736–1799) Patriota, abogado y autor estadounidense. Es conocido por un discurso que dio ante la Convención de Virginia en 1775, durante el cual declaró "¡Dadme la libertad o dadme la muerte!". Sirvió en el comité de correspondencia de Virginia y como delegado de Virginia en el Primer Congreso Continental. Luchó durante la Guerra de Independencia y luego fue gobernador del estado de Virginia y legislador estatal.

Hepburn Act > Ley Hepburn Ley de 1906 que otorgó al gobierno la autoridad de fijar y limitar las tarifas ferroviarias y fijar los precios máximos para trasbordadores, peaje de puentes y oleoductos.

Hiss, Alger > Hiss, Alger (1904–1996) Funcionario de alto rango del Departamento de Estado investigado por el Comité de la Casa de Representantes de Actividades Anti Estadounidenses (HUAC, por sus siglas en inglés) como espía comunista y más tarde condenado por perjurio, pero no por espionaje. Los documentos liberados en la década de 1990 apoyaron las acusaciones en su contra.

Hitler, Adolf > Hitler, Adolfo (1889–1945) Líder del Partido Nacionalsocialista (Nazi) y dictador alemán de 1933 a 1945. Subió al poder promoviendo puntos de vista racistas y nacionalistas. En 1939 invadió Polonia, lo cual comenzó la Segunda Guerra Mundial. Estableció un sistema de campos de concentración que llevó al Holocausto, un asesinato sistemático y brutal de millones de judíos y otros.

Ho Chi Minh > Ho Chi Minh (1890–1969) Uno de los líderes anticolonialistas más influyentes de Asia. Ho dirigió la lucha de Vietnam del Norte para reunificar Vietnam del Norte y del Sur, sirviendo como presidente de la República Democrática de Vietnam (Vietnam del Norte) de 1945 a 1969.

Hollywood Ten > diez de Hollywood Grupo de guionistas, directores y productores que se rehusaron a contestar preguntas del HUAC sobre vínculos comunistas.

Holocaust > Holocausto Nombre que se usa actualmente para describir el asesinato sistemático de judíos y otros por los nazis.

Homestead Act > Ley de Repartición de Tierras Ley de 1862 que otorgó 160 acres de terreno a los ciudadanos deseosos de habitarlo y cultivarlo por cinco años.

Homestead Strike > Huelga de Homestead Huelga en 1892 en contra de las plantas siderúrgicas de Carnegie en Homestead, Pennsylvania.

Hoover Dam > Represa Hoover Represa en el río Colorado construida durante la Gran Depresión.

Hoover, Herbert > Hoover, Herbert (1874–1964) Sirvió como secretario de Comercio y más tarde como presidente de los Estados Unidos de 1929 a 1933, durante la Gran Depresión. La respuesta de su administración a la Gran Depresión fue ampliamente criticada por su ineficacia.

Hooverville > Hooverville Término usado para describir las barriadas de casuchas establecidas por los desposeídos durante la Gran Depresión.

horizontal integration > integración horizontal Sistema de consolidación de muchas empresas en el mismo ramo de negocios.

hot line > línea directa Línea de comunicación telefónica directa entre la Casa Blanca y el Kremlin establecida luego de la crisis de los misiles de Cuba.

House of Burgesses > Cámara de los Burgueses Asamblea de representantes en la Virginia colonial formada en 1619.

House Un-American Activities Committee (HUAC) > Comité de la Cámara de Representantes contra Actividades Antiestadounidenses Comité del Congreso que investigó posibles actividades subversivas dentro de los Estados Unidos.

Houston, Sam > Houston, Sam (1793–1863) El único estadounidense en servir como gobernador de dos estados diferentes "primero Tennessee, luego Texas". Entre estos cargos, fue comandante del ejército de Texas, presidente de la República de Texas y senador de los Estados Unidos por Texas. Aunque era esclavista, Houston se oponía a la expansión de la esclavitud en el Oeste. Fue retirado de la gobernación de Texas después de hablar en contra de la separación de Texas de la Unión.

Howe, William > Howe, William (1729–1814) General que sirvió como comandante en jefe del ejército británico de 1776 a 1778, durante la Guerra de Independencia. Aunque llevó a las tropas británicas a la victoria en diferentes misiones, entre ellas Bunker Hill, Brandywine y Germantown, renunció a su mando después de no haber podido derrotar al ejército del general Washington en Valley Forge.

Huerta, Dolores > Huerta, Dolores (1930–) Creció en Stockton, California, y llegó a ser maestra de escuela elemental. Después de ver la pobreza de sus estudiantes, muchos de ellos hijos de agricultores, se involucró en defender el trabajo de los obreros y sus familias. En 1962, fundó junto con César Chávez el sindicato de los trabajadores del campo que se convertiría en Unión de Campesinos (UFW, por sus siglas en inglés). Aunque Chávez era la cara de la organización, fue Huerta quien empleó sus habilidades de organización y negociación para ayudar a que UFW tuviera éxito en nombre de sus miembros.

Hughes, Langston > Hughes, Langston (1902–1967) Influente poeta y escritor que consideraba que su obra era un medio de comunicar la experiencia de las personas de raza negra de los Estados Unidos.

human rights > derechos humanos Derechos básicos que tiene todo ser humano por el hecho de serlo y que incluyen la libertad religiosa, la educación y la igualdad.

Hurston, Zora Neale > Hurston, Zora Neale (1891–1960) Escritora asociada con el Renacimiento de Harlem que tenía formación de antropóloga y siguió enseñando durante años. Una de sus obras más influyentes fue *Sus ojos miraban a Dios,* publicada en 1935.

Hutchinson, Anne > Hutchinson, Anne (1591–1643) Líder religiosa estadounidense. Llegó a Massachusetts en 1634, donde mantuvo reuniones en su casa para promover con valentía su idea de que solo la gracia de Dios era la clave de la salvación. Pero los líderes de la colonia se opusieron a que una mujer predicara y consideraron peligrosas muchas de sus creencias. En 1637 fue desterrada y más tarde se fue a Rhode Island y después a Long Island Sound, en lo que actualmente es Nueva York. En 1643, ella y gran parte de su familia fueron asesinadas por indígenas norteamericanos.

hydraulic mining > minería hidráulica Uso de agua para erosionar la grava de las laderas y hacer que corra hacia largas esclusas para atrapar el oro.

I

ice age > era del hielo Periodo en la historia de la Tierra caracterizado por bajas temperaturas globales y glaciares que cubrieron grandes áreas.

Immigration Act of 1990 > Ley de Migración de 1990 Ley que aumenta el número de inmigrantes permitidos en los Estados Unidos cada año.

Immigration and Nationality Act of 1965 > Ley de Migración y Nacionalidad de 1965 Ley que cambió el sistema de cuotas nacionales para limitar a 170,000 por año los inmigrantes del hemisferio oriental y 120,000 por año los del hemisferio occidental.

Immigration Reform and Control Act of 1986 > Ley de Migración y Control de 1986 Legislación que otorgó la condición de residentes a los inmigrantes ilegales que vivían en los Estados Unidos desde 1982 y penaliza a los patrones que contratan inmigrantes ilegales.

impeach > enjuiciar políticamente Acusar a un funcionario público de un delito cometido en el ejercicio de su cargo.

impeachment > juicio político Acción de encausar a un funcionario público para determinar si debe ser retirado del cargo.

imperialism > imperialismo Dominio político, militar y económico de naciones poderosas sobre territorios más débiles.

impressment > reclutamiento forzado Política de capturar personas o propiedades para el servicio militar o público.

income tax > impuesto sobre la renta Impuesto que deben pagar tanto individuos como corporaciones de acuerdo a los ingresos devengados.

indentured servant > siervo por contrato Persona que aceptaba trabajar sin salario por un tiempo a cambio de transporte a las colonias.

Indian New Deal > Nuevo Trato Indígena Legislación de 1930 que otorgó mayor control a los indígenas estadounidenses sobre asuntos y financió escuelas y hospitales.

Indian Removal Act > Ley de Expulsión de Indígenas Ley aprobada por el Congreso en 1830 que permitió al gobierno federal negociar intercambios de tierras con los indígenas estadounidenses del Sureste.

Industrial Revolution > Revolución Industrial Cambio del trabajo manual al trabajo mecanizado que empezó en Gran Bretaña durante el siglo XVIII y llegó a los Estados Unidos a principios del siglo XIX.

inflation > inflación Aumento de los precios.

influenza > influenza Virus de la gripe.

information industry > industria de la información Empresa que brinda servicios de información.

initiative > iniciativa Proceso en el que los ciudadanos proponen directamente una nueva ley en la papeleta de una elección.

installment buying > compras a plazos Método de compra mediante el cual el comprador paga un pequeño enganche y luego paga el resto de la deuda con abonos mensuales regulares.

insurrection > insurrección Rebelión.

integration > integración Proceso de unir personas de diferentes razas, religiones y clases sociales.

interchangeable parts > piezas reemplazables Componentes idénticos que pueden usarse en lugar de otros.

Internet > Internet Red de computadoras que enlaza a personas de todo el mundo, también llamada Red Mundial.

internment > reclusión Encarcelamiento temporal para miembros de un grupo específico.

Interstate Commerce Commission (ICC) > Comisión Interestatal de Comercio Primera agencia federal en vigilar las operaciones comerciales, creada en 1887 para supervisar los procedimientos del ferrocarril interestatal.

Interstate Highway Act > Ley de Carreteras Interestatales Ley de 1956 que autorizó el gasto de $32 mil millones para construir 41,000 millas de carreteras.

Intolerable Acts > Leyes Intolerables Nombre estadounidense para las Leyes Coercitivas que el Parlamento aprobó en 1774 para controlar las colonias.

Iran-Contra affair > asunto Irán-Contra Incidente Irán-Contras escándalo político en la administración del presidente Reagan que involucró el uso de dinero procedente de la venta secreta de armas a Irán para apoyar ilegalmente a los Contras en Nicaragua.

iron curtain > cortina de hierro Término acuñado por Winston Churchill para describir la frontera entre los estados satélites soviéticos y Europa occidental.

Iroquois > iroqueses También conocidos como los *haudenosaunee,* los iroqueses eran un grupo de pueblos indígenas estadounidenses que vivieron al norte del estado de Nueva York y tierras vecinas. Incluían a los cayugas, cheroquíes, hurones, mohawks, oneidas, onondagas, sénecas y tuscacoras, quienes compartían un idioma común y ciertas formas de vida.

Iroquois League > Liga Iroquesa Confederación compuesta por los cinco pueblos iroqueses: los mohawks, oneidas, onondagas, cayugas y sénecas.

irreconcilables > irreconciliables Senadores aislacionistas opuestos a cualquier tratado para finalizar la Primera Guerra Mundial que tuviera alguna conexión con la Liga de las Naciones.

island-hopping > salto entre islas Estrategia aliada durante la Segunda Guerra Mundial de retomar algunas de las islas ocupadas por los japoneses e ignorar y pasar de largo de otras.

J

Jackson, Andrew > Jackson, Andrew (1767–1845) Fue Oficial estadounidense antes de servir en la Cámara de Representantes y en el Senado, y finalmente como el séptimo Presidente de 1829 a 1837. Como general del Ejército de los Estados Unidos durante la Guerra de 1812, Jackson defendió con éxito Nueva Orleans. Como Presidente, vetó la renovación de la carta del Banco de los Estados Unidos, que se oponía al tema de anulación de Carolina del Sur y comenzó un sistema de prebendas.

Jackson, Stonewall > Jackson, Stonewall (1824–1863) Thomas Jonathan Jackson, también conocido como Stonewall Jackson, fue uno de los generales confederados más renombrados de la Guerra Civil. Llevó a sus tropas a una sorprendente victoria en la Batalla de Bull Run en 1861, sorprendiendo a la Unión por su liderazgo y la fuerza de la resistencia sureña. Murió de neumonía después de que sus propios hombres le dispararan por accidente cerca de Chancellorsville, Virginia.

Jacksonian Democracy > Democracia de Jackson Andrew Jackson y los partidarios de su filosofía política se preocuparon de los intereses de la gente común y de limitar las funciones del gobierno federal.

Japanese American Citizens League > Liga de Ciudadanos Japoneses-Americanos Organización que trabajaba para proteger los derechos civiles de los japoneses americanos.

Jay, John > Jay, John (1745–1829) Abogado de Nueva York, se unió a la causa patriota durante la Guerra de Independencia y sirvió en el Congreso Continental. Fue presidente del Congreso Continental y diplomático en España y Francia. Ayudó a lograr términos favorables para la nueva nación en el Tratado de París. Después de la guerra, siguió en el servicio público y se dedicó intensamente a la ratificación de la Constitución. Como federalista, escribió cinco de los ensayos incluidos en *The Federalist, bajo* el seudónimo Publius. George Washington lo nombró el primer presidente de la Corte Suprema de los Estados Unidos.

jazz > jazz Forma musical estadounidense creada por los afroamericanos , basada en la improvisación y la mezcla del blues, ragtime y música popular de origen europeo.

Jazz Singer, The > *Jazz Singer, The* Musical estadounidense estrenado en 1927 que fue la primera película de cine de larga duración con diálogo sincronizado.

Jefferson, Thomas > Jefferson, Thomas (1743–1826) Granjero, hacendado, autor, arquitecto, abogado y estadista estadounidense. Se unió a la Cámara de los Burgueses de Virginia en 1768 y en la década de 1770 comenzó a abogar a favor de la independencia de los Estados Unidos. Jefferson representó a Virginia en el Segundo Congreso Continental; durante ese tiempo redactó y revisó la Declaración de Independencia. Sirvió como diplomático en Francia y como primer secretario de estado, segundo vicepresidente y tercer presidente de la nación. También fundó la Universidad de Virginia.

Jiang Jieshi > Jiang Jieshi (1887–1975) También conocido como Chiang Kai-shek, fue un líder nacionalista chino que se opuso al ejército comunista de Mao Zedong durante la guerra civil china. Después de la caída de la China continental, Jiang se convirtió en el líder del gobierno nacionalista en la isla de Taiwán.

Jim Crow laws > Leyes Jim Crow Leyes segregacionistas implantadas en el Sur después de la Reconstrucción.

jingoism > patrioterismo Nacionalismo agresivo; apoyo a una política exterior belicosa.

Johnson, Andrew > Johnson, Andrew (1808–1875) Sastre de Tennessee que ascendió hasta llegar a ser el 17° presidente de los Estados Unidos. En 1864, Johnson ocupó el cargo de vicepresidente bajo el presidente Lincoln. Menos de un año después, llegó a ser Presidente después del asesinato de Lincoln. Sus disputas con los republicanos radicales sobre La Reconstrucción llevaron a su juicio político en 1868. Después de su presidencia, Johnson regresó a Tennessee. Ocupó el cargo de senador de los Estados Unidos hasta su muerte.

Johnson, Lyndon B.> Johnson, Lyndon B. (1908–1973) Legislador en la Cámara de Representantes y en el Senado antes de su elección como vicepresidente junto con John Kennedy para presidente. El 22 de noviembre de 1963, asumió el cargo como 36° Presidente inmediatamente después del asesinato del presidente Kennedy. Estuvo en funciones de 1963 a 1969. En 1964, promulgó la Ley de los Derechos Civiles. Fue el principal impulsor del programa social Great Society y se esforzó, sin éxito, por poner fin a la Guerra de Vietnam.

Johnson, Robert > Johnson, Robert Empezando a mediados de la década de 1970, Robert Johnson (1946–) trabajaba en Washington, D.C. para la Corporation for Public Broadcasting y como activista en un grupo de presión para la nueva y creciente industria de la televisión por cable. En 1980, usó su experiencia y conexiones para comenzar BET, una compañía de red por cable dirigida a una amplia audiencia afroamericana marginada. Después de muchos años de crecimiento y éxito, Johnson y los socios de la inversión vendieron BET en 1998, por $3 mil millones de dólares. El trato hizo de Johnson el primer afroamericano multimillonario del país.

joint-stock company > sociedad comanditaria por acciones Compañía dirigida por un grupo de inversionistas que se reparten las ganancias y pérdidas de la empresa.

Joseph, Chief > Joseph, jefe (1840–1904) El jefe Joseph sucedió a su padre como jefe de los nez percé en 1871. Seis años más tarde dirigió a sus seguidores en una huida sin éxito para escapar de su confinamiento en una reserva. Primero fueron enviados a Oklahoma y finalmente a una nueva reserva en el estado de Washington. Sin embargo, Joseph no pudo asegurar el regreso de su tribu a su tierra natal.

judicial interpretation > interpretación jurídica Práctica por la cual los tribunales desarrollan y aplican el propósito de la Constitución más allá del significado de sus palabras escritas.

judicial review > revisión judicial Poder que le permite a la Corte Suprema decidir si los actos de un Presidente o las leyes aprobadas por el Congreso son constitucionales.

K

kamikaze > kamikaze Pilotos japoneses que deliberadamente chocaban aviones contra buques estadounidenses durante la Segunda Guerra Mundial.

Kansas-Nebraska Act > Ley Kansas-Nebraska Ley de 1854 que dividió el territorio de Nebraska en Kansas y Nebraska, dándole a cada territorio el derecho de decidir si permitiría la esclavitud o no.

Kelley, Florence > Kelley, Florence (1859–1932) Desempeñó un papel importante en Hull House al llamar la atención sobre las condiciones de trabajo de las mujeres y los niños. En 1899, encabezó la recién fundada Liga Nacional de Consumidores (NCL, por sus siglas en inglés). En 1909 Kelley ayudó a fundar la Asociación Nacional para el Progreso de la Gente de Color (NAACP, por sus siglas en inglés).

Kelley, Oliver H. Kelley > Kelley, Oliver H. Kelley (1826–1913) Empleado en el Departamento de Agricultura de los Estados Unidos que trabajó para mejorar la vida de los trabajadores y de la industria agrícola. Reconoció la necesidad de unir a los granjeros para proteger su subsistencia. Kelly sirvió como el primer secretario de la Grange de 1867 a 1878.

Kellogg-Briand Pact > Pacto Kellogg-Briand Acuerdo de 1928 en el que los delegados de muchas naciones estuvieron anuentes a prohibir la guerra.

Kennan, George F. > Kennan, George F. (1904–2005) Diplomático estadounidense que pasó varios años sirviendo en Europa del este y la Unión Soviética. Sus observaciones sobre las actitudes y acciones políticas soviéticas contribuyeron a la formación de la política de contención de los Estados Unidos.

Kennedy, John F. > Kennedy, John F. (1917–1963) Sirvió en la Cámara de Representantes y en el Senado antes de convertirse en el 35° Presidente en 1961. Enfrentó una serie de crisis en el extranjero, especialmente en Cuba y Berlín, y logró asegurar logros como el Tratado de Prohibición de Pruebas de Armas Nucleares y la Alianza para el Progreso. Fue asesinado en Dallas, Texas.

Kennedy, Robert > Kennedy, Robert (1925–1968) Candidato presidencial antibélico por el Partido Demócrata en 1968 y que fue asesinado.

Kerner Commission > Comisión Kerner Grupo que se formó para investigar las causas de los disturbios raciales en las ciudades estadounidenses en la década de 1960.

Key, Francis Scott > Key, Francis Scott (1779–1843) Abogado y poeta aficionado estadounidense, mejor conocido por ser el autor de "The Star-Spangled Banner", que en 1931 se convirtió en el himno nacional de los Estados Unidos.

Keynes, John Maynard > Keynes, John Maynard (1883–1946) Economista británico mejor conocido por su defensa de la intervención del gobierno para proteger la economía de los efectos negativos de las recesiones, depresiones y auges. Esbozó sus ideas en la obra *Teoría general del empleo,* el interés y el dinero, publicada en 1936.

Khomeini, Ayatollah Ruhollah > Jomeini, ayatolá Ruhollah (1902–1989) Influyente erudito y clérigo iraní. Después de liderar sin éxito una rebelión en contra del sah de Irán en 1963, huyó a Francia donde sus ideas religiosas y políticas se hicieron más radicales. Después del derrocamiento del sah en 1979, Jomeini regresó a Irán y, apoyado por las fuerzas revolucionarias, se hizo con el poder que mantuvo hasta su muerte en 1989.

Khrushchev, Nikita > Khrushchev, Nikita (1894–1971) Líder del Partido Comunista que sirvió como presidente de la Unión Soviética de 1958 a 1964. Khrushchev lideró la Unión Soviética durante la crisis de los misiles cubanos, pero perdió poder poco después.

King Philip's War > Guerra del Rey Philip Conflicto entre los colonos ingleses y los indígenas norteamericanos en Nueva Inglaterra.

King, Martin Luther, Jr. > King, Martin Luther, Jr. (1929–1968) Defendía los métodos no violentos de protesta mientras se convertía quizá en el líder más influyente del movimiento de los derechos civiles. Dirigió la Marcha a Washington en 1963, donde dio su famoso discurso "Tengo un sueño". Fue asesinado en 1968.

Kings Mountain > *Kings Mountain* Batalla de la Guerra de Independencia de 1780 en Carolina del Norte en la cual los patriotas derrotaron a una milicia leal a la corona.

Kissinger, Henry > Kissinger, Henry (1923–) Sirvió como asesor de política exterior a los presidentes Kennedy y Johnson. En 1969, el presidente Nixon lo nombró asesor en Seguridad Nacional y secretario de Estado en 1973. Kissinger recibió el Premio Nobel de la Paz en 1973 por su papel en el fin de la Guerra de Vietnam.

Knights of Labor > Caballeros del Trabajo Sindicato de trabajadores que procuró organizar a todos los trabajadores y se enfocó en reformas sociales amplias.

Know-Nothings > partido Know-Nothing partido político de la década de 1850, llamado oficialmente el Partido americano, que era anticatólico y antiinmigrante

Kristallnacht > *Kristallnacht* "Noche de los cristales rotos", ataques organizados contra comunidades judías en Alemania, el 9 de noviembre de 1938.

Ku Klux Klan > Ku Klux Klan Organización que promueve el odio y la discriminación contra determinados grupos étnicos, raciales y religiosos.

L

labor union > sindicato Organización de trabajadores.

Lafayette, Marquis de > Lafayette, marqués de (1757–1834) Aristócrata francés que se unió a la causa patriota en 1777. Luchó bajo las órdenes del general Washington y regresó a Francia en 1779 para convencer al rey de que enviara tropas para ayudar a los estadounidenses. En 1780, regresó para dirigir al ejército patriota de Virginia. En 1781, ayudó a atrapar a los británicos bajo el mando del general Cornwallis en Yorktown.

laissez-faire > *laissez-faire* Teoría que aboga por una mínima injerencia gubernamental en la economía.

Land Grant College Act > Ley de Cesión de Terrenos para Universidades Ley de 1862 que puso dinero a disposición de los estados para que establecieran universidades que enseñaran agricultura e ingeniería mecánica.

land grants > concesión de tierra Terrenos designados por el gobierno federal para construir escuelas, carreteras o ferrocarriles.

Land Ordinance of 1785 > Decreto de Tierras de 1785 Ley que diseñó un sistema para administrar y fijar tierras en el territorio del Noroeste.

Lange, Dorothea > Lange, Dorothea (1895–1965) Fotógrafa documentalista estadounidense conocida por sus retratos de agricultores desplazados y otros que sufrieron las dificultades económicas durante la Gran Depresión.

Las Gorras Blancas > Las Gorras Blancas Grupo de estadounidenses de origen mexicano radicados en Nuevo México que intentaron proteger sus tierras y estilo de vida de la expansión de los terratenientes blancos.

Lauder, Estee > Lauder, Estée (1908?–2004) Mujer de negocios y filántropa estadounidense que fundó un imperio de perfumes y cosméticos.

League of Nations > Liga de las Naciones Organización mundial establecida después de la Primera Guerra Mundial para promover la cooperación pacífica entre los países.

Lee, Robert E. > Lee, Robert E. (1807–1870) General de Virginia que llegó a comandante del ejército confederado durante la Guerra Civil. El 9 de abril de 1865, Lee rindió su ejército ante el ejército de la Unión dirigido por el general Grant en Appomattox Court House. Después de la guerra, fue el presidente de Washington College, actualmente conocido como Washington and Lee University, en Lexington, Virginia.

Lend-Lease Act > Ley de Préstamo y Arriendo Ley aprobada en 1941 que permitió al presidente Franklin Roosevelt vender o prestar suministros bélicos a cualquier país cuya defensa se considerara vital para la seguridad de los Estados Unidos.

Lenin, Vladimir > Lenin, Vladimir (1870–1924) Fundó el Partido Comunista en Rusia y dirigió la Revolución Rusa. Se convirtió en dictador de la Rusia soviética y promovía el comunismo siempre que podía. Lenin creía que para lograr revoluciones comunistas exitosas era necesario un partido dedicado de revolucionarios, en oposición a la población engeneral.

Lewis and Clark Expedition > expedición de Lewis y Clark Expedición de 1804 enviada por el presidente Jefferson para explorar el recién adquirido territorio de Luisiana.

liberal > liberal Persona que tiende a apoyar la intervención gubernamental en la ayuda a los necesitados y favorece las leyes que protegen los derechos de las mujeres y las minorías.

Liluokalani, Queen > Liluokalani, reina (1838–1917) Sucedió a su hermano el rey Kalakaua en 1891 como líder del pueblo de Hawái. Fue la primera y única reina hawaiana y la última soberana en gobernar las islas. Aunque Liluokalani trató de recuperar el control de las tierras propiedad de los dueños de las plantaciones, fue derrocada en 1893 y los Estados Unidos se anexaron Hawái en 1898.

limited government > gobierno limitado Principio que declara que el gobierno solo tiene tanta autoridad como la que le otorga el pueblo y, por tanto, su poder es limitado.

limited war > guerra limitada Guerra peleada para alcanzar objetivos específicos.

Lincoln, Abraham > Lincoln, Abraham (1809–1865) Nació en una granja de Kentucky. Fue autodidacta y llegó a ser abogado. Se unió al partido Whig y fue elegido para servir en la legislatura estatal de Illinois. En 1858, se presentó sin éxito como candidato a un cargo en el Senado de los Estados Unidos ante Stephen A. Douglas. Durante esa campaña obtuvo reconocimiento nacional por su desempeño en una serie de debates y por su firme postura en contra de la expansión de la esclavitud. Aunque perdió la carrera hacia el Senado, llegó a ser Presidente en 1861. Dirigió al país durante la Guerra Civil y fue asesinado en abril de 1865.

Lindbergh, Charles > Lindbergh, Charles (1902–1974) Piloto estadounidense que se convirtió en un héroe internacional cuando hizo el primer vuelo sin escalas en solitario a través del Océano Atlántico en 1927. Antes de que Estados Unidos entrara a la Segunda Guerra Mundial, Lindbergh se convirtió en una voz líder aislacionista, que argumentó firmemente que los Estados Unidos deberían permanecer neutrales y evitar ser arrastrados a la guerra.

literacy test > prueba de alfabetismo Prueba de lectura y escritura antiguamente usada en algunos estados sureños para evitar que los afroamericanos votaran.

Little Turtle > Little Turtle (c.1752–1812) Jefe indígena del pueblo miami. Al resistir la expansión de los estadounidenses hacia el territorio del Noroeste, el ejército de Little Turtle logró varias victorias contra el ejército de los Estados Unidos en 1790 y 1791. Little Turtle firmó el Tratado de Greenville en 1795 en el que cedía a los Estados Unidos gran parte de Ohio y partes de Illinois, Indiana y Michigan.

localism > localismo Política de la que dependió el presidente Hoover a principios de la Depresión para que los gobiernos locales y estatales actuaran como los principales agentes de asistencia económica.

Lodge, Henry Cabot > Lodge, Henry Cabot (1850–1924) Destacado senador republicano que dirigió con éxito la lucha para evitar que los Estados Unidos se unieran a la Liga de las Naciones después de la Primera Guerra Mundial. Antes de ser senador había servido en el Congreso. Previamente había trabajado como editor de revistas e historiador.

Lone Star Republic > República de la Estrella Solitaria Nación formada en 1835 por los texanos que declararon la Independencia de México.

Long, Huey > Long, Huey (1893–1935) Elegido gobernador de Luisiana en 1928, donde ganó por una amplia mayoría al proporcionar reformas para ayudar a los pobres durante la Depresión. Mientras servía en el Senado de los Estados Unidos (1932–1935), llegó a ser un crítico vehemente del Nuevo Trato de Roosevelt y pidió la redistribución de la riqueza de la nación. En 1935, anunció su plan para postularse a la presidencia pero fue asesinado ese mismo año.

loose construction > interpretación libre Creencia de que el gobierno tiene cualquier poder que no le prohíba la Constitución.

Lost Generation > Generación Perdida Término usado para referirse a escritores estadounidenses de la década de 1920 marcados por su desilusión con la Primera Guerra Mundial y la búsqueda de un nuevo sentido de la vida.

Louisiana Purchase > Compra de Luisiana Compra que hicieran los Estados Unidos a Francia en 1803 del territorio entre el río Mississippi y las montañas Rocosas.

Lowell girls > Chicas Lowell Mujeres jóvenes que trabajaban en las fábricas textiles de Lowell, Massachusetts, a principios del siglo XIX.

Lowell, Francis Cabot > Lowell, Francis Cabot (1775–1817) Hombre de negocios estadounidense que desarrolló la primera fábrica textil del mundo en la cual todas las operaciones para convertir algodón en tela se realizaban dentro de una sola instalación.

Loyalists > leales al rey Colonos que permanecieron leales a Gran Bretaña durante la Guerra de Independencia.

Lusitania > *Lusitania* Trasatlántico británico hundido por un submarino alemán durante la Primera Guerra Mundial.

M

MacArthur, Douglas > MacArthur, Douglas (1880–1964) Dirigió las tropas estadounidenses en la Primera Guerra Mundial, donde desarrolló su reputación de valor. Como comandante supremo de las fuerzas aliadas del Pacífico (1942–1945) aceptó la rendición de Japón al final de la Segunda Guerra Mundial. En 1950 se convirtió en comandante de las fuerzas de la ONU en la Guerra de Corea. Se jubiló después de su controvertida retirada del mando en 1951, después de una discusión con el presidente Harry Truman.

Maddox, Lester > Maddox, Lester (1915–2003) Nació en Atlanta, Georgia. Desertor escolar, dirigió un restaurante en la ciudad de 1947 a 1964, cuando lo cerró porque se rehusó a servir a afroamericanos. Elegido gobernador (1967–1971), luchó en contra de la desagregación escolar.

Madison, James > Madison, James (1751–1836) Patriota que representó a Virginia en el Congreso Continental. En 1787 participó en la Convención Constitucional y fue una voz destacada en el reemplazo de los Artículos de la Confederación por un nuevo plan de gobierno. Por su contribución al ganar la aprobación de la Constitución de 1787, fue conocido como el Padre de la Constitución. Madison siguió ejerciendo como secretario de Estado de Thomas Jefferson y luego fue el cuarto presidente de los Estados Unidos.

Magellan, Ferdinand > Magallanes, Fernando de (1480–1521) Navegante y explorador, hijo de un noble portugués. En 1519, Magallanes y su flota de 5 barcos y aproximadamente 270 hombres salieron hacia el oeste desde España. Al navegar alrededor de América del Sur, Magallanes descubrió el estrecho que lleva su nombre y luego se dirigió hacia el Pacífico. Después de ser asesinado en las islas Filipinas, solo uno de sus barcos y 17 de los primeros marineros continuaron viaje hacia el oeste hacia España. Esta fue la primera circunnavegación de la Tierra.

Magna Carta > Carta Magna Documento inglés de 1215 que limitó el poder del rey y dio derechos básicos a los ciudadanos.

Mahan, Alfred T. > Mahan, Alfred T. (1840–1914) Oficial de la Marina e historiador estadounidense que instó a los líderes estadounidenses a construir una armada más fuerte y obtener bases navales en Cuba, Hawái y Filipinas. Mahan fue también de los primeros en proponer la construcción de un canal en América Central para permitir que los navíos estadounidenses se movieran rápidamente entre los océanos Atlántico y Pacífico.

Malcolm X > Malcolm X (1925–1965) Sirvió como portavoz y ministro de la Nación del Islam. Cuando fue liberado de prisión en 1952, su trabajo ayudó a la Nación del Islam, que tenía solo 400 miembros, a crecer hasta los 40,000 miembros para 1960. Dejó el grupo poco antes de su asesinato en 1965.

Mali > Malí Imperio de África occidental que existió desde aproximadamente el año 1200 hasta el año 1450 y que prosperó gracias al comercio del oro.

Mandela, Nelson > Mandela, Nelson (1918–2013) Hijo de un jefe de la tribu africana de los tembús, se convirtió en el primer presidente negro de Sudáfrica en 1994. Como abogado, Mandela comenzó su lucha en contra del apartheid en 1952. En 1964, fue condenado a cárcel de por vida por su activismo anti-apartheid. Fue liberado en 1990. En trabajo conjunto con el presidente sudafricano F.W. de Klerk, Mandela ayudó a terminar con el sistema de segregación racial del país. Compartió el Premio Nobel de la Paz en 1993.

Manhattan Project > Proyecto Manhattan Nombre en clave del proyecto que desarrolló la bomba atómica.

Manifest Destiny > Destino Manifiesto Doctrina del siglo XIX que establecía que la expansión hacia el Oeste de los Estados Unidos no sólo era inevitable sino un derecho divino.

Mann, Horace > Mann, Horace Creció en la pobreza pero gracias a su duro trabajo se graduó en la Universidad de Brown con el título de abogado. Finalmente sirvió en la Cámara de Representantes de Massachusetts y como presidente del Senado del estado. Renunció a su cargo en el Senado para ser el primer presidente del concejo estatal de educación. Trabajó para establecer escuelas públicas gratuitas a las que, por ley, todos los niños debían asistir.

Mansa Musa > Mansa Musa (?–1332?) Emperador del imperio de Malí, en África occidental, desde aproximadamente el año 1307. En esa época, el imperio de Malí era uno de los más grandes del mundo. Conocido por su generosidad y devoción religiosa, Musa estableció un histórico peregrinaje a El Cairo y luego a La Meca acompañado por una caravana de 60,000 hombres. Su peregrinaje mostró al mundo la enorme riqueza de Malí.

manumission > manumisión Acto de liberar a un esclavo.

Mao Zedong > Mao Zedong (1893–1976) Líder chino que dirigió con éxito una revolución comunista en China continental. Fue presidente de la comunista República Popular China de 1949 a 1959 y jefe del Partido Comunista del país hasta 1976.

Marbury* v. *Madison* > *Marbury* contra *Madison Caso de la Corte Suprema de 1803 que estableció el principio de la revisión judicial.

March on Washington > Marcha en Washington Manifestación de más de 200,000 personas que en 1963 marcharon a favor de la igualdad económica y los derechos civiles.

Married Women's Property Act > Ley sobre la propiedad de las mujeres casadas Ley aprobada en 1848 en el estado de Nueva York que otorgaba mayores derechos a las mujeres sobre la propiedad. Esta ley sirvió de modelo en otros estados.

Marshall Plan > Plan Marshall Política económica y exterior que ofreció ayuda a los países de Europa Occidental después de la Segunda Guerra Mundial.

Marshall, George > Marshall, George (1880–1959) Llegó a ser el jefe del ejército en 1939. Marshall usó su fuerza tranquila, habilidades de negociación y genio en la planeación para desarrollar un ejército combatiente lo más rápidamente posible. Como secretario de Estado después de la guerra, aconsejó un plan de ayuda, llamado el Plan Marshall, para ayudar a la recuperación de Europa Occidental. En 1950, regresó como secretario de Defensa al comienzo de la Guerra de Corea y ayudó a preparar el ejército una vez más.

Marshall, John > Marshall, John (1755–1835) Cuarto presidente de la Corte Suprema de los Estados Unidos. Después de servir bajo George Washington en la Guerra de Independencia, incluyendo el invierno en Valley Forge, Marshall ocupó varios puestos jurídicos y políticos. Como presidente de la Corte Suprema, participó en más de 1,000 fallos, redactando él mismo más de 500 de ellos, a menudo promoviendo y defendiendo el poder judicial y los principios del federalismo estadounidense.

Marshall, Thurgood > Marshall, Thurgood (1908–1993) Llegó a ser consejero de la Asociación Nacional para el Progreso de la Gente de Color (NAACP, por sus siglas en inglés) en 1938 y ganó 29 de los 32 principales casos de derechos civiles que discutió en los siguientes 23 años. En 1967, fue el primer afroamericano en sentarse en la Corte Suprema y ocupar un cargo hasta que algunos problemas de salud le obligaron a retirarse en 1991.

Martí, José > Martí, José (1853–1895) Escritor cubano exilado que se convirtió en el símbolo de la lucha de Cuba por su independencia de España. Martí ayudó a establecer el Partido Revolucionario Cubano y fue elegido su líder en 1892. En 1895 ayudó a comenzar la guerra de la independencia contra España. Murió un mes más tarde en batalla en las llanuras de Dos Ríos.

mass culture > cultura de masas Patrones similares de cultura en una sociedad como resultado de la propagación del transporte, comunicación y publicidad.

mass production > producción en masa Producción de bienes en grandes cantidades mediante el uso de maquinaria y líneas de montaje.

mass transit > transporte de masas Sistemas de transporte público que llevan a grandes cantidades de personas.

massive retaliation > represalia masiva Política de amenazar con el uso de fuerza masiva en respuesta a una agresión.

matrilineal > matrilineal Cuando los bienes se heredan por el lado materno de la familia.

Maya > maya Pueblo indígena americano del área de Yucatán al sur de México, Guatemala y Belice, cuya civilización alcanzó su máximo auge entre los años 300–900 d. C.

Mayflower Compact > Pacto del Mayflower Documento para establecer el sistema de autogobierno de la colonia de Plymouth firmado en el barco *Mayflower* en 1620.

McCarthy, Eugene > McCarthy, Eugene (1916–2005) Candidato presidencial demócrata antibelicista en 1968.

McCarthy, Joseph R. > McCarthy, Joseph R. (1908–1957) Senador de los Estados Unidos que llevó a una serie de investigaciones de alto perfil a los estadounidenses a quienes él acusaba de ser desleales a los Estados Unidos. Sus tácticas, conocidas como macartismo, ayudaron a definir el Temor Rojo de la década de 1950.

McCarthyism > macartismo Lema negativo que expresa acusaciones extremas e irresponsables de deslealtad.

McClellan, George B. > McClellan, George B. (1826–1885) Soldado de Pennsylvania que asistió a la Academia Militar de West Point y sirvió en la Guerra con México antes de regresar a West Point a enseñar. Durante la Guerra Civil, sirvió primero en Ohio y luego fue nombrado comandante del Ejército del Potomac. Su estilo precavido lo llevó a tener conflictos con el presidente Lincoln, y después de varias derrotas clave en Richmond y Antietam fue destituido del mando.

McKay, Claude > McKay, Claude (1890–1948) Poeta y novelista jamaiquino cuya obra, de gran influencia durante y después del Renacimiento de Harlem, buscó definir una identidad negra distintiva.

McKinley, William > McKinley, William (1843–1901) El 25° presidente de los Estados Unidos, sirviendo de 1897 a 1901. En 1898 lideró a los Estados Unidos durante la Guerra Hispano-Estadounidense. Su segundo mandato como presidente fue breve porque fue asesinado en 1901.

Meat Inspection Act > Ley de Inspección de Carnes Ley de 1906 que permitió al gobierno federal inspeccionar la carne vendida entre los estados y que exigió la inspección federal de las plantas de procesamiento de carne.

median family income > mediana del ingreso familiar Medida del ingreso familiar promedio.

Medicaid > Medicaid Programa federal creado en 1965 para brindar seguro de salud de bajo costo a los estadounidenses de escasos recursos de cualquier edad.

Medicare > Medicare Programa federal creado en 1965 para brindar seguro hospitalario básico a la mayoría de los estadounidenses mayores de sesenta y cinco de edad.

Mellon, Andrew > Mellon, Andrew (1835–1937) Fungió como secretario del Tesoro desde 1921 hasta 1932. Desempeñó un papel importante en la reforma de la estructura fiscal de los Estados Unidos al disminuir las tasas fiscales marginales para individuos y empresas.

melting pot > crisol de razas Sociedad en la que las personas de diferentes nacionalidades se asimilan para formar una cultura.

mercantilism > mercantilismo Filosofía económica que sostiene que una nación acumula riquezas al exportar más bienes de los que importa.

mercenary > mercenario Soldado profesional a quien se le paga por pelear en un ejército extranjero.

Meredith, James > Meredith, James (1933–) Asistió a una universidad para personas negras antes de ser el primer estudiante negro en la Universidad de Mississippi en 1962. Después de graduarse, obtuvo una licenciatura en leyes y participó en la política del Partido Republicano. En 1966 le dispararon durante una manifestación en Mississippi. Después de recuperarse, continuó siendo un miembro activo en el movimiento de los derechos civiles.

mestizos > mestizo En la Hispanoamérica colonial, persona descendiente de europeo e indígena.

Metacom > Metacom (c.1638–1676) Jefe indígena wampanoag, a quien los ingleses llamaban rey Philip, que lanzó los primeros ataques indígenas que comenzaron la Guerra del Rey Philip de 1675–1676.

metis > metis Habitante de las colonias francesas en América descendiente de francés e indígena.

Middle Ages > Edad Media Período en la historia de Europa que se inicia en el siglo V y termina en el siglo XIV.

Middle Passage > travesía intermedia Transporte forzado de esclavos desde África occidental a las Américas.

migrant farmworker > trabajador agrícola del campo Persona que viaja de una granja a otra, algunas veces de un estado a otro, para la recolección de frutas y vegetales.

migrated > migrar Mudarse de una región o hábitat a otra.

militarism > militarismo Glorificación de lo militar.

militia > milicia Ciudadanos entrenados que prestan servicio como soldados durante una emergencia.

Militia Act > Ley de Alistamiento Ley aprobada en 1862 que permitió a los soldados afroamericanos prestar servicio en las fuerzas armadas de la Unión.

minutemen > *minutemen/milicianos* Miembros de los grupos patriotas armados que iban al campo de batalla al momento de ser avisados en los días que llevaron a la Guerra de Independencia y durante ella.

missionaries > misionero Persona enviada a un país extranjero para convertir a otros a su religión.

missions > misión Asentamiento religioso generalmente manejado por sacerdotes y frailes católicos en la Hispanoamérica colonial.

Missouri Compromise > Acuerdo de Missouri Acuerdo de 1820 que hacía un llamado a la admisión de Missouri como estado esclavista y de Maine como estado libre, y prohibía la esclavitud en el territorio de la Compra de Luisiana al norte de la latitud 36° 30' N.

Moctezuma > Moctezuma (1466–1520) Noveno emperador azteca, se convirtió en el líder del imperio azteca en 1502, cuando estuvo en la cúspide de su poder. Cuando Hernán Cortés y sus tropas llegaron a Tenochtitlán en 1519, Moctezuma les dio la bienvenida. Sin embargo, fue hecho prisionero y Cortés designó la ciudad como el cuartel general de los invasores españoles. El pueblo de Moctezuma finalmente le perdió el respeto, hiriéndole cuando trataba de detener una revuelta contra los españoles. Murió poco después y en 1521 el imperio azteca llegó a su fin.

Model T > Modelo T Automóvil fabricado por Henry Ford para que fuera asequible en el mercado masivo.

modernism > modernismo Movimiento artístico y literario desencadenado por una rotura con las convenciones del pasado.

monetary policy > política monetaria Control de la oferta monetaria realizado por una autoridad central, incluyendo las tasas de interés influyentes para promover el crecimiento y la estabilidad económica.

Monmouth > Monmouth Batalla de la Guerra de Independencia de 1778 en Nueva Jersey en la cual ninguno de los bandos obtuvo una victoria clara.

monopoly > monopolio Control exclusivo de una industria por una sola compañía.

Monroe Doctrine > Doctrina Monroe Doctrina de política exterior establecida por el presidente Monroe en 1823 que desalentaba la intervención europea en el hemisferio Occidental.

"moral diplomacy" > "diplomacia moral" Aseveración de Woodrow Wilson en cuanto a que los Estados Unidos no usarían la fuerza para ejercer su influencia en el mundo, sino que trabajaría en la promoción de los derechos humanos.

Moral Majority > Mayoría Moral Organización política establecida por el reverendo Jerry Falwell en 1979 para promover objetivos religiosos.

Mormon > mormón Miembro de la Iglesia de Jesucristo de los Santos de los Últimos Días, fundada en 1830 por Joseph Smith.

Morse, Samuel F.B. > Morse, Samuel F.B. (1791–1872) Originalmente un estudiante de arte que desarrolló la idea del telégrafo eléctrico. Para 1838 había desarrollado el sistema de puntos y rayas que sería conocido en todo el mundo como el código Morse. Más tarde se convirtió en un destacado filántropo por sus donaciones a la beneficencia y su ayuda para establecer el Vassar College.

Mott, Lucretia > Mott, Lucretia (1793–1880) Profundamente comprometida con el ideal de la reforma. Conocida por su eficaz forma de hablar en público, viajó por el país promoviendo la abolición. En la década de 1840, frustrada por los intentos de limitar la participación de las mujeres en la reforma, Mott dirigió su atención a los derechos de las mujeres. Trabajó con Elizabeth Cady Stanton para organizar la Convención de Seneca Falls.

Mountain Men > montañés Trampero de los Estados Unidos que exploraba el área de las Montañas Rocosas a principios del siglo XIX.

muckraker > muckraker Escritor que descubre y expone la mala conducta de políticos o empresas.

Muir, John > Muir, John (1838–1914) Emigró con su familia desde Escocia en 1849. En 1876, instó al gobierno federal a adoptar una política de conservación de los bosques y más tarde fue un elemento clave en el establecimiento de los parques nacionales de Yosemite y Sequoia en California. En 1892, Muir fundó Sierra Club, una de las organizaciones conservacionistas líderes de la actualidad.

multinational corporation > corporación multinacional Compañía que produce y vende sus bienes y servicios alrededor del mundo.

Munich Pact > Pacto de Múnich Acuerdo de 1938 entre Alemania, Italia, Gran Bretaña y Francia que sacrificó los Sudetes para preservar la paz.

mural > mural Pintura de grandes dimensiones realizada directamente sobre una pared o cielo raso.

Mussolini, Benito > Mussolini, Benito (1883–1945) Líder y dictador fascista de Italia entre 1922–1945. Le llamaban Il Duce ("el líder") y estableció una dictadura totalitaria que promovía el nacionalismo extremo. Durante su dictadura, Italia invadió Etiopía y se asoció con Alemania durante la Segunda Guerra Mundial.

mutualistas > mutualistas Grupos organizados de mexicoamericanos para ofrecer préstamos y asistencia legal a miembros de su comunidad.

mutually assured destruction > destrucción mutua asegurada Política con la que los Estados Unidos y la Unión Soviética esperaban evitar la guerra nuclear al acumular suficientes armas para destruirse mutuamente.

My Lai > My Lai Villa en Vietnam del Sur donde en 1968 fuerzas estadounidenses dispararon contra civiles desarmados.

N

Nader, Ralph > Nader, Ralph (1934–) Abogado estadounidense y defensor de los consumidores que ha participado en una variedad de temas, entre ellos seguridad automotriz, uso de la tierra, regulación de los pesticidas y procesamiento seguro de la carne.

napalm > napalm Gasolina gelatinizada lanzada en latas que explotaban al impactar y dejaban en llamas grandes áreas; lanzadas por aviones estadounidenses durante la Guerra de Vietnam.

Nation of Islam > Nación del Islam Organización religiosa afroamericana fundada en 1930 que defendía la separación de las razas.

National Aeronautics and Space Administration (NASA) > Administración Nacional de Aeronáutica y Espacio (NASA) Agencia gubernamental formada para coordinar los esfuerzos estadounidenses en el espacio.

National American Woman Suffrage Association (NAWSA) > Asociación Nacional Americana para el Sufragio Femenino Grupo fundado en 1890 que funcionó a nivel tanto estatal como nacional para que se otorgara a las mujeres el derecho al voto.

National Association for the Advancement of Colored People (NAACP) > Asociación Nacional para el Progreso de la Gente de Color Organización fundada en 1909 para suprimir la segregación y la discriminación y avanzar en los derechos políticos y civiles de los afroamericanos.

National Consumers League (NCL) > Liga Nacional de Consumidores Grupo organizado en 1899 para investigar las condiciones en que se fabricaban y vendían los bienes, así como promover condiciones seguras de trabajo y un salario mínimo.

national debt > deuda interna Cantidad total de dinero que el gobierno federal debe a los dueños de bonos de gobierno.

National Organization for Women (NOW) > Organización Nacional para las Mujeres Organización establecida por Betty Friedan para derribar las barreras de la discriminación contra mujeres.

National Reclamation Act > Ley Nacional de Reclamaciones Ley de 1902 que otorgó al gobierno federal el poder para decidir adónde y cómo se distribuiría el agua, mediante la construcción y administración de represas y proyectos de irrigación.

National Recovery Administration (NRA) > Administración para la Recuperación Nacional Agencia del Nuevo Trato que promovió la recuperación económica al instaurar nuevos códigos para controlar la producción, precios y salarios.

National Road > Carretera Nacional Carretera construida por el gobierno federal a principios del siglo XIX que se extendía desde Maryland hasta Illinois.

nationalism > nacionalismo Lealtad y devoción hacia el país propio.

nationalize > nacionalizar Poner un recurso bajo control gubernamental.

nativism > nativismo Creencia a favor de los habitantes nativos en oposición a los inmigrantes.

nativist > nativista Persona que favorece a los habitantes nativos sobre los inmigrantes.

natural rights > derechos naturales Derechos universales, como la vida y la libertad, que según los filósofos, se derivan de la naturaleza y no de un gobierno.

Navigation Acts > Leyes de Navegación Leyes comerciales británicas establecidas por el Parlamento a mediados del siglo XVIII que regulaban el comercio con las colonias.

Nazism > nazismo Movimiento totalitario liderado por el Partido Nazi de Adolf Hitler en Alemania que instituyó discriminación legal y atrocidades en contra de los judíos.

Neutrality Act of 1939 > Ley de Neutralidad de 1939 Ley que permitía que las naciones en guerra compraran bienes y armas a los Estados Unidos si pagaban en efectivo y transportaban la mercadería en sus propios barcos.

New Deal > Nuevo Trato Programas y leyes establecidos por Franklin D. Roosevelt durante la Gran Depresión para promover la recuperación económica y reforma social.

New Deal coalition > Coalición del Nuevo Trato Fuerza política formada por grupos diversos unidos para apoyar a Franklin D. Roosevelt y su Nuevo Trato.

New Freedom > Nueva Libertad Programa de Woodrow Wilson para establecer controles gubernamentales sobre las corporaciones a fin de brindar más oportunidades a las pequeñas empresas.

New Frontier > Nueva Frontera Plan del presidente Kennedy dirigido a mejorar la economía, al combatir discriminación racial, y avanzar el programa espacial.

"new" immigrants > "nuevos" inmigrantes Inmigrantes del Sur y Este de Europa que llegaron a los Estados Unidos en una gran oleada entre 1880 y 1920.

New Jersey Plan > Plan de Nueva Jersey Propuesta de William Paterson de tener una legislatura unicameral donde cada estado tendría un voto.

New Nationalism > Nuevo Nacionalismo Plan del presidente Theodore Roosevelt para restaurar el poder del gobierno de disolver monopolios.

New Right > Nueva Derecha Movimiento político apoyado por grupos conservadores revigorizados durante la última mitad del siglo XX.

Niagara Movement > Movimiento Niágara Grupo de pensadores afroamericanos fundado en 1905 que presionó para obtener reformas raciales inmediatas, particularmente en cuanto a la educación y el voto.

Nimitz, Chester > Nimitz, Chester (1885–1966) Tomó el mando de la flota del Pacífico de los Estados Unidos poco después del ataque a Pearl Harbor en 1941. Bajo su liderazgo, el ejército de los Estados Unidos ganó las batallas de Midway, Tarawa, Marianas e Iwo Jima, entre otras. El liderazgo tranquilo de Nimitz fue clave para la victoria estadounidense en el Pacífico durante la Segunda Guerra Mundial.

Nineteenth Amendment > Decimonovena Enmienda Enmienda constitucional que otorgó a las mujeres el derecho al voto.

Nixon, Richard M. > Nixon, Richard M. (1913–1994) Sirvió como miembro republicano del Congreso y del Senado así como Vicepresidente bajo Dwight D. Eisenhower. Se presentó para Presidente en 1960 y perdió ante John F. Kennedy pero ganó el cargo en 1968. Su presidencia fue marcada por significantes logros en relaciones exteriores. En 1974, renunció en lugar de ser enjuiciado politicamente por encubrir actividades ilegales en el asunto Watergate.

No Child Left Behind Act > Ley Que Ningún Niño Se Quede Atrás Ley del año 2002 destinada a mejorar el desempeño de escuelas primarias y secundarias particularmente mediante sanciones por mandato contra las escuelas que no cumplan las normas federales de desempeño.

nonimportation agreements > acuerdos de no importación Boicots de los consumidores coloniales contra las exportaciones británicas como respuesta a los impuestos aprobados por el Parlamento.

Noriega, Manuel > Noriega, Manuel (1938–2017) Militar panameño que obtuvo el control del ejército en 1983, convirtiéndose en el líder controlador de Panamá. Acusaciones de fraude electoral, tráfico de drogas, lavado de dinero y espionaje en contra de los Estados Unidos llevó a su captura por tropas de los Estados Unidos. Fue encontrado culpable en 1992 y condenado a 40 años de prisión.

North American Free Trade Agreement (NAFTA) > Tratado de Libre Comercio de América del Norte Acuerdo firmado en 1993 para la remoción de las restricciones comerciales entre Canadá, México y los Estados Unidos.

North Atlantic Treaty Organization (NATO) > Organización del Tratado del Atlántico Norte (OTAN) Alianza militar formada para contrarrestar la expansión soviética.

Northwest Ordinance of 1787 > Decreto del Noroeste de 1787 Ley que estableció la base para el gobierno del Territorio del Noroeste.

Northwest Passage > paso del Noroeste Ruta navegable hacia Asia que muchos creían que se podía hallar a través de las frías aguas de lo que actualmente es Canadá.

Northwest Territory > Territorio del Noroeste Vasto territorio al norte del río Ohio y al oeste de Pennsylvania hasta llegar al río Mississippi.

nuclear family > núcleo familiar Hogar ideal o típico con un padre, una madre y niños.

Nuclear Test Ban Treaty > Tratado de Prohibición de Pruebas Nucleares Acuerdo de 1963 sobre armas nucleares que prohibió las pruebas nucleares en la superficie de la Tierra.

nullification > anulación Teoría de que los estados podrían anular o vetar cualquier ley federal que consideraran inconstitucional.

Nuremberg Trials > Juicios de Nuremberg Juicios en los que se acusó a los líderes nazis de crímenes de guerra.

O

Obama, Barack > Obama, Barack (1961–) Elegido el 44° Presidente de los Estados Unidos en 2008, convirtiéndose en el primer afroamericano en ocupar el cargo. Obama sirvió en la legislatura estatal de Illinois y en el Senado de los Estados Unidos antes de ser Presidente. Enfrentó las guerras en Afganistán e Irak, así como una recesión financiera después de asumir la presidencia. En 2009, fue galardonado con el Premio Nobel de la Paz.

O'Connor, Sandra Day > O'Connor, Sandra Day (1930–) Recibió su diploma en leyes de la Universidad de Stanford pero, por ser mujer, no podía encontrar trabajo en un bufete de abogados. En lugar de eso encontró trabajo como fiscal general adjunta en Carolina del Norte. Después de distinguirse durante años en una cantidad de campos, como "fiscal general adjunto, senadora, jueza de la Corte Superior y jueza de la Corte de Apelaciones (todo en el estado de Arizona)", se convirtió, en 1981, en la primera mujer en la Corte Suprema de Justicia de los Estados Unidos.

Office of War Information (OWI) > Oficina de Información de Guerra Agencia gubernamental que impulsaba el apoyo al esfuerzo bélico durante la Segunda Guerra Mundial.

Oglethorpe, James > Oglethorpe, James (1696–1785) Oficial y político inglés y fundador de la colonia británica de Georgia en América. Fue miembro del Parlamento de 1722 a 1754. Notable filántropo, Oglethorpe se opuso a la práctica de encarcelar a los deudores ingleses. También creía que las personas de cualquier religión merecían vivir en un lugar que permitiera la libertad religiosa. En 1732 recibió el estatuto para fundar la colonia de Georgia como un refugio para los deudores ingleses.

Okies > Okies Término general usado para describir a los refugiados del Dust Bowl.

Olmsted, Frederick Law > Olmsted, Frederick Law (1822–1903) Arquitecto paisajista estadounidense mejor conocido por diseñar Central Park en la Ciudad de Nueva York. Olmsted también contribuyó a la conservación del parque Yosemite en California, los espacios boscosos alrededor de las cataratas del Niágara así como un gran sistema de parques públicos en Boston.

Open Door Policy > política de puertas abiertas Declaración estadounidense que proclamaba que el gobierno no deseaba colonias en China, pero favorecía el libre comercio.

open-range system > sistema de campo abierto Método de cría en granjas en el que el ganadero permitió a su ganado pastar libremente en una vasta zona de pastizal.

Operation Desert Storm > Operación Tormenta del Desierto Ataque que comandaron los estadounidenses en 1991 contra las fuerzas iraquíes luego que Irak rehusó retirar sus tropas de Kuwait.

Oppenheimer, J. Robert > Oppenheimer, J. Robert (1904–1967) Físico estadounidense que fue el director del Proyecto Manhattan, el proyecto de investigación del gobierno de los Estados Unidos durante la Segunda Guerra Mundial que produjo las primeras bombas atómicas. Después de la guerra, fue director del Instituto para Estudios Avanzados en Nueva Jersey, un centro para la investigación teórica.

Oregon Trail > Camino de Oregón Ruta desde Independence, Missouri, hasta Oregón usada por los pioneros a mediados del siglo XIX.

Organization of Petroleum Exporting Countries (OPEC) > Organización de Países Exportadores de Petróleo (OPEP) Grupo de países que vende petróleo a otras naciones y que coopera en la regulación del precio y suministro del crudo.

Otis, Elisha > Otis, Elisha (1811–1861) Estadounidense que inventó el elevador seguro en 1852. El "montacargas de seguridad" de Otis fue primero diseñado para carga pero pronto se adaptó para el servicio de pasajeros. El primer elevador para pasajeros se instaló en una tienda de la Ciudad de Nueva York en 1857. Otis también desarrolló un elevador impulsado por vapor que llegó a ser la base de la Otis Elevator Company.

P

Paine, Thomas > Paine, Thomas (1737–1809) Autor y pensador político inglés-estadounidense que se mudó a Filadelfia en 1774, después de su encuentro con Benjamin Franklin. Es conocido por su muy influyente panfleto *Sentido común,* que ayudó a proveer apoyo para la causa patriota.

Palmer Raids > Redadas Palmer Redadas de principios de la década de 1920 iniciadas por el fiscal general del estado A. Mitchell Palmer contra personas sospechosas de ser radicales o comunistas.

Panama Canal > Canal de Panamá Vía acuática artificial que une el Atlántico y el Pacífico a través del istmo de Panamá.

pandemic > pandemia Enfermedad que se ha extendido a un área geográfica amplia, generalmente a través de continentes o en todo el mundo.

pardon > indulto Perdón oficial de un delito y su castigo.

Paris Peace Accords > Acuerdos de Paz de París Acuerdo de paz de 1973 entre los Estados Unidos, Vietnam del Sur, Vietnam del Norte y el Vietcong que finalizó efectivamente la Guerra de Vietnam.

Parks, Rosa > Parks, Rosa (1913–2005) Comenzó la protesta del autobús de Montgomery en 1955 cuando se negó a ceder su asiento a un pasajero blanco. Continuó siendo activa dentro del movimiento de los derechos civiles mientras trabajaba para un miembro del Congreso y comenzó una organización sin ánimo de lucro para ayudar a los jóvenes.

Parliament > Parlamento Cuerpo legislativo del gobierno británico.

patent > patente Derechos oficiales otorgados por el gobierno a un inventor para que tenga los derechos exclusivos y desarrolle, use y venda un invento durante un plazo establecido.

Patton, George S., Jr. > Patton, George S., hijo Con una original personalidad y siendo un líder enérgico admirado por las tropas bajo su mando, George S. Patton (1885–1945) dirigió los tanques estadounidenses durante la Primera Guerra Mundial y rápidamente demostró su habilidad para liderar unidades de combate móviles. Durante la Segunda Guerra Mundial, dirigió las tropas de los Estados Unidos en el norte de África y Europa, avanzando rápidamente por Francia y Alemania en los meses finales de la guerra.

Paul, Alice > Paul, Alice (1885–1977) Se unió al liderazgo de la Asociación Nacional Americana para el Sufragio Femenino en 1912 pero pronto lo dejó para fundar una organización más militante, que se convirtió en el Partido Nacional de las Mujeres en 1917. Después de la aprobación de la Decimonovena Enmienda, Paul amplió su trabajo a los derechos de las mujeres. En 1923 introdujo en el Congreso la primera enmienda por la igualdad de derechos.

Peace Corps > Cuerpo de Paz Organización del gobierno de los Estados Unidos que envía voluntarios para que brinden servicios técnicos, educativos y médicos en países en vías de desarrollo.

Pearl Harbor > Pearl Harbor Base militar estadounidense atacada por los japoneses el 7 de diciembre de 1941.

Pendleton Civil Service Act > Ley Pendleton del Servicio Civil Ley que creó un sistema de servicio civil para el gobierno federal en un intento por contratar empleados con un sistema de méritos en lugar del clientelismo.

penitentiary movement > movimiento penitenciario Movimiento dirigido a estructurar las prisiones para que los presos se sintieran penitentes por sus delitos.

Penn, William > Penn, William (1644–1718) Cuáquero inglés, quien después de declararse desilusionado por el proyecto de tener una religión libre en Inglaterra, fundó la colonia de Pennsylvania como un refugio para los cuáqueros y otras minorías religiosas de Europa.

Pentagon Papers > Documentos del Pentágono Estudio clasificado del gobierno de los Estados Unidos que reveló que los líderes estadounidenses intencionalmente involucraron a su nación en Vietnam sin haber informado completamente a la ciudadanía; fue filtrado al *New York Times* en 1971.

Pequot War > Guerra de Pequot Breve brote de violencia entre los colonos ingleses y los indígenas pequots en 1636, durante el cual una aldea pequot fue incendiada y en la que murieron entre 600 y 700 habitantes.

perestroika > perestroika Política de la Unión Soviética de finales de la década de 1980 que abogó por la reestructuración de la estancada economía soviética.

Perot, H. Ross > Perot, H. Ross (1930–2019) Multimillonario que hizo su fortuna por sí mismo y que fundó Electronic Data Systems en 1962. Perot se presentó como candidato independiente para Presidente de los Estados Unidos en 1992, logrando 19 por ciento de los votos. En 1995 fundó el Partido de la Reforma y se presentó a la elección presidencial de 1996, pero no ganó.

Perry, Matthew > Perry, Matthew (1794–1858) Oficial de la Marina de los Estados Unidos que dirigió una flota naval de 1853 a 1854 que obligó a Japón a entablar relaciones comerciales y diplomáticas con Occidente después de más de dos siglos de aislamiento. Su viaje abrió aún más la expansión estadounidense en el océano Pacífico.

Pershing, John J. > Pershing, John J. (1860–1948) Comandó las Fuerzas Expedicionarias Estadounidenses (AEF, por sus siglas en inglés) en Europa durante la Primera Guerra Mundial. Antes había servido en Filipinas y México. Después de la Primera Guerra Mundial, sirvió como jefe del ejército de los Estados Unidos.

personal computer > computadora personal Computadora pequeña destinada al uso personal.

personal liberty laws > Leyes de libertad individual Leyes instauradas por los estados del Norte para contrarrestar la Ley de Esclavos Fugitivos, que otorgaban derechos a los afroamericanos libres y a los que buscaban la libertad.

Pickett, George > Pickett, George (1825–1875) Soldado de Virginia y después general confederado durante la Guerra Civil. Es afamado por liderar un gran contingente llamado la Carga de Pickett en la Batalla de Gettysburg el 3 de julio de 1863.

Pilgrims > peregrinos Separatistas ingleses que buscaban la libertad religiosa y que en 1620 fundaron la colonia Plymouth.

Pinchot, Gifford > Pinchot, Gifford (1865–1946) Nombrado jefe del Servicio Forestal de los Estados Unidos, pero fue despedido en 1910 después de una discusión con el secretario del Interior del presidente Taft. En 1912, ayudó a formar el Partido Progresista que nominó a Theodore Roosevelt para Presidente. Pinchot continuó su trabajo de conservación en Pennsylvania, donde fue electo gobernador en 1922.

placer mining > minería de placer Uso de cribas de metal, picos y palas para extraer el oro de los bancos y lechos de los ríos y arroyos.

Platt Amendment > Enmienda Platt Grupo de condiciones con las que se le otorgó la independencia a Cuba en 1902, que incluían restricciones de los derechos de los cubanos y que otorgaban a los Estados Unidos el "derecho de intervenir" a fin de conservar el orden en Cuba.

political machines > máquina política Organización de un partido político que gana la lealtad de los votantes y garantiza el poder a un grupo pequeño de líderes, quienes a menudo abusan de él para su propio beneficio.

political party > partido político Organización de personas que busca ganar elecciones y ocupar puestos públicos a fin de dirigir las políticas gubernamentales.

Polk, James K. > Polk, James K. (1795–1849) Abogado y político que sirvió como el 11° presidente de los Estados Unidos de 1845 a 1849. Antes de ser elegido presidente, Polk sirvió en la legislatura de Tennessee y fue portavoz de la Cámara de Representantes de los Estados Unidos. Como presidente, Polk lideró a la nación durante la Guerra México-Estadounidense, a raíz de la cual los Estados Unidos ganaron grandes territorios a lo largo de la costa del Pacífico y en el Suroeste.

poll tax > impuesto electoral Suma de dinero a pagar antes que una persona pudiera votar.

Pontiac's Rebellion > Rebelión de Pontiac Levantamiento en 1763 de los indígenas en la región de los Grandes Lagos.

popular sovereignty > soberanía popular Principio por el cual las personas son la única fuente de poder gubernamental.

Populist Party > Partido Populista Partido del Pueblo; partido político formado en 1891 para abogar por un mayor suministro de dinero y otras reformas económicas.

Powderly, Terence V. > Powderly, Terence V. (1849–1924) Líder sindical estadounidense que dirigió a los Caballeros del Trabajo durante varios años a finales del siglo XIX, con el objetivo de sacar a los trabajadores estadounidenses de lo que él veía como la esclavitud del trabajo asalariado.

Powhatan > Powhatan (?–1618) Líder del imperio powhatan cuando los ingleses establecieron la colonia de Jamestown en 1607. Gobernó sobre más de 30 grupos indígenas y entre unas 13,000 y 34,000 personas. Las relaciones entre el pueblo powhatan y los colonos ingleses fueron ambivalentes. Después de la boda de su hija Pocahontas con el hacendado inglés John Rolfe, las relaciones fueron por lo general pacíficas, hasta su muerte en 1618.

precedent > precedente Acción o declaración que se convierte en ejemplo, regla o tradición a seguir.

presidios > presidios Fuertes construidos por los españoles en la América colonial, por lo general en lo que actualmente es el Suroeste de los Estados Unidos y California.

Presley, Elvis > Presley, Elvis (1935–1977) Músico estadounidense que llegó a ser conocido como el "rey del rock and roll". La música de Presley combinaba elementos de blues afroamericanos, gospel, canciones country y baladas de Tin Pan Alley. Su llamativa personalidad e imagen inconformista hicieron de Presley un ídolo para los adolescentes y una inspiración para los artistas futuros del rock and roll de todo el mundo.

privatizing > privatizar Transferir la propiedad o control gubernamental a intereses privados.

Proclamation of 1763 > Proclamación de 1763 Declaración por la que el rey británico ordenó a todos los colonos que permanecieran al este de los montes Apalaches.

productivity > productividad Velocidad a la que se producen bienes o se brindan servicios.

Progressive Party > Partido Progresivo Partido político surgido de la batalla Taft-Roosevelt que dividió al Partido Republicano en 1912.

Progressivism > Progresismo Movimiento surgido como respuesta a las presiones de la industrialización y urbanización, que promovía nuevas ideas y reformas políticas.

Prohibition > Prohibición Ley para prohibir la fabricación, transporte y venta de alcohol.

proprietary colonies > colonias de propietarios Colonias inglesas que la Corona otorgaba a un individuo o grupo de individuos.

protective tariffs > arancel proteccionista Impuestos sobre las mercancías importadas que hacen que el precio sea suficientemente alto para proteger los productos nacionales de la competencia extranjera.

public school movement > movimiento de educación pública Movimiento orientado a ofrecer mayores oportunidades educativas mediante la fundación de escuelas públicas financiadas con los impuestos.

Public Works Administration (PWA) > Administración de Obras Públicas Agencia del Nuevo Trato que brindó millones de empleos en la construcción de obras públicas así como en la de aeropuertos, presas y puentes.

Pulitzer, Joseph > Pulitzer, Joseph (1847–1911) Influyente editor de periódicos estadounidense. Pulitzer ayudó a dar el formato de los periódicos modernos e incluyó el reportaje de investigación, cobertura de deportes y moda, tiras cómicas e ilustraciones en sus periódicos.

Pull factor > factor de atracción Causa que atrae a las personas a una nueva ubicación.

Pullman Strike > Huelga de Pullman Violenta huelga de los trabajadores ferrocarrileros de 1894 que empezó en las afueras de Chicago y se extendió por todo el país.

pump priming > cebado de bomba Teoría económica que favorece los proyectos de obras públicas porque ponen dinero en manos de los consumidores que comprarán más bienes, estimulando así la economía.

Pure Food and Drug Act > Ley de Alimentos y Fármacos Puros Ley de 1906 que permitió la inspección federal de los alimentos y medicinas y prohibió el transporte y venta interestatal de alimentos impuros así como el rotulado erróneo de alimentos y fármacos.

Puritans > puritanos Protestantes ingleses que observaban una estricta disciplina religiosa y profesaban la simplificación del culto en un esfuerzo por purificar la Iglesia anglicana; pobladores de la colonia de la bahía de Massachusetts en 1630.

Push factor > factor de empuje Causa que hace que las personas dejen su país de origen.

Q

Quakers > cuáqueros Miembros de la Sociedad Religiosa de Amigos, un movimiento cristiano dedicado a principios pacíficos. Los cuáqueros no creen en tener ministros; en lugar de eso, confían en la doctrina de la "luz interior", o sentimiento de que Cristo trabaja directamente en el alma. Los cuáqueros son pacifistas y se rehúsan a portar armas.

Quebec > Quebec Puesto comercial fortificado construido en el río San Lorenzo, en 1608, que fue el primer asentamiento europeo permanente en Canadá.

quota system > sistema de cuotas Acuerdo que limitó el número de inmigrantes provenientes de países específicos que podían ingresar a los Estados Unidos.

R

Radical Republicans > republicanos radicales Congresistas que abogaban por derechos ciudadanos íntegros para los afroamericanos junto con una política dura de Reconstrucción en el Sur.

Randolph, A. Philip > Randolph, A. Philip (1889–1979) Destacado líder sindical y del movimiento de los derechos civiles durante décadas. En 1925, llegó a ser el jefe de la Brotherhood of Sleeping Car Porters. Después de más de una década de lucha, consiguió que la Pullman Corporation firmara el primer contrato de la historia entre una compañía importante y un sindicato predominantemente afroamericano. Después Randolph dirigió su atención a la discriminación en la industria de la guerra, convenciendo al presidente Roosevelt de que emitiera la Orden Ejecutiva 8802 en 1941. Después de la guerra, convenció al presidente Truman de que aprobara otra orden ejecutiva para prohibir la discriminación en el ejército. Randolph fue uno de los impulsores de la Marcha a Washington de 1963.

ratification > ratificación Aprobación oficial.

rationing > racionamiento Límites controlados por el gobierno sobre la cantidad de ciertos bienes que podían comprar los civiles en tiempos de guerra.

Reagan, Ronald > Reagan, Ronald (1911–2004) Logró su famoso estilo de comunicación sencillo debido a su formación como presentador de deportes en la radio, presentador de programas de televisión y lo que le hizo más famoso, de actor de cine. Aunque fue demócrata de joven, sus puntos de vista se hicieron más conservadores y cambió al Partido Republicano. Fue electo gobernador de California en 1966 donde llevó a cabo una agenda conservadora durante sus dos periodos. En 1980, Reagan fue electo para el primero de sus dos periodos como Presidente.

realpolitik > realpolitik Política exterior promovida por Henry Kissinger durante la administración Nixon con base en intereses nacionales concretos en lugar de ideologías abstractas.

recall > destitución Proceso por el cual los electores pueden remover a funcionarios electos antes de terminar su período.

reconquista > reconquista Campaña finalizada en 1492 que restablecía el gobierno español cristiano en la península Ibérica después de 700 años de dominio musulmán.

Reconstruction > Reconstrucción Programa implementado por el gobierno federal entre 1865 y 1877 para reparar los daños al Sur que causó la Guerra Civil y reincorporar los estados sureños a la Unión.

Reconstruction Finance Corporation (RFC) > Corporación de Financiamiento para la Reconstrucción Agencia federal establecida por el Congreso, en 1932, para brindar créditos gubernamentales de emergencia a los bancos, ferrocarriles y otras grandes empresas.

Red Scare > Temor Rojo Miedo a que los comunistas estuviesen empeñados en destruir la forma de vida estadounidense.

Redeemer > Redentor Término con el que denominaban a los demócratas blancos del Sur que regresaron al poder político después de 1870.

referendum > referendo Proceso que permite que los ciudadanos aprueben o rechacen una ley que ha pasado una legislatura.

Renaissance > Renacimiento Periodo en la historia de Europa que cubre desde el siglo XIV hasta el siglo XVI y que introdujo una perspectiva más secular, fomentó la libertad de pensamiento y la importancia del individuo, y renovó el interés en la educación clásica.

reparations > reparaciones Pago por los daños causados por la guerra.

repatriation > repatriación Proceso por el cual los funcionarios del gobierno regresan a las personas a sus países de origen.

republic > república Forma de gobierno en la que el pueblo elige a los funcionarios.

Republican Party > Partido Republicano Partido político establecido alrededor de una plataforma antiesclavista en 1854.

reservationists > reservasionistas Grupo de senadores encabezados por Henry Cabot que se oponía a terminar la Primera Guerra Mundial con el Tratado de Versalles a menos que éste incluyera ciertos cambios.

reservations > reservas Tierras públicas donde los indígenas norteamericanos tuvieron la obligación de vivir por orden del gobierno federal.

Revere, Paul > Revere, Paul (1735–1818) Orfebre estadounidense que vivió y trabajó en Boston. Cuando los británicos se aproximaban al puerto de Boston el 16 de abril de 1775, Revere cabalgó por el campo hasta Concord avisando a los colonos y llamando a los patriotas a las armas. Sus aventuras de esa noche fueron recordadas años más tarde por Henry Wadsworth Longfellow en el poema "La Cabalgata de Paul Revere".

revivalist > renovador de la fe Predicador que trabaja para renovar la importancia de la religión en la vida estadounidense.

Riis, Jacob > Riis, Jacob (1849–1914) Inmigrante danés que trabajó como reportero periodístico de la Ciudad de Nueva York en 1873. En 1888, como reportero de crímenes para el *New York Evening Sun,* tomó fotografías de la vida nocturna en los barrios bajos urbanos. Publicadas en su libro en 1890, *Cómo vive la otra mitad,* las fotografías conmovieron al Comisionado de Policía de Nueva York, Theodore Roosevelt, y lo llevaron a comenzar la causa de la reforma urbana.

rock-and-roll > rock-and-roll Música originada en las tradiciones del gospel y blues de los afroamericanos.

Rockefeller, John D. > Rockefeller, John D. (1839–1937) Empresario y filántropo estadounidense. Comenzó la Standard Oil Company y dominó la industria del petróleo con prácticas de negocio innovadoras y agresivas. También donó dinero para diferentes causas mediante la Rockefeller Foundation.

Roosevelt Corollary > Corolario Roosevelt Replanteamiento del presidente Theodore Roosevelt de la Doctrina Monroe, según la cual la política de los Estados Unidos era mantener al hemisferio occidental libre de la intervención de las potencias europeas.

Roosevelt, Eleanor > Roosevelt, Eleanor (1884–1962) Esposa del presidente Franklin D. Roosevelt. Con la elección de su esposo como Presidente en 1932, Eleanor Roosevelt llegó a ser una figura pública por sí misma. Viajó por el país promoviendo las causas para ayudar a las mujeres, niños y pobres. Después de la muerte de su esposo, fue delegada de los Estados Unidos ante la Organización de las Naciones Unidas (1945–1951), enfocándose en los derechos humanos y temas de la mujer.

Roosevelt, Franklin D. > Roosevelt, Franklin D. (1882–1945) Secretario Adjunto de la Marina (1913–1920), antes de postularse sin éxito para Vicepresidente en la convención demócrata en 1920. Afectado por poliomielitis el año siguiente, Roosevelt se recuperó para reasumir su carrera política como gobernador de Nueva York (1929–1933). Elegido Presidente en 1932, dirigió la nación durante la Gran Depresión y la Segunda Guerra Mundial antes de morir en el cargo en 1945.

Roosevelt, Theodore > Roosevelt, Theodore (1858–1919) Gobernador de Nueva York antes de ser vicepresidente en 1901. Roosevelt fue el hombre más joven en asumir la presidencia. Fue conocido por sus políticas antimonopolio y de conservación. Hizo un intento en 1912 para obtener otro periodo como candidato del Partido Progresista, pero no tuvo éxito.

Rosenberg, Julius and Ethel > Rosenberg, Julius y Ethel Julius (1918–1953) y Ethel Rosenberg (1915–1953) fueron dos civiles estadounidenses acusados de forma controvertida y ejecutados por espionaje durante el Temor Rojo en la década de 1950. Pruebas posteriores de los Documentos Venona confirmaron que ambos habían tenido relación con el espionaje soviético.

Rough Riders > Jinetes Rudos Grupo de hombres fuertes provenientes del Oeste y de la clase alta del Este que pelearon durante la guerra entre España y Estados Unidos.

royal colonies > colonias de la corona Colonias inglesas que estaban bajo el control directo de la corona.

rural-to-urban migrants > inmigrante del campo a la ciudad Persona que se traslada de las áreas rurales a la ciudad.

Russo-Japanese War > Guerra ruso-japonesa Guerra entre Japón y Rusia durante 1904 por la presencia de tropas rusas en Manchuria.

Ruth, Babe > Ruth, Babe (1895–1948) Jugador profesional de béisbol conocido por su talento para el espectáculo y su capacidad para marcar homeruns. Es miembro del Salón de la Fama de Béisbol.

S

Sacco, Nicola > Sacco, Nicola (1891–1927) Inmigrante italiano condenado por asesinato y ejecutado en 1927.

SALT II > SALT II Acuerdo propuesto entre los Estados Unidos y la Unión Soviética para limitar la producción de ciertos tipos de armas nucleares. También conocido como Tratado de Limitación de Armas Estratégicas II no fue ratificado nunca por el Senado de los Estados Unidos.

salutary neglect > negligencia benigna Política británica de principios del siglo XVIII que permitió que las colonias prácticamente se autogobernaran en tanto que Gran Bretaña tuviera ganancias económicas.

sanctions > sanción Penalización prevista para obligar a que la gente obedezca las leyes y normas, en particular las medidas adoptadas para obligar a un país a obedecer el derecho internacional.

Sand Creek Massacre > Masacre de Sand Creek Incidente de 1864 durante el cual una milicia de Colorado asesinó a un campamento de indígenas cheyenes y arapajos.

Sanger, Margaret > Sanger, Margaret (1879–1966) La primera en acuñar el término "control de natalidad" en un panfleto que publicó en 1914. Una organización médica que ella fundó, el Birth Control Research Bureau, se convirtió en 1942 en Planned Parenthood.

Santa Anna, Antonio López de > Santa Anna, Antonio López de (1794–1876) Militar y político mexicano que desempeñó papeles importantes en los conflictos políticos y militares en México a mediados del siglo XIX, entre ellos la revuelta de Texas en 1836 y la Guerra México-Estadounidense. Santa Anna gobernó once veces durante las turbulentas décadas que siguieron a la Independencia de México.

Santa Fe Trail > Camino de Santa Fe Camino desarrollado por los comerciantes a mediados del siglo XIX que conectaba Independence, Missouri, con Santa Fe, Nuevo México.

Saratoga > Saratoga Batalla en 1777 de la Guerra de Independencia considerada el punto crucial de la guerra porque el triunfo de los patriotas convenció a Francia de aliarse oficialmente con los Estados Unidos como nación.

satellite > satélite Dispositivo mecánico que orbita la Tierra y que recibe y envía señales de comunicación o transmite datos científicos.

satellite state > estado satélite Nación independiente bajo el control de una nación más poderosa.

saturation bombing > saturación de bombardeos Táctica de dejar caer cantidades masivas de bombas a fin de infligir el máximo daño.

Savings and Loan crisis > crisis financiera Fracaso en 1989 de cerca de 1,000 bancos de ahorro y préstamo (S&Ls, por sus siglas en inglés) como resultado de prácticas comerciales riesgosas y a veces fraudulentas.

scalawag > *scalawag* Término negativo para referirse a un blanco sureño que apoyó al Partido Republicano después de la Guerra Civil.

Schlafly, Phyllis > Schlafly, Phyllis (1924–2016) Escritora y activista política estadounidense, muy conocida y franca defensora de la familia tradicional. Es la opositora más famosa a la Enmienda de Igualdad de Derechos.

scientific management > administración científica Enfoque para mejorar la eficiencia, en el que los expertos observaban cada paso de un proceso de manufactura y buscaban formas de reducir el tiempo, esfuerzo y costo.

Scopes Trial > Juicio Scopes Juicio al que fue sometido, en 1925, un maestro de Tennessee por enseñar la teoría de Darwin sobre la evolución.

Scott, Dred > Scott, Dred (c.1800–1857) Afroamericano nacido en condición de esclavo que entabló una demanda para lograr su libertad con base en que había vivido durante un tiempo en un estado donde la esclavitud estaba prohibida. En el caso *Dred Scott contra Sandford,* la Corte Suprema falló en contra de Scott declarando que su tiempo en un estado libre no anulaba su estatus de persona esclavizada y que como un esclavo era una propiedad no podía demandar en los tribunales. Después del fallo, los hijos del dueño original de Scott compraron a Scott y a su esposa y los liberaron.

Scott, Winfield > Scott, Winfield (1786–1866) Militar de carrera y una de las figuras militares estadounidenses más influyentes de la primera mitad del siglo XIX. Ocupó el rango de general en tres guerras y fue el comandante general del Ejército de los Estados Unidos de 1841 a 1861. Scott fue nominado como el candidato presidencial del Partido Whig en 1852, pero perdió la elección frente a Franklin Pierce.

secede > separarse Retirarse formalmente como miembro de un grupo u organización.

Second Continental Congress > Segundo Congreso Continental Asamblea de delegados con representación de cada colonia que se reunió en 1775 en Filadelfia después de las Batallas de Lexington y Concord.

Second Great Awakening > Segundo Gran Despertar Movimiento de renovación religiosa que se dio en la primera mitad del siglo XIX.

segregation > segregación Separación forzada, a menudo con base en la raza.

Selective Service Act > Ley de Servicio Selectivo Ley aprobada por el Congreso en 1917; autorizó el reclutamiento de hombres para el servicio militar.

self-determination > autodeterminación Derecho de las personas de elegir su propia forma de gobierno.

Seneca Falls Convention > Convención de Seneca Falls Primera convención sobre los derechos de la mujer realizada en los Estados Unidos, celebrada en Nueva York en 1848.

separation of powers > separación de poderes Principio que divide el poder entre los poderes ejecutivo, legislativo y judicial del gobierno.

Separatists > separatistas Protestantes ingleses que querían separarse de la Iglesia anglicana.

Serra, Junípero > Serra, Junípero (1713–1784) Sacerdote franciscano español que ayudó a establecer nueve misiones en lo que actualmente es California. Nacido en España, llegó a la Ciudad de México en 1750 para comenzar su trabajo misionero entre los indígenas americanos. Su trabajo en el establecimiento de misiones ayudó a fortalecer el control de España en su territorio de California.

service economy > economía de servicio Sistema económico enfocado en la compra y venta de servicios.

service sector > sector de servicios Empresas que brindan servicios en lugar de fabricar bienes.

settlement house > centro comunitario Centro comunal organizado a inicios del siglo XX para ofrecer servicios sociales a los pobres de la ciudad.

Seventeenth Amendment > Decimoséptima Enmienda Enmienda constitucional de 1913 que permitía que los ciudadanos eligieran de manera directa a los senadores de los Estados Unidos.

share-tenancy > arrendamiento por aparcería Similar a la aparcería, excepto que el granjero elige qué cultivar y compra sus propios insumos.

sharecropping > aparcería Sistema en el cual un granjero atiende una porción de la tierra del propietario a cambio de una parte de la cosecha.

Shays' Rebellion > Rebelión de Shays Rebelión de granjeros conducida por Daniel Shays en contra del aumento de impuestos en Massachusetts.

Sherman Antitrust Act > Ley Antimonopolios Sherman Ley de 1890 que prohibió los consorcios que restringían el comercio o negocios interestatales.

Sherman, William Tecumseh > Sherman, William Tecumseh (1820–1891) Hijo de un juez de Ohio que llegó a ser un renombrado general de la Unión durante la Guerra Civil. Luchó en las Batallas de Bull Run y Shiloh antes de unir sus tropas con las del general Grant para sitiar Vicksburg en 1863. Después de su victoria, Sherman dirigió su "Marcha hacia el mar", 250 millas al este para capturar Savannah, Georgia.

Shiloh > Shiloh Batalla de 1862 de la Guerra Civil ocurrida en el suroeste de Tennessee en la que la Unión logró una victoria pero murieron o fueron heridos casi 25,000 soldados de la Unión y la Confederación.

siege > sitio Táctica militar según la cual se rodea al enemigo cerrando por completo el acceso a su abastecimiento a fin de obligarlo a rendirse.

silent majority > mayoría silenciosa Frase introducida por el presidente Richard Nixon para referirse a un número significativo de estadounidenses que apoyaban sus políticas pero eligieron no expresar su opinión.

Sinclair, Upton > Sinclair, Upton (1878–1968) Comenzó escribiendo para periódicos y completó varias novelas exitosas poco después de graduarse en la universidad en 1897. Su obra más famosa, *The Jungle,* fue publicada en 1906. Sinclair siguió escribiendo obras de denuncia y con el tiempo participó activamente en la política de California, postulándose para gobernador en 1934, pero sin éxito. En 1942, ganó el Premio Pulitzer por su novela *Los dientes del dragón.*

sit-down strike > huelga de brazos caídos Protesta laboral en que los trabajadores dejan de trabajar y ocupan el lugar de trabajo hasta que se satisfacen sus demandas.

sit-in > sentada Tipo de protesta en que los participantes se sientan y rehúsan moverse.

Sitting Bull > Toro Sentado (1831?–1890) Jefe guerrero y un importante líder espiritual que se convirtió en el primer jefe de todas las tribus sioux en la década de 1860. Después de rendirse al ejército en 1881, vivió en una reserva donde fue asesinado por la policía indígena enviada a arrestarlo.

Sixteenth Amendment > Decimosexta Enmienda Enmienda constitucional de 1913 que otorgó al Congreso la autoridad para establecer un impuesto a los ingresos.

skyscrapers > rascacielos Edificio muy alto.

Slater, Samuel > Slater, Samuel (1768–1835) Industrial inglés que usó sus conocimientos sobre la manufactura del algodón y la maquinaria textil para construir en 1793 el primer telar impulsado por agua de la nación en Pawtucket, Rhode Island.

Smith Act > Ley Smith Ley que prohibió la enseñanza o defensa de un derrocamiento violento del gobierno estadounidense.

Smith, Bessie > Smith, Bessie (1898?–1937) Cantante de blues conocida como la "Emperatriz del Blues". Cantó con algunos de los grandes músicos del jazz de la época, entre ellos Louis Armstrong.

Smith, John > Smith, John (c.1580–1631) Explorador inglés y uno de los líderes promotores de la colonización inglesa en los Estados Unidos. En 1607 ayudó a fundar la colonia de Jamestown y fue su líder de 1608 a 1609. También contribuyó creando mapas y descripciones de Virginia y Nueva Inglaterra.

Smith, Joseph > Smith, Joseph (1805–1844) Fundador de Iglesia de Jesucristo de los Santos de los Últimos Días. Después de afirmar que había tenido diversas revelaciones, Smith publicó el *Book of Mormon* (*Libro del mormón*) en 1830. Junto con sus seguidores mormones construyeron asentamientos en Ohio, Missouri e Illinois. Al establecerse en Nauvoo, Illinois, ciudadanos en contra de los mormones encarcelaron a Smith y a su hermano, quienes recibieron balazos y fueron asesinados por una muchedumbre en 1844.

Social Darwinism > darwinismo social Creencia de algunos a finales del siglo XIX según la que algunas naciones o razas eran superiores a otras y por lo tanto estaban destinadas a gobernar.

Social Gospel > evangelio social Movimiento reformista surgido a finales del siglo XIX cuyo fin era mejorar la sociedad por principios cristianos.

Social Security Act > Ley de Seguridad Social Ley de 1935 que establecía un sistema de pensiones para los jubilados, un seguro de desempleo y un seguro para las víctimas de accidentes laborales; proporcionaba ayuda a las madres y los niños afectados por la pobreza, los ciegos y los discapacitados.

socialism > socialismo Sistema o teoría según la cual los medios de producción son controlados y regulados públicamente en lugar de ser propiedad de individuos.

Songhai > Songhai Gran imperio de África occidental que duró aproximadamente desde el año 1460 d. C. hasta el año 1600 d. C.

Sons of Liberty > Hijos de la Libertad Organización de colonos formada para oponerse a la Ley del Timbre y a otras leyes e impuestos británicos.

Sosa, Lionel > Sosa, Lionel (1939–) Ejecutivo de publicidad que tuvo éxito al ayudar a las compañías a comercializar sus productos para los consumidores latinos. Pero es más famoso por ayudar a los candidatos republicanos a lograr el voto de los latinos. En la elección de 2004, con la ayuda de Sosa, George W. Bush pudo conseguir un estimado de 40% de los votos latinos, un aumento considerable a los anteriores candidatos presidenciales republicanos.

Southeast Asia Treaty Organization (SEATO) > Organización del Tratado del Sudeste Asiático Alianza defensiva orientada a prevenir la agresión comunista en Asia.

southern strategy > estrategia para el Sur Táctica del Partido Republicano para ganar las elecciones presidenciales al asegurarse los votos electorales de los estados del Sur.

space race > carrera espacial Competencia entre los Estados Unidos y la Unión Soviética para aterrizar exitosamente en la Luna.

Spanish Civil War > Guerra Civil Española Conflicto en España en el que las fuerzas nacionalistas dirigidas por el general Francisco Franco se rebelaron contra el gobierno democrático republicano.

speculation > especulación Práctica de hacer inversiones de alto riesgo con la esperanza de obtener grandes ganancias.

spheres of influence > esfera de influencia Región dominada y controlada por un poder externo.

Spock, Benjamin > Spock, Benjamin (1903–1998) Pediatra y autor estadounidense cuyo libro *Common Sense Book of Baby and Child Care,* publicado en 1946, fue uno de los libros más influyentes en la crianza infantil del siglo XX. Spock rompió la tradición al aconsejar a los padres que mostraran afecto, comprensión y flexibilidad y que promovieran y apreciaran la individualidad de cada niño.

spoils system > sistema de prebendas Práctica del partido político en el poder de asignar los puestos y nombramientos a sus seguidores en lugar de basarlos en las calificaciones.

Square Deal > Trato Justo Programa de reformas del presidente Theodore Roosevelt para evitar que los ricos y poderosos se aprovecharan de los propietarios de pequeñas empresas y de los pobres.

stagflation > estanflación Término para la condición económica creada a finales de las décadas de 1960 y 1970 por una alta inflación combinada con el estancamiento del crecimiento económico y el alto desempleo.

Stalin, Joseph > Stalin, Joseph (1878–1953) Líder de la comunista Unión de Repúblicas Socialistas Soviéticas (U.R.S.S.) de 1924 a 1953. Sus esfuerzos para transformar la Unión Soviética en una potencia industrial y formar granjas colectivas operadas por el estado provocó penurias extremas y millones de muertes. Asociado con Alemania en 1939, Stalin se unió más tarde a los Aliados en la Segunda Guerra Mundial. Después de la guerra, Stalin se convirtió en un participante agresivo de la Guerra Fría.

Stamp Act > Ley del Timbre Ley promulgada en 1765 por el Parlamento que exigía a los colonos que pagaran impuestos sobre el material impreso.

Stanton, Elizabeth Cady > Stanton, Elizabeth Cady (1815–1902) Vivaz y a menudo feroz defensora de los derechos de la mujer. Mientras criaba a una familia cada vez más numerosa, trabajaba con Lucretia Mott y otras para organizar la Convención de Seneca Falls. Desde el principio, impulsó a las mujeres para que lucharan por su derecho al voto, ayudando a establecer la dirección que seguiría el movimiento en los años posteriores.

Staple crop > cultivo principal Cultivo que está en constante demanda.

"Star-Spangled Banner, The" > ***"Star-Spangled Banner, The"*** Poema escrito por Francis Scott Key en 1814 que se convirtió en el himno nacional en 1931.

Starr, Kenneth > Starr, Kenneth (1946–) Abogado estadounidense que sirvió como consejero independiente a cargo de la investigación que intentó obtener la destitución del presidente Bill Clinton en 1998.

steerage > entrecubierta Alojamiento de tercera clase en un buque de vapor.

Steffens, Lincoln > Steffens, Lincoln (1866–1936) Reportero y editor del *New York Post* y más tarde de la revista de denuncias *McClure's*. Escribió artículos y libros exponiendo la corrupción del gobierno en los niveles estatales y municipales.

Steinbeck, John > Steinbeck, John (1902–1968) Novelista estadounidense que escribió con frecuencia sobre los trabajadores agrígolas temporales y otros trabajadores durante la Gran Depresión.

Steinem, Gloria > Steinem, Gloria (1934–) Feminista estadounidense, activista política y escritora-editora, que tuvo un papel influyente en el Movimiento de las Mujeres de finales del siglo XX. En 2013, Steinem fue galardonada con la Medalla Presidencial de la Libertad.

Stowe, Harriet Beecher > Stowe, Harriet Beecher (1811–1896) Autora abolicionista estadounidense mejor conocida por su novela antiesclavista *Uncle Tom's Cabin*, (*La cabaña del tío Tom*), publicada en 1852. Comenzó a escribir su novela como una serie de historias, las cuales aparecieron por primera vez entre 1851 y 1852 en el periódico abolicionista *National Era*.

Strategic Arms Limitation Treaty (SALT I) > Tratado de Limitación de Armas Estratégicas Acuerdo de 1972 entre los Estados Unidos y la Unión Soviética para suspender el despliegue de misiles balísticos intercontinentales y limitó los misiles antibalísticos.

strategic bombing > bombardeo estratégico Táctica de dejar caer bombas en blancos políticos e industriales clave.

Strategic Defense Initiative (SDI) > Iniciativa de Defensa Estratégica Plan del presidente Reagan, apodado "Star Wars" para desarrollar defensas innovadoras con el fin de salvaguardar a los Estados Unidos contra ataques de misiles nucleares.

strict construction > interpretación estricta Creencia en que el gobierno está limitado a los poderes claramente establecidos en la Constitución.

Student Nonviolent Coordinating Committee > Comité Estudiantil Coordinador de la No Violencia Movimiento de base fundado en 1960 por jóvenes activistas a favor de los derechos humanos.

Students for a Democratic Society (SDS) > Estudiantes a Favor de una Sociedad Democrática Organización fundada en 1960 en la Universidad de Michigan para combatir el racismo y la pobreza.

suburbs > suburbios Áreas residenciales que rodean una ciudad.

Suez crisis > crisis de Suez Intento de Francia y Gran Bretaña por apoderarse del control del canal de Suez en 1956.

suffrage > sufragio Derecho al voto.

Sunbelt > Sun Belt Nombre dado a la región de los estados del Sur y Suroeste.

superpowers > superpotencias Naciones suficientemente poderosas para influir en los actos y políticas de otras naciones.

supply-side economics > economía de la oferta Teoría económica que dice que reducir las tasas tributarias estimula el crecimiento económico.

suspension bridges > puentes colgantes Puentes cuya carretera está suspendida por cables.

sweatshops > maquilas Pequeñas fábricas donde los empleados tienen que trabajar largas horas en malas condiciones y por poco dinero.

T

Taft-Hartley Act > Ley Taft Hartley Ley que restringió el poder de los sindicatos de trabajadores.

Taft, William Howard > Taft, William Howard (1857–1930) El 27° Presidente de los Estados Unidos de 1909 a 1913. En 1901, se convirtió en el primer gobernador civil de Filipinas. Bajo ese cargo, trabajó para reconstruir la economía y restablecer el orden. En 1921, el presidente Harding nombró a Taft el 10° jefe de justicia de los Estados Unidos, donde sirvió durante 9 años.

Taliban > talibán Fracción fundamentalista islámica que controló la mayor parte de Afganistán entre 1996 y 2001.

Taney, Roger B. > Taney, Roger B. (1777–1864) Sirvió como el quinto presidente de la Corte Suprema de los Estados Unidos. Es más conocido por su decisión en el caso *Dred Scott contra Sandford*, en la que establecía que los esclavos no tenían acceso a los derechos garantizados por la Constitución y que el Congreso no estaba facultado para prohibir la esclavitud en ningún territorio, ya que tales leyes privarían a los dueños de esclavos de su propiedad.

tariff > arancel Impuesto sobre bienes importados.

Tariff of 1816 > Arancel de 1816 Arancel protector establecido por el Congreso para estimular a los estadounidenses a comprar bienes hechos en los Estados Unidos.

Tariff of Abominations > Arancel de Abominaciones Arancel protector de 1828, llamado así por sus oponentes sureños.

Taylor, Susie King > Taylor, Susie King (1848–1912) Enfermera durante la Guerra Civil nacida de padres afroamericanos esclavizados. A los 7 años fue enviada a vivir con su abuela. Durante la Guerra Civil, viajó junto con otros afroamericanos a territorio ocupado por la Unión. Escribió sus memorias donde describió sus experiencias como enfermera y como maestra.

Taylor, Zachary > Taylor, Zachary (1784–1850) Creció en la frontera de Kentucky y se alistó en el ejército en 1806. Sirvió en la Guerra de 1812, la Guerra de los Halcones y las Guerras de los seminolas en Florida. Fue aclamado como héroe por su liderazgo del ejército de los Estados Unidos en la Guerra México-Estadounidense. En 1848 fue elegido el 12° presidente de los Estados Unidos, pero murió 16 meses después de asumir el cargo.

Tea Party Movement > movimiento del Tea Party Movimiento informal conformado por grupos locales que quieren reducir el tamaño y el alcance del gobierno federal.

Teapot Dome scandal > Escándalo Teapot Dome Escándalo durante la administración Harding en el cual el secretario del interior arrendó las reservas de petróleo del gobierno a petroleros privados a cambio de un soborno.

Tecumseh > Tecumseh (1768–1813) Guerrero shawnee del valle de Ohio que encabezó un movimiento de resistencia militar y espiritual entre los indígenas norteamericanos a principios del siglo XIX. Tecumseh resistió activamente a los Estados Unidos, luchando en batallas, rechazando tratados y viajando ampliamente para convencer a los otros grupos indígenas de que todos eran un pueblo y que ningún grupo tenía el derecho de hacer un tratado.

televangelist > telepredicadores Ministros que utilizan la televisión para predicar.

temperance movement > movimiento por la templanza Movimiento encauzado a eliminar el abuso del alcohol y los problemas que éste genera.

tenant farmer > granjero arrendatario Alguien que paga un alquiler a un señor para poder cultivar la tierra.

tenant farming > agricultura de arrendamiento Sistema en el que un agricultor paga un alquiler por el uso de la tierra a un propietario.

tenements > vecindades Edificios de varios pisos divididos en apartamentos para alojar a tantos residentes como sea posible.

Tennessee Valley Authority (TVA) > Autoridad del Valle del Tennessee Agencia gubernamental creada durante el Nuevo Trato, para construir represas en el valle del río Tennessee con el fin de controlar las inundaciones y generar energía eléctrica.

termination policy > política de terminación Política que cerró todos los programas a cargo de la Oficina de Asuntos Indígenas. También dio por terminada la responsabilidad federal en cuanto a la salud y el bienestar de los indígenas estadounidenses.

Tet Offensive > Ofensiva Tet Asalto comunista contra un gran número de ciudades de Vietnam del Sur a principios de 1968.

Thirteenth Amendment > Decimotercera Enmienda Enmienda constitucional de 1865 que abolió la esclavitud en los Estados Unidos.

38th parallel > paralelo 38 Línea divisoria entre Corea del Norte y Corea del Sur.

Thoreau, Henry David > Thoreau, Henry David (1817–1862) Ensayista, poeta y filósofo estadounidense y una figura líder del movimiento trascendentalista. Entre sus obras más influyentes están *Walden,* una serie de 18 ensayos que describen su experimento en vivir con sencillez, y el ensayo "Desobediencia Civil", en el cual argumenta que una persona debe ser fiel a su propia conciencia, aun si eso supone infringir la ley.

Three-Fifths Compromise > Acuerdo de los Tres Quintos Acuerdo en el que un esclavo de un estado contaría como tres quintas partes de una persona para propósitos de representación legislativa.

Tiananmen Square > Plaza de Tiananmen Lugar en Pekín donde las protestas de los estudiantes chinos a favor de la democracia fueron aplacadas por el gobierno chino en 1989.

time zones > husos horarios Cualquiera de las veinticuatro zonas longitudinales del mundo en las que se usa la misma hora.

Tin Pan Alley > Tin Pan Alley Sección de la Calle 28 de la Ciudad de Nueva York que llegó a ser el centro de la industria musical a finales del siglo XIX; género de una música popular estadounidense.

Tinker* v. *Des Moines School District* > *Tinker* contra *Des Moines School District Caso de la Corte Suprema de 1969 en el que la Corte dictaminó que el derecho a la libre expresión se ampliaba a otros tipos de expresión además de la palabra hablada.

Tojo, Hideki > Tojo, Hideki (1884–1948) Nombrado primer ministro de Japón en octubre de 1941 cuando los planes de atacar a la Marina de los Estados Unidos en Pearl Harbor estaban en marcha. Lideró Japón hasta julio de 1944. Después de la guerra, fue juzgado por crímenes de guerra y ahorcado en diciembre de 1948.

total war > guerra total Estrategia militar en la cual, además de atacar a las tropas enemigas, un ejército arremete también contra los recursos económicos y civiles que las sostienen.

totalitarianism > totalitarismo Teoría de gobierno según la cual un solo partido o líder controla la vida económica, social y cultural de la población.

toxic waste > desechos tóxicos Productos venenosos de desecho; resultantes de la actividad humana.

trade protectionism > proteccionismo comercial Política que protege a las industrias nacionales de la competencia desleal injusta de las extranjeras, generalmente utilizando métodos como aranceles o cuotas para la importación de ciertos bienes.

Trail of Tears > Camino de Lágrimas Marcha forzada de los indígenas cherokee para mudarlos al oeste del Mississippi en la década de 1830.

Transcendentalist > trascendentalista Persona que sigue el movimiento literario y filosófico basado en encontrar la realidad espiritual mediante la naturaleza y la conciencia del propio ser.

Transcontinental Railroad > ferrocarril transcontinental Enlace ferroviario entre el Este y el Oeste de los Estados Unidos.

Treaty of Fort Laramie > Tratado del Fuerte Laramie Tratado de 1851 que restringía a los indígenas norteamericanos a áreas específicas alejadas de los principales caminos.

Treaty of Ghent > Tratado de Ghent Acuerdo de 1814 que finalizó la Guerra de 1812.

Treaty of Guadalupe Hidalgo > Tratado de Guadalupe Hidalgo Tratado de 1848 que finalizó la Guerra México-Estadounidense.

Treaty of Paris > Tratado de París Tratado de paz de 1783 que dio por finalizada la Guerra de Independencia y estableció la independencia de los Estados Unidos.

triangular trade > comercio triangular Patrón trilateral de comercio que involucró a Inglaterra, las colonias inglesas en las Américas y África occidental.

trickle-down economics > economía por goteo Teoría económica que sostiene que el dinero prestado a los bancos y empresas llegará a los pequeños negocios y a los consumidores.

Tripartite Pact > Pacto Tripartito Acuerdo que creó una alianza entre Alemania, Italia y Japón durante la Segunda Guerra Mundial.

Truman Doctrine > Doctrina Truman Promesa del presidente Truman de ayudar a las naciones en lucha contra los movimientos comunistas.

Truman, Harry S. > Truman, Harry S. (1884–1972) Presidente de los Estados Unidos de 1945 a 1953. Truman asumió el cargo después de la muerte de Franklin Roosevelt y dirigió la nación durante los últimos meses de la Segunda Guerra Mundial, tomando la decisión de usar armas atómicas en contra de Japón. Durante los primeros años de la Guerra Fría, Truman trabajó para reconstruir Europa y oponerse a la expansión del comunismo. Cuando en 1950 la comunista Corea del Norte invadió Corea del Sur y comenzó la Guerra de Corea, Truman envió tropas estadounidenses al conflicto.

Trump, Donald J. > Trump, Donald J. (1946–) Elegido el 45° presidente de los Estados Unidos en 2016 y a los 70 años fue el presidente con mayor edad en ser elegido para el cargo. Nacido en Queens, Nueva York, Trump era un hombre de negocios y una personalidad de la televisión antes de entrar a la política. Como presidente, Trump renegoció acuerdos comerciales con naciones extranjeras y cambió las relaciones de la nación con aliados y enemigos extranjeros. En 2019, Trump fue el tercer presidente en ser enjuiciado políticamente por la Cámara de Representantes. El Senado lo absolvió en 2020.

trust > trust Grupo de empresas independientes que se colocan bajo el control de un único consejo de administración con el fin de formar un monopolio.

Truth, Sojourner > Truth, Sojourner (1797?–1883) Nació en condición de esclava con el nombre de Isabella Van Wagener. Obtuvo su libertad en 1827 y se convirtió en una evangelista y reformadora afroamericana líder de la abolición y el movimiento por los derechos de las mujeres. Cuenta su biografía en su libro, *The Narrative of Sojourner Truth*.

Tubman, Harriet > Tubman, Harriet (1820–1913) Nació esclava en Maryland. En 1849 se escapó y viajó a Filadelfia. Luego se convirtió en "conductora" del Tren Clandestino y llevó al Norte, y a la libertad, a cientos de esclavos, entre ellos sus padres y hermanos.

Turner, Frederick Jackson > Turner, Frederick Jackson (1861–1932) Historiador estadounidense cuyos trabajos influyeron mucho en los escritos posteriores sobre la historia de los Estados Unidos. Turner promovió el uso de las ciencias sociales en los escritos históricos e hizo hincapié en el empleo de conceptos como inmigración, urbanización, desarrollo económico e historia social y cultural cuando se intenta entender los acontecimientos históricos.

Turner, Nat > Turner, Nat (1800–1831) Nació en condición de esclavo en una pequeña plantación en Virginia. De adulto, aseguró haber sido llamado por Dios para ayudar a liberar a los esclavos afroamericanos de su cautiverio. En 1831, organizó y dirigió el único levantamiento armado de personas esclavizadas de la historia estadounidense, por lo cual fue juzgado y ahorcado.

turnpike > camino de peaje Carretera que exige el pago de una cuota a sus usuarios.

Tuskegee Airmen > Aviadores de Tuskegee Escuadrón de afroamericanos que escoltaba a los bombarderos en la guerra aérea en cielos de Europa durante la Segunda Guerra Mundial.

Twain, Mark > Twain, Mark Mark Twain (1835–1910) Pseudónimo de Samuel Langhorne Clemons, un novelista y humorista estadounidense que escribió obras famosas como *Vida en el Mississippi, Las aventuras de Tom Sawyer y Las aventuras de Huckleberry Finn.* Las historias de Twain reflejaban la vida estadounidense como él la veía.

Twenty-fifth Amendment > Vigésimoquinta Enmienda Enmienda constitucional ratificada en 1967 que trata de la sucesión presidencial, vacantes de vicepresidentes e incapacidad presidencial.

Twenty-fourth Amendment > Vigésimocuarta Enmienda Enmienda constitucional que prohibió el impuesto electoral como requisito para votar.

U

U-boats > U-boot Submarino alemán.

unconditional surrender > rendición incondicional Darse por vencido completamente sin concesiones.

Underground Railroad > Tren Clandestino Sistema que existía antes de la Guerra Civil en el que los afroamericanos y los blancos abolicionistas ayudaban a las personas que trataban de escapar de la esclavitud a llegar a zonas seguras del Norte y de Canadá.

unfunded mandate > mandato sin fondos Programa o acción requerido pero que no paga el gobierno federal.

unicameral legislature > legislatura unicameral Cuerpo legislativo compuesto de una sola cámara.

Unitarian > unitario Miembro del unitarismo, una religión basada en la creencia de que Dios es un ser divino único y no una trinidad.

United Farm Workers (UFW) > Unión de Campesinos Sindicato de trabajadores agrícolas que usó tácticas pacíficas, incluyendo una huelga de trabajadores y un boicot por los consumidores de uvas.

United Nations (UN) > Naciones Unidas (ONU) Organización fundada en 1945 para promover la paz.

Universal Declaration of Human Rights > Declaración Universal de los Derechos Humanos Documento emitido por la ONU para promover los derechos y libertades humanos básicos.

Urban League > Liga Urbana Red de iglesias y clubes que estableció agencias de empleo y ofreció asistencia para que los afroamericanos se asentaran y encontraran empleo en las ciudades.

urban renewal > renovación urbana Programas gubernamentales para el desarrollo de las áreas urbanas.

urbanization > urbanización Expansión de ciudades y/o aumento del número de sus habitantes.

USA PATRIOT Act > Ley Patriótica Ley aprobada después del 11 de septiembre de 2001 que da a las fuerzas de seguridad amplios poderes para monitorear posibles actividades terroristas.

utopian community > comunidad utópica Asentamiento aislado establecido para lograr el objetivo de la perfección moral.

V

Valley Forge > Valley Forge Lugar en Pennsylvania donde el ejército del general Washington pasó un invierno difícil de 1777 a 1778.

Van Buren, Martin > Van Buren, Martin (1782–1862) Octavo presidente de los Estados Unidos, de 1837 a 1841. Enfrentó un pánico financiero nacional resultado en parte de la transferencia de fondos federales desde el Banco de los Estados Unidos a bancos estatales. También fue presidente durante la Segunda Guerra Seminola, una costosa guerra que finalmente llevó a la expulsión de la mayoría de las tribus seminolas de partes de la Florida.

Vanzetti, Bartolomeo > Vanzetti, Bartolomeo (1888–1927) Inmigrante italiano condenado por asesinato y ejecutado en 1927.

vaudeville > vodevil Tipo de espectáculo que incluye baile, canto y comedia, que se popularizó a finales del siglo XIX.

Venona Papers > Documentos Venona Serie de documentos secretos soviéticos de la era de la Guerra Fría interceptados y más tarde liberados por oficiales de inteligencia de los Estados Unidos.

vertical integration > integración vertical Sistema de consolidación de empresas involucradas en todos los pasos de la manufactura de un producto.

Vespucci, Amerigo > Vespucio, Américo (1454?–1512) Explorador y comerciante italiano que realizó los primeros viajes a las Américas en 1499 y 1501. Exploró parte suficiente de la costa de América del Sur para considerarla un continente. El nombre de América deriva de su nombre.

viceroy > virrey En la Hispanoamérica colonial, funcionario designado por el rey para gobernar una provincia, colonia o país.

Vicksburg > Vicksburg Baluarte confederado a lo largo del río Mississippi; lugar de un sitio del ejército de la Unión que duró más de un mes en 1863 y terminó con la victoria de la Unión, dividiendo la Confederación.

Vietcong > Vietcong Rebeldes comunistas sudvietnamitas que hicieron guerra de guerrillas contra el gobierno de Vietnam del Sur durante la Guerra Vietnamita.

Vietnamization > vietnamización Plan del presidente Nixon para terminar gradualmente la participación estadounidense en Vietnam, a medida que las tropas sudvietnamitas asumían más deberes de combate.

vigilantes > vigilante Persona autonombrada para hacer cumplir la ley.

Villa, Francisco "Pancho" > Villa, Francisco "Pancho" (1878–1923) Revolucionario mexicano líder de la guerrilla. En 1916, su ejército mató a 18 estadounidenses en Nuevo México, lo que hizo que el general estadounidense John J. Pershing liderara una expedición a México con 10,000 soldados para capturarlo y castigarlo. Esta expedición no tuvo éxito.

Violence Against Women Act > Ley Contra la Violencia hacia las Mujeres Ley aprobada en 1994 que aumentó los recursos federales para arrestar y enjuiciar a los hombres culpables de actos violentos contra las mujeres.

Virginia and Kentucky resolutions > resoluciones de Virginia y Kentucky Resoluciones estatales aprobadas en 1798 que declararon inconstitucionales las Leyes de Extranjeros y de Sedición.

Virginia Plan > Plan de Virginia Propuesta de James Madison para formar una legislatura bicameral con representación basada en la cantidad de habitantes.

Volstead Act > Ley Volstead Ley impuesta por el Congreso para hacer cumplir la Decimoctava Enmienda.

Voting Rights Act > Ley de Derechos Electorales Ley que prohibió las pruebas de alfabetismo y dió poder al gobierno federal de vigilar el empadronamiento de los votantes.

voucher > vales educativos Certificados u otros documentos que pueden ser usados como dinero.

W

Wade-Davis Bill > proyecto de ley de Wade-Davis Proyecto de ley que requería a los votantes de los estados confederados de antes de la guerra jurar lealtad a la Unión para que comenzara la Restauración.

Wagner Act > Ley Wagner Ley del Nuevo Trato que abolió las prácticas laborales injustas, reconoció el derecho de los trabajadores de organizar sindicatos, y dio a los trabajadores el derecho a las negociaciones colectivas.

Wallace, George > Wallace, George (1919–1998) Gobernador de Alabama de 1963 a 1967. Se postuló para la presidencia en 1968 en la convención del Partido Independiente de los Estados Unidos, abogando por los derechos de los estados y ganando cinco de los estados del sur en la elección. Sirvió tres periodos más como gobernador (1971–1979, 1983–1987), y finalmente renunció a sus creencias segregacionistas.

Walton, Sam > Walton, Sam (1918–1992) Pionero estadounidense de la venta minorista que fundó Wal-Mart Stores, Inc., la cual llegó a ser la cadena de venta minorista más grande de los Estados Unidos.

war bond > bono de guerra Bono que se compra para financiar una campaña de guerra, redimible por interés después de un periodo determinado de tiempo.

War Hawks > Halcones (de guerra) Miembros del Congreso que presionaron por una guerra contra Gran Bretaña en los años que llevaron a la Guerra de 1812.

War of 1812 > Guerra de 1812 Guerra entre los Estados Unidos y Gran Bretaña que duró de 1812 a 1815.

War on Poverty > Guerra Contra la Pobreza Programas del presidente Johnson enfocados en ayudar a los pobres de la nación mediante la educación, entrenamiento laboral, servicios de salud y nutrición adecuados.

War Powers Act > Ley de Poderes Bélicos Ley aprobada por el Congreso en 1973 que restringió los poderes bélicos del presidente; exigía que el presidente consultara con el Congreso antes de comprometer fuerzas estadounidenses en un conflicto extranjero.

War Refugee Board > Junta de Refugiados de Guerra Agencia del gobierno de los Estados Unidos fundada en 1944 para salvar a los judíos de Europa oriental.

Warren Commission > Comisión Warren Comité que investigó el asesinato del presidente Kennedy.

Warren Court > "Corte Warren" Corte Suprema de la década de 1960 bajo el mandato del presidente de los magistrados Earl Warren, cuyas decisiones apoyaron los derechos civiles.

Warren, Earl > Warren, Earl (1891–1974) Gobernador de California durante tres periodos antes de servir como Jefe de Justicia de la Corte Suprema de 1953 a 1969. Bajo su liderazgo, la Corte falló sobre varios casos emblemáticos que afectaron los derechos civiles, los procedimientos criminales, los derechos al voto y la separación de iglesia y estado.

Warsaw Pact > Pacto de Varsovia Alianza militar de la Unión Soviética y sus estados satélite.

Washington Naval Disarmament Conference > Conferencia de Desarme Naval de Washington Reunión realizada en 1921 y 1922 durante la cual los líderes mundiales acordaron limitar la construcción de buques de guerra.

Washington, Booker T. > Washington, Booker T. (1856–1915) Nació esclavo y creció en la pobreza después de la emancipación. En 1881, Washington fue escogido para dirigir la Tuskegee Normal and Industrial Institution, donde promovió la educación vocacional para los estudiantes afroamericanos. Animó a los ciudadanos afroamericanos a aceptar la segregación y a enfocarse en mejorarse a sí mismos a través de la educación y de las oportunidades económicas.

Washington, George > Washington, George (1732–1799) Trabajó como topógrafo de la colonia de Virginia. Washington se interesó en la expansión occidental del Territorio de Ohio e invirtió en la Compañía de Ohio. En 1752, aceptó un nombramiento militar como oficial. Dos años después, dirigió una compañía para expulsar a los franceses del Fuerte Duquesne. Más tarde, pasó a servir como comandante en jefe del Ejército Continental de las colonias y fungió como el primer Presidente de los Estados Unidos.

Watergate > Watergate Escándalo político que involucró actividades ilegales que al final condujeron a la renuncia del presidente Nixon en 1974.

weapons of mass destruction (WMD) > armas de destrucción masiva (ADM) Armas biológicas, nucleares o químicas destinadas a matar o causar daño a gran escala.

welfare state > estado de bienestar Gobierno que asume la responsabilidad de velar por el bienestar de los pobres, ancianos, enfermos y desempleados.

Wells, Ida B. > Wells, Ida B. (1862–1931) Periodista afroamericana que trabajó toda su vida para terminar con los linchamientos en el Sur. Colaboró con varios periódicos, entre ellos *Memphis Free Speech, New York Age* y *Chicago Conservator*. En 1895 publicó una detallada investigación sobre los linchamientos titulada *A Red Record*.

Western Front > Frente Occidental Frente de batalla entre los Aliados y los Poderes Centrales en Europa occidental durante la Primera Guerra Mundial.

Westmoreland, William > Westmoreland, William De 1964 a 1968, el general William Westmoreland (1914–2005) fue el comandante del ejército de los Estados Unidos en la Guerra de Vietnam. Westmoreland había servido antes en la Segunda Guerra Mundial y en la Guerra de Corea.

Wheatley, Phillis > Wheatley, Phillis (1753?–1784) Primera afroamericana en publicar un libro de poemas. Como sirvienta de John Wheatley y su familia, Phyllis aprendió a leer, escribir y estudiar. Phillis y los Wheatley encontraron un editor de Londres que imprimió su volumen de poesía, *Poems on Various Subjects, Religious and Moral* (*Poemas sobre varios temas, religiosos y morales*), en 1773.

Whigs > Whigs Miembros del partido político nacionalista formado en 1832 en oposición a los demócratas.

Whiskey Rebellion > Rebelión del Whiskey Levantamiento en 1794 al oeste de Pennsylvania en oposición al impuesto federal indirecto sobre el whiskey.

Whitney, Eli > Whitney, Eli (1765–1825) Inventor estadounidense mejor conocido por su invento de la desmotadora de algodón que patentó en 1794, para automatizar la remoción de las semillas del algodón. Sin embargo, su mayor contribución fue desarrollar la idea de la producción en serie de piezas intercambiables. Lo hizo en 1797 para cumplir un contrato que suministraba mosquetes al gobierno.

Willard, Frances > Willard, Frances (1839–1898) Catedrática que se interesó en el movimiento de la templanza en 1874. Se unió a la Unión Cristiana de Mujeres por la Templanza (WCTU, por sus siglas en inglés), donde estuvo en desacuerdo con otros miembros al insistir en unir objetivos con el sufragio de las mujeres. Para 1879, había obtenido apoyo suficiente para ser elegida presidenta de la WCTU, un cargo que ocupó de por vida.

William II > Guillermo II (1859–1941) Emperador alemán y rey de Prusia hasta el final de la Segunda Guerra Mundial en 1918.

Williams, Roger > Williams, Roger (1603–1683) Colono inglés de Nueva Inglaterra que fundó la colonia de Rhode Island. Creía que los colonos ingleses no tenían derecho a quitarles sus tierras a los indígenas norteamericanos. Expulsado de Massachusetts junto con sus seguidores, Williams fundó Providence, Rhode Island, en 1636, sobre territorio comprado a los indígenas norteamericanos. La nueva colonia de Williams estableció la libertad religiosa y la separación de Iglesia y estado.

Wilmot Proviso > Cláusula de Wilmot Ley propuesta pero rechazada de 1846 que habría prohibido la esclavitud en los territorios ganados a México en la Guerra México-Estadounidense.

Wilson, Woodrow > Wilson, Woodrow (1856–1924) Entró en política en 1910 cuando fue electo gobernador de Nueva Jersey. Sus reformas atrajeron la atención nacional y la nominación presidencial demócrata en 1912. Como Presidente guió a la nación durante la Primera Guerra Mundial y negoció el Tratado de Versalles.

Winfrey, Oprah > Winfrey, Oprah Ophrah Winfrey (1954–) Trabajó como reportera de noticias y presentadora antes de trabajar como presentadora en su programa matutino de entrevistas. Su show de Chicago, *The Oprah Winfrey Show*, comenzó en 1985 y fue vendido a nivel nacional al año siguiente. El programa tuvo un gran éxito y generó su imperio en los medios y el entretenimiento, que incluye una revista y un canal de televisión por cable. Winfrey es un pilar de la lista de la revista *Forbes* de las personas más ricas de los Estados Unidos. Su valor neto en 2013 fue estimado en $2.9 mil millones de dólares.

Winthrop, John > Winthrop, John (1588–1649) Abogado puritano y primer gobernador de la colonia de la bahía de Massachusetts después de su fundación en 1630. Su objetivo fue establecer un piadoso estado puritano piadoso. Al enfatizar la disciplina del grupo y la responsabilidad individual, la colonia de Winthrop prosperó, pero su intolerancia de las nuevas ideas llevó al descontento.

Wisconsin* v. *Yoder* > *Wisconsin* contra *Yoder Veredicto de la Corte Suprema en 1972 que ampliaba la libertad de religión para permitir que los padres amish, con base en cuestiones religiosas, retiraran a su hijos de las escuelas públicas después del octavo grado.

Women's Army Corps (WAC) > Cuerpo Femenino del Ejército Grupo del Ejército de los Estados Unidos establecido durante la Segunda Guerra Mundial para que las mujeres pudieran dar servicio en papeles no combativos.

women's movement > movimiento por los derechos de la mujer Campaña por la igualdad de derechos para las mujeres.

Works Progress Administration (WPA) > Administración para el Avance de Obras Públicas Agencia clave del Nuevo Trato que brindó ayuda laboral a través de varios proyectos de obras públicas.

World Trade Organization (WTO) > Organización Mundial del Comercio Organización internacional formada en 1995 para estimular la expansión del comercio mundial.

Wounded Knee > Wounded Knee Enfrentamiento de 1890 entre la caballería de los Estados Unidos y los sioux que marcó el fin de la resistencia indígena.

X

XYZ Affair > Caso XYZ Controversia diplomática en 1798 en la que oficiales franceses exigieron sobornos a los negociadores estadounidenses.

Y

Yalta Conference > Conferencia de Yalta Reunión sobre estrategia realizada en 1945 entre Roosevelt, Churchill y Stalin.

Yellow Press > prensa amarillista Periódicos que utilizaban titulares sensacionales e historias exageradas para promover su circulación.

Yorktown > Yorktown Lugar en Virginia donde en 1781 el ejército británico del general Cornwallis se rindió ante George Washington.

Young, Brigham > Young, Brigham (1801–1877) Líder religioso estadounidense que ejerció como segundo presidente de la Iglesia mormona. Después del asesinato de Joseph Smith, líder mormón, en junio de 1844, Young se hizo cargo de la Iglesia y llevó a los mormones hacia el Oeste de Illinois. También fue el primer gobernador del nuevo territorio estadounidense de Utah.

Z

Zhou Enlai > Zhou Enlai (1898–1976) Vivió de joven en el extranjero antes de regresar a su China nativa en 1924 para ayudar a Mao Zedong a liderar la revolución comunista allí. Cuando Mao estableció la República Popular China en 1949, Zhou fue primer ministro y ministro de Asuntos Exteriores y más tarde el principal artífice de la política china de la distensión con los Estados Unidos en 1972.

Zimmermann note > Telegrama de Zimmermann Telegrama escrito por el ministro del exterior alemán, Arthur Zimmermann, en el que proponía una alianza entre Alemania y México contra los Estados Unidos en la Primera Guerra Mundial.

Note: Page numbers followed by *c* refer to chart; *g* to graph; *m* to map; *p* to picture/illustration; *t* to tables, *q* to quotations

A

C

F

G

J

N

O

P

Q

S

T

W

X

Y

Z

[Photography]

Front Matter:

v: Letter from Harold Porter. Courtesy of Dwight D. Eisenhower Library and Museum; Pictorial Press Ltd/Alamy Stock Photo, Goodluz/Shutterstock; **vii:** Fuse/Getty Images; **xT:** Carver Mostardi/Alamy Stock Photo; **xB:** Mellish, Thomas (18th century)/Ferens Art Gallery, Hull Museums, UK/ The Bridgeman Art Library; **xiT:** Brad Mitchell/Alamy Stock Photo; **xiB:** Justasc/Shutterstock; **xiiT:** Classix/Getty Images; **xiiB:** Jeffrey M. Frank/ Shutterstock; **xiiiT:** Everett Collection Inc/Alamy Stock Photo; **xiiiB:** 7 Continents History/Everett Collection Inc; **xivT:** Akg Images/The Image Works; **xivB:** Driving the Golden Spike on 10th May, 1869 (colour litho), American School, (19th century)/Private Collection/Peter Newark American Pictures/The Bridgeman Art Library; **xv:** Everett Collection Inc/Alamy Stock Photo; **xvi:** Dancing the Charleston during the 'Roaring Twenties', cover of Life magazine, 18th February, 1928 (colour litho), American School, (20th century)/Private Collection/Peter Newark American Pictures/The Bridgeman Art Library; **xvii:** Dorothea Lange/Stringer/Getty Images; **xviii:** Photos 12/Alamy Stock Photo; **xixT:** Bettmann/Corbis; **xixB:** Francis Miller/ The Life Picture Collection/Getty Images; **xxT:** Christian Simonpietri/ Sygma/Corbis; **xxB:** Cynthia Hart Designer/Corbis; **xxiT:** Dirck Halstead/ The Life Images Collection/Getty Images; **xxiB:** Lain Masterton/Age Fotostock; **xlii:** Michael Flippo/Fotolia; **xliii:** Pat Benic/UPI/Newscom

Topic 1:

001: CarverMostardi/Alamy Stock Photo; **002L:** KKulikov/Shutterstock; **002R:** Peter Dennis/Dorling Kindersley Limited; **003:** JT Vintage/ Glasshouse Images/Alamy Stock Photo; **004:** Kravka/Shutterstock; **009:** Library of Congress Prints and Photographs Division [LC-USZ62-101261]; **010:** Sarin Images/© The Granger Collection Ltd.; **012:** Kankou Mousa, King of Mali, from the Map of Charles V, Map of Mecia de Viladestes, a portulan of Europe and North Africa, 1413 (vellum), Spanish School, (15th century)/Bibliotheque Nationale, Paris, France/Giraudon/The Bridgeman Art Library; **016:** Mary Evans Picture Library/Alamy Stock Photo; **017:** GL Archive/Alamy Stock Photo; **018T:** Prisma/UIG/Getty Images; **018B:** Akg-images/Jerome me da Cunha/Newscom; **020T:** Hulton Archive/ Getty Images; **020B:** Time & Life Pictures/Getty Images; **021:** Andreja Kovac/Shutterstock; **023:** Iberfoto/SuperStock; **024:** Peter Dennis/Dorling Kindersley Limited; **027:** JT Vintage/Glasshouse Images/Alamy Stock Photo; **029T:** Album/Alamy Stock Photo; **029B:** Richard Maschmeyer/ Robertharding/Alamy Stock Photo; **032T:** Alamy Stock Photo; **032B:** Bettmann/Corbis; **033:** Erich Lessing/Art Resource, NY; **035:** Encyclopaedia Britannica/UIG/Getty Images; **036:** Patrick Frilet/Marka/Alamy Stock Photo; **038L:** Heritage Images/Corbis; **038R:** The Art Gallery Collection/ Alamy Stock Photo; **040:** Peter Horree/Alamy Stock Photo; **041T:** Doromonic/123RF; **041B:** Ann Ronan Picture Library/Heritage-Images/The Print Collector/Alamy Stock Photo

Topic 2:

042: Mellish, Thomas (18th century)/Ferens Art Gallery, Hull Museums, UK/The Bridgeman Art Library; **044TL:** Stock Montage/Archive Photos/ Getty Images; **044TR:** Library of Congress; **044B:** North Wind Picture Archives/Alamy Stock Photo; **045:** North Wind Picture Archives/Alamy Stock Photo; **046:** Glasshouse Images/Alamy Stock Photo; **051:** North Wind Picture Archives/Alamy Stock Photo; **052:** Stock Montage/Archive Photos/ Getty Images; **058:** Archive Photos/Getty Images; **060:** North Wind/North Wind Picture Archives; **063T:** North Wind Picture Archives/Alamy Stock Photo; **063B:** Edward Hicks/Getty Images/The Bridgeman Art Library; **065:** Library of Congress Prints and Photographs Division Washington, D.C[LC-USZ62-54026]; **066:** North Wind Picture Archives/Alamy Stock Photo; **068:** Print Collector/Getty Images; **070:** North Wind Picture Archives/Alamy Stock Photo; **073T:** Archive Photos/Getty Images; **073B:** North Wind Picture Archives/Alamy Stock Photo; **075T:** North Wind Picture Archives/ Alamy Stock Photo; **075B:** Library of Congress Prints and Photographs Division Washington[LC-USZ62-60943]; **077:** North Wind Picture Archives/ Alamy Stock Photo; **079T:** Stapleton Historical Collection/Heritage Image Partnership Ltd/Alamy Stock Photo; **079B:** North Wind Picture Archives; **080:** Georgios Kollidas/Fotolia; **081T:** Falkensteinfoto/Alamy Stock Photo; **081B:** John Collet/Getty Images/The Bridgeman Art Library; **082:** Library of Congress; **083:** Fareed Khan/AP Images; **084:** Print Collector/Getty Images; **087:** Edward Hicks/Getty Images/The Bridgeman Art Library

Topic 3:

088: Brad Mitchell/Alamy Stock Photo; **090T:** North Wind Picture Archives/ Alamy Stock Photo; **090B:** World History Archive/Alamy Stock Photo; **091:** JT Vintage/Glasshouse Images/Alamy Stock Photo; **092:** Interfoto/ History/Alamy Stock Photo; **094:** North Wind Picture Archives/Alamy Stock Photo; **098:** North Wind Picture Archives/Alamy Stock Photo; **101T:** The Colonial Williamsburg Foundation. Museum Purchase.; **101B:** North Wind Picture Archives/Alamy Stock Photo; **102T:** Everett Collection/Newscom; **102B:** JT Vintage/Glasshouse Images/Alamy Stock Photo; **103:** Bettmann/ Corbis; **106:** Everett Historical/Shutterstock; **108:** World History Archive/ Alamy Stock Photo; **111:** Interfoto/Alamy Stock Photo; **113:** Signing the Declaration of Independence, July 4th, 1776 (oil on canvas), Trumbull, John (1756-1843)/Capitol Collection, Washington, USA/The Bridgeman Art Library; **115:** Painting/Alamy Stock Photo; **116T:** Lebrecht Music and Arts Photo Library/Alamy Stock Photo; **116B:** North Wind Picture Archives/ Alamy Stock Photo; **117T:** Hulton Archive/Getty Images; **117B:** Art Resource, NY; **118:** SuperStock; **120:** Prisma Archivo/Alamy Stock Photo; **122:** Terra Foundation for American Art, Chicago/Art Resource, NY; **124:** Gonzales Photo/Alamy Stock Photo; **126:** North Wind Picture Archives/ Alamy Stock Photo; **128:** Lebrecht Music and Arts Photo Library/Alamy Stock Photo

Topic 4:

130: Justasc/Shutterstock; **132T:** National Portrait Gallery, Smithsonian Institution/Art Resource, NY; **132B:** Joseph Sohm/Visions of America, LLC/ Alamy Stock Photo; **133:** ClassicStock/Alamy Stock Photo; **134:** National Portrait Gallery, Smithsonian Institution/Art Resource, NY; **141:** Niday Picture Library/Alamy Stock Photo; **143:** Joseph Sohm/Visions of America, LLC/Alamy Stock Photo; **145T:** Library of Congress Prints and Photographs Division[LC-DIG-ds-04435]; **145B:** American School, (19th century)/ The London Art Archive/Alamy Stock Photo; **147T:** North Wind Picture Archives/Alamy Stock Photo; **147B:** ClassicStock/Alamy Stock Photo; **149:** Courtesy Everett Collection/Shutterstock; **150:** North Wind Picture Archives/Alamy Stock Photo; **153:** Ian Dagnall/Alamy Stock Photo; **157:** Stockbroker/MBI/Alamy Stock Photo; **158:** Courtesy Everett Collection/ Shutterstock; **160:** Bettmann/Corbis

Topic 5:

162: Classix/Getty Images; **164T:** Everett Collection Inc/Alamy Stock Photo; **164BL:** Image Asset Management Ltd./Alamy Stock Photo; **164BR:** National Gallery of Art/Alamy Stock Photo; **165:** Wavebreak Media Ltd/123RF; **166:** Image Asset Management Ltd./Alamy Stock Photo; **167:** Library of Congress Prints and photographs division [LC-USZ62-1306]; **174T:** Library of Congress Prints and Photographs Division[LC-DIG-ppmsca-31832]; **174B:** Library of Congress Prints and Photographs Division [LC-DIG-ppmsca-31156]; **176:** World History Archive/Alamy Stock Photo; **183:** Smithsonion Institute/KRT/Newscom; **184T:** King, Charles Bird (1785-1862) (attr.) John Caldwell Calhoun (1782-1850), Statesman. ca. 1818-25. Oil on canvas. 76.2 x 63.5 cm./National Portrait Gallery, Smithsonian Institution/Art Resource, NY; **184B:** Recruitment Poster for the War of 1812 (litho), American School, (19th century)/© Chicago History Museum, USA/ The Bridgeman Art Library; **185T:** Image Asset Management Ltd./Alamy Stock Photo; **185B:** Library of Congress Prints and Photographs Division [LC-USZ62-48101]; **186:** Library of Congress Prints and Photographs Division [LC-USZC4-992]; **188:** Mary Evans Picture Library/The Image Works; **190:** The first cotton mill in America, established by Samuel Slater on the Blackstone River at Pawtucket, Rhode Island, c.1790 (oil on canvas), American School, (18th century)/Smithsonian Institution, Washington DC, USA/The Bridgeman Art Library; **191:** North Wind Picture Archives; **193:** North Wind Picture Archives/Alamy Stock Photo; **194:** Christie's Images/ Corbis; **197:** Owaki Kulla/Corbis/Glow Images; **199:** National Gallery of Art/ Alamy Stock Photo; **201:** Leonard de Selva/Corbis; **204:** Library of Congress Prints and Photographs Division [LC-USZ62-1562]; **206:** SuperStock; **207T:** Bettmann/Historical/Corbis; **207B:** Corbis; **210:** Library of Congress Prints and Photographs Division [LC-USZ62-42778]; **211:** Library of Congress Prints and Photographs Division [LC-USZ62-1563]; **212:** Bettmann/Corbis; **213:** SuperStock; **215:** © The Granger Collection Ltd.; **217:** Don Mennig/ Alamy Stock Photo; **218:** Mary Evans Picture Library/The Image Works; **221:** Bettmann/Getty Images

Topic 6:

222: Jeffrey M. Frank/Shutterstock; **224T:** Library of Congress; **224BL:** Bettmann/Corbis; **224BR:** Bettmann/Corbis; **225:** Library of Congress; **226:** Library of Congress; **228:** North Wind Picture Archives/Alamy Stock Photo; **229T:** North Wind Picture Archives/Alamy Stock Photo; **229B:** North Wind Picture Archives; **231:** Pictorial Press Ltd/Alamy Stock Photo; **232:** Library of Congress; **236:** Paris Pierce/Alamy Stock Photo; **237:** Bettmann/Corbis; **240:** Paris Pierce/Alamy Stock Photo; **241:** North Wind Picture Archives/Alamy Stock Photo; **245T:** Library of Congress; **245B:** Library of Congress (Photoduplication); **246T:** Library of Congress; **246B:** Images & Stories/Alamy Stock Photo; **247T:** World History Archive/Alamy Stock Photo; **247B:** Hulton Archive/Getty Images; **249T:** Library of Congress; **249B:** Library of Congress; **250:** North Wind Picture Archives/Alamy Stock Photo; **251:** © Samuel J. Miller/Corbis; **255T:** Lebrecht Music and Arts Photo Library/Alamy Stock Photo; **255B:** Bettmann/Corbis; **256:** Fotosearch/Getty Images; **257:** National Archives and Records Administration; **258:** Incamerastock/Alamy Stock Photo; **260:** Bettmann/Corbis; **262T:** Library of Congress; **262B:** Library of Congress; **265:** David Grossman/Alamy Stock Photo; **266:** Library of Congress; **269:** Snark/Art Resource, NY

Topic 7:

270: Everett Collection Inc/Alamy Stock Photo; **272TL:** GL Archive/Alamy Stock Photo; **272TR:** Everett Collection/Newscom; **272B:** Library of Congress; **273:** Library of Congress Prints and Photographs Division[Gibson, James F/LC-DIG-cwpb-01005]; **274:** GL Archive/Alamy Stock Photo; **275T:** Art Commission of the City of New York/AP Images; **275B:** GL Archive/Alamy Stock Photo; **276:** Everett Collection/Newscom; **278T:** North Wind Picture Archives/Alamy Stock Photo; **278B:** Library of Congress Prints and Photographs Division/Highsmith, Carol M., 1946[LC-DIG-highsm-18022]; **280T:** North Wind Picture Archives/Alamy Stock Photo; **280B:** Library of Congress Prints and Photographs Division[LC-DIG-ppmsca-34495]; **282:** Library of Congress Prints and Photographs Division[LC-USZC4-1298]; **283:** Bettmann/Corbis; **284T:** North Wind Picture Archives/Alamy Stock Photo; **284B:** North Wind Picture Archives/Alamy Stock Photo; **286:** David J. & Janice L. Frent Collection/Corbis; **288:** Library of Congress Prints and Photographs Division Washington, D.C. [LC-USZ62-16378]; **290:** Peter Horree/Alamy Stock Photo; **291:** Niday Picture Library/Alamy Stock Photo; **294T:** Library of Congress Prints and Photographs Division[LC-USZ62-132563]; **294B:** Library of Congress; **298:** Library of Congress Prints and Photographs Division [LC-DIG-ppmsca-32641]; **300T:** Library of Congress Prints and Photographs Division [LC-DIG-ppmsca-31277]; **300B:** Matthew Brady/Buyenlarge/Getty Images; **301:** Library of Congress Prints and Photographs Division [LC-DIG-ds-03251]; **302:** Library of Congress Prints and Photographs Division[LC-DIG-cwpb-04294]; **303T:** Everett Collection Historical/Alamy Stock Photo; **303B:** Library of Congress Prints and Photographs Division[Gibson, James F/LC-DIG-cwpb-01005]; **304T:** GL Archive/Alamy Stock Photo; **304B:** Library of Congress Prints and Photographs Division [LC-DIG-pga-03898]; **305T:** Kean Collection/Archive Photos/Getty Images; **305B:** Akg-images/Newscom; **306:** Library of Congress Prints and Photographs Division [LC-DIG-cwpb-02004]; **308:** Library of Congress Prints and Photographs Division[LC-DIG-ppmsca-19911]; **310T:** Library of Congress; **310B:** Library of Congress Prints and Photographs Division Washington, D.C. [LC-DIG-cwpb-04035]; **311:** CMSP Education/Newscom; **312T:** Library of Congress Prints and Photographs Division Washington, D.C[LC-DIG-cwpb-00156]; **312B:** JT Vintage/Glasshouse Images/Alamy Stock Photo; **313:** World History Archive/Alamy Stock Photo; **314:** MPI/Stringer/Archive Photos/Getty Images; **315T:** Library of Congress Prints and Photographs Division[LC-DIG-pga-01871]; **315B:** Library of Congress Prints and Photographs Division [LC-DIG-ppmsca-32889]; **316T:** Corbis; **316B:** Library of Congress Prints and Photographs Division[LC-DIG-cwpb-04003]; **319T:** Niday Picture Library/Alamy Stock Photo; **319B:** Library of Congress Prints and Photographs Division; **322:** Everett Collection/Newscom; **323T:** Library of Congress Prints and Photographs Division[LC-DIG-ppmsca-32420]; **323B:** Library of Congress; **325:** Library of Congress Prints & Photographs Division[LC-DIG-ppmsca-19305]; **327:** The Print Collector/Heritage Images/Alamy Stock Photo; **329:** Wim Wiskerke/Alamy Stock Photo; **330:** Library of Congress Prints and Photographs Division Washington, D.C[LC-DIG-cwpb-00156]; **332:** Nsf/Alamy Stock Photo; **333:** Historical/Corbis Historical/Getty Images

Topic 8:

334: 7 Continents History/Everett Collection; **336T:** Picture History/Newscom; **336B:** Library of Congress; **337:** Nsf/Alamy Stock Photo; **338:** Library of Congress; **339T:** Corbis; **339B:** Seibert/Corbis; **340T:** Picture History/Newscom; **340B:** Library of Congress; **342T:** MPI/Getty Images; **342B:** Picture History/Newscom; **345:** Everett Collection Inc/Alamy Stock Photo; **347:** Library of Congress; **348T:** Library of Congress; **348B:** North Wind Picture Archives/Alamy Stock Photo; **349:** North Wind Picture Archives; **350T:** North Wind Picture Archives/AP Images; **350B:** ArtPix/Alamy Stock Photo; **353T:** Library of Congress Prints and Photographs Division [LC-USZ62-119565]; **353B:** Library of Congress; **355:** Niday Picture Library/Alamy Stock Photo; **357:** North Wind Picture Archives; **364:** Everett Collection Historical/Alamy Stock Photo; **365:** Schomburg Center, NYPL/Art Resource, NY; **366:** Ariel Skelley/DigitalVision/Getty Images; **368:** Seibert/Corbis; **371:** Library of Congress

Topic 9:

372: Akg Images/The Image Works; **374T:** North Wind Picture Archives/Alamy Stock Photo; **374B:** Fotosearch/Archive Photos/Getty Images; **375:** Bain News Service/Library of Congress; **376:** Chris Hellier/Alamy Stock Photo; **378:** DIZ Muenchen GmbH, Sueddeutsche Zeitung Photo/Alamy Stock Photo; **381:** National Child Labor Committee Collection/Library of Congress; **383T:** Corbis; **383B:** Three Lions/Stringer/Hulton Archive/Getty Images; **384:** Detroit Photographic Company/Corbis; **385:** Library of Congress Prints and Photographs Division Washington, D.C. 20540 USA [LC-USZ62-57883]; **387:** Mary Evans Picture Library/The Image Works; **390:** Everett Collection/SuperStock; **391T:** Library of Congress; **391B:** Luther Daniels Bradley/Corbis; **392M:** Minnesota Historical Society; **392U:** The New York Public Library/Art Resource, NY; **392Y:** Library of Congress Prints and Photographs Division Washington, D.C. [03582r]; **393:** Niday Picture Library/Alamy Stock Photo; **394T:** Library of Congress; **394B:** Library of Congress; **395:** Sean Sexton/Contributor/Hulton Archive/Getty Images; **396T:** Special Collections and Archives/Georgia State University Library; **396B:** Archive Photos/Getty Images; **399:** Fotosearch/Getty Images; **400:** Minnesota Historical Society; **402:** Jeff Greenberg/Alamy Stock Photo; **403:** Fotosearch/Archive Photos/Getty Images; **404:** The Art Archive/Art Resource, NY; **405:** Ann Ronan Picture Library/HIP/The Image Works; **407:** Jacob A. Riis/Museum of the City of New York/Getty Images; **409:** The New York Public Library/Art Resource, NY; **410:** FPG/Archive Photos/Getty Images; **412T:** ClassicStock/Alamy Stock Photo; **412B:** Chicago History Museum/Archive Photos/Getty Images; **413:** The Protected Art Archive/Alamy Stock Photo; **414:** North Wind Picture Archives/Alamy Stock Photo; **415:** Library of Congress Prints and Photographs Division Washington, D.C. [03582r]; **416:** Camerique/Corbis; **417:** Hulton Archive/Archive Photos/Getty Images; **418T:** Buyenlarge/Getty Images; **418B:** Library of Congress; **419:** Library of Congress; **420:** Library of Congress; **421:** www.eddie-hernandez.com/Shutterstock; **422:** National Child Labor Committee Collection/Library of Congress; **425:** Everett Collection/SuperStock

Topic 10:

426: Driving the Golden Spike on 10th May, 1869 (colour litho), American School, (19th century)/Private Collection/Peter Newark American Pictures/The Bridgeman Art Library; **428T:** MPI/Getty Images; **428B:** Library of Congress; **429:** Trailing Texas Longhorns (oil on canvas), Remington, Frederic (1861-1909)/Private Collection/Peter Newark American Pictures/The Bridgeman Art Library; **430:** Library of Congress; **432:** Dea Picture Library/DeAgostini/Getty Images; **434T:** Art Resource, NY; **434B:** Bettmann/Corbis; **435T:** The Art Archive/Alamy Stock Photo; **435B:** Smithsonian Institution/Corbis; **436:** Library of Congress; **437:** Everett Collection/SuperStock; **438:** MPI/Getty Images; **442T:** S.D. Butcher/Historical/Corbis; **442B:** North Wind Picture Archives; **444:** M.E. Jacobson/Corbis; **445:** Private Collection/The Bridgeman Art Library; **447:** Library of Congress; **448:** Everett Collection/Newscom; **450:** Library of Congress; **452:** Bettmann/Corbis; **454T:** Library of Congress Prints and Photographs Division [LC-USZC4-769]; **454B:** Library of Congress; **455T:** Bettmann/Corbis; **455B:** Library of Congress; **457T:** AP Images; **457B:** Library of Congress; **459:** Bettmann/Corbis; **461:** Clarence Holmes Photography/Alamy Stock Photo; **462:** Library of Congress; **465:** Library of Congress Prints and Photographs Division [LC-USZC4-769]

Topic 11:

466: Everett Collection Inc/Alamy Stock Photo; **468T:** Akg Images/Newscom; **468B:** Library of Congress; **469:** Niday Picture Library/Alamy Stock Photo; **470:** Library of Congress; **471T:** Library of Congress; **471B:** Bettmann/Corbis; **472T:** Library of Congress; **472B:** Library of Congress; **473:** Corbis; **475T:** AP Images; **475B:** Underwood & Underwood/Corbis; **476:** Library of Congress; **478:** Everett Collection Inc/Alamy Stock Photo; **480:** Akg Images/Newscom; **481T:** Lewis W. Hine/Archive Photos/Getty Images; **481B:** Minnesota Historical Society/Corbis; **482:** Everett Collection Historical/Alamy Stock Photo; **485T:** Everett Collection/Newscom; **485B:** Library of Congress; **487:** Everett Collection Inc/Alamy Stock Photo; **489:** Schomburg Center, NYPL/Art Resource, NY; **490:** Buyenlarge/Archive Photos/Getty Images; **492:** Everett Collection Historical/Alamy Stock Photo; **494:** Rockwood Photo Co., photographer/Library of Congress; **495:** Collection Dagli Orti/The Art Archive/Alamy Stock Photo; **497T:** Clifford Kennedy Berryman/Corbis; **497B:** The Art Archive/Alamy Stock Photo; **499:** Everett Collection Inc./Age Fotostock; **505:** Corbis; **507:** Alamy Stock Photo; **508:** William Vander Weyde/George Eastman House/Getty Images; **509:** North Wind Picture Archives; **510T:** Everett Collection/Newscom; **510B:** Akg-images/Newscom; **512:** J. F. Jarvis/Corbis; **513T:** Chronicle/Alamy Stock Photo; **513B:** Niday Picture Library/Alamy Stock Photo; **517T:** Corbis; **517B:** Library of Congress Prints and Photographs Division[LC-DIG-hec-12736]; **520:** Bettmann/Corbis; **522:** AP Images; **527:** Hulton-Deutsch Collection/Corbis; **529:** Planetpix/Alamy Live News/US Marines Photo/Alamy Stock Photo; **530:** AP Images; **533:** Clifford Kennedy Berryman/Corbis

Topic 12:

534M: The Henry Ford; **534R:** Minnesota Historical Society/Corbis Historical/Getty Images; **534W:** Chicago History Museum/Getty Images; **534AA:** The New York Public Library/Art Resource, NY; **534:** Dancing the Charleston during the 'Roaring Twenties', cover of Life magazine, 18th February, 1928 (colour litho), American School, (20th century)/Private Collection/Peter Newark American Pictures/The Bridgeman Art Library; **536T:** Bettmann/Corbis; **536B:** Library of Congress Prints and Photographs Division[LC-USZ62-22847]; **537:** Hulton-Deutsch Collection/Corbis; **538:** Akg Images/Alamy Stock Photo; **543T:** Photo12/The Image Works; **543B:** WW/Alamy Stock Photo; **544T:** Press Association/The Image Works; **544B:** Library of Congress; **546:** National Archives and Records Administration; **547:** Akg Images/Newscom; **549:** Bettmann/Corbis; **551:** Popperfoto/Getty Images; **553:** Bettmann/Corbis; **554:** American Stock/Archive Photos/Getty Images; **555T:** Lightroom/US Army/PhotoShot; **555B:** SOTK2011/Alamy Stock Photo; **557T:** AP Images; **557B:** Niday Picture Library/Alamy Stock Photo; **559T:** TopFoto/The Image Works; **559B:** Library of Congress Prints and Photographs Division[LC-USZ62-36185]; **560T:** Hulton-Deutsch Collection/Corbis; **560B:** AFIP''S National Museum Of Health KRT/Newscom; **562:** Bettmann/Corbis; **563:** TopFoto/The Image Works; **565:** The Henry Ford; **566:** Everett Collection/Newscom; **567:** Science and Society/SuperStock; **569:** Jeff Morgan 13/Alamy Stock Photo; **570T:** Riveters attaching a beam, Empire State Building, 1931 (gelatin silver print), Hine, Lewis Wickes (1874-1940)/New York Public Library, USA/Stephen A. Schwarzman Building/Photography Collection, Miriam and Ira D. Wallach Division of Art, Prints and Photogr; **570B:** Bettmann/Corbis; **571:** American Stock Archive /Getty Images; **572:** Bettmann/Corbis; **574:** Everett Collection/Newscom; **578:** Minnesota Historical Society/Corbis Historical/Getty Images; **579T:** Cond Nast Archive/Corbis; **579B:** Bettmann/Corbis; **581T:** Akg-images/Newscom; **581B:** Everett Collection/Newscom; **582:** DIZ Muenchen GmbH, Sueddeutsche Zeitung Photo/Alamy Stock Photo; **584:** The Protected Art Archive/Alamy Stock Photo; **586:** AP Images; **587:** Chicago History Museum/Getty Images; **589T:** Everett Collection; **589B:** Blank Archives/Getty Images; **590:** DIZ Muenchen GmbH, Sueddeutsche Zeitung Photo/Alamy Stock Photo; **591:** DaZo Vintage Stock Photos/Images.com/Alamy Stock Photo; **592:** Francis G. Mayer/Corbis; **593:** Snark/Art Resource, NY; **594:** Everett Collection; **595:** Lordprice Collection/Alamy Stock Photo; **597:** The New York Public Library/Art Resource, NY; **598T:** Everett Collection/Newscom; **598B:** Underwood & Underwood/Corbis; **600T:** Michael Ochs Archives/Corbis; **600B:** Hulton Archive/Stringer/Getty Images; **601T:** Bettmann/Corbis; **601B:** Robert W. Kelley/Time Life Pictures/Getty Images; **602:** Everett Collection/Newscom; **603:** Schomburg Center, NYPL/Art Resource, NY; **605:** Tomas Rodriguez/Getty Images; **606:** Francis G. Mayer/Corbis; **609:** Bettmann/Corbis

Topic 13:

610I: The New York Public Library/Art Resource, NY; **610O:** Barry, M. B., photographer. (ca. 1934) "Depression". Haddon Heights New Jersey, ca. 1934. [Photograph] Retrieved from the Library of Congress, https://www.loc.gov/item/2013647257/; **610S:** The National Archives; **610W:** The National Archives; **610:** Dorothea Lange/Stringer/Getty Images; **612L:** DIZ Muenchen GmbH, Sueddeutsche Zeitung Photo/Alamy Stock Photo; **612R:** AP Images; **613:** Ho/AP Images; **614:** Bettmann/Corbis; **615T:** FPG/Getty Images; **615B:** AP Images; **616T:** Buyenlarge/Getty Images; **616B:** ClassicStock/Alamy Stock Photo; **618T:** Superstock/Glow Images; **618B:** DIZ Muenchen GmbH, Sueddeutsche Zeitung Photo/Alamy Stock Photo; **620:** Underwood Photo Archives/SuperStock; **622:** The New York Public Library/Art Resource, NY; **623T:** Rolls Press/Popperfoto/Getty Images; **623B:** Everett Collection/Newscom; **625T:** DIZ Muenchen GmbH, Sueddeutsche Zeitung Photo/Alamy Stock Photo; **625B:** Arthur Rothstein/Corbis; **626:** Everett Collection/Newscom; **627T:** George E. Marsh/NOAA/AP Images; **627B:** Heritage Image Partnership/Alamy Stock Photo; **628:** FPG/Hulton Archive/Getty Images; **630:** University of Washington Libraries, Special Collections, Lee10546; **632:** Barry, M. B., photographer. (ca. 1934) "Depression". Haddon Heights New Jersey, ca. 1934. [Photograph] Retrieved from the Library of Congress, https://www.loc.gov/item/2013647257/.; **633T:** MPI/Getty Images; **633B:** Satirical cartoon comment on Herbert Hoover's reaction to the Great Depression, 1935 (litho), Fitzpatrick, Daniel Robert (1891–1969)/Private Collection/Peter Newark American Pictures/The Bridgeman Art Library; **635:** MPI/Getty Images; **638:** Everett Collection/Newscom; **640:** Universal Images Group/Getty Images; **641:** AP Images; **643:** The National Archives; **644:** AP Images; **649:** Fotosearch/Archive Photos/Getty Images; **650:** National Archives; **651T:** AP Images; **651B:** Corbis; **652:** AP Images; **655:** Ho/AP Images; **657:** Everett Collection/Alamy Stock Photo; **658:** Texas Parks and Wildlife; **660:** Dorothea Lange/Getty Images; **661T:** AP Images; **661B:** Hulton Archive/Getty Images; **662:** Bernard Hoffman/Time & Life Pictures/Getty Images; **663T:** Carol M. Highsmith/Library of Congress Prints and Photographs Division Washington[LC-DIG-highsm-58651]; **663B:** Heritage Image Partnership Ltd/Alamy Stock Photo; **664:** Hulton Archive/Getty Images; **665:** Xinhua/Alamy Stock Photo; **666:** George E. Marsh/NOAA/AP Images; **669:** Universal Images Group/Getty Images

Topic 14:

670K: National Archives; **670O:** U.S. Marine Corps; **670S:** Library of Congress Prints and Photographs Division[LC-DIG-fsa-8d35482]; **670Y:** National Archives; **670:** Photos 12/Alamy Stock Photo; **672L:** Hulton Archive/Getty Images; **672R:** Corbis; **673:** The Life Picture Collection/Getty Images; **674:** World History Archive/Newscom; **675T:** Daily Mirror/Mirrorpix/Newscom; **675B:** Underwood Archives/The Image Works; **676T:** Bettmann/Corbis; **676B:** Henry Guttmann/Getty Images; **677T:** Akg Images; **677B:** Hulton Archive/Getty Images; **678:** Getty Images; **680T:** Fox Photos/Hulton Archive/Getty Images; **680B:** Private Collection/Peter NewarkMilitary Pictures/The Bridgeman Art Library; **681:** Hulton-Deutsch Collection/Corbis; **682:** RW/AP/Corbis; **683T:** Central Press/Hulton Archive/Getty Images; **683B:** Popperfoto/Getty Images; **685T:** Bettmann/Corbis; **685B:** Time Life Pictures/Pictures Inc./The Life Picture Collection/Getty Images; **686T:** DIZ Muenchen GmbH,Sueddeutsche Zeitung Photo/Alamy Stock Photo; **686B:** AP Images; **687:** Scherl/Sueddeutsche Zeitung Photo/The Image Works; **688T:** Bettmann/Corbis; **688B:** Swim Ink 2, LLC/Corbis; **690:** Bettmann/Corbis; **691:** Swim Ink 2, LLC/Corbis; **693:** National Archives; **694:** Corbis; **695T:** Bettmann/Corbis; **695B:** Time Life Pictures/US Navy/The Life Picture Collection/Getty Images; **696T:** Stocktrek Images, Inc./Alamy Stock Photo; **696B:** Hulton Archive/Getty Images; **697T:** Bettmann/Corbis; **697B:** Hulton Archive/Getty Images; **698T:** Corbis; **698B:** Everett Collection Inc/Alamy Stock Photo; **700T:** PubImages/Newscom; **700B:** Corbis; **702:** U.S. Marine Corps; **703T:** Dpa/Corbis; **703B:** Corbis; **704T:** Akg images/The Image Works; **704B:** Corbis; **705:** Curt Teich Archives/HIP/The Image Works; **708:** Ralph Morse/The Life Picture Collection/Getty Images; **709:** Library of Congress Prints and Photographs Division[LC-DIG-fsa-8d35482]; **710:** Newberry Library/SuperStock; **711T:** Bettmann/Corbis; **711B:** Bettmann/Corbis; **712T:** Everett Collection/Newscom; **712B:** Lucy Pemoni/Corbis; **713:** Time Life Pictures/National Archives/The Life Picture Collection/Getty Images; **714T:** MPI/Getty Images; **714B:** National Archives at College Park Still Pictures; **715T:** Al Gretz/FPG/Hulton Archive/Getty Images; **715B:** Corbis; **716:** Corbis; **717:** National Archives; **719:** National Archives; **720T:** Paul Popper/Popperfoto/

Getty Images; **720B:** Bettmann/Corbis; **722:** Popperfoto/Getty Images; **725T:** Corbis; **725B:** Keystone/Getty Images; **726T:** Science Source/ Getty Images; **726B:** Bettmann/Corbis; **727:** Corbis; **728:** Pictorial Press Ltd/Alamy Stock Photo; **729T:** Private Collection/Peter Newark Historical Pictures/The Bridgeman Art Library; **729B:** Fox Photos/Hulton Archive/ Getty Images; **731T:** Schultz Reinhard/Prisma/Dukas Presseagentur GmbH/ Alamy Stock Photo; **731B:** Corbis Historical/Getty Images; **732:** Bettmann/ Corbis; **733:** Ullstein bild/Akg Images; **734:** Anne Frank Fonds Basel/Getty Images; **736:** Corbis; **737:** AF archive/Alamy Stock Photo; **738:** Buy Prints/ The Image Works; **739T:** Bettmann/Corbis; **739B:** David Coleman/Alamy Stock Photo; **740:** Carl Mydans/The Life Picture Collection/Getty Images; **741:** Private Collection/Photo Barbara Singer/The Bridgeman Art Library; **743:** Bettmann/Corbis; **745:** Giulio Marcocchi/Sipa Press/Newscom; **746:** The Life Picture Collection/Getty Images; **749:** Everett Collection Inc/Alamy Stock Photo

Topic 15:

750: Bettmann/Corbis; **752T:** Sovfoto/Universal Images Group/Getty Images; **752B:** J. R. Eyerman/The Life Picture Collection/Getty Images; **753:** CBS Photo Archive/Getty Images; **754:** Dpa/picture-alliance/dpa/AP Images; **755T:** Sovfoto/Universal Images Group/Getty Images; **755B:** George Skadding/The Life Picture Collection/Getty Images; **756:** AP Images; **757T:** John Rooney/AP Images; **757B:** Bettmann/Corbis; **760:** Photo12/Archives Snark/Alamy Stock Photo; **762:** Harold M. Lambert/Archive Photos/Getty Images; **763T:** AP Images; **763B:** Bettmann/Corbis; **764:** William C. Allen/ AP Images; **766:** Park Jin-hee/Xinhua Press/Corbis; **767:** Corbis; **768:** Everett Collection/Newscom; **770T:** Bettmann/Corbis; **770B:** Jack Esten/Hulton-Deutsch Collection/Corbis; **772:** Bettmann/Corbis; **773:** CBS Photo Archive/ Getty Images; **774T:** David Pollack/Corbis; **774B:** Eileen Darby/The Life Images Collection/Getty Images; **775:** Everett Collection/Glow Images; **776:** New York Daily News Archive/Getty Images; **777:** Advertising Archive/ Everett Collection; **779:** Marka/Alamy Stock Photo; **781T:** Yale Joel/The Life Picture Collection/Getty Images; **781B:** FPG/Archive Photos/Getty Images; **783:** Bettmann/Corbis; **784:** Everett Collection/Newscom; **785:** Bettmann/ Corbis; **786:** Popperfoto/Getty Images; **787:** J. R. Eyerman/The Life Picture Collection/Getty Images; **788:** J. R. Eyerman/The Life Picture Collection/Getty Images; **790:** H. Armstrong Roberts/Corbis; **791:** Akg Images/Newscom; **792:** Curt Teich Archives/HIP/The Image Works; **794:** Bettmann/Corbis; **795T:** Warner Brothers/Album/Newscom; **795B:** Tony Frank/Sygma/Corbis; **796:** Keystone Pictures USA/Alamy Stock Photo; **799T:** Keystone Features/Hulton Archive/Getty Images; **799B:** Keystone-France/Gamma-Keystone/Getty Images; **800:** Klaus Vedfelt/DigitalVision/Getty Images; **802:** FPG/Archive Photos/Getty Images; **805:** Advertising Archive/Everett Collection

Topic 16:

806G: Bettmann/Getty Images; **806M:** Robert W. Kelley/The Life Picture Collection/Getty Images; **806Q:** Danny Lyon/Magnum Photos; **806:** Francis Miller/The Life Picture Collection/Getty Images; **808L:** Bettmann/Corbis; **808R:** Joseph Louw/The Life Images Collection/Getty Images; **809:** Ivan Massar/Newscom; **810:** Bettmann/Getty Images; **811T:** Bettmann/Corbis; **811B:** Everett Collection; **814T:** St Petersburg Times/Zumapress/Newscom; **814B:** Everett Collection Inc/Alamy Stock Photo; **815:** Bettmann/Corbis; **816:** AP Images; **817:** Bettmann/Getty Images; **819:** Robert W. Kelley/ The Life Picture Collection/Getty Images; **820:** Al Fenn/The Life Picture Collection/Getty Images; **821T:** AP Images; **821B:** File/AP Images; **822:** Bettmann/Corbis; **823:** Buyenlarge/Archive Photos/Getty Images; **824:** The Birmingham News/AP Images; **826:** Francis Miller/The Life Picture Collection/Getty Images; **828:** Danny Lyon/Magnum Photos; **831T:** Rolls Press/Popperfoto/Getty Images; **831B:** Everett Collection/Newscom; **832:** Bettmann/Getty Images; **833T:** Everett Collection/Newscom; **833B:** Bettmann/Corbis; **834T:** AP Images; **834B:** Joseph Louw/The Life Images Collection/Getty Images; **836:** HWC/AP Images; **837:** Popperfoto/Getty Images; **839T:** Byron Rollins/AP Images; **839B:** Keystone View/FPG/Hulton Archive/Getty Images; **842:** King Victor Hugo/Library of Congress; **843:** Popperfoto/Getty Images; **845:** Bettmann/Corbis; **847:** Keystone Pictures USA/Alamy Stock Photo; **848:** ClassicStock/Corbis; **850:** AP Images; **851:** Kim Kulish/Corbis; **852:** Todd Bannor/Alamy Stock Photo; **854:** St Petersburg Times/Zuma Press/Newscom; **857:** ClassicStock/Corbis

Topic 17:

858G: American Photo Archive/Alamy Stock Photo; **858K:** USMC Archives; **858O:** Keystone-France/Gamma-Keystone/Getty Images; **858U:** Bill Ingraham/AP Images; **858:** Christian Simonpietri/Sygma/Corbis; **860T:** Michael Boyer/AP Images; **860B:** AP Images; **861:** Bettmann/Corbis; **862:** American Photo Archive/Alamy Stock Photo; **863T:** AP Images; **863B:** Corbis; **865T:** AP Images; **865B:** World History Archive/Alamy Stock Photo; **867:** Akg-Images/Newscom; **869T:** Akg-images/Newscom; **869B:** Everett Collection Inc/Alamy Stock Photo; **870:** Bettmann/Corbis; **871:** American Photo Archive/Alamy Stock Photo; **873:** USMC Archives; **876:** Everett_Glow/Glow Images; **879:** Agence France Presse/Getty Images; **881:** National Archives; **882T:** Pictorial Parade/Archive Photos/Getty Images; **882B:** Bettmann/Corbis; **883:** CBS Photo Archive/Getty Images; **885T:** Tim Page/Corbis; **885B:** NY Daily News/Getty Images; **886:** Michael Boyer/ AP Images; **888:** Bill Ingraham/AP Images; **889T:** White House via CNP/ Newscom; **889B:** Block Herbert/Library of Congress; **890:** John Filo/Getty Images; **891T:** World History Archive/Newscom; **891B:** Everett Collection Historical/Alamy Stock Photo; **893:** Bettmann/Corbis; **894:** Bill Peters/The Denver Post/Getty Images; **896:** Porter Binks/EPA-EFE/Shutterstock; **898:** Tim Page/Corbis; **901:** Michael Boyer/AP Images

Topic 18:

902: Cynthia Hart Designer/Corbis; **904T:** AP Images; **904B:** Anonymous/ File/AP Images; **905:** AP Images; **906:** Henry Diltz/Corbis; **907T:** CBS/Getty Images; **907B:** Henry Diltz/Corbis; **908T:** Underwood & Underwood/Corbis; **908B:** ZUMA Press, Inc./Alamy Stock Photo; **909:** Henry Diltz/Corbis; **910:** Bettmann/Corbis; **911T:** Bettmann/Corbis; **911B:** Bettmann/Corbis; **912:** Arthur Grace/Zuma Press/Newscom; **913T:** Jerry Cooke/Sports Illustrated/ Getty Images; **913B:** David Dow/NBAE/Getty Images; **916:** Wally Fong/ AP Images; **918:** Laramie Daily Boomerang/Andy Carpenean/AP Images; **919:** Bettmann/Corbis; **921:** Nikolas Georgiou/Alamy Stock Photo; **922:** AP Images; **925:** Block Herbert/Library of Congress; **926:** Pittsburgh Post-Gazette/Zuma Press/Newscom; **928:** Xinhua/Landov; **929T:** Benjamin E. "Gene" Forte - CNP/Newscom; **929B:** ChinaFotoPress/Getty Images; **932T:** CSU Archives/Everett Collection; **932B:** Jean-Claude Sauer/Paris Match/Getty Images; **936:** Wally McNamee/Corbis; **937:** Akg Images/ Newscom; **939:** Anonymous/AP Images; **940T:** Bill Pierce/Time & Life Pictures Collection/Getty Images; **940B:** Dirck Halstead/Time & Life Images Collection/Getty Images; **941T:** AP Images; **941B:** JP Laffont/Sygma/ Corbis; **942:** Everett Collection/Newscom; **944T:** Bettmann/Corbis; **944B:** AP Images; **945:** RDA/Hulton Archive/Getty Images; **947:** Panthera/Alamy Stock Photo; **949:** Posteriori/Shutterstock; **950:** Arthur Grace/Zuma Press/ Newscom; **953:** Akg Images/Newscom

Topic 19:

954: Dirck Halstead/The Life Images Collection/Getty Images; **956T:** Ira Schwarz/AP Images; **956B:** Ira Schwarz/AP Images; **957:** Dirck Halstead/ Time Life Pictures/Getty Images; **958:** Arthur Grace/Zuma Press/Newscom; **961:** Lifestyle pictures/Alamy Stock Photo; **964:** Ira Schwarz/AP Images; **967:** Yvonne Hemsey/Hulton Archive/Getty Images; **968T:** PF-(usna)/Alamy Stock Photo; **968B:** Lennox McLendon/AP Images; **969T:** Barry Thumma/ AP Images; **969B:** Cond Nast Archive/Corbis; **970:** NASA Archive/Alamy Stock Photo; **971:** Everett Collection/Alamy Stock Photo; **972:** AFP/Getty Images; **974:** Bettmann/Corbis; **976T:** Bettmann/Corbis; **976B:** Lana Harris/AP Images; **978:** Ira Schwartz/AP Images; **980:** Alamy Stock Photo; **981T:** Wally McNamee/Corbis; **981B:** Kevin Larkin/Afp/Getty Images; **982:** Keystone Pictures USA/Alamy Stock Photo; **987:** Nana Buxani/ Bloomberg/Getty Images; **990:** Kevin Larkin/Afp/Getty Images; **992:** Steve Eason/Hulton Archive/Getty Images; **993T:** Charles Porter IV/Zuma Press/ Newscom; **993B:** John Duricka/AP Images; **996:** Clu/E+/Getty Images; **999:** Shutterstock; **1001:** PR Archive/Alamy Stock Photo; **1002:** Wally McNamee/ Corbis; **1005:** AFP/Getty Images

Topic 20:

1006: Lain Masterton/Age Fotostock; **1008:** Chuck Kennedy/Mct/ Newscom;**1009:** Anthony Behar/Sipa USA/Newscom; **1010:** Ed Reinke/ AP Images; **1012T:** Win McNamee/Reuters; **1012B:** Carmen Taylor/AP Images; **1013T:** Tom Horan/AP Images; **1013B:** Al-Jazeera/Zumapress/

Newscom; **1014:** Justin Sullivan/Getty Images; **1015:** Eric Feferberg/AFP/Newscom; **1019:** Chuck Kennedy/Mct/Newscom; **1021:** Joe Raedle/Getty Images; **1024:** Steve Eberhardt/ZUMA Press, Inc./Alamy Stock Photo; **1026:** Yoan Valat/EPA/Shutterstock; **1027:** Drew Angerer/Getty Images; **1029:** NiKreative/Alamy Stock photo; **1032:** Planetpix/Alamy Stock Photo; **1033:** Michael Schwenk/Planetpix/National Guard/Alamy Stock Photo; **1034:** Larry W Smith/EPA-EFE/Shutterstock; **1035:** Andrew Harnik/Pool/EPA-EFE/Shutterstock; **1036:** Halfpoint/Shutterstock; **1038:** Tony Freeman/PhotoEdit; **1039:** Annedde/E+/Getty Images; **1042:** Jerry and Marcy Monkman/EcoPhotography.com/Alamy Stock Photov; **1043:** Seth Wenig/AP Images; **1045:** Erin Clark/The Boston Globe/Getty Images; **1047:** LeoPatrizi/+E/Getty Images; **1048:** Tony Freeman/PhotoEdit; **1051:** Eric Feferberg/AFP/Newscom

End Matter:

1050: Stock Connection Blue/Alamy Stock Photo; **1092:** The New York Historical Society/Archive Photos/Getty Images

[Text Acknowledgements]

Topic 1:

Excerpt from *The Constitution of the Five* Nations by Arthur Caswell Parker, 1916.; Excerpt from *Memorandum from Jean Talon on Canada*, 1669, translated from the original French by Savvas Learning Company, LLC; Quote from *Popol Vuh* by Francisco Ximenez. Published by Plantin Press, 1954.; Quote from The Book of Chilam Balam of Chumayel translated by Ralph L. Roys. Carnegie Institution, 1933.

Topic 2:

Excerpt from: *Of Plymouth Plantation* by William Bradford. Published by Wright & Potter Printing, 1898.; Excerpt from: Nova Britannia: Offering *Most Excellent fruites by Planting in Virginia*. Printed for Samuel Macham, 1609; Excerpt from letter to Peter Stuyvesant. From the statement of the residents of Flushing, New York, in resistance to Governor Stuyvesant's order to refuse entry to Quakers, 1657.; For we must consider that we shall be as a City upon a hill. The eyes of all people are upon us. [So] that if we shall deal falsely with our God in this work we have undertaken, and so cause him to withdraw his present help from us, we shall be made a story and a byword throughout the world. —John Winthrop, 1630

Topic 3:

Excerpt: Letter from Abigail Adams to Mercy Otis Warren, December 5, 1773. Warren-Adams papers, Massachusetts Historical Society. Reprinted with permission.; Quote from Anne Hulton letter, June 20, 1768. Printed in Letters of a Loyalist Lady, Harvard University Press, 1927.; Excerpt from speech by Patrick Henry given on May 29, 1765.; Quote from Letter from Abigail Adams to John Adams, 22 September 1774.; Quote from Letter from Phillis Wheatley to Samuel Occom, February 11, 1774; Quote from Proclamation by Governor Dunmore of Virginia, November 7, 1775; Declaration by the Virginia General Convention, December 14, 1775

Topic 4:

Excerpt from Letter from George Washington to Reverend William Gordon, 8th July 1783.; Excerpt from Federalist No. 5, Essay by James Madison, 1788.; Quote from John Adams to James Sullivan, 26 May 1776.; Cato. Letter V. The New-York Journal, November 22, 1787.; Speech by Amos Singletary at Massachusetts convention on ratification of the Constitution, 1788.; Quote from —Jonathan Smith, farmer, speech at the Massachusetts ratification convention, 1788; **141:** Founding Father, Richard Brookhiser, The Free Press, 1996; pp. 42–44; Washington: A Life, Ron Chernow, Penguin Books, 2010; 434-6.

Topic 5:

Excerpt from Address of the Committee and Council of the Cherokee Nation, in General Council Convened, to the People of the United States Lewis Ross et al. (1830); Transcript of President Andrew Jackson's Message to Congress 'On Indian Removal' (1830); George Washington's Farewell Address.; James Monroe, address to Congress, December 2, 1823; Excerpt from Speech to Congress by President James Monroe, 1823.; Excerpt from "Thomas Jefferson, letter to James Monroe, October 24, 1823.

Topic 6:

Excerpt from Frederick Douglass Independence Day Speech, July 5, 1852.; Excerpt from speech given by Mr. T. Marshall, a delegate at the Virginia legislature, Niles' Weekly Register, vol. 43, Sept. 8, 1832.; Quote from Appeal to the Coloured Citizens of the World by David Walker, 1829.; Fitzhugh, George. CANNIBALS ALL! OR, SLAVES WITHOUT MASTERS. (A Morris, 1857).

Topic 7:

Excerpt from *My Cave Life in Vicksburg*, Mary Ann Webster Loughborough, 1864; **328:** Excerpt from Letter by William G. Christie, Before Vicksburg, June the 6th 1863.; **332:** Quote from Jonathan C. Gibbs, January 1, 1863; **333:** Quote from *The Reader's Companion to American History*, William L. Barney. Houghton Mifflin, 1991.; Quote from *Battle Cry of Freedom* by James M. McPherson. Published by Oxford University Press, 1988.; Quote from "What 'Marching Through Georgia' Means", Milford Overley, 1904.

Topic 8:

Excerpt from Speech by Rev. E.J. Adams, "These are Revolutionary Times" 1867. Published by Blackpast.org. Reprinted with permission.; Excerpt Speech from Hiram R. Revels, March 16, 1870.

Topic 9:

The Story of Sadie Frowne: A Sweatshop Girl. New York Independent, (Sept 25, 1902); **386:** Excerpt from *The Gospel of Wealth* by Andrew Carnegie, 1889.; Excerpts from "The Promised Land: The Autobiography of Mary Antin" by Mary Antin

Topic 13:

Excerpt from Jesse Jackson, *The Story of Hooverville*, from Social Trends in Seattle by Calvin P. Schmid, October 1944.; *A Negro in the CCC* by Luther C. Wandall. August, 1935". The publisher wishes to thank the Crisis Publishing Co., Inc., the publisher of the magazine of the National Association for the Advancement of Colored People, for the use of this material first published in the August 1935 issue of Crisis." Reprinted with permission.; Excerpt from Letter from CCC director Robert Fechner to the president of the National Association for the Advancement of Colored People (NAACP), September 1935

Topic 14:

What My Job Means to Me, essay by Leotha Hackshaw, printed in Opportunity (magazine), 1943. Copyright © National Urban League. Reprinted with permission.; Sylvia Tucker Letter to Eleanor Roosevelt From ONE BLOOD:THE DEATH AND RESURRECTION OF CHARLES R. DREW by Spencie Love. Copyright ©1996 by the University of North Carolina Press. Used by permission of the publisher.

Topic 15:

Winston Churchill's "Sinews of Peace" speech, 1946. Reproduced with permission of Curtis Brown, London on behalf of The Estate of Winston S. Churchill. © The Estate of Winston S. Churchill; **751:** Quote from "Defining generations: Where Millennials end and Generation Z begins" by Michael Dimock; January 17, 2019; Pew Research Center.

Topic 16:

Quote from Thomas Jefferson, 1801, First Inaugural Address.

Topic 17:

Letter from Bobbie Lou Pendergress to President Kennedy, 1963; President Kennedy's Response to Bobbie Lou Pendergress, 1963; **879–880:** Excerpt(s) from PATRIOTS: THE VIETNAM WAR REMEMBERED FROM ALL SIDES by Christian Appy, copyright © 2003 by Christian G. Appy. Used by permission of Viking Books, an imprint of Penguin Publishing Group, a division of Penguin Random House LLC. All rights reserved.; Excerpts from: Peter N. Swisher, *A Vietnam Diary* (1975).

Topic 19:

State of the Union Address, Bill Clinton, 1998; **999:** Bill Clinton, 2012 Democratic National Convention speech.

Topic 20:

Tamar Weinberg, I tested positive for coronavirus. Here's what I would like you to know, March 21, 2020, Used with Permission by Medium. (https://medium.com/@tamar/i-tested-positive-for-coronavirus-heres-what-i-would-like-you-to-know-74eeffd909ae)